THE NEW INTERPRETER'S® BIBLE

IN TWELVE VOLUMES

VOLUME I	General Articles on the Bible; General Articles on the Old Testament; Genesis; Exodus; Leviticus
VOLUME II	Numbers; Deuteronomy; Introduction to Narrative Literature; Joshua; Judges; Ruth; 1 & 2 Samuel
VOLUME III	1 & 2 Kings; 1 & 2 Chronicles; Ezra; Nehemiah; Esther; Additions to Esther; Tobit; Judith
VOLUME IV	1 & 2 Maccabees; Introduction to Hebrew Poetry; Job; Psalms
VOLUME V	Introduction to Wisdom Literature; Proverbs; Ecclesiastes; Song of Songs; Book of Wisdom; Sirach
VOLUME VI	Introduction to Prophetic Literature; Isaiah; Jeremiah; Baruch; Letter of Jeremiah; Lamentations; Ezekiel
VOLUME VII	Introduction to Apocalyptic Literature; Daniel; Additions to Daniel; Hosea; Joel; Amos; Obadiah; Jonah; Micah; Nahum; Habakkuk; Zephaniah; Haggai; Zechariah; Malachi
VOLUME VIII	General Articles on the New Testament; Matthew; Mark
VOLUME IX	Luke; John
VOLUME X	Acts; Introduction to Epistolary Literature; Romans; 1 Corinthians
VOLUME XI	2 Corinthians; Galatians; Ephesians; Philippians; Colossians; 1 & 2 Thessalonians; 1 & 2 Timothy; Titus; Philemon
VOLUME XII	Hebrews; James; 1 & 2 Peter; 1, 2, & 3 John; Jude; Revelation

VOLUME THREE

THE FIRST AND SECOND BOOKS OF KINGS

THE FIRST AND SECOND BOOKS OF CHRONICLES

THE BOOK OF EZRA

THE BOOK OF NEHEMIAH

THE BOOK OF ESTHER

ADDITIONS TO ESTHER

THE BOOK OF TOBIT

THE BOOK OF JUDITH

Editorial Board

THE NEW INTERPRETER'S® BIBLE

GENERAL ARTICLES
&
INTRODUCTION, COMMENTARY, & REFLECTIONS
FOR EACH BOOK OF THE BIBLE
INCLUDING
THE APOCRYPHAL/DEUTEROCANONICAL BOOKS
IN
TWELVE VOLUMES

VOLUME
III

ABINGDON PRESS
Nashville

THE NEW INTERPRETER'S® BIBLE
VOLUME III

This book is printed on recycled, acid-free paper.

Library of Congress Cataloging-in-Publication Data

The New Interpreter's Bible: general articles & introduction, commentary, & reflections for each book of the Bible, including the Apocryphal/Deuterocanonical books.
p. cm.
Full texts and critical notes of the New International Version and the New Revised Standard Version of the Bible in parallel columns.
Includes bibliographical references.
ISBN 0-687-27816-3 (v. 3: alk. paper)
1. Bible—Commentaries. 2. Abingdon Press. I. Bible. English. New International. 1994. II. Bible. English. New Revised Standard. 1994.
BS491.2.N484 1994
220.7'7—dc20
ISBN 13: 978-0-687-27816-9

94-21092
CIP

The Hebraica® and Graeca® fonts used to print this work are available from Linguist's Software, Inc., PO Box 580, Edmonds, WA 98020-0580. Tel (206) 775-1130. Web www.linguistsoftware.com

PUBLICATION STAFF
President and Publisher: Neil M. Alexander
Editorial Director: Harriett Jane Olson
Project Director: Jack A. Keller, Jr.
Production Editor: Linda S. Allen
Hebrew and Greek Editor/Assistant Editor: Emily Cheney
Production and Design Manager: Walter E. Wynne
Designer: J. S. Laughbaum
Copy Processing Manager: Sylvia S. Street
Composition Specialist: Kathy M. Harding
Publishing Systems Analyst: Glenn R. Hinton
Prepress Manager: Billy W. Murphy
Prepress Systems Technicians: Thomas E. Mullins
J. Calvin Buckner
Phillip D. Elliott
Director of Production Processes: James E. Leath
Scheduling: Laurene M. Brazzell
Tracey D. Evans
Print Procurement Coordinator: Martha K. Taylor

09 10 11 12 13 14 15 16 17 18—14 13 12 11 10 9 8 7 6 5

MANUFACTURED IN THE UNITED STATES OF AMERICA

Consultants

Neil M. Alexander
President and Publisher
The United Methodist Publishing House
Nashville, Tennessee

Owen F. Campion
Associate Publisher
Our Sunday Visitor
Huntington, Indiana

Minerva G. Carcaño
Director
Mexican American Program
Perkins School of Theology
Southern Methodist University
Dallas, Texas

V. L. Daughtery, Jr.
Pastor
Park Avenue United Methodist Church
Valdosta, Georgia

Sharon Neufer Emswiler
Co-pastor and Co-director
Wesley United Methodist Church & Foundation
University of Illinois
Urbana, Illinois

Juan G. Feliciano Valera
Pastor
Iglesia Metodista "Juan Wesley"
Arecibo, Puerto Rico

Celia Brewer Marshall
Lecturer
University of North Carolina at Charlotte
Charlotte, North Carolina

Nancy C. Miller-Herron
Attorney and clergy member of the Tennessee Conference
The United Methodist Church
Dresden, Tennessee

Robert C. Schnase
Pastor
First United Methodist Church
McAllen, Texas

Bill Sherman
Pastor Emeritus
Woodmont Baptist Church
Nashville, Tennessee

Rodney T. Smothers
Pastor
Ousley United Methodist Church
Lithonia, Georgia

William D. Watley
Pastor
St. James African Methodist Episcopal Church
Newark, New Jersey

Tallulah Fisher Williams†
Superintendent
Chicago Northwestern District
The United Methodist Church
Chicago, Illinois

Suk-Chong Yu
Pastor
San Francisco Korean United Methodist Church
San Francisco, California

† *deceased*

Contributors

Elizabeth Achtemeier
Adjunct Professor of Bible and Homiletics
Union Theological Seminary in Virginia
Richmond, Virginia
(Presbyterian Church [U.S.A.])
Joel

Leslie C. Allen
Professor of Old Testament
Fuller Theological Seminary
Pasadena, California
(Baptist)
1 & 2 Chronicles

Gary A. Anderson
Associate Professor of Religious Studies
University of Virginia
Charlottesville, Virginia
(The Roman Catholic Church)
Introduction to Israelite Religion

David L. Bartlett
Lantz Professor of Preaching and Communication
The Divinity School
Yale University
New Haven, Connecticut
(American Baptist Churches in the U.S.A.)
1 Peter

Robert A. Bennett, Ph.D.
Cambridge, Massachusetts
(The Episcopal Church)
Zephaniah

Adele Berlin
Robert H. Smith Professor of Hebrew Bible
Associate Provost for Faculty Affairs
University of Maryland
College Park, Maryland
Introduction to Hebrew Poetry

Bruce C. Birch
Dean and Professor of Old Testament
Wesley Theological Seminary
Washington, DC
(The United Methodist Church)
1 & 2 Samuel

Phyllis A. Bird
Associate Professor of Old Testament Interpretation
Garrett-Evangelical Theological Seminary
Evanston, Illinois
(The United Methodist Church)
The Authority of the Bible

C. Clifton Black
Professor of New Testament
Perkins School of Theology
Southern Methodist University
Dallas, Texas
(The United Methodist Church)
1, 2, & 3 John

Joseph Blenkinsopp
John A. O'Brien Professor of Biblical Studies
Department of Theology
University of Notre Dame
Notre Dame, Indiana
(The Roman Catholic Church)
Introduction to the Pentateuch

M. Eugene Boring
I. Wylie and Elizabeth M. Briscoe Professor of New Testament
Brite Divinity School
Texas Christian University
Fort Worth, Texas
(Christian Church [Disciples of Christ])
Matthew

WALTER BRUEGGEMANN
William Marcellus McPheeters Professor of Old Testament
Columbia Theological Seminary
Decatur, Georgia
(United Church of Christ)
Exodus

DAVID G. BUTTRICK
Professor of Homiletics and Liturgics
The Divinity School
Vanderbilt University
Nashville, Tennessee
(United Church of Christ)
The Use of the Bible in Preaching

RONALD E. CLEMENTS
Samuel Davidson Professor of Old Testament
King's College
University of London
London, England
(Baptist Union of Great Britain and Ireland)
Deuteronomy

RICHARD J. CLIFFORD, S.J.
Professor of Old Testament
Weston Jesuit School of Theology
Cambridge, Massachusetts
(The Roman Catholic Church)
Introduction to Wisdom Literature

JOHN J. COLLINS
Professor of Hebrew Bible
The Divinity School
University of Chicago
Chicago, Illinois
(The Roman Catholic Church)
Introduction to Early Jewish Religion

ROBERT B. COOTE
Professor of Old Testament
San Francisco Theological Seminary
San Anselmo, California
(Presbyterian Church [U.S.A.])
Joshua

FRED B. CRADDOCK
Bandy Distinguished Professor of Preaching and New Testament, Emeritus
Candler School of Theology
Emory University
Atlanta, Georgia
(Christian Church [Disciples of Christ])
Hebrews

SIDNIE WHITE CRAWFORD
Associate Professor of Hebrew Bible and Chair of the Department of Classics
University of Nebraska—Lincoln
Lincoln, Nebraska
(The Episcopal Church)
Esther; Additions to Esther

JAMES L. CRENSHAW
Robert L. Flowers Professor of Old Testament
The Divinity School
Duke University
Durham, North Carolina
(Baptist)
Sirach

KEITH R. CRIM
Pastor
New Concord Presbyterian Church
Concord, Virginia
(Presbyterian Church [U.S.A.])
Modern English Versions of the Bible

R. ALAN CULPEPPER
Dean
The School of Theology
Mercer University
Atlanta, Georgia
(Southern Baptist Convention)
Luke

KATHERYN PFISTERER DARR
Associate Professor of Hebrew Bible
The School of Theology
Boston University
Boston, Massachusetts
(The United Methodist Church)
Ezekiel

ROBERT DORAN
Professor of Religion
Amherst College
Amherst, Massachusetts
1 & 2 Maccabees

THOMAS B. DOZEMAN
Professor of Old Testament
United Theological Seminary
Dayton, Ohio
(Presbyterian Church [U.S.A.])
Numbers

JAMES D. G. DUNN
Lightfoot Professor of Divinity
Department of Theology
University of Durham
Durham, England
(The Methodist Church [Great Britain])
1 & 2 Timothy; Titus

ELDON JAY EPP
Harkness Professor of Biblical Literature and Chairman of the Department of Religion
Case Western Reserve University
Cleveland, Ohio
(The Episcopal Church)
Ancient Texts and Versions of the New Testament

KATHLEEN A. ROBERTSON FARMER
Professor of Old Testament
United Theological Seminary
Dayton, Ohio
(The United Methodist Church)
Ruth

CAIN HOPE FELDER
Professor of New Testament Language and Literature
The School of Divinity
Howard University
Washington, DC
(The United Methodist Church)
Philemon

TERENCE E. FRETHEIM
Professor of Old Testament
Luther Seminary
Saint Paul, Minnesota
(Evangelical Lutheran Church in America)
Genesis

FRANCISCO O. GARCÍA-TRETO
Professor of Religion and Chair of the Department of Religion
Trinity University
San Antonio, Texas
(Presbyterian Church [U.S.A.])
Nahum

CATHERINE GUNSALUS GONZÁLEZ
Professor of Church History
Columbia Theological Seminary
Decatur, Georgia
(Presbyterian Church [U.S.A.])
The Use of the Bible in Hymns, Liturgy, and Education

JUSTO L. GONZÁLEZ
Adjunct Professor of Church History
Columbia Theological Seminary
Decatur, Georgia
(The United Methodist Church)
How the Bible Has Been Interpreted in Christian Tradition

DONALD E. GOWAN
Robert Cleveland Holland Professor of Old Testament
Pittsburgh Theological Seminary
Pittsburgh, Pennsylvania
(Presbyterian Church [U.S.A.])
Amos

DANIEL J. HARRINGTON
Professor of New Testament
Weston School of Theology
Cambridge, Massachusetts
(The Roman Catholic Church)
Introduction to the Canon

RICHARD B. HAYS
Professor of New Testament
The Divinity School
Duke University
Durham, North Carolina
(The United Methodist Church)
Galatians

THEODORE HIEBERT
Professor of Old Testament
McCormick Theological Seminary
Chicago, Illinois
(Mennonite Church)
Habakkuk

CARL R. HOLLADAY
Professor of New Testament
Candler School of Theology
Emory University
Atlanta, Georgia
Contemporary Methods of Reading the Bible

MORNA D. HOOKER
Lady Margaret's Professor of Divinity, Emeritus
The Divinity School
University of Cambridge
Cambridge, England
(The Methodist Church [Great Britain])
Philippians

DAVID C. HOPKINS
Professor of Old Testament
Wesley Theological Seminary
Washington, DC
(United Church of Christ)
Life in Ancient Palestine

LUKE T. JOHNSON
Robert W. Woodruff Professor of New Testament and Christian Origins
Candler School of Theology
Emory University
Atlanta, Georgia
(The Roman Catholic Church)
James

WALTER C. KAISER, JR.
President and Colman M. Mockler Distinguished Professor of Old Testament
Gordon-Conwell Theological Seminary
South Hamilton, Massachusetts
(The Evangelical Free Church of America)
Leviticus

LEANDER E. KECK
Winkley Professor of Biblical Theology, Emeritus
The Divinity School
Yale University
New Haven, Connecticut
(Christian Church [Disciples of Christ])
Introduction to The New Interpreter's Bible

CHAN-HIE KIM
Professor of New Testament and Director of Korean Studies
The Claremont School of Theology
Claremont, California
(The United Methodist Church)
Reading the Bible as Asian Americans

RALPH W. KLEIN
Dean and Christ Seminary-Seminex Professor of Old Testament
Lutheran School of Theology at Chicago
Chicago, Illinois
(Evangelical Lutheran Church in America)
Ezra; Nehemiah

MICHAEL KOLARCIK, S.J.
Assistant Professor
Regis College
Toronto, Ontario
Canada
(The Roman Catholic Church)
Book of Wisdom

ANDREW T. LINCOLN
Professor of New Testament
Wycliffe College
University of Toronto
Toronto, Ontario
Canada
(The Church of England)
Colossians

J. CLINTON MCCANN, JR.
Evangelical Associate Professor of Biblical Interpretation
Eden Theological Seminary
St. Louis, Missouri
(Presbyterian Church [U.S.A.])
Psalms

ABRAHAM J. MALHERBE
Buckingham Professor of New Testament Criticism and Interpretation, Emeritus
The Divinity School
Yale University
New Haven, Connecticut
(Church of Christ)
The Cultural Context of the New Testament: The Greco-Roman World

W. EUGENE MARCH
Dean and Arnold Black Rhodes Professor of Old Testament
Louisville Presbyterian Theological Seminary
Louisville, Kentucky
(Presbyterian Church [U.S.A.])
Haggai

JAMES EARL MASSEY
Dean Emeritus and Distinguished Professor-at-Large
The School of Theology
Anderson University
(Church of God [Anderson, Ind.])
Reading the Bible from Particular Social Locations: An Introduction;
Reading the Bible as African Americans

J. MAXWELL MILLER
Professor of Old Testament
Candler School of Theology
Emory University
Atlanta, Georgia
(The United Methodist Church)
Introduction to the History of Ancient Israel

PATRICK D. MILLER
Charles T. Haley Professor of Old Testament Theology
Princeton Theological Seminary
Princeton, New Jersey
(Presbyterian Church [U.S.A.])
Jeremiah

PETER D. MISCALL
Adjunct Faculty
The Iliff School of Theology
Denver, Colorado
(The Episcopal Church)
Introduction to Narrative Literature

FREDERICK J. MURPHY
Professor
Department of Religious Studies
College of the Holy Cross
Worcester, Massachusetts
(The Roman Catholic Church)
Introduction to Apocalyptic Literature

CAROL A. NEWSOM
Associate Professor of Old Testament
Candler School of Theology
Emory University
Atlanta, Georgia
(The Episcopal Church)
Job

GEORGE W. E. NICKELSBURG
Professor of Christian Origins and Early Judaism
School of Religion
University of Iowa
Iowa City, Iowa
(Evangelical Lutheran Church in America)
The Jewish Context of the New Testament

IRENE NOWELL, O.S.B.
Community Formation Director
Mount St. Scholasticas
Atchison, Kansas
(The Roman Catholic Church)
Tobit

KATHLEEN M. O'CONNOR
Professor of Old Testament Language, Literature, and Exegesis
Columbia Theological Seminary
Decatur, Georgia
(The Roman Catholic Church)
Lamentations

GAIL R. O'DAY
Almar H. Shatford Associate Professor of Homiletics
Candler School of Theology
Emory University
Atlanta, Georgia
(United Church of Christ)
John

BEN C. OLLENBURGER
Professor of Biblical Theology
Associated Mennonite Biblical Seminary
Elkhart, Indiana
(Mennonite Church)
Zechariah

DENNIS T. OLSON
Associate Professor of Old Testament
Princeton Theological Seminary
Princeton, New Jersey
(Evangelical Lutheran Church in America)
Judges

CAROLYN OSIEK
Professor of New Testament
Department of Biblical Languages and Literature
Catholic Theological Union
Chicago, Illinois
(The Roman Catholic Church)
Reading the Bible as Women

SAMUEL PAGÁN
President
Evangelical Seminary of Puerto Rico
San Juan, Puerto Rico
(Christian Church [Disciples of Christ])
Obadiah

SIMON B. PARKER
Associate Professor of Hebrew Bible and Harrell F. Beck Scholar in Hebrew Scripture
The School of Theology
Boston University
Boston, Massachusetts
(The United Methodist Church)
The Ancient Near Eastern Literary Background of the Old Testament

PHEME PERKINS
Professor of New Testament
Boston College
Chestnut Hill, Massachusetts
(The Roman Catholic Church)
Mark; Ephesians

DAVID L. PETERSEN
Clifford E. Baldridge Professor of Biblical Studies
The Iliff School of Theology
Denver, Colorado
(Presbyterian Church [U.S.A.])
Introduction to Prophetic Literature

CHRISTOPHER C. ROWLAND
Dean Ireland's Professor of the Exegesis of Holy Scripture
The Queen's College
Oxford, England
(The Church of England)
Revelation

ANTHONY J. SALDARINI
Professor of Biblical Studies
Boston College
Chestnut Hill, Massachusetts
(The Roman Catholic Church)
Baruch; Letter of Jeremiah

J. PAUL SAMPLEY
Professor of New Testament and Christian Origins
The School of Theology and The Graduate Division
Boston University
Boston, Massachusetts
(The United Methodist Church)
1 Corinthians; 2 Corinthians

JUDITH E. SANDERSON
Assistant Professor of Hebrew Bible
Department of Theology and Religious Studies
Seattle University
Seattle, Washington
Ancient Texts and Versions of the Old Testament

EILEEN M. SCHULLER, O.S.U.
Professor
Department of Religious Studies
McMaster University
Hamilton, Ontario
Canada
(The Roman Catholic Church)
Malachi

FERNANDO F. SEGOVIA
Associate Professor of New Testament and Early Christianity
The Divinity School
Vanderbilt University
Nashville, Tennessee
(The Roman Catholic Church)
Reading the Bible as Hispanic Americans

CHRISTOPHER R. SEITZ
Professor of Old Testament and Theological Studies and Pro-Dean of the Divinity Faculty
The Divinity School
University of St. Andrews
Fife, Scotland
(The Episcopal Church)
Isaiah 40–66

CHOON-LEONG SEOW
Henry Snyder Gehman Professor of Old Testament Language and Literature
Princeton Theological Seminary
Princeton, New Jersey
(Presbyterian Church [U.S.A.])
1 & 2 Kings

MICHAEL A. SIGNER
Abrams Professor of Jewish Thought and Culture
Department of Theology
University of Notre Dame
Notre Dame, Indiana
How the Bible Has Been Interpreted in Jewish Tradition

MOISÉS SILVA
Professor of New Testament
Westminster Theological Seminary
Philadelphia, Pennsylvania
(The Orthodox Presbyterian Church)
Contemporary Theories of Biblical Interpretation

DANIEL J. SIMUNDSON
Professor of Old Testament
Luther Seminary
Saint Paul, Minnesota
(Evangelical Lutheran Church in America)
Micah

ABRAHAM SMITH
Associate Professor of New Testament
Andover Newton Theological School
Newton Centre, Massachusetts
(The National Baptist Convention, USA, Inc.)
1 & 2 Thessalonians

DANIEL L. SMITH-CHRISTOPHER
Associate Professor of Theological Studies
Department of Theology
Loyola Marymount University
Los Angeles, California
(The Society of Friends [Quaker])
Daniel; Bel and the Dragon; Prayer of Azariah; Susannah

ROBERT C. TANNEHILL
Academic Dean and Harold B. Williams Professor of Biblical Studies
Methodist Theological School in Ohio
Delaware, Ohio
(The United Methodist Church)
The Gospels and Narrative Literature

GEORGE E. TINKER
Associate Professor of Cross-Cultural Ministries
The Iliff School of Theology
Denver, Colorado
(Evangelical Lutheran Church in America)
Reading the Bible as Native Americans

W. SIBLEY TOWNER
The Reverend Archibald McFadyen Professor of Biblical Interpretation
Union Theological Seminary in Virginia
Richmond, Virginia
(Presbyterian Church [U.S.A.])
Ecclesiastes

PHYLLIS TRIBLE
Professor of Biblical Studies
The Divinity School
Wake Forest University
Winston-Salem, North Carolina
Jonah

GENE M. TUCKER
Professor of Old Testament, Emeritus
Candler School of Theology
Emory University
Atlanta, Georgia
(The United Methodist Church)
Isaiah 1–39

CHRISTOPHER M. TUCKETT
Rylands Professor of Biblical Criticism and Exegesis
Faculty of Theology
University of Manchester
Manchester, England
(The Church of England)
Jesus and the Gospels

RAYMOND C. VAN LEEUWEN
Professor of Religion and Theology
Eastern College
Saint Davids, Pennsylvania
(Christian Reformed Church in North America)
Proverbs

ROBERT W. WALL
Professor of Biblical Studies
Department of Religion
Seattle Pacific University
Seattle, Washington
(Free Methodist Church of North America)
Acts; Introduction to Epistolary Literature

DUANE F. WATSON
Associate Professor of New Testament Studies
Department of Religion and Philosophy
Malone College
Canton, Ohio
(The United Methodist Church)
2 Peter; Jude

RENITA J. WEEMS
Associate Professor of Hebrew Bible
The Divinity School
Vanderbilt University
Nashville, Tennessee
(African Methodist Episcopal Church)
Song of Songs

LAWRENCE M. WILLS
Associate Professor of Biblical Studies
The Episcopal Divinity School
Cambridge, Massachusetts
(The Episcopal Church)
Judith

VINCENT L. WIMBUSH
Professor of New Testament and Christian Origins
Union Theological Seminary
New York, New York
(Progressive National Baptist Convention, Inc.)
The Ecclesiastical Context of the New Testament

N. THOMAS WRIGHT
Dean of Lichfield
Lichfield Cathedral
Staffordshire, England
(The Church of England)
Romans

GALE A. YEE
Associate Professor of Old Testament
Department of Theology
University of Saint Thomas
Saint Paul, Minnesota
(The Roman Catholic Church)
Hosea

VINCENT L. WIMBUSH
Professor of New Testament and Christian Origins
Union Theological Seminary
New York, New York
(Progressive National Baptist Convention, Inc.)
The Ecclesiastical Context of the New Testament

N. THOMAS WRIGHT
Dean of Lichfield
Lichfield Cathedral
Staffordshire, England
(The Church of England)
Romans

GALE A. YEE
Associate Professor of Old Testament
Department of Theology
University of Saint Thomas
Saint Paul, Minnesota
(The Roman Catholic Church)
Hosea

FEATURES OF THE NEW INTERPRETER'S® BIBLE

The general aim of *The New Interpreter's Bible* is to bring the best in contemporary biblical scholarship into the service of the church to enhance preaching, teaching, and study of the Scriptures. To accomplish that general aim, the design of *The New Interpreter's Bible* has been shaped by two controlling principles: (1) form serves function, and (2) maximize ease of use.

General articles provide the reader with concise, up-to-date, balanced introductions and assessments of selected topics. In most cases, a brief bibliography points the way to further exploration of a topic. Many of the general articles are placed in volumes 1 and 8, at the beginning of the coverage of the Old and New Testaments, respectively. Others have been inserted in those volumes where the reader will encounter the corresponding type of literature (e.g., "Introduction to Prophetic Literature" appears in Volume 6 alongside several of the prophetic books).

Coverage of each biblical book begins with an "Introduction" that acquaints the reader with the essential historical, sociocultural, literary, and theological issues necessary to understand the biblical book. A short bibliography and an outline of the biblical book are found at the end of each Introduction. The introductory sections are the only material in *The New Interpreter's Bible* printed in a single wide-column format.

The biblical text is divided into coherent and manageable primary units, which are located within larger sections of Scripture. At the opening discussion of any large section of Scripture, readers will often find material identified as "Overview," which includes remarks applicable to the large section of text. The primary unit of text may be as short as a few verses or as long as a chapter or more. This is the point at which the biblical text itself is reprinted in *The New Interpreter's Bible.* Dealing with Scripture in terms of these primary units allows discussion of important issues that are overlooked in a verse-by-verse treatment. Each scriptural unit is identified by text citation and a short title.

The full texts and critical notes of the New International Version and the New Revised Standard Version of the Bible are presented in parallel columns for quick reference. (For the Apocryphal/Deuterocanonical works, the NIV is replaced by The New American Bible.) Since every translation is to some extent an interpretation as well, the inclusion of these widely known and influential modern translations provides an easy comparison that in many cases will lead to a better understanding of a passage. Biblical passages are set in a two-column format and placed in green tint-blocks to make it easy to recognize them at a glance. The NAB, NIV, and NRSV material is clearly identified on each page on which the text appears.

Immediately following each biblical text is a section marked "Commentary," which provides an exegetical analysis informed by linguistic, text-critical, historical-critical, literary, social-scientific, and theological methods. The Commentary serves as a reliable, judicious guide through the text, pointing out the critical problems as well as key interpretive issues.

The exegetical approach is "text-centered." That is, the commentators focus primarily on the text in its final form rather than on (a) a meticulous rehearsal of problems of scholarship associated with a text, (b) a thorough reconstruction of the pre-history of the text, or (c) an exhaustive rehearsal of the text's interpretive history. Of course, some attention to scholarly problems, to the pre-history of a text, and to historic interpretations that have shaped streams of tradition is important in particular cases precisely in order to illumine the several levels of meaning in the final form of the text. But the *primary* focus is on the canonical text itself. Moreover, the Commentary not only describes pertinent aspects of the text, but also teaches the reader what to look for in the text so as to develop the reader's own capacity to analyze and interpret the text.

Commentary material runs serially for a few paragraphs or a few pages, depending on what is required by the biblical passage under discussion.

Commentary material is set in a two-column format. Occasional subheads appear in a bold green font. The next level of subdivisions appears as bold black fonts and a third level as black italic fonts. Footnotes are placed at the bottom of the column in which the superscripts appear.

Key words in Hebrew, Aramaic, or Greek are printed in the original-language font, accompanied by a transliteration and a translation or explanation.

Immediately following the Commentary, in most cases, is the section called "Reflections." A detailed exposition growing directly out of the discussion and issues dealt with in the Commentary, the Reflections are geared specifically toward helping those who interpret Scripture in the life of the church by providing "handles" for grasping the significance of Scripture for faith and life today. Recognizing that the text has the capacity to shape the life of the Christian community, this section presents multiple possibilities for preaching and teaching in light of each biblical text. That is, instead of providing the preacher or teacher full illustrations, poems, outlines, and the like, the Reflections offer *several* trajectories of possible interpretation that connect with the situation of the contemporary listeners. Recognizing the power of Scripture to speak anew to diverse situations, not all of the suggested trajectories could be appropriated on any one occasion. Preachers and teachers want some specificity about the implications of the text, but not so much specificity that the work is done for them. The ideas in the Reflections are meant to stimulate the thought of preachers and teachers, not to replace it.

Three-quarter width columns distinguish Reflections materials from biblical text and Commentary.

Occasional excursuses have been inserted in some volumes to address topics of special importance that are best treated apart from the flow of Commentary and Reflections on specific passages. Set in three-quarter width columns, excursuses are identified graphically by a green color bar that runs down the outside margin of the page.

Occasional maps, charts, and illustrations appear throughout the volumes at points where they are most likely to be immediately useful to the reader.

CONTENTS

VOLUME III

THE FIRST AND SECOND BOOKS OF KINGS

INTRODUCTION, COMMENTARY, AND REFLECTIONS

BY

CHOON-LEONG SEOW

THE FIRST AND SECOND BOOKS OF KINGS

INTRODUCTION

The books of 1 and 2 Kings cover more than four hundred years of Israelite history, from the death of David and the accession of Solomon in the tenth century, to the release of Judah's exiled king Jehoiachin in the sixth century BCE. The story begins with the court intrigues that propelled Solomon to power, dwells on his many worldly accomplishments and his widespread reputation, and focuses on the terrible precedent for syncretism that he set for other kings after him. From the start, one discerns the inevitable interplay of divine will and human will in history. That interplay of wills continues to be evident in the rest of the story of the monarchy, from the division of the kingdom into Judah and Samaria, through the reigns of various kings of Israel and Judah, to the fall of Samaria and, eventually, to the fall of Jerusalem. In the chaotic arena of history and amid the court intrigues, internecine warfare, and international conflicts, the story relentlessly conveys the confidence that God's will is being worked out. The story as a whole testifies to divine purposefulness in the messiness of history. Despite the impression that the affairs of the world are determined by political maneuverings and military strivings of rogues and scoundrels, it is God who will have the final say when all is said and done. History moves inexorably according to the will of the sovereign God.

THE UNITY OF 1 AND 2 KINGS

The two biblical books now known as 1 and 2 Kings originally constituted a single work. The artificial division into two books was first made in the Greek version, where the materials now known as 1–2 Samuel and 1–2 Kings are broken up into four manageable portions called the "books of Reigns/Kingdoms" (chapter and verse divisions were not introduced into biblical manuscripts until the medieval period). Thus the point of division between the books appears to be purely arbitrary; the end of 1 Kings (1 Kgs 22:51-53) and the beginning of 2 Kings (2 Kgs 1:1-18) together constitute a single literary unit, a report on the reign of King Ahaziah of Israel. The Hebrew tradition, in fact, assumed a single literary work, and it was only in the late Middle Ages when, under the influence of the Greek and Latin versions, the division began appearing in Hebrew manuscripts as well. Hence, from a literary viewpoint at least, it is more accurate to speak of a "book of Kings" rather than the "books of Kings."

In the Jewish tradition, the book of Kings belongs—together with the books of Joshua, Judges, and Samuel—to the Former Prophets, a collection of works that provide a prophetic interpretation of Israel's history from the conquest of Canaan to the end of the monarchy. Modern scholars call this biblical corpus "the deuteronomistic history" because the narratives therein share a common vocabulary, literary style, and theological perspective that is heavily influenced by the book of Deuteronomy, which many scholars now regard as the introduction to the corpus. Although it appears likely that there were earlier editions of the deuteronomistic history—in the reigns of Hezekiah (c. 715–686 BCE) and Josiah (c. 640–609 BCE)—it seems clear that the work was given its final form sometime during the exilic period (c. 586–539 BCE). The precise identification of the various stages of redaction, however, is too complicated a task to be pursued in a commentary like this one. Thus, although it may be more accurate to speak of several deuteronomists, I will presume that the final form of the text is broadly coherent and will refer to the final editor as "the (deuteronomistic) narrator." While acknowledging the likelihood of a complex compositional and redactional history behind the present form of the text, the primary focus in this commentary will be on the interpretation of the text as we have it now.

STRUCTURE

The book may be divided into three parts. The first part (1 Kings 1–11) is focused on the kingdom under Solomon. The narrator explains how Solomon succeeded David, even though Solomon was not the heir apparent to the throne (1 Kings 1–2). This succession, to the narrator, was according to the will of God, for God's promise to David was being fulfilled in Solomon's accession to the throne. From the start, therefore, the reader gets the message that God's purpose was being worked out behind all the scandals and human schemes. God's will was fulfilled despite, and even through, human devices and plots. Then the reader is introduced to Solomon the king, and the picture of him is mixed (1 Kgs 3:1-15). Solomon loved God, but he had other loves as well, and his priorities were not always right (1 Kgs 3:1-3). Still, God responded to Solomon's imperfect love and graciously granted him a gift—a gift on which Solomon's reputation would be built. The rest of the account of Solomon's reign depicts him as a king who was successful in all the worldly ways: He was famous, rich, and powerful. Among his many accomplishments was his building of the Temple in Jerusalem. Clearly the dedication of the Temple (1 Kings 8) was a highpoint within the structure of the story, for the Temple was the very symbol of God's presence in the midst of the people, and God's presence was assured, as long as God's people were faithful. Yet, to the narrator, Solomon was no ideal king. Indeed, in many ways, Solomon violated the expectations of faithful kingship laid out in Deuteronomy (Deut 17:14-20). Above all, Solomon's many loves opened the doors to all kinds of compromises to faith in the Lord. Hence, God promised to divide the kingdom into two.

Narratives about the divided kingdom constitute the bulk of the second part of the book of Kings (1 Kings 12–2 Kings 17). It begins with the secession of the ten northern tribes under Jeroboam, who established two heterodox sanctuaries at Bethel and Dan to rival the Temple of the Lord in Jerusalem (1 Kgs 12:25-33). To the narrator, this was blatant apostasy, and Jeroboam had provided a horrible precedent for all his successors to follow. Henceforth, all the kings of Israel (the northern kingdom) would be judged according to their failure to depart from "the way of Jeroboam," and all of them would fail miserably (1 Kgs 15:30, 34; 16:2, 7, 19, 26, 31; 21:22; 22:52; 2 Kgs 3:3; 9:9; 10:29, 31; 13:2, 6, 11; 14:24; 15:9, 18, 24, 28; 17:21-22). Jeroboam had set an indelible pattern of apostasy in the north; it remained possible for each of his successors to turn back to the Lord, but none would do so. Hence, the destruction of the north was inevitable. Throughout the account of the kings of the north, the imperative of obedience to God's demands is emphasized, and the narrator makes the point that destruction is the consequence of Israel's will to disobey.

Meanwhile in Judah, God's promise of an enduring dynasty for David was being preserved by the sheer grace of God. Unlike Israel, there was continuity on the throne of David in Judah, as God had promised. Yet, there was the expectation of faithfulness to the Lord. Just as the kings of the north were judged according to failure to depart from the apostate ways of Jeroboam, so also the kings of the south were judged according to the standard of piety set by David (1 Kgs 14:8; 15:3-5, 11; 2 Kgs 14:3; 16:2). Unlike the northern kingdom, however, there were a few good kings in the south, reformists like Asa (1 Kgs 15:9-15), Jehoshaphat (1 Kgs 22:41-50), and Joash (2 Kgs 12:1-21). Yet, even these reformist kings failed to do all that was necessary to ensure the centralization of worship in Jerusalem. Hence, even though Judah would last a little longer than Israel, it was also set on a path of destruction.

The third major portion of the book focuses on the kingdom of Judah (2 Kings 18–25), the northern kingdom's having been destroyed because of its persistent will to disobey God (2 Kings 17). There is hope when one reads about the reign of reformist King Hezekiah. Indeed, when the Assyrians besieged Jerusalem, they were unable to take the city and had to turn back (2 Kings 18–19). The destiny of Judah appeared to be embodied in the person of Hezekiah, who was on the brink of death, but because of his piety was miraculously granted a reprieve and recovered to live for a while longer (2 Kgs 20:1-11). Yet, all was not well, because Hezekiah, who has been portrayed as one who trusted the Lord, instead trusted the Babylonians and finally cared most about preserving his own well-being (2 Kgs 20:12-21). Even worse for Judah, Hezekiah was succeeded by Manasseh, who thoroughly undid what good Hezekiah had done (2 Kings 21:1-18). Indeed, Manasseh's heretical counterreformation was so horrifying to the narrator that he portrayed this king as Judah's equivalent of Jeroboam of Israel: Just as Jeroboam had caused Israel to sin, so also Manasseh caused Judah to sin. On account of his offenses, the fate of Judah was sealed. The pious reforms of Hezekiah were rendered as nothing. Even the all-encompassing reformation of Josiah could not save Judah (2 Kgs 22:1–23:30). So Judah was finally destroyed; Jerusalem was devastated; the Temple, the symbol of God's presence, was razed to the ground; and the people of Judah were exiled.

THE BOOK OF KINGS AS THEOLOGICAL NARRATIVE

Arguably the most challenging task for the interpreter of Kings is to make sense of it in one's own day and age. To be sure, there are the memorable stories that warm our hearts, like the story of Solomon's receipt of the gift of wisdom from God (1 Kgs 3:4-15) or his swift and simple administration of justice in a complex case (1 Kgs 3:16-28). There are also stories that obviously testify to the power of God and God's prophets, like Elijah's victory on Mt. Carmel (1 Kgs 18:1-46) or Elisha's healing of the leprous Aramean general through a cleansing at the Jordan River (2 Kgs 5:1-19). These are the passages that one finds repeatedly in lectionaries. Yet, there is much in the narratives that is difficult to appropriate as Scripture. The book is filled with all kinds of peculiar details, not only the unfamiliar names of many kings and the dates of their reigns, but also administrative lists (e.g., 1 Kgs 4:1-34) and pedantic descriptions of the Temple and its appurtenances (e.g., 1 Kgs 6:1–7:51). Many of the stories seem tedious and repetitive (cf. 1 Kgs 15:1–16:28), horribly violent (e.g., 2 Kgs 9:1–10:36), ethically challenging (e.g., 1 Kgs 1:1–2:46; 13:1-33), or just plain odd (e.g., 2 Kgs 6:1-7; 13:14-21). Our challenge in reading these texts—indeed, all of Kings—is to make theological sense of them. That will be the primary focus of the commentary.

At one level, the book of Kings reads like a historical document. By presenting the events in a chronological sequence, by its frequent chronological notices and synchronisms (coordination of the reigns of the kings of Israel with the reigns of the kings of Judah), and by its use of and references to historical sources ("the Book of the Acts of Solomon"; "the Book of the Annals of the Kings of Israel"; "the Book of the Annals of the Kings of Judah"), the book of Kings seems to present itself as a work of history. Much of what we know of the history of Israel in this period is, indeed, derived from this source; some of its information has been corroborated by extra-biblical inscriptions and other archaeological sources.

Yet, the purpose of the book is not to present a comprehensive history of the period, as if it were written for general information about the period in question. Rather, by its frequent references to fuller accounts elsewhere (e.g., 1 Kgs 14:19, 29), the text implicitly admits to the selectivity of its data. Rather, the history is a decisively theological one. It has to do with the working out of God's will. Other historical data are of secondary interest to the narrator or, indeed, of no interest at all. So, for instance, Omri, who is known from extra-biblical sources to have been a powerful monarch, warrants only passing notice, for to the narrator he was merely an unfaithful king who was a failure in the eyes of God. Likewise, Ahab is known to have accomplished much politically and militarily, but the narrator presents him as a bungling and rather weak king. By the same token, there are many tantalizing historical allusions that cannot be verified from other records, historical details that cannot be easily reconciled with what we know from other sources, synchronisms that contradict one another, and places that cannot be identified and the significance of which cannot be discerned. Although the pursuit of such historical questions may yield satisfying results, the reader must keep in mind that the purpose of the book of Kings is to impart a theological message. That is what this commentary will strive to highlight.

BIBLIOGRAPHY

Brueggemann, Walter. *1 Kings.* KPG. Atlanta: John Knox, 1983. A preaching guide, full of homiletical ideas.

———. *2 Kings.* KPG. Atlanta: John Knox, 1982. A helpful preaching guide.

Cogan, Mordechai, and Hayim Tadmor. *2 Kings.* AB 11. Garden City, N.Y.: Doubleday, 1988. A detailed commentary, especially helpful on philological and historical issues.

De Vries, Simon J. *1 Kings.* WBC 12. Waco, Tex.: Word, 1985. Detailed attention to the compositional history of the text and to text-critical matters.

Gray, John. *I & II Kings, A Commentary.* OTL. Philadelphia: Westminster, 1970. Especially good on ancient Near Eastern background.

Hobbs, T. R. *II Kings.* WBC 13. Waco, Tex.: Word, 1985. An insightful commentary, especially on literary and historical issues.

Jones, Gwilym. H. *1 and 2 Kings.* NCB. 2 vols. Grand Rapids: Eerdmans, 1984. A commentary that pays careful attention to historical-critical issues.

Long, Burke O. *1 Kings, with an Introduction to Historical Literature.* FOTL 9. Grand Rapids: Eerdmans, 1984. An insightful work that focuses on literary forms. Especially good on literary matters.

———. *2 Kings.* FOTL 10. Grand Rapids: Eerdmans, 1991. See preceding annotation.

Montgomery, James A., and Henry Snyder Gehman. *A Critical and Exegetical Commentary on the Book of Kings.* ICC. Edinburgh: T. & T. Clark, 1986. Originally published in 1951. A technical commentary designed for specialists.

Nelson, Richard D. *First and Second Kings.* Interpretation. Atlanta: John Knox, 1987. An excellent commentary written with pastors in mind. It is rich with theological insights.

Rice, G. *1 Kings: Nations Under God.* ITC. Grand Rapids: Eerdmans, 1990. A good commentary written with the laity in mind.

Walsh, Jerome T. *1 Kings.* Berit Olam. Collegeville, Minn.: Liturgical Press, 1996. Emphasis on a literary reading of the text.

OUTLINE OF FIRST AND SECOND KINGS

I. 1 Kings 1:1–11:43, The Reign of Solomon

A. 1:1-53, How Solomon Became Heir to David's Throne
1:1-4, The Demise of King David
1:5-40, Succession Is in Question
1:41-53, Solomon's Succession Is Ensured

B. 2:1-46, Solomon Consolidates Power
2:1-12, Solomon's Kingship Is Firmly Established
2:13-46, The Kingdom Is Consolidated Under Solomon

C. 3:1-15, Solomon's Priorities and His Gifts from God
3:1-3, Solomon's Alliance with Egypt
3:4-15, God's Self-revelation and Gifts to Solomon

D. 3:16-28, Solomon's Wisdom in Judgment

E. 4:1-34, Solomon's Record
4:1-6, Solomon's Cabinet
4:7-19, Solomon's Other Appointees
4:20-28, Solomon's Domains and His Provisions
4:29-34, Solomon's Reputation for Wisdom

F. 5:1-18, Shady Deals and Oppressive Policies

G. 6:1-38, The Temple Is Built

H. 7:1-51, A Digression on Solomon's Handiwork

I. 8:1-66, The Dedication of the Temple
8:1-13, Commencement of the Ceremony
8:14-21, Solomon's Preliminary Remarks
8:22-53, Solomon's Dedicatory Prayer
8:54-61, Solomon's Closing Remarks
8:62-66, Conclusion of the Ceremony

J. 9:1-9, A Second Revelation

K. 9:10–10:29, Solomon in All His Glory
9:10-28, Solomon's Commercial Forays
10:1-29, Solomon's Other Successes

L. 11:1-43, The Demise of Solomon
11:1-13, Solomon's Unfaithfulness
11:14-43, God Ends Solomon's Kingship

II. 1 Kings 12:1–2 Kings 17:41, The Divided Kingdom

A. 12:1-33, Fragmentation of the Kingdom

12:1-24, Ahijah's Prophecy Is Fulfilled
12:25-33, Jeroboam's Priorities

B. 13:1-34, When One Does Not Obey the Word of the Lord
13:1-10, Consequences of Jeroboam's Disobedience
13:11-32, No Excuse Is Acceptable for Disobedience
13:33-34, Jeroboam Continues His Disobedience

C. 14:1-20, Judgment on the House of Jeroboam

D. 14:21–15:24, Rehoboam, Abijah, and Asa of Judah
14:21-31, The Reign of Rehoboam
15:1-8, The Reign of Abijah
15:9-24, The Reign of Asa

E. 15:25–16:34, Israel's Kings from Nadab to Ahab
15:25-32, The Reign of Nadab, Son of Jeroboam
15:33–16:7, The Reign of Baasha of the House of Issachar
16:8-14, The Reign of Elah, Son of Baasha
16:15-20, The Reign of Zimri, Commander of the Chariotry
16:21-28, The Beginning of the House of Omri
16:29-34, Ahab the Son of Omri

F. 17:1-24, The Living God Who Sustains and Revives
17:1-7, Elijah Is Fed by Ravens
17:8-16, Elijah Is Fed by a Sidonian Widow
17:17-24, The Resurrection of a Dead Boy

G. 18:1-46, Equivocal Faith
18:1-2*a*, Introduction
18:2*b*-16, Obadiah's Equivocation
18:17-40, The Summit Challenge
18:41-46, Conclusion of the Contest

H. 19:1-21, The Prophet's Plight
19:1-3*a*, Why Elijah Is on the Run
19:3*b*-8*a*, Two Epiphanies in the Desert
19:8*b*-18, Encounter with God on Mount Horeb
19:19-21, The Call of Elisha

I. 20:1-43, Ahab's Handling of a Foreign-Policy Crisis
20:1-12, How the War Begins
20:13-34, How Quickly the Tide Turns
20:35-43, Assessment of Ahab's Performance

J. 21:1-29, Ahab's Domestic Policy
21:1-16, Ahab Takes Possession of Naboth's Vineyard
21:17-29, Elijah Brings the Word of the Lord

K. 22:1-40, The End of Ahab's Reign

22:1-5, Ahab Decides to Go to War
22:6-12, Ahab Finds Prophetic Consensus
22:13-28, The Lone Voice of Micaiah, Son of Imlah
22:29-40, Ahab Dies

L. 22:41-53, Jehoshaphat of Judah and Ahaziah of Israel
22:41-50, The Reign of Jehoshaphat of Judah
22:51-53, The Reign of Ahaziah of Israel

M. 1:1-18, Ahaziah's Apostasy
1:1, The Rebellion of Moab
1:2-4, Ahaziah Turns to Baal-Zebub
1:5-8, The Messengers Report Their Encounter
1:9-18, Ahaziah Challenges Elijah

N. 2:1-25, Prophetic Succession
2:1-18, Elisha Succeeds Elijah
2:19-25, Elisha's Power Illustrated

O. 3:1-27, Jehoram's Campaign Against Moab
3:1-3, Regnal Résumé of Jehoram
3:4-8, Jehoram Forms an Alliance Against Moab
3:9-19, Attack, Setback, and Prophetic Prediction
3:20-27, Fulfillment of Prophecies

P. 4:1-44, Elisha's Ministry of Life
4:1-7, The Miracle of Abundant Oil
4:8-37, Elisha Ministers to a Wealthy Woman
4:8-17, The Gift of a Son
4:18-37, Death and Resurrection
4:38-44, Elisha Feeds the Hungry
4:38-41, Death in the Pot
4:42-44, Feeding Many with Little

Q. 5:1-27, Naaman and Gehazi
5:1-7, Naaman Seeks Help in Israel
5:8-14, Naaman Is Healed
5:15-19*a*, Naaman's Conversion
5:19*b*-27, Gehazi's Treachery

R. 6:1-23, More Miracles of Elisha
6:1-7, Elisha Raises a Sunken Ax Head
6:8-23, Elisha Overcomes the Troops of Aram

S. 6:24–7:20, The Siege of Samaria
6:24-31, The Siege and Its Effects
6:32–7:2, Confrontation Between the King and Elisha
7:3-20, How the Siege Was Lifted

T. 8:1-29, A Few Loose Ends

8:1-6, Reprise of the Woman from Shunem
8:7-15, Elisha Plays Kingmaker
8:16-29, The Reigns of Jehoram and Ahaziah of Judah

U. 9:1–10:36, The Reign of Jehu
9:1-13, Jehu Is Anointed King
9:14-29, Joram and Ahaziah Are Killed
9:30-37, Jezebel Is Killed
10:1-17, Ahab's Descendants Are Killed
10:18-27, Jehu's Zeal
10:28-36, Summary Assessment of Jehu's Reign

V. 11:1–12:21, The Accession and Reign of Joash
11:1-3, Athaliah's Usurpation of the Davidic Throne
11:4-21, The Davidic Monarchy Is Restored
12:1-16, The Reign of Joash
12:17-21, Hazael Threatens and Joash Dies

W. 13:1–14:29, The Dynasty of Jehu Thrives
13:1-13, Jehoahaz and Jehoash Reign in Israel
13:14-21, Elisha Dies, But His Ministry Lives On
13:22-25, Victories over Aram
14:1-22, The Reign of Amaziah of Judah
14:23-29, The Reign of Jeroboam II of Israel

X. 15:1–16:20, Kings of Israel and Judah
15:1-7, Azariah/Uzziah of Judah
15:8-31, A Succession of Kings of Israel
15:32-38, Jotham of Judah
16:1-20, Ahaz of Judah

Y. 17:1-41, The Fall of Samaria
17:1-6, How Samaria Fell
17:7-23, Why Samaria Fell
17:24-41, The Resettlement of Samaria and Its Consequences

III. 2 Kings 18:1–25:30, The Last Days of Judah

A. 18:1–20:21, Hezekiah, the Trusting King
18:1-8, Introduction to Hezekiah the Reformer
18:9-12, Perspective on the Fall of Samaria
18:13–19:7, Sennacherib's First Challenge
19:8-37, Sennacherib's Second Challenge
20:1-11, Hezekiah's Illness and Recovery
20:12-21, From Assyria to Babylon

B. 21:1-26, Irreparable Damage to Judah
21:1-18, The Reign of Manasseh

21:19-26, The Reign of Amon

C. 22:1–23:30, The Josianic Reformation

22:1-2, Introduction to Josiah's Reign

22:3-11, Rediscovery of the Book of the Law

22:12-20, A Prophetic Oracle

23:1-25, Josiah's Reforms

23:26-30, The Failure of Josiah to Stem the Tide of Destruction

D. 23:31–25:30, The End

23:31-35, The Reign of Jehoahaz

23:36–24:7, The Reign of Jehoiakim

24:8-17, The Reign of Jehoiachin

24:18–25:21, The Reign of Zedekiah

25:22-26, Gedaliah Becomes Governor

25:27-30, Jehoiachin Is Released from Prison

1 KINGS 1:1–11:43

THE REIGN OF SOLOMON

1 KINGS 1:1-53, HOW SOLOMON BECAME HEIR TO DAVID'S THRONE

OVERVIEW

The narrative in the book of Kings begins with the demise of King David, the focal character in 2 Samuel. For much of the twentieth century, there has been something of a consensus among scholars that this account of the power struggle and transfer of authority at the end of David's reign is properly part of the conclusion of an originally unified "succession narrative," a Davidic court history comprised of 2 Samuel 9–20 and 1 Kings 1–2, with 2 Samuel 21–24 as a secondary addition. There are, to be sure, tantalizing literary and thematic links between the opening two chapters of 1 Kings and much of 2 Samuel. Some scholars have maintained, however, that these chapters in 1 Kings were never part of an original succession narrative. Rather, 1 Kings 1–2 may be better viewed as part of a Solomonic *apologia,* composed not as the conclusion of some Davidic court document but as a part of a separate work that, nevertheless, drew on Davidic court history.[1]

Indeed, the very reference to the old age of David in v. 1 ("King David was old and advanced in years") presupposes knowledge of some tradition about David's reign. The introductory words sound very much like the continuation of a story that the reader is supposed to know already. Similar words are found in Gen 18:11; 24:1; Josh 13:1; 23:1; and 1 Sam 17:12, and in all those cases the words appear in continuation of a story. One may contrast, for instance, the opening of the books of Samuel ("There was a certain man . . . " [1 Sam 1:1]), or the book of Ruth ("In the days when the judges ruled . . . " [Ruth 1:1]), or the book of Job ("There was a man in the land of Uz . . . " [Job 1:1]), none of which assumes an antecedent account. Be that as it may, the report of David's demise in this opening chapter functions now—in its present literary and canonical contexts—as an appropriate introduction to a *new* story: The passing of an old era is the beginning of a new one. The copulative ו (*wĕ*) at the very beginning of the first verse (RSV, "Now") suggests that this introduction should be read with the preceding story in mind, although it also signals a turning point. The RSV's rendering ("Now King David was old . . ."), correctly understanding the copulative *wĕ* to be disjunctive rather than conjunctive, conveys well the sense that one is at a narrative juncture.

1. So P. K. McCarter, "Plots, True or False," *Int* 35 (1981) 355-67.

1 Kings 1:1-4, The Demise of King David

NIV

1 When King David was old and well advanced in years, he could not keep warm
even when they put covers over him. 2So his
servants said to him, "Let us look for a young
virgin to attend the king and take care of him.
She can lie beside him so that our lord the king
may keep warm."
3Then they searched throughout Israel for a beautiful girl and found Abishag, a Shunammite, and
brought her to the king. 4The girl was very beautiful;
she took care of the king and waited on him, but
the king had no intimate relations with her.

NRSV

1 King David was old and advanced in years;
and although they covered him with clothes,
he could not get warm. 2So his servants said to him,
"Let a young virgin be sought for my lord the king,
and let her wait on the king, and be his attendant;
let her lie in your bosom, so that my lord the king
may be warm." 3So they searched for a beautiful
girl throughout all the territory of Israel, and found
Abishag the Shunammite, and brought her to the
king. 4The girl was very beautiful. She became the
king's attendant and served him, but the king did
not know her sexually.

COMMENTARY

King David is now old (about seventy years old, according to 2 Sam 5:4-5; 1 Kgs 2:11) and infirm. Like one suffering from arteriosclerosis, he is unable to keep warm despite the best efforts of his courtiers. At their behest, a young virgin is brought to attend to him. She would be his סכנת (*sōkenet*, "governess"), a term that has been variously interpreted to mean "nurse," "companion," "concubine," or "queen" (NRSV, "his attendant"; NIV, "take care of him").[2] This maiden is supposed to "lie in [his] bosom" (v. 2), an expression that recalls Nathan's parable in reference to the ewe lamb, a metaphor for Bathsheba, the wife of Uriah: "She used to lie in his bosom" (2 Sam 12:3). The translation in the NIV ("lie beside him") misses the subtle allusion. It is important to keep that allusion in mind, for one will soon encounter Bathsheba again.

The woman in view now is not Bathsheba, however, but Abishag "the Shunammite"—that is, one from the town of Shunem, where the prophet Elisha would later revive a dead child by lying on him and warming the dead body (2 Kgs 4:32-37). But there is no miraculous healing in the case of David. Even when the most beautiful young virgin in all the territory of Israel is brought, the old man simply cannot be warmed. Despite David's oft-noticed penchant for beautiful women (e.g., 1 Sam 25:3; 2 Sam 11:2), the aged king apparently did not have sexual relations with her; literally, "he did not know her" (v. 4).

The implicit inability of David to respond to the beautiful virgin in his bosom suggests his impotence in more ways than one. At the beginning of his career, in contrast to his predecessor Saul, he had grown "stronger and stronger," and his increasing strength in those days was reflected in the increase in the number of his wives (see 2 Sam 3:1-5). Even though he had been given Saul's house and Saul's women to be in his bosom (בחיקך *bĕḥêqekā*, "in your bosom," 2 Sam 12:8), David still desired someone who was in the bosom of another man, Uriah (2 Sam 12:3). Yet, the aged David is unable to respond now. He is also no longer in control of his house. Rather, he appears to be at the mercy of his courtiers and requires a "governess" to take care of him. The stage is set, then, for the transfer of power and authority from David to a successor. The reader, who is assumed to be familiar with the story of King David, is implicitly presented with a predicament at this critical juncture in history: Who will be heir to the throne of David, which God had promised would be established forever (see 2 Sam 7:1-17)? (See Reflections at 1:5-40.)

2. The masculine form of the term is found in Hebrew and other Semitic languages for people in positions of power and responsibility.

1 Kings 1:5-40, Succession Is in Question

NIV

5Now Adonijah, whose mother was Haggith, put himself forward and said, "I will be king." So he got chariots and horses[a] ready, with fifty men to run ahead of him. 6(His father had never interfered with him by asking, "Why do you behave as you do?" He was also very handsome and was born next after Absalom.)

7Adonijah conferred with Joab son of Zeruiah and with Abiathar the priest, and they gave him their support. 8But Zadok the priest, Benaiah son of Jehoiada, Nathan the prophet, Shimei and Rei[b] and David's special guard did not join Adonijah.

9Adonijah then sacrificed sheep, cattle and fattened calves at the Stone of Zoheleth near En Rogel. He invited all his brothers, the king's sons, and all the men of Judah who were royal officials, 10but he did not invite Nathan the prophet or Benaiah or the special guard or his brother Solomon.

11Then Nathan asked Bathsheba, Solomon's mother, "Have you not heard that Adonijah, the son of Haggith, has become king without our lord David's knowing it? 12Now then, let me advise you how you can save your own life and the life of your son Solomon. 13Go in to King David and say to him, 'My lord the king, did you not swear to me your servant: "Surely Solomon your son shall be king after me, and he will sit on my throne"? Why then has Adonijah become king?' 14While you are still there talking to the king, I will come in and confirm what you have said."

15So Bathsheba went to see the aged king in his room, where Abishag the Shunammite was attending him. 16Bathsheba bowed low and knelt before the king.

"What is it you want?" the king asked.

17She said to him, "My lord, you yourself swore to me your servant by the LORD your God: 'Solomon your son shall be king after me, and he will sit on my throne.' 18But now Adonijah has become king, and you, my lord the king, do not know about it. 19He has sacrificed great numbers of cattle, fattened calves, and sheep, and has invited all the king's sons, Abiathar the priest and Joab

a 5 Or *charioteers* b 8 Or *and his friends*

NRSV

5Now Adonijah son of Haggith exalted himself, saying, "I will be king"; he prepared for himself chariots and horsemen, and fifty men to run before him. 6His father had never at any time displeased him by asking, "Why have you done thus and so?" He was also a very handsome man, and he was born next after Absalom. 7He conferred with Joab son of Zeruiah and with the priest Abiathar, and they supported Adonijah. 8But the priest Zadok, and Benaiah son of Jehoiada, and the prophet Nathan, and Shimei, and Rei, and David's own warriors did not side with Adonijah.

9Adonijah sacrificed sheep, oxen, and fatted cattle by the stone Zoheleth, which is beside En-rogel, and he invited all his brothers, the king's sons, and all the royal officials of Judah, 10but he did not invite the prophet Nathan or Benaiah or the warriors or his brother Solomon.

11Then Nathan said to Bathsheba, Solomon's mother, "Have you not heard that Adonijah son of Haggith has become king and our lord David does not know it? 12Now therefore come, let me give you advice, so that you may save your own life and the life of your son Solomon. 13Go in at once to King David, and say to him, 'Did you not, my lord the king, swear to your servant, saying: Your son Solomon shall succeed me as king, and he shall sit on my throne? Why then is Adonijah king?' 14Then while you are still there speaking with the king, I will come in after you and confirm your words."

15So Bathsheba went to the king in his room. The king was very old; Abishag the Shunammite was attending the king. 16Bathsheba bowed and did obeisance to the king, and the king said, "What do you wish?" 17She said to him, "My lord, you swore to your servant by the LORD your God, saying: Your son Solomon shall succeed me as king, and he shall sit on my throne. 18But now suddenly Adonijah has become king, though you, my lord the king, do not know it. 19He has sacrificed oxen, fatted cattle, and sheep in abundance, and has invited all the children of the king, the priest Abiathar, and Joab the commander of the army; but your servant Solomon he has not invited. 20But you, my lord the king—the eyes of

NIV

the commander of the army, but he has not invited Solomon your servant. [20]My lord the king, the eyes of all Israel are on you, to learn from you who will sit on the throne of my lord the king after him. [21]Otherwise, as soon as my lord the king is laid to rest with his fathers, I and my son Solomon will be treated as criminals."

[22]While she was still speaking with the king, Nathan the prophet arrived. [23]And they told the king, "Nathan the prophet is here." So he went before the king and bowed with his face to the ground.

[24]Nathan said, "Have you, my lord the king, declared that Adonijah shall be king after you, and that he will sit on your throne? [25]Today he has gone down and sacrificed great numbers of cattle, fattened calves, and sheep. He has invited all the king's sons, the commanders of the army and Abiathar the priest. Right now they are eating and drinking with him and saying, 'Long live King Adonijah!' [26]But me your servant, and Zadok the priest, and Benaiah son of Jehoiada, and your servant Solomon he did not invite. [27]Is this something my lord the king has done without letting his servants know who should sit on the throne of my lord the king after him?"

[28]Then King David said, "Call in Bathsheba." So she came into the king's presence and stood before him.

[29]The king then took an oath: "As surely as the LORD lives, who has delivered me out of every trouble, [30]I will surely carry out today what I swore to you by the LORD, the God of Israel: Solomon your son shall be king after me, and he will sit on my throne in my place."

[31]Then Bathsheba bowed low with her face to the ground and, kneeling before the king, said, "May my lord King David live forever!"

[32]King David said, "Call in Zadok the priest, Nathan the prophet and Benaiah son of Jehoiada." When they came before the king, [33]he said to them: "Take your lord's servants with you and set Solomon my son on my own mule and take him down to Gihon. [34]There have Zadok the priest and Nathan the prophet anoint him king over Israel. Blow the trumpet and shout, 'Long live King Solomon!' [35]Then you are to go up with him, and he is to come and sit on my throne and

NRSV

all Israel are on you to tell them who shall sit on the throne of my lord the king after him. [21]Otherwise it will come to pass, when my lord the king sleeps with his ancestors, that my son Solomon and I will be counted offenders."

22While she was still speaking with the king, the prophet Nathan came in. [23]The king was told, "Here is the prophet Nathan." When he came in before the king, he did obeisance to the king, with his face to the ground. [24]Nathan said, "My lord the king, have you said, 'Adonijah shall succeed me as king, and he shall sit on my throne'? [25]For today he has gone down and has sacrificed oxen, fatted cattle, and sheep in abundance, and has invited all the king's children, Joab the commander[a] of the army, and the priest Abiathar, who are now eating and drinking before him, and saying, 'Long live King Adonijah!' [26]But he did not invite me, your servant, and the priest Zadok, and Benaiah son of Jehoiada, and your servant Solomon. [27]Has this thing been brought about by my lord the king and you have not let your servants know who should sit on the throne of my lord the king after him?"

28King David answered, "Summon Bathsheba to me." So she came into the king's presence, and stood before the king. [29]The king swore, saying, "As the LORD lives, who has saved my life from every adversity, [30]as I swore to you by the LORD, the God of Israel, 'Your son Solomon shall succeed me as king, and he shall sit on my throne in my place,' so will I do this day." [31]Then Bathsheba bowed with her face to the ground, and did obeisance to the king, and said, "May my lord King David live forever!"

32King David said, "Summon to me the priest Zadok, the prophet Nathan, and Benaiah son of Jehoiada." When they came before the king, [33]the king said to them, "Take with you the servants of your lord, and have my son Solomon ride on my own mule, and bring him down to Gihon. [34]There let the priest Zadok and the prophet Nathan anoint him king over Israel; then blow the trumpet, and say, 'Long live King Solomon!' [35]You shall go up following him. Let him enter and sit on my throne; he shall be king in my place; for I have appointed him to be ruler over

[a] Gk: Heb *the commanders*

NIV

reign in my place. I have appointed him ruler over
Israel and Judah."
36Benaiah son of Jehoiada answered the king,
"Amen! May the LORD, the God of my lord the
king, so declare it. 37As the LORD was with my
lord the king, so may he be with Solomon to
make his throne even greater than the throne of
my lord King David!"
38So Zadok the priest, Nathan the prophet,
Benaiah son of Jehoiada, the Kerethites and the
Pelethites went down and put Solomon on King
David's mule and escorted him to Gihon. 39Zadok
the priest took the horn of oil from the sacred
tent and anointed Solomon. Then they sounded
the trumpet and all the people shouted, "Long
live King Solomon!" 40And all the people went up
after him, playing flutes and rejoicing greatly, so
that the ground shook with the sound.

NRSV

Israel and over Judah." 36Benaiah son of Jehoiada
answered the king, "Amen! May the LORD, the
God of my lord the king, so ordain. 37As the LORD
has been with my lord the king, so may he be
with Solomon, and make his throne greater than
the throne of my lord King David."
38So the priest Zadok, the prophet Nathan, and
Benaiah son of Jehoiada, and the Cherethites and
the Pelethites, went down and had Solomon ride
on King David's mule, and led him to Gihon.
39There the priest Zadok took the horn of oil from
the tent and anointed Solomon. Then they blew
the trumpet, and all the people said, "Long live
King Solomon!" 40And all the people went up
following him, playing on pipes and rejoicing with
great joy, so that the earth quaked at their noise.

COMMENTARY

1:5-6. Immediately after the account of David's pathetic conditions (vv. 1-4), we learn that Adonijah the son of Haggith is elevating himself. Neither the NRSV nor the NIV adequately captures the emphasis in the Hebrew, for Adonijah says, literally, "I, I will be king." This story of an ambitious prince attempting to seize power is reminiscent of the Canaanite *Legend of King Keret,* where we read of an effort by a prince—the heir-presumptive by the custom of primogeniture—to depose his old and infirm father on the grounds of the old man's ineffectiveness and impotence.[3] The prince tells the old king to abdicate (Ugaritic *yrd,* "to come down," semantically opposite to Hebrew נשׂא [*nāśā'*, "to elevate"]) so that he himself might become king: "Come down from kingship [and] I will be king, from your rule [and] I will sit enthroned, even I" (author's trans.). The prince is trying to elevate himself at the expense of his impotent father.

The narrative about Adonijah's attempted *coup d'état* also recalls a previous abortive putsch by another son of David, Absalom (2 Samuel 15–18). Indeed, the narrator probably intends the linkage between these two sons. Like Absalom (2 Sam 14:25-26), Adonijah is said to be very handsome; like Absalom (2 Sam 15:1), Adonijah gathers to himself chariots, horses (not "horsemen" as the NRSV has it),[4] and royal escorts (cf. 1 Sam 8:11); like Absalom (2 Sam 15:12), Adonijah invites others to a sacrificial feast. The narrator notes that Adonijah was born "next after Absalom," meaning probably that Adonijah is the heir-presumptive by primogeniture (see 2:15, 22).

Adonijah is the fourth of David's sons who were born to him in the Judean town of Hebron (2 Sam 3:2-5).[5] David's firstborn, Amnon, had raped his half sister Tamar and was killed by Absalom, Tamar's full brother (2 Samuel 13). Absalom, the third son, was banished for the murder and killed when trying to usurp the throne (2 Samuel 18). We know virtually nothing of Chileab, the second son (2 Sam 3:3; 1 Chr 3:1); one can only conjecture that he had died in

3. *The Legend of King Keret,* in *Ancient Near Eastern Texts,* ed. J. B. Pritchard (Princeton: Princeton University Press, 1969) 142-49.

4. We should probably repoint the text to read פרשׁים (*pĕrāšîm,* "horses"), rather than פרשׁים (*pārāšîm,* "horsemen"). Cf. Jer 46:4; Ezek 27:14; Joel 2:4, where פרשׁ (*pārāš*) is used as a parallel term for סוס (*sûs*), the common word for "horse." The word refers to horses used for pulling chariots (e.g., Gen 50:9; Josh 24:6; 1 Sam 8:11). The cavalry, with horsemen riding horses, was not known in Palestine until the ninth century BCE.

5. See Josephus *Antiquities of the Jews* 7.14.4.

childhood. In any case, Adonijah is the oldest surviving son of David and, now, the presumed heir. He is seen as someone who has not been disciplined by his father (v. 6).[6] One recalls, again, the prophecy of Nathan, in which it is predicted that because of David's adultery with Bathsheba (the "ewe lamb" that used to lie in the bosom of her master), trouble would plague David from within his own house, initiated by those very people closest to him (2 Sam 12:11).

1:7-8. In his usurpation of power, Adonijah turns to people who had been with David before he became king in Jerusalem. Joab was a commander of the Judean militia when David ruled in Hebron (2 Samuel 2). Abiathar the priest had served David in his early struggle against Saul (1 Sam 22:20-23; 23:6). These are the conservative elements, the "old guard" in David's regime based in Hebron. Opposing them are Zadok the priest;[7] Benaiah, the captain of the royal bodyguards, comprised of mercenaries; and Nathan the prophet, all of whom came to prominence only after David began ruling in Jerusalem (2 Sam 7:2; 8:17-18), along with Shimei (perhaps "Shimei the son of Ela," 4:18) and Rei (of whom nothing else is known), and David's own special corps of elite warriors.

David's choice of Jerusalem as capital had been a calculated one, for the city had belonged neither to the tribes of Judah nor to the tribes of Israel. It was in Jerusalem that David united the various tribal confederacies, north and south. There he had ruled with a coalition of old guards from Judah and new personnel in Jerusalem drawn from a variety of backgrounds. Hence, he had two high priests (Abiathar and Zadok) and two military commanders (Joab and Benaiah), one apparently in charge of the militia and the other commanding the professional troops. Yet now, in David's last days, the fragile coalition appears to be disintegrating.

1:9-14. The usurper Adonijah hosts a sacrificial feast, an act fraught with political symbolism (see vv. 18-19, 24-25; cf. 2 Sam 15:7-12), and he invites other sons of the king and the court officials who are Judeans. The event is held at a landmark known as "the Stone of Zohelet" near En-Rogel in the Kidron Valley, on the boundary between Benjaminite and Judean territories, just beyond the capital city. Solomon and his supporters are not invited to Adonijah's exclusive gathering (v. 10). Although Adonijah is the heir apparent, he obviously does not trust Solomon, who was not born, as he was, in the Judean town of Hebron but in the new capital city of Jerusalem and who has the support of the more cosmopolitan officials in that city. Nathan the prophet, always a supporter of Solomon (see 2 Sam 7:1-17; 12:25), brings the matter to the attention of Bathsheba, the mother of Solomon, identifying Adonijah as "the son of Haggith"—that is, the son of a rival wife to Bathsheba—and charging that "Adonijah has become king" (v. 11; cf. 2 Sam 15:10, "Absalom has become king"). Nathan presents the attempted takeover as something that has already happened (מלך *mālak*, "has become king," v. 11), and he warns that Solomon and Bathsheba will be in mortal danger if Adonijah remains unchallenged (v. 12). He lays out their strategy for dealing with the problem: First, Bathsheba will approach David and "remind" him of an oath that he had made to name Solomon as his successor, and then Nathan would appear to "confirm" (מלא *millē'*, in the piel; lit., "fill out") her words (vv. 13-14).

1:15-19. Bathsheba appears before David, not in the court of the palace, but in his private bedroom (v. 15). The narrator reiterates at this point that David is very old, thus bringing us back to the introductory words about the king's old age and infirmity (vv. 1-4). Bathsheba, who had been desired by David even though she was in the bosom of another man, now speaks to the old king in front of the young and beautiful Abishag, who was brought to lie in his bosom. Bathsheba tells David that Adonijah has become king without his knowledge (v. 18); David is not "in the know," as it were. Even as he does not *know* Abishag (v. 4), he does not *know* that Adonijah is plotting to take over the throne (vv. 11, 18). This lack of knowledge on his part is telling, for the king was once assumed to have had great wisdom and the ability "to know all things that are on earth" (2 Sam 14:20). Here, however, David is clearly in his waning years, and he does not seem to know very much at all.

6. David is elsewhere seen as an indulgent father. See 2 Sam 13:21 (an addition in the Greek) and 2 Sam 19:1-8.

7. There is much confusion surrounding the background of Zadok (see 2 Sam 8:17, a problematic text; 15:24-29), but he is almost certainly not Judean.

Nathan and Bathsheba seem to be taking advantage of the old man's senility. The prophet suggests that Bathsheba ask David if the king himself had not sworn to her that Solomon would be his successor. In Bathsheba's own rendering, however, the leading question posed by Nathan turns into an indicative statement, an outright reminder of the king's supposed commitment to her: "My lord, you yourself swore to me" (v. 17). It is in Nathan's prompting of Bathsheba (v. 13) that the reader first learns of this putative commitment on David's part; nothing is said of such an oath in earlier narratives or, indeed, anywhere else in the Bible, which would be completely surprising, given the importance of such a tradition to the Davidic monarchy. If such a decisive oath had actually been made, or if it had been made in private between David and Bathsheba (perhaps as "pillow talk"), it would be very strange that she should have to be reminded of it by Nathan. Moreover, when Nathan appears to "confirm" (*millē*ʾ) Bathsheba's words (v. 14), he makes no mention at all of such a promise (vv. 22-27). He asks only if David has, in fact, designated Adonijah to be the successor, implicitly conceding that to be a legitimate option (cf. 1 Kgs 2:15).

Bathsheba and Nathan both draw attention to the political implication of Adonijah's sacrificial feast. They also indirectly implicate all those who joined Adonijah (vv. 19, 25). At the same time, both Bathsheba and Nathan subtly turn Adonijah's snub into a political virtue for Solomon. She points out that Solomon is not among those invited by Adonijah, thus exonerating her own son from complicity in the treasonous plot. The Hebrew word order is emphatic in its exclusion of Solomon from the reported conspiracy, and Bathsheba deliberately calls attention to Solomon's allegiance to David by referring to her son as David's "servant" and not just his "son": "But as for Solomon, your servant, [Adonijah] did not invite" (v. 19). In other words, Abiathar and Joab are complicitous in the plot, but Solomon is the king's servant.

1:20-27. No doubt to rouse David to action, Bathsheba tells him that "the eyes of all Israel" are on him to see who he will designate as his heir (v. 20). What is at stake here in Bathsheba's plea is not merely David's prestige and credibility, as many commentators have observed, but the unity of the country. The reference to the opinion of "all Israel" is poignant in the light of the fact that all of Adonijah's supporters were Judean and the emphasis in the narrative that Adonijah had specifically invited "all the men of *Judah* who are royal officials" (v. 9). The eyes of the whole nation ("all Israel"), she warns, are watching to see how David will respond to the crisis.

Bathsheba speaks as a mother whose primary interest is to protect her son; if Adonijah's actions are not negated, she points out to David, she and Solomon will be in trouble. Filling out her account, the prophet Nathan adds that Adonijah has already been acclaimed king by the rebels (v. 25) and that Nathan himself ("your servant"), Zadok the priest, and Benaiah the son of Jehoiada have not been party to Adonijah's plot (v. 26). Thereby he identifies for David the non-conspirators who could be trusted to counter Adonijah's gang.

The climax of Nathan's speech before David is an indignant question: Has David indeed chosen Adonijah as his successor without ever informing his loyal servants? Nathan's real purpose here is not so much to indict David for his ignorance and the violation of "due process," as some have suggested. Rather, he means to point out that those who are *not* with Adonijah are still loyal to David—they are truly *his servants.*

1:28-31. This time David speaks and acts decisively. Perhaps not trusting his own memory, he is simply accepting the case made by Bathsheba. Or perhaps he is genuinely moved by the plea of Bathsheba and the arguments of Nathan, and so decides to act. Whereas the reader has only heard questionable references to a previous commitment that David made to Bathsheba regarding the succession to his throne, one now hears the oath in David's own words that Solomon is indeed the heir-designate (v. 30). If one does not know whether there had really been an oath before this occasion, one certainly hears the oath sworn now in David's own words, an oath made in the name of "the LORD, the God of Israel." Bathsheba responds with gratitude, saying, "May my lord King David live forever!" (v. 31). This is surely not an expression of hope for David's physical immortality, but a wish that David would live on through his lineage upon the throne, as promised by the deity in Nathan's oracle (2 Sam 7:12-16).

With David's oath explicitly designating Solomon (vv. 28-30) and Bathsheba's benediction (v. 31), the story takes a decisive turn. Medieval Hebrew scholars noticed the shift and placed the strongest marker of a paragraph division after the words of Bathsheba (v. 31)—the only such marker in the chapter. Leading to this pivotal moment, the narrative speaks of Adonijah's elevation of himself, followed by the intervention of Nathan and Bathsheba on Solomon's behalf. Beyond this point we read of the acclamation of Solomon as king and the fall of Adonijah, ending in his humiliation before Solomon.

1:32-40. David instructs Zadok the priest, Nathan the prophet, and Benaiah the commander of the royal guards—three persons who are not implicated in the conspiracy—to install Solomon as king (מלך *melek*) and as designated ruler (נגיד *nāgîd*). In stark contrast to the divisive and provincial assembly of Adonijah, which was attended by Judeans only, Solomon is said to have been installed amid pomp and circumstance, all marking the legitimacy of his accession over the whole country ("over Israel," v. 34; "over Israel and over Judah," v. 35).

Solomon is thus presented as a duly designated and legitimate heir in the dynasty and as a ruler accepted by all the people. He is placed upon David's own mule, the mule having become a status symbol in those days (cf. 2 Sam 13:29; 18:9). He is publicly anointed with "the oil from the tent," no doubt referring here to the movable "tent of meeting" or "tent of YHWH" that had been the symbol of divine presence in the midst of Israel (2:28; 2 Sam 7:2, 7). In this way, then, he is anointed just as Saul (1 Sam 10:1) and David (1 Sam 16:1, 13) had been.

The ceremony takes place near the spring of Gihon, beneath the City of David, whereas Adonijah's feast is held at another spring outside the city. Moreover, throughout the account, the narrator presents Adonijah's actions as having arisen from ambition and personal will. Adonijah exalted himself, openly declared his wish to be king, prepared for himself the trappings of kingship, and approached his co-conspirators himself. By contrast, Solomon's accession is not his own doing. He is presented as a passive figure throughout the process: Others plot and plead his case, others cause him to ride the mule, others bring him to Gihon and anoint him. They blow the *shophar*—the ram's horn—and proclaim him king amid joyous public fanfare, rather than in an exclusive ceremony, as was the case with Adonijah. Accordingly, then, "all the people" (v. 40)—not just a select group of Judeans—follow Solomon and celebrate his accession publicly.

1 Kings 1:41-53, Solomon's Succession Is Ensured

NIV

41Adonijah and all the guests who were with him heard it as they were finishing their feast. On hearing the sound of the trumpet, Joab asked, "What's the meaning of all the noise in the city?"

42Even as he was speaking, Jonathan son of Abiathar the priest arrived. Adonijah said, "Come in. A worthy man like you must be bringing good news."

43"Not at all!" Jonathan answered. "Our lord King David has made Solomon king. 44The king has sent with him Zadok the priest, Nathan the prophet, Benaiah son of Jehoiada, the Kerethites and the Pelethites, and they have put him on the king's mule, 45and Zadok the priest and Nathan the prophet have anointed him king at Gihon.

NRSV

41Adonijah and all the guests who were with him heard it as they finished feasting. When Joab heard the sound of the trumpet, he said, "Why is the city in an uproar?" 42While he was still speaking, Jonathan son of the priest Abiathar arrived. Adonijah said, "Come in, for you are a worthy man and surely you bring good news." 43Jonathan answered Adonijah, "No, for our lord King David has made Solomon king; 44the king has sent with him the priest Zadok, the prophet Nathan, and Benaiah son of Jehoiada, and the Cherethites and the Pelethites; and they had him ride on the king's mule; 45the priest Zadok and the prophet Nathan have anointed him king at Gihon; and they have gone up from there rejoic-

NIV

From there they have gone up cheering, and the
city resounds with it. That's the noise you hear.
[46]Moreover, Solomon has taken his seat on the
royal throne. [47]Also, the royal officials have come
to congratulate our lord King David, saying, 'May
your God make Solomon's name more famous
than yours and his throne greater than yours!'
And the king bowed in worship on his bed [48]and
said, 'Praise be to the LORD, the God of Israel,
who has allowed my eyes to see a successor on
my throne today.' "

[49]At this, all Adonijah's guests rose in alarm and
dispersed. [50]But Adonijah, in fear of Solomon,
went and took hold of the horns of the altar.
[51]Then Solomon was told, "Adonijah is afraid of
King Solomon and is clinging to the horns of the
altar. He says, 'Let King Solomon swear to me
today that he will not put his servant to death
with the sword.' "

[52]Solomon replied, "If he shows himself to be
a worthy man, not a hair of his head will fall to
the ground; but if evil is found in him, he will
die." [53]Then King Solomon sent men, and they
brought him down from the altar. And Adonijah
came and bowed down to King Solomon, and
Solomon said, "Go to your home."

NRSV

ing, so that the city is in an uproar. This is the
noise that you heard. [46]Solomon now sits on the
royal throne. [47]Moreover the king's servants came
to congratulate our lord King David, saying, 'May
God make the name of Solomon more famous
than yours, and make his throne greater than your
throne.' The king bowed in worship on the bed
[48]and went on to pray thus, 'Blessed be the LORD,
the God of Israel, who today has granted one of
my offspring[a] to sit on my throne and permitted
me to witness it.' "

49Then all the guests of Adonijah got up trembling and went their own ways. [50]Adonijah, fearing Solomon, got up and went to grasp the horns
of the altar. [51]Solomon was informed, "Adonijah
is afraid of King Solomon; see, he has laid hold
of the horns of the altar, saying, 'Let King Solomon swear to me first that he will not kill his
servant with the sword.' " [52]So Solomon responded, "If he proves to be a worthy man, not
one of his hairs shall fall to the ground; but if
wickedness is found in him, he shall die." [53]Then
King Solomon sent to have him brought down
from the altar. He came to do obeisance to King
Solomon; and Solomon said to him, "Go home."

[a] Gk: Heb *one*

COMMENTARY

Adonijah and his guests hear the loud noise in town (v. 41), for En-Rogel, although outside the city limits, is less than half a mile away. The significance of the sound is reported by an intelligence scout, Jonathan, the son of Abiathar the priest (see 2 Sam 15:27, 36; 17:17-20). Adonijah apparently expects the noise to indicate the success of his *coup d'état,* for he assumes that Jonathan is a harbinger of "good news." He expects a positive word from Jonathan because the messenger is "a man of substance" (v. 42; NRSV and NIV, "worthy man"), here meaning that he is a loyal subject (cf. v. 52; 1 Sam 18:17; 2 Sam 2:7; 13:28). Furthermore, the Hebrew root used here for the bringing of good news (בשׂר *bśr*, in the piel) is related to the one used in Canaanite mythology for the announcement of Baal-Hadad's successful bid for kingship (Ugaritic, *bšr*). Upon Baal-Hadad's victory over Mot (deified Death), his brother and rival for cosmic kingship, the consort of the former brought "good news" (*tbšr . . . bšrt*) that a palace befitting Baal's kingship would be constructed for him.[8]

In Adonijah's case, however, there is no good news. In fact, the messenger reports that David has already designated Solomon as heir, that Solomon has already been installed upon the throne, that the subordinates of the king have accepted the succession as legitimate, and that David himself has affirmed that Solomon's accession is in accordance with divine will (see 2 Sam 7:12). The hopelessness of the situation for Adonijah is con-

8. *ANET,* 133.

veyed in the messenger's speech through the threefold repetition of the particle גם (*gam*, "also," "moreover"), a particle that is not consistently represented in the English translations. The text says, literally: *"Moreover* Solomon has sat enthroned" (v. 46), *"moreover* the king's servants came to bless our lord" (v. 47), *"moreover* thus said the king . . . " (v. 48). Adonijah's failure is indicated in other ways, as well, for not only does Jonathan relate the cold facts of Solomon's success, but also his language betrays his shifting loyalty: Twice he refers to David as "our lord" (vv. 43, 47). Adonijah's guests, too, are quick to abandon him; they "rose in alarm and dispersed" (v. 49).

Fearing for his life, then, Adonijah seeks temporary asylum in the sanctuary: He "went and grasped the horns of the altar" (v. 50). The "horns of the altar" refers to the four horn-like protuberances at the four corners of the altar, on which sacrificial blood is smeared and atonement is symbolically effected (Exod 27:2; 29:12; 30:10; Lev 4:7; Ezek 43:20). Hence, the grasping of these horns came to signal an appeal for asylum. The prophet Amos would later threaten Israel that the horns of the altar at Bethel—one of two national sanctuaries of the northern kingdom—would be cut off (Amos 3:14), meaning that the Israelites would have no place to go when their pursuers sought their lives. The mere grasping of the horns of the altar does not, however, guarantee one safety forever (Exod 21:14). Adonijah has to secure Solomon's agreement, sealed by an oath, that Solomon would spare him. He refers to himself as Solomon's servant (v. 51) and pays homage to Solomon. But he is simply dismissed with the words, "Go to your house" (v. 53). Thus the story of Adonijah's *coup d'état* comes full circle, as Solomon agrees to spare him, but only if Adonijah behaves like a loyal citizen.

REFLECTIONS

The story in 1 Kings 1 may be read in different ways. It may be read as an ancient historical document. Insofar as it presents the characters "warts and all," it may be viewed as an attempt—despite the inevitability of its particular biases—to present a factual record of the past, an account so detailed that some have surmised that the author must have been an eyewitness in the Davidic court. Hence, the narrator has been characterized as an early historian writing "history for history's sake," a sort of Israelite forerunner of classical writers of history like Thucydides and Herodotus. The narrative may, at the same time, be read most readily as a political document, a (re)telling of the events primarily for propagandistic reasons—most commentators say to legitimize the reign of Solomon, to justify his elevation from among his brothers, and to praise the superiority of his reign over against that of David. Others argue that the narrative is part of a larger novella told and written primarily for entertainment. The text contains all the elements that make a good story: contrast of characters, dialogue, conflict, suspense, humor, irony, colorful details, and pathos. It is a fascinating account that sounds remarkably contemporary, with factional strifes among groups with different political views (conservative and liberal), from different branches of the armed forces, belonging to different religious factions, and having different agendas.

There is validity to each of the approaches to the chapter, and they are not mutually exclusive. The text is a historical narrative, written from a particular sociopolitical viewpoint probably for political purposes at first, and it is constructed aesthetically. These perspectives all seem rather obvious when one reads the chapter. What is not so immediately evident in the story itself, however, is its theological message. There is little suggestion of direct divine intervention in the text. There is no divine manifestation, no direct word from on high, not even communication from God delivered by a messenger. Indeed, God is not mentioned very frequently in the text, only in connection with oaths, whether putative or real (1:17, 29-30), and in a couple of blessing and prayer formulas (1:36-37, 47-48). The narrative seems more concerned with human plots, schemes, and machinations.

It is difficult to find moral lessons here. The pro-Solomonic narrator discredits Adonijah as overly ambitious, impatient, and divisive. With that assessment, one might readily agree. Adonijah cannot wait until the king has passed away or given his official word about the succession, but tries to seize power by turning to certain factions in the country. Yet, his opponents do not seem morally much more compelling. Bathsheba and Nathan conspire to deny Adonijah the throne and to win it for Solomon. One may even charge that they were taking advantage of David's senility and pride, apparently fabricating an oath that David was supposed to have made and casting aspersions on Adonijah. Through their manipulation of the aged king, Solomon is designated and publicly anointed as the successor to the throne. This outcome the narrator dares to put in theological terms: God's promise to David is being fulfilled (1:36-37, 47-48). The story is utterly scandalous.

Yet there is a subtle, even subliminal, message throughout the story.[9] Quietly conveyed in this very entertaining story is a conviction that the will of God is somehow being worked out behind all the scandals and human schemes. In the first place, the elevation of Solomon may be contrary to what people might expect. Adonijah was handsome, confident, and influential. He is just the kind of person whom we would choose to rule over us. He had become first in line to the throne. Had he waited a little while longer, one wonders, might he not have been properly enthroned? Adonijah, however, was self-willed and undisciplined. He tried to impose his will and achieve kingship in his own way. He tried to seize the throne for himself. History would not be dictated by human will, however. God's promise to David would not be fulfilled by the priority of birth or by personal ambition. God's promise would be fulfilled in God's own way, through one whom God had chosen for reasons that may not be revealed to humanity. This is what one learns, too, from other stories in the Bible. God's promise to Abraham, for example, would be fulfilled, not by Ishmael, who was born to Abraham by Hagar, nor by Eliezer, the Damascan slave whom Abraham had adopted. Rather, the promise would come only through Isaac, whom God had chosen (Genesis 12–22). Divine election is a mysterious thing.

In contrast to Adonijah, Solomon is elevated despite all human odds. He was not the obvious choice, according to the custom of primogeniture. Indeed, there is no reason given for the choice of Solomon, save the sense that it was the will of God. Through him the promise of God is somehow fulfilled. To be sure, others did plot and scheme on his behalf, but the narrative puts Solomon above the fray for the time being. Throughout the intrigues, Solomon remains a passive figure. Whereas Adonijah exalted himself, Solomon was exalted by others—and by God. That is the simple conclusion of the story: One who tries to elevate himself is brought down, but one who does nothing to promote himself is exalted. It is God's will that will be done, not the will of an ambitious prince.

The case the narrator makes for Solomon as David's heir is not a logically compelling one. There is still much that is ambiguous, even questionable. Still, the reader is implicitly given the choice: whether or not to concur with the judgment of those who confessed that God's will is somehow being worked out in human reality *despite,* and sometimes even *through,* human plots.

In the end, one must recognize that this is not a tale with a moral lesson. One is not asked to emulate any of the characters in the story—not a king like David, not a prophet like Nathan, not a queen like Bathsheba, not priests like Abiathar and Zadok, not even the blessed Solomon. It is, rather, a simple but memorable story, one that the modern reader may appreciate for no other gain but enjoyment. For one who comes to the text as Scripture, however, this captivating story is more than entertainment. It poses a peculiar dilemma of faith: Whether to believe that there is divine purpose behind, and despite, such scandalous events in history. The Bible

9. On the subliminal nature of the theological message, see S. E. McEvenue, "The Basis of Empire, A Study of the Succession Narrative," *Ex Auditu* 2 (1986) 34-45, esp. 41-45.

is full of such accounts of God's surprises: the exaltation of Jacob over his elder brother, Esau—indeed, through human duplicity and deceit; the election of an enslaved people over a powerful nation; the triumph of a small shepherd boy over a giant; the choice of David over his elder brothers; the birth of Solomon through David's marriage with Bathsheba following their adultery and his murder of her husband. One may even perceive this to be at the heart of the Bible: God's purpose is constantly worked out as history moves along and human beings scheme. But human plots cannot derail God's plan. Ambitious politicians cannot stand in the way: Their purposes, if contrary to God's, will only be thwarted; their actions, if consonant with the fulfillment of God's promises, will be allowed to take place, whether they know the full consequences or not (Acts 4:27-28). God's will is worked out even though human conspirators may have personal and political agendas in mind. For the narrator of 1 Kings, Solomon's succession is just part of the mysterious working out of God's eternal promise made to David (2 Sam 7:1-17).

For the Christian believer, the scandals that attend Solomon's succession to the throne of David is part of the gospel story—the good news that God comes to us through the very arena of human history, through ordinary human beings—sinners all (see Matt 1:1-17). The scandalous story of Solomon's succession is only part of a larger story of God's plan being worked out. The climax of this biblical (hi)story comes in the scandal of the gospel—the coming of Jesus, who is called "the son of David," despite the adverse circumstances attending his birth. It is this one, this son of David, whom God has ultimately exalted as king, and now he sits enthroned "at the right hand of the Majesty on high" (Heb 1:3). The subliminal message in 1 Kings 1 is that God is at work—despite the plots of Adonijah and his supporters and even through the wicked plots of Solomon's supporters. One who so believes may be prompted to respond with the narrator, in the words spoken by Benaiah: "Amen! May the LORD, the God of my lord the king, so ordain!" (v. 36). May God's will be done.

1 KINGS 2:1-46, SOLOMON CONSOLIDATES POWER

OVERVIEW

The preceding chapter ends with the elevation of Solomon to the throne of David and the simultaneous debasement of Adonijah. Some loose ends are still untied, however. Although Solomon has already been designated, anointed, and acclaimed "king," it is clear that David is still alive, suggesting that there was some sort of co-regency during the transition from one reign to the next. Moreover, Solomon had spared Adonijah, his brother and rival, only if Adonijah would show himself to be a "person of substance" (1:52; NRSV, NIV, "worthy man"). Despite the turn of events narrated in chap. 1, there is still some uncertainty about the future of the kingdom. Now, in this new literary unit, the reader will be told how that kingdom came to be consolidated under Solomon's rule.

1 Kings 2:1-12, Solomon's Kingship Is Firmly Established

NIV

2 When the time drew near for David to die, he gave a charge to Solomon his son.

[2]“I am about to go the way of all the earth,” he said. “So be strong, show yourself a man, [3]and observe what the LORD your God requires: Walk in his ways, and keep his decrees and commands, his laws and requirements, as written in the Law of Moses, so that you may prosper in all you do and wherever you go, [4]and that the LORD may keep his promise to me: ‘If your descendants watch how they live, and if they walk faithfully before me with all their heart and soul, you will never fail to have a man on the throne of Israel.’

[5]“Now you yourself know what Joab son of Zeruiah did to me—what he did to the two commanders of Israel's armies, Abner son of Ner and Amasa son of Jether. He killed them, shedding their blood in peacetime as if in battle, and with that blood stained the belt around his waist and the sandals on his feet. [6]Deal with him according to your wisdom, but do not let his gray head go down to the grave[a] in peace.

[7]“But show kindness to the sons of Barzillai of Gilead and let them be among those who eat at your table. They stood by me when I fled from your brother Absalom.

[8]“And remember, you have with you Shimei son of Gera, the Benjamite from Bahurim, who called down bitter curses on me the day I went to Mahanaim. When he came down to meet me at the Jordan, I swore to him by the LORD: ‘I will not put you to death by the sword.’ [9]But now, do not consider him innocent. You are a man of wisdom; you will know what to do to him. Bring his gray head down to the grave in blood.”

[10]Then David rested with his fathers and was buried in the City of David. [11]He had reigned forty years over Israel—seven years in Hebron and thirty-three in Jerusalem. [12]So Solomon sat on the throne of his father David, and his rule was firmly established.

a 6 Hebrew *Sheol*; also in verse 9

NRSV

2 When David's time to die drew near, he charged his son Solomon, saying: [2]“I am about to go the way of all the earth. Be strong, be courageous, [3]and keep the charge of the LORD your God, walking in his ways and keeping his statutes, his commandments, his ordinances, and his testimonies, as it is written in the law of Moses, so that you may prosper in all that you do and wherever you turn. [4]Then the LORD will establish his word that he spoke concerning me: ‘If your heirs take heed to their way, to walk before me in faithfulness with all their heart and with all their soul, there shall not fail you a successor on the throne of Israel.’

5“Moreover you know also what Joab son of Zeruiah did to me, how he dealt with the two commanders of the armies of Israel, Abner son of Ner, and Amasa son of Jether, whom he murdered, retaliating in time of peace for blood that had been shed in war, and putting the blood of war on the belt around his waist, and on the sandals on his feet. [6]Act therefore according to your wisdom, but do not let his gray head go down to Sheol in peace. [7]Deal loyally, however, with the sons of Barzillai the Gileadite, and let them be among those who eat at your table; for with such loyalty they met me when I fled from your brother Absalom. [8]There is also with you Shimei son of Gera, the Benjaminite from Bahurim, who cursed me with a terrible curse on the day when I went to Mahanaim; but when he came down to meet me at the Jordan, I swore to him by the LORD, ‘I will not put you to death with the sword.’ [9]Therefore do not hold him guiltless, for you are a wise man; you will know what you ought to do to him, and you must bring his gray head down with blood to Sheol.”

10Then David slept with his ancestors, and was buried in the city of David. [11]The time that David reigned over Israel was forty years; he reigned seven years in Hebron, and thirty-three years in Jerusalem. [12]So Solomon sat on the throne of his father David; and his kingdom was firmly established.

COMMENTARY

2:1-4. On his deathbed, David delivers his final testament in the form of instructions to his son and successor. The introduction of David's valedictory oration ("when the time drew near for David to die . . .") is reminiscent of the opening of the account of the patriarch Jacob/Israel's final testament in Gen 47:29–50:14: "when the time drew near for Israel to die . . ." (Gen 47:29). The antiquity of the latter tradition is suggested by the archaic language in Gen 49:1*b*-27, a poem that is widely regarded by Hebraists as being among the oldest in the Bible. It is possible, too, that the original core of David's final valediction may have been quite ancient, possibly going back to the Solomonic era. Certainly the genre of the final testament of the king is already well attested in the ancient Near East by the third millennium BCE, as is evident in the Egyptian *Instruction for King Merikare* (c. 2100 BCE) and the *Instruction of King Amenemhet I* (c. 1970 BCE).[10] Both are presented as pragmatic advice of a dying king to his successor on political survival.[11] Each was intended to legitimate the new king and justify the elimination of any opposition that may yet remain. In the light of the sapiential character of the Egyptian royal testaments, it is not amiss to note that Solomon is expected to show "wisdom" in his dealings with those who may be a threat to his rule (see vv. 6, 9).

Despite the formal and thematic analogies with the Egyptian royal testaments, however, one should not assume that the text in 1 Kings 2, as we have it, is from the united monarchy. Indeed, the hand of the deuteronomist is most readily evident in vv. 2-4, for the text is replete with deuteronomistic idioms and themes (see Introduction). First of all, valedictory orations are one of the hallmarks of deuteronomistic style. Thus, just as Moses (Deuteronomy 33), Joshua (Joshua 23), and Samuel (1 Samuel 12) all made farewell speeches exhorting faithfulness to the way of the Lord, so, too, David utters a final oration for posterity. In the *Instruction for King Merikare,* the new king is exhorted to be observant of the teachings of the ancestors, as they have been written and passed down. Similarly, Solomon is charged to be faithful to the legacy of Moses, here expressed in deuteronomistic terms (v. 3): "statutes" (חקות *ḥuqqôt*; NIV, "decrees"), "commandments" (מצות *miṣwōt*), "rules" (משפטים *mišpāṭîm*; NRSV, "ordinances"; NIV, "laws"), and "stipulations" (עדות *ʿēdôt*; NRSV, "testimonies"; NIV, "requirements"). All these are said to be "as written in the תורה (*tôrâ*) of Moses," referring here essentially to the materials in the book of Deuteronomy, the constitutive document for Israel's existence as a political entity.[12]

Moshe Weinfeld makes the astute observation that the editor has superimposed a deuteronomistic theology on the original royal testament, thereby subsuming the original (largely political) intention of the account to its own *theological* agenda.[13] This is part of the theological framework within which one is now meant to understand the account as a whole. The theologian affirms that God will keep the promise made to David (v. 4), no doubt referring to the promise of an ongoing dynasty in Nathan's oracle (2 Sam 7:12-16), with the proviso that the successors of David are unwaveringly faithful. Implicitly, then, Solomon's place in history will be judged by his faithfulness, or the lack thereof, to the Mosaic standards hereby reiterated through the authority of the founder of the dynasty.

2:5-9. As the narrative has it, it was David who ordered the pre-emptive moves against any threat to his successor's absolute hegemony. Solomon's violent expurgation of his rivals is thus justified as filial and proper obedience to the will of his father. This is the same perspective that one sees in the Egyptian royal testaments, essentially apologies for the successor to the throne; the

10. See M. Lichtheim, *Ancient Egyptian Literature,* 3 vols. (Berkeley: University of California Press, 1975) 1:97-109, 134-39.

11. See L. G. Perdue, "The Testament of David and Egyptian Royal Inscriptions," in W. W. Hallo et al., eds., *Scripture in Context II: More Essays on the Comparative Method* (Winona Lake, Ind.: Eisenbrauns, 1983) 79-96.

12. Both the NIV and the NRSV translate תורה (*tôrâ*) as "law," which, given the dominance of the later Pauline notion of "law," is unsatisfactory. The Hebrew word may be taken variously to mean "teaching," "instruction," "direction," or even, as S. D. McBride has suggested, "polity" or "constitution." See McBride, "The Polity of the Covenant People: The Book of Deuteronomy," *Int* 41 (1987) 229-44.

13. Moshe Weinfeld, *Deuteronomy and the Deuteronomic School* (Oxford: Clarendon, 1972) 11. This does not mean that the old document was pro-Solomonic, whereas the deuteronomistic perspective was anti-Solomonic. Rather, it means that the deuteronomistic editor has theologically reappropriated the original account.

Figure 1: Jerusalem at the Time of Solomon

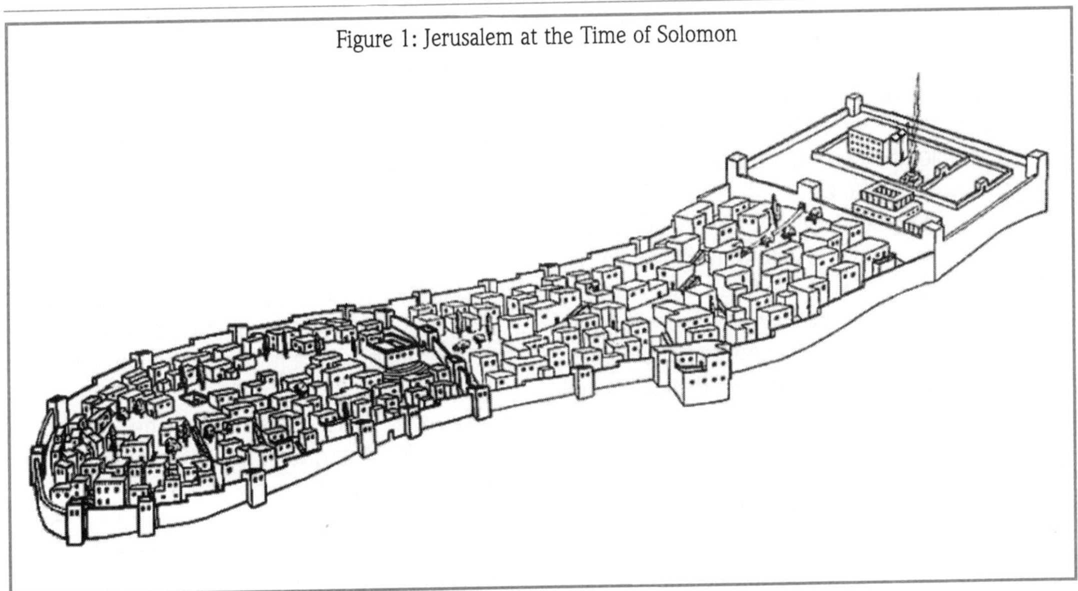

radical changes of the new king are legitimated in the name of his predecessor.

First, David orders the extermination of Joab, the commander of Adonijah's military forces. The basis for this sentence is Joab's previous actions against two military officers Abner and Amasa, both of whom Joab had killed. The incidents in question are reported in 2 Sam 3:6-39 and 20:4-10. Abner was a commander in Saul's army when David battled the house of Saul. But Abner later negotiated with David to defect, promising to rally support for him. David granted Abner safe passage, and Joab was specifically informed (2 Sam 3:21-23). Still, Joab murdered Abner to avenge his brother, whom Abner had actually killed in self-defense (2 Sam 2:18-23; 3:37). In consequence, Joab is said to have brought blood guilt upon David's house (see 1 Kgs 2:31). Hence, David supposedly took personal offense, claiming that Joab "did it to me" (1 Kgs 2:5). One wonders, however, why David himself had not punished Joab all those years since that incident. Or was the pro-Solomonic apologist attributing to David the decision to eliminate Joab, who posed a threat to Solomon?[14] Whatever the original intention, the point in the text as we have it now seems to be that David is weak, but Solomon is strong and courageous—even as David in his last testament had urged him to be. In the account of Abner's murder in 2 Samuel 3, one learns of David's weakness and, in particular, his inability to deal decisively with "the sons of Zeruiah" (2 Sam 3:39). In contrast to David, Solomon will have the character to do the things that need to be done to secure the kingdom. He will deal appropriately with Joab, "the son of Zeruiah."

Amasa was a kinsman both of Joab (2 Sam 17:25) and of David (2 Sam 19:13). He was appointed by Absalom in place of Joab as commander of the army during Absalom's rebellion against David. Although retained by David as an officer in the Judean army after the rebellion had been quelled, Amasa was later treacherously and brutally murdered by his rival, Joab (2 Sam 20:4-10). The precise point that is being made about the murder of Amasa in David's last testament, however, is unclear. The Hebrew text itself is uncertain. All one knows is that Joab's murder of Amasa is in view and, since Amasa was retained as an officer by David, Joab's offense supposedly injured David. One wonders, again, if the pro-Solomonic apologist was attempting to exonerate Solomon from the execution of Joab or if the point is that Solomon is truly bolder and stronger than David was.

On account of his "wisdom," Solomon is expected to dispose of Joab properly (v. 6). The Hebrew word חכמה (*ḥokmâ*), translated as "wisdom" (true also of the related Hebrew adjective for "wise" and the verb "to be wise") is used

14. Cf. the insistence in 2 Sam 3:28 that David and his kingdom are *not* guilty for the blood of Abner, shed by Joab.

much more broadly than the English implies. It may be used of any skill one may have, including skill in magic, divination, interpretation of dreams, handicrafts, social etiquette, sailing, military maneuvers, diplomacy, political craft, survival instincts, or even duplicity (2 Sam 13:3) and wickedness in general (Jer 4:22). In Solomon's case, "wisdom" should enable him to handle the delicate political crisis at hand. In the Egyptian royal testaments, too, the king is expected to be a "wise" person who knows how to handle those surrounding him, neutralizing his adversaries and rewarding his allies.

In contrast to the retaliatory measure that Solomon is to take against Joab, the descendants of Barzillai the Gileadite are to be "among those who eat at [the king's] table," meaning that they are to be pensioned by the government. This is a dubious honor, for those who "eat at the king's table" are often so privileged in order that they may be kept under surveillance (2 Sam 9:7, 13; 1 Kgs 18:19; 2 Kgs 25:29 = Jer 52:33). The expressed basis for this decision is the help that David received from Barzillai when he was fleeing from Absalom. In return for the hospitality and assistance that he received (2 Sam 17:27-29), David later offered Barzillai permanent residence in Jerusalem. The latter declined, citing his old age, and sent his son to take his place (2 Sam 19:31-40). Now Solomon is to continue keeping the family in Jerusalem through the government's largess.

The wealthy Barzillai (2 Sam 19:32), whose name is derived from the word for "iron" (ברזל *barzel*), probably made his fortune in the iron business. The region of ancient Gilead was rich in iron ores, and archaeologists have uncovered evidence of an extensive and technologically advanced iron industry at the end of the second millennium BCE at various sites in that region, in present-day Jordan. Mahanaim, the Gileadite administrative center where David had met Barzillai, has, in fact, been convincingly identified with iron-rich Telul edh-Dhahab. One may speculate, therefore, that the king's interest in securing the presence of the Barzillai family in Jerusalem may have arisen not simply out of gratitude for the earlier hospitality of the Gileadite. There may have been pecuniary and strategic motivations as well. Iron was the metal of choice in the production of military materiel in that period, and success in warfare depended on knowledge of iron technology, as the Israelites had learned in their earlier wars with the Philistines (1 Sam 13:19-22).

As David was on his way to Mahanaim, he was confronted by a Benjaminite kinsman of Saul, Shimei the son of Gera, who cursed David grievously (v. 8; see 2 Sam 16:5-13). On his way back to Jerusalem, however, the victorious David was met again by Shimei, now apologetic and thoroughly obsequious, although not insignificantly backed by a force of a thousand. Thereupon, perhaps to gain the loyalty of Shimei's Benjaminite kinfolks at a time when his own power had not yet been consolidated, David swore that Shimei's life would be spared (2 Sam 19:16-23). It is peculiar, therefore, that David should now include vengeance on Shimei in his last testament, contrary to his reported earlier belief that Shimei had cursed him because God had asked him to do so (2 Sam 16:11), as well as his own oath to spare him.[15] At least, the pro-Solomonic apologist would have the reader believe that it was David who told Solomon to punish Shimei. Solomon is supposed to handle the situation with the shrewdness ("wisdom") that is expected of him as king (v. 9).

2:10-12. A concluding regnal summary marks the transition between the reign of David and the reign of Solomon. Similar formulae are found throughout the book of Kings (so, e.g., 1 Kgs 11:41-43; 14:19-20, 29-31; 15:23-24, 31-32). This is an editorial device used by the Deuteronomist in his periodization of monarchical history. Here, the editor notes that David "rested with his ancestors," a formula certifying the peaceful passing of the king. Also noted in the regnal summary is the length of David's reign, rounded to forty years—seven years in Hebron and thirty-three in Jerusalem (cf. 2 Sam 5:4-5).

The establishment of Solomon as the successor to David is verified through David's charge to him (so 2:1-12). There may be a slight nuance in the Hebrew of v. 12*b* as opposed to v. 46*b,* an

15. If the record in 2 Sam 19:23[24] is accurate, David made a general promise to spare Shimei's life: "You shall not die!" In David's last testament, however, the promise is stated much more narrowly: "*I* [David] will not put you to death *by the sword*" (italics added). So Shimei's death by some other person or by some other means would still be a fulfillment of the "original" promise.

indication of progression in the story that is lost in the translation of NRSV: Solomon's *kingship* (מלכות *malkût*) is firmly established (v. 12), and then the *kingdom* (ממלכה *mamlākâ*) was established in his power. (See Reflections at 2:13-16.)

1 Kings 2:13-46, The Kingdom Is Consolidated Under Solomon

NIV

13Now Adonijah, the son of Haggith, went to Bathsheba, Solomon's mother. Bathsheba asked him, "Do you come peacefully?"

He answered, "Yes, peacefully." 14Then he added, "I have something to say to you."

"You may say it," she replied.

15"As you know," he said, "the kingdom was mine. All Israel looked to me as their king. But things changed, and the kingdom has gone to my brother; for it has come to him from the LORD. 16Now I have one request to make of you. Do not refuse me."

"You may make it," she said.

17So he continued, "Please ask King Solomon—he will not refuse you—to give me Abishag the Shunammite as my wife."

18"Very well," Bathsheba replied, "I will speak to the king for you."

19When Bathsheba went to King Solomon to speak to him for Adonijah, the king stood up to meet her, bowed down to her and sat down on his throne. He had a throne brought for the king's mother, and she sat down at his right hand.

20"I have one small request to make of you," she said. "Do not refuse me."

The king replied, "Make it, my mother; I will not refuse you."

21So she said, "Let Abishag the Shunammite be given in marriage to your brother Adonijah."

22King Solomon answered his mother, "Why do you request Abishag the Shunammite for Adonijah? You might as well request the kingdom for him—after all, he is my older brother—yes, for him and for Abiathar the priest and Joab son of Zeruiah!"

23Then King Solomon swore by the LORD: "May God deal with me, be it ever so severely, if Adonijah does not pay with his life for this request! 24And now, as surely as the LORD lives—he who has established me securely on the throne of my father David and has founded a dynasty for

NRSV

13Then Adonijah son of Haggith came to Bathsheba, Solomon's mother. She asked, "Do you come peaceably?" He said, "Peaceably." 14Then he said, "May I have a word with you?" She said, "Go on." 15He said, "You know that the kingdom was mine, and that all Israel expected me to reign; however, the kingdom has turned about and become my brother's, for it was his from the LORD. 16And now I have one request to make of you; do not refuse me." She said to him, "Go on." 17He said, "Please ask King Solomon—he will not refuse you—to give me Abishag the Shunammite as my wife." 18Bathsheba said, "Very well; I will speak to the king on your behalf."

19So Bathsheba went to King Solomon, to speak to him on behalf of Adonijah. The king rose to meet her, and bowed down to her; then he sat on his throne, and had a throne brought for the king's mother, and she sat on his right. 20Then she said, "I have one small request to make of you; do not refuse me." And the king said to her, "Make your request, my mother; for I will not refuse you." 21She said, "Let Abishag the Shunammite be given to your brother Adonijah as his wife." 22King Solomon answered his mother, "And why do you ask Abishag the Shunammite for Adonijah? Ask for him the kingdom as well! For he is my elder brother; ask not only for him but also for the priest Abiathar and for Joab son of Zeruiah!" 23Then King Solomon swore by the LORD, "So may God do to me, and more also, for Adonijah has devised this scheme at the risk of his life! 24Now therefore as the LORD lives, who has established me and placed me on the throne of my father David, and who has made me a house as he promised, today Adonijah shall be put to death." 25So King Solomon sent Benaiah son of Jehoiada; he struck him down, and he died.

26The king said to the priest Abiathar, "Go to Anathoth, to your estate; for you deserve death. But I will not at this time put you to death,

NIV

me as he promised—Adonijah shall be put to death today!" [25]So King Solomon gave orders to Benaiah son of Jehoiada, and he struck down Adonijah and he died.

[26]To Abiathar the priest the king said, "Go back to your fields in Anathoth. You deserve to die, but I will not put you to death now, because you carried the ark of the Sovereign LORD before my father David and shared all my father's hardships." [27]So Solomon removed Abiathar from the priesthood of the LORD, fulfilling the word the LORD had spoken at Shiloh about the house of Eli.

[28]When the news reached Joab, who had conspired with Adonijah though not with Absalom, he fled to the tent of the LORD and took hold of the horns of the altar. [29]King Solomon was told that Joab had fled to the tent of the LORD and was beside the altar. Then Solomon ordered Benaiah son of Jehoiada, "Go, strike him down!"

[30]So Benaiah entered the tent of the LORD and said to Joab, "The king says, 'Come out!'"

But he answered, "No, I will die here."

Benaiah reported to the king, "This is how Joab answered me."

[31]Then the king commanded Benaiah, "Do as he says. Strike him down and bury him, and so clear me and my father's house of the guilt of the innocent blood that Joab shed. [32]The LORD will repay him for the blood he shed, because without the knowledge of my father David he attacked two men and killed them with the sword. Both of them—Abner son of Ner, commander of Israel's army, and Amasa son of Jether, commander of Judah's army—were better men and more upright than he. [33]May the guilt of their blood rest on the head of Joab and his descendants forever. But on David and his descendants, his house and his throne, may there be the LORD's peace forever."

[34]So Benaiah son of Jehoiada went up and struck down Joab and killed him, and he was buried on his own land[a] in the desert. [35]The king put Benaiah son of Jehoiada over the army in Joab's position and replaced Abiathar with Zadok the priest.

[36]Then the king sent for Shimei and said to him, "Build yourself a house in Jerusalem and live

[a] 34 Or *buried in his tomb*

NRSV

because you carried the ark of the Lord GOD before my father David, and because you shared in all the hardships my father endured." [27]So Solomon banished Abiathar from being priest to the LORD, thus fulfilling the word of the LORD that he had spoken concerning the house of Eli in Shiloh.

28When the news came to Joab—for Joab had supported Adonijah though he had not supported Absalom—Joab fled to the tent of the LORD and grasped the horns of the altar. [29]When it was told King Solomon, "Joab has fled to the tent of the LORD and now is beside the altar," Solomon sent Benaiah son of Jehoiada, saying, "Go, strike him down." [30]So Benaiah came to the tent of the LORD and said to him, "The king commands, 'Come out.'" But he said, "No, I will die here." Then Benaiah brought the king word again, saying, "Thus said Joab, and thus he answered me." [31]The king replied to him, "Do as he has said, strike him down and bury him; and thus take away from me and from my father's house the guilt for the blood that Joab shed without cause. [32]The LORD will bring back his bloody deeds on his own head, because, without the knowledge of my father David, he attacked and killed with the sword two men more righteous and better than himself, Abner son of Ner, commander of the army of Israel, and Amasa son of Jether, commander of the army of Judah. [33]So shall their blood come back on the head of Joab and on the head of his descendants forever; but to David, and to his descendants, and to his house, and to his throne, there shall be peace from the LORD forevermore." [34]Then Benaiah son of Jehoiada went up and struck him down and killed him; and he was buried at his own house near the wilderness. [35]The king put Benaiah son of Jehoiada over the army in his place, and the king put the priest Zadok in the place of Abiathar.

36Then the king sent and summoned Shimei, and said to him, "Build yourself a house in Jerusalem, and live there, and do not go out from there to any place whatever. [37]For on the day you go out, and cross the Wadi Kidron, know for certain that you shall die; your blood shall be on your own head." [38]And Shimei said to the king, "The sentence is fair; as my lord the king has

NIV

there, but do not go anywhere else. [37]The day you leave and cross the Kidron Valley, you can be sure you will die; your blood will be on your own head."

[38]Shimei answered the king, "What you say is good. Your servant will do as my lord the king has said." And Shimei stayed in Jerusalem for a long time.

[39]But three years later, two of Shimei's slaves ran off to Achish son of Maacah, king of Gath, and Shimei was told, "Your slaves are in Gath." [40]At this, he saddled his donkey and went to Achish at Gath in search of his slaves. So Shimei went away and brought the slaves back from Gath.

[41]When Solomon was told that Shimei had gone from Jerusalem to Gath and had returned, [42]the king summoned Shimei and said to him, "Did I not make you swear by the LORD and warn you, 'On the day you leave to go anywhere else, you can be sure you will die'? At that time you said to me, 'What you say is good. I will obey.' [43]Why then did you not keep your oath to the LORD and obey the command I gave you?"

[44]The king also said to Shimei, "You know in your heart all the wrong you did to my father David. Now the LORD will repay you for your wrongdoing. [45]But King Solomon will be blessed, and David's throne will remain secure before the LORD forever."

[46]Then the king gave the order to Benaiah son of Jehoiada, and he went out and struck Shimei down and killed him. The kingdom was now firmly established in Solomon's hands.

NRSV

said, so will your servant do." So Shimei lived in Jerusalem many days.

39But it happened at the end of three years that two of Shimei's slaves ran away to King Achish son of Maacah of Gath. When it was told Shimei, "Your slaves are in Gath," [40]Shimei arose and saddled a donkey, and went to Achish in Gath, to search for his slaves; Shimei went and brought his slaves from Gath. [41]When Solomon was told that Shimei had gone from Jerusalem to Gath and returned, [42]the king sent and summoned Shimei, and said to him, "Did I not make you swear by the LORD, and solemnly adjure you, saying, 'Know for certain that on the day you go out and go to any place whatever, you shall die'? And you said to me, 'The sentence is fair; I accept.' [43]Why then have you not kept your oath to the LORD and the commandment with which I charged you?" [44]The king also said to Shimei, "You know in your own heart all the evil that you did to my father David; so the LORD will bring back your evil on your own head. [45]But King Solomon shall be blessed, and the throne of David shall be established before the LORD forever." [46]Then the king commanded Benaiah son of Jehoiada; and he went out and struck him down, and he died.

So the kingdom was established in the hand of Solomon.

COMMENTARY

Despite David's final testament and the accession of Solomon to the throne, the latter's kingship having been "firmly established" (v. 12*b*), the narrator now calls attention to various threats that remain within the kingdom.

2:13-25. Adonijah, the deposed heir apparent and the chief contender for the throne, is still around. Highlighting the blood rivalry between the two brothers, the narrator refers to the former as "the son of Haggith," whereas Solomon is identified with his mother, Bathsheba. Adonijah comes to Bathsheba with a proposition that is apparently so delicate and audacious that he dares not broach it with Solomon directly. Bathsheba seems, once again, to be a conduit for the dangerous petitions of men—first of Nathan before David (1:11-27), and now of Adonijah before Solomon (vv. 13-18).

Adonijah and Bathsheba encounter each other ever so cautiously. Despite the successful enthronement of her son, she continues to be suspicious of Adonijah, the son of Haggith. In their conversation, Adonijah manages to slip in his own view that the kingdom was his to begin with and that all Israel had fully expected him to be king (v. 15), a gross exaggeration at best. He concedes, though, that there has been a turnaround in the matter and that this happened because the kingdom was meant by the Lord for his younger brother. Only in his final turn of the conversation does Adonijah state his "one request": that Abishag the Shunammite be given to him for a wife. She is, of course, the beautiful young virgin who was brought to David to lie in his bosom.

Bathsheba promises to speak to the king, although what she says may be double-edged. She does not say that she will relay the petition itself to the king, but that she will speak to Solomon "about you" (עליך *ʿāleykā*). Accordingly, she comes to the royal court and speaks to Solomon "about" Adonijah. In her mouth, Adonijah's "one request" (v. 16) becomes "one small request" (v. 20). One cannot tell if the characterization of the request as a small one is intended to suggest that Bathsheba actually sees no harm in granting it or if she means it ironically. One also cannot be sure if her reference to Adonijah as "your brother" (v. 21) is intended as an argument in favor of the petition or if it is meant to signal the danger of it. Solomon certainly does not take the matter lightly; it is not just "one small request" to him. He recognizes, too, that Adonijah is not just a brother but, indeed, his *elder* brother (v. 22). Despite the propriety of Solomon's etiquette before the queen mother, and his initial assurance to her that he will not reject her request, he is thoroughly indignant. "Ask for him the kingdom also," he retorts, betraying a sense of insecurity over his domain.

Behind Solomon's paranoia is, perhaps, the notion that a king's harem may become a trophy for his challenger or successor. So David, having succeeded Saul, is said to have been given "your master's house and your master's wives into your bosom" (2 Sam 12:8). By the same token, because of David's own illicit affair with Bathsheba, Nathan predicted that God would bring about a tragedy in David's house and give his wives to someone else (2 Sam 12:11). One thinks, too, of Ishbaal's accusation that Abner was trying to take one of Saul's concubines, a charge tantamount to treason, to which Abner responded in rage (2 Sam 3:6-11). Most poignantly, when Absalom was rebelling against David, he was counseled by Ahitophel, his shrewd adviser: "Have intercourse with your father's concubines, whom he has left to keep the house, and all Israel will hear that you have become odious to your father, and all your supporters will be encouraged" (2 Sam 16:20-21).[16]

Moreover, Adonijah has the support of two influential Judean officials, Abiathar the priest and Joab the military commander.[17] Both of them are supported by the free elements in the kingdom, whereas Zadok and Benaiah are feudal retainers appointed by the authoritarian power of the king.

Solomon swears in the name of the Lord and invokes the Lord's promise to David (yet another allusion to Nathan's oracle, 2 Samuel 7), promising that Adonijah will be put to death for his conduct. The reader is supposed to remember at this point that Adonijah was earlier spared his life only on condition of his loyalty (1:52). But now the deal is off, his present quest being evidence to Solomon that Adonijah is not "a person of substance," after all. So Solomon sends Benaiah, his hatchet man, to kill Adonijah, thus putting an end to whatever claims his brother may have had to the throne. Whereas David had been weak and indulgent to Adonijah (1:5), Solomon is strong and acts boldly.

The narrator leaves many questions unanswered in this story. Is Adonijah a hopeless "romantic," who naively believes that Abishag is legitimately available to him because her relationship with David was never consummated? Or has he really been exposed as a desperate and deceitful manipulator, trying to use two women (Abishag and Bathsheba) to achieve his political ambition? Is Adonijah's concession of defeat (v. 15*b*) merely a sinister ploy verbalized only to get

16. On the political implications of the marriage of royal consorts in these texts, see M. Tsevat, "Marriage and Monarchical Legitimacy in Ugarit and Israel," *JSS* 3 (1958) 237-43.

17. The Hebrew has, literally, "and for him and for Abiathar the priest and for Joab the son of Zeruiah," a reading adopted by the NRSV and the NIV. That is possibly corrupt, however. One should read with other ancient versions, with only a slight emendation of the Hebrew: "and for him is Abiathar the priest and for him is Joab the son of Zeruiah." The point is that they are on his side. For the idiom, see Exod 32:26; Josh 5:13; 2 Kgs 10:6.

what he really wants? Or does his action reflect a genuine, if bitter, recognition that the kingdom is truly beyond him now and only a consolation prize is possible? Is Bathsheba merely a nice old woman who is easily manipulated? Or is she coldly calculating and shrewder than she seems at first blush? Does she, in fact, know her son so well that she could anticipate his reaction and the dire consequences for Adonijah and, possibly, also for young and lovely Abishag? What about Abishag's role? Is she merely a pawn, the silent object of other people's schemes? Is Solomon so astute that he sees through the true (political) agenda of Adonijah? Or is he merely paranoid or, even worse, wicked in using Adonijah's innocent, if unwise, request as a pretext to eliminate his brother? Whatever the truth, the outcome is a death sentence for Adonijah, and Solomon justifies it as the fulfillment of God's promise that he himself will be the heir to David's throne.

2:26-46. Having already mentioned the threat posed by Abiathar and Joab (v. 22), the narrator proceeds to explain how they are also neutralized. The priest is exiled to his estate in the Benjaminite town of Anathoth, three and a half miles northeast of Jerusalem. Unlike all the others who are punished, no charge is explicitly leveled against Abiathar; the only reason why he is sentenced, one gathers, is his complicity in the anti-Solomon conspiracy; this is implied in v. 22. Abiathar deserves death, but extenuating circumstances are cited for the supposed leniency of his sentence: He had carried the ark before David and had shared in David's afflictions (v. 26). During the rebellion of Absalom, Abiathar was with Zadok and the Levites in carrying the ark back into Jerusalem (2 Sam 15:24-29), the ark having presumably been brought out of the city when David fled. This is probably the incident that the narrator has in mind when he links the carrying of the ark with David's hardships (cf. Ps 132:1).

The narrator notes that the rustification of Abiathar fulfills an oracle against the priestly family of Eli in Shiloh (v. 27; see 1 Sam 2:27-36).[18] Abiathar is thus identified with the old guard associated with the shrine at Shiloh, the central sanctuary of the tribal confederacy before the construction of the Temple in Jerusalem. The way is now clear for the elevation of Zadok as the sole high priest in Jerusalem (v. 35), and his descendants will control the Jerusalem Temple continuously until the end of the monarchy. These two priests are representatives of two traditions of divine dwelling: Abiathar stood for the tent-shrine in Shiloh, and Zadok, in time, the Jerusalem Temple. Now the latter is promoted at the expense of the former. In the light of this background, it is interesting to note that the prophet Jeremiah, who was born of a priestly family in Anathoth, would appear centuries later, delivering scathing critiques of the Temple and its establishment (Jer 3:16-17; 7:1-15; 26:1-6).

The next target in Solomon's purge is Joab, the chief military commander who had supported Adonijah (v. 28). The news of Solomon's intention comes to the general, "because Joab had supported Adonijah and had not supported Absalom" (v. 28). Taken at face value, the Hebrew suggests that Joab receives the news *because* he has supported Adonijah (the heir apparent to the throne of David), but he has not supported Absalom, who had rebelled against David. That is, Joab is a Davidide loyalist through and through and, as such, is a beneficiary of the pro-Adonijah underground network.[19] Thus forewarned, he flees. Like his patron, Adonijah, he seeks asylum by coming to the tent of the Lord and grasping the horns of the altar (see Commentary on 1:50).

Given Adonijah's experience, Joab must surely expect no more than temporary reprieve. Even so, he refuses to leave the sanctuary and apparently gets away with it for a while. Benaiah, who is sent after him, dares not pursue him into the sanctuary but reports the standoff to Solomon. In effect, Joab dares Solomon and his hatchet man, Benaiah, to violate the law of sanctuary: If anyone wants to kill him, it will have to be there, right by the altar in the sanctuary! The fact that Benaiah has to try to get Joab to leave the sanctuary first suggests that Joab probably has a case. Nonetheless, Solomon orders the execution, citing not so much Joab's disloyalty or his political affiliation (v. 22), for which asylum in the sanctuary is provided

18. Abiathar's father was Ahimelech (1 Sam 30:7), one of the priests of Nob and a son Ahitub (1 Sam 22:9), the brother of Ichabod, the grandson of Eli (1 Sam 14:3).

19. So Jerome T. Walsh, *1 Kings*, Berit Olam (Collegeville, Minn.: Liturgical Press, 1996) 57.

for by law, but his murder of Abner and Amasa, the intentional and treacherous nature of which annuls any right of refuge (Exod 21:12-14). On this pretext, which is already set forth in the last testament of David, Joab is killed. Solomon goes to great lengths to place the guilt squarely on the head of Joab, emphasizing that, while Joab had killed Abner and Amasa treacherously, David had not known of it and is, therefore, not complicitous. Hence, David and his successors are free from guilt for putting Joab to death, even death in the sanctuary. Accordingly, even as Zadok becomes the sole high priest, taking over the position of Abiathar, Benaiah is appointed the commander in chief, taking over the position of his rival. Adonijah and his most important allies (1:7) have all been eliminated.

Besides the two principal supporters of Adonijah, the narrator accounts for the elimination of Shimei, who embodies the threat of Saulide loyalists, notably the Benjaminites.[20] Shimei is put under house arrest in Jerusalem and, on pain of death, forbidden to leave the Kidron Valley, east of Jerusalem. He accepts the conditions and does in fact live in Jerusalem for some time. The restriction given to Shimei, a Benjaminite from Bahurim, was no doubt to undermine his influence at home,[21] the actual weakening of which is evident in the escape of two of his slaves to Gath, one of the five principal Philistine cities. Gath is the Philistine city closest to the territory of Davidic Judah (1 Sam 17:52). The narrator notes that the slaves had escaped to "Achish, the son of Maacah, king of Gath," thus emphasizing that they are in Philistine domain. Solomon apparently does not even know of Shimei's trip until after he returns to Jerusalem. One can only speculate as to what must have been in Shimei's mind—whether he had flagrantly violated the letter of the law but not the spirit of it, as one might say. The elaborative restriction of the house arrest stipulates the Kidron Valley as the limit. That stipulation, however, might have been interpreted by Shimei to mean that Gath, which lies west of Jerusalem, was actually permissible to visit. What is clear is that he was already beyond Solomon's orbit, having reached Philistine Gath. He returns in any case. But Solomon interprets the restriction narrowly and claims to have made Shimei take a sacred oath and that the penalty for going anywhere at all from Jerusalem is death. Such details, curiously enough, are not found in the account of their agreement earlier in the passage; no oath is mentioned, and the death penalty is stipulated only for crossing the Kidron Valley, not for leaving Jerusalem per se. In fact, Shimei did not cross the Kidron, for the valley is to the east of Jerusalem, whereas Philistine Gath is to the west. It is, perhaps, in recognition of the disputable nature of the accusation that Solomon adds the charge of Shimei's offense against David long ago, a wrong that Shimei is supposed to know "in his own heart" (v. 44). Shimei must have denied the charge—that is with his lips—because Solomon accuses him of lying. The excuse for the execution of Shimei is flimsy at best, but the whole setup is precisely what one might expect, for David had expressed confidence that Solomon would know just what to do with that tricky situation, since he is a "wise" man. So Shimei is put to death, Solomon is blessed, and the kingdom is, finally, consolidated in his hand.

20. The possibility of a Benjaminite secession from the kingdom is evidenced earlier in the revolt of Sheba (2 Samuel 20).

21. This is evident in the specific prohibition for leaving the Kidron Valley, which provides access to Bahurim, where Shimei has his ancestral home.

REFLECTIONS

This passage of Scripture has come to us through a long process of transmission, the details of which are still elusive, perhaps irrecoverably so. From a moral viewpoint, the passage is difficult to appropriate. Herein one finds attitudes and actions that are utterly deplorable. We see examples of human cunning, vindictiveness, pettiness, insecurity, and sheer dishonesty. David and Solomon, God's anointed ones, are just as guilty of questionable ethics as are the others—if not more so. They are no role models for righteous conduct, except in negative ways. One might attempt a defense of their conduct in the light of ancient Near Eastern cultures, arguing that their actions sprang from culturally specific and antiquated attitudes about the power of curses, the abiding consequences of blood guilt, and the like. Still, the text remains morally problematic in the light of the totality of Scripture's teachings about right relationships among human beings.

The text "will not preach," if its primary message is ethics. When one discerns its deeper theological message, however, this passage of Scripture offers rich lessons. One may begin with the precedent set by the deuteronomistic editor-narrator, who wrestles theologically with history. David's charge to Solomon is couched in deuteronomistic idioms: Courageous and uncompromising obedience to the way of the Lord is the king's obligation (2:2-3). No doubt, for the deuteronomist, the actions of Solomon are to be judged according to this requirement of obedience to the will of God, as written in the Torah of Moses.

One might argue that the narrator is glossing over the ruthless pragmatism of ancient politicians by recourse to the language of Torah piety. That is to say, the narrator considers Solomon's unscrupulous elimination of his adversaries to be in accordance with the manifestation of courageous and uncompromising obedience. Indeed, just as Moses had charged Israel and Joshua to "be strong and courageous" in following the way of the Lord (Deut 31:1-6; Josh 1:1-9), a charge that mandated the extermination of all those who opposed Israel's possession of the promised land, so also David charges Solomon to be "strong and courageous" (2:2), a charge that is taken to mean the elimination of every threat to the fulfillment of God's promise. In an earlier period, the nations that opposed Israel's taking of God's gift of the land were defeated, and only those who did not stand in their way were spared. Now, similarly, the individuals who opposed Solomon are neutralized, while benefactors of the government are treated well. Just as God's promise of the land brooks no compromise, so, too, God's promise of succession in the Davidic kingdom brooks no compromise. Solomon did whatever it took to bring about God's promise.

That is surely not what we are to get out of the text, however. Indeed, in the light of the rest of Scripture, Solomon's actions—even if politically and legally justifiable—are morally reprehensible. It is significant that the narrator quotes Nathan's oracle, where the promise of God to David is, ironically, *unconditional* (2 Sam 7:12-16); the enduring character of the Davidic dynasty is ensured by unilateral divine decision. We see profound theology at work here. The unconditionality of promise, as we know it in Nathan's oracle, is now *conditioned* by a demand for faithfulness, introduced by the conditional particle "if": *"If* your descendants take heed to their way, to walk before me in faithfulness with all their heart and with all their being, [then] there shall not fail you a person for the throne of Israel" (2:4).

The narrator-editor insists on obedience to the Torah, and that is what we must proclaim. At the same time, however, the modern reader must ask what it means to be faithful in our time. In other words, one may accept the theological mandate of the text without necessarily agreeing with the culturally conditioned application of it. The text highlights the importance of obedience. At the same time, however, it indicates how people might use the letter of the Torah to realize their personal ambition and to justify their fundamentally unscrupulous actions. The Christian believer has to honor the "letter of the law" in ways that are always true to the "spirit of the law," as it were (see 2 Cor 3:4-18).

There is, indeed, tension and ambiguity throughout the narrative. On the one hand, one detects a certain inevitability in the accession of Solomon, for the Lord has willed the succession to be just so (see 2:15, 24). All this happens in fulfillment of God's promise. On the other hand, Solomon has to be uncompromisingly faithful to the way of the Lord in order that the promise might be fulfilled. As the narrative has it, he tries to be true to the charge by guarding the house of David against the blood guilt, curses, and disloyalties that threaten it. The tension is never resolved.

Here one encounters two seemingly irreconcilable truths about the relationship between God and people. On the one hand, there is faith in the sovereignty of God to bring about the divine will apart from human decisions and despite human failures. On the other hand, there is the insistence upon unwavering faithfulness to God's way. It is a dialectic of the absolute control of God in history as one pole, and the freedom of the human will to respond or not to respond to God as the other. That is a dialectic that persists even today in various theologies within the communities of faith, with some traditions emphasizing the absolute sovereignty of God to bring about the divine will despite human responses or lack thereof and others stressing the divinely granted freedom of humanity to respond or refuse to respond to God. But both theological realities—of God's sovereignty and human freedom—must be preserved, as they are in this passage of Scripture.

Even as the promise is relativized and made provisional by the condition of obedience, the limitations of human ability to be truly faithful are also relativized by the failures and mortality of humanity. God brings about the promise despite the questionable and presumptuous conduct of human beings.

It is, in fact, the deity who ensures that the succession is worked out as promised. This is the significance of the concluding regnal summary in 2:10-12. David dies, but history moves on inexorably to the inevitable end that God has determined. The kingdom of God is, indeed, guaranteed by God, and Solomon's enthronement is indisputably a result of divine intention. By God's will and, somehow, through the coincidence of human manipulation, the kingdom is established in the hand of Solomon. The promise of God transcends the historical presence and activities of David and Solomon. There is no letup on the demand of obedience, but the fulfillment of God's promise is not dependent on human will but on the will of God. Hence, even if mortals fail and behave as mortals only can, the will of God is nevertheless brought about.

In a similar manner, the death and burial of David are interpreted theologically in the New Testament. David's mortality only points to the transcendence of divine will, as manifested in the person of Jesus Christ (Acts 2:29; 13:36). The promise of God did not die with David. Nor would it die with Solomon. Rather, the promise of God lives on by the will of God.

1 KINGS 3:1-15, SOLOMON'S PRIORITIES AND HIS GIFTS FROM GOD

1 Kings 3:1-3, Solomon's Alliance with Egypt

NIV

3 Solomon made an alliance with Pharaoh king of Egypt and married his daughter. He brought her to the City of David until he finished building his palace and the temple of the LORD, and the wall around Jerusalem. [2]The people, however, were still sacrificing at the high places, because a temple had not yet been built for the Name of the LORD. [3]Solomon showed his love for the LORD by walking according to the statutes of his father David, except that he offered sacrifices and burned incense on the high places.

NRSV

3 Solomon made a marriage alliance with Pharaoh king of Egypt; he took Pharaoh's daughter and brought her into the city of David, until he had finished building his own house and the house of the LORD and the wall around Jerusalem. [2]The people were sacrificing at the high places, however, because no house had yet been built for the name of the LORD.

3Solomon loved the LORD, walking in the statutes of his father David; only, he sacrificed and offered incense at the high places.

COMMENTARY

This episode comes on the heels of Solomon's takeover from the now-deceased David. The new literary unit begins immediately with Solomon's marriage alliance with an unnamed king of Egypt, probably Pharaoh Siamun (c. 978–959 BCE). It was a diplomatic deal sealed by Egypt's cession of the newly conquered city of Gezer to Solomon as a dowry, according to the historical notation of 9:16. Politically, the marriage signaled Solomon's rise to prominence in the international arena. He was leading his tiny new nation into the realm of world-class diplomacy, and the ruler of the powerful Egyptian Empire had to come to terms with him, even giving the Egyptian princess to him. That was a remarkable achievement since, according to one of the Amarna letters, the Egyptians did not like to make such concessions on their part: "From time immemorial no daughter of the king of Egy[pt] is given to anyone."[22]

In terms of the overall agenda of the narrator, however, this alliance surely foreshadows problems in which Solomon and his kingdom would soon become embroiled. The narrator hints at this by mentioning the Temple of the Lord that is still to be built and the fact that the people were sacrificing at the "high places" (local cultic installations) because the Temple had not yet been built.[23] The narrative presents Solomon's marriage alliance with Egypt as the first of his acts after the kingdom was firmly established in his hand.

The Egyptian princess is brought into the City of David. Solomon apparently could not wait to bring her in, for he had not yet built his own palace and certainly not the Temple, which would have made possible the centralization of worship in Jerusalem according to the stipulations in Deuteronomy (Deut 12:13-14). The defense of the city, too, had been put off. The implication is that the consequent syncretism had compromised the security of the nation, so much so that no walls could ever shield it from destruction in the end.

The narrator no doubt intends the reader to come to the story with the Torah of Moses in mind. Thus the episode may be viewed against the backdrop of the deuteronomistic prohibition against marriages with foreigners, for such alliances would cause the people to turn away from following the Lord and, consequently, lead to destruction (Deut 7:3-4; Josh 23:11-13; 2 Kgs 8:18). It is probable, too, that one is to think of the warning in Deut 17:16, put in the mouth of Moses, that a king must not "cause the people to return to Egypt." Indeed, Israel's return to Egypt is an inevitable outcome of Solomon's action, and the division of the kingdom would be a prelude to its complete disintegration (see 11:26-40).

The Temple of the Lord in Jerusalem is said to be a temple (בית *bayit*; lit., "a house") built for "the name of the LORD" (v. 2). For the deuteronomist, the "name of the LORD" is a virtually independent entity that stands in place of the actual presence of the deity in the sanctuary (so NIV: "Name" rather than "name"). By recourse to the notion of the "Name" that represents God's presence, the theologian is able to associate the deity's presence with the sanctuary without ever implying that the deity is confined to that physical structure (see 8:27-30). The Temple is a place where God's name may be invoked, and so that presence may be brought about as and when God wills, but the Temple is not the house of God per se.

Solomon "loved the LORD," the editor tells us in characteristic deuteronomic language (Deut 6:5; 10:12; 30:16, 20), inasmuch as he was "walking in the statutes of David his father" (v. 3). Yet, that positive judgment seems to be tempered by the observation that he also offered sacrifices and burnt incense at the high places (v. 3*b*). Again, to the narrator, Solomon is setting a dangerous precedent. Indeed, by the end of the account of Solomon's reign, what is emphasized in the narrative is not his love of the Lord but his love of foreign women, the result of which was the syncretism that ultimately led to the destruction of the kingdom (see 11:1). (See Reflections at 3:4-15.)

22. Amarna letter no. 4, line 4, in W. L. Moran, trans., *The Amarna Letters* (Baltimore: Johns Hopkins University Press, 1997) 8. Although there are exceptions under certain conditions, the pharaoh's boast does reflect official Egyptian double standards in the practice of diplomatic marriage. The Egyptians typically demanded the hand of foreign princesses, but they themselves would not give up their princesses in such arrangements. The concession to Solomon indicates the weakness of Egypt and the strength of Israel in the 10th century BCE.

23. The NIV partially exonerates Solomon by introducing the word "still" (not in the Hebrew) before "sacrificing," thus placing the blame before Solomon's time; the people had already been worshiping at the high places and only continued to do so because of Solomon's negligence. The Hebrew may, in fact, be taken to mean that the people were sacrificing at the local high places precisely because of Solomon's delay in building the Temple.

1 Kings 3:4-15, God's Self-revelation and Gifts to Solomon

NIV

[4]The king went to Gibeon to offer sacrifices, for that was the most important high place, and Solomon offered a thousand burnt offerings on that altar. [5]At Gibeon the LORD appeared to Solomon during the night in a dream, and God said, "Ask for whatever you want me to give you."

[6]Solomon answered, "You have shown great kindness to your servant, my father David, because he was faithful to you and righteous and upright in heart. You have continued this great kindness to him and have given him a son to sit on his throne this very day.

[7]"Now, O LORD my God, you have made your servant king in place of my father David. But I am only a little child and do not know how to carry out my duties. [8]Your servant is here among the people you have chosen, a great people, too numerous to count or number. [9]So give your servant a discerning heart to govern your people and to distinguish between right and wrong. For who is able to govern this great people of yours?"

[10]The Lord was pleased that Solomon had asked for this. [11]So God said to him, "Since you have asked for this and not for long life or wealth for yourself, nor have asked for the death of your enemies but for discernment in administering justice, [12]I will do what you have asked. I will give you a wise and discerning heart, so that there will never have been anyone like you, nor will there ever be. [13]Moreover, I will give you what you have not asked for—both riches and honor—so that in your lifetime you will have no equal among kings. [14]And if you walk in my ways and obey my statutes and commands as David your father did, I will give you a long life." [15]Then Solomon awoke—and he realized it had been a dream.

He returned to Jerusalem, stood before the ark of the Lord's covenant and sacrificed burnt offerings and fellowship offerings.[a] Then he gave a feast for all his court.

[a] *15* Traditionally *peace offerings*

NRSV

[4]The king went to Gibeon to sacrifice there, for that was the principal high place; Solomon used to offer a thousand burnt offerings on that altar. [5]At Gibeon the LORD appeared to Solomon in a dream by night; and God said, "Ask what I should give you." [6]And Solomon said, "You have shown great and steadfast love to your servant my father David, because he walked before you in faithfulness, in righteousness, and in uprightness of heart toward you; and you have kept for him this great and steadfast love, and have given him a son to sit on his throne today. [7]And now, O LORD my God, you have made your servant king in place of my father David, although I am only a little child; I do not know how to go out or come in. [8]And your servant is in the midst of the people whom you have chosen, a great people, so numerous they cannot be numbered or counted. [9]Give your servant therefore an understanding mind to govern your people, able to discern between good and evil; for who can govern this your great people?"

10It pleased the Lord that Solomon had asked this. [11]God said to him, "Because you have asked this, and have not asked for yourself long life or riches, or for the life of your enemies, but have asked for yourself understanding to discern what is right, [12]I now do according to your word. Indeed I give you a wise and discerning mind; no one like you has been before you and no one like you shall arise after you. [13]I give you also what you have not asked, both riches and honor all your life; no other king shall compare with you. [14]If you will walk in my ways, keeping my statutes and my commandments, as your father David walked, then I will lengthen your life."

15Then Solomon awoke; it had been a dream. He came to Jerusalem where he stood before the ark of the covenant of the LORD. He offered up burnt offerings and offerings of well-being, and provided a feast for all his servants.

COMMENTARY

Solomon goes to sacrifice at Gibeon, a Benjaminite city, identified with the modern village of el-Jib, on a hill about seven miles northwest of Jerusalem. Gibeon is chosen because "that was the great high place" (NRSV, "that was the principal high place"; NIV, "that was the most important high place"), its reputation as a sacred location is corroborated by the chronicler, who portrays it as a place where "the tabernacle of the LORD" or "the tent of meeting of God" was (1 Chr 16:39; 21:29; 2 Chr 1:3, 6, 13). Yet, it is peculiar that Solomon should seek to worship at the high places or the particular one in Gibeon, for the ark, the very symbol of the Lord's presence, was in Jerusalem, as v. 15 confirms. He went to Gibeon to worship, even though the ark was already in Jerusalem! Solomon cannot be easily exonerated for having gone to that great high place.

The account of Solomon's encounter of God at Gibeon has been compared with other dream accounts in the ancient Near East, especially that of Tuth-mose IV of Egypt (c. 1421–1413 BCE), a dream in which the crown prince receives a divine promise of kingship.[24] As in the report of Tuth-Mose IV and a number of other royal dream accounts, this episode in the book of 1 Kings provides divine legitimation for the ruler in question. Not only does the very appearance of the deity confirm Solomon's favored position in this case, but it is also implied in the narrative that he is king of all Israel, both because he is the scion of David, as southern (Judean) dynastic ideology dictates, and because he is divinely endowed with charisma, as northern (Israelite) notions of leadership would have it.

Solomon's request is sometimes viewed as part of an ancient Near Eastern royal coronation ritual, where the king is given the privilege of a special petition to the deity (see the royal psalms, Pss 2:8; 20:4-6; 21:2). This is suggested by the litany-like reply of God (v. 11):

"Because you asked for yourself this thing,
 but you did not ask for yourself longevity,
 you did not ask for yourself wealth,
 you did not ask for yourself the life of your enemies,
but you ask for yourself discernment to hear what is just."

24. *ANET,* 449.

Moreover, the king's reference to his youth should be seen not as a chronological datum, a historically reliable indication of Solomon's actual age at the time of his accession. Rather, it is to be understood as a formulaic assertion of divine election, suggesting that Solomon is chosen despite overwhelming odds; although he is only a youth (cf. Jer 1:6) and incapable of leading his people (see Num 27:17; Deut 31:2; Josh 14:11; 1 Sam 18:13; 29:6; 2 Kgs 11:8). References to one's youth are quite common in ancient Near Eastern propaganda, where kings, especially those who come to the throne as usurpers, frequently call attention to divine election in and despite of their youth. So the original dream account may have been a part of a larger propagandistic work composed to legitimate the kingship of Solomon.

Accepting this pro-Solomonic perspective, modern interpreters have observed that the king's request for wisdom to govern (שׁפט *šāpaṭ*; lit., "to judge") his people (v. 9), rather than for the more selfish and worldly desires of longevity, riches, honor, and victory over enemies, indicates the depth of his character. Here is, as it were, a model of faith that seeks first the good of God's kingdom, the just and proper rule of God's chosen multitudes, rather than one's private interests, and because of that righteous attitude, Solomon is richly blessed (vv. 13-14; cf. Matt. 6:33; Rom 8:28-30). Yet, the elevation of wisdom over against other values is hardly unique in the Hebrew Bible. Indeed, in the wisdom tradition, longevity, honor, and material possessions are all seen as benefits that derive from wisdom (Prov 3:13-18). These things are given to anyone who acquires wisdom. So it only makes practical sense that one should seek wisdom first; all the other benefits will follow.

The account of Solomon's experience at Gibeon makes clear, however, that his wisdom was not something that he acquired through his own efforts. Nor was it an innate quality he was born with. Rather, wisdom was given by God upon Solomon's proper response to God's invitation. All the other benefits, too, were not merely the derivatives of wisdom. They were, rather, also graciously given by God without

Solomon's asking, the only condition being, according to the narrator, obedience to God's way (v. 14).

Then Solomon awoke from the dream and returned to Jerusalem. Whereas he had been worshiping at the high places and had gone to Gibeon to worship, he returned in the end to Jerusalem, where the ark was (v. 15). And there, in addition to the burnt offerings that he offered at Gibeon and other high places, he offered שׁלמים (*šĕlāmîm*; NRSV, "offerings of well-being"; NIV, "fellowship offerings"), probably referring to communal sacrifices accompanied by public feasting.

REFLECTIONS

Solomon's fame is legendary. Most modern readers know, as the ancient reader also did, that his reign was long and exceedingly prosperous and that he was well known for his wisdom. This account seems to confirm all that. Indeed, the original account may historically have served as political propaganda—an account to aggrandize Solomon.

Whatever the original intention of the episode, however, the editor-narrator now sets forth his own explanation. Neither Solomon's legendary wisdom, which made him an effective ruler in the eyes of all the world, nor his other attainments of longevity, wealth, honor, and victory over his enemies, is due to his own righteousness. It is true that he loved the Lord, and it is true that he came before God with the proper attitude of humility. That is neither the beginning nor the end of the story, however. In fact, it was God who came to Solomon first, despite the fact that the king had endangered the integrity of the kingdom by bringing it into alliance with Egypt. Solomon, too, was slow to build the Temple and the defenses of the city, because he was more interested in his own marriage to the Egyptian princess and in building his own palace. He worshiped at the high places, which faithful reformers like Josiah later on had to eliminate. Yet, God came to him with an open invitation. God took the initiative, while Solomon was yet in sin and darkness, as it were.

The passage as a whole seems to convey mixed messages about Solomon. It appears to vacillate between commendation and condemnation of him. On the one hand, Solomon seems to be favorably portrayed, as the builder of the Temple of the Lord in Jerusalem, as one who loves the Lord, who walks in "the statutes of David his father," who has his priorities right inasmuch as he asks for wisdom rather than worldly attainments for himself. And this attitude is explicitly affirmed by God (3:10-14). On the other hand, the salutary character and actions of Solomon are colored by the unsavory effects of his decisions. He built the Temple to be sure, but not before he had brought a foreign wife into the City of David, in contravention of deuteronomic law. He planned to construct the Lord's house only after he had built his own, and, in the meantime, his people burned incense and offered sacrifices at the local cultic installations—something that the establishment of the Jerusalem Temple would have obviated. He loved the Lord, yet Solomon offered sacrifices and incense at the high places, again in violation of deuteronomic law. The pious Solomon, who is given wisdom by God to be a wise ruler, stands in stark contrast to the unscrupulous Solomon of the earlier chapters, who is supposed to be already "wise" enough to know how to deal with all who might threaten his place (see esp. 2:6, 9).

Many commentators are inclined to see Solomon's approach to the Lord as something of a paradigm for faithful prayer. In his petition before God, he first acknowledges God's grace to him (3:6), recognizes that he is undeserving of God's special favor (3:7), and then asks for God's gift of wisdom so that he can carry out his duty as ruler of God's people, the chosen people (3:8-9). His thoughts are, it seems, noble; his primary desire is to seek the good of the kingdom. Accordingly, because of his appropriate attitude, God grants his wish for that gift, along with other benefits that he does not explicitly request. In other words, because he seeks first the kingdom of God, all these things are added unto him (see Matt 6:33).

Solomon's attitude of humility before God is admirable, and there is, indeed, a practical lesson about faith and prayer that one may learn from this story. Yet, the most salient point of the passage is surely *not* that one should emulate Solomon. If it were so, the passage would be theologically banal. Those who view the story as exemplary are, in fact, forced to concede that the picture of Solomon here, contradictory as it is to other characterizations in other passages, represents only "the ideal Solomon . . . as he ought to have been, not necessarily as he was in historical reality."[25] Moreover, that interpretation would make sense only if one were to isolate the episode of Solomon's encounter at Gibeon from the opening subunit about the more selfish and thoughtless first acts of his reign (3:1-3). Whereas the words of his prayer may indicate that his priorities were right in that he put God and duty before self, there is hardly any way to exonerate him in his marriage with the Egyptian princess and in his putting the building of his own house ahead of the construction of the centralized Temple in Jerusalem and the defenses of the city. Finally, such a reading makes no sense in the light of the larger context of chapters 1–11, for the devastating effects of Solomon's selfishness for the kingdom as a whole are plainly laid out at the end.

The lectionaries typically include only 3:5-15 (omitting even v. 4, which should properly be included on literary grounds), but not the preceding verses. Thus truncated, the text calls attention only to the self-revelation of God, the divine invitation, Solomon's admirable response, and the fact of God's gifts. Such a truncation, however, misses the theological tensions that the juxtaposition of these accounts poses: It is the very human, selfish, negligent Solomon who benefits from God's self-revelation and gifts. Solomon loved God only in a qualified way. Still, the deity appeared to him. Such is the nature of God in Scripture: God responds to the *imperfect love* (3:4), the sincere if inadequate response of mortals, with undeserved blessings, only to summon one yet again to love and to obey (3:14).

25. Simon J. De Vries, *1 Kings,* WBC (Waco, Tex.: Word, 1985) 55. De Vries notes, however, that "the two [portrayals] were not irreconcilably divorced, for elements of the real and the ideal are present in every person."

1 KINGS 3:16-28, SOLOMON'S WISDOM IN JUDGMENT

NIV

[16]Now two prostitutes came to the king and stood before him. [17]One of them said, "My lord, this woman and I live in the same house. I had a baby while she was there with me. [18]The third day after my child was born, this woman also had a baby. We were alone; there was no one in the house but the two of us.

[19]"During the night this woman's son died because she lay on him. [20]So she got up in the middle of the night and took my son from my side while I your servant was asleep. She put him by her breast and put her dead son by my breast. [21]The next morning, I got up to nurse my son—

NRSV

16Later, two women who were prostitutes came to the king and stood before him. [17]The one woman said, "Please, my lord, this woman and I live in the same house; and I gave birth while she was in the house. [18]Then on the third day after I gave birth, this woman also gave birth. We were together; there was no one else with us in the house, only the two of us were in the house. [19]Then this woman's son died in the night, because she lay on him. [20]She got up in the middle of the night and took my son from beside me while your servant slept. She laid him at her breast, and laid her dead son at my breast. [21]When

NIV	NRSV
and he was dead! But when I looked at him closely in the morning light, I saw that it wasn't the son I had borne." 22The other woman said, "No! The living one is my son; the dead one is yours." But the first one insisted, "No! The dead one is yours; the living one is mine." And so they argued before the king. 23The king said, "This one says, 'My son is alive and your son is dead,' while that one says, 'No! Your son is dead and mine is alive.' " 24Then the king said, "Bring me a sword." So they brought a sword for the king. 25He then gave an order: "Cut the living child in two and give half to one and half to the other." 26The woman whose son was alive was filled with compassion for her son and said to the king, "Please, my lord, give her the living baby! Don't kill him!" But the other said, "Neither I nor you shall have him. Cut him in two!" 27Then the king gave his ruling: "Give the living baby to the first woman. Do not kill him; she is his mother." 28When all Israel heard the verdict the king had given, they held the king in awe, because they saw that he had wisdom from God to administer justice.	I rose in the morning to nurse my son, I saw that he was dead; but when I looked at him closely in the morning, clearly it was not the son I had borne." 22But the other woman said, "No, the living son is mine, and the dead son is yours." The first said, "No, the dead son is yours, and the living son is mine." So they argued before the king. 23Then the king said, "The one says, 'This is my son that is alive, and your son is dead'; while the other says, 'Not so! Your son is dead, and my son is the living one.' " 24So the king said, "Bring me a sword," and they brought a sword before the king. 25The king said, "Divide the living boy in two; then give half to the one, and half to the other." 26But the woman whose son was alive said to the king—because compassion for her son burned within her—"Please, my lord, give her the living boy; certainly do not kill him!" The other said, "It shall be neither mine nor yours; divide it." 27Then the king responded: "Give the first woman the living boy; do not kill him. She is his mother." 28All Israel heard of the judgment that the king had rendered; and they stood in awe of the king, because they perceived that the wisdom of God was in him, to execute justice.

COMMENTARY

Immediately following the account of Solomon's encounter with the deity at Gibeon is an anecdote of his sagacious judgment in an extremely difficult case involving two prostitutes (3:16-28). This episode is a sequel to the Gibeon encounter (3:3-15). It is a sequel that does not appear in the parallel account in Chronicles, and one can only speculate as to reasons why it is in one history but not the other.

The temporal adverb אז (*'āz,* "then"; NRSV, "later"; NIV, "now") marks the transition from one passage to the next. It indicates that we have a new turn in the narrative, an event taking place in a specific temporal context, in this case, the reign of Solomon. To some commentators, the story originally had nothing to do with Solomon. Accordingly, it is argued, Solomon is not mentioned by name anywhere in the story; indeed, none of the characters is named. Thus "the king" mentioned throughout the story (vv. 16, 22-28) is a typical figure, but that type has been secondarily applied to Solomon within this literary context. In support of this view, it is often pointed out that there are folkloristic elements in the narrative and parallels found in other cultures, both in the Levant and as far away as India and eastern Asia.

In the light of such parallels, many view the story of the king's judgment of the two prostitutes as an Israelite version of a cross-cultural folktale, one that was originally told for pedagogical reasons (perhaps as an example-story of wisdom) or for pure entertainment, but that folktale was later incorporated as a part of Solomonic propaganda. Debates about the origins of such texts and the related issues of their historicity are, of course, impossible to resolve. Whatever its provenance, the story must now be read in the aftermath of Solomon's receipt of the gift of wisdom and its ancillary benefits. In its context, the story serves as an illustration of either the efficacy of Solomon's wisdom or its limitations or, as I would contend, *both.*

The Hebrew has it that two "women, prostitutes" (נשים זנות *nāšîm zōnôt*) came and stood before the king. Earlier on in the book, we read of Bathsheba, who appeared first before David (1:11-21) and then before Solomon (2:13-22) to persuade the king to do her bidding. Here, however, are two women who are related to the king neither by marriage (as Bathsheba was to David) nor by birth (as Bathsheba was to Solomon). Rather, they are commoners. Not only that—they are prostitutes. This detail is important, for the sociocultural assumptions about prostitutes are such that their credibility is immediately in question. They are women of "ill-repute" or women who "turn tricks," so to speak—deceitful women who simply cannot be trusted. That is a large part of the king's problem; the credibility of both the complainant and the respondent is in question from the beginning. The fact that they are prostitutes probably also means that no man is likely to come forward to claim their children. Only the words of these women of disrepute—the charge of the one and the denial of the other—are to be considered in the judgment.

The circumstances are laid out largely through the petition of the complainant, "the one woman," as she is called in v. 17. The two were apparently living in the same house when they each gave birth to a son at about the same time—three days apart, according to the Hebrew text and most ancient witnesses. The fact that they were at home is stressed repeatedly in the Hebrew text (four times in vv. 17-18, a fact reflected in the NRSV but not in the NIV), suggesting that there were no eyewitnesses who could have been passing by. Indeed, there were apparently no witnesses at all, for there was no one (lit., "no stranger") in the house.[26] Since the two prostitutes were "together" (so NRSV), they were the only ones responsible for the happenings therein; no one else could be blamed for any mishap (so NIV, "we were alone"). Without witnesses, there was also no one to verify or to challenge their words. Ironically, the fact that they were together alone meant that they must now be separated: One of them had suffered an injustice, and the other had to be culpable.

According to the complainant, they were both asleep when the respondent smothered her own baby by sleeping on it. So in the middle of the night, the mother of the deceased baby exchanged the dead child for the living one. The crime in darkness came to light only with the break of day, according to the complainant, when she arose to nurse her child and, upon closer examination, discovered that the dead child on her bosom was not hers.

The account is flatly denied by the respondent, without any elaboration (v. 22). A simple denial is all that it takes to bring about the legal impasse. Since no evidence whatsoever is here offered by the complainant, it is the word of one woman against another, indeed, one prostitute against another.

The Hebrew text is vivid, even tedious, in its portrayal of the impasse (vv. 22-23). As indicated below, the words of the respondent (A) reverse those of the complainant (B), and Solomon adds to the repetitiveness by summarizing the arguments of the one (C) and then the other (D):

A: "*My son is the living one,* and **your son is the dead one.**"

B: "**Your son is the dead one,** and *my son is the living one.*"

C: "*My son is the living one,* and **your son is the dead one.**"

D: "**Your son is the dead one,** and *my son is the living one.*"

The argument appears to be going around in circles, with no end in sight.

Then the king calls for a sword and orders that the living infant be cut in two and each half be

26. We expect אין־איש (*'ên-'îš*), the normal idiom for "no one." That אין־זר (*'ên-zār*; lit., "no stranger") is used may well mean that no clients of the prostitutes were present, as some scholars believe. It may simply mean, however, that there was no objective witness, no one who is not kin or friend of either of the two prostitutes.

given to one of the women. Thereupon, the mother of the living child yields, because her tender emotions are stirred up for her son (NRSV, "because compassion for her son burned within her"; NIV, she was "filled with compassion for her son"). Although it is obvious in the context that it is "mother love" that is meant, some interpreters go too far to make the case on etymological grounds, noting that the term for the mother's emotions (רחמיה *raḥămeyhā*, "her compassion") is the plural form of רחם (*reḥem*, "womb"). Yet the word, either in the singular or the plural, was never meant to be anatomically specific; it may refer to the uterus or the womb (e.g., Gen 29:31; 30:22; Job 38:8; Jer 1:5; 20:18; Job 38:8), but it is certainly not limited to that. It is, rather, a generic term for one's "gut." Accordingly, the Hebrew word may be used of male and female emotions alike, and cognates in other Semitic languages have the same wide range. Indeed, the very Hebrew idiom "emotions stirred up" (נכמרו רחמים *nikmĕrû raḥămîm*) is used of Joseph's emotional breakdown as he is being reconciled with his brothers: "his emotions stirred" (נכמרו רחמיו *nikmĕrû raḥămāyw*, Gen 43:30). It is the context that suggests that motherly love is at issue, not the etymology of the Hebrew term.

It is usually presumed that the woman whose compassion is so stirred is the complainant, perhaps because she seems utterly hysterical, as it were, whereas the respondent, with only one line of her response recorded, seems cool and detached. The text in v. 26, however, is ambiguous. It states merely that the mother of the child was so stirred by the impending threat to her son's life that she conceded the case. This "woman whose son is the living one" may, indeed, be the complainant, but she may also be the respondent.

The real mother's "gut reaction" is to give up her claim to the living child: "Give her the boy who is alive and by no means kill him!" The text is still ambiguous when it refers to the true mother's rival, who is not called "the second woman" or even "the other woman," but simply "this one" (זאת *zōʾt*), a term the king uses to refer to each of the women (v. 23). "This one" (NRSV, NIV: "the other") replies in a startlingly matter-of-fact way: "It shall be neither mine nor yours! Divide [him]!" It seems sensible that the one who so coldly responds to the threat of the boy's life is not the true mother—"the woman whose son is the living one"—but it is not absolutely clear whether she is the complainant or the respondent. At best, given one's assumptions about the normal psychology of mothers, one may conclude that the mother is *probably* the complainant. The one who is selflessly concerned about the infant's well-being is the "real" mother, one presumes. Mothers are not supposed to be willing to kill their own children. Yet, we know that there are exceptions to the rule, as many well-publicized cases of the murder of infants and young children by their own mothers have shown. Complicating one's evaluation, too, is the obvious caricature of the monstrosity of the woman who is willing to let the baby be killed and divided. This is not a case that the readers, if they were the jury, could decide beyond a reasonable doubt.

Unfortunately, the judgment of the just king is questionable. He never interrogates the two women. He accepts at face value the complainant's claim that there were no other witnesses. He does not point to the obvious gaps in her version of events and the purely circumstantial nature of her charge. He does not notice that she claimed to have been so soundly asleep that she did not know that her infant had been taken from her and another placed in her bosom, and yet she is able to report on all that was happening that night. He does not point to the inconsistency of her statement, inasmuch as she herself admits that she did not know the child was already dead until the morning. Neither does the king question the respondent, choosing merely to accept her denial as adequate. Neither woman is required to take an oath or undergo some kind of test, as the law stipulates for disputes involving no witnesses (see Exod 22:10-11; Deut 19:15-18; Num 5:11-15). He does not visit the site of the crime, nor does he send investigators to look for possible clues that may have been overlooked. Instead, he threatens the life of an innocent child, expecting the horrendous threat to provoke the responses he expects from his own stereotypes of the good mother and the deceptive woman. He does not consider the possibility that one or both women might be calling his bluff. So he pronounces one of them to be the mother of the child, curiously echoing the very words of the unspecified "woman whose son is the living one": "Give her the boy who is alive and by no means kill him!" (vv. 26-27). Most translators are uncomfortable with the ambiguity of the king's words, and so they substitute "the first woman" (i.e., the complainant) for the confusing pronoun "her" (so NRSV and NIV). The Greek translators tried to clarify the text even further: "Give her, the one who says 'Give her the living child' "—leading a few commentators to assume that some words were omitted accidentally and to emend the text. All Hebrew witnesses assume the more ambiguous reading, however. What is more, the immediate antecedent of the pronoun "her" is not the complainant, but the one who calls for the splitting of the baby. Is this intentional on the narrator's part, or is it just sloppy narrative style?

Perhaps the king was pointing to the "real" mother when he ordered that the boy who is alive be given to *her,* because "she is his mother!" The reader is not given any clarity of vision, however, only the words of the verdict that are, in fact, couched in the very words of the mother's concession. Are we to take it that the king is ironically using the words of the mother to grant her the living child—that is, she asks that the boy be given to "her" (the liar), but the king is ordering that he be given to "her" (the truth teller)? Is he, as it were, granting the unspoken desires of the mother's heart but not the words of her petition? Or is he doing what she has suggested, sparing the baby and giving him to the other woman? Moreover, if the judge is proclaiming the complainant to be the mother here, as the NRSV and the NIV have it ("to the first woman"), is he perhaps being too hasty? Should he not have considered the possibility that the one who seems to be telling the truth is merely more astute than the other in catching on to his judicial hoax and, hence, is giving him precisely the response that Solomon is expecting of a true mother? Is she merely countering his hoax with her own? And what if the other woman had not been so naive as the narrator caricatures her to be? What if she, too, sensing that the king is trying to trick them, is cool enough to play along?[27] What if she is merely trying to call Solomon's bluff, daring him to take responsibility for his threat of violence? What would the king have done if both mothers had said the "motherly thing" that he expects? Has the king's shock tactic, in fact, proved irrefutably who the real mother is?

Most interpreters seem to come down on the side of the complainant, assuming that she is the real mother and that justice has been done. That assessment is not based on the specifics of the report, however. Not only is the account lacking in details, but also one is left to interpret the words according to one's perception of the truth. Much is left to the reader's imagination and personal inclination.

The passage concludes by taking the reader outside the court of the royal arbiter to the outside world, as it were. All Israel, we are told, heard of the king's judgment and, the Hebrew text says, literally, "they feared the king, for they saw that divine wisdom was in him to do justice" (see v. 28). The most obvious interpretation of the narrator's concluding observation about the effect of the king's judgment is that it was unquestionably the correct one; divine wisdom was "in him" (NRSV, correctly, rather than NIV, "he had"), and so the entire nation stood in awe of him. This is the interpretation reflected in the translations of both the NRSV ("they stood in awe of the king") and the NIV ("they held the king in awe"). Yet, if one is cynical, if doubt lingers still in the reader's mind about the limitations of human wisdom, one might hear the text differently—that is, when all Israel heard of the judgment, *they were afraid of the king,* because they saw that this judgment was the outcome of his "divine wisdom," which was internal to him alone—"in him," as the Hebrew text ambiguously has it.

Even if one grants the first interpretation, however, history has not been as sanguine about the wisdom of the king's judgment as all Israel is supposed to have been. Josephus, who felt the case was so complicated that he had to report it in detail, says that there were those present in Solomon's time who were not convinced that he had acted wisely. On the contrary, "all the people secretly made fun of the king as of a boy."[28] That tradition is partially corroborated in a midrashic

27. In recognition of this possibility, some early interpreters suggested that Solomon finally knew who the real mother was only because a "heavenly voice" (בת קול *bat qôl*) revealed it to him: "How did Solomon know? Perhaps the woman had spoken craftily, so that Solomon would award the child to her? But it was a heavenly voice that came forth and said: *She is the mother thereof.*" See *Midr. Teh.* 72:2; cf. 17A.17. Translation in W. G. Braude, *The Midrash on Psalms,* Yale Judaica Series (New Haven: Yale University Press, 1959) 1:226, 560.

28. Josephus *Antiquities of the Jews* VIII.2.32.

passage that tells of how witnesses to the event initially pitied the country because its ruler was just a boy: "Woe to you, O Land, whose king is a boy!"[29] The same negative assessment of Solomon's judgment is said to have been made by Rabbi Judah, the son of Rabbi Ilai, who thought that Solomon's decision was contemptible: "If I had been there, I would put a rope around Solomon's neck, for one dead child was apparently not enough for him—no, he had to command that the second be divided in two."[30] More recent interpreters have been similarly critical of Solomon's failure to interrogate the women involved, to look for possible unnoticed witnesses, to consider possible clinical clues, such as the differences between the navels and the stools of babies born three days apart, and so forth.[31] Others, too, have faulted Solomon for allowing his ends to justify his means—that is, for threatening the life of a child in order to make what he thought would be a correct decision. Finally, Brueggemann points out that the story shows no indication of the king's compassion at all and, if anything, should serve to warn one "about the gift and the danger of public power, about cold objectivity as a stern form of compassion, about the practice of justice being very close to cold cynicism."[32]

29. *M. Teh.* 72.2, quoting Eccl 10:16. Translation in Braude, *The Midrash on Psalms* I, 559.

30. Ibid.

31. See S. Lasine, "The Riddle of Solomon's Judgment and the Riddle of Human Nature in the Hebrew Bible," *JSOT* 45 (1989) 65-86; S. Levin, "The Judgment of Solomon: Legal and Medical," *Judaism* 32 (1982) 463-65.

As with other passages in the book of 1 Kings, it seems possible for one to view Solomon here either in a positive or a negative light. Neither perspective can be easily dismissed. On the one hand, the story may have been intended at one time as a positive example of Solomon's wisdom. This is just the sort of account that could have been circulating as part of the legend of the great Solomon. It may be, therefore, that the narrator is merely conceding the reality of Solomon's fame and material successes. On the other hand, it is conceivable that the narrator is exploiting the gaps and ambiguities in the story to subvert the legend. The wisdom of Solomon, its divine origin and its much-vaunted fame notwithstanding, is finally limited. Wisdom, even if divinely imbued, can take one only so far. Solomon's gifts and successes are limited after all.

32. Walter Brueggemann, *1 Kings*, KPG (Atlanta: John Knox, 1983) 14.

REFLECTIONS

This section of 1 Kings contains the quintessential example-story of Solomon's wisdom. This legendary judicial decision of King Solomon has been celebrated throughout history: It is retold in medieval manuscript illustrations, oratorios, plays, paintings, sculptures, and literature.[33] In the Middle Ages, the scene was frequently depicted in law courts, and Solomon's decision was held out as a model of true justice.

At one level, the memorable story tells of the possibility of justice for people who are not in positions of power, even for people whom society has marginalized and whose credibility is not generally accepted. A modern-day attorney, whether prosecuting or defending, would probably have a field day cross-examining these prostitutes as witnesses. Perhaps these women would not even be called upon to speak for themselves, for aspects of their private and professional lives not directly relevant to the litigation at hand might surface that would cause them more harm than good. Essentially, the case revolves around the words of one "whore" against another. One of these "whores" is telling the truth, however, and she is a compassionate mother who is more concerned about the infant's welfare than with her rights. She would be called a "slut" in contemporary moralistic parlance, but she also happens to be a loving mother. And the latter character seems to be the one that matters most.

Romantic idealists are probably inclined to side with the "real" mother, despite any moral

33. For a convenient overview, see the article on Solomon in *Encyclopedia Judaica* XV, cols. 108-11.

reservations about her profession. Perhaps some would even identify emotionally with her. Yet, the other woman may actually have the law on her side. Her demand that the infant be divided equally between herself and her adversary may have some basis in Israelite property law. In the event of an unprovable dispute over property, the parties are supposed to divide the property equally (Exod 21:35; 2 Sam 19:29). In the absence of evidence, she demands that each person be given the "same pain and same gain." Many jurists today would argue the same way in disputes over custody of children and family property: When there is no clear evidence in favor of one or the other party, the fairest, safest settlement may be to divide everything down the middle and "split the baby"—a cliché still popularly used in legal circles in the United States.

In such a reading of the story, the narrator ventures a judgment in the name of Solomon. The king shocks the women into two kinds of responses: a response of love that favors life for the child over against a response that insists on one's legal rights. The true mother in this interpretation is the one who chooses life over death, love over right. Biological relationship is perhaps assumed, but it does not appear to be at issue here. Love is at issue.

The real mother is willing to surrender her right to be with her son in order that he might live. If that is true, the story makes an ironic point: Because the mother is willing to give up her son, she receives him back. Her emotionally wrenching words of surrender turn out to be the king's words of justice: "Give *her* the baby!"

This story may be compared to another famous Old Testament story involving the life of another beloved son: Abraham's sacrifice of Isaac in Genesis 22. In that story, the father is also willing to give up his son—in this case, in obedience to God. Like the unnamed living son of the unnamed mother, the life of Abraham's son Isaac, too, hangs in the balance as Abraham prepares to sacrifice him in order to be faithful to God's command. Yet, because Abraham is willing to give up the son whom he loves, he receives the boy back *as a gift.* In obedience, he is willing to surrender his beloved son.

In contrast to the story of Abraham's sacrifice of Isaac, the mother of the boy who is alive in this story is not prepared to have her son killed. That is not her sacrifice. Yet, she is prepared to sacrifice her son in the sense of losing him for herself. She would surrender him for the sake of his life. In love, she is willing to surrender her beloved son. Supreme love sometimes prompts a parent to give up his or her child in order that life—perhaps even an abundant life—might be possible for that child.

The king in our story seems to present a commonsense solution, one that especially appeals to modern readers frustrated by the slow turns of the wheels of justice. In view of legal cases that take months, if not years, of judicial hairsplitting, millions of dollars spent on teams of high-priced jurists, flamboyant prosecutors, expert testimonies, jury-selection consultations, reams of legal depositions, and extensive media coverage, only to reach decisions that are dubious and divisive, "Solomonic justice" may seem very appealing to us. A number of sensational cases in the United States in the late 1990s may come to mind. In each of these judgments, some observers came away believing that justice had been served by the tedious and expensive legal process, but others were equally convinced that there had been a gross miscarriage of justice. And often one's opinion about the verdict is colored by one's ethnic background and socioeconomic context. The tedium of due process in the American judicial system yields no certain results, it seems. It is understandable, then, to find an American interpreter of this passage suggesting that the story means "that the community of faith has a stake in letting justice in the public domain be nine parts simplicity and one part common sense."[34]

Yet, such "Solomonic justice" may be more of an ideal than a reality that can be achieved in our world of sin and darkness. In our most cautious moments, most of us would not be

34. Brueggemann, *1 Kings,* 14.

willing to sacrifice the rule of law and due process for such a brand of justice. How many of us living in a free and open society would trust a single individual to have that kind of power, no matter how "wise" that person may appear to be? That is why, in democratic societies, we have built into our systems of government a series of checks and balances. Perhaps the often frustrating system could be eliminated, we think, if only our rulers would have divine wisdom and rule just as Solomon did. Or would we? The wisdom of Solomon's judgment turns out to be a debatable matter upon a closer consideration of the account. At best, we may view him as a benign dictator, like many rulers throughout the world today, who simply demand that their citizens trust them alone to do what is right for everyone. Some of these rulers, too, use propaganda and appeal to special divine privileges, just as Solomon did. Some are truly intellectually gifted and have brought genuine benefits to their people—possibly better administration of justice, better management of the economy, more respectable international standing, perhaps even better opportunities for religion, just as Solomon gave to Israel (so we read in 1 Kings 3–10). These rulers dismiss the ability of the general populace to decide matters for themselves. They spurn the legal processes as unnecessarily complicated, and they hold themselves to be the sole trustworthy custodians of right. They think themselves wiser than others. For such leaders as these, the story of Solomon may provide scriptural sanction for dictatorship and oppression.

So, too, Solomon may have been viewed, and may continue to be perceived, as a gifted ruler. Perhaps his citizens were truly awed by him, as most English translations (including the NRSV and the NIV) would have it. Yet, the ambiguities in the text, perhaps deliberately left there by the narrator, subtly subvert any purely positive image one might have of the king. Thereby, it warns us that his dictatorship may not have been so benign after all, and it foreshadows the dire consequences of his reign for his kingdom. Even under the best of circumstances, human beings must contend with the limitations of wisdom—even wisdom given by God.

1 KINGS 4:1-34, SOLOMON'S RECORD

OVERVIEW

This passage is at once tantalizing and frustrating. It is especially intriguing to historians, for the two registers of officials (vv. 2-6, 7-19) and the commissary inventory (vv. 22-28) resemble records from a royal archive. References to two of Solomon's otherwise unknown sons-in-law (vv. 11, 15) also lend an air of authenticity to the report. Here, then, is a possible window—a broken window though it is—into the administration of the early Israelite monarchy, its various offices, perhaps even the specific names of the officials, and its administrative districts.

The task of historical reconstruction is, however, severely hampered by a number of obstacles. Most problematic are the text-critical problems: The readings in the Hebrew text are often called into question by other ancient versions, and it is almost impossible to reconstruct what the original account might have been. Moreover, while some of the place-names are readily identifiable (like Beth-shemesh, Naphath-dor, Taanach, Megiddo, and Bethshean), others are uncertain (like Elon Beth-Hanan) or even obscure (like Makaz, Arubboth, and Bealoth).

In terms of form, parallels may be drawn with numerous ancient Near Eastern royal inscriptions that boast of the successes of specific kings and their superiority over other rulers. Some Egyptian records contain precisely the sorts of administrative details that we find here. Indeed, so suggestive are some of these parallels that scholars have argued that Solomon's government may have been modeled after its Egyptian counterpart.[35]

35. See T. N. D. Mettinger, *Solomonic State Officials*, ConBOT 5 (Lund: Gleerup, 1971).

This is likely, given the alliance Solomon made with Egypt, an alliance the narrator has noted at the outset (3:1).

Other commentators have noticed continuities between this passage and various Assyrian royal inscriptions, including the itemizing of the daily provisions of the palace. Some annals boast of the king's literacy and wisdom, which surpass those of his rivals. Parallels may also be drawn with the Phoenician inscription of Azitawadda, which calls attention to the ruler's accomplishments, including the subjugation of neighboring countries, his reputation for wisdom, and peace and plenty in the land.[36] The inscription specifically observes that because of Azitawadda's benevolent rule, his people "ate and drank."

The resemblance of the account to other royal inscriptions cannot be gainsaid. Ostensibly, Solomon is being compared to other rulers in his efficiency, power, wealth, and wisdom. Despite the rhetoric of superiority that is typical of royal propaganda, however, the reader comes away with the feeling that Solomon's kingship was becoming just like that of his neighbors. In this account, we find a despotic and imperial Solomon—just as imposing and glorious as the others, to be sure, but also no less repressive, self-serving, and ostentatious.

36. *ANET,* 653-54.

1 Kings 4:1-6, Solomon's Cabinet

NIV

4 So King Solomon ruled over all Israel. [2]And these were his chief officials:

Azariah son of Zadok—the priest;
[3]Elihoreph and Ahijah, sons of Shisha—secretaries;
Jehoshaphat son of Ahilud—recorder;
[4]Benaiah son of Jehoiada—commander in chief;
Zadok and Abiathar—priests;
[5]Azariah son of Nathan—in charge of the district officers;
Zabud son of Nathan—a priest and personal adviser to the king;
[6]Ahishar—in charge of the palace;
Adoniram son of Abda—in charge of forced labor.

NRSV

4 King Solomon was king over all Israel, [2]and
these were his high officials: Azariah son
of Zadok was the priest; [3]Elihoreph and Ahijah
sons of Shisha were secretaries; Jehoshaphat son
of Ahilud was recorder; [4]Benaiah son of Jehoiada
was in command of the army; Zadok and Abiathar
were priests; [5]Azariah son of Nathan was over the
officials; Zabud son of Nathan was priest and
king's friend; [6]Ahishar was in charge of the palace;
and Adoniram son of Abda was in charge of the
forced labor.

COMMENTARY

As the Hebrew text has it, there were eleven officers in Solomon's administrative inner circle. They included a number of holdovers from the reign of David, such as Benaiah (v. 4*a*), the officer of the mercenary guards under David (2 Sam 8:18; 20:23; 1 Chr 18:17) who was promoted by Solomon to be the supreme commander of the army (2:35), and the old priests Zadok and Abiathar (v. 4*b*). Indeed, Abiathar, who had earlier been exiled by Solomon (2:26-27), seems to have been brought back. Jehoshaphat, the son of Ahilud (v. 3), "the recorder," appears to have been a minister in David's cabinet (2 Sam 8:16; 20:24; 1 Chr 18:15), and Adoniram (v. 6), chief of the corvée laborers, may be the same as "Adoram, the chief of the corvée" under David

(2 Sam 20:24). In addition, there are a few cabinet members who may have been related to former officials of the Davidic court—namely, Azariah, the son of Zadok (v. 2), who had apparently taken over his father's function as high priest, and the two sons of Nathan (v. 5)—possibly Nathan, the court prophet who helped Solomon seize power, or Nathan, a son of David (2 Sam 5:14). The two "secretaries" are identified in the Hebrew as sons of Shisha (v. 3), a name that looks suspiciously like that of variant names of the secretary in David's cabinet (2 Sam 8:17; 20:25). With the exception of Ahishar (v. 6), then, the entire cabinet seems to be composed of people with long-standing connections to the center of power in Judah.

The responsibilities of some of the officials seem clear enough, including a commander of the army, an official supervising the corvée workers, and an overseer of the royal palace. Benaiah the commander is already known to the reader, and there is no explanation needed for his title. As for the chief of the corvée ("in charge of forced labor," NRSV and NIV) and the chief steward of the palace, both are attested elsewhere in the Bible and in Hebrew inscriptions. We gather from references elsewhere that the chief of the palace was a powerful position in the monarchical period, perhaps something comparable to the Chief of Staff in the executive branch of United States government.

The duties of the two "secretaries" are more ambiguous. Since they are included in a list of "officials" (v. 2), and since they are juxtaposed with other powerful functionaries, one might consider it likely that they were secretaries of state rather than mere scribes assigned to transcribe diplomatic correspondence or royal records. In this connection, one notes that "the royal secretary" is mentioned along with other high court officials—the high priest (2 Kgs 12:10 = 2 Chr 24:11) or the royal steward in charge of the palace (2 Kgs 18:18; 19:2; Isa 36:3, 22; 37:2). Moreover, in 2 Kgs 25:19, we find a reference to "the secretary, the official of the army."

The NRSV and the NIV take the office of Jehoshaphat, son of Ahilud, to be "recorder" (v. 3), but other scholars have argued that the term מזכיר (*mazkîr*) designates a "herald"—that is, one who makes proclamations on behalf of the king or makes known the name of the king.[37] It is also possible that the word refers to one who mentions legal matters to the king, hence, a chief attorney or the like. This meaning is perhaps corroborated by the forensic use of the same Hebrew root in Isa 43:26.

Finally, the role of the "king's friend" (v. 5) is also unclear. The designation recalls Hushai's role as a "friend" of David (2 Sam 15:37; 16:16; 1 Chr 27:33). Hushai was clearly an ally and personal adviser of David, although he does not appear in any list of David's court officials. Scholars have called attention to analogies for the designation "king's friend" in Mesopotamia, Egypt, and Canaan. Still, since the title does not occur again after the reign of Solomon, one cannot be sure what the functions of such an official might have been in the Israelite-Judean context.

There remains much that is uncertain in the text. What seems clear, however, is that Solomon has surrounded himself with old-timers and insiders, no doubt to secure his own kingship. (See Reflections at 4:29-34.)

37. Mettinger, *Solomonic State Officials*, 29-30.

1 Kings 4:7-19, Solomon's Other Appointees

NIV

7Solomon also had twelve district governors over all Israel, who supplied provisions for the king and the royal household. Each one had to provide supplies for one month in the year. 8These are their names:

Ben-Hur—in the hill country of Ephraim;

NRSV

7Solomon had twelve officials over all Israel, who provided food for the king and his household; each one had to make provision for one month in the year. 8These were their names: Ben-hur, in the hill country of Ephraim; 9Ben-deker, in Makaz, Shaalbim, Beth-shemesh, and Elon-beth-hanan;

NIV

[9]Ben-Deker—in Makaz, Shaalbim, Beth Shemesh and Elon Bethhanan;
[10]Ben-Hesed—in Arubboth (Socoh and all the land of Hepher were his);
[11]Ben-Abinadab—in Naphoth Dor[a] (he was married to Taphath daughter of Solomon);
[12]Baana son of Ahilud—in Taanach and Megiddo, and in all of Beth Shan next to Zarethan below Jezreel, from Beth Shan to Abel Meholah across to Jokmeam;
[13]Ben-Geber—in Ramoth Gilead (the settlements of Jair son of Manasseh in Gilead were his, as well as the district of Argob in Bashan and its sixty large walled cities with bronze gate bars);
[14]Ahinadab son of Iddo—in Mahanaim;
[15]Ahimaaz—in Naphtali (he had married Basemath daughter of Solomon);
[16]Baana son of Hushai—in Asher and in Aloth;
[17]Jehoshaphat son of Paruah—in Issachar;
[18]Shimei son of Ela—in Benjamin;
[19]Geber son of Uri—in Gilead (the country of Sihon king of the Amorites and the country of Og king of Bashan). He was the only governor over the district.

[a] *11* Or *in the heights of Dor*

NRSV

[10]Ben-hesed, in Arubboth (to him belonged Socoh
and all the land of Hepher); [11]Ben-abinadab, in all
Naphath-dor (he had Taphath, Solomon's daughter, as his wife); [12]Baana son of Ahilud, in
Taanach, Megiddo, and all Beth-shean, which is beside Zarethan below Jezreel, and from Beth-shean to Abel-meholah, as far as the other side of
Jokmeam; [13]Ben-geber, in Ramoth-gilead (he had the villages of Jair son of Manasseh, which are in Gilead, and he had the region of Argob, which is in Bashan, sixty great cities with walls and bronze
bars); [14]Ahinadab son of Iddo, in Mahanaim; [15]Ahimaaz, in Naphtali (he had taken Basemath, Solomon's daughter, as his wife); [16]Baana son of
Hushai, in Asher and Bealoth; [17]Jehoshaphat son
of Paruah, in Issachar; [18]Shimei son of Ela, in
Benjamin; [19]Geber son of Uri, in the land of Gilead, the country of King Sihon of the Amorites and of King Og of Bashan. And there was one official in the land of Judah.

COMMENTARY

In this section, there is a list of twelve individuals who are said to be "over all Israel" (v. 7). Since Solomon is also said to be king "over all Israel" (v. 1), we understand these twelve to be representatives of the king throughout the country. These individuals are called "officials" in the NRSV and "district governors" in the NIV. The Hebrew term נצבים (*niṣṣābîm*) literally means something like "one set in place," hence "appointee."

There are still a number of problems. First of all, a number of these appointees are known only by their fathers' names (thus, lit., "Son of So-and-So"): Ben-Hur, Ben-Deker, Ben-Hesed, Ben-Abinadab, and Ben-Geber. The emphasis on the patronyms may indicate that the appointments were made primarily on the basis of family ties.

The fact that two of the appointees in Solomon's list are identified as his sons-in-law (vv. 11, 15) indicates the extent of nepotism and favoritism in his administration. Baana, the son of Ahilud, is possibly the brother of the entrenched court "recorder," Jehoshaphat, the son of Ahilud (v. 2; cf. 2 Sam 8:16; 20:24). Ahimaaz may be the son of Zadok (2 Sam 15:27; 18:27). Baana, the son of Hushai, may be the son of David's friend (2 Sam 15:32-37). Abinadab, the son of Iddo, may be the son of the same Iddo who ruled Gileadite Manasseh during David's reign (1 Chr 27:21). All these men are apparently connected to the Judean court. Yet, they are all appointed to rule over non-Judean districts.

This observation is all the more poignant when one takes the Hebrew text in v. 19 as it is, without emendation. If this is correct, Judah is not mentioned at all in the register (so NIV), suggesting that it was exempt from the tax system. Indeed, if one adds "Judah" with the Greek, as the NRSV does, one ends up with a list of thirteen officials—twelve for "all Israel" (v. 7) and an unnamed appointee for Judah. One would have to argue that "all Israel" in v. 7 means only the north, thus different from "all Israel" in v. 1, which refers to Israel and Judah.

The NIV takes the appointee in v. 19 to be Geber, son of Uri: "He was the only governor over the district." But that is a free reading of the Hebrew, and it is somewhat misleading, since the appointees in vv. 5 and 7 are called *"district* governors," where the word "district" is supplied by the translators. The Hebrew may better be rendered: "and one prefect who was in all the land."[38] We may take this cryptic notation as the narrator's summary assessment on the administration of "all Israel" (v. 7); although there are twelve appointees over various regions, there is only one prefect, a stand-in for the king, as it were, in the whole country. If that is the case, then the reference here is to Azariah, the son of Nathan, who is in charge of all the regional appointees (v. 5). Power ultimately resides in Solomon's court.

Traditionally, it has been assumed that the twelve districts correspond roughly to the territories of the twelve tribes of Israel. Yet, the only tribal names that appear are Ephraim, Benjamin, Naphtali, Issachar, and Asher. Moreover, the first district is not called simply "Ephraim" but "the hill country of Ephraim" (v. 8), a designation that elsewhere includes portions of Manasseh (see Josh 17:14-18). In addition, a number of the other districts seem to have been administered in cities that had been beyond Israelite tribal control: Naphath-dor, a stronghold of the Sea Peoples, was outside the tribal allotment (Josh 17:11-12; Judg 1:27); Taanach, Megiddo, and Bethshean were Canaanite strongholds. One can only speculate on the reasons for the choice of these centers. Solomon may have simply incorporated the more recently acquired domains and capitalized on the superior facilities that the old urban centers now afforded. Still, the choice of these traditionally non-Israelite centers may have been politically motivated as well.

It has been proposed that Solomon's restructuring was done largely for fiscal reasons. Instead of the conservative tribal system, he radically reorganized his kingdom into twelve districts of roughly comparable economic capacities.[39] The Samaria Ostraca from the eighth century BCE may provide a glimpse at the workings of the system as it continued in the north after the division of the kingdom. These inscriptions are apparently receipts recording the delivery of produce to the northern capital of Samaria from various administrative regions, including not a few sites from the district of Hepher (see "land of Hepher" in v. 10). Other archaeological discoveries also confirm that there were government fiscal centers throughout the monarchical period, centers to which taxes-in-kind were delivered. This is not to say that Solomon's motivation in the restructuring is purely economic. Indeed, economics and politics are inextricably intertwined; the economic restructuring no doubt undermined the political claims of the individual tribes.

The political implication of the restructuring is evident in the emphasis on the appointees rather than on the districts themselves, and in the fact that a number of these appointees are Judeans with old connections to the Davidic dynasty. If analogies with other administrative texts from the Levant are any indication, Solomon probably granted control over land to his family, friends, and other favorites in return for periodic taxes, the contribution of labor for the military and the corvée laborers, and, of course, loyalty. This connectedness may explain the emphasis on the appointees and the fact that their family ties seem more important than their personal names.

The irony in the passage should not be overlooked: Solomon is king over "all Israel" (v. 1); yet, his officials in the cabinet and his appointees over the districts are not representative of all Israel. Solomon may have the gift of administrative wisdom, a genius for organization, but his record shows that he has a penchant for taking care of himself and his favorites first. (See Reflections at 4:29-34.)

38. The word נִצָּבִים (*niṣṣābîm*), translated as "prefects" here, is a variant of the word for "appointees." For its usage, see 1 Sam 10:5; 13:3-4; 2 Sam 8:6, 14.

39. See G. E. Wright, "The Provinces of Solomon (I Kings 4:7-19)," *EI* 8 (1967) 58*-68*.

1 Kings 4:20-28, Solomon's Domains and His Provisions

NIV

[20]The people of Judah and Israel were as numerous as the sand on the seashore; they ate, they drank and they were happy. [21]And Solomon ruled over all the kingdoms from the River[a] to the land of the Philistines, as far as the border of Egypt. These countries brought tribute and were Solomon's subjects all his life.

[22]Solomon's daily provisions were thirty cors[b] of fine flour and sixty cors[c] of meal, [23]ten head of stall-fed cattle, twenty of pasture-fed cattle and a hundred sheep and goats, as well as deer, gazelles, roebucks and choice fowl. [24]For he ruled over all the kingdoms west of the River, from Tiphsah to Gaza, and had peace on all sides. [25]During Solomon's lifetime Judah and Israel, from Dan to Beersheba, lived in safety, each man under his own vine and fig tree.

[26]Solomon had four[d] thousand stalls for chariot horses, and twelve thousand horses.[e]

[27]The district officers, each in his month, supplied provisions for King Solomon and all who came to the king's table. They saw to it that nothing was lacking. [28]They also brought to the proper place their quotas of barley and straw for the chariot horses and the other horses.

[a] *21* That is, the Euphrates; also in verse 24 [b] *22* That is, probably about 185 bushels (about 6.6 kiloliters) [c] *22* That is, probably about 375 bushels (about 13.2 kiloliters) [d] *26* Some Septuagint manuscripts (see also 2 Chron. 9:25); Hebrew *forty* [e] *26* Or *charioteers*

NRSV

20Judah and Israel were as numerous as the sand by the sea; they ate and drank and were happy. [21a]Solomon was sovereign over all the kingdoms from the Euphrates to the land of the Philistines, even to the border of Egypt; they brought tribute and served Solomon all the days of his life.

22Solomon's provision for one day was thirty cors of choice flour, and sixty cors of meal, [23]ten fat oxen, and twenty pasture-fed cattle, one hundred sheep, besides deer, gazelles, roebucks, and fatted fowl. [24]For he had dominion over all the region west of the Euphrates from Tiphsah to Gaza, over all the kings west of the Euphrates; and he had peace on all sides. [25]During Solomon's lifetime Judah and Israel lived in safety, from Dan even to Beer-sheba, all of them under their vines and fig trees. [26]Solomon also had forty thousand stalls of horses for his chariots, and twelve thousand horsemen. [27]Those officials supplied provisions for King Solomon and for all who came to King Solomon's table, each one in his month; they let nothing be lacking. [28]They also brought to the required place barley and straw for the horses and swift steeds, each according to his charge.

[a] Ch 5.1 in Heb

COMMENTARY

In these verses we have something of a commentary on the economic and political consequences of Solomon's reign. The text seems at first blush to exalt Solomon unequivocally. Yet there are startling contradictions within it that give one pause. Solomon's administrative reorganization includes plans for forced labor and taxes that were explicitly to support the king's household and cronies. The king's appointees abundantly provided for the government, ensuring that nothing was left out (v. 27). Yet, the citizens are characterized in typically propagandistic terms: "They ate and drank and were happy" (v. 20). Solomon's reign is portrayed in idealistic and exaggerated terms; his domain is said to have included all the kingdoms from the Euphrates to the border of Egypt. Yet, we know that Solomon did not, in fact, have such control. The Phoenicians of Tyre, at least, were independent, as we know from Solomon's dealings with Hiram in the next chapter. Further, the populace is said to have dwelt securely (v. 25). Yet, that seems an unlikely environment, given the fact that this passage has to do with tax burdens for each district. These burdens are all the more onerous given the preposterous daily provisions expected for the court and the military. (In v. 26, the Hebrew records that Solomon has "forty thousand" stalls for horses [so NRSV], but that figure is played down to four thousand in the Greek [so NIV], perhaps because the figure seems too exaggerated. Yet, the extraordinarily high figure may have been intentional.)

Despite the overall impression of benevolent rule, there are subtle indications that not all is well. It is apparent that the economy is healthy, the military is strong, the country is efficiently run, and the ruler's authority is widely recognized. Still, there are implicit questions about who is served and exalted in all of this. Clearly, it is Solomon whose interests are protected, whose coffers are full. It is he who receives "offering" (NRSV, NIV, "tribute") and he who is "served" (v. 21). The text refers ambiguously to the charge to bring goods to "the place," but what the officials bring are not offerings for God but supplies for the military (v. 28).

One might argue that the similarities of Solomon's record to royal inscriptions from elsewhere in the ancient Near East point to the influence of other cultures upon Israel or to the mutuality of cultural influences. That may or may not be the case. What seems clear is that the account here is stereotypical. It is evident that Solomon was becoming a king just like the other kings of the region. This is precisely what some had warned would be the consequence of establishing a monarchy in Israel: The king might become just like the other rulers of the region, demanding forced labor, taxes for imperial expansions and the maintenance of the royal court, and the glorification of the king at the expense of the populace (Deut 17:14-20; 1 Sam 8:10-18). Indeed, the resemblance of Solomon's administration to other self-serving and repressive regimes may be the very point of the passage. The fate of the kingdom—the fate of God's people—is not secured despite Solomon's efficiency, wealth, and power. With the machinery for imposition of the king's will as regards the resources of the country, one wonders whether the narrator is being a little ironic to concede that the people were happy or that they could, indeed, live securely. One is impelled to ask questions about the benefits of Solomon's successes in the light of larger issues about what God may intend for God's people. (See Reflections at 4:29-34.)

1 Kings 4:29-34, Solomon's Reputation for Wisdom

NIV

29God gave Solomon wisdom and very great insight, and a breadth of understanding as measureless as the sand on the seashore. 30Solomon's wisdom was greater than the wisdom of all the men of the East, and greater than all the wisdom of Egypt. 31He was wiser than any other man, including Ethan the Ezrahite—wiser than Heman, Calcol and Darda, the sons of Mahol. And his fame spread to all the surrounding nations. 32He spoke three thousand proverbs and his songs numbered a thousand and five. 33He described plant life, from the cedar of Lebanon to the hyssop that grows out of walls. He also taught about animals and birds, reptiles and fish. 34Men of all nations came to listen to Solomon's wisdom, sent by all the kings of the world, who had heard of his wisdom.

NRSV

29God gave Solomon very great wisdom, discernment, and breadth of understanding as vast as the sand on the seashore, 30so that Solomon's wisdom surpassed the wisdom of all the people of the east, and all the wisdom of Egypt. 31He was wiser than anyone else, wiser than Ethan the Ezrahite, and Heman, Calcol, and Darda, children of Mahol; his fame spread throughout all the surrounding nations. 32He composed three thousand proverbs, and his songs numbered a thousand and five. 33He would speak of trees, from the cedar that is in the Lebanon to the hyssop that grows in the wall; he would speak of animals, and birds, and reptiles, and fish. 34People came from all the nations to hear the wisdom of Solomon; they came from all the kings of the earth who had heard of his wisdom.

COMMENTARY

The narrative returns explicitly to the subject of God's gift of wisdom to Solomon (see 3:1-28). The king's wisdom surpassed that of all others, and he became internationally famous for it. Like the ideal sage of the ancient Near East, he had a reputation for his aesthetic interests. He was a patron of the arts—indeed, a prolific composer himself. He also delved into nature, discussing various botanical and zoological matters. From the narrator's point of view, Solomon's successes are well known and beyond dispute. Yet, nowhere does the narrator equate giftedness with character or faithfulness. There is possibly a hint in the text as to an unsavory side to his enormous gift, for he is said to have had a phenomenal "broadness of heart/mind" (v. 29; NRSV, NIV: "breadth of understanding"). In the choice of words here is perhaps a warning, a foreshadowing of the troubles in which Solomon will be caught. The Hebrew idiom for "broadness of heart/mind" (רחב לב *rōḥab lēb*) may, if the context requires, also be interpreted as intellectual arrogance. So in Prov 21:4 and Ps 101:5, the expression "broad of heart/mind" is used for the arrogance of the wicked. Similarly, the expression "largeness of heart/mind" is used for arrogance (Isa 9:9; 10:12). Solomon's gift of wisdom may have a dangerous side as well.

REFLECTIONS

Solomon is in an enviable position. We were told earlier that he was blessed by God with the gift of wisdom and all the trappings of a good life (3:3-15). Now we get a sense of his power, wealth, intellectual capacity, and fame. One would like to think that Solomon has received all these because he came before God with unimpeachable character, the right attitude, or sincere prayer. Yet, that does not appear to be a point that the passage makes; nothing about Solomon here suggests that he deserves to have it so good.

One may well envy Solomon, but this is not someone whom most of us would like. Apparently insecure in his power, he surrounds himself with people he trusts, promoting his cronies, ensuring his own comfort. He seems to undermine traditional sociopolitical structures in order to ensure his influence throughout his domain, now reorganized into fiscal regions to support the prodigious expenses of his palace and his military machinery.

Inasmuch as the passage concerns government, one might be tempted to find scriptural warrant here for one's own political agenda. Arguably, we have a paradigm for a proactive central government; through Solomon's capital initiatives the people prosper, live securely, and have peace on every side. Political appointees provide the central government with every provision, making sure that nothing is lacking.

Other readers may not be so sanguine about the governmental interventions, however, particularly if the story is read within its larger literary context. The presence of a secretary of labor only foreshadows problems that the people will encounter later. That "tax-and-spend government" would, after all, lead the nation to destruction. To be sure, the economy may have been doing well under Solomon's administration so that other questions pertaining to his character do not seem to matter. Yet all that will change as the story progresses. Character matters, after all, and the fate of the country does depend, at least in part, on the faithful responses of its leaders.

The Bible is dangerous that way. It is easy to justify our political and personal agendas therein. That is not the purpose of Scripture, however. The story has power, not because of any political or social paradigm it may provide, but because of its affirmation that God does act in the arena of history with all its limitations, through real human beings with all their gifts and despite their failings. One is at once puzzled and amazed.

There is no question that Solomon is capable. He is efficient, savvy, and cosmopolitan. Still, this man who has been anointed by God is no perfect soul. We have the distinct impression that he is insecure, self-indulgent, and vain. It does not help that the passage ends with affirmation of his extraordinary giftedness. It paints a picture of Solomon as a person incomparable in the scope of his intellectual and creative ability. He is something of a genius, a veritable Leonardo da Vinci or Mozart of his time, with an abiding international reputation. But one wonders why it is *this* ruthless, self-centered, and vain man whom God has blessed with such extraordinary gifts. Why is it not someone else more deserving, less rapacious, more faithful, less pompous?

The difficult truth for us in this story is that it has no easy answers to our questions about the seeming arbitrariness of God's election. It is a mystery that God's purpose in history should be fulfilled through people who have their own biases, political agendas, and limited visions. It is a mystery, too, that God should bless some who are so unworthy or even unfaithful, more than those who seem to us more deserving. That same mystery of God's surprising grace, however, is the good news in the story. The instruments of God are at best imperfect. So are we.

1 KINGS 5:1-18, SHADY DEALS AND OPPRESSIVE POLICIES

NIV

5 When Hiram king of Tyre heard that Solomon had been anointed king to succeed
his father David, he sent his envoys to Solomon,
because he had always been on friendly terms
with David. 2Solomon sent back this message to
Hiram:

3"You know that because of the wars
waged against my father David from all sides,
he could not build a temple for the Name of
the LORD his God until the LORD put his
enemies under his feet. 4But now the LORD
my God has given me rest on every side, and
there is no adversary or disaster. 5I intend,
therefore, to build a temple for the Name of
the LORD my God, as the LORD told my father
David, when he said, 'Your son whom I will
put on the throne in your place will build the
temple for my Name.'

6"So give orders that cedars of Lebanon be
cut for me. My men will work with yours,
and I will pay you for your men whatever
wages you set. You know that we have no
one so skilled in felling timber as the
Sidonians."

7When Hiram heard Solomon's message, he

NRSV

5[a] Now King Hiram of Tyre sent his servants
to Solomon, when he heard that they had
anointed him king in place of his father; for Hiram
had always been a friend to David. 2Solomon sent
word to Hiram, saying, 3"You know that my father
David could not build a house for the name of
the LORD his God because of the warfare with
which his enemies surrounded him, until the LORD
put them under the soles of his feet.[b] 4But now
the LORD my God has given me rest on every side;
there is neither adversary nor misfortune. 5So I
intend to build a house for the name of the LORD
my God, as the LORD said to my father David,
'Your son, whom I will set on your throne in your
place, shall build the house for my name.' 6There-
fore command that cedars from the Lebanon be
cut for me. My servants will join your servants,
and I will give you whatever wages you set for
your servants; for you know that there is no one
among us who knows how to cut timber like the
Sidonians."

7When Hiram heard the words of Solomon, he
rejoiced greatly, and said, "Blessed be the LORD
today, who has given to David a wise son to be
over this great people." 8Hiram sent word to

[a] Ch 5.15 in Heb [b] Gk Tg Vg: Heb *my feet* or *his feet*

NIV

was greatly pleased and said, "Praise be to the
LORD today, for he has given David a wise son to
rule over this great nation."
8So Hiram sent word to Solomon:

"I have received the message you sent me
and will do all you want in providing the
cedar and pine logs. 9My men will haul them
down from Lebanon to the sea, and I will
float them in rafts by sea to the place you
specify. There I will separate them and you
can take them away. And you are to grant
my wish by providing food for my royal
household."

10In this way Hiram kept Solomon supplied
with all the cedar and pine logs he wanted, 11and
Solomon gave Hiram twenty thousand cors[a] of
wheat as food for his household, in addition to
twenty thousand baths[b, c] of pressed olive oil.
Solomon continued to do this for Hiram year after
year. 12The LORD gave Solomon wisdom, just as
he had promised him. There were peaceful relations between Hiram and Solomon, and the two
of them made a treaty.

13King Solomon conscripted laborers from all
Israel—thirty thousand men. 14He sent them off
to Lebanon in shifts of ten thousand a month, so
that they spent one month in Lebanon and two
months at home. Adoniram was in charge of the
forced labor. 15Solomon had seventy thousand
carriers and eighty thousand stonecutters in the
hills, 16as well as thirty-three hundred[d] foremen
who supervised the project and directed the workmen. 17At the king's command they removed from
the quarry large blocks of quality stone to provide
a foundation of dressed stone for the temple.
18The craftsmen of Solomon and Hiram and the
men of Gebal[e] cut and prepared the timber and
stone for the building of the temple.

[a] *11* That is, probably about 125,000 bushels (about 4,400 kiloliters)
[b] *11* Septuagint (see also 2 Chron. 2:10); Hebrew *twenty cors* [c] *11* That is, about 115,000 gallons (about 440 kiloliters) [d] *16* Hebrew; some Septuagint manuscripts (see also 2 Chron. 2:2, 18) *thirty-six hundred*
[e] *18* That is, Byblos

NRSV

Solomon, "I have heard the message that you
have sent to me; I will fulfill all your needs in
the matter of cedar and cypress timber. 9My
servants shall bring it down to the sea from the
Lebanon; I will make it into rafts to go by sea to
the place you indicate. I will have them broken
up there for you to take away. And you shall meet
my needs by providing food for my household."
10So Hiram supplied Solomon's every need for
timber of cedar and cypress. 11Solomon in turn
gave Hiram twenty thousand cors of wheat as
food for his household, and twenty cors of fine
oil. Solomon gave this to Hiram year by year. 12So
the LORD gave Solomon wisdom, as he promised
him. There was peace between Hiram and Solomon; and the two of them made a treaty.

13King Solomon conscripted forced labor out
of all Israel; the levy numbered thirty thousand
men. 14He sent them to the Lebanon, ten thousand a month in shifts; they would be a month
in the Lebanon and two months at home; Adoniram was in charge of the forced labor. 15Solomon
also had seventy thousand laborers and eighty
thousand stonecutters in the hill country, 16besides
Solomon's three thousand three hundred supervisors who were over the work, having charge of
the people who did the work. 17At the king's
command, they quarried out great, costly stones
in order to lay the foundation of the house with
dressed stones. 18So Solomon's builders and Hiram's builders and the Gebalites did the stonecut-
ting and prepared the timber and the stone to
build the house.

COMMENTARY

The chapter begins with Solomon's ties to the Phoenicians, represented here by Hiram (a variant form of Phoenician "Ahiram"), king of Tyre. The alliance is not a new one, for it had been established already since the reign of David (2 Sam 5:11-12). This reference to David provides the narrator with an opportunity to place Solomon's intention to build the Temple within the larger history of the Davidic dynasty. Alluding to Nathan's oracle (2 Sam 7:1-17), the narrator asserts that David had not been able to carry out his desire to construct a temple because he had been beset by wars. Solomon is not similarly troubled by political problems, and so he could carry out the project as the anointed successor to David.

A deal is cut between Solomon and Hiram, on terms that are more favorable to the Phoenicians than to the Israelites. In chap. 4, we learned that Solomon had taxed his people in order to support the royal palace. Foreign nations, too, supposedly supplied provisions for him. Yet, he is now agreeing to provide for the household of the Tyrian king and gives him 20,000 cors (approx. 125,000 bushels) of wheat and, according to the Hebrew text, 2,000 cors (almost 700,000 gallons) of refined oil "year after year" (v. 11),[40] and he will do so for a couple of decades (9:10-11).

Hiram agrees to supply the materials and the professional expertise. Solomon conscripts people from Israel—not just outsiders, as with the permanent corvée that was engaged in the fortification projects (9:20-21)—for a term of three months each. In addition, there are 150,000 burden bearers and hewers of stone, supervised by a force of 3,300, all under the charge of Adoniram, a cabinet minister, chief of the levy (4:6).

Despite the allusion to Solomon's wisdom (vv. 7, 12), the alliance foreshadows the problems the kingdom will soon face. Solomon notes that God has given him peace and that he has neither adversaries nor misfortunes. Yet, because of his alliances with outsiders, his kingdom will soon be threatened by one adversary after another (11:14, 23). Solomon has turned to foreigners for his most public religious project, paying an exorbitant price and even promising that his servants will be with the Phoenicians: "My servants/slaves will be with your servants/slaves" (v. 6). He has also conscripted forced labor out of Israel, probably referring to those from the north. That forced conscription of Israelites (as opposed to Judeans) will later be the cause of the kingdom's division.

40. So the Hebrew text. The Greek, followed by the NIV, has "20,000 baths" instead of "2,000 cors."

REFLECTIONS

Solomon had an ambition, one that his father, David, had but was unable to fulfill. David proposed to build a permanent house for the Lord in Jerusalem, for he himself already had a cedar palace there (2 Sam 7:2). So, too, Solomon wants to build a temple in the capital city as a symbol of God's abiding presence there.

The peace and prosperity of his time made it feasible for him to carry out this plan, and he prepared for it by making a pact with a Phoenician wheeler-dealer who was insistent that his own wishes be carried out. Solomon seemed willing to compromise with anyone in order to achieve his own goals, which is admittedly stated in traditional religious terms (5:3-5). He was also willing to impose his will on his citizens. Although the project may have legitimated his place as the designated successor to the Davidic throne, he had to sell out his people in order to achieve it. The plan is articulated in theological terms, but its consequences for God's people were dire: They had to bear the burdens and suffer injustices for the sake of Solomon's Temple.

In this story one is prompted to consider the price that others have to pay for *our* pet projects that may be motivated by a mixture of true religious conviction and personal vision and ambition. Even in a worthwhile project done in the name of God, one must consider the possibility that one's personal agenda may get in the mix, and that the questionable deals that one has to make and the oppressive costs one has to pay may compromise the integrity of the project. How often has a church building, the symbol of divine presence, involved such costs!

1 KINGS 6:1-38, THE TEMPLE IS BUILT

NIV

6 In the four hundred and eightieth[a] year after the Israelites had come out of Egypt, in the fourth year of Solomon's reign over Israel, in the month of Ziv, the second month, he began to build the temple of the LORD.

2The temple that King Solomon built for the LORD was sixty cubits long, twenty wide and thirty high.[b] 3The portico at the front of the main hall of the temple extended the width of the temple, that is twenty cubits,[c] and projected ten cubits[d] from the front of the temple. 4He made narrow clerestory windows in the temple. 5Against the walls of the main hall and inner sanctuary he built a structure around the building, in which there were side rooms. 6The lowest floor was five cubits[e] wide, the middle floor six cubits[f] and the third floor seven.[g] He made offset ledges around the outside of the temple so that nothing would be inserted into the temple walls.

7In building the temple, only blocks dressed at the quarry were used, and no hammer, chisel or any other iron tool was heard at the temple site while it was being built.

8The entrance to the lowest[h] floor was on the south side of the temple; a stairway led up to the middle level and from there to the third. 9So he built the temple and completed it, roofing it with beams and cedar planks. 10And he built the side rooms all along the temple. The height of each was five cubits, and they were attached to the temple by beams of cedar.

11The word of the LORD came to Solomon: 12"As for this temple you are building, if you follow my decrees, carry out my regulations and keep all my

a *1* Hebrew; Septuagint *four hundred and fortieth* b *2* That is, about 90 feet (about 27 meters) long and 30 feet (about 9 meters) wide and 45 feet (about 13.5 meters) high c *3* That is, about 30 feet (about 9 meters) d *3* That is, about 15 feet (about 4.5 meters) e *6* That is, about 7 1/2 feet (about 2.3 meters); also in verses 10 and 24 f *6* That is, about 9 feet (about 2.7 meters) g *6* That is, about 10 1/2 feet (about 3.1 meters) h *8* Septuagint; Hebrew *middle*

NRSV

6 In the four hundred eightieth year after the Israelites came out of the land of Egypt, in the fourth year of Solomon's reign over Israel, in the month of Ziv, which is the second month, he began to build the house of the LORD. 2The house that King Solomon built for the LORD was sixty cubits long, twenty cubits wide, and thirty cubits high. 3The vestibule in front of the nave of the house was twenty cubits wide, across the width of the house. Its depth was ten cubits in front of the house. 4For the house he made windows with recessed frames.[a] 5He also built a structure against the wall of the house, running around the walls of the house, both the nave and the inner sanctuary; and he made side chambers all around. 6The lowest story[b] was five cubits wide, the middle one was six cubits wide, and the third was seven cubits wide; for around the outside of the house he made offsets on the wall in order that the supporting beams should not be inserted into the walls of the house.

7The house was built with stone finished at the quarry, so that neither hammer nor ax nor any tool of iron was heard in the temple while it was being built.

8The entrance for the middle story was on the south side of the house: one went up by winding stairs to the middle story, and from the middle story to the third. 9So he built the house, and finished it; he roofed the house with beams and planks of cedar. 10He built the structure against the whole house, each story[c] five cubits high, and it was joined to the house with timbers of cedar.

11Now the word of the LORD came to Solomon, 12"Concerning this house that you are building, if you will walk in my statutes, obey my ordinances, and keep all my commandments by walking in

a Gk: Meaning of Heb uncertain b Gk: Heb *structure* c Heb lacks *each story*

NIV

commands and obey them, I will fulfill through you the promise I gave to David your father. 13And I will live among the Israelites and will not abandon my people Israel."

14So Solomon built the temple and completed it. 15He lined its interior walls with cedar boards, paneling them from the floor of the temple to the ceiling, and covered the floor of the temple with planks of pine. 16He partitioned off twenty cubits[a] at the rear of the temple with cedar boards from floor to ceiling to form within the temple an inner sanctuary, the Most Holy Place. 17The main hall in front of this room was forty cubits[b] long. 18The inside of the temple was cedar, carved with gourds and open flowers. Everything was cedar; no stone was to be seen.

19He prepared the inner sanctuary within the temple to set the ark of the covenant of the LORD there. 20The inner sanctuary was twenty cubits long, twenty wide and twenty high.[c] He overlaid the inside with pure gold, and he also overlaid the altar of cedar. 21Solomon covered the inside of the temple with pure gold, and he extended gold chains across the front of the inner sanctuary, which was overlaid with gold. 22So he overlaid the whole interior with gold. He also overlaid with gold the altar that belonged to the inner sanctuary.

23In the inner sanctuary he made a pair of cherubim of olive wood, each ten cubits[d] high. 24One wing of the first cherub was five cubits long, and the other wing five cubits—ten cubits from wing tip to wing tip. 25The second cherub also measured ten cubits, for the two cherubim were identical in size and shape. 26The height of each cherub was ten cubits. 27He placed the cherubim inside the innermost room of the temple, with their wings spread out. The wing of one cherub touched one wall, while the wing of the other touched the other wall, and their wings touched each other in the middle of the room. 28He overlaid the cherubim with gold.

29On the walls all around the temple, in both the inner and outer rooms, he carved cherubim, palm trees and open flowers. 30He also covered the floors of both the inner and outer rooms of the temple with gold.

[a] *16* That is, about 30 feet (about 9 meters) [b] *17* That is, about 60 feet (about 18 meters) [c] *20* That is, about 30 feet (about 9 meters) long, wide and high [d] *23* That is, about 15 feet (about 4.5 meters)

NRSV

them, then I will establish my promise with you, which I made to your father David. 13I will dwell among the children of Israel, and will not forsake my people Israel."

14So Solomon built the house, and finished it. 15He lined the walls of the house on the inside with boards of cedar; from the floor of the house to the rafters of the ceiling, he covered them on the inside with wood; and he covered the floor of the house with boards of cypress. 16He built twenty cubits of the rear of the house with boards of cedar from the floor to the rafters, and he built this within as an inner sanctuary, as the most holy place. 17The house, that is, the nave in front of the inner sanctuary, was forty cubits long. 18The cedar within the house had carvings of gourds and open flowers; all was cedar, no stone was seen. 19The inner sanctuary he prepared in the innermost part of the house, to set there the ark of the covenant of the LORD. 20The interior of the inner sanctuary was twenty cubits long, twenty cubits wide, and twenty cubits high; he overlaid it with pure gold. He also overlaid the altar with cedar.[a] 21Solomon overlaid the inside of the house with pure gold, then he drew chains of gold across, in front of the inner sanctuary, and overlaid it with gold. 22Next he overlaid the whole house with gold, in order that the whole house might be perfect; even the whole altar that belonged to the inner sanctuary he overlaid with gold.

23In the inner sanctuary he made two cherubim of olivewood, each ten cubits high. 24Five cubits was the length of one wing of the cherub, and five cubits the length of the other wing of the cherub; it was ten cubits from the tip of one wing to the tip of the other. 25The other cherub also measured ten cubits; both cherubim had the same measure and the same form. 26The height of one cherub was ten cubits, and so was that of the other cherub. 27He put the cherubim in the innermost part of the house; the wings of the cherubim were spread out so that a wing of one was touching the one wall, and a wing of the other cherub was touching the other wall; their other wings toward the center of the house were touching wing to wing. 28He also overlaid the cherubim with gold.

[a] Meaning of Heb uncertain

NIV

31For the entrance of the inner sanctuary he
made doors of olive wood with five-sided jambs.
32And on the two olive wood doors he carved
cherubim, palm trees and open flowers, and overlaid the cherubim and palm trees with beaten
gold. 33In the same way he made four-sided jambs
of olive wood for the entrance to the main hall.
34He also made two pine doors, each having two
leaves that turned in sockets. 35He carved cherubim, palm trees and open flowers on them and
overlaid them with gold hammered evenly over
the carvings.

36And he built the inner courtyard of three
courses of dressed stone and one course of
trimmed cedar beams.

37The foundation of the temple of the LORD was
laid in the fourth year, in the month of Ziv. 38In
the eleventh year in the month of Bul, the eighth
month, the temple was finished in all its details
according to its specifications. He had spent seven
years building it.

NRSV

29He carved the walls of the house all around
about with carved engravings of cherubim, palm
trees, and open flowers, in the inner and outer
rooms. 30The floor of the house he overlaid with
gold, in the inner and outer rooms.

31For the entrance to the inner sanctuary he
made doors of olivewood; the lintel and the
doorposts were five-sided.[a] 32He covered the two
doors of olivewood with carvings of cherubim,
palm trees, and open flowers; he overlaid them
with gold, and spread gold on the cherubim and
on the palm trees.

33So also he made for the entrance to the nave
doorposts of olivewood, four-sided each, 34and
two doors of cypress wood; the two leaves of the
one door were folding, and the two leaves of the
other door were folding. 35He carved cherubim,
palm trees, and open flowers, overlaying them
with gold evenly applied upon the carved work.
36He built the inner court with three courses of
dressed stone to one course of cedar beams.

37In the fourth year the foundation of the
house of the LORD was laid, in the month of Ziv.
38In the eleventh year, in the month of Bul, which
is the eighth month, the house was finished in all
its parts, and according to all its specifications. He
was seven years in building it.

a Meaning of Heb uncertain

COMMENTARY

Solomon's temple project is dated, according to the Hebrew text, to the 480th year of the exodus, meaning probably twelve generations of forty years each. (The Greek version, however, corrects the date to read "four hundred and fourtieth year.") The project is said to have begun in the fourth year of Solomon's reign, in the month of Ziv (according to the obsolete Canaanite calendar), which is explained as the second month (according to the more current Babylonian calendar, which begins its reckoning in the spring). The narrative thus recalls the time when Israel was enslaved under foreign oppressors. Long after Israel had been liberated, when the nation is supposed to be at the peak of its power, its own king is placing an enormous burden upon it through his alliance with another foreigner. Solomon endangers the freedom of his people and puts them under servitude with the slaves of Hiram; ironically, he does so in an effort to bring about and to ensure divine presence.

The Temple is described in all its ornate architectural detail, with all its dimensions. It is 60 cubits (90 feet) long, 20 cubits (30 feet) wide, and thirty cubits (45 feet) high; if one includes the portico, it is even larger, for a total area of about 100 feet long and 50 feet wide.[41] This would make the Jerusalem Temple larger than any

41. A cubit is the distance from the elbow to the tip of the index finger on the hand of an average-size man. It is about 17.5 inches in length.

Figure 2: Solomon's Temple

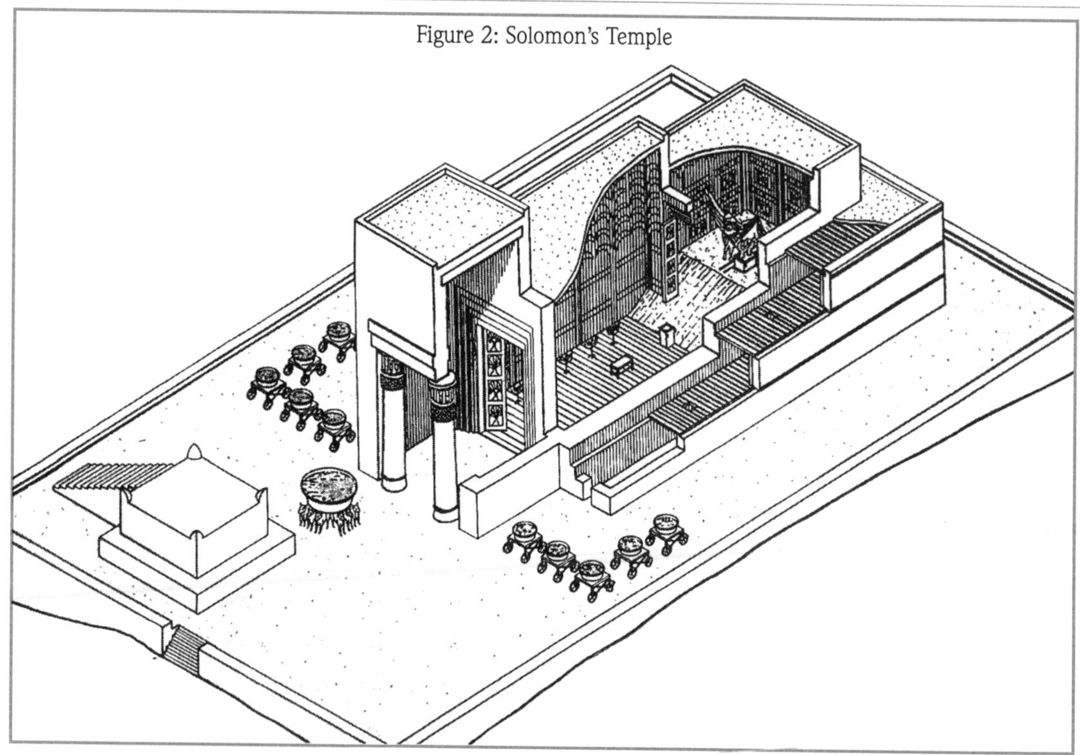

temple known in Palestine. The tripartite structure—with the porch (NIV, "portico"; NRSV, "vestibule"), the main hall (NRSV, "nave"), and the inner sanctuary—corresponds, however, to other exemplars from the region. Indeed, the Temple that Solomon built may well have been constructed after Canaanite and, especially, Phoenician models.

In the midst of the structural details comes an important theological condition, which is perhaps deliberately intrusive. It is a "word of the LORD" for Solomon regarding the building of the Temple (vv. 11-13). As if disregarding all the structural and decorative specifications, the divine word emphasizes obedience to God and the freedom of God's presence. The validity of the project is qualified by an explicit condition: *If* God's commandments are obeyed, *then* the promise to David will be made good; God will "dwell" in the midst of the people and not abandon them. The presence of the Temple will not ensure the dynasty's stability, nor will it bring about God's presence in Israel's midst. Only obedience will. Moreover, the verb used for God's dwelling is not the typical one used for the inhabitation of a house, ישב (*yāšab*, "sit," "live"), as is the case when the narrator speaks later of Solomon's residency in his palace (7:8). Rather, the verb is שכן (*šākan*, "tabernacle," "stay over"). For all its splendor, the Temple will not house the presence of God per se, but, provided that the people keep faith, God will somehow be present with them and not forsake them. One has to keep this condition in mind as one reads the rest of the details about the Temple and its furnishings.

The Temple is said to have been completed according to its elaborate specifications after seven years, in the month of Bul (according to the old Canaanite calendar), which is explained as the eighth month of the year (according to the Babylonian calendar), around the end of August and early September.

REFLECTIONS

Richard Nelson makes an apt analogy between the description of the Temple's architectural and decorative details and the commentary that one might get from a tour guide when visiting a famous building.[42] In this case, the reader is "guided" through the historic complex, the Temple, which is visible only in the imagination of the reader, for the physical structure no longer exists. The meticulous description accounts for the various measurements, structural peculiarities, architectural techniques, blend of materials, and so forth.

For some, such a tour may be utterly fascinating, if not awe-inspiring. At one level, that may have been the original intent of this commentary; the core of it may have been an official source that promoted the glories of the Temple. For many modern readers, however, the pedantic details may be overwhelming, particularly since the edifice exists no longer. The Temple is a relic that seems to be of interest primarily to history buffs.

There are many texts like that in the Bible. They seem to have a museum-like quality about them, and one wonders what all this has to do with the life of contemporary believers. Sometimes the length and pedantic character of the text drive one to ask in frustration: "So what?" The believer might and, perhaps, should ask: "What is the word of God in all of this?" This is what preachers struggle to answer with every text in Holy Scripture.

In this case, however, the text provides the answer. Intruding into the imagined visit to the historical edifice comes the divine word: "As for this temple . . . if you walk . . . then I will . . ." (6:12-13). The intrusive word of God seems to be a non sequitur in the midst of the architectural and decorative details. The received Hebrew text presents this word of the Lord despite its apparent discord. It is the imposing voice of another guide that points one beyond the glories of the edifice to another interrelation of parts, the excellence of which is measured neither in cubits nor in aesthetics. Rather, the significance of the Temple is tied to faithfulness: *If* people are faithful to the commandments, *then* God will be faithful to God's promises. The validity of the structure is dependent on the validity of the interrelationship between God and people. This is the word of the Lord about the sanctuary wherein we are to worship God.

42. Richard D. Nelson, *First and Second Kings,* Interpretation (Atlanta: John Knox, 1987) 43-46.

1 KINGS 7:1-51, A DIGRESSION ON SOLOMON'S HANDIWORK

NIV

7 It took Solomon thirteen years, however, to
complete the construction of his palace. 2He
built the Palace of the Forest of Lebanon a hundred
cubits long, fifty wide and thirty high,[a] with four
rows of cedar columns supporting trimmed cedar
beams. 3It was roofed with cedar above the beams
that rested on the columns—forty-five beams, fifteen
to a row. 4Its windows were placed high in sets of
three, facing each other. 5All the doorways had
rectangular frames; they were in the front part in
sets of three, facing each other.[b]

6He made a colonnade fifty cubits long and
thirty wide.[c] In front of it was a portico, and in

[a] 2 That is, about 150 feet (about 46 meters) long, 75 feet (about 23 meters) wide and 45 feet (about 13.5 meters) high [b] 5 The meaning of the Hebrew for this verse is uncertain. [c] 6 That is, about 75 feet (about 23 meters) long and 45 feet (about 13.5 meters) wide

NRSV

7 Solomon was building his own house thirteen years, and he finished his entire
house.

2He built the House of the Forest of the Lebanon one hundred cubits long, fifty cubits wide,
and thirty cubits high, built on four rows of cedar
pillars, with cedar beams on the pillars. 3It was
roofed with cedar on the forty-five rafters, fifteen
in each row, which were on the pillars. 4There
were window frames in the three rows, facing
each other in the three rows. 5All the doorways
and doorposts had four-sided frames, opposite,
facing each other in the three rows.

6He made the Hall of Pillars fifty cubits long
and thirty cubits wide. There was a porch in front
with pillars, and a canopy in front of them.

NIV

front of that were pillars and an overhanging roof.

[7]He built the throne hall, the Hall of Justice, where he was to judge, and he covered it with cedar from floor to ceiling.[a] [8]And the palace in which he was to live, set farther back, was similar in design. Solomon also made a palace like this hall for Pharaoh's daughter, whom he had married.

[9]All these structures, from the outside to the great courtyard and from foundation to eaves, were made of blocks of high-grade stone cut to size and trimmed with a saw on their inner and outer faces. [10]The foundations were laid with large stones of good quality, some measuring ten cubits[b] and some eight.[c] [11]Above were high-grade stones, cut to size, and cedar beams. [12]The great courtyard was surrounded by a wall of three courses of dressed stone and one course of trimmed cedar beams, as was the inner courtyard of the temple of the LORD with its portico.

[13]King Solomon sent to Tyre and brought Huram,[d] [14]whose mother was a widow from the tribe of Naphtali and whose father was a man of Tyre and a craftsman in bronze. Huram was highly skilled and experienced in all kinds of bronze work. He came to King Solomon and did all the work assigned to him.

[15]He cast two bronze pillars, each eighteen cubits high and twelve cubits around,[e] by line. [16]He also made two capitals of cast bronze to set on the tops of the pillars; each capital was five cubits[f] high. [17]A network of interwoven chains festooned the capitals on top of the pillars, seven for each capital. [18]He made pomegranates in two rows[g] encircling each network to decorate the capitals on top of the pillars.[h] He did the same for each capital. [19]The capitals on top of the pillars in the portico were in the shape of lilies, four cubits[i] high. [20]On the capitals of both pillars, above the bowl-shaped part next to the network, were

[a] *7* Vulgate and Syriac; Hebrew *floor* [b] *10* That is, about 15 feet (about 4.5 meters) [c] *10* That is, about 12 feet (about 3.6 meters) [d] *13* Hebrew *Hiram,* a variant of *Huram;* also in verses 40 and 45 [e] *15* That is, about 27 feet (about 8.1 meters) high and 18 feet (about 5.4 meters) around [f] *16* That is, about 7 1/2 feet (about 2.3 meters); also in verse 23 [g] *18* Two Hebrew manuscripts and Septuagint; most Hebrew manuscripts *made the pillars, and there were two rows* [h] *18* Many Hebrew manuscripts and Syriac; most Hebrew manuscripts *pomegranates* [i] *19* That is, about 6 feet (about 1.8 meters); also in verse 38

NRSV

7He made the Hall of the Throne where he was to pronounce judgment, the Hall of Justice, covered with cedar from floor to floor.

8His own house where he would reside, in the other court back of the hall, was of the same construction. Solomon also made a house like this hall for Pharaoh's daughter, whom he had taken in marriage.

9All these were made of costly stones, cut according to measure, sawed with saws, back and front, from the foundation to the coping, and from outside to the great court. [10]The foundation was of costly stones, huge stones, stones of eight and ten cubits. [11]There were costly stones above, cut to measure, and cedarwood. [12]The great court had three courses of dressed stone to one layer of cedar beams all around; so had the inner court of the house of the LORD, and the vestibule of the house.

13Now King Solomon invited and received Hiram from Tyre. [14]He was the son of a widow of the tribe of Naphtali, whose father, a man of Tyre, had been an artisan in bronze; he was full of skill, intelligence, and knowledge in working bronze. He came to King Solomon, and did all his work.

15He cast two pillars of bronze. Eighteen cubits was the height of the one, and a cord of twelve cubits would encircle it; the second pillar was the same.[a] [16]He also made two capitals of molten bronze, to set on the tops of the pillars; the height of the one capital was five cubits, and the height of the other capital was five cubits. [17]There were nets of checker work with wreaths of chain work for the capitals on the tops of the pillars; seven[b] for the one capital, and seven[c] for the other capital. [18]He made the columns with two rows around each latticework to cover the capitals that were above the pomegranates; he did the same with the other capital. [19]Now the capitals that were on the tops of the pillars in the vestibule were of lily-work, four cubits high. [20]The capitals were on the two pillars and also above the rounded projection that was beside the latticework; there were two hundred pomegranates in rows all around; and so with the other capital.

[a] Cn: Heb *and a cord of twelve cubits encircled the second pillar;* Compare Jer 52.21 [b] Heb: Gk *a net* [c] Heb: Gk *a net*

NIV

the two hundred pomegranates in rows all around. 21He erected the pillars at the portico of the temple. The pillar to the south he named Jakin[a] and the one to the north Boaz.[b] 22The capitals on top were in the shape of lilies. And so the work on the pillars was completed.

23He made the Sea of cast metal, circular in shape, measuring ten cubits[c] from rim to rim and five cubits high. It took a line of thirty cubits[d] to measure around it. 24Below the rim, gourds encircled it—ten to a cubit. The gourds were cast in two rows in one piece with the Sea.

25The Sea stood on twelve bulls, three facing north, three facing west, three facing south and three facing east. The Sea rested on top of them, and their hindquarters were toward the center. 26It was a handbreadth[e] in thickness, and its rim was like the rim of a cup, like a lily blossom. It held two thousand baths.[f]

27He also made ten movable stands of bronze; each was four cubits long, four wide and three high.[g] 28This is how the stands were made: They had side panels attached to uprights. 29On the panels between the uprights were lions, bulls and cherubim—and on the uprights as well. Above and below the lions and bulls were wreaths of hammered work. 30Each stand had four bronze wheels with bronze axles, and each had a basin resting on four supports, cast with wreaths on each side. 31On the inside of the stand there was an opening that had a circular frame one cubit[h] deep. This opening was round, and with its basework it measured a cubit and a half.[i] Around its opening there was engraving. The panels of the stands were square, not round. 32The four wheels were under the panels, and the axles of the wheels were attached to the stand. The diameter of each wheel was a cubit and a half. 33The wheels were made like chariot wheels; the axles, rims, spokes and hubs were all of cast metal.

34Each stand had four handles, one on each corner, projecting from the stand. 35At the top of the stand there was a circular band half a cubit[j]

[a] *21 Jakin* probably means *he establishes.* [b] *21 Boaz* probably means *in him is strength.* [c] *23* That is, about 15 feet (about 4.5 meters) [d] *23* That is, about 45 feet (about 13.5 meters) [e] *26* That is, about 3 inches (about 8 centimeters) [f] *26* That is, probably about 11,500 gallons (about 44 kiloliters); the Septuagint does not have this sentence. [g] *27* That is, about 6 feet (about 1.8 meters) long and wide and about 4 1/2 feet (about 1.3 meters) high [h] *31* That is, about 1 1/2 feet (about 0.5 meter) [i] *31* That is, about 2 1/4 feet (about 0.7 meter); also in verse 32 [j] *35* That is, about 3/4 foot (about 0.2 meter)

NRSV

21He set up the pillars at the vestibule of the temple; he set up the pillar on the south and called it Jachin; and he set up the pillar on the north and called it Boaz. 22On the tops of the pillars was lily-work. Thus the work of the pillars was finished.

23Then he made the molten sea; it was round, ten cubits from brim to brim, and five cubits high. A line of thirty cubits would encircle it completely. 24Under its brim were panels all around it, each of ten cubits, surrounding the sea; there were two rows of panels, cast when it was cast. 25It stood on twelve oxen, three facing north, three facing west, three facing south, and three facing east; the sea was set on them. The hindquarters of each were toward the inside. 26Its thickness was a handbreadth; its brim was made like the brim of a cup, like the flower of a lily; it held two thousand baths.[a]

27He also made the ten stands of bronze; each stand was four cubits long, four cubits wide, and three cubits high. 28This was the construction of the stands: they had borders; the borders were within the frames; 29on the borders that were set in the frames were lions, oxen, and cherubim. On the frames, both above and below the lions and oxen, there were wreaths of beveled work. 30Each stand had four bronze wheels and axles of bronze; at the four corners were supports for a basin. The supports were cast with wreaths at the side of each. 31Its opening was within the crown whose height was one cubit; its opening was round, as a pedestal is made; it was a cubit and a half wide. At its opening there were carvings; its borders were four-sided, not round. 32The four wheels were underneath the borders; the axles of the wheels were in the stands; and the height of a wheel was a cubit and a half. 33The wheels were made like a chariot wheel; their axles, their rims, their spokes, and their hubs were all cast. 34There were four supports at the four corners of each stand; the supports were of one piece with the stands. 35On the top of the stand there was a round band half a cubit high; on the top of the stand, its stays and its borders were of one piece with it. 36On the surfaces of its stays and on its borders he carved cherubim, lions, and palm trees,

[a] A Heb measure of volume

NIV

deep. The supports and panels were attached to the top of the stand. 36He engraved cherubim, lions and palm trees on the surfaces of the supports and on the panels, in every available space, with wreaths all around. 37This is the way he made the ten stands. They were all cast in the same molds and were identical in size and shape.

38He then made ten bronze basins, each holding forty baths[a] and measuring four cubits across, one basin to go on each of the ten stands. 39He placed five of the stands on the south side of the temple and five on the north. He placed the Sea on the south side, at the southeast corner of the temple. 40He also made the basins and shovels and sprinkling bowls.

So Huram finished all the work he had undertaken for King Solomon in the temple of the LORD:

41the two pillars;
the two bowl-shaped capitals on top of the pillars;
the two sets of network decorating the two bowl-shaped capitals on top of the pillars;
42the four hundred pomegranates for the two sets of network (two rows of pomegranates for each network, decorating the bowl-shaped capitals on top of the pillars);
43the ten stands with their ten basins;
44the Sea and the twelve bulls under it;
45the pots, shovels and sprinkling bowls.

All these objects that Huram made for King Solomon for the temple of the LORD were of burnished bronze. 46The king had them cast in clay molds in the plain of the Jordan between Succoth and Zarethan. 47Solomon left all these things unweighed, because there were so many; the weight of the bronze was not determined.

48Solomon also made all the furnishings that were in the LORD's temple:

the golden altar;
the golden table on which was the bread of the Presence;
49the lampstands of pure gold (five on the right and five on the left, in front of the inner sanctuary);
the gold floral work and lamps and tongs;

[a] *38* That is, about 230 gallons (about 880 liters)

NRSV

where each had space, with wreaths all around. 37In this way he made the ten stands; all of them were cast alike, with the same size and the same form.

38He made ten basins of bronze; each basin held forty baths,[a] each basin measured four cubits; there was a basin for each of the ten stands. 39He set five of the stands on the south side of the house, and five on the north side of the house; he set the sea on the southeast corner of the house.

40Hiram also made the pots, the shovels, and the basins. So Hiram finished all the work that he did for King Solomon on the house of the LORD: 41the two pillars, the two bowls of the capitals that were on the tops of the pillars, the two latticeworks to cover the two bowls of the capitals that were on the tops of the pillars; 42the four hundred pomegranates for the two latticeworks, two rows of pomegranates for each latticework, to cover the two bowls of the capitals that were on the pillars; 43the ten stands, the ten basins on the stands; 44the one sea, and the twelve oxen underneath the sea.

45The pots, the shovels, and the basins, all these vessels that Hiram made for King Solomon for the house of the LORD were of burnished bronze. 46In the plain of the Jordan the king cast them, in the clay ground between Succoth and Zarethan. 47Solomon left all the vessels unweighed, because there were so many of them; the weight of the bronze was not determined.

48So Solomon made all the vessels that were in the house of the LORD: the golden altar, the golden table for the bread of the Presence, 49the lampstands of pure gold, five on the south side and five on the north, in front of the inner sanctuary; the flowers, the lamps, and the tongs, of gold; 50the cups, snuffers, basins, dishes for incense, and firepans, of pure gold; the sockets for the doors of the innermost part of the house, the most holy place, and for the doors of the nave of the temple, of gold.

51Thus all the work that King Solomon did on the house of the LORD was finished. Solomon brought in the things that his father David had dedicated, the silver, the gold, and the vessels, and stored them in the treasuries of the house of the LORD.

[a] A Heb measure of volume

NIV

50the pure gold basins, wick trimmers, sprinkling bowls, dishes and censers;
and the gold sockets for the doors of the innermost room, the Most Holy Place, and also for the doors of the main hall of the temple.

51When all the work King Solomon had done for the temple of the LORD was finished, he brought in the things his father David had dedicated—the silver and gold and the furnishings—and he placed them in the treasuries of the LORD's temple.

COMMENTARY

7:1-12. In contrast to the Temple, which had taken seven years to build (6:38), we are told that Solomon's own house took nearly twice as long—thirteen years. The contrast is all the more striking when we keep in mind the fact that the original text had no chapter divisions, which were introduced only in medieval times. Disregarding the chapter division, then, one discerns possibly a criticism of Solomon, a criticism that is subtle and more evident in the Hebrew than in the English translations: literally, "He built it [the Temple] seven years, but as for his own house, he built [it] thirteen years and completed all of it." Moreover, the royal complex, which comprised several buildings, appears to be considerably larger than the Temple. The "House of the Forest of Lebanon," apparently the palace treasury and armory (10:17, 21; Isa 22:8), is alone larger than the Temple. It is 100 cubits (150 feet) long, fifty cubits (75 feet) wide, and 30 cubits (45 feet) high (cf. 6:2). The narrator also makes special mention of Solomon's construction of a house for Pharaoh's daughter whom he had married (lit., "received," v. 8).

7:13-51. Solomon not only "received" (לקח *lāqaḥ*) the daughter of Pharaoh (7:8), something he did early in his reign (3:1-3), but he also "received" (*lāqaḥ*) Hiram, a professional bronzesmith from Tyre, who is said to have done all of Solomon's work (v. 14). The smith's mother was a widow from the Israelite tribe of Naphtali, and perhaps this tie was once used to emphasize his legitimacy as the builder of the Lord's Temple in Jerusalem. Yet, the narrator seems to take pains to point out that Hiram was "received" from Tyre, that his father was a Tyrian, and that he had acquired his skills from his father. It is noteworthy, too, that he has the same name as the king of Tyre, with whom Solomon is dealing in order to attain materials to build the Temple.

The passage makes it clear throughout that it was the Phoenician who had done all the work: He cast, he made, he set, and "he finished all the work" (v. 40). The emphasis on his handiwork is tedious. Solomon, too, is responsible: He did all the work of the Temple and finished it (v. 51). The Temple here is clearly the product of human hands. Perhaps the narrator means for us to keep this in mind as we read about the dedication of the Temple.

REFLECTIONS

This chapter stands out mainly as an intrusion. The preceding chapter ends with the completion of the Temple. The next chapter will give an account of its dedication. In between the two stands this odd chapter highlighting Solomon's construction of his own palace and the emphasis that the building is the work of Hiram, the Tyrian artisan, and Solomon. It was they who made it; it was they who completed it.

The digression is, perhaps, not accidental. In any case, whether or not it has been deliberately put in this context, this intrusion is theologically important. It serves at once as a postscript to the account of the completion of the Temple and a preface to the account of the Temple's dedication.

If only in an implicit way, the text raises some questions about Solomon's worldly ambition (7:1-12). It was not for purely altruistic and pious reasons that the Temple was built so gloriously. It is a reflection of the vanity of Solomon and the dangerously compromising character of his reign.

Most important, the passage also stresses the Temple and its furnishings as human handiwork, just as the palace complex is. This is the perspective of the martyr Stephen: "It was Solomon who built a house for [God]. Yet the Most High does not dwell in houses made with human hands" (Acts 7:47-48 NRSV). Jesus, too, notes that while human beings may be enamored of the physical beauty of a temple, it is, in fact, a destructible edifice (Luke 21:5-6). By contrast, the metaphorical "temple" that God brought about on earth, culminating in the resurrection of Jesus from the dead, is not a temple made with human hands (Mark 14:58; John 2:19-22).

1 KINGS 8:1-66, THE DEDICATION OF THE TEMPLE

OVERVIEW

This literary unit, the end product of generations of theological struggles, is structured around the prayer of Solomon at the ceremonial dedication of the Temple (see also 2 Chronicles 5–7). The passage begins with the assembling of the people (v. 1), and it concludes with their departure (v. 66). The tensions between the various traditions about divine presence are still discernible; the seams are still evident. The present unit is carefully quilted, broadly patterned to focus on the dedicatory prayer:

A Commencement of the ceremony, vv. 1-13
  B Solomon's preliminary remarks, vv. 14-21
    C Solomon's prayer, vv. 22-53
  B′ Solomon's closing remarks, vv. 54-61
A′ Conclusion of the festival, vv. 62-66

1 Kings 8:1-13, Commencement of the Ceremony

NIV

8 Then King Solomon summoned into his
presence at Jerusalem the elders of Israel,
all the heads of the tribes and the chiefs of the
Israelite families, to bring up the ark of the LORD's
covenant from Zion, the City of David. [2]All the
men of Israel came together to King Solomon at
the time of the festival in the month of Ethanim,
the seventh month.

[3]When all the elders of Israel had arrived, the
priests took up the ark, [4]and they brought up the

NRSV

8 Then Solomon assembled the elders of
Israel and all the heads of the tribes, the
leaders of the ancestral houses of the Israelites,
before King Solomon in Jerusalem, to bring up
the ark of the covenant of the LORD out of the
city of David, which is Zion. [2]All the people of
Israel assembled to King Solomon at the festival
in the month Ethanim, which is the seventh
month. [3]And all the elders of Israel came, and the
priests carried the ark. [4]So they brought up

NIV

ark of the LORD and the Tent of Meeting and all
the sacred furnishings in it. The priests and Levites
carried them up, 5and King Solomon and the
entire assembly of Israel that had gathered about
him were before the ark, sacrificing so many
sheep and cattle that they could not be recorded
or counted.

6The priests then brought the ark of the LORD's
covenant to its place in the inner sanctuary of the
temple, the Most Holy Place, and put it beneath
the wings of the cherubim. 7The cherubim spread
their wings over the place of the ark and overshadowed the ark and its carrying poles. 8These
poles were so long that their ends could be seen
from the Holy Place in front of the inner sanctuary, but not from outside the Holy Place; and they
are still there today. 9There was nothing in the
ark except the two stone tablets that Moses had
placed in it at Horeb, where the LORD made a
covenant with the Israelites after they came out
of Egypt.

10When the priests withdrew from the Holy
Place, the cloud filled the temple of the LORD.
11And the priests could not perform their service
because of the cloud, for the glory of the LORD
filled his temple.

12Then Solomon said, "The LORD has said that
he would dwell in a dark cloud; 13I have indeed
built a magnificent temple for you, a place for you
to dwell forever."

NRSV

the ark of the LORD, the tent of meeting, and all
the holy vessels that were in the tent; the priests
and the Levites brought them up. 5King Solomon
and all the congregation of Israel, who had assembled before him, were with him before the ark,
sacrificing so many sheep and oxen that they
could not be counted or numbered. 6Then the
priests brought the ark of the covenant of the
LORD to its place, in the inner sanctuary of the
house, in the most holy place, underneath the
wings of the cherubim. 7For the cherubim spread
out their wings over the place of the ark, so that
the cherubim made a covering above the ark and
its poles. 8The poles were so long that the ends
of the poles were seen from the holy place in
front of the inner sanctuary; but they could not
be seen from outside; they are there to this day.
9There was nothing in the ark except the two
tablets of stone that Moses had placed there at
Horeb, where the LORD made a covenant with the
Israelites, when they came out of the land of
Egypt. 10And when the priests came out of the
holy place, a cloud filled the house of the LORD,
11so that the priests could not stand to minister
because of the cloud; for the glory of the LORD
filled the house of the LORD.

12Then Solomon said,

"The LORD has said that he would dwell in
thick darkness.
13 I have built you an exalted house,
a place for you to dwell in forever."

COMMENTARY

8:1-2. Solomon's temple building project culminates in the dedication of the edifice in the month of Ethanim (v. 2), the seventh month—that is, late September and early October. Since the Temple was already completed according to all its specifications in the month of Bul, the eighth month (6:38), this means that the official dedication was held off for nearly a year, possibly to coincide with the festival known as the Feast of Tabernacles (Lev 23:34, 39; Num 29:12-34), in the seventh month, when a large crowd of people would have come into the city. The Feast of Tabernacles was recognized as the time for the ceremonial renewal of the covenant (Deut 31:9-13), and this may be significant as well. Some scholars also believe that the festival was associated with the autumn new year and the celebration of divine enthronement.

8:3-5. The leaders of the nation gather in Jerusalem, together with the multitudes for that occasion. The ark of the covenant, at once a symbol of divine presence in the midst of God's people and a tangible reminder of Israel's covenant relationship with the Lord, is brought in procession from its location in the City of David, called by its ideologically loaded name "Zion" (2

Sam 5:7; Pss 2:6; 9:11; 14:7; 48:2; 50:2; 74:2; 78:68; 99:2). Clearly, it was believed that God was somehow present in the procession, for the ark of the covenant was brought with the "tent of meeting" (v. 4), and generous sacrifices were made "before the ark" (v. 5).

8:6-11. In some ways, the ritual is reminiscent of the dedication of cultic images elsewhere in ancient Canaan and Mesopotamia, even though the ark is not a divine image. At the climax of the ceremony, it is placed under the cherubim (v. 6), a pair of sphinx-like creatures with their wings spread across the inner sanctuary. Some scholars who have reconstructed the scene argue that the cherubim with outstretched wings represented a gigantic throne, smaller versions of which have been found in ancient Near Eastern iconography. Accordingly, the cherubim symbolized the royal seat on which the deity was thought to have been invisibly enthroned, and the ark was viewed as the footstool. An ivory plaque excavated at Megiddo and a sarcophagus of the Phoenician king Ahiram (a form to which the name "Hiram" is related) both depict a cherubim-throne with a seated king, whose feet rest upon a box-like footstool.[43] Elsewhere in the ancient Near East, treaty documents were sometimes placed in boxes that doubled as footstools for the kings. So it is interesting to note that the ark is said to have contained the two tablets placed in it by Moses when the covenant was made on Mt. Horeb.

The narrative emphasizes, too, that the ark comes with carrying poles, although that fact may not be obvious to everyone, since the poles could not be seen outside the inner sanctuary. The poles indicate the mobility of the ark and, hence, also the freedom of the deity from the sanctuary; this was no footstool of a deity permanently enthroned in the building. In Israel's persistent sanctions against the use of cultic images, the ark was merely a reminder of God's suzerainty and the covenant that bound Israel to the deity. Here, as elsewhere in the deuteronomistic tradition, the ark is called "the ark of the covenant of the LORD" (vv. 1, 6) and, lest there be any doubt, it is observed that there is nothing else in the box except the tablets that have represented God's covenant with Israel since the time of Moses (v. 9; cf. Deut 10:1-5). In these ways, the ark is demythologized, and the mention of the poles for carrying it (vv. 7-8) is part of a theological effort to move away from any misunderstanding of God as a king permanently enthroned in the Temple.

8:12-13. Still, the notion of the deity as a king lies in the background. In an archaic poetic fragment retained in these verses,[44] Solomon declares that he has built the Lord "an exalted house" (or, perhaps, "a princely house"). Both the NRSV and the NIV have "dwell." There are, in fact, two different verbs in these two verses. Whereas the verb in v. 12 (שׁכן *šākan*) refers to the settling of the "thick darkness" that accompanies the Lord's theophany (see Deut 4:11; 5:22; Ps 18:10-11; 97:2), the verb in v. 13 (ישׁב *yāšab*) may also mean "sit" and, more specifically, "sit [enthroned]." So here, again, the imagery of divine kingship is in the background.

One should pay attention to the fact that two different words are used here to describe God's presence in relation to the Temple. Subtle theological nuances may, in fact, have been intended. We should translate the Hebrew of the poetic fragment as follows:

> The LORD has said he would tabernacle in thick
> darkness.
> I [Solomon] have, indeed, built you a royal house,
> an establishment of your enthroning. (author's trans.)

The notion of God's tabernacling presence is prominent in some theological traditions in Israel. It is a way of conveying the free presence of the deity, an avoidance of the language of an enthroned and entrenched deity. So Ezekiel and the Priestly tradition of the Torah speak not of God enthroned in the Temple, but of God's *glory*, represented by a cloud that "tabernacles" at the sanctuary, coming and going as God wills (Exod 25:8; 29:45; Ezek 10:19, 22; 43:1-12). The use of imagery of the Temple's being filled with the cloud of the Lord's "glory" (vv. 10-11) and the tabernacling of the Lord through thick darkness is a way of expressing the mysterious and free presence of the deity.

As for the Temple, the "princely house" itself, it is an establishment of God's "enthroning." In-

43. See J. B. Pritchard, *The Ancient Near East in Pictures*, 2nd ed. (Princeton: Princeton University Press, 1969) 111, 157-58.

44. According to the Greek text, these words are from "The Book of the Song," probably an allusion to the lost "Book of Yashar," mentioned in Josh 10:13; 2 Sam 1:18.

asmuch as the verb for "enthroning" (לשבתך *lĕšibtĕkā*) is used for all kinds of sitting and residing, it is easy to see how that view might have led to an understanding of the Temple as God's actual dwelling place. This is a notion, a theological misinterpretation, that the present narrative about the dedication tries to dispel. In combination with the language of the tabernacling presence of God through the mysterious "thick darkness," one ought to understand the Temple not as the earthly dwelling place *for* God, but as a tangible establishment *of* (the fact of) divine enthroning. One might say that the Temple is a concrete representation of the reality of the sovereignty of God. The Temple is God's "princely house" only in this sense. (See Reflections at 8:62-66.)

1 Kings 8:14-21, Solomon's Preliminary Remarks

NIV

14While the whole assembly of Israel was standing there, the king turned around and blessed them. 15Then he said:

"Praise be to the LORD, the God of Israel, who with his own hand has fulfilled what he promised with his own mouth to my father David. For he said, 16'Since the day I brought my people Israel out of Egypt, I have not chosen a city in any tribe of Israel to have a temple built for my Name to be there, but I have chosen David to rule my people Israel.'

17"My father David had it in his heart to build a temple for the Name of the LORD, the God of Israel. 18But the LORD said to my father David, 'Because it was in your heart to build a temple for my Name, you did well to have this in your heart. 19Nevertheless, you are not the one to build the temple, but your son, who is your own flesh and blood—he is the one who will build the temple for my Name.'

20"The LORD has kept the promise he made: I have succeeded David my father and now I sit on the throne of Israel, just as the LORD promised, and I have built the temple for the Name of the LORD, the God of Israel. 21I have provided a place there for the ark, in which is the covenant of the LORD that he made with our fathers when he brought them out of Egypt."

NRSV

14Then the king turned around and blessed all the assembly of Israel, while all the assembly of Israel stood. 15He said, "Blessed be the LORD, the God of Israel, who with his hand has fulfilled what he promised with his mouth to my father David, saying, 16'Since the day that I brought my people Israel out of Egypt, I have not chosen a city from any of the tribes of Israel in which to build a house, that my name might be there; but I chose David to be over my people Israel.' 17My father David had it in mind to build a house for the name of the LORD, the God of Israel. 18But the LORD said to my father David, 'You did well to consider building a house for my name; 19nevertheless you shall not build the house, but your son who shall be born to you shall build the house for my name.' 20Now the LORD has upheld the promise that he made; for I have risen in the place of my father David; I sit on the throne of Israel, as the LORD promised, and have built the house for the name of the LORD, the God of Israel. 21There I have provided a place for the ark, in which is the covenant of the LORD that he made with our ancestors when he brought them out of the land of Egypt."

COMMENTARY

In the early monarchical period, such a dedicatory ceremony would have been fraught with political symbolism. The public ritual signified at once the election of the Davidic dynasty (in this case the choice of Solomon) and also the election of Zion (see v. 1). This dual election, especially important in Judah, is affirmed. Despite echoes of the notion of God's kingship, the Temple is not the place in which God is enthroned. Indeed, the Temple is not the Lord's palace, but is very deliberately identified as a house for the Name of the Lord. The theology of divine presence as regards the Temple is carefully nuanced. In this context, the biblical writer-theologian is able to affirm simultaneously the transcendence (remoteness) and immanence (nearness) of God. The deity is not enthroned in the Temple per se, yet divine presence is somehow represented by the Name of God in the Temple. The authority of God is there, whether or not God is personally present. Additionally, despite Solomon's words in vv. 12-13, the Temple is specifically identified as a place for the chest that contains the tangible symbols of the covenant, namely, the covenant documents (the tablets). Here the theologian moves beyond the promise to David that undergirds much of Judean theology to point to the exodus from Egypt and the covenant that God made with Israel. It is the salvific presence of God, culminating in the covenant with Israel, that the Temple affirms. The Temple is not so much the *locus* of God's presence as it is a reminder of God's free presence that is made good in the covenant. (See Reflections at 8:62-66.)

1 Kings 8:22-53, Solomon's Dedicatory Prayer

NIV

22Then Solomon stood before the altar of the
LORD in front of the whole assembly of Israel,
spread out his hands toward heaven 23and said:

"O LORD, God of Israel, there is no God
like you in heaven above or on earth below—
you who keep your covenant of love with
your servants who continue wholeheartedly
in your way. 24You have kept your promise
to your servant David my father; with your
mouth you have promised and with your
hand you have fulfilled it—as it is today.

25"Now LORD, God of Israel, keep for your
servant David my father the promises you
made to him when you said, 'You shall never
fail to have a man to sit before me on the
throne of Israel, if only your sons are careful
in all they do to walk before me as you have
done.' 26And now, O God of Israel, let your
word that you promised your servant David
my father come true.

27"But will God really dwell on earth? The
heavens, even the highest heaven, cannot
contain you. How much less this temple I
have built! 28Yet give attention to your servant's prayer and his plea for mercy, O LORD
my God. Hear the cry and the prayer that
your servant is praying in your presence this
day. 29May your eyes be open toward this
temple night and day, this place of which you

NRSV

22Then Solomon stood before the altar of the
LORD in the presence of all the assembly of Israel,
and spread out his hands to heaven. 23He said,
"O LORD, God of Israel, there is no God like you
in heaven above or on earth beneath, keeping
covenant and steadfast love for your servants who
walk before you with all their heart, 24the covenant that you kept for your servant my father
David as you declared to him; you promised with
your mouth and have this day fulfilled with your
hand. 25Therefore, O LORD, God of Israel, keep for
your servant my father David that which you
promised him, saying, 'There shall never fail you
a successor before me to sit on the throne of
Israel, if only your children look to their way, to
walk before me as you have walked before me.'
26Therefore, O God of Israel, let your word be
confirmed, which you promised to your servant
my father David.

27"But will God indeed dwell on the earth?
Even heaven and the highest heaven cannot contain you, much less this house that I have built!
28Regard your servant's prayer and his plea,
O LORD my God, heeding the cry and the prayer
that your servant prays to you today; 29that your
eyes may be open night and day toward this
house, the place of which you said, 'My name
shall be there,' that you may heed the prayer that
your servant prays toward this place. 30Hear the
plea of your servant and of your people Israel

NIV

said, 'My Name shall be there,' so that you will hear the prayer your servant prays toward this place. 30Hear the supplication of your servant and of your people Israel when they pray toward this place. Hear from heaven, your dwelling place, and when you hear, forgive.

31"When a man wrongs his neighbor and is required to take an oath and he comes and swears the oath before your altar in this temple, 32then hear from heaven and act. Judge between your servants, condemning the guilty and bringing down on his own head what he has done. Declare the innocent not guilty, and so establish his innocence.

33"When your people Israel have been defeated by an enemy because they have sinned against you, and when they turn back to you and confess your name, praying and making supplication to you in this temple, 34then hear from heaven and forgive the sin of your people Israel and bring them back to the land you gave to their fathers.

35"When the heavens are shut up and there is no rain because your people have sinned against you, and when they pray toward this place and confess your name and turn from their sin because you have afflicted them, 36then hear from heaven and forgive the sin of your servants, your people Israel. Teach them the right way to live, and send rain on the land you gave your people for an inheritance.

37"When famine or plague comes to the land, or blight or mildew, locusts or grasshoppers, or when an enemy besieges them in any of their cities, whatever disaster or disease may come, 38and when a prayer or plea is made by any of your people Israel—each one aware of the afflictions of his own heart, and spreading out his hands toward this temple—39then hear from heaven, your dwelling place. Forgive and act; deal with each man according to all he does, since you know his heart (for you alone know the hearts of all men), 40so that they will fear you all the time they live in the land you gave our fathers.

41"As for the foreigner who does not belong to your people Israel but has come from a distant land because of your name— 42for

NRSV

when they pray toward this place; O hear in heaven your dwelling place; heed and forgive.

31"If someone sins against a neighbor and is given an oath to swear, and comes and swears before your altar in this house, 32then hear in heaven, and act, and judge your servants, condemning the guilty by bringing their conduct on their own head, and vindicating the righteous by rewarding them according to their righteousness.

33"When your people Israel, having sinned against you, are defeated before an enemy but turn again to you, confess your name, pray and plead with you in this house, 34then hear in heaven, forgive the sin of your people Israel, and bring them again to the land that you gave to their ancestors.

35"When heaven is shut up and there is no rain because they have sinned against you, and then they pray toward this place, confess your name, and turn from their sin, because you punish[a] them, 36then hear in heaven, and forgive the sin of your servants, your people Israel, when you teach them the good way in which they should walk; and grant rain on your land, which you have given to your people as an inheritance.

37"If there is famine in the land, if there is plague, blight, mildew, locust, or caterpillar; if their enemy besieges them in any[b] of their cities; whatever plague, whatever sickness there is; 38whatever prayer, whatever plea there is from any individual or from all your people Israel, all knowing the afflictions of their own hearts so that they stretch out their hands toward this house; 39then hear in heaven your dwelling place, forgive, act, and render to all whose hearts you know—according to all their ways, for only you know what is in every human heart— 40so that they may fear you all the days that they live in the land that you gave to our ancestors.

41"Likewise when a foreigner, who is not of your people Israel, comes from a distant land because of your name 42—for they shall hear of your great name, your mighty hand, and your outstretched arm—when a foreigner comes and prays toward this house, 43then hear in heaven your dwelling place, and do according to all that the foreigner calls to you, so that all the peoples

[a] Or *when you answer* [b] Gk Syr: Heb *in the land*

NIV

men will hear of your great name and your
mighty hand and your outstretched arm—
when he comes and prays toward this temple,
43then hear from heaven, your dwelling place,
and do whatever the foreigner asks of you, so
that all the peoples of the earth may know
your name and fear you, as do your own
people Israel, and may know that this house
I have built bears your Name.

44"When your people go to war against
their enemies, wherever you send them, and
when they pray to the LORD toward the city
you have chosen and the temple I have built
for your Name, 45then hear from heaven their
prayer and their plea, and uphold their cause.

46"When they sin against you—for there is
no one who does not sin—and you become
angry with them and give them over to the
enemy, who takes them captive to his own
land, far away or near; 47and if they have a
change of heart in the land where they are
held captive, and repent and plead with you
in the land of their conquerors and say, 'We
have sinned, we have done wrong, we have
acted wickedly'; 48and if they turn back to
you with all their heart and soul in the land
of their enemies who took them captive, and
pray to you toward the land you gave their
fathers, toward the city you have chosen and
the temple I have built for your Name; 49then
from heaven, your dwelling place, hear their
prayer and their plea, and uphold their cause.
50And forgive your people, who have sinned
against you; forgive all the offenses they have
committed against you, and cause their conquerors to show them mercy; 51for they are your
people and your inheritance, whom you brought
out of Egypt, out of that iron-smelting furnace.

52"May your eyes be open to your servant's
plea and to the plea of your people Israel, and
may you listen to them whenever they cry
out to you. 53For you singled them out from
all the nations of the world to be your own
inheritance, just as you declared through your
servant Moses when you, O Sovereign LORD,
brought our fathers out of Egypt."

NRSV

of the earth may know your name and fear you,
as do your people Israel, and so that they may
know that your name has been invoked on this
house that I have built.

44"If your people go out to battle against their
enemy, by whatever way you shall send them,
and they pray to the LORD toward the city that
you have chosen and the house that I have built
for your name, 45then hear in heaven their prayer
and their plea, and maintain their cause.

46"If they sin against you—for there is no one
who does not sin—and you are angry with them
and give them to an enemy, so that they are
carried away captive to the land of the enemy,
far off or near; 47yet if they come to their senses
in the land to which they have been taken captive, and repent, and plead with you in the land
of their captors, saying, 'We have sinned, and
have done wrong; we have acted wickedly'; 48if
they repent with all their heart and soul in the
land of their enemies, who took them captive,
and pray to you toward their land, which you
gave to their ancestors, the city that you have
chosen, and the house that I have built for your
name; 49then hear in heaven your dwelling place
their prayer and their plea, maintain their cause
50and forgive your people who have sinned against
you, and all their transgressions that they have
committed against you; and grant them compassion in the sight of their captors, so that they may
have compassion on them 51(for they are your
people and heritage, which you brought out of
Egypt, from the midst of the iron-smelter). 52Let
your eyes be open to the plea of your servant,
and to the plea of your people Israel, listening to
them whenever they call to you. 53For you have
separated them from among all the peoples of the
earth, to be your heritage, just as you promised
through Moses, your servant, when you brought
our ancestors out of Egypt, O Lord GOD."

COMMENTARY

8:22-30. Solomon's prayer is at the heart of the entire account of the dedication ceremony. The theological disposition of the narrative is nowhere more evident than in this long prayer. We are told that Solomon comes "before the altar" and "before the assembled people" and that he "spread his hands out to heaven" (v. 22; in v. 22 Solomon is standing, but in v. 54 he is kneeling). The wording is particularly poignant when one compares this account with Isaiah's description of Hezekiah in prayer at the Temple (Isa 37:14-16). The southern prophet, who stands in the Judean tradition that emphasizes God's presence as King in the Jerusalem Temple (see Pss 46:4-5; 76:2), speaks of Hezekiah's coming to the house of the Lord, spreading his petition "before the LORD," and praying to the God enthroned upon the cherubim (Isa 37:14-16). Hezekiah's posture is that of a lone petitioner appearing before an enthroned, though invisible, King. This is not what we have here in 1 Kings. Rather, the narrator is careful to say that Solomon stood "before *the altar* of the LORD," rather than "before the LORD." This account also emphasizes the covenant, entirely appropriate if the festival does, indeed, coincide with the Feast of Tabernacles. God is confessed as an incomparable One both in heaven and on earth, thus unlike the other deities of Israel's neighbors. The Lord, Israel's God, is the suzerain who keeps covenant promises. Perhaps the narrator also means that the deity is not locally enthroned, as the images of the other deities would be depicted. There is no denial of God's kingship, to be sure, but the focus is on the keeping of God's promise and on the obligation of the vassals to conduct themselves properly before their suzerain.

The movement away from the notion of God's enthroned presence in the Temple is especially clear in the rhetorical question posed in v. 27: "Will God indeed sit [enthroned] on the earth?" The verb here is the one used in v. 13, and, again, the NRSV and the NIV both translate it as "dwell." That is the same verb used in the old divine epithet associated with the ark at Shiloh: "The ark of the LORD of Hosts, who sits [enthroned] upon the cherubim" (1 Sam 4:4; 2 Sam 6:2). That is the epithet used by Hezekiah when he comes to pray to the Lord as King (Isa 37:16). The perspective in 1 Kings, however, offers a corrective to any such misunderstandings of divine presence. If there was any doubt as to the nature of God's "enthroning" presence before (v. 13), it is clarified here. Even the heaven and the highest heaven cannot contain God; how much less, then, can the Temple that a mere mortal has built? One cannot help reading this rhetorical question with v. 13 in mind. The Temple is a reminder of God's kingship; it is an establishment of God's eternal "enthroning." That enthroning is not limited by any place; it is certainly not limited to the Temple, for Solomon pleads that God's attention be turned toward it.

A curious convergence on the Temple is created by the repetition of the preposition "toward" in v. 29: Solomon asks God to respond "toward this house," while prayer is simultaneously directed "toward this place" (see also vv. 35, 38, 42), even though the petitioner may also actually be praying "in" the Temple (cf. vv. 31, 33). The Temple is neither God's residence nor the place where the petitioner personally encounters the deity. Rather, it is a place at which the needs of the petitioner coincide with the willingness of the deity to respond. The Temple is not the place where the very person of God is; rather, it is merely the place where God's presence may be known, where the authority of God is proclaimed.

Prayer is directed toward the Temple, while God's realm is associated with "heaven." One might argue that the reference to God's "enthroning" in heaven is a polemic against the notion of God's "enthroning" in the Temple. This is anti-Temple theology, as it were: God is enthroned, not in the earthly Temple, but in heaven. Yet, the biblical writer confesses that not even the heaven and the highest heaven can contain the deity. Locality is not at issue in all this talk of God's realm. God's transcendence and sovereignty are.

The translations in the NRSV and the NIV locate God's residence in heaven: "in heaven your dwelling place" (NRSV); "from heaven, your dwelling place" (NIV). The Hebrew is admittedly strained, as perhaps any reference to God's realm must be, and one should perhaps retain the ambiguity of the text: "Hear, unto your dwelling/enthroning, unto heaven" (v. 30).

8:31-53. There follows a series of circumstances in which God's "enthroned" presence is desired, including individual sins and corporate sins, prayers offered within the Temple and without the Temple, prayers from near and far, prayers for deliverance from natural disasters and from war, prayers by the people of Israel and prayers by outsiders. The disasters mentioned in the litany are reminiscent of the covenant curses that we read in Deuteronomy 28 and in various vassal treaties from elsewhere in the ancient Near East. They are tragedies that would befall covenant violators.

The details of these circumstances are probably less significant than the fact that there seven situations are identified, seven being the number of completeness in the ancient Near East. One notes, too, the comprehensive coverage: "whatever plague, whatever sickness" (v. 37); "whatever prayer, whatever plea" (v. 38); "whenever the foreigner comes and prays toward this house" (v. 42); "whenever they call" (v. 52). The seventh situation, the longest and most detailed one, is the climax of the series, and there is reason to believe that the text intends to convey the idea of completeness. Humanity will always be in need of divine presence, for "there is no one who does not sin" (v. 46).

In vv. 46-50, there is a tantalizing wordplay involving the Semitic roots suggesting captivity (שבי *šĕbî*) and repentance or turning around (שוב *šûb*) and, perhaps, also the Hebrew word for God's "enthroning" presence (שבת *šebet*). The English translations do not adequately convey this wordplay. The litany suggests the way by which one may avert disasters that inevitably come with the violation of the covenant, calamities expressed by the metaphor of captivity (*šĕbî*). The hope lies in a change of heart, or repentance (*šûb*). Only with such a turnaround may the captive offender appeal for the forgiveness that is possible because God's presence is both heavenly (transcendent) and "enthroning" (sovereign). The litany appeals to God's compassion in the face of captivity (v. 50), and the basis for that appeal is God's sovereign grace manifested in salvation from bondage, God's election of a particular people, and God's promise made long ago. (See Reflections at 8:62-66.)

1 Kings 8:54-61, Solomon's Closing Remarks

NIV

54When Solomon had finished all these prayers
and supplications to the LORD, he rose from before
the altar of the LORD, where he had been kneeling
with his hands spread out toward heaven. 55He
stood and blessed the whole assembly of Israel in
a loud voice, saying:

56"Praise be to the LORD, who has given rest
to his people Israel just as he promised. Not one
word has failed of all the good promises he gave
through his servant Moses. 57May the LORD our
God be with us as he was with our fathers; may
he never leave us nor forsake us. 58May he turn
our hearts to him, to walk in all his ways and
to keep the commands, decrees and regulations
he gave our fathers. 59And may these words of
mine, which I have prayed before the LORD, be
near to the LORD our God day and night, that
he may uphold the cause of his servant and the

NRSV

54Now when Solomon finished offering all this
prayer and this plea to the LORD, he arose from
facing the altar of the LORD, where he had knelt
with hands outstretched toward heaven; 55he
stood and blessed all the assembly of Israel with
a loud voice:

56"Blessed be the LORD, who has given rest to
his people Israel according to all that he promised;
not one word has failed of all his good promise,
which he spoke through his servant Moses. 57The
LORD our God be with us, as he was with our
ancestors; may he not leave us or abandon us,
58but incline our hearts to him, to walk in all his
ways, and to keep his commandments, his statutes, and his ordinances, which he commanded
our ancestors. 59Let these words of mine, with
which I pleaded before the LORD, be near to the
LORD our God day and night, and may he maintain
the cause of his servant and the cause of his

NIV

cause of his people Israel according to each day's need, [60]so that all the peoples of the earth may know that the LORD is God and that there is no other. [61]But your hearts must be fully committed to the LORD our God, to live by his decrees and obey his commands, as at this time."

NRSV

people Israel, as each day requires; [60]so that all the peoples of the earth may know that the LORD is God; there is no other. [61]Therefore devote yourselves completely to the LORD our God, walking in his statutes and keeping his commandments, as at this day."

COMMENTARY

Together with vv. 14-21, these remarks of Solomon bracket his prayer. The two subsections are approximately the same length—seven verses each, according to all modern editions of the Bible. The preliminary remarks (vv. 14-21) are preceded by an account of the commencement of the festival (vv. 1-13); the final remarks (vv. 54-61) are followed by an account of the end of the celebration (vv. 62-66). In the king's opening remarks, reference is made to the promise of God made through David, a promise that is sustained by God alone and marked by the dual election of David and Zion. This dual election is stressed in Judean theology. Now, in this post-prayer public commentary, Solomon calls attention to God's blessing of the people of Israel through Moses (Deut 12:10), a tradition that predominated in the north. Moreover, just as the opening emphasis on the Judean covenant theology is balanced with allusions to the exodus and the Mosaic covenant, so also the closing remarks stress obedience to the covenant, even while assuring the people of God's presence in language that echoes Judean theology, with its emphasis on the abiding presence of God: "The LORD our God is with us" (cf. Isa 7:14). (See Reflections at 8:62-66.)

1 Kings 8:62-66, Conclusion of the Ceremony

NIV

[62]Then the king and all Israel with him offered sacrifices before the LORD. [63]Solomon offered a sacrifice of fellowship offerings[a] to the LORD: twenty-two thousand cattle and a hundred and twenty thousand sheep and goats. So the king and all the Israelites dedicated the temple of the LORD.

[64]On that same day the king consecrated the middle part of the courtyard in front of the temple of the LORD, and there he offered burnt offerings, grain offerings and the fat of the fellowship offerings, because the bronze altar before the LORD was too small to hold the burnt offerings, the grain offerings and the fat of the fellowship offerings.

[65]So Solomon observed the festival at that time, and all Israel with him—a vast assembly, people from Lebo[b] Hamath to the Wadi of Egypt. They celebrated it before the LORD our God for seven days and seven days more, fourteen days in all.

[a] 63 Traditionally *peace offerings*; also in verse 64 [b] 65 Or *from the entrance to*

NRSV

62Then the king, and all Israel with him, offered sacrifice before the LORD. [63]Solomon offered as sacrifices of well-being to the LORD twenty-two thousand oxen and one hundred twenty thousand sheep. So the king and all the people of Israel dedicated the house of the LORD. [64]The same day the king consecrated the middle of the court that was in front of the house of the LORD; for there he offered the burnt offerings and the grain offerings and the fat pieces of the sacrifices of well-being, because the bronze altar that was before the LORD was too small to receive the burnt offerings and the grain offerings and the fat pieces of the sacrifices of well-being.

65So Solomon held the festival at that time, and all Israel with him—a great assembly, people from Lebo-hamath to the Wadi of Egypt—before the LORD our God, seven days.[a] [66]On the eighth

[a] Compare Gk: Heb *seven days and seven days, fourteen days*

NIV	NRSV
66On the following day he sent the people away. They blessed the king and then went home, joyful and glad in heart for all the good things the LORD had done for his servant David and his people Israel.	day he sent the people away; and they blessed the king, and went to their tents, joyful and in good spirits because of all the goodness that the LORD had shown to his servant David and to his people Israel.

COMMENTARY

Like the Feast of Tabernacles elsewhere (Lev 23:39; Num 29:35), the temple-dedication celebration ends on the eighth day. Solomon, who had convened the assembly at the beginning (vv. 1-2), now dismisses the people. They all "went to their tents," happy and united. Reflecting a convergence of northern and southern covenant traditions, the narrator says that the people were glad for the goodness that God had shown both to the Davidic dynasty and to the people of Israel. At a later time, however, a call for the people to return to their tents will signal the division of the kingdom into two—Judah and Israel (12:16).

REFLECTIONS

Theologically, this is one of the richest passages in the book of Kings, and there are a number of issues one might highlight in the context of a faith community.

1. God tabernacles in "thick darkness," the text says (8:12). One might think of this as a metaphor for the mystery of God's presence. The text is strained at a number of points, at times even sounding contradictory as it tries to characterize the divine presence. One may wish for more clarity, more specificity, more certainty about that reality, but there is none. What we have, rather, is something of a collage of various articulations, various imageries of that mysterious but undeniable presence: Temple, ark, cloud, glory, name, deep darkness. Faith speaks with only a limited vocabulary. It paints impressionistic pictures. Together these idioms convey a sense of divine nearness that is only God's to give.

2. The Temple is an establishment of God's "enthroning" (8:13). This is biblical language for what we might call God's sovereignty. The sanctuary is but a human establishment that represents that sovereignty of God. God's rule is not tied to any one locale on earth or even in heaven or the highest heaven. God is transcendent and free of human manipulation.

Like the Temple that Solomon built, the existence of any sanctuary is a concrete representation of the possibility of God's presence amid a community in worship, but God's freedom transcends any building made by human hands—or any structure, any institution, for that matter (see Mark 11:15-19). In the New Testament, the presence of God is made manifest most decisively through Jesus. More than any building, it is in Jesus that the presence of God is "fleshed out," as it were. He "dwelled [lit., "tabernacled," "stayed over"] among us" and the "glory" of God is manifest in him (John 1:14; cf. 1 Kgs 8:10-12). The New Testament even uses the analogy of the Temple to speak of the death and resurrection of Jesus, relativizing the existence of any other temple (Mark 14:58; John 2:19-22). The point is that the living presence of God is known in the salvific acts of God, not in any structure or in any institution. With this in mind, we dare not take lightly the apostle Paul's reference to the church as God's temple (1 Cor 3:16-17; 2 Cor 6:16).

3. God, though wholly transcendent, will nevertheless hear the prayers of human beings

and will respond accordingly. Solomon's prayer portrays human desperation in terms of their personal, political, social, and natural circumstances. People will always be in desperate need of divine attention because of their sins, both small and large, against other people and against God (8:31, 33-36, 46-48). No one escapes the captivity of sin, since "there is no one who does not sin" (8:46). Yet, with faithful response, including obedience and repentance, there is hope of relief. There is hope because of God's enthroning presence—that is, divine sovereignty and freedom to intervene. Because of that "enthroning," people may come to God in the face of "whatever plague, whatever sickness" with "whatever prayer, whatever plea" (8:38). Because of that "enthroning," even the foreigners—those who are not from Israel—may come to God in prayer. The existence of the "temple" of God in every sense of the term is a testimony to the hope that the sovereign God will freely forgive, freely save.

1 KINGS 9:1-9, A SECOND REVELATION

NIV

9 When Solomon had finished building the temple of the LORD and the royal palace, and had achieved all he had desired to do, [2]the LORD appeared to him a second time, as he had appeared to him at Gibeon. [3]The LORD said to him:

"I have heard the prayer and plea you have made before me; I have consecrated this temple, which you have built, by putting my Name there forever. My eyes and my heart will always be there.

[4]"As for you, if you walk before me in integrity of heart and uprightness, as David your father did, and do all I command and observe my decrees and laws, [5]I will establish your royal throne over Israel forever, as I promised David your father when I said, 'You shall never fail to have a man on the throne of Israel.'

[6]"But if you[a] or your sons turn away from me and do not observe the commands and decrees I have given you[a] and go off to serve other gods and worship them, [7]then I will cut off Israel from the land I have given them and will reject this temple I have consecrated for my Name. Israel will then become a byword and an object of ridicule among all peoples. [8]And though this temple is now imposing, all who pass by will be appalled and will scoff and say, 'Why has the LORD done such a thing to this land and to this temple?' [9]People will answer, 'Because they have forsaken

[a] *6* The Hebrew is plural.

NRSV

9 When Solomon had finished building the house of the LORD and the king's house and all that Solomon desired to build, [2]the LORD appeared to Solomon a second time, as he had appeared to him at Gibeon. [3]The LORD said to him, "I have heard your prayer and your plea, which you made before me; I have consecrated this house that you have built, and put my name there forever; my eyes and my heart will be there for all time. [4]As for you, if you will walk before me, as David your father walked, with integrity of heart and uprightness, doing according to all that I have commanded you, and keeping my statutes and my ordinances, [5]then I will establish your royal throne over Israel forever, as I promised your father David, saying, 'There shall not fail you a successor on the throne of Israel.'

6"If you turn aside from following me, you or your children, and do not keep my commandments and my statutes that I have set before you, but go and serve other gods and worship them, [7]then I will cut Israel off from the land that I have given them; and the house that I have consecrated for my name I will cast out of my sight; and Israel will become a proverb and a taunt among all peoples. [8]This house will become a heap of ruins;[a] everyone passing by it will be astonished, and will hiss; and they will say, 'Why has the LORD done such a thing to this land and to this house?' [9]Then they will say, 'Because they have forsaken the LORD their God, who brought their ancestors out

[a] Syr Old Latin: Heb *will become high*

NIV	NRSV
the LORD their God, who brought their fathers out of Egypt, and have embraced other gods, worshiping and serving them—that is why the LORD brought all this disaster on them.'"	of the land of Egypt, and embraced other gods, worshiping them and serving them; therefore the LORD has brought this disaster upon them.'"

COMMENTARY

The narrative beginning of Solomon's reign is marked by a divine revelation to him at the greatest high place of that time, Gibeon (3:4-15). Following that encounter, the king proceeds to use the gift of wisdom that God has given him to judge his people (3:16-28), to administer his domain (4:1-34), to deal with his allies (5:1-18), and, above all, to build the Temple and his palace (6:1–7:51). Now, after the completion of the construction projects that culminated in the dedication of the Temple (8:1-66), Solomon has another revelatory encounter, this time presumably in Jerusalem. The account of the second revelation in 9:1-9 thus forms a literary bracket, together with the first revelation (3:4-15).

In direct response to Solomon's prayer at the dedication of the Temple (8:22-53), God acknowledges the special place of the Temple Solomon had built: It has been "consecrated"—set apart as a holy place—and God promises that God's name and attention will be there "forever" (v. 3). That "forever" is immediately qualified, however, by two "if . . . then" conditions (vv. 4-5, 6-7). In the Hebrew, the addressee shifts from the singular in vv. 4-5, referring to Solomon ("as for you," v. 4), to the plural in vv. 6-7, referring to all the Davidic kings ("you and your children," v. 6), although the people of Israel as a whole are also implicated (v. 9). Interestingly, the first condition is stated in terms of the validity of the promise of God to David (v. 5; cf. 2 Sam 7:13; 1 Kgs 8:25-26); that promise is good, provided that Solomon is faithful. The second condition is expressed as a threat that extends far beyond the dynasty: Israel will be exiled (vv. 7-9). The preservation of the Davidic dynasty "over Israel," the continuation of Israel in the land that God has given them, and the survival of the Temple are all at stake. Disobedience and disloyalty to the covenant will bring destruction. Even the Temple, set apart as a holy place, will be cast from God's sight (v. 7), thus negating Solomon's plea and God's promise to focus God's attention on it forever (v. 3; cf. 8:29-30). Israel, God's elect, will become the object of scorn and ridicule among the nations. This is one of the curses for disobedience (Deut 28:37). The destruction of the Temple (the NRSV emends the text at 9:8 ["shall be a heap of ruins"], following some ancient witnesses; the NIV is closer to the Hebrew text here; see also 2 Chr 7:21), too, will lead onlookers to conclude that it is the Lord who has brought destruction and exile on Israel, but they will rightly conclude that the Lord is entirely justified (cf. Deut 29:22-28).

Conditionality of the covenant is nothing new in the story. It is present already in the account of God's first revelation to Solomon (3:14). Still, whereas the emphasis in the first revelation is on divine initiative and grace shown to Solomon, indicated especially by God's gift of wisdom and its corollary benefits to Solomon while he loved God only in a compromising way (see Commentary on 3:1-15), the emphasis in this second revelation seems to be on the conditions for him and his successors. The two accounts are, in fact, meant to be read as complementary to each other: The first is clarified and balanced by the second. God has freely given, but the validity of the covenant relationship with God is indicated not so much by the gifts of God already received but by loyalty to God's demands.

REFLECTIONS

The second revelation to Solomon makes a theological counterpoint to the message of God's abundant grace manifest in the first revelation (3:1-15). God first came to Solomon while Solomon was "yet in sin and darkness," as it were. Although he loved God only in a limited way, God freely blessed Solomon. The narrator makes plain that God's blessing is the reason for Solomon's fame and success. Yet the magnitude of God's grace does not mean that there are no conditions for Solomon.

The passage makes a connection between human suffering in exile and destruction with the people's unfaithfulness. Israel's suffering in exile comes because of the people's disobedience to God, because of their disloyalty to the covenant. The same attitude toward suffering is evident also in Solomon's prayer, where natural calamities like drought and famine, along with defeat in war and exile (8:33-53), are also associated with sin. That cause-and-effect explanation is applied by the deuteronomistic theologian to Israel's experience in 587 BCE. Such explanations cannot be generalized for all human suffering, however, and other parts of the Bible (such as the book of Job) resist this blanket association. The abiding theological message in the text, however, is not that God is justified for human suffering. Read together with its counterpart in the literary bracket, this revelation can be understood as expounding on the *implications* of God's grace. The recipient of God's promise and consequent blessings is not to "sin the more that grace may abound" (cf. Rom 6:1). By no means! Rather, we need to remember that God's grace makes possible a divine-human relationship and, as in any relationship, there are demands and responsibilities. Those who are blessed are called to be faithful to God in worship and in conduct. If that relationship with God is not maintained and nurtured, no tangible symbol of divine presence, not even the sanctuary, has any abiding value.

1 KINGS 9:10–10:29, SOLOMON IN ALL HIS GLORY

OVERVIEW

After the balancing of perspectives provided in the account of God's second revelation to Solomon (9:1-9; cf. 3:1-15), the narrator proceeds to give an awe-inspiring review of Solomon's reign in all its glitter and glory. Our separation of this scriptural portion from the preceding unit is largely for practical reasons. We should, in fact, read the passage in the light of 9:1-9, keeping in mind the conditions stipulated in that passage as we assess this overview of Solomon's reign.

There is no apparent order of presentation; indeed, the order varies in different ancient versions. Logical order seems secondary to the overall impression that the collage makes. The report of Solomon's deal with Hiram (9:10-14), which revolves around Solomon's ambitious building projects, probably prompted thoughts about the use of forced labor and the supervision of the workforce (9:15-23; cf. 5:13-18). The mention of the fortification at Gezer (9:15) necessitated a parenthetical explanation regarding the acquisition of the city from the Egyptians as a dowry for Solomon's marriage to the pharaoh's daughter (9:16), which then led to an aside about Solomon's devotion to her (9:24). There is a digression about Solomon's public religious performance (9:25) before the narrator returns to Solomon's alliance with Hiram, this time to their joint maritime ventures to Ophir, a rich and exotic land probably somewhere in East Africa (9:26-28). That reference to a distant land then leads to an account of the historic visit of the queen of Sheba, an enchanting ruler from another faraway place (10:1-10). The author then returns briefly to the joint Israelite-Phoenician expedition to Ophir (10:11-12), then back again to the queen of Sheba (10:13), before going on to Solomon's other transactions with the nations at the far reaches of the then-known world: Arabia, Egypt, Kue (Cilicia) in Asia Minor, the Hittite kingdom and Aram/Syria (10:14-29). Aspects of the account are no doubt historically accurate; claims of fortifications at Hazor, Megiddo, and Gezer may be confirmed by archaeological excavations, and trade with Ophir is corroborated by an eighth-century BCE inscription from Tell Qasile, a port on the estuary of the Yarkon River (just north of modern Tel Aviv) since the twelfth century BCE. Other aspects, however, sound like the stuff of which legends are made: unprecedented amounts of spices (10:2, 10, 25), silver's being as common as stones in Jerusalem (10:27), and cedar as plentiful as the sycamore/fig trees of the Judean hill country (10:27). There are staggering amounts of treasures (gold, silver, precious gems, ivory), rare wood (cedar, cypress, "almugwood"), and quaint creatures (apes and תכיים [*tukkiyyîm*], an unknown Hebrew word interpreted as "baboons" in the NIV and "peacocks" in the NRSV). And Solomon's brilliance was without match.

1 Kings 9:10-28, Solomon's Commercial Forays

NIV

[10]At the end of twenty years, during which Solomon built these two buildings—the temple of the LORD and the royal palace— [11]King Solomon gave twenty towns in Galilee to Hiram king of Tyre, because Hiram had supplied him with all the cedar and pine and gold he wanted. [12]But when Hiram went from Tyre to see the towns that Solomon had given him, he was not pleased with them. [13]"What kind of towns are these you have given me, my brother?" he asked. And he called them the Land of Cabul,[a] a name they have to this day. [14]Now Hiram had sent to the king 120 talents[b] of gold.

[15]Here is the account of the forced labor King Solomon conscripted to build the LORD's temple, his own palace, the supporting terraces,[c] the wall of Jerusalem, and Hazor, Megiddo and Gezer. [16](Pharaoh king of Egypt had attacked and captured Gezer. He had set it on fire. He killed its Canaanite inhabitants and then gave it as a wedding gift to his daughter, Solomon's wife. [17]And Solomon rebuilt Gezer.) He built up Lower Beth Horon, [18]Baalath, and Tadmor[d] in the desert, within his land, [19]as well as all his store cities and the towns for his chariots and for his horses[e]—whatever he desired to build in Jerusalem, in Lebanon and throughout all the territory he ruled.

[a] *13 Cabul* sounds like the Hebrew for *good-for-nothing.* [b] *14* That is, about 4 1/2 tons (about 4 metric tons) [c] *15* Or *the Millo;* also in verse 24 [d] *18* The Hebrew may also be read *Tamar.* [e] *19* Or *charioteers*

NRSV

10At the end of twenty years, in which Solomon had built the two houses, the house of the LORD and the king's house, [11]King Hiram of Tyre having supplied Solomon with cedar and cypress timber and gold, as much as he desired, King Solomon gave to Hiram twenty cities in the land of Galilee. [12]But when Hiram came from Tyre to see the cities that Solomon had given him, they did not please him. [13]Therefore he said, "What kind of cities are these that you have given me, my brother?" So they are called the land of Cabul[a] to this day. [14]But Hiram had sent to the king one hundred twenty talents of gold.

15This is the account of the forced labor that King Solomon conscripted to build the house of the LORD and his own house, the Millo and the wall of Jerusalem, Hazor, Megiddo, Gezer [16](Pharaoh king of Egypt had gone up and captured Gezer and burned it down, had killed the Canaanites who lived in the city, and had given it as dowry to his daughter, Solomon's wife; [17]so Solomon rebuilt Gezer), Lower Beth-horon, [18]Baalath, Tamar in the wilderness, within the land, [19]as well as all of Solomon's storage cities, the cities for his chariots, the cities for his cavalry, and whatever Solomon desired to build, in Jerusalem, in Lebanon, and in all the land of his dominion. [20]All the people who were left of the Amorites, the Hittites, the Perizzites, the Hivites, and the Jebusites, who

[a] Perhaps meaning *a land good for nothing*

NIV

[20]All the people left from the Amorites, Hittites, Perizzites, Hivites and Jebusites (these peoples were not Israelites), [21]that is, their descendants remaining in the land, whom the Israelites could not exterminate[a]—these Solomon conscripted for his slave labor force, as it is to this day. [22]But Solomon did not make slaves of any of the Israelites; they were his fighting men, his government officials, his officers, his captains, and the commanders of his chariots and charioteers. [23]They were also the chief officials in charge of Solomon's projects—550 officials supervising the men who did the work.

[24]After Pharaoh's daughter had come up from the City of David to the palace Solomon had built for her, he constructed the supporting terraces.

[25]Three times a year Solomon sacrificed burnt offerings and fellowship offerings[b] on the altar he had built for the LORD, burning incense before the LORD along with them, and so fulfilled the temple obligations.

[26]King Solomon also built ships at Ezion Geber, which is near Elath in Edom, on the shore of the Red Sea.[c] [27]And Hiram sent his men—sailors who knew the sea—to serve in the fleet with Solomon's men. [28]They sailed to Ophir and brought back 420 talents[d] of gold, which they delivered to King Solomon.

[a] *21* The Hebrew term refers to the irrevocable giving over of things or persons to the LORD, often by totally destroying them. [b] *25* Traditionally *peace offerings* [c] *26* Hebrew *Yam Suph*; that is, Sea of Reeds [d] *28* That is, about 16 tons (about 14.5 metric tons)

NRSV

were not of the people of Israel— [21]their descendants who were still left in the land, whom the Israelites were unable to destroy completely—these Solomon conscripted for slave labor, and so they are to this day. [22]But of the Israelites Solomon made no slaves; they were the soldiers, they were his officials, his commanders, his captains, and the commanders of his chariotry and cavalry.

23These were the chief officers who were over Solomon's work: five hundred fifty, who had charge of the people who carried on the work.

24But Pharaoh's daughter went up from the city of David to her own house that Solomon had built for her; then he built the Millo.

25Three times a year Solomon used to offer up burnt offerings and sacrifices of well-being on the altar that he built for the LORD, offering incense[a] before the LORD. So he completed the house.

26King Solomon built a fleet of ships at Ezion-geber, which is near Eloth on the shore of the Red Sea,[b] in the land of Edom. [27]Hiram sent his servants with the fleet, sailors who were familiar with the sea, together with the servants of Solomon. [28]They went to Ophir, and imported from there four hundred twenty talents of gold, which they delivered to King Solomon.

[a] Gk: Heb *offering incense with it that was* [b] Or *Sea of Reeds*

COMMENTARY

Solomon has ruled for twenty years (v. 10), during which period he completed the Temple (7 years, according to 6:38) and the palace complex (13 years, according to 7:1). This is the midpoint, perhaps the peak, of his forty-year career (11:42). Now, in addition to all the positive and negative reports about his reign in the narrative thus far, we get a summary assessment of his reign. The overall impression one receives is that Solomon was an extraordinarily gifted ruler, just as one might expect from the account of the first revelation (3:4-15): Solomon's God-given wisdom has brought him untold riches, power, and honor.

The king was able to deal shrewdly with the cunning Hiram, king of Tyre (9:10-14). Although Solomon had to make territorial concessions (which were not entirely to the Tyrian ruler's satisfaction), he managed to gain some material benefits from that transaction.[45] The narrator cites

45. The parallel account in 2 Chr 8:2 says that it was Huram (Hiram) who conceded territories to Solomon. Since the chronicler's account does not specify the "twenty cities of Galilee," we may think of both accounts as different perspectives on a historic territorial exchange.

an unknown and evidently derogatory explanation for the ceded territory, which is called "the land of Cabul" (v. 13), meaning somehow that Solomon had taken advantage of his ally.[46] This advantage Solomon gained over the Phoenician king stands in contrast to an earlier report about the hard bargain driven by the Tyrian Hiram (5:1-18). Here we find Hiram paying Solomon 120 talents of gold in addition to whatever other exchanges they may have made to seal their treaty.[47] Solomon gained some and lost some, as it were, all within the bounds of international law. What he gained was prestige and wealth for himself, symbolized above all by the completion of the Temple and his palace. What he gave up was territory that God had granted to Israel (see v. 7). The reference to the surrender of northern (Israelite) territories also foreshadows the division of the kingdom into north and south in the near future.

Solomon undertook significant public constructions, including the Temple, the palace complex, the "Millo" (probably some kind of terraced structure), storage cities, fortifications at various locations, and other military installations. Indeed, he reportedly "built whatever he desired in Jerusalem, Lebanon, and all his domain" (v. 19). He was able to carry out these projects through a combination of power and administrative know-how; his labor force came from a permanent levy of foreign slaves in his domain, Israelite laborers who were drafted for three months each (cf. 5:13-18), and, presumably, paid warriors, all under a trusted corps of his officers. He engaged in all sorts of diplomatic deals, international trade, and other foreign ventures. He attended to his public religious duties, offering sacrifices at the central sanctuary three times a year, thus fulfilling the law (Deut 16:16-17). (See Reflections at 10:1-29.)

46. The reading and the etymology of the name are disputed in the ancient versions and by commentators. Notes in the NRSV and the NIV suggest the meaning "as nothing," but that assumes a Hebrew word that is not attested elsewhere. In any case, the reference is probably to the towns of Asher in the northern coastal plain. See Josh 19:27.

47. According to the Babylonian standard currency throughout the ancient Near East in the sixth century BCE, a talent was the equivalent of 3,600 shekels.

1 Kings 10:1-29, Solomon's Other Successes

NIV

10 When the queen of Sheba heard about the fame of Solomon and his relation to the name of the LORD, she came to test him with hard questions. [2]Arriving at Jerusalem with a very great caravan—with camels carrying spices, large quantities of gold, and precious stones—she came to Solomon and talked with him about all that she had on her mind. [3]Solomon answered all her questions; nothing was too hard for the king to explain to her. [4]When the queen of Sheba saw all the wisdom of Solomon and the palace he had built, [5]the food on his table, the seating of his officials, the attending servants in their robes, his cupbearers, and the burnt offerings he made at[a] the temple of the LORD, she was overwhelmed.

[6]She said to the king, "The report I heard in my own country about your achievements and your wisdom is true. [7]But I did not believe these things until I came and saw with my own eyes. Indeed, not even half was told me; in wisdom

[a] 5 *Or the ascent by which he went up to*

NRSV

10 When the queen of Sheba heard of the fame of Solomon (fame due to[a] the name of the LORD), she came to test him with hard questions. [2]She came to Jerusalem with a very great retinue, with camels bearing spices, and very much gold, and precious stones; and when she came to Solomon, she told him all that was on her mind. [3]Solomon answered all her questions; there was nothing hidden from the king that he could not explain to her. [4]When the queen of Sheba had observed all the wisdom of Solomon, the house that he had built, [5]the food of his table, the seating of his officials, and the attendance of his servants, their clothing, his valets, and his burnt offerings that he offered at the house of the LORD, there was no more spirit in her.

6So she said to the king, "The report was true that I heard in my own land of your accomplishments and of your wisdom, [7]but I did not believe the reports until I came and my own eyes had

[a] Meaning of Heb uncertain

NIV

and wealth you have far exceeded the report I heard. [8]How happy your men must be! How happy your officials, who continually stand before you and hear your wisdom! [9]Praise be to the LORD your God, who has delighted in you and placed you on the throne of Israel. Because of the LORD's eternal love for Israel, he has made you king, to maintain justice and righteousness."

[10]And she gave the king 120 talents[a] of gold, large quantities of spices, and precious stones. Never again were so many spices brought in as those the queen of Sheba gave to King Solomon.

[11](Hiram's ships brought gold from Ophir; and from there they brought great cargoes of almugwood[b] and precious stones. [12]The king used the almugwood to make supports for the temple of the LORD and for the royal palace, and to make harps and lyres for the musicians. So much almugwood has never been imported or seen since that day.)

[13]King Solomon gave the queen of Sheba all she desired and asked for, besides what he had given her out of his royal bounty. Then she left and returned with her retinue to her own country.

[14]The weight of the gold that Solomon received yearly was 666 talents,[c] [15]not including the revenues from merchants and traders and from all the Arabian kings and the governors of the land.

[16]King Solomon made two hundred large shields of hammered gold; six hundred bekas[d] of gold went into each shield. [17]He also made three hundred small shields of hammered gold, with three minas[e] of gold in each shield. The king put them in the Palace of the Forest of Lebanon.

[18]Then the king made a great throne inlaid with ivory and overlaid with fine gold. [19]The throne had six steps, and its back had a rounded top. On both sides of the seat were armrests, with a lion standing beside each of them. [20]Twelve lions stood on the six steps, one at either end of each step. Nothing like it had ever been made for any other kingdom. [21]All King Solomon's goblets were gold, and all the household articles in the Palace of the Forest of Lebanon were pure gold. Nothing was

[a] *10* That is, about 4 1/2 tons (about 4 metric tons) [b] *11* Probably a variant of *algumwood*; also in verse 12 [c] *14* That is, about 25 tons (about 23 metric tons) [d] *16* That is, about 7 1/2 pounds (about 3.5 kilograms) [e] *17* That is, about 3 3/4 pounds (about 1.7 kilograms)

NRSV

seen it. Not even half had been told me; your wisdom and prosperity far surpass the report that I had heard. [8]Happy are your wives![a] Happy are these your servants, who continually attend you and hear your wisdom! [9]Blessed be the LORD your God, who has delighted in you and set you on the throne of Israel! Because the LORD loved Israel forever, he has made you king to execute justice and righteousness." [10]Then she gave the king one hundred twenty talents of gold, a great quantity of spices, and precious stones; never again did spices come in such quantity as that which the queen of Sheba gave to King Solomon.

11Moreover, the fleet of Hiram, which carried gold from Ophir, brought from Ophir a great quantity of almug wood and precious stones. [12]From the almug wood the king made supports for the house of the LORD, and for the king's house, lyres also and harps for the singers; no such almug wood has come or been seen to this day.

13Meanwhile King Solomon gave to the queen of Sheba every desire that she expressed, as well as what he gave her out of Solomon's royal bounty. Then she returned to her own land, with her servants.

14The weight of gold that came to Solomon in one year was six hundred sixty-six talents of gold, [15]besides that which came from the traders and from the business of the merchants, and from all the kings of Arabia and the governors of the land. [16]King Solomon made two hundred large shields of beaten gold; six hundred shekels of gold went into each large shield. [17]He made three hundred shields of beaten gold; three minas of gold went into each shield; and the king put them in the House of the Forest of Lebanon. [18]The king also made a great ivory throne, and overlaid it with the finest gold. [19]The throne had six steps. The top of the throne was rounded in the back, and on each side of the seat were arm rests and two lions standing beside the arm rests, [20]while twelve lions were standing, one on each end of a step on the six steps. Nothing like it was ever made in any kingdom. [21]All King Solomon's drinking vessels were of gold, and all the vessels of the House of the Forest of Lebanon were of pure gold;

[a] Gk Syr: Heb *men*

NIV

made of silver, because silver was considered of little value in Solomon's days. 22The king had a fleet of trading ships[a] at sea along with the ships of Hiram. Once every three years it returned, carrying gold, silver and ivory, and apes and baboons.

23King Solomon was greater in riches and wisdom than all the other kings of the earth. 24The whole world sought audience with Solomon to hear the wisdom God had put in his heart. 25Year after year, everyone who came brought a gift—articles of silver and gold, robes, weapons and spices, and horses and mules.

26Solomon accumulated chariots and horses; he had fourteen hundred chariots and twelve thousand horses,[b] which he kept in the chariot cities and also with him in Jerusalem. 27The king made silver as common in Jerusalem as stones, and cedar as plentiful as sycamore-fig trees in the foothills. 28Solomon's horses were imported from Egypt[c] and from Kue[d]—the royal merchants purchased them from Kue. 29They imported a chariot from Egypt for six hundred shekels[e] of silver, and a horse for a hundred and fifty.[f] They also exported them to all the kings of the Hittites and of the Arameans.

a *22* Hebrew *of ships of Tarshish* b *26* Or *charioteers* c *28* Or possibly *Muzur,* a region in Cilicia; also in verse 29 d *28* Probably *Cilicia* e *29* That is, about 15 pounds (about 7 kilograms) f *29* That is, about 3 3/4 pounds (about 1.7 kilograms)

NRSV

none were of silver—it was not considered as anything in the days of Solomon. 22For the king had a fleet of ships of Tarshish at sea with the fleet of Hiram. Once every three years the fleet of ships of Tarshish used to come bringing gold, silver, ivory, apes, and peacocks.[a]

23Thus King Solomon excelled all the kings of the earth in riches and in wisdom. 24The whole earth sought the presence of Solomon to hear his wisdom, which God had put into his mind. 25Every one of them brought a present, objects of silver and gold, garments, weaponry, spices, horses, and mules, so much year by year.

26Solomon gathered together chariots and horses; he had fourteen hundred chariots and twelve thousand horses, which he stationed in the chariot cities and with the king in Jerusalem. 27The king made silver as common in Jerusalem as stones, and he made cedars as numerous as the sycamores of the Shephelah. 28Solomon's import of horses was from Egypt and Kue, and the king's traders received them from Kue at a price. 29A chariot could be imported from Egypt for six hundred shekels of silver, and a horse for one hundred fifty; so through the king's traders they were exported to all the kings of the Hittites and the kings of Aram.

a Or *baboons*

COMMENTARY

Indicative of the worldwide prestige Solomon had gained is the historic visit of the mysterious queen of Sheba, a place identified in the NT as a land in the southern reaches of the world (Matt 12:42; Luke 11:31).[48] Scholars suspect that it was for political and economic reasons that the queen of Sheba journeyed to Jerusalem—it was a historic trade mission. She had come to Jerusalem to resolve difficult diplomatic issues surrounding the expanding world economy—perhaps the "hard questions" mentioned in v. 1. Whatever the reason for her visit, the narrator makes plain that it was a personal triumph for Solomon. The queen had heard of this king's reputation (v. 1), and she came to Jerusalem to verify these reports personally. She came bearing splendrous tributes and tested the king's intellect. She was so impressed by his brilliance, wealth, and the luxury of his palace that she was left breathless (v. 5; NRSV, NIV, "she was overwhelmed").

Through the persona of the queen of Sheba, we are presented with the deuteronomistic narrator's perspective on Solomon. According to this version of the story, she came to Jerusalem to confirm for herself "the reputation of Solomon as regards the name of the Lord," or, more literally,

48. Josephus, *Antiquities of the Jews* 8.6.5-6, calls her "the Queen of Egypt and Ethiopia," and later traditions also identify her as Ethiopian.

"the hearing of Solomon as regards the NAME of the Lord" (v. 1). The reference to the name of the Lord is an additional deuteronomistic twist that one does not find in the parallel account in 2 Chr 9:1, which has the queen visiting only to authenticate the rumors. Regardless of the evidence of Solomon's personal successes, reported in the review, the narrator points to what is theologically crucial in all of this: It is Solomon's conduct as regards the name of the Lord that is in question.

Moreover, through the congratulatory words of the queen of Sheba (vv. 6-9), the narrator reiterates that it is God's will (חפץ *ḥāpēṣ*) that Solomon sit on the throne and that it is for the love of the people of Israel that God has so willed (v. 9). Solomon is to execute justice and righteousness. The mention of God's will (*ḥēpeṣ*) is especially poignant in the light of the allusions elsewhere in the report to the desire of Solomon (*ḥēpeṣ*, 9:11) or the desire of the queen of Sheba (10:13).

The communiqué of the queen of Sheba may be just the sort of rhetorical nicety one might expect in a diplomatic mission. No one who has followed the account of Solomon's reign so far will take her words as anything but empty flattery that does not quite fit the Solomon we know. To be sure, Solomon is recognized as a brilliant and glamorous ruler. There is no question about his fame or the splendor of his reign. He has also carried out his public religious duties in accordance with the law (9:25; Deut 16:16-17). Still, the reader is prompted by the diplomatic words of the foreign queen to wonder about his support for "justice and righteousness," which are supposed to accompany divine election (see Deut 16:18-20). The choice of Solomon is supposed to have been by the will of God and for the sake of the people—in order that justice and righteousness might be brought about. The reader may even remember that Solomon had asked for wisdom so that he could govern his people properly (see 3:9, 11). Yet, what we read about in this review is the expression of Solomon's will, the will of the queen of Sheba, the enrichment of the king and his allies, and the pomp that surrounds him. We read about the alliance with Hiram, which resulted in the concession of land to the foreign leader that God had given to the people of Israel. We read about Solomon's prejudicial exploitation of forced labor to build all the projects that "he desired" (9:11, 21). We read about the non-Israelite people who remained in the land, who should have been eliminated by the law of the ban (Deut 7:1-5; 20:16-18). Even though Solomon was then in control, he did not eliminate them in accordance with the law. Instead, he compromised by distinguishing them from the Israelites, while he exploited them for his own purposes. We read about the increased contacts Solomon established with foreigners from the farthest corners of the world and, especially, his marriage alliance with the Egyptian pharaoh, whose daughter Solomon married and brought into his capital. We read of his appointment of officials to run his workforce, just like the kings of the other nations (1 Sam 8:12). We read about all the gold that went into the making of Solomon's throne, and we wonder about a particular detail that is pointed out in the report. According to the Greek text, a calf's head (the NRSV, following the Hebrew tradition, has "rounded top") was on the back of Solomon's throne. We read about his accumulation of wealth for himself and his acquisition of horses. Indeed, Solomon had become a king *just like those of the other nations,* thus contrary to the deuteronomic ideal of the faithful king (Deut 17:14-20; 1 Sam 8:1-18).

REFLECTIONS

It is difficult not to be overawed by King Solomon "in all his glory." He seems to have it all: personal abilities, enormous wealth, international prestige, and power. From the beginning of the book of 1 Kings, the reader has been told that Solomon was chosen by God to be the successor to the throne of David and that the king was blessed with wisdom, riches, honor, and victory over his adversaries. There is no doubt regarding the initiative and concern of God: It was God who invited Solomon to request whatever he wanted, God who granted his request and even more. The characterization of Solomon throughout the narrative is, however, ambiguous. At times he is portrayed positively as one who loves God, is humble in acknowledging the grace of God, is desirous of wisdom to fulfill his responsibilities to his people, and is capable of composing a dedicatory prayer so beautiful and profound that it still provides the church with material for liturgy and for theological reflection on divine presence. At the same time, however, Solomon is depicted as ruthless, scheming, self-absorbed, oppressive, greedy, and vain. This unusually gifted king is, after all, like all of other mortals: imperfect and sinful. The mystery in the story is that God should choose such a one and bless him so richly. That mystery is also the good news, however: God's grace overcomes human limitations, and the transcendent God is free to forgive when sinners repent.

The tension between the grace of God and the demand of faith, distinctly framed between two divine revelations (3:1-15; 9:1-9), is evident throughout the narrative. The grace of God is never intended to be without demands on the part of humanity: God's promise is good, *provided* that the king and his people are faithful to God's demands. This is stated as the word of God in Solomon's first revelation (3:14); it is acknowledged by Solomon himself in his prayer at the dedication of the Temple (8:25); and it is reiterated in the second revelation to him (9:4-7). Indeed, the deuteronomist tells us that even the Queen of Sheba, a foreign woman from a distant land, knew that what mattered in terms of Solomon's reputation was his conduct regarding the name of the Lord (10:1). Even this foreign woman understood that it was God's will that mattered, not Solomon's or that of any other ruler; that Solomon was chosen because of God's love for Israel; and that the king was to do justice and righteousness. In the end, the question one must ask about Solomon in his glory is this: Has he been faithful to the will of God? Has he been obedient to God's demands?

The author of Ecclesiastes, writing in the guise of the king who had it all, raises questions about the abiding value of human desire to take control of one's future and worldly accomplishments (Eccl 1:12–2:26). The author says that he, as king, surpassed all others (Eccl 1:16, 2:9; cf. 1 Kgs 10:23). He built all that he desired and accumulated enormous wealth. He indulged in pleasure, and he was gifted in wisdom. Still, he comes to realize that all these things are ephemeral—they are as futile as trying to chase the wind. For the writer of Ecclesiastes, all wisdom, wealth, success, pleasure, and fame are finally unreliable. All is "vanity" in this sense.

The words of Ecclesiastes are echoed in the New Testament parable of the rich fool who accumulates wealth and is concerned only with his material successes (Luke 12:13-21). Jesus, however, cautions against covetousness, for "one's life does not consist in the abundance of possessions" (Luke 12:15 NRSV), and there are those "who store up treasures for themselves but are not rich toward God" (Luke 12:21 NRSV). Whereas people strive to assure their own successes, Jesus points out that the lilies of the field do not so strive and yet, "even Solomon in all his glory was not clothed like one of these" (Luke 12:27 NRSV). Jesus observes that some people are too much like the unbelievers, "like the nations of the world," who are concerned with material things. Instead of living such a life-style, he urges his disciples to seek first the kingdom of God and God's righteousness (cf. 1 Kgs 10:9), promising that God's blessings will then be granted to them (Matt 6:33).

1 KINGS 11:1-43, THE DEMISE OF SOLOMON

OVERVIEW

The preceding passage (9:10–10:29) depicts Solomon as a ruler just like those of other nations, even surpassing them all in his accumulation of wealth and horses, especially horses acquired from

Egypt. He had clearly violated deuteronomistic law (Deut 17:14-17; 1 Sam 8:1-21). Now the narrator goes on to point out how Solomon had been unfaithful to the Lord.

1 Kings 11:1-13, Solomon's Unfaithfulness

NIV

11 King Solomon, however, loved many foreign women besides Pharaoh's daughter—Moabites, Ammonites, Edomites, Sidonians and Hittites. 2They were from nations about which the LORD had told the Israelites, "You must not intermarry with them, because they will surely turn your hearts after their gods." Nevertheless, Solomon held fast to them in love. 3He had seven hundred wives of royal birth and three hundred concubines, and his wives led him astray. 4As Solomon grew old, his wives turned his heart after other gods, and his heart was not fully devoted to the LORD his God, as the heart of David his father had been. 5He followed Ashtoreth the goddess of the Sidonians, and Molech[a] the detestable god of the Ammonites. 6So Solomon did evil in the eyes of the LORD; he did not follow the LORD completely, as David his father had done.

7On a hill east of Jerusalem, Solomon built a high place for Chemosh the detestable god of Moab, and for Molech the detestable god of the Ammonites. 8He did the same for all his foreign wives, who burned incense and offered sacrifices to their gods.

9The LORD became angry with Solomon because his heart had turned away from the LORD, the God of Israel, who had appeared to him twice. 10Although he had forbidden Solomon to follow other gods, Solomon did not keep the LORD's command. 11So the LORD said to Solomon, "Since this is your attitude and you have not kept my covenant and my decrees, which I commanded you, I will most certainly tear the kingdom away from you and give it to one of your subordinates. 12Nevertheless, for the sake of David your father, I will not do it during your lifetime. I will tear it out of the hand of your son. 13Yet I will not tear the whole kingdom from him, but will give him one tribe for the sake of David my servant and for the sake of Jerusalem, which I have chosen."

[a] 5 Hebrew *Milcom*; also in verse 33

NRSV

11 King Solomon loved many foreign women along with the daughter of Pharaoh: Moabite, Ammonite, Edomite, Sidonian, and Hittite women, 2from the nations concerning which the LORD had said to the Israelites, "You shall not enter into marriage with them, neither shall they with you; for they will surely incline your heart to follow their gods"; Solomon clung to these in love. 3Among his wives were seven hundred princesses and three hundred concubines; and his wives turned away his heart. 4For when Solomon was old, his wives turned away his heart after other gods; and his heart was not true to the LORD his God, as was the heart of his father David. 5For Solomon followed Astarte the goddess of the Sidonians, and Milcom the abomination of the Ammonites. 6So Solomon did what was evil in the sight of the LORD, and did not completely follow the LORD, as his father David had done. 7Then Solomon built a high place for Chemosh the abomination of Moab, and for Molech the abomination of the Ammonites, on the mountain east of Jerusalem. 8He did the same for all his foreign wives, who offered incense and sacrificed to their gods.

9Then the LORD was angry with Solomon, because his heart had turned away from the LORD, the God of Israel, who had appeared to him twice, 10and had commanded him concerning this matter, that he should not follow other gods; but he did not observe what the LORD commanded. 11Therefore the LORD said to Solomon, "Since this has been your mind and you have not kept my covenant and my statutes that I have commanded you, I will surely tear the kingdom from you and give it to your servant. 12Yet for the sake of your father David I will not do it in your lifetime; I will tear it out of the hand of your son. 13I will not, however, tear away the entire kingdom; I will give one tribe to your son, for the sake of my servant David and for the sake of Jerusalem, which I have chosen."

COMMENTARY

Contrary to the law (Deut 17:14-17), Solomon loved many foreign women (v. 1). The daughter of the pharaoh of Egypt is singled out, but the narrator mentions also Moabites, Ammonites, Edomites, Sidonians (Phoenicians), and Hittites—women from the nations surrounding Israel. Indeed, Solomon had seven hundred royal wives and three hundred concubines (v. 3). For the narrator, the problem was not with the multiplicity of women per se, but that these foreign women had led Solomon's heart astray (vv. 2-4, 9). David also had many wives and concubines (2 Sam 3:2-5; 5:13-16; 11:27; 1 Chr 3:1-9), but, unlike Solomon, David's heart remained true to his God (vv. 4, 6). The danger of intermarriage with the foreign women lies in one's deviation from the worship of the Lord alone. The narrator says, literally, if somewhat ambiguously, "Solomon held fast [דבק *dābaq*] to loving" (v. 2). The context suggests that the objects of Solomon's love were these foreign women and their foreign gods; he held fast to them. The language is theologically loaded, for elsewhere in the deuteronomistic tradition, the love of the Lord requires one to "hold fast" (*dābaq*) to God (Deut 11:22; 30:20; Josh 22:5) and to God alone (Deut 4:4; 10:20; 13:4). It must be noted, too, that in deuteronomistic literature, "love" is more than a term to express an emotion. As the concept is used elsewhere in ancient Near Eastern treaties, "love" is an idiom for committed relationship. So Israel is exhorted to love the Lord without wavering: "Love the LORD your God with all your heart, and with all your soul, and with all your might" (Deut 6:5 NRSV).

At the beginning of Solomon's reign, we are told, he "loved the LORD" (3:3) and was blessed with wisdom (3:4-14). Even at that time, however, his actions presaged his later troubles. His first act after ascending to the throne was to enter into a marriage alliance with Egypt, taking the daughter of the pharaoh as bride (3:1). That marriage seems particularly irksome to the narrator, who mentions it repeatedly, sometimes even digressing from his story to do so (7:8; 9:16, 24). The theological problem for the narrator is that Solomon's love of the foreign women compromised his allegiance to the Lord; these foreign women caused his heart to turn from devotion to God, so that he did not follow his Suzerain wholeheartedly (vv. 4, 6).

Before the construction and completion of the Temple, Solomon had worshiped at the local high places: "Solomon loved the LORD, walking in the statutes of his father David, except that he sacrificed and offered incense at the high places" (3:3). Now, despite the presence of the Temple, Solomon built high places for the gods of his foreign wives. Some of these high places were even blatantly raised on the hill facing (על־פני *'al-pĕnê*, "to the face of") Jerusalem—that is, on the Mount of Olives.

Solomon's unfaithfulness is especially disconcerting because God had appeared to him twice (v. 9), once graciously giving him gifts (3:1-15) and another time firmly reiterating the demand for faithfulness (9:1-19). On account of Solomon's flagrant violation of the covenant, God promises to tear the kingdom from him and to give it to one of his servants (v. 11). In this way, the narrator anticipates the rise of Jeroboam, son of Nebat (vv. 26-40). Still, the deity was apparently reluctant to undo the promise to David by giving the kingdom entirely to an outsider, a servant. Referring to the dual election of David and Jerusalem, the narrator speaks of God's assurance to let hope for the Davidic promise stay alive by giving one tribe to Solomon's successor. (See Reflections at 11:14-43.)

1 Kings 11:14-43, God Ends Solomon's Kingship

NIV

14Then the LORD raised up against Solomon an adversary, Hadad the Edomite, from the royal line of Edom. 15Earlier when David was fighting with Edom, Joab the commander of the army, who had gone up to bury the dead, had struck down all the men in Edom. 16Joab and all the Israelites stayed there for six months, until they had destroyed all the men in Edom. 17But Hadad, still only a boy, fled to Egypt with some Edomite officials who had served his father. 18They set out from Midian and went to Paran. Then taking men from Paran with them, they went to Egypt, to Pharaoh king of Egypt, who gave Hadad a house and land and provided him with food.

19Pharaoh was so pleased with Hadad that he gave him a sister of his own wife, Queen Tahpenes, in marriage. 20The sister of Tahpenes bore him a son named Genubath, whom Tahpenes brought up in the royal palace. There Genubath lived with Pharaoh's own children.

21While he was in Egypt, Hadad heard that David rested with his fathers and that Joab the commander of the army was also dead. Then Hadad said to Pharaoh, "Let me go, that I may return to my own country."

22"What have you lacked here that you want to go back to your own country?" Pharaoh asked.

"Nothing," Hadad replied, "but do let me go!"

23And God raised up against Solomon another adversary, Rezon son of Eliada, who had fled from his master, Hadadezer king of Zobah. 24He gathered men around him and became the leader of a band of rebels when David destroyed the forces[a] ⌊of Zobah⌋; the rebels went to Damascus, where they settled and took control. 25Rezon was Israel's adversary as long as Solomon lived, adding to the trouble caused by Hadad. So Rezon ruled in Aram and was hostile toward Israel.

26Also, Jeroboam son of Nebat rebelled against the king. He was one of Solomon's officials, an Ephraimite from Zeredah, and his mother was a widow named Zeruah.

27Here is the account of how he rebelled against the king: Solomon had built the supporting terraces[b] and had filled in the gap in the wall of the

[a] 24 Hebrew *destroyed them* [b] 27 Or *the Millo*

NRSV

14Then the LORD raised up an adversary against Solomon, Hadad the Edomite; he was of the royal house in Edom. 15For when David was in Edom, and Joab the commander of the army went up to bury the dead, he killed every male in Edom 16(for Joab and all Israel remained there six months, until he had eliminated every male in Edom); 17but Hadad fled to Egypt with some Edomites who were servants of his father. He was a young boy at that time. 18They set out from Midian and came to Paran; they took people with them from Paran and came to Egypt, to Pharaoh king of Egypt, who gave him a house, assigned him an allowance of food, and gave him land. 19Hadad found great favor in the sight of Pharaoh, so that he gave him his sister-in-law for a wife, the sister of Queen Tahpenes. 20The sister of Tahpenes gave birth by him to his son Genubath, whom Tahpenes weaned in Pharaoh's house; Genubath was in Pharaoh's house among the children of Pharaoh. 21When Hadad heard in Egypt that David slept with his ancestors and that Joab the commander of the army was dead, Hadad said to Pharaoh, "Let me depart, that I may go to my own country." 22But Pharaoh said to him, "What do you lack with me that you now seek to go to your own country?" And he said, "No, do let me go."

23God raised up another adversary against Solomon,[a] son of Eliada, who had fled from his master, King Hadadezer of Zobah. 24He gathered followers around him and became leader of a marauding band, after the slaughter by David; they went to Damascus, settled there, and made him king in Damascus. 25He was an adversary of Israel all the days of Solomon, making trouble as Hadad did; he despised Israel and reigned over Aram.

26Jeroboam son of Nebat, an Ephraimite of Zeredah, a servant of Solomon, whose mother's name was Zeruah, a widow, rebelled against the king. 27The following was the reason he rebelled against the king. Solomon built the Millo, and closed up the gap in the wall[b] of the city of his

[a] Heb *him* [b] Heb lacks *in the wall*

NIV

city of David his father. [28]Now Jeroboam was a man of standing, and when Solomon saw how well the young man did his work, he put him in charge of the whole labor force of the house of Joseph.

[29]About that time Jeroboam was going out of Jerusalem, and Ahijah the prophet of Shiloh met him on the way, wearing a new cloak. The two of them were alone out in the country, [30]and Ahijah took hold of the new cloak he was wearing and tore it into twelve pieces. [31]Then he said to Jeroboam, "Take ten pieces for yourself, for this is what the LORD, the God of Israel, says: 'See, I am going to tear the kingdom out of Solomon's hand and give you ten tribes. [32]But for the sake of my servant David and the city of Jerusalem, which I have chosen out of all the tribes of Israel, he will have one tribe. [33]I will do this because they have[a] forsaken me and worshiped Ashtoreth the goddess of the Sidonians, Chemosh the god of the Moabites, and Molech the god of the Ammonites, and have not walked in my ways, nor done what is right in my eyes, nor kept my statutes and laws as David, Solomon's father, did.

[34]" 'But I will not take the whole kingdom out of Solomon's hand; I have made him ruler all the days of his life for the sake of David my servant, whom I chose and who observed my commands and statutes. [35]I will take the kingdom from his son's hands and give you ten tribes. [36]I will give one tribe to his son so that David my servant may always have a lamp before me in Jerusalem, the city where I chose to put my Name. [37]However, as for you, I will take you, and you will rule over all that your heart desires; you will be king over Israel. [38]If you do whatever I command you and walk in my ways and do what is right in my eyes by keeping my statutes and commands, as David my servant did, I will be with you. I will build you a dynasty as enduring as the one I built for David and will give Israel to you. [39]I will humble David's descendants because of this, but not forever.' "

[40]Solomon tried to kill Jeroboam, but Jeroboam fled to Egypt, to Shishak the king, and stayed there until Solomon's death.

[41]As for the other events of Solomon's reign—

[a] *33* Hebrew; Septuagint, Vulgate and Syriac *because he has*

NRSV

father David. [28]The man Jeroboam was very able, and when Solomon saw that the young man was industrious he gave him charge over all the forced labor of the house of Joseph. [29]About that time, when Jeroboam was leaving Jerusalem, the prophet Ahijah the Shilonite found him on the road. Ahijah had clothed himself with a new garment. The two of them were alone in the open country [30]when Ahijah laid hold of the new garment he was wearing and tore it into twelve pieces. [31]He then said to Jeroboam: Take for yourself ten pieces; for thus says the LORD, the God of Israel, "See, I am about to tear the kingdom from the hand of Solomon, and will give you ten tribes. [32]One tribe will remain his, for the sake of my servant David and for the sake of Jerusalem, the city that I have chosen out of all the tribes of Israel. [33]This is because he has[a] forsaken me, worshiped Astarte the goddess of the Sidonians, Chemosh the god of Moab, and Milcom the god of the Ammonites, and has[a] not walked in my ways, doing what is right in my sight and keeping my statutes and my ordinances, as his father David did. [34]Nevertheless I will not take the whole kingdom away from him but will make him ruler all the days of his life, for the sake of my servant David whom I chose and who did keep my commandments and my statutes; [35]but I will take the kingdom away from his son and give it to you—that is, the ten tribes. [36]Yet to his son I will give one tribe, so that my servant David may always have a lamp before me in Jerusalem, the city where I have chosen to put my name. [37]I will take you, and you shall reign over all that your soul desires; you shall be king over Israel. [38]If you will listen to all that I command you, walk in my ways, and do what is right in my sight by keeping my statutes and my commandments, as David my servant did, I will be with you, and will build you an enduring house, as I built for David, and I will give Israel to you. [39]For this reason I will punish the descendants of David, but not forever." [40]Solomon sought therefore to kill Jeroboam; but Jeroboam promptly fled to Egypt, to King Shishak of Egypt, and remained in Egypt until the death of Solomon.

41Now the rest of the acts of Solomon, all that

[a] Gk Syr Vg: Heb *they have*

NIV	NRSV
all he did and the wisdom he displayed—are they not written in the book of the annals of Solomon? 42Solomon reigned in Jerusalem over all Israel forty years. 43Then he rested with his fathers and was buried in the city of David his father. And Rehoboam his son succeeded him as king.	he did as well as his wisdom, are they not written in the Book of the Acts of Solomon? 42The time that Solomon reigned in Jerusalem over all Israel was forty years. 43Solomon slept with his ancestors and was buried in the city of his father David; and his son Rehoboam succeeded him.

COMMENTARY

The epitome of Solomon's achievements was his construction of the Temple of the Lord in Jerusalem. Whereas his father, David, had been preoccupied with warfare and was unable to carry out the project, Solomon boasted to Hiram, the Tyrian king, that he himself was able to do so because he had neither disasters nor adversaries (5:3-5). His good fortunes would be reversed, however, for God would raise up against him two adversaries from without (11:14-25) and one from within his kingdom (11:26-40).

11:14-22. In the time of David, the Israelites had defeated the Edomites in war, virtually annihilating the population (2 Sam 8:13-14). The young Edomite crown prince, Hadad, managed to escape and was brought to Egypt. The story of the Edomite's sojourn in Egypt provides some details that initially seem tangential to the point that he would be an adversary of Solomon: The refugees fled with the young crown prince to Egypt by way of Midian and Paran, desert locations important in the history of the Israelite nation. In Egypt, the Edomite married into the house of the pharaoh and produced a son who was taken in by the Egyptian queen and raised among the Egyptian royal children. Elements of the story—the reference to Midian, the birth of a child in Egypt, the raising of the child by an Egyptian queen in the Egyptian palace—find echo in the story of Moses, the mediator through whom God had freed the Israelites. The allusion to the exodus is unmistakable in the plea of the Edomite prince for freedom from Egypt: "Let me go (שלחני *šallĕḥēnî*), that I may return to my country" (v. 21; cf. v. 22). These are words that recall God's own words, uttered through Moses, in demand of Israel's release by the pharaoh of Egypt: "Let my son/people go" (see Exod 4:23; 5:1; 7:16; 8:1; 9:1; 10:3). The deuteronomistic narrator is not so sanguine about the Edomites as to suggest that the worship of the Lord would be the consequence of their release, as was the argument made before Pharaoh for Israel's freedom. Still, the text leaves no doubt that it was the Lord who raised up Hadad, despite the initial adversity of Hadad's circumstances. By a tissue of verbal allusions to the exodus experience, the narrator touches the core of Israelite belief in the particularity of their election. The text does not go so far as to state that the Edomites were liberated by the Lord and chosen by the Lord, as Israel had been. The universalism of God's salvation is not a point that the deuteronomistic narrator makes. The Lord had raised Hadad not so much to be the savior of the Edomites as to be an adversary to Solomon, who had sealed his alliance with Egypt through marrying the pharaoh's daughter. In any case, the text is clear that the will of God was being worked out even through foreigners.

11:23-25. Besides Hadad the Edomite, God also raised up Rezon. This was a man who had rebelled against his master, Hadadezer king of Zobah (an Aramaic state; see v. 23). Although the defeat of Hadadezer of Zobah is recounted elsewhere in the Bible (2 Sam 8:3-8; 10:1-19 // 1 Chr 18:3-8; 19:1-19), there is no hint anywhere else in the OT of Rezon's role. In the 1 Kings account, however, Rezon is given prominence. He is seen as the leader of a marauding band in rebellion against their overlord, just as David had led a band of men against King Saul. Rezon went on to capture Damascus, which he made the capital of a new Aramean dynasty, even as David captured Jerusalem and made it the capital of the Israelite kingdom. To the reader who knows the tradition of David's rise and the taking of Jerusalem as evidence of God's dual election of the king and the capital, the allusions cannot be missed. Again, the narrator does not make any claim that Rezon or Damascus were chosen in the same way that David and Zion had been. Still, the deliberate analogies are astounding. The narrator touches the very core of Israel's covenant theology. He points ironically to God's use of foreigners to undermine the Israelites' special relationship with God—the relationship established in the election of Israel (evident in the exodus experience) and the dual election of David and Zion.[49] There is no claim of God's universal salvation in the story here, but it is clear that history is being worked out completely under the will of the Lord—even if foreigners were used against God's chosen one!

11:26-43. Like Rezon the Aramean and David, Jeroboam rebelled against his king. Jeroboam is identified as the son of Nebat, who is called an אפרתי (*'eprātî*), a word that may be taken to mean either "Ephraimite" (as opposed to "Judean") or "Ephrathite" (someone from Ephrathah). The NIV and the NRSV both take the designation to mean that Jeroboam's father was an "Ephraimite," and that is probably correct. Still, the gentilic form *'eprātî* recalls David as the "son of an *'eprātî*" (1 Sam 17:12). The narrator acknowledges that Jeroboam the son of Nebat was no biological scion of the Davidic dynasty; yet, there are hints of other connections with David. Jeroboam is called by his patronym, perhaps to allow the cryptic note about his connection with the *'eprātî*: "son of Nebat, the *'eprātî*" (v. 26). He is also identified as a son of the widow Zeruah (meaning "leprous"?), perhaps in derogation, and he is called Solomon's "servant" (the NIV, less satisfactorily, has "one of Solomon's officials"). It may be significant that up to this point in the narrative of 1 Kings, every contender to the Davidic throne is associated with his mother: Adonijah, whose mother was Haggith (1:5, 11; 2:13), and Solomon, whose mother was Bathsheba (1:11; 2:13). Moreover, Jeroboam was a "servant" of Solomon (v. 26), just as David was a "servant" of Saul (1 Sam 17:32).

The connections with David pile up as the story continues. Jeroboam's rebellion against Solomon was set in motion by a "word" (דבר *dābār*, v. 27), possibly a reference to the divine word (NIV, "account"; NRSV, "reason"), just as the rejection of King Saul and the rise of David were set in motion by a (divine) "word" (1 Sam 15:10). Indeed, Jeroboam was encouraged in his rebellion by the word of God through Ahijah, a Shilonite prophet, even as David was encouraged to rise against Saul by God's word through Samuel, a prophet from the central sanctuary at Shiloh. Jeroboam was a youngster when he was called to service by Solomon, just as David was chosen by Saul when David was a youngster (1 Sam 17:33, 42). Despite his youth, Jeroboam is said to have been "a substantial hero" (גבור חיל *gibbôr ḥayil*, v. 28; NIV, "man of standing"; NRSV, "very able"), just as David was recommended to Saul as "a substantial hero" (*gibbôr ḥayil*) while he was still a youth (1 Sam 16:18; cf. 17:33). Jeroboam initially impressed Solomon (v. 28), just as David initially impressed Saul (1 Sam 16:21-22). The tragic fate of Saul was sealed by the tearing of a garment that symbolized the tearing of the kingdom from him, a kingdom that would be given to David (1 Sam 15:27-28). The rejection of Solomon, too, was marked by the symbolic act of the rending of a garment, in this case a *new* garment, ten fragments of which were given to Jeroboam (vv. 12, 30-31). The prophet Samuel interpreted the torn garment as God's rejection of Saul for his disobedience to the Lord. So, too, the prophet Ahijah interpreted the new torn garment as symbolic of the deity's rejection of Solomon. The rejected and jealous Saul tried to kill David (1 Sam 18:1–19:17), whom he initially favored. So, too, Solomon tried to kill Jeroboam, who had impressed him earlier (v. 40). David escaped to seek the protection of the Philistines (1 Sam 27:1-12), and he remained a fugitive until Saul's death. Likewise, Jeroboam escaped and received the protection of the Egyptians, and he remained there until Solomon died (v. 40). Most important, God promised to build Jeroboam an enduring dynasty, just as God had done for David—provided that Jeroboam keep the covenant (v. 38).

Despite the unmistakable allusions to the fall of Saul and the consequent rise of David, there are important differences between that story and

49. The exodus experience was central in the northern traditions ("Israel," as opposed to "Judah"), while the dual election of David and Zion was basic in Judean ideology. So the narrator of Kings is thorough in responding to the traditions of the north and the south.

the story of Solomon's fall and Jeroboam's rise. In Saul's case, the kingdom of Israel was torn from him and given to another, who was said to be better than he (1 Sam 15:28). In Jeroboam's case, the text is explicit that the kingdom would not be taken in its entirety out of Solomon's hand (vv. 13, 34). Nor is Jeroboam praised as a better person than Solomon. Only ten of the twelve fragments, symbolizing the ten tribes that belonged to the north, were given to Jeroboam. God's dual election of David and Jerusalem would not be violated, for one tribe will be retained for the "son of David" in order that there will always be "a lamp" in Jerusalem (v. 36; cf. 2 Sam 21:17). The narrator performs a remarkable balancing act here, at once preserving hope in God's promise that the Davidic dynasty would endure forever and maintaining the threat of severe punishment for any violation of the covenant stipulations. David had received assurance through Nathan's oracle that God's "covenant loyalty" (חסד *ḥesed*) would never be removed from his dynasty, as God had removed it from Saul (2 Sam 7:16). Now, through the rebellion of Jeroboam, it appears that God is removing the "kingdom of Israel" from the Davidides. By the allusions to God's action with regard to the fall of Saul, the narrator impels the reader to think of that incident, thus making the difference between the two cases stark: "But I will not take all the kingdom from his hand" (v. 34); "Only I will not tear away all the kingdom" (vv. 11-13). The promise to David is still good, inasmuch as Solomon will remain king until his death, and hope will remain in Jerusalem, for there will remain one tribe over which a scion of David will rule.

The careful reader will no doubt notice that the math does not add up in this passage. Ahijah had torn twelve fragments of the new garment to represent the twelve tribes. If ten tribes were given to Jeroboam and one to the Davidides, only eleven are accounted for. Ancient interpreters noticed the discrepancy as well, and, indeed, the Greek translation reflects a tradition that says two tribes were given to the Davidides—probably an attempt to harmonize the math. Commentators sometimes argue that the author did not care much about the precise figures. Yet, the narrator states in 12:20 that, while Jeroboam was given control over "all Israel" (the ten tribes of the north), only the tribe of Judah remained faithful to the house of David. Even though the Benjaminites did ally themselves with Judah under Rehoboam, Solomon's son (see 12:21-24), the unity of the south remains an open question.

REFLECTIONS

These passages raise a number of interesting theological issues that confront the faith community.

1. The negative role foreign women seem to play in Solomon's demise is troubling to the reader. Although Solomon was the one who was ultimately punished for his unfaithfulness, the story puts the blame on the foreign women. It was they who caused his heart to turn astray, as if he would not have strayed on his own or on account of other foreign alliances, such as his economic and political compromises with Phoenicia and Egypt. No, he had strayed because the women had led him to do so. To be sure, that is how the Torah sees it: The Israelites must not marry foreigners because their hearts would be turned away from loving the Lord (Deut 7:3-5; cf. Exod 34:15-16; Josh 23:12). That law was taken at face value in the post-exilic period, when, in the face of the community's losses through intermarriage, the leaders of the Jewish community called for reforms that would enforce the old prohibition against foreign marriages, the divorce of foreign wives, and the abandonment of the children of such marriages (Ezra 9–10). To modern readers, that approach to outsiders smacks of xenophobia, and its enforcement, with its demand for keeping "the race" pure (Ezra 9:2), sounds dangerously similar to what is now euphemistically called "ethnic cleansing." It is also troubling that only marriages of Israelite men to foreign women were at issue in the reforms of Ezra. No explicit sanction is made against Israelite women marrying foreign men.

Whatever the cultural, social, political, and economic circumstances that generated such laws in the Bible, it is important to understand that the biblical theologians were ultimately interested in the issue of faithfulness to the Lord alone. That is finally what is at stake in these laws. The critical theological issue in the condemnation of Solomon is his unfaithfulness to God, manifested in his love for other gods. The fundamental problem here is not the multiplicity of women or their foreignness or even their particular religions. For modern readers, Ashtoreth, Milcom, Chemosh, or other gods of Israel's neighbors are probably not serious threats. These cults have roundly been condemned for their promotion of fertility rites, their use of idols, and so on. Reading the stories in their historical contexts alone, we may be smug that we are no longer subservient to those sorts of "primitive" beliefs. The key theological issue that this text raises, however, is absolute devotion to our God. The fate of Solomon warns us against allegiance to other gods—and their names are still legion. The love of God in the biblical sense is an exclusivistic one. It brooks no compromise; it allows allegiance to no other "gods," whatever their names, whatever their forms.

2. In the light of the particularistic view in 11:11-13, with its polemic against Solomon's devotion to his foreign wives with their gods, 11:14-25 sounds almost universalistic. The particularity of Israel's claims—of God's election of the people as attested by their experience of liberation from Egypt and of the dual election of David and Zion—is astoundingly relativized. The story implies that even the Edomites had experiences of liberation analogous to those of Israel in Egypt. The narrator does not explicitly state that the liberation of the Edomites from Egypt was also the Lord's doing, but it does say that the Lord is the one who raised up Hadad, presumably the Edomite liberator, as an adversary to Solomon. The foreigner was used by God—negatively, in this case—to fulfill the divine plan as regards Israel.

By the same token, the Arameans also had a story to tell about the rise of their king that has parallels to David's rise and the taking of Jerusalem. The narrator of 1 Kings does not make the positive case that the rise of the enduring dynasty that Rezon brought and the choice of Damascus as the center of Aramean influence are evidence of God's election of the Arameans. Yet, the narrator does not doubt that it is the Lord who has raised up this Aramean—if only to be an adversary to Solomon, God's chosen king.

The narrator speaks of God's use of the foreigners only as foils for Israel. The implicitly universalistic assertion is that God is in control of all human history, not only of Israel's particular history. The passage does not make an explicit case for God's involvement in the positive experiences of the foreigners that are analogous to those of Israel, but biblical theologians do. In the face of Israel's flagrant violation of the covenant, the prophet Amos points to the liberation experiences of other nations that are, like Israel's exodus from Egypt, evidence of God's handiwork (Amos 9:7). The book of Jonah makes the case for God's love extending well beyond the boundaries of Israel to include foreigners in distant lands. Above all, the persistent message of the New Testament is that God breaks down the boundaries of ethnicity, gender, class, and nationality to proclaim the power of the love of God for all human beings, Jew and Gentile alike. The passage in 1 Kings recognizes the inclusivity of God's will alongside the claims of exclusivity that the covenant makes. So, too, the church must be exclusively devoted to the Lord and, at the same time, be open to the possibility that God might act much more inclusively than we may imagine.

3. The punishment of Solomon is a testimony to the integrity of God's demands as Suzerain. Violations of the covenant will have their consequences. This is a standard expectation in ancient Near Eastern treaties. The good news that is proclaimed throughout the Bible and that goes beyond standard covenant ideologies—the *good news* that is reiterated in this passage—is God's faithfulness to God's promises. The threat of God's punishment for sin is real, and so

is the promise, even if the signs of God's judgment and God's faithfulness do not quite add up. Mathematicians cannot resolve the mystery of that tension.

The validity of God's promise will be made manifest in the endurance of the Davidic line through the tribe of Judah. That persistence of hope through the scion of David will be the "lamp" ever before God. For many believers, that lamp shining in the midst of the darkness is most decisively manifested in the ministry of Jesus (see John 1:4-9). He is the "son of David" and a descendant from the tribe of Judah (Matt 1:1-17). That light will, by the divine promise and freedom, always be before God. In that promise, we dare to believe that God will be faithful forever.

1 KINGS 12:1–2 KINGS 17:41

THE DIVIDED KINGDOM

1 KINGS 12:1-33, FRAGMENTATION OF THE KINGDOM

OVERVIEW

In the preceding chapter, Ahijah the Shilonite had prophesied the fragmentation of the kingdom, with ten tribes given to Jeroboam, son of Nebat, an Ephraimite (11:26-40). Now in chap. 12, we see how that prophecy is fulfilled (12:1-24) and what Jeroboam's priorities were when he became king (12:25-33). Although Rehoboam has a prominent role to play in the first part of the chapter, his reign is not at issue here—that will come later (14:21-31). The point the narrator makes, rather, is that Rehoboam's oppressive and arrogant ways were instrumental in the fulfillment of the will of God, announced through Ahijah's prophecy (v. 15). By the same token, Rehoboam's surprising obedience to the word of God spoken through Shemaiah, the man of God, was decisive in the fulfillment of the will of God (v. 24). Jeroboam is ironically silent in this story of his rise to power; throughout the account in vv. 1-24, he does not speak or act, except as part of the assembly that petitioned Rehoboam (vv. 3, 12). In this way, the narrative effectively conveys the message that Jeroboam's rise to power is in accordance with the will of God; it has nothing to do with Jeroboam's ability or character. When Jeroboam does finally act and speak (vv. 25-29), it is in his own selfish interest, and his initiatives are unsavory.

1 Kings 12:1-24, Ahijah's Prophecy Is Fulfilled

NIV

12 Rehoboam went to Shechem, for all the Israelites had gone there to make him king. 2When Jeroboam son of Nebat heard this (he was still in Egypt, where he had fled from King Solomon), he returned from[a] Egypt. 3So they sent for Jeroboam, and he and the whole assembly of Israel went to Rehoboam and said to him: 4"Your father put a heavy yoke on us, but now lighten the harsh labor and the heavy yoke he put on us, and we will serve you."

5Rehoboam answered, "Go away for three days and then come back to me." So the people went away.

6Then King Rehoboam consulted the elders

[a] 2 Or *he remained in*

NRSV

12 Rehoboam went to Shechem, for all Israel had come to Shechem to make him king. 2When Jeroboam son of Nebat heard of it (for he was still in Egypt, where he had fled from King Solomon), then Jeroboam returned from[a] Egypt. 3And they sent and called him; and Jeroboam and all the assembly of Israel came and said to Rehoboam, 4"Your father made our yoke heavy. Now therefore lighten the hard service of your father and his heavy yoke that he placed on us, and we will serve you." 5He said to them, "Go away for three days, then come again to me." So the people went away.

[a] Gk Vg Compare 2 Chr 10.2: Heb *lived in*

NIV

who had served his father Solomon during his lifetime. "How would you advise me to answer these people?" he asked.

7They replied, "If today you will be a servant to these people and serve them and give them a favorable answer, they will always be your servants."

8But Rehoboam rejected the advice the elders gave him and consulted the young men who had grown up with him and were serving him. 9He asked them, "What is your advice? How should we answer these people who say to me, 'Lighten the yoke your father put on us'?"

10The young men who had grown up with him replied, "Tell these people who have said to you, 'Your father put a heavy yoke on us, but make our yoke lighter'—tell them, 'My little finger is thicker than my father's waist. 11My father laid on you a heavy yoke; I will make it even heavier. My father scourged you with whips; I will scourge you with scorpions.' "

12Three days later Jeroboam and all the people returned to Rehoboam, as the king had said, "Come back to me in three days." 13The king answered the people harshly. Rejecting the advice given him by the elders, 14he followed the advice of the young men and said, "My father made your yoke heavy; I will make it even heavier. My father scourged you with whips; I will scourge you with scorpions." 15So the king did not listen to the people, for this turn of events was from the LORD, to fulfill the word the LORD had spoken to Jeroboam son of Nebat through Ahijah the Shilonite.

16When all Israel saw that the king refused to listen to them, they answered the king:

"What share do we have in David,
what part in Jesse's son?
To your tents, O Israel!
Look after your own house, O David!"

So the Israelites went home. 17But as for the Israelites who were living in the towns of Judah, Rehoboam still ruled over them.

18King Rehoboam sent out Adoniram,[a] who was in charge of forced labor, but all Israel stoned him

[a] *18* Some Septuagint manuscripts and Syriac (see also 1 Kings 4:6 and 5:14); Hebrew *Adoram*

NRSV

6Then King Rehoboam took counsel with the older men who had attended his father Solomon while he was still alive, saying, "How do you advise me to answer this people?" 7They answered him, "If you will be a servant to this people today and serve them, and speak good words to them when you answer them, then they will be your servants forever." 8But he disregarded the advice that the older men gave him, and consulted with the young men who had grown up with him and now attended him. 9He said to them, "What do you advise that we answer this people who have said to me, 'Lighten the yoke that your father put on us'?" 10The young men who had grown up with him said to him, "Thus you should say to this people who spoke to you, 'Your father made our yoke heavy, but you must lighten it for us'; thus you should say to them, 'My little finger is thicker than my father's loins. 11Now, whereas my father laid on you a heavy yoke, I will add to your yoke. My father disciplined you with whips, but I will discipline you with scorpions.' "

12So Jeroboam and all the people came to Rehoboam the third day, as the king had said, "Come to me again the third day." 13The king answered the people harshly. He disregarded the advice that the older men had given him 14and spoke to them according to the advice of the young men, "My father made your yoke heavy, but I will add to your yoke; my father disciplined you with whips, but I will discipline you with scorpions." 15So the king did not listen to the people, because it was a turn of affairs brought about by the LORD that he might fulfill his word, which the LORD had spoken by Ahijah the Shilonite to Jeroboam son of Nebat.

16When all Israel saw that the king would not listen to them, the people answered the king,

"What share do we have in David?
We have no inheritance in the son of Jesse.
To your tents, O Israel!
Look now to your own house, O David."

So Israel went away to their tents. 17But Rehoboam reigned over the Israelites who were living in the towns of Judah. 18When King Rehoboam sent Adoram, who was taskmaster over the forced labor, all Israel stoned him to death.

NIV

to death. King Rehoboam, however, managed to get into his chariot and escape to Jerusalem. 19So Israel has been in rebellion against the house of David to this day.

20When all the Israelites heard that Jeroboam had returned, they sent and called him to the assembly and made him king over all Israel. Only the tribe of Judah remained loyal to the house of David.

21When Rehoboam arrived in Jerusalem, he mustered the whole house of Judah and the tribe of Benjamin—a hundred and eighty thousand fighting men—to make war against the house of Israel and to regain the kingdom for Rehoboam son of Solomon.

22But this word of God came to Shemaiah the man of God: 23"Say to Rehoboam son of Solomon king of Judah, to the whole house of Judah and Benjamin, and to the rest of the people, 24'This is what the LORD says: Do not go up to fight against your brothers, the Israelites. Go home, every one of you, for this is my doing.' " So they obeyed the word of the LORD and went home again, as the LORD had ordered.

NRSV

King Rehoboam then hurriedly mounted his chariot to flee to Jerusalem. 19So Israel has been in rebellion against the house of David to this day.

20When all Israel heard that Jeroboam had returned, they sent and called him to the assembly and made him king over all Israel. There was no one who followed the house of David, except the tribe of Judah alone.

21When Rehoboam came to Jerusalem, he assembled all the house of Judah and the tribe of Benjamin, one hundred eighty thousand chosen troops to fight against the house of Israel, to restore the kingdom to Rehoboam son of Solomon. 22But the word of God came to Shemaiah the man of God: 23Say to King Rehoboam of Judah, son of Solomon, and to all the house of Judah and Benjamin, and to the rest of the people, 24"Thus says the LORD, You shall not go up or fight against your kindred the people of Israel. Let everyone go home, for this thing is from me." So they heeded the word of the LORD and went home again, according to the word of the LORD.

COMMENTARY

12:1-19. Upon the death of Solomon, his son Rehoboam went to Shechem to be crowned king (922–915 BCE). Political considerations seem to have been at play in previous choices of coronation sites—David at Hebron (2 Sam 5:1-5), Adonijah at En Rogel (1 Kgs 1:9-10), Solomon at Gihon (1 Kgs 1:32-37). Shechem was perhaps a politically sensible choice for the kingdom that threatens to disintegrate. It has pride of place as the first locale Abram visited when he migrated from Haran (Gen 12:6). It was also the site of a covenant ceremony involving the whole Israelite confederacy (Joshua 24). Set in "the hill country of Ephraim" (v. 25), it was an important city for the northern tribes. So its selection may be viewed as a conciliatory overture to the northern tribes by the Judean successor to the throne. Rehoboam, however, is not portrayed by the narrator as a tactful and compromising man. It is more likely that his coronation at Shechem was a deliberate assertion of his authority over the northern tribes.

Whatever the case may have been historically, the mention of a coronation at Shechem recalls a similar event that occurred before the establishment of the Davidic monarchy. In the days of the judges, a certain Abimelech, son of Jerubbaal, tried to make himself king there. He viciously murdered all his rivals and ruled over Israel for three years, contrary to the antimonarchical tradition of the northern tribal confederacy (Judg 9:1-57). That early experiment in monarchical rule failed, however, and the Lord again raised up judges to deliver Israel (Judg 10:1-2). Rehoboam apparently had not learned a lesson from history, for history would soon repeat itself: His assumption of kingship at Shechem would be immediately challenged.

Ahijah the Shilonite had dramatized in a sign-act that Jeroboam, son of Nebat, would be instru-

Figure 3: Chronology of the Kings of the Divided Monarchy*

Judah	*Israel*
Rehoboam (922–915 BCE)	Jeroboam I (922–901 BCE)
	Abijam (915–913)
Asa (915–873)	Nadab (901–900)
	Baasha (900–877)
	Elah (877–876)
	Zimri (876)
Jehoshaphat (873–849)	Omri (876–869)
	Ahab (869–850)
	Ahaziah (850–849)
Jehoram (849–843)	Jehoram (849–843/2)
Ahaziah (843/2)	
Athaliah (843–837)	
Jehoash (837–800)	Jehu (843/2–815)
	Jehoahaz (815–802)
Amaziah (800–783)	Joash (802–786)
Azariah/Uzziah (783–742)	Jeroboam II (786–746)
	Zechariah (746–745)
	Shallum (745)
Jotham (742–735)	Menahem (745–737)
	Pekahiah (737–736)
	Pekah (736–732)
Ahaz (735–715)	Hoshea (732–724)
	Fall of Samaria (722/1 BCE)
Hezekiah (715–687/6)	
Manasseh (687/6–642)	
Amon (642–640)	
Josiah (640–609)	
Jehoahaz (609)	
Jehoiakim (609–598)	
Jehoiachin (598/7)	
Babylonian conquest of Jerusalem and for deportation (597 BCE)	
Zedekiah (597–587/6)	
Destruction of Jerusalem and second deportation (587/6 BCE)	

*Dates following the kings' names are approximate years of their rule.

mental in the dismantling of the kingdom (11:26-46). Solomon had temporarily removed that threat by driving Jeroboam into exile in Egypt. According to the Hebrew text, Jeroboam was still in Egypt at this time.[50] He was immediately summoned back, no doubt by the northerners because of his previous experience as leader of the corvée (11:28). The northern leaders appeared before the newly crowned king to ask that the workload be lightened, for they had borne the brunt of Solomon's demands for corvée workers for his various projects (see 4:1-17). Apparently there is still a chance that Ahijah's prophesied fragmentation might be averted; the decision lay in the hands of Rehoboam to follow the path of oppression set by his father or to take a different course.

Rehoboam managed to buy some time in order

50. The NRSV and the NIV both emend the Hebrew text to read "and he returned from Egypt," following the parallel text in 2 Chr 10:2, the Greek, and the Vulgate.

to seek advice. The veterans who had served Solomon counseled a conciliatory approach. Despite their links with Solomon, they advocated a reversal of policy. Their sage advice was to take a long view of the matter: If the king would accommodate the request of the Israelites now, then they would be beholden to him forever. Rehoboam, however, rejected the advice and turned instead to his peers "who had grown up with him." His bias is evident in the fact that he identifies himself with them: "What do you advise that *we* answer this people . . . ?" (v. 9; cf., "How do you advise *me* . . . ?" in v. 6). His companions—derogatorily called "the boys" (הילדים *haylādîm*), even though they must have been about forty years old (see 21:14; hence, the NRSV and the NIV have "the young men")—advocated an uncompromising approach, even urging Rehoboam to use what is probably a vulgar idiom: "My little [thing] is thicker than my father's loins!" (Most translators supply the word "finger" to clarify the substantive קטן [*qĕṭōn*, "little one," "little thing"], but that only obscures the idiom.) They encouraged Rehoboam to increase the burden and the scourge—to use "scorpions" (perhaps a reference to spiked lashes) instead of ordinary whips.

Like Pharaoh, whose heart was hardened when he was asked to grant the Israelite slaves some reprieve from their oppressive burdens, Rehoboam was recalcitrant. Just as Pharaoh did with the Israelites, so also Rehoboam promised even more hardship and more painful afflictions (Exod 5:1-23). Here, again, Rehoboam has apparently not learned from history; he "did not listen to the people" (v. 15). The narrator portrays this turn of events as something brought about in accordance with God's will in order that the prophecy of Ahijah might be fulfilled.

The northern tribes sounded the cry of rebellion with words that echo the revolt of Sheba the Benjaminite in the time of Saul (2 Sam 20:1). Again, history repeats itself, and Rehoboam is still not learning from it.

The consequence is the division of the kingdom. "All Israel" (presumably ten tribes, as Ahijah had predicted) were led by Jeroboam. Rehoboam remained in control over only the Israelites living in the Judean towns. Still, he did not appear to have learned his lesson. Of all people, he sent Adoram, the minister of forced labor, to the Israelites, possibly the same Adoram or a descendant of the Adoram who was in charge of the forced labor in the days when Sheba revolted (see 2 Sam 20:24)! The taskmaster was stoned to death, and Rehoboam had to flee to Jerusalem. The division of the kingdom had become a fact "to this day" (v. 19)—that is, in the generation of the editor.

12:20-24. While Jeroboam, son of Nebat, was made king over the ten tribes of Israel (922–901 BCE), only the tribe of Judah remained loyal to the house of David, just as Ahijah had prophesied. The tribe of Benjamin apparently did not join the northern group, but neither did they pledge allegiance to the Davidides. Despite the fact that he was in the minority, Rehoboam was willing to take up arms to restore the kingdom. Obviously, he had the seasoned military units under his command. He was on the verge of bringing the Benjaminites over to his side when he was stopped by Shemaiah, "the man of God," who declared that the division of the kingdom was in accordance with the will of the Lord. The word of the Lord somehow prevailed, and Rehoboam gave up his fight. Instead of trying "to restore" (להשיב *lĕhāšîb*, in the hiphil) the kingdom by force, the people "returned" (שוב *šûb*) to their homes. The foolish young king who began by insisting on his way finally obeyed the word of God. The will of God, as conveyed in the prophecy of Ahijah, was thus fulfilled. (See Reflections at 12:25-33.)

1 Kings 12:25-33, Jeroboam's Priorities

NIV

25Then Jeroboam fortified Shechem in the hill country of Ephraim and lived there. From there he went out and built up Peniel.[a]

26Jeroboam thought to himself, "The kingdom will now likely revert to the house of David. 27If these people go up to offer sacrifices at the temple of the LORD in Jerusalem, they will again give their allegiance to their lord, Rehoboam king of Judah. They will kill me and return to King Rehoboam."

28After seeking advice, the king made two golden calves. He said to the people, "It is too much for you to go up to Jerusalem. Here are your gods, O Israel, who brought you up out of Egypt." 29One he set up in Bethel, and the other in Dan. 30And this thing became a sin; the people went even as far as Dan to worship the one there.

31Jeroboam built shrines on high places and appointed priests from all sorts of people, even though they were not Levites. 32He instituted a festival on the fifteenth day of the eighth month, like the festival held in Judah, and offered sacrifices on the altar. This he did in Bethel, sacrificing to the calves he had made. And at Bethel he also installed priests at the high places he had made. 33On the fifteenth day of the eighth month, a month of his own choosing, he offered sacrifices on the altar he had built at Bethel. So he instituted the festival for the Israelites and went up to the altar to make offerings.

[a] *25* Hebrew *Penuel,* a variant of *Peniel*

NRSV

25Then Jeroboam built Shechem in the hill country of Ephraim, and resided there; he went out from there and built Penuel. 26Then Jeroboam said to himself, "Now the kingdom may well revert to the house of David. 27If this people continues to go up to offer sacrifices in the house of the LORD at Jerusalem, the heart of this people will turn again to their master, King Rehoboam of Judah; they will kill me and return to King Rehoboam of Judah." 28So the king took counsel, and made two calves of gold. He said to the people,[a] "You have gone up to Jerusalem long enough. Here are your gods, O Israel, who brought you up out of the land of Egypt." 29He set one in Bethel, and the other he put in Dan. 30And this thing became a sin, for the people went to worship before the one at Bethel and before the other as far as Dan.[b] 31He also made houses[c] on high places, and appointed priests from among all the people, who were not Levites. 32Jeroboam appointed a festival on the fifteenth day of the eighth month like the festival that was in Judah, and he offered sacrifices on the altar; so he did in Bethel, sacrificing to the calves that he had made. And he placed in Bethel the priests of the high places that he had made. 33He went up to the altar that he had made in Bethel on the fifteenth day in the eighth month, in the month that he alone had devised; he appointed a festival for the people of Israel, and he went up to the altar to offer incense.

[a] Gk: Heb *to them* [b] Compare Gk: Heb *went to the one as far as Dan* [c] Gk Vg Compare 13.32: Heb *a house*

COMMENTARY

Jeroboam is largely a passive figure in the preceding verses, even though his rise to power is at issue. Except for his presence with the rest of his people before Rehoboam, he is silent. Twice he had to be summoned to the scene of action (vv. 2, 20). Yet, he has come into power because it is the will of God. It is only after the division of the kingdom has become a fact that we see Jeroboam in an active role.

Shechem, an ancient city that once was the site of a covenant renewal ceremony for all Israel (Joshua 24), was rebuilt and established as Jeroboam's capital. Penuel, a sacred site in the Jacob tradition (Gen 32:24-31) and, hence, also among the northern tribes, was also rebuilt. Now the narrator lets the reader in on the private thoughts of Jeroboam so that his true intentions may be known. Fearing that the dedication to the

Jerusalem cultus would lead to disloyalty to him, he established royal sanctuaries at Bethel, a sacred site long associated with Jacob, and at Dan, near the northern border of Israel. The reader gathers from Jeroboam's soliloquy that his interests were purely political and selfish; they had nothing to do with faith in the Lord, even though he cast the issue in religious terms before his people (v. 28). He made two golden calves at these sanctuaries and called for worship there.

Like the rebuilding of Shechem and Penuel, Jeroboam's initiative at Bethel and Dan was a political one: He wanted to retain the loyalty of the populace and, no doubt, also the wealth that their offerings would bring into the state coffers. It was probably not his purpose to have the calves set up as idols to be worshiped; politically, it would have been exceedingly foolhardy for him to try to found a new religion when the country was in such turmoil. Rather, the calves were probably symbols of God, who was known from antiquity as "the Bull of Jacob" (see Gen 49:24; Ps 132:2, 5). In one tradition at least, the calf imagery was probably associated with the god of the exodus: "These are your gods, O Israel, who brought you up out of the land of Egypt" (Exod 32:4, 8 NRSV; see TNK and NAB). Thus, just as the ark and the cherubim in the Jerusalem Temple were thought to have been the symbols of an invisibly enthroned deity, so also the calf was probably intended as the pedestal for an invisible God. Accordingly, the TNK renders the Hebrew of v. 28 thus: "This is your god, O Israel, who brought you up from the land of Egypt." The allusion to the exodus experience is not accidental, for the experience of the northern tribes under the rule of the southerners was analogous to the bondage of Israel in Egypt.

Whatever the original intention of Jeroboam, from the perspective of the deuteronomistic editor, who is vehement that the Jerusalem Temple is the only acceptable one, the initiative of Jeroboam was nothing but sin, and the fact that there were two calves allows the editor to imply the polytheistic nature of Jeroboam's innovations. He feared that his people would continue to go to "the house of the LORD" (v. 27), so he built an alternative "house of high places" (v. 31; NRSV, "houses on high places"; NIV, "shrines on high places") and he appointed non-Levites to serve as priests, both actions in contravention of deuteronomistic law (Deut 12:5-7; 18:1-8). Jeroboam is also accused of changing the festal calendar; he ordered the celebration of a festival just like *the* festival in Judah—that is, the Feast of Booths (Sukkot) on the fifteenth day of the eighth month, rather than the fifteenth day of the seventh month, as stipulated in the law (Lev 23:33-36). The charge of heresy is perhaps unfair in the light of Jeroboam's original intention. Yet, it is true that his initiatives at Bethel and Dan did lead to idolatry; the calves did become objects of worship (Hos 10:5; 13:2), and the northern shrines did become centers of heterodoxy (Amos 5:4-5), in which the priests were more interested in protecting the political establishment than in following the demands of the Lord (Amos 7:10-17). By letting the reader in on the thoughts of Jeroboam, the narrator makes it clear that Jeroboam's actions were for his own political goals.

REFLECTIONS

The narrator paints a caricature of a despicable dictator in Rehoboam: He is foolish, tactless, crass, recalcitrant, and oppressive. We can name many modern dictators who would fit this description perfectly. Inevitably our sympathy lies with the oppressed people they rule. We rejoice at the people's liberation, and we are not at all surprised to learn that it is the will of God that their revolution should succeed.

The story in 1 Kings 12, however, warns us not to romanticize revolution. Jeroboam, the acknowledged leader of the liberated people, is no ideal figure himself. He has his own political agenda and is perfectly willing to manipulate religious symbols to fit it. He speaks the language of liberation theology ("who brought you out of the land of Egypt"), but his allegiance is to himself.

On the one hand, the passage teaches us that it is the will of God to liberate the oppressed.

On the other hand, we learn not to idealize every liberation movement.[51] In the end, it is the will of God that really matters (12:15), and it is not too late for even the worst of sinners to obey the will of God (12:24).

51. See Richard D. Nelson, *First and Second Kings,* Interpretation (Atlanta: John Knox, 1987) 82.

1 KINGS 13:1-34, WHEN ONE DOES NOT OBEY THE WORD OF THE LORD

OVERVIEW

This chapter is a continuation of the preceding account of Jeroboam's heterodox innovations. The account of Jeroboam's encounter with an unnamed man of God from Judah (vv. 1-10) seems logical enough in the context. It is followed, however, by a peculiar report of the fate of this man of God that seems to be entirely intrusive in the narrative (vv. 11-32). Yet, the unity of the chapter is not in doubt. The phrase "the word of the LORD" is repeated throughout the chapter (vv. 1-2, 5, 9, 17-18, 20-21, 26 [twice], 32). Various forms of the Hebrew root שׁוב (*šûb*, with its range of meanings) appear sixteen times (vv. 4, 6 [twice], 9, 10, 16, 17, 18, 19, 20, 22, 23, 26, 29, 33 [twice]), and the word for "way" or "road" also appears repeatedly (vv. 9, 10 [twice], 17, 24 [twice], 26, 33). The story of the man of God is, in fact, not an insignificant diversion. Rather, it is an illustration of what might happen when one does not obey the word of the Lord. Even a man of God, who is scrupulously obedient most of the time and who falls short on just one seemingly understandable situation, is punished. Yet, the recalcitrant Jeroboam did not seem to learn that lesson (vv. 33-34). Thus the chapter as a whole is about Jeroboam's disobedience of the word of the Lord and the predicted consequences of that disobedience.

1 Kings 13:1-10, Consequences of Jeroboam's Disobedience

NIV

13 By the word of the LORD a man of God came from Judah to Bethel, as Jeroboam was standing by the altar to make an offering. 2He cried out against the altar by the word of the LORD: "O altar, altar! This is what the LORD says: 'A son named Josiah will be born to the house of David. On you he will sacrifice the priests of the high places who now make offerings here, and human bones will be burned on you.'" 3That same day the man of God gave a sign: "This is the sign the LORD has declared: The altar will be split apart and the ashes on it will be poured out."

4When King Jeroboam heard what the man of God cried out against the altar at Bethel, he stretched out his hand from the altar and said, "Seize him!" But the hand he stretched out to-

NRSV

13 While Jeroboam was standing by the altar to offer incense, a man of God came out of Judah by the word of the LORD to Bethel 2and proclaimed against the altar by the word of the LORD, and said, "O altar, altar, thus says the LORD: 'A son shall be born to the house of David, Josiah by name; and he shall sacrifice on you the priests of the high places who offer incense on you, and human bones shall be burned on you.'" 3He gave a sign the same day, saying, "This is the sign that the LORD has spoken: 'The altar shall be torn down, and the ashes that are on it shall be poured out.'" 4When the king heard what the man of God cried out against the altar at Bethel, Jeroboam stretched out his hand from the altar, saying, "Seize him!" But the hand that he stretched out

NIV

ward the man shriveled up, so that he could not pull it back. [5]Also, the altar was split apart and its ashes poured out according to the sign given by the man of God by the word of the LORD.

[6]Then the king said to the man of God, "Intercede with the LORD your God and pray for me that my hand may be restored." So the man of God interceded with the LORD, and the king's hand was restored and became as it was before.

[7]The king said to the man of God, "Come home with me and have something to eat, and I will give you a gift."

[8]But the man of God answered the king, "Even if you were to give me half your possessions, I would not go with you, nor would I eat bread or drink water here. [9]For I was commanded by the word of the LORD: 'You must not eat bread or drink water or return by the way you came.'" [10]So he took another road and did not return by the way he had come to Bethel.

NRSV

against him withered so that he could not draw it back to himself. [5]The altar also was torn down, and the ashes poured out from the altar, according to the sign that the man of God had given by the word of the LORD. [6]The king said to the man of God, "Entreat now the favor of the LORD your God, and pray for me, so that my hand may be restored to me." So the man of God entreated the LORD; and the king's hand was restored to him, and became as it was before. [7]Then the king said to the man of God, "Come home with me and dine, and I will give you a gift." [8]But the man of God said to the king, "If you give me half your kingdom, I will not go in with you; nor will I eat food or drink water in this place. [9]For thus I was commanded by the word of the LORD: You shall not eat food, or drink water, or return by the way that you came." [10]So he went another way, and did not return by the way that he had come to Bethel.

COMMENTARY

The story actually begins at 12:32. Among the heretical religious innovations of Jeroboam was the celebration of a feast, probably the Feast of Booths (Sukkot), on the fifteenth day of the eighth month. This was in contrast to the rule in Judah, where the feast was celebrated in the seventh month.

Jeroboam had apparently come to Bethel to inaugurate the festival by offering sacrifices at the altar—sacrifices offered to the golden calves he had set up, according to the narrator (12:32). He was standing by the altar to offer incense when an unnamed man of God came from Judah "by the word of the LORD" (v. 1). It is clear that the Lord was not at Bethel. Rather, the word of the Lord was brought by someone from Judah.

As the present text has it, the man of God predicted the coming of Josiah, a descendent of David, almost three centuries later. Reflecting the events related in 2 Kgs 23:15-20, the man of God predicted Josiah's desecration of the altar by slaughtering the priests of the high places and burning their bones upon the Bethel altar. To confirm the prophecy, the man of God proclaimed an accompanying sign—namely, the splitting apart of the altar. Jeroboam stretched out his hand to order the arrest of the man, but his hand withered and his arm became paralyzed and the altar was split apart accordingly (v. 5). Jeroboam had earlier successfully "raised his hand" against Solomon (11:26, 27), but his hand is now stretched out in an attempt to prevent a sign from the Lord. His hand is dramatically stopped.

Jeroboam pleaded for the man of God to intercede for him. When the man did so, Jeroboam's hand was restored. Clearly, it was the Lord who granted the restoration. The king appeared not to get that point either, however. He invited the man of God to dine with him, promising him a gift. The holy man declined the invitation, stating that he had been commanded "by the word of the LORD" not to eat or drink or to return by the way he had come. No reason is given for this injunction. Whatever the rationale for that commandment, there is no question that the man of God knew that he was so charged. (See Reflections at 13:33-34.)

1 Kings 13:11-32, No Excuse Is Acceptable for Disobedience

NIV

11Now there was a certain old prophet living in Bethel, whose sons came and told him all that the man of God had done there that day. They also told their father what he had said to the king. 12Their father asked them, "Which way did he go?" And his sons showed him which road the man of God from Judah had taken. 13So he said to his sons, "Saddle the donkey for me." And when they had saddled the donkey for him, he mounted it 14and rode after the man of God. He found him sitting under an oak tree and asked, "Are you the man of God who came from Judah?"

"I am," he replied.

15So the prophet said to him, "Come home with me and eat."

16The man of God said, "I cannot turn back and go with you, nor can I eat bread or drink water with you in this place. 17I have been told by the word of the LORD: 'You must not eat bread or drink water there or return by the way you came.' "

18The old prophet answered, "I too am a prophet, as you are. And an angel said to me by the word of the LORD: 'Bring him back with you to your house so that he may eat bread and drink water.' " (But he was lying to him.) 19So the man of God returned with him and ate and drank in his house.

20While they were sitting at the table, the word of the LORD came to the old prophet who had brought him back. 21He cried out to the man of God who had come from Judah, "This is what the LORD says: 'You have defied the word of the LORD and have not kept the command the LORD your God gave you. 22You came back and ate bread and drank water in the place where he told you not to eat or drink. Therefore your body will not be buried in the tomb of your fathers.' "

23When the man of God had finished eating and drinking, the prophet who had brought him back saddled his donkey for him. 24As he went on his way, a lion met him on the road and killed him, and his body was thrown down on the road, with both the donkey and the lion standing beside it. 25Some people who passed by saw the body thrown down there, with the lion standing beside

NRSV

11Now there lived an old prophet in Bethel. One of his sons came and told him all that the man of God had done that day in Bethel; the words also that he had spoken to the king, they told to their father. 12Their father said to them, "Which way did he go?" And his sons showed him the way that the man of God who came from Judah had gone. 13Then he said to his sons, "Saddle a donkey for me." So they saddled a donkey for him, and he mounted it. 14He went after the man of God, and found him sitting under an oak tree. He said to him, "Are you the man of God who came from Judah?" He answered, "I am." 15Then he said to him, "Come home with me and eat some food." 16But he said, "I cannot return with you, or go in with you; nor will I eat food or drink water with you in this place; 17for it was said to me by the word of the LORD: You shall not eat food or drink water there, or return by the way that you came." 18Then the other[a] said to him, "I also am a prophet as you are, and an angel spoke to me by the word of the LORD: Bring him back with you into your house so that he may eat food and drink water." But he was deceiving him. 19Then the man of God[a] went back with him, and ate food and drank water in his house.

20As they were sitting at the table, the word of the LORD came to the prophet who had brought him back; 21and he proclaimed to the man of God who came from Judah, "Thus says the LORD: Because you have disobeyed the word of the LORD, and have not kept the commandment that the LORD your God commanded you, 22but have come back and have eaten food and drunk water in the place of which he said to you, 'Eat no food, and drink no water,' your body shall not come to your ancestral tomb." 23After the man of God[a] had eaten food and had drunk, they saddled for him a donkey belonging to the prophet who had brought him back. 24Then as he went away, a lion met him on the road and killed him. His body was thrown in the road, and the donkey stood beside it; the lion also stood beside the body.

[a] Heb *he*

NIV

the body, and they went and reported it in the
city where the old prophet lived.

[26]When the prophet who had brought him back
from his journey heard of it, he said, "It is the
man of God who defied the word of the LORD.
The LORD has given him over to the lion, which
has mauled him and killed him, as the word of
the LORD had warned him."

[27]The prophet said to his sons, "Saddle the
donkey for me," and they did so. [28]Then he went
out and found the body thrown down on the
road, with the donkey and the lion standing
beside it. The lion had neither eaten the body nor
mauled the donkey. [29]So the prophet picked up
the body of the man of God, laid it on the donkey,
and brought it back to his own city to mourn for
him and bury him. [30]Then he laid the body in his
own tomb, and they mourned over him and said,
"Oh, my brother!"

[31]After burying him, he said to his sons, "When
I die, bury me in the grave where the man of
God is buried; lay my bones beside his bones.
[32]For the message he declared by the word of the
LORD against the altar in Bethel and against all the
shrines on the high places in the towns of Samaria
will certainly come true."

NRSV

[25]People passed by and saw the body thrown in
the road, with the lion standing by the body. And
they came and told it in the town where the old
prophet lived.

26When the prophet who had brought him
back from the way heard of it, he said, "It is the
man of God who disobeyed the word of the LORD;
therefore the LORD has given him to the lion,
which has torn him and killed him according to
the word that the LORD spoke to him." [27]Then he
said to his sons, "Saddle a donkey for me." So
they saddled one, [28]and he went and found the
body thrown in the road, with the donkey and
the lion standing beside the body. The lion had
not eaten the body or attacked the donkey. [29]The
prophet took up the body of the man of God, laid
it on the donkey, and brought it back to the city,[a]
to mourn and to bury him. [30]He laid the body in
his own grave; and they mourned over him,
saying, "Alas, my brother!" [31]After he had buried
him, he said to his sons, "When I die, bury me
in the grave in which the man of God is buried;
lay my bones beside his bones. [32]For the saying
that he proclaimed by the word of the LORD
against the altar in Bethel, and against all the
houses of the high places that are in the cities of
Samaria, shall surely come to pass."

[a] Gk: Heb *he came to the town of the old prophet*

COMMENTARY

The encounter was reported to an unnamed old prophet who lived in Bethel. His response is immediate. He hastens to find the man of God from Judah to invite him to dine with him. We are not told the reason for this eager invitation, but one recognizes the similarity to Jeroboam's bidding in v. 7. In any case, it is plain now that Jeroboam was not motivated by gratitude for the healing of his withered hand. When the man of God declined the invitation of the old prophet, as he did that of Jeroboam, the old man blatantly lied, saying that he had been visited by an angel who told him to issue the invitation. So, despite his own certainty of what the Lord had commanded him earlier (vv. 9, 17), the Judean man of God was lured home by the unnamed prophet from Bethel.

It is clear by now that the old man from Bethel was a false prophet. Yet it is he who received and prounounced the word of the Lord against the man of God from Judah. For his disobedience, the latter would be deprived of burial in his ancestral tomb. Then, on his way home after the forbidden communion, the man of God was met by a lion and killed. Contrary to expectations, the lion merely stood beside the corpse instead of mauling it, a fact that is reiterated by the narrator (vv. 24-25, 28). It also did not attack the man's donkey (vv. 24, 28), as would be natural. The narrator thus makes the point that the killing was divinely ordained.

The old prophet declared that it was the Lord who had slain the man of God because of the man's disobedience. He buried the man in the grave that he had apparently reserved for himself, and he mourned for the man of God, calling him "my brother" (v. 30). Then, he instructed his sons that he, too, should be buried in that grave with the man of God. Apparently, the false prophet wanted to be associated with the man whose prophecy he knew would certainly come to pass and, according to the Greek, because he knew that the tomb of the man of God would not be desecrated. (See Reflections at 13:33-34.)

1 Kings 13:33-34, Jeroboam Continues His Disobedience

NIV

33Even after this, Jeroboam did not change his evil ways, but once more appointed priests for the high places from all sorts of people. Anyone who wanted to become a priest he consecrated for the high places. 34This was the sin of the house of Jeroboam that led to its downfall and to its destruction from the face of the earth.

NRSV

33Even after this event Jeroboam did not turn from his evil way, but made priests for the high places again from among all the people; any who wanted to be priests he consecrated for the high places. 34This matter became sin to the house of Jeroboam, so as to cut it off and to destroy it from the face of the earth.

COMMENTARY

The deuteronomistic editor concludes that Jeroboam did not repent despite the preceding story. The introductory words are ambiguous in Hebrew: אחר הדבר הזה (*'aḥar haddābār hazzeh*), "after this word/matter/event." We cannot be sure if the preceding incident itself or the account of it or the word of the Lord is meant. To the deuteronomistic editor, the fate of the man of God should have been an object lesson to Jeroboam; the story was the word of the Lord. The man of God who had prophesied the truth, who had tried so assiduously to obey the Lord but was finally tricked into disobedience, was slain for his disobedience. How much more certainly would a blatant sinner like Jeroboam be punished? Yet, Jeroboam remained unrepentant. Rather, he continued to appoint priests at the local sanctuaries—indeed, appointing anyone who wished to be a priest, without regard for lineage. Through the prophecy of Ahijah the Shilonite, the Lord had promised Jeroboam that he would reign over Israel (the ten tribes of the north) and that he would have an enduring house like that of David, provided that he remain obedient to the Lord's commandments (11:37-38). Jeroboam, however, sealed his own fate through his disobedience, and he set Israel on the course for destruction. By contrast, Rehoboam and the house of Judah, "obeyed the word of the LORD" (12:24), and so there would remain "a lamp" before the Lord in Jerusalem (11:36).

REFLECTIONS

1. This passage raises a number of awkward theological and ethical questions. It offends our moral sensibilities to think that God might actually have allowed a deceitful prophet to lure a sincere, but naive, man of God to sin. Not only that, but as if to rub salt in the wound, God then uses that false prophet to proclaim a word of judgment against the man of God. Nothing is said of the punishment of the false prophet, and, indeed, he was able to make arrangements regarding the proper interment of his own remains. The poor man of God from

Judah seems to suffer more than the other characters in the story, all because of one naive error in judgment. Even Jeroboam lived to see another day.

Despite such an offending issue, the main point of the narrative seems clear enough: God demands obedience without compromise. From beginning to end, Jeroboam seemed oblivious to this truth. Even the frightening account of the fate of the man of God did not seem to have fazed him, and so he did not turn from his evil ways. The consequences of his disobedience are dire, however—not for him alone but for an entire nation. Disobedience to God can have devastating consequences that affect more than the disobedient person. This is the primary issue that the narrative raises.

2. Still, there is a lesson for us in the fate of the man of God. Whatever the author's intention might have been, we cannot help being drawn to that peculiar story. It is, after all, with that man of God that most of us readily identify. Most of us probably do not see ourselves as flagrant sinners like Jeroboam. Nor are we deliberately deceptive like the old prophet from Bethel. Rather, like the man of God, most of us probably are sincere in our desire to obey God and do try our best to do so. For us, the lesson is, perhaps, that we should not be too quick to cast the proverbial stones. Even as we proclaim the word of the Lord to the likes of Jeroboam in our time, we must recognize that we, too, are susceptible to the same tendency to be disobedient (see 1 Cor 10:12). The danger may, indeed, lie in the fact that our sins are usually not quite so blatant as Jeroboam's or that they seem so much more excusable. Most of us do not have the kind of clout to commit sins that so affect the nation as a king in Israel might have had, or as an American president might have. Our offenses are not "high crimes and misdemeanors." Lacking an exalted post, most of us are faithful, decent people. In the fate of the man of God, however, we find a warning not to be too complacent and not to be too sure that we are on the side of God. Jeroboam did not heed this word (13:33), but we must.

3. Finally, we have to admit that the moral problems we have with the text cannot be explained away and that we may have no answers to them. We recognize that the word of God comes to us through this culturally conditioned and imperfect story. That is the amazing thing about the way God works. The word of God may be heard despite the story's limitations. So, too, the word of God was proclaimed through the man of God who was imperfect—as we all are.

1 KINGS 14:1-20, JUDGMENT ON THE HOUSE OF JEROBOAM

NIV

14 At that time Abijah son of Jeroboam became ill, [2]and Jeroboam said to his wife,
"Go, disguise yourself, so you won't be recognized as the wife of Jeroboam. Then go to Shiloh.
Ahijah the prophet is there—the one who told
me I would be king over this people. [3]Take ten
loaves of bread with you, some cakes and a jar
of honey, and go to him. He will tell you what
will happen to the boy." [4]So Jeroboam's wife did
what he said and went to Ahijah's house in
Shiloh.

NRSV

14 At that time Abijah son of Jeroboam fell
sick. [2]Jeroboam said to his wife, "Go, disguise yourself, so that it will not be known that
you are the wife of Jeroboam, and go to Shiloh;
for the prophet Ahijah is there, who said of me
that I should be king over this people. [3]Take with
you ten loaves, some cakes, and a jar of honey,
and go to him; he will tell you what shall happen
to the child."

4Jeroboam's wife did so; she set out and went
to Shiloh, and came to the house of Ahijah. Now

NIV

Now Ahijah could not see; his sight was gone because of his age. [5]But the LORD had told Ahijah, "Jeroboam's wife is coming to ask you about her son, for he is ill, and you are to give her such and such an answer. When she arrives, she will pretend to be someone else."

[6]So when Ahijah heard the sound of her footsteps at the door, he said, "Come in, wife of Jeroboam. Why this pretense? I have been sent to you with bad news. [7]Go, tell Jeroboam that this is what the LORD, the God of Israel, says: 'I raised you up from among the people and made you a leader over my people Israel. [8]I tore the kingdom away from the house of David and gave it to you, but you have not been like my servant David, who kept my commands and followed me with all his heart, doing only what was right in my eyes. [9]You have done more evil than all who lived before you. You have made for yourself other gods, idols made of metal; you have provoked me to anger and thrust me behind your back.

[10]" 'Because of this, I am going to bring disaster on the house of Jeroboam. I will cut off from Jeroboam every last male in Israel—slave or free. I will burn up the house of Jeroboam as one burns dung, until it is all gone. [11]Dogs will eat those belonging to Jeroboam who die in the city, and the birds of the air will feed on those who die in the country. The LORD has spoken!'

[12]"As for you, go back home. When you set foot in your city, the boy will die. [13]All Israel will mourn for him and bury him. He is the only one belonging to Jeroboam who will be buried, because he is the only one in the house of Jeroboam in whom the LORD, the God of Israel, has found anything good.

[14]"The LORD will raise up for himself a king over Israel who will cut off the family of Jeroboam. This is the day! What? Yes, even now.[a] [15]And the LORD will strike Israel, so that it will be like a reed swaying in the water. He will uproot Israel from this good land that he gave to their forefathers and scatter them beyond the River,[b] because they provoked the LORD to anger by making Asherah poles.[c] [16]And he will give Israel up because of the

[a] *14* The meaning of the Hebrew for this sentence is uncertain.
[b] *15* That is, the Euphrates [c] *15* That is, symbols of the goddess Asherah; here and elsewhere in 1 Kings

NRSV

Ahijah could not see, for his eyes were dim because of his age. [5]But the LORD said to Ahijah, "The wife of Jeroboam is coming to inquire of you concerning her son; for he is sick. Thus and thus you shall say to her."

When she came, she pretended to be another woman. [6]But when Ahijah heard the sound of her feet, as she came in at the door, he said, "Come in, wife of Jeroboam; why do you pretend to be another? For I am charged with heavy tidings for you. [7]Go, tell Jeroboam, 'Thus says the LORD, the God of Israel: Because I exalted you from among the people, made you leader over my people Israel, [8]and tore the kingdom away from the house of David to give it to you; yet you have not been like my servant David, who kept my commandments and followed me with all his heart, doing only that which was right in my sight, [9]but you have done evil above all those who were before you and have gone and made for yourself other gods, and cast images, provoking me to anger, and have thrust me behind your back; [10]therefore, I will bring evil upon the house of Jeroboam. I will cut off from Jeroboam every male, both bond and free in Israel, and will consume the house of Jeroboam, just as one burns up dung until it is all gone. [11]Anyone belonging to Jeroboam who dies in the city, the dogs shall eat; and anyone who dies in the open country, the birds of the air shall eat; for the LORD has spoken.' [12]Therefore set out, go to your house. When your feet enter the city, the child shall die. [13]All Israel shall mourn for him and bury him; for he alone of Jeroboam's family shall come to the grave, because in him there is found something pleasing to the LORD, the God of Israel, in the house of Jeroboam. [14]Moreover the LORD will raise up for himself a king over Israel, who shall cut off the house of Jeroboam today, even right now![a]

15"The LORD will strike Israel, as a reed is shaken in the water; he will root up Israel out of this good land that he gave to their ancestors, and scatter them beyond the Euphrates, because they have made their sacred poles,[b] provoking the LORD to anger. [16]He will give Israel up because of the sins of Jeroboam, which he sinned and which he caused Israel to commit."

[a] Meaning of Heb uncertain [b] Heb *Asherim*

NIV

sins Jeroboam has committed and has caused
Israel to commit."

17Then Jeroboam's wife got up and left and
went to Tirzah. As soon as she stepped over the
threshold of the house, the boy died. 18They
buried him, and all Israel mourned for him, as
the LORD had said through his servant the prophet
Ahijah.

19The other events of Jeroboam's reign, his wars
and how he ruled, are written in the book of the
annals of the kings of Israel. 20He reigned for
twenty-two years and then rested with his fathers.
And Nadab his son succeeded him as king.

NRSV

17Then Jeroboam's wife got up and went
away, and she came to Tirzah. As she came to
the threshold of the house, the child died. 18All
Israel buried him and mourned for him, according
to the word of the LORD, which he spoke by his
servant the prophet Ahijah.

19Now the rest of the acts of Jeroboam, how
he warred and how he reigned, are written in the
Book of the Annals of the Kings of Israel. 20The
time that Jeroboam reigned was twenty-two years;
then he slept with his ancestors, and his son
Nadab succeeded him.

COMMENTARY

Chapter 13 ends by noting the recalcitrance of Jeroboam, despite the word of the Lord. Therefore, it is stated as a matter of fact that the house of Jeroboam will be "cut off" and destroyed from the face of the earth (13:33-34). Immediately, then, we are told of the illness of Jeroboam's son (probably his firstborn) "at that time" (14:1; Abijah's position as the heir apparent is, perhaps, indicated by the fact that all Israel mourned for him when he died [v. 18]). The reader knows that this is the beginning of the end of the house of Jeroboam. The king, too, must have had an inkling of what his son's illness portended, for he sent his wife to the prophet Ahijah at Shiloh.

It was Ahijah, of course, who had prophesied Jeroboam's coming to power. This fact is noted by Jeroboam himself in his instruction to his wife. What he does not mention, but the reader already knows (11:33-34), is that the prophecy included the promise of an enduring dynasty for him, provided that Jeroboam was obedient to the Lord (11:38). It is probably his recognition of this fact that prevents him from going to see the prophet himself; it is probably this fact that necessitates his wife's disguise and bringing of offerings of gifts that commoners might bring—only ten loaves, some cakes, and a jar of honey. Apparently Jeroboam did not want to remind the prophet of what had been prophesied in regard to him, but he wanted to know what would happen to his son and no doubt hoped to receive a different word from the prophet.

The ploy fails. Ahijah is now old and cannot see, so the disguise of Jeroboam's queen is for nought. Indeed, the Lord tells the prophet what to expect and what to say. The narrator thus makes the point that it is not so much the predictive ability of Ahijah that is at issue but the will of the Lord. The disguised queen does not get a chance to go through with her charade. As soon as Ahijah hears her footsteps, he identifies her and tells her that he has bad news for her. Even though he is blind, he hears and he sees through the disguise. He sends an oracle to Jeroboam through her, reiterating the word of the Lord that was first delivered to Jeroboam (vv. 7-8; see 12:27-38). Jeroboam's sins are enumerated (v. 9), sins that have provoked the anger of God. And that terrible anger is evident as the punishment for the house of Jeroboam is spelled out in harsh, even vulgar, terms (vv. 10-11).[52] Not only will the men of the dynasty be killed, but they will be left unburied as well, abandoned to the dogs in the city and to the birds of prey in the countryside. The immediate consequence of this oracle is that Abijah will die as soon as the queen returns

52. Most modern translations use euphemisms, but the Hebrew for "male" (משתין בקיר *maštîn bĕqîr*) is literally "one who pisses against the wall" (see KJV). The idiom עצור ועזוב (*ʿāṣûr wĕʿāzûb*) is obscure (NRSV, "bond or free"; NIV, "slave or"). The idiom may refer to those who are still under parental control (lit., "restrained") and those who have been left to their own devices, hence "minors [or] adult" or the like.

to the capital. This is the direct answer to the question that Jeroboam never had a chance to ask.

The oracle points beyond familial questions, however. It points to the destiny of the entire kingdom, from the disastrous succession to Jeroboam's throne (v. 14), through the instability of the kingdom (they will be shaken like a reed in the water), to their destruction and exile by the Assyrians ("beyond the Euphrates," v. 15). Clearly, the sins of Jeroboam affect not only his family and his generation, but also the future of his people. Accordingly, Abijah dies as soon as the queen returns. Jeroboam himself dies and is succeeded by Nadab (901–900 BCE), although the reader already knows that the fate of the kingdom has been sealed.

The story of Jeroboam's reign has been told in a fast-paced manner in 1 Kings 11–14. Events occur one after another: Israel breaks free of the oppression of Rehoboam, Jeroboam comes to power, he strengthens his position in the north and establishes rival sanctuaries there, his actions are condemned, and judgment is proclaimed upon his house. The editorial note in vv. 19-20 jolts the reader into the realization that these events, in fact, took place over a twenty-two-year period. There are other details regarding Jeroboam—"how he warred and how he reigned"—that were supposedly in the "Book of the Annals of the Kings of Israel," readily available for the original readers to consult. Modern readers interested in various historical details may, likewise, turn to other sources for such details and reconstruct other explanations for the demise of Jeroboam's dynasty. The narrative in 1 Kings provides only the theological rationale for the fall of Jeroboam and the eventual destruction of his kingdom. The focus of the narrative, therefore, is judgment on the house of Jeroboam for the sins that he committed.

Yet, there are elements that cannot be easily harmonized with the harsh and decisive judgment. Despite the certainty of Abijah's death as the first installment in the fulfillment of the prophecy of doom, he would apparently not be denied a burial, as the word of judgment had proclaimed for all males in the house of Jeroboam. Not only would he be accorded proper burial, but also he would even be mourned by all Israel. Amid the reality of divine anger there was ever so slight an indication of God's favor: "There is found in him [Abijah] something pleasing to the LORD" (v. 13). Jeroboam himself does not suffer the fate prophesied for all the males in his family, and the dynasty does not end immediately; Nadab, another son of Jeroboam, comes to power as one "raised up" by the Lord (v. 14). As for Jeroboam's people, their punishment would come not strictly because of Jeroboam's sins but because their own idolatrous acts (v. 15): Jeroboam caused them to sin, but they would do so themselves. Hence, despite their destined destruction, a question comes that almost invites a response—a question that makes no logical sense in its context and, accordingly, baffles all translators: "This is the day! What, then, even now?" (14:14). The question—perhaps a later gloss—leaves open the possibility that the Israelite reader might alter the inevitable destiny with death after all.[53]

53. On the hermeneutical function of this "gloss," see Nelson, *First and Second Kings,* 96-97.

REFLECTIONS

The most obvious lesson of this chapter, of course, is the importance of faithfulness and obedience: God's punishment is inevitable in the face of the persistence of sin. The passage makes plain, too, that one's sin may have deadly consequences for others as well. Jeroboam sinned, but others died because of it or were drawn also to sin and, thus, to bring destruction upon themselves. Still, there are other important insights that the text raises for the reader.

1. God is in charge, even though people may be inclined to think that they can resolve their problems at the human level. Jeroboam sees his problem in purely human terms and tries to resolve it by manipulating others to give him the answers he seeks. God, however, intervenes with a word of judgment. The passage makes the point that our true intentions are

known to God, even if we try to hide them. God sees through our pretenses, our charades, our attempts to cover up our sins.

2. Human sins bring the inevitable judgment of God; yet, God may still provide signs of grace and glimmers of hope amid the darkness of sin and death. Despite the certainty of doom that sin brings, God persistently holds out the possibility of an appropriate response from those whom God so loves.

1 KINGS 14:21–15:24, REHOBOAM, ABIJAH, AND ASA OF JUDAH

OVERVIEW

The preceding unit ends with the death of Jeroboam and the accession of his son Nadab to the throne in Israel (14:19-20). As if to reinforce the point about the end of the house of Jeroboam, the narrative focus shifts immediately to the house of David in the south, where the Davidic dynasty continues in relative peace and apparently without regard for the characters of the kings in Jerusalem: Rehoboam, the son of Solomon, is succeeded by his son Abijah, who is succeeded by his own son Asa. Whereas the fate of Israel is sealed by the disobedience of Jeroboam, hope remains in Judah because of the dual election of Jerusalem and David.

1 Kings 14:21-31, The Reign of Rehoboam

NIV

21Rehoboam son of Solomon was king in Judah.
He was forty-one years old when he became king,
and he reigned seventeen years in Jerusalem, the
city the LORD had chosen out of all the tribes of
Israel in which to put his Name. His mother's
name was Naamah; she was an Ammonite.
22Judah did evil in the eyes of the LORD. By the
sins they committed they stirred up his jealous
anger more than their fathers had done. 23They
also set up for themselves high places, sacred
stones and Asherah poles on every high hill and
under every spreading tree. 24There were even
male shrine prostitutes in the land; the people
engaged in all the detestable practices of the
nations the LORD had driven out before the
Israelites.
25In the fifth year of King Rehoboam, Shishak
king of Egypt attacked Jerusalem. 26He carried off
the treasures of the temple of the LORD and the
treasures of the royal palace. He took everything,
including all the gold shields Solomon had made.

NRSV

21Now Rehoboam son of Solomon reigned in
Judah. Rehoboam was forty-one years old when
he began to reign, and he reigned seventeen years
in Jerusalem, the city that the LORD had chosen
out of all the tribes of Israel, to put his name
there. His mother's name was Naamah the Ammonite. 22Judah did what was evil in the sight of
the LORD; they provoked him to jealousy with
their sins that they committed, more than all that
their ancestors had done. 23For they also built for
themselves high places, pillars, and sacred poles[a]
on every high hill and under every green tree;
24there were also male temple prostitutes in the
land. They committed all the abominations of the
nations that the LORD drove out before the people
of Israel.
25In the fifth year of King Rehoboam, King
Shishak of Egypt came up against Jerusalem; 26he
took away the treasures of the house of the LORD
and the treasures of the king's house; he took

[a] Heb *Asherim*

NIV

27So King Rehoboam made bronze shields to replace them and assigned these to the commanders of the guard on duty at the entrance to the royal palace. 28Whenever the king went to the LORD's temple, the guards bore the shields, and afterward they returned them to the guardroom.

29As for the other events of Rehoboam's reign, and all he did, are they not written in the book of the annals of the kings of Judah? 30There was continual warfare between Rehoboam and Jeroboam. 31And Rehoboam rested with his fathers and was buried with them in the City of David. His mother's name was Naamah; she was an Ammonite. And Abijah[a] his son succeeded him as king.

[a] *31* Some Hebrew manuscripts and Septuagint (see also 2 Chron. 12:16); most Hebrew manuscripts *Abijam*

NRSV

everything. He also took away all the shields of gold that Solomon had made; 27so King Rehoboam made shields of bronze instead, and committed them to the hands of the officers of the guard, who kept the door of the king's house. 28As often as the king went into the house of the LORD, the guard carried them and brought them back to the guardroom.

29Now the rest of the acts of Rehoboam, and all that he did, are they not written in the Book of the Annals of the Kings of Judah? 30There was war between Rehoboam and Jeroboam continually. 31Rehoboam slept with his ancestors and was buried with his ancestors in the city of David. His mother's name was Naamah the Ammonite. His son Abijam succeeded him.

COMMENTARY

The reader has already been introduced to Solomon's son Rehoboam in 12:1-24. There, however, Rehoboam is not the main interest of the narrator. Rather, he is a foil for Jeroboam; Rehoboam's arrogant and oppressive ways provided the immediate cause for the rebellion of the ten tribes of Israel. Now in this section of the text, the report is focused on Rehoboam's own reign in Judah (922–915 BCE).

Rehoboam is said to be king not only "in Judah" but also, specifically, *in Jerusalem.* His successors are also typically said to reign over Judah in Jerusalem (15:2, 10). This detail is significant, for Jerusalem is identified as a city that the Lord "had chosen out of all the tribes of Israel" (v. 21). The divine election of Jerusalem stands over against the absence of an acceptable shrine for the Lord in the northern kingdom. It is partly for this reason that Judah appears to be judged less harshly than Israel.

At the beginning and the end of the unit (vv. 21, 31), Rehoboam is identified as the son of Naamah, an Ammonite woman. Solomon had married many foreign women who had led him away from complete devotion to the Lord (11:1-8). Accordingly, he had "followed" various foreign gods, including "Milcom the abomination of the Ammonites," and he also built high places for these gods, including one for Milcom of the Ammonites in the mountain opposite Jerusalem—namely, the Mount of Olives. The stage had been set for Judah to sin, and this is what they did. In Rehoboam's reign, Judah even sinned "more than all their ancestors" (v. 22). Along with the high places that they built for themselves, they erected מצבות (*maṣṣēbôt*; NRSV, "pillars"; NIV, "sacred stones") and אשרים (*'ăšērîm*; NRSV, "sacred poles"; NIV, "Asherah poles"), various Canaanite cultic objects that the people of God were supposed to smash and cut down (Deut 7:5; 12:2-5). They committed "all the abominations of the nations" that the Lord had driven out of the land for Israel's sake. The implication, of course, is that they themselves deserved to be driven out of the land.

Pharaoh Shishak's invasion and the consequent plunder of the Temple in Jerusalem are inevitably seen as the results of the sins of Judah. They foreshadow future plunder and the eventual destruction of the Temple in the chosen city. The glory of Solomon's Temple is tarnished in the hands of his son. Rehoboam replaced Solomon's shields of gold with shields made of bronze. Even so, the Temple survived Shishak's raid because it was the place that the Lord had chosen.

Despite the sins of Judah in the reign of Rehoboam, there is no oracle of doom corresponding to the lengthy one that Jeroboam received (vv. 7-16). For his sins, the house of Jeroboam will be cut off; his dynasty will be brought to an end. By contrast, the house of Rehoboam survives, despite the chastisement that God brought by way of Shishak's invasion and plunder. Thus, whereas Abijah the son of Jeroboam dies prematurely, Abijah the son of Rehoboam lives to succeed him (v. 31).[54] (See Reflections at 15:9-24.)

54. The NRSV, following most Hebrew MSS, has the name as "Abijam" (a unique and improbable name in Hebrew), whereas the NIV follows some Hebrew MSS and the parallel account in 2 Chr 12:16 in reading the name as "Abijah," a name reflected also in the Greek translation and in Josephus *Antiquities of the Jews* 8.9.1.

1 Kings 15:1-8, The Reign of Abijah

NIV

15 In the eighteenth year of the reign of Jeroboam son of Nebat, Abijah[a] became king of Judah, 2and he reigned in Jerusalem three years. His mother's name was Maacah daughter of Abishalom.[b]

3He committed all the sins his father had done before him; his heart was not fully devoted to the LORD his God, as the heart of David his forefather had been. 4Nevertheless, for David's sake the LORD his God gave him a lamp in Jerusalem by raising up a son to succeed him and by making Jerusalem strong. 5For David had done what was right in the eyes of the LORD and had not failed to keep any of the LORD's commands all the days of his life—except in the case of Uriah the Hittite.

6There was war between Rehoboam[c] and Jeroboam throughout ⌊Abijah's⌋ lifetime. 7As for the other events of Abijah's reign, and all he did, are they not written in the book of the annals of the kings of Judah? There was war between Abijah and Jeroboam. 8And Abijah rested with his fathers and was buried in the City of David. And Asa his son succeeded him as king.

[a] *1* Some Hebrew manuscripts and Septuagint (see also 2 Chron. 12:16); most Hebrew manuscripts *Abijam*; also in verses 7 and 8 [b] *2* A variant of *Absalom*; also in verse 10 [c] *6* Most Hebrew manuscripts; some Hebrew manuscripts and Syriac *Abijam* (that is, Abijah)

NRSV

15 Now in the eighteenth year of King Jeroboam son of Nebat, Abijam began to reign over Judah. 2He reigned for three years in Jerusalem. His mother's name was Maacah daughter of Abishalom. 3He committed all the sins that his father did before him; his heart was not true to the LORD his God, like the heart of his father David. 4Nevertheless for David's sake the LORD his God gave him a lamp in Jerusalem, setting up his son after him, and establishing Jerusalem; 5because David did what was right in the sight of the LORD, and did not turn aside from anything that he commanded him all the days of his life, except in the matter of Uriah the Hittite. 6The war begun between Rehoboam and Jeroboam continued all the days of his life. 7The rest of the acts of Abijam, and all that he did, are they not written in the Book of the Annals of the Kings of Judah? There was war between Abijam and Jeroboam. 8Abijam slept with his ancestors, and they buried him in the city of David. Then his son Asa succeeded him.

COMMENTARY

According to a parallel text (2 Chr 11:20-22), Abijah was the son of Rehoboam and his favorite wife, Maacah, and resigned around 915–913 BCE.[55] This Abijah sinned as his father had done. Yet, he did not suffer the fate of the other Abijah, Jeroboam's son, who died prematurely. Clearly, the continuation of the house of David was not due to the righteousness of David's successors in Jerusalem, but simply because of the will of the sovereign God. Despite the sins of David's successors, there will always be a lamp in Jerusalem for David's sake (v. 4; see 11:36). This everlasting promise was given because David did what was right in the eyes of the Lord. Yet, it is acknowledged that David's righteousness, which is regarded by the narrator as paradigmatic for the Judean kings, was not without blemish: David did not turn aside from what the Lord had commanded him, "except in the matter of Uriah the Hittite"—i.e., the murder of Uriah to cover up David's scandalous affair with Bathsheba, Uriah's wife. God's acceptance of David and his house was from beginning to end an act of sheer grace. (See Reflections at 15:9-24.)

55. This, however, contradicts 2 Chr 13:2, which gives Abijah's mother's name as "Micaiah the daughter of Uriel of Gibeah." For a discussion of this crux, see S. Japhet, *I & II Chronicles,* OTL (Louisville: Westminster/John Knox, 1993) 670-72.

1 Kings 15:9-24, The Reign of Asa

NIV

9In the twentieth year of Jeroboam king of Israel, Asa became king of Judah, 10and he reigned in Jerusalem forty-one years. His grandmother's name was Maacah daughter of Abishalom.

11Asa did what was right in the eyes of the LORD, as his father David had done. 12He expelled the male shrine prostitutes from the land and got rid of all the idols his fathers had made. 13He even deposed his grandmother Maacah from her position as queen mother, because she had made a repulsive Asherah pole. Asa cut the pole down and burned it in the Kidron Valley. 14Although he did not remove the high places, Asa's heart was fully committed to the LORD all his life. 15He brought into the temple of the LORD the silver and gold and the articles that he and his father had dedicated.

16There was war between Asa and Baasha king of Israel throughout their reigns. 17Baasha king of Israel went up against Judah and fortified Ramah to prevent anyone from leaving or entering the territory of Asa king of Judah.

18Asa then took all the silver and gold that was left in the treasuries of the LORD's temple and of his own palace. He entrusted it to his officials and sent them to Ben-Hadad son of Tabrimmon, the son of Hezion, the king of Aram, who was ruling in Damascus. 19"Let there be a treaty between me

NRSV

9In the twentieth year of King Jeroboam of Israel, Asa began to reign over Judah; 10he reigned forty-one years in Jerusalem. His mother's name was Maacah daughter of Abishalom. 11Asa did what was right in the sight of the LORD, as his father David had done. 12He put away the male temple prostitutes out of the land, and removed all the idols that his ancestors had made. 13He also removed his mother Maacah from being queen mother, because she had made an abominable image for Asherah; Asa cut down her image and burned it at the Wadi Kidron. 14But the high places were not taken away. Nevertheless the heart of Asa was true to the LORD all his days. 15He brought into the house of the LORD the votive gifts of his father and his own votive gifts—silver, gold, and utensils.

16There was war between Asa and King Baasha of Israel all their days. 17King Baasha of Israel went up against Judah, and built Ramah, to prevent anyone from going out or coming in to King Asa of Judah. 18Then Asa took all the silver and the gold that were left in the treasures of the house of the LORD and the treasures of the king's house, and gave them into the hands of his servants. King Asa sent them to King Ben-hadad son of Tabrimmon son of Hezion of Aram, who resided in Damascus, saying, 19"Let there be an alliance

NIV

and you," he said, "as there was between my
father and your father. See, I am sending you a
gift of silver and gold. Now break your treaty with
Baasha king of Israel so he will withdraw
from me."
20Ben-Hadad agreed with King Asa and sent the
commanders of his forces against the towns of
Israel. He conquered Ijon, Dan, Abel Beth Maacah
and all Kinnereth in addition to Naphtali. 21When
Baasha heard this, he stopped building Ramah and
withdrew to Tirzah. 22Then King Asa issued an
order to all Judah—no one was exempt—and
they carried away from Ramah the stones and
timber Baasha had been using there. With them
King Asa built up Geba in Benjamin, and also
Mizpah.
23As for all the other events of Asa's reign, all
his achievements, all he did and the cities he built,
are they not written in the book of the annals of
the kings of Judah? In his old age, however, his
feet became diseased. 24Then Asa rested with his
fathers and was buried with them in the city of
his father David. And Jehoshaphat his son succeeded him as king.

NRSV

between me and you, like that between my father
and your father: I am sending you a present of
silver and gold; go, break your alliance with King
Baasha of Israel, so that he may withdraw from
me." 20Ben-hadad listened to King Asa, and sent
the commanders of his armies against the cities of
Israel. He conquered Ijon, Dan, Abel-beth-maacah,
and all Chinneroth, with all the land of Naphtali.
21When Baasha heard of it, he stopped building
Ramah and lived in Tirzah. 22Then King Asa made
a proclamation to all Judah, none was exempt:
they carried away the stones of Ramah and its
timber, with which Baasha had been building;
with them King Asa built Geba of Benjamin and
Mizpah. 23Now the rest of all the acts of Asa, all
his power, all that he did, and the cities that he
built, are they not written in the Book of the
Annals of the Kings of Judah? But in his old age
he was diseased in his feet. 24Then Asa slept with
his ancestors, and was buried with his ancestors
in the city of his father David; his son Jehoshaphat
succeeded him.

COMMENTARY

Abijah is succeed by his son Asa (913–873 BCE), who came to the throne in Jerusalem while Jeroboam was still in power in Israel and reigned forty-one years. Accordingly, his reign overlapped with seven of his counterparts in the north: Jeroboam, Nadab, Baasha, Elah, Zimri, Omri, and Ahab (see 16:29). He was, by all accounts (see 2 Chr 14:1-8), a reformist king who (1) expelled the cult prostitutes,[56] (2) removed all the idols that his predecessors had set up, (3) deposed the idolatrous queen mother,[57] and (4) destroyed the queen mother's cult image of Asherah. Although the high places of the land were not eliminated, Asa's heart was true to the Lord until the day of his death. He returned the votive gifts of his father to the Temple and he himself brought votive gifts.

In contrast to his father, Abijah, Asa is depicted in relatively positive terms. Indeed, his attitudes and actions anticipate those of reformist kings Hezekiah (2 Kgs 18:3-6) and Josiah (2 Kgs 23:1-26). Yet, all was not well in Judah. Conflict with Israel prompted Asa to take drastic action. He removed the temple and palace treasures to bribe the Arameans to break off their alliance with Israel. Ironically, he did to the Temple and the palace what Pharaoh Shishak had done during the reign of Rehoboam (14:26). While Asa brought in votive gifts for the Temple, he also removed treasures from it.

56. The masculine plural in Hebrew (קדשים *qĕdēšîm*) is probably intended to be inclusive of male and female cult prostitutes (see NIV; NRSV).

57. Assuming the correctness of 15:2, we should probably follow the NIV in taking the word אם (*'ēm*) in 15:10 to mean "grandmother," instead of " mother" (so NRSV).

REFLECTIONS

The accounts in this unit are poignant in their contrast to the preceding story of Jeroboam's demise (12:25–14:20). Whereas the emphasis in the latter is on the essentiality of obedience to the Lord, the underlying emphasis in the accounts of the reigns of David's successors in Jerusalem is the election of Jerusalem and the eternal promise of God to David. The sovereign God who demands obedience uncompromisingly also mysteriously saves without regard for one's character.

1 KINGS 15:25–16:34, ISRAEL'S KINGS FROM NADAB TO AHAB

OVERVIEW

Following the account of the long reign of the Judean king Asa (15:9-24), we find a series of reports on six of his contemporaries in the northern kingdom: (1) Nadab (15:25-32); (2) Baasha (15:33–16:7); (3) Elah (16:8-14); (4) Zimri (16:16-20); (5) Omri (16:21-28); and (6) Ahab (16:29-34). On the one hand, the reports read like a historical work: The duration of each reign is specified and synchronized with the reign of the Judean counterpart. At the end of each report, the reader is referred to the further materials in the archives, as it were. On the other hand, the accounts are rather formulaic: The overriding criterion for evaluation of the kings is their wickedness, notably how they have followed the way of Jeroboam. Consequently, the reports are all more or less of the same length: Baasha's twenty-two-year reign receives about the same amount of space as the two-year span of Nadab and Elah, or even the seven-day rule of Zimri. Likewise, Omri, who reigned twelve years and began a powerful dynasty, gets the same brief and negative evaluation. Despite the chronological notices, cross-referencing, historical details, and the mention of archival materials, these reports are not intended to be read as a disinterested history of these kings. Their purpose is, rather, primarily theological: to show the consequences of unfaithfulness to the Lord.

1 Kings 15:25-32, The Reign of Nadab, Son of Jeroboam

NIV

25Nadab son of Jeroboam became king of Israel in the second year of Asa king of Judah, and he reigned over Israel two years. 26He did evil in the eyes of the LORD, walking in the ways of his father and in his sin, which he had caused Israel to commit.

27Baasha son of Ahijah of the house of Issachar plotted against him, and he struck him down at Gibbethon, a Philistine town, while Nadab and all Israel were besieging it. 28Baasha killed Nadab in the third year of Asa king of Judah and succeeded him as king.

NRSV

25Nadab son of Jeroboam began to reign over Israel in the second year of King Asa of Judah; he reigned over Israel two years. 26He did what was evil in the sight of the LORD, walking in the way of his ancestor and in the sin that he caused Israel to commit.

27Baasha son of Ahijah, of the house of Issachar, conspired against him; and Baasha struck him down at Gibbethon, which belonged to the Philistines; for Nadab and all Israel were laying siege to Gibbethon. 28So Baasha killed Nadab[a] in

[a] Heb *him*

NIV

[29]As soon as he began to reign, he killed Jeroboam's whole family. He did not leave Jeroboam anyone that breathed, but destroyed them all, according to the word of the LORD given through his servant Ahijah the Shilonite— [30]because of the sins Jeroboam had committed and had caused Israel to commit, and because he provoked the LORD, the God of Israel, to anger.

[31]As for the other events of Nadab's reign, and all he did, are they not written in the book of the annals of the kings of Israel? [32]There was war between Asa and Baasha king of Israel throughout their reigns.

NRSV

the third year of King Asa of Judah, and succeeded him. [29]As soon as he was king, he killed all the house of Jeroboam; he left to the house of Jeroboam not one that breathed, until he had destroyed it, according to the word of the LORD that he spoke by his servant Ahijah the Shilonite— [30]because of the sins of Jeroboam that he committed and that he caused Israel to commit, and because of the anger to which he provoked the LORD, the God of Israel.

31Now the rest of the acts of Nadab, and all that he did, are they not written in the Book of the Annals of the Kings of Israel? [32]There was war between Asa and King Baasha of Israel all their days.

COMMENTARY

The predicted end of the house of Jeroboam did not come immediately with Jeroboam's demise. Ahijah the Shilonite had prophesied the annihilation of all males in the family, and accordingly Abijah, presumably the firstborn of Jeroboam, died prematurely. Upon Jeroboam's death, however, his son Nadab succeeded him on the throne. The accession and reign of Jeroboam's son might have raised the possibility of hope in Israel. Nadab, however, did nothing to warrant the reversal of the doom prophesied against the house of Jeroboam; he acted wickedly and followed the way of his father. Accordingly, he was assassinated by Baasha of the house of Issachar; Nadab and all his family were killed, thus fulfilling the prophecy of Ahijah (14:10-11). Despite the harsh judgment against Jeroboam's house, the narrator makes it clear that Nadab paid for his own sins, and not for the sins of his father. (See Reflections at 16:29-34.)

1 Kings 15:33–16:7, The Reign of Baasha of the House of Issachar

NIV

[33]In the third year of Asa king of Judah, Baasha son of Ahijah became king of all Israel in Tirzah, and he reigned twenty-four years. [34]He did evil in the eyes of the LORD, walking in the ways of Jeroboam and in his sin, which he had caused Israel to commit.

16 Then the word of the LORD came to Jehu son of Hanani against Baasha: [2]"I lifted you up from the dust and made you leader of my people Israel, but you walked in the ways of Jeroboam and caused my people Israel to sin and to provoke me to anger by their sins. [3]So I am

NRSV

33In the third year of King Asa of Judah, Baasha son of Ahijah began to reign over all Israel at Tirzah; he reigned twenty-four years. [34]He did what was evil in the sight of the LORD, walking in the way of Jeroboam and in the sin that he caused Israel to commit.

16 The word of the LORD came to Jehu son of Hanani against Baasha, saying, [2]"Since I exalted you out of the dust and made you leader over my people Israel, and you have walked in the way of Jeroboam, and have caused my people Israel to sin, provoking me to anger with their

NIV

about to consume Baasha and his house, and I will make your house like that of Jeroboam son of Nebat. 4Dogs will eat those belonging to Baasha who die in the city, and the birds of the air will feed on those who die in the country."

5As for the other events of Baasha's reign, what he did and his achievements, are they not written in the book of the annals of the kings of Israel? 6Baasha rested with his fathers and was buried in Tirzah. And Elah his son succeeded him as king.

7Moreover, the word of the LORD came through the prophet Jehu son of Hanani to Baasha and his house, because of all the evil he had done in the eyes of the LORD, provoking him to anger by the things he did, and becoming like the house of Jeroboam—and also because he destroyed it.

NRSV

sins, 3therefore, I will consume Baasha and his house, and I will make your house like the house of Jeroboam son of Nebat. 4Anyone belonging to Baasha who dies in the city the dogs shall eat; and anyone of his who dies in the field the birds of the air shall eat."

5Now the rest of the acts of Baasha, what he did, and his power, are they not written in the Book of the Annals of the Kings of Israel? 6Baasha slept with his ancestors, and was buried at Tirzah; and his son Elah succeeded him. 7Moreover the word of the LORD came by the prophet Jehu son of Hanani against Baasha and his house, both because of all the evil that he did in the sight of the LORD, provoking him to anger with the work of his hands, in being like the house of Jeroboam, and also because he destroyed it.

COMMENTARY

Despite being in power for nearly a quarter of a century (900–877 BCE), Baasha receives a report of about the same length as that of Nadab, who had reigned only two years. The main point that the deuteronomistic historian wants to make is that Baasha also did what was evil in the sight of the Lord and that he perpetuated the sin of Jeroboam. Just as the end of the house of Jeroboam had been proclaimed by the prophet Ahijah, so also the fate of Baasha was proclaimed by the prophet Jehu, in language reminiscent of Ahijah's words (16:2-4; see 14:9-12). Baasha was killed because he, like Jeroboam, sinned (15:34; 16:2-3, 7) and because he had murdered the family of Jeroboam (15:29; 16:7). (See Reflections at 16:29-34.)

1 Kings 16:8-14, The Reign of Elah, Son of Baasha

NIV

8In the twenty-sixth year of Asa king of Judah, Elah son of Baasha became king of Israel, and he reigned in Tirzah two years.

9Zimri, one of his officials, who had command of half his chariots, plotted against him. Elah was in Tirzah at the time, getting drunk in the home of Arza, the man in charge of the palace at Tirzah. 10Zimri came in, struck him down and killed him in the twenty-seventh year of Asa king of Judah. Then he succeeded him as king.

11As soon as he began to reign and was seated on the throne, he killed off Baasha's whole family. He did not spare a single male, whether relative

NRSV

8In the twenty-sixth year of King Asa of Judah, Elah son of Baasha began to reign over Israel in Tirzah; he reigned two years. 9But his servant Zimri, commander of half his chariots, conspired against him. When he was at Tirzah, drinking himself drunk in the house of Arza, who was in charge of the palace at Tirzah, 10Zimri came in and struck him down and killed him, in the twenty-seventh year of King Asa of Judah, and succeeded him.

11When he began to reign, as soon as he had seated himself on his throne, he killed all the house of Baasha; he did not leave him a single

NIV

or friend. [12]So Zimri destroyed the whole family of Baasha, in accordance with the word of the LORD spoken against Baasha through the prophet Jehu— [13]because of all the sins Baasha and his son Elah had committed and had caused Israel to commit, so that they provoked the LORD, the God of Israel, to anger by their worthless idols.

[14]As for the other events of Elah's reign, and all he did, are they not written in the book of the annals of the kings of Israel?

NRSV

male of his kindred or his friends. [12]Thus Zimri destroyed all the house of Baasha, according to the word of the LORD, which he spoke against Baasha by the prophet Jehu— [13]because of all the sins of Baasha and the sins of his son Elah that they committed, and that they caused Israel to commit, provoking the LORD God of Israel to anger with their idols. [14]Now the rest of the acts of Elah, and all that he did, are they not written in the Book of the Annals of the Kings of Israel?

COMMENTARY

As with the house of Jeroboam, Baasha was succeeded by his son. Here, again, there is ever so slight a sign of hope that the prophetic prediction of the end of the house of Baasha might be stayed. Elah, the son and successor of Baasha (877–876 BCE), did nothing to warrant that hope, however. He acted faithlessly. Hence, he was assassinated by a usurper after having reigned only two years. Elah paid for his own sins, and not for the sins of his father. (See Reflections at 16:29-34.)

1 Kings 16:15-20, The Reign of Zimri, Commander of the Chariotry

NIV

[15]In the twenty-seventh year of Asa king of Judah, Zimri reigned in Tirzah seven days. The army was encamped near Gibbethon, a Philistine town. [16]When the Israelites in the camp heard that Zimri had plotted against the king and murdered him, they proclaimed Omri, the commander of the army, king over Israel that very day there in the camp. [17]Then Omri and all the Israelites with him withdrew from Gibbethon and laid siege to Tirzah. [18]When Zimri saw that the city was taken, he went into the citadel of the royal palace and set the palace on fire around him. So he died, [19]because of the sins he had committed, doing evil in the eyes of the LORD and walking in the ways of Jeroboam and in the sin he had committed and had caused Israel to commit.

[20]As for the other events of Zimri's reign, and the rebellion he carried out, are they not written in the book of the annals of the kings of Israel?

NRSV

15In the twenty-seventh year of King Asa of Judah, Zimri reigned seven days in Tirzah. Now the troops were encamped against Gibbethon, which belonged to the Philistines, [16]and the troops who were encamped heard it said, "Zimri has conspired, and he has killed the king"; therefore all Israel made Omri, the commander of the army, king over Israel that day in the camp. [17]So Omri went up from Gibbethon, and all Israel with him, and they besieged Tirzah. [18]When Zimri saw that the city was taken, he went into the citadel of the king's house; he burned down the king's house over himself with fire, and died— [19]because of the sins that he committed, doing evil in the sight of the LORD, walking in the way of Jeroboam, and for the sin that he committed, causing Israel to sin. [20]Now the rest of the acts of Zimri, and the conspiracy that he made, are they not written in the Book of the Annals of the Kings of Israel?

COMMENTARY

The usurper Zimri reigned only seven days, committing suicide in the palace when he knew that he had been defeated. He, too, is judged to have done evil in the sight of the Lord, perpetuating the sin of Jeroboam. (See Reflections at 16:29-34.)

1 Kings 16:21-28, The Beginning of the House of Omri

NIV

[21]Then the people of Israel were split into two factions; half supported Tibni son of Ginath for king, and the other half supported Omri. [22]But Omri's followers proved stronger than those of Tibni son of Ginath. So Tibni died and Omri became king.

[23]In the thirty-first year of Asa king of Judah, Omri became king of Israel, and he reigned twelve years, six of them in Tirzah. [24]He bought the hill of Samaria from Shemer for two talents[a] of silver and built a city on the hill, calling it Samaria, after Shemer, the name of the former owner of the hill.

[25]But Omri did evil in the eyes of the LORD and sinned more than all those before him. [26]He walked in all the ways of Jeroboam son of Nebat and in his sin, which he had caused Israel to commit, so that they provoked the LORD, the God of Israel, to anger by their worthless idols.

[27]As for the other events of Omri's reign, what he did and the things he achieved, are they not written in the book of the annals of the kings of Israel? [28]Omri rested with his fathers and was buried in Samaria. And Ahab his son succeeded him as king.

a *24* That is, about 150 pounds (about 70 kilograms)

NRSV

21Then the people of Israel were divided into two parts; half of the people followed Tibni son of Ginath, to make him king, and half followed Omri. [22]But the people who followed Omri overcame the people who followed Tibni son of Ginath; so Tibni died, and Omri became king. [23]In the thirty-first year of King Asa of Judah, Omri began to reign over Israel; he reigned for twelve years, six of them in Tirzah.

24He bought the hill of Samaria from Shemer for two talents of silver; he fortified the hill, and called the city that he built, Samaria, after the name of Shemer, the owner of the hill.

25Omri did what was evil in the sight of the LORD; he did more evil than all who were before him. [26]For he walked in all the way of Jeroboam son of Nebat, and in the sins that he caused Israel to commit, provoking the LORD, the God of Israel, to anger by their idols. [27]Now the rest of the acts of Omri that he did, and the power that he showed, are they not written in the Book of the Annals of the Kings of Israel? [28]Omri slept with his ancestors, and was buried in Samaria; his son Ahab succeeded him.

COMMENTARY

From the standpoint of secular history, Omri's reign (876–869 BCE) was a significant one. We know from the Moabite Stone that in his reign Israel extended its influence over its neighboring states.[58] Indeed, with Omri we have a dynasty that lasted through the reigns of his son Ahab and his grandsons Ahaziah and Joram. His influence was so great that even after his dynasty had come to an end, the Assyrians continued to refer to the Israelites as "the house of Omri." Yet, Omri's secular successes were of little interest to the deuteronomistic historian, who simply refers the reader to the archival materials for Omri's acts, not mentioned in this account. Of his

58. See *ANET,* 320.

achievements, only the establishment of Samaria as the capital of the northern kingdom is noted. Otherwise, Omri is dismissed with the other kings who sinned against the Lord and continued in the idolatrous ways of Jeroboam. (See Reflections at 16:29-34.)

1 Kings 16:29-34, Ahab the Son of Omri

NIV

[29]In the thirty-eighth year of Asa king of Judah, Ahab son of Omri became king of Israel, and he reigned in Samaria over Israel twenty-two years. [30]Ahab son of Omri did more evil in the eyes of the LORD than any of those before him. [31]He not only considered it trivial to commit the sins of Jeroboam son of Nebat, but he also married Jezebel daughter of Ethbaal king of the Sidonians, and began to serve Baal and worship him. [32]He set up an altar for Baal in the temple of Baal that he built in Samaria. [33]Ahab also made an Asherah pole and did more to provoke the LORD, the God of Israel, to anger than did all the kings of Israel before him.

[34]In Ahab's time, Hiel of Bethel rebuilt Jericho. He laid its foundations at the cost of his firstborn son Abiram, and he set up its gates at the cost of his youngest son Segub, in accordance with the word of the LORD spoken by Joshua son of Nun.

NRSV

29In the thirty-eighth year of King Asa of Judah, Ahab son of Omri began to reign over Israel; Ahab son of Omri reigned over Israel in Samaria twenty-two years. [30]Ahab son of Omri did evil in the sight of the LORD more than all who were before him.

31And as if it had been a light thing for him to walk in the sins of Jeroboam son of Nebat, he took as his wife Jezebel daughter of King Ethbaal of the Sidonians, and went and served Baal, and worshiped him. [32]He erected an altar for Baal in the house of Baal, which he built in Samaria. [33]Ahab also made a sacred pole.[a] Ahab did more to provoke the anger of the LORD, the God of Israel, than had all the kings of Israel who were before him. [34]In his days Hiel of Bethel built Jericho; he laid its foundation at the cost of Abiram his firstborn, and set up its gates at the cost of his youngest son Segub, according to the word of the LORD, which he spoke by Joshua son of Nun.

[a] Heb *Asherah*

COMMENTARY

These verses introduce the reader to Ahab (869–850 BCE), whose reign becomes the focus through the end of 1 Kings. Like his father, Omri, Ahab is recognized in extra-biblical sources as a powerful king. He is mentioned in the "Monolith Inscription" of the Assyrian king Shalmanezer III as having contributed a substantial force to the anti-Assyrian coalition at the Battle of Qarqar in 853 BCE.[59] His secular success, however, is of little interest to the deuteronomistic historian. Rather, the deuteronomist is primarily concerned with the religious implications of Ahab's activities. Accordingly, the first notice of his reign concerns his marriage to Jezebel, a Sidonian princess and devotee of the Canaanite god Baal. Ahab reportedly erected an altar for Baal in the temple of Baal that he had built in Samaria. He also built an אשרה (*'ăšērâ*; NRSV, "a sacred pole"; NIV, "Asherah pole") in the city, in contravention of deuteronomic law. Thus he is judged to have done more to provoke the anger of God than had all his predecessors (vv. 30, 33).

59. Ibid., 279.

REFLECTIONS

It is a commonplace in modern scholarship to point to the incompleteness of the historical records in the book of Kings. Particularly in the accounts of the reigns of Omri and Ahab, there are extra-biblical records that show that the kings who are summarily dismissed as unfaithful leaders of Israel may, in fact, turn out to have been powerful and influential rulers according to secular criteria. Yet, the lesson in this version of history is that God judges leaders not by popular measures of success but by their faithfulness to divine will. These stories prompt us to consider history beyond the interplay of social, economic, and political factors to the issues of faith and obedience. Beyond this general lesson, the accounts also convey two theological truths that are not easily reconciled: the will of God, on the one hand, and human responsibility, on the other hand.

1. God's will is being worked out in history. Even though human beings seem to be the principal actors in the historical arena, it is God who works behind the scenes to bring about events. Leaders owe their positions to God, for it is God who exalts them and grants them their place in history (16:2). It is the same God, however, who brings them down. The reader already knows that the tumultuous events were brought about in Israel because it was God's will to punish Jeroboam for his apostasy.

2. Despite the will of God, human beings are responsible for their actions. Nadab was punished, not because of the sins of his father, Jeroboam, but because of his own sins. Elah was not punished because of the sins of his father, Baasha, but because of his own sins. Even though it was the will of God to destroy the house of Jeroboam, Baasha was held responsible for their destruction (16:7).

1 KINGS 17:1-24, THE LIVING GOD WHO SUSTAINS AND REVIVES

OVERVIEW

In this chapter, the reader encounters the prophet Elijah for the very first time. This prophet will be the focus of the narrator's interest in 1 Kings 17–19, 21 and 2 Kings 1–2. The chapter itself may be divided into three subunits: (1) vv. 1-7, God's provision for Elijah through the ravens; (2) vv. 8-16, God's provision for Elijah through a Sidonian widow; and (3) vv. 17-24, God's resuscitation of the widow's dead child. Unifying the literary unit are two themes: *Life* is made possible by the Lord alone, and the importance of the *word,* meaning the word of the Lord as spoken through the prophet. Accordingly, various forms of the Hebrew verb חיה (*ḥāyâ,* "to live") recur (vv. 1, 12, 22-23), alongside repeated occurrences of the Hebrew term דבר (*dābār,* "word," vv. 1-2, 5, 8, 13, 15, 24). Over against Baal, the Canaanite god of life, it is affirmed that Israel's God is the true Lord of life, with power over the forces of nature and even over death itself.

1 Kings 17:1-7, Elijah Is Fed by Ravens

NIV

17 Now Elijah the Tishbite, from Tishbe[a] in
Gilead, said to Ahab, "As the LORD, the
God of Israel, lives, whom I serve, there will be
neither dew nor rain in the next few years except
at my word."
[2]Then the word of the LORD came to Elijah:
[3]"Leave here, turn eastward and hide in the Kerith
Ravine, east of the Jordan. [4]You will drink from
the brook, and I have ordered the ravens to feed
you there."
[5]So he did what the LORD had told him. He
went to the Kerith Ravine, east of the Jordan, and
stayed there. [6]The ravens brought him bread and
meat in the morning and bread and meat in the
evening, and he drank from the brook.
[7]Some time later the brook dried up because
there had been no rain in the land.

[a] *1* Or *Tishbite, of the settlers*

NRSV

17 Now Elijah the Tishbite, of Tishbe[a] in
Gilead, said to Ahab, "As the LORD the God
of Israel lives, before whom I stand, there shall
be neither dew nor rain these years, except by
my word." [2]The word of the LORD came to him,
saying, [3]"Go from here and turn eastward, and
hide yourself by the Wadi Cherith, which is east
of the Jordan. [4]You shall drink from the wadi, and
I have commanded the ravens to feed you there."
[5]So he went and did according to the word of the
LORD; he went and lived by the Wadi Cherith,
which is east of the Jordan. [6]The ravens brought
him bread and meat in the morning, and bread
and meat in the evening; and he drank from the
wadi. [7]But after a while the wadi dried up,
because there was no rain in the land.

[a] Gk: Heb *of the settlers*

COMMENTARY

Elijah appears on the scene abruptly. Apart from his name, he is identified only as "the Tishbite," an obscure designation that the ancient versions understood to be a reference to his place of origin, an unknown site somewhere in Gilead called "Tishbe" (so NIV, NRSV).[60] His first utterance is an oath in the name of the Lord: "As the LORD the God of Israel lives . . ." (v. 2). Although this oath formula is quite common in the Hebrew Bible, its usage in this context is particularly suggestive, for the issue at hand is the Lord as the source of life. The formula is especially poignant inasmuch as it is addressed to Ahab, who, we learned in 16:31-33, has married Jezebel, a devotee of the Canaanite god Baal, and has built an altar and a temple for Baal in Samaria, thus provoking the anger of "the LORD, the God of Israel." In Canaanite religion, Baal the storm god is the one who brings rain and, thus, the possibility of life on earth. When there is drought, it is presumed that death (which is deified in Canaanite mythology) has been victorious and that Baal is dead. Conversely, when there is rain, it is presumed that Baal is alive and that death has been defeated:

Let the heavens rain oil,
The wadis run with honey
Then I will know that Mightiest B[aal] lives,
The Prince, Lord of the earth is alive.[61]

Elijah's oath, however, affirms that it is the Lord who lives, and the rest of the narrative will make plain that it is the Lord who makes life possible (see, esp., v. 23). Elijah, as the servant of the Lord ("before whom I stand," v. 1), also dares to declare that there will be "neither dew nor rain," except by his word. The servant of the

60. Whereas the Greek translations read "the Tishbite from Tishbe," the Hebrew has Elijah as one "among the sojourners of Gilead," and "Tishbe" does not appear as a place-name anywhere.

61. Translated by Mark S. Smith in *Ugaritic Narrative Poetry,* ed. Simon B. Parker, SBL Writings from the Ancient World Series, vol. 9 (Atlanta: Scholars, 1997) 157, col. III, ll. 6-9. In this text, Baal is known as the prince (Ugaritic *zbl,* an element in the name "Jezebel").

Lord thus challenges the power of Baal directly, for drought is a sign of the powerlessness of Baal, according to Canaanite lore:

Seven years Baal is absent,
Eight, the Rider of Clouds:
No dew, no downpour,
No swirling of the deeps,
No welcome voice of Baal.[62]

The narrator does not tell us the reaction of King Ahab, but it is obvious that Elijah's life is in danger, for he is instructed by the Lord to flee to the Wadi Cherith, presumably one of the many deep and wide ravines east of the Jordan. Elijah is called to leave the promised land, as it were, and to go east of the Jordan, whence Israel came. There he is to drink from the wadi, and the Lord ordains ravens to feed him. The latter element is ironic in two important ways: Ravens are regarded in the Torah as unclean birds (Lev 11:15; Deut 14:14), and they are birds of prey (Job 38:41; Prov 30:17; Isa 34:11). These unclean birds of prey miraculously feed Elijah, and he is, indeed, fed well—with bread and meat twice a day. The narrator is clear that this feeding is done at the command of the Lord. The water in the wadi, however, dries up because there is no rain. In other words, the provision that might possibly be construed as having come from Baal, who is understood in Canaanite religion to be the lord of the rain, ends. In contrast, the provision that is explicitly a consequence of the Lord's command is abundant. The Lord provides miraculously and in ways that people might not expect—even through creatures that are deemed unclean. (See Reflections at 17:17-24.)

62. Translation by Simon B. Parker in ibid., 69, col. I, ll. 42-46.

1 Kings 17:8-16, Elijah Is Fed by a Sidonian Widow

NIV

8Then the word of the LORD came to him: 9"Go at once to Zarephath of Sidon and stay there. I have commanded a widow in that place to supply you with food." 10So he went to Zarephath. When he came to the town gate, a widow was there gathering sticks. He called to her and asked, "Would you bring me a little water in a jar so I may have a drink?" 11As she was going to get it, he called, "And bring me, please, a piece of bread."

12"As surely as the LORD your God lives," she replied, "I don't have any bread—only a handful of flour in a jar and a little oil in a jug. I am gathering a few sticks to take home and make a meal for myself and my son, that we may eat it—and die."

13Elijah said to her, "Don't be afraid. Go home and do as you have said. But first make a small cake of bread for me from what you have and bring it to me, and then make something for yourself and your son. 14For this is what the LORD, the God of Israel, says: 'The jar of flour will not be used up and the jug of oil will not run dry until the day the LORD gives rain on the land.'"

15She went away and did as Elijah had told her. So there was food every day for Elijah and for the

NRSV

8Then the word of the LORD came to him, saying, 9"Go now to Zarephath, which belongs to Sidon, and live there; for I have commanded a widow there to feed you." 10So he set out and went to Zarephath. When he came to the gate of the town, a widow was there gathering sticks; he called to her and said, "Bring me a little water in a vessel, so that I may drink." 11As she was going to bring it, he called to her and said, "Bring me a morsel of bread in your hand." 12But she said, "As the LORD your God lives, I have nothing baked, only a handful of meal in a jar, and a little oil in a jug; I am now gathering a couple of sticks, so that I may go home and prepare it for myself and my son, that we may eat it, and die." 13Elijah said to her, "Do not be afraid; go and do as you have said; but first make me a little cake of it and bring it to me, and afterwards make something for yourself and your son. 14For thus says the LORD the God of Israel: The jar of meal will not be emptied and the jug of oil will not fail until the day that the LORD sends rain on the earth." 15She went and did as Elijah said, so that she as well as he and her household ate for many days. 16The jar of meal was not emptied, neither did the jug

NIV

woman and her family. [16]For the jar of flour was not used up and the jug of oil did not run dry, in keeping with the word of the LORD spoken by Elijah.

NRSV

of oil fail, according to the word of the LORD that he spoke by Elijah.

COMMENTARY

Elijah is ordered by the Lord to go to the city of Zarephath ("Sarepta" in the Greek), a Phoenician commercial capital known for its exporting of various goods, including wine, grain, and oil. Yet, this city in Baal's territory is ironically in dire straits because of a drought. Just as the Lord ordained the ravens to feed Elijah, so also the Lord now ordains a widow to feed him. Although she apparently does not know it, this Sidonian woman is to be used by the Lord for salvific purposes. In this she stands in contrast to the other Sidonian woman, Jezebel, the Sidonian princess whom Ahab married (16:31) and who would be a champion for Baal in Israel. Again, it is ironic that the Lord would have a Phoenician, presumably a worshiper of Baal, to feed Elijah. Not only that, but she is a widow, which in ancient Near Eastern cultures means that she is probably destitute. In the OT, widows are typically associated with the neediest elements of society, the orphans and the poor (Job 24:3-4; 31:16-17; Isa 10:2; Zech 7:10). Yet, it is this widow in a land devastated by drought who is to feed Elijah, and it is to her that he turns for sustenance. She who has such scarce means is instrumental in God's plan to provide for others (cf. Mark 12:41-44).

The widow swears that she has little to spare, using the very oath formula that is put in the mouth of Elijah at the beginning of the passage: "As the LORD your God lives . . ." (v. 12; see also v. 1). According to Elijah, the Lord gives assurance that the provisions at hand will not be diminished: "The jar of meal will not be emptied and the jug of oil will not fail until the LORD sends rain on the earth." If it had not been clear before in the narrative, it is certainly clear now that it is the Lord who gives rain, not Baal. This is, indeed, the word of the Lord proclaimed to a worshiper of Baal in the territory of Baal, the homeland of Jezebel. (See Reflections at 17:17-24.)

1 Kings 17:17-24, The Resurrection of a Dead Boy

NIV

[17]Some time later the son of the woman who owned the house became ill. He grew worse and worse, and finally stopped breathing. [18]She said to Elijah, "What do you have against me, man of God? Did you come to remind me of my sin and kill my son?"

[19]"Give me your son," Elijah replied. He took him from her arms, carried him to the upper room where he was staying, and laid him on his bed. [20]Then he cried out to the LORD, "O LORD my God, have you brought tragedy also upon this widow I am staying with, by causing her son to die?" [21]Then he stretched himself out on the boy

NRSV

17After this the son of the woman, the mistress of the house, became ill; his illness was so severe that there was no breath left in him. [18]She then said to Elijah, "What have you against me, O man of God? You have come to me to bring my sin to remembrance, and to cause the death of my son!" [19]But he said to her, "Give me your son." He took him from her bosom, carried him up into the upper chamber where he was lodging, and laid him on his own bed. [20]He cried out to the LORD, "O LORD my God, have you brought calamity even upon the widow with whom I am staying, by killing her son?" [21]Then he stretched himself upon the child three times, and cried out

NIV

three times and cried to the LORD, "O LORD my God, let this boy's life return to him!"

22The LORD heard Elijah's cry, and the boy's life returned to him, and he lived. 23Elijah picked up the child and carried him down from the room into the house. He gave him to his mother and said, "Look, your son is alive!"

24Then the woman said to Elijah, "Now I know that you are a man of God and that the word of the LORD from your mouth is the truth."

NRSV

to the LORD, "O LORD my God, let this child's life come into him again." 22The LORD listened to the voice of Elijah; the life of the child came into him again, and he revived. 23Elijah took the child, brought him down from the upper chamber into the house, and gave him to his mother; then Elijah said, "See, your son is alive." 24So the woman said to Elijah, "Now I know that you are a man of God, and that the word of the LORD in your mouth is truth."

COMMENTARY

The final crisis in the chapter involves the fate of the Sidonian woman's son, who had become so severely ill that "there was no more breath left in him" (v. 17). The stakes are raised higher in this instance than in the other two vignettes in the chapter. Whereas the Lord has been able to avert death by providing first for Elijah through the ravens (vv. 1-7) and then through the widow (vv. 8-16), the challenge is now posed in the form of a boy who has already died. Elijah, who has apparently been received as a guest in the house of the woman, intercedes on the boy's behalf. The Lord hears his intercession, and the boy is miraculously revived. Thus the story claims that Elijah's deity, the God of Israel, is truly the Lord of life, for even one who has already died could be brought to life again by that deity's power. Important, too, is the claim that the miracle was accomplished as a result of the prophetic word (v. 24).

REFLECTIONS

1. Along with other stories pertaining to Elijah, the miracles in this chapter have been commemorated in music and in art. In these re-creations of the story, attention is invariably drawn to the supramundane origin of Elijah's experiences. That is, indeed, the main point of the passage: It is the Lord, the God of Israel, who brings about these wonders. So, too, we dare to believe that things that seem impossible to human beings can be brought about by the Lord: Birds of prey may provide nourishment; the poor may have their victuals wondrously replenished; and even the dead may be resurrected. It is the Lord and no other god who performs such miracles. So we are called to believe as well.

2. The wonder of these stories resides not merely in their supernatural character, however. One is amazed, too, at the wondrous freedom and sovereignty of God. The deity uses even creatures that are regarded as ritually unclean to fulfill the divine purpose. So, too, the sovereign God is free to act beyond the borders of Israel, even through Gentile worshipers of foreign gods. This point is picked up by Jesus in his inaugural sermon in his hometown synagogue (Luke 4:25-26). Jesus observes that there were many widows in Israel in Elijah's time; yet, the man of God went to a foreign land and sought out the foreign woman. The Sidonian woman is apparently not a worshiper of Elijah's God, for she refers to Elijah's deity as "your God" (17:12). Yet, she is the recipient of God's miraculous provision. In receiving divine favor, the Phoenician woman becomes a prototype for other Gentile women who receive God's grace through their encounters with Jesus (see Matt 15:21-28; Mark 7:24-30). God's universal love reaches beyond the boundaries of nationality, ethnicity, and even religious affiliation.

3. Elijah is seen in the New Testament as a forerunner of Jesus. Explicitly and implicitly, Elijah's ministry is seen as a model for the ministry of Jesus. Appropriately, therefore, most lectionaries that list 1 Kgs 17:17-24 juxtapose the passage with the account of Jesus' raising of the son of the widow of Nain (Luke 7:11-17). There are, indeed, suggestive parallels between the two accounts: the city gate, the plight of a widow, a son who has died, the miraculous resuscitation, the return of the son to his mother. The miraculous resuscitation of life in each case leads to the recognition that God has acted through an earthly intermediary.

In the New Testament, however, Jesus surpasses Elijah. Whereas Elijah is the beneficiary of God's miraculous provision of nourishment and he proclaims that God will sustain the hungry despite the meagerness of what is available, Jesus himself would miraculously feed a multitude with a seemingly meager amount of food (Matt 14:13-21; 15:32-39). Whereas Elijah appeals to God to revive the widow's son, Jesus himself commands the dead to rise again. Indeed, the culmination of the story of Jesus in the New Testament is that he represents the power of God to grant and sustain life, his own resurrection from the dead being the ultimate testimony to the triumph of God over death (1 Cor 15:20-26).

1 KINGS 18:1-46, EQUIVOCAL FAITH

OVERVIEW

This chapter concerns the reemergence of Elijah from hiding and his face-to-face confrontation with Ahab, which results in a contest on Mt. Carmel to demonstrate the power of the Lord and the powerlessness of Baal. The dramatic contest on Mt. Carmel was prompted by the people's religious equivocation as a result of Ahab's troubling patronage of Baal religion within Israel.

1 Kings 18:1-2*a*, Introduction

NIV

18 After a long time, in the third year, the word of the LORD came to Elijah: "Go and present yourself to Ahab, and I will send rain on the land." 2So Elijah went to present himself to Ahab.

NRSV

18 After many days the word of the LORD came to Elijah, in the third year of the drought,[a] saying, "Go, present yourself to Ahab; I will send rain on the earth." 2So Elijah went to present himself to Ahab.

[a] Heb lacks *of the drought*

COMMENTARY

The introductory words of chapter 18 indicate continuity with the preceding literary unit. A long time has passed since the drought had come by the word of the Lord given through Elijah (see 17:1). Now the word of the Lord comes again to Elijah "in the third year," presumably the third year of the drought (the NRSV supplies "of the drought" in v. 1). This notice of the drought's duration is important, for it establishes the fact that at least one full cycle of the seasons has come and gone, with no sign of the timely return of rejuvenating rain, which in Canaanite mythology would have been a testimony to Baal's resurrection.[63] To the narrator, the deadly dry spell would end neither by the power of Baal nor by the ritual manipulation of his worshipers, but by the word of the Lord through the prophet. There will be no rain except by the Lord's word (see 17:1). So that is why Elijah has to emerge from hiding: He is to effect the return of life-giving rain by the word of the Lord. Of the various English translations, the NAB best captures the purposeful nature of the Lord's command: " 'Go, present yourself to Ahab,' [the Lord] said, '*that* I may send rain upon the earth' " (italics added). Accordingly, Elijah obeys, and so the reader should now expect the rain to come.

63. The "third year" may imply three actual years or just one full year with a part of the preceding and part of the succeeding year.

1 Kings 18:2*b*-16, Obadiah's Equivocation

NIV

Now the famine was severe in Samaria, [3]and Ahab had summoned Obadiah, who was in charge of his palace. (Obadiah was a devout believer in the LORD. [4]While Jezebel was killing off the LORD's prophets, Obadiah had taken a hundred prophets and hidden them in two caves, fifty in each, and had supplied them with food and water.) [5]Ahab had said to Obadiah, "Go through the land to all the springs and valleys. Maybe we can find some grass to keep the horses and mules alive so we will not have to kill any of our animals." [6]So they divided the land they were to cover, Ahab going in one direction and Obadiah in another.

[7]As Obadiah was walking along, Elijah met him. Obadiah recognized him, bowed down to the ground, and said, "Is it really you, my lord Elijah?"

[8]"Yes," he replied. "Go tell your master, 'Elijah is here.' "

[9]"What have I done wrong," asked Obadiah, "that you are handing your servant over to Ahab to be put to death? [10]As surely as the LORD your God lives, there is not a nation or kingdom where my master has not sent someone to look for you. And whenever a nation or kingdom claimed you were not there, he made them swear they could not find you. [11]But now you tell me to go to my master and say, 'Elijah is here.' [12]I don't know where the Spirit of the LORD may carry you when I leave you. If I go and tell Ahab and he doesn't find you, he will kill me. Yet I your servant have worshiped the LORD since my youth. [13]Haven't you heard, my lord, what I did while Jezebel was killing the prophets of the LORD? I hid a hundred

NRSV

The famine was severe in Samaria. [3]Ahab summoned Obadiah, who was in charge of the palace. (Now Obadiah revered the LORD greatly; [4]when Jezebel was killing off the prophets of the LORD, Obadiah took a hundred prophets, hid them fifty to a cave, and provided them with bread and water.) [5]Then Ahab said to Obadiah, "Go through the land to all the springs of water and to all the wadis; perhaps we may find grass to keep the horses and mules alive, and not lose some of the animals." [6]So they divided the land between them to pass through it; Ahab went in one direction by himself, and Obadiah went in another direction by himself.

[7]As Obadiah was on the way, Elijah met him; Obadiah recognized him, fell on his face, and said, "Is it you, my lord Elijah?" [8]He answered him, "It is I. Go, tell your lord that Elijah is here." [9]And he said, "How have I sinned, that you would hand your servant over to Ahab, to kill me? [10]As the LORD your God lives, there is no nation or kingdom to which my lord has not sent to seek you; and when they would say, 'He is not here,' he would require an oath of the kingdom or nation, that they had not found you. [11]But now you say, 'Go, tell your lord that Elijah is here.' [12]As soon as I have gone from you, the spirit of the LORD will carry you I know not where; so, when I come and tell Ahab and he cannot find you, he will kill me, although I your servant have revered the LORD from my youth. [13]Has it not been told my lord what I did when Jezebel killed the prophets of the LORD, how I hid a hundred of the

NIV	NRSV
of the LORD's prophets in two caves, fifty in each, and supplied them with food and water. [14]And now you tell me to go to my master and say, 'Elijah is here.' He will kill me!" [15]Elijah said, "As the LORD Almighty lives, whom I serve, I will surely present myself to Ahab today." [16]So Obadiah went to meet Ahab and told him, and Ahab went to meet Elijah.	LORD's prophets fifty to a cave, and provided them with bread and water? [14]Yet now you say, 'Go, tell your lord that Elijah is here'; he will surely kill me." [15]Elijah said, "As the LORD of hosts lives, before whom I stand, I will surely show myself to him today." [16]So Obadiah went to meet Ahab, and told him; and Ahab went to meet Elijah.

COMMENTARY

18:2b-6. The narrator does not immediately report on the expected encounter between Elijah and Ahab, however. Instead, the reader is introduced to Obadiah, who is said to be the chief steward in Ahab's palace, the ancient Israelite equivalent of the chief of staff in the U.S. White House. Like its modern American counterpart, the position of chief steward of the palace in ancient Israel and Judah was a powerful and prestigious one. Obadiah would have had to earn Ahab's complete trust, and the extent of that trust is evident in the fact that it is to Obadiah alone that Ahab turns to deal with the national crisis at hand. Yet, Obadiah, whose name means "servant/worshiper of the LORD" in Hebrew, also "feared the LORD greatly" (so we should read with the KJV, rather than the NRSV's "revered the LORD greatly" and the NIV's "was a devout believer"). Hence, when Jezebel tried to have all the prophets of the Lord killed off, Obadiah hid a hundred of them and sustained them with food and water. On the one hand, his furtive action is reminiscent of the Hebrew midwives in Egypt, who "feared God" (so the NRSV and the NIV correctly have it) and helped to save the infant boys whom Pharaoh had ordered to be killed (Exod 1:15-29). On the other hand, his feeding of the prophets who were in hiding (v. 4) recalls the feeding of Elijah by the ravens (17:4) and by the widow in Zarephath (17:9); the Hebrew verb (כול *kûl*) is the same in all these instances. Obadiah is seen as an instrument of the Lord, even though he is also a trusted official in Ahab's government.

The severity of the famine in the capital forces Ahab to act. His first priority, it seems, is the care of his "horses and mules"—that is, animals used for the convenience of military personnel, nobles, and members of the royal family.[64] Famine and drought are in the land, but the king is concerned, not about his people, but about the stables. The prophets of the Lord are being killed off (v. 4), but the king is more worried about his animals being killed off (v. 5). So he sends Obadiah to assist him in looking for fodder and water, the two of them dividing the country between them.

18:7-16. On his way, Obadiah meets Elijah, whom he recognizes (although he is surprised to see him) and before whom he, despite his office, does obeisance. It is interesting to note the number of times the word "lord" appears in the conversation between Elijah and Obadiah. Even though Obadiah is a high-ranking official in Ahab's government, he refers to Elijah as "my lord" (vv. 7, 13) and calls himself Elijah's "servant" (vv. 9, 12). At the same time, however, Elijah refers to Ahab as Obadiah's "lord" (vv. 8, 11, 14), and Obadiah himself acknowledges Ahab as "my lord" (v. 10). Thus the narrator paints a picture of Obadiah as one who pays allegiance to two lords at the same time.

There is more at stake here, however, than loyalty to king or to prophet. Obadiah is said to be a fearer of the Lord, Elijah's God (vv. 3-4, 12-13), secretly saving and sustaining the Lord's prophets from Jezebel's pogrom. Yet, his conversation with Elijah makes it clear that he also fears Ahab immensely. He is unwilling to announce Elijah's emergence without some assurance from

64. Commoners who could afford beasts of transport ordinarily used donkeys or camels.

the latter that it would be safe for him to do so. Elijah's charge to Obadiah is repeated three times in the passage (vv. 8, 11, 14), which is an interesting detail in the light of the Hebrew; the announcement "Elijah is here" (הנה אליהו *hinnēh ʾēliyyāhû*) may also be heard in Hebrew to mean "Lo, the LORD is my God!"[65] Obadiah's reluctance to make the announcement is, therefore, tantamount to a denial of his allegiance to the Lord. Indeed, in an oath formula (v. 10), Obadiah goes so far as to refer to the Lord as Elijah's God ("your God"), thus echoing the oath formula as used by the Sidonian woman from Zarephath (17:12). He, like the Sidonian woman, fears that Elijah's presence might bring death (see 17:18). Ironically, the foreign woman, no doubt a worshiper of Baal, helped Elijah in public—at the city gate (see 17:10)—and even brought him home as a guest in her house. Meanwhile, Obadiah, who is supposed to be a fearer of the Lord and whose name in Hebrew means "servant/worshiper of the LORD," would only help the Lord's prophets secretly, and he is obsequious to Elijah when they encounter each other away from the public eye. The account of Obadiah's equivocation anticipates Elijah's accusation that the people of Israel are trying to keep all their options open (v. 21). (See Reflections at 18:41-46.)

65. See Jerome T. Walsh, *1 Kings*, Berit Olam (Collegeville, Minn.: Michael Glazier, 1996) 241.

1 Kings 18:17-40, The Summit Challenge

NIV

17When he saw Elijah, he said to him, "Is that
you, you troubler of Israel?"
18"I have not made trouble for Israel," Elijah
replied. "But you and your father's family have.
You have abandoned the LORD's commands and
have followed the Baals. 19Now summon the people from all over Israel to meet me on Mount
Carmel. And bring the four hundred and fifty
prophets of Baal and the four hundred prophets
of Asherah, who eat at Jezebel's table."
20So Ahab sent word throughout all Israel and
assembled the prophets on Mount Carmel. 21Elijah
went before the people and said, "How long will
you waver between two opinions? If the LORD is
God, follow him; but if Baal is God, follow him."
But the people said nothing.
22Then Elijah said to them, "I am the only one
of the LORD's prophets left, but Baal has four
hundred and fifty prophets. 23Get two bulls for us.
Let them choose one for themselves, and let them
cut it into pieces and put it on the wood but not
set fire to it. I will prepare the other bull and put
it on the wood but not set fire to it. 24Then you
call on the name of your god, and I will call on
the name of the LORD. The god who answers by
fire—he is God."
Then all the people said, "What you say is
good."
25Elijah said to the prophets of Baal, "Choose

NRSV

17When Ahab saw Elijah, Ahab said to him,
"Is it you, you troubler of Israel?" 18He answered,
"I have not troubled Israel; but you have, and
your father's house, because you have forsaken
the commandments of the LORD and followed the
Baals. 19Now therefore have all Israel assemble for
me at Mount Carmel, with the four hundred fifty
prophets of Baal and the four hundred prophets
of Asherah, who eat at Jezebel's table."
20So Ahab sent to all the Israelites, and assembled the prophets at Mount Carmel. 21Elijah then
came near to all the people, and said, "How long
will you go limping with two different opinions?
If the LORD is God, follow him; but if Baal, then
follow him." The people did not answer him a
word. 22Then Elijah said to the people, "I, even
I only, am left a prophet of the LORD; but Baal's
prophets number four hundred fifty. 23Let two
bulls be given to us; let them choose one bull for
themselves, cut it in pieces, and lay it on the
wood, but put no fire to it; I will prepare the
other bull and lay it on the wood, but put no fire
to it. 24Then you call on the name of your god
and I will call on the name of the LORD; the god
who answers by fire is indeed God." All the
people answered, "Well spoken!" 25Then Elijah
said to the prophets of Baal, "Choose for yourselves one bull and prepare it first, for you are
many; then call on the name of your god, but put

NIV

one of the bulls and prepare it first, since there are so many of you. Call on the name of your god, but do not light the fire." 26So they took the bull given them and prepared it.

Then they called on the name of Baal from morning till noon. "O Baal, answer us!" they shouted. But there was no response; no one answered. And they danced around the altar they had made.

27At noon Elijah began to taunt them. "Shout louder!" he said. "Surely he is a god! Perhaps he is deep in thought, or busy, or traveling. Maybe he is sleeping and must be awakened." 28So they shouted louder and slashed themselves with swords and spears, as was their custom, until their blood flowed. 29Midday passed, and they continued their frantic prophesying until the time for the evening sacrifice. But there was no response, no one answered, no one paid attention.

30Then Elijah said to all the people, "Come here to me." They came to him, and he repaired the altar of the LORD, which was in ruins. 31Elijah took twelve stones, one for each of the tribes descended from Jacob, to whom the word of the LORD had come, saying, "Your name shall be Israel." 32With the stones he built an altar in the name of the LORD, and he dug a trench around it large enough to hold two seahs[a] of seed. 33He arranged the wood, cut the bull into pieces and laid it on the wood. Then he said to them, "Fill four large jars with water and pour it on the offering and on the wood."

34"Do it again," he said, and they did it again.

"Do it a third time," he ordered, and they did it the third time. 35The water ran down around the altar and even filled the trench.

36At the time of sacrifice, the prophet Elijah stepped forward and prayed: "O LORD, God of Abraham, Isaac and Israel, let it be known today that you are God in Israel and that I am your servant and have done all these things at your command. 37Answer me, O LORD, answer me, so these people will know that you, O LORD, are God, and that you are turning their hearts back again."

38Then the fire of the LORD fell and burned up the sacrifice, the wood, the stones and the soil, and also licked up the water in the trench.

39When all the people saw this, they fell pros-

a *32* That is, probably about 13 quarts (about 15 liters)

NRSV

no fire to it." 26So they took the bull that was given them, prepared it, and called on the name of Baal from morning until noon, crying, "O Baal, answer us!" But there was no voice, and no answer. They limped about the altar that they had made. 27At noon Elijah mocked them, saying, "Cry aloud! Surely he is a god; either he is meditating, or he has wandered away, or he is on a journey, or perhaps he is asleep and must be awakened." 28Then they cried aloud and, as was their custom, they cut themselves with swords and lances until the blood gushed out over them. 29As midday passed, they raved on until the time of the offering of the oblation, but there was no voice, no answer, and no response.

30Then Elijah said to all the people, "Come closer to me"; and all the people came closer to him. First he repaired the altar of the LORD that had been thrown down; 31Elijah took twelve stones, according to the number of the tribes of the sons of Jacob, to whom the word of the LORD came, saying, "Israel shall be your name"; 32with the stones he built an altar in the name of the LORD. Then he made a trench around the altar, large enough to contain two measures of seed. 33Next he put the wood in order, cut the bull in pieces, and laid it on the wood. He said, "Fill four jars with water and pour it on the burnt offering and on the wood." 34Then he said, "Do it a second time"; and they did it a second time. Again he said, "Do it a third time"; and they did it a third time, 35so that the water ran all around the altar, and filled the trench also with water.

36At the time of the offering of the oblation, the prophet Elijah came near and said, "O LORD, God of Abraham, Isaac, and Israel, let it be known this day that you are God in Israel, that I am your servant, and that I have done all these things at your bidding. 37Answer me, O LORD, answer me, so that this people may know that you, O LORD, are God, and that you have turned their hearts back." 38Then the fire of the LORD fell and consumed the burnt offering, the wood, the stones, and the dust, and even licked up the water that was in the trench. 39When all the people saw it, they fell on their faces and said, "The LORD indeed is God; the LORD indeed is God." 40Elijah said to them, "Seize the prophets of Baal; do not let one

NIV	NRSV
trate and cried, "The LORD—he is God! The LORD—he is God!" 40Then Elijah commanded them, "Seize the prophets of Baal. Don't let anyone get away!" They seized them, and Elijah had them brought down to the Kishon Valley and slaughtered there.	of them escape." Then they seized them; and Elijah brought them down to the Wadi Kishon, and killed them there.

COMMENTARY

18:17-19. Elijah finally confronts Ahab, who immediately accuses him of being "the troubler of Israel." The Hebrew word for "troubler" (עכר *'ōkēr*) suggests someone whose action or presence is destructive to others. Jacob's sons Simeon and Levi "brought trouble" to their father by an act of vengeance that resulted in Jacob's becoming *persona non grata* to his neighbors (Gen 34:30). Achan "brought trouble" to the rest of Israel by his violation of the ban (Josh 6:18; 7:25). So Ahab's charge is that Elijah is an unsavory influence in Israel. Ahab does not spell out the charge, however. Perhaps he means that Elijah's uncompromising polemics against Baal have caused the god to be angry and, hence, have brought the drought. Perhaps he means that Elijah has disturbed the interreligious harmony that Ahab has been trying to promote. In any case, Elijah replies that it is Ahab himself who has troubled Israel by following his father's idolatrous ways, specifically, by following "the Baals"—a reference to various local manifestations of the Canaanite deity. The decisions of Ahab as king adversely affect his people's fate. The reader already knows what "trouble" Ahab has been even to a fearer of the Lord like Obadiah. Elijah will soon demonstrate the infection of Ahab's ways upon his people's faith. He issues a challenge, asking Ahab to assemble all Israel on Mt. Carmel, along with 450 prophets of Baal and 400 prophets of Asherah.

18:20-24. Elijah asks the people how long they will continue to equivocate (v. 21). The NRSV has them "limping *with* two opinions," while the NIV says that they "waver *between* two opinions" (italics added in both cases). Other modern English translations similarly interpret the idiom to mean "hopping between two opinions" (TNK), "limping between the two sides" (ASV), "straddle the issue" (NAB), "sit on the fence" (NEB), or the like. The Hebrew idiom פסחים על שתי הסעפים (*pōsĕḥîm 'al-štê hassĕ'ippîm*) means, literally, "hobbling upon two branches."[66] The imagery is probably that of a bird hopping from branch to branch or of a person hobbling on two crutches made of branches. Whatever the literal meaning of the metaphor, however, there is no doubt about Elijah's point, for he challenges the people to choose between the Lord and Baal. To this challenge, they do not respond.

Elijah proposes a test to see whether the Lord or Baal is the true God, and he gives Baal every opportunity to succeed, every advantage. On the one side of the contest would be the 450 prophets of Baal. On the other side would be the lone figure of Elijah, representing the Lord. Each side would offer a bull on an altar, and each side would invoke the name of its deity. The one who responded by fire would be the true God.

18:25-29. With the consent of the audience, the contest gets under way. Baal's representatives go first. They call on their god from morning until noon, but they get no response. They perform some kind of a ritual dance, hobbling around the altar, but, again, there is no response. Their failure prompts Elijah to taunt them by suggesting that perhaps their god, not being omnipotent and omnipresent, is preoccupied with other matters, mundane things. The prophets of Baal fall into a frenzy, lacerating themselves and desperately calling upon Baal to respond. There is, however, "no voice, no one who answers, no notice" (v. 29).

18:30-40. For his part, Elijah begins by repairing the Lord's altar, which had been destroyed. The impropriety of setting up an altar for the Lord outside of Jerusalem is momentarily forgotten as

66. On the meaning of the noun for "branches," see Isa 10:33; 17:6; 27:10; Ezek 31:6, 8.

Elijah restores the altar to vindicate his God in this contest. Twelve stones are used to represent the twelve tribes of Israel, thereby recalling the unity of the tribes before the monarchy (Josh 4:3, 8-9, 20)—indeed, the time of Moses (Exod 28:21; 39:14). That act symbolically represents Elijah's claim of authority over against Ahab. Around the altar, the prophet digs a trench that has the capacity for two *seah*-measures of seed.[67] Wood is piled upon the altar, and the sacrificial bull is laid upon it. Then Elijah gives instructions to have the entire setup thoroughly drenched with water—twelve pitchers in all.

Thus ensuring that any fire that comes upon the altar would not be accidental, Elijah calls upon the Lord as the God of Israel's ancestors. Accordingly, the Lord's fire consumes not only the burnt offering, but also the water-drenched wood, the stones, the dust, and even the water that is in the trench. The people are duly awed, for they fall down in worship and acknowledge that it is the Lord who is God, echoing Elijah's name ("The LORD is my God," v. 39). Elijah orders that the prophets of Baal be killed in the Kishon Valley, where Israel's judge Deborah had battled and slain the Canaanites long ago (Judg 4:7, 13; 5:21; Ps 83:9). (See Reflections at 18:41-46.)

67. The NRSV and the NIV both take the text to mean that the trench is capable of holding two *seah*-measures of seed (approximately seven gallons), which would be too small for an altar large enough to hold a sacrificial bull. If, however, one takes the capacity to refer to the area of land required for sowing that amount of seed (see Lev 27:16; Isa 5:10), then the area around the altar would need to be about 1,800 square yards, which seems too large for twelve pitchers of water to fill.

1 Kings 18:41-46, Conclusion of the Contest

NIV

[41]And Elijah said to Ahab, "Go, eat and drink, for there is the sound of a heavy rain." [42]So Ahab went off to eat and drink, but Elijah climbed to the top of Carmel, bent down to the ground and put his face between his knees.

[43]"Go and look toward the sea," he told his servant. And he went up and looked.

"There is nothing there," he said.

Seven times Elijah said, "Go back."

[44]The seventh time the servant reported, "A cloud as small as a man's hand is rising from the sea."

So Elijah said, "Go and tell Ahab, 'Hitch up your chariot and go down before the rain stops you.'"

[45]Meanwhile, the sky grew black with clouds, the wind rose, a heavy rain came on and Ahab rode off to Jezreel. [46]The power of the LORD came upon Elijah and, tucking his cloak into his belt, he ran ahead of Ahab all the way to Jezreel.

NRSV

41Elijah said to Ahab, "Go up, eat and drink; for there is a sound of rushing rain." [42]So Ahab went up to eat and to drink. Elijah went up to the top of Carmel; there he bowed himself down upon the earth and put his face between his knees. [43]He said to his servant, "Go up now, look toward the sea." He went up and looked, and said, "There is nothing." Then he said, "Go again seven times." [44]At the seventh time he said, "Look, a little cloud no bigger than a person's hand is rising out of the sea." Then he said, "Go say to Ahab, 'Harness your chariot and go down before the rain stops you.'" [45]In a little while the heavens grew black with clouds and wind; there was a heavy rain. Ahab rode off and went to Jezreel. [46]But the hand of the LORD was on Elijah; he girded up his loins and ran in front of Ahab to the entrance of Jezreel.

COMMENTARY

The passage concludes with the coming of rain, as the Lord had promised through Elijah at the beginning (v. 1): "the sound of the rumbling of rain" (v. 41), "rain" (v. 44), "heavy rain" (v. 45). Throughout these concluding verses, Elijah is in charge, while Ahab merely takes his cues from him. Elijah hears the sound of approaching rain and orders Ahab to ascend the mountain and to eat and drink. The summit meal no doubt signals the end of drought and famine. More important, however, it recalls the covenant meal that Moses and Aaron and the seventy elders of Israel partook at the mountain of God long ago (see Exod 24:9-14). For all his offenses, Ahab is apparently still included as a member of the covenant community, but he is clearly under prophetic authority. Elijah, then, goes off to the very peak of Mt. Carmel, just as Moses had left the rest of the party to wait for him while he retreated high up the mountain of God to commune with the deity. Elijah crouches on the ground, placing his face between his knees in what must have been a posture of intense prayer. He has an assistant with him, just as Moses had an assistant with him when he left the rest of the group waiting at the mountain of God. The unnamed servant is to look toward the sea, and he does so without result until the symbolically signficant seventh time. Then the servant sees a little cloud "no bigger than a person's hand" arising from the horizon. The approaching cloud, though appearing small in the distance, is reminiscent of the cloud of glory that represented the Lord's presence at the mountain of God in the time of Moses.

Through his servant, Elijah then instructs Ahab to leave in his chariot before the rain comes and he will be unable to do so. The long-awaited rain that would end the drought, the rain that is supposed to be a blessing, would be an obstacle for Ahab. Just as surely as Elijah had said, the sky turns dark and heavy rain falls, while the king flees on his chariot to Jezreel, Ahab and Jezebel's winter palace some seventeen miles away. Empowered by the Lord, however, Elijah outpaces him on foot.

REFLECTIONS

This is an enormously entertaining chapter. Here we find a story of a high government official furtively subverting a quasi-state-sponsored pogrom and paying homage to the most wanted dissident in the country. We have an account, too, of a confrontation between a king and a prophet, with each accusing the other of culpability in the suffering of others—a veritable power struggle between "church" and "state." Above all, we have the high drama of a mountaintop contest between the representatives of two different religions, each trying to prove the superiority of its deity.

These stories are recounted not just for entertainment, however; they are narrated for theological reasons. Herein one finds important theological lessons that continue to be instructive for the community of faith.

1. The passage obviously asserts the power of Israel's God, who is omnipotent and sovereign over the world. Just as important, although conveyed more subtly, however, are God's persistent grace and mercy. Despite the blatant unfaithfulness of human beings, God nevertheless responds to human needs even when people do not ask. In the case the text discusses, it is God who initiates the end of the drought and the return of rain. God may act wondrously and publicly—whether in the liberation of slaves from oppression, in sending fire from heaven, in the resurrection, or in some other salvific event in order to bring people to faith.

2. At the heart of biblical faith is the demand for allegiance to only one God. For most people who are already in the community of faith, however, the challenge is not theism per se, for few would deny God outright. Rather, the greatest challenge lies in faithfulness to one God and no other; it lies in the willingness to trust that one God, even in times when other alternatives seem more practical, more immediately relevant, or more popular. Human needs and wants are so great that there is always the temptation to keep one's theological options open to hedge against the possibility that our God may not adequately provide for our needs. Polytheism allows one to so hedge, but that is not the case with the religion of Moses (see Exod 20:3; Deut 5:7), after whose ministry Elijah's own is modeled. For Elijah, then, there

can be no theological compromise; we have to choose to be on one side or the other. In this perspective, *not* to choose is already to choose an alternative other than the way of the Lord. It is not only in genuine polytheism that such a threat exists, however, for even people who do not believe in the actual existence of other gods might have other equally pernicious delusions of alternative powers. Jesus called attention to one such alternative in his generation, pointing out that the command to love God allows no other allegiance: "No one can serve two masters; for a slave will either hate the one and love the other, or be devoted to one and despise the other. You cannot serve God and wealth" (Matt 6:24 NRSV).

3. The chapter illustrates the demand of Mosaic religion quite well—not only in Elijah's call to the people to choose either the Lord or Baal, but also in the realistic example of Obadiah. In Obadiah we have someone with whom most people in the community of faith might identify much more readily than with Ahab or even the people of Israel assembled on Mt. Carmel. Obadiah is a believer, a fearer of God. His loyalty to the Lord is attested by his name ("servant/worshiper of the LORD"). He is even instrumental in saving the lives of others, secretly undermining the will of the queen. Obadiah, however, has other allegiances and fears, as well: He has his boss to serve, his career to protect, his own life to preserve. He is one with whom we readily sympathize, and we wonder whether the narrator had been a tad too harsh in comparing him implicitly with the Sidonian widow, a woman outside the community of faith. The text warns us, however, of the dangers of the insidious or the seemingly excusable compromises, as well as the blatant ones. Herein lies the threat to faith for most of us.

1 KINGS 19:1-21, THE PROPHET'S PLIGHT

OVERVIEW

The chapter is anticlimactic. On the heels of the great victory on Mt. Carmel, the reader may be surprised to find the protagonist of that contest now on the run for his life. In chaps. 17–18, Elijah is a bona fide hero of faith. He is larger than life—faithful, confident, and authoritative. He is able to bring about miracles through prayer, even raising the dead and calling fire down from heaven. He is able to confront a powerful king and accuse him of sin, and he dares to challenge a large crowd of Baalists. He is able to outrun Ahab's chariot in a seventeen-mile race. So we certainly would not expect to find an easily intimidated, suicidal, self-doubting yet self-righteous Elijah in chap. 19. Indeed, the tone of this chapter is so different from the previous ones that most critics assume that the link to the preceding units of thought suggested by vv. 1-3 is artificial; the rest of the chapter, it is sometimes argued, does not return to Jezebel or to her death threat. There are, moreover, a number of elements in the chapter that suggest a complex compositional history.

All that may be true. Yet, there are signs that the text as we have it is intended to be read as a whole and, indeed, to be read as a sequel to the Mt. Carmel episode.

1 Kings 19:1-3*a*, Why Elijah Is on the Run

NIV

19 Now Ahab told Jezebel everything Elijah had done and how he had killed all the prophets with the sword. [2]So Jezebel sent a messenger to Elijah to say, "May the gods deal with me, be it ever so severely, if by this time tomorrow I do not make your life like that of one of them."

[3]Elijah was afraid[a] and ran for his life.

[a] 3 Or *Elijah saw*

NRSV

19 Ahab told Jezebel all that Elijah had done, and how he had killed all the prophets with the sword. [2]Then Jezebel sent a messenger to Elijah, saying, "So may the gods do to me, and more also, if I do not make your life like the life of one of them by this time tomorrow." [3]Then he was afraid; he got up and fled for his life,

COMMENTARY

As the preceding chapter ended, Ahab was rushing off to Jezreel (18:45), presumably to the winter palace that he and his queen have there (see 21:1). As the new chapter begins, we find him reporting to his wife, Jezebel, a princess from Sidon (16:31) and a fanatical devotee of Baal (see 18:4, 13), all the details of what Elijah had done. Specifically, Ahab reports on Elijah's killing of "all the prophets," meaning the 450 prophets of Baal (18:40) and perhaps the 400 prophets of Asherah who have been supported by the queen (18:19).

Jezebel immediately reacts by sending a message to Elijah, vowing to kill him. Yet, if that is what she really wants to do, it seems strange that she does not simply send an assassin to finish him off or a bailiff to arrest him. Instead, she tips him off, giving him time to escape. One must not press the details too hard, however, for this is not so much a historical report as it is literature. This introductory account simply sets up the rest of the story. It explains why it is that Elijah is fleeing despite his triumph on Mt. Carmel: He is persecuted for doing the Lord's work; his life threatened. Duly warned, he is frightened and flees for his life (v. 3*a*). (See Reflections at 19:19-21.)

1 Kings 19:3*b*-8*a*, Two Epiphanies in the Desert

NIV

When he came to Beersheba in Judah, he left his servant there, [4]while he himself went a day's journey into the desert. He came to a broom tree, sat down under it and prayed that he might die. "I have had enough, LORD," he said. "Take my life; I am no better than my ancestors." [5]Then he lay down under the tree and fell asleep.

All at once an angel touched him and said, "Get up and eat." [6]He looked around, and there by his head was a cake of bread baked over hot coals, and a jar of water. He ate and drank and then lay down again.

[7]The angel of the LORD came back a second

[a] 3 Or *Elijah saw*

NRSV

and came to Beer-sheba, which belongs to Judah; he left his servant there.

4But he himself went a day's journey into the wilderness, and came and sat down under a solitary broom tree. He asked that he might die: "It is enough; now, O LORD, take away my life, for I am no better than my ancestors." [5]Then he lay down under the broom tree and fell asleep. Suddenly an angel touched him and said to him, "Get up and eat." [6]He looked, and there at his head was a cake baked on hot stones, and a jar of water. He ate and drank, and lay down again. [7]The angel of the LORD came a second time, touched him, and said, "Get up and eat, otherwise

NIV	NRSV
time and touched him and said, "Get up and eat, for the journey is too much for you." 8So he got up and ate and drank.	the journey will be too much for you." 8He got up, and ate and drank;

COMMENTARY

Elijah goes to Beersheba, the southernmost town in the land of the Lord's people, as we know from the cliché "from Dan to Beersheba" (Judg 20:1; 1 Sam 3:20; 2 Sam 17:11; 24:2, 15). The narrator reminds the reader that Beersheba was at that time under Judah's control. So Elijah is legally well beyond the reach of Jezebel. Still, he does not remain there. Whereas on Mt. Carmel he had counted on his servant to help him look out for sign of impending rain (18:43-44), now he leaves the lad in Beersheba, while he himself ventures into the wilderness beyond Judah. He takes shelter under a solitary desert bush ("broom tree," NRSV and NIV) and cries out, presumably to the Lord. "Too much [רב *rab*; NIV, "I have had enough, LORD"; NRSV, "It is enough"]!" he says summarily, and asks to die because he is no better than his forebears (אבות *'ābôt*; NRSV, NIV, "ancestors"). His requesting that the Lord let him die ("for I am no better than my forebears") is usually understood to mean that he thinks his life is no better than those of his dead ancestors. It is also possible, however, that the "forebears" refers, not to his ancestors per se, but to his predecessors in the prophetic ministry. That is, despite his stupendous success on Mt. Carmel, he is no better than his vocational predecessors after all. Perhaps he has in mind Moses, who also complained to the Lord in the wilderness that his burden was too heavy to bear alone, and so he asked the Lord to let him die (Num 11:14-15). So, too, Elijah goes into the wilderness to complain that he is bearing too much and asks to die. He would later insist that he is by himself ("I alone am left," vv. 10, 14). Elijah, in other words, is in no better situation than were his forebears inasmuch as he, like them, is left with too much to bear on his own.

Elijah is then touched by an angel and provided with a cake baked on hot coals and a jug of water, hardly things one should expect to find in the desert. The Hebrew word used for "hot coals" (רצפים *rĕṣāpîm*) is a rare one. It is found elsewhere only in Isa 6:6 for a hot coal that a seraph takes from the altar of the Lord's Temple and with which he touches the lips of Isaiah in response to the prophet's expression of unworthiness to accept the Lord's commission. The word used for "jar" (צפחת *ṣappaḥat*) is also uncommon. It is found in two other passages, 1 Sam 26:10-16 and 1 Kgs 17:8-16, the latter having to do with the Lord's provision for Elijah's needs through the widow of Zarephath when Elijah was hiding from Ahab.

Through the device of a second epiphany, the narrator is able to identify the angel specifically as an angel of the Lord and to give a reason for the provision and the command to eat. In the account of the first epiphany, we read only of "an angel," which is noteworthy because the word for "angel" (מלאך *mal'āk*) is the same one used for Jezebel's "messenger" in v. 2. Rhetorically, this ambiguity heightens the tension, for the reader is momentarily uncertain whether the mysterious intermediary will bring death, which Jezebel had promised and which Elijah had self-piteously requested, or whether the intermediary will somehow deliver Elijah from his persecutor and from himself.

The account of the second epiphany clarifies that the intermediary is, in fact, from the Lord. It explains, too, that Elijah is to eat because "the way is too much for you" (רב ממך הדרך *rab mimmĕkā haddārek*, v. 7). NRSV understands the text to be referring to the journey ahead of Elijah ("the journey will be too much for you"), but the text is ambivalent. Moreover, the reference to the excessive difficulty of "the way" harks back to Elijah's own complaint in v. 4: "too much!" (br rab). Elijah has to accept the nourishment that the Lord provides in the wilderness because "the way" is "too much" for him. So he complies. (See Reflections at 19:19-21.)

1 Kings 19:8*b*-18, Encounter with God on Mount Horeb

NIV

Strengthened by that food, he traveled forty days
and forty nights until he reached Horeb, the
mountain of God. 9There he went into a cave and
spent the night.

And the word of the LORD came to him: "What
are you doing here, Elijah?"

10He replied, "I have been very zealous for the
LORD God Almighty. The Israelites have rejected
your covenant, broken down your altars, and put
your prophets to death with the sword. I am the
only one left, and now they are trying to kill me
too."

11The LORD said, "Go out and stand on the
mountain in the presence of the LORD, for the
LORD is about to pass by."

Then a great and powerful wind tore the mountains apart and shattered the rocks before the
LORD, but the LORD was not in the wind. After
the wind there was an earthquake, but the LORD
was not in the earthquake. 12After the earthquake
came a fire, but the LORD was not in the fire. And
after the fire came a gentle whisper. 13When Elijah
heard it, he pulled his cloak over his face and
went out and stood at the mouth of the cave.

Then a voice said to him, "What are you doing
here, Elijah?"

14He replied, "I have been very zealous for the
LORD God Almighty. The Israelites have rejected
your covenant, broken down your altars, and put
your prophets to death with the sword. I am the
only one left, and now they are trying to kill me
too."

15The LORD said to him, "Go back the way you
came, and go to the Desert of Damascus. When
you get there, anoint Hazael king over Aram.
16Also, anoint Jehu son of Nimshi king over Israel,
and anoint Elisha son of Shaphat from Abel Meholah to succeed you as prophet. 17Jehu will put
to death any who escape the sword of Hazael,
and Elisha will put to death any who escape the
sword of Jehu. 18Yet I reserve seven thousand in
Israel—all whose knees have not bowed down to
Baal and all whose mouths have not kissed him."

NRSV

then he went in the strength of that food forty
days and forty nights to Horeb the mount of God.
9At that place he came to a cave, and spent the
night there.

Then the word of the LORD came to him,
saying, "What are you doing here, Elijah?" 10He
answered, "I have been very zealous for the LORD,
the God of hosts; for the Israelites have forsaken
your covenant, thrown down your altars, and
killed your prophets with the sword. I alone am
left, and they are seeking my life, to take it away."

11He said, "Go out and stand on the mountain
before the LORD, for the LORD is about to pass by."
Now there was a great wind, so strong that it
was splitting mountains and breaking rocks in
pieces before the LORD, but the LORD was not in
the wind; and after the wind an earthquake, but
the LORD was not in the earthquake; 12and
after the earthquake a fire, but the LORD was not
in the fire; and after the fire a sound of sheer
silence. 13When Elijah heard it, he wrapped his
face in his mantle and went out and stood at the
entrance of the cave. Then there came a voice to
him that said, "What are you doing here, Elijah?"
14He answered, "I have been very zealous for the
LORD, the God of hosts; for the Israelites have
forsaken your covenant, thrown down your altars,
and killed your prophets with the sword. I alone
am left, and they are seeking my life, to take it
away." 15Then the LORD said to him, "Go, return
on your way to the wilderness of Damascus; when
you arrive, you shall anoint Hazael as king over
Aram. 16Also you shall anoint Jehu son of Nimshi
as king over Israel; and you shall anoint Elisha
son of Shaphat of Abel-meholah as prophet in your
place. 17Whoever escapes from the sword of
Hazael, Jehu shall kill; and whoever escapes from
the sword of Jehu, Elisha shall kill. 18Yet I will
leave seven thousand in Israel, all the knees that
have not bowed to Baal, and every mouth that
has not kissed him."

COMMENTARY

19:8b-10. Elijah goes on a journey of forty days and forty nights to "Horeb the mount of God," an alternate name for Mt. Sinai (see Exod 3:1). The period of forty days and forty nights, significantly, also echoes the time Moses spent on the same mountain, where he encountered God (see Exod 24:18; 34:28; Deut 9:9, 11, 18, 25; 10:10). On that mountain, Elijah comes to a cave (so NIV, NRSV); the Hebrew has the definite article, "the cave" (המערה *hammĕʿārâ*, v. 9), which is perhaps a reference to the "cleft of the rock" where Moses stood as the Lord "passed by" (Exod 33:22).

In response to the Lord's question as to his purpose on Horeb, Elijah replies that he has been "very zealous for the LORD" because the people of Israel have forsaken the covenant, torn down the altars of the Lord, and killed the Lord's prophets. The term used for Elijah's zeal here (קנא קנאתי *qannōʾ qinnēʾtî*), however, is used most frequently for God's "jealousy" as regards Israel's loyalty (Exod 20:5; 34:14; Deut 4:24; 5:9; 6:15; 32:16, 19, 21; Josh 24:19). Elijah, in other words, is jealous on behalf of the Lord, and he is angry because he has been left by himself to do God's work and because he is persecuted for it. So he has come to this mountain where Moses long ago had encountered God, indeed, spoken to God "face to face" (Deut 5:4).

Elijah appears to be overly zealous, however. He does not seem to recall the affirmative response of the people of Israel on Mt. Carmel (18:39). He charges them with having torn down the altars of the Lord, perhaps thinking of the altar that he had to repair to offer the sacrificial bull in the contest with Baal's prophets (18:30). Yet, the destruction of altars outside Jerusalem would be in accordance with the deuteronomic program of centralization. The reference to the killing of the Lord's prophets is also puzzling, because the only record of such killing is that ordered by Jezebel (18:4, 13), and not by the people of Israel. Elijah also does not seem to remember that Obadiah had rescued a hundred prophets of the Lord, so he is not technically left by himself.

19:11-14. The Lord tells him to go out and stand on the mountain, for the Lord is "about to pass by" (so the NIV correctly has it in v. 11). The words are probably meant to evoke the tradition of Moses standing at the "cleft of the rock"—perhaps this very cave—where he encountered the Lord's passing by (Exod 33:19-23). Signs that typically accompany theophanies appear in succession: the accompaniments of a rainstorm, an earthquake, fire (e.g., Exod 19:16-19; Judg 5:4-5; Pss 18:13; 68:9; Nah 1:3-5; Hab 3:4-6). In particular, in the preceding chapter rainstorm and fire are associated with the power of God. Yet, in each case now, Elijah discovers that the Lord is not present despite the familiar signs.

Finally, after the fire, there is an eerie calm, literally "a sound of fine silence" (קול דממה דקה *qôl dĕmāmâ daqqâ*). The traditional translation of the phrase as "a still small voice" (so KJV) has been popularized in hymns, but it does not convey the oxymoron. The NRSV takes it to be "a sound of sheer silence," which is what the words mean, and yet, Elijah is able to hear something (v. 13). The Hebrew words for "sound" and "silence," in fact, occur together in Job 4:16, where that combination is generally taken as an expression for a barely audible sound (NIV, "a gentle whisper"). That is probably what is meant by the "sound of fine silence"—that is, a hushed sound. The Hebrew word for "silence" (דממה *dĕmāmâ*) is attested in Ps 107:29 as well, where it refers to the end of a storm. What Elijah hears, apparently, is the calm that comes after the storm. Perhaps the narrator means to contrast this hushed sound with the sound of the rumbling before the storm, קול המון הגשם (*qôl hămôn haggāšem*; see 18:41). In any case, the structure of the text implies that it is in this stillness that Elijah somehow encounters the Lord: The Lord was not in the storm, not in the earthquake, not in the fire, but after the fire there is this "sound." Thereupon, Elijah covers his face with his mantle, a gesture that suggests that he is, indeed, encountering the numinous in that stillness (cf. Exod 3:6; 33:22).

Elijah then hears a sound (v. 13)—perhaps another sound, perhaps the same sound. In any case, this time the sound is clearly a personal voice, and the reader knows from the query the voice poses that it is the voice of the Lord. To that question, Elijah gives the same answer as before. The manifestation of divine presence described in the preceding verses apparently has made no difference in Elijah's understanding; he apparently does not get the point of the "sound of fine silence."

19:15-18. The Lord speaks to him a symbolically significant third time, telling him, literally, "Go, return to your way [לך שׁוב לדרכך *lēk šûb lĕdarkĕkā*]" (v. 15). The last reference in the passage to a "way" (דרך *derek*) is in v. 7, in reference to the way that would be "too much" for Elijah without divine sustenance in the wilderness. This time, however, the wilderness is not in the south, but in the north: the wilderness of Damascus. Elijah is to anoint Hazael as king of Aram (the Syrians), Jehu as king of Israel, and Elisha as his successor. The reference to Hazael and Jehu anticipates events recorded in 2 Kgs 8:7–10:31, only there it is not Elijah who is the principal prophetic figure but Elisha. It is Elisha who announces to Hazael that he will be king (2 Kgs 8:7-15), and it is Elisha who indirectly anoints Jehu as king (2 Kgs 9:1-15). Critics discern here a complex redactional process, perhaps a secondary insertion at this point of a reworked fragment from the Elisha cycle. Whatever the reality, the charge to Elijah in vv. 11-21 in its present literary context stands as an explication of the "sound of fine silence" that Elijah heard on Mt. Horeb. It also provides a conclusion to the story of Elijah's flight. The answer to the threat posed by Jezebel will not come in the spectacular and immediate manner, as on Mt. Carmel. It does not come by way of a fire from on high. It does not come by way of a rainstorm. Rather, it is to come in a quiet fashion, through the rather unspectacular fact of prophetic succession. The answer will come through the working out of divine will in the historical process. The anointing of Elisha will lead, if only indirectly, to the anointing of Hazael and Jehu. The seemingly mundane event of the ordination of Elijah's successor will turn out to be the resolution to the problem of Jezebel. Eventually, in the reign of Jehu years later, Jezebel will be killed (2 Kgs 9:30-37), as will her fellow devotees of Baal (2 Kgs 10:18-28). Moreover, contrary to the view of Elijah that he alone is left, the Lord will leave "seven thousand" (a symbolic figure) who will not bend their knees to Baal or give him their allegiance. In contrast to the events on Mt. Carmel, these events are unspectacular. They are even difficult to perceive, for they occur indirectly and over a period of time in history. Yet, that is how the Lord may appear—in "a sound of fine silence" that comes after the fire (see chap. 18). (See Reflections at 19:19-21.)

1 Kings 19:19-21, The Call of Elisha

NIV

19So Elijah went from there and found Elisha son of Shaphat. He was plowing with twelve yoke of oxen, and he himself was driving the twelfth pair. Elijah went up to him and threw his cloak around him. 20Elisha then left his oxen and ran after Elijah. "Let me kiss my father and mother good-by," he said, "and then I will come with you."

"Go back," Elijah replied. "What have I done to you?"

21So Elisha left him and went back. He took his yoke of oxen and slaughtered them. He burned the plowing equipment to cook the meat and gave it to the people, and they ate. Then he set out to follow Elijah and became his attendant.

NRSV

19So he set out from there, and found Elisha son of Shaphat, who was plowing. There were twelve yoke of oxen ahead of him, and he was with the twelfth. Elijah passed by him and threw his mantle over him. 20He left the oxen, ran after Elijah, and said, "Let me kiss my father and my mother, and then I will follow you." Then Elijah[a] said to him, "Go back again; for what have I done to you?" 21He returned from following him, took the yoke of oxen, and slaughtered them; using the equipment from the oxen, he boiled their flesh, and gave it to the people, and they ate. Then he set out and followed Elijah, and became his servant.

[a] Heb *he*

COMMENTARY

Elijah does not respond by going to the wilderness of Damascus to anoint Hazael, as one might expect from a surface reading of his commission in vv. 11-18. Rather, he responds to the essence of the divine charge, quietly beginning the process of fulfilling the Lord's word by passing on the mantle of prophetic authority to Elisha. Elijah leaves Horeb, the Mount of God, and finds Elisha, presumably in the latter's hometown of Abel-meholah (v. 16), in the western Jordan valley. Elisha is plowing the field with twelve teams of oxen, suggesting an extremely large operation and, hence, considerable wealth. Strangely, as Elijah passes him by, he throws his mantle upon Elisha and keeps on going. The cultural significance of this admittedly bizarre action is unknown. Some scholars discern a literary allusion to the Lord's "passing by" before Elijah in front of the cave in Mt. Horeb—that is, Elijah passes by Elisha, just as the Lord had passed by Elijah.[68] The mantle is presumably the one that Elijah used to cover his face from the theophany at Horeb (v. 13). With this mantle, Elijah would later strike the water of a river and cause it to miraculously part (2 Kgs 2:8), and Elisha would follow suit (2 Kgs 2:13-14). So the mantle is to Elijah what the staff was to Moses (Exod 7:17-18; 14:16). Elisha must have had a sense of the symbolic significance of that gesture, whatever that might have been, for he leaves his oxen to follow Elijah, asking only to return home first to bid his parents farewell. Elijah tells him to do so, using words that echo the Lord's commission to him in v. 15, "Go, return [לך שׁוב *lēk šûb*]." The remark that immediately follows this call to return is, however, enigmatic: "What have I done to you?" It is often understood to be a rhetorical question: "What have I done to prevent you?" (NEB) or "Have I done anything to you?" (NAB). Elijah, however, may be alluding to the symbolic meaning of the gesture—that is, what the tossing of the mantle to Elisha implies. He means, perhaps, that Elisha's acceptance of the call would entail a radical break from his familial and social moorings. Elisha clearly understands that his farewell will be more than a ritual kiss. He sacrifices the capital and tools of his trade, slaughtering the oxen and using the equipment that comes with them for fuel. Duly severed from his past, then, he sets out to follow Elijah "and attended to him" (וישׁרתהו *wayšārĕtēhû*), the Hebrew recalling the role that Joshua, Moses' successor, played before Moses passed on (Num 11:28; Josh 1:1). Elisha plays Joshua to Elijah's Moses.

68. See Robert B. Coote, "Yahweh Recalls Elijah," in *Traditions in Transformation: Turning Points in Biblical Faith,* ed. Baruch Halpern and Jon D. Levenson (Winona Lake, Ind.: Eisenbrauns, 1981) 115-20.

REFLECTIONS

It is for good reason that chapter 19 is one of the most frequently preached sections in the book of Kings. There are a number of New Testament allusions to it, and all subsections in the unit appear in various lectionaries. There is no question that this is a theologically rich passage.

1. Arguably the most memorable words in the entire chapter are the oxymoronic expression "sound of fine silence," famous in the traditional rendering, "a still small voice." The passage is perhaps theologically most important as a counterpoint to the high drama of chapter 18. There the Lord is known in spectacular manifestations of fire from heaven and sudden rainstorm after a drought. Here, however, the point is made quite deliberately that God is not locked into any one mode of appearing. Sometimes God is not made known to us through flashy theophanies. Sometimes God is known in unspectacular ways, through the quiet working out of history. For Elijah, who had known the presence of God through God's providence and through miraculous acts that clearly demonstrated God's power, divine will was also manifested in his role in the ordination of his successor. Unbeknownst to him at that time, that one act

in the countryside would lead to other events in the fulfillment of God's will in history. Elsewhere in Scripture, we learn that God's "voice" is sometimes present in unspectacular events and ordinary people. Indeed, God's "voice" may be present even amid God's silence, as in the birth of a child to an unwed mother amid scandalous circumstances or in the death of an innocent man on the cross.

2. A second lesson is related to the first. We learn that the ministry may take many forms. We may recognize Elijah's tasks in chapter 18 as traditional forms of ministry: He confronts a powerful leader with his sins; he calls on people to be faithful to God's demands; he acts to convert others by the powerful word of God. Here in chapter 19, however, we learn that ministry may include the passing on of the mantle of leadership. Faithfulness to God's calling may entail the preparation of others for their own ministries.

3. The chapter is blatantly honest about the humanity of God's servants. Even the prophet who has experienced God's providence and power has his moments of darkness. Elijah has been blessed with much success, but at the slightest sign of a reversal of fortune, he is ready to quit. In this story we find all the signs of ministerial burnout. Those who are psychologically inclined might point out that Elijah manifests all the signs of depression. He appears to be totally worn out, fatigued. This prophet who used to refer to himself as one standing before the Lord (17:1; 18:15) seems to be sleeping a lot in this passage. He complains. He is suicidal. He needs to be told to eat. His view of reality is distorted. He is quick to blame others for the situation in which he has found himself. He feels all alone. Given his attitude, one should expect a divine rebuke. There is not one, however. Instead, there is a series of epiphanies. Elijah is touched by a divine intermediary and, when he fails to get the point, the Lord speaks to him a third time. Elijah's perspective is strongly challenged, and a lesson is offered to him; but he is never rebuked for showing weakness. Rather, Elijah is accepted as he is and is merely called back to his ministry: "Go, return to your way!" God does not let him go simply because he is burned out and depressed.

4. God's persistence with Elijah does not at all imply that God's will can be carried only through him. Indeed, Elijah is assured that there are many others—unnamed heroes of faith—who have "not bent their knees to Baal." In the New Testament, this "remnant" that God has left untainted is evidence of the enormousness of divine grace (see Rom 11:3-5).

5. The account of Elisha's calling says something about the kind of commitment that it would take to accept the call to ministry. Elisha returns to bid farewell to his family and sacrifices the essential equipment of his trade. This view of faithfulness logically follows upon the call in the preceding chapter for unequivocal commitment to the way of the Lord. In the New Testament, the demand for absolute commitment in following Jesus is stated even more radically: "No one who puts a hand to the plow and looks back is fit for the kingdom of God" (Luke 9:57-62 NRSV, esp. v. 62; see also Matt 8:18-22; 19:23-30; Mark 10:23-31). Discipleship can be costly!

1 KINGS 20:1-43, AHAB'S HANDLING OF A FOREIGN-POLICY CRISIS

OVERVIEW

This chapter purports to be about a foreign-policy crisis Ahab had to face—namely, the war that Israel was forced to fight with Aram (Syria) under a certain King Ben-Hadad. Critics point out, however, that there are a number of discrepancies in the historical details, and they argue compellingly that it is more likely that the story originally concerned events that occurred later, in the reign of Jehoahaz (see 2 Kgs 13:1-9).[69] The account here is not to be read as a historical record, however, but as theological literature. Whatever its origin and compositional history, the story in its present context needs to be read as a theological assessment of Ahab's faithfulness—or lack thereof.

The story's literary context poses a problem as well. Whereas Elijah is the conduit of the Lord's word in the preceding three chapters and will make a comeback in the next chapter, he is completely absent from chap. 20. To some scholars, that fact again indicates that we have intrusive material here. Yet, we may read the text in the light of the preceding materials. Here the deity does not work in the foreground—through supernatural acts and theophanies, as in chaps. 17–19—but only in the background, through the unfolding of history. This is, in fact, the point of the "sound of fine silence" in 19:12. Moreover, the fact that Elijah is silent while several other prophetic figures convey the will of God (see vv. 13-14, 22, 28, 35-43) is testimony to the truth of the claim in 19:18 that there are numerous other people in Israel who are still loyal to the Lord (the "seven thousand in Israel who have not bent their knees to Baal"), despite Elijah's claim to be the only one left. Moreover, countering Ahab's charge that Elijah was Israel's "troubler," Elijah replied that it was Ahab who was the real "troubler," the word implying that his presence and actions would bring trouble upon others (18:17). Now the narrator will show how Ahab did, indeed, bring trouble to his people (see v. 42).

Finally, in terms of the overall flow of the passage, vv. 1-34 seem to be a self-contained unit: War turns to peace; the king of Israel is victorious over the king of Aram. Thus the final section (vv. 35-43) seems to have been tacked on. The coherence of vv. 1-34, however, is a literary setup by the narrator. One might read the end of this section with some satisfaction, only to be surprised by the two prophetic episodes in vv. 35-43. These concluding verses are, in fact, crucial for the passage, for they provide a theological lens through which to view Ahab's overall performance in his handling of the crisis.

69. See, e.g., the careful study of Wayne T. Pitard, *Ancient Damascus* (Winona Lake, Ind.: Eisenbrauns, 1987) 114-25.

1 Kings 20:1-12, How the War Begins

NIV

20 Now Ben-Hadad king of Aram mustered his entire army. Accompanied by thirty-two kings with their horses and chariots, he went up and besieged Samaria and attacked it. 2He sent messengers into the city to Ahab king of Israel, saying, "This is what Ben-Hadad says: 3'Your silver and gold are mine, and the best of your wives and children are mine.'"

NRSV

20 King Ben-hadad of Aram gathered all his army together; thirty-two kings were with him, along with horses and chariots. He marched against Samaria, laid siege to it, and attacked it. 2Then he sent messengers into the city to King Ahab of Israel, and said to him: "Thus says Ben-hadad: 3Your silver and gold are mine; your fairest wives and children also are mine." 4The king of

NIV

[4]The king of Israel answered, "Just as you say, my lord the king. I and all I have are yours."

[5]The messengers came again and said, "This is what Ben-Hadad says: 'I sent to demand your silver and gold, your wives and your children. [6]But about this time tomorrow I am going to send my officials to search your palace and the houses of your officials. They will seize everything you value and carry it away.'"

[7]The king of Israel summoned all the elders of the land and said to them, "See how this man is looking for trouble! When he sent for my wives and my children, my silver and my gold, I did not refuse him."

[8]The elders and the people all answered, "Don't listen to him or agree to his demands."

[9]So he replied to Ben-Hadad's messengers, "Tell my lord the king, 'Your servant will do all you demanded the first time, but this demand I cannot meet.'" They left and took the answer back to Ben-Hadad.

[10]Then Ben-Hadad sent another message to Ahab: "May the gods deal with me, be it ever so severely, if enough dust remains in Samaria to give each of my men a handful."

[11]The king of Israel answered, "Tell him: 'One who puts on his armor should not boast like one who takes it off.'"

[12]Ben-Hadad heard this message while he and the kings were drinking in their tents,[a] and he ordered his men: "Prepare to attack." So they prepared to attack the city.

[a] *12* Or *in Succoth*; also in verse 16

NRSV

Israel answered, "As you say, my lord, O king, I am yours, and all that I have." [5]The messengers came again and said: "Thus says Ben-hadad: I sent to you, saying, 'Deliver to me your silver and gold, your wives and children'; [6]nevertheless I will send my servants to you tomorrow about this time, and they shall search your house and the houses of your servants, and lay hands on whatever pleases them,[a] and take it away."

7Then the king of Israel called all the elders of the land, and said, "Look now! See how this man is seeking trouble; for he sent to me for my wives, my children, my silver, and my gold; and I did not refuse him." [8]Then all the elders and all the people said to him, "Do not listen or consent." [9]So he said to the messengers of Ben-hadad, "Tell my lord the king: All that you first demanded of your servant I will do; but this thing I cannot do." The messengers left and brought him word again. [10]Ben-hadad sent to him and said, "The gods do so to me, and more also, if the dust of Samaria will provide a handful for each of the people who follow me." [11]The king of Israel answered, "Tell him: One who puts on armor should not brag like one who takes it off." [12]When Ben-hadad heard this message—now he had been drinking with the kings in the booths—he said to his men, "Take your positions!" And they took their positions against the city.

[a] Gk Syr Vg: Heb *you*

COMMENTARY

The story begins with the naked aggression of Ben-hadad of Aram, who led a coalition of foreign rulers against Samaria. At first, he seems to demand a declaration of submission from Ahab. At least that is how Ahab chooses to interpret the demand, and he concedes to it. Ben-hadad, however, is not satisfied with that. Although it is unclear in the initial command (v. 3), Ben-hadad insists that he had asked Ahab to deliver the personal tribute (v. 5). Indeed, he expands his demand now to include freedom for his representatives to enter the capital to plunder it at will.

Ahab consults with the elders of the land and receives popular support. With that, he reiterates his willingness to give a personal tribute but asserts that he cannot comply with the amended demand. Already looking for any pretext to invade Israel, Ben-hadad swears that he will so devastate Samaria that when he is finished there will not even be enough dust in the city for his troops to bring home a handful each (v. 10). Ahab retorts

(v. 11), citing a proverb that says essentially that one who is only getting dressed for combat (lit., "one who girds") should not boast like one who is removing the battle gear.[70] In other words, one must not presume to know the results of the battle. Or, as we might say in contemporary parlance, "It ain't over until it's over!" Thereupon, Ben-hadad orders the Aramean troops to prepare for battle. (See Reflections at 20:35-43.)

70. For the idioms used here, see 1 Sam 17:39; Isa 45:1.

1 Kings 20:13-34, How Quickly the Tide Turns

NIV

13Meanwhile a prophet came to Ahab king of Israel and announced, "This is what the LORD says: 'Do you see this vast army? I will give it into your hand today, and then you will know that I am the LORD.'"

14"But who will do this?" asked Ahab.

The prophet replied, "This is what the LORD says: 'The young officers of the provincial commanders will do it.'"

"And who will start the battle?" he asked.

The prophet answered, "You will."

15So Ahab summoned the young officers of the provincial commanders, 232 men. Then he assembled the rest of the Israelites, 7,000 in all. 16They set out at noon while Ben-Hadad and the 32 kings allied with him were in their tents getting drunk. 17The young officers of the provincial commanders went out first.

Now Ben-Hadad had dispatched scouts, who reported, "Men are advancing from Samaria."

18He said, "If they have come out for peace, take them alive; if they have come out for war, take them alive."

19The young officers of the provincial commanders marched out of the city with the army behind them 20and each one struck down his opponent. At that, the Arameans fled, with the Israelites in pursuit. But Ben-Hadad king of Aram escaped on horseback with some of his horsemen. 21The king of Israel advanced and overpowered the horses and chariots and inflicted heavy losses on the Arameans.

22Afterward, the prophet came to the king of Israel and said, "Strengthen your position and see what must be done, because next spring the king of Aram will attack you again."

23Meanwhile, the officials of the king of Aram advised him, "Their gods are gods of the hills. That is why they were too strong for us. But if

NRSV

13Then a certain prophet came up to King Ahab of Israel and said, "Thus says the LORD, Have you seen all this great multitude? Look, I will give it into your hand today; and you shall know that I am the LORD." 14Ahab said, "By whom?" He said, "Thus says the LORD, By the young men who serve the district governors." Then he said, "Who shall begin the battle?" He answered, "You." 15Then he mustered the young men who served the district governors, two hundred thirty-two; after them he mustered all the people of Israel, seven thousand.

16They went out at noon, while Ben-hadad was drinking himself drunk in the booths, he and the thirty-two kings allied with him. 17The young men who served the district governors went out first. Ben-hadad had sent out scouts,[a] and they reported to him, "Men have come out from Samaria." 18He said, "If they have come out for peace, take them alive; if they have come out for war, take them alive."

19But these had already come out of the city: the young men who served the district governors, and the army that followed them. 20Each killed his man; the Arameans fled and Israel pursued them, but King Ben-hadad of Aram escaped on a horse with the cavalry. 21The king of Israel went out, attacked the horses and chariots, and defeated the Arameans with a great slaughter.

22Then the prophet approached the king of Israel and said to him, "Come, strengthen yourself, and consider well what you have to do; for in the spring the king of Aram will come up against you."

23The servants of the king of Aram said to him, "Their gods are gods of the hills, and so they were stronger than we; but let us fight against them in the plain, and surely we shall be stronger than

[a] Heb lacks *scouts*

NIV

we fight them on the plains, surely we will be stronger than they. 24Do this: Remove all the kings from their commands and replace them with other officers. 25You must also raise an army like the one you lost—horse for horse and chariot for chariot—so we can fight Israel on the plains. Then surely we will be stronger than they." He agreed with them and acted accordingly.

26The next spring Ben-Hadad mustered the Arameans and went up to Aphek to fight against Israel. 27When the Israelites were also mustered and given provisions, they marched out to meet them. The Israelites camped opposite them like two small flocks of goats, while the Arameans covered the countryside.

28The man of God came up and told the king of Israel, "This is what the LORD says: 'Because the Arameans think the LORD is a god of the hills and not a god of the valleys, I will deliver this vast army into your hands, and you will know that I am the LORD.'"

29For seven days they camped opposite each other, and on the seventh day the battle was joined. The Israelites inflicted a hundred thousand casualties on the Aramean foot soldiers in one day. 30The rest of them escaped to the city of Aphek, where the wall collapsed on twenty-seven thousand of them. And Ben-Hadad fled to the city and hid in an inner room.

31His officials said to him, "Look, we have heard that the kings of the house of Israel are merciful. Let us go to the king of Israel with sackcloth around our waists and ropes around our heads. Perhaps he will spare your life."

32Wearing sackcloth around their waists and ropes around their heads, they went to the king of Israel and said, "Your servant Ben-Hadad says: 'Please let me live.'"

The king answered, "Is he still alive? He is my brother."

33The men took this as a good sign and were quick to pick up his word. "Yes, your brother Ben-Hadad!" they said.

"Go and get him," the king said. When Ben-Hadad came out, Ahab had him come up into his chariot.

34"I will return the cities my father took from your father," Ben-Hadad offered. "You may set up

NRSV

they. 24Also do this: remove the kings, each from his post, and put commanders in place of them; 25and muster an army like the army that you have lost, horse for horse, and chariot for chariot; then we will fight against them in the plain, and surely we shall be stronger than they." He heeded their voice, and did so.

26In the spring Ben-hadad mustered the Arameans and went up to Aphek to fight against Israel. 27After the Israelites had been mustered and provisioned, they went out to engage them; the people of Israel encamped opposite them like two little flocks of goats, while the Arameans filled the country. 28A man of God approached and said to the king of Israel, "Thus says the LORD: Because the Arameans have said, 'The LORD is a god of the hills but he is not a god of the valleys,' therefore I will give all this great multitude into your hand, and you shall know that I am the LORD." 29They encamped opposite one another seven days. Then on the seventh day the battle began; the Israelites killed one hundred thousand Aramean foot soldiers in one day. 30The rest fled into the city of Aphek; and the wall fell on twenty-seven thousand men that were left.

Ben-hadad also fled, and entered the city to hide. 31His servants said to him, "Look, we have heard that the kings of the house of Israel are merciful kings; let us put sackcloth around our waists and ropes on our heads, and go out to the king of Israel; perhaps he will spare your life." 32So they tied sackcloth around their waists, put ropes on their heads, went to the king of Israel, and said, "Your servant Ben-hadad says, 'Please let me live.'" And he said, "Is he still alive? He is my brother." 33Now the men were watching for an omen; they quickly took it up from him and said, "Yes, Ben-hadad is your brother." Then he said, "Go and bring him." So Ben-hadad came out to him; and he had him come up into the chariot. 34Ben-hadad[a] said to him, "I will restore the towns that my father took from your father; and you may establish bazaars for yourself in Damascus, as my father did in Samaria." The king of Israel responded,[b] "I will let you go on those terms." So he made a treaty with him and let him go.

[a] Heb *He* [b] Heb lacks *The king of Israel responded*

NIV

your own market areas in Damascus, as my father did in Samaria."

⌊Ahab said,⌋ "On the basis of a treaty I will set you free." So he made a treaty with him, and let him go.

COMMENTARY

20:13-21. An unnamed prophet—apparently one of the "seven thousand" who remain loyal to the Lord (see 19:18)—comes to Ahab with an oracle. The Lord will deliver the vast Aramean army into the hand of Ahab as a self-revelatory act, says the prophet. Indeed, the promise "that you may know that I am the LORD" echoes similar promises given by God in connection with the exodus (Exod 6:6-7; 7:17; 10:2; 16:12). Ahab does not dispute the theological basis of the promise of deliverance, but he seems most interested in the pragmatic questions of strategy: Who will be the key players, and who will direct the battle? Ahab asks, literally, "Who will bind the battle?" The meaning of the idiom is, unfortunately, not clarified by its only other occurrence, in 2 Chr 20:3. The NRSV and the NIV both take it to mean "to begin the battle," but the idiom may simply refer to the control of battle strategy.

Although the Israelites attack in broad daylight ("at noon"), they still catch the enemy in a drunken stupor. Moreover, despite advance warning, Ben-hadad apparently does not have any strategy and merely gives a vague order to take the attackers alive (v. 18). The result is a rout of the Arameans, and Ben-hadad himself has to flee.

20:22-25. The prophet urges Ahab to strengthen his position and to strategize carefully because the Arameans will attack again. Meanwhile, Ben-hadad also gets advice from his counselors. They suggest to him that the coalition army lost the battle because Israel's "gods are gods of the hills" (v. 23). So they propose that the next battle be fought in the plain where the Arameans would presumably be more at home. They also urge that the conglomeration of kings in the coalition be replaced by commissioned officers (lit., "governors"), thus revealing the coalition to be the sham that it is. Ben-hadad should, of course, rebuild his army before going into battle again.

Military strategists will no doubt agree that the recommendations make perfect sense. The point about the advantage of fighting the Israelites in the plain instead of in the hill country is sound and probably well known in regional military history (see Josh 17:16-18; Judg 1:19). The problem, as the narrator sees it, is that the issue is framed in ignorant theological terms. The Aramean advisers comically presume that Israel is supported by gods whose power is geographically defined. For the narrator, this is no mere battle for the kings. It is the Lord's holy war.

20:26-30a. As the prophet predicted (v. 22), the Arameans attack again. This time, the battle takes place at Aphek. There are a number of places known as Aphek in the Hebrew Bible. Most notable is a site on the plain of Philistia, where the Philistines defeated the Israelites and carried away the ark of the covenant as a trophy, an emblem of their god's victory over the God of Israel (1 Sam 4:1-11). This time, however, there will be no victory for Israel's enemy, even though the Israelites are significantly outnumbered (v. 27). A man of God—another one of those who have not bent their knees to Baal—delivers another oracle of the Lord that repeats the divine promise in the beginning and its theological rationale: the self-disclosure of the Lord. Accordingly, the Arameans are roundly defeated; their troops are slaughtered, and those who escape into the city are killed by a collapsing wall. The implication is that the wall falls by divine will and so 27,000 are killed thereby. The collapsing of the wall in connection with a battle that is fought after a seven-day waiting period (v. 29) reminds one of the wall of Jericho, which miraculously fell because the Lord was fighting for Israel (Josh

6:15-27). This is an important clue that the narrator sees this as a holy war, a battle in which the Lord fights.

20:30b-34. Once again, Ben-hadad is able to escape. His advisers suggest that they go to Ahab with symbols of surrender: sackcloth around their waists, a sign of sorrow, and a rope around their heads, perhaps to symbolize captivity. The story faintly echoes the ploy of the Gibeonites in the time of the conquest, who tricked the Israelites into sparing them from slaughter and entering into a treaty with them instead (Josh 9:1-27). In any case, when Ahab learns that Ben-hadad is alive, he is exceedingly magnanimous. Whereas Ben-hadad refers to himself as "your servant," Ahab is quick to come to terms with him as a peer ("my brother"; cf. 9:13). The Israelite king brings Ben-hadad up on a chariot (lit., "caused him to go up on a chariot") and makes a treaty with him. In political and economic terms, Ahab's deal is sagacious: He gets his towns restored and gains trading privileges for Israel in Damascus, one of the most important trading centers in the ancient Near East.

Despite the negative portrayal of Ahab in chaps. 16–18, we here find a picture of Ahab as a shrewd politician. In practical terms, he has managed the entire foreign-policy crisis remarkably well. Faced with a demand for personal tribute from his enemy, he was willing to concede. Yet, when the demands escalated unreasonably, he did not yield. Rather, he consulted with the elders and gained popular backing for resistance. Still, he tried to keep the diplomatic solution alive. He sent word that he was willing to give what he could, but steadfastly refused to give an unconditional surrender. Indeed, in contrast to the pompous and impulsive Ben-hadad, Ahab is the model of a judicious king. He is, moreover, a pragmatic strategist. He listened to the advice of others, but he quickly cut to the chase to establish his plan of action. Then, when he is finally victorious, he looks ahead. Instead of annihilating his enemy, he makes a deal that brings material advantages for his country. The portrayal of Ahab in the chapter thus far is positive. (See Reflections at 20:35-43.)

1 Kings 20:35-43, Assessment of Ahab's Performance

NIV

35By the word of the LORD one of the sons of the prophets said to his companion, "Strike me with your weapon," but the man refused.

36So the prophet said, "Because you have not obeyed the LORD, as soon as you leave me a lion will kill you." And after the man went away, a lion found him and killed him.

37The prophet found another man and said, "Strike me, please." So the man struck him and wounded him. 38Then the prophet went and stood by the road waiting for the king. He disguised himself with his headband down over his eyes. 39As the king passed by, the prophet called out to him, "Your servant went into the thick of the battle, and someone came to me with a captive and said, 'Guard this man. If he is missing, it will be your life for his life, or you must pay a talent[a] of silver.' 40While your servant was busy here and there, the man disappeared."

[a] *39* That is, about 75 pounds (about 34 kilograms)

NRSV

35At the command of the LORD a certain member of a company of prophets[a] said to another, "Strike me!" But the man refused to strike him.
36Then he said to him, "Because you have not obeyed the voice of the LORD, as soon as you have left me, a lion will kill you." And when he had left him, a lion met him and killed him. 37Then
he found another man and said, "Strike me!" So the man hit him, striking and wounding him.
38Then the prophet departed, and waited for the king along the road, disguising himself with a bandage over his eyes. 39As the king passed by,
he cried to the king and said, "Your servant went out into the thick of the battle; then a soldier turned and brought a man to me, and said, 'Guard this man; if he is missing, your life shall be given for his life, or else you shall pay a talent of silver.'
40While your servant was busy here and there, he was gone." The king of Israel said to him, "So

[a] Heb *of the sons of the prophets*

NIV

"That is your sentence," the king of Israel said. "You have pronounced it yourself."

41Then the prophet quickly removed the headband from his eyes, and the king of Israel recognized him as one of the prophets. 42He said to the king, "This is what the LORD says: 'You have set free a man I had determined should die.[a] Therefore it is your life for his life, your people for his people.'" 43Sullen and angry, the king of Israel went to his palace in Samaria.

a *42* The Hebrew term refers to the irrevocable giving over of things or persons to the LORD, often by totally destroying them.

NRSV

shall your judgment be; you yourself have decided it." 41Then he quickly took the bandage away from his eyes. The king of Israel recognized him as one of the prophets. 42Then he said to him, "Thus says the LORD, 'Because you have let the man go whom I had devoted to destruction, therefore your life shall be for his life, and your people for his people.'" 43The king of Israel set out toward home, resentful and sullen, and came to Samaria.

COMMENTARY

Following the apparently glowing account of Ahab's leadership are a couple of related prophetic episodes that put Ahab in perspective. The first of these (vv. 35-36) is enigmatic, and its meaning is unclear until one gets to the end of the second episode (vv. 37-43).

Yet another unknown prophetic figure, a member of a guild of prophets (lit., "sons of prophets"), approaches a colleague at the command of the Lord with a strange request to be attacked. When that colleague declines to do so, the first prophet pronounces a death sentence upon him for disobeying the Lord's command, promising him a fate reminiscent of the unnamed man of God who was killed for what seems like very reasonable and faithful conduct (13:11-32): A lion will attack him. Accordingly, the prophecy comes to pass.

The man who had received the command of the Lord then approaches a second colleague, who does as he is told: He strikes and wounds the prophet. The prophet then disguises himself as a wounded soldier. He waits at the roadside until he sees Ahab and then approaches him with a petition, something every citizen has the right to do (see 3:16-28; 2 Sam 14:1-20; 2 Kgs 6:26-31; 8:3-6). No doubt Ahab thinks that this is one of the soldiers who fought with him in his victory over the Arameans. The "soldier" claims that he was in the thick of battle when he was approached by a colleague to guard a prisoner, likely one seized as personal booty of the captor. It was stipulated that if the prisoner were missing, the "soldier" would be killed or pay an exorbitant cash penalty.[71] While the "soldier" was "busy here and there," the prisoner disappears. The "soldier" implies that the loss was excusable, since he was in the midst of a battle and busy with other things.

The case seems straightforward to Ahab, who thinks that the "soldier" already knows the answer: The "soldier" deserves whatever punishment has been stipulated because he understood full well what he was supposed to do. Thereupon, the prophet removes his disguise and the king recognizes him for who he is, suggesting that there must have been some identifying marks of prophetic authority on the prophet's person. Like the prophet Nathan, who told the parable of the unfairly appropriated ewe (meaning Bathsheba) to condemn David (2 Sam 12:1-15), and like the wise woman of Tekoa, who tricked David into sparing Absalom's life (2 Sam 14:4-20), the prophet now informs the king that the parable was about him. The prophet proclaims the Lord's judgment on Ahab for his release of Ben-hadad, contrary to the custom of the ban, whereby all persons and property seized in a holy war were to be utterly destroyed (see Deut 7:2; 20:16-18; 1 Sam 15:1-35). Ahab is condemned by his own words, for he did not realize that the "soldier" was a cipher for himself. Only Ben-hadad did not escape on his own; Ahab had released him,

71. A talent of silver would be about a hundred times the average price of a slave. Such a penalty on a poor soldier, then, would be tantamount to a death sentence, for he would surely be enslaved for life.

even though it was not within his authority to do so. The battle was the Lord's, and Ben-hadad was reserved for the Lord. Ahab and, along with him, his people are condemned. Elijah was correct to say that it was Ahab who brought trouble to Israel. Like Achan, a troubler from an earlier time (Joshua 7), Ahab violated the ban and, in doing so, has brought condemnation upon not only himself but his people as well.

The meaning of the strange episode of vv. 35-36 is now clarified. Like the story of the man of God who was tricked into disobeying the Lord (13:11-32), the current story makes the point that there is no excuse for disobeying the Lord's command. Like the wounded "soldier," Ahab is not excused because of his preoccupation with the matters of war or of the state. Death is his punishment for disobedience to the Lord.

REFLECTIONS

Modern readers will no doubt read the story in this chapter with much sympathy for Ahab. By most criteria of leadership, he would be judged an able king. He may even be admired for the way he stood up to a vain foreign dictator and aggressor. Ahab was diplomatic and courageous under duress, and he is magnanimous in victory. What is more, his deal with his erstwhile enemy allowed him to open trade with that country, thus ensuring new opportunities of economic prosperity for his nation. Were a modern leader to have the kind of foreign policy successes Ahab achieved, one might be inclined to overlook his or her minor offenses. If the country is strong and the economy is sound, we are content to overlook the personal flaws and excusable infractions of our leaders. Yet, Ahab is condemned for what seems to us like a very humane and farsighted deed: the sparing of his enemy.

The notion of the ban that is associated with the assumptions of holy war is difficult for us to understand today. It is one of those regulations in the Bible to which we must say no. Yet, this passage of Scripture warns against our tendency to place pragmatic considerations ahead of a right relationship with God. It also warns us against making excuses for shunning our responsibility to the Lord—against claiming that we are too "busy here and there," too preoccupied with matters that seem more pressing than do matters of faith.

1 KINGS 21:1-29, AHAB'S DOMESTIC POLICY

OVERVIEW

The preceding chapter concerns Ahab's handling of a particular foreign-policy crisis. The present chapter concerns an incident that illustrates his performance in the domestic arena. Taken together, both chapters show him to be an unacceptable king according to the standards of deuteronomic law. Accordingly, then, this chapter anticipates Ahab's death (vv. 19, 21-24; see also 20:41-42).

Most scholars agree that the story of the judicial murder of Naboth (vv. 1*b*-14) must have originally circulated independently. Its artificial placement in its present context is evident from the presence of the obvious redactional link to the preceding material ("after these events") in addition to the circumstantial introduction ("Naboth the Jezreelite had a vineyard in Jezreel"). Some would also argue that the story as a whole fits better in a later period, while others speculate that there may have been different versions of the story that are conflated in the present account. These and other historical-critical issues, however, need not detain us in the necessary task of interpreting the passage in its present form and in its larger literary context.

The literary unit may be divided into two halves. The first half (vv. 1-16) outlines the story in considerable detail; the second half (vv. 17-29) provides the prophetic perspective on the offense.

1 Kings 21:1-16, Ahab Takes Possession of Naboth's Vineyard

NIV

21 Some time later there was an incident involving a vineyard belonging to Naboth the Jezreelite. The vineyard was in Jezreel, close to the palace of Ahab king of Samaria. 2Ahab said to Naboth, "Let me have your vineyard to use for a vegetable garden, since it is close to my palace. In exchange I will give you a better vineyard or, if you prefer, I will pay you whatever it is worth."

3But Naboth replied, "The LORD forbid that I should give you the inheritance of my fathers."

4So Ahab went home, sullen and angry because Naboth the Jezreelite had said, "I will not give you the inheritance of my fathers." He lay on his bed sulking and refused to eat.

5His wife Jezebel came in and asked him, "Why are you so sullen? Why won't you eat?"

6He answered her, "Because I said to Naboth the Jezreelite, 'Sell me your vineyard; or if you prefer, I will give you another vineyard in its place.' But he said, 'I will not give you my vineyard.' "

7Jezebel his wife said, "Is this how you act as king over Israel? Get up and eat! Cheer up. I'll get you the vineyard of Naboth the Jezreelite."

8So she wrote letters in Ahab's name, placed his seal on them, and sent them to the elders and nobles who lived in Naboth's city with him. 9In those letters she wrote:

> "Proclaim a day of fasting and seat Naboth in a prominent place among the people. 10But seat two scoundrels opposite him and have them testify that he has cursed both God and the king. Then take him out and stone him to death."

11So the elders and nobles who lived in Naboth's city did as Jezebel directed in the letters she had written to them. 12They proclaimed a fast and seated Naboth in a prominent place among the people. 13Then two scoundrels came and sat opposite him and brought charges against Naboth before the people, saying, "Naboth has cursed both God and the king." So they took him outside

NRSV

21 Later the following events took place: Naboth the Jezreelite had a vineyard in Jezreel, beside the palace of King Ahab of Samaria. 2And Ahab said to Naboth, "Give me your vineyard, so that I may have it for a vegetable garden, because it is near my house; I will give you a better vineyard for it; or, if it seems good to you, I will give you its value in money." 3But Naboth said to Ahab, "The LORD forbid that I should give you my ancestral inheritance." 4Ahab went home resentful and sullen because of what Naboth the Jezreelite had said to him; for he had said, "I will not give you my ancestral inheritance." He lay down on his bed, turned away his face, and would not eat.

5His wife Jezebel came to him and said, "Why are you so depressed that you will not eat?" 6He said to her, "Because I spoke to Naboth the Jezreelite and said to him, 'Give me your vineyard for money; or else, if you prefer, I will give you another vineyard for it'; but he answered, 'I will not give you my vineyard.' " 7His wife Jezebel said to him, "Do you now govern Israel? Get up, eat some food, and be cheerful; I will give you the vineyard of Naboth the Jezreelite."

8So she wrote letters in Ahab's name and sealed them with his seal; she sent the letters to the elders and the nobles who lived with Naboth in his city. 9She wrote in the letters, "Proclaim a fast, and seat Naboth at the head of the assembly; 10seat two scoundrels opposite him, and have them bring a charge against him, saying, 'You have cursed God and the king.' Then take him out, and stone him to death." 11The men of his city, the elders and the nobles who lived in his city, did as Jezebel had sent word to them. Just as it was written in the letters that she had sent to them, 12they proclaimed a fast and seated Naboth at the head of the assembly. 13The two scoundrels came in and sat opposite him; and the scoundrels brought a charge against Naboth, in the presence of the people, saying, "Naboth

NIV

the city and stoned him to death. 14Then they
sent word to Jezebel: "Naboth has been stoned
and is dead."
15As soon as Jezebel heard that Naboth had
been stoned to death, she said to Ahab, "Get up
and take possession of the vineyard of Naboth the
Jezreelite that he refused to sell you. He is no
longer alive, but dead." 16When Ahab heard that
Naboth was dead, he got up and went down to
take possession of Naboth's vineyard.

NRSV

cursed God and the king." So they took him
outside the city, and stoned him to death. 14Then
they sent to Jezebel, saying, "Naboth has been
stoned; he is dead."
15As soon as Jezebel heard that Naboth had
been stoned and was dead, Jezebel said to Ahab,
"Go, take possession of the vineyard of Naboth
the Jezreelite, which he refused to give you for
money; for Naboth is not alive, but dead." 16As
soon as Ahab heard that Naboth was dead, Ahab
set out to go down to the vineyard of Naboth the
Jezreelite, to take possession of it.

COMMENTARY

21:1-2. The Hebrew of v. 1 is awkward. It reads literally: "It came to pass after these events, Naboth the Jezreelite had a vineyard in Jezreel." This may suggest that the story originally circulated independently, introduced by the words "Naboth the Jezreelite had a vineyard in Jezreel" (cf. the introduction of the Song of the Vineyard in Isa 5:1*b,* "My beloved had a vineyard on a very fertile hill"). That story has been appropriated by the narrator in this particular context and placed temporally after the events just presented.[72]

At the end of chap. 20, Ahab is said to have returned home to Samaria, "resentful and sullen" (20:43). Here, too, he is called "King of Samaria" (v. 1) and later is said to return home "resentful and sullen" (v. 4). Whatever the provenance, the narrator apparently wants the reader to think of the preceding events when reading this story.

Although Ahab has returned home to Samaria (20:43), he is thinking about a piece of real estate adjacent to his winter palace in Jezreel. Its considerably lower elevation makes Jezreel a warmer location than Samaria and, hence, a suitable site for a winter palace. The narrator refers to him as "King of Samaria," an unusual designation (found elsewhere only in 2 Kgs 1:3), perhaps to emphasize that his primary residence is in that city or to allude to the fact that Samaria was acquired as crown property only a generation earlier and has no Israelite tradition associated with it (see 16:23-24). In contrast, the desired property in Jezreel is owned by a local, "Naboth the Jezreelite."

Ahab wants to acquire the property in order to plant a vegetable garden because it is adjacent to his seasonal residence. He already has a palace in Samaria and one in Jezreel, but now he covets additional property (see Isa 5:8; Mic 2:1-2). Yet, the narrator may not merely have Ahab's covetousness in mind. He tells us that Ahab intends to convert the vineyard into a "vegetable garden" (גן ירק *gan yārāq*), using an expression that occurs only one other time in the Hebrew Bible, in Deut 11:10. That passage contrasts the land that God has promised Israel's ancestors with the land of Egypt, where people have to depend on irrigation in order to grow a vegetable garden, whereas the promised land would be watered by rain from the sky. Moreover, elsewhere in Deuteronomy the promised land is described as a place where vineyards thrive naturally (Deut 6:10-12; 8:8-10). It is not surprising, therefore, that vineyards are often viewed in the Bible as a sign of God's blessings (Hos 2:15) and that Israel is sometimes depicted through the metaphor of a vineyard or a vine (Isa 3:13-15; 5:1-7; Jer 2:21; 12:10; Ezek 19:10-14; Hos 10:1). The proposed conversion of the vineyard into a vegetable garden, then, is ominous. It signals that there may be more at stake than a private real estate transaction. Indeed, this story is especially poignant when one recalls that the promised land is regarded as an inheritance given by the Lord (see, e.g., Exod 15:17;

72. That is, assuming the Hebrew tradition. The Greek text places the story after chapter 19 and before the account of the war with Aram.

32:13; Lev 20:2), and that portions of that land are but portions of this divinely given inheritance (Num 34:1-29; 35:8). Moreover, the term for Ahab's seizure of the land, ירשׁ (*yāraš*, "take possession," vv. 15-16, 18), is the term used for Israel's possessing of the inheritance given by the Lord (Lev 20:24; Num 33:53; 35:2, 8; Deut 1:39).

21:3-4. Ahab's offer seems fair enough. He gives Naboth a choice of a better vineyard or a fair market price for the property. Naboth declines the offer: "the LORD forbid!" What he utters here is not a belligerent or indignant exclamation, however. The Hebrew expression means something like, "It is profanation for me because of the LORD!" The vineyard, Naboth says, is an ancestral inheritance. Israelite laws stipulate that ancestral estates should remain within the family or the clan; these rights are generally inalienable (Num 27:8-11; 36:1-12). Such laws were intended to preserve the territorial integrity of the original tribal assignments; that is the reason why, for example, intermarriages were not allowed in Israel, for such compromises would inevitably result in the loss of Israelite property to foreigners. The laws guard against the loss of Israelite territory for economic or other reasons. Thus it is not merely for sentimental reasons that Naboth wants to hold on to his inheritance; it is a religious obligation for him to do so, and it would literally be profanation for him simply to trade it away. As one text puts it, in the mouth of the Lord, "The land shall not be sold in perpetuity, for the land is mine; with me you are but aliens and tenants" (Lev 25:23). One wonders, too, if the mixed marriage of Ahab and Jezebel does not makes the transaction so much more unacceptable. In any case, the land (which ultimately belongs to the Lord) is not for Ahab to take, just as the booty of holy war is not for him to spare. Hence, just as he returned home "resentful and sullen" because of the Lord's condemnation of his release of Ben-hadad (19:43), so also he now returns home "resentful and sullen" (v. 4), having had his offer to purchase Naboth's ancestral estate rejected. Naboth's invocation of the Lord's name makes further negotiations impossible. Ahab sulks and acts rather peevish, but he does not force the issue at this point, probably because he knows that he, even as king, is subject to the law. Not so Jezebel.

21:5-7. It is, perhaps, not a surprise that it is Jezebel, Ahab's Phoenician wife, who comes to the fore in the matter of the vineyard. She was the one who caused him to turn to patronize the Baal cult. It was she who tried to massacre the prophets of the Lord. It was to her that Ahab fled to report on Elijah's annihilation of Baal's prophets, and it was she who threatened Elijah's life. Now she mocks Ahab for not exercising his royal power, which suggests that she has no knowledge of or regard for the sort of constraints that Israelite law places on the king (Deut 17:14-20). So she arrogantly promises that she herself will give him the vineyard, as if it is within her rights to do so.

21:8-14. Jezebel literally takes over Ahab's royal authority. She writes letters in his name and seals them with his seal, sending them to elders and nobles who live with Naboth in his city—that is, the local leadership, charging them to proclaim a fast. In ancient Israel, a public fast may be called when there is a special need, particularly when a community faces a great distress or calamity (see, e.g., Judg 20:26; 1 Sam 14:24; 2 Chr 20:3) or when there is a grave sin that threatens the well-being of the entire community (1 Sam 7:6). The reason for the fast is not given here, but it will soon be clear that the pretext is the fabricated offenses of Naboth, which will be "exposed" at the gathering. So she instructs the elders and nobles, the latter perhaps people beholden to the crown for their wealth, to place Naboth in front of the assembly, a prominent place that Naboth probably would think is a mark of honor or indicative of his having a role in the proceedings. Opposite him would sit two "scoundrels" (בני־בליעל *bĕnê-bĕliyyaʿal*), meaning probably people without scruples, for they would commit perjury as witnesses to the trumped-up charges against Naboth. Jezebel is apparently sufficiently acquainted with Israelite law, for she knows that it would require two or three witnesses to corroborate the charges in a trial for a capital offense (Deut 17:6; 19:15). Naboth is to be charged with blasphemy and treason, both of which are subject to the death penalty (see 2:8-9; Lev 24:15-16; 2 Sam 16:9). So he is to be taken outside and stoned to death.

21:15-16. Jezebel's wishes are carried out to the last detail. Naboth is killed, and, the reader learns later, his corpse is left ignominiously unburied (v. 19). Thereupon, she tells Ahab to go and take possession of the vineyard, which he is now able to do, no doubt because there is no one left in Naboth's family to claim the inheritance; according to 2 Kgs 9:26, all the sons of Naboth were killed as well. Ahab, who released a foreign king whom he had defeated in a holy war, has allowed his queen to massacre a family of innocent Israelite citizens. Ben-hadad was not his to spare, but he spared him. Now there is no mercy for the innocent, and Ahab takes possession of a vineyard that is not his to take.

Naboth is only the human victim, the most immediate and obvious victim, of Ahab and Jezebel's malice. In one fell swoop, the very principles of Israelite society have been challenged as well. The office of the king has been usurped by a foreigner and corrupted with the king's acquiescence, if not consent. Neighbor has turned against neighbor. Those who are entrusted with the responsibility of upholding justice have perverted it. A solemn religious ritual becomes a pretext for a sham trial and, indeed, an occasion for perjury and murder. The law is manipulated to perpetrate gross injustice. The avarice of Ahab has led to the deaths of Naboth and his family, but that is by no means the only consequence of it. As one interpreter puts it, "The religious uniqueness of Israel, rooted in covenant and enshrined in law and tradition, is equally assaulted."[73] (See Reflections at 21:17-29.)

73. Jerome T. Walsh, *1 Kings*, Berit Olam (Collegeville, Minn.: Liturgical Press, 1996) 327.

1 Kings 21:17-29, Elijah Brings the Word of the Lord

NIV

17Then the word of the LORD came to Elijah the
Tishbite: 18"Go down to meet Ahab king of Israel,
who rules in Samaria. He is now in Naboth's
vineyard, where he has gone to take possession
of it. 19Say to him, 'This is what the LORD says:
Have you not murdered a man and seized his
property?' Then say to him, 'This is what the LORD
says: In the place where dogs licked up Naboth's
blood, dogs will lick up your blood—yes, yours!' "
20Ahab said to Elijah, "So you have found me,
my enemy!"
"I have found you," he answered, "because you
have sold yourself to do evil in the eyes of the
LORD. 21'I am going to bring disaster on you. I will
consume your descendants and cut off from Ahab
every last male in Israel—slave or free. 22I will
make your house like that of Jeroboam son of
Nebat and that of Baasha son of Ahijah, because
you have provoked me to anger and have caused
Israel to sin.'
23"And also concerning Jezebel the LORD says:
'Dogs will devour Jezebel by the wall of[a] Jezreel.'
24"Dogs will eat those belonging to Ahab who
die in the city, and the birds of the air will feed
on those who die in the country."

[a] *23* Most Hebrew manuscripts; a few Hebrew manuscripts, Vulgate and Syriac (see also 2 Kings 9:26) *the plot of ground at*

NRSV

17Then the word of the LORD came to Elijah
the Tishbite, saying: 18Go down to meet King
Ahab of Israel, who rules[a] in Samaria; he is now
in the vineyard of Naboth, where he has gone to
take possession. 19You shall say to him, "Thus says
the LORD: Have you killed, and also taken possession?" You shall say to him, "Thus says the LORD:
In the place where dogs licked up the blood of
Naboth, dogs will also lick up your blood."
20Ahab said to Elijah, "Have you found me,
O my enemy?" He answered, "I have found you.
Because you have sold yourself to do what is evil
in the sight of the LORD, 21I will bring disaster on
you; I will consume you, and will cut off from
Ahab every male, bond or free, in Israel; 22and I
will make your house like the house of Jeroboam
son of Nebat, and like the house of Baasha son
of Ahijah, because you have provoked me to anger
and have caused Israel to sin. 23Also concerning
Jezebel the LORD said, 'The dogs shall eat Jezebel
within the bounds of Jezreel.' 24Anyone belonging
to Ahab who dies in the city the dogs shall eat;
and anyone of his who dies in the open country
the birds of the air shall eat."
25(Indeed, there was no one like Ahab, who
sold himself to do what was evil in the sight of

[a] Heb *who is*

NIV

[25](There was never a man like Ahab, who sold himself to do evil in the eyes of the LORD, urged on by Jezebel his wife. [26]He behaved in the vilest manner by going after idols, like the Amorites the LORD drove out before Israel.)

[27]When Ahab heard these words, he tore his clothes, put on sackcloth and fasted. He lay in sackcloth and went around meekly.

[28]Then the word of the LORD came to Elijah the Tishbite: [29]"Have you noticed how Ahab has humbled himself before me? Because he has humbled himself, I will not bring this disaster in his day, but I will bring it on his house in the days of his son."

NRSV

the LORD, urged on by his wife Jezebel. [26]He acted most abominably in going after idols, as the Amorites had done, whom the LORD drove out before the Israelites.)

27When Ahab heard those words, he tore his clothes and put sackcloth over his bare flesh; he fasted, lay in the sackcloth, and went about dejectedly. [28]Then the word of the LORD came to Elijah the Tishbite: [29]"Have you seen how Ahab has humbled himself before me? Because he has humbled himself before me, I will not bring the disaster in his days; but in his son's days I will bring the disaster on his house."

COMMENTARY

Elijah, as usual, appears abruptly. It is unclear where he is when he is commanded to "go down" to meet Ahab, but that imperative suggests that Ahab is in Jezreel, which is only some 370 feet above sea level (see v. 18, where Ahab goes down to Jezreel). Accordingly, even though the Hebrew text refers to Ahab as "king of Israel, who is in Samaria," the NRSV and the NIV take it to mean that he is a king "who rules in Samaria." Like the reference to Ahab as "king of Samaria" (v. 1), however, the mention of Samaria may be an allusion to the capital mount as an Omride acquisition with no Israelite tradition. Indeed, the text tells us immediately that the king is in Naboth's vineyard, where he has gone (lit., "gone down") to take possession. Regardless of the indirect way by which Ahab has gone about acquiring the property, he is charged with murdering Naboth and taking possession of another person's property (see Exod 20:13, 17; Deut 5:17, 21). Hence, Elijah proclaims an oracle of doom against Ahab, promising him that he will receive the ignominious fate of Naboth upon his death, an oracle that is fulfilled later (see 22:38).

Even though Jezebel is the main schemer in the story, it is clear that Ahab is complicitous. Hence, when he hears Elijah's words of doom for him, he calls the prophet his enemy who has found him out (v. 20). Except for his initial offer to Naboth and the actual taking of the property, Ahab has been above the fray, allowing—perhaps even subtly manipulating—Jezebel to carry out his will. He is not innocent, however, for he has sold himself.

The reference to the death of Ahab leads the narrator to the stylized proclamation of the end of the dynasty in accordance with curses for the violation of the covenant (vv. 20-24; see also 13:33-34; 14:10-11; 16:1-4). The narrator manages, however, to work in a special word of doom for Jezebel (v. 23). There is no denial of Ahab's personal culpability, but the narrator notes that Jezebel has incited Ahab (cf. Deut 13:7). This assessment of Ahab is similar to the view of Solomon, whose marriage to foreign women caused him to stray from the way of the Lord (11:1-13). For the narrator, the issue boils down to idolatry or, to put the matter in terms of the covenant, disloyalty to the divine sovereign. Ahab has shown that he loves to possess Naboth's property more than he loves the Lord. Ahab's marriage to Jezebel, a devotee of Baal, has led to all this trouble.

At this point, one expects the story to conclude with an account of Ahab's death and how his dynasty comes to an abrupt end. That is not the case, however. Despite his use of the formulaic proclamation of the end of the dynasty, the narrator no doubt knows that Ahab's dynasty did not end with him, but would continue through the reigns of his sons Ahaziah and Jehoram. This delay of the end of Ahab's dynasty, according to the narrator, is a sign of the deity's grace. Surprisingly, Ahab acts penitently (v. 27; see also 2 Kgs 22:11, 19; Jonah 3:6), and that is enough for the Lord to turn back divine judgment, if only for a while.

REFLECTIONS

This passage paints a vivid picture of the abuse of power and social injustice. It tells of how a failed real estate transaction between a powerful king and an ordinary citizen leads to the frame-up of that citizen, a death sentence for him, and the confiscation of his property. Although the story is set in ancient Israel in the time of Ahab, it could be told with equal power and relevance in any period of human history. For those who take the passage as Scripture, this story, as well as the prophetic perspective on it, provides much material for theological reflection.

1. The issue at hand is an attempted business transaction between unequal partners, one who has all kinds of political and economic resources over against one who relies only on tradition and whatever protection society may provide through its legal and religious institutions. This is the kind of struggle that continues to take place today, not just between kings (or their modern equivalents) and their citizens, but also between large corporations and small businesses, powerful nations and nations that have only limited resources. The powerful in every generation will always have advisers who are clever enough to devise technically legal or quasi-legal means to achieve their clients' objectives. This passage lifts up a prophetic word against the manipulation of the legal and religious institutions to achieve such goals. It affirms that these activities do not take place without the notice of God. Ahab is found out, even though he has been mostly passive, allowing others to do the dirty work for him.

2. Chapter 21 is, in a sense, a profound exposition of the tenth commandment, the injunction against coveting something that belongs to another (Exod 20:17; Deut 5:21). We learn here that the problem lies not so much in our private desire to have something that another person has. The danger lies in the intensity of the greed that prompts someone to commit acts of violence against others in order to achieve his or her goals. Social order may be indirectly endangered by covetousness; on account of one individual's avarice, others may be quickly drawn into a web of betrayal and deceit. Moreover, this example shows how easily sin escalates. Covetousness leads quickly to perjury and murder; disregard for the tenth commandment leads to violation of the ninth and the sixth. It is no accident either that the narrator of this passage views Ahab's sin as idolatry—that is, violation of the first and second commandments (v. 26). Covetousness, in other words, is a form of idolatry: It is placing other priorities and desires before God; it is the elevation of material things to the status of gods. We hear the same warning in the New Testament: "Be sure of this, that no fornicator or impure person, or one who is greedy [that is, an idolater], has any inheritance in the kingdom of Christ and of God" (Eph 5:5 NRSV; see also Col 3:5).

3. The conclusion of the chapter (21:27-29) is jarring, but it is theologically profound. Ahab, having already been found out and judged harshly, goes through a ritual that suggests penitence. Given his track record, one might fairly question his motives. Is it a genuine expression of remorse, or is it an attempt to gain some reduction of sentence? Is he expressing sorrow for what he has done, or is he only sorry that he has been found out? God, however, does not second-guess Ahab's motives. Rather, despite the gravity of Ahab's offenses, God is quick to extend grace to the sinner. Ahab does not get off scot-free to be sure, but he is given the benefit of the doubt. This is the way God is: always ready to accept us, no matter how grave our sins may be, when we manifest the slightest will to repent.

1 KINGS 22:1-40, THE END OF AHAB'S REIGN

OVERVIEW

This literary unit, with the concluding regnal summary in vv. 37-40, brings the account of Ahab's reign (begun in 16:29-34) to a close. The present form of the narrative works well as a coherent unit, whatever its sources may have been. The bulk of the story has an almost verbatim parallel account in 2 Chr 18:3-34, which is somewhat surprising because the chronicler generally shows little interest in the affairs of northern kings. The 1 Kings account, however, has the additional chronological notice in vv. 1-2, the reference to Ahab's death as the fulfillment of Elijah's prophecy (vv. 37-38; see also 21:19-20), and the concluding regnal summary (vv. 37-40). The chapter is meant to be read as a part of the larger narrative, extending at least from 16:29.

1 Kings 22:1-5, Ahab Decides to Go to War

NIV

22 For three years there was no war between Aram and Israel. [2]But in the third year Jehoshaphat king of Judah went down to see the king of Israel. [3]The king of Israel had said to his officials, "Don't you know that Ramoth Gilead belongs to us and yet we are doing nothing to retake it from the king of Aram?"

[4]So he asked Jehoshaphat, "Will you go with me to fight against Ramoth Gilead?"

Jehoshaphat replied to the king of Israel, "I am as you are, my people as your people, my horses as your horses." [5]But Jehoshaphat also said to the king of Israel, "First seek the counsel of the LORD."

NRSV

22 For three years Aram and Israel continued without war. [2]But in the third year King Jehoshaphat of Judah came down to the king of Israel. [3]The king of Israel said to his servants, "Do you know that Ramoth-gilead belongs to us, yet we are doing nothing to take it out of the hand of the king of Aram?" [4]He said to Jehoshaphat, "Will you go with me to battle at Ramoth-gilead?" Jehoshaphat replied to the king of Israel, "I am as you are; my people are your people, my horses are your horses."

5But Jehoshaphat also said to the king of Israel, "Inquire first for the word of the LORD."

COMMENTARY

The narrator begins by noting that there was peace between Israel and Aram (Syria) for three years, meaning probably that the peace treaty signed by Ahab and his Aramean counterpart had been effective (20:34). The reader has already been apprised, however, of the fact that the treaty was not sanctioned by God, who, in fact, condemned Ahab for having spared the Aramean king's life and sentenced Ahab to death for that offense (20:42). It is not a surprise to the reader, therefore, to learn that the peace would not last long—only long enough, it seems, to see Ahab further seal his fate through other offenses committed in his own kingdom (21:20-24). Ironically, Ahab is the one who now breaks that peace treaty and initiates hostile action that would lead to the fulfillment of the prophecies of the unnamed prophet in 20:42 and Elijah (21:19-20) regarding his death.

After years at war with Judah (14:30; 15:6-7, 16-22), there is now peace between the two sister nations as well. It was probably Jehoshaphat of Judah who had sued for peace (v. 44), forging a new, though unequal, alliance between Israel and Judah that was sealed by the marriage of Ahab's daughter to Jehoshaphat's son (2 Kgs 8:18, 26; 2 Chr 18:1). The relatively strong position of Ahab over his Judean counterpart is indicated by the subservient role Jehoshaphat plays throughout this narrative. Here we see him appearing before Ahab (v. 2), perhaps having been summoned to hear Ahab's proposal.[74]

Ahab wants to recover from the Arameans the city of Ramoth-gilead in a region of the Transjordan that was probably assigned to Israel when the kingdom was divided in the late tenth century BCE. The city had fallen into Aramean hands at some point, possibly during the reign of Ben-hadad, son of Tabrimmon (15:20); but it had not been returned to Israel as Ahab's peace treaty with Ben-hadad stipulated (20:34). This is clearly Ahab's war to fight (see vv. 4, 6, 11-12, 15), but Jehoshaphat pledges his support, no doubt because he does not have much of a choice in the matter, only urging Ahab to get an oracle from the Lord first, which is standard practice in ancient Israel (see Judg 20:27-28; 1 Sam 14:36-37; 23:1-5; 30:7-8; 2 Sam 5:19). (See Reflections at 22:29-40.)

74. In accordance with the mythopoeic assumption of Jerusalem as being set on the highest mountain, the narrator speaks of Jehoshaphat's going down to Ahab, who is presumably in Samaria.

1 Kings 22:6-12, Ahab Finds Prophetic Consensus

NIV

6So the king of Israel brought together the prophets—about four hundred men—and asked them, "Shall I go to war against Ramoth Gilead, or shall I refrain?"

"Go," they answered, "for the Lord will give it into the king's hand."

7But Jehoshaphat asked, "Is there not a prophet of the LORD here whom we can inquire of?"

8The king of Israel answered Jehoshaphat, "There is still one man through whom we can inquire of the LORD, but I hate him because he never prophesies anything good about me, but always bad. He is Micaiah son of Imlah."

"The king should not say that," Jehoshaphat replied.

9So the king of Israel called one of his officials and said, "Bring Micaiah son of Imlah at once."

10Dressed in their royal robes, the king of Israel and Jehoshaphat king of Judah were sitting on their thrones at the threshing floor by the entrance of the gate of Samaria, with all the prophets prophesying before them.
11Now Zedekiah son of Kenaanah had made iron horns and he declared, "This is what the LORD says: 'With these you will gore the Arameans until they are destroyed.' "

12All the other prophets were prophesying the same thing. "Attack Ramoth Gilead and be victorious," they said, "for the LORD will give it into the king's hand."

NRSV

6Then the king of Israel gathered the prophets together, about four hundred of them, and said to them, "Shall I go to battle against Ramoth-gilead, or shall I refrain?" They said, "Go up; for the LORD will give it into the hand of the king."
7But Jehoshaphat said, "Is there no other prophet of the LORD here of whom we may inquire?"
8The king of Israel said to Jehoshaphat, "There is still one other by whom we may inquire of the LORD, Micaiah son of Imlah; but I hate him, for he never prophesies anything favorable about me, but only disaster." Jehoshaphat said, "Let the king not say such a thing."
9Then the king of Israel summoned an officer and said, "Bring quickly Micaiah son of Imlah."
10Now the king of Israel and King Jehoshaphat of Judah were sitting on their thrones, arrayed in their robes, at the threshing floor at the entrance of the gate of Samaria; and all the prophets were prophesying before them.
11Zedekiah son of Chenaanah made for himself horns of iron, and he said, "Thus says the LORD: With these you shall gore the Arameans until they are destroyed."
12All the prophets were prophesying the same and saying, "Go up to Ramoth-gilead and triumph; the LORD will give it into the hand of the king."

COMMENTARY

Ahab gathers "about four hundred" prophets together (the parallel account has simply "four hundred"; see 2 Chr 18:5). The narrator does not say that they are prophets of the Lord and may, indeed, be implying that they are not. The number 400 is reminiscent of the four hundred prophets of Asherah whom Ahab gathered on Mt. Carmel (18:19-20).[75] Elijah is said to have killed the 450 prophets of Baal (18:22, 40), but nothing is said about the fate of the other four hundred. After Ahab's prophetic advisers encourage him to proceed with the attack,[76] Jehoshaphat asks if there is no prophet of the Lord left who might be consulted, saying, literally, "Is there not here a prophet of the Lord anymore of whom we may inquire?" (v. 7).[77]

Ahab admits that there is still one person left whom he can consult. Taken literally, that claim would be untrue, of course, for we know that Elijah, Elisha, the hundred prophets saved by Obadiah, and other prophets are still around. The reader is probably supposed to think of the previous confrontation between a large contingent of illegitimate prophets and a single prophet of the Lord (see chap. 18). The lone prophet this time is a hitherto unknown Micaiah son of Imlah, and Ahab dislikes him, just as he disliked the other lone prophet who confronted the majority whom Ahab had earlier mustered. Still, with the encouragement of Jehoshaphat, Ahab quickly summons Micaiah.

Meanwhile, the two kings hold court at a "threshing floor" outside the city gates of Samaria, apparently an open area where a public event might be witnessed by a large audience. There, the four hundred prophets prophesy, and a certain prophet named Zedekiah, the son of Chenaanah, performs a prophetic sign-act (cf. Deut 33:17), a dramatization that is supposed to set the fulfillment of a prophecy in motion (see, e.g., 11:29-31; 2 Kgs 13:14-19; Isa 20:1-6; Jer 13:1-7; Ezek 4:1-5:4). The prophecy in this case is victory for Ahab at Ramoth-gilead![78] This message has the concurrence of all the prophets present. (See Reflections at 22:29-40.)

75. Apart from this passage and its parallel (see 2 Chr 18:5), the precise Hebrew idiom for gathering the prophets occurs only in 18:20, in connection with Ahab's assembling of the prophets of Baal and Asherah.

76. The NRSV assumes that the prophets are promising victory from "the LORD" (i.e., יהוה *Yahweh*), but the best Hebrew MSS read אדני (*'ădōnāy*). The parallel account has "God" (2 Chr 18:5).

77. The NRSV's translation ("Is there no other prophet of the LORD here?") suggests that the 400 are prophets of the Lord, but the text is ambiguous—perhaps deliberately so.

78. This time there is no question that the divine name is meant. One interpreter thinks that Ahab's prophets are now acceding to Jehoshaphat's request for an oracle from the Lord. See Jerome T. Walsh, *1 Kings*, Berit Olam (Collegeville, Minn.: Liturgical Press, 1996) 347.

1 Kings 22:13-28, The Lone Voice of Micaiah, Son of Imlah

NIV

13The messenger who had gone to summon Micaiah said to him, "Look, as one man the other prophets are predicting success for the king. Let your word agree with theirs, and speak favorably."

14But Micaiah said, "As surely as the LORD lives, I can tell him only what the LORD tells me."

15When he arrived, the king asked him, "Micaiah, shall we go to war against Ramoth Gilead, or shall I refrain?"

"Attack and be victorious," he answered, "for the LORD will give it into the king's hand."

16The king said to him, "How many times must I make you swear to tell me nothing but the truth in the name of the LORD?"

NRSV

13The messenger who had gone to summon Micaiah said to him, "Look, the words of the prophets with one accord are favorable to the king; let your word be like the word of one of them, and speak favorably."
14But Micaiah said, "As the LORD lives, whatever the LORD says to me, that I will speak."

15When he had come to the king, the king said to him, "Micaiah, shall we go to Ramoth-gilead to battle, or shall we refrain?" He answered him, "Go up and triumph; the LORD will give it into the hand of the king."
16But the king said to him, "How many times must I make you swear to tell me nothing but the truth in the name of

NIV

[17]Then Micaiah answered, "I saw all Israel scattered on the hills like sheep without a shepherd, and the LORD said, 'These people have no master. Let each one go home in peace.' "

[18]The king of Israel said to Jehoshaphat, "Didn't I tell you that he never prophesies anything good about me, but only bad?"

[19]Micaiah continued, "Therefore hear the word of the LORD: I saw the LORD sitting on his throne with all the host of heaven standing around him on his right and on his left. [20]And the LORD said, 'Who will entice Ahab into attacking Ramoth Gilead and going to his death there?'

"One suggested this, and another that. [21]Finally, a spirit came forward, stood before the LORD and said, 'I will entice him.'

[22]" 'By what means?' the LORD asked.

" 'I will go out and be a lying spirit in the mouths of all his prophets,' he said.

" 'You will succeed in enticing him,' said the LORD. 'Go and do it.'

[23]"So now the LORD has put a lying spirit in the mouths of all these prophets of yours. The LORD has decreed disaster for you."

[24]Then Zedekiah son of Kenaanah went up and slapped Micaiah in the face. "Which way did the spirit from[a] the LORD go when he went from me to speak to you?" he asked.

[25]Micaiah replied, "You will find out on the day you go to hide in an inner room."

[26]The king of Israel then ordered, "Take Micaiah and send him back to Amon the ruler of the city and to Joash the king's son [27]and say, 'This is what the king says: Put this fellow in prison and give him nothing but bread and water until I return safely.' "

[28]Micaiah declared, "If you ever return safely, the LORD has not spoken through me." Then he added, "Mark my words, all you people!"

[a] *24* Or *Spirit of*

NRSV

the LORD?" [17]Then Micaiah[a] said, "I saw all Israel scattered on the mountains, like sheep that have no shepherd; and the LORD said, 'These have no master; let each one go home in peace.' " [18]The king of Israel said to Jehoshaphat, "Did I not tell you that he would not prophesy anything favorable about me, but only disaster?"

19Then Micaiah[a] said, "Therefore hear the word of the LORD: I saw the LORD sitting on his throne, with all the host of heaven standing beside him to the right and to the left of him. [20]And the LORD said, 'Who will entice Ahab, so that he may go up and fall at Ramoth-gilead?' Then one said one thing, and another said another, [21]until a spirit came forward and stood before the LORD, saying, 'I will entice him.' [22]'How?' the LORD asked him. He replied, 'I will go out and be a lying spirit in the mouth of all his prophets.' Then the LORD[a] said, 'You are to entice him, and you shall succeed; go out and do it.' [23]So you see, the LORD has put a lying spirit in the mouth of all these your prophets; the LORD has decreed disaster for you."

24Then Zedekiah son of Chenaanah came up to Micaiah, slapped him on the cheek, and said, "Which way did the spirit of the LORD pass from me to speak to you?" [25]Micaiah replied, "You will find out on that day when you go in to hide in an inner chamber." [26]The king of Israel then ordered, "Take Micaiah, and return him to Amon the governor of the city and to Joash the king's son, [27]and say, 'Thus says the king: Put this fellow in prison, and feed him on reduced rations of bread and water until I come in peace.' " [28]Micaiah said, "If you return in peace, the LORD has not spoken by me." And he said, "Hear, you peoples, all of you!"

[a] Heb *he*

COMMENTARY

22:13-18. Pressure is put on Micaiah to go along with the consensus of Ahab's prophets and "speak favorably," but Micaiah promises only to speak what the Lord tells him. When Micaiah is first queried by Ahab, he simply repeats the answer of the majority. The king knows, however, that this is not the truth. He knows this, perhaps, because of the tone and manner of Micaiah's delivery. Or it may be that the king knows all too well that Micaiah would not say anything favorable to him (see v. 8). In any case, Ahab adjures the prophet to speak the truth "in the name of the LORD," something that Micaiah did not do in his initial response. Yet, when Micaiah prophesies disaster in the Lord's name (v. 17), Ahab says it only confirms his impression of Micaiah: that the prophet is always going to be a naysayer as far as Ahab is concerned.

Micaiah is clearly prophesying the demise of Ahab; "mountains" is probably an allusion to Ramoth-Gilead (the name in Hebrew means "the Heights of Gilead"), and "shepherd" is a commonly used metaphor throughout the ancient Near East for kings (see 2 Sam 5:2; Isa 44:28; Jer 23:4; 25:34, 36; Ezek 34:23; 37:24; Zech 13:7). Ahab, however, is not interested in a genuine oracle from the Lord. He accepts only the oracles that are favorable—namely, those that corroborate his intention and support the action that he plans to take. Perhaps he is going through the farce of getting an oracle only for political reasons—to placate his ally, Jehoshaphat, and to convince the populace to follow him, which is probably the reason for the public drama at the threshing floor outside the gates of the capital city.

22:19-25. Micaiah then describes a vision of the Lord sitting enthroned in the celestial court, surrounded by members of the divine council (the "heavenly host"). This vision, which bears some resemblance to the inaugural vision of Isaiah (Isa 6:1-8), authenticates Micaiah's role as a prophet of the Lord. It points to him as a true prophet, for a true prophet is given the opportunity to witness the proceedings in the divine council (Jer 23:18-22). The issue at stake here, as in Jeremiah 23, is the question of true prophecy versus false prophecy.

In Micaiah's vision, the Lord asks for a volunteer from the divine council to go and trick Ahab into going into battle, only to be struck down. One of the members of the council comes forward, proposing to be a "lying spirit" in the mouth of Ahab's prophets in order that they might entice him into going to war (see Jer 20:7; Ezek 14:9; see also 2 Thess 2:11). The volunteer is duly charged with the task by the Lord and is promised success. Micaiah then interprets the vision for Ahab, telling him that the false prophets who give him what he wants to hear are speaking for the lying spirit. When Zedekiah points out through a sarcastic question that it is difficult to prove the validity of one claim over the other (v. 24), Micaiah replies that it will become clear when Zedekiah will have to hide, the imagery being reminiscent of Ben-hadad's hiding to avoid being killed (see 20:30).

22:26-28. Ahab orders Micaiah's arrest and imprisonment, no doubt because his negative utterances undermine Ahab's war efforts. Yet, Ahab apparently wants the prophet alive, perhaps as insurance, in case his plan fails after all. Still, the king expects to return safely. The prophet retorts, however, that Ahab's safe return would prove that Micaiah is a false prophet, which means probably that Micaiah would be killed (see Deut 18:20-22).

1 Kings 22:29-40, Ahab Dies

NIV

[29]So the king of Israel and Jehoshaphat king of Judah went up to Ramoth Gilead. [30]The king of Israel said to Jehoshaphat, "I will enter the battle in disguise, but you wear your royal robes." So the king of Israel disguised himself and went into battle.

[31]Now the king of Aram had ordered his thirty-two chariot commanders, "Do not fight with anyone, small or great, except the king of Israel." [32]When the chariot commanders saw Jehoshaphat,

NRSV

29So the king of Israel and King Jehoshaphat of Judah went up to Ramoth-gilead. [30]The king of Israel said to Jehoshaphat, "I will disguise myself and go into battle, but you wear your robes." So the king of Israel disguised himself and went into battle. [31]Now the king of Aram had commanded the thirty-two captains of his chariots, "Fight with no one small or great, but only with the king of Israel." [32]When the captains of the chariots saw Jehoshaphat, they said, "It is surely the king of

NIV

they thought, "Surely this is the king of Israel."
So they turned to attack him, but when Jehoshaphat cried out, 33the chariot commanders
saw that he was not the king of Israel and stopped
pursuing him.

34But someone drew his bow at random and
hit the king of Israel between the sections of his
armor. The king told his chariot driver, "Wheel
around and get me out of the fighting. I've been
wounded." 35All day long the battle raged, and
the king was propped up in his chariot facing the
Arameans. The blood from his wound ran onto
the floor of the chariot, and that evening he died.
36As the sun was setting, a cry spread through the
army: "Every man to his town; everyone to his
land!"

37So the king died and was brought to Samaria,
and they buried him there. 38They washed the
chariot at a pool in Samaria (where the prostitutes
bathed),[a] and the dogs licked up his blood, as the
word of the LORD had declared.

39As for the other events of Ahab's reign, including all he did, the palace he built and inlaid
with ivory, and the cities he fortified, are they not
written in the book of the annals of the kings of
Israel? 40Ahab rested with his fathers. And Ahaziah his son succeeded him as king.

[a] *38* Or *Samaria and cleaned the weapons*

NRSV

Israel." So they turned to fight against him; and
Jehoshaphat cried out. 33When the captains of the
chariots saw that it was not the king of Israel,
they turned back from pursuing him. 34But a
certain man drew his bow and unknowingly
struck the king of Israel between the scale armor
and the breastplate; so he said to the driver of his
chariot, "Turn around, and carry me out of the
battle, for I am wounded." 35The battle grew hot
that day, and the king was propped up in his
chariot facing the Arameans, until at evening he
died; the blood from the wound had flowed into
the bottom of the chariot. 36Then about sunset a
shout went through the army, "Every man to his
city, and every man to his country!"

37So the king died, and was brought to
Samaria; they buried the king in Samaria. 38They
washed the chariot by the pool of Samaria; the
dogs licked up his blood, and the prostitutes
washed themselves in it,[a] according to the word
of the LORD that he had spoken. 39Now the rest
of the acts of Ahab, and all that he did, and the
ivory house that he built, and all the cities that
he built, are they not written in the Book of the
Annals of the Kings of Israel? 40So Ahab slept with
his ancestors; and his son Ahaziah succeeded him.

[a] Heb lacks *in it*

COMMENTARY

For all his bravado, Ahab seems to know the seriousness of Micaiah's oracle, which supports the predictions of Ahab's death by both the unnamed prophet (20:42) and Elijah (21:20-24). Ahab is determined to carry out his plan, but, as a precautionary measure, he disguises himself and asks Jehoshaphat to put on the royal garb of the Israelite king. Thereby Ahab intends not only to deceive the enemy, but also to thwart the will of the Lord. The narrator tells us that the Arameans focus all their attention on getting Ahab; he is their sole target.

Ahab's deception works initially. The Arameans go after Jehoshaphat, thinking that he is Ahab, but they turn back when they realize that they have been tricked. The Lord, however, is not duped. Someone shoots an arrow, unintentionally striking Ahab, and manages to wound him at one of the few vulnerable spots in his armor. The text does not tell us whether the arrow is shot by an enemy soldier or if it is "friendly fire," only that Ahab is hit by someone. Ahab may be able to deceive his enemies, but he is not able to outwit the Lord after all. One suspects that what seems accidental is in reality an act of God.

Ahab asks to be taken out of the battle, presumably to be treated. The fighting is too intense, however. His soldiers merely prop him up on the chariot facing the enemy to disguise the fact that he has been wounded, and he remains in the chariot that way, bleeding until his death at the end of the day. The incapacitated king does not, of course, provide any leadership, thus fulfilling the oracle of Micaiah in v. 17. The troops are able to return home safely, despite the absence of Ahab's leadership, again fulfilling the prophecy of Micaiah: "These have no masters, let them go home in safety" (v. 17). The Hebrew word בשלום (*bĕšālôm*) may mean "in safety" (so TNK) or "in peace" (so NRSV, NIV). The point is not that they will have peace but that they will return home without hindrance.

The fact that Ahab bled in the chariot for a long time also explains why the chariot is thoroughly soaked with blood, so that dogs could lick it, thus at least partially fulfilling the prophecy of Elijah (21:19; Elijah prophesied that Ahab's blood would be licked by dogs "in the place" where dogs licked up Naboth's blood. If that place refers to Jezreel, then the prophecy is only partially fulfilled). The reference to prostitutes bathing in the blood, perhaps meaning the blood that stains the pool in Samaria, is enigmatic. It seems to refer to an oracle for which there is now no record. The account of Ahab's reign, then, ends in the stereotypical manner, with references to further documentation of Ahab's performance as king and a note about his successor (v. 39).

REFLECTIONS

Chapter 22 is not a passage for anyone who comes to Scripture in search of easy moralistic lessons, for there are none. At the heart of the story is an account of God's initiative in the perpetration of a lie, the divine commissioning of a spirit that intentionally deceives people into self-destructive action. That perspective will not sit easily with the church. Yet, the story must be told and its lessons taught.

1. The first lesson is a negative one. In this story we see just how recalcitrant human beings can be. Here is Ahab, a man who has personally witnessed the manifestation of God's power, who has heard the word of the Lord through several prophets, and, despite his sins, has experienced the grace of God when he expressed penitence. Still, he does not seem to understand what it is that God demands. He has little understanding of the nature of God. He has a personal agenda that he is determined to carry out. So he musters all his resources. He gets his subordinates and allies to do his bidding and does not hesitate to manipulate the religious establishment to support his questionable goals. He ignores what he knows to be the truth and suppresses any voice of dissent. He even tries to thwart God's will by deceit in order to achieve his goal. Ahab is a model of what we can become when we are not attentive to the will of God.

2. The passage, however, acknowledges with remarkable honesty that it is not an easy thing to discern the will of God. Sometimes we are confronted with conflicting truth claims, the veracity of which can be authenticated only in retrospect, when it is too late. Even a "true prophet" (like Micaiah) sometimes speaks untruth. The passage does not provide a direct answer to the implicit question of how one may in practice discern what truth is, but it does warn against equating majority opinion, or even consensus, with truth. There are too many positive-thinking people who give us feel-good messages, proclaiming, "Peace! Peace!" when there is no peace (Jer 6:14). Or there may be some who are all too ready to pander to the powerful. Those who wish to know the will of God cannot simply find the messengers who will confirm their outlook and support their agenda but who will tell it like it is, even if the message is contrary to what we might expect or desire. Indeed, the word of God may not come through the popular majority but through those whom we may regard as troublers or enemies or naysayers. Perhaps we should listen especially carefully when the word makes us uncomfortable.

3. The most profound, if also confounding, theological message in this passage is that God may not fit our preconceived image of unimpeachable goodness. The passage jolts us into the

realization that such a notion of deity, ironically, is too limiting for God. Such a god would be an idol, a god of our own creation. Rather, the passage forces us to deal with a God who is sovereign, a God who is absolutely free to use any means—even those contrary to human reason or standards of morality—in order to bring divine purpose to fulfillment. The God of the Bible is a sovereign deity who oversees all that goes on in the world, darkness as well as light, woe as well as weal (Isa 45:7). The biblical God may harden people's hearts so that they do not respond to God aright (Exod 4:21; 9:12; 10:1, 20, 27; 11:10; 14:8; Deut 2:30; Isa 6:10; Rom 9:18), incite people to do wrong and then condemn them (2 Sam 24:1), deceive people (Jer 4:10), or send lying spirits (2 Thess 2:11). Yet, God's thoughts are not our thoughts, neither are God's ways our ways (Isa 55:8). The sovereign God will use whatever means necessary to bring about divine will—whether in judgment or in salvation.

1 KINGS 22:41-53, JEHOSHAPHAT OF JUDAH AND AHAZIAH OF ISRAEL

OVERVIEW

The remaining verses of 1 Kings concern the reigns of two rulers: Jehoshaphat of Judah (vv. 41-50) and Ahaziah of Israel (vv. 51-53). The account of Jehoshaphat is much shorter than what one finds in the chronicler's version (2 Chronicles 17–21), for the narrator of 1 Kings is not interested in much of the details of royal history, only with the performance of the kings according to the standards set forth in Deuteronomy. The brief account is, in any case, self-contained: It begins and ends with the typical regnal summaries for Judean kings. By contrast, the account of Ahaziah's reign is incomplete. It is, in fact, only the introduction of a longer account that continues through 2 Kgs 1:18.

1 Kings 22:41-50, The Reign of Jehoshaphat of Judah

NIV

[41]Jehoshaphat son of Asa became king of Judah in
the fourth year of Ahab king of Israel. [42]Jehoshaphat
was thirty-five years old when he became king, and
he reigned in Jerusalem twenty-five years. His
mother's name was Azubah daughter of Shilhi. [43]In
everything he walked in the ways of his father Asa
and did not stray from them; he did what was right
in the eyes of the LORD. The high places, however,
were not removed, and the people continued to offer
sacrifices and burn incense there. [44]Jehoshaphat was
also at peace with the king of Israel.

[45]As for the other events of Jehoshaphat's reign,
the things he achieved and his military exploits,
are they not written in the book of the annals of
the kings of Judah? [46]He rid the land of the rest
of the male shrine prostitutes who remained there

NRSV

41Jehoshaphat son of Asa began to reign over
Judah in the fourth year of King Ahab of Israel.
[42]Jehoshaphat was thirty-five years old when he
began to reign, and he reigned twenty-five years
in Jerusalem. His mother's name was Azubah
daughter of Shilhi. [43]He walked in all the way of
his father Asa; he did not turn aside from it, doing
what was right in the sight of the LORD; yet the
high places were not taken away, and the people
still sacrificed and offered incense on the high
places. [44]Jehoshaphat also made peace with the
king of Israel.

45Now the rest of the acts of Jehoshaphat, and
his power that he showed, and how he waged war,
are they not written in the Book of the Annals of
the Kings of Judah? [46]The remnant of the male

NIV

even after the reign of his father Asa. [47]There was then no king in Edom; a deputy ruled.

[48]Now Jehoshaphat built a fleet of trading ships[a] to go to Ophir for gold, but they never set sail—they were wrecked at Ezion Geber. [49]At that time Ahaziah son of Ahab said to Jehoshaphat, "Let my men sail with your men," but Jehoshaphat refused.

[50]Then Jehoshaphat rested with his fathers and was buried with them in the city of David his father. And Jehoram his son succeeded him.

a *48* Hebrew *of ships of Tarshish*

NRSV

temple prostitutes who were still in the land in the days of his father Asa, he exterminated.

47There was no king in Edom; a deputy was king. [48]Jehoshaphat made ships of the Tarshish type to go to Ophir for gold; but they did not go, for the ships were wrecked at Ezion-geber. [49]Then Ahaziah son of Ahab said to Jehoshaphat, "Let my servants go with your servants in the ships," but Jehoshaphat was not willing. [50]Jehoshaphat slept with his ancestors and was buried with his ancestors in the city of his father David; his son Jehoram succeeded him.

COMMENTARY

Jehoshaphat (873–849 BCE) has already been mentioned as the successor to Asa (15:24) and in connection with his alliance with Ahab. Now comes the formal report of his reign, and it is a relatively positive one. He is said to have "walked in all the way of his father Asa," not turning aside from it and doing what was right in the sight of the Lord (v. 43). Yet, the high places (local sanctuaries) were not removed, and people continued to sacrifice and offer incense there. He continued his father's policy of removing the cult prostitutes from the country (15:12).[79] He is also credited with making peace with Israel (v. 44), with the domination of Edom (v. 47), and with engaging in maritime activities (v. 48).

While the report echoes the assessment of Asa (15:9-24), both positively and negatively, it also calls to mind Solomon's reign in many ways. The observation that the king followed the ways of his father faithfully, except for the problem of the local sanctuaries, recalls a similar evaluation of Solomon (3:2-3). The mention of peace with Israel brings to mind the peace that Solomon wrought (4:24; 5:12) and recalls the unity of Israel and Judah under him. Like Solomon, too, Jehoshaphat was able to control Edom and, hence, gain access to the Red Sea port of Ezion-geber (see 9:26-27). Apparently, he also attempted to repeat the maritime successes of Solomon by sending expeditions to find gold in Ophir (9:28; 10:11). Yet, Jehoshaphat was unable to repeat Solomon's successes: His expeditions were aborted because the ships were wrecked at the port of Ezion-geber, and, despite the peace with Israel, he was unwilling to let the Israelites go on his ships. Jehoshaphat, in fact, was not like Solomon in giftedness or achievements. He was like Solomon, however, in that he was an heir to the Davidic throne. He ruled in Jerusalem, the Lord's chosen city, and was buried, like all his Judean predecessors, in the city of "his father David" (v. 50). (See Reflections at 22:51-53.)

79. As in 15:12, we should take the word קדשים (*qĕdēšîm*) as an inclusive term for all cult prostitutes and not just the male ones, as the NRSV and the NIV have it.

1 Kings 22:51-53, The Reign of Ahaziah of Israel

NIV

[51]Ahaziah son of Ahab became king of Israel in Samaria in the seventeenth year of Jehoshaphat king of Judah, and he reigned over Israel two

NRSV

51Ahaziah son of Ahab began to reign over Israel in Samaria in the seventeenth year of King Jehoshaphat of Judah; he reigned two years over

NIV	NRSV
years. 52He did evil in the eyes of the LORD, because he walked in the ways of his father and mother and in the ways of Jeroboam son of Nebat, who caused Israel to sin. 53He served and worshiped Baal and provoked the LORD, the God of Israel, to anger, just as his father had done.	Israel. 52He did what was evil in the sight of the LORD, and walked in the way of his father and mother, and in the way of Jeroboam son of Nebat, who caused Israel to sin. 53He served Baal and worshiped him; he provoked the LORD, the God of Israel, to anger, just as his father had done.

COMMENTARY

Just as Jehoshaphat walked in the ways of his father Asa (v. 43), so also Ahaziah (850–849 BCE) walked in the ways of his father, Ahab, and his mother, Jezebel (v. 52). Moreover, just as Jehoshaphat's reign is associated with those of Solomon and David, so also Ahaziah's reign is linked with Jeroboam's. Jehoshaphat did what was right in the sight of the Lord (v. 43), but Ahaziah did what was evil in the sight of the Lord (v. 52). Finally, Jehoshaphat was buried in the city of David "his father" (v. 50), but Ahaziah provoked the anger of the Lord "just as his father had done" (v. 53).

REFLECTIONS

Most readers of the concluding verses of 1 Kings will no doubt notice the different tones in the brief reports of the two reigns: One is generally positive, the other utterly negative. Jehoshaphat tried to be faithful, while Ahaziah was faithless. One may, of course, point to the importance of faithfulness to the Lord, surely a legitimate lesson to be drawn from the text. Yet, the larger and more important issue is that both kings came short of the Lord's demands. The real difference between the two is that one of them, by God's will alone, was heir to the throne of David. Whatever place Jehoshaphat may have in salvation history, it will not be because of his righteousness, but because of the sovereign will of God.

2 KINGS 1:1-18, AHAZIAH'S APOSTASY

OVERVIEW

The end of 1 Kings (22:51-53) begins the formal account of Ahaziah's reign. That report is continued and completed in this passage, with the stylized regnal summary at the end (vv. 17-18). The story echoes Elijah's encounter with Ahaziah's father, Ahab, on Mt. Carmel (1 Kings 18). Elijah comes into the picture, as before, on account of a summons from on high. As in the previous encounter of prophet and king as well, the initial contact between the two is through intermediaries. Above all, the presence of Elijah on top of a mount echoes the contest on Mt. Carmel, as does the descent of fire from heaven.

2 Kings 1:1, The Rebellion of Moab

NIV

1 After Ahab's death, Moab rebelled against Israel.

NRSV

1 After the death of Ahab, Moab rebelled against Israel.

COMMENTARY

The reference to Moab's rebellion is awkward, for it seems to have nothing to do with the rest of the chapter. Moab, in fact, does not become a factor in the narrative until 3:4-27. It is possible, therefore, that this verse has been misplaced (note the similar notice of Moab's rebellion in 3:5). Yet, it is not impossible to read the reference in its context. The narrator may intend to point to the loss of hegemony over Moab as a consequence of the Israelite king's unfaithfulness (see 1 Kgs 22:51-53). Moab had been subjugated since the time of David (2 Sam 8:12), but now Israel is beginning to lose control of it and will completely do so by the time of Jehoram, who is similarly unfaithful to the Lord (2 Kgs 3:4-27). By contrast, Judah gained influence over Edom in the reign of Jehoshaphat, Ahaziah's contemporary (1 Kgs 22:47).

2 Kings 1:2-4, Ahaziah Turns to Baal-Zebub

NIV

2Now Ahaziah had fallen through the lattice of his upper room in Samaria and injured himself. So he sent messengers, saying to them, "Go and consult Baal-Zebub, the god of Ekron, to see if I will recover from this injury."

3But the angel of the LORD said to Elijah the Tishbite, "Go up and meet the messengers of the king of Samaria and ask them, 'Is it because there is no God in Israel that you are going off to consult Baal-Zebub, the god of Ekron?' 4Therefore this is what the LORD says: 'You will not leave the bed you are lying on. You will certainly die!'" So Elijah went.

NRSV

2Ahaziah had fallen through the lattice in his upper chamber in Samaria, and lay injured; so he sent messengers, telling them, "Go, inquire of Baal-zebub, the god of Ekron, whether I shall recover from this injury." 3But the angel of the LORD said to Elijah the Tishbite, "Get up, go to meet the messengers of the king of Samaria, and say to them, 'Is it because there is no God in Israel that you are going to inquire of Baal-zebub, the god of Ekron?' 4Now therefore thus says the LORD, 'You shall not leave the bed to which you have gone, but you shall surely die.'" So Elijah went.

COMMENTARY

The introduction of the account of Ahaziah's reign (1 Kgs 22:51-53) casts him as a servant and worshiper of Baal, just like his father Ahab (1 Kgs 16:31). Now we see the extent and effect of Ahaziah's apostasy. When he injures himself as a result of a fall, he sends messengers to Ekron to seek an oracle from the local manifestation of Baal, called Baal-Zebub ("Baal the Fly" or, as one might say, "Baal the Pest"),[80] a deliberate distortion by the narrator of the name "Baal-Zebul" ("Baal the Prince"; cf. "Beelzebul" in the NT: Matt 10:25; 12:24, 27; Mark 3:22; Luke 11:15,

80. The Greek translators understood the name to mean "Baal the Fly." In the HB, flies are considered a nuisance (Eccl 10:1; Isa 7:18).

18-19).[81] Ekron is a Philistine town some twenty-two miles west of Jerusalem, so it appears that Ahaziah is going out of his way to seek this god rather than the Lord in Jerusalem.

Like his father, Ahab, Ahaziah is also challenged by Elijah, who, as usual, appears on the scene abruptly. "An angel" (מלאך *mal'āk*) of the Lord tells Elijah to intercept Ahaziah's "messengers" (מלאכים *mal'ākîm*) and deliver a word of judgment for the king through them. (See Reflections at 1:9-18.)

81. This designation of Baal, attested in Ugaritic mythology, is also suggested by the name "Jezebel" (איזבל *'îzebel*).

2 Kings 1:5-8, The Messengers Report Their Encounter

NIV

5When the messengers returned to the king, he asked them, "Why have you come back?"

6"A man came to meet us," they replied. "And he said to us, 'Go back to the king who sent you and tell him, "This is what the LORD says: Is it because there is no God in Israel that you are sending men to consult Baal-Zebub, the god of Ekron? Therefore you will not leave the bed you are lying on. You will certainly die!" ' "

7The king asked them, "What kind of man was it who came to meet you and told you this?"

8They replied, "He was a man with a garment of hair and with a leather belt around his waist."

The king said, "That was Elijah the Tishbite."

NRSV

5The messengers returned to the king, who said to them, "Why have you returned?" 6They answered him, "There came a man to meet us, who said to us, 'Go back to the king who sent you, and say to him: Thus says the LORD: Is it because there is no God in Israel that you are sending to inquire of Baal-zebub, the god of Ekron? Therefore you shall not leave the bed to which you have gone, but shall surely die.' " 7He said to them, "What sort of man was he who came to meet you and told you these things?" 8They answered him, "A hairy man, with a leather belt around his waist." He said, "It is Elijah the Tishbite."

COMMENTARY

Ahaziah's emissaries apparently do not complete their task for him, for they have been turned back by Elijah. They tell the king about their encounter with the prophet, without naming him. Whereas Elijah had asked them why they were going to ask for the oracle in Ekron, they interpret the problem to be Ahaziah's initiative in sending them. That is, of course, a logical conclusion on their part, since doom is pronounced not on them but on the king, an oracle that they duly repeat.

They tell Ahaziah that the man who confronted them was, literally, "a man, a possessor of hair" (איש בעל שער *'îš ba'al śē'ār*) who wore a leather belt. The first description probably alludes to a hairy mantle that may have been a mark of prophetic authority (see Zech 13:4). In any case, Ahaziah immediately recognizes the description as fitting Elijah. (See Reflections at 1:9-18.)

2 Kings 1:9-18, Ahaziah Challenges Elijah

NIV

9Then he sent to Elijah a captain with his company of fifty men. The captain went up to

NRSV

9Then the king sent to him a captain of fifty with his fifty men. He went up to Elijah, who

NIV

Elijah, who was sitting on the top of a hill, and said to him, "Man of God, the king says, 'Come down!'"

10Elijah answered the captain, "If I am a man of God, may fire come down from heaven and consume you and your fifty men!" Then fire fell from heaven and consumed the captain and his men.

11At this the king sent to Elijah another captain with his fifty men. The captain said to him, "Man of God, this is what the king says, 'Come down at once!'"

12"If I am a man of God," Elijah replied, "may fire come down from heaven and consume you and your fifty men!" Then the fire of God fell from heaven and consumed him and his fifty men.

13So the king sent a third captain with his fifty men. This third captain went up and fell on his knees before Elijah. "Man of God," he begged, "please have respect for my life and the lives of these fifty men, your servants! 14See, fire has fallen from heaven and consumed the first two captains and all their men. But now have respect for my life!"

15The angel of the LORD said to Elijah, "Go down with him; do not be afraid of him." So Elijah got up and went down with him to the king.

16He told the king, "This is what the LORD says: Is it because there is no God in Israel for you to consult that you have sent messengers to consult Baal-Zebub, the god of Ekron? Because you have done this, you will never leave the bed you are lying on. You will certainly die!" 17So he died, according to the word of the LORD that Elijah had spoken.

Because Ahaziah had no son, Joram[a] succeeded him as king in the second year of Jehoram son of Jehoshaphat king of Judah. 18As for all the other events of Ahaziah's reign, and what he did, are they not written in the book of the annals of the kings of Israel?

[a] *17* Hebrew *Jehoram,* a variant of *Joram*

NRSV

was sitting on the top of a hill, and said to him, "O man of God, the king says, 'Come down.'" 10But Elijah answered the captain of fifty, "If I am a man of God, let fire come down from heaven and consume you and your fifty." Then fire came down from heaven, and consumed him and his fifty.

11Again the king sent to him another captain of fifty with his fifty. He went up[a] and said to him, "O man of God, this is the king's order: Come down quickly!" 12But Elijah answered them, "If I am a man of God, let fire come down from heaven and consume you and your fifty." Then the fire of God came down from heaven and consumed him and his fifty.

13Again the king sent the captain of a third fifty with his fifty. So the third captain of fifty went up, and came and fell on his knees before Elijah, and entreated him, "O man of God, please let my life, and the life of these fifty servants of yours, be precious in your sight. 14Look, fire came down from heaven and consumed the two former captains of fifty men with their fifties; but now let my life be precious in your sight." 15Then the angel of the LORD said to Elijah, "Go down with him; do not be afraid of him." So he set out and went down with him to the king, 16and said to him, "Thus says the LORD: Because you have sent messengers to inquire of Baal-zebub, the god of Ekron,—is it because there is no God in Israel to inquire of his word?—therefore you shall not leave the bed to which you have gone, but you shall surely die."

17So he died according to the word of the LORD that Elijah had spoken. His brother,[b] Jehoram succeeded him as king in the second year of King Jehoram son of Jehoshaphat of Judah, because Ahaziah had no son. 18Now the rest of the acts of Ahaziah that he did, are they not written in the Book of the Annals of the Kings of Israel?

[a] Gk Compare verses 9, 13: Heb *He answered* [b] Gk Syr: Heb lacks *His brother*

COMMENTARY

The king sends "a captain of fifty with his fifty men" to Elijah. Whereas Elijah previously had to "go up" to intercept the king's messengers, Ahaziah's men now have to go up to meet Elijah, who is on top of the "mount" (הר *har*; the same Hebrew word used for *Mount* Carmel, so we should not translate it as "a hill" as in the NIV and the NRSV). The captain addresses Elijah as "man of God" and gives the king's command to "come down." Elijah's reply plays on the similarity of the term for "man" (איש *'îš*) to the word for "fire" (אש *'ēš*). Ahaziah wishes to bring the man of God down, but he succeeds only in bringing down a fire from heaven that consumes all his men—just like the consuming fire on Mt. Carmel. The king apparently has not learned the lesson from recent history. He has learned nothing from his father's mistakes. Worse still, he does not seem to learn from his own mistakes, for he sends a second squad of fifty to bring the man of God down, with the same consequences as before, and then a third squad. The captain of the third group, however, does not obey the king. Rather, he pleads with the prophet to spare his life and the lives of his men.

The angel of the Lord then reappears to order Elijah to go down with the captain to face the king and to reiterate in person the Lord's word of doom for his having turned to Baal-zebub. The command to "go down" is reminiscent of God's command to Moses to "go down" from the mount of God because the people of Israel had turned away from God and become idolatrous (see Exod 32:7; Deut 9:12).

The story ends with the death of Ahaziah as the fulfillment of prophecy and the typical regnal summary, with its references to further information on the reign.

REFLECTIONS

The fundamental issue that this passage treats is the violation of the first commandment, God's initial charge to the covenant people: "You shall have no other gods before me" (Exod 20:3 NRSV; Deut 5:7). Ahaziah's problem is that he believes that Baal-zebub, rather than Israel's God, is the lord of life. The passage makes plain, however, that life is the Lord's to give and to take away and that life is mediated through the proclamation of the word of the Lord. This is a lesson that two disciples of Jesus, James and John, had to learn (Luke 9:54-55). Angry that the Samaritans (descendants of the northern kingdom) seemed to have rejected Jesus, James and John offered to bring down fire from heaven to consume the unbelievers. In other words, they wanted to do what Elijah had done to the northerners. Jesus, however, rebuked them, and they simply went on. It is the Lord who takes away life and the Lord who spares life.

2 KINGS 2:1-25, PROPHETIC SUCCESSION

OVERVIEW

This chapter is sandwiched between the regnal summary of Ahaziah's reign (1:17-18) and the introductory résumé of Jehoram's (3:1-2). The historical accounting of the performance of the kings of Israel and Judah is interrupted by the momentous event of prophetic succession.

The chapter marks both the end of Elijah's ministry and the beginning of Elisha's. The latter has already been introduced in 1 Kgs 19:19-21, where we find an account of his calling by Elijah. Yet, Elisha is not mentioned again until now. Henceforth, however, he will be the key prophetic figure—through the reigns of the next four kings of Israel (Jehoram, Jehu, Jehoahaz, Jehoash)—that is, during the second half of the eighth century BCE (2 Kings 3–13).

The chapter may be divided into two parts: the first concerns the ascension of Elijah to heaven and Elisha's taking of the mantle of prophetic leadership (vv. 1-18); the second reports two incidents that show the power and authority of Elisha as Elijah's successor (vv. 19-25). The second portion is deliberately joined with the first and is meant to be read with it. Note, for instance, that "the city" and "this city" in v. 19 must refer to Jericho (see vv. 15-17), and the mention of "Bethel" (v. 23) takes the reader back to the beginning of the story (vv. 2-3).

2 Kings 2:1-18, Elisha Succeeds Elijah

NIV

2 When the LORD was about to take Elijah up to heaven in a whirlwind, Elijah and Elisha were on their way from Gilgal. [2]Elijah said to Elisha, "Stay here; the LORD has sent me to Bethel."

But Elisha said, "As surely as the LORD lives and as you live, I will not leave you." So they went down to Bethel.

[3]The company of the prophets at Bethel came out to Elisha and asked, "Do you know that the LORD is going to take your master from you today?"

"Yes, I know," Elisha replied, "but do not speak of it."

[4]Then Elijah said to him, "Stay here, Elisha; the LORD has sent me to Jericho."

And he replied, "As surely as the LORD lives and as you live, I will not leave you." So they went to Jericho.

[5]The company of the prophets at Jericho went up to Elisha and asked him, "Do you know that the LORD is going to take your master from you today?"

"Yes, I know," he replied, "but do not speak of it."

[6]Then Elijah said to him, "Stay here; the LORD has sent me to the Jordan."

And he replied, "As surely as the LORD lives and as you live, I will not leave you." So the two of them walked on.

[7]Fifty men of the company of the prophets went and stood at a distance, facing the place where Elijah and Elisha had stopped at the Jordan. [8]Elijah took his cloak, rolled it up and struck the water with it. The water divided to the right and to the left, and the two of them crossed over on dry ground.

[9]When they had crossed, Elijah said to Elisha, "Tell me, what can I do for you before I am taken from you?"

NRSV

2 Now when the LORD was about to take Elijah up to heaven by a whirlwind, Elijah and Elisha were on their way from Gilgal. [2]Elijah said to Elisha, "Stay here; for the LORD has sent me as far as Bethel." But Elisha said, "As the LORD lives, and as you yourself live, I will not leave you." So they went down to Bethel. [3]The company of prophets[a] who were in Bethel came out to Elisha, and said to him, "Do you know that today the LORD will take your master away from you?" And he said, "Yes, I know; keep silent."

4Elijah said to him, "Elisha, stay here; for the LORD has sent me to Jericho." But he said, "As the LORD lives, and as you yourself live, I will not leave you." So they came to Jericho. [5]The company of prophets[a] who were at Jericho drew near to Elisha, and said to him, "Do you know that today the LORD will take your master away from you?" And he answered, "Yes, I know; be silent."

6Then Elijah said to him, "Stay here; for the LORD has sent me to the Jordan." But he said, "As the LORD lives, and as you yourself live, I will not leave you." So the two of them went on. [7]Fifty men of the company of prophets[a] also went, and stood at some distance from them, as they both were standing by the Jordan. [8]Then Elijah took his mantle and rolled it up, and struck the water; the water was parted to the one side and to the other, until the two of them crossed on dry ground.

9When they had crossed, Elijah said to Elisha, "Tell me what I may do for you, before I am taken from you." Elisha said, "Please let me inherit a double share of your spirit." [10]He responded, "You have asked a hard thing; yet, if you see me as I am being taken from you, it will be granted you; if not, it will not." [11]As they continued walking and talking, a chariot of fire and horses of fire separated the two of them, and

[a] Heb *sons of the prophets*

NIV

"Let me inherit a double portion of your spirit," Elisha replied.

10"You have asked a difficult thing," Elijah said, "yet if you see me when I am taken from you, it will be yours—otherwise not."

11As they were walking along and talking together, suddenly a chariot of fire and horses of fire appeared and separated the two of them, and Elijah went up to heaven in a whirlwind. 12Elisha saw this and cried out, "My father! My father! The chariots and horsemen of Israel!" And Elisha saw him no more. Then he took hold of his own clothes and tore them apart.

13He picked up the cloak that had fallen from Elijah and went back and stood on the bank of the Jordan. 14Then he took the cloak that had fallen from him and struck the water with it. "Where now is the LORD, the God of Elijah?" he asked. When he struck the water, it divided to the right and to the left, and he crossed over.

15The company of the prophets from Jericho, who were watching, said, "The spirit of Elijah is resting on Elisha." And they went to meet him and bowed to the ground before him. 16"Look," they said, "we your servants have fifty able men. Let them go and look for your master. Perhaps the Spirit of the LORD has picked him up and set him down on some mountain or in some valley."

"No," Elisha replied, "do not send them."

17But they persisted until he was too ashamed to refuse. So he said, "Send them." And they sent fifty men, who searched for three days but did not find him. 18When they returned to Elisha, who was staying in Jericho, he said to them, "Didn't I tell you not to go?"

NRSV

Elijah ascended in a whirlwind into heaven. 12Elisha kept watching and crying out, "Father, father! The chariots of Israel and its horsemen!" But when he could no longer see him, he grasped his own clothes and tore them in two pieces.

13He picked up the mantle of Elijah that had fallen from him, and went back and stood on the bank of the Jordan. 14He took the mantle of Elijah that had fallen from him, and struck the water, saying, "Where is the LORD, the God of Elijah?" When he had struck the water, the water was parted to the one side and to the other, and Elisha went over.

15When the company of prophets[a] who were at Jericho saw him at a distance, they declared, "The spirit of Elijah rests on Elisha." They came to meet him and bowed to the ground before him. 16They said to him, "See now, we have fifty strong men among your servants; please let them go and seek your master; it may be that the spirit of the LORD has caught him up and thrown him down on some mountain or into some valley." He responded, "No, do not send them." 17But when they urged him until he was ashamed, he said, "Send them." So they sent fifty men who searched for three days but did not find him. 18When they came back to him (he had remained at Jericho), he said to them, "Did I not say to you, Do not go?"

[a] Heb *sons of the prophets*

COMMENTARY

2:1-8. The narrator tips the reader off right away that Elijah will soon be taken up to heaven in a whirlwind, an event that is recounted in vv. 11-12, the climax of the passage. Elijah has, of course, been the key prophetic voice throughout the reigns of Ahab and Ahaziah. Although there have been others speaking for the Lord during that period, he looms larger than all others and is portrayed by the narrator as a prophet like Moses (see Commentary on 1 Kgs 18:30-46; 19:4-18; 2 Kgs 1:1-15). Now that Elijah is departing the scene, the narrator takes great pains to show that there is a worthy successor to him: Elisha, who has already been chosen (1 Kgs 19:19-21).

The rite of passage begins with a journey taken

by both Elijah and Elisha (vv. 1-8). They travel from Gilgal down to Bethel,[82] then from Bethel to Jericho, and finally from Jericho to the Jordan River. At each stop, Elijah tells his disciple to remain behind while he continues on the journey, but Elisha refuses to leave him (vv. 2, 4, 6). The point is probably Elisha's profound commitment to his master and his determination to follow him to the end (cf. Ruth 1:16-17). One should perhaps also compare the initial call of Elisha and how Elijah merely tossed the mantle at him and passed on, while Elisha had to chase after him (1 Kgs 19:19-21). Elisha had sacrificed the capital and tools of his trade to follow Elijah and attend to him. Now Elisha persists in staying with his master. He has, indeed, understood the significance of Elijah's symbolic gesture of throwing the mantle of the prophet upon him (see Commentary on 19:20).

Elisha clearly knows what he is doing, as we note from his reply to the prophetic colleagues who ask him, literally, "Do you know that today the Lord is taking your master from over your head?" (vv. 3, 5).[83] They probably mean that Elijah would no longer be in charge of Elisha ("over your head"), but the reader, duly tipped off by the narrator in v. 1, knows that Elijah would be taken literally above the head of Elisha—that is, up to heaven. Elisha is not being led unwittingly into his new role, it seems. He is fully cognizant of the implication of the rite of passage, although he tells his inquirers to be silent (cf. Mark 9:9, 30).

At last, the two prophets come to the Jordan (v. 6-8). At their other stops, these prophetic witnesses spoke with Elisha, but now they remain in the distance as Elijah and Elisha come to the bank of the Jordan. There Elijah rolls up his mantle, probably into some semblance of a rod, and strikes the water of the river. Thereupon, the waters part and the two prophets cross over on dry ground. Elijah's mantle, the symbol of his authority and power, is apparently the equivalent of Moses' rod (Exod 14:16). Specifically, the event recalls Moses' parting of the water of the Sea of Reeds (Exod 14:21-22). The implication of the act is that Elijah is a prophet like Moses. That kind of prophetic leadership is now at stake.

2:9-12. Having crossed the Jordan, they are now in the region where Moses had died. There, Elisha asks to inherit a "double portion" of Elijah's spirit, an allusion to the legal right of the firstborn (Deut 21:15-17). Elisha, in other words, is asking to be treated as Elijah's principal heir. The "double portion" refers to two-thirds of the inheritance (the term שׁנים [*šĕnayim*] is used in this sense in Zech 13:8), not twice the measure of the prophetic spirit that Elijah possesses. Here the "spirit" refers to the divinely endowed charisma that may be apportioned and transferred to others (see Num 11:16-17, 24-26). Elijah says that the request is difficult, meaning that it is difficult for a human being to meet. He states, in essence, that the privilege is not his to give (cf. Mark 10:38); if Elisha witnesses Elijah's departure, then his wish will be granted.

Accordingly, as the two are busy walking and talking, "fiery chariots and fiery horses" (NEB) suddenly separate them from each other, and Elijah ascends to the heavens in a tempest.[84] Since fire is often associated with the numinous in the Bible (e.g., Exod 3:2; 19:18; 24:17; Deut 4:12; 9:3), the reader is meant to understand these chariots and horses to be vehicles of the celestial hosts. Amid the pandemonium, Elijah ascends into the sky in a tempest (cf. Job 27:20; Nah 1:3).

Witnessing the whole scene, Elisha cries out: "My father, my father! The chariots of Israel and its horsemen!" The significance of Elisha's outcry is disputed. The same expression occurs in 13:14 in reference to Elisha, almost as a title, probably an indication of the prophet's role in the holy war against Aram (see 6:8-23; 13:14-19). In any case, it is difficult to separate "the chariots of Israel and its horsemen" in v. 12 from the fiery chariots and horses in v. 11. In Israel's ideology of holy war, the Lord's celestial hosts fight along with and on behalf of the terrestrial hosts, the armies of Israel; the latter is but a microcosm of the former (see

82. There are a number of locations in the Bible known as Gilgal ("Circle"). Since the prophets *go down* from there to Bethel, it is unlikely that the Gilgal beside the Jordan (Joshua 3–4) is meant. Rather, many scholars have identified the Gilgal in 2 Kings 2 with a site seven miles north of Bethel and on a higher elevation.

83. The NIV and the NRSV both interpret the expression to mean simply that Elijah will be taken from Elisha.

84. The word רכב (*rekeb*) here probably refers not only to a single chariot (NRSV, NIV), but also, as in the next verse and frequently in the HB (see also 13:14; Exod 14:23; Dan 11:40), to a group of chariots. Elijah is taken up in the whirlwind, not in a chariot.

Num 10:35-36; Deut 33:2).[85] The vision, like Joshua's vision of the captain of the celestial host (Josh 5:13-15), is an empowering one. It foreshadows the kind of ministry that Elisha will have—he will have a role to play in Israel's wars—and hints at the source of his power. Elisha then rends his garment in two, a sign of mourning (see Gen 37:34; Josh 7:6; Judg 11:35; 2 Sam 13:31).

2:13-18. The story has reached its climax. Elisha has, indeed, seen Elijah "taken" from him. Now Elisha picks up the mantle of Elijah, first thrown on him by the master (1 Kgs 19:19), and begins the second half of his rite of passage, returning whence he came: first to the Jordan (vv. 13-14), then to Jericho (vv. 15-22), on to Bethel (vv. 23-24), and finally to Mt. Carmel and Samaria (v. 25).[86] Elisha returns to the bank of the Jordan. Once again, he plays Joshua to Elijah's Moses (see Commentary on 1 Kgs 19:21). Just as Elijah parted the water with his mantle, so also Elisha parts the water with the same mantle. Elisha's reenactment, in fact, recalls Joshua's marvelous crossing of the Jordan to enter the promised land after the death of Moses (Josh 3:7-17).

The members of the prophetic guild who had witnessed Elijah and Elisha crossing the Jordan from a distance (v. 7-8) now see Elisha, again from a distance (v. 15). They know, no doubt from Elisha's repetition of Elijah's miraculous act, that the spirit of Elijah now rests upon Elisha. Joshua, the servant and eventual successor of Moses, had also received the spirit when Moses laid his hands upon him (Num 27:18-23; Deut 34:9). So, too, Elisha is endowed with the spirit of Elijah. The company of prophets bow down to Elisha, just as Obadiah had bowed down to Elijah (1 Kgs 18:7), and offer to search for Elijah. They were apparently not privy to the vision that Elisha saw across the Jordan, although they know that something marvelous has happened (cf. Dan 10:7; Acts 9:7). Elisha, knowing what has happened, tries to discourage them from looking for Elijah, but is unable to dissuade them. They look for three days without success. The narrative purpose of the episode is to show that Elijah has, indeed, disappeared from the face of the earth without a trace. In some ways, then, he was like Moses, who left the earth without leaving a burial site that could be known to anyone (Deut 34:5-6). Elisha is aware, and the reader is likewise privileged to know, however, that Elijah had ascended to the heavens.

85. See Patrick D. Miller, *The Divine Warrior in Early Israel,* HSM 5 (Cambridge, Mass.: Harvard University Press, 1975) 134-35.

86. Cf. Elisha's trip with Elijah from Gilgal to Bethel (vv. 2-3), Jericho (vv. 4-5), and the Jordan (vv. 6-8).

2 Kings 2:19-25, Elisha's Power Illustrated

NIV

19The men of the city said to Elisha, "Look, our lord, this town is well situated, as you can see, but the water is bad and the land is unproductive."
20"Bring me a new bowl," he said, "and put salt in it." So they brought it to him.
21Then he went out to the spring and threw the salt into it, saying, "This is what the LORD says: 'I have healed this water. Never again will it cause death or make the land unproductive.'"
22And the water has remained wholesome to this day, according to the word Elisha had spoken.
23From there Elisha went up to Bethel. As he was walking along the road, some youths came out of the town and jeered at him. "Go on up, you baldhead!" they said. "Go on up, you baldhead!" 24He turned around, looked at them and

NRSV

19Now the people of the city said to Elisha, "The location of this city is good, as my lord sees; but the water is bad, and the land is unfruitful."
20He said, "Bring me a new bowl, and put salt in it." So they brought it to him. 21Then he went to the spring of water and threw the salt into it, and said, "Thus says the LORD, I have made this water wholesome; from now on neither death nor miscarriage shall come from it." 22So the water has been wholesome to this day, according to the word that Elisha spoke.
23He went up from there to Bethel; and while he was going up on the way, some small boys came out of the city and jeered at him, saying, "Go away, baldhead! Go away, baldhead!" 24When he turned around and saw them, he

NIV	NRSV
called down a curse on them in the name of the LORD. Then two bears came out of the woods and mauled forty-two of the youths. [25]And he went on to Mount Carmel and from there returned to Samaria.	cursed them in the name of the LORD. Then two she-bears came out of the woods and mauled forty-two of the boys. [25]From there he went on to Mount Carmel, and then returned to Samaria.

COMMENTARY

2:19-22. Immediately following the account of his assumption of the mantle of Elijah, the narrator illustrates the power and authority of Elisha through two episodes. The first tells of a miraculous act at Jericho (cf. the miracles wrought by Elijah at the beginning of his ministry, 1 Kgs 17:8-24). Elisha learns that the water at Jericho is not potable ("bad"), apparently causing the land to be unproductive (lit., "bringing bereavement"). Rationalistic explanations have been proffered for that situation. One theory, citing hydrological studies, suggests that geological disturbances caused a high amount of radioactive pollutants to be released into the springs of the region, yielding water that has been shown by laboratory tests to cause sterility.[87] Another hypothesis traces the problem to certain species of freshwater snails that have been found in excavations at Jericho; these snails are known to be carriers of a disease responsible for high infant mortality.[88] Whatever the explanation, Elisha miraculously purifies the water by throwing salt into it, a formula that has also tantalized rationalists. The chemical formula necessary to purify the contaminated water is, of course, of no interest to the narrator, who notes only that it is the Lord who has made the water drinkable. Despite the difference in method, the incident is reminiscent of Moses' sweetening of the bitter water at Marah by throwing wood into it (Exod 15:23-25). Elisha has even surpassed Moses. The latter had only sweetened water that was bitter, but the former has "healed" deadly water: "there will no longer be death or bereavement from there" (v. 21).[89]

87. See I. M. Blake, "Jericho (Ain es-Sultan): Joshua's Curse and Elisha's Miracle, One Possible Explanation," *PEQ* 99 (1967) 86-97.

88. E. V. Hulse, "Joshua's Curse and the Abandonment of Ancient Jericho: Schistosomiasis as a Possible Medical Explanation," *Medical History* 15 (1971) 376-86.

89. For the parallelism of "death" and "bereavement," see Lam 1:20 and cf. Theodore J. Lewis, *Ugaritic Narrative Poetry*, ed. Simon B. Parker, SBLWAW (Atlanta: Scholars Press, 1997) 208, ll. 8-9.

2:23-25. The next incident, however, is not so savory. Elisha is on his way from Jericho to Bethel when he comes across a group of young lads who deride him: "Go up, baldy! Go up, baldy!" (v. 23). Elisha curses them in the name of the Lord, whereupon two female bears appear from the woods to maul forty-two of the youngsters. Elisha's harsh reaction to the seemingly innocuous taunt seems horribly out of proportion. Interpreters through the centuries have tried to exonerate the prophet by explaining the taunt as something more than a ridiculing of the prophet's physical appearance—an attack on his prophetic office (indicated by his "tonsure"), an insult directed at the prophet that is tantamount to an attack on God, an attempt to prevent him from going to the Bethel sanctuary, a taunt that he should go to the heretical Bethel sanctuary, and the like. No explanation is convincing, however. If the taunt meant more than what it seems now, that original meaning is lost to the modern reader, who cannot even be certain if the imperative in Hebrew means "Go away!" (NRSV), "Go on up!" (NIV), or simply "Go up!" (KJV). What is evident, when all is said and done, is that the narrator has juxtaposed this episode illustrating the prophet's power to inflict deadly punishment (cf. 1:9-16) alongside the story of his power to turn away death (vv. 19-22). Perhaps the point is that Elisha's ministry, like that of Moses, offers the possibility of blessings or curses, life or death.

The story concludes with Elisha going to Mt. Carmel, the mountain best known for the manifestation of the Lord's power over Baal and his prophets, and then to Samaria, where the kings of Israel reign. These destinations signal to the reader that the prophet has truly taken up the mantle of his predecessor.

REFLECTIONS

Of all the wonders associated with Elijah, there are none that have been more important in shaping his reputation than the account of his ascension to heaven. No other story of the prophet has had a more vigorous hermeneutical "afterlife" than this one; no other account has fired the imagination of interpreters more. By contrast, no other passage in the Elisha cycle has offended the moral sensibilities of readers more than the episode of the prophet's deadly curse of the youngsters for what seems like mischievous behavior. Both portions deserve further reflection.

1. Although Enoch is said to have been "taken by God" upon his death (Gen 5:24), no other Old Testament personality has been said explicitly to have ascended to heaven. Elijah's dramatic departure has given rise to expectations of his return as the harbinger of the "day of the LORD" (Mal 4:5) and to speculations of his association with the messianic age (see Sir 48:1-11; Matt 11:10-14; 16:13-14; 17:10-13; 27:47, 49; Mark 6:14-15; 8:27-28; 9:11-13; 15:35-36; Luke 1:17; 9:7-8, 18-19). It is important, however, to note that the text is about the glorious ascension of the master as much as it is about prophetic succession. The disciple follows the master resolutely, until he has been given the gift of the spirit for his task. The main point of the passage is, in fact, the continued availability of people who would proclaim the word of the Lord. The people of God are not left forlorn, it seems. As one prophet passes on, another is immediately raised. The ministry in God's name will go on.

Elisha is given the privilege of witnessing the glorious assumption of his master. What is most significant about that experience, however, is not so much the manner of the master's departure but Elisha's vision of celestial power in the midst of human struggles, conveyed by the mirroring of the celestial and terrestrial hosts. Elisha is empowered by that knowledge. The same point is made in the New Testament accounts of the transfiguration (Matt 17:1-9; Mark 9:2-8; Luke 9:28-36). Witnessing the event, Peter is quick to focus on its glorious aspect and makes an enthusiastic proposal out of ignorance. In Luke's account, the disciples overhear the conversation about Jesus' departure (lit., "his exodus"; cf. the reenactment of the exodus by Elijah in 2 Kgs 2:8), but that departure/exodus is not one of glory but of suffering. Likewise, when Luke speaks later of Jesus' being "taken up" (Luke 9:51), the focus is on Jesus' fulfillment of his mission. We are, perhaps, inclined to focus on the glory of the ascension of Elijah and of Jesus, but what is equally important is the fulfillment of God's will.

One may note, too, that in the account of Jesus' ascension in Acts, the immediate concern of Scripture is with the continuation of the ministry, the empowering of the disciples of Jesus with the presence of the Holy Spirit (Acts 1:2, 11, 22).

2. The episode of Elisha's cursing of the youngsters is challenging for anyone who comes to the Bible as Scripture. Elisha's response seems vindictive, petty, and morally unjustifiable. The passage provides no paradigm of righteous conduct, however. Ethics is not at issue. The point, rather, is a theological one. Read in tandem with the preceding episode concerning a salvific act wrought in the name of God, it points to a dialectical understanding of the character of God. The sovereign deity is free to save and to punish, to bless and to curse, to give life and to take it away. It was probably on account of such an understanding of the sovereignty of God that Jesus rebuked his disciples who wanted, like Elijah, to call down fire from heaven to punish those who rejected their master. It is entirely up to God to bless or to curse.

2 KINGS 3:1-27, JEHORAM'S CAMPAIGN AGAINST MOAB

OVERVIEW

Elisha's vision of the celestial hosts—the fiery chariots and fiery horses (2:11)—and his connection of that vision with Israel's chariots and horsemen (2:12) signaled the fact that his ministry will involve him in Israel's wars. This chapter, which reports on his campaign against Moab, is but the first of several stories of Elisha's role in Israel's military conflicts (see also 6:24–7:20; 13:14-19).

Modern scholars have generally assumed that the regnal summary in vv. 1-3 is editorial and was not originally a part of the report on the Moabite war. That may be so. Nevertheless, the text as it stands places the Moabite campaign in the specific context of Jehoram's reign and, indeed, suggests that one should read the account of the war in the light of the ambivalent assessment of Jehoram in vv. 1-3.

2 Kings 3:1-3, Regnal Résumé of Jehoram

NIV

3 Joram[a] son of Ahab became king of Israel
in Samaria in the eighteenth year of Jehoshaphat king of Judah, and he reigned twelve
years. 2He did evil in the eyes of the LORD, but
not as his father and mother had done. He got
rid of the sacred stone of Baal that his father had
made. 3Nevertheless he clung to the sins of
Jeroboam son of Nebat, which he had caused
Israel to commit; he did not turn away from them.

[a] *1* Hebrew *Jehoram,* a variant of *Joram;* also in verse 6

NRSV

3 In the eighteenth year of King Jehoshaphat
of Judah, Jehoram son of Ahab became
king over Israel in Samaria; he reigned twelve
years. 2He did what was evil in the sight of the
LORD, though not like his father and mother, for
he removed the pillar of Baal that his father had
made. 3Nevertheless he clung to the sin of
Jeroboam son of Nebat, which he caused Israel
to commit; he did not depart from it.

COMMENTARY

Ahaziah, the son of Ahab, died as a result of his fall from the window (1:2, 17). Apparently having left no son, he is succeeded by his brother Jehoram (849–843 BCE; his name also appears in its variant form, Joram; e.g., 8:16-29; 9:14-26). The summary assessment of Jehoram's reign in this section is fairly typical for northern kings. Despite the admission that he was not as bad as his parents (Ahab and Jezebel) because he did carry out some reforms, Jehoram gets a negative evaluation overall. The problem of heterodoxy created by Jeroboam had not been eradicated.

In its present context, the regnal résumé provides a chronological setting for the narrative about the war with Moab. In its canonical context, the story of Israel's war with Moab (vv. 4-27) is to be read in the light of the assessment of Jehoram's reign in vv. 1-3. Hence, the deviation of this regnal résumé from the stereotypical form for northern kings is noteworthy. There is some ambiguity as regards Jehoram's performance, an ambiguity that is conveyed twice by the Hebrew adverb רק (*raq,* "only") and twice by the verb סור (*sûr,* "to turn aside"): "only not like his father and mother, for he turned aside the pillar of Baal that his father had made, only he clung to the sin of

Jeroboam son of Nebat, which he caused Israel to commit; he did not turn aside from it" (vv. 2-3). This ambiguity is reflected in the story that follows: in Elisha's initial reluctance ("Go to your father's prophets and your mother's") becomes consent to give the word of the Lord to Jehoram. It is also reflected in the results of the war: Israel scores a victory over Moab but has to withdraw and return to their land. (See Reflections at 3:20-27.)

2 Kings 3:4-8, Jehoram Forms an Alliance Against Moab

NIV

[4]Now Mesha king of Moab raised sheep, and he had to supply the king of Israel with a hundred thousand lambs and with the wool of a hundred thousand rams. [5]But after Ahab died, the king of Moab rebelled against the king of Israel. [6]So at that time King Joram set out from Samaria and mobilized all Israel. [7]He also sent this message to Jehoshaphat king of Judah: "The king of Moab has rebelled against me. Will you go with me to fight against Moab?"

"I will go with you," he replied. "I am as you are, my people as your people, my horses as your horses."

[8]"By what route shall we attack?" he asked.

"Through the Desert of Edom," he answered.

NRSV

4Now King Mesha of Moab was a sheep breeder, who used to deliver to the king of Israel one hundred thousand lambs, and the wool of one hundred thousand rams. [5]But when Ahab died, the king of Moab rebelled against the king of Israel. [6]So King Jehoram marched out of Samaria at that time and mustered all Israel. [7]As he went he sent word to King Jehoshaphat of Judah, "The king of Moab has rebelled against me; will you go with me to battle against Moab?" He answered, "I will; I am with you, my people are your people, my horses are your horses." [8]Then he asked, "By which way shall we march?" Jehoram answered, "By the way of the wilderness of Edom."

COMMENTARY

Much has been made of the fact that Jehoram's Moabite counterpart, Mesha, is known from a Moabite inscription, wherein Mesha acknowledged that Moab had been subjugated by Israel since the time of Omri, but claimed to have liberated his country sometime after that.[90] Despite difficulties in the interpretation of details, it seems clear that Moab did assert its independence during the reign of Mesha, and it is possible that Moab gained control of Israelite territory, as Mesha claimed. Still, there is nothing mentioned in the inscription of this particular campaign or any of its details. Our understanding of this passage as Scripture will come primarily from our reading of it as a literary and theological text, and not as a historical record.

As in the case of Ahab's war against the Arameans to win back Ramoth-gilead, it is the king of Israel who initiates the war (see 1 Kgs 22:3). As in that war, Jehoram wants to involve the Judeans, and so he asks Jehoshaphat, who had been allied with his father in the Aramean war, a question similar to the one Ahab had posed (v. 7, cf. 1 Kgs 22:4). Jehoshaphat, who is apparently still a weaker partner in the alliance, gives the same answer that he gave Ahab (v. 8, cf. 1 Kgs 22:4). (See Reflections at 3:20-27.)

90. See *ANET*, 320.

2 Kings 3:9-19, Attack, Setback, and Prophetic Prediction

NIV

9So the king of Israel set out with the king of Judah and the king of Edom. After a roundabout march of seven days, the army had no more water for themselves or for the animals with them.

10"What!" exclaimed the king of Israel. "Has the LORD called us three kings together only to hand us over to Moab?"

11But Jehoshaphat asked, "Is there no prophet of the LORD here, that we may inquire of the LORD through him?"

An officer of the king of Israel answered, "Elisha son of Shaphat is here. He used to pour water on the hands of Elijah.[a]"

12Jehoshaphat said, "The word of the LORD is with him." So the king of Israel and Jehoshaphat and the king of Edom went down to him.

13Elisha said to the king of Israel, "What do we have to do with each other? Go to the prophets of your father and the prophets of your mother."

"No," the king of Israel answered, "because it was the LORD who called us three kings together to hand us over to Moab."

14Elisha said, "As surely as the LORD Almighty lives, whom I serve, if I did not have respect for the presence of Jehoshaphat king of Judah, I would not look at you or even notice you. 15But now bring me a harpist."

While the harpist was playing, the hand of the LORD came upon Elisha 16and he said, "This is what the LORD says: Make this valley full of ditches. 17For this is what the LORD says: You will see neither wind nor rain, yet this valley will be filled with water, and you, your cattle and your other animals will drink. 18This is an easy thing in the eyes of the LORD; he will also hand Moab over to you. 19You will overthrow every fortified city and every major town. You will cut down every good tree, stop up all the springs, and ruin every good field with stones."

[a] *11* That is, he was Elijah's personal servant.

NRSV

9So the king of Israel, the king of Judah, and the king of Edom set out; and when they had made a roundabout march of seven days, there was no water for the army or for the animals that were with them. 10Then the king of Israel said, "Alas! The LORD has summoned us, three kings, only to be handed over to Moab." 11But Jehoshaphat said, "Is there no prophet of the LORD here, through whom we may inquire of the LORD?" Then one of the servants of the king of Israel answered, "Elisha son of Shaphat, who used to pour water on the hands of Elijah, is here." 12Jehoshaphat said, "The word of the LORD is with him." So the king of Israel and Jehoshaphat and the king of Edom went down to him.

13Elisha said to the king of Israel, "What have I to do with you? Go to your father's prophets or to your mother's." But the king of Israel said to him, "No; it is the LORD who has summoned us, three kings, only to be handed over to Moab." 14Elisha said, "As the LORD of hosts lives, whom I serve, were it not that I have regard for King Jehoshaphat of Judah, I would give you neither a look nor a glance. 15But get me a musician." And then, while the musician was playing, the power of the LORD came on him. 16And he said, "Thus says the LORD, 'I will make this wadi full of pools.' 17For thus says the LORD, 'You shall see neither wind nor rain, but the wadi shall be filled with water, so that you shall drink, you, your cattle, and your animals.' 18This is only a trifle in the sight of the LORD, for he will also hand Moab over to you. 19You shall conquer every fortified city and every choice city; every good tree you shall fell, all springs of water you shall stop up, and every good piece of land you shall ruin with stones."

COMMENTARY

Jehoram decides to attack Moab from the south, marching through Judean and Edomite territories in so doing. Israel and Judah were allies at this time, and Edom was a vassal of Judah (see 1 Kgs 22:47). The reason for this roundabout strategy is unclear. One can only speculate that the Moabites would have strengthened the defenses where they might have expected the attack to come, and so the long march from the south may have been a way of circumventing that defense.

The allied forces are on their way when they run into logistical problems: a shortage of water. Jehoshaphat suggests, as he did with Ahab (1 Kgs 22:5), that they seek an oracle from the Lord. One of Jehoram's ministers proposes that Elisha be called, adding that he "used to pour water on the hands of Elijah" (v. 11). The idiom here no doubt refers to Elisha as Elijah's assistant, but it also points to Elisha as the one who would be able to solve the water-shortage problem. More important, Jehoshaphat confirms that the word of the Lord is with Elisha.

The narrator's ambivalence about Jehoram is evident throughout the passage. Elisha is said to have been initially reluctant to acknowledge Jehoram, sending him instead to his father's and mother's prophets (cf. 1 Kgs 18:19). Yet, Elisha relents, reportedly because of Jehoram's ally, Jehoshaphat. Elisha needs music to be induced into a trance (cf. 1 Sam 10:5). Nevertheless, the "hand of the LORD" (v. 15; NRSV, "power of the LORD") does come upon him, whereupon he delivers to the king a promise of a divine miracle: The wadi will be filled with water, even though there will be neither wind nor rain. Ordinarily, the wadi would contain water only during the rainy season, but Elisha predicts that it will be full without wind or rain, elements that the Canaanites associated with the power of Baal. This miracle, which is but a small matter to the deity, will turn out to be salvific for the allies; it will be the means by which God will deliver Moab into the "hand" of the allies (v. 18).

According to Elisha's prediction, the allies will not only conquer all the cities, but will also totally devastate the land, destroying the good trees and ruining every arable plot, in contravention of deuteronomic law (Deut 20:19-20). This is probably to be read, not as a promise of what the Lord will give to the allies, but as a prediction of what they will do. God will give them victory (so vv. 17-18), but they will carry out unacceptable atrocities. (See Reflections at 3:20-27.)

2 Kings 3:20-27, Fulfillment of Prophecies

NIV

20The next morning, about the time for offering the sacrifice, there it was—water flowing from the direction of Edom! And the land was filled with water.

21Now all the Moabites had heard that the kings had come to fight against them; so every man, young and old, who could bear arms was called up and stationed on the border. 22When they got up early in the morning, the sun was shining on the water. To the Moabites across the way, the water looked red—like blood. 23"That's blood!" they said. "Those kings must have fought and slaughtered each other. Now to the plunder, Moab!"

24But when the Moabites came to the camp of

NRSV

20The next day, about the time of the morning offering, suddenly water began to flow from the direction of Edom, until the country was filled with water.

21When all the Moabites heard that the kings had come up to fight against them, all who were able to put on armor, from the youngest to the oldest, were called out and were drawn up at the frontier. 22When they rose early in the morning, and the sun shone upon the water, the Moabites saw the water opposite them as red as blood. 23They said, "This is blood; the kings must have fought together, and killed one another. Now then, Moab, to the spoil!" 24But when they came to the camp of Israel, the Israelites rose up and

NIV

Israel, the Israelites rose up and fought them until they fled. And the Israelites invaded the land and slaughtered the Moabites. 25They destroyed the towns, and each man threw a stone on every good field until it was covered. They stopped up all the springs and cut down every good tree. Only Kir Hareseth was left with its stones in place, but men armed with slings surrounded it and attacked it as well.

26When the king of Moab saw that the battle had gone against him, he took with him seven hundred swordsmen to break through to the king of Edom, but they failed. 27Then he took his firstborn son, who was to succeed him as king, and offered him as a sacrifice on the city wall. The fury against Israel was great; they withdrew and returned to their own land.

NRSV

attacked the Moabites, who fled before them; as they entered Moab they continued the attack.[a] 25The cities they overturned, and on every good piece of land everyone threw a stone, until it was covered; every spring of water they stopped up, and every good tree they felled. Only at Kir-hareseth did the stone walls remain, until the slingers surrounded and attacked it. 26When the king of Moab saw that the battle was going against him, he took with him seven hundred swordsmen to break through, opposite the king of Edom; but they could not. 27Then he took his firstborn son who was to succeed him, and offered him as a burnt offering on the wall. And great wrath came upon Israel, so they withdrew from him and returned to their own land.

[a] Compare Gk Syr: Meaning of Heb uncertain

COMMENTARY

The predictions of Elisha come to pass the next day, specifically, "when the tribute is offered up" (v. 20). One wonders whether it is only a coincidence that the decisive moment corresponds to the time of the day when Elijah called down the fire of heaven in the contest with the prophets of Baal (1 Kgs 18:36), a contest that led to the annihilation of all those prophets.

Water flows from the direction of Edom until the country is filled with water. Through Elisha, "who used to pour water upon the hand of Elijah" (v. 11), comes this miracle of abundant water that more than resolves the problem of water shortage that the allies face.

The Moabites, arrayed for battle, see the water opposite them "as red as blood," leading them to think that the allies are killing one another. Thus misled, they proceed to take the spoil and, consequently, suffer defeat. Rationalistic explanations have been proffered for the bloodred water: redness caused by the laterite soil of the region, reflection of the sun, or the like. Water becoming blood, of course, recalls the first of the plagues that led to the exodus from Egypt (Exod 7:14-25, esp. v. 21). There is, in any case, a wordplay on the name "Edom" (אדום *ʾĕdôm*) in the phrase "red as blood" (אדמים כדם *ʾădummîm kaddām*, v. 22). Whatever the explanation, the water that is a blessing for some turns out to be a curse for others.

The Israelites, as Elisha predicted, carry their victory to its extreme conclusion, destroying good trees and arable land, in contravention of deuteronomic law. In desperate straits, the king of Moab sacrifices his firstborn son, the crown prince to the Moabite throne. One expects this to be the denouement of the story, an indication of decisive victory for Israel. Instead, we find a surprising conclusion: a great wrath comes upon Israel, and so they withdraw and return home. The text is ambiguous about the source of the "great wrath." We might take the sudden withdrawal of Israel as indicative of the efficacy of the human sacrifice and, hence, take the "great wrath" as coming from Chemosh, Moab's patron deity. Some interpreters, however, have proposed that the "wrath" (קצף *qeṣep*) refers to human passion: the outrage of the Moabites that prompted them to muster all their resources to beat back the coalition, the anger of the attackers because of the protracted battle, and so on. It should be noted that the Hebrew expression for "good wrath" (קצף גדול *qeṣep gādôl*) is used in the Bible only for the wrath of the Lord (Deut 29:27; Jer 21:5; 32:37; Zech 1:15; 7:12). Moreover, the expression היה קצף על (*hāyâ qeṣep ʿal*, "there was a wrath against") is always used in reference to divine wrath. It seems most probable, therefore, that the text is referring to the wrath of the Lord for the violation of the deuteronomic prohibition of the scorched-earth policy in war. For the narrator, the Lord gave victory to Jehoram—but not a complete victory.

REFLECTIONS

This chapter reflects the conviction that God responds to people who come to the deity in time of need, even when they have been undeserving of God's help. Here we have a story of a king who is judged a sinner, a man who has embarked upon a course with nary a thought of the will of God. Yet, in his moment of need, God comes through with a promise of salvation for him. The freedom of God to save does not mean, however, that one has received a "blank check." The passage does not provide a prooftext for a triumphalistic theology—that God will fight for us, come what may. The very last words (v. 27), in fact, offer the most profound theological truth, a warning that God's salvation may instantly turn to wrath in the face of human excesses and mercilessness.

2 KINGS 4:1-44, ELISHA'S MINISTRY OF LIFE

OVERVIEW

Following the chapter on Elisha's role in Israel's war with Moab, we have a chapter on the prophet's ministry of life. It is likely, as most critics believe, that the legends contained herein originally circulated independently or as parts of various collections. Still, the various pieces in this literary collage seem to fit together rather well. They all revolve around the issue of life and death, Elisha in each case acting to bring, sustain, or restore life and avert death. The following subunits may be discerned:

I. The miracle of abundant oil (vv. 1-7)
II. Elisha ministers to a wealthy woman (vv. 8-37)
   A. The gift of a son (vv. 8-17)
   B. Death and resurrection (vv. 18-37)
III. Elisha feeds the hungry (vv. 38-44)
   A. Death in the pot (vv. 38-41)
   B. Feeding many with little (vv. 42-44)

2 Kings 4:1-7, The Miracle of Abundant Oil

NIV

4 The wife of a man from the company of the prophets cried out to Elisha, "Your servant my husband is dead, and you know that he revered the LORD. But now his creditor is coming to take my two boys as his slaves."

2Elisha replied to her, "How can I help you? Tell me, what do you have in your house?"

NRSV

4 Now the wife of a member of the company of prophets[a] cried to Elisha, "Your servant my husband is dead; and you know that your servant feared the LORD, but a creditor has come to take my two children as slaves." 2Elisha said to her, "What shall I do for you? Tell me, what do you have in the house?" She answered, "Your

[a] Heb *the sons of the prophets*

NIV

"Your servant has nothing there at all," she said, "except a little oil."

[3]Elisha said, "Go around and ask all your neighbors for empty jars. Don't ask for just a few. [4]Then go inside and shut the door behind you and your sons. Pour oil into all the jars, and as each is filled, put it to one side."

[5]She left him and afterward shut the door behind her and her sons. They brought the jars to her and she kept pouring. [6]When all the jars were full, she said to her son, "Bring me another one."

But he replied, "There is not a jar left." Then the oil stopped flowing.

[7]She went and told the man of God, and he said, "Go, sell the oil and pay your debts. You and your sons can live on what is left."

NRSV

servant has nothing in the house, except a jar of oil." [3]He said, "Go outside, borrow vessels from all your neighbors, empty vessels and not just a few. [4]Then go in, and shut the door behind you and your children, and start pouring into all these vessels; when each is full, set it aside." [5]So she left him and shut the door behind her and her children; they kept bringing vessels to her, and she kept pouring. [6]When the vessels were full, she said to her son, "Bring me another vessel." But he said to her, "There are no more." Then the oil stopped flowing. [7]She came and told the man of God, and he said, "Go sell the oil and pay your debts, and you and your children can live on the rest."

COMMENTARY

The first story in this chapter concerns Elisha's miraculous rescue of the family of a member of the prophetic guild, probably one of his followers (see v. 1: "You yourself know that your servant feared the LORD"). The man had died, leaving his widow and two children liable for debts that he had incurred. According to the law, if a man's debt is unpaid at his death, the creditor may seize the debtor's property and children (see Exod 21:7; Isa 50:1; Amos 2:6; 8:6; Mic 2:9; Neh 5:3-5). Like the widow of Zarephath, whom Elijah had encountered (1 Kgs 17:8-16), this widow is in desperate straits. Elisha cannot legally prevent the creditor from seizing the children, so if he is to help the widow, it will have to be through some other means.

The widow has nothing in her house save one cruse of oil. So Elisha instructs her to borrow containers from her neighbors. Just as Elijah had provided the widow of Zarephath with an unending supply of oil, so also Elisha miraculously provides this widow with an abundant amount of oil, instructing her to sell it to pay off her debt. She and her children may live on what is left over, he says. The episode thus moves from the problem that death has caused (v. 1) to the renewed possibility of life through the miracle wrought by Elisha (v. 7). (See Reflections at 4:42-44.)

2 Kings 4:8-37, Elisha Ministers to a Wealthy Woman

2 Kings 4:8-17, The Gift of a Son

NIV

[8]One day Elisha went to Shunem. And a well-to-do woman was there, who urged him to stay for a meal. So whenever he came by, he stopped there to eat. [9]She said to her husband, "I know

NRSV

8One day Elisha was passing through Shunem, where a wealthy woman lived, who urged him to have a meal. So whenever he passed that way, he would stop there for a meal. [9]She said to her

NIV

that this man who often comes our way is a holy man of God. 10Let's make a small room on the roof and put in it a bed and a table, a chair and a lamp for him. Then he can stay there whenever he comes to us."

11One day when Elisha came, he went up to his room and lay down there. 12He said to his servant Gehazi, "Call the Shunammite." So he called her, and she stood before him. 13Elisha said to him, "Tell her, 'You have gone to all this trouble for us. Now what can be done for you? Can we speak on your behalf to the king or the commander of the army?'"

She replied, "I have a home among my own people."

14"What can be done for her?" Elisha asked.

Gehazi said, "Well, she has no son and her husband is old."

15Then Elisha said, "Call her." So he called her, and she stood in the doorway. 16"About this time next year," Elisha said, "you will hold a son in your arms."

"No, my lord," she objected. "Don't mislead your servant, O man of God!"

17But the woman became pregnant, and the next year about that same time she gave birth to a son, just as Elisha had told her.

NRSV

husband, "Look, I am sure that this man who regularly passes our way is a holy man of God. 10Let us make a small roof chamber with walls, and put there for him a bed, a table, a chair, and a lamp, so that he can stay there whenever he comes to us."

11One day when he came there, he went up to the chamber and lay down there. 12He said to his servant Gehazi, "Call the Shunammite woman." When he had called her, she stood before him. 13He said to him, "Say to her, Since you have taken all this trouble for us, what may be done for you? Would you have a word spoken on your behalf to the king or to the commander of the army?" She answered, "I live among my own people." 14He said, "What then may be done for her?" Gehazi answered, "Well, she has no son, and her husband is old." 15He said, "Call her." When he had called her, she stood at the door. 16He said, "At this season, in due time, you shall embrace a son." She replied, "No, my lord, O man of God; do not deceive your servant."

17The woman conceived and bore a son at that season, in due time, as Elisha had declared to her.

COMMENTARY

The second episode concerns the promise and birth of a son to a Shunammite woman who has shown hospitality to the prophet. Unlike the widow of the first episode, this woman is said to be a woman of status (lit., "a great woman"; cf. 5:2; 10:6, 11; 1 Sam 25:2; 2 Sam 19:33). In contrast to the first woman, too, she does not come to Elisha with a request for help. Indeed, she has the resources to invite the prophet to dine with her family whenever he passes though her town, and she and her husband even build and furnish a guest room for him.

On his own accord, Elisha offers to peddle influence on her behalf, but the woman says she has no need of that. She seems to have everything she needs. It is pointed out to Elisha, however, that the couple have no son and that there is no prospect of their having one, since the husband is old. Elisha, therefore, tells her that she will have a son "in due time"—that is, within the year. Accordingly, the woman conceives and gives birth to a son. The prophet is able to bring the blessing of new life, even when that possibility is dimmed by biological realities. (See Reflections at 4:42-44.)

2 Kings 4:18-37, Death and Resurrection

NIV

18The child grew, and one day he went out to his father, who was with the reapers. 19"My head! My head!" he said to his father.

His father told a servant, "Carry him to his mother." 20After the servant had lifted him up and carried him to his mother, the boy sat on her lap until noon, and then he died. 21She went up and laid him on the bed of the man of God, then shut the door and went out.

22She called her husband and said, "Please send me one of the servants and a donkey so I can go to the man of God quickly and return."

23"Why go to him today?" he asked. "It's not the New Moon or the Sabbath."

"It's all right," she said.

24She saddled the donkey and said to her servant, "Lead on; don't slow down for me unless I tell you." 25So she set out and came to the man of God at Mount Carmel.

When he saw her in the distance, the man of God said to his servant Gehazi, "Look! There's the Shunammite! 26Run to meet her and ask her, 'Are you all right? Is your husband all right? Is your child all right?' "

"Everything is all right," she said.

27When she reached the man of God at the mountain, she took hold of his feet. Gehazi came over to push her away, but the man of God said, "Leave her alone! She is in bitter distress, but the LORD has hidden it from me and has not told me why."

28"Did I ask you for a son, my lord?" she said. "Didn't I tell you, 'Don't raise my hopes'?"

29Elisha said to Gehazi, "Tuck your cloak into your belt, take my staff in your hand and run. If you meet anyone, do not greet him, and if anyone greets you, do not answer. Lay my staff on the boy's face."

30But the child's mother said, "As surely as the LORD lives and as you live, I will not leave you." So he got up and followed her.

31Gehazi went on ahead and laid the staff on the boy's face, but there was no sound or response. So Gehazi went back to meet Elisha and told him, "The boy has not awakened."

32When Elisha reached the house, there was

NRSV

18When the child was older, he went out one day to his father among the reapers. 19He complained to his father, "Oh, my head, my head!" The father said to his servant, "Carry him to his mother." 20He carried him and brought him to his mother; the child sat on her lap until noon, and he died. 21She went up and laid him on the bed of the man of God, closed the door on him, and left. 22Then she called to her husband, and said, "Send me one of the servants and one of the donkeys, so that I may quickly go to the man of God and come back again." 23He said, "Why go to him today? It is neither new moon nor sabbath." She said, "It will be all right." 24Then she saddled the donkey and said to her servant, "Urge the animal on; do not hold back for me unless I tell you." 25So she set out, and came to the man of God at Mount Carmel.

When the man of God saw her coming, he said to Gehazi his servant, "Look, there is the Shunammite woman; 26run at once to meet her, and say to her, Are you all right? Is your husband all right? Is the child all right?" She answered, "It is all right." 27When she came to the man of God at the mountain, she caught hold of his feet. Gehazi approached to push her away. But the man of God said, "Let her alone, for she is in bitter distress; the LORD has hidden it from me and has not told me." 28Then she said, "Did I ask my lord for a son? Did I not say, Do not mislead me?" 29He said to Gehazi, "Gird up your loins, and take my staff in your hand, and go. If you meet anyone, give no greeting, and if anyone greets you, do not answer; and lay my staff on the face of the child." 30Then the mother of the child said, "As the LORD lives, and as you yourself live, I will not leave without you." So he rose up and followed her. 31Gehazi went on ahead and laid the staff on the face of the child, but there was no sound or sign of life. He came back to meet him and told him, "The child has not awakened."

32When Elisha came into the house, he saw the child lying dead on his bed. 33So he went in and closed the door on the two of them, and prayed to the LORD. 34Then he got up on the bed[a]

[a] Heb lacks *on the bed*

NIV

the boy lying dead on his couch. [33]He went in, shut the door on the two of them and prayed to the LORD. [34]Then he got on the bed and lay upon the boy, mouth to mouth, eyes to eyes, hands to hands. As he stretched himself out upon him, the boy's body grew warm. [35]Elisha turned away and walked back and forth in the room and then got on the bed and stretched out upon him once more. The boy sneezed seven times and opened his eyes.

[36]Elisha summoned Gehazi and said, "Call the Shunammite." And he did. When she came, he said, "Take your son." [37]She came in, fell at his feet and bowed to the ground. Then she took her son and went out.

NRSV

and lay upon the child, putting his mouth upon his mouth, his eyes upon his eyes, and his hands upon his hands; and while he lay bent over him, the flesh of the child became warm. [35]He got down, walked once to and fro in the room, then got up again and bent over him; the child sneezed seven times, and the child opened his eyes. [36]Elisha[a] summoned Gehazi and said, "Call the Shunammite woman." So he called her. When she came to him, he said, "Take your son." [37]She came and fell at his feet, bowing to the ground; then she took her son and left.

[a] Heb *he*

COMMENTARY

This episode is related to the preceding one, although some time has now passed. In the preceding scene, Elisha is in the house of the woman in Shunem (v. 11), but he is now at Mt. Carmel (v. 25), about fifteen miles from Shunem. The boy is now old enough to look for his father among the reapers and to complain of a headache. The father orders the boy to be carried to his mother, perhaps because he is too old to carry him there himself. The child, however, dies on his mother's lap. The woman puts the boy on Elisha's bed (in the room that the family had built for him, v. 10) and rushes off to see the "man of God" who had promised her the son without her having asked. Oddly, her husband does not seem to share her sense of urgency; indeed, he asks her why she is visiting the prophet when it is not a holiday. She presses on, however, with only one word to him: "It is all right!" (שלום *šālôm*).

Elisha's servant, Gehazi, is sent to greet her first, but she is eager to see the prophet face-to-face. She brushes aside his questions of her family's well-being with the same word she spoke to her husband as she left home: *šālôm* ("It is all right!"). There is no time for explanations to her husband and no time for a perfunctory exchange of greetings with the prophet, it seems. All is, in fact, not well, but she is pressing on to seek that *šālôm* from the one who can give it to her.

Elisha recognizes that she is greatly distressed, but admits that he has not been apprised of the situation by the Lord. When he learns what the problem is, he immediately dispatches Gehazi to go to the boy to place his staff on him. The mother's instincts and love for the child are great, for she will not settle for anything less than the personal attention of Elisha. Sure enough, Gehazi is not successful in reviving the boy. Indeed, several times in the text, it is asserted that the boy is dead (vv. 20, 31-32). Still, Elisha comes and prays to the Lord, just as Elijah had done when he revived the son of the widow of Zarephath (1 Kgs 17:20). After applying a technique similar to that Elijah used, Elisha gets off the boy and paces around the house once. Then, he hears the boy sneezing seven times and, returning to the room, notices him opening his eyes. He gives the boy back to his mother, who bows down to the man of God, presumably in gratitude. (See Reflections at 4:42-44.)

2 Kings 4:38-44, Elisha Feeds the Hungry

2 Kings 4:38-41, Death in the Pot

NIV

38Elisha returned to Gilgal and there was a famine in that region. While the company of the prophets was meeting with him, he said to his servant, "Put on the large pot and cook some stew for these men."

39One of them went out into the fields to gather herbs and found a wild vine. He gathered some of its gourds and filled the fold of his cloak. When he returned, he cut them up into the pot of stew, though no one knew what they were. 40The stew was poured out for the men, but as they began to eat it, they cried out, "O man of God, there is death in the pot!" And they could not eat it.

41Elisha said, "Get some flour." He put it into the pot and said, "Serve it to the people to eat." And there was nothing harmful in the pot.

NRSV

38When Elisha returned to Gilgal, there was a famine in the land. As the company of prophets was[a] sitting before him, he said to his servant, "Put the large pot on, and make some stew for the company of prophets."[b] 39One of them went out into the field to gather herbs; he found a wild vine and gathered from it a lapful of wild gourds, and came and cut them up into the pot of stew, not knowing what they were. 40They served some for the men to eat. But while they were eating the stew, they cried out, "O man of God, there is death in the pot!" They could not eat it. 41He said, "Then bring some flour." He threw it into the pot, and said, "Serve the people and let them eat." And there was nothing harmful in the pot.

[a] Heb *sons of the prophets were* [b] Heb *sons of the prophets*

COMMENTARY

The next story is reminiscent of the episode of Elisha's "healing" of the contaminated water at Jericho (2:19-22). When Elisha returns to Gilgal (see 2:1), he discovers that there is a famine. Still, he is able to provide for "the company of prophets." However, the servant assigned to prepare a stew inadvertently includes some poisonous ingredients. Those who taste it realize immediately that "there is death in the pot." Elisha then orders that flour be thrown into the pot, thereby detoxifying the stew. (See Reflections at 4:42-44.)

2 Kings 4:42-44, Feeding Many with Little

NIV

42A man came from Baal Shalishah, bringing the man of God twenty loaves of barley bread baked from the first ripe grain, along with some heads of new grain. "Give it to the people to eat," Elisha said.

43"How can I set this before a hundred men?" his servant asked.

But Elisha answered, "Give it to the people to eat. For this is what the LORD says: 'They will eat and have some left over.'" 44Then he set it before them, and they ate and had some left over, according to the word of the LORD.

NRSV

42A man came from Baal-shalishah, bringing food from the first fruits to the man of God: twenty loaves of barley and fresh ears of grain in his sack. Elisha said, "Give it to the people and let them eat." 43But his servant said, "How can I set this before a hundred people?" So he repeated, "Give it to the people and let them eat, for thus says the LORD, 'They shall eat and have some left.'" 44He set it before them, they ate, and had some left, according to the word of the LORD.

COMMENTARY

The final scene in the chapter concerns Elisha's miraculous feeding of one hundred people with a relatively small amount of food. The servant is initially skeptical, but Elisha repeats the order to feed the group, declaring that the Lord will provide more than enough food for everyone.

REFLECTIONS

What we have in this chapter is a collage of Elisha's extraordinary deeds: miraculously filling empty vessels with oil, granting a childless couple a son, raising a person from the dead, neutralizing poisonous food, and feeding a multitude with food for but a few. In his role as a wonder-worker, Elisha foreshadows the miracle worker of whom the New Testament speaks, the one whose marvelous deeds would surpass Elisha's (see Matt 9:18-26; 14:13-21; Mark 5:21-43; 6:34-44; Luke 7:11-17; 8:40-56; John 2:1-11). Although these acts all serve to demonstrate that the one who performs them does so by the power of God, they are not performed merely for their awe-inspiring effects. Rather, in each case, the marvelous deed is for the sake of others, specifically to bring, to sustain, or to restore life and avert death. The power of the "man of God" to carry out these miraculous deeds testifies to the power of God over life and death.

For all its emphasis on the miraculous nature of these acts of Elisha, however, this passage is noteworthy that the needs to which he ministered are remarkably mundane: freedom and life for the destitute, hope for the childless, restoration of a dead child to a desperate mother, food for the hungry. The man of God acts on more than just a grand political scale, bringing the word of God to kings about God's will as regards the nations (as in chap. 3). The man of God also acts to address the mundane, personal needs of people living life day to day. That is at the heart of the ministry. To be sure, one may not have the power of Elisha to fill empty vessels with oil. Yet, in the face of the desperate plight of the destitute, one may take a cue from Elisha about the economic enablement of the poor. Elisha provides a means by which the destitute widow is able to resolve her economic problem and save her children from enslavement. Indeed, the miracle of economic enablement may take many forms—it only takes the eyes of faith to discern those forms in our day and age. By the same token, one may not be able to resurrect a dead child, as Elisha did. Yet, the story makes a poignant point that there are critical moments in the ministry that may demand our immediate, personal, direct, and prayerful involvement in the problem at hand. The grieving mother in desperate need of the senior minister's attention will not be comforted by "passing the buck" to an associate with a mere emblem of the senior pastor's authority. We may not have the technical know-how to detoxify poisonous food or to cause limited quantities of food to multiply. Yet, it is imperative that we feed the hungry with whatever resources we may find. Proclamation of the word of the Lord involves much more than words; it involves reactive and proactive action to bring life and to give hope to others. As one New Testament writer puts it: "If a brother or sister is naked and lacks daily food, and one of you says to them, 'Go in peace; keep warm and eat your fill,' and yet you do not supply their bodily needs, what is the good of that?" (Jas 2:15-16 NRSV).

2 KINGS 5:1-27, NAAMAN AND GEHAZI

OVERVIEW

The issue of the unity of the passage primarily revolves around the place of the episode about Gehazi's greed (vv. 19*b*-27). For many interpreters, this account is entirely secondary, constituting an appendix of sorts to the story of the healing of Naaman (vv. 1-19*a*). Yet, there are strong indications of the coherence of the chapter or, at least, indications that the narrator intends the Gehazi episode to be read with the preceding material. Most poignantly, the present form of the text begins with the skin affliction of Naaman (v. 1) and ends with the skin affliction of Gehazi (v. 27): The "outsider" is healed, while the "insider" is afflicted. Moreover, the faithfulness of Naaman's slave girl at the beginning of the story stands in stark contrast to the treachery of Elisha's servant at the end of the chapter.

2 Kings 5:1-7, Naaman Seeks Help in Israel

NIV

5 Now Naaman was commander of the army of the king of Aram. He was a great man in the sight of his master and highly regarded, because through him the LORD had given victory to Aram. He was a valiant soldier, but he had leprosy.[a]

2Now bands from Aram had gone out and had taken captive a young girl from Israel, and she served Naaman's wife. 3She said to her mistress, "If only my master would see the prophet who is in Samaria! He would cure him of his leprosy."

4Naaman went to his master and told him what the girl from Israel had said. 5"By all means, go," the king of Aram replied. "I will send a letter to the king of Israel." So Naaman left, taking with him ten talents[b] of silver, six thousand shekels[c] of gold and ten sets of clothing. 6The letter that he took to the king of Israel read: "With this letter I am sending my servant Naaman to you so that you may cure him of his leprosy."

7As soon as the king of Israel read the letter, he tore his robes and said, "Am I God? Can I kill and bring back to life? Why does this fellow send someone to me to be cured of his leprosy? See how he is trying to pick a quarrel with me!"

[a] *1* The Hebrew word was used for various diseases affecting the skin—not necessarily leprosy; also in verses 3, 6, 7, 11 and 27. [b] *5* That is, about 750 pounds (about 340 kilograms) [c] *5* That is, about 150 pounds (about 70 kilograms)

NRSV

5 Naaman, commander of the army of the king of Aram, was a great man and in high favor with his master, because by him the LORD had given victory to Aram. The man, though a mighty warrior, suffered from leprosy.[a] 2Now the Arameans on one of their raids had taken a young girl captive from the land of Israel, and she served Naaman's wife. 3She said to her mistress, "If only my lord were with the prophet who is in Samaria! He would cure him of his leprosy."[a] 4So Naaman[b] went in and told his lord just what the girl from the land of Israel had said. 5And the king of Aram said, "Go then, and I will send along a letter to the king of Israel."

He went, taking with him ten talents of silver, six thousand shekels of gold, and ten sets of garments. 6He brought the letter to the king of Israel, which read, "When this letter reaches you, know that I have sent to you my servant Naaman, that you may cure him of his leprosy."[a] 7When the king of Israel read the letter, he tore his clothes and said, "Am I God, to give death or life, that this man sends word to me to cure a man of his leprosy?[a] Just look and see how he is trying to pick a quarrel with me."

[a] A term for several skin diseases; precise meaning uncertain [b] Heb *he*

COMMENTARY

The story begins with Naaman, the chief military commander of the Aramean army. He is a "great man" (איש גדול *'îš gādôl,* v. 1; cf. אשה גדולה *'iššâ gĕdôlâ* in 4:8) who is favored by the king of Aram (ancient Syria) because of his victory over Israel, here perhaps an allusion to the Aramean victory in the conflict over Ramoth-gilead (1 Kgs 22:19-23).[91] That victory by the Aramean army is said to have been granted by the Lord, a standard way in Israelite writings of explaining the defeat of Israel as God's people (see, e.g., Judg 6:1; 13:1; 2 Chr 28:5; Dan 1:2), for in Israelite theology no foreign army can be victorious over Israel unless it is by the will of the Lord. Indeed, as we read the story in 2 Kings 5, we gather that Israel's defeat must have been in accordance with the will of the Lord, for that defeat would result in the conversion of a powerful Gentile and the glorification of the Lord. This is no doubt the sort of story that the Israelites, particularly those in exile, liked to tell. Despite the tragedy of defeat and captivity, it seems, greater good may be achieved.

In spite of all his accomplishments and greatness, Naaman has a problem: He suffers from a terrible skin disease,[92] one that carries with it a social stigma and is associated with death (see Num 12:10-12). Ironically, salvation for this "great man" would come by way of "a young girl" from Israel, captured by the Arameans on one of their raids. This Israelite captive would bring hope for her Aramean captor. She suggests that Naaman might be healed of his disease were he to seek help from "the prophet who is in Samaria" (v. 3)—that is, Elisha, who has apparently already gained a reputation for performing miracles, doubtless because of the kinds of legends that we read in chap. 4. The young girl's proposal makes it all the way to the king of Aram, who sends a letter to his counterpart in Israel, presumably Jehoram (see 3:1). No doubt, a visit to Samaria by the Aramean general who was responsible for the defeat of Israel in their previous military engagement could not proceed in peacetime without at least some diplomatic arrangements.

Armed with extravagant gifts and a letter from his king, the general comes to the king of Israel. The letter dictates that the king of Israel is to cure Naaman of his disease. The king is in despair, for he takes the content of the letter literally as a demand for him to perform the miracle himself. He realizes that curing such a terrible affliction is not something that any human being can accomplish. It is only God who gives death or life (see Deut 32:39; 1 Sam 2:6; Hos 6:2). The faithless king sees the challenge as a political problem, a pretext on the part of the Arameans for war. That may, indeed, be the real motive for the Aramean king's letter, which, curiously, does not mention the prophet. Whatever the Aramean king's intentions, however, the narrative will show that things would work out according to God's will. Ironically, the king of Israel does not seem to know what the captive slave girl in Damascus knows: that there is a prophet in Samaria who could perform the miracle. He sees only the impossibility of the case; she sees its possibility. (See Reflections at 5:19*b*-27.)

91. There is even a tradition that Naaman was the one who shot the arrow that "accidentally" killed Ahab in that battle. See Josephus *Antiquities of the Jews* 15.5. See also the Targum on 2 Chronicles 18.

92. Most translations retain the traditional rendering of the disease as "leprosy," more as a convenient term rather than a medically accurate one. Most scholars now agree that the Hebrew word does not refer to leprosy as we know it (i.e., Hansen's disease), but to skin afflictions of various sorts, here probably psoriasis or vitiligo. See David P. Wright and Richard N. Jones, "Leprosy," in *ABD,* 4:277-82.

2 Kings 5:8-14, Naaman Is Healed

NIV

8When Elisha the man of God heard that the king of Israel had torn his robes, he sent him this message: "Why have you torn your robes? Have the man come to me and he will know that there

NRSV

8But when Elisha the man of God heard that the king of Israel had torn his clothes, he sent a message to the king, "Why have you torn your clothes? Let him come to me, that he may learn

NIV

is a prophet in Israel." 9So Naaman went with his horses and chariots and stopped at the door of Elisha's house. 10Elisha sent a messenger to say to him, "Go, wash yourself seven times in the Jordan, and your flesh will be restored and you will be cleansed."

11But Naaman went away angry and said, "I thought that he would surely come out to me and stand and call on the name of the LORD his God, wave his hand over the spot and cure me of my leprosy. 12Are not Abana and Pharpar, the rivers of Damascus, better than any of the waters of Israel? Couldn't I wash in them and be cleansed?" So he turned and went off in a rage.

13Naaman's servants went to him and said, "My father, if the prophet had told you to do some great thing, would you not have done it? How much more, then, when he tells you, 'Wash and be cleansed'!" 14So he went down and dipped himself in the Jordan seven times, as the man of God had told him, and his flesh was restored and became clean like that of a young boy.

NRSV

that there is a prophet in Israel." 9So Naaman came with his horses and chariots, and halted at the entrance of Elisha's house. 10Elisha sent a messenger to him, saying, "Go, wash in the Jordan seven times, and your flesh shall be restored and you shall be clean." 11But Naaman became angry and went away, saying, "I thought that for me he would surely come out, and stand and call on the name of the LORD his God, and would wave his hand over the spot, and cure the leprosy![a] 12Are not Abana[b] and Pharpar, the rivers of Damascus, better than all the waters of Israel? Could I not wash in them, and be clean?" He turned and went away in a rage. 13But his servants approached and said to him, "Father, if the prophet had commanded you to do something difficult, would you not have done it? How much more, when all he said to you was, 'Wash, and be clean'?" 14So he went down and immersed himself seven times in the Jordan, according to the word of the man of God; his flesh was restored like the flesh of a young boy, and he was clean.

[a] A term for several skin diseases; precise meaning uncertain [b] Another reading is *Amana*

COMMENTARY

Elisha hears of the king's despair and comes forward to help, in order that Naaman "may learn that there is a prophet in Israel" (v. 8). So Naaman comes to the entrance of the prophet's house with his impressive entourage. Although his visit brought grave anxiety to the king, the prophet does not even deign to come out to meet the "great man." A more subtle point, perhaps, is the power of the prophet. Without ever seeing Naaman, he is able to bring about Naaman's healing. Elisha merely sends instructions through a messenger, telling Naaman to wash himself seven times in the Jordan River and promising that his flesh will be restored as a result and that he will be clean (for the significance of "seven times," see Lev 14:7, 16, 27, 51; cf. 2 Kgs 4:35).

Naaman is indignant at his treatment by Elisha, for the general had already imagined how it would all work, perhaps because he had seen healing rituals being performed before. He probably expects Elisha to come out, call on the name of the Lord, wave his hand over the problem area, and heal it. Although it is not readily evident in the English translations, the Hebrew word order suggests a wounded ego: "I thought, 'Unto me he would surely come out and stand. . . .' " Naaman's national pride is also insulted, it seems. If he has to wash himself in a river, he does not see why he has to come all the way from his own country, for he deems the local rivers of Damascus, the Abana (properly, the Amanah) and the Pharpar, better than all the waters of Israel. So he turns away in rage. His servants point out that he would no doubt go to great lengths to do what Elisha says, if it had been something difficult, so he should give the simple formula a chance to succeed. For all his greatness and pride, Naaman is able to listen to the advice of his servants. The words of the Israelite servant girl caused him to come to Israel in the first place, and now, his own servants are prompting him to heed the Israelite prophet. Accordingly, Naaman follows the instructions of Elisha and is healed, just as Elisha had promised. The flesh of the "great man" is restored (שׁוּב *šûb*) like that of a "young boy" (v. 14). Naaman is now in some sense like the "young girl" from Israel whom he had enslaved. (See Reflections at 5:19*b*-27.)

2 Kings 5:15-19*a*, Naaman's Conversion

NIV

[15]Then Naaman and all his attendants went back to the man of God. He stood before him and said, "Now I know that there is no God in all the world except in Israel. Please accept now a gift from your servant."

[16]The prophet answered, "As surely as the LORD lives, whom I serve, I will not accept a thing." And even though Naaman urged him, he refused.

[17]"If you will not," said Naaman, "please let me, your servant, be given as much earth as a pair of mules can carry, for your servant will never again make burnt offerings and sacrifices to any other god but the LORD. [18]But may the LORD forgive your servant for this one thing: When my master enters the temple of Rimmon to bow down and he is leaning on my arm and I bow there also—when I bow down in the temple of Rimmon, may the LORD forgive your servant for this."

[19]"Go in peace," Elisha said.

NRSV

15Then he returned to the man of God, he and all his company; he came and stood before him and said, "Now I know that there is no God in all the earth except in Israel; please accept a present from your servant." [16]But he said, "As the LORD lives, whom I serve, I will accept nothing!" He urged him to accept, but he refused. [17]Then Naaman said, "If not, please let two mule-loads of earth be given to your servant; for your servant will no longer offer burnt offering or sacrifice to any god except the LORD. [18]But may the LORD pardon your servant on one count: when my master goes into the house of Rimmon to worship there, leaning on my arm, and I bow down in the house of Rimmon, when I do bow down in the house of Rimmon, may the LORD pardon your servant on this one count." [19]He said to him, "Go in peace."

COMMENTARY

Naaman returns to Elisha and stands before the prophet (v. 15). Unlike the previous occasion, when Elisha merely instructed him through a messenger, the prophet now speaks to him directly. Whereas Naaman had previously expected the prophet to come to him and "stand" (עמד *ʿāmad*, v. 11), it is now Naaman who stands (*ʿāmad*, v. 15) before Elisha. Moreover, whereas Naaman previously referred to the Lord as Elisha's God (v. 11), now he himself confesses the uniqueness of the Lord. Elisha had come forward to heal Naaman in order that Naaman might "know that there is a prophet in Israel"; now we hear Naaman's confession that "there is no other god in all the earth except in Israel."

Naaman offers Elisha a gift (ברכה *bĕrākâ*; lit., "a blessing"), but Elisha steadfastly refuses it, even when pressed upon to do so (cf. Num 22:18; Dan 5:17; Amos 7:12; Mic 3:5, 11). Naaman then asks that he might be allowed to take home soil from Israel. Like any new convert, Naaman's theology is apparently unsophisticated. He properly confesses that "there is no God in all the earth except in Israel," perhaps because that is what he has been taught. He takes the confession literally, however, assuming that the Lord is to be worshiped only on Israelite soil. Hence his proposal to take some of that soil home, because he does not want to offer burnt offerings or sacrifices to other gods. At the same time, however, he realizes that his position will entail certain expectations; as the king's right-hand man (see 7:2, 17), as it were, he would have to accompany the king to worship Rimmon, the storm deity Hadad-Rimmon ("Hadad the Thunderer"), the patron god of the Arameans (Zech 12:11). For that anticipated compromise of his allegiance to the Lord, he asks for forgiveness in advance (cf. 1 Kgs 8:41-43). He is clearly aware that such an act would be contrary to expectations of him in his newfound faith; thus the awkward repetition about his anticipated obeisance in the temple of Rimmon in v. 18 may indicate some embarrassment on his part about the request. Elisha replies with neither condemnation nor permission, but he tells Naaman to "go in peace" (cf. Exod 4:18; 1 Sam 1:17; 20:42; see also Mark 5:34; Luke 7:50; 8:48; Acts 16:36). (See Reflections at 5:19*b*-27.)

2 Kings 5:19*b*-27, Gehazi's Treachery

NIV

After Naaman had traveled some distance,
20Gehazi, the servant of Elisha the man of God,
said to himself, "My master was too easy on
Naaman, this Aramean, by not accepting from him
what he brought. As surely as the LORD lives, I
will run after him and get something from him."

21So Gehazi hurried after Naaman. When
Naaman saw him running toward him, he got
down from the chariot to meet him. "Is everything all right?" he asked.

22"Everything is all right," Gehazi answered.
"My master sent me to say, 'Two young men
from the company of the prophets have just come
to me from the hill country of Ephraim. Please
give them a talent[a] of silver and two sets of
clothing.'"

23"By all means, take two talents," said
Naaman. He urged Gehazi to accept them, and
then tied up the two talents of silver in two bags,
with two sets of clothing. He gave them to two
of his servants, and they carried them ahead of
Gehazi. 24When Gehazi came to the hill, he took
the things from the servants and put them away
in the house. He sent the men away and they
left. 25Then he went in and stood before his
master Elisha.

"Where have you been, Gehazi?" Elisha asked.

"Your servant didn't go anywhere," Gehazi answered.

26But Elisha said to him, "Was not my spirit
with you when the man got down from his
chariot to meet you? Is this the time to take
money, or to accept clothes, olive groves, vine-

[a] *22* That is, about 75 pounds (about 34 kilograms)

NRSV

But when Naaman had gone from him a short
distance, 20Gehazi, the servant of Elisha the man
of God, thought, "My master has let that Aramean
Naaman off too lightly by not accepting from him
what he offered. As the LORD lives, I will run after
him and get something out of him." 21So Gehazi
went after Naaman. When Naaman saw someone
running after him, he jumped down from the
chariot to meet him and said, "Is everything all
right?" 22He replied, "Yes, but my master has sent
me to say, 'Two members of a company of
prophets[a] have just come to me from the hill
country of Ephraim; please give them a talent of
silver and two changes of clothing.'" 23Naaman
said, "Please accept two talents." He urged him,
and tied up two talents of silver in two bags, with
two changes of clothing, and gave them to two
of his servants, who carried them in front of
Gehazi.[b] 24When he came to the citadel, he took
the bags[c] from them, and stored them inside; he
dismissed the men, and they left.

25He went in and stood before his master; and
Elisha said to him, "Where have you been, Gehazi?" He answered, "Your servant has not gone
anywhere at all." 26But he said to him, "Did I not
go with you in spirit when someone left his
chariot to meet you? Is this a time to accept
money and to accept clothing, olive orchards and
vineyards, sheep and oxen, and male and female
slaves? 27Therefore the leprosy[d] of Naaman shall
cling to you, and to your descendants forever."
So he left his presence leprous,[d] as white as snow.

[a] Heb *sons of the prophets* [b] Heb *him* [c] Heb lacks *the bags*
[d] A term for several skin diseases; precise meaning uncertain

NIV

yards, flocks, herds, or menservants and maidservants? [27]Naaman's leprosy will cling to you and to your descendants forever." Then Gehazi went from Elisha's presence and he was leprous, as white as snow.

COMMENTARY

Elisha has been firm that he will not receive any remuneration from Naaman. His servant Gehazi, however, thinks that Elisha has been too easy on Naaman, whom he obviously regards as still an outsider (נעמן הארמי הזה [*na'ămān hā'ărammî hazzeh*, "Naaman, that Aramean"], v. 20). Elisha had sworn ("as the LORD lives") that he would accept nothing from Naaman (v. 16). Gehazi, however, swears ("as the LORD lives") that he will get something out of Naaman (v. 20). He lies that Elisha has changed his mind about the gift because two prophets have suddenly shown up. The lie is credible because the request is relatively modest, only a small fraction of what Naaman had brought (see v. 5). Gehazi's deviousness stands in contrast to the graciousness of Naaman, who urges him (v. 16; cf. v. 23) to take twice the amount of cash requested, packages it nicely, and has his servants carry the packages for Gehazi. As soon as Gehazi returns to the capital, he sends away the helpers and conceals the loot. One deception leads to another, for Gehazi then lies to Elisha, saying that he has not gone anywhere. The prophet, however, has extraordinary powers of knowledge and knows that Gehazi has been "on the take" (the verb לקח [*lāqaḥ*, "to take"] appears twice in v. 26). So he condemns Gehazi and his descendants with Naaman's disease. Thus Gehazi, who contrives to take the "blessing" that Naaman had meant for Elisha, is cursed.

REFLECTIONS

The story of the healing of Naaman is surely one of the most fascinating in the book of Kings. It is a remarkably entertaining drama with a rich cast of characters, a well-developed plot, many ironic twists and turns, comic relief (like the image of the panicky king), keen insights into human flaws (a war hero's ego and ethnocentrism; a servant's avarice and deceitfulness), and a satisfying conclusion. Here are the essential materials for a compelling church play—one that offers many theological vignettes.

1. The most important message is, of course, the inclusivity of God's saving activity. The reader is told from the beginning that it is God who gives victory (the Hebrew word also means "deliverance" or "salvation") to Naaman. It is God's will from the start, it seems, to bring "salvation" to Naaman, even though Naaman was not among God's chosen people. This message is all the more poignant when one considers the ironic reversal that the chapter as a whole conveys: The Gentile Naaman is restored, while the Israelite Gehazi is cursed. It is appropriate, therefore, that Jesus should later point to this story to justify the inclusivity of his ministry (Luke 4:27). Just as Elijah ministered to the Phoenician widow of Zarephath, and just as Elisha ministered to Naaman the Aramean, so, too, Jesus proclaimed good news to the outcasts of Jewish society as well as to some Gentiles.

2. Naaman's path to restoration was by no means a straightforward one. He was amenable to heeding the suggestion of a captive slave and desperate enough to travel all the way from Damascus to find the prophet at his home in Samaria. Naaman had, however, his own idea

of how the restoration of health would be carried out. Elisha's instructions sounded ridiculous to Naaman, and his pride was wounded. Yet, he was restored only when he submitted himself to the seemingly silly ritual of taking a bath. He expected something dramatic, but salvation came to him through the words of a prophet, conveyed to him by a messenger—and it entailed a baptism. This is the way God cleanses people of their afflictions, it seems—not through the dramatic performance of a human healer, but through a simple act of obedience. Salvation comes mysteriously when we submit to God's script and not our own.

3. Naaman's experience of restoration leads to his confession of faith in the Lord. One might have expected the reverse (confession before restoration), but that is not the case. God initiated the entire process of salvation for Naaman—while the Aramean was yet afflicted with the deadly disease—by giving him victory (also meaning "deliverance" or "salvation"). God restored Naaman and cleansed him when he obeyed, without understanding anything of the mystery of that experience (see Titus 3:4-5). Even when Naaman finally confessed the Lord, his theology was simplistic, his notion of God's presence inadequate, his allegiance to God not without distractions. The reader may be inclined to be impatient with Naaman for his bad theology and his unwillingness to risk all that he has for the Lord. Elisha did not, however, condemn him. Rather, Elisha sent him away with a benediction: "Go in peace!" There was much room for grace in Elisha's theology.

4. Unlike Elisha, Gehazi was not so gracious. There is something disdainful, too—perhaps even exclusivistic—in the way he spoke of Naaman ("Naaman, this Aramean," 5:20). He thought that Naaman was getting off easy when he should have had to pay a price, and so he tried to squeeze something out of Naaman. Gehazi tried to make a profit from Naaman's experience of healing, and for that he was condemned (see also Acts 8:18-24). There are people in every era who are so terribly afflicted with diseases and other ailments, who are desperate to find any word of hope from spiritual leaders. And there are always opportunists like Gehazi who are ready to make a quick profit in the name of the Lord. This text sternly warns against such opportunism.

5. In stark contrast to Gehazi is the unnamed Israelite slave at the beginning of the chapter. Despite her lowly status and her captivity in a foreign land, she is faithful. Although far from her homeland, her eyes of faith perceive hope for her Aramean master. The king of Israel, on the other hand, could only despair, even though salvation was at hand in Samaria.

2 KINGS 6:1-23, MORE MIRACLES OF ELISHA

OVERVIEW

There are two stories concerning Elijah's ministry in 2 Kgs 6:1-23. The first, taking place in a somewhat private and domestic setting, tells of the prophet's raising of a sunken ax head (6:1-7). As with the preceding story concerning the healing of Naaman, the event in this account is set at the Jordan River, and that setting perhaps explains its place in this literary context. The miracle of healing at the river is followed by the miracle of the floating iron ax head. The second story concerns an international incident in which Elisha effectively neutralizes certain acts of aggression by the Arameans against Israel (6:8-23). The account may have been placed here because of the reference to a large Aramean army in Israel (see 5:9) and the allusion to Elisha's gift of "second sight" (vv. 8-10; cf. 5:26).

2 Kings 6:1-7, Elisha Raises a Sunken Ax Head

NIV

6 The company of the prophets said to Elisha, "Look, the place where we meet with you is too small for us. 2Let us go to the Jordan, where each of us can get a pole; and let us build a place there for us to live."

And he said, "Go."

3Then one of them said, "Won't you please come with your servants?"

"I will," Elisha replied. 4And he went with them.

They went to the Jordan and began to cut down trees. 5As one of them was cutting down a tree, the iron axhead fell into the water. "Oh, my lord," he cried out, "it was borrowed!"

6The man of God asked, "Where did it fall?" When he showed him the place, Elisha cut a stick and threw it there, and made the iron float. 7"Lift it out," he said. Then the man reached out his hand and took it.

NRSV

6 Now the company of prophets[a] said to Elisha, "As you see, the place where we live under your charge is too small for us. 2Let us go to the Jordan, and let us collect logs there, one for each of us, and build a place there for us to live." He answered, "Do so." 3Then one of them said, "Please come with your servants." And he answered, "I will." 4So he went with them. When they came to the Jordan, they cut down trees. 5But as one was felling a log, his ax head fell into the water; he cried out, "Alas, master! It was borrowed." 6Then the man of God said, "Where did it fall?" When he showed him the place, he cut off a stick, and threw it in there, and made the iron float. 7He said, "Pick it up." So he reached out his hand and took it.

[a] Heb *sons of the prophets*

COMMENTARY

A group of Elisha's prophetic disciples realize that they have outgrown their meeting place (NIV, "the place where we meet with you") or quarters (NRSV, "the place where we live under your charge"). The Hebrew may be taken to mean, literally, "the place where they were sitting before him" (cf. 4:38)—that is, as his disciples. So they decide to go to the Jordan to cut down trees to build a new one, and they invite Elisha to come along. As one of them is working, his iron ax head slips off the handle and falls into the river, causing him great consternation because the ax had been borrowed. Elisha, however, saves the day. When he finds the spot where the ax head fell into the river, he cuts a piece of wood and throws it into the water, causing the iron ax head to float and thus be easily retrieved.

Commentators have been tempted to see this feat as an illustration of "sympathetic magic" or to offer rationalistic explanations of what might have happened. The text is silent about the details, however. It merely reports it as a wondrous deed that was brought about on account of Elisha's presence and intervention on behalf of the man in distress. Whereas axes were relatively inexpensive in modern times, they were not so in ancient Israel, where iron was scarce and, in time of war, largely reserved for military use. The members of "the company of prophets" seem to have been quite poor (see 4:38-41; 5:22), and this story is set in a context of famine and war, so the loss of a borrowed ax was no trivial matter. Elisha's intervention probably saved the poor man from incurring a debt that he could not afford to pay. This miracle thus ranks with others that Elisha performed on behalf of individuals in dire need (see 2:19-22; 4:1-7, 38-41). Sandwiched between accounts of the prophet's role in the international arena, the story of his attention to the plight of an individual disciple is testimony to the range of Elisha's prophetic ministry. He does not save only mighty generals like Naaman (5:1-19*a*). He is concerned not only with the affairs of kings and nations (6:8–7:20). Elisha's salvific activity touches the daily and mundane needs of individual persons as well. (See Reflections at 6:8-23.)

2 Kings 6:8-23, Elisha Overcomes the Troops of Aram

NIV

8Now the king of Aram was at war with Israel. After conferring with his officers, he said, "I will set up my camp in such and such a place."

9The man of God sent word to the king of Israel: "Beware of passing that place, because the Arameans are going down there." 10So the king of Israel checked on the place indicated by the man of God. Time and again Elisha warned the king, so that he was on his guard in such places.

11This enraged the king of Aram. He summoned his officers and demanded of them, "Will you not tell me which of us is on the side of the king of Israel?"

12"None of us, my lord the king," said one of his officers, "but Elisha, the prophet who is in Israel, tells the king of Israel the very words you speak in your bedroom."

13"Go, find out where he is," the king ordered, "so I can send men and capture him." The report came back: "He is in Dothan." 14Then he sent horses and chariots and a strong force there. They went by night and surrounded the city.

15When the servant of the man of God got up and went out early the next morning, an army with horses and chariots had surrounded the city. "Oh, my lord, what shall we do?" the servant asked.

16"Don't be afraid," the prophet answered. "Those who are with us are more than those who are with them."

17And Elisha prayed, "O LORD, open his eyes so he may see." Then the LORD opened the servant's eyes, and he looked and saw the hills full of horses and chariots of fire all around Elisha.

18As the enemy came down toward him, Elisha prayed to the LORD, "Strike these people with blindness." So he struck them with blindness, as Elisha had asked.

19Elisha told them, "This is not the road and this is not the city. Follow me, and I will lead you to the man you are looking for." And he led them to Samaria.

NRSV

8Once when the king of Aram was at war with Israel, he took counsel with his officers. He said, "At such and such a place shall be my camp." 9But the man of God sent word to the king of Israel, "Take care not to pass this place, because the Arameans are going down there." 10The king of Israel sent word to the place of which the man of God spoke. More than once or twice he warned such a place[a] so that it was on the alert.

11The mind of the king of Aram was greatly perturbed because of this; he called his officers and said to them, "Now tell me who among us sides with the king of Israel?" 12Then one of his officers said, "No one, my lord king. It is Elisha, the prophet in Israel, who tells the king of Israel the words that you speak in your bedchamber." 13He said, "Go and find where he is; I will send and seize him." He was told, "He is in Dothan." 14So he sent horses and chariots there and a great army; they came by night, and surrounded the city.

15When an attendant of the man of God rose early in the morning and went out, an army with horses and chariots was all around the city. His servant said, "Alas, master! What shall we do?" 16He replied, "Do not be afraid, for there are more with us than there are with them." 17Then Elisha prayed: "O LORD, please open his eyes that he may see." So the LORD opened the eyes of the servant, and he saw; the mountain was full of horses and chariots of fire all around Elisha. 18When the Arameans[b] came down against him, Elisha prayed to the LORD, and said, "Strike this people, please, with blindness." So he struck them with blindness as Elisha had asked. 19Elisha said to them, "This is not the way, and this is not the city; follow me, and I will bring you to the man whom you seek." And he led them to Samaria.

20As soon as they entered Samaria, Elisha said, "O LORD, open the eyes of these men so that they may see." The LORD opened their eyes, and they

[a] Heb *warned it* [b] Heb *they*

NIV

[20]After they entered the city, Elisha said, "LORD, open the eyes of these men so they can see." Then the LORD opened their eyes and they looked, and there they were, inside Samaria.

[21]When the king of Israel saw them, he asked Elisha, "Shall I kill them, my father? Shall I kill them?"

[22]"Do not kill them," he answered. "Would you kill men you have captured with your own sword or bow? Set food and water before them so that they may eat and drink and then go back to their master." [23]So he prepared a great feast for them, and after they had finished eating and drinking, he sent them away, and they returned to their master. So the bands from Aram stopped raiding Israel's territory.

NRSV

saw that they were inside Samaria. [21]When the king of Israel saw them he said to Elisha, "Father, shall I kill them? Shall I kill them?" [22]He answered, "No! Did you capture with your sword and your bow those whom you want to kill? Set food and water before them so that they may eat and drink; and let them go to their master." [23]So he prepared for them a great feast; after they ate and drank, he sent them on their way, and they went to their master. And the Arameans no longer came raiding into the land of Israel.

COMMENTARY

Unlike the preceding story regarding Elisha's ministry among his own disciples, this account concerns his role in the arena of international politics. It is set in a time of war between Israel and Aram; the peace assumed by the story of the healing of Naaman (5:1-27) no longer held.

The unnamed Aramean king repeatedly devised secret plans to attack Israel, but each time Elisha learned of the plans through his extraordinary powers (cf. 5:26) and passed on the secret to the Israelites, who used the information to thwart the Arameans.[93] This was not a coincidence, the narrator implies, for the same thing recurred (v. 10). The king of Aram suspects treason (v. 11), but he was told that it was Elisha who had been responsible for the security leaks (cf. Eccl 10:20). Thereupon, he orders the prophet's capture (v. 13).

The single prophet apparently caused such concern to the Aramean king that the latter dispatches a huge force—"horses and chariots and a great army" (v. 14)—to capture him in Dothan (10 miles north of Samaria), where Elisha is reported to be (v. 13). Moreover, despite the fact that Elisha had previously known of the king's secret plans through his extrasensory powers, the Arameans think it would make a difference for them to approach under the cover of darkness (v. 13). At dawn, Elisha's attendant expresses consternation upon seeing the Aramean troops, his cry echoing the distressful cry of the disciple whose ax head had fallen into the river Jordan: "Alas! My master!" (v. 15; cf. v. 5). The prophet assures him cryptically that "there are more with us than there are with them" (v. 16). The meaning of this assurance is made plain when, upon the prayer of Elisha, the servant is given to see something of what Elisha himself had seen at his inauguration as Elijah's successor (2:11). The servant apparently sees a celestial host ("the mountains full of horses and chariots of fire") surrounding Elisha. This will be the secret of Elisha's success. The Arameans, who obviously are not privy to this vision, attack. Elisha prays for them to be struck by "a blinding light" (TNK). The NRSV and the NIV take the word סנורים (*sanwērîm*) to mean "blindness." Yet, the troops were not completely blinded, for they were able to follow Elisha to Samaria. The Hebrew word, which occurs elsewhere in the Bible only in Gen 19:11, is probably a loan word from Akkadian *šunwurum* ("having dazzling brightness"). The humor of the narrator surfaces again as one reads of Elisha's encounter

93. Josephus identified the Aramean king as Ben-hadad and the Israelite king as Joram, but that is entirely speculative. See Josephus *Antiquities of the Jews* IX.51-78.

with the Aramean troops. The very prophet whom they were sent to capture tells them that they are going in the wrong direction. When he volunteers to lead them to the man they seek to capture, they blindly follow him. Accordingly, Elisha brings them to Samaria, where the Israelites presumably had military superiority. Then he prays for their ability to see (v. 20), even as he had prayed for his servant to see (v. 17), and they realize where they are.

The Israelite king reacts as an excited child might. "Father, shall I kill them? Shall I kill them?" he asks the prophet. Elisha demurs, noting that these troops were not brought into Samaria by Israel's military might but by the will of God alone. Instead of doing violence to them, then, Elisha tells the king to extend hospitality to the enemy troops and then to release them. There is perhaps nothing more humiliating than for the great invading army to be fed and then sent on its way. In consequence, according to the narrator, the Arameans no longer harassed Israel (v. 23).

REFLECTIONS

The juxtaposition of the two stories highlights dramatically the range of Elisha's ministry. In one instance, he is involved in the daily activities of his disciples, their concern to have a suitable place for their group, the panic of a person who has lost something expensive. In the next instance, the prophet is involved in international politics, as it were, working to thwart the naked aggression of the Arameans, on the one hand, and preventing violence on the part of the Israelites, on the other hand. The ministry in God's name can be like that.

1. Richard Nelson has observed that the miracle of the floating ax head is "something of an embarrassment for modern readers" and that "it seems trivial and pointless."[94] That is especially the case when one reads it after the account of the dramatic healing of Naaman in 5:1-28 and before the story of Elisha's dazzling of the massive Aramean army in 6:8-23. Yet its very domestic and mundane character may itself be instructive. The presence of stories like this one is a powerful reminder to us that ministry involves attending to the seemingly ordinary needs and anxieties of people coping with life's routines.

2. Elisha's ministry calls attention to the fact that the battles of the world are not fought by the great armies of the earth alone. In the face of overwhelming odds, the prophet prays for his servant to see that there are celestial forces fighting on the side of God's people against those who threaten them, "for there are more with us than with them" (v. 16).

3. Against those who may be eager to annihilate their enemy, the narrator elevates a response of hospitality and kindness instead of violence. This passage offers a perspective that is different from the harsh demands of holy war ideology (cf. 1 Kgs 20:31-42).

94. Richard D. Nelson, *First and Second Kings*, Interpretation (Atlanta: John Knox, 1987) 184.

2 KINGS 6:24–7:20, THE SIEGE OF SAMARIA

OVERVIEW

This literary unit contains an account of another of Israel's encounters with the Arameans. The story is loosely linked to the preceding one by the temporal expression אחרי־כן (*'aḥărê-kēn*, "afterward"; NRSV, NIV, "sometime later"). The unit is, however, quite different from the preceding one. Whereas the preceding passage ends with the cessation of Aramean hostilities, the new unit concerns a direct attack on Samaria (v. 24). Whereas the king of Aram is not named in the preceding unit, he is now identified as Ben-hadad, the name of several Aramean kings in the ninth century BCE. Given the relative weakness of Israel and the might of Aram, it is likely that Ben-hadad, son of Hazael, is meant. He ruled in Damascus at the end of the ninth century BCE and the beginning of the eighth. Cf. 2 Kgs 8:15; 13:3-7; 22–25.

Whereas 6:1-23 contains stories of miracles performed by Elisha, 6:24–7:20 highlights a prophetic oracle and its fulfillment. Despite the chapter division in most modern Bibles, it seems clear that the original unit included not only the description of the siege and its consequences (6:24-33), but also Elisha's prediction of the end of the siege and the fulfillment of the prophecy (7:1-20). Moreover, whatever its origin might have been, 7:18-20 now appears as a final reiteration of the fulfillment of the oracle in 7:1-2, for 8:1 clearly begins a brand-new story.

2 Kings 6:24-31, The Siege and Its Effects

NIV

24Some time later, Ben-Hadad king of Aram mobilized his entire army and marched up and laid siege to Samaria. 25There was a great famine in the city; the siege lasted so long that a donkey's head sold for eighty shekels[a] of silver, and a quarter of a cab[b] of seed pods[c] for five shekels.[d]

26As the king of Israel was passing by on the wall, a woman cried to him, "Help me, my lord the king!"

27The king replied, "If the LORD does not help you, where can I get help for you? From the threshing floor? From the winepress?" 28Then he asked her, "What's the matter?"

She answered, "This woman said to me, 'Give up your son so we may eat him today, and tomorrow we'll eat my son.' 29So we cooked my son and ate him. The next day I said to her, 'Give up your son so we may eat him,' but she had hidden him."

30When the king heard the woman's words, he tore his robes. As he went along the wall, the people looked, and there, underneath, he had sackcloth on his body. 31He said, "May God deal with me, be it ever so severely, if the head of Elisha son of Shaphat remains on his shoulders today!"

[a] 25 That is, about 2 pounds (about 1 kilogram) [b] 25 That is, probably about 1/2 pint (about 0.3 liter) [c] 25 Or *of dove's dung* [d] 25 That is, about 2 ounces (about 55 grams)

NRSV

24Some time later King Ben-hadad of Aram mustered his entire army; he marched against Samaria and laid siege to it. 25As the siege continued, famine in Samaria became so great that a donkey's head was sold for eighty shekels of silver, and one-fourth of a kab of dove's dung for five shekels of silver. 26Now as the king of Israel was walking on the city wall, a woman cried out to him, "Help, my lord king!" 27He said, "No! Let the LORD help you. How can I help you? From the threshing floor or from the wine press?" 28But then the king asked her, "What is your complaint?" She answered, "This woman said to me, 'Give up your son; we will eat him today, and we will eat my son tomorrow.' 29So we cooked my son and ate him. The next day I said to her, 'Give up your son and we will eat him.' But she has hidden her son." 30When the king heard the words of the woman he tore his clothes—now since he was walking on the city wall, the people could see that he had sackcloth on his body underneath— 31and he said, "So may God do to me, and more, if the head of Elisha son of Shaphat stays on his shoulders today."

COMMENTARY

According to the conclusion of the preceding unit, the Arameans "no longer came raiding into the land of Israel" (v. 23). In the new story, set in a different time, however, Ben-hadad of Aram succeeds in laying siege to Samaria (v. 24). The Aramean siege causes such a severe famine in the city that even an unappetizing item like a donkey's head and a very small amount ("one-fourth of a kab" is about a quarter of a quart) of "dove dung" fetch exorbitant prices (v. 25). The NIV interprets the "dove dung" (חרי יונים *ḥărê yônîm*) to be a popular term for some kind of "seed pods" (NJV, "carob pods"; NEB and REB, "locust-beans"); there is some evidence for this interpretation in an Akkadian lexical text, in which "dove dung" is defined as "seed of the false carob."[95] Even such inedible husks (cf. Luke 15:16) were scarce during the siege.

Jehoram, the king of Samaria, apparently is surveying the devastation, when a distressed woman approaches him for deliverance (v. 26). The king recognizes that it is beyond his ability to alleviate the situation, for he is unable to supply any grain from the threshing floor or wine from the vats (6:27; cf. Num 18:27, 30; Deut 15:14; 16:13). Unwittingly, he points to the true source of their salvation: the Lord (v. 27; see 7:6). Nevertheless, he listens to the woman's complaint; through that complaint, the reader learns of the extreme horrors the famine has produced (vv. 28-29). Cases of cannibalism in times of siege are known from the Bible (Deut 28:56-57; Lam 2:20; 4:10; Ezek 5:10) and are corroborated by extra-biblical sources.[96]

In some ways, the case that this woman presents before the king, in which she and another woman agreed to cannibalize each other's son, but one reneges, echoes the case of the two harlots who came before Solomon in 1 Kgs 3:16-28.[97] Yet, there are stark differences. Whereas the "real" mother in the case before Solomon was overwhelmed by sorrow and moved by compassion for her dead child, the mother who presents her case to Jehoram does not express her sense of loss or her guilt at having killed her son. Instead, she complains that the other woman has reneged on their agreement so that she, the plaintiff, is being deprived of her right to have the child of the other woman as food. The famine has brought about savage desperation and callousness.

The king goes into public mourning (v. 30), another indication of the severity of the national crisis (cf. 19:1-2; 1 Kgs 20:32; 21:27). He blames Elisha for the situation (v. 31). One might speculate that the king thought the problem would not exist if he had been allowed to kill the Aramean army that had been trapped in Samaria (vv. 22-23). Perhaps he reckoned that Elisha could have performed a miracle to provide food for the people (cf. 4:42-44). The king does not give any reason, however, for placing the blame on Elisha, and that is perhaps the point that we are meant to get. The king takes no responsibility whatsoever for the situation, preferring to find a scapegoat and to divert attention from the problem by killing someone, as if the famine had not already caused death enough. (See Reflections at 7:3-20.)

95. See Mordecai Cogan and Hayim Tadmor, *II Kings*, AB 11 (New York: Doubleday, 1988) 79. Josephus, too, long ago suggested that "dove dung" might have been some sort of food, specifically something used as a salt substitute. See Josephus *Antiquities of the Jews* IX.62.

96. See *ANET*, 298.

97. See Stuart Lasine, "Jehoram and the Cannibal Mothers (2 Kings 6:24-33): Solomon's Judgment in an Inverted World," *JSOT* 50 (1991) 27-53.

2 Kings 6:32–7:2, Confrontation Between the King and Elisha

NIV

[32]Now Elisha was sitting in his house, and the elders were sitting with him. The king sent a messenger ahead, but before he arrived, Elisha said to the elders, "Don't you see how this murderer is sending someone to cut off my head? Look, when the messenger comes, shut the door and hold it shut against him. Is not the sound of his master's footsteps behind him?"

NRSV

[32]So he dispatched a man from his presence.

Now Elisha was sitting in his house, and the elders were sitting with him. Before the messenger arrived, Elisha said to the elders, "Are you aware that this murderer has sent someone to take off my head? When the messenger comes, see that you shut the door and hold it closed against him. Is not the sound of his master's feet

NIV

33While he was still talking to them, the messenger came down to him. And ⌞the king⌟ said,
"This disaster is from the LORD. Why should I wait
for the LORD any longer?"

7 Elisha said, "Hear the word of the LORD.
This is what the LORD says: About this time
tomorrow, a seah[a] of flour will sell for a shekel[b]
and two seahs[c] of barley for a shekel at the gate
of Samaria."

2The officer on whose arm the king was leaning
said to the man of God, "Look, even if the LORD
should open the floodgates of the heavens, could
this happen?"

"You will see it with your own eyes," answered
Elisha, "but you will not eat any of it!"

[a] *1* That is, probably about 7 quarts (about 7.3 liters); also in verses 16 and 18 [b] *1* That is, about 2/5 ounce (about 11 grams); also in verses 16 and 18 [c] *1* That is, probably about 13 quarts (about 15 liters); also in verses 16 and 18

NRSV

behind him?" 33While he was still speaking with
them, the king[a] came down to him and said, "This
trouble is from the LORD! Why should I hope in
the LORD any longer?"

7 1But Elisha said, "Hear the word of the
LORD: thus says the LORD, Tomorrow about
this time a measure of choice meal shall be sold
for a shekel, and two measures of barley for a
shekel, at the gate of Samaria." 2Then the captain
on whose hand the king leaned said to the man
of God, "Even if the LORD were to make windows
in the sky, could such a thing happen?" But he
said, "You shall see it with your own eyes, but
you shall not eat from it."

[a] See 7.2: Heb *messenger*

COMMENTARY

The confusing sequence of events in 6:32-33 is difficult to sort out. The king sends a man to Elisha (v. 32*a*), but the mission of that man is not spelled out in the narrative. One expects him to be an assassin or a bailiff, but, as in another instance involving a threat to the life of a prophet, he may be a messenger who is sent to issue the death threat (1 Kgs 19:2-3). The narrator here identifies the man as a messenger (v. 32*b*).

Elisha is at home with the elders of the city who had come to visit him. Through his extraordinary power of perception (cf. 5:26; 6:8-10), the prophet knows that the man is coming and that his life is in danger. Still, Elisha refers to the man as a messenger and expects the king to come behind him. The scene is thoroughly comical. Elisha calls on a bunch of old men to hold the door shut as the message from the king is delivered, either by the messenger (so the Hebrew text, followed by the NIV) or by the king in person (so NRSV, with a slight emendation of the text). In any case, the king is apparently present when the message was delivered (7:2). Just as he had held Elisha responsible in some way for the tragedy (v. 31), so also the king blames the Lord and expresses a loss of faith in the Lord (v. 33). As the Targum would have it, he was so disheartened that he even refused to pray.

Elisha responds with a surprisingly positive oracle issued in classical prophetic style (7:1). He predicts that the dire circumstances will end the very next day; the prices of food will be back to the usual levels one might expect at the marketplace ("at the gate of Samaria").[98] Nothing is said of the king's reaction. Jehoram's right-hand man, however, is skeptical that there could be such an instant turnaround. Even if the Lord were to open the floodgates of heaven (cf. Gen 7:11; Mal 3:10), the officer suggests, there could not be an immediate reversal such as Elisha predicted (v. 2). No doubt, he meant that it would take some time for the new growth to bear fruit. The officer cannot conceive of another way for deliverance to come, except by the natural process. For that lack of faith, the prophet declares, the officer will witness the miracle but not be able to partake of its benefits. (See Reflections at 7:3-20.)

98. The "measure" (סאה *sĕʾâ*) was six times larger than the קב (*qab*, "dove dung"). Yet a *sĕʾâ* of choice meal would sell for only a fifth of the price of a *qab* during the siege, and the same amount of money would buy two סאים (*sĕʾîm*) of barley.

2 Kings 7:3-20, How the Siege Was Lifted

NIV

3Now there were four men with leprosy[a] at the entrance of the city gate. They said to each other, "Why stay here until we die? 4If we say, 'We'll go into the city'—the famine is there, and we will die. And if we stay here, we will die. So let's go over to the camp of the Arameans and surrender. If they spare us, we live; if they kill us, then we die."

5At dusk they got up and went to the camp of the Arameans. When they reached the edge of the camp, not a man was there, 6for the Lord had caused the Arameans to hear the sound of chariots and horses and a great army, so that they said to one another, "Look, the king of Israel has hired the Hittite and Egyptian kings to attack us!" 7So they got up and fled in the dusk and abandoned their tents and their horses and donkeys. They left the camp as it was and ran for their lives.

8The men who had leprosy reached the edge of the camp and entered one of the tents. They ate and drank, and carried away silver, gold and clothes, and went off and hid them. They returned and entered another tent and took some things from it and hid them also.

9Then they said to each other, "We're not doing right. This is a day of good news and we are keeping it to ourselves. If we wait until daylight, punishment will overtake us. Let's go at once and report this to the royal palace."

10So they went and called out to the city gatekeepers and told them, "We went into the Aramean camp and not a man was there—not a sound of anyone—only tethered horses and donkeys, and the tents left just as they were." 11The gatekeepers shouted the news, and it was reported within the palace.

12The king got up in the night and said to his officers, "I will tell you what the Arameans have done to us. They know we are starving; so they have left the camp to hide in the countryside, thinking, 'They will surely come out, and then we will take them alive and get into the city.' "

13One of his officers answered, "Have some men take five of the horses that are left in the

[a] *3* The Hebrew word is used for various diseases affecting the skin—not necessarily leprosy; also in verse 8.

NRSV

3Now there were four leprous[a] men outside the city gate, who said to one another, "Why should we sit here until we die? 4If we say, 'Let us enter the city,' the famine is in the city, and we shall die there; but if we sit here, we shall also die. Therefore, let us desert to the Aramean camp; if they spare our lives, we shall live; and if they kill us, we shall but die." 5So they arose at twilight to go to the Aramean camp; but when they came to the edge of the Aramean camp, there was no one there at all. 6For the Lord had caused the Aramean army to hear the sound of chariots, and of horses, the sound of a great army, so that they said to one another, "The king of Israel has hired the kings of the Hittites and the kings of Egypt to fight against us." 7So they fled away in the twilight and abandoned their tents, their horses, and their donkeys leaving the camp just as it was, and fled for their lives. 8When these leprous[a] men had come to the edge of the camp, they went into a tent, ate and drank, carried off silver, gold, and clothing, and went and hid them. Then they came back, entered another tent, carried off things from it, and went and hid them.

9Then they said to one another, "What we are doing is wrong. This is a day of good news; if we are silent and wait until the morning light, we will be found guilty; therefore let us go and tell the king's household." 10So they came and called to the gatekeepers of the city, and told them, "We went to the Aramean camp, but there was no one to be seen or heard there, nothing but the horses tied, the donkeys tied, and the tents as they were." 11Then the gatekeepers called out and proclaimed it to the king's household. 12The king got up in the night, and said to his servants, "I will tell you what the Arameans have prepared against us. They know that we are starving; so they have left the camp to hide themselves in the open country, thinking, 'When they come out of the city, we shall take them alive and get into the city.' " 13One of his servants said, "Let some men take five of the remaining horses, since those left here will suffer the fate of the whole multitude of Israel that have perished already;[b] let us

[a] A term for several skin diseases; precise meaning uncertain [b] Compare Gk Syr Vg: Meaning of Heb uncertain

NIV

city. Their plight will be like that of all the
Israelites left here—yes, they will only be like all
these Israelites who are doomed. So let us send
them to find out what happened."
14So they selected two chariots with their
horses, and the king sent them after the Aramean
army. He commanded the drivers, "Go and find
out what has happened." 15They followed them
as far as the Jordan, and they found the whole
road strewn with the clothing and equipment the
Arameans had thrown away in their headlong
flight. So the messengers returned and reported
to the king. 16Then the people went out and
plundered the camp of the Arameans. So a seah
of flour sold for a shekel, and two seahs of barley
sold for a shekel, as the LORD had said.
17Now the king had put the officer on whose
arm he leaned in charge of the gate, and the
people trampled him in the gateway, and he died,
just as the man of God had foretold when the
king came down to his house. 18It happened as
the man of God had said to the king: "About this
time tomorrow, a seah of flour will sell for a
shekel and two seahs of barley for a shekel at the
gate of Samaria."
19The officer had said to the man of God, "Look,
even if the LORD should open the floodgates of the
heavens, could this happen?" The man of God had
replied, "You will see it with your own eyes, but
you will not eat any of it!" 20And that is exactly
what happened to him, for the people trampled him
in the gateway, and he died.

NRSV

send and find out." 14So they took two mounted
men, and the king sent them after the Aramean
army, saying, "Go and find out." 15So they went
after them as far as the Jordan; the whole way
was littered with garments and equipment that
the Arameans had thrown away in their haste. So
the messengers returned, and told the king.
16Then the people went out, and plundered
the camp of the Arameans. So a measure of choice
meal was sold for a shekel, and two measures of
barley for a shekel, according to the word of the
LORD. 17Now the king had appointed the captain
on whose hand he leaned to have charge of the gate;
the people trampled him to death in the gate, just
as the man of God had said when the king came
down to him. 18For when the man of God had
said to the king, "Two measures of barley shall
be sold for a shekel, and a measure of choice meal
for a shekel, about this time tomorrow in the gate
of Samaria," 19the captain had answered the man
of God, "Even if the LORD were to make windows
in the sky, could such a thing happen?" And he
had answered, "You shall see it with your own
eyes, but you shall not eat from it." 20It did indeed
happen to him; the people trampled him to death
in the gate.

COMMENTARY

The miracle is fulfilled through unexpected agents. Four starving "lepers" (see Commentary on 5:1) outside the city are pondering their options. They could go into the city, where there was a famine and where they were not permitted to go (see Lev 13:11, 46; Num 12:14-16), or they could face death outside the city (vv. 3-4). With nothing to lose, they decide to defect to the Aramean camp, where there is food aplenty. When they come to the Aramean camp, however, they find it deserted, with all the supplies left intact.

The narrator pauses at this point to explain how that situation came about. The Lord had caused the Arameans to hear a huge commotion like the sound of an enormous host, perhaps the sound of the celestial host (2:11-12; 6:17). Assuming that the Israelites must have forged an alliance with the mighty Hittites and Egyptians, the Arameans fled for their lives, ironically leaving the very vehicles of transport—the horses and donkeys—that would have aided their hasty flight. The lepers enter the camp and help themselves to its abundance, but they quickly decide, both out of guilt and out of fear of punishment, that they are not acting appropriately "on the day of good news" (v. 9). So they decide to report to the Israelite king that the Arameans have deserted their camp.

The practical, but faithless, king suspects a trap, which is not an unreasonable conclusion. After all, such tactics had been used before (cf. Joshua 8; Judges 9). One of his advisers, however, proposes that they risk sending scouts on five of the remaining horses that will probably starve anyway. Accordingly, the scouts discover that the Arameans really have fled in haste, for their clothing and equipment litter their escape route. Accordingly, the good news is brought to the Israelite king.

The Israelites plunder the Aramean camp, which was so well stocked with food that the instant increase in supply causes the prices of food to drop immediately, just as Elisha had predicted. The king's right-hand man, who earlier expressed skepticism about the possibility of an instant economic recovery, is assigned to have charge at the gate, the marketplace, and is trampled to death by the mob. Thus the prophecy of Elisha is fulfilled, and, in case the reader should somehow miss the point, the narrator clarifies it (vv. 18-20).

REFLECTIONS

The story related in this section of 2 Kings tells of the power of God to bring hope in the face of overwhelming odds, even though human authorities cannot deliver salvation.

1. For the king of Israel, expression of confidence in the ability of God to save had become a cliché, a convenient way of abdicating his responsibility (6:27). He might have led his people in seeking God's deliverance. He might have turned to the prophet for a word from the Lord. He might have prayed. He might have done any number of things that a faithful leader should have done. But he did not. Instead, he was quick to blame others and to blame God. Even worse, he was prepared to give up hope in God's ability to save.

2. Given the king's murderous intent, his bitter words, and his lack of faith, it is rather remarkable that Elisha did not react adversely to the king's message. Instead of proclaiming a word of judgment upon the king, the prophet offered a surprising, unsolicited word of hope from God. That is the marvelous testimony to the grace of God. To one who could wait no longer, the word of God was the promise of an almost immediate reversal of the adverse circumstances.

3. Curiously, the text does not report the reaction of the king to Elisha's proclamation of hope. That is apparently left to the reader's imagination. The story is horribly graphic in its description of the famine. Encountering such a portrayal of human tragedy, the reader may furtively share the perspective of the angry king, who asked the question that we may not dare to ask: "Why should I hope in the LORD?" Taken in that light, the silence regarding the king's reaction (surely he had one!) is an invitation to readers to fill in the blanks with their own responses.

4. Whereas there is no response from the king, the narrator does report one reaction—namely, the skepticism of the king's right-hand man. The officer was a realist. He thought only in pragmatic terms, considering the possibility of a reversal of Israel's economic condition to come only through the natural processes. To him, the power of God could be manifested only within the scope of his limited vision. He could not see the power of God beyond what he thought was possible. However, the story here, like other stories in the Elisha cycle, makes the point that God's ways are not necessarily the ways of human beings (cf. Isa 55:8-9). Just as God may act through forces ordinarily invisible to human eyes (see 6:16), so also God may act in ways that do not conform to human experience and expectations.

5. Certainly one of the surprises in the story is the key role that the lepers play. These outcasts of society appear out of nowhere, starving and desperate. Yet, they were given the privilege of discovering the good news that the Arameans have deserted their camp. They were concerned first and foremost with their own needs, but they decided to pass the news on to the authorities out of a twinge of guilt and a large amount of fear. Still, it is through them that the good news was conveyed, while those in power doubted the possibility of divine deliverance. By the same token, while the faithless king was slow to accept the good news for what it was, a nameless servant provided a viable solution that led eventually to the fulfillment of prophecy. This is the way of the God of the Bible, who may bring about great miracles—indeed, salvation for people—through the outcasts and the lowly ones of society.

2 KINGS 8:1-29, A FEW LOOSE ENDS

OVERVIEW

The reigns of the kings of Israel's powerful Omride dynasty have been in focus since the accession of its founder, Omri (1 Kgs 16:21-28). During the reign of Ahab, the son of Omri, Elijah had prophesied the end of the dynasty (1 Kgs 21:21-24). Now, the narrator is about to tell the story of the end of the house of Omri (chaps. 9–10). Before he gets to that, however, there are a few loose ends to be tied up.

Chapter 8 consists of three passages that appear to be unrelated to one another. The first unit (vv. 1-6) returns to the woman from Shunem, to whom Elisha had previously ministered in wondrous ways (4:8-37). An unspecified amount of time seems to have lapsed since the earlier story, for the woman now appears to be the head of her household, and the hitherto wealthy woman is now vulnerable to the threat of an impending famine. Perhaps the story of the terrible famine in the preceding chapter prompted the placing of this account here. Famine is not the principal problem in this case, however. We know already from previous accounts that threat of famine can be miraculously averted (see 4:38-44) or overturned (6:24–7:20). The narrative purpose of the famine in the present account is to explain how the woman had lost her property and is now in need of powerful intervention on her behalf. That situation provides occasion for the demonstration of the power of the traditions about the prophet's mighty deeds; the traditions affect life and cause justice to be brought about, even when the prophet is physically absent. The story begins with the threat of famine, which turned out to have been rather easily avoided (the woman only had to take refuge in the land of the Philistines, not far away), but it ends with the demonstration of prophetic authority, even when the prophet is not present.

The second passage (vv. 7-15) does not appear to be related to the first. It takes place in a completely different setting, concerns a different subject matter, and, save for Elisha, involves different characters. It begins with the illness of the Aramean king and his attempt to discover whether he would recover. The king's illness and his inquiry turn out, however, to be a pretext for the narrator to tell of Elisha's role in the rise of the usurper Hazael. If only in an indirect fashion, Elisha now fulfills the word of the Lord given to Elijah in 1 Kgs 19:15-18. To be sure, Elijah is no longer present to anoint Hazael, but Elijah's role in the calling of Elisha as his successor has brought about this expected possibility of Hazael's accession through the word of an Israelite prophet. So the story begins with the illness of the king and his inquiry, but it ends with a demonstration of prophetic authority, even when the prophet Elijah is no longer present.

The third passage consists of the reports of the reigns of two Judean kings, Jehoram (vv. 16-24) and Ahaziah (vv. 25-29). These accounts may be seen as necessary "asides," inserted here for the sake of completeness in the overall history of both kingdoms. Still, both kings are presented as having such intimate ties with Israel that the two kingdoms are practically merged as one. Ahaziah is said to have reigned only one year, but during that brief reign, he managed to join Israel in its war with Hazael and even joined his Israelite counterpart in Jezreel, where Jehu would seize power and put an end to the Omride dynasty, thus fulfilling the prophecy of 1 Kgs 19:15-18.

2 Kings 8:1-6, Reprise of the Woman from Shunem

NIV

8 Now Elisha had said to the woman whose
son he had restored to life, "Go away with
your family and stay for a while wherever you
can, because the LORD has decreed a famine in
the land that will last seven years." 2The woman
proceeded to do as the man of God said. She and
her family went away and stayed in the land of
the Philistines seven years.
3At the end of the seven years she came back
from the land of the Philistines and went to the
king to beg for her house and land. 4The king
was talking to Gehazi, the servant of the man of
God, and had said, "Tell me about all the great
things Elisha has done." 5Just as Gehazi was
telling the king how Elisha had restored the dead
to life, the woman whose son Elisha had brought
back to life came to beg the king for her house
and land.
Gehazi said, "This is the woman, my lord the
king, and this is her son whom Elisha restored to
life." 6The king asked the woman about it, and
she told him.
Then he assigned an official to her case and
said to him, "Give back everything that belonged
to her, including all the income from her land
from the day she left the country until now."

NRSV

8 Now Elisha had said to the woman whose
son he had restored to life, "Get up and
go with your household, and settle wherever you
can; for the LORD has called for a famine, and it
will come on the land for seven years." 2So the
woman got up and did according to the word of
the man of God; she went with her household
and settled in the land of the Philistines seven
years. 3At the end of the seven years, when the
woman returned from the land of the Philistines,
she set out to appeal to the king for her house
and her land. 4Now the king was talking with
Gehazi the servant of the man of God, saying,
"Tell me all the great things that Elisha has done."
5While he was telling the king how Elisha had
restored a dead person to life, the woman whose
son he had restored to life appealed to the king
for her house and her land. Gehazi said, "My lord
king, here is the woman, and here is her son
whom Elisha restored to life." 6When the king
questioned the woman, she told him. So the king
appointed an official for her, saying, "Restore all
that was hers, together with all the revenue of
the fields from the day that she left the land until
now."

COMMENTARY

The narrator makes it clear that the woman who is the focus of this account is the one "whose son [Elisha] had restored to life" (4:8-37). In the earlier story, one gathers that she was a wealthy woman who, together with her husband, provided a guest room for Elisha's use whenever his itinerary brought him to their town. The prophet now warns her of an impending seven-year famine called forth by the Lord and urges her to leave the country with her household. The language suggests that she is head of her family, with her husband now presumably dead. The coming famine, then, is not the same one that is mentioned in 4:38, immediately following the account of Elisha's miraculous resurrection of the boy (4:18-37). It is also apparently not the famine that occurred during the siege of Samaria, mentioned in the preceding chapter (6:24–7:20). In any case, this famine does not appear to be widespread, for she goes only as far as the land of the Philistines, in the coastal region southwest of Judah.

When the woman returns home at the end of the seven-year period, she has to petition the king that her property be restored to her. The reader is not told why she had lost her property. Perhaps some unscrupulous neighbor had seized it during her absence. Perhaps it had been taken over and held in trust by the crown. Whatever the case, she is now in need of royal attention. In the earlier story, Elisha had offered to peddle influence on her behalf, but she declined his offer because she was dwelling among her own people (4:13). Now, having lost her home, she comes to the king on her own accord. Elisha has not sent her, and he is absent in this sequence. Fortunately for her, however, the king has become a fan of Elisha (cf. 6:31) and is eager to hear Elisha's attendant Gehazi tell stories about the wondrous deeds of the master. Indeed, Gehazi is telling the story of the resurrection of the woman's son when she arrives with her petition before the king. Perhaps because of her connection to the prophet, she easily wins the king's favor. He appoints an officer to settle her case, returning her property to her, together with whatever revenue it may have accrued during her absence.

The story illustrates the abiding effect of Elisha's mighty deeds. In this instance, Elisha himself is absent, but the mere retelling of his wonders, particularly the story of the resurrection of the dead child, is enough to affect the king, causing him to bring about justice. (See Reflections at 8:16-29.)

2 Kings 8:7-15, Elisha Plays Kingmaker

NIV

[7]Elisha went to Damascus, and Ben-Hadad king of Aram was ill. When the king was told, "The man of God has come all the way up here," [8]he said to Hazael, "Take a gift with you and go to meet the man of God. Consult the LORD through him; ask him, 'Will I recover from this illness?' "

[9]Hazael went to meet Elisha, taking with him as a gift forty camel-loads of all the finest wares of Damascus. He went in and stood before him, and said, "Your son Ben-Hadad king of Aram has sent me to ask, 'Will I recover from this illness?' "

[10]Elisha answered, "Go and say to him, 'You will certainly recover'; but[a] the LORD has revealed to me that he will in fact die." [11]He stared at him with a fixed gaze until Hazael felt ashamed. Then the man of God began to weep.

[12]"Why is my lord weeping?" asked Hazael.

"Because I know the harm you will do to the Israelites," he answered. "You will set fire to their fortified places, kill their young men with the sword, dash their little children to the ground, and rip open their pregnant women."

[13]Hazael said, "How could your servant, a mere dog, accomplish such a feat?"

[a] *10* The Hebrew may also be read *Go and say, 'You will certainly not recover,' for.*

NRSV

7Elisha went to Damascus while King Ben-hadad of Aram was ill. When it was told him, "The man of God has come here," [8]the king said to Hazael, "Take a present with you and go to meet the man of God. Inquire of the LORD through him, whether I shall recover from this illness." [9]So Hazael went to meet him, taking a present with him, all kinds of goods of Damascus, forty camel loads. When he entered and stood before him, he said, "Your son King Ben-hadad of Aram has sent me to you, saying, 'Shall I recover from this illness?' " [10]Elisha said to him, "Go, say to him, 'You shall certainly recover'; but the LORD has shown me that he shall certainly die." [11]He fixed his gaze and stared at him, until he was ashamed. Then the man of God wept. [12]Hazael asked, "Why does my lord weep?" He answered, "Because I know the evil that you will do to the people of Israel; you will set their fortresses on fire, you will kill their young men with the sword, dash in pieces their little ones, and rip up their pregnant women." [13]Hazael said, "What is your servant, who is a mere dog, that he should do this great thing?" Elisha answered, "The LORD has shown me that you are to be king over Aram." [14]Then he left Elisha, and went to his master

NIV

"The LORD has shown me that you will become king of Aram," answered Elisha.

[14]Then Hazael left Elisha and returned to his master. When Ben-Hadad asked, "What did Elisha say to you?" Hazael replied, "He told me that you would certainly recover." [15]But the next day he took a thick cloth, soaked it in water and spread it over the king's face, so that he died. Then Hazael succeeded him as king.

NRSV

Ben-hadad,[a] who said to him, "What did Elisha say to you?" And he answered, "He told me that you would certainly recover." [15]But the next day he took the bed-cover and dipped it in water and spread it over the king's face, until he died. And Hazael succeeded him.

[a] Heb lacks *Ben-hadad*

COMMENTARY

The scene shifts from Israel to Damascus, where Ben-hadad, the king of Aram, is sick.[99] Upon learning of Elisha's presence in the city, the king sends an officer named Hazael to inquire whether the king will recover from his illness. The Aramean king's action stands in marked contrast to that of Ahaziah, an Israelite king who in his illness preferred to seek an oracle from Baal-Zebub of Ekron (1:2-8). Moreover, whereas Elisha had previously been considered such a threat that an enormous Aramean army had to be dispatched to capture him in Israel (6:8-14), he is now portrayed as a welcome presence in the capital of Aram. Like Naaman, the Aramean general who had been healed of his affliction by Elisha (5:1-19*a*), Hazael brings generous presents from the king to the prophet and refers to the king as the prophet's "son," a term suggesting filial devotion (cf. "father" in 5:13; 6:21; 13:14). The portrayal of the king is entirely positive, and so the reader is set up to expect a positive word from the man of God.

Elisha's response in v. 10 is confusing, to say the least. The NRSV and the NIV both follow a scribal tradition that has Elisha telling Hazael to say that the king will certainly recover, while Hazael is informed that the king actually will die. The consonantal Hebrew text, however, suggests that Hazael is to say that the king will certainly *not* live. Instead of לו (*lô*, "to him"), this tradition reads לא (*lō'*, "not"), thus: "Say, you shall certainly not live!" This reading, however, probably represents resistance to the idea that the prophet might have urged Hazael to lie. Josephus, likewise, tried to exonerate the man of God by having him forbid Hazael to tell the king that he would not recover.[100] These and other moves cannot,[101] however, eliminate the problem, which goes beyond the question of truthfulness and deceit. Elisha is, in fact, deliberately setting Hazael up for his role as the usurper of the throne. A long and awkward period of silence ensues between the two men "until he was embarrassed [עד־בשׁ *'ad-bōš*]." Then Elisha breaks down. He weeps, he explains, because he knows the atrocities that Hazael will do to Israel. This is further clarified by the explanation that Hazael will become king.

Taking the cue that the prophet may (or may not) have intended to give, Hazael returns to Damascus and gives Ben-hadad the prophet's assurance that the king will live. The next morning, Hazael takes some kind of woven material (the Hebrew word מכבר [*makbēr*] is of uncertain meaning), dips it in water, and apparently suffocates the king in his sleep. Thus Hazael usurps the throne.[102] In a rather indirect fashion, the accession of Hazael is the fulfillment of 1 Kgs 19:15. To be sure, Elijah in his lifetime did not anoint Hazael. Yet, Elijah had been instrumental in the calling of Elisha to the ministry, and Elisha has been instrumental in the accession of Hazael. (See Reflections at 8:16-29.)

99. Despite the narrator's obvious belief that this Ben-hadad was the predecessor of Hazael, whose reign is known from extra-biblical sources, his identity and historicity are matters of scholarly dispute. For a possible reconstruction, see Wayne T. Pitard, *Ancient Damascus* (Winona Lake, Ind.: Eisenbrauns, 1987) 132-38.

100. Josephus *Antiquities of the Jews* IX.92.

101. For other views, see John Gray, *I & II Kings*, OTL (Philadelphia: Westminster, 1964) 530-31; C. J. Labuschagne, "Did Elisha Deliberately Lie? Notes on II Kings 8:10," *ZAW* 77 (1965) 327-28.

102. In the Akkadian inscriptions, too, Hazael is known as a usurper, "a son of a nobody."

2 Kings 8:16-29, The Reigns of Jehoram and Ahaziah of Judah

NIV

16In the fifth year of Joram son of Ahab king of Israel, when Jehoshaphat was king of Judah, Jehoram son of Jehoshaphat began his reign as king of Judah. 17He was thirty-two years old when he became king, and he reigned in Jerusalem eight years. 18He walked in the ways of the kings of Israel, as the house of Ahab had done, for he married a daughter of Ahab. He did evil in the eyes of the LORD. 19Nevertheless, for the sake of his servant David, the LORD was not willing to destroy Judah. He had promised to maintain a lamp for David and his descendants forever.

20In the time of Jehoram, Edom rebelled against Judah and set up its own king. 21So Jehoram[a] went to Zair with all his chariots. The Edomites surrounded him and his chariot commanders, but he rose up and broke through by night; his army, however, fled back home. 22To this day Edom has been in rebellion against Judah. Libnah revolted at the same time.

23As for the other events of Jehoram's reign, and all he did, are they not written in the book of the annals of the kings of Judah? 24Jehoram rested with his fathers and was buried with them in the City of David. And Ahaziah his son succeeded him as king.

25In the twelfth year of Joram son of Ahab king of Israel, Ahaziah son of Jehoram king of Judah began to reign. 26Ahaziah was twenty-two years old when he became king, and he reigned in Jerusalem one year. His mother's name was Athaliah, a granddaughter of Omri king of Israel. 27He walked in the ways of the house of Ahab and did evil in the eyes of the LORD, as the house of Ahab had done, for he was related by marriage to Ahab's family.

28Ahaziah went with Joram son of Ahab to war against Hazael king of Aram at Ramoth Gilead. The Arameans wounded Joram; 29so King Joram returned to Jezreel to recover from the wounds the Arameans had inflicted on him at Ramoth[b] in his battle with Hazael king of Aram.

Then Ahaziah son of Jehoram king of Judah went down to Jezreel to see Joram son of Ahab, because he had been wounded.

[a] *21* Hebrew *Joram,* a variant of *Jehoram;* also in verses 23 and 24
[b] *29* Hebrew *Ramah,* a variant of *Ramoth*

NRSV

16In the fifth year of King Joram son of Ahab of Israel,[a] Jehoram son of King Jehoshaphat of Judah began to reign. 17He was thirty-two years old when he became king, and he reigned eight years in Jerusalem. 18He walked in the way of the kings of Israel, as the house of Ahab had done, for the daughter of Ahab was his wife. He did what was evil in the sight of the LORD. 19Yet the LORD would not destroy Judah, for the sake of his servant David, since he had promised to give a lamp to him and to his descendants forever.

20In his days Edom revolted against the rule of Judah, and set up a king of their own. 21Then Joram crossed over to Zair with all his chariots. He set out by night and attacked the Edomites and their chariot commanders who had surrounded him;[b] but his army fled home. 22So Edom has been in revolt against the rule of Judah to this day. Libnah also revolted at the same time. 23Now the rest of the acts of Joram, and all that he did, are they not written in the Book of the Annals of the Kings of Judah? 24So Joram slept with his ancestors, and was buried with them in the city of David; his son Ahaziah succeeded him.

25In the twelfth year of King Joram son of Ahab of Israel, Ahaziah son of King Jehoram of Judah began to reign. 26Ahaziah was twenty-two years old when he began to reign; he reigned one year in Jerusalem. His mother's name was Athaliah, a granddaughter of King Omri of Israel. 27He also walked in the way of the house of Ahab, doing what was evil in the sight of the LORD, as the house of Ahab had done, for he was son-in-law to the house of Ahab.

28He went with Joram son of Ahab to wage war against King Hazael of Aram at Ramoth-gilead, where the Arameans wounded Joram. 29King Joram returned to be healed in Jezreel of the wounds that the Arameans had inflicted on him at Ramah, when he fought against King Hazael of Aram. King Ahaziah son of Jehoram of Judah went down to see Joram son of Ahab in Jezreel, because he was wounded.

[a] Gk Syr: Heb adds *Jehoshaphat being king of Judah,* [b] Meaning of Heb uncertain

COMMENTARY

8:16-24. Jehoram (Joram), the son of Jehoshaphat, has already been mentioned incidentally in 1 Kgs 22:50 and 2 Kgs 1:17. Now comes the brief report of his reign (849–843 BCE). In contrast to the reigns of his two predecessors, Asa (1 Kgs 15:9-24) and Jehoshapat (22:41-50), both of whom are portrayed in generally positive terms, Jehoram's reign receives a strongly negative evaluation. He "walked in the ways of the kings of Israel" because he married the daughter of Ahab (v. 18), a marriage made, no doubt, for political convenience (cf. 1 Kgs 22:2). Just as Solomon was corrupted by his marriages to foreign women who led him down an idolatrous path (1 Kgs 11:1-8) and just as Ahab's marriage to Jezebel, the Sidonian princess, led him to patronize the cult of Baal (1 Kgs 16:31-34), so also Jehoram's marriage to Ahab's daughter has corrupted him. Still, the pro-Judean narrator tells us, the Lord's promise to David is still binding: The dynasty will continue, and Judah will not be destroyed (see 1 Kgs 11:36; 15:4). That does not mean, however, that there are no consequences for Jehoram's sins (cf. 2 Sam 7:14-16). Edom, which had been a vassal of Judah (3:8; 1 Kgs 22:47) would become independent of Judean control, and even Libnah, a town near the border with the Philistines, would revolt (v. 22).

8:25-29. On the one hand, the promise of an enduring dynasty in Judah (8:19; 1 Kgs 11:36; 15:4) seems to hold good, for Jehoram, despite his sins, is succeeded by Ahaziah, his son (v. 25). On the other hand, it is ominous that Ahaziah reigned only one year (843/2 BCE), at the young age of twenty-two, and nothing is said about an heir to him (v. 26). The promise of an enduring Davidic dynasty now seems threatened. The threat is all the worse because of Judah's dalliance with the north. All the notices about Ahaziah's brief reign have to do with his associations with Israel. His mother was Athaliah, the granddaughter of Omri and daughter of Ahab. Ahaziah also walked in the ways of Ahab, just as his father, Ahab's son-in-law, had done. Ahaziah joined Joram, his northern counterpart, in a war against the Arameans. He visited the wounded Joram in Jezreel after the Aramean campaign.

REFLECTIONS

This chapter is fragmented and difficult to appropriate in the community of faith. Nevertheless, it does offer important theological and practical insights.

1. As we so often find in the Elisha cycle, the prophet is involved in the lives of individuals in domestic settings immediately before and after dramatic successes in the international arena. Immediately after playing a major role in Israel's war with the Moabites (3:4-27), we find him attending to the economic and other mundane needs of various people (4:1-44). Immediately after his wondrous healing of Naaman, the Aramean general (5:1-27), we find him helping a disciple retrieve a lost ax head (6:1-7), before returning to international politics (6:8-23). Now, again, the man of God moves from playing a key role in a national crisis that is both economic and military (6:24–7:20) to turn his attention to an individual (8:1-3), before returning to play a role in international politics again. Such is the nature of the prophetic ministry: It attends to the needs of individuals as well as of nations.

2. The first story in the chapter illustrates how the wondrous acts of the past may continue to have their effects in the present through the retelling of the story. In this case, the retelling of the story of the resurrection of the son touched a king so much that he immediately moved to help a woman in need. The miracle happened not only in the resurrection itself, but also in the power that the story has to affect lives long after the event, even without the presence of the original performer of the miracle.

3. The story of Elisha's role in the demise of Ben-hadad and the accession of Hazael is troubling to many modern readers. The man of God apparently tells Hazael to lie and, whether he had intended it or not, is complicit in the assassination of the king. Within the narrator's larger view of history, however, this event fulfills the word of the Lord that promises an end to the horrible reigns of the apostate kings of the north. God's larger purpose will be worked out, it seems, even through human deceit (cf. 1 Kings 22) and unjustified death. The story defies our moral logic, but the Bible as a whole tells the story of a God whose will is accomplished in ways that sometimes defy human logic and moral categories.

2 KINGS 9:1–10:36, THE REIGN OF JEHU

OVERVIEW

In 1 Kgs 19:15-16, Elijah is told to anoint Elisha as his successor, Hazael as king of Aram, and Jehu as king of Israel. Although Elisha was not, strictly speaking, anointed, Elijah did pass the prophetic mantle on to him (1 Kgs 19:19-21). Hazael, too, was not anointed, but Elisha, duly commissioned by Elijah, was instrumental in his accession (8:7-15). There remains now only the anointing of Jehu, which will be carried out by one of the disciples of Elisha at the behest and with the authority of the master (9:1-13). Elijah had predicted the manner of death of Ahab and Jezebel and the obliteration of their descendants because of the murder of Naboth the Jezreelite (1 Kgs 21:17-24). The prophecy concerning Ahab's death has already been fulfilled (cf. 1 Kgs 22:37-38). Jezebel is still alive, however, and Ahab has been succeeded by one son and then another. Now the narrator will show how the wrong done to Naboth the Jezreelite will finally be righted. The Hebrew root שלם (*šlm*, "to be complete/whole/in order") reverberates throughout the story with different nuances of the meaning of the root (9:17-19, 22, 31), most notably in the question, "Is all well?" (השלום *hăšālôm*; 9:11). The root occurs, too, in the word of the Lord to Ahab regarding the murder of Naboth: "And I will repay [ושלמתיע *wĕšillamtî*] you" (9:26); there can be no שלום (*šālôm*), no closure, as it were, until Naboth's murder has been fully avenged. Jehu states that there can be no *šālôm* until all the "whoredoms and sorceries" of Jezebel are eliminated (9:22). And that justifies the massacre of the worshipers of Baal (10:18-22). Finally, the root appears in the admission of Ahaziah's kin, who tell Jehu that they have come to Israel "to salute" (לשלום *lišlôm*, 10:13; NRSV, "to visit"; NIV, "to greet") him. They would be put to death, no doubt because they are related to Ahaziah, who is related to Ahab through his mother, Athaliah. Only with the death of the last descendant of Ahab will the wrong committed against Naboth the Jezreelite be righted. Only with the complete destruction of the cult of Baal can there be *šālôm*. So complete is the judgment of God against the sins of the house of Ahab.

2 Kings 9:1-13, Jehu Is Anointed King

NIV

9 The prophet Elisha summoned a man from the company of the prophets and said to him, "Tuck your cloak into your belt, take this flask of oil with you and go to Ramoth Gilead.
2When you get there, look for Jehu son of

NRSV

9 Then the prophet Elisha called a member of the company of prophets[a] and said to him, "Gird up your loins; take this flask of oil in your hand, and go to Ramoth-gilead. 2When you

[a] Heb *sons of the prophets*

NIV

Jehoshaphat, the son of Nimshi. Go to him, get
him away from his companions and take him into
an inner room. 3Then take the flask and pour the
oil on his head and declare, 'This is what the LORD
says: I anoint you king over Israel.' Then open
the door and run; don't delay!"
4So the young man, the prophet, went to Ramoth Gilead. 5When he arrived, he found the
army officers sitting together. "I have a message
for you, commander," he said.
"For which of us?" asked Jehu.
"For you, commander," he replied.
6Jehu got up and went into the house. Then
the prophet poured the oil on Jehu's head and
declared, "This is what the LORD, the God of
Israel, says: 'I anoint you king over the LORD's
people Israel. 7You are to destroy the house of
Ahab your master, and I will avenge the blood of
my servants the prophets and the blood of all the
LORD's servants shed by Jezebel. 8The whole house
of Ahab will perish. I will cut off from Ahab every
last male in Israel—slave or free. 9I will make the
house of Ahab like the house of Jeroboam son of
Nebat and like the house of Baasha son of Ahijah.
10As for Jezebel, dogs will devour her on the plot
of ground at Jezreel, and no one will bury her.' "
Then he opened the door and ran.
11When Jehu went out to his fellow officers,
one of them asked him, "Is everything all right?
Why did this madman come to you?"
"You know the man and the sort of things he
says," Jehu replied.
12"That's not true!" they said. "Tell us."
Jehu said, "Here is what he told me: 'This is
what the LORD says: I anoint you king over Israel.' "
13They hurried and took their cloaks and spread
them under him on the bare steps. Then they
blew the trumpet and shouted, "Jehu is king!"

NRSV

arrive, look there for Jehu son of Jehoshaphat, son
of Nimshi; go in and get him to leave his companions, and take him into an inner chamber.
3Then take the flask of oil, pour it on his head,
and say, 'Thus says the LORD: I anoint you king
over Israel.' Then open the door and flee; do not
linger."
4So the young man, the young prophet, went
to Ramoth-gilead. 5He arrived while the commanders of the army were in council, and he
announced, "I have a message for you, commander." "For which one of us?" asked Jehu. "For
you, commander." 6So Jehu[a] got up and went
inside; the young man poured the oil on his head,
saying to him, "Thus says the LORD the God of
Israel: I anoint you king over the people of the
LORD, over Israel. 7You shall strike down the house
of your master Ahab, so that I may avenge on
Jezebel the blood of my servants the prophets,
and the blood of all the servants of the LORD. 8For
the whole house of Ahab shall perish; I will cut
off from Ahab every male, bond or free, in Israel.
9I will make the house of Ahab like the house of
Jeroboam son of Nebat, and like the house of
Baasha son of Ahijah. 10The dogs shall eat Jezebel
in the territory of Jezreel, and no one shall bury
her." Then he opened the door and fled.
11When Jehu came back to his master's officers, they said to him, "Is everything all right?
Why did that madman come to you?" He answered them, "You know the sort and how they
babble." 12They said, "Liar! Come on, tell us!" So
he said, "This is just what he said to me: 'Thus
says the LORD, I anoint you king over Israel.' "
13Then hurriedly they all took their cloaks and
spread them for him on the bare[b] steps; and they
blew the trumpet, and proclaimed, "Jehu is king."

[a] Heb *he* [b] Meaning of Heb uncertain

COMMENTARY

Joram, king of Israel, is wounded in the course of battle at Ramoth-gilead, and so he withdraws to Jezreel to recuperate (8:28-29), leaving some of his troops behind. Elisha sees an opportunity to anoint Jehu as king, according to the word of the Lord spoken to Elijah (1 Kgs 19:16). He does not, however, personally anoint the king. Rather, he tells one of his disciples to go immediately to Ramoth-gilead (v. 1), where Ahab had been killed earlier (1 Kgs 22:1-40), and to anoint Jehu as king in place of Joram. The idiom "gird up your loins" (NRSV) or "tuck your coat into your belt" (NIV) probably suggests urgency (see 1 Kgs 18:46; 2 Kgs 4:29). Elisha apparently wants to seize the moment and anoint Jehu before Joram recovers and returns to take control. Whereas 1 Kgs 19:16 has it that Elijah was to anoint Jehu, that is accomplished only indirectly, through Elijah's commissioning of Elisha (1 Kgs 19:19-21), who now charges one of his disciples to do the anointing. The gradual and indirect fulfillment of the word of the Lord in history is part of what Elijah was intended to understand by the almost imperceptible silence he heard on Mt. Horeb (1 Kgs 19:12). The task the young disciple of Elisha has is, in any case, a dangerous one, for he is told by Elisha to do the job and then to flee immediately (v. 3), but the precise nature of that danger is not spelled out.

Jehu, who is elsewhere called "the son of Nimshi" (v. 20; 1 Kgs 19:16; 2 Chr 22:7), is here called "son of Jehoshaphat the son of Nimshi" (vv. 2, 14). The inclusion of the grandfather's name in the patronym is rather unusual. Hence, some scholars surmise that Nimshi might have been Jehu's clan name or that Jehu's grandfather must have been better known than his father.[103] It is possible, however, that the grandfather's name is provided to make it clear that Jehu is not the son of Jehoshaphat, the son of Asa, king of Judah. The point is that Jehu is not of royal descent. He is, in fact, though a high-ranking military officer in the Israelite army stationed at Ramoth-gilead, a commoner.

When the young prophet arrives at the camp, the officers are sitting in council (v. 5). Perhaps they are already plotting a coup. If that is the case, then Jehu's official anointing by the authority of the prophet (cf. 1 Sam 9:16; 10:1; 15:1; 16:1-13) would no doubt have given the rebellion prophetic legitimation. As the narrator would have it (v. 7), Jehu is to destroy the house of Ahab as a retribution against Jezebel (Ahab is already dead!) for her role in the killing of the prophets and other servants of the Lord (1 Kgs 18:4; 19:10, 14). The elimination of the descendants of Ahab would also fulfill the prophecy of Elijah regarding the matter of Naboth the Jezreelite (vv. 9-10; 1 Kgs 21:21-24). Despite the secretive ceremony (see vv. 2, 6) and the private conversation between the young prophet and Jehu, the other officers at Ramoth-gilead are quick to pledge their allegiance to the new king-designate (vv. 11-13; unlike the elevation of Omri [1 Kgs 16:16], this acclamation of Jehu to king appears not to have had universal support of the military). Although they disparage the prophet, referring to him as a madman (v. 11; cf. Jer 29:26; Hos 9:7), they do not hesitate to use his prophetic authority to support their cause. So Jehu is proclaimed king (cf. 11:9-12; 1 Kgs 1:38-40; Matt 21:8-11).

103. See, e.g., John Gray, *I & II Kings*, OTL (Philadelphia: Westminster, 1976) 540.

2 Kings 9:14-29, Joram and Ahaziah Are Killed

NIV

[14]So Jehu son of Jehoshaphat, the son of Nimshi, conspired against Joram. (Now Joram and all Israel had been defending Ramoth Gilead against Hazael king of Aram, [15]but King Joram[a] had returned to Jezreel to recover from the wounds the Arameans had inflicted on him in the battle with Hazael king of Aram.) Jehu said, "If this is the way you feel, don't let anyone slip out of the city to go and tell the news in Jezreel." [16]Then he got into his chariot and rode to Jezreel, because Joram

a *15* Hebrew *Jehoram,* a variant of *Joram;* also in verses 17 and 21-24

NRSV

14Thus Jehu son of Jehoshaphat son of Nimshi conspired against Joram. Joram with all Israel had been on guard at Ramoth-gilead against King Hazael of Aram; [15]but King Joram had returned to be healed in Jezreel of the wounds that the Arameans had inflicted on him, when he fought against King Hazael of Aram. So Jehu said, "If this is your wish, then let no one slip out of the city to go and tell the news in Jezreel." [16]Then Jehu mounted his chariot and went to Jezreel, where Joram was lying ill. King Ahaziah of Judah had come down to visit Joram.

NIV

was resting there and Ahaziah king of Judah had gone down to see him.

17When the lookout standing on the tower in Jezreel saw Jehu's troops approaching, he called out, "I see some troops coming."

"Get a horseman," Joram ordered. "Send him to meet them and ask, 'Do you come in peace?'"

18The horseman rode off to meet Jehu and said, "This is what the king says: 'Do you come in peace?'"

"What do you have to do with peace?" Jehu replied. "Fall in behind me."

The lookout reported, "The messenger has reached them, but he isn't coming back."

19So the king sent out a second horseman. When he came to them he said, "This is what the king says: 'Do you come in peace?'"

Jehu replied, "What do you have to do with peace? Fall in behind me."

20The lookout reported, "He has reached them, but he isn't coming back either. The driving is like that of Jehu son of Nimshi—he drives like a madman."

21"Hitch up my chariot," Joram ordered. And when it was hitched up, Joram king of Israel and Ahaziah king of Judah rode out, each in his own chariot, to meet Jehu. They met him at the plot of ground that had belonged to Naboth the Jezreelite. 22When Joram saw Jehu he asked, "Have you come in peace, Jehu?"

"How can there be peace," Jehu replied, "as long as all the idolatry and witchcraft of your mother Jezebel abound?"

23Joram turned about and fled, calling out to Ahaziah, "Treachery, Ahaziah!"

24Then Jehu drew his bow and shot Joram between the shoulders. The arrow pierced his heart and he slumped down in his chariot. 25Jehu said to Bidkar, his chariot officer, "Pick him up and throw him on the field that belonged to Naboth the Jezreelite. Remember how you and I were riding together in chariots behind Ahab his father when the LORD made this prophecy about him: 26'Yesterday I saw the blood of Naboth and the blood of his sons, declares the LORD, and I will surely make you pay for it on this plot of ground, declares the LORD.'[a] Now then, pick him

[a] *26* See 1 Kings 21:19.

NRSV

17In Jezreel, the sentinel standing on the tower spied the company of Jehu arriving, and said, "I see a company." Joram said, "Take a horseman; send him to meet them, and let him say, 'Is it peace?'" 18So the horseman went to meet him; he said, "Thus says the king, 'Is it peace?'" Jehu responded, "What have you to do with peace? Fall in behind me." The sentinel reported, saying, "The messenger reached them, but he is not coming back." 19Then he sent out a second horseman, who came to them and said, "Thus says the king, 'Is it peace?'" Jehu answered, "What have you to do with peace? Fall in behind me." 20Again the sentinel reported, "He reached them, but he is not coming back. It looks like the driving of Jehu son of Nimshi; for he drives like a maniac."

21Joram said, "Get ready." And they got his chariot ready. Then King Joram of Israel and King Ahaziah of Judah set out, each in his chariot, and went to meet Jehu; they met him at the property of Naboth the Jezreelite. 22When Joram saw Jehu, he said, "Is it peace, Jehu?" He answered, "What peace can there be, so long as the many whoredoms and sorceries of your mother Jezebel continue?" 23Then Joram reined about and fled, saying to Ahaziah, "Treason, Ahaziah!" 24Jehu drew his bow with all his strength, and shot Joram between the shoulders, so that the arrow pierced his heart; and he sank in his chariot. 25Jehu said to his aide Bidkar, "Lift him out, and throw him on the plot of ground belonging to Naboth the Jezreelite; for remember, when you and I rode side by side behind his father Ahab how the LORD uttered this oracle against him: 26'For the blood of Naboth and for the blood of his children that I saw yesterday, says the LORD, I swear I will repay you on this very plot of ground.' Now therefore lift him out and throw him on the plot of ground, in accordance with the word of the LORD."

27When King Ahaziah of Judah saw this, he fled in the direction of Beth-haggan. Jehu pursued him, saying, "Shoot him also!" And they shot him[a] in the chariot at the ascent to Gur, which is by Ibleam. Then he fled to Megiddo, and died there. 28His officers carried him in a chariot to Jerusalem, and buried him in his tomb with his ancestors in the city of David.

[a] Syr Vg Compare Gk: Heb lacks *and they shot him*

NIV

up and throw him on that plot, in accordance with the word of the LORD."

27When Ahaziah king of Judah saw what had happened, he fled up the road to Beth Haggan.[a] Jehu chased him, shouting, "Kill him too!" They wounded him in his chariot on the way up to Gur near Ibleam, but he escaped to Megiddo and died there. 28His servants took him by chariot to Jerusalem and buried him with his fathers in his tomb in the City of David. 29(In the eleventh year of Joram son of Ahab, Ahaziah had become king of Judah.)

a 27 Or *fled by way of the garden house*

NRSV

29In the eleventh year of Joram son of Ahab, Ahaziah began to reign over Judah.

COMMENTARY

9:14-20. Jehu leaves instructions for his fellow officers to keep their proceedings a secret in Ramoth-gilead (v. 15), while he rushes off to Jezreel with some troops, no doubt intending to get there before word gets to the king of the conspiracy. A sentinel in Jezreel, seeing the troops approaching from afar, reports to Joram. The king sends two scouts out in succession, apparently to discover the intentions of the encroaching party. In each case, the scout is instructed to inquire of Jehu, and each in turn asks: "Is all well?" (השלום *hăšālôm*, vv. 17-19; cf. NJV, NAB). The question is the same one that Gehazi asked the Shunammite woman who was going to see Elisha because her child had died (4:26), the question only highlighting the fact that all was not well. It is the same question Naaman asked Gehazi when the latter ran after him to extract a gift from him; in that episode as well the question highlighted the fact that all was not well for Gehazi (5:21). It is also the same question that Jehu's comrades asked him when he emerged from his meeting with Elisha's emissary (v. 11). The NRSV and the NIV apparently understand the king and his scouts to be asking whether Jehu is coming in peace. While that is certainly a meaning of the question, the narrator may intend more—indeed, implying that in reality all is not well.[104] This is suggested by Jehu's question to the scouts and his invitation for them to join him on the side of שלום (*šālôm*): "What do you have to do with *šālôm*? Get around behind me!" (vv. 18-19). Each of the scouts does get behind Jehu, and the sentinel duly reports the fact to Joram. The reckless pace of the encroaching party suggests to the sentinel that it must be Jehu, "for he drives like a madman" (v. 20), a designation that prompts the reader to associate Jehu with Elisha, who is earlier also called a madman (v. 11). The reader is given a signal that Jehu is on the side of Elisha.

9:21-22. At last, Joram sets forth, accompanied by Ahaziah of Judah in a separate chariot, to meet Jehu. Poignantly, the parties meet at the property of Naboth the Jezreelite. This is probably the very plot of land where Elijah had earlier proclaimed judgment on the house of Ahab for his murder of Naboth (1 Kings 21). Joram now asks Jehu directly if all is well (*hăšālôm*), perhaps meaning the military situation at the battlefront in Ramoth-gilead. To that question Jehu replies that there can be no שלום (*šālôm*) so long as the "whoredoms and sorceries" of Jezebel continue (v. 22). The "whoredoms" here should not be taken literally; the language of promiscuity is often used in the Bible for association with other gods (cf. Exod 34:16; Lev 17:7; Deut 31:16; Judg 2:17; 8:33; Jer 2:1-13; Hosea 1–3). Likewise, "sorceries" should be taken as a metaphor for general wickedness (cf. Isa 47:9, 12; Nah 3:4).

104. On the polyvalence of the root שלום (*šlwm*) and its use in this passage, see Saul Olyan, "*Hăšālôm*: Some Literary Considerations of 2 Kings 9," *CBQ* 46 (1984) 652-68.

9:23-26. Joram now recognizes the rebellion for what it is and shouts a warning to Ahaziah: "Treason!" (מרמה *mirmâ*) (v. 23)[105] and then tries to flee. Ahab had already paid for his crime when, in the heat of the battle at Ramoth-gilead, an archer shot an arrow that struck and killed him while he was in his chariot (1 Kgs 22:34). Now Jehu shoots an arrow that kills Joram in his chariot (v. 24). Joram is then thrown onto Naboth's plot, thus fulfilling the prophecy of Elijah against Ahab (1 Kgs 21:19) and against his descendants (1 Kgs 21:21-22). Specifically, the death of Joram is seen as the Lord's righting of the wrong that Ahab and Jezebel had done to Naboth the Jezreelite: "And I will repay [ושלמתי *wěšillamtî*] you on this very plot of ground." To the narrator, then, this is the reason for Jehu's mission, hinted at by the repetition of the question, "Is it well?" (vv. 11, 17-19, 22). All is, in fact, not well. There can be no *šālôm* as long as Jezebel lives, and there can be no *šālôm* until wrong is righted (שלם *šillēm*, in the piel).

105. Olyan, ibid., 667, has pointed out that מרמה (*mirmâ*) is the opposite of (*šālôm*). See also Burke O. Long, *2 Kings*, FOTL (Grand Rapids: Eerdmans, 1991) 121-22.

9:27-29. Ahaziah of Judah, who has already cast his lot with Joram, flees south in the direction of Beth-haggan (ancient Jenin), apparently trying to return to Judah. He, too, is shot by an arrow and dies in Megiddo (v. 27), but his corpse is brought back to Jerusalem to be buried with his ancestors (v. 28; 2 Chr 22:9, however, suggests that Ahaziah was hiding in Samaria). It is unclear why Jehu wants to have Ahaziah killed. We may surmise that it is because of Ahaziah's various ties with Ahab and that Jehu wants to eliminate all threats to his own power in Israel and Judah.

2 Kings 9:30-37, Jezebel Is Killed

NIV

[30]Then Jehu went to Jezreel. When Jezebel heard about it, she painted her eyes, arranged her hair and looked out of a window. [31]As Jehu entered the gate, she asked, "Have you come in peace, Zimri, you murderer of your master?"[a]

[32]He looked up at the window and called out, "Who is on my side? Who?" Two or three eunuchs looked down at him. [33]"Throw her down!" Jehu said. So they threw her down, and some of her blood spattered the wall and the horses as they trampled her underfoot.

[34]Jehu went in and ate and drank. "Take care of that cursed woman," he said, "and bury her, for she was a king's daughter." [35]But when they went out to bury her, they found nothing except her skull, her feet and her hands. [36]They went back and told Jehu, who said, "This is the word of the LORD that he spoke through his servant Elijah the Tishbite: On the plot of ground at Jezreel dogs will devour Jezebel's flesh.[b] [37]Jezebel's body will be like refuse on the ground in the plot at Jezreel, so that no one will be able to say, 'This is Jezebel.'"

[a] *31* Or *"Did Zimri have peace, who murdered his master?"* [b] *36* See 1 Kings 21:23.

NRSV

30When Jehu came to Jezreel, Jezebel heard of it; she painted her eyes, and adorned her head, and looked out of the window. [31]As Jehu entered the gate, she said, "Is it peace, Zimri, murderer of your master?" [32]He looked up to the window and said, "Who is on my side? Who?" Two or three eunuchs looked out at him. [33]He said, "Throw her down." So they threw her down; some of her blood spattered on the wall and on the horses, which trampled on her. [34]Then he went in and ate and drank; he said, "See to that cursed woman and bury her; for she is a king's daughter." [35]But when they went to bury her, they found no more of her than the skull and the feet and the palms of her hands. [36]When they came back and told him, he said, "This is the word of the LORD, which he spoke by his servant Elijah the Tishbite, 'In the territory of Jezreel the dogs shall eat the flesh of Jezebel; [37]the corpse of Jezebel shall be like dung on the field in the territory of Jezreel, so that no one can say, This is Jezebel.'"

COMMENTARY

With Joram now dead, Jehu turns next to Jezebel. She is, however, defiant. She puts on her makeup, adorns her head, and comes to the window, probably in order to be viewed as queen. When Jehu appears, she also asks him the question that pervades the narrative: “Is it well?” (v. 31). Here she is surely not wondering whether Jehu is coming in peace, as the translations of the NIV and the NRSV would have it, for she has already heard of what he has done (cf. v. 30). Her question is a bitingly sarcastic one, implying that all is not well for Jehu, despite his triumphs thus far.[106] Her sarcastic intention is corroborated by her insult of Jehu, for she calls him “Zimri,” referring to the usurper of the Israelite throne who managed to rule for only seven days (1 Kgs 16:9-16). Zimri, too, was an officer in the army and had murdered his master, but he was not accepted by the troops. In fact, it was Omri, the father of Ahab, who had replaced that usurper!

At the behest of Jehu, two palace officials throw Jezebel down from the window, perhaps onto the very plot of ground once owned by Naboth the Jezreelite (vv. 36-37; cf. 1 Kgs 21:1). Her blood spatters on the wall, and her corpse is trampled by horses. Jehu celebrates his victory and only as an afterthought orders her burial (because she is a princess), but his henchmen find that there is not much left of her body to be interred. This event is recognized as a fulfillment of the prophecy of Elijah (cf. v. 10), although Jehu’s quote expands on the original oracle as we know it in 1 Kgs 21:23.

106. Olyan, “Some Literary Considerations,” 668.

2 Kings 10:1-17, Ahab’s Descendants Are Killed

NIV

10 Now there were in Samaria seventy sons of the house of Ahab. So Jehu wrote letters and sent them to Samaria: to the officials of Jezreel,[a] to the elders and to the guardians of Ahab’s children. He said, 2“As soon as this letter reaches you, since your master’s sons are with you and you have chariots and horses, a fortified city and weapons, 3choose the best and most worthy of your master’s sons and set him on his father’s throne. Then fight for your master’s house.”

4But they were terrified and said, “If two kings could not resist him, how can we?”

5So the palace administrator, the city governor, the elders and the guardians sent this message to Jehu: “We are your servants and we will do anything you say. We will not appoint anyone as king; you do whatever you think best.”

6Then Jehu wrote them a second letter, saying, “If you are on my side and will obey me, take the heads of your master’s sons and come to me in Jezreel by this time tomorrow.”

Now the royal princes, seventy of them, were

[a] *1* Hebrew; some Septuagint manuscripts and Vulgate *of the city*

NRSV

10 Now Ahab had seventy sons in Samaria. So Jehu wrote letters and sent them to Samaria, to the rulers of Jezreel,[a] to the elders, and to the guardians of the sons of[b] Ahab, saying, 2“Since your master’s sons are with you and you have at your disposal chariots and horses, a fortified city, and weapons, 3select the son of your master who is the best qualified, set him on his father’s throne, and fight for your master’s house.” 4But they were utterly terrified and said, “Look, two kings could not withstand him; how then can we stand?” 5So the steward of the palace, and the governor of the city, along with the elders and the guardians, sent word to Jehu: “We are your servants; we will do anything you say. We will not make anyone king; do whatever you think right.” 6Then he wrote them a second letter, saying, “If you are on my side, and if you are ready to obey me, take the heads of your master’s sons and come to me at Jezreel tomorrow at this time.” Now the king’s sons, seventy persons, were with the leaders of the city, who were charged with their upbringing. 7When the letter reached

[a] Or *of the city*, Vg Compare Gk [b] Gk: Heb lacks *of the sons of*

NIV

with the leading men of the city, who were rearing them. 7When the letter arrived, these men took the princes and slaughtered all seventy of them. They put their heads in baskets and sent them to Jehu in Jezreel. 8When the messenger arrived, he told Jehu, "They have brought the heads of the princes."

Then Jehu ordered, "Put them in two piles at the entrance of the city gate until morning."

9The next morning Jehu went out. He stood before all the people and said, "You are innocent. It was I who conspired against my master and killed him, but who killed all these? 10Know then, that not a word the LORD has spoken against the house of Ahab will fail. The LORD has done what he promised through his servant Elijah." 11So Jehu killed everyone in Jezreel who remained of the house of Ahab, as well as all his chief men, his close friends and his priests, leaving him no survivor.

12Jehu then set out and went toward Samaria. At Beth Eked of the Shepherds, 13he met some relatives of Ahaziah king of Judah and asked, "Who are you?"

They said, "We are relatives of Ahaziah, and we have come down to greet the families of the king and of the queen mother."

14"Take them alive!" he ordered. So they took them alive and slaughtered them by the well of Beth Eked—forty-two men. He left no survivor.

15After he left there, he came upon Jehonadab son of Recab, who was on his way to meet him. Jehu greeted him and said, "Are you in accord with me, as I am with you?"

"I am," Jehonadab answered.

"If so," said Jehu, "give me your hand." So he did, and Jehu helped him up into the chariot. 16Jehu said, "Come with me and see my zeal for the LORD." Then he had him ride along in his chariot.

17When Jehu came to Samaria, he killed all who were left there of Ahab's family; he destroyed them, according to the word of the LORD spoken to Elijah.

NRSV

them, they took the king's sons and killed them, seventy persons; they put their heads in baskets and sent them to him at Jezreel. 8When the messenger came and told him, "They have brought the heads of the king's sons," he said, "Lay them in two heaps at the entrance of the gate until the morning." 9Then in the morning when he went out, he stood and said to all the people, "You are innocent. It was I who conspired against my master and killed him; but who struck down all these? 10Know then that there shall fall to the earth nothing of the word of the LORD, which the LORD spoke concerning the house of Ahab; for the LORD has done what he said through his servant Elijah." 11So Jehu killed all who were left of the house of Ahab in Jezreel, all his leaders, close friends, and priests, until he left him no survivor.

12Then he set out and went to Samaria. On the way, when he was at Beth-eked of the Shepherds, 13Jehu met relatives of King Ahaziah of Judah and said, "Who are you?" They answered, "We are kin of Ahaziah; we have come down to visit the royal princes and the sons of the queen mother." 14He said, "Take them alive." They took them alive, and slaughtered them at the pit of Beth-eked, forty-two in all; he spared none of them.

15When he left there, he met Jehonadab son of Rechab coming to meet him; he greeted him, and said to him, "Is your heart as true to mine as mine is to yours?"[a] Jehonadab answered, "It is." Jehu said,[b] "If it is, give me your hand." So he gave him his hand. Jehu took him up with him into the chariot. 16He said, "Come with me, and see my zeal for the LORD." So he[c] had him ride in his chariot. 17When he came to Samaria, he killed all who were left to Ahab in Samaria, until he had wiped them out, according to the word of the LORD that he spoke to Elijah.

[a] Gk: Heb *Is it right with your heart, as my heart is with your heart?*
[b] Gk: Heb lacks *Jehu said* [c] Gk Syr Tg: Heb *they*

COMMENTARY

Jehu sets out next to deal with Ahab's "seventy sons" (v. 1), a figurative expression referring to all possible claimants to the throne (Judg 8:30; 9:5; 12:14). Just as Jezebel had written a letter to the elders of Jezreel in order to frame Naboth (1 Kgs 21:8), so also Jehu writes a letter to the local authorities—the commanders, the elders, and the guardians of Ahab's family—inviting them to select one of the descendants of Ahab as heir to the throne. The leaders, of course, perceive the dare implied in the invitation. They quickly pledge their allegiance to Jehu. He is not satisfied with words of allegiance, however, and demands that they present, literally, "the heads of the men of your master's sons" and to come to him in Jezreel the next day (v. 6). The word "heads" (ראשים *rā'šîm*) is ambiguous, for it could refer literally to anatomical heads or figuratively to leaders. The officials assume the literal meaning and decapitate the remaining descendants of Ahab. Instead of going to Jezreel, however, as they have been ordered, they send the heads in a basket to Jehu, who has the heads put in heaps at the city gate until the next morning.[107]

The precise intent of Jehu's public statement is unclear (vv. 9-10). It is evident that he accepts responsibility for the death of the king, and he implies that he had not ordered the killing of the rest of the Omrides. There is great ambiguity, however, in his initial words, when he calls the people "righteous" (צדקים *ṣaddiqîm*). Does he mean to exonerate them from guilt in the king's murder, as the translation in the NRSV and the NIV suggests ("you are innocent")? Does he mean that they are impartial witnesses who would surely recognize that he is not responsible for this atrocity (REB, "you are fair-minded judges")? Does he imply that they are, in fact, implicated in the offense (NJV, "Are you blameless?").[108] Whatever the case, the narrator sees the slaughter of the descendants of Ahab as the fulfillment of the prophecy of Elijah (1 Kgs 21:21-22, 24). With this theological legitimation, then, Jehu proceeds to kill all those who may still be associated with the house of Ahab in any way, until there are no survivors left (v. 11).

With his rivals thus eliminated, Jehu proceeds to the capital city, Samaria, no doubt to claim the throne formally (v. 12). On his way, he comes to Beth-eked of the Shepherds (an unknown location), where he meets associates of Ahaziah of Judah, who apparently do not seem to have been aware of what has happened to their king. Ironically, they inform Jehu that they are on their way "to salute" (לשלום *lišlôm*) the royal princes and the sons of the queen mother, Jezebel. Jehu has them arrested and killed—forty-two men in all (cf. 2:24). Thus he has eliminated all supporters of the house of Ahab, including those from Judah. (See Reflections at 10:28-36.)

107. The Assyrian kings did similar things as a warning to the general populace of the kings' willingness to resort to violence to achieve their goals. See *ANET*, 276-77.

108. See Long, *2 Kings*, 136; Gray, *I & II Kings*, 555.

2 Kings 10:18-27, Jehu's Zeal

NIV

[18]Then Jehu brought all the people together and said to them, "Ahab served Baal a little; Jehu will serve him much. [19]Now summon all the prophets of Baal, all his ministers and all his priests. See that no one is missing, because I am going to hold a great sacrifice for Baal. Anyone who fails to come will no longer live." But Jehu was acting deceptively in order to destroy the ministers of Baal.

[20]Jehu said, "Call an assembly in honor of

NRSV

18Then Jehu assembled all the people and said to them, "Ahab offered Baal small service; but Jehu will offer much more. [19]Now therefore summon to me all the prophets of Baal, all his worshipers, and all his priests; let none be missing, for I have a great sacrifice to offer to Baal; whoever is missing shall not live." But Jehu was acting with cunning in order to destroy the worshipers of Baal. [20]Jehu decreed, "Sanctify a solemn assembly for Baal." So they proclaimed it. [21]Jehu sent

NIV

Baal." So they proclaimed it. [21]Then he sent word throughout Israel, and all the ministers of Baal came; not one stayed away. They crowded into the temple of Baal until it was full from one end to the other. [22]And Jehu said to the keeper of the wardrobe, "Bring robes for all the ministers of Baal." So he brought out robes for them.

[23]Then Jehu and Jehonadab son of Recab went into the temple of Baal. Jehu said to the ministers of Baal, "Look around and see that no servants of the LORD are here with you—only ministers of Baal." [24]So they went in to make sacrifices and burnt offerings. Now Jehu had posted eighty men outside with this warning: "If one of you lets any of the men I am placing in your hands escape, it will be your life for his life."

[25]As soon as Jehu had finished making the burnt offering, he ordered the guards and officers: "Go in and kill them; let no one escape." So they cut them down with the sword. The guards and officers threw the bodies out and then entered the inner shrine of the temple of Baal. [26]They brought the sacred stone out of the temple of Baal and burned it. [27]They demolished the sacred stone of Baal and tore down the temple of Baal, and people have used it for a latrine to this day.

NRSV

word throughout all Israel; all the worshipers of Baal came, so that there was no one left who did not come. They entered the temple of Baal, until the temple of Baal was filled from wall to wall. [22]He said to the keeper of the wardrobe, "Bring out the vestments for all the worshipers of Baal." So he brought out the vestments for them. [23]Then Jehu entered the temple of Baal with Jehonadab son of Rechab; he said to the worshipers of Baal, "Search and see that there is no worshiper of the LORD here among you, but only worshipers of Baal." [24]Then they proceeded to offer sacrifices and burnt offerings.

Now Jehu had stationed eighty men outside, saying, "Whoever allows any of those to escape whom I deliver into your hands shall forfeit his life." [25]As soon as he had finished presenting the burnt offering, Jehu said to the guards and to the officers, "Come in and kill them; let no one escape." So they put them to the sword. The guards and the officers threw them out, and then went into the citadel of the temple of Baal. [26]They brought out the pillar[a] that was in the temple of Baal, and burned it. [27]Then they demolished the pillar of Baal, and destroyed the temple of Baal, and made it a latrine to this day.

[a] Gk Vg Syr Tg: Heb *pillars*

COMMENTARY

Jehu next meets an enigmatic figure, Jehonadab "son of Rechab." Apart from this passage, the latter is mentioned in Jeremiah 35, where he is remembered as the ancestor or founder of the house of the Rechabites. According to Jer 35:6-7, Jehonadab "son of Rechab" forbade the drinking of wine, viticulture, or, indeed, sedentary life in general. This is commonly seen as a rejection of all aspects of life in Canaan, and so Jehonadab is viewed by many scholars as a conservative worshiper of the Lord who advocated a return to the faith in its pristine purity, as in the wilderness days. Other interpreters, however, noting that the "house of Rechab" is associated with the Kenites or "smiths" in 1 Chr 2:55, argue that the Rechabites were really a guild of metallurgists, specifically chariot makers.[109] If the latter is the case, then בן־רכב (*ben-rēkāb*) would not be a patronym ("son of Rechab") but an indication of Jehonadab's association with the Rechabite guild ("a chariotmaker," or the like).[110] Whatever the reasons, Jehu and Jehonadab form an immediate bond (v. 15), and Jehu treats Jehonadab as a close ally (see 1 Kgs 20:33).

With his newfound ally, Jehu sets about eliminating Baal worship in Israel. The story is told with great irony. Jehu announces that Ahab had

109. See Frank S. Frick, "The Rechabites Reconsidered," *JBL* 90 (1970) 279-87. In this view, the injunction against wine (Jer 35:6-7) is not an indication of asceticism but a rule of the guild designed to prevent accidental divulgence of metallurgic secrets.

110. See T. R. Hobbs, *2 Kings*, WBC 13 (Waco, Tex.: Word, 1985) 128-29.

served Baal a little and that Jehu would serve Baal much. There is an apparent wordplay here, for the Hebrew verb for "to serve" (עבד *ʿābad*) sounds like the verb "to destroy" (אבד *ʾābad*; cf. v. 19). So Jehu summons the worshipers of Baal to one place, just as Ahab had done on Mt. Carmel (1 Kgs 18:20), where they were eventually slaughtered by Elijah (1 Kgs 18:40). The occasion, according to Jehu, would be a great "sacrifice" (זבח *zebaḥ*) for Baal; the root for "sacrifice" is used of the slaughter of idolaters (cf. 1 Kgs 13:2). Lest the reader miss the point, however, the narrator states that Jehu is acting with cunning (v. 19).

When the Baal worshipers are assembled at the temple, no doubt the temple of Baal that Ahab had built (1 Kgs 16:32), they pack the building "from end to end" (v. 21; lit., "mouth to mouth"). The number of Baal worshipers in Israel at that time must have been considerably greater than those assembled, but the narrator heightens the drama by having the worshipers of Baal destroyed in Baal's very own temple. Ironically, too, Jehu orders the baalists to be properly attired for the occasion (v. 22) and takes steps to ensure the exclusion of "the servants of the LORD" from this special occasion (v. 23). Then he orders his officers to slaughter all of the people, and they desecrate and destroy the temple, indeed, turning it into a latrine, thus ensuring that it could never again be used as a sanctuary (vv. 24-27). (See Reflections at 10:28-36.)

2 Kings 10:28-36, Summary Assessment of Jehu's Reign

NIV

28So Jehu destroyed Baal worship in Israel. 29However, he did not turn away from the sins of Jeroboam son of Nebat, which he had caused Israel to commit—the worship of the golden calves at Bethel and Dan.

30The LORD said to Jehu, "Because you have done well in accomplishing what is right in my eyes and have done to the house of Ahab all I had in mind to do, your descendants will sit on the throne of Israel to the fourth generation." 31Yet Jehu was not careful to keep the law of the LORD, the God of Israel, with all his heart. He did not turn away from the sins of Jeroboam, which he had caused Israel to commit.

32In those days the LORD began to reduce the size of Israel. Hazael overpowered the Israelites throughout their territory 33east of the Jordan in all the land of Gilead (the region of Gad, Reuben and Manasseh), from Aroer by the Arnon Gorge through Gilead to Bashan.

34As for the other events of Jehu's reign, all he did, and all his achievements, are they not written in the book of the annals of the kings of Israel?

35Jehu rested with his fathers and was buried in Samaria. And Jehoahaz his son succeeded him as king. 36The time that Jehu reigned over Israel in Samaria was twenty-eight years.

NRSV

28Thus Jehu wiped out Baal from Israel. 29But Jehu did not turn aside from the sins of Jeroboam son of Nebat, which he caused Israel to commit—the golden calves that were in Bethel and in Dan. 30The LORD said to Jehu, "Because you have done well in carrying out what I consider right, and in accordance with all that was in my heart have dealt with the house of Ahab, your sons of the fourth generation shall sit on the throne of Israel." 31But Jehu was not careful to follow the law of the LORD the God of Israel with all his heart; he did not turn from the sins of Jeroboam, which he caused Israel to commit.

32In those days the LORD began to trim off parts of Israel. Hazael defeated them throughout the territory of Israel: 33from the Jordan eastward, all the land of Gilead, the Gadites, the Reubenites, and the Manassites, from Aroer, which is by the Wadi Arnon, that is, Gilead and Bashan. 34Now the rest of the acts of Jehu, all that he did, and all his power, are they not written in the Book of the Annals of the Kings of Israel? 35So Jehu slept with his ancestors, and they buried him in Samaria. His son Jehoahaz succeeded him. 36The time that Jehu reigned over Israel in Samaria was twenty-eight years.

COMMENTARY

Jehu's purge of baalism wins him praise from the deuteronomistic narrator (v. 28). Jehu is considered to have done so well that God rewards him with four generations on the throne; in fact, his dynasty will be the longest lived that the northern kingdom will ever know (v. 30). For all this, however, the evaluation of Jehu is negative. He is said to have failed to keep the Torah of the Lord with all his heart, and he did not turn away from the sin of Jeroboam, for the golden calves at Dan and Bethel were not destroyed (v. 31). The closing summary of Jehu's reign includes observations about the losses of Israelite territory east of the Jordan (vv. 32-36).

REFLECTIONS

This passage is surely one of the most violent portions of the Bible. The greatest difficulty for those who come to 2 Kgs 9:1–10:36 as Scripture, however, is not the reality of extensive violence per se, but the contention of the narrator that Jehu was anointed by the will of God and the implication that his massacres were a fulfillment of the will of God (see 9:7-10, 22, 26, 36-37; 10:10, 30). Jehu is unscrupulous, cunning, ruthless, and brutal. He reminds us of the most extreme kind of religious fanatic, who resorts to deceit and brutality to exterminate those who do not share his or her religious views. Yet, Jehu is affirmed as the one who has brought שלום (*šālôm*). He is praised for his elimination of the house of Ahab (v. 30) and for eradicating Baal worship (v. 28). The text is not unequivocal in its commendation of Jehu, however. He is judged negatively for not turning away from the sins of Jeroboam (v. 29) and for his failure to keep the Lord's instructions with all his heart (v. 31). Jeroboam was also the acknowledged leader of a revolution, but he served his own ambitions and was perfectly willing to manipulate religion to suit his own purposes; his idolatry was not so much the worship of statues (the golden calves) but his own agenda (see Commentary and Reflections on 1 Kgs 12:1-33). Jehu was cut from the same cloth.

1. On the one hand, then, the text affirms the judgment of God: Injustice will not be overlooked, disloyalty to God will be punished, and idolatry will have its deadly consequences. The judgment may not be carried out immediately, but it will be carried out in due time, perhaps through the complicated plots of human history and even through self-serving and wicked opportunists who are, nevertheless, unwitting agents of God's will. On the other hand, the text makes it plain that the responsibility of human beings is to obey God with all their hearts. God looks beyond the results of one's actions into the inner motivation.

2. The story in 2 Kings 9–10 is ironic in its suggestion that *šālôm* is achieved through violence. The narrator's point of view, conveyed by Jehu, is that there can be no *šālôm* as long as human atrocities are not requited. Yet, all is not well, even with the death of Ahab and Jezebel and their descendants. Jezebel's question to Jehu remains as yet unanswered: "Is all well?" (9:31). The reader has a sense that the terrible violence cannot really bring *šālôm*. Soon, in some remote site off the beaten track, the paranoid Jehu has to kill the unnamed associates of the Judean king who were seeking *šālôm* (10:13). As for Jehu himself, all was not well: His territory was trimmed, and he died with the condemnation of the Lord for his unfaithfulness. A century later, the prophet Hosea would proclaim the judgment of God against the house of Jehu for the violence committed at Jezreel (Hos 1:4-5). Still, the narrator's point that there can be no *šālôm* in the face of unrequited sin vexes, and the point that *šālôm* may paradoxically come out of violence haunts the reader. That unsettling perspective is consonant with the rest of the Bible, however, culminating in the view, central to the New Testament, that in God's mysterious dispensation, *šālôm* for sinful humanity does come about in the

aftermath of violence. That is how the will of God is worked out sometimes. Indeed, that is the paradox of the cross.

2 KINGS 11:1–12:21, THE ACCESSION AND REIGN OF JOASH

OVERVIEW

The narrator turns from the revolution in the north to a crisis in the south. The idolatrous ways of the house of Ahab had insidiously but surely infected the house of David. Jehoshaphat was forced to fight alongside Ahab and his son Jehoram, although in each case he had tried to coax the Israelite kings to turn to the Lord (1 Kgs 22:1-40; 2 Kgs 3:1-27), and he tried to do what was right in the eyes of the Lord (1 Kgs 22:41-44). His son and successor, Jehoram, however, was married to Athaliah, the daughter of Ahab, and behaved in the manner of the idolatrous northern kings (8:16-18). Still, despite his recalcitrant ways, the Lord would not destroy Judah and would continue to uphold the promise to David that one of his descendants would always sit on his throne (8:19). Jehoram's son and successor, Ahaziah, had continued in the ways of his father—indeed, associating so closely with the house of Ahab that he, in effect, tied Judah's fate with that of Israel (8:27-29). Poignantly, in the report of his reign, there is no reiteration of the Lord's promise that the Davidic line will endure. The revolution that took the life of the Israelite king also killed the king of Judah (9:27-29) and, along with him, some of his relatives (10:12-14). The foolhardy exploits of Ahaziah left him dead after having reigned only one year. The promise of God to David is now threatened as never before. The queen mother, Athaliah, an Omride princess (8:18, 26; 2 Chr 21:6; 22:2), seizes power and attempts to kill all the sons in the royal family (11:1). Although Athaliah rules for seven years, the typical regnal summaries are omitted in the report, for the narrator does not consider her to have been a legitimate ruler.

2 Kings 11:1-3, Athaliah's Usurpation of the Davidic Throne

NIV

11 When Athaliah the mother of Ahaziah saw that her son was dead, she proceeded to destroy the whole royal family. [2]But Jehosheba, the daughter of King Jehoram[a] and sister of Ahaziah, took Joash son of Ahaziah and stole him away from among the royal princes, who were about to be murdered. She put him and his nurse in a bedroom to hide him from Athaliah; so he was not killed. [3]He remained hidden with his nurse at the temple of the LORD for six years while Athaliah ruled the land.

[a] 2 Hebrew *Joram,* a variant of *Jehoram*

NRSV

11 Now when Athaliah, Ahaziah's mother, saw that her son was dead, she set about to destroy all the royal family. [2]But Jehosheba, King Joram's daughter, Ahaziah's sister, took Joash son of Ahaziah, and stole him away from among the king's children who were about to be killed; she put[a] him and his nurse in a bedroom. Thus she[b] hid him from Athaliah, so that he was not killed; [3]he remained with her six years, hidden in the house of the LORD, while Athaliah reigned over the land.

[a] With 2 Chr 22.11: Heb lacks *she put* [b] Gk Syr Vg Compare 2 Chr 22.11: Heb *they*

COMMENTARY

Athaliah is to Judah what Jezebel was to Israel. Jezebel, the Phoenician princess and devotee of Baal, held an unsavory influence over the house of Ahab, leading eventually to Jehu's revolution. Athaliah is a daughter of Ahab and, one presumes, of Jezebel. Like the ruthless Jezebel, Athaliah is willing to commit murder in order to have her way. She orders a purge of all possible claimants to the throne (v. 1), thus endangering the promise of God to David that there will always by a "lamp" in Jerusalem (1 Kgs 11:36). Indeed, the Omrides had been eradicated by Jehu in Jezreel and Samaria, but Athaliah threatens to continue the ways of that dynasty in Jerusalem. The purge of Ahaziah's heirs is foiled, however, by Ahaziah's sister Jehosheba, who hides the infant Joash, together with his nurse (v. 2).[111] Safe from Athaliah, the baby Joash (the form of the name alternates with its variant, "Jehoash") spends six years in the "house of the LORD" (v. 3). Indeed, the parallel account in 2 Chr 22:10-12 provides the additional information that Jehosheba is the wife of Jehoiada, the priest who will have a dominant role to play in the restoration of "the king's son" (see v. 4) to the throne.

111. Jehosheba is said to be the daughter of Joram and Ahaziah's sister, but the text does not specify whether she is also Athaliah's daughter. Not surprisingly, Josephus (*Antiquities of the Jews* IX.7) and others have speculated that Jehosheba is the daughter of Joram through another marriage and, hence, is a half sister of Joash, thus explaining her loyalty to him.

2 Kings 11:4-21, The Davidic Monarchy Is Restored

NIV

4In the seventh year Jehoiada sent for the commanders of units of a hundred, the Carites and the guards and had them brought to him at the temple of the LORD. He made a covenant with them and put them under oath at the temple of the LORD. Then he showed them the king's son. 5He commanded them, saying, "This is what you are to do: You who are in the three companies that are going on duty on the Sabbath—a third of you guarding the royal palace, 6a third at the Sur Gate, and a third at the gate behind the guard, who take turns guarding the temple— 7and you who are in the other two companies that normally go off Sabbath duty are all to guard the temple for the king. 8Station yourselves around the king, each man with his weapon in his hand. Anyone who approaches your ranks[a] must be put to death. Stay close to the king wherever he goes."

9The commanders of units of a hundred did just as Jehoiada the priest ordered. Each one took his men—those who were going on duty on the Sabbath and those who were going off duty—and came to Jehoiada the priest. 10Then he gave the commanders the spears and shields that had belonged to King David and that were in the temple of the LORD. 11The guards, each with his weapon

[a] *8* Or *approaches the precincts*

NRSV

4But in the seventh year Jehoiada summoned the captains of the Carites and of the guards and had them come to him in the house of the LORD. He made a covenant with them and put them under oath in the house of the LORD; then he showed them the king's son. 5He commanded them, "This is what you are to do: one-third of you, those who go off duty on the sabbath and guard the king's house 6(another third being at the gate Sur and a third at the gate behind the guards), shall guard the palace; 7and your two divisions that come on duty in force on the sabbath and guard the house of the LORD[a] 8shall surround the king, each with weapons in hand; and whoever approaches the ranks is to be killed. Be with the king in his comings and goings."

9The captains did according to all that the priest Jehoiada commanded; each brought his men who were to go off duty on the sabbath, with those who were to come on duty on the sabbath, and came to the priest Jehoiada. 10The priest delivered to the captains the spears and shields that had been King David's, which were in the house of the LORD; 11the guards stood, every man with his weapons in his hand, from the south side of the house to the north side of the house,

[a] Heb *the LORD to the king*

NIV

in his hand, stationed themselves around the king—near the altar and the temple, from the south side to the north side of the temple.

12Jehoiada brought out the king's son and put the crown on him; he presented him with a copy of the covenant and proclaimed him king. They anointed him, and the people clapped their hands and shouted, "Long live the king!"

13When Athaliah heard the noise made by the guards and the people, she went to the people at the temple of the LORD. 14She looked and there was the king, standing by the pillar, as the custom was. The officers and the trumpeters were beside the king, and all the people of the land were rejoicing and blowing trumpets. Then Athaliah tore her robes and called out, "Treason! Treason!"

15Jehoiada the priest ordered the commanders of units of a hundred, who were in charge of the troops: "Bring her out between the ranks[a] and put to the sword anyone who follows her." For the priest had said, "She must not be put to death in the temple of the LORD." 16So they seized her as she reached the place where the horses enter the palace grounds, and there she was put to death.

17Jehoiada then made a covenant between the LORD and the king and people that they would be the LORD's people. He also made a covenant between the king and the people. 18All the people of the land went to the temple of Baal and tore it down. They smashed the altars and idols to pieces and killed Mattan the priest of Baal in front of the altars.

Then Jehoiada the priest posted guards at the temple of the LORD. 19He took with him the commanders of hundreds, the Carites, the guards and all the people of the land, and together they brought the king down from the temple of the LORD and went into the palace, entering by way of the gate of the guards. The king then took his place on the royal throne, 20and all the people of the land rejoiced. And the city was quiet, because Athaliah had been slain with the sword at the palace.

21Joash[b] was seven years old when he began to reign.

[a] *15* Or *out from the precincts* [b] *21* Hebrew *Jehoash,* a variant of *Joash*

NRSV

around the altar and the house, to guard the king on every side. 12Then he brought out the king's son, put the crown on him, and gave him the covenant;[a] they proclaimed him king, and anointed him; they clapped their hands and shouted, "Long live the king!"

13When Athaliah heard the noise of the guard and of the people, she went into the house of the LORD to the people; 14when she looked, there was the king standing by the pillar, according to custom, with the captains and the trumpeters beside the king, and all the people of the land rejoicing and blowing trumpets. Athaliah tore her clothes and cried, "Treason! Treason!" 15Then the priest Jehoiada commanded the captains who were set over the army, "Bring her out between the ranks, and kill with the sword anyone who follows her." For the priest said, "Let her not be killed in the house of the LORD." 16So they laid hands on her; she went through the horses' entrance to the king's house, and there she was put to death.

17Jehoiada made a covenant between the LORD and the king and people, that they should be the LORD's people; also between the king and the people. 18Then all the people of the land went to the house of Baal, and tore it down; his altars and his images they broke in pieces, and they killed Mattan, the priest of Baal, before the altars. The priest posted guards over the house of the LORD. 19He took the captains, the Carites, the guards, and all the people of the land; then they brought the king down from the house of the LORD, marching through the gate of the guards to the king's house. He took his seat on the throne of the kings. 20So all the people of the land rejoiced; and the city was quiet after Athaliah had been killed with the sword at the king's house.

21 [b]Jehoash[c] was seven years old when he began to reign.

[a] Or *treaty* or *testimony*; Heb *eduth* [b] Ch 12.1 in Heb [c] Another spelling is *Joash*; see verse 19

COMMENTARY

In the seventh year of Athaliah's illegitimate reign, Jehoiada, the chief priest of the Temple of the Lord (see 2 Chr 24:6), orchestrates a return of the legitimate heir to the throne. He secures the support of the Carites, mercenaries of uncertain origin, who are charged with guarding the Temple and the palace, swearing them to secrecy and loyalty.[112] The instructions given to them are rather confusing (cf. the NIV and the NRSV of vv. 5-8), partly because of our ignorance of military organization of that time and the layout of the city and partly because the Hebrew is ambiguous.[113] It appears that the guards are divided into three detachments, one of which is further divided into three details and is assigned to three strategic stations, while the other two are to protect the boy, Joash. The troops are provided with weapons from the Temple that had belonged to King David (v. 10; cf. 2 Sam 8:7). This is a subtle but important detail inasmuch as the countercoup is seen by the narrator as an effort to restore the promise made by the Lord to David. Then these guards bring out Joash, put the crown upon his head, and give him some kind of emblem of kingship (v. 12). The Hebrew word for that emblem (עדות *'ēdût*) is used elsewhere in the Bible for covenant documents (e.g., Exod 25:16, 21; 31:18; 32:15; 34:29; 40:20) and occurs in conjunction with David's kingship in Ps 132:12. Hence the NIV interprets it as "a copy of the covenant" (NRSV, "the covenant"; REB, "the testimony"), although the word has been taken by some interpreters to refer to some sort of royal insignia.[114] In any case, Joash is proclaimed king (v. 12).

Athaliah is caught off guard; her protestations of treachery are of no avail, as Jehoiada orders her arrest and the guards kill her, but only after they have taken her away from the sacred precincts (vv. 13-16). Jehoiada then initiates a covenant renewal between the Lord and the king and his people (v. 17), a renewal necessitated by the rupture in the relationship between the Lord and the nation, caused by Ahaziah's allegiance to the house of Ahab, which seemed to have intertwined Judah's fate with Israel, and by the subsequent illegitimate rule of Athaliah. The people move to destroy the hitherto unmentioned temple of Baal (presumably built by Athaliah), its cultic appurtenances, and Mattan, its priest (v. 18). In contrast to the carnage that attended the revolution in the north, there is no massacre; only Mattan, the priest of Baal, and Athaliah are killed. Instead of the terror and uncertainty that Jehu's revolution brought, the narrator reports that all the people rejoice and that the city is quiet (v. 20).

112. The Hebrew consonantal text in 2 Sam 20:23 also speaks of the "Carites," but later scribes preferred reading "Cherethites," who may or may not be related to the Carites.

113. The "house" (בית *bayit*) at the end of v. 6, for instance, is interpreted as "palace" in the NRSV but as "temple" in the NIV. Indeed, it has even been interpreted as the "house" of Baal mentioned in v. 18. See Iain W. Provan, *1 and 2 Kings*, NIBC (Peabody, Mass.: Hendrickson, 1995) 221-22.

114. See M. Cogan and H. Tadmor, *II Kings*, AB 11 (New York: Doubleday, 1988) 128.

2 Kings 12:1-16, The Reign of Joash

NIV

12 In the seventh year of Jehu, Joash[a] became king, and he reigned in Jerusalem forty years. His mother's name was Zibiah; she was from Beersheba. [2]Joash did what was right in the eyes of the LORD all the years Jehoiada the priest instructed him. [3]The high places, however, were not removed; the people continued to offer sacrifices and burn incense there.

a *1* Hebrew *Jehoash*, a variant of *Joash*; also in verses 2, 4, 6, 7 and 18

NRSV

12 In the seventh year of Jehu, Jehoash began to reign; he reigned forty years in Jerusalem. His mother's name was Zibiah of Beer-sheba. [2]Jehoash did what was right in the sight of the LORD all his days, because the priest Jehoiada instructed him. [3]Nevertheless the high places were not taken away; the people continued to sacrifice and make offerings on the high places.

4Jehoash said to the priests, "All the money

NIV

4Joash said to the priests, "Collect all the money that is brought as sacred offerings to the temple of the LORD—the money collected in the census, the money received from personal vows and the money brought voluntarily to the temple. 5Let every priest receive the money from one of the treasurers, and let it be used to repair whatever damage is found in the temple."

6But by the twenty-third year of King Joash the priests still had not repaired the temple. 7Therefore King Joash summoned Jehoiada the priest and the other priests and asked them, "Why aren't you repairing the damage done to the temple? Take no more money from your treasurers, but hand it over for repairing the temple." 8The priests agreed that they would not collect any more money from the people and that they would not repair the temple themselves.

9Jehoiada the priest took a chest and bored a hole in its lid. He placed it beside the altar, on the right side as one enters the temple of the LORD. The priests who guarded the entrance put into the chest all the money that was brought to the temple of the LORD. 10Whenever they saw that there was a large amount of money in the chest, the royal secretary and the high priest came, counted the money that had been brought into the temple of the LORD and put it into bags. 11When the amount had been determined, they gave the money to the men appointed to supervise the work on the temple. With it they paid those who worked on the temple of the LORD—the carpenters and builders, 12the masons and stonecutters. They purchased timber and dressed stone for the repair of the temple of the LORD, and met all the other expenses of restoring the temple.

13The money brought into the temple was not spent for making silver basins, wick trimmers, sprinkling bowls, trumpets or any other articles of gold or silver for the temple of the LORD; 14it was paid to the workmen, who used it to repair the temple. 15They did not require an accounting from those to whom they gave the money to pay the workers, because they acted with complete honesty. 16The money from the guilt offerings and sin offerings was not brought into the temple of the LORD; it belonged to the priests.

NRSV

offered as sacred donations that is brought into the house of the LORD, the money for which each person is assessed—the money from the assessment of persons—and the money from the voluntary offerings brought into the house of the LORD, 5let the priests receive from each of the donors; and let them repair the house wherever any need of repairs is discovered." 6But by the twenty-third year of King Jehoash the priests had made no repairs on the house. 7Therefore King Jehoash summoned the priest Jehoiada with the other priests and said to them, "Why are you not repairing the house? Now therefore do not accept any more money from your donors but hand it over for the repair of the house." 8So the priests agreed that they would neither accept more money from the people nor repair the house.

9Then the priest Jehoiada took a chest, made a hole in its lid, and set it beside the altar on the right side as one entered the house of the LORD; the priests who guarded the threshold put in it all the money that was brought into the house of the LORD. 10Whenever they saw that there was a great deal of money in the chest, the king's secretary and the high priest went up, counted the money that was found in the house of the LORD, and tied it up in bags. 11They would give the money that was weighed out into the hands of the workers who had the oversight of the house of the LORD; then they paid it out to the carpenters and the builders who worked on the house of the LORD, 12to the masons and the stonecutters, as well as to buy timber and quarried stone for making repairs on the house of the LORD, as well as for any outlay for repairs of the house. 13But for the house of the LORD no basins of silver, snuffers, bowls, trumpets, or any vessels of gold, or of silver, were made from the money that was brought into the house of the LORD, 14for that was given to the workers who were repairing the house of the LORD with it. 15They did not ask an accounting from those into whose hand they delivered the money to pay out to the workers, for they dealt honestly. 16The money from the guilt offerings and the money from the sin offerings was not brought into the house of the LORD; it belonged to the priests.

COMMENTARY

The reign of Joash (837–800 BCE) is focused almost entirely on the renovation of the Temple, symbolic of the rededication of Judah to the Lord. The mother of Joash is identified as Zibiah of Beersheba, a site at the southern border of Judah—that is, as far south from the border with Israel as possible. The narrator seems to imply that it is this parentage, together with the fact of Jehoiada's tutelage, that accounts for the relatively faithful reign of Joash, although he, too, is criticized for failing to remove the high places.

Joash orders the priests to collect the money from the census taxes (see Exod 30:11-16) and from the voluntary offerings that are given in repayment of vows (Lev 27:1-8) and instructs them to oversee the renovation of the Temple (vv. 4-5). The fund-raising mandate seems to be a general one; it is not clear whether the funds are specifically designated for the project. Hence, more than two decades later, the repairs are still not done (v. 6). Joash dismisses the priests from the project because of the obvious conflicts of interest. Henceforth the priests are no longer to receive the contributions, and they are also released from the obligation of overseeing the temple repairs (vv. 7-8). A chest is set up to receive additional contributions, and whenever it is full, representatives of the state and the Temple together disburse the money for payment of the workers. The funds were not to be used for the maintenance of the temple appurtenances, but only for the workers commissioned to do the repairs. The priests, though, are still paid out of the funds accumulated from the guilt offerings and sin offerings (see Lev 4:1–6:7; Num 15:22-31).

2 Kings 12:17-21, Hazael Threatens and Joash Dies

NIV

17About this time Hazael king of Aram went up and attacked Gath and captured it. Then he turned to attack Jerusalem. 18But Joash king of Judah took all the sacred objects dedicated by his fathers—Jehoshaphat, Jehoram and Ahaziah, the kings of Judah—and the gifts he himself had dedicated and all the gold found in the treasuries of the temple of the LORD and of the royal palace, and he sent them to Hazael king of Aram, who then withdrew from Jerusalem.

19As for the other events of the reign of Joash, and all he did, are they not written in the book of the annals of the kings of Judah? 20His officials conspired against him and assassinated him at Beth Millo, on the road down to Silla. 21The officials who murdered him were Jozabad son of Shimeath and Jehozabad son of Shomer. He died and was buried with his fathers in the City of David. And Amaziah his son succeeded him as king.

NRSV

17At that time King Hazael of Aram went up, fought against Gath, and took it. But when Hazael set his face to go up against Jerusalem, 18King Jehoash of Judah took all the votive gifts that Jehoshaphat, Jehoram, and Ahaziah, his ancestors, the kings of Judah, had dedicated, as well as his own votive gifts, all the gold that was found in the treasuries of the house of the LORD and of the king's house, and sent these to King Hazael of Aram. Then Hazael withdrew from Jerusalem.

19Now the rest of the acts of Joash, and all that he did, are they not written in the Book of the Annals of the Kings of Judah? 20His servants arose, devised a conspiracy, and killed Joash in the house of Millo, on the way that goes down to Silla. 21It was Jozacar son of Shimeath and Jehozabad son of Shomer, his servants, who struck him down, so that he died. He was buried with his ancestors in the city of David; then his son Amaziah succeeded him.

COMMENTARY

All the efforts of Joash to do right seem to be negated, however, when Hazael of Aram threatens Jerusalem. To buy Hazael off, Joash takes from the temple treasury the votive gifts deposited there by his predecessors, Jehoshaphat, Joram, and Ahaziah. History seems to repeat itself, for the reformist king Asa had long ago taken from the same treasury in order to buy off the Arameans (1 Kgs 15:18). The temple treasury, which was depleted by Asa and slowly replenished by his successors, is again being raided by a reformist king in the face of an Aramean threat. Even reformist kings like Asa and Joash do not perform adequately in the interest of the Lord's house.

The regnal summary of Joash includes a note about his assassination by his own courtiers. No reason is given by the narrator for this murder, but the chronicler adds the information that Joash is killed for having murdered the son of his former patron, Jehoiada the priest (2 Chr 24:23-27).

REFLECTIONS

In this chapter, we see how God's promise of an enduring Davidic dynasty is threatened by a ruthless usurper determined to eliminate all the royal family. A single baby is saved, however, by a hitherto unknown and never again mentioned woman who takes it upon herself to hide him from his would-be killers. This is not the first time, of course, that a baby is saved from a royal pogrom. Pharaoh tried to have all the male infants of his Hebrew slaves killed, but Moses was secretly hidden and saved from harm, and he grew up to be an agent of God's liberation (Exod 2:1-10). Nor is the deliverance of baby Joash the last time that such a deliverance of an infant would occur. Indeed, the deliverance of Joash from death in some ways foreshadows the deliverance of another baby, another "son of David," from the efforts of King Herod to have all male infants killed (Matt 2:1-23). To be sure, God is silent in this story of the deliverance of the infant Joash. In the light of the repeated emphasis in the book of Kings on the working out of God's will in history, however, there can be little doubt that the reader is to understand that God is working behind the scenes, too, in this deliverance of an infant. God does not have to act or speak in order for God's will to be accomplished. In history there will always be agents, witting or unwitting, who will bring about the divine will.

The story also points to the potential and limitations of human beings who strive to serve God. Jehoiada, who so valiantly and efficiently orchestrated the restoration of the heir to the throne of David, does not seem to have the ability to manage the finances of the Temple efficiently enough to carry out the needed repairs. By the same token, King Joash had initiated the fund-raising campaign to repair the Temple, but he seemed so out of touch with the project that it took him more than two decades to realize that the repairs had not been done. He who had taken steps to raise funds for the Temple's renovation is the same king who robbed the temple treasury in order to pay off an outsider. He who had been rescued as an infant was struck down forty years later by his own servants, perhaps because he had betrayed the very person who had instructed him in his youth (2 Chr 24:23-27).

2 KINGS 13:1–14:29, THE DYNASTY OF JEHU THRIVES

OVERVIEW

Having addressed the crisis in Judah (chap. 12), the narrator now returns to the situation in Israel. The crisis in Judah was not merely a political one; it was also a theological crisis. The conduct of Joram of Judah and his son Ahaziah had so tied Judah to Israel that the two nations had practically become one. It was no accident, therefore, that Ahaziah was murdered along with his northern counterpart in Israel. The foolhardy actions of Ahaziah brought consequences not only to himself, but to the Davidic dynasty as well. Athaliah, a princess from the house of Ahab, seized power and moved to eradicate all legitimate claimants to the throne in Jerusalem. It looked as if the house of Ahab, annihilated in Jezreel and Samaria, would simply continue in Judah through Athaliah. Moreover, God's promise of an enduring Davidic dynasty hung in the balance for a while, thwarted only by the deliverance of a lone baby, the future King Joash, from death. At last, the crisis had blown over, as the legitimate scion of David was placed on the throne; the covenant was renewed among God, king, and people; and the Temple was refurbished. Things were as God had intended them to be for Judah. But what about Israel?

Unlike Ahaziah, who had pandered to the house of Ahab, Jehu had been effective in destroying it and eliminating Baal worship from Israel. For his accomplishments in those areas, Jehu was commended and rewarded with the promise of a relatively enduring dynasty—one that would last four generations. Now in the new unit (13:1–14:29) we find a report of how Israel fared through three generations of the descendants of Jehu. In that period, Israel seemed to have been treated in a manner more typical for Judah: The ruling dynasty endured, and Israel experienced the persistence of God's grace despite the sins of the kings.

These two chapters look like a collection of loosely connected and haphazardly placed units. The reports of the reigns of Jehoahaz (13:1-9) and Jehoash (13:10-13) appear to be already closed out, when we find Jehoash active again and performing sign-actions at the behest of Elisha (13:14-19). An account of an odd incident occurring after the death of Elisha appears in 13:20-21; it concerns the resurrection of an unknown man and seems at first blush to have nothing to do with the national and international events in the rest of these chapters. Then, the focus turns again to the international arena, with a reference in the narrative to the Aramean oppression of Israel during the reign of Jehoahaz (13:24), together with allusions to victory for Israel under Jehoash (13:25). There follows a report on the reign of Amaziah of Judah (14:1-14), with a closing summary of that reign (14:17-22). Intruding into that report, however, is a regnal summary of the reign of Jehoash that most commentators regard as anomalous (14:15-16) and some believe to be a secondary duplication of a similar summary in 13:12-13. Finally, there is a report of the reign of Jeroboam II (14:23-29). Not surprisingly, some scholars posit that a series of originally independent pieces has been brought together over a period of time and through a series of redactions.[115] That may be the case, but it is still possible to read the entire unit as one literary piece, as some scholars have attempted to do.[116] As it stands, the narrative is about the fulfillment of God's promise to Jehu that his dynasty will last four generations (10:30). Regardless of the sins of Jehu's descendants, therefore, God has continued to grant Israel salvation and victory.

115. See, e.g., the survey in Burke O. Long, *2 Kings,* FOTL 10 (Grand Rapids: Eerdmans, 1991) 163-65.

116. Long, *2 Kings,* 162-70.

2 Kings 13:1-13, Jehoahaz and Jehoash Reign in Israel

NIV

13 In the twenty-third year of Joash son of Ahaziah king of Judah, Jehoahaz son of Jehu became king of Israel in Samaria, and he reigned seventeen years. [2]He did evil in the eyes of the LORD by following the sins of Jeroboam son of Nebat, which he had caused Israel to commit, and he did not turn away from them. [3]So the LORD's anger burned against Israel, and for a long time he kept them under the power of Hazael king of Aram and Ben-Hadad his son.

[4]Then Jehoahaz sought the LORD's favor, and the LORD listened to him, for he saw how severely the king of Aram was oppressing Israel. [5]The LORD provided a deliverer for Israel, and they escaped from the power of Aram. So the Israelites lived in their own homes as they had before. [6]But they did not turn away from the sins of the house of Jeroboam, which he had caused Israel to commit; they continued in them. Also, the Asherah pole[a] remained standing in Samaria.

[7]Nothing had been left of the army of Jehoahaz except fifty horsemen, ten chariots and ten thousand foot soldiers, for the king of Aram had destroyed the rest and made them like the dust at threshing time.

[8]As for the other events of the reign of Jehoahaz, all he did and his achievements, are they not written in the book of the annals of the kings of Israel? [9]Jehoahaz rested with his fathers and was buried in Samaria. And Jehoash[b] his son succeeded him as king.

[10]In the thirty-seventh year of Joash king of Judah, Jehoash son of Jehoahaz became king of Israel in Samaria, and he reigned sixteen years. [11]He did evil in the eyes of the LORD and did not turn away from any of the sins of Jeroboam son of Nebat, which he had caused Israel to commit; he continued in them.

[12]As for the other events of the reign of Jehoash, all he did and his achievements, including his war against Amaziah king of Judah, are they not written in the book of the annals of the kings of Israel? [13]Jehoash rested with his fathers, and

[a] *6* That is, a symbol of the goddess Asherah; here and elsewhere in 2 Kings [b] *9* Hebrew *Joash,* a variant of *Jehoash;* also in verses 12-14 and 25

NRSV

13 In the twenty-third year of King Joash son of Ahaziah of Judah, Jehoahaz son of Jehu began to reign over Israel in Samaria; he reigned seventeen years. [2]He did what was evil in the sight of the LORD, and followed the sins of Jeroboam son of Nebat, which he caused Israel to sin; he did not depart from them. [3]The anger of the LORD was kindled against Israel, so that he gave them repeatedly into the hand of King Hazael of Aram, then into the hand of Ben-hadad son of Hazael. [4]But Jehoahaz entreated the LORD, and the LORD heeded him; for he saw the oppression of Israel, how the king of Aram oppressed them. [5]Therefore the LORD gave Israel a savior, so that they escaped from the hand of the Arameans; and the people of Israel lived in their homes as formerly. [6]Nevertheless they did not depart from the sins of the house of Jeroboam, which he caused Israel to sin, but walked[a] in them; the sacred pole[b] also remained in Samaria. [7]So Jehoahaz was left with an army of not more than fifty horsemen, ten chariots and ten thousand footmen; for the king of Aram had destroyed them and made them like the dust at threshing. [8]Now the rest of the acts of Jehoahaz and all that he did, including his might, are they not written in the Book of the Annals of the Kings of Israel? [9]So Jehoahaz slept with his ancestors, and they buried him in Samaria; then his son Joash succeeded him.

10In the thirty-seventh year of King Joash of Judah, Jehoash son of Jehoahaz began to reign over Israel in Samaria; he reigned sixteen years. [11]He also did what was evil in the sight of the LORD; he did not depart from all the sins of Jeroboam son of Nebat, which he caused Israel to sin, but he walked in them. [12]Now the rest of the acts of Joash, and all that he did, as well as the might with which he fought against King Amaziah of Judah, are they not written in the Book of the Annals of the Kings of Israel? [13]So Joash slept with his ancestors, and Jeroboam sat upon his throne; Joash was buried in Samaria with the kings of Israel.

[a] Gk Syr Tg Vg: Heb *he walked* [b] Heb *Asherah*

NIV

Jeroboam succeeded him on the throne. Jehoash was buried in Samaria with the kings of Israel.

COMMENTARY

Jehoahaz (variant of "Joahaz") has already been mentioned in 10:35 as the son and successor of Jehu. Now comes the formal report of his reign (vv. 1-9). He is evaluated in the manner typical for the northern kings. Accordingly, Jehoahaz followed the ways of Jeroboam, son of Nebat, causing Israel to sin, and he did not depart from them (v. 2; cf. 1 Kgs 12:26-32; 16:26; 22:52; 2 Kgs 3:3; 10:29; 13:11; 14:24; 15:9, 18, 24, 28). The account in vv. 3-6 echoes the typical cycle of events that one finds in early Israel's history: Israel sins, God sends an oppressive enemy as retribution, the people cry to God for mercy, God sends a deliverer, things return to normal for Israel, but soon the people sin again (see Judg 2:11-23; 3:7-15, 30; 4:1-3, 23; 10:6-10). Whereas the "savior" is typically named in the analogous depictions from Israel's early history (it was typically the next ruler), however, he is not explicitly identified here (v. 5). Scholars have variously suggested that the allusion is to a third-party aggressor whose pressure on the Arameans brought a reprieve for Israel (such as the Assyrian king Adad-nirari III or even Zakkur of Hamath), another Israelite king like Joash or Jeroboam (II), or Elisha.[117] Despite the fact that it is the reign of Jehoahaz that is in view, it seems clear that the narrator has in mind the problem of Aramean aggression over a considerable period of time; God repeatedly gave Israel into the hands of the Arameans during the reigns of Hazael and then of his son, Ben-hadad (v. 3), certainly a period extending well beyond the rule of Jehoahaz. The "savior" (מושיע *môšîa'*), then, would not be one specific individual, but anyone who was instrumental in the deliverance of Israel from its plight. Indeed, in the course of the narrative, the Hebrew root ישע (*yš'*, "save") is used in conjunction with Elisha (13:14-21), Joash (13:17), and Jeroboam (14:27), each of whom will in some way bring salvation/victory (the Hebrew word is the same) to Israel in its times of distress.

It is important to observe that God responds to the cry for deliverance from oppression, even when the entreaty comes from the recalcitrant Jehoahaz. Nothing is said in the text about repentance, yet God heeds the prayer of the king. Still, the people persist in following the ways of Jeroboam, and unacceptable sacred objects, like the "sacred pole," were not purged from Samaria (v. 6). Jehoahaz is left with a remnant of an army as insignificant as the dust on a threshing floor, vulnerable to every wind that blows across it (v. 7). This remnant is, paradoxically, a testimony to both God's judgment and God's grace: The army's diminution is certainly a sign of divine judgment, but the fact that a remnant survives is a sign of grace. For now, Israel is like Judah inasmuch as it is punished for its offenses against God, but there is continuity on the throne in Samaria as in Jerusalem. So when Jehoahaz dies (v. 9), he is succeeded by his son Jehoash (variant of "Joash"). The new king, too, does not depart from the ways of Jeroboam (vv. 10-11). Yet, he triumphs mightily over Judah (v. 12), and he is succeeded by his son Jeroboam (v. 3). (See Reflections at 14:23-29.)

117. See Mordecai Cogan and Hayim Tadmor, *II Kings*, AB 11 (New York: Doubleday, 1988) 143.

2 Kings 13:14-21, Elisha Dies, But His Ministry Lives On

NIV

14Now Elisha was suffering from the illness
from which he died. Jehoash king of Israel went
down to see him and wept over him. "My father!
My father!" he cried. "The chariots and horsemen
of Israel!"
15Elisha said, "Get a bow and some arrows,"
and he did so. 16"Take the bow in your hands,"
he said to the king of Israel. When he had taken
it, Elisha put his hands on the king's hands.
17"Open the east window," he said, and he
opened it. "Shoot!" Elisha said, and he shot. "The
LORD's arrow of victory, the arrow of victory over
Aram!" Elisha declared. "You will completely destroy the Arameans at Aphek."
18Then he said, "Take the arrows," and the
king took them. Elisha told him, "Strike the
ground." He struck it three times and stopped.
19The man of God was angry with him and said,
"You should have struck the ground five or six
times; then you would have defeated Aram and
completely destroyed it. But now you will defeat
it only three times."
20Elisha died and was buried.
Now Moabite raiders used to enter the country
every spring. 21Once while some Israelites were
burying a man, suddenly they saw a band of
raiders; so they threw the man's body into Elisha's
tomb. When the body touched Elisha's bones, the
man came to life and stood up on his feet.

NRSV

14Now when Elisha had fallen sick with the
illness of which he was to die, King Joash of Israel
went down to him, and wept before him, crying,
"My father, my father! The chariots of Israel and
its horsemen!" 15Elisha said to him, "Take a bow
and arrows"; so he took a bow and arrows. 16Then
he said to the king of Israel, "Draw the bow";
and he drew it. Elisha laid his hands on the king's
hands. 17Then he said, "Open the window eastward"; and he opened it. Elisha said, "Shoot";
and he shot. Then he said, "The LORD's arrow of
victory, the arrow of victory over Aram! For you
shall fight the Arameans in Aphek until you have
made an end of them." 18He continued, "Take
the arrows"; and he took them. He said to the
king of Israel, "Strike the ground with them"; he
struck three times, and stopped. 19Then the man
of God was angry with him, and said, "You should
have struck five or six times; then you would
have struck down Aram until you had made an
end of it, but now you will strike down Aram
only three times."
20So Elisha died, and they buried him. Now
bands of Moabites used to invade the land in the
spring of the year. 21As a man was being buried,
a marauding band was seen and the man was
thrown into the grave of Elisha; as soon as the
man touched the bones of Elisha, he came to life
and stood on his feet.

COMMENTARY

Given the importance of the "savior" (מושיע *môšîaʿ*) in the survival of Israel, the impending death of Elisha (אלישע *ʾĕlîšāʿ*; lit., "My God Saves") is certainly ominous, and Jehoash knows it. The king's weeping before the prophet suggests a recognition of the role that the celestial hosts have played in Israel's victories on account of Elisha's presence (see 2:11-12; 6:16-17). Elisha had cried as Elijah ascended into heaven, "My father, my father! The chariotry of Israel and its horses!" (2:12). So now Jehoash cries as Elisha lies on his deathbed, "My father, my father! The chariotry of Israel and its horses!" (v. 14). Is it conceivable, one might wonder, that Jehoash could somehow be in the position that Elisha had been in when he succeeded the great Elijah?

Elisha tells Joash to shoot an arrow eastward, out of the window (vv. 15-17). This is a prophetic sign-act, akin to Ahijah's tearing of the garments into twelve pieces to symbolize the fragmentation of the kingdom (1 Kgs 11:29-32). Such prophetic sign-acts, intended as the initial realization of the prophecy, are typically performed by prophets (e.g., Isa 7:3; 8:1-4; 20:1-6; Jer 13:1-11; 18:1-12;

27:2-11; 32:1-15; Ezek 4:1-11; 5:1-12; 12:1-20; 24:15-27). Here it is Jehoash who acts out the prophetic event under the instruction of Elisha. Then, when Jehoash shoots the arrow out the window, Elisha announces that it is the Lord's "arrow of victory, the arrow of victory over Aram," the Hebrew word for "victory" (תשועה *tĕšûʿâ*) being the same as the word for "salvation," a word consisting of the same root as the word for "savior" (*môšîaʿ*) in v. 5 and found in the name "Elisha." Poignantly, Elisha places his hand upon the hand of Jehoash after the king has shot the arrow, as if the prophet is passing on to the king his prophetic power or authority. It is as if the agency of salvation or victory made possible through the person of Elisha is now somehow passed on to the king of Israel. Even after the death of the prophet, there will be a "savior"; there will be salvation/victory through a king, even one as sinful as Jehoash. Elisha stipulates, however, that Jehoash is to fight Aram at Aphek "unto completion" (עד־כלה *ʿad-kallēh*). The mention of Aphek recalls Ahab's victory over the Arameans at that same site, although Ahab did not completely destroy the Arameans, as he was supposed to do in a holy war (1 Kgs 20:26-43). The fact that the arrow shot out of the window is called "the LORD's arrow" suggests that the battle belongs to the Lord (cf. other references to arrows of the divine warrior in Deut 32:23; Pss 77:18; 91:5; Hab 3:11; Zech 9:14). As in the case of the war Ahab had earlier fought against the king of Aram at Aphek, this war belongs to the Lord, and victory in it belongs to the Lord.

The prophet further instructs the king to strike the ground with the arrows (v. 18). The Hebrew word for "strike" (הכה *hikkâ*, in the hiphil) is also the word used in the defeat of enemies, and the word for "earth" (ארצה *ʾarṣâ*) is the same one used for "country." Given the context, therefore, one may understand the command to be a call to defeat the country of Aram. When Jehoash strikes the ground with the arrow only three times and stops, he is chided for having carried out the command inadequately (v. 19). Elisha interprets this to mean that the king should have struck "unto completion" (v. 19; cf. v. 17). Jehoash's failure is sometimes explained as evidence of his "tendency to think small,"[118] of his "vacillating character,"[119] or the like. The anger of Elisha, too, seems unreasonable to some scholars, who note that the prophet did not tell the king precisely how many times to strike the arrows on the ground.[120] In view of Elisha's call (v. 18) to "strike" (*hikkâ*) Aram "unto completion" (*ʿad-kallēh*), and in the light of the account of the earlier battle of Israel with Aram at Aphek, however, it seems clear that the issue here is not the insufficiency of Jehoash's enthusiasm, but his flagrant disregard for the will of God in holy war (see the Commentary on 1 Kgs 20:35-43). The incident anticipates the report on Israel's limited success against Aram in v. 25.

In all, the account provides an explanation for the success of Israel against Aram during the years under the house of Jehu. It explains why the dynasty endured four generations, despite the flaws of the descendants of Jehu. God somehow provides a "savior" whenever there is a need for one, whether that "savior" is a prophet or a king, a man of God or a sinner. At the same time, however, the passage provides a rationale for the impending end of that period of grace: The kings of the house of Jehu, like Jehoash, are just like the willfully disobedient Ahab after all.

As if to ensure that the point is not missed that the abiding effects of Elisha's ministry will continue even after his death, the narrator then tells a somewhat comical, but nevertheless powerful, story of an event that happened after Elisha had died and was buried. A funeral of another man is taking place when a marauding band of Moabites come to a region in Israel. In their hurry to avoid the Moabites, the people burying the man simply throw the corpse into a grave, which just happens to be Elisha's. When the corpse comes into contact with Elisha's skeleton, the dead man is revived. The possibility that this resurrection was a result of the contact of the dead man's body with that of Elisha is reminiscent of the resurrection of the dead child of the Shunammite woman in 4:32-35. The present story is even more poignant, however, for Elisha has long been dead and buried, his body having decayed until only the skeleton is left. Yet, even in death, Elisha's power lives

118. T. R. Hobbs, *2 Kings*, WBC 13 (Waco, Tex.: Word, 1985) 170.

119. Norman Snaith, "II Kings," in *The Interpreter's Bible* (Nashville: Abingdon, 1954) 3:257.

120. See, e.g., Paul J. Kissling, *Reliable Characters in the Primary History: Profiles of Moses, Joshua, Elijah, and Elisha*, JSOTSup 224 (Sheffield: Sheffield Academic, 1996) 179-80.

and enlivens, even as the mere retelling of his power empowers and enlivens, despite his absence (8:1-6). As in life, so even in death, his power not only affects kings in the international arena (vv. 14-19), but it also brings life to ordinary folk, even an unnamed dead man! (See Reflections at 14:23-29.)

2 Kings 13:22-25, Victories over Aram

NIV

[22]Hazael king of Aram oppressed Israel throughout the reign of Jehoahaz. [23]But the LORD was gracious to them and had compassion and showed concern for them because of his covenant with Abraham, Isaac and Jacob. To this day he has been unwilling to destroy them or banish them from his presence.

[24]Hazael king of Aram died, and Ben-Hadad his son succeeded him as king. [25]Then Jehoash son of Jehoahaz recaptured from Ben-Hadad son of Hazael the towns he had taken in battle from his father Jehoahaz. Three times Jehoash defeated him, and so he recovered the Israelite towns.

NRSV

22Now King Hazael of Aram oppressed Israel all the days of Jehoahaz. [23]But the LORD was gracious to them and had compassion on them; he turned toward them, because of his covenant with Abraham, Isaac, and Jacob, and would not destroy them; nor has he banished them from his presence until now.

24When King Hazael of Aram died, his son Ben-hadad succeeded him. [25]Then Jehoash son of Jehoahaz took again from Ben-hadad son of Hazael the towns that he had taken from his father Jehoahaz in war. Three times Joash defeated him and recovered the towns of Israel.

COMMENTARY

The narrator summarizes the situation during the reigns of Jehoahaz and Jehoash. The Lord had been gracious and merciful to Israel on account of the covenant with the ancestors (see Gen 15:1-21; 26:23-25; 28:10-22). Without parallel anywhere in the book of Kings, this claim explains the survival of Israel despite the sins of its kings. In effect, this appeal to the covenant with the ancestors functions as the equivalent of the appeal to the Davidic covenant (2 Sam 7:1-17) for the kings of Judah. It explains why salvation came to Israel, despite the lack of any appropriate response by Israel's kings (vv. 1-9). Hence, Israel is able to have victories over Aram, just as Elisha had predicted in the symbolic actions of Jehoash (vv. 14-19). There are hints in the text, however, that the respite God has granted Israel will not last forever, the narrator's historical viewpoint being evident in the words "until now" (v. 23). Jehoash does "strike" (הכה *hikkâ*; NRSV, NIV, "defeated") Aram three times and recovers the towns of Israel (v. 25). The reader has been apprised, however, that the victories of Jehoash will not last (v. 19). (See Reflections at 14:23-29.)

2 Kings 14:1-22, The Reign of Amaziah of Judah

NIV

14 In the second year of Jehoash[a] son of Jehoahaz king of Israel, Amaziah son of Joash king of Judah began to reign. [2]He was twenty-five years old when he became king, and he reigned in Jerusalem twenty-nine years. His

[a] *1* Hebrew *Joash,* a variant of *Jehoash;* also in verses 13, 23 and 27

NRSV

14 In the second year of King Joash son of Joahaz of Israel, King Amaziah son of Joash of Judah, began to reign. [2]He was twenty-five years old when he began to reign, and he reigned twenty-nine years in Jerusalem. His mother's name was Jehoaddin of Jerusalem. [3]He did what

NIV

mother's name was Jehoaddin; she was from Jerusalem. 3He did what was right in the eyes of the LORD, but not as his father David had done. In everything he followed the example of his father Joash. 4The high places, however, were not removed; the people continued to offer sacrifices and burn incense there.

5After the kingdom was firmly in his grasp, he executed the officials who had murdered his father the king. 6Yet he did not put the sons of the assassins to death, in accordance with what is written in the Book of the Law of Moses where the LORD commanded: "Fathers shall not be put to death for their children, nor children put to death for their fathers; each is to die for his own sins."[a]

7He was the one who defeated ten thousand Edomites in the Valley of Salt and captured Sela in battle, calling it Joktheel, the name it has to this day.

8Then Amaziah sent messengers to Jehoash son of Jehoahaz, the son of Jehu, king of Israel, with the challenge: "Come, meet me face to face."

9But Jehoash king of Israel replied to Amaziah king of Judah: "A thistle in Lebanon sent a message to a cedar in Lebanon, 'Give your daughter to my son in marriage.' Then a wild beast in Lebanon came along and trampled the thistle underfoot. 10You have indeed defeated Edom and now you are arrogant. Glory in your victory, but stay at home! Why ask for trouble and cause your own downfall and that of Judah also?"

11Amaziah, however, would not listen, so Jehoash king of Israel attacked. He and Amaziah king of Judah faced each other at Beth Shemesh in Judah. 12Judah was routed by Israel, and every man fled to his home. 13Jehoash king of Israel captured Amaziah king of Judah, the son of Joash, the son of Ahaziah, at Beth Shemesh. Then Jehoash went to Jerusalem and broke down the wall of Jerusalem from the Ephraim Gate to the Corner Gate—a section about six hundred feet long.[b] 14He took all the gold and silver and all the articles found in the temple of the LORD and in the treasuries of the royal palace. He also took hostages and returned to Samaria.

15As for the other events of the reign of

[a] *6* Deut. 24:16 [b] *13* Hebrew *four hundred cubits* (about 180 meters)

NRSV

was right in the sight of the LORD, yet not like his ancestor David; in all things he did as his father Joash had done. 4But the high places were not removed; the people still sacrificed and made offerings on the high places. 5As soon as the royal power was firmly in his hand he killed his servants who had murdered his father the king. 6But he did not put to death the children of the murderers; according to what is written in the book of the law of Moses, where the LORD commanded, "The parents shall not be put to death for the children, or the children be put to death for the parents; but all shall be put to death for their own sins."

7He killed ten thousand Edomites in the Valley of Salt and took Sela by storm; he called it Jokthe-el, which is its name to this day.

8Then Amaziah sent messengers to King Jehoash son of Jehoahaz, son of Jehu, of Israel, saying, "Come, let us look one another in the face." 9King Jehoash of Israel sent word to King Amaziah of Judah, "A thornbush on Lebanon sent to a cedar on Lebanon, saying, 'Give your daughter to my son for a wife'; but a wild animal of Lebanon passed by and trampled down the thornbush. 10You have indeed defeated Edom, and your heart has lifted you up. Be content with your glory, and stay at home; for why should you provoke trouble so that you fall, you and Judah with you?"

11But Amaziah would not listen. So King Jehoash of Israel went up; he and King Amaziah of Judah faced one another in battle at Beth-shemesh, which belongs to Judah. 12Judah was defeated by Israel; everyone fled home. 13King Jehoash of Israel captured King Amaziah of Judah son of Jehoash, son of Ahaziah, at Beth-shemesh; he came to Jerusalem, and broke down the wall of Jerusalem from the Ephraim Gate to the Corner Gate, a distance of four hundred cubits. 14He seized all the gold and silver, and all the vessels that were found in the house of the LORD and in the treasuries of the king's house, as well as hostages; then he returned to Samaria.

15Now the rest of the acts that Jehoash did, his might, and how he fought with King Amaziah of Judah, are they not written in the Book of the Annals of the Kings of Israel? 16Jehoash slept with his ancestors, and was buried in Samaria with the

NIV

Jehoash, what he did and his achievements, including his war against Amaziah king of Judah, are they not written in the book of the annals of the kings of Israel? [16]Jehoash rested with his fathers and was buried in Samaria with the kings of Israel. And Jeroboam his son succeeded him as king.

[17]Amaziah son of Joash king of Judah lived for fifteen years after the death of Jehoash son of Jehoahaz king of Israel. [18]As for the other events of Amaziah's reign, are they not written in the book of the annals of the kings of Judah?

[19]They conspired against him in Jerusalem, and he fled to Lachish, but they sent men after him to Lachish and killed him there. [20]He was brought back by horse and was buried in Jerusalem with his fathers, in the City of David.

[21]Then all the people of Judah took Azariah,[a] who was sixteen years old, and made him king in place of his father Amaziah. [22]He was the one who rebuilt Elath and restored it to Judah after Amaziah rested with his fathers.

[a] *21* Also called *Uzziah*

NRSV

kings of Israel; then his son Jeroboam succeeded him.

17King Amaziah son of Joash of Judah lived fifteen years after the death of King Jehoash son of Jehoahaz of Israel. [18]Now the rest of the deeds of Amaziah, are they not written in the Book of the Annals of the Kings of Judah? [19]They made a conspiracy against him in Jerusalem, and he fled to Lachish. But they sent after him to Lachish, and killed him there. [20]They brought him on horses; he was buried in Jerusalem with his ancestors in the city of David. [21]All the people of Judah took Azariah, who was sixteen years old, and made him king to succeed his father Amaziah. [22]He rebuilt Elath and restored it to Judah, after King Amaziah[a] slept with his ancestors.

[a] Heb *the king*

COMMENTARY

14:1-6. The attention of the narrator shifts from north to south, as we now find a report on the reign of Amaziah (800–873 BCE), a contemporary of Jehoash of Israel. The report is a typical one for Judean kings. It is a generally positive evaluation: Amaziah, like David, did what was right in the sight of God (cf. 1 Kgs 3:3; 15:11; 22:43). Yet, he was not quite like David, for Amaziah failed to destroy the local sanctuaries (vv. 1-4). To the narrator, the overall faithfulness of Amaziah is evident in the fact that he avenged the murder of his father, Joash (cf. 12:19-21)—but he did so within the limits of the law (vv. 5-6; cf. Deut 24:16).

14:7. Amaziah is relatively successful against the Edomites, killing ten thousand of them in the Valley of Salt (cf. 2 Sam 8:13) and capturing Sela (v. 7).[121] So far in the narratives of Kings, Judah's relation with Edom has been something of a gauge of the status of the Davidic king in the eyes of God. When the king has been generally faithful, Edom has been a vassal of Judah (so in the reign of Jehoshaphat, 1 Kgs 22:47; 2 Kgs 3:8). When the king has been unfaithful, however, Judah has lost control of its neighbor (so in the reign of Joram, 8:20). The implication of Amaziah's successes over Edom, therefore, is a sign of divine favor. Still, as the account that follows suggests, Israel under the descendant of Jehu is even stronger than Judah.

14:8-14. Perhaps emboldened by his triumphs over Edom, Amaziah sends emissaries to his northern counterpart, apparently in an attempt to shake off Judah's vassal status (2 Chr 25:6-16 provides a plausible explanation for Amaziah's desire to work things out with his northern counterpart before things got out of hand). His proposal for a face-to-face conference assumes parity of the two states. Jehoash, however, is disdainful of the proposal. He cites a fable, comparing Judah to an

121. Sela has traditionally been identified with Petra, although there are no remains there dated earlier than the seventh century. The site is more likely near es-Sela', where traces of a fortified city dating from the ninth to the seventh centuries have been discovered. The name "Jokthe-el" is otherwise used of a town in the Judean foothills around Lachish (Josh 15:38).

insignificant thornbush that tries to behave as an equal or even a superior to a cedar tree (v. 9), and he urges Amaziah to stay home and behave himself (v. 10).[122] When Amaziah refuses, Jehoash indeed meets him face-to-face, not in a diplomatic conference but in combat at Beth-Shemesh, not far from Jerusalem (v. 11). To distinguish the town from others with the same name (cf. Josh 19:22, 38), the narrator specifies that this town is Beth-shemesh of Judah. That is, despite the challenge issued in Samaria, the battle was fought just outside the Judean capital. In consequence, Judah is defeated, Amaziah is captured, a large portion of the wall of Jerusalem is torn down,[123] the treasuries of the palace and the Temple are raided, and hostages are seized (vv. 12-14).

14:15-16. The regnal summary of Jehoash in these verses seems out of place and, since it duplicates the regnal summary in 13:12-13, is usually regarded as an intrusive anomaly.[124] Yet, the presence of this regnal notice makes good narrative sense, for the account of Amaziah's reign is really subordinated to the larger story of Israel's period of favor under the kings of the Jehu dynasty. Not even Amaziah, with all of his attempts to do right and his triumphs over the Edomites, can stand in the way of Israel's success. Israel's victory over Judah is merely part of the larger story of the accomplishments wrought in Israel through Jehoash. The theological importance of this point necessitates the insertion of this regnal notice here, even if it duplicates the similar summary in 13:12-13.[125]

14:17-22. With that theological point now scored, the narrator returns to complete his report on Amaziah. Although still called "king," Amaziah is said to have lived for fifteen years after the death of Jehoash. Whether he was, in fact, still ruling in Jerusalem, the narrator does not say. Despite the claim that he reigned twenty-nine years in Jerusalem (vv. 1-2), there are hints that he might have been deposed (see 14:23; 15:8). Indeed, in contrast to the regnal summary for Jehoash, which speaks of the "might" of that king of Israel (v. 15), we read only of the "deeds" of Amaziah (v. 18). Even worse, the summary notes a conspiracy against him in Jerusalem, of his flight to Lachish, and of his murder (v. 19). Like that of his ancestor Ahaziah (9:28), his body had to be brought back to Jerusalem for burial (14:20). Jehoash, the descendant of Jehu, dies peacefully, while Amaziah, the descendant of David, is murdered while in enemy captivity. Despite the promise to David of an everlasting dynasty, Amaziah dies a humiliated man, succeeded by his sixteen-year-old son Azariah, during whose reign the Edomite city of Elath, on the northern coast of the Gulf of Aqaba, will be restored—only after Jehoash has passed away (v. 22; cf. v. 17). (See Reflections at 14:23-29.)

122. For other examples of plant fables, see Judg 9:7-15 and Ezek 17:1-10.
123. Although the major battle took place in Beth-Shemesh, southwest of Jerusalem, it is the northern wall that is breached. The breach was 400 cubits, approximately 600 feet, long.
124. See, e.g, T. R. Hobbs, *2 Kings*, WBC 13 (Waco, Tex.: Word, 1985) 177; John Gray, *I & II Kings*, OTL (Philadelphia: Westminster, 1970) 612.
125. Some scholars have plausibly suggested that the earlier text (13:12-13) is, in fact, the secondary text. See Cogan and Tadmor, *II Kings*, 145.

2 Kings 14:23-29, The Reign of Jeroboam II of Israel

NIV

[23]In the fifteenth year of Amaziah son of Joash king of Judah, Jeroboam son of Jehoash king of Israel became king in Samaria, and he reigned forty-one years. [24]He did evil in the eyes of the LORD and did not turn away from any of the sins of Jeroboam son of Nebat, which he had caused Israel to commit. [25]He was the one who restored the boundaries of Israel from Lebo[a] Hamath to the Sea of the Arabah,[b] in accordance with the word

[a] 25 Or *from the entrance to* [b] 25 That is, the Dead Sea

NRSV

23In the fifteenth year of King Amaziah son of Joash of Judah, King Jeroboam son of Joash of Israel began to reign in Samaria; he reigned forty-one years. [24]He did what was evil in the sight of the LORD; he did not depart from all the sins of Jeroboam son of Nebat, which he caused Israel to sin. [25]He restored the border of Israel from Lebo-hamath as far as the Sea of the Arabah, according to the word of the LORD, the God of Israel, which he spoke by his servant Jonah son

NIV

of the LORD, the God of Israel, spoken through his servant Jonah son of Amittai, the prophet from Gath Hepher.

26The LORD had seen how bitterly everyone in Israel, whether slave or free, was suffering; there was no one to help them. 27And since the LORD had not said he would blot out the name of Israel from under heaven, he saved them by the hand of Jeroboam son of Jehoash.

28As for the other events of Jeroboam's reign, all he did, and his military achievements, including how he recovered for Israel both Damascus and Hamath, which had belonged to Yaudi,[a] are they not written in the book of the annals of the kings of Israel? 29Jeroboam rested with his fathers, the kings of Israel. And Zechariah his son succeeded him as king.

[a] 28 Or *Judah*

NRSV

of Amittai, the prophet, who was from Gath-hepher. 26For the LORD saw that the distress of Israel was very bitter; there was no one left, bond or free, and no one to help Israel. 27But the LORD had not said that he would blot out the name of Israel from under heaven, so he saved them by the hand of Jeroboam son of Joash.

28Now the rest of the acts of Jeroboam, and all that he did, and his might, how he fought, and how he recovered for Israel Damascus and Hamath, which had belonged to Judah, are they not written in the Book of the Annals of the Kings of Israel? 29Jeroboam slept with his ancestors, the kings of Israel; his son Zechariah succeeded him.

COMMENTARY

The narrator has already noted that Jehoash was succeeded by his son, Jeroboam II (786–746 BCE; 13:13; 14:16). Now he gives a brief report of Jeroboam's reign. As the reader has come to expect of northern kings, the evaluation of him is basically negative: Jeroboam did evil in the sight of God and did not turn from the ways of Jeroboam, son of Nebat (v. 24). Even so, the narrator notes Jeroboam's expansion of Israel's border "from Lebo-hamath as far as the Sea of Arabah" (v. 25)—that is, to the extent of Israel's territory in the days of Solomon (1 Kgs 4:21; 8:65). This achievement was "according to the word of the LORD, the God of Israel, which he spoke by his servant Jonah son of Amittai" (v. 25). The territorial expansion is apparently understood as a fulfillment of an oracle by the prophet Jonah, son of Amittai. No such oracle has been preserved, however, and nothing else is known about Jonah, except what we may extrapolate from the biblical book that bears his name. Still, it is significant that we have an allusion to a positive prophetic word to Israel, despite the sins of its kings. Noteworthy, too, is that the Lord is called "the God of Israel" (v. 25). This "God of Israel" responded to Israel's distress (see 13:5) and, seeing that there was no one else who could help Israel, saved it through Jeroboam. The assertion that "the LORD had not said that he would blot out the name of Israel under heaven" is remarkable, for it implies that Israel is the chosen people of God (cf. Deut 9:14; 1 Sam 12:22). The summary of Jeroboam, like that of his father and predecessor (vv. 15-16), notes the main accomplishments of Jeroboam. It notes, too, that he is succeeded by Zechariah, thus bringing up the name of the last king of the Jehu dynasty (v. 29).

REFLECTIONS

These chapters of the book of Kings are remarkable for the ways they contradict and nuance the pattern that we have come to expect. One who reads through the reports of the reigns of the various kings of Israel and Judah from 1 Kings 12 to 2 Kings 14 will notice the rhythmic quality in the accounts. The kings of Israel are uniformly regarded with disdain, and reports of their reigns typically include harsh words of judgment for Israel. The kings of Judah, however, are judged much more sympathetically. Even when they are evaluated negatively, the narrator typically calls attention to the validity of God's promise to David: For the sake of David, who did what was right in the eyes of the Lord, God had promised that there would always be a scion of David on the throne in Jerusalem (see, e.g., 1 Kgs 14:21–16:34). In 2 Kings 13–14, however, Israel is the undeserving recipient of God's favor. Despite the fact that all the kings of Israel named in this context are as sinful as their predecessors, the narrator speaks of Israel in idioms that recall other texts that describe God's chosen people (see especially 13:4-5, 23; 14:26-27). At the same time, the reader gets a hint that Judah, the recipient of God's grace through the promise to David, cannot count on divine favor forever. God's dealings with humanity cannot be reduced to any easy formula, for the deity saves whomever the deity wills.

The God who delivers people from oppression does so through unexpected agents. In the first place, we are astounded to learn that God answers the prayers of people even when they show no signs of repentance. For the sake of the oppressed, God heeded the prayers of a person as sinful as Jehoahaz. Not only that, God even calls sinners to be saviors! That is a remarkable claim that this text makes. It violates our expectations, for we tend to think of saviors as heroes, and we idealize heroes as people of irreproachable character. God's salvation, however, breaks our preconceived molds. Salvation may come from prophets like Elisha, but succeeding Elisha in the role of the one who brings salvation is the sinful king Jehoash. It is through Jehoash that God brings Israel salvation from the Arameans. Then it is the sinful king Jeroboam who brought salvation to his people. What a remarkable lesson that is for those of us who tend to see good coming only from people who are perfect or, at least, generally of good character. God, however, works for good through whomever God chooses—through faithful ministers of the word (like Elisha), and even through evil people (like Jehoahaz, Jehoash, and Jeroboam)!

2 KINGS 15:1–16:20, KINGS OF ISRAEL AND JUDAH

2 Kings 15:1-7, Azariah/Uzziah of Judah

NIV

15 In the twenty-seventh year of Jeroboam king of Israel, Azariah son of Amaziah king of Judah began to reign. 2He was sixteen years old when he became king, and he reigned in Jerusalem fifty-two years. His mother's name was Jecoliah; she was from Jerusalem.
3He did what was right in the eyes of the LORD, just as his father Amaziah had done.
4The high places, however, were not removed; the people continued to offer sacrifices and burn incense there.

NRSV

15 In the twenty-seventh year of King Jeroboam of Israel King Azariah son of Amaziah of Judah began to reign. 2He was sixteen years old when he began to reign, and he reigned fifty-two years in Jerusalem. His mother's name was Jecoliah of Jerusalem. 3He did what was right in the sight of the LORD, just as his father Amaziah had done. 4Nevertheless the high places were not taken away; the people still sacrificed and made offerings on the high places. 5The LORD struck the king, so that he was

NIV

[5]The LORD afflicted the king with leprosy[a] until the day he died, and he lived in a separate house.[b] Jotham the king's son had charge of the palace and governed the people of the land.

[6]As for the other events of Azariah's reign, and all he did, are they not written in the book of the annals of the kings of Judah? [7]Azariah rested with his fathers and was buried near them in the City of David. And Jotham his son succeeded him as king.

[a] *5* The Hebrew word was used for various diseases affecting the skin—not necessarily leprosy. [b] *5* Or *in a house where he was relieved of responsibility*

NRSV

leprous[a] to the day of his death, and lived in a separate house. Jotham the king's son was in charge of the palace, governing the people of the land. [6]Now the rest of the acts of Azariah, and all that he did, are they not written in the Book of the Annals of the Kings of Judah? [7]Azariah slept with his ancestors; they buried him with his ancestors in the city of David; his son Jotham succeeded him.

[a] A term for several skin diseases; precise meaning uncertain

COMMENTARY

Azariah (783–742 BCE), the son of Amaziah, of Judah is also known as Uzziah (see vv. 13, 30, 32, 34). The former is probably his personal name, whereas the latter is his throne name (so it is used in references to his reign in Isa 1:1; 6:1; 7:1; Hos 1:1; Amos 1:1; Zech 14:5). He became king at the age of sixteen (v. 2), when his father was deposed after a humiliating defeat by Jehoash of Israel (14:1-22). According to the narrator, Azariah reigned a remarkable fifty-two years (v. 2), probably including a period of co-regency with his father. The evaluation of his reign is typical of the positive analyses of Judean kings. Like Amaziah (14:3), he did what was right in the eyes of the Lord (v. 3), except that he failed to centralize worship in Jerusalem (v. 4). The text speaks of a skin affliction ("leprosy") that he suffered—later in life, according to the parallel account in 2 Chr 26:16-21. The disease is said to have been an affliction from the Lord (v. 5). No reason is given here for that affliction, but according to the 2 Chronicles version, the king grew arrogant in his autumn years and flagrantly violated ritual regulations (2 Chr 26:16-21).[126] He was not banned from the city, as might be expected (Lev 13:11, 46; Num 12:14-16; cf. 2 Kgs 7:3), but he did live in בית החפשית (*bêt haḥopšît*), literally, "the house of freedom."[127] Since he was unable to perform his royal duties because of his condition, the king probably went into early retirement, while his son Jotham served as regent. That is perhaps the reason for the occasional reversion to his personal name. In any case, despite his disease, his long reign brought considerable stability to Judah. According to the chronicler, Azariah/Uzziah repaired the defenses of the capital, reformed the army, gained control of the trade routes to the south, and extended the borders of Judah at the expense of its Philistine and Edomite neighbors 2 Chr 26:6-15. (See Reflections at 16:1-20.)

126. See also Josephus *Antiquities of the Jews* IX.222-25.

127. The NIV and the NRSV both have "a separate house," presuming that the king was quarantined, an interpretation supported by the Targum, which has Azariah living outside the city. Another interpretation, already found in the medieval commentator Qim'i, takes "house of freedom" to mean release from all duties. See John Gray, *I & II Kings*, OTL (Philadelphia: Westminster, 1964) 619-20.

2 Kings 15:8-31, A Succession of Kings of Israel

NIV

[8]In the thirty-eighth year of Azariah king of Judah, Zechariah son of Jeroboam became king of Israel in Samaria, and he reigned six months. [9]He did evil in the eyes of the LORD, as his fathers had done. He did not turn away from the sins of Jeroboam son of Nebat, which he had caused Israel to commit.

[10]Shallum son of Jabesh conspired against Zechariah. He attacked him in front of the people,[a] assassinated him and succeeded him as king. [11]The other events of Zechariah's reign are written in the book of the annals of the kings of Israel. [12]So the word of the LORD spoken to Jehu was fulfilled: "Your descendants will sit on the throne of Israel to the fourth generation."[b]

[13]Shallum son of Jabesh became king in the thirty-ninth year of Uzziah king of Judah, and he reigned in Samaria one month. [14]Then Menahem son of Gadi went from Tirzah up to Samaria. He attacked Shallum son of Jabesh in Samaria, assassinated him and succeeded him as king.

[15]The other events of Shallum's reign, and the conspiracy he led, are written in the book of the annals of the kings of Israel.

[16]At that time Menahem, starting out from Tirzah, attacked Tiphsah and everyone in the city and its vicinity, because they refused to open their gates. He sacked Tiphsah and ripped open all the pregnant women.

[17]In the thirty-ninth year of Azariah king of Judah, Menahem son of Gadi became king of Israel, and he reigned in Samaria ten years. [18]He did evil in the eyes of the LORD. During his entire reign he did not turn away from the sins of Jeroboam son of Nebat, which he had caused Israel to commit.

[19]Then Pul[c] king of Assyria invaded the land, and Menahem gave him a thousand talents[d] of silver to gain his support and strengthen his own hold on the kingdom. [20]Menahem exacted this money from Israel. Every wealthy man had to contribute fifty shekels[e] of silver to be given to

[a] *10* Hebrew; some Septuagint manuscripts *in Ibleam* [b] *12* 2 Kings 10:30 [c] *19* Also called *Tiglath-Pileser* [d] *19* That is, about 37 tons (about 34 metric tons) [e] *20* That is, about 1 1/4 pounds (about 0.6 kilogram)

NRSV

8In the thirty-eighth year of King Azariah of Judah, Zechariah son of Jeroboam reigned over Israel in Samaria six months. [9]He did what was evil in the sight of the LORD, as his ancestors had done. He did not depart from the sins of Jeroboam son of Nebat, which he caused Israel to sin. [10]Shallum son of Jabesh conspired against him, and struck him down in public and killed him, and reigned in place of him. [11]Now the rest of the deeds of Zechariah are written in the Book of the Annals of the Kings of Israel. [12]This was the promise of the LORD that he gave to Jehu, "Your sons shall sit on the throne of Israel to the fourth generation." And so it happened.

13Shallum son of Jabesh began to reign in the thirty-ninth year of King Uzziah of Judah; he reigned one month in Samaria. [14]Then Menahem son of Gadi came up from Tirzah and came to Samaria; he struck down Shallum son of Jabesh in Samaria and killed him; he reigned in place of him. [15]Now the rest of the deeds of Shallum, including the conspiracy that he made, are written in the Book of the Annals of the Kings of Israel. [16]At that time Menahem sacked Tiphsah, all who were in it and its territory from Tirzah on; because they did not open it to him, he sacked it. He ripped open all the pregnant women in it.

17In the thirty-ninth year of King Azariah of Judah, Menahem son of Gadi began to reign over Israel; he reigned ten years in Samaria. [18]He did what was evil in the sight of the LORD; he did not depart all his days from any of the sins of Jeroboam son of Nebat, which he caused Israel to sin. [19]King Pul of Assyria came against the land; Menahem gave Pul a thousand talents of silver, so that he might help him confirm his hold on the royal power. [20]Menahem exacted the money from Israel, that is, from all the wealthy, fifty shekels of silver from each one, to give to the king of Assyria. So the king of Assyria turned back, and did not stay there in the land. [21]Now the rest of the deeds of Menahem, and all that he did, are they not written in the Book of the Annals of the Kings of Israel? [22]Menahem slept with his ancestors, and his son Pekahiah succeeded him.

23In the fiftieth year of King Azariah of Judah,

NIV

the king of Assyria. So the king of Assyria withdrew and stayed in the land no longer.

21As for the other events of Menahem's reign, and all he did, are they not written in the book of the annals of the kings of Israel? 22Menahem rested with his fathers. And Pekahiah his son succeeded him as king.

23In the fiftieth year of Azariah king of Judah, Pekahiah son of Menahem became king of Israel in Samaria, and he reigned two years. 24Pekahiah did evil in the eyes of the LORD. He did not turn away from the sins of Jeroboam son of Nebat, which he had caused Israel to commit. 25One of his chief officers, Pekah son of Remaliah, conspired against him. Taking fifty men of Gilead with him, he assassinated Pekahiah, along with Argob and Arieh, in the citadel of the royal palace at Samaria. So Pekah killed Pekahiah and succeeded him as king.

26The other events of Pekahiah's reign, and all he did, are written in the book of the annals of the kings of Israel.

27In the fifty-second year of Azariah king of Judah, Pekah son of Remaliah became king of Israel in Samaria, and he reigned twenty years. 28He did evil in the eyes of the LORD. He did not turn away from the sins of Jeroboam son of Nebat, which he had caused Israel to commit.

29In the time of Pekah king of Israel, Tiglath-Pileser king of Assyria came and took Ijon, Abel Beth Maacah, Janoah, Kedesh and Hazor. He took Gilead and Galilee, including all the land of Naphtali, and deported the people to Assyria. 30Then Hoshea son of Elah conspired against Pekah son of Remaliah. He attacked and assassinated him, and then succeeded him as king in the twentieth year of Jotham son of Uzziah.

31As for the other events of Pekah's reign, and all he did, are they not written in the book of the annals of the kings of Israel?

NRSV

Pekahiah son of Menahem began to reign over Israel in Samaria; he reigned two years. 24He did what was evil in the sight of the LORD; he did not turn away from the sins of Jeroboam son of Nebat, which he caused Israel to sin. 25Pekah son of Remaliah, his captain, conspired against him with fifty of the Gileadites, and attacked him in Samaria, in the citadel of the palace along with Argob and Arieh; he killed him, and reigned in place of him. 26Now the rest of the deeds of Pekahiah, and all that he did, are written in the Book of the Annals of the Kings of Israel.

27In the fifty-second year of King Azariah of Judah, Pekah son of Remaliah began to reign over Israel in Samaria; he reigned twenty years. 28He did what was evil in the sight of the LORD; he did not depart from the sins of Jeroboam son of Nebat, which he caused Israel to sin.

29In the days of King Pekah of Israel, King Tiglath-pileser of Assyria came and captured Ijon, Abel-beth-maacah, Janoah, Kedesh, Hazor, Gilead, and Galilee, all the land of Naphtali; and he carried the people captive to Assyria. 30Then Hoshea son of Elah made a conspiracy against Pekah son of Remaliah, attacked him, and killed him; he reigned in place of him, in the twentieth year of Jotham son of Uzziah. 31Now the rest of the acts of Pekah, and all that he did, are written in the Book of the Annals of the Kings of Israel.

COMMENTARY

Following the report of Azariah's reign comes a series of brief accounts of the reigns of a rapid succession of Israel's kings, each of whom (except for Shallum, who reigned only one month) is said to have done evil in the sight of the Lord and followed the ways of Jeroboam, son of Nebat (vv.

9, 18, 24, 28). Zechariah (746–745 BCE), the son of Jeroboam II, was the last king of the house of Jehu. He reigned only six months before being assassinated in public by a man named Shallum, "son of Jabesh" (a reference probably to his clan, Jabesh of Gilead, rather than to his parentage), who then ruled as king for only one month, before being himself assassinated (see Amos 7:9, 11; Hos 7:6-7, 16). Shallum's killer was Menahem, who reigned 747–737 BCE, during which time he sacked Tiphsah and committed atrocities there.[128] During his reign, the Assyrian king Pul (an alternate Hebrew name for Tiglath-pileser III) became a dominant force in the region. Menahem had to buy him off with increased taxes (v. 20). Menahem was succeeded by his son Pekaiah, who reigned two years (737–736 BCE) before being assassinated by Pekah, son of Remaliah (vv. 23-25). Pekah held the throne from 736 to 732 BCE, during which time Tiglath-pileser III raided the country several times, taking many cities and carrying off captives to Assyria. Pekah was killed by Hoshea, who reigned 732–724 BCE. Thus the narrator races through history, naming six kings of Israel, five of whom were assassinated. The narrator seems to be hastening toward the end of Israel's existence as an independent nation. (See Reflections at 16:1-20.)

128. Tiphsah was a city in northern Syria, on the west bank of the Euphrates. It was a border town in the days of Solomon (1 Kgs 4:24). The reading of the name, however, is uncertain. Some Greek witnesses assume the name "Tappuah," a town on the border of Ephraim and Manasseh.

2 Kings 15:32-38, Jotham of Judah

NIV

[32]In the second year of Pekah son of Remaliah king of Israel, Jotham son of Uzziah king of Judah began to reign. [33]He was twenty-five years old when he became king, and he reigned in Jerusalem sixteen years. His mother's name was Jerusha daughter of Zadok. [34]He did what was right in the eyes of the LORD, just as his father Uzziah had done. [35]The high places, however, were not removed; the people continued to offer sacrifices and burn incense there. Jotham rebuilt the Upper Gate of the temple of the LORD.

[36]As for the other events of Jotham's reign, and what he did, are they not written in the book of the annals of the kings of Judah? [37](In those days the LORD began to send Rezin king of Aram and Pekah son of Remaliah against Judah.) [38]Jotham rested with his fathers and was buried with them in the City of David, the city of his father. And Ahaz his son succeeded him as king.

NRSV

32In the second year of King Pekah son of Remaliah of Israel, King Jotham son of Uzziah of Judah began to reign. [33]He was twenty-five years old when he began to reign and reigned sixteen years in Jerusalem. His mother's name was Jerusha daughter of Zadok. [34]He did what was right in the sight of the LORD, just as his father Uzziah had done. [35]Nevertheless the high places were not removed; the people still sacrificed and made offerings on the high places. He built the upper gate of the house of the LORD. [36]Now the rest of the acts of Jotham, and all that he did, are they not written in the Book of the Annals of the Kings of Judah? [37]In those days the LORD began to send King Rezin of Aram and Pekah son of Remaliah against Judah. [38]Jotham slept with his ancestors, and was buried with his ancestors in the city of David, his ancestor; his son Ahaz succeeded him.

COMMENTARY

Uzziah's son Jotham reigned sixteen years (742–735 BCE). He gets an evaluation typical of a good Judean king: Jotham did what was right in the eyes of the Lord but failed to remove the high places (vv. 34-35). In addition, he is said to have built "the upper gate of the temple of the LORD," the location of which is unknown. (See Reflections at 16:1-20.)

2 Kings 16:1-20, Ahaz of Judah

NIV

16 In the seventeenth year of Pekah son of Remaliah, Ahaz son of Jotham king of Judah began to reign. 2Ahaz was twenty years old when he became king, and he reigned in Jerusalem sixteen years. Unlike David his father, he did not do what was right in the eyes of the LORD his God. 3He walked in the ways of the kings of Israel and even sacrificed his son in[a] the fire, following the detestable ways of the nations the LORD had driven out before the Israelites. 4He offered sacrifices and burned incense at the high places, on the hilltops and under every spreading tree.

5Then Rezin king of Aram and Pekah son of Remaliah king of Israel marched up to fight against Jerusalem and besieged Ahaz, but they could not overpower him. 6At that time, Rezin king of Aram recovered Elath for Aram by driving out the men of Judah. Edomites then moved into Elath and have lived there to this day.

7Ahaz sent messengers to say to Tiglath-Pileser king of Assyria, "I am your servant and vassal. Come up and save me out of the hand of the king of Aram and of the king of Israel, who are attacking me." 8And Ahaz took the silver and gold found in the temple of the LORD and in the treasuries of the royal palace and sent it as a gift to the king of Assyria. 9The king of Assyria complied by attacking Damascus and capturing it. He deported its inhabitants to Kir and put Rezin to death.

10Then King Ahaz went to Damascus to meet Tiglath-Pileser king of Assyria. He saw an altar in Damascus and sent to Uriah the priest a sketch of the altar, with detailed plans for its construction. 11So Uriah the priest built an altar in accordance with all the plans that King Ahaz had sent from Damascus and finished it before King Ahaz returned. 12When the king came back from Damascus and saw the altar, he approached it and presented offerings[b] on it. 13He offered up his burnt offering and grain offering, poured out his drink offering, and sprinkled the blood of his fellowship offerings[c] on the altar. 14The bronze altar that stood before the LORD he brought from the front

[a] 3 Or *even made his son pass through* [b] 12 Or *and went up*
[c] 13 Traditionally *peace offerings*

NRSV

16 In the seventeenth year of Pekah son of Remaliah, King Ahaz son of Jotham of Judah began to reign. 2Ahaz was twenty years old when he began to reign; he reigned sixteen years in Jerusalem. He did not do what was right in the sight of the LORD his God, as his ancestor David had done, 3but he walked in the way of the kings of Israel. He even made his son pass through fire, according to the abominable practices of the nations whom the LORD drove out before the people of Israel. 4He sacrificed and made offerings on the high places, on the hills, and under every green tree.

5Then King Rezin of Aram and King Pekah son of Remaliah of Israel came up to wage war on Jerusalem; they besieged Ahaz but could not conquer him. 6At that time the king of Edom[a] recovered Elath for Edom,[b] and drove the Judeans from Elath; and the Edomites came to Elath, where they live to this day. 7Ahaz sent messengers to King Tiglath-pileser of Assyria, saying, "I am your servant and your son. Come up, and rescue me from the hand of the king of Aram and from the hand of the king of Israel, who are attacking me." 8Ahaz also took the silver and gold found in the house of the LORD and in the treasures of the king's house, and sent a present to the king of Assyria. 9The king of Assyria listened to him; the king of Assyria marched up against Damascus, and took it, carrying its people captive to Kir; then he killed Rezin.

10When King Ahaz went to Damascus to meet King Tiglath-pileser of Assyria, he saw the altar that was at Damascus. King Ahaz sent to the priest Uriah a model of the altar, and its pattern, exact in all its details. 11The priest Uriah built the altar; in accordance with all that King Ahaz had sent from Damascus, just so did the priest Uriah build it, before King Ahaz arrived from Damascus. 12When the king came from Damascus, the king viewed the altar. Then the king drew near to the altar, went up on it, 13and offered his burnt offering and his grain offering, poured his drink offering, and dashed the blood of his offerings of

[a] Cn: Heb *King Rezin of Aram* [b] Cn: Heb *Aram*

NIV

of the temple—from between the new altar and the temple of the LORD—and put it on the north side of the new altar.

[15]King Ahaz then gave these orders to Uriah the priest: "On the large new altar, offer the morning burnt offering and the evening grain offering, the king's burnt offering and his grain offering, and the burnt offering of all the people of the land, and their grain offering and their drink offering. Sprinkle on the altar all the blood of the burnt offerings and sacrifices. But I will use the bronze altar for seeking guidance." [16]And Uriah the priest did just as King Ahaz had ordered.

[17]King Ahaz took away the side panels and removed the basins from the movable stands. He removed the Sea from the bronze bulls that supported it and set it on a stone base. [18]He took away the Sabbath canopy[a] that had been built at the temple and removed the royal entryway outside the temple of the LORD, in deference to the king of Assyria.

[19]As for the other events of the reign of Ahaz, and what he did, are they not written in the book of the annals of the kings of Judah? [20]Ahaz rested with his fathers and was buried with them in the City of David. And Hezekiah his son succeeded him as king.

[a] *18* Or *the dais of his throne* (see Septuagint)

NRSV

well-being against the altar. [14]The bronze altar that was before the LORD he removed from the front of the house, from the place between his altar and the house of the LORD, and put it on the north side of his altar. [15]King Ahaz commanded the priest Uriah, saying, "Upon the great altar offer the morning burnt offering, and the evening grain offering, and the king's burnt offering, and his grain offering, with the burnt offering of all the people of the land, their grain offering, and their drink offering; then dash against it all the blood of the burnt offering, and all the blood of the sacrifice; but the bronze altar shall be for me to inquire by." [16]The priest Uriah did everything that King Ahaz commanded.

17Then King Ahaz cut off the frames of the stands, and removed the laver from them; he removed the sea from the bronze oxen that were under it, and put it on a pediment of stone. [18]The covered portal for use on the sabbath that had been built inside the palace, and the outer entrance for the king he removed from[a] the house of the LORD. He did this because of the king of Assyria. [19]Now the rest of the acts of Ahaz that he did, are they not written in the Book of the Annals of the Kings of Judah? [20]Ahaz slept with his ancestors, and was buried with his ancestors in the city of David; his son Hezekiah succeeded him.

[a] Cn: Heb lacks *from*

COMMENTARY

16:1-9. Following the disastrous reigns of Jehoram (8:16-24) and Ahaziah (8:25-29) and the debacle of Athaliah's coup (11:1-3), the Judean monarchy seems to be back on track. Kings Joash, Amaziah, Azariah/Uzziah, and Jotham are all said to have done what is right in the eyes of God, even though they did not remove the local sanctuaries (12:2-3; 14:3-4; 15:3-4, 34-35). Ahaz, however, receives an overwhelmingly negative evaluation. He did not do what was right in the eyes of God, as his ancestor David had done, but instead, "walked in the ways of the kings of Israel" (v. 3; cf. 8:18, 27). The narrator accuses him of practicing child sacrifice like the nations that were driven out of the land at God's command when Israel entered it (v. 3). The narrator, no doubt, is referring here to certain religious practices of the cult of Molech (cf. 1 Kgs 11:7) that are banned by deuteronomic law (Deut 18:9-14; see also Lev 18:21; 20:2-5; Jer 7:31; 19:5; 32:35).[129] Such a horrible offense is given as one of the reasons for Israel's eventual destruction (17:17-18). The only other king of Judah who committed such a sin was Manasseh, the archrogue of the Davidic dynasty (21:6). Ahaz, of

129. See John Day, *Molech: A God of Human Sacrifice in the Old Testament,* University of Cambridge Oriental Publications (Cambridge: Cambridge University Press, 1989) 31-33.

course, is also accused of personally worshiping at the "high places" (local cultic sites condemned by the deuteronomists), the first Judean king to be so accused after the completion of the Temple in Jerusalem (v. 4; cf. 1 Kgs 14:23-24).

It was during the reign of Ahaz that the so-called Syro-Ephraimitic War was waged by a coalition of Aramean (Syrian) forces and Israel against Judah. The alliance was attempting to depose Ahaz and coerce Judah into joining in its rebellion against Assyria (cf. Isa 7:1-8, 10). During that period, the Edomites retook Elath, on the northern coast of the Gulf of Aqaba (v. 6; cf. 2 Chr 28:17), which had been seized by Judah during the reign of Azariah/Uzziah (cf. 14:22). Against Aram and Israel, Ahaz pledged vassalage to Tiglath-pileser III of Assyria (v. 7). In consequence, Judah had to pay tribute to the Assyrians, which then prompted Ahaz to draw on the temple treasury, as other kings before him had done (v. 8). Hence, the Assyrians marched against Damascus, captured it, carried its people into exile to Kir (said to be the original home of the Arameans in Amos 9:7), and killed Rezin, the Aramean king.

16:10-20. In Damascus to meet with his Assyrian suzerain, Ahaz saw an altar in that city that particularly impressed him. So he sent a model of it to Jerusalem and commissioned one just like it to be built in Jerusalem. The old bronze altar in the Temple (cf. 1 Kgs 8:64) was moved (v. 14), now for the king to seek oracles (v. 15). Some of the furnishings were removed and apparently were used as part of the bribe.

REFLECTIONS

These chapters appear to contain straight historical records that have no explicit theological messages. Indeed, when we compare various portions of this text with parallel accounts found elsewhere in the Bible, we find a strange silence in chapters 15–16 where theological implications of the stories are fleshed out in the parallel passages. Regarding Azariah/Uzziah, for instance, the chronicler tells of the king's initial faithfulness and his successes because of it. When the king became arrogant and disregarded the ritual regulations, however, he was afflicted with a skin disease. By contrast, the narrator of the passage in 2 Kgs 15:1-7 is remarkably terse in his report about Azariah/Uzziah, mentioning his skin disease as a divine affliction but not giving the cause of it. Similarly, whereas the chronicler presents Jotham as a righteous king who held firm to the ways of the Lord (2 Chr 27:1-9), the narrator in 2 Kgs 15:32-38 only makes formulaic judgments about this king, noting without comment Jotham's construction of the upper gate of the Temple. Although Isaiah observes Ahaz's dependence upon military prowess instead of trusting the Lord (Isa 7:1–8:10), the narrator in 2 Kgs 16:1-20 does not make such an explicit theological claim, even though he acknowledges Ahaz's apostasy. Ahaz's innovations at the Temple are passed over without any theological judgments. Instead of such overt theological moves, the narrator conveys a subtle, even subliminal, message: God's sovereign will is being worked out in separate tracks. On the one hand, the kingdom is moving inexorably toward destruction because its leaders will not turn the nation away from the sinful course on which it has been set. On the other hand, another nation is being preserved because of God's promise, despite the inadequacies of its rulers.

2 KINGS 17:1-41, THE FALL OF SAMARIA

OVERVIEW

This long chapter, containing an account of the fall of Samaria (722/721 BCE) and its aftermath, is widely believed to be the product of a long and complex compositional-redactional history. There is little agreement among critics, however, about the details of that history, except for the fact that the final form of it is a showcase of the deuteronomistic theology of history.[130] The fall of Samaria is, in any case, a key moment in the history of the monarchy. It is the moment anticipated since the very beginning of the divided monarchy, when Jeroboam established the sanctuaries in Dan and Bethel together with the golden calves therein (1 Kgs 12:25–14:18). Henceforth there will be only the state of Judah, the focus of the rest of 2 Kings. In any case, the present text is coherent in broad outline. The chapter may be divided into three parts: (1) an account of the fall of Samaria, vv. 1-6; (2) a lengthy theological rationale for the event, vv. 7-23; and (3) the aftermath of the destruction, vv. 24-41.

130. See T. R. Hobbs, *2 Kings*, WBC 13 (Waco, Tex.: Word, 1985) 224-25; Burke O. Long, *2 Kings*, FOTL 10 (Grand Rapids: Eerdmans, 1991) 180-82.

2 Kings 17:1-6, How Samaria Fell

NIV

17 In the twelfth year of Ahaz king of Judah, Hoshea son of Elah became king of Israel in Samaria, and he reigned nine years. [2]He did evil in the eyes of the LORD, but not like the kings of Israel who preceded him.

[3]Shalmaneser king of Assyria came up to attack Hoshea, who had been Shalmaneser's vassal and had paid him tribute. [4]But the king of Assyria discovered that Hoshea was a traitor, for he had sent envoys to So[a] king of Egypt, and he no longer paid tribute to the king of Assyria, as he had done year by year. Therefore Shalmaneser seized him and put him in prison. [5]The king of Assyria invaded the entire land, marched against Samaria and laid siege to it for three years. [6]In the ninth year of Hoshea, the king of Assyria captured Samaria and deported the Israelites to Assyria. He settled them in Halah, in Gozan on the Habor River and in the towns of the Medes.

a 4 Or *to Sais, to the*; *So* is possibly an abbreviation for *Osorkon*.

NRSV

17 In the twelfth year of King Ahaz of Judah, Hoshea son of Elah began to reign in Samaria over Israel; he reigned nine years. [2]He did what was evil in the sight of the LORD, yet not like the kings of Israel who were before him. [3]King Shalmaneser of Assyria came up against him; Hoshea became his vassal, and paid him tribute. [4]But the king of Assyria found treachery in Hoshea; for he had sent messengers to King So of Egypt, and offered no tribute to the king of Assyria, as he had done year by year; therefore the king of Assyria confined him and imprisoned him.

5Then the king of Assyria invaded all the land and came to Samaria; for three years he besieged it. [6]In the ninth year of Hoshea the king of Assyria captured Samaria; he carried the Israelites away to Assyria. He placed them in Halah, on the Habor, the river of Gozan, and in the cities of the Medes.

COMMENTARY

Hoshea, son of Elah (c. 732–724 BCE), was the last king of the northern kingdom, the king in whose reign the fall of Samaria would actually begin (v. 1). The history of Israel has been leading up to this point ever since the days of Jeroboam. On account of Jeroboam's sins, which all the succeeding kings of Israel followed, God is expected to bring the nation to an end, uprooting the people from the land given to their ancestors and sending them into exile beyond the Euphrates (1 Kgs 14:15). Hence, the reader anticipates the harshest judgment on the king's conduct as the story of the end is told. One expects the narrator to observe that things really came to a head with Hoshea, the last king, who was more sinful than all his predecessors. That is not what the text says, however. Rather, the narrator acknowledges the sinfulness of the king, but quickly adds that Hoshea was not as bad as the kings who preceded him (v. 2). This toning down of judgment is unprecedented in the history of the northern kings. Moreover, the standard negative assessment of the kings of Israel—that the king followed the ways of Jeroboam, son of Nebat—is absent here (cf. 1 Kgs 16:2, 19, 26, 31; 22:52; 2 Kgs 3:3; 9:9; 10:29; 13:2, 11; 14:24). Indeed, this evaluation of Hoshea stands in stark contrast to that of Ahaz of Judah, who is said to have "walked in the ways of the kings of Israel" (16:3). In this way, the narrator indirectly makes the point that the destruction of Samaria is not due to the conduct of its present king alone. Rather, the pattern of behavior that has led to the destruction had been set long ago. Israel's history of unfaithfulness to the Lord has led to this point, and destruction cannot now be averted.

The Assyrian king Shalmaneser—in this case Shalmaneser V (c. 727–722 BCE), the son and successor of Tiglath-pileser III—threatened Israel (v. 3). Hoshea duly paid him tribute and submitted to him as a vassal, but soon flirted with the possibility of making an alliance with Egypt (v. 4).[131] Assyrian retribution was swift. Shalmaneser besieged Samaria (vv. 5-6),[132] but one gathers from Assyrian records that he apparently died while the three-year-long siege was going on in Israel, and the city was actually taken by his successor, Sargon II (722–705 BCE).[133] The citizens of Israel were exiled to various parts of the Assyrian Empire (v. 6)—to Hallah (a region northeast of Nineveh) and to the area around the Habor (a tributary of the Euphrates), which is said to be "the river of Gozan" (Gozan being the capital of an Assyrian province and in the cities of the Medes). (See Reflections at 17:24-41.)

131. The identity of "So" has sparked vigorous debate, for no such king is known from the Egyptian records. See Mordechai Cogan and Hayim Tadmor, *II Kings*, AB 11 (New York: Doubleday, 1988) 196.

132. For some of the historical details behind this account, see John H. Hayes and Jeffery K. Kuan, "The Final Years of Samaria (730–720 B.C.)," *Bib* 72 (1991) 153-81.

133. See *ANET*, 284-85.

2 Kings 17:7-23, Why Samaria Fell

NIV

7All this took place because the Israelites had
sinned against the LORD their God, who had
brought them up out of Egypt from under the
power of Pharaoh king of Egypt. They worshiped
other gods 8and followed the practices of the
nations the LORD had driven out before them, as
well as the practices that the kings of Israel had
introduced. 9The Israelites secretly did things
against the LORD their God that were not right.
From watchtower to fortified city they built themselves high places in all their towns. 10They set
up sacred stones and Asherah poles on every high
hill and under every spreading tree. 11At every
high place they burned incense, as the nations
whom the LORD had driven out before them had
done. They did wicked things that provoked the
LORD to anger. 12They worshiped idols, though the
LORD had said, "You shall not do this."[a] 13The LORD
warned Israel and Judah through all his prophets
and seers: "Turn from your evil ways. Observe

a *12* Exodus 20:4, 5

NRSV

7This occurred because the people of Israel had
sinned against the LORD their God, who had
brought them up out of the land of Egypt from
under the hand of Pharaoh king of Egypt. They
had worshiped other gods 8and walked in the
customs of the nations whom the LORD drove out
before the people of Israel, and in the customs
that the kings of Israel had introduced.[a] 9The
people of Israel secretly did things that were not
right against the LORD their God. They built for
themselves high places at all their towns, from
watchtower to fortified city; 10they set up for
themselves pillars and sacred poles[b] on every high
hill and under every green tree; 11there they made
offerings on all the high places, as the nations did
whom the LORD carried away before them. They
did wicked things, provoking the LORD to anger;
12they served idols, of which the LORD had said
to them, "You shall not do this." 13Yet the LORD
warned Israel and Judah by every prophet and

a Meaning of Heb uncertain b Heb *Asherim*

NIV

my commands and decrees, in accordance with the entire Law that I commanded your fathers to obey and that I delivered to you through my servants the prophets."

[14]But they would not listen and were as stiff-necked as their fathers, who did not trust in the LORD their God. [15]They rejected his decrees and the covenant he had made with their fathers and the warnings he had given them. They followed worthless idols and themselves became worthless. They imitated the nations around them although the LORD had ordered them, "Do not do as they do," and they did the things the LORD had forbidden them to do.

[16]They forsook all the commands of the LORD their God and made for themselves two idols cast in the shape of calves, and an Asherah pole. They bowed down to all the starry hosts, and they worshiped Baal. [17]They sacrificed their sons and daughters in[a] the fire. They practiced divination and sorcery and sold themselves to do evil in the eyes of the LORD, provoking him to anger.

[18]So the LORD was very angry with Israel and removed them from his presence. Only the tribe of Judah was left, [19]and even Judah did not keep the commands of the LORD their God. They followed the practices Israel had introduced. [20]Therefore the LORD rejected all the people of Israel; he afflicted them and gave them into the hands of plunderers, until he thrust them from his presence.

[21]When he tore Israel away from the house of David, they made Jeroboam son of Nebat their king. Jeroboam enticed Israel away from following the LORD and caused them to commit a great sin. [22]The Israelites persisted in all the sins of Jeroboam and did not turn away from them [23]until the LORD removed them from his presence, as he had warned through all his servants the prophets. So the people of Israel were taken from their homeland into exile in Assyria, and they are still there.

[a] *17* Or *They made their sons and daughters pass through*

NRSV

every seer, saying, "Turn from your evil ways and keep my commandments and my statutes, in accordance with all the law that I commanded your ancestors and that I sent to you by my servants the prophets." [14]They would not listen but were stubborn, as their ancestors had been, who did not believe in the LORD their God. [15]They despised his statutes, and his covenant that he made with their ancestors, and the warnings that he gave them. They went after false idols and became false; they followed the nations that were around them, concerning whom the LORD had commanded them that they should not do as they did. [16]They rejected all the commandments of the LORD their God and made for themselves cast images of two calves; they made a sacred pole,[a] worshiped all the host of heaven, and served Baal. [17]They made their sons and their daughters pass through fire; they used divination and augury; and they sold themselves to do evil in the sight of the LORD, provoking him to anger. [18]Therefore the LORD was very angry with Israel and removed them out of his sight; none was left but the tribe of Judah alone.

19Judah also did not keep the commandments of the LORD their God but walked in the customs that Israel had introduced. [20]The LORD rejected all the descendants of Israel; he punished them and gave them into the hand of plunderers, until he had banished them from his presence.

21When he had torn Israel from the house of David, they made Jeroboam son of Nebat king. Jeroboam drove Israel from following the LORD and made them commit great sin. [22]The people of Israel continued in all the sins that Jeroboam committed; they did not depart from them [23]until the LORD removed Israel out of his sight, as he had foretold through all his servants the prophets. So Israel was exiled from their own land to Assyria until this day.

[a] Heb *Asherah*

COMMENTARY

The explanation for the fall of Samaria is couched in terms of violation of the covenant: The people sinned against the God of the exodus (v. 7); conducted themselves like the nations that had been driven out of the land (vv. 8, 15); constructed unacceptable sanctuaries (v. 9); set up idolatrous symbols (vv. 10, 16); worshiped idols, astral deities, and other gods (vv. 11-12, 15-16); practiced child sacrifice (v. 17); turned to divinations and auguries (v. 17); and generally violated the covenant and various stipulations laid down by God (vv. 14-16; see especially Deut 6:4-15; 7:1-6; 12:2-4; 18:9-14). God had sent them warning "by every prophet and every seer," but they did not turn back from their wicked ways (vv. 13-14). Poignantly, the narrator notes that the people had gone after things ephemeral (ההבל *hahebel*) and, hence, themselves became ephemeral (see v. 15). The Hebrew word הבל (*hebel*; NJV, "delusion"; NRSV, "false idols"; NIV, "worthless idols") literally means "wind" or "puff." It refers to things that are insubstantial, ephemeral, or unreliable. They will not last because they have chosen relationships that do not last. Against the Lord they "secretly" did things that were not right (v. 9).

Remarkably, woven into the present text is a subliminal message for Judah. Although the issue at hand is the fall of Samaria, the narrator notes that God's warning through the prophets and seers had been for Israel *and* Judah (v. 13). Israel fell because the Lord was angry, says the narrator, so that Judah alone remained (v. 18). Implicit here is a warning to the Judeans not to take the lesson of Israel's fall lightly; even though they may still be standing, the fate that befell Israel may yet await them. Indeed, as the present text has it, Judah also did not keep the commandments of God and had, in fact, followed the customs that Israel had introduced (v. 19). The theological explanation, then, seems to be directed not at Israel but at Judah. It is not only a justification of God's action against Israel, but also a theological lesson directed at the people of Judah, calling for them to turn back to God before it is too late. As one scholar sees it, the narrator "looks back on what has been to set forth what will be for the future."[134]

The narrator summarizes the issue in vv. 21-23, where we find the history of the divided kingdom in a nutshell. It all began with Jeroboam, son of Nebat, who drove the people of Israel from God and provoked them to sin (v. 21). Yet, the responsibility for proper conduct rests squarely on the shoulders of the people themselves. They continued in all the ways of Jeroboam, and they did not turn back from those ways (v. 23) until the Lord finally removed them from God's presence, thus fulfilling the proclamations of the prophets. (See Reflections at 17:24-41.)

134. Pauline A. Viviano, "2 Kings 17: A Rhetorical and Form-Critical Analysis," *CBQ* 49 (1987) 559.

2 Kings 17:24-41, The Resettlement of Samaria and Its Consequences

NIV

[24]The king of Assyria brought people from Babylon, Cuthah, Avva, Hamath and Sepharvaim and settled them in the towns of Samaria to replace the Israelites. They took over Samaria and lived in its towns. [25]When they first lived there, they did not worship the LORD; so he sent lions among them and they killed some of the people. [26]It was reported to the king of Assyria: "The people you deported and resettled in the towns of Samaria do

NRSV

24The king of Assyria brought people from Babylon, Cuthah, Avva, Hamath, and Sepharvaim, and placed them in the cities of Samaria in place of the people of Israel; they took possession of Samaria, and settled in its cities. [25]When they first settled there, they did not worship the LORD; therefore the LORD sent lions among them, which killed some of them. [26]So the king of Assyria was told, "The nations that you have carried away and

NIV

not know what the god of that country requires. He has sent lions among them, which are killing them off, because the people do not know what he requires."

27Then the king of Assyria gave this order: "Have one of the priests you took captive from Samaria go back to live there and teach the people what the god of the land requires." 28So one of the priests who had been exiled from Samaria came to live in Bethel and taught them how to worship the LORD.

29Nevertheless, each national group made its own gods in the several towns where they settled, and set them up in the shrines the people of Samaria had made at the high places. 30The men from Babylon made Succoth Benoth, the men from Cuthah made Nergal, and the men from Hamath made Ashima; 31the Avvites made Nibhaz and Tartak, and the Sepharvites burned their children in the fire as sacrifices to Adrammelech and Anammelech, the gods of Sepharvaim. 32They worshiped the LORD, but they also appointed all sorts of their own people to officiate for them as priests in the shrines at the high places. 33They worshiped the LORD, but they also served their own gods in accordance with the customs of the nations from which they had been brought.

34To this day they persist in their former practices. They neither worship the LORD nor adhere to the decrees and ordinances, the laws and commands that the LORD gave the descendants of Jacob, whom he named Israel. 35When the LORD made a covenant with the Israelites, he commanded them: "Do not worship any other gods or bow down to them, serve them or sacrifice to them. 36But the LORD, who brought you up out of Egypt with mighty power and outstretched arm, is the one you must worship. To him you shall bow down and to him offer sacrifices. 37You must always be careful to keep the decrees and ordinances, the laws and commands he wrote for you. Do not worship other gods. 38Do not forget the covenant I have made with you, and do not worship other gods. 39Rather, worship the LORD your God; it is he who will deliver you from the hand of all your enemies."

40They would not listen, however, but persisted in their former practices. 41Even while these peo-

NRSV

placed in the cities of Samaria do not know the law of the god of the land; therefore he has sent lions among them; they are killing them, because they do not know the law of the god of the land." 27Then the king of Assyria commanded, "Send there one of the priests whom you carried away from there; let him[a] go and live there, and teach them the law of the god of the land." 28So one of the priests whom they had carried away from Samaria came and lived in Bethel; he taught them how they should worship the LORD.

29But every nation still made gods of its own and put them in the shrines of the high places that the people of Samaria had made, every nation in the cities in which they lived; 30the people of Babylon made Succoth-benoth, the people of Cuth made Nergal, the people of Hamath made Ashima; 31the Avvites made Nibhaz and Tartak; the Sepharvites burned their children in the fire to Adrammelech and Anammelech, the gods of Sepharvaim. 32They also worshiped the LORD and appointed from among themselves all sorts of people as priests of the high places, who sacrificed for them in the shrines of the high places. 33So they worshiped the LORD but also served their own gods, after the manner of the nations from among whom they had been carried away. 34To this day they continue to practice their former customs.

They do not worship the LORD and they do not follow the statutes or the ordinances or the law or the commandment that the LORD commanded the children of Jacob, whom he named Israel. 35The LORD had made a covenant with them and commanded them, "You shall not worship other gods or bow yourselves to them or serve them or sacrifice to them, 36but you shall worship the LORD, who brought you out of the land of Egypt with great power and with an outstretched arm; you shall bow yourselves to him, and to him you shall sacrifice. 37The statutes and the ordinances and the law and the commandment that he wrote for you, you shall always be careful to observe. You shall not worship other gods; 38you shall not forget the covenant that I have made with you. You shall not worship other gods, 39but you shall worship the LORD your God; he will deliver you

[a] Syr Heb *them*

NIV	NRSV
ple were worshiping the LORD, they were serving their idols. To this day their children and grandchildren continue to do as their fathers did.	out of the hand of all your enemies." [40]They would not listen, however, but they continued to practice their former custom. 41So these nations worshiped the LORD, but also served their carved images; to this day their children and their children's children continue to do as their ancestors did.

COMMENTARY

While the Assyrians deported Israelites from the land to distant places, they also brought in outsiders from various parts of the empire (v. 24).[135] To the narrator, however, the land still belonged to the Lord, who sent lions to attack the foreign settlers who did not worship God (v. 25). When this was reported to the Assyrian king, he sent an exiled Israelite priest, a man from Bethel, to return to his country to teach the settlers the true religion (vv. 26-28).

The damage had been done, however, for the settlers continued to worship their foreign gods with their strange-sounding names (vv. 29-31).[136] Syncretism became the order of the day, as the settlers worshiped the Lord along with their own gods (v. 32). They even appointed all sorts of people as priests in the local sanctuaries, ironically replicating what Jeroboam had done when he founded the heterodox sanctuary at Dan and Bethel (1 Kgs 12:31). That is perhaps not surprising, since the one person whom the Assyrians found to save the situation turned out to be a priest from the heterodox sanctuary at Bethel that Jeroboam had built (v. 28). Evidently, the consequences of Jeroboam's sins were felt long after his death, for now the deuteronomic laws that were supposed to be constitutive in the land became irreparably compromised (vv. 34-41).

135. The Assyrian practice of repopulating conquered territories is well attested in extra-biblical texts. See, e.g., the record of Sargon II in *ANET,* 284-85.

136. Of the names of the gods mentioned, only Nergal may be identified with certainty.

REFLECTIONS

Most scholars recognize that 2 Kings 17 is a key passage illustrating the deuteronomistic editor's message to the exiles in the sixth century BCE. The narrator's temporal viewpoint is evident throughout the narrative, most notably in the phrase "to this day" (17:23, 34, 41). Here the theologian justifies God's destruction for disobedience and warns against syncretism in the face of the temptation to do so as the exiles dwell among foreigners in faraway places. There are theological lessons in this text, however, that are as pertinent for people in the modern community of faith as they were for those living in the sixth century BCE.

1. The text is ultimately more than a justification of the doom that God brought upon a nation long ago. It is a homily to those of us for whom there is still an opportunity to do what is right. It is a homily about what happens when we violate the first commandment and betray God, from whom no secrets can be kept (see 17:9).

2. The narrator makes the point that God's judgment in the present does not come because of what someone else did in the past. Accordingly, the destruction of Israel occurred not because of what Jeroboam, son of Nebat, had done generations before or, for that matter, because of what Hoshea did when the Assyrians came. Rather, God's judgment is against what the people themselves have been doing. Jeroboam did sin, but the people of Israel continued in his ways and did not depart from them. Moreover, the judgment is not so much against specific offenses at any one time as it is against people's refusal to turn back despite God's persistent pleas through human messengers. The problem is with the assumption that grace entails no responsibility. We cannot expect God's patience in the face of the persistence of our rejection of God's call.

3. Paradoxically, the narrator also believes that sin has consequences beyond the experiences of individuals in the present. The sins of Jeroboam, son of Nebat, did have consequences far greater and longer lasting than he could ever have imagined. Largely for pragmatic and political reasons, he had established heterodox sanctuaries in Dan and Bethel. The tradition that he began had become so entrenched that when the Assyrians decided to send someone back to Israel to teach the ways of the Lord to the settlers there, the only person who could be found to do so was a priest from Bethel; the narrator seems to imply, however, that this priest only managed to teach them unacceptable practices. The heterodoxy of "Samaria" and the "Samaritans" is an indirect result of what both Jeroboam and the people of Israel had done.

2 KINGS 18:1–25:30

THE LAST DAYS OF JUDAH

2 KINGS 18:1–20:21, HEZEKIAH, THE TRUSTING KING

OVERVIEW

This literary unit, which focuses on the reign of Hezekiah, son of Ahaz, is neatly framed by the regnal summaries at the beginning (18:1-8) and the end (20:20-21). The accounts here find extensive parallels elsewhere in the Old Testament (2 Chronicles 29–32; Isaiah 36–39), not to mention accounts in the Assyrian annals.[137] Scholars posit that the text as it stands is a compilation of a number of originally independent units, including two variant accounts of the confrontation between the representatives of the Assyrian king and Hezekiah. Whatever the reality, the entire unit as we have it reads reasonably well as a continuous report. The chronological notices scattered throughout the chapters suggest a sequential framework. The story begins with the beginning of Hezekiah's reign (18:1-8), followed by accounts of events in the fourth, sixth, and fourteenth years of his reign (18:9–19:7; 19:8-34); Hezekiah's illness and the extension of his life by fifteen years (20:1-19); and, finally, a reference to his death (20:20-21).

137. See ANET, 287-88.

2 Kings 18:1-8, Introduction to Hezekiah the Reformer

NIV

18 In the third year of Hoshea son of Elah
king of Israel, Hezekiah son of Ahaz king
of Judah began to reign. 2He was twenty-five years
old when he became king, and he reigned in
Jerusalem twenty-nine years. His mother's name
was Abijah[a] daughter of Zechariah. 3He did what
was right in the eyes of the LORD, just as his father
David had done. 4He removed the high places,
smashed the sacred stones and cut down the
Asherah poles. He broke into pieces the bronze
snake Moses had made, for up to that time the
Israelites had been burning incense to it. (It was
called[b] Nehushtan.[c])
5Hezekiah trusted in the LORD, the God of

[a] 2 Hebrew *Abi,* a variant of *Abijah* [b] 4 Or *He called it* [c] 4 *Nehushtan* sounds like the Hebrew for *bronze* and *snake* and *unclean thing.*

NRSV

18 In the third year of King Hoshea son of
Elah of Israel, Hezekiah son of King Ahaz
of Judah began to reign. 2He was twenty-five years
old when he began to reign; he reigned twenty-
nine years in Jerusalem. His mother's name was
Abi daughter of Zechariah. 3He did what was right
in the sight of the LORD just as his ancestor David
had done. 4He removed the high places, broke
down the pillars, and cut down the sacred pole.[a]
He broke in pieces the bronze serpent that Moses
had made, for until those days the people of Israel
had made offerings to it; it was called Nehushtan.
5He trusted in the LORD the God of Israel; so that
there was no one like him among all the kings of
Judah after him, or among those who were before
him. 6For he held fast to the LORD; he did not

[a] Heb *Asherah*

NIV

Israel. There was no one like him among all the kings of Judah, either before him or after him. [6]He held fast to the LORD and did not cease to follow him; he kept the commands the LORD had given Moses. [7]And the LORD was with him; he was successful in whatever he undertook. He rebelled against the king of Assyria and did not serve him. [8]From watchtower to fortified city, he defeated the Philistines, as far as Gaza and its territory.

NRSV

depart from following him but kept the commandments that the LORD commanded Moses. [7]The LORD was with him; wherever he went, he prospered. He rebelled against the king of Assyria and would not serve him. [8]He attacked the Philistines as far as Gaza and its territory, from watchtower to fortified city.

COMMENTARY

The regnal notice in v. 1 notes that Hezekiah began his reign in the third year of King Hoshea of Israel (i.e., 729/728 BCE), but that date does not square with the information in vv. 9-10 and 13. There have been many attempts to explain or harmonize the discrepancies,[138] but such moves are perhaps unnecessary, for the text is finally to be viewed, not as a historical document, but as theological literature. Most scholars now agree that Hezekiah reigned from around 715 to 687/686 BCE (the parallel text in 2 Chr 29:1-2 omits the synchronism).

Hezekiah receives an unequivocal endorsement from the narrator (v. 3), the first of its kind so far in the book of Kings. Like many of his predecessors, Hezekiah is said to have done what is right in the sight of God. However, in contrast to the others, whose failure to centralize the cult in Jerusalem in accordance with deuteronomic law is invariably noted (1 Kgs 22:43; 2 Kgs 12:3; 14:4), Hezekiah is commended for removing the "high places" (local sanctuaries) and the cultic symbols that accompanied such heterodox religious sites (see 1 Kgs 14:15, 23; 15:14; 22:43; 2 Kgs 12:3; 14:4; 15:4, 35; 17:10). He is portrayed as being faithful to the deuteronomic law (cf. Deut 7:5; 12:3), a monotheistic reformer like Gideon (Judg 6:25-32), and, perhaps, even like Moses (Exod 34:11-17; Deut 9:21). Indeed, whereas Moses had set up a bronze serpent, a cultic object for treating snakebites (Num 21:8-9), Hezekiah surpasses him by removing that object (נחשתן [*nĕḥuštān*] is a play on the words for "bronze" and "serpent"), because it had come to be venerated (v. 4).

The narrator reports that Hezekiah "trusted" the Lord as no other king before him had done (v. 5)—indeed, apart from Hezekiah (the Hebrew root occurs eight other times in this story, in vv. 19 [twice], 20, 21 [twice], 22, 24; 19:10), the verb is not used of any other ruler in the book of Kings. Unlike Solomon, who "held fast" (דבק *dābaq*) to his foreign wives (1 Kgs 11:2), Hezekiah "held fast" (*dābaq*) to the Lord and did not depart from the law of Moses (v. 6). As a result, the Lord was with Hezekiah as God was with David (v. 7; cf. 1 Sam 16:18; 18:12, 14; 2 Sam 5:10), and Hezekiah became successful, just as David had been (1 Sam 18:5, 14-15). Like David, too, he was given victory over the Philistines (v. 8; 1 Sam 18:27; 19:8). Finally, in contrast to Ahaz, who turned readily to the king of Assyria for security (16:7), Hezekiah rebelled against the Assyrians (v. 7). Hezekiah was, by all accounts, a faithful king. (See Reflections at 20:12-21.)

138. See, e.g., John Gray, *I & II Kings*, OTL (Philadelphia: Westminster, 1964) 669-70; E. Thiele, *The Mysterious Numbers of the Hebrew Kings*, 2nd ed. (Grand Rapids: Eerdmans, 1965) 132-33.

2 Kings 18:9-12, Perspective on the Fall of Samaria

NIV

[9]In King Hezekiah's fourth year, which was the seventh year of Hoshea son of Elah king of Israel, Shalmaneser king of Assyria marched against Samaria and laid siege to it. [10]At the end of three years the Assyrians took it. So Samaria was captured in Hezekiah's sixth year, which was the ninth year of Hoshea king of Israel. [11]The king of Assyria deported Israel to Assyria and settled them in Halah, in Gozan on the Habor River and in towns of the Medes. [12]This happened because they had not obeyed the LORD their God, but had violated his covenant—all that Moses the servant of the LORD commanded. They neither listened to the commands nor carried them out.

NRSV

9In the fourth year of King Hezekiah, which was the seventh year of King Hoshea son of Elah of Israel, King Shalmaneser of Assyria came up against Samaria, besieged it, [10]and at the end of three years, took it. In the sixth year of Hezekiah, which was the ninth year of King Hoshea of Israel, Samaria was taken. [11]The king of Assyria carried the Israelites away to Assyria, settled them in Halah, on the Habor, the river of Gozan, and in the cities of the Medes, [12]because they did not obey the voice of the LORD their God but transgressed his covenant—all that Moses the servant of the LORD had commanded; they neither listened nor obeyed.

COMMENTARY

The fate of the northern kingdom at the hands of the Assyrians is retold here in virtually the same detail as in 17:1-6, except for the attempt to synchronize the events with the reign of Hezekiah (vv. 9-10). It appears that Hezekiah had rebelled against the king of Assyria (v. 7) but was able to survive foreign invasion because he had been obedient and faithful, whereas Samaria was destroyed because the people of Israel were disobedient (v. 12). The narrator implies that Hezekiah's trust (v. 5) had put Judah on the side of the Lord. Thus expectation is raised on the part of the reader that Judah will survive the Assyrian threat.[139] (See Reflections at 20:12-21.)

139. Burke O. Long, *II Kings,* FOTL 10 (Grand Rapids: Eerdmans, 1991) 198. Mordechai Cogan and Hayim Tadmor, *II Kings,* AB 11 (New York: Doubleday, 1988) 221.

2 Kings 18:13–19:7, Sennacherib's First Challenge

NIV

[13]In the fourteenth year of King Hezekiah's reign, Sennacherib king of Assyria attacked all the fortified cities of Judah and captured them. [14]So Hezekiah king of Judah sent this message to the king of Assyria at Lachish: "I have done wrong. Withdraw from me, and I will pay whatever you demand of me." The king of Assyria exacted from Hezekiah king of Judah three hundred talents[a] of silver and thirty talents[b] of gold. [15]So Hezekiah gave him all the silver that was found in the

[a] *14* That is, about 11 tons (about 10 metric tons) [b] *14* That is, about 1 ton (about 1 metric ton)

NRSV

13In the fourteenth year of King Hezekiah, King Sennacherib of Assyria came up against all the fortified cities of Judah and captured them. [14]King Hezekiah of Judah sent to the king of Assyria at Lachish, saying, "I have done wrong; withdraw from me; whatever you impose on me I will bear." The king of Assyria demanded of King Hezekiah of Judah three hundred talents of silver and thirty talents of gold. [15]Hezekiah gave him all the silver that was found in the house of the LORD and in the treasuries of the king's house. [16]At that time Hezekiah stripped the gold from the doors of the temple of the LORD, and from the

NIV

temple of the LORD and in the treasuries of the royal palace.

[16]At this time Hezekiah king of Judah stripped off the gold with which he had covered the doors and doorposts of the temple of the LORD, and gave it to the king of Assyria.

[17]The king of Assyria sent his supreme commander, his chief officer and his field commander with a large army, from Lachish to King Hezekiah at Jerusalem. They came up to Jerusalem and stopped at the aqueduct of the Upper Pool, on the road to the Washerman's Field. [18]They called for the king; and Eliakim son of Hilkiah the palace administrator, Shebna the secretary, and Joah son of Asaph the recorder went out to them.

[19]The field commander said to them, "Tell Hezekiah:

> "'This is what the great king, the king of Assyria, says: On what are you basing this confidence of yours? [20]You say you have strategy and military strength—but you speak only empty words. On whom are you depending, that you rebel against me? [21]Look now, you are depending on Egypt, that splintered reed of a staff, which pierces a man's hand and wounds him if he leans on it! Such is Pharaoh king of Egypt to all who depend on him. [22]And if you say to me, "We are depending on the LORD our God"—isn't he the one whose high places and altars Hezekiah removed, saying to Judah and Jerusalem, "You must worship before this altar in Jerusalem"?
>
> [23]"'Come now, make a bargain with my master, the king of Assyria: I will give you two thousand horses—if you can put riders on them! [24]How can you repulse one officer of the least of my master's officials, even though you are depending on Egypt for chariots and horsemen[a]? [25]Furthermore, have I come to attack and destroy this place without word from the LORD? The LORD himself told me to march against this country and destroy it.'"

[26]Then Eliakim son of Hilkiah, and Shebna and Joah said to the field commander, "Please speak to your servants in Aramaic, since we understand

c 24 Or *charioteers*

NRSV

doorposts that King Hezekiah of Judah had overlaid and gave it to the king of Assyria. [17]The king of Assyria sent the Tartan, the Rabsaris, and the Rabshakeh with a great army from Lachish to King Hezekiah at Jerusalem. They went up and came to Jerusalem. When they arrived, they came and stood by the conduit of the upper pool, which is on the highway to the Fuller's Field. [18]When they called for the king, there came out to them Eliakim son of Hilkiah, who was in charge of the palace, and Shebnah the secretary, and Joah son of Asaph, the recorder.

19The Rabshakeh said to them, "Say to Hezekiah: Thus says the great king, the king of Assyria: On what do you base this confidence of yours? [20]Do you think that mere words are strategy and power for war? On whom do you now rely, that you have rebelled against me? [21]See, you are relying now on Egypt, that broken reed of a staff, which will pierce the hand of anyone who leans on it. Such is Pharaoh king of Egypt to all who rely on him. [22]But if you say to me, 'We rely on the LORD our God,' is it not he whose high places and altars Hezekiah has removed, saying to Judah and to Jerusalem, 'You shall worship before this altar in Jerusalem'? [23]Come now, make a wager with my master the king of Assyria: I will give you two thousand horses, if you are able on your part to set riders on them. [24]How then can you repulse a single captain among the least of my master's servants, when you rely on Egypt for chariots and for horsemen? [25]Moreover, is it without the LORD that I have come up against this place to destroy it? The LORD said to me, Go up against this land, and destroy it."

26Then Eliakim son of Hilkiah, and Shebnah, and Joah said to the Rabshakeh, "Please speak to your servants in the Aramaic language, for we understand it; do not speak to us in the language of Judah within the hearing of the people who are on the wall." [27]But the Rabshakeh said to them, "Has my master sent me to speak these words to your master and to you, and not to the people sitting on the wall, who are doomed with you to eat their own dung and to drink their own urine?"

28Then the Rabshakeh stood and called out in

NIV

it. Don't speak to us in Hebrew in the hearing of the people on the wall."

27But the commander replied, "Was it only to your master and you that my master sent me to say these things, and not to the men sitting on the wall—who, like you, will have to eat their own filth and drink their own urine?"

28Then the commander stood and called out in Hebrew: "Hear the word of the great king, the king of Assyria! 29This is what the king says: Do not let Hezekiah deceive you. He cannot deliver you from my hand. 30Do not let Hezekiah persuade you to trust in the LORD when he says, 'The LORD will surely deliver us; this city will not be given into the hand of the king of Assyria.'

31"Do not listen to Hezekiah. This is what the king of Assyria says: Make peace with me and come out to me. Then every one of you will eat from his own vine and fig tree and drink water from his own cistern, 32until I come and take you to a land like your own, a land of grain and new wine, a land of bread and vineyards, a land of olive trees and honey. Choose life and not death!

"Do not listen to Hezekiah, for he is misleading you when he says, 'The LORD will deliver us.' 33Has the god of any nation ever delivered his land from the hand of the king of Assyria? 34Where are the gods of Hamath and Arpad? Where are the gods of Sepharvaim, Hena and Ivvah? Have they rescued Samaria from my hand? 35Who of all the gods of these countries has been able to save his land from me? How then can the LORD deliver Jerusalem from my hand?"

36But the people remained silent and said nothing in reply, because the king had commanded, "Do not answer him."

37Then Eliakim son of Hilkiah the palace administrator, Shebna the secretary and Joah son of Asaph the recorder went to Hezekiah, with their clothes torn, and told him what the field commander had said.

19 When King Hezekiah heard this, he tore his clothes and put on sackcloth and went into the temple of the LORD. 2He sent Eliakim the palace administrator, Shebna the secretary and the leading priests, all wearing sackcloth, to the

NRSV

a loud voice in the language of Judah, "Hear the word of the great king, the king of Assyria! 29Thus says the king: 'Do not let Hezekiah deceive you, for he will not be able to deliver you out of my hand. 30Do not let Hezekiah make you rely on the LORD by saying, The LORD will surely deliver us, and this city will not be given into the hand of the king of Assyria.' 31Do not listen to Hezekiah; for thus says the king of Assyria: 'Make your peace with me and come out to me; then every one of you will eat from your own vine and your own fig tree, and drink water from your own cistern, 32until I come and take you away to a land like your own land, a land of grain and wine, a land of bread and vineyards, a land of olive oil and honey, that you may live and not die. Do not listen to Hezekiah when he misleads you by saying, The LORD will deliver us. 33Has any of the gods of the nations ever delivered its land out of the hand of the king of Assyria? 34Where are the gods of Hamath and Arpad? Where are the gods of Sepharvaim, Hena, and Ivvah? Have they delivered Samaria out of my hand? 35Who among all the gods of the countries have delivered their countries out of my hand, that the LORD should deliver Jerusalem out of my hand?' "

36But the people were silent and answered him not a word, for the king's command was, "Do not answer him." 37Then Eliakim son of Hilkiah, who was in charge of the palace, and Shebna the secretary, and Joah son of Asaph, the recorder, came to Hezekiah with their clothes torn and told him the words of the Rabshakeh.

19 When King Hezekiah heard it, he tore his clothes, covered himself with sackcloth, and went into the house of the LORD. 2And he sent Eliakim, who was in charge of the palace, and Shebna the secretary, and the senior priests, covered with sackcloth, to the prophet Isaiah son of Amoz. 3They said to him, "Thus says Hezekiah, This day is a day of distress, of rebuke, and of disgrace; children have come to the birth, and there is no strength to bring them forth. 4It may be that the LORD your God heard all the words of the Rabshakeh, whom his master the king of Assyria has sent to mock the living God, and will rebuke the words that the LORD your God has heard; therefore lift up your prayer for the rem-

NIV

prophet Isaiah son of Amoz. [3]They told him, "This is what Hezekiah says: This day is a day of distress and rebuke and disgrace, as when children come to the point of birth and there is no strength to deliver them. [4]It may be that the LORD your God will hear all the words of the field commander, whom his master, the king of Assyria, has sent to ridicule the living God, and that he will rebuke him for the words the LORD your God has heard. Therefore pray for the remnant that still survives."

[5]When King Hezekiah's officials came to Isaiah, [6]Isaiah said to them, "Tell your master, 'This is what the LORD says: Do not be afraid of what you have heard—those words with which the underlings of the king of Assyria have blasphemed me. [7]Listen! I am going to put such a spirit in him that when he hears a certain report, he will return to his own country, and there I will have him cut down with the sword.' "

NRSV

nant that is left." [5]When the servants of King Hezekiah came to Isaiah, [6]Isaiah said to them, "Say to your master, 'Thus says the LORD: Do not be afraid because of the words that you have heard, with which the servants of the king of Assyria have reviled me. [7]I myself will put a spirit in him, so that he shall hear a rumor and return to his own land; I will cause him to fall by the sword in his own land.' "

COMMENTARY

Given the auspicious start in the narrative in vv. 1-8 and the implication in vv. 9-12 that, because of Hezekiah's faithfulness, the fate of the southern kingdom would be radically different from that of the northern kingdom, the account of the fall of Judean cities at the hands of the Assyrians is utterly astounding. Suddenly we are in the fourteenth year of Hezekiah's reign (cf. Isa 36:1)—that is, 701 BCE—and the Assyrian king now is Sennacherib (705–681 BCE). Indeed, two decades have passed since the destruction of Samaria in 722/721 BCE (see vv. 9-12). Now the Assyrians are at the doorsteps of Jerusalem, Sennacherib having captured "all the fortified cities" (v. 13).

18:13-16. In its present literary context, Sennacherib's attack might be understood as Assyrian retribution for Hezekiah's rebellion (vv. 7, 20), and historians might point out that Hezekiah probably joined other anti-Assyrian states in the region in the widespread insurrection that followed the death of Sargon II in 705 BCE.[140] Hezekiah had, indeed, strengthened the defenses of Jerusalem and taken steps to ensure an adequate water supply for the city (20:20).[141] Such historical details, however, are of little interest to the narrator, for whom Sennacherib was simply an arrogant king who would not be appeased. Sennacherib was bent on humiliating Hezekiah and challenging the God of Judah.

In the face of Sennacherib's aggression, Hezekiah is as accommodating as one might expect: He admits to his wrongdoing (perhaps referring to his role in the insurrection of the vassal states in Palestine), pleads for the Assyrians to withdraw, and agrees to pay indemnity (v. 14). Although Sennacherib's price is enormous,[142] Hezekiah complies fully (v. 15), giving Sennacherib "all the silver" in the temple and palace treasuries, even stripping the temple doors and doorposts of their gold inlays in order to do so (v. 16).

18:17-18. Yet, Sennacherib would not leave Jerusalem alone. The Assyrian king sends a triumvirate to Jerusalem, including the "Tartan"

140. Mordechai Cogan and Hayim Tadmor, *II Kings,* AB 11 (New York: Doubleday, 1988) 221.

141. See Amihai Mazar, *Archaeology of the Land of the Bible,* ABRL (New York: Doubleday, 1990) 405, 420-22.

142. See *ANET,* 288, where the amount is 30 talents of gold and 800 talents of silver.

(Assyrian *turtanû,* the highest official after the king, hence, "the Viceroy"), the "Rabsaris" (Assyrian *rab ša rēši,* "the chief courtier"), and the Rabshakeh (lit., "chief cup-bearer," a reference to the adjutant). They come to Jerusalem with a sizable force and stand just outside the city walls.[143] Meeting the Assyrian delegation of three are three Judean emissaries: Eliakim, "the one over the house" (the chief of staff in the palace); Shebna, "the secretary" (keeper of royal records?); and Joah, "the recorder" (perhaps "the herald").

18:19-25. Through the speech of the Rabshakeh (vv. 19-23), the narrator calls attention to what was at stake for Hezekiah: "What is this security [הבטחון *habbiṭṭāḥôn*] on which you trust [בטחת *bāṭāḥtā*]?" (v. 19). The poignancy of the speech is more evident in Hebrew than in English, for the root בטח (*bṭḥ,* "trust") has already been used to depict Hezekiah's faith in v. 5 and is repeated several times (vv. 19-22, 24). The Assyrians accuse Hezekiah of trusting in Egypt, which was an untrustworthy alliance since Egypt was but a crushed reed that would, in fact, pierce the hand of anyone who tried to lean on it (vv. 20-21). The Rabshakeh takes the view, proffered also by the prophet Isaiah, that Judah should not turn to Egypt for help (cf. Isa 30:1-5; 31:1-3).[144] To the charge that Judah had relied on Egypt, however, the Judean delegation (the first "you" in v. 22 is plural in Hebrew) apparently assert that their trust is really in the Lord ("We trust the LORD our God"), rather than in Egypt (v. 22). Yet, the Rabshakeh, who clearly believes that the local high places are legitimate Yahwistic sanctuaries, points out that Hezekiah had removed them and so could not have been on the side of the Lord (v. 22). This was no doubt a view shared by many in Judah as well. The Assyrian officer implies that Hezekiah's decision to centralize worship in Jerusalem is so unpopular that, even if Hezekiah were given two thousand horses, he would not be able to find riders for them to fight the Assyrians (v. 23).[145] Egypt was finally what Hezekiah was really counting on, says the Rabshakeh, who suggests that Assyria might, indeed, have been sent by the Lord to punish Hezekiah (vv. 24-25).

18:26-35. The Rabshakeh made a compelling case. Certainly there would have been Judeans who would have agreed with some or all of his arguments, which were made to them in their own language. Hence, Hezekiah's negotiators request that the Assyrians speak in Aramaic (v. 26), the language of diplomacy in the Near East in those days, a language that was not accessible to the populace. The Assyrians insist, however, that the message is not just for the king and his emissaries, but is also for the people who would have to suffer the horrible consequences of a siege (v. 27; cf. 6:25-29).

Directly addressing the people in their own language, the Rabshakeh urges them not to let Hezekiah mislead them into thinking that he can deliver them or believing that the Lord can save them (vv. 28-30). The issue is now viewed in terms of the ability of the Lord to deliver the Judeans from the power of the Assyrians. Through the Rabshakeh, Sennacherib presents himself as a benevolent suzerain, inviting the Judeans literally to "make a blessing" (ברכה *bĕrākâ*) with him and to depart with him (v. 31). The Assyrian king offers himself as a suzerain in place of the Lord, urging the Judeans to choose him over their God. Whereas the Lord promised blessing to those who would obey the Lord and are brought into the promised land (cf. Deut 30:15-16; 28:8), the Assyrian king invites them out of that land, promising them abundant food to eat and water to drink (cf. the conditions of siege, 6:25). His offer to take them out of their land to a new promised land, as it were, is an indirect challenge to the Lord, implying that it is in the promised land of Sennacherib where they will find an abundant supply of food and wine and where they will live and not die (v. 32; cf. Deut 8:7-9). Hezekiah's talk of deliverance by the Lord is surely a delusion, Sennacherib maintains, for the gods of the nations that had previously been attacked by him have not been able to deliver their people from him. The gods of the other nations, too, had not been able to deliver the citizens of Samaria from Sennacherib's power, and now neither would the Lord be able to save Judah.

18:36–19:7. Hezekiah has no answer to the

143. The precise location of the conference (v. 17) is uncertain. For a survey of various options, see T. R. Hobbs, *II Kings,* WBC 13 (Waco, Tex.: Word, 1985) 260-62.

144. For the imagery of the fractured reed, cf. Isa 42:3; Ezek 29:6.

145. Indeed, Sennacherib claimed massive desertion on the part of the Judean soldiers. See *ANET,* 288.

taunts of Sennacherib's spokesman and instructs his people not to give one. The emissaries return in mourning to the king (v. 37). Hezekiah, too, goes into mourning (19:1). Then he sends a special delegation to consult with the prophet Isaiah (v. 2), calling the moment "a day of distress, of rebuke, and of disgrace" (v. 3). The king cites a proverb in v. 3*b,* suggesting that the crucial moment for deliverance has arisen but that the participants in it have not been able to bring it about. The Lord has heard the insults and challenges from the Assyrian delegation and responds through the words of Isaiah, noting Sennacherib's challenge as such and promising that a spirit will be sent into the Assyrian king that will cause him to hear a rumor and to return to his homeland, there to be killed (vv. 6-7). (See Reflections at 20:12-21.)

2 Kings 19:8-37, Sennacherib's Second Challenge

NIV

8When the field commander heard that the king of Assyria had left Lachish, he withdrew and found the king fighting against Libnah.

9Now Sennacherib received a report that Tirhakah, the Cushite[a] king ⌊of Egypt⌋, was marching out to fight against him. So he again sent messengers to Hezekiah with this word: 10"Say to Hezekiah king of Judah: Do not let the god you depend on deceive you when he says, 'Jerusalem will not be handed over to the king of Assyria.' 11Surely you have heard what the kings of Assyria have done to all the countries, destroying them completely. And will you be delivered? 12Did the gods of the nations that were destroyed by my forefathers deliver them: the gods of Gozan, Haran, Rezeph and the people of Eden who were in Tel Assar? 13Where is the king of Hamath, the king of Arpad, the king of the city of Sepharvaim, or of Hena or Ivvah?"

14Hezekiah received the letter from the messengers and read it. Then he went up to the temple of the LORD and spread it out before the LORD. 15And Hezekiah prayed to the LORD: "O LORD, God of Israel, enthroned between the cherubim, you alone are God over all the kingdoms of the earth. You have made heaven and earth. 16Give ear, O LORD, and hear; open your eyes, O LORD, and see; listen to the words Sennacherib has sent to insult the living God.

17"It is true, O LORD, that the Assyrian kings have laid waste these nations and their lands. 18They have thrown their gods into the fire and destroyed them, for they were not gods but only wood and stone, fashioned by men's hands.

[a] 9 That is, from the upper Nile region

NRSV

8The Rabshakeh returned, and found the king of Assyria fighting against Libnah; for he had heard that the king had left Lachish. 9When the king[a] heard concerning King Tirhakah of Ethiopia,[b] "See, he has set out to fight against you," he sent messengers again to Hezekiah, saying, 10"Thus shall you speak to King Hezekiah of Judah: Do not let your God on whom you rely deceive you by promising that Jerusalem will not be given into the hand of the king of Assyria. 11See, you have heard what the kings of Assyria have done to all lands, destroying them utterly. Shall you be delivered? 12Have the gods of the nations delivered them, the nations that my predecessors destroyed, Gozan, Haran, Rezeph, and the people of Eden who were in Telassar? 13Where is the king of Hamath, the king of Arpad, the king of the city of Sepharvaim, the king of Hena, or the king of Ivvah?"

14Hezekiah received the letter from the hand of the messengers and read it; then Hezekiah went up to the house of the LORD and spread it before the LORD. 15And Hezekiah prayed before the LORD, and said: "O LORD the God of Israel, who are enthroned above the cherubim, you are God, you alone, of all the kingdoms of the earth; you have made heaven and earth. 16Incline your ear, O LORD, and hear; open your eyes, O LORD, and see; hear the words of Sennacherib, which he has sent to mock the living God. 17Truly, O LORD, the kings of Assyria have laid waste the nations and their lands, 18and have hurled their gods into the fire, though they were no gods but the work of human hands—wood and stone—and

[a] Heb *he* [b] Or *Nubia*; Heb *Cush*

NIV

[19]Now, O LORD our God, deliver us from his hand, so that all kingdoms on earth may know that you alone, O LORD, are God."

[20]Then Isaiah son of Amoz sent a message to Hezekiah: "This is what the LORD, the God of Israel, says: I have heard your prayer concerning Sennacherib king of Assyria. [21]This is the word that the LORD has spoken against him:

"'The Virgin Daughter of Zion
despises you and mocks you.
The Daughter of Jerusalem
tosses her head as you flee.
[22]Who is it you have insulted and blasphemed?
Against whom have you raised your voice
and lifted your eyes in pride?
Against the Holy One of Israel!
[23]By your messengers
you have heaped insults on the Lord.
And you have said,
"With my many chariots
I have ascended the heights of the mountains,
the utmost heights of Lebanon.
I have cut down its tallest cedars,
the choicest of its pines.
I have reached its remotest parts,
the finest of its forests.
[24]I have dug wells in foreign lands
and drunk the water there.
With the soles of my feet
I have dried up all the streams of Egypt."
[25]"'Have you not heard?
Long ago I ordained it.
In days of old I planned it;
now I have brought it to pass,
that you have turned fortified cities
into piles of stone.
[26]Their people, drained of power,
are dismayed and put to shame.
They are like plants in the field,
like tender green shoots,
like grass sprouting on the roof,
scorched before it grows up.

[27]"'But I know where you stay
and when you come and go
and how you rage against me.
[28]Because you rage against me
and your insolence has reached my ears,
I will put my hook in your nose

NRSV

so they were destroyed. [19]So now, O LORD our God, save us, I pray you, from his hand, so that all the kingdoms of the earth may know that you, O LORD, are God alone."

20Then Isaiah son of Amoz sent to Hezekiah, saying, "Thus says the LORD, the God of Israel: I have heard your prayer to me about King Sennacherib of Assyria. [21]This is the word that the LORD has spoken concerning him:

She despises you, she scorns you—
virgin daughter Zion;
she tosses her head—behind your back,
daughter Jerusalem.

[22] "Whom have you mocked and reviled?
Against whom have you raised your voice
and haughtily lifted your eyes?
Against the Holy One of Israel!
[23] By your messengers you have mocked the Lord,
and you have said, 'With my many chariots
I have gone up the heights of the mountains,
to the far recesses of Lebanon;
I felled its tallest cedars,
its choicest cypresses;
I entered its farthest retreat,
its densest forest.
[24] I dug wells
and drank foreign waters,
I dried up with the sole of my foot
all the streams of Egypt.'

[25] "Have you not heard
that I determined it long ago?
I planned from days of old
what now I bring to pass,
that you should make fortified cities
crash into heaps of ruins,
[26] while their inhabitants, shorn of strength,
are dismayed and confounded;
they have become like plants of the field
and like tender grass,
like grass on the housetops,
blighted before it is grown.

[27] "But I know your rising[a] and your sitting,
your going out and coming in,
and your raging against me.

[a] Gk Compare Isa 37.27 QMs: MT lacks *rising*

NIV

and my bit in your mouth,
and I will make you return
by the way you came.'
29"This will be the sign for you, O Hezekiah:
"This year you will eat what grows by itself,
and the second year what springs from that.
But in the third year sow and reap,
plant vineyards and eat their fruit.
30Once more a remnant of the house of Judah
will take root below and bear fruit above.
31For out of Jerusalem will come a remnant,
and out of Mount Zion a band of survivors.
The zeal of the LORD Almighty will accomplish this.

32"Therefore this is what the LORD says concerning the king of Assyria:
"He will not enter this city
or shoot an arrow here.
He will not come before it with shield
or build a siege ramp against it.
33By the way that he came he will return;
he will not enter this city, declares the LORD.
34I will defend this city and save it,
for my sake and for the sake of David my servant."

35That night the angel of the LORD went out and
put to death a hundred and eighty-five thousand
men in the Assyrian camp. When the people got up
the next morning—there were all the dead bodies!
36So Sennacherib king of Assyria broke camp and
withdrew. He returned to Nineveh and stayed there.
37One day, while he was worshiping in the
temple of his god Nisroch, his sons Adrammelech
and Sharezer cut him down with the sword, and
they escaped to the land of Ararat. And Esarhaddon his son succeeded him as king.

NRSV

28 Because you have raged against me
and your arrogance has come to my ears,
I will put my hook in your nose
and my bit in your mouth;
I will turn you back on the way
by which you came.

29"And this shall be the sign for you: This year
you shall eat what grows of itself, and in the
second year what springs from that; then in the
third year sow, reap, plant vineyards, and eat their
fruit. 30The surviving remnant of the house of
Judah shall again take root downward, and bear
fruit upward; 31for from Jerusalem a remnant shall
go out, and from Mount Zion a band of survivors.
The zeal of the LORD of hosts will do this.

32"Therefore thus says the LORD concerning the
king of Assyria: He shall not come into this city,
shoot an arrow there, come before it with a
shield, or cast up a siege ramp against it. 33By the
way that he came, by the same he shall return;
he shall not come into this city, says the LORD.
34For I will defend this city to save it, for my own
sake and for the sake of my servant David."

35That very night the angel of the LORD set out
and struck down one hundred eighty-five thousand in the camp of the Assyrians; when morning
dawned, they were all dead bodies. 36Then King
Sennacherib of Assyria left, went home, and lived
at Nineveh. 37As he was worshiping in the house
of his god Nisroch, his sons Adrammelech and
Sharezer killed him with the sword, and they
escaped into the land of Ararat. His son Esar-haddon succeeded him.

COMMENTARY

19:8-13. Despite the word of the Lord spoken through Isaiah (vv. 6-7), the Rabshakeh returns to his headquarters to find that Sennacherib has already left Lachish, the principal fortress west of Jerusalem, and is now fighting against Libnah (v. 8), a smaller site probably to be located to the east of Lachish. Instead of turning back, Sennacherib appears to be pressing on toward Jerusalem. He hears word, however, that the Tirhakah of Cush (NRSV, "Ethiopia") is fighting against his armies (v. 9).[146] The Assyrian king, no doubt

146. Tirhakah, in fact, became pharaoh of Egypt, but not until 690 BCE. In 701 BCE, however, he was probably a military commander of the Egyptian army, which, according to Sennacherib's Assyrian annals, fought against the Assyrians in the Plain of Eltekeh. See Kenneth A. Kitchen, *The Third Intermediate Period in Egypt (1100–65)* (Warminster: Aris & Phillips, 1973) 157-61.

fearing that this development might encourage Hezekiah, threatens the Judean again. This time, Sennacherib intensifies his rhetoric. Whereas he had previously told the people not to let Hezekiah deceive them into trusting the Lord (18:30), Sennacherib now tells Hezekiah himself not to let the Lord deceive him into trusting the Lord (19:10). He asserts, once again, that the Lord will not be able to deliver Jerusalem any more than the gods of the other nations were able to deliver their cities (vv. 10-13; cf. 18:19-35).

19:14-19. One gathers from v. 14 that the message this time is delivered in written form. Whereas Hezekiah had previously sent representatives to the Temple to ask the prophet Isaiah to pray (v. 2), the king himself now prays to God (v. 15). In the Temple, probably facing the symbols of divine presence in the holy of holies (cf. 1 Kgs 8:6-13), the king spreads the document "before the LORD" (v. 15). He appeals to God, using an epithet that affirms the deity as king ("enthroned above the cherubim") and acknowledges that the Lord alone is God over all the kingdoms of the earth—not just over Judah, but over Assyria as well. He appeals to God as the sovereign Creator of heaven and earth and prays that God might take note of Sennacherib's blasphemous challenge, despite the fact that the Assyrian gods are but wood and stone (vv. 16-18). Then he asks God to save the Judeans from Sennacherib's hands, in order that the whole world might know that the Lord alone is God (v. 19). Nothing less than the sovereignty of God is at stake in this theological crisis.

19:20-28. Isaiah delivers an oracle of the Lord concerning Sennacherib (vv. 20-34; cf. Isa 10:12-19; 14:24-27). The word of the Lord is set over against the words of Sennacherib (vv. 20-21). Although the oracle begins by depicting personified Jerusalem as a woman scorned and mocked by personified Assyria, it quickly becomes clear that the issue is not between two women, two cities, or even two nations. Rather, it is a dispute between an arrogant king and the Lord, whom Hezekiah trusts. Sennacherib is addressed directly, for the challenge has become an intensely personal one for the Lord: It is Sennacherib against the Holy One of Israel (v. 22). The deity quotes the Assyrian king's boast—precisely the sort of boast that one finds in the Assyrian annals about how the king has ventured into the remote recesses of the world, felling the tallest trees and drying up rivers in doing so (vv. 23-24). God points out, however, that Sennacherib's victories have, in fact, been part of God's plan from long ago, meaning that Assyria is merely being used as an agent of God's plan (vv. 25-26; cf. Isa 10:5-11). The power of the Assyrian king is but a manifestation of divine will and power. God knows Sennacherib's every move, and the Assyrian will be harnessed like an animal (vv. 27-28).

19:29-37. Then Hezekiah is addressed directly and is promised a sign (vv. 29-31). The ravaged land will not recover immediately, and the people will have to eat what grows naturally. But by the third year, the agricultural routines will return fully. This cycle is a sign that the land will be repopulated from the remnant of people now left in Jerusalem. As for Sennacherib, he will not be successful in his attack of Jerusalem but will be turned back, for the Lord will personally defend the city and save it, for the Lord's own sake and for the sake of David (vv. 32-34).

That very night, the angel of the Lord attacks the Assyrian army, decimating it (v. 35). Suddenly, Sennacherib has to return to Nineveh, where he is assassinated by his own sons while he is worshiping in the temple of his god, an otherwise unknown deity named Nisroch (vv. 35-37). (See Reflections at 20:12-21.)

2 Kings 20:1-11, Hezekiah's Illness and Recovery

NIV

20 In those days Hezekiah became ill and was at the point of death. The prophet Isaiah son of Amoz went to him and said, "This is what

NRSV

20 In those days Hezekiah became sick and was at the point of death. The prophet Isaiah son of Amoz came to him, and said to him,

NIV

the LORD says: Put your house in order, because you are going to die; you will not recover."

2Hezekiah turned his face to the wall and prayed to the LORD, 3"Remember, O LORD, how I have walked before you faithfully and with wholehearted devotion and have done what is good in your eyes." And Hezekiah wept bitterly.

4Before Isaiah had left the middle court, the word of the LORD came to him: 5"Go back and tell Hezekiah, the leader of my people, 'This is what the LORD, the God of your father David, says: I have heard your prayer and seen your tears; I will heal you. On the third day from now you will go up to the temple of the LORD. 6I will add fifteen years to your life. And I will deliver you and this city from the hand of the king of Assyria. I will defend this city for my sake and for the sake of my servant David.'"

7Then Isaiah said, "Prepare a poultice of figs." They did so and applied it to the boil, and he recovered.

8Hezekiah had asked Isaiah, "What will be the sign that the LORD will heal me and that I will go up to the temple of the LORD on the third day from now?"

9Isaiah answered, "This is the LORD's sign to you that the LORD will do what he has promised: Shall the shadow go forward ten steps, or shall it go back ten steps?"

10"It is a simple matter for the shadow to go forward ten steps," said Hezekiah. "Rather, have it go back ten steps."

11Then the prophet Isaiah called upon the LORD, and the LORD made the shadow go back the ten steps it had gone down on the stairway of Ahaz.

NRSV

"Thus says the LORD: Set your house in order, for you shall die; you shall not recover." 2Then Hezekiah turned his face to the wall and prayed to the LORD: 3"Remember now, O LORD, I implore you, how I have walked before you in faithfulness with a whole heart, and have done what is good in your sight." Hezekiah wept bitterly. 4Before Isaiah had gone out of the middle court, the word of the LORD came to him: 5"Turn back, and say to Hezekiah prince of my people, Thus says the LORD, the God of your ancestor David: I have heard your prayer, I have seen your tears; indeed, I will heal you; on the third day you shall go up to the house of the LORD. 6I will add fifteen years to your life. I will deliver you and this city out of the hand of the king of Assyria; I will defend this city for my own sake and for my servant David's sake." 7Then Isaiah said, "Bring a lump of figs. Let them take it and apply it to the boil, so that he may recover."

8Hezekiah said to Isaiah, "What shall be the sign that the LORD will heal me, and that I shall go up to the house of the LORD on the third day?" 9Isaiah said, "This is the sign to you from the LORD, that the LORD will do the thing that he has promised: the shadow has now advanced ten intervals; shall it retreat ten intervals?" 10Hezekiah answered, "It is normal for the shadow to lengthen ten intervals; rather let the shadow retreat ten intervals." 11The prophet Isaiah cried to the LORD; and he brought the shadow back the ten intervals, by which the sun[a] had declined on the dial of Ahaz.

[a] Syr See Isa 38.8 and Tg: Heb *it*

COMMENTARY

The temporal introduction ("in those days") vaguely links this passage with the preceding unit (chaps. 18–19)—namely, the time of Hezekiah and Sennacherib (v. 1). The narrator becomes more precise in v. 6, however, in placing the story at the time of Sennacherib's siege of Jerusalem—that is, in the fourteenth year of Hezekiah's reign, 701 BCE (v. 6; cf. 18:13).

When Hezekiah becomes critically ill, the prophet Isaiah comes to him with the word of the Lord, telling Hezekiah to give his last injunction (cf. 1 Kgs 2:1),[147] for he will not recover (v. 2). Hezekiah does not accept that fate, however. He prays fervently for God to remember (cf. Ps 132:1) his wholehearted devotion and faithful conduct before the Lord (v. 3). Thereupon, Isaiah, who

147. See John Gray, *I & II Kings* (Philadelphia: Westminster, 1964) 397.

has scarcely left Hezekiah's presence (v. 4), is told to return to the king with the promise that God has heard his prayers and seen his tears, and thus will bring healing to the sick king so that he can go again to the Temple (v. 5). Hezekiah is given an extension of his life span: He will live fifteen more years (v. 6*a*). It is important to note here that reprieve and recovery for the king are linked to the same good fortune for Judah (v. 6*b*). The fate of the king and the fate of the city are bound together.[148] God will deliver both the king and Judah from the hands of the Assyrian king for God's own sake, as well as for the sake of David. Read in its larger literary-theological context, the deliverance of Jerusalem can be understood as being partly God's specific response to Sennacherib's blasphemous challenge and partly the manifestation of God's grace extended to David. Thus Hezekiah's personal recovery is the working out of God's will in microcosm. Isaiah then makes a poultice of figs and applies it to Hezekiah's boils to heal them (v. 7).

Hezekiah requests a sign as a confirmation of the promise of his recovery (v. 8). Unlike his father, Ahaz, who had refused to ask for a sign even when invited to do so by Isaiah (Isa 7:11-13), Hezekiah wants a sign from the Lord. Isaiah's response to the request comes not as a straightforward announcement of the sign, but initially in the form of a question: "The shadow has advanced ten steps, will it return ten steps?" (vv. 8-9; cf. Num 20:10; Ezek 37:3). The "steps" here refer to the "steps of Ahaz" in v. 11, which the NRSV, following most interpreters, takes to be a sundial ("dial of Ahaz"), presumably a series of steps on which the movement of a shadow cast by the sun marked the hours of the day. Hezekiah replies that it is natural for the shadow to lengthen ten steps, but not for it to retreat ten steps (v. 10). When a shadow has been cast, it ordinarily will not recede. Isaiah then prays to God, and the shadow on the dial miraculously retreats after it has advanced (cf. the miracle of the sun's standing still in Josh 10:12-13). The miracle is dramatized in the recovery of Hezekiah. Isaiah had already proclaimed that Hezekiah is about to die (v. 1). Yet, when Hezekiah prayed to the Lord (v. 3), Isaiah was commanded to *turn back* (v. 5) and tell Hezekiah that fifteen years had been added to his life (v. 6). So, too, even though the shadow has already advanced ten degrees on the "steps of Ahaz" (i.e., time has passed), Isaiah prays to the Lord, and the Lord turns back the shadow (v. 11). Even if the word of death or destruction has been proclaimed, it is possible, through prayer, to turn back that word of judgment. (See Reflections at 20:12-21.)

148. See Long, *2 Kings*, 238.

2 Kings 20:12-21, From Assyria to Babylon

NIV

[12]At that time Merodach-Baladan son of Baladan king of Babylon sent Hezekiah letters and a gift, because he had heard of Hezekiah's illness. [13]Hezekiah received the messengers and showed them all that was in his storehouses—the silver, the gold, the spices and the fine oil—his armory and everything found among his treasures. There was nothing in his palace or in all his kingdom that Hezekiah did not show them.

[14]Then Isaiah the prophet went to King Hezekiah and asked, "What did those men say, and where did they come from?"

"From a distant land," Hezekiah replied. "They came from Babylon."

NRSV

12At that time King Merodach-baladan son of Baladan of Babylon sent envoys with letters and a present to Hezekiah, for he had heard that Hezekiah had been sick. [13]Hezekiah welcomed them;[a] he showed them all his treasure house, the silver, the gold, the spices, the precious oil, his armory, all that was found in his storehouses; there was nothing in his house or in all his realm that Hezekiah did not show them. [14]Then the prophet Isaiah came to King Hezekiah, and said to him, "What did these men say? From where did they come to you?" Hezekiah answered, "They have come from a far country, from Baby-

[a] Gk Vg Syr: Heb *When Hezekiah heard about them*

NIV

15The prophet asked, "What did they see in your palace?"

"They saw everything in my palace," Hezekiah said. "There is nothing among my treasures that I did not show them."

16Then Isaiah said to Hezekiah, "Hear the word of the LORD: 17The time will surely come when everything in your palace, and all that your fathers have stored up until this day, will be carried off to Babylon. Nothing will be left, says the LORD. 18And some of your descendants, your own flesh and blood, that will be born to you, will be taken away, and they will become eunuchs in the palace of the king of Babylon."

19"The word of the LORD you have spoken is good," Hezekiah replied. For he thought, "Will there not be peace and security in my lifetime?"

20As for the other events of Hezekiah's reign, all his achievements and how he made the pool and the tunnel by which he brought water into the city, are they not written in the book of the annals of the kings of Judah? 21Hezekiah rested with his fathers. And Manasseh his son succeeded him as king.

NRSV

lon." 15He said, "What have they seen in your house?" Hezekiah answered, "They have seen all that is in my house; there is nothing in my storehouses that I did not show them."

16Then Isaiah said to Hezekiah, "Hear the word of the LORD: 17Days are coming when all that is in your house, and that which your ancestors have stored up until this day, shall be carried to Babylon; nothing shall be left, says the LORD. 18Some of your own sons who are born to you shall be taken away; they shall be eunuchs in the palace of the king of Babylon." 19Then Hezekiah said to Isaiah, "The word of the LORD that you have spoken is good." For he thought, "Why not, if there will be peace and security in my days?"

20The rest of the deeds of Hezekiah, all his power, how he made the pool and the conduit and brought water into the city, are they not written in the Book of the Annals of the Kings of Judah? 21Hezekiah slept with his ancestors; and his son Manasseh succeeded him.

COMMENTARY

This story is loosely connected to the present context by the temporal phrase "at that time" (v. 1). The Mesopotamian ruler with whom Hezekiah deals in this case is not the king of Assyria, as in chapters 17–18, however, but the king of Babylon, the power that within a century would defeat the Assyrians and invade Judah, capture Jerusalem, and send the Judeans into exile. According to the narrator, Babylonian emissaries had made overtures to Judah when Hezekiah was ill (v. 12), although nothing is said of the purpose for their having come to Jerusalem. The chronicler has them coming to learn about the sign that had been given to Hezekiah (2 Chr 32:31). Whatever the case, they are willingly received in Jerusalem and are shown all its resources (vv. 13, 15). When Isaiah learns what has transpired, he predicts that the day will come when the Babylonians will return to take all the wealth of the city and the king's descendants will be taken as captives to Babylon (vv. 16-18).

The king's response is somewhat enigmatic.[149] Taking the Hebrew text at face value, it appears that Hezekiah has two responses. The first is the public one that he states to Isaiah: "The word of the LORD that you have spoken is good" (v. 19*a*). That response is consonant with Hezekiah's image of a compliant, pious king who is ready to accept God's judgment. The other response, however, made known to the reader by the narrator, is Hezekiah's private response: "Why not, if there will be peace and security in my days?" (v. 19*b*). Apparently Hezekiah is willing to take the judgment, since it does not affect him directly. During his own reign, he seems to think, there will be peace and security. The publicly pious king is

149. For various interpretations of Hezekiah's response, see Peter R. Ackroyd, "An Interpretation of the Babylonian Exile: A Study of 2 Kings 20, Isaiah 38-39," *SJT* 27 (1974) 335-38.

willing to accept the judgment of God, knowing full well that it does not affect him personally.

With that shocking assessment of the private side of Hezekiah, the narrator simply moves on to give the standard closing summary of the king's reign, calling attention to his famous public project—namely, the provision of a water supply through the cutting of the Siloam tunnel.

REFLECTIONS

1. In both obvious and subtle ways, this lengthy report addresses the issue of trust, a term that appears numerous times in the text. It begins with a portrayal of a king who trusted God as no other king had done before him (18:1-8). That trust entailed bold and decisive compliance with the will of God, and it brought divine favor. In contrast, those who did not trust God did not survive (18:9-12).

2. Despite the introductory verses of the story, the narrator seems to know that such talk of trust in God and its payoffs is difficult to work out in the "real world." In the real world, even those who trust in God are confronted with political realities. For all his trust in God, Hezekiah had to suffer humiliation at the hands of a foreign invader, and he even had to strip the Temple of its wealth, removing gold from the doors and doorposts of the Lord's house in order to pay off the bully (18:13-16). Trust in God will not necessarily stave off actual political threats. Trust in God may not have immediate or manifest results.

3. The text implicitly concedes that the rhetoric of trust in an invisible God is difficult to authenticate in the nitty-gritty of worldly affairs. People may speak of trust in God while they work on political solutions, their trust being in military alliances and the like (18:19-25). By the same token, talk of God's blessings is often difficult to corroborate. In the face of war's atrocities and the deprivations that people suffer, it is tempting to respond to the invitation of the most powerful ruler in the world to "make a blessing" with him and to go on an exodus with him from one's God-given place (18:30-32). It is tempting to believe his claim that it is he who would provide us with the necessities and luxuries of life. In view of the verifiable evidence of military might, and in view of the absence of any divine resistance to such demonstrations of power, it is tempting to believe that God cannot rescue us from such political and military power (18:33-35). In such circumstances, the people of God may, indeed, have no answer and ought not to try to give one (18:36). There is no answer in human disputation. In such circumstances, the only answer, if one is forthcoming, is a word from God—difficult though that word may be to verify (19:1-7). Thus this story asserts that prayer can make a difference.

4. The silence of God may prompt arrogant individuals to believe that they are in a place to challenge God directly, to believe that they are in control of the destiny of the world. Such people miss the point, however, that even they may actually be instruments of God. Their power and their every plan may, indeed, be known to God and may be utilized in the working out of God's will in the world (9:8-34). When all is said and done, it is God who will have the last word. The text, therefore, invites the reader to believe that even in the face of the atrocious manifestation of military power—indeed, even evil, destructive power—nevertheless, the sovereign Creator of the world is in control.

5. The story of Hezekiah's recovery from a deadly illness is something of a parable about the possibility of life even when death is all too certain. The Hebrew word translated as "recover" in the NRSV (20:1, 7) is also the word for "live." Hezekiah was about to die, but his faith made the impossible possible (20:3-6). For the individual, as well as for the people of God as a larger community, there is hope in trusting God, even if no hope seems possible

(20:6). Even if the shadow has been cast and it has lengthened ten times, God can reverse it (20:8-11). This is the kind of trust that the text challenges the reader to have. The grace of God through faith makes it possible for death to be overcome (Rom 3:21-31; 4:2-4; Gal 2:1-10). This is at the heart of the gospel story in the New Testament.

6. Readers may prefer that the story of Hezekiah ended with his miraculous recovery by grace through faith, for that would make a wonderful theological denouement. That is not the final word, however. Hezekiah's trust in God does not seem so firm after all. He, who has been portrayed as a model of faith and piety, turns to the Babylonians, for reasons that the narrator does not bother to explain. When confronted with a prophetic word of judgment (a prediction of the eventual destruction of Jerusalem and the consequent exile), Hezekiah responds with appropriate humility in public, declaring the word of the Lord to be "good" (v. 19*a*). Publicly he is still the humble and obedient king. He accepted the word of the Lord. The narrator tells us, however, that his private thoughts may not have been entirely commendable. Hezekiah was more concerned, it seems, with his lame-duck reign than with the long-term consequences of his misplaced trust in the Babylonians. Interpreters from time immemorial have been uncomfortable with this negative portrayal of Hezekiah at the end of the mostly positive assessment of his reign. One must not try to exonerate Hezekiah for the sake of literary coherence, however. If anything, the presence of this story after the crescendo in 20:1-11 is a powerful reminder to the reader not to hold any human being, however attractive, however faithful, as a model. The Bible is not finally a story about faithful people but a story about a faithful God. The story of the lapse of pious Hezekiah is a lesson to us about post-recovery life: Despite one's experience of God's wondrous, life-renewing grace, there remains the possibility—indeed, the likelihood—that one may not fully trust God. As the apostle Paul warns us: "If you think you are standing, watch out that you do not fall" (1 Cor 10:12 NRSV).

2 KINGS 21:1-26, IRREPARABLE DAMAGE TO JUDAH

OVERVIEW

The preceding chapter already hinted at the impending destruction of Judah. Even faithful and pious King Hezekiah somehow lost perspective at the end of his reign, completely exposing Jerusalem and its resources to the unsavory gaze of the Babylonians (20:12-15). For that, the prophet Isaiah predicted that in time the Babylonians would invade Jerusalem and take captives to Babylon (20:16-18). For all his dedication, Hezekiah's reaction to that word of judgment was less than faithful; while he publicly accepted the word of God as "good," he privately thought only of the peace and security that his reign would enjoy (20:19). The future of God's people mattered less to him than did his own reign.

In chapter 21 the reader witnesses Judah's rapid downward spiral toward destruction and exile. Any good that was accomplished through Hezekiah's reforms is undone by the two wicked kings, his son (21:1-18) and grandson (21:19-26). Manasseh reigned for more than half a century, around 687/686 BCE–642 BCE. To the deuteronomistic narrator, this was the worst of times. Manasseh did such harm to Judah that no reform, however well intentioned, could ever save it from destruction. Manasseh was the most evil of all the kings of Judah, doing to that kingdom what Jeroboam and Ahab did to Israel. Partly because of him, Judah did everything Israel did that led to the fall of Samaria (17:7-20). Manasseh was succeeded by his son Amon, who reigned for only two years (642–640 BCE) before being assassinated in his own palace. Amon followed in his father's faithless footsteps. Thus Judah was led down the inevitable path of doom.

2 Kings 21:1-18, The Reign of Manasseh

NIV

21 Manasseh was twelve years old when he became king, and he reigned in Jerusalem fifty-five years. His mother's name was Hephzibah. 2He did evil in the eyes of the LORD, following the detestable practices of the nations the LORD had driven out before the Israelites. 3He rebuilt the high places his father Hezekiah had destroyed; he also erected altars to Baal and made an Asherah pole, as Ahab king of Israel had done. He bowed down to all the starry hosts and worshiped them. 4He built altars in the temple of the LORD, of which the LORD had said, "In Jerusalem I will put my Name." 5In both courts of the temple of the LORD, he built altars to all the starry hosts. 6He sacrificed his own son in[a] the fire, practiced sorcery and divination, and consulted mediums and spiritists. He did much evil in the eyes of the LORD, provoking him to anger.

7He took the carved Asherah pole he had made and put it in the temple, of which the LORD had said to David and to his son Solomon, "In this temple and in Jerusalem, which I have chosen out of all the tribes of Israel, I will put my Name forever. 8I will not again make the feet of the Israelites wander from the land I gave their forefathers, if only they will be careful to do everything I commanded them and will keep the whole Law that my servant Moses gave them." 9But the people did not listen. Manasseh led them astray, so that they did more evil than the nations the LORD had destroyed before the Israelites.

10The LORD said through his servants the prophets: 11"Manasseh king of Judah has committed these detestable sins. He has done more evil than the Amorites who preceded him and has led Judah into sin with his idols. 12Therefore this is what the LORD, the God of Israel, says: I am going to bring such disaster on Jerusalem and Judah that the ears of everyone who hears of it will tingle. 13I will stretch out over Jerusalem the measuring

[a] 6 Or *He made his own son pass through*

NRSV

21 Manasseh was twelve years old when he began to reign; he reigned fifty-five years in Jerusalem. His mother's name was Hephzibah. 2He did what was evil in the sight of the LORD, following the abominable practices of the nations that the LORD drove out before the people of Israel. 3For he rebuilt the high places that his father Hezekiah had destroyed; he erected altars for Baal, made a sacred pole,[a] as King Ahab of Israel had done, worshiped all the host of heaven, and served them. 4He built altars in the house of the LORD, of which the LORD had said, "In Jerusalem I will put my name." 5He built altars for all the host of heaven in the two courts of the house of the LORD. 6He made his son pass through fire; he practiced soothsaying and augury, and dealt with mediums and with wizards. He did much evil in the sight of the LORD, provoking him to anger. 7The carved image of Asherah that he had made he set in the house of which the LORD said to David and to his son Solomon, "In this house, and in Jerusalem, which I have chosen out of all the tribes of Israel, I will put my name forever; 8I will not cause the feet of Israel to wander any more out of the land that I gave to their ancestors, if only they will be careful to do according to all that I have commanded them, and according to all the law that my servant Moses commanded them." 9But they did not listen; Manasseh misled them to do more evil than the nations had done that the LORD destroyed before the people of Israel.

10The LORD said by his servants the prophets, 11"Because King Manasseh of Judah has committed these abominations, has done things more wicked than all that the Amorites did, who were before him, and has caused Judah also to sin with his idols; 12therefore thus says the LORD, the God of Israel, I am bringing upon Jerusalem and Judah such evil that the ears of everyone who hears of

[a] Heb *Asherah*

NIV

line used against Samaria and the plumb line used against the house of Ahab. I will wipe out Jerusalem as one wipes a dish, wiping it and turning it upside down. [14]I will forsake the remnant of my inheritance and hand them over to their enemies. They will be looted and plundered by all their foes, [15]because they have done evil in my eyes and have provoked me to anger from the day their forefathers came out of Egypt until this day."

[16]Moreover, Manasseh also shed so much innocent blood that he filled Jerusalem from end to end—besides the sin that he had caused Judah to commit, so that they did evil in the eyes of the LORD.

[17]As for the other events of Manasseh's reign, and all he did, including the sin he committed, are they not written in the book of the annals of the kings of Judah? [18]Manasseh rested with his fathers and was buried in his palace garden, the garden of Uzza. And Amon his son succeeded him as king.

NRSV

it will tingle. [13]I will stretch over Jerusalem the measuring line for Samaria, and the plummet for the house of Ahab; I will wipe Jerusalem as one wipes a dish, wiping it and turning it upside down. [14]I will cast off the remnant of my heritage, and give them into the hand of their enemies; they shall become a prey and a spoil to all their enemies, [15]because they have done what is evil in my sight and have provoked me to anger, since the day their ancestors came out of Egypt, even to this day."

16Moreover Manasseh shed very much innocent blood, until he had filled Jerusalem from one end to another, besides the sin that he caused Judah to sin so that they did what was evil in the sight of the LORD.

17Now the rest of the acts of Manasseh, all that he did, and the sin that he committed, are they not written in the Book of the Annals of the Kings of Judah? [18]Manasseh slept with his ancestors, and was buried in the garden of his house, in the garden of Uzza. His son Amon succeeded him.

COMMENTARY

Unlike the slightly lengthier parallel account in 2 Chr 33:1-20, which portrays Manasseh in a more favorable light (including a report of his repentance and restoration), the depiction of him in 2 Kgs 21:1-18 is entirely negative. Indeed, no other king in Judah received such an unrelentingly negative evaluation. Unlike his father, Hezekiah, who did what was right in the sight of the Lord (18:3), Manasseh did what was evil (v. 2). In violation of deuteronomic law (Deut 12:29-31), he "followed the abominable practices of the nations that the Lord had driven out" from before the people of Israel (cf. 16:3; 17:7). He rebuilt the local sanctuaries ("high places") that Hezekiah had torn down (v. 3; cf. 18:4), sanctuaries that were roundly condemned in Kings as heterodox sites, contrary to the ideal of worship centralized in Jerusalem (1 Kgs 11:7; 12:31-32; 13:32-33; 14:23; etc.; cf. Deut 12:2-7). He erected altars for Baal and other heterodox cultic symbols (v. 3), just as Ahab had done in Israel (16:11). Even worse, Manasseh introduced various foreign cultic objects into the Temple of the Lord in Jerusalem, constructing altars for astral deities and crafting an image of Asherah (consort of the high god in the Canaanite pantheon) in it (vv. 3-5). He followed Ahaz in the practice of child sacrifice (v. 6; 16:3) and sanctioned divination (v. 6; cf. Deut 18:9-14; 2 Kgs 17:17). Not only did he out-sin his predecessors and the worst kings of Israel, he even outdid the former inhabitants of the land in his atrocities (see Deut 9:5).

Despite the warning of the Lord proclaimed by unspecified prophets, Manasseh continued in his wicked ways (vv. 10-11). Hence judgment will come upon Israel as it has upon Samaria (vv. 12-13). Indeed, the deity will clean out Jerusalem as one might clean out a dish, turning it upside down to ensure that everything in it is removed (v. 13*b*).

Although Manasseh has done irreparable damage, the narrator does not mean that the destruction would come because of his sins alone. Rather, the people of Israel as a whole are culpable, for they have been provoking the Lord to anger since the time of the exodus (see v. 15). Manasseh sinned horribly and he caused Judah to sin (v. 16), even as Jeroboam son of Nebat had caused Israel to sin; but Judah is culpable because of its collective response (cf. 17:7-20). (See Reflections at 21:19-26.)

2 Kings 21:19-26, The Reign of Amon

NIV

19Amon was twenty-two years old when he became king, and he reigned in Jerusalem two years. His mother's name was Meshullemeth daughter of Haruz; she was from Jotbah. 20He did evil in the eyes of the LORD, as his father Manasseh had done. 21He walked in all the ways of his father; he worshiped the idols his father had worshiped, and bowed down to them. 22He forsook the LORD, the God of his fathers, and did not walk in the way of the LORD.

23Amon's officials conspired against him and assassinated the king in his palace. 24Then the people of the land killed all who had plotted against King Amon, and they made Josiah his son king in his place.

25As for the other events of Amon's reign, and what he did, are they not written in the book of the annals of the kings of Judah? 26He was buried in his grave in the garden of Uzza. And Josiah his son succeeded him as king.

NRSV

19Amon was twenty-two years old when he began to reign; he reigned two years in Jerusalem. His mother's name was Meshullemeth daughter of Haruz of Jotbah. 20He did what was evil in the sight of the LORD, as his father Manasseh had done. 21He walked in all the way in which his father walked, served the idols that his father served, and worshiped them; 22he abandoned the LORD, the God of his ancestors, and did not walk in the way of the LORD. 23The servants of Amon conspired against him, and killed the king in his house. 24But the people of the land killed all those who had conspired against King Amon, and the people of the land made his son Josiah king in place of him. 25Now the rest of the acts of Amon that he did, are they not written in the Book of the Annals of the Kings of Judah? 26He was buried in his tomb in the garden of Uzza; then his son Josiah succeeded him.

COMMENTARY

Manasseh is succeeded by his son Amon, who is said to have followed in his father's footsteps, doing evil in the sight of God, serving idols, and generally turning away from the God of Israel's ancestors. He is assassinated by his servants in the palace, and his son Josiah is placed on the throne.

REFLECTIONS

There is no question that the picture in this chapter is a gloomy one. Humanity seems utterly incapable of sustaining anything good. Any hope of a proper response of faith that Hezekiah might have raised is dashed against the rocks of Manasseh's and Amon's faithlessness. Doom is inevitable because human beings are bent on their destructive course, turning away from the way of God. Yet the text does not merely proclaim the inevitability of judgment. The point is not simply that people deserve punishment because they sin. Rather, woven into the account that justifies God's judgment is a subliminal message of God's grace. Even as one hears the word of judgment, one hears a message of God's persistent grace: God brought the people out of bondage (v. 15*b*), made it possible for Israel to possess the promised land (vv.

2*b,* 9*b*), gave the people rest (v. 8), promised to be present in the midst of the people (vv. 4, 7), and preserved a remnant as God's heritage (v. 14). When one considers the subliminal message of grace, one understands that judgment comes not so much because of isolated acts of disobedience, but because of a people's history of willful rejection of grace.

2 KINGS 22:1–23:30, THE JOSIANIC REFORMATION

OVERVIEW

Up to this point in Kings, the history that the narrator presents is a history of failure. From Solomon on down, the kings have failed to live up to the high standards of faithfulness that the Torah demands. Solomon began reasonably well and he received God's gift of gracious wisdom (1 Kgs 3:1-15), but he soon showed that he was not up to the standards. He turned out to be a self-serving, oppressive, and syncretistic despot (1 Kings 3–11). As a result of his unfaithfulness, the kingdom was divided into two: Israel and Judah.

Things still did not improve, however. Indeed, the kings of the northern kingdom all turned out to be complete failures. They invariably followed the idolatrous ways of Jeroboam the son of Nebat, and that history of willful disobedience led eventually to the destruction of Samaria and the dispersion of the people. Judah's kings fared somewhat better, for there were a few kings who generally did right by God, kings like Asa (1 Kgs 15:9-24), Jehoshaphat (1 Kgs 22:41-50), Jehoash (2 Kgs 12:1-16), and, above all, Hezekiah (2 Kgs 18:1–20:21). Still, the southern kingdom did not survive because of the righteousness of its kings, for none of them lived up to the standards of the Torah. Even Hezekiah, who is acknowledged as one who trusted the Lord, endangered the well-being of his people by unduly trusting the Babylonians (2 Kgs 20:12-15). Moreover, when he heard the word of judgment delivered by the prophet Isaiah, he was more concerned about his own reign than he was with the destiny of God's people (2 Kgs 20:16-19). In any case, any hopes of recovery that Judah might have had were utterly shattered by the blatantly syncretistic counter-reformation of Manasseh and by his equally impious son and successor, Amon (2 Kgs 21:1-26).

Then comes Josiah, the ideal king according to the standards of deuteronomic law, the paragon of kingly righteousness (2 Kgs 22:1–23:30). There has never been and never will be a king like him, the narrator says (23:25). Josiah earned the narrator's praise primarily because of his reform efforts based on a rediscovered "book of the תורה (*tôrâ*)," a document that, to judge by the nature of the reform, with its emphasis on the elimination of syncretism and on the centralization of worship in Jerusalem, is probably some form of the book of Deuteronomy. The parallel account of Josiah's reign traces his reform efforts to an earlier period in his career (2 Chr 34:3-7), but the narrator of Kings has no interest in all that. What he considers most important is that Josiah's reforms were based on the rediscovery of the Torah and, in that regard, Josiah was completely faithful. The narrator has nothing but positive things to say about Josiah and his reforms.

Yet, the shocking conclusion of the story is that the reforms came too late. As thorough as Josiah was, his reforms could not overcome the horrible effects of Manasseh's counter-reformation. So Judah was doomed despite the righteousness of Josiah (23:26-27).

2 Kings 22:1-2, Introduction to Josiah's Reign

NIV

22 Josiah was eight years old when he became king, and he reigned in Jerusalem thirty-one years. His mother's name was Jedidah daughter of Adaiah; she was from Bozkath. 2He did what was right in the eyes of the LORD and walked in all the ways of his father David, not turning aside to the right or to the left.

NRSV

22 Josiah was eight years old when he began to reign; he reigned thirty-one years in Jerusalem. His mother's name was Jedidah daughter of Adaiah of Bozkath. 2He did what was right in the sight of the LORD, and walked in all the way of his father David; he did not turn aside to the right or to the left.

COMMENTARY

The narrator's evaluation of Josiah (c. 640–609 BCE) is entirely positive. Like a few other reformist kings of Judah, he is judged to have done right in the sight of the Lord and to have walked in the way of his ancestor David (cf. 1 Kgs 15:11; 22:43; 2 Kgs 12:2; 18:3). Of all these kings, only Hezekiah and Josiah are praised without qualification; the rest are commended for generally doing well before God, but each is noted for failure to remove the heterodox "high places" and centralize worship in Jerusalem. Josiah alone, however, is said to have walked in *all* the ways of David, and of no one else is it said that "he did not turn aside to the right or to the left" (v. 2), an allusion to Moses' charge (Deut 5:32; 17:11, 20; 28:14) that is reiterated to and by Joshua (Josh 1:7; 23:6). In Josiah, then, we have an image of the ideal king according to deuteronomic law (Deut 17:14-20). In his utter devotion he is reminiscent of Moses, Joshua, David, and Hezekiah.

2 Kings 22:3-11, Rediscovery of the Book of the Law

NIV

3In the eighteenth year of his reign, King Josiah sent the secretary, Shaphan son of Azaliah, the son of Meshullam, to the temple of the LORD. He said: 4"Go up to Hilkiah the high priest and have him get ready the money that has been brought into the temple of the LORD, which the doorkeepers have collected from the people. 5Have them entrust it to the men appointed to supervise the work on the temple. And have these men pay the workers who repair the temple of the LORD— 6the carpenters, the builders and the masons. Also have them purchase timber and dressed stone to repair the temple. 7But they need not account for the money entrusted to them, because they are acting faithfully."

8Hilkiah the high priest said to Shaphan the

NRSV

3In the eighteenth year of King Josiah, the king sent Shaphan son of Azaliah, son of Meshullam, the secretary, to the house of the LORD, saying, 4"Go up to the high priest Hilkiah, and have him count the entire sum of the money that has been brought into the house of the LORD, which the keepers of the threshold have collected from the people; 5let it be given into the hand of the workers who have the oversight of the house of the LORD; let them give it to the workers who are at the house of the LORD, repairing the house, 6that is, to the carpenters, to the builders, to the masons; and let them use it to buy timber and quarried stone to repair the house. 7But no accounting shall be asked from them for the money that is delivered into their hand, for they deal honestly."

NIV

secretary, "I have found the Book of the Law in the temple of the LORD." He gave it to Shaphan, who read it. 9Then Shaphan the secretary went to the king and reported to him: "Your officials have paid out the money that was in the temple of the LORD and have entrusted it to the workers and supervisors at the temple." 10Then Shaphan the secretary informed the king, "Hilkiah the priest has given me a book." And Shaphan read from it in the presence of the king.

11When the king heard the words of the Book of the Law, he tore his robes.

NRSV

8The high priest Hilkiah said to Shaphan the secretary, "I have found the book of the law in the house of the LORD." When Hilkiah gave the book to Shaphan, he read it. 9Then Shaphan the secretary came to the king, and reported to the king, "Your servants have emptied out the money that was found in the house, and have delivered it into the hand of the workers who have oversight of the house of the LORD." 10Shaphan the secretary informed the king, "The priest Hilkiah has given me a book." Shaphan then read it aloud to the king.

11When the king heard the words of the book of the law, he tore his clothes.

COMMENTARY

Josiah is, first and foremost, a reformer. Just as Jehoash had refurbished the Temple after the six-year usurpation of the throne by Athaliah daughter of Ahab (12:4-16), so also Josiah, who comes to power after the disastrously syncretistic reigns of Manasseh and Amon, orders the Temple to be repaired (vv. 3-7). According to 2 Chr 34:3-7, Josiah began to seek God in the eighth year of his reign, and his reforms began in the twelfth year of his reign, information that interests many scholars because that date more or less coincides with the death of Assyria's highly effective king, Asshurbanipal. Many scholars believe that the chronicler's account may, in fact, reflect historical realities. The narrator of Kings, however, has little interest in the events prior to Josiah's eighteenth year (622 BCE), the year when the so-called book of the law was rediscovered. The reformation effort that grew out of that pivotal event is the narrator's primary focus.

During the renovation of the Temple, the high priest Hilkiah discovers a copy of the "book of the law," which, some scholars speculate, had been hidden away during the anti-deuteronomic counter-reformation of Manasseh (21:2-9). This archaeological "discovery" is reported to Shaphan the secretary, who has come to the Temple to disburse funds for the project. Shaphan reads the book (v. 8) and then informs the king of the find and reads it aloud to him (v. 10). On hearing the content of the document, Josiah is greatly distressed (v. 11; cf. Josh 7:6; Job 1:20; 2 Kgs 5:7; 6:30). His reaction suggests that he recognizes the content not merely as information about the past, but as a prophetic word for the present--not as instruction only, but as prophecy (cf. 17:13).[150]

150. See Burke O. Long, *2 Kings*, FOTL 10 (Grand Rapids: Eerdmans, 1991) 262.

2 Kings 22:12-20, A Prophetic Oracle

NIV

12He gave these orders to Hilkiah the priest, Ahikam son of Shaphan, Acbor son of Micaiah, Shaphan the secretary and Asaiah the king's attendant: 13"Go and inquire of the LORD for me and for the people and for all Judah about what is written in this book that has been found. Great is the LORD's anger that burns against us because our fathers have not obeyed the words of this book; they have not acted in accordance with all that is written there concerning us."

14Hilkiah the priest, Ahikam, Acbor, Shaphan and Asaiah went to speak to the prophetess Huldah, who was the wife of Shallum son of Tikvah, the son of Harhas, keeper of the wardrobe. She lived in Jerusalem, in the Second District.

15She said to them, "This is what the LORD, the God of Israel, says: Tell the man who sent you to me, 16'This is what the LORD says: I am going to bring disaster on this place and its people, according to everything written in the book the king of Judah has read. 17Because they have forsaken me and burned incense to other gods and provoked me to anger by all the idols their hands have made,[a] my anger will burn against this place and will not be quenched.' 18Tell the king of Judah, who sent you to inquire of the LORD, 'This is what the LORD, the God of Israel, says concerning the words you heard: 19Because your heart was responsive and you humbled yourself before the LORD when you heard what I have spoken against this place and its people, that they would become accursed and laid waste, and because you tore your robes and wept in my presence, I have heard you, declares the LORD. 20Therefore I will gather you to your fathers, and you will be buried in peace. Your eyes will not see all the disaster I am going to bring on this place.'"

So they took her answer back to the king.

a *17* Or *by everything they have done*

NRSV

12Then the king commanded the priest Hilkiah, Ahikam son of Shaphan, Achbor son of Micaiah, Shaphan the secretary, and the king's servant Asaiah, saying, 13"Go, inquire of the LORD for me, for the people, and for all Judah, concerning the words of this book that has been found; for great is the wrath of the LORD that is kindled against us, because our ancestors did not obey the words of this book, to do according to all that is written concerning us."

14So the priest Hilkiah, Ahikam, Achbor, Shaphan, and Asaiah went to the prophetess Huldah the wife of Shallum son of Tikvah, son of Harhas, keeper of the wardrobe; she resided in Jerusalem in the Second Quarter, where they consulted her. 15She declared to them, "Thus says the LORD, the God of Israel: Tell the man who sent you to me, 16Thus says the LORD, I will indeed bring disaster on this place and on its inhabitants—all the words of the book that the king of Judah has read. 17Because they have abandoned me and have made offerings to other gods, so that they have provoked me to anger with all the work of their hands, therefore my wrath will be kindled against this place, and it will not be quenched. 18But as to the king of Judah, who sent you to inquire of the LORD, thus shall you say to him, Thus says the LORD, the God of Israel: Regarding the words that you have heard, 19because your heart was penitent, and you humbled yourself before the LORD, when you heard how I spoke against this place, and against its inhabitants, that they should become a desolation and a curse, and because you have torn your clothes and wept before me, I also have heard you, says the LORD. 20Therefore, I will gather you to your ancestors, and you shall be gathered to your grave in peace; your eyes shall not see all the disaster that I will bring on this place." They took the message back to the king.

COMMENTARY

The king dispatches a delegation to seek an oracle for himself and for his people, noting that their ancestors had not obeyed the document's dictates and hence had brought the document's covenant curses upon themselves (v. 13). Like his great-grandfather before him (cf. 19:2), Josiah is portrayed as one who is willing to seek the counsel of the prophets.

Prophetic word comes from a hitherto unnamed prophetess, Huldah (v. 14). She confirms Josiah's fears, pronouncing judgment upon Jerusalem and its inhabitants because they have been disloyal to God and have served idols (vv. 15-17). The anger of the Lord will be kindled against Jerusalem ("this place") and its inhabitants (meaning the citizens of Judah), says Huldah, and it will not be quenched (v. 17). As for the king, because he has heard God (vv. 18, 19), God has also heard him (v. 19). Huldah prophesies that Josiah will "be gathered to [the] grave" with his ancestors and will be buried "in peace" (v. 20). The idioms used imply that Josiah will die a non-violent death (cf. Gen 15:15; 25:8), yet the meaning of that prophecy is clarified immediately: "Your eyes shall not see all the disaster that I will bring upon this place." In comparison to the disaster that will befall Jerusalem, Josiah's death (23:29-30) will be a peaceful one.

2 Kings 23:1-25, Josiah's Reforms

NIV

23 Then the king called together all the elders of Judah and Jerusalem. 2He went up to the temple of the LORD with the men of Judah, the people of Jerusalem, the priests and the prophets—all the people from the least to the greatest. He read in their hearing all the words of the Book of the Covenant, which had been found in the temple of the LORD. 3The king stood by the pillar and renewed the covenant in the presence of the LORD—to follow the LORD and keep his commands, regulations and decrees with all his heart and all his soul, thus confirming the words of the covenant written in this book. Then all the people pledged themselves to the covenant.

4The king ordered Hilkiah the high priest, the priests next in rank and the doorkeepers to remove from the temple of the LORD all the articles made for Baal and Asherah and all the starry hosts. He burned them outside Jerusalem in the fields of the Kidron Valley and took the ashes to Bethel. 5He did away with the pagan priests appointed by the kings of Judah to burn incense on the high places of the towns of Judah and on those around Jerusalem—those who burned incense to Baal, to the sun and moon, to the constellations and to all the starry hosts. 6He took the Asherah pole from the temple of the LORD to the Kidron Valley

NRSV

23 Then the king directed that all the elders of Judah and Jerusalem should be gathered to him. 2The king went up to the house of the LORD, and with him went all the people of Judah, all the inhabitants of Jerusalem, the priests, the prophets, and all the people, both small and great; he read in their hearing all the words of the book of the covenant that had been found in the house of the LORD. 3The king stood by the pillar and made a covenant before the LORD, to follow the LORD, keeping his commandments, his decrees, and his statutes, with all his heart and all his soul, to perform the words of this covenant that were written in this book. All the people joined in the covenant.

4The king commanded the high priest Hilkiah, the priests of the second order, and the guardians of the threshold, to bring out of the temple of the LORD all the vessels made for Baal, for Asherah, and for all the host of heaven; he burned them outside Jerusalem in the fields of the Kidron, and carried their ashes to Bethel. 5He deposed the idolatrous priests whom the kings of Judah had ordained to make offerings in the high places at the cities of Judah and around Jerusalem; those also who made offerings to Baal, to the sun, the moon, the constellations, and all the host of the

NIV

outside Jerusalem and burned it there. He ground
it to powder and scattered the dust over the
graves of the common people. 7He also tore down
the quarters of the male shrine prostitutes, which
were in the temple of the LORD and where women
did weaving for Asherah.

8Josiah brought all the priests from the towns
of Judah and desecrated the high places, from
Geba to Beersheba, where the priests had burned
incense. He broke down the shrines[a] at the
gates—at the entrance to the Gate of Joshua, the
city governor, which is on the left of the city gate.
9Although the priests of the high places did not
serve at the altar of the LORD in Jerusalem, they
ate unleavened bread with their fellow priests.

10He desecrated Topheth, which was in the
Valley of Ben Hinnom, so no one could use it to
sacrifice his son or daughter in[b] the fire to Molech.
11He removed from the entrance to the temple of
the LORD the horses that the kings of Judah had
dedicated to the sun. They were in the court near
the room of an official named Nathan-Melech.
Josiah then burned the chariots dedicated to the
sun.

12He pulled down the altars the kings of Judah
had erected on the roof near the upper room of
Ahaz, and the altars Manasseh had built in the
two courts of the temple of the LORD. He removed
them from there, smashed them to pieces and
threw the rubble into the Kidron Valley. 13The
king also desecrated the high places that were east
of Jerusalem on the south of the Hill of Corruption—the ones Solomon king of Israel had built
for Ashtoreth the vile goddess of the Sidonians,
for Chemosh the vile god of Moab, and for
Molech[c] the detestable god of the people of Ammon. 14Josiah smashed the sacred stones and cut
down the Asherah poles and covered the sites
with human bones.

15Even the altar at Bethel, the high place made
by Jeroboam son of Nebat, who had caused Israel
to sin—even that altar and high place he demolished. He burned the high place and ground it to
powder, and burned the Asherah pole also. 16Then
Josiah looked around, and when he saw the tombs

[a] *8* Or *high places* [b] *10* Or *to make his son or daughter pass through* [c] *13* Hebrew *Milcom*

NRSV

heavens. 6He brought out the image of[a] Asherah
from the house of the LORD, outside Jerusalem, to
the Wadi Kidron, burned it at the Wadi Kidron,
beat it to dust and threw the dust of it upon the
graves of the common people. 7He broke down
the houses of the male temple prostitutes that
were in the house of the LORD, where the women
did weaving for Asherah. 8He brought all the
priests out of the towns of Judah, and defiled the
high places where the priests had made offerings,
from Geba to Beer-sheba; he broke down the high
places of the gates that were at the entrance of
the gate of Joshua the governor of the city, which
were on the left at the gate of the city. 9The
priests of the high places, however, did not come
up to the altar of the LORD in Jerusalem, but ate
unleavened bread among their kindred. 10He defiled Topheth, which is in the valley of Ben-hin-
nom, so that no one would make a son or a
daughter pass through fire as an offering to
Molech. 11He removed the horses that the kings
of Judah had dedicated to the sun, at the entrance
to the house of the LORD, by the chamber of the
eunuch Nathan-melech, which was in the precincts;[b] then he burned the chariots of the sun
with fire. 12The altars on the roof of the upper
chamber of Ahaz, which the kings of Judah had
made, and the altars that Manasseh had made in
the two courts of the house of the LORD, he pulled
down from there and broke in pieces, and threw
the rubble into the Wadi Kidron. 13The king
defiled the high places that were east of Jerusalem, to the south of the Mount of Destruction,
which King Solomon of Israel had built for Astarte
the abomination of the Sidonians, for Chemosh
the abomination of Moab, and for Milcom the
abomination of the Ammonites. 14He broke the
pillars in pieces, cut down the sacred poles,[c] and
covered the sites with human bones.

15Moreover, the altar at Bethel, the high place
erected by Jeroboam son of Nebat, who caused
Israel to sin—he pulled down that altar along with
the high place. He burned the high place, crushing
it to dust; he also burned the sacred pole.[c] 16As
Josiah turned, he saw the tombs there on the

[a] Heb lacks *image of* [b] Meaning of Heb uncertain [c] Heb *Asherim*

NIV

that were there on the hillside, he had the bones removed from them and burned on the altar to defile it, in accordance with the word of the LORD proclaimed by the man of God who foretold these things.

17The king asked, "What is that tombstone I see?"

The men of the city said, "It marks the tomb of the man of God who came from Judah and pronounced against the altar of Bethel the very things you have done to it."

18"Leave it alone," he said. "Don't let anyone disturb his bones." So they spared his bones and those of the prophet who had come from Samaria.

19Just as he had done at Bethel, Josiah removed and defiled all the shrines at the high places that the kings of Israel had built in the towns of Samaria that had provoked the LORD to anger.
20Josiah slaughtered all the priests of those high places on the altars and burned human bones on them. Then he went back to Jerusalem.

21The king gave this order to all the people: "Celebrate the Passover to the LORD your God, as it is written in this Book of the Covenant." 22Not since the days of the judges who led Israel, nor throughout the days of the kings of Israel and the kings of Judah, had any such Passover been observed. 23But in the eighteenth year of King Josiah, this Passover was celebrated to the LORD in Jerusalem.

24Furthermore, Josiah got rid of the mediums and spiritists, the household gods, the idols and all the other detestable things seen in Judah and Jerusalem. This he did to fulfill the requirements of the law written in the book that Hilkiah the priest had discovered in the temple of the LORD.
25Neither before nor after Josiah was there a king like him who turned to the LORD as he did—with all his heart and with all his soul and with all his strength, in accordance with all the Law of Moses.

NRSV

mount; and he sent and took the bones out of the tombs, and burned them on the altar, and defiled it, according to the word of the LORD that the man of God proclaimed,[a] when Jeroboam stood by the altar at the festival; he turned and looked up at the tomb of the man of God who had predicted these things. 17Then he said, "What is that monument that I see?" The people of the city told him, "It is the tomb of the man of God who came from Judah and predicted these things that you have done against the altar at Bethel."
18He said, "Let him rest; let no one move his bones." So they let his bones alone, with the bones of the prophet who came out of Samaria.
19Moreover, Josiah removed all the shrines of the high places that were in the towns of Samaria, which kings of Israel had made, provoking the LORD to anger; he did to them just as he had done at Bethel. 20He slaughtered on the altars all the priests of the high places who were there, and burned human bones on them. Then he returned to Jerusalem.

21The king commanded all the people, "Keep the passover to the LORD your God as prescribed in this book of the covenant." 22No such passover had been kept since the days of the judges who judged Israel, even during all the days of the kings of Israel and of the kings of Judah; 23but in the eighteenth year of King Josiah this passover was kept to the LORD in Jerusalem.

24Moreover Josiah put away the mediums, wizards, teraphim,[b] idols, and all the abominations that were seen in the land of Judah and in Jerusalem, so that he established the words of the law that were written in the book that the priest Hilkiah had found in the house of the LORD. 25Before him there was no king like him, who turned to the LORD with all his heart, with all his soul, and with all his might, according to all the law of Moses; nor did any like him arise after him.

[a] Gk: Heb *proclaimed, who had predicted these things* [b] Or *household gods*

COMMENTARY

Despite Huldah's prophecy of doom for Judah, Josiah gathers all the people for a public reading of the "book of the law," and he leads them in a covenant renewal ceremony (vv. 1-3; cf. Deut

5:1-5; 29:2-28; 31:9-13), just as his ancestor Jehoiada had done (11:12-18). He immediately institutes sweeping reforms in accordance with the stipulations of the law. He removes all the heterodox cultic paraphernalia and structures in Jerusalem and its vicinity (vv. 4, 6-7, 10-12), deposes the idolatrous priests (vv. 5, 8-9) and diviners of various sorts (v. 24), and destroys the local sanctuaries and all things associated with them (vv. 8, 13-15). He extends his reforms beyond Judah into the northern kingdom (vv. 4, 15-20). Indeed, Josiah removes all the heterodox elements that had been introduced by preceding kings of Judah and Israel, undoing the unacceptable innovations of recent kings, like Manasseh and Ahaz (v. 12), and of kings from long ago, like Solomon (v. 13) and Jeroboam son of Nebat (v. 15). The narrator makes it clear that Josiah takes no chances and leaves no stone unturned. He removes from the Temple "all the vessels made for Baal" (v. 4), removes "all the priests" from the Judean towns "from Geba to Beersheba" (v. 8). Indeed, he does not merely remove offensive objects, he burns them, pulverizes them, and thoroughly defiles them so that they could never again be used (vv. 4, 6, 14, 20). He does not merely depose the priests from the local sanctuaries, he even goes beyond deuteronomic laws in banning these priests from sacrificing in Jerusalem (v. 9; cf. Deut 18:6-8). He does not stop his reforms in Judah but extends them into Samaria. Then he commands the celebration of the Passover (v. 21), the festival that is rooted in Israel's experience as a chosen people (Exod 12:1-28), following the prescription in "the book of the covenant" (cf. Deut 16:1-8). The festival had been neglected since the emergence of Israel as a nation (cf. Josh 5:10-12), but Josiah restores it (v. 22). To the narrator, Josiah is the quintessential good king: There has been none like him who has turned to the Lord with heart and soul and might (cf. Deut 6:5) "according to all the law of Moses," and none will arise after him who will be as faithful (v. 25).

2 Kings 23:26-30, The Failure of Josiah to Stem the Tide of Destruction

NIV

[26]Nevertheless, the LORD did not turn away from the heat of his fierce anger, which burned against Judah because of all that Manasseh had done to provoke him to anger. [27]So the LORD said, "I will remove Judah also from my presence as I removed Israel, and I will reject Jerusalem, the city I chose, and this temple, about which I said, 'There shall my Name be.'[a]"

[28]As for the other events of Josiah's reign, and all he did, are they not written in the book of the annals of the kings of Judah?

[29]While Josiah was king, Pharaoh Neco king of Egypt went up to the Euphrates River to help the king of Assyria. King Josiah marched out to meet him in battle, but Neco faced him and killed him at Megiddo. [30]Josiah's servants brought his body in a chariot from Megiddo to Jerusalem and buried him in his own tomb. And the people of the land took Jehoahaz son of Josiah and anointed him and made him king in place of his father.

[a] *27* 1 Kings 8:29

NRSV

26Still the LORD did not turn from the fierceness of his great wrath, by which his anger was kindled against Judah, because of all the provocations with which Manasseh had provoked him. [27]The LORD said, "I will remove Judah also out of my sight, as I have removed Israel; and I will reject this city that I have chosen, Jerusalem, and the house of which I said, My name shall be there."

28Now the rest of the acts of Josiah, and all that he did, are they not written in the Book of the Annals of the Kings of Judah? [29]In his days Pharaoh Neco king of Egypt went up to the king of Assyria to the river Euphrates. King Josiah went to meet him; but when Pharaoh Neco met him at Megiddo, he killed him. [30]His servants carried him dead in a chariot from Megiddo, brought him to Jerusalem, and buried him in his own tomb. The people of the land took Jehoahaz son of Josiah, anointed him, and made him king in place of his father.

COMMENTARY

Following the detailed report of Josiah's thorough reform, and especially the summary assessment of v. 25, the conclusion of the story is anticlimactic. Josiah's salutary efforts could not undo the destructive effects of Manasseh's sins. Despite what Josiah has done, Judah will fall like Israel; even Jerusalem, the place God has chosen as the site for God's Temple, will be destroyed (vv. 26-27). Repentance and reformation could not stem the tide of destruction that sin has set in motion.

Josiah's regnal summary (vv. 28-30) notes his death at the hands of Pharaoh Neco of Egypt. Historians point out that the Egyptian army was on its way to Carchemish to join forces with the Assyrians in a last-ditch effort to deny victory to the emerging power of Babylon. Josiah tried to intercept them at the strategic pass of Esdraelon, where Megiddo was the principal fortress, and there, in 609 BCE, he was killed. The details are, however, of little interest to the narrator, who notes the death only to get to the peaceful burial of the king in Jerusalem. The prophecy of Huldah is fulfilled inasmuch as Josiah is buried with his ancestors in Jerusalem and does not witness the final destruction of the city (22:20).

REFLECTIONS

The reader of Kings may be forgiven for feeling a little betrayed by the narrator. From the very beginning of this long story, the narrator has stressed the need for obedience and repentance. The history told so far has been a history of the failure of the kings to obey God fully and to repent of wrongs committed against God. Over and over again, the narrator emphasizes the need for repentance and reform. Now, near the end of the story, comes, at last, the ideal king according to the standards of deuteronomic law. This is the king who is obedient in every way. He leads his people in a renewal of the covenant. He initiates all-encompassing reforms in accordance with the stipulations of the Torah, and the narrator goes through the long catalog of the reforms. Yet the conclusion of all this is that the efforts of Josiah have come too late. The sins of Manasseh trump the righteousness of Josiah and have consequences for all his people, including those who come after him, but the righteousness of Josiah does not have salvific effects for the people. What an infuriating conclusion that is! Is there a redeeming, liberating word of God in this story? What theological lessons might one draw from this admittedly depressing conclusion?

1. The story points out that the faithful response of one good leader does not gain salvation for others. Josiah is spared because he is pious, penitent, and humble, but Judah is not spared on account of Josiah's faith. Josiah in this story evokes memories of Moses, Joshua, David, and Hezekiah. Yet his personal faithfulness cannot bring deliverance to others. The text thus invites readers to consider their own responses to God, for it implies that deliverance cannot be received without one's own response of faith.

2. It is significant that Josiah carried out his reforms despite the word of doom for Judah. He leads his people in covenant renewal, repentance, and reform. Significantly, however, there is no prayer for deliverance, no call for God to turn back the word of judgment, as one might expect. To be sure, the acts of repentance may be intended to turn back God's wrath. Yet that is not how the narrator has presented his account. Josiah's initial desire to turn back God's wrath (22:13) is met by the prophetic word stating the inevitability of destruction for Judah (22:16-17). Still, Josiah proceeds with the reforms. One gathers, then, that we obey God neither for the sake of rewards nor for the aversion of judgment. Rather, obedience to God is simply what faith brings about. Even in the face of God's judgment and without promise of relief, one is to obey and worship God, for that is what faith calls one to do.

3. The most important lesson of all that the passage offers is a negative one. It teaches that human acts of righteousness, even those as thorough and as sincere as Josiah's, are no guarantee of salvation. The story is a warning against all who dare to believe that salvation can be earned through perfect works of righteousness (cf. Romans 1–3). Here is the story of an admirable reformation, one carried out in strict accordance with "the book," and yet it ends in destruction. Josiah initiated an ancient equivalent of a "back to the Bible" movement, as it were, but the rediscovery of the law does not save. Despite his zealous adherence to "the book," there is no salvation for Judah. Salvation, if it comes at all, will be by the grace of God alone, through faith (Eph 2:8).

2 KINGS 23:31–25:30, THE END

OVERVIEW

With the death of Josiah, the thoroughly faithful reformer, all hopes of recovery appear to be dashed. The narrator now recounts the story of Judah's inevitable demise, culminating in the report of Jerusalem's destruction in 586 BCE. Four kings reigned during this period (609–586 BCE): Jehoahaz (3 months), Jehoiakim (11 years), Jehoiachin (3 months), and Zedekiah (11 years). All are judged by the narrator to have done evil in the sight of the Lord (23:32, 37; 24:9, 19). Jehoahaz is the first Judean king to be deposed by a foreign power and exiled, a foretaste of what is to come. God appears to have abandoned the Davidic dynasty, whose fate now seems to be determined by the winds of international politics. Indeed, all these kings apparently reigned at the will of foreign powers. Jehoiakim was installed as an Egyptian puppet, although he vacillated between Egypt and Babylon; he died as the Babylonians moved to punish him for rebellion. Jehoiachin, who succeeded Jehoiakim, was removed from power by the Babylonians and exiled. Zedekiah was first placed on the throne by the Babylonians, but he was eventually deposed, humiliated, and taken captive by them. The narrator tells the story in a matter-of-fact manner, focusing on the two invasions of Jerusalem in 598/597 BCE and 587/586 BCE. He does not conclude with destruction and exile, however. Rather, a surprising epilogue appears at the very end (25:27-30), with the release of Jehoiachin from prison. While still in Babylon, he is nevertheless set free and treated well, a living testimony to the fact that the house of David has not been extinguished forever.

2 Kings 23:31-35, The Reign of Jehoahaz

NIV

31Jehoahaz was twenty-three years old when he
became king, and he reigned in Jerusalem three
months. His mother's name was Hamutal daughter of Jeremiah; she was from Libnah. 32He did
evil in the eyes of the LORD, just as his fathers
had done. 33Pharaoh Neco put him in chains at
Riblah in the land of Hamath[a] so that he might

[a] 33 Hebrew; Septuagint (see also 2 Chron. 36:3) *Neco at Riblah in Hamath removed him*

NRSV

31Jehoahaz was twenty-three years old when
he began to reign; he reigned three months in
Jerusalem. His mother's name was Hamutal
daughter of Jeremiah of Libnah. 32He did what
was evil in the sight of the LORD, just as his
ancestors had done. 33Pharaoh Neco confined him
at Riblah in the land of Hamath, so that he might
not reign in Jerusalem, and imposed tribute on
the land of one hundred talents of silver and a

NIV

not reign in Jerusalem, and he imposed on Judah a levy of a hundred talents[a] of silver and a talent[b] of gold. 34Pharaoh Neco made Eliakim son of Josiah king in place of his father Josiah and changed Eliakim's name to Jehoiakim. But he took Jehoahaz and carried him off to Egypt, and there he died. 35Jehoiakim paid Pharaoh Neco the silver and gold he demanded. In order to do so, he taxed the land and exacted the silver and gold from the people of the land according to their assessments.

a *33* That is, about 3 3/4 tons (about 3.4 metric tons) b *33* That is, about 75 pounds (about 34 kilograms)

NRSV

talent of gold. 34Pharaoh Neco made Eliakim son of Josiah king in place of his father Josiah, and changed his name to Jehoiakim. But he took Jehoahaz away; he came to Egypt, and died there. 35Jehoiakim gave the silver and the gold to Pharaoh, but he taxed the land in order to meet Pharaoh's demand for money. He exacted the silver and the gold from the people of the land, from all according to their assessment, to give it to Pharaoh Neco.

COMMENTARY

On the death of Josiah in 609 BCE, his son Jehoahaz was placed on the throne by a pro-Babylonian faction in the country, the so-called "people of the land" (v. 30), even though he was not the eldest son of Josiah (compare vv. 31 and 36). He did evil in the sight of God, the narrator reports (v. 32), and reigned only three months before Pharaoh Neco deposed him and deported him first to Riblah in Syria and then to Egypt (vv. 33-34). In his place the Egyptians installed a pro-Egyptian puppet, an elder son of Josiah by the name of Eliakim ("my God will raise up"), who assumed a Yahwistic throne-name, Jehoiakim ("the LORD will raise"). That token of loyalty to the Lord would, however, make little difference in stemming the tide of destruction.

2 Kings 23:36–24:7, The Reign of Jehoiakim

NIV

36Jehoiakim was twenty-five years old when he became king, and he reigned in Jerusalem eleven years. His mother's name was Zebidah daughter of Pedaiah; she was from Rumah. 37And he did evil in the eyes of the LORD, just as his fathers had done.

24 During Jehoiakim's reign, Nebuchadnezzar king of Babylon invaded the land, and Jehoiakim became his vassal for three years. But then he changed his mind and rebelled against Nebuchadnezzar. 2The LORD sent Babylonian,[a] Aramean, Moabite and Ammonite raiders against him. He sent them to destroy Judah, in accordance with the word of the LORD proclaimed by his servants the prophets. 3Surely these things happened to Judah according to the LORD's com-

a *2* Or *Chaldean*

NRSV

36Jehoiakim was twenty-five years old when he began to reign; he reigned eleven years in Jerusalem. His mother's name was Zebidah daughter of Pedaiah of Rumah. 37He did what was evil in the sight of the LORD, just as all his ancestors had done.

24 In his days King Nebuchadnezzar of Babylon came up; Jehoiakim became his servant for three years; then he turned and rebelled against him. 2The LORD sent against him bands of the Chaldeans, bands of the Arameans, bands of the Moabites, and bands of the Ammonites; he sent them against Judah to destroy it, according to the word of the LORD that he spoke by his servants the prophets. 3Surely this came upon Judah at the command of the LORD, to remove them out of his sight, for the sins of Manasseh,

NIV

mand, in order to remove them from his presence because of the sins of Manasseh and all he had done, [4]including the shedding of innocent blood. For he had filled Jerusalem with innocent blood, and the LORD was not willing to forgive.

[5]As for the other events of Jehoiakim's reign, and all he did, are they not written in the book of the annals of the kings of Judah? [6]Jehoiakim rested with his fathers. And Jehoiachin his son succeeded him as king.

[7]The king of Egypt did not march out from his own country again, because the king of Babylon had taken all his territory, from the Wadi of Egypt to the Euphrates River.

NRSV

for all that he had committed, [4]and also for the innocent blood that he had shed; for he filled Jerusalem with innocent blood, and the LORD was not willing to pardon. [5]Now the rest of the deeds of Jehoiakim, and all that he did, are they not written in the Book of the Annals of the Kings of Judah? [6]So Jehoiakim slept with his ancestors; then his son Jehoiachin succeeded him. [7]The king of Egypt did not come again out of his land, for the king of Babylon had taken over all that belonged to the king of Egypt from the Wadi of Egypt to the River Euphrates.

COMMENTARY

Jehoiakim, who reigned eleven years (609–598 BCE), is also judged to have done evil in the sight of God (vv. 36-37). Completely at the mercy of foreign powers, he allied himself now with Egypt and now with Babylon in order to survive. Thus when the Babylonians under Nebuchadnezzar won the Battle of Carchemish (605 BCE), Jehoiakim, who had been placed on the throne by the Egyptians, threw his lot in with the Babylonians, and Judah became a vassal of Babylon for three years (604–602 BCE). When the Babylonians were later (c. 602/601 BCE) defeated, however, Jehoiakim changed sides again. Unfortunately for Jehoiakim and for Judah, Nebuchadnezzar's setback proved to be temporary. The Babylonians quickly recovered, and Nebuchadnezzar sent a coalition army from his vassal states to punish Judah for its disloyalty. To the narrator, however, God was working behind the scenes, as it were (24:2-4). The invading army was, in fact, sent by the Lord to fulfill the promised punishment of Judah for the sins of Manasseh (see 21:1-16; 23:26). Jehoiakim apparently died during the Babylonian invasion, although the details of his death are unclear (v. 5).

2 Kings 24:8-17, The Reign of Jehoiachin

NIV

[8]Jehoiachin was eighteen years old when he became king, and he reigned in Jerusalem three months. His mother's name was Nehushta daughter of Elnathan; she was from Jerusalem. [9]He did evil in the eyes of the LORD, just as his father had done.

[10]At that time the officers of Nebuchadnezzar king of Babylon advanced on Jerusalem and laid siege to it, [11]and Nebuchadnezzar himself came up to the city while his officers were besieging it. [12]Jehoiachin king of Judah, his mother, his atten-

NRSV

8Jehoiachin was eighteen years old when he began to reign; he reigned three months in Jerusalem. His mother's name was Nehushta daughter of Elnathan of Jerusalem. [9]He did what was evil in the sight of the LORD, just as his father had done.

10At that time the servants of King Nebuchadnezzar of Babylon came up to Jerusalem, and the city was besieged. [11]King Nebuchadnezzar of Babylon came to the city, while his servants were besieging it; [12]King Jehoiachin of Judah gave him-

NIV

dants, his nobles and his officials all surrendered to him.

In the eighth year of the reign of the king of Babylon, he took Jehoiachin prisoner. 13As the LORD had declared, Nebuchadnezzar removed all the treasures from the temple of the LORD and from the royal palace, and took away all the gold articles that Solomon king of Israel had made for the temple of the LORD. 14He carried into exile all Jerusalem: all the officers and fighting men, and all the craftsmen and artisans—a total of ten thousand. Only the poorest people of the land were left.

15Nebuchadnezzar took Jehoiachin captive to Babylon. He also took from Jerusalem to Babylon the king's mother, his wives, his officials and the leading men of the land. 16The king of Babylon also deported to Babylon the entire force of seven thousand fighting men, strong and fit for war, and a thousand craftsmen and artisans. 17He made Mattaniah, Jehoiachin's uncle, king in his place and changed his name to Zedekiah.

NRSV

self up to the king of Babylon, himself, his mother, his servants, his officers, and his palace officials. The king of Babylon took him prisoner in the eighth year of his reign.

13He carried off all the treasures of the house of the LORD, and the treasures of the king's house; he cut in pieces all the vessels of gold in the temple of the LORD, which King Solomon of Israel had made, all this as the LORD had foretold. 14He carried away all Jerusalem, all the officials, all the warriors, ten thousand captives, all the artisans and the smiths; no one remained, except the poorest people of the land. 15He carried away Jehoiachin to Babylon; the king's mother, the king's wives, his officials, and the elite of the land, he took into captivity from Jerusalem to Babylon. 16The king of Babylon brought captive to Babylon all the men of valor, seven thousand, the artisans and the smiths, one thousand, all of them strong and fit for war. 17The king of Babylon made Mattaniah, Jehoiachin's uncle, king in his place, and changed his name to Zedekiah.

COMMENTARY

Jehoiakim was succeeded by his son Jehoiachin (v. 6), who is also judged to have done evil in the sight of God (v. 9). The new king reigned only three months (598/597 BCE). When Nebuchadnezzar reached Jerusalem and laid siege to it, Jehoiachin surrendered himself along with his family and palace staff (vv. 10-12). Nebuchadnezzar raided the temple and palace treasuries and stripped the Temple of its gold inlay (v. 13). The elite of society were deported to Babylon, along with the king and the royal household (vv. 12, 14-16). In place of the deposed king, Nebuchadnezzar installed Mattaniah, who was an uncle of Jehoiachin (v. 17) and a younger brother of Jehoahaz (v. 18; cf. 23:31). Once again, it was an outsider who determined the one who would reign over Judah, and the pro-Babylonian puppet was not a legitimate heir to the throne. It is perhaps telling, therefore, that Mattaniah took the throne name Zedekiah ("my Legitimacy is the LORD!").

2 Kings 24:18–25:21, The Reign of Zedekiah

NIV

18Zedekiah was twenty-one years old when he became king, and he reigned in Jerusalem eleven years. His mother's name was Hamutal daughter of Jeremiah; she was from Libnah. 19He did evil in the eyes of the LORD, just as Jehoiakim had done. 20It was because of the LORD's anger that all this happened to Jerusalem and Judah, and in the end he thrust them from his presence.

Now Zedekiah rebelled against the king of Babylon.

25 So in the ninth year of Zedekiah's reign, on the tenth day of the tenth month, Nebuchadnezzar king of Babylon marched against Jerusalem with his whole army. He encamped outside the city and built siege works all around it. 2The city was kept under siege until the eleventh year of King Zedekiah. 3By the ninth day of the ⌞fourth⌟[a] month the famine in the city had become so severe that there was no food for the people to eat. 4Then the city wall was broken through, and the whole army fled at night through the gate between the two walls near the king's garden, though the Babylonians[b] were surrounding the city. They fled toward the Arabah,[c] 5but the Babylonian[d] army pursued the king and overtook him in the plains of Jericho. All his soldiers were separated from him and scattered, 6and he was captured. He was taken to the king of Babylon at Riblah, where sentence was pronounced on him. 7They killed the sons of Zedekiah before his eyes. Then they put out his eyes, bound him with bronze shackles and took him to Babylon.

8On the seventh day of the fifth month, in the nineteenth year of Nebuchadnezzar king of Babylon, Nebuzaradan commander of the imperial guard, an official of the king of Babylon, came to Jerusalem. 9He set fire to the temple of the LORD, the royal palace and all the houses of Jerusalem. Every important building he burned down. 10The whole Babylonian army, under the commander of the imperial guard, broke down the walls around Jerusalem. 11Nebuzaradan the commander of the guard carried into exile the people who remained

[a] *3* See Jer. 52:6. [b] *4* Or *Chaldeans*; also in verses 13, 25 and 26 [c] *4* Or *the Jordan Valley* [d] *5* Or *Chaldean*; also in verses 10 and 24

NRSV

18Zedekiah was twenty-one years old when he began to reign; he reigned eleven years in Jerusalem. His mother's name was Hamutal daughter of Jeremiah of Libnah. 19He did what was evil in the sight of the LORD, just as Jehoiakim had done. 20Indeed, Jerusalem and Judah so angered the LORD that he expelled them from his presence.

Zedekiah rebelled against the king of Babylon.

25 1And in the ninth year of his reign, in the tenth month, on the tenth day of the month, King Nebuchadnezzar of Babylon came with all his army against Jerusalem, and laid siege to it; they built siegeworks against it all around. 2So the city was besieged until the eleventh year of King Zedekiah. 3On the ninth day of the fourth month the famine became so severe in the city that there was no food for the people of the land. 4Then a breach was made in the city wall;[a] the king with all the soldiers fled[b] by night by the way of the gate between the two walls, by the king's garden, though the Chaldeans were all around the city. They went in the direction of the Arabah. 5But the army of the Chaldeans pursued the king, and overtook him in the plains of Jericho; all his army was scattered, deserting him. 6Then they captured the king and brought him up to the king of Babylon at Riblah, who passed sentence on him. 7They slaughtered the sons of Zedekiah before his eyes, then put out the eyes of Zedekiah; they bound him in fetters and took him to Babylon.

8In the fifth month, on the seventh day of the month—which was the nineteenth year of King Nebuchadnezzar, king of Babylon—Nebuzaradan, the captain of the bodyguard, a servant of the king of Babylon, came to Jerusalem. 9He burned the house of the LORD, the king's house, and all the houses of Jerusalem; every great house he burned down. 10All the army of the Chaldeans who were with the captain of the guard broke down the walls around Jerusalem. 11Nebuzaradan the captain of the guard carried into exile the rest of the people who were left in the city and the deserters who had defected to the king of Babylon—all the

[a] Heb lacks *wall* [b] Gk Compare Jer 39.4; 52.7: Heb lacks *the king* and lacks *fled*

NIV

in the city, along with the rest of the populace and those who had gone over to the king of Babylon. 12But the commander left behind some of the poorest people of the land to work the vineyards and fields.

13The Babylonians broke up the bronze pillars, the movable stands and the bronze Sea that were at the temple of the LORD and they carried the bronze to Babylon. 14They also took away the pots, shovels, wick rimmers, dishes and all the bronze articles used in the temple service. 15The commander of the imperial guard took away the censers and sprinkling bowls—all that were made of pure gold or silver.

16The bronze from the two pillars, the Sea and the movable stands, which Solomon had made for the temple of the LORD, was more than could be weighed. 17Each pillar was twenty-seven feet[a] high. The bronze capital on top of one pillar was four and a half feet[b] high and was decorated with a network and pomegranates of bronze all around. The other pillar, with its network, was similar.

18The commander of the guard took as prisoners Seraiah the chief priest, Zephaniah the priest next in rank and the three doorkeepers. 19Of those still in the city, he took the officer in charge of the fighting men and five royal advisers. He also took the secretary who was chief officer in charge of conscripting the people of the land and sixty of his men who were found in the city. 20Nebuzaradan the commander took them all and brought them to the king of Babylon at Riblah. 21There at Riblah, in the land of Hamath, the king had them executed.

So Judah went into captivity, away from her land.

[a] *17* Hebrew *eighteen cubits* (about 8.1 meters) [b] *17* Hebrew *three cubits* (about 1.3 meters)

NRSV

rest of the population. 12But the captain of the guard left some of the poorest people of the land to be vinedressers and tillers of the soil.

13The bronze pillars that were in the house of the LORD, as well as the stands and the bronze sea that were in the house of the LORD, the Chaldeans broke in pieces, and carried the bronze to Babylon. 14They took away the pots, the shovels, the snuffers, the dishes for incense, and all the bronze vessels used in the temple service, 15as well as the firepans and the basins. What was made of gold the captain of the guard took away for the gold, and what was made of silver, for the silver. 16As for the two pillars, the one sea, and the stands, which Solomon had made for the house of the LORD, the bronze of all these vessels was beyond weighing. 17The height of the one pillar was eighteen cubits, and on it was a bronze capital; the height of the capital was three cubits; latticework and pomegranates, all of bronze, were on the capital all around. The second pillar had the same, with the latticework.

18The captain of the guard took the chief priest Seraiah, the second priest Zephaniah, and the three guardians of the threshold; 19from the city he took an officer who had been in command of the soldiers, and five men of the king's council who were found in the city; the secretary who was the commander of the army who mustered the people of the land; and sixty men of the people of the land who were found in the city. 20Nebuzaradan the captain of the guard took them, and brought them to the king of Babylon at Riblah. 21The king of Babylon struck them down and put them to death at Riblah in the land of Hamath. So Judah went into exile out of its land.

COMMENTARY

Zedekiah was on the throne for eleven years (596–587/586 BCE). Like all other kings after Josiah, he is judged to have done evil in the sight of God, thus provoking the wrath of God and leading God to exile the Judeans (24:19-20). It is on the final devastation of Jerusalem and the consequent exile of its citizens that the narrator is focused.

The story of the final days of Judah is told elsewhere in the Bible (2 Chr 36:11-21; Jer 39:1-14; 52:1-34). Zedekiah is portrayed as a tragic figure in Jeremiah's accounts: The king desperately wanted to do what was right, turning to Jeremiah again and again for a word from the Lord (Jer 37:1-10, 16-21; 38:14-28), and yet he was unable to stand up to the officials and other leaders who opposed the prophet. The narrator of Kings, however, does not focus on Zedekiah's personal struggles, only on the tragedy of the fall of Jerusalem. Zedekiah rebelled against Babylon, the narrator reports, probably meaning that Judah was once again counting on the protection of a resurgent Egypt under Pharaoh Psammeticus II, who came to power in 592 BCE. Nebuchadnezzar's response was swift. The Babylonian siege of Jerusalem began in the ninth year of Zedekiah's reign (January 587 BCE) and lasted eighteen months (until July 586 BCE), during which time there was a famine (25:1-3). The king fled when the city walls were breached, but he was captured and brought before Nebuchadnezzar in Riblah (vv. 4-6; see 23:33). Then, his captors murdered his sons in his sight, put out his eyes and brought him in chains to Babylon (v. 7). The Temple in Jerusalem was subsequently burned, its sacred vessels were carried off to Babylon, and the elite citizens of the city were exiled (vv. 8-17).

2 Kings 25:22-26, Gedaliah Becomes Governor

NIV

[22]Nebuchadnezzar king of Babylon appointed Gedaliah son of Ahikam, the son of Shaphan, to be over the people he had left behind in Judah. [23]When all the army officers and their men heard that the king of Babylon had appointed Gedaliah as governor, they came to Gedaliah at Mizpah—Ishmael son of Nethaniah, Johanan son of Kareah, Seraiah son of Tanhumeth the Netophathite, Jaazaniah the son of the Maacathite, and their men. [24]Gedaliah took an oath to reassure them and their men. "Do not be afraid of the Babylonian officials," he said. "Settle down in the land and serve the king of Babylon, and it will go well with you."

[25]In the seventh month, however, Ishmael son of Nethaniah, the son of Elishama, who was of royal blood, came with ten men and assassinated Gedaliah and also the men of Judah and the Babylonians who were with him at Mizpah. [26]At this, all the people from the least to the greatest, together with the army officers, fled to Egypt for fear of the Babylonians.

NRSV

22He appointed Gedaliah son of Ahikam son of Shaphan as governor over the people who remained in the land of Judah, whom King Nebuchadnezzar of Babylon had left. [23]Now when all the captains of the forces and their men heard that the king of Babylon had appointed Gedaliah as governor, they came with their men to Gedaliah at Mizpah, namely, Ishmael son of Nethaniah, Johanan son of Kareah, Seraiah son of Tanhumeth the Netophathite, and Jaazaniah son of the Maacathite. [24]Gedaliah swore to them and their men, saying, "Do not be afraid because of the Chaldean officials; live in the land, serve the king of Babylon, and it shall be well with you." [25]But in the seventh month, Ishmael son of Nethaniah son of Elishama, of the royal family, came with ten men; they struck down Gedaliah so that he died, along with the Judeans and Chaldeans who were with him at Mizpah. [26]Then all the people, high and low,[a] and the captains of the forces set out and went to Egypt; for they were afraid of the Chaldeans.

[a] Or *young and old*

COMMENTARY

To bring about stability in the region, the Babylonians appointed a prominent citizen named Gedaliah as governor of Judah (v. 22; cf. also Jer 40:7–41:8). Gedaliah's grandfather, Shaphan, had been a secretary during the reign of Josiah (22:3) and his father, Ahikam, had been a part of the delegation sent to consult with the prophetess Huldah (22:12) and was a friend to Jeremiah (Jer 26:24). The officers of the remnant army came to Gedaliah at the administrative center in Mizpah (vv. 23-24), probably a site about eight miles north of Jerusalem, only to hear Gedaliah counsel cooperation with the Babylonians (a stance shared by the prophet Jeremiah [Jer 27:1-22; 40:1-6]). One of the officers, a certain Ishmael (a member of the extended royal family), led a rebellious group to assassinate the governor, along with the Judeans and Babylonians who were with him (v. 25). The assassins then fled to Egypt, apparently with other Judean citizens (v. 26). Their intended refuge is ironic, for God had once freed the people from bondage in Egypt. Indeed, only recently Jehoiakim had been captured and taken there by force (23:34). Yet it was to Egypt that "all the people" of Judah fled. The people thus willfully reversed the exodus.

2 Kings 25:27-30, Jehoiachin Is Released from Prison

NIV

27In the thirty-seventh year of the exile of
Jehoiachin king of Judah, in the year Evil-Merodach[a] became king of Babylon, he released Jehoiachin from prison on the twenty-seventh day
of the twelfth month. 28He spoke kindly to him
and gave him a seat of honor higher than those
of the other kings who were with him in Babylon.
29So Jehoiachin put aside his prison clothes and
for the rest of his life ate regularly at the king's
table. 30Day by day the king gave Jehoiachin a
regular allowance as long as he lived.

a 27 Also called *Amel-Marduk*

NRSV

27In the thirty-seventh year of the exile of King
Jehoiachin of Judah, in the twelfth month, on the
twenty-seventh day of the month, King Evil-merodach of Babylon, in the year that he began to
reign, released King Jehoiachin of Judah from
prison; 28he spoke kindly to him, and gave him a
seat above the other seats of the kings who were
with him in Babylon. 29So Jehoiachin put aside
his prison clothes. Every day of his life he dined
regularly in the king's presence. 30For his allowance, a regular allowance was given him by the
king, a portion every day, as long as he lived.

COMMENTARY

In this brief epilogue, the narrator turns to the exiled king, Jehoiachin, in Babylon (cf. Jer 52:31-34). The Davidide ruler is now in the thirty-seventh year of his exile (that is, 561 BCE) and Evil-Merodach has succeeded Nebuchadnezzar as king in Babylon. Jehoiachin is released from prison and treated well by the Babylonians. He is even exalted among the other captive kings, eats regularly at the king's table, and receives an allowance.

REFLECTIONS

The story of Judah's end is, of course, a story of God's unrelenting judgment against disobedience. For the narrator, the events were not accidental, for God was behind it all. Even Nebuchadnezzar's invading force of coalition troops was sent against Judah by none other than the Lord, in fulfillment of the prophetic word of destruction proclaimed because of the sins of Manasseh (24:2-3). The people's persistent and willful rejection of the Lord could not go unpunished, and so God had abandoned them, leaving Jerusalem and the Temple of the Lord to be destroyed and the people to be exiled. As if to underscore the point about the willfulness of the people, the story is told of how, after God had already devastated the city and sent the elite of the country into exile, "all the people, from the young to the old," fled to Egypt because of their misplaced fear (25:26). The story thus justifies God's judgment in the face of recalcitrant human will.

That is by no means the last word in Kings, however. Rather, alongside the story of God's inevitable judgment because of human will to disobey, is a hint that the last word has not yet been spoken. Despite the willful reversal of the exodus that "all the people" of Judah effected (25:26), the final word is an unexpected account of liberation, however tentative; after thirty-seven years in exile, there is the inexplicable good news of freedom for Jehoiachin. Despite the capture and humiliation of Zedekiah, the last king in Jerusalem, the final episode of Kings reports the exaltation of Jehoiachin above other kings in Babylonian captivity. It was the Lord who had sent the Babylonians to punish Judah, the narrator has asserted (23:26; 24:2-3). Though God is not mentioned in the closing words of Kings, one is invited to ponder if the reality of liberation and favor amid exile is not, finally, also a sign of divine grace. The tentative ending suggests an incomplete story that will be continued another time.

Davidic kingship, as one knows it from the book of Kings, has ended. The house of David, however, lives on. In the post-exilic period, Zerubbabel, a scion of Jehoiachin, would be called upon to join with the high priest to rebuild the Temple of Jerusalem (Hag 1:1; 2:2). Zerubbabel, though, would never become king in Jerusalem. Yet, in time, a descendant of Jehoiachin and Zerubbabel would be born (Matt 1:12-16; 2:2, 6), who would go on to play the role of king (cf. Matt 21:6-9; 27:11, 29, 37, 42), although his kingship would not be "of this world" (John 18:36 NIV). In him, God's expectations of a righteous king would finally be met (see Heb 7:1-2). Instead of leading people to sin and finally to destruction, that King would save people from darkness and bring about the forgiveness of sins (Col 1:13-14).

THE FIRST AND SECOND BOOKS OF CHRONICLES

INTRODUCTION, COMMENTARY, AND REFLECTIONS
BY
LESLIE C. ALLEN

THE FIRST AND SECOND BOOKS OF CHRONICLES

INTRODUCTION

The books of Chronicles are the Bible's best-kept secret. Pastors who base their preaching on *The Revised Common Lectionary*[1] will find Chronicles absent from its readings. In Christian tradition these books have suffered by being placed behind 1 and 2 Samuel and 1 and 2 Kings, as if they were some pale shadow instead of an epic work in their own right. In the Hebrew Bible they stand impressively at the end, at the close of the Writings, or else before Psalms and after Malachi. That canonical distance from Samuel–Kings is necessary to symbolize a later time frame and different perspective. Still, the first nine chapters of genealogies are like lions guarding the gates, driving away the fainthearted from the treasures inside. S. De Vries has testified: "I regard Chronicles as one of the richest mines of spirituality in all Scripture."[2] The assessment of an earlier commentator may be added: "Chronicles is one of the most stimulating books in the Bible, courageous and practical—a splendid achievement."[3]

THE DATING OF CHRONICLES

There is a growing tendency to regard Chronicles as distinct from Ezra–Nehemiah, over against the traditional view of the two texts as a composite document. Although more work needs to be done to establish their precise relationship, enough evidence of their

1. *The Revised Common Lectionary* (Nashville: Abingdon, 1992).
2. S. J. De Vries, *1 and 2 Chronicles,* FOTL 11 (Grand Rapids: Eerdmans, 1989) xiv.
3. W. A. Elmslie, *The First and Second Books of Chronicles,* IB, 12 vols. (New York: Abingdon, 1954) 3:341.

basic independence has emerged.[4] This discovery has released the books of Chronicles from the burden of interpretation dictated by Ezra–Nehemiah, which as a post-exilic document dealing with post-exilic events has a plainer agenda than Chronicles.

Chronicles appears to have been written after the bulk of Ezra–Nehemiah. It cites the latter, just as it does other written texts. Ezra 1:1-3 is quoted in 2 Chr 36:22-23, and Neh 11:3-19 in 1 Chr 9:2-17, while Ezra 9–10 is reflected in 2 Chr 24:26. Chronicles also depends on Zechariah 1–8, as it does on pre-exilic prophetic texts. Zechariah 1:2-4 is presupposed in 2 Chr 30:6-7, Zech 4:10 in 2 Chr 16:9, and Zech 8:10 in 2 Chr 15:5-6. Since Zechariah 1–8 was written in the early post-exilic period, Chronicles must have been written sometime later. Moreover, it is significant that Chronicles used the Pentateuch in its final form.[5]

Archaeologists have found that the Persian period of Judean history falls into two parts. The second part, from about 450 to 332 BCE, is marked by an increase in prosperity.[6] David's appeal for contributions to the Temple and prayer of praise for a generous response in 1 Chronicles 29 and the narrative of the people's provision of ample support for the temple personnel in 2 Chronicles 31 are significant in this respect. Both chapters are transparently addressed to the constituency for whom the book was intended. The difficulty to be surmounted was evidently not an inability to give but an unwillingness to do so. The motif of willingness pervades the account in 1 Chronicles 29, and it is accompanied by references to the wealthy patriarchs as models. Such references fit the relative affluence of the second part of the Persian period.

A late Persian period dating is also supported by the levitical claims made in the course of Chronicles. There seems to have been considerable development in the standing of subordinate personnel of the post-exilic Temple. At an early stage the singing musicians were not regarded as Levites (Ezra 2:41 = Neh 7:44). By Nehemiah's time they were considered as such and were composed of two groups, the descendants of Asaph and the descendants of Jeduthun (Neh 11:3-19). At a later period the choir of Heman was added; eventually it became more prominent than that of Asaph, while the choir of Jeduthun was displaced by that of Ethan.[7] The evidence of Chronicles spans both stages of the third period, the former in 1 Chr 16:37-42; 2 Chr 5:12; 29:13-14; 35:15, and the latter in 1 Chr 6:31-48; 15:16-21, while the citation of Neh 11:3-19 in 1 Chronicles 9 naturally echoes the second period. Similarly, the gatekeepers were not yet Levites at the time of Ezra 2:42 (= Neh 7:45), nor had they yet graduated to this position by Neh 11:19, cited

4. See T. C. Eskenazi, *In an Age of Prose: A Literary Approach to Ezra–Nehemiah,* SBLMS 36 (Atlanta: Scholars Press, 1988) 14-36; S. Japhet, *I & II Chronicles,* OTL (Louisville: Westminster/John Knox, 1993) 3-5.

5. See W. M. Schniedewind, *The Word of God in Transition: From Prophet to Exegete in the Second Temple Period,* JSOTSup 197 (Sheffield: Sheffield Academic, 1995) 133n. 11, 194n. 16.

6. See C. L. Myers and E. M. Myers, *Zechariah 9–14,* AB 25C (Garden City, N.Y.: Doubleday, 1993) 22-26.

7. See H. Gese, "Zur Geschichte der Kultsänger am zweiten Tempel," *Abraham unser Vater: Juden und Christen im Gespräch über die Bibel,* ed. O. Betz et al. (Leiden: Brill, 1963) 222-34 (= *Vom Sinai zum Zion. Alttestamentliche Beiträge zur biblischen Theologie,* BEvT 64 [Munich: Chr. Kaiser, 1974] 147-58); H. G. M. Williamson, "The Origins of the Twenty-four Priestly Courses: A Study of 1 Chronicles xxiii-xxvii," in *Studies in the Historical Books of the Old Testament,* ed. J. A. Emerton, VTSup 30 (Leiden: Brill, 1979) 251-68, esp. 263.

at 1 Chr 9:17. However, a later source employed in 1 Chr 9:18 firmly identifies them as such.

The same impression of a dating late in the Persian period is given by the post-exilic continuation of the Davidic genealogy in 1 Chronicles 3. The exact number of generations involved cannot be ascertained, but the genealogy extends into the fourth century BCE and was presumably meant to reflect the time of Chronicles. In the light of this and the earlier evidence, the first half of the fourth century BCE seems to be the period when it was written. No Hellenistic features are present to warrant a later date.

THE SETTING AND PURPOSE OF CHRONICLES

A dominant feature of Chronicles is an emphasis on exile and restoration, both as a historical fact and as a metaphor that providentially relates the overall success or failure of the community to its spiritual relationship to the Lord. The chronicler—the homogeneity of most of the work suggests that an individual rather than a group was responsible, and one may presume that the author was male—envisioned in 2 Chronicles 28–36 not one exile but a series of exiles toward the end of the pre-exilic period. He conceived of not only one literal and national restoration but also a royal one in the case of Manasseh and a metaphorical one under Hezekiah, which repeated the restoration represented by David's reign after the "exilic" fate of Saul and Israel.[8]

The novelty of the chronicler lies in his application of the theme and not in his creation of it. A later author (Daniel 9) would claim that the exile was to last 490 years, not seventy, and was a negative condition still experienced by the so-called post-exilic community.[9] This notion of exile as a metaphor for a continuing experience is also found in earlier post-exilic literature. Psalm 126 celebrates the Lord's restoration of Zion's fortunes in the return from exile. Yet all was not well. The worshiping community prayed afresh, "Restore our fortunes." They were still suffering a virtual exile, though they lived in the land again. The same point is made in the first half of Psalm 85, where the Lord's past restoration of Jacob's fortunes is the basis for hope of a renewed restoration (Ps 85:1, 4). The cessation of divine anger indicated by the return from literal exile needed to be repeated, since the community was still suffering from that anger (Ps 85:3, 4-5). This superimposing of an exilic condition as a way to understand the post-exilic situation also occurs in Zech 1:2-6, which as has been observed is reflected in 2 Chr 30:6-7. The Lord's anger with the pre-exilic people, which resulted in their exile, is used as a symbol of warning for the post-exilic community.

The prayers in Ezra 9 and Nehemiah 9 demonstrate the ways in which exile as a metaphor can be traced to the present. In the former case it is lamented that "from the

8. See R. Mosis, *Untersuchungen zur Theologie des chronisten Geschichtswerks,* Freiburger theologische Studien 92 (Freiburg: Herder, 1973) 31-43; P. R. Ackroyd, "The Chronicler as Exegete," *JSOT* 2 (1977) 2-32, esp. 3-9 (= *The Chronicler in His Age,* JSOTSup 101 [Sheffield: JSOT, 1991] 314-18).

9. See M. A. Knibb, "The Exile in the Literature of the Intertestamental Period," *HeyJ* 17 (1976) 253-72.

days of our ancestors to this day we have been deep in guilt, and for our iniquities we, our kings, and our priests have been handed over to the kings of the lands, to the sword, to captivity, to plundering, and to utter shame, as is now the case" (Ezra 9:7 NRSV). Divine alleviation of this condition is described in grudging terms (Ezra 9:8-9). Similarly, Nehemiah 9 speaks of the hardships endured by the community "since the time of the kings of Assyria until today" and of the "great distress" caused by foreign domination (Neh 9:32, 37). Despite domicile in the land, the people understood themselves to be "in exile."

In this connection the reader should consider the partial spiritualization of terms relating to the land in the psalms. Although the process began in the pre-exilic period, its continuing use in the post-exilic age is significant. The psalms use the levitical phrase "the LORD is my portion"—the Levites had received no portion of tribal land—to express the faith of the laity (Pss 16:5; 73:26; 142:6; cf. Lam 3:24). They also freely employ terms of inheriting the land as metaphors of blessing in store for the faithful (Pss 16:6; 25:13; 37 [5 times]; 44:4; 69:36-37).[10] The concept of a spiritual restoration to the land is reinforced by this use of language.

Chronicles acknowledges the problematic condition of metaphorical exile. The chronicler utilized this well-established imagery of exile and restoration, and he deliberately echoed it thoughout his work. He used three religious texts that deal with the literal exile and pointed forward to restoration, reapplying them to people in other conditions. These texts became guidelines for his constituency to follow, commending to them the cures advocated in the texts.

The first text is Lev 26:34-45, which reviews Israel's sin, exile, and return to the land. Leviticus 26:34 is given a structurally significant place in 2 Chr 36:21 to define the duration of the literal exile as limited to a set period of sabbath rest. According to Jeremiah 29, this exile was to last seventy years. There never was a fatalistic decree that exile should continue for centuries. The metaphorical exile was the people's fault, not the Lord's. To describe the spiritual conditions for such exile the chronicler drew upon the expression מעל מעל (*mā'al ma'al*), "practice unfaithfulness" (Lev 26:40; "committed treachery," NRSV). He used either the phrase or its separate elements of verb and noun as a key term. In the light of Lev 26:15, 43, this vocabulary is used in the general sense of breaking the covenant, though in a few contexts it gains a cultic nuance. He employed the term to define the cause of literal exile in 1 Chr 5:25 ("were unfaithful," NIV); 9:1; and 2 Chr 36:14. This same vocabulary appears elsewhere in his regular diagnosis for metaphorical exile, notably in the evaluation of the reigns of Saul and Ahaz (1 Chr 10:13; 2 Chr 29:6). The Leviticus passage also supplies one of the characteristic terms used by the chronicler when he refers to restoration, "to be humbled" (נכנע *nikna'* , in the niphal; Lev 26:41), e.g., in 2 Chr 7:14 , a text that puts in a nutshell the chronicler's remedy for spiritual exile.

10. See H. D. Preuss, *Old Testament Theology I,* trans. L. G. Perdue (Louisville: Westminster/John Knox, 1995) 123.

The second text imbued with religious authority to which the chronicler made frequent reference is Jer 29:10-19. It, too, discusses literal exile and restoration, and so might be used as a basis for comparison for their metaphorical counterparts. The description of the desolation of the land in Jer 29:18 is applied to the outworking of divine wrath inherited by Hezekiah in 2 Chr 29:8. The prophecy of seventy years of exile is used positively as a limit of the Lord's judgment of exile in 2 Chr 36:21-22. However, the passage was primarily used to define how God's people might be spiritually restored: "when you call upon me and come and pray to me, I will hear you . . . If you seek me with all your heart, I will let you find me, says the LORD, and I will restore your fortunes" (Jer 29:12-14 NRSV). The divine promise became the substance of the chronicler's own message. It is the basis of the epigrammatic 2 Chr 7:14 and of the spiritual principle, "If you seek [the Lord], he will be found by you" in 1 Chr 28:9 and 2 Chr 15:2. Most notably the Jeremian text supplies the chronicler's devotional key word דרשׁ (*dāraš*, "seek"), which is extensively used to characterize repentant return to the Lord and normative worship and way of life. The chronicler uses the parallel verb בקשׁ (*biqqēš*, "seek"), which occurs in Jer 29:13, less often.

The third text about exile and return from which the chronicler drew heavily is Ezekiel 18, which grounds an appeal to the exiles for repentance in a sequence of good and bad generations, and also generations who changed in midcourse from bad to good and from good to bad.[11] The text provides structural models for the royal narratives of both the divided kingdom in 2 Chronicles 10–28 and the reunited kingdom in chaps. 29–36. Moreover, it uses the idiom *mā ʿal maʿal*, "practice unfaithfulness" [Lev 26:40; Ezek 18:24]), in the general sense of breaking the Torah. The chronicler's teaching of immediate retribution is generally worked out at the level of individual kings, but who symbolize separate generations. We have learned to exegete Ezekiel 18 in terms of generations, and we must also do so in the case of Chronicles. The chronicler regarded members of each generation as controlling their own destiny, free to start again with or against the Lord.

A clue to the importance of each generation in Chronicles is the recurring phrase "the God of their/your/our fathers" (NIV). The NRSV, true to its inclusive concern, renders "the God of . . . ancestors," but this is rarely the meaning. The singular counterpart "the God of your/his father" in 1 Chr 28:9; 2 Chr 17:4 is significant. Each generation had the responsibility of appropriating the faith handed down by its immediate predecessors. The chronicler was calling on his own generation to pursue the path that led to spiritual restoration. It was this policy that, by God's grace, made possible a break with the oppressive past that otherwise haunted each post-exilic generation.

11. See R. B. Dillard, "Reward and Punishment in Chronicles: The Theology of Immediate Retribution," *WTJ* 46 (1984) 164-72, esp. 171.

THE DAVIDIC ERA

The literary backbone of Chronicles is the account of the joint reigns of David and Solomon, to which nearly half the work is devoted. Correspondingly their reigns constitute the theological mainstay of the book. The chronicler used the verb "choose" (בחר *bāḥar*) to indicate special agents or agencies in the Lord's long-term purposes. Of the seven entities so described, five are closely associated with these two reigns: David (2 Chr 6:6), Solomon (1 Chr 28:10), the Temple (2 Chr 7:12, 16; 33:7), Jerusalem (2 Chr 6:6, 34, 38; 12:13), and the tribe of Judah in its royal role (1 Chr 28:4). The two other entities, Israel (1 Chr 16:13) and the Levites (1 Chr 15:2; 2 Chr 29:11), are swept into this new work.

Another term for theological destiny used by the chronicler is "forever" (עד עולם *'ad 'ôlām*) or variations involving this word. Apart from two references to God, it is employed twenty-seven times in Chronicles, of which sixteen occurrences relate either to the Davidic dynasty (7 times) or to the Temple (9 times). Again the joint reigns supply the arena for the majority of cases. As for the other instances, three entities were radically affected by the two reigns, the land (3 times), Israel (twice), and the covenant love (חסד *ḥesed*, "[steadfast] love") extended by the Lord to Israel (6 times).

The way these weighty terms are used discloses the chronicler's perception of a Davidic era launched under David and Solomon and continuing until the chronicler's own time. It superseded the Mosaic dispensation and covenant, to which Israel failed to adhere. Hence Chronicles plays down, though without denying, the exodus traditions. They are given a swan song in 1 Chr 17:21-22, to be replaced, in effect, by new traditions. The concept of a new dispensation was probably suggested to the chronicler by Psalm 78, especially vv. 67-72; the chronicler alludes to Ps 78:68, 70 in 1 Chr 28:4. There was continuity with the old dispensation; the religious and general duties of the Mosaic Torah were still obligatory for Israel. Yet the Jerusalem Temple now replaced the tabernacle of the Torah, and the Levites received a new role. The chronicler indulged in a host of typological parallels to demonstrate the divine authority of the new sanctuary, over against the representations of the written Torah. And for those who broke the Torah and repented, there was a way back to the Lord.

There is also a concern to establish the permanent nature of the Davidic dynasty. It was guaranteed, the chronicler claimed, by Solomon's construction of the Temple and general obedience to the Torah (1 Chr 28:6-7). Thereby Israel's relationship to the Lord was made permanent, as especially 2 Chr 9:8 affirms. The hymnic snatch "for [the Lord's] [steadfast] love endures forever" ties Israel's covenant to the Davidic covenant (1 Chr 16:34, 41; 2 Chr 5:13; 7:3, 6; 20:21). The permanent gift of the land to the patriarchs was reinforced by the Davidic covenant (1 Chr 16:17; 2 Chr 20:7).

There is a delicate balance between the once-for-all theological privilege established under David and Solomon and the onus of covenant obedience laid on kings and commoners thereafter. These twin phenomena find common ground in 1 Chronicles 28: In v. 8 the latter responsibility is added to a declaration of the God-given privilege. Israel's future oscillates in Chronicles between objective certainty in principle (2 Chr 9:8) and subjective uncertainty in particular (2 Chr 7:19-20).

In the interests of a moral and spiritual challenge the royal narratives after David's and Solomon's reigns focus on tracing the obedience or disobedience of each king to the guidelines laid down in those reigns. Yet there are also reminders of the permanent nature of Davidic kingship (2 Chr 13:5; 21:7), reaffirming the earlier narratives. Similarly, in 1 Chronicles 2–9 the extension of the Davidic genealogy into the post-exilic period at 1 Chronicles 3 strikes a unique note of permanence. The Davidic covenant's divinely pledged permanence—and hence certainty of restoration—was also the sign of Israel's permanence. Pastoral needs loom large in the emphasis on Israel's responsibility after 2 Chronicles 9. The lack of any royal reaffirmation near or at the end of the book also reflects the historical fact of the Davidic dynasty's eclipse, an eclipse that stretched far into the post-exilic period. One suspects that the dynasty's restoration was a distant item on the chronicler's eschatological calendar, doubtless as a negative response to political and perhaps proto-apocalyptic pressures.[12] It would be restored in God's good time. Moreover, that restoration was separate from the blessings each post-exilic generation had the potential to inherit, even within the context of Persian hegemony (see 2 Chr 12:7-8).

The Temple provided a pivot between theological stability and spiritual alternatives in the chronicler's thought. Its choirs brought a constant reminder that the Lord's "[steadfast] love endures forever." The Temple was the divinely instituted setting for the normative obligations of worship and maintenance of its fabric and personnel. In the course of the royal narratives, the chronicler covered each of the Torah-based festivals in turn, the Feast of Tabernacles in 2 Chronicles 7, the Feast of Weeks in 2 Chronicles 15, and the double feast of Passover and Unleavened Bread in 2 Chronicles 30 and 35.[13] Both in these chapters and in 1 Chronicles 15–16, he affirmed the joy of celebrating regular worship. Yet the Temple was also the center of an emergency system that offered restoration to the repentant. Redemptive grace could prevail over the breaking of the Torah (see esp. 2 Chr 7:3-16; 30:18-20; 32:25-26).

AN INCLUSIVE ISRAEL

A constant issue in the teaching of Chronicles is the inclusiveness of the people of God. In this respect the work stands at a remarkable distance from Ezra and Nehemiah, who at an earlier period advocated a separatist community made up of Judeans who had returned from exile. Doubtless the chronicler judged that the time was ripe for a less rigorous policy, now that the community was more established. His insistence on the spiritual potential of a wider religious community made up of "all Israel" is integrated with his presentation

12. See H. H. Rowley's refusal to see eschatological significance in World War II in *The Relevance of Apocalyptic* (London: Lutterworth, 1944) 7-8. Very little is known of Judah's history in this period. For the unsettled political history of the later Persian period in the West, see E. Stern, *The Cambridge History of Judaism,* ed. W. D. Davies and L. Finkelstein (Cambridge: Cambridge University Press, 1984) 1:73-77.

13. See H. Cancik, "Des jüdische Fest," *TQ* 105 (1970) 335-48, esp. 338-39.

of the united kingdom of David and Solomon, and that insistence is reaffirmed under the reunited kingdom of Hezekiah. In the genealogical prologue, it is undergirded by appeals to the traditions of the twelve tribes in the wilderness period, attested by the Torah, and affirmed in the settlement of the promised land.

In this respect the chronicler steered a middle course between separatist and assimilationist parties in Jerusalem.[14] He rigorously maintained the unique role of the Jerusalem Temple in Israel's worship. The well-established traditions of a united Israel laid on Judah the obligation to attempt to win back Israelites still in the north to allegiance to the God of the Temple. Hezekiah is presented as a model for this obligation (2 Chronicles 30).

THE LEVITES

The chronicler's attitude toward the Levites breaks the pattern of his overall teaching. Certainly it is stitched neatly into the Davidic organization of the Temple, and their work is thus invested with the highest religious authority. Yet his teaching would have been coherent, theologically and spiritually, without his pervasive attention to the Levites. The chronicler acted as advocate for the Levites, regarding them as a disadvantaged group. His enthusiasm, which extends to a call for affirmative action, opens for us an otherwise closed window to the music and song provided by the singing Levites and the security system operated by the gatekeeping Levites. The chronicler urges that they be given a greater role in sacrificial worship and attaches names and pedigrees to the faceless members of these lower ranks of the temple staff.

The chronicler's advocacy of the Levites led to the redactional introduction of material emphasizing the role of the priesthood. A pro-priestly reviser was active mainly in 1 Chronicles 23–27, but also in a few passages elsewhere; he may have lived a generation later than the chronicler.[15] The redactor's aim was not to silence his predecessor's advocacy but to supplement it and so redress the balance somewhat, making Chronicles more comprehensive in its outlook.

THE FORM OF CHRONICLES

The Outline below will show that the work falls into four literary blocks. The longest and most important block deals with the reigns of David and Solomon, which established under God the institutions of the dynasty and the Temple. It is followed by accounts of the divided kingdom of Judah and of the reunited kingdom. These latter two blocks reaffirm the spiritual guidelines laid down in the main one, sometimes positively but more often negatively. The introduction to Chronicles provides a block of genealogies, which presents

14. H. G. M. Williamson, *Israel in the Books of Chronicles* (Cambridge: Cambridge University Press, 1977) 139.

15. See H. G. M. Williamson, "The Origins of the Twenty-four Priestly Courses: A Study of 1 Chronicles xxiii-xxvii," in *Studies in the Historical Books of the Old Testament,* ed. J. A. Emerton, VTSup 30 (Leiden: Brill, 1979) 251-68, esp. 266; cf. in principle A. C. Welch, *The Work of the Chronicler: Its Purpose and Date* (London: British Academy, 1939) 71-73, 85-96.

the themes of Israel's election, its inclusive nature as traditionally made up of twelve tribes, and its territorial heritage. These themes are set against a gradually emerging background of the people's unfaithfulness, exile, and restoration, which the royal narratives will repeat.

The chronicler had only a few tunes in his literary repertoire. He played them over and over again in the interests of spiritual challenge and encouragement, mainly with the present and immediate future in mind, but also on a long-term scale. It has been observed that Chronicles could "have been utilised section by section as a series of connected homilies."[16] I have traced in an article, and reproduced in this commentary, the quasi-homiletic stylization of the subdivisions in the four literary blocks of Chronicles.[17] The chronicler used standard rhetorical devices to present his material in assimilable portions in order to stimulate spiritual commitment to theological principles.

The question of the relation of Chronicles to "real" history is often raised. A thorough answer would be complex. Sometimes the chronicler evidently reproduced ancient, authentic documents, for instance in 1 Chr 27:25-31; sometimes he wrote up a grand tale out of a little incident, for example in 2 Chr 20:1-30; and once he stood an earlier narrative on its head to adapt it to his own perspective, in 2 Chr 20:35-37. In general modern readers need to be warned against false expectations. The chronicler was writing to help his own generation. Hence readers must focus on his situation and message—and not only on earlier history—if they are to do him justice. His royal narratives in 2 Chronicles 10–36 are a series of spiritual parables, and the speeches put into the mouths of his characters are vehicles by means of which he interprets these stories. The earlier narratives of Samuel–Kings, which were his sources, are put through a hermeneutical filter to convey the truths his constituency needed to learn. The particular genre of historiography exhibited in Chronicles must be considered in the light of its homiletic function.

THE TEXT OF CHRONICLES

Discussion of the Masoretic Text (MT) has been limited to explaining cases of divergence from it by the NRSV and the NIV, which are both alert to textual problems, and between these versions and also to other instances judged to be of exegetical importance. For further discussion, readers will often be directed to my earlier work, *The Greek Chronicles: The Relation of the Septuagint of I and II Chronicles to the Massoretic Text.*[18] It may be mentioned here that for convenience the English versification is followed throughout.

An important issue is what type of text of Samuel–Kings was available to the chronicler. For Kings, he had the type preserved in the MT.[19] In the case of Samuel, his text was close

16. P. R. Ackroyd, *The Age of the Chronicler* (Aukland: Colloquium, 1970) 45 (= *The Chronicler in His Age,* JSOTSup 101 [Sheffield: JSOT, 1991] 64).

17. L. C. Allen, "Kerygmatic Units in 1 and 2 Chronicles," *JSOT* 41 (1988) 21-36.

18. L. C. Allen, *The Greek Chronicles: The Relation of the Septuagint of I and II Chronicles to the Massoretic Text,* Part 1: *The Translator's Craft;* Part 2: *Textual Criticism,* VTSup 25, 27 (Leiden: Brill, 1974).

19. See S. L. McKenzie, *The Chronicler's Use of the Deuteronomistic History,* HSM 33 (Atlanta: Scholars Press, 1985) 83-84, 119-58.

to that of the first-century BCE Qumran manuscript 4QSam[a].[20] It is crucial to trace this textual relationship because a number of idiosyncratic features previously credited to the chronicler are now seen to be already part of the textual tradition of Samuel that he used.

EXEGETING AND APPLYING CHRONICLES

Chronicles is inspirational literature, and so an exegetical and hermeneutical commentary has the duty to convey with warmth the inspirational message. The chronicler had a pastor's heart and a teacher's mind, and his concern for his constituency surfaces throughout. Application depends on the particular circumstances of the modern pastor. In the Reflections, the aim will be to make general applications, especially by building a bridge to the NT and showing how the spiritual concerns of the chronicler reappear in its Christian contexts. There will also be an endeavor to note and discuss as necessary our own distance, real or perceived, from the chronicler.

In the Commentary sections the goal will be to enter into the chronicler's world by discerning his particular agenda in each passage, and to appreciate his passion. The focus will be on Chronicles itself, rather than on looking through it or behind it to historical details. The chronicler does invite us to take an interest in his literary sources (see, e.g., 2 Chr 13:22), and so some attention will be paid to this aspect. But the main endeavor will be to examine Chronicles as a work in its own right and to listen to the spiritual message it wants to bring. As we readers first overhear it and then make an effort to hear it in the context of our particular situations, we shall find that message to be both biblical and contemporary, both inspired and inspiring.[21]

20. See ibid., 33-81.

21. Portions of the treatment of the books of Chronicles in the following commentary are similar to the author's comments in Leslie C. Allen, *1, 2 Chronicles,* Communicator's Commentary 10 (Waco, Tex.: Word, 1987). Thanks ae due to my colleague Francis I. Andersen for giving me a copy of the unpublished "A Key-Word-in-Context Concordance to Chronicles," edited by himself and A. D. Forbes, which proved of inestimable help; to the staff of the word processing office of Fuller Seminary for their labors on my behalf; and to my research assistant Curtis McNeil for his careful editing of the manuscript.

BIBLIOGRAPHY

Ackroyd, P. R. *I & II Chronicles, Ezra, Nehemiah.* Torch Bible. London: SCM, 1973. A short, judicious commentary for general readers.

Braun, R. L. *1 Chronicles.* WBC 14. Waco, Tex.: Word, 1986. A technical and exegetical commentary reflecting informed scholarship.

De Vries, S. J. *1 and 2 Chronicles.* FOTL 11. Grand Rapids: Eerdmans, 1989. A form-critical analysis; an excellent contribution to this series, which lays an invaluable foundation for exegesis.

Dillard, R. B. *2 Chronicles.* WBC 15. Waco, Tex.: Word, 1987. A companion volume to Braun's book; equally helpful.

Japhet, S. *I & II Chronicles.* OTL. Louisville: Westminster/John Knox, 1993. The definitive commentary on Chronicles; embodies the author's comprehensive study, *The Ideology of the Book of Chronicles and Its Place in Biblical Thought.* Translated by A. Barber. BEATAJ 9. Frankfurt am Main: Peter Lang, 1989.

McConville, J. G. *I & II Chronicles.* Daily Study Bible. Philadelphia: Westminster, 1984. A good devotional commentary for the general reader.

Selman, M. J. *1 Chronicles; 2 Chronicles.* TOTC. Downers Grove: Inter-Varsity, 1994. A thorough commentary written from a conservative perspective and concerned to relate Chronicles to history.

Williamson, H. G. M. *1 and 2 Chronicles.* NCB. Grand Rapids: Eerdmans, 1982. A masterly, detailed commentary that incorporates his insightful *Israel in the Books of Chronicles.* Cambridge: Cambridge University Press, 1977.

OUTLINE OF FIRST AND SECOND CHRONICLES

I. 1 Chronicles 1:1–9:34, Israel: Elect and Inclusive, Unfaithful but Restored

A. 1:1–2:2, Israel's Election

B. 2:3–9:1, A Panorama of Pre-exilic Israel

- 2:3–4:23, The Royal Tribe of Judah
- 4:24–5:26, Simeon and the Transjordanian Tribes
- 6:1-81, The Religious Tribe of Levi
- 7:1-40, The Other Northern Tribes
- 8:1–9:1, The Tribe of Benjamin

C. 9:2-34, Israel's Restoration in Principle

II. 1 Chronicles 9:35–2 Chronicles 9:31, The Reigns of David and Solomon

A. 9:35–29:30, The Reign of David

- 9:35–12:40, A Decisive Change of King
  - 9:35–10:14, Saul's Infidelity and Death
  - 11:1–12:40, David Crowned by All Israel
- 13:1–16:43, Giving God Pride of Place
  - 13:1-14, David Tries to Move the Ark
  - 14:1-17, God Honors David's Intentions
  - 15:1–16:3, David Moves the Ark Properly
  - 16:4-43, Praise and Worship Inaugurated
- 17:1–20:8, Thy Kingdom Come!
  - 17:1-27, God's Program for David and Solomon
  - 18:1–20:8, A Place for God's People
- 21:1–22:19, Temple Site and Builder Announced
  - 21:1–22:1, Discovery of the Site by Grace
  - 22:2-19, Solomon's Mandate to Build
- 23:1–29:30, Preparing Personnel for the Temple
  - 23:1-32, Organization and Duties of the Levites
  - 24:1-31, The Divisions of Priests and Levites
  - 25:1-31, Temple Musicians

26:1-32, Temple Security and Secular Assignments
27:1-34, Lay Leaders
28:1-21, Solomon's Renewed Mandate to Build the Temple
29:1-30, David's Public Appeal and Prayer of Praise

B. 1:1–9:31, The Reign of Solomon
1:1-17, Seeking God and Receiving Blessing
2:1-18, Preparing for the Temple
3:1–5:1, Building the Temple
5:2–7:22, The Temple: Place of Worship and Means of Grace
8:1-16, Finding Blessing and Finishing the Temple
8:17–9:31, Solomon's Significant Prosperity

III. 2 Chronicles 10:1–28:27, The Divided Kingdom

A. 10:1–12:16, Rehoboam's Checkered Reign
10:1-19, The King Who Would Not Listen
11:1-23, Strength from Listening
12:1-16, Failure and a Fresh Start

B. 13:1–16:14, Trusting the True God in Times of Crisis
13:1–14:1*a,* Abijah's Loyal Trust Vindicated
14:1*b*–15:19, Asa's Valid Trust Vindicated
16:1-14, Asa's False Trust Punished

C. 17:1–21:1*a,* Jehoshaphat Chooses and Loses the Lord's Presence
17:1-19, Finding God in Obedience and Blessing
18:1–19:3, Collusion with a Northern King
19:4-11, Finding God in Social Reform
20:1-30, Finding God in Trust and Deliverance
20:31–21:1*a,* Collusion with Another Northern King

D. 21:1*b*–23:21, The Threat to the Dynasty Averted
21:1*b*–22:9, The Apostasy of Jehoram and Ahaziah
22:10–23:21, The Coup in Support of Joash

E. 24:1–26:23, How to Lose the Race, in Three Lessons
24:1-27, Joash Listens to the Wrong Advice
25:1-28, Amaziah Finds a New Faith
26:1-23, Uzziah Oversteps God's Limits

F. 27:1–28:27, Royal Models of Right and Wrong
27:1-9, Jotham the Good
28:1-27, Ahaz the Bad

IV. 2 Chronicles 29:1–36:23, The Reunited Kingdom

A. 29:1–32:33, Hezekiah Attains Royal Potential

29:1-36, Temple Cleansing, Atonement, and Worship
30:1–31:1, United Passover Worship
31:2-21, Temple Reorganization
32:1-33, Deliverance and Blessing

B. 33:1–35:27, Dross Into Gold

33:1-20, Manasseh, a Model of Repentance
33:21–35:27, Amon's Wrongdoing; Josiah's Repentance, Reform, and Relapse

C. 36:1-23, Recurring Exile and the Prospect of Restoration

1 CHRONICLES 1:1–9:34

ISRAEL: ELECT AND INCLUSIVE, UNFAITHFUL BUT RESTORED

OVERVIEW

This unit supplies a genealogical prologue for the chronicler's history. The latter will consist of royal narratives, the stories of the Davidic dynasty. The prologue has a wider national and chronological focus. It considers the people of Israel, first in relation to the world at large, as the elect people of God, then in terms of pre-exilic tribal records that provocatively reproduce both southern and northern traditions, and finally in the light of a provisional post-exilic restoration that hopefully would lead to bigger and better things.

Lists of names do not make for easy reading. Students of the genealogies will benefit from J. M. Myers's presentation of them in the form of charts.[22] But there is more than names here. The genealogies are used for the chronicler's literary and theological ends, both negative and positive. They exhibit close thematic links with the royal narratives, which the sectional commentaries will trace.[23] The plainer teaching of the narratives helps the reader of the genealogies to decode them.

22. J. M. Myers, *II Chronicles,* AB 13 (Garden City, N.Y.: Doubleday, 1965) 233-50.

23. See M. D. Johnson, *The Purpose of the Biblical Genealogies,* SNTSMS 8 (Cambridge: Cambridge University Press, 1969) 47-55; W. L. Osborne, "The Genealogies of 1 Chronicles 1–9" (Ph.d. diss., Dropsie University, 1979) 21-74.

Israel stood in a special relationship with the Lord. Yet what was the identity of Israel? The title could not be monopolized by the members of the post-exilic province of Yehud whose predecessors returned from Babylonian exile. They were only a nucleus of a larger entity, attested traditionally in the wilderness period, in the settlement and division of the promised land, and in the united kingdom of David and Solomon. It was with that larger Israel, for whom the sanctuary was so important, that the post-exilic community should identify and find its continuity. They must also reckon with failure, the common failure that led north and south to the divine punishment of exile (5:25-26; 6:15; 9:1). Yet beyond failure lay restoring grace, already realized in part (9:2). The path to complete restoration lay via heartfelt need and earnest prayer (4:9-10; 5:20).

The sequence of generations held a fascination for the chronicler, for whom each generation had the privilege and responsibility of commitment to the God of its predecessors. There are two examples of consecutive generations' taking opposite decisions and reaping what they severally sowed, in 5:19-22, 25-26 and 7:21-24. Which generation, the chronicler was implicitly asking, did his readers wish to take for their model?

1 CHRONICLES 1:1–2:2, ISRAEL'S ELECTION

NIV

1 Adam, Seth, Enosh, 2Kenan, Mahalalel,
Jared, 3Enoch, Methuselah, Lamech, Noah.

NRSV

1 Adam, Seth, Enosh; 2Kenan, Mahalalel,
Jared; 3Enoch, Methuselah, Lamech;
4Noah, Shem, Ham, and Japheth.

NIV

4The sons of Noah:[a]
Shem, Ham and Japheth.

5The sons[b] of Japheth:
Gomer, Magog, Madai, Javan, Tubal, Meshech and Tiras.
6The sons of Gomer:
Ashkenaz, Riphath[c] and Togarmah.
7The sons of Javan:
Elishah, Tarshish, the Kittim and the Rodanim.

8The sons of Ham:
Cush, Mizraim,[d] Put and Canaan.
9The sons of Cush:
Seba, Havilah, Sabta, Raamah and Sabteca.
The sons of Raamah:
Sheba and Dedan.
10Cush was the father[e] of
Nimrod, who grew to be a mighty warrior on earth.
11Mizraim was the father of
the Ludites, Anamites, Lehabites, Naphtuhites, 12Pathrusites, Casluhites (from whom the Philistines came) and Caphtorites.
13Canaan was the father of
Sidon his firstborn,[f] and of the Hittites, 14Jebusites, Amorites, Girgashites, 15Hivites, Arkites, Sinites, 16Arvadites, Zemarites and Hamathites.

17The sons of Shem:
Elam, Asshur, Arphaxad, Lud and Aram.
The sons of Aram[g]:
Uz, Hul, Gether and Meshech.
18Arphaxad was the father of Shelah,
and Shelah the father of Eber.
19Two sons were born to Eber:
One was named Peleg,[h] because in his time the earth was divided; his brother was named Joktan.
20Joktan was the father of
Almodad, Sheleph, Hazarmaveth, Jerah,

a4 Septuagint; Hebrew does not have *The sons of Noah:* *b5 Sons* may mean *descendants* or *successors* or *nations*; also in verses 6-10, 17 and 20. *c6* Many Hebrew manuscripts and Vulgate (see also Septuagint and Gen. 10:3); most Hebrew manuscripts *Diphath* *d8* That is, Egypt; also in verse 11 *e10 Father* may mean *ancestor* or *predecessor* or *founder*; also in verses 11, 13, 18 and 20. *f13* Or *of the Sidonians, the foremost* *g17* One Hebrew manuscript and some Septuagint manuscripts (see also Gen. 10:23); most Hebrew manuscripts do not have this line. *h19 Peleg* means *division*

NRSV

5The descendants of Japheth: Gomer, Magog,
Madai, Javan, Tubal, Meshech, and Tiras. 6The
descendants of Gomer: Ashkenaz, Diphath,[a] and
Togarmah. 7The descendants of Javan: Elishah,
Tarshish, Kittim, and Rodanim.[b]

8The descendants of Ham: Cush, Egypt, Put,
and Canaan. 9The descendants of Cush: Seba,
Havilah, Sabta, Raama, and Sabteca. The descendants of Raamah: Sheba and Dedan. 10Cush became the father of Nimrod; he was the first to be
a mighty one on the earth.

11Egypt became the father of Ludim, Anamim,
Lehabim, Naphtuhim, 12Pathrusim, Casluhim, and
Caphtorim, from whom the Philistines come.[c]

13Canaan became the father of Sidon his firstborn, and Heth, 14and the Jebusites, the Amorites,
the Girgashites, 15the Hivites, the Arkites, the
Sinites, 16the Arvadites, the Zemarites, and the
Hamathites.

17The descendants of Shem: Elam, Asshur,
Arpachshad, Lud, Aram, Uz, Hul, Gether, and
Meshech.[d] 18Arpachshad became the father of
Shelah; and Shelah became the father of Eber.
19To Eber were born two sons: the name of the
one was Peleg (for in his days the earth was
divided), and the name of his brother Joktan.
20Joktan became the father of Almodad, Sheleph,
Hazarmaveth, Jerah, 21Hadoram, Uzal, Diklah,
22Ebal, Abimael, Sheba, 23Ophir, Havilah, and Jobab; all these were the descendants of Joktan.

24Shem, Arpachshad, Shelah; 25Eber, Peleg,
Reu; 26Serug, Nahor, Terah; 27Abram, that is,
Abraham.

28The sons of Abraham: Isaac and Ishmael.
29These are their genealogies: the firstborn of
Ishmael, Nebaioth; and Kedar, Adbeel, Mibsam,
30Mishma, Dumah, Massa, Hadad, Tema, 31Jetur,
Naphish, and Kedemah. These are the sons of
Ishmael. 32The sons of Keturah, Abraham's con-
cubine: she bore Zimran, Jokshan, Medan,
Midian, Ishbak, and Shuah. The sons of Jokshan:
Sheba and Dedan. 33The sons of Midian: Ephah,
Epher, Hanoch, Abida, and Eldaah. All these were
the descendants of Keturah.

34Abraham became the father of Isaac. The
sons of Isaac: Esau and Israel. 35The sons of Esau:

a Gen 10.3 *Ripath*; See Gk Vg b Gen 10.4 *Dodanim*; See Syr Vg c Heb *Casluhim, from which the Philistines come, Caphtorim*; See Am 9.7, Jer 47.4 d *Mash* in Gen 10.23

NIV

21Hadoram, Uzal, Diklah, 22Obal,[a] Abimael, Sheba, 23Ophir, Havilah and Jobab.
All these were sons of Joktan.

24Shem, Arphaxad,[b] Shelah,
25Eber, Peleg, Reu,
26Serug, Nahor, Terah
27and Abram (that is, Abraham).

28The sons of Abraham:
Isaac and Ishmael.
29These were their descendants:
Nebaioth the firstborn of Ishmael, Kedar,
Adbeel, Mibsam, 30Mishma, Dumah,
Massa, Hadad, Tema, 31Jetur, Naphish and
Kedemah. These were the sons of
Ishmael.

32The sons born to Keturah, Abraham's
concubine:
Zimran, Jokshan, Medan, Midian, Ishbak
and Shuah.
The sons of Jokshan:
Sheba and Dedan.
33The sons of Midian:
Ephah, Epher, Hanoch, Abida and Eldaah.
All these were descendants of Keturah.

34Abraham was the father of Isaac.
The sons of Isaac:
Esau and Israel.
35The sons of Esau:
Eliphaz, Reuel, Jeush, Jalam and Korah.
36The sons of Eliphaz:
Teman, Omar, Zepho,[c] Gatam and Kenaz;
by Timna: Amalek.[d]
37The sons of Reuel:
Nahath, Zerah, Shammah and Mizzah.

38The sons of Seir:
Lotan, Shobal, Zibeon, Anah, Dishon, Ezer
and Dishan.
39The sons of Lotan:
Hori and Homam. Timna was Lotan's
sister.
40The sons of Shobal:

[a]*22* Some Hebrew manuscripts and Syriac (see also Gen. 10:28); most Hebrew manuscripts *Ebal* [b]*24* Hebrew; some Septuagint manuscripts *Arphaxad, Cainan* (see also note at Gen. 11:10) [c]*36* Many Hebrew manuscripts, some Septuagint manuscripts and Syriac (see also Gen. 36:11); most Hebrew manuscripts *Zephi* [d]*36* Some Septuagint manuscripts (see also Gen. 36:12); Hebrew *Gatam, Kenaz, Timna and Amalek*

NRSV

Eliphaz, Reuel, Jeush, Jalam, and Korah. 36The
sons of Eliphaz: Teman, Omar, Zephi, Gatam,
Kenaz, Timna, and Amalek. 37The sons of Reuel:
Nahath, Zerah, Shammah, and Mizzah.
38The sons of Seir: Lotan, Shobal, Zibeon,
Anah, Dishon, Ezer, and Dishan. 39The sons of
Lotan: Hori and Homam; and Lotan's sister was
Timna. 40The sons of Shobal: Alian, Manahath,
Ebal, Shephi, and Onam. The sons of Zibeon: Aiah
and Anah. 41The sons of Anah: Dishon. The sons
of Dishon: Hamran, Eshban, Ithran, and Cheran.
42The sons of Ezer: Bilhan, Zaavan, and Jaakan.[a]
The sons of Dishan:[b] Uz and Aran.
43These are the kings who reigned in the land
of Edom before any king reigned over the Israelites: Bela son of Beor, whose city was called
Dinhabah. 44When Bela died, Jobab son of Zerah
of Bozrah succeeded him. 45When Jobab died,
Husham of the land of the Temanites succeeded
him. 46When Husham died, Hadad son of Bedad,
who defeated Midian in the country of Moab,
succeeded him; and the name of his city was
Avith. 47When Hadad died, Samlah of Masrekah
succeeded him. 48When Samlah died, Shaul[c] of
Rehoboth on the Euphrates succeeded him.
49When Shaul[c] died, Baal-hanan son of Achbor
succeeded him. 50When Baal-hanan died, Hadad
succeeded him; the name of his city was Pai, and
his wife's name Mehetabel daughter of Matred,
daughter of Me-zahab. 51And Hadad died.
The clans[d] of Edom were: clans[d] Timna, Aliah,[e]
Jetheth, 52Oholibamah, Elah, Pinon, 53Kenaz, Teman, Mibzar, 54Magdiel, and Iram; these are the
clans[d] of Edom.

2 These are the sons of Israel: Reuben,
Simeon, Levi, Judah, Issachar, Zebulun,
2Dan, Joseph, Benjamin, Naphtali, Gad, and
Asher.

[a] Or *and Akan*; See Gen 36.27 [b] See 1.38: Heb *Dishon* [c] Or *Saul* [d] Or *chiefs* [e] Or *Alvah*; See Gen 36.40

NIV

Alvan,[a] Manahath, Ebal, Shepho and Onam.
The sons of Zibeon:
Aiah and Anah.
41The son of Anah:
Dishon.
The sons of Dishon:
Hemdan,[b] Eshban, Ithran and Keran.
42The sons of Ezer:
Bilhan, Zaavan and Akan.[c]
The sons of Dishan[d]:
Uz and Aran.

43These were the kings who reigned in Edom before any Israelite king reigned[e]:

Bela son of Beor, whose city was named Dinhabah.
44When Bela died, Jobab son of Zerah from Bozrah succeeded him as king.
45When Jobab died, Husham from the land of the Temanites succeeded him as king.
46When Husham died, Hadad son of Bedad, who defeated Midian in the country of Moab, succeeded him as king. His city was named Avith.
47When Hadad died, Samlah from Masrekah succeeded him as king.
48When Samlah died, Shaul from Rehoboth on the river[f] succeeded him as king.
49When Shaul died, Baal-Hanan son of Acbor succeeded him as king.
50When Baal-Hanan died, Hadad succeeded him as king. His city was named Pau,[g] and his wife's name was Mehetabel daughter of Matred, the daughter of Me-Zahab.
51Hadad also died.

The chiefs of Edom were:
Timna, Alvah, Jetheth, 52Oholibamah, Elah, Pinon, 53Kenaz, Teman, Mibzar, 54Magdiel and Iram. These were the chiefs of Edom.

[a] *40* Many Hebrew manuscripts and some Septuagint manuscripts (see also Gen. 36:23); most Hebrew manuscripts *Alian* [b] *41* Many Hebrew manuscripts and some Septuagint manuscripts (see also Gen. 36:26); most Hebrew manuscripts *Hamran* [c] *42* Many Hebrew and Septuagint manuscripts (see also Gen. 36:27); most Hebrew manuscripts *Zaavan, Jaakan* [d] *42* Hebrew *Dishon,* a variant of *Dishan* [e] *43* Or *before an Isralite king reigned over them* [f] *48* Possibly the Euphrates [g] *50* Many Hebrew manuscripts, some Septuagint manuscripts, Vulgate and Syriac (see also Gen. 36:39); most Hebrew manuscripts *Pai*

NIV

2 These were the sons of Israel:
Reuben, Simeon, Levi, Judah, Issachar, Zebulun, 2Dan, Joseph, Benjamin, Naphtali, Gad and Asher.

COMMENTARY

This section is a genealogical list that traces a narrowing process from the world of humanity to the founder of the twelve tribes of Israel. The chronicler's intention may be deduced from a speech in which he used a similar process. David told Israel's leaders in 28:4-5: "The LORD . . . chose Judah as leader, and from the house of Judah he chose my family, and from my father's sons he was pleased to make me king over all Israel. Of all my sons . . . he has chosen my son Solomon" (NIV). These specific references to divine selection explain the implicit purpose here. Support for this interpretation comes from 16:13, where the chronicler borrowed from Ps 105:6 the description of the "sons of Jacob" (NIV) as the Lord's "chosen ones."

Structurally the section falls into two halves. Name lists devoid of any kinship terms occur in 1:1-4 and 24-27. Each list is followed by a series of genealogies, though in the second case it is amplified by lists of kings and chiefs in 1:43-54. The genealogies fall into groups of three. In the first half of the section the descendants of the three sons of Noah are listed. In the second half, this phenomenon occurs twice, relating first to the sons of Abraham—namely Ishmael, those born to Keturah, and Isaac—and then to the family of Isaac—namely Esau, Seir, and Israel. In accord with the theme of election, the chosen line is put last, after the two other lines are disposed of. In the first case the chronicler was following the order of his Genesis source, but he reversed it in putting Israel's sons after those of Esau and Seir. His reordering suggests his intention: to conclude with the elect line.

So, apart from 1:43-54, the whole genealogical list has an ABCD/ABCDB′C′D′ pattern. There is first a dash from creation to the flood, then a lingering over the triple, postdiluvian descendants of Noah. This is followed by a further dash from the flood to the first patriarch, Abraham, and a lingering over the triple descendants of both Abraham and Isaac. The tripling enhances the principle of election. The genealogical list culminates in the sons of Jacob, or "Israel." The latter name, divinely conferred in Gen 35:10, is the chronicler's preferred name for Jacob, which occurs only in the quoted material of 1 Chr 16:13, 17. He used it to highlight the relationship between the chosen nation and its ancestor. That relationship is facilitated by the linguistic fact that the standard Hebrew phrase for Israelites is בני ישראל (*bĕnê yiśrā'ēl*), literally "sons of Israel." The phrase occurs in 1:43, so that in 2:2 the reader is made aware of an intentional ambiguity between persons and tribes. In the NT, Paul focuses on a son of Abraham as a prime figure of theological history: "You . . . like Isaac, are children of the promise" (Gal 4:28 NRSV). The chronicler's perspective moved two generations down the line, but made the same point, as if saying to his Judean contemporaries, "You, like Israel's sons, are children of the promise."

The chronicler derived his genealogical material from the book of Genesis. His principle was not to use all its genealogies, but to select only those that have the heading "These are the generations of . . ." (KJV, Gen 6:9; 10:1; 11:10, 27; 25:12, 19; 36:1, 9; also Gen 5:1, which has a longer heading). The headings in 25:12, 19 are actually cited in 1:29, in the form "These are their generations" (KJV). In the case of Jacob's sons he presumably took his cue from the heading "These are the genealogies of Jacob" in Gen 37:2 (KJV), which introduces not a genealogy but a narrative, and defined it in terms of the genealogy in Gen 35:22*b*-26. The genealogy of Keturah's sons (Gen 25:1-4) lacks such a heading, but the chronicler used it anyway, inserting it in 1:32-33 between the descendants of Ishmael and those of Isaac, in keeping with the triple structure. There are a few textual discrepancies between the Genesis lists and the readings of the MT in Chronicles, and between the MT and the LXX of Chronicles. The NIV tends to emend in line with Genesis, while the NRSV has retained the MT (apart from a small change in 1:42 and a conjectural transposition in 1:12), presumably judging that the differences were already in the text of Genesis used by the chronicler.

1:1-42. The name list from Adam to Noah has been distilled from the names given in the course of Genesis 5, minus the narrative of ages. Knowledge of the source is presupposed, so that it now functions as a linear genealogy. The last three names in v. 4 introduce what follows and were taken from a fusion of Gen 6:9 and 10:1. There is parallelism between the ten names in vv. 1-4 (as far as Noah) and the ten in vv. 24-27. The linear character of both passages contrasts with the following segmented genealogies, which branch out in the form of a family tree. Verses 5-23 continue using Genesis 10, with deletion of its historical and geographical material. Verses 24-27 are derived from Gen 11:10-27; its names overlap with those of the previous genealogy. Details of age are again omitted. The explanation of Abram as Abraham paves the way for v. 28. Verses 28-31, 34*a* are extracted from Gen 25:12-16, 19 and vv. 32-33 from Gen 25:1-4, while v. 34*b* has been distilled from Gen 25:20-26. Verses 35-42 have been compressed from Gen 36:1-4, 9-28 (bypassing vv. 15-19). Seir is nowhere given a genealogical relationship to Esau; Gen 36:20-21 states, and the chronicler assumed, that he lived in Edom. Timna in v. 36 was actually not a son of Eliphaz but his concubine (Gen 36:12). The chronicler, in compressing his material, assumed that readers would know Genesis and not be confused.

1:43-54. The structurally anomalous lists of kings and chiefs are taken practically verbatim from Gen 36:31-43, apart from the insertion of v. 51*a*. The list of chiefs is related to Edom in v. 51, as in the closing v. 54 (= Gen 36:43); in Gen 36:40, chiefs of Esau are specified. So there are standardizing references to Edom in vv. 43, 51, and 54. The NRSV renders the Hebrew term אלופים (*'allûpîm*) as "clans" both here and in Genesis 36; the NIV prefers "chiefs," which seems to reflect the chronicler's intention.

Why was this Edomite material included, with the preservation of its narrative, in the first case? It can hardly have been for the sake of completeness, since Gen 36:15-19 finds no place here. There must have been good reason for the chronicler to interrupt his structural pattern. The mate-

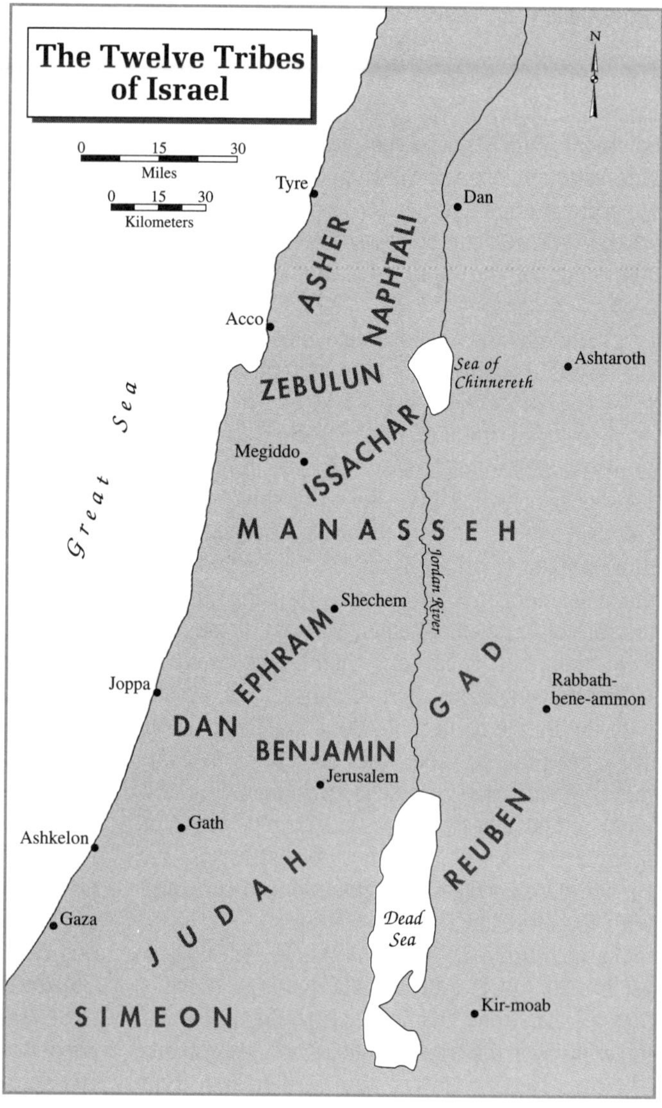

rial traces the fortunes of the Edomite monarchy. The focus of the chronicler's history will be the Davidic monarchy, and David's genealogy will begin a few verses later in 2:9. Was the chronicler influenced by the promise of Gen 35:11, that (proper) kings would spring from Jacob? In comparison to the Davidic monarchy, the Edomite one was a travesty. David's dynasty lasted in Jerusalem from generation to generation by the Lord's appointment, while Edom had a chaotic assortment of unrelated kings and different capitals. By adding a reference to the death of Hadad in 1:51*a,* the chronicler interpreted 1:51*b*-54 as a sequel to the monarchy, a series of chieftains after the monarchy collapsed. In the post-exilic period, Judah had a strong sense of grievance against Edom for various reasons, a grievance that emerges at 1 Chr 18:12-13 and 2 Chr 25:11-12. A scoring over Edom fits this historical mood. The implicit contrast assumes a future for the house of David. Although historically it was swept away at the exile and not restored, it lived on in the chronicler's heart. Its eventual restoration was guaranteed by a divine "forever" (2 Chr 13:5).

2:1-2. It has already been noted that the genealogy of Israel's sons comes from Gen 35:22*b*-26. The arrangement by maternal rank has been kept, but pruned to a list of paternal brothers. The upgrading of Dan, born to Rachel's maid Bilhah, to a position before Rachel's sons, Joseph and Benjamin, presupposes Rachel's adoption of Dan in Gen 30:6, before her natural children were born.

The chronicler has presented the book of Genesis in potted form. Its divine plan, moving from primeval history to patriarchal history, from creation to covenant, from the universal to the national, has been echoed via its genealogical lists. The principle of this section is that of Samuel's review of Jesse's sons one by one in 1 Sam 16:1-13: "The LORD has not chosen any of these. . . . This is the one" (NRSV). Israel was the elect people of God. Much important truth in Genesis has been passed over in the process, such as the divine command to multiply and be fruitful, which the table of nations in Genesis 10 illustrates, and the checkered pattern of blessing, judgment, and grace that runs through Genesis 1–11. The chronicler's constituency needed to hear their election reaffirmed. Assurance was the basic need for these subjects of the Persian Empire, to hear that "the LORD . . . chose Abram" (Neh 9:7). In due course the chronicler would have much to say by way of challenge and warning.

REFLECTIONS

Genesis is a book of beginnings and basics, with which post-exilic Judah identified. The Christian church, in prizing the Gospels and Acts, takes a similar stand. Here is decisive divine/human interaction that refuses to stay in its own historical place but chases humanity down the corridors of time, demanding recognition and response and identifying the church thereafter as "children of the promise" through Christ. We have inherited the doxology generated by divine election, "Blessed be the God and Father of our Lord Jesus Christ" for choosing us in him (Eph 1:3-4).

As we have seen, the figure of David, who will dominate Chronicles, haunts even this section, in providing a normative perspective for critiquing the Edomite monarchy and its supposed aftermath in 1:43-54. The Lord's Davidic goal in history and in hope colored the chronicler's interpretation of Genesis, just as a christological hermeneutic controls some Christians' reading of the OT.

A note of challenge creeps into the climax of the section, though its implications await spelling out in the tribal material of the following chapters. Was the little post-exilic community of Judah the true Israel? Only as a nucleus for a larger entity. The twelve sons of Israel had a relevance for the chronicler's own time. Every descendant of Jacob or Israel could claim a stake in Judah's heritage. It is the first occurrence of an "ecumenical" note that will pervade the chronicler's work, dispelling complacency. In turn, to be members of the "chosen race . . . holy nation, God's own people" (1 Pet 2:9) means grappling with different traditions and unappropriated insights. "I have other sheep," Jesus has warned us, "that do not belong to this fold" (John 10:16 NRSV).

1 CHRONICLES 2:3–9:1, A PANORAMA OF PRE-EXILIC ISRAEL

OVERVIEW

The framework of this unit is provided by the placing of the three southern tribes of Judah, Levi, and Benjamin at beginning, middle, and end. The circumference and center are used as a setting for the northern tribes, as joint members of "all Israel" (9:1): "The other tribes are not excluded, but rather enclosed by this framework."[24] The ordering of the tribes represents a chiastic pattern:

A 2:3–4:43, Judah and its ancillary tribe, Simeon
  B 5:1-26, the Transjordanian tribes
    C 6:1-81, the religious tribe of Levi
  B′ 7:1-40, the remaining northern tribes
A′ 8:1-40, the other Judean tribe, Benjamin

At the conclusion mention of "all Israel" harks back to the listing of the sons of Israel, after whom the tribes were named (2:1-2), though a schematic total of twelve tribes prevents exact correspondence.

Just as 9:2-34 will provide a post-exilic list of Israelites in Jerusalem, so also the purpose here is to present a pre-exilic survey of the tribes.[25] A striking exception is the genealogy of David's descendants in chap. 3, which pushes deep into the post-exilic period, in line with the chronicler's royalist hopes, expressed in his narratives. The blend of genealogical historical and geographical concerns exhibited in this unit corresponds to a pattern found in the Safaitic inscriptions of the first centuries BCE and CE.[26] The chronicler was able to copy comparable mixed sources for his own ends. He also drew on biblical material, especially Genesis 46, Numbers 26, and parts of Joshua 15–21, and on a military census list for the Transjordanian tribes and for Issachar, Benjamin, and Asher. The listing of tribal territories outside the post-exilic province of Yehud and the tales of vigorous expansion to adjacent areas present a paradigm of territorial hope.

24. H. W. M. Williamson, *1 and 2 Chronicles*, NCB (Grand Rapids: Eerdmans, 1982) 47.

25. See J. P. Weinberg, "Die Wesen und die funktionelle Bestimmung der Listen in 1 Chr 1–9," *ZAW* 93 (1981) 91-114.

26. See Johnson, *The Purpose of the Biblical Genealogies*, 60-62; H. G. M. Williamson, *Israel in the Books of Chronicles* (Cambridge: Cambridge University Press, 1977) 76-80.

1 Chronicles 2:3–4:23, The Royal Tribe of Judah

NIV	NRSV
3The sons of Judah: Er, Onan and Shelah. These three were born to him by a Canaanite woman, the daughter of Shua. Er, Judah's firstborn, was wicked in the LORD's sight; so the LORD put him to death. 4Tamar, Judah's daughter-in-law, bore him Perez and Zerah. Judah had five sons in all.	3The sons of Judah: Er, Onan, and Shelah; these three the Canaanite woman Bath-shua bore to him. Now Er, Judah's firstborn, was wicked in the sight of the LORD, and he put him to death. 4His daughter-in-law Tamar also bore him Perez and Zerah. Judah had five sons in all. 5The sons of Perez: Hezron and Hamul. 6The sons of Zerah: Zimri, Ethan, Heman, Calcol, and

NIV

5The sons of Perez:
Hezron and Hamul.
6The sons of Zerah:
Zimri, Ethan, Heman, Calcol and Darda[a]—five in all.
7The son of Carmi:
Achar,[b] who brought trouble on Israel by
violating the ban on taking devoted
things.[c]
8The son of Ethan:
Azariah.
9The sons born to Hezron were:
Jerahmeel, Ram and Caleb.[d]

10Ram was the father of
Amminadab, and Amminadab the father
of Nahshon, the leader of the people of
Judah. 11Nahshon was the father of
Salmon,[e] Salmon the father of Boaz,
12Boaz the father of Obed and Obed the
father of Jesse.
13Jesse was the father of
Eliab his firstborn; the second son was
Abinadab, the third Shimea, 14the fourth
Nethanel, the fifth Raddai, 15the sixth
Ozem and the seventh David. 16Their sisters were Zeruiah and Abigail. Zeruiah's
three sons were Abishai, Joab and Asahel.
17Abigail was the mother of Amasa, whose
father was Jether the Ishmaelite.

18Caleb son of Hezron had children by his wife
Azubah (and by Jerioth). These were her
sons: Jesher, Shobab and Ardon. 19When
Azubah died, Caleb married Ephrath, who
bore him Hur. 20Hur was the father of Uri,
and Uri the father of Bezalel.
21Later, Hezron lay with the daughter of Makir
the father of Gilead (he had married her
when he was sixty years old), and she
bore him Segub. 22Segub was the father
of Jair, who controlled twenty-three towns
in Gilead. 23(But Geshur and Aram captured Havvoth Jair,[f] as well as Kenath with

[a]*6* Many Hebrew manuscripts, some Septuagint manuscripts and Syriac (see also 1 Kings 4:31); most Hebrew manuscripts *Dara* [b]*7* *Achar* means *trouble*; *Achar* is called *Achan* in Joshua. [c]*7* The Hebrew term refers to the irrevocable giving over of things or persons to the LORD, often by totally destroying them. [d]*9* Hebrew *Kelubai*, a variant of *Caleb* [e]*11* Septuagint (see also Ruth 4:21); Hebrew *Salma* [f]*23* Or *captured the settlements of Jair*

NRSV

Dara,[a] five in all. 7The sons of Carmi: Achar, the
troubler of Israel, who transgressed in the matter of
the devoted thing; 8and Ethan's son was Azariah.

9The sons of Hezron, who were born to him:
Jerahmeel, Ram, and Chelubai. 10Ram became the
father of Amminadab, and Amminadab became
the father of Nahshon, prince of the sons of Judah.
11Nahshon became the father of Salma, Salma of
Boaz, 12Boaz of Obed, Obed of Jesse. 13Jesse
became the father of Eliab his firstborn, Abinadab
the second, Shimea the third, 14Nethanel the
fourth, Raddai the fifth, 15Ozem the sixth, David
the seventh; 16and their sisters were Zeruiah and
Abigail. The sons of Zeruiah: Abishai, Joab, and
Asahel, three. 17Abigail bore Amasa, and the father
of Amasa was Jether the Ishmaelite.

18Caleb son of Hezron had children by his wife
Azubah, and by Jerioth; these were her sons:
Jesher, Shobab, and Ardon. 19When Azubah died,
Caleb married Ephrath, who bore him Hur. 20Hur
became the father of Uri, and Uri became the
father of Bezalel.

21Afterward Hezron went in to the daughter
of Machir father of Gilead, whom he married
when he was sixty years old; and she bore him
Segub; 22and Segub became the father of Jair, who
had twenty-three towns in the land of Gilead.
23But Geshur and Aram took from them Havvoth-
jair, Kenath and its villages, sixty towns. All these
were descendants of Machir, father of Gilead.
24After the death of Hezron, in Caleb-ephrathah,
Abijah wife of Hezron bore him Ashhur, father of
Tekoa.

25The sons of Jerahmeel, the firstborn of
Hezron: Ram his firstborn, Bunah, Oren, Ozem,
and Ahijah. 26Jerahmeel also had another wife,
whose name was Atarah; she was the mother of
Onam. 27The sons of Ram, the firstborn of
Jerahmeel: Maaz, Jamin, and Eker. 28The sons of
Onam: Shammai and Jada. The sons of Shammai:
Nadab and Abishur. 29The name of Abishur's wife
was Abihail, and she bore him Ahban and Molid.
30The sons of Nadab: Seled and Appaim; and Seled
died childless. 31The son[b] of Appaim: Ishi. The
son[b] of Ishi: Sheshan. The son[b] of Sheshan: Ahlai.
32The sons of Jada, Shammai's brother: Jether and

[a] Or *Darda*; Compare Syr Tg some Gk Mss; See 1 Kings 4.31 [b] Heb *sons*

NIV

its surrounding settlements—sixty towns.) All these were descendants of Makir the father of Gilead.

24After Hezron died in Caleb Ephrathah, Abijah the wife of Hezron bore him Ashhur the father[a] of Tekoa.

25The sons of Jerahmeel the firstborn of Hezron:
Ram his firstborn, Bunah, Oren, Ozem and[b] Ahijah. 26Jerahmeel had another wife, whose name was Atarah; she was the mother of Onam.

27The sons of Ram the firstborn of Jerahmeel:
Maaz, Jamin and Eker.

28The sons of Onam:
Shammai and Jada.
The sons of Shammai:
Nadab and Abishur.

29Abishur's wife was named Abihail, who bore him Ahban and Molid.

30The sons of Nadab:
Seled and Appaim. Seled died without children.

31The son of Appaim:
Ishi, who was the father of Sheshan.
Sheshan was the father of Ahlai.

32The sons of Jada, Shammai's brother:
Jether and Jonathan. Jether died without children.

33The sons of Jonathan:
Peleth and Zaza.
These were the descendants of Jerahmeel.

34Sheshan had no sons—only daughters.
He had an Egyptian servant named Jarha.
35Sheshan gave his daughter in marriage to his servant Jarha, and she bore him Attai.

36Attai was the father of Nathan,
Nathan the father of Zabad,
37Zabad the father of Ephlal,
Ephlal the father of Obed,
38Obed the father of Jehu,
Jehu the father of Azariah,
39Azariah the father of Helez,
Helez the father of Eleasah,
40Eleasah the father of Sismai,

[a]24 *Father* may mean *civic leader* or *military leader*; also in verses 42, 45, 49-52 and possibly elsewhere. [b]25 Or *Oren and Ozem, by*

NRSV

Jonathan; and Jether died childless. 33The sons of
Jonathan: Peleth and Zaza. These were the descendants of Jerahmeel. 34Now Sheshan had no
sons, only daughters; but Sheshan had an Egyptian
slave, whose name was Jarha. 35So Sheshan gave
his daughter in marriage to his slave Jarha; and
she bore him Attai. 36Attai became the father of
Nathan, and Nathan of Zabad. 37Zabad became
the father of Ephlal, and Ephlal of Obed. 38Obed
became the father of Jehu, and Jehu of Azariah.
39Azariah became the father of Helez, and Helez
of Eleasah. 40Eleasah became the father of Sismai,
and Sismai of Shallum. 41Shallum became the
father of Jekamiah, and Jekamiah of Elishama.

42The sons of Caleb brother of Jerahmeel:
Mesha[a] his firstborn, who was father of Ziph. The
sons of Mareshah father of Hebron. 43The sons of
Hebron: Korah, Tappuah, Rekem, and Shema.
44Shema became father of Raham, father of
Jorkeam; and Rekem became the father of Shammai. 45The son of Shammai: Maon; and Maon was
the father of Beth-zur. 46Ephah also, Caleb's concubine, bore Haran, Moza, and Gazez; and Haran
became the father of Gazez. 47The sons of Jahdai:
Regem, Jotham, Geshan, Pelet, Ephah, and
Shaaph. 48Maacah, Caleb's concubine, bore Sheber and Tirhanah. 49She also bore Shaaph father
of Madmannah, Sheva father of Machbenah and
father of Gibea; and the daughter of Caleb was
Achsah. 50These were the descendants of Caleb.

The sons[b] of Hur the firstborn of Ephrathah:
Shobal father of Kiriath-jearim, 51Salma father of
Bethlehem, and Hareph father of Beth-gader.
52Shobal father of Kiriath-jearim had other sons:
Haroeh, half of the Menuhoth. 53And the families
of Kiriath-jearim: the Ithrites, the Puthites, the
Shumathites, and the Mishraites; from these came
the Zorathites and the Eshtaolites. 54The sons of
Salma: Bethlehem, the Netophathites, Atroth-
beth-joab, and half of the Manahathites, the
Zorites. 55The families also of the scribes that lived
at Jabez: the Tirathites, the Shimeathites, and the
Sucathites. These are the Kenites who came from
Hammath, father of the house of Rechab.

3 These are the sons of David who were
born to him in Hebron: the firstborn
Amnon, by Ahinoam the Jezreelite; the second

[a] Gk reads *Mareshah* [b] Gk Vg: Heb *son*

NIV

Sismai the father of Shallum,
41Shallum the father of Jekamiah,
and Jekamiah the father of Elishama.

42The sons of Caleb the brother of Jerahmeel:
Mesha his firstborn, who was the father of Ziph, and his son Mareshah,[a] who was the father of Hebron.

43The sons of Hebron:
Korah, Tappuah, Rekem and Shema. 44Shema was the father of Raham, and Raham the father of Jorkeam. Rekem was the father of Shammai. 45The son of Shammai was Maon, and Maon was the father of Beth Zur.

46Caleb's concubine Ephah was the mother of Haran, Moza and Gazez. Haran was the father of Gazez.

47The sons of Jahdai:
Regem, Jotham, Geshan, Pelet, Ephah and Shaaph.

48Caleb's concubine Maacah was the mother of Sheber and Tirhanah. 49She also gave birth to Shaaph the father of Madmannah and to Sheva the father of Macbenah and Gibea. Caleb's daughter was Acsah. 50These were the descendants of Caleb.

The sons of Hur the firstborn of Ephrathah:
Shobal the father of Kiriath Jearim, 51Salma the father of Bethlehem, and Hareph the father of Beth Gader.

52The descendants of Shobal the father of Kiriath Jearim were:
Haroeh, half the Manahathites, 53and the clans of Kiriath Jearim: the Ithrites, Puthites, Shumathites and Mishraites. From these descended the Zorathites and Eshtaolites.

54The descendants of Salma:
Bethlehem, the Netophathites, Atroth Beth Joab, half the Manahathites, the Zorites, 55and the clans of scribes[b] who lived at Jabez: the Tirathites, Shimeathites and Sucathites. These are the Kenites who came from Hammath, the father of the house of Recab.[c]

[a]42 The meaning of the Hebrew for this phrase is uncertain. [b]55 Or *of the Sopherites* [c]55 Or *father of Beth Recab*

NRSV

Daniel, by Abigail the Carmelite; 2the third Absalom, son of Maacah, daughter of King Talmai of
Geshur; the fourth Adonijah, son of Haggith; 3the
fifth Shephatiah, by Abital; the sixth Ithream, by
his wife Eglah; 4six were born to him in Hebron,
where he reigned for seven years and six months.
And he reigned thirty-three years in Jerusalem.
5These were born to him in Jerusalem: Shimea,
Shobab, Nathan, and Solomon, four by Bath-shua,
daughter of Ammiel; 6then Ibhar, Elishama,
Eliphelet, 7Nogah, Nepheg, Japhia, 8Elishama,
Eliada, and Eliphelet, nine. 9All these were
David's sons, besides the sons of the concubines;
and Tamar was their sister.

10The descendants of Solomon: Rehoboam,
Abijah his son, Asa his son, Jehoshaphat his son,
11Joram his son, Ahaziah his son, Joash his son,
12Amaziah his son, Azariah his son, Jotham his
son, 13Ahaz his son, Hezekiah his son, Manasseh
his son, 14Amon his son, Josiah his son. 15The sons
of Josiah: Johanan the firstborn, the second Jehoiakim, the third Zedekiah, the fourth Shallum.
16The descendants of Jehoiakim: Jeconiah his son,
Zedekiah his son; 17and the sons of Jeconiah, the
captive: Shealtiel his son, 18Malchiram, Pedaiah,
Shenazzar, Jekamiah, Hoshama, and Nedabiah;
19The sons of Pedaiah: Zerubbabel and Shimei;
and the sons of Zerubbabel: Meshullam and Hananiah, and Shelomith was their sister; 20and
Hashubah, Ohel, Berechiah, Hasadiah, and
Jushab-hesed, five. 21The sons of Hananiah: Pelatiah and Jeshaiah, his son[a] Rephaiah, his son[a]
Arnan, his son[a] Obadiah, his son[a] Shecaniah. 22The
son[b] of Shecaniah: Shemaiah. And the sons of
Shemaiah: Hattush, Igal, Bariah, Neariah, and
Shaphat, six. 23The sons of Neariah: Elioenai,
Hizkiah, and Azrikam, three. 24The sons of Elioe-
nai: Hodaviah, Eliashib, Pelaiah, Akkub, Johanan,
Delaiah, and Anani, seven.

4 The sons of Judah: Perez, Hezron, Carmi,
Hur, and Shobal. 2Reaiah son of Shobal
became the father of Jahath, and Jahath became
the father of Ahumai and Lahad. These were the
families of the Zorathites. 3These were the sons[c]
of Etam: Jezreel, Ishma, and Idbash; and the name
of their sister was Hazzelelponi, 4and Penuel was

[a] Gk Compare Syr Vg: Heb *sons of* [b] Heb *sons* [c] Gk Compare Vg: Heb *the father*

NIV

3 These were the sons of David born to him in Hebron:
The firstborn was Amnon the son of Ahinoam of Jezreel;
the second, Daniel the son of Abigail of Carmel;
2the third, Absalom the son of Maacah daughter of Talmai king of Geshur;
the fourth, Adonijah the son of Haggith;
3the fifth, Shephatiah the son of Abital;
and the sixth, Ithream, by his wife Eglah.
4These six were born to David in Hebron, where he reigned seven years and six months.

David reigned in Jerusalem thirty-three years, 5and these were the children born to him there:
Shammua,[a] Shobab, Nathan and Solomon. These four were by Bathsheba[b] daughter of Ammiel. 6There were also Ibhar, Elishua,[c] Eliphelet, 7Nogah, Nepheg, Japhia, 8Elishama, Eliada and Eliphelet—nine in all. 9All these were the sons of David, besides his sons by his concubines. And Tamar was their sister.

10Solomon's son was Rehoboam,
Abijah his son,
Asa his son,
Jehoshaphat his son,
11Jehoram[d] his son,
Ahaziah his son,
Joash his son,
12Amaziah his son,
Azariah his son,
Jotham his son,
13Ahaz his son,
Hezekiah his son,
Manasseh his son,
14Amon his son,
Josiah his son.
15The sons of Josiah:
Johanan the firstborn,
Jehoiakim the second son,
Zedekiah the third,
Shallum the fourth.

[a]5 Hebrew *Shimea,* a variant of *Shammua* [b]5 One Hebrew manuscript and Vulgate (see also Septuagint and 2 Samuel 11:3); most Hebrew manuscripts *Bathshua* [c]6 Two Hebrew manuscripts (see also 2 Samuel 5:15 and 1 Chron. 14:5); most Hebrew manuscripts *Elishama* [d]11 Hebrew *Joram,* a variant of *Jehoram*

NRSV

the father of Gedor, and Ezer the father of
Hushah. These were the sons of Hur, the firstborn
of Ephrathah, the father of Bethlehem. 5Ashhur
father of Tekoa had two wives, Helah and Naarah;
6Naarah bore him Ahuzzam, Hepher, Temeni, and
Haahashtari.[a] These were the sons of Naarah. 7The
sons of Helah: Zereth, Izhar,[b] and Ethnan. 8Koz
became the father of Anub, Zobebah, and the
families of Aharhel son of Harum. 9Jabez was
honored more than his brothers; and his mother
named him Jabez, saying, "Because I bore him in
pain." 10Jabez called on the God of Israel, saying,
"Oh that you would bless me and enlarge my
border, and that your hand might be with me,
and that you would keep me from hurt and
harm!" And God granted what he asked. 11Chelub
the brother of Shuhah became the father of Mehir,
who was the father of Eshton. 12Eshton became
the father of Beth-rapha, Paseah, and Tehinnah
the father of Ir-nahash. These are the men of
Recah. 13The sons of Kenaz: Othniel and Seraiah;
and the sons of Othniel: Hathath and Meonothai.[c]
14Meonothai became the father of Ophrah; and
Seraiah became the father of Joab father of Ge-
harashim,[d] so-called because they were artisans.
15The sons of Caleb son of Jephunneh: Iru, Elah,
and Naam; and the son[e] of Elah: Kenaz. 16The
sons of Jehallelel: Ziph, Ziphah, Tiria, and Asarel.
17The sons of Ezrah: Jether, Mered, Epher, and
Jalon. These are the sons of Bithiah, daughter of
Pharaoh, whom Mered married;[f] and she conceived and bore[g] Miriam, Shammai, and Ishbah
father of Eshtemoa. 18And his Judean wife bore
Jered father of Gedor, Heber father of Soco, and
Jekuthiel father of Zanoah. 19The sons of the wife
of Hodiah, the sister of Naham, were the fathers
of Keilah the Garmite and Eshtemoa the Maacathite. 20The sons of Shimon: Amnon, Rinnah,
Ben-hanan, and Tilon. The sons of Ishi: Zoheth
and Ben-zoheth. 21The sons of Shelah son of
Judah: Er father of Lecah, Laadah father of
Mareshah, and the families of the guild of linen
workers at Beth-ashbea; 22and Jokim, and the men
of Cozeba, and Joash, and Saraph, who married
into Moab but returned to Lehem[h] (now the

[a] Or *Ahashtari* [b] Another reading is *Zohar* [c] Gk Vg: Heb lacks *and Meonothai* [d] That is *Valley of artisans* [e] Heb *sons*
[f] The clause: *These are . . . married* is transposed from verse 18
[g] Heb lacks *and bore* [h] Vg Compare Gk: Heb *and Jashubi-lahem*

NIV

[16]The successors of Jehoiakim:
Jehoiachin[a] his son,
and Zedekiah.

[17]The descendants of Jehoiachin the captive:
Shealtiel his son, [18]Malkiram, Pedaiah, Shenazzar, Jekamiah, Hoshama and Nedabiah.

[19]The sons of Pedaiah:
Zerubbabel and Shimei.

The sons of Zerubbabel:
Meshullam and Hananiah.
Shelomith was their sister.

[20]There were also five others:
Hashubah, Ohel, Berekiah, Hasadiah and Jushab-Hesed.

[21]The descendants of Hananiah:
Pelatiah and Jeshaiah, and the sons of Rephaiah, of Arnan, of Obadiah and of Shecaniah.

[22]The descendants of Shecaniah:
Shemaiah and his sons:
Hattush, Igal, Bariah, Neariah and Shaphat—six in all.

[23]The sons of Neariah:
Elioenai, Hizkiah and Azrikam—three in all.

[24]The sons of Elioenai:
Hodaviah, Eliashib, Pelaiah, Akkub, Johanan, Delaiah and Anani—seven in all.

4 The descendants of Judah:
Perez, Hezron, Carmi, Hur and Shobal.

[2]Reaiah son of Shobal was the father of Jahath, and Jahath the father of Ahumai and Lahad. These were the clans of the Zorathites.

[3]These were the sons[b] of Etam:
Jezreel, Ishma and Idbash. Their sister was named Hazzelelponi. [4]Penuel was the father of Gedor, and Ezer the father of Hushah.

These were the descendants of Hur, the firstborn of Ephrathah and father[c] of Bethlehem.

a *16* Hebrew *Jeconiah,* a variant of *Jehoiachin*; also in verse 17   b *3* Some Septuagint manuscripts (see also Vulgate); Hebrew *father*   c *4 Father* may mean *civic leader* or *military leader*; also in verses 12, 14, 17, 18 and possibly elsewhere.

NRSV

records[a] are ancient). [23]These were the potters and
inhabitants of Netaim and Gederah; they lived
there with the king in his service.

a Or *matters*

NIV

[5]Ashhur the father of Tekoa had two wives, Helah and Naarah.

[6]Naarah bore him Ahuzzam, Hepher, Temeni and Haahashtari. These were the descendants of Naarah.

[7]The sons of Helah:

Zereth, Zohar, Ethnan, [8]and Koz, who was the father of Anub and Hazzobebah and of the clans of Aharhel son of Harum.

[9]Jabez was more honorable than his brothers.
His mother had named him Jabez,[a] saying, "I gave
birth to him in pain." [10]Jabez cried out to the God
of Israel, "Oh, that you would bless me and
enlarge my territory! Let your hand be with me,
and keep me from harm so that I will be free
from pain." And God granted his request.

[11]Kelub, Shuhah's brother, was the father of Mehir, who was the father of Eshton. [12]Eshton was the father of Beth Rapha, Paseah and Tehinnah the father of Ir Nahash.[b] These were the men of Recah.

[13]The sons of Kenaz:

Othniel and Seraiah.

The sons of Othniel:

Hathath and Meonothai.[c] [14]Meonothai was the father of Ophrah.

Seraiah was the father of Joab,

the father of Ge Harashim.[d] It was called this because its people were craftsmen.

[15]The sons of Caleb son of Jephunneh:

Iru, Elah and Naam.

The son of Elah:

Kenaz.

[16]The sons of Jehallelel:

Ziph, Ziphah, Tiria and Asarel.

[17]The sons of Ezrah:

Jether, Mered, Epher and Jalon. One of Mered's wives gave birth to Miriam, Shammai and Ishbah the father of Eshtemoa. [18](His Judean wife gave birth to Jered the father of Gedor, Heber the father of Soco, and Jekuthiel the father of Zanoah.) These were the children of Pharaoh's

[a]9 *Jabez* sounds like the Hebrew for *pain.* [b]12 Or *of the city of Nahash* [c]13 Some Septuagint manuscripts and Vulgate; Hebrew does not have *and Meonothai.* [d]14 *Ge Harashim* means *valley of craftsmen.*

NIV

daughter Bithiah, whom Mered had married.
19The sons of Hodiah's wife, the sister of Naham:
the father of Keilah the Garmite, and Eshtemoa the Maacathite.
20The sons of Shimon:
Amnon, Rinnah, Ben-Hanan and Tilon.
The descendants of Ishi:
Zoheth and Ben-Zoheth.
21The sons of Shelah son of Judah:
Er the father of Lecah, Laadah the father of Mareshah and the clans of the linen workers at Beth Ashbea, 22Jokim, the men of Cozeba, and Joash and Saraph, who ruled in Moab and Jashubi Lehem. (These records are from ancient times.) 23They were the potters who lived at Netaim and Gederah; they stayed there and worked for the king.

COMMENTARY

This section supplies a genealogical list for Judah. The key to understanding this composite text is its present structuring as a chiasm.[27] It has a large center of three concentric rings forming an ABCC′B′A′ pattern. In 2:9 we are introduced to the three sons of Hezron, Judah's grandson and Perez's son—namely Jerahmeel, Ram, and Chelubai (or Caleb). Their lineage is explored in 2:10-33. Ram's descendants are listed as far as David in 2:10-17, Caleb's descendants are presented in 2:18-24, and Jerahmeel's in 2:25-33. Then supplementary material relating to these three lineages is given in 2:34–3:24, in reverse order, Jerahmeel's in 2:34-41, Caleb's in 2:42-55, and finally Ram's in 3:1-24 in the form of David's descendants. This chiasm is provided with two outer rings concerning the lineages of Judah's sons, that of Shelah in 2:3 and 4:21-23, and a further one of Perez, Hezron's father, in 2:4-8 (including that of a third son, Zerah) and 4:1-20.

27. E. L. Curtis and A. A. Madsen, *The Books of Chronicles,* ICC (Edinburgh: T. &. T. Clark, 1910) 82-84; H. G. M. Williamson, "Sources and Redaction in the Chronicler's Genealogy of Judah," *JBL* 98 (1979) 351-59; *1 and 2 Chronicles,* 48-50; cf. the comments of R. L. Braun, *1 Chronicles,* WBC 14 (Waco, Tex.: Word, 1986) 25-28.

The overall effect of this intricate chiasm is to let David's clan dominate the center of the composition, so that it begins with his ancestors and ends with his descendants. The split conveys a sense of the overarching theological importance of David's kingship, not only as a historical phenomenon but also in terms of an expectation for its restoration.

The intention of presenting the double genealogy of Jerahmeel is to take it down to the end of the pre-exilic period. The Caleb genealogies are concerned at their close to give the traditional localities of various clans (2:50*b*-55). The reference to the royal service of the guild of potters mentioned at the end of the genealogy of Shelah (4:23) strikes an explicitly pre-exilic note. In general the chronicler understood the genealogies as pre-exilic. It is remarkable, therefore, that the second genealogy of Ram does not stop at the exile but overshoots it at 3:17 ("the captive") and takes the Davidic family down into the fourth century BCE. They were waiting in the wings, ready to take center stage again at the time of the Lord's choosing. The permanent nature of the Davidic dynasty is a theme emphasized in Chronicles ("forever," 1 Chr 17:12, 14, 23, 27; 28:4; 2 Chr 13:5). The chronicler used the genre of genealogy to reaffirm this conviction.

In 28:4-5 this genre is echoed in narrative form to express David's testimony that "the LORD God of Israel chose me from all my ancestral house to be king over Israel forever; for he chose Judah as leader, and in the house of Judah my father's house. . . . And of all my sons . . . he has chosen my son Solomon" (NRSV). Such sentiments are here expressed in a genealogical form. The leadership of Judah among the tribes and its royal associations will also be attested in 5:2: "Judah became prominent among his brothers and a ruler came from him" (NRSV). Accordingly Judah is here put first and presented as the matrix of the monarchy. In Jacob's blessing, his sons Reuben, Simeon, and Levi were virtually passed over (Gen 49:2-7), so that Judah, next in line among the sons of Judah's first wife, Leah, assumed the headship (Gen 35:23; 49:8-12).[28]

In 2:3-8, 10-17, 20; 3:1-6, the backbone of the Judah genealogy has been copied substantially from earlier biblical texts, with minor variations. This material has been interwoven with extra-biblical genealogies, three of which have been incorporated with their parallel opening and closing formulas: 2:25-33, relating to Jerahmeel; 2:42-50*a*, relating to Caleb; and 2:50*b*-55 + 4:2-4, relating to Hur (cf. the introductory 2:18-19).

2:3-4. Judah's lineage came down only through Shelah, Perez, and Zerah; his other sons, Er and Onan, died without heirs (Gen 46:12). The story of the latter, told in Gen 38:8-10, is presupposed, while in v. 3*b* the chronicler has copied out Gen 38:7 concerning Er. It corresponds to his general teaching that for each generation the wages of sin can be death. Genesis 38:11-26, a tangled tale of grievance and disappointment and of a willful attempt to get one's rights, is presupposed. It ended in the shocking fact of v. 4: "Tamar, his daughter-in-law, bore him Perez and Zerah." This relationship was incestuous according to the Torah (Lev 18:15), and both parties should have died (Lev 20:12). The chronicler has juxtaposed the striking disparity of vv. 3*b* and 4: The wicked son lost his life, while the wicked father and wife found places in the line leading to David. Elsewhere the chronicler ties such grace to prior repentance. Presumably he deduced it from Judah's declaration in Gen 38:26, on the lines of the confession attributed to him in the *Testaments of the Twelve Patriarchs*: "Before the eyes of all I turned aside to Tamar and committed a great sin."[29]

Mention of Judah's Canaanite wife initiates a recurring phenomenon in the Judah genealogy. Marrying a Canaanite defied not only Gen 24:3; 28:1, but also Ezra 9:1. In 2:17 an Ishmaelite father appears, and in 2:34 an Egyptian slave. At 3:2 one of David's wives is a princess from the Aramean state of Geshur, and in 4:18 an Egyptian princess is mentioned. The chronicler allowed these references to stand. Throughout his history he took a softer line on intermarriage than did Ezra and Nehemiah. Writing later, he evidently regarded their rigorous stand as no longer so necessary. He did not censor out from 1 Kings a portion of Solomon's prayer in 2 Chr 6:32-33, to the effect that foreigners were welcome to worship the Lord at the Temple.

2:5-8. After reflecting Gen 46:12*a*, the text cites Gen 46:12*b* at v. 5. Zerah's sons in v. 6 include Zimri, the equivalent of Zabdi in Josh 7:1, the two forms being similar in the old Hebrew script. So in v. 7 the line leads via Carmi to Achan. Mention of Ethan, Heman, Calcol, and Dara in v. 6 comes from 1 Kgs 4:31, where the fourth name is Darda. It depends on equating "[Ethan] the Ezrahite" and Zerah's clan, the Zerahites. In the headings to Psalms 88 and 89, Heman and Ethan are called Ezrahites. Temple music guilds, elsewhere levitical in Chronicles, are here adopted into the tribe of Judah. There is considerable telescoping involved in v. 6: These figures are associated with the age of Solomon, while v. 7 moves back to the period of conquest.[30] The music of the Temple is a key concern of the chronicler, and here genealogical tribute is paid to it.

Verse 7 presupposes knowledge of the story of Achan in Joshua 7. He is called "Achar" by wordplay with the Valley of Achar ("trouble") in Josh 7:26. Similarly he is branded "troubler (עוכר *'ôkēr*) of Israel," the contemptuous term Elijah threw back at Ahab in 1 Kgs 18:17-18. Here it

28. See T. J. Prewitt, "Kinship and the Genesis Genealogies," *JNES* 40 (1981) 87-98, esp. 97-98.

29. *T. Jud.* 14:5.

30. W. L. Osborne, "The Genealogies of 1 Chronicles 1–9" (Ph.D. diss., Dropsie University, 1979) 213.

alludes to his contaminating Israel by disobeying a holy war ruling: "Israel has sinned" and he "troubled us" (Josh 7:11, 25). His "being unfaithful" (NJB) reflects the text of Josh 7:1. The Hebrew expression used there (מעל מעל *mā'al ma'al,* "practice unfaithfulness") is only the first in a series within 1 Chronicles 2–9. In 5:25 and 9:1 the verb מעל (*mā'al*) and the noun מעל (*ma'al*) refer to the sin that leads to exile, a characteristic use in Chronicles derived from Lev 26:40. In 9:1, Judah's own sin is here prefigured in Achan's.

2:9-17. Verse 9 provides the framework for the central part of Judah's genealogy. "Chelubai" (NRSV) refers to Caleb later (vv. 18, 42, etc). The chronicler distinguished between this archetypal figure and "Caleb son of Yephunneh," who is mentioned in another connection in 4:15. David's genealogy recalls Num 2:3; Ruth 4:19-22; 1 Sam 16:6-9; and narratives of 1–2 Samuel. It has been telescoped into ten members. Jesse had eight sons, according to 1 Sam 16:10-11; 17:12, and 1 Chr 27:18 suggests that the name of the eighth was Elihu. The names in vv. 16-17 are included because of the role these persons played in David's rise to power.

2:18-24. The Caleb clan, who lived in the southern part of the mountains of Judah, was originally distinct from the tribe of Judah (1 Sam 25:3; 30:14), but was later incorporated into it, as this next genealogy implies. The Caleb genealogy, which basically lists children according to Caleb's two wives, reflects the amalgamation of different types of material. The Bezalel lineage in v. 20 has been inserted from Exod 31:2, though it remains unharmonized with the Hur genealogy given in 2:50*b*-55; 4:2-4. It will be cited again at 2 Chr 1:5. It pays tribute to the craftsman of the Mosaic tabernacle, the precursor of the Solomonic Temple. The chronicler will represent Solomon as his antitype, so room is made for him here. Separate information about a fourth son of Hezron in vv. 21-23 interrupts the story of the progeny of Caleb's marriages. It was presumably placed here before the mention of Hezron's death in v. 24; it records links with the Transjordanian tribe of Manasseh (see Num 27:1; 32:39-42). The loss of cities to the Arameans is not related to sin, but it paves the way for the theological association in 5:23-26. In v. 24, which continues v. 19, a preferable textual tradition yields the translation "Caleb went in to Ephrath" (cf. the RSV and REB, and see *BHS*; for intercourse with one's wife after bereavement, see 2 Sam 12:24).[31] The isolated Hebrew sentence "and Abijah [was] the wife of Hezron" may originally have been attached to v. 21, itself part of the insertion of vv. 21-23.[32] The Ashhur genealogy will be continued in 4:5-8. Ashhur was the "founder" (REB) of Tekoa, an idiomatic use of "father" that occurs several times in chaps. 2 and 4.

2:25-33. The first Jerahmeel genealogy rounds off the first half of the chiasm. Like the clan of Caleb, this group was originally distinct from Judah (see 1 Sam 27:10; 30:29) and was incorporated subsequently. Ancient genealogies reflected social relationships as well as physical descent. The Jerahmeelites lived in the Negeb, either in the northeast or in the southeast.[33]

2:34-41. Whereas in the previous segmented genealogy Sheshan has a son named Ahlai, Sheshan's own linear genealogy reflects a different tradition. Such fluidity was common in ancient genealogies.[34] The chronicler assumed that this genealogy extended to the close of the pre-exilic period. If one compares Sheshan's position as the tenth generation from Judah and the subsequent fifteen generations with David's genealogy in 2:9-17; 3:1-24, then Sheshan corresponds with Jesse, and Elishama (v. 41) with Josiah, near the end of the monarchical period.[35]

2:42-55. The second Caleb genealogy relates to an unnamed wife and two concubines, Ephah (v. 46) and Maachah (v. 48). The seemingly unconnected v. 42*a* and v. 42*b* (reflected in the NRSV, except that "and" should precede the second phrase) define the descendants of Caleb as both Mesha and the unidentified descendants of Mareshah.[36] The connection between v. 47 and

31. See L. C. Allen, *The Greek Chronicles: The Relation of the Septuagint of I and II Chronicles to the Massoretic Text,* Part 2: *Textual Criticism,* VTSup 25, 27 (Leiden: Brill, 1974) 87, 106; D. Barthélemy et al., *Critique textuelle de l'Ancien Testament,* OBO 50/1 (Fribourg: Editions Universitaires; and Göttingen: Vandenhoeck & Ruprecht, 1982) 1:431.

32. H. G. M. Williamson, *1 and 2 Chronicles,* NCB (Grand Rapids: Eerdmans, 1982) 53-54.

33. See Y. Aharoni, "The Negeb of Judah," *IEJ* 8 (1958) 26-38, esp. 30.

34. For fluidity whereby a change of genealogical function caused a change in form, see R. R. Wilson, *Genealogy and History in the Biblical World,* (New Haven: Yale University Press, 1977) 27-36.

35. S. Japhet, "The Israelite Legal and Social Reality as Reflected in Chronicles: A Case Study," in *"Shaarei Talmon": Studies in the Bible, Qumran and the Ancient Near East Presented to Shemaryahu Talmon,* ed. M. Fishbane et al. (Winona Lake: Eisenbrauns, 1992) 79-91, esp. 82-83.

36. M. Kartveit, *Motive und Schichten der Landtheologie in 1 Chronik 1–9,* ConBOT 28 (Stockholm: Almqvist & Wiksell, 1989) 46.

what precedes is not indicated by a kinship term. In v. 49 Achsah was actually the daughter of Caleb son of Yephunneh, according to Josh 15:16-17 and Judg 1:12-13. The clause may have originated as a note on v. 50*a*, which equated the two Calebs, something the chronicler himself did not do.

Hur's genealogy in vv. 50*b*-55 continues vv. 18-19, giving the descendants of Caleb and his wife, Ephrath(ah), via Hur and then via his sons Shobal and Salma. The descendants of the latter two are mainly described in terms of clans. "Haroeh" in v. 52 is called Reaiah in 4:2 and has probably been corrupted from that form (REB; see *BHS*). For "the Menuhoth" (NRSV), one should doubtless read "the Manahathites" (NIV; cf. the REB; see also *BHS*), in line with v. 54. Verse 55 probably refers to "Sophrites" (REB) rather than to "scribes" (NRSV, NIV; there is no article in the Hebrew), with reference to Kiriath-sepher southwest of Hebron. The Kenites were an independent tribe in the eastern Negeb (see 1 Sam 27:10), here affiliated with the (Judaized) Calebites.

3:1-9. David's descendants in chap. 3 provide the outer rim of the main chiastic structure. The list in vv. 1-8 is related primarily to 2 Sam 3:2-5 and 5:5, 13-16; vv. 5-8 will recur in 14:4-7 to illustrate divine blessing. The attribution of four sons to Bathshua (= Bathsheba) occurs only here, and the position of Solomon is surprising. For Elishama (NRSV) in v. 6 one expects "Elishua," as in 14:5 and 2 Sam 5:15 (the NIV has duly emended the text, assuming assimilation to the name in v. 8).

3:10-24. The linear list of Solomon's descendants up to v. 14 simply follows the order of Davidic monarchs in the books of Kings. It changes style in v. 15 by enumerating the four sons of Josiah not by succession but by age, including an otherwise unknown Johanan. From now on a segmented list is used from another source. Shallum, as in Jer 22:11, is elsewhere known as Jehoahaz. In v. 16 Jehoiachin is called Jeconiah, as in Jer 24:1; 29:2. The repeated "his son" in this verse does not refer to separate generations as in vv. 10-14, since Jeconiah's sons are listed in vv. 17-18; thus sons of Jehoiakim are meant. The Zedekiah of v. 16 will be equated with the king in 2 Chr 36:10, whereas 2 Kgs 24:17 relates him to his namesake uncle in v. 15. Zerubbabel is listed as a son of Pedaiah in v. 18; he is Shealtiel's son in Ezra 3:28; 5:2; Neh 12:1. Perhaps Pedaiah engaged in a levirate marriage with Shealtiel's widow after he died without a son. In v. 20 there is no kinship term, and so the relation of these five persons is not clarified; the reference to Hananiah in v. 21 may suggest that they were sons of Meshullam. In v. 21 the NIV reflects the MT, which may be retained. After Hananiah's two sons, four generations are represented in the form of an empty horizontal framework, introductions to name lists for which no names were available.[37] The errant arithmetic in v. 22 may be resolved by regarding "and the sons of Shemaiah" (NRSV) as an erroneous repetition of part of what precedes, so that Shemaiah is the first of the six sons of Shecaniah (REB; see *BHS*).[38] Whether Hattush is the Davidide of Ezra 8:2-3 is a moot issue. Although the number of generations involved in this genealogy is uncertain, it seems to extend well into the fourth century, down to the chronicler's period. Fecundity marks out this family as the object of divine blessing.

4:1-4. The first of the outer rings of the chiasm, 4:1-20, begins here. It corresponds to 2:4-8 and is intended as a genealogy of Perez according to the recapitulating heading in v. 1. It uses to this end supplements to various genealogies that appeared in chap. 2. In place of Carmi in v. 1 one expects a reference to Caleb; confusion with Reuben's sons Hezron and Carmi (5:3; Gen 46:9) seems to have occurred at some stage. Verse 2 restates 2:52-53 in different terms, giving more background information about the Zorathite clan. In v. 3, the NIV and the NRSV have replaced the MT's "father" (in the sense of founder) with a minority reading "sons," but some words may have dropped out earlier,[39] perhaps referring to Hur's third son, Hareph (2:51), whose genealogy is not otherwise supplied.

4:5-8. The genealogy of Caleb's son Ashhur is continued from 2:24. In v. 6 "Haahashtari" seems to refer to a clan, "the Ahashtarites" (NJB). The name is evidently Persian in origin, so that this reference is post-exilic. Verse 8 is unrelated in the MT to what precedes; the NIV, together with the

37. S. J. De Vries, *1 and 2 Chronicles*, FOTL 11 (Grand Rapids: Eerdmans, 1989) 42.

38. See Barthélemy, *Critique textuelle de l'Ancien Testament*, 1:434-35.

39. See *BHS*.

REB, has supplied "and Koz" at the end of v. 7, attested only in the Targum, a procedure that all three versions adopt in v. 13.

4:9-10. Mention of Jabez in v. 9 may be linked with the place-name in 2:55, here treated as a person associated with "territory" (v. 10 NIV). Verse 9 presents a paradox, and v. 10 resolves it. Jabez enjoyed a higher status in the community than did his brothers—surprisingly so, since he was dogged by an ill-omened name. The story engages in wordplay between עצב (*ʿōṣeb*, "pain") and the (metathesized—the name of the Hebrew consonants *b* and *ṣ* is switched) name יעבץ (*yaʿbēṣ*), assuming that the name means "he [God] inflicts pain" and commemorates his mother's painful delivery. In popular thinking such a name made Jabez a born loser. His name should have been changed for his own good, as in Gen 35:18. Yet his life turned into a success story. The secret was God's answering his prayer. What his mother "called" him (REB) was countered by his calling on God. He prayed that God bless him with territorial growth and protection from the "pain" (NIV) that would otherwise have been his lot. This little narrative must have appealed to the chronicler, since it accords with his own emphasis on prayer as the remedy for crisis. Like Asa in 2 Chr 15:2 and like Jehoshaphat in 20:17, Jabez enjoyed the protective presence of God in response to trusting prayer. Jabez's experience in desiring and obtaining an enlarged border constituted a vignette of hope for post-exilic Israel. References to the southern part of the Judean mountain country and to the Negeb, areas lost by post-exilic times to the Edomites, suggest that the chronicler intended his constitutency to identify with the prayer in v. 10.

4:11-20. The genealogy of the Recah clan in vv. 11-12 is not related to anything in the preceding context. The LXX refers instead to Rechab, linking with the Rechabites of 2:55; but that may reflect ingenuity rather than a sound tradition. In vv. 13-15 the Kenizzite genealogy refers more certainly to 2:55; it is presupposed that Othniel and Caleb son of Yephunneh were brothers associated with the conquest of Kiriath-sepher, home of the Sophrites (REB; cf. Josh 15:15-19; Judg 1:11-15). The Kenizzites were another southern group who were incorporated into the tribe of Judah. They lived in the southern mountain country of Judah in the area of Debir. Verses 16-20 present a series of fragmentary genealogies. In vv. 17-18 the NRSV, along with the REB, has transposed the order and secured better sense, while the NIV bravely struggles with the MT.

4:21-23. The Shelah genealogy rounds off the whole chiasm, harking back to Judah's oldest son in 2:3. It preserves traditions of weaving and pottery guilds, continuing a theme broached in v. 14. Since the potters worked for Judean kings, the records in which these details were preserved may have been royal ones. Reference to those "who ruled in Moab" reflects the period of the united monarchy when Moab was under Israelite control (see Ezra 2:6). If the slight emendation reflected in the NRSV's "but returned to Lehem" is correct, Lehem is short for Bethlehem.[40]

40. Y. Aharoni, *The Land of the Bible: A Historical Geography,* 2nd rev. ed., trans. A. F. Rainey (Philadelphia: Westminster, 1979) 108.

REFLECTIONS

1. The length and artistic structure of the genealogy of the tribe of Judah emphasizes its importance for the chronicler. The tribe was the bastion of Israel, shaping its religious and national traditions down through the centuries. Its value lay particularly in its role as tribal matrix of the Davidic monarchy. As in 28:4, we can observe divine election flowing from Judah to David. Two of the evangelists took a leaf out of the chronicler's book. Both Matthew and Luke prefaced their accounts of the ministry of Jesus with linear genealogies that traced Jesus' ancestry from Abraham, in the former case, and back to Adam, in the latter (Matt 1:11-17; Luke 3:23-28).

Matthew's periodization in terms of Abraham, David, the Babylonian exile, and the coming of Jesus as the Messiah is similar to the standpoint of the chronicler, for whom Jacob or Israel replaced Abraham. The interruption of exile (3:17) meant not the collapse of Davidic hopes, but an open-ended continuation of the register of the royal family, evidently down to the chronicler's own time. What the chronicler awaited, Matthew proclaimed as fulfilled in the person of Jesus. In briefer, Pauline terms, Jesus was "descended from David according to the flesh" (Rom 1:3 NRSV).

2. The genealogical open-endedness of the chronicler is matched by an ethnic openheartedness. Foreigners found an undisputed place in Judah's heritage. Clans were adopted into the family; individuals joined it by marriage. This perspective recalls the post-exilic oracle in Isa 56:2-8, which extended a welcome to foreigners who joined themselves to the Lord and aspired to worshiping in the Jerusalem Temple. Matthew's Gospel strikes a similar note by incorporating the motherhood of the Moabite Ruth into the royal genealogy of Jesus (Matt 1:5). In the framework of the Gospel, that element and the visit of the magi are matched by the commission of the risen Jesus to go and "make disciples of all nations" (Matt 28:19). This openness should not be regarded as a missiological truism, but must challenge us to its domestic implications, such as integration within local churches and fellowship between homogeneous churches of different sorts. Such applications will be true to the antidiscriminatory religious intention the chronicler himself had.

3. In 2:3-4 the chronicler knew more than he wrote, expecting his readers to reflect on the underlying Genesis narrative. Matthew picked up the implicit message of Tamar from the Chronicles genealogy and passed it on in his own (Matt 1:3). Judah and Tamar were links in the chain that led ultimately to Jesus. Grace was at work here, as the chronicler underlined by his dramatic contrast. Human failure was transcended in the ongoing purposes of a merciful God. In the Midrash Rabbah the pregnant Tamar exclaims, "I am big with kings and redeemers."[41] Matthew the Evangelist was one reader who picked up this implicit message from the Chronicles genealogy and passed it on in his own (Matt 1:3). Judah and Tamar, though they deserved to die like Er, were links in the chain that led ultimately to Jesus.

4. Achar, Mr. Trouble, is another character over whom we are invited to pause. He disobeyed a divine mandate by keeping loot for himself. The selfish act had wider consequences, as selfish acts do. It contaminated the entire community and laid it under a divine curse. Their existence was threatened almost as soon as they set foot in the promised land. Achar would have brought total disaster on them, if the Lord had not arranged a way to decontaminate Israel. It was a sad beginning, curiously like the story of greedy Ananias and Sapphira in Acts 5. Human nature soon raises its ugly head, spoiling the work of God, and it requires a quick response. If 2:3-4 points to divine forgiveness, 2:7 poses a serious warning.

5. Food for thought is provided in the reference to "Bathshua," or Bathsheba, among David's wives, through whom the blessing of a large family came from God (3:5; cf. 26:4-5). As if incest and greed were not bad enough, now the crimson threads of adultery and murder are woven into the tapestry of divine providence (see 2 Samuel 11–12). The chronicler did not have occasion to incorporate the sordid narrative into his presentation of David. He was constrained by the religious nature of that presentation to illustrate David's sin as the pride that led to the military census, which led eventually to the gracious revelation of the temple site (1 Chronicles 21). He did, however, echo a striking sentence from the Bathsheba narrative at 21:7. The incident carries a message of sin and repentance, of judgment and grace. Once more Matthew—in his own genealogy—wondered at God's graciousness, pointedly referring to Bathsheba as simply "the wife of Uriah" (Matt 1:6). Where sin abounded, divine grace superabounded.

6. One can sense the chronicler's relishing of the story of Jabez in 4:9-10. Prayer changes things, he testifies throughout his work, because the Lord answers prayer. Jabez could

41. *Gen. Rab.* 85. 11.

participate in the dynamics of change. He knew of available resources in the communal faith: He "called on the God of Israel." As in the Aaronic benediction (Num 6:24-26), blessing and keeping trouble at bay are positive and negative factors that belong together. Jabez's name created an emotional hang-up that society endorsed. It stopped him from leading a satisfying life: Only God could deal with that negative image and flood his life with blessing. He was enabled to get release from its grip and enjoy a social role beyond all expectations.

1 Chronicles 4:24–5:26, Simeon and the Transjordanian Tribes

NIV

[24]The descendants of Simeon:

Nemuel, Jamin, Jarib, Zerah and Shaul;

[25]Shallum was Shaul's son, Mibsam his son and Mishma his son.

[26]The descendants of Mishma:

Hammuel his son, Zaccur his son and Shimei his son.

[27]Shimei had sixteen sons and six daughters, but his brothers did not have many children; so their entire clan did not become as numerous as the people of Judah. [28]They lived in Beersheba, Moladah, Hazar Shual, [29]Bilhah, Ezem, Tolad, [30]Bethuel, Hormah, Ziklag, [31]Beth Marcaboth, Hazar Susim, Beth Biri and Shaaraim. These were their towns until the reign of David. [32]Their surrounding villages were Etam, Ain, Rimmon, Token and Ashan—five towns— [33]and all the villages around these towns as far as Baalath.[a] These were their settlements. And they kept a genealogical record.

[34]Meshobab, Jamlech, Joshah son of Amaziah, [35]Joel, Jehu son of Joshibiah, the son of Seraiah, the son of Asiel, [36]also Elioenai, Jaakobah, Jeshohaiah, Asaiah, Adiel, Jesimiel, Benaiah, [37]and Ziza son of Shiphi, the son of Allon, the son of Jedaiah, the son of Shimri, the son of Shemaiah.

[38]The men listed above by name were leaders of their clans. Their families increased greatly, [39]and they went to the outskirts of Gedor to the east of the valley in search of pasture for their flocks. [40]They found rich, good pasture, and the land was spacious, peaceful and quiet. Some Hamites had lived there formerly.

[41]The men whose names were listed came in the days of Hezekiah king of Judah. They attacked

[a]33 Some Septuagint manuscripts (see also Joshua 19:8); Hebrew *Baal*

NRSV

24The sons of Simeon: Nemuel, Jamin, Jarib, Zerah, Shaul;[a] [25]Shallum was his son, Mibsam his son, Mishma his son. [26]The sons of Mishma: Hammuel his son, Zaccur his son, Shimei his son. [27]Shimei had sixteen sons and six daughters; but his brothers did not have many children, nor did all their family multiply like the Judeans. [28]They lived in Beer-sheba, Moladah, Hazar-shual, [29]Bilhah, Ezem, Tolad, [30]Bethuel, Hormah, Ziklag, [31]Beth-marcaboth, Hazar-susim, Beth-biri, and Shaaraim. These were their towns until David became king. [32]And their villages were Etam, Ain, Rimmon, Tochen, and Ashan, five towns, [33]along with all their villages that were around these towns as far as Baal. These were their settlements. And they kept a genealogical record.

34Meshobab, Jamlech, Joshah son of Amaziah, [35]Joel, Jehu son of Joshibiah son of Seraiah son of Asiel, [36]Elioenai, Jaakobah, Jeshohaiah, Asaiah, Adiel, Jesimiel, Benaiah, [37]Ziza son of Shiphi son of Allon son of Jedaiah son of Shimri son of Shemaiah— [38]these mentioned by name were leaders in their families, and their clans increased greatly. [39]They journeyed to the entrance of Gedor, to the east side of the valley, to seek pasture for their flocks, [40]where they found rich, good pasture, and the land was very broad, quiet, and peaceful; for the former inhabitants there belonged to Ham. [41]These, registered by name, came in the days of King Hezekiah of Judah, and attacked their tents and the Meunim who were found there, and exterminated them to this day, and settled in their place, because there was pasture there for their flocks. [42]And some of them, five hundred men of the Simeonites, went to Mount Seir, having as their leaders Pelatiah, Neariah, Rephaiah, and Uzziel, sons of Ishi; [43]they

[a] Or *Saul*

NIV

the Hamites in their dwellings and also the Meunites who were there and completely destroyed[a] them, as is evident to this day. Then they settled in their place, because there was pasture for their flocks. 42And five hundred of these Simeonites, led by Pelatiah, Neariah, Rephaiah and Uzziel, the sons of Ishi, invaded the hill country of Seir. 43They killed the remaining Amalekites who had escaped, and they have lived there to this day.

5 The sons of Reuben the firstborn of Israel (he was the firstborn, but when he defiled his father's marriage bed, his rights as firstborn were given to the sons of Joseph son of Israel; so he could not be listed in the genealogical record in accordance with his birthright, 2and though Judah was the strongest of his brothers and a ruler came from him, the rights of the firstborn belonged to Joseph)— 3the sons of Reuben the firstborn of Israel:

Hanoch, Pallu, Hezron and Carmi.

4The descendants of Joel:

Shemaiah his son, Gog his son,
Shimei his son, 5Micah his son,
Reaiah his son, Baal his son,
6and Beerah his son, whom Tiglath-Pileser[b] king of Assyria took into exile. Beerah was a leader of the Reubenites.

7Their relatives by clans, listed according to their genealogical records:

Jeiel the chief, Zechariah, 8and Bela son of Azaz, the son of Shema, the son of Joel. They settled in the area from Aroer to Nebo and Baal Meon. 9To the east they occupied the land up to the edge of the desert that extends to the Euphrates River, because their livestock had increased in Gilead.

10During Saul's reign they waged war against the Hagrites, who were defeated at their hands; they occupied the dwellings of the Hagrites throughout the entire region east of Gilead.

11The Gadites lived next to them in Bashan, as far as Salecah:

[a]*41* The Hebrew term refers to the irrevocable giving over of things or persons to the LORD, often by totally destroying them. [b]*6* Hebrew *Tilgath-Pilneser,* a variant of *Tiglath-Pileser*; also in verse 26

NRSV

destroyed the remnant of the Amalekites that had escaped, and they have lived there to this day.

5 The sons of Reuben the firstborn of Israel. (He was the firstborn, but because he defiled his father's bed his birthright was given to the sons of Joseph son of Israel, so that he is not enrolled in the genealogy according to the birthright; 2though Judah became prominent among his brothers and a ruler came from him, yet the birthright belonged to Joseph.) 3The sons of Reuben, the firstborn of Israel: Hanoch, Pallu, Hezron, and Carmi. 4The sons of Joel: Shemaiah his son, Gog his son, Shimei his son, 5Micah his son, Reaiah his son, Baal his son, 6Beerah his son, whom King Tilgath-pilneser of Assyria carried away into exile; he was a chieftain of the Reubenites. 7And his kindred by their families, when the genealogy of their generations was reckoned: the chief, Jeiel, and Zechariah, 8and Bela son of Azaz, son of Shema, son of Joel, who lived in Aroer, as far as Nebo and Baal-meon. 9He also lived to the east as far as the beginning of the desert this side of the Euphrates, because their cattle had multiplied in the land of Gilead. 10And in the days of Saul they made war on the Hagrites, who fell by their hand; and they lived in their tents throughout all the region east of Gilead.

11The sons of Gad lived beside them in the land of Bashan as far as Salecah: 12Joel the chief, Shapham the second, Janai, and Shaphat in Bashan. 13And their kindred according to their clans: Michael, Meshullam, Sheba, Jorai, Jacan, Zia, and Eber, seven. 14These were the sons of Abihail son of Huri, son of Jaroah, son of Gilead, son of Michael, son of Jeshishai, son of Jahdo, son of Buz; 15Ahi son of Abdiel, son of Guni, was chief in their clan; 16and they lived in Gilead, in Bashan and in its towns, and in all the pasture lands of Sharon to their limits. 17All of these were enrolled by genealogies in the days of King Jotham of Judah, and in the days of King Jeroboam of Israel.

18The Reubenites, the Gadites, and the half-tribe of Manasseh had valiant warriors, who carried shield and sword, and drew the bow, expert in war, forty-four thousand seven hundred sixty, ready for service. 19They made war on the Hagrites, Jetur, Naphish, and Nodab; 20and when they received help against them, the Hagrites and

NIV

12Joel was the chief, Shapham the second,
then Janai and Shaphat, in Bashan.
13Their relatives, by families, were:
Michael, Meshullam, Sheba, Jorai, Jacan,
Zia and Eber—seven in all.
14These were the sons of Abihail son of Huri,
the son of Jaroah, the son of Gilead, the
son of Michael, the son of Jeshishai, the
son of Jahdo, the son of Buz.
15Ahi son of Abdiel, the son of Guni, was
head of their family.
16The Gadites lived in Gilead, in Bashan and
its outlying villages, and on all the pasturelands of Sharon as far as they
extended.

17All these were entered in the genealogical
records during the reigns of Jotham king of Judah
and Jeroboam king of Israel.

18The Reubenites, the Gadites and the half-tribe
of Manasseh had 44,760 men ready for military
service—able-bodied men who could handle
shield and sword, who could use a bow, and who
were trained for battle. 19They waged war against
the Hagrites, Jetur, Naphish and Nodab. 20They
were helped in fighting them, and God handed
the Hagrites and all their allies over to them,
because they cried out to him during the battle.
He answered their prayers, because they trusted
in him. 21They seized the livestock of the Hagrites—fifty thousand camels, two hundred fifty
thousand sheep and two thousand donkeys. They
also took one hundred thousand people captive,
22and many others fell slain, because the battle
was God's. And they occupied the land until the
exile.

23The people of the half-tribe of Manasseh were
numerous; they settled in the land from Bashan
to Baal Hermon, that is, to Senir (Mount
Hermon).

24These were the heads of their families: Epher,
Ishi, Eliel, Azriel, Jeremiah, Hodaviah and Jahdiel.
They were brave warriors, famous men, and heads
of their families. 25But they were unfaithful to the
God of their fathers and prostituted themselves to
the gods of the peoples of the land, whom God
had destroyed before them. 26So the God of Israel
stirred up the spirit of Pul king of Assyria (that is,
Tiglath-Pileser king of Assyria), who took the

NRSV

all who were with them were given into their
hands, for they cried to God in the battle, and he
granted their entreaty because they trusted in
him. 21They captured their livestock: fifty thousand of their camels, two hundred fifty thousand
sheep, two thousand donkeys, and one hundred
thousand captives. 22Many fell slain, because the
war was of God. And they lived in their territory
until the exile.

23The members of the half-tribe of Manasseh
lived in the land; they were very numerous from
Bashan to Baal-hermon, Senir, and Mount Hermon. 24These were the heads of their clans: Epher,[a] Ishi, Eliel, Azriel, Jeremiah, Hodaviah, and
Jahdiel, mighty warriors, famous men, heads of
their clans. 25But they transgressed against the
God of their ancestors, and prostituted themselves
to the gods of the peoples of the land, whom God
had destroyed before them. 26So the God of Israel
stirred up the spirit of King Pul of Assyria, the
spirit of King Tilgath-pilneser of Assyria, and he
carried them away, namely, the Reubenites, the
Gadites, and the half-tribe of Manasseh, and
brought them to Halah, Habor, Hara, and the river
Gozan, to this day.

[a] Gk Vg: Heb *and Epher*

NIV

Reubenites, the Gadites and the half-tribe of Manasseh into exile. He took them to Halah, Habor, Hara and the river of Gozan, where they are to this day.

COMMENTARY

The little tribe of Simeon is tucked behind Judah, into whose tribal territory it became incorporated at a very early date. However, the southern tribe and the northern tribes across the Jordan have also been blatantly juxtaposed to form a contrasting pair. The passages 4:24-43 and 5:1-26 have parallel conclusions: "to this day." Both are also matched in their formal content, exhibiting a mixture of genealogy, geography, and history. This parallelism takes an ironic turn at the end: One group survived in the land "to this day," while the other was exiled from it "to this day." The polarization throws into relief a homiletic contrast between the deportation suffered by the bad group of tribes and the territorial permanence enjoyed by the evidently good tribe, Simeon. An option confronts the people of God, exemplified by the fate and fortune of these groups. They may either stay loyal to the Lord and keep the land or stray from their allegiance and lose it. The motif of exile often functions in Chronicles as a symbol of spiritual loss that any generation was liable to suffer, should they rebel against the divine will.

Simeon's genealogy falls into three parts, a descending genealogy in 4:24-27, a list of towns and villages to define the tribal area in 4:28-33, and two reports of territorial expansion in 4:34-43, introduced by a list of clan leaders in 4:34-38, to which 4:41 refers. Historically the passage specifies a pre-David period (4:31) and dates one of the expansions in Hezekiah's reign (4:41). So what the chronicler intends is to give a pre-exilic account of the tribe.

4:24-33. The genealogy begins with a linear list that has extracted names from the catalog of Simeonite clans in Num 26:12-24, except that Jarib replaces Jachin, which may have died out. Verses 25-27*a* add a total of five more generations from an unknown source. An example of fertility is given, as also in v. 38, to pay maximum respect to a tribe so overshadowed by Judah. Historically this genealogy must have survived because of the importance of this particular clan. The geographical area they occupied was mostly in the Negeb of Judah, though it extended into the southern Shephelah and other areas of the Negeb.[42] The list of places has been taken from Josh 19:2-9, which it reflects pretty closely. A historical note has been inserted into v. 31. The towns were absorbed into Judah for administrative purposes, though local consciousness of their association with Simeonite clans survived. The last sentence in v. 33 means, "And they were placed on the muster roll," referring to a military census.[43] It is the chronicler's interpretation of "according to its families" in Josh 19:8 (NRSV).[44]

4:34-43. An example of such a census is supplied in vv. 34-38, in a partially genealogical listing of clan leaders who were officers in the tribal or regional militia. According to v. 41, this listing relates to the eighth century BCE. A campaign was mounted to secure grazing grounds for flocks, as the literary frame in vv. 39 and 41 informs us. It is not possible to locate "Gedor," read by the MT; "Gerar," attested by the LXX (cf. the NJB), would make good sense. It was a city between Beersheba and Gaza, on the edge of the Philistine coastal plain, and will be important in 2 Chr 14:13. The valley named after it, to be identified with Wadi esh-Sharieh, extends to the east.[45] The campaign may have been part of Hezekiah's expansion into Philistia (see 2 Kgs 18:8).[46] The "Meunim" or "Meunites" hardly fit such a location; Maon was in southeastern Judah.

42. See Aharoni, *The Land of the Bible,* 260-62.

43. De Vries, *1 and 2 Chronicles,* 49.

44. E. L. Curtis and A. A. Madsen, *The Books of Chronicles,* ICC (Edinburgh: T. & T. Clark, 1910) 116.

45. See Y. Aharoni, "The Land of Gerar," *IEJ* 6 (1956) 26-32.

46. See B. Oded, *Israelite and Judean History,* ed. J. H. Hayes and J. M. Miller (Philadelphia: Westminster, 1977) 444-46.

Originally there may have been a reference to "the dwellings [which]" (NJB; cf. *BHS*). Another campaign marked an expansion to the southeast, to the south of the Dead Sea. Again militia officers are named; evidently a group of Amalekites had taken refuge in the area.

Both of the battle reports are set in the context of a schema of territorial claims, which not only states how a group came into possession of an area but also affirms continuous and still-existing occupation.[47] The formula "to this day," used in vv. 41 and 43, clearly belongs to the source, as it does in 2 Chr 5:9 in dependence on 1 Kgs 8:8. In 5:26 the phrase will involve reference to the post-exilic era. Did the chronicler regard the two districts, respectively in the province of Ashdod and in Idumea by his time, as still occupied by Simeonite families? He might have assumed the contemporary validity of the source. If so, he was maintaining membership in the people of God not only of returned exiles, but also of those who were not deported. His inclusivity in other respects would accord with such a conclusion. At least the story holds out this ideal. In retrospect, after reading the drab sequence of sin and exile in 5:25-26, successful Simeon seems to exemplify an obedient people who possess the land forever (28:8). He stands for the hope that old national boundaries would one day be reestablished. The Abrahamic covenant concerning the land would find renewed and lasting fulfillment (16:15-18; cf. 2 Chr 6:25; 20:7, 11; 33:8).

The genealogical account of the two and a half eastern tribes in chap. 5 is intended as a single passage, as the comprehensive references in vv. 18-22 and 26 indicate. There is the same mixture of concerns in the individual paragraphs that we saw in the case of Simeon, though now the genealogical concern is oriented toward military registration. The function of the text is to give pre-exilic sketches of the tribes, anchored by references to domestic and foreign kings in vv. 6, 10, 17, and 26 and conscious of looming exile in vv. 6, 22, and 26.

5:1-10. The Reuben genealogy opens with a list of sons in vv. 1*a* and 3, extracted from Num 26:5-6, just as Num 26:12-14 was used in 4:24. It is broken off by an observation of the chronicler in vv. 1*b*-2 and then resumed. If Reuben was the firstborn (Num 26:5), the chronicler asks, then why did I begin my genealogy of the twelve individual tribes with Judah, rather than Reuben, whom I placed first in the list of 2:1-2? He gives the answer in v. 2*a*: "For" (KJV) Judah eclipsed Reuben. The explanation is not merely historical but scriptural. It is based on Jacob's blessing of Judah in Gen 49:8-10, which specifies his brothers' subordination to him and his royal progeny. The chronicler also interprets incestuous Reuben's loss of excellence (Gen 49:4) in terms of his loss of the birthright. He maintains that such privilege passed to Joseph, presumably deducing from Jacob's adoption of his grandsons Ephraim and Manasseh that Joseph received the double portion reserved for the firstborn (Deut 21:17). The repetition of Joseph's privilege in vv. 1-2 indicates its importance for the chronicler and reflects his tribal inclusivity. These major northern tribes were key members of the ideal community of Israel. He sometimes used "Ephraim and Manasseh" as a shorthand reference to the northern tribes in general (9:3; 2 Chr 30:10; 31:1).

The genealogy of Reuben is supplied from both ends, first moving down five generations and then providing a lineage for the exiled tribal leader Beerah for eight generations in vv. 4-6, though the two linear genealogies do not meet in the middle. "Tiglath-pilneser" is the chronicler's version of Tiglath-pileser (v. 26; 2 Chr 28:20). Other military leaders, presumably contemporary with Beerah, are listed in vv. 7-8*a*. We do not know whether the Joel of v. 8*a* is intended to be that of v. 4; if so, this genealogy is telescoped. In vv. 8*b*-9 the territory of the Reubenites is defined: In the Hebrew the singular verb agrees with the Hebrew collective term "the Reubenite" at v. 6, as the NIV (and the REB) recognizes. From south to north they occupied the area to the east of the Dead Sea. They also expanded eastward into the desert "that extends to the Euphrates River" (NIV) to gain grazing land for their cattle. A historical example of such expansion is supplied in v. 10, the taking of land from a bedouin tribe.

5:11-17. The genealogy of Gad actually gives a list of tribal chiefs (v. 12), then a list of military leaders of interrelated clans, which are traced back through Abihail nine generations to Buz (vv. 13-14), and finally the name of a further leader whose genealogy is traced to a depth of three

47. S. J. De Vries, *1 and 2 Chronicles*, FOTL 11 (Grand Rapids: Eerdmans, 1989) 51, 426.

generations (v. 15). The first list is interrupted after "the sons of Gad" by a brief description of the tribal territory, which abbreviates v. 16. Elsewhere in the OT, Gad's region is Gilead, the area to the east of the river Jordan; here it includes Bashan, the region east of the Sea of Chinnereth. The description of Bashani territory in v. 11 may be a rationalization from the description of Reubenite territory as Gilead (originally intended in a wider sense?) in v. 9. The military census material of vv. 12-15 is given a dating by the synchronism of v. 17 at about 750 BCE.

5:18-22. One gets the impression that the Gadite census details were meant to prepare for this intertribal campaign, especially as it begins with an analysis of the conscript army in terms of expertise and size. The enemies were a bedouin confederation (cf. 1:31). The style of the battle report is so typical of the chronicler that he has probably edited his source at this point. The divine initiative (v. 22), which serves to explain the great victory (vv. 21-22*a* [NIV]), finds Hebrew parallels at 2 Chr 22:7; 25:20 (cf. 10:15). Here it is grounded in the trust that motivates an appeal for divine help, very much like Asa's in 2 Chr 14:11 and Jehoshaphat's in 18:31 (cf. 26:17; 32:8, 20-22). The observation that the Transjordanian tribes occupied their foes' territory until the exile introduces a somber note. Blessing is not cast in concrete. Each generation determines its own fate or fortune under God.

5:23-24. The chronicler will present that agenda in vv. 25-26. Meanwhile, it is necessary to round off the genealogical input by referring to the half tribe of Manasseh. Instead of a genealogy proper, territorial information is initially provided (which reads better in the NIV, although it deviates from the MT's accentuation), and then a military list of clan leaders, which supplements the information of vv. 17-22, is given. The former datum locates them in Bashan, with a northward expansion. Elsewhere they are also located in the northern part of Gilead. There seems to be a trend in this chapter to push the two northern tribes farther north, so that Reuben has more space.

5:25-26. Another summary from the chronicler appears here. The unfaithfulness (NIV) that leads to exile is characteristic of the chronicler, as was observed at 2:7. So is the challenge that faces a new generation, implied in the phrase "the God of their fathers" (NIV). Such language will be combined again in 2 Chr 36:14-16 as the tragic cause of Judah's exile. In presenting the exile of the eastern tribes in 733 BCE, the chronicler blends their fate with that of the rest of the northern kingdom in 721. He draws upon 2 Kgs 15:19, 29; 17:6; 18:11 and includes a short summary of 17:7-23. Was all lost? Not necessarily. In 2 Chr 30:9 he will hold out hope that the northern exiles would return, as a consequence of the repentance of their kinsfolk still in the land. The eastern tribes, no less than the rest, belonged to the chronicler's ideal Israel. Their pre-exilic gains and losses were presented as respective incentive and challenge to his post-exilic contemporaries in Judah, both to motivate their own response to the Lord and to reinforce a larger hope.

REFLECTIONS

The basic theology of the OT is a triangle with three points: God, Israel, and the land. The theme of the land—promised, given, taken away, and given back—is a thread that weaves in and out of the OT story. The land is a barometer that registers Israel's level of obedience or disobedience to the Lord. This land-based spirituality dominates the present section. The post-exilic community, relishing the land because in their history they knew what it meant to lose it (9:1-2) and had only partially regained it, is confronted with contrasting stories of winning and losing the land as corollaries of obedience and backsliding. Such morally based contrasts are typical of the chronicler. Here the land features as prize or penalty. Israel's right to the land was conditional, according to 1 Chr 28:8. Yet, once forfeited, it could be won back by repentance, according to 2 Chr 6:24-25; 30:9.

The chronicler drew a contrast not only between Simeon's survival and the Transjordanians' loss of the land, but also between the differing attitude to the Lord in the experience of the latter group. One generation trusted in the Lord; the next was disloyal to the God of that generation (5:20, 25). God has no grandchildren. The call to allegiance comes afresh to each generation in turn. This was a conviction the chronicler habitually reaffirmed. Christians, too, are called to take the baton from their predecessors and carry it faithfully for their lap of the relay race.

> Remember your [deceased] leaders, who spoke the word of God to you. Consider the outcome of their way of life and imitate their faith. Jesus Christ is the same yesterday and today and forever. (Heb 13:7-8 NIV)
>
> So do not throw away your confidence; it will be richly rewarded. You need to persevere so that when you have done the will of God, you will receive what he has promised. (Heb 10:35-36 NIV)

The writer to the Hebrews strikingly echoes the chronicler's call to commitment, constancy, and hope.

1 Chronicles 6:1-81, The Religious Tribe of Levi

NIV

6 The sons of Levi:
Gershon, Kohath and Merari.
2The sons of Kohath:
Amram, Izhar, Hebron and Uzziel.
3The children of Amram:
Aaron, Moses and Miriam.
The sons of Aaron:
Nadab, Abihu, Eleazar and Ithamar.
4Eleazar was the father of Phinehas,
Phinehas the father of Abishua,
5Abishua the father of Bukki,
Bukki the father of Uzzi,
6Uzzi the father of Zerahiah,
Zerahiah the father of Meraioth,
7Meraioth the father of Amariah,
Amariah the father of Ahitub,
8Ahitub the father of Zadok,
Zadok the father of Ahimaaz,
9Ahimaaz the father of Azariah,
Azariah the father of Johanan,
10Johanan the father of Azariah (it was he
who served as priest in the temple Solomon built in Jerusalem),
11Azariah the father of Amariah,
Amariah the father of Ahitub,
12Ahitub the father of Zadok,
Zadok the father of Shallum,
13Shallum the father of Hilkiah,
Hilkiah the father of Azariah,
14Azariah the father of Seraiah,

NRSV

6[a] The sons of Levi: Gershom,[b] Kohath, and
Merari. 2The sons of Kohath: Amram,
Izhar, Hebron, and Uzziel. 3The children of Amram: Aaron, Moses, and Miriam. The sons of
Aaron: Nadab, Abihu, Eleazar, and Ithamar.
4Eleazar became the father of Phinehas, Phinehas
of Abishua, 5Abishua of Bukki, Bukki of Uzzi,
6Uzzi of Zerahiah, Zerahiah of Meraioth,
7Meraioth of Amariah, Amariah of Ahitub, 8Ahitub
of Zadok, Zadok of Ahimaaz, 9Ahimaaz of Azariah,
Azariah of Johanan, 10and Johanan of Azariah (it
was he who served as priest in the house that
Solomon built in Jerusalem). 11Azariah became the
father of Amariah, Amariah of Ahitub, 12Ahitub of
Zadok, Zadok of Shallum, 13Shallum of Hilkiah,
Hilkiah of Azariah, 14Azariah of Seraiah, Seraiah
of Jehozadak; 15and Jehozadak went into exile
when the LORD sent Judah and Jerusalem into
exile by the hand of Nebuchadnezzar.

16[c]The sons of Levi: Gershom, Kohath, and
Merari. 17These are the names of the sons of
Gershom: Libni and Shimei. 18The sons of Kohath:
Amram, Izhar, Hebron, and Uzziel. 19The sons of
Merari: Mahli and Mushi. These are the clans of
the Levites according to their ancestry. 20Of Ger-
shom: Libni his son, Jahath his son, Zimmah his
son, 21Joah his son, Iddo his son, Zerah his son,
Jeatherai his son. 22The sons of Kohath: Ammi-

[a] Ch 5.27 in Heb [b] Heb *Gershon*, variant of *Gershom*; See 6.16
[c] Ch 6.1 in Heb

NIV

and Seraiah the father of Jehozadak.
[15]Jehozadak was deported when the LORD sent Judah and Jerusalem into exile by the hand of Nebuchadnezzar.

[16]The sons of Levi:
Gershon,[a] Kohath and Merari.
[17]These are the names of the sons of Gershon:
Libni and Shimei.
[18]The sons of Kohath:
Amram, Izhar, Hebron and Uzziel.
[19]The sons of Merari:
Mahli and Mushi.
These are the clans of the Levites listed according to their fathers:
[20]Of Gershon:
Libni his son, Jehath his son,
Zimmah his son, [21]Joah his son,
Iddo his son, Zerah his son
and Jeatherai his son.
[22]The descendants of Kohath:
Amminadab his son, Korah his son,
Assir his son, [23]Elkanah his son,
Ebiasaph his son, Assir his son,
[24]Tahath his son, Uriel his son,
Uzziah his son and Shaul his son.
[25]The descendants of Elkanah:
Amasai, Ahimoth,
[26]Elkanah his son,[b] Zophai his son,
Nahath his son, [27]Eliab his son,
Jeroham his son, Elkanah his son
and Samuel his son.[c]
[28]The sons of Samuel:
Joel[d] the firstborn
and Abijah the second son.
[29]The descendants of Merari:
Mahli, Libni his son,
Shimei his son, Uzzah his son,
[30]Shimea his son, Haggiah his son
and Asaiah his son.

[31]These are the men David put in charge of the music in the house of the LORD after the ark came to rest there. [32]They ministered with music before

[a]*16* Hebrew *Gershom,* a variant of *Gershon;* also in verses 17, 20, 43, 62 and 71 [b]*26* Some Hebrew manuscripts, Septuagint and Syriac; most Hebrew manuscripts *Ahimoth* [26]*Wand Elkanah. The sons of Elkanah:* [c]*27* Some Septuagint manuscripts (see also 1 Samuel 1:19, 20 and 1 Chron. 6:33, 34); Hebrew does not have *and Samuel his son.* [d]*28* Some Septuagint manuscripts and Syriac (see also 1 Samuel 8:2 and 1 Chron. 6:33); Hebrew does not have *Joel.*

NRSV

nadab his son, Korah his son, Assir his son,
[23]Elkanah his son, Ebiasaph his son, Assir his son,
[24]Tahath his son, Uriel his son, Uzziah his son,
and Shaul his son. [25]The sons of Elkanah: Amasai
and Ahimoth, [26]Elkanah his son, Zophai his son,
Nahath his son, [27]Eliab his son, Jeroham his son,
Elkanah his son. [28]The sons of Samuel: Joel[a] his
firstborn, the second Abijah.[b] [29]The sons of Merari:
Mahli, Libni his son, Shimei his son, Uzzah his
son, [30]Shimea his son, Haggiah his son, and Asaiah
his son.

31These are the men whom David put in
charge of the service of song in the house of the
LORD, after the ark came to rest there. [32]They
ministered with song before the tabernacle of the
tent of meeting, until Solomon had built the house
of the LORD in Jerusalem; and they performed their
service in due order. [33]These are the men who
served; and their sons were: Of the Kohathites:
Heman, the singer, son of Joel, son of Samuel,
[34]son of Elkanah, son of Jeroham, son of Eliel, son
of Toah, [35]son of Zuph, son of Elkanah, son of
Mahath, son of Amasai, [36]son of Elkanah, son
of Joel, son of Azariah, son of Zephaniah, [37]son of
Tahath, son of Assir, son of Ebiasaph, son of
Korah, [38]son of Izhar, son of Kohath, son of Levi,
son of Israel; [39]and his brother Asaph, who stood
on his right, namely, Asaph son of Berechiah, son
of Shimea, [40]son of Michael, son of Baaseiah, son
of Malchijah, [41]son of Ethni, son of Zerah, son of
Adaiah, [42]son of Ethan, son of Zimmah, son
of Shimei, [43]son of Jahath, son of Gershom, son
of Levi. [44]On the left were their kindred the
sons of Merari: Ethan son of Kishi, son of Abdi,
son of Malluch, [45]son of Hashabiah, son of Amaziah, son of Hilkiah, [46]son of Amzi, son of Bani,
son of Shemer, [47]son of Mahli, son of Mushi, son
of Merari, son of Levi; [48]and their kindred the
Levites were appointed for all the service of the
tabernacle of the house of God.

49But Aaron and his sons made offerings on
the altar of burnt offering and on the altar of
incense, doing all the work of the most holy place,
to make atonement for Israel, according to all that
Moses the servant of God had commanded.
[50]These are the sons of Aaron: Eleazar his

[a] Gk Syr Compare verse 33 and 1 Sam 8.2: Heb lacks *Joel* [b] Heb reads *Vashni, and Abijah* for *the second Abijah,* taking *the second* as a proper name

NIV

the tabernacle, the Tent of Meeting, until Solomon built the temple of the LORD in Jerusalem.
They performed their duties according to the
regulations laid down for them.

33Here are the men who served, together with
their sons:

From the Kohathites:
Heman, the musician,
the son of Joel, the son of Samuel,
34the son of Elkanah, the son of Jeroham,
the son of Eliel, the son of Toah,
35the son of Zuph, the son of Elkanah,
the son of Mahath, the son of Amasai,
36the son of Elkanah, the son of Joel,
the son of Azariah, the son of Zephaniah,
37the son of Tahath, the son of Assir,
the son of Ebiasaph, the son of Korah,
38the son of Izhar, the son of Kohath,
the son of Levi, the son of Israel;
39and Heman's associate Asaph, who served at
his right hand:
Asaph son of Berekiah, the son of Shimea,
40the son of Michael, the son of Baaseiah,[a]
the son of Malkijah, 41the son of Ethni,
the son of Zerah, the son of Adaiah,
42the son of Ethan, the son of Zimmah,
the son of Shimei, 43the son of Jahath,
the son of Gershon, the son of Levi;
44and from their associates, the Merarites, at
his left hand:
Ethan son of Kishi, the son of Abdi,
the son of Malluch, 45the son of
Hashabiah,
the son of Amaziah, the son of Hilkiah,
46the son of Amzi, the son of Bani,
the son of Shemer, 47the son of Mahli,
the son of Mushi, the son of Merari,
the son of Levi.

48Their fellow Levites were assigned to all the
other duties of the tabernacle, the house of God.
49But Aaron and his descendants were the ones who
presented offerings on the altar of burnt offering and
on the altar of incense in connection with all that
was done in the Most Holy Place, making atonement for Israel, in accordance with all that Moses
the servant of God had commanded.

[a]40 Most Hebrew manuscripts; some Hebrew manuscripts, one Septuagint manuscript and Syriac *Maaseiah*

NRSV

son, Phinehas his son, Abishua his son, 51Bukki his
son, Uzzi his son, Zerahiah his son, 52Meraioth
his son, Amariah his son, Ahitub his son, 53Zadok
his son, Ahimaaz his son.

54These are their dwelling places according to
their settlements within their borders: to the sons
of Aaron of the families of Kohathites—for the lot
fell to them first— 55to them they gave Hebron
in the land of Judah and its surrounding pasture
lands, 56but the fields of the city and its villages
they gave to Caleb son of Jephunneh. 57To the
sons of Aaron they gave the cities of refuge:
Hebron, Libnah with its pasture lands, Jattir,
Eshtemoa with its pasture lands, 58Hilen[a] with its
pasture lands, Debir with its pasture lands,
59Ashan with its pasture lands, and Beth-shemesh
with its pasture lands. 60From the tribe of Benjamin, Geba with its pasture lands, Alemeth with
its pasture lands, and Anathoth with its pasture
lands. All their towns throughout their families
were thirteen.

61To the rest of the Kohathites were given by
lot out of the family of the tribe, out of the
half-tribe, the half of Manasseh, ten towns. 62To
the Gershomites according to their families were
allotted thirteen towns out of the tribes of Issachar, Asher, Naphtali, and Manasseh in Bashan.
63To the Merarites according to their families were
allotted twelve towns out of the tribes of Reuben,
Gad, and Zebulun. 64So the people of Israel gave
the Levites the towns with their pasture lands.
65They also gave them by lot out of the tribes of
Judah, Simeon, and Benjamin these towns that
are mentioned by name.

66And some of the families of the sons of
Kohath had towns of their territory out of the
tribe of Ephraim. 67They were given the cities of
refuge: Shechem with its pasture lands in the hill
country of Ephraim, Gezer with its pasture lands,
68Jokmeam with its pasture lands, Beth-horon with
its pasture lands, 69Aijalon with its pasture lands,
Gath-rimmon with its pasture lands; 70and out of
the half-tribe of Manasseh, Aner with its pasture
lands, and Bileam with its pasture lands, for the
rest of the families of the Kohathites.

71To the Gershomites: out of the half-tribe of
Manasseh: Golan in Bashan with its pasture lands

[a] Other readings *Hilez, Holon*; See Josh 21.15

NIV

50These were the descendants of Aaron:
Eleazar his son, Phinehas his son,
Abishua his son, 51Bukki his son,
Uzzi his son, Zerahiah his son,
52Meraioth his son, Amariah his son,
Ahitub his son, 53Zadok his son
and Ahimaaz his son.

54These were the locations of their settlements allotted as their territory (they were assigned to the descendants of Aaron who were from the Kohathite clan, because the first lot was for them):

55They were given Hebron in Judah with its surrounding pasturelands. 56But the fields and villages around the city were given to Caleb son of Jephunneh.

57So the descendants of Aaron were given Hebron (a city of refuge), and Libnah,[a] Jattir, Eshtemoa, 58Hilen, Debir, 59Ashan, Juttah[b] and Beth Shemesh, together with their pasturelands. 60And from the tribe of Benjamin they were given Gibeon,[c] Geba, Alemeth and Anathoth, together with their pasturelands.

These towns, which were distributed among the Kohathite clans, were thirteen in all.

61The rest of Kohath's descendants were allotted ten towns from the clans of half the tribe of Manasseh.

62The descendants of Gershon, clan by clan, were allotted thirteen towns from the tribes of Issachar, Asher and Naphtali, and from the part of the tribe of Manasseh that is in Bashan.

63The descendants of Merari, clan by clan, were allotted twelve towns from the tribes of Reuben, Gad and Zebulun.

64So the Israelites gave the Levites these towns and their pasturelands. 65From the tribes of Judah, Simeon and Benjamin they allotted the previously named towns.

66Some of the Kohathite clans were given as their territory towns from the tribe of Ephraim.

67In the hill country of Ephraim they were given Shechem (a city of refuge), and Gezer,[d]

[a]57 See Joshua 21:13; Hebrew *given the cities of refuge: Hebron, Libnah.* [b]59 Syriac (see also Septuagint and Joshua 21:16); Hebrew does not have *Juttah.* [c]60 See Joshua 21:17; Hebrew does not have *Gibeon.* [d]67 See Joshua 21:21; Hebrew *given the cities of refuge: Shechem, Gezer.*

NRSV

and Ashtaroth with its pasture lands; 72and out of the tribe of Issachar: Kedesh with its pasture lands, Daberath[a] with its pasture lands, 73Ramoth with its pasture lands, and Anem with its pasture lands; 74out of the tribe of Asher: Mashal with its pasture lands, Abdon with its pasture lands, 75Hukok with its pasture lands, and Rehob with its pasture lands; 76and out of the tribe of Naphtali: Kedesh in Galilee with its pasture lands, Hammon with its pasture lands, and Kiriathaim with its pasture lands. 77To the rest of the Merarites out of the tribe of Zebulun: Rimmono with its pasture lands, Tabor with its pasture lands, 78and across the Jordan from Jericho, on the east side of the Jordan, out of the tribe of Reuben: Bezer in the steppe with its pasture lands, Jahzah with its pasture lands, 79Kedemoth with its pasture lands, and Mephaath with its pasture lands; 80and out of the tribe of Gad: Ramoth in Gilead with its pasture lands, Mahanaim with its pasture lands, 81Heshbon with its pasture lands, and Jazer with its pasture lands.

[a] Or *Dobrath*

NIV

[68]Jokmeam, Beth Horon, [69]Aijalon and Gath Rimmon, together with their pasturelands.

[70]And from half the tribe of Manasseh the Israelites gave Aner and Bileam, together with their pasturelands, to the rest of the Kohathite clans.

[71]The Gershonites received the following:
From the clan of the half-tribe of Manasseh
they received Golan in Bashan and also Ashtaroth, together with their pasturelands;
[72]from the tribe of Issachar
they received Kedesh, Daberath, [73]Ramoth and Anem, together with their pasturelands;
[74]from the tribe of Asher
they received Mashal, Abdon, [75]Hukok and Rehob, together with their pasturelands;
[76]and from the tribe of Naphtali
they received Kedesh in Galilee, Hammon and Kiriathaim, together with their pasturelands.

[77]The Merarites (the rest of the Levites) received the following:

From the tribe of Zebulun
they received Jokneam, Kartah,[a] Rimmono and Tabor, together with their pasturelands;
[78]from the tribe of Reuben across the Jordan east of Jericho
they received Bezer in the desert, Jahzah, [79]Kedemoth and Mephaath, together with their pasturelands;
[80]and from the tribe of Gad
they received Ramoth in Gilead, Mahanaim, [81]Heshbon and Jazer, together with their pasturelands.

[a]77 See Septuagint and Joshua 21:34; Hebrew does not have *Jokneam, Kartah.*

COMMENTARY

In the tribal genealogies, a central place is allotted to the tribe of Levi. Moreover, a great deal of coverage is given to it, amounting to eighty-one verses, not much less than the hundred devoted to Judah. The emphasis on Levi carries both a religious and a theological message. The

Temple was of crucial importance for the post-exilic community of Judah, and the tribe of Levi, made up of priests and Levites, had been commissioned to minister to the special presence of God that it represented. From a human perspective, the size of the genealogy reflects the extensiveness of the available records. In order to officiate at the Temple, hereditary legitimacy had to be proved (see Ezra 2:62-63).

The chronicler wrote his history to promote the interests of the Temple. He leaves readers in no doubt about his convictions that the Temple merited the community's unstinting support and that worship should be conducted in a traditional and proper manner. Putting Levi at the middle of the tribal genealogies reflects the chronicler's belief that the Temple stood at the heart of the community of faith. He also uses this section as an opportunity to maintain for the first time the validity of the Temple as a religious institution. The Torah regarded the Mosaic tabernacle as the focus of the Lord's holy presence, and, true to its historical context, had nothing to say about the Temple, apart from the annotation in Gen 22:14, which the chronicler will exploit in 2 Chr 3:1, and of course Deut 12:10-11, which he so interprets in 1 Chr 22:9-10, 18-19. A new Temple-related dispensation was launched under David and Solomon (vv. 10, 31-32, 48). It continued the sacrificial system of the Mosaic era (v. 49), but gave new and permanent duties of music and song to the Levites. As the chronicler's community worshiped at the post-exilic Temple, they could be confident that it perpetuated pre-exilic ideals and reflected the will of the Lord.

The chronicler is concerned with giving a sketch of temple personnel in pre-exilic times, as v. 15 indicates with its reference to the exile. He focused on Aaron, Moses, David, and Solomon as founders of Israel's religion under God. The same concerns of genealogy, history, and geography reappear in this section, with the religious character of the tribe providing a unique slant. After a basic tribal lineage in vv. 1-3, a genealogy of the high priesthood appears in vv. 4-15, then one of the clans of Levites in vv. 16-30, and another of the levitical guilds of music in vv. 31-47, with a brief indication of the roles of the other Levites and of the priests in vv. 48-49 and a short list of high priests up to David's time in vv. 50-53. The rest of the chapter is devoted to the territorial holdings of the tribe of Levi among the other tribes (vv. 54-81). One should notice that much more space is devoted to the Levites than to priests. This inequity reflects the chronicler's perennial concern to promote the cause of the former.

6:1-15. The genealogy begins by listing the eponymous ancestors of the three tribal clans: Gershon (NIV), Kohath, and Merari. Gershom is the chronicler's preferred form; the variant Gershon used in the priestly texts of the Pentateuch appears here as a reflection of his source, reverting in v. 16 to Gershom (NRSV; the NRSV and the NIV have standardized differently in this chapter). Priests traced their descent from a branch of the tribe, through Kohath, Amram, and Aaron, and the high priests belonged to this line. The chronicler does not mention here that other priests were also descended from Ithamar (cf. 24:1-4). The genealogy takes a segmented form in vv. 1-3; its names have been extracted from the record in Exod 6:16-23, with the difference that Miriam is now included alongside Amram's sons (see Num 26:59). Her role in the pentateuchal narratives merited a place in the genealogy.

The continuation of the genealogy in vv. 4-15 takes a linear form. Although given a genealogical shaping, it is taken from an official list of high priests with a variety of family ties or even none. The list is related to that in Ezra 7:1-5. It probably belonged to a slightly longer list ending in Joshua, the first high priest after the exile (see Hag 1:1); it contained interesting symbolic features, but they were not the chronicler's concern.[48] He cut it off at the point of exile, true to his time frame in the genealogical chapters, and added two historical notes. The one in v. 15 ends with exile; the other in v. 10 draws attention to the first high priest of the Solomonic Temple, though it is misplaced and historically belongs next to the Azariah of v. 9 (see 1 Kgs 4:2).

6:16-30. The Levites are given a corresponding genealogy. The Davidic emphasis of the next paragraph, announced in v. 31, suggests that the chronicler regarded his genealogy as tracing the levitical line down to that period. The closing of the Kohathite lineage a generation after Samuel

48. For its schematic and partial character see H. G. M. Williamson, *1 and 2 Chronicles,* NCB (Grand Rapids: Eerdmans, 1982) 70-71.

in v. 28 also suggests this point. In v. 30 Asaiah nicely aligns with 15:6, where Asaiah leads the Merarites in the levitical guard of honor for the ark. But comparison with vv. 39-41 implies that the final representative of the Gershom lineage in v. 21, Jeatherai, marks a somewhat earlier stage. As in the former listing, the initial generations are segmented with reference to the three tribal clans, and the rest is supplied in a linear form. The material in vv. 16-19 has been abbreviated from Num 3:17-20, with the closing statement in v. 19*b* now serving as a heading to another, non-biblical list of clan genealogies in vv. 20-30. Gershom (NRSV) in v. 16 is doubtless an adaptation of Gershon, to accord with Gershom in the new list at v. 20.

The clan genealogies are developed from the first sons of the three eponymous clan founders, at least in the case of Gershom (Libni, vv. 17, 20) and Merari (Mahli, vv. 19, 29). In the case of Kohath, the line of the firstborn Amram has been preempted as a priestly pedigree. Izhar is expected here, as the father of Korah (cf. vv. 37-38). Instead the name of Amminadab appears. We do not know whether this is intended to refer to Aaron's father-in-law (Exod 6:23), of the same generation as Amram, and if some link was being claimed between David and the tribe of Levi via Ruth (see Ruth 4:18-22).[49] Kohath's genealogy is longer than the other two. It includes a collateral branch descended from Elkanah (v. 23) in vv. 25-28. It attests the adoption of Samuel into the levitical chain, legitimating the religious activity of this Ephraimite, to which his mother especially dedicated him (1 Sam 1:1, 11, 28). The chronicler will exploit this levitical link at 2 Chr 35:18 as part of his crusade to promote the Levites' cause. The attribution of different sons to Elkanah in vv. 23 and 25 is a clue to the fact that the vertical listing in vv. 22-23 has replaced an earlier horizontal grouping of three brothers, Assir, Elkanah and Ebiasaph, with Tahath functioning as Assir's son (see Exod 6:24).[50] Verse 28 has come down to us in a damaged form; our versions represent an attempt to repair it (see the NRSV note; cf. *BHS*). Verse 48 implies that this genealogy was meant to represent the large group of Levites responsible for assisting the priests by carrying out a range of general duties (cf. 23:4, 24, 28-29).

6:31-49. The next series of ascending genealogies in vv. 33-47 involves a specialist group of Levites, the singing musicians organized into a threefold ancestral guild. The chronicler has set it in an explanatory narrative frame, vv. 31-32 and 48-49. At the beginning of the post-exilic period, these choirs were not yet regarded as Levites, but gradually they were integrated into the levitical order and equipped with legitimating genealogies. The present arrangement of Heman, Asaph, and Ethan attests the latest historical development found in Chronicles (see 15:16-21; see also the Introduction). The three choirs are represented as they performed in the temple court, with Heman's at the center and Asaph's and Ethan's on each side. This genealogy differs from the preceding one by claiming to trace the guild from the second sons of Gershom, Kohath and Merari (vv. 16-19), at least in the cases of Izhar and Mushi. The inclusion of Shimei, now in v. 42 near the end of the Gershom list, may have the same intent. Perhaps it originally stood in v. 43, leaving Zimmah and Jahath as father and son as in v. 20. This overlap with the earlier genealogy based on first sons also occurs in the line of Kohath, which has coordinated the independent Elkanah genealogy into a vertical, and so longer, list.

Verses 31-32 possess chiastic structure.[51] The chronicler puts in the middle the overlap of dispensations, when the new choirs officiated at the old tabernacle in Gibeon (see 16:39-42). He contrasts it with the new sanctuary built by Solomon, where the choirs found their proper place, in fulfillment of preparations David had made for their role in the Temple (see 23:5; 25:1-6). He has in mind the installation of the ark in the Temple (2 Chr 5:12-13; 6:41; 7:6). They symbolized the beginning of a new era to which the chronicler's community of faith still belonged. The ending of the Levites' duties to carry the ark, reflected in the name of Asaiah at v. 31 (cf. 15:6), provided opportunities for their temple ministry, especially that of music and song (cf. 23:26, 30; 2 Chr 35:3). The Temple had the same value for

49. W. L. Osborne, "The Genealogies of 1 Chronicles 1–9" (Ph.d. diss., Dropsie University, 1979) 272.

50. See M. D. Johnson, *The Purpose of the Biblical Genealogies,* SNTSMS 8 (Cambridge: Cambridge University Press, 1969) 71-73, summarizing the contribution of A. Lefèvre.

51. John W. Kleinig, *The Lord's Song: The Basis, Function and Significance of Choral Music in Chronicles,* JSOTSup 156 (Sheffield: JSOT, 1993) 43.

Israel as had the old tabernacle, as the juxtaposition of terms in v. 48 signifies; according to 2 Chr 5:5 the tabernacle was placed inside the Temple.

Apart from the replacement of the tabernacle, featured in the Torah, with the Temple and the extension of levitical duties, the old Mosaic dispensation continued, with the perpetuation of the Levites' other responsibilities (see Num 18:1-6). The priests kept their regular duties. The latter are summarized in v. 49, first in terms of sacrificing burnt offerings and burning incense, both done twice a day (Exod 30:7; Num 28:1-8; 29:38-42; 2 Chr 2:4). Their responsibility for "the most holy things" (NJB; cf. the REB) relates to other offerings: the grain offering, the sin offering, and the guilt offering, which were regarded as especially holy (Num 18:9). Their work of atonement, associated with all animal sacrifices, refers to the blood rite of Lev 4:16-20; 17:11. This aspect of their work will come to the fore in 2 Chr 29:22-24.

6:50-53. The linear list of high priests up to David's reign is a partial repetition of the one at the head of the chapter. It appears to be a redactional addition: "Aaron's sons," an expression used for priests in general (v. 49), are here restricted to high priests.[52] The list was added to match the genealogy of levitical singers as far as David's time in vv. 33-47, but it does not involve a new role. Its intent was to illustrate from a priestly perspective the shift from tabernacle to Temple.

6:54-81. The geographical component of the Levi genealogy relates to the towns and pasturelands set aside for the tribe throughout Israel's territory according to Joshua 21, from which this passage has adapted vv. 4-39.[53] The chronicler has supplied an introduction in v. 54*a.* The earlier list summarized the towns assigned to priests and the three levitical clans in terms of tribal areas and numbers, and then itemized the particular towns in each of the four cases. Here the priestly towns in the south are itemized first in vv. 55-60 (= Josh 21:10-19). Doubtless the intent was to bunch together the priestly details with those of v. 49 (plus vv. 50-53). Then the summaries relating to the levitical clans in the north follow in vv. 61-63 and their detailed listings in vv. 66-81. Verses 64-65 provide a comprehensive summary of the towns located among the northern and the southern tribes, respectively. Verse 65 has been adapted from the heading to the specific list of priestly towns in Josh 21:9. This adaptation with an unspecified subject means that in v. 64 "Levites" now refers generally to members of the tribe of Levi rather than only to its non-priestly members.

The chronicler seems to assign the dating of the initial occupation of these areas to the end of the period of conquest, in line with a plain reading of Joshua 21. According to 1 Chr 13:2, the priests and the Levites were already settled there immediately after David's coronation. According to 2 Chr 11:14, in Rehoboam's reign the Levites abandoned their "pasturelands" (NIV) in the newly formed northern kingdom and moved to the south, evidently to all the towns in Judah (23:2). In 31:15, 19 the priestly towns and "pasture lands" (NJB) in the southern kingdom find mention in the account of Hezekiah's reign. A number of scholars regard this system as a historical fact and date it to the period of the united kingdom.[54] The chronicler took it seriously as a normative means of supporting the temple clergy.

The tribe of Levi had no land holdings comparable with those of its fellow tribes. The tribe was maintained partly by the tithes and offerings given to the Lord, as 2 Chr 31:4-19 will recount and commend, and partly by the allocation of land from the territory of the other tribes in recognition of its religious service. The Lord, not land, was Levi's inheritance (Deut 10:9). The devotional saying "The LORD is my portion" (Pss 16:5; 73:26; 119:57; 142:5; Lam 3:24) seems to have originated among the tribe of Levi in acknowledgment of this fact. In the Psalms it gained a wider, spiritualized sense as a beautiful expression of faith in the Lord as the mainstay of the believer's life. The present listing had become a dead letter

52. See Williamson, *1 and 2 Chronicles,* 74; De Vries, *1 and 2 Chronicles,* 64.

53. See R. L. Braun, *1 Chronicles,* WBC 14 (Waco, Tex.: Word, 1986) 98-100; M. Kartveit, *Motive und Schichten der Landtheologie in 1 Chronik 1–9,* ConBOT 28 (Stockholm: Almqvist & Wiksell, 1989) 69-77; E. Ben Zvi, "The List of the Levitical Cities," *JSOT* 54 (1992) 77-106, esp. 77n. 1.

54. See C. Hauer, Jr., "David and the Levites," *JSOT* 23 (1982) 33-54; Z. Kallai, *Historical Geography of the Bible: The Tribal Territories of Israel* (Jerusalem: Magnes, 1986) 447-58.

by the chronicler's time. The province of Yehud did not even match the traditional area of the state of Judah, let alone other tribal areas. It conveyed a double message to his constituency: the hope of eventual territorial restoration and a contemporary challenge to make room for priests and Levites in the priestly towns and elsewhere within their borders (cf. 2 Chr 23:2; 31:11-19, esp. vv. 15, 19; Neh 12:27). Traditionally each of the tribes gave up part of its territory to the Lord's ministers. It was like rent, surrendering part in acknowledgment of God's claim on the whole. The community of faith was still obligated to make space for the temple personnel. According to 2 Chronicles 31, they were to support them by sacrificial offerings and gifts in kind to the Temple. A firm part of Israel's understanding of the land was that it belonged to the Lord: "The land is mine" (Lev 25:23). Each tribe gave over towns for them to reside in and grazing land for their cattle (Josh 21:2).

A total of forty-eight towns was assigned for this purpose. Verse 60*b,* with its closing number of priestly towns, nicely prefaces the summaries in vv. 61-63, each of which has a numerical component for the levitical towns. Sometimes the totals do not align with the listings in the MT. Accordingly in the NIV, Juttah and Gibeon have been supplied from Joshua 21 in vv. 59-60, and Jokneam and Kartah in v. 77. It is noticeable that the tribe of Dan, included in Josh 21:23-25, is not cited in vv. 61 and 69, though two of its four towns survive in the latter verse. The omission of Dan is consistent with its absence from the tribal listings in chap. 7. Here, however, the lack of apparently vital information—the absence of Ephraim in v. 61 (contrast vv. 66-67) and of two towns in v. 69—suggests that the material has been clumsily wrenched out of the text of Chronicles, perhaps because the Danites built an idolatrous sanctuary (cf. Judges 18; see *BHS* here). Joshua 21 leans on the account of the institution of six cities of refuge in Joshua 20, by noting their inclusion in the list of towns, notably Hebron and Shechem in Josh 21:13, 21. These two references are reproduced in 1 Chr 6:57, 67, but in a plural form as if the towns were all cities of refuge. Although no variant reading occurs in the textual tradition of Chronicles, the NIV along with the REB has adopted the singulars of Joshua 21.[55] In view of the chronicler's extensive knowledge of OT sources, it is difficult to envision his sanctioning so serious a change.

55. See *BHS.*

REFLECTIONS

The centrality of Levi among the tribes implies the centrality of the Temple in Israel's culture and the centrality of the Lord in their lives. Lyonel Feininger's painting *The Church,* executed in the cubist tradition, translates this concept into a Christian idiom. In his picture of houses surrounding a church, all the lines bring the eye toward the central feature. Then the eye is taken up by the spire into the sky. It expresses the ideal of the church as the living heart of society, drawing the community to itself and then directing it to God.

One may conceive of many ways in which Christians can appropriate the chronicler's focus on the Temple, in view of the NT's multifaceted interpretation. Yet we would not represent his mind adequately if we simply spoke of putting God at the center of the individual's life. A truth faithful to his intent is the importance of institutional religion for the people of God. No church building has the theological value assigned to the Temple in the OT; yet, the Christian faith necessarily has its institutional forms. Those who seek to worship only in front of a television set or in private devotions lack a key dimension of Christian experience. Over against such a solitary form of faith we may set the testimony of Psalm 42. Enforced deprivation of corporate worship was a source of anguish for the psalmist. Times were nostalgically recalled when "I went with the throng,/ and led them in procession to the house of God,/ with glad shouts and songs of thanksgiving,/ a multitude keeping festival" (Ps 42:4 NRSV).

There is a healthy ring to the declaration of Ps 122:1:

I was glad when they said to me,
"Let us go to the house of the LORD!"

Our feet are standing
  within your gates, O Jerusalem. (NRSV)

This communal enthusiasm defies the individualism rampant in modern Western societies. The chronicler will amply illustrate in ensuing narratives about the Temple the communal aspect of putting God at the center of life. Seeking the Lord very often has for him an institutional meaning. Personal faith must find communal expression if it is to be true to the Bible. "Christianity is essentially a social religion; and . . . to turn it into a solitary religion is indeed to destroy it," affirmed John Wesley.[56] The same is true of the faith of the Old Testament. The exhortation "Let us not give up meeting together, as some are in the habit of doing" (Heb 10:25 NIV) echoes the OT's own emphasis on temple worship.

One of the chronicler's aims in his work was to establish the validity of post-exilic worship. For us, he tells his readers, the Temple corresponds to the tabernacle, which the Torah associates with the Lord's special presence. He envisioned an old order, still largely valid, and a new order that added to God's earlier revelation as to how to worship. In juggling things old and new, the chronicler offers a model for us in treating the Old Testament and the New Testament, with their respective eras of revelation and response. He knew such tension as Christian preachers feel in handling the OT, the Bible of the early church but much less so for the modern church. Fortunately for him, he could not indulge in our temptation to replace a Hebrew Bible with a Christian New Testament. He had to wrestle with the tension of development and adaptation evident in the Law and the Prophets and in the ongoing history of the community of faith. We read "Jesus" in place of David and Solomon as founders of a new spiritual era under God. Just as David's work did not cancel out the former revelation but vitally supplemented it, so also it has been the traditional conviction of the church that the New Testament is set alongside the Old Testament to form a completed revelation.

The Temple did not run itself. No magic broomstick kept its courts clean. The daily duties of sacrificing to the accompaniment of music and song and the less spectacular routines of preparation and maintenance were the responsibility of priests and Levites. The system came with a necessary price tag for Israel, including the setting aside of some of their territory directly for the Lord to be used by temple personnel. This principle correlates with the divine claim on the lives of Christians. It is not enough to speak of surrendering oneself to God or to sing "All for Jesus." Such sincere sentiments require translation into the allocation of one's resources to God and so to God's human agencies. Surrender means stewardship, part of which is to devote a portion of what one has directly to God's work and workers.

56. John Wesley, *The Works of John Wesley,* ed. A. C. Outler (Nashville: Abingdon, 1984) 1:533.

1 Chronicles 7:1-40, The Other Northern Tribes

NIV

7 The sons of Issachar:
Tola, Puah, Jashub and Shimron—four in all.

2The sons of Tola:
Uzzi, Rephaiah, Jeriel, Jahmai, Ibsam and Samuel—heads of their families. During the reign of David, the descendants of Tola listed as fighting men in their genealogy numbered 22,600.

3The son of Uzzi:

NRSV

7 The sons[a] of Issachar: Tola, Puah, Jashub,
and Shimron, four. 2The sons of Tola: Uzzi,
Rephaiah, Jeriel, Jahmai, Ibsam, and Shemuel,
heads of their ancestral houses, namely of Tola,
mighty warriors of their generations, their number
in the days of David being twenty-two thousand
six hundred. 3The son[b] of Uzzi: Izrahiah. And the
sons of Izrahiah: Michael, Obadiah, Joel, and
Isshiah, five, all of them chiefs; 4and along with

[a] Syr Compare Vg: Heb *And to the sons* [b] Heb *sons*

NIV

Izrahiah.

The sons of Izrahiah:

Michael, Obadiah, Joel and Isshiah. All five of them were chiefs. [4]According to their family genealogy, they had 36,000 men ready for battle, for they had many wives and children.

[5]The relatives who were fighting men belonging to all the clans of Issachar, as listed in their genealogy, were 87,000 in all.

[6]Three sons of Benjamin:

Bela, Beker and Jediael.

[7]The sons of Bela:

Ezbon, Uzzi, Uzziel, Jerimoth and Iri, heads of families—five in all. Their genealogical record listed 22,034 fighting men.

[8]The sons of Beker:

Zemirah, Joash, Eliezer, Elioenai, Omri, Jeremoth, Abijah, Anathoth and Alemeth. All these were the sons of Beker. [9]Their genealogical record listed the heads of families and 20,200 fighting men.

[10]The son of Jediael:

Bilhan.

The sons of Bilhan:

Jeush, Benjamin, Ehud, Kenaanah, Zethan, Tarshish and Ahishahar. [11]All these sons of Jediael were heads of families. There were 17,200 fighting men ready to go out to war.

[12]The Shuppites and Huppites were the descendants of Ir, and the Hushites the descendants of Aher.

[13]The sons of Naphtali:

Jahziel, Guni, Jezer and Shillem[a]—the descendants of Bilhah.

[14]The descendants of Manasseh:

Asriel was his descendant through his Aramean concubine. She gave birth to Makir the father of Gilead. [15]Makir took a wife from among the Huppites and Shuppites. His sister's name was Maacah.

Another descendant was named Zelophehad, who had only daughters.

[16]Makir's wife Maacah gave birth to a son and named him Peresh. His brother

[a]*13* Some Hebrew and Septuagint manuscripts (see also Gen. 46:24 and Num. 26:49); most Hebrew manuscripts *Shallum*

NRSV

them, by their generations, according to their ancestral houses, were units of the fighting force, thirty-six thousand, for they had many wives and sons. [5]Their kindred belonging to all the families of Issachar were in all eighty-seven thousand mighty warriors, enrolled by genealogy.

6The sons of Benjamin: Bela, Becher, and Jediael, three. [7]The sons of Bela: Ezbon, Uzzi, Uzziel, Jerimoth, and Iri, five, heads of ancestral houses, mighty warriors; and their enrollment by genealogies was twenty-two thousand thirty-four. [8]The sons of Becher: Zemirah, Joash, Eliezer, Elioenai, Omri, Jeremoth, Abijah, Anathoth, and Alemeth. All these were the sons of Becher; [9]and their enrollment by genealogies, according to their generations, as heads of their ancestral houses, mighty warriors, was twenty thousand two hundred. [10]The sons of Jediael: Bilhan. And the sons of Bilhan: Jeush, Benjamin, Ehud, Chenaanah, Zethan, Tarshish, and Ahishahar. [11]All these were the sons of Jediael according to the heads of their ancestral houses, mighty warriors, seventeen thousand two hundred, ready for service in war. [12]And Shuppim and Huppim were the sons of Ir, Hushim the son[a] of Aher.

13The descendants of Naphtali: Jahziel, Guni, Jezer, and Shallum, the descendants of Bilhah.

14The sons of Manasseh: Asriel, whom his Aramean concubine bore; she bore Machir the father of Gilead. [15]And Machir took a wife for Huppim and for Shuppim. The name of his sister was Maacah. And the name of the second was Zelophehad; and Zelophehad had daughters. [16]Maacah the wife of Machir bore a son, and she named him Peresh; the name of his brother was Sheresh; and his sons were Ulam and Rekem. [17]The son[a] of Ulam: Bedan. These were the sons of Gilead son of Machir, son of Manasseh. [18]And his sister Hammolecheth bore Ishhod, Abiezer, and Mahlah. [19]The sons of Shemida were Ahian, Shechem, Likhi, and Aniam.

20The sons of Ephraim: Shuthelah, and Bered his son, Tahath his son, Eleadah his son, Tahath his son, [21]Zabad his son, Shuthelah his son, and Ezer and Elead. Now the people of Gath, who were born in the land, killed them, because they came down to raid their cattle. [22]And their father

[a] Heb *sons*

NIV

was named Sheresh, and his sons were Ulam and Rakem.

[17]The son of Ulam:

Bedan.

These were the sons of Gilead son of Makir, the son of Manasseh. [18]His sister Hammoleketh gave birth to Ishhod, Abiezer and Mahlah.

[19]The sons of Shemida were:

Ahian, Shechem, Likhi and Aniam.

[20]The descendants of Ephraim:

Shuthelah, Bered his son,
Tahath his son, Eleadah his son,
Tahath his son, [21]Zabad his son
and Shuthelah his son.
Ezer and Elead were killed by the native-born men of Gath, when they went down to seize their livestock. [22]Their father Ephraim mourned for them many days, and his relatives came to comfort him. [23]Then he lay with his wife again, and she became pregnant and gave birth to a son. He named him Beriah,[a] because there had been misfortune in his family. [24]His daughter was Sheerah, who built Lower and Upper Beth Horon as well as Uzzen Sheerah.

[25]Rephah was his son, Resheph his son,[b]
Telah his son, Tahan his son,
[26]Ladan his son, Ammihud his son,
Elishama his son, [27]Nun his son
and Joshua his son.

[28]Their lands and settlements included Bethel and its surrounding villages, Naaran to the east, Gezer and its villages to the west, and Shechem and its villages all the way to Ayyah and its villages. [29]Along the borders of Manasseh were Beth Shan, Taanach, Megiddo and Dor, together with their villages. The descendants of Joseph son of Israel lived in these towns.

[30]The sons of Asher:

Imnah, Ishvah, Ishvi and Beriah. Their sister was Serah.

[31]The sons of Beriah:

Heber and Malkiel, who was the father of Birzaith.

[a]23 *Beriah* sounds like the Hebrew for *misfortune.* [b]25 Some Septuagint manuscripts; Hebrew does not have *his son.*

NRSV

Ephraim mourned many days, and his brothers came to comfort him. [23]Ephraim[a] went in to his wife, and she conceived and bore a son; and he named him Beriah, because disaster[b] had befallen his house. [24]His daughter was Sheerah, who built both Lower and Upper Beth-horon, and Uzzen-sheerah. [25]Rephah was his son, Resheph his son, Telah his son, Tahan his son, [26]Ladan his son, Ammihud his son, Elishama his son, [27]Nun[c] his son, Joshua his son. [28]Their possessions and settlements were Bethel and its towns, and eastward Naaran, and westward Gezer and its towns, Shechem and its towns, as far as Ayyah and its towns; [29]also along the borders of the Manassites, Beth-shean and its towns, Taanach and its towns, Megiddo and its towns, Dor and its towns. In these lived the sons of Joseph son of Israel.

30The sons of Asher: Imnah, Ishvah, Ishvi, Beriah, and their sister Serah. [31]The sons of Beriah: Heber and Malchiel, who was the father of Birzaith. [32]Heber became the father of Japhlet, Shomer, Hotham, and their sister Shua. [33]The sons of Japhlet: Pasach, Bimhal, and Ashvath. These are the sons of Japhlet. [34]The sons of Shemer: Ahi, Rohgah, Hubbah, and Aram. [35]The sons of Helem[d] his brother: Zophah, Imna, Shelesh, and Amal. [36]The sons of Zophah: Suah, Harnepher, Shual, Beri, Imrah, [37]Bezer, Hod, Shamma, Shilshah, Ithran, and Beera. [38]The sons of Jether: Jephunneh, Pispa, and Ara. [39]The sons of Ulla: Arah, Hanniel, and Rizia. [40]All of these were men of Asher, heads of ancestral houses, select mighty warriors, chief of the princes. Their number enrolled by genealogies, for service in war, was twenty-six thousand men.

[a] Heb *He* [b] Heb *beraah* [c] Here spelled *Non*; see Ex 33.33
[d] Or *Hotham*; see 7.32

NIV

[32]Heber was the father of Japhlet, Shomer and Hotham and of their sister Shua.
[33]The sons of Japhlet:
Pasach, Bimhal and Ashvath.
These were Japhlet's sons.
[34]The sons of Shomer:
Ahi, Rohgah,[a] Hubbah and Aram.
[35]The sons of his brother Helem:
Zophah, Imna, Shelesh and Amal.
[36]The sons of Zophah:
Suah, Harnepher, Shual, Beri, Imrah,
[37]Bezer, Hod, Shamma, Shilshah, Ithran[b] and Beera.
[38]The sons of Jether:
Jephunneh, Pispah and Ara.
[39]The sons of Ulla:
Arah, Hanniel and Rizia.
[40]All these were descendants of Asher—heads of families, choice men, brave warriors and outstanding leaders. The number of men ready for battle, as listed in their genealogy, was 26,000.

[a]34 Or *of his brother Shomer: Rohgah* [b]37 Possibly a variant of *Jether*

COMMENTARY

In the tribal genealogies the Transjordanian tribes were dovetailed between Judah and Simeon on one side and Levi on the other. Now the remaining northern tribes are placed as a bloc between Levi and Benjamin. The framework of southern tribes embraces within it the clusters of northern ones. The symbolism is clear. The southern tribes, marked by allegiance to the Jerusalem Temple and dynasty and so to the Lord, were incomplete apart from the other tribes. In the case of Issachar, mention of David (v. 2) recalls a long-lost period of unity. The northern tribes still had a place reserved for them in the ideal Israel, which they should claim by faith. Southerners must encourage them to do so, rather than stand in their way.

The tribes in this section are not listed in any special order, in relation to listings elsewhere or to geographical position. The military slant of the Issachar, Benjamin, and Asher genealogies indicates that the chronicler found them in the census source he used for the Transjordanian tribes (cf. 5:18), deliberately breaking into it by his insertion of the tribe of Levi in chap. 6. The placing of Asher after west Manasseh and Ephraim reflects the southern setting of this particular list, as we shall see.

Unlike the listing in 2:1-2, Zebulun and Dan find no place here, presumably under the constraint of the conventional schematic representation of Israel's tribes as twelve in number. The splitting of Joseph into Manasseh and Ephraim and the further division of Manasseh into its eastern and western areas meant that two others had to be dropped. In 12:24-37 the problem will be resolved by treating the eastern tribes as one group, and in 27:16-22 by omitting Asher and Gad. Here the omission was not motivated by lack of material. Some earlier genealogical material was available to the chronicler in Gen

46:14-23 and Num 26:26, 42, and geographical information, in Josh 19:10-16, 40-48. All three sources are used in his other tribal genealogies. Lack of later material was not a factor; in the case of Naphtali (v. 13) he coped without it.

7:1-5. The Issachar genealogy falls into three parts. The first in v. 1 has been extracted from the clan information in Num 26:23-24. The other two parts, in vv. 2 and 3-5, give details of a military census. In v. 5, "enrolled by genealogy" (NRSV) signifies rather "enrolled for war."[57] In vv. 2 and 4 and also in v. 9, "of/by/according to their generations" (NRSV) means "according to their genealogical divisions." In v. 2, a census list credited to the time of David names six officers in the clan descended from Tola, who commanded conscripts from their extended families. One thinks, as presumably the chronicler did, of David's census in chap. 21. The item also invites comparison with the list of tribal heads in 27:16-22, related to that census, and with the enumeration of tribal contingents in 12:24-37, where Issachar is uniquely represented not by a number but by "200 chiefs, with all their relatives" (NIV). In the next census extract, five officers, Izrahiah and his four sons, all related to the subclan of Uzzi, are listed with the number of their conscripts. The total in v. 5 seems to include troops from the other three clans of v. 1, though the Hebrew is unclear.

7:6-12. The Benjaminite listing is unexpected in view of the long entry in chap. 8, where its presence accords with the overall design of the literary unit. The listing was evidently included in the longer source used by the chronicler, and he may have appreciated its military data as providing a sense of community and chose to use it here rather than incorporating it into chap. 8. The listing may also reflect a tradition that part of Benjamin belonged to the northern kingdom, as the double listing of tribal towns in Josh 18:21-28 seems to attest.[58] Verses 6-11 are taken from a military census document; in vv. 7 and 9 enrollment for military service is again in view. Three clans are listed, first according to their eponymous founders and then in terms of the numbers and names of their commanders and the numbers of their conscripts. In v. 6, neither Num 26:38-40 nor Gen 46:21 is followed precisely. No date is supplied for the census, though the chronicler probably assumed it was Davidic. The comparatively late name Elioenai may point to the period of Hezekiah, as in 4:36. Verse 12 gives a fragment of a genealogy of Benjamin, related to Num 26:39. It betrays an awareness that Benjamin had more than three clans and supplies two more in v. 12*a*; Ir may be meant to refer to Iri in v. 7. In v. 12*b* the name of a third clan or subclan founder, Hushim, seems to be Benjaminite; it is used of a woman in 8:8, 11. Aher appears to be a variant of either Aharah in 8:1 or Ahiram in Num 26:38. There is little merit in the conjecture that a lost genealogy of Dan underlies v. 12*b* (see the REB; see also Gen 46:23).

7:13. The terse genealogy of Naphtali is derived from Gen 46:24-25*a*. It gives the founders of its four clans and calls them "descendants" of the tribal mother Bilhah. In the parent text, the reference was to Dan and Naphtali as sons of Bilhah, but the chronicler has reused it to augment his scanty source material; Num 26:48-49 could supply him with nothing more.

7:14-19. The genealogy of Manasseh is closely related to that of Ephraim in vv. 20-27, as the joint geographical description in vv. 28-29 shows. That description also makes clear that west Manasseh is in view, notwithstanding the eastern flavor of the names "Machir" and "Gilead" (cf. Josh 17:3).[59] The eastern half of the tribe has already been featured in chap. 4. This genealogy has no solid basis in biblical precedents, though a number of names overlap with Numbers 26 and Joshua 17. It makes lavish use of birth reports. In its present form it reads like a series of disjointed statements. Its lack of coherence may be overcome by assuming that (1) "Asriel" in v. 14 originated as an early annotation specifying a further clan (see Num 26:31; Josh 17:2); (2) in v. 15 Machir's wife was taken (in relation to and so) "from" (NIV) the Benjaminite family of Huppim and Shuppim in v. 12; and (3) originally it was "their" sister, Maacah, who became his wife (see v. 16; cf. *BHS*). Mention of Zelophehad as "the second" (son) presupposes the role of Machir

57. S. J. De Vries, *1 and 2 Chronicles,* FOTL 11 (Grand Rapids: Eerdmans, 1989) 74.

58. See Y. Aharoni, *Land of the Bible: A Historical Geography,* 2nd rev. ed., trans. A. F. Rainey (Philadelphia: Westminster, 1979) 315; cf. W. L. Osborne, "The Genealogies of 1 Chronicles 1–9," (Ph.D. diss. Dropsie University, 1979) 28-87; M. Oeming, *Das wahre Israel: die "genealogische Vorhalle" 1 Chronik 1-9,* BWANT 128 (Stuttgart: Kohlhammer, 1990) 161-63.

59. See D. Edelman, "The Manasseh Genealogy in 1 Chronicles 7:14-19: Form and Source," *CBQ* 53 (1991) 179-201, esp. 192-93.

as the firstborn (Josh 17:1), though in Josh 17:3 Zelophehad is placed later in the genealogical chain.

This genealogy identifies first Manasseh's two sons Machir and Zelophehad by an Aramean concubine (vv. 14-15) and then specifies the lineage of Machir and his wife, Maacah, to a depth of four generations (vv. 16-17*a*). The derivation from Gilead in v. 17*b* offers an instance of genealogical fluidity; it accords with the tradition of Josh 17:3. It is uncertain whether Machir's sister or Gilead's is in view in v. 18. The lineage in v. 19 is not coordinated with what precedes it, but Shemida is known as a clan ancestor (Num 26:32; Josh 17:2). Mention of Zelophehad's daughters in v. 15 reminds readers of their role as heirs in Josh 17:3-6 by a special dispensation that extended a male privilege to them.

7:20-27. The genealogy of Ephraim, like the former one, does not depend directly on OT sources. It provides two separate linear genealogies that are interrupted by a narrative. The first is the line from Ephraim to an unknown Zabad, traced to a depth of seven generations. The second, beginning in v. 25, is that of Joshua; it has a depth of ten generations. At the start of the first genealogy, the vertical listing is an adaptation of an earlier horizontal one, in the light of the clan founders named in Num 26:36. The second overlaps with the first to some extent, with variations in spelling. In the course of v. 21 the phrase "Shuthelah his son" resumes the reference to Ephraim's son in v. 20 as an introduction to the story of the killing of two other sons and its sequel (cf. 2:3-4). The sense is: "Now Shuthelah was Ephraim's son, and so were Ezer and Elead."[60]

Ephraim's involvement in this Palestinian narrative stands in tension with his birth in Egypt (Gen 41:50-52). Whether the narrative is set in the patriarchal period or in the period of conquest cannot be ascertained. Gath is probably Gittaim, a dozen miles west of the Beth-horons.[61] This city-state was still a Canaanite enclave early in the monarchical period (2 Sam 4:3). The death of the cattle rustlers caused grief that their father found impossible to shake off, though his "relatives" (NIV) or "kinsmen" (REB)—he had only one brother—rallied around him in sympathy. His next son was given the name Beriah to commemorate the loss: It is explained as "in disaster" or "in misfortune" (ברעה *bĕrā'â*). What was the moral of the story for the chronicler? Two contrasted generations are often juxtaposed in his narratives, and so the little success story of Ephraim's daughter Sheerah in v. 24 is significant. Building is a sign of divine blessing in Chronicles (e.g., 2 Chr 26:5-6). The message is that disaster in one generation need not hold the next generation hostage. A Saul may give way to a David, an Ahaz to a Hezekiah.

7:28-29. The territory occupied by west Manasseh and Ephraim is defined together. Ephraim's boundaries are described in v. 28 and the boundaries of the northern area of west Manasseh in v. 29. Shechem was variously aligned in different historical periods; v. 19 suggests its attachment to Manasseh.

7:30-40. In the Asher genealogy, there is a return to the military census list used for a number of the earlier genealogies, most recently Benjamin's. Its introduction in vv. 30-31*a* is taken from Gen 46:17. Verses 30-32 take the form of a segmented genealogy to a depth of four generations. The attached list of clan commanders now functions as its continuation, though the partial alignment of names betrays its independent origin; the clan in v. 39 has no counterpart in the genealogy. The phrase "enrolled by genealogies" (v. 40) refers rather to military registration. The listing refers not to the tribe in its northern setting, but to an Asherite enclave in the southern part of the hill country of Ephraim, as some of the names show.[62]

60. See W. Rudolph, *Chronikbücher,* HAT 1:21 (Tübingen: Mohr [Siebeck], 1955) 71-72.

61. See B. Mazar, "Gath and Gittaim," *IEJ* 4 (1954) 227-35.

62. See D. Edelman, "The Asherite Genealogy in 1 Chronicles 7:30-40," *BR* 33 (1988) 13-23; N. Na'aman, "Sources and Redaction in the Chronicler's Genealogies of Asher and Ephraim," *JSOT* 49 (1991) 99-111, esp. 100-105; Aharoni, *The Land of the Bible,* 244.

REFLECTIONS

1. Who belongs to the people of God? The chronicler gives a provocative answer. The earlier leaders Ezra and Nehemiah had given a minimal answer, understandable in a hard-pressed, relatively new community. The chronicler judged that a broader answer grounded in ancient tradition could be given. He endeavored to prevent a particular religious emphasis driven by temporary need from hardening into a permanent attitude. He conceived of an ideal Israel to which the northern tribes belonged in principle just as much as did the southern tribes. Such completeness would replicate the united kingdom and the allocation of the land of Israel to each of the twelve tribes. No wonder David finds mention early in the section (7:2). No wonder an honored place is given to the genealogy of Joshua, under whose leadership the land was won and allocated (7:25-27).

Each new work of God throws into focus a particular truth and creates champions for it. A new denomination builds a shrine to its truth and makes it a permanent tradition and the reason for its continued existence. Anthony Norris Groves, a nineteenth-century Christian leader, after receiving adult baptism, was informed by a Baptist pastor, "Of course, you must be a Baptist now." "No," Groves replied, "I desire to follow all in those things in which they follow Christ, but I would not by joining one party cut myself off from others."[63] There is an idealism in this response that is difficult to attain in practice. Each local church has its own emphases and affiliation with like-minded believers. The chronicler was protesting at the iron curtain that was erected between members of the Lord's people. Have we in turn built walls of partition to cut ourselves off from fellow Christians?

2. There is a Wild West flavor about the first of the two scenarios sketched in 7:21-24. It easily translates into a celluloid world of cattle rustling and lynching at the hands of a posse who galloped after the rustlers. The genre is less evident in the sequel of family mourning. The father could not get over the overwhelming loss of two grown sons, and he perpetuated his grief in the name of his infant son. The baby was made to bear the brunt of an unending grief. We have already learned from 4:9-10 the cultural consequences of such unlucky naming, which only prayer to a powerful God could avert. Here the vignette is set against a scene of blessing. Sheerah is the only woman in the Old Testament to found cities. Like Dido, traditionally the founder of Carthage, she enjoyed a rare privilege. The chronicler contrasted bane and blessing, in line with his regular teaching that each generation could beat its past and win blessing from the Lord. Elsewhere he included moral and religious factors. Here the constraint of his source produced a contrast of blessedly achieving and fatalistically putting life on hold.

To those in the chronicler's constituency with ears to hear, the question posed was, Should we cast ourselves as victims of past tragedy? Zechariah had the right answer, when asked whether fast days commemorating the onset of conquest and exile should be perpetuated. No, turn them into happy holidays, he replied, and build a community where truth and peace are cherished (Zech 7:1-7; 8:18). Sowing in tears is meant to result in reaping with shouts of joy (Ps 126:5-6). The people themselves had a part to play in shaking off the past and beginning again with the Lord. The passage served the chronicler as an illustration of one of his model texts, Ezekiel 18. Pessimism could give way to optimism. The chains of a demoralizing past could be broken. A door of hope stands open, and readers are challenged to walk through and achieve great things with God. This is a message many believers still need to hear.

63. G. H. Lang, *Anthony Norris Groves* (London: Paternoster, 1949) 279.

1 Chronicles 8:1–9:1, The Tribe of Benjamin

NIV

8 Benjamin was the father of Bela his
firstborn,
Ashbel the second son, Aharah the third,
2Nohah the fourth and Rapha the fifth.
3The sons of Bela were:
Addar, Gera, Abihud,[a] 4Abishua, Naaman,
Ahoah, 5Gera, Shephuphan and Huram.
6These were the descendants of Ehud, who
were heads of families of those living in
Geba and were deported to Manahath:
7Naaman, Ahijah, and Gera, who deported them and who was the father of
Uzza and Ahihud.
8Sons were born to Shaharaim in Moab after he
had divorced his wives Hushim and Baara.
9By his wife Hodesh he had Jobab, Zibia,
Mesha, Malcam, 10Jeuz, Sakia and Mirmah.
These were his sons, heads of families. 11By
Hushim he had Abitub and Elpaal.
12The sons of Elpaal:
Eber, Misham, Shemed (who built Ono
and Lod with its surrounding villages),
13and Beriah and Shema, who were heads
of families of those living in Aijalon and
who drove out the inhabitants of Gath.
14Ahio, Shashak, Jeremoth, 15Zebadiah, Arad,
Eder, 16Michael, Ishpah and Joha were the
sons of Beriah.
17Zebadiah, Meshullam, Hizki, Heber, 18Ish-
merai, Izliah and Jobab were the sons of
Elpaal.
19Jakim, Zicri, Zabdi, 20Elienai, Zillethai, Eliel,
21Adaiah, Beraiah and Shimrath were the
sons of Shimei.
22Ishpan, Eber, Eliel, 23Abdon, Zicri, Hanan,
24Hananiah, Elam, Anthothijah, 25Iphdeiah
and Penuel were the sons of Shashak.
26Shamsherai, Shehariah, Athaliah, 27Jaareshiah,
Elijah and Zicri were the sons of Jeroham.
28All these were heads of families, chiefs as
listed in their genealogy, and they lived in
Jerusalem.
29Jeiel[b] the father[c] of Gibeon lived in Gibeon.

[a]3 Or *Gera the father of Ehud* [b]29 Some Septuagint manuscripts (see also 1 Chron. 9:35); Hebrew does not have *Jeiel.* [c]29 *Father* may mean *civic leader* or *military leader.*

NRSV

8 Benjamin became the father of Bela his
firstborn, Ashbel the second, Aharah the
third, 2Nohah the fourth, and Rapha the fifth.
3And Bela had sons: Addar, Gera, Abihud,[a]
4Abishua, Naaman, Ahoah, 5Gera, Shephuphan,
and Huram. 6These are the sons of Ehud (they
were heads of ancestral houses of the inhabitants
of Geba, and they were carried into exile to
Manahath): 7Naaman,[b] Ahijah, and Gera, that is,
Heglam,[c] who became the father of Uzza and
Ahihud. 8And Shaharaim had sons in the country
of Moab after he had sent away his wives Hushim
and Baara. 9He had sons by his wife Hodesh:
Jobab, Zibia, Mesha, Malcam, 10Jeuz, Sachia, and
Mirmah. These were his sons, heads of ancestral
houses. 11He also had sons by Hushim: Abitub and
Elpaal. 12The sons of Elpaal: Eber, Misham, and
Shemed, who built Ono and Lod with its towns,
13and Beriah and Shema (they were heads of
ancestral houses of the inhabitants of Aijalon, who
put to flight the inhabitants of Gath); 14and Ahio,
Shashak, and Jeremoth. 15Zebadiah, Arad, Eder,
16Michael, Ishpah, and Joha were sons of Beriah.
17Zebadiah, Meshullam, Hizki, Heber, 18Ishmerai,
Izliah, and Jobab were the sons of Elpaal. 19Jakim,
Zichri, Zabdi, 20Elienai, Zillethai, Eliel, 21Adaiah,
Beraiah, and Shimrath were the sons of Shimei.
22Ishpan, Eber, Eliel, 23Abdon, Zichri, Hanan, 24Ha-
naniah, Elam, Anthothijah, 25Iphdeiah, and Penuel
were the sons of Shashak. 26Shamsherai, Shehariah, Athaliah, 27Jaareshiah, Elijah, and Zichri
were the sons of Jeroham. 28These were the heads
of ancestral houses, according to their generations,
chiefs. These lived in Jerusalem.
29Jeiel[d] the father of Gibeon lived in Gibeon,
and the name of his wife was Maacah. 30His
firstborn son: Abdon, then Zur, Kish, Baal,[e]
Nadab, 31Gedor, Ahio, Zecher, 32and Mikloth,
who became the father of Shimeah. Now these
also lived opposite their kindred in Jerusalem,
with their kindred. 33Ner became the father of
Kish, Kish of Saul,[f] Saul[f] of Jonathan, Malchishua,
Abinadab, and Esh-baal; 34and the son of Jonathan

[a] Or *father of Ehud*; see 8.6 [b] Heb *and Naaman* [c] Or *he carried them into exile* [d] Compare 9.35: Heb lacks *Jeiel* [e] Gk Ms adds *Ner*; Compare 8.33 and 9.36 [f] Or *Shaul*

NIV

His wife's name was Maacah, [30]and his firstborn son was Abdon, followed by Zur, Kish, Baal, Ner,[a] Nadab, [31]Gedor, Ahio, Zeker [32]and Mikloth, who was the father of Shimeah. They too lived near their relatives in Jerusalem.

[33]Ner was the father of Kish, Kish the father of Saul, and Saul the father of Jonathan, Malki-Shua, Abinadab and Esh-Baal.[b]

[34]The son of Jonathan:
Merib-Baal,[c] who was the father of Micah.

[35]The sons of Micah:
Pithon, Melech, Tarea and Ahaz.

[36]Ahaz was the father of Jehoaddah, Jehoaddah was the father of Alemeth, Azmaveth and Zimri, and Zimri was the father of Moza. [37]Moza was the father of Binea; Raphah was his son, Eleasah his son and Azel his son.

[38]Azel had six sons, and these were their names:
Azrikam, Bokeru, Ishmael, Sheariah, Obadiah and Hanan. All these were the sons of Azel.

[39]The sons of his brother Eshek:
Ulam his firstborn, Jeush the second son and Eliphelet the third. [40]The sons of Ulam were brave warriors who could handle the bow. They had many sons and grandsons—150 in all.

All these were the descendants of Benjamin.

9 All Israel was listed in the genealogies recorded in the book of the kings of Israel.

The people of Judah were taken captive to Babylon because of their unfaithfulness.

[a]*30* Some Septuagint manuscripts (see also 1 Chron. 9:36); Hebrew does not have *Ner.* [b]*33* Also known as *Ish-Bosheth* [c]*34* Also known as *Mephibosheth*

NRSV

was Merib-baal; and Merib-baal became the father of Micah. [35]The sons of Micah: Pithon, Melech, Tarea, and Ahaz. [36]Ahaz became the father of Jehoaddah; and Jehoaddah became the father of Alemeth, Azmaveth, and Zimri; Zimri became the father of Moza. [37]Moza became the father of Binea; Raphah was his son, Eleasah his son, Azel his son. [38]Azel had six sons, and these are their names: Azrikam, Bocheru, Ishmael, Sheariah, Obadiah, and Hanan; all these were the sons of Azel. [39]The sons of his brother Eshek: Ulam his firstborn, Jeush the second, and Eliphelet the third. [40]The sons of Ulam were mighty warriors, archers, having many children and grandchildren, one hundred fifty. All these were Benjaminites.

9 So all Israel was enrolled by genealogies; and these are written in the Book of the Kings of Israel. And Judah was taken into exile in Babylon because of their unfaithfulness.

COMMENTARY

The massive textual unit that began in 2:2 is now brought to a conclusion. Benjamin, in whose territory Jerusalem lay (according to a prominent OT claim), was one of the triumvirate of tribes that for centuries preserved Israel's religious and dynastic traditions. So in the chronicler's genealogies Judah and Benjamin stand at either end of a literary rainbow, red and violet, with Levi as the central green. The rainbow represents the whole people of God, who were given stakes in the land

and a religious center in acknowledgment of God's divine patronage and presence. The spectrum comprised many more than three colors, or four including the vestigial tribe of Simeon. The southern tribes needed the rest to complete the rainbow.

The Benjaminite genealogy reflects a compilation available to the chronicler that evidently contained a range of earlier listings. They were largely made up of local community records of a military nature. The combination of genealogical, geographical, and historical data that featured in many of the earlier genealogies reappears in this one. The Benjaminite clans who traditionally lived at Geba are represented in vv. 1-7; those associated with Moab and with Ono and Lod, in vv. 8-12; residents of Aijalon, Gath, and Jerusalem, in vv. 13-28; and others who lived in Gibeon and Jerusalem, in vv. 29-32. With this last listing is linked a genealogy of Saul in vv. 33-40*a,* while the whole section is concluded in v. 40*b.* The unit of twelve tribal genealogies is brought to a close in 9:1. The emphasis on Jerusalem in this chapter nicely anticipates a post-exilic concern in 9:3, 34 and its dynastic and religious roles inaugurated by David in 11:4-8 and chaps. 15–16.

8:1-7. The first record is associated with the town of Geba. It is prefaced in vv. 1-2 by Benjamin's sons, five eponymous founders of clans. This listing is close to that in Num 26:38-40, though the last two names are different. The genealogy is then traced from a son, Bela, to representatives of nine subclans. Some of these recur in v. 7, with Ahijah replacing Ahoah. Verse 6 indicates that these are the names of militia commanders at some point in history (cf. 7:40). There is a partial generational update at the end of v. 7. Rather awkwardly, they are also called the "descendants" of Ehud in v. 6. It is tempting to identify him with Ehud ben-Gera, the left-handed Benjaminite judge who delivered Israel from Moab (Judg 3:12-30), but the Hebrew form of the name is slightly different (אחוד [*'ēḥûd*], not אהוד [*'ēhûd*]). These commanders are located at Geba and, after migration, at Manahat, whether the Edomite one of 1:40 or the Judean one of 2:52, 54. The interpretation of the NIV and the REB in v. 7 is probably correct: Gera did lead the transplanted group.

8:8-12. The next listing is also credited with settlement outside tribal territory, in this case wholly so. A subclan descended from Shaharaim is located in Moab and is supplied with contemporary representatives. This settlement must have taken place before Moab gained independence in the middle of the ninth century BCE. "Mesha" (v. 9) is a Moabite name, shared by the king who successfully rebelled against Israel. A collateral branch, traced through an earlier wife and a second son of the union, Elpaal, is linked with the western enterprise of Shemed, rebuilding or fortifying Ono and Lod on the eastern edge of the coastal plain.

8:13-28. Verse 13 begins a new sentence (as in the NJB). Five militia leaders of Aijalon are named, the first two of whom are associated with expansion to Gath-Gittaim to the south of Lod (cf. 7:21). Their family counterparts in a later generation are named in vv. 15-21. In the latter listing, Shimei stands for Shema, and there is mention of another group under Elpaal, presumably a different person from the one in listed v. 12. Over against the Aijalon-based groups are two other groups of commanders descended from Shashak and Jeremoth (v. 14), who settled in Jerusalem (vv. 22-28). In the later list, "Jeroham" appears as the equivalent of "Jeremoth." It is clear that the later information in vv. 15-28 was originally independent of that in vv. 13-14. The two records were combined with their deviations intact, including the dropping of Ahio in v. 14, unless it really means "his brother" (NJB, following the LXX).

8:29-32. In this last localized listing, a family group moved to Jerusalem and, not surprisingly, took up residence near their fellow Benjaminites whose leaders were named in vv. 22-27. This group originally came from Gibeon; it is traced back to the Israelite "founder" (REB) of this older, Canaanite town, otherwise known in Chronicles as the honorable site of the tabernacle until Solomon's reign (16:39-40; 2 Chr 1:3). His name is not supplied, but in the parallel text at 9:35 it is given as "Jeiel," which the NIV and the NRSV have repeated here. Presumably most of the ensuing family listed in vv. 30-32*a* remained in Gibeon. Perhaps those who relocated were the families mentioned in v. 32 (cf. the REB). The name "Baal" in v. 30 implies an early dating for the list.

8:33-40a. The Gibeon-Jerusalem listing continues with a genealogy of King Saul, Benjamin's best-known scion (except for a later Saul of NT fame) and so ancestor of a prominent family. He evidently came from Gibeon.[64] This lineage connects with the preceding listing at the point of "Ner" (v. 30; cf. 1 Sam 14:50-51). The name appears at 9:36 before "Nadab" (the first part of this name, "Nadab" [נדב *nādāb*], looks very similar in the Hebrew script to "Ner" [נר *nēr*]; evidently it fell out of the text). His "brother" Kish fluidly reappears as a son. In fact, a strictly genealogical relationship is now given, over against the horizontal grouping of subclans in vv. 30-31. The genealogy basically represents the lineage of Azal (v. 37); it is mainly linear, with segmented details at three points. It has been updated by one generation and by a collateral branch of conscripts specializing in archery (vv. 38-40*a*). This genealogy was probably composed toward the end of the monarchical period.[65]

64. See J. Blenkinsopp, *Gibeon and Israel: The Role of Gibeon and the Gibeonites in the Political and Religious History of Early Israel,* SOTSMS 2 (Cambridge: Cambridge University Press, 1972) 58-59.

65. See A. Demsky, "The Genealogy of Gibeon (1 Chronicles 9:35-44): Biblical and Epigraphic Considerations," *BASOR* 202 (April 1971) 16-23.

8:40b–9:1. After the sectional summary in 8:40*b,* the chronicler looked back over the whole unit with its twelve tribal genealogies. Since the sons of Israel or Jacob (2:1-2) had been treated in principle, "all Israel" had been presented in genealogical form. This entity of twelve tribes comprised the people of God, and no lesser, sectarian definition could satisfy. The source, unlike in 2 Chr 20:34, appears to be a royal document, from which the tribal census information given for a number of the tribes, and perhaps also the guild records of 4:21-23, had been taken.

A final statement was necessary—namely, a historical and theological comment on the southern tribes. In 5:25-26 the chronicler had recorded the unfaithfulness and exile of the northern tribes. Now a precise parallel needed to be drawn; that of 6:15 was not enough. The southern tribes, who comprised the state of Judah, were no less partners in such sin and punishment. They, too, were covenant breakers (cf. Lev 26:40, where "treachery" translates מעל [*ma'al*], here rendered "unfaithfulness"). So they in turn had to lose the land. Eventually the royal narrative will return to this point at 2 Chr 36:14, 20*a.*

REFLECTIONS

If the chronicler were alive and active in the Jewish community today, he would surely be a member of Habad, encouraging assimilated Jews to appreciate their heritage and to be true to its glorious traditions. Benjamin and Judah stood for him as pre-exilic models for his own constituency, insofar as they were guardians of covenant truths centered in Jerusalem's Temple and dynasty. As guardians they had a responsibility to the other tribes, who had long ago lost their allegiance to these truths. They were not to be an inner circle, hugging to themselves their relationship with the Lord. Rather, as the structure of chaps. 2–8 indicates, they were to be an outer circle, inviting the others back into their midst and acknowledging their equality as fellow children of Israel. Although Judah was historically preeminent, the birthright still belonged to Ephraim and Manasseh (5:1-2).

How may we apply this principle, which was so important for the chronicler's time? There tends to be a denominational hierarchy in Christian circles. Traditional denominations are valued by their members for their links with the religious past. Younger denominations are dismissed to the end of the pecking order. It also works the other way. The newer groups see themselves as more open to the Holy Spirit and in touch with modernity. They look on older denominations as worn-out wineskins that held the spiritual wine of yesteryear. Either way, our denominational selves align easily with Judah and Benjamin. The chronicler would grant us our elitism, for whatever reason, yet urge that we are thereby responsible for initiating moves to express our unity with the "lesser" groups. We are the ones, he would tell us, who must work at producing a cross-fertilizing commonwealth of churches, devoted alike to worship, service, and outreach. "From everyone to whom much has been given, much will be required;

and from the one to whom much has been entrusted, even more will be demanded" (Luke 12:48 NRSV).

There is a sting in the tail at 9:1. The state of Judah fell into the same fate of exile as had the northern state earlier, victim of the same failure. Each of the two groups could come before God only as repentant sinners, saved by repeated grace in spite of the skeletons in their closets. Unity is best achieved by crowding together at the mercy seat in a common humility, aware that "God has imprisoned all in disobedience so that he may be merciful to all" (Rom 11:32 NRSV).

1 CHRONICLES 9:2-34, ISRAEL'S RESTORATION IN PRINCIPLE

NIV

2Now the first to resettle on their own property
in their own towns were some Israelites, priests,
Levites and temple servants.
3Those from Judah, from Benjamin, and from
Ephraim and Manasseh who lived in Jerusalem
were:
4Uthai son of Ammihud, the son of Omri, the
son of Imri, the son of Bani, a descendant
of Perez son of Judah.
5Of the Shilonites:
Asaiah the firstborn and his sons.
6Of the Zerahites:
Jeuel.
The people from Judah numbered 690.
7Of the Benjamites:
Sallu son of Meshullam, the son of Hodaviah, the son of Hassenuah;
8Ibneiah son of Jeroham; Elah son of Uzzi,
the son of Micri; and Meshullam son of
Shephatiah, the son of Reuel, the son of
Ibnijah.
9The people from Benjamin, as listed in
their genealogy, numbered 956. All these
men were heads of their families.
10Of the priests:
Jedaiah; Jehoiarib; Jakin;
11Azariah son of Hilkiah, the son of Meshullam, the son of Zadok, the son of
Meraioth, the son of Ahitub, the official
in charge of the house of God;
12Adaiah son of Jeroham, the son of Pashhur, the son of Malkijah; and Maasai son
of Adiel, the son of Jahzerah, the son of
Meshullam, the son of Meshillemith, the
son of Immer.

NRSV

2Now the first to live again in their possessions
in their towns were Israelites, priests, Levites, and
temple servants.
3And some of the people of Judah, Benjamin,
Ephraim, and Manasseh lived in Jerusalem: 4Uthai
son of Ammihud, son of Omri, son of Imri, son
of Bani, from the sons of Perez son of Judah. 5And
of the Shilonites: Asaiah the firstborn, and his
sons. 6Of the sons of Zerah: Jeuel and their kin,
six hundred ninety. 7Of the Benjaminites: Sallu
son of Meshullam, son of Hodaviah, son of Hassenuah, 8Ibneiah son of Jeroham, Elah son of Uzzi,
son of Michri, and Meshullam son of Shephatiah,
son of Reuel, son of Ibnijah; 9and their kindred
according to their generations, nine hundred fifty-
six. All these were heads of families according to
their ancestral houses.
10Of the priests: Jedaiah, Jehoiarib, Jachin,
11and Azariah son of Hilkiah, son of Meshullam,
son of Zadok, son of Meraioth, son of Ahitub, the
chief officer of the house of God; 12and Adaiah
son of Jeroham, son of Pashhur, son of Malchijah,
and Maasai son of Adiel, son of Jahzerah, son of
Meshullam, son of Meshillemith, son of Immer;
13besides their kindred, heads of their ancestral
houses, one thousand seven hundred sixty, qualified for the work of the service of the house of
God.
14Of the Levites: Shemaiah son of Hasshub,
son of Azrikam, son of Hashabiah, of the sons of
Merari; 15and Bakbakkar, Heresh, Galal, and Mattaniah son of Mica, son of Zichri, son of Asaph;
16and Obadiah son of Shemaiah, son of Galal, son
of Jeduthun, and Berechiah son of Asa, son of

NIV

13The priests, who were heads of families, numbered 1,760. They were able men, responsible for ministering in the house of God.

14Of the Levites:

Shemaiah son of Hasshub, the son of Azrikam, the son of Hashabiah, a Merarite; 15Bakbakkar, Heresh, Galal and Mattaniah son of Mica, the son of Zicri, the son of Asaph; 16Obadiah son of Shemaiah, the son of Galal, the son of Jeduthun; and Berekiah son of Asa, the son of Elkanah, who lived in the villages of the Netophathites.

17The gatekeepers:

Shallum, Akkub, Talmon, Ahiman and their brothers, Shallum their chief 18being stationed at the King's Gate on the east, up to the present time. These were the gatekeepers belonging to the camp of the Levites. 19Shallum son of Kore, the son of Ebiasaph, the son of Korah, and his fellow gatekeepers from his family (the Korahites) were responsible for guarding the thresholds of the Tent[a] just as their fathers had been responsible for guarding the entrance to the dwelling of the LORD. 20In earlier times Phinehas son of Eleazar was in charge of the gatekeepers, and the LORD was with him. 21Zechariah son of Meshelemiah was the gatekeeper at the entrance to the Tent of Meeting.

22Altogether, those chosen to be gatekeepers at the thresholds numbered 212. They were registered by genealogy in their villages. The gatekeepers had been assigned to their positions of trust by David and Samuel the seer. 23They and their descendants were in charge of guarding the gates of the house of the LORD—the house called the Tent. 24The gatekeepers were on the four sides: east, west, north and south. 25Their brothers in their villages had to come from time to time and share their duties for seven-day periods. 26But the four principal gatekeepers, who were Levites, were entrusted with the responsibility for the rooms and treasuries in the house of God. 27They would spend the night stationed around the house

[a]19 That is, the temple; also in verses 21 and 23

NRSV

Elkanah, who lived in the villages of the Netophathites.

17The gatekeepers were: Shallum, Akkub, Talmon, Ahiman; and their kindred Shallum was the chief, 18stationed previously in the king's gate on the east side. These were the gatekeepers of the camp of the Levites. 19Shallum son of Kore, son of Ebiasaph, son of Korah, and his kindred of his ancestral house, the Korahites, were in charge of the work of the service, guardians of the thresholds of the tent, as their ancestors had been in charge of the camp of the LORD, guardians of the entrance. 20And Phinehas son of Eleazar was chief over them in former times; the LORD was with him. 21Zechariah son of Meshelemiah was gatekeeper at the entrance of the tent of meeting. 22All these, who were chosen as gatekeepers at the thresholds, were two hundred twelve. They were enrolled by genealogies in their villages. David and the seer Samuel established them in their office of trust. 23So they and their descendants were in charge of the gates of the house of the LORD, that is, the house of the tent, as guards. 24The gatekeepers were on the four sides, east, west, north, and south; 25and their kindred who were in their villages were obliged to come in every seven days, in turn, to be with them; 26for the four chief gatekeepers, who were Levites, were in charge of the chambers and the treasures of the house of God. 27And they would spend the night near the house of God; for on them lay the duty of watching, and they had charge of opening it every morning.

28Some of them had charge of the utensils of service, for they were required to count them when they were brought in and taken out. 29Others of them were appointed over the furniture, and over all the holy utensils, also over the choice flour, the wine, the oil, the incense, and the spices. 30Others, of the sons of the priests, prepared the mixing of the spices, 31and Mattithiah, one of the Levites, the firstborn of Shallum the Korahite, was in charge of making the flat cakes. 32Also some of their kindred of the Kohathites had charge of the rows of bread, to prepare them for each sabbath.

33Now these are the singers, the heads of ancestral houses of the Levites, living in the cham-

NIV

of God, because they had to guard it; and they had charge of the key for opening it each morning.

28Some of them were in charge of the articles used in the temple service; they counted them when they were brought in and when they were taken out. 29Others were assigned to take care of the furnishings and all the other articles of the sanctuary, as well as the flour and wine, and the oil, incense and spices. 30But some of the priests took care of mixing the spices. 31A Levite named Mattithiah, the firstborn son of Shallum the Korahite, was entrusted with the responsibility for baking the offering bread. 32Some of their Kohathite brothers were in charge of preparing for every Sabbath the bread set out on the table.

33Those who were musicians, heads of Levite families, stayed in the rooms of the temple and were exempt from other duties because they were responsible for the work day and night.

34All these were heads of Levite families, chiefs as listed in their genealogy, and they lived in Jerusalem.

NRSV

bers of the temple free from other service, for they were on duty day and night. 34These were heads of ancestral houses of the Levites, according to their generations; these leaders lived in Jerusalem.

COMMENTARY

Exile was not the end of the story. Restoration to the land and so, in the light of v. 1, to the Lord's favor eventually occurred. Only here does the chronicler deal with resettlement as a fact. (In 2 Chr 36:20*b*-23 he will tantalizingly look forward to it, like Moses viewing the land from Mt. Nebo.) This section has a partial, preliminary tone, for all its solid data. Only mention of the resettlement of Judah is made in the brief note of v. 2, despite the fact that the northern tribes had "possessions" in the land (7:28 NRSV; cf. 2 Chr 31:1). The next focus is narrower still: the reoccupation of Jerusalem, stated at the beginning and the end (vv. 3, 34), though a bit more information is included in vv. 16 and 22. The singling out of Jerusalem has symbolic value—as an earnest of the eventual reoccupation of the whole land, a promise the Lord could fulfill only if the people played their part (28:8). Moreover, it surely echoes earlier prophetic hopes, from First Isaiah (Isa 1:26), via a package of promises in Second Isaiah (esp. Isa 49:14-21; 52:12; 54:1-3), and via Ezekiel (Ezek 16:53-63; 48:30-35), to Zechariah (Zech 8:1-10). The word of the Lord had begun to come true.

The chronicler affirms the continuity of the post-exilic community with the pre-exilic one, whose story is told in the ensuing narratives. The tribal groupings of chaps. 2–8 were represented in the resettlement of Jerusalem not only by the secular tribes but also by the tribe of Levi, divided into priests and Levites. Jerusalem had been chosen by the Lord to be the home of the Temple (2 Chr 6:6). The emphasis on its sacred personnel in vv. 10-34 reflects continuity of worship at the Temple, which was duly rebuilt, as 2 Chr 36:23 was to announce.

The issue of continuity, lay and religious, comes to the fore in the different form the genealogies now take. In chaps. 1–8 they had mainly been descending, apart from the levitical links between the ages of David and Moses, forged for dispensational purposes in 6:33-48 (also 5:8, 14-15). Now they are ascending, tracing the perpetuation of older lines in the post-exilic community. Provisionally at least, Israel is alive and well, and through its religious representatives is faithful to its duty to maintain the worship of the Lord. Ideals are presented here with an implicit challenge that they should be cherished.

Verses 2-17 appear to depend on Neh 11:3-11, despite substantial differences. The echoing of the editorial introduction of Neh 11:3 is a strong argument for literary dependence. Apart from textual variants and subsequent omissions in Nehemiah 11, most differences may be understood in terms of updating to a later generation, both by replacing older with more contemporary names and by increasing the numbers of figures. The Nehemiah list records those who were drafted to Jerusalem as a defensive measure after its walls were rebuilt.

9:2-9. Verse 2, adapted from Neh 11:3, views the population of Judah returning to their ancestral properties. "Again" (NRSV; "resettle," NIV) is not in the Hebrew, but is implied after v. 1 and agrees with the post-exilic nature of the source. "Israelites" refers to lay members. A tolerable tension is created by the chronicler's including in v. 3 "Ephraim and Manasseh," which is lacking in Neh 11:4. He not only relegated "Israelites" in Neh 11:3 (NIV) to lay status but also invested the term with intertribal significance, in line with "all Israel" in v. 1. The pair of tribes is a shorthand reference to all the northern tribes (as in 2 Chr 30:1; 31:4; 34:9), though no tribal representatives have been inserted into the list that follows. The spiritual reunion of Judah and members of the old northern kingdom is portrayed in 2 Chr 28:8-15; 30:11, 18; 34:9 is presupposed here. The chronicler's addition is motivated by his idealism. He may have been influenced by Ezekiel's description of the new Jerusalem as being entered by gates named after the tribes of Israel (Ezek 48:30-35).

In accord with its heading, the list details the lay population in vv. 4-9 and priests and Levites in vv. 10-34. The "temple servants" (cf. Neh 11:21), though retained in the heading, are not elaborated upon, because they never feature among the chronicler's temple personnel. As for Judah, three family heads represent the three clans of Perez, Shelah, and Zerah (see 2:3-4; in v. 5 "Shelanites" [REB] is to be read with the LXX by repointing the Hebrew). The representative of the Perez clan has been replaced. A reference to Zerah probably followed in Nehemiah 11 at an earlier stage; the low number in Neh 11:6 relates only to the Perez clan. Consistent with the source, there is no listing for the family of David (cf. Ezra 8:2). The chronicler has already supplied its post-exilic genealogy in 3:18-24.

The four Benjaminite family heads represent a considerable amplification of the parallel in Nehemiah 11, but the two officials of Neh 11:9 are not reproduced. The family heads are not distinguished by clan, though "according to their generations" (v. 9, also v. 34), which means "according to their genealogical divisions," implies clan ancestry.

9:10-13. The priestly list traces the lineage of two out of six priestly heads of families, one by telescoping to the ancient high priest Ahitub (see 6:11-12), and the other by tracing to Immer, presumably the ancestor mentioned in Ezra 2:37; Neh 7:40; 10:20. The number of priests reflects a total of the individual numbers in Neh 11:12-14 with an updating from 1,192 to 1,760.

9:14-16. The listing of Levites does not give a straightforward derivation from the three clans of Merari, Gershom, and Kohath, apart from Merari in v. 14. Two singing groups are represented in the course of vv. 15-16. That of Asaph was descended from Gershom, according to 6:39-43; that of Jeduthun is nowhere traced to a clan. The Kohath clan will feature in v. 32 and by implication in vv. 19 and 31 via its Korahite subclan. The list here has added a reference to Berechiah and his home at Netophah, where singers lived, according to Neh 12:28. Presumably his family rose to prominence later. His presence does not fit comfortably in a list of Jerusalem residents; doubtless his part-time residence when on duty is in view (see vv. 25, 33).

9:17-27. The source already regarded temple singers as Levites, unlike that of Ezra 2:41 (= Neh 7:44). Gatekeepers were not yet included, just as they were not in Ezra 2:42 (= Neh 7:45). The chronicler turns to use another source, beginning in v. 17. It overlapped with Neh 11:19, but mentioned four rather than two family heads of the gatekeepers.[66] In this later source, gatekeepers

66. H. G. M. Williamson, *1 and 2 Chronicles*, NCB (Grand Rapids: Eerdmans, 1982) 90.

are firmly identified as Levites (v. 18; cf. v. 26), as the chronicler himself identified them in 23:5 and in the primary layer of chap. 26. In the rest of the section the focus shifts from names to duties. The shortest listing, that of the Levites in vv. 14-17, receives an extensive analysis of duties in vv. 18-33, in terms of security (vv. 18-27), supplies and equipment (vv. 28-32), and singing (v. 33). This range of duties accords with three of the four categories of Levites in 23:4-5 and is amplified in subsequent chapters—namely, maintenance staff, gatekeepers, and singers. The chronicler consistently regarded Levites as the solid bedrock of temple service. He regularly championed them and encouraged appreciation of their work, which lacked the attention and honor attached to the priesthood.

The issue of continuity is treated in a distinctive way (vv. 18-33). Shallum was currently head of the security force and formerly in the prestigious position of controlling the east gate, still called the royal gate, before he was replaced by Zechariah (v. 21). Shallum is credited with a magnificent pedigree stretching back to the wilderness period of the tabernacle, to which there is a flashback in vv. 19*b*-20 (cf. Num 1:53). Then the gatekeepers came under the supervision of the chief priest Eleazar in Num 3:32 and so later of his illustrious son Phineas, who was a blessed model of temple service (Num 25:7-13; cf. 1 Chr 6:4; Ps 106:30-31). In the temple dispensation, the gatekeepers' office was renewed by no less than David and the prophet Samuel. The reference to David accords with 23:2-6. Samuel's patronage is of a vaguer nature. Although he predicted David's reign (11:3), he did not live to see it or his organization of the Temple (see 1 Sam 25:1; 28:3). Presumably young Samuel's service in the Shiloh temple (1 Sam 3:2-18) was a levitical precedent; his adoption into the family tree of the Levites in 6:28, 33 is noteworthy.

Direct reference to the ancient tabernacle in v. 19*b* is accompanied by typological allusions to it in vv. 18*b*, 19*a*, 21, and 23; in the first case, "the camp of the LORD" refers to the temple precincts, as in 2 Chr 31:2. The Temple was the dispensational counterpart of the tabernacle, featured in the Torah. So the post-exilic gatekeepers, bridging the two dispensations in their ancient and current work, had a double validity. As in v. 16, their commuting "for seven-day periods" in vv. 22 and 25 (cf. Neh 12:28-29) does not fit the impression of permanent residence in the context. As if aware of this, v. 26*a* states that "the four head gatekeepers were on permanent duty" (NJB) and thus were residents.

There seems to be a shift in the course of v. 26 to another source or to another part of the same source (see the new paragraph in the NJB). The Hebrew clause "they were Levites" may be intended to indicate that a range of levitical categories is in view hereafter, and not just gatekeepers. First, security work continues to be in mind. The reference in v. 28*b* is not to the administrative posts of 26:20-28 but to sentry duty, like that at "the storehouse" in 26:15, 17. Their crucial responsibilities are highlighted in v. 27.

9:28-32. Another group of Levites comes into view: the maintenance workers of 23:4, 6-24 (cf. 23:28-29). They worked faithfully behind the scenes, caring as conscientiously for mundane utensils as for the sacred vessels used in temple services. The aside in v. 30 may be attributed to the pro-priestly reviser who embellished Chronicles at various points to redress the balance.[67] The "flat cakes" (v. 31) were for the daily grain offerings (see Lev 6:19-23).

9:33-34. Another source break occurs at v. 33, which must have been the heading or conclusion for a list of family heads of levitical singers. The chronicler used this extract for the light it shed on their duties, especially their dedication in serving by night as well as by day (cf. Ps 134:1). Before the chronicler turns to repeat in vv. 35-44 the genealogy of Saul from 8:29-38, he puts 8:28 to new use by slipping in a reference to Levites. It becomes a conclusion both to vv. 14-33 and to the whole section, corresponding to v. 3.

67. Ibid., 91.

REFLECTIONS

Exile gave way to return. Although the wording stays at the human level, there were divine overtones for the chronicler in the light of Solomon's prayers that the sinning and repentant people might be restored to their God-given land (2 Chr 6:24-25, 36-39) and the reference to Jeremiah's prediction of restoration at 2 Chr 36:21-22. The story is symbol as well as event, since it is related to the chronicler's use of return from exile as a metaphor for the spiritual and complete restoration available to the post-exilic people of God. The historical return has a provisional character, limited as it was to Judah and Jerusalem. The tribal boundaries and towns covered in chapters 2–8 are woefully contracted. Yet that return was consistent with earlier prophetic words, and the concentration on Jerusalem seems to underline the implicit theme of prophecy's coming true.

These are themes the New Testament also celebrates. The gospel of Christ is no novelty but was promised by God through the prophets in the Holy Scriptures (Rom 1:2). The Christian church enjoys both present grace and the prospect of final salvation foretold by the prophets (1 Pet 1:3-12). We, too, have a "pledge of our inheritance as God's own people" (Eph 1:14 NRSV) and are challenged to make every effort to enter it (Heb 4:1, 10; 12:1-2).

The chronicler insists that Israel was present in the post-exilic capital, in its wider, grander sense. North and south, sinners both (5:26-27; 9:1-2), found in Jerusalem a big enough umbrella of divine grace to cover them all in token of their common heritage and future enjoyment of it on a larger scale. Paul expressed a remarkably similar conviction in his defense before Agrippa, when he testified of his "hope in the promise made by God to our ancestors, a promise that our twelve tribes hope to attain" (Acts 26:6-7 NRSV). The theme is repeated in a typological sense at Rev 21:12-14 in borrowing from Ezekiel 48 the vision of the new Jerusalem's twelve gates inscribed with the names of the twelve tribes (see Rev 7:4-8). All of God's people were to be represented there. Accordingly here and now we are to extend the right hand of fellowship that transcends different spheres of the faith as James, Cephas, and John did to Paul and Barnabas (Gal 2:9).

For the chronicler, the restored Jerusalem was home to the Temple. He used the opportunity to extol the work of the Levites. His exuberant description is reminiscent of C. S. Lewis's depiction of Sarah Smith, who used to live in Golders Green, now radiantly transformed into a veritable Queen of Heaven.[68] The message there is to respect and honor people like Mrs. Smith, whose labors for good and for God will redound to surprising fame in heaven. So here a glorious picture of heritage and devotion is painted in honor of these lesser members of the temple staff. We may apply this call for appreciation to our particular ecclesiastical settings and elsewhere.

The chronicler is also concerned to validate post-exilic worship, for which the work of the Levites is used as a test case. Their heritage stretched back to the wilderness period of Israel's history, when their predecessors worked for the tabernacle. Their work was validated afresh by Samuel and by David. Along the chain of generations, God's work went on. We do not readily warm to this saga of hereditary succession. It clashes with a cultural commitment to modernity and a strange disdain for the past. Yet it is a necessary message for Christians, if we are to stand on solid spiritual foundations, true to a historically given revelation. The call comes in turn to us to maintain the traditions of the ancient faith handed on to us, proudly and appropriately (see 1 Cor 11:2; 15:1-2).

68. C. S. Lewis, *The Great Divorce* (New York: Macmillan, 1946) 108-23.

1 CHRONICLES 9:35–
2 CHRONICLES 9:31

THE REIGNS OF DAVID AND SOLOMON

OVERVIEW

The chronicler highlighted the reigns of David and Solomon as a key period of theological history. During that time, there was a special manifestation of the covenant goodness of the Lord and a revelation of guidelines for Israel thereafter. The chronicler set the period inside its own literary frame, which serves to isolate it from the comparative mundaneness of history before and after. The frame occurs in 10:14, "the LORD . . . turned the kingdom over to David," and in 2 Chr 10:15, the "turn" in events predicted for Rehoboam. These two turning points in sacred history, at the end of Saul's reign and at the beginning of Rehoboam's, draw attention to the intervening reigns of David and Solomon as a period when God's will for Israel then and thereafter was supremely realized. First Chronicles 11–2 Chronicles 9, prefaced by 1 Chr 9:35–10:14, is a single overarching unit and nearly half the chronicler's work. We must listen carefully to his presentation of the double reign, if we want to catch his message.

1 CHRONICLES 9:35–29:30, THE REIGN OF DAVID

OVERVIEW

The account of David's reign is dominated by two religious enterprises: his moving the ark to Jerusalem (chaps. 13–16) and his preparations for the building of the Temple, where the ark was to be housed (chaps. 23–29). The accomplishment of each task is marked by public praise of God (16:7-36; 29:10-19). Chapters 17–22 are introduced by a prophetic oracle in chap. 17. It sets out the divine program for the reigns of David and Solomon—David's preparatory role as a warrior king and Solomon's as temple builder—and announces a Davidic dynasty. David's role is discharged in chaps. 18–20. Chapters 21–22 are concerned with the temple site, which is essentially linked with divine grace, and with Solomon's double mandate as temple builder and guarantor of the dynasty. These latter themes are revisited in chap. 28. The initial section, chaps. 9–12, by recounting the disastrous end of Saul's reign and the beginning of David's blessed one, contrasts the motifs of spiritual exile and the restoration begun by David's coronation and his occupation of Jerusalem.

1 Chronicles 9:35–12:40, A Decisive Change of King

OVERVIEW

Saul and David are like night and day. They function as models of right and wrong, of defeat and victory. The chronicler has given a pointer to their typological meaning by speaking plainly of Judah as first unfaithful to God and so exiled, and then returning to live again in their cities, especially in Jerusalem (9:1-3). Now Saul is unfaithful and dies; his subjects are scattered from their homes. But David is raised up as the new king of a united people and comes to live in Jerusalem. So David becomes a pledge that exile will finally be put behind the people of God and that full restoration will eventually come, if only they will follow in David's footsteps and not Saul's.

1 Chronicles 9:35–10:14, Saul's Infidelity and Death

NIV

35Jeiel the father[a] of Gibeon lived in Gibeon.
His wife's name was Maacah, 36and his
firstborn son was Abdon, followed by Zur,
Kish, Baal, Ner, Nadab, 37Gedor, Ahio,
Zechariah and Mikloth. 38Mikloth was the
father of Shimeam. They too lived near
their relatives in Jerusalem.
39Ner was the father of Kish, Kish the father
of Saul, and Saul the father of Jonathan,
Malki-Shua, Abinadab and Esh-Baal.[b]
40The son of Jonathan:
Merib-Baal,[c] who was the father of Micah.
41The sons of Micah:
Pithon, Melech, Tahrea and Ahaz.[d]
42Ahaz was the father of Jadah, Jadah[e] was
the father of Alemeth, Azmaveth and
Zimri, and Zimri was the father of Moza.
43Moza was the father of Binea; Rephaiah
was his son, Eleasah his son and Azel his
son.
44Azel had six sons, and these were their
names:
Azrikam, Bokeru, Ishmael, Sheariah,
Obadiah and Hanan. These were the sons
of Azel.

10 Now the Philistines fought against Israel;
the Israelites fled before them, and many
fell slain on Mount Gilboa. 2The Philistines

[a]35 *Father* may mean *civic leader* or *military leader.* [b]39 Also known as *Ish-Bosheth* [c]40 Also known as *Mephibosheth* [d]41 Vulgate and Syriac (see also Septuagint and 1 Chron. 8:35); Hebrew does not have *and Ahaz.* [e]42 Some Hebrew manuscripts and Septuagint (see also 1 Chron. 8:36); most Hebrew manuscripts *Jarah, Jarah*

NRSV

35In Gibeon lived the father of Gibeon, Jeiel,
and the name of his wife was Maacah. 36His
firstborn son was Abdon, then Zur, Kish, Baal,
Ner, Nadab, 37Gedor, Ahio, Zechariah, and Mikloth; 38and Mikloth became the father of
Shimeam; and these also lived opposite their kindred in Jerusalem, with their kindred. 39Ner became the father of Kish, Kish of Saul, Saul of
Jonathan, Malchishua, Abinadab, and Esh-baal;
40and the son of Jonathan was Merib-baal; and
Merib-baal became the father of Micah. 41The sons
of Micah: Pithon, Melech, Tahrea, and Ahaz;[a]
42and Ahaz became the father of Jarah, and Jarah
of Alemeth, Azmaveth, and Zimri; and Zimri became the father of Moza. 43Moza became the
father of Binea; and Rephaiah was his son, Eleasah
his son, Azel his son. 44Azel had six sons, and
these are their names: Azrikam, Bocheru, Ishmael,
Sheariah, Obadiah, and Hanan; these were the
sons of Azel.
10 Now the Philistines fought against Israel;
and the men of Israel fled before the Philistines, and fell slain on Mount Gilboa. 2The
Philistines overtook Saul and his sons; and the
Philistines killed Jonathan and Abinadab and Malchishua, sons of Saul. 3The battle pressed hard on
Saul; and the archers found him, and he was
wounded by the archers. 4Then Saul said to his
armor-bearer, "Draw your sword, and thrust me
through with it, so that these uncircumcised may
not come and make sport of me." But his armor-

[a] Compare 8.35: Heb lacks *and Ahaz*

NIV

pressed hard after Saul and his sons, and they killed his sons Jonathan, Abinadab and Malki-Shua. [3]The fighting grew fierce around Saul, and when the archers overtook him, they wounded him.

[4]Saul said to his armor-bearer, "Draw your sword and run me through, or these uncircumcised fellows will come and abuse me."

But his armor-bearer was terrified and would not do it; so Saul took his own sword and fell on it. [5]When the armor-bearer saw that Saul was dead, he too fell on his sword and died. [6]So Saul and his three sons died, and all his house died together.

[7]When all the Israelites in the valley saw that the army had fled and that Saul and his sons had died, they abandoned their towns and fled. And the Philistines came and occupied them.

[8]The next day, when the Philistines came to strip the dead, they found Saul and his sons fallen on Mount Gilboa. [9]They stripped him and took his head and his armor, and sent messengers throughout the land of the Philistines to proclaim the news among their idols and their people. [10]They put his armor in the temple of their gods and hung up his head in the temple of Dagon.

[11]When all the inhabitants of Jabesh Gilead heard of everything the Philistines had done to Saul, [12]all their valiant men went and took the bodies of Saul and his sons and brought them to Jabesh. Then they buried their bones under the great tree in Jabesh, and they fasted seven days.

[13]Saul died because he was unfaithful to the LORD; he did not keep the word of the LORD and even consulted a medium for guidance, [14]and did not inquire of the LORD. So the LORD put him to death and turned the kingdom over to David son of Jesse.

NRSV

bearer was unwilling, for he was terrified. So Saul took his own sword and fell on it. [5]When his armor-bearer saw that Saul was dead, he also fell on his sword and died. [6]Thus Saul died; he and his three sons and all his house died together. [7]When all the men of Israel who were in the valley saw that the army[a] had fled and that Saul and his sons were dead, they abandoned their towns and fled; and the Philistines came and occupied them.

8The next day when the Philistines came to strip the dead, they found Saul and his sons fallen on Mount Gilboa. [9]They stripped him and took his head and his armor, and sent messengers throughout the land of the Philistines to carry the good news to their idols and to the people. [10]They put his armor in the temple of their gods, and fastened his head in the temple of Dagon. [11]But when all Jabesh-gilead heard everything that the Philistines had done to Saul, [12]all the valiant warriors got up and took away the body of Saul and the bodies of his sons, and brought them to Jabesh. Then they buried their bones under the oak in Jabesh, and fasted seven days.

13So Saul died for his unfaithfulness; he was unfaithful to the LORD in that he did not keep the command of the LORD; moreover, he had consulted a medium, seeking guidance, [14]and did not seek guidance from the LORD. Therefore the LORD[b] put him to death and turned the kingdom over to David son of Jesse.

[a] Heb *they* [b] Heb *he*

COMMENTARY

For the chronicler, the monarchy was important because it provided models for the contemporary people of God, against which they could evaluate their own spiritual lives. Saul functions as a negative model, as 10:13-14 will show.

9:35-44. The genealogy is a reprise of 8:29-38, part of the listing relating to the tribe of Benjamin. This genealogy is presented in a slightly better form than was the earlier one. A few names are spelled a little differently; the NRSV and the NIV rightly restore "and Ahaz" at the end of v. 41, as in 8:35, to prepare for Ahaz's own genealogy in

v. 42. The genealogy is intended to pave the way for the narrative of chap. 10. It traces Saul's ancestry back four generations and his posterity to a depth of twelve generations, down to late pre-exilic times. The genealogy intersects in v. 39 with 10:2, with the cluster of names of Saul and his sons. At first sight mention of Saul's posterity awkwardly conflicts with the statement in 10:6 that "all" of Saul's "house" perished in battle. The reference is to Saul's royal house or dynasty, in the light of v. 14*b*. The short-lived reign of Eshbaal (2 Samuel 2–4) did not count for the chronicler; he mentions Saul's daughter Michal as living at a later time (15:29). What did the genealogy signify for the chronicler, for whom Saul was a villain of the deepest dye? It illustrated his characteristic view of separate generations. Each generation enjoyed a fresh start before God and was not doomed by the wickedness of its predecessors. While royal status passed to David's house, Saul's descendant Azel received rich blessing in the gift of six sons (see Ps 127:3).

10:1-14. The narrative in these verses concentrates on Saul's death and its implications. It falls into two roughly parallel halves, vv. 1-7 and vv. 8-14. Each half has three parts in an ABCA′C′B′ order. A series of Philistine-related actions concerning Saul is presented in vv. 1-5 and 8-10. They trigger reactions in Israel (v. 7, "saw"; vv. 11-12, "heard") and are given an evaluative summary in both v. 6 and vv. 13-14.

The chronicler does not linger over Saul's reign in its own right, but abruptly passes to its lamentable outcome. He will interpret it (vv. 13-14) as the grim harvest of wrong choices previously made. He repeats the narrative of 1 Samuel 31, which describes Israel's luckless stand against the Philistines on Mt. Gilboa. The source used by the chronicler appears to have been a shorter version than we read in the MT of Samuel.[69] The chronicler has amplified his source into a new structure by expanding "together" in 1 Sam 31:6 with an evaluative element, "and all his house," in v. 6 and by matching this evaluative summary with his own longer interpretive conclusion in vv. 13-14.

69. See the comparative textual analyses of P. K. McCarter, *I Samuel*, AB 8 (Garden City, N.Y.: Doubleday, 1980) 440-42, and S. L. McKenzie, *The Chronicler's Use of the Deuteronomistic History*, HSM 33 (Atlanta: Scholars Press, 1985) 58-60.

10:1-7. The first half of the chapter may be viewed not only as a succession of statements moving toward a conclusion, but also as a series of concentric circles. The center of the account is Saul's face-saving death by his own hand in vv. 4-6*a*. From this center the story spreads out to the fate of others bound up with the king's own death in vv. 2*a* and 6*b*. The boundaries of the story are marked in vv. 1 and 7 by the flight of such Israelites as survived, both soldiers from the battlefield and local citizens from their homes. Saul dragged down with him both his sons and his subjects.

Verse 6 provides a crucial statement. The chronicler has not merely added to his source a negative reference to a possible dynasty, but has highlighted the verse by creating a chiasm.[70] This he has done by adding "they died" at the end of the verse, which matches the initial "and he died" in the Hebrew.

10:8-10. The chronicler underscores the deaths of Saul and his sons, to which v. 6 has drawn particular attention. The burial of their bodies reinforces the fact of their deaths. These verses have their own agenda: The humiliation Saul evaded in life (v. 4) overtook him in death. So when the chronicler refers again to Saul's death (vv. 13-14), the reference now carries with it an allusion to this humiliation. Whereas he has generalized the original reference to Ashtaroth (1 Sam 31:10), in whose temple Saul's armor was placed, replacing it with "their gods," the chronicler has evidently imported mention of the temple of Dagon as the repository of Saul's severed head. Once the ark was taken as a prize of war to this very temple—and the idol of Dagon fell flat on its face in virtual homage (1 Sam 5:1-4)! And when David slew Goliath, the Philistines fled and Goliath's head was taken to Jerusalem (1 Sam 17:50-54). Now the boot was very much on the other foot. The allusions highlight by contrast the grimness of the present situation as one of utter defeat.[71]

70. H. G. M. Williamson, *1 and 2 Chronicles*, NCB (Grand Rapids: Eerdmans, 1982) 93.

71. Ibid., 92-95, with reference to R. Mosis, *Untersuchungen zur Theologie des chronisten Geschichtswerks*, Freiburger theologische Studien 92 (Freiburg: Herder, 1973) 17-43, though he recognizes that not all of his argumentation is valid; P.R. Ackroyd, "The Chronicler As Exegete," *JSOT* 2 (1977) 2-32, esp. 3-9 (= *The Chronicler in His Age*, JSOTSup 101 [Sheffield: JSOT, 1991] 313-23). All these authors see a paradigmatic reference to exile, which will be considered below.

10:11-12. The only glimmer of hope was the loyal bravery of the citizens of Jabesh-Gilead, who had good reason to be grateful to Saul (see 1 Sam 11:1-11). But even this incident differentiates disparagingly between Saul's early promise and his tragic end. How the mighty are fallen!

10:13-14. The chronicler writes his own obituary for Saul. He develops the dynastic reference of his previous summary (v. 6), which becomes an appropriate transition to David's dynasty. So tragic and humiliating a death narrated in vv. 1-12 could only be due to cardinal sins committed in Saul's lifetime. These sins are first summarized as "unfaithfulness." This key term (מעל *ma'al*), here used with the cognate verb, has occurred earlier at significant points. In 5:25 the verb (NIV, "were unfaithful"; NRSV, "transgressed") described the sins of the northern tribes, which led to exile. In 9:1 the noun defined the sins of the southern kingdom of Judah, which likewise caused their exile (see 2 Chr 36:14). These previous cases suggest that here the chronicler found in his narrative about Saul a picture of Israel's fate of military defeat and exile (see vv. 7, 10), a paradigm for the sorry state of the contemporary people of God.

The reader's knowledge of Samuel–Kings is assumed, as is often the case in Chronicles. Two damning reasons from earlier places in the Samuel narrative are discovered, to unpack the charge of unfaithfulness.[72] (A third sin, neglecting the ark, will be added in 13:3; cf. 15:29.) The first sin is rejection of the prophetic word narrated in 1 Samuel 13 and 15. In 1 Sam 13:13-14, the verb "keep" is negatively associated with Saul's loss of kingship, as here, in a framework of accusation and punishment. The "word" (NIV; NRSV, "command") that Saul disobeyed is the prophet's message in 1 Sam 10:8. In 1 Sam 15:23, 26 the divine "word" that is flouted is that given through Samuel in 1 Sam 15:1-3. The chronicler is echoing Samuel's judgment oracles in 1 Samuel 13 and 15 and finds their fulfillment here. The second sin occurs in the incident narrated by 1 Sam 28:6-14: consulting the witch of Endor, which is interpreted as a religious sin, as 1 Sam 28:3 implies (cf. 2 Chr 33:6, in the light of Lev 19:31; Deut 18:11). It was no less than disobedience of the Torah. Those conversant with the Samuel narrative will recall that Saul tried to consult the Lord and turned to a medium only when he received no answer (1 Sam 28:6). The chronicler found no room for this gray detail in his black and white presentation.

The verb דרשׁ (*dāraš*), rendered "seek guidance" (NRSV; NIV, "guidance," "inquire") is another key term in the chronicler's religious vocabulary. It stands for a spiritual commitment that takes God's revealed will as normative for life (see 2 Chr 14:4). By consulting the witch of Endor, Saul showed himself essentially unspiritual, hostile to the Torah as well as to the Prophets.

The chronicler states baldly that "the LORD put him to death," recalling Samuel's forecast in 1 Sam 28:19 of the divinely instigated defeat of Israel's army and the death of the royal family. Behind the hand of Saul in taking his own life and behind the Philistine victory that occasioned it stood the figure of the divine judge as agent of warranted punishment. The loss of Saul's kingship necessitated a new king, David, the man after the Lord's own heart (1 Sam 13:14). For the transfer from one royal house to another, the chronicler uses a verb (סבב *sābab*) derived from 1 Kgs 12:15 (= 2 Chr 10:15). His intention is to demarcate structurally the special reigns of David and Solomon from preceding and subsequent history. The last clause of v. 14 is a theological interpretation of the human events of 11:1-3, as the final wording of 11:3, repeated in 12:23, shows. It may be taken as a heading for the next section, 11:1–12:40.

72. לשׁאול (*liš'ôl*) continues the previous על (*'al*), "because of [the word] . . . and because he consulted." See W. Rudolph, *Chronikbücher*, HAT 1:21 (Tübingen: Mohr [Siebeck], 1955) 94.

REFLECTIONS

If we compare this section with the long and complex account of Saul's reign in 1 Samuel 9–31, we see the starkness of the Chronicles version standing out. There is no room in it for his victories mentioned in 1 Chr 26:28, only for a story of shocking death and national defeat and a sketch of the personal defeats that led to them. Here is an illustration of the chronicler's use of narrative as a sermon to his contemporaries. Historiography has become a source of spiritual reflection. Particulars of one human life have been used as a window onto general issues that confront any reader who belongs to the community of faith in a later age. The New Testament uses this same approach. In 1 Cor 10:1-11, Paul interpreted the destruction of the Israelites in the wilderness as warnings not to sin against God: "These things happened to them as examples and were written down as warnings for us" (1 Cor 10:11 NIV).

At first sight, one might think of adducing as a New Testament parallel to this passage the text "the wages of sin is death, but the gift of God is eternal life" (Rom 6:23 NIV). Yet the widespread use of that text in an evangelistic context may lead us away from an understanding of what the chronicler intended. He was a spiritual director to the community of faith. So a better parallel would be Rom 8:13, clearly addressed to believers: "If you live according to the flesh, you will die; but if . . . you put to death the deeds of the body, you will live" (NRSV). We are meant to read the text as a challenge, to measure our own lives against the parable of Saul's experience and so to keep away from the broad road that leads to destruction (Matt 7:13).

While the narrative gives a good deal of space to Saul's death as a deterrent, the climax of the narrative looks back briefly to the seeds that yielded such a terrible harvest. The chronicler could appeal to his contemporaries' knowledge of the Saul narratives in 1 Samuel as background to his summary, while we modern readers are at a disadvantage unless we turn back to read them. The chronicler did not merely presuppose them, but imposed his own generalizing vocabulary of spirituality upon them. The key to the divine will was found in the revelation of the Law and the Prophets. Correspondingly, the teaching of our own canon of Scripture provides standards for our own spirituality. By such means we shall avoid, in Paul's terms, sowing to our own flesh and reaping corruption. Instead we will sow to the Spirit by doing what is right and contributing to the good of others (Gal 6:7-10).

1 Chronicles 11:1–12:40, David Crowned by All Israel

NIV

11 All Israel came together to David at Hebron and said, "We are your own flesh and blood. [2]In the past, even while Saul was king, you were the one who led Israel on their military campaigns. And the LORD your God said to you, 'You will shepherd my people Israel, and you will become their ruler.' "

[3]When all the elders of Israel had come to King David at Hebron, he made a compact with them at Hebron before the LORD, and they anointed David king over Israel, as the LORD had promised through Samuel.

NRSV

11 Then all Israel gathered together to David at Hebron and said, "See, we are your bone and flesh. [2]For some time now, even while Saul was king, it was you who commanded the army of Israel. The LORD your God said to you: It is you who shall be shepherd of my people Israel, you who shall be ruler over my people Israel." [3]So all the elders of Israel came to the king at Hebron, and David made a covenant with them at Hebron before the LORD. And they anointed David king over Israel, according to the word of the LORD by Samuel.

NIV

[4]David and all the Israelites marched to Jerusalem (that is, Jebus). The Jebusites who lived there [5]said to David, "You will not get in here." Nevertheless, David captured the fortress of Zion, the City of David.

[6]David had said, "Whoever leads the attack on the Jebusites will become commander-in-chief." Joab son of Zeruiah went up first, and so he received the command.

[7]David then took up residence in the fortress, and so it was called the City of David. [8]He built up the city around it, from the supporting terraces[a] to the surrounding wall, while Joab restored the rest of the city. [9]And David became more and more powerful, because the LORD Almighty was with him.

[10]These were the chiefs of David's mighty men—they, together with all Israel, gave his kingship strong support to extend it over the whole land, as the LORD had promised— [11]this is the list of David's mighty men:

Jashobeam,[b] a Hacmonite, was chief of the officers[c]; he raised his spear against three hundred men, whom he killed in one encounter.

[12]Next to him was Eleazar son of Dodai the Ahohite, one of the three mighty men. [13]He was with David at Pas Dammim when the Philistines gathered there for battle. At a place where there was a field full of barley, the troops fled from the Philistines. [14]But they took their stand in the middle of the field. They defended it and struck the Philistines down, and the LORD brought about a great victory.

[15]Three of the thirty chiefs came down to David to the rock at the cave of Adullam, while a band of Philistines was encamped in the Valley of Rephaim. [16]At that time David was in the stronghold, and the Philistine garrison was at Bethlehem. [17]David longed for water and said, "Oh, that someone would get me a drink of water from the well near the gate of Bethlehem!" [18]So the Three broke through the Philistine lines, drew water from the well near the gate of Bethlehem and carried it back to David. But he refused to drink it; instead, he poured it out before the LORD. [19]"God forbid that I should do this!" he said.

[a]8 Or *the Millo* [b]11 Possibly a variant of *Jashob-Baal* [c]11 Or *Thirty; some Septuagint manuscripts Three* (see also 2 Samuel 23:8)

NRSV

4David and all Israel marched to Jerusalem, that is Jebus, where the Jebusites were, the inhabitants of the land. [5]The inhabitants of Jebus said to David, "You will not come in here." Nevertheless David took the stronghold of Zion, now the city of David. [6]David had said, "Whoever attacks the Jebusites first shall be chief and commander." And Joab son of Zeruiah went up first, so he became chief. [7]David resided in the stronghold; therefore it was called the city of David. [8]He built the city all around, from the Millo in complete circuit; and Joab repaired the rest of the city. [9]And David became greater and greater, for the LORD of hosts was with him.

10Now these are the chiefs of David's warriors, who gave him strong support in his kingdom, together with all Israel, to make him king, according to the word of the LORD concerning Israel. [11]This is an account of David's mighty warriors: Jashobeam, son of Hachmoni,[a] was chief of the Three;[b] he wielded his spear against three hundred whom he killed at one time.

12And next to him among the three warriors was Eleazar son of Dodo, the Ahohite. [13]He was with David at Pas-dammim when the Philistines were gathered there for battle. There was a plot of ground full of barley. Now the people had fled from the Philistines, [14]but he and David took their stand in the middle of the plot, defended it, and killed the Philistines; and the LORD saved them by a great victory.

15Three of the thirty chiefs went down to the rock to David at the cave of Adullam, while the army of Philistines was encamped in the valley of Rephaim. [16]David was then in the stronghold; and the garrison of the Philistines was then at Bethlehem. [17]David said longingly, "O that someone would give me water to drink from the well of Bethlehem that is by the gate!" [18]Then the Three broke through the camp of the Philistines, and drew water from the well of Bethlehem that was by the gate, and they brought it to David. But David would not drink of it; he poured it out to the LORD, [19]and said, "My God forbid that I should do this. Can I drink the blood of these men? For at the risk of their lives they brought it." Therefore

[a] Or *a Hachmonite* [b] Compare 2 Sam 23.8: Heb *Thirty* or *captains*

NIV

"Should I drink the blood of these men who went at the risk of their lives?" Because they risked their lives to bring it back, David would not drink it.

Such were the exploits of the three mighty men.

20Abishai the brother of Joab was chief of the Three. He raised his spear against three hundred men, whom he killed, and so he became as famous as the Three. 21He was doubly honored above the Three and became their commander, even though he was not included among them.

22Benaiah son of Jehoiada was a valiant fighter from Kabzeel, who performed great exploits. He struck down two of Moab's best men. He also went down into a pit on a snowy day and killed a lion. 23And he struck down an Egyptian who was seven and a half feet[a] tall. Although the Egyptian had a spear like a weaver's rod in his hand, Benaiah went against him with a club. He snatched the spear from the Egyptian's hand and killed him with his own spear. 24Such were the exploits of Benaiah son of Jehoiada; he too was as famous as the three mighty men. 25He was held in greater honor than any of the Thirty, but he was not included among the Three. And David put him in charge of his bodyguard.

26The mighty men were:
Asahel the brother of Joab,
Elhanan son of Dodo from Bethlehem,
27Shammoth the Harorite,
Helez the Pelonite,
28Ira son of Ikkesh from Tekoa,
Abiezer from Anathoth,
29Sibbecai the Hushathite,
Ilai the Ahohite,
30Maharai the Netophathite,
Heled son of Baanah the Netophathite,
31Ithai son of Ribai from Gibeah in Benjamin,
Benaiah the Pirathonite,
32Hurai from the ravines of Gaash,
Abiel the Arbathite,
33Azmaveth the Baharumite,
Eliahba the Shaalbonite,
34the sons of Hashem the Gizonite,
Jonathan son of Shagee the Hararite,

[a]23 Hebrew *five cubits* (about 2.3 meters)

NRSV

he would not drink it. The three warriors did these things.

20Now Abishai,[a] the brother of Joab, was chief of the Thirty.[b] With his spear he fought against three hundred and killed them, and won a name beside the Three. 21He was the most renowned[c] of the Thirty,[b] and became their commander; but he did not attain to the Three.

22Benaiah son of Jehoiada was a valiant man[d] of Kabzeel, a doer of great deeds; he struck down two sons of[e] Ariel of Moab. He also went down and killed a lion in a pit on a day when snow had fallen. 23And he killed an Egyptian, a man of great stature, five cubits tall. The Egyptian had in his hand a spear like a weaver's beam; but Benaiah went against him with a staff, snatched the spear out of the Egyptian's hand, and killed him with his own spear. 24Such were the things Benaiah son of Jehoiada did, and he won a name beside the three warriors. 25He was renowned among the Thirty, but he did not attain to the Three. And David put him in charge of his bodyguard.

26The warriors of the armies were Asahel brother of Joab, Elhanan son of Dodo of Bethlehem, 27Shammoth of Harod,[f] Helez the Pelonite, 28Ira son of Ikkesh of Tekoa, Abiezer of Anathoth, 29Sibbecai the Hushathite, Ilai the Ahohite, 30Maharai of Netophah, Heled son of Baanah of Netophah, 31Ithai son of Ribai of Gibeah of the Benjaminites, Benaiah of Pirathon, 32Hurai of the wadis of Gaash, Abiel the Arbathite, 33Azmaveth of Baharum, Eliahba of Shaalbon, 34Hashem[g] the Gizonite, Jonathan son of Shagee the Hararite, 35Ahiam son of Sachar the Hararite, Eliphal son of Ur, 36Hepher the Mecherathite, Ahijah the Pelonite, 37Hezro of Carmel, Naarai son of Ezbai, 38Joel the brother of Nathan, Mibhar son of Hagri, 39Zelek the Ammonite, Naharai of Beeroth, the armor-bearer of Joab son of Zeruiah, 40Ira the Ithrite, Gareb the Ithrite, 41Uriah the Hittite, Zabad son of Ahlai, 42Adina son of Shiza the Reubenite, a leader of the Reubenites, and thirty with him, 43Hanan son of Maacah, and Joshaphat

[a] Gk Vg Tg Compare 2 Sam 23.18: Heb *Abshai* [b] Syr: Heb *Three* [c] Compare 2 Sam 23.19: Heb *more renowned among the two* [d] Syr: Heb *the son of a valiant man* [e] See 2 Sam 23.20: Heb lacks *sons of* [f] Compare 2 Sam 23.25: Heb *the Harorite* [g] Compare Gk and 2 Sam 23.32: Heb *the sons of Hashem*

NIV

[35]Ahiam son of Sacar the Hararite,
Eliphal son of Ur,
[36]Hepher the Mekerathite,
Ahijah the Pelonite,
[37]Hezro the Carmelite,
Naarai son of Ezbai,
[38]Joel the brother of Nathan,
Mibhar son of Hagri,
[39]Zelek the Ammonite,
Naharai the Berothite, the armor-bearer of Joab son of Zeruiah,
[40]Ira the Ithrite,
Gareb the Ithrite,
[41]Uriah the Hittite,
Zabad son of Ahlai,
[42]Adina son of Shiza the Reubenite, who was chief of the Reubenites, and the thirty with him,
[43]Hanan son of Maacah,
Joshaphat the Mithnite,
[44]Uzzia the Ashterathite,
Shama and Jeiel the sons of Hotham the Aroerite,
[45]Jediael son of Shimri,
his brother Joha the Tizite,
[46]Eliel the Mahavite,
Jeribai and Joshaviah the sons of Elnaam,
Ithmah the Moabite,
[47]Eliel, Obed and Jaasiel the Mezobaite.

12 These were the men who came to David at Ziklag, while he was banished from the presence of Saul son of Kish (they were among the warriors who helped him in battle; [2]they were armed with bows and were able to shoot arrows or to sling stones right-handed or left-handed; they were kinsmen of Saul from the tribe of Benjamin):

[3]Ahiezer their chief and Joash the sons of Shemaah the Gibeathite; Jeziel and Pelet the sons of Azmaveth; Beracah, Jehu the Anathothite, [4]and Ishmaiah the Gibeonite, a mighty man among the Thirty, who was a leader of the Thirty; Jeremiah, Jahaziel, Johanan, Jozabad the Gederathite, [5]Eluzai, Jerimoth, Bealiah, Shemariah and Shephatiah the Haruphite; [6]Elkanah, Isshiah, Azarel, Joezer and Jashobeam the Korahites; [7]and Joelah and Zebadiah the sons of Jeroham from Gedor.

NRSV

the Mithnite, [44]Uzzia the Ashterathite, Shama and Jeiel sons of Hotham the Aroerite, [45]Jediael son of Shimri, and his brother Joha the Tizite, [46]Eliel the Mahavite, and Jeribai and Joshaviah sons of Elnaam, and Ithmah the Moabite, [47]Eliel, and Obed, and Jaasiel the Mezobaite.

12 The following are those who came to David at Ziklag, while he could not move about freely because of Saul son of Kish; they were among the mighty warriors who helped him in war. [2]They were archers, and could shoot arrows and sling stones with either the right hand or the left; they were Benjaminites, Saul's kindred. [3]The chief was Ahiezer, then Joash, both sons of Shemaah of Gibeah; also Jeziel and Pelet sons of Azmaveth; Beracah, Jehu of Anathoth, [4]Ishmaiah of Gibeon, a warrior among the Thirty and a leader over the Thirty; Jeremiah,[a] Jahaziel, Johanan, Jozabad of Gederah, [5]Eluzai,[b] Jerimoth, Bealiah, Shemariah, Shephatiah the Haruphite; [6]Elkanah, Isshiah, Azarel, Joezer, and Jashobeam, the Korahites; [7]and Joelah and Zebadiah, sons of Jeroham of Gedor.

8From the Gadites there went over to David at the stronghold in the wilderness mighty and experienced warriors, expert with shield and spear, whose faces were like the faces of lions, and who were swift as gazelles on the mountains: [9]Ezer the chief, Obadiah second, Eliab third, [10]Mishmannah fourth, Jeremiah fifth, [11]Attai sixth, Eliel seventh, [12]Johanan eighth, Elzabad ninth, [13]Jeremiah tenth, Machbannai eleventh. [14]These Gadites were officers of the army, the least equal to a hundred and the greatest to a thousand. [15]These are the men who crossed the Jordan in the first month, when it was overflowing all its banks, and put to flight all those in the valleys, to the east and to the west.

16Some Benjaminites and Judahites came to the stronghold to David. [17]David went out to meet them and said to them, "If you have come to me in friendship, to help me, then my heart will be knit to you; but if you have come to betray me to my adversaries, though my hands have done no wrong, then may the God of our ancestors see and give judgment." [18]Then the spirit came upon Amasai, chief of the Thirty, and he said,

[a] Heb verse 5 [b] Heb verse 6

NIV

[8]Some Gadites defected to David at his stronghold in the desert. They were brave warriors, ready for battle and able to handle the shield and spear. Their faces were the faces of lions, and they were as swift as gazelles in the mountains.

[9]Ezer was the chief,
Obadiah the second in command, Eliab the third,
[10]Mishmannah the fourth, Jeremiah the fifth,
[11]Attai the sixth, Eliel the seventh,
[12]Johanan the eighth, Elzabad the ninth,
[13]Jeremiah the tenth and Macbannai the eleventh.

[14]These Gadites were army commanders; the least was a match for a hundred, and the greatest for a thousand. [15]It was they who crossed the Jordan in the first month when it was overflowing all its banks, and they put to flight everyone living in the valleys, to the east and to the west.

[16]Other Benjamites and some men from Judah also came to David in his stronghold. [17]David went out to meet them and said to them, "If you have come to me in peace, to help me, I am ready to have you unite with me. But if you have come to betray me to my enemies when my hands are free from violence, may the God of our fathers see it and judge you."

[18]Then the Spirit came upon Amasai, chief of the Thirty, and he said:

"We are yours, O David!
We are with you, O son of Jesse!
Success, success to you,
and success to those who help you,
for your God will help you."

So David received them and made them leaders of his raiding bands.

[19]Some of the men of Manasseh defected to David when he went with the Philistines to fight against Saul. (He and his men did not help the Philistines because, after consultation, their rulers sent him away. They said, "It will cost us our heads if he deserts to his master Saul.") [20]When David went to Ziklag, these were the men of Manasseh who defected to him: Adnah, Jozabad, Jediael, Michael, Jozabad, Elihu and Zillethai, leaders of units of a thousand in Manasseh. [21]They helped David against raiding bands, for all of them were brave warriors, and they were commanders

NRSV

"We are yours, O David;
and with you, O son of Jesse!
Peace, peace to you,
and peace to the one who helps you!
For your God is the one who helps you."

Then David received them, and made them officers of his troops.

19Some of the Manassites deserted to David when he came with the Philistines for the battle against Saul. (Yet he did not help them, for the rulers of the Philistines took counsel and sent him away, saying, "He will desert to his master Saul at the cost of our heads.") [20]As he went to Ziklag these Manassites deserted to him: Adnah, Jozabad, Jediael, Michael, Jozabad, Elihu, and Zillethai, chiefs of the thousands in Manasseh. [21]They helped David against the band of raiders,[a] for they were all warriors and commanders in the army. [22]Indeed from day to day people kept coming to David to help him, until there was a great army, like an army of God.

23These are the numbers of the divisions of the armed troops who came to David in Hebron to turn the kingdom of Saul over to him, according to the word of the LORD. [24]The people of Judah bearing shield and spear numbered six thousand eight hundred armed troops. [25]Of the Simeonites, mighty warriors, seven thousand one hundred. [26]Of the Levites four thousand six hundred. [27]Jehoiada, leader of the house of Aaron, and with him three thousand seven hundred. [28]Zadok, a young warrior, and twenty-two commanders from his own ancestral house. [29]Of the Benjaminites, the kindred of Saul, three thousand, of whom the majority had continued to keep their allegiance to the house of Saul. [30]Of the Ephraimites, twenty thousand eight hundred, mighty warriors, notables in their ancestral houses. [31]Of the half-tribe of Manasseh, eighteen thousand, who were expressly named to come and make David king. [32]Of Issachar, those who had understanding of the times, to know what Israel ought to do, two hundred chiefs, and all their kindred under their command. [33]Of Zebulun, fifty thousand seasoned troops, equipped for battle with all the weapons of war, to help David[b] with singleness of purpose.

[a] Or *as officers of his troops* [b] Gk: Heb lacks *David*

NIV

in his army. [22]Day after day men came to help David, until he had a great army, like the army of God.[a]

[23]These are the numbers of the men armed for battle who came to David at Hebron to turn Saul's kingdom over to him, as the LORD had said:

[24]men of Judah, carrying shield and spear—
6,800 armed for battle;
[25]men of Simeon, warriors ready for battle—
7,100;
[26]men of Levi—4,600, [27]including Jehoiada,
leader of the family of Aaron, with 3,700
men, [28]and Zadok, a brave young warrior,
with 22 officers from his family;
[29]men of Benjamin, Saul's kinsmen—3,000,
most of whom had remained loyal to
Saul's house until then;
[30]men of Ephraim, brave warriors, famous in
their own clans—20,800;
[31]men of half the tribe of Manasseh, designated by name to come and make David king—18,000;
[32]men of Issachar, who understood the times
and knew what Israel should do—200
chiefs, with all their relatives under their
command;
[33]men of Zebulun, experienced soldiers prepared for battle with every type of weapon, to help David with undivided loyalty—50,000;
[34]men of Naphtali—1,000 officers, together
with 37,000 men carrying shields and
spears;
[35]men of Dan, ready for battle—28,600;
[36]men of Asher, experienced soldiers prepared
for battle—40,000;
[37]and from east of the Jordan, men of Reuben,
Gad and the half-tribe of Manasseh, armed
with every type of weapon—120,000.

[38]All these were fighting men who volunteered to serve in the ranks. They came to Hebron fully determined to make David king over all Israel. All the rest of the Israelites were also of one mind to make David king. [39]The men spent three days there with David, eating and drinking, for their families had supplied provisions for them. [40]Also, their neighbors from as far away as Issachar, Zebulun and

[a]22 Or *a great and mighty army*

NRSV

[34]Of Naphtali, a thousand commanders, with whom there were thirty-seven thousand armed with shield and spear. [35]Of the Danites, twenty-eight thousand six hundred equipped for battle. [36]Of Asher, forty thousand seasoned troops ready for battle. [37]Of the Reubenites and Gadites and the half-tribe of Manasseh from beyond the Jordan, one hundred twenty thousand armed with all the weapons of war.

38All these, warriors arrayed in battle order, came to Hebron with full intent to make David king over all Israel; likewise all the rest of Israel were of a single mind to make David king. [39]They were there with David for three days, eating and drinking, for their kindred had provided for them. [40]And also their neighbors, from as far away as Issachar and Zebulun and Naphtali, came bringing food on donkeys, camels, mules, and oxen—abundant provisions of meal, cakes of figs, clusters of raisins, wine, oil, oxen, and sheep, for there was joy in Israel.

NIV

Naphtali came bringing food on donkeys, camels, mules and oxen. There were plentiful supplies of flour, fig cakes, raisin cakes, wine, oil, cattle and sheep, for there was joy in Israel.

COMMENTARY

These next two chapters make up a literary unit. Its theme is the transfer of royal power to David, as the end of chap. 10 has announced. There David's kingship was represented as the Lord's work. Here the narrative emphasizes its human outworking; yet, at crucial points there are indications that God's will was being done.

At first sight the narrative hops disconcertingly from period to period, from place to place. David is anointed king at Hebron (11:1-3) and at once marches off to capture Jerusalem (11:4-9). A list of the high-ranking soldiers who participated in the coronation at Hebron (11:10-47) follows. Then there are flashbacks to tribal groups who threw in their lot with David at two earlier periods in his life (12:1-22). David's coronation at Hebron is again the topic of 12:23-40, with lists of the tribal contingents who attended (12:23-37), followed by an account of the celebrations (12:38-40).

There is method in this seeming randomness. A chiastic structuring dominates the section and gives it coherence, in an ABCDD′C′B′A′ pattern.[73] The coronation and the celebratory meal that seals it make up the Hebron-based outer framework (A, 11:1-3; A′, 12:38-40). Next to it are placed lists of the officers and conscript soldiers who attended (B, 11:10-47; B′, 12:23-37). Military support for David at an earlier period, when he was based at Ziklag, is presented in an inner ring (C, 12:1-7; C′, 12:19-22). At the double center stand reports of backing for David at an even earlier stage, while he was an outlaw in the wilderness, at "the stronghold" (D, 12:8-15; D′, 12:16-18). The chiasm is used to present growing support for David and his transformation from a nervous victim of harassment (12:1, 17) to the secure bearer of power at the time of his coronation (11:9; 12:22).

Alongside this structural concern is another, in part independent, scheme: a roll call of David's army, from its commander Joab (11:6) and the Three and the Thirty and other leaders (11:10-47), to veterans who were "mighty warriors" (12:1-21), and finally down to the rank and file of this "great army" (12:22-37).[74]

The end of chap. 10 left the people of God defenseless, at the mercy of their enemies, and, in principle, bereft of land and liberty. Now they are portrayed as militarily strong. Over against the flight narrated in chap. 10, occasioned by Saul, strength and unity surround the figure of David. By the end of 1 Chronicles 12, king and people stand together, ready to win freedom under God. The Israel of David's days was intended to be an inspirational example. The unity of God's people was an ideal for which contemporary Judah must begin training! In 11:1-9 and 12:23-40 unity was finally achieved, but only gradually as one group after another pledged its allegiance to the new king, who had a divine claim on their support.

In 11:1-3 the chronicler rushes from Saul's death to the anointing of his successor as king of Israel in order to point out the contrast. In his biblical source four traumatic chapters elapsed between 1 Samuel 31 and 2 Samuel 5, on which latter chapter he relies in 11:1-9. He leaps to its eventual outcome. Afterward, however, he goes back to portray the hard climb to the top and the outstretching of hands that enabled David to get there. So this material is not so triumphalist as it first appears. An impressionistic contrast is drawn between the defeated, leaderless nation and a united, virile people under a God-given leader. It accentuates the slow but sure triumph of divine grace and also functions as a vision for the chronicler's constituency.

11:1-3. This paragraph is taken from 2 Sam

73. H. G. M. Williamson, " 'We Are Yours, O David': The Setting and Purpose of 1 Chronicles xii 1-23," *OTS* 21 (1981) 168-70; *1 and 2 Chronicles*, 105.

74. T. Willi, *Die Chronik als Auslegung* (Göttingen: Vandenhoeck & Ruprecht, 1972) 224n. 30.

5:1-3, in which Israel confirms David's divine right to the throne (v. 2). At the end of v. 3, the chronicler adds his own theological commentary, as he often does. What has been narrated was a fulfillment of "the word of the LORD by Samuel" (NRSV). He has in mind the prophet's message of judgment to Saul in 1 Sam 15:28 and his mission to anoint David in advance in 1 Sam 16:1-13. He presupposes knowledge of this material. This accent on the divine "word" will reappear later, in his comments at 11:10 and 12:23 (NRSV).

The chronicler emphasizes the involvement of "all Israel" in this event (v. 1; cf. v. 3). In 2 Samuel 5 the context shows that the original phrase "all the tribes of Israel" (2 Sam 5:1) refers only to the northern tribes, and "all the elders of Israel" (2 Sam 5:3) to a northern delegation. The chronicler adapts the passage to reflect one of his favorite motifs. He will unpack the phrase "all Israel" as essentially composed of members of all the traditional tribes of Israel, northern and southern, in 12:38.

The chronicler also glosses over the fact that David had earlier been made king over Judah, before the northerners recognized him. In fact, the distinction drawn in 2 Sam 5:4-5 between Hebron as David's capital while king of Judah, and Jerusalem as his capital while he reigned over all Israel may not have been present in the text of Samuel used by the chronicler. It was evidently lacking in the Hebrew scroll 4QSam[a], as it is in the Old Latin.[75] Mention of "the king" in 11:3 is a clue that the chronicler was aware of the two stages of kingship, but preferred not to draw further attention to it, as a distraction from his main theme.

11:4-9. The report of the capture of Jerusalem derives from 2 Sam 5:6-10. The material was significant for the chronicler in several ways.[76] For later readers, Jerusalem would automatically have been associated with David as his capital, and so crown and capital are naturally paired. It was also an opportunity to introduce Israel's army commander, as we have seen, initiating a review of David's army. Most significantly, it fits neatly into a larger scheme broached in chap. 9. After the unfaithfulness that caused Judah's exile, representatives of Judah returned and dwelt in their cities again and sacramentally, as it were, in Jerusalem, the traditional capital (9:1-3). For the chronicler, Saul and David were archetypes of exile and restoration. After Saul's unfaithfulness (10:13), David comes to dwell in Jerusalem (11:7; unlike the NRSV and the NIV, the RSV uses "dwell" in both chap. 9 and chap. 11 for ישב [*yāšab*]). This passage allows the chronicler to express the paradigmatic parallel. The union of Israel centered around David in Jerusalem was an ideal the chronicler hoped would again be realized eventually.

He once more introduces the concept of a united Israel into his text at v. 4. The 2 Samuel text has "his men," referring to David's mercenary troops. From the chronicler's ideal perspective it is "all Israel," who had just sworn allegiance to David and marched off with him to capture Jerusalem as a national undertaking in token of their allegiance. The city is graced with an antiquarian note, "that is Jebus," a literary borrowing from Judg 19:10-11.

In v. 5, the chronicler leaves out the rather obscure taunting from the Jebusites in 2 Sam 5:6. We do not know whether or how the novel reference to Joab related to the 2 Samuel text; 2 Sam 5:8 contains quite different material. Did it originate in a textual variant? Was it derived from an amplified text? It fits well into the overall text of 1 Chronicles, which otherwise mentions only the names of Joab's brothers, identifying them as such (11:20, 26). The reference may depend on a historical tradition. Joab was already commander in 2 Sam 2:13, but perhaps permanently so only from this time on.

In v. 7 the chronicler introduces the conjunction "therefore," so that not conquest but residence—important for him—explained the title "city of David." In v. 8, "the city" reflects a reading different from the Samuel text, shared by 4QSam[a] and the Greek Codex Vaticanus in place of the MT's "David." The relation of v. 8*b* to the text the chronicler used is uncertain, and so is the meaning of the verb rendered "restored" or "repaired" (יחיה *yĕḥayyeh*). A building reference links well with the earlier part of the verse. It would also reflect a regular motif in the books of Chronicles, where building is often a mark of

75. See P. K. McCarter, *II Samuel*, AB 9 (Garden City, N.Y.: Doubleday, 1984) 130-31; S. L. McKenzie, *The Chronicler's Use of the Deuteronomistic History*, HSM 33 (Atlanta: Scholars Press, 1985) 42-43.

76. See D. A. Glatt, *Chronological Displacement in Biblical and Related Literatures* (Atlanta: Scholars Press, 1993) 174-78.

blessing that comes to faithful kings. So it is a fitting illustration of the divine presence bestowing favor on David (v. 9).

11:10-47. For vv. 10-41 the chronicler depends on the appendix in 2 Sam 23:8-39. The passage was meant to illustrate the exploits of David's military heroes, but he reinterprets it as a list of supporters present at the coronation, as v. 10 makes clear. So the list of names now gives examples of "all Israel," who recognized the divinely willed kingship of David. At the end of v. 10, the NIV and the NRSV reflect different renditions: either to follow the accentuation in the MT and render "concerning Israel" (NRSV), which accords with 15:2, or to relate the phrase to the verb, "[make king] over Israel," paraphrased in the NIV as "over the whole land," an option that agrees with 12:38.

There seems to be some textual confusion between the Three and the Thirty, two high-ranking groups, in v. 11 and again in vv. 20-21. It is difficult to be sure, but it seems logical at least to find reference to the Thirty (NRSV) in v. 21 in the light of the seemingly parallel v. 25 (cf. 27:6) and then so to read in v. 20*a*, as again the NRSV does. Similarly a reference to the Three is contextually fitting in v. 11 and has some support from 2 Sam 23:8, over against the MT, which the NIV reflects with "the officers."

11:10-14. Exploits of two of the Three are related. Comparison with 2 Samuel 23 shows that a chunk of text has fallen out. Two separate feats of the second and third of the Three have been telescoped. It is often suggested that this omission occurred only within the Chronicles tradition, but it may already have befallen the text of Samuel used by the chronicler. Certainly there is a coherent structural pattern in the present text of vv. 11-25. The exploits of two heroes, each introduced with an emphatic "he" (הוא *hû'*), form an outer framework in vv. 11-14 and 20-25.[77] The reference to God-given victory at the end of v. 14 is in tune with the chronicler's own thinking, as is the similar refrain in 18:6, 13. Military victory was for him evidence of divine blessing on obedient kings.

11:15-19. This episode encapsulates both the devotion of David's supporters and his own devotion to God. It is taken from 2 Sam 23:13-17. David, with a soldier's nostalgia for home, longs for a drink from the well of enemy-occupied Bethlehem. For three anonymous members of the Thirty, his wish is their command, and they break through enemy lines to get the water for him. David cannot bring himself to drink it. He pours it on the ground as a sort of libation to God, regarding it as significant as the blood of those who had risked their lives for him. By this dramatic gesture, David both acknowledges his appreciation of their self-sacrificial loyalty and gives God the glory.

11:20-25. The "sons of Ariel" in v. 22 are better translated "champions" (REB). In v. 23 the chronicler evidently had a fuller text than the MT of 2 Sam 23:21, which is also reflected in some Greek traditions of 2 Samuel. The expansion recalls Goliath's height and his having a spear "like a weaver's beam" (1 Sam 17:4, 7; the ancient texts differ concerning the giant's stature).

11:26-47. At v. 26 the chronicler makes a break in the 2 Samuel 23 list by supplying a short heading before Asahel's name. Although "among the Thirty" in 2 Sam 23:24 is omitted here, he probably took the following names up to v. 41*a* as an enumeration of the Thirty, so warranting a separate heading. They are ranked with those from the Bethlehem area placed first, and include officers of mercenary contingents, notably "Uriah the Hittite" (v. 41). Verses 41*b*-47 comprise an independent list evidently available to the chronicler from another source. It is stylistically different from the preceding list and appears to enumerate a group of soldiers from the Transjordan.

12:1-7. There is a glance back to David's stay at Ziklag, a Philistine city in which the king of Gath established David in return for his military support (1 Sam 27:6). There is no parallel text in 1 or 2 Samuel. The chronicler depended to a greater or lesser extent on independent material for vv. 1-21, using it to promote his "all Israel" theme.[78] Irony is present in that, while Saul restricted David's movements, members of Saul's own tribe of Benjamin joined David's militia. A motif of help proffered to David at a time of weakness by various tribal groups comes to the fore in each of the next three paragraphs (vv. 1-22). The verbal forms in vv. 1, 17-19, 21-22

77. S. J. De Vries, *1 and 2 Chronicles*, FOTL 11 (Grand Rapids: Eerdmans, 1989) 128.

78. See S. Japhet, *I & II Chronicles*, OTL (Louisville: Westminster/John Knox, 1993) 257-58.

relating to "help" (עזר *ʿāzar*) are supplemented by some names in the lists: Ahiezer (v. 3), Joezer (v. 6), and Ezer (v. 9), the first and third receiving emphasis from the accompanying epithet "the chief."[79] We can now see that preparation for the wordplay was made in the list of names in chap. 11; i.e., Eleazar (v. 12) and Abiezer (v. 28).

12:8-15. David had received such support before. During his preceding period as an outlaw, when he had established a base in the wilds of Judah, a contingent of commandos from the tribe of Gad in the Transjordan "defected" (NIV) and threw in their lot with him. A number of such bases are mentioned in 1–2 Samuel: Adullam (1 Sam 22:14; 2 Sam 23:13-14), Ziph (1 Sam 23:14), Maon (1 Sam 23:24), and En-gedi (1 Sam 23:29). Perhaps the last one is in view here, since it is closest to the Transjordan.

12:16-18. These early days are now featured again. Two groups from Benjamin and Judah arrived at one of the bases. David's weakness, evidenced in his political circumstances in v. 1, is now expressed in terms of lack of morale. Friend or foe? All he can do is to appeal to God to expose them and bring about their downfall, if they are spies. The appeal, spoken out of human helplessness, receives a gracious answer from God. On the spot, Amasai, no regular prophet, is endowed with the spirit of prophecy to give a reassuring pledge of support from the new arrivals and from God.[80] The triple greeting of "peace" (NRSV), woven into his answer, is meant to give encouragement to David. It picks up a term used by David himself in v. 17: "peace" (NIV). He is surrounded by helpers and is even aided by God as patron of his cause, and so victory is assured. In fact, the complex term שׁלום (*šālôm*) here takes on the flavor of "success" (NIV). In the overall context this oracle of salvation reinforces Samuel's prophecy of kingship for David, mentioned in 11:3, 10.

12:19-22. The narrative revisits Ziklag to show how fresh followers were added, this time from the northern tribe of Manasseh, doubtless along with their contingents. David would have approached or even entered Manassite territory while accompanying the Philistine army, marching to its decisive encounter with Saul at Mt. Gilboa (cf. 1 Sam 29:1, 11), before he was dismissed and spared fighting against his own nation. They were able to aid him as he rescued prisoners from Amalekite raiders, who had sacked Ziklag in David's absence (1 Sam 30:1-20).

Verse 22 provides a transition to a new section, which reverts to the coronation at Hebron. The trickle of support in the early days turned into a stream and then a river, until each of Israel's tribes was amply represented in the army present at Hebron. He enthusiastically compares it to "an army of God," an army even by God's definition, "a camp of prodigious size" (NJB).

12:23-37. The tribal list is presented idealistically as the report of a muster of David's troops at Hebron.[81] Again the fulfillment of the Lord's prophetic word is brought to the fore, and the divinely formulated language of 10:14*b* is echoed in human terms. The list suits well the chronicler's intention, being a catalog of all the tribes with enormous numbers attached. Mention of "help" in v. 33 (here עדר *ʿādar*, an Aramaism) reiterates the earlier emphasis. He evidently made use of an existing list based on a military census. The grand total of 340,822 may be contrasted with the national conscript army of 30,000 in 2 Sam 6:1. It is possible to rationalize the numbers by regarding a "thousand" as a nominal term for what was a much smaller contingent.[82] However, the chronicler himself wanted to take the numbers at their maximum value, as an exuberant expression of an "army of God" (v. 22).

The list enumerates first the tribes associated with the kingdom and province of Judah (Judah, Simeon, Levi, Benjamin), and then the tribes to the north and in the Transjordan. The traditional number of twelve tribal groups is here achieved by amalgamating the two and a half Transjordanian tribes in v. 37. The numbers assigned to Judah and Benjamin are comparatively small, and an apology is felt to be necessary in the latter case.[83] The overall impression is to play up the contribution of the remaining tribes.

79. Willi, *Die Chronik als Auslegung,* 224n. 30.

80. See W. M. Schniedewind, *The Word of God in Transition: From Prophet to Exegete in the Second Temple Period,* JSOTSup 197 (Sheffield: Sheffield Academic, 1995) 70-74.

81. De Vries, *1 and 2 Chronicles,* 131.

82. For details see G. E. Mendenhall, "The Census Lists of Numbers 1 and 26," *JBL* 77 (1958) 61-63.

83. See Braun's suggestion that two separate lists have been joined. R. L. Braun, *1 Chronicles,* WBC 14 (Waco, Tex.: Word, 1986) 169.

In v. 26 the Levites would naturally refer to the tribe of Levi, if vv. 27-28 did not add priestly contingents, so that now the Levites relate to the non-priestly part of the tribe. It is probable that the latter verses represent a supplement from the pro-priestly reviser to make room for the participation of priests on this great occasion. The twenty-two commanders of Zadok's house may be a link with the twenty-two priestly families in the late list of Neh 12:1-7.

12:38-40. The chronicler rounds off the unit with his own fervent description of the climactic coronation event. The phrase "arrayed in battle order" (NRSV) is better rendered "helping [עֹדְרֵי *'ōdĕrê*] in battle" (cf. v. 11), echoing the prominent motif used earlier.[84] The narrative continues where 11:1-3 left off, repeating the understanding of the previous list (v. 23) as Israel's conscript army, which represented "all Israel" (11:1-2) at the coronation. The chronicler typically refers to the feasting and joy that befitted this national occasion. The resolution and unanimity of David's support are emphasized. The covenant between king and people (11:3) is capped with a covenant meal by way of commitment and celebration (cf. Gen 26:30; Josh 9:11-15). It is an expression of solidarity and fellowship. The chronicler cannot resist a reference to three far-flung northern tribes among those who brought supplies for the potluck meal. They, too, belonged to Israel, he insists, and thus had a vital contribution to make.

84. H. G. M. Williamson, *1 and 2 Chronicles*, NCB (Grand Rapids: Eerdmans, 1982) 111.

REFLECTIONS

The chronicler highlights the reigns of David and Solomon as a special manifestation of divine blessing and as a revelation of guidelines for God's people thereafter. Saul's death was a graphic illustration of the road to exile, leading away from God. Yet it did not spell the demise of the divine purpose. From the ashes of failure and judgment arose a new flame of achievement. The Lord raised up a new king for Israel. God's redemptive grace stooped to the lowest point of human failure, lifting its victims to new life.

1. Both 11:1-3 and 11:4-9 start with one of the chronicler's beloved phrases, "all Israel"; and much of this literary unit amplifies its meaning. Just as the genealogies of chapters 1–9 were intended to teach, and as the renewed listing of tribal units in 12:23-37 will reinforce, so also the chronicler refused to identify the spiritual heirs of God's pre-exilic people as merely the tribes of Judah, Benjamin, Levi, and Simeon. Although many in post-exilic Judah so defined the latter-day Israel (see Ezra 4:1-3), the chronicler represents a broader view.

Many Christians belong to a particular group with which they strongly identify. They look over its walls with suspicion and distrust at other, unfamiliar manifestations of the Christian faith. And many more of us have such a background from which we have reached a wider standpoint. If the chronicler could have read John's Gospel, one of his favorite texts may have been from the prayer of Jesus: "that they may all be one . . . so that the world may believe that you sent me" (John 17:21). The way forward is not via the holy huddle that nervously finds security in its own rarefied traditions of the faith and pays lip service to some hidden, mystical unity that only God can see. Needed in each denomination are intrepid visionaries who are open to the potential of rich fellowship with others of God's flock outside their particular fold. If the Gospel of John was originally composed for the church to whom the First Letter of John was written—a dispirited group who had been victims of dissension and schism (see 1 John 2:18-19)—then one of the Evangelist's aims was to encourage them not to be so embittered by the experience as to withdraw into their shells, but to maintain a broad perspective.

The chronicler used David's coronation as an opportunity to encourage his fellow Judeans to think big about the dimensions of the community of faith. However, he had no vague, amorphous view of the spiritual traditions he espoused. God's revelation for him stood firmly within the tradition of the Davidic dynasty and of Jerusalem as its capital, which was to be the home of the Temple. "All Israel" travels to Jerusalem in David's company (11:4), and in spirit God's people had to continue making that journey. The chronicler had convictions that many "separated brethren" of his own day would have opposed (see 2 Chr 30:10-11). With evangelical fervor he was urging narrower believers in his constituency to invite them back to the purity of the traditional faith (12:17) and to regard themselves as incomplete until that task was achieved.

2. The chronicler acknowledged that his vision outstrips present realities—frustratingly so. The leap from chapter 10 to 11:1-9 did not occur overnight. In the middle of the unit readers are taken back to David at his wilderness base. Superficially it had a Robin Hood glamour (see 1 Sam 22:1-2), but the reality was far different. David was emotionally low, forced to flee from court and hounded by a psychotic king, his former patron turned foe. He did not know whom to trust or which of his companions might turn traitor. Politically there was a rival cause: the house of Saul, which enjoyed the support especially of his own tribe for a long time (12:29). It was an act of religious and political courage to throw in one's lot with David, daring to believe in God's prophetic word. Until that cause triumphed, it meant swimming against the tide and anticipating the "trouble" in this world that Jesus promised his own followers, with the encouragement that in principle he had already "overcome the world" (John 16:33 NIV).

The chronicler meant to echo the comparative weakness and discouragement of post-exilic Judah. Even as he did so, he laid before his readers the vision of David's ascent from weakness to strength. He skillfully wove it into his larger plan for a united Israel, challenging them to make it their own and advising them that the task would be arduous but worthwhile.

3. The divine thread that holds these two chapters together is the prophetic word of promise (11:3, 10; 12:23; cf. 12:18). Saul fatally ignored the word of the Lord (10:13) when it came in the form of a command. Now "all Israel" took as their command the divine promise of David's kingship (11:2). The chronicler placed a high value on the words of the prophets as divine revelation. To believe in the Lord involved believing the prophets (2 Chr 20:20). The prophetic word will often be quoted and applied in the so-called sermons scattered throughout Chronicles, but its fundamental role here is to affirm the new era of David and Solomon as a dispensation that stretched down to the chronicler's day and beyond. In New Testament terms, his perspective finds a parallel in the gospel about the Son of God descended from David, promised beforehand through God's prophets in the Holy Scriptures (Rom 1:2-3). In both cases the prophetic word functions as a warranty that a new era of divine grace has dawned, destined to reverberate through human history and challenge it to its core.

Working within the parameters of Old Testament history and theology, the chronicler promised that if God's people threw in their lot with David and the divine revelation associated with him, they would experience fully the restoration that lay beyond their "exile" of failure and frustration. Jerusalem, David's new home, was part and pledge of the whole land. United under a restored Davidic monarchy ruling from Jerusalem, Israel would win back the land in part of which they now lived by the grace of the Persian emperor. The patriarchs, too, were prophets, through whom the land of Israel was promised to Israel (16:15-18, 22). And salvation oracles in prophetic texts provided promises that the judgment of exile would one day be fully over and that the day of salvation, anticipated and inaugurated in the era of David and Solomon, would dawn for Israel. The chronicler, like the Christian, saw himself as standing in the middle of time, looking back in faith to the beginning of God's great work and looking forward in hope to its blessed fulfillment.

Meanwhile the believing, hoping community was not to sit idly, but to prepare for that day by embracing the unity that was theirs in principle and living in the light of their faith and hope. In New Testament terms, the chronicler brought a challenge to encompass in their vision the panorama of "all the saints" (Eph 3:18) and to make every effort "to maintain the unity of the Spirit in the bond of peace" as "one body" (Eph 4:3-4 NRSV). This single body could only progress as each part was working properly (Eph 4:16). Accordingly, the chronicler not only surveys the army of Israel en masse and enumerates its tribal dimensions, but also gives examples of individual commitment to the cause of David and his kingdom.

4. This emphasis is also served by the motif of help, which runs throughout these two chapters and elsewhere in the books of Chronicles. It is a comprehensive motif, covering not only help from other members of God's people, but also help from God and an obligation not to help the ungodly.[85] The element of divine help appears plainly in 12:18. The God who made promises did not stand aside, but provided gracious help, ensuring that the promises came true. David's role was not only to obey the revelation but also to accept divine help to that end. And such is always the case, as Paul attested in Acts 26:22. The element of divine help is accentuated by some of the names of David's supporters: Eleazar ("God helps," 11:12), Abiezer ("the [divine] father helps," 11:28), Ahiezer ("the [divine] brother helps," 12:3), and Joezer ("the Lord helps," 12:6).

The factor of not helping the enemy emerges in 12:19 in principle and will reappear in 2 Chr 19:2 (cf. 28:16, 23). There are boundaries that separate God's people from the world. The wise will discern occasions when they apply, lest they be "mismatched with unbelievers" (2 Cor 6:14 NRSV). Mostly, however, the motif of help is associated with cooperation, as we have seen. Behind David stood an army of active supporters. They rallied around their leader and so promoted God's work. The Letter to the Romans joins Chronicles in featuring at least two of these aspects of help. Paul celebrated the Spirit of God who "helps us in our weakness" (Rom 8:26) and also honored Phoebe as "a great help to many people, including me" (Rom 16:2 NIV).

5. Chapters 10–12 laid before post-exilic Judah two possibilities. For the chronicler, the current generation stood at a crossroads, to decide either for or against God. Saul still lurked in contemporary hearts, seeking to drag them down the path that led to continued exile from God and God's blessing. Yet David beckoned, challenging them to a breadth of spirit, exemplifying commitment to God and to Israel, and summoning them to a hope that the Lord would again work in such a fashion. It is helpful for us later readers to formulate this positive appeal in terms of Heb 12:1-2. The chronicler, taking David as pioneer, urged all of his readers, including us, to run with perseverance this arduous but rewarding race. Only of those who do so can it be truly said that they have "understanding of the times, to know what Israel ought to do" (12:32 NRSV).

85. H. G. M. Williamson, " 'We Are Yours, O David': The Setting and Purpose of 1 Chronicles xii 1-23," *OTS* 21 (1981) 166-67; *1 and 2 Chronicles*, 105.

1 Chronicles 13:1–16:43, Giving God Pride of Place

OVERVIEW

David's two attempts to install the ark in Jerusalem, the first unsuccessful and the second successful, are the narrative framework that binds these chapters together. The section is united structurally by two series of repeated Hebrew terms. The English reader is made aware of two instances in the first series by the transliterated place-names "Perez Uzzah," or "outburst against Uzzah" (13:11), and "Baal Perazim," or "Lord of breakthroughs" (14:11). Both place-names are explained with the verbal form פרץ (*pāraṣ*), rendered "burst/broken out." These two cases are taken over from the source material in 2 Samuel 5–6, but are presented in reverse order. The chronicler uses the verb in two other ways. The first is in 13:2, rendered together with a second verb as "Let us send abroad" (NRSV) or "let us send word far and wide" (NIV). The other is in 15:13, which picks up 13:11. This fourfold wordplay will be investigated as it is encountered.

The other series of repetitions is more straightforward, except that both of the English versions lack consistency. One of the chronicler's key verbs, דרש (*dāraš*, "seek"), which was used twice in 10:13-14, surfaces again three times in this section. In 16:11 there is a call to "seek the LORD" (NRSV). It echoes two references to seeking the ark in 13:3 ("inquire of," NIV; "turn to," NRSV) and 15:13 ("inquire of [him]," NIV; "give proper care," NRSV). Here is a clue that seeking God and doing so by proper means constitute the message of this section.

1 Chronicles 13:1-14, David Tries to Move the Ark

NIV

13 David conferred with each of his officers, the commanders of thousands and commanders of hundreds. 2He then said to the whole assembly of Israel, "If it seems good to you and if it is the will of the LORD our God, let us send word far and wide to the rest of our brothers throughout the territories of Israel, and also to the priests and Levites who are with them in their towns and pasturelands, to come and join us. 3Let us bring the ark of our God back to us, for we did not inquire of[a] it[b] during the reign of Saul." 4The whole assembly agreed to do this, because it seemed right to all the people.

5So David assembled all the Israelites, from the Shihor River in Egypt to Lebo[c] Hamath, to bring the ark of God from Kiriath Jearim. 6David and all the Israelites with him went to Baalah of Judah (Kiriath Jearim) to bring up from there the ark of God the LORD, who is enthroned between the cherubim—the ark that is called by the Name.

7They moved the ark of God from Abinadab's house on a new cart, with Uzzah and Ahio guiding it. 8David and all the Israelites were celebrating with all their might before God, with songs and with harps, lyres, tambourines, cymbals and trumpets.

9When they came to the threshing floor of Kidon, Uzzah reached out his hand to steady the ark, because the oxen stumbled. 10The LORD's anger burned against Uzzah, and he struck him down because he had put his hand on the ark. So he died there before God.

[a]3 Or *we neglected* [b]3 Or *him* [c]5 Or *to the entrance to*

NRSV

13 David consulted with the commanders of the thousands and of the hundreds, with every leader. 2David said to the whole assembly of Israel, "If it seems good to you, and if it is the will of the LORD our God, let us send abroad to our kindred who remain in all the land of Israel, including the priests and Levites in the cities that have pasture lands, that they may come together to us. 3Then let us bring again the ark of our God to us; for we did not turn to it in the days of Saul." 4The whole assembly agreed to do so, for the thing pleased all the people.

5So David assembled all Israel from the Shihor of Egypt to Lebo-hamath, to bring the ark of God from Kiriath-jearim. 6And David and all Israel went up to Baalah, that is, to Kiriath-jearim, which belongs to Judah, to bring up from there the ark of God, the LORD, who is enthroned on the cherubim, which is called by his[a] name. 7They carried the ark of God on a new cart, from the house of Abinadab, and Uzzah and Ahio[b] were driving the cart. 8David and all Israel were dancing before God with all their might, with song and lyres and harps and tambourines and cymbals and trumpets.

9When they came to the threshing floor of Chidon, Uzzah put out his hand to hold the ark, for the oxen shook it. 10The anger of the LORD was kindled against Uzzah; he struck him down because he put out his hand to the ark; and he died there before God. 11David was angry because the LORD had burst out against Uzzah; so that

[a] Heb lacks *his* [b] Or *and his brother*

NIV

[11]Then David was angry because the LORD's wrath had broken out against Uzzah, and to this day that place is called Perez Uzzah.[a]

[12]David was afraid of God that day and asked, "How can I ever bring the ark of God to me?" [13]He did not take the ark to be with him in the City of David. Instead, he took it aside to the house of Obed-Edom the Gittite. [14]The ark of God remained with the family of Obed-Edom in his house for three months, and the LORD blessed his household and everything he had.

[a]*11 Perez Uzzah* means *outbreak against Uzzah.*

NRSV

place is called Perez-uzzah[a] to this day. [12]David was afraid of God that day; he said, "How can I bring the ark of God into my care?" [13]So David did not take the ark into his care into the city of David; he took it instead to the house of Obed-edom the Gittite. [14]The ark of God remained with the household of Obed-edom in his house three months, and the LORD blessed the household of Obed-edom and all that he had.

[a] That is *Bursting Out Against Uzzah*

COMMENTARY

God has been present behind the scenes in chaps. 10–12. The Lord was responsible for both Saul's death (10:14) and for David's growth to greatness (11:9). Now there is a national resolve to give God a central place in the community. This was to be achieved by paying tribute to the ark, the religious symbol of God's presence.

The chronicler draws a pointed contrast (v. 3) between the negative attitude toward the ark during Saul's reign and the positive one now displayed at the beginning of David's.[86] By using his spiritual key word דרשׁ (*dāraš*), the chronicler recalls to his readers Saul's failure to "seek" the Lord (10:14) and offers another example of such behavior. To neglect the ark by leaving it in Kiriath-jearim (cf. 1 Sam 7:2) was symptomatic of Saul's neglect of God. The chronicler assumes that his readers know the history of the ark from 1 Samuel 4–7. For a generation the ark had languished at Kiriath-jearim, some eight miles west of Jerusalem. Now that a new era had dawned with David, this aberration could be tolerated no longer. It was necessary to restore the ark as a way of putting God at the heart of the community's life.

13:1. Verses 6-14 correspond to 2 Sam 6:2-11. The chronicler has supplied his own introduction in vv. 1-5. David consults first with the leaders of tribal contingents and then with the rank and file as an assembly that represents the nation. Both groups were present at Hebron for the coronation (12:23, 38), so that the narrative runs on without a break. David proposes to bring the ark to Jerusalem (cf. v. 13). The conquest of Jerusalem lies in the past (11:4). The chronicler loosely implies that the national army, gathered at Hebron, marched to Jerusalem to conquer it and then returned to continue the coronation celebrations. David's residence in Jerusalem (11:7; 13:13) does not square with this overall impression.

In 2 Samuel, the moving of the ark follows the two victories over the Philistines, but here it precedes them. One reason for this reordering is to make David's first act after the coronation a religious one, the transportation of the ark. The chronicler claims that the city of David (11:7; 13:13) soon becomes the city of God. The residence of the human king becomes that of the divine king (cf. v. 6).

13:2-4. In v. 2 a change in the MT's accentuation would supply an impersonal verb in the second condition, with the force "and if there is a breakthrough brought about by the LORD our God." The LXX understood it similarly: "and if success is brought about by the LORD our God."[87] So does the REB: "and if the LORD our God opens a way." This is the first instance of one of the key words in the section, פרץ (*pāraṣ*). The chronicler appears to be anticipating the third, positive

86. For 1 Sam 14:18, see P. K. McCarter, *I Samuel*, AB 8 (Garden City, N.Y.: Doubleday, 1980) 237, 240.

87. See L. C. Allen, *The Greek Chronicles: The Relation of the Septuagint of I and II Chronicles to the Massoretic Text*, Part 1: *The Translator's Craft*, VTSup 25, 27 (Leiden: Brill, 1974) 128.

instance in 14:11, God's breaking through the Philistines and giving David victory. This evidence of blessing will encourage the king to continue his quest to bring the ark to Jerusalem. In the chronicler's narrative it acquires the value of a divine affirmation that David may go ahead. This wordplay supplies a further reason why the chronicler places David's victories over the Philistines after his initial attempt to transport the ark.

First, however, there has to be a full assembling of the people. "The whole assembly" (v. 2) and "all the people" (v. 4) were in fact the representative body of tribal contingents. The new enterprise merits even greater representation than David's coronation, as God is greater than the human king. So the rest of Israel, absent in 12:38, is now summoned. Along with the laity, the presence of the priests and the Levites is sought for this religious occasion (the NIV's "and also" is better than the NRSV's "including"). They will feature prominently in the chronicler's narrative in chap. 15, but allusion will also be made to them at 13:8. Reference to the cities and pasturelands of the priests and Levites directs the reader back to the list in 6:50-81.

13:5-6. The chronicler's inclusive term "all Israel" in v. 5 is pointedly repeated in v. 6 and also in v. 8. This threefold occurrence shows its importance for the passage. In v. 6, as the chronicler joins the 2 Samuel text, he makes this point by replacing with the idealized "all Israel" the limited reference to a representative group of 30,000 conscripts. This theme of "all Israel" is underscored by making the northern and southern frontiers of Israel as wide as possible. They are evidently defined in terms of the Davidic Empire and accord with the frontiers of Solomon's kingdom in 2 Chr 7:8.[88] Accordingly, "Shihor," the easternmost branch of the Nile, is used loosely for Wadi el-Arish, corresponding to "the Wadi of Egypt" at 2 Chr 7:8. It is significant that such boundaries are drawn for the ideal Israel in Num 34:2-12 (cf. Ezek 47:15-19), while in Josh 13:1-7 the promised land is similarly defined, with precise mention of Shihor, which clearly inspired the present reference.[89] The Davidic Empire and the promised land are fused in the chronicler's mind as the ideal shape of Israel's territory. The land that belonged to Israel by divine gift would one day be restored to the people of God, who now occupied far less (see 16:15-20, 35).

13:7-10. In v. 7 the chronicler has omitted the second verbal form in 2 Sam 6:3, "and they brought it." This verb, נשׂא (*nāśā'*), bears religious connotation, as its use with reference to the Levites in 15:2, 15 (rendered "carry") will make clear.[90] To keep the word here would have brought confusion into the story. Another significant change occurs in v. 8, with the addition of "trumpets" to the list of musical instruments (2 Sam 6:5) that were used to celebrate the transportation of the ark. The lyres, harps, and cymbals have now implicitly become the instruments played by the Levites of v. 2, while the trumpets are blown by the priests, as the description of the second ceremony will explicitly mention (15:16, 24; cf. 15:28). In the chronicler's own day, music had an official religious setting, and he sees the ancient ceremony through contemporary lenses.

On the other hand, it is unlikely that the difference in v. 9 between the infinitive "to hold" or "to steady" and the past tense in the text of 2 Sam 6:6 is an intensification on the chronicler's part. The infinitive was probably already in the text he used.[91] Nor is the immediacy of the phrase "before God" in v. 10 a heightening of the chronicler's narrative. His text of 2 Samuel seems to have had the same reading, rather than "beside the ark of God," which appears in the MT of 2 Samuel.[92]

13:11-14. To a large extent the story follows the contours it has in 2 Samuel. The introduction (vv. 1-4) increases the sense of shock and anticlimax at the failure of the venture. The chronicler will explain it in chap. 15, but one must respect the narrative sequence and wait until then. The mission is disastrously short-circuited. The numinous holiness of which the ark partook has here a dangerous physical quality like an electrical

88. H. G. M. Williamson, *Israel in the Books of Chronicles* (Cambridge: Cambridge University Press, 1977) 123-24; *1 and 2 Chronicles,* 115.

89. See S. Japhet, "Conquest and Settlement," 209-10; *I & II Chronicles,* OTL (Louisville: Westminster/John Knox, 1993) 277-78.

90. M. Fishbane, *Biblical Interpretation in Ancient Israel* (Oxford: Clarendon, 1985) 393.

91. See S. L. McKenzie, *The Chronicler's Use of the Deuteronomistic History,* HSM 33 (Atlanta: Scholars Press, 1985) 49. For the name variants "Chidon" in Chronicles and "Nacon" in the MT of 2 Samuel, see McCarter, *II Samuel,* who regards both as secondary to "Nodan" in 4QSam[a].

92. McCarter, *II Samuel,* 165; McKenzie, *The Chronicler's Use of the Deuteronomistic History,* 49-50. Cf. v. 8 and the parallel 2 Sam 6:5.

charge (cf. Num 4:18-20; 1 Sam 6:19-20). As with the parallel in 2 Samuel, the episode is an installment of a larger story, but the chronicler's insertion of chap. 14 increases the tension. He tantalizingly leaves loose ends dangling until, like a mystery writer, he finally explains its twists and turns. The narrative does end with a glimmer of hope, blessing enjoyed by the family of Obed-edom, which will be explained in terms of a large family in 26:4-5. The ark is left with him for three months.

REFLECTIONS

1. The chronicler's introduction brings David's good intentions to the fore—not the good intentions the proverb tells us the road to hell is paved with, mental aspirations that die before seeing the light of day. David's intentions are matched with an energetic endeavor to realize them and are backed with sincere integrity. This dedication makes the subsequent failure hard to handle. Who has not known the consternation of a serious setback, when all seemed to be going well in a life committed, one thought, to God's will? It is at this realistic midpoint that the chapter ends.

2. Another favorite theme of the chronicler appears here: seeking God. Verse 3 mentions seeking the Lord via the ark. To neglect the ark was to neglect God, a symptom of the way to exile chosen by Saul. The road to restoration calls for an active concern for God and so for the discharge of religious duties that serve to express it. Whatever denomination we belong to, we all have religious rites and forms that are part of that denominational tradition, whether high or low, traditional or contemporary. Of course, any means of grace can degenerate into "a human commandment learned by rote," if "the hearts" of those who perform it are "far from" the Lord (Isa 29:13 NRSV). There is an opposite danger when religious habits are disregarded. As the Jewish scholar Israel Abrahams shrewdly observed, "What can be done at any time and in any manner is liable to be done at no time and in no manner."[93]

The chronicler's ordering of his material gives top priority to the things of God. Here David seeks first the kingdom of God (cf. Matt 6:33) in seeking the ark that celebrated God's kingship ("enthroned on/between the cherubim," 13:6). For the chronicler and his first readers, just as for us, the story needed mental reinterpretation. The ark no longer rested as a nucleus of worship in the holy of holies of the Second Temple. Although the ark was gone, what it stood for remained. There was still a conviction of the vital presence of God with the worshiping community, and still a need to acknowledge the Lord as King of kings.

3. As the story proceeds, these ideals shatter into (as yet) inexplicable fragments. David reacts in two ways to this crisis. First, he is angry. It is the anger of frustration hammering impotently at a slammed door. Such anger underlies the laments in the psalms, expressing the disappointment and resentment with which we typically respond to crisis. Second, David is afraid (cf. Acts 5:11), realizing that he is in the presence of a mysterious power he can neither control nor comprehend. He has lost the rapport with God he seemed to enjoy up to 13:8. One might regard this fear as a more appropriate response than anger, but the human frame is too weak to attain to spirituality at a single leap. One must work steadily through emotions triggered by crisis. David and reader alike can only wait, clinging to such redeeming features as bolster faith and hope.

93. I. Abrahams, *Studies in Pharisaism and the Gospels,* 2nd ser. (Cambridge: Cambridge University Press, 1924) 84.

1 Chronicles 14:1-17, God Honors David's Intentions

NIV

14 Now Hiram king of Tyre sent messengers
to David, along with cedar logs, stonema-
sons and carpenters to build a palace for him.
2And David knew that the LORD had established
him as king over Israel and that his kingdom had
been highly exalted for the sake of his people
Israel.

3In Jerusalem David took more wives and became the father of more sons and daughters.
4These are the names of the children born to him
there: Shammua, Shobab, Nathan, Solomon, 5Ib-
har, Elishua, Elpelet, 6Nogah, Nepheg, Japhia,
7Elishama, Beeliada[a] and Eliphelet.

8When the Philistines heard that David had
been anointed king over all Israel, they went up
in full force to search for him, but David heard
about it and went out to meet them. 9Now the
Philistines had come and raided the Valley of
Rephaim; 10so David inquired of God: "Shall I go
and attack the Philistines? Will you hand them
over to me?"

The LORD answered him, "Go, I will hand them
over to you."

11So David and his men went up to Baal
Perazim, and there he defeated them. He said,
"As waters break out, God has broken out against
my enemies by my hand." So that place was called
Baal Perazim.[b] 12The Philistines had abandoned
their gods there, and David gave orders to burn
them in the fire.

13Once more the Philistines raided the valley;
14so David inquired of God again, and God answered him, "Do not go straight up, but circle
around them and attack them in front of the
balsam trees. 15As soon as you hear the sound of
marching in the tops of the balsam trees, move
out to battle, because that will mean God has
gone out in front of you to strike the Philistine
army." 16So David did as God commanded him,
and they struck down the Philistine army, all the
way from Gibeon to Gezer.

17So David's fame spread throughout every
land, and the LORD made all the nations fear him.

[a]7 A variant of *Eliada* [b]11 *Baal Perazim* means *the lord who breaks out.*

NRSV

14 King Hiram of Tyre sent messengers to
David, along with cedar logs, and masons
and carpenters to build a house for him. 2David
then perceived that the LORD had established him
as king over Israel, and that his kingdom was
highly exalted for the sake of his people Israel.

3David took more wives in Jerusalem, and
David became the father of more sons and daughters. 4These are the names of the children whom
he had in Jerusalem: Shammua, Shobab, and
Nathan; Solomon, 5Ibhar, Elishua, and Elpelet;
6Nogah, Nepheg, and Japhia; 7Elishama, Beeliada,
and Eliphelet.

8When the Philistines heard that David had
been anointed king over all Israel, all the Philistines went up in search of David; and David heard
of it and went out against them. 9Now the Philistines had come and made a raid in the valley of
Rephaim. 10David inquired of God, "Shall I go up
against the Philistines? Will you give them into
my hand?" The LORD said to him, "Go up, and I
will give them into your hand." 11So he went up
to Baal-perazim, and David defeated them there.
David said, "God has burst out[a] against my enemies by my hand, like a bursting flood." Therefore
that place is called Baal-perazim.[b] 12They abandoned their gods there, and at David's command
they were burned.

13Once again the Philistines made a raid in the
valley. 14When David again inquired of God, God
said to him, "You shall not go up after them; go
around and come on them opposite the balsam
trees. 15When you hear the sound of marching in
the tops of the balsam trees, then go out to battle;
for God has gone out before you to strike down
the army of the Philistines." 16David did as God
had commanded him, and they struck down the
Philistine army from Gibeon to Gezer. 17The fame
of David went out into all lands, and the LORD
brought the fear of him on all nations.

[a] Heb *paraz* [b] That is *Lord of Bursting Out*

COMMENTARY

Chapter 14 fills the three-month gap—a literary device that conveys a sense of waiting—between the two attempts to bring the ark to Jerusalem. Material from 2 Sam 5:11-23, placed there before the first attempt, is used here to fill the intervening period, though historically the reports of both David's involvement with Hiram and the birth of thirteen children in Jerusalem belong much later in his reign.

Three incidents are borrowed from 2 Samuel 5: Hiram's gifts to David, his growing family, and his double victory over the Philistines. They represent a flood of divine blessings filling David's life. For the chronicler such blessings result from David's seeking God via the ark (see 13:3). Later in Chronicles he will present King Asa as seeking God and victorious (2 Chr 14:4, 7, 9-15) and King Jehoshaphat as receiving tribute and riches after seeking the Lord (2 Chr 17:4-5). David's reversal of Saul's bad example meant that he could receive divine approval.[94]

14:1-2. God's blessing is first traced in the area of foreign tribute. The chronicler appears to have understood the gifts of the king of Tyre as tribute from a vassal. In 2 Chr 2:14, in a letter from Hiram to Solomon, David is referred to as "my lord." In v. 2 he gladly takes over the interpretation of this event given in 2 Samuel. Behind the human honor was the Lord's providential purpose to confirm David's royal power, as will also be the case for Jehoshaphat (2 Chr 17:5). Whereas Saul lost his kingship (10:14), David's was put on a firm footing. It was "exalted," as Hezekiah's will be, another good king (2 Chr 32:23). The chronicler adds a characteristic word, למעלה (*lĕmaʿlâ*, "highly"), to recognize David's imperial greatness. Such recognition is balanced with an acknowledgment of the Lord as the power behind the throne and the source of David's success, and also with an awareness of his role as servant to his subjects. The king's function was to serve the interests of the God who supported him and the people he ruled (cf. 13:6; 17:14).

The chronicler doubtless saw a deeper significance in v. 2*b* than social justice or economic prosperity enjoyed by David's subjects. His monarchy was the means by which God's will was being realized for the people of Israel. The hint of a continuing dynasty broached in vv. 3-7 fits this broader horizon. The chronicler could not conceive of Israel's ultimate future without a descendant of David (cf. 3:1-24).

14:3-7. Sons and daughters born to David are understood as a further indication of divine blessing. The chronicler has retained "more" from his text of 2 Samuel in v. 3, indicating that he was aware of the earlier list of children born at Hebron (2 Sam 3:2-5), which in fact he cited in 3:1-4. Mention of concubines in the master text, alongside wives, is omitted, presumably to safeguard the legitimacy of the children.[95] There is an implicit contrast with Saul's loss of his sons in 10:6. David's family raises dynastic hopes. Solomon will turn out to be the chosen successor (22:9-10; 28:6).

14:8-12. The rest of the chapter is devoted to David's victories over the Philistines. Again Saul's negative experience lies in the background, as one defeated by them. Whereas the king who did not seek God became a loser, this king who put the Lord first is a winner. In the chronicler's hands the Samuel text takes on new significance.

There is a slight harmonization with chaps. 11–12. "Israel" in the text of 2 Samuel becomes "all Israel," in line with the chronicler's earlier emphasis. "Baal-perazim" in v. 11 and David's accompanying interpretation also reflect a previous concern of Chronicles. Perez-Uzzah, God's outbreak against Uzzah (13:11), is compensated for by a breakthrough against David's enemies. Divine curse gives way to blessing. This use of the key word פרץ (*pāraṣ*) recalls the first use in 13:2. The Lord has now broken through in a clear demonstration of favor. The initial condition is satisfied. Now David can resume his honorable attempt to move the ark to Jerusalem.

This seeker after God lived up to his reputation. He "inquired of God" before both campaigns (vv. 10, 14). It is no accident that this verb (שׁאל *šāʾal*) occurred with reference to Saul in 10:13

94. H. G. M. Williamson, *1 and 2 Chronicles*, NCB (Grand Rapids: Eerdmans, 1982) 116-19, judiciously following R. Mosis, *Untersuchungen zur Theologie des chronisten Geschichtswerks*, Freiburger theolische Studien 92 (Freiburg: Herder, 1973) 55-79.

95. P. K. McCarter, *II Samuel*, AB9 (Garden City, N.Y.: Doubleday, 1984) 147.

("consulted," NRSV, NIV), where he inquired of a medium instead of the Lord. The burning of the captured images of the Philistines' gods (v. 12) conspicuously differs from their being taken back as trophies of war in the MT of 2 Sam 5:21. There is disagreement as to whether the chronicler's text of 2 Samuel already had this different reading.[96] Anyway, it was probably significant for the chronicler that David follows in such matters the dictate of the Torah, as laid down in Deut 7:5, 25.

14:13-16. In the second campaign an attack from the rear evidently made it impossible for the Philistines to withdraw at the western end of the valley of Rephaim, to the southwest of Jerusalem. They are forced to retreat by a northern route. In Chronicles the retreat is made by way of Gibeon, rather than Geba (so 2 Sam 5:25 MT). The LXX of 2 Samuel reflects the same reading as does Chronicles, and so it may already have been present in the chronicler's text of 2 Samuel, unless the LXX reading is simply the result of textual assimilation. The variant is often explained as an allusion to Isa 28:21.[97] That text celebrates great victories wrought by the Lord on Israel's behalf at Mt. Perazim and in the valley of Gibeon, with the latter probably referring to Joshua 10. The chronicler, no stranger to prophetic literature, may have had Isa 28:21 in mind and hence intended to glorify David's victories.

14:17. This observation is found only in 1 Chronicles. The historian is meditating on David's foreign relations, most particularly those with Tyre and the Philistines. He regards them as striking examples of general international renown, doubtless thinking of chaps. 18–20 (esp. 18:11). He interprets this phenomenon in line with the reflection he took over from 2 Samuel in v. 2. These international dealings reflect the Lord at work, providentially bestowing blessing, and will find echoes in the reigns of David's faithful heirs Jehoshaphat and Hezekiah (2 Chr 17:10-11; 20:29; 32:22-23). Such weal in the foreign affairs of the Davidic dynasty created an expectation that an illustrious king would be restored in God's good time.

96. See W. E. Lemke, "The Synoptic Problem in the Chronicler's History," *HTR* 58 (1965) 352; S. L. McKenzie, *The Chronicler's Use of the Deuteronomistic History,* HSM 33 (Atlanta: Scholars Press, 1985) 62; but note Williamson's reply, *1 and 2 Chronicles,* 1982) 118-19.

97. Notably by Mosis, *Untersuchungen zur Theologie des chronisten Geschichtswerks,* 65. See also Williamson, *1 and 2 Chronicles,* 119.

REFLECTIONS

1. The chronicler's new placement of this material has made it serve his own concerns, functioning as a literary interlude. Its present message is that God has honored David's good intentions, though not Uzzah's, unfortunately. Did the ancient writer, too, experience a sense of unfairness that well-intentioned Uzzah should die? Life, like war, is often so unfair. One person, too close to the catastrophe, is engulfed by it. Another survives, shell-shocked and wondering at the randomness of providence. At last there comes the signal of God's will, expressed in terms of the wordplay of the section (13:2; 14:11). David's efforts at seeking God brought an appreciative response, for the Lord stood behind these human experiences, we are told in 14:2 and 17. God measures spiritual progress by endeavors, not by results.

2. The chronicler wanted his readers to find in these happy consequences an incentive for their own spiritual lives. Jesus also proclaimed such an incentive in his exhortation, "Seek first [God's] kingdom and his righteousness, and all these things will be given to you as well" (Matt 6:33 NIV; cf. Heb. 6:10). David's heart was in the right place. There is a close parallel in 2 Chr 30:19, where again the chronicler traces the blessed outcome of seeking God. Hezekiah prayed that Israelites who had unavoidably failed to undergo proper purification rites might participate with impunity in the Passover celebrations. The ground of his prayer is that they had "set their hearts to seek God . . . even though not in accordance with the sanctuary's rules of cleanness" (NRSV). David, too, it will be revealed in chapter 15, had made a ritual mistake, but he had certainly set his heart to seek God. In his case he had to go through the whole ceremony again, but his efforts did not go unrewarded. The chronicler's emphasis on motivation shows how far from legalism his concept of spirituality was.

3. David has taken the high road, while Saul took the low road to failure. Chapter 10 must reverberate in readers' ears as they study chapter 14. Where foreigners were concerned, David was the head, and Saul was the tail (Deut 28:13, 44). The chronicler is posing a warning: Along which road are you traveling, my readers—a road of backsliding and virtual exile or a road of restoration and blessing? As we identify with the things of God and live accordingly, the chronicler's purpose will be honored.

4. The reflection borrowed in 14:2 sets before us ideals of human leaders, who are to be subject to God and sensitive to the needs of subordinates. David is empowered not for his own sake, but to do the will of God and to promote the interests of the nation. Power tends to corrupt, but as David's star reaches its zenith, his resolve is that God should be glorified and the people should profit. His consultation with national representatives and concern for the divine will in 13:1-2 already illustrated such ideals.

5. The reflections in 14:2 and 17 also point toward the future by tracing the inauguration of eschatological ideals. The establishment of the dynasty, at which 14:3-7 hints, gave birth to a hope still dear to the chronicler's heart centuries later and shaped his understanding of Israel's future under God. The David of 14:2 and 17 finds a parallel in the Christ of Eph 1:21-22. God has made him "the head over all things for the church" and already placed him "above every name that is named, not only in this age but also in the age to come" (NRSV). Here "all lands" and "all nations" (NRSV) in 14:17 hint at the universal submission promised to David's line from "the nations" and "the ends of the earth" in Ps 2:8-9, a psalm that has an eschatological function in the psalter and to which the christology of the NT is no stranger. A divine arc is drawn for both the chronicler and the Christian between past revelation and future hope. Both stand in the gap between those two points, looking forward to a hope stamped by that past.

1 Chronicles 15:1–16:3, David Moves the Ark Properly

NIV

15 After David had constructed buildings for
himself in the City of David, he prepared
a place for the ark of God and pitched a tent for
it. 2Then David said, "No one but the Levites may
carry the ark of God, because the LORD chose
them to carry the ark of the LORD and to minister
before him forever."
3David assembled all Israel in Jerusalem to bring
up the ark of the LORD to the place he had
prepared for it. 4He called together the descendants of Aaron and the Levites:
5From the descendants of Kohath,
Uriel the leader and 120 relatives;
6from the descendants of Merari,
Asaiah the leader and 220 relatives;

NRSV

15 David[a] built houses for himself in the city
of David, and he prepared a place for the
ark of God and pitched a tent for it. 2Then David
commanded that no one but the Levites were to
carry the ark of God, for the LORD had chosen
them to carry the ark of the LORD and to minister
to him forever. 3David assembled all Israel in
Jerusalem to bring up the ark of the LORD to its
place, which he had prepared for it. 4Then David
gathered together the descendants of Aaron and
the Levites: 5of the sons of Kohath, Uriel the chief,
with one hundred twenty of his kindred; 6of the
sons of Merari, Asaiah the chief, with two hundred twenty of his kindred; 7of the sons of Gershom, Joel the chief, with one hundred thirty of

[a] Heb *He*

NIV

7from the descendants of Gershon,[a]
Joel the leader and 130 relatives;
8from the descendants of Elizaphan,
Shemaiah the leader and 200 relatives;
9from the descendants of Hebron,
Eliel the leader and 80 relatives;
10from the descendants of Uzziel,
Amminadab the leader and 112 relatives.

11Then David summoned Zadok and Abiathar the priests, and Uriel, Asaiah, Joel, Shemaiah, Eliel and Amminadab the Levites. 12He said to them, "You are the heads of the Levitical families; you and your fellow Levites are to consecrate yourselves and bring up the ark of the LORD, the God of Israel, to the place I have prepared for it. 13It was because you, the Levites, did not bring it up the first time that the LORD our God broke out in anger against us. We did not inquire of him about how to do it in the prescribed way." 14So the priests and Levites consecrated themselves in order to bring up the ark of the LORD, the God of Israel. 15And the Levites carried the ark of God with the poles on their shoulders, as Moses had commanded in accordance with the word of the LORD.

16David told the leaders of the Levites to appoint their brothers as singers to sing joyful songs, accompanied by musical instruments: lyres, harps and cymbals.

17So the Levites appointed Heman son of Joel; from his brothers, Asaph son of Berekiah; and from their brothers the Merarites, Ethan son of Kushaiah; 18and with them their brothers next in rank: Zechariah,[b] Jaaziel, Shemiramoth, Jehiel, Unni, Eliab, Benaiah, Maaseiah, Mattithiah, Eliphelehu, Mikneiah, Obed-Edom and Jeiel,[c] the gatekeepers.

19The musicians Heman, Asaph and Ethan were to sound the bronze cymbals; 20Zechariah, Aziel, Shemiramoth, Jehiel, Unni, Eliab, Maaseiah and Benaiah were to play the lyres according to *alamoth*,[d] 21and Mattithiah, Eliphelehu, Mikneiah, Obed-Edom, Jeiel and Azaziah were to play the harps, directing according to *sheminith*.[d]

a*7* Hebrew *Gershom*, a variant of *Gershon* b*18* Three Hebrew manuscripts and most Septuagint manuscripts (see also verse 20 and 1 Chron. 16:5); most Hebrew manuscripts *Zechariah son and* or *Zechariah, Ben and* c*18* Hebrew; Septuagint (see also verse 21) *Jeiel and Azaziah* d*20, 21* Probably a musical term

NRSV

his kindred; 8of the sons of Elizaphan, Shemaiah the chief, with two hundred of his kindred; 9of the sons of Hebron, Eliel the chief, with eighty of his kindred; 10of the sons of Uzziel, Amminadab the chief, with one hundred twelve of his kindred.

11David summoned the priests Zadok and Abiathar, and the Levites Uriel, Asaiah, Joel, Shemaiah, Eliel, and Amminadab. 12He said to them, "You are the heads of families of the Levites; sanctify yourselves, you and your kindred, so that you may bring up the ark of the LORD, the God of Israel, to the place that I have prepared for it. 13Because you did not carry it the first time,[a] the LORD our God burst out against us, because we did not give it proper care." 14So the priests and the Levites sanctified themselves to bring up the ark of the LORD, the God of Israel. 15And the Levites carried the ark of God on their shoulders with the poles, as Moses had commanded according to the word of the LORD.

16David also commanded the chiefs of the Levites to appoint their kindred as the singers to play on musical instruments, on harps and lyres and cymbals, to raise loud sounds of joy. 17So the Levites appointed Heman son of Joel; and of his kindred Asaph son of Berechiah; and of the sons of Merari, their kindred, Ethan son of Kushaiah; 18and with them their kindred of the second order, Zechariah, Jaaziel, Shemiramoth, Jehiel, Unni, Eliab, Benaiah, Maaseiah, Mattithiah, Eliphelehu, and Mikneiah, and the gatekeepers Obed-edom and Jeiel. 19The singers Heman, Asaph, and Ethan were to sound bronze cymbals; 20Zechariah, Aziel, Shemiramoth, Jehiel, Unni, Eliab, Maaseiah, and Benaiah were to play harps according to Alamoth; 21but Mattithiah, Eliphelehu, Mikneiah, Obed-edom, Jeiel, and Azaziah were to lead with lyres according to the Sheminith. 22Chenaniah, leader of the Levites in music, was to direct the music, for he understood it. 23Berechiah and Elkanah were to be gatekeepers for the ark. 24Shebaniah, Joshaphat, Nethanel, Amasai, Zechariah, Benaiah, and Eliezer, the priests, were to blow the trumpets before the ark of God. Obed-edom and Jehiah also were to be gatekeepers for the ark.

25So David and the elders of Israel, and the

a Meaning of Heb uncertain

NIV

[22]Kenaniah the head Levite was in charge of the singing; that was his responsibility because he was skillful at it.

[23]Berekiah and Elkanah were to be doorkeepers for the ark. [24]Shebaniah, Joshaphat, Nethanel, Amasai, Zechariah, Benaiah and Eliezer the priests were to blow trumpets before the ark of God. Obed-Edom and Jehiah were also to be doorkeepers for the ark.

[25]So David and the elders of Israel and the commanders of units of a thousand went to bring up the ark of the covenant of the LORD from the house of Obed-Edom, with rejoicing. [26]Because God had helped the Levites who were carrying the ark of the covenant of the LORD, seven bulls and seven rams were sacrificed. [27]Now David was clothed in a robe of fine linen, as were all the Levites who were carrying the ark, and as were the singers, and Kenaniah, who was in charge of the singing of the choirs. David also wore a linen ephod. [28]So all Israel brought up the ark of the covenant of the LORD with shouts, with the sounding of rams' horns and trumpets, and of cymbals, and the playing of lyres and harps.

[29]As the ark of the covenant of the LORD was entering the City of David, Michal daughter of Saul watched from a window. And when she saw King David dancing and celebrating, she despised him in her heart.

16 They brought the ark of God and set it inside the tent that David had pitched for it, and they presented burnt offerings and fellowship offerings[a] before God. [2]After David had finished sacrificing the burnt offerings and fellowship offerings, he blessed the people in the name of the LORD. [3]Then he gave a loaf of bread, a cake of dates and a cake of raisins to each Israelite man and woman.

[a]*1* Traditionally *peace offerings*; also in verse 2

NRSV

commanders of the thousands, went to bring up the ark of the covenant of the LORD from the house of Obed-edom with rejoicing. [26]And because God helped the Levites who were carrying the ark of the covenant of the LORD, they sacrificed seven bulls and seven rams. [27]David was clothed with a robe of fine linen, as also were all the Levites who were carrying the ark, and the singers, and Chenaniah the leader of the music of the singers; and David wore a linen ephod. [28]So all Israel brought up the ark of the covenant of the LORD with shouting, to the sound of the horn, trumpets, and cymbals, and made loud music on harps and lyres.

29As the ark of the covenant of the LORD came to the city of David, Michal daughter of Saul looked out of the window, and saw King David leaping and dancing; and she despised him in her heart.

16 They brought in the ark of God, and set it inside the tent that David had pitched for it; and they offered burnt offerings and offerings of well-being before God. [2]When David had finished offering the burnt offerings and the offerings of well-being, he blessed the people in the name of the LORD; [3]and he distributed to every person in Israel—man and woman alike—to each a loaf of bread, a portion of meat,[a] and a cake of raisins.

[a] Compare Gk Syr Vg: Meaning of Heb uncertain

COMMENTARY

Chapter 14 left unresolved the issue of bringing the ark to Jerusalem, though it did establish favorable conditions for doing so. Now the narrative reaches a climax, explaining what went wrong the first time and how it was to be done. The ark is duly moved, and worship is offered in Jerusalem—worship that constitutes a spiritual landmark. The passage is based on the account of the second, successful attempt to convey the ark in 2 Sam 6:12*a*-19*a*. The chronicler expands these eight verses fourfold, making the episode especially important. He turns it into an injunction to honor the Torah, specifically its guidelines for worship.

15:1-24. Reproduction of the 2 Samuel narrative is left until the end of the passage (15:25–16:3). What precedes is concerned with preparations for and clarification of the ark narrative, which will itself be correspondingly amplified as it is quoted. First, 2 Sam 6:17 (= 1 Chr 16:1) mentions a tent David had set up for the ark in Jerusalem. Room needed to be made, so in v. 1 the king carefully prepares a site for the ark and erects the tent, in addition to engaging in his own building projects (14:1). This preparation is underlined in vv. 3 and 12. It is a key motif of the passage, revealing David's active concern for the ark, which is the opposite of the neglect shown by Saul (13:3). Did the chronicler have in mind Ps 132:3-5, which mentions David's vow not to enter his own home or rest until he had found "a place for the LORD," by bringing the ark to Jerusalem? Although David builds houses for himself (v. 1), it is not stated until 17:1, after the installation of the ark in the place prepared for it, that David took up residence in his house. Here is diligence, indeed, for the things of God and a spiritual lesson for others to emulate.

Second, the story in 2 Samuel speaks first of David's bringing up the ark and then of "David and all the house of Israel" (the latter group is also mentioned at the end of the account, 2 Sam 6:12, 15, 19). This information calls for an explanation about another assembling of "all Israel" after the three months time lag. This explanation duly appears in v. 3. The chronicler is alluding to 13:5, the total participation of the believing community envisioned there. When, however, he quotes 2 Sam 5:12*b* in v. 25, David is joined by "the elders of Israel and the commanders of thousands" as his fellow participants, echoing the partial representation in 11:3 and 13:1. Did the chronicler have in view a representational procession over to Obed-edom's house and a comprehensive one back to the temple site? Perhaps, but the main point is a literary one, that earlier threads of the coronation celebration and of deliberations to move the ark are being drawn together in order to convey its climactic importance.

The chronicler's third and crucial clarification concerns the preparing of personnel for the procession and its aftermath. The ark narrative in 2 Samuel no longer spoke of "transporting" (הרכיב *hirkîb*) the ark on a new cart. Instead, it mentioned those who were "carrying" (נשׂא *nāśā'*) the ark in 2 Sam 6:13, with which 1 Chr 15:26 is parallel.[98] This information provides the chronicler with a clue that David had to pursue his seeking of God at a deeper level. In v. 13 there is an admission from David that, literally, "we did not seek (דרשׁ *dāraš*) it in the proper way." So they had to search the Torah to discover the appropriate manner to transport the ark. The chronicler found it in Deut 10:8, which stipulated that the tribe of Levi is to "carry [*nāśā'*] the ark of the covenant of the LORD." In the priestly writings of the Pentateuch, this work was allocated to the associate clergy, the Levites, and so it is in Chronicles (v. 2). The exact procedure is spelled out in v. 15. The Levites were to carry on their shoulders poles that supported the suspended ark. In this case explicit reference to the Torah is made, presumably to Exod 25:13-15 (cf. Num 7:9; בדים [*baddîm*] is used for poles in Exodus 25, but here a different word, מטות [*mōṭôt*]; cf. the use of מוט [*môṭ*] as a flat carrying frame for vessels in Num 4:10, 12). These priestly texts already have the Levites in view, specifically the Kohathite clan. The poles kept the carriers at a safe distance from the ark, respecting its holiness: "They must not touch the holy things, or they will die" (Num 4:15 NIV). Repetition of poor Uzzah's fate is avoided by maintaining an insulating space around the holy ark.

The "word of the LORD" (v. 15) was of paramount importance for the chronicler. In chaps. 10–12 it had been a prophetic word. Now it stands for the Torah, "as Moses had commanded." The Lord was honored by obeying Scripture. The chronicler highlights this solution by recalling the negative use of the section's key word: פרץ (*pāraṣ*, "burst/broken out") in 13:11 and explaining in David's speech that the judgment on Uzzah had been evidence of the Lord's displeasure for disobeying the Torah's prescription.

98. This verb also occurred in a general sense ("brought") at 2 Sam 6:3 and was omitted in 1 Chr 13:7.

The chronicler understood this event to have affected later levitical responsibilities. In v. 2 he fused Deut 10:8 with the overlapping Deut 18:5, where the tribe of Levi, including the Levites, is given a divine commission to "minister in the LORD's name always" (NIV). The chronicler found in the ark narratives a definition of part of the Levites' ministry. He will argue in 16:4, 37 that this ministry entailed choral music. He associated the first attempt to move the ark with their musical participation, as the list of musical instruments in 13:8 is meant to convey (cf. 13:2). Now they come into their own, again implicitly playing the cymbals, harps, and lyres in v. 28 as well as conveying the ark. In vv. 16-24 the chronicler will take the opportunity to trace back to David's initiative the organization of the levitical singing musicians, which developed in post-exilic times. It is uncertain whether these verses represent the stage of development in the chronicler's day or a little later. They represent the latest post-exilic stage, with Heman in first place, before Asaph, and the third group associated not with Jeduthun but with Ethan, as in 6:31-48. In 16:37-41, however, a slightly earlier stage, probably a generation earlier, is reflected, with Asaph in first place, Heman in second, and Jeduthun in third (see the Introduction).[99]

In vv. 5-10 a list of Levites available to the chronicler is applied to the present situation by means of the heading in v. 4 and the summary in v. 11. It cites representatives of the three clans of Levites, the clans of Kohath, Merari, and Gershom, together with their family heads at the particular time when the list was composed. In addition, three Kohathite subclans, those of Elizaphan, Hebron, and Uzziel (cf. 6:18; Num 3:30) are here elevated to independent status, as in the case of Elizaphan in 2 Chr 29:13. Mention is also made of priests who participated in vv. 4, 11, 14, and 24, in the last case as trumpeters. This last reference presupposes Num 10:10. Otherwise, their presence may stem from an awareness of Num 4:5, where they are to be responsible for covering the ark. Their normative role in sacrifices (15:26; 16:1) and their responsibility to place the ark in the tent (16:1) may also be in view.[100]

So vv. 1-24 are concerned with preparations for the ceremony of 15:25–16:3. The passage is structurally governed by the two commands of David in vv. 2 and 16 for Levites to carry the ark and to be responsible for the choral music. There are two subdivisions, vv. 2-15 and vv. 16-24. Verse 15 has an anticipatory role, as a comment on v. 26. This text presents arrangements that would guide the procession of the ark.

Verse 16 announces the second great preparation, with a double list of participants and the instruments they were to play provided in vv. 17-21.[101] The religious musicians of the post-exilic period were only gradually given levitical status, which they lacked at the early stage represented by the list preserved in Ezra 2:41; Neh 7:44. The chronicler typically projects later customs back to an earlier period. Obed-edom, presumably the naturalized Gittite who took care of the ark in 13:14, is adopted into the musicians' ranks in vv. 18, 21 (and in 16:5). Footnotes incorporated into the text at v. 18 ("gatekeepers") and v. 24 ("Obed-edom . . . ark") about his status as a gatekeeper seem to reflect different claims about the post-exilic role of Obed-edom's descendants. Two brief items concerning the musical director and the "gatekeepers" are supplied in vv. 22-23. Presumably the latter were responsible for security during the ceremony.

15:25-28. The chronicler now joins the text of 2 Samuel. In v. 26 the same number of sacrificial animals appears in 4QSam[a] (cf. 2 Sam 6:13 MT). In v. 27 the aberrant first clause represents probably the chronicler's attempt to deal with an indistinct text, reading the verb מכרכר (*mĕkarkēr*, "was dancing") in 2 Sam 6:14*a*

99. Williamson, *1 and 2 Chronicles,* 120-25, attributes the list in 15:16-24 to the chronicler, rather than to a redactor.

100. See John W. Kleinig, *The Lord's Song: The Basis, Function and Significance of Choral Music in Chronicles,* JSOTSup 156 (Sheffield: JSOT, 1993) 50n. 3. Kleinig's understanding of 15:16-24 in terms of a processional order at the ark ceremony can hardly stand without consideration of diachronic factors. Williamson, *1 and 2 Chronicles,* 123, among others, has taken the references to priests as the work of the pro-priestly reviser. Some mention of priestly participation by the chronicler is not unexpected; see 13:2 and the pointed reference to trumpets in 13:8. In v. 4, however, the sole designation of the priests as "the descendants of Aaron" is characteristic of secondary passages, and the context refers only to the Levites' duties. 15:24*a* is set in a secondary context and may be an addition developed from 16:6, designed to restore a priestly balance.

101. The terms "Alamoth" and "Sheminith" in vv. 20-21 are transliterated because they are no longer understood. They refer to musical modes or melodies.

as מכרבל (*mĕkurbāl,* "was clothed"), an interpretation influenced by v. 14*b.* Certain additions are made to harmonize the text with his own earlier perceptions. The Levites are duly given a prominent part in vv. 26-27. The success of the new mode of moving the ark is credited to divine help, an echo of 12:18. This time God did not hinder, but blessed human compliance with the divine will. In a major change from the 2 Samuel text, the ark is now repeatedly called "the ark of the covenant of the LORD/God" (vv. 25-26, 28-29; also 16:6, 37). This designation has been formally triggered by Deut 10:8, cited earlier. The ark was a symbol of the covenant relationship between God and Israel. When the chronicler thought of the ark, he was reminded that Israel was God's people, the object of divine care and claim. These instances cluster around the three references to the covenant (16:15-17). Overall, the chronicler seems to have taken the Lord's covenant with David as a new, once-for-all arrangement that subsumed within it all that was best in God's earlier relations with Israel (cf. 2 Chr 13:5; 21:7). We shall observe the development of this thought in chap. 16.

15:29. The incident of Michal's scorn takes on new meaning in this context. It becomes a reminder of Saul's neglect of the ark. This "daughter of Saul" was the odd person out that day. She was the would-be killjoy in this atmosphere of communal joy. As David and "all Israel" honored the ark and worshiped God, she failed to perceive the significance of the event. It was a case of "like father, like daughter." Michal chose to follow Saul's path away from God and God's people.

REFLECTIONS

1. The chronicler's resolution of the failure of the first attempt to move the ark to Jerusalem is achieved by recourse to the Torah. The new, unprofaned cart and the willing helpers in chapter 13 were not good enough. Seeking God was not to be an arbitrary human endeavor (cf. 1 Sam 6:7), but was to follow a sacred pattern already revealed in the Torah. Christians have not been furnished in the New Testament such detailed information about institutional aspects of their faith. "If every church must be built on the exact model of the Church at Corinth, at Ephesus or at Antioch, we are in hopeless difficulties. The plans have been lost, and the specifications destroyed."[102] The New Testament does not echo the Old Testament's prescriptions of institutional order. The sacraments of baptism and communion and such general principles as unity, faith, love, and the need that "all things be done decently and in order" (see 1 Corinthians 10–14) are what the church has received as its heritage. Denominational traditions have variously clothed with culturally appropriate flesh and blood the skeletons of these practices and principles.

From a broader perspective, however, the chronicler and the Christian think alike. The new order, originated under David and commended by the chronicler as still relevant to believers in his own day, continued to take its cue from the Torah. Each new revelation of God in the Bible takes a step forward in one or a few great respects, and otherwise preserves the older faith. In chapters 10–12, the "word of the LORD" was prophetic. Now, in 15:15, it is from the Torah. The chronicler regarded the Law and the Prophets as the divine word for contemporary Israel. In them was to be sought expression of God's will for each generation. This emphasis on the Scriptures is an essential trait of the books of Chronicles. Invested with divine authority, Scripture was to be the basis of Judah's self-understanding and life-style. Similarly the New Testament church was later to echo this value attached to the Old Testament scriptures, now composed of a greater canonical whole, and to find in them positive and negative guidelines as to what to believe and how to behave (2 Tim 3:16).

2. If the chronicler turned back to the Torah to hear a recording of the divine voice, here

102. R. W. Dale, *Essays and Addresses* (London: Hodder and Stoughton, 1909) 31.

about religious practice, then he also had a dynamic conception of the living presence of God at work in the community of faith. "God [had] helped the Levites" who were carrying the ark (15:26). The Lord is envisioned not as the inspirer of the Torah who then left Israel to obey ancient commands as best they could, but as providentially present with them and promoting their participation in the divine will. The same sentiments will reappear in David's prayer in 28:18-19—namely, that God would turn Israel's hearts toward the light and help Solomon keep the Torah. Similarly, according to Psalm 119, where God's "law" or Torah is more than the Pentateuch and included at least Isaiah, Jeremiah, and Proverbs, Israel is to depend not only on written revelation but also on the living God, whose constant help is sought in prayer.

3. The new era associated with David and Solomon meant a step forward, supremely in the building of the Temple, for which a vital beginning is made here. The Second Temple had the same value as the First for the chronicler. These pre-temple chapters implicitly present a message about temple worship for God's people in the chronicler's time to heed. Solomon duly incorporated the Davidic innovations into temple practice, especially "the Levites for their offices of praise . . . for so David the man of God had commanded" (2 Chr 8:14 NRSV). Chapter 15 is one key place where we read of this new practice. As the chronicler and his generation enjoyed listening to the Levites singing to their own music at temple services, he encouraged them to prize the tradition as ultimately grounded in the glorious work of David, "the man of God" and so agent of divine revelation. This spanning of the centuries corresponds to the way Christians look back to the dawn of a new era in Christ and celebrate it as the revelation of God (Heb 1:1-2).

4. The note of joy struck at the end of the previous section (12:40) also comes to the fore in 15:16, 25. Comparison of these two verses shows that the chronicler regarded the Levites' music and song as inspiring the people's joy. Such joy was not a spontaneous phenomenon but was promoted by this new institutional practice. Likewise, every church has the task of translating the spirit of worship into appropriate religious forms. Forms there must be, and their character should be a constant challenge. Forms can turn into formality, and so new Christian groups appear with fresh and "informal" forms, for the eventual edification of the church at large. Tradition and adaptability are the two poles within which the church legitimately moves. Worship is to be alive and joyful, ascending to God from hearts and minds in culturally appropriate language and modes.

5. The Saul/David antithesis returns to haunt this passage. Saul is typical of those who do not seek the things of God and are blind to such endeavors. The challenge came, as ever, to the next generation. Michal took the wrong direction by siding with her father. In the chronicler's thinking, every generation in turn is confronted with the need to make a fresh decision for God. He here poses an implicit warning as to which direction his own generation wants to take at its own crossroads: the low road away from God or the high road of spiritual commitment. Michal had the same chance we all have, but she made the wrong choice.

1 Chronicles 16:4-43, Praise and Worship Inaugurated

NIV

4He appointed some of the Levites to minister
before the ark of the LORD, to make petition, to
give thanks, and to praise the LORD, the God of
Israel: 5Asaph was the chief, Zechariah second,
then Jeiel, Shemiramoth, Jehiel, Mattithiah, Eliab,
Benaiah, Obed-Edom and Jeiel. They were to play

NRSV

4He appointed certain of the Levites as ministers before the ark of the LORD, to invoke, to
thank, and to praise the LORD, the God of Israel.
5Asaph was the chief, and second to him
Zechariah, Jeiel, Shemiramoth, Jehiel, Mattithiah,
Eliab, Benaiah, Obed-edom, and Jeiel, with harps

NIV

the lyres and harps, Asaph was to sound the cymbals, [6]and Benaiah and Jahaziel the priests were to blow the trumpets regularly before the ark of the covenant of God.

[7]That day David first committed to Asaph and his associates this psalm of thanks to the LORD:

[8]Give thanks to the LORD, call on his name;
make known among the nations what he has done.
[9]Sing to him, sing praise to him;
tell of all his wonderful acts.
[10]Glory in his holy name;
let the hearts of those who seek the LORD rejoice.
[11]Look to the LORD and his strength;
seek his face always.
[12]Remember the wonders he has done,
his miracles, and the judgments he pronounced,
[13]O descendants of Israel his servant,
O sons of Jacob, his chosen ones.

[14]He is the LORD our God;
his judgments are in all the earth.
[15]He remembers[a] his covenant forever,
the word he commanded, for a thousand generations,
[16]the covenant he made with Abraham,
the oath he swore to Isaac.
[17]He confirmed it to Jacob as a decree,
to Israel as an everlasting covenant:
[18]"To you I will give the land of Canaan
as the portion you will inherit."

[19]When they were but few in number,
few indeed, and strangers in it,
[20]they[b] wandered from nation to nation,
from one kingdom to another.
[21]He allowed no man to oppress them;
for their sake he rebuked kings:
[22]"Do not touch my anointed ones;
do my prophets no harm."

[23]Sing to the LORD, all the earth;
proclaim his salvation day after day.

[a]*15* Some Septuagint manuscripts (see also Psalm 105:8); Hebrew *Remember* [b]*18-20* One Hebrew manuscript, Septuagint and Vulgate (see also Psalm 105:12); most Hebrew manuscripts *inherit, / [19]though you are but few in number, / few indeed, and strangers in it." / [20]They*

NRSV

and lyres; Asaph was to sound the cymbals, [6]and the priests Benaiah and Jahaziel were to blow trumpets regularly, before the ark of the covenant of God.

7Then on that day David first appointed the singing of praises to the LORD by Asaph and his kindred.

[8] O give thanks to the LORD, call on his name,
make known his deeds among the peoples.
[9] Sing to him, sing praises to him,
tell of all his wonderful works.
[10] Glory in his holy name;
let the hearts of those who seek the LORD rejoice.
[11] Seek the LORD and his strength,
seek his presence continually.
[12] Remember the wonderful works he has done,
his miracles, and the judgments he uttered,
[13] O offspring of his servant Israel,[a]
children of Jacob, his chosen ones.

[14] He is the LORD our God;
his judgments are in all the earth.
[15] Remember his covenant forever,
the word that he commanded, for a thousand generations,
[16] the covenant that he made with Abraham,
his sworn promise to Isaac,
[17] which he confirmed to Jacob as a statute,
to Israel as an everlasting covenant,
[18] saying, "To you I will give the land of Canaan
as your portion for an inheritance."

[19] When they were few in number,
of little account, and strangers in the land,[b]
[20] wandering from nation to nation,
from one kingdom to another people,
[21] he allowed no one to oppress them;
he rebuked kings on their account,
[22] saying, "Do not touch my anointed ones;
do my prophets no harm."

[23] Sing to the LORD, all the earth.
Tell of his salvation from day to day.
[24] Declare his glory among the nations,
his marvelous works among all the peoples.

[a] Another reading is *Abraham* (compare Ps 105.6) [b] Heb *in it*

NIV

24Declare his glory among the nations,
his marvelous deeds among all peoples.
25For great is the LORD and most worthy of praise;
he is to be feared above all gods.
26For all the gods of the nations are idols,
but the LORD made the heavens.
27Splendor and majesty are before him;
strength and joy in his dwelling place.
28Ascribe to the LORD, O families of nations,
ascribe to the LORD glory and strength,
29 ascribe to the LORD the glory due his name.
Bring an offering and come before him;
worship the LORD in the splendor of his[a] holiness.
30Tremble before him, all the earth!
The world is firmly established; it cannot be moved.
31Let the heavens rejoice, let the earth be glad;
let them say among the nations, "The LORD reigns!"
32Let the sea resound, and all that is in it;
let the fields be jubilant, and everything in them!
33Then the trees of the forest will sing,
they will sing for joy before the LORD,
for he comes to judge the earth.

34Give thanks to the LORD, for he is good;
his love endures forever.
35Cry out, "Save us, O God our Savior;
gather us and deliver us from the nations,
that we may give thanks to your holy name,
that we may glory in your praise."
36Praise be to the LORD, the God of Israel,
from everlasting to everlasting.

Then all the people said "Amen" and "Praise the LORD."

37David left Asaph and his associates before the
ark of the covenant of the LORD to minister there
regularly, according to each day's requirements.
38He also left Obed-Edom and his sixty-eight associates to minister with them. Obed-Edom son
of Jeduthun, and also Hosah, were gatekeepers.
39David left Zadok the priest and his fellow
priests before the tabernacle of the LORD at the
high place in Gibeon 40to present burnt offerings

d29 Or *LORD with the splendor of*

NRSV

25 For great is the LORD, and greatly to be praised;
he is to be revered above all gods.
26 For all the gods of the peoples are idols,
but the LORD made the heavens.
27 Honor and majesty are before him;
strength and joy are in his place.

28 Ascribe to the LORD, O families of the peoples,
ascribe to the LORD glory and strength.
29 Ascribe to the LORD the glory due his name;
bring an offering, and come before him.
Worship the LORD in holy splendor;
30 tremble before him, all the earth.
The world is firmly established; it shall never be moved.
31 Let the heavens be glad, and let the earth rejoice,
and let them say among the nations, "The LORD is king!"
32 Let the sea roar, and all that fills it;
let the field exult, and everything in it.
33 Then shall the trees of the forest sing for joy
before the LORD, for he comes to judge the earth.
34 O give thanks to the LORD, for he is good;
for his steadfast love endures forever.

35Say also:
"Save us, O God of our salvation,
and gather and rescue us from among the nations,
that we may give thanks to your holy name,
and glory in your praise.
36 Blessed be the LORD, the God of Israel,
from everlasting to everlasting."
Then all the people said "Amen!" and praised the LORD.
37David left Asaph and his kinsfolk there before the ark of the covenant of the LORD to
minister regularly before the ark as each day
required, 38and also Obed-edom and his[a] sixty-
eight kinsfolk; while Obed-edom son of Jeduthun
and Hosah were to be gatekeepers. 39And he left
the priest Zadok and his kindred the priests before
the tabernacle of the LORD in the high place that
was at Gibeon, 40to offer burnt offerings to the
LORD on the altar of burnt offering regularly,
morning and evening, according to all that is

a Gk Syr Vg: Heb *their*

NIV	NRSV
to the LORD on the altar of burnt offering regularly, morning and evening, in accordance with everything written in the Law of the LORD, which he had given Israel. [41]With them were Heman and Jeduthun and the rest of those chosen and designated by name to give thanks to the LORD, "for his love endures forever." [42]Heman and Jeduthun were responsible for the sounding of the trumpets and cymbals and for the playing of the other instruments for sacred song. The sons of Jeduthun were stationed at the gate. [43]Then all the people left, each for his own home, and David returned home to bless his family.	written in the law of the LORD that he commanded Israel. [41]With them were Heman and Jeduthun, and the rest of those chosen and expressly named to render thanks to the LORD, for his steadfast love endures forever. [42]Heman and Jeduthun had with them trumpets and cymbals for the music, and instruments for sacred song. The sons of Jeduthun were appointed to the gate. 43Then all the people departed to their homes, and David went home to bless his household.

COMMENTARY

The chronicler brings to a close his convoluted account of the installation of the ark in Jerusalem, the first step toward the goal of building a temple. The only point of contact with his 2 Samuel text is the quotation of 2 Sam 6:19*b*-20 in 16:43. He uses it as his conclusion, having no use on this celebratory occasion for Michal's bitter confrontation with David (2 Sam 6:20*b*-23). Verse 43*b* has an important anticipatory role in the Chronicles narrative, paving the way for chap. 17. David returns home to pray for divine blessing on his "household" or "family." His prayer will be answered in the prophetic announcement of a Davidic dynasty.

16:4-7, 37-42. Apart from this borrowed conclusion, the prose narrative falls into two parts: David's appointment of personnel to be responsible for choral music at the site of the ark (vv. 4-6) and the implementation of these arrangements (vv. 37-42). The chronicler was concerned to trace the ministry of levitical musicians back to the establishment of the ark in Jerusalem, before the Temple was built. He had expressed this concern in 6:31-32. However, he had to address another issue: Solomon's sacrificing at Gibeon in 2 Chr 1:2-6. To be sure, the ark was safely installed at Jerusalem. However, the chronicler also affirmed that at one time the tabernacle was located at Gibeon, along with the altar of burnt offering on which sacrifices were regularly offered. We do not know whether he reasoned to this end or had recourse to an older tradition that attested the later history of the tabernacle after its stay in Shiloh (Josh 18:1; cf. 19:51). The chronicler describes the sacrificial calendar of the Pentateuch for the tabernacle as in full operation at Gibeon (see Exod 29:38-42; Num 28:2-8). In v. 40, he emphasizes that all ritual activity is based on what was written in the Torah, as was the case in 15:15 with respect to the carrying of the ark. At Gibeon the newly appointed levitical musicians were to play a supporting role, as later they would in the Temple.

The description of sacrifice in Gibeon (v. 39) helps to explain vv. 4-6. A key word in the prose narrative is "regularly" (תמיד *tāmîd*, vv. 6, 37, 40). Its most natural usage occurs in v. 37, where it is used to describe the regular morning and evening sacrifices. In v. 37 the chronicler transfers this term to the Levites' music and song in the vicinity of the ark, and in v. 6 to the priests' trumpet blasts there. Evidently the simultaneous accompaniment of the sacrificial procedure with musical songs in the Temple, envisioned in 23:30-31, was to happen even now. The singing element was to take place together, at the same time, with the sacrificial element in Gibeon, but by itself in Jerusalem.[103] Proper worship could occur in two places: Gibeon and Jerusalem.

The comprehensive choral arrangements re-

103. John W. Kleinig, *The Lord's Song: The Basis, Function and Significance of Chroal Music in Chronicles,* JSOTSup 156 (Sheffield: JSOT, 1993) 53.

corded as having been set up in the list of personnel and instruments in 15:16-21 are now implemented. There is a slight inconsistency, noted earlier, in that the scheme reflected in vv. 5, 37, 41-42 does not quite accord with the previous arrangements. It attests an earlier stage of post-exilic development. The two stages are loosely treated as the same. In v. 41, five of the fourteen names in 15:20-21 are presupposed ("the rest of those . . . expressly named," NRSV), after the citation of the other nine in v. 5. The same dispute in 15:18, 24—over whether Obed-edom was a musician or a gatekeeper—reappears in v. 38.

The task of the singing musicians was to praise God, as v. 4 indicates with an enthusiastic amassing of synonymous verbs. The first verb, rendered "invoke" (להזכיר *lĕhazkîr*) in the NRSV, is a general term for making mention of the Lord's name either in praise or in prayer. The NIV opts for the latter sense ("make petition"), but here the former is preferable. The second verb (להודות *lĕhôdôt*), involves primarily the thanksgiving song of an individual delivered from a crisis. By post-exilic times, however, it had also become part of the vocabulary for hymnic praise, as in v. 7, where *lĕhôdôt* reappears ("psalm of thanks," NIV). So the chronicler is concerned about the singing of hymns, as vv. 8-36 will illustrate. The chronicler introduces this sacred poetry in v. 7; afterward he resumes his narrative in v. 37.[104]

16:8-43. The poem is an anthology of elements drawn from three post-exilic psalms: Ps 105:1-15 in vv. 8-22, Ps 96:1*b*-13*a* in vv. 23-33, and Ps 106:1, 47-48 in vv. 4-36. Psalm 105 is a hymn that reviews the Lord's saving work on Israel's behalf. Psalm 96 is an eschatological hymn celebrating divine kingship, already grounded in creation and one day to be consummated worldwide. Psalm 106 is best understood as a communal lament; it praises God for past acts of grace because they provide hope of renewed help for Israel. The chronicler uses his anthology as an example of what the guild of singers contributed to public worship. Still the content of the psalm extracts was also important for him. The overlap of vocabulary with the narrative context shows that he anchored the medley to his story of David. The process is akin to that which underlies historicizing headings in the book of Psalms, which apply a psalm to a particular incident in David's life.[105] The anthology constitutes a complex hymn that at the end weaves petition into its praise. It is used as a song of adoration for what God had done thus far in David's career and as an appeal that the Lord will bring it to a successful conclusion.

The Temple is presupposed in the source behind vv. 27 and 29 (Ps 96:6, "in his sanctuary"; Ps 96:8, "to his courts"). The chronicler adapts these historically unsuitable phrases to "in his place" and "before him" respectively. In doing so, he achieves references to "the place" David had prepared for the ark (15:1, 3, 12) and to God's presence through the ark (13:8, 10; 16:1). The regular system of music and song just set up before the ark (vv. 6, 37) to synchronize with the sacrifices and songs offered at Gibeon (v. 40) is echoed in v. 11 ("continually" [*tāmîd*]). It occurs in a summons to resort to the Lord's "presence" (NRSV), now via the ark. The call in v. 11*a* to "seek" (דרשׁ *dāraš*) the Lord reinforces the motivation of David and the believing community in bringing the ark to Jerusalem (cf. 13:3; 15:13). The thrice-mentioned patriarchal "covenant" comprising the promise of the land of Canaan (vv. 15-17) relates to the frequent designation of the ark as the ark of the covenant in recent narrative (vv. 6, 37; see also 15:25-26, 28-29). The chronicler is aware of the close links between the patriarchal and the Davidic covenants. Reference to the land echoes the imperial frontiers of 13:5, while the everlastingness of the covenant (vv. 15, 17) alludes to the permanency of the Davidic dynasty in 17:13-14. The covenant with the patriarchs was taken up into the Davidic one and through David became Israel's heritage. Similarly, the Lord's "[steadfast] love," which "endures for ever" (v. 34, echoed in v. 41), presupposes the divine blessing promised to the Davidic line through Solomon in 17:13.

The accent on rejoicing in v. 10 reflects the festive joy of 15:16, 25; the hearers are urged to share it in v. 31 ("rejoice," NRSV). Hebrew synonyms for "rejoice" appear in vv. 27, 31-33 in an

104. See T. C. Butler, "A Forgotten Passage from a Forgotten Era (1 Chr xvi 8-36)," *VT* 28 (1978) 146; J. W. Watts, *Inset Hymns in Hebrew Narrative*, JSOTSup 139 (Sheffield: JSOT, 1992) 163 and nn. 4-5.

105. For the intricate intertextuality involved in this procedure, see E. Slomovic, "Toward an Understanding of the Formation of Historical Titles in the Book of Psalms," *ZAW* 91 (1979) 350-80.

outflowing of joy that spreads throughout the world. Likewise, the "strength" of v. 27 harks back to Israel's celebrating "with all their might" in 13:8 (עֹז *ʿōz* in both cases). Here are Asaph and his fellow choristers doing their work, singing and encouraging song (vv. 9, 23). Called to "thank" (v. 4), they promote thanksgiving in vv. 8, 34-35. Summoned to "praise," they stimulate it in vv. 10 (rendered "glory"), 25, 35-36.

If the new psalm majors in David's present, it also looks back to his past. The small number of David's followers in his wilderness and mercenary periods, when God protected them (see 12:18), is paralleled in vv. 19-22. God's "wonders" (v. 12 NIV; v. 24, "marvelous works/deeds") are now the exploits wrought by the Lord through David and his troops in chaps. 11–12 and 14. The divine causation of these exploits will be emphasized in 17:8*a*. The kingship of the Lord (v. 31) had recently been shown to be reflected in the ark (13:6), while David's kingdom will turn out to be God's own kingdom (17:14). This psalm medley also has in view the future of David. Appeal is made to the God who had already proved to be "our savior" (v. 35 NIV; cf. the related noun for "victory" in 11:14), for further feats of salvation. They will duly be accomplished in 18:6, 13.

The historicizing Davidic titles in the psalms were designed to present David as a model for post-exilic Judah.[106] The chronicler also had his contemporaries in mind in the new entity he created. Hermeneutical application pervades its stanzas. It falls into four stanzas: a call to Israel to praise God (vv. 8-22), a call for praise throughout the earth (vv. 23-30), a call for cosmic praise (vv. 31-33), and a call for Israel not only to praise but also to pray that fresh potential for praise may be theirs (vv. 34-36).[107] The clarion call to seek the Lord (v. 11) rings through the ages from Asaph to post-exilic readers. Contemporary Judah is meant to heed the double call to remember God's intervention in history to launch the new Davidic era (v. 12) and the everlasting patriarchal covenant received anew by David and passed on to Israel (vv. 15-18; the NRSV's imperative "Remember" in v. 15 suits the chronicler's exhortatory intent, while the NIV's "He remembers" has harmonized with the parent text, Ps 105:8). These old truths assure post-exilic Judah that it is only part of a wider Israel and that the whole land would one day be theirs. In v. 13 the chronicler has changed "Abraham" in Ps 105:6 to "Israel," thereby achieving the same parallelism as in v. 17. He sought to draw attention to the ancestor of the twelve tribes, whom he calls Israel rather than Jacob. As to the promise of the land, the patriarchs were God's veritable "prophets" (v. 22). Verses 19-22 had relevance for post-exilic Judah, territorially cramped yet assured of God's protection. In v. 19 the MT has "you" rather than "they." One wonders whether the "you" is directed to the chronicler's audience or if it implies reference to a continuation of direct speech from v. 18, as the NJB takes it.

Psalm 96, which underlies vv. 23-33, is an eschatological hymn, urging confident praise for what the Lord is yet to do. The chronicler still wanted the psalm to be understood this way. Judah's witness to the nations about the Lord's purposes (v. 18) would one day trigger an echoing response (v. 23). The world belongs to the Lord by virtue of creation, and so the fear inspired by God in all nations (14:17) would eventually issue into universal submission. The final clause in v. 29 is probably to be rendered "Worship the LORD for his holy splendor."[108] One day the universe would dance in honor of the ultimate outworking of Davidic kingship, when the whole earth welcomed the Lord coming to reign and to establish justice.

But not yet. The nations still jostled the people of God, who were "strangers" in their own "land" (v. 19). God's everlasting "[steadfast] love" (v. 34), like the covenant promises (vv. 15-18), was assurance enough that the full salvation celebrated in anticipation in v. 23 would eventually be theirs. Even now Israel should begin to give God everlasting praise to match that everlasting love. In v. 35 the vocative "O God, our savior" is provided

106. See B. S. Childs, "Psalm Titles and Midrashic Exegesis," *JSS* 16 (1971) 137-50; *Introduction to the OT as Scripture* (Philadelphia: Fortress, 1979) 520-22. David is presented in the psalter both as a model of ethical spirituality and as a source of eschatological hope.

107. Kleinig, *The Lord's Song,* 65n. 1, has cited C. Becker's observation that pushing Ps 96:11*a* into a leading place in 16:31*a* was intended to highlight the cosmic reference. He also draws attention to the use of "all the earth" as a framework in vv. 23, 30 (p. 142). Verse 36 (= Ps 106:48), originally a redactional doxology to the fourth book of the psalter, is here partly woven into the poem and partly made a narrative response.

108. See ibid., 176n. 2.

by the chronicler, and so is the imperative "and deliver us" (the two verbal forms for "and gather us" [not reflected in the LXX] and "and deliver us" probably reflect a conflated text in the MT). He probably took both elements from Ps 79:9, attracted by the potential of a new generation in Ps 79:8.[109] The focus changes from a concern of the diaspora to the needs of the returned exiles.

109. See L. C. Allen, *The Greek Chronicles: The Relation of the Septuagint of I and II Chronicles to the Massoretic Text,* Part 1: *The Translator's Craft,* VTSup 25, 27 (Leiden: Brill, 1974) 217.

REFLECTIONS

1. The chronicler has used his psalm extracts as hermeneutical stepping-stones from a unique but incomplete past to an inadequate, still incomplete present. David's growth from weakness to power has turned into an omen that post-exilic Judah's own prayers would be answered. Israel's glorious past is held up as a mirror to Israel's future. Partial restoration would give way to full rehabilitation. God's kingdom was to come on earth. The secret is the spiritual lesson the chronicler has been teaching since chapter 10: to seek the Lord. This means giving God the rightful place of honor in the religious life of the community, as the journey of the ark had symbolized. It also means expressing appreciative praise for what God had already done and would yet do.

"Let the hearts of those who seek the LORD" (16:10) rejoice over the purposes God had for them. The believing community in the chronicler's time, as in David's, was God's "chosen ones" (v. 13), as recipients of the divine promise, good for a thousand generations (v. 16). We are the chosen people, affirms the chronicler in healthy pride, in order to convey to his contemporaries a necessary continuity and destiny. When pride is the opposite of humility, it is bad; when it is the opposite of shame, it is good. At a time when so much in Judah's environment shouted no at their claims, the chronicler's faith dared to shout yes. They were tantalizingly close to and yet so far from the promise, like the patriarchs and like outlawed David. Yet they stood under the same protection of God (16:21-22). Promise, privation, protection—such was the dappled pattern of light and shade that covered the Judean community. We Christians recognize this clash of perspectives. Our hope is veiled: "We walk by faith, not by sight" (2 Cor 5:7 NRSV).

2. Accordingly, 16:23-33 presents a vision of victorious hope. Verse 23*b* has a remarkably Christian ring: It may be rendered "Proclaim . . . the good news that [the LORD] has saved us" (GNB). It was a mark of the new age God had established through David. It replaced the defeatism of the way of exile, which encouraged the impression that the Lord had lost and other powers had won. The same verb occurs in 10:9, where messengers were sent all through Philistine territory "to convey the good news" of Israel's defeat "to their idols and to the people." Underlying David's great power in 11:9 and 12:2 was the Lord's own greatness (16:25). Divine kingship in the psalms is often associated with the Lord's work as creator and maintainer of the world (16:26, 30). The Judeans, like us, could entrust themselves to a faithful creator (1 Pet 4:19). Psalm 96, used here, reflects the faith of post-exilic Judah in a universal God of creation and its hope that this universal role would be matched by a future intervention, when the Lord was to lay redemptive claim to the world and set it right (see Acts 17:31; 2 Pet 3:13). For the chronicler, there had already been a significant revelation of this God in the period of David, which confirmed the earlier disclosure to the patriarchs. The first chapter of 1 Chronicles had begun with the world, and so this message about its destiny is appropriate. To the post-exilic community living in "a day of small things" (Zech 4:10) are offered the narratives of a great David as encouraging signs of a great hope. "Sit at my right hand, until I make your enemies your footstool" (Ps 110:1) was the Lord's similar word to David elsewhere, and it came to pervade the New Testament, now addressed to Jesus enthroned in token of a greater throne hereafter.

3. The ambivalence of 16:8-22 returns in 16:34-36. On the one hand, the believing community is the recipient of God's goodness and love forever. On the other hand, they pray to the Lord for deliverance. Full restoration is conspicuous by its absence. The chronicler opens his contemporaries' eyes to their great traditions and urges this small community to appropriate these traditions, to live in the good of them and to make them the basis of a sure hope in the God who is preserving them for a purpose.

Here is theology set to music. As the hearts of God's people open in praise, divine truths take root. This theology functions as encouragement, giving renewed strength to the weary: "The LORD is great" and "the LORD is coming" (16:25, 33). The chronicler's old, yet new, psalm is matched in the New Testament by Rom 5:1-11 and 8:18-39. The church is represented as subject to limitations. Yet its members raise joyful voices because they look beyond brute facts to see God at work, preparing future glory. They feel the rain, but see a rainbow. God's electing love embraces them in its strong grip. That love brings assurance of victory, even now enjoyed in spirit. The work of God in Christ is the guarantee of their own destiny.

Doxology is here used as an antidote to despair. On other occasions both Paul and the chronicler challenged their constituencies. However, the need of this hour was to ensure that they were strengthened in faith and hope, with a power that came from God: "Seek the LORD and his strength" (16:11 NRSV).

1 Chronicles 17:1–20:8, Thy Kingdom Come!

OVERVIEW

This section presents the divine program for the reigns of David and Solomon. First, it is revealed in chap. 17 that David is to play the part of a warrior king. He will bring about stability and thus provide the people of Israel with a place of freedom and security. Second, Solomon (as yet unnamed) may then do his own work, building the Temple in Jerusalem. Solomon's accomplishment of this task will win lasting blessing from the Lord, the foundation of a permanent dynasty, which will be an inaugural manifestation of the kingdom of God. In chaps. 18–20, David duly fulfills the role assigned to him, in accord with the promise that God "will subdue all his enemies" (17:10). The verb "subdue" (הכניע *hiknîʿa*, in the hiphil) becomes a key word of the unit. It is echoed at the beginning of the first and third subunits in chaps. 18–20. At 18:1 David "subdued" the Philistines, and at 20:4 they "were subdued" (NRSV) again.

1 Chronicles 17:1-27, God's Program for David and Solomon

NIV

17 After David was settled in his palace, he said to Nathan the prophet, "Here I am, living in a palace of cedar, while the ark of the covenant of the LORD is under a tent."

2Nathan replied to David, "Whatever you have in mind, do it, for God is with you."

3That night the word of God came to Nathan, saying:

4"Go and tell my servant David, 'This is

NRSV

17 Now when David settled in his house, David said to the prophet Nathan, "I am living in a house of cedar, but the ark of the covenant of the LORD is under a tent." 2Nathan said to David, "Do all that you have in mind, for God is with you."

3But that same night the word of the LORD came to Nathan, saying: 4Go and tell my servant David: Thus says the LORD: You shall not build

NIV

what the LORD says: You are not the one to build me a house to dwell in. [5]I have not dwelt in a house from the day I brought Israel up out of Egypt to this day. I have moved from one tent site to another, from one dwelling place to another. [6]Wherever I have moved with all the Israelites, did I ever say to any of their leaders[a] whom I commanded to shepherd my people, "Why have you not built me a house of cedar?" '

[7]"Now then, tell my servant David, 'This is what the LORD Almighty says: I took you from the pasture and from following the flock, to be ruler over my people Israel. [8]I have been with you wherever you have gone, and I have cut off all your enemies from before you. Now I will make your name like the names of the greatest men of the earth. [9]And I will provide a place for my people Israel and will plant them so that they can have a home of their own and no longer be disturbed. Wicked people will not oppress them anymore, as they did at the beginning [10]and have done ever since the time I appointed leaders over my people Israel. I will also subdue all your enemies.

" 'I declare to you that the LORD will build a house for you: [11]When your days are over and you go to be with your fathers, I will raise up your offspring to succeed you, one of your own sons, and I will establish his kingdom. [12]He is the one who will build a house for me, and I will establish his throne forever. [13]I will be his father, and he will be my son. I will never take my love away from him, as I took it away from your predecessor. [14]I will set him over my house and my kingdom forever; his throne will be established forever.' "

[15]Nathan reported to David all the words of this entire revelation.

[16]Then King David went in and sat before the LORD, and he said:

"Who am I, O LORD God, and what is my family, that you have brought me this far? [17]And as if this were not enough in your sight, O God, you have spoken about the future of

[a]6 Traditionally *judges*; also in verse 10

NRSV

me a house to live in. [5]For I have not lived in a house since the day I brought out Israel to this very day, but I have lived in a tent and a tabernacle.[a] [6]Wherever I have moved about among all Israel, did I ever speak a word with any of the judges of Israel, whom I commanded to shepherd my people, saying, Why have you not built me a house of cedar? [7]Now therefore thus you shall say to my servant David: Thus says the LORD of hosts: I took you from the pasture, from following the sheep, to be ruler over my people Israel; [8]and I have been with you wherever you went, and have cut off all your enemies before you; and I will make for you a name, like the name of the great ones of the earth. [9]I will appoint a place for my people Israel, and will plant them, so that they may live in their own place, and be disturbed no more; and evildoers shall wear them down no more, as they did formerly, [10]from the time that I appointed judges over my people Israel; and I will subdue all your enemies.

Moreover I declare to you that the LORD will build you a house. [11]When your days are fulfilled to go to be with your ancestors, I will raise up your offspring after you, one of your own sons, and I will establish his kingdom. [12]He shall build a house for me, and I will establish his throne forever. [13]I will be a father to him, and he shall be a son to me. I will not take my steadfast love from him, as I took it from him who was before you, [14]but I will confirm him in my house and in my kingdom forever, and his throne shall be established forever. [15]In accordance with all these words and all this vision, Nathan spoke to David.

16Then King David went in and sat before the LORD, and said, "Who am I, O LORD God, and what is my house, that you have brought me thus far? [17]And even this was a small thing in your sight, O God; you have also spoken of your servant's house for a great while to come. You regard me as someone of high rank,[b] O LORD God! [18]And what more can David say to you for honoring your servant? You know your servant. [19]For your servant's sake, O LORD, and according to your own heart, you have done all these great deeds, making known all these great things. [20]There is

[a] Gk 2 Sam 7.6: Heb *but I have been from tent to tent and from tabernacle* [b] Meaning of Heb uncertain

NIV

the house of your servant. You have looked on me as though I were the most exalted of men, O LORD God.

18"What more can David say to you for honoring your servant? For you know your servant, 19O LORD. For the sake of your servant and according to your will, you have done this great thing and made known all these great promises.

20"There is no one like you, O LORD, and there is no God but you, as we have heard with our own ears. 21And who is like your people Israel—the one nation on earth whose God went out to redeem a people for himself, and to make a name for yourself, and to perform great and awesome wonders by driving out nations from before your people, whom you redeemed from Egypt? 22You made your people Israel your very own forever, and you, O LORD, have become their God.

23"And now, LORD, let the promise you have made concerning your servant and his house be established forever. Do as you promised, 24so that it will be established and that your name will be great forever. Then men will say, 'The LORD Almighty, the God over Israel, is Israel's God!' And the house of your servant David will be established before you.

25"You, my God, have revealed to your servant that you will build a house for him. So your servant has found courage to pray to you. 26O LORD, you are God! You have promised these good things to your servant. 27Now you have been pleased to bless the house of your servant, that it may continue forever in your sight; for you, O LORD, have blessed it, and it will be blessed forever."

NRSV

no one like you, O LORD, and there is no God besides you, according to all that we have heard with our ears. 21Who is like your people Israel, one nation on the earth whom God went to redeem to be his people, making for yourself a name for great and terrible things, in driving out nations before your people whom you redeemed from Egypt? 22And you made your people Israel to be your people forever; and you, O LORD, became their God.

23"And now, O LORD, as for the word that you have spoken concerning your servant and concerning his house, let it be established forever, and do as you have promised. 24Thus your name will be established and magnified forever in the saying, 'The LORD of hosts, the God of Israel, is Israel's God'; and the house of your servant David will be established in your presence. 25For you, my God, have revealed to your servant that you will build a house for him; therefore your servant has found it possible to pray before you. 26And now, O LORD, you are God, and you have promised this good thing to your servant; 27therefore may it please you to bless the house of your servant, that it may continue forever before you. For you, O LORD, have blessed and are blessed[a] forever."

[a] Or *and it is blessed*

COMMENTARY

This chapter falls into three parts: David's plan to build a temple to house the ark (vv. 1-2), the Lord's negative and positive answers (vv. 3-15), and David's prayer of thanksgiving and petition (vv. 16-27). What binds the chapter together is a series of wordplays on the term "house" (בית *bayit*). David, now residing in his house or palace (v. 1), wants to build a comparable house for the Lord, a temple (v. 6). God has other plans: to build a house or dynasty for David (vv. 11, 17-27) and for one of David's sons to build a house or temple for the Lord (vv. 12, 14).

The chapter follows 2 Samuel 7 fairly closely; differences will be pointed out as they are encountered. The major convictions associated with the deuteronomistic form of the oracle in 2 Sam 7:5-16 (= 1 Chr 17:4-14) are that David's reign is a period of promise and preparation, looking forward to the establishment of the royal dynasty and to the building of the Temple in Solomon's reign. David was to prepare for this period of fulfillment by pacifying the land, as 2 Samuel 8 records.[110] All this was grist for the chronicler's mill, and he took it over with a few refinements.

The reader of 1 Chronicles will recognize here another version of chaps. 13–15. A spiritual proposal is followed first by a divine setback and then by divine blessing as a reward for the previous spiritual intention. This was how the chronicler perceived the episode, in the light of 2 Chr 6:8 (= 1 Kgs 8:18). In these circumstances even a divine no can be worth having. God prizes spiritual initiatives, even if they eventually prove impracticable for reasons beyond the initiator's knowledge. David is still seeking the Lord with all his heart, and he is presented as an implicit model for later believers.

17:1-2. The king is concerned by the imbalance between his own palace and a mere tent for the ark. Why should he be better housed (cf. Hag 1:4)? The chronicler has been building up to this point in his narrative by mentioning David's palace at structurally significant points (v. 1; 14:1; 15:1). In v. 2, he makes a pregnant statement in calling "the ark of God" (2 Sam 7:2) "the ark of the covenant of the LORD." The issue of housing the ark will involve a divine covenant as the chapter progresses, the all-important covenant with David (cf. 2 Sam 23:5; Ps 89:3, 28, 34). As in chaps. 15–16, the value of the ark as a symbol of the Davidic covenant comes to the fore.

17:3-6. Nathan's general promise of divine support for building the Temple is countermanded by a detailed and complex oracle, which includes the ruling that on God's calendar the time for such a venture has not yet arrived. The oracle's initial sentence forms the first side of a triangle of statements. "You are not the one to build me a house to dwell in" (v. 4), says God. Instead, "the LORD will build you a house" (v. 10). And of one of David's sons, it is said, "He is the one who will build a house for me" (v. 12). In 2 Sam 7:5, the first statement appears in the form of a question. Here it is rephrased as a statement, as in 1 Kgs 8:19, and it looks forward to the two other contrasting ones. Verses 5-6 begin to explain the refusal in terms of the divine program for the reigns of David and Solomon. The long-standing precedent of housing the ark in a tent was to continue for a little longer. The ark had gone "from tent to tent and from tabernacle" (MT, which the NRSV has emended according to the parallel 2 Sam 7:6, following the harmonistic LXX, while the NIV has implicitly indulged in a popular conjectural addition, for which some have claimed support from the Targum). Once located in the tabernacle of the tent of meeting according to Exod 39:32 (cf. 1 Chr 6:32), it had now been moved to another tent, David's tent.[111] This distinction between the tabernacle and the tent provided by David follows naturally that made by the chronicler in 15:1; 16:1, 39.

17:7-10a. The initial "And now" ("Now then," NIV; "Now therefore," NRSV) in v. 7 typically signals that the main point is to be announced after introductory material. The renewed messenger formula "thus says the LORD of Hosts" lends further emphasis. In God's program, David's role was to be a warrior king. David's reign was to be the Lord's means of providing a secure land for Israel. To accomplish this goal, David is guaranteed complete victory. Whereas 2 Sam 7:11 promises David rest from all his enemies, here in v. 10 a verb of subjection is substituted. The chronicler associated Solomon with rest and David with warfare, and so found this reference to rest inappropriate (see Commentary on 22:9).[112] Both the deuteronomist and the chronicler presumed the condition laid down in Deut 12:10-11 that only after God had given Israel rest from all their enemies could they offer worship, at the place of the Lord's choosing. They differed as to when that rest occurred. The chronicler associated David with necessary warfare as his role in a pre-Temple program. Accordingly, he replaced the verb of rest, borrowing his new verb

110. P. K. McCarter, *II Samuel*, AB 9 (Garden City, N.Y.: Doubleday, 1984) 217-20, 241.

111. R. E. Friedman, *The Exile and Biblical Narrative*, HSM 22 (Chico, Calif.: Scholars Press, 1981) 54. In the priestly literature the inner curtains of the tabernacle structure are referred to as the tabernacle, and the outer curtains as the tent. See Exod 26:1-13.

112. R. L. Braun, "Solomon, the Chosen Temple Builder: The Significance of 1 Chronicles 22, 28, and 29 for the Theology of the Chronicler," *JBL* 95 (1976) 582-86; and *1 Chronicles*, WBC 14 (Waco, Tex.: Word, 1986) 198-99.

of subjection from 2 Sam 8:1 (= 1 Chr 18:1). By so doing, he created a structural marker for the section, using it yet again in 20:4.

17:10b-15. The second half of the program is presented in these verses. It supplies the other two sides of the triangle of statements in quick succession. Dynasty building and temple building are intertwined. The chronicler and his first readers knew what it was not yet time to say, that Solomon was in view as temple builder.[113] A temple was indeed to be built, but not yet, and by Solomon, not by David. His building of the Temple was to constitute a guarantee of the Davidic dynasty and its perpetuity. For the chronicler, the two halves of v. 12 constitute cause and effect. Another condition Solomon must keep will be presented in 28:7 (cf. 2 Chr 7:17-18). The divine side of the agreement was that the "[steadfast] love" forfeited by Saul would be permanently bestowed on Solomon. The post-exilic community often sang of the Lord's "[steadfast] love" in their hymns (see 16:34, 41). The chronicler traced it back to God's covenant with David and Solomon, which he regarded as the foundation of a permanent relationship with Israel. The reference to divine punishment in 2 Sam 7:14*b* is omitted as irrelevant after 1 Chr 17:13*a*. At this point the chronicler focuses solely on Solomon, whom he regarded as fulfilling the condition of obedience, the other factor that was to seal the dynastic promise. So Solomon was not liable to punishment at the hands of the divine patron of the monarchy.[114]

Solomon's dual role is summed up in v. 14. God would "set him over" the Temple and the theocracy, giving him a once-for-all supervisory role in these two areas. Second Samuel 7:16*a* reads "your house and your kingdom," but the chronicler prefers a concluding summary that repeats the substance of vv. 11*b*-12*a*. The new reference to God's kingdom introduces a motif characteristic of the books of Chronicles (28:5; 29:23; 2 Chr 9:8; 13:8). The Lord was to reign not only via the religious symbolism of the ark (13:6), but also from the palace itself. The human king would be regent, responsible to the heavenly king. It is difficult not to recognize an eschatological reference, especially after 16:31, in the sense of an inaugurated rather than a realized eschatology. The character of v. 14 as a recapitulating conclusion extends to the last clause. Instead of David's throne being established forever (2 Sam 7:16), Solomon's would be, in repetition of v. 12.

The portrayal of a new era founded on the Jerusalem Temple and dynasty finds a parallel in Psalm 78. Its review of the twists and turns of Israelite history culminates in the opening of a new age. This age is marked by God's building on Mt. Zion "his sanctuary," as secure as heaven and earth, and by choosing "his servant David" as Israel's shepherd (Ps 78:69-71; cf. 1 Chr 28:4 and Commentary on 28:4-7). Israel's history was to witness many more twists and turns after the basic 2 Samuel 7 and Psalm 78 were composed. The Temple would be destroyed, as Psalm 79 attests, and David's house with it, as Psalm 89 laments. Yet from those ruins, the Temple had now been rebuilt, and the chronicler rejoiced in the Davidic era of God's grace, which still continued. One element was missing: a restored house of David. Spiritual logic required that it would be only a matter of time before that, too, occurred. The perpetuity of vv. 12 and 14 was God's pledge.

17:16-19. David's response of prayer closely reflects the source, 2 Sam 7:18-29. The chronicler's version falls into two parts, vv. 16-22 and 23-27. The second part is introduced by "And now," which indicates a transition to the main part of the prayer, just as in the prophetic oracle at v. 7. The first part is devoted to thanksgiving. There is a convention in the OT that a person endowed with a divine revelation and mission responds in tones disparaging to oneself and one's family. Moses did so in Exod 3:11 ("Who am I . . . ?"), and so did Gideon in Judg 6:11. David continues this healthy tradition (see 1 Sam 8:18). Here the prayer strikes a note of surprise at God's gracious initiative, both in advancing David's career thus far, as the oracle had mentioned in vv. 7-8*a*, and in making the dynastic promise of vv. 10*b*-14. David's heart is too full for words, but God could read his gratitude there (v. 18). The "great thing" the Lord had done (v. 19), as the continuation

113. For the slight change in 17:11, "one of your own sons" in place of "[one] who will come from your own body" (2 Sam 7:12 NIV), see H. G. M. Williamson, "The Dynastic Oracle in the Books of Chronicles," *I. L. Seeligmann Volume*, ed. A. Rofé and Y. Zakovitch (Jerusalem: Rubinstein, 1983) 305-9.

114. See H. G. M. Williamson, *1 and 2 Chronicles*, NCB (Grand Rapids: Eerdmans, 1982) 135-36.

explains, is the revelation of God's great promise of a dynasty.

17:20-22. The thanksgiving moves into general praise, rehearsing the past work of God on Israel's behalf, which religious tradition had handed down, and deducing from it a conviction of the Lord's uniqueness. Redemption from Egypt (cf. v. 5) and divinely aided entry into the promised land were evidence of God's praiseworthiness. Associated with such crucial demonstrations of grace was the covenant bonding of God and people. The *forever*ness of the Mosaic covenant strikes a late, deuteronomistic note (cf. Deut 4:30-31; 30:4-6), which for the chronicler was taken up and confirmed in the Davidic covenant.

17:23-24. The second half of the prayer moves from thanksgiving to petition. Nathan has initially encouraged the king to do what he had in mind (v. 2), and David would have been glad to do so. Now he bows to God's better will: "Do as you [have] promised." David adds his amen to the Lord's revelation. Behind the verb "be established," used three times, is the verb יאמן (*yē'āmēn*). He prays that God will keep the promises about himself (vv. 8-10*a*) and the ensuing dynasty (vv. 10*b*-14). For the promises to come true, the Lord's help was necessary. And such help would redound to continuing and greater praise.

17:25-27. The dynastic promise becomes the closing focus. David would never have dared invent such a pretentious-sounding petition. Two present factors (v. 26, "now," NRSV; v. 27, "Now," NIV) encourage David to envision its fulfillment. The first is the oracular promise made by God through Nathan. The second factor is the blessing already experienced by the royal house (cf. chap. 14), a guarantee that it would, indeed, enjoy God's perennial favor.[115] The Lord had already blessed it, and so "it will be blessed forever" (NIV, similarly REB; see NRSV note). The chronicler alters slightly the ending in the prayer in 2 Samuel 7 so that cognizance may be taken of the previous establishment of David's kingship (1 Chr 14:2). God had laid a good foundation, as the oracle itself observed in vv. 7-8*a*. The chronicler draws a little tighter the threads between the prayer, the oracle, and the preceding narrative.

Oracle and prayer fit the chronicler's purposes well. The oracle announces the divine program for David and Solomon and establishes the once-for-all character of their reigns for the future of God's people. For the deuteronomist, the theology of grace fits imperfectly a historical context of failure and exile. From the chronicler's post-exilic perspective it could be embraced afresh as grounds of hope for a partially restored people.

Accordingly, mention of the exodus and entry into the land of promise in David's prayer (v. 21) becomes a swan song for the old Mosaic era. Divine revelation had taken a dynamic step forward. Just as David looked back to the exodus and the Mosaic covenant, so also thereafter Israel should look back to the Davidic covenant and its establishment by Solomon. It subsumed the best of what had gone before, but marked a real and irreversible advance. The prayer of 2 Sam 7:24, paralleled here in v. 22, speaks of the Mosaic covenant as revealing the triumph of divine grace and so is everlasting like the patriarchal covenant. The chronicler took over this concept, but would have explained it differently, in the light of chap. 16. He saw in God's relationship with Israel a reflection of the promise of perpetuity associated with the Davidic dynasty. This promise, celebrated in vv. 12, 14, 23, and 27 (cf. v. 13), resumed God's everlasting "[steadfast] love" in 16:24, 41, which itself echoed the "everlasting covenant" with the patriarchs in 16:17.

One might be surprised that there is no mention of the Temple in David's response. While it is possible to explain this lack in 2 Samuel 7 as a pre-redactional phenomenon, it is significant that the chronicler did not add such a reference, though he had augmented the allusion to the Temple in the oracle. Many scholars view David's and Solomon's kingship as a means to an end in the chronicler's thought, a step toward the establishment of the Temple as the divinely authorized place of worship. Here, however, the Davidic dynasty stands in its own right. The chronicler intended his readers to add their own amen to David's, that in God's good time the Davidic house would be reestablished.

115. הואלת (*hô'altā*) is rendered "you have been pleased" in the NIV and as a precative perfect, "may it please you" in the NRSV. The context suggests a different sense, "you have begun." See Braun, *1 Chronicles,* 196, 199; BDB 384a.

REFLECTIONS

1. The chronicler took over without a qualm the discrepancy between the prophet's initial *yes* and later *no,* or rather *not yet.* It is reassuring to us less inspired humans that even a prophet apprehended God's will in stages. Nathan's general awareness that a temple should be built was correct, but he did not initially know when and by whom. God's servants in every age have experienced this slow progress in the right direction. Paul had a similar experience in seeking where to go on his first missionary journey (Acts 16:6-10). He wanted to go west to the Roman province of Asia, but found his way blocked by the Holy Spirit. He turned north to Bithynia, with the same result. He traveled west to the port of Troas and at last received clear guidance to catch a boat to Macedonia. In 1 Chronicles 17 and in Acts 16, guidance comes through a sincere desire to be led by God. In spite of our best intentions, we may sometimes be mistaken initially in perceiving what the Lord wants of us. We are to act boldly in accordance with what we believe to be God's purpose, putting that belief to the test even as we wait for clarification.

David was not to build the Temple, after all. A need was there, but it did not constitute a call, eager volunteer though he was. He might have been resentful that another was to do what he wanted to do. Unlike in 13:11, there is no outburst of anger at the overruling of his well-intentioned wishes. David's prayer shows that he accepted his different preparatory role. Here is the generous spirit of 1 Cor 3:6, "I planted the seed, Apollos watered it, but God made it grow" (NIV).

2. We encounter here for the first time the chronicler's emphasis that the earthly kingdom was a manifestation of the *kingdom of God.* Henceforth the truth that "the LORD reigns" (16:31) was to take on new meaning. God would rule in Israel through the Davidic throne. The chronicler seems to have regarded the eschatological kingdom of God (see Dan 7:14, 27; Obad 21; Mic 4:7; Zech 14:9) as having been inaugurated in Israel's past history. The end time had been anticipated in principle, in a historical manifestation that fostered hope that its consummation was no less certain. Readers of the New Testament are no strangers to the idea of a once-for-all revelation. It is not difficult to draw parallels between the new era of David and Solomon and the new age manifested in Christ. The manifestation of the eschatological kingdom of God was proclaimed in the ministry of Jesus (Luke 11:20; see also Luke 7:22; 17:21). In Christ we meet a new Son of God, heir of the royal promise and more besides. He has provided a spiritual temple, giving us access to God so that we may approach the throne of grace with confidence and through him offer sacrifices of praise (Heb 4:16; 13:15). He has established the kingdom of God in fact and in hope. We are in the process of receiving "a kingdom that cannot be shaken" (Heb 12:28).

3. A notable feature of David's prayer is the reflection of elements of the prophetic oracle. The term "servant" occurs twice in the oracle, in the messenger formula of 17:4 and 17:7. The term occurs no less than ten times in the prayer. David affirms his subordinate role in the divine program. A response of humility is made to the honor of stabilizing the land and to the privilege of founding a dynasty, firmly keeping down the peacock's feathers that the human heart loves to display. "All who exalt themselves will be humbled, and all who humble themselves will be exalted" (Matt 23:12 NRSV).

The plea for God to keep the promises relating to David and his dynasty (17:23) is grounded in human need. The divine commission could be carried out only with the Lord's help. Beyond necessary human endeavors there must be dependence on God to fulfill the promises. Prayer is a means by which believers may acknowledge their sense of weakness and ask for divine strength to accomplish the tasks they have been given.[116]

116. R. E. Clements, *In Spirit and in Truth: Insights from Biblical Prayers* (Atlanta: John Knox, 1985) 76-77, 79.

1 Chronicles 18:1–20:8, A Place for God's People

NIV

18 In the course of time, David defeated the Philistines and subdued them, and he took Gath and its surrounding villages from the control of the Philistines.

2David also defeated the Moabites, and they became subject to him and brought tribute.

3Moreover, David fought Hadadezer king of Zobah, as far as Hamath, when he went to establish his control along the Euphrates River. 4David captured a thousand of his chariots, seven thousand charioteers and twenty thousand foot soldiers. He hamstrung all but a hundred of the chariot horses.

5When the Arameans of Damascus came to help Hadadezer king of Zobah, David struck down twenty-two thousand of them. 6He put garrisons in the Aramean kingdom of Damascus, and the Arameans became subject to him and brought tribute. The LORD gave David victory everywhere he went.

7David took the gold shields carried by the officers of Hadadezer and brought them to Jerusalem. 8From Tebah[a] and Cun, towns that belonged to Hadadezer, David took a great quantity of bronze, which Solomon used to make the bronze Sea, the pillars and various bronze articles.

9When Tou king of Hamath heard that David had defeated the entire army of Hadadezer king of Zobah, 10he sent his son Hadoram to King David to greet him and congratulate him on his victory in battle over Hadadezer, who had been at war with Tou. Hadoram brought all kinds of articles of gold and silver and bronze.

11King David dedicated these articles to the LORD, as he had done with the silver and gold he had taken from all these nations: Edom and Moab, the Ammonites and the Philistines, and Amalek.

12Abishai son of Zeruiah struck down eighteen thousand Edomites in the Valley of Salt. 13He put garrisons in Edom, and all the Edomites became subject to David. The LORD gave David victory everywhere he went.

14David reigned over all Israel, doing what was just and right for all his people. 15Joab son of

[a]8 Hebrew *Tibhath,* a variant of *Tebah*

NRSV

18 Some time afterward, David attacked the Philistines and subdued them; he took Gath and its villages from the Philistines.

2He defeated Moab, and the Moabites became subject to David and brought tribute.

3David also struck down King Hadadezer of Zobah, toward Hamath,[a] as he went to set up a monument at the river Euphrates. 4David took from him one thousand chariots, seven thousand cavalry, and twenty thousand foot soldiers. David hamstrung all the chariot horses, but left one hundred of them. 5When the Arameans of Damascus came to help King Hadadezer of Zobah, David killed twenty-two thousand Arameans. 6Then David put garrisons[b] in Aram of Damascus; and the Arameans became subject to David, and brought tribute. The LORD gave victory to David wherever he went. 7David took the gold shields that were carried by the servants of Hadadezer, and brought them to Jerusalem. 8From Tibhath and from Cun, cities of Hadadezer, David took a vast quantity of bronze; with it Solomon made the bronze sea and the pillars and the vessels of bronze.

9When King Tou of Hamath heard that David had defeated the whole army of King Hadadezer of Zobah, 10he sent his son Hadoram to King David, to greet him and to congratulate him, because he had fought against Hadadezer and defeated him. Now Hadadezer had often been at war with Tou. He sent all sorts of articles of gold, of silver, and of bronze; 11these also King David dedicated to the LORD, together with the silver and gold that he had carried off from all the nations, from Edom, Moab, the Ammonites, the Philistines, and Amalek.

12Abishai son of Zeruiah killed eighteen thousand Edomites in the Valley of Salt. 13He put garrisons in Edom; and all the Edomites became subject to David. And the LORD gave victory to David wherever he went.

14So David reigned over all Israel; and he administered justice and equity to all his people. 15Joab son of Zeruiah was over the army;

[a] Meaning of Heb uncertain [b] Gk Vg 2 Sam 8.6 Compare Syr: Heb lacks *garrisons*

NIV

Zeruiah was over the army; Jehoshaphat son of Ahilud was recorder; 16Zadok son of Ahitub and Ahimelech[a] son of Abiathar were priests; Shavsha was secretary; 17Benaiah son of Jehoiada was over the Kerethites and Pelethites; and David's sons were chief officials at the king's side.

19 In the course of time, Nahash king of the Ammonites died, and his son succeeded him as king. 2David thought, "I will show kindness to Hanun son of Nahash, because his father showed kindness to me." So David sent a delegation to express his sympathy to Hanun concerning his father.

When David's men came to Hanun in the land of the Ammonites to express sympathy to him, 3the Ammonite nobles said to Hanun, "Do you think David is honoring your father by sending men to you to express sympathy? Haven't his men come to you to explore and spy out the country and overthrow it?" 4So Hanun seized David's men, shaved them, cut off their garments in the middle at the buttocks, and sent them away.

5When someone came and told David about the men, he sent messengers to meet them, for they were greatly humiliated. The king said, "Stay at Jericho till your beards have grown, and then come back."

6When the Ammonites realized that they had become a stench in David's nostrils, Hanun and the Ammonites sent a thousand talents[b] of silver to hire chariots and charioteers from Aram Naharaim,[c] Aram Maacah and Zobah. 7They hired thirty-two thousand chariots and charioteers, as well as the king of Maacah with his troops, who came and camped near Medeba, while the Ammonites were mustered from their towns and moved out for battle.

8On hearing this, David sent Joab out with the entire army of fighting men. 9The Ammonites came out and drew up in battle formation at the entrance to their city, while the kings who had come were by themselves in the open country.

10Joab saw that there were battle lines in front of him and behind him; so he selected some of the best troops in Israel and deployed them against the Arameans. 11He put the rest of the

a*16* Some Hebrew manuscripts, Vulgate and Syriac (see also 2 Samuel 8:17); most Hebrew manuscripts *Abimelech* b*6* That is, about 37 tons (about 34 metric tons) c*6* That is, Northwest Mesopotamia

NRSV

Jehoshaphat son of Ahilud was recorder; 16Zadok son of Ahitub and Ahimelech son of Abiathar were priests; Shavsha was secretary; 17Benaiah son of Jehoiada was over the Cherethites and the Pelethites; and David's sons were the chief officials in the service of the king.

19 Some time afterward, King Nahash of the Ammonites died, and his son succeeded him. 2David said, "I will deal loyally with Hanun son of Nahash, for his father dealt loyally with me." So David sent messengers to console him concerning his father. When David's servants came to Hanun in the land of the Ammonites, to console him, 3the officials of the Ammonites said to Hanun, "Do you think, because David has sent consolers to you, that he is honoring your father? Have not his servants come to you to search and to overthrow and to spy out the land?" 4So Hanun seized David's servants, shaved them, cut off their garments in the middle at their hips, and sent them away; 5and they departed. When David was told about the men, he sent messengers to them, for they felt greatly humiliated. The king said, "Remain at Jericho until your beards have grown, and then return."

6When the Ammonites saw that they had made themselves odious to David, Hanun and the Ammonites sent a thousand talents of silver to hire chariots and cavalry from Mesopotamia, from Aram-maacah and from Zobah. 7They hired thirty-two thousand chariots and the king of Maacah with his army, who came and camped before Medeba. And the Ammonites were mustered from their cities and came to battle. 8When David heard of it, he sent Joab and all the army of the warriors. 9The Ammonites came out and drew up in battle array at the entrance of the city, and the kings who had come were by themselves in the open country.

10When Joab saw that the line of battle was set against him both in front and in the rear, he chose some of the picked men of Israel and arrayed them against the Arameans; 11the rest of his troops he put in the charge of his brother Abishai, and they were arrayed against the Ammonites. 12He said, "If the Arameans are too strong for me, then you shall help me; but if the Ammonites are too strong for you, then I will help

NIV

men under the command of Abishai his brother, and they were deployed against the Ammonites. [12]Joab said, "If the Arameans are too strong for me, then you are to rescue me; but if the Ammonites are too strong for you, then I will rescue you. [13]Be strong and let us fight bravely for our people and the cities of our God. The LORD will do what is good in his sight."

[14]Then Joab and the troops with him advanced to fight the Arameans, and they fled before him. [15]When the Ammonites saw that the Arameans were fleeing, they too fled before his brother Abishai and went inside the city. So Joab went back to Jerusalem.

[16]After the Arameans saw that they had been routed by Israel, they sent messengers and had Arameans brought from beyond the River,[a] with Shophach the commander of Hadadezer's army leading them.

[17]When David was told of this, he gathered all Israel and crossed the Jordan; he advanced against them and formed his battle lines opposite them. David formed his lines to meet the Arameans in battle, and they fought against him. [18]But they fled before Israel, and David killed seven thousand of their charioteers and forty thousand of their foot soldiers. He also killed Shophach the commander of their army.

[19]When the vassals of Hadadezer saw that they had been defeated by Israel, they made peace with David and became subject to him.

So the Arameans were not willing to help the Ammonites anymore.

20 In the spring, at the time when kings go off to war, Joab led out the armed forces. He laid waste the land of the Ammonites and went to Rabbah and besieged it, but David remained in Jerusalem. Joab attacked Rabbah and left it in ruins. [2]David took the crown from the head of their king[b]—its weight was found to be a talent[c] of gold, and it was set with precious stones—and it was placed on David's head. He took a great quantity of plunder from the city [3]and brought out the people who were there, consigning them to labor with saws and with iron picks and axes. David did this to all the Ammonite

[a]*16* That is, the Euphrates [b]*2* Or *of Milcom,* that is, Molech [c]*2* That is, about 75 pounds (about 34 kilograms)

NRSV

you. [13]Be strong, and let us be courageous for our people and for the cities of our God; and may the LORD do what seems good to him." [14]So Joab and the troops who were with him advanced toward the Arameans for battle; and they fled before him. [15]When the Ammonites saw that the Arameans fled, they likewise fled before Abishai, Joab's brother, and entered the city. Then Joab came to Jerusalem.

16But when the Arameans saw that they had been defeated by Israel, they sent messengers and brought out the Arameans who were beyond the Euphrates, with Shophach the commander of the army of Hadadezer at their head. [17]When David was informed, he gathered all Israel together, crossed the Jordan, came to them, and drew up his forces against them. When David set the battle in array against the Arameans, they fought with him. [18]The Arameans fled before Israel; and David killed seven thousand Aramean charioteers and forty thousand foot soldiers, and also killed Shophach the commander of their army. [19]When the servants of Hadadezer saw that they had been defeated by Israel, they made peace with David, and became subject to him. So the Arameans were not willing to help the Ammonites any more.

20 In the spring of the year, the time when kings go out to battle, Joab led out the army, ravaged the country of the Ammonites, and came and besieged Rabbah. But David remained at Jerusalem. Joab attacked Rabbah, and overthrew it. [2]David took the crown of Milcom[a] from his head; he found that it weighed a talent of gold, and in it was a precious stone; and it was placed on David's head. He also brought out the booty of the city, a very great amount. [3]He brought out the people who were in it, and set them to work[b] with saws and iron picks and axes.[c] Thus David did to all the cities of the Ammonites. Then David and all the people returned to Jerusalem.

4After this, war broke out with the Philistines at Gezer; then Sibbecai the Hushathite killed Sippai, who was one of the descendants of the giants; and the Philistines were subdued. [5]Again there was war with the Philistines; and Elhanan

[a] Gk Vg See 1 Kings 11.5, 33: MT *of their king* [b] Compare 2 Sam 12.31: Heb *and he sawed* [c] Compare 2 Sam 12.31: Heb *saws*

NIV

towns. Then David and his entire army returned
to Jerusalem.
4In the course of time, war broke out with the
Philistines, at Gezer. At that time Sibbecai the
Hushathite killed Sippai, one of the descendants
of the Rephaites, and the Philistines were
subjugated.
5In another battle with the Philistines, Elhanan
son of Jair killed Lahmi the brother of Goliath the
Gittite, who had a spear with a shaft like a
weaver's rod.
6In still another battle, which took place at
Gath, there was a huge man with six fingers on
each hand and six toes on each foot—twenty-four
in all. He also was descended from Rapha. 7When
he taunted Israel, Jonathan son of Shimea, David's
brother, killed him.
8These were descendants of Rapha in Gath, and
they fell at the hands of David and his men.

NRSV

son of Jair killed Lahmi the brother of Goliath the
Gittite, the shaft of whose spear was like a
weaver's beam. 6Again there was war at Gath,
where there was a man of great size, who had
six fingers on each hand, and six toes on each
foot, twenty-four in number; he also was descended from the giants. 7When he taunted Israel,
Jonathan son of Shimea, David's brother, killed
him. 8These were descended from the giants in
Gath; they fell by the hand of David and his
servants.

COMMENTARY

This long passage develops the Davidic part of the divine program, laid down in 17:8*b*-10*a,* the promise that the Lord "will subdue all" David's "enemies" (17:10). This verb becomes a key word in the section. It is repeated in 18:1 from 2 Sam 8:1: David "subdued" (יכניעם *yaknî'ēm*) The Philistines. The chronicler also worked it into the final narrative at 20:4: The Philistines "were subdued" (NRSV). Another structural marker is present at both the beginning and the end of the present passage. We have to turn to the KJV, however, to find it. In 18:1, David takes the Philistine city of Gath and its villages "out of *the hand* of the Philistines." In 20:8, the Philistine giants "fell by *the hand* of David and by *the hand* of his servants." This rhetorical framework expresses well the loss of Philistine control and its passing to David. Both the first paragraph (18:1) and the final, longer one (20:4-8) relate to the Philistines as archetypal enemies of Israel. They were the ones who defeated Saul and the Israelite army. Now the tide turns. Where there was once divinely instigated failure, there is now God-given victory. The Philistines, who had sought to conquer the Israelite interior (chap. 14) and were defeated, lose control of some of their own territory. God, through David, is providing a place for the covenant people and putting an end to external oppression (17:9).

The sequence of subunits within chaps. 18–20 is indicated structurally by a common opening formula. The NIV reproduces the repeated Hebrew phrase as "In the course of time" in 18:1; 19:1; and 20:4. These three initial markers indicate separate blocks of material taken over from 2 Samuel. First Chronicles 18:1-17 comes from 2 Sam 8:1-18; 1 Chr 19:1–20:3 from 2 Sam 10:1–11:1; 1 Chr 12:26, 30-31; and 20:4-8 from 2 Sam 21:18-22. The chronicler has selected three blocks from 2 Samuel dealing with military victories, which provided him with a set of initial markers. The combination of material from 2 Samuel 8 and 21 also furnished him with the framework for the transfer of power from the Philistines to David. As for 1 Chr 20:4-8, one might ask why the chronicler did not include 2 Sam 21:15-17. The chronicler's eye lighted on the introductory phrase in 2 Sam 21:18. His desire for structural symmetry committed him to beginning the last of his three subunits at that point, which became 2 Chr 20:4.

Mention may also be made of a pervasive and appropriate key word in the passage, the verb הכה (*hikkâ*, in the hiphil), which occurs seven times in chap. 18 (vv. 1, 2, 3, 5, 9, 10, 12), once in 19:1–20:3 (20:1), and three times in 20:4-8 (vv. 4, 5, 7). It has a wide range of meanings, such as "attack," "defeat," and "kill." The useful archaic verb "smite" allowed the KJV closer reproduction of this drumbeat of doom for Israel's enemies. Apart from 18:10, the Hebrew verb supplies a marker for the separate military episodes.

The chronicler vigorously ransacked 2 Samuel for material relating to David's military victories and, as a result of this single-mindedness, refrained from using a lot of other material in 2 Samuel. In particular he pruned 2 Samuel 10–12 of David's affair with Bathsheba and murder of her husband. One can hardly accuse the chronicler of tendentiously cutting out conduct unbefitting the gentleman he wanted David to be; he fully acknowledges David's sin over the census in chap. 21. The difference is that it fits the chronicler's emphasis on the Temple.

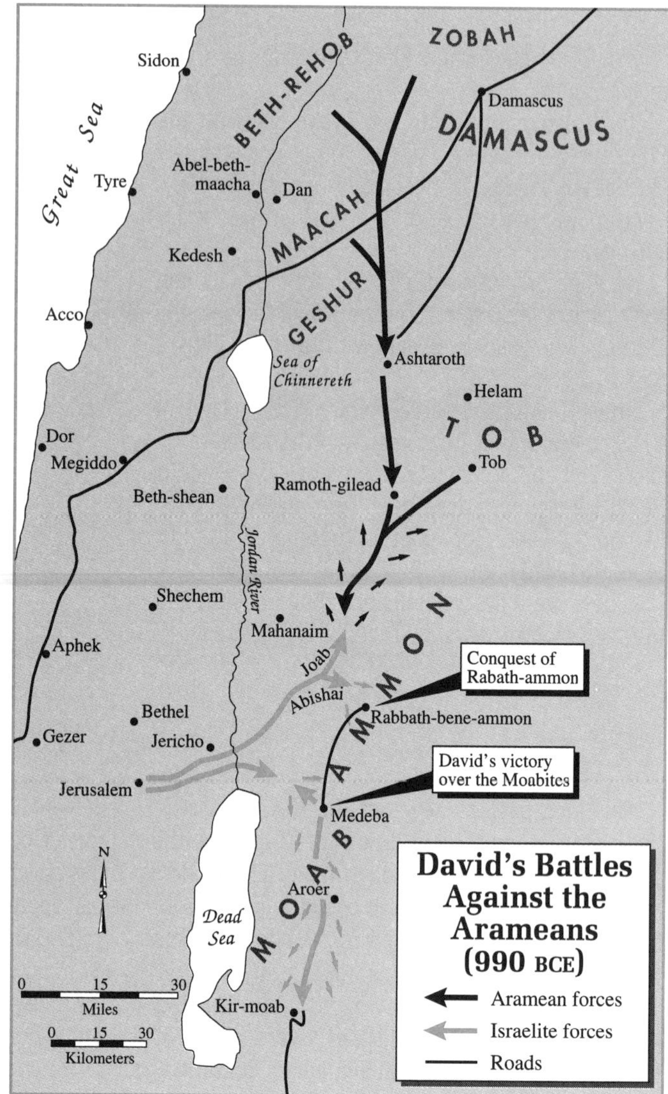

The series of victories (18:1-12) already had in 2 Samuel 8 an all-encompassing character. The victories fan out in all directions. The Philistines were subdued to the west, Moab to the east, Hadadezer of Zobah to the north (and in the far north Tou of Hamath became an ally), and in the south Edom was defeated. Second Samuel 8 presents a spectrum of victory throughout the land, and it fit the chronicler's own purposes to take it over. In fulfilling the pre-temple program, David was pushing out to the ideal limits of the land expressed in 13:5.

18:1-6. A number of battle reports are presented. In the defeat of the Philistines (v. 1) the capture of "Gath and its villages" is pinpointed. The corresponding phrase in 2 Sam 8:1, "Metheg-ammah," is obscure. In order to make sense out of this dubious text, the chronicler was probably influenced by the occurrence of Gath in 2 Sam 21:20, 22 (= 1 Chr 20:6, 8). Transposition of the last two Hebrew consonants of "Metheg" (מתג *mtg*) produced "Gath" (גת *gt*). In turn, אמה (*'ammâ*) suggested to him a mother city, and so "daughter settlements," as the Hebrew term for "villages" may be more literally rendered.

The executions meted out to the Moabite army (2 Sam 8:2) are not reproduced here, perhaps simply for the sake of brevity.[117] The Moabite campaign is the first of a series of victorious battles waged in the Transjordan, which the chronicler

117. S. L. McKenzie, *The Chronicler's Use of the Deuteronomistic History*, HSM 33 (Atlanta: Scholars Press, 1985) 64, suggests simply a textual oversight. He is probably correct in considering idealization of David an unlikely cause for the omission.

narrates according to the sequence in 2 Samuel, before he comes full circle to fresh Philistine episodes in 20:4-8.

Zobah was the strongest of the Aramean states in David's period, and David was a threat to their sphere of power in the north Transjordan, just as he was to the Philistines in the west. The chronicler was not responsible for the increase of military numbers of v. 4. The LXX of 2 Sam 8:4 and, probably, 4QSam^a have the same reading.

The series of battle reports is brought to a close in v. 6*b* with a statement attributing such victories to the Lord. This generalizing conclusion will recur at the end of the next series, in v. 13*b*. These refrains were gladly reproduced by our historian, since they fit his reports about God subduing David's enemies and then David doing so himself (v. 1; 17:10; see also 20:4). The divine program relating to David's battles was being realized, as God crowned all his campaigns with blessing.

18:7-11. The spoils of war and related tribute are now the topic. The city of "Berothai" in 2 Sam 8:8 is replaced in v. 8*a* with "Cun," perhaps a place better known to post-exilic readers. Verse 8*b* represents an addition to the MT of 2 Samuel. The text 4QSam^a is not extant at this point, but the addition is present in the LXX of 2 Samuel, possibly by assimilation to the text of Chronicles. Whether the chronicler found it or added it, it suits his overall theme from chap. 17, in pointing to the Solomonic Temple on the horizon of his thought (see 2 Chr 4:12, 15-16). The gifts of metals from Tou of Hamath and similar spoils from the campaigns are "dedicated to the LORD," as an acknowledgment that the glory should go to David's patron. The dedication corresponds in placing and purport to the refrain of God's help in vv. 6 and 12. Within 1 Chronicles the dedication is picked up in 26:26 and then in 2 Chr 5:1 (= 1 Kgs 7:51). Verses 8*b* and 11 anticipate the theme of David's preparations for the Temple, to be announced in 22:5.

18:12-13. A second, shorter battle report is supplied, followed by a refrain that gives the Lord credit for the victories. There is a lack of concord between v. 12 and v. 13*a*. In the latter verse, David is the subject, and one expects him to be so in v. 12, as in the parallel 2 Sam 8:13. But Abishai appears in v. 12. Perhaps Abishai's victory was regarded the same as David's, like the killing of the giants in 1 Chr 20:4-8. The heading to Psalm 60 attributes the slaughter to Joab, another son of Zeruiah. So both the MT of 2 Samuel and the text of 1 Chronicles may have preserved different parts of a longer narrative.[118] The initial clause in 2 Sam 8:13, concerning David's making a name for himself, is not included. It would have accorded with 17:8. The fact that David is the subject here, while the Lord is the subject there, may have encouraged its omission.

18:14-17. The chronicler continues to use the 2 Samuel text, describing the stability enjoyed by "all Israel" as a result of David's military successes. The secure place God was to create through David is now realized. The terms "Israel" and "people" in v. 14 are links with 17:9. The list of members of the royal administration in vv. 15-17*a* exhibits a chiastic order of military/civilian/religious/civilian/military leadership.[119] The bureau provides yet another indication that David's kingdom has been set on a firm footing. His imperial reign, marked by "justice," constitutes the inauguration of the kingdom in which the Lord will come to judge the earth (16:31-33).

In v. 16, the NRSV and the NIV, in place of the MT's "Abimelech," have followed a minority reading, "Ahimelech," as the name of the second priest, which accords with 2 Sam 8:17. The reconstructed reading underlying both texts may have been "Abiathar son of Ahimelech" (Ahitub may have been the grandfather of Abiathar).[120] But the chronicler knows nothing of this (see 6:12; the REB's "Zadok and Abiathar son of Ahimelech, son of Ahitub" represents a hypercorrection in which historical reconstruction has triumphed over respect for the text of Chronicles). David's sons are called "priests" in 2 Sam 8:19, and the change is generally credited to the chronicler's reluctance, in a post-exilic context, to envision any priesthood other than the Aaronic one.[121] Verses 15-17 have

118. McCarter, *II Samuel,* 246.

119. S. J. De Vries, *1 and 2 Chronicles,* FOTL 11 (Grand Rapids: Eerdmans, 1989) 162.

120. See the discussion in McCarter, *II Samuel,* 253-54.

121. Armerding has observed that Israel knew of several orders of priesthood, citing 2 Sam 20:26; 1 Kgs 4:5. See C. E. Armerding, "Were David's Sons Really Priests?" in *Current Issues in Biblical and Patristic Interpretation,* ed. G. F. Hawthorne (Grand Rapids: Eerdmans, 1975) 75-86. Alternatively, Wenham has suggested that the chronicler has paraphrased a term for administrators of royal estates, סכנים (*sknym*), found in his text of 2 Samuel, which was subsequently corrupted to כהנים (*khnym*), "priests." See G. J. Wenham, "Were David's Sons Priests?" *ZAW* 87 (1975) 79-82.

a new, prospective role. They reintroduce readers to Joab, who is to play a prominent role in the next three chapters. In referring to the priests Zadok and Ahimelech, the verses anticipate David's organization of temple personnel with their help (24:3, 6, 31).

19:1–20:3. The narrative, like that in 2 Samuel but to a much lesser extent, functions as an extended note, explaining the defeat of Ammon, briefly mentioned in 18:11. It also supplies further information on the defeat of Hadadezer, covered in 18:3-4. The narrative has been pruned of the complication of David's adultery and murder in 2 Samuel; otherwise, it follows that text by and large. It tells of the new Ammonite king's provocation of David (19:1-5) and both sides' preparations for battle (19:6-13), reports the defeat of the Aramean mercenary troops and withdrawal of the Ammonite army to the capital (19:14-19), and reports the next season's victorious campaign (20:1-3). The chronicler must have appreciated the way 19:11 mentions "all Israel" as being conscripted to fight under David, an echo for him of the concerted campaign against Jerusalem in 11:4-6. He would also have liked the fresh affirmation in 19:13 that, when victory comes, God is the giver. Both Israelite companies were to do their best and leave the rest to the Lord, who "will do [rather than "may the Lord do," NRSV] what is good in his sight" (NIV). A greater role is given to David in a few places. He takes the initiative in 19:17*b,* over against 2 Sam 10:17*b,* and in 19:19 peace is made with him, not with Israel, as in 2 Sam 10:19. On the other hand, in 20:1 the 2 Samuel text has been roughly condensed, and Joab's concern to give David the glory by capturing Rabbah in 2 Sam 12:27-30 has been dropped.

In 19:6-7 there are a few differences from the MT of 2 Samuel. The chronicler's reference to "Mesopotamia" in place of "Beth-Rehob" in 2 Sam 10:6 probably reflects a later readership's unfamiliarity with that Aramean state, and so does the dropping of "the men of Tob." The sum of 1,000 talents of silver in 19:6 is not an embellishment by the chronicler. It also occurs in 4QSam[a] and so was shared by the chronicler's 2 Samuel text. Apparently 4QSam[a] also read "thirty-two thousand chariots," which explains its presence in 19:7, over against 2 Sam 10:6. The final sentence in 19:7, absent from the MT of 2 Sam 10:7, also occurs in 4QSam[a], though in a slightly different form. The penultimate Hebrew sentence in 19:7 ("who . . . Medeba"), which does not occur in 4QSam[a], presents a logistical problem. Moabite Medeba is too far to the south to permit the reciprocal emergency arrangements envisioned in 19:12 for the two obviously adjacent Israelite companies. An underlying מי רבה (*my rbh*), "waters of Rabbah," has been conjectured for מידבא (*mydb'*) with reference to 2 Sam 12:27.[122]

In 19:19 the "servants" (NRSV) of Hadadezer are his "vassals" (NIV), the junior Aramean kings who had committed their armies to the enterprise (cf. 2 Sam 10:19). With their capitulation only the Ammonite sector had still to be overcome, which duly takes place in 20:1. The English versions attest the ambiguity of the consonantal Hebrew text in 20:2. Was it the crown of "their king" (מלכם *malkām*, NIV) or of "Milcom" (מלכם *milkōm*, NRSV), the Ammmonite god in iconic form? In 20:3 both versions emend the verb of sawing to one of setting or consigning to work, in line with 2 Sam 12:31. However, the MT may refer, not to a gruesome act of cruelty, but to dismantling fortifications.[123]

20:4-8. The narrative returns to the Philistines. They are the A and Z of opposition to God's people, who typically needed to be "subdued," as representatives of all of David's enemies (17:10). These agents of defeat in chap. 10 now meet their match. Whereas Saul lost, David won and won again. Power passed from Israel's enemies to David and his troops (18:1; 20:8).

Three Israelite exploits against aboriginal "giants" (NRSV) or "Rephaim" (REB) who were allied with the Philistines are recounted. The perpetrators of these exploits are assumed in v. 8*b* (as in the parallel 2 Sam 21:22) to be soldiers in David's service, though he was not personally involved. "Gezer" in v. 4 corresponds to "Gob" in 2 Sam 21:18. Whatever the reason for the variant, in the overall narrative of Chronicles it nicely picks up where the campaign against the Philistines in 14:16 left off.[124] Verse 5 appears to

122. W. Rudolph, *Chronikbücher,* HAT 1:21 (Tübingen: Mohr [Siebeck], 1955) 137, following Rothstein and *BHS.*

123. McCarter, *II Samuel,* 313.

124. McCarter considers the 1 Chronicles reading superior and the MT of 2 Samuel the product of assimilation to the city in 2 Sam 21:19. See K. McCarter, *II Samuel,* 448.

be the result of an exegetical crux that confronted the chronicler, a crux that presupposes knowledge of 1 Samuel 17 (cf. 11:23). Who killed Goliath: Elhanan (2 Sam 21:19) or David (1 Samuel 17)? The chronicler may have been making the best of a corrupt text (בית-הלחמי [*bêt-hallaḥmî*, "the Bethlehemite"] is represented as את-לחמי [*'et-laḥmî*], now the slain giant's name, and the sign of the direct object את [*'ēt*] has become אחי [*'ăḥî*, "brother of"]). However, the reconciliation of rival traditions seems to have played a part in the history of this text.

These territorial victories gave Israel room to dwell in all directions. There were also respectful overtures from Tou, king of Hamath, who is Huram of Tyre all over again (14:1). David's fame was, indeed, going out into all lands (14:17). The chronicler finds here evidence of God's immediate purpose: to give Israel a secure place, free of the oppression that has dogged them since the days of the Judges (17:9-10*a*). It was part of the Lord's overall plan, which required a peaceful setting for the building of the Temple, which in turn would guarantee the continuance of the Davidic dynasty (17:10*b*-14). The goal of the Temple has received some minor attention in 18:8 and, implicitly, in 18:11.

The forward-looking prayer in 16:35, "Save us from the nations," which fuses historical and contemporary concerns, raises the issue of an implicit eschatological agenda in these chapters, according to which David won victories over "all the nations" (18:11 NRSV). Judah's territorial weakness in the post-exilic period must have filled the chronicler's first readers with nostalgia. The relish with which he narrates royal victories suggests that this victorious past was intended to point toward Israel's own future.

REFLECTIONS

1. A triangle dominates Old Testament theology: the Lord, Israel, and the land. In the New Testament, the issue of the land falls away. The Old Testament promise of the land as Abraham's inheritance is transformed into the world in Rom 4:13 and into a heavenly country in Heb 11:16. Moreover, prophetic and apocalyptic talk of warfare largely gives way to a sublimated and spiritualized form of cosmic struggle, which occasions impressive imagery for the development of Christian virtues, as Eph 6:10-17 illustrates. Perhaps we modern readers need a stronger sense of the supernatural conflict of which the later chapters of Daniel and such New Testament writings as Ephesians are so conscious in order to draw a fair typological parallel with the chronicler's concerns.

His portrayal of the warrior king fighting at God's behest and with God's help was associated with the inauguration of a new age. There is a close spiritual rapport at this point between 1 Chronicles and the Letter to the Colossians. God has rescued us believers (1 Chr 16:35 NRSV) from the power of darkness and transferred us into the kingdom of Christ (Col 1:13; cf. 1 Chr 10:14). Peace has been won through the cross (Col 1:19). Christ has triumphed, disarming hostile powers (Col 2:15).

The chronicler lived in an age much less glorious than David's. While desiring eschatological fulfillment, the chronicler seems to have perceived that it would not be manifested soon. Yet, he wished his readers to sense that they were on God's side and identified with a cause that would ultimately enjoy victory. Likewise, the Christian affirmation that "we are more than conquerors" was spoken in defiance of present tribulation (Rom 8:35, 37).

The New Testament speaks of the Christian life in tones agreeable to the pacifism, implicit or radical, of modern Christians. It must not be forgotten, however, that Christianity also directly inherits the theme of eschatological warfare from the Old Testament and intertestamental writings. The theological sublimation of an inaugurated eschatology, expressed in the once-for-all achievement of Christ and the ongoing struggle of Christians in an alien universe, does not exclude a coming showdown. The old language of military violence is dramatically revived for this event (see 2 Thess 1:7-9; 2:8; Rev 19; 20:7-9).

2. The section glides easily from God's subduing of David's enemies to David's doing it himself, and back again (17:10; 18:1; 20:4). The chronicler borrows from the description of the king's victories in 2 Samuel 8 the conviction that they were the gifts of the Lord (18:6, 13). He both borrows and enhances David's own desire to give God the credit (18:8, 11). In the same vein, Paul, returning from his third missionary trip, reported to the church leaders in Jerusalem "what God had done . . . through his ministry," and the hearers "praised God" (Acts 21:19-20). Both David and Paul were God's responsible agents in their different spheres. There is an exaggerated type of spirituality that makes God big by making humans small, urging them to be nothing so that God may be everything. David and Paul were individuals with their own identities, which they used for God even as God was using them.

3. Just as the verb of subduing has both divine and human subjects, so also human and divine factors are coordinated in Joab's battle speech (19:12-13). Each has its place, as in the not insincere summons to "put your trust in God and keep your powder dry." One human factor through which the Lord worked was mutual help. The motif of human help is reminiscent of chaps. 11–12, where it is associated with God's own help. Here it makes use of proven ability, in the sphere of shrewd military tactics. The second factor is sheer courage, the grit that is necessary to pursue doggedly an endeavor to its close. The third is loyal commitment to those for whom one is laboring and to God ("our people," "our God"). The expression of the divine factor conveys a calm sense of the Lord's sovereignty. Entrusting the venture to God releases us from crippling anxiety and enables us to do our best in God's service.

1 Chronicles 21:1–22:19, Temple Site and Builder Announced

OVERVIEW

Chapters 17–29 all relate to the Temple. The purpose of chap. 21 is to designate the site of the Temple, and of chap. 22 to specify Solomon as the son of David who will build it (cf. 17:11-12, 14). Solomon's name is mentioned in this connection for the first time. Both chapters use at their close the chronicler's key term for spirituality: "seek" (דרשׁ *dāraš*; 21:30; 22:19). In this new era, the Lord is to be sought in the Temple, which is about to be built in Jerusalem. Both chapters focus on human failure or weakness as a means of bringing glory to God and highlighting God's own role.

1 Chronicles 21:1–22:1, Discovery of the Site by Grace

NIV

21 Satan rose up against Israel and incited
David to take a census of Israel. [2]So David
said to Joab and the commanders of the troops,
"Go and count the Israelites from Beersheba to
Dan. Then report back to me so that I may know
how many there are."
[3]But Joab replied, "May the LORD multiply his
troops a hundred times over. My lord the king, are
they not all my lord's subjects? Why does my lord
want to do this? Why should he bring guilt on Israel?"

NRSV

21 Satan stood up against Israel, and incited
David to count the people of Israel. [2]So
David said to Joab and the commanders of the
army, "Go, number Israel, from Beer-sheba to
Dan, and bring me a report, so that I may know
their number." [3]But Joab said, "May the LORD
increase the number of his people a hundredfold!
Are they not, my lord the king, all of them my
lord's servants? Why then should my lord require
this? Why should he bring guilt on Israel?" [4]But

NIV

4The king's word, however, overruled Joab; so Joab left and went throughout Israel and then came back to Jerusalem. 5Joab reported the number of the fighting men to David: In all Israel there were one million one hundred thousand men who could handle a sword, including four hundred and seventy thousand in Judah.

6But Joab did not include Levi and Benjamin in the numbering, because the king's command was repulsive to him. 7This command was also evil in the sight of God; so he punished Israel.

8Then David said to God, "I have sinned greatly by doing this. Now, I beg you, take away the guilt of your servant. I have done a very foolish thing."

9The LORD said to Gad, David's seer, 10"Go and tell David, 'This is what the LORD says: I am giving you three options. Choose one of them for me to carry out against you.' "

11So Gad went to David and said to him, "This is what the LORD says: 'Take your choice: 12three years of famine, three months of being swept away[a] before your enemies, with their swords overtaking you, or three days of the sword of the LORD—days of plague in the land, with the angel of the LORD ravaging every part of Israel.' Now then, decide how I should answer the one who sent me."

13David said to Gad, "I am in deep distress. Let me fall into the hands of the LORD, for his mercy is very great; but do not let me fall into the hands of men."

14So the LORD sent a plague on Israel, and seventy thousand men of Israel fell dead. 15And God sent an angel to destroy Jerusalem. But as the angel was doing so, the LORD saw it and was grieved because of the calamity and said to the angel who was destroying the people, "Enough! Withdraw your hand." The angel of the LORD was then standing at the threshing floor of Araunah[b] the Jebusite.

16David looked up and saw the angel of the LORD standing between heaven and earth, with a drawn sword in his hand extended over Jerusalem. Then David and the elders, clothed in sackcloth, fell facedown.

17David said to God, "Was it not I who ordered the fighting men to be counted? I am the one who has sinned and done wrong. These are but

[a]*12* Hebrew; Septuagint and Vulgate (see also 2 Samuel 24:13) *of fleeing* [b]*15* Hebrew *Ornan,* a variant of *Araunah*; also in verses 18-28

NRSV

the king's word prevailed against Joab. So Joab departed and went throughout all Israel, and came back to Jerusalem. 5Joab gave the total count of the people to David. In all Israel there were one million one hundred thousand men who drew the sword, and in Judah four hundred seventy thousand who drew the sword. 6But he did not include Levi and Benjamin in the numbering, for the king's command was abhorrent to Joab.

7But God was displeased with this thing, and he struck Israel. 8David said to God, "I have sinned greatly in that I have done this thing. But now, I pray you, take away the guilt of your servant; for I have done very foolishly." 9The LORD spoke to Gad, David's seer, saying, 10"Go and say to David, 'Thus says the LORD: Three things I offer you; choose one of them, so that I may do it to you.' " 11So Gad came to David and said to him, "Thus says the LORD, 'Take your choice: 12either three years of famine; or three months of devastation by your foes, while the sword of your enemies overtakes you; or three days of the sword of the LORD, pestilence on the land, and the angel of the LORD destroying throughout all the territory of Israel.' Now decide what answer I shall return to the one who sent me." 13Then David said to Gad, "I am in great distress; let me fall into the hand of the LORD, for his mercy is very great; but let me not fall into human hands."

14So the LORD sent a pestilence on Israel; and seventy thousand persons fell in Israel. 15And God sent an angel to Jerusalem to destroy it; but when he was about to destroy it, the LORD took note and relented concerning the calamity; he said to the destroying angel, "Enough! Stay your hand." The angel of the LORD was then standing by the threshing floor of Ornan the Jebusite. 16David looked up and saw the angel of the LORD standing between earth and heaven, and in his hand a drawn sword stretched out over Jerusalem. Then David and the elders, clothed in sackcloth, fell on their faces. 17And David said to God, "Was it not I who gave the command to count the people? It is I who have sinned and done very wickedly. But these sheep, what have they done? Let your hand, I pray, O LORD my God, be against me and against my father's house; but do not let your people be plagued!"

NIV

sheep. What have they done? O LORD my God, let your hand fall upon me and my family, but do not let this plague remain on your people."

18Then the angel of the LORD ordered Gad to tell David to go up and build an altar to the LORD on the threshing floor of Araunah the Jebusite.
19So David went up in obedience to the word that Gad had spoken in the name of the LORD.

20While Araunah was threshing wheat, he turned and saw the angel; his four sons who were with him hid themselves. 21Then David approached, and when Araunah looked and saw him, he left the threshing floor and bowed down before David with his face to the ground.

22David said to him, "Let me have the site of your threshing floor so I can build an altar to the LORD, that the plague on the people may be stopped. Sell it to me at the full price."

23Araunah said to David, "Take it! Let my lord the king do whatever pleases him. Look, I will give the oxen for the burnt offerings, the threshing sledges for the wood, and the wheat for the grain offering. I will give all this."

24But King David replied to Araunah, "No, I insist on paying the full price. I will not take for the LORD what is yours, or sacrifice a burnt offering that costs me nothing."

25So David paid Araunah six hundred shekels[a] of gold for the site. 26David built an altar to the LORD there and sacrificed burnt offerings and fellowship offerings.[b] He called on the LORD, and the LORD answered him with fire from heaven on the altar of burnt offering.

27Then the LORD spoke to the angel, and he put his sword back into its sheath. 28At that time, when David saw that the LORD had answered him on the threshing floor of Araunah the Jebusite, he offered sacrifices there. 29The tabernacle of the LORD, which Moses had made in the desert, and the altar of burnt offering were at that time on the high place at Gibeon. 30But David could not go before it to inquire of God, because he was afraid of the sword of the angel of the LORD.

22 Then David said, "The house of the LORD God is to be here, and also the altar of burnt offering for Israel."

[a]25 That is, about 15 pounds (about 7 kilograms) [b]26 Traditionally *peace offerings*

NRSV

18Then the angel of the LORD commanded Gad to tell David that he should go up and erect an altar to the LORD on the threshing floor of Ornan the Jebusite. 19So David went up following Gad's instructions, which he had spoken in the name of the LORD. 20Ornan turned and saw the angel; and while his four sons who were with him hid themselves, Ornan continued to thresh wheat.
21As David came to Ornan, Ornan looked and saw David; he went out from the threshing floor, and did obeisance to David with his face to the ground. 22David said to Ornan, "Give me the site of the threshing floor that I may build on it an altar to the LORD—give it to me at its full price—so that the plague may be averted from the people." 23Then Ornan said to David, "Take it; and let my lord the king do what seems good to him; see, I present the oxen for burnt offerings, and the threshing sledges for the wood, and the wheat for a grain offering. I give it all." 24But King David said to Ornan, "No; I will buy them for the full price. I will not take for the LORD what is yours, nor offer burnt offerings that cost me nothing." 25So David paid Ornan six hundred shekels of gold by weight for the site. 26David built there an altar to the LORD and presented burnt offerings and offerings of well-being. He called upon the LORD, and he answered him with fire from heaven on the altar of burnt offering.
27Then the LORD commanded the angel, and he put his sword back into its sheath.

28At that time, when David saw that the LORD had answered him at the threshing floor of Ornan the Jebusite, he made his sacrifices there. 29For the tabernacle of the LORD, which Moses had made in the wilderness, and the altar of burnt offering were at that time in the high place at Gibeon; 30but David could not go before it to inquire of God, for he was afraid of the sword of the angel of the LORD.

22 1Then David said, "Here shall be the house of the LORD God and here the altar of burnt offering for Israel."

COMMENTARY

The climax of this episode comes in 22:1: the announcement of the site chosen by God for the future Temple, where Israel was to worship the Lord. For the chronicler and his post-exilic readers, it was a story full of spiritual relevance. It laid the foundation for their own worship of God in the Second Temple on the same site. Incongruously, it seems at first, the discovery was the result of a shameful act of presumption, narrated in chap. 21. Yet the very association of human sin with the Temple will turn out to be crucial for the chronicler's concept of spirituality.

The chronicler is sometimes accused of triumphalism and idealism in his depiction of David. He passed over the Bathsheba affair and the Uriah cover-up, narrated in 2 Samuel 11–12, which in 1 Chronicles is telescoped into a single, blame-free verse (20:1). That criticism is hardly fair. Those chapters in 2 Samuel belong to narrative about the royal succession and were designed to show that the Davidic dynasty was rooted in divine grace that overcame human sinfulness. As for the succession, the chronicler's interests in the dynasty were better served, he judged, by concentrating on the outcome, the passing of the crown to Solomon. The temple-building project was a major concern for the chronicler, and he wanted to establish from the outset its grounding in divine grace, the "mercy" of God, which is "very great" (21:13). At one point in the narrative, he departs from the basic text of 2 Samuel 24 and inserts a clause borrowed from the Bathsheba episode, "But God was displeased with this thing" (21:7 NRSV), in the Hebrew a virtual copy of 2 Sam 11:27*b*. The chronicler's awareness of Bathsheba is shown by 3:5, where she is called Bathshua. The echo in 21:7 is tantamount to saying that in his estimation this was an equivalent story. His David, too, had feet of clay. The chronicler wanted to affirm, in principle, that the Temple afforded the opportunity for the forgiveness of sins not only in David's case, but also for all the people of God during the centuries-long dispensation launched under David and Solomon (cf. 2 Chr 7:14-16).

The original story in 2 Samuel 24 reflected the conviction that the altar built at the threshing floor was the altar of burnt offering at the Temple. The story implicitly looked beyond David's reign to Solomon's building of the Temple.[125] The chronicler makes this conviction his own in the interpretive conclusion he adds at 22:1. His version of the story depends heavily on literary flashbacks. David's transgression in having taken a military census is narrated straightforwardly in 21:1-6; 21:7 is a summary statement of consequent divine punishment, which is explained in 21:8-14, with 21:14 eventually catching up with 21:7*b*. Another summary is found in 21:15*a*, now about God's relenting, which is told in 21:15*b*-27, with 21:27 giving actual expression to the divine change of heart. Finally, 21:28–22:1 represents the chronicler's own ending to the story. It explains the divine legitimacy of the altar David had built.

The narrative of 1 Chronicles deviates from that in the MT of 2 Samuel 24 at a number of places. The discovery of 4QSam[a], fragmentary though it is, shows that many of these variants were inherited by the chronicler from the text he used, an important factor in assessing his own contribution. However, 4QSam[a] is extant only for 21:15-21 (= 2 Sam 24:16-20).

21:1-2. A fascinating change occurs in v. 1, with mention of Satan as the initiating factor behind David's sin. Whether the chronicler made the change or it had already occurred in his text, it clearly represents theological rewriting. The Lord's anger is referred to in 2 Sam 24:1 as the reason for inciting David to sin. Sometimes in the psalms divine anger is not a reaction to human sinning, but an amoral violent force beyond human control (e.g., Pss 6:1; 74:1; 88:16; 102:10-11). It corresponds in some respects to the modern term used by insurance companies, "act of God." Old Testament theology often traces human experience directly back to God. Here the directness illustrates a logical difficulty occasioned by a monotheistic faith. Polytheism can simply assign misfortune to one or another god or goddess. Both Jews and Christians can appreciate that a later generation of believers required a more indirect explanation of both the divine anger and the entrapment policy, here associated with it.

125. Ibid., 517.

Divine enticement finds parallels in 1 Sam 26:19 and 1 Kgs 22:21-22, paralleled as well in 2 Chr 18:19-21, although a different verb is used. The latter reference was not changed, presumably because Ahab was regarded as already wicked (2 Chr 19:2) and so ripe for punishment.

Here, by way of explanation, help is obtained from Job 1–2 and Zech 3:1-5, where the שׂטן (*śāṭān*), "accuser," a supernatural member of the heavenly council, is represented as the malicious prosecutor in the celestial law court, gloating over human weakness and exploiting it. He has a mysterious role in God's purposes, but the harm he is permitted to do is limited by the Lord's control. The use of the verb "incite" with him as subject in Job 2:3 underlies the usage here. In Zech 3:1, he stood to accuse the high priest, and this expression, too, is borrowed as a posture of hostility. Both of these texts have been used to shed light on 2 Sam 24:1. In addition to borrowing, there is also development, in that here for the first time "Satan" appears as a name instead of a descriptive noun.[126]

The test relates to the taking of a military "census." Its military intent is indicated by the report of the results (v. 5) and by its being organized by army officers (v. 2). Here it is regarded as a sinful act to ascertain the precise number of the Israelite conscripts. In the context of 1 Chronicles it indicates a lack of trust in God as the giver of victory (cf. 18:6, 13). The Lord is able to achieve victory with an insignificant force (2 Chr 14:10-15). Chapters 18–20 described David's military successes as part of the overall divine plan for building the Temple. David gave God the glory and acknowledged that his success reflected God's blessing (17:8, 24; 18:1). Now his decision to take a census betrays a trust in human resources, rather than in God as their giver and user.

21:3. Joab objects that David is trespassing on God's prerogatives. Divine blessing is what counts. The 1 Chronicles text adduces another factor: that David has the whole people behind him (cf. 12:38), a boon with which the king should be content. It also intensifies Joab's objection by adding the warning that Israel would be imperiled by the guilt triggered by the census. The warning points the reader to v. 1, Satan's aim to attack Israel, and then forward to v. 7, the divine punishment of Israel, another adaptation in the text of 1 Chronicles. For the negative cultural presuppositions of census taking, one may compare Exod 30:12.

21:4-5. The detailed itinerary in 2 Sam 24:5-8 is omitted, and the chronicler moves quickly to the total obtained. He engages in two mathematical sums to revise the numbers given in 2 Sam 24:9. Instead of listing separately the totals for the northern tribes ("Israel") and the later southern state ("Judah"), he gives a grand total for "all Israel," over which David reigns, according to chaps. 11–12. He also provides a separate, partial sum ("including," NIV) for the tribe of Judah. The grand total of 1,100,000 represents the addition of 800,000 and 500,000, the numbers in 2 Samuel, minus the two omitted tribes of v. 6, assuming 100,000 per tribe. The numbers in 2 Samuel may reflect a use of אלף (*'elep*), not numerically as 1,000, but as a smaller contingent.[127] The chronicler, however, would have appreciated enormous numbers as reflecting the glory of David's reign. The total of 470,000 for the tribe of Judah inconsistently presupposes the subtraction of only 30,000 for the tribe of Benjamin, which belonged to the state of Judah.

21:6. In this supplement to the text of 2 Samuel, Joab refuses to include all the tribes. The exclusion of Levi reflects the pentateuchal precedent in Num 1:49; 2:33, with which בתוכם (*bĕtôkām*; lit., "among them") provides an intertextual link.[128] The reason for the exclusion of Benjamin is less obvious. It is probably because of the presence of the tabernacle in Gibeon within its tribal territory (cf. Josh 18:25). The 1 Chronicles text assigns to Joab, in his abhorrence and greater vehemence, the role of spokesperson for the Lord's displeasure.

21:7. The text turns to the divine reaction. A

126. Day, observing that the name does not occur until c. 168 BCE, takes the noun as "a *satan*," an unspecified celestial accuser. See P. Day, *An Adversary in Heaven: Satan in the Hebrew Bible,* HSM 43 (Atlanta: Scholars Press, 1988) 128-29, 142-44. Japhet interprets it as a human figure. See S. Japhet, *I & II Chronicles,* OTL (Louisville: Westminster/John Knox, 1993) 374-75. And Wright takes it as a national enemy. See J. W. Wright, "The Innocence of David in 1 Chronicles 21," *JSOT* 60 (1993) 93. However, the intertextual links with Job and Zechariah suggest hermeneutical dependence on both passages.

127. See P. K. McCarter, *II Samuel,* AB 9 (Garden City, N.Y.: Doubleday, 1984) 510.

128. R. Mosis, *Untersuchungen zur Theologie des chronisten Geschichtswerks,* Freiburger theologische Studien 92 (Freiburg: Herder, 1973) 108.

direct reference to God is necessary after the adaptation of v. 1. "This thing" or "command" refers to the taking of the census, in the light of vv. 8 and 17. The clause is borrowed from 2 Sam 11:27, the Lord's reaction to David's murder of Uriah after having committed adultery with his wife. There is only a loose connection between 2 Sam 24:10 and v. 7, the verb of striking. Israel, the object of David's selfish pride, is punished, and Satan's initial aim of attacking Israel (v. 1) is achieved. By using the verb "to strike" (הכה *hikkâ*, in the hiphil) in this new way, the text has anticipated v. 14. Hence, vv. 8-14 function as a detailed flashback. Moreover, David's prayer (v. 8) lacks the introduction of repentance it has in the parent text.

21:8-14. The king prays for the alleviation of the burden of guilt that his sin has brought upon Israel (v. 3). The flow of the narrative and a comparison with Num 14:19-23 suggest that what David sought was mitigation of punishment, escape from the crushing weight of merited annihilation (cf. 2 Sam 12:13-14). The court prophet Gad gives David a choice—not as to whether Israel is to suffer, but as to how they should suffer: by famine, foreign invasion, or pestilence. The Lord is represented as being capable of using nature and humanity as instruments of moral providence (cf. Amos 4:6-11). David opts for the shorter form of direct punishment from God as a judge who has the quality of mercy, rather than for punishment mediated through human agents, who might cruelly overstep the divine mandate (see Isa 10:5-12; 37:26-29). The 1 Chronicles text has been amplified in v. 12 by polarizing two new elements, "the sword of your enemies" and "the sword of the Lord," which paves the way for the contrast drawn in v. 13. The second phrase also prepares for the angelic sword in vv. 16 and 27. This is the role of a further amplification: the reference to the angel of the Lord destroying the land, which also anticipates v. 15. The great sin (v. 8) was to be mitigated through God's very great mercy. The chronicler draws an arc between these two points by adding "very" (מאד *mĕ'ōd*) in v. 13, the term rendered "greatly" in v. 8. Verse 14 reports the pestilence as the method by which the Lord duly "struck" or "punished" Israel (v. 7), thus reducing sizably the large forces in which David trusted.

21:15-17. Once again an initial statement summarizes the whole and traces a process that is eventually reached in v. 27. The chronicler's own conclusion to the episode is in 21:26*b*–22:1. The addition of v. 27 achieves the eventual resolution of the threat posed in v. 15*a*. In the 2 Samuel text the parallel v. 16*a* does not have an anticipatory role. However, the drawn sword of 1 Chr 21:16 is found in 4QSam[a]. Here, in vv. 16 and 27, the angel's sword begins and ends the episode as a symbol of destruction. It is brandished in threat until finally it is sheathed in implicit response to the Lord's command (v. 15*a*). The 1 Chronicles text adds a reference to the Lord's seeing (NIV) or taking note (NRSV). It anticipates David's response, physical and verbal, of repentance and intercession (vv. 16*b*-17). The verb is used as in Ps 106:44, where God "regarded their distress [with compassion] when he heard their cry" (NRSV). The contingent nature of the divine word of judgment is expounded well in Jer 18:1-11 and illustrated even better in Jonah 3:1–4:2. The prophetic word of judgment assumes that the sinners threatened at the outset remain identified with their sin. If they distance themselves from it, the situation changes and the message of judgment does not apply. This prophetic contingency stands in tension with the emphasis on the absoluteness of the divine word in other parts of the OT (e.g., Isa 55:11). The chronicler does not employ the motif of divine relenting apart from this citation of 2 Sam 24:16, but the motif is similar to his regular message of divine forgiveness for the repentant, which appears in a classic formulation at 2 Chr 7:14.

The threshing floor, which will be the site for the Temple, is mentioned for the first time in v. 15*b*. It plays an increasingly prominent role throughout the paragraph, here simply as the angel's location, in v. 18 as the place where David is told to build an altar, in vv. 21-22 as the scene of David's negotiations to purchase it, and finally as the site of the duly built altar ("there," v. 26).

Verse 16 is much longer than the parallel text in 2 Sam 24:17. It was already in the chronicler's parent text, for it appears in almost identical form in 4QSam[a] and may well have been largely lost in the MT.[129] The angel of destruction, hovering

129. See S. L. McKenzie, *The Chronicler's Use of the Deuteronomistic History*, HSM 33 (Atlanta: Scholars Press, 1985) 55-56.

in midair, threatened Jerusalem with his drawn sword, ready to strike it. The drawn sword provides a counterpoint to the soldiers of the sinister census, "who drew the sword" (v. 5 NRSV). The punishment fits the crime.

David, together with the nation's representatives (cf. 11:3; 15:25), responds to the threat with renewed submission and repentant prayer. He now urges that he, as the instigator of the census, should bear the punishment—and not only he, but his family as well, despite the high expectations that were forecast for it in chap. 17 (note "my God," as in 17:25). The Lord's people, sheep in God's covenant flock who are innocently led to the slaughter (cf. Jer 11:19), should not suffer. Such seems to be the force of the metaphor in the present text. The LXX of Samuel and 4QSam[a] develop the metaphor with reference to David as a shepherd, responsible for the sheep. This was surely the original text there.[130] The REB, indulging in hypercorrection, imports this longer text into 1 Chr 21:17, "It is I who have sinned, I, the shepherd who have committed wrong."

21:18-19. The chronicler introduces the angel of the Lord as the originator of the command to build an altar. He had in mind the story of Balaam, where the angel of the Lord first confronts Balaam with a drawn sword, causing him to fall to the ground in submission, and then reveals a message to him (Num 22:31, 35). Arrangements for a means of reconciliation now begin. In terms of the summary in v. 15*a,* they happen between the Lord's relenting and the restraint of the angel (v. 27). God listens, not to the logic, but to the spirit of David's prayer. A new prophetic word has come to David through God, as v. 19 underlines—a word as momentous as that which came through Samuel for him to become king (11:3, 10; 12:23). This word constitutes a significant step toward the implementation of the building of the Temple, as 22:1 will affirm. The erection of an altar is the task assigned to David as an act of penance and the means of his reconciliation to God, which would lead to the cessation of the pestilence (cf. v. 22).

21:20-21. Verses 20-21*a* reflect a conflated text (cf. 2 Sam 24:20). The first part may reflect a rewriting of an illegible text, as in 15:27, which has subsequently had a correction added. But the detail of Ornan's threshing wheat, absent from the MT of 2 Samuel, is confirmed by 4QSam[a].[131] The hiding of Ornan's sons reflects a fear that looking at the angel of the Lord would be fatal (cf. Judg 6:22-23).

21:22-25. The negotiations have been flavored with several details drawn from Abraham's bargaining for a burial place for Sarah in Genesis 23. In v. 22, David's taking the initiative echoes Gen 23:3-4, and the two instances of the verb "give" (נתן *nātan*) reflect Gen 23:4, 9. The insistence on paying "the full price" in vv. 22, 24*a* corresponds to Gen 23:9. Abraham's purchase was a landmark in Israel's history, since it was the first piece of real estate owned in the promised land. The purchase of the threshing floor was a comparable landmark for the chronicler. Ornan's throwing in the wheat he had been threshing as part of the deal (v. 23), to be used as a grain offering, is a new touch. The citing of a grain offering alongside burnt offerings meant that David's foundational sacrifices in v. 26 included the statutory pair of offerings laid down in the Torah (see Exod 29:38-41; Num 15:2-10; 2 Chr 7:7). The fine or choice flour of the grain offering was ground from wheat (Exod 29:2).

David's insistence that he will not offer free burnt offerings is reinforced in 1 Chronicles with the prefatory statement that he will not use for the Lord another person's property (v. 24). Since David is sacrificing on Israel's behalf, he must bear the cost. In v. 25 the price of 600 gold shekels contrasts with that of 50 silver shekels in 2 Sam 24:24. There it is the cost of the threshing floor and oxen, here it is the price for "the site" (vv. 22, 25), which covers a larger area, sufficient for the Temple (cf. 2 Chr 3:1). The change from silver to gold may reflect the lavish use of gold for the Temple. The medieval commentator Rashi suggested that the number 600 had symbolic value as a multiple of twelve: Whereas the 50 shekels of 2 Samuel were paid by David as a member of the tribe of Judah, 600 were sufficient for the twelve tribes.

21:26-27. Verse 26*a* marks the completion of the commission to erect an altar in v. 18. It is sealed by the inaugural sacrificing of the two standard types of offerings, as in 16:1. We were

130. Ibid., 56.

131. See ibid., 57.

not told on what altar the offerings in 16:1 were sacrificed (cf. 29:21). The chronicler simply took over the rite from his 2 Samuel text. What the chronicler adds begins in v. 26*b* and extends to 22:1. First, the narrative is brought to a close in vv. 26*b*-27. David presumably asked that this inaugural rite of worship be accepted as a sign of forgiveness. The prayer appears to be modeled on Elijah's prayer in 1 Kgs 18:36-37. That earlier prayer appealed for an answer, which came in the form of fire devouring the sacrifice on the altar Elijah had built. Here God "answered" similarly. Acceptance by divine fire will reappear in 2 Chr 7:1, in another addition made by the chronicler, after the inaugural sacrificial rite in Solomon's Temple. Both instances depend on Lev 9:24, which associates the fire of acceptance with the inauguration of Aaron's priesthood. The fire puts David's altar on a par with the altar of the old tabernacle, featured in the Torah. It also marks the reconciliation and reinstatement of David and Israel before God. Verse 27 returns to this more immediate concern. The crisis is over.

21:28–22:1. The chronicler regularly appends an interpretive conclusion to a narrative. The Hebrew syntax of this passage is complex, and the English versions simplify it into a series of separate sentences. The main clause consists of David's pronouncement in 22:1. Verse 28 is best understood as a two-part temporal clause. It recapitulates the two significant facts of v. 26 in reverse order, mentioning first David's appreciation of the divine answer of v. 26*b* and then continuing "and he had [earlier] sacrificed there," with reference to v. 26*a*.[132] Verses 29-30 are in parenthesis between the temporal clause and the main clause. But first v. 28, recapitulating v. 26, underscores the divine endorsement of David's sacrifice by means of supernatural fire. His sacrifice was a trial offer, one might say. God's acceptance proved that the altar bore a greater significance: It was good enough for both God and the king, so it would be good enough for Israel. The national dimensions of the event have been hinted at in v. 22: Relief of Israel's present suffering was at stake. Now sacrifices and altar are hailed as possessing "a once-for-all" value. Israel had a new altar of burnt offering; it had been prophetically commissioned (21:18). It was the nucleus of a new sanctuary, which in terms of chap. 17 may be called God's "house," the temple that David's successor was to build (cf. 2 Chr 3:1).

The parenthesis in vv. 29-30 raises the question of the old altar and the old sanctuary at Gibeon (cf. 16:39-40) and implies that its days were numbered. For all its traditional authenticity, traced back to Moses (cf. Exodus 26), it could not for long remain Israel's religious center. The Torah had been superseded in this respect. The chronicler could have appealed to the prophetic warrant of 21:18. In fact, he appeals to a higher authority; the revelation of the angel of the Lord, whose intervention the chronicler had claimed, lay behind the prophetic oracle in 21:18. This remarkable figure appears with his full title in the MT of 2 Sam 24:16*b*, and also as "the angel" in 2 Sam 24:16*a*, 17. In 1 Chronicles, however, he is called "the angel of the LORD" five times (21:12, 15*b*, 16 [= 4QSam[a]], 18, and 30) and four times "the [or an] angel" (21:15[twice], 20, and 27). The chronicler, encouraged by 2 Sam 24:16, echoes older traditions in crediting the figure with divine authority.[133] He stands at a distance from them; they have lost their original complex significance. He has little interest in angelology elsewhere. Here a greater significance is assigned to this figure, and the punch line in v. 30 explains why. It refers back to 21:16, now interpreted as a supernatural, deliberate barring of the way. The chronicler again had in mind Num 22:21, where the angel of the Lord is described in similar language and has this role. David's temporary inability to "seek" (דרשׁ *dāraš*; NRSV and NIV, "inquire [of]") God, here not only in a formal religious sense, but also tinged with a sense of repentance and finding God anew, is invested with a once-for-all significance. This event points forward to the Temple to be built in Jerusalem as the divinely intended place at which Israel would seek the Lord. The Temple was to be dedicated especially to bringing repentant sinners, like David, back to God. The divinely nominated place is associated with a theology of grace, as 2 Chr 7:14 will explain.[134] David serves as a model for every backslider.

132. For inverse order in recapitulation as a Hebrew literary technique, see S. Talmon, "The Textual Study of the Bible—A New Outlook," in *Qumran and the History of the Biblical Text*, ed. F. M. Cross and S. Talmon (Cambridge, Mass.: Harvard University Press, 1975) 359-62.

133. For these traditions see T. Fretheim, *The Suffering of God*, OBT 14 (Philadelphia: Fortress, 1989) 93-95.

134. T.-S. Im, *Das Davidbild in den Chronikbüchern*, Europäische Hochschulschriften 23:263 (Frankfurt am Main: Peter Lang, 1985) 152.

REFLECTIONS

The altar David is commanded to build is, for the chronicler, a monument to God's forgiving grace. Hitherto the narrative had witnessed to a David dedicated to the will of God whose only fault was an unwitting ritual ignorance that he gladly resolved. But sooner or later forgiving grace cannot stay out of any divine/human relationship. There is a need for a "God who is rich in mercy," who redirects misused energies into new and wholesome channels (see Eph 2:1-10).

1. The reference to Satan in 21:1 is a milestone in the development of the theological explanation of human wrongdoing in the Bible. The echoing of phraseology from passages in Job and Zechariah reflects a constructive use of Scripture to grapple with issues of theodicy. Second Samuel 24:1 had referred simply to the mysterious will of the sovereign Lord, using the category of divine wrath, to which a number of the psalms attribute human suffering. However, in this context it involves David's being tempted to do wrong. So a means was sought to avoid associating God directly with such temptation. James 1:13-15 bears witness to a similar endeavor, but grounds temptation in the human self. The text of 1 Chronicles retains a supernatural reference. As in the book of Job, Satan is an angelic member of the divine administration who is permitted to initiate moral challenges and to appeal to what is base in human nature. He is permitted to inflict suffering and to provoke his victim to sin against God. The text has not reached the stage of an open rival to God's sovereignty that appears in the New Testament, for instance in Eph 2:2, where "the ruler of the power/kingdom of the air" is considered to be the agent of evil.

At no stage in the biblical development is there any denial of human responsibility for human actions. There is never a suggestion that the buck may be passed back with the excuse, "The devil made me do it." Moreover, the text of 1 Chronicles, like the underlying texts in Job and Zechariah, firmly encloses evil in a larger framework of divine providence. As in Zechariah 3, it is ultimately eclipsed by forgiving grace. In turn, the New Testament regards the celestial powers of evil as already being defeated in principle at the crucifixion and doomed finally to submit to God's benevolent sovereignty (see Rom 16:20; Col 2:15; Rev 20:10).

2. According to the chronicler, David's demand for a military census betrayed a lack of faith, an ungodly determination to walk by sight, not by faith, to adapt the language of 2 Cor 5:7. Joab's protest implies that David's sin was an act of presumption against the Lord as giver of national blessing. If we consider the chronicler's standpoint out of place in the real world, we may compare it to the warning of Jesus not to worry over such mundane matters as food and clothing, but to "seek first" God's "kingship over you" (Matt 6:33 NAB).

3. The social consequences of a person's sinning come to the fore in 21:1–22:1. Israel features as the object of Satan's challenge and the victim of God's displeasure. David did not function simply as an individual. He was Israel's representative before God and the agent of the whole people's destiny. He will magnanimously plead to bear the punishment alone (21:17)—a noble offer and an appropriate sign of remorse, but unrealistic nevertheless. Self-centered willfulness begins with oneself, but ends by dragging others down. This truth applies to commoners as well as to kings. Apparently private acts, such as personal infidelity or substance abuse, have social consequences. It was too late for David to say he did not want others to be involved as victims of his folly.

4. The king pleaded to be forgiven (21:8), but the forgiveness is not straightforward. In 21:10-15, as often in the Old Testament, God's grace is displayed after an experience of judgment. In the New Testament, the peace that spells reconciliation with God could only be

made through the blood of the cross (Col 1:20). On the human plane this principle is also true to life. Sinning tends to unleash unchecked suffering. Repentance cannot undo the results of drunk driving. Confession of sin and recognition of accountability before God do not turn the clock back.

5. Divine grace is celebrated in 21:1–22:1. David opts to "fall into the hand[s] of the LORD, for his mercy is very great." The reader of the New Testament is superficially reminded of the grim words and grimmer context of Heb 10:31 that it is "a terrifying thing to fall into the hands of the living God" (REB). The contrast warns against the all-too-common generalization that the Old Testament is full of God's wrath, but the New Testament of God's love. Here the chronicler takes over from 2 Samuel a message that stands at the heart of his own overall presentation: Forgiving grace predominates in the Lord's attitude to the covenant people. The combination of divine mercy and relenting accords with a version of part of the great theological proposition in Exod 34:6-7, which appears in Joel 2:13 and Jonah 4:2, "The LORD is merciful . . . and relents from punishing" (NRSV). It is the theme of Psalm 103, a hymn celebrating God's forgiving grace: "The LORD is merciful. . . . He does not deal with us according to our sins" (Ps 103:8, 10 NRSV).

6. Personal cost is an essential factor in biblical spirituality. David's protest that he must pay for the threshing floor and its accoutrements (21:24) is prefaced in the text by the extra clause, "I will not take for the LORD what is yours." The offering of sacrifices had to reflect personal spirituality. Malachi complained that some of the sacrificial animals that worshipers were bringing to the Temple had been misappropriated, while others were blind or lame (Mal 1:8, 13). For integrity's sake, an offering had to be of true value. This is a principle worth pondering by the Christian in offering to God the spiritual sacrifices of praise and shared resources (Heb 13:15-16). The ostensible price tags do not necessarily represent the value, as Jesus shrewdly taught in contrasting the respective donations of the widow and the wealthy (Luke 21:1-4).

1 Chronicles 22:2-19, Solomon's Mandate to Build

NIV

2So David gave orders to assemble the aliens living in Israel, and from among them he appointed stonecutters to prepare dressed stone for building the house of God. 3He provided a large amount of iron to make nails for the doors of the gateways and for the fittings, and more bronze than could be weighed. 4He also provided more cedar logs than could be counted, for the Sidonians and Tyrians had brought large numbers of them to David.

5David said, "My son Solomon is young and inexperienced, and the house to be built for the LORD should be of great magnificence and fame and splendor in the sight of all the nations. Therefore I will make preparations for it." So David made extensive preparations before his death.

NRSV

2David gave orders to gather together the aliens who were residing in the land of Israel, and he set stonecutters to prepare dressed stones for building the house of God. 3David also provided great stores of iron for nails for the doors of the gates and for clamps, as well as bronze in quantities beyond weighing, 4and cedar logs without number—for the Sidonians and Tyrians brought great quantities of cedar to David. 5For David said, "My son Solomon is young and inexperienced, and the house that is to be built for the LORD must be exceedingly magnificent, famous and glorified throughout all lands; I will therefore make preparation for it." So David provided materials in great quantity before his death.

6Then he called for his son Solomon and charged him to build a house for the LORD, the

NIV

[6]Then he called for his son Solomon and charged him to build a house for the LORD, the God of Israel. [7]David said to Solomon: "My son, I had it in my heart to build a house for the Name of the LORD my God. [8]But this word of the LORD came to me: 'You have shed much blood and have fought many wars. You are not to build a house for my Name, because you have shed much blood on the earth in my sight. [9]But you will have a son who will be a man of peace and rest, and I will give him rest from all his enemies on every side. His name will be Solomon,[a] and I will grant Israel peace and quiet during his reign. [10]He is the one who will build a house for my Name. He will be my son, and I will be his father. And I will establish the throne of his kingdom over Israel forever.'

[11]"Now, my son, the LORD be with you, and may you have success and build the house of the LORD your God, as he said you would. [12]May the LORD give you discretion and understanding when he puts you in command over Israel, so that you may keep the law of the LORD your God. [13]Then you will have success if you are careful to observe the decrees and laws that the LORD gave Moses for Israel. Be strong and courageous. Do not be afraid or discouraged.

[14]"I have taken great pains to provide for the temple of the LORD a hundred thousand talents[b] of gold, a million talents[c] of silver, quantities of bronze and iron too great to be weighed, and wood and stone. And you may add to them. [15]You have many workmen: stonecutters, masons and carpenters, as well as men skilled in every kind of work [16]in gold and silver, bronze and iron—craftsmen beyond number. Now begin the work, and the LORD be with you."

[17]Then David ordered all the leaders of Israel to help his son Solomon. [18]He said to them, "Is not the LORD your God with you? And has he not granted you rest on every side? For he has handed the inhabitants of the land over to me, and the land is subject to the LORD and to his people. [19]Now devote your heart and soul to seeking the LORD your God. Begin to build the sanctuary of the LORD God, so that you may bring the ark of

[a]*9 Solomon* sounds like and may be derived from the Hebrew for *peace.* [b]*14* That is, about 3,750 tons (about 3,450 metric tons) [d]*14* That is, about 37,500 tons (about 34,500 metric tons)

NRSV

God of Israel. [7]David said to Solomon, "My son, I had planned to build a house to the name of the LORD my God. [8]But the word of the LORD came to me, saying, 'You have shed much blood and have waged great wars; you shall not build a house to my name, because you have shed so much blood in my sight on the earth. [9]See, a son shall be born to you; he shall be a man of peace. I will give him peace from all his enemies on every side; for his name shall be Solomon,[a] and I will give peace[b] and quiet to Israel in his days. [10]He shall build a house for my name. He shall be a son to me, and I will be a father to him, and I will establish his royal throne in Israel forever.' [11]Now, my son, the LORD be with you, so that you may succeed in building the house of the LORD your God, as he has spoken concerning you. [12]Only, may the LORD grant you discretion and understanding, so that when he gives you charge over Israel you may keep the law of the LORD your God. [13]Then you will prosper if you are careful to observe the statutes and the ordinances that the LORD commanded Moses for Israel. Be strong and of good courage. Do not be afraid or dismayed. [14]With great pains I have provided for the house of the LORD one hundred thousand talents of gold, one million talents of silver, and bronze and iron beyond weighing, for there is so much of it; timber and stone too I have provided. To these you must add more. [15]You have an abundance of workers: stonecutters, masons, carpenters, and all kinds of artisans without number, skilled in working [16]gold, silver, bronze, and iron. Now begin the work, and the LORD be with you."

17David also commanded all the leaders of Israel to help his son Solomon, saying, [18]"Is not the LORD your God with you? Has he not given you peace on every side? For he has delivered the inhabitants of the land into my hand; and the land is subdued before the LORD and his people. [19]Now set your mind and heart to seek the LORD your God. Go and build the sanctuary of the LORD God so that the ark of the covenant of the LORD and the holy vessels of God may be brought into a house built for the name of the LORD."

[a] Heb *Shelomoh* [b] Heb *shalom*

NIV

the covenant of the LORD and the sacred articles belonging to God into the temple that will be built for the Name of the LORD."

COMMENTARY

According to 17:11-12, one of David's sons would build the Temple. Now that son is identified as Solomon, who duly receives a commission from David to undertake his divinely assigned task. The identification of the site for the Temple (v. 1) made it possible to proceed with plans for its construction. The passage is structurally bound together as a threefold series of instructions toward this end, vv. 2-5, 6-16, and 17-19.

22:2-5. David's provision of materials for the future Temple was an ongoing task that he pursued for many years (v. 5*b*). The Hebrew verb "to provide" (הכין *hēkîn,* in the hiphil) is the key word, occurring three times (v. 3, "provided"; v. 5*a,* "make provision," REB; "make preparation[s]," NRSV, NIV; v. 5*b,* "provided," NRSV). These verses function as narrative background for David's mention of his provision (v. 14). The stone had to be hewn, and so stonecutters were procured from among the resident aliens, who were used for forced labor. The chronicler has transferred back to David's reign material he has also used for Solomon's (cf. 1 Kgs 5:15; 9:20-21; 2 Chr 2:17-18; 8:7-8). Bronze, which was used extensively in Solomon's Temple, had been obtained in David's wars and would be used for the molten sea, the pillars in front of the Temple, and temple vessels (18:8; cf. 1 Kgs 7:15-47; 2 Chr 4:11-18). The Phoenicians' supply of cedar anticipates Solomon's own request for cedar from King Huram of Tyre (2 Chr 2:8 = 1 Kgs 5:6). The chronicler does not specify its use, but the 1 Kings account mentions the cedar paneling of the main walls and roof of the Temple and the inner wall of the holy of holies (1 Kgs 6:9, 15-16). The note of hyperbole sounded in vv. 3-4 concerning the amounts of bronze and cedar used, which v. 14 repeats to a greater degree, is explained in v. 5.

David's reflection in v. 5*a* provides the reader with two inter-related reasons for his policy of preparation: Solomon's youthfulness and inexperience. The gist of it will recur in 29:1. Mention of Solomon's youth is a wisdom motif (cf. 1 Kgs 3:7, where the motif refers to his ruling), applied here to his role as temple builder. David's building experience (cf. 14:1; 15:1) could be put to good use, not for building the Temple, from which he had been debarred (17:4), but for amassing appropriate materials and for other preparations listed in 28:11-19. The chronicler gives the Temple greater legitimacy by closely associating it with David, already a theological hero and a role model for Israel.

The end product had to be worthy of God. It would be a showpiece commanding universal admiration and reflect its divine patron. One of the Songs of Zion, with the Temple in mind, celebrates Mount Zion as "beautiful in elevation . . . the joy of all the earth" (Ps 48:2 NRSV); another psalm calls Zion "the perfection of beauty" (Ps 50:2), and Lam 2:15 echoes both these accolades. The chronicler's actual vocabulary, "fame" (שׁם *šēm*) and "glory" (תפארת *tif'eret*), is borrowed from the description of Israel's eschatological supremacy (*šēm, tif'eret* [Deut 26:19; Jer 13:11]; *šēm* [Zeph 3:19-20]). In Jer 33:9 *tif'eret* is applied to Jerusalem, which probably encouraged the chronicler's reapplication of it to the Temple. Indeed, in 29:11 similar language appears in an effusive description of God. The Temple was to be as adequately as possible a reflection of divine glory. This idealistic representation explains the language of limitlessness in vv. 3-4 and in v. 14 below. Verse 5 reaffirms the complementary nature of the respective work of David and Solomon. Their reigns represented a joint venture in completing the institution that thereafter in Israel's experience would be the channel of divine grace and human worship.

22:6-10. Chapter 28 will contain the public charge to Solomon to build the Temple. This charge is a preliminary, private commissioning. In

David's speech the previous divine warrant for Solomon to be temple builder (17:4-14) is repeated in vv. 7-10, and Solomon is encouraged to assume this role in vv. 11-16. Each half of the speech is introduced by the vocative "my son" (vv. 7, 11). Verses 7-10 obviously depend on Nathan's oracle in 17:4-14. However, the chronicler takes the opportunity to import some fresh nuances. He leans on Solomon's retelling of the event in his letter to Hiram at 1 Kgs 5:3-4 and in his prayer at 1 Kgs 8:17. First, Solomon's words in 1 Kgs 8:17, which the chronicler uses directly in 2 Chr 6:7, are put back into David's mouth in v. 7, to give expression to his own frustrated ambition to build the Temple. Then in vv. 8-9*a* David's leadership in war is presented as that which disqualifies him from building the Temple (cf. 1 Kgs 5:3), while the absence of warfare qualifies Solomon as the temple builder (cf. 1 Kgs 5:4). In Samuel–Kings, both David and Solomon are created with enjoying rest from war (2 Sam 7:11; 1 Kgs 5:4), which was a precondition for building the Temple (Deut 12:10-11; cf. 2 Chr 7:12). The chronicler tended to view David as a warrior, and to that end edited the reference to rest (2 Sam 7:11) out of 17:10, as we saw. Here the NRSV and NIV conceal the connection with 1 Kgs 5:4 by rendering שׁלוֹם (*šālôm*) as "peace" instead of as "rest" twice in v. 9*a*. The Chronicler clinches his attribution of rest to Solomon by a wordplay between his name (שׁלמה *šĕlōmōh*) and *šālôm* in v. 9*b*.

The description of David as a warrior king in v. 8*a* has a different nuance from that in 17:8*b*-10*a*. There it has a positive ring, as the result of divine initiative and blessing. This interpretation of David's warfare is actually echoed in v. 18 below. Here David's actions are his own, while God is a comparative bystander. The basis for the change may be Shimei's accusation that David was "a man of blood" (2 Sam 16:7 NIV), though it has been completely reapplied, if so. The repeated mention of shedding much blood suggests that it had a polluting effect (cf. Num 35:33; Ps 106:38-39). This dual interpretation of David's fighting finds a parallel in Numbers 31.[135] There, on the one hand, Israelite troops engaged in a divinely initiated campaign to execute the Lord's vengeance on Midian (Num 31:3); yet, on the other hand, any who killed became unclean and had to purify themselves (Num 31:20, 24). In Israelite culture uncleanness was differentiated from moral culpability.[136] The unclean were debarred from approaching the temple (2 Chr 23:19). It was an easy step for the chronicler to extend the ban to David's building the Temple, after repeated bouts of uncleanness. Such a firm ban enhanced Solomon's legitimacy as temple builder.

Verse 10 is paralleled in 17:12-13*a*, but is closer to 2 Sam 7:13-14*a*. The last three clauses are inverted so that greater emphasis falls on Solomon's divinely backed kingship. David's son (v. 9) would also be the Lord's son, adopted into divine patronage (cf. Ps 2:7). Modern versions are much more staccato than the Hebrew; the KJV's "*and* he shall be my son" expresses the consequence. The building of the Temple would clinch Solomon's special relation to the Lord, which in turn would lead to a further consequence: the perpetuity of the dynasty descended from him.

22:11-16. Verse 11 moves to the imminent task of temple building. The commissioning proper begins at this point. It typically consists of three elements.[137] One is the assurance that the Lord's presence will bring success to the task. Expressed as a wish, it is placed at the beginning and repeated at the end, functioning as a framework in the commissioning (vv. 11, 16). The second element is the description of the task (v. 11). The third element is one of encouragement, to be strong and free of needless fears (v. 13). In v. 12, God's supporting presence is reformulated as a divine gift of wisdom, which David covets for Solomon (cf. 1 Kgs 3:12). Here Solomon's general task of ruling appears to be in view. Solomon had a double duty: to be Israel's king and to build the Temple (vv. 10-12; these general and specific duties are also combined in 29:19). Wisdom here refers to the Torah, which Solomon must use to rule well. The NRSV differentiates between "succeed" in the temple project (v. 11) and "prosper" generally (v. 13). Although the same Hebrew verb (צלח *ṣālēaḥ*) is used, the con-

135. See ibid., 139.

136. See T. Frymer-Kensky, "Pollution, Purification, and Purgation in Biblical Israel," in *The Word of the Lord Shall Go Forth*, ed. C. L. Myers et al. (Winona Lake: Eisenbrauns, 1983) 399-404.

137. See D. McCarthy, "An Installation Genre?" *JBL* 90 (1971) 31-41.

text indicates different references. This advice to obey the Torah echoes David's charge to Solomon just before his death in 1 Kgs 2:2-3. The exhortation to be strong in v. 13*b* reverts to the building of the Temple. The new link forged by the chronicler between the wise rule of 1 Kings 3 and obedience to the Torah in 1 Kings 2 reflects a late development in wisdom thinking, which defined wisdom in terms of the Torah (see Psalms 19; 119).

David grounds the encouragement in a further factor: his own provision of resources for the task. Solomon would not have to start from scratch, but could use materials and workers that have already been supplied. The NIV and the NRSV rightly take v. 16*a* closely with v. 15, so that "without number" refers to the workers. The chiastic order confirms this connection: metals, timber, stone, stoneworkers, timberworkers, metalworkers.[138]

A striking feature of David's description of his provision is the incredibly large amounts mentioned in v. 14. The qualifications "beyond weighing" and "without number" in vv. 14-15 echo those of vv. 3-4, where the divine associations of the Temple encouraged hyperbole. Here the same motivation is implicitly at work. According to 1 Kgs 10:14, Solomon's annual income was 666 gold talents, which was intended to be a breathtaking amount. This comparison enables the reader to judge the colossal nature of the present figures and calls into question a literal interpretation. Earlier figures in 1 Chronicles all seemed to have had some rational basis in relation to the literary source or context. Here, as elsewhere, the chronicler resorts to his own branch of mathematics, rhetorical mathematics, which must be respected for its intention. English idioms can use mathematical language to express hyperbole, as when we say, "Thanks a million" or "A thousand pardons." Here the exaggeration is akin to the extravagant language of praise in the hymns and thanksgiving songs of the psalms. Just as they attempt to convey in words God's incomparability, so also these incredible numbers express in material terms the magnificence of this God of the Temple.

A further agenda is found in this commissioning speech: The double charge to Solomon, private and public, in chaps. 22 and 28 recalls the commissioning of Joshua in Deut 31:7-8, where Moses addresses him, and in Josh 1:2-9, where the Lord communicates to him directly (cf. Deut 31:23). All three of the formal elements are found in both passages: (1) the call for courage and the banishing of fear (Deut 31:7-8; Josh 1:6-7, 9); (2) the description of the new task (Deut 31:7; Josh 1:2, 6); and (3) the assurance of divine aid (Deut 31:8; Josh 1:5, 9). The duty of obeying the Torah reappears in Josh 1:7-8, with mention of general prosperity (*ṣālēaḥ*), the same verb used in 1 Chr 22:13. A deliberate parallel is being drawn between Joshua as successor to Moses and Solomon as successor to David.[139] Just as Joshua, rather than Moses, crossed the Jordan as the divinely appointed leader to win the land (Deut 31:2-3), so also Solomon, rather than David, is commissioned to build the Temple. The chronicler affirms a dispensational relationship of type and antitype between the old pair of God's servants and this new pair. This typologizing functioned as an argument that a temple age had succeeded the tabernacle era of Moses and Joshua. The Lord was doing a comparable new work and resetting the stopwatch of theological history.

22:17-19. David now urges Israel's leaders to support Solomon in the project. This charge was meant as a private lobbying meeting before the public one in 28:1-8. The speech in vv. 18-19 falls into the same double pattern found in vv. 7-16. In v. 18, David concentrates on God's work (rather than God's Word, vv. 7-10), and in v. 19 on building the Temple (as in vv. 11-16). The leaders, too, receive a charge, with two of the standard three elements represented: the Lord's presence and the task. The Lord's presence had been manifested in the momentous achievements of David's reign, which had by its close brought about "rest" from warfare. So, implicitly, it was time to build the Temple, according to the divine calendar of Deut 12:10-11. Their task is first defined in general terms in a call to "devote your heart and soul" to seeking the Lord. As "your God" (vv. 18-19), the Lord had a claim on their lives. Again the chronicler's key term for spirituality is used ("seek," דרשׁ *dāraš*; cf. 10:13-14; 13:3; 15:13; 21:30). Spirituality is worked out in

138. E. L. Curtis and A. A. Madsen, *The Books of Chronicles,* ICC (Edinburgh: T. &. T. Clark, 1910) 258.

139. R. L. Braun, "Solomon, the Chosen Temple Builder: The Significance of 1 Chronicles 22, 28, and 29 for the Theology of the Chronicler," *JBL* 95 (1976) 586-88; *1 Chronicles,* WBC 14 (Waco, Tex.: Word, 1986) 221-23; H. G. M. Williamson, "The Accession of Solomon in the Books of Chronicles," *VT* 26 (1976) 351-61.

various ways in 1 Chronicles; here it takes the specific form of assisting in building the Temple, so that the ark and the holy vessels (2 Chr 5:5) might receive due honor. To respect the things of God in this way was to honor God.

REFLECTIONS

1. David and Solomon have complementary roles in their great work for God, David as a warrior king and a provider and Solomon as a king in peacetime and a builder. Each brought to his particular tasks his personal qualities, resources, and opportunities. Paul, in turn, testified to this principle of complementarity in Christian service: "I planted the seed, Apollos watered it, but God made it grow . . . and each will be rewarded according to his own labor" (1 Cor 3:6, 8 NIV). While Paul "laid a foundation," others had opportunities to build on it with such resources as they were able to contribute, "gold, silver, costly stones" (1 Cor 3:10-12).

According to the chronicler, the overall criterion in building the Temple was that the end product should be worthy of the Lord and reflect divine glory. Likewise, the high appreciation of God we voice in our hymns and prayers should emerge from our commitment to God as we work and live for God.

2. A new era of divine revelation dawned with David's and Solomon's reigns. David had the role of being the forerunner, and Solomon was the fulfiller in a glorious outworking of God's Word in Deut 12:10-11. This day of grace, though old in time, was still operating for the chronicler, since God had promised David that Solomon's throne would be forever (22:10). In the New Testament, there is a comparable ring about the advent of Christ: "When the fullness of time had come, God sent his son" (Gal 4:4 NRSV). Like Solomon for Israel, Christ is "our peace," a claim that echoes the royal prophecy of Mic 5:5, "and he shall be the one of peace" (NRSV).

The typological comparison between Joshua and Solomon as fellow fulfillers of a task begun by others also affirms that a new epoch of revelation had arrived, authentically like the old, but superseding it. Second Isaiah engaged in this theological argumentation, for instance with the language of a new exodus in Isa 43:16-21; 52:12, over against Deut 16:3.[140] The Christian is reminded of the way temple language is reapplied to Jesus and the church in the New Testament, with similar claims that the God of former revelation has now moved on further (see John 2:19-22; 1 Cor 3:16; 6:19; Eph 2:21). The Bible urges us to appreciate the continuity and development of God's purposes. Old and new elements are intermingled in the New Testament. Their significance cannot be understood, however, until the Old Testament is taken seriously, rather than slighted as an antiquarian millstone around the neck of the modern church.

3. Verses 11-13 have an obvious value for the commissioning of any servant of God to a new work. Fears are admitted and faced, and God's enabling presence is offered as an antidote. Especially important is the truth that a special task does not exempt any believer from the general standards of God's will. The lesson was taken over from the deuteronomist in Josh 1:7-8. In this respect, also, Solomon was meant to be a latter-day Joshua. None of God's servants is ever placed in a privileged position above the moral law. That is a much-needed lesson, because in the shadow of prestige and power lurks the temptation to consider oneself untrammeled by ordinary conventions. However special the task, it grants no immunity from standards laid on all the people of God.

The new temple-oriented age was not exempt from the moral claims of the Torah in the

140. See B. W. Anderson, "Exodus Typology in Second Isaiah," in *Israel's Prophetic Heritage,* ed. B. W. Anderson and W. Harrelson (New York: Harper, 1962) 177-95.

old one. The Christian, in turn, rejoicing over God's grace in Christ, dares not dispense with the New Testament's affirmation that to love God still involves keeping God's commandments (1 John 5:3), as truly as in Exod 20:6. To live in the Spirit means to meet fully "the righteous requirements of the law" (Rom 8:4 NIV).

The "help" sought from Israel's leaders for Solomon in his task of building the Temple echoes the help David himself received in chaps. 11–12. God's servant does not stand alone or even receive help only from God directly, but is encouraged to look around for support from others. These leaders, however, especially needed the assurance of the Lord's presence with them. Their eyes are directed back to what their God had done. This recollection is to be equated, not with a proud self-congratulation for one's own efforts, which one may easily duplicate in the future, but with a sober assessment of what God has accomplished through one's ministry (see Acts 21:19). It functions as encouragement to the anxious that the same God will also be with them at the next stage.

1 Chronicles 23:1–29:30, Preparing Personnel for the Temple

OVERVIEW

The structural bookends holding these chapters together are the partly parallel sentences of 23:1 and 29:28. First, David, "full of days," makes Solomon king, and finally David dies, "full of days," and Solomon becomes king. Co-regency was followed by sole rule. In chap. 28, David publicly commissions Solomon as temple builder, after the private ceremony in chap. 22. The bulk of chap. 29 is taken up with David's prayer of praise. This prayer is formally parallel to the psalm of praise and petition in chap. 16. The two great religious events of David's life, the installation of the ark in Jerusalem and preparation for the Temple, are both concluded with appropriate praise of God (16:8-36; 29:10-22).

The account of the private commissioning of Solomon as temple builder in chap. 22 was closely associated with David's material preparations for the Temple. This motif reappears in 29:2-5. Similarly, a little earlier David presents Solomon with a set of plans for the Temple and its furnishings (28:11-19), and also for the personnel (28:13; cf. 28:21). The preceding chapters in this unit pave the way for this last statement by tracing back to David the complex organization of Levites at the Temple in the period of the chronicler. As De Vries comments on 28:13, "Now we know why [the chronicler] has insisted on inserting his regulations for the clergy into his narrative of the investiture."[141] Readers have been prepared for such a comprehensive ordering by the account of David's appointment of levitical and priestly musicians and security officers for the ark procession, for the ark installed in Jerusalem, and for the tabernacle in Gibeon (15:16-24; 16:4-6, 37-42).

141. S. J. De Vries, *1 and 2 Chronicles*, FOTL 11 (Grand Rapids: Eerdmans, 1989) 219.

1 Chronicles 23:1-32, Organization and Duties of the Levites

NIV

23 When David was old and full of years, he made his son Solomon king over Israel.

[2]He also gathered together all the leaders of Israel, as well as the priests and Levites. [3]The Levites thirty years old or more were counted, and the total number of men was thirty-eight

NRSV

23 When David was old and full of days, he made his son Solomon king over Israel.

2David assembled all the leaders of Israel and the priests and the Levites. [3]The Levites, thirty years old and upward, were counted, and the total was thirty-eight thousand. [4]"Twenty-four thou-

NIV

thousand. 4David said, "Of these, twenty-four thousand are to supervise the work of the temple of the LORD and six thousand are to be officials and judges. 5Four thousand are to be gatekeepers and four thousand are to praise the LORD with the musical instruments I have provided for that purpose."

6David divided the Levites into groups corresponding to the sons of Levi: Gershon, Kohath and Merari.

7Belonging to the Gershonites:
Ladan and Shimei.
8The sons of Ladan:
Jehiel the first, Zetham and Joel—three in all.
9The sons of Shimei:
Shelomoth, Haziel and Haran—three in all.
These were the heads of the families of Ladan.
10And the sons of Shimei:
Jahath, Ziza,[a] Jeush and Beriah.
These were the sons of Shimei—four in all.
11Jahath was the first and Ziza the second, but Jeush and Beriah did not have many sons; so they were counted as one family with one assignment.

12The sons of Kohath:
Amram, Izhar, Hebron and Uzziel—four in all.
13The sons of Amram:
Aaron and Moses.
Aaron was set apart, he and his descendants forever, to consecrate the most holy things, to offer sacrifices before the LORD, to minister before him and to pronounce blessings in his name forever. 14The sons of Moses the man of God were counted as part of the tribe of Levi.
15The sons of Moses:
Gershom and Eliezer.
16The descendants of Gershom:
Shubael was the first.
17The descendants of Eliezer:
Rehabiah was the first.

[a] *10* One Hebrew manuscript, Septuagint and Vulgate (see also verse 11); most Hebrew manuscripts *Zina*

NRSV

sand of these," David said, "shall have charge of the work in the house of the LORD, six thousand shall be officers and judges, 5four thousand gatekeepers, and four thousand shall offer praises to the LORD with the instruments that I have made for praise." 6And David organized them in divisions corresponding to the sons of Levi: Gershon,[a] Kohath, and Merari.

7The sons of Gershon[b] were Ladan and Shimei. 8The sons of Ladan: Jehiel the chief, Zetham, and Joel, three. 9The sons of Shimei: Shelomoth, Haziel, and Haran, three. These were the heads of families of Ladan. 10And the sons of Shimei: Jahath, Zina, Jeush, and Beriah. These four were the sons of Shimei. 11Jahath was the chief, and Zizah the second; but Jeush and Beriah did not have many sons, so they were enrolled as a single family.

12The sons of Kohath: Amram, Izhar, Hebron, and Uzziel, four. 13The sons of Amram: Aaron and Moses. Aaron was set apart to consecrate the most holy things, so that he and his sons forever should make offerings before the LORD, and minister to him and pronounce blessings in his name forever; 14but as for Moses the man of God, his sons were to be reckoned among the tribe of Levi. 15The sons of Moses: Gershom and Eliezer. 16The sons of Gershom: Shebuel the chief. 17The sons of Eliezer: Rehabiah the chief; Eliezer had no other sons, but the sons of Rehabiah were very numerous. 18The sons of Izhar: Shelomith the chief. 19The sons of Hebron: Jeriah the chief, Amariah the second, Jahaziel the third, and Jekameam the fourth. 20The sons of Uzziel: Micah the chief and Isshiah the second.

21The sons of Merari: Mahli and Mushi. The sons of Mahli: Eleazar and Kish. 22Eleazar died having no sons, but only daughters; their kindred, the sons of Kish, married them. 23The sons of Mushi: Mahli, Eder, and Jeremoth, three.

24These were the sons of Levi by their ancestral houses, the heads of families as they were enrolled according to the number of the names of the individuals from twenty years old and upward who were to do the work for the service of the house of the LORD. 25For David said, "The

[a] Or *Gershom*; See 1 Chr 6.1, note, and 23.15 [b] Vg Compare Gk Syr: Heb *to the Gershonite*

NIV

Eliezer had no other sons, but the sons of Rehabiah were very numerous.

18The sons of Izhar:
Shelomith was the first.

19The sons of Hebron:
Jeriah the first, Amariah the second, Jahaziel the third and Jekameam the fourth.

20The sons of Uzziel:
Micah the first and Isshiah the second.

21The sons of Merari:
Mahli and Mushi.

The sons of Mahli:
Eleazar and Kish.

22Eleazar died without having sons: he had only daughters. Their cousins, the sons of Kish, married them.

23The sons of Mushi:
Mahli, Eder and Jerimoth—three in all.

24These were the descendants of Levi by their
families—the heads of families as they were
registered under their names and counted individually, that is, the workers twenty years old
or more who served in the temple of the LORD.
25For David had said, "Since the LORD, the God
of Israel, has granted rest to his people and has
come to dwell in Jerusalem forever, 26the
Levites no longer need to carry the tabernacle
or any of the articles used in its service." 27Ac-
cording to the last instructions of David, the
Levites were counted from those twenty years
old or more.

28The duty of the Levites was to help Aaron's
descendants in the service of the temple of the
LORD: to be in charge of the courtyards, the side
rooms, the purification of all sacred things and the
performance of other duties at the house of God.
29They were in charge of the bread set out on the
table, the flour for the grain offerings, the unleavened wafers, the baking and the mixing, and all
measurements of quantity and size. 30They were
also to stand every morning to thank and praise
the LORD. They were to do the same in the
evening 31and whenever burnt offerings were presented to the LORD on Sabbaths and at New Moon
festivals and at appointed feasts. They were to
serve before the LORD regularly in the proper
number and in the way prescribed for them.

32And so the Levites carried out their responsi-

NRSV

LORD, the God of Israel, has given rest to his
people; and he resides in Jerusalem forever. 26And
so the Levites no longer need to carry the tabernacle or any of the things for its service"— 27for
according to the last words of David these were
the number of the Levites from twenty years old
and upward— 28"but their duty shall be to assist
the descendants of Aaron for the service of the
house of the LORD, having the care of the courts
and the chambers, the cleansing of all that is holy,
and any work for the service of the house of God;
29to assist also with the rows of bread, the choice
flour for the grain offering, the wafers of unleavened bread, the baked offering, the offering mixed
with oil, and all measures of quantity or size.
30And they shall stand every morning, thanking
and praising the LORD, and likewise at evening,
31and whenever burnt offerings are offered to the
LORD on sabbaths, new moons, and appointed
festivals, according to the number required of
them, regularly before the LORD. 32Thus they shall
keep charge of the tent of meeting and the sanctuary, and shall attend the descendants of Aaron,
their kindred, for the service of the house of the
LORD."

NIV

bilities for the Tent of Meeting, for the Holy Place and, under their brothers the descendants of Aaron, for the service of the temple of the LORD.

COMMENTARY

23:1-6a. Verse 1 briefly alludes to the narrative of 1 Kings 1–2, characteristically omitting the struggle for succession to the throne described there, and presents the destined conclusion. Verse 2 refers to a preliminary meeting in which David gives assignments and instructions in preparation for Solomon's succession and commission as temple builder. The verse has often been regarded as a duplicate of 28:1, but the two meetings, for which different Hebrew verbs are used, are distinct. This meeting is an informal briefing, while the meeting in 28:1 is a formal convocation.[142] In vv. 3-6*a,* the chronicler has used a list older than his own time, related to a census of the Levites and to their proportionate division of duties. It appears to be post-exilic, since it regards gatekeepers and singers as Levites, a phenomenon that developed after the return from exile. It is attributed to the reign of David and had the function of legitimating the roles the Levites had in the Temple just before the time of the chronicler. Unlike the ill-fated military census of chap. 21, no exception is taken to this census, which has a different purpose. A similar census of Levites that assigns duties is found in Num 3:14-39; 4:1-49. The total of 38,000 Levites is generally regarded as exaggerated. The value of the list for the chronicler is the fourfold division of duties, which he uses as a framework for the presentation of Levites in the following chapters. Here the groups are listed in descending numerical order, but in the expanded analysis their contribution to temple worship determines their order. Those responsible for maintenance of the Temple are featured in 23:6*b*-24. The Levites involved in administration and those assigned to secular work, here loosely called "officials and judges," are dealt with in 26:20-32. The gatekeepers appear in 26:1-19, and the musicians in 25:1-31. The tradition that David made the instruments used for sacred music also occurs in 2 Chr 7:6; 29:26; Neh 12:36. That it is an old tradition is indicated by its presence in Amos 6:5.

23:6b-24. The chronicler now uses another list, structured not according to total numbers of individuals involved but by family heads. The NIV uses a reader-friendly layout. One might judge it to be a general list of Levites, but it relates to the first category, as v. 24 shows by its echo of temple work. This group was probably the oldest of the levitical groups, which gradually adopted others into its ranks. The list begins in v. 6*b,* "The sons of Levi: Gershon, Kohath and Merari" (TNK). It is not a proper genealogy, but a representative list of family heads current when it was composed, with narrative explanations where the list was incomplete. It runs from clan founder to a second or third generation and then jumps to contemporary heads of families. So "sons" with reference to these heads is used in the loose sense of descendants, as the NIV renders sketchily in vv. 16-17 and 24. Twenty-two family heads are listed.[143] Verses 10-11 regard Shimei's four sons as constituting only three families; v. 22 incorporates Eleazar's family into that of Kish. It is uncertain whether the law of inheritance in Numbers 27 would have been applied to exclusively male families of serving Levites. Japhet admits that in 24:28 Eleazar has no father's house.[144]

In vv. 7-8 (and 26:21), "Ladan" appears in place of "Libni" elsewhere (6:16-17; Exod 6:17; Num 3:18). Mention of "Shimei" in v. 9 seems to anticipate v. 10. The general structure of the list, in which the eldest son's children begin the

142. See J. W. Wright, "The Legacy of David in Chronicles: The Narrative Function of 1 Chronicles 23-27," *JBL* 110 (1991) 229-42, esp. 229-31.

143. Japhet finds 24, including 10 from Gershon and 5 from Merari. Her total, however, disregards conclusions the text itself draws. See S. Japhet, *I & II Chronicles,* OTL (Louisville: Westminster/John Knox, 1993) 413-17.

144. Ibid., 433-34.

listing of the next generation, leads one to expect the name "Jehiel" at this point.[145] Moses (v. 15) is a necessary exception to this pattern. In vv. 10-11, "Zina" and "Ziza(h)" must be the same person; the NIV and the REB emend the first name. The chronicler adds his own conclusion to the list in v. 24, relating this list of family heads to the previous total of individuals in v. 4*a*. The final phrase in the Hebrew, "from twenty years old and upwards," seems to be an annotation correcting the thirty-year lower limit of v. 3 (cf. Num 4:3). The lower limit evidently fluctuated according to supply and demand, and another limit was cited, which accords with 2 Chr 31:17; Ezra 3:8. A further annotation entered the text at v. 27, crediting the change of the minimum age of service to a later ruling by David.

Two aberrant factors of this levitical list are the aside in v. 13*b* and the complementary information of v. 14, concerning Aaron's status as a priest distinct from Moses and other Levites. This report apparently emanated from a pro-priestly redactor who wanted to present a more balanced view of the temple personnel than the rather one-sided approach of the chronicler.[146] Since this summary of the priests' work is best understood as sketching their duties, the word לשרתו (*lĕšortô*) ought to be translated as "in serving him."[147] The first duty involved "the most holy things"—that is, things to be sacrificed. They were consecrated or kept holy through the following of proper sacrificial rituals. The second duty was that of communicating the Lord's blessing to the people (cf. Num 6:22-27). The benediction formed a bridge between temple worship and the worshipers' lives, promising fulfillment and satisfaction to those who had met with God at the Temple.

23:25-32. These verses, apart from the annotation in v. 27, should also be attributed to a pro-priestly redactor. They complement v. 13*b* by giving a review of the work of the Levites. The redactor stresses the Levites' subordination in rank to the priesthood. Their essential duty to "assist" and to "attend" the priests in a number of respects is stated emphatically at the beginning (v. 28) and the end (v. 32). In the temple age, they were no longer porters, as they had been in the earlier period of the portable tabernacle. In 15:2, the chronicler traced the Levites' old task back to Deut 10:8; 18:5, whereas here it is related to Num 3:6-9; 4:15, 27, 33 and is replaced by tasks that demonstrate their continued subordination to the priests.[148] Now some had become temple janitors, responsible for keeping everything clean. Others were bakers, scrupulously preparing various items for the standard offerings made by the priests. Yet others were musicians, accompanying the priests' regular sacrifices of burnt offerings with their music and songs of worship.

One can appreciate the redactor's desire to present a more balanced view of the Levites' work. What brands these verses as supplementary is the misunderstanding of the role of vv. 6*b*-24. Verse 24 harks back to v. 4*a* and indicates that only the first category of Levites is in view in the preceding list. Verses 25-32 assume that the list referred to all the categories in vv. 4-5 and so may include the musicians in vv. 30-31. The phrase "for the service of the house of the LORD" is deliberately repeated three times (vv. 24, 28, 32), but inclusion of the musicians shows that the phrase is related to the Levites generally. Verses 25-32 function as an explanation of this "service." The accent on God's gift of rest to Israel in v. 25 recalls 22:18. There is a hint that the Lord also shared the rest, which anticipates the chronicler's perspective in 28:2; 2 Chr 6:41. The "forever" in v. 25 assumes continuity of worship despite the hiatus of the exile. It matches the double "forever" associated with the priests' duties in v. 13. Verse 32 gives the gist of Num 18:3-5, with the phrase "service of the tent" updated as "service of the house of the LORD" to fit the new context. This change suggests that in v. 32 the expression "tent of meeting," another term that could refer to the tabernacle, is used metaphorically for the Temple, which is the new counterpart of and replacement for the tabernacle.

145. K. Hognesius, "A Note on 1 Chr 23," *SJOT* 1 (1987) 123-27.

146. See H. G. M. Williamson, "The Origins of the Twenty-Four Priestly Courses: A Study of 1 Chronicles xxiii-xxvii," in *Studies in the Historical Books of the Old Testament,* ed. J. A. Emerton, VTSup 30 (Leiden: Brill, 1979) 257n. 18; *1 and 2 Chronicles,* NCB (Grand Rapids: Eerdmans, 1982) 161.

147. John W. Kleinig, *The Lord's Song: The Basis, Function and Significance of Choral Music in Chronicles,* JSOTSup 156 (Sheffield: JSOT, 1993) 105-6.

148. W. Rudolph, *Chronikbücher,* HAT 1:21 (Tübingen: Mohr [Siebeck], 1955) 157.

REFLECTIONS

1. Chapter 23 begins a series of lists concerning temple administration. They are perhaps the most difficult part of Chronicles for Christian readers to apply. When the ark was brought to Jerusalem, lists of religious personnel and their roles were presented in chaps. 15–16. Now sacred history had moved on, and a more extensive organization was necessary. David is credited with having set up a complex system involving classes of Levites in the areas of maintenance, security, music, and secular duties. There is an outworking of a principle affirmed in the New Testament: "All things should be done decently and in order" (1 Cor 14:40 NRSV).

2. Essentially, the chronicler is investing the temple organization of his own day with the glory of past tradition. The chronicler belonged to a community of relatively little political importance. Thus he endeavored to give it a spiritual identity by postulating the Temple as the center of the community's life. To this end he used David and Solomon as religious models. This ideology brought meaning into life and crowned contemporary worship with the past glory. The thread of Davidic organization that runs through this chapter and succeeding ones helped the community to understand that the expression of post-exilic faith in worship rested on ancient, divinely sponsored foundations.

Modern Christians have to juggle cultural pressures and biblical roots and, as citizens of one world and heirs of another, try to find what to stand for. Aversion to modern-day bureaucracy has made us weary of organization and highly developed structures. Many Christians want to start again with smaller groups that can relate heart to heart and to shrug off the burden of large religious institutions with top-heavy appendages. Nevertheless, each religious group develops its own traditions, if only to differentiate itself from other groups, and needs organization in order to function effectively in worship, teaching, and faith development. The Christian who visits a church on vacation and enjoys a Sunday service knows nothing about the labors of love that lie behind it. In thanking the pastor, one should add thanks for others who have contributed behind the scenes. Commitment to the Lord necessarily means commitment to many details. They become windows through which others may glimpse the Lord. This is the chronicler's attitude as he takes us into a hive of religious industry.

3. The second half of the chapter (23:25-32, and also the earlier vv. 13*b*-14) reflects a need to redress the emphasis placed on the Levites. Nothing the chronicler has said is denied, but an editor considered a different perspective necessary. The chronicler wrote as an enthusiast, with the lopsidedness that often goes with zeal for a beloved cause. He crusaded for recognition and appreciation of the Levites. The editor also wanted the contribution made by priests to be prized. He wanted Chronicles to be more widely representative of temple traditions. We need the enthusiast, especially the champion of unappreciated worth. We also need the generalist who restores the balance. May God give us wisdom to know which to be and when.

4. The brief job description of the priests (23:13*b*) focuses on their roles in bringing the people's sacrifices to God and in bringing God's blessing to the people. Like the priest, the pastor stands in the middle, representative of earth to heaven and of heaven to earth.

1 Chronicles 24:1-31, The Divisions of Priests and Levites

NIV

24 These were the divisions of the sons of Aaron:

The sons of Aaron were Nadab, Abihu, Eleazar and Ithamar. 2But Nadab and Abihu died before their father did, and they had no sons; so Eleazar and Ithamar served as the priests. 3With the help of Zadok a descendant of Eleazar and Ahimelech a descendant of Ithamar, David separated them into divisions for their appointed order of ministering. 4A larger number of leaders were found among Eleazar's descendants than among Ithamar's, and they were divided accordingly: sixteen heads of families from Eleazar's descendants and eight heads of families from Ithamar's descendants. 5They divided them impartially by drawing lots, for there were officials of the sanctuary and officials of God among the descendants of both Eleazar and Ithamar.

6The scribe Shemaiah son of Nethanel, a Levite, recorded their names in the presence of the king and of the officials: Zadok the priest, Ahimelech son of Abiathar and the heads of families of the priests and of the Levites—one family being taken from Eleazar and then one from Ithamar.

7The first lot fell to Jehoiarib,
the second to Jedaiah,
8the third to Harim,
the fourth to Seorim,
9the fifth to Malkijah,
the sixth to Mijamin,
10the seventh to Hakkoz,
the eighth to Abijah,
11the ninth to Jeshua,
the tenth to Shecaniah,
12the eleventh to Eliashib,
the twelfth to Jakim,
13the thirteenth to Huppah,
the fourteenth to Jeshebeab,
14the fifteenth to Bilgah,
the sixteenth to Immer,
15the seventeenth to Hezir,
the eighteenth to Happizzez,
16the nineteenth to Pethahiah,
the twentieth to Jehezkel,
17the twenty-first to Jakin,

NRSV

24 The divisions of the descendants of Aaron were these. The sons of Aaron: Nadab, Abihu, Eleazar, and Ithamar. 2But Nadab and Abihu died before their father, and had no sons; so Eleazar and Ithamar became the priests. 3Along with Zadok of the sons of Eleazar, and Ahimelech of the sons of Ithamar, David organized them according to the appointed duties in their service. 4Since more chief men were found among the sons of Eleazar than among the sons of Ithamar, they organized them under sixteen heads of ancestral houses of the sons of Eleazar, and eight of the sons of Ithamar. 5They organized them by lot, all alike, for there were officers of the sanctuary and officers of God among both the sons of Eleazar and the sons of Ithamar. 6The scribe Shemaiah son of Nethanel, a Levite, recorded them in the presence of the king, and the officers, and Zadok the priest, and Ahimelech son of Abiathar, and the heads of ancestral houses of the priests and of the Levites; one ancestral house being chosen for Eleazar and one chosen for Ithamar.

7The first lot fell to Jehoiarib, the second to Jedaiah, 8the third to Harim, the fourth to Seorim, 9the fifth to Malchijah, the sixth to Mijamin, 10the seventh to Hakkoz, the eighth to Abijah, 11the ninth to Jeshua, the tenth to Shecaniah, 12the eleventh to Eliashib, the twelfth to Jakim, 13the thirteenth to Huppah, the fourteenth to Jeshebeab, 14the fifteenth to Bilgah, the sixteenth to Immer, 15the seventeenth to Hezir, the eighteenth to Happizzez, 16the nineteenth to Pethahiah, the twentieth to Jehezkel, 17the twenty-first to Jachin, the twenty-second to Gamul, 18the twenty-third to Delaiah, the twenty-fourth to Maaziah. 19These had as their appointed duty in their service to enter the house of the LORD according to the procedure established for them by their ancestor Aaron, as the LORD God of Israel had commanded him.

20And of the rest of the sons of Levi: of the sons of Amram, Shubael; of the sons of Shubael, Jehdeiah. 21Of Rehabiah: of the sons of Rehabiah, Isshiah the chief. 22Of the Izharites, Shelomoth; of the sons of Shelomoth, Jahath. 23The sons of

NIV

the twenty-second to Gamul,
18the twenty-third to Delaiah
and the twenty-fourth to Maaziah.

19This was their appointed order of ministering when they entered the temple of the LORD, according to the regulations prescribed for them by their forefather Aaron, as the LORD, the God of Israel, had commanded him.

20As for the rest of the descendants of Levi:
from the sons of Amram: Shubael;
from the sons of Shubael: Jehdeiah.
21As for Rehabiah, from his sons:
Isshiah was the first.
22From the Izharites: Shelomoth;
from the sons of Shelomoth: Jahath.
23The sons of Hebron: Jeriah the first,[a] Amariah the second, Jahaziel the third and Jekameam the fourth.
24The son of Uzziel: Micah;
from the sons of Micah: Shamir.
25The brother of Micah: Isshiah;
from the sons of Isshiah: Zechariah.
26The sons of Merari: Mahli and Mushi.
The son of Jaaziah: Beno.
27The sons of Merari:
from Jaaziah: Beno, Shoham, Zaccur and Ibri.
28From Mahli: Eleazar, who had no sons.
29From Kish: the son of Kish:
Jerahmeel.
30And the sons of Mushi: Mahli, Eder and Jerimoth.

These were the Levites, according to their families. 31They also cast lots, just as their brothers the descendants of Aaron did, in the presence of King David and of Zadok, Ahimelech, and the heads of families of the priests and of the Levites. The families of the oldest brother were treated the same as those of the youngest.

a23 Two Hebrew manuscripts and some Septuagint manuscripts (see also 1 Chron. 23:19); most Hebrew manuscripts *The sons of Jeriah:*

NRSV

Hebron:[a] Jeriah the chief,[b] Amariah the second,
Jahaziel the third, Jekameam the fourth. 24The
sons of Uzziel, Micah; of the sons of Micah,
Shamir. 25The brother of Micah, Isshiah; of the
sons of Isshiah, Zechariah. 26The sons of Merari:
Mahli and Mushi. The sons of Jaaziah: Beno.[c]
27The sons of Merari: of Jaaziah, Beno,[c] Shoham,
Zaccur, and Ibri. 28Of Mahli: Eleazar, who had no
sons. 29Of Kish, the sons of Kish: Jerahmeel. 30The
sons of Mushi: Mahli, Eder, and Jerimoth. These
were the sons of the Levites according to their
ancestral houses. 31These also cast lots corresponding to their kindred, the descendants of Aaron, in
the presence of King David, Zadok, Ahimelech,
and the heads of ancestral houses of the priests
and of the Levites, the chief as well as the
youngest brother.

a See 23.19: Heb lacks *Hebron* b See 23.19: Heb lacks *the chief*
c Or *his son*: Meaning of Heb uncertain

COMMENTARY

The priests were organized into divisions in order to establish a rotational system of temple service, "their appointed order of ministering" (v. 3). These divisions correspond to the organization of Levites into four divisions (credited to David in 23:6*a*). Those levitical divisions related to different functions, but these twenty-four priestly divisions refer to different periods of temple duty. In Jewish practice, each division served for a week twice in a year of forty-eight weeks, based on a lunar calendar. Since 24:1 closely follows the mention of "the descendants of Aaron" in 23:32, the passage appears to be part of the same redactional complex. Like 23:25-32, 24:1-19 interrupts the exposition of the four divisions of Levites, announced in 23:4-6*a*.

This system of twenty-four divisions based on priestly families continued throughout the rest of the period of the Second Temple, and so it constitutes an important development. It reflects an overabundance of priests, who had to take their turn to exercise their right to serve in the Temple. Here this arrangement is attributed to David's supervision, but it appears to have occurred within the post-exilic period. At the beginning of that period, a time reflected in Ezra 2:36-39, there were only four priestly families. In Neh 12:12-31, an original fifteen or sixteen families at the time of the high priest Joiakim (Neh 12:12-18) had been editorially augmented with an extra six, which corresponded to a later situation (Neh 12:19-21).[149] By then the present twenty-four divisions had nearly been attained; ten names appearing here overlap with those in Neh 12:12-21, sometimes in slightly different forms.[150] This final stage of development probably took place near the end of the Persian period, a little later than the chronicler's own time.

24:1-19. The numbered list (vv. 7-18) reflects this later development. It was inserted to amplify the description of priestly divisions in 28:13, 21, together with the divisions of Levites (cf. 2 Chr 8:14; 23:18; 31:2). Presumably these references were related to different priestly functions, although the original block of material contained within chaps. 23–27 does not contain such information. David was regarded as simply endorsing the functions of priests in the Torah and ordering that they be put into operation in the Temple.

The method for selecting the priests is reported in vv. 1*b*-6. They are described as descendants of only two of the four sons of Aaron: Eleazar and Ithamar. The scandal of the sacrilege committed by Nadab and Abihu, which led to their deaths (Num 3:4), is treated with reserve (v. 2), out of respect for the priesthood. In the Torah, Eleazar and Ithamar are mentioned as sharing certain responsibilities for transporting the tabernacle (Num 4:16, 28, 33). The presence of the names of the two leading priests in David's reign, Zadok and Ahimelech, reflects literary dependence on 18:16; these two priests are credited to the two surviving lines of priestly descent. Zadok's descent from Eleazar was derived from 6:8, 53, where his adoption into that priestly group is evidently in view. One may infer that Ahimelech was associated with the remaining line of Ithamar. The numerical dominance of Eleazar's line presumably corresponds to the situation in the period of the redactor. The necessary adjustments to create twenty-four divisions are legitimated by tracing them back to David. Both groups win approval by having among them "sacred officers" (REB) and "officers of God" (NRSV). These titles do not refer to particular offices but are general descriptions of qualification for the priesthood.

The order of shifts is achieved by casting lots.[151] Apparently, one each of the families belonging to Eleazar's line and those of Ithamar's were chosen in turn, until the latter's families were exhausted. Then, the last eight families were confined to the line of Eleazar. A parallel for this pattern occurs in chap. 25. Accordingly, Ithamar's line is made up of numbers 2, 4, 6, 8, 10, 12, 14, and 16. The resulting roster by families is presented in vv. 7-18. Verse 19 carefully observes that the functions of the priests had been laid down in the Torah, presented by the Lord via Aaron, the priests' ancestor (see, e.g., Lev 10:8-11; 17:1-7). Only the number and order of the shifts were established by the present system.

24:20-31. A corresponding roster of Levites is given. The heading in v. 20*a* differentiates between the priestly line of Aaron, dealt with in vv. 1-19, and the rest of the "descendants" of Levi,

149. See H. G. M. Williamson, *Ezra, Nehemiah,* WBC 16 (Waco, Tex.: Word, 1985) 358-62.

150. See S. Japhet, *I & II Chronicles,* OTL (Louisville: Westminster/John Knox, 1993) 429.

151. In v. 6*b**a* slight emendation is followed implicitly by both the NIV and the NRSV. See the notes in the REB and *BHS.*

the Levites. The list that follows in vv. 20*b*-30 bears a close relationship to that of the maintenance staff, grouped by family heads in 23:12-23. Once again, however, as in the redactional addition (23:25-32), it is assumed that the list represents Levites generally, and not just one group of them. The system of levitical divisions parallel to that of the priests presupposes the role of the Levites as assistants to the priests (23:28-32), which is here developed into a corresponding roster.

This list makes no mention of the Gershonites, who were featured in 23:7-11. It begins with the clan of Kohath, who is not actually mentioned in vv. 20*b*-25, and continues with the clan of Merari in vv. 26-30. It represents a slightly later stage of the previous list of family heads. In most cases, it is advanced one generation. Thus Shubael (= Shebuel, 23:16 NRSV) is replaced by Jehdeiah (v. 20*b*). Other replacements are Isshiah (v. 21), Jahath (v. 22), Shamir (v. 24), Zechariah (v. 25), and Jerahmeel (v. 29). The descendants of Merari stay the same in v. 27 as in 23:21. Another recapitulation occurs in v. 23 concerning the family heads descended from Hebron, reference to which needs to be restored in line with 23:19, as the NRSV and the NIV recognize. The mixture of recapitulation and replacement indicates that the updated list reflects a period shortly after that of the preceding one. This phenomenon suggests that the pro-priestly reviser was at work one generation later than the chronicler.[152]

In vv. 26-27, "Beno" is simply a transliteration of the Hebrew term בנו (*bĕnô*, "his son"). The consequent rendering in v. 26, "the sons of Jaaziah, his son," refers to a newly recognized descendant of Merari, now included by adoption into the clan. In v. 27*a*, an explanatory annotation has probably been incorporated, with the sense "the descendants of Merari via Jaaziah were" (cf. the NJB).

After a closing summary in v. 30*b*, the procedure of casting lots is narrated in v. 31, with material from vv. 1, 3, and 5-6 included. The comparisons with the priests chosen by lot implies twenty-four divisions. We are not told how this number was attained. Presumably, in addition to the nine family heads credited to the clan of Kohath and the seven allocated to the clan of Merari, eight of the nine family heads associated with the clan of Gershon in 23:7-11 must be included.[153] The recapitulation of the earlier list in vv. 23 and 30 supports this explanation, and a reason is supplied for the omission of the Gershon clan members, who are assumed to stay the same. The principle of equality, which in the case of the priests related to the two priestly houses, is here applied to a lack of preferential treatment of closely related family heads. A "chief" (cf. vv. 21, 23; 23:8, 11) received no different treatment from his juniors. All "were treated the same."

152. Williamson, "The Origins of the Twenty-Four Priestly Courses," 266.

153. Japhet, *I & II Chronicles,* 433.

REFLECTIONS

1. Mention of Abijah in 24:10 spans the testaments. Zechariah, the father of John the Baptist, belonged to the eighth division (according to Luke 1:5). He was on duty in the Temple, burning incense, when he received an angelic vision and message about the birth of John and his mission. Struck dumb, Zechariah was unable to deliver the priestly benediction in the temple court. Thus 1 Chr 23:13 and 24:10 may be understood as background material for that New Testament passage.

2. This system of twenty-four divisions became an established custom until the Temple fell in 70 CE. The system gradually evolved after the exile; 24:1-19 is the first evidence that it reached its final form. The attribution to the period of David reflects a sincere and evidently successful attempt to have its value recognized and its permanence guaranteed. Christian denominations and movements that honestly claim New Testament support for their distinctive teachings work in a similar fashion.

The passage gives the impression that "all things should be done decently and in order" (1 Cor 14:40 NRSV). To worship in spirit and in truth is not incompatible with the implementation of a mass of necessary details.

The principle of equality achieved by casting lots (24:5) was, presumably, to prevent more powerful priestly families from controlling the system. While the most desirable case is for the best people do the work, a principle of fair sharing is also required in order that no one becomes too heavily burdened and that the gifts of other persons may be developed.

3. The parallel levitical roster (24:20-31) presupposes the role of the Levites as assistants to the priests, outlined in 23:28-32. The priest depended on the partnership of the lesser staff member, if the job was to be done. The significant difference between the new list and the old one in 23:7-21 is that time had moved on. While some of the heads of families were still in office, others had been succeeded by the next generation. The principle of a new generation taking over from the preceding one has a major part to play in 1 Chronicles. The work can only go on insofar as younger persons take over ministry in God's service.

Again the principle of equality is featured. We tend to assume that the biblical tradition ascribes honor to age. Here, however, age plays no part. The chronicler envisions that these family heads stood on a level playing field and gained no advantage from their degree of maturity. Seniority is a prized ingredient of many aspects of our culture. The notion of equality that has been running through recent passages represents a challenge. We need to ask ourselves when this factor should reasonably prevail and when it should be discarded in the name of God.

1 Chronicles 25:1-31, Temple Musicians

NIV

25 David, together with the commanders of the army, set apart some of the sons of Asaph, Heman and Jeduthun for the ministry of prophesying, accompanied by harps, lyres and cymbals. Here is the list of the men who performed this service:

[2]From the sons of Asaph:

Zaccur, Joseph, Nethaniah and Asarelah. The sons of Asaph were under the supervision of Asaph, who prophesied under the king's supervision.

[3]As for Jeduthun, from his sons:

Gedaliah, Zeri, Jeshaiah, Shimei,[a] Hashabiah and Mattithiah, six in all, under the supervision of their father Jeduthun, who prophesied, using the harp in thanking and praising the LORD.

[4]As for Heman, from his sons:

Bukkiah, Mattaniah, Uzziel, Shubael and Jeri-

[a]3 One Hebrew manuscript and some Septuagint manuscripts (see also verse 17); most Hebrew manuscripts do not have *Shimei.*

NRSV

25 David and the officers of the army also set
apart for the service the sons of Asaph, and
of Heman, and of Jeduthun, who should prophesy
with lyres, harps, and cymbals. The list of those
who did the work and of their duties was: [2]Of
the sons of Asaph: Zaccur, Joseph, Nethaniah, and
Asarelah, sons of Asaph, under the direction of
Asaph, who prophesied under the direction of the
king. [3]Of Jeduthun, the sons of Jeduthun:
Gedaliah, Zeri, Jeshaiah, Shimei,[a] Hashabiah, and
Mattithiah, six, under the direction of their father
Jeduthun, who prophesied with the lyre in thanksgiving and praise to the LORD. [4]Of Heman, the
sons of Heman: Bukkiah, Mattaniah, Uzziel, Shebuel, and Jerimoth, Hananiah, Hanani, Eliathah,
Giddalti, and Romamti-ezer, Joshbekashah, Mallothi, Hothir, Mahazioth. [5]All these were the sons
of Heman the king's seer, according to the promise of God to exalt him; for God had given Heman
fourteen sons and three daughters. [6]They were all

[a] One Ms: Gk: MT lacks *Shimei*

NIV

moth; Hananiah, Hanani, Eliathah, Giddalti
and Romamti-Ezer; Joshbekashah, Mallothi,
Hothir and Mahazioth. 5All these were sons
of Heman the king's seer. They were given
him through the promises of God to exalt
him.[a] God gave Heman fourteen sons and
three daughters.

6All these men were under the supervision of
their fathers for the music of the temple of the
LORD, with cymbals, lyres and harps, for the ministry at the house of God. Asaph, Jeduthun and
Heman were under the supervision of the king.
7Along with their relatives—all of them trained
and skilled in music for the LORD—they numbered
288. 8Young and old alike, teacher as well as
student, cast lots for their duties.

9The first lot, which was for Asaph, fell to
Joseph,
his sons and relatives,[b] 12[c]
the second to Gedaliah,
he and his relatives and sons, 12
10the third to Zaccur,
his sons and relatives, 12
11the fourth to Izri,[d]
his sons and relatives, 12
12the fifth to Nethaniah,
his sons and relatives, 12
13the sixth to Bukkiah,
his sons and relatives, 12
14the seventh to Jesarelah,[e]
his sons and relatives, 12
15the eighth to Jeshaiah,
his sons and relatives, 12
16the ninth to Mattaniah,
his sons and relatives, 12
17the tenth to Shimei,
his sons and relatives, 12
18the eleventh to Azarel,[f]
his sons and relatives, 12
19the twelfth to Hashabiah,
his sons and relatives, 12
20the thirteenth to Shubael,
his sons and relatives, 12
21the fourteenth to Mattithiah,

[a]*5* Hebrew *exalt the horn* [b]*9* See Septuagint; Hebrew does not have *his sons and relatives.* [c]*9* See the total in verse 7; Hebrew does not have *twelve.* [d]*11* A variant of *Zeri* [e]*14* A variant of *Asarelah* [f]*18* A variant of *Uzziel*

NRSV

under the direction of their father for the music
in the house of the LORD with cymbals, harps, and
lyres for the service of the house of God. Asaph,
Jeduthun, and Heman were under the order of
the king. 7They and their kindred, who were
trained in singing to the LORD, all of whom were
skillful, numbered two hundred eighty-eight. 8And
they cast lots for their duties, small and great,
teacher and pupil alike.

9The first lot fell for Asaph to Joseph; the
second to Gedaliah, to him and his brothers and
his sons, twelve; 10the third to Zaccur, his sons
and his brothers, twelve; 11the fourth to Izri, his
sons and his brothers, twelve; 12the fifth to
Nethaniah, his sons and his brothers, twelve; 13the
sixth to Bukkiah, his sons and his brothers,
twelve; 14the seventh to Jesarelah,[a] his sons and
his brothers, twelve; 15the eighth to Jeshaiah, his
sons and his brothers, twelve; 16the ninth to
Mattaniah, his sons and his brothers, twelve; 17the
tenth to Shimei, his sons and his brothers, twelve;
18the eleventh to Azarel, his sons and his brothers,
twelve; 19the twelfth to Hashabiah, his sons and
his brothers, twelve; 20to the thirteenth, Shubael,
his sons and his brothers, twelve; 21to the fourteenth, Mattithiah, his sons and his brothers,
twelve; 22to the fifteenth, to Jeremoth, his sons
and his brothers, twelve; 23to the sixteenth, to
Hananiah, his sons and his brothers, twelve; 24to
the seventeenth, to Joshbekashah, his sons and
his brothers, twelve; 25to the eighteenth, to Hanani, his sons and his brothers, twelve; 26to the
nineteenth, to Mallothi, his sons and his brothers,
twelve; 27to the twentieth, to Eliathah, his sons
and his brothers, twelve; 28to the twenty-first, to
Hothir, his sons and his brothers, twelve; 29to the
twenty-second, to Giddalti, his sons and his brothers, twelve; 30to the twenty-third, to Mahazioth,
his sons and his brothers, twelve; 31to the twenty-
fourth, to Romamti-ezer, his sons and his brothers,
twelve.

[a] Or *Asarelah*; see 25.2

NIV

his sons and relatives,	12
[22]the fifteenth to Jerimoth,	
his sons and relatives,	12
[23]the sixteenth to Hananiah,	
his sons and relatives,	12
[24]the seventeenth to Joshbekashah,	
his sons and relatives,	12
[25]the eighteenth to Hanani,	
his sons and relatives,	12
[26]the nineteenth to Mallothi,	
his sons and relatives,	12
[27]the twentieth to Eliathah,	
his sons and relatives,	12
[28]the twenty-first to Hothir,	
his sons and relatives,	12
[29]the twenty-second to Giddalti,	
his sons and relatives,	12
[30]the twenty-third to Mahazioth,	
his sons and relatives,	12
[31]the twenty-fourth to Romamti-Ezer,	
his sons and relatives,	12

COMMENTARY

Exposition of the four divisions of Levites, announced in 23:4-5 and begun with the maintenance staff in 23:6*b*-24, now continues with attention devoted to the singing musicians.[154] According to 15:16-24, these musicians attended David's second and successful attempt to install the ark in Jerusalem. They were appointed by the chiefs of the Levites at David's command. Then, according to 16:4-6, 41-42, the king also appointed two groups: one led by Asaph to sing and play at the tent of the ark and another led by Heman and Jeduthun to serve at the tabernacle in Gibeon. The chronicler emphasizes David's initiation of the levitical system of sacred music and song. The same claim is made in the course of the genealogy of Levi at 6:31-48.

25:1a. The singers were set apart from other levitical duties. The army officers were presumably present to add formality to the occasion, occasion, as "all the leaders of Israel" were in 23:2. It is possible, however, that the term צבא (*ṣābā'*) refers to the "host" of Levites, as both the noun and its cognate verb are used in Numbers 4 and 8, rather than "army."[155] Then these officers are the equivalent of "the chiefs of the Levites" in 15:16 (NRSV). The listing of the choir heads as Asaph, Heman, and Jeduthun permits us to place this account within the post-exilic developments of the singers' role. This list reflects the penultimate stage, but is already leaning toward the final stage listing Heman, Asaph, and Ethan, in that Heman is pushed to the fore (v. 5; see the Introduction).

Their ministry is strikingly defined as prophesying. It refers to the oral aspect of their combined music and song. The description is repeated for each of the guild leaders in the list of vv. 1*b*-6. Asaph "prophesied" (v. 2), and so did Jeduthun as he praised with the lyre (v. 3), while Heman is called "the king's seer" (v. 5). In v. 1*a*, however, it is the rank and file who are said to

154. Williamson, "The Origins of the Twenty-four Priestly Courses," 255-57.

155. E. L. Curtis and A. A. Madsen, *The Books of Chronicles,* ICC (Edinburgh: T. &. T. Clark, 1910) 279.

prophesy. Much discussion has been devoted to the nature of this prophesying.[156] It is best taken as being related to the nature of their songs, the texts of the psalms regarded as the words of God given by inspiration.[157] The guild leaders are reckoned as inspired authors of certain psalms. Indeed, in 2 Chr 29:30 Hezekiah ordered the Levites to worship "with the words of David and of the seer Asaph" (NRSV). This phrase refers to the collections of psalms ascribed to David and to Asaph in the psalter. Heman features in the heading to Psalm 88, and Jeduthun in those to Psalms 39, 62, and 77. In the NT, one may add, David is considered a prophet in Mark 12:36 and Acts 2:25-35; 4:25, and Asaph in Matt 13:35.

25:1b-6. The chronicler supplies a list of the three-part guild and its members. The founders are regarded as contemporary with David, whom vv. 2 and 6 identify as their patron, which is consistent with his setting aside their families in v. 1*a.* The list in vv. 9-31 and the need for an extra name to make up the stated total of six (v. 3) indicate that the name "Shimel," preserved in the LXX, has accidentally fallen out of v. 3 in the MT. Heman is singled out because of the exceptional size of his family, which is viewed as the object of divine blessing. There is a deliberate intent to promote him as the leading figure among the guild founders. The repeated "All these" at the beginning of vv. 5 and 6 accentuates this singular emphasis. There is some question about the translation of v. 5*a.* The TNK takes the words following "seer" as descriptive of Heman's prophetic role: "who uttered the prophecies of God for His greater glory." The latter part of this rendering is doubtful, since elsewhere the Hebrew phrase "raise the horn" is used with a human object. Rather, the phrase seems to qualify Heman's sons, whose numbers give him prominence. It is attractive to take the earlier part of the phrase as qualifying "seer," with the sense "the king's seer with [= using] the words of God." Reference is then made to the psalms he was regarded as having composed for future use in the Temple.[158]

The names after Jerimoth in v. 4 have a strange, exotic ring. They do not look like Hebrew names at all, but ordinary words. It is possible to regard them as slightly adapted in form from a snatch of psalm poetry, specifically an individual lament or, since the sequence of clauses becomes rather ragged as it continues, a series of beginning phrases (incipits) used as psalm titles.[159] One feasible rendering of v. 4*b* is "Have mercy on me, O LORD, have mercy. You are my God. I magnify and exalt [your] help. As one living in adversity, I speak. Give an abundance of visions." An attempt has been made to find a Sumerian parallel for using quotations from religious songs as names, but it is unconvincing.[160] The latter part of the list of Heman's fourteen sons seems to be a literary formulation rather than a historical report.

The list of names "Asaph, Jeduthun, and Heman" is abrupt in the Hebrew of v. 6*b.* It is often taken as an annotation indicating that v. 6 refers to the descendants of all three founders, so that "their father" functions as a distributive singular. If so, the reference to the king in v. 6*b* relates to the royal patronage of the Heman group; likewise, the reference to the king in v. 2 relates to the royal patronage of the Asaph group. "All these" at the start of v. 6 (NIV) brackets the verse with v. 5, which begins identically. Moreover, one does expect a general statement relating to the Heman group, parallel with those in vv. 2 and 3*b,* which refer to the other Asaph and Jeduthun groups. The only reason for considering v. 6 a summary of vv. 1*b*-5 is the repetition of the instruments of v. 1*a,* but the repetition only rounds off the paragraph with a rhetorical inversion.

25:7-31. This roster is based on the preceding list of names. Although the term "division" is not used, the roster is modeled on the twenty-four priestly divisions of 24:1-19. This rotation of shifts was motivated by the reviser's description of the levitical singers who accompanied with music and song the priests' sacrificing of the regular burnt offerings (23:30-31). The priestly divisions are given a matching roster of twenty-four choirs,

156. See esp. D. L. Petersen, *Late Israelite Prophecy,* SBLMS 23 (Missoula, Mont.: Scholars Press, 1977) 62-87; John W. Kleinig, *The Lord's Song: The Basis, Function and Significance of Choral Music in Chronicles,* JSOTSup 156 (Sheffield: JSOT, 1993) 154-57; W. M. Schniedewind, *The Word of God in Transition: From Prophet to Exegete in the Second Temple Period,* JSOTSup 197 (Sheffield: Sheffield Academic, 1995) 170-88.

157. S. Zalewski, cited in Kleinig, *The Lord's Song,* 155. See also A. H. J. Gunneweg, *Leviten und Priester,* FRLANT 89 (Göttingen: Vandenhoeck & Ruprecht, 1965) 215; S. Japhet, *I & II Chronicles,* OTL (Louisville: Westminster/John Knox, 1993) 440.

158. See Petersen, *Late Israelite Prophecy,* 64 and n. 43.

159. J. M. Myers, *I Chronicles,* AB 12 (Garden City, N.Y.: Doubleday, 1965) 173.

160. See Petersen, *Late Israelite Prophecy,* 65-66.

each led by one of the named persons. This arrangement depends on the work of the pro-priestly reviser and, since it ministers to priestly ends, was probably added by him. It is possible that the names of the extra sons of Heman were added along with the roster, which depends on their presence to make up the required number.

An introduction to the roster is given in vv. 7-8. It uses as a catchword מספר (*mispār*), with which the former list opened (v. 16), therein the sense of "list" and now meaning "number." Emphasis is laid on the professional standards of the singers, which included a training program. The total number of 288 is made up of twenty-four choirs of twelve members each. According to the Mishnah, in later times such a musical choir would comprise nine lyre players, two harp players, and one cymbal player.[161] The casting of lots accords with redactional elements (24:5, 31). Based on vv. 9-31, one expects selection of the order of choirs to be the object of the lot, but v. 8 has individuals in view, from whom the choirs were formed. So not one but two separate lot castings are envisioned. The principle of equality characteristic of the other selections by lot is at work here, so that experience ("young and old," NIV) and expertise are not of particular value at this stage.

The form of the roster is remarkably full and repetitive. Some of the names vary slightly from those in vv. 2-4. In v. 9 one expects a reference to the choir, which the LXX attests in an abbreviated and misplaced note.[162] Both the analogy of the following verses and the total of 288 in v. 7 suggest its original presence (the NIV has restored it). At each round of lots a choice was made between two previously selected candidates for two positions.[163]

The chronicler has given three extended treatments of the levitical singing musicians: 6:31-48 in a genealogy, chaps. 15–16 in the narrative of the installation of the ark, and here. Other parts of his narrative will feature them further. This aspect of levitical duties was especially dear to the chronicler's heart as a mark of the new dispensation associated with David and still valid in his own day.

161. *b. 'Arak.* 13*b.*

162. See L. C. Allen, *The Greek Chronicles: The Relation of the Septuagint of I and II Chronicles to the Massoretic Text,* Part 2: *Textual Criticism,* VTSup 25, 27 (Leiden: Brill, 1974) 140.

163. See the table in Kleinig, *The Lord's Song,* 59.

REFLECTIONS

1. A striking characteristic of the chronicler's description of the choirs' ministry is the use of the concept of prophecy. The temple choirs were so credited because they sang items from the authoritative psalms and also because the composition of inspired psalms was attributed to the choirs' founders. The medley of psalm extracts in chapter 16 is an example of the Levites' contribution to temple worship. With divinely inspired words, they lifted up to God the hearts and minds of the congregation and stimulated them to a loftier spirituality. They led the worship and voiced the praises and prayers to which the congregation added their amens and hallelujahs (16:36). No choir could be paid a greater tribute. Ideals are presented that church choirs today may want to take seriously.

2. In 25:7-8 the high standards expected of the choirs' ministry are mentioned. Evidently a general training scheme tested and improved professional competence, and rehearsals were designed to teach accomplished renderings of the psalms. According to the Talmud,[164] in later times temple choristers underwent five years of training. These references, tantalizingly brief though they are, suggest that Christian churches should have high standards of music and song.

3. The book of Revelation describes the hymns sung to the music of the harp (Rev 5:8; 15:2), mentioning "harps of God" (Rev 15:2 NRSV), presumably harps used in the worship of

164. *b. Ḥul.* 24*a.*

God. Music appeals to the emotions, with the accompanying words appealing more to the intellect. Thereby the whole person is brought nearer to God. Martin Luther testified to the power of music: "With all my heart I would extol the precious gift of God in the noble art of music. . . . Music is to be praised as second only to the Word of God, because by her are all the emotions swayed. Nothing on earth is more mighty . . . to hearten the downcast, mellow the overweening, temper the exuberant, or mollify the vengeful. . . . When natural music is sharpened and polished by art, then one begins to see with amazement the great and perfect wisdom of God."[165]

165. Martin Luther, cited in R. H. Bainton, *Here I Stand* (Nashville: Abingdon, 1950) 343.

1 Chronicles 26:1-32, Temple Security and Secular Assignments

NIV

26 The divisions of the gatekeepers:

From the Korahites: Meshelemiah son of Kore, one of the sons of Asaph.
2Meshelemiah had sons:
Zechariah the firstborn,
Jediael the second,
Zebadiah the third,
Jathniel the fourth,
3Elam the fifth,
Jehohanan the sixth
and Eliehoenai the seventh.
4Obed-Edom also had sons:
Shemaiah the firstborn,
Jehozabad the second,
Joah the third,
Sacar the fourth,
Nethanel the fifth,
5Ammiel the sixth,
Issachar the seventh
and Peullethai the eighth.
(For God had blessed Obed-Edom.)

6His son Shemaiah also had sons, who were leaders in their father's family because
they were very capable men. 7The sons of
Shemaiah: Othni, Rephael, Obed and Elzabad; his relatives Elihu and Semakiah
were also able men. 8All these were descendants of Obed-Edom; they and their sons and their relatives were capable men with the strength to do the work—descendants of Obed-Edom, 62 in all.

NRSV

26 As for the divisions of the gatekeepers: of the Korahites, Meshelemiah son of Kore,
of the sons of Asaph. 2Meshelemiah had sons:
Zechariah the firstborn, Jediael the second, Zebadiah the third, Jathniel the fourth, 3Elam the
fifth, Jehohanan the sixth, Eliehoenai the seventh.
4Obed-edom had sons: Shemaiah the firstborn,
Jehozabad the second, Joah the third, Sachar the
fourth, Nethanel the fifth, 5Ammiel the sixth,
Issachar the seventh, Peullethai the eighth; for
God blessed him. 6Also to his son Shemaiah sons
were born who exercised authority in their ancestral houses, for they were men of great ability.
7The sons of Shemaiah: Othni, Rephael, Obed,
and Elzabad, whose brothers were able men,
Elihu and Semachiah. 8All these, sons of Obed-edom with their sons and brothers, were able men
qualified for the service; sixty-two of Obed-edom.
9Meshelemiah had sons and brothers, able men,
eighteen. 10Hosah, of the sons of Merari, had sons:
Shimri the chief (for though he was not the
firstborn, his father made him chief), 11Hilkiah the
second, Tebaliah the third, Zechariah the fourth:
all the sons and brothers of Hosah totaled thirteen.

12These divisions of the gatekeepers, corresponding to their leaders, had duties, just as their
kindred did, ministering in the house of the LORD;
13and they cast lots by ancestral houses, small and
great alike, for their gates. 14The lot for the east
fell to Shelemiah. They cast lots also for his son
Zechariah, a prudent counselor, and his lot came
out for the north. 15Obed-edom's came out for the
south, and to his sons was allotted the storehouse.

NIV

[9]Meshelemiah had sons and relatives, who were able men—18 in all.

[10]Hosah the Merarite had sons: Shimri the first (although he was not the firstborn, his father had appointed him the first), [11]Hilkiah the second, Tabaliah the third and Zechariah the fourth. The sons and relatives of Hosah were 13 in all.

[12]These divisions of the gatekeepers, through their chief men, had duties for ministering in the temple of the LORD, just as their relatives had. [13]Lots were cast for each gate, according to their families, young and old alike.

[14]The lot for the East Gate fell to Shelemiah.[a] Then lots were cast for his son Zechariah, a wise counselor, and the lot for the North Gate fell to him. [15]The lot for the South Gate fell to Obed-Edom, and the lot for the storehouse fell to his sons. [16]The lots for the West Gate and the Shalleketh Gate on the upper road fell to Shuppim and Hosah.

Guard was alongside of guard: [17]There were six Levites a day on the east, four a day on the north, four a day on the south and two at a time at the storehouse. [18]As for the court to the west, there were four at the road and two at the court itself.

[19]These were the divisions of the gatekeepers who were descendants of Korah and Merari.

[20]Their fellow Levites were[b] in charge of the treasuries of the house of God and the treasuries for the dedicated things.

[21]The descendants of Ladan, who were Gershonites through Ladan and who were heads of families belonging to Ladan the Gershonite, were Jehieli, [22]the sons of Jehieli, Zetham and his brother Joel. They were in charge of the treasuries of the temple of the LORD.

[23]From the Amramites, the Izharites, the Hebronites and the Uzzielites:

[24]Shubael, a descendant of Gershom son of Moses, was the officer in charge of the treasuries. [25]His relatives through Eliezer: Rehabiah his son, Jeshaiah his son, Joram his son, Zicri his son and Shelomith his son. [26]Shelomith and his relatives were in charge of all the treasuries for the things dedicated by King David, by the heads of

[a]*14* A variant of *Meshelemiah* [b]*20* Septuagint; Hebrew *As for the Levites, Ahijah was*

NRSV

[16]For Shuppim and Hosah it came out for the west, at the gate of Shallecheth on the ascending road. Guard corresponded to guard. [17]On the east there were six Levites each day,[a] on the north four each day, on the south four each day, as well as two and two at the storehouse; [18]and for the colonnade[b] on the west there were four at the road and two at the colonnade.[b] [19]These were the divisions of the gatekeepers among the Korahites and the sons of Merari.

20And of the Levites, Ahijah had charge of the treasuries of the house of God and the treasuries of the dedicated gifts. [21]The sons of Ladan, the sons of the Gershonites belonging to Ladan, the heads of families belonging to Ladan the Gershonite: Jehieli.[c]

22The sons of Jehieli, Zetham and his brother Joel, were in charge of the treasuries of the house of the LORD. [23]Of the Amramites, the Izharites, the Hebronites, and the Uzzielites: [24]Shebuel son of Gershom, son of Moses, was chief officer in charge of the treasuries. [25]His brothers: from Eliezer were his son Rehabiah, his son Jeshaiah, his son Joram, his son Zichri, and his son Shelomoth. [26]This Shelomoth and his brothers were in charge of all the treasuries of the dedicated gifts that King David, and the heads of families, and the officers of the thousands and the hundreds, and the commanders of the army, had dedicated. [27]From booty won in battles they dedicated gifts for the maintenance of the house of the LORD. [28]Also all that Samuel the seer, and Saul son of Kish, and Abner son of Ner, and Joab son of Zeruiah had dedicated—all dedicated gifts were in the care of Shelomoth[d] and his brothers.

29Of the Izharites, Chenaniah and his sons were appointed to outside duties for Israel, as officers and judges. [30]Of the Hebronites, Hashabiah and his brothers, one thousand seven hundred men of ability, had the oversight of Israel west of the Jordan for all the work of the LORD and for the service of the king. [31]Of the Hebronites, Jerijah was chief of the Hebronites. (In the fortieth year of David's reign search was made, of whatever genealogy or family, and men of great ability among them were found at Jazer

[a] Gk: Heb lacks *each day* [b] Heb *parbar*: meaning uncertain [c] The Hebrew text of verse 21 is confused [d] Gk Compare 26.28: Heb *Shelomith*

NIV

families who were the commanders of
thousands and commanders of hundreds,
and by the other army commanders.
[27]Some of the plunder taken in battle they
dedicated for the repair of the temple of
the LORD. [28]And everything dedicated by
Samuel the seer and by Saul son of Kish,
Abner son of Ner and Joab son of Zeruiah,
and all the other dedicated things were in
the care of Shelomith and his relatives.
[29]From the Izharites: Kenaniah and his sons
were assigned duties away from the temple, as officials and judges over Israel.
[30]From the Hebronites: Hashabiah and his relatives—seventeen hundred able men—
were responsible in Israel west of the
Jordan for all the work of the LORD and
for the king's service. [31]As for the Hebronites, Jeriah was their chief according
to the genealogical records of their families. In the fortieth year of David's reign
a search was made in the records, and
capable men among the Hebronites were
found at Jazer in Gilead. [32]Jeriah had
twenty-seven hundred relatives, who
were able men and heads of families, and
King David put them in charge of the
Reubenites, the Gadites and the half-tribe
of Manasseh for every matter pertaining
to God and for the affairs of the king.

NRSV

in Gilead.) [32]King David appointed him and his
brothers, two thousand seven hundred men of
ability, heads of families, to have the oversight of
the Reubenites, the Gadites, and the half-tribe of
the Manassites for everything pertaining to God
and for the affairs of the king.

COMMENTARY

This chapter completes the exposition of the various groups of Levites appointed by David, which had been announced in 23:4-5. In vv. 1-19 the chronicler deals with the gatekeepers and in vv. 20-32 with the miscellaneous group called "officials and Judges" (23:4 NIV). Verse 1*a* provides a heading for vv. 1*b*-19, and v. 19 a summary of the two levitical clans involved. The term "division" refers here to the assignment of personnel to particular tasks of gatekeeping. Somewhat surprisingly, David is not mentioned in this passage, whereas in 9:22 the organization of the temple gatekeepers is credited to David and Samuel. The earliest layer in this material is probably vv. 1-3, 9-11, and 19.[166] In the early post-exilic period, gatekeepers were not regarded as Levites. Indeed, they are not so viewed in the source from Neh 11:19, which is used in 9:17. By the chronicler's time they were classed as Levites and their descent was traced from Levi.

26:1-3, 9-11. Here the Levites are traced back to Merari, a son of Levi, and to Korah, who in Num 16:1 is descended from Kohath, another son of Levi. Meshelemiah, called Shelemiah in v. 14, is possibly the Shallum of 9:17 and Ezra 2:42

166. See Williamson, "The Origins of the Twenty-four Priestly Courses: A Study of 1 Chronicles xxiii-xxvii," in *Studies in Historical Books of the Old Testament*, ed. J. A. Emerton, VTSup 30 (Leiden: Brill, 1979) 253-54.

(= Neh 7:45). The appearance of Asaph, head of one of the branches of the singing guild, is unexpected here. He belongs to a different part of the family tree of Levi, one who descended from Gershom, another son of Levi (6:39-43). By comparison with 9:19, we expect "Ebiasaph" at this point, which is found in the LXX in a corrupted form and is restored in the REB.

26:4-8. The information about Obed-edom cuts across the data about Meshelemiah in vv. 1*b*-3 and 9. In the primary tradition present in chaps. 15–16, Obed-edom was regarded as a singer; references to his status as a gatekeeper in 15:18, 24; 16:38*b* are secondary. His reappearance here represents a redactional addition, since a genealogical link is lacking. He has been adopted into the Kohathite clan and is identified with the Gittite who was temporary keeper of the ark (13:14). The Lord's blessing mentioned there is here defined in terms of an abundance of children. The emphasis on the ability of his family (v. 6) reflects an attempt to have them accepted as members of the guild of gatekeepers. Another motivation for the insertion at this point is the goal of attaining a total of twenty-four divisions, on the model of the priests in chap. 24. The total of twenty-four family heads is achieved by adding the seven sons of Meshelemiah, the four of Hosah, seven of the sons of Obed-edom, and the six sons of his firstborn son, Shemaiah. Hosah features outside this passage only in 16:38. His role with Obed-edom there suggests that verse depends on the expanded 1 Chronicles 26.

26:12-19. The duties of the gatekeepers rely on the expanded text of vv. 1-11. The term מחלקות (*maḥlĕqôt*, "divisions," v. 1) is related to "shifts" in v. 12. The use of lots has been a redactional feature in the accounts of the priestly and derivative divisions. The lots are cast according to ancestral houses. Presumably the twenty-four family heads of the previous expanded paragraph are in view. The principle of equality achieved by taking the lot is here applied to the family groups, whether "small or great." In this case, the casting of lots is related, not to the order of divisions on duty, as elsewhere, but to the particular gates to which the three major groups were assigned. Since there were four gates, one group had to take charge of two gates. One might have expected Obed-edom's family to qualify, but, upstart that he was, this was not to be the case. The east gate, which was the most important, honored by the title "the king's gate" (9:18), was manned by the greatest number of guards (v. 17). The "storehouse" refers to a temple treasury (cf. 2 Chr 25:24). In v. 16, the name of a newcomer to the passage, "Shuppim," should be deleted (so REB); a marginal variant reading for ולאספים (*wĕlā-ʾăsuppîm*, "and for the storehouses") in v. 17 was wrongly related to the noun האספים (*hāʾăsuppîm*) in v. 15 and was incorporated into the text. The west gate was approached from the Tyropoeon Valley; its name, "Shallecheth," does not occur elsewhere.

Verse 16*b* functions as a heading for the distribution of guards in vv. 17-18, as the paragraphing in the NIV indicates. The total of twenty-four guards on duty at any one time is a permutation of the dominant priestly number, to which v. 12 refers in its echo of 24:31 ("just as their kindred did," NRSV). Extensive topographical knowledge of the temple area is displayed here, knowledge to which, unfortunately, we do not have access. In v. 17, "each day" needs to be restored to the MT, as the NIV does implicitly and the NRSV explicitly.[167] The rare term פרבר (*parbār*) in v. 18, long unexplained, has been clarified by its use in the *Temple Scroll,* found at Qumran. In the form פרור (*prwr*) it is there used of a porch with columns at the west side of the Temple, in connection with priests' sin offerings and guilt offerings.[168] This context suggests the rendering "colonnade" (NRSV, REB; the first instance of "colonnade" in v. 18 should be deleted with *BHS* as an erroneous anticipation of the second).

The temple gatekeepers were security police, as their placement at the storehouse indicates.[169] Much of the security for which they were responsible had a religious motivation. According to 2 Chr 23:19, they ensured that anyone unclean would not enter the temple grounds. The temple gates were evidently ritual checkpoints. Psalm 15 seems to be based on an interchange between a pilgrim and a gatekeeper about God's moral standards for the would-be worshiper (see also Pss 24:3-6; 118:19-20; Isa 33:14-16). The condemna-

167. The *BHS* apparatus is a better guide than the note in the NRSV.
168. 11QTemple 35:10-15.
169. For the paramilitary role of gatekeepers, see J. W. Wright, "Guarding the Gates: 1 Chronicles 26.1-19 and the Roles of Gatekeepers in Chronicles," *JSOT* 48 (1990) 69-81, esp. 69-74.

tion of temple worshipers in Isa 1:10-17 implies that in Isaiah's day this check was a perfunctory one, if done at all. Isaiah, speaking as a substitute gatekeeper, challenges pilgrims to "cease to do evil, learn to do good" (Isa 1:16-17 NRSV). Zechariah's qualification as "a prudent counselor" (v. 14 NRSV) apparently legitimated him in his role at the gate.

26:20-32. The last levitical category of "officials and judges" (NIV) in 23:4 is defined in terms of personnel and duties in these verses. At first sight, one might think that this section deals with two distinct groups, temple treasurers (vv. 20-28) and secular officials (vv. 29-32). But it has a common genealogical framework, at least from v. 23 on. The diverse Levites mentioned in vv. 24-32 were all Kohathites, attributed to the subclans of Amram, Izhar, Hebron, and Uzziel (cf. 23:16). The Uzzielites do not feature in the detailed presentation extracted by the chronicler from a longer list.

Apart from the genealogical framework that binds this passage together, in terms of temple duties it falls into two distinct parts, vv. 20-28 and vv. 29-32. The first part is supplied with an introduction in v. 20, referring to two types of treasuries. Then vv. 21-22 deal with those in charge of the temple treasuries, and vv. 25-28 with the staffing of the treasuries of dedicated gifts. Verse 23 is a genealogical heading for vv. 24-32 (see the NIV). Verse 24 specifies Shebuel as the overall supervisor of both kinds of treasuries. So there is no room for "Ahijah" (NRSV = MT) in this role (v. 20). This name has arisen from misunderstanding of an abbreviated form of "their brothers" or "their fellow [Levites]" (NIV).[170]

The first type of treasury stored sacred vessels and sacrificial materials, such as fine flour, wine, and oil (9:29).[171] Verses 21-22 should be read together, as in the NIV. These storerooms were staffed not by Kohathites but by Gershonites, who are traced through Ladan, as in 23:7-9. "Jehieli" is probably the same person as "Jehiel" there.

The other type of treasury was a combined bank and museum. Ancient temples regularly contained valuable objects that had been accumulated over centuries. These treasuries contained spoils of war and could be used as necessary for the "maintenance" (NRSV) or upkeep of the Temple. According to 18:11, David contributed to such a treasury. Objects associated with various military campaigns were placed in this treasury, presented as trophies to God's grace.

In vv. 29-32, the genealogical framework introduced in v. 23 is developed in terms of another group of Levites, who had been relieved of temple duties to play a role in the community at large. The Izharites (v. 29) had a judicial role as judges and "officials" or "officers"; their responsibilities fell somewhere between those of clerks and the police (see Deut 17:8-13; 2 Chr 29:11). Levitical experience in interpreting the Torah (see 2 Chr 17:7-9) and in security work was used for a broader purpose. According to vv. 30-32, the Hebronites had a national role, on both sides of the Jordan. This tradition evidently goes back to the period of the united monarchy. Their duties, on behalf of palace and Temple, probably involved the collection of taxes, in which case these Levites were appropriately listed alongside the temple treasurers. In v. 31, the chronicler assigns to David's last year a search for Hebronites at the levitical city of Jazer (cf. 6:81), who were given the same role among the Transjordanian tribes as their western counterparts had in v. 30.

170. See Allen, *The Greek Chronicles,* 2:89.

171. In Ezra 8:33-34, we get a glimpse of activity there on a special day, when Ezra arrived from Babylonia with a consignment of money and vessels.

REFLECTIONS

1. The lists of traditional groups responsible for gates, goods, and gifts and for trials and taxes described in chapter 26 illustrate the extensive organization of the Levites. They are concerned with security in many forms. The sacred grounds of the Temple had to be protected from ritually unclean people. In Rev 21:27, this concept is developed with reference to the heavenly Jerusalem. That holy city *par excellence* can have nothing unclean entering it, and a strict demarcation is drawn between faith and immorality. The temple gatekeepers were evidently responsible for setting worship standards. In the Sermon on the Mount (Matt 5:23-24),

Jesus echoed the entrance liturgy of Psalm 15. He counseled that his disciples be their own gatekeepers in monitoring their approach to the altar of the Temple. Anyone who brought offerings in worship was to examine the self about his or her treatment of others. If a problem existed for which one bore responsibility, the offering was not to be completed until the matter had been put right. Consistency between worship and way of life is as necessary for the Christian as it was for the people of God in the Old Testament.

2. De Vries thinks it is significant that two brothers were in charge of the temple stores (26:22): "We take note of Zetham's and Joel's joint tenure, as though the one was needed to keep check on the other."[172] God's property must receive good care, not least so as to keep faith with the donors. Occasionally we hear of church treasurers embezzling funds or otherwise using them improperly. We, too, require a foolproof system of precautions to protect church funds from misappropriation and their stewards from temptation.

3. The wider ministry described in 26:29-32 will not be found in countries that strictly separate church and state. In the British House of Lords, the Anglican archbishops and bishops sit as "lords spiritual." This civil appointment is a traditional part of their overall duties as servants of God. On a less grandiose scale, many ordained pastors sit on social committees concerned with welfare work or education. Although nation and people of God are not coterminous as they were for ancient Israel, Christian love and concern cannot stay in the church, but must overflow into a needy world and seek to give direction in societies where so many people lack moral and spiritual bearings. Only thus will Christians fulfill their mandate to be salt of the earth and light of the world.

172. S. J. De Vries, *1 and 2 Chronicles*, FOTL 11 (Grand Rapids: Eerdmans, 1989) 210.

1 Chronicles 27:1-34, Lay Leaders

NIV

27 This is the list of the Israelites—heads of families, commanders of thousands and commanders of hundreds, and their officers, who served the king in all that concerned the army divisions that were on duty month by month throughout the year. Each division consisted of 24,000 men.

2In charge of the first division, for the first month, was Jashobeam son of Zabdiel. There were 24,000 men in his division. 3He was a descendant of Perez and chief of all the army officers for the first month.

4In charge of the division for the second month was Dodai the Ahohite; Mikloth was the leader of his division. There were 24,000 men in his division.

5The third army commander, for the third month, was Benaiah son of Jehoiada the priest. He was chief and there were 24,000 men in his division. 6This was the Benaiah who was

NRSV

27 This is the list of the people of Israel, the heads of families, the commanders of the thousands and the hundreds, and their officers who served the king in all matters concerning the divisions that came and went, month after month throughout the year, each division numbering twenty-four thousand:

2Jashobeam son of Zabdiel was in charge of the first division in the first month; in his division were twenty-four thousand. 3He was a descendant of Perez, and was chief of all the commanders of the army for the first month. 4Dodai the Ahohite was in charge of the division of the second month; Mikloth was the chief officer of his division. In his division were twenty-four thousand. 5The third commander, for the third month, was Benaiah son of the priest Jehoiada, as chief; in his division were twenty-four thousand. 6This is the Benaiah who was a mighty man of the Thirty and in command of the Thirty; his son Ammizabad was in charge

NIV

a mighty man among the Thirty and was over the Thirty. His son Ammizabad was in charge of his division.

7The fourth, for the fourth month, was Asahel the brother of Joab; his son Zebadiah was his successor. There were 24,000 men in his division.

8The fifth, for the fifth month, was the commander Shamhuth the Izrahite. There were 24,000 men in his division.

9The sixth, for the sixth month, was Ira the son of Ikkesh the Tekoite. There were 24,000 men in his division.

10The seventh, for the seventh month, was Helez the Pelonite, an Ephraimite. There were 24,000 men in his division.

11The eighth, for the eighth month, was Sibbecai the Hushathite, a Zerahite. There were 24,000 men in his division.

12The ninth, for the ninth month, was Abiezer the Anathothite, a Benjamite. There were 24,000 men in his division.

13The tenth, for the tenth month, was Maharai the Netophathite, a Zerahite. There were 24,000 men in his division.

14The eleventh, for the eleventh month, was Benaiah the Pirathonite, an Ephraimite. There were 24,000 men in his division.

15The twelfth, for the twelfth month, was Heldai the Netophathite, from the family of Othniel. There were 24,000 men in his division.

16The officers over the tribes of Israel:

over the Reubenites: Eliezer son of Zicri;
over the Simeonites: Shephatiah son of Maacah;
17over Levi: Hashabiah son of Kemuel;
over Aaron: Zadok;
18over Judah: Elihu, a brother of David;
over Issachar: Omri son of Michael;
19over Zebulun: Ishmaiah son of Obadiah;
over Naphtali: Jerimoth son of Azriel;
20over the Ephraimites: Hoshea son of Azaziah;
over half the tribe of Manasseh: Joel son of Pedaiah;
21over the half-tribe of Manasseh in Gilead: Iddo son of Zechariah;
over Benjamin: Jaasiel son of Abner;

NRSV

of his division.[a] 7Asahel brother of Joab was fourth,
for the fourth month, and his son Zebadiah after
him; in his division were twenty-four thousand.
8The fifth commander, for the fifth month, was
Shamhuth, the Izrahite; in his division were
twenty-four thousand. 9Sixth, for the sixth month,
was Ira son of Ikkesh the Tekoite; in his division
were twenty-four thousand. 10Seventh, for the
seventh month, was Helez the Pelonite, of the
Ephraimites; in his division were twenty-four
thousand. 11Eighth, for the eighth month, was
Sibbecai the Hushathite, of the Zerahites; in his
division were twenty-four thousand. 12Ninth, for
the ninth month, was Abiezer of Anathoth, a
Benjaminite; in his division were twenty-four
thousand. 13Tenth, for the tenth month, was Maharai of Netophah, of the Zerahites; in his division
were twenty-four thousand. 14Eleventh, for the
eleventh month, was Benaiah of Pirathon, of the
Ephraimites; in his division were twenty-four
thousand. 15Twelfth, for the twelfth month, was
Heldai the Netophathite, of Othniel; in his division were twenty-four thousand.

16Over the tribes of Israel, for the Reubenites,
Eliezer son of Zichri was chief officer; for the
Simeonites, Shephatiah son of Maacah; 17for Levi,
Hashabiah son of Kemuel; for Aaron, Zadok; 18for
Judah, Elihu, one of David's brothers; for Issachar,
Omri son of Michael; 19for Zebulun, Ishmaiah son
of Obadiah; for Naphtali, Jerimoth son of Azriel;
20for the Ephraimites, Hoshea son of Azaziah; for
the half-tribe of Manasseh, Joel son of Pedaiah;
21for the half-tribe of Manasseh in Gilead, Iddo
son of Zechariah; for Benjamin, Jaasiel son of
Abner; 22for Dan, Azarel son of Jeroham. These
were the leaders of the tribes of Israel. 23David
did not count those below twenty years of age,
for the LORD had promised to make Israel as
numerous as the stars of heaven. 24Joab son of
Zeruiah began to count them, but did not finish;
yet wrath came upon Israel for this, and the
number was not entered into the account of the
Annals of King David.

25Over the king's treasuries was Azmaveth son
of Adiel. Over the treasuries in the country, in
the cities, in the villages and in the towers, was
Jonathan son of Uzziah. 26Over those who did the

[a] Gk Vg: Heb *Ammizabad was his division*

NIV

22over Dan: Azarel son of Jeroham.

These were the officers over the tribes of Israel.

23David did not take the number of the men twenty years old or less, because the LORD had promised to make Israel as numerous as the stars in the sky. 24Joab son of Zeruiah began to count the men but did not finish. Wrath came on Israel on account of this numbering, and the number was not entered in the book[a] of the annals of King David.

25Azmaveth son of Adiel was in charge of the royal storehouses.

Jonathan son of Uzziah was in charge of the storehouses in the outlying districts, in the towns, the villages and the watchtowers.

26Ezri son of Kelub was in charge of the field workers who farmed the land.

27Shimei the Ramathite was in charge of the vineyards.

Zabdi the Shiphmite was in charge of the produce of the vineyards for the wine vats.

28Baal-Hanan the Gederite was in charge of the olive and sycamore-fig trees in the western foothills.

Joash was in charge of the supplies of olive oil.

29Shitrai the Sharonite was in charge of the herds grazing in Sharon.

Shaphat son of Adlai was in charge of the herds in the valleys.

30Obil the Ishmaelite was in charge of the camels.

Jehdeiah the Meronothite was in charge of the donkeys.

31Jaziz the Hagrite was in charge of the flocks.

All these were the officials in charge of King David's property.

32Jonathan, David's uncle, was a counselor, a man of insight and a scribe. Jehiel son of Hacmoni took care of the king's sons.

33Ahithophel was the king's counselor.

Hushai the Arkite was the king's friend.
34Ahithophel was succeeded by Jehoiada son of Benaiah and by Abiathar.

Joab was the commander of the royal army.

[a]24 Septuagint; Hebrew *number*

NRSV

work of the field, tilling the soil, was Ezri son of
Chelub. 27Over the vineyards was Shimei the
Ramathite. Over the produce of the vineyards for
the wine cellars was Zabdi the Shiphmite. 28Over
the olive and sycamore trees in the Shephelah was
Baal-hanan the Gederite. Over the stores of oil
was Joash. 29Over the herds that pastured in
Sharon was Shitrai the Sharonite. Over the herds
in the valleys was Shaphat son of Adlai. 30Over
the camels was Obil the Ishmaelite. Over the
donkeys was Jehdeiah the Meronothite. Over the
flocks was Jaziz the Hagrite. 31All these were
stewards of King David's property.

32Jonathan, David's uncle, was a counselor,
being a man of understanding and a scribe; Jehiel
son of Hachmoni attended the king's sons.
33Ahithophel was the king's counselor, and Hushai
the Archite was the king's friend. 34After Ahithophel came Jehoiada son of Benaiah, and Abiathar.
Joab was commander of the king's army.

COMMENTARY

This chapter consists of four secular lists, two relating to Israel's tribes and two to Israel's king, though David is also associated with the first two (vv. 1, 23). The lists tend to supplement the religious, temple-related lists of the previous four chapters. Levitical involvement in secular work (chap. 26) has eased the transition. These four lists are inserted with a consciousness that with David's reign drawing to a close this was the only place to insert such information. This feeling surfaces especially in the last pair of lists, the stewards of royal property (vv. 25-31) and the members of the privy council (vv. 32-34).

However, the first two lists, the tribal divisions (vv. 1-15) and the tribal leaders (vv. 16-24), are motivated by priestly interests. The basic structure of chaps. 23–27 was dictated by the skeleton list of Levites in 23:4-5, and a pro-priestly editor took the opportunity to add material. By this token not only does chap. 27 have no place in the original levitical structuring of chaps. 24–27, but also one expects priestly interests to surface in it, as they do in the first two lists.

27:1-15. Verse 1 functions as a heading for the first list. "The people of Israel [בני ישׂראל *bĕnê yiśrā'ēl*]" here refers to the laity, as distinct from the religious personnel of previous chapters. The list consists of twelve heads of monthly divisions. The introduction provides information about levels of leadership in these divisions and their monthly royal service. The list postulates twelve divisions of conscripts, each consisting of 24,000 men, amounting to 288,000 in all. This idealistic presentation was probably inspired by the list of twelve district leaders who supplied Solomon's court with food each month of the year (1 Kgs 4:7-19, 27). It not only adopts a military format, but also reflects the influence of the twenty-four divisions of priests in 24:1-19. Israel is made to march to a priestly tune, like the levitical groups in earlier chapters. This microcosm of divine order provides a pattern for society.

The names of the divisional leaders are closely related to the list of David's prominent warriors in 11:11-31, particularly to names appearing in 11:11-12, 26-31. These individual warriors receive an administrative role in the present list. In fact, Asahel (v. 7) was already dead before David became king of all Israel (2 Sam 2:18-32); mention of his son's succession shows a recognition, though hardly a resolution, of the difficulty. The assigning of Benaiah to the priesthood (v. 5) reflects 12:27, itself an addition of the pro-priestly reviser. Other features of the list seem to supply older information independent of the list of warriors in chap. 11. Benaiah is credited with leadership of the Thirty, a role only Abishai has in 11:21. This list knows the names of Benaiah's and Asahel's sons (vv. 6-7), and in general more family information is given.[173]

27:16-24. The list of tribal leaders in vv. 16-22 has been taken from older material associated with David's census, as the closing material in the list shows. The narrative is more closely linked with the list than either the NIV or the NRSV indicates. The Hebrew for "their number" (KJV; מספרם *mispārām*, v. 23) refers to the number of the tribes of Israel mentioned in v. 22. This account of the census has a different tone from the story in chap. 21. The account shows that David did no wrong in ordering the census. It makes the implicit claim that David followed the procedure of the Torah by not including those under twenty years old (Num 1:3), thus respecting the Lord's sovereignty. The full number of Israelites would be known only to God and would be allowed to grow as indefinitely large as divine promises to the patriarchs had foretold (see Gen 15:5; 22:17; 26:4). As in chap. 21, Joab was evidently assigned the task of taking the census, but according to this account he was interrupted by divine wrath (v. 24). According to chap. 21, he reluctantly obeyed David's orders and completed the census, but registered a protest by omitting two tribes, Levi and Benjamin, though here their leaders are included (vv. 17, 21). The narrative is terse, but the reviser evidently wants to exonerate David of any blame and implicitly to cast some blame on Joab. Joab ceases to be the

173. The clause relating to Mikloth in v. 4, omitted in the RSV, probably originated as an explanatory gloss. See W. Rudolph, *Chronikbücher,* HAT 1:21 (Tübingen: Mohr [Siebeck], 1955) 178; L. C. Allen, *The Greek Chronicles: The Relation of the Septuagint of I and II Chronicles to the Massoretic Text,* Part 2: *Textual Criticism,* VTSup 25, 27 (Leiden: Brill, 1974) 144-45.

good guy, and his respect for God (21:3) is transferred to David. This account represents an idealized view of David that the chronicler did not share. Since the census was broken off, only the tribal leaders were inserted in the Davidic record, not the full numbers. In taking over the narrative appended to the list, the editor may have wanted to highlight the list as authentically Davidic.

The touch of the priestly editor appears in the reference to Zadok as head of (the house of) Aaron (v. 17). The point of the insertion was the same as in 12:27-28: to make room for explicit participation, on the assumption that "Levi" represented not the tribe but merely the non-priestly members.

Apart from this insertion, the nominal number of twelve tribes for Israel is here achieved by taking the two halves of Manasseh separately and then omitting Gad and Asher. The list of Jacob's sons in Gen 35:23-26 provides the basis for the ordering of the tribes. The first six tribes (vv. 16-19*a*) correspond to the order of the sons born to Jacob by Leah. Those in vv. 20-21 represent his sons by Rachel. Dan and Naphtali, here strangely separated in vv. 22*a* and 19*b* respectively, were sons of Bilhah, Rachel's maid, while those by Leah's maid Zilpah, Gad and Asher, are omitted as being outside the traditional number of twelve. Judah's representative "Elihu" (v. 18) is not otherwise known as a brother of David. He may have been the unnamed eighth brother in 1 Sam 16:10 (in addition to the seven names in 1 Chr 2:13-15). The emphasis on the twelve tribes of Israel accords with the chronicler's own concern for the traditional unity of north and south, a concern for all Israel. The redactor, by including this list, was adding his own "amen" to this element of the chronicler's agenda.

27:25-31. The list of David's administrators of crown property is generally recognized as historically reliable. It is arranged in three groups, according to storage places in the capital (implicitly) and in the country (v. 25), agriculture and agricultural products (vv. 26-28), and livestock (vv. 29-31*a*). A descriptive summary in v. 31*b* concludes the list. The royal property was spread throughout the united kingdom, as vv. 28-29 attest. The list illustrates David's riches (29:28), painting a beautiful picture of God's blessing on the land and a nostalgic ideal that implicitly included economic and political hopes for full restoration.

27:32-34. The final list, which is also viewed as historically authentic, presents David's inner circle of confidants. It complements the list of members of his administration (18:15-17). The inclusion of Joab, defined by his administrative role and not by a counseling function, has been regarded as secondary. He was certainly a member of the old guard; in 2 Sam 19:5-8, he speaks candidly as an intimate adviser. The tutor of the royal princes is given a place in the list. Replacements for Ahithophel were necessary in view of his suicide after supporting Absalom's rebellion (2 Sam 17:23). Hushai's epithet, "the king's friend," was an official title, which 2 Sam 15:37 uses of him and to which 2 Sam 16:17 ironically alludes.

REFLECTIONS

The first list in chap. 27 is dedicated to order, which, as closely as it can, takes its cue from the organization of the priesthood into divisions. Each family took its turn serving at the Temple. This modeling of a secular list on a religious background means that the Temple is regarded as a pattern for society. It resembles attempts to set up a civil community based on Christian principles, such as Calvin's Geneva and the colonies established by the Puritans in New England.

The second list, here garnished with an extra, priestly flavor, reinforces the chronicler's own ecumenical concern. It challenges readers to endorse the larger dimensions of the people of God and to recognize as separatist any smaller grouping that claims to be the whole. A second point of interest in the list is a redeeming feature claimed for the ill-fated census in 27:23. Israelites under the age of twenty were not included in the census, in order that the full number of God's people should not be known. In this way a balance was struck between human practicality and divine promise.

The third list may be read in the light of the Old Testament theology of the land. It finds an echo in Uzziah's love of the soil and devotion to agricultural enterprises (2 Chr 26:10). Such a concern has a theological basis in Deut 8:7-10, which describes the gift of a good land that provides food for God's people. From Paul's perspective, "the earth and its fullness are the Lord's," and so they are to be enjoyed, affirms 1 Cor 10:26 (NRSV) in an application of Ps. 24:1.

The fourth list in the chapter sets out the members of David's privy council. In terms of the themes to be found elsewhere in the books of Chronicles, it recalls the help given by the people of God, which came to the fore in 1 Chronicles 11–12. David, in his rise to power, did not stand alone. Here, in his heyday, he still leaned on others to help him rule. The help is defined in terms of counseling (27:32-33*a,* 34*a*). Joab's unpalatable advice in 2 Sam 19:5-8 encouraged David to act like a king when he was tempted to withdraw into private grief, just as Queen Victoria did at the death of her husband, Prince Albert. Counseling is especially prized in the wisdom traditions of the Old Testament: "Without counsel plans go wrong, but with many advisers they succeed" (Prov 15:22 NRSV; cf. Prov 11:14; 13:10; 24:6; Eccl 4:13). Second Chronicles 10 and 22 will develop this motif in terms of both good and bad advice.

1 Chronicles 28:1-21, Solomon's Renewed Mandate to Build the Temple

NIV

28 David summoned all the officials of Israel to assemble at Jerusalem: the officers over the tribes, the commanders of the divisions in the service of the king, the commanders of thousands and commanders of hundreds, and the officials in charge of all the property and livestock belonging to the king and his sons, together with the palace officials, the mighty men and all the brave warriors.

2King David rose to his feet and said: "Listen to me, my brothers and my people. I had it in my heart to build a house as a place of rest for the ark of the covenant of the LORD, for the footstool of our God, and I made plans to build it. 3But God said to me, 'You are not to build a house for my Name, because you are a warrior and have shed blood.'

4"Yet the LORD, the God of Israel, chose me from my whole family to be king over Israel forever. He chose Judah as leader, and from the house of Judah he chose my family, and from my father's sons he was pleased to make me king over all Israel. 5Of all my sons—and the LORD has given me many—he has chosen my son Solomon to sit on the throne of the kingdom of the LORD over Israel. 6He said to me: 'Solomon your son is the one who will build my house and my courts,

NRSV

28 David assembled at Jerusalem all the officials of Israel, the officials of the tribes, the officers of the divisions that served the king, the commanders of the thousands, the commanders of the hundreds, the stewards of all the property and cattle of the king and his sons, together with the palace officials, the mighty warriors, and all the warriors. 2Then King David rose to his feet and said: "Hear me, my brothers and my people. I had planned to build a house of rest for the ark of the covenant of the LORD, for the footstool of our God; and I made preparations for building. 3But God said to me, 'You shall not build a house for my name, for you are a warrior and have shed blood.' 4Yet the LORD God of Israel chose me from all my ancestral house to be king over Israel forever; for he chose Judah as leader, and in the house of Judah my father's house, and among my father's sons he took delight in making me king over all Israel. 5And of all my sons, for the LORD has given me many, he has chosen my son Solomon to sit upon the throne of the kingdom of the LORD over Israel. 6He said to me, 'It is your son Solomon who shall build my house and my courts, for I have chosen him to be a son to me, and I will be a father to him. 7I will establish his kingdom forever if he continues resolute in keep-

NIV

for I have chosen him to be my son, and I will be his father. 7I will establish his kingdom forever if he is unswerving in carrying out my commands and laws, as is being done at this time.'

8"So now I charge you in the sight of all Israel and of the assembly of the LORD, and in the hearing of our God: Be careful to follow all the commands of the LORD your God, that you may possess this good land and pass it on as an inheritance to your descendants forever.

9"And you, my son Solomon, acknowledge the God of your father, and serve him with wholehearted devotion and with a willing mind, for the LORD searches every heart and understands every motive behind the thoughts. If you seek him, he will be found by you; but if you forsake him, he will reject you forever. 10Consider now, for the LORD has chosen you to build a temple as a sanctuary. Be strong and do the work."

11Then David gave his son Solomon the plans for the portico of the temple, its buildings, its storerooms, its upper parts, its inner rooms and the place of atonement. 12He gave him the plans of all that the Spirit had put in his mind for the courts of the temple of the LORD and all the surrounding rooms, for the treasuries of the temple of God and for the treasuries for the dedicated things. 13He gave him instructions for the divisions of the priests and Levites, and for all the work of serving in the temple of the LORD, as well as for all the articles to be used in its service. 14He designated the weight of gold for all the gold articles to be used in various kinds of service, and the weight of silver for all the silver articles to be used in various kinds of service: 15the weight of gold for the gold lampstands and their lamps, with the weight for each lampstand and its lamps; and the weight of silver for each silver lampstand and its lamps, according to the use of each lampstand; 16the weight of gold for each table for consecrated bread; the weight of silver for the silver tables; 17the weight of pure gold for the forks, sprinkling bowls and pitchers; the weight of gold for each gold dish; the weight of silver for each silver dish; 18and the weight of the refined gold for the altar of incense. He also gave him the plan for the chariot, that is, the cherubim of gold that spread

NRSV

ing my commandments and my ordinances, as he is today.' 8Now therefore in the sight of all Israel, the assembly of the LORD, and in the hearing of our God, observe and search out all the commandments of the LORD your God; that you may possess this good land, and leave it for an inheritance to your children after you forever.

9"And you, my son Solomon, know the God of your father, and serve him with single mind and willing heart; for the LORD searches every mind, and understands every plan and thought. If you seek him, he will be found by you; but if you forsake him, he will abandon you forever. 10Take heed now, for the LORD has chosen you to build a house as the sanctuary; be strong, and act."

11Then David gave his son Solomon the plan of the vestibule of the temple, and of its houses, its treasuries, its upper rooms, and its inner chambers, and of the room for the mercy seat;[a] 12and the plan of all that he had in mind: for the courts of the house of the LORD, all the surrounding chambers, the treasuries of the house of God, and the treasuries for dedicated gifts; 13for the divisions of the priests and of the Levites, and all the work of the service in the house of the LORD; for all the vessels for the service in the house of the LORD, 14the weight of gold for all golden vessels for each service, the weight of silver vessels for each service, 15the weight of the golden lampstands and their lamps, the weight of gold for each lampstand and its lamps, the weight of silver for a lampstand and its lamps, according to the use of each in the service, 16the weight of gold for each table for the rows of bread, the silver for the silver tables, 17and pure gold for the forks, the basins, and the cups; for the golden bowls and the weight of each; for the silver bowls and the weight of each; 18for the altar of incense made of refined gold, and its weight; also his plan for the golden chariot of the cherubim that spread their wings and covered the ark of the covenant of the LORD.

19"All this, in writing at the LORD's direction, he made clear to me—the plan of all the works."

20David said further to his son Solomon, "Be strong and of good courage, and act. Do not be afraid or dismayed; for the LORD God, my God, is with you. He will not fail you or forsake you,

a Or *the cover*

NIV

their wings and shelter the ark of the covenant of the LORD.

[19]"All this," David said, "I have in writing from the hand of the LORD upon me, and he gave me understanding in all the details of the plan."

[20]David also said to Solomon his son, "Be strong and courageous, and do the work. Do not be afraid or discouraged, for the LORD God, my God, is with you. He will not fail you or forsake you until all the work for the service of the temple of the LORD is finished. [21]The divisions of the priests and Levites are ready for all the work on the temple of God, and every willing man skilled in any craft will help you in all the work. The officials and all the people will obey your every command."

NRSV

until all the work for the service of the house of the LORD is finished. [21]Here are the divisions of the priests and the Levites for all the service of the house of God; and with you in all the work will be every volunteer who has skill for any kind of service; also the officers and all the people will be wholly at your command."

COMMENTARY

In chap. 22 David gave Solomon a private charge to build the Temple as the chief task of his reign. Now David assembles representatives of the people and delivers a public charge, rehearsing Solomon's divinely authored qualifications (vv. 1-10). Then David ceremoniously hands over a set of plans for the Temple (vv. 11-19) and adds words of encouragement, as he commissions Solomon to undertake the task and carry it through (vv. 20-21). David's speech primarily recapitulates themes announced earlier (chaps. 17 and 22). The speech falls into the regular pattern of explanatory introduction (vv. 2*b*-7) and a main exhortatory part headed by "So now" (vv. 8-10).

28:1. This meeting is different from that in 23:2, which was of a preparatory, private nature. Here David summons the leaders of the nation and of the court and members of the army, as representatives of "all Israel" (v. 8), to present Solomon to them as his successor. An editor has introduced five titles for leaders of the groups mentioned in 27:1-31, in order to integrate that later material into the Chronicles history. The fifth group, the royal stewards, strictly belongs with the palace officials. The complex organization associated with David's successful reign is impressive.

28:2-3. David's addressing the assembly as both his brothers (cf. 13:2) and his people paves the way for the statement in v. 4 that God had promoted him up from the ranks (cf. Deut 17:20). God's declaration to David (v. 3; see also v. 6) is the primary theme. The contrast between the veto of the father's building of the Temple and the mandate to the son to do so instead is based on 17:4, 12, while the disqualification summarizes 22:8 and the specification of Solomon repeats 22:9-10.

Reference to David's original plan in v. 2 builds on 17:1 and 22:7, putting the motif of rest to new use. There it was rest for Israel achieved by David's victories (22:9, 18). Now it has a religious sense with the ark as subject. The chronicler reflects Ps 132:8 (cf. Ps 132:14): the description of the ark as God's "footstool" occurs elsewhere only in Ps 132:7. In Ps 132:8 the permanent installation of the ark in Jerusalem is dramatically represented as an invitation to the Lord to go to "your resting place," the Temple. David's "preparations" sound like those made by the king in 22:2-5; yet, the text reads as if they occurred before the prophetic oracle of chap. 17. The clause "and I made preparations for building" (v. 2) probably breaks the continuity and has the sense "and [subsequently] I have in fact . . ." (see the GNB).

28:4-7. David's roles as founder of the dynasty and father of the builder of the Temple are drawn from 17:7-14. This repetition emphasizes the divine purpose, which would affect Israel thereafter. God's choosing of David from within his family recalls the narrative of his being anointed in 1 Samuel 16 (cf. 2 Sam 6:21). A narrowing process has transpired. First, Judah was chosen as "ruling tribe" (REB), then David's family was chosen (1 Samuel 16). The choice of Judah echoes Ps 78:68-69, where it is associated with God's choice of "his servant David" (Ps 78:70).[174] God's word through Nathan pointed to Solomon's election from among David's many sons, repeating the process of a generation earlier. As in chap. 22, with hindsight the chronicler cuts through the complex succession narrative in 2 Samuel 9–1 Kings 2. Here a new factor, the divine election of Solomon, is introduced, indicated by the term "chosen" (בחר *bāḥar*) in vv. 5-6 and 10.[175] Solomon stood alongside David as elected by God. They are twin agents of the divine purpose, joint founders of a new era under God, an era that was to last "forever" (vv. 4, 7).

As in 17:14 and later in 29:23, Solomon was to represent the Lord's own kingship (v. 5). We may compare Solomon's throne to the description of the ark as the "footstool" of God (v. 2). A parallel is drawn between the Temple and the palace as two disclosures of God's kingship (cf. 16:31). The "ark of the covenant of the LORD" is mentioned twice in this chapter (vv. 2, 18). In chaps. 16 and 17, the ark was associated with the Davidic covenant, as it is in this chapter. God's earlier covenant with Israel was now subsumed under the present one and thus guaranteed "forever" for the community of faith.

Solomon is assigned the double role of temple builder and guarantor of the dynasty. Although the Temple is the focus of David's speech (vv. 2*b*-3, 6*a*, 10), much space is devoted to the dynasty, which was important for Israel's future. Verse 7 lays down a condition for the permanence of the dynasty: Solomon's overall obedience to the Torah.[176] The issue had been introduced in a lower key at 22:12-13*a*. Now it is elevated to a condition, supplementing the earlier condition of building the Temple (17:12; 22:10). Obedience is envisioned as humanly possible, as in Deut 30:11-14. The chronicler's account of Solomon's reign never contradicts this statement. That reign ends on the laudatory notes of wisdom and wealth as implicit signs of God's blessing and approval (2 Chronicles 9). The chronicler thus insists that Solomon's adherence to God's general requirements was still sufficient to guarantee the dynasty (see 2 Chr 13:5; 21:7; 23:3). He is implicitly challenging the deuteronomist's perspective in 1 Kings 11 (see esp. 1 Kgs 11:31-34, 38) and also the strict line taken against intermarriage in Ezra–Nehemiah, which was partially grounded in 1 Kings 11 (see Neh 13:26). The chronicler undoubtedly found a basis for the condition in 1 Kgs 6:11-13; 9:4-5 (see also 1 Kgs 3:14), which he interpreted in terms of a general dynastic promise that would hold good after Solomon had successfully undergone a probationary period.

28:8-10. Solomon received two mandates, one of general obedience and the specific one of building the Temple. This part of the speech focuses on exhortations to carry out these mandates. The reader expects Solomon to be addressed throughout, and v. 8*a* encourages this expectation. But v. 8*b*, with its plural verbs and pronouns in the Hebrew, goes off on a tangent. David turns for a moment to address the representative assembly, applying Solomon's role homiletically to the people. In obeying the Torah, he would not only secure the dynasty but also become a role model for the people. The appeal borrows from Deuteronomy the association of obedience to the Torah and enjoyment of "the good land" (see Deut 4:22-23; 6:17-18), but the chronicler slips in his own spiritual key word, דרש (*dāraš*), "seek" ("search out," NRSV; "follow," NIV). Seeking God meant the people must obey the Torah. God's covenant with Israel through David included the land as a vital component, but Israel's prayers to this end (16:35) had to be backed by lives dedicated to the Lord's requirement. Verse 8*b* is intended to transcend its his-

174. See R. J. Clifford, "In Zion and David a New Beginning: An Interpretation of Psalm 78," in *Traditions in Transformation,* ed. F. M. Cross (Winona Lake: Eisenbrauns, 1981) 121-41, esp. 137-41.

175. The application of the concept of election to Solomon (28:5-6) is unparalleled in the OT. See R. L. Braun, "Solomon, the Chosen Temple Builder: The Significance of 1 Chronicles 22, 28, and 29 for the Theology of the Chronicler," *JBL* 95 (1976) 588-90.

176. See H. G. M. Williamson, "The Dynastic Oracle in the Books of Chronicles," *I. E. Seeligmann Volume,* ed. A. Rofé and Y. Zakovitch (Jerusalem: Rubinstein, 1983) 313-18.

torical context. Every reader's mind rushes to the disappointing fact that the people failed in this obligation and lost the land. Yet the chronicler and his first readers rejoiced in the partial renewal of the gift. He was challenging them to qualify for full restoration.

In the charge to Solomon (vv. 9-10), the condition of v. 7 is reiterated in a fervent call to spiritual commitment. The reference to a devoted heart and mind again borrows from Deuteronomy (Deut 4:29; 10:12). The chronicler includes his own emphasis: the obligation of each generation to appropriate the faith of the preceding one. The call is undergirded by a reference to divine omniscience, a motif that will recur in 29:17.

The pair of conditional statements that follows is based on Jer 29:13-14, as is indicated by the passive form "be found" (or "let himself be found"; cf. the active verb in Deut 4:29), so that in this respect, too, Solomon turns out to be a model for later generations. In this context, however, the idea of "being found" gives expression to the unique responsibility that rests on Solomon to "make" his "election sure," to use a NT phrase (2 Pet 1:10 NIV). The exhortations and dire warning stress the human side of the matter. In 29:19, as already in 22:12, they are balanced by David's request that God empower Solomon. At its end, the speech returns to Solomon's other mandate. The chosen king was also the chosen temple builder. He is encouraged in this future task, in anticipation of the charge in vv. 20-21.

28:11-19. The chronicler narrates a ceremonial handing over of a set of plans for the Temple, drawn up by David as a further part of his preparations. Although he could not build the Temple, David did everything he could to help Solomon achieve that goal. According to the chronicler, David was not only the supplier of materials but also the designer of the Temple and its furnishings. The Temple's legitimacy was thus enhanced by such close association with this traditional hero of the faith.

Verse 12 probably refers to David's own planning, as an amplification of v. 2 (NRSV; cf. the NIV). Verse 19 will trace these plans, evidently in the form of a written description, to divine inspiration. The Lord's "hand . . . upon me" is a prophetic expression (cf. Ezek 1:3; 3:14). The chronicler intends to prove that the Temple is the product of divine revelation. Even "the details" were divinely inspired.

The description moves from architectural layout and ritual procedure to particular vessels and furnishings and the amounts of gold and silver required in each case. In v. 18, the ark is singled out for special mention. The golden cherubim on each side are related to a chariot, which alludes to Ezekiel's visions (Ezekiel 1; 10–11; 43); both v. 18 and v. 19 depend on the book of Ezekiel. The cherubim are part of what Ezekiel experienced of the divine presence, which rested in the earthly temple (cf. Ezek 10:4, 18-19).

The chronicler's enthusiasm shines through. Although he lived many centuries later and knew only the Second Temple, he rejoiced in the wonder of it all. The ark and the gold-plated cherubim were no more, nor was Solomon's Temple standing in all its glory (cf. Ezra 3:10-13; Hag 2:3). Still, the Second Temple was its successor in spiritual, if not material, terms. The temple "vessels" (vv. 13-14) provided continuity between the old and the new buildings.[177] Some were recovered, others took on the aura of the old (Ezra 1:6-11).

The legitimacy of the old temple, inherited by the new one, was confirmed by the plans (תבנית *tabnît*) of vv. 11, 18-19. The same Hebrew word is used of the revealed "pattern" of the tabernacle and its furnishings in Exod 25:1-40, which contains a list very similar to the one supplied here. David is represented as a second Moses, doing for the Temple what Moses had done for the tabernacle. Another allusion to the tabernacle will appear in v. 21, where the skilled volunteers who work on the Temple reflect Exod 35:10. The Temple corresponded to the tabernacle and would function as a divine replacement for it. There was a new era of worship, which authentically corresponded to the old one prescribed in the Torah, but represented a fresh, prophetic revelation. David was a prophet for the new age, in which the chronicler and his contemporaries still lived.

28:20-21. The formal public commissioning of Solomon to build the Temple, like the private one in 22:11-16, includes three standard elements:

177. See P. R. Ackroyd, "The Temple Vessels: A Continuity Theme," in *Studies in the Religion of Ancient Israel,* ed. G. W. Anderson et al., VTSup 23 (Leiden: Brill, 1972) 166-81 (= *Studies in the Religious Tradition of Ancient Israel* [London: SCM, 1987] 46-60.

exhortations of encouragement, including the facing and overcoming of natural fears, an assurance of the Lord's enabling presence, and a description of the job to be done. The Lord is David's own God (v. 20). David is testifying that God had seen him through every problem (see 2 Sam 4:9; 1 Kgs 1:29) and would be there to help Solomon to the end. Such a privilege accompanied the responsibility to appropriate a parent's faith (v. 9). This incentive was accompanied by another: the cooperation of qualified personnel. Yet another was the good will of "all the people," for whom Solomon's word was to be their command. The motif of help, from human beings and from God, proclaimed earlier in chaps. 11–12, reappears here.

Another agenda, repeated from chap. 22, is pursued in this commissioning speech. No one who has read Deut 31:7-8 and Josh 1:2-9 can be blind to the intertextual themes in vv. 20-21, including the assurance that the Lord would not fail or forsake this new servant (cf. Deut 31:8; Josh 1:5). The transition of leadership from Moses to Joshua is used as a model. On the human plane, David and Solomon belong together, with the second taking over from the first and completing the unfinished business he left. Theologically, activity in the Second Temple period was a comparable work of God. The new age that continued until the chronicler's time was as divinely authentic as the age launched by the exodus and entry into the promised land.

REFLECTIONS

1. The chronicler devoted three speeches to the Davidic covenant, the prophetic oracle in chap. 17, and the royal speeches in chapters 22 and 28. A new element found here is the motif of election applied not only to David but also to Solomon. The motif reinforces the theological principles of the earlier speeches. The Lord worked through both David and Solomon on behalf of the people's future. Matthew and Luke identified Jesus as God's chosen servant of Isa 42:1 (cf. Matt 12:18; Luke 9:35). In Eph 1:4, 6, God's election of the church is grounded in that of Christ, the beloved. Karl Barth well observed that "as elected man, He is the Lord and Head of all the elect, the revelation and reflection of their election, and the organ and instrument of all divine electing."[178] In the Christian era, the spotlight of revelation has singled out Christ as the embodiment of the divine purposes.

2. The aside in 28:8*b* makes Solomon a model for God's people. They also are called to obey, if they are to enjoy the Lord's continued blessing. The royal "if" (28:7 and 9) is implicitly transferred to the king's subjects as beneficiaries of the royal covenant. The chronicler's readers were meant to overhear the challenge, generation by generation. Likewise, we need to hear the somber conditions of Rom 11:22 and Col 1:23.

3. Commitment comes to the fore in 28:9 as David addresses Solomon. It would be difficult to find in Scripture a more fervent call to spiritual commitment. The chronicler's echoing of Deuteronomy and his use of similar language elsewhere indicates that here, too, Solomon is meant to be a model for all believers, especially as they receive the torch of faith from the preceding generation. The call to consciously live a life that is an open book to God is repeated in Heb 4:13: "Before him no creature is hidden" (NRSV). The ill-fated attempt of Ananias and Sapphira to deceive the church (Acts 5:1-11) is a dire example of the need to hear as a challenge the message of God's insight.

4. A love for the Temple and a pride even in its bygone glory shine through the descriptive list in 28:11-18. It is true that today's means of grace may become tomorrow's superstition (see 2 Kgs 18:4). Yet a spiritual beauty emanates from sacred use. In the most austere of churches a communion table, given pride of place at the front, has a sacred role attached to

178. Karl Barth, *Church Dogmatics,* ed. G. W. Bromiley and T. F. Torrance (Edinburgh: T. & T. Clark, 1957) 2:2.117.

it. We could empathize with the chronicler as he listed the objects that spoke to him of God and mostly still functioned for him as a means of grace.

5. The typological move from tabernacle to Temple is reminiscent of the careful arguments in the Letter to the Hebrews. The tabernacle described in the Torah was a foreshadowing of the heavenly sanctuary into which the ascended Christ had entered (Hebrews 5–10). Writing for Hellenistic Jews who were more oriented to the Torah than to the Temple, the author of Hebrews needed to start with the Torah. For us modern Christians, the New Testament and its revelation have gained a venerable authenticity of their own, but originally it was necessary to trace the consistency and consecutiveness of the work of God by balancing things old and new. The Old Testament and the New Testament together represent the total Word of God, and their mutual relationship deserves careful evaluation. The chronicler had a similar task in his own day. He valued the law, but was aware that it had been supplemented by the prophets, here by a prophetic type of revelation for his own age. Diligent study and careful discrimination were necessary to show their complexity and the contemporary value of each part of God's revelation. Let us, as heirs of both testaments, listen to the chronicler.

A similar message is carried by the comparison of David and Solomon with Moses and Joshua. The old was a model for the new, and the new was an updated, revised version of the old. Typology, properly understood, traces correspondences with former phases of divine revelation in order to recognize the subsequent work of God. The New Testament follows in the wake of the books of Chronicles by making much use of typology. The New Testament knows of a last Adam, a heavenly Jerusalem, and a new sacrifice for sins.

1 Chronicles 29:1-30, David's Public Appeal and Prayer of Praise

NIV

29 Then King David said to the whole assembly: "My son Solomon, the one whom God
has chosen, is young and inexperienced. The task
is great, because this palatial structure is not for
man but for the LORD God. 2With all my resources
I have provided for the temple of my God—gold
for the gold work, silver for the silver, bronze for
the bronze, iron for the iron and wood for the
wood, as well as onyx for the settings, turquoise,[a]
stones of various colors, and all kinds of fine stone
and marble—all of these in large quantities. 3Be-
sides, in my devotion to the temple of my God I
now give my personal treasures of gold and silver
for the temple of my God, over and above everything I have provided for this holy temple: 4three
thousand talents[b] of gold (gold of Ophir) and seven
thousand talents[c] of refined silver, for the overlaying of the walls of the buildings, 5for the gold
work and the silver work, and for all the work

a2 The meaning of the Hebrew for this word is uncertain. *b4* That is, about 110 tons (about 100 metric tons) *c4* That is, about 260 tons (about 240 metric tons)

NRSV

29 King David said to the whole assembly,
"My son Solomon, whom alone God has
chosen, is young and inexperienced, and the work
is great; for the temple[a] will not be for mortals
but for the LORD God. 2So I have provided for the
house of my God, so far as I was able, the gold
for the things of gold, the silver for the things of
silver, and the bronze for the things of bronze,
the iron for the things of iron, and wood for the
things of wood, besides great quantities of onyx
and stones for setting, antimony, colored stones,
all sorts of precious stones, and marble in abundance. 3Moreover, in addition to all that I have
provided for the holy house, I have a treasure of
my own of gold and silver, and because of my
devotion to the house of my God I give it to
the house of my God: 4three thousand talents of
gold, of the gold of Ophir, and seven thousand
talents of refined silver, for overlaying the walls
of the house, 5and for all the work to be done by

a Heb *fortress*

NIV

to be done by the craftsmen. Now, who is willing
to consecrate himself today to the LORD?"
6Then the leaders of families, the officers of the
tribes of Israel, the commanders of thousands and
commanders of hundreds, and the officials in
charge of the king's work gave willingly. 7They
gave toward the work on the temple of God five
thousand talents[a] and ten thousand darics[b] of gold,
ten thousand talents[c] of silver, eighteen thousand
talents[d] of bronze and a hundred thousand talents[e]
of iron. 8Any who had precious stones gave them
to the treasury of the temple of the LORD in the
custody of Jehiel the Gershonite. 9The people
rejoiced at the willing response of their leaders,
for they had given freely and wholeheartedly to
the LORD. David the king also rejoiced greatly.

10David praised the LORD in the presence of the
whole assembly, saying,

"Praise be to you, O LORD,
God of our father Israel,
from everlasting to everlasting.
11Yours, O LORD, is the greatness and the power
and the glory and the majesty and the
splendor,
for everything in heaven and earth is yours.
Yours, O LORD, is the kingdom;
you are exalted as head over all.
12Wealth and honor come from you;
you are the ruler of all things.
In your hands are strength and power
to exalt and give strength to all.
13Now, our God, we give you thanks,
and praise your glorious name.

14"But who am I, and who are my people, that
we should be able to give as generously as this?
Everything comes from you, and we have given
you only what comes from your hand. 15We are
aliens and strangers in your sight, as were all our
forefathers. Our days on earth are like a shadow,
without hope. 16O LORD our God, as for all this
abundance that we have provided for building you
a temple for your Holy Name, it comes from your
hand, and all of it belongs to you. 17I know, my
God, that you test the heart and are pleased with

[a]7 That is, about 190 tons (about 170 metric tons) [b]7 That is, about 185 pounds (about 84 kilograms) [c]7 That is, about 375 tons (about 345 metric tons) [d]7 That is, about 675 tons (about 610 metric tons) [e]7 That is, about 3,750 tons (about 3,450 metric tons)

NRSV

artisans, gold for the things of gold and silver for
the things of silver. Who then will offer willingly,
consecrating themselves today to the LORD?"
6Then the leaders of ancestral houses made
their freewill offerings, as did also the leaders of
the tribes, the commanders of the thousands and
of the hundreds, and the officers over the king's
work. 7They gave for the service of the house of
God five thousand talents and ten thousand darics
of gold, ten thousand talents of silver, eighteen
thousand talents of bronze, and one hundred
thousand talents of iron. 8Whoever had precious
stones gave them to the treasury of the house of
the LORD, into the care of Jehiel the Gershonite.
9Then the people rejoiced because these had given
willingly, for with single mind they had offered
freely to the LORD; King David also rejoiced
greatly.
10Then David blessed the LORD in the presence
of all the assembly; David said: "Blessed are you,
O LORD, the God of our ancestor Israel, forever
and ever. 11Yours, O LORD, are the greatness, the
power, the glory, the victory, and the majesty; for
all that is in the heavens and on the earth is yours;
yours is the kingdom, O LORD, and you are exalted as head above all. 12Riches and honor come
from you, and you rule over all. In your hand are
power and might; and it is in your hand to make
great and to give strength to all. 13And now, our
God, we give thanks to you and praise your
glorious name.
14"But who am I, and what is my people, that
we should be able to make this freewill offering?
For all things come from you, and of your own
have we given you. 15For we are aliens and
transients before you, as were all our ancestors;
our days on the earth are like a shadow, and there
is no hope. 16O LORD our God, all this abundance
that we have provided for building you a house
for your holy name comes from your hand and is
all your own. 17I know, my God, that you search
the heart, and take pleasure in uprightness; in the
uprightness of my heart I have freely offered all
these things, and now I have seen your people,
who are present here, offering freely and joyously
to you. 18O LORD, the God of Abraham, Isaac, and
Israel, our ancestors, keep forever such purposes
and thoughts in the hearts of your people, and

NIV

integrity. All these things have I given willingly
and with honest intent. And now I have seen
with joy how willingly your people who are here
have given to you. [18]O LORD, God of our fathers
Abraham, Isaac and Israel, keep this desire in the
hearts of your people forever, and keep their
hearts loyal to you. [19]And give my son Solomon
the wholehearted devotion to keep your commands, requirements and decrees and to do everything to build the palatial structure for which I
have provided."

[20]Then David said to the whole assembly,
"Praise the LORD your God." So they all praised
the LORD, the God of their fathers; they bowed
low and fell prostrate before the LORD and the
king.

[21]The next day they made sacrifices to the LORD
and presented burnt offerings to him: a thousand
bulls, a thousand rams and a thousand male
lambs, together with their drink offerings, and
other sacrifices in abundance for all Israel. [22]They
ate and drank with great joy in the presence of
the LORD that day.

Then they acknowledged Solomon son of David
as king a second time, anointing him before the
LORD to be ruler and Zadok to be priest. [23]So
Solomon sat on the throne of the LORD as king in
place of his father David. He prospered and all
Israel obeyed him. [24]All the officers and mighty
men, as well as all of King David's sons, pledged
their submission to King Solomon.

[25]The LORD highly exalted Solomon in the sight
of all Israel and bestowed on him royal splendor
such as no king over Israel ever had before.

[26]David son of Jesse was king over all Israel.
[27]He ruled over Israel forty years—seven in Hebron and thirty-three in Jerusalem. [28]He died at a
good old age, having enjoyed long life, wealth and
honor. His son Solomon succeeded him as king.

[29]As for the events of King David's reign, from
beginning to end, they are written in the records
of Samuel the seer, the records of Nathan the
prophet and the records of Gad the seer, [30]to-
gether with the details of his reign and power,
and the circumstances that surrounded him and
Israel and the kingdoms of all the other lands.

NRSV

direct their hearts toward you. [19]Grant to my son
Solomon that with single mind he may keep your
commandments, your decrees, and your statutes,
performing all of them, and that he may build the
temple[a] for which I have made provision."

20Then David said to the whole assembly,
"Bless the LORD your God." And all the assembly
blessed the LORD, the God of their ancestors, and
bowed their heads and prostrated themselves before the LORD and the king. [21]On the next day
they offered sacrifices and burnt offerings to the
LORD, a thousand bulls, a thousand rams, and a
thousand lambs, with their libations, and sacrifices
in abundance for all Israel; [22]and they ate and
drank before the LORD on that day with great joy.

They made David's son Solomon king a second
time; they anointed him as the LORD's prince, and
Zadok as priest. [23]Then Solomon sat on the throne
of the LORD, succeeding his father David as king;
he prospered, and all Israel obeyed him. [24]All the
leaders and the mighty warriors, and also all the
sons of King David, pledged their allegiance to
King Solomon. [25]The LORD highly exalted Solomon
in the sight of all Israel, and bestowed upon him
such royal majesty as had not been on any king
before him in Israel.

26Thus David son of Jesse reigned over all
Israel. [27]The period that he reigned over Israel
was forty years; he reigned seven years in Hebron,
and thirty-three years in Jerusalem. [28]He died in
a good old age, full of days, riches, and honor;
and his son Solomon succeeded him. [29]Now the
acts of King David, from first to last, are written
in the records of the seer Samuel, and in the
records of the prophet Nathan, and in the records
of the seer Gad, [30]with accounts of all his rule
and his might and of the events that befell him
and Israel and all the kingdoms of the earth.

[a] Heb *fortress*

COMMENTARY

In his last speech, David appeals for contributions so that the community of faith may share in the cost of building the Temple (vv. 1-5). They respond positively to his appeal (vv. 6-9). Then the king gives thanks to the Lord (vv. 10-19), and the whole community responds by celebrating in worship (vv. 20-22*a*). Both passages of public response end on notes of joy (vv. 9, 22*a*). Solomon is duly made king and is eulogized by the chronicler (vv. 22*b*-25). David's reign is concluded with a formal epilogue (vv. 26-30).

The key word that begins the first of David's speeches and closes the second is the verb הכינותי (*hăkînôtî*), denoting the preparation that pervaded 22:2-5 and is here rendered "provided" or "made provision" (vv. 2-3, 16, 19). It primarily refers to David, appropriately summing up his role as the human author of the temple project, while Solomon would finish it. Under God both kings established the religious institution that would be the channel of Israel's faith and worship down to the chronicler's day and beyond. The chronicler uses another term for the Temple in vv. 1 and 19, בירה (*bîrâ*), "fortress," rendered "palatial structure" in the NIV. It evokes the Temple's imposing grandeur.

29:1-5. David makes an appeal to the representative assembly convened in 28:1 (cf. 28:8). The purpose of the speech is disclosed at the end. The flow of the passage from 28:21 to 29:5 suggests that there was a practical way in which the people could help Solomon fulfill the mandate for which he had been chosen (v. 1; cf. 28:10). Just as the formidable nature of this task encouraged David to make advance preparations (22:5), so also here it motivates contributions from the people as well as from David. David led with his pocket, giving not public money but his own (v. 3), thus setting an example of generosity. His provision for the Temple in 22:14 was expressed in a colossal number of talents. The same rhetorical use of numbers occurs here in v. 4, though the figures are smaller than before. Still, the motivation is the same; his provisions reflect the worth of the God for whom the Temple was to be built (v. 1).

The king's appeal for voluntary contributions (v. 5) contains a striking phrase. It is employed in Exod 28:41 (also in 2 Chr 13:9) when a newly ordained priest offered his first sacrifice. The exact sense of the phrase "fill one's hand" (מלא יד *millēʾ yād*) is unclear, but it seems to invest the sacrifice with symbolic value, ratifying the offerer's admission to the priesthood. Here it is used as a spiritual metaphor. It is not simply the gift that is consecrated to God but also the giver to God's service. The financial sponsors declared themselves committed to the Lord's work and its success.

29:6-9. The representatives of the people, inspired by David's example and moved by his appeal, gave unstintingly. The storage of precious stones (v. 8) reflects personnel created by 26:21-22. In v. 7, fabulous sums are also mentioned. The reference to "ten thousand darics" (a Persian unit of currency) breaks the pattern in v. 7. It amounts to about 185 pounds, whereas one talent weighed about 75 pounds. The conversion is an admission that the chronicler's constituency was unable to give such vast sums, but was affluent enough to give substantially. The chronicler was appealing to his contemporaries to give according to their means (cf. Deut 16:17). An impression of overwhelming generosity is conveyed by their "single mind" (NRSV) or "wholeheartedness" (NIV; בלב שלם *bĕlēb šālēm*). This virtue marked spiritual service of God in 28:9, and here it represents an outworking of that service.

In Exod 35:4-9, Moses appealed for similar contributions to the construction of the tabernacle and its contents, and the people willingly responded (Exod 35:20-29; see also Exod 25:1-7). The chronicler has written vv. 1-9 with one eye on these Exodus passages. Again the Temple is being put on a par with the tabernacle. The chronicler is announcing a new era launched by the same God of Israel.

29:10-19. The chronicler's account of David's reign consists of two phases: bringing the ark to Jerusalem and preparing for the Temple. Each phase ends in praise, in chap. 16 and here. This magnificent prayer reflects the joy of David and the people over the leaders' generous giving (v. 9) and turns it Godward. Not surprisingly, the prayer has an exuberant tone, reflected in its expressions of totality. "All" (כל *kōl*) occurs no less than ten times. The prayer falls into three parts, each introduced by a fresh address of God: praise in vv. 10*b*-12, thanksgiving in vv. 13-17, and petition in vv. 18-19. Thanksgiving is the main element. It is prefaced by hymnic praise, which seems to reflect liturgical language of the chronicler's period.

29:10-12. David functions as spokesperson for the worshiping community. God deserves their never-ending praise. The reference to the patriarch Jacob, pointedly called Israel in Chronicles, reflects the fact that he, too, was blessed with wealth for which he gave God the credit (Gen 30:43; 31:7; 33:11). The doxology (v. 11*a*) effusively piles up terms for God's sovereign power. Four reasons for praise are given in vv. 11*b*-12: (1) the Lord, as creator, owns the world; (2) as its king, the Lord is supreme over the world; (3) the Lord is the source of all human wealth; and (4) the Lord is the providential supplier of human power.

29:13-15. "And now" (ועתה *wĕʿattâ*) typically marks a transition to the main point, here to thanksgiving directed to the God who acts not only on a universal plane but also as "our God," dispensing wealth to Israel. King and people could claim no credit for their own generous giving. They were channels of resources first given by God, "what comes from your hand" (v. 14). Everything depended on God's prevenient grace. The people of Israel, like the patriarchs, lived as aliens in the promised land (cf. 16:19-20). The land—and all the resources in it—"is mine," declared the Lord; "with me you are but aliens and tenants" (Lev 25:23 NRSV) or "aliens and transients," as the NRSV renders the same Hebrew nouns. Whereas in 16:19-20, the term "alien" had a political sense and in Lev 25:23 a socioeconomic connotation, here גרים (*gērîm*) involves a spiritual meaning.[179] Although David and Israel were firmly in possession of the land, nothing belonged to them by right. They were stewards of God's property, spiritual counterparts of the royal stewards in 27:25-31. This generation must seize the opportunity while it can (see Job 8:9; 14:2).

29:16-17. Wealth, God-given to the last penny, had been returned to God for work on the Temple. In the end, the offering was more than a material one, for its substance already belonged to the Lord. The real offerings were spiritual, matters of "the heart": a sincere motivation to honor God and a readiness to give.

29:18-19. The passage ends with petitions, asking that God's help continue into the future. As at the start, there is a reference to the patriarchs. Not only Jacob but also Abraham and Isaac depended on the Lord for the resources they enjoyed (Gen 13:2; 24:1; 26:12-14). They are no longer models of weakness and hope, as in chap. 16, but of stewardship. The Lord both gives resources and inspires the heart to part with them. So David prays for God to keep fresh and sweet the people's devotion in this area. It was a prayer the chronicler meant his own generation to hear.

The final petitions transcend the immediate context. They revert to a concern of chap. 28: the two mandates, general and particular, that pressed heavily on Solomon's shoulders. The survival of the dynasty depended on his obedience to God in the areas of Torah and Temple (17:12; 22:12; 28:7). How could he maintain the required compliance? The Lord, who gave these duties, also is asked to give Solomon "wholehearted devotion" so that he might live for God and "do everything" necessary for the building of the Temple. Only the Lord's help could make this possible (cf. 1 Kgs 8:58; Ps 119:33-36, 133). The chronicler acknowledged that "there is no one who does not sin" (2 Chr 6:36 = 1 Kgs 8:46). Here, David asks God to give special grace to Solomon.

29:20-22a. Then David urges the assembly to praise God. They worship in word and gesture and also offer homage to the king as a mark of respect and of appreciation for his long reign. They also worship with sacrifices. With meat from the sacrifices other than burnt offerings, they engage in a sacred meal to celebrate their spiritual "joy." The united worship of "all Israel" was an ideal the chronicler coveted for his own generation.

29:22b-25. The coronation of Solomon as co-regent is an idealistic version of the material in 1 Kings. The intertwining of David's and Solomon's reigns is a hook-and-eye bonding into a single whole. Royal appointment functions as an outer framework for David's reign, which started with Israel's anointing David king in chaps. 11–12 and then with their anointing of Solomon as king

179. D. J. Estes, "Metaphorical Sojourning in 1 Chronicles 29:15," *CBQ* 53 (1991) 45-49.

here. The "second" coronation may reflect the chronicler's view that the ceremony in 1 Kgs 1:38-40 was a hasty, improvised affair, followed by this more formal event. The anointing of Zadok, presumably as (sole) high priest (15:11; 16:39) seems to reflect Solomon's act early in his reign (1 Kgs 2:35). His sitting on God's throne is a typical rewriting of 1 Kgs 1:46; 2:12 (cf. 1 Chr 17:14; 28:5). Solomon's prosperity represents a fulfillment of 22:13, and so the implicit guarantee of the Davidic dynasty. The obedience of "all Israel" characterized the reigns of both David and Solomon. Solomon won the support of all the other sons of David; thereby hangs a long tale, told in the succession narrative of 2 Samuel 9–20 and 1 Kings 1–2. As in the case of David's accession, the chronicler was not concerned with this tangled process but instead passed to the outcome. Solomon is even presented as greater than David (v. 25; cf. 1 Kgs 1:47).

The reader will be reminded of Joshua in the chronicler's depiction of Solomon. Joshua was the object of Israel's obedience (Deut 34:9; Josh 1:17), and the Lord exalted him in the sight of all Israel (Josh 3:7; 4:14). Solomon was a second Joshua, as David was another Moses. God's new age had the authenticating hallmarks of the previous one.

29:26-30. The chronicler recapitulates David's reign in the course of a royal epilogue, an expanded version of the one in 1 Kgs 2:10-12. Tribute is paid to the blessings he enjoyed from God's hand: a long life, riches, and honor (cf. v. 12; 23:1). The chronicler copies other royal epilogues in 1–2 Kings by closing with a reference to the literary sources (v. 29) he used for his digest in chaps. 10–29. He casts 1 and 2 Samuel as a series of prophetic narratives (cf. 2 Chr 29:25). In Samuel's case, he had particularly in mind 1 Samuel 16 (cf. 1 Chr 28:4); for Nathan, 2 Samuel 7 (= 1 Chronicles 17); and for Gad, 2 Samuel 24 (= 1 Chronicles 21). In the Jewish canon, 1–2 Samuel are included in the Former Prophets and carry prophetic authority. Even in the chronicler's day they appear to have been invested with a prophetic role.

REFLECTIONS

1. David's appeal for contributions to the building of the Temple reminds the Christian reader of the emergency fund Paul set up on behalf of the needy church in Jerusalem, for which he appealed in 2 Corinthians 8–9. For both Paul and the chronicler, cheerful giving was a measure of spirituality. While in 1 Chronicles David is the model, in 2 Cor 8:9 the "generous act" (NRSV) of Christ in choosing human poverty is the example. If the people and the king rejoiced at the willingness of the giving, God, too, "loves a cheerful giver" (2 Cor 9:7), as 1 Chr 29:17 hints. Consumers experience self-gratification in their spending, and so do misers in their saving; but givers know a deeper joy and a greater gain.

2. The thanksgiving prayer (29:14-17) wrestles reverently with the paradox that one cannot give to God, who is the prior giver of everything. C. S. Lewis expressed this problem well:

> It is like a small child going to its father and saying, "Daddy, give me sixpence to buy you a birthday present." Of course, the father does and is pleased with the present. It is all very nice and proper, but only an idiot would think that the father is sixpence to the good in the transaction.[180]

Israel was like a child without sixpence to call its own. It could be asked of them, "What do you have that you did not receive?" (1 Cor 4:7 NRSV). There could be no self-congratulation on the part of the donors. The thanksgiving emphasizes this point as it traces all giving back to the Lord. As well, God's prior giving constrains Christian giving. As one version of a popular hymn declares, "The gifts we have to offer are what thy love imparts, but chiefly thou desirest our humble, thankful hearts."[181]

180. C. S. Lewis, *Mere Christianity* (New York: Macmillan, 1952) 110-11.
181. From "We Plow the Fields and Scatter" by M. Claudius, trans. J. M. Campbell, an altered version in *The Hymnal 1982* (New York: Church Hymnal Corporation) 291.

Dependence on God is given a twist in the petitions of 29:18-19. If the means of giving is given first by God, we humans depend on God also for a continuing sense of motivation. We need the prodding of the Holy Spirit to stimulate our self-centered hearts Godward.

3. The second petition is conscious of the burdens resting on young Solomon. God never gives burdens for us to bear alone, but wants to share them. In fact, "we do not have to do any carrying without remembering that we *are* carried."[182] There is a beautiful prayer in the *bar mitzvah* service used in Great Britain, when a thirteen-year-old Jewish boy assumes the yoke of the Torah. It speaks, rightly, of duty and resolve, but it manifests throughout a sense of utter dependence on God's help, as in this extract: "I pray humbly and hopefully before thee, to grant me thy gracious help, so that I have the will and the understanding to walk firmly in thy ways all the days of my life. Implant [literally "create"] in me a spirit of sincere devotion to thy service."[183] Christians, too, are called to trust and obey—to trust in God's enabling even as they obey. "It is God who is at work in you, enabling you both to will and to work for his good pleasure" (Phil 2:13 NRSV).

4. David's thanksgiving and praise in vv. 10-19 provide a counterpart to the praise and petitioning taken from the psalms in 1 Chr 16:7-36. Both have similar themes: The Lord is the sovereign King. The people, insignificant in and of themselves, are caught up in God's great purposes. There are also differences. According to 1 Chr 16:7-36, the patriarchs are models for a needy Israel as they wander through the land and receive the divine promise of a future inheritance. Here the patriarchs and Israel are recipients of God-given assets, which are humbly owned as such. Whereas in 1 Chr 16:7-36 Israel's appeal is brought to God, in David's prayer the chronicler implicitly brings the Lord's appeal to contemporary Israel and stakes God's claim on their lives and especially their monetary resources. Challenge rather than assurance is the dominant note. In these prayers of praise, different facets of theology are presented, and both end in petitions. In the psalm it was an eschatological petition, while here it is an existential plea for God's help in life's divinely assigned duties. We need both types of prayer, for life is both performance and preparation.

182. Karl Barth, *Ethics*, trans. G. W. Bromiley (New York; Seabury, 1981) 516.
183. *The Authorised Daily Prayer Book of the United Hebrew Congregations of the British Commonwealth of Nations*, 2nd ed., trans. S. Singer (London: Eyre and Spottiswoode, 1962) 407.

2 CHRONICLES 1:1–9:31, THE REIGN OF SOLOMON

OVERVIEW

The account of Solomon's reign has been analyzed as if it were a complex chiasm.[184] More probably it falls into two parallel halves, 1:1–5:1 and 5:2–9:31. Each half is initiated by the king's organizing a national assembly to worship at a sanctuary and receiving a nocturnal theophany in which a prayer of Solomon is answered (1:1-13; 5:2–7:22). The fact that the first sanctuary visited is the old one at Gibeon and the second is the new Temple in Jerusalem shows the crucial development that the reign of Solomon brought. While much of the material is devoted to temple matters, the focus on Solomon's prosperous reign in chaps. 1 and 9 provides a different framework for the unit. Chapter 2 is concerned with his

184. R. B. Dillard, *2 Chronicles*, WBC 15 (Waco, Tex.: Word, 1987) 5-7. See also John W. Kleinig, *The Lord's Song: The Basis, Function and Significance of Choral Music in Chronicles*, JSOTSup 156 (Sheffield: JSOT, 1993) 159-60.

preparations for building the Temple and 3:1–5:1 with the actual building. Chapter 8 looks backward and forward: 8:1-11 anticipates the royal initiatives of 8:17–9:31, while 8:12-16 rounds off a description of temple ritual.

2 Chronicles 1:1-17, Seeking God and Receiving Blessing

NIV

1 Solomon son of David established himself firmly over his kingdom, for the LORD his God was with him and made him exceedingly great.

2Then Solomon spoke to all Israel—to the commanders of thousands and commanders of hundreds, to the judges and to all the leaders in Israel, the heads of families— 3and Solomon and the whole assembly went to the high place at Gibeon, for God's Tent of Meeting was there, which Moses the LORD's servant had made in the desert. 4Now David had brought up the ark of God from Kiriath Jearim to the place he had prepared for it, because he had pitched a tent for it in Jerusalem. 5But the bronze altar that Bezalel son of Uri, the son of Hur, had made was in Gibeon in front of the tabernacle of the LORD; so Solomon and the assembly inquired of him there. 6Solomon went up to the bronze altar before the LORD in the Tent of Meeting and offered a thousand burnt offerings on it.

7That night God appeared to Solomon and said to him, "Ask for whatever you want me to give you."

8Solomon answered God, "You have shown great kindness to David my father and have made me king in his place. 9Now, LORD God, let your promise to my father David be confirmed, for you have made me king over a people who are as numerous as the dust of the earth. 10Give me wisdom and knowledge, that I may lead this people, for who is able to govern this great people of yours?"

11God said to Solomon, "Since this is your heart's desire and you have not asked for wealth, riches or honor, nor for the death of your enemies, and since you have not asked for a long life but for wisdom and knowledge to govern my people over whom I have made you king, 12therefore wisdom and knowledge will be given you. And I will also give you wealth, riches and honor,

NRSV

1 Solomon son of David established himself in his kingdom; the LORD his God was with him and made him exceedingly great.

2Solomon summoned all Israel, the commanders of the thousands and of the hundreds, the judges, and all the leaders of all Israel, the heads of families. 3Then Solomon, and the whole assembly with him, went to the high place that was at Gibeon; for God's tent of meeting, which Moses the servant of the LORD had made in the wilderness, was there. 4(But David had brought the ark of God up from Kiriath-jearim to the place that David had prepared for it; for he had pitched a tent for it in Jerusalem.) 5Moreover the bronze altar that Bezalel son of Uri, son of Hur, had made, was there in front of the tabernacle of the LORD. And Solomon and the assembly inquired at it. 6Solomon went up there to the bronze altar before the LORD, which was at the tent of meeting, and offered a thousand burnt offerings on it.

7That night God appeared to Solomon, and said to him, "Ask what I should give you." 8Solomon said to God, "You have shown great and steadfast love to my father David, and have made me succeed him as king. 9O LORD God, let your promise to my father David now be fulfilled, for you have made me king over a people as numerous as the dust of the earth. 10Give me now wisdom and knowledge to go out and come in before this people, for who can rule this great people of yours?" 11God answered Solomon, "Because this was in your heart, and you have not asked for possessions, wealth, honor, or the life of those who hate you, and have not even asked for long life, but have asked for wisdom and knowledge for yourself that you may rule my people over whom I have made you king, 12wisdom and knowledge are granted to you. I will also give you riches, possessions, and honor, such as none of the kings had who were before you, and none after you shall have the like." 13So

NIV

such as no king who was before you ever had and none after you will have."

[13]Then Solomon went to Jerusalem from the high place at Gibeon, from before the Tent of Meeting. And he reigned over Israel.

[14]Solomon accumulated chariots and horses; he had fourteen hundred chariots and twelve thousand horses,[a] which he kept in the chariot cities and also with him in Jerusalem. [15]The king made silver and gold as common in Jerusalem as stones, and cedar as plentiful as sycamore-fig trees in the foothills. [16]Solomon's horses were imported from Egypt[b] and from Kue[c]—the royal merchants purchased them from Kue. [17]They imported a chariot from Egypt for six hundred shekels[d] of silver, and a horse for a hundred and fifty.[e] They also exported them to all the kings of the Hittites and of the Arameans.

[a]*14* Or *charioteers* [b]*16* Or possibly *Muzur,* a region in Cilicia; also in verse 17 [c]*16* Probably Cilicia [d]*17* That is, about 15 pounds (about 7 kilograms) [e]*17* That is, about 3 3/4 pounds (about 1.7 kilograms)

NRSV

Solomon came from[a] the high place at Gibeon, from the tent of meeting, to Jerusalem. And he reigned over Israel.

14Solomon gathered together chariots and horses; he had fourteen hundred chariots and twelve thousand horses, which he stationed in the chariot cities and with the king in Jerusalem. [15]The king made silver and gold as common in Jerusalem as stone, and he made cedar as plentiful as the sycamore of the Shephelah. [16]Solomon's horses were imported from Egypt and Kue; the king's traders received them from Kue at the prevailing price. [17]They imported from Egypt, and then exported, a chariot for six hundred shekels of silver, and a horse for one hundred fifty; so through them these were exported to all the kings of the Hittites and the kings of Aram.

[a] Gk Vg: Heb *to*

COMMENTARY

This chapter has two agendas. The first involves its relationship with chap. 9, as one of two literary bookends for this unit. Although the theme of the Temple dominates most of the account of Solomon's reign, his kingship is pushed to the fore at the beginning and the end. The root מלך (*mlk*), which denotes aspects of kingship, occurs no fewer than six times in vv. 1-13 and twice more in vv. 14-17. And this repetition is not surprising: Solomon's role in establishing the Davidic dynasty has been emphasized in 1 Chronicles 17; 22; and 28. Both his building of the Temple and his overall obedience to God were the conditions that had to be fulfilled if the dynasty were to last. Prosperity, it had been hinted, would be the signal that he had been obedient (1 Chr 22:13; cf. 1 Chr 29:23). So his reign is pointedly described as a success story at both its beginning and its ending. At the outset, his reign is grounded in his spirituality—namely, seeking the Lord. This fits the prescription for finding God that David gave him: "If you seek him, he will be found by you" (1 Chr 28:9). The second agenda of the chapter involves a description of the old pre-Temple religious order, in preparation for the claim in later chapters that it had been superseded by the new Temple.

1:1. Solomon's accession to the throne carries with it a suggestion of opposition. The negative undercurrents are probed in 1 Kings 2, while 2 Chronicles sums up their resolution in a sentence. Solomon succeeded, as 1 Kgs 2:46*b* records, but only because he had divine backing. It is 1 Chr 11:9 all over again: "David became greater and greater, for the Lord of hosts was with him" (NRSV). The boon of the Lord's presence with Solomon begins to fulfill David's encouraging wish and affirmation in 1 Chr 22:11; 28:20. There the temple project was in view, but here it is the wider matter of Solomon's reign, as was the case with David (1 Chr 11:9). The statement that the Lord "made him exceedingly great" is a recapitulation of the same Hebrew wording in 1 Chr 29:25*a* (cf. KJV; TNK).

1:2-6. The chronicler makes clear that Solomon's first act as king was to seek the Lord. The writer of 1 Kgs 3:2-3 is apologetic about Solomon's visit to the high place at Gibeon, excusing him grudgingly.[185] The chronicler had no such misgivings. Elsewhere he distinguishes between sincere worship of the Lord and idolatrous religion at high places (33:17). What made Solomon's visit to Gibeon unimpeachably legitimate was the claim, already encountered in 1 Chr 16:39-40; 21:29, that Gibeon was the national sanctuary for sacrifice, complete with the accoutrements of Mosaic religion. In 1 Kings 3, the sanctuary is of importance only as the place of ensuing theophany. In 2 Chronicles, Solomon's private visit is developed into a national pilgrimage. "All Israel" and "the whole assembly" are descriptions of a representative group of leaders, as v. 2 suggests.

According to 1 Chronicles, the first thing David had done after becoming king was to seek out the ark (1 Chr 13:3; cf. 1 Chr 15:13) with a national pilgrimage to its location (1 Chr 13:6). It was a case of like father, like son. Solomon and Israel "sought" (דרשׁ *dāraš*; NRSV, "inquired at it," a more likely interpretation than the NIV's "inquired of him," in view of the intended reminiscence of 1 Chr 13:3 and the fact that in the Hebrew single compound sentence of v. 5 the object of the verb is naturally the subject of the first clause, "the altar") the bronze altar for burnt offerings.[186] Verses 3 and 5 paint a beautiful picture of a united people worshiping together under God's chosen king. This expression of Solomon's spiritual faithfulness to God boded well for the perpetuity of the dynasty. It also sent reverberations of challenge and hope down through the centuries.

The legitimacy of the enterprise is painstakingly spelled out. The Mosaic "tent of meeting" (v. 3) or "tabernacle" (v. 5) had been preserved at Gibeon. The presence of the ancient altar at Gibeon (v. 5) made sacrificial worship there legitimate. Yet, there are hints of changes to come, heralded already by the installation of the ark in David's new tent in Jerusalem. The reference to Bezalel (cf. Exod 31:2; 1 Chr 2:20) prepares readers for a typological application in chap. 2, which will authorize a new order of worship. In 1 Kgs 3:4, the "thousand burnt offerings" on the altar (v. 6) refer to Solomon's general custom. Here they are applied to this event and constitute a grand farewell to the tabernacle in its old setting. This moment marked the phasing out of Torah-based tabernacle worship, before the launching of the temple age.

1:7-9. In a private theophany, the Lord's invitation, "Ask what I should give you," has a royal flavor. In Ps 2:8, God offers to the king universal rule and in Ps 21:4 long life. Verse 8 is an abbreviation of 1 Kgs 3:6-7. One missing element, Solomon's inexperience, has been transferred to 1 Chr 22:5; 29:1. Two elements have been added. The first, an appeal for the Lord to keep the promise made to David, has been borrowed from 1 Kgs 8:26, which reappears in 2 Chr 6:17. We hear an echo of David's own prayer (1 Chr 17:23-24). These other contexts show that Solomon is requesting realization of that dynasty. This dynastic reference suggests that here Solomon's obedience is in view as a condition for the dynastic continuity. In fact, the motif of royal obedience accompanies the references to the divine promises in 1 Kgs 8:26 and the parallel 2 Chr 6:17. The second addition is the interpretation of the vast number of the people in terms of dust, recalling the promise made to Jacob in Gen 28:14.[187] So this interpretation represents an idealization of Solomon's reign as the keeping of a much older divine promise.

1:10-12. The king's request for wisdom in governing God's people, a purpose underlined by the chronicler in v. 12, is granted with the bonus of great riches and status. Whereas 1 Kgs 3:12 focuses on Solomon's imcomparable wisdom, here his wealth is brought to the fore, as vv. 14-17 will illustrate.

1:13. Solomon returns to Jerusalem "from the high place" (rightly emended in the NRSV with a note and implicitly in the NIV).[188] His celebratory sacrificing in Jerusalem (1 Kgs 3:15) is not mentioned here. Did the chronicler consider Gibeon the only rightful place of sacrifice at the time (cf. 1 Chr 16:39-40)? No, the presence of an altar in Jerusalem (1 Chr 21:26–22:1; cf. 1 Kgs 2:28) would have satisfied him, and he even

185. See the comparative analysis of D. M. Carr, *From D to Q: A Study of Early Jewish Interpretations of Solomon's Dream at Gibeon,* SBLMS 44 (Atlanta: Scholars Press, 1991) 90-114.

186. S. Japhet, *I & II Chronicles,* OTL (Louisville: Westminster/John Knox, 1993) 529.

187. See H. G. M. Williamson, *Israel in the Books of Chronicles* (Cambridge: Cambridge University Press, 1977) 64.

188. See L. C. Allen, *The Greek Chronicles: The Relation of the Septuagint of I and II Chronicles to the Massoretic Text,* Part 2: *Textual Criticism,* VTSup 25, 27 (Leiden: Brill, 1974) 131.

took over the earlier reference to sacrificing there in 1 Chr 15:26. But the omission did underline the legitimacy of Gibeon.[189]

1:14-17. The cluster of items about horses has been taken from 1 Kgs 10:26-29. One expects to find it in the parallel 2 Chr 9:25-28. What does appear there has been influenced by the similar report in 1 Kgs 4:26. The chronicler regarded the 1 Kings texts as two separate summaries of Solomon's chariotry at the beginning and end of his reign. He put the smaller number first, encouraged by the verb "gathered together."[190] The paragraph was put here to illustrate the fulfillment of the promise of riches in v. 12; it represents divine blessing for Solomon's seeking the things of God. Mention of "silver and gold" in v. 15, over against "silver" in 1 Kgs 10:27 and 2 Chr 9:27, paves the way for 2:7, as "cedar" does for 2:8, though here temple building is not yet in view. Readers may consult the 1 Kings commentary for the details of vv. 16-17. For the chronicler, the broad picture was sufficient.

189. H. G. M. Williamson, *1 and 2 Chronicles*, NCB (Grand Rapids: Eerdmans, 1982) 196.

190. E. L. Curtis and A. A. Madsen, *The Books of Chronicles*, ICC (Edinburgh: T. &. T. Clark, 1910) 318.

REFLECTIONS

Like the account of David's reign, the chapters devoted to Solomon are vibrant with the excitement of change. These were times of transition from an old order to a new one. A royal dynasty was in the process of being founded, which was to reverberate through later history and become the basis of eschatological hope. A temple was to be built as the focus of offering worship and finding God's love thereafter for Israel. As Christian readers enter into the chronicler's excitement, they will appreciate in turn Jesus' claim that "something [even] greater than Solomon is here" (Matt 12:42 NRSV).

Solomon is represented as a model of spirituality. His first royal act was to urge "all Israel" to "seek" the Lord with him at a national sanctuary, replete with religious objects endorsed by the Torah. "Seek first . . ." is the chronicler's message, like that of Jesus (Matt 6:33 NIV). As a consequence, the king was rewarded with divine blessing. Solomon gained wealth (and also wisdom, but the chapter concentrates on the wealth) as a prize for seeking the Lord.

"Wealth . . . and honor" (1:12 NIV) come from God, according to 1 Chr 29:12. In the books of Chronicles these are the blessings poured out on good kings: David (1 Chr 29:28), Jehoshaphat (2 Chr 17:5; 18:1), Hezekiah (32:27), and here Solomon (also 9:22). In Jehoshaphat's case, it is also the result of seeking God (2 Chr 17:4). In Proverbs, wealth and honor are held out as incentives for seeking wisdom (Prov 8:17-18; see also Prov 22:4). Other parts of the Old Testament are not so sanguine in their attitude to wealth. While it fits snugly into the Old Testament's land-oriented theology, there are warnings about confusing material blessings and materialism (Deut 8:12-14, 17-18; Jer 9:23). The prophets complain of the wealth of the wicked (Jer 5:27; Hos 12:7-8; Mic 6:12; Zech 11:5), while Ecclesiastes is dubious about a providential explanation of wealth (Eccl 9:11). We are uneasily aware of such caveats. Yet, the chronicler was careful to take over the emphasis in 1 Kings that no self-seeking was involved and that it was in the context of discharging difficult responsibilities and seeking help in so doing that blessing came.

The one who seeks is invited to ask (1:7). Verses 5 and 7 of this chapter are reminiscent of the promise-laden invitations in the Sermon on the Mount: "Ask and it will be given to you; seek and you will find. . . . For everyone who asks receives; he who seeks finds" (Matt 7:7-8 NIV). Indeed, seeking God's kingdom results in the meeting of material needs (Matt 6:33) and the receipt of benefits ironically comparable with those enjoyed by "Solomon in all his glory" (Matt 6:29 NRSV). Again, we modern readers find it easier to separate spirituality from material things and to psychologize by focusing on the peace of mind we forfeit by not seeking God. Nevertheless, there is a refreshing simplicity about the link between body and spirit that often underlies biblical thinking and that we still honor when we pray at mealtime.

If, during Solomon's reign, gold was as common as stone in Jerusalem, in the new Jerusalem the very streets are to be paved with gold (Rev 21:21). One can hardly exclude an eschatological dimension from the text of 2 Chronicles (cf. Isa 60:5, 11; 61:6; 66:12). Here was the inauguration of future hope; here was a fitting earthly manifestation of God's kingdom (cf. 1 Chr 29:11-12). Jesus, too, received gold as an implicit pledge of his royal glory (Matt 2:11; 25:31).

2 Chronicles 2:1-18, Preparing for the Temple

NIV

2 Solomon gave orders to build a temple for
the Name of the LORD and a royal palace
for himself. [2]He conscripted seventy thousand
men as carriers and eighty thousand as stonecutters in the hills and thirty-six hundred as foremen
over them.

[3]Solomon sent this message to Hiram[a] king of
Tyre:

"Send me cedar logs as you did for my
father David when you sent him cedar to
build a palace to live in. [4]Now I am about to
build a temple for the Name of the LORD my
God and to dedicate it to him for burning
fragrant incense before him, for setting out
the consecrated bread regularly, and for making burnt offerings every morning and evening
and on Sabbaths and New Moons and at the
appointed feasts of the LORD our God. This is
a lasting ordinance for Israel.

[5]"The temple I am going to build will be
great, because our God is greater than all
other gods. [6]But who is able to build a temple
for him, since the heavens, even the highest
heavens, cannot contain him? Who then am
I to build a temple for him, except as a place
to burn sacrifices before him?

[7]"Send me, therefore, a man skilled to
work in gold and silver, bronze and iron, and
in purple, crimson and blue yarn, and experienced in the art of engraving, to work in
Judah and Jerusalem with my skilled craftsmen, whom my father David provided.

[8]"Send me also cedar, pine and algum[b] logs
from Lebanon, for I know that your men are

[a]3 Hebrew *Huram,* a variant of *Hiram;* also in verses 11 and 12
[b]8 Probably a variant of *almug;* possibly juniper

NRSV

2[a] Solomon decided to build a temple for the
name of the LORD, and a royal palace for
himself. [1b]Solomon conscripted seventy thousand
laborers and eighty thousand stonecutters in the
hill country, with three thousand six hundred to
oversee them.

3Solomon sent word to King Huram of Tyre:
"Once you dealt with my father David and sent
him cedar to build himself a house to live in. [4]I
am now about to build a house for the name of
the LORD my God and dedicate it to him for
offering fragrant incense before him, and for the
regular offering of the rows of bread, and for burnt
offerings morning and evening, on the sabbaths
and the new moons and the appointed festivals
of the LORD our God, as ordained forever for Israel.
[5]The house that I am about to build will be great,
for our God is greater than other gods. [6]But who
is able to build him a house, since heaven, even
highest heaven, cannot contain him? Who am I
to build a house for him, except as a place to
make offerings before him? [7]So now send me an
artisan skilled to work in gold, silver, bronze, and
iron, and in purple, crimson, and blue fabrics,
trained also in engraving, to join the skilled workers who are with me in Judah and Jerusalem,
whom my father David provided. [8]Send me also
cedar, cypress, and algum timber from Lebanon,
for I know that your servants are skilled in cutting
Lebanon timber. My servants will work with your
servants [9]to prepare timber for me in abundance,
for the house I am about to build will be great
and wonderful. [10]I will provide for your servants,
those who cut the timber, twenty thousand cors
of crushed wheat, twenty thousand cors of barley,

[a]Ch 1.18 in Heb [b]Ch 2.1 in Heb

NIV

skilled in cutting timber there. My men will
work with yours [9]to provide me with plenty
of lumber, because the temple I build must
be large and magnificent. [10]I will give your
servants, the woodsmen who cut the timber,
twenty thousand cors[a] of ground wheat,
twenty thousand cors of barley, twenty thousand baths[b] of wine and twenty thousand
baths of olive oil."

[11]Hiram king of Tyre replied by letter to
Solomon:

"Because the LORD loves his people, he has
made you their king."

[12]And Hiram added:

"Praise be to the LORD, the God of Israel,
who made heaven and earth! He has given
King David a wise son, endowed with intelligence and discernment, who will build a
temple for the LORD and a palace for himself.

[13]"I am sending you Huram-Abi, a man of
great skill, [14]whose mother was from Dan and
whose father was from Tyre. He is trained to
work in gold and silver, bronze and iron,
stone and wood, and with purple and blue
and crimson yarn and fine linen. He is experienced in all kinds of engraving and can
execute any design given to him. He will
work with your craftsmen and with those of
my lord, David your father.

[15]"Now let my lord send his servants the
wheat and barley and the olive oil and wine
he promised, [16]and we will cut all the logs
from Lebanon that you need and will float
them in rafts by sea down to Joppa. You can
then take them up to Jerusalem."

[17]Solomon took a census of all the aliens who
were in Israel, after the census his father David
had taken; and they were found to be 153,600.
[18]He assigned 70,000 of them to be carriers and
80,000 to be stonecutters in the hills, with 3,600
foremen over them to keep the people working.

[a] *10* That is, probably about 125,000 bushels (about 4,400 kiloliters)
[b] *10* That is, probably about 115,000 gallons (about 440 kiloliters)

NRSV

twenty thousand baths[a] of wine, and twenty thousand baths of oil."

11Then King Huram of Tyre answered in a
letter that he sent to Solomon, "Because the LORD
loves his people he has made you king over
them." [12]Huram also said, "Blessed be the LORD
God of Israel, who made heaven and earth, who
has given King David a wise son, endowed with
discretion and understanding, who will build a
temple for the LORD, and a royal palace for himself.

13"I have dispatched Huram-abi, a skilled artisan, endowed with understanding, [14]the son of
one of the Danite women, his father a Tyrian. He
is trained to work in gold, silver, bronze, iron,
stone, and wood, and in purple, blue, and crimson
fabrics and fine linen, and to do all sorts of
engraving and execute any design that may be
assigned him, with your artisans, the artisans of
my lord, your father David. [15]Now, as for the
wheat, barley, oil, and wine, of which my lord
has spoken, let him send them to his servants.
[16]We will cut whatever timber you need from
Lebanon, and bring it to you as rafts by sea to
Joppa; you will take it up to Jerusalem."

17Then Solomon took a census of all the aliens
who were residing in the land of Israel, after the
census that his father David had taken; and there
were found to be one hundred fifty-three thousand six hundred. [18]Seventy thousand of them he
assigned as laborers, eighty thousand as stonecutters in the hill country, and three thousand six
hundred as overseers to make the people work.

[a] A Hebrew measure of volume

COMMENTARY

2:1. Now the king can make the necessary arrangements for carrying out his God-appointed task of building the Temple. This verse is a headline for the chapter. It brings the Temple project to the fore and only glances at matters of royalty. Such side glances also occur in 2:12; 7:11; 8:1; 9:11, and presuppose knowledge of the account of building the palace in 1 Kgs 7:1-12. The chronicler turns into a narrative introduction Solomon's statement in his message to Hiram (Huram in Chronicles) at 1 Kgs 5:5 about the intention to build the Temple.

2:2. Two factors were necessary for building the Temple. The first is treated in this verse: personnel. The need for personnel provides a literary framework for the chapter. It is mentioned here and given fuller treatment in vv. 17-18. The need for a particular artisan appears in vv. 7 and 13-14. In ancient times, building projects were labor-intensive. An adequate labor force had to be prepared. This recruitment parallels the work of Solomon to that of David in 1 Chr 22:2.

2:3-16. Materials were also needed to build the Temple. Although David had provided much, 1 Chr 22:14 indicated the need for more. Verse 9 suggests that the splendor of Solomon's project made more materials required, harking back to 1 Chr 22:5. His negotiations with the Phoenician king Huram take up most of the chapter (vv. 3-16). They open with a message that falls into two parts: an introduction in vv. 3*b*-6 and its substance in vv. 7-10. Verses 3*b*-9 are bound together as a single meandering sentence in the Hebrew, with the core meaning "As you sent David cedar . . . send me also cedar" (vv. 3, 8).

2:3-6. Solomon's message to Huram is based on 1 Kgs 5:2-6, but here the Israelite king takes the initiative, and Hiram's prior congratulations in 1 Kgs 5:1 are relegated to his reply at v. 11. The text of 1 Kgs 5:3-5 consists of Solomon's preliminary statements before his request in 1 Kgs 5:6. The chronicler had already used the motif of David's disqualifying warfare in 1 Chr 22:8-9, and has moved Solomon's intention to build the Temple back to 2 Chr 2:1.

That intention is repeated in v. 4*a*, but the rest of the introductory passage in vv. 3*b*-6 is given over to the chronicler's own concerns. First, a parallel is drawn between David and Solomon to call attention to their joint status. The chronicler deems Solomon to be as great a king as his father, since Solomon asked Huram for tribute (see vv. 14-15; cf. 1 Chr 14:1-2). Verse 7 will discriminate between the respective roles of David and Solomon vis-à-vis the Temple by presenting David as provider (cf. 1 Chr 22:15) and Solomon as executor.

Second, before the building narrative begins, the chronicler takes the opportunity to define the function of the Temple as a place of sacrificial worship (vv. 4*b*, 6; cf. 7:12). Although the Temple was a religious innovation, it was to operate on traditional lines laid down in the Lord's earlier revelation. The new era was to be marked by religious conformity to the old tabernacle era, as the priestly material in the Torah presented it. The offerings of incense (Exod 30:7-8), the bread of the presence (Exod 25:30; Lev 24:5-8), and the regular burnt offerings (Numbers 28–29) were to be maintained as permanent obligations for God's people to honor. These regular rites became a feature of the macrostructure of the chronicler's narrative as a yardstick by which to measure the spiritual loyalty of future kings.[191] In the divided kingdom, temple duties are reaffirmed at the outset as at least still being honored in Judah (13:10-11). At the end they are recorded as being tragically neglected even in Judah (29:7). In the reunited kingdom, Hezekiah reestablished these rites (29:18; 31:2-3), restoring the Temple to the religious standards of the Torah (31:3).

Third, in vv. 5-6 the theology of the Temple's structure and decor is discussed, in a development of David's statements at 1 Chr 22:5; 29:1. If Israel's "God is greater than all other gods" (1 Chr 16:25 NIV), then an edifice to honor such a God must itself be correspondingly great. It must be a visible witness to the wonderful glory of the Lord (v. 9). Yet too much should not be claimed for the Temple. It was only in a limited sense God's house (cf. Exod 25:8), though it did enjoy the partial presence of the Lord ("before him," vv. 4, 6). The chronicler borrows material from

191. H. G. M. Williamson, *1 and 2 Chronicles*, NCB (Grand Rapids: Eerdmans, 1982) 198.

Solomon's prayer in 1 Kgs 8:27 that he will use again in its proper place at 6:18. It is an assertion of divine omnipresence by which the Lord is shown to be beyond all manipulation (cf. Ps 139:7-12).

2:7-10. Solomon asks for a master craftsman (v. 7) and for lumber (vv. 8-10). In a letter Huram will consent to both requests (vv. 13-16). The chronicler's source is 1 Kgs 7:13-14, a separate narrative whose gist he weaves into Solomon's message. There the craftsman was called simply Hiram and is a bronzesmith, while ethnically he was a Phoenician with an Israelite mother from the tribe of Naphtali. Here he is called Huram-abi and is an artisan skilled in many crafts, and his mother's tribe is Dan.

As elsewhere, the chronicler writes with one eye on the historical source and the other on the tabernacle account, specifically the description of its construction in Exodus 35. Its chief craftsman was Bezalel, from the tribe of Judah. He was mentioned in 2 Chr 1:5 in anticipation of this passage (cf. 1 Chr 2:20). Bezalel had an assistant named Aholiab (Exod 35:34), from the tribe of Dan, and between them they had the manifold skills of vv. 7 and 14. Solomon is regarded typologically as a second Bezalel from Judah, and Huram-abi as a second Aholiab from Dan. In the latter case, the longer name "Huram-abi" is a clue to the typologizing. We shall read repeatedly in chaps. 3–4 the statement "and he made" (ויעש *wayya'aś*) about Solomon's work for the Temple. It is used much more often than in the 1 Kings source and echoes the same frequent refrain concerning Bezalel in Exodus 36–39. With these echoes, the chronicler affirms theologically that the Temple is a second tabernacle. In 1 Kgs 7:14, Hiram had been modeled in part on Bezalel (cf. Exod 35:3-35),[192] while the temple furnishings in 1 Kgs 7:40, 48-50 reflected those of the tabernacle.[193] The chronicler takes these hints seriously and develops them in his own way. Typological comparison serves to describe the new era as comparable to and succeeding the old one.

2:11-16. Huram's reply is cast in the form of a letter. It corresponds closely to Solomon's message, both in content and in structure, which consists of introduction and main part (vv. 13-16). The introduction, like Solomon's, is theologically oriented. The description of Solomon as the Lord's love gift to Israel is borrowed from another foreign testimony (1 Kgs 10:9), which will be used again in 2 Chr 9:8. It fits Solomon's role as the chosen agent of a new era for Israel (cf. 1 Chr 28:5-7). It is adapted from Hiram's love for David, mentioned in the narrative of 1 Kgs 5:1 (KJV). The shift was encouraged by the pair of blessing formulas in 1 Kgs 5:7 and 10:9.

Huram's praise in v. 12 changes 1 Kgs 5:7*b* in two ways. First, it adds a reference to the Lord as creator (cf. Ps 78:69), which is consistent with Solomon's witness to God (vv. 5-6). Second, and in accord with the literary context, it envisions Solomon's wisdom as being manifested in his building of the Temple rather than in his reign. The theological program of 1 Chr 16:25-30 finds partial realization here. The Phoenician king represents Gentile peoples who were urged to "ascribe to the LORD the glory due to his name," as the God who "made the heavens." The new era inaugurated by David and Solomon awaited the consummation, the Gentiles' acknowledgment of the praiseworthiness of Israel's God (cf. Ps 22:27-28; 102:21-22; Isa 45:14; 66:18-23). King Huram is also represented as vassal of David and Solomon ("my lord," vv. 14-15). Solomon receives foreign homage on the Lord's behalf, sitting as he does on God's throne (1 Chr 29:23). This is an aspect of Solomon's reign that chap. 9 will develop.

The NRSV and the NIV omit the transitional "And now" (v. 13 KJV), which is repeated in v. 15. Huram assents to Solomon's two requests and agrees with the wages to be paid Huram's woodcutters, offered in v. 10. In 1 Kgs 5:6, Solomon left it to the king of Tyre to fix the wages, but here Solomon again takes the initiative. The quantities involved are loosely based on the annual contribution specified in 1 Kgs 5:11, but here a single fee is envisioned.

2:17-18. The issue of local workers, broached in v. 2, is elaborated in a resumptive conclusion. The chronicler is now following the order of his parent text, 1 Kgs 5:13-18. The numbers and job descriptions of 1 Kgs 5:15-16 are closely followed and supplied with a total (v. 17). There is one other passage about forced labor in 1 Kgs 9:20-22,

192. See S. L. McKenzie, *The Chronicler's Use of the Deuteronomistic History,* HSM 33 (Atlanta: Scholars Press, 1985) 107.

193. R. D. Nelson, *First and Second Kings,* Interpretation (Louisville: John Knox, 1987) 47.

which states categorically that Solomon used no Israelites for the labor gangs, but only indigenous groups. The chronicler, who will make explicit use of 1 Kgs 9:20-22 in 2 Chr 8:7-9, follows that tradition, encouraged by his view of Solomon as one who follows the Torah. He is mindful of Lev 25:39-45 and Deut 20:11, which prohibit harsh rule over Israelites and permit the use of indigenous subjects as forced labor.[194] Accordingly, both here and in 1 Chr 22:2, to which he refers (אחרי [*'aḥărê*] is better rendered "similar to," with the REB, than "after"), he interpreted "out of all Israel" in 1 Kgs 5:13 not nationally but territorially, as "the aliens who were residing in the land of Israel" (NRSV). The chronicler's interpretation seems forced. It does not accord with Jeroboam's position as overseer of the forced labor of the house of Joseph (1 Kgs 11:28). Moreover, the antipathy of the northern tribes to Rehoboam and their stoning of the administrator of the forced labor program (1 Kgs 12:3-4, 18), both of which are taken over in 2 Chr 10:3-4, 18, are left unexplained.[195]

194. See Williamson, *1 and 2 Chronicles*, 202.

195. For further study see R. H. Lowery, *The Reforming Kings: Cults and Society in First Temple Judah*, JSOTSup 120 (Sheffield: JSOT, 1991) 80-88.

REFLECTIONS

The chronicler has used Solomon's preparations for building the Temple as an opportunity to express a number of theological themes relating to the Temple and to Solomon himself. The Torah is honored both as a continuing model for temple worship (2:4) and implicitly as a guide for Solomon's use of labor gangs for construction (2:17). The chronicler was sensitive to the blend of old and new. The new era, even as it forged ahead in certain areas, respected older norms and took them seriously. One covets for the Christian similar conscientiousness in honoring the Old Testament as God's Word and carefully tracing the New Testament's relation to it.

1. The greatness of God is reflected in two ways. First, it is reflected through Solomon, who receives the homage of the Phoenician king and takes the initiative to procure lumber and an artisan from him. Moreover, the aliens in Israel also served him (2:17). The Lord gives Solomon greatness (1:1) in a Gentile setting, such as David before him had enjoyed (1 Chr 14:17). Solomon, builder of a palace and a temple (v. 1), was God's viceroy. His reign represented the inauguration of an era that was to be consummated in the future, when the Lord was revealed fully as king over the nations (1 Chr 16:31). Would not God's future king of David's line be "great to the ends of the earth" (Mic 5:4 NRSV)? History and hope are intertwined in the theology of the new era. Likewise, according to the New Testament, God has already highly exalted the risen Jesus, with the eventual purpose that "every knee should bow" at the supreme name given to him (Phil 2:9-10). In Christian worship, we find God's work in past and future time having an impact on our present lives.

Second, the Lord's greatness would be reflected in the Temple. It, too, would be "great" (2:5, 9). Solomon's principle of a great building for a great God was taken over by the medieval church, which channeled immense economic resources into magnificent cathedrals that were showpieces of artistic beauty. The modern church, poorer and also alert to human need, can hardly emulate such architectural masterpieces. Yet, church buildings are silent witnesses to the faith of those who worship inside them. Outsiders receive from these buildings a visual impression of the God who is worshiped there. The role of the church building committee, therefore, is to communicate theology.

2. The magnificence of the Temple was to be only a relative reflection of God's greatness. The Lord was near, yet also enthroned beyond the stars. The God of the covenant was also the God of creation (2:11-12). There are Christians whose conceptions of God are too limited,

yet who are confident about their version of the Christian faith and God's predictability. Here, by contrast, is a conception of God that testifies to the mystery of God's being. God is never so accessible as to be caged. The Lord could only be worshiped with a regularity that created its own calendar. Only by that *forever*ness (see 2:4) could Israel hope to reflect the truth that God is great and greatly to be praised (1 Chr 16:25).

3. Typological comparisons, like the one manifested in the description of the craftsman Huram-abi, appear in the New Testament. The phenomenon of a new revelation, echoing language relevant to an older one, even as it supersedes it, is found in the description of Christ as "the last Adam" (1 Cor 15:45), head of a new humanity. There is the same painstaking concern as here in 2 Chronicles to trace continuity between revelations both old and new. Theological history is a series of divine interventions, with each new one bearing the familiar signature of the earlier intervention in token of its authenticity.

2 Chronicles 3:1–5:1, Building the Temple

NIV

3 Then Solomon began to build the temple of the LORD in Jerusalem on Mount Moriah, where the LORD had appeared to his father David. It was on the threshing floor of Araunah[a] the Jebusite, the place provided by David. 2He began building on the second day of the second month in the fourth year of his reign.

3The foundation Solomon laid for building the temple of God was sixty cubits long and twenty cubits wide[b] (using the cubit of the old standard). 4The portico at the front of the temple was twenty cubits[c] long across the width of the building and twenty cubits[d] high.

He overlaid the inside with pure gold. 5He paneled the main hall with pine and covered it with fine gold and decorated it with palm tree and chain designs. 6He adorned the temple with precious stones. And the gold he used was gold of Parvaim. 7He overlaid the ceiling beams, doorframes, walls and doors of the temple with gold, and he carved cherubim on the walls.

8He built the Most Holy Place, its length corresponding to the width of the temple—twenty cubits long and twenty cubits wide. He overlaid the inside with six hundred talents[e] of fine gold. 9The gold nails weighed fifty shekels.[f] He also overlaid the upper parts with gold.

[a]*1* Hebrew *Ornan,* a variant of *Araunah* [b]*3* That is, about 90 feet (about 27 meters) long and 30 feet (about 9 meters) wide [c]*4* That is, about 30 feet (about 9 meters); also in verses 8, 11 and 13 [d]*4* Some Septuagint and Syriac manuscripts; Hebrew *and a hundred and twenty* [e]*8* That is, about 23 tons (about 21 metric tons) [f]*9* That is, about 1 1/4 pounds (about 0.6 kilogram)

NRSV

3 Solomon began to build the house of the LORD in Jerusalem on Mount Moriah, where the LORD had appeared to his father David, at the place that David had designated, on the threshing floor of Ornan the Jebusite. 2He began to build on the second day of the second month of the fourth year of his reign. 3These are Solomon's measurements[a] for building the house of God: the length, in cubits of the old standard, was sixty cubits, and the width twenty cubits. 4The vestibule in front of the nave of the house was twenty cubits long, across the width of the house;[b] and its height was one hundred twenty cubits. He overlaid it on the inside with pure gold. 5The nave he lined with cypress, covered it with fine gold, and made palms and chains on it. 6He adorned the house with settings of precious stones. The gold was gold from Parvaim. 7So he lined the house with gold—its beams, its thresholds, its walls, and its doors; and he carved cherubim on the walls.

8He made the most holy place; its length, corresponding to the width of the house, was twenty cubits, and its width was twenty cubits; he overlaid it with six hundred talents of fine gold. 9The weight of the nails was fifty shekels of gold. He overlaid the upper chambers with gold.

10In the most holy place he made two carved cherubim and overlaid[c] them with gold. 11The wings of the cherubim together extended twenty

[a] Syr: Heb *foundations* [b] Compare 1 Kings 6.3: Meaning of Heb uncertain [c] Heb *they overlaid*

NIV

10In the Most Holy Place he made a pair of sculptured cherubim and overlaid them with gold. 11The total wingspan of the cherubim was twenty cubits. One wing of the first cherub was five cubits[a] long and touched the temple wall, while its other wing, also five cubits long, touched the wing of the other cherub. 12Similarly one wing of the second cherub was five cubits long and touched the other temple wall, and its other wing, also five cubits long, touched the wing of the first cherub. 13The wings of these cherubim extended twenty cubits. They stood on their feet, facing the main hall.[b]

14He made the curtain of blue, purple and crimson yarn and fine linen, with cherubim worked into it.

15In the front of the temple he made two pillars, which ⌊together⌋ were thirty-five cubits[c] long, each with a capital on top measuring five cubits. 16He made interwoven chains[d] and put them on top of the pillars. He also made a hundred pomegranates and attached them to the chains. 17He erected the pillars in the front of the temple, one to the south and one to the north. The one to the south he named Jakin[e] and the one to the north Boaz.[f]

4 He made a bronze altar twenty cubits long, twenty cubits wide and ten cubits high.[g] 2He made the Sea of cast metal, circular in shape, measuring ten cubits from rim to rim and five cubits[h] high. It took a line of thirty cubits[i] to measure around it. 3Below the rim, figures of bulls encircled it—ten to a cubit.[j] The bulls were cast in two rows in one piece with the Sea.

4The Sea stood on twelve bulls, three facing north, three facing west, three facing south and three facing east. The Sea rested on top of them, and their hindquarters were toward the center. 5It was a handbreadth[k] in thickness, and its rim was like the rim of a cup, like a lily blossom. It held three thousand baths.[l]

a *11* That is, about 7 1/2 feet (about 2.3 meters); also in verse 15
b *13* Or *facing inward*
c *15* That is, about 52 feet (about 16 meters)
d *16* Or possibly *made chains in the inner sanctuary*; the meaning of the Hebrew for this phrase is uncertain.
e *17 Jakin* probably means *he establishes.*
f *17 Boaz* probably means *in him is strength.*
g *1* That is, about 30 feet (about 9 meters) long and wide, and about 15 feet (about 4.5 meters) high
h *2* That is, about 7 1/2 feet (about 2.3 meters)
i *2* That is, about 45 feet (about 13.5 meters)
j *3* That is, about 1 1/2 feet (about 0.5 meter)
k *5* That is, about 3 inches (about 8 centimeters)
l *5* That is, about 17,500 gallons (about 66 kiloliters)

NRSV

cubits: one wing of the one, five cubits long, touched the wall of the house, and its other wing, five cubits long, touched the wing of the other cherub; 12and of this cherub, one wing, five cubits long, touched the wall of the house, and the other wing, also five cubits long, was joined to the wing of the first cherub. 13The wings of these cherubim extended twenty cubits; the cherubim[a] stood on their feet, facing the nave. 14And Solomon[b] made the curtain of blue and purple and crimson fabrics and fine linen, and worked cherubim into it.

15In front of the house he made two pillars thirty-five cubits high, with a capital of five cubits on the top of each. 16He made encircling[c] chains and put them on the tops of the pillars; and he made one hundred pomegranates, and put them on the chains. 17He set up the pillars in front of the temple, one on the right, the other on the left; the one on the right he called Jachin, and the one on the left, Boaz.

4 He made an altar of bronze, twenty cubits long, twenty cubits wide, and ten cubits high. 2Then he made the molten sea; it was round, ten cubits from rim to rim, and five cubits high. A line of thirty cubits would encircle it completely. 3Under it were panels all around, each of ten cubits, surrounding the sea; there were two rows of panels, cast when it was cast. 4It stood on twelve oxen, three facing north, three facing west, three facing south, and three facing east; the sea was set on them. The hindquarters of each were toward the inside. 5Its thickness was a handbreadth; its rim was made like the rim of a cup, like the flower of a lily; it held three thousand baths.[d] 6He also made ten basins in which to wash, and set five on the right side, and five on the left. In these they were to rinse what was used for the burnt offering. The sea was for the priests to wash in.

7He made ten golden lampstands as prescribed, and set them in the temple, five on the south side and five on the north. 8He also made ten tables and placed them in the temple, five on the right side and five on the left. And he made one hundred basins of gold. 9He made the court of the priests, and the great court, and doors for the

a Heb *they*
b Heb *he*
c Cn: Heb *in the inner sanctuary*
d A Hebrew measure of volume

NIV

[6]He then made ten basins for washing and placed five on the south side and five on the north. In them the things to be used for the burnt offerings were rinsed, but the Sea was to be used by the priests for washing.

[7]He made ten gold lampstands according to the specifications for them and placed them in the temple, five on the south side and five on the north.

[8]He made ten tables and placed them in the temple, five on the south side and five on the north. He also made a hundred gold sprinkling bowls.

[9]He made the courtyard of the priests, and the large court and the doors for the court, and overlaid the doors with bronze. [10]He placed the Sea on the south side, at the southeast corner.

[11]He also made the pots and shovels and sprinkling bowls.

So Huram finished the work he had undertaken for King Solomon in the temple of God:

[12]the two pillars;
the two bowl-shaped capitals on top of the pillars;
the two sets of network decorating the two bowl-shaped capitals on top of the pillars;
[13]the four hundred pomegranates for the two sets of network (two rows of pomegranates for each network, decorating the bowl-shaped capitals on top of the pillars);
[14]the stands with their basins;
[15]the Sea and the twelve bulls under it;
[16]the pots, shovels, meat forks and all related articles.

All the objects that Huram-Abi made for King Solomon for the temple of the LORD were of polished bronze. [17]The king had them cast in clay molds in the plain of the Jordan between Succoth and Zarethan.[s] [18]All these things that Solomon made amounted to so much that the weight of the bronze was not determined.

[19]Solomon also made all the furnishings that were in God's temple:

the golden altar;
the tables on which was the bread of the Presence;

[a]*17* Hebrew *Zeredatha,* a variant of *Zarethan*

NRSV

court; he overlaid their doors with bronze. [10]He set the sea at the southeast corner of the house.

11 And Huram made the pots, the shovels, and the basins. Thus Huram finished the work that he did for King Solomon on the house of God: [12]the two pillars, the bowls, and the two capitals on the top of the pillars; and the two latticeworks to cover the two bowls of the capitals that were on the top of the pillars; [13]the four hundred pomegranates for the two latticeworks, two rows of pomegranates for each latticework, to cover the two bowls of the capitals that were on the pillars. [14]He made the stands, the basins on the stands, [15]the one sea, and the twelve oxen underneath it. [16]The pots, the shovels, the forks, and all the equipment for these Huram-abi made of burnished bronze for King Solomon for the house of the LORD. [17]In the plain of the Jordan the king cast them, in the clay ground between Succoth and Zeredah. [18]Solomon made all these things in great quantities, so that the weight of the bronze was not determined.

19 So Solomon made all the things that were in the house of God: the golden altar, the tables for the bread of the Presence, [20]the lampstands and their lamps of pure gold to burn before the inner sanctuary, as prescribed; [21]the flowers, the lamps, and the tongs, of purest gold; [22]the snuffers, basins, ladles, and firepans, of pure gold. As for the entrance to the temple: the inner doors to the most holy place and the doors of the nave of the temple were of gold.

5 Thus all the work that Solomon did for the house of the LORD was finished. Solomon brought in the things that his father David had dedicated, and stored the silver, the gold, and all the vessels in the treasuries of the house of God.

NIV

[20]the lampstands of pure gold with their lamps,
to burn in front of the inner sanctuary as
prescribed;
[21]the gold floral work and lamps and tongs
(they were solid gold);
[22]the pure gold wick trimmers, sprinkling
bowls, dishes and censers; and the gold
doors of the temple: the inner doors to
the Most Holy Place and the doors of the
main hall.

5 When all the work Solomon had done for
the temple of the LORD was finished, he
brought in the things his father David had dedicated—the silver and gold and all the furnishings—and he placed them in the treasuries of
God's temple.

COMMENTARY

These two chapters follow a clearly marked route defined by Solomon's beginning and finishing the construction of the Temple (3:1-2; 5:1) and by a series of literary milestones along the way, the repeated "and he made" (ויעש *wayya'aś*) from 3:8 onward. The chronicler has considerably shortened his source, 1 Kings 6–7, to about half its length. He does not attach precise significance to each detail. The details were evidently regarded as a means to a more important end, the worship of God. The theology of the Temple had been broached in chap. 2 and will be treated further in chaps. 5–7; it finds little expression here.

Second Chronicles 3:1–4:9 represents an integral block of material. The location of the Temple and the date for starting its construction are the concerns of 3:1-2; 3:3-14 presents the dimensions and ornamentation of the temple building, as a whole and in its parts. Details of the items with which the Temple was furnished are provided in 3:15–4:8, while 4:9 takes in the courts around the Temple.

3:1-2. The chronicler omits the exodus dating found in 1 Kgs 6:1, since a new religious era had dawned for Israel with the Davidic monarchy. He inserts fresh evidence of its divine authenticity, reminding readers of the choice of the Temple site in 1 Chronicles 21. David's encounter with the angel of the Lord and the supernatural fire are described as divine revelation. The translation "the LORD has appeared" stands for a Hebrew verb lacking a subject (נראה *nir'â*). It may more properly be regarded as an impersonal passive, "revelation was made." The chronicler alludes to Gen 22:14, which associates the place where Abraham almost sacrificed Isaac with a future revelation. There is wordplay in Gen 22:14—between God's provision of an alternative sacrifice and a future theophany. The Hebrew verb rendered "see" also means "see to," "provide." So the promise that "on the mount of the LORD it shall be provided" (Gen 22:14 NRSV) could also mean "revelation shall be made." The phrase "the mountain of the LORD" is used of the Jerusalem Temple in Ps 24:3; Isa 2:3. The chronicler took over a tradition in the book of Genesis and claimed that this omen associated with a patriarchal experience had now come true. Here was "Mount Moriah" (cf. Gen 22:2), understood by popular etymology as "the mountain of the revelation of the LORD." It was David who received the promised revelation. So there was further good reason for David to pass over the Gibeon sanctuary in 1 Chr 21:28–22:1, even though it contained the tabernacle. In the Torah there was a warrant for worship that was more ancient than the tabernacle and pointed beyond the tabernacle to the Temple.

3:3-14. This passage is concerned with the overall size and appearance of the Temple. It was an opulent and artistically ornamented structure. Here was splendor and beauty as worthy of God as any funded and fashioned by human hands (cf. 1 Chr 29:1-9; 2 Chr 2:5-9). Verse 3 presents a ground plan (the NIV's "foundation" [הוּסַד *hûsad*; cf. the REB] need not be emended with the NRSV; the plural "these" [אֵלֶּה *'ēlleh*] is attracted to the dimensions). The chronicler observes that the size of the cubit was obsolete by his time; it was seven handbreadths rather than six (cf. Ezek 43:13). The height of the vestibule or portico in the MT, and preserved in the NRSV, is surprising. Some 180 feet high, it was an enormous tower. The height of the vestibule of the Herodian Temple was 100 cubits high. The writers of 1 Kgs 6:3 are silent about the height; the rest of the Temple was thirty cubits high according to 1 Kgs 6:2. The textual evidence for "twenty cubits," to which the NIV and the REB appeal, is not impressive.[196]

The rest of the Temple was divided into the nave, or main hall, and the "most holy place," or holy of holies, with its gold-plated cherubim (see 1 Kgs 6:15-30). The rear room in which the ark was to be placed is described as the "most holy place," the ultimate in gradations of holiness. It symbolizes the sovereign mystery of the Lord, whose gracious fellowship with Israel was never to be interpreted as familiarity. The chronicler highlights the presence of the images of cherubim in the Temple, which the Second Temple no longer contained. They were featured not only as statues in the most holy place, but also as engravings on the wood lining the Temple's walls (v. 7; cf. 1 Kgs 6:29); figures of cherubim were also embroidered on the curtain covering the "most holy place" (v. 14; cf. Ezek 36:25). They functioned as symbols of the divine presence. As in 1 Chr 28:18, these cherubim reflect the chronicler's fascination with the visions of Ezekiel 1; 8–10; and 43. Mention of the cherubim also drew implicit attention to "the ark of God the Lord who is enthroned between the cherubim" (1 Chr 13:6) and served as a reminder that the Temple was to house the ark (5:7).

The repeated "And he made" (*wayya'aś*), which occurs thirteen times between 3:8 and 4:9, systematically demarcates the progression of the narrative. The chronicler develops the four instances of *wayya'aś* in 1 Kgs 6:23; 7:23, 38, 48, in line with the description of the tabernacle and its furnishings (Exodus 36–39). The chronicler is teaching his Torah-versed readers that what Solomon made corresponds to what Bezalel had made. There are further features borrowed from the tabernacle in this account. The small weight of gold for the nails in the most holy place (v. 9) indicates the use of gold plating. These golden nails correspond to the gold hooks used for the screen of the tabernacle in Exod 26:32, 37; 36:36. The curtain between the rear room and the nave (v. 14) was a feature of the Herodian Temple, but is not mentioned in the 1 Kings narrative, which has doors instead (1 Kgs 7:50; cf. 2 Chr 4:22), though 1 Kgs 8:8 may presuppose it.[197] The chronicler again has the tabernacle screen in mind, as the verbal parallelism with Exod 36:35 (and 26:31) indicates.

3:15-17. The chronicler draws attention to the two ornate pillars at the entrance to the vestibule, abbreviating 1 Kgs 7:15-22, to which he jumps in his source from 1 Kgs 6:29. Did their names, "Jachin" and "Boaz," have any special meaning for the chronicler? "Jachin" means "he establishes," or "he prepares." The related verb הכין (*hēkîn*, in the hiphil) has been used of God's permanent establishment of the Davidic dynasty once the condition of erecting the Temple had been met (1 Chr 17:11-12; 22:10; cf. 1 Chr 28:7). On the human plane the verb was used when the chronicler described David's preparations for the Temple. Boaz, if the vocalization suggests "in him is strength," attests the Lord's power, mentioned in 1 Chr 16:11, 27-28; 2 Chr 6:41, which is associated with the sanctuary in 1 Chr 16:27. Both names resonate with literary connotations.

In v. 16, in place of the MT's בדביר (*baddĕbîr*, "in the rear room") the NRSV and the NIV rightly adopt the conjectural emendation כרביד (*kĕrābîd*, "encircling," "interwoven," or "like a necklace" [REB];

196. See Williamson, *1 and 2 Chronicles,* 206-7; D. Barthélemy et al., *Critique textuelle de l'Ancien Testament,* OBO 50/1 (Fribourg: Editions Universitaires; and Göttingen: Vandenhoeck & Ruprecht, 1982) 1:477-78.

197. See J. A. Montgomery and H. S. Gehman, *The Books of Kings,* ICC (Edinburgh: T. & T. Clark, 1951) 189.

see the REB; the MT probably arose from a displacing gloss that loosely compared it to 1 Kgs 6:21).[198] The pillars are said to be thirty-five cubits "high" (NRSV), literally "long" (NIV). This dimension clashes with the eighteen cubits of 1 Kgs 7:15; 2 Kgs 25:17; Jer 52:21. The change recalls the increased height of the vestibule in v. 4; in this case it may have arisen from the chronicler's confused understanding of the numbers in 1 Kgs 7:15.[199]

4:1-8. The chronicler continues describing the items installed in the Temple and its court. The bronze altar is not mentioned in the MT of 1 Kings 6–7, but 1 Kgs 9:25 (= 2 Chr 8:12) states that Solomon built it, and 1 Kgs 8:22, 64; 2 Kgs 16:14 presuppose it. It was probably in the chronicler's text of 1 Kings between 1 Kgs 7:22 and 23, and was lost from the MT.[200] Its presence here is consonant with the emphasis on the sacrificial function of the Temple in 2:4, 6. Whereas religious items were brought from Gibeon (5:5), the altar of 2 Chr 1:5-6 (cf. 1 Chr 21:29) is not mentioned there. Solomon, a second Bezalel (Exod 38:1-7), made a fresh altar for the new era of temple worship. David's altar in 1 Chr 21:26 was presumably regarded as provisional, so that the altar announced in 1 Chr 22:1 anticipates this one, made by Solomon.

The description of the vast bronze "sea" or "tank" (GNB) in vv. 2-5 is taken closely from 1 Kgs 7:23-26. In v. 6*b,* its function is defined in terms of the bronze laver of the tabernacle in Exod 30:19-21, linking it with sacrificial ritual. Mathematicians will notice that in v. 2 π is given the numerical value of 3, rather than 3.14. The circumference is given as a round figure; possibly it was measured with a line more easily placed beneath the flared rim.[201] The "gourds" (NIV) of 1 Kgs 7:24, embossed under the rim, have here become "figures of bulls." The chronicler probably misread or misunderstood his source. The capacity of 3,000 baths contrasts with the 2,000 in 1 Kgs 7:26, either because of a textual error or because of the conversion to a smaller, post-exilic unit of capacity.[202]

The material about lampstands is taken from 1 Kgs 7:49*a,* to which the chronicler leaps. The appeal to earlier prescription hardly refers to the Torah, as it usually does in Chronicles, since only one lampstand stood in the tabernacle, as in the Second Temple (cf. Exod 25:31-40; 37:17-24). But the use of the lampstands does allude to the plans for the Temple and its furnishings that were drawn up by David and presented to Solomon (see 1 Chr 28:15).[203] The burning of the Temple lamps, an element of special importance to the chronicler, was the fourth traditional medium of worship that belonged with the other three listed in 2:4. All four are enumerated in 13:11; 29:7.

What were the ten tables used for? The reference in 1 Chr 28:16 to a number of tables used for the bread of the presence (cf. v. 19) suggests that this was their purpose, though only one table is mentioned in 2 Chr 13:11; 29:18, as in 1 Kgs 7:48. One hundred gold "sprinkling bowls" (NIV) were used to dash sacrificial blood against the altar (see 1 Kgs 7:50, where the number of bowls is unspecified).

4:9. The closing reference to the two courts has been loosely derived from 1 Kgs 6:36; 7:12. There the temple court, or "inner court," was distinguished from the "great court" that surrounded the complex of palace buildings and the temple area. The chronicler, however, in accord with Second Temple practice and with Ezekiel 40–48, conceives of two temple courts, an inner one restricted to priests and Levites and an outer one for laity. The bronze doors are not mentioned in 1 Kings.

4:10-22. This passage is a close copy of 1 Kgs 7:39*b*-50. It does not match the earlier material in 3:1–4:9, which was marked by selectivity, summarizing, and precise copying of short passages. The lampstands of 1 Kgs 7:49*a* (2 Chr 4:20) have already been dealt with in 4:7, and the "sprinkling bowls" of 1 Kgs 7:50 (= 2 Chr 4:22) have been mentioned in v. 8*b.* One does not expect a return to the pillars of 3:15-17 in such detail as is found in vv. 12-13. Renewed mention of the basins and the sea (vv. 14-15) is also sur-

198. See Williamson, *1 and 2 Chronicles,* 210.

199. See S. Japhet, *I & II Chronicles,* OTL (Louisville: Westminster/John Knox, 1993) 557.

200. See W. Rudolph, *Chronikbücher,* HAT 1:21 (Tübingen: Mohr [Siebeck], 1955) 207; McKenzie, *The Chronicler's Use of the Deuteronomistic History,* 88.

201. A. Zuidhof, "King Solomon's Molten Sea and (π)," *BA* 45 (1982) 179-84, esp. 181.

202. Ibid., 181.

203. S. J. De Vries, "Moses and David as Cult Founders in Chronicles," *JBL* 107 (1988) 619-39, esp. 630.

prising, as is mention of the stands for the basins, since the chronicler appeared to have chosen to omit reference to them in v. 6. The overall impression is that the passage has been subsequently inserted to fill a gap between citation of 1 Kgs 7:39*a* in v. 7 and of 1 Kgs 7:51 in 5:1.[204] One may explain the abrupt resumption of the topic of the sea in 4:10 (= 1 Kgs 7:39*b*) in this fashion.

This new material improves the earlier text of Chronicles by incorporating the work of Huram-abi, which 2:13-14 led the reader to expect. The unweighed amounts of bronze in v. 18 recall the same factor in David's preparations at 1 Chr 22:3, 14 and so reintroduce the pervasive theme of the Temple's grandeur. The golden altar (v. 19) refers to the incense altar in the nave. Its presence builds a literary bridge between David's prescription in 1 Chr 28:18 and the narrative about Uzziah's misuse of it in 2 Chr 26:16-20. There are a few departures from 1 Kings 7. In v. 19 the table for the bread of the presence is made plural, in line with v. 8. In v. 22 "entrance" or "door" (פתח *petaḥ*) represents a different reading; 1 Kgs 7:50 has "sockets" (פתות *pōtôt*). In v. 20, the prescriptive formula of v. 7 has been added and supplied with a new basis, the use of the lampstands rather than their form, corresponding more precisely to 13:11; 29:7.

5:1. The chronicler uses 1 Kgs 7:51 to round off his narrative of the Temple's construction. In 1 Chr 22:9 we observed a Hebrew wordplay on Solomon's name (שׁלמה *šĕlōmōh*) and "peace" (שׁלום *šālôm*). Another wordplay seems to occur here, with reference to Solomon's work having been finished (ותשׁלם *wattišlam*). Both wordplays underline the divine program for Solomon's reign, in this case as temple builder. However, in another sense, there was more to be done. The empty Temple had yet to be filled with the personnel and rites of regular worship; this dynamic aspect will be covered in 8:12-16. Here a finishing touch is supplied by the installation of David's victory trophies (cf. 1 Chr 18:10-11), in tribute to the labors of the warrior king who had earlier played his part in the Lord's program. David's and Solomon's joint work is affirmed here, as at the beginning of the passage (3:1). Mention of the "treasuries" also helps the reader to recall David's work in 1 Chr 26:20-28. The treasuries have not been mentioned in the account of building the Temple. Presumably they were on the first floor of the structure surrounding three sides of the Temple, described in 1 Kgs 6:5-10, while the "upper rooms" of 1 Chr 28:11 and 2 Chr 3:9 were its second and third stories.

204. See T. Willi, *Die Chronik als Auslegung* (Göttingen: Vandenhoeck & Ruprecht, 1972) 94n. 78; Williamson, *1 and 2 Chronicles,* 211-12; R. B. Dillard, *2 Chronicles,* WBC 15 (Waco, Tex.: Word, 1987) 34. See also Japhet, *I & II Chronicles,* 560-64.

REFLECTIONS

1. The completion of the Temple (5:1) was a decisive step forward, laying a divine foundation for the future. At the outset of construction, the reader is reminded that the human activity is based on the purposes of God. According to 3:1, David's preparatory work in designating the Temple site had been grounded in a divine revelation, which the Torah itself had forecast. Thus the divine authenticity of the Temple was doubly established as successor to the Mosaic tabernacle, first in the Torah and then in a new revelation to David. In appealing to the Torah the chronicler is giving a solid theological argument for the importance of the contemporary Temple.

The argument is similar to that used in Hebrews 7. How may Jesus, a member of the non-priestly tribe of Judah, be high priest of the heavenly tabernacle? The answer lies in Gen 14:18-20 and Ps 110:4: Jesus, in inheriting this royal role, also became an heir of the priest-king Melchizedek. Another example is Paul's grounding of justification by faith in Gen 15:6 at Romans 4 and Galatians 3. The authors of the New Testament used the Old Testament as a theological dictionary, turning to it for clarification and finding special authority in the Torah. Sometimes we modern Christians hide behind an appeal to blind faith and ignore such unashamedly intellectual concerns to gain a hearing for what was held to be the truth by culturally relevant arguments. The Bible constantly appeals to the mind, with careful argumentation to support its claims. Faith has to find corroboration if it is to satisfy and survive. Such corroboration is worth seeking, both in the theological reasoning of the Bible and in contemporary theological and ethical reflection.

2. The accent on gold and precious stones, which the redactional supplement enhances in 4:19-22, envisions a past glory that the chronicler's contemporaries could not copy. Even for David the qualification "so far as I was able" (1 Chr 29:2 NRSV) posed a limit as well as a target. Only the best—always a relative best—that particular human hands can give and do is good enough for God. Neither more nor less is sought. It was that human best that was to be graciously filled with divine glory (5:14).

3. The ever-burning lampstands, singled out in 4:7 and editorially underlined in 4:20, were a vital element of worship for the chronicler, according to 13:11. In 29:7, he will deplore their temporary absence. Worship is grounded in certain traditional sacred acts that transcend the present and the personal concerns of worshipers. They remind us that we are part of a sacred entity much greater than ourselves.

4. The completion of Solomon's task (5:1) recalls David's work as pioneer, as the rest of the verse suggests. We are reminded of another who became both "pioneer and perfecter" (Heb 12:2 NRSV) and who was to cry, "It is finished" (John 19:30 NIV). In both eras, a solid foundation was being laid for future believers to stand on before God.

5. Paul, reading 2 Chronicles 3–4, may have reflected on its relevance for his own ministry and incorporated his reflections into a letter to the church he had recently planted in Corinth (1 Cor 3:10-17). He would have been reading the 2 Chronicles account rather than the one in 1 Kings, since the chronicler's account refers to laying a foundation and to precious stones. Paul was probably reading the Hebrew text because the LXX does not mention laying a foundation. The apostle represented himself as another Solomon for the Christians in Corinth, a temple builder who had laid a foundation in evangelism and basic teaching. Now each member was responsible for continuing the work, making his or her contribution to the fellowship, like Huram-abi and like the craftsmen of 2 Chr 2:13. The latter contributed a golden bowl and a silver dish or jeweled ornamentation, each item skillfully and lovingly made—no hay or stubble, ludicrous examples of the ephemeral, but contributions of solid and lasting worth. The apostle was typologizing, using elements of the old era to teach principles of the new era. If 2 Chronicles 3–4 strikes us as unpromising preaching material, Paul's hermeneutical creativity is worth studying.

2 Chronicles 5:2–7:22, The Temple: Place of Worship and Means of Grace

NIV

[2]Then Solomon summoned to Jerusalem the elders of Israel, all the heads of the tribes and the chiefs of the Israelite families, to bring up the ark of the LORD's covenant from Zion, the City of David. [3]And all the men of Israel came together to the king at the time of the festival in the seventh month.

NRSV

2Then Solomon assembled the elders of Israel and all the heads of the tribes, the leaders of the ancestral houses of the people of Israel, in Jerusalem, to bring up the ark of the covenant of the LORD out of the city of David, which is Zion. [3]And all the Israelites assembled before the king at the festival that is in the seventh month. [4]And all the

NIV

4When all the elders of Israel had arrived, the Levites took up the ark, 5and they brought up the ark and the Tent of Meeting and all the sacred furnishings in it. The priests, who were Levites, carried them up; 6and King Solomon and the entire assembly of Israel that had gathered about him were before the ark, sacrificing so many sheep and cattle that they could not be recorded or counted.

7The priests then brought the ark of the LORD's covenant to its place in the inner sanctuary of the temple, the Most Holy Place, and put it beneath the wings of the cherubim. 8The cherubim spread their wings over the place of the ark and covered the ark and its carrying poles. 9These poles were so long that their ends, extending from the ark, could be seen from in front of the inner sanctuary, but not from outside the Holy Place; and they are still there today. 10There was nothing in the ark except the two tablets that Moses had placed in it at Horeb, where the LORD made a covenant with the Israelites after they came out of Egypt.

11The priests then withdrew from the Holy Place. All the priests who were there had consecrated themselves, regardless of their divisions. 12All the Levites who were musicians—Asaph, Heman, Jeduthun and their sons and relatives—stood on the east side of the altar, dressed in fine linen and playing cymbals, harps and lyres. They were accompanied by 120 priests sounding trumpets. 13The trumpeters and singers joined in unison, as with one voice, to give praise and thanks to the LORD. Accompanied by trumpets, cymbals and other instruments, they raised their voices in praise to the LORD and sang:

"He is good;
his love endures forever."

Then the temple of the LORD was filled with a cloud, 14and the priests could not perform their service because of the cloud, for the glory of the LORD filled the temple of God.

6 Then Solomon said, "The LORD has said that he would dwell in a dark cloud; 2I have built a magnificent temple for you, a place for you to dwell forever."

3While the whole assembly of Israel was standing there, the king turned around and blessed them. 4Then he said:

NRSV

elders of Israel came, and the Levites carried the ark. 5So they brought up the ark, the tent of meeting, and all the holy vessels that were in the tent; the priests and the Levites brought them up. 6King Solomon and all the congregation of Israel, who had assembled before him, were before the ark, sacrificing so many sheep and oxen that they could not be numbered or counted. 7Then the priests brought the ark of the covenant of the LORD to its place, in the inner sanctuary of the house, in the most holy place, underneath the wings of the cherubim. 8For the cherubim spread out their wings over the place of the ark, so that the cherubim made a covering above the ark and its poles. 9The poles were so long that the ends of the poles were seen from the holy place in front of the inner sanctuary; but they could not be seen from outside; they are there to this day. 10There was nothing in the ark except the two tablets that Moses put there at Horeb, where the LORD made a covenant[a] with the people of Israel after they came out of Egypt.

11Now when the priests came out of the holy place (for all the priests who were present had sanctified themselves, without regard to their divisions), 12all the levitical singers, Asaph, Heman, and Jeduthun, their sons and kindred, arrayed in fine linen, with cymbals, harps, and lyres, stood east of the altar with one hundred twenty priests who were trumpeters. 13It was the duty of the trumpeters and singers to make themselves heard in unison in praise and thanksgiving to the LORD, and when the song was raised, with trumpets and cymbals and other musical instruments, in praise to the LORD,

"For he is good,
for his steadfast love endures forever,"

the house, the house of the LORD, was filled with a cloud, 14so that the priests could not stand to minister because of the cloud; for the glory of the LORD filled the house of God.

6 Then Solomon said, "The LORD has said that he would reside in thick darkness. 2I have built you an exalted house, a place for you to reside in forever."

3Then the king turned around and blessed all the assembly of Israel, while all the assembly of

[a] Heb lacks *a covenant*

NIV

"Praise be to the LORD, the God of Israel, who with his hands has fulfilled what he promised with his mouth to my father David. For he said, [5]'Since the day I brought my people out of Egypt, I have not chosen a city in any tribe of Israel to have a temple built for my Name to be there, nor have I chosen anyone to be the leader over my people Israel. [6]But now I have chosen Jerusalem for my Name to be there, and I have chosen David to rule my people Israel.'

[7]"My father David had it in his heart to build a temple for the Name of the LORD, the God of Israel. [8]But the LORD said to my father David, 'Because it was in your heart to build a temple for my Name, you did well to have this in your heart. [9]Nevertheless, you are not the one to build the temple, but your son, who is your own flesh and blood—he is the one who will build the temple for my Name.'

[10]"The LORD has kept the promise he made. I have succeeded David my father and now I sit on the throne of Israel, just as the LORD promised, and I have built the temple for the Name of the LORD, the God of Israel. [11]There I have placed the ark, in which is the covenant of the LORD that he made with the people of Israel."

[12]Then Solomon stood before the altar of the LORD in front of the whole assembly of Israel and spread out his hands. [13]Now he had made a bronze platform, five cubits[a] long, five cubits wide and three cubits[b] high, and had placed it in the center of the outer court. He stood on the platform and then knelt down before the whole assembly of Israel and spread out his hands toward heaven. [14]He said:

"O LORD, God of Israel, there is no God like you in heaven or on earth—you who keep your covenant of love with your servants who continue wholeheartedly in your way. [15]You have kept your promise to your servant David my father; with your mouth you have promised and with your hand you have fulfilled it—as it is today.

[16]"Now LORD, God of Israel, keep for your

[a]*13* That is, about 7 1/2 feet (about 2.3 meters) [b]*13* That is, about 4 1/2 feet (about 1.3 meters)

NRSV

Israel stood. [4]And he said, "Blessed be the LORD, the God of Israel, who with his hand has fulfilled what he promised with his mouth to my father David, saying, [5]'Since the day that I brought my people out of the land of Egypt, I have not chosen a city from any of the tribes of Israel in which to build a house, so that my name might be there, and I chose no one as ruler over my people Israel; [6]but I have chosen Jerusalem in order that my name may be there, and I have chosen David to be over my people Israel.' [7]My father David had it in mind to build a house for the name of the LORD, the God of Israel. [8]But the LORD said to my father David, 'You did well to consider building a house for my name; [9]nevertheless you shall not build the house, but your son who shall be born to you shall build the house for my name.' [10]Now the LORD has fulfilled his promise that he made; for I have succeeded my father David, and sit on the throne of Israel, as the LORD promised, and have built the house for the name of the LORD, the God of Israel. [11]There I have set the ark, in which is the covenant of the LORD that he made with the people of Israel."

12Then Solomon[a] stood before the altar of the LORD in the presence of the whole assembly of Israel, and spread out his hands. [13]Solomon had made a bronze platform five cubits long, five cubits wide, and three cubits high, and had set it in the court; and he stood on it. Then he knelt on his knees in the presence of the whole assembly of Israel, and spread out his hands toward heaven. [14]He said, "O LORD, God of Israel, there is no God like you, in heaven or on earth, keeping covenant in steadfast love with your servants who walk before you with all their heart— [15]you who have kept for your servant, my father David, what you promised to him. Indeed, you promised with your mouth and this day have fulfilled with your hand. [16]Therefore, O LORD, God of Israel, keep for your servant, my father David, that which you promised him, saying, 'There shall never fail you a successor before me to sit on the throne of Israel, if only your children keep to their way, to walk in my law as you have walked before me.' [17]Therefore, O LORD, God of Israel, let your word be confirmed, which you promised to your servant David.

[a] Heb *he*

NIV

servant David my father the promises you
made to him when you said, 'You shall never
fail to have a man to sit before me on the
throne of Israel, if only your sons are careful
in all they do to walk before me according to
my law, as you have done.' 17And now,
O Lord, God of Israel, let your word that you
promised your servant David come true.

18"But will God really dwell on earth with
men? The heavens, even the highest heavens,
cannot contain you. How much less this temple I have built! 19Yet give attention to your
servant's prayer and his plea for mercy,
O Lord my God. Hear the cry and the prayer
that your servant is praying in your presence.
20May your eyes be open toward this temple
day and night, this place of which you said
you would put your Name there. May you
hear the prayer your servant prays toward this
place. 21Hear the supplications of your servant
and of your people Israel when they pray
toward this place. Hear from heaven, your
dwelling place; and when you hear, forgive.

22"When a man wrongs his neighbor and
is required to take an oath and he comes and
swears the oath before your altar in this
temple, 23then hear from heaven and act.
Judge between your servants, repaying the
guilty by bringing down on his own head
what he has done. Declare the innocent not
guilty and so establish his innocence.

24"When your people Israel have been defeated by an enemy because they have sinned
against you and when they turn back and
confess your name, praying and making supplication before you in this temple, 25then
hear from heaven and forgive the sin of your
people Israel and bring them back to the land
you gave to them and their fathers.

26"When the heavens are shut up and there
is no rain because your people have sinned
against you, and when they pray toward this
place and confess your name and turn from
their sin because you have afflicted them,
27then hear from heaven and forgive the sin
of your servants, your people Israel. Teach
them the right way to live, and send rain on

NRSV

18"But will God indeed reside with mortals on
earth? Even heaven and the highest heaven cannot contain you, how much less this house that
I have built! 19Regard your servant's prayer and
his plea, O Lord my God, heeding the cry and
the prayer that your servant prays to you. 20May
your eyes be open day and night toward this
house, the place where you promised to set your
name, and may you heed the prayer that your
servant prays toward this place. 21And hear the
plea of your servant and of your people Israel,
when they pray toward this place; may you hear
from heaven your dwelling place; hear and forgive.

22"If someone sins against another and is required to take an oath and comes and swears
before your altar in this house, 23may you hear
from heaven, and act, and judge your servants,
repaying the guilty by bringing their conduct on
their own head, and vindicating those who are in
the right by rewarding them in accordance with
their righteousness.

24"When your people Israel, having sinned
against you, are defeated before an enemy but
turn again to you, confess your name, pray and
plead with you in this house, 25may you hear from
heaven, and forgive the sin of your people Israel,
and bring them again to the land that you gave
to them and to their ancestors.

26"When heaven is shut up and there is no
rain because they have sinned against you, and
then they pray toward this place, confess your
name, and turn from their sin, because you punish
them, 27may you hear in heaven, forgive the sin
of your servants, your people Israel, when you
teach them the good way in which they should
walk; and send down rain upon your land, which
you have given to your people as an inheritance.

28"If there is famine in the land, if there is
plague, blight, mildew, locust, or caterpillar; if
their enemies besiege them in any of the settlements of the lands; whatever suffering, whatever
sickness there is; 29whatever prayer, whatever plea
from any individual or from all your people Israel,
all knowing their own suffering and their own
sorrows so that they stretch out their hands toward this house; 30may you hear from heaven,
your dwelling place, forgive, and render to all

NIV

the land you gave your people for an
inheritance.

28“When famine or plague comes to the
land, or blight or mildew, locusts or grasshoppers, or when enemies besiege them in any
of their cities, whatever disaster or disease
may come, 29and when a prayer or plea is
made by any of your people Israel—each one
aware of his afflictions and pains, and spreading out his hands toward this temple— 30then
hear from heaven, your dwelling place. Forgive, and deal with each man according to all
he does, since you know his heart (for you
alone know the hearts of men), 31so that they
will fear you and walk in your ways all the
time they live in the land you gave our
fathers.

32“As for the foreigner who does not belong
to your people Israel but has come from a
distant land because of your great name and
your mighty hand and your outstretched
arm—when he comes and prays toward this
temple, 33then hear from heaven, your dwelling place, and do whatever the foreigner asks
of you, so that all the peoples of the earth
may know your name and fear you, as do
your own people Israel, and may know that
this house I have built bears your Name.

34“When your people go to war against
their enemies, wherever you send them, and
when they pray to you toward this city you
have chosen and the temple I have built for
your Name, 35then hear from heaven their
prayer and their plea, and uphold their cause.

36“When they sin against you—for there is
no one who does not sin—and you become
angry with them and give them over to the
enemy, who takes them captive to a land far
away or near; 37and if they have a change of
heart in the land where they are held captive,
and repent and plead with you in the land of
their captivity and say, ‘We have sinned, we
have done wrong and acted wickedly’; 38and
if they turn back to you with all their heart
and soul in the land of their captivity where
they were taken, and pray toward the land
you gave their fathers, toward the city you
have chosen and toward the temple I have

NRSV

whose heart you know, according to all their
ways, for only you know the human heart. 31Thus
may they fear you and walk in your ways all the
days that they live in the land that you gave to
our ancestors.

32“Likewise when foreigners, who are not of
your people Israel, come from a distant land
because of your great name, and your mighty
hand, and your outstretched arm, when they
come and pray toward this house, 33may you hear
from heaven your dwelling place, and do whatever the foreigners ask of you, in order that all
the peoples of the earth may know your name
and fear you, as do your people Israel, and that
they may know that your name has been invoked
on this house that I have built.

34“If your people go out to battle against their
enemies, by whatever way you shall send them,
and they pray to you toward this city that you
have chosen and the house that I have built for
your name, 35then hear from heaven their prayer
and their plea, and maintain their cause.

36“If they sin against you—for there is no one
who does not sin—and you are angry with them
and give them to an enemy, so that they are
carried away captive to a land far or near; 37then
if they come to their senses in the land to which
they have been taken captive, and repent, and
plead with you in the land of their captivity,
saying, ‘We have sinned, and have done wrong;
we have acted wickedly’; 38if they repent with all
their heart and soul in the land of their captivity,
to which they were taken captive, and pray toward their land, which you gave to their ancestors, the city that you have chosen, and the house
that I have built for your name, 39then hear from
heaven your dwelling place their prayer and their
pleas, maintain their cause and forgive your people who have sinned against you. 40Now, O my
God, let your eyes be open and your ears attentive
to prayer from this place.

41 “Now rise up, O LORD God, and go to your
resting place,
you and the ark of your might.
Let your priests, O LORD God, be clothed with
salvation,
and let your faithful rejoice in your
goodness.

NIV

built for your Name; 39then from heaven, your dwelling place, hear their prayer and their pleas, and uphold their cause. And forgive your people, who have sinned against you.

40"Now, my God, may your eyes be open and your ears attentive to the prayers offered in this place.

41"Now arise, O LORD God, and come to your resting place,
you and the ark of your might.
May your priests, O LORD God, be clothed with salvation,
may your saints rejoice in your goodness.
42O LORD God, do not reject your anointed one.
Remember the great love promised to David your servant."

When Solomon finished praying, fire came down from heaven and consumed the burnt offering and the sacrifices, and the glory of the LORD filled the temple. 2The priests could not enter the temple of the LORD because the glory of the LORD filled it. 3When all the Israelites saw the fire coming down and the glory of the LORD above the temple, they knelt on the pavement with their faces to the ground, and they worshiped and gave thanks to the LORD, saying,

"He is good;
his love endures forever."

4Then the king and all the people offered sacrifices before the LORD. 5And King Solomon offered a sacrifice of twenty-two thousand head of cattle and a hundred and twenty thousand sheep and goats. So the king and all the people dedicated the temple of God. 6The priests took their positions, as did the Levites with the LORD's musical instruments, which King David had made for praising the LORD and which were used when he gave thanks, saying, "His love endures forever." Opposite the Levites, the priests blew their trumpets, and all the Israelites were standing.

7Solomon consecrated the middle part of the courtyard in front of the temple of the LORD, and there he offered burnt offerings and the fat of the fellowship offerings,[a] because the bronze altar he had made could not hold the burnt offerings, the grain offerings and the fat portions.

a7 Traditionally *peace offerings*

NRSV

42 O LORD God, do not reject your anointed one.
Remember your steadfast love for your servant David."

7 When Solomon had ended his prayer, fire came down from heaven and consumed the burnt offering and the sacrifices; and the glory of the LORD filled the temple. 2The priests could not enter the house of the LORD, because the glory of the LORD filled the LORD's house. 3When all the people of Israel saw the fire come down and the glory of the LORD on the temple, they bowed down on the pavement with their faces to the ground, and worshiped and gave thanks to the LORD, saying,

"For he is good,
for his steadfast love endures forever."

4Then the king and all the people offered sacrifice before the LORD. 5King Solomon offered as a sacrifice twenty-two thousand oxen and one hundred twenty thousand sheep. So the king and all the people dedicated the house of God. 6The priests stood at their posts; the Levites also, with the instruments for music to the LORD that King David had made for giving thanks to the LORD—for his steadfast love endures forever—whenever David offered praises by their ministry. Opposite them the priests sounded trumpets; and all Israel stood.

7Solomon consecrated the middle of the court that was in front of the house of the LORD; for there he offered the burnt offerings and the fat of the offerings of well-being because the bronze altar Solomon had made could not hold the burnt offering and the grain offering and the fat parts.

8At that time Solomon held the festival for seven days, and all Israel with him, a very great congregation, from Lebo-hamath to the Wadi of Egypt. 9On the eighth day they held a solemn assembly; for they had observed the dedication of the altar seven days and the festival seven days. 10On the twenty-third day of the seventh month he sent the people away to their homes, joyful and in good spirits because of the goodness that the LORD had shown to David and to Solomon and to his people Israel.

11Thus Solomon finished the house of the LORD and the king's house; all that Solomon had

NIV

[8]So Solomon observed the festival at that time for seven days, and all Israel with him—a vast assembly, people from Lebo[a] Hamath to the Wadi of Egypt. [9]On the eighth day they held an assembly, for they had celebrated the dedication of the altar for seven days and the festival for seven days more. [10]On the twenty-third day of the seventh month he sent the people to their homes, joyful and glad in heart for the good things the LORD had done for David and Solomon and for his people Israel.

[11]When Solomon had finished the temple of the LORD and the royal palace, and had succeeded in carrying out all he had in mind to do in the temple of the LORD and in his own palace, [12]the LORD appeared to him at night and said:

"I have heard your prayer and have chosen this place for myself as a temple for sacrifices.

[13]"When I shut up the heavens so that there is no rain, or command locusts to devour the land or send a plague among my people, [14]if my people, who are called by my name, will humble themselves and pray and seek my face and turn from their wicked ways, then will I hear from heaven and will forgive their sin and will heal their land. [15]Now my eyes will be open and my ears attentive to the prayers offered in this place. [16]I have chosen and consecrated this temple so that my Name may be there forever. My eyes and my heart will always be there.

[17]"As for you, if you walk before me as David your father did, and do all I command, and observe my decrees and laws, [18]I will establish your royal throne, as I covenanted with David your father when I said, 'You shall never fail to have a man to rule over Israel.'

[19]"But if you[b] turn away and forsake the decrees and commands I have given you[b] and go off to serve other gods and worship them, [20]then I will uproot Israel from my land, which I have given them, and will reject this temple I have consecrated for my Name. I will make it a byword and an object of ridicule among all peoples. [21]And though this temple is now so imposing, all who pass by will be appalled and say, 'Why has the LORD done

[a]*8* Or *from the entrance to* [b]*19* The Hebrew is plural.

NRSV

planned to do in the house of the LORD and in his own house he successfully accomplished.

12Then the LORD appeared to Solomon in the night and said to him: "I have heard your prayer, and have chosen this place for myself as a house of sacrifice. [13]When I shut up the heavens so that there is no rain, or command the locust to devour the land, or send pestilence among my people, [14]if my people who are called by my name humble themselves, pray, seek my face, and turn from their wicked ways, then I will hear from heaven, and will forgive their sin and heal their land. [15]Now my eyes will be open and my ears attentive to the prayer that is made in this place. [16]For now I have chosen and consecrated this house so that my name may be there forever; my eyes and my heart will be there for all time. [17]As for you, if you walk before me, as your father David walked, doing according to all that I have commanded you and keeping my statutes and my ordinances, [18]then I will establish your royal throne, as I made covenant with your father David saying, 'You shall never lack a successor to rule over Israel.'

19"But if you[a] turn aside and forsake my statutes and my commandments that I have set before you, and go and serve other gods and worship them, [20]then I will pluck you[b] up from the land that I have given you;[b] and this house, which I have consecrated for my name, I will cast out of my sight, and will make it a proverb and a byword among all peoples. [21]And regarding this house, now exalted, everyone passing by will be astonished, and say, 'Why has the LORD done such a thing to this land and to this house?' [22]Then they will say, 'Because they abandoned the LORD the God of their ancestors who brought them out of the land of Egypt, and they adopted other gods, and worshiped them and served them; therefore he has brought all this calamity upon them.'"

[a] The word *you* in this verse is plural [b] Heb *them*

NIV

such a thing to this land and to this temple?'
22People will answer, 'Because they have forsaken the LORD, the God of their fathers, who brought them out of Egypt, and have embraced other gods, worshiping and serving them—that is why he brought all this disaster on them.'"

COMMENTARY

The reign of Solomon is divided into two halves in 2 Chronicles (1:1–5:1; 5:2–9:31). Each half begins with the king's organizing a national assembly to worship at a sanctuary and his receiving a theophany in which one of his prayers is answered at night. The second half of Solomon's reign is addressed in this section. The main agenda of the first half was the construction and equipping of the Temple. Now the chronicler fills the building with the Lord's presence and with Israel's worship and prayers. The Temple comes to life and becomes a dynamic element in maintaining the relationship between Israel and their God.

5:2-10. This spiritual landmark in Israel's history is appropriately initiated by a representative assembly at the Temple. The installation of the ark in the Temple fittingly launches the new section, because the ark symbolized the divine presence. Housed in the Temple, it became the implicit focus of Israel's prayers ("in your presence," 6:19) and sacrificial worship ("before the LORD," 7:4). The chronicler used 1 Kgs 8:1-9 as his source for the account of the ark's installation, only supplementing it with the role of the Levites in carrying the ark, evidently for the last time. There is a grand procession from "the city of David," where the ark had stood in David's tent (1 Chr 13:13; 16:1), to the Temple, a few hundred yards to the north. The occasion was the Feast of Tabernacles (v. 3; cf. Lev 23:34). The account in 1 Kings 8 uses the generic term "priests" (כהנים *kōhănîm*) for those who carried the ark (1 Kgs 8:3), as in Joshua 3, and then adds the note that both priests and Levites were involved (1 Kgs 8:4). The chronicler scrupulously changes "priests" (*kōhănîm*) to "Levites" (לוים *lĕwiyyim*) in v. 4, to conform with the emphasis on the Levites in 1 Chronicles 15. The text in v. 5 is not certain; both "the Levitical priests" and "the priests and the Levites" appear in ancient manuscripts.

The installation of the ark and its "vessels" (NRSV) marks a fulfillment of David's directions (1 Chr 22:19). The presence of the "tent of meeting," or tabernacle, presumably brought earlier from Gibeon, builds on the dual system of worship set up by David (1 Chronicles 16). In v. 7, the priests install the ark in the Temple (see Num 4:5-15, 20). In v. 9 "the ark" (הארון *hā'ārôn*) accords with the Masoretic Text. More probably "the ark" represents a gloss that has displaced the NRSV's "the holy place" (הקדש *haqqōdeš*), which appears in the parallel text, 1 Kgs 8:8.[205] The phrase "to this day" is retained in 2 Chronicles as an antiquarian reference. The Second Temple had no ark, but it did possess the ritual vessels (v. 5), which provided essential continuity with the First Temple and affirmed its legitimacy. The contents of the ark, the tablets inscribed with the Ten Commandments, represented the Torah, a continuing mandate for king and people (6:16; 7:17, 19). The new, temple-oriented revelation did not eclipse the obligations of the old, though it did demonstrate a remarkably qualified perspective toward them (6:24-39; 7:14).

5:11-14. The chronicler interrupts the account of the priests' leaving the Temple and the supernatural cloud that fills it (1 Kgs 8:10) with his own snapshot of the scene. He enthusiastically portrays the massed presence of the priests exiting the Temple and the levitical singing musicians in

205. See L. C. Allen, *The Greek Chronicles: The Relation of the Septuagint of I and II Chronicles to the Massoretic Text,* Part 2: *Textual Criticism,* VTSup 25, 27 (Leiden: Brill, 1974) 145.

white robes in front of the altar in the temple court, accompanied by the priestly trumpeters. The choirs, formerly separated at different sanctuaries (1 Chr 16:37-42), were now united at the new Temple. The chronicler envisions a service of music and song to complement the sacrificial worship (v. 6).

The hymn fragment, sung earlier in 1 Chr 16:41, offers praise for the permanent "[steadfast] love" (חסד *ḥesed*) which is the Lord's attribute as God of the covenant. It fits the inauguration of the new age, founded on the Davidic covenant and centered in Temple and dynasty. Although the Torah was associated first with the Mosaic covenant (v. 10; 6:11), that covenant was now taken up into the new Davidic covenant (cf. 6:14, 42; 7:18), and so was secured with a fresh guarantee: God's "[steadfast] love endures forever." For the chronicler, this song results in the appearance of the cloud of glory in the Temple, which marks an intensified mode of the divine presence.[206] It constitutes an implicit parallel with the cloud in Exod 40:34-35, as God's seal of approval on the Temple.

6:1-11. 6:1-2. In two speeches (vv. 1-11), Solomon takes stock of the situation and comments on its theological significance, consistent with 1 Kgs 8:12-21. Facing the Temple, the king formally presents it to the Lord. The theophanic cloud, which concealed even as it revealed, is implicitly compared with the dark holy of holies in which the ark had been placed. The holy of holies marked the permanent presence of the transcendent and mysterious God.

6:3-11. The second speech is made to the assembled Israel, whom Solomon turns to face. It opens with a formula of praise ("Blessed be . . ." NRSV); the verb "blessed" (ויברך *wayyĕbārek*) in v. 3 refers to the use of this formula in the address. Solomon explains why he built the Temple and installed the ark in it. The speech is constructed around two divine promises to David (vv. 5-6 and vv. 8*b*-9). David was to be king, but the privilege of being temple builder was reserved for one of his sons, who would succeed him and would build the sanctuary. The Lord's promise had been kept, and for that Solomon gave praise (v. 4). The speech here does not have the force it has in 1 Kings 8, since, according to 1 Chr 22:9, David had already disclosed Solomon's identity as the divinely revealed successor and temple builder, while 1 Kings 8 knows of no such disclosure. Here the speech endorses the earlier revelation. The emphasis on the Lord's name being in the Temple (vv. 5-6, preserving a longer text than the MT of 1 Kgs 8:16) identified the Temple as the legitimate sanctuary—*the* place at which invoking the divine name was authorized (cf. Exod 20:24 REB: "wherever I cause my name to be invoked"; see also 2 Chr 6:24, 26).[207]

Verse 11 recalls 5:10. The ark is again identified as the container for the tablets summarizing the Torah, here briefly called "the covenant." It conveyed for the chronicler the importance of the Torah as a basis for the covenant relationship (see vv. 16, 27). In the books of Chronicles, "the ark of the covenant" appears prominently in passages that celebrate the Davidic covenant. The chronicler regarded the Mosaic covenant as substantially taken up into the Davidic one (see also 1 Chr 16:15-22).

6:12-42. The prayer in vv. 12-42 primarily introduces a fresh topic: the ongoing function of the Temple in Israel's relationship with the Lord. The text of 1 Kgs 8:22-53 is followed closely in vv. 12-42, except for the addition of minimal material in the initial narrative and a change in the ending of the prayer. There is also unfinished business concerning the dynasty, left over from Solomon's second speech. The opening part of the prayer is devoted to this matter.

6:12-13. Solomon's position is clarified (v. 13) by an addition to 1 Kgs 8:22, which may antedate the chronicler.[208] First, the king does not stand in the inner court, "the court of the priests," but in "the great court" of 4:9, and so "the outer court." Holy space was thus safeguarded even from this distinguished layperson. Second, Solomon stands on a platform so that he can be seen and heard by the large company, "the whole assembly of Israel." Third, the chronicler carefully notes that

206. T. Fretheim, *The Suffering of God,* OBT 14 (Philadelphia: Fortress, 1984) 64.

207. See A. S. van der Woude, "שם *šēm,* Name," *Theologische Handwörterbuch zum Alten Testament,* ed. E. Jenni and C. Westermann (Munchen: Kaiser, 1976) 2:935-63, esp. 951-55; E. Talstra, *Solomon's Prayer,* Contributions to Biblical Exegesis and Theology 3, trans. G. Runia-Deenick (Kampen: Pharos, 1993) 139-40.

208. See S. Japhet, *I & II Chronicles,* OTL (Louisville: Westminster/John Knox, 1993) 586.

Solomon knelt to pray, which his source states later (1 Kgs 8:54). After the addition, 1 Kgs 8:22*b* is recapitulated.

6:14-17. The unfinished business is an issue high on the chronicler's agenda: the guarantee of a permanent dynasty, secured by Solomon's building the Temple and his keeping the Torah (cf. 1:9; 1 Chr 17:12-14; 22:10; 28:5-7). The introductory praise (vv. 14-15) echoes the king's testimony of praise (vv. 4-10). The Lord is faithful to those who are faithful to the Lord. This theological proposition is taken from Exod 20:4; Deut 7:9 (cf. 1 Sam 2:30*b*; see also Matt 10:32-33). It leads on to a particular example: The completed Temple testifies to God's faithfulness to David as a keeper of promises. (The praise is a preamble to the petition of vv. 16-17: "Now . . . And now" [NIV].) And there was a further promise. For the chronicler, who has Solomon in mind, it was the promise of a permanent Davidic dynasty, hedged by the condition of human faithfulness. David's own petition to this end (1 Chr 17:23) is echoed in v. 17. The chronicler relates the reference to David's "sons" in 1 Kgs 8:25 explicitly to Solomon (see 1 Chr 28:7-10; 2 Chr 7:17-18). The outworking of the theological proposition of v. 14, relating to God's faithfulness, implied that the survival, and so restoration, of the Davidic dynasty was grounded in the character of God.

Instead of simply repeating the phrase "walking before God" (vv. 14, 16; cf. 1 Kgs 8:23, 25), the chronicler offers a stylistic variation, "walk in my law." To walk before the Lord is to adopt a way of life that complies with God's will. This spelled Torah for the chronicler. Indeed, the very word תורה (*tôrâ*) suggests a metaphor that pictures life as a journey. The related verb הורה (*hôrâ*, in the hiphil), which occurs in v. 27, can mean to give directions to a place (Gen 46:28 NIV). So the Torah constitutes God's guiding principles for the journey of life. The chronicler may have been influenced by v. 27, which can be translated "when you give directions to the good way in which they should walk," to make the change here.

6:18-21. The rest of Solomon's prayer is about prayer. It envisions seven scenarios of prayer (vv. 22-39). By way of introduction, these verses explore the relationship between the Temple and prayer in an all-embracing petition that is resumed in v. 40 after the intervening examples. As in v. 14, a theological proposition is the starting point and qualifies the concept of the Temple as God's residence, expressed in v. 2. Those who came to the Temple area to pray did indeed find the Lord there. Solomon was praying "in your presence" (v. 19; cf. 7:4). Certainly God's "heart" was there (7:16), but the chronicler reaffirms the principle, already expressed in 2:6, that divine immanence had to be held in tension with divine transcendence. Here the text reflects the traditional OT dialectic that the Lord is present both in heaven and in an earthly counterpart, the Temple in Jerusalem (see Pss 14:2, 7; 20:2, 6; 76:2, 8; Isa 31:4, 9).

The outer court of the Temple was the place where the laity prayed facing the Temple. The only exception was when those who prayed were detained outside the country (vv. 34, 38). Daniel fits this category; he compensated for being outside Jerusalem by praying in his upper room with the window shutters open toward Jerusalem (Dan 6:10). As the location of God's earthly presence, the Temple was a means of access to the heavenly God.

6:22-23. The framework of Solomon's prayer makes forgiveness the keynote of the divine response. The following seven petitions are grounded in basic conditions of human sin and so function as penitential prayers. Four of the seven fall into this category. The first, fifth, and sixth do not. The first petition is for social justice. It has in view a self-cursing oath sworn at the sanctuary (cf. Num 5:11-31; Ps 7:3-5). Solomon's request that the sinner be exposed and the one sinned against be vindicated by the curse parallels the standard covenant relationship between the Lord and Israel (v. 14). Most of the other petitions postulate emergency situations in which the usual order has irretrievably broken down so that people no longer call for justice but for grace instead. In human failure, which turns out to be the rule rather than the exception, the Temple is the place to go to find forgiveness and a new start in life.

6:24-27. The second to seventh petitions fall, basically, into three pairs.[209] The first pair occurs in vv. 24-25 and vv. 26-27. Verses 24-25 reflect

209. See Talstra, *Solomon's Prayer,* 112-26.

a covenant curse of a military defeat coming true (cf. Lev 26:17; Deut 28:25). The nation finds itself collectively in the role of the sinner (v. 22), whose self-curse has become effective. Is there a way back to the Lord? The king asks God to make it possible. Part of the population is regarded as being in exile; the rest are still in the land and able to come to the Temple. The gift of the land is understood in v. 25 as made not only to Israel's "ancestors," as in 1 Kgs 8:34, but also to the generation featured in this scenario. It was not automatically inherited; each generation had to prove itself worthy of it.[210] Solomon dares to pray for resolution of this hopeless sitation and for restoration of the land. The scenario of vv. 26-27 envisions the covenant curse of Deut 28:24. The king prays that the God who justly punishes sinners may be further revealed as the one who saves from crisis and restores the relationship, pointing the people back to "the right way to live" (v. 27).

6:28-33. The second pair of scenarios has substantial differences; both stress, however, the importance of fearing God. The first continues the theme of Israel's experience of covenant curses (v. 28*a*; cf. Deut 28:21-22, 38, 48, 52). The situations reflect a variety of dire possibilities. Humans can respond in both communal and individual laments. These particular laments affirm an awareness of human guilt (cf. Pss 25:7; 38:3-4; 39:8-11; 51:1-4, 9; 106:6; Jer 14:7). Forgiveness after sincere repentance is meant to lead to respectful obedience (cf. Jer 32:39). "The foreigner too" (REB) is given a place in these scenarios. Here divine forgiveness extends to one who cannot claim the help offered to God's covenant people. The prospect of international respect for the Lord is reminiscent of 1 Chr 14:17 and 2 Chr 20:29, except that here it is a response to answered prayer.

6:34-39. The sixth petition recalls the first in the way it prepares for and contrasts with the following one. It presents the situation of a holy war obediently undertaken at God's command and so warranting divine help (cf. 1 Sam 15:20). Such respectability is replaced by culpable crisis in the contrasting seventh scenario. Now defeat and deportation function as instruments of divine punishment. It is the second scenario blown up to horrendous proportions. Solomon dares to hope that the Lord will acknowledge Israel as covenant partner again, if the people will repent of their apostasy. Sinning is no longer an option, but has become inevitable and fateful. So there is an emphasis on a complete "change of heart" (v. 37). A communal lament is put on the people's lips, addressed to the God of the Temple, who has driven them from the land.

A glance ahead at the divine response in 7:12-16 (cf. 1 Kgs 9:2-3) shows that Solomon's prayer is meant to contribute to a theological manifesto for the Temple. The chronicler uses the prayer and its answer to develop the thesis he propounded in 1 Chronicles 21 that the Temple was based on divine grace. He copied out this long prayer from 1 Kings 8 because it illustrates so well that the Temple provided a means of grace for the people of God. When the Torah had been broken, the Lord honored the prayers of individuals or the community. But sinning was not condoned. Repentance features not only in vv. 37-38 but also in the "turning back" of v. 24 and the turning from sin in v. 26. In v. 37, the "change of heart" (NIV) or "coming to one's senses" (NRSV) means recalling what one did when carried away by self-will and reconsidering it in the cold light of day. An ethical life-style is anticipated as the sequel to repentance in vv. 27 and 31.

6:40-42. After reverting to the framework of the prayer in v. 40, the chronicler's version ends on a different note. Both the exodus as the basis of Israel's covenant relationship and the Lord's assurance given "through Moses your servant" were recalled in 1 Kgs 8:51-53. For the chronicler, this recollection turned the clock back to an earlier era of revelation. The time had come to concentrate on "David your servant" (v. 42), in line with the emphasis at the start of the prayer (vv. 15-17). What follows in vv. 41-42 is largely drawn from Ps 132:8-10. Psalm 132 associates the transportation of the ark with the establishment of the Davidic dynasty, which the chronicler found congenial to his own interests. He may initially have been attracted to it by its motif of rest. He omitted the speech to Israel (1 Kgs 8:56-61), probably because it began by again harking back to the Lord's "servant Moses." But its reference to divine rest for Israel may have reminded him of the rest the Lord achieved with the installation of the ark (cf. 1 Chr 28:2).

210. Japhet, *I & II Chronicles*, 595.

The quotation of Ps 132:8-10 associates God with the ark as a symbol of the divine presence. The invitation to the Lord to take up residence in the Temple by means of the ark could more appropriately have accompanied 5:2-11, but the remainder of the block of quoted material made it a suitable conclusion to Solomon's prayer. The three added vocatives, "O LORD God," though turning the poetry into prose, now recall the opening of the prayer, with its triple "O LORD, God of Israel" (6:14-17 NRSV), and so welds the quotation to its new context.

God's presence in the Temple inaugurated a new era in which its priests would be mediators of divine "salvation" (תשועה *tĕšu'â*), a term borrowed from Ps 132:16. The term is used here, as it is in the psalter (in psalms of lament and thanksgiving), to signify the Lord's rescuing humans from situations of crisis (cf. 20:9). It alludes to the granting of the petitions in the body of Solomon's prayer. Priests, it is hoped, would pass on God's favorable answers and promises of restoration (see Pss 28:6; 85:8-9). The final clause, "and let your faithful rejoice in your goodness," paraphrases "and let the faithful exult" (Ps 132:9), intended to provide intertextual links with 7:10. The reference to God's "faithful ones" (חסידים *ḥăsîdîm*) may refer to the Levites whose role required them to sing of the Lord's goodness and (steadfast) love (5:13). However, the term *ḥăsîdîm*, which connotes those who are faithful or who evince steadfast love, probably refers to the people. In v. 14, the related word חסד (*ḥesed*) was used to describe the covenant relationship between the Lord and Israel. Not only the combination of the people's joy and God's goodness in 7:10, but also the people's singing of the levitical chorus in 7:3 will indicate the fulfillment of the prayerful wish of 6:41.

The final verse of the prayer blends part of Ps 132:10 with a phrase taken from Isa 55:3. The chronicler may have been attracted to the prophetic oracle because Isa 55:6-7 issues an invitation to "seek the LORD . . . call upon him. . . . Let the wicked forsake his way. . . . Let him turn to the LORD . . . for he will freely pardon" (NIV). Such motifs have been the burden of Solomon's prayer earlier in the chapter, while "seeking the LORD" is the chronicler's key term for spirituality. The citation of Isa 55:3 becomes Solomon's appeal to God to fulfill the dynastic promise made to David, as the paraphrase in the NIV suggests.[211] The temple prayer ends as it began in 6:16-17. Solomon's building of the Temple for the Lord and the establishment of a permanent dynasty were intertwined in the purposes of God.

According to Isa 55:3, the Davidic covenant is made with Israel. In the light of Second Isaiah's overall message, this represents a democratization of the royal covenant. Royal benefits were to be transferred to the people as a whole. The chronicler understood the text differently. From his perspective, the Davidic covenant enlarged the divine relationship with Israel, undergirding with divine permanence what is often in the Torah represented as perishable. The everlasting nature of the covenant was bound up with the permanence of the dynasty (cf. 13:5; 21:7; 23:3).

7:1-3. Solomon's prayer, apart from its dynastic framing, has been concerned with the religious functioning of the Temple, now that the ark had been installed in it and it had been graced with a special manifestation of God's presence (5:2-14). The Temple has two functions in the books of Chronicles: to be a place of prayer and "a house of sacrifice" (v. 12). The latter element is missing from the account in 1 Kings 8; sacrifices are offered there without explicit divine warrant (1 Kgs 8:62-64). So the chronicler has supplied it in these verses.

"Fire came down from heaven," which symbolizes acceptance of the sacrifices (5:6) that were made in conjunction with the ark's installation. The miracle echoes 1 Chr 21:26, where the temple site was divinely sanctioned for worship in this way. The Temple, approved then in principle, is now formally designated as the legitimate place of worship. This fire adds to the endorsement of 5:13-14. The circumstantial clause in v. 1*b* is better translated "and the glory of the LORD was [still] filling the temple."[212] However, a new note is introduced in v. 3. Whereas the revelation in 5:13-14 affected only the priests, as 7:2 reminds us, now God's people were witnesses. Seeing the fire on the altar of burnt offering and now also an aura of glory "on" the Temple, they received

211. See H. G. M. Williamson, " 'The Sure Mercies of David': Subjective or Objective Genitive?" *JSS* 23 (1978) 31-49. Cf. S. Japhet, *I & II Chronicles*, OTL (Louisville: Westminster/John Knox, 1993) 604-5.

212. H. G. M. Williamson, *1 and 2 Chronicles*, NCB (Grand Rapids: Eerdmans, 1982) 222.

assurance of the Lord's commitment to the Temple. The chronicler has in mind Lev 9:23-24, where the tabernacle sacrifices were authenticated by supernatural fire before all the people. This repetition teaches that the Temple had taken over the role of the tabernacle.

The people responded to the divine revelation with vocal worship. If in chap. 5 revelation was a gracious response to the singing of praise, here it inspires praise in a service of dedication (cf. 7:5*b*). Israel takes over the Levites' chorus (5:13), duly enabled to rejoice in the Lord's goodness, as Solomon had asked in 6:41. They celebrate God's "[steadfast] love" (*ḥesed*) as a feature not merely of the Mosaic covenant (6:14) but of the Davidic covenant, which inaugurated a new era of grace for Israel (6:42; 7:10).

7:4-11. In vv. 4-5 the text of 1 Kgs 8:62-63 is rejoined, while vv. 7-10 are based on 1 Kgs 8:64-66. In v. 6 the chronicler introduces the component of worship, which for him necessarily supplemented sacrifice, the blasts of the priestly trumpeters, and the music and song of the Levites. Appeal is made to David's traditional association with musical instruments, which enhances the prestige of temple music (cf. 1 Chr 23:5). For the first time, sacrifice and song were offered together in Jerusalem, as formerly had been done in Gibeon (1 Chr 16:37-42). The service of dedicating the "house" (v. 5) or the "altar" (v. 9) was so lavishly supplied with sacrificial animals that the altar proved too small to accommodate the burnable parts, and the celebrations lasted a week. Then the Feast of Tabernacles provided a further week of worship, which reached a finale on the eighth day. The narrative in 1 Kgs 8:65-66 (in the emended form of the NRSV) follows the seven-day festival of Deut 16:13-15. The chronicler carefully realigns it with the Torah's detailed requirements for an eight-day festival in Lev 23:34-36, 39-43 (cf. Num 29:15-38). The "eighth day" of dismissal in 1 Kgs 8:66 now becomes the ninth day as the twenty-third day of the month, after the dedication of the altar from the eighth to the fourteenth day and the Feast of Tabernacles from the fifteenth to the twenty-second.[213] The Torah's festivals, in their priestly form, as practiced in the post-exilic period, continued into the new era, with a new rendezvous. The chronicler made the dedicatory celebrations separate from the Feast of Tabernacles. Accordingly, pilgrims were summoned a week before the feast (5:3 is now implicitly revised).

The reference in 1 Kgs 8:65 to Israel's north and south frontiers as Lebo-hamath and the Wadi of Egypt serves as a parallel to David's assembly for the original transportation of the ark (1 Chr 13:5) and underlines the significance of "all Israel." It also alludes to the joint nature of David's and Solomon's reigns. The reference to Solomon, added by the chronicler (v. 10), reminds the reader that their reigns were two halves of a single episode of divine revelation (cf. 11:17; 35:4). Verse 11 is also added as a development of 1 Kgs 9:1. Here was a further stage in the completion of the Temple, now that its sacrificial system had been representatively inaugurated. The success for which David had prayed concerning the building of the Temple (1 Chr 22:11) was duly attained. "Mission accomplished," reports the chronicler.

7:12-22. 7:12. The account of the personal theophany in 7:12-22 amplifies 1 Kgs 9:2-9. Verse 12*b* embraces Solomon's prayer in 6:14-42 and the ensuing narrative in 7:1. The Lord had heard the prayer and chose the Temple as "a house of sacrifice." What was expressed in symbol (v. 1) is now put into words. Sacrifice was of prime importance at the Temple, so much so that its dedication (v. 5) could be called a dedication of the altar (v. 9); Solomon had summed up the Temple's function thus in 2:4, 6. By means of the distinctive verb "chosen" (בחר *bāḥar*; cf. 6:6), the Temple was now accredited as the place to sacrificially worship the Lord. Now, at last, the promise of the Lord's choosing such a place in Deut 12:4-6, 11 had come true.

7:13-14. This section returns to the other great role of the Temple: It was a place of prayer, the topic of most of Solomon's prayer. A digest of that prayer is provided in vv. 13-14, especially in terms of the third and fourth scenarios (6:26, 28). They dealt with crisis suffered by the land in reprisal for the people's sinning and so were relevant to the chronicler's post-exilic constituency. The other key scenarios that depict exile (the second and especially the seventh), now function as metaphors for their spiritual state: They are still alienated from the Lord and so

213. See J. R. Shaver, *Torah and the Chronicler's History Work*, BJS 196 (Atlanta: Scholars Press, 1989) 99-100.

deprived of blessing. In response, the Lord first acknowledges the truth of the phrase "your people" in the king's prayer, reaffirming it with an idiom of ownership, "called by my name" (נִקְרָא־שְׁמִי *niqrā˒-šĕmî*). Israel was still the object of God's care and claim. Prayer—humble prayer (cf. Lev 26:41) that abandoned the brazenness of disobedience—is endorsed as the means of triggering divine love. This prayer was to be an expression of seeking God's face. Instead of the standard term for "spirituality" (דרשׁ *dāraš*; lit., "seek"), a synonym (בִּקֵּשׁ *biqqēš*) appears, which had occurred alongside it in one of the chronicler's basic texts, Jer 29:13-14. The word *biqqēš* is appropriate in 2 Chr 7:14 because to seek God's face was a religious idiom for worship at the Temple (see also Pss 24:6; 27:8; 105:4). The chronicler used Ps 105:4 in 1 Chr 16:11. Here it relates not to standard worship, but to prodigal sons and daughters returning to the Lord.

The Lord promised to honor such prayer and to wipe the slate clean in forgiveness, as Solomon had asked. Curses resting on the land would be removed. Rain would fall again on the drought-stricken land (6:26-27). The locusts of 6:28 would be banished, as in the book of Joel. Where there had been failure and loss, healing would be given. In Solomon's prayer, the land of Israel had featured as an area of both deprivation and blessing (6:25, 27-28, 31). As generally in the OT, the land functioned as a spiritual barometer, registering the people's loyalty to the Lord. The chronicler's exposition of the Lord's response to the king's prayer sums up a crucial aspect of his message: Through worship at the Temple, God had provided a way of ending guilt and the spiritual and material crises it caused. Beyond a broken covenant lay divine resources of healing and restoration. The chronicler will weave this divine promise into the narratives that follow in order to reinforce a message of human guilt and divine love for the people of God.[214]

7:15-16. These verses substantially return to 1 Kgs 9:3*b*, making God's response apply to the royal request in 6:40 and adding the motif of divine choice, repeated from 6:6; 7:12. The new parallelism with v. 12 brackets the two roles of the Temple, a normative one of worship and praise and a special one of finding a welcome after falling away. God waits, ever ready to hear Temple-centered prayers of repentance.

7:17-18. God responds to the initial and final requests of Solomon's prayer, concerning the dynastic succession of Davidic kings. The chronicler follows 1 Kgs 9:4-5 but with his own emphases. The dynastic condition of building the Temple, laid down in 1 Chr 17:12, has been met. The other proviso, Solomon's general obedience, reported by David as having been met thus far in 1 Chr 28:7, was still ahead. It was the chronicler's conviction that Solomon did meet the latter condition, and the next section will address this issue. The account of Solomon's reign will end with glorious tributes to him and to his God. The omission of "over Israel forever" (1 Kgs 9:5) from v. 18 may indicate an expansion in the MT of 1 Kings.[215] At the end of the verse, the chronicler makes a significant change, upgrading the verb "promised" (דבר *dibber*, in the piel) in the 1 Kings text to "covenanted" (כרת *kārat*) here. The change recalls the divine faithfulness to David in 6:14 and advances the Mosaic reference in 5:10. The Mosaic covenant had been amplified by the Davidic covenant, which strengthened Israel's relationship with the Lord. The new verb, "covenanted" (כרתי *kārattî*), is also a pun on God's assurance that the people would never "lack" (יכרת *yikkārēt*) a Davidic successor. The pun reinforces the promise. The promise to David, as found in the MT of 1 Kings, "on the throne of Israel," is replaced by (literally) "ruling in Israel." The reading is shared by the LXX of 1 Kings, and the MT may reflect assimilation to 1 Kgs 2:4; 8:25.[216]

7:19-22. The text takes over the dire warning of 1 Kgs 9:6-9, which not only amplifies 1 Kgs 8:46 (= 2 Chr 6:36), but also spells out the possibility of withdrawing the Temple-centered relationship between Israel and the Lord. In v. 19, both the king and the people are addressed together with plural verbs, while in vv. 20-22 the people are in view. Solomon could have been punished (cf. 1 Chr 28:9*b*), but he eluded it, at least according to the chronicler. For the people such punishment was a recurring threat. Accord-

214. See Williamson, *1 and 2 Chronicles*, 226.

215. See S. L. McKenzie, *The Chronicler's Use of the Deuteronomistic History*, HSM 33 (Atlanta: Scholars Press, 1985) 97.

216. S. J. De Vries, *1 Kings*, WBC 12 (Waco, Tex.: Word, 1985) 119.

ing to 1 Chr 28:8, continued possession of the land was tied to obedience. Here its loss is envisioned as a result of disobedience. The exodus, if forgotten, could give way to exile. The rhetorical device of question and answer in vv. 21-22 conveys in a dramatic way the folly of turning one's back on the Lord. The stark warning alludes to Judah's fate in 587 BCE.

There are two redeeming features, however, in the 2 Chronicles presentation. First, there is no suggestion that the dynastic promise would die. Once Solomon's reign was over, it became a guarantee for the long-term future of God's people. Second, the post-exilic Temple had arisen from the ashes of the first, and so the Temple-related promise of forgiveness and a fresh start still stood. Yet, each generation had the threat of spiritual exile hanging over it (cf. 1 Chr 10:7, 13; 16:19-20), if they turned their backs on "the God of their fathers" (v. 22). On the other hand, obedience or doom-laden disobedience were not the only options open to Israel. Repentance leading to restoration and blessing was a third alternative that still was made available, as ensuing narratives in 2 Chronicles will amply testify. The chronicler chose not to end on this note. He knew that the repentance of heart and soul sought by the Lord (6:38) did not come about easily. A hefty stick was needed to break down human willfulness and induce a healthy fear of God (6:31).

REFLECTIONS

Much of the chronicler's theology is showcased in these chapters. The concentration on the Temple and its dynamic roles in the life of God's people is at first alien to the Christian reader. However, the chronicler offers a clue about why the Temple features so prominently in spiritual metaphors in the New Testament. The chronicler was proud to live in a temple age. The narrative of Solomon's work under God resonates with new beginnings. The chronicler looked back over the centuries to a significant, sacred moment in history. In the same vein, we read of "the beginning of the gospel" in Mark 1:1 and join the Evangelist in investing particular incidents with profound meaning.

1. The older covenant between the Lord and Israel attested mutual commitment (cf. 6:14), to which the ark's contents testified. The Lord's redeeming love in the exodus established an obligation for Israel to adopt a particular life-style, reflected in the Ten Commandments. The Torah, to which 6:11 alludes, surfaces again as a continuing mandate for king and people in 7:17-22. The new revelation did not suspend the broader obligations of the old. In eighteenth-century Jewish history, the charismatic Hasidim emerged in Poland, emphasizing joy and God's presence in one's heart and mind every waking moment. This movement within Judaism was a dynamic reaction against religious scholarship, which had not gloried in the joy of Torah study. It was left to the second generation of Hasidim to restore the balance and learn again that the Torah comprised God-given guidelines for living.

In the early Christian church, there were those who identified the new wine of Christianity with antinomianism and made divine grace an argument for human licentiousness (see Jude 4). Paul himself was so accused (Rom 3:8; 6:1-2). Firmly rebutting the charge, he insisted on obedience "from the heart to the standard of teaching" to which Christians had been "committed" (Rom 6:17 RSV) and even on the fulfilling of "the righteous requirements of the law" in the power of the Spirit (Rom 8:4 NIV). The metaphor of the Torah as the basis for "the good way" of life (2 Chr 6:27) finds a parallel in the New Testament at Eph 2:10. God has prepared in advance "good works" for Christians to "walk in" (KJV) or "to be our way of life" (NRSV).

2. Temple and covenant were linked by more than the Torah inside the ark. Temple worship testified to the covenant love of the Lord, present in the songs of the levitical choirs and repeated by the congregation (5:13; 7:3, 6). Such worship had been revealed in a richer way in the promises to David, which trickled down to Israel (6:41-42; 7:10). A new, "forever" age was dawning for God's people with a fresh manifestation of covenant grace as its keynote, a "[steadfast] love" so deep and wide that it met their repentance with forgiveness and renewed blessing (7:14). Christian readers can draw parallels of their own. In Rom 5:1-11, the beginning of a new era is celebrated ("at the right time," Rom 5:6 NRSV). God's love had been demonstrated toward sinners in Christ's death, so that they are friends of God and are blessed with everlasting salvation. No wonder joy is the response that frames this passage! Christians have fresh grounds to join in Israel's worship in 7:3.

3. The typological parallel drawn between tabernacle and Temple in the descent of the cloud of glory upon the sanctuary is repeated in John 1:14: "The Word became flesh and made his dwelling among us. We have seen his glory . . . full of grace and truth" (NIV). In Jesus there was a new manifestation of divine presence. The Fourth Gospel develops that imagery by assigning to the risen Jesus the role of a miraculously rebuilt temple, like Ezekiel's new temple (John 2:19-22).

Solomon's first speech (6:1-2) compares the cloud to the home of the unseen ark. Although the New Testament rejoices in the rending of the veil and in fuller access to God, there will always be a sense of divine mystery. It is a feature of traditional Jewish theology to maintain from an intellectual standpoint, though not from a spiritual one, that God is unknowable. Paul also affirmed such human inadequacy of knowledge of God in stating that "we know only in part" (1 Cor 13:9 NRSV).

This section of 2 Chronicles is full of theological tension, between the concealing and revealing of the deity in the cloud of glory, between the Lord's dwelling in earthly and heavenly temples, and between the latter and a divine presence that spills everywhere. Such divine paradoxes defy our tidy systems.

4. Solomon's sanctuary was meant to be a great temple for a great God (2:5); yet, it could not contain the Lord (6:18). Likewise, God is too magnificent to fit snugly into our church, our denomination, our present conception of deity. God is a veritable Gulliver in our Lilliputian world.

5. The petitions in Solomon's prayer move primarily from a situation of existential crisis caused by human sinning to Temple-centered prayer. They look forward to divine hearing, forgiveness, and reversal of the crisis. Solomon is concerned that the spiritual relationship between the Lord and the believing community (or individual, 7:29) be restored and reflected sacramentally in land-related blessing. The repeated emphasis on human sinning, which necessitates divine forgiveness (7:21 onward), stands in conflict with the calm, orderly situation of 6:14. An adequate theology must recognize and deal with the abnormal, because "there is no one who does not sin" (7:36), and sooner or later everybody falls into a self-inflicted predicament. In order to address such situations realistically, the chronicler took over the deuteronomistic emphasis on temple prayer as a means of forgiveness. It conformed to his Davidic prototype of a sinner's plea that found a divine response (1 Chr 21:26). Sin was not thereby condoned, but it was confronted and held at a distance (6:24, 26, 29, 37-38). We modern worshipers find such an opportunity in our own corporate prayer, especially in the confession of sins and the laying hold of forgiveness in Christ.

6. The fifth scenario (7:32-33) makes those of us who are Gentiles feel at home. The chronicler, no xenophobe and no hoarder of divine grace, took over this scenario gladly. A foreigner, Naaman-like, is drawn to the Temple because of God's exploits on Israel's behalf. Isaiah 56:7 likewise speaks of the Temple as "a house of prayer for all nations." According to Mark 11:17, Jesus cited that text when he condemned blatant commercialization in the Court of the Gentiles. Such behavior presented a poor testimony to Gentiles who frequented that part of the Temple that was open to them. We inherit Scripture that invites all to come, and so we must ensure that all groups in our community find a welcome in our church.

7. When normal life collapsed, the Temple had a role other than that of a "house of sacrifice," as the channel of penitential prayer and restorative love. This latter role is developed in 2 Chr 7:13-14. Solomon's prayer laid the foundation by identifying the need. Now the forgiveness he sought is duly pledged. The pall of judgment, guilt, and frustration that hung over the post-exilic community (cf. Neh 9:32-37; Dan 9:4-14) could be dispelled. When the Torah had been broken and covenant curses rested on people and land, there was a way forward. The low road from sin to disaster could be left by a new track winding back to the high road from obedience to blessing, according to 7:14. God's people find two divine claims on their lives. The first is for obedience to the divine will. However, if they go down a path of their own choosing, they find the Lord standing in the way, ready to make a second claim and offer another chance.

The chronicler articulates an evangelical theology, meeting sin with forgiveness, while safeguarding morality by means of repentance and renewed commitment. Some Christians want to see a theology of grace in the New Testament and deny its presence in the Old, but the chronicler attests otherwise. The God of the Torah coped with failure, picking up the broken pieces as soon as the covenant was broken (Exodus 32–34; note Exod 34:6). The chronicler, too, found in the Temple a means to reaffirm God's compassion.

Those who would not accept the carrot of 7:14, the chronicler consigned to the stick of 7:19-22. The divine presentations stand as alternatives. The broken covenant, apart from the Lord's provision, must lead to an intensification of the curses in the Torah. There is a tension in this section that the New Testament expresses and every pastor knows. On the one hand, the Lord issues a solemn call for compliance and integrity, backed by due warnings. On the other hand, there is fervent assurance of forgiveness and a fresh chance. Untidy as this double message is, it is realistic. The logic of the double message is supplied in 1 John 2:1, "I write this to you so that you will not sin. But if anybody does sin . . ." (NIV). The literary movement from grace to judgment at the end of 2 Chronicles 7 finds a parallel in the Letter to the Galatians. From justification by grace through faith (Gal 2:20–3:25), the apostle moved to a threatening message of judgment: "God is not mocked, for you reap whatever you sow" (Gal 6:7 NRSV).

For the chronicler, as for the deuteronomist, the moral issue was resolved by an emphasis on repentance. As a second best, God is prepared to take the thought for the deed and to accept conscience in place of constancy, if commitment to the good ensued (6:27). It is not only talking the talk of penitential prayer that is envisioned, but also walking a corresponding walk thereafter. The grim either/or of 7:17-22 is not God's last word. The post-exilic community had seen that beyond "just deserts" lay God's helping hand. Sometimes, like the chronicler's constituency, even we need to hear strident threats, in the hope that we may be saved from willful apathy.

2 Chronicles 8:1-16, Finding Blessing and Finishing the Temple

NIV

8 At the end of twenty years, during which
Solomon built the temple of the LORD and
his own palace, [2]Solomon rebuilt the villages that
Hiram[a] had given him, and settled Israelites in

[a]2 Hebrew *Huram*, a variant of *Hiram*; also in verse 18

NRSV

8 At the end of twenty years, during which
Solomon had built the house of the LORD
and his own house, [2]Solomon rebuilt the cities
that Huram had given to him, and settled the
people of Israel in them.

NIV

them. 3Solomon then went to Hamath Zobah and captured it. 4He also built up Tadmor in the desert and all the store cities he had built in Hamath. 5He rebuilt Upper Beth Horon and Lower Beth Horon as fortified cities, with walls and with gates and bars, 6as well as Baalath and all his store cities, and all the cities for his chariots and for his horses[a]—whatever he desired to build in Jerusalem, in Lebanon and throughout all the territory he ruled.

7All the people left from the Hittites, Amorites, Perizzites, Hivites and Jebusites (these peoples were not Israelites), 8that is, their descendants remaining in the land, whom the Israelites had not destroyed—these Solomon conscripted for his slave labor force, as it is to this day. 9But Solomon did not make slaves of the Israelites for his work; they were his fighting men, commanders of his captains, and commanders of his chariots and charioteers. 10They were also King Solomon's chief officials—two hundred and fifty officials supervising the men.

11Solomon brought Pharaoh's daughter up from the City of David to the palace he had built for her, for he said, "My wife must not live in the palace of David king of Israel, because the places the ark of the LORD has entered are holy."

12On the altar of the LORD that he had built in front of the portico, Solomon sacrificed burnt offerings to the LORD, 13according to the daily requirement for offerings commanded by Moses for Sabbaths, New Moons and the three annual feasts—the Feast of Unleavened Bread, the Feast of Weeks and the Feast of Tabernacles. 14In keeping with the ordinance of his father David, he appointed the divisions of the priests for their duties, and the Levites to lead the praise and to assist the priests according to each day's requirement. He also appointed the gatekeepers by divisions for the various gates, because this was what David the man of God had ordered. 15They did not deviate from the king's commands to the priests or to the Levites in any matter, including that of the treasuries.

16All Solomon's work was carried out, from the day the foundation of the temple of the LORD was laid until its completion. So the temple of the LORD was finished.

[a] 6 Or *charioteers*

NRSV

3Solomon went to Hamath-zobah, and captured it. 4He built Tadmor in the wilderness and all the storage towns that he built in Hamath. 5He also built Upper Beth-horon and Lower Beth-horon, fortified cities, with walls, gates, and bars, 6and Baalath, as well as all Solomon's storage towns, and all the towns for his chariots, the towns for his cavalry, and whatever Solomon desired to build, in Jerusalem, in Lebanon, and in all the land of his dominion. 7All the people who were left of the Hittites, the Amorites, the Perizzites, the Hivites, and the Jebusites, who were not of Israel, 8from their descendants who were still left in the land, whom the people of Israel had not destroyed—these Solomon conscripted for forced labor, as is still the case today. 9But of the people of Israel Solomon made no slaves for his work; they were soldiers, and his officers, the commanders of his chariotry and cavalry. 10These were the chief officers of King Solomon, two hundred fifty of them, who exercised authority over the people.

11Solomon brought Pharaoh's daughter from the city of David to the house that he had built for her, for he said, "My wife shall not live in the house of King David of Israel, for the places to which the ark of the LORD has come are holy."

12Then Solomon offered up burnt offerings to the LORD on the altar of the LORD that he had built in front of the vestibule, 13as the duty of each day required, offering according to the commandment of Moses for the sabbaths, the new moons, and the three annual festivals—the festival of unleavened bread, the festival of weeks, and the festival of booths. 14According to the ordinance of his father David, he appointed the divisions of the priests for their service, and the Levites for their offices of praise and ministry alongside the priests as the duty of each day required, and the gatekeepers in their divisions for the several gates; for so David the man of God had commanded. 15They did not turn away from what the king had commanded the priests and Levites regarding anything at all, or regarding the treasuries.

16Thus all the work of Solomon was accomplished from[a] the day the foundation of the house of the LORD was laid until the house of the LORD was finished completely.

[a] Gk Syr Vg: Heb *to*

COMMENTARY

This section takes its cue from 1 Kgs 9:10-25. The chronicler follows the order of its twists and turns tenaciously and at times puts his own spin on the material. The key word is the verb "build" (בנה *bānâ*), which occurs seven times here and only five times in the source. The building of the Temple and the altar (vv. 1, 12) is the pervasive theme for Solomon's reign up to this point. The rest of the references to building reflect another agenda. The chronicler will regularly use building in later narratives as a symbol of divine blessing for a king's obedience (cf. 1 Chr 11:8). For example, Asa's building program is a sign of prosperity after seeking the Lord and keeping the Torah (14:1*b*-7). The terms "fortified cities," "walls," and "gates and bars" in v. 5 occur again in 2 Chronicles only in 14:6-7. The motif of rest also links the reigns of Solomon and Asa. The Lord gave Asa rest because he had sought God (14:6-7 NIV). Rest is especially associated in the books of Chronicles with Solomon's reign (1 Chr 22:9).

Building also belongs to a network of other motifs: seeking the Lord, keeping the Torah, and so enjoying divine blessing. These motifs appear in the account of Asa's reign and are implicit here. The chronicler is answering the question set against Solomon's reign in 7:17-18: Would Solomon keep the Torah and so fulfill the dynastic condition of 1 Chr 28:7? The answer is yes, because the prosperity enjoyed by Asa and linked with building (14:7*b*) was also enjoyed by Solomon, which would fulfill the promise of 1 Chr 22:13. The prosperity credited to Solomon in 1 Chr 29:23 finds illustration here.

8:1-6. The account of Huram's cities in v. 2 reads differently from the longer one in 1 Kgs 9:10-14. It is unlikely that the chronicler contradicted the 1 Kings account, though he would have wanted to put his own construction on the text.[217] His copy may have had a corrupted text, so that in 1 Kgs 9:12 he read "the cities which he had given Solomon" and took that as the basis for his own account, omitting the rest as irrelevant to his agenda.[218] Some scholars have objected that the chronicler must have been well aware of the Samuel–Kings narratives, since he often presupposes them.[219] However, one may question whether he would have known such precise details as to be able to override a divergent text.

The motif of (re)building is imported from the context. The addition about settling Israelites in the Galilean cities introduces the motif of restoration from exile (see Isa 54:3; Jer 32:37; Ezek 36:33; cf. 1 Chr 10:7). Perhaps the insertion of both topics was inspired by the information about Gezer in 1 Kgs 9:16-17*a*. It was a little step forward in the enjoyment of the land promised in 1 Chr 16:18, an earnest of future hope. Both here and in 2 Chr 8:9 Israel's interests are represented as a goal of Solomon's rule.

In v. 4, the reference to Tadmor follows a variant tradition reflected in the oral text (the Qere) of 1 Kgs 9:17 and in the LXX at 3 Kgdms 2:46*d*, though both may depend on Chronicles. The context shows that Tamar in the Negeb was original in the 1 Kings text. However, the chronicler alludes to the northern Tadmor or Palmyra in the Syrian desert, and so it is separated from the building projects in Israel. The reference to its storage towns as well as to Baalath's in v. 6 represents a double use of 1 Kgs 9:19*a*. The reading "Tadmor" encouraged another textual variant, the earlier reference to Hamath-Zobah. Again a damaged parent text appears responsible, with the "wall" in 1 Kgs 9:15 (חומת [*ḥômat*], read defectively as חמת [*ḥmt*]), being understood as Hamath.[220] Zobah was also added, which reflected the later administrative system of provinces set up by the Assyrians and retained under the Persians.

8:7-11. The chronicler follows in a straightforward fashion the narrative concerning forced labor in 1 Kgs 9:20-23. As was observed at 2:17, the chronicler preferred this aspect of the double tradition preserved in 1 Kings. He presupposes knowledge of Solomon's wife, provided in 1 Kgs 3:1; 7:8; 9:16. The information that she was moved up from the city of David reminds the chronicler that the ark had also been brought up

217. McKenzie, *The Chronicler's Use of the Deuteronomistic History,* 108.

218. T. Willi, *Die Chronik als Auslegung* (Göttingen: Vandenhoeck & Ruprecht, 1972) 77.

219. R. B. Dillard, *2 Chronicles,* WBC 15 (Waco, Tex.: Word, 1987) 63.

220. S. J. De Vries, *1 and 2 Chronicles,* FOTL 11 (Grand Rapids: Eerdmans, 1989) 238.

from there (5:2). He thinks in terms of a residual holiness at its former site, with which a woman's regular states of impurity would clash (see Lev 12:1-4; 15:19-31*a*).[221] Unlike the deuteronomist, the chronicler finds her gender greater cause for concern than her foreignness. His Torah-based reasoning accords with a presupposition of the preceding narrative, Solomon's spiritual qualification for divine blessing.

8:12-16. This passage expands 1 Kgs 9:25. For the chronicler, preoccupied with the Torah, it represents the last of the various stages of the completion of the Temple project (cf. 5:1; 7:11). Whereas the ritual festivities of chap. 7 mark the inauguration of the religious calendar, the lapse of time permits the institution of the whole calendar, in line with Solomon's intention in 2:4. The priestly calendar of Numbers 28–29 is in view, but whereas it stipulates five annual festivals, the chronicler is limited by the reference to three in the parent text and so reflects the deuteronomic system of three feasts (Deut 16:1-16; cf. Exod 23:14-17; 34:18-24).[222] The Torah's program of sacrificial worship is transferred from the tabernacle to the Temple.

The revelation given to Moses had been supplemented by that granted to David. The new temple order had been enriched by specifications for its administrative staffing (see 1 Chr 24-26; 28:13, 21). Moses was not the only "man of God" (1 Chr 23:14; 2 Chr 30:16). David, too, possessed such inspiration, as he had claimed in 1 Chr 28:19 (cf. 2 Sam 23:1-2). A prophetic type of revelation had been added to that of the Torah. The chronicler found in both of them binding models for contemporary temple worship. Now Solomon's command puts into operation for the first time David's commands, while perpetuating those of Moses. The NRSV and the NIV are correct in reading "from the day" in place of "to the day" at v. 16. The ungrammatical MT has in initial view the period of preparation in chap. 2 before the actual building began in 3:1-3.[223] Verse 16 marks the fulfillment of David's blessing in 1 Chr 28:20*b*. The Lord had, indeed, brought Solomon through to the end.

The information that Solomon had finished his God-given work was no matter-of-fact statement for the chronicler. It involved the start of a new era of temple worship. Solomon had started religious worship, which would operate into post-exilic times, transcending the brief silence of the exile. Day after day, year after year it would continue to glorify God, in a tradition of worship that gave the Lord pride of place in the community.

221. W. Rudolph, *Chronikbüker,* HAT 121 (Tubingen: J. C. B. Mohr [Siebeck], 1955) 220.

222. Shaver, *Torah and the Chronicler's History Work,* 94-96.

223. See D. Barthélemy et al., *Critique textuelle de l'Ancien Testament,* OBO 50/1 (Fribourg: Editions Universitaires; and Göttingen: Vandenhoeck & Ruprecht, 1982) 1:486-87; Allen, *The Greek Chronicles,* 2:97.

REFLECTIONS

1. Israel's religious faith stood firmly on a double foundation: the revelations to Moses and David. Likewise, the church must never forget that its faith is based on God's double revelation in the Old Testament and the New Testament. Christians are offered assurance of God's revelation when they attend services that include readings from both testaments and so are taken back to the roots of their faith.

Those roots are as person-centered today as they were in the chronicler's teaching. A firm foundation was laid by Christ's "finishing the work" that God "gave" him "to do" (John 17:4). In the Chronicles program, Solomon's obedience to God, which underlies the prosperity of his building projects, sealed the dynasty and so undergirded the covenant relationship between Israel and the Lord. In Christ's prayer of John 17, too, there is a strong sense that the community would last, committed to God's safekeeping. The theological history the chronicler recognized as being made in Solomon, John the Evangelist saw reproduced in Jesus Christ for the church.

2. The explanation the chronicler gives for Solomon's removal of his Egyptian wife from

Jerusalem is unwelcome to modern ears. It perpetuates the Torah's reference to ritual (rather than moral) uncleanness, here associated with the female gender. For the chronicler, however, Solomon's action meant that he was honoring the Torah. His first readers might have disliked his refusal to attack racially mixed marriages (see Neh 13:23-27). In such a debate, the chronicler would have taken the side of the writer of the book of Ruth. We should applaud the chronicler for denying the need to end ethnically mixed marriages. Not even much of what is in the New Testament lives up to the great affirmation of Gal 3:28, which calls for men and women to be treated as equally by others as they are regarded in God's sight.

2 Chronicles 8:17–9:31, Solomon's Significant Prosperity

NIV

17Then Solomon went to Ezion Geber and Elath
on the coast of Edom. 18And Hiram sent him ships
commanded by his own officers, men who knew
the sea. These, with Solomon's men, sailed to
Ophir and brought back four hundred and fifty
talents[a] of gold, which they delivered to King
Solomon.
9 When the queen of Sheba heard of Solomon's fame, she came to Jerusalem to test
him with hard questions. Arriving with a very
great caravan—with camels carrying spices, large
quantities of gold, and precious stones—she came
to Solomon and talked with him about all she had
on her mind. 2Solomon answered all her questions; nothing was too hard for him to explain to
her. 3When the queen of Sheba saw the wisdom
of Solomon, as well as the palace he had built,
4the food on his table, the seating of his officials,
the attending servants in their robes, the cupbearers in their robes and the burnt offerings he
made at[b] the temple of the LORD, she was
overwhelmed.
5She said to the king, "The report I heard in
my own country about your achievements and
your wisdom is true. 6But I did not believe what
they said until I came and saw with my own eyes.
Indeed, not even half the greatness of your wisdom was told me; you have far exceeded the
report I heard. 7How happy your men must be!
How happy your officials, who continually stand
before you and hear your wisdom! 8Praise be to
the LORD your God, who has delighted in you and
placed you on his throne as king to rule for the
LORD your God. Because of the love of your God
for Israel and his desire to uphold them forever,

[a] *18* That is, about 17 tons (about 16 metric tons) [b] *4* Or *the ascent by which he went up to*

NRSV

17Then Solomon went to Ezion-geber and
Eloth on the shore of the sea, in the land of Edom.
18Huram sent him, in the care of his servants,
ships and servants familiar with the sea. They
went to Ophir, together with the servants of
Solomon, and imported from there four hundred
fifty talents of gold and brought it to King Solomon.
9 When the queen of Sheba heard of the
fame of Solomon, she came to Jerusalem
to test him with hard questions, having a very
great retinue and camels bearing spices and very
much gold and precious stones. When she came
to Solomon, she discussed with him all that was
on her mind. 2Solomon answered all her questions; there was nothing hidden from Solomon
that he could not explain to her. 3When the queen
of Sheba had observed the wisdom of Solomon,
the house that he had built, 4the food of his table,
the seating of his officials, and the attendance of
his servants, and their clothing, his valets, and
their clothing, and his burnt offerings[a] that he
offered at the house of the LORD, there was no
more spirit left in her.
5So she said to the king, "The report was true
that I heard in my own land of your accomplishments and of your wisdom, 6but I did not believe
the[b] reports until I came and my own eyes saw
it. Not even half of the greatness of your wisdom
had been told to me; you far surpass the report
that I had heard. 7Happy are your people! Happy
are these your servants, who continually attend
you and hear your wisdom! 8Blessed be the LORD
your God, who has delighted in you and set you
on his throne as king for the LORD your God.

[a] Gk Syr Vg 1 Kings 10.5: Heb *ascent* [b] Heb *their*

NIV

he has made you king over them, to maintain justice and righteousness."

[9]Then she gave the king 120 talents[a] of gold, large quantities of spices, and precious stones. There had never been such spices as those the queen of Sheba gave to King Solomon.

[10](The men of Hiram and the men of Solomon brought gold from Ophir; they also brought algumwood[b] and precious stones. [11]The king used the algumwood to make steps for the temple of the LORD and for the royal palace, and to make harps and lyres for the musicians. Nothing like them had ever been seen in Judah.)

[12]King Solomon gave the queen of Sheba all she desired and asked for; he gave her more than she had brought to him. Then she left and returned with her retinue to her own country.

[13]The weight of the gold that Solomon received yearly was 666 talents,[c] [14]not including the revenues brought in by merchants and traders. Also all the kings of Arabia and the governors of the land brought gold and silver to Solomon.

[15]King Solomon made two hundred large shields of hammered gold; six hundred bekas[d] of hammered gold went into each shield. [16]He also made three hundred small shields of hammered gold, with three hundred bekas[e] of gold in each shield. The king put them in the Palace of the Forest of Lebanon.

[17]Then the king made a great throne inlaid with ivory and overlaid with pure gold. [18]The throne had six steps, and a footstool of gold was attached to it. On both sides of the seat were armrests, with a lion standing beside each of them. [19]Twelve lions stood on the six steps, one at either end of each step. Nothing like it had ever been made for any other kingdom. [20]All King Solomon's goblets were gold, and all the household articles in the Palace of the Forest of Lebanon were pure gold. Nothing was made of silver, because silver was considered of little value in Solomon's day. [21]The king had a fleet of trading ships[f] manned by Hiram's[g] men. Once every three years it returned, carrying gold, silver and ivory, and apes and baboons.

[a]*9* That is, about 4 1/2 tons (about 4 metric tons) [b]*10* Probably a variant of *almugwood* [c]*13* That is, about 25 tons (about 23 metric tons) [d]*15* That is, about 7 1/2 pounds (about 3.5 kilograms) [e]*16* That is, about 3 3/4 pounds (about 1.7 kilograms) [f]*21* Hebrew *of ships that could go to Tarshish* [g]*21* Hebrew *Huram,* a variant of *Hiram*

NRSV

Because your God loved Israel and would establish them forever, he has made you king over them, that you may execute justice and righteousness." [9]Then she gave the king one hundred twenty talents of gold, a very great quantity of spices, and precious stones: there were no spices such as those that the queen of Sheba gave to King Solomon.

10Moreover the servants of Huram and the servants of Solomon who brought gold from Ophir brought algum wood and precious stones. [11]From the algum wood, the king made steps[a] for the house of the LORD and for the king's house, lyres also and harps for the singers; there never was seen the like of them before in the land of Judah.

12Meanwhile King Solomon granted the queen of Sheba every desire that she expressed, well beyond what she had brought to the king. Then she returned to her own land, with her servants.

13The weight of gold that came to Solomon in one year was six hundred sixty-six talents of gold, [14]besides that which the traders and merchants brought; and all the kings of Arabia and the governors of the land brought gold and silver to Solomon. [15]King Solomon made two hundred large shields of beaten gold; six hundred shekels of beaten gold went into each large shield. [16]He made three hundred shields of beaten gold; three hundred shekels of gold went into each shield; and the king put them in the House of the Forest of Lebanon. [17]The king also made a great ivory throne, and overlaid it with pure gold. [18]The throne had six steps and a footstool of gold, which were attached to the throne, and on each side of the seat were arm rests and two lions standing beside the arm rests, [19]while twelve lions were standing, one on each end of a step on the six steps. The like of it was never made in any kingdom. [20]All King Solomon's drinking vessels were of gold, and all the vessels of the House of the Forest of Lebanon were of pure gold; silver was not considered as anything in the days of Solomon. [21]For the king's ships went to Tarshish with the servants of Huram; once every three years the ships of Tarshish used to come bringing gold, silver, ivory, apes, and peacocks.[b]

22Thus King Solomon excelled all the kings of

[a] Gk Vg: Meaning of Heb uncertain [b] Or *baboons*

NIV

[22]King Solomon was greater in riches and wisdom than all the other kings of the earth. [23]All the kings of the earth sought audience with Solomon to hear the wisdom God had put in his heart. [24]Year after year, everyone who came brought a gift—articles of silver and gold, and robes, weapons and spices, and horses and mules.

[25]Solomon had four thousand stalls for horses and chariots, and twelve thousand horses,[a] which he kept in the chariot cities and also with him in Jerusalem. [26]He ruled over all the kings from the River[b] to the land of the Philistines, as far as the border of Egypt. [27]The king made silver as common in Jerusalem as stones, and cedar as plentiful as sycamore-fig trees in the foothills. [28]Solomon's horses were imported from Egypt[c] and from all other countries.

[29]As for the other events of Solomon's reign, from beginning to end, are they not written in the records of Nathan the prophet, in the prophecy of Ahijah the Shilonite and in the visions of Iddo the seer concerning Jeroboam son of Nebat? [30]Solomon reigned in Jerusalem over all Israel forty years. [31]Then he rested with his fathers and was buried in the city of David his father. And Rehoboam his son succeeded him as king.

[a]*25* Or *charioteers* [b]*26* That is, the Euphrates [c]*28* Or possibly *Muzur,* a region in Cilicia

NRSV

the earth in riches and in wisdom. [23]All the kings of the earth sought the presence of Solomon to hear his wisdom, which God had put into his mind. [24]Every one of them brought a present, objects of silver and gold, garments, weaponry, spices, horses, and mules, so much year by year. [25]Solomon had four thousand stalls for horses and chariots, and twelve thousand horses, which he stationed in the chariot cities and with the king in Jerusalem. [26]He ruled over all the kings from the Euphrates to the land of the Philistines, and to the border of Egypt. [27]The king made silver as common in Jerusalem as stone, and cedar as plentiful as the sycamore of the Shephelah. [28]Horses were imported for Solomon from Egypt and from all lands.

29Now the rest of the acts of Solomon, from first to last, are they not written in the history of the prophet Nathan, and in the prophecy of Ahijah the Shilonite, and in the visions of the seer Iddo concerning Jeroboam son of Nebat? [30]Solomon reigned in Jerusalem over all Israel forty years. [31]Solomon slept with his ancestors and was buried in the city of his father David; and his son Rehoboam succeeded him.

COMMENTARY

The account of Solomon's reign draws to a close with an emphasis on his wealth, wisdom, and international fame. As far as 9:28, the narrative has been largely a straightforward transcription of 1 Kgs 9:26–10:29. What was the point of copying out so much material? The only other king for whom such details of wealth are given is Hezekiah (32:27-29). His international fame also aligns him with Solomon (32:23). In Hezekiah's case, wealth and fame illustrate God-given success or prosperity that accrued to him after having sought the Lord by observing the Torah (31:21; 32:30). Prosperity that follows obedience implicitly ties the present section into the overall presentation of Solomon's reign in 2 Chronicles. The same verb used in the Hezekiah account (הצליח *hiṣlîaḥ*, in the hiphil) occurs in the programmatic 1 Chr 22:13: Solomon would "prosper" or "succeed" if he observed the Torah. This condition was elevated into a stipulation for guaranteeing the dynasty in 1 Chr 28:7. This section, as does the preceding one, answers with a resounding yes the vital question of whether the king obeyed the Torah (cf. 11:17; 12:1). Not only did he carry out the other, specific stipulation of building the Temple (1 Chr 22:11; 2 Chr 7:11), but also in this general area he set the dynasty on a permanent foundation, as was also affirmed in 2 Chr 1:1-13. The chronicler has framed his account of Solomon's reign with this good news, in elaboration of his preliminary claim in 1 Chr 29:23.

Solomon's maritime ventures appear at the circumference and center of 8:17–9:21 (8:17-18; 9:10, 21). They present an exotic backdrop to the narrative, especially for Judean landlubbers who, throughout most of their history, had no direct territorial access to the sea. The sea and ships are balanced by the mention of land (9:5, 11-12, 14) and overland caravans, and this theme is generalized in 9:22-28 ("earth," vv. 22-23; "land," v. 26; "lands," v. 28). A term that cascades through 8:17–9:21 is "gold": how much gold Solomon received and from whom, to what uses he put it in the Temple. The chronicler emphasizes unique elements that distinguish Solomon's reign (cf. 1:12; 1 Chr 29:25). Exuberant denials minister to this theme. There was nothing Solomon could not explain to the queen of Sheba (9:2). No breath was left in her, so breathtaking were Solomon's wisdom and flair (9:4). Statements of the same type appear in 9:9, 11, 19-20.

Use of the word "all" also underlines the magnificence of Solomon's reign. The beginning and end of the narrative concerning the queen of Sheba is especially so marked. Wise Solomon listened to all her questions and could answer them all (9:1*b*-2). He gave her everything she wanted (9:12). The word "all" also forms a frame for the next passage, 9:13-21, in 9:14, and 20. The final passage, 9:22-28, even more stresses this element, at the beginning, the middle, and the end: 9:22-23, "all the kings of the earth"; 9:26, "all the kings"; and 9:28, "all lands."

Both wealth and wisdom are featured, as 9:22 summarizes. The definition of wisdom as God's gift in 9:23 echoes the endowment in the theophany in 1:11-12. Whereas in 2:12 it was diverted to the service of the Temple, here such wisdom returns to its initial regal setting. The emphasis placed on wisdom in the story of the queen of Sheba (9:22-23) illustrates the Lord's spectacular blessing on Solomon's reign.

8:17–9:12. In its context, "house" (9:3 NRSV) refers to the "palace" (NIV), rather than the Temple. The context also makes it a little more likely that the "burnt offerings" in the Temple, which the English versions envision in 9:4, (adopting the reading of the ancient versions and of the parallel 1 Kgs 10:5), should be rejected in favor of the MT's reference to "the procession with which he went up" to the Temple (TNK; cf. NIV). A characteristic change is made at 9:8. Israel's throne (1 Kgs 10:9) becomes the throne of God (cf. 13:8; 1 Chr 17:14; 28:5; 29:23). Solomon in all his glory had no independent role but was the Lord's viceroy, pointing beyond himself to the divine rule for whose final establishment on earth the chronicler yearned (1 Chr 16:31). The queen's reference to Solomon's reign as evidence of God's love for Israel matches Huram's testimony in 2:11. Whether the phrase "to uphold them" is a part of the original text or is a later addition is debatable, but the phrase does represent a thought high on the agenda of 2 Chronicles: The permanent dynastic covenant brought a payoff for the people of God. In its permanence, they enjoyed their own and found a warranty of the Lord's continuing purposes for Israel and so of their eventual vindication.

The translations of 9:12 in both the NRSV and the NIV are doubtful. The text seems to refer to Solomon's gifts of exotic articles, far different from the type of gifts brought by the queen. It represents a misunderstanding of "besides what he gave her according to king Solomon's [generous] hand" in 1 Kgs 10:13 as "besides what she gave into the hand of king Solomon (נתנה ביד *nātĕnâ bĕyad* in place of נתן-לה כיד *nātan-lāh kĕyad*))."[224]

9:13-21. The text of v. 14 probably reflects the already corrupted MT of 1 Kgs 10:15 (the NIV ["revenues"] implicitly and the REB ["tolls"] explicitly have emended the awkward אנשי [ʾ*anšê*, "men"] to ענשי [ʿ*onšê*).[225] The amount of gold used for each type of ceremonial shield in vv. 15-16 is represented in 1 Kgs 10:16-17 as 600 shekels for each large, body-length shield and three minas for each small round shield. The unit of weight is not expressed in the first case, but common use requires shekels. Here the weights are given as 600 and 300 shekels respectively (NRSV). The NIV of 1 Kgs 10:16 and 2 Chr 9:15-16 has assumed that the unexpressed unit of weight is the beka, or half shekel. This produces a solution for the discrepancy, since a mina is fifty shekels, and so three minas are 150 shekels, or 300 bekas. Dillard has rightly judged the harmonization ingenious, but not conforming to standard use; he

224. D. Barthélemy et al., *Critique textuelle de l'Ancien Testament,* OBO 50/1 (Fribourg: Editions Universitaires; and Göttingen: Vandenhoeck & Ruprecht, 1982) 1:488.

225. So *BHS.* See ibid., 1:358-59.

prefers to think in terms of a heavy mina of 100 shekels.[226]

Solomon's throne, "inlaid with ivory" (v. 17) and overlaid with gold, had "the top . . . rounded in the back" according to 1 Kgs 10:19 (NRSV), but in v. 18 a "footstool" is "attached" to it. Of the two textual differences involved, the second probably reflects an indistinct text in the chronicler's source, but there is no convincing reason for the first.[227] In v. 21, the royal fleet is presumably that based in the Red Sea port of Ezion-geber (8:17). Mention of Tarshish as a destination is embarrassing; it is mentioned as a Mediterranean port elsewhere in the OT. The writer of 1 Kgs 10:22 speaks simply of "ships of Tarshish," in the sense of large oceangoing vessels. The chronicler's change, reflected in the NRSV, suggests that the chronicler knew less than we do about the location of Tarshish. The NIV's rendering is a harmonization with the parallel text.

9:22-28. The mention of "weaponry" or "weapons" in v. 24 is more likely a reference to "perfumes" (REB), as the LXX rendered it. The association with spices favors this explanation. Verse 25*a* reflects an abandoning of the parallel 1 Kgs 10:26*a* in favor of 1 Kgs 4:26, except that the 40,000 horse stalls are 4,000 here. The change is bound up with the chronicler's choice to make use of 1 Kgs 10:26*a* in 2 Chr 1:14. A numerical progression is assumed, so that Solomon had more stalls/chariots at the end of his reign than at the beginning. Another deviation from the parent text occurs in v. 26, which reflects an insertion from 1 Kgs 4:21*a*. The chronicler sometimes uses Solomonic material at different points. Here the added material provides an impressive generalization for the close of Solomon's reign. Moreover, it ministers to the element of comprehensiveness that pervades this paragraph. Verses 26*b*-28 (parallel to 1 Kgs 10:27-29) have already been used in 1:14*b*-17. The repetition seems to be more a matter of rhetoric than of redaction, providing a roughly parallel framework for Solomon's reign.[228] So v. 28 does not repeat the details of the source but gives the gist, adapting it stylistically to the context by mentioning "all lands."

9:29-31. The epilogue makes use of the end of 1 Kings 11. There is a blatant jump from 1 Kgs 10:29. Every commentator, given the chance to put one question to the chronicler, would choose to interrogate him on his omission of the deuteronomist's negative material concerning Solomon in 1 Kgs 11:1-40. In both 9:29 and 10:15, the chronicler reflects the prophet Ahijah's oracle of judgment in 1 Kgs 11:29-40, though the chronicler blames Rehoboam for the division of the kingdom. The omission contrasts with the condemnation of Solomon's sin in marrying foreign women in Neh 13:26 as a supporting argument against a post-exilic practice. The chronicler evidently sided with the leading figures in Judah who had engaged in mixed marriages (see Ezra 9:2), or at least regarded intermarriage as permissible in his own later time. He refers to the practice without qualm in the course of his history (1 Chr 2:3, 17, 34-35; 3:1; 4:17; 7:14; 8:8; 2 Chr 2:14; 8:11; 12:13; 24:26). While he was bitterly opposed to foreign alliances, he does not seem to have felt so strongly about foreign marriages. Only such acts by northern royalty provoked his anger (18:1; 21:6; 22:2-3, 10) as a threat to the Davidic dynasty.

The chronicler appears to have been motivated by two factors: his opposition to the rigorism advocated by Ezra and Nehemiah as a policy for his own period, and his theological contention that Solomon was not guilty of alleged apostasy but had met the requirements laid down for the perpetuation of the dynasty. In his story, Solomon did nothing to threaten this consequence. Special grace was given him by the Lord (see the Commentary on 1 Chr 29:19). The king rode into a golden sunset, his double mission accomplished in the building of the Temple and the securing of the dynasty (13:5-8; 21:7). The chronicler leaned heavily on 2 Samuel 7 (= 1 Chronicles 17) and 1 Kings 1–10, which consistently share his conviction that Solomon discharged his obligations and guaranteed the dynasty.[229] So he considered himself justified in silencing the discordant voice of 1 Kings 11, just as he dropped one of the two traditions concerning forced labor.

The epilogue to Solomon's reign is adapted

226. R. B. Dillard, *2 Chronicles,* WBC 15 (Waco, Tex.: Word, 1987) 73.

227. See S. L. McKenzie, *The Chronicler's Use of the Deuteronomistic History,* HSM 33 (Atlanta: Scholars Press, 1985) 98.

228. S. J. De Vries, *1 and 2 Chronicles,* FOTL 11 (Grand Rapids: Eerdmans, 1989) 238.

229. Baruch Halpern, *The Constitution of the Monarchy in Israel,* HSM 25 (Chico, Calif.: Scholar's Press, 1981) 40.

from 1 Kgs 11:41-43. Here the chronicler refers to 1 Kings in terms of prophetic announcement, with the initial involvement of Nathan (1 Kings 1) and the final prophecy of Ahijah (1 Kgs 11:29-39). According to Josephus, "Iddo," who prophesied about Rehoboam's rival Jeroboam, was the name of the anonymous prophet of 1 Kgs 13:1-10.[230] The last reference was important to the chronicler, since it affirmed the continuation of the Davidic dynasty and the importance of the Temple in Jerusalem as Israel's religious center (1 Kgs 13:2; cf. 1 Kgs 13:32). Like Ahijah's oracle, it dealt primarily with Jeroboam, but also provided a comment on his picture of Solomon. The chronicler understood the reign of Solomon from a prophetic perspective, as he did that of David (1 Chr 29:29). The later view of Joshua–Kings as the Former Prophets is anticipated here. The chronicler stood foursquare on the foundation of the Law and the Prophets, faithful to the revelation associated with Moses, on the one hand, and with David and Solomon, on the other.

230. Josephus *Antiquities of the Jews* VIII.8.5 231.

REFLECTIONS

1. The picture of Solomon in all his glory, master of land and sea, ruling over an independent, enlarged Israel and receiving tribute and respect from the kings of the earth must have aroused nostalgia in the chronicler's post-exilic constituency. The chronicler mainly used Solomon's glory as a window through which to view a theological truth. It was proof of the Lord's love for Israel (9:8*b*), an affirmation that the anticipatory declaration in 2:11 shows to be crucial for the chronicler. It laid a foundation for Israel's security and brought guarantees to the dynasty and so to the Lord's covenant with Israel, since Israel was heir to the permanent royal covenant.

In turn the faith of Christian believers is continually strengthened as they remind themselves of the guarantees God has given in Christ. God's love, revealed through Jesus, has embraced generations of Christians (John 17:20, 23). The love of God in Christ is so strong that nothing can separate us from it (Rom 8:35-39). The work of Christ mediates God's love and guarantees for the church the success already told in the resurrection and ascension of Christ (Eph 2:4-7). The Lord's purpose of establishing Israel forever was a concept Paul took seriously, wrestling with it in Romans 9–11 and finally affirming it.

2. Also evident in this narrative of Solomon's royal glory is an eschatological dimension. Here the kingdom of God (9:8*a*) was glimpsed, and so the veil of the future was drawn back when, as the prophets encouraged the chronicler to believe, God's king would "be great to the ends of the earth" (Mic 5:4 NRSV; cf. 2 Chr 20:20). Solomon's establishment of justice and righteousness within Israel's frontiers (9:8*b*) prefigured the just society to be set up by the coming Davidic king (see 1 Chr 16:3; 18:14; Isa 9:7; 11:1-5). Indeed, royal tribute from Sheba was promised in one of the royal psalms (Ps 72:10, 15), which already in the post-exilic psalter was imbued with hope: "Let all kings pay him homage" was the hope set in the Davidic dynasty (Ps 72:11 REB).

The reader of the first Gospel is familiar with prodigious history of this type. The magi from the east brought gifts of gold, frankincense, and myrrh to the infant Jesus in homage to him in his role as King of the Jews (Matt 2:1-11). Implicit in Matthew's account is a fulfillment of Psalm 72 and the related Isa 60:5-6. It was an anticipatory fulfillment, just as the triumphal entry of Jesus proclaimed his kingship in principle (Matt 21:1-11). Something even greater than Solomon was manifested in Christ, which so many of Jesus' generation could not see, though the queen of Sheba had recognized Solomon's worth (Matt 12:42 NRSV). For both the chronicler and Christians, eschatology puts the present into perspective and challenges its limitations with ideals to work for.

3. The chronicler's discriminating dependence on the Law and the Prophets is attested in this section. The ancient texts spoke to him with religious authority. The church is called to study a larger canon of Scripture and to make it their own in a modern age that has experienced a crisis of authority in so many ways. The chronicler invites us to follow in his tracks, assuring us from his productive example that the human mind is not thereby locked passively into thinking about the past but may find stimulation for creative theological reflection.

4. Solomon's wisdom plays a prime role as the object of the queen's adulation. The resumption of this motif on a wider scale in 9:22-23 gives the chronicler the opportunity to affirm a truth associated with 1:1-12: The wisdom of Solomon was a divine gift, and so credit for it must go to the Lord. Since Solomon is the "patron saint" of wisdom in the Old Testament, it is not surprising that this divine origination is also found in the wisdom literature, notably at Prov 2:6, "The LORD gives wisdom;/ from his mouth come knowledge and understanding" (NRSV). The virtues so prized in wisdom teaching, one's own experience and learning from the experience of others, were the very means by which the Lord communicated truth and provided answers to perplexing questions that life poses. In the New Testament, Solomon's gift is offered in principle to all believers: "If any of you is lacking in wisdom, ask God . . . and it will be given you" (Jas 1:5 NRSV).

2 CHRONICLES 10:1–28:27

THE DIVIDED KINGDOM

OVERVIEW

These chapters make up the third block of the chronicler's history: the period of the divided kingdom. A new age marked by a permanent dynasty and temple worship had been inaugurated in the reigns of David and Solomon (7:10). The continued enjoyment of these privileges by the southern kingdom and their forfeiture by the northern kingdom are affirmed in a royal speech in 13:5-12. The dynastic privilege is reaffirmed at a significant moment of threat in 21:7, whose passing is celebrated at 23:3. Davidic kingship was restored against all odds, and its survival then spelled hope thereafter.

David and Solomon function as role models (11:17). The reigns of the kings of Judah are used in this literary block to illustrate the spiritual principle propounded to Solomon by David, the principle of seeking rather than forsaking the Lord (1 Chr 28:9), which finds full expression in 15:2. Such normative spirituality is worked out with reference to both the Temple and the Torah, maintaining the worship and fabric of the Temple and complying with the guidelines of the Torah. These obligations, previously the two conditions for the establishment of the dynasty, now operate as criteria for blessing or bane for successive Judean kings. Blessing shows itself in the gift of children, building operations, and victory over invaders, while military defeat, illness, and premature death are reaped by sinners.

The Temple was built not only for worship but also for prayer in time of trouble. Judah's kings, like any believer, needed the sort of help outlined in 7:14. God's help comes into operation in chaps. 12; 15 (momentarily); and 20 and, surprisingly, in the northern kingdom in chap. 28. However, appropriate human humility is tragically missing in the pride exhibited in chaps. 25–26.

The varying levels of virtue and vice registered in the kings' lives seem to function as royal versions of the successive scenarios listed in Ezekiel 18: a good king, a bad king, a good king who degenerates, and a sinning king who reforms. The principle of each generation's standing or falling on its own showing, which Ezekiel attested, also finds explicit illustration in these chapters, signaled by the chronicler's phrase "the God of one's fathers" or predecessors.

The ecumenical ideal cherished by the chronicler is particularly evident at both the beginning and the end of this literary block. The status of the two kingdoms as "brothers" before the Lord is affirmed in chaps. 11 and 28. Yet their roles become skewed. The people of the north, the straying sheep of the family of God in chap. 13, become models of restoration and reconciliation in chap. 28. Conversely, the people of the south, pillars of orthodoxy in chap. 13, degenerate into religious apostasy in chap. 28. This leveling was the chronicler's challenge to the separatism of post-exilic Judah.

The text falls into six units: (1) lessons from Rehoboam's reign, 10:1–12:26; (2) three examples of trust, 13:1–16:14; (3) lessons of fellowship with the Lord from Jehoshaphat's reign, 17:1–21:1*a*; (4) the averting of a threat to the Davidic dynasty, 21:1*b*–23:21; (5) three examples of good kings who became apostate, 24:1–26:23; and (6) examples of a good king and a bad king, 27:1–28:27.

2 CHRONICLES 10:1–12:16, REHOBOAM'S CHECKERED REIGN

OVERVIEW

Rehoboam's reign is presented as a spiritual roller coaster. First, he plunges deep into failure. His immature folly is responsible for the loss of most of his kingdom. The only good that emerges from the disaster is that the Lord is glorified by vindication of an earlier prophetic word. The king's paying heed to another prophetic revelation is made the basis of a high period of blessing. Then he falls into apostasy and experiences further loss. A third prophetic intervention brings a challenge that is heeded, and utter disaster is averted. Prophecy is assigned a role in each of the three sections of the chronicler's narrative of the reign of Rehoboam. This prophetic message was addressed to his contemporaries, that they heed God's written prophetic revelation and, for their own good, apply to their own lives its challenge and warning as an alternative to experiencing its judgment.

2 Chronicles 10:1-19, The King Who Would Not Listen

NIV

10 Rehoboam went to Shechem, for all the Israelites had gone there to make him king. 2When Jeroboam son of Nebat heard this (he was in Egypt, where he had fled from King Solomon), he returned from Egypt. 3So they sent for Jeroboam, and he and all Israel went to Rehoboam and said to him: 4"Your father put a heavy yoke on us, but now lighten the harsh labor and the heavy yoke he put on us, and we will serve you."

5Rehoboam answered, "Come back to me in three days." So the people went away.

6Then King Rehoboam consulted the elders who had served his father Solomon during his lifetime. "How would you advise me to answer these people?" he asked.

7They replied, "If you will be kind to these people and please them and give them a favorable answer, they will always be your servants."

8But Rehoboam rejected the advice the elders gave him and consulted the young men who had grown up with him and were serving him. 9He asked them, "What is your advice? How should we answer these people who say to me, 'Lighten the yoke your father put on us'?"

10The young men who had grown up with him replied, "Tell the people who have said to you, 'Your father put a heavy yoke on us, but make

NRSV

10 Rehoboam went to Shechem, for all Israel had come to Shechem to make him king. 2When Jeroboam son of Nebat heard of it (for he was in Egypt, where he had fled from King Solomon), then Jeroboam returned from Egypt. 3They sent and called him; and Jeroboam and all Israel came and said to Rehoboam, 4"Your father made our yoke heavy. Now therefore lighten the hard service of your father and his heavy yoke that he placed on us, and we will serve you." 5He said to them, "Come to me again in three days." So the people went away.

6Then King Rehoboam took counsel with the older men who had attended his father Solomon while he was still alive, saying, "How do you advise me to answer this people?" 7They answered him, "If you will be kind to this people and please them, and speak good words to them, then they will be your servants forever." 8But he rejected the advice that the older men gave him, and consulted the young men who had grown up with him and now attended him. 9He said to them, "What do you advise that we answer this people who have said to me, 'Lighten the yoke that your father put on us'?" 10The young men who had grown up with him said to him, "Thus should you speak to the people who said to you, 'Your father

NIV

our yoke lighter'—tell them, 'My little finger is thicker than my father's waist. 11My father laid on you a heavy yoke; I will make it even heavier. My father scourged you with whips; I will scourge you with scorpions.'"

12Three days later Jeroboam and all the people returned to Rehoboam, as the king had said, "Come back to me in three days." 13The king answered them harshly. Rejecting the advice of the elders, 14he followed the advice of the young men and said, "My father made your yoke heavy; I will make it even heavier. My father scourged you with whips; I will scourge you with scorpions." 15So the king did not listen to the people, for this turn of events was from God, to fulfill the word the LORD had spoken to Jeroboam son of Nebat through Ahijah the Shilonite.

16When all Israel saw that the king refused to listen to them, they answered the king:

"What share do we have in David,
what part in Jesse's son?
To your tents, O Israel!
Look after your own house, O David!"

So all the Israelites went home. 17But as for the Israelites who were living in the towns of Judah, Rehoboam still ruled over them.

18King Rehoboam sent out Adoniram,[a] who was in charge of forced labor, but the Israelites stoned him to death. King Rehoboam, however, managed to get into his chariot and escape to Jerusalem. 19So Israel has been in rebellion against the house of David to this day.

a18 Hebrew *Hadoram,* a variant of *Adoniram*

NRSV

made our yoke heavy, but you must lighten it for us'; tell them, 'My little finger is thicker than my father's loins. 11Now, whereas my father laid on you a heavy yoke, I will add to your yoke. My father disciplined you with whips, but I will discipline you with scorpions.'"

12So Jeroboam and all the people came to Rehoboam the third day, as the king had said, "Come to me again the third day." 13The king answered them harshly. King Rehoboam rejected the advice of the older men; 14he spoke to them in accordance with the advice of the young men, "My father made your yoke heavy, but I will add to it; my father disciplined you with whips, but I will discipline you with scorpions." 15So the king did not listen to the people, because it was a turn of affairs brought about by God so that the LORD might fulfill his word, which he had spoken by Ahijah the Shilonite to Jeroboam son of Nebat.

16When all Israel saw that the king would not listen to them, the people answered the king,

"What share do we have in David?
We have no inheritance in the son of Jesse.
Each of you to your tents, O Israel!
Look now to your own house, O David."

So all Israel departed to their tents. 17But Rehoboam reigned over the people of Israel who were living in the cities of Judah. 18When King Rehoboam sent Hadoram, who was taskmaster over the forced labor, the people of Israel stoned him to death. King Rehoboam hurriedly mounted his chariot to flee to Jerusalem. 19So Israel has been in rebellion against the house of David to this day.

COMMENTARY

The chronicler used from the 1 Kings account a contrast between Rehoboam's refusal to listen to the people, mentioned twice in 10:15-16, and his and Judah's willingness to listen to the Lord in 11:4 ("They listened to the word of the Lord," REB). In each case the verb שמע (*šāma'*) is used. The prophet's name, Shemaiah, in 11:2 must have suggested to the chronicler the sense of "listening to the LORD," and so it accentuates the contrast.

The chronicler follows the MT of 1 Kgs 12:1-19 closely. Scholars disagree over the role of Jeroboam in the original form of the 1 Kings narrative and whether its present text is the result of assimilation to the Chronicles form of the story. Whether the chronicler was the first to push Jeroboam to the fore or not, his interest in the rival king was not his culpability, at this stage at least, but as a historical sequel to Ahijah's prophecy concerning Jeroboam in 9:29, which finds a subsequent echo at 10:15. Jeroboam's seizure of power on justifiable grounds had been predicted by the Lord. The chronicler omitted 1 Kgs 12:20 because of the redundancy of its first half and because political information about the northern kingdom is filtered out as much as possible in this book.

The section begins with Rehoboam's expectation of becoming king over "all Israel" (v. 1), which in 1 Kgs 12:1 meant the northern tribes, but here signifies all twelve. His reign concludes with a report about his reign over Judah (v. 17). So ended an eighty-year-old bond between king and unified nation (cf. 9:30; 1 Chr 29:26-27). The chronicler does not let the shattering of this ideal pass without comment, but makes small adaptations later in the narrative to express his viewpoint.

10:1-14. The coronation at Shechem never took place. The people, weary of conscription and subscription to Solomon's projects, laid down conditions, which delayed the ceremony. Wisely, Rehoboam consulted Solomon's counselors. Foolishly, he rejected their counsel of conciliation, preferring the tough policy urged by his contemporaries. The royal wisdom of chap. 9 is conspicuous by its absence. The divine purpose that the monarchy should minister to the people's interests, advocated in 9:8 and in 1 Chr 14:2, finds no place now. The chronicler cannot stomach the two references to the king's serving the people in 1 Kgs 12:7, replacing them in v. 7 with a reference to treating them kindly and pleasing them. In fact, the omission of "today" (1 Kgs 12:7) advocates a policy, not of temporary blandishment, but of permanent benevolence.

10:15. The word of the Lord had dominated David's coronation in 1 Chr 11:1-3, 10; 12:23 in a positive way. Here the Lord's word controls the absence of a coronation for Rehoboam, providing a framework for the coronation narrative (vv. 1-15*a*) at 9:29 and 10:15*b*. The chronicler retains without explanation the theological comment that the Lord's prophetic revelation was realized. The narrative in 1 Kgs 11:29-39 is more lucid, but one can read into the present reference only Ahijah's prediction that Jeroboam would reign over ten of Israel's tribes. In 1 Kings that prediction constitutes a reprisal for Solomon's wrongdoing, whereas the chronicler's concern in his presentation of Solomon's reign was to avoid such negative factors, so that the accusation in v. 4, with which he could hardly dispense, now stands in tension with his earlier account. God's prediction is here a reprisal for Rehoboam's willful folly. The chronicler's propensity for giving a clean slate to each generation, and so control over its own destiny, favors this explanation, though some adaptation of the language of 1 Kgs 12:15 might have made it clearer. Ironically, Rehoboam had more power in his "little finger" (v. 10) than even he realized. The resumption of v. 15*a* in v. 16*a* shows how the divine purpose was realized in human experience.

This expression of the divine will has an overarching function in the narrative. At 1 Chr 10:14, mention was made of the Lord's turning Saul's kingdom over to David. Similar language was used in 1 Chr 12:23, with a reference to the Lord's predictive word. A noun relating to the verb used there occurs here: "It was a turn of affairs brought about by God" (NRSV). These parallel statements isolate the reigns of David and Solomon from earlier and later history. Prophets bore witness that they constituted a special period. With David's accession, the outgoing tide turned and brought special revelation on its crest. With Solomon's death, the tide turned again. It left on Israel's shores three witnesses to God's dynamic will: the Temple, the Davidic dynasty, and, in memory at least, the union of God's people. The Temple that stood in the chronicler's day had been rebuilt on the same site as the First Temple and had the same validity as its predecessor. Restoration of the dynasty and a united people belonged to his vision of a divinely ordered future.

10:16-19. To this last ideal the chronicler testifies in v. 17 (cf. 11:3) in referring to "the people of Israel who were living in the cities of Judah." They matched "the people of Israel" in the north (v. 18).[231] He never forgot that twelve tribes, not two, were the Lord's ideal. He was implicitly calling for a halt to the separatism of Ezra and Nehemiah.

Rehoboam underestimated the power of his constituents. Their anti-Davidic slogan (v. 16) functions as a reversal of the affirmation of loyalty in 1 Chr 12:18. With one stroke he had undone the achievement of David and decimated his subjects. Still expecting business as usual, he dispatched the administrator of national conscription.

231. See H. G. M. Williamson, *Israel in the Books of Chronicles* (Cambridge: Cambridge University Press, 1977) 108-10.

His lynching forced him, so rigidly standing on his dignity hitherto, to retreat to the safety of Jerusalem.[232] He "managed to get into his chariot and escape" (NIV). The northern kingdom's rebellion against the Davidic dynasty remained an unresolved issue. Sadly, the chronicler had no reason to correct the time limit of 1 Kgs 12:19, "to this day." The renunciation of David's house reverberated through the centuries—but would not be forever, the chronicler hoped and prayed.

232. See L. Koehler and W. Baumgartner, *The Hebrew and Aramaic Lexicon of the Old Testament* (Leiden: Brill, 1994) 1:65.

REFLECTIONS

The text sides with the rejected counsel of Solomon's old advisers and so with the people's demand for their national burdens to be lightened. We can understand the chronicler's reluctance to reflect on the significance of this demand to Solomon's reign. Not even the deuteronomist gave a clear lead in this respect. For both historians, it carried a message about the new reign, the folly of inexperience that refuses conciliation and blunders into alienation. Power went to Rehoboam's head, and he listened to advice to put his foot down from the start, as if he were a novice schoolteacher. He lacked respect for those over whom he had been given authority. His threats were an overreaction born of insecurity. He heard the weary people's conditions as threats to his power and reacted with counterthreats. Power was misconstrued as force to be exercised "harshly" (10:13) without regard for human feelings or any real understanding of the situation. The chapter should be required reading for persons embarking on new tasks involving authority over others.

Rehoboam's brash threat to increase his subjects' yoke contrasts with the offer Jesus made to the weary and burdened: "Take my yoke upon you and learn from me . . . for I am gentle and humble in heart, and you will find rest for your souls. For my yoke is easy, and my burden is light" (Matt 11:29-30). The tension between challenge and assurance is a delicate one for pastors and church authorities to hold in balance. The Scylla of a lax attitude with regard to the spiritual and moral lives of members is as reprehensible as the Charybdis of tyranny that some groups exercise over their adherents. This passage is concerned with the Charybdis, just as in religious terms the yoke of the Torah is deplored in Acts 15:10. More generally, and with a different metaphor, lording it over the flock is deprecated in 1 Pet 5:3, an echo of Ezek 34:4. Yet there must be a yoke. The invitation of Jesus spoke not only of rest but also of discipline, learning to change the way we would otherwise live.

2 Chronicles 11:1-23, Strength from Listening

NIV

11 When Rehoboam arrived in Jerusalem, he mustered the house of Judah and Benjamin—a hundred and eighty thousand fighting men—to make war against Israel and to regain the kingdom for Rehoboam.
2But this word of the LORD came to Shemaiah
the man of God: 3"Say to Rehoboam son of
Solomon king of Judah and to all the Israelites in
Judah and Benjamin, 4'This is what the LORD says:
Do not go up to fight against your brothers. Go
home, every one of you, for this is my doing.'"

NRSV

11 When Rehoboam came to Jerusalem, he assembled one hundred eighty thousand chosen troops of the house of Judah and Benjamin to fight against Israel, to restore the kingdom to
Rehoboam. 2But the word of the LORD came to
Shemaiah the man of God: 3Say to King Rehoboam of Judah, son of Solomon, and to all Israel
in Judah and Benjamin, 4"Thus says the LORD: You
shall not go up or fight against your kindred. Let
everyone return home, for this thing is from me."

NIV

So they obeyed the words of the LORD and turned
back from marching against Jeroboam.
5Rehoboam lived in Jerusalem and built up
towns for defense in Judah: 6Bethlehem, Etam,
Tekoa, 7Beth Zur, Soco, Adullam, 8Gath,
Mareshah, Ziph, 9Adoraim, Lachish, Azekah,
10Zorah, Aijalon and Hebron. These were fortified
cities in Judah and Benjamin. 11He strengthened
their defenses and put commanders in them, with
supplies of food, olive oil and wine. 12He put
shields and spears in all the cities, and made them
very strong. So Judah and Benjamin were his.
13The priests and Levites from all their districts
throughout Israel sided with him. 14The Levites
even abandoned their pasturelands and property,
and came to Judah and Jerusalem because
Jeroboam and his sons had rejected them as
priests of the LORD. 15And he appointed his own
priests for the high places and for the goat and
calf idols he had made. 16Those from every tribe
of Israel who set their hearts on seeking the LORD,
the God of Israel, followed the Levites to Jerusalem to offer sacrifices to the LORD, the God of
their fathers. 17They strengthened the kingdom of
Judah and supported Rehoboam son of Solomon
three years, walking in the ways of David and
Solomon during this time.
18Rehoboam married Mahalath, who was the
daughter of David's son Jerimoth and of Abihail,
the daughter of Jesse's son Eliab. 19She bore him
sons: Jeush, Shemariah and Zaham. 20Then he
married Maacah daughter of Absalom, who bore
him Abijah, Attai, Ziza and Shelomith. 21Re-
hoboam loved Maacah daughter of Absalom more
than any of his other wives and concubines. In
all, he had eighteen wives and sixty concubines,
twenty-eight sons and sixty daughters.
22Rehoboam appointed Abijah son of Maacah
to be the chief prince among his brothers, in order
to make him king. 23He acted wisely, dispersing
some of his sons throughout the districts of Judah
and Benjamin, and to all the fortified cities. He
gave them abundant provisions and took many
wives for them.

NRSV

So they heeded the word of the LORD and turned
back from the expedition against Jeroboam.
5Rehoboam resided in Jerusalem, and he built
cities for defense in Judah. 6He built up Bethlehem, Etam, Tekoa, 7Beth-zur, Soco, Adullam,
8Gath, Mareshah, Ziph, 9Adoraim, Lachish,
Azekah, 10Zorah, Aijalon, and Hebron, fortified
cities that are in Judah and in Benjamin. 11He
made the fortresses strong, and put commanders
in them, and stores of food, oil, and wine. 12He
also put large shields and spears in all the cities,
and made them very strong. So he held Judah
and Benjamin.
13The priests and the Levites who were in all
Israel presented themselves to him from all their
territories. 14The Levites had left their common
lands and their holdings and had come to Judah
and Jerusalem, because Jeroboam and his sons had
prevented them from serving as priests of the
LORD, 15and had appointed his own priests for the
high places, and for the goat-demons, and for the
calves that he had made. 16Those who had set
their hearts to seek the LORD God of Israel came
after them from all the tribes of Israel to Jerusalem
to sacrifice to the LORD, the God of their ancestors.
17They strengthened the kingdom of Judah, and
for three years they made Rehoboam son of Solomon secure, for they walked for three years in
the way of David and Solomon.
18Rehoboam took as his wife Mahalath daughter of Jerimoth son of David, and of Abihail
daughter of Eliab son of Jesse. 19She bore him
sons: Jeush, Shemariah, and Zaham. 20After her
he took Maacah daughter of Absalom, who bore
him Abijah, Attai, Ziza, and Shelomith. 21Re-
hoboam loved Maacah daughter of Absalom more
than all his other wives and concubines (he took
eighteen wives and sixty concubines, and became
the father of twenty-eight sons and sixty daughters). 22Rehoboam appointed Abijah son of Maacah
as chief prince among his brothers, for he intended to make him king. 23He dealt wisely, and
distributed some of his sons through all the districts of Judah and Benjamin, in all the fortified
cities; he gave them abundant provisions, and
found many wives for them.

COMMENTARY

Rehoboam had closed his ears to his northern constituents' demands for a lighter load. He responded to their cries of good riddance with an arrogant and vain dispatch of Hadoram. The lesson was not learned until 11:4, when king and southerners listened to a prophetic word and desisted from any attempt to take back the kingdom by force. In vv. 1-4 the text of 1 Kgs 12:21-24 is followed, but the chronicler makes it a preliminary to a receipt of blessing. By means of his extra narrative in vv. 5-23, he preaches a message to his contemporaries advocating obedience to the Lord's written prophetic word and offering incentives for so doing.

11:1-4. The intervention of Shemaiah is typical of prophetic behavior before a battle—inquiry about the military campaign's success (cf. 18:4-27; 25:7-8; 1 Chr 14:10, 14). Whereas Ahijah had pronounced judgment in advance on Rehoboam's highhandedness (10:15), here a new prophecy intrudes, banning Rehoboam's military reprisal. Just as that "turn of events was from God" (10:15 NIV), so also "this thing is from me," declares the Lord (v. 4). The division of the kingdom, and so Jeroboam's reign over the ten tribes, was God's will—for the moment at least. Civil war was not the answer. "Brothers" in the family of God were not to be treated as enemies. For the chronicler, this appeal to brotherhood had a special attraction. It belonged to his agenda for a complete Israel, to which he draws attention in v. 3 by importing a reference to Israel into 1 Kgs 10:23: "all Israel in Judah and Benjamin" (NRSV). The new southern kingdom was only a partial representation of the true Israel.

The king who would not hear what his constituents were saying now listens to the Lord. "The courage, flexibility and humility which were so urgently needed in the preceding episode suddenly appear here in full bloom."[233] Rehoboam's compliance with the divine will motivates three responses of divine blessing: vv. 5-12*a,* vv. 12*b*-17, and vv. 18-23. The first two responses have strength as their keynote, the strength of the fortified cities in vv. 11-12 and the strengthening of the kingdom by an influx of believers from the north in v. 17. In the third paragraph, the king's vigor in producing a huge family strikes a similar

233. S. Japhet, *I & II Chronicles,* OTL (Louisville: Westminster/John Knox, 1993) 660.

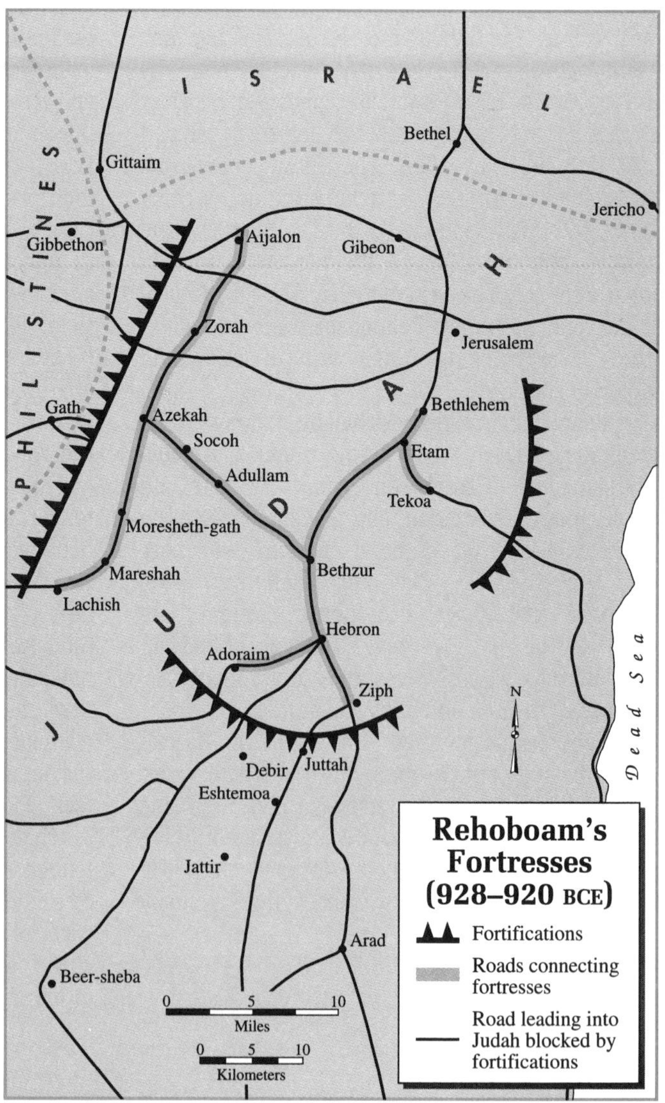

chord. In a retrospective summary he is described as strong. The chronicler's perspective at 12:1 is the same as that expressed in 16:9: The Lord's policy was to "strengthen those whose hearts are fully committed to him" (NIV). Rehoboam and the later Uzziah are a parallel pair of kings, obedient and strong in the early parts of their reigns (see 26:8, 15-16; cf. 27:6). Moreover, the three paragraphs are deliberately modeled on 1 Kgs 12:25–13:10; 14:1-18.[234] If Jeroboam resided in his own capital and built a frontier fortress, Rehoboam did likewise. If Jeroboam engaged in religious reforms and encountered adverse reactions to them, such reactions involved Judah too. If Jeroboam's royal house was cursed, Rehoboam's family was blessed, and an ordered succession was secured.

11:5-12a. It is generally acknowledged that in vv. 6-10*a* the chronicler had available a source other than 1 Kings: a list of Judah's military defenses. If it did originally relate to Rehoboam's reign, at least in part the list seems to reflect a period after Shishak's invasion in chap. 12. The lines of fortification were set up in the east, south, and west along important roads.[235] The northern side was left unprotected, either because the king anticipated no invasion from that quarter or because he expected to recover the lost territory to the north.

In the books of Chronicles, building operations symbolize God's blessing as a response to obedient behavior (see 8:2-6). The Lord was building and guarding through Rehoboam, on the principle of Ps 127:1: "Unless the LORD builds the house, those who build it labor in vain" (NRSV). The security of having a good defense system was not regarded as inconsistent with trust in God, a perspective that suits in principle the land-based theology of the OT. Elsewhere in the OT, prophets criticize the presence of military power in the OT as a sinister shift whereby it became a substitute object of faith (see Isa 31:1). Occasionally biblical perspectives clash. Hezekiah's defense measures against Assyria were, for Isaiah, evidence of a lack of faith, but they were proof of faith for the chronicler (Isa 22: 8*b*-11; 2 Chr 32:1-8).

11:12b-17. Verse 12*b* introduces the next paragraph.[236] Extra support was forthcoming from the north, initially in the form of religious personnel, who "sided with" Rehoboam. The chronicler deduces from Jeroboam's appointing of his own priesthood that the former ones who officiated at the Jerusalem Temple and lived in the northern kingdom had been expelled (cf. 13:9). The account of the division of the kingdom in chap. 10 had laid little, if any, blame on Jeroboam. Rehoboam had been the foolish villain and Jeroboam the divinely specified agent in an oracle of judgment (9:29; 10:15). Now the roles of saint and sinner are reversed. The role of sinner is even extended to all succeeding kings of the north, as "sons" in v. 14 appears to signify. Not only is the idolatrous interpretation of Jeroboam's calves taken over from the deuteronomist and Hosea (Hos 8:4-6; 10:5; 13:2), but also his pernicious innovations are intensified by a new mention of "goat-demons," an infringement of the Torah's prohibition at Lev 17:7. Priests and Levites defected to the south, prepared to lose their land holdings for the sake of maintaining their religious integrity (cf. 1 Chr 6:54-81; 13:2).

Whether the northern laity who came to Jerusalem to worship are meant as pilgrims or as immigrants is uncertain; the parallel of 15:9 suggests the latter. Verse 16 is redolent with the chronicler's language of religious faith. The Temple is recognized as the only "house of sacrifice" (7:12) authorized for worship of the Lord. People came to "seek" (בקשׁ *biqqēš*) the Lord, a term associated especially with going to the Temple. They "set their hearts" or "were resolved" (REB) to do so, a phrase used earlier at 1 Chr 22:19; 29:19 and part of the chronicler's vocabulary of spiritual zeal. Their devotion to "the God of their fathers" indicates the stand taken by this particular generation in converting their parents' faith into their own. The chronicler has in mind an ideal for his own day: the status of the Temple as a place of worship for all the tribes of Israel. He lavishes the riches of his spiritual vocabulary on northerners, hoping for an influx of northern pilgrims who recognize the Temple as God's ap-

234. Ibid., 663.

235. See Y. Aharoni, *The Land of the Bible: A Historical Geography,* trans. A. F. Rainey, 2nd rev. ed. (Philadelphia: Westminster, 1979) 330. For the dating and the strange order of place-names see H. G. M. Williamson, *1 and 2 Chronicles,* NCB (Grand Rapids: Eerdmans, 1982) 240-42.

236. P. R. Ackroyd, *I & II Chronicles, Ezra, Nehemiah,* Torch Bible (London: SCM, 1973) 128.

pointed sanctuary. In doing so, he appeals to his fellow Judeans to open their hearts to their neighbors.

The southern kingdom, bolstered by such northern saints, basked in the Lord's blessing. The early period of Rehoboam's reign is presented as a spiritual heyday. The three-year duration of security for the land (v. 17) appears to have been calculated by counting back from the fifth year of his reign (12:2) and by allowing one year for backsliding. The period allows room for the blessings of military defense and a family for Rehoboam. David and Solomon are portrayed as ideals of obedience. The chronicler conceives of a joint era of blessing, finding no room for the deuteronomist's toppling of Solomon from his pedestal of faith in 1 Kgs 11:4-6.

11:18-23. The third paragraph presents Rehoboam's enormous family as an implicit sign of divine blessing, in line with 1 Chr 25:5; 26:4-5; it accords with the reference to David's family in 1 Chr 14:3-7. Solomon's harem was passed over because of the sinister interpretation the deuteronomist had put on it. We have no parallel for the description of Rehoboam's family in 1 Kings, gleaning only the name of Abijah's mother, Maacah daughter of Absalom (1 Kgs 15:2), who now turns out to be the king's second wife. The list presumably came from a source at the chronicler's disposal.[237] This special material explains why the firstborn son did not become king, though Deut 21:15-17 was thereby contravened. The list obviously relates to Rehoboam's whole reign and has been placed here to fit the chronicler's agenda of obedience and blessing. The first wife was the king's second cousin, another grandchild of David. It is unlikely that the Absalom mentioned here as the father of Rehoboam's second wife was David's son; the link would have been expressed, as in v. 18. Another tradition about Abijah's mother is followed in 13:2 (see also 1 Kgs 15:10).[238] In ancient royal circles, sons of the harem were trained as civil and military leaders (v. 23). Family bonds ensured the loyalty of persons in high places, and so the king acted "wisely." At the end of the verse both the NIV and the NRSV have implicitly followed a common conjectural emendation made by textual critics.

237. S. L. McKenzie, *The Chronicler's Use of the Deuteronomistic History,* HSM 33 (Atlanta: Scholars Press, 1985) 89-90.

238. See Japhet, *I & II Chronicles,* 670-71.

Reflections

1. At the close of the account of the divided kingdom the chronicler shows that calling the people of the north "brothers" was a very important concern (28:8-15 NIV). His heart ached over a truncated people of God, as Paul's had over his unconverted Jewish brothers and sisters in Rom 9:1. Like Paul in Romans 9–11, the chronicler dreamed that one day God would be glorified by a reunited covenant people. The separated "brothers" of the north were "brothers" still and even potential saints, as the chronicler suggests with some irony in 11:16.

The New Testament bids us take the family relationship seriously in our treatment of fellow Christians (Matt 5:22; Rom 14:10, 21; 1 Thess 4:6-10; 1 John 3:17; 4:20-21; see also Acts 7:26). The chronicler's concern, however, translates less readily into fellowship within the local church, as most of these texts envision, but more into a wider fellowship of God's people that transcends denominational barriers. Recent overtures between evangelicals and Roman Catholics in the United States are a beautiful example of the melting of traditional antagonism.

2. This story of polygamy and concubinage, including Rehoboam's intent to make a son of his favorite wife his heir, strikes a discordant note for the modern reader. One must try to rise above cultural prejudices, even when they may seem well founded, and appreciate the concerns of the text. In the Old Testament, polygamy was an accepted form of marriage, and concubines did not lack legal rights. Indeed, Judaism has sometimes permitted polygamy for Jews residing in Muslim countries. In practice, economic factors probably made monogamy more expedient. However, the cultural ethos of polygamy is so ingrained in the Old Testament that the Lord is symbolically represented as having two wives in the allegory of Ezekiel 23 (see also Jer 3:6-10). Similarly, in the New Testament the cultural phenomenon of slavery can be used as a model for Christian service (Rom 6:16-22; Gal 5:13).

3. This particular text refers to God's gift of children. In the Old Testament fertility is traced directly back to God's providential blessing (see Job 10:8-12; Ps 139:13-15), while infertility is regarded as an unnatural and divinely wrought situation, as 1 Sam 1:6, 11 illustrates. Many people in the ancient world equated nature and deity, while Israel viewed nature as the arena by which the Lord's will was worked out. Too close and too remote a correlation between God and the natural world is dangerous, but that there is some relation is a necessary Christian belief, in tune with the biblical concept of God as creator and sustainer of the natural world. Parents rejoicing over a new baby respond to a wise spiritual instinct when they praise God for the gift.

2 Chronicles 12:1-16, Failure and a Fresh Start

NIV

12 After Rehoboam's position as king was established and he had become strong, he
and all Israel[a] with him abandoned the law of the
LORD. 2Because they had been unfaithful to the
LORD, Shishak king of Egypt attacked Jerusalem in
the fifth year of King Rehoboam. 3With twelve
hundred chariots and sixty thousand horsemen
and the innumerable troops of Libyans, Sukkites
and Cushites[b] that came with him from Egypt,
4he captured the fortified cities of Judah and came
as far as Jerusalem.

5Then the prophet Shemaiah came to Rehoboam and to the leaders of Judah who had
assembled in Jerusalem for fear of Shishak, and
he said to them, "This is what the LORD says, 'You
have abandoned me; therefore, I now abandon
you to Shishak.'"

6The leaders of Israel and the king humbled
themselves and said, "The LORD is just."

7When the LORD saw that they humbled themselves, this word of the LORD came to Shemaiah:
"Since they have humbled themselves, I will not
destroy them but will soon give them deliverance.
My wrath will not be poured out on Jerusalem
through Shishak. 8They will, however, become
subject to him, so that they may learn the difference between serving me and serving the kings
of other lands."

9When Shishak king of Egypt attacked Jerusalem, he carried off the treasures of the temple of

[a]*1* That is, Judah, as frequently in 2 Chronicles [b]*3* That is, people from the upper Nile region

NRSV

12 When the rule of Rehoboam was established and he grew strong, he abandoned
the law of the LORD, he and all Israel with him.
2In the fifth year of King Rehoboam, because they
had been unfaithful to the LORD, King Shishak of
Egypt came up against Jerusalem 3with twelve
hundred chariots and sixty thousand cavalry. A
countless army came with him from Egypt—Libyans, Sukkiim, and Ethiopians.[a] 4He took the fortified cities of Judah and came as far as Jerusalem.
5Then the prophet Shemaiah came to Rehoboam
and to the officers of Judah, who had gathered at
Jerusalem because of Shishak, and said to them,
"Thus says the LORD: You abandoned me, so I
have abandoned you to the hand of Shishak."
6Then the officers of Israel and the king humbled
themselves and said, "The LORD is in the right."
7When the LORD saw that they humbled themselves, the word of the LORD came to Shemaiah,
saying: "They have humbled themselves; I will
not destroy them, but I will grant them some
deliverance, and my wrath shall not be poured
out on Jerusalem by the hand of Shishak. 8Nev-
ertheless they shall be his servants, so that they
may know the difference between serving me and
serving the kingdoms of other lands."

9So King Shishak of Egypt came up against
Jerusalem; he took away the treasures of the
house of the LORD and the treasures of the king's
house; he took everything. He also took away the
shields of gold that Solomon had made; 10but King

[a] Or *Nubians*; Heb *Cushites*

NIV

the LORD and the treasures of the royal palace. He took everything, including the gold shields Solomon had made. 10So King Rehoboam made bronze shields to replace them and assigned these to the commanders of the guard on duty at the entrance to the royal palace. 11Whenever the king went to the LORD's temple, the guards went with him, bearing the shields, and afterward they returned them to the guardroom.

12Because Rehoboam humbled himself, the LORD's anger turned from him, and he was not totally destroyed. Indeed, there was some good in Judah.

13King Rehoboam established himself firmly in Jerusalem and continued as king. He was forty-one years old when he became king, and he reigned seventeen years in Jerusalem, the city the LORD had chosen out of all the tribes of Israel in which to put his Name. His mother's name was Naamah; she was an Ammonite. 14He did evil because he had not set his heart on seeking the LORD.

15As for the events of Rehoboam's reign, from beginning to end, are they not written in the records of Shemaiah the prophet and of Iddo the seer that deal with genealogies? There was continual warfare between Rehoboam and Jeroboam. 16Rehoboam rested with his fathers and was buried in the City of David. And Abijah his son succeeded him as king.

NRSV

Rehoboam made in place of them shields of bronze, and committed them to the hands of the officers of the guard, who kept the door of the king's house. 11Whenever the king went into the house of the LORD, the guard would come along bearing them, and would then bring them back to the guardroom. 12Because he humbled himself the wrath of the LORD turned from him, so as not to destroy them completely; moreover, conditions were good in Judah.

13So King Rehoboam established himself in Jerusalem and reigned. Rehoboam was forty-one years old when he began to reign; he reigned seventeen years in Jerusalem, the city that the LORD had chosen out of all the tribes of Israel to put his name there. His mother's name was Naamah the Ammonite. 14He did evil, for he did not set his heart to seek the LORD.

15Now the acts of Rehoboam, from first to last, are they not written in the records of the prophet Shemaiah and of the seer Iddo, recorded by genealogy? There were continual wars between Rehoboam and Jeroboam. 16Rehoboam slept with his ancestors and was buried in the city of David; and his son Abijah succeeded him.

COMMENTARY

The chronicler uses the passages in 1 Kgs 14:22-28 about Judah's religious sins and Shishak's invasion and exaction of tribute from palace and Temple as the basis for his narrative in vv. 1-12. Whereas the 1 Kings story places apostasy and foreign invasion side by side without comment, it implicitly invites its readers to draw a moral. The chronicler is one reader who does moralize. He summarizes the detailed circumstances of 1 Kgs 14:22-24 in his own way in vv. 1-2 and 5 as forsaking the Torah and being unfaithful to the Lord. The first verb, here rendered "abandon" (עזב *'āzab*) in order to capture the wordplay in v. 5, was used earlier (1 Chr 28:9) in a polarized proposition of spirituality versus apostasy: "If you seek [the LORD], he will be found by you, but if you forsake him, he will reject you forever" [NIV]). The other verb (מעל *mā'al,* "to be unfaithful") or a related noun was used of the dire cause of the exile in 1 Chr 5:25; 9:1 and was applied to Saul's apostasy in 1 Chr 10:13. Like Saul, Rehoboam, scion of David though he was, found that unfaithfulness exposed him to military defeat.

12:1. Whereas the MT of 1 Kgs 14:22-24 puts the blame on the people of Judah, our text includes the king in that blame. In the LXX of 1 Kgs 14:22 Rehoboam is made the subject of v.

22*a,* as indeed in v. 14 of the Chronicles text, and the plural verb "they provoked him to jealousy" in v. 22*b* is correspondingly singular. The chronicler may have read a complex text, with a singular verb in v. 22*a,* like the LXX, and a plural verb at the start of v. 22*b,* like the MT. The reference to "all Israel with him" refers to the representatives of the total Israel to be found in the southern kingdom.

What did he mean by saying that the Torah had been abandoned by Rehoboam? In view of the details in 1 Kgs 14:23, the chronicler probably had in view Deut 12:1-14. Such pagan worship contrasts with worship of the true God in the chosen sanctuary. For the chronicler, as for the deuteronomist, this was the Jerusalem Temple (2 Chr 7:12). To seek the Lord meant to worship at the Temple (11:16). Conversely, to forsake the Lord was to forsake the Torah (cf. 7:19, 22).

Verse 1 draws an arc between becoming "strong," the key word of 11:5-23, and forsaking the Torah. As in the later case of Uzziah (26:16), Rehoboam fell into a trap of self-sufficiency, believing that "my power and the might of my own hand have gotten me this wealth" or strength (Deut 8:17 NRSV). Behind the blatant sins of religious perversity, the chronicler glimpsed an intellectual sin of failing to interpret success as the Lord's blessing.

12:2-4. Punishment for apostasy comes in the form of military attack and defeat. Shishak's own description of the campaign is extant today; it lists cities in southern Judah throughout the northern kingdom. Only the mention of Aijalon overlaps with the list of Rehoboam's fortress cities in 11:6-10. Demand for a heavy tribute from Jerusalem must have been issued from Gibeon, which is also mentioned in Shishak's account. The chronicler magnifies the effect on the southern kingdom to make his point. The mention of 60,000 cavalry (v. 3) seems to be a further example of his rhetorical use of mathematics, as his use of "innumerable" or "countless" suggests. The chronicler paints a sensational picture as a deterrent to such behavior. It gives him the opportunity to revisit the fortified cities of chap. 11. They had been tokens of divine blessing and expressions of the king's trust in the Lord to protect Judah. Only as strong as their builder's faith, they became houses built on sand. Rehoboam could no longer expect God's positive presence.

12:5. To make the religious point, Shemaiah, the prophet active in 11:2-4, steps onstage again. His one-sentence message, expressed in a powerful chiastic style, is delivered to the king and the government officials huddled in Jerusalem. After vv. 2-4 the Lord had providentially treated Judah as they had treated the Lord (see the NRSV; the rendering in the NIV and the REB, "I now abandon you," takes the perfect as performative).

A typical role for a prophet in 2 Chronicles is that of a sentry posted to warn of trouble ahead. Thus in 24:19 prophets are sent to bring the people back to the Lord, while in 36:15 they are dispatched out of the Lord's compassion to prevent the destruction of people and sanctuary. Prophets feature as well as agents of the redemptive policy disclosed in 7:14.

12:6. Rehoboam had let himself be sucked into the fatal vortex of 1 Chr 10:13 and 28:9. Death and utter dereliction loomed ominously near. Help came in the form of the gracious option announced in 2 Chr 7:14, set against the scenario of 6:24-25. Rehoboam and the officials escaped judgment by humbling themselves and confessing the Lord's name (6:24; 7:14); the officials acted as representatives of the people of God ("Israel," v. 6). God had offered a way back to spiritual security and a new lease on life. Four times the chronicler mentions people humbling themselves (vv. 6-7, 12). It is his call to those with ears to hear that the good news of 7:14 can work for anybody. The liturgical formula "The LORD is righteous" works as a confession of sin, implying that the Lord is in the right and correspondingly the people are in the wrong and thus are receiving their just deserts (cf. Exod 9:27; Dan 9:14).

12:7-8. The people's admission that the Lord was in the right made possible a reprieve, announced in Shemaiah's further message. Yet it came with a condition. Just as Jacob was left with a limp as a poignant reminder of having fought with God (Gen 32:25, 31), so also Rehoboam became Shishak's vassal, which left Rehoboam the capital and the throne. King and country were to be taught a lesson by this partial deliverance ("some," NRSV, fits the context better than "soon," NIV). They would find that the Lord's yoke was light in comparison with being in the service of a foreign power. Experience of both alternatives would enable them to appreciate the former. These verses are transparent. Rehoboam under Shishak is a mirror for post-exilic Judah, restored to the land but still subject to Persia (Ezra 9:8-9; Neh 9:36-37; see also 2 Chr 36:20). The healing envisioned in 7:14 does not materialize fully in this presentation. The chronicler hints that spiritual return to the Lord would not necessarily spell immediate liberation. This cautious scenario indicates that the glorious descriptions elsewhere in 2 Chronicles were meant to serve as incentives to appropriate behavior.

12:9-12. Verses 9-11 are a copy of 1 Kgs 14:25-28. The ceremonial gold shields of 9:15 had to be replaced with bronze copies for the palace escort. Did the chronicler think ironically of the prophetic promise, "Instead of bronze I will bring gold" (Isa 60:17)? Verse 12 sums up the situation positively. Rehoboam's self-humbling was the factor that "under God" saved the day. The king had climbed down from the daredevil stance of v. 1 and so averted utter destruction from the Lord's indignation. The last clause has a religious reference, as the parallel in 19:3 suggests. Once again "conditions were good in Judah." That comment paves the way for the favorable portrayal of Judean religion in 13:10-11. The cultic aberrations of 1 Kgs 14:23-24 had been eliminated. The chronicler's introduction of Rehoboam's repentance was intended both to teach its own spiritual lesson and to build a literary bridge back to the religious orthodoxy to be portrayed in chap. 13.

12:13-14. In vv. 13*b*-14 the chronicler cites part of the royal prologue to Rehoboam's reign in 1 Kgs 14:21*b*-22*a*, using it for his own ends. He prefaces it with the statement that Rehoboam "grew strong" (TNK) and "continued as king" (NIV). He introduces the actual citation with "because" (כִּי *kî*, "for," KJV), left untranslated in modern English versions. The king must have regained the sorts of strength described in 11:5-23, which indicated divine blessing, because according to 1 Kings he went on to enjoy twelve more years on the throne. Mention of his ruling in Jerusalem takes on special significance; it confirms the Lord's promise to spare the capital in v. 7.[239] Verse 14, which he relates to the king, is a reflective flashback to v. 1*b*, itself a paraphrase of 1 Kgs 14:22-23. Why did Rehoboam commit such evil deeds? Because he did not persevere in the seeking of the Lord to which 11:16-17 had referred. He "did not make a practice of" seeking God (REB; for the sense of perseverance, see 19:3; Ps 78:8). Rehoboam did eventually get back on track, but how much better it would have been had he followed the high road of chap. 11 without the detour of 12:1-12!

12:15-16. The epilogue is modeled on 1 Kgs 14:29-31, which the chronicler has adapted to his prophetic format. The Shemaiah story of 1 Kgs 12:21-24 (= 2 Chr 11:1-4) is singled out, and (as in 9:29) the oracle of the prophet in 1 Kgs 13:1-3 is mentioned as significant. The reference to a genealogy, or muster, is awkward in the Hebrew and may be a gloss.[240] It relates either to a genealogical source for the royal family in 11:18-22 (cf. 1 Chr 9:1) or to a military source for 11:5-12 and possibly 12:3-4.

239. J. M. Myers, *II Chronicles,* AB 13 (Garden City, N.Y.: Doubleday, 1965) 75.

240. Cf. the REB and *BHS.*

REFLECTIONS

1. The spiritual mountaintop of 11:5-23 brings its own temptations. The chronicler sees in Rehoboam the pride that would ruin the later kings Amaziah and Uzziah and that marred for a time Hezekiah's spiritual journey (25:19; 26:16; 32:25). As in 32:26, spiritual humbling is a reversal of such pride that demoted the Lord from rightful sovereignty. There was a flouting of the Torah, the expression of the divine will, "that pattern of teaching" to which God's people had been "made subject" (Rom 6:17 REB). There was no longer a resolve to "obey [God's] commandments and do what pleases him" (1 John 3:22).

The chronicler affirms that there was still hope beyond such disobedience, according to the provision of 7:14. Yet he has a pastoral concern not to minimize the seriousness of Rehoboam's departure from the divine norm. In 12:14 he deplores this abandoning of the Torah. There is a risk that leaving an opportunity for repentance may lull believers into carelessness. John was sensitive to this danger in emphasizing that his prime purpose was to encourage Christians not to sin and that God's emergency system should not be trivialized (1 John 2:1-2). This is why the chronicler deplores the king's lack of spiritual stamina. Similarly, Christian believers are urged to "remain faithful to the Lord with steadfast devotion" (Acts 11:23 NRSV) and to "continue securely established and steadfast in the faith" (Col 1:23 NRSV). Redeeming grace can put Humpty Dumpty together again, but it is better for him not to fall.

2. In Shemaiah's first oracle there is a dire pronouncement, a quid pro quo that deals in direct retribution. Repentance is the intention, and so a second chance for king and country. Human intransigence ties even God's hands, but a humble heart permits the Lord to work miracles.

3. The divinely sanctioned vassalage of 12:8 serves as a reminder that frustrating hindrances may teach spiritual lessons, if only by directing us toward God in prayer and a renewed sense of dependence. Paul came to regard his "thorn in the flesh" as not merely necessary but a fresh opportunity to appreciate God's power and grace (2 Cor 12:7-10).

2 CHRONICLES 13:1–16:14, TRUSTING THE TRUE GOD IN TIMES OF CRISIS

OVERVIEW

The accounts of Abijah's and Asa's reigns are dominated by the theme of reliance on God. Forms of the key term "rely" (נשען *nis̆ʿan*, in the niphal) occur here five times and nowhere else in Chronicles, though the general motif of turning to God in emergencies and to God alone is common elsewhere. The repetition creates a literary unit with three sections. The first occurrence of the word (13:18) helps us to identify the first section, 13:1–14:1*a*, in which Abijah's and Judah's trust in the Lord is vindicated over against the infidelity of Jeroboam and the people of the northern kingdom. The second case (14:11) is set within the section 14:1*b*–15:19, in which Asa's initial trust is vindicated. The remaining three instances (16:7-8) occur in the third section, 16:1-14, where Asa's counterfeit trust is punished.

The chronicler uses the two reigns to preach a series of sermons that are variations on a single theme: trust in the Lord. Moreover, if trust in the Lord is the main thread that runs through these chapters, it is interwoven with two other threads taken from the general religious vocabulary of Chronicles: forsaking the Lord (13:10-11) and its polar opposite, seeking the Lord (14:4, 7; 15:2, 4, 12, 15; 16:12). Also, in each of the first two sections the chronicler refers to the Lord twice as "God of your/their fathers" (NIV, 13:12, 18; 14:4; 15:3).

2 Chronicles 13:1–14:1*a*, Abijah's Loyal Trust Vindicated

NIV

13 In the eighteenth year of the reign of Jeroboam, Abijah became king of Judah,
[2]and he reigned in Jerusalem three years. His

NRSV

13 In the eighteenth year of King Jeroboam, Abijah began to reign over Judah. [2]He
reigned for three years in Jerusalem. His mother's name was Micaiah daughter of Uriel of Gibeah.

NIV

mother's name was Maacah,[a] a daughter[b] of Uriel of Gibeah.

There was war between Abijah and Jeroboam. 3Abijah went into battle with a force of four hundred thousand able fighting men, and Jeroboam drew up a battle line against him with eight hundred thousand able troops.

4Abijah stood on Mount Zemaraim, in the hill country of Ephraim, and said, "Jeroboam and all Israel, listen to me! 5Don't you know that the LORD, the God of Israel, has given the kingship of Israel to David and his descendants forever by a covenant of salt? 6Yet Jeroboam son of Nebat, an official of Solomon son of David, rebelled against his master. 7Some worthless scoundrels gathered around him and opposed Rehoboam son of Solomon when he was young and indecisive and not strong enough to resist them.

8"And now you plan to resist the kingdom of the LORD, which is in the hands of David's descendants. You are indeed a vast army and have with you the golden calves that Jeroboam made to be your gods. 9But didn't you drive out the priests of the LORD, the sons of Aaron, and the Levites, and make priests of your own as the peoples of other lands do? Whoever comes to consecrate himself with a young bull and seven rams may become a priest of what are not gods.

10"As for us, the LORD is our God, and we have not forsaken him. The priests who serve the LORD are sons of Aaron, and the Levites assist them. 11Every morning and evening they present burnt offerings and fragrant incense to the LORD. They set out the bread on the ceremonially clean table and light the lamps on the gold lampstand every evening. We are observing the requirements of the LORD our God. But you have forsaken him. 12God is with us; he is our leader. His priests with their trumpets will sound the battle cry against you. Men of Israel, do not fight against the LORD, the God of your fathers, for you will not succeed."

13Now Jeroboam had sent troops around to the rear, so that while he was in front of Judah the ambush was behind them. 14Judah turned and saw that they were being attacked at both front and rear. Then they cried out to the LORD. The priests

[a]2 Most Septuagint manuscripts and Syriac (see also 2 Chron. 11:20 and 1 Kings 15:2); Hebrew *Micaiah* [b]2 Or *granddaughter*

NRSV

Now there was war between Abijah and Jeroboam. 3Abijah engaged in battle, having an army of valiant warriors, four hundred thousand picked men; and Jeroboam drew up his line of battle against him with eight hundred thousand picked mighty warriors. 4Then Abijah stood on the slope of Mount Zemaraim that is in the hill country of Ephraim, and said, "Listen to me, Jeroboam and all Israel! 5Do you not know that the LORD God of Israel gave the kingship over Israel forever to David and his sons by a covenant of salt? 6Yet Jeroboam son of Nebat, a servant of Solomon son of David, rose up and rebelled against his lord; 7and certain worthless scoundrels gathered around him and defied Rehoboam son of Solomon, when Rehoboam was young and irresolute and could not withstand them.

8"And now you think that you can withstand the kingdom of the LORD in the hand of the sons of David, because you are a great multitude and have with you the golden calves that Jeroboam made as gods for you. 9Have you not driven out the priests of the LORD, the descendants of Aaron, and the Levites, and made priests for yourselves like the peoples of other lands? Whoever comes to be consecrated with a young bull or seven rams becomes a priest of what are no gods. 10But as for us, the LORD is our God, and we have not abandoned him. We have priests ministering to the LORD who are descendants of Aaron, and Levites for their service. 11They offer to the LORD every morning and every evening burnt offerings and fragrant incense, set out the rows of bread on the table of pure gold, and care for the golden lampstand so that its lamps may burn every evening; for we keep the charge of the LORD our God, but you have abandoned him. 12See, God is with us at our head, and his priests have their battle trumpets to sound the call to battle against you. O Israelites, do not fight against the LORD, the God of your ancestors; for you cannot succeed."

13Jeroboam had sent an ambush around to come on them from behind; thus his troops[a] were in front of Judah, and the ambush was behind them. 14When Judah turned, the battle was in front of them and behind them. They cried out to the LORD, and the priests blew the trumpets.

[a] Heb *they*

NIV

blew their trumpets [15]and the men of Judah raised the battle cry. At the sound of their battle cry, God routed Jeroboam and all Israel before Abijah and Judah. [16]The Israelites fled before Judah, and God delivered them into their hands. [17]Abijah and his men inflicted heavy losses on them, so that there were five hundred thousand casualties among Israel's able men. [18]The men of Israel were subdued on that occasion, and the men of Judah were victorious because they relied on the LORD, the God of their fathers.

[19]Abijah pursued Jeroboam and took from him the towns of Bethel, Jeshanah and Ephron, with their surrounding villages. [20]Jeroboam did not regain power during the time of Abijah. And the LORD struck him down and he died.

[21]But Abijah grew in strength. He married fourteen wives and had twenty-two sons and sixteen daughters.

[22]The other events of Abijah's reign, what he did and what he said, are written in the annotations of the prophet Iddo.

14 And Abijah rested with his fathers and was buried in the City of David.

NRSV

[15]Then the people of Judah raised the battle shout. And when the people of Judah shouted, God defeated Jeroboam and all Israel before Abijah and Judah. [16]The Israelites fled before Judah, and God gave them into their hands. [17]Abijah and his army defeated them with great slaughter; five hundred thousand picked men of Israel fell slain. [18]Thus the Israelites were subdued at that time, and the people of Judah prevailed, because they relied on the LORD, the God of their ancestors. [19]Abijah pursued Jeroboam, and took cities from him: Bethel with its villages and Jeshanah with its villages and Ephron[a] with its villages. [20]Jeroboam did not recover his power in the days of Abijah; the LORD struck him down, and he died. [21]But Abijah grew strong. He took fourteen wives, and became the father of twenty-two sons and sixteen daughters. [22]The rest of the acts of Abijah, his behavior and his deeds, are written in the story of the prophet Iddo.

14 [b]So Abijah slept with his ancestors, and they buried him in the city of David.

[a] Another reading is *Ephrain* [b] Ch 13.23 in Heb

COMMENTARY

Abijah is called Abijam in 1 Kgs 15:1-8. We do not know why the names are different; they may represent a throne name and a personal name. According to 1 Kings 15, this king is a worthless nonentity who does so little to enhance the Davidic line that its survival is credited to the Lord's gracious covenant with David. One of the few significant contacts between the 1 Kings account and the text in 2 Chronicles is the mention of warfare between Abijah and Jeroboam, of which the chronicler indulges in an example in vv. 3-19. There is controversy over whether he invented it or wrote it up from a historical source that specified the territorial gains of v. 19. It has been argued that the place-names have been borrowed from a longer text of Josh 18:21-24 that is preserved in the LXX.[241] Others find it difficult to believe that the chronicler reversed the verdict of 1 Kings 15 on Abijah's reign without a written tradition of even a fleeting victory over the north.[242] The evidence of 1 Kgs 15:19 (= 2 Chr 16:3) concerning an alliance between Abijah and Aram to secure dominance over their common neighbor Jeroboam, lends support to this judgment. The chronicler appears to have written up such a tradition into a holy war type of narrative akin to that in chap. 20. Victory in warfare is a standard motif in the books of Chronicles to show divine favor for obedience. The chronicler found support for this positive assessment in another available tradition concerning Abijah's large family (v. 21).

These traditions gave him grounds for his description of the healthy state of the southern

241. R. W. Klein, "Abijah's Campaign Against the North (II Chr 13)—What Were the Chronicler's Sources?" *ZAW* 95 (1983) 210-17. See the critique of D. G. Deboys, "History and Theology in the Chronicler's Portrayal of Abijah," *Bib* 71 (1990) 48-62, esp. 60-61.

242. W. Rudolph, *Chronikbücher,* HAT 1:21 (Tübingen: Mohr [Siebeck], 1955) 235-36, with reference to M. Noth.

kingdom at this time. He assumed the continuing orthodoxy of temple worship, which he had affirmed in 11:16, and wove both this factor and the issue of the Davidic dynasty (specified in 1 Kgs 15:4) into a pre-battle type of speech in vv. 4-12. They became the basis for miraculous victory and remarkable blessing that come later in the chapter. Tension was thereby created with Asa's reforming zeal in 2 Chr 14:3-5*a* (what was there to reform?), but the chronicler was not concerned to iron out such inconsistencies, as his retention of the negotiations between the northerners and Rehoboam in chap. 10 illustrated.

13:1. Only here is a synchronism with a northern king repeated from 1–2 Kings. Its presence reflects the fact that the whole chapter hangs on the respective relations of the two kingdoms to the Lord. The people of God had radically split in two. The initial split was ratified by prophetic prediction, while on the human plane Rehoboam's folly was warrant enough for the bulk of his subjects to reject his rule. The chronicler knew from 1 Kgs 11:37-38 that the perpetuation of the northern line of kings depended on Jeroboam's fidelity to the Lord. He had failed in this respect, as his religious innovations proved (2 Chr 11:14-15). Accordingly, the death of foolish Rehoboam and the accession of a new Judean king afforded an opportunity for the northerners to reject Jeroboam and revert to allegiance to the true Davidic king and temple worship.[243]

13:2. Abijah's mother was Maacah (LXX and NIV), as mentioned in 11:20-22 and the parallel 1 Kgs 15:2, rather than Micaiah (MT and NRSV).[244] The different patronymic represents another tradition.

13:3. The numbers are a further example of the rhetorical mathematics in which the chronicler sometimes indulged for dramatic effect. The size of the northern army may symbolize the total commitment of available forces, corresponding to the northern census number in 2 Sam 24:9. Then Judah's forces were a mere half, a feature that enhances their eventual victory. It is possible to rationalize the figures by interpreting them as 400 and 800 units, but such an approach destroys the intended grandiose effect.

13:4-12. The unidentified Mount Zemaraim was evidently in the region of Bethel (see Josh 18:22). The royal speech, like other speeches that have no parallel in 1–2 Kings, is a vehicle of the chronicler's theological interpretation.[245] The punch line at the end of v. 12 gives the main point of the king's speech: The northerners should recognize that the Lord is on the other side, so to fight Judah is to fight Judah's divine patron. What precedes is a two-pronged argument for this conclusion (vv. 5-8*a* and vv. 8*b*-12*a*). The first prong is the legitimacy of the Davidic dynasty, which earlier chapters have already established for the reader, and the second is the authenticity of the worship offered only at the Jerusalem Temple.

The expression "covenant of salt" is borrowed from Num 18:19 (cf. Lev 2:13) and has been reapplied to the Davidic covenant. Whatever its original meaning, the phrase clearly reinforces the notion of a perpetual covenant. In the light of the chronicler's overall presentation, his description of Jeroboam's rebellion (v. 6) probably has in view not the narrative of 1 Kgs 11:26-27, 40, which is set in Solomon's reign, but that of 2 Chronicles 10, in Rehoboam's reign (see esp. 10:19), so that "his master" is in fact Rehoboam. Then v. 7 reflects mitigating circumstances: the bad influence of younger counselors on Rehoboam, who persuaded him to adopt a high-handed attitude and so prevailed over him (התאמץ *hit'ammēṣ;* cf. the Qal in v. 18, rather than the NRSV's "defied" or the NIV's "opposed").[246] Josephus interpreted the text in this way,[247] and a small group seems more apposite than "Jeroboam and all Israel" (10:3). According to 10:15, the chronicler respected the necessity of Jeroboam's rebellious role in the light of Rehoboam's conduct. His successor apologizes for Rehoboam's immature mistake and its tragic consequences. There was now no reason to persist in secession. The rule of David's sons had been approved by God (cf. 1 Chr 17:14;

243. See H. G. M. Williamson, *Israel in the Books of Chronicles* (Cambridge: Cambridge University Press, 1977) 110-14.

244. See L. C. Allen, *The Greek Chronicles: The Relation of the Septuagint of I and II Chronicles to the Massoretic Text,* Part 2: *Textual Criticism,* VTSup 25, 27 (Leiden: Brill, 1974) 99.

245. See Deboys, "History and Theology in the Chronicler's Portrayal of Abijah," 55-59.

246. Williamson, *Israel in the Books of Chronicles,* 112-13; *1 and 2 Chronicles,* NCB (Grand Rapids: Eerdmans, 1982) 252-53; S. J. De Vries, *1 and 2 Chronicles,* FOTL 11 (Grand Rapids: Eerdmans, 1989) 292. See also G. N. Knoppers, "Rehoboam in Chronicles: Villain or Victim?" *JBL* 109 (1990) 423-44, esp. 437-39.

247. Josephus *Antiquities of the Jews* 8.11.2 277.

29:23). As the speech progresses, Abijah increasingly bypasses Jeroboam. He is jointly addressed in v. 4, but is mentioned obliquely in vv. 6, 8; by the end of the speech, only the people are addressed (v. 12). Jeroboam was no longer in the picture, just as Rehoboam had ceased to be a material factor in the contemporary situation. The reason for Jeroboam's exclusion is given in v. 8*b* : He had appointed his own priests and had encouraged idol worship (11:15).

In formal structure, the speech consists of a historical introduction (vv. 5-7) and contemporary consequences (vv. 8-12), with a recapitulation of the argument of vv. 5-7 in v. 8*a.* Verses 10-12*a* form a smaller section counterpointing at beginning and end Judah's not having forsaken the Lord and Israel's having done so.

The new era established by David and Solomon determined criteria of worship for the people of God. The reader of the books of Chronicles is no stranger to these criteria: proper personnel and four archetypical features of worship. Their presence or absence defined the seeking or forsaking of the Lord. Implicit conformity of temple worship with the Torah determined which elements should be mentioned here, as a citation of Lev 24:6 in v. 11 ("table of pure gold") and an appeal to Num 10:8-9 (cf. Num 31:6) for the priestly trumpets in v. 12 indicate. So the role of levitical singers went unnoticed, and the single lampstand of the tabernacle surreptitiously replaced the ten that were actually present in the Temple, according to 4:7 (cf. Exod 25:31-39; 37:17-24).

Abijah's challenge to the northerners not to fight the southerners is a counterpart to the call to Rehoboam and his army not to attack the northerners in 11:4. Now the shoe was on the other foot. Any justification for the secession of the northern kingdom had disappeared. Abijah appeals for reunification under the banner of "the God of your fathers." The parents of these northerners had worshiped the Lord as citizens of a united kingdom. Now it was the new generation's turn to make such a decision and break with recent religious aberrations. Accordingly, the term "Israelites" or "sons of Israel" carries theological overtones. Prodigal children are invited back into God's family. If they had forsaken the Lord, so

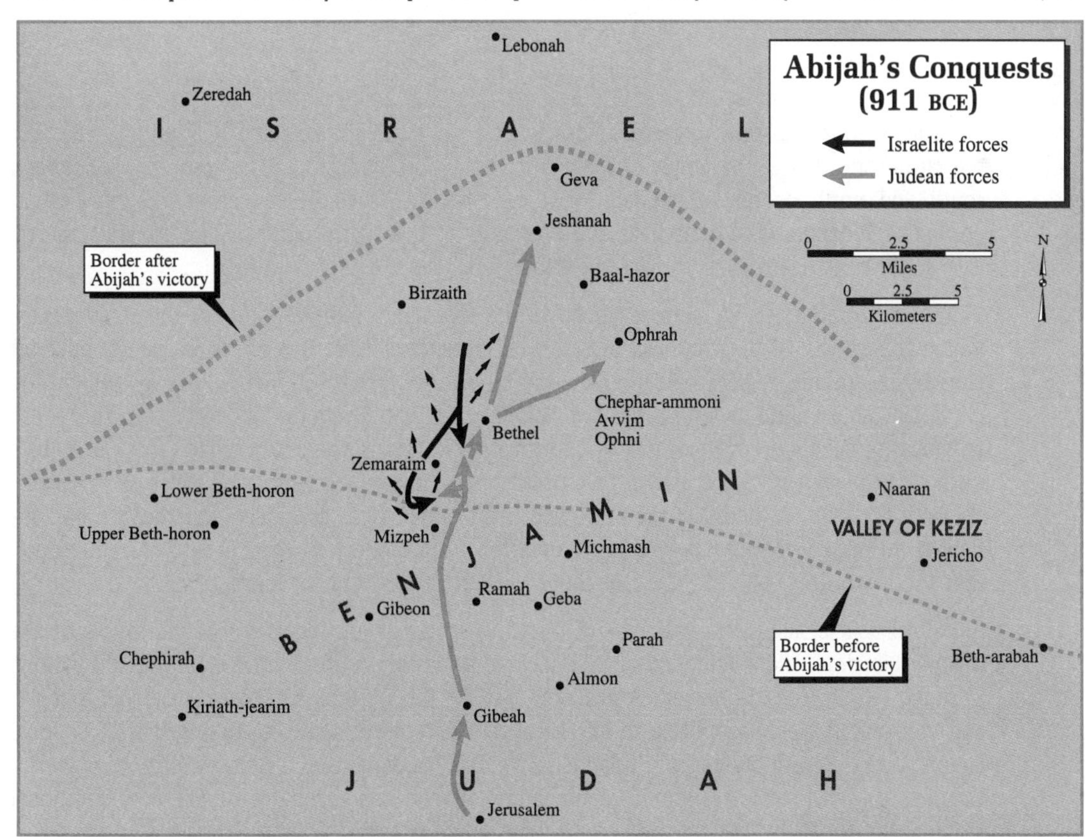

had Rehoboam earlier, and a door of repentance had stood open for him (12:5-6).

13:13-18. No such hopes prevailed. The huge northern army, surrounding the Judean troops with a pincer movement, expected victory. But neither strategy nor statistics won the day against the Lord. The claim and challenge of v. 12 are translated into narrative in vv. 14 and 18. The priestly trumpets sounded an alarm to summon divine aid (cf. Num 10:9), and it was the new generation in the south that prevailed. Unlike those in the north, the southern army had laid hold of their parents' faith (vv. 12, 18). The battle is described in an archaic fashion, in the style of holy war used in the military narratives of Joshua and Judges. The secret of the southern army's success is revealed in the verb "relied" (נשׁען *niš'an*, in the niphal) in v. 18, the first appearance of this key word in this literary unit. Its use harks back to the shout of allegiance in v. 15 (cf. Judg 7:18), which the Lord honored. "To rely" is literally "to lean." A related noun (משׁען *miš'ān*) occurs in Ps 18:18, where the victorious king testifies that "the LORD was my support." The contexts of both v. 18 and Ps 18:18 are situations of desperate crisis, and in each case there is a divine acknowledgment of human fidelity (cf. Ps 18:19-27). The victory confirmed Abijah's arguments that the southern kingdom had remained loyal.

13:19-21. The frontier between the kingdoms was redrawn to the north of Bethel. As in 2 Kgs 19:37, the battle report concludes by looking ahead to the premature death of the enemy king, which stands in contrast to Abijah's fruitful reign. The point is a religious rather than a chronological one; Abijah died before Jeroboam, according to 1 Kgs 14:20; 15:9, though the chronicler may have overlooked these texts. The path of fidelity is paved with blessing, while infidelity leads to destruction (cf. Deut 30:15-20).

13:22–14:1a. The royal epilogue is based on 1 Kgs 15:7*a,* 8. By referring to Iddo, the chronicler appeals to 1 Kgs 13:1-10 to bolster his case. That oracle denounced Jeroboam's religious innovations and affirmed the Davidic dynasty. Such an allusion adds an authoritative "amen" to Abijah's speech.

REFLECTIONS

Abijah's appeal to the northerners has at first sight the ring of civil war propaganda. For the chronicler, it was not simply a reconstruction of ancient history. The controversy between south and north opened a window on contemporary issues. It concerned the warrant of post-exilic Judah to regard itself as the preserver of true faith and worship. Abijah's speech lays down basic theological convictions about Judah's status before the Lord.

1. The Torah-based worship practiced in the Jerusalem Temple is one of the standards by which the fidelity of the southern kingdom is measured. Faith was no vague belief, but was clothed in specific religious forms. A striking feature typical of the culture of which the chronicler spoke and to which he still belonged is that for both the north and the south religious forms stood at the center of controversy. Religious worship loomed large, as it does in most ages—but less so our own. Very many who sincerely regard themselves as Christians consider their faith a matter of the mind and heart rather than essentially expressed in religious habits, private or communal. We need to listen with respect to the chronicler's affirmation that those who rely on God are also those who prize institutional forms of faith.

2. Abijah's challenge at the end of 13:12 is virtually an appeal for reunification of the divided kingdom under one God and king. Prodigal children are invited back into the family. Through Abijah, the chronicler's voice rang out for the Judeans to accept their role as hosts and welcome the prodigals back. In an age of religious resentment, not untinged with political factors, he refused to budge from this inclusive ideal, undergirding it with even more powerful arguments in chapter 28. Within his ecumenicity, he had non-negotiable standards of traditional religion and theology; but his arms were wide open to religious union.

But subsequent generations paid no heed to history. They followed a downward path to the point where some Jews did "not associate with Samaritans" (John 4:9 NIV). In principle, Jesus was affirming the chronicler's stand when he built bridges between himself and the Samaritan community of Sychar (John 4:39-41). He insisted on the historical priority of Jerusalem, just as the chronicler had done: "salvation is from the Jews" (John 4:21). Jesus went on to announce a new era of worship, based on criteria of "spirit and truth" (John 4:22-26). These criteria, while denying a single religious center, by no means promote an amorphous religion. The phrase "spirit and truth" does not replace the solid verb "worship," but rather qualifies it.

3. The warning against fighting God in 13:12 has a striking parallel in Gamaliel's caution to the Sanhedrin, who wanted to kill the apostles: "If it is from God, you will not be able to stop these men; you will only find yourselves fighting against God" (Acts 5:39 NIV). Just as the apostles were bravely determined to "obey God rather than any human authority" (Acts 5:29 NRSV), so also Abijah, at the head of an outnumbered army, stood staunchly by his principles. The spirit of Martin Luther sums up both scenarios: "Here I stand, I can do not other."[248]

4. The winners relied on "the God of their fathers" (13:18 NIV). The chronicler saw himself as an upholder of tradition. He defined tradition not as a dead thing to be mechanically perpetuated for its own sake, but in terms of a reincarnation of the living faith of previous generations. To each generation the call of God comes afresh to take a positive stand as champions of the faith their parents held.

5. The chronicler conjures up a scenario of faith vindicated in time of crisis. In the case of Abijah and Judah, it was no foxhole religion. Their cry of trust drew credit from a spiritual bank account that had already been set up and was regularly used. Crisis can befall sincere believers as well as backsliders. For the former, the chronicler envisioned the certainty of divine help. Times of crisis, which may seem beyond human ability to resolve, can be a challenge to faith and an opportunity to rely on God.

248. See R. H. Bainton, *Here I Stand: A Life of Martin Luther* (Nashville: Abingdon, 1950) 185.

2 Chronicles 14:1*b*–15:19, Asa's Valid Trust Vindicated

NIV

Asa his son succeeded him as king, and in his days the country was at peace for ten years.

[2]Asa did what was good and right in the eyes of the LORD his God. [3]He removed the foreign altars and the high places, smashed the sacred stones and cut down the Asherah poles.[a] [4]He commanded Judah to seek the LORD, the God of their fathers, and to obey his laws and commands. [5]He removed the high places and incense altars in every town in Judah, and the kingdom was at peace under him. [6]He built up the fortified cities of Judah, since the land was at peace. No one was at war with him during those years, for the LORD gave him rest.

[a]3 That is, symbols of the goddess Asherah; here and elsewhere in 2 Chronicles

NRSV

His son Asa succeeded him. In his days the land had rest for ten years. [2a]Asa did what was good and right in the sight of the LORD his God. [3]He took away the foreign altars and the high places, broke down the pillars, hewed down the sacred poles,[b] [4]and commanded Judah to seek the LORD, the God of their ancestors, and to keep the law and the commandment. [5]He also removed from all the cities of Judah the high places and the incense altars. And the kingdom had rest under him. [6]He built fortified cities in Judah while the land had rest. He had no war in those years, for the LORD gave him peace. [7]He said to Judah, "Let us build these cities, and surround them with walls and towers, gates and bars; the land is still

[a] Ch 14.1 in Heb [b] Heb *Asherim*

NIV

[7]"Let us build up these towns," he said to Judah, "and put walls around them, with towers, gates and bars. The land is still ours, because we have sought the LORD our God; we sought him and he has given us rest on every side." So they built and prospered.

[8]Asa had an army of three hundred thousand men from Judah, equipped with large shields and with spears, and two hundred and eighty thousand from Benjamin, armed with small shields and with bows. All these were brave fighting men.

[9]Zerah the Cushite marched out against them with a vast army[a] and three hundred chariots, and came as far as Mareshah. [10]Asa went out to meet him, and they took up battle positions in the Valley of Zephathah near Mareshah.

[11]Then Asa called to the LORD his God and said, "LORD, there is no one like you to help the powerless against the mighty. Help us, O LORD our God, for we rely on you, and in your name we have come against this vast army. O LORD, you are our God; do not let man prevail against you."

[12]The LORD struck down the Cushites before Asa and Judah. The Cushites fled, [13]and Asa and his army pursued them as far as Gerar. Such a great number of Cushites fell that they could not recover; they were crushed before the LORD and his forces. The men of Judah carried off a large amount of plunder. [14]They destroyed all the villages around Gerar, for the terror of the LORD had fallen upon them. They plundered all these villages, since there was much booty there. [15]They also attacked the camps of the herdsmen and carried off droves of sheep and goats and camels. Then they returned to Jerusalem.

15 The Spirit of God came upon Azariah son of Oded. [2]He went out to meet Asa and said to him, "Listen to me, Asa and all Judah and Benjamin. The LORD is with you when you are with him. If you seek him, he will be found by you, but if you forsake him, he will forsake you. [3]For a long time Israel was without the true God, without a priest to teach and without the law. [4]But in their distress they turned to the LORD, the God of Israel, and sought him, and he was found

[a]9 Hebrew *with an army of a thousand thousands* or *with an army of thousands upon thousands*

NRSV

ours because we have sought the LORD our God; we have sought him, and he has given us peace on every side." So they built and prospered. [8]Asa had an army of three hundred thousand from Judah, armed with large shields and spears, and two hundred eighty thousand troops from Benjamin who carried shields and drew bows; all these were mighty warriors.

9Zerah the Ethiopian[a] came out against them with an army of a million men and three hundred chariots, and came as far as Mareshah. [10]Asa went out to meet him, and they drew up their lines of battle in the valley of Zephathah at Mareshah. [11]Asa cried to the LORD his God, "O LORD, there is no difference for you between helping the mighty and the weak. Help us, O LORD our God, for we rely on you, and in your name we have come against this multitude. O LORD, you are our God; let no mortal prevail against you." [12]So the LORD defeated the Ethiopians[b] before Asa and before Judah, and the Ethiopians[b] fled. [13]Asa and the army with him pursued them as far as Gerar, and the Ethiopians[b] fell until no one remained alive; for they were broken before the LORD and his army. The people of Judah[c] carried away a great quantity of booty. [14]They defeated all the cities around Gerar, for the fear of the LORD was on them. They plundered all the cities; for there was much plunder in them. [15]They also attacked the tents of those who had livestock,[d] and carried away sheep and goats in abundance, and camels. Then they returned to Jerusalem.

15 The spirit of God came upon Azariah son of Oded. [2]He went out to meet Asa and said to him, "Hear me, Asa, and all Judah and Benjamin: The LORD is with you, while you are with him. If you seek him, he will be found by you, but if you abandon him, he will abandon you. [3]For a long time Israel was without the true God, and without a teaching priest, and without law; [4]but when in their distress they turned to the LORD, the God of Israel, and sought him, he was found by them. [5]In those times it was not safe for anyone to go or come, for great disturbances afflicted all the inhabitants of the lands. [6]They were broken in pieces, nation against nation

[a] Or *Nubian*; Heb *Cushite* [b] Or *Nubians*; Heb *Cushites* [c] Heb *They* [d] Meaning of Heb uncertain

NIV

by them. 5In those days it was not safe to travel about, for all the inhabitants of the lands were in great turmoil. 6One nation was being crushed by another and one city by another, because God was troubling them with every kind of distress. 7But as for you, be strong and do not give up, for your work will be rewarded."

8When Asa heard these words and the prophecy of Azariah son of[a] Oded the prophet, he took courage. He removed the detestable idols from the whole land of Judah and Benjamin and from the towns he had captured in the hills of Ephraim. He repaired the altar of the LORD that was in front of the portico of the LORD's temple.

9Then he assembled all Judah and Benjamin and the people from Ephraim, Manasseh and Simeon who had settled among them, for large numbers had come over to him from Israel when they saw that the LORD his God was with him.

10They assembled at Jerusalem in the third month of the fifteenth year of Asa's reign. 11At that time they sacrificed to the LORD seven hundred head of cattle and seven thousand sheep and goats from the plunder they had brought back. 12They entered into a covenant to seek the LORD, the God of their fathers, with all their heart and soul. 13All who would not seek the LORD, the God of Israel, were to be put to death, whether small or great, man or woman. 14They took an oath to the LORD with loud acclamation, with shouting and with trumpets and horns. 15All Judah rejoiced about the oath because they had sworn it wholeheartedly. They sought God eagerly, and he was found by them. So the LORD gave them rest on every side.

16King Asa also deposed his grandmother Maacah from her position as queen mother, because she had made a repulsive Asherah pole. Asa cut the pole down, broke it up and burned it in the Kidron Valley. 17Although he did not remove the high places from Israel, Asa's heart was fully committed ⌞to the LORD⌟ all his life. 18He brought into the temple of God the silver and gold and the articles that he and his father had dedicated.

19There was no more war until the thirty-fifth year of Asa's reign.

[a]8 Vulgate and Syriac (see also Septuagint and verse 1); Hebrew does not have *Azariah son of.*

NRSV

and city against city, for God troubled them with every sort of distress. 7But you, take courage! Do not let your hands be weak, for your work shall be rewarded."

8When Asa heard these words, the prophecy of Azariah son of Oded,[a] he took courage, and put away the abominable idols from all the land of Judah and Benjamin and from the towns that he had taken in the hill country of Ephraim. He repaired the altar of the LORD that was in front of the vestibule of the house of the LORD.[b] 9He gathered all Judah and Benjamin, and those from Ephraim, Manasseh, and Simeon who were residing as aliens with them, for great numbers had deserted to him from Israel when they saw that the LORD his God was with him. 10They were gathered at Jerusalem in the third month of the fifteenth year of the reign of Asa. 11They sacrificed to the LORD on that day, from the booty that they had brought, seven hundred oxen and seven thousand sheep. 12They entered into a covenant to seek the LORD, the God of their ancestors, with all their heart and with all their soul. 13Whoever would not seek the LORD, the God of Israel, should be put to death, whether young or old, man or woman. 14They took an oath to the LORD with a loud voice, and with shouting, and with trumpets, and with horns. 15All Judah rejoiced over the oath; for they had sworn with all their heart, and had sought him with their whole desire, and he was found by them, and the LORD gave them rest all around.

16King Asa even removed his mother Maacah from being queen mother because she had made an abominable image for Asherah. Asa cut down her image, crushed it, and burned it at the Wadi Kidron. 17But the high places were not taken out of Israel. Nevertheless the heart of Asa was true all his days. 18He brought into the house of God the votive gifts of his father and his own votive gifts—silver, gold, and utensils. 19And there was no more war until the thirty-fifth year of the reign of Asa.

[a] Compare Syr Vg: Heb *the prophecy, the prophet Obed* [b] Heb *the vestibule of the LORD*

COMMENTARY

In 1 Kgs 15:10-11, 15, Asa is judged to be a consistently good king who reigned for forty-one years. The picture presented in 2 Chronicles 14–16 is different. Two contrasting vignettes of a long good period and a short bad one are sketched in a schematic fashion. The first period did justice to his long reign, interpreted as a recompense for goodness. But there were negative features in 1 Kings 15 to be explained: his alliance with Aram and illness in old age. Interpreting these features providentially, the chronicler reasoned back to a radical change in Asa's spiritual stance, as 16:7-8 explains.

There are chronological difficulties in the different presentations of Asa's reign. According to 1 Kgs 16:6, 8, the northern king Baasha died in Asa's twenty-sixth year, yet 2 Chr 16:1 presents him as still active in Asa's thirty-sixth year. The best way to explain this chronological anomaly is to assume that the chronicler reshuffled the events and timing in 1 Kings 15 in order to create a clear-cut division into a very long period of blessing for fidelity and a short period of infidelity. His account of Asa's reign reads as a powerful two-part lesson of spiritual greatness and a tragic fall, bringing messages of both assurance and challenge.

14:1b-8. The phrase "at peace" (vv. 1*b,* 5) provides a framework for vv. 1-5. In vv. 6-7, which describe the building of fortified cities, it is repeated in v. 6*a* and is modified by the Lord's gift of "rest" in vv. 6*b*-7. Rest from enemies was an ancient promise (Deut 12:10), associated with the land, which is mentioned three times (vv. 1*b,* 6, 7). The designation of certain periods as times of peace for the land recalls Judg 3:11, 30; 5:31; 8:28, all of which use the same Hebrew verb (שׁקט *šāqaṭ,* "to be quiet") and punctuate periods of backsliding and providential punishment by invasion.[249] The chronicler imposed on Asa's reign the periodization of Judges. His allusion to the judges era in 15:3-6 develops this parallel.

For the chronicler, rest had been realized in Solomon's reign, marking the onset of a new era of grace (1 Chr 22:9). It was a heritage that each succeeding king had the potential to enjoy, but its enjoyment depended on meeting two God-given responsibilities relating to the Temple and to the Torah, both of which Solomon had successfully discharged (1 Chr 28:7-10). Asa is portrayed in vv. 1*b*-7 as another Solomon. The material in vv. 1*b*-5 does not appear in the 1 Kings account, apart from the accolade of v. 2, which reproduces 1 Kgs 15:11*a,* though the reform measures of vv. 3 and 5*a* are thematically related to those in 1 Kgs 15:12. The chronicler has developed the motif of peace by arguing back from his dating of warfare between the two kingdoms in the latter part of Asa's reign in 15:19. He has shortened the period of warfare of 1 Kgs 15:16. Aware of open conflict only in the Ramah incident of 1 Kgs 15:17-22 (= 2 Chr 16:1-6), he assumed a state of cold war in the preceding period.[250]

Divinely given rest and peace provide a frame for Asa's loyal discharge of the obligations relating to Temple and Torah. The accolade of v. 2, taken over from 1 Kings, is unpacked in vv. 3-5*a.* Asa's concern for the Temple is illustrated in vv. 3 and 5*a.* Only Solomon could build the Temple; his successors were to maintain it as the sole focus of worship. This concern dictated the rewriting of the religious reform in 1 Kgs 15:12. The vocabulary of cultic perversions is implicitly antithetical to pure temple worship. The chronicler echoes the language of Lev 26:30 and Deut 12:2-3 and anticipates the pro-temple reforms of Hezekiah and Josiah in 2 Chr 21:1 (cf. 2 Kgs 18:4*a*) and 34:3-7. Mention of the idols in 1 Kgs 15:2 is held over until Asa's second reform in 15:8. "Incense altars" (חמנים *ḥammānîm*), not to be confused with the altar in the Temple, bore pagan associations, as Isa 17:7-8 illustrates. The removal of high places conflicts with the explicit statement of 1 Kgs 15:14. The chronicler will deal with this inconsistency later in his own way. He leaves unsettled the matter of when such deviations occurred; in his view, Asa's predecessor was a saint, and not the sinner of 1 Kgs 15:3.

If the Temple was important, so was the Torah (v. 4). The spiritual catchword of Chronicles, "seeking [דרשׁ *dāraš*] the LORD," reappears here.

249. H. G. M. Williamson, *1 and 2 Chronicles,* NCB (Grand Rapids: Eerdmans, 1982) 259.

250. Ibid., 272.

Traditional faith and personal commitment are correlated in the phrase "seek the LORD, the God of their fathers" or predecessors. Here is the chronicler's ideal, for a new generation to appropriate their spiritual heritage, so that the community would be renewed from age to age. Such spiritual renewal is here measured by an adherence to the Torah.

The references to building fortified cities in vv. 6-7 and later to the army in v. 8 represent in the idiom of Chronicles God's blessings in response to the king's faithfulness. The building of the cities is derived from 1 Kgs 15:23 (cf. Jer 41:9), while the details of Asa's conscript army seem to depend on a military census list available to the chronicler.[251] When did these military developments take place? The chronology of chaps. 14–15 is left hazy. Verses 1*b*-8 read as if they relate to a ten-year period. Yet the battle of vv. 9-15 took place in Asa's fifteenth year, according to 15:10-11. De Vries seems to be right in assigning vv. 6-7 to a period of five years of special blessing after the initial ten years of reform and rest.[252] He has drawn attention to the stylistic differentiation of vv. 1*b*-5 and 6-7 as separate passages. In v. 6, "while" in the NRSV is confusing; the NIV's "since" is preferable. Verse 7 distinguishes a phase of seeking the Lord and finding rest from a phase of building (in v. 7*b* the MT may be retained, instead of emending with the REB and NJB).[253] The royal speech reinforces the narrative, implicitly conveying to the chronicler's contemporaries an incentive for their own seeking of God in Temple and Torah. The prophetic speech in chap. 15 will develop this message.

14:9-15. Verse 8 marks a transition, capping the blessings of vv. 6-7, yet ironically preparing for the anticlimax of v. 9, which rudely shatters the peace of the earlier passage. The story of vv. 9-15 appears to be an extravagant rewriting of an extant historical tradition about the defeat of a semi-nomadic group based in the region of Gerar but originally from Cush to the south of the Dead Sea (cf. 21:16).[254] A raid on Mareshah was repulsed, and the raiders were chased back to Gerar. The Judeans "killed the herdsmen" (v. 15 REB; cf. *BHS*) and captured livestock, which will reappear in 15:11. The chronicler transformed history to story, enlarging the raiders into a huge exotic force from Cush in Africa ("Ethiopians," NRSV), as the reference to "Libyans" in 16:8 makes clear. The chronicler had in mind an invasion like that in 12:3. In his hands, the account became a spiritual call to faith and a portrayal of the Lord as able to meet any need, however great the human odds. The odds are grandiloquently presented as "a thousand thousand men" ("million," NRSV). The NIV's less colorful rendering, "vast," recognizes the rhetoric of this figure.

Had not the Lord already provided the answer to Asa's problem in vv. 7-8? The capture of Abijah's fortified cities in 12:4 has prepared for a negative answer here. There had to be a fresh turning of the heart to the Lord, rather than trusting in earlier provision. In fact, God proved to be a very present help in trouble. That help is triggered by prayer, which admits to human helplessness and claims the Lord's patronage ("our God" twice) and unique power. Asa's prayer opens with praise of the Lord's incomparable protective power: "There is no one like you to help the powerless against the mighty" (NIV, rightly interpreting the literal "help [in a conflict] between the mighty and the powerless"). Appeals for that help surround avowals of trust.

The account of God-given victory, laden with holy war motifs, reinforces the message of its twin in chap. 13. The key word of the literary unit, "rely" (נשען *niš'an*, niphal), is used in the royal prayer, alongside a claim that the people are the Lord's representatives ("in your name"; cf. 1 Sam 17:45). The trust of the faithful is vindicated.

15:1-7. Azariah's prophetic message builds an interpretative bridge between the preceding and the following accounts of Asa's reign. In the ungrammatical MT of v. 8, the prophet seems disconcertingly to turn into his father ("the prophecy, Oded the prophet"). The text is in disorder; the NIV and the NRSV have taken over an attested, but secondary, reading in an attempt to correct it. "Oded the prophet" seems to be a misplaced marginal annotation to v. 1, intending to add "the prophet," qualifying Azariah, to the phrase ending in "Oded" there. Azariah is men-

251. See ibid., 261-63.

252. S. J. De Vries, *1 and 2 Chronicles,* FOTL 11 (Grand Rapids: Eerdmans, 1989) 297-98.

253. See R. B. Dillard, *2 Chronicles,* WBC 15 (Waco, Tex.: Word, 1987) 114.

254. See Y. Aharoni, *The Land of the Bible: A Historical Geography,* trans. A. F. Rainey, 2nd rev. ed. (Philadelphia: Westminster, 1979) 146.

tioned only here. Whether the chronicler knew of him from a historical tradition or invented him along with his religious message, the name, which means "Yahweh has helped," fits the situation of 14:9-15. The Lord answers the petition for help in 14:11. Such help had been shown in the Lord's protective presence "with" them (cf. 20:17; "you" and "your" are plural throughout the address). God's continued presence in blessing was possible only if the people remained committed to the Lord.

Two alternative prospects are presented, underlined by prophetic authority. The chronicler has already introduced them to his readers in David's challenge to Solomon in 1 Chr 28:9: "If you seek him, he will be found by you; but if you forsake him, he will reject you forever" (NIV). The first alternative is taken from one of the chronicler's favorite texts, Jer 29:13-14, while the second is his own formulation, a negative foil to reinforce the first. This pair of alternatives expresses what has been called mirror-image theology.[255] It sums up the Lord's normal dealings with Israel according to the Torah, though God also has an emergency system of restoration, proclaimed in 7:14. Here it serves to point forward to Asa's remaining years, which split into two contrasting periods. The clause "The LORD is with you while you are with him" will work itself out in vv. 8-19. While Asa and the people engaged in God's work, "the LORD . . . was with him" (v. 9). The opposite scenario, being forsaken by the forsaken God, will appear in chap. 16. A contrast between the two narratives is afforded by the double reference to commitment of heart in 15:17 and 16:19. Asa's commitment proved temporary.

Azariah gives a historical illustration in vv. 3-6. The alternatives of seeking and finding or leaving and losing the Lord were not foreign to Israel's pre-monarchical history. The book of Judges presents that period as a revolving wheel of fortune, a wheel segmented into declension, invasion, cry for help, divine deliverance, and peace (Judg 2:11-16; 3:7-11; 10:6-16). These segments are used to illustrate the alternatives facing Asa. In declension, Israel forsook the Lord, the legitimate priestly order, and the Torah for pagan religion (see Judg 2:12; 17:5-6). Yet, they were able to bypass the divine law of cause and effect by crying to God for help.

In Judges, the wheel turned on, and punitive crisis soon loomed again, with danger lurking on every journey, so prevalent was the enemy (cf. Judg 5:6; 6:2). In the absence of a true return, things went from bad to worse under God's chastising hand. If 2 Chr 15:3-4 illustrates the first alternative of v. 2, the vehemently negative vv. 5-6 function as a warning to Asa not to become embroiled in the second alternative. This rhetorical stick is replaced by a carrot in the concluding direct appeal to king and people. They are encouraged to keep up the good "work" and are urged not to rest on their laurels.

The chronicler wove into vv. 5-6 material from Zech 8:10. It is his way of challenging his post-exilic readers. Was not the return from exile marked by national distress? Was not this a case of forsaking God and incurring punishment? Such a history teaches one to seek the Lord and find in God the answer to one's needs. Just as Azariah was exhorting pre-exilic Judah by referring to past history, so also the chronicler was challenging post-exilic Judah and using Azariah's address as his own.

15:8-15. The rest of the chapter presents the development of the first of the two scenarios of v. 2. These verses are marked by positive answers to the prophetic word. In v. 8, "took courage" echoes the imperative in v. 7, an echo captured in the NRSV. The seeking and finding of vv. 12 and 15 pick up the principle laid down in v. 2 and illustrated in v. 4. King and people constitute a model congregation, taking the message to heart and living it out. Their behavior triggers a revival, a deepening of the nation's spiritual life. Further temple-related reform took place, and maintenance work was carried out on the altar. The Feast of Weeks evidently provided an opportunity for a special service of recommitment to the Lord (cf. Lev 23:15-21; there seems to be a wordplay between the root שׁבע [*šāba'*, "swore," "oath"] and שׁבועת [*šābu'ôt*, "weeks"]). Verses 9-15 are awash with expressions of totality and enthusiasm. Verse 9 mentions the representative wholeness of God's people, continuing the trend of 11:13-17. The sacrificial worship of v. 11 indicates their indebtedness to the Lord in the earlier battle.

This feast provided an incentive for the com-

255. J. G. McConville, *I & II Chronicles,* Daily Study Bible (Philadelphia: Westminster, 1984) 168-69.

munity to dedicate themselves to the Lord afresh. The royal command of 14:4 is now enthusiastically endorsed. Whereas the king was the subject there, now the people are actively involved. The total commitment of v. 12 echoes Jer 29:13 (cf. Deut 4:29). The obligation of each generation to decide anew for the God of earlier generations was honored in this communal pledge ("covenant"). It was an experience the chronicler yearned for his contemporaries to share. The somber note of v. 13 only adds to the impression of solidarity. It borrows from Deut 13:1-10; 17:2-7 a negative consequence of group solidarity (see Ezra 7:16; see also 1 Cor 5:5). The community's oath of allegiance, sealing the pledge of v. 12, is made to the accompaniment of hallelujahs and musical blasts, which expresses the fervor of human hearts. The chronicler was presenting a model of temple worship, a joyful celebration of spiritual commitment in which religious forms reflected the adoration of the heart. The paragraph ends on the satisfying note that the people had found the Lord and had, consequently, been given rest in the land.

15:16-19. These verses provide a fitting sequel, with their motifs of reform, thankfulness to the Lord, and peace. Apart from v. 19 they are cited en bloc from 1 Kgs 15:13-15, to capture the theme of Asa's reforming zeal. The presence of the high places, which in 1 Kings clashes with the chronicler's claim in 14:3, is harmonized by locating them in the northern kingdom (in cities captured, according to v. 8). The chronicler may have had in view the extension of the frontier as far north as Mizpah, recorded in 16:6 (cf. 17:2), despite the chronological anomaly. In the light of Asa's backsliding (chap. 16) the chronicler must have understood Asa's lifelong commitment as a reference to his life up to this point. The continual warfare of 1 Kgs 15:16 is deliberately adapted to accord with his periodization of Asa's reign.

REFLECTIONS

1. The chronicler presents his religious ideals in this section. The seeking of the Lord is its basic theme, mentioned no less than eight times. Seeking the Lord, in our idiom, refers to uncommitted persons' feeling their way toward faith. Here it stands for commitment that is worked out in positive ways. One prime way related to the Temple: worshiping there and not elsewhere, worshiping in the traditional monotheistic way and according to standard rites, and maintaining the fabric of the Temple. Such fidelity to the Temple in 14:3, 5*a* and 15:8 was a measure of fidelity to the Lord. Christian readers may be tempted to dismiss this focus as a typical Old Testament stress on the material, which in the New Testament gives way to spiritual concerns. This conclusion would ignore the coexistence of the material and the spiritual. Although John 4:21-26 announces a new era in which the Temple is superseded, the spirit of worship can be demonstrated only in material ways, and the inner attitude of the heart only in external forms. Belonging to the spiritual temple of the church carries with it the obligations of communal worship and commitment to a local congregation of believers (Heb 13:15; 1 Pet 2:5).

2. Each generation in turn was called to be a steward of temple worship. In seeking the Lord, they were also called to commitment to the Torah, to its revealed guidelines for life. John's appeal, in his first letter, to Christians to keep God's commandments in token of their love for God (1 John 5:2-3; see also 2:3-5), may be regarded as a renewed application of the message of 2 Chronicles. In the church to which John wrote, there were people claiming to love God, whose bluff he called by demanding that spiritual claims be grounded in keeping God's commandments.

3. The violent turn the narrative takes at 14:9 shows the chronicler's awareness that crisis is a fact of life that does not always discriminate between the worthy and the unworthy in its choice of victims. If it could not be explained in terms of moral providence, the pragmatic answer was that the Lord had provided resources so that one could deal with the situation. In the laments and thanksgiving songs in the book of Psalms, there is a turning to the Lord, even in the voicing of doubt and anger. In turn, we Christians are urged to "approach the throne of grace with confidence" and to find through prayer "grace to help us in our time of need" (Heb 4:16 NIV).

4. Asa's prayer in 14:11 is well known to Christian congregations in the form of the beautiful hymn written by Edith G. Cherry, "We rest on thee, our shield and our defender," happily set to Sibelius's *Finlandia.* As in 13:18, this kind of faith is not the everyday variety. It is trust exercised in crisis. Again in the laments of the psalms such faith is heard in ardent prayer, when life had inflicted bleeding wounds.

5. The mirror-image formula of spirituality in 15:2 reappears in principle in the teaching of Jesus, as an incentive to fulfill God-given obligations. It always has an unexpected ring, jolting readers out of complacency. In the Lord's prayer, God is asked with some irony to "forgive us our debts, as we also have forgiven our debtors" (Matt 6:12). Yes, God does take the initiative in forgiveness, but God sets up an obligation for us to forgive in turn, which if not heeded can damage our relationship with God and impede further forgiveness. So Jesus taught in his parable of forgiveness in Matt 18:21-35, which explains the petition in the prayer he gave the church. Mirror-image spirituality is the norm in God's dealings with believers (see Ps 18:25-26). The New Testament equivalent of 2 Chr 15:2 is the solemn either/or message of Gal 6:7-9 about sowing and reaping. Paul could use it along with the doctrine of justification by faith earlier in the letter, ill matched though the association may look in terms of human logic.

6. The use of Judges in Azariah's address (15:3-6) offers an instance of the use of past history in Scripture as a spur to the life of faith. It is a microcosm of what the books of Chronicles as a whole were meant to convey. The practice occurs elsewhere in the Bible as a means of conveying moral and spiritual lessons. Psalm 95 harks back to the wilderness period and is reused in Heb 3:7–4:13. Paul also employed that period for "examples" and "warnings" to believers (1 Cor 10:1-11 NIV). As we read scriptural narratives, we will find their relevance to our lives.

2 Chronicles 16:1-14, Asa's False Trust Punished

NIV

16 In the thirty-sixth year of Asa's reign Baasha king of Israel went up against Judah and fortified Ramah to prevent anyone from leaving or entering the territory of Asa king of Judah.

2Asa then took the silver and gold out of the
treasuries of the LORD's temple and of his own
palace and sent it to Ben-Hadad king of Aram,
who was ruling in Damascus. 3"Let there be a
treaty between me and you," he said, "as there
was between my father and your father. See, I
am sending you silver and gold. Now break your
treaty with Baasha king of Israel so he will withdraw from me."

4Ben-Hadad agreed with King Asa and sent the

NRSV

16 In the thirty-sixth year of the reign of Asa,
King Baasha of Israel went up against
Judah, and built Ramah, to prevent anyone from
going out or coming into the territory of[a] King
Asa of Judah. 2Then Asa took silver and gold from
the treasures of the house of the LORD and the
king's house, and sent them to King Ben-hadad
of Aram, who resided in Damascus, saying, 3"Let
there be an alliance between me and you, like
that between my father and your father; I am
sending to you silver and gold; go, break your
alliance with King Baasha of Israel, so that he may
withdraw from me." 4Ben-hadad listened to King

[a] Heb lacks *the territory of*

NIV

commanders of his forces against the towns of Israel. They conquered Ijon, Dan, Abel Maim[a] and all the store cities of Naphtali. 5When Baasha heard this, he stopped building Ramah and abandoned his work. 6Then King Asa brought all the men of Judah, and they carried away from Ramah the stones and timber Baasha had been using. With them he built up Geba and Mizpah.

7At that time Hanani the seer came to Asa king of Judah and said to him: "Because you relied on the king of Aram and not on the LORD your God, the army of the king of Aram has escaped from your hand. 8Were not the Cushites[b] and Libyans a mighty army with great numbers of chariots and horsemen[c]? Yet when you relied on the LORD, he delivered them into your hand. 9For the eyes of the LORD range throughout the earth to strengthen those whose hearts are fully committed to him. You have done a foolish thing, and from now on you will be at war."

10Asa was angry with the seer because of this; he was so enraged that he put him in prison. At the same time Asa brutally oppressed some of the people.

11The events of Asa's reign, from beginning to end, are written in the book of the kings of Judah and Israel. 12In the thirty-ninth year of his reign Asa was afflicted with a disease in his feet. Though his disease was severe, even in his illness he did not seek help from the LORD, but only from the physicians. 13Then in the forty-first year of his reign Asa died and rested with his fathers. 14They buried him in the tomb that he had cut out for himself in the City of David. They laid him on a bier covered with spices and various blended perfumes, and they made a huge fire in his honor.

a4 Also known as *Abel Beth Maacah* b8 That is, people from the upper Nile region c8 Or *charioteers*

NRSV

Asa, and sent the commanders of his armies against the cities of Israel. They conquered Ijon, Dan, Abel-maim, and all the store-cities of Naphtali. 5When Baasha heard of it, he stopped building Ramah, and let his work cease. 6Then King Asa brought all Judah, and they carried away the stones of Ramah and its timber, with which Baasha had been building, and with them he built up Geba and Mizpah.

7At that time the seer Hanani came to King Asa of Judah, and said to him, "Because you relied on the king of Aram, and did not rely on the LORD your God, the army of the king of Aram has escaped you. 8Were not the Ethiopians[a] and the Libyans a huge army with exceedingly many chariots and cavalry? Yet because you relied on the LORD, he gave them into your hand. 9For the eyes of the LORD range throughout the entire earth, to strengthen those whose heart is true to him. You have done foolishly in this; for from now on you will have wars." 10Then Asa was angry with the seer, and put him in the stocks, in prison, for he was in a rage with him because of this. And Asa inflicted cruelties on some of the people at the same time.

11The acts of Asa, from first to last, are written in the Book of the Kings of Judah and Israel. 12In the thirty-ninth year of his reign Asa was diseased in his feet, and his disease became severe; yet even in his disease he did not seek the LORD, but sought help from physicians. 13Then Asa slept with his ancestors, dying in the forty-first year of his reign. 14They buried him in the tomb that he had hewn out for himself in the city of David. They laid him on a bier that had been filled with various kinds of spices prepared by the perfumer's art; and they made a very great fire in his honor.

a Or *Nubians*; Heb *Cushites*

COMMENTARY

In the macrostructure of the unit (13:1–16:14), Asa's new trust in human allies stands as a negative counterpart to the trust in the Lord, expressed in the two earlier sections. From a narrower perspective, this section describes the outworking of the second of the two scenarios offered by Azariah in 15:2-7, to abandon the Lord and suffer the bitter consequences. So, as the illustration in 15:6 warned, Asa will find himself troubled by God with every kind of distress. The section is a hellish reversal of the previous two. Victory is now won by unworthy means, the Lord's word is rejected, and, in contrast to earlier fidelity, infidelity is compounded. Asa becomes for the chronicler's readers a dramatic warning against backsliding (cf. Ezek 18:24).

16:1-6. The chronicler substantially repeats 1 Kgs 15:17-22 in vv. 1*b*-6. "Abel-maim" (v. 4) was probably the post-exilic name for "Abel-beth-maacah" (1 Kgs 15:20). The reference in v. 5 to Asa's having abandoned his work is probably the chronicler's attempt to make sense of a partially illegible text in 1 Kgs 15:21. He lets the 1 Kings passage speak for itself, reserving comment until the speech of Hanani in vv. 7-10. However, his underlying sense of outrage is easily appreciated. Where now is the faith expressed in 14:11? How can treasures consecrated to the Lord, including Asa's own votive gifts put in the Temple in the halcyon days of 15:18, be seized and used as payment for foreign aid?

The chronological notice added in v. 1*a* corresponds to the previous one in 15:19. The chronicler appears to have envisioned Asa's forty-one-year reign as being divided into two long periods of spirituality and blessing (15 + 20 years) and two short periods of unspirituality and misfortune (3 + 3 years). Some scholars have attempted to relate the thirty-fifth and thirty-sixth years to the length of time since the division of the monarchy, equating them with the fifteenth and sixteenth years of Asa's reign.[256] However, Asa's death in the forty-first year of his reign is a given, taken over from 1 Kgs 15:10, and the earlier numbers are more likely the product of the chronicler's schematization. He probably overlooked the chronological discrepancy with 1 Kgs 15:33; 16:8.

The chronicler did not view Baasha's aggressive move into Judean territory as providential retaliation for disobedience (cf. 12:1-2). Rather, he saw it as a counterpart to Zerah's invasion earlier in the reign (14:19) and as an opportunity to put renewed trust in the Lord, whereupon Baasha would have been repulsed by supernatural means.

16:7-9. Whereas in 1 Kings Asa is not blamed for his alliance with Aram, the chronicler uses the prophetic speech of Hanani to condemn it as a breach of faith in the Lord. He derives the name from the reference to the prophet "Jehu the son of Hanani" in 1 Kgs 16:1, 7, an opponent of Baasha, and he will make use of the son's name in 19:2; 20:34 in his account of Jehoshaphat's reign. Hanani's address is made up of essentially an initial accusation followed by an announcement of punishment, with the accusation enhanced by an elaboration of Asa's folly. In prophetic oracles, the accusation is at times made to appear more shocking by setting it against a background of divine grace (e.g., Isa 5:4; Amos 2:9-11; Mic 6:3-5). Asa's folly was to disregard the gracious aid he had enjoyed previously and that would still have been available to him. If the king was congratulating himself on the success of his stratagem, he needed to hear how shortsighted he had been. Not only would he have secured the retreat of Baasha, but also the Aramean army would have fallen into his lap![257]

The reference to Asa's earlier victory is described in terms of reliance on the Lord, and by contrast the alliance with Aram is regarded as a switch of allegiance. The key word of the literary unit, "rely," bombards Asa's ears and the reader's eyes, recalling 14:11. Again crisis gave an opportunity to prove the Lord, but this time trust was put in human aid. The chronicler seems to have had Isa 10:20 in mind, which mentions relying (NIV; NRSV, "lean") on the Lord instead of on Assyria. Isaiah had considered reliance on foreign aid a besetting sin of the Judean monarchy (Isa 30:1-2; 31:1), while earlier Hosea had berated the northern kingdom for such improper action (Hos 7:8-12; 14:3). Such is the prophetic standpoint that the chronicler puts in the mouth of the prophet Hanani.

Verse 9 cites Zech 4:10, affirming the universality of the Lord's protection. God could cope with crisis from any quarter, ever ready to respond to faith with a demonstration of divine power. In fact, narratives of divine deliverance throughout chaps. 13–25 illustrate victory over the north in chap. 13, the west in chap. 14, the east in chap. 20, and the south in chap. 25. In this case, however, faith had been replaced by folly. In reprisal, Asa's lot would be warfare, not peace as before. The chronicler found a providential role for the warfare of 1 Kgs 15:16, which for him

256. E.g., H. G. M. Williamson, *1 and 2 Chronicles*, NCB (Grand Rapids: Eerdmans, 1982) 256-58; S. J. De Vries, *1 and 2 Chronicles*, FOTL 11 (Grand Rapids: Eerdmans, 1989) 296.

257. E. L. Curtis and A. A. Madsen, *The Books of Chronicles*, ICC (Edinburgh: T. &. T. Clark, 1910) 389.

lasted the remaining five or six years of Asa's reign. This final period was no longer a test of faith but retribution for lack of faith.

16:10. Asa had responded in model fashion to a sermon in chap. 15. Now he compounds his errant spiritual attitude by rejecting the divine message. He takes out on God's messenger his resentment against God, putting the messenger in the prison "stocks," a fate for a prophet that the chronicler derived from the book of Jeremiah (Jer 20:3; 29:26). Some of the people were tortured. The ideal of a king's proper rule (2:1; 9:8; see also 1 Chr 14:2) has been left far behind. Presumably the chronicler adduced this persecution of prophet and people as the reason for Asa's illness in v. 12, which we are not given enough information to identify.

16:11-14. The royal epilogue in 1 Kgs 15:23-24 is used, with extra focus on the king's illness and burial and specifying the length of his reign from 1 Kgs 15:10. The chronicler identifies his main source as a document identified with the canonical books of 1–2 Kings, blocks of which have been used in his account, though he seems to have had access to other written traditions. If Asa failed to rely on the Lord in his military crisis, he also failed to "seek the LORD" in a personal crisis generated by his own wrongdoing, and instead turned to physicians. Asa did not take the opportunity to resort to God in prayer in his sickness (6:28), humbling himself and turning from his wicked ways (7:14). We are meant to understand that Asa's lack of repentance led to his death.

The report of an elaborate funeral, with lavish burning of spices (cf. 21:19; Jer 34:5), is a device the chronicler often used to give an overall evaluation of a reign. In fairness he wanted readers to remember that even if Asa fell from grace in his final six years, for thirty-five years he had been a good king. The chronicler so characterized him in 20:32 and 21:12 (cf. 17:3-4). Yesterday's scandals were not allowed to obliterate the integrity of yesteryear. The chronicler could not bring himself to apply the rigorous standard offered as a deterrent in Ezek 18:24, that "none of the righteous deeds . . . shall be remembered" (NRSV).

REFLECTIONS

1. Asa exemplifies a good person who turns bad. His story warns against spiritual complacency. In the terms of 1 Tim 1:19, Asa suffered a shipwreck in the faith. What counts is for the believer to have a steady walk with God in ordinary days, finding resources from God to cope with emergencies, and, if sin intrudes, repairing the damage by humbly seeking divine forgiveness. Asa failed the third test, fool that he was (16:9).

2. The heart of the chapter is Hanani's interpretive message. He is another Isaiah, contrasting recourse to foreign military aid with reliance on God. In a crisis, Asa looked around rather than up, forgetting the proven help the Lord gives to committed believers. Lessons of trust, once we have learned them, are to be reapplied when crisis strikes again. According to Paul: God, "who rescued us from so deadly a peril will continue to rescue us; on him we have set our hope that he will rescue us again" (2 Cor 1:10 NRSV).

3. Hanani, like Jeremiah, suffered persecution for his faithful witness for the Lord. The chronicler will return to the motif of persecution in 18:26 and 24:20-22; it stands out starkly against the mellow background of his standard teaching that loyalty to God spells blessing. Jesus echoes the motif in one of his ironical beatutitudes: "Blessed are you when people . . . persecute you. In the same way they persecuted the prophets" (Matt 5:11-12). It takes courage to witness for God in a hostile or potentially hostile environment. The writer of the Letter to the Hebrews, addressing a group who had previously suffered persecution and were likely to do so again, challenged them to recall the persecution that God's people in the Old Testament had endured (Heb 10:32-35; 11:35-37). He pointed them to the supreme example of Jesus (Heb 12:3).

4. Healing is a perennial topic on which Christians seek spiritual enlightenment. This passage gives only part of the biblical answer. The chronicler brackets recourse to physicians together with an alliance with a foreign king as a further example of resorting to human aid, rather than divine. Morally lapsed as Asa was, his disease should have been a warning of the Lord's displeasure. This malady went too deep for doctors to cure, irrespective of the limitations of ancient medical lore. Asa's reaction represented an evasive tactic, dealing with a symptom instead of going to the root of the problem and seeking God in the spirit of 7:14. It was like treating a decayed tooth with a pain reliever. In the New Testament, too, are envisioned cases of sickness linked with unfaithfulness to God (1 Cor 11:30). According to Paul's diagnosis, the sick Christians at Corinth would have been remiss to seek medical help rather than putting their spiritual malady aright. This text is not the only biblical tradition concerning medical help; Paul's reference to Luke as "the beloved physician" (Col 4:14 NRSV) reflects positive appreciation, while the intertestamental Ben Sira taught God's healing through the agency of doctors (Sir 38:1-15).

2 CHRONICLES 17:1–21:1*a*, JEHOSHAPHAT CHOOSES AND LOSES THE LORD'S PRESENCE

OVERVIEW

The four chapters devoted to Jehoshaphat indicate his importance in the chronicler's eyes. He has used the motif of divine presence, expressed by means of the preposition "with" (עם *'im*), to describe the reigns of David (1 Chr 11:9; 17:2, 8) and Solomon (1 Chr 22:11, 16; 28:20; 2 Chr 1:1). It has previously surfaced in important passages (13:12; 15:2, 9; cf. 13:8). Now it takes on a structural role in this literary unit, concerned with Jehoshaphat's reign. He and his subjects had opportunities to enjoy the Lord's presence in blessing that followed obedience (17:3), in the maintenance of social justice (19:6, 11) and in help against an external threat (20:17). This positive motif is interspersed with a negative one, alliance with sinners, represented by the northern kings Ahab and Ahaziah (18:3; 20:35-37). So the chronicler's account of the reign of Jehoshaphat provides a challenging sermon on the alternatives of association with God or with human allies, somewhat on the lines of a NT text: "As God has said, 'I will live with them. . . . Therefore come out from them and be separate, says the Lord' " (2 Cor 6:16-17 NIV).

At one point the chronicler slightly alters his source in order to highlight the motif. The word אתי (*'ittî*, "with me") in 1 Kgs 22:4 is standardized to עמי (*'immî*) in 2 Chr 18:3, and "we will be with you in the war" (NRSV) is added. The use of the key word establishes five sections in an ABAAB pattern. These sections accord with the five narratives that make up the unit: 17:1-19; 18:1–19:3; 19:4-11; 20:1-30; and 20:31–21:1*a*. Three of the sections are also graced with the chronicler's prime term for spirituality, "seek" (דרש *dāraš*), in 17:3-4; 18:4 (NIV; NRSV, "inquire"); 19:3; and 20:3 (cf. the use of בקש [*biqqēš*, "seek"] in v. 4). In the fourth section, verbal phrases with the same role appear (20:32-33).

2 Chronicles 17:1-19, Finding God in Obedience and Blessing

NIV

17 Jehoshaphat his son succeeded him as king and strengthened himself against Israel. 2He stationed troops in all the fortified cities of Judah and put garrisons in Judah and in the towns of Ephraim that his father Asa had captured.

3The LORD was with Jehoshaphat because in his early years he walked in the ways his father David had followed. He did not consult the Baals 4but sought the God of his father and followed his commands rather than the practices of Israel. 5The LORD established the kingdom under his control; and all Judah brought gifts to Jehoshaphat, so that he had great wealth and honor. 6His heart was devoted to the ways of the LORD; furthermore, he removed the high places and the Asherah poles from Judah.

7In the third year of his reign he sent his officials Ben-Hail, Obadiah, Zechariah, Nethanel and Micaiah to teach in the towns of Judah. 8With them were certain Levites—Shemaiah, Nethaniah, Zebadiah, Asahel, Shemiramoth, Jehonathan, Adonijah, Tobijah and Tob-Adonijah—and the priests Elishama and Jehoram. 9They taught throughout Judah, taking with them the Book of the Law of the LORD; they went around to all the towns of Judah and taught the people.

10The fear of the LORD fell on all the kingdoms of the lands surrounding Judah, so that they did not make war with Jehoshaphat. 11Some Philistines brought Jehoshaphat gifts and silver as tribute, and the Arabs brought him flocks: seven thousand seven hundred rams and seven thousand seven hundred goats.

12Jehoshaphat became more and more powerful; he built forts and store cities in Judah 13and had large supplies in the towns of Judah. He also kept experienced fighting men in Jerusalem. 14Their enrollment by families was as follows:

From Judah, commanders of units of 1,000:
Adnah the commander, with 300,000 fighting men;
15next, Jehohanan the commander, with 280,000;

NRSV

17 His son Jehoshaphat succeeded him, and strengthened himself against Israel. 2He placed forces in all the fortified cities of Judah, and set garrisons in the land of Judah, and in the cities of Ephraim that his father Asa had taken. 3The LORD was with Jehoshaphat, because he walked in the earlier ways of his father;[a] he did not seek the Baals, 4but sought the God of his father and walked in his commandments, and not according to the ways of Israel. 5Therefore the LORD established the kingdom in his hand. All Judah brought tribute to Jehoshaphat, and he had great riches and honor. 6His heart was courageous in the ways of the LORD; and furthermore he removed the high places and the sacred poles[b] from Judah.

7In the third year of his reign he sent his officials, Ben-hail, Obadiah, Zechariah, Nethanel, and Micaiah, to teach in the cities of Judah. 8With them were the Levites, Shemaiah, Nethaniah, Zebadiah, Asahel, Shemiramoth, Jehonathan, Adonijah, Tobijah, and Tob-adonijah; and with these Levites, the priests Elishama and Jehoram. 9They taught in Judah, having the book of the law of the LORD with them; they went around through all the cities of Judah and taught among the people.

10The fear of the LORD fell on all the kingdoms of the lands around Judah, and they did not make war against Jehoshaphat. 11Some of the Philistines brought Jehoshaphat presents, and silver for tribute; and the Arabs also brought him seven thousand seven hundred rams and seven thousand seven hundred male goats. 12Jehoshaphat grew steadily greater. He built fortresses and storage cities in Judah. 13He carried out great works in the cities of Judah. He had soldiers, mighty warriors, in Jerusalem. 14This was the muster of them by ancestral houses: Of Judah, the commanders of the thousands: Adnah the commander, with three hundred thousand mighty warriors, 15and next to him Jehohanan the commander, with two hundred eighty thousand, 16and next to him Amasiah son of Zichri, a volunteer for the service

[a] Another reading is *his father David* [b] Heb *Asherim*

NIV

[16]next, Amasiah son of Zicri, who volunteered himself for the service of the LORD, with 200,000.

[17]From Benjamin:

Eliada, a valiant soldier, with 200,000 men armed with bows and shields;

[18]next, Jehozabad, with 180,000 men armed for battle.

[19]These were the men who served the king, besides those he stationed in the fortified cities throughout Judah.

NRSV

of the LORD, with two hundred thousand mighty warriors. [17]Of Benjamin: Eliada, a mighty warrior, with two hundred thousand armed with bow and shield, [18]and next to him Jehozabad with one hundred eighty thousand armed for war. [19]These were in the service of the king, besides those whom the king had placed in the fortified cities throughout all Judah.

COMMENTARY

The presentation of Jehoshaphat's reign in 1–2 Kings often involves relations with the northern kingdom (1 Kgs 15:24*b*; 22:1-50; 2 Kgs 3:4-27). Here he is considered in his own right as a Judahite king. This chapter functions as an introduction describing his rule. The following chapters either endorse the high assessment of Jehoshaphat or provide exceptions to the general tenor of his reign. Only at 17:1, 3 is there use of the 1 Kings narrative (1 Kgs 15:24; 22:43).

17:1-5. The gist of the section is provided here in summary form. It is structured with a spiritual center (vv. 3*b*-4) and a framework of divinely authored success (vv. 1-3*a,* 5). Jehoshaphat's life was characterized by loyalty to God. The accolade of spirituality is bestowed on him: He "sought" the Lord. An even more glowing testimony will be given in 22:9: "He sought the LORD with all his heart."

The observation is clarified by a comparison and a contrast. Jehoshaphat lived up to the chronicler's ideal of appropriating his father's faith, keeping the spiritual flag flying in the next generation. The chronicler follows 1 Kgs 22:43 in comparing him with Asa. But his own representation of Asa required him to distinguish between Asa's "earlier" period of faith, described in chaps. 14–15, and his later period of decline in chap. 16 (NRSV, following the shorter reading of the LXX [cf. v. 4*a*]; the NIV retains the MT's "David" and then gives the unlikely rendering "in his [= Jehoshaphat's] early years"). Jehoshaphat is compared to his sinful northern contemporary Ahab in oblique terms. The chronicler presupposes knowledge of the final chapters of 1 Kings, where Ahab's devotion to Canaanite religion is narrated. By contrast, Jehoshaphat exemplifies devotion to the Torah. Such spirituality invited the Lord's presence in blessing, which is described in terms of military defense in vv. 1*b*-2. As in 11:5-12, the royal defense system was a mark of divine help, making Judah a strong nation. Blessing is further elaborated in v. 5, in terms of consolidation of his rule and riches and honor.

17:6-9. Verses 1-5 offer a digest of the rest of the chapter, where its themes are amplified. Jehoshaphat's adherence to the religious purity of the Torah, and so to that of the Temple, is illustrated in v. 6*b* with loose reference to Deut 7:5; 12:2-3. As in 14:3, the chronicler is writing idealistically and so does not use 1 Kgs 22:43, which he will cite later in 20:33. The compliment in v. 6*a* refers literally to a high heart. Elsewhere it connotes pride ("He took pride in the service of the Lord" [REB]). It here refers to high ideals and serves as a headline for both v. 6*b* and vv. 7-9. The king's wider commitment to the Torah finds illustration in vv. 7-9. The dating in Jehoshaphat's third year may be simply a literary device for the close of a short period of time.[258] An itinerant team of teachers is envisioned as

258. M. Cogan, "The Chronicler's Use of Chronology as Illuminated by Neo-Assyrian Royal Inscription," in *Empirical Models for Biblical Criticism,* ed. J. H. Tigay (Philadelphia: University of Pennsylvania Press, 1980) 197-209, esp. 207-8.

having been commissioned by the king. Here and in the related 19:4-11 the chronicler appears to have drawn from a source describing Jehoshaphat's judicial reforms. In this case, the promulgation of the royal law code was doubtless in view, and the chronicler adapted it anachronistically into a concern for the Torah, or Pentateuch.[259] In the light of 15:3, teaching and Torah went together—naturally so, since Torah relates to directions for life's journey, as was noted at 6:16, 27. A team of Levites and priests, backed by royal officials to lend authority to the enterprise, was dispatched throughout Judah on a teaching mission. There are post-exilic similarities with Ezra's commission from the Persian king in Ezra 7:6, 11-26 and with the expository task of the Levites in Neh 8:7-8. Here was a further example of Jehoshaphat's high ideals, instructing the people in divine revelation so that it might govern their lives. Such activity corresponds to Asa's concerns expressed in 14:4.

17:10-12a. The blessing mentioned in v. 5*b* is amplified in vv. 10-11. The gift of Solomonic peace, enjoyed by Asa in 14:1, 6-7, is combined with fear typical of a holy war, such as foreigners had of Asa (14:14). Another of Solomon's blessings, tribute from other nations (9:14, 23-24), appears in v. 11, while the increasing prominence of the king echoes that of David in 1 Chr 11:9, where it is accompanied by the formula of divine presence. Here was a noble scion of the Davidic dynasty.

17:12b-19. The theme of troops and fortified cities, broached in v. 2, is now expanded. Fortresses and military "supplies" were part of the defense system, which was manned by a standing army (vv. 13, 19*b*). As backup there was a large conscript army, whose commanding officers are listed in vv. 14-18. Along with the notice in 14:8, vv. 14-18 probably derive from a royal military census list that was available to the chronicler.[260] Doubtless the word אלף (*'elep*), here rendered in terms of thousands, referred there to much smaller units, though the chronicler has maximized them. In v. 14, the conscript army available in wartime seems to be equated with the standing army stationed in Jerusalem. The list was not adequately coordinated with its new context.

259. See H. G. M. Williamson, *1 and 2 Chronicles*, NCB (Grand Rapids: Eerdmans, 1982) 282-83.

260. See ibid., 261-63.

REFLECTIONS

1. The blessings of the divine presence enjoyed by a spiritually minded king are the topic of this chapter. In principle this theme corresponds to Paul's promise that the presence of the God of love and peace would attend in blessing those who pursued such virtues among their fellow Christians (2 Cor 13:11). A similar promise appears in Phil 4:9, that continuance in apostolic teaching and practice would secure the presence of the God of peace. We who want God to be with us in our lives are here given clues as to how to achieve such a blessing.

2. The theme of 17:1-5 is seeking and finding. The narrative develops the spiritual principle enunciated by Azariah in 15:2, "The LORD is with you, while you are with him. If you seek him, he will be found by you" (NRSV). The chronicler encourages his own constituency to commit themselves to God. The king's success is traced back to his dedication to the Lord. Seeking God, he found evidence of God's goodness flooding his life. For the chronicler, a living faith and well-being went together, and exceptions only proved the rule. Jehoshaphat stands as a spiritual role model for the chronicler.

3. The developments described in 17:6-19 are prefaced by a reference to Jehoshaphat's high ideals or spiritual ambitions. A strikingly similar reference occurs in the New Testament in the exhortation of Col 3:2, which literally may be rendered, "Think high things." Ambition is a virtue when practiced within the guidelines of "the ways of the LORD." The king's high aims were achieved in the twin areas of love of God and love of neighbor (17:6*b*, 7-9). The

community was encouraged to take seriously the standards of the Torah for their lives. The chronicler's own communal ideal is transparent here.

4. The muster list at the close of the chapter describes one of the officers as "a volunteer for the service of the LORD" (17:16 NRSV). He evidently volunteered and rose to a responsible rank, but interestingly his work is described in religious terms. A word with the same root occurs in a royal psalm at Ps 110:3, which speaks of the king's subjects as volunteers to serve him in his divinely authorized campaigns. Similarly, the New Testament urges Christian slaves as they serve their masters to "work willingly for the sake of the Lord" (Eph 6:7 NJB; cf. Col 3:23). Happy is the person whose job is his or her hobby, to paraphrase George Bernard Shaw. Even happier is the person whose daily work is dedicated to God and done to please the Lord.

2 Chronicles 18:1–19:3, Collusion with a Northern King

NIV

18 Now Jehoshaphat had great wealth and
honor, and he allied himself with Ahab by
marriage. 2Some years later he went down to visit
Ahab in Samaria. Ahab slaughtered many sheep
and cattle for him and the people with him and
urged him to attack Ramoth Gilead. 3Ahab king
of Israel asked Jehoshaphat king of Judah, "Will
you go with me against Ramoth Gilead?"

Jehoshaphat replied, "I am as you are, and my
people as your people; we will join you in the
war." 4But Jehoshaphat also said to the king of
Israel, "First seek the counsel of the LORD."

5So the king of Israel brought together the
prophets—four hundred men—and asked them,
"Shall we go to war against Ramoth Gilead, or
shall I refrain?"

"Go," they answered, "for God will give it into
the king's hand."

6But Jehoshaphat asked, "Is there not a prophet
of the LORD here whom we can inquire of?"

7The king of Israel answered Jehoshaphat,
"There is still one man through whom we can
inquire of the LORD, but I hate him because he
never prophesies anything good about me, but
always bad. He is Micaiah son of Imlah."

"The king should not say that," Jehoshaphat
replied.

8So the king of Israel called one of his officials
and said, "Bring Micaiah son of Imlah at once."

9Dressed in their royal robes, the king of Israel
and Jehoshaphat king of Judah were sitting on
their thrones at the threshing floor by the entrance
to the gate of Samaria, with all the prophets
prophesying before them. 10Now Zedekiah son of

NRSV

18 Now Jehoshaphat had great riches and
honor; and he made a marriage alliance
with Ahab. 2After some years he went down to
Ahab in Samaria. Ahab slaughtered an abundance
of sheep and oxen for him and for the people
who were with him, and induced him to go up
against Ramoth-gilead. 3King Ahab of Israel said
to King Jehoshaphat of Judah, "Will you go with
me to Ramoth-gilead?" He answered him, "I am
with you, my people are your people. We will be
with you in the war."

4But Jehoshaphat also said to the king of Israel,
"Inquire first for the word of the LORD." 5Then
the king of Israel gathered the prophets together,
four hundred of them, and said to them, "Shall
we go to battle against Ramoth-gilead, or shall I
refrain?" They said, "Go up; for God will give it
into the hand of the king." 6But Jehoshaphat said,
"Is there no other prophet of the LORD here of
whom we may inquire?" 7The king of Israel said
to Jehoshaphat, "There is still one other by whom
we may inquire of the LORD, Micaiah son of Imlah;
but I hate him, for he never prophesies anything
favorable about me, but only disaster." Jehoshaphat said, "Let the king not say such a
thing." 8Then the king of Israel summoned an
officer and said, "Bring quickly Micaiah son of
Imlah." 9Now the king of Israel and King Jehoshaphat of Judah were sitting on their thrones,
arrayed in their robes; and they were sitting at
the threshing floor at the entrance of the gate of
Samaria; and all the prophets were prophesying
before them. 10Zedekiah son of Chenaanah made
for himself horns of iron, and he said, "Thus says

NIV

Kenaanah had made iron horns, and he declared,
"This is what the LORD says: 'With these you will
gore the Arameans until they are destroyed.'"

11All the other prophets were prophesying the
same thing. "Attack Ramoth Gilead and be victorious," they said, "for the LORD will give it into
the king's hand."

12The messenger who had gone to summon
Micaiah said to him, "Look, as one man the other
prophets are predicting success for the king. Let
your word agree with theirs, and speak favorably."

13But Micaiah said, "As surely as the LORD lives,
I can tell him only what my God says."

14When he arrived, the king asked him, "Micaiah, shall we go to war against Ramoth Gilead,
or shall I refrain?"

"Attack and be victorious," he answered, "for
they will be given into your hand."

15The king said to him, "How many times must
I make you swear to tell me nothing but the truth
in the name of the LORD?"

16Then Micaiah answered, "I saw all Israel
scattered on the hills like sheep without a shepherd, and the LORD said, 'These people have no
master. Let each one go home in peace.'"

17The king of Israel said to Jehoshaphat, "Didn't
I tell you that he never prophesies anything good
about me, but only bad?"

18Micaiah continued, "Therefore hear the word
of the LORD: I saw the LORD sitting on his throne
with all the host of heaven standing on his right
and on his left. 19And the LORD said, 'Who will
entice Ahab king of Israel into attacking Ramoth
Gilead and going to his death there?'

"One suggested this, and another that. 20Fi-
nally, a spirit came forward, stood before the LORD
and said, 'I will entice him.'

"'By what means?' the LORD asked.

21"'I will go and be a lying spirit in the mouths
of all his prophets,' he said.

"'You will succeed in enticing him,' said the
LORD. 'Go and do it.'

22"So now the LORD has put a lying spirit in the
mouths of these prophets of yours. The LORD has
decreed disaster for you."

23Then Zedekiah son of Kenaanah went up and
slapped Micaiah in the face. "Which way did the

NRSV

the LORD: With these you shall gore the Arameans
until they are destroyed." 11All the prophets were
prophesying the same and saying, "Go up to
Ramoth-gilead and triumph; the LORD will give it
into the hand of the king."

12The messenger who had gone to summon
Micaiah said to him, "Look, the words of the
prophets with one accord are favorable to the
king; let your word be like the word of one of
them, and speak favorably." 13But Micaiah said,
"As the LORD lives, whatever my God says, that
I will speak."

14When he had come to the king, the king
said to him, "Micaiah, shall we go to Ramoth-
gilead to battle, or shall I refrain?" He answered,
"Go up and triumph; they will be given into your
hand." 15But the king said to him, "How many
times must I make you swear to tell me nothing
but the truth in the name of the LORD?" 16Then
Micaiah[a] said, "I saw all Israel scattered on the
mountains, like sheep without a shepherd; and
the LORD said, 'These have no master; let each
one go home in peace.'" 17The king of Israel said
to Jehoshaphat, "Did I not tell you that he would
not prophesy anything favorable about me, but
only disaster?"

18Then Micaiah[a] said, "Therefore hear the
word of the LORD: I saw the LORD sitting on his
throne, with all the host of heaven standing to
the right and to the left of him. 19And the LORD
said, 'Who will entice King Ahab of Israel, so that
he may go up and fall at Ramoth-gilead?' Then
one said one thing, and another said another,
20until a spirit came forward and stood before the
LORD, saying, 'I will entice him.' The LORD asked
him, 'How?' 21He replied, 'I will go out and be a
lying spirit in the mouth of all his prophets.' Then
the LORD[a] said, 'You are to entice him, and you
shall succeed; go out and do it.' 22So you see, the
LORD has put a lying spirit in the mouth of these
your prophets; the LORD has decreed disaster for
you."

23Then Zedekiah son of Chenaanah came up
to Micaiah, slapped him on the cheek, and said,
"Which way did the spirit of the LORD pass from
me to speak to you?" 24Micaiah replied, "You will
find out on that day when you go in to hide in

[a] Heb *he*

NIV

spirit from[a] the LORD go when he went from me to speak to you?" he asked.

24Micaiah replied, "You will find out on the day you go to hide in an inner room."

25The king of Israel then ordered, "Take Micaiah and send him back to Amon the ruler of the city and to Joash the king's son, 26and say, 'This is what the king says: Put this fellow in prison and give him nothing but bread and water until I return safely.'"

27Micaiah declared, "If you ever return safely, the LORD has not spoken through me." Then he added, "Mark my words, all you people!"

28So the king of Israel and Jehoshaphat king of Judah went up to Ramoth Gilead. 29The king of Israel said to Jehoshaphat, "I will enter the battle in disguise, but you wear your royal robes." So the king of Israel disguised himself and went into battle.

30Now the king of Aram had ordered his chariot commanders, "Do not fight with anyone, small or great, except the king of Israel." 31When the chariot commanders saw Jehoshaphat, they thought, "This is the king of Israel." So they turned to attack him, but Jehoshaphat cried out, and the LORD helped him. God drew them away from him, 32for when the chariot commanders saw that he was not the king of Israel, they stopped pursuing him.

33But someone drew his bow at random and hit the king of Israel between the sections of his armor. The king told the chariot driver, "Wheel around and get me out of the fighting. I've been wounded." 34All day long the battle raged, and the king of Israel propped himself up in his chariot facing the Arameans until evening. Then at sunset he died.

19 When Jehoshaphat king of Judah returned safely to his palace in Jerusalem, 2Jehu the seer, the son of Hanani, went out to meet him and said to the king, "Should you help the wicked and love[b] those who hate the LORD? Because of this, the wrath of the LORD is upon you. 3There is, however, some good in you, for you have rid the land of the Asherah poles and have set your heart on seeking God."

a23 Or *Spirit of* b2 Or *and make alliances with*

NRSV

an inner chamber." 25The king of Israel then ordered, "Take Micaiah, and return him to Amon the governor of the city and to Joash the king's son; 26and say, 'Thus says the king: Put this fellow in prison, and feed him on reduced rations of bread and water until I return in peace.'" 27Micaiah said, "If you return in peace, the LORD has not spoken by me." And he said, "Hear, you peoples, all of you!"

28So the king of Israel and King Jehoshaphat of Judah went up to Ramoth-gilead. 29The king of Israel said to Jehoshaphat, "I will disguise myself and go into battle, but you wear your robes." So the king of Israel disguised himself, and they went into battle. 30Now the king of Aram had commanded the captains of his chariots, "Fight with no one small or great, but only with the king of Israel." 31When the captains of the chariots saw Jehoshaphat, they said, "It is the king of Israel." So they turned to fight against him; and Jehoshaphat cried out, and the LORD helped him. God drew them away from him, 32for when the captains of the chariots saw that it was not the king of Israel, they turned back from pursuing him. 33But a certain man drew his bow and unknowingly struck the king of Israel between the scale armor and the breastplate; so he said to the driver of his chariot, "Turn around, and carry me out of the battle, for I am wounded." 34The battle grew hot that day, and the king of Israel propped himself up in his chariot facing the Arameans until evening; then at sunset he died.

19 King Jehoshaphat of Judah returned in safety to his house in Jerusalem. 2Jehu son of Hanani the seer went out to meet him and said to King Jehoshaphat, "Should you help the wicked and love those who hate the LORD? Because of this, wrath has gone out against you from the LORD. 3Nevertheless, some good is found in you, for you destroyed the sacred poles[a] out of the land, and have set your heart to seek God."

a Heb *Asheroth*

COMMENTARY

The moral of this story is spelled out in the prophet Jehu's interpretation in 19:2: Jehoshaphat ended up in the wrong camp, helping the Lord's enemies. The king entered into an alliance with the northern king Ahab. The story is taken from 1 Kgs 22:2, 4-35, which is closely followed in 18:2*a,* 3-34. The focus of the narrative in 1 Kings 22 lies in the fate of the wicked king Ahab, unable to evade God's punishment. Here Jehoshaphat is the center of the story, as new material at the beginning, partway through, and at the end indicates (18:1, 2*b,* 31*b;* 19:1-3). If improper association with the Lord's enemies is the point of the story in the larger literary context (17:1–20:37), then such behavior also carries its own message, as is indicated by the chronicler's addition of the verb הסית (*hēsît,* in the hiphil, "entice") with a human subject at 18:2 (NRSV, "induced"; NIV, "urged") and with God as subject at 18:31 ("drew away"). This new verb acts as a counterfoil to the synonymous divine enticing of 18:19-21 (= 1 Kgs 22:20-22: יפתה [*yĕpatteh*]). The story becomes a study in manipulation, both human and divine. The three appearances of the verb, taken over from 1 Kings, are set in a new framework of enticement. The celestial scheme of enticing Ahab to his death is presented as a reprisal for Ahab's own scheming in 18:2. Ahab is outmaneuvered, and the punishment is shown to fit his recent crime. As for 18:31, Ahab's further plotting against Jehoshaphat is foiled. The Lord manipulated the tactics of the enemy charioteers to save Jehoshaphat. So justice was done by punishing the bad king and protecting the good but gullible king.

18:1-3. Verse 1*a* repeats 17:5*b* as a critical comment on Jehoshaphat's marriage alliance in v. 1*b,* which anticipates 21:6 (= 2 Kgs 8:18). Although the Lord had lavished "great riches and honor" on him, he ventured into the marriage treaty, which was contracted among royalty for political and economic advantage. Ahab's name is introduced into the narrative from the start, whereas in the parent text it is delayed until 1 Kgs 22:20. The name spoke volumes to anyone who knew the account of his reign in 1 Kings, which the chronicler presupposes. His own comments in 21:6; 22:2-3 indicate his low estimate of Ahab. Earlier Jehoshaphat had resolutely followed a path of spiritual purity. Now he entangled himself with the apostate Ahab. The text drops a hint of the theme of the next unit, chaps. 21–23: the danger posed to the Davidic dynasty by this marriage alliance. The marriage of the crown prince Jehoram and Athaliah, daughter of Ahab and Jezebel, introduced a viper into the Judean nest.

This negative account of the association with Ahab is also colored by the theological judgment of chap. 13, where the chronicler distinguished between the people of the northern kingdom and the kings who led them astray from the Lord's chosen dynasty and sanctuary. Ahab had aggravated the sins of his royal predecessors by sanctioning an alien religion (17:3-4). So the northern troops and Jehoshaphat, both misled, were eventually to return home in peace, but Ahab had to die on the battlefield (18:16, 27, 34; 19:1).

Verse 1*a* also serves as an interpretative foil for v. 2 and judges Jehosaphat's agreement with Ahab to fight against the Arameans to be an act of folly. Jehoshaphat was dazzled by the extravagance of his state visit to Samaria, falling a naive victim to Ahab's wishes. As noted above, the verb of enticement (*hēsît*) becomes a key word in the chronicler's version of the story. It is used in Deut 13:6 of enticement to apostasy and so connotes leading someone spiritually astray. Such manipulation would not go unchecked.

The key word of the unit occurs in this section (v. 3). The chronicler stated in 15:2 that "the LORD is with you, while you are with him" (NRSV). Now Jehoshaphat promised to be with Ahab, the Lord's enemy. The chronicler adds the last clause of v. 3: *with* him. At least Jehoshaphat insisted on a prophetic seeking (דרש *dāraš*) of the Lord's will, with a spark of his old spiritual fire. Yet, when his request was honored and defeat was foretold, he persisted in the military enterprise, a campaign to capture Ramoth-gilead, a border town in the north Transjordan.

18:4-8. The scene of prophetic inquiry concerning the success or otherwise of the campaign is a variant of a conventional type scene illustrated in Judg 4:12-16 and 1 Kgs 20:26-30. The campaign is presented as a fiasco from beginning to end. It is a game Ahab wrongly thought he had won, ignoring the checkmate moves of his prophetic opponent. Jehoshaphat, again displaying a modicum of spiritual insight, was not satisfied with the glib replies of Ahab's seeming yes-men and asked for a second opinion. Ahab, with a cynical comment, had Micaiah brought to Jehoshaphat.

18:9-17. Zedekiah's symbolic action of vv. 9-11 affirms the sincerity of Ahab's prophets—a disconcerting affirmation, on reflection—and fills the time it takes for Micaiah to arrive. Zedekiah at first refuses to speak other than God's truth, then confirms the previous promises of victory—another disconcerting element. Ahab draws attention to it in v. 15, finding it out of character (cf. v. 7). How can these tensions in the story find resolution? The reader is disappointed by Micaiah's parroting of the court prophets' assurances of victory. Yet Micaiah had to do this: He was affirming that it was a divinely given word. The sequel will show that it was deliberately deceptive, a genuine but wrong prophecy.[261] His provocative reply in v. 14 is justified by two reports of prophetic visions. The first, described and given a divine interpretation in v. 16, envisions a leaderless rout. The troops' trudging home unscathed implicitly contrasts with Ahab's fate.

18:18-22. The second vision is narrated and given a prophetic interpretation, resolving the paradox of Micaiah's two answers in vv. 14 and 16. It features the heavenly council, whose traditional role in war was to muster a celestial army to fight for Israel. Here its role is reversed, and it plans Ahab's providential defeat and death.[262] The heavenly court is the counterpart of the human court depicted in v. 9. The heavenly court has higher authority and greater power[263] and controls not only the outcome of the battle but also the means by which the prophets of the earthly court enticed Ahab to his fate. In the context of 1 Kings 22, the entrapment is regarded as morally justified, as the punishment of a wicked king. In 2 Chronicles the justification of this entrapment is reinforced by Ahab's reaping the harvest of enticement he had sown. The Machiavellian manipulator of v. 2 was lured by a countermanipulation to the doom he deserved. Ahab was told the truth (vv. 15-16), but the narrator can safely gamble that he would consider himself master of his own fate. In effect, the Lord gave him up to his own perversity (cf. Rom 1:24, 26, 28).

18:23-27. Zedekiah killed the moment of truth by refusing to believe Micaiah's sophisticated explanation. He rejected that complex kind of inspiration, genuine as to source but deceptive in content. In the wake of this convenient attack, Ahab ordered the prophet's incarceration, somewhat like that of Asa in 16:10, until Ahab returned "in peace," thus defying the prophetic vision in v. 16 and the oracle of judgment in v. 22. Micaiah's confident answer to both Zedekiah and Ahab was, "Wait and see," a deuteronomic test of prophecy (Deut 18:22). His final word of appeal to the nations (NRSV, "peoples") is a gloss citing Mic 1:2 in the text of 1 Kgs 22:28, which the chronicler found and took over; its omission in the REB is a textual hypercorrection. It becomes an appeal for the chronicler's readers to listen open-mindedly, after Ahab had refused to listen in v. 18, and to be witness to Micaiah's vision of judgment and eventual vindication.

18:28-34. The text now takes the form of a battle report. Ahab still had a card to play, donning a disguise so that Jehoshaphat would be the only royal figure in sight. The two kings are deceitful and naive to the last. The rest of the battle story is devoted to the undoing of Ahab's ruse to endanger Jehoshaphat and save his own skin. Jehoshaphat was duly mistaken for Ahab, but had only a close shave with death. His cry, left undefined in 1 Kgs 22:32, is here interpreted as a prayer (cf. 13:14; 14:10). The prayer of this believer, though the trouble was of his own making, was charitably answered with divine help. The chronicler understands the efficacy of prayer to trigger the gracious help of the Lord. He also draws attention to the divine manipulation of events. Ahab had wanted to make Jehoshaphat the fall guy. God foiled him by showing the Aramean charioteers that this royal figure was not their intended quarry, enticing them away from him. The human manipulator of v. 2 met

261. R. D. Nelson, *First and Second Kings*, Interpretation (Louisville: John Knox, 1987) 146, 148.

262. R. B. Dillard, *2 Chronicles*, WBC 15 (Waco, Tex.: Word, 1987) 142.

263. S. J. De Vries, *Prophet Against Prophet: The Role of the Micaiah Narrative (1 Kings 22) in the Development of Early Prophetic Tradition* (Grand Rapids: Eerdmans, 1978) 42.

his match in the Lord. Ahab, still safe from overt Aramean attack, had the bad luck to be hit by a stray arrow, which found its way between the plates of his armor. Readers are invited to recognize divine intervention at work here.[264]

19:1-3. The chronicler skips details crucial for the Ahab-centered account of 1 Kgs 22:36-38, leaping to his own account of Jehoshaphat's safe return. The motif of peaceful return in 2 Chr 18:16, 26-27 parallels the account in 1 Kgs 22:17, 27-28; now it is extended and applied to the Judean king "in peace" (בשלום *bĕšālôm*; NRSV, "in safety"; NIV, "safely"). In accordance with the divine word, only Ahab died. The chronicler puts an interpretive message in Jehu's mouth, retrieving him from a northern context in 1 Kgs 16:1, 7. The prophetic postmortem begins with an accusatory question (as later in 24:20; 25:15). Jehoshaphat is taken to task for his association with Ahab. Divine mercy does not condone wrongdoing. "Love" (אהב *'āhēb*) is used in the Hebrew idiomatic sense of alliance, but the contrasted hating of the Lord gives it a nuance of unspirituality. The reference to divine "wrath" lacks a verb, so its tense may be past (NRSV), present (NIV), or future (REB, "will strike you"). The NRSV is probably right; it relates to Jehoshaphat's humiliating defeat (18:16; cf. 20:37).[265] Many commentators find a forward-looking reference, to a kind of sword of Damocles poised over the king's head and kept aloft by his repentant deeds in 19:14–20:30, but eventually falling on him in 20:1 or 20:35-37. In the latter passage, however, the judgment has its own adequate reasons, while Jehoshaphat's prayer in 20:6-12 lacks a corresponding confession of sin.

The divine deliverance (18:31) had taken into account the king's "good" qualities, his reform (17:6), and his spiritual commitment (17:3-4). He had "made a practice" (REB) of seeking the Lord. So God's rescue falls into the category of normative help, rather than redemptive help of the variety described in 7:14. Jehoshaphat had been more simpleton than sinner.

264. This reference to divine help is an addition of the chronicler.The Lucianic recension of the LXX of 1 Kings has it, but by assimilation to the LXX of 2 Chronicles, since the distinctive Greek rendering is the same and the motif of divine help is so typical of the chronicler.

265. See W. M. Schniedewind, *The Word of God in Transition: From Prophet to Exegete in the Second Temple Period,* JSOTSup 197 (Sheffield: Sheffield Academic, 1995) 94, 96.

REFLECTIONS

1. Should one lie if lying leads to a good end? This question makes us uneasy. Doubtless we would become even more uneasy at the suggestion that God might give false messages to prophets, to lure the recipient to his or her death. Yet, that is what we find in these chapters. The chronicler himself was a little uneasy at taking over the story from 1 Kings 22 and so made a few changes. Does the New Testament contain any parallels to the chronicler's presentation of God's punitive providence in 2 Chronicles 18–19? A close parallel may be presented in 2 Thess 2:11: A fate reserved for those who refuse to love the truth and be saved is that "God sends them a powerful delusion, leading them to believe what is false" (NRSV; similarly NIV). If chapters 18–19 pose a problem, it is a biblical problem. "Can one trust God? Maybe, but only at the price of obedience and a genuine love for the truth, no matter how unpleasant that truth may be. Without these ingredients in one's response to God, the divine lie remains a distinct and terrifying possibility."[266]

We must examine how far our difficulties are due to an idealized, static conception of God, which may make us uneasy with the portrayal of a dynamic player in the ever-changing game of life, who responds to each new move with an appropriate countermove. Certainly the chronicler's view of moral contingency accords with the last of the theological propositions expressed in Ps 18:26, "with the crooked you show yourself perverse" (NRSV; unconscionably toned down in the NIV). If the thesis of a just war is granted, one may compare this divine

266. J. J. M. Roberts, "Does God Lie? Divine Deceit as a Theological Problem in Israelite Prophetic Literature," *Congress Volume Jerusalem 1986,* ed. J. A. Emerton, VTSup 40 (Leiden: Brill, 1988) 211-20, esp. 220.

deception to the cracking of encoded messages sent by the enemy and the consequent feeding of misinformation to them to bring about their necessary defeat. In 2 Sam 17:14, there is a similar incident: Hushai misrepresents the truth at Absalom's court in order that the rightful king might be restored to his throne; Hushai's deception is then credited to the Lord's providential overruling. Ahab's death by entrapment is similar, as a case of his reaping what he had sown.

A theological protest against such a presentation of God arose within the Old Testament itself. Habakkuk complained that the Lord, in using the Chaldeans to punish Judean immorality, was using a thief to catch a thief (Hab 1:13). Yet the answer offered in Hab 2:1-13 appears to be that this was a necessary part of a long process of gradually establishing justice in the world. The mills of God grind slowly; yet, they grind exceedingly small.

2. Did the chronicler have in mind a post-exilic situation comparable to Jehoshaphat's ill-advised venture? He would not have taken the narrow stance of Ezra and Nehemiah with regard to mixed marriages, especially since he differentiated between members of the northern kingdom and their leaders. Perhaps political involvement with Samaria was an equivalent temptation (see 19:2). He leaves his readers with a black-and-white picture to apply for themselves. This principle comes to us through 2 Cor 6:14, "Do not be mismatched with unbelievers. . . . What fellowship is there between light and darkness?" (NRSV). May the Spirit help us to apply this principle aright, remembering that in this impure world the Christian cause is not necessarily advanced by insulation from sinners (see 1 Cor 5:9-13).

2 Chronicles 19:4-11, Finding God in Social Reform

NIV

[4]Jehoshaphat lived in Jerusalem, and he went out again among the people from Beersheba to the hill country of Ephraim and turned them back to the LORD, the God of their fathers. [5]He appointed judges in the land, in each of the fortified cities of Judah. [6]He told them, "Consider carefully what you do, because you are not judging for man but for the LORD, who is with you whenever you give a verdict. [7]Now let the fear of the LORD be upon you. Judge carefully, for with the LORD our God there is no injustice or partiality or bribery."

[8]In Jerusalem also, Jehoshaphat appointed some of the Levites, priests and heads of Israelite families to administer the law of the LORD and to settle disputes. And they lived in Jerusalem. [9]He gave them these orders: "You must serve faithfully and wholeheartedly in the fear of the LORD. [10]In every case that comes before you from your fellow countrymen who live in the cities—whether bloodshed or other concerns of the law, commands, decrees or ordinances—you are to warn them not to sin against the LORD; otherwise his wrath will come on you and your brothers. Do this, and you will not sin.

NRSV

4Jehoshaphat resided at Jerusalem; then he went out again among the people, from Beersheba to the hill country of Ephraim, and brought them back to the LORD, the God of their ancestors. [5]He appointed judges in the land in all the fortified cities of Judah, city by city, [6]and said to the judges, "Consider what you are doing, for you judge not on behalf of human beings but on the LORD's behalf; he is with you in giving judgment. [7]Now, let the fear of the LORD be upon you; take care what you do, for there is no perversion of justice with the LORD our God, or partiality, or taking of bribes."

8Moreover in Jerusalem Jehoshaphat appointed certain Levites and priests and heads of families of Israel, to give judgment for the LORD and to decide disputed cases. They had their seat at Jerusalem. [9]He charged them: "This is how you shall act: in the fear of the LORD, in faithfulness, and with your whole heart; [10]whenever a case comes to you from your kindred who live in their cities, concerning bloodshed, law or commandment, statutes or ordinances, then you shall instruct them, so that they may not incur guilt

NIV

[11]"Amariah the chief priest will be over you in any matter concerning the LORD, and Zebadiah son of Ishmael, the leader of the tribe of Judah, will be over you in any matter concerning the king, and the Levites will serve as officials before you. Act with courage, and may the LORD be with those who do well."

NRSV

before the LORD and wrath may not come on you and your kindred. Do so, and you will not incur guilt. [11]See, Amariah the chief priest is over you in all matters of the LORD; and Zebadiah son of Ishmael, the governor of the house of Judah, in all the king's matters; and the Levites will serve you as officers. Deal courageously, and may the LORD be with the good!"

COMMENTARY

The keynote of the unit, the Lord's presence, appears in two places: as a cautionary assurance at the beginning of the king's first speech (v. 6) and as a prayerful wish at the end of his second speech (v. 11). We are led out of the shadows of chap. 18 and back into the sunshine of chap. 17. The chronicler split Jehoshaphat's reign into two periods of social reform, as he did with Asa's reign and his religious reforms (14:3-5; 15:8-15). He seems to have followed a source other than 1 Kings in his description of a judicial reform instigated by Jehoshaphat.[267] Underlying the reform was a shift from the old tribal system of justice to a centralized royal administration.[268] This shift is reproduced in vv. 5, 8, and 11*a,* which frame the section. The chronicler supplied the two speeches, drawing on Deuteronomy for the content, and furnished the section with a headline in v. 4. He was doubtless conscious of the wordplay of Jehoshaphat's name, which means "the LORD judges," and it probably influenced v. 6. This unit is an amalgamation of a historical tradition, material from Deuteronomy, and post-exilic judicial practice, all wrapped up in the chronicler's distinctive vocabulary.[269]

19:4-7. Jehoshaphat learned his lesson, at least initially. He did not return to the northern kingdom, but devoted himself to Judean affairs. He set up a nationwide system of social reform from the southern to the northern frontier (17:7-9; cf. 15:8). This reform was enacted through judicial administration. To effect justice for the people was a king's divinely sanctioned duty; it had Davidic and Solomonic precedents (1 Chr 18:14; 2 Chr 9:8). It was a way in which the king could show concern for the people's welfare, as in 17:9. Earlier, Jehoshaphat had taken seriously the responsibility to affirm his faith as a member of a new generation (17:4). Now he encourages the people to respond to the challenge in the area of social ethics.

The national system of law courts is described in v. 5, and the king's commissioning of the judges is presented in vv. 6-7. The system included fortified cities as locations for courts. We are meant to think of Rehoboam's defense network in 11:5-10, situated along major roads, thus accessible to the surrounding areas. The commissioning speech is concerned with maintaining high standards in these local courts. Its form falls into the chronicler's pattern for speeches: an introduction (v. 6) and a main part prefaced with "And now" (v. 7 [ועתה *wĕʿattâ*]). In content both parts run on parallel lines, arguing that divine considerations should affect human practice. Deuteronomy 1:17 influences v. 6. The local judges were to regard themselves as the Lord's representatives in their communities. Answerable to God, they were to be conscientiously aware of the divine presence with them, guiding their decisions. In v. 7, the influence of Deut 16:19 is evident in the warning against unjust decisions, especially when made under the influence of partiality or bribery. Such scrupulous standards are grounded in the Lord's character, portrayed as it is in Deut 10:17.

19:8-11. A higher court is set up in Jerusalem, and it, too, is launched with a commissioning

267. See K. W. Whitelam, *The Just King: Monarchical Judicial Authority in Ancient Israel,* JSOTSup 12 (Sheffield: JSOT, 1979) 185-206. See also Knoppers, "Jehoshaphat's Judiciary and 'the Scroll of YHWH's Torah,' " *JBL* 113 (1994) 59-80.

268. See Williamson, *1 and 2 Chronicles,* 287-89; S. Japhet, *I & II Chronicles,* OTL (Louisville: Westminster/John Knox, 1993) 770-74.

269. See R. R. Wilson, "Israel's Judicial System in the Pre-exilic Period," *JQR* 74 (1983) 229-48, esp. 245-48.

speech. The MT at the end of v. 8 has "and they returned [וישבו *wayyāšubû*] to Jerusalem," which can hardly be right. If it refers to returning from the mission of v. 4, which is not consistent with the plural verb, this expression should have come at the beginning of v. 8. The reading of the phrase in the LXX, which the NEB adopted, is more reasonable: "[and the disputed cases of] the citizens of Jerusalem." This reading of ישבי (*yōšĕbê*) as "citizens" envisions the Jerusalem court not only as having an appellate function but also as serving as a lower court for the area of the capital. However, in v. 10 the reference to "every case" seems to resume the concern "to settle cases" at the end of v. 8. This resumption suggests that, as in v. 10, provincial cases are in view, rather than local cases from the Jerusalem area. Accordingly another option is to be followed, revocalizing the verb as the NRSV and the NIV have done (וישבו *wayyēšĕbû*; NIV, "lived"; NRSV, "had their seat at").

This higher court was made up of three groups: Levites, priests, and laypersons ("Israel") who were clan chiefs. In specifying Levites, the chronicler had in mind the Davidic appointment of levitical "officials and judges" (1 Chr 23:4; 26:29). The spiritual aspect of their role is spelled out: "to give judgment for the LORD," like the judges of the lower courts (v. 6).

In form the commissioning speech is like the one David addressed to Solomon in 1 Chr 28:20-21. It has a formula of encouragement (v. 11*b*). It gives a job description, which in this case is lengthy and given pride of place (vv. 9-10). It also mentions the provision of personnel, here chairpersons and supporting staff, beginning (as in 1 Chr 28:21) with והנה (*wĕhinnēh*, "And behold" [KJV]). Verses 9-10 are framed in the Hebrew with the same clause, "thus you shall act." The speech includes norms to be followed as well as judicial procedures. The motive, "the fear of the LORD," is repeated from v. 7 and is coupled with virtues found elsewhere in 2 Chronicles: devotion to their work (cf. 31:12, 15; 34:12) and integrity (e.g., 15:17; 16:9). The procedures in v. 10 depend on Deut 17:8-13. The superior court was to review difficult cases referred by the judges of the lower courts, with the tasks of specifying types of homicide and establishing which laws were applicable. The issue of motivation recurs in the latter part of v. 10. For both the superior judges and their provincial colleagues, handing down ("instruct," NRSV; cf. Exod 18:20 for הזכיר [*hizkîr*, in the hiphil] in a forensic sense) and receiving verdicts was a serious matter. The Lord would hold both groups responsible for doing justice, repaying unjust verdicts with reprisals. The superior court was to have two departments, religious and secular, the former headed by the chief priest (presumably the Amariah of 1 Chr 6:11) and the latter by the senior elder of the tribe of Judah. Levites were to function as court officers, with clerical and policing duties. At the end, the judges are encouraged to work well and are blessed with the incentive of enjoying the beneficent presence of the Lord.

REFLECTIONS

Uncontrolled power is frightening, and sanctions are necessary if it is not to be abused. The lower courts established by Jehoshaphat are presented as being free to make their own decisions, though if they referred cases to the higher court its verdicts were binding. Both types of courts were still subject to a higher mandate: the divine will. Since the Lord was the supreme judge, God's moral character was to be shared by the human judges. They were on trial even as they tried others.

Such spiritual ethics are worthy of Christian judges and of any believer who makes authoritative evaluations. In the New Testament, such considerations are applied to Christian slave owners. In Eph 6:9, both masters and slaves are told that they have "the same Master in heaven, and with him there is no partiality" (NRSV). Another perspective relating to Christian respect for secular authority may be found in Rom 13:1-7. In principle, officers of the state are God's ministers in enforcing law and order. God is the Lord of social order in the secular world. So Christians, for example, who cheat on their taxes are obstructing God's purposes for society. A commitment to social justice must be a prime concern of the church, even in the midst of a secular society.

2 Chronicles 20:1-30, Finding God in Trust and Deliverance

NIV

20 After this, the Moabites and Ammonites with some of the Meunites[a] came to make war on Jehoshaphat.

2Some men came and told Jehoshaphat, "A vast army is coming against you from Edom,[b] from the other side of the Sea.[c] It is already in Hazazon Tamar" (that is, En Gedi). 3Alarmed, Jehoshaphat resolved to inquire of the LORD, and he proclaimed a fast for all Judah. 4The people of Judah came together to seek help from the LORD; indeed, they came from every town in Judah to seek him.

5Then Jehoshaphat stood up in the assembly of Judah and Jerusalem at the temple of the LORD in the front of the new courtyard 6and said:

"O LORD, God of our fathers, are you not the God who is in heaven? You rule over all the kingdoms of the nations. Power and might are in your hand, and no one can withstand you. 7O our God, did you not drive out the inhabitants of this land before your people Israel and give it forever to the descendants of Abraham your friend? 8They have lived in it and have built in it a sanctuary for your Name, saying, 9'If calamity comes upon us, whether the sword of judgment, or plague or famine, we will stand in your presence before this temple that bears your Name and will cry out to you in our distress, and you will hear us and save us.'

10"But now here are men from Ammon, Moab and Mount Seir, whose territory you would not allow Israel to invade when they came from Egypt; so they turned away from them and did not destroy them. 11See how they are repaying us by coming to drive us out of the possession you gave us as an inheritance. 12O our God, will you not judge them? For we have no power to face this vast army that is attacking us. We do not know what to do, but our eyes are upon you."

13All the men of Judah, with their wives and

a1 Some Septuagint manuscripts; Hebrew *Ammonites* b2 One Hebrew manuscript; most Hebrew manuscripts, Septuagint and Vulgate *Aram* c2 That is, the Dead Sea

NRSV

20 After this the Moabites and Ammonites, and with them some of the Meunites,[a] came against Jehoshaphat for battle. 2Messengers[b] came and told Jehoshaphat, "A great multitude is coming against you from Edom,[c] from beyond the sea; already they are at Hazazon-tamar" (that is, En-gedi). 3Jehoshaphat was afraid; he set himself to seek the LORD, and proclaimed a fast throughout all Judah. 4Judah assembled to seek help from the LORD; from all the towns of Judah they came to seek the LORD.

5Jehoshaphat stood in the assembly of Judah and Jerusalem, in the house of the LORD, before the new court, 6and said, "O LORD, God of our ancestors, are you not God in heaven? Do you not rule over all the kingdoms of the nations? In your hand are power and might, so that no one is able to withstand you. 7Did you not, O our God, drive out the inhabitants of this land before your people Israel, and give it forever to the descendants of your friend Abraham? 8They have lived in it, and in it have built you a sanctuary for your name, saying, 9'If disaster comes upon us, the sword, judgment,[d] or pestilence, or famine, we will stand before this house, and before you, for your name is in this house, and cry to you in our distress, and you will hear and save.' 10See now, the people of Ammon, Moab, and Mount Seir, whom you would not let Israel invade when they came from the land of Egypt, and whom they avoided and did not destroy— 11they reward us by coming to drive us out of your possession that you have given us to inherit. 12O our God, will you not execute judgment upon them? For we are powerless against this great multitude that is coming against us. We do not know what to do, but our eyes are on you."

13Meanwhile all Judah stood before the LORD, with their little ones, their wives, and their children. 14Then the spirit of the LORD came upon Jahaziel son of Zechariah, son of Benaiah, son of Jeiel, son of Mattaniah, a Levite of the sons of Asaph, in the middle of the assembly. 15He said, "Listen, all Judah and inhabitants of Jerusalem,

a Compare 26.7: Heb *Ammonites* b Heb *They* c One Ms: MT *Aram* d Or *the sword of judgment*

NIV

children and little ones, stood there before the LORD.

14Then the Spirit of the LORD came upon Jahaziel son of Zechariah, the son of Benaiah, the son of Jeiel, the son of Mattaniah, a Levite and descendant of Asaph, as he stood in the assembly.

15He said: "Listen, King Jehoshaphat and all who live in Judah and Jerusalem! This is what the LORD says to you: 'Do not be afraid or discouraged because of this vast army. For the battle is not yours, but God's. 16Tomorrow march down against them. They will be climbing up by the Pass of Ziz, and you will find them at the end of the gorge in the Desert of Jeruel. 17You will not have to fight this battle. Take up your positions; stand firm and see the deliverance the LORD will give you, O Judah and Jerusalem. Do not be afraid; do not be discouraged. Go out to face them tomorrow, and the LORD will be with you.'"

18Jehoshaphat bowed with his face to the ground, and all the people of Judah and Jerusalem fell down in worship before the LORD. 19Then some Levites from the Kohathites and Korahites stood up and praised the LORD, the God of Israel, with very loud voice.

20Early in the morning they left for the Desert of Tekoa. As they set out, Jehoshaphat stood and said, "Listen to me, Judah and people of Jerusalem! Have faith in the LORD your God and you will be upheld; have faith in his prophets and you will be successful." 21After consulting the people, Jehoshaphat appointed men to sing to the LORD and to praise him for the splendor of his[a] holiness as they went out at the head of the army, saying:

"Give thanks to the LORD,
  for his love endures forever."

22As they began to sing and praise, the LORD set ambushes against the men of Ammon and Moab and Mount Seir who were invading Judah, and they were defeated. 23The men of Ammon and Moab rose up against the men from Mount Seir to destroy and annihilate them. After they finished slaughtering the men from Seir, they helped to destroy one another.

24When the men of Judah came to the place that overlooks the desert and looked toward the

[a]21 Or *him with the splendor of*

NRSV

and King Jehoshaphat: Thus says the LORD to you: 'Do not fear or be dismayed at this great multitude; for the battle is not yours but God's. 16Tomorrow go down against them; they will come up by the ascent of Ziz; you will find them at the end of the valley, before the wilderness of Jeruel. 17This battle is not for you to fight; take your position, stand still, and see the victory of the LORD on your behalf, O Judah and Jerusalem.' Do not fear or be dismayed; tomorrow go out against them, and the LORD will be with you."

18Then Jehoshaphat bowed down with his face to the ground, and all Judah and the inhabitants of Jerusalem fell down before the LORD, worshiping the LORD. 19And the Levites, of the Kohathites and the Korahites, stood up to praise the LORD, the God of Israel, with a very loud voice.

20They rose early in the morning and went out into the wilderness of Tekoa; and as they went out, Jehoshaphat stood and said, "Listen to me, O Judah and inhabitants of Jerusalem! Believe in the LORD your God and you will be established; believe his prophets." 21When he had taken counsel with the people, he appointed those who were to sing to the LORD and praise him in holy splendor, as they went before the army, saying,

"Give thanks to the LORD,
  for his steadfast love endures forever."

22As they began to sing and praise, the LORD set an ambush against the Ammonites, Moab, and Mount Seir, who had come against Judah, so that they were routed. 23For the Ammonites and Moab attacked the inhabitants of Mount Seir, destroying them utterly; and when they had made an end of the inhabitants of Seir, they all helped to destroy one another.

24When Judah came to the watchtower of the wilderness, they looked toward the multitude; they were corpses lying on the ground; no one had escaped. 25When Jehoshaphat and his people came to take the booty from them, they found livestock[a] in great numbers, goods, clothing, and precious things, which they took for themselves until they could carry no more. They spent three days taking the booty, because of its abundance. 26On the fourth day they assembled in the Valley of Beracah, for there they blessed the LORD; there-

[a] Gk: Heb *among them*

NIV

vast army, they saw only dead bodies lying on the ground; no one had escaped. [25]So Jehoshaphat and his men went to carry off their plunder, and they found among them a great amount of equipment and clothing[a] and also articles of value—more than they could take away. There was so much plunder that it took three days to collect it. [26]On the fourth day they assembled in the Valley of Beracah, where they praised the LORD. This is why it is called the Valley of Beracah[b] to this day.

[27]Then, led by Jehoshaphat, all the men of Judah and Jerusalem returned joyfully to Jerusalem, for the LORD had given them cause to rejoice over their enemies. [28]They entered Jerusalem and went to the temple of the LORD with harps and lutes and trumpets.

[29]The fear of God came upon all the kingdoms of the countries when they heard how the LORD had fought against the enemies of Israel. [30]And the kingdom of Jehoshaphat was at peace, for his God had given him rest on every side.

a25 Some Hebrew manuscripts and Vulgate; most Hebrew manuscripts *corpses* b26 *Beracah* means *praise.*

NRSV

fore that place has been called the Valley of Beracah[a] to this day. [27]Then all the people of Judah and Jerusalem, with Jehoshaphat at their head, returned to Jerusalem with joy, for the LORD had enabled them to rejoice over their enemies. [28]They came to Jerusalem, with harps and lyres and trumpets, to the house of the LORD. [29]The fear of God came on all the kingdoms of the countries when they heard that the LORD had fought against the enemies of Israel. [30]And the realm of Jehoshaphat was quiet, for his God gave him rest all around.

a That is *Blessing*

COMMENTARY

The unit's motif of divine presence surfaces as the climax of a prophet's speech of assurance, "and the LORD will be with you" (v. 17). The prophet refers to rescue from crisis, which God provides for faithful believers. That issue is closely tied to the secondary theme of the unit, "seeking the LORD" (v. 3, דרש *dāraš*; v. 4, בקש *biqqēš*, twice), here turning to God in religious rites as a response to an overwhelming attack. Once again the spiritual presupposition of 15:2 finds illustration: "The LORD is with you, while you are with him. If you seek him, he will be found by you" (NRSV).

The chronicler uses again the type scene of Asa and Zerah (14:9-15), but the narrative here is more complex. The chronicler breaks away from 1 Kings, evidently following a tradition of a successful military engagement—perhaps a minor conflict—at the northwest of the Dead Sea. The use of local names and locations in vv. 16, 20, and 24, the modernizing reinterpretation of Hazazon-tamar as En-gedi in v. 2, and the etymologizing of the Valley of Berachah in v. 26 appear to reflect a written tradition.[270] The present narrative reflects a rewriting in the grand style of holy war. According to De Vries, "Chapter 20 represents the ultimate in idealization" and brings "together a wide variety of formulae and motifs from the Holy War tradition, being surpassed in rigid stylization only by 1QM."[271]

20:1-5. Judah's enemies are described (vv. 10, 22-23) as a coalition of Moab, Ammon, and Mount Seir or Edom. This tripartite grouping suggests that in place of the impossible repetition of the Ammonites in v. 1, the MT should be emended to "Meunites" in line with the LXX, as is commonly done (cf. 26:7). This name survives

270. See H. G. M. Williamson, *1 and 2 Chronicles,* NCB (Grand Rapids: Eerdmans, 1982) 291-93.

271. S. J. De Vries, "Temporal Terms as Structural Elements in the Holy War Tradition," *VT* 25 (1975) 80-105, esp. 103.

in the later place-name Ma'an, twelve miles southeast of Petra. The chronicler understood it in this way, though in the original story Ma'on in the southeast of Judah, ten miles south of Hebron, may have been in view (see 1 Sam 23:24-26; 25:2). Moreover, the inappropriate "Aram" in the MT of v. 2 is generally emended to "Edom."[272]

Jehoshaphat's initial reaction of fear (v. 3) leads to a chain of religious events that culminate in his receiving the divine message "Do not fear" in vv. 15, 17. The cause of this fear, the "great multitude" of v. 2, is given an important role in the lament at v. 12, in the positive answer at v. 15, and in the battle report at v. 24, where, however, "the multitude" is no longer great (despite the NIV) but is diminished in death. The secret of the reversal is disclosed in v. 3: Jehoshaphat seeks the Lord in a series of religious measures that bring the whole community to the Temple to implore God's help, complete with wives and children (v. 13; cf. Joel 2:16). King and people adopt a united front in an all-out mobilization, not for war, but for worship. As in the story of Asa in chap. 14, Jehoshaphat's vast army (17:14-18) was not to be used as a surrogate for faith in the Lord. The enormity of the crisis required all the people's involvement, by fasting to show the earnestness of the ensuing prayer and by offering communal prayer in front of the Temple. Jehoshaphat's location as he leads the prayer, "before the new court," reflects the post-exilic Temple. This court replaced the pre-exilic royal court outside the temple area. When the Second Temple was built, it was recognized as new and the name stuck.[273]

20:6-12. The prayer is a beautiful expression of human despair and dependence on the Lord. It follows the general structure of the communal laments in the psalter, such as Psalms 44 and 83.[274] Jehoshaphat recounts the Lord's past favors, which exemplify divine praiseworthiness (vv. 6-7), affirms the people's grounds for confidence in God (vv. 8-9), narrates the human predicament (vv. 10-11), and closes with a petition for divine intervention and an affirmation of total trust (v. 12). The barrage of rhetorical questions in which the initial praise of v. 6 is cast is unusual. It expresses well the customary role of praise in laments—namely, to challenge the Lord to live up to earlier saving help.

Two issues were at stake: the promised land as the gift of God (vv. 7, 11; cf. Ps 44:1-3) and the Temple as the place where God answers prayer. The Lord's people were heirs to two dispensations, inheriting two blessings to which they could lay claim. The promise of the land to God's "friend" Abraham (cf. Isa 41:8), realized in the initial occupation, still played a part in the Lord's ongoing will for Israel, as 1 Chr 16:14-22 had reaffirmed. The temple promise of 2 Chr 7:14, in response to the prayers of 6:28, 34, was valid as long as the Temple stood. In this context the somber background of human sin requiring divine forgiveness (6:30) is less relevant than the optimistic scenario of compliance with the Lord's will in 6:34-35. So in v. 9 the translation "the sword, judgment" (NRSV) is preferable to "the sword of judgment" (NIV).

The prayer takes a new turn with the "But now" of v. 10. What preceded was theological preamble; here the main point is a crisis that required the Lord's presence. (A continuing element is the persuasive argumentation that persists into vv. 10-12*a*.) The invasion not only violated the Lord's will, but also constituted an act of ingratitude after Israel had spared their territory at God's bidding (cf. Deut 2:1-19; Judg 11:15-18). So there was a host of reasons for the Lord to intervene in the role of "our God" (vv. 7, 12), whose care extended to the present generation of Israel. Their powerlessness stands in contrast to God's "power" in v. 6. The final affirmation of trust, looking to the Lord for help, is a lovely expression of hope and faith, reminiscent of Ps 123:2.

20:13-17. In the temple system, prayer was sometimes answered by a prophetic message (as Joel 2:18-27 illustrates). This religious tradition appears here as a response to the expectantly waiting people. This message introduces the literary tradition of holy war that pervades vv. 14-29. The inspired oracle of the Levite stands in contrast to the travesty and confusion of 18:4-27. The pedigree of the temple singer Jahaziel is traced back four generations, presumably to David's time as a reminder of that new era of temple worship,

272. See *BHS*.

273. E. L. Curtis and A. A. Madsen, *The Books of Chronicles*, ICC (Edinburgh: T. &. T. Clark, 1910) 406.

274. See D. L. Petersen, *Late Israelite Prophecy*, SBLMS 23 (Missoula, Mont.: Scholars Press, 1977) 72.

which also anticipates vv. 19 and 21. The use of the possession formula "the spirit of the LORD came upon" indicates that Jahaziel was not a regular prophet.[275]

Jehaziel's message is a summons to holy war.[276] It has the three basic elements of assignments to a task: a call to fearless courage, a detailed description of the task, and an assurance of the Lord's enabling presence, like Solomon's commissioning in 1 Chr 28:20-21. The message also fulfills more specific functions appropriate to the context. The call not to fear is typical of the oracle of salvation that responds to a prayer of lament (e.g., Lam 3:57). The call is backed with a promise of divine help, which also characterizes this form (see Isa 41:8-14). The call not to fear is also a holy war motif (see Exod 14:13-14; Josh 11:6). So a variety of literary traditions is blended into this prophetic answer. The description of the task (v. 16) was presumably derived from details of the underlying historical tradition. Verse 17 has a resumptive role; it is reinforced with an appeal to Exod 14:13. The God who could defeat Pharaoh was still Israel's God.

20:18-19. The reassuring message is followed by worship and praise. In usual worship practice, a prayer of lament was later followed by a song of thanksgiving, when the crisis was over. Praise after the prayer might anticipate this song, if the prayer received an affirmative response (cf. Ps 28:6-7). Such praise took the divine answer on trust, unresolved though the crisis was. This type of praise, which dared to take the Lord's promise seriously, is featured here. The group of levitical singers is presented: "Kohathites and [specifically] Korahites." In terms of the customary choral designations in the books of Chronicles, this group appears to be related to the later clan of Heman (cf. 1 Chr 6:33-38). In the post-exilic development of temple music, the appellation "Korahites" reflects a stage just before the singling out of the Heman group, which subsequently took a dominant role in the choral guild.[277] The chronicler here made use of a tradition older than his own time, which is also reflected in the Korahite collection of psalms (Psalms 42–49; 84–85; 87–88; in Psalm 88, Heman also appears in the heading). This use of an older tradition may indicate that, in chap. 20, the chronicler employed a source that had been written a little before his own period.

20:20-25. The narrative moves to an account of the battle. The "morrow" of vv. 16-17 had dawned. The royal speech of encouragement places a premium on faith. It echoes Isaiah's message from God in a similar context of military threat, a message sharpened by Hebrew wordplay: "If you will not take your stand on me, you will not stand firm" (Isa 7:9 NJB). There the oracle was presented negatively as a challenge; here it is recast into a word of assurance. Historically Isaiah belonged to the century after Jehoshaphat. The speech, as elsewhere, is the work of the chronicler, communicating spiritual issues to his own constituency. This function becomes transparent in the following exhortation, "Have faith in his prophets, and you will be successful" (NIV; the last clause is unaccountably omitted in the NRSV). The message was to be found not only in Isaiah's prophecy but also in a larger collection of prophetic works that looked beyond judgment to salvation.

In an outworking of such faith, Jehoshaphat ordered anticipatory praise to be sung again, as on the previous day in the temple court. No particular choir is specified. Positioned as the army's vanguard, they were to praise the Lord for "the splendor of his holiness" (NIV, REB; cf. 1 Chr 16:29)—that is, for the radiant power they hoped would be demonstrated. From another perspective, the Lord's "[steadfast] love" in deliverance was anticipated. Promised "forever," it was claimed for that day. The praise here replaces the shout in holy war contexts (13:14-15; Judg 7:20; cf. Isa 30:29-32) or the trumpet blast of Num 10:9 (cf. 2 Chr 13:12, 14). The focus on the Lord accentuates the conviction that the battle was not theirs but God's (v. 15). The people were not to fight but were to watch the Lord defeating the enemy, as v. 17 had promised. Divine intervention duly came in v. 22, which is interpreted in v. 23 in terms of an act of self-destruction on the part of Judah's enemies. It is a conventional holy war motif, illustrated in Judg 7:22; 1 Sam 14:20; Ezek 38:21; and Hag 2:22. The enormous amount of booty reflects both the magnitude of the Lord's victory and the blessing enjoyed by the believing

275. W. M. Schniedewind, *The Word of God in Transition: From Prophet to Exegete in the Second Temple Period,* JSOTSup 197 (Sheffield: Sheffield Academic, 1995) 70-74, 116-17.

276. R. A. Mason, *Preaching the Tradition: Homily and Hermeneutics After the Exile* (Cambridge: Cambridge University Press, 1990) 64.

277. See Petersen, *Late Israelite Prophecy,* 75-76.

people. "Livestock" and "clothing" represent neccessary emendations.[278]

20:26-30. While anticipatory praise was featured in vv. 19 and 21, this passage represents standard praise celebrating what the Lord had done. The army, assembled to march back to Jerusalem, first engaged in a service of thanksgiving. The site, Berachah, which can mean "praise," is associated with a testimony to the God-given victory. Further celebration followed their return to the capital, in a processional service in which levitical music and song and priestly trumpets stimulated praise. As in 1 Chr 15:25, 28, the jubilation took a religious form. The passage closes by mentioning a further consequence of the Lord's intervention in the battle (v. 29), while the whole section concludes with a notice of the cessation of warfare (v. 30).[279] The king who had trusted the Lord now receives the blessing of rest and quiet, like Asa before him.

In the chronicler's accounts of David's victories and of Solomon's power and prestige, it could be inferred that another agenda was being pursued: presenting a model of Israel's future hope. That agenda now reappears. Here was an earnest of prophetic salvation (v. 20). The hymn in 1 Chronicles 16 had offered the hope of enjoying to the full the Lord's gift of the land and the realization of God's kingship over the earth. Fulfillment of this double hope was inaugurated in the reigns of David and Solomon. According to Jehoshaphat's prayer, Israel's divine right to the land was at stake and so was the Lord's "rule over all of the kingdoms of the nations" (v. 6), while the aftermath attested to the fear of God falling on "all the kingdoms of the countries" (v. 29). The victory was intended as an anticipatory pledge of an eschatological kingdom.

The post-exilic community prized the message of salvation they found in the prophetic books. Correspondingly, the chronicler's message to his own generation is unmistakable in the exhortation, "Believe [the LORD's] prophets." The divine hope revealed there gave shape to Israel's future. Yet, even as the holy war narrative was a parable of eschatological hope, it issued a call for quietism, to wait in faith for divine intervention. Herein lies the relevance of the holy war theme, which leaves everything to God. The Lord's good time would surely come. Meanwhile, Judah was not to plunge into apocalyptic battles of its own devising.[280]

278. See *BHS.* See also Allen, *Greek Chronicles,* 2:89, 98.

279. S. J. De Vries, *1 and 2 Chronicles,* FOTL 11 (Grand Rapids: Eerdmans, 1989) 326.

280. See P. R. Ackroyd, *I & II Chronicles, Ezra, Nehemiah,* Torch Bible (London: SCM, 1973) 151-52.

REFLECTIONS

1. This is a classic story of faith, gripping in its portrayal of commitment to God as ally when life wages war against us and "we do not know what to do" (20:2). It carries an existential message as well as an eschatological one. It is a beautiful paradigm of taking seriously grounds for fear and yet transcending them by a conviction of the divine presence that could cope with the monster and bring God's people safely through the crisis. Believers are not exempt from fear, but they have a God to whom to take their fears. Fear is like a smoke detector, warning that appropriate action should be taken against a fiery disaster. Recourse to God must be one such action; here it was the only option. Fear banishes our self-sufficiency, driving us to "seek" God by resorting to religious measures. At times of crisis, we need religious forms as vehicles of divine comfort. The temple laments in the book of Psalms were the Lord's provision for believers in need (2 Chr 20:9).

2. Using praise to challenge God is no part of ordinary prayer, but when crisis strikes it can express human frustration. It is a cry for God to become real in our situation, to live up to the creeds and hymns we tend to take for granted in calmer times. The chronicler had spiritual insight in linking faith with periods of crisis.

3. Apocalyptic fervor brought a temptation to take matters into one's own hands. Centuries later in Jewish history, orthodox Jews opposed the rise of Zionism as usurping the Messiah's role in taking the people of Israel back to their land. The chronicler used the model of the holy war, which left everything to the Lord as a warning not to try to help God by abortive rebellion against the secular powers. Meanwhile, there was plenty to be done for the Lord by inculcating the standards of the Torah in Judah's social life (17:9) and by promoting law and order as the divine will for the comunity the Lord had set in their own land (19:5-11; 20:7).

In a similar vein, the New Testament has distinguished between the work God has done and will do in Christ and the work to be done by the church. It looks forward to the second advent as a dynamic breaking into human history, like a thief in the night. In Rev 19:11-21, it is the King of kings and a celestial army who fight against human and superhuman forces of evil. There is a distinction in the books of Chronicles between the type of war a king fought with the Lord's help (e.g., 1 Chr 18:1-6, 9-14; 2 Chr 6:34-35) and the form presented in chapter 20, in which God fought without their participation. The New Testament speaks of the once-for-all campaign Christ fought against evil principalities and powers (Col 2:15). It also proclaims the ongoing fight of Christians in the Lord's strength against those very forces (Eph 6:10-17). The church trusts in a work only its Lord can do and that God will consummate. Within these parameters, Christians strenuously "fight the good fight of the faith" (1 Tim 6:12).

2 Chronicles 20:31–21:1*a*, Collusion with Another Northern King

NIV

[31]So Jehoshaphat reigned over Judah. He was thirty-five years old when he became king of Judah, and he reigned in Jerusalem twenty-five years. His mother's name was Azubah daughter of Shilhi. [32]He walked in the ways of his father Asa and did not stray from them; he did what was right in the eyes of the LORD. [33]The high places, however, were not removed, and the people still had not set their hearts on the God of their fathers.

[34]The other events of Jehoshaphat's reign, from beginning to end, are written in the annals of Jehu son of Hanani, which are recorded in the book of the kings of Israel.

[35]Later, Jehoshaphat king of Judah made an alliance with Ahaziah king of Israel, who was guilty of wickedness. [36]He agreed with him to construct a fleet of trading ships.[a] After these were built at Ezion Geber, [37]Eliezer son of Dodavahu of Mareshah prophesied against Jehoshaphat, saying, "Because you have made an alliance with Ahaziah, the LORD will destroy what you have made." The ships were wrecked and were not able to set sail to trade.[b]

21 Then Jehoshaphat rested with his fathers and was buried with them in the City of David.

[a]36 Hebrew *of ships that could go to Tarshish* [b]37 Hebrew *sail for Tarshish*

NRSV

31So Jehoshaphat reigned over Judah. He was thirty-five years old when he began to reign; he reigned twenty-five years in Jerusalem. His mother's name was Azubah daughter of Shilhi. [32]He walked in the way of his father Asa and did not turn aside from it, doing what was right in the sight of the LORD. [33]Yet the high places were not removed; the people had not yet set their hearts upon the God of their ancestors.

34Now the rest of the acts of Jehoshaphat, from first to last, are written in the Annals of Jehu son of Hanani, which are recorded in the Book of the Kings of Israel.

35After this King Jehoshaphat of Judah joined with King Ahaziah of Israel, who did wickedly. [36]He joined him in building ships to go to Tarshish; they built the ships in Ezion-geber. [37]Then Eliezer son of Dodavahu of Mareshah prophesied against Jehoshaphat, saying, "Because you have joined with Ahaziah, the LORD will destroy what you have made." And the ships were wrecked and were not able to go to Tarshish.

21 Jehoshaphat slept with his ancestors and was buried with his ancestors in the city of David;

COMMENTARY

The religious message of 20:1-30 was an application of the positive side of the proposition in 15:2. Now the alternative implicitly comes to the fore, "But if you forsake him, he will forsake you" (NIV). Jehoshaphat, no longer "with" the Lord, was "with" the northern king Ahaziah instead. The preposition occurs three times in the MT in the course of vv. 35-37, as the NIV attests. The dynamics of chap. 18 appear again.

20:31-34. The section depends on 1 Kgs 22:41-51 and takes it over as a block, though with a few small omissions and adaptations. The review of Jehoshaphat's reign in vv. 31-33 stands in some tension with the representation in earlier chapters. Presumably the chronicler regarded the positive assessment of v. 32 as a generalization, as in the more blatant case of Asa (14:2), which was also taken over from 1 Kings. The chronicler's view of Jehoshaphat's relation to Asa was more adequately expressed in 17:3. The king's life was good despite some temporary lapses. More seriously, v. 33*a* contradicts the statement in 17:6 as well as the tone of 19:3. The rewriting of the last part of 1 Kgs 22:43 in v. 33*b* shows that pagan high places are in view as they were in 17:6. The chronicler differentiated between the king and the people; the spiritual language of v. 33*b* was used positively of the king in 19:3. The chronicler may have meant that the people resisted the king's efforts at reform. Certainly the reference to traditional faith directs the reader to Jehoshaphat's endeavors in 19:4. The mention of Jehu in the source formula of v. 34 picks up his prophetic speech in 19:2-3, where he condemned Jehoshaphat's participation with Ahab. The reference leads nicely to a similar misadventure in vv. 35-37. The chronicler put the source formula to a new use in order to remind readers of 1 Kgs 16:1-4, 7, 12, an instance in which Jehu condemned the northern king Baasha for having led his people astray religiously. The text has nothing to do with Jehoshaphat, but in this way the chronicler justified his use of Jehu's name to condemn the alliance with a northern king.

20:35–21:1a. The disastrous enterprise is not military this time but commercial. The 1 Kings account has been stood on its head. The chronicler evidently took Ahaziah's offer to Jehoshaphat in 1 Kgs 22:49 as having taken place prior to the shipwreck by interpreting the verb "said" as a pluperfect.[281] He construed it in terms of seeking a human ally instead of the Lord and assumed that Jehoshaphat's unwillingness to agree to Ahaziah's offer in 1 Kgs 22:49 was overridden in the light of the expedition in 1 Kgs 22:48. Then he gave his interpretation of the narrative by adding an oracle of judgment. The prophet Eliezer is not otherwise known, but his very name, which means "God is help," reinforces the rebuke and ties in with Jehu's complaint that Jehoshaphat had helped wicked Ahab (19:2). The reference to acting wickedly, added by the chronicler in v. 35, is ambiguous. Is the subject Jehoshaphat, as the REB, the NJB, and the TNK take it to be? The answer may seem more obvious, but the labeling of Ahab as wicked in 19:2 suggests that the NRSV and the NIV are correct in referring to Ahaziah. As in 9:21, the chronicler seems not to have known where in the world Tarshish was; the NIV again tones down the tenor of the Hebrew.

281. T. Willi, *Die Chronik als Auslegung* (Göttingen: Vandenhoeck & Ruprecht, 1972) 219; Williamson, *1 and 2 Chronicles,* 303.

REFLECTIONS

The chronicler allowed Solomon to go through life unscathed by failure, although he took seriously Solomon's own testimony that "there is no one who does not sin" (1 Kgs 8:46 = 2 Chr 6:36). Jehoshaphat was basically good (20:32), but he had a blind spot, a besetting sin to which he surrenders again in 20:35-37. Yet, despite temporary lapses, the tenor of his life was positive. God was "not unjust" so as "to overlook" his "work" (Heb 6:10 NRSV). The reassurance brings comfort to us all.

The people's unspiritual behavior contrasts with the king's own spirituality and efforts to encourage the people in this direction in 19:3-4. Jehoshaphat had shown the people the right way; it was their fault and not his that they failed to follow. This situation is in line with the principle of Ezek 33:7-9 that the wicked must be warned to repent even if they decide not to repent. Parents can find reassurance in this passage, when they are tempted to blame themselves for the actions of adult children who stray from the good ways they were taught.

2 CHRONICLES 21:1*b*–23:21, THE THREAT TO THE DYNASTY AVERTED

OVERVIEW

The accounts of the reigns of Jehoram, Ahaziah, and Athaliah make up a single unit. It traces in two sections the annulling of threats that the Davidic dynasty would be extinguished in spirit and in fact. The reigns of Jehoram and Ahaziah are presented as a pair, correlated in 21:2 and 22:3 with the linking "also" or "too." So the first section is 21:1*b*–22:9. Its first half, 21:1*b*-20, introduces the pernicious influence of "the house of Ahab" through "the daughter of Ahab" (21:6 = 2 Kgs 8:18). A fresh reference to it is created at 21:13.[282] That "house" stands in contrast with "the house of David" (21:7), which replaces "Judah" in 2 Kgs 8:19, a variation that strengthens the theological assertion of the permanence of the Davidic dynasty. The contrasting fates of their houses was suggested by "David" (2 Kgs 8:19), which is retained in 2 Chr 21:7. A new reference to "David" appears in 21:12, a challenge to the current Davidic king to live up to his royal heritage. That reference is matched by another comment about "the house of Ahab" in 21:13. The alternating references to rival dynasties sum up the passage's agenda.

The second half of the first section (22:1-9) contains two references to "the house of Ahab" (22:3-4), which are derived from 2 Kgs 8:27. They are echoed in 22:7-8 by two final references unparalleled in 2 Kings. Two intervening references to J(eh)oram son of Ahab in 22:5-6 (= 2 Kgs 8:28-29) reinforce the ominous phrase. But the allusions to David in chap. 21 are absent. This stylistic monopoly prepares the reader for the despairing final sentence, "And the house of Ahaziah had no one able to rule the kingdom" (NRSV).

The second section, 22:10–23:21, records the reversal of this sinister situation. The house of Ahab receives no comment now. Restoration of Davidic rule is celebrated by two references introduced by the chronicler: an affirmation of the Lord's promise about the dynasty (23:3) and an account of the reintroduction of cultic worship inaugurated by David (23:18). The triumph of the Judean dynasty gave the chronicler an opportunity to draw attention to the permanence of the Davidic covenant and to the temple worship associated closely with it.

Jehoshaphat's reign marked a zenith in the fortunes of the Judean monarchy during the period of the divided kingdom. The next two reigns registered an all-time low. The chronicler polarizes the two periods in 21:12 and 22:9. Northern kingship, camel-like, poked its nose into the Davidic tent in Jehoshaphat's reign. Now it made its presence felt so blatantly that the Judean dynasty was almost wiped out by a combination of divine judgment (21:14, 16, 18; 22:7) and human sin. Almost, for the Lord's promise guaranteed its survival.

282. For the epigrammatic nature of this phrase in the OT, see T. Ishida, "The House of Ahab," *IEJ* 25 (1975) 135-37.

2 Chronicles 21:1*b*–22:9, The Apostasy of Jehoram and Ahaziah

NIV

And Jehoram his son succeeded him as king. [2]Jehoram's brothers, the sons of Jehoshaphat, were Azariah, Jehiel, Zechariah, Azariahu, Michael and Shephatiah. All these were sons of Jehoshaphat king of Israel.[a] [3]Their father had given them many gifts of silver and gold and articles of value, as well as fortified cities in Judah, but he had given the kingdom to Jehoram because he was his firstborn son.

[4]When Jehoram established himself firmly over his father's kingdom, he put all his brothers to the sword along with some of the princes of Israel. [5]Jehoram was thirty-two years old when he became king, and he reigned in Jerusalem eight years. [6]He walked in the ways of the kings of Israel, as the house of Ahab had done, for he married a daughter of Ahab. He did evil in the eyes of the LORD. [7]Nevertheless, because of the covenant the LORD had made with David, the LORD was not willing to destroy the house of David. He had promised to maintain a lamp for him and his descendants forever.

[8]In the time of Jehoram, Edom rebelled against Judah and set up its own king. [9]So Jehoram went there with his officers and all his chariots. The Edomites surrounded him and his chariot commanders, but he rose up and broke through by night. [10]To this day Edom has been in rebellion against Judah.

Libnah revolted at the same time, because Jehoram had forsaken the LORD, the God of his fathers. [11]He had also built high places on the hills of Judah and had caused the people of Jerusalem to prostitute themselves and had led Judah astray.

[12]Jehoram received a letter from Elijah the prophet, which said:

> "This is what the LORD, the God of your father David, says: 'You have not walked in the ways of your father Jehoshaphat or of Asa king of Judah. [13]But you have walked in the ways of the kings of Israel, and you have led Judah and the people of Jerusalem to prostitute themselves, just as the house of Ahab did

[a]*2* That is, Judah, as frequently in 2 Chronicles

NRSV

his son Jehoram succeeded him. [2]He had brothers, the sons of Jehoshaphat: Azariah, Jehiel, Zechariah, Azariah, Michael, and Shephatiah; all these were the sons of King Jehoshaphat of Judah.[a] [3]Their father gave them many gifts, of silver, gold, and valuable possessions, together with fortified cities in Judah; but he gave the kingdom to Jehoram, because he was the firstborn. [4]When Jehoram had ascended the throne of his father and was established, he put all his brothers to the sword, and also some of the officials of Israel. [5]Jehoram was thirty-two years old when he began to reign; he reigned eight years in Jerusalem. [6]He walked in the way of the kings of Israel, as the house of Ahab had done; for the daughter of Ahab was his wife. He did what was evil in the sight of the LORD. [7]Yet the LORD would not destroy the house of David because of the covenant that he had made with David, and since he had promised to give a lamp to him and to his descendants forever.

8In his days Edom revolted against the rule of Judah and set up a king of their own. [9]Then Jehoram crossed over with his commanders and all his chariots. He set out by night and attacked the Edomites, who had surrounded him and his chariot commanders. [10]So Edom has been in revolt against the rule of Judah to this day. At that time Libnah also revolted against his rule, because he had forsaken the LORD, the God of his ancestors.

11Moreover he made high places in the hill country of Judah, and led the inhabitants of Jerusalem into unfaithfulness, and made Judah go astray. [12]A letter came to him from the prophet Elijah, saying: "Thus says the LORD, the God of your father David: Because you have not walked in the ways of your father Jehoshaphat or in the ways of King Asa of Judah, [13]but have walked in the way of the kings of Israel, and have led Judah and the inhabitants of Jerusalem into unfaithfulness, as the house of Ahab led Israel into unfaithfulness, and because you also have killed your brothers, members of your father's house, who

[a] Gk Syr: Heb *Israel*

NIV

You have also murdered your own brothers, members of your father's house, men who were better than you. 14So now the LORD is about to strike your people, your sons, your wives and everything that is yours, with a heavy blow. 15You yourself will be very ill with a lingering disease of the bowels, until the disease causes your bowels to come out.'"

16The LORD aroused against Jehoram the hostility of the Philistines and of the Arabs who lived near the Cushites. 17They attacked Judah, invaded it and carried off all the goods found in the king's palace, together with his sons and wives. Not a son was left to him except Ahaziah,[b] the youngest.

18After all this, the LORD afflicted Jehoram with an incurable disease of the bowels. 19In the course of time, at the end of the second year, his bowels came out because of the disease, and he died in great pain. His people made no fire in his honor, as they had for his fathers.

20Jehoram was thirty-two years old when he became king, and he reigned in Jerusalem eight years. He passed away, to no one's regret, and was buried in the City of David, but not in the tombs of the kings.

22 The people of Jerusalem made Ahaziah, Jehoram's youngest son, king in his place, since the raiders, who came with the Arabs into the camp, had killed all the older sons. So Ahaziah son of Jehoram king of Judah began to reign.

2Ahaziah was twenty-two[a] years old when he became king, and he reigned in Jerusalem one year. His mother's name was Athaliah, a granddaughter of Omri.

3He too walked in the ways of the house of Ahab, for his mother encouraged him in doing wrong. 4He did evil in the eyes of the LORD, as the house of Ahab had done, for after his father's death they became his advisers, to his undoing. 5He also followed their counsel when he went with Joram[b] son of Ahab king of Israel to war against Hazael king of Aram at Ramoth Gilead. The Arameans wounded Joram; 6so he returned to Jezreel to recover from the wounds they had

a17 Hebrew *Jehoahaz,* a variant of *Ahaziah* b2 Some Septuagint manuscripts and Syriac (see also 2 Kings 8:26); Hebrew *forty-two* c5 Hebrew *Jehoram,* a variant of *Joram*; also in verses 6 and 7

NRSV

were better than yourself, 14see, the LORD will bring a great plague on your people, your children, your wives, and all your possessions, 15and you yourself will have a severe sickness with a disease of your bowels, until your bowels come out, day after day, because of the disease."

16The LORD aroused against Jehoram the anger of the Philistines and of the Arabs who are near the Ethiopians.[a] 17They came up against Judah, invaded it, and carried away all the possessions they found that belonged to the king's house, along with his sons and his wives, so that no son was left to him except Jehoahaz, his youngest son.

18After all this the LORD struck him in his bowels with an incurable disease. 19In course of time, at the end of two years, his bowels came out because of the disease, and he died in great agony. His people made no fire in his honor, like the fires made for his ancestors. 20He was thirty-two years old when he began to reign; he reigned eight years in Jerusalem. He departed with no one's regret. They buried him in the city of David, but not in the tombs of the kings.

22 The inhabitants of Jerusalem made his youngest son Ahaziah king as his successor; for the troops who came with the Arabs to the camp had killed all the older sons. So Ahaziah son of Jehoram reigned as king of Judah. 2Ahaziah was forty-two years old when he began to reign; he reigned one year in Jerusalem. His mother's name was Athaliah, a granddaughter of Omri. 3He also walked in the ways of the house of Ahab, for his mother was his counselor in doing wickedly. 4He did what was evil in the sight of the LORD, as the house of Ahab had done; for after the death of his father they were his counselors, to his ruin. 5He even followed their advice, and went with Jehoram son of King Ahab of Israel to make war against King Hazael of Aram at Ramoth-gilead. The Arameans wounded Joram, 6and he returned to be healed in Jezreel of the wounds that he had received at Ramah, when he fought King Hazael of Aram. And Ahaziah son of King Jehoram of Judah went down to see Joram son of Ahab in Jezreel, because he was sick.

7But it was ordained by God that the downfall of Ahaziah should come about through his going

a Or *Nubians*; Heb *Cushites*

NIV

inflicted on him at Ramoth[a] in his battle with Hazael king of Aram.

Then Ahaziah[b] son of Jehoram king of Judah went down to Jezreel to see Joram son of Ahab because he had been wounded.

7Through Ahaziah's visit to Joram, God brought about Ahaziah's downfall. When Ahaziah arrived, he went out with Joram to meet Jehu son of Nimshi, whom the LORD had anointed to destroy the house of Ahab. 8While Jehu was executing judgment on the house of Ahab, he found the princes of Judah and the sons of Ahaziah's relatives, who had been attending Ahaziah, and he killed them. 9He then went in search of Ahaziah, and his men captured him while he was hiding in Samaria. He was brought to Jehu and put to death. They buried him, for they said, "He was a son of Jehoshaphat, who sought the LORD with all his heart." So there was no one in the house of Ahaziah powerful enough to retain the kingdom.

[a]6 Hebrew *Ramah,* a variant of *Ramoth* [b]6 Some Hebrew manuscripts, Septuagint, Vulgate and Syriac (see also 2 Kings 8:29); most Hebrew manuscripts *Azariah*

NRSV

to visit Joram. For when he came there he went out with Jehoram to meet Jehu son of Nimshi, whom the LORD had anointed to destroy the house of Ahab. 8When Jehu was executing judgment on the house of Ahab, he met the officials of Judah and the sons of Ahaziah's brothers, who attended Ahaziah, and he killed them. 9He searched for Ahaziah, who was captured while hiding in Samaria and was brought to Jehu, and put to death. They buried him, for they said, "He is the grandson of Jehoshaphat, who sought the LORD with all his heart." And the house of Ahaziah had no one able to rule the kingdom.

COMMENTARY

21:1-7. Jehoram's reign is the first to be judged in totally negative terms. His successor's reign will be the next. These reigns form a dark backdrop to the Lord's redeeming purpose, described in v. 7. The citing of 1 Kgs 22:50 in v. 1 is followed in vv. 2-4 by a grim tale of fratricide, which is generally attributed to the chronicler's use of another source. A flashback (see the NIV of v. 3) establishes Jehoshaphat's generosity to his other sons. Not content with the throne, the new king had all of his brothers murdered for their possessions. So the chronicler implies that Jehoram's punishment would affect his own possessions (vv. 14, 17; the Hebrew word for "possessions" is different in vv. 14, 17). This fratricide introduces the theme that runs throughout the unit: a threat to the royal family that puts at risk the very purposes of God. Here it is a threat from within, a multiplication of Cain's primeval sin.

Jehoram chalked up further crimes on his slate. The chronicler cites 2 Kgs 8:17-22 in vv. 5-10*a,* significantly varied by importing "the house of David" into v. 7. Mention of Jehoshaphat's marriage alliance in 18:1 warned readers of the grim legacy of the influence of the ill-famed house of Ahab. The house of David, chameleon-like, assumed the morally and religiously evil character of the house of Ahab so that it deserved the same fate (see 1 Kgs 21:22, 29; 2 Kgs 9:7-9). Divine grace, in the form of the covenant promise made to David, intervened, replacing the wages of sin with everlasting life for the dynasty (see 1 Chr 17:12; 28:7). It was a lamp that would keep burning, however dark and long the night (cf. Ps 132:17). It might even be extinguished for a time, like the temple lamps (cf. 2 Chr 29:7), but it would eventually be relit. This assurance looks beyond the coup of chap. 23 to a hope that the Davidic monarchy would one day be restored.

21:8-10. Verse 9*b* takes over the uncertain

text of 2 Kgs 8:20, which speaks first in terms of victory and then of defeat. Here it presumably means that the king escaped by the skin of his teeth. The NIV paraphrases to this effect, while the NRSV gives a literal rendering. The narrative of the loss of Edom and of Libnah on the Philistine border spelled for the chronicler the providential punishment of Jehoram. The chronicler added his own theological interpretation of these territorial losses in v. 10*b,* using his term "forsake" and so reminding readers of the proposition in 15:2. In 2 Chronicles, the Lord keeps short accounts in claiming moral debts, if a new generation disdains the spiritual baton passed down from its predecessors.

21:11-20. Except for parts of v. 20, vv. 11-20 are unique to 2 Chronicles.

21:11. The chronicler drives another nail into Jehoram's coffin by accusing him of disparaging the Temple by constructing high places as alternative sanctuaries. This new sin is an example of assimilation to the northern kingdom (v. 6), specifically in its adoption of Canaanite religion. The mention of religious prostitution echoes 1 Chr 5:25, where the same verb is used of the northern tribes. Likewise, the Lord's stirring up the "spirit" (TNK) of foreign groups (v. 16) repeats the phrase used in 1 Chr 5:26 with reference to Assyria's deportation of the northerners. Judah under Jehoram sank as low morally as had its northern neighbor. This theme will be developed in chap. 28.

21:12-15. A letter from Elijah, the great prophet to the northern kingdom (1 Kings 17–19; 21; 2 Kings 1–2), is cited. The letter's historicity is questionable. It is implied in 2 Kgs 3:11 that Elijah was dead by the time Jehoram came to the throne, while 2 Kgs 1:17 suggests that he died early in his reign. The chronicler's recourse to a northern prophet reinforces his equation of the two kingdoms. He honored the tradition represented by the prophet, a tradition of opposition in the Lord's name to Ahab's immorality and Jezebel's patronage of pagan worship. Who better than Elijah to be the vehicle of this theology of providential retribution? The notes of accusation and punishment that run through the surrounding narratives are given a distinctively theological orientation in the letter, which takes the classic two-part form of a prophetic oracle of judgment. A general accusation of choosing a wrong role model, the house of Ahab, is followed by the specific one of murdering innocent brothers. "Better" is used in a judicial sense.[283] A double punishment is announced, a "heavy blow" to befall the people and the royal household and a serious illness for the king.

21:16-17. The narrative traces the detailed fulfillment of both reprisals. The chronicler evidently drew on historical traditions, which he also incorporated into the letter. The first concerned a local border raid, typically magnified by the chronicler.[284] The rendering "Cushites" (NIV) represents the standpoint of the tradition and "Ethiopians" (NRSV) that of the chronicler (see the Commentary on 14:9-15). A conquest of Jerusalem is not envisioned even by the chronicler, as 22:1 confirms. In v. 17, "the goods found in the king's palace" (NIV) are not in view, but those "that belonged to the king's house" (NRSV), meaning crown property. Ahaziah is called "Jehoahaz" with a reversal of the two elements of his name; perhaps this was his personal name, which was replaced by a throne name. Justice had been done. The killing of Jehoram's brothers was repaid by the killing of all but one of his sons (cf. 22:1). When he gained his brothers' possessions, he forfeited his own. The survival of a single son to ensure Davidic succession is consistent with the principle that the house of David would survive (v. 7). The motif of the dynasty's hanging by a single thread will be repeated in 22:10-11. In 2 Chronicles, as is also probably the case in 2 Kings 11, collateral lines may not provide an heir.[285]

21:18-20. The outworking of the second prophetic curse follows in vv. 18-19*a.* As in 16:12 (and in 1 Cor 11:30) fatal sickness is the mode of punishment, a premature and painful death that satisfies the chronicler's sense of outrage over Jehoram's evil reign. The repetition of v. 5 (= 2 Kgs 8:17) in v. 20*a* draws attention to the providential brevity of his reign. The quotation continues in the following verb, which repeats "He walked" (v. 6 = 2 Kgs 8:18), but now in a new, fatal sense, "He departed" or "passed away." It is

283. S. J. De Vries, *1 and 2 Chronicles,* FOTL 11 (Grand Rapids: Eerdmans, 1989) 334.

284. See S. Japhet, *I & II Chronicles,* OTL (Louisville: Westminster/John Knox, 1993) 814-15.

285. De Vries, *1 and 2 Chronicles,* 333.

as if the chronicler were saying, "There is a way that seems right to a person, but its end is the way to death" (Prov 14:12 NRSV). As he often does, the chronicler uses as an obituary the final circumstances, here the lack of a fire in his honor (cf. 16:14) and of burial in the royal cemetery. It may be significant that there is no reference to a literary source corresponding to 2 Kgs 8:23. Jehoram was best forgotten.

22:1-9. The attack of 21:16-17 is rounded off in the course of 22:1*a.* The chronicler follows 2 Kgs 8:26-29 fairly closely in vv. 1*b*-6. Ahaziah's age is given as twenty-two in 2 Kgs 8:26 (thus the NIV and the REB are preferred here, following the Lucanic recension of the LXX and the Syriac, whose reading is probably due to synoptic assimilation). The king could hardly have been forty-two (NRSV with the MT), which would make him older than his father, according to 21:5, 20. The LXX has "twenty"; the MT may have arisen from conflation of twenty and twenty-two.[286] Ahaziah is another Jehoram in treading "the ways of the house of Ahab." The chronicler introduces three references to evil counsel in vv. 3-5. The NRSV has preserved the first two ("counselor," "counselors"), and the NIV the third ("counsel"). Ahaziah took the wrong advice, which led first to moral wrongdoing and then to the king's ruin. This reference to unethical behavior is here interwoven with the overarching theme, the influence of the house of Ahab. The queen mother, who *ex officio* had an influential role in the Judean monarchy (see 1 Kgs 2:19), was Athaliah, a member of the northern royal family.

The writing was on the wall for the northern dynasty, and Ahaziah was caught up in its destruction. His joining in a campaign at Ramoth-gilead resembles the story about Jehoshaphat's campaign at Ramoth-gilead in chap. 18, and it carries the same negative overtones as that account. In vv. 7*b*-9*a* the chronicler assumes knowledge of 2 Kgs 9:1-28; 10:12-14, abbreviating his source and concentrating on the southern royal family. In v. 8, reference to "the sons of Ahaziah's brothers" involves a harmonistic addition. Either the chronicler or a later copyist took "brothers" literally and adjusted the text to their having died earlier. At 2 Kgs 10:13-14, Ahaziah's "relatives" are the ones killed.

The chronicler supplies an interpretive framework in vv. 7*a* and 9*b.* The former verse brings to the fore the providential work of God, effecting the destruction that must lie at the end of Ahaziah's self-chosen path. Mention of Jehoshaphat's spirituality, which allows the corpse decent burial, widens the gap between grandfather and grandson (like 21:12). The reforming zeal of Jehu, commissioned by Elisha to crusade in the Lord's name against the house of Ahab, extended not only to the southern ally Ahaziah but also to other princes. It meant the radical depletion of the house of David. There was nobody of sufficient maturity and influence to take over. Was all lost?

286. J. M. Myers, *II Chronicles,* AB 13 (Garden City, N.Y.: Doubleday, 1965) 125. See also D. Barthélemy et al., *Critique textuelle de l'Ancien Testament,* OBO 50/1 (Fribourg: Editions Universitaires; and Göttingen: Vandenhoeck & Ruprecht, 1982) 1:499-500.

REFLECTIONS

1. Divine grace and justice clash in this section. On one side stood the "lamp" (21:7), which in 13:5, 8 the chronicler had interpreted as the sons of David perpetually ruling over the kingdom of the Lord (see also 1 Kgs 15:4). Confronting this promise of irrevocable grace was Jehoram's and Ahaziah's defiance of basic religious and ethical standards. The Lord had promised to wipe out the house of Ahab. Logically one expects the same fate for David's house, now that it had sunk as low as its northern counterpart. In the way, however, stood the promise of 21:7. Yet divine judgment brought the chosen royal family to the verge of extinction by the end of the section (22:1, 8-9). The story was a parable for the chronicler. The days of the post-exilic period without a king were an interim phase. The Lord's royal promises, affirmed in the prophetic books, could not be gainsaid. No less sure is the hope of the church, which has its own "lamp shining in a dark place, until . . . the morning star rises in your hearts" (2 Pet 1:19 NRSV). This hope is centered in "the root and the descendant of David, the bright morning star" (Rev 22:16 NRSV).

2. The spiritual correlation between north and south implied in the language of 21:11 represents a call for humility at this point. He was preaching against the Judah of his day, a proud elder brother who despised the northern prodigal. He reminded them that in their own past they, too, had been prodigal sons and daughters, needing the same grace from a forgiving Parent. Paul had a similar word of rebuke for Jew-despising Gentile Christians in Rom 11:17-22.

3. The motif of bad counsel, added in 22:3-5, builds on the precedent of Rehoboam in chapter 10. Ahaziah might have pleaded that he was not to blame, as the pawn of stronger personalities. But his plea would have been to no avail: The buck stopped here, in the decisions of the leader. The dice of heredity and environment were loaded against Ahaziah, but it was his own succumbing that plunged the dynasty into danger. The chronicler teaches personal responsibility here. Ahaziah forfeited the beatitude of those who do "not walk in the counsel of the wicked" (Ps 1:1 NIV). He was no Job, who testified, "I stand aloof from the counsel of the wicked" (Job 21:16 NIV).

2 Chronicles 22:10–23:21, The Coup in Support of Joash

NIV

10When Athaliah the mother of Ahaziah saw that her son was dead, she proceeded to destroy the whole royal family of the house of Judah. 11But Jehosheba,[a] the daughter of King Jehoram, took Joash son of Ahaziah and stole him away from among the royal princes who were about to be murdered and put him and his nurse in a bedroom. Because Jehosheba,[a] the daughter of King Jehoram and wife of the priest Jehoiada, was Ahaziah's sister, she hid the child from Athaliah so she could not kill him. 12He remained hidden with them at the temple of God for six years while Athaliah ruled the land.

23 In the seventh year Jehoiada showed his strength. He made a covenant with the commanders of units of a hundred: Azariah son of Jeroham, Ishmael son of Jehohanan, Azariah son of Obed, Maaseiah son of Adaiah, and Elishaphat son of Zicri. 2They went throughout Judah and gathered the Levites and the heads of Israelite families from all the towns. When they came to Jerusalem, 3the whole assembly made a covenant with the king at the temple of God.

Jehoiada said to them, "The king's son shall reign, as the LORD promised concerning the descendants of David. 4Now this is what you are to do: A third of you priests and Levites who are going on duty on the Sabbath are to keep watch at the doors, 5a third of you at the royal palace and a third at the Foundation Gate, and all the

[a]*11* Hebrew *Jehoshabeath,* a variant of *Jehosheba*

NRSV

10Now when Athaliah, Ahaziah's mother, saw that her son was dead, she set about to destroy all the royal family of the house of Judah. 11But Jehoshabeath, the king's daughter, took Joash son of Ahaziah, and stole him away from among the king's children who were about to be killed; she put him and his nurse in a bedroom. Thus Jehoshabeath, daughter of King Jehoram and wife of the priest Jehoiada—because she was a sister of Ahaziah—hid him from Athaliah, so that she did not kill him; 12he remained with them six years, hidden in the house of God, while Athaliah reigned over the land.

23 But in the seventh year Jehoiada took courage, and entered into a compact with the commanders of the hundreds, Azariah son of Jeroham, Ishmael son of Jehohanan, Azariah son of Obed, Maaseiah son of Adaiah, and Elishaphat son of Zichri. 2They went around through Judah and gathered the Levites from all the towns of Judah, and the heads of families of Israel, and they came to Jerusalem. 3Then the whole assembly made a covenant with the king in the house of God. Jehoiada[a] said to them, "Here is the king's son! Let him reign, as the LORD promised concerning the sons of David. 4This is what you are to do: one-third of you, priests and Levites, who come on duty on the sabbath, shall be gatekeepers, 5one-third shall be at the king's house, and one-third at the Gate of the Foundation; and all

[a] Heb *He*

NIV

other men are to be in the courtyards of the temple of the LORD. 6No one is to enter the temple of the LORD except the priests and Levites on duty; they may enter because they are consecrated, but all the other men are to guard what the LORD has assigned to them.[a] 7The Levites are to station themselves around the king, each man with his weapons in his hand. Anyone who enters the temple must be put to death. Stay close to the king wherever he goes."

8The Levites and all the men of Judah did just as Jehoiada the priest ordered. Each one took his men—those who were going on duty on the Sabbath and those who were going off duty—for Jehoiada the priest had not released any of the divisions. 9Then he gave the commanders of units of a hundred the spears and the large and small shields that had belonged to King David and that were in the temple of God. 10He stationed all the men, each with his weapon in his hand, around the king—near the altar and the temple, from the south side to the north side of the temple.

11Jehoiada and his sons brought out the king's son and put the crown on him; they presented him with a copy of the covenant and proclaimed him king. They anointed him and shouted, "Long live the king!"

12When Athaliah heard the noise of the people running and cheering the king, she went to them at the temple of the LORD. 13She looked, and there was the king, standing by his pillar at the entrance. The officers and the trumpeters were beside the king, and all the people of the land were rejoicing and blowing trumpets, and singers with musical instruments were leading the praises. Then Athaliah tore her robes and shouted, "Treason! Treason!"

14Jehoiada the priest sent out the commanders of units of a hundred, who were in charge of the troops, and said to them: "Bring her out between the ranks[b] and put to the sword anyone who follows her." For the priest had said, "Do not put her to death at the temple of the LORD." 15So they seized her as she reached the entrance of the Horse Gate on the palace grounds, and there they put her to death.

[a]*6* Or *to observe the LORD's command ⌊not to enter⌋* [b]*14* Or *out from the precincts*

NRSV

the people shall be in the courts of the house of the LORD. 6Do not let anyone enter the house of the LORD except the priests and ministering Levites; they may enter, for they are holy, but all the other[a] people shall observe the instructions of the LORD. 7The Levites shall surround the king, each with his weapons in his hand; and whoever enters the house shall be killed. Stay with the king in his comings and goings."

8The Levites and all Judah did according to all that the priest Jehoiada commanded; each brought his men, who were to come on duty on the sabbath, with those who were to go off duty on the sabbath; for the priest Jehoiada did not dismiss the divisions. 9The priest Jehoiada delivered to the captains the spears and the large and small shields that had been King David's, which were in the house of God; 10and he set all the people as a guard for the king, everyone with weapon in hand, from the south side of the house to the north side of the house, around the altar and the house. 11Then he brought out the king's son, put the crown on him, and gave him the covenant;[b] they proclaimed him king, and Jehoiada and his sons anointed him; and they shouted, "Long live the king!"

12When Athaliah heard the noise of the people running and praising the king, she went into the house of the LORD to the people; 13and when she looked, there was the king standing by his pillar at the entrance, and the captains and the trumpeters beside the king, and all the people of the land rejoicing and blowing trumpets, and the singers with their musical instruments leading in the celebration. Athaliah tore her clothes, and cried, "Treason! Treason!" 14Then the priest Jehoiada brought out the captains who were set over the army, saying to them, "Bring her out between the ranks; anyone who follows her is to be put to the sword." For the priest said, "Do not put her to death in the house of the LORD." 15So they laid hands on her; she went into the entrance of the Horse Gate of the king's house, and there they put her to death.

16Jehoiada made a covenant between himself and all the people and the king that they should be the LORD's people. 17Then all the people went

[a] Heb lacks *other* [b] Or *treaty*, or *testimony*; Heb *eduth*

NIV

[16]Jehoiada then made a covenant that he and
the people and the king[a] would be the LORD's
people. [17]All the people went to the temple of
Baal and tore it down. They smashed the altars
and idols and killed Mattan the priest of Baal in
front of the altars.

[18]Then Jehoiada placed the oversight of the
temple of the LORD in the hands of the priests,
who were Levites, to whom David had made
assignments in the temple, to present the burnt
offerings of the LORD as written in the Law of
Moses, with rejoicing and singing, as David had
ordered. [19]He also stationed doorkeepers at the
gates of the LORD's temple so that no one who
was in any way unclean might enter.

[20]He took with him the commanders of hundreds, the nobles, the rulers of the people and all
the people of the land and brought the king down
from the temple of the LORD. They went into the
palace through the Upper Gate and seated the
king on the royal throne, [21]and all the people of
the land rejoiced. And the city was quiet, because
Athaliah had been slain with the sword.

a16 Or *covenant between ⌊the LORD⌋ and the people and the king that they* (see 2 Kings 11:17)

NRSV

to the house of Baal, and tore it down; his altars
and his images they broke in pieces, and they
killed Mattan, the priest of Baal, in front of the
altars. [18]Jehoiada assigned the care of the house
of the LORD to the levitical priests whom David
had organized to be in charge of the house of the
LORD, to offer burnt offerings to the LORD, as it is
written in the law of Moses, with rejoicing and
with singing, according to the order of David. [19]He
stationed the gatekeepers at the gates of the house
of the LORD so that no one should enter who was
in any way unclean. [20]And he took the captains,
the nobles, the governors of the people, and all
the people of the land, and they brought the king
down from the house of the LORD, marching
through the upper gate to the king's house. They
set the king on the royal throne. [21]So all the people
of the land rejoiced, and the city was quiet after
Athaliah had been killed with the sword.

COMMENTARY

This thrilling section depends on 2 Kgs 11:1-20, though the chronicler has left his fingerprints all over 23:1-21.

22:10-12. This episode stays rather close to the 2 Kings narrative. Athaliah usurped the throne, a double shock because she did not belong to the Davidic line and was Ahab's daughter (21:6), with a history of leading the former kings astray (v. 3; 21:6). In four centuries of southern rule, this was the only break in the Davidic succession, brief though it was. The divine principle of the permanence of the house of David, enunciated in 21:7, invites readers to see the Lord's hand in events. At first, the situation became more hopeless. The queen tried to kill off the remaining male heirs, in reprisal for her family members' deaths. The theme of the royal family's being whittled down reaches a climax.

This first passage is a tale of two women. Athaliah was in control, indulging to the full her opposition to the true God (cf. 24:7) and thinking she has dealt the same death blow to the house of David that Jehu had to the house of Ahab. She met her match in Jehoshabeath (a feminine form of "Jehosheba" in 2 Kgs 11:2), a Davidic princess born to Jehoram by another wife, according to Josephus.[287] The chronicler adds that she was the wife of the chief priest, which would explain her hiding Joash in the married priest's quarters in the temple compound. It is not known whether this statement was the chronicler's inference or was based on a historical tradition. The princess kidnapped the baby Joash with his wet nurse, taking on herself the hazardous mission of preserving the Davidic line. The mission will pass to her husband in chap. 23, but she spent six long years guarding her secret.

287. Josephus *Antiquities of the Jews* IX.7.1-141.

23:1-21. Another contrast is posed, between the usurper and the baby king. Even before the boy Joash was crowned, the chronicler honored him with the title of king (v. 3), regarding him as the legitimate Davidic king during the queen mother's interregnum. In his version of the coup to restore the Davidic monarch, the chronicler closely followed 2 Kings 11, apart from working into its narrative three particular interests. The first is a concern to replace the foreign palace guards by Levites; by his time temple security was the responsibility of Levites.[288] The change was given theological warrant in Ezek 44:6-14: The intrusion of "foreigners uncircumcised in heart and flesh" profaned holy space. So the palace guards have been edited out of the text, and an idealized account has been put in its place in the interest of religious propriety. The plot fomented by Jehoiada with the officers of the palace guard now involved officers of the levitical security force. They mobilized Levites to carry out the plot, which was evidently planned to take place on a particular sabbath.

The proposed deployment of different groups of guards in various areas of the palace and temple complex described in 2 Kgs 11:5-8 is given a religious coloring in vv. 4-7. The orders are complicated in the 2 Kings account because of the addition of v. 6*a* to 2 Kings, which the chronicler appropriated. The 2 Kings account includes one set of instructions for those coming off duty who were to guard the palace in three groups, and another set for those coming on duty, consisting of two platoons, who were to guard the Temple and the boy king. "The probability is that the chronicler neither understood nor cared about the details of the arrangements."[289] He identified the first group with priests and Levites and made the orders include a specific ban on anybody else entering the Temple (vv. 4, 6). The second watch is identified with Levites (v. 7).

The chronicler took the reference to "whoever approaches the ranks [of the palace guards] is to be killed" in 2 Kgs 11:8 (NRSV) to refer to the temple precincts, and he chose to elaborate this order to kill in the anticipatory ban of v. 6. The same term (שׂדרות *śĕdērôt*) occurs in 2 Kgs 11:15 and the parallel 2 Chr 23:14. Was Athaliah to be brought out "between the ranks" or "out from the precincts" (NIV note; cf. the REB)? The chronicler's interpretation (v. 7) suggests that he interpreted this phrase in the latter sense. Jehoiada's command not to profane the temple area with homicide in v. 14*b* is closely related to his instructions about where to take her in v. 14*a*. In both v. 6 and v. 14, a concern to protect holy space comes to the fore.

The second feature the chronicler worked into the narrative is the pervasive inclusion of the people in the plot. He took the mention of "the people" or "the people of the land," who suddenly appear in 2 Kgs 11:13-14, 17-20 (= 2 Chr 23:12-13, 16-17, 20-21), as his cue to project them back into the earlier narrative for both logical and theological reasons. Whatever political flavor "the people of the land" may have had in 2 Kings, in 2 Chronicles the phrase simply refers to the covenant nation, as the use of "the people" in v. 17 indicates. The first new reference to the people occurs in v. 2, where "the heads of families of Israel" are gathered from Judah. They form the representative members of "the whole assembly" (v. 3). The compact with the officers of the guard (according to 2 Kgs 11:4) is doubled, thus also becoming a pact with the representative assembly of God's people. The chronicler found warrant for this pact in 2 Kgs 11:17*b*, which he transposed here.[290] This compact with the people repeats on a smaller scale the pact that the newly crowned Solomon made with the nation gathered in 2 Chr 1:2-3. Moreover, the unity of king and people under God, which had characterized David's coronation in 1 Chronicles 11–12, finds its first echo in this chapter. Just as David depended on the help of his supporters who pledged themselves to him and to the Lord, so also the boy king Joash was backed by a loyal populace, or at least a representative group. The pact marks the triumph of the Lord's word concerning "the sons of David," the promise of a perpetual dynasty made to David "and to his sons" (21:7 NJB).

The presentation to the people assumed in the NRSV, "Here is the king's son," presupposes and puts into direct speech the narrative detail in 2

288. For the paramilitary role of the Levites, see J. W. Wright, "Guarding the Gates: 1 Chronicles 26.1-19 and the Roles of Gatekeepers in Chronicles," *JSOT* 48 (1990) 69-74.

289. E. L. Curtis and A. A. Madsen, *The Books of Chronicles,* ICC (Edinburgh: T. &. T. Clark, 1910) 427.

290. Japhet, *I & II Chronicles,* 835.

Kgs 11:4 that Jehoiada showed them the king's son. This translation is preferable to the more low-key rendering of the NIV, which reflects the punctuation in the MT and leaves the presentation to the people until v. 11. The former interpretation fits the popular sequence of the plot, injected into the text by the chronicler. The people are next introduced at v. 5, posing as ordinary worshipers. According to v. 10, "all the people" were to share in guarding the king, positioned in the temple court, while in v. 6 "all the people" (REB) were to observe religious protocol by staying out of the temple building. A careful distinction is drawn between the people's theological inclusion and religious exclusion, though in this emergency they are allowed access to the temple court.

The chronicler appears to have had a hermeneutical basis for introducing the people in vv. 2, 5-6. In the 2 Kings story "the guards" or "the runners" (2 Kgs 11:13) is a term that, in the Hebrew, stands in apposition to "the people." The chronicler understood the two terms as a single entity, "the people running," and also as objective warrant for changing "the guards" in 2 Kgs 11:4, 6 (in the standard Hebrew form הרצים [*hārāṣîm*]) into "the people," as the group who were running when the plot was put into action (cf. v. 20*a,* where this expedient was impossible and he converted them into "governors/rulers of the people"; in v. 20*b,* "the gate of the guards" [2 Kgs 11:19] became simply "the upper gate"). The renderings "all the other men" and "all the men" in the NIV at vv. 5-6, 10 and also "all the other people" in the NRSV at v. 6 miss the point. The unambiguous mention of "all [the men of] Judah" in v. 8 shows how the chronicler's mind was working.

The third concern in the chronicler's version is to parade the religious music and song he prized and associated with the temple era founded by David. The reference to trumpeters in 2 Kgs 11:14 suggested to him the priestly trumpeters. While he allowed the next mention of the people trumpeting to stand, he quickly followed it up with a reference to levitical singers, who were leading the cheers with religious songs (v. 13; cf. 1 Chr 15:16, 27-28). The destruction of the temple of Baal, along with its altars, images, and priest invited the promotion of the interests of the true Temple. The setting of "guards" at the Temple (2 Kgs 11:18) gave him an opportunity. The chronicler first applied פקדות (*pĕquddôt*) to the levitical gatekeepers, ascribing to them the role of protecting holy space, which is a strong theme of the section (v. 19). He also understood *pĕquddôt* as "oversight" and explained it in terms of the double system planned by David, who retained the Mosaic order of priestly sacrifice and supplemented it with his own order of levitical music and song (v. 18). It was a reestablishment of Solomon's institution in 8:12-15. The restoration of Davidic rule and of David's worship in the Temple meant the fulfillment of ideals cherished by the chronicler.

The preliminary "covenant" made with the people to carry out the enthronement of the Davidic claimant (v. 3) is fittingly followed by renewed commitment to the covenant with the Lord (v. 16). For the chronicler, it was a repetition of the people's covenant pledge in Asa's reign (15:12) and a model of spiritual devotion to God, which he commended to his own generation. The language of 2 Kgs 11:17, involving both people and king, and with the priest now acting as the Lord's representative, suited the chronicler's conception of covenant. The Lord's covenant with David (21:7) and the covenant with Israel overlapped, with the former providing a guarantee of the continuance of the covenant. The quiet of the city after the coup carried political overtones in 2 Kgs 11:21; in 2 Chr 23:21 it connotes divine blessing on the faithful (as in 15:15).

REFLECTIONS

1. The dramatic contrast in 22:10-12 is a link in a biblical chain. It begins with the hiding of baby Moses in the bulrushes and culminates in the spiriting away of the infant Jesus from the wrath of King Herod. Whether it was a pharaoh, an Athaliah, or a Herod, the wicked ruler met his or her match in the providential working of God. They did their worst and thought they had triumphed, unaware of the loophole that spelled their failure. In this episode,

a seminal victory is won, which, like the moral victory of Dunkirk in World War II, allows a decisive encounter to be mounted at a later stage. It crystallizes the theme that runs throughout the Bible and throughout the history of the church and the synagogue: the triumph of the remnant. It speaks to the people of God whenever they find themselves a beleaguered minority.

2. The *leitmotif* of the two royal houses runs through this unit, with that of the house of Ahab rising to a savage crescendo until it is silenced and followed by a resurgence of the sweeter melody. This saga of an overwhelming threat to the Davidic dynasty and its eventual removal is reminiscent of Rimsky-Korsakov's arrangement of Mussorgsky's *A Night on Bald Mountain.* The increasingly strident music represented in the dance of the witches of the power of evil is stilled by the dawning of a new day and the tolling of a church bell. Corresponding to that finale is the closing paragraph, 23:16-21, which speaks of the triumph of good and the enjoyment of rest. God is the ultimate winner in this terrible struggle. The Davidic line, the Temple, and the community of faith are all beneficiaries of the divine victory. The story became for the chronicler a parable of hope. All who live in dark days and labor for a good cause can read it as such for themselves as well.

3. The tale of the two women presents contrasted cameos of self-seeking evil and unselfish heroism in the Lord's service. Athaliah stands for a regime of cruel oppression. Jehoshabeath is the heroine of a resistance movement, risking her life in order that good may eventually triumph. She is a role model for all who take a stand with God when evil is rampant (cf. Heb 11:33).

4. The rivalry of royal houses comes to a poignant interim climax in the course of this section. The house of David lives on in a baby. Is this the King? Yes, the chronicler claims, as surely as Matthew does in his birth narrative. In Matt 2:1-18, King Herod pits his power against one who is born King of the Jews. In both narratives, weakness and power are polarized. As in a later age, here "God chose what is weak in the world to shame the strong" (1 Cor 1:27 NRSV). Christians still know of hiddenness, awaiting the revelation of the Son of David as the key to truth and right (Col 3:1-10).

5. Restoration of royalty and of right religion is intertwined in chapter 23. Its most obvious feature is the protection of holy space devoted to the Lord. So gatekeepers are stationed to keep out those of the people who are unclean (23:19). The chronicler acts as a literary gatekeeper throughout the story, taking Ezekiel 44 to heart and idealistically expelling the foreign palace guard from the original narrative. In fact, the old guard is replaced not only by the Torah-accredited priests and Levites (cf. Numbers 18), but also by the covenant people, who had an essential stake in the vindication of King and Temple. The New Testament, especially in the Letter to the Hebrews, fuses the themes of holiness and the people still further. Now "we have confidence to enter the Most Holy Place . . . by a new and living way" (Heb 10:19-20 NIV). Yet, just as the chronicler's story is a paradigm of promise and hope to work toward, so, too, this new spiritual access has been inaugurated but not yet consummated: "Let us hold unswervingly to the hope we profess, for he who promised is faithful" (Heb 10:23 NIV).

6. Many themes cherished by the chronicler crowd into this section. It is a glorious moment of revelation and attained potential. It portrays ideals concerning what ought to be and what was yet to be. No wonder the section closes with notes of joy and peace, inspired by the recognition of the true King. In like spirit, Luke's Gospel lets us hear the angels' song of peace and joy at the birth of the Davidic Messiah, in fulfillment of God's ancient word of covenant promise (Luke 1:69-75; 2:4-14).

2 CHRONICLES 24:1–26:23, HOW TO LOSE THE RACE, IN THREE LESSONS

OVERVIEW

These chapters present three Jekyll and Hyde scenarios of initial obedience to God and subsequent apostasy. They preach in narrative form a triple warning against abandoning the true faith. In each case, the first half opens with a commendatory "did what was right in the sight of the LORD" (NRSV), followed by a negative qualifying clause about the king's short-lived virtue (24:2, from 2 Kgs 12:3; 25:2; 26:4-5). In the first and third of the three reigns described, virtue is credited to heeding a wise old counselor (24:17; 26:5), and in the first and second wise counsel is rejected (24:21-22; 25:16, 20). In the second and third reigns, the second phase features pride (25:19, from 2 Kgs 14:10; 26:16).

Each of the three kings was "running well" for a time, to use the metaphor of Gal 5:7 (NRSV), but each failed to finish the race. The chronicler seems to be using them to illustrate the case in Ezek 18:24, 26 (cf. 33:12-13), where "the righteous turn away from their righteousness and commit iniquity" (NRSV) and are punished with premature death. He wrote from a pastor's heart, providing spiritual case studies for his own generation to heed.

2 Chronicles 24:1-27, Joash Listens to the Wrong Advice

NIV

24 Joash was seven years old when he became king, and he reigned in Jerusalem forty years. His mother's name was Zibiah; she was from Beersheba. [2]Joash did what was right in the eyes of the LORD all the years of Jehoiada the priest. [3]Jehoiada chose two wives for him, and he had sons and daughters.

[4]Some time later Joash decided to restore the temple of the LORD. [5]He called together the priests and Levites and said to them, "Go to the towns of Judah and collect the money due annually from all Israel, to repair the temple of your God. Do it now." But the Levites did not act at once.

[6]Therefore the king summoned Jehoiada the chief priest and said to him, "Why haven't you required the Levites to bring in from Judah and Jerusalem the tax imposed by Moses the servant of the LORD and by the assembly of Israel for the Tent of the Testimony?"

[7]Now the sons of that wicked woman Athaliah had broken into the temple of God and had used even its sacred objects for the Baals.

[8]At the king's command, a chest was made and placed outside, at the gate of the temple of the

NRSV

24 Joash was seven years old when he began to reign; he reigned forty years in Jerusalem; his mother's name was Zibiah of Beer-sheba. [2]Joash did what was right in the sight of the LORD all the days of the priest Jehoiada. [3]Jehoiada got two wives for him, and he became the father of sons and daughters.

4Some time afterward Joash decided to restore the house of the LORD. [5]He assembled the priests and the Levites and said to them, "Go out to the cities of Judah and gather money from all Israel to repair the house of your God, year by year; and see that you act quickly." But the Levites did not act quickly. [6]So the king summoned Jehoiada the chief, and said to him, "Why have you not required the Levites to bring in from Judah and Jerusalem the tax levied by Moses, the servant of the LORD, on[a] the congregation of Israel for the tent of the covenant?"[b] [7]For the children of Athaliah, that wicked woman, had broken into the house of God, and had even used all the dedicated things of the house of the LORD for the Baals.

[a] Compare Vg: Heb *and* [b] Or *treaty,* or *testimony;* Heb *eduth*

NIV

LORD. 9A proclamation was then issued in Judah and Jerusalem that they should bring to the LORD the tax that Moses the servant of God had required of Israel in the desert. 10All the officials and all the people brought their contributions gladly, dropping them into the chest until it was full. 11Whenever the chest was brought in by the Levites to the king's officials and they saw that there was a large amount of money, the royal secretary and the officer of the chief priest would come and empty the chest and carry it back to its place. They did this regularly and collected a great amount of money. 12The king and Jehoiada gave it to the men who carried out the work required for the temple of the LORD. They hired masons and carpenters to restore the LORD's temple, and also workers in iron and bronze to repair the temple.

13The men in charge of the work were diligent, and the repairs progressed under them. They rebuilt the temple of God according to its original design and reinforced it. 14When they had finished, they brought the rest of the money to the king and Jehoiada, and with it were made articles for the LORD's temple: articles for the service and for the burnt offerings, and also dishes and other objects of gold and silver. As long as Jehoiada lived, burnt offerings were presented continually in the temple of the LORD.

15Now Jehoiada was old and full of years, and he died at the age of a hundred and thirty. 16He was buried with the kings in the City of David, because of the good he had done in Israel for God and his temple.

17After the death of Jehoiada, the officials of Judah came and paid homage to the king, and he listened to them. 18They abandoned the temple of the LORD, the God of their fathers, and worshiped Asherah poles and idols. Because of their guilt, God's anger came upon Judah and Jerusalem. 19Although the LORD sent prophets to the people to bring them back to him, and though they testified against them, they would not listen.

20Then the Spirit of God came upon Zechariah son of Jehoiada the priest. He stood before the people and said, "This is what God says: 'Why do you disobey the LORD's commands? You will

NRSV

8So the king gave command, and they made a chest, and set it outside the gate of the house of the LORD. 9A proclamation was made throughout Judah and Jerusalem to bring in for the LORD the tax that Moses the servant of God laid on Israel in the wilderness. 10All the leaders and all the people rejoiced and brought their tax and dropped it into the chest until it was full. 11Whenever the chest was brought to the king's officers by the Levites, when they saw that there was a large amount of money in it, the king's secretary and the officer of the chief priest would come and empty the chest and take it and return it to its place. So they did day after day, and collected money in abundance. 12The king and Jehoiada gave it to those who had charge of the work of the house of the LORD, and they hired masons and carpenters to restore the house of the LORD, and also workers in iron and bronze to repair the house of the LORD. 13So those who were engaged in the work labored, and the repairing went forward at their hands, and they restored the house of God to its proper condition and strengthened it. 14When they had finished, they brought the rest of the money to the king and Jehoiada, and with it were made utensils for the house of the LORD, utensils for the service and for the burnt offerings, and ladles, and vessels of gold and silver. They offered burnt offerings in the house of the LORD regularly all the days of Jehoiada.

15But Jehoiada grew old and full of days, and died; he was one hundred thirty years old at his death. 16And they buried him in the city of David among the kings, because he had done good in Israel, and for God and his house.

17Now after the death of Jehoiada the officials of Judah came and did obeisance to the king; then the king listened to them. 18They abandoned the house of the LORD, the God of their ancestors, and served the sacred poles[a] and the idols. And wrath came upon Judah and Jerusalem for this guilt of theirs. 19Yet he sent prophets among them to bring them back to the LORD; they testified against them, but they would not listen.

20Then the spirit of God took possession of[b] Zechariah son of the priest Jehoiada; he stood above the people and said to them, "Thus says

[a] Heb *Asherim* [b] Heb *clothed itself with*

NIV

not prosper. Because you have forsaken the LORD,
he has forsaken you.'"
21But they plotted against him, and by order of
the king they stoned him to death in the courtyard
of the LORD's temple. 22King Joash did not remember the kindness Zechariah's father Jehoiada had
shown him but killed his son, who said as he lay
dying, "May the LORD see this and call you to
account."
23At the turn of the year,[a] the army of Aram
marched against Joash; it invaded Judah and Jerusalem and killed all the leaders of the people.
They sent all the plunder to their king in Damascus. 24Although the Aramean army had come with
only a few men, the LORD delivered into their
hands a much larger army. Because Judah had
forsaken the LORD, the God of their fathers, judgment was executed on Joash. 25When the Arameans withdrew, they left Joash severely
wounded. His officials conspired against him for
murdering the son of Jehoiada the priest, and they
killed him in his bed. So he died and was buried
in the City of David, but not in the tombs of the
kings.
26Those who conspired against him were
Zabad,[b] son of Shimeath an Ammonite woman,
and Jehozabad, son of Shimrith[c] a Moabite
woman. 27The account of his sons, the many
prophecies about him, and the record of the
restoration of the temple of God are written in
the annotations on the book of the kings. And
Amaziah his son succeeded him as king.

[a]*23* Probably in the spring [b]*26* A variant of *Jozabad* [c]*26* A variant of *Shomer*

NRSV

God: Why do you transgress the commandments
of the LORD, so that you cannot prosper? Because
you have forsaken the LORD, he has also forsaken
you." 21But they conspired against him, and by
command of the king they stoned him to death
in the court of the house of the LORD. 22King Joash
did not remember the kindness that Jehoiada,
Zechariah's father, had shown him, but killed his
son. As he was dying, he said, "May the LORD see
and avenge!"
23At the end of the year the army of Aram
came up against Joash. They came to Judah and
Jerusalem, and destroyed all the officials of the
people from among them, and sent all the booty
they took to the king of Damascus. 24Although
the army of Aram had come with few men, the
LORD delivered into their hand a very great army,
because they had abandoned the LORD, the God
of their ancestors. Thus they executed judgment
on Joash.
25When they had withdrawn, leaving him severely wounded, his servants conspired against
him because of the blood of the son[a] of the priest
Jehoiada, and they killed him on his bed. So he
died; and they buried him in the city of David,
but they did not bury him in the tombs of the
kings. 26Those who conspired against him were
Zabad son of Shimeath the Ammonite, and Jehozabad son of Shimrith the Moabite. 27Accounts of
his sons, and of the many oracles against him,
and of the rebuilding[b] of the house of God are
written in the Commentary on the Book of the
Kings. And his son Amaziah succeeded him.

[a] Gk Vg: Heb *sons* [b] Heb *founding*

COMMENTARY

For the most part, the chronicler followed the account of Joash's reign in 2 Kings 12, but he interpreted it differently. He understood in a restrictive sense the statement in 2 Kgs 12:3 about lifelong loyalty to the Lord because of Jehoiada's influence, taking it like the NIV's (harmonistic) rendering, "All the years Jehoiada the priest instructed him." The chronicler's report of regular sacrificing while Jehoiada was alive (v. 14) provides a summary for vv. 2-13 and reinforces his understanding of v. 2. This latter end is also served by Jehoiada's involvement in organizing the temple repairs (vv. 12, 14). Why did the chronicler split Joash's reign into good and bad periods? He was encouraged to do so by the misfortunes at the end of his reign, foreign invasion, and an internal conspiracy that led to his assassination. He conceived of two providentially coherent phases, before and after Jehoiada's demise, the first marked by obedience and blessing and the second by disobedience and unmitigated disaster.[291] This structuring made it expedient to omit, or at least postpone, 2 Kgs 12:3 with its negative mention of worship at the high places.

Chapter 23 has left readers with a sense of relief that now all was well in the palace and the Temple and throughout the land. And so it was at first under Jehoiada's tutelage. In 24:3, the chronicler adds a vignette of divine blessing to cap the obedience of 24:2. After the decimation of the royal family in the previous unit, their increase is a welcome sign that the threat to the dynasty was now over.

24:1-14. The account of the temple repairs in 2 Kgs 12:14-16 has been used loosely to illustrate Joash's obedience, which relates both to the Torah and to the Temple. The theme of repairing the Temple, which runs throughout the 2 Kings account in speech and narrative (2 Kgs 12:5-7, 12, 14), is precisely paralleled only at vv. 5 and 12 (= 2 Kgs 12:5, 12), but the chronicler begins his account by announcing Joash's plans for restoration in v. 4 and ends it by adding a long sentence about its having been accomplished in v. 13. This generalized packaging suggests that he intended to inspire his contemporaries to maintain the Temple—joyfully (v. 10). This idealistic perspective explains in part the reversal of 2 Kgs 12:13 in v. 14; so liberal was the funding that vessels could be provided for the Temple (cf. Ezra 8:25). The chronicler also wanted to supply a positive counterpart to the note he had added in v. 7 about the misappropriation of consecrated articles in Athaliah's reign. Moreover, the chronicler has in mind the tabernacle tax, part of which was used to furnish the sanctuary (Exod 38:24-31). The tabernacle had been replaced by the Temple as the sanctuary Israel was obliged to maintain and keep equipped.

The chronicler was concerned to honor the Torah stipulations that related to the sanctuary. In Israel's wilderness period, the tabernacle had been maintained by an annual tax of half a shekel (see Exod 30:11-16). Scholars differ as to whether 2 Kgs 12:4 refers to this tax, but the chronicler explicitly cites it. He characteristically emphasized the Torah by twice naming "Moses the servant of the LORD/God" (vv. 6, 9) as the venerable author of the tax. In mentioning the initial hesitation of the temple personnel (a simplification of the religious politics in 2 Kgs 12:5-8) and the eventual glad giving of leaders and people, strong hints were dropped to his own generation.[292] In the post-exilic period, there seems to have been a reluctance to pay the temple tax, perhaps due to economic difficulties in the early part of the period. A pledge to pay the tax is written into the covenant of rededication to the Lord in Neh 10:32-33. The chronicler used both 1 Chronicles 29 and the present narrative, notably v. 10, to provide models for his readers of joyful giving to God's work. Whereas in the former passage it was presented as a Davidic ideal, here it has the backing of the Torah.

Two aspects of proper religious practice are introduced. First, in v. 8 the location of the chest is specified as being outside the temple gate—that is, outside the inner or temple court. In deference to the Temple's sanctity, the laity was restricted to the outer court, though in the emergency of 23:5 the chronicler had relaxed this ruling. Second, in v. 14*b* the regular sacrifices of burnt offering align with both the Torah and Solomon's institution of them at the Temple (2:4; 8:12-13).

24:15-16. The chronicler pauses to note the honorable burial of Joash's mentor, after a patricharchal-like longevity that reflected God's blessing on his good work on behalf of the Temple and the dynasty. This latter work is defined in terms of "Israel," so close were the respective covenants in the chronicler's thinking. Jehoiada's burial in the royal cemetery, unlike that of his royal protégé (v. 25), communicates his high regard for the priest's achievements.

24:17-19. The rest of Joash's reign takes a shockingly different turn. As with Asa in chap. 16, the chronicler reasoned back from the military and political crises of 2 Kgs 13:17-18, 20-21 and thought that Asa had forsaken the Lord. The king's life-style degenerated into a vicious cycle of wrongdoing. Joash lent his ear to less worthy counselors who hankered after precedents set by

291. See the parallel reversal found in the two phrases by M. P. Graham, "The Composition of 2 Chronicles 24," in *Christian Teaching: Studies in Honor of LeMoine G. Lewis,* ed. E. Ferguson (Abilene: Abilene Christian University, 1981) 138-55, esp. 140.

292. For the non-secondary nature of 24:5*b*-6, see R. B. Dillard, *2 Chronicles,* WBC 15 (Waco, Tex.: Word, 1987) 189-90.

Athaliah. Verse 18*a* is the chronicler's elaboration of the worship at high places in 2 Kgs 12:3, moved here for schematic reasons. Asa had rejected the religious orthodoxy of vv. 4-14, abandoning the Temple. This time also spells a generational shift from "the God of their fathers." Jehoiada's piety was forgotten. Divine "wrath" was incurred, to which Zechariah would give vent. Yet, the Lord gave a second chance by sending prophets to urge repentance. In the Hebrew the phrase "bring them back" (להשׁיבם *lahăšîbām*) is the causative form of the verb "turn" (שׁוב *šûb*) in 7:14. It was a cue for the people to claim that divine provision for backsliders. Their refusal augments the wrong listening of v. 17.

24:20-22. When these warnings went unheeded, the Lord gave a third chance through Zechariah, the son of the venerable Jehoiada, not willing that any should perish (Ezek 33:11; see also 2 Pet 3:9). The chronicler may have known a prophetic tradition referring to Zechariah; here Zechariah's words reflect the perspective of the chronicler. The message of judgment was not final but was intended to bring repentance (cf. 12:5-6). The accusation is framed in a rhetorical question, as in 19:3 and 25:15. It draws on Num 14:41, citing the Torah even as it charges its breach as worshiping at the pagan high places (cf. Deut 12:2-6). The grim mirror-image principle of 1 Chr 28:9; 2 Chr 12:5; 15:2 is repeated, but to no avail. Zechariah's patronym did not protect him from lynching, at the king's urging. This inspired priest, standing on a platform inside the temple court, was an easy target for rocks hurled by a mob undeterred by the sanctity of the location. The chronicler lays the responsibility on the king's shoulders, finding it a shocking response to Jehoiada's loyal service. His failure to remember provides a play on the victim's name, which means "The LORD remembers." The Lord did indeed remember, by answering Zechariah's prayer. The dying priest had the last word, indicating that the fate of king and priest was now sealed. Judgment incurred after prophetic warnings had been rejected is a repeated theme until it culminates in exile (16:7-10; 25:15-16; 33:10-11; 36:15-16).

24:23-27. Now the moral stage has been set for the calamities described in 2 Kgs 12:17-18, 20-21. The divine wrath (v. 18) is realized through foreign invasion and a palace coup. Precise correspondence between fault and fate is traced. The national leaders, Joash's misleaders, are targeted for death (vv. 17, 23). Conspiracy against Zechariah, in which the king was involved, is requited by a court conspiracy against him (vv. 21, 25-26). The king who killed God's messenger is himself killed; the chronicler interprets the conspiracy as divine judgment for the murder of Zechariah (see vv. 22, 25, where "sons" in the MT is rightly emended to "son"). Forsaking the Lord is duly repaid (vv. 20, 24). So the tables are turned. Ironically, a small Aramean force defeated "a very great army" (v. 24). The Lord sided with the outnumbered, as in 13:3-18 and 14:8-15, this time backing Judah's foes. Mention of the king's dishonorable burial place is a last word of evaluation, though it formally disagrees with 2 Kgs 12:21. The common grave contrasts with the honor paid to the non-royal Jehoiada in v. 16. In v. 26, the extra information that the conspirators were sons of Ammonite and Moabite women may be due to the chronicler's having associated their names with their presence in a list relating to interracial marriages in Ezra 10:22-23, 27, 33, 43.[293]

At the close, the chronicler tries to find a good word to say about Joash concerning the repair of the Temple, but it enhances the heinousness of his idolatry and his execution of Zechariah in vv. 18 and 21. The reference to a literary source in v. 27 is probably a device to sum up key aspects of Joash's reign.[294]

The figure of Jehoiada not only dominates the first half of the chapter, but also haunts the second half (vv. 17, 20, 22, 25) as a symbolic measure of the king's degeneration. A term that pervades the second half is the verb "forsake" or "abandon" (עזב *ʿāzab*), in a literary pattern of wrongdoing and retribution. Each of the four parts into which it falls, vv. 17-19, vv. 20-22, vv. 23-24, and vv. 25-26, uses this verb. In v. 18, the forsaking of the Temple marks the abandoning of true, traditional faith. In v. 20, it is interpreted as forsaking

293. M. P. Graham, "A Connection Proposed Between II Chr 24, 26, and Ezra 9–10," *ZAW* 97 (1985) 256-58.

294. See H. G. M. Williamson, *1 and 2 Chronicles,* NCB (Grand Rapids: Eerdmans, 1982) 326. See also S. L. McKenzie, *The Chronicler's Use of the Deuteronomistic History,* HSM 33 (Atlanta: Scholars Press, 1985) 111-12.

the Lord, which incurs the curse of being forsaken in turn. Verse 24 reiterates the sin of vv. 18 and 20, now as the reason for Judah's punishment, with repetition of the generational implications of v. 18. The last case, in v. 25, is concealed by the English translations. Half dead, Joash was abandoned by his enemies, left to die. The verb traces the final outworking of the king's God-forsakenness. It is the polar opposite of the fellowship with the Lord, highlighted in the Jehoshaphat unit.

REFLECTIONS

1. Joash's spirituality is illustrated in his efforts to repair the Temple. His is a down-to-earth piety, concerned with renovation of fabric and woodwork. The instruments of human faith have a built-in obsolescence. Maintaining a practical faith is like going up a down escalator. One has to move to stay in the same place on the escalator, in order to offset a downward pull. A church, understood in terms of place or people, needs effort to counteract natural wear and tear.

In the case of the Temple, a special factor made repairs necessary: damage and defilement caused in the interregnum of the "wicked" queen (24:7). The repair work was an implementation of the king's and the people's rededication to the Lord (23:16). It was a positive counterpart to the negative work of 23:17: the tearing down of Baal's images and altars. The undoing of wrong had to be succeeded by doing "what was right in the sight of the LORD" (24:2). Only thus is true spirituality attained.

2. Joash was also alert to the relevance of the Torah. The chronicler emphasizes the Torah's stipulation of the tabernacle tax and reapplies it to the Temple. Similarly, Paul appears to have translated the temple tax into a corresponding obligation laid on the churches he planted to support the poor church in Jerusalem (Rom 15:25-28; 2 Corinthians 8–9).[295] Both the chronicler and Paul were using a typological principle. Each transferred a responsibility in the old dispensation to another in the new. This typologizing insists that dipping regularly into pocket and purse remains a measure of the believer's spirituality.

3. The spiritual shift after Jehoiada's death provides the chronicler with an opportunity to dwell on the generational aspect of his doctrine. "The LORD, God of their fathers" (24:18, 24 NIV) had been abandoned. Jehoiada's faith was not taken over by the next generation. So in the person of the king they reaped what they had sown, as the precise parallels drawn between offense and punishment show. A positive counterpart to this lesson occurs in Heb 13:7-9: "Remember your leaders, those who spoke the word of God to you; consider the outcome of their way of life, and imitate their faith. Jesus Christ is the same yesterday and today and forever. Do not be carried away by all kinds of strange teachings" (NRSV).

4. Justice and grace tussled in the divine heart. The opportunity of 7:14 stayed open longer than one might have expected. Eventually Zechariah had to utter a grim prayer of requital. Christian readers may be tempted to contrast the gracious prayer of Jesus on the cross, "Father, forgive them, for they do not know what they are doing" (Luke 23:34), or the cry of Stephen, the first Christian martyr, "Lord, do not hold this sin against them" (Acts 7:60). But one may not contrast New Testament grace with Old Testament wrath; Luke 11:47-51 and Rev 6:10; 19:2 are worth comparing with Zechariah's stern prayer (2 Chr 24:22). The inspired priest was not praying a personal prayer of vengeance. Divine overtures had been spurned time after time, and this last refusal sealed the people's fate. They had lost their last chance. It could hardly be said that they did not know what they were doing. The Lord's hands were tied, as if to say, "What else can I do?" (see Jer 9:7).[296] The redeeming feature in the chronicler's

295. See K. F. Nickle, *The Collection: A Study in Paul's Strategy*, SBT 48 (Naperville, Ill.: Allenson, 1966) 87-93.
296. Cf. T. Fretheim, *The Suffering of God*, OBT 14 (Philadelphia: Fortress, 1989) 122-26.

program is that God gives each generation a fresh opportunity to respond. God offers chance after chance, but these moments leave us in God's debt, accountable if we fail to respond.

The assassination of Zechariah finds a place in a woe uttered by Jesus that discerns a crimson thread "from the blood of Abel to the blood of Zechariah, who perished between the altar and the sanctuary" (Luke 11:51 NRSV: cf. Matt 23:35). This incident in Chronicles is regarded as the culmination of the Old Testament record of human rejection of God.

2 Chronicles 25:1-28, Amaziah Finds a New Faith

NIV

25 Amaziah was twenty-five years old when he became king, and he reigned in Jerusalem twenty-nine years. His mother's name was Jehoaddin[a]; she was from Jerusalem. 2He did what was right in the eyes of the LORD, but not wholeheartedly. 3After the kingdom was firmly in his control, he executed the officials who had murdered his father the king. 4Yet he did not put their sons to death, but acted in accordance with what is written in the Law, in the Book of Moses, where the LORD commanded: "Fathers shall not be put to death for their children, nor children put to death for their fathers; each is to die for his own sins."[b]

5Amaziah called the people of Judah together and assigned them according to their families to commanders of thousands and commanders of hundreds for all Judah and Benjamin. He then mustered those twenty years old or more and found that there were three hundred thousand men ready for military service, able to handle the spear and shield. 6He also hired a hundred thousand fighting men from Israel for a hundred talents[c] of silver.

7But a man of God came to him and said, "O king, these troops from Israel must not march with you, for the LORD is not with Israel—not with any of the people of Ephraim. 8Even if you go and fight courageously in battle, God will overthrow you before the enemy, for God has the power to help or to overthrow."

9Amaziah asked the man of God, "But what about the hundred talents I paid for these Israelite troops?"

The man of God replied, "The LORD can give you much more than that."

[a]*1* Hebrew *Jehoaddan,* a variant of *Jehoaddin* [b]*4* Deut. 24:16
[c]*6* That is, about 3 3/4 tons (about 3.4 metric tons); also in verse 9

NRSV

25 Amaziah was twenty-five years old when he began to reign, and he reigned twenty-nine years in Jerusalem. His mother's name was Jehoaddan of Jerusalem. 2He did what was right in the sight of the LORD, yet not with a true heart. 3As soon as the royal power was firmly in his hand he killed his servants who had murdered his father the king. 4But he did not put their children to death, according to what is written in the law, in the book of Moses, where the LORD commanded, "The parents shall not be put to death for the children, or the children be put to death for the parents; but all shall be put to death for their own sins."

5Amaziah assembled the people of Judah, and set them by ancestral houses under commanders of the thousands and of the hundreds for all Judah and Benjamin. He mustered those twenty years old and upward, and found that they were three hundred thousand picked troops fit for war, able to handle spear and shield. 6He also hired one hundred thousand mighty warriors from Israel for one hundred talents of silver. 7But a man of God came to him and said, "O king, do not let the army of Israel go with you, for the LORD is not with Israel—all these Ephraimites. 8Rather, go by yourself and act; be strong in battle, or God will fling you down before the enemy; for God has power to help or to overthrow." 9Amaziah said to the man of God, "But what shall we do about the hundred talents that I have given to the army of Israel?" The man of God answered, "The LORD is able to give you much more than this." 10Then Amaziah discharged the army that had come to him from Ephraim, letting them go home again. But they became very angry with Judah, and returned home in fierce anger.

NIV

10So Amaziah dismissed the troops who had
come to him from Ephraim and sent them home.
They were furious with Judah and left for home
in a great rage.

11Amaziah then marshaled his strength and led
his army to the Valley of Salt, where he killed ten
thousand men of Seir. 12The army of Judah also
captured ten thousand men alive, took them to
the top of a cliff and threw them down so that
all were dashed to pieces.

13Meanwhile the troops that Amaziah had sent
back and had not allowed to take part in the war
raided Judean towns from Samaria to Beth Horon.
They killed three thousand people and carried off
great quantities of plunder.

14When Amaziah returned from slaughtering
the Edomites, he brought back the gods of the
people of Seir. He set them up as his own gods,
bowed down to them and burned sacrifices to
them. 15The anger of the LORD burned against
Amaziah, and he sent a prophet to him, who said,
"Why do you consult this people's gods, which
could not save their own people from your hand?"

16While he was still speaking, the king said to
him, "Have we appointed you an adviser to the
king? Stop! Why be struck down?"

So the prophet stopped but said, "I know that
God has determined to destroy you, because you
have done this and have not listened to my
counsel."

17After Amaziah king of Judah consulted his
advisers, he sent this challenge to Jehoash[a] son of
Jehoahaz, the son of Jehu, king of Israel: "Come,
meet me face to face."

18But Jehoash king of Israel replied to Amaziah
king of Judah: "A thistle in Lebanon sent a message to a cedar in Lebanon, 'Give your daughter
to my son in marriage.' Then a wild beast in
Lebanon came along and trampled the thistle
underfoot. 19You say to yourself that you have
defeated Edom, and now you are arrogant and
proud. But stay at home! Why ask for trouble and
cause your own downfall and that of Judah also?"

20Amaziah, however, would not listen, for God
so worked that he might hand them over to
⌊Jehoash⌋, because they sought the gods of Edom.

[a] *17* Hebrew *Joash,* a variant of *Jehoash*; also in verses 18, 21, 23 and 25

NRSV

11Amaziah took courage, and led out his people; he went to the Valley of Salt, and struck
down ten thousand men of Seir. 12The people of
Judah captured another ten thousand alive, took
them to the top of Sela, and threw them down
from the top of Sela, so that all of them were
dashed to pieces. 13But the men of the army
whom Amaziah sent back, not letting them go
with him to battle, fell on the cities of Judah from
Samaria to Beth-horon; they killed three thousand
people in them, and took much booty.

14Now after Amaziah came from the slaughter
of the Edomites, he brought the gods of the people
of Seir, set them up as his gods, and worshiped
them, making offerings to them. 15The LORD was
angry with Amaziah and sent to him a prophet,
who said to him, "Why have you resorted to a
people's gods who could not deliver their own
people from your hand?" 16But as he was speaking
the king[a] said to him, "Have we made you a royal
counselor? Stop! Why should you be put to
death?" So the prophet stopped, but said, "I know
that God has determined to destroy you, because
you have done this and have not listened to my
advice."

17Then King Amaziah of Judah took counsel
and sent to King Joash son of Jehoahaz son of
Jehu of Israel, saying, "Come, let us look one
another in the face." 18King Joash of Israel sent
word to King Amaziah of Judah, "A thornbush on
Lebanon sent to a cedar on Lebanon, saying, 'Give
your daughter to my son for a wife'; but a wild
animal of Lebanon passed by and trampled down
the thornbush. 19You say, 'See, I have defeated
Edom,' and your heart has lifted you up in boastfulness. Now stay at home; why should you
provoke trouble so that you fall, you and Judah
with you?"

20But Amaziah would not listen—it was God's
doing, in order to hand them over, because they
had sought the gods of Edom. 21So King Joash of
Israel went up; he and King Amaziah of Judah
faced one another in battle at Beth-shemesh,
which belongs to Judah. 22Judah was defeated by
Israel; everyone fled home. 23King Joash of Israel
captured King Amaziah of Judah, son of Joash,
son of Ahaziah, at Beth-shemesh; he brought him

[a] Heb *he*

NIV

[21]So Jehoash king of Israel attacked. He and Amaziah king of Judah faced each other at Beth Shemesh in Judah. [22]Judah was routed by Israel, and every man fled to his home. [23]Jehoash king of Israel captured Amaziah king of Judah, the son of Joash, the son of Ahaziah,[a] at Beth Shemesh. Then Jehoash brought him to Jerusalem and broke down the wall of Jerusalem from the Ephraim Gate to the Corner Gate—a section about six hundred feet[b] long. [24]He took all the gold and silver and all the articles found in the temple of God that had been in the care of Obed-Edom, together with the palace treasures and the hostages, and returned to Samaria.

[25]Amaziah son of Joash king of Judah lived for fifteen years after the death of Jehoash son of Jehoahaz king of Israel. [26]As for the other events of Amaziah's reign, from beginning to end, are they not written in the book of the kings of Judah and Israel? [27]From the time that Amaziah turned away from following the LORD, they conspired against him in Jerusalem and he fled to Lachish, but they sent men after him to Lachish and killed him there. [28]He was brought back by horse and was buried with his fathers in the City of Judah.

a23 Hebrew *Jehoahaz,* a variant of *Ahaziah* b23 Hebrew *four hundred cubits* (about 180 meters)

NRSV

to Jerusalem, and broke down the wall of Jerusalem from the Ephraim Gate to the Corner Gate, a distance of four hundred cubits. [24]He seized all the gold and silver, and all the vessels that were found in the house of God, and Obed-edom with them; he seized also the treasuries of the king's house, also hostages; then he returned to Samaria.

25King Amaziah son of Joash of Judah, lived fifteen years after the death of King Joash son of Jehoahaz of Israel. [26]Now the rest of the deeds of Amaziah, from first to last, are they not written in the Book of the Kings of Judah and Israel? [27]From the time that Amaziah turned away from the LORD they made a conspiracy against him in Jerusalem, and he fled to Lachish. But they sent after him to Lachish, and killed him there. [28]They brought him back on horses; he was buried with his ancestors in the city of David.

COMMENTARY

Once again the reign is split down the middle with an initial period of favor and then a fall from grace. The chronicler's added reference to Amaziah's lack of wholeheartedness (v. 2) relates to this spiritual inconsistency. This verse anticipates the judgment in vv. 14-16, but also alludes to the lesser flaw (v. 6), which at least the king was prepared to put right.

The chronicler found in the account of Amaziah's reign in 2 Kgs 14:1-20 four pieces of an incomplete jigsaw, two relating to positive events and two to negative ones. They dictated his schematic division of the reign, but failed to give a complete theological picture. The chronicler supplied vv. 14-16 as the missing piece, which explained the following two negative incidents. He harked back to it in the material he added at vv. 20*b* and 27*a*.[297]

25:1-4. The first episode (vv. 3-4) is taken over, along with vv. 1-2*a*, from 2 Kgs 14:1-3, 5-6. The reference to compliance with the Torah (v. 4) obviously coincides with one of the chronicler's interests. Honoring the Torah illustrates the king's having done right in the Lord's sight. Although Joash's murderers had been agents of divine providence (according to 24:25), their recourse to illegality could not be condoned. The Torah citation about limiting reprisals is taken from Deut 24:16, which states that parents and children will

297. See M. P. Graham, "Aspects of the Structure and Rhetoric of 2 Chronicles 25," in *History and Interpretation: Essays in Honour of John H. Hayes,* ed. M. P. Graham et al., JSOTSup 123 (Sheffield: JSOT, 1993) 78-89, who finds in 25:14-16 a pivot for the concentric structure of this chapter.

not be punished for each other's offenses. Appeal is also made to the law in Ezek 18:20 that only the offender will receive punishment. The judicial principle provided the prophet's theological tenet that the Lord operated providentially within a single generation, a tenet that finds ample illustration in the chronicler's narratives about kings.

25:5-13. The second episode concerns a successful campaign against Edom. It is an expansion of a single verse, 2 Kgs 14:7, which is reflected at v. 11. In vv. 5-6, the chronicler was probably able to amplify it with a detail from military census lists arranged according to the reigns of kings (see 14:8; 17:14-17). The damage that the Emphraimite mercenaries inflicted on Judah probably also had an objective basis; its inconsistency with the promise of v. 9 is an argument against free composition at this point. Amaziah's having supplemented the national army with northerners draws a rebuke from an unnamed prophet. The type of alliance that Jehoshapat made with Ahab in chap. 18 is repeated here. Defeat is forecast as the price to pay for such reliance on the northern kingdom. As long as that nation persisted in rejecting the Lord, it was out of fellowship with God, as the chronicler explained in 13:4-12 (see also 15:2).

The first half of v. 8 is a textual crux. A feasible reconstruction is, "For if with these you act strongly in war, God . . .," which underlies the REB's paraphrase, "For, if you make these people your allies in war . . ." (cf. the LXX).[298] The issue was not numerical superiority but the will of God, who could grant victory or defeat irrespective of numbers. It is a trust-oriented argument we have heard from the chronicler before (14:11 and esp. chap. 20). The rueful inquiry for an oracle in v. 9*a* leads to a repetition of the motif of divine power, now to compensate for loss incurred out of loyalty to the Lord. We have not heard the last of the mercenaries. Deprived of the customary spoils of war, they returned home bent on reprisal and launched their own attack on Judean territory (vv. 10, 13). Verse 13 is not clearly expressed, since Samaria was in no way a Judean town.[299]

The account of the successful Edomite campaign (vv. 11-12) has a bloodthirsty ring. While v. 11 is based on 2 Kgs 14:7, v. 12 may have arisen as a variant interpretation of it. One must take into account the long-standing hostility between Judah and Edom, which in post-exilic times was exacerbated by the failure of Edom to support its ally Judah in the disaster of 587 BCE and by their infiltration of Judah's southern territory during the exile. The prophecy of Obadiah reflects this animosity, and so does the passionate Psalm 137. Consequently, the subjugation of Edom played a key role in the conception of the coming kingdom of God, as Amos 9:12 and Obad 21 indicate. Edom became a symbol for human opposition to God's people and so to God, which required that justice be done. This prophetic, eschatologically tinged way of thinking is the animating force behind the hostility of the text.

25:14-19. After 20:20-28, the sequel to the campaign is a shocking disappointment to the reader; worship from grateful hearts is given to the wrong deities. The worship of other people's gods becomes a new negative pivot for the rest of the chapter and explains the reversals copied from 2 Kings 14. The unusual character of the incident, to which v. 15*b* will refer, has an ideological basis in the ancient Near Eastern notion that gods abandoned a conquered nation and joined the conquerors' side, to whose country their images were duly transferred.[300] So it may have had some historical basis.

The chronicler uses the intervention of another unnamed prophet to express an adverse theological perspective. The divine anger, expressed in the prophet's accusation, functions as a warning to Amaziah to turn from his folly and reverts implicitly to the motif of divine power, used by the earlier prophet in v. 8. The dire charge of "seeking" (דרשׁ *dāraš*; NIV, "consult"; NRSV, "resorted to") gods other than the Lord is a denial of true spirituality, which will be echoed in v. 20 ("sought"). Now the royal response is not assent but protest and threat. For the chronicler, the greater sin was the spurning of a second chance.

298. See L. C. Allen, *The Greek Chronicles: The Relation of the Septuagint of I and II Chronicles to the Massoretic Text,* Part 2: *Textual Criticism,* VTSup 25, 27 (Leiden: Brill, 1974) 85-86.

299. See *BHS.*

300. See M. Cogan, *Imperialism and Religion: Assyria, Judah and Israel in the Eighth and Seventh Centuries* BCE, SBLMS 19 (Missoula, Mont.: Scholars Press, 1974) 9-21; R. B. Dillard, *2 Chronicles,* WBC 15 (Waco, Tex.: Word, 1987) 201.

The king's fate was sealed by his refusal to heed the prophet's counsel.

Verses 16-17*a* contain a fourfold Hebrew play on the word "counsel" (יעץ *yā'aṣ*). Amaziah rejected the prophet's right to take part in royal deliberations and threatened death. In reply, the prophet blamed the king for refusing to listen to his sound deliberation and retorted that in reprisal God had deliberated Amaziah's destruction. Finally, the king proceeded to deliberate a foolish military confrontation with the northern kingdom, which is the chronicler's preface to his citation of 2 Kgs 14:8-14. This episode was intended as an ironic echo of the divine decision and marks a significant stage in its providential outworking. Divine and human wisdom are contrasted, with the latter shown to be arrogant folly in this political fable of the northern king—"God has made the wisdom of this world look foolish!" (1 Cor 1:20 NRSV). It is a tragic antithesis of the humble repentance that the prophet's accusation was meant to elicit (cf. 7:14; 24:19).

25:20-24. Capital, palace, and Temple all suffered, their destruction foreshadowing the later conquests of 597 and 587 BCE that led to exile. Twice in quick succession, in 24:23 and here, the chronicler has mentioned Jerusalem's exposure to enemy attack, both deliberately repeated from 2 Kings. The taking of hostages sounds an exilic note. The chronicler regarded such exile-related disaster as a recurring phenomenon, rather than a unique climax. It functions as a theological image of divine punishment confronting any generation who turns away from the Lord. The insertion of v. 20*b* into the 2 Kings narrative interprets the disaster as providential punishment for apostasy. Another addition, this time redactional, appears in v. 24, referring to Obed-edom's liability for religious artifacts that had been looted (NIV: cf. 1 Chr 26:15). It is a breach of temple security, while the looting marks a reversal of 2 Chr 24:14*a*.

25:25-28. A further block of material from 2 Kgs 14:17-22 is quoted in 25:25–26:2, spilling over into Uzziah's reign. Amaziah lived on, only to fall victim to a conspiracy, as had his predecessor. His flight from fatality just postponed it, for the wages of sin is death. The chronicler adds a theological comment in v. 27*a*. He regards Amaziah's steps as being dogged thereafter by a resistance movement that issued into conspiracy. Apostasy was a slippery slope toward destruction; his remaining fifteen years were not blessed but blighted. Such is the fate of those who turn away from the Lord. There are extra-biblical parallels for calling Jerusalem "the City of Judah," a variant of "the city of David" in the 2 Kings text.[301]

301. See M. J. Selman, *2 Chronicles,* TOTC (Downers Grove: InterVarsity, 1994) 464 and n. 1.

REFLECTIONS

1. The chronicler relished the citation of Deut 24:16 in 2 Chr 25:4 (taken over from 2 Kings), because it favored his concept of the independence of each generation before God. He was not always consistent; in 22:9, Ahaziah was permitted a decent burial for his grandfather's sake. But that incident leans positively on the side of graciousness, recalling good qualities and forgetting bad ones. The chronicler was not such a stickler for logical consistency as was Ezekiel, who held that God remembered neither the good of those who turned away from righteousness nor the bad of those who turned back to righteousness (Ezek 18:22, 24). Human memories tend to be less charitable, holding on to grudges more readily than to good opinions.

Amaziah's moderation speaks to all persons in positions of authority. Parents know the temptation to crack the nut of a child's offense with a sledgehammer of fury. Police, eyeing a surging crowd of demonstrators, need to decide whether or when to resort to a crack down. Who does not sympathize with James and John, who wanted to call down fire from heaven when the Samaritan villager rejected Jesus? And who does not agree on reflection with Jesus' branding their impulse as an overreaction (Luke 9:25-56; cf. 2 Sam 16:5-13)?

2. The king's complaint in 25:8 also hits home. Virtue and an appropriate grace do not always go together. We can all look back and regret the expenditure of resources to no good purpose. Hopefully, we are wiser as a result, though sadder. The prophet's reply that God can compensate for losses is not neatly worked out in the ensuing narrative. A lesson learned has value in itself. In fact, Amaziah incurred further losses. Even when amends have been made, mistakes sometimes cast long shadows and dim future potential.

3. The vehemence underlying 25:12 is something we all find abhorrent but need to try to understand. In the same vein it is too easy to read only Ps 137:1-6 and to silence its last three verses. Implicit in both post-exilic passages are a deep sense that injustice has been done and a passionate craving for justice to prevail (cf. 1 Chr 16:33). The same aggrieved vehemence reappears in 2 Thess 1:5-10 and the book of Revelation.

4. Is the emphasis in the second half of the chapter on a working out of providential punishment the shadow side of Rom 8:28? If eventual good is the prospect of those who love God, what awaits those who go on to repudiate that love? The chronicler intended his moral narrative to be a warning. He was pleading with his readers not to "abandon" their "confidence." His message resonates with the New Testament affirmation that "we are not among those who shrink back and so are lost, but among those who have faith and so are saved" (Heb 10:35, 39 NRSV).

2 Chronicles 26:1-23, Uzziah Oversteps God's Limits

NIV

26 Then all the people of Judah took Uzziah,[a] who was sixteen years old, and made him king in place of his father Amaziah. 2He was the one who rebuilt Elath and restored it to Judah after Amaziah rested with his fathers.

3Uzziah was sixteen years old when he became king, and he reigned in Jerusalem fifty-two years. His mother's name was Jecoliah; she was from Jerusalem. 4He did what was right in the eyes of the LORD, just as his father Amaziah had done. 5He sought God during the days of Zechariah, who instructed him in the fear[b] of God. As long as he sought the LORD, God gave him success.

6He went to war against the Philistines and broke down the walls of Gath, Jabneh and Ashdod. He then rebuilt towns near Ashdod and elsewhere among the Philistines. 7God helped him against the Philistines and against the Arabs who lived in Gur Baal and against the Meunites. 8The Ammonites brought tribute to Uzziah, and his fame spread as far as the border of Egypt, because he had become very powerful.

9Uzziah built towers in Jerusalem at the Corner Gate, at the Valley Gate and at the angle of the

[a]*1* Also called *Azariah* [b]*5* Many Hebrew manuscripts, Septuagint and Syriac; other Hebrew manuscripts *vision*

NRSV

26 Then all the people of Judah took Uzziah, who was sixteen years old, and made him king to succeed his father Amaziah. 2He rebuilt Eloth and restored it to Judah, after the king slept with his ancestors. 3Uzziah was sixteen years old when he began to reign, and he reigned fifty-two years in Jerusalem. His mother's name was Jecoliah of Jerusalem. 4He did what was right in the sight of the LORD, just as his father Amaziah had done. 5He set himself to seek God in the days of Zechariah, who instructed him in the fear of God; and as long as he sought the LORD, God made him prosper.

6He went out and made war against the Philistines, and broke down the wall of Gath and the wall of Jabneh and the wall of Ashdod; he built cities in the territory of Ashdod and elsewhere among the Philistines. 7God helped him against the Philistines, against the Arabs who lived in Gur-baal, and against the Meunites. 8The Ammonites paid tribute to Uzziah, and his fame spread even to the border of Egypt, for he became very strong. 9Moreover Uzziah built towers in Jerusalem at the Corner Gate, at the Valley Gate, and at the Angle, and fortified them. 10He built towers in the wilderness and hewed out many cisterns,

NIV

wall, and he fortified them. [10]He also built towers in the desert and dug many cisterns, because he had much livestock in the foothills and in the plain. He had people working his fields and vineyards in the hills and in the fertile lands, for he loved the soil.

[11]Uzziah had a well-trained army, ready to go out by divisions according to their numbers as mustered by Jeiel the secretary and Maaseiah the officer under the direction of Hananiah, one of the royal officials. [12]The total number of family leaders over the fighting men was 2,600. [13]Under their command was an army of 307,500 men trained for war, a powerful force to support the king against his enemies. [14]Uzziah provided shields, spears, helmets, coats of armor, bows and slingstones for the entire army. [15]In Jerusalem he made machines designed by skillful men for use on the towers and on the corner defenses to shoot arrows and hurl large stones. His fame spread far and wide, for he was greatly helped until he became powerful.

[16]But after Uzziah became powerful, his pride led to his downfall. He was unfaithful to the LORD his God, and entered the temple of the LORD to burn incense on the altar of incense. [17]Azariah the priest with eighty other courageous priests of the LORD followed him in. [18]They confronted him and said, "It is not right for you, Uzziah, to burn incense to the LORD. That is for the priests, the descendants of Aaron, who have been consecrated to burn incense. Leave the sanctuary, for you have been unfaithful; and you will not be honored by the LORD God."

[19]Uzziah, who had a censer in his hand ready to burn incense, became angry. While he was raging at the priests in their presence before the incense altar in the LORD's temple, leprosy[a] broke out on his forehead. [20]When Azariah the chief priest and all the other priests looked at him, they saw that he had leprosy on his forehead, so they hurried him out. Indeed, he himself was eager to leave, because the LORD had afflicted him.

[21]King Uzziah had leprosy until the day he died. He lived in a separate house[b]—leprous, and excluded from the temple of the LORD. Jotham his

a19 The Hebrew word was used for various diseases affecting the skin—not necessarily leprosy; also in verses 20, 21 and 23. *b21* Or *in a house where he was relieved of responsibilities*

NRSV

for he had large herds, both in the Shephelah and in the plain, and he had farmers and vinedressers in the hills and in the fertile lands, for he loved the soil. [11]Moreover Uzziah had an army of soldiers, fit for war, in divisions according to the numbers in the muster made by the secretary Jeiel and the officer Maaseiah, under the direction of Hananiah, one of the king's commanders. [12]The whole number of the heads of ancestral houses of mighty warriors was two thousand six hundred. [13]Under their command was an army of three hundred seven thousand five hundred, who could make war with mighty power, to help the king against the enemy. [14]Uzziah provided for all the army the shields, spears, helmets, coats of mail, bows, and stones for slinging. [15]In Jerusalem he set up machines, invented by skilled workers, on the towers and the corners for shooting arrows and large stones. And his fame spread far, for he was marvelously helped until he became strong.

16But when he had become strong he grew proud, to his destruction. For he was false to the LORD his God, and entered the temple of the LORD to make offering on the altar of incense. [17]But the priest Azariah went in after him, with eighty priests of the LORD who were men of valor; [18]they withstood King Uzziah, and said to him, "It is not for you, Uzziah, to make offering to the LORD, but for the priests the descendants of Aaron, who are consecrated to make offering. Go out of the sanctuary; for you have done wrong, and it will bring you no honor from the LORD God." [19]Then Uzziah was angry. Now he had a censer in his hand to make offering, and when he became angry with the priests a leprous[a] disease broke out on his forehead, in the presence of the priests in the house of the LORD, by the altar of incense. [20]When the chief priest Azariah, and all the priests, looked at him, he was leprous[a] in his forehead. They hurried him out, and he himself hurried to get out, because the LORD had struck him. [21]King Uzziah was leprous[a] to the day of his death, and being leprous[a] lived in a separate house, for he was excluded from the house of the LORD. His son Jotham was in charge of the palace of the king, governing the people of the land.

22Now the rest of the acts of Uzziah, from first

[a] A term for several skin diseases; precise meaning uncertain

NIV

son had charge of the palace and governed the
people of the land.
[22]The other events of Uzziah's reign, from
beginning to end, are recorded by the prophet
Isaiah son of Amoz. [23]Uzziah rested with his
fathers and was buried near them in a field for
burial that belonged to the kings, for people said,
"He had leprosy." And Jotham his son succeeded
him as king.

NRSV

to last, the prophet Isaiah son of Amoz wrote.
[23]Uzziah slept with his ancestors; they buried him
near his ancestors in the burial field that belonged
to the kings, for they said, "He is leprous."[a] His
son Jotham succeeded him.

[a] A term for several skin diseases; precise meaning uncertain

COMMENTARY

Amaziah, his father before him, and his son after him were all tarred with the same brush, first faithful to the Lord and then faithless. The royal trilogy is meant to function as a powerful sermon to believers to "hold" their "first confidence firm to the end" (Heb 3:14 NRSV).

The royal name "Uzziah" appears to be an alternative form of "Azariah," which this king bears in the Davidic genealogy of 1 Chr 3:12 and, most of the time, in 2 Kings 14–15. The chronicler may have preferred "Uzziah" to avoid confusion with the high priest Azariah (vv. 17, 20). He was aware of both names and provides wordplays on their meanings, "Yahweh helps" (Azariah) and "Yahweh is my strength" (Uzziah) in vv. 7-8, 13, 15. Only about seven verses of the section have been copied from 2 Kings, at the beginning and at the end of the chapter. Verses 1-2 were taken over from 2 Kgs 14:21-22, and vv. 3-4 from 2 Kgs 15:2-3. Verses 20*b*-22 were supplied from 2 Kgs 15:5-6, apart from the temple reference, and v. 23 from 2 Kgs 15:7, except for mention of the royal burial field.

26:1-5. Uzziah's military success, long reign, and approbation, echoed in vv. 2-4, and the Lord's afflicting him with leprosy in his final years provided scaffolding for a further sequence of blessing and backsliding. The comparison with Amaziah in v. 4 gave the chronicler, though not the deuteronomist, support for this structuring. The high and low points of the section are featured by two contrasting statements, "God gave him success" (v. 5) and "the LORD had afflicted him" (v. 20).

26:6-15. The good period of the reign is elaborated with three examples of divine blessing: military success, vv. 6-8; building projects, vv. 9-10; and an army and armaments, vv. 11-15. At beginning and end, God's help is celebrated (vv. 7, 15). In the latter case, the passive verb and the adverb point to the Lord as the source of the help. Historians regard Uzziah's long reign as a prosperous one, though the deuteronomist took little interest in it. Control of the port of Eloth or Elath (v. 2) gave access to Arabia, Africa, and India via maritime trade. The accounts of Uzziah's enterprise in vv. 6-15 are all feasible in principle and appear to depend on solid tradition, the last item doubtless relying on a royal military source. The chronicler also seems to have known from elsewhere a mentor called Zechariah (v. 5) and the king's officiating in the Temple (v. 16).

The chronicler introduces Uzziah's period of blessing in v. 5. It spells out the spiritual accolade of v. 4 and adds its corollary of prosperity, limited though it was. This period reiterates the situation of the pious Jehoiada's mentoring of Joash (24:2-16).[302] Uzziah was like Joash, too, in that his prosperity lasted only as long as did a positive attitude toward God (24:20). This attitude is typically defined as seeking (דרש *dāraš*) the Lord and is closely linked with a successful life. The link, loosely made in 14:7, will be repeated in Hezekiah's case (31:21). The pattern of obedience and prosperity finds a parallel in 1 Chr 22:13 and is a more tangible version of the basic proposition that to seek the Lord leads to a manifestation of

302. For the "fear" of God sees *BHS* and S. Japhet, *I & II Chronicles*, OTL (Louisville: Westminster/John Knox, 1993) 878.

the divine presence (15:2; 1 Chr 28:9). The list of military victories draws an impressive semicircle, west, southwest, south, and east. The lack of such activity to the north reflects détente with the northern kinigdom. The campaign against the Philistines was followed by the building of Judean settlements in the area. The reference to Gur-baal is textually and exegetically uncertain and may conceal mention of Gerar;[303] in that case the Arabs are the Cushites (cf. 14:13-14). The Meunites are to be located in Edom (see 20:1). The mention of Ammonites is uncertain; the LXX refers instead to the Meunites, which suits better the directional reference to the border of Egypt. Uzziah's power and prestige are traced to the backing of his divine patron, directly in v. 7 and indirectly in v. 8, where his strength alludes to the meaning of his name, "Yahweh is my strength."

The triple themes of vv. 6-15 fall into two paragraphs, vv. 6-8 and vv. 9-15, each ending in the same refrain of fame and divinely given strength. The first paragraph highlights external success, and the other internal. Building work is always an indication of blessing in the books of Chronicles; here it embraces both urban and rural enterprises. The latter relate to livestock and crops in the development of the royal estates (cf. 1 Chr 27:25-31), for which there is considerable archaeological support.[304] The description of Uzziah as a lover of the soil reflects the chronicler's own regard for the good land of Israel (cf. Deut 8:7-10). The details of the conscript army include a list of weapons provided by the king, which have an impression of increasing sophistication and include a description of a new invention for defense against a siege. This innovation consisted of attaching to towers and battlements wooden frames into which round shields were inserted to form a protective barrier behind which archers and stone throwers could safely stand instead of crouching awkwardly. These devices were used at Lachish at the end of the eighth century, according to the scenes of the siege depicted on Sennacherib's reliefs.[305]

All this military power illustrated for the chronicler not simply Judah's defensive capability (v. 13) but also further signs of divine blessing. Old Testament theology often involves a triangle made up of God, the land, and Israel. So land-related work and territorial security were necessarily drawn into the sphere of the divine/human relationship. In v. 15, the developments in military technology are linked to miraculous assistance ("marvelously helped"), which is an aspect of the protective power of God (cf. Ps 127:1).

26:16-21. Uzziah's sudden fall from grace, anticipated in the qualification of v. 5, serves to explain his leprosy late in life. The chronicler has in view the apostasy of the good person in Ezek 18:24, borrowing from there the term for "unfaithfulness" (מעל *mā'al*), which is twice used for the royal sin (vv. 16, 18). It fits well here because it can have a religious nuance as well as referring to breaking of the covenant (cf. Lev 5:15; 26:40). The chronicler may have known a tradition of Uzziah's officiating in the Temple and then imaginatively wrote it up from the post-exilic perspective that only Aaronic priests might "burn incense" (v. 18), which is reflected in the Torah at Exod 30:7 and Num 16:39-40. In 1 Kgs 9:25, there is a reference to Solomon's burning incense, which the chronicler left out of his account. The Davidic king evidently engaged in certain religious rituals apart from those restricted to the regular priesthood (see Ps 110:4). The incense altar stood in the nave of the Temple near the holy of holies (see 1 Kgs 6:22). So, for the chronicler, there was a violation of sacred space and sacred ritual, a double trespass. Biblical evidence is insufficient to reconstruct the precise ceremony, in this case involving both the incense altar and use of a censer.[306]

In the story of Rehoboam, royal strength led to an abandoning of the Torah, which was followed by a prophetic challenge and subsequent repentence (12:1, 6-7; cf. 7:14). A less happy permutation of such motifs appears here. Strength leads to pride, which is unrelieved by repentance, even when the king is challenged by the high priest. Uzziah displayed his father's sin of pride (25:19), now demonstrated against the Lord. Yet v. 19 emphasizes that judgment struck only after Azariah's warning had been rejected. In each of the

303. See *BHS*.

304. See H. G. M. Williamson, *1 and 2 Chronicles*, NCB (Grand Rapids: Eerdmans, 1982) 336-37.

305. See Y. Yadin, *The Art of Warfare in Biblical Lands* (New York: McGraw-Hill, 1963) 2:324-26, 431, 434.

306. See D. L. Petersen, *Late Israelite Prophecy*, SBLMS 23 (Missoula, Mont.: Scholars Press, 1977) 80-81; K. Nielsen, *Incense in Ancient Israel*, VTSup 38 (Leiden: Brill, 1986) 57, 79.

cases of the three apostate kings, the chronicler was concerned to highlight the Lord's patience in giving an opportunity for a change of heart. Punishment came as a last resort, after a challenge had fallen on deaf ears (24:19-21; 25:15-16; 26:18-19).

The first part of v. 20 is colored by Aaron's reaction to Miriam's leprosy (Num 12:10). The term for "leprosy" (מצרע *mĕṣōrā'*) carried emotive overtones, reflected in its fivefold occurrence in vv. 19-21 and in the chronicler's addition at v. 23. The annotations in the NRSV and the NIV remind us that in the Bible leprosy is not the same malady we think of as leprosy today. It was a severe skin disease, dire in that it rendered its victim ritually unclean (cf. Lev 13:44-46). So, commented the chronicler with Lev 13:46 in mind, Uzziah was excluded from worship in the temple area and so was stripped of the religious privilege of every believer. He also lost his right to rule, surrendering it to his son as regent.

26:22-23. The chronicler writes Uzziah's obituary in consigning him in death, not to the royal cemetery, but to adjoining crown property. In referring to the underlying 2 Kings narrative, the chronicler assumes that Isaiah was the author, since the prophet lived during part of Uzziah's reign (Isa 6:1) and because the same material concerning Hezekiah appears in both his book and 2 Kings. Once more the basic narrative is invested with prophetic authority.

REFLECTIONS

1. The chronicler tended to work with a theology of prosperity—that is, a conviction that God would materially reward the virtuous in their lifetime. True, the chronicler allowed for crisis to break into the life of obedient believers, as precursor to a new experience of trust in the Lord, who saves and blesses them (see 20:1-30). His prosperity theology had a pastoral intent, using the prospect of well-being as an incentive for his fellow believers to adopt a spirituality that honored the Torah and the Temple. We human beings all seem to require incentives. The New Testament writers sometimes retain such a material, this-worldly perspective. When they enlarge the scale of life to encompass a heavenly reward, they are still within the scope of giving an incentive. Disciples are urged to lay up for themselves treasures in heaven (Matt 6:20). An ideal of virtue for virtue's sake is intellectually appealing, but inadequate for most of us. A practicable system of ethics needs to argue long-term expediency—for example, warning couples who enjoy the stolen waters of premarital sex not to be surprised if they find marital sex disappointing.

2. Chapters 24–26 depict a shift from spirituality to willful disobedience. The chronicler's positive aim was that of the writer of the Letter to the Hebrews in its passages of grim warning. The kindly intent of both authors was the same: The writer of Hebrews cautioned: "Take care, brothers and sisters, that none of you may have an evil, unbelieving heart that turns away from the living God" (Heb 3:12 NRSV). The chronicler, too, wrote sadly of such turning away (25:27).

One has to ask whether the well-intentioned assurance current in some circles that the Christian is "once saved always saved" does not show a false kindness, evading the tension of the challenges that balance the assurances of Scripture. The somber proviso "if only we hold our first confidence firm to the end" (Heb 3:14 NRSV) is part of a chorus of New Testament conditions. It is heard not only in the "if" of Heb 3:6 but also in the Pauline caution of Rom 11:22 ("provided you continue in [God's] kindness"), of 1 Cor 15:2 ("if you hold firmly to the word I preached to you" [NIV]), and of Col 1:23 ("if you continue in your faith, established and firm" [NIV]). In such texts, Paul added his "amen" to the message of 2 Chronicles.

2 CHRONICLES 27:1–28:27, ROYAL MODELS OF RIGHT AND WRONG

OVERVIEW

Two reigns are set back-to-back as polar opposites of right and wrong. Jotham the good is presented alongside Ahaz the bad. The assessments of their reigns function as rhetorical markers: Jothan "did what was right in the sight of the LORD," while Ahaz "did not do what was right in the sight of the LORD" (27:2 [= 2 Kgs 15:34]; 28:1 [= 2 Kgs 16:2]). The chronicler seems to have had in mind the case histories of Ezek 18:5-13, in which a good father is succeeded by a wretch of a son. Chapter 28 also has its own agenda. It marks the end of the narrative of the divided kingdom in chaps. 10–28, which accounts for its greater length and special features.

2 Chronicles 27:1-9, Jotham the Good

NIV

27 Jotham was twenty-five years old when he became king, and he reigned in Jerusalem sixteen years. His mother's name was Jerusha daughter of Zadok. [2]He did what was right in the eyes of the LORD, just as his father Uzziah had done, but unlike him he did not enter the temple of the LORD. The people, however, continued their corrupt practices. [3]Jotham rebuilt the Upper Gate of the temple of the LORD and did extensive work on the wall at the hill of Ophel. [4]He built towns in the Judean hills and forts and towers in the wooded areas.

[5]Jotham made war on the king of the Ammonites and conquered them. That year the Ammonites paid him a hundred talents[a] of silver, ten thousand cors[b] of wheat and ten thousand cors of barley. The Ammonites brought him the same amount also in the second and third years.

[6]Jotham grew powerful because he walked steadfastly before the LORD his God.

[7]The other events in Jotham's reign, including all his wars and the other things he did, are written in the book of the kings of Israel and Judah. [8]He was twenty-five years old when he became king, and he reigned in Jerusalem sixteen years. [9]Jotham rested with his fathers and was buried in the City of David. And Ahaz his son succeeded him as king.

[a]5 That is, about 3 3/4 tons (about 3.4 metric tons) [b]5 That is, probably about 62,000 bushels (about 2,200 kiloliters)

NRSV

27 Jotham was twenty-five years old when he began to reign; he reigned sixteen years in Jerusalem. His mother's name was Jerushah daughter of Zadok. [2]He did what was right in the sight of the LORD just as his father Uzziah had done—only he did not invade the temple of the LORD. But the people still followed corrupt practices. [3]He built the upper gate of the house of the LORD, and did extensive building on the wall of Ophel. [4]Moreover he built cities in the hill country of Judah, and forts and towers on the wooded hills. [5]He fought with the king of the Ammonites and prevailed against them. The Ammonites gave him that year one hundred talents of silver, ten thousand cors of wheat and ten thousand of barley. The Ammonites paid him the same amount in the second and the third years. [6]So Jotham became strong because he ordered his ways before the LORD his God. [7]Now the rest of the acts of Jotham, and all his wars and his ways, are written in the Book of the Kings of Israel and Judah. [8]He was twenty-five years old when he began to reign; he reigned sixteen years in Jerusalem. [9]Jotham slept with his ancestors, and they buried him in the city of David; and his son Ahaz succeeded him.

COMMENTARY

The first story with a moral is short and sweet, if unexciting. Jotham's reign is presented as a compact vignette of obedience and blessing. The chapter is structured in a symmetrical fashion. At its center lie two pieces of evidence of the Lord's favor (vv. 3-5). This pair of elements is surrounded by statements revealing the secret of Jotham's success (vv. 2, 6). They are encircled by the royal prologue and epilogue to his reign (vv. 1, 7-9), the latter echoing the former by repeating v. 1*a* in v. 8. This presentation is as neat as a piece of embroidery, each stitch carefully sewn. On a smaller scale, the neatness is reflected in the Hebrew by chiastic sentences at vv. 3-4 and in parallel beginnings at vv. 3 and 5 (הוא . . . והוא *hû'* . . . *wĕhû'*, "he . . . and he"). The chronicler has stressed, using such literary technique, his admiration for Jotham.

27:1-5. The chronicler cites the short account of Jotham's reign, found in 2 Kgs 15:32-38. He amplified that account with details of further building operations (vv. 3*b*-4) and with a reference to an Ammonite victory (v. 5). The lavish presence of literary features often used by the chronicler means that if he was depending on sources, he edited heavily, though the report remains reasonable.[307] An Ammonite victory would imply the weakening of the northern kingdom's control over the Transjordan. The chronicler held over the reference to the Syro-Ephraimite war in 2 Kgs 15:37 until Ahaz's reign (26:5), which was more appropriate to his polarized conception. The accounts of tribute are presented in an inflated form.

307. See Williamson, *1 and 2 Chronicles*, 342; Japhet, *I & II Chronicles*, 892.

At the heart of the chapter lie two forms of evidence of the security given by the Lord. Building operations and military victory belong to the chronicler's code for divine blessing. If the Lord is the unnamed benefactor in vv. 3-5, such blessing is grounded explicitly in the king's honoring of God (v. 2). The blanket affirmation of 2 Kgs 15:34 had to be adjusted by reference to Uzziah's lack of respect for holy space in 26:16. The verbal echo of that verse in Hebrew (בא *bā'*) favors "enter" (NIV) rather than the vehement "invade" (NRSV). The paraphrase of 2 Kgs 15:35*a* in v. 2*b* seems to reflect a continuing agenda to discredit the people of Judah. It began in 20:33, will come to a head in 28:6, and will be reversed in 30:12 and 31:1, only to rise to a fatal climax in 36:14-17. Neither Jehoshaphat nor Jotham could force them into paths of righteousness. Jotham's goodness shines all the brighter against the background of the people's unspirituality.

27:6-9. The elements given in vv. 2*a* and 3-5 are combined in v. 6. Jotham's strength echoes that of Uzziah (26:6-15) and also of Rehoboam (12:2). The key was Jotham's consistency, which both Rehoboam and Uzziah lacked: "He maintained a steady course of obedience" (REB; cf. the NIV; see 12:14). The reference in v. 7 to "all his wars and all his ways" may simply be an impressionistic way of alluding to a supposed wealth of military and spiritual exploits. Amid the details of v. 8, the chronicler focuses on the length of Jotham's reign. He cited a similar block of material at the close of the reigns of Rehoboam and Jehoshaphat to focus on their length (12:13; 20:31). Here the material is repeated from v. 1*a*, as in the case of Jehoram (21:5, 20).

REFLECTIONS

Chapters 24–26 warned three times over that human fortunes can plummet when spirituality ceases to be a priority. In chaps. 27–28, the chronicler uses a different format to preach the same message, setting two reigns side by side. We shall see that chap. 28, similar in form to chap. 27 but diverse in content, functions as its negative counterpart. Yet chap. 27 poses its own contrast with chaps. 24–26. Verse 6 puts the chapter in a nutshell: The Lord honors consistent commitment to moral and spiritual excellence. So the chronicler's challenge to his constituency to continue all their days in a living faith, presented negatively in the preceding unit, is now repeated in a positive package. In New Testament terms, it corresponds to Paul's missionary concern that newly planted churches should remain faithful to the Lord (Acts 11:23; 13:43; 14:22). In the ups and downs of human experience, we are called to stay on an even keel in living out our faith.

2 Chronicles 28:1-27, Ahaz the Bad

NIV

28 Ahaz was twenty years old when he became king, and he reigned in Jerusalem sixteen years. Unlike David his father, he did not do what was right in the eyes of the LORD. 2He walked in the ways of the kings of Israel and also made cast idols for worshiping the Baals. 3He burned sacrifices in the Valley of Ben Hinnom and sacrificed his sons in the fire, following the detestable ways of the nations the LORD had driven out before the Israelites. 4He offered sacrifices and burned incense at the high places, on the hilltops and under every spreading tree.

5Therefore the LORD his God handed him over to the king of Aram. The Arameans defeated him and took many of his people as prisoners and brought them to Damascus.

He was also given into the hands of the king of Israel, who inflicted heavy casualties on him. 6In one day Pekah son of Remaliah killed a hundred and twenty thousand soldiers in Judah—because Judah had forsaken the LORD, the God of their fathers. 7Zicri, an Ephraimite warrior, killed Maaseiah the king's son, Azrikam the officer in charge of the palace, and Elkanah, second to the king. 8The Israelites took captive from their kinsmen two hundred thousand wives, sons and daughters. They also took a great deal of plunder, which they carried back to Samaria.

9But a prophet of the LORD named Oded was there, and he went out to meet the army when it returned to Samaria. He said to them, "Because the LORD, the God of your fathers, was angry with Judah, he gave them into your hand. But you have slaughtered them in a rage that reaches to heaven. 10And now you intend to make the men and women of Judah and Jerusalem your slaves. But aren't you also guilty of sins against the LORD your God? 11Now listen to me! Send back your fellow countrymen you have taken as prisoners, for the LORD's fierce anger rests on you."

NRSV

28 Ahaz was twenty years old when he began to reign; he reigned sixteen years in Jerusalem. He did not do what was right in the sight of the LORD, as his ancestor David had done, 2but he walked in the ways of the kings of Israel. He even made cast images for the Baals; 3and he made offerings in the valley of the son of Hinnom, and made his sons pass through fire, according to the abominable practices of the nations whom the LORD drove out before the people of Israel. 4He sacrificed and made offerings on the high places, on the hills, and under every green tree.

5Therefore the LORD his God gave him into the hand of the king of Aram, who defeated him and took captive a great number of his people and brought them to Damascus. He was also given into the hand of the king of Israel, who defeated him with great slaughter. 6Pekah son of Remaliah killed one hundred twenty thousand in Judah in one day, all of them valiant warriors, because they had abandoned the LORD, the God of their ancestors. 7And Zichri, a mighty warrior of Ephraim, killed the king's son Maaseiah, Azrikam the commander of the palace, and Elkanah the next in authority to the king.

8The people of Israel took captive two hundred thousand of their kin, women, sons, and daughters; they also took much booty from them and brought the booty to Samaria. 9But a prophet of the LORD was there, whose name was Oded; he went out to meet the army that came to Samaria, and said to them, "Because the LORD, the God of your ancestors, was angry with Judah, he gave them into your hand, but you have killed them in a rage that has reached up to heaven. 10Now you intend to subjugate the people of Judah and Jerusalem, male and female, as your slaves. But what have you except sins against the LORD your God? 11Now hear me, and send back the captives whom you have taken from your kindred, for the

NIV

[12]Then some of the leaders in Ephraim—Azariah son of Jehohanan, Berekiah son of Meshillemoth, Jehizkiah son of Shallum, and Amasa son of Hadlai—confronted those who were arriving from the war. [13]"You must not bring those prisoners here," they said, "or we will be guilty before the LORD. Do you intend to add to our sin and guilt? For our guilt is already great, and his fierce anger rests on Israel."

[14]So the soldiers gave up the prisoners and plunder in the presence of the officials and all the assembly. [15]The men designated by name took the prisoners, and from the plunder they clothed all who were naked. They provided them with clothes and sandals, food and drink, and healing balm. All those who were weak they put on donkeys. So they took them back to their fellow countrymen at Jericho, the City of Palms, and returned to Samaria.

[16]At that time King Ahaz sent to the king[a] of Assyria for help. [17]The Edomites had again come and attacked Judah and carried away prisoners, [18]while the Philistines had raided towns in the foothills and in the Negev of Judah. They captured and occupied Beth Shemesh, Aijalon and Gederoth, as well as Soco, Timnah and Gimzo, with their surrounding villages. [19]The LORD had humbled Judah because of Ahaz king of Israel,[b] for he had promoted wickedness in Judah and had been most unfaithful to the LORD. [20]Tiglath-Pileser[c] king of Assyria came to him, but he gave him trouble instead of help. [21]Ahaz took some of the things from the temple of the LORD and from the royal palace and from the princes and presented them to the king of Assyria, but that did not help him.

[22]In his time of trouble King Ahaz became even more unfaithful to the LORD. [23]He offered sacrifices to the gods of Damascus, who had defeated him; for he thought, "Since the gods of the kings of Aram have helped them, I will sacrifice to them so they will help me." But they were his downfall and the downfall of all Israel.

[24]Ahaz gathered together the furnishings from the temple of God and took them away.[d] He shut the doors of the LORD's temple and set up altars

[a]*16* One Hebrew manuscript, Septuagint and Vulgate (see also 2 Kings 16:7); most Hebrew manuscripts *kings* [b]*19* That is, Judah, as frequently in 2 Chronicles [c]*20* Hebrew *Tilgath-Pilneser,* a variant of *Tiglath-Pileser* [d]*24* Or *and cut them up*

NRSV

fierce wrath of the LORD is upon you." [12]Moreover, certain chiefs of the Ephraimites, Azariah son of Johanan, Berechiah son of Meshillemoth, Jehizkiah son of Shallum, and Amasa son of Hadlai, stood up against those who were coming from the war, [13]and said to them, "You shall not bring the captives in here, for you propose to bring on us guilt against the LORD in addition to our present sins and guilt. For our guilt is already great, and there is fierce wrath against Israel." [14]So the warriors left the captives and the booty before the officials and all the assembly. [15]Then those who were mentioned by name got up and took the captives, and with the booty they clothed all that were naked among them; they clothed them, gave them sandals, provided them with food and drink, and anointed them; and carrying all the feeble among them on donkeys, they brought them to their kindred at Jericho, the city of palm trees. Then they returned to Samaria.

16At that time King Ahaz sent to the king[a] of Assyria for help. [17]For the Edomites had again invaded and defeated Judah, and carried away captives. [18]And the Philistines had made raids on the cities in the Shephelah and the Negeb of Judah, and had taken Beth-shemesh, Aijalon, Gederoth, Soco with its villages, Timnah with its villages, and Gimzo with its villages; and they settled there. [19]For the LORD brought Judah low because of King Ahaz of Israel, for he had behaved without restraint in Judah and had been faithless to the LORD. [20]So King Tilgath-pilneser of Assyria came against him, and oppressed him instead of strengthening him. [21]For Ahaz plundered the house of the LORD and the houses of the king and of the officials, and gave tribute to the king of Assyria; but it did not help him.

22In the time of his distress he became yet more faithless to the LORD—this same King Ahaz. [23]For he sacrificed to the gods of Damascus, which had defeated him, and said, "Because the gods of the kings of Aram helped them, I will sacrifice to them so that they may help me." But they were the ruin of him, and of all Israel. [24]Ahaz gathered together the utensils of the house of God, and cut in pieces the utensils of the house of God. He shut up the doors of the house of the LORD and

[a] Gk Syr Vg Compare 2 Kings 16.7: Heb *kings*

NIV	NRSV
at every street corner in Jerusalem. [25]In every town in Judah he built high places to burn sacrifices to other gods and provoked the LORD, the God of his fathers, to anger. [26]The other events of his reign and all his ways, from beginning to end, are written in the book of the kings of Judah and Israel. [27]Ahaz rested with his fathers and was buried in the city of Jerusalem, but he was not placed in the tombs of the kings of Israel. And Hezekiah his son succeeded him as king.	made himself altars in every corner of Jerusalem. [25]In every city of Judah he made high places to make offerings to other gods, provoking to anger the LORD, the God of his ancestors. [26]Now the rest of his acts and all his ways, from first to last, are written in the Book of the Kings of Judah and Israel. [27]Ahaz slept with his ancestors, and they buried him in the city, in Jerusalem; but they did not bring him into the tombs of the kings of Israel. His son Hezekiah succeeded him.

COMMENTARY

Alongside Jotham's good reign is set Ahaz's shockingly bad one. The chronicler wants his readers to view them together as alternative role members, as if saying, "See, I . . . set before you . . . life and prosperity, death and adversity" (Deut 30:15 NRSV). Jotham's sixteen worthy years are succeeded by Ahaz's sixteen wasted years (27:1, 8; 28:1). Jotham's strength through spirituality is contrasted with Ahaz's lack of strength after turning to a secular power for help (27:6; 28:20 in the NRSV). The structure of concentric rings in chap. 27 is matched in chap. 28. The opening and closing formulas appear in vv. 1*a* and 26-27. The next ring (vv. 1*b*-4, 22-25) involves religious apostasy; each features sacrificing and making offerings and specifies high places. Further into the chapter appear two pairs of divinely instigated military defeats suffered by Judah at the hands of Aram and Israel (vv. 5-7) and of Edom and Philistia (vv. 17-19). The latter pair of disasters is set in its own framework, Ahaz's turning to Assyria for help (vv. 16, 20-21). At the heart of the chapter (vv. 8-15), stands a prophetic appeal to the northern troops to repatriate their Judean prisoners of war. Their affirmative response shows up, in an even worse light, in the unspirituality of Ahaz and Judah.

The chronicler has based his version of Ahaz's reign on the unsavory account in 2 Kings 16. He follows it primarily at the beginning and the end (vv. 1-4, 26-27) and loosely echoes it (vv. 5, 16*a*, 21*a*, 24*a*). The general outline of 2 Kings 16 is maintained: religious apostasy, the invasion of Aram and Israel, and cultic innovations. The details of v. 7 point to a tradition other than 2 Kings, and so does the second pair of invasions (vv. 17-19). The specification of personal names in v. 2 and the evident suppression of names (cf. "men nominated for this duty," NEB) and the place-name "Jericho" in v. 15 also appear to reflect a separate source. The chronicler has woven various items into a powerful piece of writing that makes liberal use of his own interpretive language.

The war waged by Israel and Aram Judah provides the historical background. It sprang from an attempt to form a multinational alliance against attack from the eastern power Assyria. Judah, nestling in its out-of-the-way hills, refused to cooperate, judging discretion to be the better part of valor and unwilling to antagonize Assyria, should an attack materialize. This policy provoked its northern neighbors to increasing pressure, culminating in an attack on Jerusalem. There are various divergent accounts of this complex conflict in the OT (see 2 Kgs 15:37; 16:5; Isaiah 7; Hos 5:8–6:6). Each account is written from a specific perspective; the 2 Chronicles account complements the others with its own theological emphasis.[308] The conflict led to Judah's loss of independence and vassalage under Assyria, to which vv. 20-21 allude. It also brought about the end of the northern kingdom and the exile of many of its citizens at Assyria's hands. This catastrophe is not mentioned here (cf. 30:6; 1 Chr 5:6,

308. See M. E. W. Thompson, *Situation and Theology: OT Interpretations of the Syro-Ephraimite War* (Sheffield: Almond, 1982) 91-124.

26), but the chronicler presupposes that it occurred in Ahaz's reign, leaving Judah as the only kingdom in which the Lord is worshiped. The chronicler calls Ahaz king of Israel and speaks of his subjects as all Israel (vv. 19, 23).

28:1-4. The contrast between David and the kings of Israel in vv. 1-2 (= 2 Kgs 16:2-3) recalls Abijah's speech in 13:4-12, in which the ideals of Davidic worship were set against Jeroboam's innovations. This similarity signals the close relationship between the present chapter and chap. 13. The chronicler has added in v. 2*b* the sentence about casting images for the Baals. That addition evokes Jeroboam's sin of making images in 1 Kgs 14:9 and, even more closely, the indictment of the northern kingdom in 2 Kgs 17:16 that they cast images of two calves and served Baal, sins that merited exile. Ahaz is painted in northern hues. In the addition of v. 3*a,* local coloring is provided by specifying the Valley of Hinnom as the site of a cult of child sacrifice (cf. 2 Kgs 23:10). The change from "his son" (2 Kgs 16:3) to "his sons" probably marks an intentional rhetorical intensification—i.e., a general practice rather than a single occurrence. The reference to "the kings of Assyria" in the MT of v. 16, rather than the singular at 2 Kgs 16:7, reflects similar intensification.

28:5-7. The chronicler links religious apostasy and military defeat as cause and effect. He portrays separately the attacks of the allies (vv. 5*a,* 5*b*-7) to prepare for his focus on Israel's Judean prisoners (vv. 8-15). Israel's sword, ranging wide and high, is described as the Lord's reprisal for Judah's apostasy. They had failed the test confronting each new generation and had to face the consequences. Similarly, the disaster is credited to the Lord's anger against the southern kingdom (v. 9). The number of the casualties, whether or not they can be rationally reduced to 120 units, reflects the rhetorical mathematics we have noticed the chronicler using elsewhere. Together with the phrase "in one day," it contributes to a dramatic effect intended as a deterrent. A NT parallel occurs in 1 Cor 10:6-10.

28:8-15. A defeat leads into this narrative and prophetic speech. Its key word is "brothers," at beginning, middle, and end (vv. 8, 11, 15 NJB). An otherwise unknown prophet, Oded urges the release of the families of Judean conscripts, rather than enslavement. His main argument seems to be based on the mandate in Lev 25:39-43, 46 that "brother-Israelites" (NJB) should not be enslaved. He also offers a supporting argument: Although the victory was theologically justified, the slaughter had exceeded what the Lord had intended (cf. Isa 10:5-19). There is also a hint at a backlog of guilt: "Aren't you also [as well as Judah] guilty?" (NIV).

The message hits home to four leading Ephraimites, who add their own warning to Oded's, grounded in a confession of the sins of which he had accused them. It works. The prisoners and the spoils are given up—not only that, but a task force is also designated to meet the immediate needs of the naked, hungry, wounded prisoners and to escort them compassionately back to the border town of Jericho for repatriation. In a structurally central place, this message of sensitivity to the Lord's will forms a sharp contrast to Ahaz's growing intransigence.

28:16-21. The rest of the chapter returns to that latter theme. Attacks by Edomites (cf. 2 Kgs 16:6) and Philistines are framed with an appeal to Assyria, help that was not forthcoming (vv. 16, 21). By putting the appeal in the context of the defeats at the hands of Aram and Israel ("At that time," v. 16), the chronicler implies that their attacks, as well as these new ones from the south and west, motivated the appeal. The Philistine incursions are illustrated by a list of towns in the northern Shephelah that were captured and occupied.

The chronicler supplies a theological interpretation of these attacks (v. 19) in terms of providential punishment. Ahaz's loss of "restraint" in Judah looks back to v. 4. "Faithlessness" or "unfaithfulness" (מעל *mā'al*) is the chronicler's key term for describing sin that leads straight to exile (1 Chr 5:25 NIV; *ma'al* in 9:1), which had found illustration in Saul's experience (1 Chr 10:10-14, esp. v. 13). Indeed, the Philistines' attack and their occupation of Judean towns reads like a rerun of 1 Chr 10:1-2, 7. The note of exile is sounded elsewhere in the chapter in the deportation of Judean prisoners of war to Aram, Israel, and Edom (vv. 5, 8, 17). Post-exilic Judah looked back to the Babylonian exile as the ultimate of woe, in tune with the representation of national defeat in 2 Kings and pre-exilic prophecy of divine

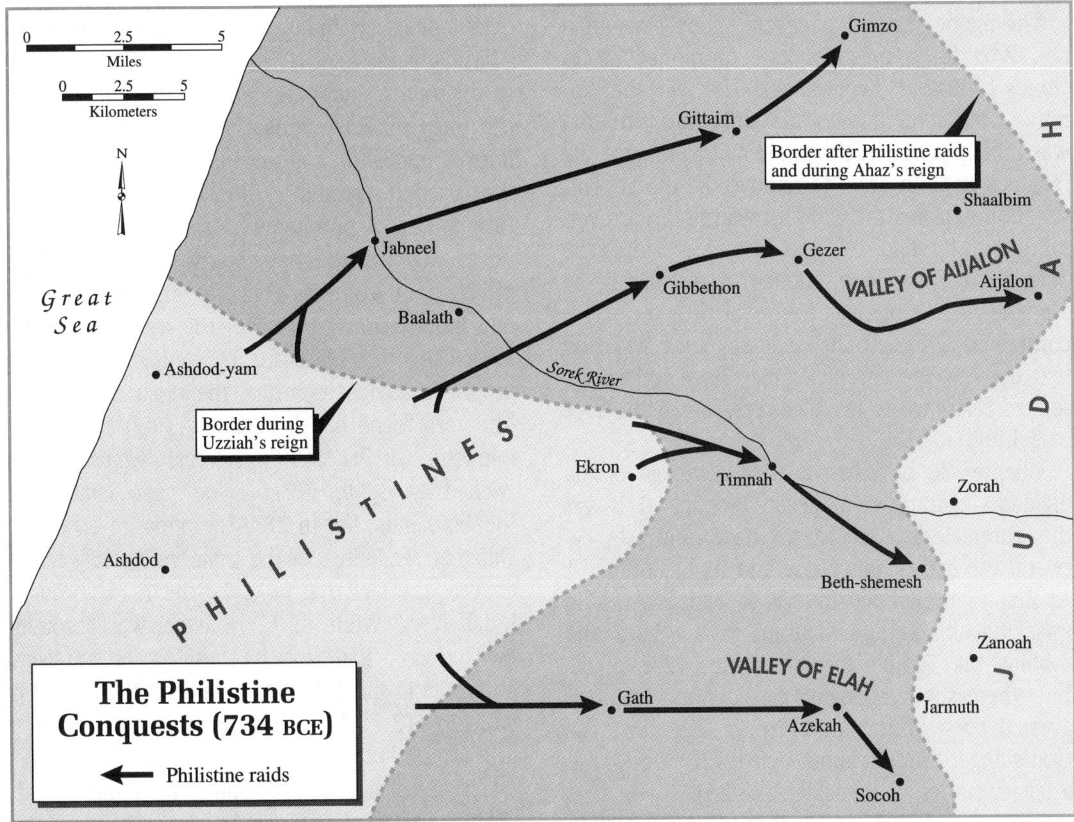

judgment in terms of exile. The chronicler also regarded exile as the worst of calamities, but he refused to see it as a chasm separating pre-exilic and post-exilic Judah. He found that exile was repeated in Judean history, and each time the Lord created a new beginning as its positive aftermath. Each generation contained within itself seeds of exile, which it could cultivate into fast-growing weeds or firmly suppress with God's help.

Judah so disdained the Lord's help that they put the Assyrian monarchy in God's place. It was no help, the chronicler concludes with grim satisfaction. In the short term, the ploy did get Aram and Israel off Judah's back. However, the chronicler has in mind the long-term consequences of becoming entangled with an oppressive empire (so Isa 7:17; 8:7-8). How could robbing the Temple (v. 21) turn out otherwise?

28:22-27. The faithlessness of vv. 2-4 (and referred to in v. 19), is now surpassed. There is also development of the motif of inappropriate help, broached in vv. 16 and 21. Now help was being sought from other gods (v. 23). Ahaz turned everywhere for help except to the Lord. The chronicler interprets Ahaz's having a copy made of an altar seen in Damascus and installing it in the temple court (2 Kgs 16:10-16) as worship of the gods of Damascus (cf. v. 5 and the different theological explanation there). The 2 Kings narrative is written in such neutral terms that its interpretation is uncertain, though it implies that the altar was used for sacrifice to the Lord (2 Kgs 16:13, 15). The chronicler found the narrative sinister, not only because of Ahaz's bad reputation even in 2 Kings, but also because for him Solomon's temple arrangements were cast in concrete (cf. 4:1; 7:9; 8:12-13), and not to be changed. With 2 Kings 16:17*a* in mind, the chronicler thought of desecration as he wrote of cutting holy implements into pieces. He extrapolated the complete closing of the temple doors from Ahaz's closing of the royal entrance to the Temple (2 Kgs 16:18) and from Hezekiah's later plating of its doorposts (2 Kgs 18:16).[309]

309. See S. Japhet, *I & II Chronicles,* OTL (Louisville: Westminster/John Knox, 1993) 918.

The theme of worshiping other gods is resumed (vv. 24*b*-25), a practice that summoned storm clouds of further divine anger. The way the narrative breaks off implies that this dire situation was inherited by Hezekiah. He had to reverse the religious trend in order to remove the threat. This situation explains the careful tracking of its reversal, drawn in chap. 29. The chronicler writes the obituary of Ahaz in his notice of the burial, by denying Ahaz a place in the royal cemetery. This contradicts 2 Kgs 16:20 (at least in the MT; the text used by the chronicler may have lacked the second reference to his ancestors, as did the LXX of 2 Kings).

Chapter 28 brings to a close coverage of the divided kingdom, which began in chap. 10. It was the chronicler's concern to draw contrasts between the end of this phase and its beginning.[310] At first sight, Rehoboam was as bad as Ahaz in forsaking and being unfaithful to the Lord and robbing the Temple to pay tribute (12:2, 5, 9). But whereas in Rehoboam's case divine wrath was averted by self-humbling (12:6, 7, 12), for Ahaz God's anger brought about defeat (28:9) and was a legacy he left to Hezekiah (28:25).

In 11:4 and 28:11, a prophet takes an army to task for improper treatment of their "brothers," first a southern army preparing to fight the north, then a northern army that had captured southerners. Now the northern kingdom is given an opportunity to celebrate the wholeness of the covenant people, and takes it. The stereotype of the southerners as good guys and the northerners as bad guys, which the chronicler has tended to accept, is discarded and even reversed in some respects. In v. 5 the "great slaughter" (NRSV) experienced by Judah was the fate of Israel at Abijah's hands in 13:17. In 12:5-6, Judah listened to a prophet and repented in self-humbling (on the lines of 7:1), while Israel rejected Abijah's implicit appeal to stop turning away from the God they used to worship (13:8). Now it was Israel's turn to hear a prophet who spoke of their traditional God (v. 9). They took a step in the right direction by confessing the backlog of sins they had inherited and retained, the dynastic and religious sins of 13:8-9, and by complying with the prophet's advice to return the prisoners (v. 11). The verb "send back" (השׁיבו *hāšîbû*) echoes the injunction of 7:14 to "turn" (ישׁבו *yāšubû*) from wicked ways. In 13:16, God gave Israel into Judah's hands, but in 28:9 the opposite occurred. Different renderings of the same verb (כנע *kāna'*) conceal the fact that in v. 19 the Lord "brought Judah low," while in 13:18 Israel was "brought low." Judah had lost its position of privilege, grounded in the Temple as the center of orthodox worship (13:10-11). Now its doors were closed (28:24; 29:7).

The note of exile is sounded for Judah in this chapter, a note that will be developed in later chapters. Israel was now exiled, and a mere remnant was left; but in principle Judah had undergone a similar experience (29:9; 30:6). Judah was leveled to the same low state of unworthiness before the Lord that Israel had reached. The chronicler was bidding post-exilic Judah to remember the skeletons in its closet when it thought of disowning brothers and sisters in the north. He was also urging them to take seriously a provocative potential for confession and conciliation, taught here by northern role models.

310. See H. G. M. Williamson, *Israel in the Books of Chronicles* (Cambridge: Cambridge University Press, 1977) 114-18.

REFLECTIONS

1. The chronicler regards Ahaz as a despicable traitor, although the deuteronomist reserved that role for Manasseh. No other Davidic king is portrayed in such disparaging tones; he is as bad as Saul or Athaliah, neither of whom was part of David's house. Through Ahaz, the chronicler warns of the terrible fate that overwhelms apostates. This account is a lesson "written down to instruct later readers" (1 Cor 10:11 NRSV).

2. In comparison to chapters 11–13, Judah's role vis-à-vis Israel has been stood on its head. The message is like that of the parable of the prodigal son in Luke 15:11-32, where the older

brother stands for the Judean establishment as he objects to the welcome extended to the prodigal, who represents repentant tax collectors and sinners (Luke 15:1-2). The former, faithful to God in their own eyes, are portrayed in a bad light for criticizing the claims of Jesus that his work of love was a God-given mission. The chronicler was playing a similar tune. Judah should be prepared to make warm advances to their northern kinsfolk. They stood in the same needy position before the Lord as did their neighbors.

Paul had occasion to condemn such a spirit of arrogant distancing (Rom 11:13-22). Gentile Christians were proud of their own response to the gospel and of their role as members of the people of God. They snobbishly looked down on Jews as spiritual has-beens—they had become God's favorites. For the apostle, it was a dangerous perspective. Privilege never warrants pride, let alone prejudice. Do not boast, Paul warned, or else you will find yourself outside the circle of God's active favor. Every group of believers is prone to arrogance, letting new wine go to their heads. Jesus had to correct John, when he and the other disciples forbade a man they saw casting out demons in his name, "because he is not one of us" (Luke 9:49-50 NIV).

3. Christians, when reading 28:15, may recall the parable of the good Samaritan (Luke 10:25-37). In fact, this passage may have been the literary inspiration for the parable.[311] Jesus told it at a time when religious relations between Jerusalem and Samaria had degenerated much further. Yet, in the parable the good Samaritan, as we ironically call him, shows up the Judean priest and the Levite, who each passed by on the other side of the injured man. There is the same reversal of expected roles as in the chronicler's narrative. The northerners' actions were "deeds consistent with repentance" (Acts 26:20 NRSV) or "fruit in keeping with repentance" (Matt 3:8 NIV).

4. Another part of the ministry of Jesus may have been influenced by this passage: his teaching on the last judgment in Matt 25:31-46. Those who gave food and drink or clothing to others were themselves honored and credited with having also done it to Jesus. It is a measure of the premium the Bible places on loving actions.

311. See F. S. Spencer, "2 Chronicles 28:5-15 and the Parable of the Good Samaritan," *WTJ* 46 (1984) 317-49, though some of his treatment is a little forced.

2 CHRONICLES 29:1–36:23

THE REUNITED KINGDOM

OVERVIEW

This is the last and shortest of the four literary blocks that make up the chronicler's selective retelling of Israel's history. It mirrors on a smaller scale the two preceding blocks. Hezekiah is portrayed as a second David and Solomon, reenacting their devotion to the ideals of Temple and Torah, and so reversing the degenerate state of Judah in chap. 28. He also availed himself of the Solomonic revelation (7:14) in his appeal for self-humbling, in his own recourse to it (30:11; 32:26), and in his prayer on behalf of unclean worshipers (30:18-20). In the second case, he became another Rehoboam, averting divine wrath by humbling himself (12:6-7; 32:25-26). Like Abijah, he laid the claims of the Jerusalem sanctuary before the people of the north (13:8-12; 30:5-9).

The kaleidoscope of good and bad royal models in the previous block continues to flash before our eyes, as we are shown a good reign, a bad one that turns good, an utterly bad one, a good one that turns bad at the end, and then a series of utterly bad reigns. The variety of options offered in Ezekiel 18 is illustrated once more in the interests of spiritual challenge and encouragement.

In the previous block, we noticed a sharp contrast between Judah's spiritual well-being near the beginning and its sorry state by the end, as bad as and, in fact, worse than that of the northern kingdom. The same impression is given here. Zedekiah's people scorned the prophetic messengers the Lord sent to warn and coax them, as had the northern tribes earlier in reaction to Hezekiah's courier (30:10; 36:16). Some of the latter did humble themselves (7:14), but not Zedekiah (30:11; 36:12). In this respect, he was no Hezekiah, whose example had been followed by Manasseh and Josiah; Zedekiah took after Amon (32:26; 33:12, 19, 23; 34:27). Both the northerners and Zedekiah are called stiff-necked (30:8; 36:13), and both they and his subjects are confronted with the divinely consecrated role of the Temple (30:8; 36:14).

The fall of the northern kingdom at the end of the preceding block removed a stumbling block of wicked alliance from Judah's kings, leaving the Davidic dynasty unchallenged and giving the opportunity for good kings of Judah to make spiritual overtures to the members of the tribes of Israel left in the north. Hezekiah, in line with his Davidic and Solomonic orientation, went to great lengths to hold a festival for all Israelites, whereupon religious reform ensued in north and south (30:1–31:1). Josiah, a paler reflection of Hezekiah, is credited with similar, if less vigorously stated, roles (34:33; 35:17-18).

This final block resembles the first in moving at its close from exile to restoration (1 Chr 9:1-34; 2 Chr 36:20-23). Punishment was not the Lord's last word. A day of opportunity dawned for a new generation. Solomon's petition that a repentant people might return to the land found a gracious hearing (2 Chr 6:24-25; cf. Zech 1:4-6). For the chronicler, such restoration created a precedent still available to any generation aware of their spiritual exile from the Lord. "Return to me . . . and I will return to you" (Zech 1:3 NIV) was the divine word to an earlier post-exilic generation, and it was still the Lord's gracious invitation, this last block affirms (30:8-9).

The block is made up of three units: (1) 29:1–32:33 presents Hezekiah's model reign; (2) 33:1–35:27 portrays two dramatic shifts from apostasy to spirituality, though flawed at the close in the latter case; and (3) 36:1-23 contrasts the finale of decline and destruction with the divinely endorsed hope of a fresh beginning.

2 CHRONICLES 29:1–32:33, HEZEKIAH ATTAINS ROYAL POTENTIAL

OVERVIEW

This unit divides Hezekiah's reign into two unequal halves, 29:1–31:21 and 32:1-33. In the first, the king is held up as a model of loyalty to the Lord. This section is introduced by the statement that he did right in the Lord's sight (29:2), which reuses a standard element of the deuteronomistic prologue to a monarch's reign (2 Kgs 18:3). Hezekiah's behavior is described at length and then recapitulated in a longer sentence, including "he did what was . . . right . . . before the LORD" (31:20 NRSV). The second half also uses a framing device. Now Hezekiah is presented as a paradigm for the prosperity that follows faithfulness to the Lord. The chronicler announces his theme in 31:21, "In everything that he undertook . . . he prospered" (NIV). He reinforces it with a final summary in 32:30, "He succeeded in everything he undertook" (NIV).

Throughout the account, Hezekiah is represented as reestablishing royal ideals associated with the reigns of David and Solomon.[312] The founders of a new era of revelation found a worthy heir in Hezekiah, in his honoring of the Lord's chosen shrine and in his efforts to unite the people of God in worship. When the accounts of his reign in 2 Kings and 2 Chronicles are compared, a shift of emphasis becomes apparent. For the writer of the books of Kings, deliverance from crisis was the primary theme, in a context of political threat and military invasion. The chronicler found room for this theme as well, but inserted it in a panorama of spiritual restoration, united worship, religious reformation, and divine blessing. In reliving such Davidic and Solomonic ideals, Hezekiah became a role model for the post-exilic community.

312. See M. A. Throntveit, *When Kings Speak: Royal Speech and Royal Prayer in Chronicles,* SBLDS 93 (Atlanta: Scholars Press, 1987) 121-24.

2 Chronicles 29:1-36, Temple Cleansing, Atonement, and Worship

NIV

29 Hezekiah was twenty-five years old when
he became king, and he reigned in Jerusalem twenty-nine years. His mother's name was Abijah daughter of Zechariah. 2He did what was right in the eyes of the LORD, just as his father David had done.

3In the first month of the first year of his reign, he opened the doors of the temple of the LORD and repaired them. 4He brought in the priests and the Levites, assembled them in the square on the east side 5and said: "Listen to me, Levites! Consecrate yourselves now and consecrate the temple of the LORD, the God of your fathers. Remove all defilement from the sanctuary. 6Our fathers were unfaithful; they did evil in the eyes of the LORD our God and forsook him. They turned their faces

NRSV

29 Hezekiah began to reign when he was
twenty-five years old; he reigned twenty-nine years in Jerusalem. His mother's name was Abijah daughter of Zechariah. 2He did what was right in the sight of the LORD, just as his ancestor David had done.

3In the first year of his reign, in the first month, he opened the doors of the house of the LORD and repaired them. 4He brought in the priests and the Levites and assembled them in the square on the east. 5He said to them, "Listen to me, Levites! Sanctify yourselves, and sanctify the house of the LORD, the God of your ancestors, and carry out the filth from the holy place. 6For our ancestors have been unfaithful and have done what was

NIV

away from the LORD's dwelling place and turned
their backs on him. 7They also shut the doors of
the portico and put out the lamps. They did not
burn incense or present any burnt offerings at the
sanctuary to the God of Israel. 8Therefore, the
anger of the LORD has fallen on Judah and Jerusalem; he has made them an object of dread and
horror and scorn, as you can see with your own
eyes. 9This is why our fathers have fallen by the
sword and why our sons and daughters and our
wives are in captivity. 10Now I intend to make a
covenant with the LORD, the God of Israel, so that
his fierce anger will turn away from us. 11My sons,
do not be negligent now, for the LORD has chosen
you to stand before him and serve him, to minister
before him and to burn incense."

12Then these Levites set to work:
from the Kohathites,
Mahath son of Amasai and Joel son of Azariah;
from the Merarites,
Kish son of Abdi and Azariah son of Jehallelel;
from the Gershonites,
Joah son of Zimmah and Eden son of Joah;
13from the descendants of Elizaphan,
Shimri and Jeiel;
from the descendants of Asaph,
Zechariah and Mattaniah;
14from the descendants of Heman,
Jehiel and Shimei;
from the descendants of Jeduthun,
Shemaiah and Uzziel.

15When they had assembled their brothers and
consecrated themselves, they went in to purify
the temple of the LORD, as the king had ordered,
following the word of the LORD. 16The priests went
into the sanctuary of the LORD to purify it. They
brought out to the courtyard of the LORD's temple
everything unclean that they found in the temple
of the LORD. The Levites took it and carried it out
to the Kidron Valley. 17They began the consecration on the first day of the first month, and by
the eighth day of the month they reached the
portico of the LORD. For eight more days they
consecrated the temple of the LORD itself, finishing
on the sixteenth day of the first month.

18Then they went in to King Hezekiah and

NRSV

evil in the sight of the LORD our God; they have
forsaken him, and have turned away their faces
from the dwelling of the LORD, and turned their
backs. 7They also shut the doors of the vestibule
and put out the lamps, and have not offered
incense or made burnt offerings in the holy place
to the God of Israel. 8Therefore the wrath of the
LORD came upon Judah and Jerusalem, and he has
made them an object of horror, of astonishment,
and of hissing, as you see with your own eyes.
9Our fathers have fallen by the sword and our
sons and our daughters and our wives are in
captivity for this. 10Now it is in my heart to make
a covenant with the LORD, the God of Israel, so
that his fierce anger may turn away from us. 11My
sons, do not now be negligent, for the LORD has
chosen you to stand in his presence to minister
to him, and to be his ministers and make offerings
to him."

12Then the Levites arose, Mahath son of
Amasai, and Joel son of Azariah, of the sons of
the Kohathites; and of the sons of Merari, Kish
son of Abdi, and Azariah son of Jehallelel; and of
the Gershonites, Joah son of Zimmah, and Eden
son of Joah; 13and of the sons of Elizaphan, Shimri
and Jeuel; and of the sons of Asaph, Zechariah
and Mattaniah; 14and of the sons of Heman, Jehuel
and Shimei; and of the sons of Jeduthun, Shemaiah and Uzziel. 15They gathered their brothers,
sanctified themselves, and went in as the king had
commanded, by the words of the LORD, to cleanse
the house of the LORD. 16The priests went into the
inner part of the house of the LORD to cleanse it,
and they brought out all the unclean things that
they found in the temple of the LORD into the
court of the house of the LORD; and the Levites
took them and carried them out to the Wadi
Kidron. 17They began to sanctify on the first day
of the first month, and on the eighth day of the
month they came to the vestibule of the LORD;
then for eight days they sanctified the house of
the LORD, and on the sixteenth day of the first
month they finished. 18Then they went inside to
King Hezekiah and said, "We have cleansed all
the house of the LORD, the altar of burnt offering
and all its utensils, and the table for the rows of
bread and all its utensils. 19All the utensils that
King Ahaz repudiated during his reign when he

NIV

reported: "We have purified the entire temple of
the LORD, the altar of burnt offering with all its
utensils, and the table for setting out the consecrated bread, with all its articles. 19We have prepared and consecrated all the articles that King
Ahaz removed in his unfaithfulness while he was
king. They are now in front of the LORD's altar."

20Early the next morning King Hezekiah gathered the city officials together and went up to the
temple of the LORD. 21They brought seven bulls,
seven rams, seven male lambs and seven male
goats as a sin offering for the kingdom, for the
sanctuary and for Judah. The king commanded
the priests, the descendants of Aaron, to offer
these on the altar of the LORD. 22So they slaughtered the bulls, and the priests took the blood and
sprinkled it on the altar; next they slaughtered
the rams and sprinkled their blood on the altar;
then they slaughtered the lambs and sprinkled
their blood on the altar. 23The goats for the sin
offering were brought before the king and the
assembly, and they laid their hands on them.
24The priests then slaughtered the goats and presented their blood on the altar for a sin offering
to atone for all Israel, because the king had
ordered the burnt offering and the sin offering for
all Israel.

25He stationed the Levites in the temple of the
LORD with cymbals, harps and lyres in the way
prescribed by David and Gad the king's seer and
Nathan the prophet; this was commanded by the
LORD through his prophets. 26So the Levites stood
ready with David's instruments, and the priests
with their trumpets.

27Hezekiah gave the order to sacrifice the burnt
offering on the altar. As the offering began, singing
to the LORD began also, accompanied by trumpets
and the instruments of David king of Israel. 28The
whole assembly bowed in worship, while the
singers sang and the trumpeters played. All this
continued until the sacrifice of the burnt offering
was completed.

29When the offerings were finished, the king
and everyone present with him knelt down and
worshiped. 30King Hezekiah and his officials ordered the Levites to praise the LORD with the
words of David and of Asaph the seer. So they

NRSV

was faithless, we have made ready and sanctified;
see, they are in front of the altar of the LORD."

20Then King Hezekiah rose early, assembled
the officials of the city, and went up to the house
of the LORD. 21They brought seven bulls, seven
rams, seven lambs, and seven male goats for a sin
offering for the kingdom and for the sanctuary
and for Judah. He commanded the priests the
descendants of Aaron to offer them on the altar
of the LORD. 22So they slaughtered the bulls, and
the priests received the blood and dashed it
against the altar; they slaughtered the rams and
their blood was dashed against the altar; they also
slaughtered the lambs and their blood was dashed
against the altar. 23Then the male goats for the
sin offering were brought to the king and the
assembly; they laid their hands on them, 24and
the priests slaughtered them and made a sin
offering with their blood at the altar, to make
atonement for all Israel. For the king commanded
that the burnt offering and the sin offering should
be made for all Israel.

25He stationed the Levites in the house of the
LORD with cymbals, harps, and lyres, according to
the commandment of David and of Gad the king's
seer and of the prophet Nathan, for the commandment was from the LORD through his prophets.
26The Levites stood with the instruments of David,
and the priests with the trumpets. 27Then
Hezekiah commanded that the burnt offering be
offered on the altar. When the burnt offering
began, the song to the LORD began also, and the
trumpets, accompanied by the instruments of King
David of Israel. 28The whole assembly worshiped,
the singers sang, and the trumpeters sounded; all
this continued until the burnt offering was finished. 29When the offering was finished, the king
and all who were present with him bowed down
and worshiped. 30King Hezekiah and the officials
commanded the Levites to sing praises to the LORD
with the words of David and of the seer Asaph.
They sang praises with gladness, and they bowed
down and worshiped.

31Then Hezekiah said, "You have now consecrated yourselves to the LORD; come near, bring
sacrifices and thank offerings to the house of the
LORD." The assembly brought sacrifices and thank
offerings; and all who were of a willing heart

NIV

sang praises with gladness and bowed their heads and worshiped.

[31]Then Hezekiah said, "You have now dedicated yourselves to the LORD. Come and bring sacrifices and thank offerings to the temple of the LORD." So the assembly brought sacrifices and thank offerings, and all whose hearts were willing brought burnt offerings.

[32]The number of burnt offerings the assembly brought was seventy bulls, a hundred rams and two hundred male lambs—all of them for burnt offerings to the LORD. [33]The animals consecrated as sacrifices amounted to six hundred bulls and three thousand sheep and goats. [34]The priests, however, were too few to skin all the burnt offerings; so their kinsmen the Levites helped them until the task was finished and until other priests had been consecrated, for the Levites had been more conscientious in consecrating themselves than the priests had been. [35]There were burnt offerings in abundance, together with the fat of the fellowship offerings[a] and the drink offerings that accompanied the burnt offerings.

So the service of the temple of the LORD was reestablished. [36]Hezekiah and all the people rejoiced at what God had brought about for his people, because it was done so quickly.

[a]*35* Traditionally *peace offerings*

NRSV

brought burnt offerings. [32]The number of the burnt offerings that the assembly brought was seventy bulls, one hundred rams, and two hundred lambs; all these were for a burnt offering to the LORD. [33]The consecrated offerings were six hundred bulls and three thousand sheep. [34]But the priests were too few and could not skin all the burnt offerings, so, until other priests had sanctified themselves, their kindred, the Levites, helped them until the work was finished—for the Levites were more conscientious[a] than the priests in sanctifying themselves. [35]Besides the great number of burnt offerings there was the fat of the offerings of well-being, and there were the drink offerings for the burnt offerings. Thus the service of the house of the LORD was restored. [36]And Hezekiah and all the people rejoiced because of what God had done for the people; for the thing had come about suddenly.

[a] Heb *upright in heart*

COMMENTARY

29:1-2. This passage is taken from 2 Kgs 18:1-3. Verse 2 now functions as a basic statement about Hezekiah's reign. The comparison with David reminds us of his religious devotion, both to the ark of the covenant and to preparations for the building of the Temple. The chronicler saw this spirit reborn in Hezekiah. Taking his cue from the single verse concerning religious reform, 2 Kgs 18:4, he divided his definition of the king's spirituality into three parts, all relating to the Temple. The first (vv. 3-35) is concerned with the cleansing of the Temple, desecrated and discounted by Ahaz (chap. 28). This narrative matches the schematic interpretation of Ahaz's religious measures in 28:24 and serves as a positive counterpart.

29:3-11. The divine wrath that threatened Judah (28:25) demanded an immediate response (vv. 8, 10). So top priority was given to opening up the Temple, which Ahaz had closed down. This task had to fall on its official personnel, and the first opportunity is taken to summon them to a meeting. Comparison with 30:2-3 suggests that the first calendar month of Hezekiah's first official year as king is in view (v. 3), rather than the first month he came to the throne. The date was chosen to accord with priestly tradition, in the light of the sin offering on that date (see Ezek 45:18-19).[313] Verse 3 functions as an initial sum-

313. S. Japhet, *I & II Chronicles*, OTL (Louisville: Westminster/John Knox, 1993) 922-23.

mary; v. 17 suggests that the doors were opened on the eighth day of the project.

The speech ascribed to Hezekiah gives the chronicler a chance to provide a theological interpretation. He understood the "square" from a post-exilic perspective, situating Hezekiah, as he gave his speech, outside the uncleansed temple area, between that and the eastern wall of the city. The Levites are addressed in v. 5, which accords with their response in vv. 12-15. Yet priests, too, were summoned (v. 4) to hear the speech. The double reference to ministering (v. 11) embraces both groups, while mention of making offerings or burning incense relates to priests. So both are in view throughout. The singling out of the Levites accords with the chronicler's special interest in them and may also stem from the fact that they would do most of the work. There is a parallel in 1 Chr 15:11-14, where again a mainly levitical task is in view.

The speech uses calls for action (vv. 5, 11) as a frame for interpreting Ahaz's reign in terms of communal sin and punishment (vv. 6-9) and announcing Hezekiah's positive intent, for which the action will prepare (v. 10). The new generation had the responsibility of relating spiritually to the God of the previous generation ("fathers," NIV; the NRSV's "ancestors" is patently wrong in vv. 5-6; see v. 19 and its rendering of "fathers" in v. 9). Now their turn had come, and the Lord had become "our God" (v. 6). That meant correcting the abuses of their predecessors and making a total change, like the good son of the wicked father in Ezek 18:14-18. Their parents' sins are described in terms of general spirituality (v. 6) and more specifically (v. 7). Their unfaithfulness (מעל *mā'al*) echoes that of 28:19, 22, with reference to the Temple-related offenses of 28:2-4, 23-25. Their having forsaken the Lord picks up the reference in 28:6. Their rejection of the Lord's earthly home had been a token of their rejection of God. The specific sins begin with the datum in 28:24. They continue with the cessation of the Temple's archetypal functions, initiated by Solomon and affirmed by Abijah (2:4; 4:7; 13:11). Judah could no longer claim that, in Adijah's words, "we are observing the requirements of the Lord our God" (NIV).

The consequent wrath of the Lord recalls the divine anger depicted in 24:18, which was a response to temple-related sins. The chronicler here describes the divine motivation for surrendering Judah to Aram and Israel (28:5, 9). Verse 8*b* cites part of Jer 29:18*b*, essentially a description of the Judean exile of 587 BCE. The program of restoration in Jer 29:12-14 was dear to the chronicler, and he related it metaphorically to post-exilic Judah. Here he does the same with a verse in the context, reapplying it to the exile-like conditions of Hezekiah's reign, after many of the people had been killed or deported by their enemies. Verse 9 describes this very situation, echoing 28:5-8, 17-18. Although most Judeans still occupied the land, they had undergone a virtual exile. It was the situation of Saul's time all over again (1 Chr 10:1, 7). From this perspective, the reference to unfaithfulness in v. 6 takes on new significance. In 1 Chr 10:13, the chronicler made it the trigger for metaphorical exile, echoing Lev 26:40, where it describes the sin of covenant breaking, which leads to exile. Hezekiah was another David whose reign brought spiritual restoration. His task was to re-call the people from their exile.

Hezekiah's eventual aim of making a covenant pledge to the Lord is reminiscent of the pledges in Asa's (15:12) and Jehoiada's (23:16) reigns, and it anticipates Josiah's (34:31; cf. Ezra 10:3). It suggests a service at which this sinful state would be renounced, which is presumably reflected in vv. 20-31 (see also v. 31). This goal required preparation: the cleansing of the neglected and defiled Temple, including the removal of pagan objects (implied in v. 16). The task fell to the priests and Levites. The former alone had access to the temple building (cf. 5:7), while the latter had access to the temple court and were responsible for maintenance work. Challenged to do their God-given duty and coaxed by the epithet "my sons," they are encouraged to get on with the work.

In this address, the chronicler uses Hezekiah's situation as a means of preaching to his contemporaries. They were heirs of the message of the Torah (Lev 26:40) and of the prophetic message in Jer 29:18, to the effect that sin had caused the Babylonian exile, which still haunted the descendants of the returnees (see Neh 9:32-37). The chronicler offers the success story of Hezekiah's reign as a model for escape from such frustration.

The Temple was the key to appropriate religion, and the priests and especially the Levites—the workhorses of the Temple—had a vital role in its worship. Only thus could worship be given pride of place in the community's life. "Do not be negligent" is his appeal to the temple personnel of his day.

29:12-17. The historical response was positive. All the main groups of the Levites were represented, even the choral families (cf. 1 Chr 15:5-8; 28:1). The priests were not unresponsive; they worked in areas inaccessible to the Levites. They all worked with devotion, heeding not only the king's appeal but also the inspired messages implicitly brought to their notice (cf. 30:12). They spent a week in the temple court and another in the sanctuary, where the priests first became involved, and by day sixteen the task was done. The references to beginning and ending are a faint but proud echo of Solomon's basic work in 3:1-2; 5:1. As in Asa's reign (15:16), pagan religious objects were burned in the Kidron Valley. The cleansing rites had to be repeated on successive days (cf. Exod 29:37; Ezek 43:18-27) and carried out on different items. Evidently the priests who performed this task were insufficiently represented (cf. 30:3). Consequently, the date of the passover, the fourteenth of Nisan, was overshot and had to be reset (30:5).

29:18-19. In this conclusion of Hezekiah's appeal, the chronicler focuses first on the altar of burnt offering in the temple court and the table for the bread of the presence in the Temple, and then on the replacement of utensils that had been "removed" or discarded by faithless Ahaz (see 28:22, 24). The first case presupposes knowledge of Ahaz's having displaced the altar in 2 Kgs 16:14-15 (see "the altar of the LORD," instead of "the pagan one," in vv. 19, 21). Mention of the table together with the altar recalls their archetypal role in 2:4; 13:11. The "utensils" (NRSV) or "vessels" (REB) in vv. 18-19 were important for the chronicler. In the post-exilic Temple, the vessels were especially prized as providing continuity with the pre-exilic sanctuary; extra ones came to share their pristine sanctity (cf. Ezra 1:6-11; 6:5; 8:30, 33).

29:20-35a. With the preliminary work of cleansing completed, it was now time for the pledge of loyalty to the Lord to deflect the divine anger of 28:25, in accordance with the program of v. 10. The pledge takes the form of a service involving complex ritual, narrated in vv. 20-35*a*. It gave the chronicler an opportunity to portray a post-exilic service of ritual reconsecration for the spiritual enlightenment of his constituency. The course of the service is demarcated by four stages, beginning with Hezekiah's command in vv. 21, 27, 30-31. The service, conducted by priests and Levites, was organized by the king and the city officials (vv. 20, 30; 30:12; see also 18:25; 34:8). As the service proceeds, there is also mention of "the assembly" (vv. 23, 28, 31-32) and "all the people" (v. 36). Moreover, in v. 29 "all who were present" refers to the congregation, as in 30:21; 31:1; 34:32-33; 35:7, 17-18.[314] In the light of 30:2, these terms refer to a body of Jerusalem residents who represented the people of Judah (cf. v. 21). The leaders provided the sacrificial animals (see 30:24), as did the prince in Ezekiel 45–46. The details given in vv. 22-24 show that the first three sets of seven animals were to be burnt offerings, and only the goats were to be used as sin offerings. The groups on whose behalf they were to be sacrificed were "the royal house" (NJB), the temple personnel, and Judah.

The first royal command initiates the general sacrificial procedure (v. 21*b*). Thereafter the ritual is divided into two separate stages: the blood rite (vv. 22-24) and the actual sacrificing of the public burnt offerings (vv. 25-30).[315] Then a third stage of voluntary private offerings is given by individual members of the congregation (v. 31). The whole ritual sequence follows a standard pattern of atonement and then worship.[316] The various parts of the burnt offering ritual for animals from the herd and flock are laid down in the priestly source at Lev 1:3-9, 10-13. The present account, though shorter, seems to presuppose that procedure. In vv. 22-24, the chronicler focuses on the treatment of the blood (cf. Lev 1:5, 11). After the offerers had slaughtered the animals, the blood was drained out of the carcasses and collected in a basin. The blood was then splashed against the

314. John W. Kleinig, *The Lord's Song: The Basis, Function and Significance of Choral Music in Chronicles,* JSOTSup 156 (Sheffield: JSOT, 1993) 121 n. 1.

315. D. L. Petersen, *Late Israelite Prophecy,* SBLMS 23 (Missoula, Mont.: Scholars Press, 1977) 83.

316. See A. F. Rainey, "The Order of Sacrifices in OT Ritual Texts," *Bib* 51 (1970) 485-98; note the modification of Kleinig, *The Lord's Song,* 101 n. 2.

sides of the altar in the temple court. Blood had an atoning role in the sacrificial ritual. The subject of the verbs of slaughtering (v. 22) are the king and officials depicted in vv. 20-21*a.* Such a picture differentiates the priests' dealing with the blood in the first two cases, which is consistent with Lev 1:5, 11. The NRSV, unlike the NIV, allows for this interpretation.

Next came the sin offerings. The Hebrew term חטאת (*ḥaṭṭāʾt*) is literally a de-sinning offering or "purification-offering" (REB). The full ritual is described in Lev 4:1–5:13, though there it is prescribed for inadvertent sins and sins of omission. Here it involves much more, as it does in the Day of Atonement ceremony of Leviticus 16. The theory behind the sin offering in Leviticus is related, in part at least, to the sanctuary. Human sins had a polluting effect on it, "defiling [God's] tabernacle that is in their midst" (Lev 15:31 NRSV). The effect of the sin offering was "to cleanse it and consecrate it from the uncleanness of the Israelites" (Lev 16:19 NIV). Leviticus knows two types of sin offering: One type had the specific role of cleansing the altar (Lev 4:30), which is the one envisioned here.[317] Again, the treatment of the blood was the important element for the chronicler, but there was a different procedure in the case of the sin offering. After the blood was drained, most of it was poured out at the bottom of the altar and a little was put in a basin and smeared on the altar. As in vv. 18-19, 21, continuing emphasis is placed on the altar of burnt offering, which had suffered at Ahaz's hands.

Mention is made of the rite of the laying on of hands in v. 23. This is specified at Lev 4:24 in the case of the sin offering, in which each worshiper pressed one hand on the goat's head. This action represented the self-identification of the offerer with the victim[318] and was a personal affirmation of a sinful status before the Lord and of the sincere desire to mend the broken relationship. In this case, the king and the congregation represented not only themselves but the rest of the people as well, "to make atonement for all Israel." In the light of the clarification in v. 24*b,* his reference to "all Israel" functions as a correction made by the king, so that not only Judah was covered, as v. 21 envisions, but all the tribes as well.[319] Hezekiah's sense of responsibility for the northern tribes, evidenced in the next chapter, is already in view here. He would not rest until separated members of the covenant family were visibly reunited in worship of their one God.

Much scholarly ink has been spilled to determine the meaning of the verb כפר (*kipper*), rendered "atone" or "make atonement." An explanation that is widely preferred is a denominative sense, "pay a ransom." Sacrificial animals were a ransom, the alternative to the sinful offerers' losing their own lives. In the overall context, a propitiatory value for these atoning sacrifices can hardly be avoided. They function as God's answer to the question of what will appease the divine wrath (v. 10). A novel feature of v. 24, in comparison with earlier verses, is that the priests carry out the slaughtering. The solemnity of the occasion may have led the chronicler to base this stage on the Day of Atonement ritual, in which the high priest killed the goat for the people's sin offering (Lev 16:15).[320]

Verses 25-30 are concerned with the placing of burnt offerings on the altar (cf. Lev 1:6-9, 12-13). This stage is inaugurated by royal command in v. 27*a.* Its being accompanied by sacred music and song is narrated in v. 27*b,* as in 1 Chr 23:30-31. Verses 25-26 describe a preliminary procedure for v. 27*b,* placing the levitical singing musicians and the priestly trumpeters in position. It gives the chronicler another chance to reaffirm the ancient authority vested in the post-exilic musical guilds of Levites. In vv. 26-27, David's traditional association with musical instruments is applied to those played by the Levites, as earlier in 1 Chr 23:5; 2 Chr 7:6. This link enhanced the venerability with which the chronicler invested levitical music. Moreover, in v. 25 the use of music is traced back to David's organization of the Temple. Readers are meant to read this text from the perspective of 1 Chr 15:16-21; 25:1-6. However, in v. 25 David's authority as founder of this aspect of the temple era is backed by the prophetic sanction of Gad and Nathan and

317. See J. Milgrom, "Two Kings of *Ḥaṭṭāʾt,*" *VT* 26 (1976) 333-37.

318. See D. P. Wright, "Hands, Laying on of. Old Testament," *ABD,* 3:47-48.

319. See H. G. M. Williamson, *Israel in the Books of Chronicles* (Cambridge: Cambridge University Press, 1977) 126-27.

320. H. G. M. Williamson, *1 and 2 Chronicles,* NCB (Grand Rapids: Eerdmans, 1982) 357.

through them by divine warrant.[321] A prophetic role also appears in 1 Chronicles 25, but there it is associated with the musical choirs and especially their leaders. Here the wider God-given mission of Nathan and Gad as prophets involved in the location and building of the Temple (1 Chr 17:3-15; 21:18-19) is invoked. Hezekiah honored the Davidic command, as did Solomon in 8:14.

The accompaniment of burnt offerings with song and trumpet blasts accords with and clarifies the representations of 1 Chr 23:30-31; 2 Chr 8:12-14; 23:18. Worship ascended to the Lord in both ritual and music. It was echoed by the prostration of the congregation at beginning and end and also of the singers at the end after having laid down their instruments.[322] The royal command to the Levites (v. 30) is not chronologically placed, but serves as a footnote qualifying v. 27*b* and as a parallel to the ritual command of v. 27*a*. The command provides a fitting climax, with its further affirmation of the Levites' venerable role, which dominates the paragraph. Here the chronicler focuses on the content of the singing—namely, the psalms attributed to David and Asaph in the psalter. This reference to inspired songs is closest to 1 Chr 25:1-6, where Asaph is also mentioned in prophetic terms (1 Chr 25:2). The chronicler's message is that the Lord had authorized practices and texts that were to be perpetuated in temple worship. For post-exilic Judeans, remote from the origins of their faith, this was to be an anchor securing them to divine revelation and, hence, keeping them true to the Lord. The chronicler was particularly concerned to endorse the Levites' ministry as an indispensable part of temple worship.

The last stage of this model service of temple cleansing and spiritual restoration occurs in vv. 31-35*a*. The accent thus far has been on bridging the gap between the community and the Lord. The praise of v. 30 is a welcome indication that the gap had been closed. The previous public sacrifices of worship represented self-dedication on the part of the worshiping congregation. The Hebrew verbal phrase usually refers to the consecration of a new priest by offering his first sacrifice. In 1 Chr 29:5, it was used metaphorically of commitment to the Lord's work by giving money. Here מלא יד (*mālē' yād*) relates to reconsecration to God's service after the burden of guilt had been lifted. While the "covenant," or pledge, of v. 10 looked forward to the service of atonement, this phrase looks back to it.

The "sacrifices and thank offerings" (v. 31) are better taken as idiomatic for "thanksgiving sacrifices" (NJB). Such sacrifices celebrated the end of a crisis for an individual. Here these private offerings reflect individuals' gratitude for deliverance from the divine wrath that had loomed over the community. These offerings took the form of שלמים (*šĕlāmîm*, "offerings of well-being" or "fellowship offerings," v. 35), of which only the fat and a few other parts of the animal were sacrificed (Lev 3:3-4, 16*b*). Yet other parts were donated to the priests, and the rest was returned to the worshiper for a sacred meal with his family (Lev 7:15-17, 29-36). In v. 33, these are called "consecrated offerings" because they could be eaten only at the sanctuary (cf. Lev 19:8). People could elect to present a burnt offering instead, which was completely given over to the Lord with nothing returned to the individual. It expressed a generosity of devotion beyond that of the other offering (see Ps 66:15). Of course, all the private offerings were given out of "a willing heart," but the chronicler was issuing a challenge to his own constituency to go the extra mile in their worship. The data in vv. 32-33 suggest that about a tenth of the heads of households present elected to do so.

Staffing the temple became a problem. The responsibility of priests to skin burnt offerings may reflect the custom in the chronicler's day; in Lev 1:6 it is the duty of the lay offerer. The co-opting of Levites for this task is used as an opportunity not only to highlight their spiritual alacrity but also to advocate a policy change. In the narrative of sacrificial procedures during Josiah's reign, the Levites are reported in a more matter-of-fact way to have engaged in skinning sacrificial animals (35:11). The emergency measures described in this story become virtually the norm in the next. By such means, the chronicler was urging that Levites be given a greater role in sacrificial ritual. Further reasons why the priests were hard-pressed

321. See W. M. Schniedewind, *The Word of God in Transition: From Prophet to Exegete in the Second Temple Period,* JSOTSup 197 (Sheffield: Sheffield Academic, 1995) 197-98.

322. See Kleinig, *The Lord's Song,* 122.

are supplied in v. 35*a*. They had to burn the fat of the offerings of well-being with the burnt offerings and to make the drink offerings that accompanied the burnt offerings (see Exod 29:40; 1 Chr 9:29; Ezra 7:17).

29:35b-36. This catalog of priestly duties serves as a glad reminder that normal services at the Temple had resumed. A restored Temple and a restored people worshiping their God constituted spiritual normality. This switch from apostasy to piety had occurred "so quickly," in less than three weeks. King and congregation took none of the credit. God must have been at work among them, they concluded. They gave thanks for this miracle of grace.

REFLECTIONS

1. The Temple had a sacramental value in the life of God's people, for it mediated the blessing of God. It was the touchstone of their reverence, the place where God's honor was most obviously acknowledged. A right regard for the Lord was grounded in pure and regular worship at the sanctuary. Hezekiah found the Temple to be in a shocking state of neglect and disuse. It mirrored the people's condition before God. Restoration from the spiritual exile of Ahaz's reign required cleansing rites and reestablishment of Torah-based patterns of worship. These patterns were to be supplemented with levitical music and song attributed to David's inspired institution. The reorganization of the Temple is presented as normative for later generations, a model for the chronicler's constituency. "Go and do likewise" is his message, one that we in turn must try to hear as we search for principles to govern our own worship.

A locked Temple was unthinkable for God's people; the Temple provided regular access to the Lord. The New Testament uses this function of the Temple as a spiritual metaphor. In Eph 2:18-22, access to God and status within the new Temple-church are mentioned side by side. Hebrews 10:19-22 celebrates the privilege of entering the heavenly sanctuary won by Jesus for his followers.

Only priests could enter the temple building, but they did so on the people's behalf. Israel's supreme task was to worship the Lord both indirectly through the regular rites of the Temple and directly by their participating presence in the temple area. This priority of worship comes over into the Christian era. In 1 Pet 2:5, 9, the role of believers in a local church is described as "offering spiritual sacrifices acceptable to God through Jesus Christ" and declaring "the praises" of a gracious God (NIV). The "prayers of the saints" are represented as incense in a vision at Rev 5:8 (cf. 2 Chr 29:7). Christians are to offer their whole selves as "living sacrifices, holy and pleasing to God—this is your spiritual act of worship" (Rom 12:1 NIV). Here religious worship spills over into the rest of life. First, however, those of us who culturally tend to shy away from the institutional and the congregational must hear the more literal side of the message. Psalm 133:1, 3 suggests that the communal experience of temple worship was a prime source of blessing and vitality for ancient Israelites. In turn, the writer to the Hebrews could not conceive of exercising the privilege of access to God apart from the responsibility of loyal attendance at Christian meetings for mutual encouragement (Heb 10:19, 25).

2. In Hezekiah's appeal to the temple clergy to play their preliminary role in restoring the sanctuary, we hear the chronicler addressing the temple personnel of his own day. His message may be updated as a call to pastors of the church for continued consecration. Thus their example of spiritual living and reverent service can work to prompt lay Christians to turn their own hearts toward God.

3. The post-exilic community prized the vessels of the Temple, highlighted in 29:18-19. They were heirlooms that could be traced back to the temple builder, Solomon, and even to David (1 Chr 28:13-17; 2 Chronicles 4). In a spiritual sense, we Christians receive the communion cup ultimately from our Lord, who first passed it to his disciples' hands. In validation of our faith we take the morsel of bread broken first by Jesus and by faith hear his voice across the centuries, "Do this in remembrance of me."

4. At first sight, 29:21-24 gives an account of antiquated rites irrelevant to Christians today. On the contrary, however, they provide a necessary background to the thinking of the New Testament. The New Testament depends heavily on the concept of sacrifice in the Old Testament, especially as a way of expressing the meaning of the crucifixion. The problem of sin had not gone away by the first century CE, nor has it vanished in our own day. The early church lived and thought in a period when religious sacrifice was still common, not least in a Jewish context, as a means of dealing with sinfulness. Although such rituals are absent from modern culture, the church's theology—if it is to be a biblical one—cannot dispense with this dynamic concept, whose roots delve deep into the Old Testament. The New Testament's description of the death of Jesus in terms of "blood" takes its readers back to the blood rite described here. The atoning value of the burnt offering is echoed in important New Testament passages, even though the precise term is not used. In Mark 10:45, it partly underlies the explanation that Jesus came "to give his life [as] a ransom for many." The definition of the devoted love of Christ in Eph 5:2 refers to it: He "gave himself up for us [as] a fragrant offering and sacrifice to God" (cf. Lev 1:9). In 1 Pet 1:18-19, Christians are similarly described as "ransomed . . . with the precious blood of Christ, like that of a lamb without defect or blemish" (NRSV; cf. Lev 1:10).

The sense of propitiation implied in 2 Chronicles 29 is matched in the Letter to the Romans. Just as atoning sacrifices were the God-given answer to the divine wrath that loomed over the people, so also "God put forward" Jesus "as a sacrifice of atonement by his blood," as God's own solution to the wrath that threatened humanity (Rom 3:25 NRSV: cf. Rom 1:18; 2:5; 3:5-6; 4:15). Divine wrath coexists with divine love (Rom 5:8-9), just as in 2 Chronicles escaping it was possible because of the Lord's gracious provision of a means of atonement.

As for the purification offering, the writer to the Hebrews was aware of its importance in the Old Testament economy (Heb 9:22). He used its function on the Day of Atonement in Hebrews 9–10 to explain the work of Christ in dying and ascending alive to heaven. Just as the sanctuary was sprinkled with the blood of the purification offering, so also in the earthly counterpart of the heavenly sanctuary, elements have been purified through the sacrificial death of Christ—namely, the bad consciences and sinful hearts of those who have availed themselves of God's provision (Heb 9:14, 23; 10:22; cf. 1 John 1:7, 9).

In 1 Chr 29:23, this appropriation is symbolized by the laying of the offerer's right hand on the sacrificial victim. Such acts of self-identification touch the heart of the Christian gospel as the personal means of turning the bad news of human sinfulness into the good news of divine forgiveness. In 1 John 1:9, the verbal aspect of such appropriation is made explicit: "If we confess our sins, he who is faithful and just will forgive us our sins and cleanse us from all unrighteousness" (NRSV). Significantly, this New Testament promise is related not to the beginning of the Christian life, but to its continuation, as a means of maintaining pre-existing fellowship with God. In this respect, it aligns itself with the perspective of 2 Chronicles.

5. In 29:25-30 the chronicler values greatly following a Davidic blueprint for the use of music and song in worship. No such biblical blueprint is available to the local church. The New Testament principles of proclaiming Christ and worshiping both in spirit and truth, "and decently and in order" (1 Cor 14:40) apply to every Christian gathering, though the more liturgical churches have filled the gap with ancient traditions. The singing of psalms, or at least hymnic paraphrases, has been a healthy tradition, presumably based partly on the authority of Eph 5:19, which could be described as a New Testament counterpart to 2 Chr 29:25-30.

6. Worship in this chapter accents the public burnt offerings. This communal function underlies the reference to the burnt offering as a metaphor for Christian living in Rom 12:1.

Worship was also offered by means of the private offerings of 29:30-35. These offerings comprise a large category of voluntary sacrifices, brought not because they were mandatory but to express personal devotion. Some churches use the phrase "tithes and offerings" for the collection; those offerings correspond to this type of sacrifice. Christians who categorize Old Testament religion as being marked by joyless formality and compulsion must reckon with the offerings and with the enthusiasm of 29:30, 36. Such offerings were the expression of willing hearts, and the chronicler placed a premium on voluntary contributions. The offerings of well-being are invested with a metaphorical interpretation in Heb 13:15-16, as vocal praise, doing good, and sharing one's resources with others: "Such sacrifices are pleasing to God" (NRSV).

2 Chronicles 30:1–31:1, United Passover Worship

NIV

30 Hezekiah sent word to all Israel and Judah and also wrote letters to Ephraim and Manasseh, inviting them to come to the temple of the LORD in Jerusalem and celebrate the Passover to the LORD, the God of Israel. [2]The king and his officials and the whole assembly in Jerusalem decided to celebrate the Passover in the second month. [3]They had not been able to celebrate it at the regular time because not enough priests had consecrated themselves and the people had not assembled in Jerusalem. [4]The plan seemed right both to the king and to the whole assembly. [5]They decided to send a proclamation throughout Israel, from Beersheba to Dan, calling the people to come to Jerusalem and celebrate the Passover to the LORD, the God of Israel. It had not been celebrated in large numbers according to what was written.

[6]At the king's command, couriers went throughout Israel and Judah with letters from the king and from his officials, which read:

> "People of Israel, return to the LORD, the God of Abraham, Isaac and Israel, that he may return to you who are left, who have escaped from the hand of the kings of Assyria. [7]Do not be like your fathers and brothers, who were unfaithful to the LORD, the God of their fathers, so that he made them an object of horror, as you see. [8]Do not be stiff-necked, as your fathers were; submit to the LORD. Come to the sanctuary, which he has consecrated forever. Serve the LORD your God, so that his fierce anger will turn away from you. [9]If you return to the LORD, then your brothers and your children will be shown compassion by their captors and will come back to this land,

NRSV

30 Hezekiah sent word to all Israel and Judah, and wrote letters also to Ephraim and Manasseh, that they should come to the house of the LORD at Jerusalem, to keep the passover to the LORD the God of Israel. [2]For the king and his officials and all the assembly in Jerusalem had taken counsel to keep the passover in the second month [3](for they could not keep it at its proper time because the priests had not sanctified themselves in sufficient number, nor had the people assembled in Jerusalem). [4]The plan seemed right to the king and all the assembly. [5]So they decreed to make a proclamation throughout all Israel, from Beer-sheba to Dan, that the people should come and keep the passover to the LORD the God of Israel, at Jerusalem; for they had not kept it in great numbers as prescribed. [6]So couriers went throughout all Israel and Judah with letters from the king and his officials, as the king had commanded, saying, "O people of Israel, return to the LORD, the God of Abraham, Isaac, and Israel, so that he may turn again to the remnant of you who have escaped from the hand of the kings of Assyria. [7]Do not be like your ancestors and your kindred, who were faithless to the LORD God of their ancestors, so that he made them a desolation, as you see. [8]Do not now be stiff-necked as your ancestors were, but yield yourselves to the LORD and come to his sanctuary, which he has sanctified forever, and serve the LORD your God, so that his fierce anger may turn away from you. [9]For as you return to the LORD, your kindred and your children will find compassion with their captors, and return to this land. For the LORD your

NIV

for the LORD your God is gracious and compassionate. He will not turn his face from you
if you return to him."

[10]The couriers went from town to town in
Ephraim and Manasseh, as far as Zebulun, but the
people scorned and ridiculed them. [11]Neverthe-
less, some men of Asher, Manasseh and Zebulun
humbled themselves and went to Jerusalem.
[12]Also in Judah the hand of God was on the
people to give them unity of mind to carry out
what the king and his officials had ordered, following the word of the LORD.

[13]A very large crowd of people assembled in
Jerusalem to celebrate the Feast of Unleavened
Bread in the second month. [14]They removed the
altars in Jerusalem and cleared away the incense
altars and threw them into the Kidron Valley.

[15]They slaughtered the Passover lamb on the
fourteenth day of the second month. The priests
and the Levites were ashamed and consecrated
themselves and brought burnt offerings to the
temple of the LORD. [16]Then they took up their
regular positions as prescribed in the Law of
Moses the man of God. The priests sprinkled the
blood handed to them by the Levites. [17]Since
many in the crowd had not consecrated themselves, the Levites had to kill the Passover lambs
for all those who were not ceremonially clean and
could not consecrate ⌞their lambs⌟ to the LORD.
[18]Although most of the many people who came
from Ephraim, Manasseh, Issachar and Zebulun
had not purified themselves, yet they ate the
Passover, contrary to what was written. But
Hezekiah prayed for them, saying, "May the LORD,
who is good, pardon everyone [19]who sets his heart
on seeking God—the LORD, the God of his fathers—even if he is not clean according to the
rules of the sanctuary." [20]And the LORD heard
Hezekiah and healed the people.

[21]The Israelites who were present in Jerusalem
celebrated the Feast of Unleavened Bread for
seven days with great rejoicing, while the Levites
and priests sang to the LORD every day, accompanied by the LORD's instruments of praise.[a]

[22]Hezekiah spoke encouragingly to all the
Levites, who showed good understanding of the

[a]21 Or *priests praised the LORD every day with resounding instruments belonging to the LORD*

NRSV

God is gracious and merciful, and will not turn
away his face from you, if you return to him."

10So the couriers went from city to city
through the country of Ephraim and Manasseh,
and as far as Zebulun; but they laughed them to
scorn, and mocked them. [11]Only a few from
Asher, Manasseh, and Zebulun humbled themselves and came to Jerusalem. [12]The hand of God
was also on Judah to give them one heart to do
what the king and the officials commanded by the
word of the LORD.

13Many people came together in Jerusalem to
keep the festival of unleavened bread in the
second month, a very large assembly. [14]They set
to work and removed the altars that were in
Jerusalem, and all the altars for offering incense
they took away and threw into the Wadi Kidron.
[15]They slaughtered the passover lamb on the fourteenth day of the second month. The priests and
the Levites were ashamed, and they sanctified
themselves and brought burnt offerings into the
house of the LORD. [16]They took their accustomed
posts according to the law of Moses the man of
God; the priests dashed the blood that they received[a] from the hands of the Levites. [17]For there
were many in the assembly who had not sanctified themselves; therefore the Levites had to
slaughter the passover lamb for everyone who was
not clean, to make it holy to the LORD. [18]For a
multitude of the people, many of them from
Ephraim, Manasseh, Issachar, and Zebulun, had
not cleansed themselves, yet they ate the passover
otherwise than as prescribed. But Hezekiah
prayed for them, saying, "The good LORD pardon
all [19]who set their hearts to seek God, the LORD
the God of their ancestors, even though not in
accordance with the sanctuary's rules of cleanness." [20]The LORD heard Hezekiah, and healed the
people. [21]The people of Israel who were present
at Jerusalem kept the festival of unleavened bread
seven days with great gladness; and the Levites
and the priests praised the LORD day by day,
accompanied by loud instruments for the LORD.
[22]Hezekiah spoke encouragingly to all the Levites
who showed good skill in the service of the LORD.
So the people ate the food of the festival for seven

[a] Heb lacks *that they received*

NIV

service of the LORD. For the seven days they ate their assigned portion and offered fellowship offerings[a] and praised the LORD, the God of their fathers.

23The whole assembly then agreed to celebrate the festival seven more days; so for another seven days they celebrated joyfully. 24Hezekiah king of Judah provided a thousand bulls and seven thousand sheep and goats for the assembly, and the officials provided them with a thousand bulls and ten thousand sheep and goats. A great number of priests consecrated themselves. 25The entire assembly of Judah rejoiced, along with the priests and Levites and all who had assembled from Israel, including the aliens who had come from Israel and those who lived in Judah. 26There was great joy in Jerusalem, for since the days of Solomon son of David king of Israel there had been nothing like this in Jerusalem. 27The priests and the Levites stood to bless the people, and God heard them, for their prayer reached heaven, his holy dwelling place.

31 When all this had ended, the Israelites who were there went out to the towns of Judah, smashed the sacred stones and cut down the Asherah poles. They destroyed the high places and the altars throughout Judah and Benjamin and in Ephraim and Manasseh. After they had destroyed all of them, the Israelites returned to their own towns and to their own property.

a22 Traditionally *peace offerings*

NRSV

days, sacrificing offerings of well-being and giving thanks to the LORD the God of their ancestors.

23Then the whole assembly agreed together to keep the festival for another seven days; so they kept it for another seven days with gladness. 24For King Hezekiah of Judah gave the assembly a thousand bulls and seven thousand sheep for offerings, and the officials gave the assembly a thousand bulls and ten thousand sheep. The priests sanctified themselves in great numbers. 25The whole assembly of Judah, the priests and the Levites, and the whole assembly that came out of Israel, and the resident aliens who came out of the land of Israel, and the resident aliens who lived in Judah, rejoiced. 26There was great joy in Jerusalem, for since the time of Solomon son of King David of Israel there had been nothing like this in Jerusalem. 27Then the priests and the Levites stood up and blessed the people, and their voice was heard; their prayer came to his holy dwelling in heaven.

31 Now when all this was finished, all Israel who were present went out to the cities of Judah and broke down the pillars, hewed down the sacred poles,[a] and pulled down the high places and the altars throughout all Judah and Benjamin, and in Ephraim and Manasseh, until they had destroyed them all. Then all the people of Israel returned to their cities, all to their individual properties.

a Heb *Asherim*

COMMENTARY

This section provides the second example of Hezekiah's having acted properly in the Lord's sight (29:2). He was intended as a model for the post-exilic community to follow. Already in 29:24 we noticed the chronicler's interest in showing the king's concern for "all Israel." The joint celebration of passover and the Feast of Unleavened Bread provided an opportunity to invite all members of the covenant people to Jerusalem to worship at the Temple. The repentance of the northerners in 28:13 and their overtures to Judah in 28:14-15 had paved the way for such a united venture. The phrase "all Israel" in this comprehensive sense occurs at significant points in the narrative (30:5; 31:1). Unity meant for the chronicler a religious unity, worshiping "the God of Israel" (30:1, 5). He affirmed it over against the exclusivism associated with Ezra and Nehemiah.

This section lays stress not only on a common faith but on a continuity of faith from generation to generation as well. The present generation was to become a living link in the chain of faith. The Lord was the God of their common ancestors, Abraham, Isaac, and Israel (v. 6), and the God of their immediate predecessors (NIV, "fathers," vv. 7, 19, 22; cf. 28:9, 22; 29:6) and now "your

God" (v. 9). The challenge went out to northerners and southerners alike in Hezekiah's day to live up to God's claims and to honor the common roots of their faith by worshiping together. Hezekiah is the chronicler's hero in his refusal to write off the people of the north as apostates, but recognizing them instead as brothers and sisters in the faith who were to be welcomed in God's name.

The chronicler has left 2 Kings far behind, citing it last in 29:1-2 and about to echo it briefly in 31:1, 21. We do not know what sources he had available for these three chapters or to what extent they are simply his own reconstruction. An appeal to the north is historically fitting. The northern kingdom, earlier diminished territorially by the Assyrians, was brought to an end in 721 BCE; its land was incorporated into their provincial system. Hezekiah's naming of his son Manasseh, after the northern tribe, indicates his interest in the citizens of the old northern state halfway through his reign. Moreover, scholars now recognize that the deuteronomists had their own agenda. Religious information about Hezekiah may have been suppressed in order to promote the stock of Josiah, their own hero of the faith. Certainly the chronicler did not take over his account of a combined passover and Festival of Unleavened Bread from Josiah's celebration in 2 Kings 23. The irregularities of its timing and the admission of unclean participants look authentic. Yet the section is so full of expressions and concerns typical of the chronicler that it is difficult to disentangle his own contribution from older elements.[323]

The Pentateuch contains a number of different traditions concerning the passover and whether and in what respects it was linked with the Festival of Unleavened Bread.[324] Although the present account alludes freely to a variety of these traditions, it seems to come closest to the representation in the holiness code of Lev 23:5-8 and the later Num 28:16-25, in which the two are closely associated as sanctuary-based celebrations; the passover is held on the evening of Nisan 14, and the seven-day Festival of Unleavened Bread is held from Nisan 15.

30:1-5. Verse 1 provides a summary of a verbal proclamation accompanied by a letter, while the details are unpacked in vv. 2-9. "Ephraim and Mannasseh" refer to the northern tribes, as in 1 Chr 9:3. The failure to keep the passover in the first month could have been explained simply: It was now too late (cf. 29:17). The chronicler was concerned to relate the issue to the permission granted in Num 9:6-12 for an individual to hold it in the second month on grounds of uncleanness or absence. Numbers 9:6 is quoted in v. 3: "They could not keep the passover on that day" (cf. the REB; the renderings of the NRSV and the NIV are paraphrases that obscure the allusion).[325] Justification is found in the Torah in a provision for an individual, which is here applied more broadly. The grounds of ritual impurity and absence are hermeneutically applied to the priests' failure to purify themselves in adequate numbers, a circumstance borrowed from 29:34, and to the absence of "the people," which here refers not to the representative assembly of 29:36 but to the larger, ideal assembly. Its territorial extent from Beer-sheba to Dan, as in the Davidic narrative at 1 Chr 21:2, reflects the ideal boundaries of the united kingdom, now existing, in principle, under the reign of a Davidic king. The chronicler makes another reference to the Torah (v. 5), now to Deut 16:1-8, where a pilgrimage festival of sacrifice at the central sanctuary is envisioned, rather than the home-based celebration of Exodus 12. Temple worship had to be grounded in the Torah. The nature of the celebration as pilgrimage will be affirmed in v. 13.

30:6-9. The message is presented at the center, an invitation to come to the divinely accredited Temple, echoing the narrative of vv. 1 and 5. The rest of the proclamation alludes to restoration after exile. Accordingly, the chronicler borrows from Zech 1:2-4, an appeal to an early post-exilic constituency to live up to the spiritual ideals of returning to the land by returning to the Lord. Then the Lord would return to them in the fullness of a restoration blessing. The message transcends its explicit audience in the narrative

323. See J. Rosenbaum, "Hezekiah's Reform and the Deuteronomistic Tradition," *HTR* 72 (1979) 23-43; S. L. McKenzie, *The Chronicler's Use of the Deuteronomistic History*, HSM 33 (Atlanta: Scholars Press, 1985) 170-72; R. H. Lowery, *The Reforming Kings: Cults and Society in First Temple Judah*, JSOTSup 120 (Sheffield: JSOT, 1991) 162-67.

324. See the survey in J. R. Shaver, *Torah and the Chronicler's History Work*, BJS 196 (Atlanta: Scholars Press, 1989) 105-9.

325. See M. Fishbane, *Biblical Interpretation in Ancient Israel* (Oxford: Clarendon, 1984) 154-57.

and speaks also to the chronicler's contemporaries, setting out conditions for their enjoying the fulfillment of divine promises. There was a way to escape from a perpetuation of exile, a way outlined in the prophetic text. Not only the Law but also the Prophets provide biblical models for the chronicler to commend to his constituency. The appeals to "return to the LORD . . . that he may return to you" and "Do not be like your fathers" (NIV) are cited from Zech 1:2-4. They are given backing from the Torah by the warning "Do not be stiff-necked," taken from Deut 10:16, which is set in a context of the Lord's renewed grace to Israel after their disobedience.

The proclamation involves a series of appeals backed by incentives and reasons. Although it is addressed to both Judah and the northern tribes, it is angled toward the latter, as the references to Assyrian destruction at the hands of Tiglath-pileser III and Shalmaneser V (see 2 Kgs 15:29; 17:3; 18:9) and exile make clear. Judah, too, is in view: It was described in similar terms in Hezekiah's speech at 29:6, 8-10. The leveling down to the fate of the northern kingdom, implied in chaps. 28–29, now becomes explicit. South and north stood before their God as sinners and as victims of the Lord's fair judgment. They all stood in an exilic situation after unfaithfulness to God. The spirit of 7:14 permeates the speech. The people are virtually called to humble themselves, seek the Lord's face, and turn from their wicked ways, so that God may accept them back. In fact, the chronicler has reserved until now Solomon's petition that the Lord may arrange compassionate treatment for the exiles (1 Kgs 8:50). In the light of 2 Chr 7:14, petition becomes promise, a promise of response to Israel's repentance. Although explicit vocabulary links with 7:14 are scanty, the repeated motif of turning or returning is important. In the narrative of response, however, the reference to self-humbling in v. 11 provides an intratextual echo. The definition of God as "gracious and merciful" is inspired by Exod 34:6, a text from the same narrative setting as Deut 10:16, cited earlier. The definition commemorates forgiveness that was originally extended to those who had broken a brand-new covenant by worshiping the golden calf. Just as the old dispensation of the Torah offered a second chance, so, too, did the new, temple-based dispensation. History repeated itself, bringing new hope to victims of exile in Hezekiah's time and also to their counterparts in the chronicler's age.

30:10-12. The response to Hezekiah's proclamation was mixed. In v. 11, "some men" (NIV) is a superior rendering to "only a few" (NRSV) in describing the northern pilgrims. The religious unity rejected by the north in chap. 13 was again rejected by most, but at least the offer had been made in good faith. The tribal list is only representative, in the light of v. 18. Mention of Zebulun as the tribe farthest north contrasts with Dan (v. 5). The discrepancy may point to use of a historical detail here, though consistency is not the chronicler's strong suit. Judah's unanimous response is sensitively presented, not as a feather in its cap, but as the result of the Lord's gracious nudging. The chronicler, himself a Judean, will not allow his fellow Judeans to take the credit, as if they were doing God a favor. The unanimity is a partial echo of a Davidic phenomenon in 1 Chr 12:38. The "word of the LORD" refers to Zech 1:2-4, which was used in the king's message (cf. 2 Chr 29:15).

30:13-14. The spiritual commitment of the pilgrims to the God of the Temple led to reform in Jerusalem and the destruction of altars built at Ahaz's behest (28:24). Just as the Levites and priests had cleansed the Temple, so also the people purified the city of pagan worship paraphernalia, each group acting in its own sphere.

30:15-20. The chronicler describes the combined festivals of passover and Unleavened Bread. The laity's slaughtering of the passover lambs (v. 15*a*) is followed by a statement that the Levites took over this task (v. 17*b*). What precedes in vv. 15*b*-17*a* parenthetically explains v. 17*b* and should be translated with pluperfect verbs (as in the NJB). Criticism of the religious professionals, confined in 29:34; 30:3 to priests, is now extended to the Levites (cf. 24:5-6). Stung by the laity's enthusiasm, they now prepared for their ritual roles. Opposition to the united festival, and perhaps to Hezekiah's reform, was found not only among the northerners but also at home among the temple staff. Some priests and even Levites stood aloof until their hardness of heart was melted by the devotion of the pilgrims. They duly joined in, after offering their purificatory burnt offerings (cf. 29:21). The reference to the Torah is a general one, as a reference to the prominence of priests in the ritual.[326] The description also demarcates the non-traditional role to be adopted by the Levites in v. 17*b.* Just as penitential pilgrimage gave honor to the prophetic word (v. 12), so also the ritual paid tribute to the Torah. The passover lambs slain in a temple setting were naturally subject to the blood rite. The innovation to which the chronicler draws attention is the Levites' taking over from the laity the rite of slaughtering the sacrificial animals. It is explained in v. 18 as an emergency procedure, like the skinning in 29:34. In chap. 35, such levitical participation will be presented as normative. A subplot runs through these chapters, to give Levites new roles in the sacrificial procedure.

The explanation concerns especially the northern pilgrims as lacking ritual purity and so unable to slaughter their own passover lambs. The Levites stood in for the pilgrims, while the priests cooperated in the arrangements. Yet it was not enough, for the essence of the passover was eating the lamb. In 30:18-19, Hezekiah availed himself of the provision of 7:14, conscious that the provisions about the passover in Numbers 9 had been exhausted. The Torah was not God's last word, though it was the norm, as v. 16 makes clear and the rest of 2 Chronicles overwhelmingly testifies. In the temple dispensation, there was a higher principle of grace, a Solomonic ideal whereby the sanctuary was a house of prayer as well as a place of sacrifice. Moreover, the Lord had shown that spiritual intentions are honored in the blessing that followed David's first attempt to bring the ark to Jerusalem (1 Chronicles 13–14). So Hezekiah prayed, treading in the noble tradition of Solomon, who prayed on the people's behalf in chap. 6. In Hezekiah's prayer that the Lord may "provide atonement" (v. 18 TNK) there is minimal verbal contact with 7:14, but again the ensuing narrative expresses the link, the divine hearing and healing. The golden text was gloriously fulfilled. The verb of healing had to be stretched. The chronicler used it to refer to some objective evidence of the Lord's affirmative answer. Doubtless he extrapolated from Num 9:13 (cf. Lev 15:31) a punishment of being cut off from the people for improper eating (cf. Ezek 14:8-9; Acts 5:5, 10; 1 Cor 11:29-30). He envisioned for them a fate like Uzzah's in 1 Chr 13:10. Instead, the Lord left them unharmed, like the household of Obed-edom in 1 Chr 13:14.[327] It was a divine tribute to the spirituality of the northern pilgrims. The language used to describe an earlier generation of such pilgrims, setting hearts to seek the Lord (2 Chr 11:16), has been reused here.

30:21-22. This is a short description of the weeklong Festival of Unleavened Bread, which concentrates on the private offerings brought by the people rather than on the official sacrifices of Lev 23:8 and Num 28:19-24. The chiastic structure of these verses highlights the link between the people's daily praise and the contribution of levitical music and song and priestly trumpet blasts, which stimulated their praise.[328] Hezekiah congratulated the Levites; their standard of choral and musical excellence was not something to be taken for granted. "Hear, hear!" is the chronicler's implicit comment. The "offerings of well-being" (NRSV) were brought by individuals, as in 29:31, 35. They were tokens of willing worship and expressions of personal thanksgiving.

30:23–31:1. The festivities spilled into a second week. In this paragraph, the theme of the united people of God is prominent once more. The chronicler bids his readers to think of Solomon, who also engaged in two weeks of enthusiastic celebration (v. 26; 7:8-10). So generous were the king and the officials and so ample now the supply of priests identifying themselves with Hezekiah's vision that sacrifices abounded and sacred meals of veal and lamb lasted through the second week. The inclusion of resident aliens or non-Israelite proselytes from north and south echoes their presence at the passover laid down in Num 9:14 (also Exod 12:19, 48-49). In this section, the chronicler has used Numbers 9 both to exemplify obedience to the Torah and to expose its limitations, which further divine revelation had made good. The aliens from the north presumably included the foreigners brought into Israel (the chronicler presupposes and counters 2 Kgs 17:24-41).[329]

326. H. G. M. Williamson, *1 and 2 Chronicles,* NCB (Grand Rapids: Eerdmans, 1982) 369-70.

327. See S. Japhet, *I & II Chronicles,* OTL (Louisville: Westminster/John Knox, 1993) 953.

328. John W. Kleinig, *The Lord's Song: The Basis, Function and Significance of Choral Music in Chronicles,* JSOTSup 156 (Sheffield: JSOT, 1993) 76, 88.

329. See M. Cogan, "For We, Like You, Worship Your God: Three Biblical Portrayals of Samaritan Origins," *VT* 38 (1988) 286-92, esp. 290-91.

The united gathering was dismissed by the "levitical priests" (NJB with the MT, similarly the TNK; the NIV and the NRSV insert "and" with some ancient MSS, but only priests gave the blessing). They offered the priestly benediction of Num 6:24-26 (cf. Lev 9:22; 1 Chr 23:13). It was no magic formula but a prayer, which God duly heard and answered in the agricultural blessing of 31:10 and also in the protection and prosperity of chap. 32. The use of the deuteronomic term "levitical priests" and the linguistic echoes of the divine blessing of Israel in the tithe-related Deut 26:15 at v. 27*b* suggest that the chronicler's mind was already moving on to the deuteronomic topic of the tithe in the next section. The removal of Judean pagan shrines (v. 1) reflects 2 Kgs 18:4 (cf. 2 Kgs 18:22), but enthusiastically extends the reform to northern territory in keeping with the dominant theme of the section. It spelled the last undoing of Ahaz's pernicious work (28:25). The Temple now stood in solitary splendor, unchallenged in its testimony to the Lord as God of a bigger Israel.

REFLECTIONS

This section provides food for thought for translating the truth of a universal church into a practical demonstration of unity among various Christian traditions. Hezekiah used the common origins of now diverse groups (30:6) as the basis for his call to joint celebration of worship and fellowship.

1. The chronicler's account of Ahaz's reign revealed the privations suffered by Judah. So Hezekiah's message in 30:6-10 could appeal to needs shared by north and south, and so to a common yearning for renewal and grace. All the people must humble themselves before the Lord. A call for renewed commitment is likely to be heard by people when it is addressed to a sense of spiritual dissatisfaction. Dietrich Bonhoeffer wrote eloquently about a formal brand of Christianity into which we can all fall. Cheap grace, as he called it, is "the preaching of forgiveness without requiring repentance, baptism without church discipline, Communion without confession. . . . Cheap grace is grace without discipleship, grace without the cross, grace without Jesus Christ living and incarnate."[330]

2. What if the enthusiasm of one group is largely snubbed by another group (30:10)? Pessimists would have forecast such a rejection and deplored the enterprise as a waste of time. But that is no reason not to make the effort, urged the chronicler. The powerful presence of separatist traditions and conventions must not be minimized. Hezekiah reaffirmed as non-negotiable Abijah's claim that the Jerusalem Temple was the true focus of the ancestral faith (13:10-11), claiming that the decisive sign of fellowship with the Lord was to share in worship there. For the north, it meant going against a religious current that had been flowing the other way for centuries. It meant abandoning an entrenched position. Concessions had to be made on Judah's side by lowering temporarily the standards of the Temple and the Torah (30:18-19). The need to build bridges across Christian divisions may press us to surrender what is emotionally dear and challenge us to reexamine cherished convictions.

What if one group's feelings of superiority are well founded? The chronicler refuses to give credit to Judah, but says, "Thanks to God," to divine enabling, which alone brings us where we are in our best moments. The whole section concerning divisions in the local church in 1 Corinthians 3–5 is applicable on a larger scale. It is a sad irony that the mocking of the northern tribes will become Judah's response in 36:16.

3. United worship is excellent, but it cannot stand alone. Changes follow, in areas for which different groups realize themselves to be responsible (30:14; 31:1). Circles of reform gradually widened. Lives that know God's blessing must banish that which is alien to the true

330. Dietrich Bonhoeffer, *The Cost of Discipleship,* 2nd ed., trans. R. H. Fuller (New York: Macmillan, 1959) 36.

God. Further steps of faith grant new insights for bringing our lives more into line with God's will.

4. Irony appears in the reluctance of religious professionals to commit themselves to Hezekiah's efforts at religious integration. Put to shame by lay enthusiasm, they eventually joined in the revival movement. For Christian ecumenism to flourish, it must light its fire in the hearts of all believers and in local churches that go out of their way to bear a common witness to their Lord.

5. When people work together, concessions have to be made to ensure amicable relations. The chronicler shows the lengths he was prepared to go to in the cause of religious reunification, presenting a scene in which the temple rules of purity were waived for northern worshipers. There were times when the Torah had to stay broken in the interests of a higher ideal and God's greater glory. We may welcome this distinction between law and spirit. Or it may leave us murmuring uneasily about compromise, relativism, and situational ethics. May God give us insight as to how and when to apply this risky principle.

The chronicler's teaching on this point is part of a wider paradigm of a divine double standard. On the one hand, believers had a normative relationship with the Lord, governed by responsibilities and expectations determined by the Torah. On the other hand, there were emergency situations when the Torah hindered rather than helped. In such cases, there had to be a redemptive breakthrough if the momentum of spiritual life was to be restored. Here the Lord looked at people's motives and took the spiritual thought for the deed and the repentant spirit for obedience (30:11, 19). This shift cannot be equated with the move from the law to the gospel. The parallel for Christian believers appears in the First Letter of John, in the tension between obeying God's commandments and finding a fresh start in divine forgiveness and renewal (1 John 2:1; 5:2-3) after moral breakdown.

2 Chronicles 31:2-21, Temple Reorganization

NIV

2Hezekiah assigned the priests and Levites to divisions—each of them according to their duties as priests or Levites—to offer burnt offerings and fellowship offerings,[a] to minister, to give thanks and to sing praises at the gates of the LORD's dwelling. 3The king contributed from his own possessions for the morning and evening burnt offerings and for the burnt offerings on the Sabbaths, New Moons and appointed feasts as written in the Law of the LORD. 4He ordered the people living in Jerusalem to give the portion due the priests and Levites so they could devote themselves to the Law of the LORD. 5As soon as the order went out, the Israelites generously gave the firstfruits of their grain, new wine, oil and honey and all that the fields produced. They brought a great amount, a tithe of everything. 6The men of Israel and Judah who lived in the towns of Judah

a2 Traditionally *peace offerings*

NRSV

2Hezekiah appointed the divisions of the priests and of the Levites, division by division, everyone according to his service, the priests and the Levites, for burnt offerings and offerings of well-being, to minister in the gates of the camp of the LORD and to give thanks and praise. 3The contribution of the king from his own possessions was for the burnt offerings: the burnt offerings of morning and evening, and the burnt offerings for the sabbaths, the new moons, and the appointed festivals, as it is written in the law of the LORD. 4He commanded the people who lived in Jerusalem to give the portion due to the priests and the Levites, so that they might devote themselves to the law of the LORD. 5As soon as the word spread, the people of Israel gave in abundance the first fruits of grain, wine, oil, honey, and of all the produce of the field; and they brought in abundantly the tithe of everything. 6The people of

NIV

also brought a tithe of their herds and flocks and a tithe of the holy things dedicated to the LORD their God, and they piled them in heaps. [7]They began doing this in the third month and finished in the seventh month. [8]When Hezekiah and his officials came and saw the heaps, they praised the LORD and blessed his people Israel.

[9]Hezekiah asked the priests and Levites about the heaps; [10]and Azariah the chief priest, from the family of Zadok, answered, "Since the people began to bring their contributions to the temple of the LORD, we have had enough to eat and plenty to spare, because the LORD has blessed his people, and this great amount is left over."

[11]Hezekiah gave orders to prepare storerooms in the temple of the LORD, and this was done. [12]Then they faithfully brought in the contributions, tithes and dedicated gifts. Conaniah, a Levite, was in charge of these things, and his brother Shimei was next in rank. [13]Jehiel, Azaziah, Nahath, Asahel, Jerimoth, Jozabad, Eliel, Ismakiah, Mahath and Benaiah were supervisors under Conaniah and Shimei his brother, by appointment of King Hezekiah and Azariah the official in charge of the temple of God.

[14]Kore son of Imnah the Levite, keeper of the East Gate, was in charge of the freewill offerings given to God, distributing the contributions made to the LORD and also the consecrated gifts. [15]Eden, Miniamin, Jeshua, Shemaiah, Amariah and Shecaniah assisted him faithfully in the towns of the priests, distributing to their fellow priests according to their divisions, old and young alike.

[16]In addition, they distributed to the males three years old or more whose names were in the genealogical records—all who would enter the temple of the LORD to perform the daily duties of their various tasks, according to their responsibilities and their divisions. [17]And they distributed to the priests enrolled by their families in the genealogical records and likewise to the Levites twenty years old or more, according to their responsibilities and their divisions. [18]They included all the little ones, the wives, and the sons and daughters of the whole community listed in these genealogical records. For they were faithful in consecrating themselves.

[19]As for the priests, the descendants of Aaron,

NRSV

Israel and Judah who lived in the cities of Judah also brought in the tithe of cattle and sheep, and the tithe of the dedicated things that had been consecrated to the LORD their God, and laid them in heaps. [7]In the third month they began to pile up the heaps, and finished them in the seventh month. [8]When Hezekiah and the officials came and saw the heaps, they blessed the LORD and his people Israel. [9]Hezekiah questioned the priests and the Levites about the heaps. [10]The chief priest Azariah, who was of the house of Zadok, answered him, "Since they began to bring the contributions into the house of the LORD, we have had enough to eat and have plenty to spare; for the LORD has blessed his people, so that we have this great supply left over."

11Then Hezekiah commanded them to prepare store-chambers in the house of the LORD; and they prepared them. [12]Faithfully they brought in the contributions, the tithes and the dedicated things. The chief officer in charge of them was Conaniah the Levite, with his brother Shimei as second; [13]while Jehiel, Azaziah, Nahath, Asahel, Jerimoth, Jozabad, Eliel, Ismachiah, Mahath, and Benaiah were overseers assisting Conaniah and his brother Shimei, by the appointment of King Hezekiah and of Azariah the chief officer of the house of God. [14]Kore son of Imnah the Levite, keeper of the east gate, was in charge of the freewill offerings to God, to apportion the contribution reserved for the LORD and the most holy offerings. [15]Eden, Miniamin, Jeshua, Shemaiah, Amariah, and Shecaniah were faithfully assisting him in the cities of the priests, to distribute the portions to their kindred, old and young alike, by divisions, [16]except those enrolled by genealogy, males from three years old and upwards, all who entered the house of the LORD as the duty of each day required, for their service according to their offices, by their divisions. [17]The enrollment of the priests was according to their ancestral houses; that of the Levites from twenty years old and upwards was according to their offices, by their divisions. [18]The priests were enrolled with all their little children, their wives, their sons, and their daughters, the whole multitude; for they were faithful in keeping themselves holy. [19]And for the descendants of Aaron, the priests, who were in the fields

NIV	NRSV
who lived on the farm lands around their towns or in any other towns, men were designated by name to distribute portions to every male among them and to all who were recorded in the genealogies of the Levites.	of common land belonging to their towns, town by town, the people designated by name were to distribute portions to every male among the priests and to everyone among the Levites who was enrolled.
20This is what Hezekiah did throughout Judah, doing what was good and right and faithful before the LORD his God. 21In everything that he undertook in the service of God's temple and in obedience to the law and the commands, he sought his God and worked wholeheartedly. And so he prospered.	20Hezekiah did this throughout all Judah; he did what was good and right and faithful before the LORD his God. 21And every work that he undertook in the service of the house of God, and in accordance with the law and the commandments, to seek his God, he did with all his heart; and he prospered.

COMMENTARY

This section is the third and last result of Hezekiah's spiritual activity, introduced in 29:2 and enthusiastically recapitulated in 31:20*b*-21. The theme of this section reverts to Ahaz's closing down of the Temple (28:4), which is envisioned as having been reopened (chap. 29). Still, more remained to be done. Presumably the system of staffing the Temple had collapsed. Hezekiah had to reorganize it, just as Jehoiada had done (23:18-19).

31:2. Hezekiah implemented the system of coordinating personnel and duties, set up by David and administered by Solomon, after the Temple was built (1 Chr 28:21; 2 Chr 8:14; cf. 1 Chr 16:37-42; 23:5). This moment gave the chronicler an opportunity to instruct his own generation, urging them to make the Temple services run like clockwork. This was part of what it meant to "seek" God (v. 21). David's and Solomon's system of sacrifice, security, and singing was the Lord's way for them to follow. Moreover, there is an allusion to an even older heritage. Temple procedure stood in line with gatekeeping duties for the tabernacle. This role had passed to the Temple, so that its precincts in turn became the Lord's "camp" (v. 2 NRSV, which implicitly adopts the order of words in the LXX; cf. 1 Chr 9:18).[331] Moreover, the sacrificial calendar followed the one laid down in the Torah (v. 3; see Numbers 28–29), duly transferred to the Temple by Solomon (8:13). Sanctions regarding the tabernacle constituted a religious mandate "ordained forever for Israel" (2:4). Each generation of the Lord's people was responsible for maintaining these commands. The chronicler is here expanding in a religious direction the information that Hezekiah "kept the commandments that the Lord commanded Moses" (2 Kgs 18:6 NRSV; cf. 2 Chr 31:21).[332]

31:3. The king undertook to provide the regular burnt offerings that made up regular worship practice. It was a costly responsibility, such as Josiah was to assume in the case of passover lambs (35:7). Such support echoes the gifts of sacrificial victims made by Hezekiah and the officials (30:24). There was a precedent in Solomon's special gift of offerings in 7:5, while 8:12-13 implies his responsibility for the regular sacrifices. Presumably the chronicler, writing when the monarchy no longer existed, was arguing that such burdens should be borne by the private resources of the governor and leading officials or by state funds (see Ezra 6:9-10), not, at any rate, by the people (cf. Neh 10:32-33).

31:4-10. The people had their own responsibility: to provide consistent financial support for the temple staff (see Neh 10:35-39). Administrative ramifications will occupy the text up to v. 19. The amount of space the chronicler devoted to this concern reflects the difficulty of maintain-

331. L. C. Allen, *The Greek Chronicles: The Relation of the Septuagint of I and II Chronicles to the Massoretic Text,* Part 2: *Textual Criticism,* VTSup 25, 27 (Leiden: Brill, 1974) 108.

332. J. R. Shaver, *Torah and the Chronicler's History Work,* BJS 196 (Atlanta: Scholars Press, 1989) 91.

ing full staffing in the Temple of the post-exilic period (see Neh 13:10-13; Mal 3:8-10). In the early days, economic stringency was a significant factor (cf. Hag 1:2-11). By the more settled time of the chronicler, it was a question of unwillingness rather than want, as he implied in 1 Chronicles 29. The message of these verses is threefold: that such support was (1) a divine mandate, (2) a human obligation to be discharged with good grace, and (3) a source of divine blessing. The chronicler leaned heavily on the Torah for his terminology, expecting his Torah-versed readers to catch the allusions and hear the solemn call of duty. His prime source was Num 18:8-32, whose phrases, including the verb "bring [in]," are echoed in vv. 5-6, 12.[333] The "portion due to the priests and the Levites" bought them time for Torah-mandated duties by releasing them from the need to work to support themselves and their families (v. 4; cf. Neh 13:10).

The royal command came first to the citizens of Jerusalem. As soon as it went out, there was a generous response from these Israelites, or members of God's people. Then others responded, those of the community of faith living in Judean towns.[334] The responses took the form of offerings of firstfruits and tithes. According to Numbers 18, the former went to priests and the latter to Levites. A tithe of honey is mentioned in Lev 2:11-12, and a tithe of livestock in Lev 27:32. The "holy things" (NIV; NRSV, "dedicated things") refer generally to these donations in v. 6 and in v. 12 (see Num 18:8, "holy gifts/offerings"), while they are called "contributions" in vv. 10, 12-13 (see Num 18:8, 11 REB). These holy things were tithes and were not themselves tithed, as v. 6 seems to imply. The phrase there must mean "and [the rest of] the tithes consisting of holy things." The third and seventh months were key agricultural periods, marking respectively the grain harvest and the grape and other fruit harvest.

The lavishness of the people's response, strategically mentioned in vv. 5 and 10, carries a message of challenge to readers. The copious contributions evoke exclamations of blessing upon God and the people. They refer to two formulas of blessing, "Blessed be the LORD who . . ." (see Ruth 4:14) and "May you be blessed by the LORD for . . ." (see Ruth 2:20). In fact, the Lord had already provided a bumper harvest, so that the people lost nothing by their gifts. The windows of heaven had been opened for them (Mal 3:10)!

31:11-19. Arrangements had to be made for storing the contributions (vv. 11-13) and then for allocating them (vv. 14-19). Two Levites with ten assistants were given charge of the stored items, for which the chronicler in v. 12 loosely piles up three earlier terms. A high-ranking security officer (see Commentary on 1 Chr 26:14, 17) was given the responsibility of distributing the mandated items, "the contributions made to the LORD" (v. 14). These were supplemented, we are now told, with voluntary gifts. The chronicler took the opportunity to mention further priestly dues, "the most holy offerings." He had in view their definition in Num 18:9-10 as food derived from the grain offering, the sin offering, and the guilt offering, which had to be eaten in the sacred precincts. The distribution officer had six assistants, posted in the tribal areas where the priests and Levites lived when not on duty (cf. 1 Chr 6:54-81).

Verses 16-18 define more exactly the regulations for distribution to serving personnel, specifying who was eligible, though the definition is not crystal clear. Registration for receiving food differed for priests and Levites (v. 17 NRSV, REB, NJB; the NIV interprets otherwise, following the punctuation of the MT, which does not fit the context so well). Priests were registered according to their ancestral families. For v. 18, the NRSV appears to be correct in taking priests as the implicit subject. The family members of priests were also eligible to receive food; evidently priests brought their immediate families to Jerusalem. Verse 18*b* may mean that the priests had greater holiness (cf. Lev 21:1-15; Ezek 44:15-31), which isolated them from the rest of society so that they needed their families there for companionship. In the case of Levites, who apparently did not bring their families, only (male) serving staff were registered, according to their particular duties (see 1 Chr 23:4-5).

The limitation at the beginning of v. 16 is best attached to the end of v. 15 as an elaboration of "old and young alike." Verse 16*a* implies that, in the case of off-duty staff, registration was not

333. Fishbane, *Biblical Interpretation*, 214-15.

334. The inclusion of "and Judah" in 32:6 is difficult to construe and may be an addition. See *BHS*.

necessary for the young (see the REB's "irrespective of their registration"). The reason was that all males ages three and over (children were breast-fed up to that age) were automatically eligible for food from the sanctuary. After that a new topic begins, the procedures for serving priests and Levites. The arrangements for off-duty staff resume in v. 19. The assistants mentioned in v. 15 allocated food to every male of the priestly line and to every registered Levite. We may deduce that the beginning of v. 16 applies only to priestly males, as in fact the phrase "the cities/towns of the priests" in v. 15 suggests (cf. 1 Chr 6:54-60). Evidently females within priests' families could not obtain food when the priests were not on duty, while the families of registered Levites were never recipients. In both cases, there was opportunity to provide food by other means.

Overall, vv. 14-19 give the impression of being angled toward priests, with levitical regulations inserted somewhat awkwardly as necessary. This suggests that the chronicler adapted a post-exilic priestly document. All these details, whatever their precise meaning, indicate scrupulous thoroughness and conscientious stewardship. Contributions given in good faith (v. 12) had to be allocated in good faith (v. 15). So rules had to be followed for responsible allocation.

31:20-21. The chronicler loosely followed 2 Kgs 18:6-7*a* in these verses to create a summary of chaps. 29–31. Verse 20*a* summarizes vv. 4-19, and vv. 20*b*-21 enthusiastically develop 29:2 as a sweeping résumé of the intervening material. Hezekiah's devotion to God in matters pertaining to Temple and Torah was exemplary. His ambition was to apply himself to the revealed will of God and to the right worship of God. In seeking the Lord with all his heart, Hezekiah was a king like Jehoshaphat (22:9). The king's ensuing prosperity opens a window to the next section.

Reflections

The theme of chapter 31 is the maintenance of temple worship. Sacrifices did not appear on the altar by themselves, nor could the staff live on air. Human resources and organization were necessary to keep the system going to the glory of God. There is a type of piety that regards efficient methods as carnal. The chronicler adduced Hezekiah's organizational acumen as one fine way in which he was able to seek the Lord, thereby endowing the most mundane of religious tasks with an aura of devotion. The chronicler was encouraged to think this way because he inherited the details of the priestly strata of the Torah. Every church requires efficient administration and coordination, of which the visitor is hardly aware unless they are lacking.

Most of the section 31:2-21 is concerned with funding. The chronicler's portrayal of the king as the donor-patron of the Temple uses a pre-exilic ideal to take some of the burden off the worshiping people. We may compare tax concessions, such as the exemption of church buildings from property taxes and the parsonage allowance for pastors, that apply to churches in the United States (cf. Ezra 7:24).

Yet much of the burden had to fall on the people. Every church or parachurch organization knows the time and energy that must be devoted to fund-raising. A few Christian organizations operate on the lofty principle that "the Lord will provide." Yet the chronicler's axiom is reasonable. Paul expressed it thus: "Those who work in the temple get their food from the temple, and those who serve at the altar share in what is offered on the altar" (1 Cor 9:13 NIV). The apostle deduced from this axiom a corresponding Christian tenet that "those who preach the gospel should receive their living from the gospel" (1 Cor 9:14 NIV; cf. Luke 10:7; 1 Tim 5:18). There need be no embarrassment in soliciting funds for Christian work from the Christian public, nor should it be resented as unspiritual, provided that fitting approaches are used. And, the chronicler would add, there must be scrupulous integrity in the allocation of funds. The gospel has not been advanced by tales of the lavish spending of countless widows' mites.

The chronicler, never slow to provide incentives for his challenges, gives an agricultural blessing (31:10). Paul used a similar argument when he wrote that God is generous to those who were generous to support the poor church in Jerusalem: "God is able to provide you with every blessing in abundance, so that by always having enough of everything you may share abundantly in every good work" (2 Cor 9:8 NRSV; cf. Phil 4:19). Obviously his words are intended not to provide a selfish motivation for giving, but as an assurance that God is nobody's debtor and blesses even the disinterested giver (cf. Luke 6:32-38). Another incentive appears at the end of the chapter: The one who seeks the Lord finds success also (31:21). We may think once more of the spiritual arithmetic of Matt 6:33, "Seek first [the Father's] kingdom . . . and all these things will be given to you as well" (NIV).

2 Chronicles 32:1-33, Deliverance and Blessing

NIV

32 After all that Hezekiah had so faithfully done, Sennacherib king of Assyria came and invaded Judah. He laid siege to the fortified cities, thinking to conquer them for himself. 2When Hezekiah saw that Sennacherib had come and that he intended to make war on Jerusalem, 3he consulted with his officials and military staff about blocking off the water from the springs outside the city, and they helped him. 4A large force of men assembled, and they blocked all the springs and the stream that flowed through the land. "Why should the kings[a] of Assyria come and find plenty of water?" they said. 5Then he worked hard repairing all the broken sections of the wall and building towers on it. He built another wall outside that one and reinforced the supporting terraces[b] of the City of David. He also made large numbers of weapons and shields.

6He appointed military officers over the people and assembled them before him in the square at the city gate and encouraged them with these words: 7"Be strong and courageous. Do not be afraid or discouraged because of the king of Assyria and the vast army with him, for there is a greater power with us than with him. 8With him is only the arm of flesh, but with us is the LORD our God to help us and to fight our battles." And the people gained confidence from what Hezekiah the king of Judah said.

9Later, when Sennacherib king of Assyria and all his forces were laying siege to Lachish, he sent his officers to Jerusalem with this message for Hezekiah king of Judah and for all the people of Judah who were there:

[a]4 Hebrew; Septuagint and Syriac *king* [b]5 Or *the Millo*

NRSV

32 After these things and these acts of faithfulness, King Sennacherib of Assyria came and invaded Judah and encamped against the fortified cities, thinking to win them for himself. 2When Hezekiah saw that Sennacherib had come and intended to fight against Jerusalem, 3he planned with his officers and his warriors to stop the flow of the springs that were outside the city; and they helped him. 4A great many people were gathered, and they stopped all the springs and the wadi that flowed through the land, saying, "Why should the Assyrian kings come and find water in abundance?" 5Hezekiah[a] set to work resolutely and built up the entire wall that was broken down, and raised towers on it,[b] and outside it he built another wall; he also strengthened the Millo in the city of David, and made weapons and shields in abundance. 6He appointed combat commanders over the people, and gathered them together to him in the square at the gate of the city and spoke encouragingly to them, saying, 7"Be strong and of good courage. Do not be afraid or dismayed before the king of Assyria and all the horde that is with him; for there is one greater with us than with him. 8With him is an arm of flesh; but with us is the LORD our God, to help us and to fight our battles." The people were encouraged by the words of King Hezekiah of Judah.

9After this, while King Sennacherib of Assyria was at Lachish with all his forces, he sent his servants to Jerusalem to King Hezekiah of Judah and to all the people of Judah that were in Jerusalem, saying, 10"Thus says King Sennacherib

[a] Heb *He* [b] Vg: Heb *and raised on the towers*

NIV

10"This is what Sennacherib king of Assyria says: On what are you basing your confidence, that you remain in Jerusalem under siege? 11When Hezekiah says, 'The LORD our God will save us from the hand of the king of Assyria,' he is misleading you, to let you die of hunger and thirst. 12Did not Hezekiah himself remove this god's high places and altars, saying to Judah and Jerusalem, 'You must worship before one altar and burn sacrifices on it'?

13"Do you not know what I and my fathers have done to all the peoples of the other lands? Were the gods of those nations ever able to deliver their land from my hand? 14Who of all the gods of these nations that my fathers destroyed has been able to save his people from me? How then can your god deliver you from my hand? 15Now do not let Hezekiah deceive you and mislead you like this. Do not believe him, for no god of any nation or kingdom has been able to deliver his people from my hand or the hand of my fathers. How much less will your god deliver you from my hand!"

16Sennacherib's officers spoke further against the LORD God and against his servant Hezekiah. 17The king also wrote letters insulting the LORD, the God of Israel, and saying this against him: "Just as the gods of the peoples of the other lands did not rescue their people from my hand, so the god of Hezekiah will not rescue his people from my hand." 18Then they called out in Hebrew to the people of Jerusalem who were on the wall, to terrify them and make them afraid in order to capture the city. 19They spoke about the God of Jerusalem as they did about the gods of the other peoples of the world—the work of men's hands.

20King Hezekiah and the prophet Isaiah son of Amoz cried out in prayer to heaven about this. 21And the LORD sent an angel, who annihilated all the fighting men and the leaders and officers in the camp of the Assyrian king. So he withdrew to his own land in disgrace. And when he went into the temple of his god, some of his sons cut him down with the sword.

22So the LORD saved Hezekiah and the people of Jerusalem from the hand of Sennacherib king

NRSV

of Assyria: On what are you relying, that you undergo the siege of Jerusalem? 11Is not Hezekiah misleading you, handing you over to die by famine and by thirst, when he tells you, 'The LORD our God will save us from the hand of the king of Assyria'? 12Was it not this same Hezekiah who took away his high places and his altars and commanded Judah and Jerusalem, saying, 'Before one altar you shall worship, and upon it you shall make your offerings'? 13Do you not know what I and my ancestors have done to all the peoples of other lands? Were the gods of the nations of those lands at all able to save their lands out of my hand? 14Who among all the gods of those nations that my ancestors utterly destroyed was able to save his people from my hand, that your God should be able to save you from my hand? 15Now therefore do not let Hezekiah deceive you or mislead you in this fashion, and do not believe him, for no god of any nation or kingdom has been able to save his people from my hand or from the hand of my ancestors. How much less will your God save you out of my hand!"

16His servants said still more against the Lord GOD and against his servant Hezekiah. 17He also wrote letters to throw contempt on the LORD the God of Israel and to speak against him, saying, "Just as the gods of the nations in other lands did not rescue their people from my hands, so the God of Hezekiah will not rescue his people from my hand." 18They shouted it with a loud voice in the language of Judah to the people of Jerusalem who were on the wall, to frighten and terrify them, in order that they might take the city. 19They spoke of the God of Jerusalem as if he were like the gods of the peoples of the earth, which are the work of human hands.

20Then King Hezekiah and the prophet Isaiah son of Amoz prayed because of this and cried to heaven. 21And the LORD sent an angel who cut off all the mighty warriors and commanders and officers in the camp of the king of Assyria. So he returned in disgrace to his own land. When he came into the house of his god, some of his own sons struck him down there with the sword. 22So the LORD saved Hezekiah and the inhabitants of Jerusalem from the hand of King Sennacherib of Assyria and from the hand of all his enemies; he

NIV

of Assyria and from the hand of all others. He
took care of them[a] on every side. 23Many brought
offerings to Jerusalem for the LORD and valuable
gifts for Hezekiah king of Judah. From then on
he was highly regarded by all the nations.

24In those days Hezekiah became ill and was
at the point of death. He prayed to the LORD, who
answered him and gave him a miraculous sign.
25But Hezekiah's heart was proud and he did not
respond to the kindness shown him; therefore the
LORD's wrath was on him and on Judah and
Jerusalem. 26Then Hezekiah repented of the pride
of his heart, as did the people of Jerusalem;
therefore the LORD's wrath did not come upon
them during the days of Hezekiah.

27Hezekiah had very great riches and honor,
and he made treasuries for his silver and gold and
for his precious stones, spices, shields and all kinds
of valuables. 28He also made buildings to store the
harvest of grain, new wine and oil; and he made
stalls for various kinds of cattle, and pens for the
flocks. 29He built villages and acquired great numbers of flocks and herds, for God had given him
very great riches.

30It was Hezekiah who blocked the upper outlet
of the Gihon spring and channeled the water
down to the west side of the City of David. He
succeeded in everything he undertook. 31But
when envoys were sent by the rulers of Babylon
to ask him about the miraculous sign that had
occurred in the land, God left him to test him
and to know everything that was in his heart.

32The other events of Hezekiah's reign and his
acts of devotion are written in the vision of the
prophet Isaiah son of Amoz in the book of the
kings of Judah and Israel. 33Hezekiah rested with
his fathers and was buried on the hill where the
tombs of David's descendants are. All Judah and
the people of Jerusalem honored him when he
died. And Manasseh his son succeeded him as
king.

[a]22 Hebrew; Septuagint and Vulgate *He gave them rest*

NRSV

gave them rest[a] on every side. 23Many brought
gifts to the LORD in Jerusalem and precious things
to King Hezekiah of Judah, so that he was exalted
in the sight of all nations from that time onward.

24In those days Hezekiah became sick and was
at the point of death. He prayed to the LORD, and
he answered him and gave him a sign. 25But
Hezekiah did not respond according to the benefit
done to him, for his heart was proud. Therefore
wrath came upon him and upon Judah and Jerusalem. 26Then Hezekiah humbled himself for the
pride of his heart, both he and the inhabitants of
Jerusalem, so that the wrath of the LORD did not
come upon them in the days of Hezekiah.

27Hezekiah had very great riches and honor;
and he made for himself treasuries for silver, for
gold, for precious stones, for spices, for shields,
and for all kinds of costly objects; 28storehouses
also for the yield of grain, wine, and oil; and stalls
for all kinds of cattle, and sheepfolds.[b] 29He likewise provided cities for himself, and flocks and
herds in abundance; for God had given him very
great possessions. 30This same Hezekiah closed the
upper outlet of the waters of Gihon and directed
them down to the west side of the city of David.
Hezekiah prospered in all his works. 31So also in
the matter of the envoys of the officials of Babylon, who had been sent to him to inquire about
the sign that had been done in the land, God left
him to himself, in order to test him and to know
all that was in his heart.

32Now the rest of the acts of Hezekiah, and
his good deeds, are written in the vision of the
prophet Isaiah son of Amoz in the Book of the
Kings of Judah and Israel. 33Hezekiah slept with
his ancestors, and they buried him on the ascent
to the tombs of the descendants of David; and all
Judah and the inhabitants of Jerusalem did him
honor at his death. His son Manasseh succeeded
him.

[a] Gk Vg: Heb *guided them* [b] Gk Vg: Heb *flocks for folds*

COMMENTARY

We have seen that, when compared with the writer of 2 Kings, the chronicler gave much more space to temple matters in his account of Hezekiah's reign. Correspondingly, he reduced the amount of material devoted in 2 Kgs 18:13–19:37 to the Assyrian crisis of 701 BCE. Besides 2 Kings, he seems also to have had at his disposal another source concerning his measures taken to defend Jerusalem (vv. 2-6) and his projects (vv. 27-30). The narrative is set within a framework that interprets Hezekiah's success as a direct result of his spirituality. The summary of the latter in 31:21, repeated at the start of chap. 32, introduces the theme of the king's success. Hezekiah is commended as a spiritual model. His spirituality, already demonstrated in his zeal for the Temple, now takes on new dimensions: trust when attacked and repentance. The chronicler's hero is realistically unexempt from threats and scars.

The section covers the king's deliverance (vv. 1-26) and his general success (vv. 27-33), though the latter also breaks into vv. 5-6 and 22*b*-23. Three examples of deliverance at God's hands are given: from Assyrian invasion (vv. 1-22), from deadly sickness (v. 24), and from divine wrath (vv. 25-26; cf. v. 31). Most attention is paid to the first. The 2 Kings account celebrates Hezekiah's reign by highlighting Sennacherib's failure to capture Jerusalem, interpreting it as a tribute to the power of the Lord. The chronicler echoed this interpretation, but wove it into his own literary tapestry of holy war, in which supernatural deliverance comes when committed believers demonstrate fresh trust in God. Again, war comes as a providential surprise, unprovoked by previous sin on the king's part. The Lord's protective presence is itself a blessing bestowed on the good king. The catchword that marked Jehoshaphat's and Asa's God-given victories, the Lord's being "with" each king at a time of unprovoked attack, recurs in v. 8, echoing 15:2 and 20:17 (see also 13:12).

32:1-6a. The chronicler begins with Sennacherib's invasion of Judah in 2 Kgs 18:13, but, in line with his overall perspective, regards the capture of fortified cities as a threat rather than a fact, presumably by interpreting the verbal form differently from the MT (as "in order that he might capture them"). Verses 2-6 have no counterpart in 2 Kings. The topics of v. 5 also appear in Isa 22:8-11, but the blatantly different treatment and lack of intertextual correspondence suggest that the chronicler knew them from another written tradition. Hezekiah's practical measures concerning Jerusalem's water supply (vv. 3-4, 30) give the same impression, while the organization of a conscript army, mentioned obliquely in v. 6, aligns with more specific information supplied for earlier reigns.

The king took defensive measures against a siege. Isaiah condemned such precautions as indications of lack of faith (Isa 22:8-11). The chronicler regularly gave defensive building and conscription a positive significance. Such actions were associated with divine blessing in the cases of Asa and Jehoshaphat (14:6-8; 17:12-19). In each instance, such measures were not used in the ensuing war. The divine and human help (vv. 3 and 8) echoes a Davidic pattern in 1 Chronicles 11–12. The first measure was control of the water supply. It was a separate procedure from the construction of the Siloam tunnel (v. 30), an extensive enterprise that must have occurred earlier. The water supply from the Gihon Spring had been channeled into outlets to irrigate the cultivated terraces on the western slope of the Kidron Valley, which then produced a runoff stream at the bottom of the valley. These outlets were now blocked off to prevent Assyrian access to the water.[335] A second measure was the improvement of Jerusalem's fortifications ("and raised towers on it," NRSV, similarly NIV; this rendering involves a slight change; see *BHS*). The other wall built by Hezekiah is probably that of which a portion was found in 1969–71. It enclosed part of the western hill of Jerusalem, which had become populated.[336] The third measure was the organization and arming of a defensive force.

32:6b-8. It was the chronicler's practice to preface a battle report with a speech or prayer or

335. J. Simons, *Jerusalem in the OT* (Leiden; Brill, 1952) 177.

336. See N. Avigad, "Excavations in the Jewish Quarter of the Old City 1968-1974," in *Jerusalem Revealed: Archaeology in the Holy City 1968–1974,*" ed. Y. Yadin (Jerusalem: Israel Exploration Society, 1975) 41-51, esp. 43-44.

both in which trust in the Lord was affirmed in reaction to the military crisis. The speech in vv. 7-8, perhaps set in the square (mentioned in 29:4), takes the form of an encouragement for a task, here adapted to a pre-battle speech.[337] It has the standard elements of a call for courage and an assurance of the divine presence, but it does so as a vehicle for expressing trust in the Lord's power to save. Such trust could put natural fears to flight and impart strength to face opposition unflinchingly. The motif of the divine presence in a military context was borrowed from 2 Kgs 18:7*a,* already echoed more generally in 31:21. The belittling phrase "arm of flesh" reflects biblical language (e.g., Isa 31:3; Jer 17:5), while v. 7*b* recalls such texts as 2 Kgs 6:16 and Isa 7:14.

32:9-15. The shift from v. 8 to v. 9 brings to the fore a contrast that runs throughout vv. 1-22, that between the God-honoring believer and the blasphemous infidel. The counterpointing is accentuated by the parallel titles "King Hezekiah of Judah" and "King Sennacherib of Assyria." To be for or against the Lord is the basic issue for the chronicler. The shocking nature of Sennacherib's blasphemies, underlined in v. 19, is an implicit call to faith, intended to put Judean readers on their mettle and to transform nominal faith into keenness. The core of Israel's faith was under attack.

As v. 16 hints, the chronicler selectively condensed the composite account of 2 Kgs 18:13–19:37 into a single narrative to express a barrage of threats via an oral message (vv. 9-16), a letter (v. 17), and intimidating shouts (v. 18). He omitted and adapted material that did not fit his holy war perspective. Already the calm, resolute believer of vv. 7-8 looks different from the desperate figure of 2 Kgs 19:1-4. Jehoshaphat was allowed his fear in 2 Chr 20:3, 12, but Hezekiah was not, though he will be presented as more human in vv. 25-26. The very form of the speech made the transformation inevitable.

Hezekiah's speech deactivates the verbal warheads launched by Sennacherib, reducing them to fireworks. The Assyrian king was only accumulating providential grounds for his eventual disgrace and premature death (v. 21). Although the chronicler imagines the worst, going beyond 2 Kings in representing Jerusalem as already under siege (v. 10), Sennacherib turned out to be a paper tiger. His speech follows the Chronicles pattern of introductory arguments (vv. 10-14) and a main challenge prefaced by "And now" (v. 15). The arguments consist of a series of sneering questions. As in the 2 Kings presentation, there is a shift in Sennacherib's denials from the divine will to save to the power to do so. The speech amalgamates Rabshakeh's first speech in 2 Kgs 18:19-25 (vv. 10, 12) with his second speech in 2 Kgs 18:28-35 (vv. 11, 13-14) and anticipates Sennacherib's letter in 2 Kgs 19:10-13 (v. 13; "predecessors" would be a better rendering than the NRSV's "ancestors" in vv. 13-15). References to Judah's alliance with Egypt in 2 Kgs 18:21, 24*b* are understandably filtered out. So, too, are the now unnecessary warnings to Hezekiah about trusting in his own strength in 2 Kgs 18:20, 23, 24*a.*

32:16-19. If Sennacherib was counterpointed with Hezekiah in vv. 8-9, he is the arrogant rival of the Lord in v. 16, where his "servants" match God's "servant Hezekiah." The chronicler expresses the same royal ideology as that found in Psalm 2, where the kings of the earth "set themselves . . . against the LORD and his anointed" (Ps 2:2 NRSV). Here, too, the Lord is the unseen power behind the Judean throne, guaranteeing the eventual triumph of king and people and the downfall of their blasphemous foes. The mention of "the gods of the nations" (v. 17) focuses on 2 Kgs 19:12 and develops it into a plain statement of denial. Its "insulting" nature is derived from Hezekiah's reaction in 2 Kgs 19:16 (חרף *ḥērēp,* in the piel; NRSV, "mock"; NIV, "insult"; cf. 2 Kgs 19:4, 22-23). The intimidating shouts of v. 18 come from 2 Kgs 18:26, 28, transposed in order to form a climactic conclusion. The chronicler has the last word in v. 19, derived from Hezekiah's prayer in 2 Kgs 19:18. If in v. 16 he echoed a royal tradition, in referring to "the God of Jerusalem" he draws on Zion ideology, in which it is celebrated as God's own city (see Psalms 46; 48; 87). Such thinking would be dealt a cruel blow in 36:19 (cf. Lam 4:12), but it could spring to new life in post-exilic times. Jerusalem was an essential ingredient in the chronicler's restoration hope (cf. 6:6; 12:13; 1 Chr 9:3, 34; 11:4-9).

32:20-23. The prayers of trust (v. 20) echo 2

337. R. A. Mason, *Preaching the Tradition: Homily and Hermeneutics After the Exile* (Cambridge: Cambridge University Press, 1990) 110.

Kgs 19:4, 15, 30. They are the human factor that tipped the scales from defeat to deliverance. Jehoshaphat had said about prayer to a powerful God at a time of crisis: "You will hear and save" (20:9; cf. 13:15; 14:11; 18:31). The Lord did save (v. 22). The verb הציל (*hiṣṣîl*, in the hiphil, "rescue"), variously rendered in the NRSV and the NIV, has run negatively through vv. 11-17, but now a synonym celebrates its positive truth. Deliverance takes two appropriate forms, abbreviated from 2 Kgs 19:35-37: the supernatural defeat of Sennacherib's forces and the ironic failure of a pagan god to protect his devotee from providential punishment. The menacing "hand" so blatantly brandished in Sennacherib's speech was rendered powerless.

The chronicler used the event as an example of numerous victories (cf. 2 Kgs 18:7-8). He deduced that, like Jehoshaphat in 20:30, Hezekiah entered into the Solomonic heritage of divinely given "rest" (NRSV, following the LXX, the Old Latin, and the Vulgate; the MT's "guided" in the sense of "took care" [so NIV; cf. Gen 47:17] is contextually less likely).[338] Another of his blessings, he infers, was the international prestige like that which Solomon (9:23-24) and Jehoshaphat (17:10-11) had enjoyed. The indemnity Hezekiah paid to Assyria in 2 Kgs 18:14-16 finds no place in the chronicler's idealistic narrative. He had a bigger agenda to promote, one with eschatological implications. Solomon's golden age had represented for him one end of a rainbow, while its other end rested out of sight in a coming age. In the same way, Hezekiah's glory was a sign pointing to eschatological splendor. Sacred traditions pertaining to the dynasty and to Zion found anticipatory fulfillment in his reign (see Pss 72:10; 76:11).

32:24-26. If deliverance from Sennacherib was the chronicler's main example of deliverance, he now offers instances in other areas. Hezekiah is now brought down to earth as a fallible mortal. The chronicler assumes that his readers know the account of the king's sickness and the visit of envoys from Babylon (2 Kgs 20:1-9). At death's door, Hezekiah once more offers a trusting prayer, which the Lord not only answers but confirms with a miraculous sign. In spite of this favor, the king ostentatiously displays all his wealth to the envoys. In the 2 Kings narrative, Isaiah had judged this a reprehensible act. It is characterized here as an exhibition of pride that left God out of account. The sin of Amaziah and Uzziah all over again (25:19; 26:16), it could have led to terrible punishment such as those kings had incurred. Instead, Hezekiah resorted to the Solomonic principle of 7:14, not for others (as in 30:18-20) but for himself. The chronicler regarded the royal submission of 2 Kgs 20:19*a* as an example of the self-humbling required by the gracious provision of 7:14. So the king avoided the divine wrath expressed in Isaiah's oracles of judgment in 2 Kgs 20:16-18, which would have overwhelmed the palace and implicitly the capital and the country.

God's grace opened a new chapter of life for Hezekiah and his people. The threat of exile was averted. The chronicler used the story to hold out to his contemporaries the divinely authored way out of the metaphorical exile that loomed over them as a manifestation of God's wrath. He gave it a communal slant in vv. 25*b*-26. Each generation had to decide for or against the Lord, and its fate was decided accordingly. A later generation would sin and face exile as an expression of wrath (36:16, 20), but this one was spared, according to 2 Kgs 20:19*b*.

32:27-31. The chronicler recounts Hezekiah's blesings. Verse 27 elaborates 2 Kgs 20:13. His possessions are recognized as God's gifts (v. 29*b*), unlike his own denial of stewardship (v. 25). Verses 28-29*a* and 30*a* probably depend on an independent source. Evidence of his storage cities has survived, directly or indirectly, in the royal seal impressions on jars dating from his reign.[339] The description of the Siloam tunnel is too detailed to depend on 2 Kgs 20:20. The chronicler concluded by recapitulating the theme of the section, which is that Hezekiah experienced the success that follows spirituality. The chronicler could not resist adding "even in the affair of the envoys" (REB), assuming that the Babylonians came as astronomical experts to investigate the sun-related sign of v. 24. It was a different kind of success, however—a victory over himself. The

338. See D. Barthélemy et al., *Critique textuelle de l'Ancien Testament,* OBO 50/1 (Fribourg: Editions Universitaires; and Göttingen: Vandenhoeck & Ruprecht, 1982) 1:511.

339. See Y. Aharoni, *The Land of the Bible: A Historical Geography,* trans. A. F. Rainey, 2nd rev. ed. (Philadelphia: Westminster, 1979) 394-400.

king's relations with the Lord reached a critical point. God had to confront him with wrath and forsake him (cf. 15:2). In the end, his "heart" was loyal, as was demonstrated by his return to the Lord's way of thinking. He had passed the test. The notion of testing recalls Deut 8:2, but there it was to determine whether Israel would obey the Torah, whereas here it relates to response to the divine provision of 7:14. The chronicler drew renewed attention to this incident, inviting his readers to ponder it.

32:32-33. The standard conclusion to the reign was inspired by 2 Kgs 20:20-21. There is a focus on the king's "acts of devotion," doubtless with 2 Kgs 18:3-6 in mind. Isaiah's vision refers to 2 Kings 19–20, in which the prophet played a key role and issued oracles. The chronicler treats the funeral report as an obituary by adding references to a special burial place and the honor his people paid him (cf. 16:14; 21:19-20). He commended Hezekiah as a positive role model so that his readers would honor this king in turn by emulating his acts of devotion.

REFLECTIONS

1. The chronicler was a good student of human nature in refusing to let virtue be its own reward but ever dangling incentives before his readers. He also recognized the mystery of life and admitted that disaster strikes even the virtuous, here in the forms of invasion and sickness (cf. 2 Kgs 20:3). He devoted more space to the blessing of deliverance from such random ills than to the blessing of material prosperity. The virtuous could overcome such disasters. The secret was trust in the Lord. The Assyrian invasion was another opportunity to preach this message, highlighted in the affirmation of faith in 32:7-8. If it left no room for the human fear found in the basic narrative, at least Hezekiah comes over as an encourager in 32:6*b*, 8*b*. Leaders had to rise above the crisis and direct God's people to God's "grace to help in time of need" (Heb 4:16 NRSV).

The chronicler may irritate us by reducing complex issues to simplistic and seemingly unrealistic terms. Isaiah has the same effect on us. In fact, so do any number of biblical writers. They want us to take the simple message more seriously. We are invited to look beyond the crisis and its array of factors that fill us with justifiable fear. The testimony that God saves believers from existential crisis is reiterated in the New Testament at 2 Cor 1:8-10; 2 Tim 4:17-18; and 2 Pet 2:7-9.

2. Hezekiah's deliverance from a potentially fatal illness is the next blessing. James would have approved: "The prayer of faith will save the sick. . . . The prayer of the righteous is powerful and effective" (Jas 5:15-16 NRSV). Such miraculous healing does not always happen—or saints would never die—but at least we are encouraged to pray and leave the result to God in faith (see 2 Cor 12:7-10). It is ironic, then, that this seeming supersaint responded to his deliverance from fatal illness by falling into pride. The king received a warning about this fall from favor. The fuller narrative in 2 Kings shows that the chronicler had in mind the gracious role of the prophet as the bearer of divine wrath, which had the goal of turning the backslider from erring ways (cf. 36:15-16).

3. One could forsake—and so be forsaken by—God not only by breaking the Torah or adopting another religion but also by simply putting oneself in God's place as the provider of all one's assets. It is the sin of Deut 8:17: "My power and the might of my own hand have gotten me this wealth" (NRSV). The chronicler noticed the five third-person and two first-person pronouns relating to Hezekiah's pride of ownership in 2 Kgs 20:13, 15 and exegeted accordingly. He interpreted the aftermath in terms of a key element in his own message, the divine provision in 7:14, and was sufficiently impressed by the incident to remind his readers about it in 32:31. True believers are not those who never sin, "for there is no one who does

not sin" (6:36), in the sense of falling into grave sin that upsets the even tenor of spiritual life. No, the true believer is the person who repents sincerely. Drawing on divine grace, one may continue along the spiritual path, chastened but not devastated by the experience. To "walk in the light" includes bringing into God's light willful mistakes one makes and finding forgiveness and new confidence to carry on (1 John 1:7–2:2). Such is God's provision—and from another perspective God's test as to whether we appropriate it. "With the testing he will also provide the way out" (1 Cor 10:13 NRSV)—whether we take the way out is up to us.

2 CHRONICLES 33:1–35:27, DROSS INTO GOLD

OVERVIEW

Like chaps. 21–23 and 24–26, this unit features three kings. In 33:1-20, Manasseh is portrayed as a renegade who makes good. The chronicler then parallels his apostasy and reformation with the next two reigns. In 33:21-25, Amon is a carbon copy of Manasseh in his pre-reformation period, while Josiah's reign in chaps. 34–35 reflects the later, better part of his grandfather's life. The two phases of Manasseh's reign, degenerate and regenerate, are paired with Amon's negative reign and Josiah's positive one.

The negative parallels are threefold, the first two of which were taken from 2 Kings 21. Manasseh did evil in the Lord's sight, and Amon copied him (33:2 = 2 Kgs 21:2; 33:22 = 2 Kgs 21:20). Manasseh "worshiped all the host of heaven and served them," and Amon "served" his father's gods (33:3 = 2 Kgs 21:3; 33:23 = 2 Kgs 21:21). The chronicler reinforced this parallelism with his own third case: Manasseh set up "images," and in turn Amon "sacrificed to all the images that his father Manasseh had made" (33:19, 22 NRSV). The positive parallels the chronicler drew between the redeemed Manasseh and Josiah are also threefold. First, he found a precedent for Josiah's self-humbling at 34:27, based on 2 Kgs 22:19, in Manasseh's own submission in 33:12, 19, 23; in the last case, he differentiated it from Amon's negative attitude. Second, he provided a parallel for the Lord's hearing Josiah's repentant prayer at 34:27 (= 2 Kgs 22:19) in Manasseh's experience at 33:13. In both cases, features of Josiah's reign were transferred to Manasseh's by way of anticipation. Third, he credited both Manasseh and Josiah with having established true worship and for commending it to the people (33:16; 34:33; 35:16). Josiah's reign reinforces the lessons of Manasseh's regenerate phase.

The chronicler found in these three kings two paradigms of the way back to the Lord from apostasy via repentance. Once more he seems to have had in view the range of vignettes in Ezekiel 18. Manasseh lived out the instructions in Ezek 18:21-23, a trophy to the grace of a God who forgives repentant sinners, forgets their past, and inspires a new integrity. Amon is the sinner who never detached himself from his sins, like the person in Ezek 18:10-13. Josiah's reversal of Amon's evil reign captures in story form Ezek 18:14-18, the case of the son who rises above an evil family background. His unexpected relapse brings him closer to the character of Ezek 18:24.

2 Chronicles 33:1-20, Manasseh, a Model of Repentance

NIV

33 Manasseh was twelve years old when he became king, and he reigned in Jerusalem fifty-five years. 2He did evil in the eyes of the LORD, following the detestable practices of the nations the LORD had driven out before the Israelites. 3He rebuilt the high places his father Hezekiah had demolished; he also erected altars to the Baals and made Asherah poles. He bowed down to all the starry hosts and worshiped them. 4He built altars in the temple of the LORD, of which the LORD had said, "My Name will remain in Jerusalem forever." 5In both courts of the temple of the LORD, he built altars to all the starry hosts. 6He sacrificed his sons in[a] the fire in the Valley of Ben Hinnom, practiced sorcery, divination and witchcraft, and consulted mediums and spiritists. He did much evil in the eyes of the LORD, provoking him to anger.

7He took the carved image he had made and put it in God's temple, of which God had said to David and to his son Solomon, "In this temple and in Jerusalem, which I have chosen out of all the tribes of Israel, I will put my Name forever. 8I will not again make the feet of the Israelites leave the land I assigned to your forefathers, if only they will be careful to do everything I commanded them concerning all the laws, decrees and ordinances given through Moses." 9But Manasseh led Judah and the people of Jerusalem astray, so that they did more evil than the nations the LORD had destroyed before the Israelites.

10The LORD spoke to Manasseh and his people, but they paid no attention. 11So the LORD brought against them the army commanders of the king of Assyria, who took Manasseh prisoner, put a hook in his nose, bound him with bronze shackles and took him to Babylon. 12In his distress he sought the favor of the LORD his God and humbled himself greatly before the God of his fathers. 13And when he prayed to him, the LORD was moved by his entreaty and listened to his plea; so he brought him back to Jerusalem and to his kingdom. Then Manasseh knew that the LORD is God.

[a]6 Or *He made his sons pass through*

NRSV

33 Manasseh was twelve years old when he began to reign; he reigned fifty-five years in Jerusalem. 2He did what was evil in the sight of the LORD, according to the abominable practices of the nations whom the LORD drove out before the people of Israel. 3For he rebuilt the high places that his father Hezekiah had pulled down, and erected altars to the Baals, made sacred poles,[a] worshiped all the host of heaven, and served them. 4He built altars in the house of the LORD, of which the LORD had said, "In Jerusalem shall my name be forever." 5He built altars for all the host of heaven in the two courts of the house of the LORD. 6He made his son pass through fire in the valley of the son of Hinnom, practiced soothsaying and augury and sorcery, and dealt with mediums and with wizards. He did much evil in the sight of the LORD, provoking him to anger. 7The carved image of the idol that he had made he set in the house of God, of which God said to David and to his son Solomon, "In this house, and in Jerusalem, which I have chosen out of all the tribes of Israel, I will put my name forever; 8I will never again remove the feet of Israel from the land that I appointed for your ancestors, if only they will be careful to do all that I have commanded them, all the law, the statutes, and the ordinances given through Moses." 9Manasseh misled Judah and the inhabitants of Jerusalem, so that they did more evil than the nations whom the LORD had destroyed before the people of Israel.

10The LORD spoke to Manasseh and to his people, but they gave no heed. 11Therefore the LORD brought against them the commanders of the army of the king of Assyria, who took Manasseh captive in manacles, bound him with fetters, and brought him to Babylon. 12While he was in distress he entreated the favor of the LORD his God and humbled himself greatly before the God of his ancestors. 13He prayed to him, and God received his entreaty, heard his plea, and restored him again to Jerusalem and to his kingdom. Then Manasseh knew that the LORD indeed was God.

[a] Heb *Asheroth*

NIV

14Afterward he rebuilt the outer wall of the City of David, west of the Gihon spring in the valley, as far as the entrance of the Fish Gate and encircling the hill of Ophel; he also made it much higher. He stationed military commanders in all the fortified cities in Judah.

15He got rid of the foreign gods and removed the image from the temple of the LORD, as well as all the altars he had built on the temple hill and in Jerusalem; and he threw them out of the city. 16Then he restored the altar of the LORD and sacrificed fellowship offerings[a] and thank offerings on it, and told Judah to serve the LORD, the God of Israel. 17The people, however, continued to sacrifice at the high places, but only to the LORD their God.

18The other events of Manasseh's reign, including his prayer to his God and the words the seers spoke to him in the name of the LORD, the God of Israel, are written in the annals of the kings of Israel.[b] 19His prayer and how God was moved by his entreaty, as well as all his sins and unfaithfulness, and the sites where he built high places and set up Asherah poles and idols before he humbled himself—all are written in the records of the seers.[c] 20Manasseh rested with his fathers and was buried in his palace. And Amon his son succeeded him as king.

[a] *16* Traditionally *peace offerings* [b] *18* That is, Judah, as frequently in 2 Chronicles [c] *19* One Hebrew manuscript and Septuagint; most Hebrew manuscripts *of Hozai*

NRSV

14Afterward he built an outer wall for the city of David west of Gihon, in the valley, reaching the entrance at the Fish Gate; he carried it around Ophel, and raised it to a very great height. He also put commanders of the army in all the fortified cities in Judah. 15He took away the foreign gods and the idol from the house of the LORD, and all the altars that he had built on the mountain of the house of the LORD and in Jerusalem, and he threw them out of the city. 16He also restored the altar of the LORD and offered on it sacrifices of well-being and of thanksgiving; and he commanded Judah to serve the LORD the God of Israel. 17The people, however, still sacrificed at the high places, but only to the LORD their God.

18Now the rest of the acts of Manasseh, his prayer to his God, and the words of the seers who spoke to him in the name of the LORD God of Israel, these are in the Annals of the Kings of Israel. 19His prayer, and how God received his entreaty, all his sin and his faithlessness, the sites on which he built high places and set up the sacred poles[a] and the images, before he humbled himself, these are written in the records of the seers.[b] 20So Manasseh slept with his ancestors, and they buried him in his house. His son Amon succeeded him.

[a] Heb *Asherim* [b] One Ms Gk: MT *of Hozai*

COMMENTARY

In 2 Kings 21, Manasseh is an unmitigated villain, the king at whose doorstep liability for Judah's exile is laid (cf. Jer 15:4). The chronicler put Zedekiah in the dastardly role of Judas-like betrayer, true to his tenet that each generation was master of its own fate. Instead, Manasseh became a counterpart to Simon Peter, restored through repentance. It is reasonable to assume that the king's long reign influenced the chronicler, who took it as divine blessing for obedience. It is difficult to imagine, however, that this was the sole justification for the crucial episode in vv. 11 and 13, though we may only surmise how the otherwise unknown incident might fit into Assyrian history, in which Manasseh had the role of a vassal king.[340] There was political unrest in much of the western sector of the empire at a certain point, and the otherwise loyal Manasseh could have been caught up in it. If that was the case, Ashurbanipal's attested leniency toward defiant vassals makes Manasseh's restoration to his throne credible. However, we do not know whether or to what extent the chronicler was

340. See H. G. M. Williamson, *1 and 2 Chronicles,* NCB (Grand Rapids: Eerdmans, 1982) 391-93; S. Japhet, *I & II Chronicles,* OTL (Louisville: Westminster/John Knox, 1993) 1002-4, 1009.

extrapolating from Isaiah's forecast in 2 Kgs 20:18 that Hezekiah's sons would end up in Babylon. He did sometimes hold material over, for instance reserving 1 Kgs 8:50 until 2 Chr 30:9. But the 2 Kings reference does not account for the king's return or for his having built the city walls, specifically described in vv. 13-14. Whatever the political background, the spiritual significance of Manasseh's adventure was what mattered for the chronicler. He saw in the incident a pattern of exile and return and in Manasseh's reign generally an outworking of the temple theology broached in chap. 7.

The section is artistically structured with a chiastic framework. Between the royal prologue and epilogue in vv. 1 and 18-20 are set narratives of apostasy and reformation in vv. 2-9 and 14-17, which have as their pivot Manasseh's change of heart in vv. 10-13.[341]

33:1-9. This passage is taken over practically verbatim from 2 Kgs 21:1-9, an impassioned piece of writing that was well worth repeating. The double declaration of the flouting of the Lord's express will (vv. 4, 7-8) is enveloped in a refrain of Manasseh's wrongdoing, escalating from "evil" to "much evil" to "more evil" than what the destroyed Canaanites perpetrated (vv. 2, 6, 9). Whereas the formula of v. 2*a* refers in the parent text to the whole reign, here it is limited in duration. The chronicler seems to have divided the paragraph into vv. 2-3, vv. 4-6, and vv. 7-9, applying the evil of v. 2*a* to pagan worship at the high places in vv. 2*b*-3 and summarizing the offenses in the environs of the temple building in vv. 4-6*a* as "much evil" in v. 6*b*, and the temple sin of v. 7*a* as egregiously evil in v. 9. In the light of v. 19, v. 3 refers wholly to the high places, which explains the plural versions of the singular "Baal" and "sacred pole" at 2 Kgs 21:3 (NRSV).[342] Manasseh's child sacrifice in v. 6 is brought into line with that of Ahaz in 28:3 by specification of the place and by the plural "sons" (NIV; the NRSV unaccountably has a singular).

Mention of the Lord's will concerning the Temple (vv. 4, 7-8) reminds the chronicler of God's revelation to Solomon in chap. 7, which represented for him the theological basis of the era in which he and his contemporaries lived. The deuteronomist's "In Jerusalem I will put my name" (2 Kgs 21:4) becomes the chronicler's "In Jerusalem shall my name be forever" (v. 4) to align with the divine statement of 7:16. "Forever" recurs in v. 7, affirming the permanence of the temple age. Chapter 7 went on to speak of human behavior that could interfere with the promise—namely, abandoning the Torah and exclusive worship of the Lord. Manasseh became guilty of those very sins. Verse 6*a* evokes a directive in Deut 18:10-11 in the reference to "sorcery" or "witchcraft." Moreover, the reference to the Torah in v. 8 has been expanded. The NIV captures the flagrancy of Manasseh's apostasy (v. 7), taken from the basic text: Manasseh "put" the image of the idol in the very sanctuary where the Lord had "put" the divine name, as if to assert, "Not thy will but mine be done."

The king had fallen into the traps of 7:19 and shown himself at odds with the Lord's Temple-centered revelation. The fate prescribed in 7:20 was exile from the land, to which v. 8 also refers. Verse 2 had already let us hear the rumbling of this volcano in its flashback to the dispossessed nations, warning that the king was even then walking a road that led to exile. By v. 9, he has qualified for a further flashback to the destruction of those nations. Now his subjects had fallen under his pernicious spell: Loss of life would be fitting reprisal for the way the king and the people had spurned their religious heritage.

33:10-13. This core part of the section relates Manasseh's roundabout return to the Lord. At first matters got worse, with the Lord setting punishment in motion after divine warnings went unheeded. Verse 10*a* encapsulates the prophetic revelation of 2 Kgs 21:10-15, while v. 10*b* relocates 2 Kgs 21:9*a*, "But they did not listen" (NRSV), retaining the plural reference of v. 9. The chronicler now leaves the 2 Kings account until vv. 18 and 20, staying under the influence of 2 Chronicles 7. The oracle of 2 Kgs 21:10-15 sealed the nation's fate by predicting national calamity. The chronicler has a different perspective, inspired by his understanding of prophecy as meant to bring the people back to the Lord (see 24:19; 36:15) and so as a warning to the people to turn from their wicked ways, which is consistent with 7:14. Here, as in 24:19, this second chance was

341. See K. A. D. Smelik's more complex structuring in *Converting the Past, OTS* 28 (Leiden: Brill, 1992) 169-74.

342. E. L. Curtis and A. A. Madsen, *The Books of Chronicles,* ICC (Edinburgh: T. &. T. Clark, 1910) 495.

rejected. The Assyrian invaders whom the Lord "brought upon them" (KJV) were marching in step with the negative part of chap. 7: "He has brought all this calamity upon them" (7:22 NRSV). The punishment actually fell on Manasseh, presumably to comply with the source followed by the chronicler. The king functions theologically as the representative victim of providential punishment. The specification of Babylon, at a time when Nineveh was the Assyrian capital, may reflect a summons in 648 BCE, after the emperor suppressed in Babylon the rebellion of his brother, who had also fomented unrest in the western provinces.

For the chronicler, the "exile" of Manasseh was an anticipation of Judah's own exile in Babylon. Return from exile was envisioned in Solomon's prayer in the scenario of 6:24-25, after prayer offered by penitents still in the land, and implicitly in 6:36-39, where the exiles themselves repent. Those scenarios were affirmed by the divine promise of 7:14. The promise finds verbal echoes in Manasseh's humbling himself and praying to the Lord for help. The king is represented as a textbook case of fulfillment of the golden promise. In 6:24, the chronicler refers to the confession of the divine name before return to the land. Here the perception that the Lord was the true God is a testimony inspired by Manasseh's return. Human intermediaries had fallen away; it was God who restored him, rather than the Assyrians. An experience interpreted by faith as divine deliverance created the Lord's exclusive claims on his life. Even before that experience he put his trust in the Lord as "his God" (v. 12). Manasseh now became a living link in the chain of believers by owning "the God of his fathers." The chronicler was speaking to his post-exilic contemporaries here. Exile did not constitute a great gulf whereby pre-exilic Judah had to give way to a second-rate community that perpetuated exile in failing to realize full restoration. The Lord's redemptive power was just one earnest prayer away for each generation of God's people. Even a religious renegade like Manasseh could be restored to blessing. Exile is used as a parable of alienation from God and a temporary precursor of restoration, in line with the gracious promise the Lord gave Solomon in launching the temple era.[343]

343. R. Mosis, *Untersuchungen zur Theologie des chronisten Geschichtswerks,* Freiburger theologische Studien 92 (Freiburg: Herder, 1973) 192-94; Williamson, *1 and 2 Chronicles,* 389-90.

33:14-17. The repentant sinner lives a saintly life. He steps into the shoes of Rehoboam, who after obedience found blessing in the form of building operations (11:5-12). To repent was to obey, and to obey was to be eligible for blessing. Manasseh's repentance bore religious fruit: The Lord's exclusive role in the Temple and in the city was now honored. The idolatry of vv. 4-5, 7 was reversed because of the truth he had learned (v. 13*b*). A directive to the people "to serve the LORD God of Israel" now countermanded the commending of his own service of other gods (v. 9). Outside the capital, the high places of v. 3, though not removed, were restricted to worship of the Lord. Step by step, religious aberrations were replaced by reforms.

The chronicler appears to be writing idealistically in penning such reforms. He will preserve evidence from 2 Kings that Amon perpetuated his father's religious deviations and that only Josiah removed them, even as he transfers back to Manasseh's reign Josiah's own reforms (2 Kgs 23:12, echoed in 2 Chr 33:15). The symmetrical grid into which he divided the three reigns encouraged him to preserve this impression. Narrative consistency was sacrificed in presenting religious models that created their own logic.

33:18-20. The customary source citation formula of 2 Kgs 21:17 has been reconstructed to describe Manasseh's checkered life. The chronicler's elaboration made it expedient to split his usual citation of the deuteronomistic narrative in prophetic terms into two parallel parts.[344] The basic text spoke only of the king's sin, in line with its uniformly negative presentation. The chronicler granted its presence and reinforced it with the qualifying "all" and with his key term for unspirituality: "being unfaithful" or "being faithless" (מעל *ma'al*). He also recapitulates the religious deviations of vv. 3 and 7. Yet, he wanted to make clear that divine grace triumphed over godlessness. The Lord would not let Manasseh alone, but tried to coax him back through "seers" (see v. 10; see also 2 Kgs 21:10-15). Eventually Manasseh succumbed to this persistent tough love and found in 7:14 a prescription for returning to the Lord. Prayer is mentioned twice as a spiritual

344. See *BHS* for the end of 33:19, where the conjectured "his seers" is an abbreviated reference to "the seers who spoke to him" in 33:18.

key to securing a favorable response from God. The elaboration of his sin serves as a pastoral reminder that no one is too bad to be welcomed back to divine favor.

REFLECTIONS

The chronicler's account of Hezekiah's reign had given him the opportunity to present the best possible spiritual life for his own constituency to emulate. Best possible, because to err is human. Now he presented another potential: The worst apostates may turn their lives around and find blessing. It starts as a worst-case scenario, in which sinning against God is turned into a major element. It is said that the Christian journalist Hugh Redwood used to say that God is able to save "from the guttermost to the uttermost." Manasseh was an ideal candidate for this presentation.

There is a beautiful inconsistency in the temple theology of chapter 7. It sets up high standards of obedience, but provides a loophole for those who fail to meet them (cf. 1 John 1:5–2:2). This illogicality is a concession to human infirmity made by a gracious God. It is celebrated in the thanksgiving hymn, Psalm 103: "[The LORD] does not treat us as our sins deserve . . . for he knows how we are formed, he remembers that we are dust" (Ps 103:10, 14 NIV).

When Manasseh rejected his second chance, the Lord reluctantly had to activate providential judgment. He had failure written all over him (33:11), but God had not given him up, using "distress" as a megaphone to appeal to the unhearing king. Manasseh's positive reaction contrasts with that of Ahaz, who plunged into deeper sin (28:22). These alternative responses to suffering are true to life. Manasseh availed himself of the promise of 7:14, as any backslider may. Jesus taught this perspective in the parable of the fig tree (Luke 13:6-9). For three years, the owner looked for figs in vain. Even then he was prevailed upon not to cut the tree down but to give it another chance—after which it did produce fruit. This divine opportunity may not be restricted to an evangelistic setting; it also belongs to Christian counseling. It is significant that Jewish theology uses the metaphor of being born again for any occasion of repentance.

Restoration to divine favor also requires becoming sensitive to divine claims on one's life. Manasseh rectified those areas where he had erred. After failure, there is first a call to rest in God's acceptance and then to rise to God's expectations, and thereby find blessing.

2 Chronicles 33:21–35:27, Amon's Wrongdoing; Josiah's Repentance, Reform, and Relapse

NIV

[21]Amon was twenty-two years old when he became king, and he reigned in Jerusalem two years. [22]He did evil in the eyes of the LORD, as his father Manasseh had done. Amon worshiped and offered sacrifices to all the idols Manasseh had made. [23]But unlike his father Manasseh, he did not humble himself before the LORD; Amon increased his guilt.

[24]Amon's officials conspired against him and assassinated him in his palace. [25]Then the people

NRSV

21Amon was twenty-two years old when he began to reign; he reigned two years in Jerusalem. [22]He did what was evil in the sight of the LORD, as his father Manasseh had done. Amon sacrificed to all the images that his father Manasseh had made, and served them. [23]He did not humble himself before the LORD, as his father Manasseh had humbled himself, but this Amon incurred more and more guilt. [24]His servants conspired against him and killed him in his house. [25]But the

NIV

of the land killed all who had plotted against King Amon, and they made Josiah his son king in his place.

34 Josiah was eight years old when he became king, and he reigned in Jerusalem thirty-one years. [2]He did what was right in the eyes of the LORD and walked in the ways of his father David, not turning aside to the right or to the left.

[3]In the eighth year of his reign, while he was still young, he began to seek the God of his father David. In his twelfth year he began to purge Judah and Jerusalem of high places, Asherah poles, carved idols and cast images. [4]Under his direction the altars of the Baals were torn down; he cut to pieces the incense altars that were above them, and smashed the Asherah poles, the idols and the images. These he broke to pieces and scattered over the graves of those who had sacrificed to them. [5]He burned the bones of the priests on their altars, and so he purged Judah and Jerusalem. [6]In the towns of Manasseh, Ephraim and Simeon, as far as Naphtali, and in the ruins around them, [7]he tore down the altars and the Asherah poles and crushed the idols to powder and cut to pieces all the incense altars throughout Israel. Then he went back to Jerusalem.

[8]In the eighteenth year of Josiah's reign, to purify the land and the temple, he sent Shaphan son of Azaliah and Maaseiah the ruler of the city, with Joah son of Joahaz, the recorder, to repair the temple of the LORD his God.

[9]They went to Hilkiah the high priest and gave him the money that had been brought into the temple of God, which the Levites who were the doorkeepers had collected from the people of Manasseh, Ephraim and the entire remnant of Israel and from all the people of Judah and Benjamin and the inhabitants of Jerusalem. [10]Then they entrusted it to the men appointed to supervise the work on the LORD's temple. These men paid the workers who repaired and restored the temple. [11]They also gave money to the carpenters and builders to purchase dressed stone, and timber for joists and beams for the buildings that the kings of Judah had allowed to fall into ruin.

[12]The men did the work faithfully. Over them to direct them were Jahath and Obadiah, Levites descended from Merari, and Zechariah and Meshullam,

NRSV

people of the land killed all those who had conspired against King Amon; and the people of the land made his son Josiah king to succeed him.

34 Josiah was eight years old when he began to reign; he reigned thirty-one years in Jerusalem. [2]He did what was right in the sight of the LORD, and walked in the ways of his ancestor David; he did not turn aside to the right or to the left. [3]For in the eighth year of his reign, while he was still a boy, he began to seek the God of his ancestor David, and in the twelfth year he began to purge Judah and Jerusalem of the high places, the sacred poles,[a] and the carved and the cast images. [4]In his presence they pulled down the altars of the Baals; he demolished the incense altars that stood above them. He broke down the sacred poles[a] and the carved and the cast images; he made dust of them and scattered it over the graves of those who had sacrificed to them. [5]He also burned the bones of the priests on their altars, and purged Judah and Jerusalem. [6]In the towns of Manasseh, Ephraim, and Simeon, and as far as Naphtali, in their ruins[b] all around, [7]he broke down the altars, beat the sacred poles[a] and the images into powder, and demolished all the incense altars throughout all the land of Israel. Then he returned to Jerusalem.

8In the eighteenth year of his reign, when he had purged the land and the house, he sent Shaphan son of Azaliah, Maaseiah the governor of the city, and Joah son of Joahaz, the recorder, to repair the house of the LORD his God. [9]They came to the high priest Hilkiah and delivered the money that had been brought into the house of God, which the Levites, the keepers of the threshold, had collected from Manasseh and Ephraim and from all the remnant of Israel and from all Judah and Benjamin and from the inhabitants of Jerusalem. [10]They delivered it to the workers who had the oversight of the house of the LORD, and the workers who were working in the house of the LORD gave it for repairing and restoring the house. [11]They gave it to the carpenters and the builders to buy quarried stone, and timber for binders, and beams for the buildings that the kings of Judah had let go to ruin. [12]The people did the work faithfully. Over them were appointed the

[a] Heb *Asherim* [b] Meaning of Heb uncertain

NIV

descended from Kohath. The Levites—all who were skilled in playing musical instruments—13had charge of the laborers and supervised all the workers from job to job. Some of the Levites were secretaries, scribes and doorkeepers.

14While they were bringing out the money that had been taken into the temple of the LORD, Hilkiah the priest found the Book of the Law of the LORD that had been given through Moses. 15Hilkiah said to Shaphan the secretary, "I have found the Book of the Law in the temple of the LORD." He gave it to Shaphan.

16Then Shaphan took the book to the king and reported to him: "Your officials are doing everything that has been committed to them. 17They have paid out the money that was in the temple of the LORD and have entrusted it to the supervisors and workers." 18Then Shaphan the secretary informed the king, "Hilkiah the priest has given me a book." And Shaphan read from it in the presence of the king.

19When the king heard the words of the Law, he tore his robes. 20He gave these orders to Hilkiah, Ahikam son of Shaphan, Abdon son of Micah,[a] Shaphan the secretary and Asaiah the king's attendant: 21"Go and inquire of the LORD for me and for the remnant in Israel and Judah about what is written in this book that has been found. Great is the LORD's anger that is poured out on us because our fathers have not kept the word of the LORD; they have not acted in accordance with all that is written in this book."

22Hilkiah and those the king had sent with him[b] went to speak to the prophetess Huldah, who was the wife of Shallum son of Tokhath,[c] the son of Hasrah,[d] keeper of the wardrobe. She lived in Jerusalem, in the Second District.

23She said to them, "This is what the LORD, the God of Israel, says: Tell the man who sent you to me, 24'This is what the LORD says: I am going to bring disaster on this place and its people—all the curses written in the book that has been read in the presence of the king of Judah. 25Because they have forsaken me and burned incense to other gods and provoked me to anger by all that their hands have made,[e] my anger will be poured

a20 Also called *Acbor son of Micaiah* b22 One Hebrew manuscript, Vulgate and Syriac; most Hebrew manuscripts do not have *had sent with him.* c22 Also called *Tikvah* d22 Also called *Harhas* e25 Or *by everything they have done*

NRSV

Levites Jahath and Obadiah, of the sons of Merari, along with Zechariah and Meshullam, of the sons of the Kohathites, to have oversight. Other Levites, all skillful with instruments of music, 13were over the burden bearers and directed all who did work in every kind of service; and some of the Levites were scribes, and officials, and gatekeepers.

14While they were bringing out the money that had been brought into the house of the LORD, the priest Hilkiah found the book of the law of the LORD given through Moses. 15Hilkiah said to the secretary Shaphan, "I have found the book of the law in the house of the LORD"; and Hilkiah gave the book to Shaphan. 16Shaphan brought the book to the king, and further reported to the king, "All that was committed to your servants they are doing. 17They have emptied out the money that was found in the house of the LORD and have delivered it into the hand of the overseers and the workers." 18The secretary Shaphan informed the king, "The priest Hilkiah has given me a book." Shaphan then read it aloud to the king.

19When the king heard the words of the law he tore his clothes. 20Then the king commanded Hilkiah, Ahikam son of Shaphan, Abdon son of Micah, the secretary Shaphan, and the king's servant Asaiah: 21"Go, inquire of the LORD for me and for those who are left in Israel and in Judah, concerning the words of the book that has been found; for the wrath of the LORD that is poured out on us is great, because our ancestors did not keep the word of the LORD, to act in accordance with all that is written in this book."

22So Hilkiah and those whom the king had sent went to the prophet Huldah, the wife of Shallum son of Tokhath son of Hasrah, keeper of the wardrobe (who lived in Jerusalem in the Second Quarter) and spoke to her to that effect. 23She declared to them, "Thus says the LORD, the God of Israel: Tell the man who sent you to me, 24Thus says the LORD: I will indeed bring disaster upon this place and upon its inhabitants, all the curses that are written in the book that was read before the king of Judah. 25Because they have forsaken me and have made offerings to other gods, so that they have provoked me to anger with all the works of their hands, my wrath will

NIV

out on this place and will not be quenched.' 26Tell
the king of Judah, who sent you to inquire of the
LORD, 'This is what the LORD, the God of Israel,
says concerning the words you heard: 27Because
your heart was responsive and you humbled yourself before God when you heard what he spoke
against this place and its people, and because you
humbled yourself before me and tore your robes and
wept in my presence, I have heard you, declares
the LORD. 28Now I will gather you to your fathers,
and you will be buried in peace. Your eyes will not
see all the disaster I am going to bring on this place
and on those who live here.'"

So they took her answer back to the king.

29Then the king called together all the elders
of Judah and Jerusalem. 30He went up to the
temple of the LORD with the men of Judah, the
people of Jerusalem, the priests and the Levites—
all the people from the least to the greatest. He
read in their hearing all the words of the Book of
the Covenant, which had been found in the
temple of the LORD. 31The king stood by his pillar
and renewed the covenant in the presence of the
LORD—to follow the LORD and keep his commands, regulations and decrees with all his heart
and all his soul, and to obey the words of the
covenant written in this book.

32Then he had everyone in Jerusalem and Benjamin pledge themselves to it; the people of Jerusalem did this in accordance with the covenant
of God, the God of their fathers.

33Josiah removed all the detestable idols from
all the territory belonging to the Israelites, and he
had all who were present in Israel serve the LORD
their God. As long as he lived, they did not fail
to follow the LORD, the God of their fathers.

35 Josiah celebrated the Passover to the LORD
in Jerusalem, and the Passover lamb was
slaughtered on the fourteenth day of the first
month. 2He appointed the priests to their duties
and encouraged them in the service of the LORD's
temple. 3He said to the Levites, who instructed
all Israel and who had been consecrated to the
LORD: "Put the sacred ark in the temple that
Solomon son of David king of Israel built. It is
not to be carried about on your shoulders. Now
serve the LORD your God and his people Israel.
4Prepare yourselves by families in your divisions,

NRSV

be poured out on this place and will not be
quenched. 26But as to the king of Judah, who sent
you to inquire of the LORD, thus shall you say to
him: Thus says the LORD, the God of Israel:
Regarding the words that you have heard, 27be-
cause your heart was penitent and you humbled
yourself before God when you heard his words
against this place and its inhabitants, and you have
humbled yourself before me, and have torn your
clothes and wept before me, I also have heard
you, says the LORD. 28I will gather you to your
ancestors and you shall be gathered to your grave
in peace; your eyes shall not see all the disaster
that I will bring on this place and its inhabitants."
They took the message back to the king.

29Then the king sent word and gathered together all the elders of Judah and Jerusalem. 30The
king went up to the house of the LORD, with all
the people of Judah, the inhabitants of Jerusalem,
the priests and the Levites, all the people both
great and small; he read in their hearing all the
words of the book of the covenant that had been
found in the house of the LORD. 31The king stood
in his place and made a covenant before the LORD,
to follow the LORD, keeping his commandments,
his decrees, and his statutes, with all his heart
and all his soul, to perform the words of the
covenant that were written in this book. 32Then
he made all who were present in Jerusalem and
in Benjamin pledge themselves to it. And the
inhabitants of Jerusalem acted according to the
covenant of God, the God of their ancestors.
33Josiah took away all the abominations from all
the territory that belonged to the people of Israel,
and made all who were in Israel worship the LORD
their God. All his days they did not turn away
from following the LORD the God of their ancestors.

35 Josiah kept a passover to the LORD in Jerusalem; they slaughtered the passover lamb
on the fourteenth day of the first month. 2He
appointed the priests to their offices and encouraged them in the service of the house of the LORD.
3He said to the Levites who taught all Israel and
who were holy to the LORD, "Put the holy ark in
the house that Solomon son of David, king of
Israel, built; you need no longer carry it on your
shoulders. Now serve the LORD your God and his

NIV

according to the directions written by David king of Israel and by his son Solomon.

5"Stand in the holy place with a group of Levites for each subdivision of the families of your fellow countrymen, the lay people. 6Slaughter the Passover lambs, consecrate yourselves and prepare ⌊the lambs⌋ for your fellow countrymen, doing what the LORD commanded through Moses."

7Josiah provided for all the lay people who were there a total of thirty thousand sheep and goats for the Passover offerings, and also three thousand cattle—all from the king's own possessions.

8His officials also contributed voluntarily to the people and the priests and Levites. Hilkiah, Zechariah and Jehiel, the administrators of God's temple, gave the priests twenty-six hundred Passover offerings and three hundred cattle. 9Also Conaniah along with Shemaiah and Nethanel, his brothers, and Hashabiah, Jeiel and Jozabad, the leaders of the Levites, provided five thousand Passover offerings and five hundred head of cattle for the Levites.

10The service was arranged and the priests stood in their places with the Levites in their divisions as the king had ordered. 11The Passover lambs were slaughtered, and the priests sprinkled the blood handed to them, while the Levites skinned the animals. 12They set aside the burnt offerings to give them to the subdivisions of the families of the people to offer to the LORD, as is written in the Book of Moses. They did the same with the cattle. 13They roasted the Passover animals over the fire as prescribed, and boiled the holy offerings in pots, caldrons and pans and served them quickly to all the people. 14After this, they made preparations for themselves and for the priests, because the priests, the descendants of Aaron, were sacrificing the burnt offerings and the fat portions until nightfall. So the Levites made preparations for themselves and for the Aaronic priests.

15The musicians, the descendants of Asaph, were in the places prescribed by David, Asaph, Heman and Jeduthun the king's seer. The gatekeepers at each gate did not need to leave their posts, because their fellow Levites made the preparations for them.

16So at that time the entire service of the LORD

NRSV

people Israel. 4Make preparations by your ancestral houses by your divisions, following the written directions of King David of Israel and the written directions of his son Solomon. 5Take position in the holy place according to the groupings of the ancestral houses of your kindred the people, and let there be Levites for each division of an ancestral house.[a] 6Slaughter the passover lamb, sanctify yourselves, and on behalf of your kindred make preparations, acting according to the word of the LORD by Moses."

7Then Josiah contributed to the people, as passover offerings for all that were present, lambs and kids from the flock to the number of thirty thousand, and three thousand bulls; these were from the king's possessions. 8His officials contributed willingly to the people, to the priests, and to the Levites. Hilkiah, Zechariah, and Jehiel, the chief officers of the house of God, gave to the priests for the passover offerings two thousand six hundred lambs and kids and three hundred bulls. 9Conaniah also, and his brothers Shemaiah and Nethanel, and Hashabiah and Jeiel and Jozabad, the chiefs of the Levites, gave to the Levites for the passover offerings five thousand lambs and kids and five hundred bulls.

10When the service had been prepared for, the priests stood in their place, and the Levites in their divisions according to the king's command. 11They slaughtered the passover lamb, and the priests dashed the blood that they received[b] from them, while the Levites did the skinning. 12They set aside the burnt offerings so that they might distribute them according to the groupings of the ancestral houses of the people, to offer to the LORD, as it is written in the book of Moses. And they did the same with the bulls. 13They roasted the passover lamb with fire according to the ordinance; and they boiled the holy offerings in pots, in caldrons, and in pans, and carried them quickly to all the people. 14Afterward they made preparations for themselves and for the priests, because the priests the descendants of Aaron were occupied in offering the burnt offerings and the fat parts until night; so the Levites made preparations for themselves and for the priests, the descendants of Aaron. 15The singers, the descendants

[a] Meaning of Heb uncertain [b] Heb lacks *that they received*

NIV

was carried out for the celebration of the Passover and the offering of burnt offerings on the altar of the LORD, as King Josiah had ordered. [17]The Israelites who were present celebrated the Passover at that time and observed the Feast of Unleavened Bread for seven days. [18]The Passover had not been observed like this in Israel since the days of the prophet Samuel; and none of the kings of Israel had ever celebrated such a Passover as did Josiah, with the priests, the Levites and all Judah and Israel who were there with the people of Jerusalem. [19]This Passover was celebrated in the eighteenth year of Josiah's reign.

[20]After all this, when Josiah had set the temple in order, Neco king of Egypt went up to fight at Carchemish on the Euphrates, and Josiah marched out to meet him in battle. [21]But Neco sent messengers to him, saying, "What quarrel is there between you and me, O king of Judah? It is not you I am attacking at this time, but the house with which I am at war. God has told me to hurry; so stop opposing God, who is with me, or he will destroy you."

[22]Josiah, however, would not turn away from him, but disguised himself to engage him in battle. He would not listen to what Neco had said at God's command but went to fight him on the plain of Megiddo.

[23]Archers shot King Josiah, and he told his officers, "Take me away; I am badly wounded." [24]So they took him out of his chariot, put him in the other chariot he had and brought him to Jerusalem, where he died. He was buried in the tombs of his fathers, and all Judah and Jerusalem mourned for him.

[25]Jeremiah composed laments for Josiah, and to this day all the men and women singers commemorate Josiah in the laments. These became a tradition in Israel and are written in the Laments.

[26]The other events of Josiah's reign and his acts of devotion, according to what is written in the Law of the LORD— [27]all the events, from beginning to end, are written in the book of the kings of Israel and Judah.

NRSV

of Asaph, were in their place according to the command of David, and Asaph, and Heman, and the king's seer Jeduthun. The gatekeepers were at each gate; they did not need to interrupt their service, for their kindred the Levites made preparations for them.

16So all the service of the LORD was prepared that day, to keep the passover and to offer burnt offerings on the altar of the LORD, according to the command of King Josiah. [17]The people of Israel who were present kept the passover at that time, and the festival of unleavened bread seven days. [18]No passover like it had been kept in Israel since the days of the prophet Samuel; none of the kings of Israel had kept such a passover as was kept by Josiah, by the priests and the Levites, by all Judah and Israel who were present, and by the inhabitants of Jerusalem. [19]In the eighteenth year of the reign of Josiah this passover was kept.

20After all this, when Josiah had set the temple in order, King Neco of Egypt went up to fight at Carchemish on the Euphrates, and Josiah went out against him. [21]But Neco[a] sent envoys to him, saying, "What have I to do with you, king of Judah? I am not coming against you today, but against the house with which I am at war; and God has commanded me to hurry. Cease opposing God, who is with me, so that he will not destroy you." [22]But Josiah would not turn away from him, but disguised himself in order to fight with him. He did not listen to the words of Neco from the mouth of God, but joined battle in the plain of Megiddo. [23]The archers shot King Josiah; and the king said to his servants, "Take me away, for I am badly wounded." [24]So his servants took him out of the chariot and carried him in his second chariot[b] and brought him to Jerusalem. There he died, and was buried in the tombs of his ancestors. All Judah and Jerusalem mourned for Josiah. [25]Jeremiah also uttered a lament for Josiah, and all the singing men and singing women have spoken of Josiah in their laments to this day. They made these a custom in Israel; they are recorded in the Laments. [26]Now the rest of the acts of Josiah and his faithful deeds in accordance with what is written in the law of the LORD, [27]and his acts, first and last, are written in the Book of the Kings of Israel and Judah.

[a] Heb *he* [b] Or *the chariot of his deputy*

COMMENTARY

This section reiterates the truth that a situation of spiritual failure can be redeemed. The transition from Amon to Josiah repeats the good news, but now it spreads the process over two generations.

33:21-25. The chronicler based his account of Amon's reign on 2 Kgs 21:19-24. The epilogue in 2 Kgs 21:25-26 is not represented. Either his eye slipped over it because of the similar endings in vv. 24 and 26 or this omission had already occurred in his text. His concern was to present the reign as a parallel rerun of Manasseh's first, evil period. So he adapted the vocabulary of apostasy in 2 Kgs 21:21-22 by echoing the "images" and self-humbling of v. 19. In hindsight, that verse has another agenda, to recapitulate negative elements that would resurface in Amon's reign in order to facilitate the comparison. Now self-humbling before the Lord, the back door to blessing, was conspicuous by its absence (v. 23).

The convoluted political maneuverings of vv. 24-25 are intended as providential retribution and reordering, like the regicidal conspiracies of 24:25; 25:27. The "people of the land," duly copied from 2 Kings, here has no special meaning; it picks up the reference to the people in v. 17. Under Manasseh they had been the willing dupes of his evil genius. By v. 17, they lagged somewhat behind the momentum of his new spirituality. Now they have gotten the message and instigated a turn for the better.

Spirituality is restored in 34:1–35:19. The people retained and developed their new commitment, as 34:33*b* attests. In this exemplary pilgrimage, they now had the encouragement and role modeling of Josiah (v. 33*a*), whose reign is now described. It was a more elaborate parallel of Manasseh's new lease on life. While Manasseh's first period was marked by failure to keep the Torah (33:8), Josiah's reign is characterized not only by an admission of such failure but also by a resolve to give the Torah priority and to subordinate communal life to the Lord's revealed will (34:14, 21, 31; cf. 35:26). There was a devout spirit of self-humbling before God and a desire to honor the Temple as the center of proper worship.

34:1-13. Amon had negatively modeled exile from the Lord and from the divine will for Israel's worship. Now Josiah became an example of restoration and religious renewal. The chronicler took over the introduction to the reign he found in 2 Kgs 22:1-2 and used v. 2 as a headline for 34:3–35:19, which provides four examples of its outworking. The Davidic idealism of v. 2 is reinforced in v. 3 with the help of the term for spirituality, "seek" (דרשׁ *dāraš*).

In 2 Kings the record of Josiah's reforms clusters around the eighteenth year of his reign, 622 BCE, and his discovery of the Torah book, so that reform took its motivation and direction from it. Here, however, the reform is staggered over two stages and the book has a lesser role. Did the chronicler know more than we do from reading 2 Kings? It is significant that the data of vv. 3*b*-7, applied to Josiah's twelfth year (628 BCE), are borrowed from the phase of reform after the discovery of the book, described in 2 Kgs 23:4-20, as is shown by the quotation of "Then he went back/returned to Jerusalem" (v. 7 = 2 Kgs 23:20).

There is no objective indication in the chronicler's material that he was using a different source at this point. Suggestions to the contrary stem from uneasiness felt by readers of the account of the reform in 2 Kings 22–23. There reforms are all squeezed into a single year, and the Torah book is given enormous weight in providing impetus for the religious reform. The deuteronomists had a vested interest in the discovery and impact of the book, evidently a form of Deuteronomy, and so the emphasis placed on it is not necessarily to be taken at face value. For the chronicler, the book was largely important because its discovery led to Huldah's prophetic oracle and then to a communal pledge of renewal. He represents the reform as a long process, begun in the twelfth year (v. 3*b*), continued in the eighteenth (v. 8; better translated "in the course of purifying the land and the temple"), and resumed after the book turned up (v. 33). This spacing looks more feasible than the one presented in 2 Kings, but it must be weighed against the fact that the chronicler retained Huldah's accusation of contemporary backsliding in 34:24-25 (= 2 Kgs 22:16-17) and praise of Josiah for his repentance in response to the book. In 2 Chronicles, the prophet is still allowed to speak as if no reform had occurred in Jerusalem. Moreover, Josiah's panic over the dire message of the book has been robbed of justification by the earlier account of reforms. As elsewhere, and indeed in this very unit, the chronicler has evidently sacrificed the consistency he found in 2 Kings to a more atomistic presentation of spiritual themes.

A further factor is a historical one: whether Assyria's growing loss of control over the west had reached by 628 BCE a point of allowing the northern religious measures described in vv. 6-7. It is questionable whether there was a political vacuum sufficient for Josiah to exercise such control until after Ashurbanipal's death in 627. Two factors emerge from the chronicler's presentation. First, he has left no objective evidence that he was following an independent historical tradition. Second, there are a number of signs that he took his cue from 2 Kings, adapting it to accord with his own concerns.[345]

David, with whom Josiah is compared in v. 2, had put religious matters first, capturing Jerusalem and planning the installation of the ark there in the very context of his coronation (1 Chr 11:4-8; 13:1-4). Josiah showed a similar alacrity, also like Jehoshaphat, who was spiritually active in the third year of his reign, and like Hezekiah, who set to work in the first month of his (official) first year (17:7; 29:3).[346] When still a minor, Josiah determined to walk spiritually in David's footsteps and make David's religious devotion his own. At the first opportunity, presumably as soon as a regent no longer ruled on his behalf, he used his new royal power to this end. The twelfth year of his reign, when he became twenty years old, appears to function as the age of majority, as in the case of the Levites at 31:17.

A start was made to undo Amon's religious apostasy. "Carved images" or "idols" (פסלים *pĕsilîm,* vv. 3-4) had been a mark of Amon's backsliding, renewed from Manasseh's early period and set up at high places (33:19, 22). So the pagan high places had to go, along with their other furnishings, including incense altars (vv. 4, 7; cf. 14:5), whether in Jerusalem (cf. 2 Kgs 23:8*b,* 13) or in Judah (cf. 2 Kgs 23:5, 8*a*). In this period of the reunited kingdom, beginning with Hezekiah, Josiah also removed high places from the former northern kingdom (cf. 2 Kgs 23 15-20; in v. 6, בער בתיהם [*bi'ēr bātêhem,* "he destroyed their sanctuaries"] is the best emendation of the corrupt MT, here rendered "in the/their ruins"; cf. the REB).[347] The general reference to purging the Temple (v. 8) presupposes and sums up Josiah's measures, narrated in 2 Kgs 23:4, 6-7, 11-12, though the chronicler had already borrowed 2 Kgs 23:6, 12 for Manasseh's reforms at 33:15.

The 2 Kings account focuses on the discovery of the Torah book, and the issue of temple repairs is relegated to a preliminary royal speech. Here the repairs are given their own narrative as further evidence of Josiah's religious enthusiasm. The commands of 2 Kgs 23:3-7 become the basis of the account in 2 Chr 34:8-13. The topic is woven into this unit by citing impairment in the reigns of "the kings of Judah," meaning Manasseh and Amon (v. 11). In v. 8, the details about the royal delegation are striking; they may preserve information that has fallen out of 2 Kgs 22:3 as we know it.

The chronicler takes the opportunity to repeat and develop lessons he has taught in chaps. 24 and 31 about the responsibility of God's people to contribute to the upkeep of the sanctuary. The new emphasis here is that they all participated, including members of northern tribes. Whether "the remnant of Israel" refers to non-exiled members of the northern kingdom or includes southerners (in the light of chap. 28), as the longer definition in v. 21 certainly does, the chronicler was expressing a viewpoint at variance with that of Ezra 4:1-3. Both groups had a stake in the Temple, he insisted, and there was no room for a separatist claim that only survivors of the Judean exile could comprise the Lord's people. In his account of Hezekiah's reign, he had asserted that all of them have a right and duty to worship at the Jerusalem Temple (30:1-12), though evidently Judeans were assigned the responsibility of sup-

345. See H. G. M. Williamson, *1 and 2 Chronicles,* NCB (Grand Rapids: Eerdmans, 1982) 397-98; S. Japhet, *I & II Chronicles,* OTL (Louisville: Westminster/John Knox, 1993) 1018-20.

346. See M. Cogan, "The Chronicler's Use of Chronology as Illuminated by Neo-Assyrian Royal Inscription," in *Empirical Models for Biblical Criticism,* ed. J. H. Tigay (Philadelphia: University of Pennsylvania Press, 1980) 203-5; D. A. Glatt, *Chronological Displacement in Biblical and Related Literatures* (Atlanta: Scholars Press, 1993) 68-72.

347. See Williamson, *1 and 2 Chronicles,* 399; R. B. Dillard, *2 Chronicles,* WBC 15 (Waco, Tex.: Word, 1987) 275.

porting its workers (31:4-6; cf. 24:9). Here the overall theme of the reunited kingdom is taken a step further. If the instigation of repairs was the king's responsibility, its financing rested on the whole people of God. In the chronicler's day, Judah's religious policy meant a higher financial burden than was necessary!

In the 2 Chronicles version, another opportunity is taken to give maximum visibility to the contribution of the Levites. The "keepers of the threshold" (2 Kgs 22:24), who are priests in 2 Kgs 12:9, are identified here as Levites (cf. 24:6, 11; 1 Chr 9:19). They are also given a supervisory role in the repairs. The clans of Merari and Kohath are specified in v. 12, though not that of Gershom, unlike in 29:12. The levitical arrangements of the chronicler's day are projected back. The temple musicians evidently provided timing and rhythm for the workers' tasks, as regularly happened in ancient times, while other levitical skills were harnessed to this work (cf. 1 Chr 23:4-5).

34:14-33. Communal commitment to the Lord is the overall theme of these verses. The chronicler has repeatedly mentioned the habit of good kings to hold a special service in which they and the people pledged their lives to the Lord. It occurred in Asa's reign and during Jehoiada's regency; most recently Hezekiah had instigated it (15:9-12; 23:16; 29:10). Josiah took his place in this noble succession. In 2 Chronicles such a pledge is always part of a larger reform program and is preceded or followed by corrective measures. Verses 15-32*a* have been largely copied from 2 Kgs 22:8–23:3, with the chronicler supplying his own introduction and conclusion at vv. 14 and 32*b*-33. Verse 14 serves as a recapitulation after the expanded narrative of vv. 10-13, synchronizing the mission of vv. 8-9 and 15. The chronicler used this long extract because it fit his pattern of making pledges of covenant renewal, which he considered a spiritual ideal relevant to his own time.

The striking prelude to the ceremony must also have intrigued him because it coincided with his own spiritual program in three other respects. First, it showed a healthy respect for the Torah and its demand for exclusive worship of the Lord (v. 25). Second, the prelude featured an inquiry for God's will through a prophet. This inquiry or seeking (vv. 21, 23) echoes and develops in a specific direction the seeking that characterized the king's early commitment (v. 3). Third, the divine revelation of Torah and the prophetic oracle are associated with a response of self-humbling, which accords with a goal of prophecy elsewhere (12:5-7; 36:12; cf. 32:24-26). The single reference to self-humbling in 2 Kgs 22:19 is doubled in v. 27, perhaps to highlight Josiah's parallel role to that of Manasseh (33:12, 19). Self-humbling in 33:12, 19 was a pointer to the divine provision of 7:14, and it functions here in the same way.

The negative side of the revelation in chap. 7 emerges in the forsaking of the Lord and the espousal of other gods (v. 25; cf. 7:19, 22), which result in "all the disaster" of v. 28 (cf. v. 24 and 7:22 NIV). However, the positive side surfaces not only in self-humbling but also in the Lord's hearing the king's penitent plea (v. 27; cf. 7:14). As a result, king and people resolved to keep the Lord's "commandments" and "statutes" (v. 31), in line with 7:19, acutely aware that they had been disobedient. Once more grace provided a way back to God.

The book of the Torah, found in the Temple before the repairs had started, is generally identified with some form of Deuteronomy. The account of its discovery in 2 Kings furnishes evidence to support this identification. The chronicler replaces "all the words of the book" (2 Kgs 22:16) with "all the curses [that are] written in the book" (v. 24). This formulation forges an intertextual link with Deut 29:21, "all the curses . . . written in this book of the law," with reference to the lists of curses in Deut 28:15-68; 29:19-28. It is likely, however, that the chronicler had the entire Pentateuch in mind. It has been claimed that the issue turns on v. 18, where Josiah's reading "of the book" (2 Kgs 22:10) is replaced in the Hebrew by his reading "in the book." Does this imply a complete Torah, read partially in v. 18? The NIV's "read from it" might so indicate, over against the NRSV's "read it." The Hebrew diction of the chronicler is also found in Jer 36:6, 8, 10, 13, where the reading of a whole document is meant.[348] It is significant, however, that in 2 Chr 34:19 the book is referred to as

348. P. R. Ackroyd, *I & II Chronicles, Ezra, Nehemiah,* Torch Bible (London: SCM, 1973) 202.

"the law," rather than "the book of the law" (cf. 2 Kgs 22:11). Moreover, in 35:6, 12 "the word of the LORD by Moses" (NRSV) and "the book of Moses," to which appeal is made in an echo of the reference in 2 Kgs 23:21 to "this book of the covenant," seems to have contained both deuteronomic and priestly material.

An interesting change occurs in the comprehensive description of the participants in the ceremony of rededication (v. 30). Whereas 2 Kgs 23:2 mentions "priests and prophets," the chronicler has "priests and Levites." In view of the chronicler's special interest in Levites, it is hardly likely that we are to conclude from the presence of this reading in a few MT manuscripts of 2 Kings that he found it in his source.[349] The change can be explained as his furnishing a description in terms of the post-exilic scene he knew, rather than a conscious identification of Levites with earlier prophets.[350]

Verses 32*b*-33 are the chronicler's own finale to this passage. It shows how king and people alike lived up to the pledge of obedience. As for the king, there is further use of 2 Kgs 23:4-20 to illustrate his reforms throughout the area of the old northern kingdom. The chronicler achieved maximum mileage out of the passage, having used it also for describing Manasseh's reforms and for Josiah's early endeavors. He singled out "the inhabitants of Jerusalem" as participants, as he will do later in the course of the passover (35:18). After all, they had been the target of Huldah's oracle of judgment (vv. 24-25, 27-28). He demoted her pronouncement of inexorable wrath to a warning to draw back from the brink of destruction. They heeded the threat and were spared. The same impression is given in v. 33, where the people are responsive to Josiah's efforts. The "God of their fathers" became "their God." The chronicler was countering the intergenerational pronouncement copied from 2 Kings in 2 Chr 34:21 (cf. v. 25). There was a sure way to escape divine wrath that was open to every generation: a new and continuing allegiance to the Lord "all [Josiah's] days." Divine wrath was intended to be a provocative precursor to grace and a new spiritual start, and so it proved in this chapter not only for Josiah but also for the people.

35:1-19. The chronicler found three pieces of evidence that Josiah had acted properly in the Lord's sight (34:2): his religious reforms throughout the land, his arrangements to repair the Temple with public money, and his service of spiritual renewal (34:3-7, 8-13, 14-33). Now the chronicler adds a fourth, Josiah's celebration of the passover as a token of his respect for traditional temple procedure (35:1-19). This fourth element also illustrates the spirituality of the reunited people in general and of the inhabitants of Jerusalem in particular (vv. 17-18; 34:32-33). The 2 Kings account had devoted three verses to the celebration (2 Kgs 23:21-23). The chronicler expanded it to nineteen verses, incorporating its material into the beginning and the end (vv. 1*a,* 18*a,* 19). He altered the royal directive of 2 Kgs 23:21 into narrative in v. 1*a,* but referred to it as such in v. 16. "This book of the covenant" has been transmuted into "the word of the LORD by Moses" and "the book of Moses" as the basis for the festival (vv. 6, 12). Its content begins to be unfolded in v. 1.

This passover was held at the sanctuary, which is consistent with Deut 16:5-6, while its precise dating accords with later priestly texts (Exod 12:6; Lev 23:5; Num 9:3) and conforms with the cultic calendar, over against Hezekiah's emergency, dating in 30:2, 13.[351] The accent on slaughtering the passover lamb, which echoes the terminology of Exodus 12, anticipates an issue that will loom large in the chronicler's account (esp. vv. 6, 11) and as an implicit element in the preparations of vv. 14-15.

This is the final description of a festival given in the royal narratives. In Hezekiah's reign, the Festival of Unleavened Bread received greater emphasis than it does here; in this case, the passover is brought to the fore and the festival that followed is mentioned in passing (v. 17). The passage falls into four paragraphs: preparation of the Temple staff (vv. 2-6), donations of sacrificial victims (vv. 7-9), details of the ritual (vv. 10-15), and closing observations (vv. 16-19). The third paragraph has its own summarizing frame, "So the service was arranged" and "so the whole

349. Contra S. L. McKenzie, *The Chronicler's Use of the Deuteronomistic History,* HSM 33 (Atlanta: Scholars Press, 1985) 166.

350. See W. M. Schniedewind, *The Word of God in Transition: From Prophet to Exegete in the Second Temple Period,* JSOTSup 197 (Sheffield: Sheffield Academic, 1995) 184-86.

351. J. R. Shaver, *Torah and the Chronicler's History Work,* BJS 196 (Atlanta: Scholars Press, 1989) 115.

service of Yahweh was arranged that day" (vv. 10, 16 NJB). There are two agendas in the account. First, the grounding of worship in the Lord's past revelation is emphasized. The ceremony took over the rulings for sacrificial worship laid down in the Torah (vv. 6*b,* 12-13) and also the organizational prescriptions established by David and Solomon with prophetic authorization (vv. 4, 15, reading "the king's seers" [REB], whether by emendation [see *BHS*] or by giving a plural sense to the Hebrew singular form).[352] This celebration honored a blend of truths imparted in the old and new eras of revelation and paid tribute to both the Law and the Prophets.

This passover celebration reflects a number of different traditions preserved in the Torah.[353] As in the case of Hezekiah's festival, described in chap. 30, in principle Deuteronomy 16 is followed, with its prescription of a centralized service of sacrifice, rather than the home celebration of Exodus 12. Taking the passover animals from the flock and the herd accords with Deut 16:2, whereas Exod 12:5 ruled that only a lamb or a kid should be used. In v. 13, the cooking of the passover offerings over fire reflects a harmonization of the two traditions. The verb בשׁל (*biššēl*) means primarily "boil" and more generally "cook." It is used in the latter sense in Deut 16:7. However, Exod 12:9 creates tension: The passover lamb was not to be "boiled" (בשׁל מבשׁל *bāšēl mĕbuššāl*) in water, but "roasted" (צלי *ṣĕlî*) over fire. The chronicler harmonized the double mandate by using the verb of one tradition with the qualifying phrase of the other. The "holy offerings" that were boiled rather than roasted are not explained. They seem to refer to the bulls, which for some reason were treated differently from the other passover animals. The tradition of boiling sacrificial animals is attested outside the Pentateuch in 1 Sam 2:13-14 and 1 Kgs 19:21 (cf. Ezek 46:20, 24; Zech 14:21), but in the priestly material of the Pentateuch only in connection with certain other rituals (Exod 29:31; Lev 6:28; 8:31; Num 6:19). Temple custom in the chronicler's day may be reflected here, but it may also express his desire to honor Deut 16:7 in another way, by retaining the primary sense of its Hebrew verb "boil."

Observing the passover in the sanctuary necessitated a degree of institutionalization not previously encountered in the Torah. In 30:16, the blood rite associated with all animal offerings was applied to the passover animals, and so it is in v. 11. In terms of temple sacrifices, the passover offering was justifiably put in the category of the שׁלמים (*šĕlāmîm*), the "offerings of well-being" or "fellowship offerings," which were partly eaten by the worshiper and partly burned on the altar. The latter parts are called "burnt offerings" in vv. 12 and 14 and are given a prominent place in the summary at v. 16. This label is defined as "the fat parts" of the victims (v. 14; "and" is explicative, meaning "namely," as in 29:31). This phrase also referred to the kidneys and the heart of sheep and goats (Lev 3:9-11, 14-15) and cattle (Lev 3:3-4). The rules of Leviticus 3 seem to be reflected in the formula "as it is written in the book of Moses."[354] The process relating to the lambs or kids (vv. 11-12*a*) was repeated for the bulls (v. 12*b*).

The chronicler had another message, a more sensitive one, to deliver in his passover story. The Levites are assigned a strikingly prominent role, which was his way of proposing innovations in the range of their ministry. Josiah's speech (vv. 3-5) sets the scene. The introduction to the speech boosts the Levites' image, after the priests have been organized and given their own word of encouragement (cf. 1 Chr 28:20).[355] The Levites are honored as teachers, as they were represented in 17:8-9 (cf. Neh 8:7, 9-12), and are given the epithet "holy" by virtue of their right of access to the temple court, which they were to exercise in the ensuing ceremony (v. 5).[356] The opening command is puzzling, since there has been no prior notice of the removal of the ark from the Temple. The MT may have been corrupted from a past tense,[357] with reference to the ark's installation at Solomon's dedication of the Temple, when the

352. D. Barthélemy et al., *Critique textuelle de l'Ancien Testament,* OBO 50/1 (Fribourg: Editions Universitaires; and Göttingen: Vandenhoeck & Ruprecht, 1982) 1:618-19.

353. M. Fishbane, *Biblical Interpretation in Ancient Israel* (Oxford: Clarendon, 1984) 136-38.

354. H. G. M. Williamson, "History," in *It Is Written: Scripture Citing Scripture: Essays in Honour of Barnabas Lindars SSR,* ed. D. A. Carson and H. G. M. Williamson (Cambridge: Cambridge University Press, 1988) 25-38, esp. 29.

355. See *BHS.* See also Mason, *Preaching the Tradition in Ancient Israel,* 115.

356. See John W. Kleinig, *The Lord's Song: The Basis, Function and Significance of Choral Music in Chronicles,* JSOTSup 156 (Sheffield: JSOT, 1993) 94.

357. See *BHS.*

Levites carried it and the priests actually installed it in the inner room (5:4-7). Their Mosaic task of carrying the "holy" ark was over. What was their new ritual role to be?

Already in the temple era, the Levites had been assigned the roles of musicians and gatekeepers; in vv. 4 and 10 the reference to their divisions relates to their assignments in 1 Chr 23:4-5, two of which are mentioned in v. 15. The "written directions" of David and Solomon (v. 4) pose a problem in the latter case. The chronicler seems to refer to the David narrative and the Solomon narrative in his own writings, in the first case to 1 Chronicles 16 and to the primary layer of 1 Chronicles 23–27 and in the second to 2 Chr 8:14.[358] As for the Levites, v. 5 proposes a new role for the third group of Levites, the temple workers—namely, to take over the tasks of slaughtering and skinning the passover animals. The latter task is stated in v. 11 and alluded to in v. 6, while in vv. 14-15 the preparations also include slaughtering and cooking. Ordinarily the first two tasks were carried out by the lay worshiper, according to Lev 1:5-6 and to 2 Chr 29:22 in the case of slaughtering. Verse 6 implies as much: The Levites were to "prepare for" their "brothers to fulfill the word of the Lord given through Moses" (REB)—that is, it was their duty to help laypeople carry out their religious responsibilities by doing them on their behalf. In v. 11, it can only be the Levites who did the slaughtering, in view of v. 6.[359] In 29:34 and 30:16-17, the skinning and slaughtering respectively were assigned to Levites as emergency measures. Now the chronicler was urging that such preparatory work should be their regular prerogative in recognition of their holy status.

To this end Levites were assigned to lay family groups as their representatives in v. 5, and also in vv. 12-13, where their duties include delivering the meat for the passover meal. Respect was thereby paid to the family setting of Exod 12:3-4. The Levites' haste may be a reenactment of the haste of Exod 12:11; Deut 10:3. These new arrangements presuppose that in post-exilic times laypeople were not usually admitted into the temple court. The chronicler's proposal rationalized this situation, though it did not become normative for later Judaism. Ezra 6:20 is the only other place where the Levites slaughter the passover animals. The role of the Levites as the people's representatives is also prominent in Ezek 44:11; 46:24, though in other respects the chronicler goes further. Verses 11-15 portray the Levites as duly discharging these preliminary activities and so playing a key role in the passover ritual. It was a facilitating role, allowing other personnel—priests and gatekeepers—to carry out their duties uninterrupted. This observation functions as a further argument adduced by the chronicler.

The other levitical groups—musicians and gatekeepers—also played their part. The former group is described in terms of the same developmental stage as in 1 Chr 16:37-42 and 2 Chr 5:12; 29:13-14, which prevailed in the chronicler's period or just before. The musicians are assigned to the Asaph group, perhaps here only a shorthand reference to all three groups.[360] Their music accompanied the burning of the fat, which accords with their having played at the regular burnt offerings in 1 Chr 23:30-31; 2 Chr 29:27, and they performed at the place specified in 2 Chr 5:12.

The donations of the king and the members of the civil and religious administration (vv. 7-9) recall 30:24 and the regular royal contributions of 31:3. The leaders' having given "willingly" (v. 8) and the rhetorical number of the king's gift function as an exhortation to leaders in the chronicler's day.

The closing observations in vv. 16-19 mention the unified nature of the celebration, but do not belabor the point, which was adequately covered in the account of Hezekiah's passover in chap. 30. The same brevity extends to mention of the accompanying Festival of Unleavened Bread. The notice in 2 Kgs 23:22 that an ancient precedent from "the days of the judges" was revived is changed to "since the days of the prophet Samuel." At first glance, the alteration says little: Samuel was the last of the judges. However, in 1 Chr 6:26-28, 33-38 Samuel was represented as an adoptee of the levitical clan. A Levite once led Israel's worship! Here was precedent for Levites

358. S. J. De Vries, *1 and 2 Chronicles,* FOTL 11 (Grand Rapids: Eerdmans, 1989) 415.

359. For the text of 35:11, see D. Barthélemy et al., *Critique textuelle de l'Ancien Testament,* OBO 50/1 (Fribourg: Editions Universitaires; and Göttingen: Vandenhoeck & Ruprecht, 1982) 1:518.

360. S. Japhet, *I & II Chronicles,* OTL (Louisville: Westminster/John Knox, 1993) 1053.

to take a more prominent role in sacrificial worship. The chronicler used this narrative to argue a cause dear to his heart—the Levites' leadership—and to advocate their importance in his own day.

35:20-27. Josiah's observance of the festival is interpreted in v. 20 as his reorganization of the temple worship and functioned as an example of his reinstating of services, as Manasseh had done (33:16). The resumption of the religious calendar was evidence of a response to the Lord on the part of king and people (34:2, 33). However, the chronicler now has a less happy incident to record, jumping thirteen years to the time of Josiah's death. The disappointment of "after all this" recalls 20:35. The brief account of his tragic death in 2 Kgs 23:29-30, tucked into an appendix there, appears here in a longer version, integrated into the ongoing narrative, which thus culminates in his death and burial. The chronicler writes independently of the 2 Kings account, avoiding its erroneous statement that Pharaoh Neco was campaigning "against the king of Assyria" (TNK), specifying Carchemish as the place of battle and adding such objective details as Josiah's being moved to another chariot and dying in Jerusalem. These and perhaps other points appear to have been taken from another account, though the reference to Carchemish may have come from Jer 46:2 and the details of Josiah's death may have been influenced in part by Ahaziah's in 2 Kgs 9:27-28. The chronicler wove it into a theological explanation of Josiah's unexpected end, employing as usual a speech for this purpose.

Josiah had been caught up in the death throes of a superpower, Assyria, and collided with the efforts of Egypt, the other superpower, to preserve its ally Assyria from the vigorous attacks of the Babylonians for as long as possible.[361] The chronicler had an ideological framework into which the incident could be slotted. Surprise attacks on good kings did happen, as opportunities for them to put their faith in the Lord and thus be victorious. Such a category does not fit here. Josiah initiated the conflict, and his death meant that he was culpable. He was like Rehoboam, who was ready to fight and encountered a prophet who warned him that it was not the Lord's will. Unlike Josiah, Rehoboam was dissuaded and won divine blessing as a consequence (11:1-12). Josiah was close to Jeroboam I of Israel, whom Abijah urged not to fight against the Judean army because the Lord was with Judah and whose refusal led to military defeat and an early death (13:3-20). Here, too, the opposing king claims the advantage of the divine presence as a foreigner speaking more appropriately of "God." The story may also have been influenced by the divine revelation to Abimelech, king of Gerar, in Gen 20:3-7. We are meant to take the claim of revelation at face value and not stray outside the boundaries of the story by asking how it could have been recognized as such (cf. 2 Kgs 18:25).

Reformers do not stay the course in 2 Chronicles. Josiah went the way of Joash and Hezekiah, more like the former in not listening to the warning sent by God (24:19; cf. 32:26). The chronicler went so far as to present Josiah as a second Ahab, who disguised himself in an attempt to prevent the wound from the predicted arrow that necessitated his removal from the fray (18:19, 29, 33). The king's having died in Jerusalem instead of Megiddo seems to reflect Huldah's oracle (34:28) and may have already featured in the chronicler's independent source. This issue would not have caused him concern: If repentance could cancel out oracles of judgment, presumably, then, defiance could annul an oracle of salvation (so Jer 18:9-10). From the chronicler's perspective, the incident constituted a warning that to disregard God's revealed will was dire folly and that, if one of the most spiritual of kings was not immune from backsliding, constant vigilance was required by all believers.

Yet he did not want the aberration of Josiah's premature and humiliating end to overshadow this king's extremely positive contribution to the life of God's people. The threefold reference to mourning takes the place of the funeral fires (16:14; 21:19) as a tribute. Jeremiah's laments (v. 25) have not been preserved, but they are consistent with his high regard for Josiah (see Jer 22:11, 15-16). The chronicler used v. 26 as an obituary notice to express his conviction that Josiah was a spiritually good king whose reign was characterized by honoring the Torah. The chronicler ranged over the narrative and alluded to such passages as 34:19, 27, 31; 35:6, 12. On the scales of history, Josiah's obedience to the divine Word far outweighed his final, fatal disobedience.

361. See A. Malamat, "Josiah's Bid for Armageddon," *JANESCU* 5 (1973) 267-79.

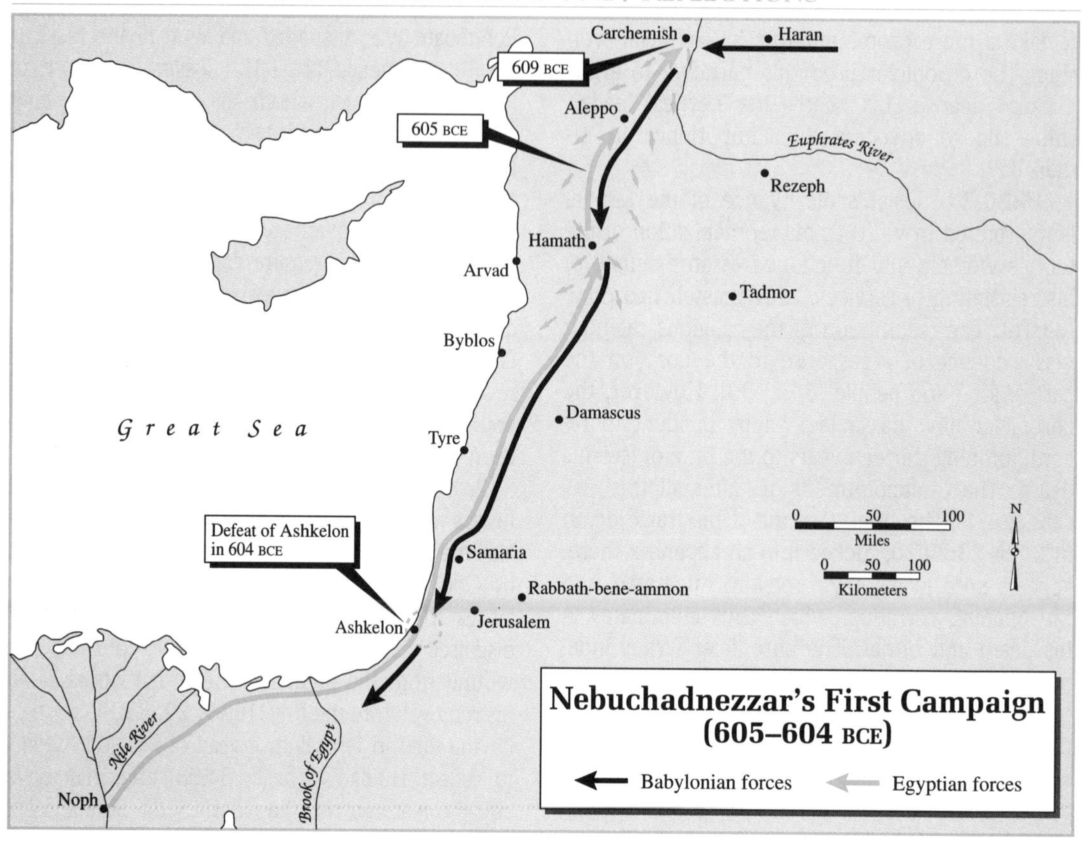

REFLECTIONS

1. The homiletic melodies the chronicler played in this part of his composition are by now familiar. By dint of repetition, he wanted his hearers to go away humming them and taking them to heart, especially the second half of the two-part unit, which compares Amon and Josiah to Manasseh's "before and after" life. If a single generation could experience transformation from apostasy to spirituality, then equally so a wicked generation, doomed to failure, could be succeeded by a reforming, virtuous one. The chains of the past could be unshackled; lives dedicated to the Lord could find freedom. It is the quintessential message of Ezekiel 18, a denial that when parents ate sour grapes the children's teeth were inevitably set on edge (Ezek 18:2). The wrath of God was no fatalistic process engulfing generation after generation. The Lord had provided an opportunity for people to live new, unfettered lives. Yet, a note of challenge is mixed with this encouragement. If the story of Manasseh taught, over against 2 Kings, that failure need not be final, then Josiah's tale reinforces the truth that failure dogs the steps of any believer (cf. 1 Cor 10:12).

2. "First things first" is a principle the chronicler has preached before. Josiah's reign teaches a lesson of spiritual priorities. His religious aspirations appear in his eighth year, when he was sixteen. Many Christians look back to their teenage years or even earlier as the period when faith in God first found a place in their hearts and decisions were made that set a course for the rest of their lives. Church work among young people has a tremendous potential in urging them to "begin to seek" the God of their parents' generation and gain a living faith for themselves, a faith that fits their new circumstances.

3. Josiah's resolve to repair the Temple reinforces the message of chapter 24 that the people were responsible for providing funds, with no group being exempt (34:9). The chronicler's spirituality included such a down-to-earth element, which he hoped would not fall on unlistening ears in his own day. Routine maintenance of church premises is not the most glamorous of calls on the Christian's resources, but it belongs to the needs of real life, which we disregard at our peril.

4. The chronicler also found room for the extraordinary—here a special service of rededication to the Lord—confronting human lives with divine revelation and calling for deep commitment to God's Word and an enthusiastic embrace of the obligations it brought (34:29-32). It caused changes in the religious life of the nation (35:33*a*) and reflected on a larger scale Josiah's having come to terms with his sense of failure and remorse (35:27). Once again, the message is that grace can triumph over human failure and that disappointing lives can be rechanneled into satisfying paths of allegiance to God. Josiah influenced the nation for good, bringing others to the point he had reached earlier: appropriation of a traditional faith.

5. Traditions of worship are brought to the fore in the description of Josiah's passover celebration. Revelation mediated both through Moses and through David and Solomon (35:6, 12, 19) is emphasized. Guidelines had been provided in the old and the new eras of revelation, in the Law and in the (Former) Prophets. To worship God meant to stay respectfully within the parameters of revelation and to grapple conscientiously with different traditions reflected in it. These traditions had been developed over the centuries and reflect the stage they had reached by the chronicler's time. He belongs to those who raise their voices today in favor of traditional forms of worship.

6. Inconsistently, but at the same time healthily, the chronicler also fought for innovation and used his narrative as a platform for religious development. The role of the Levites, he believed, should be extended because its expansion would be advantageous, both for other temple personnel and for worshipers. Levites were held back from the ministry of which they were capable, which in fact the editorial material in 1 Chr 23:25-32 served to reinforce. One cannot help comparing the movement at work in Christian denominations, with varying success, to promote the ministry of women.

7. Unlike the deuteronomist, the chronicler could take in stride Josiah's tragic end, though it spoiled somewhat the structural agenda of the literary unit. It took little adaptation, helped doubtless by another version of the story available to him, to weave it into a pattern of spiritual experience. Josiah had to be a lesser king than Hezekiah in 2 Chronicles because Josiah fatally succumbed to his flaw, whereas Hezekiah came successfully through his. As for an inspired pharaoh, the lesson is that God's message, however unlikely the medium, must be sensitively recognized as such by the believer and taken seriously after testing whether such a spirit is from God (see 1 John 4:1). This section challenges us in a number of respects to decide when to change course and when to stand our ground. The principle at stake is that changing is not expediency but rather reasonable openness to adaptability.

2 CHRONICLES 36:1-23, RECURRING EXILE AND THE PROSPECT OF RESTORATION

NIV

36 And the people of the land took Jehoahaz
son of Josiah and made him king in Jerusalem in place of his father.

2Jehoahaz[a] was twenty-three years old when he
became king, and he reigned in Jerusalem three
months. 3The king of Egypt dethroned him in
Jerusalem and imposed on Judah a levy of a
hundred talents[b] of silver and a talent[c] of gold.
4The king of Egypt made Eliakim, a brother of
Jehoahaz, king over Judah and Jerusalem and
changed Eliakim's name to Jehoiakim. But Neco
took Eliakim's brother Jehoahaz and carried him
off to Egypt.

5Jehoiakim was twenty-five years old when he
became king, and he reigned in Jerusalem eleven
years. He did evil in the eyes of the LORD his God.
6Nebuchadnezzar king of Babylon attacked him
and bound him with bronze shackles to take him
to Babylon. 7Nebuchadnezzar also took to Babylon
articles from the temple of the LORD and put them
in his temple[d] there.

8The other events of Jehoiakim's reign, the
detestable things he did and all that was found
against him, are written in the book of the kings
of Israel and Judah. And Jehoiachin his son succeeded him as king.

9Jehoiachin was eighteen[e] years old when he
became king, and he reigned in Jerusalem three
months and ten days. He did evil in the eyes of
the LORD. 10In the spring, King Nebuchadnezzar
sent for him and brought him to Babylon, together
with articles of value from the temple of the LORD,
and he made Jehoiachin's uncle,[f] Zedekiah, king
over Judah and Jerusalem.

11Zedekiah was twenty-one years old when he
became king, and he reigned in Jerusalem eleven
years. 12He did evil in the eyes of the LORD his
God and did not humble himself before Jeremiah
the prophet, who spoke the word of the LORD.

[a]2 Hebrew *Joahaz,* a variant of *Jehoahaz;* also in verse 4 [b]3 That is, about 3 3/4 tons (about 3.4 metric tons) [c]3 That is, about 75 pounds (about 34 kilograms) [d]7 Or *palace* [e]9 One Hebrew manuscript, some Septuagint manuscripts and Syriac (see also 2 Kings 24:8); most Hebrew manuscripts *eight* [f]10 Hebrew *brother,* that is, relative (see 2 Kings 24:17)

NRSV

36 The people of the land took Jehoahaz son
of Josiah and made him king to succeed
his father in Jerusalem. 2Jehoahaz was twenty-
three years old when he began to reign; he
reigned three months in Jerusalem. 3Then the king
of Egypt deposed him in Jerusalem and laid on
the land a tribute of one hundred talents of silver
and one talent of gold. 4The king of Egypt made
his brother Eliakim king over Judah and Jerusalem, and changed his name to Jehoiakim; but
Neco took his brother Jehoahaz and carried him
to Egypt.

5Jehoiakim was twenty-five years old when he
began to reign; he reigned eleven years in Jerusalem. He did what was evil in the sight of the
LORD his God. 6Against him King Nebuchadnezzar
of Babylon came up, and bound him with fetters
to take him to Babylon. 7Nebuchadnezzar also
carried some of the vessels of the house of the
LORD to Babylon and put them in his palace in
Babylon. 8Now the rest of the acts of Jehoiakim,
and the abominations that he did, and what was
found against him, are written in the Book of the
Kings of Israel and Judah; and his son Jehoiachin
succeeded him.

9Jehoiachin was eight years old when he began
to reign; he reigned three months and ten days
in Jerusalem. He did what was evil in the sight
of the LORD. 10In the spring of the year King
Nebuchadnezzar sent and brought him to Babylon, along with the precious vessels of the house
of the LORD, and made his brother Zedekiah king
over Judah and Jerusalem.

11Zedekiah was twenty-one years old when he
began to reign; he reigned eleven years in Jerusalem. 12He did what was evil in the sight of the
LORD his God. He did not humble himself before
the prophet Jeremiah who spoke from the mouth
of the LORD. 13He also rebelled against King Nebuchadnezzar, who had made him swear by God;
he stiffened his neck and hardened his heart
against turning to the LORD, the God of Israel.
14All the leading priests and the people also were
exceedingly unfaithful, following all the abomina-

NIV

13He also rebelled against King Nebuchadnezzar,
who had made him take an oath in God's name.
He became stiff-necked and hardened his heart
and would not turn to the LORD, the God of Israel.
14Furthermore, all the leaders of the priests and
the people became more and more unfaithful,
following all the detestable practices of the nations
and defiling the temple of the LORD, which he had
consecrated in Jerusalem.

15The LORD, the God of their fathers, sent word
to them through his messengers again and again,
because he had pity on his people and on his
dwelling place. 16But they mocked God's messengers, despised his words and scoffed at his prophets
until the wrath of the LORD was aroused against his
people and there was no remedy. 17He brought up
against them the king of the Babylonians,[a] who
killed their young men with the sword in the
sanctuary, and spared neither young man nor young
woman, old man or aged. God handed all of them
over to Nebuchadnezzar. 18He carried to Babylon all
the articles from the temple of God, both large and
small, and the treasures of the LORD's temple and
the treasures of the king and his officials. 19They set
fire to God's temple and broke down the wall of
Jerusalem; they burned all the palaces and destroyed
everything of value there.

20He carried into exile to Babylon the remnant,
who escaped from the sword, and they became
servants to him and his sons until the kingdom of
Persia came to power. 21The land enjoyed its sabbath
rests; all the time of its desolation it rested, until the
seventy years were completed in fulfillment of the
word of the LORD spoken by Jeremiah.

22In the first year of Cyrus king of Persia, in
order to fulfill the word of the LORD spoken by
Jeremiah, the LORD moved the heart of Cyrus king
of Persia to make a proclamation throughout his
realm and to put it in writing:

23"This is what Cyrus king of Persia says:

"'The LORD, the God of heaven, has given
me all the kingdoms of the earth and he has
appointed me to build a temple for him at
Jerusalem in Judah. Anyone of his people
among you—may the LORD his God be with
him, and let him go up.'"

a17 Or *Chaldeans*

NRSV

tions of the nations; and they polluted the house
of the LORD that he had consecrated in Jerusalem.

15The LORD, the God of their ancestors, sent
persistently to them by his messengers, because
he had compassion on his people and on his
dwelling place; 16but they kept mocking the messengers of God, despising his words, and scoffing
at his prophets, until the wrath of the LORD against
his people became so great that there was no
remedy.

17Therefore he brought up against them the
king of the Chaldeans, who killed their youths
with the sword in the house of their sanctuary,
and had no compassion on young man or young
woman, the aged or the feeble; he gave them all
into his hand. 18All the vessels of the house of
God, large and small, and the treasures of the
house of the LORD, and the treasures of the king
and of his officials, all these he brought to Babylon. 19They burned the house of God, broke down
the wall of Jerusalem, burned all its palaces with
fire, and destroyed all its precious vessels. 20He
took into exile in Babylon those who had escaped
from the sword, and they became servants to him
and to his sons until the establishment of the
kingdom of Persia, 21to fulfill the word of the LORD
by the mouth of Jeremiah, until the land had
made up for its sabbaths. All the days that it lay
desolate it kept sabbath, to fulfill seventy years.

22In the first year of King Cyrus of Persia, in
fulfillment of the word of the LORD spoken by
Jeremiah, the LORD stirred up the spirit of King
Cyrus of Persia so that he sent a herald throughout all his kingdom and also declared in a written
edict: 23"Thus says King Cyrus of Persia: The LORD,
the God of heaven, has given me all the kingdoms
of the earth, and he has charged me to build him
a house at Jerusalem, which is in Judah. Whoever
is among you of all his people, may the LORD his
God be with him! Let him go up."

COMMENTARY

The chronicler insisted that the Judean exile of 587 BCE was not a unique or final event; it had counterparts in earlier generations. The motifs of death, deportation, and deprivation of temple worship had materialized at the end of the divided kingdom, in the reign of Ahaz (28:5-6, 8, 17; 29:8-9), and had been succeeded by a spiritual restoration under Hezekiah. In turn, Manasseh was exiled to Babylon and after his repentance was restored to the throne (33:11-13). The last four reigns, summarized in this last section of the book, are also sketched in terms of as many exiles. The first three of the four kings were deported, and in the reign of the last the people suffered exile. The cessation of temple worship at the conclusion is anticipated by the removal of temple vessels by foreigners in two of the three preceding reigns. None of the earlier royal exiles is reversed, but the continuity of people and monarchy in the land does not give a repeated impression of finality. At the end, this impression bursts into an explicit announcement of restoration, with the dawn of the Persian Empire. So the last nine chapters of the book major in presenting exile as a judgment borne by generation after generation, yet one that can be followed by renewal.

The vignettes of successive reigns function as parables of a potential for good or evil confronting each generation. The chronicler took up the metaphor of a prolonged exile that dominated Judean thinking after the Babylonian exile had ended, both accepting it and pointing beyond it. His royal parables of exile and restoration all presuppose and reinforce his master plot of exile under Saul and restoration under David and Solomon. Davidic kings though these last monarchs were, they were spiritual Sauls. Each generation could take Saul's low road of unfaithfulness to the Lord, which led to failure. With such warnings came an implicit challenge to lay hold of restoring grace and to embrace in heart and life the positive purposes God had for the people. At the end of the chapter, the chronicler had Jer 29:10 in view. He would have agreed with the representation of the divine purpose in Jer 29:11: "I know the plans I have for you, says the LORD, plans for your welfare and not for harm, to give you a future with hope" (NRSV).

36:1-10. The pace of the narrative quickens. Kings tumble into exile like lemmings into the sea. The pace of the source (2 Kgs 23:30*b*–24:17) is rapid, but the chronicler's account is still much more accelerated than that in 2 Kings, cut to less than half. The chronicler's account emphasizes the fate of exile suffered by each king. It is like a series of clips of automobile crashes shown in a public service announcement.

The message of the reigns of Jehoiakim and Jehoiachin in vv. 5-10 is that the wages of sin is exile. In Jehoahaz's case, the expected formula of wrongdoing, which appears in 2 Kgs 23:32, is missing—not because of his short reign; Jehoiachin's was little longer. Did the chronicler think of him as being caught up in Josiah's catastrophe, which politically was in fact the case? He does not usually work with the deuteronomistic concept of transgenerational punishment. The wham-bam style he adopted here may have run away with him, making him prune his source overmuch. The account of the first two reigns reflects Egypt's brief period of control over Syria and Palestine, until Babylonia took over Assyria's western provinces and vassal states. Judah's payment of tribute and enforced change of king were a far cry from the glorious reigns of David and Solomon, when tribute flowed into Jerusalem. Neco's heavy fine reminds the reader of another pharaoh who rode roughshod over Judah as an agent of divine punishment (12:1-12). With Jehoahaz being held hostage in Egypt to ensure his people's loyalty, Judah's new puppet king was devoid of power. He had trappings of traditional royalty, his new throne name "Jehoiakim" emptily honoring Yahweh. Ironically, though, the Lord was in control through Neco.

The account of Jehoiakim's reign (vv. 5-8) is a truncated version of 2 Kgs 23:36–24:7, with a new item inserted about his exile to Babylon and the closing source formula expanded. He noticeably stands and falls as an individual, unshackled by the inherited ball and chain so prominent in the 2 Kings account. It is possible that the 2 Chronicles version depends on the chronicler's understanding of that source. He found in it a record of Jehoiakim's "abominations" and "what happened to him in consequence" (NJB). The latter clause refers to the divinely instigated military attacks of 2 Kgs 24:2. The "sins of Manasseh," related in 2 Kgs 24:3-4, became Jehoiakim's own abominations that providentially triggered the attacks. The chronicler apparently took the king, rather than Judah, as the object of the Lord's command "to remove from his face because of the sins of Manasseh" and interpreted the last phrase as sins such as Manasseh had committed. Then he understood the sequel as "according to all that he [the Lord] did [to Manasseh]." What the Lord did was to arrange that the Assyrian king "bound him with fetters" (33:11). So the same fate, including subsequent removal to Babylon, could be predicated of Jehoiakim. The infinitive form, "to take him" (להליכו *lĕhōlîkô*), does not imply unfulfilled purpose; it may echo the infinitive defining the Lord's command in 2 Kings, "to remove [him] from his face." The plausibility of this interpretation is shown by the partial parallel in the LXX, which here uses a longer Hebrew text assimilated to that of 2 Kings. It specifies Jehoiakim as the object of "to remove from his face" (2 Kgs 24:3) and also as the subject of "filled Jerusalem with innocent blood" (2 Kgs 24:4).

What is left unexplained by this hypothesis is Nebuchadnezzar's having taken temple vessels and putting them in his palace (v. 7; or "temple," KJV; cf. Dan 1:2). It is possible that the incidents of vv. 6-7 are associated with the king's appropriation of these vessels, which the chronicler magnified into a long-term exile.[362] If so, the chronicler found extra support for deportation and its spiritual cause in his treatment of 2 Kings. Mention of the loss of temple vessels symbolizes the Lord's abandonment of the sanctuary. It is a theme of this chapter, rising to a crescendo in the destruction of the Temple. In each case (vv. 7, 10, 18), the chronicler added the plundering of its vessels, which prevented true worship.[363] It is a divinely authored action that works out the threat against the Temple, "I will cast [it] out of my sight" (7:20 = 1 Kgs 9:7).

The account of Jehoiachin's short reign is abbreviated from 2 Kgs 24:8-17 to correspond to the triple pattern of the section: evil, exile, and looting of the Temple. The chronicler leaves out the partial deportation of the people (2 Kgs 24:14-16), preferring for literary effect to continue the motif of royal exile and to reserve national exile as a terrible climax. In 2 Kgs 24:17, Zedekiah is identified with Jehoiachin's uncle, but here he is equated with his "brother" (NRSV; the NIV harmonistically has "relative" and so "uncle").[364] Both persons with the same name are featured in a royal genealogy (1 Chr 3:15-16).

36:11-20a. The chronicler's account of Zedekiah's rule in vv. 11-12*a,* 13*a,* 19-20*a* is based on 2 Kgs 24:18–25:11. The account falls into two parts: (1) the willful sins of Zedekiah and other leaders, including their rejection of opportunities to repent (vv. 12-16), and, as a consequence, (2) inexorable punishment (vv. 17-20*a*). This climactic passage is written in an emotional vein, indicated in Hebrew narrative by a poetic piling up of terms and clauses in parallel arrangements. Thus the totality of the catastrophe in vv. 17-18 is described in two parallel, three-beat clauses at the end of adjacent sentences: "all he gave into his hand" (such is the Hebrew order) and "all he brought to Babylon."

Mention of the prophet Jeremiah provides a frame in vv. 12 and 21. The first case met with rejection, as the middle part (vv. 15-16) elaborates. In Jeremiah 37–38, Zedekiah is portrayed as two-faced, but his dominant attitude is summed up at the outset of that narrative:

> Neither he nor his attendants nor the people of the land paid any attention to the words the Lord had spoken through Jeremiah the prophet. (Jer 37:2 NIV)

The chronicler echoes that sentiment in the double indictment of vv. 12-16, blaming the king in vv. 12-13 and the religious and civil leaders in v. 14.

The chronicler brings together a number of his spiritual principles in this passage. The first is the offer of a fresh start, enshrined in 7:14. Zedekiah's

362. See H. G. M. Williamson, *1 and 2 Chronicles,* NCB (Grand Rapids: Eerdmans, 1982) 413-14.

363. P. R. Ackroyd, "The Temple Vessels: A Continuity Theme," in *Studies in the Religion of Ancient Israel,* ed. G. W. Anderson et al., VTSup 23 (Leiden: Brill, 1972) 56-57.

364. See Barthélemy et al., *Critique textuelle de l'Ancien Testament,* 1:520-21.

attitude is defined in terms of its vocabulary in vv. 12-13. He "did not humble himself" before the Lord's agent and in that respect took after Amon rather than Manasseh or Josiah (33:12, 19, 23; 34:27). He also resisted "turning" from his wicked ways. Zedekiah's twofold rejection of the Lord's overtures was reproduced in the community. "His people" (vv. 15-16) poignantly echoes "my people" in the promise of 7:14. Their blatant refusal blocked the promise; there could be "no remedy," or more literally, "healing" (מרפא *marpē'*). Reluctantly, divine wrath had to prevail over grace.

Chapter 7 also has a shadow side: the sinister consequences of opposing the Lord (7:19-22). It would mean the divine uprooting of the people and rejection of the Temple, "consecrated" to God though it was. Verse 14, where Judah defiled what the Lord had consecrated, opens the floodgates to those disasters. The Temple was indeed reduced to a shocking condition (7:21-22), first despoiled and then burned, while exile awaited the people left alive.

Exile is the result of unfaithfulness, in the general sense of breaking the covenant, as the chronicler had learned from Lev 26:40. It was a historical lesson he often taught (1 Chr 5:25-26; 9:1; 2 Chr 33:19) and also applied metaphorically (1 Chr 10:13; 2 Chr 28:19, 22; 29:6-9, 19). The ominous term occurs in v. 14. In the absence of a response to God's overtures, unfaithfulness led inexorably to exile (v. 20). It was the chronicler's custom to link those overtures with prophetic warnings (as in 24:19; 33:18) and to regard prophets as those who announced the promise of 7:14. He makes such a link in vv. 12, 15-16 for the last time.

He evidently had in mind particular oracles that forecast the calamity of 587 BCE. As was noted above, Jer 37:2 seems to be in view in v. 12. The phrase "stiffen one's neck" (v. 13) and the term "persistently" or "again and again" (v. 15) are characteristic of Jeremiah. Since they occur together in Jer 7:25-26, it is likely that the chronicler was principally thinking of that oracle, forecasting the destruction of the Temple. Moreover, "defiling the temple" (v. 14) and "abominations" (v. 14) are mentioned in Jer 7:30. The chronicler also made use of the book of Ezekiel. In v. 13 he referred to the charge of Ezek 17:18-19 that Zedekiah's political rebellion involved breaking an oath made in the name of the Lord. It is likely, too, that the abominations of v. 14 echo not only Jer 7:30 but also the abominations that are repeated in Ezek 8:6, 13, 15. The chronicler was drawing on Ezekiel's vision of the destruction of the Temple. Certainly the carnage in the Temple (v. 17) depends on the visionary slaughter carried out by angelic executioners (Ezek 9:5-6), who were to show no compassion, and the killing was to begin at the sanctuary and to embrace old men, young men, and young women.[365] The destroying angels turned into flesh and blood, wearing Babylonian uniforms. The chronicler has used prophetic texts involving the Temple to illustrate his account of the fall of Judah.

The slaughter spelled the withdrawal of the earlier divine compassion (v. 15). Invasion similar to that of Shishak was occurring all over again, when palace and royal treasuries were completely emptied and Judah became his servant (12:8-9). Now the city felt the full force of that wrath against the covenant people (vv. 16, 19). The curses of an empty land and a ruined Temple made in 7:20-22 now had come true.

36:20b-21. The narrative glides into a positive aftermath. The Lord never intended that the exile would go on interminably, but set limits for its duration. The divine purpose and human history, in the form of Persian seizure of power, coalesced in the interests of God's people. The "until" of history in v. 20 finds a parallel in the "until" set by the Torah at v. 21, while the human "until" fulfills the prophetic "word of the LORD." This word might be that of Jer 25:11-12, which continues the western nations' service of Babylon with a seventy-year limit to Babylonian control. More likely, Jer 29:10 is in view, which is addressed specifically to Judean exiles. The chronicler regularly employed Jer 29:12-14 as a spiritual formula for conditional release from a metaphorical exile. Here his use of an adjacent verse involves the same theme. The divine judgment of Babylonian exile had ended long ago. There was no barrier to blessing on God's side; the onus rested on the covenant people. So the seventy years—how one reckoned them was not the

365. C. Begg, "Babylon and Judah in Chronicles," *ETL* 64 (1988) 142-52, esp. 149-50.

chronicler's concern—were not simply a historical datum but a divine closure.

With the prophetic word, the chronicler intertwined the covenant curse of the Torah at Lev 26:34, a reprisal for sabbath breaking (cf. Lev 26:2). He cited it word for word, simply changing the tenses from future to past to indicate fulfillment. The Torah, too, set a time limit to the exile. It spoke of a sabbath year, a seventh year of letting the land lie fallow after six years of cultivation. As many years as were missed before the exile were to be "made up" (NRSV) or else "enjoyed" (NIV) by the land, in the latter case by way of recuperation for the new life of the post-exilic period.[366] The chronicler read the Torah text in the light of Jer 29:10 and envisioned a period of disobedience lasting 490 years, though he does not develop this point. Exile was the punishment for unfaithfulness (Lev 26:40, 43; cf. 2 Chr 36:14). Yet, like Jer 29:10, the word of judgment was given in a context of conditional restoration: "If . . . their . . . heart . . . is humbled . . . then will I remember my covenant" (Lev 26:41-42 NRSV).

36:22-23. A quotation from Ezra 1:1-3, broken off at the end, expresses in plain terms the promise of v. 21. Scholars dispute whether it is a redactional addition.[367] It is probably the chronicler's own quotation from the earlier book of Ezra–Nehemiah, just as he quoted Nehemiah 11 in 1 Chronicles 9. He had intruded into the later period in 1 Chr 9:2-34, so as to bring out the continuity of God's purposes. The concentration on Temple and people in the quotation develops the negative emphasis in vv. 15-20*a* in a positive direction, while vv. 20*b*-21 are a typical theological summary introducing a quotation. The royal speech of v. 23 coincides with the chronicler's own pattern of speechmaking as an encouragement to a task.[368]

As in the case of many of his citations of earlier material, there is a measure of reinterpretation in these verses. The prophetic oracle, originally related to Jer 51:1, 11, was understood in terms of the promises of Second Isaiah.[369] Here it refers to Jer 29:10, echoing v. 21. The seventy years were over, and Cyrus functioned as agent of divine grace. In Ezra 1:3, the Judeans' return to Jerusalem was in view. Here restoration of "all" the Lord's "people" residing throughout "all" Cyrus's "kingdom" reads like a comprehensive reference to displaced northern as well as southern tribes and as an implicit call for them to return to the land (cf. 1 Chr 5:26; 17:5; 2 Chr 30:9; 34:9, 21).

Cyrus's recognition of the Lord meant that God's kingship was acknowledged among the nations and that God's people were in principle rescued from among the nations, as 1 Chr 16:31, 35 had hoped (cf. 2 Chr 20:6). It was an earnest of greater blessing yet to come. As in 35:21, a non-Israelite king was steward of divine power. Ultimately a Davidic king was to wield such universal influence (cf. 1 Chr 14:17; 2 Chr 9:23-24, 26; 17:10; 20:29; 32:17). History had witnessed a lesser restoration, akin to that of Rehoboam, though with only fleeting Davidic control under Zerubbabel (cf. 1 Chr 3:19). Yet, the returning exiles were to enjoy the presence of the Lord. The prayerful wish of Cyrus is turned into a ringing affirmation, "The LORD will be with him."[370] The promise functions as an echo of the great model of restoration under Solomon: "and the LORD his God was with him" (1:1; cf. 1 Chr 28:20). David had known such a blessing, and other good kings, such as Abijah, Asa, Jehoshaphat, and Hezekiah, were no stranger to it (2 Chr 13:12; 15:2; 17:3; 20:17; 32:8).

As in 13:10-12, the Lord's supportive presence with the covenant people would be mediated through temple worship. The Temple, destroyed under Nebuchadnezzar, was to be rebuilt under Cyrus by divine behest. The temple age would continue, and so the grace associated with the Temple would still be available. Solomon's temple prayer—that the Lord bring Israel back to the land (6:25)—was now to be answered. All that remained was for each Israelite generation to respond to divine grace and to honor divine revelation in their worship and way of life. Each

366. See P. R. Ackroyd, *Exile and Restoration* (London: SCM, 1968) 241-42.

367. For opposing viewpoints, see H. G. M. Williamson, *Israel in the Books of Chronicles* (Cambridge: Cambridge University Press, 1977) 7-10; W. Riley, *King and Cultus in Chronicles: Worship and the Reinterpretation of History,* JSOTSup 160 (Sheffield: JSOT, 1993) 149-55.

368. See Mason, *Preaching the Tradition in Ancient Israel,* 118.

369. Williamson, *Ezra and Nehemiah,* 9-10.

370. Cf. 1 Chr 28:20; 2 Chr 20:17 for the Hebrew ellipsis. The NRSV and the NIV presuppose a jussive sense, but the change from יהי (*yĕhî,* "may he be") to the divine name יהוה (*yhwh*) seems to have been intended to change the meaning. See also the LXX, which reflects יהיה (*yihyeh,* "will be") in place of *yhwh.*

had to "go up," embracing the proferred inheritance. The prerequisite was repentance, specified at the beginning of this literary unit (30:8-9; cf. Zech 1:3).

REFLECTIONS

1. John Bunyan ended the first part of *Pilgrim's Progress* with Ignorance being turned away from the gate of the celestial city. The shining ones were commanded "to bind him hand and foot and have him away." "Then I saw," added Christian, "that there was a way to hell even from the gates of heaven, as well as from the city of destruction."[371] The Sermon on the Mount, addressed to disciples, concludes with the same warning: "and it fell—and great was its fall" (Matt 7:27 NRSV). The chronicler ends his work on the same warning note, speaking of expulsion from Jerusalem in language close to Bunyan's. The last two decades of the monarchy provided the chronicler with a series of spiritual parables of the consequences of being out of fellowship with the Lord. To do evil meant to lose God's favor and land-centered blessings. The New Testament speaks just as bluntly: "Do you not know that wrongdoers will not inherit the kingdom of God? Do not be deceived!" (1 Cor 6:9; cf. Gal 6:7-8*a*). In Romans 8, the message of liberation, life, and divine love realistically includes a warning: "If you live according to the flesh, you will die" (Rom 8:13 NRSV).

2. Zedekiah and his generation function as the ultimate of negative role models. The chronicler typically works with a double definition of *sin*, a basic sin of rejecting the Lord's revealed will and compounding that sin by rejecting the Lord's call to repent. This doubling is emphasized in this chapter, receiving three parallel statements in 36:12-16, twice with reference to the king and once with reference to his people. After the normative standard of obedience had been abandoned, all was not lost, however. Sinners could qualify for God's grace. The emergency system enunciated in 7:14 could rescue them from merited destruction. Unfortunately, prophetic overtures intended to foster that promise found no welcome, and so the promise could not work. The parable of the fig tree in Luke 13:6-9 acknowledges such a point of no return.

3. The chronicler was not tied to a legalistic mode of thought. The doom of exile came about not primarily because of broken laws but because of the rejection of the Lord's prophetic warnings and offers of forgiveness and a further chance. Spurning this initiative is the sin of sins in the chronicler's book, just as in John 16:9 sin is defined as not believing in Christ. Lesser sins do not drive anyone beyond the pale—only the sinner's refusal to repent and start over again with God. In case Christian readers complacently agree, contrasting their security with the fate of unbelievers, it is wise to recall that the chronicler had in mind a falling away from within the believing community.

4. The worst of fates befell Zedekiah's generation. Yet by setting *the* exile against a background of earlier exiles, it became just *an* exile. That generation had to be written off, but the Lord's purposes for the covenant people continued. In no way did the exile of 587 BCE represent a divine intention to "destroy them and blot out their name from under heaven" (Deut 9:14). Nor by an extension of deuteronomistic doctrine did it leave in the Lord's heart a lingering grudge such as parents sometimes inflict on their children long after an offense has been dealt with. As in Ezekiel 18, each generation is given a nontransferable ticket. Human responsibility is real; humanity has a free choice for good, which the Lord encourages. A balanced theological presentation would tinker with this partial truth, but it was the message that the chronicler's generation, like Ezekiel's, badly needed to hear.

371. John Bunyan *Pilgrim's Progress* in *The Complete Works of John Bunyan* (Philadelphia: Bradley, Garretson, 1873) 170.

5. A picture of restoration is displayed in 36:20*b*-23. The chronicler appealed to the Law and the Prophets to substantiate his affirmation that from the Lord's perspective the historical exile was long over. His encouraging message is akin to that of Second Isaiah, for whom ruined Jerusalem, a cipher for the exiled people, "has served her term . . . her penalty is paid" (Isa 40:2 NRSV). The Lord was ready to "renew [Zion] in his love" (Zeph 3:17 NRSV). The wrath of 36:16 was spent, and healing was once again a live option. A hallmark of restoration for the chronicler was God's enabling presence with the recommitted people. It has passed as a rich blessing into the Christian era. An Immanuel, "God with us," is enthroned at the heart of the Christian faith. The Gospel of Matthew exults in this powerful truth at its beginning, middle, and end (Matt 1:23; 18:20; 28:20). An assurance of the divine presence was the old message given Israel on the verge of entering the promised land: "It is the LORD your God who goes with you; he will not fail you or forsake you" (Deut 31:6 NRSV). It became the chronicler's new message for each generation of God's people, as he urged them to commit themselves to pilgrimage with the Lord. In turn, this challenge and assurance pass to us and then to those who will take our place.

THE BOOKS OF EZRA & NEHEMIAH

INTRODUCTION, COMMENTARY, AND REFLECTIONS
BY
RALPH W. KLEIN

THE BOOKS OF
EZRA & NEHEMIAH

INTRODUCTION

The books of Ezra and Nehemiah were originally considered a single literary work called Ezra. Although this work was already separated into two books by Origen and Jerome, the division does not appear in the Hebrew Bible until the fifteenth century, and the statistics traditionally given at the end of a biblical book ("final massorah") come only at the end of the twenty-three chapters of Ezra–Nehemiah.

Ezra and Nehemiah consistently turn up in all canonical lists of Judaism and of Western Christianity, though they and 1–2 Chronicles are lacking in canonical lists of the Syrian church. In modern Hebrew Bibles the third section of the canon, the Writings, ends with Ezra–Nehemiah and then the books of Chronicles.

EXTENT AND DATE OF THE ORIGINAL WORK

A principal issue in studies of Ezra and Nehemiah is whether they were once part of a longer chronicler's history or whether they formed from the beginning an independent work. Since the time of Leopold Zunz (1832) until the 1960s, the vast majority of scholars believed that the chronicler's history consisted of (all or most of) Chronicles and (all or parts of) Ezra–Nehemiah. Objections to this hypothesis were first raised by Sara Japhet on linguistic grounds, although subsequent discussion has questioned whether linguistic arguments alone can decide the question one way or the other.[1]

1. Sara Japhet, "The Supposed Common Authorship of Chronicles and Ezra-Nehemiah, Investigated Anew," *VT* 18 (1968) 330-71. See also the response and review of subsequent research in Mark Throntveit, "Linguistic Analysis and the Question of Authorship in Chronicles, Ezra and Nehemiah," *VT* 32 (1982) 201-16.

Other scholars have focused more on theological differences between Chronicles and Ezra–Nehemiah: (1) the concept of retribution and the terms related to it in Chronicles are almost entirely lacking in Ezra–Nehemiah; (2) the two works differ in their attitude toward the northern tribes, in particular the Samaritans; (3) Chronicles places a greater emphasis on the Davidic monarchy; (4) Ezra–Nehemiah mentions the election of Abraham and the exodus, whereas Chronicles concentrates on the patriarch Jacob (who is always called Israel) and de-emphasizes the exodus; (5) the frequent references to prophets in Chronicles make it a prophetic history; in Ezra–Nehemiah, by contrast, the prophetic influence has virtually ceased; (6) the נתינים (*nĕtînîm*, "temple servants") and the sons of Solomon's servants appear throughout Ezra–Nehemiah, but are absent from Chronicles, with the exception of 1 Chr 9:2; (7) in Chronicles, Israel comprises all twelve tribes, whereas in Ezra–Nehemiah Israel is limited to Judah and Benjamin.[2] This commentary assumes that Chronicles and Ezra–Nehemiah are separate works.

While Tamara Eskenazi, through a literary reading, has made a strong case for the unity of Ezra–Nehemiah, including even the originality of the repetition of Ezra 2 in Nehemiah 7, David Kraemer and James VanderKam have proposed that Ezra and Nehemiah should be read as separate books.[3] Kraemer argues that Ezra is the work of the priesthood and limits the realm of the sacred to the Temple and the priests. Nehemiah, by way of contrast, is a lay composition that sees Torah as the focus of the sacred. VanderKam notes numerous minor differences in language between the two books, their different use of sources, and, most important, the alternate themes of the two books: Ezra focuses entirely on the restoration of the Temple and the people; Nehemiah centers on the rebuilding of the wall and the repopulating of Jerusalem. It is unclear whether these differences are due to the editor or to the sources (such as the Ezra and Nehemiah Memoirs) that were incorporated into the work. Perhaps the most suggestive aspect of this proposal is to understand Ezra's reading of the law in Nehemiah 8 within the literary context of Nehemiah, rather than in a reconstructed, "more original" position after Ezra 8 or Ezra 10. In this commentary, Ezra's reading of the law will be interpreted in the context of Nehemiah 8, but I believe that Sara Japhet's proposed structure for Ezra–Nehemiah undercuts the proposals to read the books separately.

Scholars unanimously locate the author of this work in Palestine, but are somewhat more uncertain about the book's date. If we follow the traditional dates for Ezra (458 BCE) and Nehemiah (445–432?), then the composition must have taken place sometime later, but presumably well within the Persian period, since a favorable attitude is displayed

2. See Kent Harold Richards, "Reshaping Chronicles and Ezra-Nehemiah Interpretation," in *Old Testament Interpretation: Past, Present, and Future,* ed. James Luther Mays, David L. Petersen, and Kent Harold Richards (Nashville: Abingdon, 1995) 211-24.

3. Tamara C. Eskenazi, *In an Age of Prose: A Literary Approach to Ezra–Nehemiah,* SBLMS 36 (Atlanta: Scholars Press, 1988); David Kraemer, "On the Relationship of the Books of Ezra and Nehemiah," *JSOT* 59 (1993) 73-92; James C. VanderKam, "Ezra–Nehemiah or Ezra and Nehemiah?" *Priests, Prophets and Scribes: Essays on the Formation and Heritage of Second Temple Judaism in Honour of Joseph Blenkinsopp,* ed. Eugene Ulrich, John W. Wright, and Robert P. Carroll, JSOTSup 149 (Sheffield: Sheffield Academic, 1992) 55-75.

toward the Persians nearly everywhere in the book (except for Neh 9:37). A date in the first quarter of the fourth century, before the weakening of the Persian Empire, seems reasonable.

STRUCTURE OF EZRA–NEHEMIAH

Sara Japhet detects a historical periodization in Ezra–Nehemiah and divides the book into two units.[4] The first, Ezra 1–6, lasting one generation from the decree of Cyrus to the dedication of the Temple, includes two leaders, Zerubbabel and Jeshua, heads of the secular and religious establishments respectively. The building of the Temple is the main event in this unit, with events happening only in the first two and last two years of the unit. The intervening years, when work on the Temple was stopped, are described in one verse (Ezra 4:24). The status of the leaders is left undefined throughout the unit. Neither is present at the beginning of the unit, and neither was there at the Temple's dedication.

The second unit, Ezra 7–Nehemiah 13, again lasts one generation, from the arrival of Ezra in 458 BCE to the second term of Nehemiah in 432. This period is defined by its leaders, not by its projects. Ezra at first works by himself, then Nehemiah by himself, then the two together, and then Nehemiah again by himself. The two figures are active in 458 BCE (Ezra 7–10), 445 (Nehemiah 1–12), and 432 (Nehemiah 13), with nothing reported about the spaces between these activities. Nehemiah alone directs work on the walls, the social reform, and the repopulating of Jerusalem, but in the reading of the Torah and the dedication of the wall both Ezra and Nehemiah are present (Neh 8:1-2, 9; 12:26, 36).

For the first unit the author did not have a continuous literary source, but combined existing documents with his own narrative. For the second unit he was able to incorporate the memoirs of Ezra and Nehemiah, and he assigned both of them to the era of Artaxerxes I. By alternating between the two sources (Ezra 7–10; Nehemiah 1–7; Nehemiah 8 [Ezra material]; Neh 13:4-31), he created a synchronicity between the two leaders. Nehemiah 9–10 was added as material pertaining to the reading of Torah, and the lists in 11:1–12:26 provide information about the inhabitants of Jerusalem and Judah. Nehemiah 10; 11:1-2; and 12:27-43 are also excerpts from the Nehemiah Memoir (for more on the Nehemiah Memoir, see the Overview to Nehemiah 1:1–7:73*a*; parts of 12:27-43; and 13:4-31). The author in the second unit did not include much of his own writing, but assigned the borrowed material to a chronological and historical framework he had created.

Throughout the work the author affirms that change and renewal in the life of Judah were the result of initiative on the part of the Persian kings—Cyrus, Darius, and Artaxerxes—and the Jews who had returned from exile in Babylon. God extended grace to those who returned from exile by means of the kings of Persia. Because of the author's method of composition, it is impossible to fully reconstruct his sources or the events they report.

4. Sara Japhet, "Composition and Chronology in the Book of Ezra–Nehemiah," in *Temple Community in the Persian Period,* ed. Tamara C. Eskenazi and Kent Harold Richards, JSOTSup 175 (Sheffield: Sheffield Academic, 1994) 189-216.

HISTORICAL BACKGROUND

General Historical Outline. After Cyrus and the Persians conquered Babylon in 539 BCE, the king issued a decree that commanded the Jews, who had been exiled in 597 and 586, to return home and rebuild the Temple. Sheshbazzar led the first group home, and he was replaced at an unknown time by the governor (?) Zerubbabel and the high priest Jeshua. Their initial efforts to rebuild the Temple were interrupted by opposition from the peoples of the land, until Darius I reaffirmed the decree of Cyrus and ordered the rebuilding of the Temple to continue. The Temple was dedicated in 516 BCE.

About fifty-eight years later, Artaxerxes I (465–424) sent Ezra, the priest and scribe of the law of the God of heaven, to Jerusalem. The king's Aramaic decree (Ezra 7:12-26) commanded Ezra to lead Jews to Jerusalem, deliver gifts offered by the Persian authorities and by the people to the Temple, make inquiry about conformity to the law in Judah and Jerusalem, and appoint magistrates and judges to teach the law. Within his first year Ezra led the people in a public confession of sin because of their intermarriage with foreigners and saw the creation of a commission that carried out the removal of the foreign wives and their children.

In 445 BCE Artaxerxes I sent Nehemiah to rebuild the walls of Jerusalem, a task completed within fifty-two days. Nehemiah also corrected abuses in the making of loans and the charging of interest and generously provided for others at his table without drawing on the taxes enjoyed by former governors (Neh 5:14-19). Before Nehemiah could carry out the repopulation of Jerusalem, Ezra reappeared and read the law to the people, who resolved to study it and then celebrated the Feast of Tabernacles. In a public ceremony, the people separated themselves from foreigners and confessed their sins and those of their parents. Next they entered a firm agreement to amend a number of activities with regard to mixed marriages, the sabbath, the wood offering, first fruits, levitical tithes, and proper care of the Temple.

The community also decided to relocate 10 percent of the population to Jerusalem, followed by a joyful celebration at the dedication of the city walls. The final chapter of the book lists specific corrections of abuses during Nehemiah's second stay in Jerusalem.

Perhaps the most contested historical question has been the date of Ezra's arrival (see further the Overview to Ezra 7:1–10:44). The order of the canonical texts suggests that Ezra came before Nehemiah, and since Nehemiah is firmly dated to the reign of Artaxerxes I, Ezra is traditionally assigned to this king as well. But Ezra and Nehemiah actually have little to do with each other in the book, and a number of Nehemiah's reforms do not seem to presuppose Ezra's establishment of the law in the land. Hence a number of scholars redate Ezra to the time of Artaxerxes II (404–358), although the traditional date has gained in favor. If Japhet is correct in her analysis of the compositional techniques of the editor who intentionally periodized the history, scholarship may never be able to decide definitively about the date of Ezra. Lester Grabbe even questions his existence![5]

5. Lester Grabbe, *Judaism from Cyrus to Hadrian,* vol. 1: *The Persian and Greek Periods* (Minneapolis: Fortress, 1992) 93.

Other debated historical issues include the following:

(1) The relationship of Sheshbazzar and Zerubbabel—Sheshbazzar's descent is unknown, and the transition between him and Zerubbabel, his successor, cannot be dated. According to data outside the corpus of Ezra–Nehemiah, Zerubbabel was both a son of David and a governor of the Persian province of Yehud, but neither of these facts is affirmed in Ezra–Nehemiah. Japhet believes this silence is ideological.

(2) The establishment of Judah as an independent province—Albrecht Alt contended that Judah was part of the province of Samaria under a Samarian governor until the coming of Nehemiah, but Nehemiah refers to his predecessors in Jerusalem as governors. The discovery of a group of bullae and seals from Yehud that identify several individuals as "governors," has permitted a reconstruction of a list of Judean governors in the fifth–fourth centuries, prior to Nehemiah.[6]

(3) Ezra's book of the law—the canonical text of Ezra–Nehemiah suggests that Ezra's law book was the Pentateuch, but scholars differ in their assessment of what that law may have been historically. Some identify it as the source P, others as an undefined group of laws now contained in the Pentateuch, others as Deuteronomy, and still others believe that the law of Ezra has been lost. Where the book seems to differ from the Pentateuch, we do not know whether the book cites the Pentateuch inexactly or whether it has reinterpreted ancient laws to meet the demands of the day.

(4) The Citizen-Temple community (Bürger Tempel Gemeinde)—Joel Weinberg describes the post-exilic community as a citizen-temple community, consisting of an assembly made up of free, property-owning citizens and temple personnel.[7] Weinberg distinguishes this type of community from that of the Persian province of Judah, even believing Nehemiah to be governor of the citizen-temple community and not of the province. Land belonged to the "fathers' houses" (בית אבות *bêt ʾābôt*), the household units that came to prominence in the post-exilic period. This community was loyal to the Persian government and was controlled by the people who had returned from exile in Babylon, much to the disadvantage of those who had remained in the land after 586. Weinberg has been criticized for his use of Ezra 2 and Nehemiah 7 to create artificially high population numbers, and his model departs somewhat from the extra-biblical parallels in which land was owned by the Temple. What we do not know—and what surely must have been one of the most bitter sources of division within the community—was the way land ownership was transferred from those who had never left the land to those who had returned from exile. In any case, the books of Ezra and Nehemiah thoroughly back those who had returned from exile (the Golah) and virtually ignore those who had remained in the land.

6. Albrecht Alt, "Die Rolle Samarias bei der Entstehung des Judentums," *Kleine Schriften* 2 (Munich: Beck, 1953) 316-37; Nahman Avigad, *Bullae and Seals from a Post-Exilic Judean Archive,* Qedem 4 (Jerusalem: The Hebrew University Press, 1966).

7. Joel Weinberg, *The Citizen-Temple Community,* JSOTSup 151 (Sheffield: Sheffield Academic, 1992).

MESSAGE

The main theological message of Ezra–Nehemiah may be summarized as (1) the return from exile and the rebuilding of the Temple; (2) the initial activities of Ezra; (3) Nehemiah and the rebuilding of the walls; (4) the climax of the work of Ezra and Nehemiah; and (5) the final acts of Nehemiah.

The Return from Exile and the Rebuilding of the Temple (Ezra 1–6). At the beginning (1:1-3) and end (6:22) of this section, the text asserts that Yahweh had brought about both the return of the exiles to Judah and Jerusalem and the rebuilding of the Temple through the favorable actions of the Persian kings toward Israel. Cyrus's decree permitted the rebuilding of the Temple and the restoration of its vessels (6:5), and Darius reinforced these privileges and added to them a curse against anyone who would attempt to countermand them (6:6-12).

The book fails to mention the Davidic ancestry of Sheshbazzar and Zerubbabel or the governors of Judah except in materials drawn from the author's sources, themes that might lead to a more eschatological or revolutionary orientation. Instead, the work of Cyrus fulfills the prophecy of Jeremiah (1:1), and contemporary prophets like Haggai and Zechariah merely encourage the building of the Temple (Ezra 5:2; 6:14) without setting forth any additional eschatological promises.

According to the books of Ezra and Nehemiah, the community in Jerusalem is made up only of those who returned from the exile (Ezra 2:1-70), who constitute the true Israel. In order to maintain continuity with the great pre-exilic traditions, all the temple vessels captured by Nebuchadnezzar are returned to Jerusalem through the agency of Sheshbazzar (Ezra 1:7-11; 5:14-15; 6:5), and both the altar (Ezra 3:3) and the Temple (Ezra 6:7) are re-erected on their former sites. The return from the exile (Ezra 1:5) and the rebuilding of the Temple (Ezra 3:7-13) show similarities to accounts of the first exodus and the construction of the First Temple respectively. The celebration of the Feast of Tabernacles after the completion of the altar (Ezra 3:4-5) anticipates the joyful dedication of the Temple (Ezra 6:16-18) and the equally joyful observation of the Passover a few months thereafter (Ezra 6:19-22).

The delay in the completion of the Temple is blamed not on the people's concern for their own comforts (as in Hag 1:4), but on the actions of the people of the land, who persistently opposed the work in Jerusalem and disheartened the returned exiles (Ezra 3:3; 4:1-24) and who later enlisted Artaxerxes I in their efforts to stop the building of the walls (Ezra 4:21-22). The laying of the foundation for the Temple was also a time for weeping for the older members of the community, who compared the foundation to that of the First Temple. The great noise produced by these emotions (Ezra 3:13) was heard by the adversaries, and it spurred them on to a deceptive offer to help with the temple building.

The Initial Activities of Ezra (Ezra 7–10). The second scene in Ezra–Nehemiah is formed by the initial activities of Ezra some fifty-eight years later (Ezra 7–10). Like

Sheshbazzar and Zerubbabel, Ezra, too, led a group of exiles home (8:1-14; 8:15-34). His lineage is traced back to Aaron, the high priest (7:1-5), and his own attitude toward the law parallels that of Moses (7:10). The authority of the law is underscored by the decree of Artaxerxes (7:12-26).

After the leaders raise the problem of mixed marriages (9:1-5), the prayer of Ezra in 9:6-15 makes clear that the community is not yet the complete embodiment of Yahweh's will since it is still under bondage to Persian power. Yet, Yahweh's love for the community in these circumstances is considered a sign of God's favor and evidence for hope of a little reviving (Ezra 9:8-9). Ezra articulates the people's confession of sin, accompanied by public weeping (10:1) and fasting (10:6).

The people gathered together in a mass assembly during inclement weather to express their contrition publicly (10:6-12), and requested the creation of a special commission to carry out the removal of the foreign wives and their children (10:13-17). Within a year of Ezra's departure from Babylon (cf. 7:9 with 10:17), a purified community was created in Jerusalem.

Nehemiah and the Rebuilding of the Walls (Neh 1:1–7:73a [HB 7:72*a*]). Nehemiah, too, led exiles home (cf. Sheshbazzar, Zerubbabel, and Ezra). Opposition from Sanballat and his allies was met by Nehemiah's defensive maneuvers (Neh 4:21-23 [HB 4:15-17]). Because he saw through the opponents' plots and their false charges about his desire for the office of king (6:1-14), he prayed for deliverance from them and placed an imprecation upon them (Neh 4:4-5 [HB 3:36-37]). The nations lost self-esteem when they perceived that the completion of the wall was the work of God (Neh 6:16). Nehemiah's work, then, authorized by Persian authorities (2:6-8), was ultimately successful: The purified community (Ezra 7–10) completed the building of walls (Neh 6:15) around the holy city (Ezra 1–6). Nehemiah corrected abuses in the making of loans and charging of interest (Neh 5:1-13) and generously provided for others at his table without drawing on the taxes enjoyed by former governors (5:14-19).

After the threefold restoration of the community and the city reported in Ezra 1–6; 7–10; and Nehemiah 1–6, Nehemiah decided to remedy the low population in the city by selecting people for relocation there whose genealogy could be correlated with the list of those who had returned with Zerubbabel (Neh 7:73*a*; HB 7:5, 6-72*a*).

The Climax of the Work of Ezra and Nehemiah (Neh 7:73*b* [HB 7:72*b*]–10:39 [HB 40]). Before the actual repopulation of Jerusalem began, the people unanimously requested that Ezra read the law to them (Neh 8:1). Ezra reassured them that the joy of the Lord would offer protection against the judgments of the law against transgressors (Neh 8:10).

The people resolved to study the law (Neh 8:13) just as Ezra had done (Ezra 7:10). On the basis of this study, they held a unique celebration of the Feast of Tabernacles, unparalleled since the days of Joshua (Neh 8:17). This celebration in Nehemiah 8 recalls the Tabernacles celebration at the erection of the altar (Ezra 3:4) and the dedication celebration (Ezra 6:16-18) and Passover (Ezra 6:19-22) observed at the completion of the Temple.

Next the people separated themselves from foreigners and confessed their sins and those of their parents (Neh 9:2-3). A speech by an unnamed speaker (Neh 9:6; attributed by LXX to Ezra), which rehearses the sinfulness of Israel in the days of the wilderness wandering (9:16-18) and the people's stay in the land (9:26-30) includes the sinfulness of the present generation (9:33). Nevertheless, they had received Yahweh's repeated benefactions in creation (9:6); in the time of Abraham (9:7-8); in the exodus from Egypt and the giving of the law on Mt. Sinai (9:9-14); in the provision of food, water, and guidance in the wilderness (9:15, 19-21); in the gift of the land (9:22-25); and in the patient warning through the prophets in the land (9:27-30). Even the defeats at the time of the exile did not bring Yahweh's mercies to an end (9:31).

The confession concludes with an acknowledgment that the present Persian rulership, accepted elsewhere with equanimity in Ezra–Nehemiah, leaves the community in a less than perfect situation: "We are slaves this day . . . and we are in great distress" (9:36-37; cf. Ezra 9:8-9).

The community entered into a covenant to walk in God's law and to do all the commandments (10:28 [HB 10:29]; cf. Ezra 7:10). The community obligated itself to correct certain practices that later in the book require Nehemiah's direct actions.

Nehemiah 8–10, therefore, sets forth an ideal picture of the community. Made joyful by the reading of the law, after an initial reaction of grief, the people celebrated Tabernacles and confessed their previous sins and God's constant deliverance—and their less than perfect current status. The appropriate sequel to reading the law and offering a confession was a community-wide commitment to keep the proscriptions of the law.

Final Acts of Nehemiah (Neh 11:1–13:31). The perfected community decided to relocate one of every ten persons from the local towns to Jerusalem, thus carrying out what Nehemiah had begun in Neh 7:1-5. Subsequent lists identify those who lived in Jerusalem (11:3-24) and in the villages (11:25-36) and provide the names of priests, Levites, and high priests at various times of the restoration period (12:1-26). The dedication of the city's wall features a double procession in which both Ezra and Nehemiah play a role. The joy at the dedication (12:43) recalls the joy experienced at the reading of the law (Neh 8:12, 17), at the beginning of the rebuilding of the Temple (Ezra 3:12-13), and at its dedication (Ezra 6:16). The sounds of exaltation at the dedication of the wall were heard at a great distance (Neh 12:43; cf. Ezra 3:13).

After the appointment of supervisors of contributions, following the command and example of David (Neh 12:44-47), and a decision to separate from all foreigners (13:1-3), the rest of the book consists of specific corrections of abuses during Nehemiah's second stay in Jerusalem. He removed the Ammonite Tobiah from a chamber in the Temple (Neh 13:4-9), restored the portions due to the Levites (Neh 13:10-14), reinstituted proper observance of the sabbath (Neh 13:15-22), remonstrated with those who had married foreign women and whose children could not speak Hebrew (Neh 13:23-27), chased away the son of the high priest who had married the daughter of Nehemiah's arch-rival Sanballat (Neh 13:28-29), cleansed the community from foreign contamination and established the duties of the priests and Levites (Neh 13:30), and provided for the wood offering and first fruits (Neh 13:31). These reforms were precisely in those areas in which the community had undertaken covenantal obligations according to Nehemiah 10.

The plea "Remember me, O my God, for good" (Neh 13:31) and similar expressions in Neh 13:14, 22, and 29, call attention in the canonical context to the virtue of Nehemiah, the wall builder and reformer of the community. At the same time, Nehemiah 13 reminds the reader that even the best intentions of the perfect community, under ideal leadership (see the ceremonies in Nehemiah 8–10), can fail and the people can lapse into sin. While the people confessed in chapter 9 that God's saving goal for them had not yet been achieved, the final chapter of Nehemiah concedes that the behavior of the restored community, too, was never fully perfected and often was in need of reform. The real circumstances in which people live—still under Persian rulership and in imperfection—set limits to the salvation that God gives in fulfillment of promises. The author leaves unresolved the relationship between the present and the future in the divine plan of salvation.

BIBLIOGRAPHY

Commentaries:

Blenkinsopp, Joseph. *Ezra–Nehemiah.* OTL. Philadelphia: Westminster, 1988. A thorough interpretation of the books as part of the chronicler's history; well informed about the social, economic, and political affairs of the Persian Empire.

Clines, David J. A. *Ezra, Nehemiah, Esther.* NCB. Grand Rapids: Eerdmans, 1984. An insightful commentary based on the RSV.

Gunneweg, A. H. J. *Esra.* KAT 19, 1. Gütersloh: Gütersloher Verlagshaus Gerd Mohn, 1985.

———. *Nehemia.* KAT 19, 2. Gütersloh: Gütersloher Verlagshaus Gerd Mohn, 1987. The best current German commentary, it attempts to interpret the present form of the biblical text while acknowledging its complex literary history.

Myers, Jacob. *Ezra–Nehemiah.* AB 14. Garden City, N.Y.: Doubleday, 1965. Especially helpful information on lists and archaeological finds; now somewhat dated.

Rudolph, Wilhelm. *Esra und Nehemia, samt 3. Esra.* HAT 20. Tübingen: J. C. B. Mohr [Paul Siebeck], 1949. The best commentary of the previous generation.

Throntveit, Mark A. *Ezra–Nehemiah.* Interpretation. Louisville: John Knox, 1992. Hermeneutical resources for the church's didactic and homiletical tasks; proposed identification of a number of chiasms.

Williamson, H. G. M. *Ezra, Nehemiah.* WBC 16. Waco, Tex.: Word, 1985. The best interpretation of the books as a work independent of Chronicles, with meticulous discussion of contemporary scholarship. Conservative on historical issues.

Other recent literature:

Eskenazi, Tamara C. *In an Age of Prose: A Literary Approach to Ezra–Nehemiah.* SBLMS 36. Atlanta: Scholars Press, 1988. A pioneering effort to read these books holistically, using literary and rhetorical methods.

Hoglund, Kenneth G. *Achaemenid Imperial Administration in Syria-Palestine and the Missions of Ezra and Nehemiah.* SBLDS 125. Atlanta: Scholars Press, 1992. An important effort to clarify what it meant to live within and under the Persian Empire, drawing on and synthesizing recent archaeological research.

Klein, Ralph W. "Ezra–Nehemiah, Books of." In *Anchor Bible Dictionary.* Garden City, N.Y.: Doubleday, 1992, 2:731-42. A survey of the current state of research on Ezra–Nehemiah.

Stern, Ephraim. *Material Culture and the Land of the Bible in the Persian Period 538–322 B.C.* Jerusalem: Israel Exploration Society, 1982. A convenient and accessible handbook on archaeological research relating to the period of Ezra–Nehemiah.

Weinberg, Joel P. *The Citizen-Temple Community.* JSOTSup 151. Sheffield: JSOT, 1992. A significant collection of essays, originally published in Latvia, that outline a hypothesis for understanding political and economic features of the post-exilic religious community.

OUTLINE OF EZRA–NEHEMIAH

I. Ezra 1:1–6:22, Return from Exile and Rebuilding of the Temple

A. 1:1-11, Imperial Permission to Go Home

B. 2:1-70, The List of Those Who Returned

C. 3:1-13, Altar and Temple

D. 4:1-24, Opposition to the Jewish Community
- 4:1-5, Opposition Breaks Out
- 4:6-24, Opposition Continues

E. 5:1-17, A Challenge to the Temple Rebuilding
- 5:1-2, Work on the Temple Resumes
- 5:3-17, Tattenai Visits Jerusalem and Writes a Report to the King

F. 6:1-22, The Temple Is Authorized and Completed
- 6:1-5, The Decree of Cyrus
- 6:6-12, The Decree of Darius
- 6:13-22, Completion of the Temple and Celebration of Passover

II. Ezra 7:1–10:44, The Initial Work of Ezra

A. 7:1-10, Ezra Comes to Jerusalem

B. 7:11-28, The Authorization of Ezra

C. 8:1-36, Ezra's Trip to Jerusalem
- 8:1-14, The Group That Returned with Ezra
- 8:15-20, The Search for Levites
- 8:21-30, Final Preparations for Ezra's Trip
- 8:31-36, Ezra's Arrival in Jerusalem

D. 9:1-15, Ezra Faces a Severe Community Crisis
- 9:1-5, A Complaint About Intermarriage

9:6-15, Ezra's Prayer

E. 10:1-44, The Great Divorce Proceedings
    10:1-17, A Decision to Divorce Foreign Women
    10:18-44, The List of Those Who Divorced Their Wives

III. Nehemiah 1:1–7:73*a*, Return of Nehemiah and Rebuilding of the Walls of Jerusalem

A. 1:1-11, Nehemiah Prays for Help

B. 2:1-20, The Beginning of Nehemiah's Efforts in Jerusalem
    2:1-10, Artaxerxes Authorizes Nehemiah's Trip Home
    2:11-20, Nehemiah's Inspection of the Wall

C. 3:1-32, Workers on Nehemiah's Wall

D. 4:1-23, Nehemiah's Provisions for the Defense of Jerusalem
    4:1-12, External and Internal Threats
    4:13-23, Nehemiah's Response

E. 5:1-19, Internal Threats to the Community
    5:1-13, A Social and Economic Crisis
    5:14-19, Nehemiah's Personal Generosity as Governor

F. 6:1-19, The Wall Is Completed Despite Repeated Attempts to Intimidate Nehemiah
    6:1-9, Sanballat and Geshem as Antagonists
    6:10-14, Tobiah and Sanballat as Antagonists
    6:15-19, The Nobles of Judah and Tobiah as Antagonists

G. 7:1-73*a*, Next Steps After the Completion of the Wall

IV. Nehemiah 7:73*b*–10:39, Torah, Confession, and Firm Agreement

A. 7:73*b*–8:18, Ezra Reads the Law to the People

B. 9:1-37, A Great Day of Repentance
    9:1-5*a*, Preparations for Confession
    9:5*b*-37, The Great Prayer of Repentance

C. 9:38–10:39, A Firm Agreement to Keep the Law
    9:38–10:29, Sealing of the Agreement
    10:30-39, Requirements of the Firm Agreement

V. Nehemiah 11:1–13:31, The Climax of Nehemiah's Work and Related Matters

A. 11:1-36, The New Settlers in Jerusalem

B. 12:1-26, Lists of Priests, Levites, and High Priests

C. 12:27-43, The Dedication of the City Wall
D. 12:44–13:3, The People Solidify the Reform Measures
E. 13:4-31, Nehemiah's Corrective Measures

EZRA 1:1–6:22

RETURN FROM EXILE AND REBUILDING OF THE TEMPLE

OVERVIEW

Ezra 1–6 focuses on the first generation after the return from the Babylonian exile, in which Zerubbabel and Joshua played the leading roles. The principal event in these chapters, in addition to the return itself, is the rebuilding and dedication of the Temple, despite the opposition of the peoples of the land. The decisive importance of the Persian royal favor is noted at the beginning and the end of this unit, and this favor is attributed to divine intervention. The text expresses a political stance of collaboration with the Persian Empire, and it acts as if the community in its entirety consisted of those who had returned from exile. The author seems to have had available the following source documents, which will be further described in the commentary:

1:2-4, a Hebrew copy of the decree of Cyrus
1:9-11, an inventory of temple vessels
2:1–3:1, a list of those who returned from the exile
4:6-7, summaries of letters from Jewish adversaries in the time of Xerxes and Artaxerxes
4:8-16, a letter in Aramaic from Rehum to Artaxerxes
4:17-22, Artaxerxes' reply, in Aramaic
5:6-17, a letter from Tattenai, in Aramaic, to Darius
6:3-12, Darius's reply, in Aramaic, including an Aramaic copy of the decree of Cyrus (vv. 3-5)

Aramaic was the *lingua franca* of the Persian Empire and so was undoubtedly the language in which official correspondence and official records were written. Letters to and from the Persian authorities are presented in 4:8-16, 17-22; 5:6-17; and 6:3-12, including in the latter case a copy of the original decree by Cyrus (6:3-5; also paraphrased in 5:13-15). The question is whether the narrative in Aramaic that surrounds these documents (4:23–5:5; 6:1-2, 13-18) was written by the author of Ezra–Nehemiah[8] or by the author of Ezra 1–6[9], or whether the author of Ezra–Nehemiah incorporated a previously existing Aramaic Chronicle, consisting of both narrative and documents, into his work.[10] Those who believe the author of Ezra–Nehemiah incorporated an Aramaic Chronicle seek to discover differences between the views of the author of Ezra–Nehemiah and the views expressed in the Aramaic Chronicle. They also conclude that the narrative portions of Ezra 4:8–6:18 contain additional historical information. Neither of these approaches seems particularly fruitful. In fact, all the information in the narrative portions can be derived from the letters themselves or from information gleaned from Haggai and Zechariah. We may find it strange that an author who wrote in one language switched to another in the middle of his book, but the Aramaic narrative in Dan 2:4–7:28 serves as a parallel. Thus one may conclude that the author composed an Aramaic narrative that incorporated Aramaic documents and that he continued to write in the Aramaic language until a plausible break-off point was reached. The concluding verses of chap. 6 (vv. 19-22) were written in Hebrew, perhaps as a transition to the Hebrew narrative in the following excerpt from the Ezra Memoir.

Modern scholars are more inclined to accept the authenticity of the decree of Cyrus in 6:3-5

8. Joseph Blenkinsopp, *Ezra–Nehemiah,* OTL (Philadelphia: Westminster, 1988) 42-44.
9. H. G. M. Williamson, "The Composition of Ezra i-vi," *JTS* 33 (1983) 1-30.
10. David J. A. Clines, *Ezra, Nehemiah, Esther,* NCB (Grand Rapids: Eerdmans, 1984) 8; A. H. J. Gunneweg, *Esra,* KAT 19, 1 (Gütersloh: Gütersloher Verlagshaus Gerd Mohn, 1985) 85.

over that in 1:2-4, primarily because Aramaic was the international diplomatic language of the day, much like English is in the late twentieth century. Jewish elements in these and the other documents are often attributed to the role that Jews played within the Persian royal court, although allusions to the exodus and references to the return from exile as the fulfillment of prophecy may show that the author modified the Persian documents theologically when he included them in his text.

Ezra 1–6 was written as an introduction to chaps. 7–10, and probably also to Nehemiah, if indeed Ezra–Nehemiah are to be considered as one book. In both Ezra 1–6 and Ezra 7–Nehemiah 13, the author concentrated on a single generation, with two outstanding leaders in each period (Zerubbabel and Joshua for Ezra 1–6; Ezra and Nehemiah for Ezra 7–Nehemiah 13). The completion and dedication of the Temple serve as a fitting introduction to the establishing of the community in Ezra 7–10, the rebuilding of the walls of Jerusalem in Nehemiah 1–7, and the dedication of the community to the Torah in Nehemiah 8–10. Williamson (see note 9) dates Ezra 1–6 to a period a century later than the combination of Ezra 7–Nehemiah 13 and proposes that the author sought to justify the Jerusalem Temple and its cult after a possible split in its priesthood, the establishment of the Samaritan community, and the first moves to build a temple on Mount Gerizim. This supposed critique of the Samaritan temple and its alternative priesthood, however, seems excessively subtle, and it seems highly unlikely that the pro-Persian orientation of Ezra 1–6 would have been written after the Persian Empire had fallen to Alexander the Great. The final schism between Jerusalem and the Samaritan community, in any case, is best dated to the second century BCE.

EZRA 1:1-11, IMPERIAL PERMISSION TO GO HOME

NIV

1 In the first year of Cyrus king of Persia, in order to fulfill the word of the LORD spoken by Jeremiah, the LORD moved the heart of Cyrus king of Persia to make a proclamation throughout his realm and to put it in writing:

2“This is what Cyrus king of Persia says:

“‘The LORD, the God of heaven, has given me all the kingdoms of the earth and he has appointed me to build a temple for him at Jerusalem in Judah. 3Anyone of his people among you—may his God be with him, and let him go up to Jerusalem in Judah and build the temple of the LORD, the God of Israel, the God who is in Jerusalem. 4And the people of any place where survivors may now be living are to provide him with silver and gold, with goods and livestock, and with freewill offerings for the temple of God in Jerusalem.’”

5Then the family heads of Judah and Benjamin, and the priests and Levites—everyone whose heart God had moved—prepared to go up and build the house of the LORD in Jerusalem. 6All

NRSV

1 In the first year of King Cyrus of Persia, in order that the word of the LORD by the mouth of Jeremiah might be accomplished, the LORD stirred up the spirit of King Cyrus of Persia so that he sent a herald throughout all his kingdom, and also in a written edict declared:

2“Thus says King Cyrus of Persia: The LORD, the God of heaven, has given me all the kingdoms of the earth, and he has charged me to build him a house at Jerusalem in Judah. 3Any of those among you who are of his people—may their God be with them!—are now permitted to go up to Jerusalem in Judah, and rebuild the house of the LORD, the God of Israel—he is the God who is in Jerusalem; 4and let all survivors, in whatever place they reside, be assisted by the people of their place with silver and gold, with goods and with animals, besides freewill offerings for the house of God in Jerusalem.”

5The heads of the families of Judah and Benjamin, and the priests and the Levites—everyone whose spirit God had stirred—got ready to go up

NIV

their neighbors assisted them with articles of silver and gold, with goods and livestock, and with valuable gifts, in addition to all the freewill offerings. 7Moreover, King Cyrus brought out the articles belonging to the temple of the LORD, which Nebuchadnezzar had carried away from Jerusalem and had placed in the temple of his god.[a] 8Cyrus king of Persia had them brought by Mithredath the treasurer, who counted them out to Sheshbazzar the prince of Judah.

9This was the inventory:

gold dishes	30
silver dishes	1,000
silver pans[b]	29
10gold bowls	30
matching silver bowls	410
other articles	1,000

11In all, there were 5,400 articles of gold and of silver. Sheshbazzar brought all these along when the exiles came up from Babylon to Jerusalem.

a 7 Or *gods* b 9 The meaning of the Hebrew for this word is uncertain.

NRSV

and rebuild the house of the LORD in Jerusalem. 6All their neighbors aided them with silver vessels, with gold, with goods, with animals, and with valuable gifts, besides all that was freely offered. 7King Cyrus himself brought out the vessels of the house of the LORD that Nebuchadnezzar had carried away from Jerusalem and placed in the house of his gods. 8King Cyrus of Persia had them released into the charge of Mithredath the treasurer, who counted them out to Sheshbazzar the prince of Judah. 9And this was the inventory: gold basins, thirty; silver basins, one thousand; knives,[a] twenty-nine; 10gold bowls, thirty; other silver bowls, four hundred ten; other vessels, one thousand; 11the total of the gold and silver vessels was five thousand four hundred. All these Sheshbazzar brought up, when the exiles were brought up from Babylonia to Jerusalem.

a Vg: Meaning of Heb uncertain

COMMENTARY

1:1-4. The return from the Babylonian exile took place primarily because of the intervention of divine and human agents: Yahweh "stirred up" (העיר *hēʿîr*, in the hiphil) the spirit of Cyrus II, king of Persia, who issued a decree authorizing the Jews' return to Jerusalem and the rebuilding of the Temple. Whether or not the book of Ezra is a continuation of the books of Chronicles, it presupposes the story told there, including the burning of the Temple and the exiling of all those who had survived Babylon's sword (2 Chr 36:19-20). Twice previously, according to Chronicles, the Lord "had stirred up" the spirit of foreign kings or nations to carry out judgment against Israel (1 Chr 5:26; 2 Chr 21:16).

Cyrus had come to power already in 559 BCE and had rapidly extended his control from Anshan (Elam) to Persia, Media, Lydia, and Assyria. In October 539 BCE, he had conquered Babylon and assumed authority over the exiled Jews; this event, from the point of view of the author, inaugurated a new era, the "first year" of Cyrus (v. 1). By issuing a royal proclamation backed by a written copy, the king became part of a larger plan that fulfilled a prophetic word of Jeremiah. Although the books of Chronicles limit that promise to a seventy-year captivity (2 Chr 36:21; cf. Jer 25:11-12), the author of Ezra may also have thought of Yahweh's promise to bring Israel back to Jerusalem (Jer 29:10; 51:1, 11). Perhaps the author also saw here the fulfillment of the prophecies of Second Isaiah, who had hailed the Lord's commissioning of Cyrus and predicted that Cyrus would set the exiles free and rebuild Jerusalem and the Temple (Isa 41:2, 25; 44:28; 45:1, 13).

The edict of Cyrus is also cited in Aramaic in 6:3-5, often taken to be a more authentic source, and it is paraphrased in 5:13-15. The proclamation recorded in chap. 1 is more suspect historically because it is written in Hebrew, refers to Yahweh by name, orders gifts for the Temple and its cult, and in general describes an exodus-like return from exile.[11] After his conquest of Babylon, Cyrus did not use the title "King of Persia" (v. 2) for himself in any of his extant inscriptions. While commentators are divided on the authenticity of the document cited in vv. 2-4, they agree that at least in some details it was shaped by Jewish advisers in the Persian court or by the biblical author. The attribution of his worldwide rule to the Lord (v. 2) does not mean that the king had become a Yahwist, but only that he was accommodating himself to Jewish religious presuppositions. Similarly, in the famous Cyrus cylinder, Cyrus reported that Marduk, the god of Babylon, had chosen him and declared him to be ruler of all the world.[12] The title "the God of Heaven" was attributed to Baal Hadad in pre-exilic times. After the exile it was occasionally used also by Jews with reference to their own God, especially when they were speaking to foreigners (Neh 1:4-5; Dan 2:37-44; Jonah 1:9). Because Yahweh was the God of heaven, Yahweh's actions had effects well beyond the geographical borders of Israel.

In distinction to the version of the decree in 6:3-5, the proclamation in chap. 1 grants permission for the Jews to return to Jerusalem—a possible argument for its authenticity. Cyrus's wish that God would be with them, however, may echo Jerusalemite traditions (Ps 46:7, 11; Isa 7:14). To "go up" (עלה *'ālâ*) to Jerusalem is multivalent; it could connote a pilgrimage, compare the return home to the exodus (in both cases the people "go up" [*'ālâ*] to the land; this usage is preserved in the modern term עליה [*aliyah*], used for Jews who emigrate to modern-day Israel), or it may indicate that in leaving Babylon one would follow the course of the Euphrates toward the north before descending to Israel.

The term "survivors" (הנשאר *hanniš'ār*, v. 4), with reference to the exiles, has the theological connotation of "remnant" (1 Chr 13:2; 2 Chr 30:6; 34:21; 36:20; Neh 1:2-3). These survivors were to be supported by their non-Jewish neighbors, much as the Israelites of the first exodus received aid from the Egyptians (Exod 3:21-22; 11:2; 12:35-36). Second Isaiah also drew a typological comparison between the first exodus and the return to the land as a second exodus, but he suggested that those leaving for home should not accept gifts from the Babylonians (Isa 52:11). In addition to financial aid and logistic supplies for the returnees, Cyrus included voluntary offerings for the Temple itself (see 1:4; 3:5; 2 Chr 31:14; 35:8).

1:5-8. Verse 5 recognizes that not all the exiles did return, but only those "whose spirit God had stirred" (העיר האלהים את-רוחו *hē'îr hā'ĕlōhîm et-rûḥô*), a clause that echoes the Lord's stirring up of Cyrus in v. 1. The exact number of those who returned is unknown (see Commentary on 2:1-70), but it is likely that the majority of the exiles stayed in Babylon. Josephus noted that many did not want to exchange what they had acquired in exile for a more uncertain future in the land.[13] The list of returnees in v. 5 begins with the "heads of families," who are sometimes called "elders" in Ezra–Nehemiah. "Families" (בית אבות *bêt 'ābôt*; lit., "fathers' [houses]") were an important sociological subdivision within the tribal system, to which an individual would be related by genealogical descent. In pre-exilic times a "family" referred to a group composed of all living persons, except married women, who were descended from a person who was still living. During the restoration period, however, the term was used to refer to conglomerates of such households, more like the "clans" of pre-exilic times.[14] The families in 2:3-19 averaged about 900 people apiece.

The tribes of Judah and Benjamin (v. 5) comprised the primary population groups of the province called Yehud (2:20-35). Among the clergy who returned were the priests and the Levites. In the Pentateuch, the priests were descendants of Aaron (Num 3:10), to whom the Levites were assigned as helpers or clergy of a secondary rank (Num 3:5-9). Verse 6 presents an idealized picture that again echoes themes of the first exodus: Non-Jewish neighbors readily followed the invita-

11. The authenticity of the decrees in chaps. 1 and 6 was defended by Elias J. Bickerman, "The Edict of Cyrus in Ezra 1," *JBL* 65 (1946) 249-75. He distinguished between an oral proclamation addressed to the Jews and published by heralds in Hebrew, and an official Aramaic firman, or royal decree. Chapter 1 of Ezra says that the Temple is to be rebuilt by private contributions while chap. 6 promises government funds. See also Roland de Vaux, "The Decrees of Cyrus and Darius on the Rebuilding of the Temple," in *The Bible and the Ancient Near East* (London: Darton, Longman & Todd, 1976) 63-96.

12. *ANET*, 315.

13. Josephus *Antiquities of the Jews* XI.1-3.

14. Daniel L. Smith, *The Religion of the Landless: The Social Context of the Babylonian Exile* (Bloomington, Ind.: Meyer-Stone Books, 1989) 99. See also Joel Weinberg, *The Citizen-Temple Community*, JSOTSup 151 (Sheffield: Sheffield Academic, 1992).

tion of Cyrus by providing material aid and voluntary gifts for the Temple. The provision of animals (NIV, "livestock") recalls the numerous livestock that accompanied Israel at the first exodus (Exod 12:38).

Cyrus contributed to the return by restoring to the Jews the temple vessels that Nebuchadnezzar had taken from Jerusalem (v. 7; cf. 2 Chr 36:10, 18) and placed in the temple of his god (so NIV; NRSV, "gods"), Marduk. The restoration of the vessels is part of the king's decree in 6:5. These vessels provide real and symbolic continuity between the new Temple and the destroyed Temple (cf. 2 Chr 13:11). The return of the vessels may be compared with Cyrus's restoration of divine statues to their original temple cities in other countries. Israel's aniconic tradition meant that there were no statues of Yahweh that could be returned. Temple vessels are mentioned again during Ezra's return (7:19; 8:25-30, 33-34). "Mithredath," the treasurer to whom Cyrus handed the vessels, is a typical Persian name meaning "the gift of [the god] Mithra." The word "treasurer" is also a Persian rather than a Hebrew word. Jerome transliterated it freely as "Gabazar" in the Vulgate, and this eventually led to the creation of the name "Caspar" and its assignment to one of the magi (Matthew 2).

Mithredath relayed the vessels to Sheshbazzar, the prince of Judah. Sheshbazzar, although a Jew, has a Babylonian name with the meaning "May Shamash protect the father [of this child]." Outside of this chapter Sheshbazzar is mentioned only in 5:14-16, where he is given the title of governor and is credited with laying the "foundations of the house of God." Sheshbazzar is not to be identified with Shenazzar, one of the five sons of King Jehoiachin, listed in 1 Chr 3:18. Since he is called governor and since Nehemiah refers to a number of his predecessors as governors (Neh 5:15), it seems that the province of Judah may have been independent and may have had an officially designated Persian governor right from the start. Albrecht Alt, however, proposed that until the time of Nehemiah Jerusalem was under the governorship of Samaria.[15] No one knows what happened to Sheshbazzar or when he was replaced by Zerubbabel. Some commentators conclude that the author of Ezra, like Josephus, identified these two governors as one person since he mentions Zerubbabel without introductory comment in 2:2. The term "prince" (נשׂיא *nāśî'*; v. 8) does not necessarily designate a descendant of the Davidic line, even though Ezekiel used the term to refer to the royal leader of the eschatological Israelite community in Ezekiel 40–48. "Prince" is used in Exod 22:28 (cf. Num 7:84) to refer to a leader of one of the tribes. The more general meaning of "leader" fits the context in Ezra 1:8.

1:9-11. The inventory of temple vessels probably comes from a source available to the author. The varying translations in the NRSV ("basins," "knives," "other silver bowls") and the NIV ("dishes," "silver pans," "matching silver bowls") reflect scholarly uncertainty about the correct meaning of these words. The first of these words (אגרטלי *'ăgarṭĕlê*, "basins"/"dishes") has five consonants (an unusually long word in Hebrew) and may be a Persian loan word. The term "knives" (מחלפים *maḥălāpîm*) follows the translation provided by the Vulgate.[16] Instead of "other silver bowls" the RSV reads "two thousand four hundred and ten bowls of silver," based on 1 Esdr 2:13, but it is unclear how the word משׁנים (*mišnîm*), now preserved in the HB, could be understood as 2,000. In any, case the total for all the vessels given in v. 11 (5,400) does not equal the total of the figures given in vv. 9-10 (2,499). The individual figures in the RSV differ from the MT (1,000, 1,000, 29, 30, 2,410, 1,000) and total 5,469 (see 1 Esdr 2:14), which is close to the number 5,400 given in Ezra 1:11. Only vessels of gold or silver are mentioned in v. 11; perhaps articles of bronze, such as the bronze sea (2 Kgs 25:14-17), had been melted down during the destruction or were not considered valuable enough to be included in this list.

Verse 11 emphasizes that Sheshbazzar "brought up" (העלה *he'ĕlâ*, in the hiphil) the vessels, but along with them were "brought up" (העלות *he'ālôt*) the exiles from Babylon to Jerusalem. The term "exiles" (גולה *gôlâ*; sometimes "children of the exile") is used frequently in Ezra

15. Albrecht Alt, "Die Rolle Samarias bei der Entstehung des Judentums," *Kleine Schriften* 2 (Munich: Beck, 1953).

16. In his commentary and in *BHS* note 9[b], Rudolph interpreted this word, which he revocalizes, as a marginal gloss meaning "to be corrected," which was mistakenly entered into the text. See Wilhelm Rudolph, *Esra und Nehemia, Samt 3. Esra.* HAT 20 (Tübingen: J. B. C. Mohr [Paul Siebeck], 1949).

and Nehemiah as a designation for the post-exilic community. According to the chronicler, the land had been vacant during the exile (2 Chr 36:20-21).

REFLECTIONS

In many respects the restoration of the Jewish community in Palestine was a more or less insignificant event in one corner of the vast Persian Empire, which stretched from Greece toward the east, beyond modern Afghanistan. The account in this chapter ignores the contributions to the post-exilic community of those who had never gone into exile and who had maintained worship of the Lord in the meantime back home (Jer 41:5; Zech 7:5). Instead, the author saw in the return of the exiles the providential hand of the Lord, the same Lord who had been the power behind Israel's captors. In judgment and in grace, the author experienced the same God, who had been faithful in both of these actions.

The restoration of the community was a sign that the prophetic word of God remained true and reliable. That word had also been important for the deuteronomistic historian (Deut 31:16-17, 20; Josh 21:45) and especially for Second Isaiah, who affirmed that the word or promise of God would stand forever (Isa 40:8). When church and government are as impermanent as the grass that withers and the flower that decays, there is sometimes no evident reason why faith should still be the best alternative and why God's promises should be trusted. But the author of Ezra–Nehemiah confessed that Yahweh had faithfully fulfilled the word spoken through Jeremiah and had enlisted the great Emperor Cyrus in the divine plan.

God's actions and God's word lent legitimacy to the struggling and tiny community in Judah, whose uneven history is recounted in the following chapters of Ezra and Nehemiah. Despite all its warts and blemishes, despite failures by leadership and individual members, this little community, gathered around its Temple, was God's people. In going up to Jerusalem it had repeated symbolically the trip out of Egypt taken by its forebears. Unbelieving neighbors back at the time of the exodus and now at this return from exile recognized the legitimacy of the community through financial and material support. While continuity is established theologically by God's words and actions, human faith also needs tangible signs or cultural expressions to experience true continuity and a feeling of being at home. The temple vessels, so familiar and yet obscure enough to have the meaning of most of their technical terms forgotten, linked together the pre-exilic and the post-exilic communities.

The imperial government permitted, even encouraged, the return home. Sometimes Cyrus has been hailed as a unique individual, a cultural breakthrough, whose generosity toward the captive Jews went beyond any expectations. As Amélie Kuhrt has shown, however, his policies of restoring people and cults were also in his own best interest and were designed to keep peace within the empire.[17] All the restored gods were to "pray daily to Bel and Nabu for my [Cyrus's] length of days." In a number of ways his imperial policies continued those of the Assyrians, who have a well-deserved, almost universally negative public reputation. Still, without Persian state support—humanly speaking—the restoration would never have happened. There were dangers in the cooperation between the Persians and the Judeans, of course, as there always are in the interplay of church and state. The priestly community was willing to go along with the status quo and to live dependently within the Persian Empire. Perhaps that was a wise course; perhaps it was the only feasible course. But one wonders what had happened to belief in the old promises of the land or the promises to David. Acceptance of the political status quo can also be a sign of little faith.

Those who returned were affected by public displays of divine initiative and political

17. Amélie Kuhrt, "The Cyrus Cylinder and Achaemenid Imperial Policy," *JSOT* 25 (1983) 83-97.

permission, but they were also people whose inner spirit God had stirred up. Some of their colleagues stayed behind in Babylon to retain their acquired status, perhaps because they had lost the vision. Some—how large a number we do not know—said yes to the invitation to go home. In this combination of divine empowerment and human decision among those who returned is reflected the paradox that Paul expressed so memorably: "Work out your own salvation with fear and trembling; for it is God who is at work in you, enabling you both to will and to work for his good pleasure" (Phil 2:12*b*-13 NRSV). Our claim to being saved by grace alone carries with it the correlary assumption that God's grace empowers us actively to do justice, love kindness, and walk humbly with God (Mic 6:8).

Sheshbazzar, the leader of this returning group, was no Moses. Whether appointed by the king or elected by the people, he had achieved leadership and responsibility. He was "prince" and "governor"; he was the person responsible for receiving the temple vessels and carrying them home, and his tasks included initial work on the Temple. But Sheshbazzar never makes a speech in the Bible, apparently delivered no law or performed any miracle. We do not even know how his career ended. And yet, without him, would the community in Judah have ever restarted at all? Such nondescript leadership is often significant for the people of God today. Each week Christians gather in congregations across the land, without fanfare or public notice, and then go forth into ministry in daily life to turn the other cheek, to care for the lonely and the marginalized, to forgive as they have been forgiven, to love their enemies. A stanza in a hymn by Daniel March points out the significance of such Sheshbazzars (cf. Exod 17:11-13):

> If you cannot be a watchman,
> Standing high on Zion's wall,
> Pointing out the path to heaven,
> Off'ring life and peace to all,
> With your prayers and with your bounties
> You can do what God demands;
> You can be like faithful Aaron,
> Holding up the prophet's hands.

EZRA 2:1-70, THE LIST OF THOSE WHO RETURNED

NIV

2 Now these are the people of the province
who came up from the captivity of the
exiles, whom Nebuchadnezzar king of Babylon
had taken captive to Babylon (they returned to
Jerusalem and Judah, each to his own town, 2in
company with Zerubbabel, Jeshua, Nehemiah,
Seraiah, Reelaiah, Mordecai, Bilshan, Mispar,
Bigvai, Rehum and Baanah):

The list of the men of the people of Israel:

3the descendants of Parosh	2,172
4of Shephatiah	372
5of Arah	775

NRSV

2 Now these were the people of the province
who came from those captive exiles whom
King Nebuchadnezzar of Babylon had carried cap-
tive to Babylonia; they returned to Jerusalem and
Judah, all to their own towns. 2They came with
Zerubbabel, Jeshua, Nehemiah, Seraiah, Reelaiah,
Mordecai, Bilshan, Mispar, Bigvai, Rehum, and
Baanah.

The number of the Israelite people: 3the descendants of Parosh, two thousand one hundred
seventy-two. 4Of Shephatiah, three hundred seventy-two. 5Of Arah, seven hundred seventy-five.
6Of Pahath-moab, namely the descendants of

NIV

6of Pahath-Moab (through the line of Jeshua and Joab)	2,812
7of Elam	1,254
8of Zattu	945
9of Zaccai	760
10of Bani	642
11of Bebai	623
12of Azgad	1,222
13of Adonikam	666
14of Bigvai	2,056
15of Adin	454
16of Ater (through Hezekiah)	98
17of Bezai	323
18of Jorah	112
19of Hashum	223
20of Gibbar	95
21the men of Bethlehem	123
22of Netophah	56
23of Anathoth	128
24of Azmaveth	42
25of Kiriath Jearim,[a] Kephirah and Beeroth	743
26of Ramah and Geba	621
27of Micmash	122
28of Bethel and Ai	223
29of Nebo	52
30of Magbish	156
31of the other Elam	1,254
32of Harim	320
33of Lod, Hadid and Ono	725
34of Jericho	345
35of Senaah	3,630

36The priests:

the descendants of Jedaiah (through the family of Jeshua)	973
37of Immer	1,052
38of Pashhur	1,247
39of Harim	1,017

40The Levites:

the descendants of Jeshua and Kadmiel (through the line of Hodaviah)	74

41The singers:

the descendants of Asaph	128

42The gatekeepers of the temple:

a 25 See Septuagint (see also Neh. 7:29); Hebrew *Kiriath Arim.*

NRSV

Jeshua and Joab, two thousand eight hundred
twelve. 7Of Elam, one thousand two hundred
fifty-four. 8Of Zattu, nine hundred forty-five. 9Of
Zaccai, seven hundred sixty. 10Of Bani, six hundred forty-two. 11Of Bebai, six hundred twenty-
three. 12Of Azgad, one thousand two hundred
twenty-two. 13Of Adonikam, six hundred sixty-six.
14Of Bigvai, two thousand fifty-six. 15Of Adin, four
hundred fifty-four. 16Of Ater, namely of Hezekiah,
ninety-eight. 17Of Bezai, three hundred twenty-
three. 18Of Jorah, one hundred twelve. 19Of
Hashum, two hundred twenty-three. 20Of Gibbar,
ninety-five. 21Of Bethlehem, one hundred twenty-
three. 22The people of Netophah, fifty-six. 23Of
Anathoth, one hundred twenty-eight. 24The descendants of Azmaveth, forty-two. 25Of
Kiriatharim, Chephirah, and Beeroth, seven hundred forty-three. 26Of Ramah and Geba, six hundred twenty-one. 27The people of Michmas, one
hundred twenty-two. 28Of Bethel and Ai, two
hundred twenty-three. 29The descendants of
Nebo, fifty-two. 30Of Magbish, one hundred fifty-
six. 31Of the other Elam, one thousand two hundred fifty-four. 32Of Harim, three hundred twenty.
33Of Lod, Hadid, and Ono, seven hundred twenty-
five. 34Of Jericho, three hundred forty-five. 35Of
Senaah, three thousand six hundred thirty.

36The priests: the descendants of Jedaiah, of
the house of Jeshua, nine hundred seventy-three.
37Of Immer, one thousand fifty-two. 38Of Pashhur,
one thousand two hundred forty-seven. 39Of
Harim, one thousand seventeen.

40The Levites: the descendants of Jeshua and
Kadmiel, of the descendants of Hodaviah, seventy-
four. 41The singers: the descendants of Asaph, one
hundred twenty-eight. 42The descendants of the
gatekeepers: of Shallum, of Ater, of Talmon, of
Akkub, of Hatita, and of Shobai, in all one hundred thirty-nine.

43The temple servants: the descendants of
Ziha, Hasupha, Tabbaoth, 44Keros, Siaha, Padon,
45Lebanah, Hagabah, Akkub, 46Hagab, Shamlai,
Hanan, 47Giddel, Gahar, Reaiah, 48Rezin, Nekoda,
Gazzam, 49Uzza, Paseah, Besai, 50Asnah, Meunim,
Nephisim, 51Bakbuk, Hakupha, Harhur, 52Bazluth,
Mehida, Harsha, 53Barkos, Sisera, Temah, 54Nez-
iah, and Hatipha.

55The descendants of Solomon's servants: Sotai,

NIV

the descendants of
Shallum, Ater, Talmon,
Akkub, Hatita and Shobai 139

[43]The temple servants:

the descendants of
Ziha, Hasupha, Tabbaoth,
[44]Keros, Siaha, Padon,
[45]Lebanah, Hagabah, Akkub,
[46]Hagab, Shalmai, Hanan,
[47]Giddel, Gahar, Reaiah,
[48]Rezin, Nekoda, Gazzam,
[49]Uzza, Paseah, Besai,
[50]Asnah, Meunim, Nephussim,
[51]Bakbuk, Hakupha, Harhur,
[52]Bazluth, Mehida, Harsha,
[53]Barkos, Sisera, Temah,
[54]Neziah and Hatipha

[55]The descendants of the servants of Solomon:

the descendants of
Sotai, Hassophereth, Peruda,
[56]Jaala, Darkon, Giddel,
[57]Shephatiah, Hattil,
Pokereth-Hazzebaim and Ami

[58]The temple servants and the descendants
of the servants of Solomon 392

[59]The following came up from the towns of Tel Melah, Tel Harsha, Kerub, Addon and Immer, but they could not show that their families were descended from Israel:

[60]The descendants of
Delaiah, Tobiah and Nekoda 652

[61]And from among the priests:

The descendants of
Hobaiah, Hakkoz and Barzillai (a man who had married a daughter of Barzillai the Gileadite and was called by that name).

[62]These searched for their family records, but they could not find them and so were excluded from the priesthood as unclean. [63]The governor ordered them not to eat any of the most sacred food until there was a priest ministering with the Urim and Thummim.

[64]The whole company numbered 42,360,

NRSV

Hassophereth, Peruda, [56]Jaalah, Darkon, Giddel, [57]Shephatiah, Hattil, Pochereth-hazzebaim, and Ami.

58All the temple servants and the descendants of Solomon's servants were three hundred ninety-two.

59The following were those who came up from Tel-melah, Tel-harsha, Cherub, Addan, and Immer, though they could not prove their families or their descent, whether they belonged to Israel: [60]the descendants of Delaiah, Tobiah, and Nekoda, six hundred fifty-two. [61]Also, of the descendants of the priests: the descendants of Habaiah, Hakkoz, and Barzillai (who had married one of the daughters of Barzillai the Gileadite, and was called by their name). [62]These looked for their entries in the genealogical records, but they were not found there, and so they were excluded from the priesthood as unclean; [63]the governor told them that they were not to partake of the most holy food, until there should be a priest to consult Urim and Thummim.

64The whole assembly together was forty-two thousand three hundred sixty, [65]besides their male and female servants, of whom there were seven thousand three hundred thirty-seven; and they had two hundred male and female singers. [66]They had seven hundred thirty-six horses, two hundred forty-five mules, [67]four hundred thirty-five camels, and six thousand seven hundred twenty donkeys.

68As soon as they came to the house of the LORD in Jerusalem, some of the heads of families made freewill offerings for the house of God, to erect it on its site. [69]According to their resources they gave to the building fund sixty-one thousand darics of gold, five thousand minas of silver, and one hundred priestly robes.

70The priests, the Levites, and some of the people lived in Jerusalem and its vicinity;[a] and the singers, the gatekeepers, and the temple servants lived in their towns, and all Israel in their towns.

[a] 1 Esdras 5.46: Heb lacks *lived in Jerusalem and its vicinity*

NIV

65besides their 7,337 menservants and maidservants; and they also had 200 men and
women singers. 66They had 736 horses, 245
mules, 67435 camels and 6,720 donkeys.

68When they arrived at the house of the LORD
in Jerusalem, some of the heads of the families
gave freewill offerings toward the rebuilding of
the house of God on its site. 69According to their
ability they gave to the treasury for this work
61,000 drachmas[a] of gold, 5,000 minas[b] of silver
and 100 priestly garments.

70The priests, the Levites, the singers, the gatekeepers and the temple servants settled in their
own towns, along with some of the other people,
and the rest of the Israelites settled in their towns.

[a] *69* That is, about 1,100 pounds (about 500 kilograms) [b] *69* That is, about 3 tons (about 2.9 metric tons)

COMMENTARY

The list of those who returned in Ezra 2:1-67 is almost exactly duplicated by Neh 7:6-69, although there are many differences in spelling, numerical totals, and other textual matters, for which 1 Esdras and Nehemiah often preserve jointly more original readings.[18] A paragraph following this list and forming a transition to the next chapter is also largely the same in both chapters (Ezra 2:68–3:1//Neh 7:70–8:1). Three questions have dominated the scholarly discussion of this chapter and remain in large part unresolved: Was the list of returnees originally located in Ezra 2 or in Nehemiah 7? What does this list really describe? What is its date?

Nehemiah cited this list in his efforts to move 10 percent of the population of Judah to Jerusalem, apparently using it as a way of evaluating the purity of their descent (Neh 7:5), but after the list has been presented, Nehemiah 8–10 deals with the reading of the law and the making of a covenant, before returning to the process of population transfer in chap. 11. At the end of Ezra 1, where we would expect to find a report of Sheshbazzar's return from Babylon to Jerusalem (1:11), "the list of those who returned" now serves in lieu of that account, and Sheshbazzar's absence is notable. Hence the list is awkward or secondary in both Ezra 2 and Nehemiah 7.

Many scholars argue that the list was first included in Nehemiah and was then copied from Nehemiah 7 into Ezra 2. They think that the seventh month in Neh 7:73 fits its context better than the same reference in Ezra 3:1 and that Ezra 2:69 is an abbreviation of Neh 7:70-72, rather than Nehemiah's being an expansion of Ezra. Williamson proposes that Ezra 2:68 is an addition designed to fit its present context in Ezra and that Neh 7:73*a* is an original sentence from the Nehemiah Memoir that has now been expanded in Ezra 2:70.[19] Blenkinsopp, however, has countered that the syntax in Neh 7:70 is awkward because the list is secondary in Nehemiah and that the reference to the seventh month in Ezra 3:1 is altogether appropriate because of the mention of the Feast of Tabernacles later in the chapter (3:4, 6). He opts for Ezra 2 as the original location for the list.[20] The question about the original location

18. Ralph W. Klein, "Old Readings in 1 Esdras: The List of Returnees from Babylon (Ezra 2//Nehemiah 7)," *HTR* 61 (1969) 99-107.

19. H. G. M. Williamson, *Ezra, Nehemiah,* WBC 16 (Waco, Tex.: Word, 1985) 29-30.

20. Joseph Blenkinsopp, *Ezra–Nehemiah,* OTL (Philadelphia: Westminster, 1988) 43-44.

of the list is still open, and attention will focus on how the list now functions in each of its canonical contexts.

Since the numbers in the list are too large for the initial return—they far exceed the number of those who had been deported according to 2 Kgs 24:14 (10,000); 2 Kgs 24:16 (8,000), and Jer 52:28-30 (4,600)—commentators face a baffling question: What was the purpose of this list originally in its pre-canonical context? Note that Sheshbazzar is not included in the list despite expectations raised by his leadership in chap. 1 and that the references to people from various towns seem to presuppose settled life in the land. Galling proposed that the list was designed to prove to the Samarians that the true Israel had sufficient material and human resources to rebuild the Temple without any outside help.[21] Hölscher believed it was a Persian tax list.[22] Albrecht Alt thought it was a list made by Zerubbabel to determine the right of returning exiles to the land.[23] Albright understood it as a census of the community from the time of Nehemiah.[24] Weinberg believed it contains a list of the "fathers' houses" (בית אבות *bêt 'ābôt*), which made up the civic temple community in the mid-fifth century BCE.[25] These collectives consisted of a number of families that were related, in fact or by genealogical invention, and arose in the context of exile and restoration. The solidarity of these groups was based on their communal ownership of the land, and the name of the *bêt 'ābôt* was included in the full name of each of its members. Several recent commentators interpret the list either as a combined summary of several returns from exile or as a census record from approximately the time of Nehemiah.

21. Kurt Galling, "Die Liste der aus dem Exil Heimgekehrten," *Studien zur Geschichte Israels im persischen Zeitalter* (Tübingen: Mohr, 1964) 89-108.

22. Hölscher, "Die Bücher Esra und Nehemia." *Die heilige Schrift des Alten Testaments,* ed. E. Kautzsch and A. Bertholet, 4th ed. (Tübingen: Mohr, 1923) 503-4.

23. Albrecht Alt, *Kleine Schriften,* (Munich: Beck, 1953) 2:34-35.

24. William F. Albright, *The Biblical Period from Abraham to Ezra,* 2nd ed. (New York: Harper and Bros., 1963) 110-11.

25. Joel Weinberg, *The Citizen-Temple Community,* JSOTSup 151 (Sheffield: Sheffield Academic, 1992) esp. 49-61. There are 17 lay collectives named after various ancestors in Ezra 2:3-19 (= Neh 7:8-24) and some additional lay collectives named after localities in Ezra 2:20-35 (= Neh 7:25-38). Joseph Blenkinsopp writes approvingly about Weinberg's sociological analysis, but believes that the figures in Ezra 2//Nehemiah 7 are much too large for the civic temple community itself. See Joseph Blenkinsopp, "Temple and Society in Achemenid Judah" in *Persian Period,* ed. P. R. Davies, Second Temple Studies 1 (Sheffield: Sheffield Academic, 1991) 22-53.

The unclarity about the genre of the list affects the discussion of its date. The major options are the first two decades of the restoration period (538–515 BCE) if it is the list of several returns, or the mid-fifth century if it is some kind of census document. On two issues there is agreement: The list was available in a source document, and its use in Ezra 2 and Nehemiah 7 is secondary to the original intention of the list. In Ezra the list gives the impression of a wholehearted response to Cyrus's permission to go home; in Nehemiah it provides background for transferring 10 percent of the population to Jerusalem, and it shows that the entire community was present for the reading of the law in Nehemiah 8.

2:1-2. The author does not supply an account of the exiles' arrival home, but inserts instead a list of the members of the community who had been saved from exile. The reader thust concludes that the community that returned home was authentic, relatively large, and a complete expression of Israel. We can be fairly certain that not all the people were able to return to their towns of origin (despite 2:1), since some of the settlements lay outside the old territory of Judah and, no doubt, many destroyed towns were never restored. Those who returned made up the "province" (v. 1) called Yehud in Persian documents. Yehud was at first a part of a large satrapy, Beyond the River (see 4:10), which originally included Babylon and all of Syro-Palestine. During the reign of Xerxes, Babylon became an independent satrapy because of the frequent disturbances that took place in it, but the rest of the western satrapy continued to be called Beyond the River.

Before the list itself begins, the author names the leaders of the community over a considerable span of time (v. 2). The insertion of Nahamani after Reeliah (following Neh 7:7; cf. 1 Esdr 5:8, Eneneus) brings the number of leaders to twelve, symbolic of all Israel. Zerubbabel and Nehemiah were governors, while Jeshua was the high priest. The fourth name, "Seraiah," is sometimes replaced with "Azariah" (Neh 7:7; cf. 1 Esdr 5:8), an alternate spelling of the name "Ezra." The Persian name "Bigvai" is sometimes spelled "Bagoas" or "Bagohi"; this Bigvai may be identified with a governor of Yehud after Nehemiah. All the other names are unknown.

2:3-35. The list begins with the laity (vv. 3-35) before the clergy (vv. 36-58), an unusual order for the books of Ezra and Nehemiah and probably a further indication that the author was using a list drawn up for another purpose. The list of laity is broken down into two subdivisions: a list of people according to family names ("the descendants of," vv. 3-20) and a list of residents according to city names ("the people of," vv. 21-35).

2:3-20. Many of the family names reappear among the signers of the firm agreement in Nehemiah 10, among those who returned with Ezra in Ezra 8, or among those who divorced their wives in Ezra 10. "Pahath-Moab" (v. 6) is not a name, but a title meaning "governor of Moab." Moab was ruled from Judah during the united monarchy, and the founder of this family may have stemmed from that era. An additional 418 members of this family returned with Ezra (8:4, 9). "Bigvai" (v. 14; cf. 2:2) has one of the largest families. "Gabbar" (v. 20) appears as "Gibeon" in Neh 7:25. If the latter reading is correct, this verse should be included among the city names. The total in the list of family names is 15,604.

2:21-35. The first two city names are the only ones indisputably from Judah; almost all of the rest are from Benjamin. Bethlehem (v. 21) and Netophah (v. 22) are located just south of Jerusalem. Anathoth (v. 23), the birthplace of Jeremiah, is located three miles northeast of Jerusalem. Just to the north of it is (Beth)-azmaveth (v. 24; see Neh 7:28). Kiriatharim (probably the same as Kiriath Jearim, NIV), Chephirah, and Beeroth were among the towns allied with Gibeon at the time of Joshua (Josh 9:17; 18:25-28). Ramah and Geba (v. 26) were border cities, sometimes disputed between the northern and southern kingdoms (Josh 18:24-25; 1 Kgs 15:17, 22), with Michmas (v. 27) lying just north of Geba. Josiah annexed the Benjaminite (Josh 18:22) cities of Bethel and Ai (v. 28) to the southern kingdom; originally they had belonged to the northern kingdom. The identity of Nebo (v. 29) is unsure, but may be a hill in the northern environs of Jerusalem, the home of the Elide priesthood (1 Sam 22:11; cf. Neh 11:32). Magbish (v. 30), unknown, is lacking in Nehemiah 7. Elam (v. 31) is also recorded among the family names where it is more appropriate (v. 7). In both places the group has the same number of members. Harim (v. 32) is unknown. Lod, Hadid, and Ono (v. 33) are roughly twenty-five miles northwest of Jerusalem and so are more remote than the other towns. Jericho (v. 34) was originally part of Benjamin (Josh 18:21), but during much of its history belonged to the northern kingdom. The location of Senaah (סנאה *sĕnāʾâ*, v. 35) is uncertain. The most probable site, eight miles north of Jericho, seems too remote for so large a group of people. Some commentators parse (שׂנאה *śĕnāʾâ*) as a noun meaning "hated one" so that its people would be the "despised" or "rejected"—that is, members of the lower class. The total of the numbers in this list of city names is 8,540.

2:36-39. The priests comprise roughly 10 percent of the total list. Three of the four names also appear in the list of twenty-four priestly courses in 1 Chr 24:7-18. Only Pashhur is missing there, perhaps because this group of priests later lost its priestly status. Jeshua, the son of Jozadak (2:3; 3:2), is the high priest.

2:40-42. The number of Levites (v. 40), 74, is exceedingly small (1 Chr 23:3 lists 38,000 at David's time!), and Ezra later finds none among those scheduled to return with him (8:15). After a diligent search he does come up with an additional 38 (8:18-19). Perhaps relatively few Levites had gone into exile because of their low social status, or perhaps Levites were reluctant to return to the land, since they knew their rights would be restricted in the Golah community (see Ezek 44:10-14). Neither the singers nor the gatekeepers had yet risen to full levitical status (cf. 3:10; 1 Chr 9:18, 26, 33-34). The only singers identified by name are the descendants of Asaph (v. 41), traditionally associated with Psalms 50; 73–83. The gatekeepers had been set aside in the time of David and were responsible for guarding the ritual purity of the Temple and taking charge of the temple stores (see Neh 11:19).

2:43-58. Moving further down the hierarchical scale we come to the temple servants (those "given" [נתינים *nĕtînîm*] to the Levites as servants; vv. 43-54) and the servants of Solomon (vv. 55-57). These groups are not known before the exile, but are mentioned in 1 Chr 9:2, in Ezra 7:24 and 8:20, and several times in Nehemiah. As full members of the Golah assembly, they are clearly distinguished from the slaves in v. 65. The temple servants, but apparently not the servants of Solomon, had the right to sign the firm agreement in Neh 10:28-29. The totals for these two groups are given together as 392 (v. 58).

2:59-63. Finally, the document notes groups of laypeople and priests who were unable to establish their genealogical relationship to the assembly. The laity included the descendants of Delaiah, Tobiah, and Nekoda, the first two of whom have Yahwistic names (a Nekoda also appears among the temple servants in v. 48). The relationship between this Tobiah and Nehemiah's opponent (Neh 2:10) or the later Tobiad group of priests is unknown. The Babylonian towns are also unknown, but the "Tel" prefix on two of them may indicate that these exiles had been settled at abandoned sites. Note that the prophet Ezekiel was located at Tel Abib (Ezek 3:15).

Three priestly families were also unable to prove their genealogical connections to established families (v. 61). Hakkoz (cf. 1 Chr 24:10) appears to have regained his status later since his descendants were among the builders of Nehemiah's wall (Neh 3:4, 21; cf. Ezra 8:33). Barzillai acquired the name for his priestly family by marrying the daughter of a priest at the time of David (2 Sam 17:27-29; 19:31-39; 1 Kgs 2:7). He had defended David when he fled from Absalom, and the king asked Solomon to treat him kindly. There are no parallels for acquiring a family name through one's wife. The priests without proper genealogies were excluded from their duties lest they bring ritual impurity on the cultic community. In addition, the governor told them not to eat the most sacred food, reserved for the sons of Aaron (see Lev 7:1-10), though they could presumably eat ordinary holy food that had been set aside for the priests and the Levites (Neh 12:44, 47). The term "governor" (תרשׁתא *tiršātā'*) is related to an Old Persian word meaning "revered." This governor (cf. Neh 7:65, 70; 8:9; 10:1; 12:26) cannot be identified by name because the date of the list is unclear; 1 Esdr 5:40 adds the word "Nehemiah" to the text. The banning of these priests was only to be temporary—that is, until a priest using the Urim and the Thummim could make an appropriate decision. The Urim and the Thummim could provide a postive or negative answer to a question—or provide no answer (Exod 28:30; Lev 8:8; 1 Sam 14:36-37, 41-42; 28:6). No other use of this device is attested after the time of King Saul.

2:64-70. The whole assembly of the exiles (v. 64) numbered 42,360, though the total of the individual numbers comes to only 29,818 in Ezra (31,089 in Nehemiah, and 30,142 in 1 Esdras). Williamson and Rudolph propose that the difference between the grand total and the sum of individual numbers resulted from including women in the calculation, though Clines notes that this would mean that men outnumbered women by about 3 to 1.[26] In any case, the numbers seem too high for any single return to the land from exile. The 200 singers (v. 65) were apparently attached to certain families as entertainers (2 Sam 19:35; Eccl 2:8), since female singers were not permitted inside the Temple. The animals listed in v. 66 may be another allusion to the exodus (cf. Exod 12:38 and Ezra 1:4, 6), or they may be an attempt to provide a full account of what would comprise a caravan that went from Babylon to Jerusalem.

The heads of families made a contribution for the Temple as soon as they came from Babylon to Jerusalem (v. 68; cf. Exod 25:2-7; 35:21-29, where the congregation in the wilderness made a freewill offering for the tabernacle). The returning exiles wanted to erect the Temple on its former site—note again the theme of continuity with pre-exilic tradition. Whereas David and Solomon had endowed the First Temple, the whole community backed the Second Temple with generous financial gifts. It has been estimated that the gold and silver gifts mentioned in v. 69 would weigh 1,133 pounds and 6,250 pounds respectively. To take these figures literally would be to imagine the returnees as a very rich community. If taken metaphorically, these totals express the wholehearted support of the returnees for the Temple, and they imply criticism of any who would oppose this building project (such as the critical words about the Temple in Isa 66:1-2).

Ezra 2:70 and Neh 7:73*a* show slight and apparently insignificant differences in word order (the NIV recasts the verses in a way that hides this issue). The NRSV has added "in Jerusalem

26. Williamson, *Ezra–Nehemiah,* 37-38; Wilhelm Rudolph, *Esra und Nehemia, samt 3. Esra,* HAT 20 (Tübingen: J. C. B. Mohr [Paul Siebeck], 1949) 25; David J. A. Clines, *Ezra, Nehemiah, Esther,* NCB (Grand Rapids: Eerdmans, 1984) 60.

and its vicinity" to 2:70 on the basis of a reading in 1 Esdras. The translation of 2:70, however, should not contain the first "in their towns," which is lacking in both 1 Esdras and the Septuagint. These words are probably a marginal correction (cf. 3:1) that was wrongly added to the text. Accordingly, the priests, the Levites, and some of the people lived in Jerusalem, while everyone else lived in the towns scattered throughout the countryside.

REFLECTIONS

The legitimacy of the clergy and of the worship site, the continuity of the community with its pre-exilic forebears, and a deep need to have a sense of belonging are frequent themes in the books of Ezra and Nehemiah. These are all identity issues, and a modern reader will surely empathize with the question about identity even if the answer for us in another age and another culture has a completely different shape than it did in this ancient Jewish community. Many questions, now as before, must remain unanswered about a document like Ezra 2. We do not know whether the list was used first in Ezra or first in Nehemiah; we have only educated guesses about its original purpose, and its date is limited to almost any time within a hundred-year time frame.

And yet this list functioned in an important way for this community that put so much stock in genealogy and lists. The narrator could have told us about all the troubles of the returnees on the way home, the excitement—or even disappointment—of those who waited for them in Judah, the self-confidence or self-doubt of the participants. Instead, he included an old list that makes it perfectly clear that there was a unified and wholehearted response to the Persian king's permission for the Jews to go home. The list identifies twelve leaders in the community, altogether appropriate and reassuring for a small group that considered itself a remnant of the twelve tribes of Israel. This list represents nothing less than Israel entire. Laity make up a large portion of the list—their role then and now is essential for the people of God—and they are given a very prominent position within that list. The community that returned gave generously for the Temple, recalling King David's generosity at the founding of the First Temple and offering subtle criticism of anyone who did not support this project enthusiastically.

People in antiquity kept lists and remembered genealogies because they wanted to know who they were and how they related to one another and to people outside their families. Our identity and our relationship to others are perhaps two of the biggest religious questions we have today. Too often our identity comes from our association with those who are like us. Genealogy may severely limit and crimp our identity. Our true identity as Christians comes through a God who knows our names and the number of the hairs on our head, who accepts us and reconciles us, and who includes us among the children of God through the sacrament of baptism. The more diverse the church, the more we should feel at home.

And how do we relate to people outside our families, to the other gender, to persons of another color or language or class? That has become the most significant question in the new, fractious world (dis)order after the peaceful end of the cold war. In this new context we sense the limits of lists and genealogies, of bloodlines and status and lineage. "Welcome one another, therefore," Paul wrote, "just as Christ has welcomed you, for the glory of God" (Rom 15:7 NRSV).

EZRA 3:1-13, ALTAR AND TEMPLE

NIV

3 When the seventh month came and the Israelites had settled in their towns, the people assembled as one man in Jerusalem. 2Then Jeshua son of Jozadak and his fellow priests and Zerubbabel son of Shealtiel and his associates began to build the altar of the God of Israel to sacrifice burnt offerings on it, in accordance with what is written in the Law of Moses the man of God. 3Despite their fear of the peoples around them, they built the altar on its foundation and sacrificed burnt offerings on it to the LORD, both the morning and evening sacrifices. 4Then in accordance with what is written, they celebrated the Feast of Tabernacles with the required number of burnt offerings prescribed for each day. 5After that, they presented the regular burnt offerings, the New Moon sacrifices and the sacrifices for all the appointed sacred feasts of the LORD, as well as those brought as freewill offerings to the LORD. 6On the first day of the seventh month they began to offer burnt offerings to the LORD, though the foundation of the LORD's temple had not yet been laid.

7Then they gave money to the masons and carpenters, and gave food and drink and oil to the people of Sidon and Tyre, so that they would bring cedar logs by sea from Lebanon to Joppa, as authorized by Cyrus king of Persia.

8In the second month of the second year after their arrival at the house of God in Jerusalem, Zerubbabel son of Shealtiel, Jeshua son of Jozadak and the rest of their brothers (the priests and the Levites and all who had returned from the captivity to Jerusalem) began the work, appointing Levites twenty years of age and older to supervise the building of the house of the LORD. 9Jeshua and his sons and brothers and Kadmiel and his sons (descendants of Hodaviah[a]) and the sons of Henadad and their sons and brothers—all Levites—joined together in supervising those working on the house of God.

10When the builders laid the foundation of the temple of the LORD, the priests in their vestments and with trumpets, and the Levites (the sons of

[a] 9 Hebrew *Yehudah,* probably a variant of *Hodaviah*

NRSV

3 When the seventh month came, and the Israelites were in the towns, the people gathered together in Jerusalem. 2Then Jeshua son of Jozadak, with his fellow priests, and Zerubbabel son of Shealtiel with his kin set out to build the altar of the God of Israel, to offer burnt offerings on it, as prescribed in the law of Moses the man of God. 3They set up the altar on its foundation, because they were in dread of the neighboring peoples, and they offered burnt offerings upon it to the LORD, morning and evening. 4And they kept the festival of booths,[a] as prescribed, and offered the daily burnt offerings by number according to the ordinance, as required for each day, 5and after that the regular burnt offerings, the offerings at the new moon and at all the sacred festivals of the LORD, and the offerings of everyone who made a freewill offering to the LORD. 6From the first day of the seventh month they began to offer burnt offerings to the LORD. But the foundation of the temple of the LORD was not yet laid. 7So they gave money to the masons and the carpenters, and food, drink, and oil to the Sidonians and the Tyrians to bring cedar trees from Lebanon to the sea, to Joppa, according to the grant that they had from King Cyrus of Persia.

8In the second year after their arrival at the house of God at Jerusalem, in the second month, Zerubbabel son of Shealtiel and Jeshua son of Jozadak made a beginning, together with the rest of their people, the priests and the Levites and all who had come to Jerusalem from the captivity. They appointed the Levites, from twenty years old and upward, to have the oversight of the work on the house of the LORD. 9And Jeshua with his sons and his kin, and Kadmiel and his sons, Binnui and Hodaviah[b] along with the sons of Henadad, the Levites, their sons and kin, together took charge of the workers in the house of God.

10When the builders laid the foundation of the temple of the LORD, the priests in their vestments were stationed to praise the LORD with trumpets, and the Levites, the sons of Asaph, with cymbals, according to the directions of King David of Israel;

[a] Or *tabernacles*; Heb *succoth* [b] Compare 2.40; Neh 7.43; 1 Esdras 5.58: Heb *sons of Judah*

NIV

Asaph) with cymbals, took their places to praise the LORD, as prescribed by David king of Israel. [11]With praise and thanksgiving they sang to the LORD:

"He is good;
his love to Israel endures forever."

And all the people gave a great shout of praise to the LORD, because the foundation of the house of the LORD was laid. [12]But many of the older priests and Levites and family heads, who had seen the former temple, wept aloud when they saw the foundation of this temple being laid, while many others shouted for joy. [13]No one could distinguish the sound of the shouts of joy from the sound of weeping, because the people made so much noise. And the sound was heard far away.

NRSV

[11]and they sang responsively, praising and giving thanks to the LORD,

"For he is good,
for his steadfast love endures forever toward Israel."

And all the people responded with a great shout when they praised the LORD, because the foundation of the house of the LORD was laid. [12]But many of the priests and Levites and heads of families, old people who had seen the first house on its foundations, wept with a loud voice when they saw this house, though many shouted aloud for joy, [13]so that the people could not distinguish the sound of the joyful shout from the sound of the people's weeping, for the people shouted so loudly that the sound was heard far away.

COMMENTARY

The chapter divides neatly into two sections: the rebuilding of the altar (vv. 1-6) and the laying of the foundations of the Temple (vv. 7-13). In both sections the community's leaders are Jeshua and Zerubbabel, whom Haggai and Zechariah help us to date to the late 520s, in the reign of Darius I (521–486 BCE). Some commentators assign the building of the altar historically to the early 530s and the laying of the foundations of the Temple to c. 520. The author of Ezra, however, seems to place both events in the early 530s, apparently to emphasize the immediate and faithful cultic action of the returned exiles. The rebuilding of the altar in this view took place in the seventh month of the year of the return, and the Temple foundations were laid in the second month of the second year after the return. This commentary will follow the chronology of the biblical text. Those primarily interested in reconstructing the history of the post-exilic community, of course, may need to seek alternative dates, especially for the founding of the Temple.

3:1-6, Rebuilding the Altar. In the seventh month (Tishri), the people gathered together to restore the altar "as one person" (the NRSV strangely omits the last three words). Just as there had been no chronological gap between the fall of Babylon and Cyrus's permission for the return (1:2-4), so also there was no hiatus between the new settlement in the land and the reestablishment of the altar. Elsewhere in Chronicles and Ezra–Nehemiah officials call the people together for cultic celebration (1 Chr 13:1-5; 2 Chr 5:2-3; 20:3-4; 30:1-13; 34:20-32; Ezra 10:7-9), but here the people come together of their own volition, just as they did for Ezra's reading of the law in Neh 8:1. While the altar from the First Temple had continued in use in the land during the exile (Jer 41:5), such use would not have sanctified it for the author of Ezra, who ascribed legitimacy only to the community that had returned from Babylon and who acted as if Palestine were vacant during the exile (see 2 Chr 36:20-21). This ideological loyalty to the group that returned from exile should not be turned into historical evidence for the actual state of the land during the exile.

Among the leaders was the priest Jeshua, a Zadokite and a descendant of Jehozadak, who had been the high priest at the time Judah went into exile (1 Chr 6:1-15). Jeshua's grandfather Seraiah, the last high priest before the exile, was executed by the Babylonians (2 Kgs 25:18-21; Jer 52:24-27). Although Ezra gives Jeshua no title, Haggai frequently calls him the high priest, and both Haggai and Zechariah spell his name "Joshua." When Jeshua appears in the Bible with Zerubbabel, he is usually listed second (cf. v. 8), but in v. 2 he is given first position because of the emphasis on the altar.

Zerubbabel was appointed governor of Judah either by Darius or by his predecessor, Cambyses, in connection with his Egyptian campaign of 525 BCE. Zerubbabel disappears mysteriously from the biblical account before the dedication of the Temple. In Ezra, Nehemiah, and Haggai, Zerubbabel is identified as the son of Shealtiel, but 1 Chr 3:19 names Pedaiah as his father. Perhaps Shealtiel's widow had married her brother-in-law Pedaiah, according to the provisions of levirate marriage (Deut 25:5-10). Although Shealtiel and Pedaiah were both descendants of David, and although Zechariah speaks of Zerubbabel in messianic tones, Ezra makes no mention of his Davidic descent or the fact that he was governor, although he may be the unnamed governor mentioned in 6:7 (this identification is explicitly made in 1 Esdr 6:27). A reference to the genealogical heritage of Jeshua and Zerubbabel would have provided another point of continuity with the pre-exilic community, but the author is more interested in stressing the wholehearted participation of the entire community than in recording the titles of its leaders. Jeshua was supported by his fellow priests and Zerubbabel by his lay kin.

The altar conformed to the law of Moses (v. 2), whose authority is recognized by the expression "man of God" added to his name (cf. the same designation for Moses in 1 Chr 23:14; 2 Chr 30:16; for David in 2 Chr 8:14; Neh 12:24, 36). Moses had instructed the early Israelites to build an altar as soon as they came into the land at Mt. Ebal (Shechem) and had forbidden the use of an iron tool on the altar stones (Deut 27:6-7; cf. Exod 20:25; 1 Macc 4:47). The post-exilic community put the altar on its old foundations (plural, though both the NRSV and the NIV have the singular in v. 3), thus underscoring the continuity with the First Temple. Opposition to the community's project came from the outside, from the "neighboring peoples" (v. 3), and not, as Haggai would have it, from internal resistance within the community itself. The neighbors who caused fear may have lived within the province of Judah or in its vicinity, and they may have included the Edomites as well as foreigners, such as those mentioned in 4:9-10. As in the time of David, the sacrificial cult began before the actual building of the Temple (2 Sam 24:18-25; 1 Chr 21:28–22:1).

The community's first sacrifices were the regular morning and evening burnt offerings (see Exod 29:38-42; Num 28:3-8), which the reforming kings Joash and Hezekiah had also restored (2 Chr 24:14; 29:7, 27-29). Next came the community's celebration of the Feast of Tabernacles, usually held from the 15th to the 22nd of the seventh month (Lev 23:39-43). Tabernacles was a fall harvest festival, commemorating Israel's having lived in booths during the wilderness period (Lev 23:42-43; cf. Neh 8:13-18); the First Temple had been dedicated in connection with this festival (2 Chr 5:3). The total number of animals needed for this festival was 71 bulls, 15 rams, 105 lambs, and 7 goats, although the specific number of required sacrificial animals varied from day to day (Num 29:12-38). The community also reinstituted sacrifices for sabbaths (adding this word to the text of v. 5 from 1 Esdr 5:52; cf. Num 28:9-10) and for new moons (Num 28:9-15; cf. 2 Chr 2:4; 8:13; Neh 10:33; Isa 1:14; Hos 2:11; Amos 8:5), in addition to the freewill or votive offerings (Lev 22:17-25; Num 15:1-20; Deut 12:17). The "sacred festivals of the LORD" (v. 5) included Passover, Weeks, Tabernacles, and the Day of Atonement. The latter festival would not have been included in the celebrations recounted in Ezra 3, however, since its observance presupposed the existence of the Temple.

The mention of the seventh month in v. 6—actually the first day of that month, or new year's day (cf. Lev 23:23-25)—forms an inclusio with the same month in v. 1. Hence vv. 1-6 are a unit, dated by the author to the earliest period of the restoration. The text notes that the reinstitution of sacrifices was not accompanied by the laying of the Temple's foundations. Fear caused by neighboring peoples accounted for this delay.

3:7-13, Laying the Foundation of the Temple. The account continues immediately with the work on the foundations of the Temple. While this activity probably took place historically in the time of Darius, the text suggests it was much earlier, in the time of Cyrus. Blenkinsopp claims that events are backdated to emphasize the role played by the Golah group immediately after its return.[27]

27. Joseph Blenkinsopp, *Ezra–Nehemiah,* OTL (Philadelphia: Westminster, 1988) 96.

The similarity of the terminology used to describe the hiring of workers and the acquisition of supplies (v. 7) to the description of work on the First Temple suggests that the Second Temple was the typological double of the first. The community paid silver (coins were probably not yet in use) for skilled construction workers (both the terms "masons" and "carpenters" may refer to people who work with stone), just as David had done in preparation for the First Temple (1 Chr 22:2, 4, 15). They paid the Sidonians and Tyrians, who were to provide lumber, with agricultural products just as Solomon had paid Huram (2 Chr 2:15). Now as then, the Phoenicians brought cedar from Lebanon to Jerusalem via the port of Joppa (cf. 2 Chr 2:16). The divine promise that cedar would come to Jerusalem from Lebanon, delivered through the words of an anonymous prophet (Isa 60:13), was fulfilled in the experience of the Golah community. The "grant" (רשיון *rišyôn*) from Cyrus, though not mentioned in the decrees of Cyrus in 1:2-4 or 6:3-5, gave official authorization to this international trade and underscored once more the Persian king's approval of the Temple building project.

In the second month of the second year (v. 8), a brief seven months after the building of the altar and the same month in which Solomon had begun work on the First Temple (2 Chr 3:2), the officials—indeed, the whole exilic group—appointed the Levites who were at least twenty years old to oversee the reconstruction work. According to Chronicles, David had set the entry age for Levites at thirty in conformity with pentateuchal law (1 Chr 23:3; cf. Num 4:3, 23, 30), though one pentateuchal text lowered the age for levitical service to twenty-five (Num 8:24). The community's reduction of the age limit to twenty in v. 8 may have been necessitated by the very small number of Levites who were available (cf. 2:40). Precedent for this young age is provided by 1 Chr 23:24-27 and 2 Chr 31:17.

The NRSV and the NIV replace the name of the Levite "Judah" in v. 9 with "Hodaviah" following 2:40; the NRSV, probably correctly, further replaces the MT's "descendants of" with the name "Binnui," again adjusting the text to agree with the text of 2:40, which has in turn been emended on the basis of 1 Esdr 5:26. The levitical sons of Henadad (v. 9) are mentioned again in Neh 3:18, 24; and 10:9. The Levite Jeshua in this verse, of course, is to be distinguished from the high priest of the same name mentioned in v. 2.

David Petersen has proposed that the "founding" of the Temple in this chapter and in Hag 2:18 and Zech 4:7-10 refers to a foundation deposit ceremony, or *kalû*, known elsewhere in the ancient Near East.[28] Through the ritual of this festival a site of a destroyed temple was purified so that it could once again function as a holy space. A stone taken from the foundations of the old temple was installed in the new temple during this ceremony (cf. Zech 4:7-10). Hence, Sheshbazzar worked on the Temple footings (5:16), but the Golah community in Ezra 3 carried out the foundation deposit ceremony.

The appropriate clergy participated in this ceremony (v. 10). First mentioned are the priests who were clothed in "linen" vestments, according to a common addition to the text that brings it in line with the apparel of the levitical singers in 2 Chr 5:12. The word "linen" (בוץ *bûṣ*) may have been lost by homoioarchton (a scribe's omission of words between two words that have the same beginning syllables) in Ezra. These priests played (silver) trumpets (Num 10:1-10; 31:6; 1 Chr 15:24; 2 Chr 5:12-13; 7:6; 13:12; Neh 12:35) while the levitical descendants of Asaph played cymbals (cf. 1 Chr 15:19, the ceremony in which the ark is brought to Jerusalem; 2 Chr 29:25-26). Again affirming continuity with the past, the author notes that the musicians followed the directions of David, king of Israel (cf. 8:20). Thus the sacrifices themselves followed the pattern of Moses, but the duties of the Levites reflected changes David had instituted when it was no longer necessary for them to carry the ark, once it had been brought permanently to Jerusalem.

In a responsive song (v. 11; the verb ענה [*ʿānâ*] means both "sing" and "answer"), the clergy recited a line from the psalter appropriate to the occasion (Pss 100:5; 106:1; 107:1; 118:1; 136; Jer 33:11), indeed, a verse that is a favorite in the books of Chronicles (1 Chr 16:3; 2 Chr 5:13; 7:3). The author of Ezra–Nehemiah, however, makes a significant addition: God's steadfast love is not a graciousness for all people; rather, God's loyalty is directed especially to Israel. The great

28. David L. Petersen, *Haggai, Zechariah 1–8*, OTL (Louisville: Westminster/John Knox, 1984) 88-90.

shout of all the people (note again the unanimous participation of the community in the temple-founding ceremony) was the kind of acclaim given to God as King in the enthronement psalms (Pss 47:5; 93; 95–99).

Some of the older clergy and family heads, who had seen the pre-exilic Temple, broke into tears during the foundation deposit ceremony (v. 12; the NIV, which connects the word "foundation" to the new Temple, is better). It had been forty-nine years since that Temple was burned, if the ceremony took place in 538, sixty-seven years if the ceremony was held in 520—hence those who cried were elderly. Commentators have proposed various reasons for the crying: The elderly people knew they would not live to see the Temple's completion, the new Temple was not up to the splendor of the previous one, or the tears were tears of joy. Haggai quotes an apposite divine oracle: "Who is left among you that saw this house in its former glory? How does it look to you now? Is it not in your sight as nothing?" (Hag 2:3 NRSV). Other clergy and family heads shouted loudly with joy, and it was impossible to distinguish those who rejoiced from those who wept. "The sound was heard far away" (v. 13). This comment not only expresses the loudness of the ceremony's sound, but it also provides a hint that some who heard these sounds would be very unhappy about them.

REFLECTIONS

Worship is the center of any thriving community of believers. Before the first year had passed in Jerusalem, the community of former exiles managed to restart sacrificial offerings, and five months later initiated work on the Temple itself. They followed laws and precedents that stemmed from Moses, David, Asaph, and Solomon. The logs riding the waves of commerce from Phoenicia not only recalled the way in which Solomon had acquired workers and materials for his Temple, but they also were prophecies being fulfilled before the eyes of the faithful—cedar was being brought to Jerusalem and the words of the book of the prophet Isaiah were coming true. Worship is a response to God's prior actions; it is nourished through God's words of promise.

The form and substance of worship must change to meet the challenges of each new generation, but worship needs also to continue and maintain the heritage of mothers and fathers in the faith. The community set up the altar on its old foundations, and in the foundation deposit ceremony they probably brought a stone from the old Temple and deposited it in the new one. Worship must be a blend of innovation and tradition. In the words of the poet, "Be not the first by whom the new is tried. Nor yet the last to lay the old aside."

Restoring altar and Temple was a community project. Leaders like Jeshua and Zerubbabel appear without any genealogy and without the titles they might rightly have claimed. They are at the most first among equals. No one called this assembly together; the people gathered unanimously and at their own volition. Laity and common priests joined with the governor and the high priest—here called only by their names, Zerubbabel and Jeshua—in the tasks.

God's redemptive activities are never just for individuals and individual salvation. God wants to establish new worshiping communities that will seek peace and justice throughout the world. God's loyalty for Israel—the people, the post-exilic community, the congregation of laity and clergy—lasts forever. Words of thanksgiving and praise echoed back in antiphonal rhythm from the restored community.

We are not surprised that the high joy of those days was mixed with sorrow. Some shouted loudly for joy while others cried so loudly that it was hard for listeners to distinguish one emotion from the other. No wonder. It seems not unlikely that some of the very ones who shouted most in thanksgiving and praise broke down and wept moments later; still others praised God amid their tears. This was a model community, though not an ideal one. We are not saved from the world and its problems, but for them. And life even at its best is lived out in great peril. Christians seek joy but experience death, broken relationships, sickness, and loss of jobs. The gospel is not about success and perpetual victory, but about a God who in Jesus Christ is good and whose loyalty toward God's people lasts forever.

EZRA 4:1-24, OPPOSITION TO THE JEWISH COMMUNITY

Ezra 4:1-5, Opposition Breaks Out

NIV

4 When the enemies of Judah and Benjamin heard that the exiles were building a temple for the LORD, the God of Israel, [2]they came to Zerubbabel and to the heads of the families and said, "Let us help you build because, like you, we seek your God and have been sacrificing to him since the time of Esarhaddon king of Assyria, who brought us here."

[3]But Zerubbabel, Jeshua and the rest of the heads of the families of Israel answered, "You have no part with us in building a temple to our God. We alone will build it for the LORD, the God of Israel, as King Cyrus, the king of Persia, commanded us."

[4]Then the peoples around them set out to discourage the people of Judah and make them afraid to go on building.[a] [5]They hired counselors to work against them and frustrate their plans during the entire reign of Cyrus king of Persia and down to the reign of Darius king of Persia.

[a] 4 Or *and troubled them as they built*

NRSV

4 When the adversaries of Judah and Benjamin heard that the returned exiles were building a temple to the LORD, the God of Israel, [2]they approached Zerubbabel and the heads of families and said to them, "Let us build with you, for we worship your God as you do, and we have been sacrificing to him ever since the days of King Esar-haddon of Assyria who brought us here." [3]But Zerubbabel, Jeshua, and the rest of the heads of families in Israel said to them, "You shall have no part with us in building a house to our God; but we alone will build to the LORD, the God of Israel, as King Cyrus of Persia has commanded us."

4Then the people of the land discouraged the people of Judah, and made them afraid to build, [5]and they bribed officials to frustrate their plan throughout the reign of King Cyrus of Persia and until the reign of King Darius of Persia.

COMMENTARY

The community's fear of the peoples of the land during the building of the altar (3:3) is explained by the persistent hostility of their neighbors from the time of Cyrus to Artaxerxes (4:5, 7, 11). The author paints the situation in stark contrasts. On the one side stand those whom he calls adversaries (NRSV) or enemies (NIV), and on the other side are Judah and Benjamin, the returned exiles, who are building a temple to the Lord, the God of Israel (4:1). The group of adversaries approached Zerubbabel, Jeshua (added with 1 Esdr 5:65; cf. v. 3), and the family heads with a seemingly innocent proposition: "Let us build with you" (vv. 1-2). They based this offer on the fact that they worshiped the same God; in fact, they claimed that they had been sacrificing to God since the days of the Assyrian

King Esarhaddon (681–669), who had deported them from their homeland to Palestine.[29]

Such a forced repopulation of Palestine by Esarhaddon is otherwise unattested, though not improbable. After the destruction of the northern kingdom and the exiling of its leadership in 721 BCE, the Assyrian King Sargon II had brought a number of people from Mesopotamia and settled them in the cities of Samaria. These people eventually began to worship Yahweh, but they also continued to worship a number of their own gods. Such syncretistic practices continued at least until the time of the writing of the deuteronomistic history (2 Kgs 17:24-41). Esarhaddon may have settled other people in the former northern kingdom during the course of his campaign against Syria.[30] Some commentators find a reference to this in Isa 7:8, where the prophetic book indicates, somewhat obscurely, that within sixty-five years—roughly 670 BCE—the northern kingdom would be destroyed.

The leaders of the Golah community—Zerubbabel, Jeshua, and the rest of the family heads—sharply rejected the seemingly innocent request to help with the building: "You shall have no part with us" (lit., "There is nothing to you and to us" [see Josh 22:22-24; 2 Kgs 3:13; John 2:4]). Rather, they were determined to build the Temple alone, just as Cyrus, king of Persia, had commanded them to do. The Persian decree that gave the community permission to rebuild the Temple is here interpreted as if it gave them the exclusive right to build. Since the author considered the Golah group to be the true people of God, all others were by definition apostate. This exclusivistic attitude is the negative side of the author's preference for the returned community.

The rejection of the adversaries' offer to help by no means ended the problem. Rather, the people of the land "discouraged" (מרפים ידי *mĕrappîm yĕdê*; lit., "weakened the hands of"; cf. Neh 6:4; Jer 38:4) the people of Yahweh and intimidated them so that they could not build (v. 4). In pre-exilic times, "people of the land" designated a conservative part of the upper class in Judah. In post-exilic times, and especially in Ezra and Nehemiah, it refers to those who had not been exiled, who were not considered to be Jews, and who therefore were not full members of the Golah community. A more positive meaning of the expression "people of the land," however, still appears in Hag 2:4 and Zech 7:5.

Chapter 4 does not make clear how these peoples discouraged the Golah or even intimidated them, but v. 5 charges that the people of the land bribed Persian officials at the royal court in an effort to frustrate the plan of the returned exiles. These harassments or frustrations lasted throughout the time of Cyrus (539–530) and even into the time of Darius I (522–486).

In vv. 1-5, the author attributes the delay in the completion of the Temple to outside interference. This is quite different from the position of the early post-exilic prophets, who ascribed the delay to the indifference and self-centeredness of the people themselves, to strife in the community, to bad social and economic conditions, and even to internal opposition to the whole idea of rebuilding the Temple (cf. Isa 58:4; 66:1-2; Hag 1:2-4). Some of the difficult political and theological questions connected with the rebuilding of the Temple are reflected in these verses, but they are also an apology for the Golah, attempting to absolve this group of the charges of neglecting the Temple, made specifically in the book of Haggai. The leaders of the peoples of the land apparently saw the building of the Temple as a threat to their security, but their offer to share in labor and material costs threatened the integrity of the temple community. After all, if the people of the land shared in the cost, they might expect to share in control of the Temple as well.

Williamson, following Talmon, separates vv. 1-5 into two paragraphs. He dates vv. 1-3 to the time of Darius, but understands vv. 4-5 as a "summary notation," with v. 4 recapitulating the earlier statement about the neighboring peoples from 3:3, while v. 5*b* refers to the cessation of the building under Darius. These verses accordingly suggest that 3:1-6 reports events from the time of Cyrus, while 3:7–4:3 describes the beginning of the work under Darius. In this view, the enemies of Judah and Benjamin in v. 1 (under Darius) are not the same as the people of the land

29. Though unnoted by the NRSV and the NIV, the MT puts an unbelieving, arrogant statement into the mouths of the adversaries by changing the original ולו (*wĕlô*) to ולא (*wĕlōʾ*) in v. 2, which changes the translation to "We have not been sacrificing to him since the days of Esarhaddon." This variant may have arisen through a hearing error (the words are pronounced identically in Hebrew), but it is more likely a tendentious change.

30. *ANET*, 290-91.

in v. 4 (under Cyrus).[31] It seems more natural, however, to interpret 3:1–4:5 as an account of the work on the altar *and* the Temple that was backdated by the author to the time of Cyrus so that his account described the community's moving directly to the restoration of its worship life and its sanctuary as soon as it reached home, even though historically no major work on the Temple was done until the reign of Darius. The reference to Darius in v. 5 (cf. v. 24) prepares the reader for events in the days of Darius in chaps. 5–6. Before describing these events, however, the author picks up the theme of outside opposition and follows it through the reigns of Xerxes and Artaxerxes I. (See Reflections at 4:6-24.)

31. H. G. M. Williamson, *Ezra, Nehemiah,* WBC 16 (Waco, Tex.: Word, 1985) 43-45; S. Talmon, "Ezra and Nehemiah (Books and Men)," IDBSup, 322.

Ezra 4:6-24, Opposition Continues

NIV

[6]At the beginning of the reign of Xerxes,[a] they lodged an accusation against the people of Judah and Jerusalem.

[7]And in the days of Artaxerxes king of Persia, Bishlam, Mithredath, Tabeel and the rest of his associates wrote a letter to Artaxerxes. The letter was written in Aramaic script and in the Aramaic language.[b, c]

[8]Rehum the commanding officer and Shimshai the secretary wrote a letter against Jerusalem to Artaxerxes the king as follows:

[9]Rehum the commanding officer and Shimshai the secretary, together with the rest of their associates—the judges and officials over the men from Tripolis, Persia,[d] Erech and Babylon, the Elamites of Susa, [10]and the other people whom the great and honorable Ashurbanipal[e] deported and settled in the city of Samaria and elsewhere in Trans-Euphrates.

[11](This is a copy of the letter they sent him.)

To King Artaxerxes,

From your servants, the men of Trans-Euphrates:

[12]The king should know that the Jews who came up to us from you have gone to Jerusalem and are rebuilding that rebellious and wicked city. They are restoring the walls and repairing the foundations.

[13]Furthermore, the king should know that if this city is built and its walls are restored,

a *6* Hebrew *Ahasuerus,* a variant of Xerxes' Persian name b *7* Or *written in Aramaic and translated* c *7* The text of Ezra 4:8—6:18 is in Aramaic. d *9* Or *officials, magistrates and governors over the men from* e *10* Aramaic *Osnappar,* a variant of *Ashurbanipal*

NRSV

6In the reign of Ahasuerus, in his accession year, they wrote an accusation against the inhabitants of Judah and Jerusalem.

7And in the days of Artaxerxes, Bishlam and Mithredath and Tabeel and the rest of their associates wrote to King Artaxerxes of Persia; the letter was written in Aramaic and translated.[a] [8]Rehum the royal deputy and Shimshai the scribe wrote a letter against Jerusalem to King Artaxerxes as follows [9](then Rehum the royal deputy, Shimshai the scribe, and the rest of their associates, the judges, the envoys, the officials, the Persians, the people of Erech, the Babylonians, the people of Susa, that is, the Elamites, [10]and the rest of the nations whom the great and noble Osnappar deported and settled in the cities of Samaria and in the rest of the province Beyond the River wrote—and now [11]this is a copy of the letter that they sent):

"To King Artaxerxes: Your servants, the people of the province Beyond the River, send greeting. And now [12]may it be known to the king that the Jews who came up from you to us have gone to Jerusalem. They are rebuilding that rebellious and wicked city; they are finishing the walls and repairing the foundations. [13]Now may it be known to the king that, if this city is rebuilt and the walls finished, they will not pay tribute, custom, or toll, and the royal revenue will be reduced. [14]Now because we share the salt of the palace and it is not fitting for us to witness the king's dishonor, therefore we send and inform the king, [15]so that

a Heb adds *in Aramaic,* indicating that 4.8-6.18 is in Aramaic. Another interpretation is *The letter was written in the Aramaic script and set forth in the Aramaic language*

NIV

no more taxes, tribute or duty will be paid, and the royal revenues will suffer. [14]Now since we are under obligation to the palace and it is not proper for us to see the king dishonored, we are sending this message to inform the king, [15]so that a search may be made in the archives of your predecessors. In these records you will find that this city is a rebellious city, troublesome to kings and provinces, a place of rebellion from ancient times. That is why this city was destroyed. [16]We inform the king that if this city is built and its walls are restored, you will be left with nothing in Trans-Euphrates.

[17]The king sent this reply:

To Rehum the commanding officer, Shimshai the secretary and the rest of their associates living in Samaria and elsewhere in Trans-Euphrates:

Greetings.

[18]The letter you sent us has been read and translated in my presence. [19]I issued an order and a search was made, and it was found that this city has a long history of revolt against kings and has been a place of rebellion and sedition. [20]Jerusalem has had powerful kings ruling over the whole of Trans-Euphrates, and taxes, tribute and duty were paid to them. [21]Now issue an order to these men to stop work, so that this city will not be rebuilt until I so order. [22]Be careful not to neglect this matter. Why let this threat grow, to the detriment of the royal interests?

[23]As soon as the copy of the letter of King Artaxerxes was read to Rehum and Shimshai the secretary and their associates, they went immediately to the Jews in Jerusalem and compelled them by force to stop.

[24]Thus the work on the house of God in Jerusalem came to a standstill until the second year of the reign of Darius king of Persia.

NRSV

a search may be made in the annals of your ancestors. You will discover in the annals that this is a rebellious city, hurtful to kings and provinces, and that sedition was stirred up in it from long ago. On that account this city was laid waste. [16]We make known to the king that, if this city is rebuilt and its walls finished, you will then have no possession in the province Beyond the River."

17The king sent an answer: "To Rehum the royal deputy and Shimshai the scribe and the rest of their associates who live in Samaria and in the rest of the province Beyond the River, greeting. And now [18]the letter that you sent to us has been read in translation before me. [19]So I made a decree, and someone searched and discovered that this city has risen against kings from long ago, and that rebellion and sedition have been made in it. [20]Jerusalem has had mighty kings who ruled over the whole province Beyond the River, to whom tribute, custom, and toll were paid. [21]Therefore issue an order that these people be made to cease, and that this city not be rebuilt, until I make a decree. [22]Moreover, take care not to be slack in this matter; why should damage grow to the hurt of the king?"

23Then when the copy of King Artaxerxes' letter was read before Rehum and the scribe Shimshai and their associates, they hurried to the Jews in Jerusalem and by force and power made them cease. [24]At that time the work on the house of God in Jerusalem stopped and was discontinued until the second year of the reign of King Darius of Persia.

COMMENTARY

These verses report a series of accusations against the restored community made during the reigns of Xerxes I (486–465; v. 6) and Artaxerxes I (465–424; vv. 7-23), before describing the cessation of work on the Temple in the reign of Darius I (522–486; v. 24). This narrative illustrates the persistent opposition from the community's neighbors, even though the opposition in these verses was directed against the building of the walls rather than the building of the Temple. At first the chronology in the text is confusing since the text moves from Darius I (v. 5) to Xerxes and to Artaxerxes I, before returning to the cessation of temple building under Darius I in v. 24. The latter verse, however, is a repetitive resumption of v. 5, indicating that the author was not confused about Persian chronology. Beginning with v. 8 and continuing through 6:18, the text is written in Aramaic instead of Hebrew (see the Overview to chaps. 1–6).

4:6-7. The author refers to two accusatory letters sent to Persian authorities, but he does not supply the text of the letters themselves or indicate specifically what the accusations were. (Did he consider the information in them incriminating?) Ahasuerus is the king's Persian name; he is more commonly known to us as Xerxes because that is the way his name was transliterated into Greek. Note that the NIV substitutes the Greek for the Persian name. We know that Egypt rebelled against Xerxes in 486 (Khabasha's revolt) and that this revolt lasted until 483. In 484 a revolt broke out also in Babylon. It is possible that the Judean community sided with the opposition in one of these revolts and thus precipitated a letter from its neighbors to Xerxes in his accession year (486–485), charging the community with infidelity.

It is not clear who sent the letter in v. 7 because of uncertainties about the name "Bishlam," for which there is no convincing etymology. If בשלם (*bišlām*) is translated as a prepositional phrase ("in peace") instead of as a name, then the letter sent by Tabeel and Mithredath was favorable (that is, it was sent with peaceful intent).[32] But why would reference to such a positive letter be is preserved in this context? Blenkinsopp translates *bišlām* as "in accord with," and believes that different from the man referred to in 1:8. As the NRSV and the NIV indicate, it is also possible to identify three principal authors of this letter, all of whom are otherwise unknown.

The varying translations of the second half of v. 7 in the NIV and the NRSV (cf. also the alternative translations in the footnotes of both versions) reflect two interpretative possibilities. If we follow the NIV, then the document was written in the square, or Aramaic, script and was translated (from Hebrew?) into Aramaic. The square script replaced the original Phoenician-Hebrew script in post-exilic times. If we follow the NRSV, then the letter was written in the Aramaic language and translated into another language, presumably Persian. In this understanding, the second occurrence of the Aramaic word, left untranslated in the NRSV, merely indicates that the next section, 4:8–6:18, is in Aramaic. While 4:7 is now in Hebrew, a few of its words seem to be Aramaic in origin.

4:8-16. The first official charges are contained in a letter from Rehum, whom the Persian king had appointed "royal deputy" (בעל-טעם *bĕʿēl ṭĕʿēm*; not "commanding officer," as in the NIV), and Shimshai the scribe, a person who would write out or translate official letters. Verse 8 may represent a message put on the outside of ancient letters that gave the names of the sender(s), the addressee, and a brief summary of the content. As officials in the satrapy, Rehum and Shimshai conveyed the objections of the local populace to the proper authorities. Joining in this accusation were a series of officials and other people who had been deported to Palestine from Mesopotamia, but who hailed originally from Uruk (NRSV, "Erech," a city in southern Babylon), Babylon, and Susa (the residence of the Persian kings in Elam). Because of the endings on the Aramaic names, a number of commentators have interpreted some of the officials listed in v. 9 as misunderstood hometown names of people now living in Samaria. These would include people from Dina (unknown; NRSV, "judges"), Afarsach (NRSV, "envoys"), Tripoli or Tarpal/Tarpel (NRSV, "officials"), or Sippar (NRSV, "Persians").

After naming the Persian officials and the peo-

32. Blenkinsopp, *Ezra-Nehemiah*, 110-12.

ple who have been exiled to Samaria and the rest of the satrapy Beyond the River (see Commentary on 2:1-2), the document mentions others whom the Assyrian king Osnappar, or Asshurbanipal (669–c. 630 BCE), had sent there. Asshurbanipal defeated Erech in 642 and Susa in 641, after putting down a revolt in Babylon in 648. It is plausible, though nowhere else documented, that he transferred people from the defeated cities to the west during his campaign there in 640–639. The words "and now" (וכענת *ûkĕʿenet*) at the end of v. 11 are a typical transition marker to the body of a letter. The word *ûkĕʿenet* has been mistakenly added to the Aramaic text also at the end of v. 10. The NIV omits this expression in both verses. "Send greeting" in v. 11 of the NRSV is a paraphrastic addition to the text, making explicit the intention of the verse. Note that the writers designate themselves as loyal servants of the king.

Although the chapter began with the enemies trying to intimidate the people from continuing their work on the Temple, the accusation in v. 12 deals with those who are rebuilding the city and its walls. The letter refers to Jerusalem as a perpetually rebellious and evil city, and it charges that the Jews were rebuilding the city and completing the city wall, after having repaired or reinforced its foundations (the last verb in v. 12 is in the perfect tense). Was this wall the one that Nehemiah heard had been broken down (Neh 1:3)? Was it built in connection with Ezra's trip to Jerusalem, or in connection with a revolt against Persian authority? Many commentators link this incident to the supposed revolt of the satrap Megabyzus in 448, but Hoglund has raised serious questions about the historicity of this revolt.[33]

The accusers introduce their conclusion with a dramatic "now" (כען *kĕʿan*, v. 13). If the building projects go on, they aver, the Jews will not pay tribute (a semi-voluntary gift), custom (a fixed tax), or toll (corvée labor). The last part of v. 13 may be translated: "And finally this will cause harm to the kings" (the last word is written with a Hebrew rather than an Aramaic plural noun ending). The NIV and the NRSV speak correctly, if paraphrastically, about damage to the royal revenue.

By claiming that the salt of the palace is their salt (v. 14), the accusers indicate that they are under obligation to the king, or that they are in mutual partnership with him. Their liaison with him has been ratified by some kind of salt ceremony (cf. the covenant of salt in Lev 2:13; Num 18:19; 2 Chr 13:5). Since they do not want to see Artaxerxes dishonored (lit., they do not want to see his nakedness) by having him lose out on his revenues, they advise the king to search through his ancestors' archives so that he may discover the record of Jerusalem's constant rebelliousness and the destruction it experienced as a consequence. The king's "ancestors" in this context may include the kings of Assyria and Babylonia, of whom the Persians thought they were the rightful heirs. While the prophets interpreted Jerusalem's destruction as being due to the wrath of the Lord, the enemies here see it as punishment for the city's rebellious character, and they exaggerate the effects of a possible revolt in Jerusalem. Would a rebellion in a small province of some 800 square miles really deprive Persia of the whole satrapy of Beyond the River? Of course, the domino theory is not limited to modern times.

4:17-22. In his reply, Artaxerxes first sends "peace" or "greetings" (see the NRSV at v. 11) and then acknowledges the previous letter of the accusers. Both the NIV and the NRSV interpret the word מפרש *mĕpāraš* in v. 18 to mean "translate extemporaneously." This interpretation goes back to a suggestion by H. H. Schaeder, which unfortunately cannot be proved philologically.[34] The etymology of the Aramaic word suggests that the letter was read "completely" or "word for word"—that is, not in summary. Remarkably, a search through the files discovered evidence for Jerusalem's rebellious character, as its enemies had alleged. In v. 20 the king refers to powerful kings in Jerusalem—presumably David and Solomon—who had ruled over the whole province of Beyond the River. This echoes the Bible's own estimate of Solomon's domain ("Solomon was sovereign over all the kingdoms from the Euphrates to the land of the Philistines, even to the border of Egypt; they brought tribute and served Solomon all the days of his life" [1 Kgs 4:21]) and may have been added to the letter by the author of Ezra. Since these kings collected

33. Kenneth G. Hoglund, *Achaemenid Imperial Administration in Syria-Palestine and the Missions of Ezra and Nehemiah,* SBLDS 125 (Atlanta: Scholars Press, 1992) 123-27.

34. H. H. Schaeder, *Esra der Schreiber,* BHT 5 (Tübingen: J. C. B. Mohr, 1939) 51-53.

tribute, custom, and toll, Artaxerxes infers that their contemporary successors are likely to try to renew the same policy.

Hence, the king ordered work on the city to stop and that it should not be restarted until he gave orders to do so. Is this an allusion to the permission granted to Nehemiah to rebuild the walls (Neh 2:4-8)? And if so, is this reference secondary, as suggested by the footnote in *BHS*?[35] The king concludes his letter by agreeing with the accusers that no damage should be done to the royal coffers (lit., "kings," v. 22; cf. v. 13).

35. *BHS* note 21[a-a].

4:23-24. As soon as Rehum and his associates heard the letter, they rushed to Jerusalem and stopped the work that was going on by force and power. Perhaps they also destroyed what had been built thus far (cf. Neh 1:3). Verse 24, by repetitive resumption, picks up the narrative from v. 5, shifting the focus back to the harassment of the temple builders. Work on the Temple itself stopped until the second year of Darius I (520 BCE).

REFLECTIONS

Did the Golah act too negatively in turning down their neighbors' offer to help with the rebuilding of the Temple? The author's identification of the neighbors as the "adversaries of Judah" (4:1) may already prejudice the case. He is so passionately in favor of the Golah community as the true Israel that one suspects that he sees every tactic of the neighbors in the worst possible light. Should not there have been some investigation of the adversaries' claim to have worshiped the God of Israel for more than 150 years?

Western Christians have surely known the danger of being so sure of their correctness that they see those with other views as being divisive. Consider the bane of denominationalism and the fact that the Lord's supper has often been as much a point of division as of unity in the church. We can rejoice that the ecumenical slogan, "Unity in Reconciled Diversity," suggests that the oneness of the faith far transcends differences in details of doctrine, liturgy, or polity. This slogan also recognizes that ecumenically minded denominations at their best nurture and preserve distinct forms of piety, liturgy, and doctrine that enrich the whole.

Psychological warfare and intimidation (4:4) and the use of bribes to high Persian officials (4:5) are not gestures that make for friendship. Were these real happenings, or were they only paranoid justifications for the earlier decision of the Golah to say no to their neighbors' offer to work with them?

Over the long haul, of course, the neighbors did prove to be untrustworthy, as 4:6-23 amply documents. Three times the neighbors had appealed to Persian authorities against the members of the community, and in the one exchange of letters that has been preserved for us, the character of the opponents becomes clear. The accusers' expressions of loyalty to Artaxerxes are much too self-serving. Their concern was not that the king lose taxes; they really wanted to thwart the wall building in Jerusalem because for some reason that seemed to work to their own disadvantage.

There might be some truth in the charge that Jerusalem was a rebellious city. After all, the revolts of Jehoiakim and Zedekiah played a major role in bringing the Babylonian attacks of 597 and 586 BCE. But was the current rebuilding of the walls really the first step of the Jews toward refusing to pay taxes? The Golah community in Ezra was painfully subservient to the Persian government and saw Cyrus as a person whose spirit had been stirred up by Yahweh. Rebellion by kings more than 150 years earlier is hardly a precedent for what this community might do politically. The charge becomes even more absurd when Artaxerxes compares the post-exilic community to the power of David and Solomon.

Was the community's rejection of help hasty and premature, or was it justified? Both conclusions deserve consideration. With the all-too-willing use of force and violence by Rehum and Shimshai, however, injustice was in fact perpetrated. Construction of both the Temple and the walls was stopped. Reversal would come only through further decrees of Darius (6:1-12) and Artaxerxes (Neh 2:8).

The reader knows, of course, that in spite of these reverses and new decrees the open-ended word of the prophet Jeremiah (Jer 29:10-11) was being fulfilled. These Persians, too, had hearts that needed to be stirred up by Yahweh. Once again God would help servant Israel, in remembrance of God's mercy (Luke 2:54). In a conflicted situation, when the very life of the community is at stake, it is hard to keep focused on God's promises.

EZRA 5:1-17, A CHALLENGE TO THE TEMPLE REBUILDING

Ezra 5:1-2, Work on the Temple Resumes

NIV

5 Now Haggai the prophet and Zechariah the prophet, a descendant of Iddo, prophesied to the Jews in Judah and Jerusalem in the name of the God of Israel, who was over them. 2Then Zerubbabel son of Shealtiel and Jeshua son of Jozadak set to work to rebuild the house of God in Jerusalem. And the prophets of God were with them, helping them.

NRSV

5 Now the prophets, Haggai[a] and Zechariah son of Iddo, prophesied to the Jews who were in Judah and Jerusalem, in the name of the God of Israel who was over them. 2Then Zerubbabel son of Shealtiel and Jeshua son of Jozadak set out to rebuild the house of God in Jerusalem; and with them were the prophets of God, helping them.

[a] Aram adds *the prophet*

COMMENTARY

The author credits Haggai and Zechariah with getting work on the Temple started again after a long interruption (4:5, 24). Haggai delivered his first oracle on August 29, 520 BCE (first day of the sixth month of the second year of Darius [Hag 1:2]), and work on the Temple had begun again by October 17 of the same year (seventh month, twenty-first day of the month [Hag 2:1]). After the upheavals during the first two years of Darius I, when Gaumata, the alleged brother of Cambyses, contested with Darius for the throne,[36] peace and order had settled over the empire by 520. This would be a plausible time for building projects to commence.

No genealogy is provided for Haggai either in the prophetic book or in the references to him in Ezra (5:1; 6:14). While other post-exilic figures depended greatly on their ability to show a genealogical connection to a specific family (cf. 2:59-63), Haggai's authority lay in the Word of the Lord. In the book of Zechariah, the prophet is called the son of Berechiah son of Iddo, instead of merely the son of Iddo as in Ezra. The word "son" (בֵּן *bēn*) in Hebrew can also mean "grandson" or "descendant" (so NIV).[37] The expectation of an eschatological appearance of Yahweh, contained in both prophetic books, does not occur here. While the superscriptions to both prophetic works mention the word of Yahweh, the deity is called simply "the God of Israel" in Ezra. This God validated the prophetic message and the legitimacy and the necessity of rebuilding the Temple.

36. Cf. *ABD* 5:238. Darius recorded his account of these events in the Behistun inscription.

37. Zechariah from the house of Iddo appears among the priests in the time of Joiakim, the second high priest after the return from exile (Neh 12:16).

Apparently prophetic encouragement triumphed over the "hand-weakening" efforts of the people of the land (4:4), because Zerubbabel, the governor of Yehud (Hag 1:1, 14; 2:2, 21), and Jeshua began to rebuild the Temple. The authority of the prophets and of their God stood behind the renewed work on the Temple (v. 2). According to the chronology of the book, Sheshbazzar began the first repairs on the Temple just after the return (5:16), and Zerubbabel and Jeshua also had worked on this task during Cyrus's reign (3:8) before a long interruption. Commentators suspect, of course, that Zerubbabel and Jeshua did not work on the Temple at all until the time of Darius I. (See Reflections at 5:3-17.)

Ezra 5:3-17, Tattenai Visits Jerusalem and Writes a Report to the King

NIV

[3]At that time Tattenai, governor of Trans-Euphrates, and Shethar-Bozenai and their associates went to them and asked, "Who authorized you to rebuild this temple and restore this structure?" [4]They also asked, "What are the names of the men constructing this building?"[a] [5]But the eye of their God was watching over the elders of the Jews, and they were not stopped until a report could go to Darius and his written reply be received.

[6]This is a copy of the letter that Tattenai, governor of Trans-Euphrates, and Shethar-Bozenai and their associates, the officials of Trans-Euphrates, sent to King Darius. [7]The report they sent him read as follows:

To King Darius:

Cordial greetings.

[8]The king should know that we went to the district of Judah, to the temple of the great God. The people are building it with large stones and placing the timbers in the walls. The work is being carried on with diligence and is making rapid progress under their direction.

[9]We questioned the elders and asked them, "Who authorized you to rebuild this temple and restore this structure?" [10]We also asked them their names, so that we could write down the names of their leaders for your information.

[11]This is the answer they gave us:

"We are the servants of the God of heaven and earth, and we are rebuilding the temple

[a] 4 See Septuagint; Aramaic [4]*We told them the names of the men constructing this building.*

NRSV

3At the same time Tattenai the governor of the province Beyond the River and Shethar-bozenai and their associates came to them and spoke to them thus, "Who gave you a decree to build this house and to finish this structure?" [4]They[a] also asked them this, "What are the names of the men who are building this building?" [5]But the eye of their God was upon the elders of the Jews, and they did not stop them until a report reached Darius and then answer was returned by letter in reply to it.

6The copy of the letter that Tattenai the governor of the province Beyond the River and Shethar-bozenai and his associates the envoys who were in the province Beyond the River sent to King Darius; [7]they sent him a report, in which was written as follows: "To Darius the king, all peace! [8]May it be known to the king that we went to the province of Judah, to the house of the great God. It is being built of hewn stone, and timber is laid in the walls; this work is being done diligently and prospers in their hands. [9]Then we spoke to those elders and asked them, 'Who gave you a decree to build this house and to finish this structure?' [10]We also asked them their names, for your information, so that we might write down the names of the men at their head. [11]This was their reply to us: 'We are the servants of the God of heaven and earth, and we are rebuilding the house that was built many years ago, which a great king of Israel built and finished. [12]But because our ancestors had angered the God of heaven, he gave them into the hand of King Nebuchadnezzar of Babylon, the Chaldean, who destroyed this house and carried away the people

[a] Gk Syr: Aram *We*

NIV

that was built many years ago, one that a great king of Israel built and finished. [12]But because our fathers angered the God of heaven, he handed them over to Nebuchadnezzar the Chaldean, king of Babylon, who destroyed this temple and deported the people to Babylon.

[13]"However, in the first year of Cyrus king of Babylon, King Cyrus issued a decree to rebuild this house of God. [14]He even removed from the temple[a] of Babylon the gold and silver articles of the house of God, which Nebuchadnezzar had taken from the temple in Jerusalem and brought to the temple[a] in Babylon.

"Then King Cyrus gave them to a man named Sheshbazzar, whom he had appointed governor, [15]and he told him, 'Take these articles and go and deposit them in the temple in Jerusalem. And rebuild the house of God on its site.' [16]So this Sheshbazzar came and laid the foundations of the house of God in Jerusalem. From that day to the present it has been under construction but is not yet finished."

[17]Now if it pleases the king, let a search be made in the royal archives of Babylon to see if King Cyrus did in fact issue a decree to rebuild this house of God in Jerusalem. Then let the king send us his decision in this matter.

[a] *14* Or *palace*

NRSV

to Babylonia. [13]However, King Cyrus of Babylon, in the first year of his reign, made a decree that this house of God should be rebuilt. [14]Moreover, the gold and silver vessels of the house of God, which Nebuchadnezzar had taken out of the temple in Jerusalem and had brought into the temple of Babylon, these King Cyrus took out of the temple of Babylon, and they were delivered to a man named Sheshbazzar, whom he had made governor. [15]He said to him, "Take these vessels; go and put them in the temple in Jerusalem, and let the house of God be rebuilt on its site." [16]Then this Sheshbazzar came and laid the foundations of the house of God in Jerusalem; and from that time until now it has been under construction, and it is not yet finished.' [17]And now, if it seems good to the king, have a search made in the royal archives there in Babylon, to see whether a decree was issued by King Cyrus for the rebuilding of this house of God in Jerusalem. Let the king send us his pleasure in this matter."

COMMENTARY

5:3-5. Tattenai was the governor of the western half of the Persian satrapy called Beyond the River, which at this time still included Babylon. His supervisor, the satrap Ushtannu, had his headquarters in Babylon; Tattenai himself may have made Damascus his administrative center. Shethar-bozenai may have been Tattenai's secretary, much as Shimshai was Rehum's secretary (4:8), though this is not stated explicitly and other functions could have been assigned to him.

For unspecified reasons Tattenai and his entourage made a visit to the post-exilic community. The investigating team first asked the Golah community who had given them authority to rebuild the Temple and to complete its woodwork (v. 3*b;* NRSV and NIV, "structure"). Wood was used within the walls and on the roof of the Temple. Second, the investigators asked for a list of the people working on the project (v. 4). In introducing the second question, both the NRSV and the NIV correctly emend the text of v. 4, changing "we spoke to them" into "they spoke to them."

The faulty reading apparently arose because of assimilation to the first-person plural form of the same verb in the report to the king about this visit (v. 9).

Despite the critical connotations of the investigators' questions, divine protection kept the work from being interrupted. Elsewhere Ezra and Nehemiah use "the hand of God" to connote divine support (7:6, 9, 28; 8:18, 22, 31); here the author refers to God's "eye" (עין *'ayin*), as does the psalmist: "Truly the eye of the LORD is on those who fear him, on those who hope in his steadfast love" (Ps 33:18 NRSV; cf. Job 36:7). Ironically, inspectors or investigators in Persia were known as the king's eye. The eye of God was countering the eye of the king! The leaders of the Jewish community are referred to in this context as its elders (5:5, 8 [restored from 1 Esdr 6:8], 9; 6:7-8. 14; cf. 10:8, 14). Neither Zerubbabel nor Jeshua is mentioned again in the rest of the book of Ezra. While many commentators speculate that Zerubbabel was removed from office because of royal or messianic pretensions, there is no clear evidence for this. In fact, the Persian king reaffirmed the work of the Jewish governor—presumably Zerubbabel—in 6:7. The decision of the investigating team not to stop the work on the Temple was only temporary. Their strategy was to send a letter to Darius and to wait for his official reply before acting.

5:6-10. Verses 6-7*a* introduce the transcript of the letter to the king. The greeting at the end of the address (NRSV, "all peace"; NIV, "cordial greetings") may be an abbreviation of a longer formula, although parallels to this shorter form have also been found. The first paragraph in the letter (vv. 8-10) recounts the visit to Jerusalem described in vv. 3-5. First Esdras 6:8 preserves an extra clause after "the house of the great God" in v. 8: "We discovered that it was being rebuilt by the Jewish elders in the city of Jerusalem." Most likely this clause is original since without it the references to "those elders" in v. 9 would come as a surprise. The NIV obscures this difficulty by omitting the word "these" in v. 9.

Tattenai and his associates refer to Yahweh in a positive way: "the great God." They also supply a short glimpse into what was happening in the reconstruction of the Temple, again stated in positive terms. The masons working on the Temple used smoothed or polished hewn stones, perhaps ashlars, and wood was being placed into the walls. Commentators suggest that the mixture of wood and stone was designed to prevent damage by earthquakes or to hold the building together. Wood was also used in the construction of the First Temple (1 Kgs 6:36, inner court; 7:12, great court) and is mentioned in the decree of Cyrus (6:4). The Persian officials note that the work of the Jews was being done perfectly or exactly (NRSV, "diligently") and was, in fact, meeting with great success. The two questions addressed to the elders in vv. 3-4 are repeated in vv. 9-10: Who authorized this? What are your names? The desire of the investigators to report the names of the Jewish leaders to the king has an ominous ring.[38]

5:11-16. Almost all of the rest of Tattenai's letter consists of a quotation of the Jewish elders' response to his visit. Instead of listing their names, as Tattenai had demanded in his second question, the elders confessed who they were theologically: "We are the servants [worshipers] of the God of heaven and earth." Cyrus had also invoked the "God of heaven" in his decree authorizing the building of the Temple (1:2; cf. 6:9-10; 7:12, 21, 23). The elders' seemingly small expansion of the divine name—the God of heaven *and earth*—claims for their God total sovereignty. Heaven *and* earth (the figure of speech is called a merismus) stand for the totality of conceivable spaces (cf. God's rule over the whole world defined as "the sea and the dry land" in Jonah 1:9). By answering the request for names in their own way, the Jewish leaders took the offensive. The omnidominant God, whom they worship, is the authority behind their building project. Their Temple's legitimacy has existed for centuries ("many years ago," v. 11). In describing the builder and finisher (cf. 4:12-13; 5:3) of the First Temple as a great king, they are referring, of course, to Solomon.

Verse 12 serves in this context as a defense against the investigation of Tattenai and a rebuttal of the charge, made by Rehum and his associates in 4:15, that Jerusalem had been a perpetually

38. If the antecedent of the first "their" in v. 10 is the elders of v. 9, Galling's hypothesis that the original purpose of Ezra 2 and Nehemiah 7 was to supply a list for Tattenai fails, since that list clearly contains many more names than the elders of the community. See Kurt Galling, "Die Liste der aus dem Exil Heimgekehrten," *Studien zur Geschichte Israels im persischen Zeitalter* (Tübingen: Mohr, 1964).

rebellious city. The elders confess that their ancestors had provoked the God of heaven, through some unspecified evil deeds, and that the God of heaven had handed them over to Nebuchadnezzar, who had torn down the Temple and exiled the people to Babylon. Thus their defeat had resulted neither from Nebuchadnezzar's own intrinsic strength nor from Babylonian reprisals for their rebellious character. Their confession accepts implicitly the conclusion of the prophets and the deuteronomistic history—namely, that the exile was the Lord's righteous judgment for Israel's misdeeds. An earlier generation had tried to dissociate itself from the consequences of the sins of the ancestors (Jer 31:29-30; Ezek 18:2).

Since the leaders are writing from Palestine, the return to the land is presupposed, and no attention is given to the exile itself. Instead, they note in his very first year that Cyrus, the king of Babylon,[39] had authorized the rebuilding of the Temple.

Verses 13-16 are a paraphrase of the edict of Cyrus in 6:2-5 (cf. 1:2-4). All three versions of the decree agree on the date of the decree and on the fact that it authorized the temple building and the restoration of the temple vessels to Jerusalem. Nebuchadnezzar had taken the vessels to the temple of his own god in Babylon (Esagila), and Cyrus removed them from there and entrusted them to Sheshbazzar for their return. Clines argues that the way Sheshbazzar is referred to in v. 14 ("a man named Sheshbazzar") is a form of address used elsewhere mostly with reference to slaves (cf. "this Sheshbazzar," v. 16).[40] This may indicate that Sheshbazzar had lost favor with the Persian authorities and that the Jewish leaders sought to distance themselves from him in their defense to Tattenai. Sheshbazzar's loss of favor would also explain why Haggai and Zechariah do not mention this important post-exilic leader. Still, the leaders do claim that Sheshbazzar had been appointed governor, a title attested for him only here (cf. 1:8, however, where he is called "prince of Judah"). Verse 15 turns things around chronologically since Cyrus commands Sheshbazzar to deposit the vessels in the Temple and only then to restore the Temple itself. The point of this verse, of course, is to affirm that both the restoration of vessels and the building of the Temple had the full support of Cyrus.

The elders claim that Sheshbazzar came right away to Jerusalem ("then") and laid the temple foundations, or repaired the platform that formed the base for the Temple. Elsewhere in Ezra (3:8-10) and in Zech 4:9, Zerubbabel is credited with "founding" (יסד *yāsad*) the Temple. Some commentators say that only one person could have laid the temple foundations and so that one of these traditions—presumably the one with regard to Sheshbazzar—is secondary and not historical. In one example of this view, the altar was reconsecrated at the time of Sheshbazzar in 3:1-6, but the work on the Temple itself began in the time of Darius (3:7-13). As noted in this commentary, the text of Ezra 3 places both the dedication of the altar and the initial work on the Temple in the second year of Cyrus. Other commentators have tried to distinguish philologically between the preliminary work done by Sheshbazzar ("laid the foundations"[יהב אשיא *yĕhab 'uššayyā'*]) and the completion of the foundation stone ceremony (*kalû*) by Zerubbabel. Still others conclude that any preliminary work done by Sheshbazzar in 538 BCE would have had to be redone eighteen years later by Zerubbabel. The text permits no final decision.

Even more puzzling is the claim in v. 16*b* that the work in Jerusalem had been going on uninterrupted from the time of Sheshbazzar until the time this defense was written in 520, and in all that time the Temple had not been completed. Historically, this notion of uninterrupted work on the Temple is simply untrue, as Haggai (1:2, 4, 9) and the book of Ezra elsewhere make abundantly clear (4:4, 24). Viewed as a part of the Jewish defense, however, this statement makes sense. Question: Who authorized the building of the Temple? Answer: Cyrus. Question: What was the Jewish response to the king's permission to rebuild the Temple? Answer: Sheshbazzar immediately went home, taking the temple vessels with him, and began working on the Temple: In the intervening years the post-exilic community had responded obediently to the king's charge. Hence they argued that the authorization of Cyrus should not be reversed because of Jewish indifference.

5:17. With "and now" Tattenai continues his

39. See *ANET*, 316, for the use of this title with Cyrus.

40. David J. A. Clines, *Ezra, Nehemiah, Esther*, NCB (Grand Rapids: Eerdmans, 1984) 87-88.

own part of the letter, after quoting the lengthy Jewish defense. Tattenai wanted to know from Darius whether, in fact, such a decree had been issued or whether this was only a specious Jewish claim. So he urged the king to search through the royal archives in Babylon to discover whether a copy of the order by Cyrus could be found. Surprisingly, as the next chapter will show, the record turned up in Ecbatana, the former capital of Media and the summer residence for Persian kings. Finally, and quite formally, Tattenai's letter refers to the royal addressee in the third person: "Let the king send us his pleasure"—his decision—"in this matter."

REFLECTIONS

What gives authority to a person's message or meaning to one's life? Too often we rely on the office we hold or on the power we can claim by virtue of that office. Ezra 5 discusses the basis for the authority of Jewish leaders, such as Haggai, Zechariah, Zerubbabel, Jeshua, the Jewish elders, and Sheshbazzar, as well as the authority claimed by Tattenai and his associates. In the case of the Jewish leaders, their authority lay not in themselves, in the prophets, or even in the Persian king whom God had sent, but in God. For all the bluster of Tattenai and his associates, the author of Ezra 5 discounted them, since they were also subject to the greater authority of God.

The prophets Haggai and Zechariah had an authority based on the God of Israel, who was over them and who authorized their message. The reference to Israel in the title they used for God expressed God's solidarity with the people to whom they prophesied.

Zerubbabel and Jeshua, as we know from elsewhere in the Bible, could have claimed the titles of governor and high priest. But as they set out to lead the people in the rebuilding of the Temple, their authority lay in the fact that the prophets of God were helping them.

Tattenai and his associates were the secular "authorities"; they had the office and the access to imperial power that could nip in the bud the rebuilding of the Temple in Jerusalem. They were the king's eye. But they were also under a greater authority, since the eye of God looked favorably on the elders of the Jews.

The elders were asked by Tattenai and his associates to provide the names of their leaders, which might serve as evidence in the leaders' undoing. "We are the servants of the God of heaven and earth," the elders replied. "Servants" has the right mixture of humility, status (as in the honored title "servant of the king" [2 Kgs 22:12]), and commitment to the worship of God. Just as a Christian's identity may be better expressed by the fact that she or he is baptized than by the name recorded at city hall, so also the elders did better to describe themselves as servants of God than to express exactly who they were; they refused to supply the noose for their own necks. They confessed the power of their God, the ruler of everything, both heaven and earth.

Who had given permission to build this house? To this question the elders replied with a recital of their nation's history. The great king Solomon had built the Temple centuries earlier, but when their ancestors angered the God of heaven, God turned them over to devastating judgment under Nebuchadnezzar, who burned the Temple and took its vessels to Babylon. But then arose Cyrus, whose spirit God had stirred up, and he authorized the rebuilding of the Temple and the return of its vessels as soon as he came to power.

Sheshbazzar, whom Cyrus had appointed governor, took these vessels home and started to rebuild the Temple. By using the title "governor" in speaking of him, the Jewish elders aim to show that their leader, Sheshbazzar, had been treated favorably by the Persians. Even Paul knew when it was appropriate to claim political rights and privileges (Acts 22:25).

Haggai would have had trouble with the claim that the temple building had been going on without interruption in the last two decades. And we may be tempted to join him and to see in this claim a reliance on self-accomplishment rather than on the authorization of God and of those officials through whom God works. But this claim to uninterrupted work may be like other statements of innocence in the Bible. They are not so much claims of perfection, but declarations of loyalty, in which believers commit themselves to live in obedience to God.[41] In such loyalty lies freedom and authority.

41. See Gerhard von Rad, *Old Testament Theology I* (New York: Harper & Row, 1962–65) 380-82.

EZRA 6:1-22, THE TEMPLE IS AUTHORIZED AND COMPLETED

Ezra 6:1-5, The Decree of Cyrus

NIV

6 King Darius then issued an order, and they searched in the archives stored in the treasury at Babylon. [2]A scroll was found in the citadel of Ecbatana in the province of Media, and this was written on it:

Memorandum:

[3]In the first year of King Cyrus, the king issued a decree concerning the temple of God in Jerusalem:

Let the temple be rebuilt as a place to present sacrifices, and let its foundations be laid. It is to be ninety feet[a] high and ninety feet wide, [4]with three courses of large stones and one of timbers. The costs are to be paid by the royal treasury. [5]Also, the gold and silver articles of the house of God, which Nebuchadnezzar took from the temple in Jerusalem and brought to Babylon, are to be returned to their places in the temple in Jerusalem; they are to be deposited in the house of God.

a 3 Aramaic *sixty cubits* (about 27 meters)

NRSV

6 Then King Darius made a decree, and they searched the archives where the documents were stored in Babylon. [2]But it was in Ecbatana, the capital in the province of Media, that a scroll was found on which this was written: "A record. [3]In the first year of his reign, King Cyrus issued a decree: Concerning the house of God at Jerusalem, let the house be rebuilt, the place where sacrifices are offered and burnt offerings are brought;[a] its height shall be sixty cubits and its width sixty cubits, [4]with three courses of hewn stones and one course of timber; let the cost be paid from the royal treasury. [5]Moreover, let the gold and silver vessels of the house of God, which Nebuchadnezzar took out of the temple in Jerusalem and brought to Babylon, be restored and brought back to the temple in Jerusalem, each to its place; you shall put them in the house of God."

a Meaning of Aram uncertain

COMMENTARY

After an unsuccessful search of the records in Babylon, Darius' officials found a copy of the decree of Cyrus deposited at Ecbatana, the former Median capital, which had been captured by Cyrus in 550. Because of its high elevation, Ecbatana was the summer residence for the Persian kings. Known today as Hamadan, Ecbatana is located between Tehran and Baghdad. While many of the records of the Persians are preserved on clay tablets, the memorandum of Cyrus was written on a scroll in Aramaic. The word "record" (דכרונה *dikrônâ*) at the end of v. 2 is the first word in the document.

As in 1:1, the "first year of Cyrus" refers to his first year as ruler over Babylon. The document cited in vv. 3-5 may have contained provisions for various countries, but only the information about the Temple in Jerusalem is provided. The text begins a bit awkwardly, perhaps because it is an extract from a longer document, and the word "concerning" is added to translate the Aramaic *casus pendens* grammatical structure. A contemporary letter from Bagohi, governor of Judah, and Delaiah, governor of Samaria, gives a similar authorization to the Jews at Elephantine to build a temple: "You may say in Egypt . . . about the Altar-house of the God of Heaven . . . to rebuild it on its site as it was formerly and they shall offer the meal-offering and the incense upon that altar just as formerly was done."[42] The Udjahorresnet inscription also reports Persian financing of local cults.[43] The document in Ezra 6 makes no explicit reference to the return from the exile (cf. 1:3), but it sets aside funds from the royal treasury for the building project and gives measurements and a few other details about how the Temple is to be built.

By identifying the Temple as a place where sacrifices are offered (v. 3), the document expresses observations that Persians indeed might make, since they did not practice animal sacrifice in their own worship. The Jews, during their exile in Babylon, also did not perform sacrifices. The difference between "its foundations" (אשׁוהי *'uššôhî*, MT and NIV) and "[its] burnt offerings" (אשׁוהי *'eššôhî*) results from the change of the first vowel. The reading in the NRSV seems preferable because of the verb סבל (*sābal*), which means "bring" rather than "lay."[44]

The dimensions for the Temple are defective, since only the height and the width are given. If the length is supplied from 1 Kgs 6:2 as sixty cubits, then the Temple emerges as a gigantic cube of 216,000 cubic cubits, exactly six times the volume of Solomon's Temple, with its 36,000 cubic cubits. But a text with numbers is prone to accidental omissions (by homoioteleuton) or misreading of numbers. In the following translation, brackets indicate words that have been supplied and quotation marks indicate a number that has been changed, both of these made on the basis of Kings:

The Temple's height in cubits = [30]
The Temple's length in cubits = [60]
The Temple's breadth in cubits = [20]

These measurements are the same as those for Solomon's Temple and would indicate continuity between the First and Second temples. Regular cubits were 17.5", and royal cubits were 20.4" (Ezek 40:5; 43:13). Using the regular cubit, the Temple measured 87.5′ by 29.16′; its height was 43.75′. The same numbers, according to the royal cubit, would be 102′, 34′, and 51′.[45] The alternation between three courses of stone and one of wood resembles the construction technique for the inner and great courts of Solomon's Temple (1 Kgs 6:36; 7:12).[46]

It is strange that the Golah community had done no work on the Temple for about twenty years, if all their building expenses were covered by the Persian government (v. 4*b*). Haggai complained bitterly that some of the people were living in luxurious houses while neglecting the temple ruins (1:4) and indicated that attention to self-interests lay behind the delay in rebuilding. The decree of Cyrus confirms that the gold and silver vessels, taken from Jerusalem by Nebuchadnezzar, were to be returned to their appropriate places in the Jerusalem Temple (cf. 1:7-11; 5:14-15).[47] (See Reflections at 6:13-22.)

42. AP 32:2-11. See Bezalel Porten, *Textbook of Documents from Ancient Egypt*, vol. 1: *Letters* (Winona Lake, Ind.: Eisenbrauns, 1986) 76. The letter is dated c. 407 BCE.

43. Joseph Blenkinsopp, "The Mission of Udjahorresnet and Those of Ezra and Nehemiah," *JBL* 106 (1987) 409-21.

44. For the opposite opinion, see H. G. M. Williamson, *Ezra, Nehemiah*, WBC 16 (Waco, Tex.: Word, 1985) 71, who proposes the translation "and let its foundations be retained."

45. Tamara C. Eskenazi, *In an Age of Prose: A Literary Approach to Ezra–Nehemiah*, SBLMS (Atlanta: Scholars Press, 1988) 57, follows the MT and suggests that the dimensions indicate that Cyrus granted permission for a house of God that was larger than the Temple. But surely the purpose of the dimensions is to limit the size of the king's obligation—a temple as big as the first, but no more.

46. "One" (חד *ḥad*) comes from emendation; the Aramaic text reads "new" (חדת *ḥădat*).

47. The passive construction in the NIV, "they are to be deposited," is based on an emendation (see *BHS* 5[b]) and is preferable to the NRSV translation.

Ezra 6:6-12, The Decree of Darius

NIV

[6]Now then, Tattenai, governor of Trans-Euphrates, and Shethar-Bozenai and you, their fellow officials of that province, stay away from there. [7]Do not interfere with the work on this temple of God. Let the governor of the Jews and the Jewish elders rebuild this house of God on its site.

[8]Moreover, I hereby decree what you are to do for these elders of the Jews in the construction of this house of God:

The expenses of these men are to be fully paid out of the royal treasury, from the revenues of Trans-Euphrates, so that the work will not stop. [9]Whatever is needed—young bulls, rams, male lambs for burnt offerings to the God of heaven, and wheat, salt, wine and oil, as requested by the priests in Jerusalem—must be given them daily without fail, [10]so that they may offer sacrifices pleasing to the God of heaven and pray for the well-being of the king and his sons.

[11]Furthermore, I decree that if anyone changes this edict, a beam is to be pulled from his house and he is to be lifted up and impaled on it. And for this crime his house is to be made a pile of rubble. [12]May God, who has caused his Name to dwell there, overthrow any king or people who lifts a hand to change this decree or to destroy this temple in Jerusalem.

I Darius have decreed it. Let it be carried out with diligence.

NRSV

6"Now you, Tattenai, governor of the province Beyond the River, Shethar-bozenai, and you, their associates, the envoys in the province Beyond the River, keep away; [7]let the work on this house of God alone; let the governor of the Jews and the elders of the Jews rebuild this house of God on its site. [8]Moreover I make a decree regarding what you shall do for these elders of the Jews for the rebuilding of this house of God: the cost is to be paid to these people, in full and without delay, from the royal revenue, the tribute of the province Beyond the River. [9]Whatever is needed—young bulls, rams, or sheep for burnt offerings to the God of heaven, wheat, salt, wine, or oil, as the priests in Jerusalem require—let that be given to them day by day without fail, [10]so that they may offer pleasing sacrifices to the God of heaven, and pray for the life of the king and his children. [11]Furthermore I decree that if anyone alters this edict, a beam shall be pulled out of the house of the perpetrator, who then shall be impaled on it. The house shall be made a dunghill. [12]May the God who has established his name there overthrow any king or people that shall put forth a hand to alter this, or to destroy this house of God in Jerusalem. I, Darius, make a decree; let it be done with all diligence."

COMMENTARY

The command for Tattenai and his colleagues to stay away from the Temple implied that they should not interfere with or thwart the building project (cf. v. 7). The reference to the governor of the Jews (v. 7; identified as Zerubbabel in 1 Esdr 6:27) is surprising because he had not been mentioned in the report of Tattenai. Perhaps this is a secondary harmonization with Ezra 5:2.[48]

48. cf. *BHS.*

Darius further ordered (v. 8), in accord with the decree of Cyrus (v. 4*b*), that building costs for the Temple should be paid from royal resources—that is, the taxes received from the Beyond the River satrapy. This would guarantee that the work could go on without interruption (v. 8; so correctly NIV; NRSV, "without delay"). The king also supplied many animals to the Jews for their sacrifices. Bulls, rams, and sheep (v. 9;

cf. v. 17) would be needed for burnt offerings for the God of heaven (cf. 1:2). Such offerings were often supplemented by various agricultural products: wheat (Lev 2:1-7; 5:11), salt (Lev 2:13; Ezek 43:24), wine (Exod 29:38-41; Lev 23:13), and oil (Lev 2:1-7). The specificity of the items needed for the cult suggests either that the king had a Jewish adviser who helped him draft his decree or that the author of Ezra–Nehemiah has added these details. The king's mandate was open-ended—"whatever is needed," everything the priests require "day by day without fail." These sacrifices are to be "pleasing" (v. 10), a favorite and favorable description of God-approved offerings in the Bible (e.g., Exod 29:18; Lev 1:9; 6:8). A modern North American reader, accustomed to the separation of church and state, may be surprised to hear that these sacrifices were to be accompanied by prayers for the king and his sons (v. 10). This instruction, however, helps us to understand why the king would financially support Jewish sacrifices. The Cyrus Cylinder has a similar provision: "May all the gods whom I have resettled to their sacred cities ask daily Bel and Nebo for a long life for me."[49] An Elephantine papyrus contains a prayer of the Jews in Egypt for their Persian governor Bagohi: "They [your servants Jedaniah and his colleagues] will offer the meal-offering and the incense, and the holocaust on the altar of YHWH the God in your name and we shall pray for you at all times—we and our wives and our children and the Jews."[50] The author of Ezra was willing to live in a harmonious relationship with the Persians, without threat of revolt (cf. 1:1). Even Jeremiah had urged Jews in exile to pray for the welfare of Babylon (Jer 29:7; cf. 1 Macc 7:33; 12:11; Bar 1:10-12).

Darius placed heavy sanctions on anyone who would change or disobey this document (vv. 11-12). Both the NIV and the NRSV state that any such person would be impaled on a piece of wood taken from the person's own house. Because the verb מחא (*mĕḥā'*), translated "impaled," means "beaten" in other contexts, some scholars believe that the perpetrator was to be tied upright to a pole taken from his house and flogged. Impaling was a practice that the Persians may have taken over from the Assyrians.[51] Darius makes reference to such punishment in the Behistun inscription. Darius also ordered the person's house to be torn down and turned into a public lavatory (NRSV, "dunghill").[52] The NIV's "pile of rubble" (v. 11) is based on an Akkadian etymology that has been discredited. When the king refers to "God who has established his name there," he is using a biblical, Yahwistic formula used in reference to Jerusalem and found repeatedly in deuteronomic and deuteronomistic contexts (Deut 12:5, 11). A Jewish adviser of Darius or the author of the book himself is probably responsible for this expression. Darius commands Yahweh to overthrow any king or people who would change this Persian document or who would put a stop to the building of the Temple. The king's final words in v. 12 function like a signature. (See Reflections at 6:13-22.)

49. *ANET,* 316.
50. AP 30:25-26. See Porten, *Textbook of Documents from Ancient Egypt,* 71. The letter is dated to November 25, 407 BCE.
51. *ANEP,* 131, fig. 373.
52. The book of Daniel refers to threats of home destruction under the Babylonians (2:5; 3:29). King Jehu and his fellow reformers turned the temple of Baal in Samaria into a latrine (2 Kgs 10:27).

Ezra 6:13-22, Completion of the Temple and Celebration of Passover

NIV

13Then, because of the decree King Darius had sent, Tattenai, governor of Trans-Euphrates, and Shethar-Bozenai and their associates carried it out with diligence. 14So the elders of the Jews continued to build and prosper under the preaching of Haggai the prophet and Zechariah, a descendant

NRSV

13Then, according to the word sent by King Darius, Tattenai, the governor of the province Beyond the River, Shethar-bozenai, and their associates did with all diligence what King Darius had ordered. 14So the elders of the Jews built and prospered, through the prophesying of the prophet

NIV

of Iddo. They finished building the temple according to the command of the God of Israel and the decrees of Cyrus, Darius and Artaxerxes, kings of Persia. 15The temple was completed on the third day of the month Adar, in the sixth year of the reign of King Darius.

16Then the people of Israel—the priests, the Levites and the rest of the exiles—celebrated the dedication of the house of God with joy. 17For the dedication of this house of God they offered a hundred bulls, two hundred rams, four hundred male lambs and, as a sin offering for all Israel, twelve male goats, one for each of the tribes of Israel. 18And they installed the priests in their divisions and the Levites in their groups for the service of God at Jerusalem, according to what is written in the Book of Moses.

19On the fourteenth day of the first month, the exiles celebrated the Passover. 20The priests and Levites had purified themselves and were all ceremonially clean. The Levites slaughtered the Passover lamb for all the exiles, for their brothers the priests and for themselves. 21So the Israelites who had returned from the exile ate it, together with all who had separated themselves from the unclean practices of their Gentile neighbors in order to seek the LORD, the God of Israel. 22For seven days they celebrated with joy the Feast of Unleavened Bread, because the LORD had filled them with joy by changing the attitude of the king of Assyria, so that he assisted them in the work on the house of God, the God of Israel.

NRSV

Haggai and Zechariah son of Iddo. They finished their building by command of the God of Israel and by decree of Cyrus, Darius, and King Artaxerxes of Persia; 15and this house was finished on the third day of the month of Adar, in the sixth year of the reign of King Darius.

16The people of Israel, the priests and the Levites, and the rest of the returned exiles, celebrated the dedication of this house of God with joy. 17They offered at the dedication of this house of God one hundred bulls, two hundred rams, four hundred lambs, and as a sin offering for all Israel, twelve male goats, according to the number of the tribes of Israel. 18Then they set the priests in their divisions and the Levites in their courses for the service of God at Jerusalem, as it is written in the book of Moses.

19On the fourteenth day of the first month the returned exiles kept the passover. 20For both the priests and the Levites had purified themselves; all of them were clean. So they killed the passover lamb for all the returned exiles, for their fellow priests, and for themselves. 21It was eaten by the people of Israel who had returned from exile, and also by all who had joined them and separated themselves from the pollutions of the nations of the land to worship the LORD, the God of Israel. 22With joy they celebrated the festival of unleavened bread seven days; for the LORD had made them joyful, and had turned the heart of the king of Assyria to them, so that he aided them in the work on the house of God, the God of Israel.

COMMENTARY

The description of the building of the Temple in vv. 13-15 is very short. Because Tattenai and his associates thoroughly carried out the king's positive orders with regard to the Temple, some commentators conclude that they had not originally been hostile to the Jews, but had appealed to Darius because they were unclear about what they should do. The elders of the Jews—without any mention of Zerubbabel (cf. 6:7)—executed the king's decree with great success. The author notes also that their work prospered because of the prophesying of Haggai and Zechariah. References to these prophets at the beginning (5:1) and now at the end of the temple building account indicate that the entire enterprise was supported by prophetic authority. The building's completion benefited from the explicit commands of the God of Israel and of the Persian kings (v. 14). For the first time in this chapter, Yahweh is called the God of Israel (cf. 5:1), a name perhaps highlighting the inalienable connection between Israel and the Temple. Before the end of the chapter the word "Israel" will be used exactly seven times. While the same Aramaic consonants (טעם *ṭʿm*) are used to denote the commands of God and those of the king in v. 14, the Masoretic vocalization is different (טעם *ṭaʿam* vs. טעם *ṭĕʿēm*), perhaps to indicate the significant difference between the two usages. This distinction is nicely observed by the NRSV and the NIV, which speak of the "command" of God and the "decree(s)" of three Persian kings. The decree of Cyrus appears in vv. 3-5; that of Darius, supporting his predecessor, in vv. 6-12. The reference to Artaxerxes in v. 14 seems out of place, since he did not come to the throne until about fifty years after the building of the Temple. Rudolph, therefore, suggests that this reference be deleted and refers the reader to Ezra 7:11-27.[53] It is unlikely, however, that we need to resort to such surgery, let alone attribute ignorance of Persian history to the author of Ezra. Rather, the mention of Artaxerxes alerts the reader to the fact that this Persian king, too, will offer financial support for the Temple and its worship program (7:12-26; cf. 9:9). As the author approached the end of the Aramaic section, he may have inserted a positive reference to Artaxerxes to balance out the complaints made to him at the beginning of the Aramaic account in 4:7-16 and his order to stop the building of the walls in 4:17-23.

The Temple was completed by the third day of Adar—or the twenty-third day if we follow 1 Esdr 7:5. Some scholars have calculated that the third day of Adar, March 12, 515 BCE, would have been a sabbath day and hence inappropriate for the completion of the work. They see this as the reason behind the recalculation in 1 Esdras to April 1, 515. Others have remarked, however, that creation itself was "completed" on the seventh day without contradicting God's decision to rest on that day (Gen 2:2-3). They suggest that the reading in 1 Esdras is original and that the number "twenty" fell out of the MT by accident. Note that in 2 Chr 7:9-10 the dedication of Solomon's Temple lasted until the twenty-third day of the month (cf. 1 Kgs 8:66, where it ended on the eighth day). In any case, the Second Temple was completed in fewer than five years (Solomon's Temple took seven years to build [1 Kgs 8:38]), but it would stand for almost five hundred years, until it was lavishly rebuilt by Herod in the first century BCE. The date of the Second Temple's completion was seventy-two years after the destruction of the First Temple, thus fulfilling Jer 25:11-12; 29:10 (cf. 2 Chr 36:21-22).

In the description of the dedication of the Temple, the author refers to the community as "the people of Israel" (v. 16), just as he had called Yahweh the God of Israel in v. 14. Elsewhere in the Aramaic account he had called members of the community "the Jews" (4:12, 23; 5:1, 5; 6:7-8, 14; "elders" are mentioned in 5:5, 8 [by emendation], 9; 6:7-8, 14). Priests and laity together celebrated the dedication of the Temple with joy (v. 16; cf. 1 Kgs 8:66). This account resembles the dedication of Solomon's Temple in a variety of ways (see 1 Kings 8; 2 Chr 7:4-7), as well as the celebration that was held when the foundations of the Temple were laid (Ezra 3:10-13). For the dedication of the post-exilic Temple the people offered generous gifts: 100 bulls, 200 rams, 400 lambs, and 12 male goats. To sacrifice 712 animals for one occasion may seem excessive, but this report pales before the account of the dedication of Solomon's Temple, when the king offered 22,000 oxen and 120,000 sheep (1 Kgs 8:5, 63). The twelve male goats for the sin offering (v. 17) correspond to the number of the tribes in Israel as a whole, even though the people present were restricted to the tribes of Judah, Benjamin, and Levi. The sin offering cleansed the Temple or the altar of any impurity picked up during the period of reconstruction (Lev 4:22-26; 9:1-7; Numbers 7; Ezek 43:18-27). The group that later returned with Ezra also offered twelve goats as a sin offering (Ezra 8:35). The new Temple required the stationing of the priests and the Levites, following the prescriptions of the Pentateuch (here called "the book of Moses," v. 18; cf. 3:2; 7:6; Neh 8:1, 14; 10:29; 13:1). While the priests and the Levites are mentioned extensively in the Pentateuch (Exodus 29; Leviticus 8; Numbers 3; 4; 8), there is no reference there to separation into "divisions" or "courses." According to 1 Chronicles 23–26, these divisions stem traditionally from the time of King David, who is mentioned only twice in Ezra (3:10; 8:20; cf. Neh 12:24, 45), although historically the development of

53. *BHS* note 14[d-d].

the twenty-four Priestly courses probably came in the fourth century BCE.[54] Note that the "divisions," the "courses," and the "service of the house[55] of God" are also mentioned in the chronicler's account of Josiah's Passover (2 Chr 35:2-5).

In the final paragraph (vv. 19-22), the writer returns to the Hebrew language. Chapters 1–6 begin with Cyrus's decree to build the Temple and conclude with its dedication of the Temple and the subsequent Passover account. Exodus and temple building are connected in Exod 15:17-18, and here in Ezra, temple building is joined with Passover, the great celebration of Israel's deliverance from Egypt. Passover, of course, played a major role in the reforms of Hezekiah and Josiah, according to Chronicles (2 Chr 30:13-22; 35:1-19).

By the time of Ezra, Passover was celebrated on a fixed day, the fourteenth day of the first month (Lev 23:5; cf. Exod 12:6). Verse 20 in the NRSV suggests that the priests and the Levites killed the Passover lamb for the rest of the congregation, whereas elsewhere we read that the priests did not do the slaughtering but manipulated the blood and performed burnt offerings (2 Chr 30:16-17; 35:3-6, 10-14; in Exod 12:6 and Deut 16:2 the whole congregation slaughters the lamb). The NIV solves the problem by adding the word "Levites" midway through the verse. Williamson proposes a creative, but unconvincing, construal of the Hebrew text: "The priests had purified themselves, and the Levites were all pure to a man, and they [i.e., the Levites] slaughtered the Passover."[56] Perhaps it is best to follow Rudolph's advice and delete "the priests and" from the first part of v. 20.[57] The purification of the clergy symbolized that an era of sin and guilt was over and that now a new era was beginning.

The makeup of the group celebrating the Passover is unexpectedly broad (v. 21). In addition to those who had returned from exile, the text mentions those who had separated themselves from the uncleanness of the nations of the land. "Uncleanness" (טמאה *ṭumʾâ*) is generally connected with the worship of foreign gods (cf. 9:11). "Those who had separated themselves" may have been Gentiles who had become proselytes or Jews who had not gone into exile, but who had now become members of the new community. The use of the phrase "nations of the land" instead of "peoples of the land"—this is the only mention of the nations in the whole book of Ezra—favors the gentile interpretation. In either case, the author does not restrict the community only to those who came back from the captivity as he seems to do elsewhere (e.g., 1:5). According to pentateuchal law, sojourners were allowed to participate in the Passover if they were circumcised (Exod 12:43-49; cf. Num 9:14).

Following the one-day observance of Passover came the weeklong Feast of Unleavened Bread. Originally the latter festival had been a harvest festival at which one ate bread that had not been leavened by sour dough left over from the previous year's crop. Early on, however, the Festival of Unleavened Bread was connected to the exodus (see the old calendars in Exod 23:14-15; 34:18). Since Unleavened Bread and Passover both occurred in the spring of the year, they were eventually joined into one festival (cf. Exod 12:15-20; Lev 23:6-8; Num 28:17; Deut 16:1-8). This festival was celebrated with joy, much like the Passover of Hezekiah (2 Chr 30:21) or the celebration at the founding of the Temple (Ezra 3:10-13). God was the source of this joy. God made them rejoice just as God had turned the heart of the foreign king (v. 22). While the reader is inclined to identify this king with either Cyrus (1:1) or Darius (6:6-12), kings of Persia, the author calls him the king of Assyria. Perhaps he wanted to say that Cyrus and Darius, heirs of the Assyrian rule, had finally undone the evil against Israel that had been committed by Assyrian kings (cf. Neh 9:32). Blenkinsopp calls attention to 2 Chr 30:6, which mentions a remnant of Israel at the time of Hezekiah that had escaped the hands of the king of Assyria. That remnant was now embodied in the post-exilic community.[58] The people of the land, who had weakened the hands of the people of Judah and made them afraid to build (4:4), had now been trumped by a God who strengthened the hands of the community of returned exiles. This God is the God of Israel, whose name reflects what this small community is: Israel.

54. H. G. M. Williamson, "The Origins of the Twenty-Four Priestly Courses," *VTSup* 30 (1979) 251-68.

55. Perhaps the word "house" should be inserted after "service" in 6:18. See the Syriac and the Lucianic recension of the Septuagint.

56. H. G. M. Williamson, *Ezra, Nehemiah,* WBC 16 (Waco, Tex.: Word, 1985) 69, 72.

57. *BHS* note 20[a-a].

58. Joseph Blenkinsopp, *Ezra–Nehemiah,* OTL (Philadelphia: Westminster, 1988) 133.

REFLECTIONS

Chapters 1–6 report how the favor of Yahweh and of the Persian kings led to the return from exile and the rebuilding of the Temple. Both authorizations were necessary and frequently noted, though at the beginning (1:1) and at the end (6:22) of these chapters the text makes clear that the Persian king's favor was effected by the graciousness of Yahweh. The king clearly expected that a people favored by him would pray for him and his descendants (6:10), and the author seems willing to pay this price to ensure peaceful existence. Jeremiah urged exilic Israel to pray for the peace of Babylon; Babylon's prosperity would mean prosperity for Israel (Jer 29:7). A high tide raises all boats. No doubt there were voices that chafed under such foreign domination (Neh 9:36-37), and it would be a mistake to derive from these chapters a universal principle of passivity or quietism. The God of the exodus and the Magnificat is One who puts down the mighty from their thrones and exalts the lowly, and God invites us to live with the expectation of God's preferential option for the weak and to implement these divine commitments in our roles as caretakers in charge of God's estate. But for the author of Ezra–Nehemiah, having a fully functioning Temple was indispensable, something to be achieved at all costs. If God chooses to mediate such a reality through the Persian emperor, why should anyone begrudge God's generosity or restrict God's freedom?

The author has insisted throughout these chapters that the temple community in Palestine is the true Israel. The Temple was rebuilt by the command of the God of Israel (6:14), whose name also brings closure to these chapters in 6:22. And the group that worships in this God's house has the right to call itself Israel. Although painfully small, and with representatives of only three of the tribes, this community is nevertheless completely Israel, it is all Israel in this place. The twelve goats for the sin offering express this catholicity. However much these chapters have favored those who returned over those who never left the land, the Passover celebration following the dedication of the Temple has a more inclusive tone: All those who separated themselves from the uncleannesses of the nations were welcome to join in the joyful celebration. A community turned in on itself, closed to outsiders, is no community.

In the Song of Moses/Miriam, Israel confessed that the final goal of the exodus was life in God's presence:

> You brought them in and planted
> them on the mountain of your own possession,
> the place, O LORD, that you
> made your abode,
> the sanctuary, O LORD, that
> your hands have established. (Exod 15:17 NRSV)

Ezra 6 links the Temple again to the exodus by celebrating Passover soon after the dedication of the Temple. When one reads Ezra in the context of the books of Chronicles, one sees a clear pattern begin to emerge. Once worship had been purified or restored, it was time to celebrate Passover—so it was with Hezekiah, with Josiah, and with late sixth-century Israel.

Joy is more than a human emotion. Joyful celebration is more than a standing ovation for God. When God makes us joyful, only then can we rejoice. Through the many stories in Ezra 1–6 of hard work, of frequent reversals, of internal disappointment, and of outside opposition, the author remained clear about the divine source of joy, both his and ours. He also knew that joy was not achieved solely in the religious sphere. God made the Judean community joyful by guiding the political events of the day, even by turning the heart of the king of Assyria to the exiled people. As the church today lives in, with, and for the larger society, it contributes to the common good of that society and prospers when society creates a favorable climate for the church's mission. Both joy and the favorable climate are finally God's benefactions.

EZRA 7:1–10:44

THE INITIAL WORK OF EZRA

OVERVIEW

This section is usually called the Ezra Memoir, an analogy with the more famous Nehemiah Memoir that immediately follows it. This part of the Ezra Memoir consists of narratives told by Ezra (or by someone who wrote in his name) in the first person (7:27–8:34; 9:1-15), as well as third-person narratives about Ezra in 7:1-11; 8:35-36; and 10:1-44. Many commentators would also include among the third-person parts of the Ezra Memoir Neh 7:73*b*–8:18 (perhaps also Neh 9:1-5), which deal with Ezra's reading of the law (and the subsequent day of penitence) in the time of Nehemiah. It is argued by many that Ezra would not have waited thirteen years to read the law and that therefore these materials belonged "originally" between chaps. 8 and 9,[59] after 10:44 (cf. 1 Esdras; other even more complex rearrangements have been proposed). In any one of these hypothetical positions Ezra would have completed his mission within a year. Historically there is very little evidence that Ezra and Nehemiah were exact contemporaries.

These historical arguments are, indeed, persuasive, but the alleged "original" position of Nehemiah 8–9 in Ezra is very uncertain, with no consensus in sight. What is more, Neh 7:73*b*–9:5 has now been incorporated into the book of Nehemiah, where it is part of a unit extending from Neh 7:73*b* to Neh 10:39. This section of the Ezra Memoir is interpreted in that literary context, where, regardless of its original position, it is now well integrated. Japhet's proposal on the structure of Ezra–Nehemiah fully incorporates these Ezra materials into the book of Nehemiah.[60]

The third-person materials about Ezra may have been recast from an original first-person narrative, they may represent an alternative source about Ezra, or they may be the author's own composition. No great difference in viewpoint between the first- and the third-person accounts has been convincingly demonstrated, but within the Ezra Memoir these documents can be identified:

7:12-26: the firman of Artaxerxes, an Aramaic document giving the Persian king's commission to Ezra
8:1-14: of those who returned with Ezra
10:8-43, the list of those who had been involved in mixed marriages.

Questions about Ezra's identity, his origins, and the book of the Law he brought with him from exile have dominated Ezra scholarship. According to the edict of Artaxerxes, Ezra was an official sent by the king with a series of specific assignments. In addition to being a priest, he is called a "scribe of law of the God of heaven" (7:12). Does the title "scribe" mean only that he had the literary skills of a scribe and was an expert in the law? Or was he also a commissioner for Jewish affairs in the Persian government? The Commentary on 7:1-20 will address these issues. Blenkinsopp has compared Ezra's mission to that of Udjahorresnet, an Egyptian priest and scribe who was sent back to his home country by the Persians to restore the cult and to reorganize the institutions of scribalism and religious learning.[61]

The date of Ezra's arrival in Jerusalem is either 458 BCE, if he came under Artaxerxes I, or 398 BCE, if he came under Artaxerxes II. The present arrangement of Ezra–Nehemiah, which puts Ezra before Nehemiah, favors the earlier date. Detailed arguments in favor of this date have been pres-

59. Blenkinsopp, *Ezra–Nehemiah*, 45; Williamson, *Ezra–Nehemiah*, 308.

60. Sara Japhet, "Composition and Chronology in the Book of Ezra–Nehemiah," in *Temple Community in the Persian Period*, ed. Tamara C. Eskenazi and Kent Harold Richards, JSOTSup 175 (Sheffield: Sheffield Academic, 1994) 189-216. See also Introduction.

61. J. Blenkinsopp, "The Mission of Udjahorresnet and Those of Ezra and Nehemiah," *JBL* 106 (1987) 409-21.

ented in recent commentaries.[62] The second date has been proposed because Ezra and Nehemiah, with only three exceptions (Neh 8:9 [Nehemiah is not found in 1 Esdr 9:49]; 12:26, 36), are not mentioned together and ignore each other completely. Since their powers and responsibilities are similar, it seems unlikely that they would have played their respective roles in the Jewish community at the same time. The reference to a "wall" in Ezra 9:9 has sometimes been taken to refer to the wall of Nehemiah, though many scholars, including myself in this commentary, understand Ezra 9:9 metaphorically. If the Jehohanan, son of Eliashib, mentioned in Ezra 10:6 is high priest, this also would require a later date for Ezra because Eliashib was the high priest at the time of Nehemiah. Finally, it seems unlikely that Ezra would have waited thirteen years after his arrival to read the law. But if Neh 7:73*b*–9:5 belongs historically to the materials in Ezra 7:1–10:44, then all of Ezra's actions took place within one year, long before Nehemiah. If we could be sure that Ezra's law was the Pentateuch and that his actions gave it canonical status, the arguments for his priority would be even stronger. The structure of the books of Ezra and Nehemiah make it appropriate for us to choose the earlier date in any case.

The text of Ezra–Nehemiah suggests that the book of the law that Ezra brought in Ezra 7 and from which he read in Nehemiah 8 was the Pentateuch. While many modern scholars share this opinion, others think the law book of Ezra was the Priestly source in the Pentateuch (P), a more or less undefined group of laws now included in the Pentateuch, or some form of Deuteronomy. Most conclude that a law that proved so crucial in the restoration community would not be lost and, therefore, must be somewhere in the present canon. The Commentary on Ezra 7:11-28 will address the question of why certain practices in Ezra–Nehemiah are not in accord with the Pentateuch.

Ezra, like all the other major figures in Ezra–Nehemiah—Zerubbabel, Jeshua, and Nehemiah—disappears without a trace or without any clear endpoint in his career. His most controversial action was the divorce proceedings initiated among those who had married women from the peoples of the land (chaps. 9–10). Some have speculated that negative reaction to this action would have brought his career to an end.

62. For a thorough discussion of the dating question see David J. A. Clines, *Ezra, Nehemiah, Esther*, NCB (Grand Rapids: Eerdmans, 1984) 16-24; Williamson, *Ezra, Nehemiah*, xxxix-xliv; Blenkinsopp, *Ezra–Nehemiah*, 139-44; Lester Grabbe, *Judaism from Cyrus to Hadrian*, vol. 1: *The Persian and Greek Periods* (Minneapolis: Fortress, 1992) 88-93. Albright and John Bright proposed a date in 428 BCE, in the thirty-seventh year of Artaxerxes, but this now is generally viewed as an unlikely conjecture. See W. F. Albright, *The Biblical Period from Abraham to Ezra* (New York: Harper and Bros., 1963) 93-94; John Bright, *A History of Israel*, 3rd ed. (Philadelphia: Westminster, 1981) 391-402.

EZRA 7:1-10, EZRA COMES TO JERUSALEM

NIV

7 After these things, during the reign of
Artaxerxes king of Persia, Ezra son of
Seraiah, the son of Azariah, the son of Hilkiah,
2the son of Shallum, the son of Zadok, the son of
Ahitub, 3the son of Amariah, the son of Azariah,
the son of Meraioth, 4the son of Zerahiah, the son
of Uzzi, the son of Bukki, 5the son of Abishua,
the son of Phinehas, the son of Eleazar, the son
of Aaron the chief priest— 6this Ezra came up
from Babylon. He was a teacher well versed in
the Law of Moses, which the LORD, the God of
Israel, had given. The king had granted him

NRSV

7 After this, in the reign of King Artaxerxes
of Persia, Ezra son of Seraiah, son of Azariah, son of Hilkiah, 2son of Shallum, son of
Zadok, son of Ahitub, 3son of Amariah, son of
Azariah, son of Meraioth, 4son of Zerahiah, son of
Uzzi, son of Bukki, 5son of Abishua, son of Phinehas, son of Eleazar, son of the chief priest Aaron—
6this Ezra went up from Babylonia. He was a
scribe skilled in the law of Moses that the LORD
the God of Israel had given; and the king granted
him all that he asked, for the hand of the LORD
his God was upon him.

NIV

everything he asked, for the hand of the LORD his God was on him. [7]Some of the Israelites, including priests, Levites, singers, gatekeepers and temple servants, also came up to Jerusalem in the seventh year of King Artaxerxes.

[8]Ezra arrived in Jerusalem in the fifth month of the seventh year of the king. [9]He had begun his journey from Babylon on the first day of the first month, and he arrived in Jerusalem on the first day of the fifth month, for the gracious hand of his God was on him. [10]For Ezra had devoted himself to the study and observance of the Law of the LORD, and to teaching its decrees and laws in Israel.

NRSV

7Some of the people of Israel, and some of the priests and Levites, the singers and gatekeepers, and the temple servants also went up to Jerusalem, in the seventh year of King Artaxerxes. [8]They came to Jerusalem in the fifth month, which was in the seventh year of the king. [9]On the first day of the first month the journey up from Babylon was begun, and on the first day of the fifth month he came to Jerusalem, for the gracious hand of his God was upon him. [10]For Ezra had set his heart to study the law of the LORD, and to do it, and to teach the statutes and ordinances in Israel.

COMMENTARY

Fifty-eight years intervene between the dedication of the Temple in 516 BCE and the second great event in Ezra–Nehemiah: the arrival of Ezra in Jerusalem in 458 BCE, the seventh year of Artaxerxes I, King of Persia (v. 7; see the Overview of 7:1–10:44 for a discussion of this date). The words "After this" at the beginning of v. 1 pass over these fifty-eight years in silence, and yet they connect the coming of Ezra to the completion of the Temple and the initiation of the cult. Artaxerxes' title, "King of Persia" (v. 1), was previously used for Cyrus (1:1-2), in whose reign the first turn toward salvation took place. Although the dedication of the Temple had made it possible for the community to carry on its cultic life, Isaiah 56–66 and the book of Malachi indicate that the years after the Temple's rededication were largely times of failure and/or division in the community.

7:1-5. The priestly genealogy of Ezra repeats in large part the line of high priests from Aaron to Seraiah in 1 Chr 6:3-15. A copyist's error in v. 3 was apparently responsible for the omission of Johanan, Azariah, Ahimaaz, Zadok, Ahitub, and Amariah between Azariah and Meraioth (cf. 1 Chr 6:7-9). The Azariah omitted from the list served as priest in the Temple Solomon had built, according to 1 Chr 5:35-36 as corrected in the footnotes in *BHS* (1 Chr 6:9 follows the MT). There is a second gap in the genealogy, between Ezra and Seraiah (v. 1). Seraiah himself was executed by the Babylonians (2 Kgs 25:18-21), and his son Jehozadak was taken into exile by Nebuchadnezzar in 586 BCE (1 Chr 6:15), some 128 years before the arrival of Ezra. Rudolph suggested that Ezra's actual father was named Seraiah, and that a copyist skipped all the names from the first Seraiah to the second Seraiah.[63] Although Ezra is identified numerous times as a priest (7:11, 12, 21; 10:10, 16), he was not part of the post-exilic line of high priests, which included at least Jeshua (cf. 5:2), Joiakim, Eliashib, Joiada, Jonathan/Johanan, and Jaddua (see the Commentary on Neh 12:10-11, 22). Some commentators believe that the high priestly genealogy was supplied by a later hand in an attempt to enhance Ezra's credentials. This secondary addition created the somewhat awkward and repetitious beginning of v. 6. (Note the use of a dash between v. 5 and v. 6 in both the NRSV and the NIV.) A long genealogy for the main character in the second phase of the post-exilic community, however, is appropriate. By connecting Ezra directly to Seraiah, the author created an unbroken continuity between the pre-exilic high priesthood and Ezra.

7:6-10. Ezra came to deal with questions about the law of Moses. He is the prototype of

63. Wilhelm Rudolph, *Esra und Nehemia, samt 3. Esra,* HAT 20 (Tübingen: J. C. B. Mohr [Paul Siebeck], 1949) 66.

the later scribes, who were laypeople. The name "Ezra" is a shorter form of Azariah, a name that appears three times in the (reconstructed) genealogy. Ezra was a scribe skilled in the law of Moses (v. 6). Here and in Nehemiah 8: 1, 4, 9, 13 the word "scribe" (סֹפֵר *sōpēr*) seems to refer to a person who knew and could expound the written word of the Pentateuch. Verse 6 ascribes to the first five books of the Bible the authority of the Lord God of Israel.

Did Ezra play a role in the Persian bureaucracy? Scribes are listed among Israelite officials in monarchical times (e.g., Seraiah, 2 Sam 8:17; Elihoreph and Ahijah, 1 Kgs 4:3). In addition to their ability to write and edit, scribes had financial (2 Kgs 12:11) and diplomatic (2 Kgs 19:2-7; 22:14-20) responsibilities; they could even carry on negotiations in foreign languages (2 Kgs 18:18-27). Shimshai was a scribe who co-authored a letter with the satrapal official Rehum to Artaxerxes (Ezra 4:8). H. H. Schaeder believed that Ezra was a kind of secretary of state or high commissioner for Jewish affairs at the Persian court (cf. 7:12, 21; Neh 8:9; 12:26).[64] It is possible, however, that the author's understanding of Ezra as a priest and scribal expert in the law led him to put his own understanding of Ezra's office into the wording of the Aramaic decree of Artaxerxes.[65] Since Ezra's role as priest is not due to the Persians, the title "scribe" may represent only his role among the Jews. Regardless of the Persian understanding of the word "scribe," Ezra had three responsibilities with regard to the Torah: He studied it, he lived or obeyed it, and he taught it to others (v. 10; cf. Neh 8:13-18). Ezra eagerly picked up this assignment ("he set his heart," v. 10) to study, to do, and to teach the law; he was a true scribe (cf. Sir 38:24–39:11). "Statutes" and "ordinances" may at times refer to apodeictic and casuistic forms of law, but in v. 10 the terms are probably to be taken more inclusively as a reference to the entirety of Israelite law.

Ezra—as well as Nehemiah—was supported throughout his career by the gracious and providential hand of God (7:6, 9, 28; 8:18, 22, 31; cf. Neh 2:8, 18). The Persian king's generosity to him (v. 6; cf. 1 Kgs 10:13; Esth 1:6; 2:18) was the channel through which the Lord's benefaction came to Ezra. None of Ezra's specific requests made to Artaxerxes is identified in v. 6, and we read later that he refused the king's offer of a bodyguard (8:22).

Ezra was accompanied by a group consisting of lay Israelites ("people of Israel," NRSV; "Israelites," NIV; the NIV mistakenly makes the priests, etc., subgroups within the Israelites, a term here designating laity; see 6:16), priests, Levites, singers (cf. 2:41, 65, 70), gatekeepers (cf. 2:42, 70), and temple servants (נְתִינִים *nĕtînîm*; cf. 2:43, 58, 70)—the categories resemble those of chapter 2. Singers and gatekeepers, as distinct categories within the Levites, are not included in the list of returnees in chap. 8, though the names "Hashabiah" and "Jeshaiah" from that list (8:19) do occur in lists of pre-exilic musicians (1 Chr 6:45, Hashabiah; 25:3, Jeshaiah and Hashabiah). The laity are mentioned first in v. 7, as in 2:2. The group arrived in Jerusalem on the first of Ab (August 4, 458 BCE), after the decision to make the journey was made on the first day of the first month (April 8, 458). According to 8:31 the actual start was delayed until the twelfth day of the first month (April 19). The fourteen-week journey proceeded at a pace of about ten miles per day. The dates given for the start of Ezra's journey may have symbolic importance. The original exodus had taken place in the first month (Exod 12:2; cf. Num 33:3), which is also the month of Passover. The journey of Ezra's group up to Jerusalem may be considered a new exodus event, with a celebration of Passover quite early in the trip, on the fourteenth day of the first month. Just as the first exodus was followed by the giving of the law on Sinai, so also the new exodus with Ezra was followed by his seeking the law. The word יְסֻד (*yĕsud* "[was] begun") in v. 9 should be repointed as *yissad* ("he had fixed" or "he had arranged for" the journey up from Babylon).[66] Klaus Koch suggested that 458 BCE was a "sabbatical year" (cf. 1 Macc 6:49, 53).[67] (See Reflections at 7:11-28.)

64. H. H. Schaeder, *Esra der Schreiber,* BHT 5 (Tübingen: J. C. B. Mohr, 1939) 45-49.

65. Blenkinsopp, *Ezra–Nehemiah,* 137. Further discussion may be found in Grabbe, *Judaism from Cyrus to Hadrian,* 1:94-98, who not only doubts that Ezra was a Persian scribe, but also questions whether Ezra's mission took place at all. Williamson, *Ezra, Nehemiah,* 100, is basically favorable to Schaeder's proposal.

66. "Journey up" (הַמַּעֲלָה *hammaʿălâ*) may be another allusion to the exodus; compare the word עליה (*aliyah*), which connotes emigration to the modern state of Israel.

67. Klaus Koch, "Ezra and the Origins of Judaism," *JJS* 19 (1974) 173-97.

EZRA 7:11-28, THE AUTHORIZATION OF EZRA

NIV

11This is a copy of the letter King Artaxerxes had given to Ezra the priest and teacher, a man learned in matters concerning the commands and decrees of the LORD for Israel:

12[a]Artaxerxes, king of kings,

To Ezra the priest, a teacher of the Law of the God of heaven:

Greetings.

13Now I decree that any of the Israelites in my kingdom, including priests and Levites, who wish to go to Jerusalem with you, may go. 14You are sent by the king and his seven advisers to inquire about Judah and Jerusalem with regard to the Law of your God, which is in your hand. 15Moreover, you are to take with you the silver and gold that the king and his advisers have freely given to the God of Israel, whose dwelling is in Jerusalem, 16together with all the silver and gold you may obtain from the province of Babylon, as well as the freewill offerings of the people and priests for the temple of their God in Jerusalem. 17With this money be sure to buy bulls, rams and male lambs, together with their grain offerings and drink offerings, and sacrifice them on the altar of the temple of your God in Jerusalem.

18You and your brother Jews may then do whatever seems best with the rest of the silver and gold, in accordance with the will of your God. 19Deliver to the God of Jerusalem all the articles entrusted to you for worship in the temple of your God. 20And anything else needed for the temple of your God that you may have occasion to supply, you may provide from the royal treasury.

21Now I, King Artaxerxes, order all the treasurers of Trans-Euphrates to provide with diligence whatever Ezra the priest, a teacher of the Law of the God of heaven, may ask of you— 22up to a hundred talents[b] of silver, a hundred cors[c] of wheat, a hundred baths[d] of

[a] *12* The text of Ezra 7:12-26 is in Aramaic. [b] *22* That is, about 3 3/4 tons (about 3.4 metric tons) [c] *22* That is, probably about 600 bushels (about 22 kiloliters) [d] *22* That is, probably about 600 gallons (about 2.2 kiloliters)

NRSV

11This is a copy of the letter that King Artaxerxes gave to the priest Ezra, the scribe, a scholar of the text of the commandments of the LORD and his statutes for Israel: 12"Artaxerxes, king of kings, to the priest Ezra, the scribe of the law of the God of heaven: Peace.[a] And now 13I decree that any of the people of Israel or their priests or Levites in my kingdom who freely offers to go to Jerusalem may go with you. 14For you are sent by the king and his seven counselors to make inquiries about Judah and Jerusalem according to the law of your God, which is in your hand, 15and also to convey the silver and gold that the king and his counselors have freely offered to the God of Israel, whose dwelling is in Jerusalem, 16with all the silver and gold that you shall find in the whole province of Babylonia, and with the freewill offerings of the people and the priests, given willingly for the house of their God in Jerusalem. 17With this money, then, you shall with all diligence buy bulls, rams, and lambs, and their grain offerings and their drink offerings, and you shall offer them on the altar of the house of your God in Jerusalem. 18Whatever seems good to you and your colleagues to do with the rest of the silver and gold, you may do, according to the will of your God. 19The vessels that have been given you for the service of the house of your God, you shall deliver before the God of Jerusalem. 20And whatever else is required for the house of your God, which you are responsible for providing, you may provide out of the king's treasury.

21"I, King Artaxerxes, decree to all the treasurers in the province Beyond the River: Whatever the priest Ezra, the scribe of the law of the God of heaven, requires of you, let it be done with all diligence, 22up to one hundred talents of silver, one hundred cors of wheat, one hundred baths[b] of wine, one hundred baths[b] of oil, and unlimited salt. 23Whatever is commanded by the God of heaven, let it be done with zeal for the house of the God of heaven, or wrath will come upon the realm of the king and his heirs. 24We also notify you that it shall not be lawful to impose tribute,

[a] Syr Vg 1 Esdras 8.9: Aram *Perfect* [b] A Heb measure of volume

NIV

wine, a hundred baths[a] of olive oil, and salt without limit. 23Whatever the God of heaven has prescribed, let it be done with diligence for the temple of the God of heaven. Why should there be wrath against the realm of the king and of his sons? 24You are also to know that you have no authority to impose taxes, tribute or duty on any of the priests, Levites, singers, gatekeepers, temple servants or other workers at this house of God.

25And you, Ezra, in accordance with the wisdom of your God, which you possess, appoint magistrates and judges to administer justice to all the people of Trans-Euphrates—all who know the laws of your God. And you are to teach any who do not know them. 26Whoever does not obey the law of your God and the law of the king must surely be punished by death, banishment, confiscation of property, or imprisonment.

27Praise be to the LORD, the God of our fathers, who has put it into the king's heart to bring honor to the house of the LORD in Jerusalem in this way 28and who has extended his good favor to me before the king and his advisers and all the king's powerful officials. Because the hand of the LORD my God was on me, I took courage and gathered leading men from Israel to go up with me.

a *22* That is, probably about 600 gallons (about 2.2 kiloliters)

NRSV

custom, or toll on any of the priests, the Levites, the singers, the doorkeepers, the temple servants, or other servants of this house of God.

25"And you, Ezra, according to the God-given wisdom you possess, appoint magistrates and judges who may judge all the people in the province Beyond the River who know the laws of your God; and you shall teach those who do not know them. 26All who will not obey the law of your God and the law of the king, let judgment be strictly executed on them, whether for death or for banishment or for confiscation of their goods or for imprisonment."

27Blessed be the LORD, the God of our ancestors, who put such a thing as this into the heart of the king to glorify the house of the LORD in Jerusalem, 28and who extended to me steadfast love before the king and his counselors, and before all the king's mighty officers. I took courage, for the hand of the LORD my God was upon me, and I gathered leaders from Israel to go up with me.

COMMENTARY

Verse 11 is a Hebrew introduction to the Aramaic edict or letter of Artaxerxes in vv. 12-26. In v. 11*a* Ezra is described as the priest, the scribe, but v. 11*b*, which may be secondary, identifies him as a student (lit., "scribe") of the words of the commandments of the Lord and the statutes for Israel (cf. v. 10). The Aramaic edict is either an authentic document of Artaxerxes that has been revised by a Jewish scribe or a Jewish composition in Aramaic putting Ezra's commission into the mouth of Artaxerxes. Clines attributes the Jewish coloring of the letter to the influence of a Jewish official at work in Artaxerxes' court, perhaps Ezra himself, while Williamson proposes that the edict was drafted in response to a written request by Ezra.[68]

The title "king of kings" for Artaxerxes (v. 12) expresses the fullness of his authority; this phrase appears elsewhere in the Bible as a title for Nebuchadnezzar (Ezek 26:7; Dan 2:37). Outside the Bible, Darius I and Artaxerxes both use this title. The translations "peace" (NRSV) and "greetings" (NIV) in v. 12 follow 1 Esdr 8:9; the MT has an Aramaic word, גמיר (*gĕmîr*), meaning "complete" or "perfect." Some commentators understand this word in the sense of "etc."—that is, as an abbreviation

68. David J. A. Clines, *Ezra, Nehemiah, Esther,* NCB (Grand Rapids: Eerdmans, 1984); H. G. M. Williamson, *Ezra, Nehemiah,* WBC 16 (Waco, Tex.: Word, 1985) 99.

for a standard greeting formula. "And now" forms a transition to the body of the letter.

In the edict Artaxerxes first authorizes Israelites—laity, priests, and Levites—to return to Jerusalem with Ezra. Cyrus made a similar decree early in his reign (1:2-4), and a number of such returns took place between 538 and 520 BCE.

Second, Artaxerxes and his seven counselors instruct Ezra to determine whether the community in Judah and Jerusalem was in conformity with the law of their God (v. 14). The issue of mixed marriages plays a major role in this inquiry (cf. chaps. 9–10). Ezra had mastery over the law, or he was entrusted with it, for it was "in his hand." Since v. 25 seems to presuppose the existence of the law throughout the province of Beyond the River, it is unlikely that "in your hand" refers to a new law that Ezra brought with him from Babylon.

Ezra's law is usually thought to be a collection of laws more or less conforming to the Pentateuch. Blenkinsopp notes clear connections with Deuteronomy 12–26 as well as with portions of the Holiness Code and the priestly writing. He also observes that certain practices in Ezra–Nehemiah are not in accord with the Pentateuch and concludes that pentateuchal law had not yet reached its final form by the mid-fifth century, even if it was well on its way to doing so. The day of repentance in Neh 9:1, for instance, takes place on the twenty-fourth instead of on the tenth day of Tishri (Lev 16:29; 23:27-32), and the temple tax is set at a third of a shekel in Neh 10:33-34 rather than at a half shekel (Exod 30:11-16).[69] The discrepancies between the Pentateuch and the practices in Ezra–Nehemiah, however, may result at least in part from attempts to update or harmonize the law in the fifth century.[70] It is impossible to say whether or how much the decree of Artaxerxes contributed to the codification of biblical law (see the Commentary on 7:26).

Third, the king ordered Ezra to take a series of contributions to Jerusalem and spend them on sacrificial offerings (vv. 15-18). The king and his counselors made the first contribution of gold and silver. The references to "the God of Israel" and to "whose dwelling is in Jerusalem" (v. 15) are expressions that are not likely to have been used by a Persian king. The people of the province of Babylon made the second contribution, or, rather, Ezra "found" or collected money among them. Gifts from such non-Jews (cf. 8:25) recall the theme of the despoiling of the Egyptians during the exodus from Egypt (cf. 1:4, 6). Finally, the Jewish people and the priests in Babylon made freewill offerings for the Temple of their God (v. 16). Artaxerxes instructed Ezra to use these funds to acquire a number of animals for a special sacrifice—the types of animals are the same as those in 6:9-10, 17 although the goats, which played a symbolic role in chap. 6, are not mentioned here. The king also ordered Ezra to buy the cereal offerings and drink offerings that accompany these sacrifices. This clear reference to the details of the sacrificial system (cf. Num 15:1-16) provides further evidence for Jewish influence on the present wording of the letter of Artaxerxes. This financial support of sacrifices was only for a single occasion, possibly a ceremony of thanksgiving for Ezra's safe arrival. Any funds left over after the purchase of sacrificial animals could be spent at the discretion of Ezra and his colleagues, though only for cultic purposes ("according to the will of your God," v. 18).

The king's rescript also mentions cultic vessels that had been given to Ezra (v. 19). These must be distinguished from the vessels from the First Temple, which had been taken from Jerusalem by Nebuchadnezzar and were returned through the authority of Cyrus (1:7-11; 6:5). The vessels Ezra took home, which are itemized in 8:26-27, 33-34, are special votive offerings contributed by Artaxerxes. The title "God of Jerusalem" is used only here in the Bible.[71] The temple vessels make the first return (in chap. 1) and Ezra's return parallel events. Any additional cultic needs of the Jerusalem Temple were to be supplied from the Persian treasuries (v. 20).

Verses 21-24 are directly addressed to the Persian satrapal authorities and suggest maximum amounts that they should contribute to Ezra. Perhaps a copy of this paragraph was made available for them, or they read their instructions from the edict of Artaxerxes to Ezra. It is not stated

69. Joseph Blenkinsopp, *Ezra–Nehemiah,* OTL (Philadelphia: Westminster, 1988) 152-57. See also Judson Shaver, *Torah and the Chronicler's History,* BJS 196 (Atlanta: Scholars Press, 1989).

70. So H. G. M. Williamson, *Ezra and Nehemiah* (Sheffield: JSOT, 1987) 93-98.

71. *BHS* emends unnecessarily to "the God of Israel who is in Jerusalem."

whether these were one-time requirements or regular expectations. The materials given for the Jerusalem cult, with the exception of the silver, seem generous, but not implausible: 650 bushels of wheat; 600 gallons of wine; 600 gallons of oil. Alfred Bertholet estimated that these commodities would have met the Temple's needs for about two years.[72] The contribution of salt, on which the Persians had a monopoly, was to be made without limit. The amount of silver, 100 talents—roughly 3.75 tons—is totally out of proportion. The whole kingdom of Judah gave only 100 talents of silver to Necho (2 Kgs 23:33), and Herodotus reports that the total tax raised from all of Beyond the River in one year was 350 talents, of which 28 percent in this case would have been used as a kind of church tax.[73] Perhaps the vastness of the amount is designed to show the true generosity of the Persians. Clines suggests emending "talents" to "minas," which would reduce the total to 1/60 of the amount stated in the biblical text—still 125 pounds.[74] The rescript announces serious consequences for the subjects of the empire if the financial needs of Israel's God are not met. The threat of "wrath" (the word קְצַף [*qeṣep*] is used only of divine wrath [Num 1:53; 18:5; Josh 9:20; 2 Kgs 3:27; 2 Chr 19:10]) and is probably a reference to God's intervention in some future battle.

The treasurers of the satrapy were empowered to raise these funds through taxes, but with one significant exception: No taxes could be imposed on any of the temple personnel in Jerusalem (v. 24). The list of clergy (cf. v. 7) follows very closely the list of cultic personnel in 2:36-57, except that "the servants of this house of God" have replaced Solomon's servants (2:55). If the purpose of the missions of Ezra and Nehemiah was to solidify Yehud as a Persian province because of the turmoil in Egypt and its threat of revolt, aided by the Greeks, then it would make sense for the king to appeal to local provincial deities, such as Yahweh in Yehud, by excusing their temple personnel from taxation. In the Gadatas inscription, Darius II tells one of his officials that the priests of Apollo are free from taxes and service on labor gangs.[75]

Finally, Artaxerxes ordered Ezra to appoint judges for the province Beyond the River, in accordance with the wisdom he possessed (vv. 25-26). "Wisdom" probably refers here to the intelligence or judgment God has given to Ezra, and it is not an early identification of wisdom with law (as in Sir 24:23, 25; Bar 4:1). These judges were to regulate Jewish life outside Jerusalem in an appropriate manner. "All the people in Beyond the River" refers to Jewish people, both those Jews who acknowledge the laws of God and those who do not. The latter group is to be brought into active participation in Judaism through teaching them the law. Ezra, as a representative of the Jewish community in Babylon, which had learned to live without the Temple and sacrifice during their exile, would be well prepared to help Jews widely removed from the Temple continue their life as Jews in conformity with the law. Two laws seem to be distinguished in v. 26, "the law of God" and "the law of the king." Frei has concluded, however, that the Persian king was in fact authorizing Ezra's religious law book to serve also as the law of the empire.[76] The king took disobedience to this doubly authorized law very seriously. Penalties for violation included capital punishment, deportation (banishment), confiscation of goods, and imprisonment. Some commentators see connotations of physical punishment or flogging in לִשְׁרֹשִׁו (*lišrōšiw*), the Aramaic word for "banishment." Imprisonment for breaches of OT law is not prescribed elsewhere in any biblical law code, though some kings did imprison political enemies (1 Kgs 22:27; Jer 37:15–38:13). The threatened sentences indicate that the full authority of the Persian penal system has been put behind Ezra's law.

Ezra expresses his own doxology in Hebrew in response to the letter of Artaxerxes, in which he refers to himself in the first person (vv. 27-28*a*). Ezra praises God for putting into the heart of the king of Persia plans for beautifying and glorifying the Temple at Jerusalem "in this way"—by commissioning Ezra to make inquiries about the conformity of the community to the law, by providing lavishly for a thank offering and for other needs

72. As cited in Wilhelm Rudolph, *Esra und Nehemiah, samt 3. Esra,* HAT 20 (Tübingen: J. C. B. Mohr [Paul Siebeck], 1949) 75.

73. Herodotus III.91.

74. Clines, *Ezra, Nehemiah, Esther,* 104.

75. See Lester Grabbe, *Judaism from Cyrus to Hadrian,* vol. 1: *The Persian and Greek Periods* (Minneapolis: Fortress, 1992) 59. Grabbe also calls attention to the debate over this inscription's authenticity.

76. Peter Frei, "Zentralgewalt und Lokalautonomie im Achämenidenreich," *Reichsidee und Reichsorganisation im Perserreich,* OBO (Göttingen: Vandenhoeck & Ruprecht, 1984) 17. Frei calls the recognition of local norms by the empire "Reichsautorisation" (13). The best parallel is provided by the Xanthos inscription.

of the Temple, by giving votive offerings, and by making available ongoing finances for the sacrificial system. The hand of the Lord was indeed with him (v. 28; cf. vv. 6, 9), and God had shown him steadfast, covenantal love, before no one less than the Persian king, his seven counselors, and all his powerful officials, who served as sure witnesses (v. 28; cf. v. 14). Ezra took courage—like one who had been commissioned by God (Joshua 1)—and set immediately to the task.

REFLECTIONS

Ezra's life was motivated by praise for God. He praised God especially for moving the heart of the king to glorify the house of Yahweh in Jerusalem. Artaxerxes had given gifts that permitted a rich cultic life at Jerusalem, including sacrifices of thanksgiving for Ezra's safe arrival and provisions for the ongoing worship life of Israel.

But the "house of God" in Ezra, much like the church, is more than a building. The house of God is the whole company of those who hear and confess the words and ways of God. They practice the presence of God by doing God's will both in the sanctuary and away from it. God's will is expressed in Torah, which specifies the ethical demands of the faith within the context of the story of God with the world and with Israel. Today we call that Torah the Pentateuch—it is the Torah of Moses, given by the God of Israel. We concede its authority because we recognize its self-authenticating power.

Although sent with an assignment to bring Israel into conformity with Torah and to extend its authority to those living away from Jerusalem, Ezra embodied what it means to be a child of God in any age. He studied Torah, he did it, and he taught it to Israel.

Study of Torah is necessary for at least two reasons. First, it is necessary to harmonize its diverse requirements or to bring them up to date with the ethical and moral needs of the day. The books of Ezra and Nehemiah are replete with attempts to understand the implications of Torah for the fifth-century BCE community living under Persian domination. Communities today faced with societal collapse, environmental disaster, and the ravages of violence and war also need to reflect on their responsibility for the created world, the biblically mandated love for strangers, and the implications of the faith for peace and justice throughout the world.

Second, it is important to correlate one's own story with the larger salvation history. Ezra personally experienced God's steadfast love in his dealings with the authorities of the Persian Empire, and he was protected by the gracious hand of God upon him (7:6, 9, 28). But this gracious hand and steadfast love were only tokens of that grace and providence that Israel had experienced as a nation and recorded in its Torah.

Study of Torah is no objective, dispassionate science. Ezra was also assigned to do Torah, to live it. God's self-disclosure and the revelation of God's will are invitations to take up the burden of Torah, the yoke of the kingdom (Deut 6:4). Ezra "set his heart" to do this; he gladly assumed this burden. He is both the father of Judaism and its best example.

Those who have seen God's goodness must necessarily bear witness to it. Ezra was instructed to teach the statutes and ordinances in Israel. His teaching ministry embraced those who participated in the daily life of the Temple as well as those who lived far away from the Temple and who wished to remain faithful in that diaspora setting.

The burning center of Christianity is the impulse to bear witness. To witness is not a gimmick or a marketing technique to ensure church growth. Rather, to witness is to tell and teach what one has experienced so that others might be led to study Torah, to practice it, and to teach it to others.

Each life should be a high doxology, a life of praise for God. Claus Westermann drew a clear distinction between thanksgiving and praise.[77] Thanksgiving is often too individualistic, a private communication between an individual and God. Too often we express our thanks grudgingly, almost out of obligation. But praise in the Bible and today is offered willingly and joyfully before the whole community. It recites one's experiences of God and relates them to the community's wider experience of God's grace and will, to Torah. We praise God in the presence of others so that they might be encouraged and strengthened by what we have discovered or experienced. In this way, the whole house of God is glorified.

77. Claus Westermann, *The Praise of God in the Psalms* (Richmond: John Knox, 1965) 25-30.

EZRA 8:1-36, EZRA'S TRIP TO JERUSALEM

Ezra 8:1-14, The Group That Returned with Ezra

NIV

8 These are the family heads and those registered with them who came up with me from Babylon during the reign of King Artaxerxes:

2of the descendants of Phinehas, Gershom;
of the descendants of Ithamar, Daniel;
of the descendants of David, Hattush 3of the descendants of Shecaniah;
of the descendants of Parosh, Zechariah, and with him were registered 150 men;
4of the descendants of Pahath-Moab, Eliehoenai son of Zerahiah, and with him 200 men;
5of the descendants of Zattu,[a] Shecaniah son of Jahaziel, and with him 300 men;
6of the descendants of Adin, Ebed son of Jonathan, and with him 50 men;
7of the descendants of Elam, Jeshaiah son of Athaliah, and with him 70 men;
8of the descendants of Shephatiah, Zebadiah son of Michael, and with him 80 men;
9of the descendants of Joab, Obadiah son of Jehiel, and with him 218 men;
10of the descendants of Bani,[b] Shelomith son of Josiphiah, and with him 160 men;
11of the descendants of Bebai, Zechariah son of Bebai, and with him 28 men;
12of the descendants of Azgad, Johanan son of Hakkatan, and with him 110 men;

[a] *5* Some Septuagint manuscripts (also 1 Esdras 8:32); Hebrew does not have *Zattu.* [b] *10* Some Septuagint manuscripts (also 1 Esdras 8:36); Hebrew does not have *Bani.*

NRSV

8 These are their family heads, and this is
the genealogy of those who went up with
me from Babylonia, in the reign of King Artaxerxes: 2Of the descendants of Phinehas, Gershom.
Of Ithamar, Daniel. Of David, Hattush, 3of the
descendants of Shecaniah. Of Parosh, Zechariah,
with whom were registered one hundred fifty
males. 4Of the descendants of Pahath-moab, Eliehoenai son of Zerahiah, and with him two hundred males. 5Of the descendants of Zattu,[a]
Shecaniah son of Jahaziel, and with him three
hundred males. 6Of the descendants of Adin, Ebed
son of Jonathan, and with him fifty males. 7Of the
descendants of Elam, Jeshaiah son of Athaliah, and
with him seventy males. 8Of the descendants of
Shephatiah, Zebadiah son of Michael, and with
him eighty males. 9Of the descendants of Joab,
Obadiah son of Jehiel, and with him two hundred
eighteen males. 10Of the descendants of Bani,[b]
Shelomith son of Josiphiah, and with him one
hundred sixty males. 11Of the descendants of
Bebai, Zechariah son of Bebai, and with him
twenty-eight males. 12Of the descendants of
Azgad, Johanan son of Hakkatan, and with him
one hundred ten males. 13Of the descendants of
Adonikam, those who came later, their names
being Eliphelet, Jeuel, and Shemaiah, and with
them sixty males. 14Of the descendants of Bigvai,
Uthai and Zaccur, and with them seventy males.

[a] Gk 1 Esdras 8.32: Heb lacks *of Zattu* [b] Gk 1 Esdras 8.36: Heb lacks *Bani*

NIV

13of the descendants of Adonikam, the last ones, whose names were Eliphelet, Jeuel and Shemaiah, and with them 60 men;
14of the descendants of Bigvai, Uthai and Zaccur, and with them 70 men.

COMMENTARY

The list of the heads of families who had been gathered by Ezra for his trip to Jerusalem begins with two priestly families and one Davidic family, and then continues with a list of twelve lay family heads and the number of males belonging to each family. The total for the list comes to 1,513 men (1 Esdras, 1,690), which, when supplemented with estimates for women and children, might add up to about 5,000. The whole assembly from chap. 2 numbered 42,360 (2:64).

The inclusion of this list produced a slight overlap of 7:28 and 8:1 and led to a repetitive resumption of 7:28 in 8:15 ("I gathered"). The repetition of some of the families from chap. 2 in this list means that certain members of these families returned early in the restoration period while others came only at the time of Ezra.

Both Gershom (Phinehas) and Daniel (Ithamar), the priests mentioned in v. 2, traced their ancestry back to Aaron's immediate family (Phinehas was Aaron's grandson and Ithamar his son; the priests listed in 2:36-39 are not identified as descendants of Aaron). This verse indicates the increasing preeminence of the Aaronides in post-exilic times, a development also reflected in the Pentateuch (Exod 6:23-25; 28:1; Num 3:2-4; 25:6-13). Among Aaron's four sons, only Eleazar and Ithamar had children; Nadab and Abihu were killed because they had kindled "strange fire" (Lev 10:1-7; 1 Chr 24:2).

The chronicler assigned eight of the twenty-four priestly courses to Ithamar's descendants, while Eleazar's descendants supervised sixteen of these courses (1 Chr 24:4). The chronicler also traces Eli, the priest at Shiloh, and Abiathar, one of David's high priests, back to Ithamar (1 Chr 18:16). The names "Gershom" and "Daniel" actually represent priestly families rather than individual persons, since Ezra is able to select twelve priests from his entourage to carry home gifts from Babylon (v. 24).

Hattush, a descendant of David, was the son of Shecaniah, rather than one of his descendants, as in the NRSV and the NIV (8:2-3).[78] Hattush is related to David through Zerubbabel according to 1 Chr 3:15-22. The prominence given to the Davidic line in this list suggests that the author has incorporated a source, since David is not prominent elsewhere in the Ezra materials.

The twelve lay families listed in vv. 3-14 follow a consistent pattern, exemplified by v. 6: the name of the extended family or father's house (descendants of Adin), the name of the current head of the family (Ebed), the father of the current head (Jonathan), and the number of people in the family (50). The pattern is broken in v. 13, where three members of the Adonikam family, without patronymics, are identified as the last of that family to remain in Babylon. The frequent use of the number twelve in this chapter (vv. 3-14, 24, 35; cf. Neh 8:4) indicates that Ezra's group is to be seen as representative of all Israel. All twelve of these lay families are also present in chap. 2, assuming that Joab (v. 9), formerly part of Pahath-Moab (2:6), has now become an independent family. The family of Parosh (v. 3) and those families listed in vv. 10-14 appear in the same order in chap. 2 (2:3, 10-14). Members of seven of these twelve lay families pledge to divorce their wives in chap. 10, and all the families except Shephatiah are among those who sign the firm agreement in Nehemiah 10. "Shelomith" (v. 10), a woman's name (1 Chr 3:19), should be amended to "Shelomoth" (1 Chr 23:9; 24:22;

78. Cf. *BHS* note 3^{a-a}. This parentage contrasts with 1 Chr 3:22, where Hattush is identified as the son of Shemaiah and, therefore, the grandson of Shecaniah; but that text, too, may be in need of emendation.

26:25-26).[79] Verse 14 should be emended to read: "Of the descendants of Bigvai, Uthai son of Zaccur [or Zabbud], and with him seventy men."[80] (See Reflections at 8:31-36.)

79. Cf. *BHS*

80. Cf. ibid.

Ezra 8:15-20, The Search for Levites

NIV

[15]I assembled them at the canal that flows toward Ahava, and we camped there three days. When I checked among the people and the priests, I found no Levites there. [16]So I summoned Eliezer, Ariel, Shemaiah, Elnathan, Jarib, Elnathan, Nathan, Zechariah and Meshullam, who were leaders, and Joiarib and Elnathan, who were men of learning, [17]and I sent them to Iddo, the leader in Casiphia. I told them what to say to Iddo and his kinsmen, the temple servants in Casiphia, so that they might bring attendants to us for the house of our God. [18]Because the gracious hand of our God was on us, they brought us Sherebiah, a capable man, from the descendants of Mahli son of Levi, the son of Israel, and Sherebiah's sons and brothers, 18 men; [19]and Hashabiah, together with Jeshaiah from the descendants of Merari, and his brothers and nephews, 20 men. [20]They also brought 220 of the temple servants—a body that David and the officials had established to assist the Levites. All were registered by name.

NRSV

15I gathered them by the river that runs to Ahava, and there we camped three days. As I reviewed the people and the priests, I found there none of the descendants of Levi. [16]Then I sent for Eliezer, Ariel, Shemaiah, Elnathan, Jarib, Elnathan, Nathan, Zechariah, and Meshullam, who were leaders, and for Joiarib and Elnathan, who were wise, [17]and sent them to Iddo, the leader at the place called Casiphia, telling them what to say to Iddo and his colleagues the temple servants at Casiphia, namely, to send us ministers for the house of our God. [18]Since the gracious hand of our God was upon us, they brought us a man of discretion, of the descendants of Mahli son of Levi son of Israel, namely Sherebiah, with his sons and kin, eighteen; [19]also Hashabiah and with him Jeshaiah of the descendants of Merari, with his kin and their sons, twenty; [20]besides two hundred twenty of the temple servants, whom David and his officials had set apart to attend the Levites. These were all mentioned by name.

COMMENTARY

Ezra's entourage stopped at Ahava (an unknown place-name and also the name of a river or canal connected to the Euphrates, vv. 21, 31) for three days, and it made a pause of the same length of time upon its arrival in Jerusalem (v. 32; cf. Neh 2:11). During the stay at Ahava, Ezra discovered that no Levites were among his group, a shortage reminiscent of the small numbers of Levites in the first return (cf. 2:40). Koch suggests that Levites were needed so that Ezra's group could re-create the "order of march" through the desert as in the original exodus, but Levites were also needed to fulfill the requirements of Artaxerxes (7:13).[81] Ezra appointed a commission to go to an unknown sanctuary called Casiphia[82] and talk to its head priest Iddo, in order to remedy this shortage of Levites.

Eleven members of this commission are listed in v. 16, including three Elnathans and a Nathan, and the similar names Jarib and Joiarib. The NRSV indicates that some members of the commission were leaders and others were wise (v. 16; cf. NIV). Other commentators translate the word מבינים (*mĕbînîm,* "wise") as "teachers" (1 Chr 15:22; 25:7-8; 2 Chr 34:2; 35:3; Neh 8:8-9), thus distinguishing between the nine leading men and

81. Klaus Koch, "Ezra and the Origins of Judaism," *JJS* 19 (1974) 187.

82. In the Hebrew text Casiphia is called a "place" (מקום *māqôm*) both times it is mentioned in v. 17, a technical term for a sanctuary (cf. Gen 28:11, 16-17). The Jews at Elephantine erected a temple for Yahu (= Yahweh) in the Egyptian diaspora. See AP 30, 32 in *ANET,* 491-92.

the two teachers. Still other commentators put the two words together ("wise leaders") and omit a number of the names, including the last two, as needlessly repetitious. The kinsmen (or colleagues) of Iddo were apparently his fellow Levites (or priests); they are to be distinguished from the temple servants in v. 17 (נתינים *nĕtînîm*).[83] Hence the commission was sent by Ezra to talk to Iddo, his fellow Levites (or priests?), and the Nethinim. Because of divine providence (the gracious hand of God), the Casiphia group sent Sherebiah and other Levites of the Mahli group, plus Hashabiah and Jeshaiah and other Levites of the Merari group, or a total of 38 men (41 if the three people named in vv. 18-19 were not included in the group totals).[84] Seventy-four Levites are listed in 2:40. Perhaps the term "skilled man" (שׂכל *śekel,* v. 18; NRSV, "a man of discretion"; NIV, "a capable man") applies to all 38 Levites. Their skill consisted in their ability to give the sense of the text of the law (Neh 8:8) or to study the words of the law (Neh 8:13). The people of Casiphia also sent 220 Nethinim, or temple servants, a group related to the Levites (cf.2:43-58, where the totals of the Nethinim and the servants of Solomon are given as 392). Verse 20 ascribes the origin of the Nethinim to David (cf. 1 Chronicles 15–16; 23–27), who gave them as helpers to the Levites.[85] Perhaps we should follow a conjecture recorded in *BHS* and replace "and his officials" (v. 20) with the word "ministers" and read: "whom David had set apart as ministers to attend the Levites." The author of this account also claims that he had a full list of the names of the Nethinim, or temple servants.

83. Mahli was a subgroup among the Merarites. In Levitic genealogies Mahli is listed as the son of Merari the son of Levi (Exod 6:19; Num 3:20; 1 Chr 6:19; 24:26). The Merarites were responsible for carrying the tabernacle and caring for other holy objects in the wilderness (Num 3:33-37; 4:29-33). Levi's father is called Israel in 8:18, the only reference to the patriarch Jacob/Israel in the books of Ezra–Nehemiah.

84. "Gave" and "Nethinim" come from the same verbal root, נתן (*nātan*).

85. See note [d] in *BHS.*

Ezra 8:21-30, Final Preparations for Ezra's Trip

NIV

[21]There, by the Ahava Canal, I proclaimed a fast, so that we might humble ourselves before our God and ask him for a safe journey for us and our children, with all our possessions. [22]I was ashamed to ask the king for soldiers and horsemen to protect us from enemies on the road, because we had told the king, "The gracious hand of our God is on everyone who looks to him, but his great anger is against all who forsake him." [23]So we fasted and petitioned our God about this, and he answered our prayer.

[24]Then I set apart twelve of the leading priests, together with Sherebiah, Hashabiah and ten of their brothers, [25]and I weighed out to them the offering of silver and gold and the articles that the king, his advisers, his officials and all Israel present there had donated for the house of our God. [26]I weighed out to them 650 talents[a] of silver, silver articles weighing 100 talents,[b] 100 talents[b] of gold, [27]20 bowls of gold valued at 1,000 darics,[c]

[a] *26* That is, about 25 tons (about 22 metric tons) [b] *26* That is, about 3 3/4 tons (about 3.4 metric tons) [c] *27* That is, about 19 pounds (about 8.5 kilograms)

NRSV

21Then I proclaimed a fast there, at the river Ahava, that we might deny ourselves[a] before our God, to seek from him a safe journey for ourselves, our children, and all our possessions. [22]For I was ashamed to ask the king for a band of soldiers and cavalry to protect us against the enemy on our way, since we had told the king that the hand of our God is gracious to all who seek him, but his power and his wrath are against all who forsake him. [23]So we fasted and petitioned our God for this, and he listened to our entreaty.

24Then I set apart twelve of the leading priests: Sherebiah, Hashabiah, and ten of their kin with them. [25]And I weighed out to them the silver and the gold and the vessels, the offering for the house of our God that the king, his counselors, his lords, and all Israel there present had offered; [26]I weighed out into their hand six hundred fifty talents of silver, and one hundred silver vessels worth . . . talents,[b] and one hundred talents of gold, [27]twenty gold bowls worth a thousand

[a] Or *might fast* [b] The number of talents is lacking

NIV	NRSV
and two fine articles of polished bronze, as precious as gold. [28]I said to them, "You as well as these articles are consecrated to the LORD. The silver and gold are a freewill offering to the LORD, the God of your fathers. [29]Guard them carefully until you weigh them out in the chambers of the house of the LORD in Jerusalem before the leading priests and the Levites and the family heads of Israel." [30]Then the priests and Levites received the silver and gold and sacred articles that had been weighed out to be taken to the house of our God in Jerusalem.	darics, and two vessels of fine polished bronze as precious as gold. [28]And I said to them, "You are holy to the LORD, and the vessels are holy; and the silver and the gold are a freewill offering to the LORD, the God of your ancestors. [29]Guard them and keep them until you weigh them before the chief priests and the Levites and the heads of families in Israel at Jerusalem, within the chambers of the house of the LORD." [30]So the priests and the Levites took over the silver, the gold, and the vessels as they were weighed out, to bring them to Jerusalem, to the house of our God.

COMMENTARY

The text describes only the spiritual preparations for the return home. We read nothing about acquiring beasts of burden, wagons, food supplies, clothing, or the like. Before setting out on the trip home, Ezra called for a fast so that his group could "humble" (להתענות *lĕhit'annôt*; NRSV, "deny") itself before God and pray for a safe journey.[86] "Safe journey" might be rendered as "a level way," an expression that recalls Isa 40:3 and may be an attempt to interpret Ezra's trip as a fulfillment of prophecy. Despite dangers that threatened, Ezra refused to ask the king for any kind of military accompaniment because he had told the king that the people were under God's providential care. Surprisingly, the Persians did not insist on providing Ezra with such protection, although Ezra carried with him contributions that they had made. Both Udjahorresnet[87] and Nehemiah (Neh 2:9) were provided with such protection. Ezra states his rationale for refusing secular assistance in a poetic, psalm-like couplet (v. 22). The community's fasting and self-humiliation exemplify what is meant by seeking the Lord; trusting in a military escort would express that they had abandoned God. The report that their prayer had been heard (v. 23) is written from the perspective of someone who had experienced the safe outcome of the trip, but the author may also want us to infer that Ezra's entourage started out with full confidence that their prayer had already been heard, even if there was as yet no evidence for that.

Ezra chose twelve from the leaders of the priests and twelve Levites—both numbers symbolizing all Israel, even if they all came from only the tribe of Levi—to convey that money to Jerusalem (v. 24). Among the Levites were Sherebiah (cf. v. 19) and Hashabiah (cf. v. 20). The punctuation of v. 24 in the NRSV incorrectly suggests that the commission consisted only of priests. The money had come from the king and other members of the Persian administration as well as from those Israelites in Babylon who were not returning home (v. 25). The 650 talents of silver weighed in excess of twenty-four tons, but the one hundred silver vessels weighed only about two talents, or 130 pounds.[88] One hundred talents of gold would be 3.75 tons. The twenty gold bowls (v. 27) weighed about twenty-one pounds (1,000 darics). The weight of the final two bowls is not given. The exorbitant tonnage of silver and gold in v. 26 may have arisen through a copyist's error, or it may be only the author's way of showing

86. On fasting, see Judg 20:26; Ezra 10:6; Neh 9:1; Esth 4:3, 16; Isa 58:3-9; Joel 1-2.

87. See Joseph Blenkinsopp, "The Mission of Udjahorresnet and Those of Ezra and Nehemiah," *JBL* 106 (1987) 411.

88. The MT reads only "talents," without specifying the number. *BHS* suggests that the word ככרים (*kikkārîm*) be vocalized as a dual (*kikkĕrayim*) without any change in the consonantal text. The NRSV leaves the number of talents blank; the NIV emends it to 100 talents, or somewhere between three and four tons.

how God had moved the hearts of the Persian people to give generously and how God had demonstrated the legitimacy of the Jerusalemite shrine (cf. 7:22). In comparison with the gifts brought back by the first returnees—61,000 darics of gold (1,133 pounds), 5,000 minas of silver (6,250 pounds), and 100 priestly garments—the gifts brought back by Ezra's group are considerably larger, emphasizing the great importance of Ezra's mission. It has been estimated that the precious metals would have amounted to the total annual income of somewhere between 100,000 and 500,000 people.[89]

Ezra designated the members of the group carrying the contributions and the freewill offerings (cf. 7:13, 15-16) as holy to the Lord, the God of the ancestors (7:27; 10:11). To call something holy means that it has been transferred from the secular realm to divine service. Perhaps Ezra believed that God would protect the holy treasures because they had been entrusted to holy men, or he thought that such a designation might deter members of his group from stealing these contributions. The mention of the God of the ancestors again underscored the legitimacy and continuity of the temple cult in Jerusalem.

Ezra urged diligent protection of the contributions until they were "weighed" before the appropriate officials in Jerusalem (v. 29). The word "weighed" (שׁקל *šāqal*) is used six times in this chapter (vv. 25, 26, 29, 30, 33, 34), perhaps indicating to Persian officials that Ezra was making an honest accounting. The "chambers" where the contributions were weighed were storage bins around the main hall and the inner hall of the First Temple, and presumably were also a part of the Second Temple (cf. 1 Kgs 6:5-10; cf. Ezra 10:6; Neh 10:38-39; 13:5, 8). (See Reflections at 8:31-36.)

89. Clines, *Ezra, Nehemiah, Esther,* 113.

Ezra 8:31-36, Ezra's Arrival in Jerusalem

NIV

[31]On the twelfth day of the first month we set out from the Ahava Canal to go to Jerusalem. The hand of our God was on us, and he protected us from enemies and bandits along the way. [32]So we arrived in Jerusalem, where we rested three days.

[33]On the fourth day, in the house of our God, we weighed out the silver and gold and the sacred articles into the hands of Meremoth son of Uriah, the priest. Eleazar son of Phinehas was with him, and so were the Levites Jozabad son of Jeshua and Noadiah son of Binnui. [34]Everything was accounted for by number and weight, and the entire weight was recorded at that time.

[35]Then the exiles who had returned from captivity sacrificed burnt offerings to the God of Israel: twelve bulls for all Israel, ninety-six rams, seventy-seven male lambs and, as a sin offering, twelve male goats. All this was a burnt offering to the LORD. [36]They also delivered the king's orders to the royal satraps and to the governors of Trans-Euphrates, who then gave assistance to the people and to the house of God.

NRSV

31Then we left the river Ahava on the twelfth day of the first month, to go to Jerusalem; the hand of our God was upon us, and he delivered us from the hand of the enemy and from ambushes along the way. [32]We came to Jerusalem and remained there three days. [33]On the fourth day, within the house of our God, the silver, the gold, and the vessels were weighed into the hands of the priest Meremoth son of Uriah, and with him was Eleazar son of Phinehas, and with them were the Levites, Jozabad son of Jeshua and Noadiah son of Binnui. [34]The total was counted and weighed, and the weight of everything was recorded.

35At that time those who had come from captivity, the returned exiles, offered burnt offerings to the God of Israel, twelve bulls for all Israel, ninety-six rams, seventy-seven lambs, and as a sin offering twelve male goats; all this was a burnt offering to the LORD. [36]They also delivered the king's commissions to the king's satraps and to the governors of the province Beyond the River; and they supported the people and the house of God.

COMMENTARY

Ezra's entourage left Babylon on the twelfth day of the first month, eleven days behind schedule (cf. 7:9). This departure means that the start of the trip home (their exodus) would have been followed very quickly by the need to observe Passover on the fourteenth day of the first month. Ezra again calls attention to God's gracious and providential care (v. 31), which did not allow any harm to fall on them. It is unclear from the verb "delivered" (נצל *nāṣal*) in v. 31 whether they faced no adversaries on the way or whether they had been rescued by God from hostile attacks. On their arrival in Jerusalem they "rested" (ישׁב *yāšab*; the NIV is correct) three days (cf. v. 15). Joshua, too, paused for three days after crossing the Jordan River before continuing with the conquest of the promised land (Josh 3:1-2). In addition to whatever ceremonial duties are implied by this three-day rest, Ezra and his entourage would have needed at least that much time to recuperate from their 900-mile journey and to find suitable housing for about 5,000 people. Ezra's arrival in Jerusalem occurred in the same month in which the Temple had been burned down 129 years earlier (2 Kgs 25:8).

On the first day after their pause, and as their very first act, the group weighed out the contributions to a contingent of two priests and two Levites (v. 33). Meremoth, the son of Uriah, belonged to the Hakkoz family, which had not been able to prove its ancestry and, therefore, had been barred from exercising its office (2:61). In v. 33, Meremoth is identified as a priest, apparently indicating that his difficulty in proving his priestly identity had been cleared up and that he had even been given important financial responsibilities. He later is one of those who (as a priest?) worked on the wall with Nehemiah (Neh 3:4, 21; cf. Neh 10:6; 12:3).[90] The other priest who received the contributions was Eleazar, whom some identify with Eliezer in 10:18, one of the people who had married a foreign wife; but this name is extremely common, and there may be no connection between these two persons. The Levite Jozabad was also one of those who had married a foreign wife (10:23), and his role as overseer of the "outside work of the house of God" in Neh 11:16 may indicate a subsequent demotion.

In vv. 35-36 the exiles, including Ezra, are once again referred to in the third person. At the time when the contributions were presented at the Temple (the division between vv. 34 and 35 is better in the NRSV than in the NIV), Ezra's entourage joined in the sacrificial worship at Jerusalem and offered twelve bulls for all Israel, ninety-six (8×12) rams, and seventy-two lambs (6×12; cf. 1 Esdr 8:65; the MT has 77) as a burnt offering to the Lord (cf. 7:17). The twelve male goats of the sin offering atoned for the ritual pollution the group had picked up in Babylon or during the course of their long trip home through the desert (cf. 6:17). The multiples of the number twelve are meant to show that Ezra's group is the heir of all Israel.

The king's "orders" (NRSV, "commissions"; cf. 7:21-24) were delivered to the satraps and governors of Beyond the River. Since there was only one satrap per satrapy, the plural "satraps" in v. 36 is a copyist's mistake, or the word "satrap" here, like the word "governor" in many parts of the book of Ezra, is to be understood in a less specific or broader sense. These Persian officials (following the NIV's superior interpretation of the second "they" in v. 36) gave their ongoing support to the people of Israel and to the house of God. Ezra's assignment was not yet complete because there still remained dangers from the peoples of the land, as the next chapters will demonstrate. A number of commentators believe that Ezra's reading of the law in Nehemiah 8 followed immediately after this paragraph in an earlier form of the Ezra tradition (see the Introduction).

90. Koch, "Ezra and the Origins of Judaism," 190-94, proposed that Meremoth was the high priest when Ezra arrived and was replaced by Ezra in that office. Outside of the genealogy in 7:1-5, however, there is no reason to think that Ezra served as high priest, since he is not listed among the high priests of post-exilic times. Cf. Neh 12:10-11, 22.

REFLECTIONS

Although Ezra is remembered most of all for his efforts on behalf of the Torah (Ezra 9–10; Nehemiah 8), the account of his trip to Jerusalem is not without theological significance. The author mentions the good (or gracious) hand of God that helped to solve the problem of the shortage of Levites and that also led Ezra to refuse a military escort. The hand of God delivered Ezra and his entourage from dangers on the way, particularly those represented by the hand of the enemy. The book of Ezra is not naive about the power of evil at work in the world, nor does it underestimate the threat posed by the enemy's evil hand. In this case, Ezra relied completely on God for deliverance.

Ezra's faith and his teaching office are well represented in this chapter. God is gracious to seekers; God's wrath is against all who abandon the Lord. Abandoning God can take many forms, from the individual sins of the prodigal son to the rich and oppressive opponents of the prophets. For Ezra, abandoning God included trusting in military power for safety. His embarrassment in asking the king for protection is consistent with his teaching office. What would the Persians think if he asked for help? Would that not undercut his testimony that the good hand of God was upon them and thus make his own testimony hard to believe? How easily our reliance on human power can reveal our failure to trust God's almighty power!

The theology of community in this chapter is also remarkable. The author delights in ringing out the changes on the number 12 and its multiples to express his passion for the community as a whole. Twelve lay families went with Ezra, groups of twelve priests and Levites to carry the contributions to Jerusalem, sacrificial animals in numbers of 12, 72, and 96, not to mention the fact that the trip to Jerusalem started on the twelfth day of the month. The number twelve implies that the Israel of Ezra's time is the true Israel, the complete Israel. Even Levi is known as the son of Israel. The true community for us exists wherever the gospel is preached and the sacraments are administered, and the marks of that community are such things as the presence of the Spirit, the inclusion of the other, a concern for peace and justice, and the honoring of tradition and of difference. That true community is one—holy, catholic, and apostolic.

It is unclear why no Levites at first signed up for the trip home. Perhaps not many of them had been exiled in the first place, and those who had been feared the secondary status they would experience back in Jerusalem. But for Ezra to go home without even a token number of them was intolerable. The trip was delayed until a commission—with the help of God's good hand—secured 38 Levites and 220 Nethinim.

The story of Meremoth is also part of this healthy theology of community. His family was unable to prove its right to the priesthood and was even excluded as unclean at the beginning of the restoration period. Although the details of his rehabilitation are unknown to us, Meremoth not only was restored to the official priesthood, but he was given a responsible financial position as well.

With this chapter, Ezra is well on his way to fulfilling the mission on which he had been sent, and along the way he *did* Torah. With his group he prayed and fasted, and he faithfully brought sacrifices in Jerusalem. His personal experience became part of the ongoing story of Israel. He did Torah, and the account of his trip to Jerusalem teaches that Torah to others (7:10). "Doing Torah" for us means to do the will of God—in worship, in family life, in business, in neighborhood. Just as God teaches us through Torah, so also we proclaim to ourselves and to one another God's story with Israel and with ourselves. The way we journey through the routine challenges of life is not without theological significance.

EZRA 9:1-15, EZRA FACES A SEVERE COMMUNITY CRISIS

Ezra 9:1-5, A Complaint About Intermarriage

NIV

9 After these things had been done, the
leaders came to me and said, "The people
of Israel, including the priests and the Levites,
have not kept themselves separate from the neighboring peoples with their detestable practices, like
those of the Canaanites, Hittites, Perizzites, Jebusites, Ammonites, Moabites, Egyptians and Amorites. 2They have taken some of their daughters
as wives for themselves and their sons, and have
mingled the holy race with the peoples around
them. And the leaders and officials have led the
way in this unfaithfulness."
3When I heard this, I tore my tunic and cloak,
pulled hair from my head and beard and sat down
appalled. 4Then everyone who trembled at the
words of the God of Israel gathered around me
because of this unfaithfulness of the exiles. And I
sat there appalled until the evening sacrifice.
5Then, at the evening sacrifice, I rose from my
self-abasement, with my tunic and cloak torn, and
fell on my knees with my hands spread out to
the LORD my God

NRSV

9 After these things had been done, the
officials approached me and said, "The
people of Israel, the priests, and the Levites have
not separated themselves from the peoples of the
lands with their abominations, from the Canaanites, the Hittites, the Perizzites, the Jebusites, the
Ammonites, the Moabites, the Egyptians, and the
Amorites. 2For they have taken some of their
daughters as wives for themselves and for their
sons. Thus the holy seed has mixed itself with
the peoples of the lands, and in this faithlessness
the officials and leaders have led the way." 3When
I heard this, I tore my garment and my mantle,
and pulled hair from my head and beard, and sat
appalled. 4Then all who trembled at the words of
the God of Israel, because of the faithlessness of
the returned exiles, gathered around me while I
sat appalled until the evening sacrifice.
5At the evening sacrifice I got up from my
fasting, with my garments and my mantle torn,
and fell on my knees, spread out my hands to the
LORD my God,

COMMENTARY

It is possible that the events in Nehemiah 8 took place between those reported in Ezra 8 and 9. Ezra arrived in Jerusalem on the first day of the fifth month (7:9), and in the ninth month a great assembly was convened in Jerusalem in order to deal with the issue of mixed marriages (10:9). Since Ezra's reading of the law took place in the seventh month (Neh 7:73), a reconstruction that puts Nehemiah 8 after Ezra 8 makes sense both chronologically and theologically. The actions of Ezra 9–10 are based on the very pentateuchal law that had been given renewed authority by Ezra. Whatever the value of this historical proposal, the words "After these things" (Ezra 9:1) bridge the four-month gap in the canonical text between the arrival of Ezra's entourage and the crisis dealing with foreign marriages. The exegesis of Nehemiah 8, therefore, can be deferred to its literary context within the book of Nehemiah.

9:1. The leaders of the community, perhaps representing the governance of the administrative districts into which the province of Judah was divided (Neh 3:9-19), complained to Ezra that the three principal groups in Israel—laity, priests, and Levites—had not separated themselves from "the peoples of the lands." Their formal complaint seems to have followed earlier efforts by Ezra to advise the people on this issue (10:3). The NRSV and the NEB interpret these peoples of the lands as foreigners—namely, the pre-Israelite inhabitants of the land. The translation in the TNK clarifies the situation considerably: "The people of Israel and the priests and Levites have not separated themselves from the peoples of the land whose abhorrent practices are like those of the Canaanites." The "peoples of the land," therefore, are those who are not considered to be full members of the community, perhaps referring to those who had not been in exile and those who had not been fully accepted into the Golah community for other reasons. The behavior of these non-members of the community was like that of the pre-Israelite inhabitants of the land; the accusation of "abominations" (cf. vv. 11, 14) may suggest that they worshiped other gods (cf. Neh 13:26-27), practiced sexual immorality, or followed a detestable diet.[91] The list of nations resembles nine other lists of the pre-Israelite inhabitants of the land (Gen 15:19-20; Exod 3:8, 17; 33:2; 34:11; Deut 7:1; 20:17; Judg 3:5; Neh 9:8). The list in v. 1 shares with all the others the names of the Canaanites, the Hittites, the Perizzites, the Jebusites, and the Amorites. The Ammonites, the Moabites, and the Egyptians, however, appear only in this list and provide links to passages in the Pentateuch that provide legal grounds for the complaint about intermarriage. Ammonites and Moabites had been barred from membership in the assembly of Israel for ten generations (Deut 23:3-6). Leviticus warns the Israelites not to practice those things done by the Egyptians (Lev 18:3) and discusses the case of a blasphemous son who came from the marriage of an Israelite woman with an Egyptian man (Lev 24:10-16, 23). Deuteronomy, however, counsels Israel not to abhor the Egyptians and the Edomites[92] and permits their children in the third generation to become part of the assembly of the Lord (Deut 23:7).

9:2. Failure to separate from the peoples of the land is further defined as intermarriage with women from these nations. Joseph (Gen 41:50), Moses (Num 12:1), and Mahlon and Chilion, the sons of Elimelech (Ruth 1), married foreign women when they were in foreign lands without much apparent criticism. When Miriam and Aaron criticized Moses for having married a foreigner, they were punished for it. Lay leaders and temple officials at Elephantine also married women who were not Jews, if we can judge by the use of non-Hebrew names for their wives. Marriages to foreigners are prohibited in the Torah because they could lead to the worship of the gods of the foreign women (Deut 7:4). Passages such as Exod 34:11-16 and Deut 20:10-18 see great dangers in such liaisons, especially if the women are from Palestine. Foreign women led to Solomon's theological undoing (1 Kgs 11:1-11). Mixing the holy seed—that is, the elect members of the community—with outsiders runs the risk of apostasy or sacrilege (see Isa 6:13: "The holy seed is its stump"; the promised "seed," Gen 12:7; 13:15-16; 17:17; only in deuteronomic tradition is Israel considered a "holy people," Deut 7:6; 14:2, 21; 26:19; 28:9). Marriages outside the community were *prima facie* evidence of "faithlessness" (v. 2; cf. 9:4; 10:2, 6, 10; Neh 1:8; 13:27), and the leaders of the post-exilic community, presumably those who had returned in migrations before the time of Ezra, were prominent among the offenders.

9:3-5. Ezra immediately went into public mourning on behalf of the entire community and tore both his inner garment and his outer mantle (v. 3). The tearing of garments in grief may have its roots in ritual nakedness (cf. Gen 37:34; 2 Sam 11:1; Job 1:20; 2:12; Ezek 16:39; Mic 1:8). Shaving one's head was a frequent means of expressing grief (Job 1:20; Isa 22:12; Jer 16:6; 41:5; Ezek 7:18; Amos 8:10), though some biblical texts prohibit it because of possible pagan connotations (Lev 19:27; 21:5; Deut 14:1). Perhaps because of such laws, Ezra limited himself to pulling the hair of his head and of his beard. He sat in stunned silence (cf. Job 2:13; Ezek 3:15; 26:16), from an unspecified starting time until the evening sacrifice at 3:00 P.M. (cf. 1 Kgs 18:36; Acts 3:1). It is not clear whether the mourning rites in v. 5 included "fasting" (NRSV; cf. 1 Esdr 8:73) or only "self-abasement" (NIV).

Joining him in this public display of grief was a group of those who trembled at the words of the God of Israel (v. 4). These people seemed to

91. Bezalel Porten, *Archives from Elephantine* (Berkeley: University of California Press, 1968) 249.

92. One Hebrew manuscript and 1 Esdr 8:69 read "Edomites" instead of "Amorites" in Ezra 9:1, but marriage with Edomites is not explicitly prohibited in the Pentateuch (see Deut 23:7, which rules only that they cannot be admitted to the assembly of the Lord until the third generation), even though hatred toward them is expressed in many post-exilic passages (Ps 137:7-9; Isa 63:1-6; Lam 4:21-22; Mal 1:2-5).

have formed a kind of support group around Ezra, and they shared his views on the mixed marriages (cf. 10:3). On the basis of these verses in Ezra and similar texts in Isa 66:2, 5, Blenkinsopp has identified a post-exilic movement that opposed syncretism and espoused a rigorist interpretation of the law.[93] Isaiah 66:5 indicates that these people may have been out of favor with the religious leadership of the province. (See Reflections at 9:6-15.)

93. Joseph Blenkinsopp, Ezra–Nehemiah, OTL (Philadelphia: Westminster, 1988) 178-79.

Ezra 9:6-15, Ezra's Prayer

NIV

[6]and prayed:

"O my God, I am too ashamed and disgraced to lift up my face to you, my God, because our sins are higher than our heads and our guilt has reached to the heavens. [7]From the days of our forefathers until now, our guilt has been great. Because of our sins, we and our kings and our priests have been subjected to the sword and captivity, to pillage and humiliation at the hand of foreign kings, as it is today.

[8]"But now, for a brief moment, the LORD our God has been gracious in leaving us a remnant and giving us a firm place in his sanctuary, and so our God gives light to our eyes and a little relief in our bondage. [9]Though we are slaves, our God has not deserted us in our bondage. He has shown us kindness in the sight of the kings of Persia: He has granted us new life to rebuild the house of our God and repair its ruins, and he has given us a wall of protection in Judah and Jerusalem.

[10]"But now, O our God, what can we say after this? For we have disregarded the commands [11]you gave through your servants the prophets when you said: 'The land you are entering to possess is a land polluted by the corruption of its peoples. By their detestable practices they have filled it with their impurity from one end to the other. [12]Therefore, do not give your daughters in marriage to their sons or take their daughters for your sons. Do not seek a treaty of friendship with them at any time, that you may be strong and eat the good things of the land and leave it to your children as an everlasting inheritance.'

[13]"What has happened to us is a result of our evil deeds and our great guilt, and yet,

NRSV

[6]and said,

"O my God, I am too ashamed and embarrassed to lift my face to you, my God, for our iniquities have risen higher than our heads, and our guilt has mounted up to the heavens. [7]From the days of our ancestors to this day we have been deep in guilt, and for our iniquities we, our kings, and our priests have been handed over to the kings of the lands, to the sword, to captivity, to plundering, and to utter shame, as is now the case. [8]But now for a brief moment favor has been shown by the LORD our God, who has left us a remnant, and given us a stake in his holy place, in order that he[a] may brighten our eyes and grant us a little sustenance in our slavery. [9]For we are slaves; yet our God has not forsaken us in our slavery, but has extended to us his steadfast love before the kings of Persia, to give us new life to set up the house of our God, to repair its ruins, and to give us a wall in Judea and Jerusalem.

10"And now, our God, what shall we say after this? For we have forsaken your commandments, [11]which you commanded by your servants the prophets, saying, 'The land that you are entering to possess is a land unclean with the pollutions of the peoples of the lands, with their abominations. They have filled it from end to end with their uncleanness. [12]Therefore do not give your daughters to their sons, neither take their daughters for your sons, and never seek their peace or prosperity, so that you may be strong and eat the good of the land and leave it for an inheritance to your children forever.' [13]After all that has come upon us for our evil deeds and for our great guilt, seeing that you, our God, have punished us less than our iniquities deserved and have given us such a remnant as this, [14]shall we break your

[a] Heb *our God*

NIV	NRSV
our God, you have punished us less than our sins have deserved and have given us a remnant like this. [14]Shall we again break your commands and intermarry with the peoples who commit such detestable practices? Would you not be angry enough with us to destroy us, leaving us no remnant or survivor? [15]O LORD, God of Israel, you are righteous! We are left this day as a remnant. Here we are before you in our guilt, though because of it not one of us can stand in your presence."	commandments again and intermarry with the peoples who practice these abominations? Would you not be angry with us until you destroy us without remnant or survivor? [15]O LORD, God of Israel, you are just, but we have escaped as a remnant, as is now the case. Here we are before you in our guilt, though no one can face you because of this."

COMMENTARY

The time of the evening sacrifice was known as the time of prayer (Acts 3:1). Ezra prayed on his knees,[94] with his hands extended as a sign of helplessness or need.[95] While this prayer is a communal confession of sin, it seems also to be an effort to persuade those who had married foreign women to divorce them.

9:6-7. Ezra begins his recital of the community's sinful history by speaking in the first-person singular, but he soon switches to the first-person plural and thereby shows solidarity with the community. Although personally innocent, Ezra expresses embarrassment over the people's sins (v. 7; cf. 8:22) and a reluctance even to raise his face toward God. Iniquities are piled higher than their heads; guilt reaches up to the sky! Ezra's prayer makes no distinction between the sins of the ancestors and the behavior of the present generation (in contrast to the popular theology cited in Jer 31:29; Ezek 18:2). Ezekiel had retold the history of Israel and traced its fatal sin back to those who lived in Egypt before the exodus (Ezekiel 20), but Ezra dates apostasy even earlier, to the time of Israel's patriarchs and matriarchs and concedes that these sins have persisted to the present day. So Ezra does not blame the troubles of his generation on the ancestors, nor does he imagine an earlier, more innocent generation. Instead, he sees a sinful continuum from earliest times until the present. Because of these accumulated iniquities, he and the rest of Israel, including their kings and priests, had been handed over to the military ravages of the kings of the lands. One thinks immediately not only of Assyrian and Babylonian rulers who waged war against Israel and Judah, but also of the Persians, who allowed Israel no independent government even if their rule was relatively benign. Capture by foreign kings meant death ("sword"), exile ("captivity"), plundering, and utter shame—in the past as in the present. Though the book of Ezra often sees in Persian rule the good hand of God, the book is keenly aware of the difference between being a client nation and being completely free.

9:8-9. The second paragraph of the prayer, beginning with "but now," confesses in amazement the benefactions of Yahweh subsequent to and in spite of the long history of sin. The recent period of grace, only some eighty years, has been brief compared to the centuries of Mesopotamian attack and oppression. Ezra advances from personal to corporate faith: "Yahweh my God" in v. 5 becomes "Yahweh our God" in v. 8. His reference in v. 8 to God in the third person, however, may indicate that his prayer was addressed as much to members of the community as to God.

In a first act of divine favor, God preserved the community as a remnant. The word "remnant" (שְׁאָר *šĕʾār*) can refer to the survivors of a disaster whose small numbers serve as grim evidence of the severity of the disaster (Amos 3:12), or, more positively, it can refer, as here, to a small com-

94. See *ANEP*, 204, fig. 622; 1 Kgs 8:54.
95. See Esarhaddon, Prism B, *ANET*, 289.

munity that has been delivered and that is the down payment on a greater future to come (cf. 2 Chr 12:7, where the people humbled themselves and were granted "some deliverance" [lit., "remnant," פליטה *pĕlêṭâ*] so that the Lord's wrath would not be poured out on Jerusalem by Shishak).

Second, the Lord gave the community a "stake" or a "tent peg" in the holy place (v. 8). Ezra's prayer thus underscores the significance of the restored Temple ("his holy place"), the subject of chaps. 1–6. Driving a peg into the ground is a way of staking a claim, of providing a stable tent for people to live in (Isa 54:2), or of securing a tight fit as when a nail is driven into a hard medium (Isa 22:23). Clines suggests that this tent peg, like the pegs or nails placed in ancient foundation deposits, shows the stability of the building or the fixed agreement between the devout builder and the deity.[96] Regardless of the exact connotation of the tent peg metaphor, Ezra's prayer interprets the Temple and the cult as a sure promise of even greater divine beneficence.

Third, divine favor gave cheer to the sinful community. Just as the eyes of an exhausted Jonathan brightened when he ate honey on the battlefield, so also Israel in its exile had been rejuvenated and given hope (1 Sam 14:27, 29; cf. Ps 13:3; 19:8).

Finally, God gave them a little sustenance right in the midst of their slavery (cf. 2 Chr 12:8). The word "sustenance" (מחיה *miḥyâ*) is related etymologically to the word "life" (חיה *ḥayyâ*). The prayer acknowledges that the people are slaves, but confesses that God will not abandon them in their slavery. The psalmist cried out in innocence and amazement, "My God, why have you abandoned me?" (see Ps 22:1). The chronicler believed in sure and immediate retribution: "If you abandon him, he will abandon you" (2 Chr 15:2 NRSV). But the post-exilic community was not innocent—slavery was the result of their sins—nor had it been abandoned despite its sin. Instead, "our God"—the first of five straight uses of this divine epithet in vv. 8-13—had extended to them loyal, covenantal love (lit., "steadfast love" [חסד *ḥesed*]), in the presence of and, one might add, with the cooperation and willing participation of the kings of Persia (v. 9). When the foundation of the Temple had been laid, the Levites had sung, "His steadfast love for Israel endures forever" (3:11). Ezra had also personally experienced such loyal love in the presence of Artaxerxes (7:28). Four specific benefits give concreteness to this divine love mediated through the Persian kings: relief in bondage (cf. vv. 8-9), erection of the Temple, restoration of the ruined city, and a wall of protection in Judah and Jerusalem (v. 9).

The reference to a wall has played a major role in discussions of the date of Ezra and Nehemiah. Some commentators conclude that if a wall existed at the time of Ezra, then he must have come to Jerusalem after Nehemiah. But the Hebrew word used here for "wall" (גדר *gādēr*) usually refers to a fence around something like a vineyard rather than to a city wall (Mic 7:11 may be an exception). Furthermore, this wall is "in Judea and Jerusalem," not just around the city itself. This wall, therefore, stands metaphorically for the protection supplied by the Persians from the surrounding enemies.

9:10-12. The words "And/but now" (ועתה *wĕʿattâ*, v. 10) mark the transition between the past and the present. Ezra asks the community what its present ethical response should be in the light of its long history of sin (vv. 6-7) and its recent experience of divine grace (vv. 8-9). Ezra and the community jointly confess that they have abandoned the commandments given by God's servants the prophets.[97] He alludes in vv. 11-12 to both pentateuchal and prophetic texts, with the former far exceeding the latter. Clearly for Ezra, Moses is to be numbered among the prophets (see Deut 18:15; 34:10; Hos 12:13), and the words attributed to him in the Pentateuch are prophetic words. The following texts may have provided Ezra with the vocabulary for articulating the prophetic commandments, given by God's graciousness, which the people had disobeyed by associating with the nations:

> Lev 18:24, "By all these practices the nations I am casting out before you have defiled themselves [טמא (*ṭimmēʾ*), a synonym of נדה (*niddâ*); both words are used in Ezra 9:11]." (NRSV)

96. David J. A. Clines, *Ezra, Nehemiah, Esther,* NCB (Grand Rapids: Eerdmans, 1984) 123.

97. "Servants the prophets" is a technical term frequently used in deuteronomistic and other texts. See 2 Kgs 17:23; Jer 26:5.

Deut 1:39, "Your children . . . to them I will give [the land], and they shall take possession of it." (NRSV)

Deut 7:1, "The land that you are about to enter and occupy." (NRSV)

Deut 7:3, "Do not intermarry with them, giving your daughters to their sons or taking their daughters for your sons." (NRSV)

Deut 11:8, "Keep, then, this entire commandment . . . that you may have strength to go in and occupy the land." (NRSV)

Deut 18:9, "You must not learn to imitate the abhorrent practices of those nations." (NRSV)

Deut 23:6, "You shall never promote their welfare or their prosperity [referring to the Ammonites and Moabites]." (NRSV)

2 Kgs 21:16, "Manasseh shed very much innocent blood, until he had filled Jerusalem from one end to another." (NRSV; cf. 2 Kgs 10:21)

Isa 1:19, "You shall eat the good of the land." (NRSV)

9:13. Since the land was full of the detestable practices of the nations, marriage with non-Israelite inhabitants was forbidden. Ezra applied these ethical principles to his own time, some eight centuries after Moses, and urged the community not to intermarry with the peoples of the lands, presumably meaning with those Jews in the land who had not experienced the exile in Babylon or who for some other reason were not considered full members of the community. Because of the interruption caused by the summation of the law in vv. 11*b*-12, v. 13 restates the context in which Israel stands and the urgent question it faces. In Ezra's opinion, God has inflicted less punishment on the community than their iniquities have deserved—a striking contrast to Isa 40:2: "[Jerusalem] has received from the LORD's hand double for all her sins" (NRSV). And God also has spared a remnant. In the words "like this," one can almost see Ezra gesturing toward this little community.

9:14. What should the community do after this long history of guilt and this more recent, paradoxical experience of divine mercy? Should they once more break the commandments, as they and their forebears had done from the very start (v. 7)? Should they intermarry with the "peoples of these abominations," as the Hebrew text puts it? The expression "the peoples of these abominations" articulates the danger perceived in intermarriage and replaces "the peoples of the lands" (vv. 1, 2, 11). Any future breach of the commandments (v. 14; cf. v. 10) would call forth a renewed outburst of divine anger that would again leave only a "remnant" or "survivor."

9:15. Ezra's final plea begins with an appeal to Yahweh, who had been hailed as "my God" (v. 5) and "our God" (v. 8), but is now designated "the God of Israel." Ezra seems to use this title to appeal to Yahweh's commitment to Israel and to confess once more that "we" are still God's people (cf. "all who trembled at the words of the God of Israel," v. 4). Ezra insists that this Yahweh is righteous, faithful to the relationships in which God stands. Even Pharaoh had been finally forced to admit this fact (Exod 9:27; cf. 2 Chr 12:6; Neh 9:33). The NRSV correctly adds the word "but" in v. 15 after the word "just." Although Yahweh is righteous and just—and therefore should have destroyed the people utterly for their sins—nevertheless a remnant perseveres up to this very day (v. 15), despite its persistent guilt (v. 7). The community presents itself before God in its guilt, knowing that no one is able to insist upon innocence or be acquitted because of the intermarriage problem. This final affirmation of community humility echoes that of Ezra himself in v. 6.

REFLECTIONS

Ezra's prayer is a masterly presentation of sin and grace. Granted, it is difficult to affirm the condemnation of the specific sin of marrying with "the peoples of the lands," but we can surely understand the dangers of going against the prophetic word and of transgressing thereby the first and greatest commandment. Perhaps we would be more sympathetic to the concern about intermarriage if we understood exactly the danger that was perceived in it (see further discussion of the underlying issues in the Commentary on 10:1-44).

What made the sin most shocking to the Golah community was that the officials and leaders had led the way (9:2). Those who were called to be role models and examples had failed at their task. Many church members today are shaken to the core when church leaders violate the trust of the members, engage in abusive behavior toward those whom they serve, or otherwise lack integrity.

What should religious leaders do when a public sin has been identified? Those who call for repentance dare not stand apart from the people they accuse. Ezra had not married a foreign woman, but in his confessional prayer he identified himself as a participant in the community's guilt. Ezra's generation could have joined their ancestors from the exilic period and blamed their fate on the sins of their ancestors. But chap. 9 acknowledges that the grievous sins of the mothers and fathers continued right up to the present moment. God had even punished them less than they deserved.

Ezra's prayer is also a masterly presentation of God's grace. Ezra saw in his weak and dependent community a true sign of divine mercy. This grace was only for a brief moment, and it granted only a little sustenance (9:8), but God had not forsaken them. Even in their political servitude God had continued to love them. This remnant was a down payment on a greater salvation that was to come. The divine presence in the Temple was a tent peg one could hold on to.

God is righteous, and a righteous or just God must judge. According to Ezra, God is righteous, but the community's remnant status is a sign of hope. No one at Ezra's time could really face God with the sense of guilt they had; yet, they did address God, and they acknowledged in numerous ways God's great "nevertheless," God's contradiction of wrath by mercy. God's great "nevertheless" for us is pronounced through the life, death, and resurrection of Jesus Christ. Such a theology takes seriously the depth of our fallenness and the lavishness of God's grace.

To rehearse the history of sin and grace, however, necessitates some kind of response on the part of the believing community. Should the people continue to intermarry and run the risk of participating in the abominations of idolatry or syncretism? Of course not. Neither should they continue to sin so that grace might abound. While unexpressed in this chapter, two other options stood before the community. First, they could decide to cease and desist from any future mixed marriages. Second, they could dissolve the mixed marriages they had already entered into.

While the latter option will require further reflection in the next chapter, for now this is enough: Sin is never totally individualistic, because it almost always involves the community in some way. Leaders and even the innocent need to share in the responsibility for it. Grace and forgiveness are always miracles. Sometimes these are little miracles, but miracles even so, such as a remnant, a temple, life, and punishment that is less than one deserves. Good news is always preached with the goal of change. What shall we do? That is always the believer's question.

EZRA 10:1-44, THE GREAT DIVORCE PROCEEDINGS

Ezra 10:1-17, A Decision to Divorce Foreign Women

NIV

10 While Ezra was praying and confessing, weeping and throwing himself down before the house of God, a large crowd of Israelites—men, women and children—gathered around him. They too wept bitterly. 2Then Shecaniah son of Jehiel, one of the descendants of Elam, said to Ezra, "We have been unfaithful to our God by marrying foreign women from the peoples around us. But in spite of this, there is still hope for Israel. 3Now let us make a covenant before our God to send away all these women and their children, in accordance with the counsel of my lord and of those who fear the commands of our God. Let it be done according to the Law. 4Rise up; this matter is in your hands. We will support you, so take courage and do it."

5So Ezra rose up and put the leading priests and Levites and all Israel under oath to do what had been suggested. And they took the oath. 6Then Ezra withdrew from before the house of God and went to the room of Jehohanan son of Eliashib. While he was there, he ate no food and drank no water, because he continued to mourn over the unfaithfulness of the exiles.

7A proclamation was then issued throughout Judah and Jerusalem for all the exiles to assemble in Jerusalem. 8Anyone who failed to appear within three days would forfeit all his property, in accordance with the decision of the officials and elders, and would himself be expelled from the assembly of the exiles.

9Within the three days, all the men of Judah and Benjamin had gathered in Jerusalem. And on the twentieth day of the ninth month, all the people were sitting in the square before the house of God, greatly distressed by the occasion and because of the rain. 10Then Ezra the priest stood up and said to them, "You have been unfaithful; you have married foreign women, adding to Israel's guilt. 11Now make confession to the LORD, the God of your fathers, and do his will. Separate

NRSV

10 While Ezra prayed and made confession, weeping and throwing himself down before the house of God, a very great assembly of men, women, and children gathered to him out of Israel; the people also wept bitterly. 2Shecaniah son of Jehiel, of the descendants of Elam, addressed Ezra, saying, "We have broken faith with our God and have married foreign women from the peoples of the land, but even now there is hope for Israel in spite of this. 3So now let us make a covenant with our God to send away all these wives and their children, according to the counsel of my lord and of those who tremble at the commandment of our God; and let it be done according to the law. 4Take action, for it is your duty, and we are with you; be strong, and do it." 5Then Ezra stood up and made the leading priests, the Levites, and all Israel swear that they would do as had been said. So they swore.

6Then Ezra withdrew from before the house of God, and went to the chamber of Jehohanan son of Eliashib, where he spent the night.[a] He did not eat bread or drink water, for he was mourning over the faithlessness of the exiles. 7They made a proclamation throughout Judah and Jerusalem to all the returned exiles that they should assemble at Jerusalem, 8and that if any did not come within three days, by order of the officials and the elders all their property should be forfeited, and they themselves banned from the congregation of the exiles.

9Then all the people of Judah and Benjamin assembled at Jerusalem within the three days; it was the ninth month, on the twentieth day of the month. All the people sat in the open square before the house of God, trembling because of this matter and because of the heavy rain. 10Then Ezra the priest stood up and said to them, "You have trespassed and married foreign women, and so increased the guilt of Israel. 11Now make con-

[a] 1 Esdras 9.2: Heb *where he went*

NIV

yourselves from the peoples around you and from your foreign wives."

12The whole assembly responded with a loud voice: "You are right! We must do as you say. 13But there are many people here and it is the rainy season; so we cannot stand outside. Besides, this matter cannot be taken care of in a day or two, because we have sinned greatly in this thing. 14Let our officials act for the whole assembly. Then let everyone in our towns who has married a foreign woman come at a set time, along with the elders and judges of each town, until the fierce anger of our God in this matter is turned away from us." 15Only Jonathan son of Asahel and Jahzeiah son of Tikvah, supported by Meshullam and Shabbethai the Levite, opposed this.

16So the exiles did as was proposed. Ezra the priest selected men who were family heads, one from each family division, and all of them designated by name. On the first day of the tenth month they sat down to investigate the cases, 17and by the first day of the first month they finished dealing with all the men who had married foreign women.

NRSV

fession to the LORD the God of your ancestors, and do his will; separate yourselves from the peoples of the land and from the foreign wives." 12Then all the assembly answered with a loud voice, "It is so; we must do as you have said. 13But the people are many, and it is a time of heavy rain; we cannot stand in the open. Nor is this a task for one day or for two, for many of us have transgressed in this matter. 14Let our officials represent the whole assembly, and let all in our towns who have taken foreign wives come at appointed times, and with them the elders and judges of every town, until the fierce wrath of our God on this account is averted from us." 15Only Jonathan son of Asahel and Jahzeiah son of Tikvah opposed this, and Meshullam and Shabbethai the Levites supported them.

16Then the returned exiles did so. Ezra the priest selected men,[b] heads of families, according to their families, each of them designated by name. On the first day of the tenth month they sat down to examine the matter. 17By the first day of the first month they had come to the end of all the men who had married foreign women.

[b] 1 Esdra 9.16: Syr: Heb *And there were selected Ezra,*

COMMENTARY

10:1. Another section of the story of Ezra told in the third person begins with this verse (cf. 7:1-11; 8:35-36; Nehemiah 8; see the Overview to Ezra 7:1–10:44). Ezra's public display of grief in front of the Temple may sound more vigorous in translation than it was in reality. "Falling down" (v. 1) may only be another way of saying that he knelt down during his prayer (cf. 9:5). His behavior in any case drew a very large and inclusive crowd or "assembly" (see the use of the word "assembly" [קהל *qāhāl*] also at critical occasions in 2 Chr 29:28, 31-32; 30:2). Women also participated in the reading of the law in Neh 8:2 and the making of the firm agreement (Neh 10:28); Joshua read the law to men, women, and children (Josh 8:35). The translation of the last clause of v. 1 in the NRSV is unclear, and the NIV is misleading; both use, but do not mention, a small emendation proposed by *BHS* (ויבכו *wayyibkû*). It is better to retain the MT—"for the people [around Ezra] wept bitterly"—and conclude that the crying of Ezra's support group (9:4) helped to attract the large crowd. The writer makes clear throughout this chapter that the community strongly supported the decision to separate from the "nations"; Ezra articulated their consensus and served as agent of their decisions.

10:2-5. A layperson, Shecaniah, from the family of Elam (2:7, 31; 8:7), supported Ezra and added a concrete suggestion. Although he himself had apparently not married a foreign wife (he is absent from the list of offenders from the family of Elam in v. 26), he expressed solidarity with the people in their guilt (v. 2).[98] Ezra had also identified with the people in their sin (9:7), but

98. The word "foreign" (נכריות *nokriyyôt*) occurs seven times in this chapter, but not at all in chap. 9. These foreign women are said to be from the "peoples of the land" in 10:2, 11. The Judean rivals to the Golah and the neighboring non-Judean peoples were equally alien to Israel. Anyone who is not a member of the Golah belongs to the peoples of the lands.

Shecaniah moved beyond Ezra's position to see hope beyond judgment.[99] Shecaniah proposed that the people swear an oath to God to expel their foreign wives and the children born to these unions. Thus he endorsed an earlier proposal made by Ezra and his support group ("those who tremble at the commandment of our God," 9:4), and his initiative put Ezra in a less isolated situation than Nehemiah was in when faced with a similar crisis (Neh 13:23-27). In the last part of his proposal, Shecaniah suggested that all this should be done in accordance with the law—that is, with the Pentateuch. The Pentateuch does not mandate divorce for people who have married foreigners, but it forbids marriage to certain foreigners (the pre-Israelite inhabitants of the land, Deut 7:3-4) and permits men to divorce when they find "something objectionable" in their wives (Deut 24:1). Such divorces were often based on evidence of adultery. Shecaniah's rigorist proposal understands "something objectionable" to include the foreignness of women, and so he links the divorce passage in Deut 24:1 with those forbidding marriage with the native population of Israel (Deut 7:1-4).

Shecaniah is otherwise unknown, although his father's name, "Jehiel," is the same as one of the men who had married a foreign woman (v. 26). Both men hail from the family of Elam. It seems quite unlikely, however, that these two Jehiels are the same person. The name is quite common, and if Shecaniah's father had been one of the offenders, Shecaniah would have been advocating his own excommunication from the community. Shecaniah urged Ezra to take up his responsibilities, and his words of encouragement at the end of v. 4 resemble those used by God when Joshua succeeded Moses (Deut 31:23; Josh 1:9; cf. 1 Chr 28:10, 20; 2 Chr 19:11). The burden of responsibility indeed rested on Ezra, but he had the full support of the community. Ezra rose from his position of prayer and placed the leaders of the priests, the Levites, and the laity of Israel under oath to carry out Shecaniah's proposal.[100] His actions seem to anticipate what will be done by the community in more detail in vv. 12-17.

10:6. Ezra moved to the chamber of Jehohanan, where he continued to fast and mourn because of the unfaithfulness of the people. Such private grief calls into question those who criticize Ezra's previous actions as things done only for show (e.g., 9:3-5; 10:1). The reference to Jehohanan has precipitated much discussion because his father, Eliashib, has the same name as the high priest at the time of Nehemiah (Neh 3:1) and because a high priest Jehohanan is mentioned in the Elephantine Papyri of 407 BCE.[101] The equation of the two Eliashibs and the identification of Jehohanan as a high priest have been two of the principal reasons for concluding that Ezra must have come after Nehemiah during the reign of Artaxerxes II. Is it likely, however, that if Ezra had lived after Nehemiah, he would have taken up residence in the room of this family? Nehemiah had chased away one of the grandsons of Eliashib, who had married the daughter of the hated Samaritan governor Sanballat (Neh 13:28). In addition Neh 12:22, a list of high priests, makes Johanan (note the slight spelling difference) the grandson of Eliashib instead of his son, as in Ezra 10:6 (but see Neh 12:23). A further complication comes in Neh 12:10-11, where the grandson of Eliashib is called Jonathan, not Johanan.

Two alternative interpretations of Jehohanan in v. 6 make it possible to retain the traditional chronological order of Ezra and Nehemiah. Frank M. Cross has suggested that the lists of priests in Neh 12:10-11, 22-23 are defective and that the gaps can be filled in because the high priesthood followed the practice of papponomy, in which a high priest is named after his grandfather. Thus he inserts an additional Eliashib and Johanan into the list: [Eliashib I—Johanan I (contemporary of Ezra)]—Eliashib II (contemporary of Nehemiah)—Johanan II. The people mentioned in v. 6, according to this reconstruction, are Eliashib I and Johanan I.[102]

A second interpretation questions whether Eliashib and his son Jehohanan were actually members of the high priestly family, since v. 6 does

99. Note the contrast in connotation between Shecaniah's affirmation of hope "in spite of this" in 10:2 and Ezra's confession of guilt "because of this" at the end of his prayer in 9:15.

100. Kenneth G. Hoglund, *Achaemenid Imperial Administration in Syria-Palestine and the Missions of Ezra and Nehemiah,* SBLDS 125 (Atlanta: Scholars Press, 1992) 233, notes that Ezra forced the people to take an oath, which suggests a more aggressive leadership style than Tamara C. Eskenazi proposes in *In an Age of Prose: A Literary Approach to Ezra–Nehemiah,* SBLMS 36 (Atlanta: Scholars Press, 1988).

101. AP 30.18.

102. Frank M. Cross, "A Reconstruction of the Judean Restoration," *JBL* 94 (1975) 4-18. This reconstruction is evaluated more thoroughly in the Commentary on Nehemiah 12:1-26.

not explicitly make this identification. If they are not members of the high priestly family, the passage becomes irrelevant to the question of the dating of Ezra and Nehemiah. However this problem of the identity of Eliashib and Jehohanan is resolved, v. 6 provides evidence for a close working relationship between the officials of the Temple and Ezra.

10:7-9. A proclamation sent throughout the province required that the whole post-exilic community convene in Jerusalem within three days. The "returned exiles" (v. 7) can be identified with the "people of Israel" in 9:1, with the "Israelites" in 10:2, or with the "men of Judah and Benjamin" in 10:9. The "officials and elders" (v. 8) endorsed this demand—thus exonerating Ezra from sole responsibility—and attached to it severe penalties for noncompliance. All those who did not show up in three days would forfeit their property and would be banned from the community. The root of the word "forfeited" (יחרם *yāḥāram,* in the hophal) is used in holy war contexts to indicate property that has been put under the "ban" and so transferred from the secular to the sacred realm. In some cases a transfer to the sacred realm meant that the property was burned or destroyed (Josh 6:21; 7:25); in other cases the ban meant that the material was given to the priests (Num 18:14; Ezek 44:29; see also 1 Esdr 9:4).[103] People could also be put under the ban (Exod 22:20). Banishment from the community seems to have replaced capital punishment in some biblical laws (Exod 12:15). The two punishments threatened in v. 8 correspond to the second and third penalties authorized in the rescript of Artaxerxes (7:26). Banishment and confiscation of goods as punishments are interrelated because only people who were members of the temple community were entitled to hold property within it. The three-day deadline does not seem improbable, since the whole province measured only thirty-five miles north to south and twenty-five miles west to east. The people of Judah and Benjamin came together by the twentieth day of the ninth month (Chislev, Neh 1:1) and assembled in the square before the Temple, where they may have gathered two months earlier to hear Ezra read the law (Neh 8:1). This event assumes that Nehemiah 8 belongs historically between Ezra 8 and Ezra 9. They trembled because of two seemingly unrelated factors: the matter under discussion and the rain. Chislev 20 is the third week in December, when the weather in Jerusalem can be cold and rainy.

10:10-12. Ezra the priest (the title indicates the basis of his authority within Israel) underscores the faithlessness of the community's behavior and says that the marriages with foreign women have added to the guilt of Israel (v. 10). Some of the people were guilty because they had married foreign women; others were guilty for having tolerated this practice. He urges the guilty to confess their sin (lit., "give thanks" [תנו תודה *tĕnû tôdâ*]; cf. Josh 7:19) and to do what would be pleasing to Yahweh (the only reference to Yahweh in this chapter), the God of their ancestors—that is, to separate from the "peoples of the land" in general (Lev 20:22-26) and to divorce their foreign wives in particular. The community gives its unanimous consent to Ezra's proposals, showing that Ezra is not the sole actor in this matter and that his viewpoint is not forced on the people against their will.

10:13-17. Verses 13-14 indicate, however, that the situation was quite complicated, with the people proposing the appointment of a special commission composed of laypeople to conduct an investigation. A number of possible extenuating circumstances might have prevented their taking action on the day of the assembly—too many people, the rainy weather, the fact that the problem of intermarriage was widespread in the community. We can also imagine that there would have been disagreements about which women were "foreigners" or about the legitimacy of some of the criticized marriages. The people, in any case, propose that representative officials examine at an appropriate time all those who had married foreign women and that local elders and judges (v. 14) participate in the inquiry (v. 16), perhaps presenting information they had acquired by personal observation or from local reports. The purpose of this commission was to remedy the situation "so that" (v. 14; not "until") God's anger over these marriages might be averted.[104]

Four members of the community opposed this plan (v. 15). It seems unlikely that they opposed

103. Josephus *Antiquities of the Jews* XI.148.

104. H. G. M. Williamson, *Ezra, Nehemiah,* WBC 16 (Waco, Tex.: Word, 1985) 143.

the idea of divorcing the foreign women, because there were severe penalties for failure to attend the assembly (v. 8), let alone failure to agree with its central agenda. Did they oppose the appointment of the commission, the resultant delays, and the possible compromises it might lead to? The four opponents may have been more dedicated to an exclusivist policy than were the majority. Jonathan and Jahzeiah are not identified; most likely they were lay leaders. Supporting them were Meshullam and Shabbethai. A Meshullam was one of the leaders Ezra had commissioned to work on the problem of the small number of Levites in his entourage (8:16), though one cannot be sure that these are the same person. He needs to be distinguished in any case from the Meshullam listed in v. 29 who had married a foreign wife. Shabbethai was a Levite (NIV; cf. Neh 11:16), as was also Meshullam, according to the NRSV (following some Hebrew and Greek MSS; see *BHS*). The etymology of Shabbethai's name may imply a special fidelity to the sabbath requirements (see Isa 58:13, which announces a blessing on those who keep the sabbath). Both Meshullam and Shabbethai are listed in Neh 8:4, 7 as supporters of Ezra.

The community agreed to the proposed commission, and Ezra appointed people to it from the heads of the families (Ezra's role in the appointment results from an emendation of the Hebrew text of v. 16, though this is not mentioned in the NIV). The author of this chapter claims that he had access to the names of these commissioners, but he does not supply them. The first session of the commission was held on the first day of the tenth month (December 29, 458 BCE); three months later, on the first day of the first month (March 27, 457 BCE), it completed the task of investigating all the men who had married foreign women. Exactly one year had elapsed since Ezra's journey from Babylon was supposed to have started (7:9). Since the events in Nehemiah 8 may have taken place in the seventh month of that first year, and since all other references to Ezra in Nehemiah are probably secondary, we may conclude that Ezra's mission to Jerusalem was really quite brief. Some commentators conjecture that Ezra's mission failed, especially because of reaction to the forced divorces, and that he was recalled to Babylon. This argument is based on silence, however, and may need to be reconsidered once the reasons for opposition to intermarriage have been considered. (See Reflections at 10:18-44.)

Ezra 10:18-44, The List of Those Who Divorced Their Wives

NIV

18Among the descendants of the priests, the following had married foreign women:

From the descendants of Jeshua son of Jozadak, and his brothers: Maaseiah, Eliezer, Jarib and Gedaliah. 19(They all gave their hands in pledge to put away their wives, and for their guilt they each presented a ram from the flock as a guilt offering.)

20From the descendants of Immer:
Hanani and Zebadiah.

21From the descendants of Harim:
Maaseiah, Elijah, Shemaiah, Jehiel and Uzziah.

22From the descendants of Pashhur:
Elioenai, Maaseiah, Ishmael, Nethanel, Jozabad and Elasah.

NRSV

18There were found of the descendants of the priests who had married foreign women, of the descendants of Jeshua son of Jozadak and his brothers: Maaseiah, Eliezer, Jarib, and Gedaliah. 19They pledged themselves to send away their wives, and their guilt offering was a ram of the flock for their guilt. 20Of the descendants of Immer: Hanani and Zebadiah. 21Of the descendants of Harim: Maaseiah, Elijah, Shemaiah, Jehiel, and Uzziah. 22Of the descendants of Pashhur: Elioenai, Maaseiah, Ishmael, Nethanel, Jozabad, and Elasah.

23Of the Levites: Jozabad, Shimei, Kelaiah (that is, Kelita), Pethahiah, Judah, and Eliezer. 24Of the singers: Eliashib. Of the gatekeepers: Shallum, Telem, and Uri.

25And of Israel: of the descendants of Parosh:

NIV

[23]Among the Levites:
Jozabad, Shimei, Kelaiah (that is, Kelita), Pethahiah, Judah and Eliezer.
[24]From the singers:
Eliashib.
From the gatekeepers:
Shallum, Telem and Uri.

[25]And among the other Israelites:

From the descendants of Parosh:
Ramiah, Izziah, Malkijah, Mijamin, Eleazar, Malkijah and Benaiah.
[26]From the descendants of Elam:
Mattaniah, Zechariah, Jehiel, Abdi, Jeremoth and Elijah.
[27]From the descendants of Zattu:
Elioenai, Eliashib, Mattaniah, Jeremoth, Zabad and Aziza.
[28]From the descendants of Bebai:
Jehohanan, Hananiah, Zabbai and Athlai.
[29]From the descendants of Bani:
Meshullam, Malluch, Adaiah, Jashub, Sheal and Jeremoth.
[30]From the descendants of Pahath-Moab:
Adna, Kelal, Benaiah, Maaseiah, Mattaniah, Bezalel, Binnui and Manasseh.
[31]From the descendants of Harim:
Eliezer, Ishijah, Malkijah, Shemaiah, Shimeon,
[32]Benjamin, Malluch and Shemariah.
[33]From the descendants of Hashum:
Mattenai, Mattattah, Zabad, Eliphelet, Jeremai, Manasseh and Shimei.
[34]From the descendants of Bani:
Maadai, Amram, Uel, [35]Benaiah, Bedeiah,
Keluhi, [36]Vaniah, Meremoth, Eliashib,
[37]Mattaniah, Mattenai and Jaasu.
[38]From the descendants of Binnui:[a]
Shimei, [39]Shelemiah, Nathan, Adaiah,
[40]Macnadebai, Shashai, Sharai, [41]Azarel,
Shelemiah, Shemariah, [42]Shallum,
Amariah and Joseph.
[43]From the descendants of Nebo:
Jeiel, Mattithiah, Zabad, Zebina, Jaddai, Joel and Benaiah.

[44]All these had married foreign women, and some of them had children by these wives.[b]

[a] *37,38* See Septuagint (also 1 Esdras 9:34); Hebrew *Jaasu* [38]and Bani and Binnui, [b] *44* Or *and they sent them away with their children*

Ramiah, Izziah, Malchijah, Mijamin, Eleazar,
Hashabiah,[a] and Benaiah. [26]Of the descendants of
Elam: Mattaniah, Zechariah, Jehiel, Abdi, Jeremoth, and Elijah. [27]Of the descendants of Zattu:
Elioenai, Eliashib, Mattaniah, Jeremoth, Zabad,
and Aziza. [28]Of the descendants of Bebai: Jehohanan, Hananiah, Zabbai, and Athlai. [29]Of the de-
scendants of Bani: Meshullam, Malluch, Adaiah,
Jashub, Sheal, and Jeremoth. [30]Of the descendants
of Pahath-moab: Adna, Chelal, Benaiah, Maaseiah,
Mattaniah, Bezalel, Binnui, and Manasseh. [31]Of
the descendants of Harim: Eliezer, Isshijah, Malchijah, Shemaiah, Shimeon, [32]Benjamin, Malluch,
and Shemariah. [33]Of the descendants of Hashum:
Mattenai, Mattattah, Zabad, Eliphelet, Jeremai,
Manasseh, and Shimei. [34]Of the descendants of
Bani: Maadai, Amram, Uel, [35]Benaiah, Bedeiah,
Cheluhi, [36]Vaniah, Meremoth, Eliashib, [37]Mat-
taniah, Mattenai, and Jaasu. [38]Of the descendants
of Binnui:[b] Shimei, [39]Shelemiah, Nathan, Adaiah,
[40]Machnadebai, Shashai, Sharai, [41]Azarel, Shelemiah,
Shemariah, [42]Shallum, Amariah, and Joseph. [43]Of
the descendants of Nebo: Jeiel, Mattithiah, Zabad,
Zebina, Jaddai, Joel, and Benaiah. [44]All these had
married foreign women, and they sent them away
with their children.[c]

[a] 1 Esdras 9.26 Gk: Heb *Malchijah* [b] Gk: Heb *Bani, Binnui*
[c] 1 Esdras 9.36; Meaning of Heb uncertain

COMMENTARY

The text supplies a relatively short list of names of those who had to divorce their wives and send away their children, a total of 110 (or 111).[105] This is 0.58 percent of the clergy and 0.67 percent or 0.68 percent of the laity (based on the figures in chap. 2). Perhaps some people were able to convince the commission that their marriage to a foreigner did not require them to follow through with a divorce. Galling suggested that the list contained offenders only from the upper economic and political classes, and he noted there are no offenders from the Nethinim, the servants of Solomon (cf. 2:43-58), or any of the provincial towns (cf. 2:20-35).[106]

Priests and Levites are mentioned before the laity in chap. 10, as in chap. 8. Verse 19 indicates that the members of the high priestly family of Jeshua were treated differently from the other transgressors because they pledged to send away their wives and also to contribute a ram of the flock as a guilt or reparation offering. According to Lev 5:14-16, a guilt offering was required when one had been remiss with regard to a holy thing.[107] Four heads of priestly families are listed as being involved in intermarriages: Jeshua (in Ezra 2:36, Jeshua is listed under the descendants of Jedaiah; cf. 1 Chr 24:7), Immer, Harim, and Pashhur (vv. 18-22). In 1 Chronicles 24, Jeshua heads the ninth course of priests, Immer the sixteenth course, and Harim the third course; Pashhur is not part of the twenty-four priestly courses. The number of those who divorced from the family of Pashhur is the largest among the priests.

The following chart indicates the family names of priests and Levites in vv. 18-24, the number of those who divorced their wives from each family, the location of the name in chap. 2, the number of returnees given for the family in chap. 2, and the percentage of that number who divorced their wives.

105. The reduction from 111 to 110 results from the emendation of the personal name "Machnadebai" (v. 40) to "Of the descendants of Azzur" or "Of the descendants of Zaccai," following 1 Esdr 9:34 (cf. *BHS*). The advantage of this emendation is that it creates an additional, twelfth family, implying that all Israel participated in this event (cf. 8:35-36).

106. Kurt Galling, *Die Bücher der Chronik, Esra, Nehemia*, ATD (Göttingen: Vandenhoeck & Ruprecht) 215.

107. Jacob Milgrom, *Leviticus 1–16*, AB 3 (Garden City, N.Y.: Doubleday, 1991) 359-61, argues that a reparation offering was required because they had committed a sacrilege (מעל *ma' al*) against the holy seed by inadvertent intermarriage. That is, they had not been aware that the marriages they had contracted were forbidden by the law.

Ezra 10 Name	Divorced	Ezra 2	Total	Percentage
Jeshua	4	v. 36	973	0.41
Immer	2	v. 37	1,052	.19
Harim	5	v. 39	1,017	.49
Passhur	6	v. 38	1,247	.48
Levites	6	v. 40	74	8.10
Singers	1	v. 41	128	.78
Gatekeepers	3	v. 42	139	2.15
Totals	27		4,630	0.58

A study of the 83 lay names indicates that a number of names from early Israel were used again in post-exilic times: e.g., Benjamin, Joseph, Judah, Manasseh, and Simeon. Over thirty of these names are Yahwistic—that is, they incorporate some form of the word "Yahweh." None of the family names is Yahwistic.[108]

The chart on page 746 indicates the lay family names in vv. 25-43, the number of those from a particular family who divorced their wives, the location of the name of the family in chap. 2, the numbers given for the returnees from the family in that chapter, and the percentage of that number who divorced their wives. The percentages range from 0.28 to 13.4!

108. "Bani" in v. 34 should be emended to "Bigvai," since Bani is listed already in v. 29. I have provided alternative figures for the families of Azzur (based on 1 Esdr 5:15) and Zaccai (based on Ezra 2:9). See also Kurt Galling, *Die Bücher der Chronik, Esra, Nehemia*, ATD (Göttingen: Vandenhoeck & Ruprecht) 215.

Ezra 10 Name	Divorced	Ezra 2	Total	Percentage
Parosh	7	v. 3	2,172	0.32
Elam	6	v. 7	1,254	0.48
Zattu	6	v. 8	945	0.63
Bebai	4	v. 11	623	0.64
Bani	6	v. 10	642	0.93
Pahath-Moab	8	v. 6	2,812	0.28
Harim	8	v. 32	320	2.50
Hashum	7	v. 19	223	3.13
Bigvai	12	v. 14	2,056	0.58
Binnui	4	Neh 7:15	648	0.61
Azzur	8	v. 16	432	1.85
or				
Zaccai	8	v. 9	760	1.05
Nebo	7	v. 29	52	13.40
Totals with Azzur	83		12,127	0.68
Totals with Zaccai	83		12,455	0.67

The NRSV and the NIV have divergent translations for v. 44. The NRSV emends the text according to 1 Esdr 9:36 and indicates that both the women and their children were sent away (cf. v. 3). The NIV follows the MT, which notes only that some of the women had children. Since there are numerous grammatical questions about the five Hebrew words in the second half of the verse, no confidence can be gained about any translation.

REFLECTIONS

It is difficult to find redeeming theological value in this chapter. The cruelty involved in the forcible divorcing of more than one hundred women and the possible sending away of their children must also have created economic and personal misery for many. While divorce was permitted, at least for men, in ancient Israel (Deut 24:1-4), there are strong voices critical of divorce in the Bible. According to Malachi, God hates divorce (Mal 2:16), and Jesus severely restricted the circumstances in which he was ready to permit divorce (Matt 5:31-32; 19:9; Mark 10:11-12; Luke 16:18).

Shemaryahu Talmon has pointed out that the problem of mixed marriages did not arise in the first decades after the return of the exiles, when they no doubt viewed any symbiosis with the native inhabitants as anathema. They even refused to allow the people of the land to participate in the rebuilding of the Temple.[109] Three quarters of a century later, intermarriage was indeed taking place, and it was believed that such marriages would inevitably lead to apostasy (9:1); in Ezra's mind they were already evidence of unfaithfulness (9:2; 10:6). If the list of those who divorced their wives in chapter 10 is more or less complete, the problem involved slightly more than half of 1 percent of the people, but it was a persistent problem that would also haunt Nehemiah (Neh 6:18; 10:30; 13:23-28).

While issues of religious identity and the danger of apostasy were the explicit cause of the divorces in Ezra 9–10, scholars suspect that there may have been other, more covert reasons for this controversy. Kenneth Hoglund notes that political factors may have played a role in the criticism of foreign marriages. If the purpose of the Persians' sending Ezra and Nehemiah was to enhance their control over Yehud and neighboring territories, then it was crucial to define who was part of the assembly of the exiles and who was not.[110] Right of access to the land was not based on past land allotment systems, but the exiles were allowed to dwell in

109. Shemaryahu Talmon, "Esra-Nehemia: Historiographie oder Theologie?" *Ernten was man sät. Festschrift für Klaus Koch zu seinem 65. Geburtstag* (Neukirchen-Vluyn: Neukirchener Verlag, 1991) 344-47.

110. Hoglund, *Achaemenid Imperial Administration in Syria-Palestine and the Missions of Ezra and Nehemiah,* 238-40.

their homeland at the dispensation of the Persian Empire. If a province like Yehud was in a perilous condition, it would become important to know who could function in it and who could not, and the empire would take action to control issues of assimilation. Ezra and Nehemiah were sent in part to clarify these issues. Intermarriage under these circumstances might threaten the future of the Persian-authorized community in Yehud. The exiles might lose their land if they did not maintain themselves as a distinct community.

Harold C. Washington argues that women in post-exilic times were able to own property and even pass it on to heirs (e.g., the daughters of Zelophehad in Numbers 27 and the rights of women at Elephantine).[111] Exogamous marriages could threaten encroachment on the land holdings of the congregation, since "foreign" women and their children might claim land belonging to the temple collective. There was an interconnection of genealogical lineage, land tenure, and membership in the cult: Legal right to the land accrued to those who had access to the cult, and having the appropriate genealogy assured one's right to membership in the cult. Judeans outside the temple community were classed together with the traditional enemies of Israel.[112]

These proposals for understanding the social setting of the intermarriage crisis in Ezra–Nehemiah help us to see that much more was involved here than religious sectarianism. Ezra was no tyrant or fanatic, and he did not fail in this undertaking.

It is important to note that post-exilic Jews did not always have such a hostile attitude to outsiders. Ezra 1–6 lacks the theme entirely, and all those who had separated themselves from the uncleannesses of the nations were allowed to participate in the Passover (6:21; cf. Neh 10:28). Even "Golah" changed from being a term used to refer to returned exiles to a designation for all recognized members of the community.

The canon seen as a whole is more welcoming to the outsider. Already as early as the Book of the Covenant, biblical texts prohibited oppression of resident aliens, with the reminder that Israel, too, had been a resident alien nation in the land of Egypt (Exod 22:21). The book of Ruth celebrates the character and piety of a remarkable Moabite woman (e.g., Ruth 2:11-12) and sees her incorporation in the ancestry of David as a decided credit to Israel's greatest king (Ruth 4:17-22). Some scholars, past and present, believe that the book of Ruth was written precisely to be a counterweight to the actions of Ezra and Nehemiah. Even if it was written much earlier, as some scholars affirm, it would have offered a decidedly different perspective on Moabites and other foreigners in the fifth century BCE. The narrator in Genesis 34 shows ambivalence about the relationship to outsiders by having Jacob scold Simeon and Levi for making his name odious to the inhabitants of the land, but then ending the chapter with a question by Simeon and Levi, "Should our sister be treated like a whore?" (NRSV). The reader, in effect, is asked by the author to choose between two conflicting attitudes toward outsiders. In short, the canon leaves the reader with conflicting opinions and options. There are texts that welcome outsiders, and there are texts that warn of the dangers of outsiders. In our modern context, the definitions of "insiders" and "outsiders" are vastly different from those of biblical times. Almost all contemporary Christians would agree that moving toward gender and ethnic diversity is a radical imperative for the church. But how should we to respond to the difficult interfaith questions facing us today? What is the Christian response to other religions? What is the boundary between witness and dialogue? The biblical ambivalence toward outsiders and the excesses recounted in Ezra 10 call us to serious reflection on these questions today. Ignoring interfaith questions is irresponsible. But in addressing these issues we should not be surprised by different approaches at different people, or even by conflict within ourselves. How do we maintain the integrity of the faith without excluding others?

111. See Tamara C. Eskenazi, "Out from the Shadows: Biblical Women in the Postexilic Era," *JSOT* 54 (1992) 25-43. Eskenazi and Judd have compared the actions in Ezra 9–10 with the opposition to various forms of intermarriage in the modern state of Israel. See Tamara C. Eskenazi and Eleanor P. Judd, "Marriage to a Stranger in Ezra 9–10," in *Temple Community in the Persian Period,* ed. Tamara C. Eskenazi and Kent H. Richards, vol. 2 of Second Temple Studies, JSOTSup 175 (Sheffield: Sheffield Academic, 1994) 266-85.

112. Harold C. Washington, "The Strange Woman (אשה זרה/נכריה) of Proverbs 1–9 and Post Exilic Judean Society," in ibid., 217-42. Washington argues that the polemic against the strange/foreign woman in Proverbs 1–9 is based on the fear that Judean property would fall under the control of alien families via marriages to women outside the community.

NEHEMIAH 1:1–7:73*a*

RETURN OF NEHEMIAH AND REBUILDING OF THE WALLS OF JERUSALEM

OVERVIEW

Whereas the book of Ezra focuses on the rebuilding of the Temple, the book of Nehemiah provides an account of the rebuilding of the walls of Jerusalem. For the relationship between the books of Ezra and Nehemiah, see the Introduction (pp. 666-71).

Much of the book of Nehemiah consists of a first-person narrative, traditionally called the Nehemiah Memoir, recounting Nehemiah's role in constructing the walls of Jerusalem, expanding its population, correcting social abuses, supporting the worship life of the community, and guarding against any mixing with foreigners.[113] The actions leading up to the dedication of the walls in Neh 12:27-43 took place during Nehemiah's first year in Jerusalem, while the events in chap. 13 took place some twelve years later, during the governor's second term in office. Chapters 3 and 7 (= Ezra 2), composed in the third person, were not written by Nehemiah, but may have been included by him in the Nehemiah Memoir. The paragraph in Neh 11:1-2 reports the completion of the repopulation of Jerusalem, initiated by Nehemiah in chap. 7, but it is not written in the first person and does not mention Nehemiah.

Scholars have searched vigorously for formal parallels to this memoir in ancient Near Eastern royal inscriptions narrating the king's deeds in the first person; in Egyptian tomb and temple inscriptions in which officials report their faithful carrying out of duties; and in the biblical prayers of the falsely accused. None of the parallels is completely satisfying, and the search is hampered by the fact that the memoir has not been preserved in its original form. There are supplementary materials in Neh 7:73*b*–12:26 and 12:44–13:1-3 (and perhaps elsewhere), and it is generally agreed that Nehemiah's spirited defense of himself in 5:14-19 belongs historically with the materials in chap. 13. Blenkinsopp has argued that an editor has incorporated only parts of the Nehemiah Memoir into his own third-person account, making conclusions about the original extent of the Nehemiah Memoir impossible.[114]

One of the most striking characteristics of the memoir is a series of four formulaic prayers containing the word "remember" (זכר *zākar*): "Remember for my good, O my God, all that I have done for this people" (5:19; cf. 13:14, 22, 31). Williamson notes that the formula in 5:19 belongs at the end of Nehemiah's service as governor and that none of these formulas mentions the rebuilding of the wall. Therefore, he ascribes 5:14-19 and 13:4-31 to a second edition of the Nehemiah Memoir, in which Nehemiah was claiming credit for actions attributed elsewhere to others. The original memoir, in Williamson's opinion, was a report to the Persian king about the rebuilding and rededication of the wall, but in its present state it is an appeal for God to remember Nehemiah's good deeds. Williamson has to admit, however, that the original memoir was probably written in Aramaic rather than in Hebrew and lacked the prayers now included in it (1:4-11;

113. Clines notes that this is the only historiographical document in the OT written within a decade of the events described and by an eyewitness and principal actor in the events. Nevertheless, he calls the veracity of the account into question because of its self-serving character, because the narrator claims to know the inner feelings and motivations of others, and for other literary and historical reasons. See David J. A. Clines, "Nehemiah: The Perils of Autobiography," in *What Does Eve Do to Help? and Other Readerly Questions to the Old Testament,* JSOTSup 94 (Sheffield: Sheffield Academic, 1990) 124-64.

114. "The Nehemiah Autobiographical Narrative," in *Language, Theology, and the Bible: Essays in Honour of James Barr,* ed. Samuel E. Balentine and John Barton (Oxford: Clarendon, 1994) 199-212. Third-person sections include Neh 3:1-32; 11:1-2; 12:27-30, 44-47; and 13:1-3.

4:4-5; 6:14).[115] We should also note that in its present form the memoir does not address the king at all.

Blenkinsopp concedes that 5:14-19 is chronologically out of place, but observes that short invocations are quite prevalent throughout the Nehemiah Memoir in addition to the four already cited (see 3:36-37; 6:9, 14; 13:29). Three of these prayers use the word "remember" (*zākar*) in imprecations against Nehemiah's adversaries, while the fourth (Neh 6:9) uses different terminology in the invocation: "But now, O God, strengthen my hands." Blenkinsopp finds a parallel to the Nehemiah Memoir in the contemporary inscription of the Egyptian Udjahorresnet, who was, like Nehemiah, sent back to his homeland by the Persians to accomplish a number of social, economic, and religious tasks. Through this memoir, Nehemiah was trying to keep his own memory alive with God and with his readers by recounting all of his activities on behalf of the restored community. Blenkinsopp also notes the close parallels between Nehemiah's activities in chap. 13 and the firm agreement in 9:38–10:39, but he concludes, contrary to Williamson, that the firm agreement builds on the Nehemiah Memoir rather than vice versa.

Whatever the original purpose and extent of the Nehemiah Memoir, which cannot be determined in a decisive way, this commentary will attempt to understand it within its present context, as an integral part of the book of Nehemiah.

115. Williamson, *Ezra, Nehemiah,* xxiv-xxviii.

NEHEMIAH 1:1-11, NEHEMIAH PRAYS FOR HELP

NIV

1 The words of Nehemiah son of Hacaliah:

In the month of Kislev in the twentieth year, while I was in the citadel of Susa, 2Hanani, one of my brothers, came from Judah with some other men, and I questioned them about the Jewish remnant that survived the exile, and also about Jerusalem.

3They said to me, "Those who survived the exile and are back in the province are in great trouble and disgrace. The wall of Jerusalem is broken down, and its gates have been burned with fire."

4When I heard these things, I sat down and wept. For some days I mourned and fasted and prayed before the God of heaven. 5Then I said:

"O LORD, God of heaven, the great and awesome God, who keeps his covenant of love with those who love him and obey his commands, 6let your ear be attentive and your eyes open to hear the prayer your servant is praying before you day and night for your servants, the people of Israel. I confess the sins we Israelites, including myself and my father's house, have committed against you.

NRSV

1 The words of Nehemiah son of Hacaliah.
In the month of Chislev, in the twentieth
year, while I was in Susa the capital, 2one of my
brothers, Hanani, came with certain men from
Judah; and I asked them about the Jews that
survived, those who had escaped the captivity,
and about Jerusalem. 3They replied, "The survivors there in the province who escaped captivity
are in great trouble and shame; the wall of Jerusalem is broken down, and its gates have been
destroyed by fire."
4When I heard these words I sat down and
wept, and mourned for days, fasting and praying
before the God of heaven. 5I said, "O LORD God
of heaven, the great and awesome God who keeps
covenant and steadfast love with those who love
him and keep his commandments; 6let your ear
be attentive and your eyes open to hear the prayer
of your servant that I now pray before you day
and night for your servants, the people of Israel,
confessing the sins of the people of Israel, which
we have sinned against you. Both I and my family
have sinned. 7We have offended you deeply, failing to keep the commandments, the statutes, and
the ordinances that you commanded your servant

NIV

7We have acted very wickedly toward you. We have not obeyed the commands, decrees and laws you gave your servant Moses.

8"Remember the instruction you gave your servant Moses, saying, 'If you are unfaithful, I will scatter you among the nations, 9but if you return to me and obey my commands, then even if your exiled people are at the farthest horizon, I will gather them from there and bring them to the place I have chosen as a dwelling for my Name.'

10"They are your servants and your people, whom you redeemed by your great strength and your mighty hand. 11O Lord, let your ear be attentive to the prayer of this your servant and to the prayer of your servants who delight in revering your name. Give your servant success today by granting him favor in the presence of this man."

I was cupbearer to the king.

NRSV

Moses. 8Remember the word that you commanded your servant Moses, 'If you are unfaithful, I will scatter you among the peoples; 9but if you return to me and keep my commandments and do them, though your outcasts are under the farthest skies, I will gather them from there and bring them to the place at which I have chosen to establish my name.' 10They are your servants and your people, whom you redeemed by your great power and your strong hand. 11O Lord, let your ear be attentive to the prayer of your servant, and to the prayer of your servants who delight in revering your name. Give success to your servant today, and grant him mercy in the sight of this man!"

At the time, I was cupbearer to the king.

COMMENTARY

After he had received a report about the terrible conditions in Jerusalem (vv. 1-4), Nehemiah prayed for success in his forthcoming petition to Artaxerxes (vv. 5-11). That prayer, which is composed largely of deuteronomistic quotations and allusions, has the following outline:

- v. 5, address to God
- v. 6*a,* appeal for God to hear
- vv. 6*b*-7, confession of sins by the people and by Nehemiah
- vv. 8-9, remembrance of God's promise to Israel
- v. 10, identification of the people who are the recipients of the promise
- v. 11, petition for an answer and for the success of Nehemiah's mission

The prayer does not correspond exactly to any known genre, including the somewhat similar communal prayers of lament, since there is no explicit complaint section. There are, however, similarities to other late prayers, especially in the speaker's identification with the sins of the whole people (cf. 9:6-37; Ezra 9:6-15; Dan 9:4-19; Bar 1:15–3:8; 1 QS I.24–II.1). Numerous short prayers of Nehemiah appear elsewhere in the Nehemiah Memoir (4:4-5; 4:9; 5:19; 6:9, 14).

Because of the prayer's formulaic language and because of a number of minor tensions with its present context, the prayer may be secondary in the Nehemiah Memoir. The prayer deals extensively, for example, with the question of exile and return, which was no longer a main concern at the time of Nehemiah. Verse 11 speaks of one specific day of prayer, whereas v. 4 from the memoir indicates that Nehemiah prayed over a considerable period of time. Some consider the awkward reference to "this man" in v. 11 a sign of the prayer's secondary character. All agree, however, that some kind of prayer must always have stood after 1:4. It seems senseless to reconstruct a purely hypothetical and supposedly more original prayer for this place.

1:1-4, Bad News from Jerusalem. The book of Nehemiah begins with a reference to the words, or chronicles, of Nehemiah. Nehemiah (meaning, "Yahweh has comforted") was the son of Hacaliah (10:2), whose name remains unexplained etymologically. Nehemiah was employed in the Persian court as a cupbearer (v. 11), responsible for selecting the king's wine, tasting it as a defense against assassination, and providing the king companionship.[116] A few manuscripts of the Septuagint call him a eunuch, but this seems to have resulted from a miswriting of the first letters of the Greek word for "cupbearer." It is hard to imagine how Nehemiah could have served as an effective Jewish religious leader, especially in cultic matters, if he had been a eunuch (see Deut 23:2; the promise to include eunuchs in the community in Isa 56:4-5 would hardly have silenced critics of Nehemiah).

The dates mentioned in the first two chapters are difficult. Chislev is the ninth month of the year (November–December), and the twentieth year (v. 1), used here without reference to a king's name, is presumably the twentieth year of Artaxerxes I. But the next event, in 2:1, takes place in Nisan, or the first month, of the twentieth year of Artaxerxes. Commentators have tried to remove this confusion by emending the text of 1:1 to the nineteenth year (of Artaxerxes), or they have proposed various chronological schemes to understand the MT, such as dating the new year to the fall instead of to the spring. Bickerman suggested that Nehemiah reckoned years not according to the normal calendar, but from the day of Artaxerxes' accession. This method of dating would place Chislev of the twentieth regnal year of Artaxerxes in December 445 BCE, and Nisan of the twentieth regnal year in the spring of 445 BCE.[117] Commentators note how abruptly the book of Nehemiah begins and suggest that the editor has not incorporated the beginning of the Nehemiah Memoir into his account (see the Overview). There is no transition after the tragic events of Ezra 10, nor is there a full explanation of who Nehemiah is. This abrupt beginning may also account for the confusion about the twentieth year.

The Persian king whom Nehemiah served must have been Artaxerxes I (464–424 BCE). An Elephantine papyrus mentions that two sons of Sanballat, the governor of Samaria at the time of Nehemiah, had succeeded him by 408 BCE,[118] placing Sanballat in the mid-fifth century, during the reign of Artaxerxes I. Artaxerxes II began to reign in 404 BCE. Since Ezra is also dated to the reign of Artaxerxes I (Ezra 7:1, 11), the chronology implicit in Ezra–Nehemiah makes a narrative connection between Ezra and Nehemiah. The "citadel" or the "capital" of Susa (v. 1) was the winter residence of the Achaemenid kings in southwest Iran, where Artaxerxes spent a good part of his reign.

Nehemiah's account begins with his interrogation of Hanani and his associates. Hanani, who was probably a brother of Nehemiah and not just his kinsman, was later put in charge of Jerusalem (7:2). It is unclear whether Hanani had been sent from Mesopotamia to investigate Jerusalem or whether Nehemiah merely questioned him about conditions in Jerusalem, since he had recently been there. It is also unclear whether Hanani reported about Jews who had never left the land to go into exile or about those who had returned from the exile or about both groups. The Hebrew word נשארו (*nišă'rû*; NRSV, the Jews "that survived"; NIV, the Jewish "remnant") and other forms of its root are used elsewhere with a strong theological overtone (1 Chr 4:43; 2 Chr 12:7; 20:24; 30:6; Ezra 9:8, 13-15). The Jerusalem delegation reported that conditions back in the land were bad, even disgraceful: The city wall had been broken down, and the gates had been burned. This destruction may refer to the effects of the events in Ezra 4:23, when Rehum and his companions had forcibly carried out the order of Artaxerxes to stop the rebuilding of Jerusalem. Perhaps Rehum not only stopped the building program, but also destroyed what had already been built. Nehemiah's deep and dramatic mourning must have been over such a recent reversal rather than over the Babylonian destruction of Jerusalem nearly 150 years before. He sat in mourning, like the friends of Job (Job 2:8, 13) and fasted and prayed.

1:5-11. Nehemiah's Prayer. The following list of quotations from or allusions to other parts of the Bible in Nehemiah's prayer shows how deeply the author of the prayer was shaped by traditional language.

116. See E. M. Yamauchi, "Was Nehemiah the Cupbearer a Eunuch?" *ZAW* 92 (1989) 132-42.

117. E. J. Bickerman, "En marge de l'écriture. I.—Le comput des années de régne des Achéménides (Néh., i, 2; ii, 1 et Thuc., viii, 58," *RB* 88 (1981) 19-23.

118. AP 30.

Neh 1:5
"The faithful God who maintains covenant loyalty with those who love him and keep his commandments." (Deut 7:9 NRSV; cf. Dan 9:4)
"A great and awesome God." (Deut 7:21 NRSV)
"God of gods and Lord of lords, the great God, mighty and awesome." (Deut 10:17 NRSV)
". . . keeping covenant and steadfast love for your servants." (1 Kgs 8:23 NRSV)

Neh 1:6
". . . that your eyes may be open night and day toward this house." (1 Kgs 8:28-29 NRSV)
"Let your eyes be open to the plea of your servant, and to the plea of your people Israel." (1 Kgs 8:52 NRSV)
"Let your eyes be open and your ears attentive to prayer from this place." (2 Chr 6:40 NRSV; cf. 2 Chr 7:15)
"Let your ears be attentive/ to the voice of my supplications." (Ps 130:2 NRSV)

Neh 1:7
"I will tell you all the commandments, the statutes and the ordinances." (Deut 5:31 NRSV)
"Moses, the servant of the LORD." (Deut 34:5 NRSV)

Neh 1:8
"The LORD will scatter you among the peoples." (Deut 4:27 NRSV; cf. Deut 28:64)

Neh 1:9
"The place that the LORD your God will choose out of all your tribes as his habitation to put his name there." (Deut 12:5 NRSV; cf. 12:11)
"When all these things have happened to you, the blessings and the curses that I have set before you, if you call them to mind among all the nations where the LORD your God has driven you, and return to the LORD your God, and you and your children obey him with all your heart and with all your soul, just as I am commanding you today, then the LORD your God will restore your fortunes and have compassion on you, gathering you again from all the peoples among whom the LORD your God has scattered you. Even if you are exiled to the ends of the world, from there the LORD your God will gather you, and from there he will bring you back." (Deut 30:1-4 NRSV)

Neh 1:10
". . . whom you brought out of the land of Egypt with great power and with a mighty hand." (Exod 32:11 NRSV)
". . . whom you brought out by your great power, and by your outstretched arm." (Deut 9:29 NRSV)
". . . whom you redeemed from Egypt." (1 Chr 17:21 NRSV)

1:5-7. This verse has a rare reference to Yahweh in the Nehemiah Memoir (see the references to the divine name in vv. 9 and 11; see also 5:13), and this is the only time it is used as an invocation. The epithet "God of heaven" was frequently used by the Jews in conversation with the Persians (cf. 2:20; Ezra 1:2), although it is not used exclusively in such contexts. Here it designates Israel's God as the sole and universal God. This God and the king of the Persian Empire had authorized Nehemiah for his mission. This verse reminds "the great and awesome" God of the covenantal promise and implicitly includes Nehemiah and the Jews among those who love God and keep the commandments. Nehemiah expresses appropriate piety as God's servant who prays around the clock (v. 6). As in many post-exilic prayers, the author of the prayer acknowledges his solidarity with the people's confession of their sins. Nehemiah includes his whole family—that is, his father's house—in this confession.

1:8. No exact biblical equivalent can be found

for the "word that you commanded to your servant Moses," referred to in this verse, although the substance of this promise is reflected in Deut 30:1-4. Note, however, that a key verb in v. 8, "to be unfaithful" (מעל *mā'al*), never appears in Deuteronomy, although it is used frequently in the books of Chronicles (cf. Ezra 9:4). It represents an adaptation of the traditional deuteronomistic language to a new context.

1:9-10. True "returning" to God in repentance (v. 9) necessarily means keeping and doing God's commandments. The "farthest skies," from which outcasts may return, are the most distant points on the horizon (see NIV). The place God has chosen, where God's name dwells and to which the exiles will return, is Jerusalem. Nehemiah reminds God that the exiled people are at the same time God's obedient servants and the elect people, whom God won (redeemed) by the warlike acts of the exodus ("your power," "your strong hand").

1:11. This petition is clear but only implicit: Nehemiah asks God to restore the exiled Israelites who have turned to God in repentance and obedience. Understood narrowly, this request for a return may be a sign that this prayer was originally written for another, earlier context. But it may imply in the present context that God has not fully restored the repentant and obedient people as long as the broken-down walls and the burned gates of Jerusalem have been left unattended to.

This verse notes a distinction between Nehemiah ("your servant") and the people ("your servants"), as well as the latter's profound unity as servants of God, who find delight in reverencing God's name. Nehemiah prays for success in his approach to "this man," a veiled and somewhat awkward allusion to Artaxerxes I, in whose court Nehemiah was serving. If God wanted to, Nehemiah implies, God could change the will of the king, who was only a man.

REFLECTIONS

Nehemiah's name means something like "Yahweh has given comfort." That name recalls the famous opening to the book of Second Isaiah, "Give comfort to my people Israel" (Isa 40:1). It also reminds us that comfort includes more than sympathy; it can also denote complete restoration of the people, as in Isa 52:9.

The conditions in Jerusalem at Nehemiah's time stood in contradiction to the promise inherent in his own name. Yahweh had not, in fact, given comfort. Hence Nehemiah turned to Yahweh in prayer and invoked the divine name for the only time in the Nehemiah Memoir. Yahweh's name provided the means by which God's presence was realized in Jerusalem; to reverence this name committed the one offering reverence to full and true obedience.

Nehemiah speaks of God paradoxically. On the one hand, God is the God of heaven, the great and awesome God, whose power had been experienced in the awful judgment of exile. But this God is also the one who keeps covenant and steadfast love with those who love God and keep the commandments. That self-contradictory God had promised already through words attributed to Moses to restore from distant exile those who turned to God in repentance. No banishment, no exile, no sin is too great for the God whose unique characteristic is to trump wrath with forgiveness.

Those for whom Nehemiah prayed also had a special name. They were the servants of Yahweh, or even more concretely, the people of Israel (this otherwise common designation is used only in 1:6 in the entire Nehemiah Memoir). Nehemiah prays for these people of Israel, and he confesses their sins—for them and with them.

Perhaps the most crucial theological part of this prayer, for Nehemiah and also for us, is that it holds God to God's promises. From Nehemiah's point of view, Israel had not yet been restored out of its exile into its homeland. How could one talk of restoration when the walls of the city had gaps in them and when the gates had been burned down? Nehemiah reminds God that the "outcasts," who should be restored and of whom Moses had spoken, are the servants of God. More than that, they are the very people whom God had won through the saving and warlike deed of the exodus. Thus both the verbal promise and the implications of earlier saving deeds put God under obligation to the people of Israel. Nehemiah wanted God to continue as redeemer and fulfill the promise. Holding God to God's promises is a way of describing how we do not fail or lose heart or faith in bleak situations. God does not need to be reminded of promises, but we need to remind ourselves that God's promises are true, all evidence to the contrary notwithstanding.

It would be demeaning to God's reputation to imagine that God could be persuaded by a catalog of human arguments, no matter how long and eloquent. But God is not the only one who needs to be convinced. Through this recitation of benefactions, Nehemiah also reminds the readers of his memoir of the character of the God who supports them. The doubting reader can be made strong and faithful again, and so become the polar opposite of the faithless people referred to in 1:8. Readers are implicitly urged to join the chorus of those who love God, who keep God's commandments, and who delight to revere God's name. Trust is always accompanied by transformation and personal renewal, which result in newness of life and in worship that celebrates and declares God's name.

NEHEMIAH 2:1-20, THE BEGINNING OF NEHEMIAH'S EFFORTS IN JERUSALEM

Nehemiah 2:1-10, Artaxerxes Authorizes Nehemiah's Trip Home

NIV

2 In the month of Nisan in the twentieth
year of King Artaxerxes, when wine was
brought for him, I took the wine and gave it to
the king. I had not been sad in his presence
before; [2]so the king asked me, "Why does your
face look so sad when you are not ill? This can
be nothing but sadness of heart."

I was very much afraid, [3]but I said to the king,
"May the king live forever! Why should my face
not look sad when the city where my fathers are
buried lies in ruins, and its gates have been
destroyed by fire?"

[4]The king said to me, "What is it you want?"

Then I prayed to the God of heaven, [5]and I
answered the king, "If it pleases the king and if
your servant has found favor in his sight, let him
send me to the city in Judah where my fathers
are buried so that I can rebuild it."

[6]Then the king, with the queen sitting beside
him, asked me, "How long will your journey take,
and when will you get back?" It pleased the king
to send me; so I set a time.

NRSV

2 In the month of Nisan, in the twentieth
year of King Artaxerxes, when wine was
served him, I carried the wine and gave it to the
king. Now, I had never been sad in his presence
before. [2]So the king said to me, "Why is your face
sad, since you are not sick? This can only be
sadness of the heart." Then I was very much
afraid. [3]I said to the king, "May the king live
forever! Why should my face not be sad, when
the city, the place of my ancestors' graves, lies
waste, and its gates have been destroyed by fire?"
[4]Then the king said to me, "What do you request?" So I prayed to the God of heaven. [5]Then
I said to the king, "If it pleases the king, and if
your servant has found favor with you, I ask that
you send me to Judah, to the city of my ancestors'
graves, so that I may rebuild it." [6]The king said
to me (the queen also was sitting beside him),
"How long will you be gone, and when will you
return?" So it pleased the king to send me, and
I set him a date. [7]Then I said to the king, "If it
pleases the king, let letters be given me to the

NIV	NRSV
[7]I also said to him, "If it pleases the king, may I have letters to the governors of Trans-Euphrates, so that they will provide me safe-conduct until I arrive in Judah? [8]And may I have a letter to Asaph, keeper of the king's forest, so he will give me timber to make beams for the gates of the citadel by the temple and for the city wall and for the residence I will occupy?" And because the gracious hand of my God was upon me, the king granted my requests. [9]So I went to the governors of Trans-Euphrates and gave them the king's letters. The king had also sent army officers and cavalry with me. [10]When Sanballat the Horonite and Tobiah the Ammonite official heard about this, they were very much disturbed that someone had come to promote the welfare of the Israelites.	governors of the province Beyond the River, that they may grant me passage until I arrive in Judah; [8]and a letter to Asaph, the keeper of the king's forest, directing him to give me timber to make beams for the gates of the temple fortress, and for the wall of the city, and for the house that I shall occupy." And the king granted me what I asked, for the gracious hand of my God was upon me. 9Then I came to the governors of the province Beyond the River, and gave them the king's letters. Now the king had sent officers of the army and cavalry with me. [10]When Sanballat the Horonite and Tobiah the Ammonite official heard this, it displeased them greatly that someone had come to seek the welfare of the people of Israel.

COMMENTARY

2:1-3. Nehemiah skillfully asks the Persian king for permission to go home to rebuild Jerusalem. When the king asks about the reason for his sadness, Nehemiah proposes a schedule for his trip and requests safe passage and a supply of timber for rebuilding the Temple in Jerusalem.

Throughout his memoir, Nehemiah faces numerous forms of opposition, beginning with this pericope. Many of the pericopes in the memoir end with accounts of opposition or with Nehemiah's prayers or expressions of trust.[119]

2:1-10, Permission to return home; opposition of Sanballat and Tobiah
2:11-20, Return home and inspection of walls; accusations of sedition; Nehemiah's expression of trust
3:1–4:5, Rebuilding of wall; opposition by Sanballat and Tobiah; imprecatory prayer by Nehemiah
4:6-9, Wall building continues; plots against Nehemiah; prayer and defensive measures
6:1-9, Accusation of rebellion; Nehemiah's prayer for strength
6:10-15, Attempt by false prophet to trap Nehemiah; wall completed; enemy nations ashamed in answer to Nehemiah's prayer

In the month of Nisan (March-April), four months after learning about Jerusalem's sorry condition, Nehemiah found an opportunity during a banquet to request help from Artaxerxes. The Persian kings were famous for their opulent banquets (Esth 1:1-12; Dan 5:1-4; 1 Esdr 3:1-3; Herodotus 9:110-11), and on some of these occasions they were accustomed to grant special requests to those in attendance. At an appropriate moment during this banquet, Nehemiah, in his role as cupbearer, brings wine to the king and conducts himself as if in deep mourning. In his previous audiences before the king he had managed to mask his discouragement. This time the king sees what Nehemiah intends for him to see and recognizes at once that Nehemiah is not physically sick, but only depressed or discouraged. Nehemiah had anxieties about this deceptive role. He knew that a courtier acting morose in the king's presence might be suspected of sedition, but he also realized that the welfare of Jerusalem depended on the skill of his negotiations. In his reply to Artaxerxes, therefore, he wishes the king

119. Joseph Blenkinsopp, *Ezra–Nehemiah*, OTL (Philadelphia: Westminster, 1988) 225.

a long and prosperous life (cf. 1 Kgs 1:31; Dan 2:4) and reports to the king a problem that he knew might evoke the king's sympathy: The city where Nehemiah's ancestors had been buried was falling into ruin, and its gates had been damaged by fire. Nehemiah carefully avoids discussing the present political circumstances of Jerusalem or even mentioning the city's name. He may have known that Artaxerxes had stopped the rebuilding of Jerusalem because of the charge that it had been a notoriously rebellious city (Ezra 4:12-23).

2:4-5. The king responds to Nehemiah with an open-ended question: What do you want (v. 4)? Nehemiah prays silently (cf. 1 Sam 1:13), signaling that he is at the crucial point of his negotiations with the king. By using the title "God of heaven" in the prayer, the Nehemiah Memoir reminds the reader of the things for which Nehemiah had prayed to the same God in chap. 1. Nehemiah displays diplomatic courtesy by recognizing the king's right to make decisions, but he also reminds the king of his own faithfulness as his trusted wine steward and servant. His first request was simple and straightforward: He wanted the king to appoint him to go to Judah—again no explicit mention of Jerusalem—to rebuild the city of his ancestral graves, again without mention of the wall.

2:6-7. As Artaxerxes continues the dialogue in v. 6, the narrator notes that the king's consort was sitting beside him. This may be a reference to his wife, Damaspia, or, since the ordinary Hebrew word for "queen" (מלכה *malkâ*) is not used, "consort" (שׁגל *šēgal*; see Ps 45:9), may refer to a favorite woman from his harem. This woman may have been favorably disposed toward Nehemiah or he may even have plotted with her in advance. It would be unusual for such a woman to appear with the king at a public banquet (cf. Esther 1).

When asked about the length of the proposed journey and a date for his return, Nehemiah names a time. Since his assignment is only to repair the city, it is unlikely that the length of time would have been anywhere close to the twelve years Nehemiah actually served in Jerusalem (5:14). He also makes two further requests: for a letter that would guarantee him safe passage and a requisition to Asaph (the word is either Jewish or the Hebrew form of a non-Jewish word), the king's forester, for timber for the construction projects in Jerusalem. The location of this forest is unknown; it may have been a forest in Lebanon, but a site in the Shephelah is also possible, since 1 Chronicles mentions olive and sycamore trees in the area just west of Jerusalem at the time of David (1 Chr 27:28). Jepsen proposed a site southeast of Jerusalem, near Tekoa and the Herodium.[120] Its Arabic name, Jebel Fardes, seems to preserve the word פרדס (*pardēs*, "royal forest"; cf. Eccl 2:5; Cant 4:13).

2:8. To justify this request for timber, Nehemiah spells out more fully his building plans. The fortress or citadel was a defensive structure north of the Temple, probably to be identified with the Tower of Hananel and the Tower of the Hundred in 3:1. Later the Hasmoneans had a citadel at the same spot (1 Macc 13:52), and Herod built the Antonia Fortress there.[121] Nehemiah also mentioned for the first time the far more politically sensitive issue of the city wall. Most of the wall was built of stone, but its gates and towers were made of wood (see Ezra 5:8). The mention of his own house suggests that Nehemiah may have come from a family of some means. Only such a family would have their graves within the city walls (vv. 3, 5).

The king grants all of Nehemiah's requests. Theologically speaking, this resulted from the gracious and powerful hand of God, which rested on Nehemiah as it had on Ezra (see Ezra 7:6, 9, 28; 8:18). We can also imagine that Artaxerxes may have seized this opportunity to use his trusted cupbearer as a building commissioner in Jerusalem. By fortifying Jerusalem, he would provide a defense against Egypt, which had revolted shortly before this time with the assistance of the Greeks. While the Persians were famous for never changing their decrees (Esth 1:19; 8:8; Dan 6:8), the order of Artaxerxes to stop building in Ezra 4:21 had a built-in escape clause. It was valid only "until I make a[nother] decree."

2:9-10. Nehemiah takes his letter of safe passage to the satrap, who probably lived in Damascus, and to the governors of Beyond the River. The king also had given him a military escort to guarantee his safety (v. 9; Ezra had declined a similar offer; see Ezra 8:22). Whatever the satraps and governors thought about Nehemiah, other offi-

120. Alfred Jepsen, "*Pardēs*," *ZDPV* 74 (1958) 64-68.
121. Josephus *Antiquities of the Jews* XV.11.4; 18.4.3

cials in the land did not welcome him warmly. Sanballat (v. 10) was the governor of Samaria, although the book of Nehemiah never gives him this title. Sanballat may also have become a caretaker over Judah after the decree of Artaxerxes stopped the Jewish building project (Ezra 4:21). He had influential contacts in Jerusalem (6:10-14), and his daughter married into the high priest's family (13:28). Despite his Babylonian name ("May Sin [the moon god] give life"), he was probably a follower of Yahweh. Two of his children mentioned in the Elephantine Papyri had Yahwistic names: Delaiah and Shemaiah.[122] Zerubbabel, too, was an Israelite in spite of his Babylonian name. Sanballat's title, "the Horonite," may be contemptuous (cf. 2:19; 13:28); since his father's name is not given, we may surmise that he was the first in his family to hold the office of governor. Etymologically, "Horonite" may refer to his hometown, possibly one of the Beth-horons, small towns in the Shephelah, five miles northwest of Jerusalem (Josh 16:3, 5). Later Sanballat and Geshem will try to trap Nehemiah in this vicinity (6:2). Alternatively, the title may refer to Harran, a city of the moon god in Mesopotamia, or even Horonaim in Moab (Isa 15:5; Jer 48:3). If the latter were intended, however, the memoir might have called him a Moabite just as it called Tobiah an Ammonite.[123]

122. AP 30:29.
123. The Samaria Papyri mention another Sanballat (Sanballat II) as governor, and Cross proposes that there was a Sanballat III on the basis of Josephus (*Antiquities of the Jews* 11.8, 2.306-12). See Frank M. Cross, "A Reconstruction of the Jewish Restoration," *JBL* 94 (1975) 5-6.

Tobiah, who had ties to the Jerusalem nobility and the priesthood (6:17-19; 13:4), took offense that anyone was coming to help the Israelites (v. 10). He was probably a royal official (judging by the technical term "servant" used of him; cf. 2 Kgs 24:10-11; 25:24), though his title may have a contemptuous second connotation in the book of Nehemiah: He was "the slave." Tobiah was probably the governor of Ammon, whether as an Ammonite himself (4:3) or as a Jew who rose to power in the Persian system.[124] He and his son Jehohanan (6:18) had Yahwistic names. It is unclear how Tobiah is related to the Transjordanian Tobiads of the third century BCE and later, a powerful group connected to the high priestly family (see 1 Macc 5:10-13; 2 Macc 3:11; 12:17).[125] He may have had some kind of temporary authority over Judah in cooperation with, or under the supervision of, the Samaritans. The well-known hostility between the Ammonites and the Israelites is probably reflected in the wording of v. 10: This "Ammonite" begrudged anyone who sought the welfare of the "Israelites." The Pentateuch banned Moabites and Ammonites from the cultic assembly (Deut 23:3-6; cf. Neh 13:1).

124. H. G. M. Williamson, *Ezra, Nehemiah,* WBC 16 (Waco, Tex.: Word, 1985) 183-84, argues that "Ammonite" refers only to his ancestry and that he was in fact a junior colleague of Sanballat in Samaria.
125. See also Josephus *Antiquities of the Jews* XI.4; 12.160-236; Zeno Papyri.

REFLECTIONS

Many a social justice project in the church has failed because those involved in it did not display political savvy or know-how. People of goodwill are sometimes politically naive. Jesus urged his followers to be wise as serpents and innocent as doves and noted that no one builds a tower without first figuring out the cost. The children of light need at least to be as wise as the children of darkness.

Nehemiah did not make the mistake of underestimating the difficulty of his assignment. He carefully chose a favorable time to approach Artaxerxes with his concerns about Jerusalem, using all the tricks of body language and tact that he could muster. He may have known that the mention of Jerusalem would raise the king's hackles, and so he referred to the city as the place of his ancestors' graves, never once mentioning the city by name. He recognized that the king had the right to make his own decision ("If it pleases the king," 2:5). But he also knew that timing was everything, and he may even have enlisted one of the king's favorite women to help with his plan. He did not ask for too much too soon, but instead seized the opportunities granted by the king's open-ended questions. Nehemiah had gained the king's confidence over the years and used that trust now to good effect.

But Nehemiah did not settle for vague generalities. He mentioned specific building projects for which he needed timber from the royal forest, and he asked the king for a guaranteed safe passage. There is nothing wrong with using the structures and laws of society to bring about that which is good. The king backed up his word of safe passage with a protective military contingent.

Nehemiah's tact and political savvy were also matched by his profound faith in God. At the turning point in his conversation with the king, he uttered a silent prayer to the God of heaven, and he recognized in his memoir that it was the gracious hand of God that gave him success.

Sometimes the faithful get tripped up because they do not take evil seriously enough and do not recognize that the "powers that be" can thwart well-intentioned plans. Nehemiah's Memoir recognizes that more than personality conflicts were involved in the opposition of Sanballat and Tobiah. This was finally a confrontation between an Ammonite and the Israelites, between the forces of evil and the God of heaven.

Nehemiah 2:11-20, Nehemiah's Inspection of the Wall

NIV

11I went to Jerusalem, and after staying there three days 12I set out during the night with a few men. I had not told anyone what my God had put in my heart to do for Jerusalem. There were no mounts with me except the one I was riding on.

13By night I went out through the Valley Gate toward the Jackal[a] Well and the Dung Gate, examining the walls of Jerusalem, which had been broken down, and its gates, which had been destroyed by fire. 14Then I moved on toward the Fountain Gate and the King's Pool, but there was not enough room for my mount to get through; 15so I went up the valley by night, examining the wall. Finally, I turned back and reentered through the Valley Gate. 16The officials did not know where I had gone or what I was doing, because as yet I had said nothing to the Jews or the priests or nobles or officials or any others who would be doing the work.

17Then I said to them, "You see the trouble we are in: Jerusalem lies in ruins, and its gates have been burned with fire. Come, let us rebuild the wall of Jerusalem, and we will no longer be in disgrace." 18I also told them about the gracious hand of my God upon me and what the king had said to me.

[a] *13* Or *Serpent* or *Fig*

NRSV

11So I came to Jerusalem and was there for three days. 12Then I got up during the night, I and a few men with me; I told no one what my God had put into my heart to do for Jerusalem. The only animal I took was the animal I rode. 13I went out by night by the Valley Gate past the Dragon's Spring and to the Dung Gate, and I inspected the walls of Jerusalem that had been broken down and its gates that had been destroyed by fire. 14Then I went on to the Fountain Gate and to the King's Pool; but there was no place for the animal I was riding to continue. 15So I went up by way of the valley by night and inspected the wall. Then I turned back and entered by the Valley Gate, and so returned. 16The officials did not know where I had gone or what I was doing; I had not yet told the Jews, the priests, the nobles, the officials, and the rest that were to do the work.

17Then I said to them, "You see the trouble we are in, how Jerusalem lies in ruins with its gates burned. Come, let us rebuild the wall of Jerusalem, so that we may no longer suffer disgrace." 18I told them that the hand of my God had been gracious upon me, and also the words that the king had spoken to me. Then they said, "Let us start building!" So they committed themselves to the common good. 19But when Sanballat the Horonite and Tobiah the Ammonite official,

NIV

They replied, "Let us start rebuilding." So they began this good work.

[19]But when Sanballat the Horonite, Tobiah the Ammonite official and Geshem the Arab heard about it, they mocked and ridiculed us. "What is this you are doing?" they asked. "Are you rebelling against the king?"

[20]I answered them by saying, "The God of heaven will give us success. We his servants will start rebuilding, but as for you, you have no share in Jerusalem or any claim or historic right to it."

NRSV

and Geshem the Arab heard of it, they mocked and ridiculed us, saying, "What is this that you are doing? Are you rebelling against the king?" [20]Then I replied to them, "The God of heaven is the one who will give us success, and we his servants are going to start building; but you have no share or claim or historic right in Jerusalem."

COMMENTARY

Upon arrival in Jerusalem, Nehemiah takes no action for the first three days (cf. Ezra 8:32). Then, under cover of darkness, he makes a secret inspection of the walls of Jerusalem. He is accompanied by only a few men, whom he has not informed of his mission, but who presumably can provide information about Jerusalem and its defenses. Nehemiah alone rides on an unidentified animal, probably not a horse or a mule, lest it raise the suspicion that he was politically ambitious, as his opponents later charge (6:6-7; cf. 1 Kgs 1:38-40).

Jerusalem in Nehemiah's time consisted of the Temple Mount and the hill of Ophel (or City of David), extending south from it. He left the city by the Valley Gate (v. 13),[126] on the west side of Ophel, leading to the Tyropoeon Valley (see "Nehemiah's Reconstruction of the Wall of Jerusalem," p. 760). He turned left, or south, and passed the Dragon's Spring, a water source that can no longer be identified on the east side of the Tyropoeon Valley. As he proceeded counterclockwise around the city, he came to the Dung Gate, some 1,000 cubits from the Valley Gate (3:13). Located at the southern end of Ophel, the Dung (or Rubbish) Gate got its name because excrement and other refuse from the sacrificial system were taken out through this gate; it is probably the same as the Potsherd Gate (Jer 19:2). Then he turned north and passed between the Fountain Gate, in the southeast corner of the city, and the King's Pool (cf. the Pool of Shelah in 3:15). We may identify this pool with the waters of Shiloah (Isa 8:6) or the lower pool (Isa 22:9) in the Kidron Valley. Josephus mentions a pool of Solomon.[127] At this point in his inspection tour, Nehemiah had to dismount because the rubble was too difficult for his animal to manuever, and he walked northward in the Kidron Valley as he inspected the wall. The eastern side of Ophel had been terraced in preexilic times, and the destruction of the city wall in 587 BCE may have precipitated considerable collapsing and erosion of the terrace system. Nehemiah later abandoned the part of the former city wall that lay on the northern half of the eastern slope and created a new stretch of wall on the crest. Finally, he retraced his steps and entered the city through the Valley Gate. He did not inspect the northern wall. Perhaps he could do that during daylight hours without arousing suspicion.

The "officials" (or "administrators" [סגנים *sĕgānîm*]) of the city did not know what Nehemiah was up to, nor had he told the Jews in general or their authorities (priests, nobles, and officials) his plans. "Officials" (*sĕgānîm*) and "nobles" (חרים *ḥōrîm*) seem to be used more or less interchangeably in Nehemiah, although Gunneweg proposes that the officials had authority because of their office while the nobles could claim authority because of their birth or their

126. Uzziah had built towers here and at other gates (2 Chr 26:9).

127. Josephus *The Jewish War* V.145.

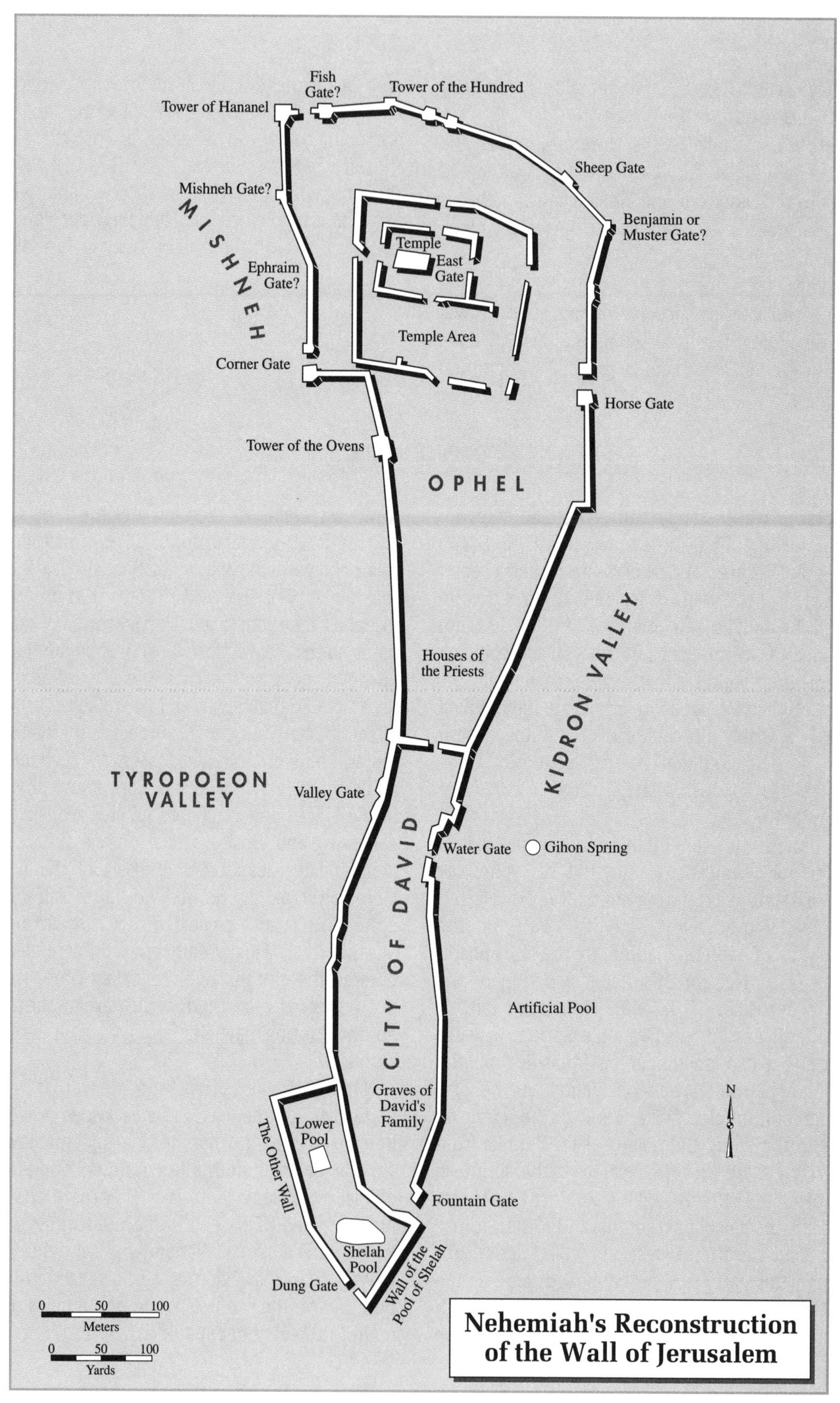

Fish Gate?
Tower of the Hundred
Tower of Hananel
Sheep Gate
Mishneh Gate?
MISHNEH
Benjamin or Muster Gate?
Temple
East Gate
Ephraim Gate?
Temple Area
Corner Gate
Horse Gate
Tower of the Ovens
OPHEL
KIDRON VALLEY
Houses of the Priests
TYROPOEON VALLEY
Valley Gate
CITY OF DAVID
Water Gate
Gihon Spring
Artificial Pool
Graves of David's Family
N
Lower Pool
The Other Wall
Fountain Gate
Shelah Pool
Wall of the Pool of Shelah
Dung Gate
0 50 100
Meters
0 50 100
Yards
Nehemiah's Reconstruction of the Wall of Jerusalem

place of origin.[128] "Jews" in v. 16 may refer to a wealthy elite who had returned from Babylon (cf. 5:1, 17).

After his inspection trip is over, Nehemiah reminds his supporters of the bad state of the city and its gates and urges them to rebuild the wall. His inspection had confirmed Hanani's report: Jerusalem was in a state of disgrace (v. 17; cf. 1:3; 3:36; 5:9). Nehemiah insisted that he was under divine commission and protection (v. 18; cf. v. 8; Ezra 7:6) and that the Persian king had also authorized his mission. The people quickly agree to rebuild the city wall, and they encourage one another in this good work. God, king, Nehemiah, and the people were in agreement.

Sanballat and Tobiah, joined by Geshem the Arab, mock the project and accuse Nehemiah and the people of rebelling against the king by rebuilding the city wall (v. 19). Geshem, or Gashmu, is also among the opponents of Nehemiah in 6:1-2, 6. His name appears in several inscriptions, especially in a fifth-century Aramaic inscription from Tell el-Maskhuṭa in Lower Egypt, where he is identified as the king of Kedar, a tribal people living between the Transjordanian plateau and the Nile Delta.[129] Nehemiah replies firmly to his critics, insisting that the God of heaven, the God with worldwide sovereignty and the God to whom he had prayed at Susa (1:5; 2:4) would give success to the wall-building project and that Nehemiah and his associates, who were loyal servants of this God, would build despite the opposition they were experiencing. He also declares that his opponents will have no political share in Jerusalem (cf. 2 Sam 20:1; 1 Kgs 12:16), no claim to exercise jurisdiction or citizenship there, and no right to participate in the worship at the Jerusalem Temple (cf. Ezra 4:3).

128. Antonius H. J. Gunneweg, *Nehemia,* KAT 19, 2 (Gütersloh: Gütersloher Verlagshaus Gerd Mohn, 1987).

129. W. J. Dumbrell, "The Tell el-Maskhuṭa Bowls and the 'Kingdom' of Qedar in the Persian Period," *BASOR* 203 (1971) 33-44.

REFLECTIONS

Nehemiah continued to act wisely after he arrived in Jerusalem. He needed firsthand knowledge of the lay of the land, and so he made his own secret nocturnal inspection of the walls. He took along only those people he needed and kept his plan secret even from these few. "All power corrupts," the proverb goes; but Nehemiah made no effort to gain political power in this project. He even carefully chose his beast of burden lest some think that he was on a power trip.

For Nehemiah it was a shame and a disgrace for Jerusalem, God's chosen city, to lie in ruins. After all, this was the city God had chosen "to put his name there" (1:9). Nehemiah also knew who he was. Despite the boastful tone of some portions of the Nehemiah Memoir, Nehemiah confessed that his authority rested in the fact that God's gracious hand was upon him and that the king had supported this project with words and deeds (2:8). God, king, Nehemiah, and the people—all were agreed on this project. Nehemiah was so convincing that the people committed themselves to the common good.

Sanballat and Tobiah, and their new colleague Geshem, still tried to thwart Nehemiah's mission, even resorting to political propaganda. They charged that this project was an act of rebellion against the king of Persia. Nehemiah relied, however, on the God of heaven, to whom he had prayed for many days (1:5-11) and during his crucial moment before Artaxerxes (2:4). Nehemiah knew that success depended on God's intervening power, but he and his colleagues were not easily deterred. They confessed: "We are God's servants, God's obedient ones. We worship God. We are going to start building."

Nehemiah did not underestimate the evil that was present in his three opponents, and so he made a decision not to compromise and not to negotiate. Anyone who opposes the plans of God and of God's servants, according to this strategy, forfeits his or her rights in the society and in the cult. One cannot come to praise Yahweh or sacrifice in the Temple if one stands opposed to the Lord's will and way. One cannot serve both God and mammon. The only difficulty we have with this strategy is that it is often exceedingly difficult to be as sure as Nehemiah was in knowing that those opposing us are at the same time opposing God. In fact, we grow rightly suspicious of anyone who too easily confuses his or her views alone with the views of God. But in those cases where we can be sure, we, like Nehemiah, have no reason to compromise.

NEHEMIAH 3:1-32, WORKERS ON NEHEMIAH'S WALL

NIV

3 Eliashib the high priest and his fellow
priests went to work and rebuilt the Sheep
Gate. They dedicated it and set its doors in place,
building as far as the Tower of the Hundred,
which they dedicated, and as far as the Tower of
Hananel. 2The men of Jericho built the adjoining
section, and Zaccur son of Imri built next to them.

3The Fish Gate was rebuilt by the sons of
Hassenaah. They laid its beams and put its doors
and bolts and bars in place. 4Meremoth son of
Uriah, the son of Hakkoz, repaired the next section. Next to him Meshullam son of Berekiah, the
son of Meshezabel, made repairs, and next to him
Zadok son of Baana also made repairs. 5The next
section was repaired by the men of Tekoa, but
their nobles would not put their shoulders to the
work under their supervisors.[a]

6The Jeshanah[b] Gate was repaired by Joiada son
of Paseah and Meshullam son of Besodeiah. They
laid its beams and put its doors and bolts and bars
in place. 7Next to them, repairs were made by
men from Gibeon and Mizpah—Melatiah of
Gibeon and Jadon of Meronoth—places under the
authority of the governor of Trans-Euphrates.
8Uzziel son of Harhaiah, one of the goldsmiths,
repaired the next section; and Hananiah, one of
the perfume-makers, made repairs next to that.
They restored[c] Jerusalem as far as the Broad Wall.
9Rephaiah son of Hur, ruler of a half-district of
Jerusalem, repaired the next section. 10Adjoining
this, Jedaiah son of Harumaph made repairs opposite his house, and Hattush son of Hashabneiah
made repairs next to him. 11Malkijah son of Harim
and Hasshub son of Pahath-Moab repaired another

[a] 5 Or *their Lord* or *the governor* [b] 6 Or *Old* [c] 8 Or *They left out part of*

NRSV

3 Then the high priest Eliashib set to work
with his fellow priests and rebuilt the
Sheep Gate. They consecrated it and set up its
doors; they consecrated it as far as the Tower of
the Hundred and as far as the Tower of Hananel.
2And the men of Jericho built next to him. And
next to them[a] Zaccur son of Imri built.

3The sons of Hassenaah built the Fish Gate;
they laid its beams and set up its doors, its bolts,
and its bars. 4Next to them Meremoth son of
Uriah son of Hakkoz made repairs. Next to them
Meshullam son of Berechiah son of Meshezabel
made repairs. Next to them Zadok son of Baana
made repairs. 5Next to them the Tekoites made
repairs; but their nobles would not put their
shoulders to the work of their Lord.[b]

6Joiada son of Paseah and Meshullam son of
Besodeiah repaired the Old Gate; they laid its
beams and set up its doors, its bolts, and its bars.
7Next to them repairs were made by Melatiah the
Gibeonite and Jadon the Meronothite—the men
of Gibeon and of Mizpah—who were under the
jurisdiction of[c] the governor of the province Beyond the River. 8Next to them Uzziel son of
Harhaiah, one of the goldsmiths, made repairs.
Next to him Hananiah, one of the perfumers,
made repairs; and they restored Jerusalem as far
as the Broad Wall. 9Next to them Rephaiah son
of Hur, ruler of half the district of[d] Jerusalem,
made repairs. 10Next to them Jedaiah son of
Harumaph made repairs opposite his house; and
next to him Hattush son of Hashabneiah made
repairs. 11Malchijah son of Harim and Hasshub
son of Pahath-moab repaired another section and
the Tower of the Ovens. 12Next to him Shallum

[a] Heb *him* [b] Or *lords* [c] Meaning of Heb uncertain [d] Or *supervisor of half the portion assigned to*

NIV

section and the Tower of the Ovens. 12Shallum
son of Hallohesh, ruler of a half-district of Jerusalem, repaired the next section with the help of
his daughters.

13The Valley Gate was repaired by Hanun and
the residents of Zanoah. They rebuilt it and put
its doors and bolts and bars in place. They also
repaired five hundred yards[a] of the wall as far as
the Dung Gate.

14The Dung Gate was repaired by Malkijah son
of Recab, ruler of the district of Beth Hakkerem.
He rebuilt it and put its doors and bolts and bars
in place.

15The Fountain Gate was repaired by Shallun
son of Col-Hozeh, ruler of the district of Mizpah.
He rebuilt it, roofing it over and putting its doors
and bolts and bars in place. He also repaired the
wall of the Pool of Siloam,[b] by the King's Garden,
as far as the steps going down from the City of
David. 16Beyond him, Nehemiah son of Azbuk,
ruler of a half-district of Beth Zur, made repairs
up to a point opposite the tombs[c] of David, as far
as the artificial pool and the House of the Heroes.

17Next to him, the repairs were made by the
Levites under Rehum son of Bani. Beside him,
Hashabiah, ruler of half the district of Keilah,
carried out repairs for his district. 18Next to him,
the repairs were made by their countrymen under
Binnui[d] son of Henadad, ruler of the other half-
district of Keilah. 19Next to him, Ezer son of
Jeshua, ruler of Mizpah, repaired another section,
from a point facing the ascent to the armory as
far as the angle. 20Next to him, Baruch son of
Zabbai zealously repaired another section, from
the angle to the entrance of the house of Eliashib
the high priest. 21Next to him, Meremoth son of
Uriah, the son of Hakkoz, repaired another section, from the entrance of Eliashib's house to the
end of it.

22The repairs next to him were made by the
priests from the surrounding region. 23Beyond
them, Benjamin and Hasshub made repairs in
front of their house; and next to them, Azariah
son of Maaseiah, the son of Ananiah, made repairs

[a] *13* Hebrew *a thousand cubits* (about 450 meters) [b] *15* Hebrew *Shelah,* a variant of *Shiloah,* that is, Siloam [c] *16* Hebrew; Septuagint, some Vulgate manuscripts and Syriac *tomb* [d] *18* Two Hebrew manuscripts and Syriac (see also Septuagint and verse 24); most Hebrew manuscripts *Bavvai*

NRSV

son of Hallohesh, ruler of half the district of[a]
Jerusalem, made repairs, he and his daughters.

13Hanun and the inhabitants of Zanoah repaired the Valley Gate; they rebuilt it and set up
its doors, its bolts, and its bars, and repaired a
thousand cubits of the wall, as far as the Dung
Gate.

14Malchijah son of Rechab, ruler of the district
of[b] Beth-haccherem, repaired the Dung Gate; he
rebuilt it and set up its doors, its bolts, and its
bars.

15And Shallum son of Col-hozeh, ruler of the
district of[b] Mizpah, repaired the Fountain Gate;
he rebuilt it and covered it and set up its doors,
its bolts, and its bars; and he built the wall of the
Pool of Shelah of the king's garden, as far as the
stairs that go down from the City of David. 16After
him Nehemiah son of Azbuk, ruler of half the
district of[a] Beth-zur, repaired from a point opposite
the graves of David, as far as the artificial pool
and the house of the warriors. 17After him the
Levites made repairs: Rehum son of Bani; next to
him Hashabiah, ruler of half the district of[a] Keilah,
made repairs for his district. 18After him their kin
made repairs: Binnui,[c] son of Henadad, ruler of
half the district of[a] Keilah; 19next to him Ezer son
of Jeshua, ruler[d] of Mizpah, repaired another section opposite the ascent to the armory at the
Angle. 20After him Baruch son of Zabbai repaired
another section from the Angle to the door of the
house of the high priest Eliashib. 21After him
Meremoth son of Uriah son of Hakkoz repaired
another section from the door of the house of
Eliashib to the end of the house of Eliashib. 22After
him the priests, the men of the surrounding area,
made repairs. 23After them Benjamin and Hasshub
made repairs opposite their house. After them
Azariah son of Maaseiah son of Ananiah made
repairs beside his own house. 24After him Binnui
son of Henadad repaired another section, from the
house of Azariah to the Angle and to the corner.
25Palal son of Uzai repaired opposite the Angle
and the tower projecting from the upper house of
the king at the court of the guard. After him
Pedaiah son of Parosh 26and the temple servants

[a] Or *supervisor of half the portion assigned to* [b] Or *supervisor of the portion assigned to* [c] Gk Syr Compare verse 24, 10.9: Heb *Bavvai* [d] Or *supervisor*

NIV

beside his house. [24]Next to him, Binnui son of Henadad repaired another section, from Azariah's house to the angle and the corner, [25]and Palal son of Uzai worked opposite the angle and the tower projecting from the upper palace near the court of the guard. Next to him, Pedaiah son of Parosh [26]and the temple servants living on the hill of Ophel made repairs up to a point opposite the Water Gate toward the east and the projecting tower. [27]Next to them, the men of Tekoa repaired another section, from the great projecting tower to the wall of Ophel.

[28]Above the Horse Gate, the priests made repairs, each in front of his own house. [29]Next to them, Zadok son of Immer made repairs opposite his house. Next to him, Shemaiah son of Shecaniah, the guard at the East Gate, made repairs. [30]Next to him, Hananiah son of Shelemiah, and Hanun, the sixth son of Zalaph, repaired another section. Next to them, Meshullam son of Berekiah made repairs opposite his living quarters. [31]Next to him, Malkijah, one of the goldsmiths, made repairs as far as the house of the temple servants and the merchants, opposite the Inspection Gate, and as far as the room above the corner; [32]and between the room above the corner and the Sheep Gate the goldsmiths and merchants made repairs.

NRSV

living[a] on Ophel made repairs up to a point opposite the Water Gate on the east and the projecting tower. [27]After him the Tekoites repaired another section opposite the great projecting tower as far as the wall of Ophel.

28Above the Horse Gate the priests made repairs, each one opposite his own house. [29]After them Zadok son of Immer made repairs opposite his own house. After him Shemaiah son of Shecaniah, the keeper of the East Gate, made repairs. [30]After him Hananiah son of Shelemiah and Hanun sixth son of Zalaph repaired another section. After him Meshullam son of Berechiah made repairs opposite his living quarters. [31]After him Malchijah, one of the goldsmiths, made repairs as far as the house of the temple servants and of the merchants, opposite the Muster Gate,[b] and to the upper room of the corner. [32]And between the upper room of the corner and the Sheep Gate the goldsmiths and the merchants made repairs.

[a] Cn: Heb *were living* [b] Or *Hammiphkad Gate*

COMMENTARY

This list of those who worked on Nehemiah's wall is important for the topography of Jerusalem and the administration of Yehud in the Persian period, even if not all the gates and other topographical features can now be identified with absolute certainty. It is unlikely that Nehemiah himself wrote this chapter, since it is cast in the third person instead of in the first person. The writer mentions a group called "nobles" (אדירים *'addîrîm,* v. 5), a social class not referred to elsewhere in the Nehemiah Memoir (except in 10:30, where it should be emended into an adjective modifying "brothers"), and refers to Nehemiah as "lord" (v. 5). Nehemiah may have included this list in his memoir despite the fact that the list presupposes the completion of the wall, including the installation of doors, bolts, and bars (vv. 1, 3, 6, 13-15), whereas chap. 4 reports events that took place during the building of the wall and 6:1 and 7:1 reveal that the doors were hung later. Chapter 3 gives impressive evidence of Nehemiah's organizational and administrative skills and shows the widespread support for the wall-building project. The original purpose of the list is unknown.[130]

The importance of the list for understanding the administration of Yehud results from the men-

130. Kurt Galling, *Die Bücher der Chronik, Esra, Nehemia,* ATD 12 (Göttingen: Vandenhoeck & Ruprecht, 1954) 222, and Ulrich Kellermann, *Nehemia, Quellen, Überlieferung und Geschichte,* BZAW 102 (Berlin: de Gruyter, 1967) 14-16, believe it was some kind of administrative document. They also follow Rudolph's lead in concluding that Nehemiah included this document in his memoir. See Wilhelm Rudolph, *Esra und Nehemia,* HAT 20 (Tübingen: J. C. B. Mohr [Paul Siebeck], 1949) 113.

tion of a number of rulers over a "district" (פלך *pelek*) among the builders:

v. 9, ruler of half the district of Jerusalem
v. 12, ruler of half the district of Jerusalem
v. 14, ruler of the district of Beth-haccherem
v. 15, ruler of the district of Mizpah (see 3:19)
v. 16, ruler of half the district of Beth-Zur
v. 17, ruler of half the district of Keilah
v. 18, ruler of half the district of Keilah
v. 19, ruler of Mizpah (see 3:15)

Mention of only one half district of Beth-Zur suggests that the list may be incomplete, lacking the other half district named after this town. Beth-haccherem is the only clearly "whole" district mentioned. Neither of the references to Mizpah follows the expected pattern (ruler of half the district of); perhaps textual error has crept in during the course of transmission. The districts seem to be administrative units into which Yehud was divided. It is not clear whether the rulers of the half districts connected with Jerusalem, Keilah, and Mizpah (plus Beth-Zur?) lived in the cities named in their title and presided over separate subdistricts or whether a major administrative center (such as Jerusalem) had a secondary administrative center connected to it. Aharoni followed the first option and assumed that the other cities mentioned in this chapter were subdistricts, leading him to reconstruct the following administrative chart:[131]

City of Residence	**Subdistricts**
Keilah	Keilah, Zanoah
Beth-Zur	Beth-Zur, Tekoa
Beth-haccherem	Beth-haccherem
Jerusalem	Jerusalem, Gibeon
Mizpah	Mizpah, Jericho

Blenkinsopp followed the second option and reconstructed a list of six districts, with each divided into a principal and a secondary administrative center and a secondary one, which can be charted in the following manner:[132]

Principal Administrative Center	**Secondary Center**
Jerusalem	Netophah
Beth-zur	Tekoa
Keilah	Adullam
Beth-haccherem	Zanoah
Mizpah	Gibeon
Jericho	Senaah

Both of these proposals are conjectural. More cautious textual changes would allow the reconstruction of two half districts connected with Jerusalem, Keilah, Mizpah (the readings in vv. 15 and 19 are adjusted to the predominant pattern), and Beth-zur (mention of one half district implies that there were two half districts associated with this city), and a one-part district at Beth-haccherem, for a total of nine districts or subdistricts. The province of Yehud was only about half as big as pre-exilic Judah.

The use of the word "built" (בנה *bānâ*, vv. 1-3, with reference to the north side of the city) suggests that this area was severely damaged by the Babylonian invasion of 587 BCE (cf. 2 Kgs 25:4, 9-10). The list distinguishes between areas that had to be built (*bānâ;* 7 times in vv. 1-3, 13-15) and those that had only to be repaired (החזיק *heḥĕzîq*, in the hiphil; 35 times in vv. 4-24; 27-32). For the western and southern walls Nehemiah may only have needed to carry further the work that had been interrupted by the earlier decree of Artaxerxes (Ezra 4:7-24). Despite the use of the word "repaired" (*heḥĕzîq*) in vv. 16-32, the northern half of the eastern wall must have been all new construction, since archaeological findings have shown that the destruction of the pre-exilic city wall on the eastern slope of the hill caused catastrophic erosion to the terraced hillside.[133] The references to urban features other than gates and the high number of work gangs noted in vv. 16-32 may also show that the most severe damage was on the east side. Note the uneven distribution of work gangs:

north wall	8 work gangs	vv. 1-5
west wall	10 work gangs	vv. 6-13
south wall	2 work gangs	vv. 14-15
east wall	21 work gangs	vv. 16-32

131. Yohanan Aharoni, *The Land of the Bible: A Historical Geography*, trans. A. F. Rainey (Philadelphia: Westminster, 1979).

132. Joseph Blenkinsopp, *Ezra–Nehemiah*, OTL (Philadelphia: Westminster, 1988) 235-36.

133. Kathleen Kenyon, *Digging up Jerusalem* (London: Benn, 1974) 183-84.

There are significant differences in form and content between vv. 1-15 and vv. 16-32. In the first half of the list (vv. 1-15), the work gangs are separated by the expression "next to him/them,"[134] whereas in the rest of the list (vv. 16-32; vv. 17 and 19 are exceptions to the rule) the work gangs are separated by the words "after him." The "next to" formula seems to be used when an old wall is being repaired or rebuilt, whereas the "after him" formula appears when the builders are erecting a new stretch of wall on the crest of Ophel. When gates or topographical features are mentioned on the east side, it is only for purposes of orientation rather than for rebuilding or repairing. A worker or the work gangs are said to be "opposite" a given feature (vv. 16-31; cf. v. 10). All six gates mentioned in vv. 1-15 from the north, west, and south are rebuilt or repaired, including the installation of new doors. The additional topographical features that are mentioned on the north, west, and south are part of the wall itself. The chapter does not seem to be a combination of separate lists, since there is no overlapping of data and since there are gangs that worked on two sections, one of them appearing in each half of the list.

The list of those gangs that worked on two sections do not seem to have been completely preserved. The Masoretic Text (MT) offers the following information on those who worked on "another section":

Verses	Heads of Work Gangs	Locations
4	Meremoth son of Uriah son of Hakkoz	N wall
21	Meremoth son of Uriah son of Hakkoz	E wall (another section)
5	Tekoites	N wall
27	Tekoites	E wall (another section)
*11	Malchijah son of Harim and Hasshub son of Pahath-Moab	W wall (another section)
18	Binnui son of Hedad	E wall
24	Binnui son of Hedad	E wall (another section)
*19	Ezer son of Jeshua	W wall (another section)
*20	Baruch	E wall (another section)
*30	Hananiah son of Shecaniah and Hanun sixth son of Zalaph	E wall (another section

134. The suffixes on אחר ('*aḥar*) are frequently inaccurate. Singular suffixes appear for plurals and vice versa. In v. 23 (twice) and v. 29 the NRSV and the NIV have changed "after him" to "after them."

In four of the seven references to a second wall section (marked with an asterisk), the MT does not supply the information for the first section. Half of this defect, however, can be repaired. A man named Hasshub (v. 23; cf. v. 11) is mentioned among those who worked on the E wall, and Hananiah (v. 8) and Hanun (v. 13) are mentioned as being among the workers on the W wall (cf. v. 30). Hence information on both sections is probably attested in the list. We cannot tell on which other sections the gangs of Ezer and Baruch worked. The list is also defective in not identifying explicitly all the groups that worked on two sections. Verse 30 should note that Meshullam, son of Berechiah, worked on "another section," since information about his first work gang is supplied in v. 4.

Ten gates are referred to in a counterclockwise direction in this chapter. The first six are "built" or "repaired"; the last four are mentioned only to supply topographical orientation. The following identifications can be made (see "Nehemiah's Reconstruction of the Wall of Jerusalem," 760):

1. Sheep Gate (vv. 1, 32; see also 12:39 and perhaps Ezek 9:2 [upper gate, which faces north]). A city gate in the eastern half of the northern wall, this gate was probably next to a market that sold sacrificial sheep. It is in the vicinity of the later Pool of Bethesda (John 5:2) and the Crusader church of St. Anne.

2. Fish Gate (v. 3; see also 12:38-39). This gate in the northwest corner of the city got its name from the fish markets in the immediate vicinity (see also 13:16). The Fish Gate is mentioned in the chronicler's account of Manasseh (2 Chr 33:14; see also Zeph 1:10).

3. Mishneh Gate (v. 6; see also 12:39). The name of this gate is based on a simple emendation of the Hebrew text: המשנה (*hammišāneh*, "Mishneh") replaces הישנה (*hayěšnâ*, "Old"). "Old Gate" (NRSV) is an impossible combination of a feminine adjective and a masculine noun. "Jeshanah Gate" (NIV), while grammatically possible, is quite unusual; Jeshanah (see 2 Chr 13:19) is a relatively insignificant town near Bethel, and a gate leading to it should be on the north side of the city instead of on the west, as is this gate. The Mishneh Gate would have led into the Second Quarter of the city, or Mishneh (2 Kgs 22:14; 2 Chr 34:22; Zeph 1:10), although its exact location is unknown. Some identify it with the Corner Gate, where Uzziah built towers after Jehoash of Israel had broken down the wall (2 Kgs 14:13; 2 Chr 25:23; 26:9).[135] In 12:3, however, the Mishneh Gate is north of the Ephraim Gate, itself 200 yards north of the Corner Gate.

4. Valley Gate (v. 13; see Commentary on 2:13)—a gate on the west side of Ophel, overlooking the Tyropoeon Valley. It had been fortified by Uzziah, according to 2 Chr 26:9.

5. Dung Gate (vv. 13-14; see Commentary on 2:13)—a gate at the southern end of the city, about 500 yards (1,000 cubits) south of the Valley Gate.

6. Fountain Gate (v. 15; see Commentary on 2:14). This gate was in the southeastern corner of the city, leading apparently to En Rogel, a spring about 215 yards south of where the Hinnom and Kidron valleys meet. This is the only gate that was given a new roof.

7. Water Gate (v. 26; see also 12:37). This was a city gate in pre-exilic Jerusalem, located near the Gihon Spring. Since Nehemiah built his city wall farther up on Ophel at this point, the Water Gate was not included in his defensive works. Thus the text mentions only the Water Gate on the east, without reporting any work on it.

8. Horse Gate (v. 28). A gate in the outer defensive wall, also mentioned in Jer 31:40, this was located in the temple area, near the southeast corner of present-day Haram esh-Sharif. Thus priests were assigned to repair this gate. It should be distinguished from "the horses' entrance to the king's house" (2 Kgs 11:16; 2 Chr 23:15).

9. East Gate (v. 29)—a gate of the temple court, not the city (see Ezek 10:19; 11:1; 40:6). It was repaired by Shemaiah, apparently a Levite.

10. Muster Gate (v. 31; NIV, "Inspection Gate"). This may be either another gate of the temple court, before which the assembly dealing with mixed marriages was held (Ezra 10:9), or another city gate. Williamson suggests that it should be identified with the Benjamin Gate at the northernmost point of the eastern side of the city (Jer 37:13; 38:7; Zech 14:10; see also 2 Chr 32:6).[136]

3:1-2, The Sheep Gate. Eliashib the high priest headed the first work gang (v. 1; see also 12:10, 22; 13:28). Although he and his priestly crew "consecrated" the Sheep Gate, he is strangely absent at the dedication of the wall in 12:27-43. The Tower of the Hundred and the Tower of Hananel (Jer 31:38; Zech 14:10) were apparently part of the fortress located northwest of the Temple (2:8; cf. 7:2). This was also the site of the Hasmonean baris (the Greek word for "fortress") and Herod's Antonia Fortress. These towers were just east of the Fish Gate (12:39) or even framed that gate. The "men of Jericho" (v. 2) are also mentioned in Ezra 2:34, where 345 people were counted from that city. Zaccur (v. 2) is probably not to be identified with one of the men with the same name listed in 8:14; 10:12; and 13:13.

3:3-5, The Fish Gate. The sons of Hassenaah (v. 3) may be people from Senaah, a town eight miles northeast of Jericho. This place is also mentioned in Ezra 2:35, where 3,630 residents are counted. Blenkinsopp believes that the people of Jericho and Senaah staffed one district with two administrative centers in the Jordan Valley.[137] The "bolts" on the doors were metal brackets into which wooden or bronze bars were dropped on the inside (cf. vv. 6, 13-15). The family of Hakkoz, an ancestor of Meremoth (v. 4), had been unable to prove its ancestry in the early post-exilic period (7:63; Ezra 2:61), although by the time of Ezra, Meremoth had become a trusted cultic official in charge of the temple treasury (Ezra 8:33). The daughter of Meshullam (v. 4) later married Jehohanan, the son of Nehemiah's rival Tobiah (6:18; cf. the marriage of Eliashib's grandson to the daughter of Sanballat in 13:28). Zadok's father, Baana, appears among the families who signed the

135. Dale C. Liid, "Corner Gate," *ABD* (1992) 1:1156, however, locates the Corner Gate at the western end of the eighth-century "broad wall," which, of course, was not included in the city of Nehemiah's time.

136. H. G. M. Williamson, *Ezra, Nehemiah,* WBC 16 (Waco, Tex.: Word, 1985) 211.

137. Blenkinsopp, *Ezra–Nehemiah,* 233

firm agreement in 10:27. Another Zadok appears in this list in v. 29. The people of Tekoa (v. 5; cf. v. 27, where a second work gang of Tekoites is mentioned despite the failure of their leadership noted in v. 5) came from the hometown of Amos, about twelve miles south of Jerusalem and three and three-quarters miles north of Hebron. The inhabitants of Tekoa are not listed among those who returned from exile in Ezra 2 and Nehemiah 7. Perhaps they had never been in exile. (None of the district administrative centers are mentioned in the list of those who returned in Ezra 2:21-35.) Their "nobles" dissented from the work of Nehemiah. Had they been influenced by Geshem (2:19), who was active in the south? Instead of "their Lord" (NRSV) or "their supervisors" (NIV) in v. 5, we should probably translate the word אדניהם (*'ădōnêhem*) as "their lord," understanding the noun as a majestic plural referring to Nehemiah.

3:6-12, The Mishneh Gate. The first work gang on the west wall was led by Joiada son of Paseah (v. 6), perhaps a descendant of one of the temple servants who returned from Babylon (Ezra 2:49). Meshullam (v. 6) is unknown. Melatiah and Jadon, from Gibeon and Meronoth (a town near Gibeon; cf. 1 Chr 27:30), respectively, worked with the people from Gibeon (five miles northwest of Jerusalem) and Mizpah (eight miles north of Jerusalem). The last clause of v. 7 (after the dash in the NRSV and the NIV) should be translated, "the seat of the governor of Beyond the River." That is, Mizpah was the place where the governor of the satrapy stayed when he visited Yehud. Gedaliah, appointed governor by the Babylonians after the fall of Jerusalem, also had his residence there (2 Kgs 25:23, 25; Jeremiah 40–41). Uzziel and Hananiah (v. 8) are unknown, but they were part of the goldsmiths' and the perfumers' guilds, who plied their trade in the region just west of the Mishneh Gate. Both the NRSV and the NIV follow Ugaritic and Sabaean etymologies when they translate יעזבו (*ya'azĕbû*), the last verb in v. 8, as "restored" (cf. 4:2).[138] The "Broad Wall" (v. 8; cf. 12:38) may refer to the point where the portion of the city wall that has been excavated by Avigad in the modern-day Jewish Quarter rejoined the old western city wall. Rephaiah (v. 9), judging by his ancestor's name Hur, stemmed from an old Calebite (1 Chr 2:19-20) or Judahite (1 Chr 4:1) family that may never have gone into exile. Harumaph (v. 10) is a nickname meaning "mutilated nose" or "cleft nose." His son Jedaiah and a number of others worked on the portion of the wall facing their own house (vv. 10, 23-24, 28-30; cf. vv. 16, 20-21, 31). Hattush (v. 10) may be one of those who signed the firm agreement in 10:4. Malchijah son of Harim (v. 11; see also vv. 14, 31) is mentioned among those who divorced their wives in Ezra 10:31, though both names are common, and Harim may be a distant ancestor rather than his immediate father. Pahath-Moab (v. 11) is one of the families that returned from exile (Ezra 2:6). The Tower of the Ovens (v. 11; 12:38), exact site unknown, designates bakery ovens (cf. Jer 37:21) or pottery kilns. Shallum (v. 12) was the descendant of Hallohesh (the "whisperer," the "charmer"), a person named among those who signed the firm agreement (10:24). Note that Shallum's daughters made up his work crew. No other women are mentioned in the list, but this does not permit us to emend "daughters" to "sons," as was done in one medieval Hebrew manuscript and the Syriac.

3:13-14, The Valley Gate and the Dung Gate. Hanun and the inhabitants of Zanoah (located fourteen miles southwest of Jerusalem; see also 11:30) repaired a long stretch of wall, some 1,000 cubits (500 yards) between the Valley Gate and the Dung Gates, suggesting that this part of the wall may have needed only minor repairs.

Malchijah (v. 14), a descendant of the Kenite family of Rechab (1 Chr 2:55), was in charge of the work on the Dung Gate at the south end of the city (see 2:13; 12:31). Beth-haccherem, an administrative center, is usually identified with Ramat Rachel, two miles south of Jerusalem.

3:15-24, The Fountain Gate. The ancestor of Shallum (v. 15; MT and NIV, "Shallun"), ruler of Mizpah, was "Col-hozeh" ("one who sees all," a mantic?), a name found also in 11:5. The wall of the Pool of Shelah (NIV, "Siloam") of the king's garden (2 Kgs 25:4; Jer 39:4; 52:7) may be the

138. H. G. M. Williamson, "Nehemiah's Wall Revisited," *PEQ* 116 (1984) 81-88, defends the translation "left out," suggesting that Nehemiah left out part of Jerusalem as far as the Broad Wall. Blenkinsopp, *Ezra–Nehemiah,* 230, rightly insists that (*ya' azĕbû*) cannot have this meaning and supports "restored."

same as the Pool of Shiloah (Isa 8:6), located by Wilkinson at modern-day Birket el-Hamra, to the south of the Fountain Gate.[139] The stairs going down from the City of David (v. 15) may have led into the Kidron Valley from the Fountain Gate.

The portion of the east wall north of the Fountain Gate was probably built at a new, much higher location on the crest of Ophel, as archaeological findings have shown. Azbuk, the ancestor of the Nehemiah mentioned in v. 16, has a non-Israelite name ("[The god] Buk is mighty"). The district administrative center at Beth-zur is located three and three-quarter miles north of Hebron (see Josh 15:58). Opposite Nehemiah's repair site were "the graves of David" (v. 16). This notice may reflect the pre-exilic tradition of locating royal burials within the City of David (e.g., 1 Kgs 2:10; 11:43; 14:31; see also Acts 2:29). The artificial pool (v. 16) is probably the same as the King's Pool (2:14), outside the city wall and north of the Fountain Gate. The "house of the warriors" is unknown (cf. 2 Sam 23:8-39).

Levites form the next series of work gangs, beginning in v. 17, although it is not clear how far the list of Levites extends. Bani, the ancestor of Rehum (v. 17), is listed among the Levites in 10:13 (see also 8:7; 9:5; 11:22). Hashabiah (v. 17) appears among the Levites in 10:11; 11:15, 22; 12:24; and Ezra 8:19. Keilah, his administrative center, is located about seventeen miles southwest of Jerusalem (see Josh 15:44). Binnui (v. 18; MT, "Bavvai") son of Hedad is unknown, though both the name "Binnui" and the sons of Henadad occur in Ezra 3:9. "Their kin" (v. 18) suggests that the names in this verse are still Levites. Jeshua, father of Ezer (v. 19), may be the person mentioned in Ezra 2:40 and 3:9. The location of Ezer's work on the wall is unclear; the "Angle" may refer to a buttress or an escarpment (v. 19; see also vv. 20, 24-25; 2 Chr 26:9). The "armory" (v. 19) is unknown.

Zabbai, father of Baruch (v. 20), may be the layperson mentioned in Ezra 10:28 or, if his name is to be read as "Zaccai,"[140] he may be identified with the family named in Ezra 2:9. The house of the high priest Eliashib serves as an orientation point in vv. 20-21. The word translated "zealously" in the NIV (v. 20) is most uncertain; it is deleted as a dittography (the accidental repetition of letters or words), in the NRSV (without notifying the reader).[141] Meremoth's second work assignment (v. 21; see also v. 4) seems very narrow—less than a house wide!

The priests for the next work gang (v. 22) were drawn from towns in the surrounding area, perhaps, from the Jordan Valley (the usual meaning of כִּכָּר [*kikkār*]; see, e.g., Gen 13:10-12; 19:28). Benjamin and Hasshub (v. 23) shared a house, and their names are common and hence unidentifiable with persons named elsewhere (for Benjamin, see Ezra 10:32; for Hasshub, see Ezra 3:11; 11:15). Azariah's genealogy (v. 23) is given for two previous generations, but the three names are so common that little can be derived from a study of them, except to note that all of them contain the divine name "Yahweh." For Binnui (v. 24), see v. 18. The mention of a "corner" in v. 24 suggests a change in the direction of the wall, although it still ran more or less south to north. Palal (v. 25) is unknown, but Parosh, the ancestor of Pedaiah, appears as a layperson in Ezra 2:3 and Neh 10:14, and Pedaiah himself is listed as a lay leader in Neh 8:4. The "projecting tower" in vv. 25-27 is part of the "upper house of the king at the court of the guard" (v. 25). The court of the guard is part of the palace, according to Jer 32:2. The topographical notices in these verses still seem to be south of the Gihon Spring and, therefore, farther south than we would expect the palace to be.[142]

3:25-27, The Water Gate. In pre-exilic Jerusalem, this gate was down the slope of Ophel, near the Gihon Spring. The text of v. 26 locates Pedaiah's workstation to the west of the gate, in the direction of the projecting tower, without suggesting that a water gate was included in Nehemiah's wall. For the Tekoites (v. 27), see v. 5. Their work extended from the projecting tower up to the wall of Ophel, an east-west wall around the northern part of the Ophel, which had been rebuilt in the days of Jotham (2 Chr 27:3).

3:28-30, The Horse Gate. This gate was in the temple area, and so a group of priests (cf. vv. 1, 22) did the repair work opposite their own

139. J. Wilkinson, "The Pool of Siloam," *Levant* 10 (1978) 116-25.
140. See *BHS* 20[b].

141. Cf. *BHS* 20[a].
142. Blenkinsopp, *Ezra–Nehemiah,* 238, considers "from the upper house of the king" to be an incorrect gloss. He also deletes "and the temple servants living on Ophel" from v. 26 as a mistaken gloss drawn from 11:21.

houses. The priests worked above this pre-exilic gate—that is, the line of Nehemiah's wall was still along the crest. Immer, the father of Zadok (v. 29), is mentioned among the ancestors of the priests in Ezra 2:37; 1,052 people traced their lineage to him. A priest named Zadok appears in Neh 10:21. Shemaiah (v. 29), otherwise unknown, was a gatekeeper (cf. 10:28; 11:19; Ezra 2:42; see also Ezek 44:11) and repaired the area around the East Gate. For Hananiah (v. 30), see v. 8. Hanun (v. 30), who may be the same person who worked with the people of Zanoah (v. 13), is identified by the unusual designation "sixth son." For Meshullam (v. 30), see v. 4. His living quarters were one of the priestly apartments in the Temple (see 12:44; 13:7; Ezra 10:6).

3:31-32, The Muster Gate. Malchijah is unknown; two others in the list also bear this name (vv. 11, 14). For goldsmiths, see v. 8. "The house of the temple servants [Nethinim] and the merchants" may indicate the symbiotic relationship between the Nethinim, who had to supply various provisions for the sacrificial system (like the Gibeonites in Josh 9:27) and those who did business with worshipers coming to the Temple. Since the Nethinim actually lived on Ophel (11:26; see also the gloss in 3:26), their "house" was apparently the place where they carried out their cultic activities. In the northeast corner of the city (v. 32), there were also goldsmiths and merchants to provide services to temple visitors. The "upper room at the corner" may refer to a watch tower on the northeast point of the city. Between this watch tower and the Sheep Gate the last gang did its work. Note that the chapter begins and ends with the Sheep Gate (vv. 1, 32).

REFLECTIONS

Lists in Ezra and Nehemiah often take the place of narrative accounts. Cyrus's authorization for the Jews to return home in Ezra 1 is followed by a list of those who returned home from exile in Ezra 2. With such a full list, there was no need for a narrative account of the arduous journey home. After Ezra 7:1-5 reports the priestly genealogy of Ezra and the king's commissioning of Ezra (Ezra 7:12-26), there follows a list of all those who came home with Ezra (Ezra 8:1-20), including some Levites whom he had to recruit energetically. The actual return home is reported rather laconically in Ezra 8:21-36. So it is with the great third act in these books, the building of the wall. Nehemiah 1–2 reports that Nehemiah came to Jerusalem and discovered the poor condition of the city's defenses. There follows immediately a list of those who worked on the wall, anticipating the work and the rededication that would come.

Instead of telling of Nehemiah's efforts to recruit workers and coordinate the building of the wall, chapter 3 indicates through a list that all segments of the community supported the project and completed it. The high priest Eliashib headed the list of workers, followed closely by Meshullam, even though both of them would later offend Nehemiah through intermarriages between their descendants and descendants of some of Nehemiah's opponents. Priests and Levites participated as well, and laypeople were hardly underrepresented. Nehemiah was apparently able and willing to work with all the structures of society. Eight rulers from the administrative districts (counties or townships?) of Yehud did their share on the wall, as well as did people from other cities, like Tekoa, Jericho, Seenah, Zanoach, and Gibeon. Plotting the cities on a map shows us the size and shape of the post-exilic province. Merchants were there, too, not to mention the guilds of skilled workers, especially goldsmiths and the perfumers. One ruler even enlisted his daughters for the work crew.

It has been noted that the list seems to appear too early in the account, that it was not written by Nehemiah, and that it may well be incomplete. But the fact that it reports a complete circumvalation of the city and describes gates fully fitted out with doors, bars, and bolts signifies a mission that has been accomplished. This relativizes the threats from Sanballat, Tobiah, the Arabs, the Ammonites, and the Ashdodites—the foes who will completely surround the little community in chapter 4. Their threats and mockeries can be taken somewhat dispassionately by the reader who has already seen the list of those who successfully completed the wall.

Even though God and the Temple are never mentioned, no sacrifices are offered, and there are no prayers or hymns in this chapter, we see in this list how God works with work gangs from every segment of society to realize fully the divine plans and promises. Hard as it is for us today to identify gates, topographical features, and even the people in this chapter, chapter 3 clearly consists of a list that has not been invented—no one who forged a list would leave so many obscurities and ambiguities. Nehemiah's leadership is clear, without his name's ever being mentioned and without his having to tout his own accomplishments.

The whole community participated; the task was in fact completed. We know the outcome of Nehemiah's mission before he tells us about it. God's grace and Persian kindness enabled Nehemiah and the entire population to rebuild the wall of Jerusalem, which had lain waste since 587 BCE. All attempts to stop this wall are characterized in advance as useless.

NEHEMIAH 4:1-23, NEHEMIAH'S PROVISIONS FOR THE DEFENSE OF JERUSALEM

Nehemiah 4:1-12, External and Internal Threats

NIV

4 When Sanballat heard that we were rebuilding the wall, he became angry and
was greatly incensed. He ridiculed the Jews, 2and
in the presence of his associates and the army of
Samaria, he said, "What are those feeble Jews
doing? Will they restore their wall? Will they offer
sacrifices? Will they finish in a day? Can they
bring the stones back to life from those heaps of
rubble—burned as they are?"

3Tobiah the Ammonite, who was at his side,
said, "What they are building—if even a fox
climbed up on it, he would break down their wall
of stones!"

4Hear us, O our God, for we are despised. Turn
their insults back on their own heads. Give them
over as plunder in a land of captivity. 5Do not
cover up their guilt or blot out their sins from
your sight, for they have thrown insults in the
face of[a] the builders.

6So we rebuilt the wall till all of it reached half
its height, for the people worked with all their heart.

[a] 5 Or *have provoked you to anger before*

NRSV

4[a] Now when Sanballat heard that we were
building the wall, he was angry and greatly
enraged, and he mocked the Jews. 2He said in
the presence of his associates and of the army of
Samaria, "What are these feeble Jews doing? Will
they restore things? Will they sacrifice? Will they
finish it in a day? Will they revive the stones out
of the heaps of rubbish—and burned ones at
that?" 3Tobiah the Ammonite was beside him, and
he said, "That stone wall they are building—any
fox going up on it would break it down!" 4Hear,
O our God, for we are despised; turn their taunt
back on their own heads, and give them over as
plunder in a land of captivity. 5Do not cover their
guilt, and do not let their sin be blotted out from
your sight; for they have hurled insults in the face
of the builders.

6So we rebuilt the wall, and all the wall was
joined together to half its height; for the people
had a mind to work.

7[b]But when Sanballat and Tobiah and the Arabs
and the Ammonites and the Ashdodites heard that
the repairing of the walls of Jerusalem was going

[a] Ch 3.33 in Heb [b] Ch 4.1 in Heb

NIV

7But when Sanballat, Tobiah, the Arabs, the Ammonites and the men of Ashdod heard that the repairs to Jerusalem's walls had gone ahead and that the gaps were being closed, they were very angry. 8They all plotted together to come and fight against Jerusalem and stir up trouble against it. 9But we prayed to our God and posted a guard day and night to meet this threat.

10Meanwhile, the people in Judah said, "The strength of the laborers is giving out, and there is so much rubble that we cannot rebuild the wall."

11Also our enemies said, "Before they know it or see us, we will be right there among them and will kill them and put an end to the work."

12Then the Jews who lived near them came and told us ten times over, "Wherever you turn, they will attack us."

NRSV

forward and the gaps were beginning to be closed, they were very angry, 8and all plotted together to come and fight against Jerusalem and to cause confusion in it. 9So we prayed to our God, and set a guard as a protection against them day and night.

10But Judah said, "The strength of the burden bearers is failing, and there is too much rubbish so that we are unable to work on the wall." 11And our enemies said, "They will not know or see anything before we come upon them and kill them and stop the work." 12When the Jews who lived near them came, they said to us ten times, "From all the places where they live[a] they will come up against us."[d]

[a] Cn: Heb *you return* [d] Compare Gk Syr: Meaning of Heb uncertain

COMMENTARY

This chapter identifies external and internal threats to the building project and the measures taken by Nehemiah to counter these threats. The chapter division in English Bibles is superior because all the material in the passage comes from the Nehemiah Memoir and is not a continuation of the list in chap. 3. In the Hebrew Bible, the fourth chapter begins with what is v. 7 in English versions.

The first external threat to the wall-building process was posed by Sanballat and Tobiah. When Sanballat heard about the progress on the wall, he was angry and mocked the Jews (v. 1; see also 2:19). In the presence of his allies (lit., brothers) and the army of Samaria he posed five questions designed to deprecate the building project in Jerusalem (v. 2). Both his anger and these threatening words show his desperation.

Sanballat's questions are loaded with sarcasm, even if the fine nuances of his words are not always clear to us. First he asked what the "feeble" Jews were doing. A connotation of "forlorn" or "impotent" should be included in the adjective "feeble." Both the NRSV and the NIV assign a rare meaning, "restore," to the verb עזב (*ʿāzab*) in the second question (see also 3:8). It may be better to use the common meaning "abandon" and emend להם (*lāhem*) in 4:2[3:34] to לאלהים (*lĕʾlōhîm*).[143] The question then can be translated: "Will they leave everything to God" (cf. Ps 10:14)? That is, do they expect a miracle to aid them in building the wall? The reference to sacrifices in the third question again mocks the community's dependence on God, expressed through their liturgical practices. The fourth question makes fun of the Jews for thinking they can finish this project in record time—in one day. Sanballat's fifth question discredits the building materials the Jews are using. We might paraphrase it: "Do they think they can bring to life stones from the ruined wall so that the wall will build itself?" The stones showed soot marks from the destruction of 587 BCE, and such fire damage, in Sanballat's judgment, called into question the stability of the stones.

Tobiah also verbally attacked the Jews' workmanship and the quality of their building materials. He suggested that if a nimble fox, traditionally associated with city ruins (Ps 63:10; Lam 5:18) were to jump up on their wall, it would knock

143. *BHS* 34[c].

the wall over (v. 3). The wall Kathleen Kenyon identified as Nehemiah's in her excavations is in fact of second-rate quality![144] Tobiah's words contain an implicit threat: If he were to attack the wall, it would surely fall.

Nehemiah's response to these verbal threats is also only verbal, an imprecatory prayer (cf. 6:14; 13:29; and the frequent use of such prayers elsewhere: Pss 10:15; 35; 58:6-9; 59:5; 69:22-28; 79:12; 109:6-19; Jer 15:15; 18:21-23). The opening of the prayer indicates that God ought to hear and respond, just as Sanballat had heard and responded (4:1; cf. 4:7). The words "our God" express the faith of Nehemiah, and he reminds God of the despised (2:19) and taunted (1:3; 2:17) condition of the post-exilic community. He wants God's punishment to fit the crime of the enemies: They should receive taunts on their own heads (cf. Ps 7:16; Ezek 9:10; Joel 3:4) and be despised in a land of captivity, just as the Jewish community had recently been despised in Babylon. His petition for God not to forgive the enemies' sins is remarkably similar to Jer 18:23. He based these harsh requests on the actions of the enemies (cf. 1 Kgs 21:22): "They have hurled insults against you in the presence of the builders." "You" is not explicit in the Hebrew text, but the context clearly implies this reference to God. Both the NRSV and the NIV misconstrue v. 5 as a diatribe against the builders (but see the NIV footnote). Verse 5 also offers a clarification of the setting indicated in v. 2: The words of Sanballat and Tobiah, while delivered first of all to their own supporters, were meant to be heard by the Jews working on the wall (cf. 2 Kgs 18:26). Their verbal threats were psychological warfare. Nehemiah concludes that any enemy of his project is an enemy of God.

The first external threat (vv. 1-3), countered by an imprecatory prayer (vv. 4-5), is followed by a report of continuing progress on the wall (v. 6). In fact, the whole wall had now been "joined together" up to half of its expected height. The speeches of Sanballat and Tobiah, which were somehow reported to the builders, do not succeed in undermining Jewish morale. Nehemiah notes that the people have worked on the wall with all their heart.

The second external threat comes from Sanballat in the north and a group of hostile peoples surrounding Judah on the other three sides: the Arabs, under the influence of Geshem, to the south; the Ammonites to the east; and the Ashdodites to the west. The Ashdodites had been part of a separate Philistine province since 711 BCE, when they had been defeated by the Assyrians under Sargon. All of these enemies are described as exceedingly angry over the news that the walls of Jerusalem were being repaired (lit., "healed," referring to flesh growing over a wound [Isa 58:8; Jer 8:22; 30:17; 33:6]; in 2 Chr 24:13 the word is also used of wall repairs), and the gaps were beginning to be closed. The (closed) "gaps" (הפרצים *happĕruṣîm*, 4:1) form an ironic pun with the verb describing how a fox would "knock over" (פרץ *pāraṣ*, 4:3) the wall in Tobiah's threat. The walls were not broken down as Tobiah had threatened, but their gaps were being closed up. All the adversaries, therefore, "conspired" (יקשרו [*yiqšĕrû*, "plotted together"] in v. 8[4:2] forms an ironic contrast to תקשר [*tiqqāšēr*, "joined together"] in v. 6[3:38]) to fight against Jerusalem and to create social havoc (cf. Isa 32:6, where the people's "error" results in social injustice). Their verbal threats had been transformed into mobilization for violence.

Nehemiah and the Judeans again resort to prayer (v. 9), but because the character of the threat has changed, they also appoint a guard against these adversaries day and night. Deeds had been added to words on both sides.

In addition to these two external threats, the community was in danger of collapsing internally. Judah began to recite a depressing little poem or song (v. 10), written in the lament, or Qinah, meter (neither the NRSV nor the NIV parses the quotation as poetry).[145] "Burden bearers" (הסבל *hassabbāl*) and "we are unable" (לא נוכל *lōʾ nûkal*) have end rhyme in Hebrew. The people had grown tired of carrying rocks and rubble, and the remaining tasks seemed overwhelming. They felt incapable of completing the wall.

Another internal threat is reflected in the remarks of the enemies in v. 11. They describe the Judeans as not being alert, unable to see an attack until the enemies had fallen upon them, killed

144. See K. Kenyon, *Jerusalem: Excavating 3000 Years of History* (London: Benn, 1974) 54.

145. Cf. *BHS*.

them, and stopped the work. A lack of concentration threatened doom for Judah.

A third internal threat came from those Jews who lived near the enemies (v. 12). Although the NRSV and the NIV emend the text of v. 12 in different ways, plausible sense can be gained from the MT: "When the Jews who lived near them came to us, they said to us ten times from all their places, 'Won't you return to us?' " That is, the people living near the border of Judah feared that enemy attack would hit them first and so begged their colleagues to desert the wall-building project and come home. "Ten times" is a conventional way of saying "time after time" (e.g., Gen 31:7, 41; Lev 26:26; Num 14:22; 1 Sam 1:8; Job 19:3). (See Reflections at 4:13-23.)

Nehemiah 4:13-23, Nehemiah's Response

NIV

13Therefore I stationed some of the people behind the lowest points of the wall at the exposed places, posting them by families, with their swords, spears and bows. 14After I looked things over, I stood up and said to the nobles, the officials and the rest of the people, "Don't be afraid of them. Remember the Lord, who is great and awesome, and fight for your brothers, your sons and your daughters, your wives and your homes."

15When our enemies heard that we were aware of their plot and that God had frustrated it, we all returned to the wall, each to his own work.

16From that day on, half of my men did the work, while the other half were equipped with spears, shields, bows and armor. The officers posted themselves behind all the people of Judah 17who were building the wall. Those who carried materials did their work with one hand and held a weapon in the other, 18and each of the builders wore his sword at his side as he worked. But the man who sounded the trumpet stayed with me.

19Then I said to the nobles, the officials and the rest of the people, "The work is extensive and spread out, and we are widely separated from each other along the wall. 20Wherever you hear the sound of the trumpet, join us there. Our God will fight for us!"

21So we continued the work with half the men holding spears, from the first light of dawn till the stars came out. 22At that time I also said to the people, "Have every man and his helper stay inside Jerusalem at night, so they can serve us as guards by night and workmen by day." 23Neither I nor my brothers nor my men nor the guards

NRSV

13So in the lowest parts of the space behind the wall, in open places, I stationed the people according to their families,[a] with their swords, their spears, and their bows. 14After I looked these things over, I stood up and said to the nobles and the officials and the rest of the people, "Do not be afraid of them. Remember the LORD, who is great and awesome, and fight for your kin, your sons, your daughters, your wives, and your homes."

15When our enemies heard that their plot was known to us, and that God had frustrated it, we all returned to the wall, each to his work. 16From that day on, half of my servants worked on construction, and half held the spears, shields, bows, and body-armor; and the leaders posted themselves behind the whole house of Judah, 17who were building the wall. The burden bearers carried their loads in such a way that each labored on the work with one hand and with the other held a weapon. 18And each of the builders had his sword strapped at his side while he built. The man who sounded the trumpet was beside me. 19And I said to the nobles, the officials, and the rest of the people, "The work is great and widely spread out, and we are separated far from one another on the wall. 20Rally to us wherever you hear the sound of the trumpet. Our God will fight for us."

21So we labored at the work, and half of them held the spears from break of dawn until the stars came out. 22I also said to the people at that time, "Let every man and his servant pass the night inside Jerusalem, so that they may be a guard for us by night and may labor by day." 23So neither

[a] Meaning of Heb uncertain

NIV

with me took off our clothes; each had his weapon, even when he went for water.[a]

[a] 23 The meaning of the Hebrew for this clause is uncertain.

NRSV

I nor my brothers nor my servants nor the men of the guard who followed me ever took off our clothes; each kept his weapon in his right hand.[a]

[a] Cn: Heb *each his weapon the water*

COMMENTARY

4:13. The last eleven verses of chap. 4 report a variety of countermeasures taken by Nehemiah to meet all of these threats. Unfortunately, the text of this verse is corrupt; therefore, Nehemiah's strategy is not completely clear, even if the NRSV and the NIV make passable sense of the passage. Nehemiah seems to have posted armed guards at the lowest points of the wall that was being built. The hope was that, when the enemies saw these men armed with swords, spears, and bows at these exposed sites, they would conclude that more similarly armed forces were stationed at other points along the wall. Hence they would fear that they faced a sizable army. The Midianites once panicked because they concluded that Gideon must have had an enormous army, since he had a 300-person army band (Judges 7)! By stationing these troops, Nehemiah was acting like a governor, though this office has not yet been mentioned in the book (cf. 5:14-15).

4:14-15. Significantly, Nehemiah begins v. 14 with the words "I saw" (NRSV and NIV, "I looked these things over"). That is, the enemies were wrong when they thought the Jews would not know or see an impending enemy attack (v. 11). Nehemiah did indeed see what they were doing. The paraphrastic translations in the NRSV and the NIV obscure the function of Nehemiah's remark. His subsequent speech to the leaders of the people and to the people as a whole appeals to holy war traditions (v. 14; cf. 2 Chr 13:2-20; 14:10-16; 20:1-30; 25:5-13; 32:1-23). In these traditions the people, when faced with an enemy attack, would draw up in battle lines according to their tribal families and be told by an official not to fear because God would fight for them and defeat their enemies. Already arranged by families (v. 13), the people here are told by Nehemiah not to be afraid (cf. Exod 14:13-14). He also urges them to think about their great and awesome Lord (cf. 1:5) and to fight united. His actions were enough to convince the enemy that their hostile plans had indeed been discovered. From Nehemiah's perspective, it was clear that God had frustrated the enemies' plans as God had often confused the Israelites' enemies in the past (Exod 15:14-16; 23:27-28; Deut 2:25; 11:25). Instead of deserting the project and returning home (cf. v. 12), the people unanimously returned to work on the wall.

4:16. Just as prayer was supplemented by the setting up of a guard in v. 9, so also Nehemiah now initiates concrete security measures in addition to his reliance on the holy war traditions. First he appoints half of his loyal troops (cf. 4:16, 23; 5:10, 16; 13:19) to work on the wall while the other half of his servants, supplied with nearly the full armor of Persian soldiers and surely better armed than the people described in v. 13, are stationed as guards just behind the whole house of Judah, who were building the wall. The word שׂרים (*śārîm*, v. 16), translated as "leaders" (NRSV) or "officers" (NIV), should be deleted as a dittograph.[146] The words "posted themselves" in the NRSV and the NIV are not in the Hebrew text but were added to incorporate "leaders" or "officers" into the translation. Nehemiah's elite troops offered protection to the builders, but they also may have served to keep people from deserting the building project.

4:17-20. In Nehemiah's second security measure, the basket carriers are not divided into two groups, as the servants had been, but are instead given a double task (v. 17). With one hand they are to steady their baskets and with the other hand carry a weapon, perhaps, judging by the Hebrew word שלח (*šālaḥ*), something that could

146. Cf. *BHS.*

be thrown at the enemy. These are the same basket carriers who had been running out of energy according to v. 10. The builders themselves needed both hands for their work, but they had a short sword strapped on their hips for emergencies (v. 18).

In a third security measure, Nehemiah sets up a makeshift warning system in case of enemy attack. He concedes that the building project is vast (cf. v. 10) and that the workers have been distributed over the entire length of the wall. If the enemy were to attack this dispersed group, the trumpeter, who was always with Nehemiah, would sound the alarm and the people would assemble at the danger point, as in a holy war (see Judg 3:27; 6:34; 7:18; 1 Sam 13:3). The system seems rather cumbersome because one first had to find Nehemiah and the trumpeter and get them to the danger point for the plan to work. It is also hard to imagine how one trumpeter could be heard throughout the city. A perfect warning system in any case was hardly necessary, since Nehemiah concluded these plans by appealing to the holy war tradition: "Our God will fight for us" (v. 20). Note the reappearance of the title "our God" (אלהינו *'ĕlōhênû*; see also vv. 4, 9) and Nehemiah's confidence in God as the real defender of Jerusalem (cf. the great and awesome LORD," v. 14; other references to God as the fighter in Israel's wars may be found in Exod 14:14; 15:3; Deut 1:30; 3:22; 20:4; Josh 10:14, 42; 23:10; 1 Sam 17:47). Neither those who would fight against Jerusalem (v. 8) nor even those who would fight for the city (v. 14) would be decisive in the battle; God's intervention would make the difference.

4:21-23. Nehemiah's security measures successfully met the external and internal threats. The people even put in a longer than usual day—from dawn to the time when the stars came out (instead of from dawn to sunset, Deut 24:15). The phrase "and half of them held the spears" in v. 21 should be deleted as an incorrect gloss based on a very similar context in v. 16.[147] Nehemiah also increased the security of the city and reduced the time it took people to reach the work site and the attendant danger of people's defecting from the task by urging everyone—including their servants when applicable—to spend their nights in the midst of Jerusalem (v. 22). He wanted to have people available for guard duty by night and for work by day (an echo of v. 9). Nehemiah and his elite troops set an example in dedication for the others. In the Hebrew text he says, "We [that is, "I, my brothers (including, perhaps, Hanani, his blood brother [1:2; 7:2]; note how these brothers are a counterpart to Sanballat's brothers in v. 2), and the people who supported me"] never took off our clothes but stayed armed at all times." In the last clause, the NRSV translation is superior to that of the NIV, although the NRSV is based on a slight emendation of the Hebrew text (reading הימינו [*hêmînû*, "kept in his right hand"] for המים [*hammāyim*, "water"]).

147. See *BHS*. Note that if the phrase were original, it should read "half of *us* held the spears."

REFLECTIONS

This chapter demonstrates that a community is often threatened as much by internal weakness as by external attack. In fact, our enemies often have no power if we individually and collectively retain our integrity. The sad little poem sung by the Judeans (4:10) not only depicts things at their worst, but also has the effect of pulling down the morale of everyone else. How much better if they had sung: "Your servants hold [Zion's] stones dear, and have pity on its dust" (Ps 102:14). Lack of concentration on the task at hand (4:11) could also erode the basis for security. Finally, the siren call of fellow members of the community, who put self-preservation above community goals, threatened to lure people to defection, weakness, and defeat.

This chapter contains a disturbing, imprecatory prayer (4:4-5), in which Nehemiah asks God to punish his adversaries with the threats they had aimed at him, and in which he asks God not to forgive his enemies. Jeremiah, in his controversial letter to the exiles, set a different example for dealing with one's enemies by urging those who were captives in Babylon to pray for their enemies (Jer 29:1-9). No doubt there is much merit in Jesus' admonition to love our enemies and to pray for those who abuse us (Matt 5:44; Luke 6:27-28, 35), not to mention following the example of Jesus in praying for one's enemies (Luke 23:34).

But we should hesitate before assigning Nehemiah's prayer too quickly to an inferior ethical domain. Nehemiah saw the attacks of Sanballat and his allies as a direct threat to God's plans for Israel. That, too, could be a dangerous attitude, often abused in the course of history when people consider all their opponents as *ipso facto* enemies of God. But there are, indeed, times when hostility is directed not only against us as people, but against us as God's people; it is designed to thwart God's purposes.

Imprecatory prayers have this to their credit: They flow from a spirit that knows it can tell God anything, even if God finally chooses the route of forgiveness and reconciliation. The greatest thing about deep human relationships is that we can share with the other person exactly what is on our mind. So it is with a good, faith-full relationship with God; we trust God enough to share our deepest pain, anguish, hurt, and anger.

From a position of power or health it is easy to pontificate on the inappropriateness of imprecatory psalms. But one needs to ask oneself: "Do I really understand the anguish this other person has gone through?" Imprecatory prayers, despite their difficult elements, may provide an opportunity for those who have really been hurt to express themselves to God and to God's people in the context of worship.

Nehemiah's role as strategist in this chapter is admirable. The community for which he was responsible was beset with external and internal threats, and he led the people as the first among equals; at times he was willing to pay an extra personal price to guarantee their safety. He willingly assigned half of his elite troops to the work detail and the other half to guarding the endangered builders. He no doubt also knew the hardships involved for the builders who spent every night in Jerusalem during the reconstruction process. As a good leader, he was not above those whom he led. He and all his closest associates never undressed for bed, but kept alert at all times.

This chapter articulates an excellent mixture of the physical and the spiritual in carrying out one's calling. Nehemiah responded to the first external threat with prayer, but to the second he responded with prayer and the setting up of a guard. Conditions had changed, and Nehemiah did not make the mistake of only praying while neglecting to take concrete actions through which God could provide deliverance. At a time of crisis, not only did he invoke the memories of holy war, but he also assigned his elite troops, the burden bearers, and the builders themselves to concrete actions of self-defense. He proved his enemies wrong when they said, "They are not prepared for what we are going to do to them."

Pray and act—*ora et labora.* Nehemiah exemplified the meaning of that old proverb. But he knew also that all his preparations would be in vain if one bottom line would not hold: God ultimately must fight for the people (4:20).

NEHEMIAH 5:1-19, INTERNAL THREATS TO THE COMMUNITY

Nehemiah 5:1-13, A Social and Economic Crisis

NIV

5 Now the men and their wives raised a great outcry against their Jewish brothers. 2Some were saying, "We and our sons and daughters are numerous; in order for us to eat and stay alive, we must get grain."

3Others were saying, "We are mortgaging our fields, our vineyards and our homes to get grain during the famine."

4Still others were saying, "We have had to borrow money to pay the king's tax on our fields and vineyards. 5Although we are of the same flesh and blood as our countrymen and though our sons are as good as theirs, yet we have to subject our sons and daughters to slavery. Some of our daughters have already been enslaved, but we are powerless, because our fields and our vineyards belong to others."

6When I heard their outcry and these charges, I was very angry. 7I pondered them in my mind and then accused the nobles and officials. I told them, "You are exacting usury from your own countrymen!" So I called together a large meeting to deal with them 8and said: "As far as possible, we have bought back our Jewish brothers who were sold to the Gentiles. Now you are selling your brothers, only for them to be sold back to us!" They kept quiet, because they could find nothing to say.

9So I continued, "What you are doing is not right. Shouldn't you walk in the fear of our God to avoid the reproach of our Gentile enemies? 10I and my brothers and my men are also lending the people money and grain. But let the exacting of usury stop! 11Give back to them immediately their fields, vineyards, olive groves and houses, and also the usury you are charging them—the hundredth part of the money, grain, new wine and oil."

12"We will give it back," they said. "And we will not demand anything more from them. We will do as you say."

NRSV

5 Now there was a great outcry of the people and of their wives against their Jewish kin. 2For there were those who said, "With our sons and our daughters, we are many; we must get grain, so that we may eat and stay alive." 3There were also those who said, "We are having to pledge our fields, our vineyards, and our houses in order to get grain during the famine." 4And there were those who said, "We are having to borrow money on our fields and vineyards to pay the king's tax. 5Now our flesh is the same as that of our kindred; our children are the same as their children; and yet we are forcing our sons and daughters to be slaves, and some of our daughters have been ravished; we are powerless, and our fields and vineyards now belong to others."

6I was very angry when I heard their outcry and these complaints. 7After thinking it over, I brought charges against the nobles and the officials; I said to them, "You are all taking interest from your own people." And I called a great assembly to deal with them, 8and said to them, "As far as we were able, we have bought back our Jewish kindred who had been sold to other nations; but now you are selling your own kin, who must then be bought back by us!" They were silent, and could not find a word to say. 9So I said, "The thing that you are doing is not good. Should you not walk in the fear of our God, to prevent the taunts of the nations our enemies? 10Moreover I and my brothers and my servants are lending them money and grain. Let us stop this taking of interest. 11Restore to them, this very day, their fields, their vineyards, their olive orchards, and their houses, and the interest on money, grain, wine, and oil that you have been exacting from them." 12Then they said, "We will restore everything and demand nothing more from them. We will do as you say." And I called the priests, and made them take an oath to do as they had promised. 13I also shook out the fold of

NIV

Then I summoned the priests and made the nobles and officials take an oath to do what they had promised. [13]I also shook out the folds of my robe and said, "In this way may God shake out of his house and possessions every man who does not keep this promise. So may such a man be shaken out and emptied!"

At this the whole assembly said, "Amen," and praised the LORD. And the people did as they had promised.

NRSV

my garment and said, "So may God shake out everyone from house and from property who does not perform this promise. Thus may they be shaken out and emptied." And all the assembly said, "Amen," and praised the LORD. And the people did as they had promised.

COMMENTARY

The first part of the chapter describes an acute socioeconomic crisis faced by many farmers during the wall-building process (vv. 1-13). Albertz suggests that this is but a single episode of a more long-term economic problem in which some members of the upper class were usurious toward those who took out loans and deprived them of their land and forced their children into labor through a ruthless application of the rules of borrowing.[148] The usual marginal financial status of many people in the community had deteriorated even further because of their work on the wall (which was apparently done without remuneration), because of drought and crop failure (v. 3), and because of the need to pay Persian taxes out of the "surplus" that could be produced from a given field (v. 4). Nehemiah had required the builders to stay in Jerusalem during the fifty-two days of wall building, and this meant that there was a shortage of labor at harvesttime, when grain farmers would acquire almost all of their income for the year, and when capital and interest payments would fall due. The nature of the initiatives undertaken by Nehemiah, with only passing appeal to the Torah, may indicate how swiftly this crisis arose. A more permanent solution to the problem is reached in 10:31, with the promise to forgo the exaction of every debt.

5:1. The women who had been left to tend to the farms during the building of the wall experienced firsthand the effects of the economic crisis. Their cries and those of the people in general were directed to God (cf. 9:4; Job 34:28). But they were also heard by Nehemiah (v. 6; see also 1 Kgs 20:39; 2 Kgs 6:26), who used words and actions—not to mention his own personal example—to alleviate at least temporarily the financial crisis. The pain of this crisis was exacerbated by the fact that the creditors were Jewish kin of those who were in debt.

5:2. Three different groups experienced severe financial difficulties. The first group, consisting apparently of poor landless farmers, complained that they were forced to pledge the labor of their sons and daughters in order to pay for essential foodstuffs. This interpretation is based on a slight emendation of the Hebrew text, reading ערבים (*ʿōrĕbîm*) for רבים (*rabbîm*; see also v. 3)[149] and translating, "We have to pledge our sons and daughters in order to get grain, so that we may eat and stay alive."

5:3. The second group of debtors complain that they have had to pledge fields, vineyards, and houses in order to get grain, and they also note that the situation has been exacerbated by drought-caused famine, a frequent problem in post-exilic Judah (see Joel 1-2; Hag 1:5-6, 10-11; 2:15-16, 19; Mal 3:9-12). The pledging of real estate may indicate their increased desperation, since land once pledged and lost would be gone forever, whereas children might eventually be redeemed.

5:4. A third group of debtors has had to bor-

148. Rainer Albertz, *A History of Israelite Religion in the Old Testament Period*, vol. 2: *From the Exile to the Maccabees*, trans. John Bowden (Louisville: Westminster/John Knox, 1994) 495-97.

149. Cf. *BHS*.

row silver in order to pay the Persian royal tax, again using their fields and vineyards as collateral. The Persians levied an annual land tax based on the average expected yield (see Ezra 4:13; 6:8), which Herodotus tells us amounted to 350 talents of silver for the fifth satrapy (Beyond the River).[150]

5:5. This verse offers bitter reflections on the fact that the creditors, who were foreclosing on loans to all three groups, were members of the Jewish community. The victims note poignantly, "Our flesh is like the flesh of our kinsmen, our children are like theirs." Creditors had seized fields and vineyards. And despite ties of blood and country, creditors forced debtors to put their children into debt slavery (see Exod 21:2-11; 22:25-27; Leviticus 25; Deut 15:1-18; 24:10-13), and some of their daughters had already been claimed by creditors, to be sexually exploited in the process (see Esth 7:8).

5:6-7. Nehemiah's reaction is spontaneous, with no explicit reference to pentateuchal law. His anger (cf. his reactions in 13:8, 21, 25) is followed by sober reflection before he initiates a direct confrontation with the upper class—the nobles and the officers—who were calling in their loans. His accusation was not, as the translation of v. 7 in the NRSV and the NIV would suggest, that the creditors were charging interest. Instead, he questioned the way they were seizing pledges that had been given to back loans: "Each of you is foreclosing against his own people" (v. 7; cf. the limitations placed on seizing pledges in Exod 22:26; Deut 24:10), and he convened a public assembly to deal with the brutal creditors.

5:8-10. Nehemiah notes ironically that the community has just bought back from debt slavery as many fellow Jews as possible after they had sold themselves to Gentile groups. Now the Jews are selling their own kinsfolk into the shame of debt slavery, requiring the community to spend additional money to redeem them out of slavery.[151] Nehemiah's blunt charges leave the creditors speechless (v. 8), and he urges them to act more justly based upon their fear of (= faith in) the God whom he also confesses ("our God"; note the appeal to the fear of God in a similar financial context at Lev 25:17, 36, 43). Strictly speaking, what the creditors were doing was not illegal, but they were using the crisis of the "brothers" to make personal gain. The people's complaints in vv. 2-4 show clearly that the process was "not good" (v. 9). Concern for Israel's reputation with the nations should have provided a reason to cease these usurious practices. What would the other nations say if they heard about Jewish creditors who were taking advantage of their own people's predicament for personal profit? Nehemiah admits that he, his brothers, and his elite companions (cf. 4:16) had also loaned out money to those in need, but he proposes that he and his close colleagues cease from seizing pledges (v. 10).

5:11. Nehemiah demands that creditors return to the original owners whatever land had been taken in pledge. He also demands that interest charged be rebated to the borrowers, although previously the discussion had not dealt with the question of interest. The NRSV's reference to an unknown rate of interest is preferable to the 1 percent monthly interest reflected in the NIV. An annual interest rate of 12 percent would have been very low in the Persian Empire! The known minimum interest was 20 percent; one contract at Elephantine sets the annual rate at 60 percent, while another sets it at 100 percent monthly.[152] While interest on loans to the poor within Israel is prohibited in pentateuchal law (Exod 22:25; Lev 25:35-37; Deut 23:19-20), incidental references elsewhere in the Bible reveal that there were always those who assessed interest on loans (Ps 15:5; Prov 28:8; Ezek 18:8, 13, 17).[153]

5:12-13. The creditors immediately agree to Nehemiah's terms, promising to restore items taken from their debtors in pledge and not to make loans in the future on the basis of people or property taken in pledge (v. 12). Nehemiah persuades the priests to enforce these promises by an oath. The promises of the creditors are referred to three times in these verses. Then, in a sym-

150 Herodotus 3.91.

151. *BHS* suggests emending ונמכרו (*wĕnimkĕrû*, "so that they will have to be sold back") in v. 8 to ונכרו (*wĕnikrû*, "so that they will have to be bought back"), and this apparently lies behind the NRSV's "be bought back by us."

152. AP 10; BMAP 11.3. Cf. R. P. Maloney, "Usury and Restrictions on Interest-Taking in the Ancient Near East," *CBQ* (1974) 1-20.

153. David J. A. Clines, *Ezra, Nehemiah, Esther,* NCB (Grand Rapids: Eerdmans, 1984) 169, and *BHS* emend the word ומאת (*ûmĕ'at*, "interest") to ומשאת (*ûmaššaʾt*, "debt"). According to this view, Nehemiah proposed canceling the "debts" of money, grain, wine, and oil.

bolically enacted curse, Nehemiah shakes out his garment's fold, which served much like pockets do today, and announces that God similarly will shake out of his or her house and property anyone who fails to keep the promise that has been made. The whole assembly (v. 13; cf. v 7) adds its "Amen" and praises Yahweh as an indication of its affirmation of this agreement. The nobles and officials—here referred to as "the people"—do follow through on their promise. (See Reflections at 5:14-19.)

Nehemiah 5:14-19, Nehemiah's Personal Generosity as Governor

NIV

[14]Moreover, from the twentieth year of King Artaxerxes, when I was appointed to be their governor in the land of Judah, until his thirty-second year—twelve years—neither I nor my brothers ate the food allotted to the governor. [15]But the earlier governors—those preceding me—placed a heavy burden on the people and took forty shekels[a] of silver from them in addition to food and wine. Their assistants also lorded it over the people. But out of reverence for God I did not act like that. [16]Instead, I devoted myself to the work on this wall. All my men were assembled there for the work; we[b] did not acquire any land.

[17]Furthermore, a hundred and fifty Jews and officials ate at my table, as well as those who came to us from the surrounding nations. [18]Each day one ox, six choice sheep and some poultry were prepared for me, and every ten days an abundant supply of wine of all kinds. In spite of all this, I never demanded the food allotted to the governor, because the demands were heavy on these people.

[19]Remember me with favor, O my God, for all I have done for these people.

[a] *15* That is, about 1 pound (about 0.5 kilogram) [b] *16* Most Hebrew manuscripts; some Hebrew manuscripts, Septuagint, Vulgate and Syriac *I*

NRSV

14Moreover from the time that I was appointed to be their governor in the land of Judah, from the twentieth year to the thirty-second year of King Artaxerxes, twelve years, neither I nor my brothers ate the food allowance of the governor. [15]The former governors who were before me laid heavy burdens on the people, and took food and wine from them, besides forty shekels of silver. Even their servants lorded it over the people. But I did not do so, because of the fear of God. [16]Indeed, I devoted myself to the work on this wall, and acquired no land; and all my servants were gathered there for the work. [17]Moreover there were at my table one hundred fifty people, Jews and officials, besides those who came to us from the nations around us. [18]Now that which was prepared for one day was one ox and six choice sheep; also fowls were prepared for me, and every ten days skins of wine in abundance; yet with all this I did not demand the food allowance of the governor, because of the heavy burden of labor on the people. [19]Remember for my good, O my God, all that I have done for this people.

COMMENTARY

The second part of this chapter reports the generosity of Nehemiah throughout his career and was written after his first term as governor was over—that is, after 433 BCE. The rest of the memoir, except for 13:4-31, deals with events in his first year in Jerusalem. Here Nehemiah tells how he entertained many people as governor on the basis of his own resources, without dipping into the income that ordinarily came to him from taxes levied on the province. These verses provide ethical support and moral encouragement for what the creditors had just done and for anyone who would face similar temptations to exploit the poor in the future.

In v. 14, the Nehemiah Memoir tells us for the first time that Nehemiah had been appointed governor by Artaxerxes I for a term lasting twelve years (445–433 BCE), after which he returned to Susa for an unspecified period of time (cf. 13:6). We do not know whether Nehemiah was sent as governor from the beginning or whether he was appointed governor shortly after his arrival in Jerusalem.

Nehemiah was the latest in a long line of governors in the province of Judah. The Bible calls both Sheshbazzar (Ezra 5:14; cf. Ezra 1:8) and Zerubbabel governor (Hag 1:1, 14), and an unnamed governor is mentioned in Ezra 6:7 and Mal 1:8. The word תרשׁתא (*tiršātā'*; Ezra 2:63; Neh 7:65, 70; see also Neh 8:9; 10:1) is the Persian equivalent for this title. Nachman Avigad has published inscriptional evidence for three additional governors, Elnathan, Yehoezer, and Azai, between Zerubbabel and Nehemiah.[154] Perhaps Artaxerxes' order to stop the rebuilding of Jerusalem (Ezra 4:23) had given the Samaritan authorities temporary authority over Jerusalem and reduced the independence of the governors of Judah. This would help to account for the hostility of Sanballat and Tobiah toward Nehemiah, since they resented the more independent stance he assumed in Judah. The biblical and inscriptional evidence, including the references to Judah as a province (Ezra 2:1 [= Neh 7:6]; 5:8; Neh 1:3; see also Neh 11:3), seems to contradict Albrecht Alt, who concluded that Nehemiah was the first governor of Judah in the Persian period and that previously Judah was part of the province of Samerina (Samaria), which had retained its identity since the Assyrian conquest in the eighth century BCE.[155] Nehemiah's governorship did not bring about a fundamentally different status for Judah in the Persian Empire.

During his term as governor Nehemiah declined the food allowance he could have taken from the taxes of the province (v. 14). His gubernatorial predecessors had received a stipend (לחם *leḥem*, "bread," "food"), from Persian tax money, of forty shekels "per day" (reading ליום אחד [*lĕyôm 'eḥād*] for ויין אחר [*wāyayin 'aḥar*] in v. 15), and their elite companions ("their servants") also had "lorded it" over the people (v. 15). Nehemiah and his staff dedicated themselves to building the wall and did not acquire property as a perquisite of the governor's office. The 150 "Jews and officials" who ate at Nehemiah's table were apparently Jewish and Persian governmental employees. Nehemiah fed all these people in addition to visitors from foreign lands who dropped by from time to time (v. 17). The food for an average day was one ox, six sheep, and an unspecified number of fowl. Every ten days many different kinds of wine were provided at Nehemiah's own expense. Solomon, by comparison, needed every day ten fat oxen, twenty pasture-fed cattle, and one hundred sheep, besides deer, gazelles, roebucks, fatted fowl, and ninety cors of meal (1 Kgs 4:22-23)! Despite his leaner budget, Nehemiah provided enough meat to feed 600-800 people.[156] Two reasons are given for his generous behavior: fear of God (v. 15; cf. v. 9) and the high tax rate already paid by the people ("the burden of labor on the people," v. 18). The "heavy burden" on the people may even allude to the misery of their ancestors in Egypt (Exod 1:14). The ability to carry out this policy over a twelve-year period implies that Nehemiah had considerable personal resources (see 2:3, 8).

In its present form the Nehemiah Memoir is an autobiographical report to God. Nehemiah repeats his prayer for God to remember favorably his own generosity (v. 19) three more times in 13:14, 22, 31. The form of this prayer resembles Egyptian votive or royal inscriptions,[157] and Blenkinsopp calls attention specifically to the inscription of Udjahorresnet at the time of Darius I: "O great gods. . . . Remember all the useful things accomplished by the chief physician Udjahorresnet."[158] Nehemiah's prayer is not so self-serving or self-righteous as it might at first appear. He knew that however great his own accomplishments and benefactions toward the people had been, God's kindness, finally, was motivated by God's own steadfast love (see 13:22).

154. See Nachman Avigad, *Bullae und Seals from a Post-exilic Judaean Archive*, Qedem 4 (Jerusalem: Hebrew University of Jerusalem, 1976); H. G. M. Williamson, "The Governors of Judah Under the Persians," *TynBul* 39 (1988) 59-82.

155. Albrecht Alt, "Die Rolle Samarias bei der Entstehung des Judentums," *Kleine Schriften zur Geschichte des Volkes Israel* (Munich: Beck, 1953) 2:316-37. See also Sean McEvenue, "The Political Structure in Judah from Cyrus to Nehemiah," *CBQ* 43 (1981) 353-64.

156. The estimate is that of Loring W. Batten, *A Critical and Exegetical Commentary on the Books of Ezra and Nehemiah*, ICC (Edinburgh: T. & T. Clark, 1913) 246-47.

157. See *ANET* 307, 316-17.

158. Joseph Blenkinsopp, "The Mission of Udjahorresnet and Those of Ezra and Nehemiah," *JBL* 106 (1987) 211.

REFLECTIONS

The inexorable pressures of economic systems today often chew people up, leaving them without work, food, clothing, health care, or housing. In a community like that of post-exilic Judah, with its economy distorted by a great public works project and by a crop failure, were all the ingredients for an economic disaster. Pledges made against loans were being called in, and people were having to surrender their children and their real estate to cover their debts and to maintain life itself. The text adds that women were foremost among those affected by this economic crisis, just as they form a disproportionate part of poor people today. What made the situation particularly bad was that the creditors were fellow Jews, kinsfolk, "brothers" (5:1, 5, 7-8). Even Nehemiah had been involved in making loans (5:10).

Despite his great personal courage in addressing this issue, Nehemiah insisted that this problem involved the whole community, and he called an assembly against the creditors. He appealed to the creditors' faith ("Should you not walk in the fear of our God?") as well as to their pride ("to prevent the taunts of the nations").

But Nehemiah also set an example. First he proposed that all seizing of pledges cease. Second, he pointed to his own generous policies as governor to illustrate hospitality toward kinsfolk. The people whom he governed were not people who owed him a living, but were in fact his "brothers" (5:8). He had hosted people generously during his term in office because he feared God (5:15) and because he had compassion for the people because of their heavy tax burdens (5:18). Such fear of God and such compassion might transform potentially ruthless creditors into people who would invest their money for the good and benefit of all.

The apostle Paul did not take a salary from his Corinthian congregation, even though he had every right to do so (1 Cor 9:12). He chose not to make use of all of his rights lest he put an obstacle in the way of the gospel. Jesus, too, did not consider equality with God something he had to maintain at any cost. Instead, he emptied himself, assumed the form of a slave, and became obedient to the point of death, even death on the cross (Phil 2:6-11).

Nehemiah did not insist on his rights. Instead he presented his life to God as a kind of living sacrifice: "Remember for my good all that I have done for this people." Nehemiah knew in the final analysis that he would be spared only because of God's great and steadfast love (13:22), but he also took holy pride in those great accomplishments God had achieved through Nehemiah's public service for the entire community and especially for the blessed poor. Would that our politicians were so proud!

NEHEMIAH 6:1-19, THE WALL IS COMPLETED DESPITE REPEATED ATTEMPTS TO INTIMIDATE NEHEMIAH

OVERVIEW

In this chapter Nehemiah plays the role of the omniscient author who knows the secret motives of all those with whom he deals. We need to remember that this is only Nehemiah's side of the story, and it is clear that a number of people in Jerusalem had a positive relationship with Tobiah, Nehemiah's arch rival. Nehemiah successfully fends off all the efforts to do him in and to frustrate the completion of the wall.

Nehemiah 6:1-9, Sanballat and Geshem as Antagonists

NIV

6 When word came to Sanballat, Tobiah, Geshem the Arab and the rest of our enemies that I had rebuilt the wall and not a gap was left in it—though up to that time I had not set the doors in the gates— 2Sanballat and Geshem sent me this message: "Come, let us meet together in one of the villages[a] on the plain of Ono."

But they were scheming to harm me; 3so I sent messengers to them with this reply: "I am carrying on a great project and cannot go down. Why should the work stop while I leave it and go down to you?" 4Four times they sent me the same message, and each time I gave them the same answer.

5Then, the fifth time, Sanballat sent his aide to me with the same message, and in his hand was an unsealed letter 6in which was written:

> "It is reported among the nations—and Geshem[b] says it is true—that you and the Jews are plotting to revolt, and therefore you are building the wall. Moreover, according to these reports you are about to become their king 7and have even appointed prophets to make this proclamation about you in Jerusalem: 'There is a king in Judah!' Now this report will get back to the king; so come, let us confer together."

8I sent him this reply: "Nothing like what you are saying is happening; you are just making it up out of your head."

9They were all trying to frighten us, thinking, "Their hands will get too weak for the work, and it will not be completed."

⌊But I prayed,⌋ "Now strengthen my hands."

[a] *2* Or *in Kephirim* [b] *6* Hebrew *Gashmu,* a variant of *Geshem*

NRSV

6 Now when it was reported to Sanballat and Tobiah and to Geshem the Arab and to the rest of our enemies that I had built the wall and that there was no gap left in it (though up to that time I had not set up the doors in the gates), 2Sanballat and Geshem sent to me, saying, "Come and let us meet together in one of the villages in the plain of Ono." But they intended to do me harm. 3So I sent messengers to them, saying, "I am doing a great work and I cannot come down. Why should the work stop while I leave it to come down to you?" 4They sent to me four times in this way, and I answered them in the same manner. 5In the same way Sanballat for the fifth time sent his servant to me with an open letter in his hand. 6In it was written, "It is reported among the nations—and Geshem[a] also says it—that you and the Jews intend to rebel; that is why you are building the wall; and according to this report you wish to become their king. 7You have also set up prophets to proclaim in Jerusalem concerning you, 'There is a king in Judah!' And now it will be reported to the king according to these words. So come, therefore, and let us confer together." 8Then I sent to him, saying, "No such things as you say have been done; you are inventing them out of your own mind" 9—for they all wanted to frighten us, thinking, "Their hands will drop from the work, and it will not be done." But now, O God, strengthen my hands.

[a] Heb *Gashmu*

COMMENTARY

All the gaps in the wall have been filled in (note the progress beyond 4:7), though the doors on the gates have not yet been installed (v. 1; see also vv. 3, 15; 7:1). When Sanballat and Geshem hear about the progress on the wall, they propose a meeting with Nehemiah in Kephirim (or Hak-kephirim), an unknown village in the plain of Ono. The NRSV and the NIV follow an alternative vocalization of the Hebrew text and substitute "one of the villages" for Kephirim.[159] Ono, where some Jews had settled after the return (Ezra 2:33 = Neh 7:37; see 1 Chr 8:12), was about

159. Cf. *BHS.*

twenty miles northwest of Jerusalem and represents one of the most remote parts of the province.[160] Although the proposed meeting sounds innocent on the surface, Nehemiah detects in it a plan to lure him away from Jerusalem to do him harm. His enemies later also attribute conspiracy to him (v. 6). Nehemiah declines their proposal courteously, noting that he is engaged in building the wall and that his absence might stop that project. Ironically, that is exactly what his enemies want. It is not clear what their goals were, since it was really too late to reverse the progress on the wall. Perhaps they hoped that by eliminating Nehemiah they would maintain their relationships (business contacts) with various sectors of the population in Jerusalem (see esp. vv. 17-18). Or were they seeking to avenge their loss of influence and power in Jerusalem because of Nehemiah's governorship?

After his opponents have extended an invitation four times, followed always by the same reply from Nehemiah, they change their tactics. Sanballat sends him an open letter, via his personal servant (cf. 4:16), which accuses Nehemiah of rebellion against the Persian Empire (see 2:19). The unsealed letter implies to Nehemiah that these politically damaging charges are now public knowledge and that its contents are designed to stir up distrust of Nehemiah's motives among the people. The letter reports that the surrounding nations (cf. 4:7) have picked up rumors of a rebellion and that these rumors have been confirmed by Geshem (here spelled in a more archaic way as Gashmu). The charge that the building of the wall was treasonous was in itself not very credible. After all, the king had given permission for this project and had even supplied building materials (2:8). Sanballat, however, further charges that the building of the wall has been given a new meaning by Nehemiah, who, according to the rumors, is about to become king. If this charge were true, the walled city of Jerusalem would not so much provide a safe outpost for the Persians as it would be a rebellious, independent city, next door to Egypt, where serious revolts had occurred in recent years.

Lest one think that these rumors are just warmed-over anxieties inherited from Rehum and the Samaritan authorities (see Ezra 4:8-23), Sanballat expands his charge by claiming that Nehemiah has appointed prophets who are announcing a coming king in Judah. Before the exile, prophets were often involved in king making: Samuel with Saul (1 Samuel 9–10) and David (1 Samuel 16); Nathan with Solomon (2 Samuel 7; 1 Kgs 1:32-40); Ahijah with Jeroboam I (1 Kings 11); and Elisha with Jehu (2 Kgs 9:1-13). More recently, but actually a full seventy-five years earlier, Haggai (Hag 2:21-23) and Zechariah (Zech 3:8; 4:6-10; 6:10-14) had expressed messianic hopes while the Second Temple was being built. Sanballat's charge probably implied that Nehemiah had bribed these prophets. Were there prophetic supporters of Nehemiah whose words would have given Sanballat's charges some credibility? Or were these charges of hired prophets meant to deflect attention from Sanballat and Tobiah's own hiring of false prophets (vv. 10-14)? If the Nehemiah Memoir were to be read by the Persian king, Nehemiah would want to leave no uncertainty about Sanballat's calumny. Kellermann tried to make Sanballat's charges more plausible by proposing that Nehemiah was a descendant of the Davidic house.[161] But neither Nehemiah's confession of the sins of his ancestral house (1:6) nor his reference to his ancestral graves at Jerusalem (2:3) provides real evidence for his Davidic pedigree.

Sanballat notes cynically at the end of his letter that this open report will surely find its way back to the king. That is, Sanballat might leak it to him, or others who had heard about the letter might report it to the authorities. For the fifth time Sanballat says, "Let's meet."

It is difficult to know whether Sanballat was doing anything more than bluffing since Nehemiah flatly denied the accusations and accused Sanballat of making them up out of his own imagination. To meet with Sanballat under these circumstances would give some validity to these dangerous accusations. If Sanballat really thought Nehemiah was traitorous, why would he want to meet with him?

From Nehemiah's point of view all of his opponents (see v. 1) were trying to intimidate him, weaken the workers' resolve, and stop work on

160. The plain of Ono may be identical with the Valley of the Craftsmen in 11:35.

161. Ulrich Kellermann, *Nehemia, Quellen, Überlieferung und Geschichte,* BZAW 102 (Berlin: de Gruyter, 1967) 179-82.

the wall even at this late date (v. 9). Nehemiah claims that he knows the secret thoughts and strategies of his opponents. Their threats, however, prove to be counterproductive and only solidify Nehemiah's resolve. The last clause in v. 9 may be translated, "But in fact I redoubled my resolve." The hands that the opponents hoped to weaken become stronger than ever. Both the NRSV and the NIV interpret this clause as a prayer, but they add the words "O God" (NRSV) or "But I prayed" (NIV) to achieve this interpretation. The verb they parse as an imperative is actually an infinitive absolute, used in this case in the place of a finite verb. (See Reflections at 6:15-19.)

Nehemiah 6:10-14, Tobiah and Sanballat as Antagonists

NIV

10One day I went to the house of Shemaiah son of Delaiah, the son of Mehetabel, who was shut in at his home. He said, "Let us meet in the house of God, inside the temple, and let us close the temple doors, because men are coming to kill you—by night they are coming to kill you."

11But I said, "Should a man like me run away? Or should one like me go into the temple to save his life? I will not go!" 12I realized that God had not sent him, but that he had prophesied against me because Tobiah and Sanballat had hired him. 13He had been hired to intimidate me so that I would commit a sin by doing this, and then they would give me a bad name to discredit me.

14Remember Tobiah and Sanballat, O my God, because of what they have done; remember also the prophetess Noadiah and the rest of the prophets who have been trying to intimidate me.

NRSV

10One day when I went into the house of Shemaiah son of Delaiah son of Mehetabel, who was confined to his house, he said, "Let us meet together in the house of God, within the temple, and let us close the doors of the temple, for they are coming to kill you; indeed, tonight they are coming to kill you." 11But I said, "Should a man like me run away? Would a man like me go into the temple to save his life? I will not go in!" 12Then I perceived and saw that God had not sent him at all, but he had pronounced the prophecy against me because Tobiah and Sanballat had hired him. 13He was hired for this purpose, to intimidate me and make me sin by acting in this way, and so they could give me a bad name, in order to taunt me. 14Remember Tobiah and Sanballat, O my God, according to these things that they did, and also the prophetess Noadiah and the rest of the prophets who wanted to make me afraid.

COMMENTARY

The second external threat to Nehemiah comes through the prophet Shemaiah. Although both the prophet and his father, Delaiah, have Yahwistic names and although Shemaiah's genealogy is traced back to his grandfather, we know nothing about his personal life (see 1 Chr 3:22 for a Davidide with this name). It is also unclear why Nehemiah went to Shemaiah's house, unless the prophet had intimated that he had an oracle for him. Commentators have worked intensively on the significance of Shemaiah's being "confined to" or "shut in at" his house (v. 10), but without any fully convincing results. He surely was not shut up because he was ritually unclean, as one might immediately surmise, because he seems free to go to the Temple.

Shemaiah's words are cast in poetic form (see the layout in *BHS*) in which there are seconding or heightening effects. He suggests that there might be danger for Nehemiah and that they should meet at the house of God, but then goes on to suggest a more specific meeting point, in the Temple building itself. Similarly, he first warns that "they," an unspecified group of enemies, are coming to kill Nehemiah, but then adds that these assassins are coming that very night. Shemaiah proposes that he and Nehemiah meet in the Temple behind closed doors.

On the surface, nothing seems wrong with this proposal, but Nehemiah rejects it categorically for three reasons. First, as governor, he does not want to be a coward and flee from his enemies (v. 11*a*). Second, as a layperson, he has no right to go inside the Temple because that space is reserved for the priests, and violation of it is a capital crime (v. 11*b*; see Num 18:7). Shemaiah does not seem to be inviting Nehemiah to seek asylum, since that was attained by grasping the horns of the altar, which stood outside the Temple (Exod 21:13-14; 1 Kgs 1:50-53; 2:25, 28-34); besides, it is not likely that assassins would pay much attention to the protection offered by asylum. Third, Nehemiah, again as the omniscient narrator, recognizes that God has not sent Shemaiah and that, therefore, he is a false prophet (see Jer 23:21; 28:15) hired by Tobiah and Sanballat to work mischief on Nehemiah. The end of v. 12 and the beginning of v. 13 show a conflation of nearly synonymous Hebrew expressions, one of which should be removed in translation: "because Tobiah and Sanballat had hired him to intimidate me." Nehemiah accuses Tobiah and Sanballat of suborning a prophet, exactly the charge that Sanballat had raised against Nehemiah in v. 7. If Nehemiah had been a coward and had fled or hidden in the Temple, which was out of bounds for laypeople, he would have sinned (v. 13; cf. Uzziah in 2 Chr 26:16-20; 27:2) and ruined his reputation among the people so that they rightly would have reproached him. Nehemiah leaves vengeance to God (Deut 32:35; Ps 94:1; Rom 12:19) and asks God to remember—that is, punish (see 13:29)—Tobiah and Sanballat for their misdeeds.

At the end of v. 14 Nehemiah refers to a woman prophet by the name of Noadiah and to other prophetic colleagues who also had tried to intimidate him. Outside of her Yahwistic name, we know nothing else about Noadiah or about this incident except that it shows that the Shemaiah incident was not isolated. Nehemiah's enemies also used other prophets to try to discredit him or to make him afraid (v. 14). Kellermann has speculated that lying behind the Noadiah story is an attempt by prophetic and messianic circles to designate Nehemiah as king in the Temple.[162] This speculation, however, seems unnecessary and unjustified. (See Reflections at 6:15-19.)

162. Ibid., 179-82.

Nehemiah 6:15-19, The Nobles of Judah and Tobiah as Antagonists

NIV

[15]So the wall was completed on the twenty-fifth of Elul, in fifty-two days. [16]When all our enemies heard about this, all the surrounding nations were afraid and lost their self-confidence, because they realized that this work had been done with the help of our God.

[17]Also, in those days the nobles of Judah were sending many letters to Tobiah, and replies from Tobiah kept coming to them. [18]For many in Judah were under oath to him, since he was son-in-law to Shecaniah son of Arah, and his son Jehohanan had married the daughter of Meshullam son of Berekiah. [19]Moreover, they kept reporting to me his good deeds and then telling him what I said. And Tobiah sent letters to intimidate me.

NRSV

15So the wall was finished on the twenty-fifth day of the month Elul, in fifty-two days. [16]And when all our enemies heard of it, all the nations around us were afraid[a] and fell greatly in their own esteem; for they perceived that this work had been accomplished with the help of our God. [17]Moreover in those days the nobles of Judah sent many letters to Tobiah, and Tobiah's letters came to them. [18]For many in Judah were bound by oath to him, because he was the son-in-law of Shecaniah son of Arah: and his son Jehohanan had married the daughter of Meshullam son of Berechiah. [19]Also they spoke of his good deeds in my presence, and reported my words to him. And Tobiah sent letters to intimidate me.

[a] Another reading is *saw*

COMMENTARY

6:15. Before narrating the third external threat, Nehemiah tells the story of the wall's completion in the amazingly fast time of fifty-two days. This figure may well be correct. The walls on the south and west of the city only needed repairing, while the wall on the east was new, erected on the crest with no necessity to clean up heavy debris. In addition, some of the restoration on the wall that had been done earlier (see Ezra 4:8-23) may not have been completely destroyed.[163] Perhaps the enthusiasm of Nehemiah and the whole-hearted cooperation of the people (cf. chap. 3) also speeded the completion of the work. Josephus claims that the wall took twenty-eight months to build, but this is not an ancient tradition and may have arisen from his attempt to calculate how long it would take to rebuild the wall of Jerusalem in his day.[164] Since the wall was completed on the twenty-fifth day of the month of Elul, the sixth month, just about half a year had passed from the time of Nehemiah's commissioning by Artaxerxes to the completion of the wall (cf. 2:1).

6:16. When the enemies of Nehemiah (see also v. 1) hear about the completion of the wall, they and their allies ("the nations") are afraid and lose their self-confidence (in the HB = 7:72*b*–10:40).[165] They recognize that the completion of the wall is the work of "our God" (cf. Ps 126:2)—again Nehemiah seems to know the innermost feelings of his opponents. They have become victims of the same terror they had wanted to impose on Nehemiah (vv. 9, 13, 14, 19).

6:17-19. Nehemiah, however, is upset by the frequent exchange of letters between Tobiah and the nobles of Judah (v. 17). Many people in Judah were under an oath of allegiance to Tobiah, who may have spent some time in Jerusalem as interim administrator after Artaxerxes had stopped the earlier building of the wall (Ezra 4:8-23). Tobiah had significant, politically important marital ties to families in Jerusalem, who seem to have been supportive in general of Nehemiah's program. Tobiah himself married the daughter of Shecaniah the son of Arah. Arah was a family of 775 people, listed among those who returned from exile (7:10; Ezra 2:5). Shemaiah, the son of Shecaniah and possibly a brother of Tobiah's wife, was a gatekeeper and headed one of the labor gangs that worked on the wall (3:29). Tobiah's son Jehohanan, presumably born to Tobiah's Jerusalemite wife, married the daughter of Meshullam the son of Berechiah, another leader of a labor gang that worked on two sections of the wall (3:4, 30). Obviously not everyone who participated in the wall building supported Nehemiah in all the other aspects of his program. The nobles may have wanted to maintain business, political, economic, and religious (13:4) ties with other rulers or regions in Palestine, while Nehemiah warded off positive relationships to Sanballat, Tobiah, and the others (see 2:20). The supporters of Tobiah constantly reminded Nehemiah of Tobiah's many virtues (טובתיו *ṭôbōtāyw*; "Tobiah" [טוביה *ṭôbiyyâ*]) and reported Nehemiah's words and deeds back to Tobiah. While Tobiah's supporters were involved in such image building and spying, he sent letters designed to intimidate Nehemiah, thus contradicting what his supporters were saying. The intentions of Sanballat, Tobiah, and Geshem throughout the chapter remain consistently hostile to Nehemiah and his program. These intentions resulted in physical threats, political charges, traps and tricks, and psychological warfare.

163. Kathleen Kenyon, *Digging Up Jerusalem* (London: Benn, 1974) 183, suggested that Nehemiah's workmanship on the wall was not of outstanding quality in any case.

164. Josephus *Antiquities of the Jews* XI.5.8 179.

165. Some commentators emend ויפלו (*wayyippĕlû*, "and fell") to ויפלא (*wayyippālē*ʾ) and translate: "It seemed a truly astonishing achievement." See Ps 118:23 and *BHS*.

REFLECTIONS

Nehemiah had to face up to significant external dangers. At times he almost seems to know too much about his opponents because he writes with narrative omniscience. Some of his colleagues in Jerusalem did not see things the same way he did, and even the words of his opponents are taken at times in the worst possible way.

Words can be deceptive and harmful. "Let's meet," an enemy may say (see. 6:2, 7, 10). But it is possible that such meetings may have a hidden and even dangerous agenda. Sanballat and Geshem wanted to harm Nehemiah at a remote site; Shemaiah's invitation to meet in the Temple was an open invitation for Nehemiah to discredit or compromise himself. Tobiah's support group sang his praises, but Nehemiah was at the same time receiving letters from Tobiah himself that contradicted the propaganda. If enough lies are told about a person, some people will conclude that they are true merely because they have been stated so often. Sanballat used an open letter to unnerve Nehemiah before his own citizens and threatened to leak the words of this letter to the king.

Sometimes attacks on another person are meant to deflect attention from one's own faults. Sanballat charged Nehemiah and the Jews with plotting rebellion (6:6), but in fact Sanballat and Geshem themselves were plotting to harm Nehemiah (6:2). Sanballat accused Nehemiah of hiring prophets to further his own royal ambitions (6:7), but in fact Tobiah and Sanballat themselves hired Shemaiah to discredit and compromise Nehemiah (6:12). Proposals for meetings, mail left open before the wrong eyes, messages leaked to the king, duplicitous offers of safety, and flattering words cannot hide the fact that the goal of these enemies with smiling faces was psychological terror from beginning to end.

How does one defend oneself in such circumstances? Nehemiah tried several approaches. He equivocated, saying he was too busy and that he just could not get away (6:3), but he also said a flat no when he had to (6:8, 11). He prayed to God to bring back the deeds of Tobiah and Sanballat on their own heads (6:14), knowing that vengeance belongs finally to God. The enemies' strategies to weaken the hands of Nehemiah and his associates in order to stop the work backfired, for Nehemiah only strengthened his hand all the more (6:9). Like Jeremiah, Nehemiah knew he was under no obligation to listen to a prophet whom God had not sent (6:12; see Jer 28:15-16). Nehemiah considered his station in life and acted correspondingly (6:11): Someone who is governor should not flee; someone who is a layperson should not claim priestly prerogatives by hiding in the Temple.

We would love to have the other side of the stories, to know what Sanballat, Tobiah, and Geshem were thinking, and to know more details about the inter-Jewish debates. However one-sided Nehemiah's report may be, it is clear that he faced dangers from outside that could have frustrated and destroyed his reputation just as much as the internal threats from ruthless creditors could have done in chapter 5. However much a historian might want the other data, Nehemiah maintains a posture that is consistent and coherent. With prayer to God and with considerable political savvy, he withstood all the dangers of the day and—with God's help—finished the wall.

NEHEMIAH 7:1-73*a*, NEXT STEPS AFTER THE COMPLETION OF THE WALL

NIV

7 After the wall had been rebuilt and I had
set the doors in place, the gatekeepers and
the singers and the Levites were appointed. 2I put
in charge of Jerusalem my brother Hanani, along
with[a] Hananiah the commander of the citadel,
because he was a man of integrity and feared God
more than most men do. 3I said to them, "The
gates of Jerusalem are not to be opened until the
sun is hot. While the gatekeepers are still on duty,
have them shut the doors and bar them. Also
appoint residents of Jerusalem as guards, some at
their posts and some near their own houses."

4Now the city was large and spacious, but there
were few people in it, and the houses had not
yet been rebuilt. 5So my God put it into my heart
to assemble the nobles, the officials and the common people for registration by families. I found
the genealogical record of those who had been
the first to return. This is what I found written
there:

> 6These are the people of the province who
> came up from the captivity of the exiles
> whom Nebuchadnezzar king of Babylon had
> taken captive (they returned to Jerusalem and
> Judah, each to his own town, 7in company
> with Zerubbabel, Jeshua, Nehemiah, Azariah,
> Raamiah, Nahamani, Mordecai, Bilshan, Mis-
> pereth, Bigvai, Nehum and Baanah):

The list of the men of Israel:

8the descendants of Parosh	2,172
9of Shephatiah	372
10of Arah	652
11of Pahath-Moab (through the line of Jeshua and Joab)	2,818
12of Elam	1,254
13of Zattu	845
14of Zaccai	760
15of Binnui	648
16of Bebai	628
17of Azgad	2,322
18of Adonikam	667

a 2 Or *Hanani, that is,*

NRSV

7 Now when the wall had been built and I
had set up the doors, and the gatekeepers,
the singers, and the Levites had been appointed,
2I gave my brother Hanani charge over Jerusalem,
along with Hananiah the commander of the citadel—for he was a faithful man and feared God
more than many. 3And I said to them, "The gates
of Jerusalem are not to be opened until the sun
is hot; while the gatekeepers[a] are still standing
guard, let them shut and bar the doors. Appoint
guards from among the inhabitants of Jerusalem,
some at their watch posts, and others before their
own houses." 4The city was wide and large, but
the people within it were few and no houses had
been built.

5Then my God put it into my mind to assemble
the nobles and the officials and the people to be
enrolled by genealogy. And I found the book of
the genealogy of those who were the first to come
back, and I found the following written in it:

6These are the people of the province who
came up out of the captivity of those exiles whom
King Nebuchadnezzar of Babylon had carried into
exile; they returned to Jerusalem and Judah, each
to his town. 7They came with Zerubbabel, Jeshua,
Nehemiah, Azariah, Raamiah, Nahamani, Mordecai, Bilshan, Mispereth, Bigvai, Nehum, Baanah.

The number of the Israelite people: 8the descendants of Parosh, two thousand one hundred
seventy-two. 9Of Shephatiah, three hundred seventy-two. 10Of Arah, six hundred fifty-two. 11Of
Pahath-moab, namely the descendants of Jeshua
and Joab, two thousand eight hundred eighteen.
12Of Elam, one thousand two hundred fifty-four.
13Of Zattu, eight hundred forty-five. 14Of Zaccai,
seven hundred sixty. 15Of Binnui, six hundred
forty-eight. 16Of Bebai, six hundred twenty-eight.
17Of Azgad, two thousand three hundred twenty-
two. 18Of Adonikam, six hundred sixty-seven. 19Of
Bigvai, two thousand sixty-seven. 20Of Adin, six
hundred fifty-five. 21Of Ater, namely of Hezekiah,
ninety-eight. 22Of Hashum, three hundred twenty-

a Heb *while they*

NIV

19of Bigvai 2,067
20of Adin 655
21of Ater (through Hezekiah) 98
22of Hashum 328
23of Bezai 324
24of Hariph 112
25of Gibeon 95
26the men of Bethlehem and Netophah 188
27of Anathoth 128
28of Beth Azmaveth 42
29of Kiriath Jearim, Kephirah and Beeroth 743
30of Ramah and Geba 621
31of Micmash 122
32of Bethel and Ai 123
33of the other Nebo 52
34of the other Elam 1,254
35of Harim 320
36of Jericho 345
37of Lod, Hadid and Ono 721
38of Senaah 3,930

39The priests:

the descendants of Jedaiah (through the family of Jeshua) 973
40of Immer 1,052
41of Pashhur 1,247
42of Harim 1,017

43The Levites:

the descendants of Jeshua (through Kadmiel through the line of Hodaviah) 74

44The singers:

the descendants of Asaph 148

45The gatekeepers:

the descendants of
Shallum, Ater, Talmon, Akkub, Hatita and Shobai 138

46The temple servants:

the descendants of
Ziha, Hasupha, Tabbaoth,
47Keros, Sia, Padon,
48Lebana, Hagaba, Shalmai,
49Hanan, Giddel, Gahar,
50Reaiah, Rezin, Nekoda,
51Gazzam, Uzza, Paseah,
52Besai, Meunim, Nephussim,

NRSV

eight. 23Of Bezai, three hundred twenty-four. 24Of
Hariph, one hundred twelve. 25Of Gibeon, ninety-
five. 26The people of Bethlehem and Netophah,
one hundred eighty-eight. 27Of Anathoth, one
hundred twenty-eight. 28Of Beth-azmaveth, forty-
two. 29Of Kiriath-jearim, Chephirah, and Beeroth,
seven hundred forty-three. 30Of Ramah and Geba,
six hundred twenty-one. 31Of Michmas, one hundred twenty-two. 32Of Bethel and Ai, one hundred
twenty-three. 33Of the other Nebo, fifty-two. 34The
descendants of the other Elam, one thousand two
hundred fifty-four. 35Of Harim, three hundred
twenty. 36Of Jericho, three hundred forty-five. 37Of
Lod, Hadid, and Ono, seven hundred twenty-one.
38Of Senaah, three thousand nine hundred thirty.

39The priests: the descendants of Jedaiah,
namely the house of Jeshua, nine hundred seventy-three. 40Of Immer, one thousand fifty-two.
41Of Pashhur, one thousand two hundred forty-
seven. 42Of Harim, one thousand seventeen.

43The Levites: the descendants of Jeshua,
namely of Kadmiel of the descendants of
Hodevah, seventy-four. 44The singers: the descendants of Asaph, one hundred forty-eight. 45The
gatekeepers: the descendants of Shallum, of Ater,
of Talmon, of Akkub, of Hatita, of Shobai, one
hundred thirty-eight.

46The temple servants: the descendants of
Ziha, of Hasupha, of Tabbaoth, 47of Keros, of Sia,
of Padon, 48of Lebana, of Hagaba, of Shalmai, 49of
Hanan, of Giddel, of Gahar, 50of Reaiah, of Rezin,
of Nekoda, 51of Gazzam, of Uzza, of Paseah, 52of
Besai, of Meunim, of Nephushesim, 53of Bakbuk,
of Hakupha, of Harhur, 54of Bazlith, of Mehida,
of Harsha, 55of Barkos, of Sisera, of Temah, 56of
Neziah, of Hatipha.

57The descendants of Solomon's servants: of Sotai, of Sophereth, of Perida, 58of Jaala, of Darkon,
of Giddel, 59of Shephatiah, of Hattil, of Pochereth-
hazzebaim, of Amon.

60All the temple servants and the descendants
of Solomon's servants were three hundred ninety-
two.

61The following were those who came up from
Tel-melah, Tel-harsha, Cherub, Addon, and Immer, but they could not prove their ancestral
houses or their descent, whether they belonged
to Israel: 62the descendants of Delaiah, of Tobiah,

NIV

[53]Bakbuk, Hakupha, Harhur,
[54]Bazluth, Mehida, Harsha,
[55]Barkos, Sisera, Temah,
[56]Neziah and Hatipha

[57]The descendants of the servants of Solomon:

the descendants of
Sotai, Sophereth, Perida,
[58]Jaala, Darkon, Giddel,
[59]Shephatiah, Hattil,
Pokereth-Hazzebaim and Amon

[60]The temple servants and the descendants of the servants of Solomon 392

[61]The following came up from the towns of Tel Melah, Tel Harsha, Kerub, Addon and Immer, but they could not show that their families were descended from Israel:

[62]the descendants of
Delaiah, Tobiah and Nekoda 642

[63]And from among the priests:

the descendants of

Hobaiah, Hakkoz and Barzillai (a man who had married a daughter of Barzillai the Gileadite and was called by that name).

[64]These searched for their family records, but they could not find them and so were excluded from the priesthood as unclean. [65]The governor, therefore, ordered them not to eat any of the most sacred food until there should be a priest ministering with the Urim and Thummim.

[66]The whole company numbered 42,360, [67]besides their 7,337 menservants and maidservants; and they also had 245 men and women singers. [68]There were 736 horses, 245 mules,[a] [69]435 camels and 6,720 donkeys.

[70]Some of the heads of the families contributed to the work. The governor gave to the treasury 1,000 drachmas[b] of gold, 50 bowls and 530 garments for priests. [71]Some of the heads of the families gave to the treasury for

[a] *68* Some Hebrew manuscripts (see also Ezra 2:66); most Hebrew manuscripts do not have this verse. [b] *70* That is, about 19 pounds (about 8.5 kilograms)

NRSV

of Nekoda, six hundred forty-two. [63]Also, of the
priests: the descendants of Hobaiah, of Hakkoz,
of Barzillai (who had married one of the daughters
of Barzillai the Gileadite and was called by their
name). [64]These sought their registration among
those enrolled in the genealogies, but it was not
found there, so they were excluded from the
priesthood as unclean; [65]the governor told them
that they were not to partake of the most holy
food, until a priest with Urim and Thummim
should come.

66The whole assembly together was forty-two
thousand three hundred sixty, [67]besides their male
and female slaves, of whom there were seven
thousand three hundred thirty-seven; and they
had two hundred forty-five singers, male and
female. [68]They had seven hundred thirty-six
horses, two hundred forty-five mules,[a] [69]four hundred thirty-five camels, and six thousand seven
hundred twenty donkeys.

70Now some of the heads of ancestral houses
contributed to the work. The governor gave to
the treasury one thousand darics of gold, fifty
basins, and five hundred thirty priestly robes.
[71]And some of the heads of ancestral houses gave
into the building fund twenty thousand darics of
gold and two thousand two hundred minas of
silver. [72]And what the rest of the people gave was
twenty thousand darics of gold, two thousand
minas of silver, and sixty-seven priestly robes.

73So the priests, the Levites, the gatekeepers,
the singers, some of the people, the temple servants, and all Israel settled in their towns.

[a] Ezra 2.66 and the margins of some Hebrew Mss: MT lacks *They had . . . forty-five mules*

NIV

the work 20,000 drachmas[a] of gold and 2,200 minas[b] of silver. [72]The total given by the rest of the people was 20,000 drachmas of gold, 2,000 minas[c] of silver and 67 garments for priests.

[73]The priests, the Levites, the gatekeepers, the singers and the temple servants, along with certain of the people and the rest of the Israelites, settled in their own towns.

[a] *71* That is, about 375 pounds (about 170 kilograms); also in verse 72 [b] *71* That is, about 1 1/3 tons (about 1.2 metric tons) [c] *72* That is, about 1 1/4 tons (about 1.1 metric tons)

COMMENTARY

The problem of the original location and the original significance of the list of returnees (7:5*b*-73*a*) is discussed in the Commentary on Ezra 2:1-70. The other verses in this chapter of Nehemiah (vv. 1-5*a*), which introduce the list, continue the first-person account of the Nehemiah Memoir. Although Nehemiah clearly did not compose the list himself, it is probable that he included it in his memoir. Verse 73*a* may once have served as a transition to Nehemiah's account of the actual transfer of people to Jerusalem to fill out the city. A third-person account of the transfer now appears in chap. 11; the original account from the Nehemiah Memoir is forever lost. It is possible, of course, that the list of returnees replaced the narrative of the transfer that we expect, just as a list replaced the expected narrative of the return in Ezra 2 and of the building of the wall in Nehemiah 3. The next extant portion of the Nehemiah Memoir is the dedication of the walls of Jerusalem in 12:27-43.

7:1-5a, Jerusalem Secured; Plans for Its Repopulation. With the wall complete (6:1, 15), Nehemiah finishes the gates by hanging the doors, and he posts appropriate guards. These gatekeepers guard the gates of the city against hostile forces, unlike other gatekeepers in the Bible who served as temple personnel intent on warding off cultic impurity (see v. 45). A later scribe missed this point, confused the two kinds of gatekeepers, and added the words "singers and Levites" in v. 1. These minor clergy are often mentioned with the liturgical gatekeepers (see vv. 43-44).

Nehemiah also appoints his brother Hanani (see 1:2) as military ruler over Jerusalem. Nehemiah apparently wanted someone in this crucial position whom he could completely trust—a faithful man who feared God more than many and a person with whom he had grown up. As ruler over Jerusalem, Hanani's office is to be distinguished from the governor of the province of Judah (Nehemiah) and from the civic rulers of the territory of Jerusalem, mentioned in 3:9, 12. The name "Hananiah" needs to be deleted as an explanatory gloss in v. 2. Hence it is Hanani, not Hananiah, who was commander of the citadel (cf. 2:8), a fortress that later developed into the Antonia Fortress of Herod's Jerusalem. Hanani and Hananiah are apparently alternative spellings of the same name, which means "Yahweh has been gracious."

Hanani gives the people instructions on how to maintain the city gates (v. 3; the NRSV and the NIV follow the Qere and ascribe this speech to Nehemiah). One can only hope that these instructions to the gatekeepers were clearer to them than they are in English translations. Why would one leave the gates closed until the temperature got hot? Perhaps we should translate: "The gates of Jerusalem are not to be opened while the sun is hot." That is, Hanani directed that the gates be shut by the guards during the hottest hours of the day when the guards would probably be taking a siesta. Hanani also conscripted supplementary guards from the inhabitants of Jerusalem. Some were to keep watch over the wall next to their own houses (see 3:10, 20-21, 23-24, 28-31), while others would guard the remaining portions of the wall (see 3:1, 11, 25-27).

Nehemiah notices at this time that the population of the city is not adequate for a city of 30-40 acres. Thus the city seemed too wide (lit., "broad of hands"; cf. Gen 34:21; 1 Chr 4:40; Ps 104:25) and too large, though it was considerably smaller than it had been in late monarchical times. It also had inadequate housing. Clearly there were some houses in the city despite the apparently categorical denial of this in v. 4 (see v. 3 and the frequent references to the houses of the leaders of the work gangs in chap. 3).

Nehemiah claims that the unprecedented idea of moving people to Jerusalem came by divine inspiration (cf. 2:12). When David, on the other hand, had numbered the people, he succumbed to the temptation of God (2 Sam 24:1) or of Satan (1 Chr 21:1). The transference of people to Jerusalem was to be regulated by genealogical records. This list of those who returned would supply some people with the opportunity to find an individual within the last century to whom they could trace their ancestry. Presumably the book of genealogy (v. 5) also contained other names of father's houses, such as those mentioned in Ezra 8:1-14. In the present context, the list of those who returned also dramatizes the fullness of the assembly that listened to Ezra's reading of the law in Ezra 9. It is this assembly of returned exiles that, after building the Temple, purifying itself internally, and building the wall, constitutes itself as the people of God. The community at the beginning of the restoration (Ezra 2) and at the completion of the wall (Nehemiah 7) is one and the same.

7:5b-73a, The List of Those Who Returned. For commentary on these verses see the Commentary on Ezra 2:1-70. The words in v. 68 are not present in the MT, but are found in Ezra 2:66, in some medieval Hebrew manuscripts of Nehemiah 7, and in some LXX manuscripts as well. The sequence of words—(two hundred) forty-five (male and female singers) at the end of v. 67 and forty-five (mules) at the end of v. 68—shows that the words of this verse were lost in the majority of manuscripts by homoioteleuton. The restoration of v. 68 gives the five subsequent verses in the chapter a higher verse number than the corresponding verses in Hebrew. Verse 70 singles out the contribution of the governor, presumably Nehemiah, for special mention. In Ezra's account, the materials from Neh 7:70-72 are combined into a single verse, Ezra 2:69.

REFLECTIONS

Much of what has been said about the list of those who returned in Ezra 2 could be repeated here. But the present context presents several new challenges that deserve mention.

Nehemiah needed administrative help if the wall he had completed was to function effectively as a defense for the community. He chose his brother for this important post and ran the risk of being charged with nepotism. Still, the man he chose had ideal credentials, with previous experience as a commander of the citadel. More important for any leader, he was faithful and feared God more than many. His name, which means "Yahweh has been gracious," was a token of that power that finally made him trustworthy, made him able to believe, and might even make him capable of transcending the temptations that come with being appointed to leadership by one's brother.

By including the list of those who returned twice, in both Ezra 2 and Nehemiah 7, the author of this book has made a most important point: The community that had built the altar and the Temple, that had separated itself from the dangers of mixed marriages and from the cancer of ruthless internal economic policies, that had built a wall giving the community protection and providing stability in the midst of grave external dangers, and that now stood ready to hear the will of God and to do it in the events of Nehemiah 8—that community, at the beginning and up until this turning point in the post-exilic period, had the same heritage and the same character. It was the community of all those who had returned from exile, including also all those who had attached themselves to it and who had accepted its values. That community had settled down in its land and in its own cities, ready for all those events in the rest of the book of Nehemiah that would solidify its previous gains. Communities of Christians today, even amid great change, strive to live up to the living tradition of their predecessors and to witness to God's fidelity and freedom in ways they imagine their predecessors would act if they faced today's challenges.

NEHEMIAH 7:73*b*–10:39[166]

TORAH, CONFESSION, AND FIRM AGREEMENT

OVERVIEW

The three units in this section are not part of the Nehemiah Memoir, but they have been artfully arranged to form a coherent theological sequence between Nehemiah's decision to repopulate Jerusalem (7:1-73*a*) and the actual transfer of people there (11:1-2).

The events in Neh 7:73*b*–8:18 took place in the seventh month, and Ezra, who last appeared in Ezra 10, is once again the leading actor. In the MT of Neh 8:9, "Nehemiah, who was the governor" is mentioned alongside Ezra, but it is fast becoming the consensus among modern commentators that Nehemiah and Ezra were not contemporaries (despite Neh 12:26, 36) and that the reference to Nehemiah is secondary, as even textual criticism suggests.[167] The words "Nehemiah" and "the governor" appear frequently in the immediate context (7:65, 70; 10:1), which may have facilitated the incorrect addition of "Nehemiah, who was the governor" in 8:9. The NIV surely errs when it adds Nehemiah's name to its translation of v. 10.

Why are Ezra and Nehemiah not considered contemporaries by modern scholars? As we have seen, Artaxerxes I, the Persian king, sent Ezra on a mission to Judah in 458 BCE (Ezra 7:12-26). Ezra set out from Babylon on the twelfth day of the first month (Ezra 8:31; see also Ezra 7:9) and arrived in Jerusalem with his entourage on the first day of the fifth month (Ezra 7:9). Ezra criticized the people for their mixed marriages on the twentieth day of the ninth month (Ezra 10:9), and the commission investigating this problem carried out its duties from the first day of the tenth month to the first day of the first month of the following year (Ezra 10:16-17). If we follow the chronology implied by the present location of Nehemiah 8, then Ezra would have delayed his most important assignment, the one dealing with the law (Ezra 7:14, 25-26), for thirteen years, until Nehemiah arrived, and the Bible would provide no information on what transpired in the intervening years. Outside of Neh 8:9 and 12:26, 36, there is no reason to think these two leaders were contemporaries. From a historical perspective the events of Nehemiah 8 make more sense between Ezra 8 and Ezra 9 (or after Ezra 10:44; see the Overview to Ezra 7:1–10:44). This would mean that Ezra arrived in Jerusalem in the fifth month, read and interpreted the law in the seventh month, and concluded his duties with the dissolution of the mixed marriages by the first day of the first month of his second year. No one knows what happened to Ezra afterward.

But if Nehemiah 8 is read in its present canonical position, as it has been for this commentary, then this pericope suggests that the people whom Nehemiah transferred to Jerusalem (7:4-5; cf. 11:1-2) consisted solely of those who had dedicated themselves to the law. This arrangement of the Ezra materials also gives the story of Ezra a more or less happy ending, instead of the tension inherent in the account of the forced divorces (Ezra 10). The theological and compositional reasons for locating Nehemiah 8 in its present position apparently overrode chronological considerations in the editor's mind.

Chapter 9 poses a variety of difficult questions about its origin and function. Why is the joyous Festival of Tabernacles (8:13-18) followed by a ceremony marked by mourning, sackcloth, and

166. In the HB = 7:72*b*–10:40.

167. 1 Esdr 9:45 reads only "Attharates" [= the governor], and the Septuagint has only "Nehemiah"; these alternative expansions have been conflated in the MT.

ashes in chap. 9, especially in the light of Ezra's and the Levites' admonition not to mourn in 8:9-11? Why does the community observe a festival of penance that is not commanded in the law, and why does the sad festival not precede the joyous one? Why is Ezra absent from chapter 9 (he next appears at 12:36)? In 9:6 the NRSV adds his name as the author of the prayer, based on the Septuagint, but few scholars would support this emendation. Why is the confession of sins in 9:5*b*-37 so lacking in specifics, saying nothing at all about intermarriage with foreign women (Ezra 10) or Israel's failure in the past to observe the Festival of Tabernacles correctly (Nehemiah 8)? Why does 9:2 report that Israel separated itself from all foreigners, since this goes beyond what transpired in Ezra 10 and anticipates what happens in Neh 13:1-3?

Commentators have tried to address these questions by finding a new place for chap. 9 within Ezra–Nehemiah. Clines decided to move Nehemiah 8–9 to a position after Ezra 9, while Williamson proposed putting an early form of Neh 9:1-5 in a position between Ezra 10:15 and 10:16, and Blenkinsopp believes Neh 9:1-5 is an alternative account of the reading of the law in Neh 8:1-12 and hence considers its present location appropriate.[168] Ulrich Kellermann and Wilhelm In der Smitten, however, have concluded that this chapter (or at least 9:1-5) was composed precisely for its present location.[169] Gunneweg has refined their observations and proposes that this whole chapter comes from a later scribe who wanted to modify the original picture contained in Nehemiah 8 without contradicting it. While "true Israel" at the time of Ezra or the author of Nehemiah 8 included primarily only those who had returned home from the exile, true Israel at the time of the later scribe consisted of all those who agreed to separate themselves from non-Israelites and who, with confession of sins and true repentance, believed in Israel's God. The day when the law was read and when the Israelites had returned from exile may have been no time for repentance (Neh 8:9-11); however, a look at Israel's past and present, at the sins of the ancestors and of themselves, would convince the author's readers that repentance is the only possible posture for Israel's encounter with God. The person who added this chapter was less able to accept with equanimity life under Persian rule (see vv. 36-37; cf. Ezra 1:1 and the general message of Ezra and Nehemiah).[170] The sequence of chap. 8 (reading of the law), chap. 9 (confession of sin), and chap. 10 (the firm agreement) is meant to depict an ideal response to the law.

Just as lament psalms often conclude with a vow, so also Nehemiah 9, whose final verses are like a lament, leads on to the "firm agreement" in chap. 10. This unit, which begins in 9:38, may be outlined as follows:

9:38, Introduction
10:1-27, A list of those who signed the firm agreement
10:28-29, Other signatories
10:30-39, The details of the legal pledge

The list of names of those who signed the agreement (10:1-27) is commonly regarded as secondary because it is unusual for names to be given at the beginning of a document, and because the order of the names in the list—priests, Levites, laity—is different from the order suggested in 9:38—laity, Levites, priests. The list of names, as will be shown in the Commentary section, seems to have been constructed by gathering names from other lists in Ezra and Nehemiah. Nehemiah 10:28-29*a* ("through a servant of God") are a (secondary?) parenthesis indicating that the rest of the people pledged their support for the firm agreement by a curse and an oath rather than by signing or sealing the document as the officials, Levites, and priests had done.

Many of the specific pledges in 10:30-39 deal with the same issues that are treated in 5:11-12 and in chap. 13 and are an attempt to make the governor's temporary rulings permanent:

10:30, mixed marriages (cf.13:23-30)
10:31*a*, the sabbath day (cf. 13:15-22)
10:31*b*, the sabbath year and debts (cf. 5:11-12)

168. David J. A. Clines, *Ezra, Nehemiah, Esther,* NCB (Grand Rapids: Eerdmans, 1984) 189; H. G. M. Williamson, *Ezra, Nehemiah,* WBC 16 (Waco, Tex.: Word, 1985) 309-10; Joseph Blenkinsopp, *Ezra–Nehemiah,* OTL (Philadelphia: Westminster, 1988) 294-95.

169. Ulrich Kellermann, *Nehemia, Quellen, Überlieferung und Geschichte,* BZAW 102 (Berlin: de Gruyter, 1967); Wilhelm In der Smitten, *Esra: Quellen, Überlieferung und Geschichte,* SSN 15 (Assen: Van Gorcum, 1973) 47-51.

170. Antonius H. J. Gunneweg, *Nehemia,* KAT 19, 2 (Gütersloh: Gütersloher Verlagshaus Gerd Mohn, 1987) 118-21.

10:32-33, one-third of a shekel offering
10:34, wood offering (cf. 13:31)
10:35-36, first fruits (cf. 13:31)
10:37-38, tithes (cf. 13:10-14)
10:39, not to neglect the house of God (cf. 13:11)

Although these pledges are logically and chronologically subsequent to Nehemiah 13, the final form of the book of Nehemiah presents them out of their chronological order. This may be because the firm agreement was needed as a sequel to the reading of the Torah and the confession of sins in Nehemiah 8–9, and because chap. 13, with its prayers for God to remember, was felt to be a fitting climax to the book.

NEHEMIAH 7:73*b*–8:18, EZRA READS THE LAW TO THE PEOPLE

NIV

When the seventh month came and the Israelites had settled in their towns,

8 1all the people assembled as one man in the square before the Water Gate. They told Ezra the scribe to bring out the Book of the Law of Moses, which the LORD had commanded for Israel.

2So on the first day of the seventh month Ezra the priest brought the Law before the assembly, which was made up of men and women and all who were able to understand. 3He read it aloud from daybreak till noon as he faced the square before the Water Gate in the presence of the men, women and others who could understand. And all the people listened attentively to the Book of the Law.

4Ezra the scribe stood on a high wooden platform built for the occasion. Beside him on his right stood Mattithiah, Shema, Anaiah, Uriah, Hilkiah and Maaseiah; and on his left were Pedaiah, Mishael, Malkijah, Hashum, Hashbaddanah, Zechariah and Meshullam.

5Ezra opened the book. All the people could see him because he was standing above them; and as he opened it, the people all stood up. 6Ezra praised the LORD, the great God; and all the people lifted their hands and responded, "Amen! Amen!" Then they bowed down and worshiped the LORD with their faces to the ground.

7The Levites—Jeshua, Bani, Sherebiah, Jamin, Akkub, Shabbethai, Hodiah, Maaseiah, Kelita, Azariah, Jozabad, Hanan and Pelaiah—instructed the people in the Law while the people were standing

NRSV

When the seventh month came—the people of Israel being settled in their towns—

8 1all the people gathered together into the square before the Water Gate. They told the scribe Ezra to bring the book of the law of Moses, which the LORD had given to Israel. 2Accordingly, the priest Ezra brought the law before the assembly, both men and women and all who could hear with understanding. This was on the first day of the seventh month. 3He read from it facing the square before the Water Gate from early morning until midday, in the presence of the men and the women and those who could understand; and the ears of all the people were attentive to the book of the law. 4The scribe Ezra stood on a wooden platform that had been made for the purpose; and beside him stood Mattithiah, Shema, Anaiah, Uriah, Hilkiah, and Maaseiah on his right hand; and Pedaiah, Mishael, Malchijah, Hashum, Hash-baddanah, Zechariah, and Meshullam on his left hand. 5And Ezra opened the book in the sight of all the people, for he was standing above all the people; and when he opened it, all the people stood up. 6Then Ezra blessed the LORD, the great God, and all the people answered, "Amen, Amen," lifting up their hands. Then they bowed their heads and worshiped the LORD with their faces to the ground. 7Also Jeshua, Bani, Sherebiah, Jamin, Akkub, Shabbethai, Hodiah, Maaseiah, Kelita, Azariah, Jozabad, Hanan, Pelaiah, the Levites,[a] helped the people to understand the law, while the people remained in their

[a] 1 Esdras 9.48 Vg: Heb *and the Levites*

NIV

there. 8They read from the Book of the Law of God, making it clear[a] and giving the meaning so that the people could understand what was being read.

9Then Nehemiah the governor, Ezra the priest and scribe, and the Levites who were instructing the people said to them all, "This day is sacred to the LORD your God. Do not mourn or weep." For all the people had been weeping as they listened to the words of the Law.

10Nehemiah said, "Go and enjoy choice food and sweet drinks, and send some to those who have nothing prepared. This day is sacred to our Lord. Do not grieve, for the joy of the LORD is your strength."

11The Levites calmed all the people, saying, "Be still, for this is a sacred day. Do not grieve."

12Then all the people went away to eat and drink, to send portions of food and to celebrate with great joy, because they now understood the words that had been made known to them.

13On the second day of the month, the heads of all the families, along with the priests and the Levites, gathered around Ezra the scribe to give attention to the words of the Law. 14They found written in the Law, which the LORD had commanded through Moses, that the Israelites were to live in booths during the feast of the seventh month 15and that they should proclaim this word and spread it throughout their towns and in Jerusalem: "Go out into the hill country and bring back branches from olive and wild olive trees, and from myrtles, palms and shade trees, to make booths"—as it is written.[b]

16So the people went out and brought back branches and built themselves booths on their own roofs, in their courtyards, in the courts of the house of God and in the square by the Water Gate and the one by the Gate of Ephraim. 17The whole company that had returned from exile built booths and lived in them. From the days of Joshua son of Nun until that day, the Israelites had not celebrated it like this. And their joy was very great.

18Day after day, from the first day to the last, Ezra read from the Book of the Law of God. They celebrated the feast for seven days, and on the eighth day, in accordance with the regulation, there was an assembly.

a *8* Or *God, translating it*   b *15* See Lev. 23:37-40.

NRSV

places. 8So they read from the book, from the law of God, with interpretation. They gave the sense, so that the people understood the reading.

9And Nehemiah, who was the governor, and Ezra the priest and scribe, and the Levites who taught the people said to all the people, "This day is holy to the LORD your God; do not mourn or weep." For all the people wept when they heard the words of the law. 10Then he said to them, "Go your way, eat the fat and drink sweet wine and send portions of them to those for whom nothing is prepared, for this day is holy to our LORD; and do not be grieved, for the joy of the LORD is your strength." 11So the Levites stilled all the people, saying, "Be quiet, for this day is holy; do not be grieved." 12And all the people went their way to eat and drink and to send portions and to make great rejoicing, because they had understood the words that were declared to them.

13On the second day the heads of ancestral houses of all the people, with the priests and the Levites, came together to the scribe Ezra in order to study the words of the law. 14And they found it written in the law, which the LORD had commanded by Moses, that the people of Israel should live in booths[a] during the festival of the seventh month, 15and that they should publish and proclaim in all their towns and in Jerusalem as follows, "Go out to the hills and bring branches of olive, wild olive, myrtle, palm, and other leafy trees to make booths,[a] as it is written." 16So the people went out and brought them, and made booths[a] for themselves, each on the roofs of their houses, and in their courts and in the courts of the house of God, and in the square at the Water Gate and in the square at the Gate of Ephraim. 17And all the assembly of those who had returned from the captivity made booths[a] and lived in them; for from the days of Jeshua son of Nun to that day the people of Israel had not done so. And there was very great rejoicing. 18And day by day, from the first day to the last day, he read from the book of the law of God. They kept the festival seven days; and on the eighth day there was a solemn assembly, according to the ordinance.

a Or *tabernacles*; Heb *succoth*

COMMENTARY

7:73b–8:8. The initiative for the public reading of the book of the law came from the congregation as a whole, who invited Ezra to present it to them (v. 1; cf. Ezra 10:7-17). While it is not possible to be certain about the exact identity of the law book ascribed to Moses, it seems to be something quite similar to our current Pentateuch.[171] Ezra and the Levites applied this law to the contemporary situation, and their hermeneutical efforts make it difficult to be sure what text was read and what was added hermeneutically (see the Commentary on 8:14-18).

The public reading took place on the day that was to become known in Judaism as new year's day (Lev 23:23-25; Num 10:10; 29:1-6), the first day of the seventh month, late in September or early in October. The seventh month was also the time when the altar had been first set up and when the community began sacrificial worship (Ezra 3:3). With the completion of the wall in the sixth month (25th of Elul, 6:15), the editor apparently considered the seventh month to be an appropriate time to bind the community to the law.

The assembly gathered in a square opposite the Water Gate (v. 1; cf. 3:26; 8:3, 16; 12:37), located on the east side of the city, perhaps outside the wall built by Nehemiah. The Water Gate may have been in the vicinity of the spring of Gihon. This nonsacral area permitted participation by laypeople as well as clergy.[172] The assembly consisted of men, women, and at least some of the children ("all who could hear with understanding," vv. 2-3). A similarly inclusive congregation is reported for other readings of the law and covenantal occasions (10:28; Deut 31:10-13; 2 Chr 20:13). Children are referred to even more explicitly at the confessional rite in Ezra 10:1. The focus in Nehemiah 8 is on the reading of the law; the sacrifices ordinarily performed at new year's are not even mentioned (Lev 23:24-25; Num 29:2-6).

Verse 3 is a summary of the activities in vv. 4-7, and v. 8 is a retrospective conclusion to these same activities. Ezra and his companions read from the book of the law for about six hours (from early morning until midday), and despite this length of time men, women, and children gave their rapt attention. Even during this long meeting only a portion of the Pentateuch could have been read, but the author gives no hint about which pericopes were chosen. Ezra and his thirteen, presumably lay, companions (v. 4) stood on a raised platform (a tower of wood), that seems to have performed the same function as did the bronze platform upon which Solomon prayed at the dedication of the First Temple (2 Chr 6:13). The raised position of Ezra and his companions may be echoed by the hierarchical seating in the later synagogue (see Matt 23:6 and the Tosephta). Attempts to use textual criticism to reduce the thirteen companions to the symbolic number twelve (cf. Ezra 8:35-36) are called into question by the fact that thirteen Levites also appear in v. 7. Perhaps one person in each group of thirteen served as leader, leaving twelve others. Since the names of the lay companions are given without patronymics (fathers' names), it is impossible to tell whether Anaiah, Maaseiah, Hasum, and Meshullam are the same men who are listed among the lay signers of the firm agreement in 10:14-27. Although laypeople share in the leadership of this service, Ezra is identified here in his role as priest. The focus on the law does not imply criticism of the sacrificial cult.

When Ezra unrolled the scroll—codexes or "books" were not used in pre-Christian times—all the people stood in reverence (cf. Job 29:8). Ezra offered a blessing to the Lord (cf. 1 Chr 16:36; 2 Chr 6:4; perhaps, "Blessed are you, O Lord, our God . . ."), who is here given the title of "the great God" (cf. 1:5; Deut 10:17; Jer 32:18). The twofold "Amen" of the people in v. 6 expresses agreement with the blessing of the Lord and acceptance of the law (a double "Amen" is frequent as an introduction to speeches by Jesus in the NT); the people's raised hands connote expec-

171. Frank Crüsemann, *Die Tora* (Munich: Chr. Kaiser, 1992) 393, observes that regardless of what the exact shape or content of Ezra's law book was, it was from this law book that our present Pentateuch developed. For an opposite opinion, see C. Houtman, who concluded that the law book presupposed in Ezra–Nehemiah was a completely separate work, citing the analogy of the Temple Scroll from Qumran. See C. Houtman, "Ezra and the Law," *OTS* 21 (1981) 111-17. See also the discussion of the book of the law at Ezra 7:14.

172. 1 Esdras 9:38 relocates the ceremony to the east gate of the Temple!

tation and dependency (cf. Ezra 9:5; Ps 28:2; 134:2). Obedience and submission are articulated by their bowed heads and by their prostration on the ground. Thirteen Levites carried out their usual teaching functions (v. 7; cf. Deut 33:10; 2 Chr 17:7-9; 35:3). Seven of these Levites also signed the firm agreement (Jeshua, Bani, Sherebiah, Hodiah, Kelita, Hanan, and Pelaiah, 10:9-13), and four participated in the confessional liturgy (Jeshua, Bani, Sherebiah, and Hodiah, 9:4-5). The Levites may have circulated through the crowd, since the people did not move from their places (v. 7).

The interpretation of v. 8 depends upon how one understands מפרש (*mĕpōrāš*). The translations "with interpretation" (NRSV) and "making it clear" (NIV) are attempts to make sense of a root meaning "divide," "separate," or "specify." Other suggested translations include: "with pauses between verses" (Clines); "distinctly" (Blenkinsopp); and "paragraph by paragraph" (Williamson). Schaeder's proposal that this word connotes extempore translation into Aramaic, comparable to the use of the Aramaic Targums in the synagogue for people who no longer understood Hebrew, remains highly speculative.[173] If Clines and Williamson are right about the basic meaning of the word, we might paraphrase v. 8 and specify who the speakers are as follows: "So Ezra and his lay companions [or perhaps Ezra and the Levites; the verb is plural] read from the book, from the law of God, paragraph by paragraph [or sentence by sentence]. The Levites, moving through the crowd, interpreted and applied the law, and the people [Hebrew: they] understood it." This verse, therefore, summarizes vv. 4-7.

Many scholars believe that vv. 1-12 provide an etiology for the synagogue service from the time of the author back to the time of Ezra.[174] They call attention to the assembling of the congregation, the procession with the scroll, the opened book with the people standing, the recital of a blessing, the double "Amen," the explanation of the sacred reading, and the dismissal. Missing are the Shema, the eighteen blessings, and the Haftorah (second lesson). Unfortunately, we have no direct evidence for synagogal liturgy until Roman times, and it is possible that Jewish liturgical practices evolved in part on the basis of this chapter.

8:9-12. Together with the Levites—but not Nehemiah—Ezra designated the day as holy (v. 9; cf. vv. 10-11). A holy object is one that has been separated from its usual setting to be dedicated to the Lord. The writer of Leviticus called the first day of the seventh month a day of complete rest, a holy convocation to be commemorated with trumpet blasts (Lev 23:24; cf. Num 29:1-6). Ezra urged the people not to mourn or cry, although that had indeed been their reaction to hearing the law, probably reflecting their guilt for failing to observe the law perfectly (cf. Josiah's reaction when the law was read to him in 2 Kgs 22:11; 2 Chr 34:19). Instead, Ezra urged the people to celebrate by eating the fat portions[175] and by drinking sweet drinks (cf. Cant 5:16). There was to be no bitterness on this day! They were also to send portions to those who had not had the opportunity, or the wherewithal, to prepare for this celebration. Joy in the Lord (objective genitive) is the best antidote for grieving (v. 10; cf. 1 Chr 16:27); it is a source of strength or defense against divine anger. The people heeded the urging of Ezra and the Levites and went home to feast and celebrate and to send portions to others. The reading of the law by Ezra and the teaching of the law by the Levites led to understanding and therefore to joy (v. 12).

8:13-18. A portion of the crowd remained in Jerusalem—heads of families, priests, and Levites—and they gathered together on the next day to continue to study the words of the law. In their study of the legislation on the Feast of Tabernacles (presumably including at least Exod 23:16; 34:22; Lev 23:33-43; Num 29:12-38; Deut 16:13-15), they noticed a series of requirements that must be followed: The Israelites must live in booths during the festival of the seventh month; they must make a proclamation throughout the land to bring home branches of various trees; and they must use these branches to construct booths.

173. H. H. Schaeder, *Esra der Schreiber,* BHT 5 (Tübingen: J. C. B. Mohr, 1930) 52-53.

174. See Ulrich Kellermann, *Nehemia, Quellen, Überlieferung und Geschichte,* BZAW 102 (Berlin: de Gruyter, 1967) 29-30. Wahl has explored the theological significance of the parts of this service for Christian worship. See Otto Wahl, "Grundelemente eines festlichen Wortgottesdienstes nach Neh 8, 1-12," in *Die Freude an Gott unsere Kraft* (Stuttgart: Katholisches Bibelwerk, 1991) 47-59.

175. A favorite food in antiquitiy. See Homer *The Iliad* 1.40, 66, 461; *The Odyssey* 3.456-458. See also Antoninus H. J. Gunneweg, *Nehemia,* KAT 19, 2 (Gütersloh: Gütersloher Verlagshaus Gerd Mohn, 1987) 114.

While they are said to be "written" in the law (vv. 14-15; cf. v. 18, "according to the ordinance"), not all of the requirements listed here are explicitly stated in the Pentateuch. The requirement to live in booths during the fall festival is contained in Lev 23:42, but might be inferred from the name of the festival as well (Deut 16:13). Nowhere does the Pentateuch mention the need for proclamation throughout the land (v. 15), but it was perhaps inferred from the requirement to proclaim all the festivals as holy convocations (Lev 23:2). Leviticus 23:40 is the source of the statement about gathering the branches, but it does not say how these branches are to be used. In the mid-second century BCE, the Maccabees celebrated the rededication of the Temple by carrying a number of branches in procession "in the manner of the festival of booths" (2 Macc 10:6-8), but apparently Ezra and his people had concluded that the branches were to be used for building the booths within which they would live. Again, as with the proclamation requirement, they had made inferences from the written law, and this exegesis was described as that which is written in the law. The requirement to celebrate the festival in Jerusalem was no doubt inferred from Deut 16:15, and Lev 23:40 states that the festival was to take place "before the LORD your God," an expression often referring to the sanctuary. The selection of the Water Gate and the Gate of Ephraim (about 200 yards from the corner gate, according to 2 Kgs 14:13) as places for assembly may have resulted from their relative proximity to the Temple. Strangely, the trees mentioned in v. 15 do not fully correspond with those mandated in Lev 23:40. While palm trees and leafy trees are identical in both passages, the olive, wild olive, and myrtle trees mentioned in Nehemiah 8 are different from the trees that are required in the Pentateuch—namely, "majestic trees" and "willows of the brook." Did Ezra and his people substitute trees that were available to them for those listed in Leviticus, and did this interpretation of the Torah's command then become known as "what is written"? While the people observed an eight-day festival (v. 18), no explicit mention is made of the fifteenth of the month as the first day of the festival (Lev 23:34).

Everyone in the assembly who had returned from captivity—the true Israel—participated in the assembly (cf. Ezra 2:1; 3:8; 6:21; 8:35). This was the first time, according to Nehemiah 8, that during the Festival of Tabernacles people had built booths and lived in them since the time of Joshua (here spelled Jeshua), the son of Nun.[176] The comparison of Joshua and Ezra may be an attempt to associate the occupation of the land with the need to observe the law, just as Joshua had made this connection at the conclusion of the first occupation of the land (Joshua 24). These booths were no longer merely the booths used by harvesters in the field; but, rather, they were now reminders of Israel's history with God during the forty years of the wilderness wandering. Failure to observe the Festival of Tabernacles correctly between the time of Joshua and that of Ezra was among Israel's many sins. According to 2 Chr 30:26, there was no Passover like Hezekiah's since the time of Solomon, while according to 2 Chr 35:18 no Passover like Josiah's had been held since the days of Samuel. Each of these incomparable festivals is related to an even earlier individual: Hezekiah is related to Solomon, Josiah to Samuel, and now Ezra to Joshua. The Festival of Tabernacles had been the occasion for the dedication of Solomon's Temple (2 Chronicles 5–7) and for the rededication of the altar for the returned exiles (Ezra 3:1-4). Thus it was not the Festival of Tabernacles in itself that was new or different, but the manner in which it was celebrated—that is, in booths commemorating the wilderness wanderings.

In the celebration of the festival there was great rejoicing (v. 17), as the law required (Deut 16:14-15; Lev 23:40). Each day Ezra read from the book of the law. While there is no biblical mandate for such daily readings, the requirement to read the law every seventh year at the Festival of Tabernacles may have provided a rough precedent (Deut 31:10-13) that could now be carried out. The solemn assembly on the eighth day follows the provisions of Lev 23:36, 39 and Num 29:35, which extend the festival beyond the seven days referred to in Deut 16:13-15.

Why does Nehemiah 8 not mention the Day of Atonement, which took place on the tenth day of the seventh month (Lev 16:29-34; 23:26-32;

176. There are frequent references to the celebration of the Festival of Tabernacles itself before the time of Ezra: Judg 21:19; 1 Sam 1:3; 1 Kgs 8:2, 65; Hos 12:9; Ezra 3:4; see also Zech 14:16.

Num 29:7-11)? Was it because Yom Kippur had not yet attained a fixed position in the liturgical calendar? (See the references to fasts and lamentations in Zech 7:5 and 8:19, which may have been predecessors of the Day of Atonement.) Had the Pentateuch not yet reached its final form? Was Ezra silent about the Day of Atonement because of his strained relationship with the high priest? Did the ceremony on the Day of Atonement take place in parts of the Temple that were not open to laypeople, and Nehemiah 8 focuses on how Ezra changed the law from a priestly concern to something that involved all the people? Or was the Day of Atonement celebrated in the usual manner, without the innovations mentioned for Tabernacles, therefore requiring no special mention?

REFLECTIONS

We live in a time when hierarchy has gained a bad reputation. We resent people who "pull rank" or who exclude those who are different from themselves. Whatever the differences between clergy and laity in our religious life, we rightly oppose any notion of superiority for those who happen to belong to the clergy. The books of Ezra and Nehemiah often struggle with who has the right to serve as priest or who has the right to be a member of the community. In this chapter, however, the writer is at pains to show that Ezra's reading of the law followed an initiative of the laypeople and that the great scribe and priest was supported by thirteen laypeople who helped him to read the law. While laws in the Bible often reflect a patriarchal culture, in this chapter the law is announced in public, before men, women, and children (see 8:2-3).

This is the first public recognition of the authority of the Pentateuch in the Bible, and, indeed, most discussions of canon indicate that by the time of Ezra the Pentateuch had achieved recognition throughout the community and was, more or less, in its final form. The Pentateuch is here called Torah, or teaching (NRSV and NIV, "law"). The Torah includes both the story of Israel and its ancestors and God's instructions, or laws, that make for a wholesome and joyful community.

Modern studies of the Pentateuch have shown that it had a complex—and not yet fully known—history. Israel's story was shaped and edited over centuries, perhaps preceded by long periods of oral transmission. Scholars conventionally talk about documents called J, E, D, and P that were addressed to specific community problems and offered a vision of God and God's people appropriate to that context. Only later were these documents woven together into the Torah or Pentateuch. The old, simple distinction between Scripture and tradition has become meaningless. Close study of Scripture shows us that it is the heir of a long period of tradition, that people reworked the tradition in a new age, and that once Scripture achieved its final form there developed traditions of understanding and interpretation. Tradition comes before Scripture—and after it.

Nehemiah 8 wrestles with the gap between Scripture and contemporary practice and calls readers to follow what is written. But when we compare the regulations for the Festival of Booths in 8:14-15 with the legislation in the Pentateuch, we see several cases in which the two do not coincide. It may be that the author wanted to bring his interpretation of the text and the text itself into close harmony and even referred to his own interpretation as "what is written." If this interpretation is not correct, and the author had a text of the Pentateuch that was somewhat different from our present copy that read much like 8:14-15, we would then have to conclude that there were competing written texts from time to time, one of which won out and became canonical.

We need guides to understand ancient texts. That is why two twentieth-century translations are placed before each Commentary section of *The New Interpreter's Bible.* Each modern version is an interpretation of the text, and we have had ample opportunity to see correct—and incorrect—interpretations in both modern versions. The need to understand ancient texts creates a market for commentaries as well, including this one. But this need for guidance and interpretation is not just because we live more than 2,000 years later. When Ezra read the Torah, the Levites had to explain it, and only then did the people understand. No doubt most people in that great assembly could not read or write; they heard the Torah reverently, but had difficulty in understanding its meaning or its significance. The Levites interpreted the text, supported the admonitions of Ezra (8:11), and shared in the study on the second day, which led to the recovery of a proper celebration of the Festival of Tabernacles.

We do well to note the theme of joy in this chapter, since we often connect law to legalism or to accusations against us. *Lex semper accusat!* (The law always accuses!) is a common theological slogan in my own religious tradition. Reading and teaching the law led to understanding (8:8), but also to great joy (8:12). The first reaction to hearing the law was mourning and weeping, and from one point of view, that was a good and correct understanding, given the gap between Torah and the people's lives. But Ezra and the Levites stressed that this day was not a day of punishment, the fearsome day of the Lord. Rather, it was a day that was considered holy, or set apart, by God. It was, therefore, a time for celebrating and banqueting and thinking generously even of those who were not in attendance on this great day.

Is it joy *in* (Blenkinsopp) the Lord or joy *of* (NRSV, NIV, Williamson) the Lord that is strength? Probably both, but especially, I think, joy in the Lord. Joy in the Lord reflects dedication to God, commitment to God's ways and to God's Torah, faith and trust in God. If one wants refuge from the accusations of the Torah, one finds it in reliance on God. But the expression is somewhat ambiguous and could also mean that God's own joy in us is the source of our strength.

On the second day of study of the Torah, people discovered some dissonance between the requirements for the Festival of Tabernacles and what they had observed over the years. But instead of letting this lead to paralyzing fear or guilt, they took action and initiated reform. The whole congregation erected their booths and held the festival. Understanding led to obedience and, therefore, to great joy (8:17). The writer saw a connection between what the post-exilic community was doing and what the community of Joshua had done. Both of these communities had entered the land from outside, as a result of God's kindness. Joshua's community and those who had returned from exile knew that understanding was not enough. Real hearing embraces both connotations of the Hebrew word שמע (*šāma'*)—hearing and obeying. Do we fully understand a text when we know the meaning of all the words and how they fit together in ancient genres and in ancient historical contexts? Or do we really understand a text only when it addresses us and calls us to joy in the Lord and to obedience to Torah? The best obedience is not that of slaves before their master. Such obedience comes from fear and hatred and raw exercise of power. The obedience described in this chapter is total, involving all the assembly, and it is spontaneous and voluntary. In the keeping of the Festival of Tabernacles there was great rejoicing.

NEHEMIAH 9:1-37, A GREAT DAY OF REPENTANCE

Nehemiah 9:1-5*a*, Preparations for Confession

NIV

9 On the twenty-fourth day of the same month, the Israelites gathered together, fasting and wearing sackcloth and having dust on their heads. 2Those of Israelite descent had separated themselves from all foreigners. They stood in their places and confessed their sins and the wickedness of their fathers. 3They stood where they were and read from the Book of the Law of the LORD their God for a quarter of the day, and spent another quarter in confession and in worshiping the LORD their God. 4Standing on the stairs were the Levites—Jeshua, Bani, Kadmiel, Shebaniah, Bunni, Sherebiah, Bani and Kenani—who called with loud voices to the LORD their God. 5And the Levites—Jeshua, Kadmiel, Bani, Hashabneiah, Sherebiah, Hodiah, Shebaniah and Pethahiah—said: "Stand up and praise the LORD your God, who is from everlasting to everlasting.[a]"

[a] 5 Or *God for ever and ever*

NRSV

9 Now on the twenty-fourth day of this month the people of Israel were assembled with fasting and in sackcloth, and with earth on their heads.[a] Then those of Israelite descent separated themselves from all foreigners, and stood and confessed their sins and the iniquities of their ancestors. 3They stood up in their place and read from the book of the law of the LORD their God for a fourth part of the day, and for another fourth they made confession and worshiped the LORD their God. 4Then Jeshua, Bani, Kadmiel, Shebaniah, Bunni, Sherebiah, Bani, and Chenani stood on the stairs of the Levites and cried out with a loud voice to the LORD their God. 5Then the Levites, Jeshua, Kadmiel, Bani, Hashabneiah, Sherebiah, Hodiah, Shebaniah, and Pethahiah, said, "Stand up and bless the LORD your God from everlasting to everlasting.

[a] Heb *on them*

COMMENTARY

After a one-day interval following the solemn assembly (8:18), the Israelites gathered for another liturgical ceremony on the twenty-fourth day of the seventh month. This day of fasting and confession is not part of the regular Jewish calendar, although periodic fasts during exilic and early post-exilic times are mentioned elsewhere (Zech 7:5; 8:19). The text reflects a mood appropriate to the Day of Atonement, unmentioned in Ezra–Nehemiah, which falls on the tenth day of the seventh month (see Lev 23:26-32). The alternative locations for this chapter proposed by Clines and Williamson would put this ceremony on the twenty-fourth day of the ninth month of Ezra's first year; Rudolph's suggested arrangement of the text would date the ceremony to the twenty-fourth day of the first month in Ezra's second year.[177] In the present context, the date was set at a time when the eight-day Festival of Tabernacles (8:18) would have been completed.

Fasting, wearing sackcloth (see 1 Chr 21:16; Dan 9:3; Jonah 3:5), and placing dirt or ashes on one's forehead (Josh 7:6; 1 Sam 4:12; 2 Sam 1:2; Esth 4:1; Job 2:12) are regular parts of mourning rites in the Old Testament and may suggest that the worshipers felt themselves to be under a sentence of death. The "seed of Israel" (v. 2; "those of Israelite descent," NRSV and NIV; cf. Ezra 9:2), who had separated themselves from *all* foreigners and not just from foreign women as in

177. David J. A. Clines, *Ezra, Nehemiah, Esther,* NCB (Grand Rapids: Eerdmans, 1984) 189; H. G. M. Williamson, *Ezra, Nehemiah,* WBC 16 (Waco, Tex.: Word, 1985) 310; Wilhelm Rudolph, *Esra und Nehemia, samt 3. Esra,* HAT 20 (Tübingen: J. C. B. Mohr [Paul Siebeck], 1949) 154.

Ezra 10, corporately confessed their own sins (see vv. 33-37) and the sins of their forebears (see vv. 16-30). The whole ceremony lasted six hours, or about as long as the reading of the law in 8:3, and this festival of penance was divided into equal sections of reading from the book of the law and confessing sins before Yahweh (v. 3). The antecedent of "they" in v. 3 would seem to be those of Israelite descent, but it could also refer to the Levites in the following verses. Five of the eight names in the two lists of Levites in vv. 4-5 are identical (though not in the same order). Did one of these groups of Levites perform public displays of grief while the other group put the community's thoughts into words? Or was there originally only one group of Levites, with the second group arising because of the conflation of variant readings? The first group stood on the "stairs of the Levites" (v. 4; so correctly NRSV against NIV); these stairs served the same function as did the raised wooden platform in 8:4. In distinction to chap. 8, these Levites do not teach the people; rather, they serve as leaders of song and prayer, as often in the books of Chronicles (1 Chr 16:8-36; 2 Chr 8:14). The second group of Levites ordered the assembly to stand and bless Yahweh (cf. Ps 106:1). (See Reflections at 9:5*b*-37.)

Nehemiah 9:5*b*-37, The Great Prayer of Repentance

NIV

"Blessed be your glorious name, and may
it be exalted above all blessing and praise.
[6]You alone are the LORD. You made the heavens, even the highest heavens, and all their
starry host, the earth and all that is on it, the
seas and all that is in them. You give life to
everything, and the multitudes of heaven worship you.
[7]"You are the LORD God, who chose Abram
and brought him out of Ur of the Chaldeans
and named him Abraham. [8]You found his
heart faithful to you, and you made a covenant
with him to give to his descendants the land
of the Canaanites, Hittites, Amorites,
Perizzites, Jebusites and Girgashites. You have
kept your promise because you are righteous.
[9]"You saw the suffering of our forefathers
in Egypt; you heard their cry at the Red Sea.[b]
[10]You sent miraculous signs and wonders
against Pharaoh, against all his officials and all
the people of his land, for you knew how
arrogantly the Egyptians treated them. You
made a name for yourself, which remains to
this day. [11]You divided the sea before them,
so that they passed through it on dry ground,
but you hurled their pursuers into the depths,
like a stone into mighty waters. [12]By day you
led them with a pillar of cloud, and by night

[a] 5 Or *God for ever and ever* [b] 9 Hebrew *Yam Suph*; that is, Sea of Reeds

NRSV

Blessed be your glorious name, which is exalted
above all blessing and praise."
6And Ezra said:[a] "You are the LORD, you alone;
you have made heaven, the heaven of heavens,
with all their host, the earth and all that is on it,
the seas and all that is in them. To all of them
you give life, and the host of heaven worships
you. [7]You are the LORD, the God who chose
Abram and brought him out of Ur of the Chaldeans and gave him the name Abraham; [8]and you
found his heart faithful before you, and made with
him a covenant to give to his descendants the
land of the Canaanite, the Hittite, the Amorite,
the Perizzite, the Jebusite, and the Girgashite; and
you have fulfilled your promise, for you are righteous.
9"And you saw the distress of our ancestors in
Egypt and heard their cry at the Red Sea.[b] [10]You
performed signs and wonders against Pharaoh and
all his servants and all the people of his land, for
you knew that they acted insolently against our
ancestors. You made a name for yourself, which
remains to this day. [11]And you divided the sea
before them, so that they passed through the sea
on dry land, but you threw their pursuers into
the depths, like a stone into mighty waters.
[12]Moreover, you led them by day with a pillar of
cloud, and by night with a pillar of fire, to give
them light on the way in which they should go.

[a] Gk: Heb lacks *And Ezra said* [b] Or *Sea of Reeds*

NIV

with a pillar of fire to give them light on the
way they were to take.

13“You came down on Mount Sinai; you
spoke to them from heaven. You gave them
regulations and laws that are just and right,
and decrees and commands that are good.
14You made known to them your holy Sabbath
and gave them commands, decrees and laws
through your servant Moses. 15In their hunger
you gave them bread from heaven and in their
thirst you brought them water from the rock;
you told them to go in and take possession
of the land you had sworn with uplifted hand
to give them.

16“But they, our forefathers, became arrogant and stiff-necked, and did not obey your
commands. 17They refused to listen and failed
to remember the miracles you performed
among them. They became stiff-necked and
in their rebellion appointed a leader in order
to return to their slavery. But you are a
forgiving God, gracious and compassionate,
slow to anger and abounding in love. Therefore you did not desert them, 18even when
they cast for themselves an image of a calf
and said, ‘This is your god, who brought you
up out of Egypt,’ or when they committed
awful blasphemies.

19“Because of your great compassion you
did not abandon them in the desert. By day
the pillar of cloud did not cease to guide them
on their path, nor the pillar of fire by night
to shine on the way they were to take. 20You
gave your good Spirit to instruct them. You
did not withhold your manna from their
mouths, and you gave them water for their
thirst. 21For forty years you sustained them in
the desert; they lacked nothing, their clothes
did not wear out nor did their feet become
swollen.

22“You gave them kingdoms and nations,
allotting to them even the remotest frontiers.
They took over the country of Sihon[a] king of
Heshbon and the country of Og king of
Bashan. 23You made their sons as numerous
as the stars in the sky, and you brought them

[a] *22* One Hebrew manuscript and Septuagint; most Hebrew manuscripts *Sihon, that is, the country of the*

NRSV

13You came down also upon Mount Sinai, and
spoke with them from heaven, and gave them
right ordinances and true laws, good statutes and
commandments, 14and you made known your
holy sabbath to them and gave them commandments and statutes and a law through your servant
Moses. 15For their hunger you gave them bread
from heaven, and for their thirst you brought
water for them out of the rock, and you told them
to go in to possess the land that you swore to
give them.

16“But they and our ancestors acted presumptuously and stiffened their necks and did not obey
your commandments; 17they refused to obey, and
were not mindful of the wonders that you performed among them; but they stiffened their
necks and determined to return to their slavery
in Egypt. But you are a God ready to forgive,
gracious and merciful, slow to anger and abounding in steadfast love, and you did not forsake
them. 18Even when they had cast an image of a
calf for themselves and said, ‘This is your God
who brought you up out of Egypt,’ and had
committed great blasphemies, 19you in your great
mercies did not forsake them in the wilderness;
the pillar of cloud that led them in the way did
not leave them by day, nor the pillar of fire by
night that gave them light on the way by which
they should go. 20You gave your good spirit to
instruct them, and did not withhold your manna
from their mouths, and gave them water for their
thirst. 21Forty years you sustained them in the
wilderness so that they lacked nothing; their
clothes did not wear out and their feet did not
swell. 22And you gave them kingdoms and peoples, and allotted to them every corner,[a] so they
took possession of the land of King Sihon of
Heshbon and the land of King Og of Bashan. 23You
multiplied their descendants like the stars of
heaven, and brought them into the land that you
had told their ancestors to enter and possess. 24So
the descendants went in and possessed the land,
and you subdued before them the inhabitants of
the land, the Canaanites, and gave them into their
hands, with their kings and the peoples of the
land, to do with them as they pleased. 25And they
captured fortress cities and a rich land, and took

[a] Meaning of Heb uncertain

NIV

into the land that you told their fathers to enter and possess. 24Their sons went in and took possession of the land. You subdued before them the Canaanites, who lived in the land; you handed the Canaanites over to them, along with their kings and the peoples of the land, to deal with them as they pleased. 25They captured fortified cities and fertile land; they took possession of houses filled with all kinds of good things, wells already dug, vineyards, olive groves and fruit trees in abundance. They ate to the full and were well-nourished; they reveled in your great goodness.

26"But they were disobedient and rebelled against you; they put your law behind their backs. They killed your prophets, who had admonished them in order to turn them back to you; they committed awful blasphemies. 27So you handed them over to their enemies, who oppressed them. But when they were oppressed they cried out to you. From heaven you heard them, and in your great compassion you gave them deliverers, who rescued them from the hand of their enemies.

28"But as soon as they were at rest, they again did what was evil in your sight. Then you abandoned them to the hand of their enemies so that they ruled over them. And when they cried out to you again, you heard from heaven, and in your compassion you delivered them time after time.

29"You warned them to return to your law, but they became arrogant and disobeyed your commands. They sinned against your ordinances, by which a man will live if he obeys them. Stubbornly they turned their backs on you, became stiff-necked and refused to listen. 30For many years you were patient with them. By your Spirit you admonished them through your prophets. Yet they paid no attention, so you handed them over to the neighboring peoples. 31But in your great mercy you did not put an end to them or abandon them, for you are a gracious and merciful God.

32"Now therefore, O our God, the great, mighty and awesome God, who keeps his covenant of love, do not let all this hardship

NRSV

possession of houses filled with all sorts of goods, hewn cisterns, vineyards, olive orchards, and fruit trees in abundance; so they ate, and were filled and became fat, and delighted themselves in your great goodness.

26"Nevertheless they were disobedient and rebelled against you and cast your law behind their backs and killed your prophets, who had warned them in order to turn them back to you, and they committed great blasphemies. 27Therefore you gave them into the hands of their enemies, who made them suffer. Then in the time of their suffering they cried out to you and you heard them from heaven, and according to your great mercies you gave them saviors who saved them from the hands of their enemies. 28But after they had rest, they again did evil before you, and you abandoned them to the hands of their enemies, so that they had dominion over them; yet when they turned and cried to you, you heard from heaven, and many times you rescued them according to your mercies. 29And you warned them in order to turn them back to your law. Yet they acted presumptuously and did not obey your commandments, but sinned against your ordinances, by the observance of which a person shall live. They turned a stubborn shoulder and stiffened their neck and would not obey. 30Many years you were patient with them, and warned them by your spirit through your prophets; yet they would not listen. Therefore you handed them over to the peoples of the lands. 31Nevertheless, in your great mercies you did not make an end of them or forsake them, for you are a gracious and merciful God.

32"Now therefore, our God—the great and mighty and awesome God, keeping covenant and steadfast love—do not treat lightly all the hardship that has come upon us, upon our kings, our officials, our priests, our prophets, our ancestors, and all your people, since the time of the kings of Assyria until today. 33You have been just in all that has come upon us, for you have dealt faithfully and we have acted wickedly; 34our kings, our officials, our priests, and our ancestors have not kept your law or heeded the commandments and the warnings that you gave them. 35Even in their own kingdom, and in the great goodness

NIV	NRSV
seem trifling in your eyes—the hardship that has come upon us, upon our kings and leaders, upon our priests and prophets, upon our fathers and all your people, from the days of the kings of Assyria until today. [33]In all that has happened to us, you have been just; you have acted faithfully, while we did wrong. [34]Our kings, our leaders, our priests and our fathers did not follow your law; they did not pay attention to your commands or the warnings you gave them. [35]Even while they were in their kingdom, enjoying your great goodness to them in the spacious and fertile land you gave them, they did not serve you or turn from their evil ways. [36]"But see, we are slaves today, slaves in the land you gave our forefathers so they could eat its fruit and the other good things it produces. [37]Because of our sins, its abundant harvest goes to the kings you have placed over us. They rule over our bodies and our cattle as they please. We are in great distress.	you bestowed on them, and in the large and rich land that you set before them, they did not serve you and did not turn from their wicked works. [36]Here we are, slaves to this day—slaves in the land that you gave to our ancestors to enjoy its fruit and its good gifts. [37]Its rich yield goes to the kings whom you have set over us because of our sins; they have power also over our bodies and over our livestock at their pleasure, and we are in great distress."

COMMENTARY

Neither the NRSV nor the NIV understands the prayer as poetry, though Rudolph and Gunneweg do, and it is printed as poetry in *BHS.*[178] The prayer displays rhythm and meter only sporadically and may be considered a kind of poetic prose, with a series of Hebrew puns in vv. 20, 24, and 27. The prayer begins with a call to praise in v. 5*b* (cf. Psalm 106) and ends with a final paragraph consisting of petition (v. 32), confession of sins (vv. 33-35), and complaint (vv. 36-37). In between comes a historical retrospect (vv. 6-31). The prayer praises Yahweh for righteousness of judgment on Israel and functions in part as a "doxology of judgment," much like the hymn whose stanzas have been distributed throughout the book of Amos (Amos 4:13; 5:8-9; 9:5-6). Its closest formal parallel in the Bible is Psalm 106 (see also the so-called historical Psalms 78; 105; 135; 136). The recital of Israel's past sin climaxes with the great distress in which the people now find themselves. Blenkinsopp finds similarities between Nehemiah 9 and the *Words of the Heavenly Luminaries* from Qumran, Baruch 1:15–3:8, and the *Prayer of Manasseh* (this text, however, is individual rather than communal).[179] The prayer is composed almost entirely of citations of or allusions to other biblical texts. The writer seems to have known the Pentateuch in its entirety.[180]

9:5b-31, Historical Retrospect. The outline of this section offers important clues to the overall meaning of the chapter. First, the prayer recites God's providential care in creation (v. 6), the election of Abraham (vv. 7-8), and the exodus from Egypt (vv. 9-11). During this time there was no hint of human infidelity. Verses 12-21 then discuss the complex divine-human relationships during Israel's wilderness wanderings: God's

178. See Rudolph, *Esra und Nehemia*, 57; Gunneweg, *Nehemia*, 124.

179. Joseph Blenkinsopp, *Ezra–Nehemiah*, OTL (Philadelphia: Westminster, 1988) 302.

180. A convenient list of parallels is provided by Jacob M. Myers, *Ezra, Nehemiah*, AB 14 (Garden City, N.Y.: Doubleday, 1965) 167-69.

providential care (vv. 12-15); the rebellions of the ancestors in the wilderness (vv. 16-18); and God's continued guidance in spite of their rebellion (vv. 19-21). Finally, vv. 22-31 review the life of the ancestors in the land. After the dramatically successful conquest (vv. 22-25), the people became disobedient and were punished, they prayed, and they received divine deliverance throughout the period of the judges (vv. 26-28). The last verses of the historical retrospect report sin and punishment during the monarchical period and bring the account down to the (implied) time of the poem's origin during the exile.[181] Despite the present captivity, God's mercy and righteousness endure (vv. 29-31).

According to this prayer, the period of the judges, just as in the book of Judges itself, consisted of a series of cycles in which sin and punishment were followed by petition and deliverance. The period of the kings in vv. 29-31, just as in the books of Kings, consisted of a truncated cycle: repeated sins that eventually led to the loss of land. At the end of the books of Kings the reader may be tempted to ask: "If we were to cry out, would there not be deliverance for us?" In other words, an implied cycle of petition and deliverance is also there. In Nehemiah 9, too, after the historical retrospect come a petition (v. 32), a confession of sins (vv. 33-35), and a complaint about their present condition that functions as a kind of appeal for God to act based on pity for them (vv. 36-37). In short, the prayer asks for the cycle of deliverance to resume.

9:5b, Hymnic Introduction. Because this verse addresses God in the second person without an appropriate introduction, and because the preceding phrase, "from everlasting to everlasting," is awkward both in Hebrew and in the literal translation of the NRSV, it seems advisable to add a clause after "your God" to solve both difficulties: "Blessed are you, O LORD, our God" (the NIV glosses over the problem by inserting the words "who is"). This original reading, which forms the first line of the prayer, was later lost by haplography, the omission of one or two identical or similar letters, groups of letters, or words found together.

9:6, Creation. The praise of the Creator should begin with the following translation: "You, O LORD, are the only God." The translations in the NRSV and the NIV suggest instead that there is only one Yahweh, which is not likely to have been a major point of dispute when this poem was composed. The Hebrew cosmos presupposed in this verse was tri-partite: heaven, earth, and sea (Pss 69:34; 96:11; cf. Rev 21:1, the new creation, in which there will be no sea). God's creative action produced this cosmos, and God created and preserves all living beings—in the heavens, on the land, and in the sea. The "host of heaven" connotes either the stars or the members of God's heavenly council (cf. Pss 103:21; 148:2). The worship performed by the host of heaven stands in sharp contrast to the disobedience of Israel.

9:7-8, The Election of Abraham. Abraham is selected by the author to represent the traditions of Israel's ancestors in Genesis 12–50. The prayer applies the word "chose" (בחר *bāḥar*) to Abraham, based no doubt on the terminology of Deut 4:37; 10:15, although his election is described with other words in Genesis. The verb "brought out" (יצא *yāṣāʾ*), used of God's guidance of Abraham from his southern Mesopotamian home in Ur of the Chaldees (cf. Gen 11:28, 31; 15:7), suggests a kind of deliverance, or exodus, also for him (see Exod 20:2; 32:11-12). The reference to the gift of the name "Abraham" recalls Genesis 17, where God changed Abram's name to Abraham and Sarai's to Sarah to mark their new covenantal status. Abraham was faithful (cf. the "righteousness" of Abram in Gen 15:6), and God made with him a covenant—the only covenant mentioned in this prayer—whose primary content was the promise of the land (see Gen 15:18-21; 17:7-8). The list of pre-Israelite inhabitants of the land in v. 8 resembles the other nine biblical lists (Gen 15:19-20; Exod 3:8, 17; 33:2; 34:11; Deut 7:1; 20:17; Judg 3:5; Ezra 9:1), but is not identical to any of them (see the Commentary on Ezra 9:1-5). Just as foreigners ruled Israel at the time of the writer, so also a multitude of foreigners had occupied the land in the ancestral period. Nevertheless, in spite of their presence, the promise to give the land to Abra-

181. H. G. M. Williamson, "Structure and Historiography in Nehemiah 9," in *Proceedings of the Ninth World Congress of Jewish Studies, 1985 Panel Session* (Jerusalem: Magnes, 1988) 129, ascribes the whole prayer to the Judean community, which was never exiled to Babylon, but continued to live in the land during the exile and afterward.

ham's descendants had been fulfilled—God kept the promise, and this fulfillment demonstrated God's righteousness, or faithfulness, to the relationship with Abraham (see Gen 15:6).[182] In the Hebrew text, v. 6 begins and v. 8 ends with the pronoun "you," referring to God, as does the whole historical retrospect in v. 31.

9:9-11, Exodus. The survey of the exodus event reports that God saw the affliction of the people's ancestors—no doubt much like their own affliction—and heard their cry. Perhaps the author is suggesting that God will soon hear the plea of the Levites, who had just cried out with a loud voice (v. 4). Through the plagues God brought judgment on Pharaoh's officials and all his people. God's reputation or name, earned through the event of the exodus and the crossing of the Sea of Reeds (v. 10), endured to the time when this prayer was offered. According to two of the pentateuchal source documents, the divine name Yahweh had been revealed to Moses in the course of the events leading to the exodus (Exod 3:13-15 [E]; 6:2 [P]). The Egyptians had acted arrogantly in the time of oppression (v. 16); the prayer gives no hint of Israelite disobedience in Egypt (cf. Ezek 20:8).

9:12-21, Wilderness Wanderings. In vv. 12-15 four providential acts of God are mentioned: the pillar of cloud and the pillar of fire (Exod 13:21); the giving of the law on Sinai (Exodus 19–24); manna from heaven for the hungry and water from the rock for the thirsty (Exod 16:4; 17:6; Num 20:8); and the command to enter and possess the promised land, based on a divine oath. Only observance of the sabbath is mentioned as a specific ethical requirement, a typical exilic and post-exilic concern (10:31; 13:15-22; Isa 56:2, 4, 6), also highlighted in the survey of Israel's history in Ezekiel 20:12-13, 16, 20-21, 24.

The confession of sins begins in v. 16 with the mention of the presumptuous acts of the ancestors (the NRSV errs in distinguishing "they" from "our ancestors in this verse"). The sins of the ancestors are compared to those of their erstwhile Egyptian oppressors in that "acted presumptuously" (v. 16, referring to the ancestors) and "acted insolently" (v. 10, referring to Pharaoh and his servants) translate the same Hebrew verb (זיד *zîd*). The ancestors even stubbornly desired to return to slavery in Egypt (v. 17).[183] Their behavior contrasts markedly with the character of Yahweh: a God ready to forgive, one who is gracious and merciful (v. 17), a theme that recurs at the end of the historical retrospect in v. 31. God's patience—slow to anger and abounding in steadfast love—continued even during the making of the golden calf (v. 18; cf. Exodus 32) and the committing of great blasphemies.

God did not abandon them (vv. 17, 19), but in fact inaugurated a second era of providential guidance in the wilderness (vv. 19-21), which repeats the themes of vv. 12-15: the pillar of cloud and the pillar of fire, the gift of God's good Spirit to instruct them (functionally the same as the giving of the law in vv. 13-14), and the provision of manna and water.

9:22-31, Life in the Land. The fourth providential act (v. 15), the command to enter the land, is developed extensively in vv. 22-25, the first part of the section dealing with life in the land. The conquest began with victories over Sihon and Og in Transjordan (Num 21:21-35; Deut 1:4; 2:16–3:11). Both the conquest and Israel's subsequent population explosion were fulfillments of promises to the ancestors (Gen 15:5; 22:17; 26:4; Deut 1:10-11). The victory over the Canaanites was solely God's doing; Joshua is not even mentioned. Only the descendants of the exodus generation were able to enter the land. The prayer does not seem to expect or call for any armed appropriation of the land in the future. The people's delight in the abundance of the land is matched by a recognition that all this stems from God's goodness. Even the words "became fat" (v. 25) denote unbroken prosperity without any of the negative connotations of Deut 32:15. Indeed, the obedience of the ancestors continued until the end of the period of the conquest (see Judg 2:7).

Verses 26-31 offer a cyclical picture of Israel's subsequent history of disobedience, and they depict a constantly downward spiral. The offenses were egregious, but the charges are not specific:

182. Some scholars find an ambivalence in Gen 15:6, referring both to the righteousness of God and the righteousness of Abraham. The prayer in Nehemiah 9 deduces the same double meaning from Gen 15:6.

183. "In Egypt," in the middle of v. 17 in the NRSV, is a correct emendation of the Hebrew text, but this change should have been recorded in the footnotes to this translation. The NIV's "in their rebellion" translates במרים (*bĕmiryām*) literally without making the emendation as in NRSV, but moves it to a different part of the verse.

rejection of the law, killing of the prophets, and doing great blasphemies. There is actually little historical evidence for violence against the prophets in the Bible (2 Chr 24:20-22; Jer 26:20-23),[184] and this charge may have grown as a rhetorical heightening of the people's rejection of the prophetic word. Two times the prayer recounts a complete cycle of sin, punishment, petition for help, and deliverance, roughly corresponding to the period of the judges (vv. 26-28); the third cycle (vv. 29-31) has not yet advanced to the people's cry (but see v. 32). God's manifold mercies had led to the raising of saviors (v. 27; cf. Judg 2:16, 18) and the sending of prophets to bring the people to repentance (v. 29; cf. v. 26 and 1 Kgs 18:4, 13; 2 Kgs 17:13). Punishment in each cycle consisted of being turned over to the power of foreign peoples (vv. 27, 28, 30).

Verse 29 returns to the idea of presumptuous behavior, but now in the monarchical period (cf. vv. 10, 16). The accusations against the people are still rather colorless—disobedience of the commandments, stubbornness, failure to listen to the admonitions of the prophets. They rejected the very commandments that would give them life (Lev 18:5; Deut 30:15-20; Ezek 20:11). Despite God's patience and the sending of the Spirit through the prophets to warn them (2 Chr 36:15-16), the people had refused to listen. But even the present punishment by the peoples of the lands did not mean a complete end, as Jeremiah had promised (Jer 5:18; 30:11), nor did it bring abandonment (v. 31; despite v. 28). God remained a gracious and merciful God until the very hour of this prayer.

9:32, Petition. The transition point between historical retrospect and petition is marked by a transitional "now" (v. 32). God is addressed, even by those under judgment, as "our God," as in the first (reconstructed) line of the poem (v. 5). God is great, mighty, and awesome, but God is also, paradoxically, the one who keeps covenant and steadfast love, a reference to the covenantal promise of the land to Abraham in v. 8. The petition is forceful in its understatement: "Do not treat lightly all the hardship that has come upon us." The term "hardship" (תלאה *tĕlā'â*) is used elsewhere to refer to Israel's troubles in Egypt (Exod 18:8; Num 20:14). That trouble has now struck people both high and low—kings, officials, priests, prophets, and the immediate ancestors of those who offer the prayer. It has lasted from the Assyrian domination until the present time (cf. vv. 10, 36).

9:33-37, Confession of Sin and Complaint. Verse 33 has led to the classification of this prayer as a doxology of judgment: "God, you have been righteous in what you have done." God has acted truthfully, the poet says, but "we" have acted wickedly. We are as guilty as our ancestors. The "we" of this confession includes various segments of society, significantly omitting the prophets from any blame (v. 34; cf. v. 32). Despite God's kingship and great goodness, manifested in the marvelous gift of the land, the speakers admit that they have not served God and so they now have become slaves (vv. 35-36). The very land God gave to the ancestors has become the place of servitude until "this very day." The writer complains that the rich yield of this land now goes—presumably through taxation and tribute—to the kings who were imposed on them as punishment. This view of the imperial power seems much harsher and much less nuanced and cautious than the usual attitude toward the Persians reflected in the books of Ezra and Nehemiah: "They have power over our bodies and over our livestock at their pleasure" (v. 37). This critical attitude toward the Persians makes Gunneweg's proposal about the later origin of this chapter quite attractive (see the Overview to 7:73*b*–10:39).[185]

The speakers of this prayer clearly include themselves among the guilty: These punishments have come on *us* because of *our* sins (v. 37); *we* are in great distress. The pronoun "we" forms the last word of the prayer in Hebrew, just as "you" (referring to God) began and ended the historical retrospect (vv. 6-31). Between those two words, and between those two characters, God and people, the hopes of those who prayed stand in the balance.

184. See Luke 11:47-51; Acts 7:52. See also Odil Hannes Steck, *Israel und das gewaltsame Geschick der Propheten,* WMANT 23 (Neukirchen-Vluyn: Neukirchener Verlag, 1967). Steck argues that the idea of the violent fate of the prophets arose over a long period of time in order to express the constant obstinacy of pre-exilic Israel, which necessitated the destruction of Israel and Judah (2 Kgs 17:13-14).

185. Antonius H. J. Gunneweg, *Nehemia,* KAT 19, 2 (Gütersloh: Gütersloher Verlagshaus Gerd Mohn, 1987) 124.

REFLECTIONS

The truth for one generation is only partly the truth for the next. All of us struggle with how to express the faith of our heritage in the language of our children. The person responsible for having written this chapter did not contest that those who returned from Babylon in the days of Ezra were faithful, nor did he doubt that the joy of the Festival of Tabernacles had drowned out their sorrow. But he wanted to add some qualifications for his own time, when faithfulness to God required separation from all foreigners and the temptations they offered. For his time, acceptance before God required coming to terms with a history of failure. Reading the law needed to be followed by confession of sins and worship of God (9:3).

But his account of Israel's history with God was not just a catalog of misery. The host of heaven worshiped the Creator right at the beginning and thereby set a pattern now echoed by the levitical leaders in the world of the text (9:3). Abraham—should we not add Sarah, too?—had a heart that was faithful to God. The central truth about God is faithfulness to the people; this makes God a promise maker and a promise keeper.

God's mercy is repeated in each generation and many times in one's own life. God's mercy is boundless and, paradoxically, has its limits. One should not expect sin and punishment, prayer to God, and deliverance to go on forever without any change in oneself. Grace is free but not cheap. But even when the cycles of deliverance came to an end in this poem, God did not make a full end, nor did God abandon the people. How many times should a person forgive sister or brother? How many times will God forgive us? Even when the cycles of deliverance come to an end, we dare to pray for the wheel of history to turn toward deliverance one more time.

What is the character of God? God is a covenant maker and therefore promises whatever God's people need for wholeness of life, here expressed as the gift of the land. God is also a covenant keeper. For many people God's awesomeness is manifested in the reversals of life and the mysteries of judgment. And yet we boldly confess in a well-known collect, "God, your almighty power is shown chiefly in showing mercy." The One to whom we pray for forgiveness is great, mighty, and awesome and, at the same time, the One who keeps covenant and steadfast love (9:32). Are not the latter virtues the surest signs of God's almighty power?

God guides us and protects us night and day, before, during, and after our sin (9:12, 19). God gives us good and just laws that sometimes can be summarized in one imperative. In the time when Nehemiah 9 was composed, observance of the sabbath day showed whether one acknowledged God. What would be a comprehensive and concrete imperative for our day? Acceptance of the stranger? Respect for the environment? Peace? Justice?

God's good Spirit comes to offer us instruction and encouragement (9:20*a*). This good Spirit appears today in our congregational leaders and fellow members, our friends and our relatives, and in all those who love us enough to tell us the truth of the faith. Hunger and thirst according to this prayer were satisfied before, during, and, most important, after sinning (9:15*a*, 20*b*-21). Even after sinning, Israel, like the psalmist, lacked nothing (9:21; cf. Ps 23:1). In addition to daily bread in the wilderness, then, God provided clothes that never wore out and ankles that never swelled. Divine beneficence after sinning was more lavish than before.

Before Israel's history of sin began, the command to possess the land required half a verse (9:15*b*). After the "ancestors acted presumptuously and stiffened their necks," that promise expanded to four verses (9:22-25)! The earthiness of God's goodness comes to full expression through fertile land, wells already dug, trees in abundance, well-nourished people, reveling in God's goodness. God continually tried to give the people the one thing they now lacked: possession of the land. Salvation must always meet our needs, or it is not salvation *for us.*

The history of sinning is not just a history of a fallen world somewhere out there or a roll call of notorious sinners. It is not that our parents erred and we are paying the consequences.

No, according to chap. 9, the history of sinning is our history; we did wrong—despite God's faithful actions. The leaders and representatives did not *serve* God, and therefore, with punishment to fit the crime, the people are now *servants,* real slaves. Some people can tolerate foreign domination and make a virtue of it, as did the principal authors of Ezra and Nehemiah. But finally, at least for some within Israel, including the author of this chapter—and for many surely today—such slavery could not be tolerated. The alien, yet God-given, kings ruled the bodies and the cattle of those who prayed in chap. 9 mostly in accord with what was pleasing to these rulers (9:37).

What moves God to act? Is it our praise, God's character, God's promises? "You are the LORD, you alone" is the way the poem begins in 9:6.

But the poem ends with "we"—we the slaves, we the exploited, we who are in great distress (9:36-37). Is not God moved by pity for us?

You, God, are one-half of the issue. We are the other half. You and us—in that connection lies our only hope.

NEHEMIAH 9:38–10:39,[186] A FIRM AGREEMENT TO KEEP THE LAW

Nehemiah 9:38–10:29, Sealing of the Agreement

NIV

38"In view of all this, we are making a binding agreement, putting it in writing, and our leaders, our Levites and our priests are affixing their seals to it."

10 Those who sealed it were:

Nehemiah the governor, the son of Hacaliah.

Zedekiah, 2Seraiah, Azariah, Jeremiah,
3Pashhur, Amariah, Malkijah,
4Hattush, Shebaniah, Malluch,
5Harim, Meremoth, Obadiah,
6Daniel, Ginnethon, Baruch,
7Meshullam, Abijah, Mijamin,
8Maaziah, Bilgai and Shemaiah.
These were the priests.

9The Levites:

Jeshua son of Azaniah, Binnui of the sons of Henadad, Kadmiel,
10and their associates: Shebaniah,
Hodiah, Kelita, Pelaiah, Hanan,
11Mica, Rehob, Hashabiah,
12Zaccur, Sherebiah, Shebaniah,
13Hodiah, Bani and Beninu.

14The leaders of the people:

NRSV

38[a]Because of all this we make a firm agreement in writing, and on that sealed document are
inscribed the names of our officials, our Levites,
and our priests.

10 [b]Upon the sealed document are the names
of Nehemiah the governor, son of Hacaliah, and Zedekiah; 2Seraiah, Azariah, Jeremiah,
3Pashhur, Amariah, Malchijah, 4Hattush, Shebaniah, Malluch, 5Harim, Meremoth, Obadiah,
6Daniel, Ginnethon, Baruch, 7Meshullam, Abijah,
Mijamin, 8Maaziah, Bilgai, Shemaiah; these are
the priests. 9And the Levites: Jeshua son of
Azaniah, Binnui of the sons of Henadad, Kadmiel;
10and their associates, Shebaniah, Hodiah, Kelita,
Pelaiah, Hanan, 11Mica, Rehob, Hashabiah, 12Zac-
cur, Sherebiah, Shebaniah, 13Hodiah, Bani,
Beninu. 14The leaders of the people: Parosh, Pahath-moab, Elam, Zattu, Bani, 15Bunni, Azgad,
Bebai, 16Adonijah, Bigvai, Adin, 17Ater, Hezekiah,
Azzur, 18Hodiah, Hashum, Bezai, 19Hariph,
Anathoth, Nebai, 20Magpiash, Meshullam, Hezir,
21Meshezabel, Zadok, Jaddua, 22Pelatiah, Hanan,
Anaiah, 23Hoshea, Hananiah, Hasshub, 24Hallo-
hesh, Pilha, Shobek, 25Rehum, Hashabnah,

[a] Ch 10.1 in Heb   [b] Ch 10.2 in Heb

186. In the HB 9:38–10:1-39 = 9:38–10:40.

NIV

Parosh, Pahath-Moab, Elam, Zattu, Bani,
15Bunni, Azgad, Bebai,
16Adonijah, Bigvai, Adin,
17Ater, Hezekiah, Azzur,
18Hodiah, Hashum, Bezai,
19Hariph, Anathoth, Nebai,
20Magpiash, Meshullam, Hezir,
21Meshezabel, Zadok, Jaddua,
22Pelatiah, Hanan, Anaiah,
23Hoshea, Hananiah, Hasshub,
24Hallohesh, Pilha, Shobek,
25Rehum, Hashabnah, Maaseiah,
26Ahiah, Hanan, Anan,
27Malluch, Harim and Baanah.

28"The rest of the people—priests, Levites,
gatekeepers, singers, temple servants and all
who separated themselves from the neighboring peoples for the sake of the Law of God,
together with their wives and all their sons
and daughters who are able to understand—
29all these now join their brothers the nobles,
and bind themselves with a curse and an oath
to follow the Law of God given through
Moses the servant of God and to obey carefully all the commands, regulations and decrees of the LORD our Lord.

NRSV

Maaseiah, 26Ahiah, Hanan, Anan, 27Malluch,
Harim, and Baanah.
28The rest of the people, the priests, the
Levites, the gatekeepers, the singers, the temple
servants, and all who have separated themselves
from the peoples of the lands to adhere to the
law of God, their wives, their sons, their daughters, all who have knowledge and understanding,
29join with their kin, their nobles, and enter into
a curse and an oath to walk in God's law, which
was given by Moses the servant of God, and to
observe and do all the commandments of the LORD
our Lord and his ordinances and his statutes.

COMMENTARY

9:38–10:1, A Human Pledge. "Because of all this" (9:38) refers to the reading of the law and the confessional prayer in chaps. 8–9, and the "we" and "our" that are used so frequently in chap. 10 follow naturally after the first-person pronouns in the prayer of chap. 9. The "firm agreement" (אמנה *'ămānâ*) is not called a "covenant," perhaps to identify it as a human pledge rather than as a divinely initiated promise (cf. 9:8). "Those who sealed it" (10:1) represents an emended text (reading החותמים [*haḥôtĕmîm*] for על החתומים [*'al haḥătûmîm*], "Upon the sealed documents"). Perhaps each of these people signed a document that was also given an official seal. Nehemiah, the governor (cf. 8:9; Ezra 2:63), was the first to sign it. Some scholars believe that Zedekiah, mentioned right after Nehemiah, may have been his secretary (Zadok, a scribe with a similar name, is mentioned in 13:13; cf. Rehum and his scribe Shimshai in Ezra 4:8-9).

10:2-8, The Priests. The list of priests in these verses is closely related to and may be derived from lists of priests in 12:1-7, 12-21. Names that probably served as a source for this chapter are marked with an asterisk in the table that follows (the six names from Joiarib to the second Jedaiah are a secondary development of the list; see the Commentary on 12:6-7, 19-21); names that appear in italic type are difficult to explain. In 12:12-21 the names of the priestly families are followed by the name of an individual, but only the family names are listed below. Nehemiah 10 clearly understands these family names as individuals.

Figure 4: The Signers of the Firm Agreement

Nehemiah 10	Neh 12:1-7	Neh 12:12-21
Seraiah	*Seraiah	*Seraiah
Azariah	*Jeremiah	*Jeremiah
Jeremiah	*Ezra	*Ezra
Pashhur	*Amariah	*Amariah
Amariah	*Malluch	*Malluchi
Malchijah	*Hattush	*Shebaniah
Hattush	*Shecaniah	*Harim
Shebaniah	*Rehum	*Meraioth
Malluch	*Meremoth	*Iddo
Harim	*Iddo	*Ginnethon
Meremoth	*Ginnethoi	*Abijah
Obadiah	*Abijah	*Miniamin
Daniel	*Mijamin	*Moadiah
Ginnethon	*Maadiah	*Bilgah
Baruch	*Bilgah	*Shemaiah
Meshullam	*Shemaiah	Joiarib
Abijah	Joiarib	Jedaiah
Mijamin	Jedaiah	Sallai
Maaziah	Sallu	Amok
Bilgai	Amok	Hilkiah
Shemaiah	Hilkiah	Jedaiah
	Jedaiah	

In addition to identical names and those that display some minor spelling variations in one or both of the lists in chap. 12 (Azariah = Ezra; Shebaniah = Shecaniah; Harim = Rehum; Meremoth = Meraioth; Obadiah = Iddo; Ginnethon = Ginnethoi; Mijamin = Miniamin; Maaziah = Maadiah or Moadiah; Bilgai = Bilgah), only five of the twenty-one priests in vv. 2-8 are unaccounted for. Of these the family of Pashhur is mentioned in Ezra 2:38; Malchijah may be an alternative form of Malluch; and Daniel and Meshullam accompanied Ezra on his return (Ezra 8:2, 16); thus only Baruch cannot be explained.

10:9-13, The Levites. The list of Levites may have been derived from other lists of Levites at 8:7; 9:4, 5; and 12:8. Names that probably served as a source for the list in chap. 10 are marked with an asterisk in the table below; italicized names in the list are difficult to explain.

Figure 5: The Levites Who Signed the Firm Agreement

Nehemiah 10	Neh 8:7	Neh 9:4	Neh 9:5	Neh 12:8
Jeshua	*Jeshua	*Jeshua	*Jeshua	*Jeshua
Binnui	*Bani	*Bani	*Kadmiel	*Binnui
Kadmiel	*Sherebiah	*Kadmiel	*Bani	*Kadmiel
Shebaniah	Jamin	*Shebaniah	*Hashabneiah	*Sherebiah
Hodiah	Akkub	Bunni	*Sherebiah	Judah
Kelita	Shabbethai	*Sherebiah	*Hodiah	Mattaniah
Pelaiah	*Hodiah	*Bani	*Shebaniah	
Hanan	Maaseiah	*Chenani	Pethahiah	
Mica	*Kelita			
Rehob	Azariah			
Hashabiah	Jozabad			
Zaccur	*Hanan			
Sherebiah	*Pelaiah			
Shebanaiah				
Hodiah				
Bani				
Beninu				

Of the fifteen Levites in these verses (Shebaniah and Hodiah appear twice in vv. 10 and 12-13), twelve are attested in one or more of the other lists (assuming that Hashabiah = Hashabneiah and Beninu = Chenani). The first three names—Jeshua, Binnui, and Kadmiel—head all lists of Levites except that in 12:24. Note how these three are distinguished from "their associates" (v. 10). Seven of the thirteen Levites who assisted in reading the law in 8:7 reappear here, as do seven of the eight Levites in 9:4, seven of the eight in 9:5, and four of the six in 12:8. Mica is listed among the levitical ancestors in 11:22; Rehob and Zaccur are the only names unknown from elsewhere. The number of Levites is much greater here proportionally than in Ezra 2:40 or 8:15-20.

10:14-27, Lay Leaders. Of the first twenty-one lay leaders of the people (vv. 14-20), twenty are known as family or place-names from Ezra 2, Nehemiah 7, and 1 Esdras 5: Parosh (Ezra 2:3); Pahath-Moab (Ezra 2:6); Elam (Ezra 2:7); Zattu (Ezra 2:8); Bani (Ezra 2:10); Bunni (Bunnui, Neh 7:15); Azgad (Ezra 2:12); Bebai (Ezra 2:11); Adonijah (Adonikam, Ezra 2:13); Bigvai (Ezra 2:14); Adin (Ezra 2:15); Ater (Ezra 2:16); Azzur (1 Esdr 5:15); Hashum (Ezra 2:19); Bezai (Ezra 2:17); Hariph (Neh 7:24); Anathoth (Ezra 2:23); Nebai (Nebo, Ezra 2:29); and Magpiash (Magbish, Ezra 2:30). Only Hodiah does not appear in the list of returnees.

Mowinckel[187] and Williamson[188] have shown that thirteen of the twenty-three leaders of the people in the second half of the list (vv. 20-27) have been derived from the list of those who worked on the wall in chap. 3, appearing in both lists in virtually the same order: Meshullam, Meshezabel, Zadok, Jaddua, Pelatiah, Hananiah, Hasshub, Hallohesh, Rehum, Hashabnah, Hanan, Anan, Malluch. A fourteenth name, Baanah (v. 27), appears out of order in 3:4 as the father of Zadok. Again there are minor spelling differences between many of the names in the two lists.

10:28-29, Others Who Endorsed the Agreement. All the names in vv. 1-27 and the lists of the categories of people in v. 28—priests, Levites, gatekeepers, singers, temple servants, those who have separated themselves from the peoples of the lands, wives, sons, and daughters—emphasize the unanimity with which the people endorsed the firm agreement. The people who did not actually sign the document—that is, the rest of the people (v. 28)—endorsed it by a curse and an oath (v. 29), and they ascribed to this interpretation of the law the authority of Moses himself (v. 29). (See Reflections at 10:30-39.)

187. Sigmund Mowinckel, *Studien zu dem Buche Ezra-Nehemia I: Die nachronistische Redaktion des Buches. Die Listen,* SUNVAO (Oslo: Universitetsforlaget, 1964) 135-45; *Studien zu dem Buche Ezra-Nehemia III: Die Ezrageschichte und das Gesetz Moses,* SUNVAO (Oslo: Universitetsforlaget, 1965) 142-55.

188. H. G. M. Williamson, *Ezra, Nehemiah,* WBC 16 (Waco, Tex.: Word, 1985) 328-30.

Nehemiah 10:30-39, Requirements of the Firm Agreement

NIV

30"We promise not to give our daughters in marriage to the peoples around us or take their daughters for our sons.

31"When the neighboring peoples bring merchandise or grain to sell on the Sabbath, we will not buy from them on the Sabbath or on any holy day. Every seventh year we will forgo working the land and will cancel all debts.

32"We assume the responsibility for carrying out the commands to give a third of a shekel[a] each year for the service of the house of our

[a] 32 That is, about 1/8 ounce (about 4 grams)

NRSV

30We will not give our daughters to the peoples of the land or take their daughters for our sons;
31and if the peoples of the land bring in merchandise or any grain on the sabbath day to sell, we will not buy it from them on the sabbath or on a holy day; and we will forego the crops of the seventh year and the exaction of every debt.

32We also lay on ourselves the obligation to charge ourselves yearly one-third of a shekel for the service of the house of our God:
33for the rows of bread, the regular grain offering, the regular burnt offering, the sabbaths, the new moons, the appointed festivals, the sacred dona-

NIV

God: [33]for the bread set out on the table; for the regular grain offerings and burnt offerings; for the offerings on the Sabbaths, New Moon festivals and appointed feasts; for the holy offerings; for sin offerings to make atonement for Israel; and for all the duties of the house of our God.

[34]"We—the priests, the Levites and the people—have cast lots to determine when each of our families is to bring to the house of our God at set times each year a contribution of wood to burn on the altar of the LORD our God, as it is written in the Law.

[35]"We also assume responsibility for bringing to the house of the LORD each year the firstfruits of our crops and of every fruit tree.

[36]"As it is also written in the Law, we will bring the firstborn of our sons and of our cattle, of our herds and of our flocks to the house of our God, to the priests ministering there.

[37]"Moreover, we will bring to the storerooms of the house of our God, to the priests, the first of our ground meal, of our ⌞grain⌟ offerings, of the fruit of all our trees and of our new wine and oil. And we will bring a tithe of our crops to the Levites, for it is the Levites who collect the tithes in all the towns where we work. [38]A priest descended from Aaron is to accompany the Levites when they receive the tithes, and the Levites are to bring a tenth of the tithes up to the house of our God, to the storerooms of the treasury. [39]The people of Israel, including the Levites, are to bring their contributions of grain, new wine and oil to the storerooms where the articles for the sanctuary are kept and where the ministering priests, the gatekeepers and the singers stay.

"We will not neglect the house of our God."

NRSV

tions, and the sin offerings to make atonement for Israel, and for all the work of the house of our God. [34]We have also cast lots among the priests, the Levites, and the people, for the wood offering, to bring it into the house of our God, by ancestral houses, at appointed times, year by year, to burn on the altar of the LORD our God, as it is written in the law. [35]We obligate ourselves to bring the first fruits of our soil and the first fruits of all fruit of every tree, year by year, to the house of the LORD; [36]also to bring to the house of our God, to the priests who minister in the house of our God, the firstborn of our sons and of our livestock, as it is written in the law, and the firstlings of our herds and of our flocks; [37]and to bring the first of our dough, and our contributions, the fruit of every tree, the wine and the oil, to the priests, to the chambers of the house of our God; and to bring to the Levites the tithes from our soil, for it is the Levites who collect the tithes in all our rural towns. [38]And the priest, the descendant of Aaron, shall be with the Levites when the Levites receive the tithes; and the Levites shall bring up a tithe of the tithes to the house of our God, to the chambers of the storehouse. [39]For the people of Israel and the sons of Levi shall bring the contribution of grain, wine, and oil to the storerooms where the vessels of the sanctuary are, and where the priests that minister, and the gatekeepers and the singers are. We will not neglect the house of our God.

COMMENTARY

While Nehemiah dramatically insisted that men from the community should not marry foreign women and that the people should not give their daughters to foreigners in marriage (13:23-27), the community now makes a firm agreement to follow these provisions (v. 30; for the chronological relationship between chaps. 10 and 13, see the Overview to 7:73*b*–10:39). This action seems to revise or update Deut 7:3-4, which forbids intermarriage with the sons or daughters of the indigenous population.[189] The old list of pre-Israelite inhabitants of the land in Deuteronomy—Hittites, Girgashites, Amorites, Canaanites, Perizzites, Hivites, and Jebusites—has been replaced in Nehemiah by "the peoples of the land" (v. 30), and so the category of forbidden marriages has been made more comprehensive so that it includes Ashdodites, Ammonites, and Moabites, against whom Nehemiah protested. In neither chap. 10 nor chap. 13 is there a requirement to dissolve existing marriages (cf. Ezra 10).

Nehemiah had also warned people against selling food or transporting goods to the market in Jerusalem on the sabbath (see the Commentary on 13:15-22). Selling on the sabbath was already considered wrong by Amos (Amos 8:5), and Jeremiah, whom Nehemiah seems to follow,[190] had expanded the sabbath commandment to include bearing burdens to Jerusalem or removing a burden from a person's home (Jer 17:21-22). Nehemiah also argued with the nobles of Judah that they should not buy food even from foreigners on the sabbath, and the signers of the firm agreement now pledge not to buy from the peoples of the land (v. 31*a*). Thus Nehemiah and the firm agreement redefined "work" to include buying and so made the sabbath laws more comprehensive.[191]

After the provisions on the sabbath day, the agreement moves on to the sabbath year (v. 31*b*). One ancient law required that all the land should lie fallow in the seventh year, with the poor allowed to eat anything that grew without cultivation (Exod 23:10-11). A second law canceled debts in the seventh year and allowed Israelite slaves to go free (Exod 21:2-6; Deut 15:1-18; Jer 34:8-16; 1 Macc 6:49, 53). The firm agreement accepts both laws, forgoing the crops of the seventh year and the exaction of every debt. Thus it makes a more comprehensive law out of existing legislation. Early in his career Nehemiah had prohibited the taking of interest from fellow Israelites or enslaving them for failure to pay their debts (5:1-13). These ad hoc measures are now made the regular practice.

According to the Pentateuch, each Israelite, whether rich or poor, had once been assessed half a shekel "as a ransom for their lives to the LORD" (Exod 30:11-16), and the silver raised in this way was dedicated to the tabernacle (Exod 38:25-26). Joash revived this tax in his efforts to secure enough cash to repair the Temple (see 2 Chr 24:4-14, esp. "the tax levied by Moses" in v. 6). During the period of the monarchy, the king was largely responsible for the financial support of temple worship, but in the Second Temple period other arrangements had to be made. Hence the post-exilic community resolved to pay a special temple tax and set it at one-third of a shekel, instead of one-half of a shekel (10:32-33; cf. Matt 17:24). Apparently the provisions for support for the cultus initiated by Darius (Ezra 6:9-10) and Artaxerxes (Ezra 7:21-72) were proving inadequate. The community also decided to set money aside for the twelve loaves of showbread, which had come to symbolize thanksgiving to the divine giver of all good things (Exod 25:23-30; Lev 24:5-9; Num 4:7; 1 Sam 21:7; 1 Kgs 7:48; 2 Kgs 25:29; 1 Chr 9:32; 23:29; 2 Chr 13:11), for the regular grain offering and burnt offerings each evening and morning (Exod 29:38-42; Num 28:1-8; 1 Kgs 18:29, 36; 2 Kgs 16:15), for sacrifices on various holy days (cf. Num 28–29; 1 Chr 23:31; 2 Chr 2:3; 8:13; 31:3), for sacred donations (2 Chr 29:33; 35:13), for sin offerings that canceled sin and undid its effects (Leviticus 4–5; 17:10-11), and for the support of the house of God in general. In this case they created a new prescription from a precedent in pentateuchal law.

A wood offering is not mentioned in the Pentateuch, although the people were required to keep a fire constantly burning on the altar ("as it is written in the law," v. 34; see Lev 6:9, 12-13). Nehemiah boasts of having provided personally for the wood offering of the community (13:31). The regular and periodic wood offering required in the firm agreement was probably a new, facilitating law, designed to make it possible for the continuous fire to be maintained on the altar.

189. For an excellent study of the five types of legal developments contained in this chapter, see David J. A. Clines, "Nehemiah as an Example of Early Jewish Exegesis," *JSOT* 21 (1981) 111-17.

190. Michael Fishbane, *Biblical Interpretation in Ancient Israel* (Oxford: Clarendon, 1985) 132-33. Jeremiah gives these innovations full Sinaitic authority.

191. The oldest sabbath law prohibited occupational work by men (Exod 34:21), and Exod 35:3 extended the ban to domestic activities, such as lighting a fire. The Decalogue includes all members of the community in the sabbath law (Exod 20:10).

Earlier in Israel's history the Gibeonites, who had been hewers of wood and drawers of water for the sanctuary (Josh 9:27), may have been responsible for supplying the wood.

Verses 35-36 make specific promises with regard to the first fruits and the firstborn. All agricultural products belonged to God until their first fruits or firstborn had been presented to God; then the rest of the product was desacralized and available for human consumption (Exod 23:19; 34:26; Num 18:12-13). Nehemiah had made provisions for first fruits at their appointed times (13:31), although it is impossible to say what innovations or specific changes he had brought about.

The firm agreement makes explicit that the first fruits are to come from "all fruit of every tree"—that is, the law is being understood more comprehensively than before. Deuteronomy had spoken only of the first of all the produce of the ground (Deut 26:2). This agreement makes clear that the offering of the first fruits and of the firstborn are intended for the priests and not just for the sanctuary. Here the agreement seems to side with Num 18:12-13 against the law of the firstborn in Deut 15:19-23. According to Deuteronomy, the worshiper and his family could eat the firstborn ox or the firstborn of the flock at the sanctuary. It is implied in Nehemiah that human firstborn and the firstborn of unclean animals (NRSV, "livestock") are to be redeemed—hence the notice that these firstborn are to be brought "as it is written in the law" (cf. Exod 13:2, 13-15; 22:29-30; 34:19-20; Num 18:15-17; Deut 15:19-23).

Verse 37*a* refers to a third type of offering in addition to first fruits and firstborn: the gift of the best or prime thing to the Lord. A distinction may be intended here between raw products and those that have been processed in some way (Num 15:20-21; 18:12; Deut 18:4; Ezek 44:30), with the latter considered the prime offering. This would fit particularly well with the references to dough and wine in this passage. These prime offerings were for the priests and were to be brought directly to their chambers (13:4-5; 2 Chr 31:11-12).

Nehemiah had complained that the tithes due to the Levites and the singers had not been paid so that they had to go back to work in the fields in order to support themselves. He remonstrates with the people, and the tithes from Judah will eventually be delivered to the proper officials with appropriate supervision (13:10-14).

The firm agreement promises that the Levites will receive their appropriate tithe of grain, wine, and oil in accord with Num 18:21-32. The detailed provisions for collecting the tithe in vv. 37-39 do not seem appropriate in a document like the firm agreement, especially since they are expressed in the third rather than the first person. They may be secondary. According to these provisions, the Levites were to collect the tithe in all the rural towns, instead of its being gathered by the laity (Amos 4:4), but an Aaronic priest was to be with them when they received the tithe, apparently to make sure that the priests would receive the tenth of the tithe to which they were entitled (Num 18:25-32). The "contribution" of the Levites (v. 39) is apparently the tithe of the tithe (Num 18:26-27).

Deuteronomy has a quite different understanding of the tithe (Deut 14:22-29; 26:12-14). For two years the tithe was to be ritually consumed by members of the household (without neglecting the Levites), but in the third year it was to be stored in the towns for the benefit of Levites, resident aliens, orphans, and widows. Thus the firm agreement again favors Numbers over Deuteronomy (see the provision for giving the firstborn to the priests in v. 36).

The chapter closes with a final strong affirmation, "We will not neglect the house of our God" (v. 39). As we have seen, the firm agreement throughout provides permanent legislative solutions to reforms or temporary measures instituted by Nehemiah. The promise not to neglect the house of God also provides an appropriate response to Nehemiah's complaint: "Why is the house of God neglected?" (13:11; NRSV, "forsaken").

REFLECTIONS

We have seen that the materials in Nehemiah 8–10 may have come from different historical contexts, not all of which can be identified with certainty. In their present canonical arrangement they make a very important point: Hearing the Torah should lead to reflection and confession, but confession also needs to lead beyond words to deeds. Sorrow for sin (contrition) and amendment of life (metanoia) go hand in hand. In chap. 10, the people promise to walk in God's law (Deut 8:6) and to observe and do all the commandments (Deut 28:15). They commit themselves to specific deeds in specific disputed circumstances. Hearing the Word can never be a mere spectator sport. Our preaching needs always to be designed to move people toward deeper faith or more perfect service.

Between the lines of this chapter one can detect serious ethical issues: How does one decide what to do when the Torah is unclear or contradictory, or when it is silent? In such uncertain times one tries to build on precedents in the tradition or to follow the example of leaders in the faith. Today we ask how we can maximize love for God and love for neighbor in new, unprecedented situations. We also need to rely on the wisdom of our communities and the consent of the faithful. Ethical decisions are never merely private matters—what *I* need or what *I* want. We also need to ask what sisters and brothers in the faith think. How can we achieve consensus? Through its long list of names (10:1-27) and by mentioning every segment of the community (10:28), this chapter shows a community consciousness that transcends the modern sin of individualism.

Consider the difficult decisions family members today must make when a loved one lies dying. There comes a time when the expense of treatment or the diminished quality of life of the person who is ill makes extraordinary measures to sustain life unnecessary or even ill-advised. Jesus' entrusting of his Spirit into the Father's loving hands offers an exemplary posture for all those who face death. His admonition that life is more than food and the body more than clothing (Luke 12:23) provides a precedent for deciding that "life" sustained only by machines, without the possibility of human interaction and with no conceivable hope for improvement or recovery, is not really life at all. As the church reflects on the ethical issues involved in the artificial extension of life merely by technological means, it helps to clarify when life is to be grasped for all it is worth, and when it is to be surrendered back into the Creator's hands. Sharing the decision to "pull the plug" with chaplains or pastors connects the family to the wider current ethical discussion and to the decisions of faithful Christians who have decided that preservation of life at all costs may be more idolatrous than faithful.

This chapter also focuses on stewardship and the support of worship. When the Temple had been a royal chapel, the king was expected to finance its daily needs. But now there were no kings, and the assistance promised by the Persians was good for a start although, clearly it was not enough for the long term. Sacrifices had to be financed for every evening and every morning; wood had to be provided to keep the flames eternal; and the clergy had to be paid. The people resolved to meet these financial needs: "We also lay on ourselves the obligation" (10:32). It is good to see how fully this was thought through in their agricultural economy. Stewardship involved what they grew in their fields, what they raised in their stalls, and what they manufactured from their raw materials.

Stewardship is much more than fund-raising. Real stewardship means a commitment to not abandon or neglect the house of our God—its worship life, its clergy, its building, its people. Such a firm agreement is real metanoia.

NEHEMIAH 11:1–13:31

THE CLIMAX OF NEHEMIAH'S WORK AND RELATED MATTERS

NEHEMIAH 11:1-36, THE NEW SETTLERS IN JERUSALEM

NIV

11 Now the leaders of the people settled in Jerusalem, and the rest of the people cast lots to bring one out of every ten to live in Jerusalem, the holy city, while the remaining nine were to stay in their own towns. [2]The people commended all the men who volunteered to live in Jerusalem.

[3]These are the provincial leaders who settled in Jerusalem (now some Israelites, priests, Levites, temple servants and descendants of Solomon's servants lived in the towns of Judah, each on his own property in the various towns, [4]while other people from both Judah and Benjamin lived in Jerusalem):

From the descendants of Judah:

Athaiah son of Uzziah, the son of Zechariah, the son of Amariah, the son of Shephatiah, the son of Mahalalel, a descendant of Perez; [5]and Maaseiah son of Baruch, the son of Col-Hozeh, the son of Hazaiah, the son of Adaiah, the son of Joiarib, the son of Zechariah, a descendant of Shelah. [6]The descendants of Perez who lived in Jerusalem totaled 468 able men.

[7]From the descendants of Benjamin:

Sallu son of Meshullam, the son of Joed, the son of Pedaiah, the son of Kolaiah, the son of Maaseiah, the son of Ithiel, the son of Jeshaiah, [8]and his followers, Gabbai and Sallai—928 men. [9]Joel son of Zicri was their chief officer, and Judah son of Hassenuah was over the Second District of the city.

[10]From the priests:

NRSV

11 Now the leaders of the people lived in Jerusalem; and the rest of the people cast lots to bring one out of ten to live in the holy city Jerusalem, while nine-tenths remained in the other towns. [2]And the people blessed all those who willingly offered to live in Jerusalem.

3These are the leaders of the province who lived in Jerusalem; but in the towns of Judah all lived on their property in their towns: Israel, the priests, the Levites, the temple servants, and the descendants of Solomon's servants. [4]And in Jerusalem lived some of the Judahites and of the Benjaminites. Of the Judahites: Athaiah son of Uzziah son of Zechariah son of Amariah son of Shephatiah son of Mahalalel, of the descendants of Perez; [5]and Maaseiah son of Baruch son of Col-hozeh son of Hazaiah son of Adaiah son of Joiarib son of Zechariah son of the Shilonite. [6]All the descendants of Perez who lived in Jerusalem were four hundred sixty-eight valiant warriors.

7And these are the Benjaminites: Sallu son of Meshullam son of Joed son of Pedaiah son of Kolaiah son of Maaseiah son of Ithiel son of Jeshaiah. [8]And his brothers[a] Gabbai, Sallai: nine hundred twenty-eight. [9]Joel son of Zichri was their overseer; and Judah son of Hassenuah was second in charge of the city.

10Of the priests: Jedaiah son of Joiarib, Jachin, [11]Seraiah son of Hilkiah son of Meshullam son of Zadok son of Meraioth son of Ahitub, officer of the house of God, [12]and their associates who did the work of the house, eight hundred twenty-two; and Adaiah son of Jeroham son of Pelaliah son of Amzi son of Zechariah son of Pashhur son of

[a] Gk Mss: Heb *And after him*

NIV

Jedaiah; the son of Joiarib; Jakin; 11Seraiah son of Hilkiah, the son of Meshullam, the son of Zadok, the son of Meraioth, the son of Ahitub, supervisor in the house of God, 12and their associates, who carried on work for the temple—822 men; Adaiah son of Jeroham, the son of Pelaliah, the son of Amzi, the son of Zechariah, the son of Pashhur, the son of Malkijah, 13and his associates, who were heads of families—242 men; Amashsai son of Azarel, the son of Ahzai, the son of Meshillemoth, the son of Immer, 14and his[a] associates, who were able men—128. Their chief officer was Zabdiel son of Haggedolim.

15From the Levites:

Shemaiah son of Hasshub, the son of Azrikam, the son of Hashabiah, the son of Bunni; 16Shabbethai and Jozabad, two of the heads of the Levites, who had charge of the outside work of the house of God; 17Mattaniah son of Mica, the son of Zabdi, the son of Asaph, the director who led in thanksgiving and prayer; Bakbukiah, second among his associates; and Abda son of Shammua, the son of Galal, the son of Jeduthun. 18The Levites in the holy city totaled 284.

19The gatekeepers:

Akkub, Talmon and their associates, who kept watch at the gates—172 men.

20The rest of the Israelites, with the priests and Levites, were in all the towns of Judah, each on his ancestral property.

21The temple servants lived on the hill of Ophel, and Ziha and Gishpa were in charge of them.

22The chief officer of the Levites in Jerusalem was Uzzi son of Bani, the son of Hashabiah, the son of Mattaniah, the son of Mica. Uzzi was one of Asaph's descendants, who were the singers responsible for the service of the house of God. 23The singers were under the king's orders, which regulated their daily activity.

24Pethahiah son of Meshezabel, one of the descendants of Zerah son of Judah, was the king's agent in all affairs relating to the people.

25As for the villages with their fields, some of

[a] *14* Most Septuagint manuscripts; Hebrew *their*

NRSV

Malchijah, 13and his associates, heads of ancestral houses, two hundred forty-two; and Amashsai son of Azarel son of Ahzai son of Meshillemoth son of Immer, 14and their associates, valiant warriors, one hundred twenty-eight; their overseer was Zabdiel son of Haggedolim.

15And of the Levites: Shemaiah son of Hasshub son of Azrikam son of Hashabiah son of Bunni; 16and Shabbethai and Jozabad, of the leaders of the Levites, who were over the outside work of the house of God; 17and Mattaniah son of Mica son of Zabdi son of Asaph, who was the leader to begin the thanksgiving in prayer, and Bakbukiah, the second among his associates; and Abda son of Shammua son of Galal son of Jeduthun. 18All the Levites in the holy city were two hundred eighty-four.

19The gatekeepers, Akkub, Talmon and their associates, who kept watch at the gates, were one hundred seventy-two. 20And the rest of Israel, and of the priests and the Levites, were in all the towns of Judah, all of them in their inheritance. 21But the temple servants lived on Ophel; and Ziha and Gishpa were over the temple servants.

22The overseer of the Levites in Jerusalem was Uzzi son of Bani son of Hashabiah son of Mattaniah son of Mica, of the descendants of Asaph, the singers, in charge of the work of the house of God. 23For there was a command from the king concerning them, and a settled provision for the singers, as was required every day. 24And Pethahiah son of Meshezabel, of the descendants of Zerah son of Judah, was at the king's hand in all matters concerning the people.

25And as for the villages, with their fields, some of the people of Judah lived in Kiriath-arba and its villages, and in Dibon and its villages, and in Jekabzeel and its villages, 26and in Jeshua and in Moladah and Beth-pelet, 27in Hazar-shual, in Beer-sheba and its villages, 28in Ziklag, in Meconah and its villages, 29in En-rimmon, in Zorah, in Jarmuth, 30Zanoah, Adullam, and their villages, Lachish and its fields, and Azekah and its villages. So they camped from Beer-sheba to the valley of Hinnom. 31The people of Benjamin also lived from Geba onward, at Michmash, Aija, Bethel and its villages, 32Anathoth, Nob, Ananiah, 33Hazor, Ramah, Gittaim, 34Hadid, Zeboim, Neballat, 35Lod,

NIV

the people of Judah lived in Kiriath Arba and its
surrounding settlements, in Dibon and its settlements, in Jekabzeel and its villages, 26in Jeshua,
in Moladah, in Beth Pelet, 27in Hazar Shual, in
Beersheba and its settlements, 28in Ziklag, in Meconah and its settlements, 29in En Rimmon, in
Zorah, in Jarmuth, 30Zanoah, Adullam and their
villages, in Lachish and its fields, and in Azekah
and its settlements. So they were living all the
way from Beersheba to the Valley of Hinnom.
31The descendants of the Benjamites from Geba
lived in Micmash, Aija, Bethel and its settlements,
32in Anathoth, Nob and Ananiah, 33in Hazor,
Ramah and Gittaim, 34in Hadid, Zeboim and Neballat, 35in Lod and Ono, and in the Valley of the
Craftsmen.
36Some of the divisions of the Levites of Judah
settled in Benjamin.

NRSV

and Ono, the valley of artisans. 36And certain
divisions of the Levites in Judah were joined to
Benjamin.

COMMENTARY

The first two verses of chap. 11 return to the question of the repopulation of Jerusalem, last mentioned at 7:5*a*. Yet these verses do not come from the Nehemiah Memoir. Note that Nehemiah is not mentioned, the account is cast in the third person, the vocabulary is different ("rulers" [שׂרים *śārîm* instead of סגנים *sĕgānîm* or חרים *ḥōrîm*]; "remainder" [שׁאר *šĕʾār* instead of יתר *yeter*]; 2:16; 4:8, 13; 6:1, 14), Jerusalem is called by the late term "holy city" (עיר הקדשׁ *ʿîr haqqōdeš*, 11:1; cf. 11:18), and the people cast lots to decide who is to move instead of following genealogical considerations.

The list of those who settled in Jerusalem at the time of Nehemiah (vv. 3-19) has a parallel in 1 Chr 9:2-17, where the list purports to document those who returned to the land right after the exile. The texts differ considerably from each other, as will be noted in the Commentary below, and 1 Chronicles 9 seems to depend on Nehemiah 11. Verses 3-4*a*, composed specifically for Nehemiah 11, are included also in 1 Chronicles 9.

This list identifies lay residents from Judah (vv. 4*b*-6) and from Benjamin (vv. 7-8), together with their leaders (v. 9) and clergy residents, including priests (vv. 10-14), Levites (vv. 15-18), and gatekeepers (v. 19). Verse 20 serves as a conclusion to the list of residents and as a transition to the list of towns in vv. 25-35. Typologically this list of residents is later than Ezra 2//Nehemiah 7, since singers are now included among the Levites (v. 17), though gatekeepers have not yet attained levitical status (v. 19; cf. 1 Chr 9:26; 23–26). Shabbethai and Jozabad (v. 16) provide an important connection to the time of Ezra and Nehemiah (Ezra 8:33; 10:15; Neh 8:7; see also the discussion of Col-hozeh in the Commentary on 11:4-9). Neither Mowinckel's attempt to date the list a generation or more later than Nehemiah[192] nor Kellermann's attempt to prove that it is a list of arrangements[193] made for the defense of Jerusalem at the time of Josiah has proved successful.

The inclusion of temple servants and Solomon's servants in v. 3 is probably influenced by 7:46-59;

192. Sigmund Mowinckel, *Studien zu dem Buche Ezra-Nehemia I: Die nachronistische Redaktion des Buches. Die Listen,* SUNVAO (Oslo: Universitetsforlaget, 1964) 48-49, 145-51, esp. 150. Mowinckel was convinced that Ezra functioned under Artaxerxes II. H. G. M. Williamson, *Ezra, Nehemiah,* WBC 16 (Waco, Tex.: Word, 1985) 347, has shown the invalidity of Mowinckel's arguments.

193. Ulrich Kellermann, "Die Listen in Nehemia 11 eine Dokumentation aus den letzten Jahren des Reiches Juda?" *ZDPV* 82 (1966) 209-27. H. G. M. Williamson, *Ezra, Nehemiah,* WBC 16 (Waco, Tex.: Word, 1985) 347-48, calls attention to five types of data that relate to the time of Ezra or Nehemiah or, more generally, to post-exilic times.

perhaps everything after the word "Jerusalem" in v. 3 comes from a secondary hand. Note that the NIV puts vv. 3-4*a* in parentheses. Verses 21-24 also appear to be secondary. Verse 21 supplies a list of the temple servants, alluded to in v. 3. Verse 22 gives further details on the Levites and contains names that are three generations later genealogically (see Commentary). Verse 23 supplements v. 22 by citing the king's authorization for the work of the Levites, and v. 24 identifies this king as a Persian.

The lists of towns in Judah (vv. 25-30) and Benjamin (vv. 31-35) are also secondary and describe a much wider territory than was occupied by the post-exilic province (see Ezra 2//Nehemiah 7 and Nehemiah 3). They also omit many towns mentioned elsewhere in the book of Nehemiah.[194]

11:1-3. Jerusalem had attracted enough leaders among its residents (v. 1), but it still lacked ordinary people. By casting lots (see 10:34) the people designated 10 percent of their number (a tithe) for the "holy city" (see Isa 48:2; 52:1; Dan 9:24; Matt 4:5). The city is now considered holy because the Temple has been built, the wall has been restored, and the law has been read publicly and responded to. The people destined for the move willingly consented to it and so set an example for anyone who would move to Jerusalem in the future. Blenkinsopp sees in the participle המתנדבים (*hammitnaddĕbîm*, "willingly offered") a military term (see also the mention of "warriors" in vv. 6, 8 [following the suggested emendation in *BHS*], and 14).[195] Perhaps the list originally documented Jerusalem's military strength. Defense needs may also explain the numbers supplied throughout the list.

11:4-9. The list of residents begins with laypeople from Judah and Benjamin (1 Chr 9:3 adds Ephraim and Manasseh). Judah had three sons who survived him: Shelah, Perez, and Zerah (Gen 38:11, 29-30; 46:12; Num 26:20; 1 Chr 2:3-6). Athaiah (v. 4) is six generations removed from Perez, and Maaseiah (v. 5) is seven generations removed from Shelah (the last word of v. 5 should be "Shelanite"). Athaiah (= Uthai in 1 Chr 9:4) has a completely different line of ancestors connecting him to Perez in Chronicles, except for Amariah (= Imri). Maaseiah's grandfather, Colhozeh, may have been the father of Shallum, ruler of Mizpeh, who worked on the wall (3:15). For "Maaseiah son of Baruch," 1 Chr 9:5 has "Asaiah the firstborn." Zerah is not mentioned in v. 5, although 1 Chr 9:6 ascribes Jeuel and 690 kinsmen to him. A reference to Zerah in Neh 11:24 (itself secondary) suggests that his name may have been lost accidentally in v. 5. The long genealogies give legitimation to the individuals in these verses. In a holy city, purity of laypeople is as important as the purity of priests.[196]

Nehemiah 11 includes only Sallu and his brothers from the tribe of Benjamin (vv. 7-8); 1 Chronicles 9 identifies Meshullam as Sallu's father, but differs in the rest of the genealogy. It also adds three other Benjaminite names: Ibneiah, Elah, and Meshullam (1 Chr 9:8). Instead of "Gabbai, Sallai" (v. 8), we should read "the warriors" (cf. vv. 6, 14; see also *BHS*). Instead of the number 928 (v. 8), 1 Chr 9:9 has 956. The total number available for military service from Judah and Benjamin was 2,356 if we include Zerah and his associates from 1 Chronicles 9. The two overseers mentioned in v. 9 may have been commanders of the reserve forces. Joel son of Zichri may have succeeded Hanani as military ruler over Jerusalem (cf. 7:2). The name "Hassenuah" (v. 9) appears in 1 Chronicles as part of the genealogy of Sallu (1 Chr 9:7).

11:10-14. The list of priests in v. 10 is unclear (note the different interpretations in the NRSV and the NIV).[197] Seraiah (v. 11; spelled "Azariah" in 1 Chr 9:11) was the last high priest before the exile (1 Chr 6:14-15), and his genealogy is the same for five generations in both Nehemiah 11 and 1 Chronicles 9. According to the standard high priestly genealogy in 1 Chr 6:13-14 (cf. Ezra 7:1), however, Seraiah was the grandson of

194. Tekoa (3:5); Meremoth, Gibeon, and Mizpah and Meronoth (3:7); Beth-haccherem (3:14); Beth-zur (3:16); Keilah (3:17); Bethlehem and Netophah (7:26); Beth-azmaveth (7:28); Kiriath-jearim, Chephirah, and Beeroth (7:29); Jericho (7:36); and Gilgal (12:29). This list has a utopian or eschatological character.

195. Joseph Blenkinsopp, *Ezra–Nehemiah*, OTL (Philadelphia: Westminster, 1988) 323.

196. Tamara C. Eskenazi, *In an Age of Prose: A Literary Approach to Ezra–Nehemiah*, SBLMS 36 (Atlanta: Scholars Press, 1988) 114.

197. Wilhelm Rudolph, *Esra und Nehemia, samt 3. Esra*, HAT 20 (Tübingen: J. C. B. Mohr [Paul Siebeck], 1949) 184, reconstructs a single long genealogy in 11:10-11 that extends from Jedaiah to Ahitub. Williamson, *Ezra, Nehemiah*, 343, identifies two priests in 11:10, Jedaiah and Joiarib, both sons of Seraiah. Blenkinsopp, *Ezra–Nehemiah*, 322, finds three priests in 11:10—Jedaiah, Joiarib, Jachin—with none of them related to Seraiah (see 1 Chr 9:10).

Hilkiah, not his son, and the name Meraioth does not appear in the standard genealogy of the high priests. The term "officer [נגיד *nāgîd*] of the house of God" (v. 11) is a synonym for "high priest" (1 Chr 9:20; 2 Chr 31:10, 13; 35:8).

There are seven names in Adaiah's genealogy (v. 12); the first two names and the last two names are also found in 1 Chr 9:12, but the middle three names are omitted there. Amashsai (v. 13) was a descendant of the priestly house of Immer. The names intervening between Amashsai and Immer differ widely in Nehemiah and Chronicles. Three of the four priestly families mentioned in Ezra 2:36-39 are attested in vv. 10-13: Jeshua, Immer, and Pashhur; only Harim is lacking, perhaps accidentally.

Each priestly family is supplied with numbers in Nehemiah 11, totalling 1,192 altogether. These numbers apparently have to do with people available for military conscription ("valiant warriors," v. 14) and not with the actual number of family heads, as v. 13 implies. Comparison with the list of returnees in Ezra 2//Nehemiah 7 shows that most of the high priestly family lived in Jerusalem (822 in v. 12 vs. a total number of 973 in Ezra 2:36), but only a minority of the other priestly families lived in Jerusalem (242 for Pashhur and 128 for Immer in vv. 13-14 vs. a total population of 1,247 and 1,052 respectively in Ezra 2:37-38). The overseer of these houses in military matters was Zabdiel (v. 14; cf. vv. 9, 22).

11:15-18. The first four generations of the Levite Shemaiah (v. 15) are the same in Nehemiah and 1 Chronicles, though for the fifth generation, "the son of Bunni" is replaced by "from the sons of Merari" in 1 Chr 9:14. Shabbethai and Jozabad (v. 16) played prominent roles in the career of Ezra, but they are absent from 1 Chr 9:15. The "outside work of the house of God" (v. 16) may include such things as care of the Temple and collection of tithes (see 10:37-39) in distinction to cultic activities in the narrow sense. Mattaniah (v. 17), one of the singers or musicians, is included here among the Levites. His genealogy goes back to Asaph, a leader of the musical guilds at the time of David (1 Chr 25:1-6; cf. Ezra 2:41). He was "the leader of [musical] praise [reading יהודה (*yĕhôdeh*); the NIV is better than the NRSV but does not indicate the emendation of the text] who gave thanks in prayer." Bakbukiah was probably the leader of a choir that sang antiphonally (12:8-9; 27-42; cf. Ezra 3:11). The levitical family of Abda traced its roots back to Jeduthun at the time of David (v. 17 and 1 Chr 9:16 with spelling variations; cf. 1 Chr 25:1-6). The Levites totaled 284, or 23.8 percent, of the priests listed in vv. 10-14 (16.1 percent of the priests listed in 1 Chr 9:10-13).

11:19-24. Of the 172 gatekeepers, who are not yet included among the Levites, only Akkub and Talmon are mentioned by name (v. 19). First Chronicles 9:17 adds an additional two names, Shallum and Ahiman, and has a total of 212 gatekeepers (1 Chr 9:22). The text of 1 Chr 9:18-32 spells out additional duties of the gatekeepers and reveals its typological lateness by including the four chief gatekeepers among the Levites (1 Chr 9:26). Six gatekeepers, including Talmon and Akkub in that order, are listed at Ezra 2:42 (cf. Neh 12:25). The use of the same names over a long period of time indicates that these are family names rather than the names of individuals.

Verse 20 forms a fitting conclusion to the list of those living in Jerusalem, and its reference to the towns of Judah forms a transition to vv. 25-35. Between v. 20 and vv. 25-35, however, there have been several expansions. Verse 21 supplies information on the Nethinim (temple servants), mentioned in the expansionist v. 3. They lived on Ophel (see 3:26, 31), where Ziha (see Ezra 2:43), and Gishpa (otherwise unknown) supervised them. Verse 22 identifies Uzzi as overseer of the Levites. Since Uzzi was the great-grandson of Mattaniah (v. 17), this verse may have been added at least fifty years after the original list had been drawn up. A supplementer added that the singers were under royal orders (v. 23), an apparent reference to David's assigning them specific tasks (12:24), unless it refers to sponsorship of Israelite music by the Persian king. Verse 24 definitely understands the word "king" as referring to the Persian ruler. Pethahiah, a descendant of Zerah (see vv. 4*b*-6; 1 Chr 9:6) was the king's adviser (lit., "at the king's hand") in all matters concerning the community.[198]

11:25-35. 11:25-30. The list of villages in

198. Williamson, *Ezra, Nehemiah,* 352-53, tentatively compares this role to that of Ezra (Ezra 7:12), while David J. A. Clines, *Ezra, Nehemiah, Esther,* NCB (Grand Rapids: Eerdmans, 1984) 219, wonders if Pethahiah was the governor of Judah at the time of the supplementer.

vv. 25-35 describes an area much larger geographically than the actual post-exilic province, and it compares this community to early Israel, which received the land through God's favor in the exodus and through conquest. The list of the cities of Judah in vv. 25-30 seems to have been taken from the Judean town list in Josh 15:20-33, almost in the same order, and forms the southern and western boundary of Judah (see Josh 15:1-12). In the following list, I have marked with an asterisk the eleven towns that almost surely lie outside the boundaries of the post-exilic community. It is uncertain whether the other six were part of Yehud.

Figure 6: Cities of Judah in Neh 11:25-30 Compared to Joshua 15

v. 25	
*Kiriath-arba	Josh 15:13, 54
*Dibon	Josh 15:22 Dimona or 15:49 Debir; cf. vv. 15-19
*Jekabzeel	Josh 15:21 Kabzeel
v. 26	
*Jeshua	Josh 15:26 Shema
*Moladah	Josh 15:26
*Beth-pelet	Josh 15:27
v. 27	
*Hazar-shual	Josh 15:28
*Beer-sheba	Josh 15:28
v. 28	
*Ziklag	Josh 15:31
*Meconah	?
v. 29	
*En-rimmon	Josh 15:32; Josh 19:7
Zorah	Josh 15:33, 41
Jarmuth	Josh 15:35
v. 30	
Zanoah	Josh 15:34
Adullam	Josh 15:35
Lachish	Josh 15:39
Azekah	Josh 15:35

Kiriath-arba (v. 25) is an older name for Hebron, which was not part of the post-exilic community. The next ten towns, from Dibon to En-Rimmon, were located south of Hebron toward the Negeb and would have been under Edomite or Arabic hegemony at the time of Nehemiah. The final six towns, from Zorah to Azekah, were located in the Shephelah. Only one of them is listed elsewhere in Ezra and Nehemiah—namely, Zanoah, in Neh 3:13.

Verse 30 notes that the people of Judah "camped" (so correctly NRSV) from Beersheba to the valley of Hinnom (see Josh 15:8). The word "camped" may imply Yahweh's presence in the land (see Deut 23:9-14; Numbers 2).

11:31-35. The relationship between the Benjaminite cities and Josh 18:11-28 is not as close as we might hope. Cities that are part of the census list in Ezra 2//Nehemiah 7 are marked with a plus sign (= 10 of the fifteen Benjaminite cities).

Figure 7: Cities of Benjamin in Neh 11:25-30 Compared to Ezra 2 or Joshua 15

Cities of Benjamin	References in Ezra 2 or Joshua 18
v. 31	
+Geba	Josh 18:24; Ezra 2:26
+Michmash	Ezra 2:27
+Aija (Ai)	Ezra 2:28
+Bethel	Josh 18:22; Ezra 2:28
v. 32	
+Anathoth	Ezra 2:23
+Nob	Ezra 2:29 Nebo
Ananiah	
v. 33	
Hazor	
+Ramah	Josh 18:25; Ezra 2:26
Gittaim	
v.34	
+Hadid	Ezra 2:33
Zeboim	
Neballat	
v. 35	
+Lod	Ezra 2:33
+Ono	Ezra 2:33
the valley of artisans	unknown

11:36. The last verse in the NRSV indicates that some divisions of the Levites from Judah were connected in some way to Benjamin. Clines believes that some levitical divisions moved from Judah to Benjamin, or, through emendation, that some levitical divisions lived in Judah and Benjamin, while others lived in Jerusalem.[199] Blenkinsopp concludes that this obscure verse states that not all levitical settlements were confined to Judah.[200]

199. Clines, *Ezra, Nehemiah, Esther,* 222.
200. Blenkinsopp, *Ezra–Nehemiah,* 332.

REFLECTIONS

The narrative content in this chapter is extremely sparse, since the chapter consists primarily of a list indicating the makeup of Jerusalem after the relocation of 10 percent of the population there and a list of towns making up Judah and Benjamin. We do not know whether or how Nehemiah followed up on his intention to expand the population of Jerusalem, but in 11:1-2 lots were cast to decide who would move to the capital. Presumably the casting of lots indicated the will of God in this matter. The people themselves, and not some kind of heroic leader, decided how some would be chosen to relocate. Those families chosen to move to Jerusalem did not consider moving a matter of winning or losing. Rather, they willingly volunteered to live in Jerusalem. Their will was attuned to the will of God. When the rest of the people blessed them for their voluntary acceptance of what might have been a disruptive decision, we sense connotations of community unity and harmony. Without adequate population, Jerusalem would have been only an orderly pile of stone and rubble. With increased population, the stage was set for the dedication of the wall. Resettling the city demonstrated that the people would not forsake the house of God (10:39). Maintaining one's membership today in a congregation challenged by racial or ethnic change also shows loyalty to the house of God—not by moving, but by staying.

The list of towns in 11:25-35 is not historical, and we are only partially able to trace the roots of this list. But it makes the important point that the post-exilic community resembles the first inhabitants of the land, who shared in the benefits of God's actions in exodus and conquest. Like their predecessors in the wilderness camps, their residence in the land was a camping around the presence of Yahweh.

But the large dimensions of the province implied in this list, far beyond anything in the time of Ezra and Nehemiah and not realized until three hundred years later in the days of Jonathan the Maccabee, conveyed a subtle eschatological hope. The tiny community, which had to stretch in order even to fill up Jerusalem, was not all that God had in store for the people. The community that confessed, "We are in great distress" (9:37) would someday inherit all the land promised through the ancestors and distributed through Joshua.

The author did not content himself with saying merely that Jerusalem was repopulated. Instead he named names, glorious names with long genealogies reaching back to storied ancestral heroes. The people who now lived in Jerusalem were fully part of Israel—you could tell it by their genealogies and by the fact that they represented the complete spectrum of laity and clergy.

NEHEMIAH 12:1-26, LISTS OF PRIESTS, LEVITES, AND HIGH PRIESTS

NIV

12 These were the priests and Levites who returned with Zerubbabel son of Shealtiel and with Jeshua:

Seraiah, Jeremiah, Ezra,
2Amariah, Malluch, Hattush,
3Shecaniah, Rehum, Meremoth,
4Iddo, Ginnethon,[a] Abijah,
5Mijamin,[b] Moadiah, Bilgah,
6Shemaiah, Joiarib, Jedaiah,
7Sallu, Amok, Hilkiah and Jedaiah.

These were the leaders of the priests and their associates in the days of Jeshua.

8The Levites were Jeshua, Binnui, Kadmiel, Sherebiah, Judah, and also Mattaniah, who, together with his associates, was in charge of the songs of thanksgiving. 9Bakbukiah and Unni, their associates, stood opposite them in the services.

10Jeshua was the father of Joiakim, Joiakim the father of Eliashib, Eliashib the father of Joiada, 11Joiada the father of Jonathan, and Jonathan the father of Jaddua.

12In the days of Joiakim, these were the heads of the priestly families:

of Seraiah's family, Meraiah;
of Jeremiah's, Hananiah;

[a] *4* Many Hebrew manuscripts and Vulgate (see also Neh. 12:16); most Hebrew manuscripts *Ginnethoi* [b] *5* A variant of *Miniamin*

NRSV

12 These are the priests and the Levites who came up with Zerubbabel son of Shealtiel, and Jeshua: Seraiah, Jeremiah, Ezra, 2Amariah, Malluch, Hattush, 3Shecaniah, Rehum, Meremoth, 4Iddo, Ginnethoi, Abijah, 5Mijamin, Maadiah, Bilgah, 6Shemaiah, Joiarib, Jedaiah, 7Sallu, Amok, Hilkiah, Jedaiah. These were the leaders of the priests and of their associates in the days of Jeshua.

8And the Levites: Jeshua, Binnui, Kadmiel, Sherebiah, Judah, and Mattaniah, who with his associates was in charge of the songs of thanksgiving. 9And Bakbukiah and Unno their associates stood opposite them in the service. 10Jeshua was the father of Joiakim, Joiakim the father of Eliashib, Eliashib the father of Joiada, 11Joiada the father of Jonathan, and Jonathan the father of Jaddua.

12In the days of Joiakim the priests, heads of ancestral houses, were: of Seraiah, Meraiah; of Jeremiah, Hananiah; 13of Ezra, Meshullam; of Amariah, Jehohanan; 14of Malluchi, Jonathan; of Shebaniah, Joseph; 15of Harim, Adna; of Meraioth, Helkai; 16of Iddo, Zechariah; of Ginnethon, Meshullam; 17of Abijah, Zichri; of Miniamin, of Moadiah, Piltai; 18of Bilgah, Shammua; of Shemaiah, Jehonathan; 19of Joiarib, Mattenai; of

NIV

[13]of Ezra's, Meshullam;
of Amariah's, Jehohanan;
[14]of Malluch's, Jonathan;
of Shecaniah's,[a] Joseph;
[15]of Harim's, Adna;
of Meremoth's,[b] Helkai;
[16]of Iddo's, Zechariah;
of Ginnethon's, Meshullam;
[17]of Abijah's, Zicri;
of Miniamin's and of Moadiah's, Piltai;
[18]of Bilgah's, Shammua;
of Shemaiah's, Jehonathan;
[19]of Joiarib's, Mattenai;
of Jedaiah's, Uzzi;
[20]of Sallu's, Kallai;
of Amok's, Eber;
[21]of Hilkiah's, Hashabiah;
of Jedaiah's, Nethanel.

[22]The family heads of the Levites in the days
of Eliashib, Joiada, Johanan and Jaddua, as well
as those of the priests, were recorded in the reign
of Darius the Persian. [23]The family heads among
the descendants of Levi up to the time of Johanan
son of Eliashib were recorded in the book of the
annals. [24]And the leaders of the Levites were
Hashabiah, Sherebiah, Jeshua son of Kadmiel, and
their associates, who stood opposite them to give
praise and thanksgiving, one section responding
to the other, as prescribed by David the man of
God.

[25]Mattaniah, Bakbukiah, Obadiah, Meshullam,
Talmon and Akkub were gatekeepers who
guarded the storerooms at the gates. [26]They
served in the days of Joiakim son of Jeshua, the
son of Jozadak, and in the days of Nehemiah the
governor and of Ezra the priest and scribe.

[a] *14* Very many Hebrew manuscripts, some Septuagint manuscripts and Syriac (see also Neh. 12:3); most Hebrew manuscripts *Shebaniah's*
[b] *15* Some Septuagint manuscripts (see also Neh. 12:3); Hebrew *Meraioth's*

NRSV

Jedaiah, Uzzi; [20]of Sallai, Kallai; of Amok, Eber;
[21]of Hilkiah, Hashabiah; of Jedaiah, Nethanel.

22As for the Levites, in the days of Eliashib,
Joiada, Johanan, and Jaddua, there were recorded
the heads of ancestral houses; also the priests until
the reign of Darius the Persian. [23]The Levites,
heads of ancestral houses, were recorded in the
Book of the Annals until the days of Johanan son
of Eliashib. [24]And the leaders of the Levites: Hashabiah, Sherebiah, and Jeshua son of Kadmiel, with
their associates over against them, to praise and
to give thanks, according to the commandment
of David the man of God, section opposite to
section. [25]Mattaniah, Bakbukiah, Obadiah,
Meshullam, Talmon, and Akkub were gatekeepers
standing guard at the storehouses of the gates.
[26]These were in the days of Joiakim son of Jeshua
son of Jozadak, and in the days of the governor
Nehemiah and of the priest Ezra, the scribe.

COMMENTARY

Nehemiah 12 presents lists of priests (vv. 1-7, 12-21) and Levites (vv. 8-9, 24-25) from two different periods, as well as important information about the post-exilic high priestly line (vv. 10-11, 22-23). Verses 12-21 consist of a master list of twenty-two priestly houses, followed in each case by the name of the head of that house in the time of the high priest Joiakim. From this list is derived the list of "priests" from the time of Jeshua in vv. 1-7, which is really a list of the priestly *houses* from vv. 12-21 interpreted as if they were *individuals.* Jeshua (v. 1) and Joiakim (v. 12) were the first two high priests after the return from exile. The list in vv. 12-21 also seems to be the basic source used to develop the roster of priestly signatories to the firm agreement in 10:2-8. The following table compares the lists in 12:12-21, 12:1-7, and 10:2-8. The assigned numbers are based on the order of the names in 12:12-21.

Figure 8: Post-Exilic Priests

Neh 12:12-21 HP Joiakim (v. 12) Priestly house/head of house	Neh 12:1-7 HP Jeshua (v. 1)	Neh 10:2-8 Signatories
1. Seraiah/Meraiah	1. Seraiah	1. Seraiah (v. 2)
2. Jeremiah/Hananiah	2. Jeremiah	3. Azariah
3. Ezra/Meshullam (v. 13)	3. Ezra	2. Jeremiah Pashhur (v. 3)
4. Amariah/Jehohanan	4. Amariah (v. 2)	4. Amariah Malchijah
5. Malluchi/Jonathan (v. 14)	5. Malluch	
6. Data missing	6. Hattush	6. Hattush (v. 4)
7. Shebaniah/Joseph	7. Shecaniah (v. 3)	7. Shebaniah 5. Malluch
8. Harim/Adna (v. 15)	8. Rehum	8. Harim (v. 5)
9. Meraioth/Helkai	9. Meremoth	9. Meremoth Obadiah Daniel (v. 6)
10. Iddo/Zechariah (v. 16)	10. Iddo (v. 4)	
11. Ginnethon/Meshullam	11. Ginnethon	11. Ginnethon Baruch Meshullam (v. 7)
12. Abijah/Zichri (v. 17)	12. Abijah	12. Abijah
13. Miniamin/name missing	13. Mijamin (v. 5)	13. Mijamin
14. Moadiah/Piltai	14. Maadiah	14. Maaziah (v. 8)
15. Bilgah/Shammua (v. 18)	15. Bilgah	15. Bilgai
16. Shemaiah/Jehnonathan	16. Shemaiah (v. 6)	16. Shemaiah
17. Joiarib/Mattenai (v. 19)	17. Joiarib	
18. Jedaiah/Uzzi	18. Jedaiah	
19. Sallai/Kallai (v. 20)	19. Sallu (v. 7)	
20. Amok/Eber	20. Amok	
21. Hilkiah/Hashabiah (v. 21)	21. Hilkiah	
22. Jedaiah/Nethanel	22. Jedaiah	

In addition to the minor spelling variations expected in such a list,[201] this list has also undergone significant supplementation. While fifteen of the first sixteen names from the master list (vv. 12-21) appear in 10:2-8, the last six names do not appear, and there is an unnecessary "and" before the name Joiarib in the Hebrew text of 12:6, 19. Apparently, an original list of sixteen priests was later expanded to twenty-two. The date of that expansion was probably relatively early because J(eh)oiarib and Jedaiah, numbers 17 and 18, are the names of the first two priestly courses in 1 Chr 24:7, which Williamson has dated to the end of the Persian period.[202] This expansion may date to the Maccabean period, when it provided genealogical support for Mattathias, who claimed membership in the priestly family of Joiarib (1 Macc 2:1). Iddo (#10) is

201. Compare these family names: Malluchi/Malluch; Shebaniah/Shecaniah; Harim/Rehum (an interchange of the first two consonants); Meraioth/Meremoth; Miniamin/Mijamin; Moadiah/Maadiah/Maaziah; Bilgah/Bilgai; and Sallai/Sallu.

202. H. G. M. Williamson, "The Origins of the Twenty-four Priestly Courses: A Study of 1 Chronicles xxiii-xxvii," *VTSup* 30 (1979) 251-68. Seven other names from the list in 12:12-21 also appear among the priestly courses: 5. Malchijah = Malluch, course 5; 7. Shecaniah, course 10; 8. Harim, course 3; 12. Abijah, course 8; 13. Mijamin, course 6; 14. Maaziah, course 24; and 15. Bilgai, course 15.

missing by accident in Neh 10:6, as is the name of the head of the priestly house of Miniamin (#13) in 12:17 (the NIV mistakenly assigns Piltai as a priestly head to houses 13 and 14). The double appearance of Jedaiah as a family name (#18 and #22) is unusual but not implausible. Ezra (#3) is not the scribe, but should be identified with Azariah (Neh 10:2).

The relationship between the two lists of Levites in vv. 8-9 and vv. 24-25 is not clear; each list consists of eight names, after the emendation of בן (*ben*, "son") to בנוי (*binnûy*) in v. 24 (cf. 10:9 with 12:8; the numbers are assigned by me, with vv. 8-9 treated as the base text):

Neh 12:8-9	Neh 12:24-25
1. Jeshua (v. 8)	Hashabiah (v. 24)
2. Binnui	4. Sherebiah
3. Kadmiel	1. Jeshua
4. Sherebiah	2. Binnui
5. Judah	3. Kadmiel
6. Mattaniah	6. Mattaniah (v. 25)
7. Bakbukiah (v. 9)	7. Bakbukiah
8. Unno	8. Obadiah

Six names in the two lists are identical (##1-4, ##6-7), and Unno may be a corruption of Obadiah. Hashabiah has replaced Judah in the second list, and he and Sherebiah, who accompanied Ezra on his trek to Jerusalem (Ezra 8:18-19), have been moved to the head of the list in vv. 24-25. The lists are dated to the time of Jeshua and Joiakim respectively (see v. 26).

Finally, this chapter contains a list of high priests in vv. 10-11 and notes on the priestly and levitical genealogies in vv. 22-23. Verse 26*b* identifies Joiakim as the high priest during the period of Nehemiah and Ezra. This synchronism is incorrect, at least for Nehemiah, whose contemporary high priest was Eliashib. The synchronism with Joiakim comes from a time when the Ezra and Nehemiah memoirs had been brought together, with Ezra and Nehemiah considered as contemporaries. It sets the stage for the role of both leaders in the dedication of the wall (vv. 27-43).

Verse 27 was once joined to 11:20, since 11:21–12:26 is a series of supplements.

12:1-9. The first lists of priests (vv. 1-7) and Levites (vv. 8-9) are dated to the time of Zerubbabel and Jeshua, the high priest (c. 520 BCE). Ezra 2//Nehemiah 7 record only four priestly families for the early period of the restoration: Jedaiah, Immer, Pashhur, and Harim. Jedaiah and Harim are families #18 (or #22) and #8 respectively in vv. 1-7. Pashhur appears among the signatories of the firm agreement in chap. 10, but he is not mentioned in chap. 12. Immer appears in neither chapter.

The Levites Jeshua and Kadmiel from the list of returnees (Ezra 2:40//Neh 7:43) became families #1 and #3 in the lists of Levites in vv. 8-9. Judah (v. 8; family #5) may be an alternative spelling of Hodaviah (Ezra 2:40//Neh 7:43). Perhaps we should reconstruct a Binnui (family #2) in Ezra 2:40 on the basis of the name "Bannas" in 1 Edsr 5:26 (cf. Ezra 3:9; Neh 10:9). The names "Mattaniah" and "Bakbukiah" (families 6-7) were derived from the list of Levites in Neh 11:17, and Unno (family #8; cf. Obadiah) may be a variant form of Abda in that same verse. Mattaniah and his brothers were in charge of the songs of thanksgiving.[203] Bakbukiah and Unno gave antiphonal responses to their colleagues (see 11:17; Ezra 3:10-11). If Sherebiah (family #4) is to be identifed with the Levite who accompanied Ezra in Ezra 8:18 (see Neh 8:7; 9:4-5; 10:12), then the list of Levites is clearly later than the time of Jeshua, as the presence of Mattaniah and Bakbukiah also suggests.

12:10-11. The list of high priests in vv. 10-11 has the same form as the list in 1 Chr 6:4-15 (X was the father of Y), but its names are subsequent to the high priests listed in 1 Chronicles. Evidence in the Bible and in Josephus provides some help in identifying the high priests listed in vv. 10-11. Josephus names Joiakim as the high priest when Ezra arrived in Jerusalem, and Eliashib is mentioned several times as the contemporary of Nehemiah (3:1, 20-21; 13:28; cf. 13:4, 7). According to 13:28, an unnamed son of Jehoiada (= Joiada), the son of Eliashib (hence a grandson of Eliashib), married the daughter of Nehemiah's rival Sanballat. Jonathan is only attested in v. 11. Finally, Josephus mentions a high priest named Jaddua as the successor of Johanan during the reign of Darius III (336–331 BCE).[204] This Jaddua met with Alexander the Great during the latter's campaign through Palestine.

These data must be correlated with information about the high priestly line in vv. 22-23. Verse

203. See *BHS* note 8[b].
204. Josephus *Antiquities of the Jews* XI.302.

22 mentions four high priestly names in a row, without the intervening expression "the father of," suggesting that these high priests were successors or descendants of one another. The succession Eliashib-Joiada has already been mentioned (12:10; see 13:28). Johanan follows Joiada, according to v. 22, and the Elephantine Papyri confirm that a man named Jehohanan (note the slight spelling difference) was high priest about 410 BCE.[205] A number of commentators emend "Jonathan" (יונתן *yônātān*) to "Johanan" (יוחנן *yôḥānān*) in v. 11, despite the fact that v. 23 identifies Johanan as the son of Eliashib, instead of his grandson, as in v. 22. The data from the four verses may be diagrammed as follows:

vv. 10-11	v. 22	v. 23
Jeshua (v. 10)		
Joiakim		
Eliashib	Eliashib	Eliashib
Joiada (v. 11)	Joiada	Johanan
Jonathan	Johanan	
Jaddua	Jaddua	

Was Johanan the son, or the grandson, of Eliashib? What is his relationship to Jonathan? How can only six high priests (vv. 10-11) have served between c. 520 (Jeshua) and 333 (Jaddua) BCE?

Through his decipherment of the Aramaic papyri, Cross discovered that papponomy (the naming of a person after a grandfather) was practiced in the family of the Samarian Sanballat, and he was able to identify a Sanballat II and a Sanballat III from that family.[206] Cross proposed that papponomy was also practiced in the Judean high priestly line, and he inserted an Eliashib and a Johanan between Joiakim and Eliashib, and another Johanan and a Jaddua after Jaddua in v. 11. He claimed that these four names were later lost by haplography. His new priests, their birth years, and the numbers he assigned to high priests with the same names are included in parentheses in the following list:

Jeshua (born c. 570)
Joiakim (born c. 545)
(Eliashib I, born c. 545)
(Johanan I, born c. 520)
Eliashib (II, born c. 495)
Joiada (I, born c. 470)
Johanan (II, born c. 445 = Jonathan)
Jaddua (II, born c. 420)
(Johanan III, born c. 395)
(Jaddua III, born c. 370)

Cross dated Ezra to the time of Johanan I, whom he identified with Jehohanan son of Eliashib in Ezra 10:6. Johanan III and Jaddua III correspond to the names mentioned above by Josephus during the reign of Darius III. Cross correlated his chronology with additional data from Josephus—namely, that a Johanan (= III) killed his brother Jesus in the time of Artaxerxes III (358–338 BCE) and that Manasseh, the brother of Jaddua (= Jaddua III) married Nikaso the daughter of Sanballat (= Sanballat III).

Critics of Cross have pointed out three main problems with his list. First, there is no evidence in the biblical text for papponomy in the high priestly line either before or after the exile. Second, his proposal to make Eliashib I the brother of Joiakim is pure conjecture and faces the difficulty that the preserved text indicates that Joiakim is the *father* of Eliashib. As was pointed out in the Commentary on Ezra 10:6, there is no need to identify the Eliashib mentioned there as the high priest. Third, by identifying Jonathan and Johanan II he has not completely solved the problem, since in v. 11 Jonathan seems to be the grandson of Eliashib, as Johanan is in v. 22, but Johanan is the son of Eliashib in v. 23 (unless Johanan II is intended in v. 22 and Johanan I in v. 23).

In short, Cross seems to be correct in concluding that the list of high priests is defective and needs to be expanded, perhaps even after Joiakim and after Jaddua, but his specific reconstruction of the list on the basis of papponomy is quite arbitrary. His proposal to insert another Johanan and another Jaddua at the end of the list of high priests is less problematical because the Johanan of the biblical text is dated securely to 410 BCE by the Elephantine data, and Josephus mentions a transition of power from Johanan to Jaddua in the high priestly office almost eighty years later.[207] In a counterhypothesis, Williamson noted that both Joiada and Johanan are sons of Eliashib (vv. 10, 23) and thus brothers, and proposed that

205. AP 30.18.

206. Frank M. Cross, "A Reconstruction of the Judaean Restoration," *JBL* 94 (1975) 4-18.

207. Josephus *Antiquities of the Jews* XI.302.

Johanan succeeded his brother Joiada as high priest. Verse 22 would then indicate merely sequence in office—Eliashib, Joiada, Johanan—rather than genealogical relationship. Williamson argued that Johanan was then succeeded by his nephew Jonathan, the son of his brother Joiada (v. 11).[208] But this proposal collapses if Jaddua is not secondary in v. 22. If the text of v. 22 is correct as it stands, Johanan, according to Williamson's argument, would have to be succeeded by Jaddua, and not by Jonathan.

James VanderKam has argued that the list of high priests in vv. 10-11 is in fact complete and does not need to be restored or expanded.[209] He stretches the six high priests in this list over the entire period of the restoration, until the arrival of Alexander the Great. His conclusions may be summarized as follows:

❖ Jeshua—first high priest after the return from Babylon; continued until first years of fifth century (495?).

❖ Joiakim —began about 495 and continued until 460 or even 450.

❖ Eliashib—evidence in the book of Nehemiah fixes the chronology of his high priesthood from at least 445 to 432; he may well have begun his term prior to 445 (perhaps 450).

❖ Joiada—seems to have become high priest early in Nehemiah's second term (c. 431; see 13:28) and to have vacated the office sometime before 410.

❖ Johanan—appears as high priest in the Elephantine Papyri in 410, the fourteenth year of Darius II (423/24–404); continued in office until the time of Artaxerxes II (404–358), perhaps until about 370 BCE; he killed his brother Jeshua.

❖ Jaddua—served as high priest when Darius III (336–330) was king of the Persians and was a contemporary of Alexander the Great; his brother married Sanballat's daughter Nikaso.

VanderKam has made great strides in understanding the list of high priests and in accepting its data as relatively complete. The lengths of term for the high priests are quite long and perhaps improbable, but not impossible: Jeshua c. 43 years; Joiakim c. 35-45 years; Eliashib c. 18 years; Joiada c. 21-22 years; Johanan c. 40 years; Jaddua c. 38-40 years. VanderKam believes that Jonathan in v. 11 is the same as Johanan in v. 22.

Two conclusions seem prudent at the end of this discussion. First, if the list of high priests in Nehemiah 12 is defective and short, no proposition to restore it is fully convincing. After many years of debate over Cross's proposals, it is exceedingly interesting that a forceful case can still be made for the integrity of the six-name list. Second, the relationship of Jonathan to Johanan is unclear, even though, in my judgment, they are probably the same person.

12:12-21. This second list of priests is the master list from which vv. 1-7 and 10:2-8 were developed. The omission of Hattush (family #6) in v. 14 is probably a textual accident. Zechariah from the family of Iddo (#10) would seem to be the post-exilic prophet of the same name (cf. Ezra 5:1; 6:14), although Zech 1:1 makes Iddo Zechariah's grandfather and Berechiah his father (cf. Isa 8:2). The prophet Zechariah should be listed under the Jeshua priests in vv. 1-7 rather than under the Joiakim priests in vv. 12-21. The names "Joseph" (v. 14; cf. Genesis 37–50) and "Eber" (v. 20; cf. Gen 10:21; 1 Chr 5:13) may indicate a revival of interest in ancestral names in this period.

12:22-23. These verses offer notes about the sources of the lists of priests and Levites. The first word in the Hebrew text of v. 22, הלוים (*halwiyyim*, "the Levites"), should be deleted as an incorrectly entered gloss on the unusual expression בני לוי *bĕnê lēwî*, "sons of Levi" [NRSV, "The Levites"]; cf. Ezra 8:15) at the start of v. 23. The conjunction "and" on the word "priests" in v. 22 should be omitted, and we should emend על (*'al*, "until") to עד (*'ad*, "up to"). The verse should then be translated: "In the days of Eliashib, Joiada, Johanan, and Jaddua, the heads of the fathers' houses of the priests were written down up to the reign of Darius the Persian." The author, therefore, claims that in addition to the priests mentioned in this chapter he knows of additional records for the priestly families extending from the time of Nehemiah (Eliashib) to the time of Darius the

208. H. G. M. Williamson, *Ezra, Nehemiah,* WBC 16 (Waco, Tex.: Word, 1985) 361-65.

209. James C. VanderKam, "Jewish High Priests of the Persian Period: Is the List Complete?" in *Priesthood and Cult in Ancient Israel,* ed. Gary A. Anderson and Saul M. Olyan, JSOTSup 125 (Sheffield: JSOT, 1991) 69-91.

Persian. This latter reference could be to Darius II Nothus (423–404) or Darius III Codomannus (336–331), depending on which Jaddua is referred to (see Commentary on 12:11). Although the author included in this chapter only lists of priests from the time of Jeshua and Joiakim at the beginning of the restoration, he had access to other lists, presumably up to his own day.[210] Verse 23 tells us that similar lists for the Levites were written down in an unknown source called the Book of the Annals until the time of the high priest Johanan.

12:24-26. The writer records in vv. 24-25*a* a list of Levites from the time of Joiakim (v. 26), which thus complements the list of priests from the period of the same high priest in vv. 12-21. (For an interpretation of this list, see the Commentary on 12:8-9.) Antiphonal singing of praise is traced back to David (see 11:22-23), who is given the honored title of "man of God" (cf. 1 Chr 25:2; 2 Chr 8:14). Moses, the founder of the Israelite cult, is called "man of God" in deuteronomistic texts (Deut 33:1; Josh 14:6). *BHS* recommends the insertion of the word "singers" (lost by haplography) after Obadiah, thus identifying Mattaniah, Bakbukiah, and Obadiah as singers (see 11:17).[211] At the end of this list the author adds the names of three gatekeepers—Meshullam, Talmon, and Akkub—whom he may have considered Levites as well (for Meshullam, cf. Shallum at 1 Chr 9:17 and Ezra 10:24; for Talmon and Akkub, see the Commentary on 11:19). The NRSV and the NIV have correctly reversed the order of the seventh and eighth words in the Hebrew text of v. 25.

210. Although Williamson rejects the above proposal as "radical emendation," he deletes the name of the high priest Jaddua and interprets the last five words of v. 22 as the incorporation of a late gloss into the text. Through these emendations he dates the list of Levites in 12:24-25 to the time of Johanan and considers the remaining fragment of 12:22 as an "artificial device to cover over the way in which [the author] composed vv 8-9 out of vv 24-25." See Williamson, *Ezra, Nehemiah,* 357, 364.

211. *BHS* 25[b].

REFLECTIONS

The person who added Neh 12:1-26 was intensely concerned with completeness and continuity. It was not enough to report the rebuilding of the wall (chap. 3), the reading of the law (chap. 8), a confessional prayer (chap. 9), a firm agreement to obey God (chap. 10), a list of those who had been resettled in Jerusalem after the completion of the walls (chap. 11), not to mention the dismissal of foreign wives (Ezra 10), the dedication of the Temple (Ezra 6), and the rebuilding of the altar (Ezra 3). For the sake of completeness, the reviser mentioned priests, high priests, and Levites of this community to show how appropriate worship in this new age would be carried out.

Continuity was also important for the reviser of the books of Ezra and Nehemiah. At this point he did not have to show how the post-exilic community corresponded to its pre-exilic counterpart, as was the concern in Ezra 1–6, but rather how *within* that post-exilic community clerical continuity remained over the generations. A full roster of priests and Levites for the first and the second post-exilic high priests was given. While we can see how 12:1-7 was derived from 12:12-21—and how some kind of relationship of dependency exists between 12:8-9 and 12:24-25—the reader of the final text of chapter 12 notices that these lists form an unbroken clerical chain over the generations, without radical change of personnel. The list of clergy during the second high priestly term reached to the period of Nehemiah and Ezra in the world of the text, if not in the world of history. All was now ready for the liturgical act that would dedicate the walls and bring the work of Nehemiah and Ezra to its climax.

But as the reviser made these theological points, he included valuable documents that were available to him. Sometimes, as in 12:1-7, we may detect his creative hand as he reconstructed a list of priests for the period of Joshua; but that means also that 12:12-21 gains in credibility and historical value. Whatever its exact age, it clearly was older than the person who added this chapter. Close study of 12:12-21 enables modern scholars to detect a major supplement at the end of this old list of priests, perhaps merely to meet the expanded worship needs of the community, but perhaps also—centuries later—to link the Maccabean line with the early post-exilic community and so enhance its credibility. Today we do not find pedigree or genealogy to be clear evidence for continuity. We are called by the same Spirit and sent by the same Lord who first dispatched the apostles and the disciples. But we do take pride in being official spokespersons of the apostolic faith.

Much progress has been made in study of the high priestly line, but many details still remain obscure to us. We would like to be able to fill in the apparent gaps, to learn the true identity of Jonathan, to know whether there was one or two Jadduas, and so forth. But despite all these maddening historical uncertainties, we should not miss the author's theological point: The clergy line was maintained during the high priesthood of Joshua and Joiakim, and it continued much longer in a series of high priests from Eliashib to Jaddua, regardless of how many high priests really stood in between. Thus not only the early returnees and those at the time of Ezra and Nehemiah have a legitimate clergy, but so also did all subsequent generations living under their high priests, regardless of how many there were, down to the time of the author. He assures us that this could all be checked out, if the reader wanted to take the trouble, in the Book of the Annals.

NEHEMIAH 12:27-43, THE DEDICATION OF THE CITY WALL

NIV

27At the dedication of the wall of Jerusalem, the Levites were sought out from where they lived and were brought to Jerusalem to celebrate joyfully the dedication with songs of thanksgiving and with the music of cymbals, harps and lyres. 28The singers also were brought together from the region around Jerusalem—from the villages of the Netophathites, 29from Beth Gilgal, and from the area of Geba and Azmaveth, for the singers had built villages for themselves around Jerusalem. 30When the priests and Levites had purified themselves ceremonially, they purified the people, the gates and the wall.

31I had the leaders of Judah go up on top[a] of the wall. I also assigned two large choirs to give thanks. One was to proceed on top[b] of the wall to the right, toward the Dung Gate. 32Hoshaiah and half the leaders of Judah followed them, 33along with Azariah, Ezra, Meshullam, 34Judah, Benjamin, Shemaiah, Jeremiah, 35as well as some priests with trumpets, and also Zechariah son of Jonathan, the son of Shemaiah, the son of Mattaniah, the son of Micaiah, the son of Zaccur, the son of Asaph, 36and his associates—Shemaiah, Azarel, Milalai, Gilalai, Maai, Nethanel, Judah and

a *31* Or *go alongside* b *31* Or *proceed alongside*

NRSV

27Now at the dedication of the wall of Jerusalem they sought out the Levites in all their places, to bring them to Jerusalem to celebrate the dedication with rejoicing, with thanksgivings and with singing, with cymbals, harps, and lyres. 28The companies of the singers gathered together from the circuit around Jerusalem and from the villages of the Netophathites; 29also from Beth-gilgal and from the region of Geba and Azmaveth; for the singers had built for themselves villages around Jerusalem. 30And the priests and the Levites purified themselves; and they purified the people and the gates and the wall.

31Then I brought the leaders of Judah up onto the wall, and appointed two great companies that gave thanks and went in procession. One went to the right on the wall to the Dung Gate; 32and after them went Hoshaiah and half the officials of Judah, 33and Azariah, Ezra, Meshullam, 34Judah, Benjamin, Shemaiah, and Jeremiah, 35and some of the young priests with trumpets: Zechariah son of Jonathan son of Shemaiah son of Mattaniah son of Micaiah son of Zaccur son of Asaph; 36and his kindred, Shemaiah, Azarel, Milalai, Gilalai, Maai, Nethanel, Judah, and Hanani, with the musical instruments of David the man of God; and the

NIV

Hanani—with musical instruments ⌊prescribed by⌋ David the man of God. Ezra the scribe led the procession. 37At the Fountain Gate they continued directly up the steps of the City of David on the ascent to the wall and passed above the house of David to the Water Gate on the east.

38The second choir proceeded in the opposite direction. I followed them on top[a] of the wall, together with half the people—past the Tower of the Ovens to the Broad Wall, 39over the Gate of Ephraim, the Jeshanah[b] Gate, the Fish Gate, the Tower of Hananel and the Tower of the Hundred, as far as the Sheep Gate. At the Gate of the Guard they stopped.

40The two choirs that gave thanks then took their places in the house of God; so did I, together with half the officials, 41as well as the priests—Eliakim, Maaseiah, Miniamin, Micaiah, Elioenai, Zechariah and Hananiah with their trumpets—42and also Maaseiah, Shemaiah, Eleazar, Uzzi, Jehohanan, Malkijah, Elam and Ezer. The choirs sang under the direction of Jezrahiah. 43And on that day they offered great sacrifices, rejoicing because God had given them great joy. The women and children also rejoiced. The sound of rejoicing in Jerusalem could be heard far away.

[a] *38* Or *them alongside* [b] *39* Or *Old*

NRSV

scribe Ezra went in front of them. 37At the Fountain Gate, in front of them, they went straight up by the stairs of the city of David, at the ascent of the wall, above the house of David, to the Water Gate on the east.

38The other company of those who gave thanks went to the left,[a] and I followed them with half of the people on the wall, above the Tower of the Ovens, to the Broad Wall, 39and above the Gate of Ephraim, and by the Old Gate, and by the Fish Gate and the Tower of Hananel and the Tower of the Hundred, to the Sheep Gate; and they came to a halt at the Gate of the Guard. 40So both companies of those who gave thanks stood in the house of God, and I and half of the officials with me; 41and the priests Eliakim, Maaseiah, Miniamin, Micaiah, Elioenai, Zechariah, and Hananiah, with trumpets; 42and Maaseiah, Shemaiah, Eleazar, Uzzi, Jehohanan, Malchijah, Elam, and Ezer. And the singers sang with Jezrahiah as their leader. 43They offered great sacrifices that day and rejoiced, for God had made them rejoice with great joy; the women and children also rejoiced. The joy of Jerusalem was heard far away.

[a] Cn: Heb *opposite*

COMMENTARY

Historically, the dedication of the city wall would seem to fit better at 7:3, but the editors of the book decided to give a full picture of the ideal Judean community in 7:4–12:26 before recording the climactic dedication. For the first time since 7:5 the Nehemiah Memoir is the source of at least part of this pericope. Note especially the use of first-person narration in vv. 31, 38, and 40. Nehemiah, to be sure, is not mentioned in vv. 27-30, nor does the narrator of these verses speak in the first person. It also seems strange for Nehemiah to list the names of priests and musicians (vv. 33-36, 41-42), since that is not his custom elsewhere. If vv. 27-30, 33-36, and 41-43 are not from the memoir (v. 43 seems to be an attempt to bring the whole book to its conclusion), they were probably added by the editor of this material or a supplementer on the basis of his own knowledge or sources available to him. Williamson's proposal that two alternative accounts of the wall dedication have been merged is not convincing.[212]

The present text may be outlined as follows:

vv. 27-29, Assembly of Levites and musicians

v. 30, Rite of purification

vv. 31, 37-39, Appointment of two choirs to lead processions around city

212. Williamson, *Ezra, Nehemiah,* 370-71.

vv. 32, 40, Prominent lay leaders, Hoshaiah and Nehemiah
vv. 33-35*a*, 41, Seven priests with trumpets
vv. 35*b*, 42*b*, Directors of levitical music, Zechariah, and Izrahiah
vv. 36, 42*a*, Eight levitical musicians
v. 43, Concluding sacrifices (cf. v. 40)

The mention of Ezra the scribe at the head of the priests and Levites in the first procession (v. 36) seems out of place and is commonly interpreted as a supplement meant to stress the contemporaneity of Ezra and Nehemiah in a unified reform movement (cf. the addition of Nehemiah in 8:9 and the secondary reference to both leaders in 12:26).

The dedication of the wall comes toward the end of the books of Ezra and Nehemiah, whereas the dedication of the Temple in Jerusalem took place near its beginning (Ezra 6:16-17; cf. the completion of the altar and the laying of the Temple's foundation in 3:4-5 and 3:11-13 respectively). As usual the Levites were leaders in the joyful musical praise (cf. 2 Chr 23:18; 29:30; 30:23; Ezra 3:11-13). Since musical instruments play an important role in v. 27, it might be better to use the word "musicians" rather than "singers" in v. 28. Although many Levites already lived in Jerusalem (see 11:15-19, where 284 Levites and 172 gatekeepers are mentioned), others now had to be brought in from their local residences. The musicians in particular came from a series of towns they had built for themselves in the immediate vicinity of Jerusalem, all less than eight miles away: Netophah was between Bethlehem and Tekoa (1 Chr 2:54; Ezra 2:22); the other three were north of Jerusalem, within the territory of Benjamin: Beth-gilgal (Josh 4:19; 15:7), Geba (listed as a levitical city in Josh 21:17; cf. Ezra 2:26), and Azmaveth (Ezra 2:24//Neh 7:28).

The clergy purified themselves (cf. Ezra 6:20), the people, the gates, and the wall (v. 30). Purification before a cultic act might include sexual abstinence, washing one's clothes, shaving the entire body, offering sacrificial animals, and sprinkling one's body or an object with ritually prepared water (see Exod 19:10, 14-15; Lev 14:4-8, 49-53; 16:28; Num 8:5-8, 19; Ps 51:7; Ezek 36:25). The walls and the gates needed purification either because of the many deaths involved in their destruction by the Babylonians (see Num 19:14-18) or because the city had been ruled by foreigners.

Verses 31-42 describe the two processions that went around Jerusalem. Nehemiah brought the religious and secular leaders of Judah to the top of the wall and appointed two choirs to head the two processional groups (v. 31). Since the priests with their trumpets and the Levites with their instruments made music at the rear, the choirs at the front provided the processions with a kind of stereophonic sound. The processions marched around the top of the walls of Jerusalem in opposite directions. The section of Nehemiah's wall excavated by Kathleen Kenyon might allow on its top for a column two or three people wide.

Although no starting point for the processions is explicitly given, the groups probably began at the Valley Gate, where Nehemiah's nighttime inspection tour had originated (2:13, 15; 3:13; see the Commentary on 3:1-32; see also "Nehemiah's Reconstruction of the Wall of Jerusalem," 760). The first column proceeded counterclockwise, moving toward the south (v. 31; NRSV and NIV, "right") in the direction of the Dung Gate (see 2:13; 3:13). Leading the procession behind the choir was a layperson, Hoshaiah, otherwise unknown, with half of the lay leaders (v. 32). A list of such lay leaders is provided in 10:14-27.

The names of six of the seven priests listed in vv. 33-34 appear among the priests recorded in chaps. 10 and 12: Azariah (10:2); Ezra (12:1, 13); Meshullam (10:17; 12:13); Mijamin (10:7; 12:5) or Miniamin (12:17) instead of Benjamin; Shemaiah (10:8; a priestly family in 12:8); and Jeremiah (10:2; a priestly family in 12:12). Azariah and Ezra are the long and short forms of the same name, and a textual error may be suspected; the Ezra mentioned in v. 33 is not to be identified with Ezra the scribe. Benjamin in the MT seems to have replaced the more original Mijamin or Miniamin because of the preceding Judah (see LXX^{L}), or Judah replaced an earlier name because of the secondary reading Benjamin. Only the name "Judah" is unknown elsewhere as a priest (see 12:8, where he is a Levite).

Zechariah (v. 35) was the leader of the musicians in the group that headed south, and his importance is seen in that his genealogy is traced back to his seventh ancestor, the Levite Asaph.

More problematic is the fact that his great-grandfather Mattaniah (11:17)[213] was apparently one of the Levites who lived in Jerusalem at this time. Perhaps this musician's name has been updated to the time of the redaction of this chapter (see the similar updating of this genealogy in 11:22). None of the eight Levites in the first group can be identified. The conjunction "and" should either be moved from the second to the last to the last name in v. 36 (so NRSV and NIV, which "correct" the HB without notice), or the two names should be reversed. The musical instruments of these Levites were authorized for worship by David (see v. 24 for the title "man of God" used of him).

The route taken by the first procession is difficult to trace after the Fountain Gate (v. 37; cf. 2:14; 3:15). The group ascended the stairs of the city of David (cf. 3:15), but we do not know what is meant by the "ascent of the wall." The "house of David" would surely have been destroyed by the Babylonians; perhaps only its location is referred to here (cf. the "graves of David" in 3:16). The group then moved toward the site of the old Water Gate, which was probably outside of Nehemiah's newly restored eastern wall (see the Commentary on 3:26 and 8:1).

The other part of the procession headed north (NRSV, "left") along the top of the wall, beginning, presumably, from the Valley Gate, with Nehemiah leading the people who came behind the choir. The procession passed the Tower of Ovens (3:11), the Broad Wall (the place where the southern line of the westward pre-exilic expansion rejoined the original walls; see 3:8), and the Gate of Ephraim. This gate apparently served as an exit from the temple area toward the central ridge that leads to the mountains of Ephraim. The gate is mentioned during Jehoash's eighth-century attack on Jerusalem (2 Kgs 14:13; 2 Chr 25:23; cf. Neh 8:16). Next the procession passed the Mishneh Gate (v. 39; read המשנה [*hammišneh*] for הישנה [*hayĕšānâ*], "Old Gate," as at 3:6), the Fish Gate (3:3), the Tower of Hananel and the Tower of the Hundred (3:1), and finally arrived at the Sheep Gate (3:1), where the rebuilding of the wall had been initiated. This second procession halted at the Gate of the Guard, which may be connected with the Court of the Guard (3:25), a bit south of the Temple. Did the first group proceed from the Water Gate area to the Court of the Guard, where, after connecting with the second group, the two processions entered the Temple together? Or did the first procession continue on to the Sheep Gate or the Muster Gate at the northeast corner of the city (3:31) and enter the temple area from one of these gates? The second suggestion assumes that the text of v. 37 is incomplete. Unless the first group went on to the Sheep Gate or the Muster Gate, however, the two groups would not have encircled the whole city.

Verse 40 finds both companies inside the temple area. Nehemiah continues his description of the makeup of the second processional group in this verse. We might have expected these details already in v. 38. Five of the seven priests in v. 41 appear in other lists of priests in Ezra 10 and Nehemiah 12: Maaseiah (Ezra 10:18, 21, 22); Miniamin (Neh 12:17, a family name; cf. Mijamin in Neh 12:5); Elioenai (Ezra 10:22); Zechariah (Neh 12:16); and Hananiah (Neh 12:12; cf. Hanani in Ezra 10:20). Only Eliakim and Micaiah are absent from those lists. Little can be said about the list of eight Levites and their leader Jezrahiah, except to note that Uzzi was identified as the overseer of the Levites in Jerusalem in Neh 11:22. It seems unlikely that Ezer is the same person as the ruler of Mizpeh (3:19).

The last verse in this pericope (v. 43) emphasizes the great joy and the inclusive character of the celebrators—women and children also participated. Five times (three verbs; two nouns) we hear of their joy, even their great joy. Joy was also the mood at the dedication of the house of God (Ezra 6:16), at the reading of the law (Neh 8:12), at the celebration of the Feast of Tabernacles (Neh 8:17), and, earlier, at David's bringing of the ark to Jerusalem (1 Chr 15:16, 25). "Joy" is connected to the service of dedication also in v. 27. The adjective "great" (גדולה *gĕdôlâ*), describing their joy, echoes the "great sacrifices"—that is, the great number of their thanksgiving sacrifices (Leviticus 3; Ezra 3:3-5; 6:17). The thanksgiving choirs were themselves described as "great" in v. 31. The noise of the rejoicing was heard far away, just as it had been, but with fateful negative consequences, in Ezra 3:13. This time the joy of the community was not mixed with any weeping.

213. Zaccur (his great-great-great-grandfather) should be identified with Zabdi (11:17) or the probably more original Zichri (LXX^L; 1 Chr 9:15).

REFLECTIONS

All things necessary for the restored community in Jerusalem to be considered complete had been achieved, and the book of Nehemiah reaches a kind of climax in this pericope. Blenkinsopp even conjectures that the book once ended at this point.[214] This unit begins and ends with affirmations of joy and thanksgiving. What had been achieved was more than skillful administration by Nehemiah. It was God who had made them rejoice. *Large* choirs, *great* joy, *many* sacrifices of thanksgiving—all three of these adjectives in this sentence are expressed with one repeated Hebrew word. Indeed, something big was happening here.

This was a ceremony of dedication. After the dedication of the Temple in 515 BCE (Ezra 6:16), it had taken a full seventy years and the work of two great leaders, Ezra and Nehemiah, to come to the next dedication. This was more than a wall they were dedicating. It was a celebration of the revived and purified community, bound to the Torah and fully outfitted with the clerical leadership necessary for such a cultic community. Everything was now present that was necessary for the community to live in blessing.

The Hebrew word for "dedication" is known to us through its English transliteration, "Hanukkah." That great Jewish festival, celebrated near Christmas by Jews even today, marks the dedication—or rather rededication—of the Second Temple after the victories of Judah the Maccabee in response to the defiling persecutions of Antiochus IV Epiphanes. Nehemiah's wall dedication and the second-century Hanukkah remind the community how vulnerable it is and how often it has been delivered.

The service as described in these verses would have been most impressive. We will, of course, never know what music they played or what words they sang. One can imagine that communal psalms of thanksgiving or hymns of praise formed part of the repertoire. Cymbals, lutes, lyres, and trumpets backed up the choral voices. Their joyful noise bore witness far and wide to what God had done.

The text does not tell us the reason for the processions, what the community was trying to "say" by its actions. Blenkinsopp quotes Mircea Eliade's interpretation of such processions as circumscribing a sacred center within which the threatening forces of chaos and disorder are brought under control.[215] The whole city, all the people it contained, and the institutions it enshrined were truly now the holy city (Neh 11:1, 18).

These processions might well recall earlier pilgrimages and processions, enshrined now also in the book of Psalms:

> Walk about Zion, go all around it,
>   count its towers,
> consider well its ramparts;
>   go through its citadels,
> that you may tell the next generation
>   that this is God,
> our God forever and ever.
>   He will be our guide forever.
> (Ps 48:12-14 NRSV)

The post-exilic community had achieved its goals, but the text knows more than that. God had made them rejoice. The time for dedication of the walls was also a time for rededication to God: "This is our God forever and ever." Celebration is more than making a lot of noise or even rendering thanks to God. It is also a time for witness and praise, in which the community shares its experience with those who are far away.

214. Joseph Blenkinsopp, *Ezra–Nehemiah,* OTL (Philadelphia: Westminster, 1988) 347.
215. Ibid., 346.

NEHEMIAH 12:44–13:3, THE PEOPLE SOLIDIFY THE REFORM MEASURES

NIV

44At that time men were appointed to be in charge of the storerooms for the contributions, firstfruits and tithes. From the fields around the towns they were to bring into the storerooms the portions required by the Law for the priests and the Levites, for Judah was pleased with the ministering priests and Levites. 45They performed the service of their God and the service of purification, as did also the singers and gatekeepers, according to the commands of David and his son Solomon. 46For long ago, in the days of David and Asaph, there had been directors for the singers and for the songs of praise and thanksgiving to God. 47So in the days of Zerubbabel and of Nehemiah, all Israel contributed the daily portions for the singers and gatekeepers. They also set aside the portion for the other Levites, and the Levites set aside the portion for the descendants of Aaron.

13 On that day the Book of Moses was read aloud in the hearing of the people and there it was found written that no Ammonite or Moabite should ever be admitted into the assembly of God, 2because they had not met the Israelites with food and water but had hired Balaam to call a curse down on them. (Our God, however, turned the curse into a blessing.) 3When the people heard this law, they excluded from Israel all who were of foreign descent.

NRSV

44On that day men were appointed over the chambers for the stores, the contributions, the first fruits, and the tithes, to gather into them the portions required by the law for the priests and for the Levites from the fields belonging to the towns; for Judah rejoiced over the priests and the Levites who ministered. 45They performed the service of their God and the service of purification, as did the singers and the gatekeepers, according to the command of David and his son Solomon. 46For in the days of David and Asaph long ago there was a leader of the singers, and there were songs of praise and thanksgiving to God. 47In the days of Zerubbabel and in the days of Nehemiah all Israel gave the daily portions for the singers and the gatekeepers. They set apart that which was for the Levites; and the Levites set apart that which was for the descendants of Aaron.

13 On that day they read from the book of Moses in the hearing of the people; and in it was found written that no Ammonite or Moabite should ever enter the assembly of God, 2because they did not meet the Israelites with bread and water, but hired Balaam against them to curse them—yet our God turned the curse into a blessing. 3When the people heard the law, they separated from Israel all those of foreign descent.

COMMENTARY

Each of the two paragraphs in this unit (12:44-47 and 13:1-3) begins with the words “in that day,” which link it to the ceremony of the dedication of the wall. The mention of Judah’s joy (12:44) provides another tie between the first paragraph and the dedication of the wall. Neither of these paragraphs, however, comes from the Nehemiah Memoir, and their similarity to chap. 10, itself judged to be part of a secondary stratum in the book, suggests that each of these paragraphs was an editor’s addition to the book. As an introduction to the final quotations from the Nehemiah Memoir in 13:4-31, the two paragraphs declare that nothing really new happened under Nehemiah, but that he only acted in conformity with the already constituted theocracy and its laws and decisions. Nehemiah merely corrected certain exceptions from the rule. Everything had proceeded from the beginning in a model way.

Verses 44-47, which report the full participation of the people in various kinds of contributions for the Temple and especially for the clergy, anticipate the action taken by Nehemiah to restore the tithe (13:10-13). The first three verses of chap.

13, on the other hand, which report the community's total separation from all foreigners, anticipate the specific action Nehemiah took against Tobiah's living in the Temple in 13:4-9 and reaffirm the decision of the community not to intermarry with the peoples of the land (10:30). Note the chiastic arrangement of 12:44–13:9:

A 12:44-47, Tithes
  B 13:1-3, Separation from foreigners
  B′ 13:4-9, Separation from Tobiah
A′ 13:10-13, Tithes

Repeated connections to the firm agreement of chap. 10 can be found in this section, thus bringing cohesion to the final four chapters of the book.

12:44-47. The first paragraph reports the appointment of officials to supervise regular donations to the Temple and its clergy (see the Commentary on 13:13) and ties these actions thematically to the dedication of the wall ("in that day"). These officials managed the "storerooms" (NRSV, "stores") in which were kept the contributions, prime offerings, and tithes required by the law (see 10:37-39 for definitions of prime offerings and tithes; "contributions" [v. 44] is clearly a separate category of donation, but its exact meaning in 10:37, 39 and here is unclear; cf. 13:5). The amount of the donations was assessed on the basis of real estate ownership or land cultivated ("fields").

The community's voluntary support of the priests and Levites is expressed by its joy over their ministry, an emotion that continues a major motif from the dedication ceremony (12:43). Here it is surely meant to encourage subsequent generations to continue that support. The service of purification (12:45) is a duty assigned specifically to the Levites in 1 Chr 23:28. Support for singers and gatekeepers followed the instructions of David (1 Chronicles 23–26; cf. Neh 11:23) and Solomon (2 Chr 8:14) that had been given when the duties of the Levites needed revising after the ark had come to rest in the Temple. Verse 46 traces the heritage of the singers back to their first leader, Asaph, in the time of David (in 1 Chr 15:16-19, three leaders are mentioned; for the focus on Asaph alone, see Ezra 2:41). Back in those ancient days "there were leaders [with the Qere; NRSV, "a leader"] of the singers and chiefs [ושׂרי *wĕśārê*; NRSV, "and there were songs," ושׁיר *wĕšîr*] of praise and thanksgiving." Verse 47 contends that the entire community gave its support for the singers and gatekeepers throughout the post-exilic period, from the time of Zerubbabel to the time of Nehemiah. Israel also gave its tithes to the Levites (not the "other Levites," as in the NIV), who in turn gave a tithe of this offering to the priests (see 10:38). The linking of Zerubbabel and Nehemiah in v. 47, in spite of the approximately seventy-five years between them, may have led later authors to place Nehemiah at the time of the first return (see 2 Macc 1:18-36).

13:1-3. The community decided to exclude from the assembly all those of foreign or mixed descent (v. 3; cf. Exod 12:38; Jer 25:20; 50:37; Ezek 30:5), without any direct mention of the problem of mixed marriages that had exercised Ezra (Ezra 9–10). This decision was based on a portion of the Book of Moses (see 8:1; 2 Chr 25:4; 35:12; Neh 8:1)—that is, Deut 23:3-6 (paraphrased here)—which banned Ammonites and Moabites permanently (to the tenth generation) from participation in Israel's cult. Both in Deuteronomy and in Nehemiah this exclusion is based on their inhospitality toward Israel in the wilderness period and the hiring of Balaam in a futile attempt to curse them (Numbers 22–24; 31:8, 16; Josh 13:22). This hiring was done by Balak (Num 22:18), who is alluded to by the third-person singular subject of the verb "hired" (v. 2; neither the NRSV nor the NIV indicates that the subject of the verb is singular). Nehemiah had charged earlier that Tobiah and Sanballat had hired the false prophet Shemaiah against him (6:12). That attempt to undo Nehemiah by hiring someone against him continued the hostile spirit of the Ammonites (Tobiah was an Ammonite; 2:10, 19) and the Moabites. The community did not demand that men who had already married foreign wives must divorce, and this may indicate that Ezra's policy had been unpopular, unsuccessful, or both. Nehemiah expelled Tobiah rather than forcing him to get a divorce (13:8), and he only required the people to take an oath not to engage in mixed marriages in the future (see 13:23-27).

REFLECTIONS

Since the editor wants us to see the post-exilic community as a model despite the many measures Nehemiah had to take to correct its failures, he played down the innovative character of Nehemiah's service and credited the changes to the community as a whole. The Torah required regular contributions for the Temple and its clergy, assessed on the basis of land use or ownership. This was a kind of church tax, or at least it could have been so interpreted, and may have led to resentment or even to attempts to avoid paying it. But the model community, portrayed by the writer, readily gave what was needed from the beginning of the restoration (Zerubbabel) until the completion of the restoration of Jerusalem (Nehemiah). Lay participation was matched by the faithfulness of the Levites, who shared 10 percent of their income with the priests. Judah rejoiced in its priests and Levites, who ministered (lit., who stood) in their stead in the presence of Yahweh. The temptation of a modern reader is to view this report of wholesale support for the clergy critically, as cult propaganda. A more sympathetic reading finds in this support respect for the clergy and a delight in fostering the worship of God. "God loves cheerful givers," the old saying goes. The editor urges us all to be such givers.

An inclusive age such as ours is rightly troubled by the fear of outsiders in the books of Ezra and Nehemiah, but we may be reading the text too much from our point of view, without appreciating the specific dangers inherent in Israel's relationships to outsiders (see 13:26-27). The Ammonites and the Moabites are mentioned here because of their inhospitality and their attempt to foil Israel by hiring Balaam to curse them. Meeting someone with bread and water or showing hospitality to the hungry and the thirsty, as Jesus reminds us, is a characteristic of those who will be blessed by the Father (Matt 25:34-35). In the wonderful alchemy of divine providence, the attempt to curse Israel had resulted in blessing for them instead.

The people heard the law and did it (13:3). In Jewish tradition, the festival called *Simḥat* Torah (Joy in the Law) is a celebration at the end of the annual reading of the entire Pentateuch. The community rejoices because once more it has experienced the fullness of the Torah. Joy in the Torah can also be expressed by the willingness to follow its teaching and advice, even in such mundane matters as ecclesiastical contributions and separating oneself from anyone whose character is flawed by inhospitality.

NEHEMIAH 13:4-31, NEHEMIAH'S CORRECTIVE MEASURES

NIV

4Before this, Eliashib the priest had been put in charge of the storerooms of the house of our God. He was closely associated with Tobiah, 5and he had provided him with a large room formerly used to store the grain offerings and incense and temple articles, and also the tithes of grain, new wine and oil prescribed for the Levites, singers and gatekeepers, as well as the contributions for the priests.

NRSV

4Now before this, the priest Eliashib, who was appointed over the chambers of the house of our God, and who was related to Tobiah, 5prepared for Tobiah a large room where they had previously put the grain offering, the frankincense, the vessels, and the tithes of grain, wine, and oil, which were given by commandment to the Levites, singers, and gatekeepers, and the contributions for the priests. 6While this was taking place I was not

NIV

6But while all this was going on, I was not in Jerusalem, for in the thirty-second year of Artaxerxes king of Babylon I had returned to the king. Some time later I asked his permission 7and came back to Jerusalem. Here I learned about the evil thing Eliashib had done in providing Tobiah a room in the courts of the house of God. 8I was greatly displeased and threw all Tobiah's household goods out of the room. 9I gave orders to purify the rooms, and then I put back into them the equipment of the house of God, with the grain offerings and the incense.

10I also learned that the portions assigned to the Levites had not been given to them, and that all the Levites and singers responsible for the service had gone back to their own fields. 11So I rebuked the officials and asked them, "Why is the house of God neglected?" Then I called them together and stationed them at their posts.

12All Judah brought the tithes of grain, new wine and oil into the storerooms. 13I put Shelemiah the priest, Zadok the scribe, and a Levite named Pedaiah in charge of the storerooms and made Hanan son of Zaccur, the son of Mattaniah, their assistant, because these men were considered trustworthy. They were made responsible for distributing the supplies to their brothers.

14Remember me for this, O my God, and do not blot out what I have so faithfully done for the house of my God and its services.

15In those days I saw men in Judah treading winepresses on the Sabbath and bringing in grain and loading it on donkeys, together with wine, grapes, figs and all other kinds of loads. And they were bringing all this into Jerusalem on the Sabbath. Therefore I warned them against selling food on that day. 16Men from Tyre who lived in Jerusalem were bringing in fish and all kinds of merchandise and selling them in Jerusalem on the Sabbath to the people of Judah. 17I rebuked the nobles of Judah and said to them, "What is this wicked thing you are doing—desecrating the Sabbath day? 18Didn't your forefathers do the same things, so that our God brought all this calamity upon us and upon this city? Now you are stirring up more wrath against Israel by desecrating the Sabbath."

19When evening shadows fell on the gates of Jerusalem before the Sabbath, I ordered the doors

NRSV

in Jerusalem, for in the thirty-second year of King Artaxerxes of Babylon I went to the king. After some time I asked leave of the king 7and returned to Jerusalem. I then discovered the wrong that Eliashib had done on behalf of Tobiah, preparing a room for him in the courts of the house of God. 8And I was very angry, and I threw all the household furniture of Tobiah out of the room. 9Then I gave orders and they cleansed the chambers, and I brought back the vessels of the house of God, with the grain offering and the frankincense.

10I also found out that the portions of the Levites had not been given to them; so that the Levites and the singers, who had conducted the service, had gone back to their fields. 11So I remonstrated with the officials and said, "Why is the house of God forsaken?" And I gathered them together and set them in their stations. 12Then all Judah brought the tithe of the grain, wine, and oil into the storehouses. 13And I appointed as treasurers over the storehouses the priest Shelemiah, the scribe Zadok, and Pedaiah of the Levites, and as their assistant Hanan son of Zaccur son of Mattaniah, for they were considered faithful; and their duty was to distribute to their associates. 14Remember me, O my God, concerning this, and do not wipe out my good deeds that I have done for the house of my God and for his service.

15In those days I saw in Judah people treading wine presses on the sabbath, and bringing in heaps of grain and loading them on donkeys; and also wine, grapes, figs, and all kinds of burdens, which they brought into Jerusalem on the sabbath day; and I warned them at that time against selling food. 16Tyrians also, who lived in the city, brought in fish and all kinds of merchandise and sold them on the sabbath to the people of Judah, and in Jerusalem. 17Then I remonstrated with the nobles of Judah and said to them, "What is this evil thing that you are doing, profaning the sabbath day? 18Did not your ancestors act in this way, and did not our God bring all this disaster on us and on this city? Yet you bring more wrath on Israel by profaning the sabbath."

19When it began to be dark at the gates of Jerusalem before the sabbath, I commanded that

NIV

to be shut and not opened until the Sabbath was over. I stationed some of my own men at the gates so that no load could be brought in on the Sabbath day. 20Once or twice the merchants and sellers of all kinds of goods spent the night outside Jerusalem. 21But I warned them and said, "Why do you spend the night by the wall? If you do this again, I will lay hands on you." From that time on they no longer came on the Sabbath. 22Then I commanded the Levites to purify themselves and go and guard the gates in order to keep the Sabbath day holy.

Remember me for this also, O my God, and show mercy to me according to your great love.

23Moreover, in those days I saw men of Judah who had married women from Ashdod, Ammon and Moab. 24Half of their children spoke the language of Ashdod or the language of one of the other peoples, and did not know how to speak the language of Judah. 25I rebuked them and called curses down on them. I beat some of the men and pulled out their hair. I made them take an oath in God's name and said: "You are not to give your daughters in marriage to their sons, nor are you to take their daughters in marriage for your sons or for yourselves. 26Was it not because of marriages like these that Solomon king of Israel sinned? Among the many nations there was no king like him. He was loved by his God, and God made him king over all Israel, but even he was led into sin by foreign women. 27Must we hear now that you too are doing all this terrible wickedness and are being unfaithful to our God by marrying foreign women?"

28One of the sons of Joiada son of Eliashib the high priest was son-in-law to Sanballat the Horonite. And I drove him away from me.

29Remember them, O my God, because they defiled the priestly office and the covenant of the priesthood and of the Levites.

30So I purified the priests and the Levites of everything foreign, and assigned them duties, each to his own task. 31I also made provision for contributions of wood at designated times, and for the firstfruits.

Remember me with favor, O my God.

NRSV

the doors should be shut and gave orders that they should not be opened until after the sabbath. And I set some of my servants over the gates, to prevent any burden from being brought in on the sabbath day. 20Then the merchants and sellers of all kinds of merchandise spent the night outside Jerusalem once or twice. 21But I warned them and said to them, "Why do you spend the night in front of the wall? If you do so again, I will lay hands on you." From that time on they did not come on the sabbath. 22And I commanded the Levites that they should purify themselves and come and guard the gates, to keep the sabbath day holy. Remember this also in my favor, O my God, and spare me according to the greatness of your steadfast love.

23In those days also I saw Jews who had married women of Ashdod, Ammon, and Moab; 24and half of their children spoke the language of Ashdod, and they could not speak the language of Judah, but spoke the language of various peoples. 25And I contended with them and cursed them and beat some of them and pulled out their hair; and I made them take an oath in the name of God, saying, "You shall not give your daughters to their sons, or take their daughters for your sons or for yourselves. 26Did not King Solomon of Israel sin on account of such women? Among the many nations there was no king like him, and he was beloved by his God, and God made him king over all Israel; nevertheless, foreign women made even him to sin. 27Shall we then listen to you and do all this great evil and act treacherously against our God by marrying foreign women?"

28And one of the sons of Jehoiada, son of the high priest Eliashib, was the son-in-law of Sanballat the Horonite; I chased him away from me. 29Remember them, O my God, because they have defiled the priesthood, the covenant of the priests and the Levites.

30Thus I cleansed them from everything foreign, and I established the duties of the priests and Levites, each in his work; 31and I provided for the wood offering, at appointed times, and for the first fruits. Remember me, O my God, for good.

COMMENTARY

This last section of Nehemiah consists of three units from the Nehemiah Memoir (vv. 4-14, 15-22, 23-29) and a concluding summary (vv. 30-31). The first of these units deals with misuse of the temple chambers to house Tobiah (vv. 4-9) and with measures taken by Nehemiah to restore the full payment of the tithes (vv. 10-14). The second and third units have a common structure throughout:

vv. 15, 23, "In those days I saw . . ."
vv. 17, 25, Nehemiah remonstrates with the people.
vv. 18, 26-27, Rhetorical questions dealing with the past.
vv. 19-22, 28, Specific reform acts.

All three units and the concluding summary end with a "Remember" formula (vv. 14, 22, 29, 31). The first reform measure (vv. 4-14) is dated sometime after Nehemiah's twelfth year, during Nehemiah's second term in Jerusalem, and the second (vv. 15-22) presupposes a date after the completion of the walls at the earliest. Perhaps both it and the third unit (vv. 23-29) should also be dated to Nehemiah's second term.

Tamara Eskenazi has described this last unit as a coda, almost an afterthought. The firm agreement in chap. 10 and the community actions in 12:44–13:3 ascribe the real reforms to the people as a whole and make Nehemiah's activities essentially the administering of communally ordained regulations. Primary significance resides in the community as a whole. Ezra subordinates himself to it; Nehemiah claims to be above it, but his claims are made relative by the final shape of the book.[216]

13:4-14. The chronological note "before this" (v. 4) indicates that historically Nehemiah did not wait for the community to come to a consensus before he took decisive action. The incident in vv. 4-9 took place before the final separation from all those of mixed descent (v. 3). The priest Eliashib (apparently different from the high priest of Nehemiah's time with the same name because he is identified only as the person in charge of the chambers of the Temple; cf. Ezra 8:29) provided Tobiah, an associate of Sanballat, one of Nehemiah's arch enemies, with housing in one of the large temple chambers. Eliashib was related in some way to Tobiah (he was not just "closely associated" as in the NIV). According to 6:18, Tobiah had two other relatives by marriage in Jerusalem: his brother-in-law Shemaiah and his son's father-in-law, Meshullam, both of whom were in charge of labor gangs that worked on the wall. The room assigned to Tobiah had formerly been used to store cereal offerings (see 10:33); frankincense (used as a supplement to the cereal offering, Lev 2:1-2); temple vessels (10:39); tithes of grain, wine, and oil designated for the Levites and related minor cultic officials (10:37, 39); and contributions for the priests.

When Eliashib gave Tobiah housing, Nehemiah was back in Mesopotamia with Artaxerxes, who is here called king of Babylon.[217] Nehemiah's return to Babylon took place in the thirty-second year of the king's reign, Nehemiah's twelfth year in office, or 433 BCE. We do not know why Nehemiah left. Was his term over? Did he have a leave as did Arsames, who was absent from Egypt for three years?[218] Had he been summoned to defend himself against the charges of Sanballat and his associates? Although Eliashib and Tobiah surely did not expect him to return soon, if at all, Nehemiah secured permission from the king to return to Judah. He leaves us in the dark, however, on how long he stayed in Mesopotamia (though he must have returned before the last year of Artaxerxes in 423 BCE). We also do not know whether he had heard reports of events in Judah that prompted his return (see 1:2-3). While the text says nothing about the capacity in which he returned, his decisive actions in vv. 11, 13, and 19 indicate that he was probably still governor. Eliashib's actions were highly offensive to Nehemiah (v. 8), and he promptly threw Tobiah and his household goods out of the chamber. Nehemiah also gave orders to purify the chambers

216. Tamara C. Eskenazi, *In an Age of Prose: A Literary Approach to Ezra–Nehemiah,* SBLMS 36 (Atlanta: Scholars Press, 1988) 125, 152.

217. See *ANET,* 316. The Persian king is called "king of Assyria" in Ezra 6:22. Elsewhere in Nehemiah, Artaxerxes is simply called "the king" (1:11; 2:1; 5:14).

218. AP 27; 30; 32.

(2 Chr 29:15-19)—presumably both the chamber of Tobiah and adjacent ones, which would have been made ritually unclean by his presence—and to restore the temple vessels, the cereal offering, and the frankincense that had been formerly kept there.

Significantly, Nehemiah does not mention the tithes for the Levites and the contributions of the priests, although we learn from v. 10 that the Levites and the musicians had indeed been deprived of their income ("portions" = tithes; see 10:37) and had fled to various settlements outside Jerusalem. Malachi indicates that this failure to pay the tithe to the Levites was not a one-time problem in the post-exilic period (Mal 3:8-9). Although Levites were not supposed to own land (Num 18:20-24; Deut 14:29; 18:1-2), several passages in Nehemiah refer to their settlements outside Jerusalem (7:73; 11:20; 12:27). The musicians, too, had villages in the vicinity of Jerusalem (12:28-29).[219] The priests may have had adequate income to meet their needs from the sacrifices given directly to them (Num 18:8-19; Deut 18:3).

Nehemiah responded to the flight of the Levites by remonstrating with the lay officials (v. 11; cf. vv. 17, 25, and 5:7) and by restoring the Levites to their appropriate posts. Then all of Judah, perhaps with the encouragement of the lay officials, brought in the tithe of grain, wine, and oil.

Nehemiah attempted to give these reforms lasting effect (v. 32 and 5:10) by setting up a four-person commission to handle the distribution of the tithes: a priest named Shelemiah, otherwise unknown; Zadok, the scribe, apparently representing the interests of the governor (cf. the Zedekiah mentioned right after Nehemiah as a signer of the firm agreement in 10:1); Pedaiah, a Levite, otherwise unknown; and Hanan, a grandson of Mattaniah, one of the leading singers at the time of the repopulation of Jerusalem (11:17).[220] Zechariah, the leader of the second Levite choir at the dedication of the wall, was a great-grandson of Mattaniah, but through a different father and grandfather (12:35).

Nehemiah's commission seems to be different in composition and function from the group of two priests and two Levites who were in charge of temple treasures at the time of Ezra (Ezra 8:33) and, therefore, should not be used in an attempt to date Nehemiah before Ezra. According to the firm agreement, the community as a whole went beyond Nehemiah's commission and decided to establish levitical depots throughout the country as a more effective way to bring in the tithes than to expect everyone to bring them to a central location (10:37-39).

The realistic account of the reform measures Nehemiah instituted with regard to the Levites stands in sharp contrast to what was added editorially in the wider context. Nehemiah had to work energetically to bring Levites to the city; the editors wrote that the installation of Levites in Jerusalem was accomplished almost effortlessly (11:1-2, 15-19). Nehemiah initiated appropriate support for the Levites; the editors insisted that the community unanimously agreed to grant them support, even from the days of Zerubbabel (10:37; 12:47). In the final form of the book, chap. 10 establishes the legal basis for the practices of the post-exilic community, and Nehemiah's work is reduced to slight corrections of errors that had exceptionally infiltrated the community.

In his prayer for God to remember him (v. 14; cf. vv. 22, 29, 31 and 5:19), Nehemiah asked God not to blot out his acts of loyalty, which were written in the divine book that records human deeds (Isa 65:6; Dan 7:10; Mal 3:16; Rev 20:12). Nehemiah's acts of loyalty included his work for the Temple itself (expelling Tobiah, vv. 4-9) and his work for its service (regulating the distribution of contributions for priests and Levites, vv. 10-13). Moses once asked God to blot him out of the divine book if there was no forgiveness for the people (Exod 32:32-33; cf. Ps 69:20).

13:15-22. Sabbath abuses prompted Nehemiah to institute additional reform measures. In September-October, at the time of the grape harvest, he saw people trampling out grapes on the sabbath. We are not told whether Nehemiah traveled to the countryside to see such forbidden work or whether such travel would have been considered a sabbath violation already at this time. On the sabbath the people also used donkeys to haul grain that had been harvested in April-June

219. This is not a reference to the levitical cities in Judah and Benjamin (Josh 21:13-19; 1 Chr 6:54-60), since they were designated only for the sons of Aaron.

220. According to 12:44 a group of men had also been chosen at the time of the dedication of the wall to collect the tithes for the priests and the Levites.

and brought it and other agricultural products to Jerusalem to sell. The NRSV and the NIV emend the text of v. 15 so that Nehemiah only warns the people not to sell food. The MT, however, is more comprehensive and may be original: "I warned them on the [next] day that they sold food." That is, on the next sabbath day, when the people were selling food, he warned them about all the violations of sabbath identified in v. 15.

Tyrians, famous throughout the ancient Near East as traders (Ezra 3:7; Isa 23:2-3, 8, 18; Ezek 27:12-25; 28:5; Amos 1:9-10; Joel 3:6), had taken up residence in Jerusalem and brought in fish and other goods to sell on the sabbath. Already at the time of Amos some people had complained that the sabbath interrupted trade (Amos 8:5). As non-Jews, the Tyrians would not be under the restraint of sabbath regulations, which prohibited selling on the sabbath, and some Jews apparently concluded that buying did not break the sabbath. Nehemiah reacted as usual by remonstrating with the nobles (cf. 5:7; 13:11, 25), thus putting them under legal pressure, and compared their actions with those pre-exilic violations of the sabbath that caused God to bring about the Babylonian destruction of the city, whose effects continued in the present foreign rule over Judah (cf. 9:26-27; Ezra 9:13). There is a similar line of argument about the effects of sabbath violation in Jer 17:19-27 (cf. Ezek 20:12-24). Nehemiah separated himself from the sins that were being committed but identified with the judgment on them: He spoke of the sins of *their* ancestors and the judgment of *our* God. He charged the nobles with adding to the divine wrath on Israel by permitting or participating in commerce on the sabbath.

Nehemiah followed up his remonstrations with specific actions aimed at temporary and more permanent reform. When it began to grow dark before the sabbath, Nehemiah ordered the gates to be closed until the sabbath day was over. He also posted his own elite servants (cf. 4:16) by the gates to make sure no burdens were carried in privately. When merchants occasionally camped outside the gates, presumably so that people who went out through a postern gate could buy from them, Nehemiah warned them and threatened them with the use of force, thus exercising the powers of the governor. This strategy worked (v. 21); he had shown what such threats might mean in the case of Tobiah. Later Nehemiah assigned levitical gatekeepers to take over permanent control of the gates (v. 22), after appropriate purification before this religious duty (cf. 12:30; Ezra 6:20). Although levitical gatekeepers usually worked as temple guards, sabbath violation threatened to destroy the holiness of the city (cf. 11:1, 18), and so their deployment as guardians of the city gates seems appropriate. In the firm agreement, the people promised not to buy items brought into the city on a sabbath day or other holy day (10:31). This provision gives community approval to Nehemiah's reform and also extends it further by including holy days in the ban.

Nehemiah asked God to remember—for Nehemiah's benefit—Nehemiah's actions in defense of the sabbath day (v. 22). He balanced the mention of his own works with a request for God to spare him in accord with God's own loyal love (cf. 1:5).

13:23-29. Nehemiah's last reform deals with mixed marriages. He noticed that half of the children of men who had married women from Ashdod spoke only Ashdodite and not Hebrew. According to 4:7, Ashdodites had joined Sanballat and others in opposing the building of the city wall.

A later hand added the words "Ammon and Moab" in v. 23 and the expression "but spoke the language of various peoples" in v. 24 (the latter clause looks like an afterthought in the sentence and is lacking in the LXX). The purpose of these additions may have been to harmonize this account with 13:1 or to show why Ashdodite marriages should be condemned. Thus marriages with Ashdodites were to be considered like marriages with Ammonites or Moabites. The Torah never explicitly forbids marriage to Ashdodites.

No one knows what language the fifth-century Ashdodites spoke. Was it Philistine? Was it the language of the Assyrians, who had been settled in Ashdod in the eighth century? Was it Aramaic (see 2 Kgs 18:26, 28)? Greek? Nabatean? Or did "Ashdodite" stand for any unintelligible language?

Nehemiah remonstrated with the offenders (v. 25; the NRSV strangely replaces its regular translation of the word ריב [*rîb*] with "contended"), cursed them, and pulled out their hair (probably in order to embarrass them; see 2 Sam 10:4, Isa

50:6; or as a sign of grief, Ezra 9:3). Such personal abuse and (threatened) assault were a regular part of Nehemiah's strategy (vv. 8, 21). He also made them take an oath that was a paraphrase of Deut 7:3, the law against intermarriage with the pre-Israelite inhabitants of the land (v. 25 is written in the second-person plural, while the law from Deuteronomy is in the second-person singular; cf. Ezra 9:2, 12). Note that the oath includes the giving of Israelite women to foreigners, which was not a problem here or in Ezra 9–10. The people's oath goes beyond Deut 7:3 in that those making this oath promised not to take foreign women for themselves as well as not to allow their sons or daughters to enter into mixed marriages. The whole community took a similar pledge, according to the firm agreement (10:30).

Deuteronomy had warned that marriages with members of the previous inhabitants of the land might lead to the worship of other gods (Deut 7:4). Nehemiah alludes to the same concern by posing a rhetorical question about Solomon. Solomon was an incomparably wise king (1 Kgs 3:12; 10:1-6), he was beloved by God, as even his name, "Jedidah" ("beloved of Yahweh") showed (2 Sam 12:24-25) and had been made king over Israel by God. Yet despite these three great qualifications, marriage to foreign women caused him to sin by following their gods (1 Kings 11). "Should we listen to you?" Nehemiah asks those who had married Ashdodite women. That is, "Should we follow your example by doing evil and acting faithlessly toward God in this way?" (cf. 1:8; Ezra 9:2; 10:2, 6, 10; Neh 1:8). If Solomon in all his greatness could be led into sin by foreign women, how much more would Nehemiah's contemporaries be endangered? While he took umbrage at the failure of some families to teach their children Hebrew, he recognized that more was at stake than ethnic identity or linguistic purity. Failure to learn the language of worship and Torah could in his view lead to idolatry or syncretism.

Verses 28-29 provide a case in point. An unnamed son of Jehoiada, the son of the high priest Eliashib (12:10, 22), had married the daughter of Sanballat the Horonite (cf. the marriage relationships of the family of Tobiah with people in Jerusalem, 6:18; 13:4). It is not clear from the text whether Eliashib was still high priest or whether he had already been succeeded by his son Jehoiada. In any case, high priests were explicitly forbidden to marry anyone except virgin Israelite women (Lev 21:13-15). Jehoiada's son, as a member of the high priest's family and, perhaps, as a future candidate for high priest himself as the son of the current high priest, had violated this law. Nehemiah simply chased him away.[221]

Nehemiah did not repeat Ezra's strategy of requiring men who had married foreign women to divorce them. Instead, he forced the citizens to take an oath that their children would not intermarry and that they themselves would also not intermarry in the future. In the case of the high priest's (grand)son, divorce also seemed to be no solution. Rather, Nehemiah expelled him from the community (cf. Ezra 7:26).

The "remember" formula in v. 29 is an imprecation (cf. 6:14). God is asked to remember "them"—that is, to consider the unnamed man and the other responsible members of the high priest's family in v. 28 with disfavor. By violating the covenant with the priests and the Levites (cf. Deut 33:9-11; Mal 2:4-8), they merited direct divine punishment. Priests were supposed to offer people instruction (Mal 2:7). How could a priest who had married someone like Sanballat's daughter teach the meaning of Deut 7:3 with credibility?

13:30-31. According to the concluding summary of Nehemiah's reform measures, the governor had purified the people from everything foreign, a possible reference to the oath not to intermarry with foreigners (v. 25) and perhaps an allusion to the community's decision to separate itself from all those of foreign descent (v. 3; 10:28). One might also cite his expulsion of Tobiah (v. 8). In a sense, all of Nehemiah's measures in chap. 13 were designed to make

221. Josephus (*Antiquities of the Jews* XI.306-13) tells a story in which Manasseh, the brother of Jaddua (= Jehoiada) married Nikaso, daughter of Sanballat. The elders of Jerusalem forced Manasseh to leave Jerusalem, and his father-in-law, Sanballat, had a temple built for him on Mt. Gerizim, where he became the first high priest of the Samaritans. Josephus dates this incident to the end of the reign of Darius III (336–330). Frank M. Cross, "A Reconstruction of the Judaean Restoration," *JBL* 94 (1975) 6, has argued that Josephus preserves here an authentic memory from about a century later than Nehemiah. Jaddua in his view is Jaddua III, and Sanballat is Sanballat III. H. G. M. Williamson, *Ezra, Nehemiah*, WBC 16 (Waco, Tex.: Word, 1985) 400-401, however, notes that Josephus omits this incident involving Jehoiada's son when he tells the story of Nehemiah (*Antiquities of the Jews* XI.182) and believes that Josephus preserves only a jumbled account of Neh 13:28.

Jerusalem a separate and distinct city. He also established rotas of duty for the priests and the Levites, each assigned to his task (vv. 10-13; cf. 12:44 and the lists of priests and Levites in the time of Jeshua [12:1-7] and Joiakim [12:12-21, 24-25]). Finally, he provided for the regular wood offering (see the community decision in 10:34) and for the offering of first fruits (see the community decision in 10:35). His final prayer for remembrance is a shortened form of 5:19. Its simplicity makes it a fitting conclusion to the Nehemiah Memoir and to the book of Nehemiah. God is asked to remember all of Nehemiah's benefactions, not just the few that are mentioned.

REFLECTIONS

Through the building of the wall and his reform measures, Nehemiah endeavored to create a separate and holy city or province. While we do not know why Eliashib gave Tobiah a room in the Temple or what Tobiah hoped to do with that room, it is easy to understand that this association of one of Nehemiah's arch enemies with the central religious institution of post-exilic Judah was intolerable.

Clearly not everyone, not even among the priests, was on the same page with Nehemiah. Eliashib's actions disrupted the purity of part of the Temple where temple vessels and contributions had once been stored; even worse, it destroyed the financial system that supported the clergy. When the Levites and singers had to go out on the land to support themselves, the Temple, in Nehemiah's view, had been abandoned (13:11).

The sabbath day, which, with circumcision, already served during the exile as a sign of allegiance to the religion of Yahweh, could be violated by those who did physical labor on it and by those who tinkered with the law's edges and tried to argue that buying was not work even if selling was. Again, Nehemiah saw foreigners as dangerous to the community's health. They could sell with impunity, since they were not under Jewish laws; they seemed insensitive to the temptations they posed by trying to sell on the sabbath. Violations of sabbath repeated the moral causes of the exile and threatened to make the present situation worse.

Mixed marriages produced children who were ignorant of Hebrew, the language of Torah, worship, and prayer. Nehemiah's anxieties come perilously close to what we would see as racial prejudice or the hatred that goes with ethnic cleansing. In his view, nevertheless, marital ties with foreigners were pernicious and dangerous precisely because they had brought down the incomparable Solomon, the king who was loved and enthroned by God. Now a member of the high priestly family, who was more obligated than the average Israelite to marry within the nation, showed similar faithlessness by intermarrying with the family of Sanballat. If kings and high priests, therefore, were vulnerable to the dangers of marriage with foreigners, how much more were the average lay members of the community? What is never completely clear, of course, is whether "foreigners" denotes truly alien peoples, like Moabites or Ammonites, or whether it refers to all those, including Jews, who were not directly related to the people who had returned from exile.

Nehemiah's actions appear intemperate to us at times. He threw Tobiah's goods out of the temple chamber, threatened Tyrian merchants with physical violence, and virtually lost all control when it came to dealing with those who had married Ashdodite women. He cursed them, beat them, and pulled out their hair. But these actions need to be seen in the light of their context. They are clear expressions of the dangers he perceived for the community. He did not take evil lightly (13:7, 27).

His leadership style was also marked by attempts to get others to fulfill their responsibilities. He remonstrated with the officials and told them—and all their successors in this office—that they should see to it that the Temple of God was not forsaken. He remonstrated with the nobles and reminded them—and all their successors in their office—that tolerating evil profaned the sabbath and threatened to make their political situation even worse. He expected those who had intermarried to commit themselves to the Torah in the future, both for themselves and for their children. All three groups were left with difficult rhetorical questions to ponder (13:11, 17-18, 27). Emergency measures had to be followed by long-term, institutional changes. By the dint of his office, Nehemiah could get Levites back on the job; his appointment of treasurers to distribute the contributions from the storehouses prevented any future abandonment of the Temple through financial exigency. He posted his elite servants for emergency duty at the city gates; eventually they had to be replaced by regular levitical gatekeepers.

But it is perhaps his prayers that are the most memorable and most theologically important part of this chapter (13:14, 22, 29, 31). He wore his accomplishments as a badge before God (cf. Job) and begged God not to let them be erased from the permanent records. He asked God to remember him, but prayed also that God would spare him because of the greatness of God's loyal love. Imprecations are hard prayers for us to understand, sometimes because we have never been in an impossible situation where the whole system seems to be against us, and sometimes because we are unwilling to say that our opponents are really trying to undercut God's reign.

Nehemiah prayed that God would remember everything for good. No doubt he included in this open-ended prayer his wall building program, the reform measures of chapter 13, and even his efforts to cancel debts in chapter 5. But ultimately he was simply confessing that God's remembrance of him was his only hope.

THE BOOK OF ESTHER

INTRODUCTION, COMMENTARY, AND REFLECTIONS
BY
SIDNIE WHITE CRAWFORD

For my mother—also a heroine.

THE BOOK OF ESTHER

INTRODUCTION

The Hebrew book of Esther is an exciting, fast-paced story that has captured the imagination of Jews over the centuries, although it has been less well-received by the Christian church. It contains all the elements of a popular romance novel: a young and beautiful heroine; a wicked, scheming villain; a wise older father figure; and an inept and laughable ruler. In the story good triumphs, evil is destroyed, and all ends happily. It is no surprise, then, that the book of Esther was so popular that, despite certain objections, including its failure to mention God even once (see below), it made its way into the Jewish canon by popular acclaim. Beneath its lighthearted surface, however, the book of Esther explores darker themes: racial hatred, the threat of genocide, and the evil of overweening pride and vanity. These layers of meaning make this book a worthwhile object of study.

DATE AND PROVENANCE

The book of Esther is set in the Jewish diaspora of the Persian Empire, during the reign of Ahasuerus, who is to be identified with Emperor Xerxes (486–465 BCE). Therefore, the book was written no earlier than the fifth century BCE. A later date is more probable, however, given the book's distance from the actual events of Xerxes' reign (see below). It is unlikely that Esther was written later than the third century BCE, since it lacks all Hellenistic coloring (including any evidence of Greek vocabulary) and displays a much more positive attitude toward Gentiles and Gentile rulers than do later works, such as

Judith or 1 Maccabees. In addition, the author's familiarity with the Persian court setting and customs suggests a date within or close to the period of the Persian Empire. Therefore, a date in the late fourth or early third century BCE seems most likely.[1]

It is probable that the book, set in the Persian diaspora, was written there as well. The characters evince no interest in the Judean homeland—not even, most strikingly, in the Jewish Temple in Jerusalem. Rather, the plot centers around the court in Susa, where Esther and Mordecai have made their lives. The author displays knowledge of the court of Susa and its immediate surroundings, as well as Persian court customs; but his knowledge about outlying provinces is quite hazy. Hence, Esther was most likely composed in the eastern diaspora of the Persian Empire for the Jews who resided there.

GENRE, STRUCTURE, AND STYLE

Any discussion of the genre of the book of Esther must begin with the acknowledgment that it is *written* literature, with no stylistic traits of oral literature. This work is meant to be read; in fact, the one rabbinic requirement concerning the Festival of Purim is the obligation to read the scroll publicly.[2] Further, although the author may have used sources in composing his work, the book is now a unified literary piece with a distinct and meaningful structure.

The genre of Esther is most easily described as an early Jewish novella (Wills) or short story (Fox).[3] Either term is acceptable if what is meant is a piece of literature with a single plot that has a clear beginning, middle, and end and whose action occurs within a specified length of time.[4] The Esther novella is related in type to the royal courtier tale, but it has a more complex plot and structure than a typical tale of that type (e.g., the stories in Daniel 2–6). As the book stands now, it is also a *Festlegende,* an explanation (or etiology) of the Festival of Purim, although the story's connection with that festival may be late and secondary. As either novella or *Festlegende,* the book is meant to be read as if it were history, even though it is clearly fictional. As Fox puts it, it is "a fictive text meant to be read by nonfictional conventions."[5]

Within the novella are several structuring elements that give the work a sense of symmetry and equilibrium. The most obvious structuring device is the use of banquets to form an elaborate envelope construction. Banquets occur in the book of Esther in pairs, with each one either opposing or complementing the other. A single banquet can belong to more than one pair, as shown in the following chart:

1. This is a revision of my previously stated position that Esther was written in the early fourth century BCE. While this date is still certainly possible, it is also possible to argue for the later date. See Sidnie A. White, "Esther," in *The Woman's Bible Commentary,* ed. Carol A. Newsom and Sharon H. Ringe (Louisville: Westminster/John Knox, 1992) 124.

2. *b. Meg.* 3.

3. Lawrence M. Wills, *The Jew in the Court of the Foreign King,* HDR 26 (Minneapolis: Fortress, 1990) 153-54; Michael V. Fox, *Character and Ideology in the Book of Esther* (Columbia: University of South Carolina Press, 1991) 146.

4. Wills, *The Jew in the Court of the Foreign King,* 153; Fox, *Character and Ideology in the Book of Esther,* 45.

5. Fox, *Character and Ideology in the Book of Esther,* 149 n. 22.

Figure 9: The Banquets in Esther

1. Xerxes' banquet for the nobility (1:2-4)
2. Xerxes' banquet for all the men in Susa (1:5-8)
3. Vashti's banquet for the women (1:9)
4. Esther's enthronement banquet (2:18)
5. Haman and Xerxes' banquet (3:15)
6. Esther's first banquet (5:4-8)
7. Esther's second banquet (7:1-9)
8. The Jews' feasting in celebration of Mordecai's glory and the counterdecree (8:17)
9. The first feast of Purim: Adar 14 (9:17, 19)
10. The second feast of Purim: Adar 15 (9:18)[6]

6. Ibid., 157.

The first two and the last two banquets form a set: Numbers 1 and 9 are empire-wide, while numbers 2 and 10 are limited to the inhabitants of Susa. Banquet 2 for the men forms a pair with banquet 3, given for the women. Banquets 3 and 4 also form an oppositional pair, with banquet 3 given by Vashti and banquet 4 given for Esther. Banquets 5 and 8 oppose each other, while 6 and 7 complement each other. The resulting structure is a pleasing envelope construction.

Banquets are not the only things in the book that occur in pairs. The main characters appear in three pairs of men and women: (1) Ahasuerus and Vashti, (2) Esther and Mordecai, and (3) Haman and Zeresh. Further, the protagonists, in groups of two, revolve around King Ahasuerus in a clear progression. The first pair is Esther-Mordecai; the second, Mordecai-Haman; the third, Haman-Esther; and the fourth, Esther-Mordecai. Note the progression through pairs and the symmetry of the envelope construction. The pairs motif recurs throughout the book: two groups of seven servants/noblemen (1:10, 14; the names of the two groups are suspiciously similar); two helpful eunuchs (2:8-9; 7:9), two meetings of Haman and Zeresh (5:10-14; 6:13); two decrees (3:12-14; 8:9-14), and a two-day celebration of Purim (9:21).

Finally, the motif of pairs lends itself to a major theme of the book: ironic reversal (peripety). Throughout the book of Esther, the expected outcome is reversed; people's status and character undergo sudden changes. Vashti is queen; then she is banished. Esther changes from humble orphan to powerful queen. Haman is forced to honor his enemy Mordecai. Haman is hanged on the gallows prepared for Mordecai. Mordecai becomes grand vizier in place of Haman. Most important, the Jews move from mourning to rejoicing. These reversals signal pivotal moments in the plot: Esther's character change in 4:15-17 enables her to save the Jews; Haman's honoring of Mordecai signals the beginning of his downfall, as recognized by Zeresh (6:13); and Mordecai's elevation (8:15-16) completes the salvation of the Jews. As Levenson nicely puts it, this theme is summarized by a single phrase in 9:1: "the reverse occurred" (נהפוך הוא *nahăpôk hû'*).[7] The theme gives the book its movement: The plot is never in stasis; something is always changing. This is also a hopeful message to Jews living in diaspora; the status quo is never such, and things can always change.

The book of Esther has received rather low marks for its prose style. Carey A. Moore comments that "the author of Esther was no master of the Hebrew language, writing timeless prose."[8] Indeed, the prose of Esther sometimes seems to sink under its own weight. There are long lists of names (1:10, 14; 9:7-9) and endless descriptions of palace procedures, such as the banquet arrangements (1:5-9) and the Persian postal system (8:9-14). The language appears repetitious; there is an extraordinary number of verbal dyads in the text, such as "Ahasuerus, the same Ahasuerus" (1:1) and "to the governors over all the provinces and to the officials of all the peoples" (3:12).[9] The text also contains verbal and nominal chains, some of which occur several times, such as "to destroy, to slay, and to annihilate" (3:13; 7:4; 8:11). All of these features tend to weigh down the prose. However, as Levenson astutely points out, this is not a matter of bad writing, but the author's attempt to convey Persian "officialese," the style of writing common to bureaucracies both ancient and modern.[10] The story, after all, takes place in the Persian court, and if the events had actually happened, this is how they would have been reported.

The sometimes pompous language of the book is also part of a larger characteristic of this author: the use of humor to convey his message. The book, which was written for Jews living in exile, consistently lampoons their Gentile overlords. Ahasuerus is less an awe-inspiring ruler than an easily manipulated buffoon. Haman is an egomaniac whose vanity leads to his humiliation and downfall. The author also uses hyperbole to point to the surreality of the Persian Empire: Ahasuerus gives a banquet that lasts 180 days (six months! 1:4); the maidens are beautified for an entire year (2:12); and even at the denouement of the plot, when the Jews defend themselves against their enemies, the number of those slain (75,000) strains credibility (9:6, 15-16). Finally, the characters' reactions to events lead the reader to laugh. For example, Vashti's refusal to obey one order is thought to threaten the stability of the empire and leads to a decree declaring, of all things, that husbands should rule in their own houses and speak their own languages (1:21-22). The irony and humor found throughout the book mask, in a pleasant way, the author's very serious intent: to teach diaspora Jews that it is possible to lead a successful life in the sometimes inexplicable Gentile world in which they find themselves.[11]

7. Jon D. Levenson, *Esther,* OTL (Louisville: Westminster/John Knox, 1997) 8.

8. Carey A. Moore, *Esther,* AB 7B (Garden City, N.Y.: Doubleday, 1971) LIV.

9. Edward L. Greenstein, "A Jewish Reading of Esther," in *Judaic Perspectives on Ancient Israel,* ed. J. Neusner et al. (Philadelphia: Fortress, 1987) 238-39.

10. Levenson, *Esther,* 11.

11. Bruce W. Jones, "Two Misconceptions About the Book of Esther," *CBQ* 39 (1977) 171-81.

HISTORICITY

Although much ink has been spilled in attempting to show that Esther, or some parts of it, is historical, it is clear that the book is a work of fiction that happens to contain some historical elements. The historical elements may be summarized as follows: Xerxes, identified as Ahasuerus, was a "great king" whose empire extended from the borders of India to the borders of Ethiopia. One of the four Persian capitals was located at Susa (the other three being Babylon, Ecbatana, and Persepolis). Non-Persians could attain to high office in the Persian court (witness Nehemiah), and the Persian Empire consisted of a wide variety of peoples and ethnic groups. The author also displays a vague familiarity with the geography of Susa, knowing, for example, that the court was separate from the city itself.[12] Here, however, the author's historical veracity ends. Among the factual errors found in the book we may list these: Xerxes' queen was Amestris, to whom he was married throughout his reign; there is no record of a Haman or a Mordecai (or, indeed, of any non-Persian) as second to Xerxes at any time; there is no record of a great massacre in which thousands of people were killed at any point in Xerxes' reign. The book of Esther is not a historical record, even though its author may have wished to present it as history, since by doing so he could claim royal sanction for the purpose of his book: establishing Purim as an official Jewish festival.

The book of Esther, as stated above, is a *Festlegende,* an etiology for Purim, a festival probably originally celebrated in the eastern diaspora and slowly accepted in Judea (e.g., it is evidently not among the festivals celebrated among the Jews at Qumran). It is possible that Purim is a Jewish adaptation of a Persian festival, its connection with the story of Esther only secondary. However, the present book's intimate connection with the festival was probably the reason why it was ultimately allowed into the canon, unlike the very similar book of Judith. As Paton states, "It is connected in the closest way with the feast of Purim; and if the events here narrated did not create the feast, then the feast probably created the story."[13] Therefore, an investigation into the origins of Purim is warranted.[14]

Only two possibilities exist for the origins of Purim: the first that its origins lie in post-exilic Judaism, the second that it is an originally pagan festival adapted by the Jews. Those commentators who suspect a Jewish origin for Purim have searched through the known persecutions of Jews in the Hellenistic period to find a suitable antecedent. The most convincing argument, first put forth by Michaelis (1772),[15] holds that Purim was founded to commemorate the victory of Judas Maccabeus over Nicanor on 13 Adar 161 BCE. This argument, however, fails on several points. The book of Esther calls for the observance of Purim on the fourteenth and fifteenth of Adar, not on the thirteenth. Second Maccabees 15:36, which calls the fourteenth of Adar the "Day of Mordecai," carefully distinguishes it from the thirteenth, the "Day of Nicanor." The later rabbis (Jewish sages who, beginning in the second century, produced commentaries on the books of the HB) make the same

12. Moore, *Esther,* 5.
13. Lewis B. Paton, *Esther,* ICC (Edinburgh: T. & T. Clark, 1908) 77.
14. The following remarks are dependent upon Paton, ibid., 77-94, and Moore, *Esther,* XLVI-XLIX.
15. Cited in Paton, *Esther,* 78.

distinction. Further, this identification, like all identifications with Jewish historical events, founders on the same rock: Purim is a feast whose character is essentially secular. Finally, the word "Purim" has no satisfactory Hebrew etymology; it appears to be a Hebrew corruption of either an original Aramaic form, פוריא (*pûrayyā'*),[16] or the Babylonian *pūrū*, meaning "fate" or "lot." It seems best, therefore, to seek the origins of Purim in a Persian or Babylonian celebration. If Purim does have a foreign origin, then the Esther/Mordecai tale is easily explained as a justification for it. It is possible that the festival was originally a Persian feast, possibly the spring new year festival, adopted by the Jews of Susa that later spread to the rest of the Jewish community. Purim may also be connected to the Babylonian new year festival (which, however, was celebrated in Nisan, not Adar). All speculations on this subject run aground on the fact that we know very little about the eastern diaspora in the Persian period. Moore rightly declares, "Scholars have suggested much but proven very little about the probable origins of the festival of Purim."[17] In the end, a Persian origin for the festival seems most likely, with the tale of Esther and Mordecai added to bring it into the Jewish orbit.

TEXTS AND VERSIONS

The book of Esther differs from other books of the Hebrew Bible in that it exists not just in its Masoretic form and more or less similar translations, but instead in three different versions, each with integrity as a separate literary piece. These versions are the Hebrew Masoretic Text (MT), the Septuagint (LXX), and the Alpha Text (AT).

The Masoretic Text, written in Hebrew in the late fourth–early third centuries BCE, used as its source a Hebrew story concerning Esther and Mordecai. The MT author added the etiology of Purim to the original story, and this version gained canonical status in Jewish Scriptures and later in Protestant Bibles.

The Alpha Text is a Greek translation of a Hebrew text similar to, but not identical with, the original Hebrew source of the MT (the AT is approximately 20 percent shorter than the MT). It contains several conspicuous differences from the MT, indicating a different author/redactor: The conspiracy of the two eunuchs (2:21-23) is missing; Persian law is not characterized as irrevocable, an important plot device in the MT; there is no mention of Purim; and, very important, the AT explicitly mentions God. The AT came into being at about the same time as the MT,[18] but never enjoyed canonical status, although it may have been popular in Egypt in the second century BCE (see Commentary on Addition F).

The Septuagint is a Greek translation of the Hebrew MT, made in the late second century BCE. It contains six long passages not found in the MT that were added to the LXX at the time of translation or later. These additions change the nature of the LXX, so that it is a

16. C. C. Torrey, "The Older Book of Esther," *HTR* XXXVII (1944) 6

17. Moore, *Esther,* XLIX.

18. See David J. A. Clines, *The Esther Scroll: The Story of the Story,* JSOTSup 30 (Sheffield: JSOT, 1984); Michael V. Fox, *The Redaction of the Books of Esther,* SBLMS 40 (Atlanta: Scholars Press, 1991); Karen H. Jobes, *The Alpha-Text of Esther: Its Character and Relationship to the Masoretic Text,* SBLDS 153 (Atlanta: Scholars Press, 1996); Carey A. Moore, *Daniel, Esther and Jeremiah: The Additions,* AB 44 (Garden City, N.Y.: Doubleday, 1977).

distinctly different literary piece from the MT. The LXX has canonical status in the Eastern (Orthodox) churches and deuterocanonical status in the Roman Catholic Church (in the Vg, the Additions appear after the end of the Hebrew text). In modern translations, these Additions often appear in the apocrypha. In this commentary they appear at the end of the Hebrew book of Esther. The Additions were added to the Alpha Text of Esther sometime after the LXX came into being, evidently to bring the two Greek texts into conformity. The following diagram illustrates the relations of the various versions, in which proto-Esther stands for the hypothetical source(s) behind the MT and the AT.

Figure 10: Texts and Versions of Esther

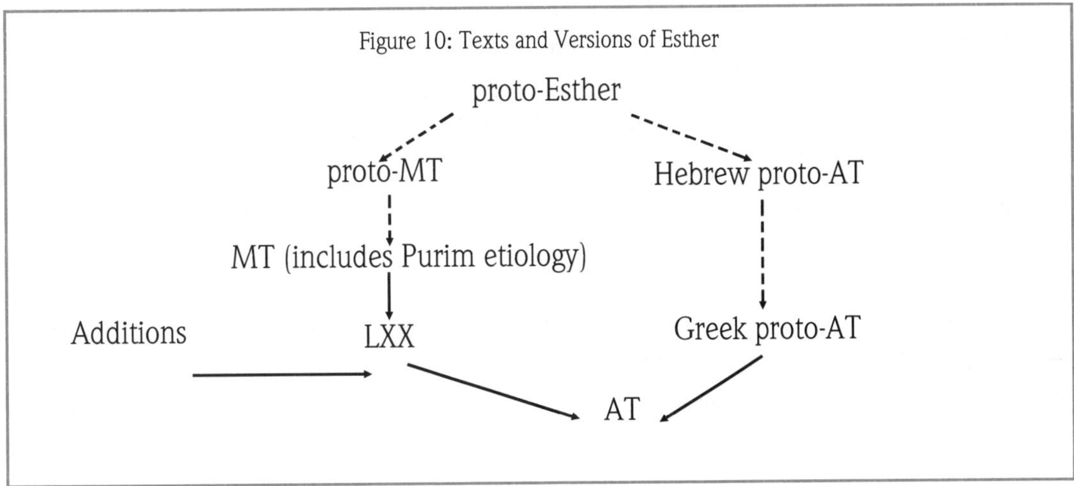

In addition, several other translations of both the MT and the LXX exist, including an Old Latin (OL) translation. The book of Esther also has two Targums (translations into Aramaic), which are more like midrashic free renderings than strict translations. Finally, the paraphrase of the first-century CE Jewish historian Josephus seems to show his familiarity with several of the versions, which he rendered freely. All of the versions will be taken into account at various points in the commentary.

THE ORIGINS OF ESTHER

It has long been suspected in the field of Esther studies that behind the three extant versions of the book of Esther (MT, LXX, and AT) lie sources that are no longer recoverable. Cazelles proposed a two-source theory for Esther. One source was liturgical, centered around Esther and the Jews in the provinces, and was concerned with the celebration of a festival. The second source was historical and centered around Mordecai and court intrigues leading to a persecution of the Jews in Susa. The two sources would have had much in common, including the two main characters and the basic plot structure, making them relatively easy to combine.[19] In a later analysis, Bardtke suggested that the author of

19. Henri Cazelles, "Note sur la composition du rouleau d'Esther," in *Lex tua veritas. Festschrift für Hubert Junker,* ed. H. Gross and F. Mussner (Trier: Paulinus Verlag, 1961) 17-29. Clines, *The Esther Scroll,* 115-26, does a masterful job of presenting both the strengths and the weaknesses of Cazelles's theory. Clines concludes that in modified form Cazelles's two-source theory is possible, but it is still not preferable to posit separate Esther and Mordecai sources.

Esther drew on a Jewish "midrashic" source, from which he reworked three tales: an apocryphal harem story about Vashti; the story of Mordecai, concerning court intrigue and the persecution of Jews in Susa; and the Esther story, about a young Jewish girl who becomes the king's favorite and saves her people from persecution.[20] Other scholars have preferred to talk about traditions lying behind the Esther story. The argument is complicated by the presence of the expanded version of the LXX, for which Semitic sources have been posited for Additions A, C, D, and F. Torrey suggested that the Greek versions of Esther are translations of Aramaic originals and that the Hebrew version is late and secondary, but his conclusions have not been widely accepted.[21] Rather, it seems most probable that the Hebrew MT, from which the LXX was translated, and the Hebrew proto-AT, from which the Greek AT was translated (this Greek text was later expanded using the LXX Additions), were constructed from a common story about Esther and Mordecai, two Jews living in the court of a foreign king who by their wits defeated the plot of Haman to destroy all the Jews of Persia. However, this story no longer exists; it may be hypothetically reconstructed from the three extant versions. A further question remains: Are there "sources" or "traditions" behind this tale and/or behind the Additions to the LXX?

Previous attempts to isolate sources, especially Cazelles's, have foundered on the attempt to assign blocks of material from the present form of MT Esther to specific sources. As shown above, the layers between MT Esther and its possible sources are too many, and the literary skill of the author too great, to allow for a convincing analysis. The search for plausible sources seemed to be stymied.

Some new light has been shed on the question. In 1992, Milik published fragments of an Aramaic manuscript(s) from Qumran Cave 4 that he entitled "4Qproto-Esther-aramaic."[22] These fragments, Milik argued, contain the Aramaic source for the Greek source of the OL translation of Esther. Milik maintains that this Greek text was the original book of Esther. The LXX is, according to him, a revision of the OL's Greek source, while the Hebrew MT is a late (post–70 CE) and secondary translation. While Milik's arguments about the textual history of Esther are not at all convincing,[23] the fragments he presents may be an example of the type of source material the author of proto-Esther may have used when composing his story.

4Qproto-Estheraramaic, or as it is better named, *4QTales of the Persian Court,* consists of six manuscript fragments (4Q550), dating paleographically from the second half of the first century BCE.[24] The fragments appear to contain three distinct blocks of material, the

20. Hans Bardtke, *Das Buch Esther,* KAT XVII/5 (Gütersloh: G. Mohn, 1963) 248-52.

21. C. C. Torrey, "The Older Book of Esther," *HTR* XXXVII (1944) 1-40.

22. J. T. Milik, "Les Modèles Araméens du Livre d'Esther dans la Grotte 4 de Qumrân," *RQ* 15 (1992) 321-99.

23. Sidnie White Crawford, "Has Esther Been Found at Qumran? 4QProto-Esther and the Esther Corpus," *RQ* 17 (1996) 307-25.

24. Milik, "Les Modèles Araméens du Livre d'Esther dans la Grotte 4 de Qumrân," 384. A paleographic date indicates only when the MS was copied. It is much more difficult to determine a date of composition; the terminus ad quem is the reign of Xerxes (486–465 BCE), in which the stories are set. The lack of animosity toward Gentiles (indeed, most of the characters may be Gentiles) may indicate a date of composition before the upheavals in the reign of Antiochus IV Epiphanes in the second century BCE.

first two of which contain clear parallels to the book of Esther. The first story, found in 4Q550[a-c], is set in the court of King Xerxes and appears to be addressed to a man whose father was named Patireza.[25] The text of frags. a-c is as follows:

Frag. a:
1. . . . o]beyed Patireza your father [. . .
2. . . . and [am]ong your servants of the royal wardrobe [. . .] to serve
3. the service of the king like all which [you have] receiv[ed . . .] at the same hour
4. the temper of the king was stretched [. . . the bo]oks of his father should be read to him and among
5. the books was found a scroll [. . .] sealed with seven seals of Darius his father entitled:
6. . . . . Dar]ius the king to the servants of the empire which is the whol[e e]arth, Peace! On being opened and read, it was found written therein: Darius the king
7. . . .]reign after me and to the servants of the empire, Pe[ac]e! Let it be known to him who violates or falsifies . . .

Frag. b:
1. nobody but the king kn[ows] if there is [. . .
2. and his good name does not perish [and his] faithful[ness . . .
3. the king come to Patireza son of ?[. . .
4. fear of the house of the scribe fell on him [. . .
5. the messenger of the king, Comm[and] and let it be given [. . .
6. my house and possessions to all who [. . .
7. being measured. And you will receive the office of your father. [. . .

Frag. c:
1. . . .]the messenger of the king, Command the princess (?) [. . .]banish[ed . . .
2. . . . Patrieza [your] father, from Ḥamaʾ who arose concerning the service of [. . .] before the king [. . .
3. . . .] and he was a faithful and tr[usty] servant before her [. . .
4. . . . and the messenger said, [. . .
5. . . . purp[le] . . .

Interesting parallels to the book of Esther may be noted: The story is set in the Persian court, it takes place during the reign of Xerxes (note "Darius his father" in frag. a, line 5); and it resembles the royal courtier tale in genre. Some parallels are even more specific: In frag. a, the king has the royal annals read to him, as in Esth 6:1. Also, Patireza's son is rewarded by the king (frag. b), as is Mordecai in Esther 6. Finally, the name *Ḥamaʾ* (חמא) in frag. c bears some resemblance to the name "Haman."

The differences between the two tales are also clear. First, the story in frags. a-c has no Jewish

25. "Patireza" is a Persian name. See Shaul Shaked, "Qumran: Some Iranian Connections," in *Solving Riddles and Untying Knots: Biblical, Epigraphic and Semitic Studies in Honor of Jonas C. Greenfield,* ed. Z. Zevit, S. Gitin, M. Sokoloff (Winona Lake: Eisenbrauns, 1995) 278.

connection at all. Second, it is Patireza's son who is the object of the king's favor. If Patireza is to be equated with Mordecai, as Milik suggests (both being the son of Jair),[26] then 4Q550 mentions three generations: the father, Patireza, and his son, with the son being the protagonist of the story. Esther, of course, focuses on Mordecai. Third, a court conflict, which is at the heart of Esther, is not reflected in these fragments. And fourth, there are no direct linguistic connections between these fragments and any of the Esther versions.

The situation with frag. d, consisting of three columns, is similar:

Column 1:
1. Behold, you know [. . .] and because of the errors of my fathers
2. who sinned before you and [. . .] I went out, a man of
3. Judah, one of the leaders of Benjam[in . . .] an exile is standing to be received [. . .] goo[d
4. a good man who serves [. . .] What may I do for you? You know [that it is not] possib[le
5. that a man like me is responsible [. . . your ki]ngdom, standing in front of you [. . .
6. . . .] that which you desire, entrust me with, and when [you d]ie, I will bury you in [
7. being the master of all. It is possible that my elevation in service bef[ore . . .

Column 2:
1. . . .] the decree [. . .] they left [. . .
2. . . .] plagues [. . .]he left [. . .] in the wardrobe [. . .
3. . . .] coronet of go[ld . . .] her [h]ead and five years passed [. . .
4. . . .] alone [. . . and the s]ixth passed [. . .
5. . . . si]lver and gold [. . . possess]ions which belong to Bagoshe, in double amount [. . .
6. and the sev[enth passed . . .] then in peace Bagasraw went up to the court of the king [. . .
7. Bagosh[e . . .] pronoun[ced . . . he was k]illed. Then Bagasraw went up to the co[ur]t of the king.
8. And he took his han[d . . .] on [his] head [. . .] kissed him, answered and said [. . .] Bagasraw, who [. . .

Column 3:
1. . . .] the Most High whom you revere and [wo]rship, it is He who rules over [all the ea]rth. Everything that he wishes is within his p[ow]er [. . .
2. . . .] any man who says anything bad against Bagasraw [. . . will] be killed, because there is nothing [. . .
3. . . .] ? for [e]ver [. . . th]at he saw [in the] two [. . .] And the king commanded that it be writt[en . . .
4. . . . em]pi[re . . .] in the court of the king's house [. . .
5. . . . a]rise after Bagasraw, those who read in this book [. . .
6. . . .] his wickedness will return on his own [head . . .
7. . . .] his des[cendants].[27]

26. Milik, "Les Modèles Araméens du Livre d'Esther dans la Grotte 4 de Qumrân," 332, restores the name of Patireza's father as Jair, thus making the connection to Esther even closer.

27. My translation has been greatly improved by study of the translation of John J. Collins and Deborah A. Green, "The Tales from the Persian Court (4Q550a-c)," in *Antikes Judentum und Frühes Christentum* (Berlin, New York: Walter de Gruyter, 1999) 39-50.

Notice that the characters are different from those in frags. a-c: Bagasraw, Bagoshe, the king (unidentified), and an unidentified woman. It, too, has parallels to Esther: Frag. d opens with a prayer, which has certain similarities to the prayer of Esther in LXX Addition C. The description of "a man of Judah, one of the leaders of Benjamin, an exile" (col. 1, ll. 2-3) corresponds to the description of Mordecai in Esth 2:5-6. There is a dialogue between the king and a female protagonist, in which an adversary is criticized. The period of five years mentioned in column 2 is the same as the time lapse between Esther's ascension to the throne and her actions to save the Jews from Haman's plot. There is evidently a power struggle between Bagoshe, a non-Jew, and Bagasraw, a Jew, like the struggle between Haman and Mordecai. Bagasraw is received by the king in a manner similar to Esther's reception in LXX Addition D (taking into account the obvious difference that Bagasraw is a man and not the spouse of the king). The king makes a proclamation praising God, as in LXX Addition E.

However, the following caveats to the comparison should be noted: The parallels are not exact. The prayer in frag. d laments "the errors of my fathers," rather than present wrongdoing, as in LXX Addition C. Many of the parallels may plausibly be regarded simply as motifs of the royal courtier tale genre; for example, the royal proclamation is equally reminiscent of those in Dan 2:46-47 and 6:25-27. Further, if Bagasraw is a seer, as suggested by col. 3, line 3, he more closely resembles Daniel than any character in the book of Esther.

Finally, frags. e-f of 4Q550:

Frag. e, frag. 1:1. . . .] before the king of Assy[ria? . . .
2. . . .] went at the summons [. . .
3. . . .] on yo[ur] faces [. . .
4. . . . Ba]gasraw [. . .

Frag. e, frag. 2:1. . . .] servant [. . .
2. . . .] remembrance [. . .

Frag. f:1. . . .] behold from the north comes evil [. . .
2. . . .] the building of Zion and in her shelter all the poor of [the] people [
3. . . .] space
4. . . .] come up upon it. They swell up between Medea and Persia and Assyria and the [Great] Sea
5. . . .] space

The only possible parallels to be noted between these fragments and the book of Esther are the phrase "on your faces" in frag. e, frag. 1, line 3, which may refer to prostrating oneself before royalty, and the mention of Medea and Persia in frag. f, line 4. On the other hand, in frag. f, lines 1-2 contain a paraphrase of Isa 14:31-32, while the book of Esther contains no allusions to any other biblical book.

In sum, *4QTales of the Persian Court* contains several intriguing parallels to the book of Esther in both its Hebrew and its Greek versions. These parallels permit us to posit some type of generic relationship between the two texts, but not enough to argue for any type of direct dependence. *4QTales of the Persian Court* may have been an example of a popular type of story—a royal courtier tale in which a Jew, against all odds, rises to success in the court of the Persian king. The author of Esther may have drawn from this type of tale when constructing his story.

THE IMPLIED THEOLOGICAL STANCE OF THE BOOK OF ESTHER

Although enjoying unwavering popularity among Jews throughout most of its existence, the book of Esther has come into its share of theological criticism. The reasons for this are the absence of religious elements in the book, and, among Christians, its perceived hostility toward Gentiles. The lack of religiosity in Esther is indeed striking. The book does not mention God even once. In addition, there is no prayer, no mention of the Temple, and no clear indication of religious activity on the part of Esther or Mordecai. The possible exception is the fast ordered by Esther in 4:16; however, that fast is not explicitly directed to God and seems to have no purpose beyond communal solidarity.[28] Furthermore, there is no indication that either Esther or Mordecai is obedient to the Torah; in fact, quite the opposite is true. Esther is married to a Gentile, eats non-kosher food, and appears to be so thoroughly assimilated that her husband and his court are unaware that she is a Jew. Jewishness, in fact, is a matter of ethnic identification rather than religious practice.

This lack of religion was noticed early on. The proto-AT, which stems from either the same or a very similar Semitic source as the MT, mentions God several times in natural places in the text (AT 5:9, 11; 7:17; 8:2, 34).[29] The LXX, which is a translation of the MT, deliberately adds long passages, as well as short references, that insert a distinct tone of religiosity and change the character of the book. Esther and Mordecai both pray (Add. C), and Esther declares that she has kept the commandments and lived as a good Jew (Add. D). Josephus and the Targums also add religious elements to the book of Esther, as do the rabbis. The rabbis speculate, for example, that Mordecai refuses to bow down to Haman because Haman wears an idol pinned to his chest.[30] These additions show that the mention of God or of religious practice would be natural in several places in the book; moreover, it is unlikely that an ancient Jewish reader, with even the vaguest familiarity with Israel's sacred history (e.g., the exodus) could have read a story of Jewish deliverance without understanding in it God's action.[31] Therefore, the lack of any theological statements in the

28. However, see Jon D. Levenson, *Esther*, OTL (Louisville: Westminster/John Knox, 1997) 19.
29. All verses of the AT are given according to the Cambridge Septuagint edition: *The Old Testament in Greek*, vol. 3, Part I: *Esther, Judith, Tobit*, ed. A. E. Brooke, N. McLean, H. S. J. Thackeray (London: Cambridge University Press, 1940).
30. For references, see Louis Ginzberg, *The Legends of the Jews* (Philadelphia: Jewish Publication Society, 1946) 6:463.
31. Richard Bauckham, *The Bible in Politics: How to Read the Bible Politically* (London: SPCK, 1989) 123.

book must be deliberate. What was the author's intention? The answer is not immediately apparent.

There are, however, two key passages in the book that contain theological implications. In the first, 4:13-14, Mordecai says to Esther:

> "Do not think that in the king's palace you will escape any more than all the other Jews. For if you keep silence at such a time as this, relief and deliverance will rise for the Jews from another quarter, but you and your father's family will perish. Who knows? Perhaps you have come to royal dignity for just such a time as this." (NRSV)

"Quarter" (מקום *māqôm*) is not a circumlocution for God, as is sometimes claimed, meaning that Mordecai is implying that if Esther does not act, God will (as God does in the book of Daniel). Rather, the passage indicates that Mordecai believes in a wider historical purpose, which includes the survival of the Jews; therefore, in this crisis, the deliverance of the Jews will occur somehow. Does this imply the hand of God in these events? It would seem so, for the only way the survival of the Jews as a historical issue makes any theological sense is for the Jews to be God's special chosen people. Therefore, for the author of Esther, there must be a God, and God must want the Jews to survive. How God will ensure their survival is unclear, however, especially to Mordecai. It is possible that Esther became queen just to fulfill God's purpose, but humans cannot know that. They must act, with profound hope that they are thereby participating in the divine scheme.

The second key passage would seem to support this interpretation. In 6:13*b,* Zeresh says to Haman: "If Mordecai, before whom your downfall has begun, is of the Jewish people, you will not prevail against him, but will surely fall before him." Why does Mordecai's Jewish identity guarantee his triumph and, consequently, Haman's downfall? It does so only if the Jews are somehow special; and in ancient Judaism their specialness is that of being God's people. Once again, belief in God and God's action in history is implied, but not directly stated. However, this implication, coupled with the Jewish context in which the book was read, probably smoothed Esther's entry into the canon.

Another feature of the book that commentators have argued may point to the author's theology is the series of remarkable coincidences moving the plot forward. These include Vashti's dethronement, Esther's enthronement, the king's insomnia (this coincidence is seemingly so obvious that both the LXX and Josephus attribute the king's sleeplessness to God), the reading of the passage concerning Mordecai in the royal annals, and Haman's early arrival in the court, just in time to honor Mordecai. According to Berg, these coincidences help to show that "the narrator believed in a hidden causality behind the surface of human history, both concealing and governing the order and significance of events."[32] However, what is equally important to note is that not one of these coincidences would mean anything without corresponding human action. Esther's enthronement means

32. Sandra Beth Berg, *The Book of Esther: Motifs, Themes, and Structure,* SBLDS 44 (Missoula, Mont.: Scholars Press, 1979) 178.

nothing if she does not choose to act for her people. The reading of the passage concerning Mordecai is meaningless unless Ahasuerus decides to reward him. Coincidences may reveal the hand of God, but, once again, humans cannot know that for sure. All they can do is act, in the hope that their action corresponds to the plan and purpose of God.

The theological implications teased out above may have more direct relevance in our secular culture than stories in which God intervenes directly and miraculously, such as that of Daniel. Along with the implicit belief that within the realm of human history God's plan includes the salvation of the Jews, the book of Esther also holds out the possibility that in the immediate circumstances things might not work out. Esther might not sway the king; Haman may succeed in his murderous scheme. However, for the author, the failure of Esther and Mordecai would not prove the absence of God (as it would by necessity in Daniel), since Esther and Mordecai can never be completely sure that they are acting in concord with God. This is certainly theologically ambiguous, but it corresponds with the modern believer's daily struggle to discern the will of God. The best anyone can do, the author of Esther implies, is to act within those circumstances in which one finds oneself and to take advantage of those opportunities with an attitude of hope, what Fox calls "an openness to the possibility of providence, even when history seems to weigh against its likelihood."[33] It is this openness that speaks to the skeptical end of the twentieth century and becomes a posture of profound faith.

The second charge, hostility toward Gentiles, is more easily disposed of. The book of Esther has never enjoyed great popularity in the Christian church, even to the present day. It had difficulty obtaining canonical status, particularly among the Eastern churches.[34] Esther is not quoted anywhere in the New Testament and is rarely mentioned by the church fathers. During the Reformation, Martin Luther was vehement in his dislike of the book. The attitude of many Christian commentators toward the book of Esther before the latter part of the twentieth century is nicely summarized by the remarks of L. B. Paton in 1908:

> There is not one noble character in this book. Xerxes is a sensual despot. Esther, for the chance of winning wealth and power, takes her place in the herd of maidens who become concubines of the King. She wins her victories not by skill or by character, but by her beauty. She conceals her origin, is relentless toward a fallen enemy, secures not merely that the Jews escape from danger, but that they fall upon their enemies, slay their wives and children, and plunder their property. Not satisfied with this slaughter, she asks that Haman's ten sons may be hanged, and that the Jews may be allowed another day for killing their enemies in Susa. The only redeeming traits in her character are her loyalty to her people and her bravery in trying to save them. Mordecai sacrifices his cousin to advance his interests, advises her to

33. Michael V. Fox, *Character and Ideology in the Book of Esther: Studies in Biblical Personalities* (Columbia: University of South Carolina Press, 1991) 242.

34. For a thorough discussion of Esther's canonical status in early Christianity, see Carey A. Moore, *Esther*, AB 7B (Garden City, N.Y.: Doubleday, 1971) xxi-xxx.

> conceal her religion, displays wanton insolence in his refusal to bow to Haman, and helps Esther in carrying out her schemes of vengeance. All this the author narrates with interest and approval. He gloats over the wealth and the triumph of his heroes and is oblivious to their moral shortcomings. Morally Esther falls far below the general level of the Old Testament and even of the Apocrypha. The verdict of Luther is not too severe: "I am so hostile to this book that I wish it did not exist, for it Judaizes too much, and has too much heathen naughtiness."[35]

With the benefit of hindsight, it is clear that Paton fell victim to his own preconceptions of what a biblical book "should" be like, rather than reading the book for what it is: an entertaining story written for an oppressed minority that ties what was probably originally a pagan holiday into a Jewish context. The tone of the book is ironic and gives the audience a chance to chuckle at those who, in the reality of day-to-day life, rule over them. Ahasuerus is less a sensuous despot than a buffoon ruled by his emotions. Esther, who receives the bulk of Paton's criticisms, actually has no choice about entering the king's harem; once there, she makes the best of the situation and acts with courage and resourcefulness to save her people, who had been endangered by the bloated revenge fantasies of the Gentile Haman. Mordecai does not "sacrifice" his cousin but acts toward her with care and concern; when his personal quarrel with Haman threatens the whole Jewish people, he acts to save them in concert with Esther. The laconic reports in chapter 9 concerning the number of enemies killed may be disconcerting, particularly to Gentile readers, but it must be remembered that they are not real, that this is a work of fiction. What is more, it is reiterated that the Jewish people fight only in self-defense against their declared enemies. In this way, Esther is much less "anti-Gentile" than, for example, the book of Joshua, in which the Israelites fight aggressive wars leading to the wholesale slaughter of the Gentile inhabitants of Canaan. In fact, the book of Esther portrays a situation in which, under normal circumstances, Jews and Gentiles live harmoniously under Persian rule. Only the threat of annihilation causes the Jews to respond aggressively. Therefore, the objections of Paton (and others) to the book of Esther can be dismissed as, at best, misunderstanding, and, at worst, anti-Semitism.

S. Talmon has suggested a solution to the objections raised against Esther, especially its lack of religious elements, in his proposal to understand the book as a "historicized Wisdom tale."[36] Talmon sees the characters of the book as "types" of wisdom characters: Mordecai is the wise courtier; Haman is the foolish courtier; Esther is the adopted heir of the wise courtier; and Ahasuerus is the king manipulated by the court intrigues. While Esther should not be classified as wisdom literature,[37] it certainly falls within the parameters of the "royal courtier tale," in which a courtier rises to prominence, is endangered by the machinations of enemies, and is eventually vindicated. However, as Wills notes, Esther is more complex in its literary structure than a simple court legend (cf., e.g., Daniel 6).[38] There are two

35. Lewis B. Paton, *Esther,* ICC (Edinburgh: T. & T. Clark, 1908) 96.
36. S. Talmon, " 'Wisdom' in the Book of Esther," *VT* 13 (1963) 419-55.
37. See the objections of James Crenshaw in "Method in Determining Wisdom Influence Upon 'Historical Literature,' " *JBL* 88 (1969) 129-42.
38. Lawrence M. Wills, *The Jew in the Court of the Foreign King,* HDR 26 (Minneapolis: Fortress, 1990) 151.

protagonists, Esther and Mordecai; there is a long subplot concerning Vashti; and the Jews act to secure their own rescue. Further, the book contains common folklore motifs—such as the stupid king, the clever court official, and the beautiful wise queen—so that the characters are not unique to wisdom literature.[39] Finally, as the book now stands, the establishment of the Festival of Purim is its *raison d'être.* Nevertheless, the book's emphasis on the ability to function well in a secular environment may point to an influence from wisdom literature (cf. Proverbs).

COMPARISON WITH JOSEPH, DANIEL, AND JUDITH

The book of Esther also lends itself to comparison with other stories of Jews in foreign courts, particularly those of Joseph (Genesis 37–50), Daniel, and Judith. The story of Joseph may have served as a model for the author of Esther.[40] Both are stories of Jews in a foreign court who overcome obstacles and achieve fabulous success. In both stories, the proximity of the protagonist to royal power results in the saving of his or her ethnic group, in Joseph's case his father's family, in Esther's the Jewish people. Both stories involve cases of concealed identity: Joseph is unrecognized by his brothers; Esther conceals her Jewishness. Most intriguing, several times the stories demonstrate almost exact linguistic correspondence, for example at Esth 6:11 and Gen 41:42-43:

Esther	*Joseph*
And he clothed Mordecai	*And he clothed him . . .*
and he caused him to ride	*and he caused him to ride*
in the square of the city	in his second chariot
and he cried out before him . . .	*and they cried out before him . . .*

However, the differences are also important, not the least of which is the fact that Joseph attributes the outcome of the story directly to God (Gen 45:5-8; 50:19), a declaration never found in Esther. Therefore, it seems best to presume that the author of Esther knew the Joseph story and used it when composing his story, but not in a relation of strict dependence.

Esther has also been compared to the book of Daniel, specifically to the cycle of royal courtier tales found in Daniel 2–6.[41] The correspondences are clear; both concern Jewish protagonists in foreign courts who, despite the machinations of enemies, rise to be trusted advisers to the king. Both stories display a tolerant attitude toward the Gentile ruler, and both assume that it is possible for Jews to lead comfortable, happy lives in the diaspora.

39. Susan Niditch, "Legends of Wise Heroes and Heroines," in *The Hebrew Bible and Its Modern Interpreters,* ed. Douglas Knight and Gene Tucker (Philadelphia: Fortress, 1985) 450.

40. For the following remarks I am dependent on the work of Berg, *The Book of Esther,* 124-42.

41. It is probable that these tales, which once circulated separately from the apocalyptic material in Daniel 7–12, were composed in the late Persian period diaspora. See John Collins, *The Apocalyptic Imagination* (New York: Crossroad, 1984) 70-72.

These similarities, however, probably do not indicate dependence one way or the other, but rather adherence to the royal courtier tale genre, adapted for a Jewish audience.[42] The differences between the stories of Esther and Daniel and the conclusions their audiences are expected to reach are very striking. The character of Daniel is a pious Jew, keeping the dietary laws (Dan 1:8-16), praying several times a day facing Jerusalem (Dan 6:10), and, with his companions, bearing his identity as an observant religious Jew proudly and openly. Further, in every misadventure Daniel and his companions survive, God actively intervenes, causing them to interpret dreams (Dan 2:19-23; 4:19-27), providing mysterious signs (Dan 5:5, 24-28), and, in extreme cases, rescuing them from the fiery furnace and the lions' den (Dan 3:24-29; 6:20-23). The message of the Daniel cycle is clear: It is possible for Jews to achieve success under Gentile rule, but only if they are careful to live a pious and observant life, causing God to intervene directly on their behalf. This is radically different from Esther, in which Jewish observance is not an issue; God, if active at all, is only so in a veiled and indirect way, and human action is the primary tool of deliverance.

The third story with which Esther may be directly compared is that of Judith, found in the apocrypha. In fact, it may be argued that the author of the book of Judith, familiar with the story of Esther, set about to create a Jewish heroine more in keeping with the pious standards of his own time.[43] Both stories are supposedly historical tales (although Judith contains even wilder historic "bloopers" than does Esther; for example, Judith makes Nebuchadnezzar, the king of Babylon in the sixth century BCE, the king of Assyria with his capital at Nineveh!) about Jewish women who save their people from destruction at the hands of Gentiles. However, the character of Judith contrasts sharply with that of Esther. Judith is a pious widow who spends her time in constant prayer and fasting (Jdt 8:4-6). She is beautiful, as Esther is beautiful; but Judith's beauty is secondary to her piety. When the people of her town, Bethuliah, are endangered by the besieging army of Nebuchadnezzar's general Holofernes, she acts on their behalf, but only after beseeching God's aid in prayer (Jdt 9:1-14; this scene closely parallels Add. C in the LXX Esther, added to give Esther the appearance of piety). Judith then arrays herself beautifully and makes her way to the enemy camp (Jdt 10:1-13, parallel to Esth 5:1, also Add. D 1-6). However, once Judith is in the Gentile realm, she is careful to eat only kosher food (Jdt 12:1-2), and she prays and purifies herself daily (Jdt 12:5-9). This is in direct contrast to Esther, who does none of those things. Finally, when Judith is confronted by Holofernes' desire to sleep with her, she does not defile herself by having intercourse with a Gentile; rather, she waits until he is drunk, then cuts off his head and carries it back to Bethuliah in a sack (Jdt 13:1-10)! MT Esther marries the Gentile Ahasuerus without a qualm; the most the LXX author can do to repair the situation is to have Esther declare that she "abhors the bed of

42. Many similar correspondences could be cited for the *Tale of Ahiqar,* a royal courtier tale set in the Assyrian Empire, in which the protagonist is not Jewish. However, the tale was evidently popular with Jewish audiences, since a copy of Ahiqar was found in the Jewish colony of Elephantine. See W. Lee Humphreys, "A Life-Style for Diaspora: A Study of the Tales of Esther and Daniel," *JBL* 92 (1973) 211-23.

43. It is probable that Judith was written during the period of the Hasmoneans. See Carey A. Moore, *Judith,* AB 40 (Garden City, N.Y.: Doubleday, 1985) 67-70.

the uncircumcised" (Add. C 26). So, although Esther and Judith are often compared to each other,[44] it is their differences that are most striking. The pious Judith seems to be created as a foil for the perceived defects in the character of Esther.

How, then, can the book of Esther be understood by a contemporary audience? For the Jew, the function of the book of Esther as an etiology for the Festival of Purim takes priority. For the Christian, the question is harder to answer. I would suggest two related paths for entering the book of Esther. The first sees the character of Esther as a feminine model for the Jewish diaspora. The second sees the book of Esther as the story of an oppressed minority struggling for recognition, and for life itself, in a majority culture that is indifferent, or even hostile, to its existence.

ESTHER AS HEROINE

Although the book of Esther takes its name from its chief female protagonist, the character of Esther has suffered much in the history of interpretation, especially Christian interpretation. Mainstream scholars have insisted on seeing Mordecai as the primary hero of the book, in spite of the fact that at the moment of crisis, Mordecai (who has brought the situation into being by his refusal to bow before Haman) can only go to Esther and ask her to intercede with the king.[45] Esther then devises a plan, carries it out with admirable skill, and, in the end, arranges for Mordecai to inherit Haman's position. Without Esther there would be no story.

Feminist scholars as well find little to admire in Esther, often preferring the deposed Vashti. Alice Laffey sums up the position: "In contrast to Vashti, who refused to be men's sexual object and her husband's toy, Esther is the stereotypical woman in a man's world."[46] Esther, it seems, is neither "woman" enough nor "man" enough to satisfy any of her critics.

Neither of these positions does justice to the character of Esther as she appears within the cultural confines of the book named after her.[47] As will be shown in the Reflections, Esther serves as a model of the successful Jew living in diaspora, and she is able to function as a model precisely because she is a woman. Within the culture we call "Western" or "Judeo-Christian," a culture that is admittedly male-dominated and patriarchal, women have been the constantly marginalized and oppressed gender. Lacking public power, women have historically been able to gain individual or private strength only by successfully

44. Moore notes that the Church Fathers especially made this connection. See C. F. Moore, "Why Wasn't the Book of Judith Included in the Hebrew Bible?" in *No One Spoke Ill of Her: Essays on Judith,* ed. James C. VanderKam (Atlanta: Scholars Press, 1992) 66.

45. See Moore, *Esther,* lii, who states, "Between Mordecai and Esther the greater hero in the Hebrew is Mordecai, who supplied the brains while Esther simply followed his directions."

46. Alice Laffey, *An Introduction to the Old Testament: A Feminist Perspective* (Philadelphia: Fortress, 1988) 216.

47. Sidnie White, "Esther: A Feminine Model for Jewish Diaspora," in *Gender and Difference in Ancient Israel,* ed. Peggy L. Day (Philadelphia: Fortress) 161-77; Sidnie A. White, "Esther," in *The Women's Bible Commentary,* ed. Carol A. Newsom and Sharon H. Ringe (Louisville: Westminster/John Knox, 1992). See also Michael V. Fox, *Character and Ideology in the Book of Esther* (Columbia: University of South Carolina Press, 1991).

exploiting the male power structure around them, as Esther does so well. Her actions are presented as a model to the Jews who, living in exile, are marginalized and powerless minority members of Persian society. Esther also attains her success without the element of the miraculous, which is so often a part of these royal courtier tales (e.g., Daniel). Rather, the oblique references to the providential action of God are so subtle that they might be missed by the casual reader. God is on the side of the oppressed, but works through human instruments to achieve the divine purpose. Esther is a human heroine for a human situation and, as such, speaks powerfully to all oppressed people through the centuries.

ANTI-SEMITISM, OPPRESSION, AND GENOCIDE

Although the book of Esther is entertaining and thought-provoking in many respects, its most salient theme for a modern theological understanding of the book is the fact that it is the story of an attempt by a Gentile to exterminate the Jewish people. Its importance to both Christians and Jews resides in the survival of the Jews in the face of the threats posed by the Gentile characters' active anti-Semitism or, at best, indifference. The relevance of this theme to a modern audience lies in a fact of history that responsible readers are compelled to acknowledge: the sorry history of Western Christianity's anti-Semitism, culminating in the murder of six million Jews in the Holocaust.[48] In the light of that history, arguments concerning Esther's "anti-Gentile" bias seem self-serving, to say the least. The book of Esther is about Jewish survival in the face of Gentile threat, and an enlightened interpretation in the post-Holocaust period must acknowledge the reality of that threat.

The book of Esther, with its theological underpinning of belief in the providence of God manifest in human events, also offers a message of hope to other minorities living in majority cultures, such as African Americans in the white-dominated United States. To those who are oppressed the book gives a message of active faith and hope in the face of threat, and to those who rule that the rights of minorities are as important as the rulers' self-interest. For both groups, the greatest societal rewards come through tolerance and cooperation. Further, the book of Esther teaches that in every situation God is able to work through willing human agents (not by miraculous intervention) to ensure that justice is done. The message of the book of Esther is thus easily translatable to our contemporary situation.[49]

48. Richard Bauckham, *The Bible in Politics: How to Read the Bible Politically* (London: SPCK, 1989) chap. 8.

49. I would like to thank the following institutions and people: Albright College, especially the staff of the Gingrich Library; The W. F. Albright Institute of Archaeological Research, my scholarly home in Jerusalem; Katheryn Pfisterer Darr, Thomas G. Long, John R. Spencer, and Benjamin G. Wright III for their helpful comments on earlier drafts; and my husband, Dan D. Crawford, for his constant support.

BIBLIOGRAPHY

Berg, Sandra Beth. *The Book of Esther: Motifs, Themes, and Structure.* SBLDS 44. Missoula, Mont.: Scholars Press, 1979. A study of the literary structure of Esther.

Clines, David J. A. *The Esther Scroll: The Story of the Story.* JSOTSup 30. Sheffield: JSOT, 1984. Concerned mainly with a discussion of the sources of Esther.

Fox, Michael V. *Character and Ideology in the Book of Esther.* Studies in Biblical Personalities. Columbia: University of South Carolina Press, 1991. A commentary that focuses on Esther as a literary work.

Laniak, Timothy S. *Shame and Honor in the Book of Esther.* SBLDS 165. Atlanta: Scholars Press, 1998. A study of Esther using the anthropological categories of shame and honor.

Levenson, Jon D. *Esther: A Commentary.* OTL. Louisville: Westminster/John Knox, 1997. A commentary that makes extensive use of rabbinic material in addition to the standard historical-critical works.

Moore, Carey A. *Daniel, Esther, and Jeremiah: The Additions.* AB 44. Garden City, N.Y.: Doubleday, 1977. Focuses almost entirely on the LXX Additions to Esther.

———. *Esther.* AB 7B. Garden City, N.Y.: Doubleday, 1971. A standard historical-critical and linguistic commentary.

White, Sidnie A. "Esther." In *The Woman's Bible Commentary.* Edited by Carol A. Newsom and Sharon H. Ringe. Louisville: Westminster/John Knox, 1992, 124-29. A brief commentary from a feminist perspective.

OUTLINE OF ESTHER

I. Esther 1:1-22, The Deposition of Queen Vashti

A. 1:1-9, Introduction to the Court of Susa
B. 1:10-22, The Downfall of Vashti

II. Esther 2:1-23, Esther Becomes Queen

A. 2:1-4, The Search for a New Queen
B. 2:5-7, The Introduction of Esther and Mordecai
C. 2:8-18, Esther Is Chosen Queen
D. 2:19-23, Mordecai Discovers the Eunuchs' Plot

III. Esther 3:1-15, Haman's Plot to Destroy the Jews

A. 3:1-6, Conflict Between Mordecai and Haman
B. 3:7-11, Haman's Plot
C. 3:12-15, Haman's Plot Is Carried Out

IV. Esther 4:1-17, Mordecai Turns to Esther

A. 4:1-3, Mordecai's Reaction to Haman's Decree
B. 4:4-17, Dialogue Between Esther and Mordecai

V. Esther 5:1–8:2, Haman's Plans Are Thwarted

A. 5:1-8, Esther Acts: The First Banquet
B. 5:9-14, Haman Builds a Gallows for Mordecai
C. 6:1-11, Haman's Humiliation
D. 6:12-13, Haman Is Warned by His Advisers
E. 6:14–7:10, Esther's Second Banquet
F. 8:1-2, Esther's Triumph

VI. Esther 8:3-17, The Undoing of Haman's Plot

A. 8:3-8, Esther Petitions the King
B. 8:9-14, Mordecai Writes an Edict
C. 8:15-17, Mordecai's Appearance

VII. Esther 9:1–10:3, The Battles of Adar and the Festival of Purim

A. 9:1-5, The First Battle
B. 9:6-10, The Battle in Susa
C. 9:11-15, The Fourteenth of Adar
D. 9:16-19, The Jews Celebrate
E. 9:20-32, The Letters of Purim
  9:20-28, Mordecai's Letter
  9:29-32, Esther's Letter
F. 10:1-3, Appendix Concerning Mordecai

ESTHER 1:1-22

THE DEPOSITION OF QUEEN VASHTI

OVERVIEW

The function of this opening chapter is to set the story within the framework of the Persian Empire, to introduce several prominent themes, and to foreshadow important events in the main plot. The author also adopts an ironic and even satirical tone, which he will rarely relinquish. The careful reader will note that the only character from chapter 1 who appears in the rest of the story is King Ahasuerus, giving rise to the claim that the story of Vashti comes from a source separate from that of the following chapters, a source originally unrelated to the Esther story.[50] While this theory may be true (see Introduction), here the story of Vashti serves the important function of providing background and framework for the story of Esther.

50. See Hans Bardtke, *Das Buch Esther, Kommentar zum Alten Testament* (Gütersloh: Mohn, 1963) 248-52.

ESTHER 1:1-9, INTRODUCTION TO THE COURT OF SUSA

NIV

1 This is what happened during the time of
Xerxes,[a] the Xerxes who ruled over 127
provinces stretching from India to Cush[b]: 2At that
time King Xerxes reigned from his royal throne
in the citadel of Susa, 3and in the third year of
his reign he gave a banquet for all his nobles and
officials. The military leaders of Persia and Media,
the princes, and the nobles of the provinces were
present.
4For a full 180 days he displayed the vast
wealth of his kingdom and the splendor and glory
of his majesty. 5When these days were over,
the king gave a banquet, lasting seven days, in
the enclosed garden of the king's palace, for all
the people from the least to the greatest, who
were in the citadel of Susa. 6The garden had
hangings of white and blue linen, fastened with
cords of white linen and purple material to silver
rings on marble pillars. There were couches of

[a]*1* Hebrew *Ahasuerus,* a variant of Xerxes' Persian name; here and throughout Esther [b]*1* That is, the upper Nile region

NRSV

1 This happened in the days of Ahasuerus,
the same Ahasuerus who ruled over one
hundred twenty-seven provinces from India to
Ethiopia.[a] 2In those days when King Ahasuerus sat
on his royal throne in the citadel of Susa, 3in the
third year of his reign, he gave a banquet for all
his officials and ministers. The army of Persia and
Media and the nobles and governors of the provinces were present, 4while he displayed the great
wealth of his kingdom and the splendor and pomp
of his majesty for many days, one hundred eighty
days in all.
5When these days were completed, the king
gave for all the people present in the citadel of
Susa, both great and small, a banquet lasting for
seven days, in the court of the garden of the king's
palace. 6There were white cotton curtains and
blue hangings tied with cords of fine linen and
purple to silver rings[b] and marble pillars. There
were couches of gold and silver on a mosaic

[a] Or *Nubia*; Heb *Cush* [b] Or *rods*

NIV

gold and silver on a mosaic pavement of porphyry, marble, mother-of-pearl and other costly stones. 7Wine was served in goblets of gold, each one different from the other, and the royal wine was abundant, in keeping with the king's liberality. 8By the king's command each guest was allowed to drink in his own way, for the king instructed all the wine stewards to serve each man what he wished.

9Queen Vashti also gave a banquet for the women in the royal palace of King Xerxes.

NRSV

pavement of porphyry, marble, mother-of-pearl, and colored stones. 7Drinks were served in golden goblets, goblets of different kinds, and the royal wine was lavished according to the bounty of the king. 8Drinking was by flagons, without restraint; for the king had given orders to all the officials of his palace to do as each one desired. 9Furthermore, Queen Vashti gave a banquet for the women in the palace of King Ahasuerus.

COMMENTARY

1:1. The book of Esther, which purports to be a historical work (but see Introduction), begins by placing its story in a historical place and time, the court of an actual Persian king. The reader is introduced to King Ahasuerus, who ruled "from India to Ethiopia." "Ahasuerus" is not the name of a known Persian king; however, the author seems to assume that his audience will know which Persian king is meant. Many candidates have been proposed, from Cambyses, son of Cyrus, to Artaxerxes III Ochus, the last Persian emperor before the conquest of Alexander the Great. The LXX and Josephus understand Ahasuerus to be Artaxerxes, and Josephus specifically identifies the king in Esther as Artaxerxes I Longimanus (465–424 BCE). The AT at 10:3 identifies Ahasuerus as Xerxes as well. Linguistic and historical evidence indicate that Xerxes, the fourth Persian emperor (486–465 BCE), is meant. "Ahasuerus" is the Hebrew rendering of the Persian title *xšayāršā*, "mighty man," a title that Xerxes used on his monumental inscriptions. Further, Xerxes' kingdom extended from India to the borders of Egypt (inclusive) and from the Ionian coast to the Arabian desert, thus including most of the known world and agreeing with v. 1 (see Map, figure XX, for the extent of Xerxes' kingdom). Finally, one of Xerxes' four capitals was at Susa.[51] The number of provinces (127; Dan 6:2 mentions 120 satraps, while 1 Esdr 3:1-2 has 127 satraps) is not attested in Persian sources and seems to be an inflated number, perhaps in keeping with the author's hyperbolic tone.

1:2-4. Now that a historical time frame has been established, v. 2 introduces the actual story of the book. The phrase "sat on his royal throne" or "reigned from his royal throne" has the sense of "sat securely" and implies that Xerxes had established his rule securely enough by his third year to give a banquet to celebrate. The AT supplies the phrase "of his deliverance," and indeed the historical Xerxes did face rebellion in both Egypt and Babylon, which he swiftly quelled, at the beginning of his reign. However, the LXX states that the banquet is to celebrate his marriage to Vashti. The banquet takes place in Susa, the former capital of Elam and one of the four capitals of the Persian Empire (see the map on p. 879). According to Herodotus, the Persian court wintered in Babylon and then, to escape the scorching heat, spent the spring in Susa and the summers in Ecbatana. The text differentiates between the city of Susa and its citadel (בירה *bîrâ*), the royal palace excavated by M. Dieulafoy in 1884–86, who discovered an acropolis containing the royal buildings.[52] This first banquet includes all the officials, both military and civic, of the entire Persian Empire, and lasts 180 days, or half a year. Xerxes must have indeed been secure on his throne to allow his government to grind to a halt while his officials banqueted for six months! A suspicion of hyperbole is raised.

51. For a good discussion of the evidence for the identification of Ahasuerus with Xerxes, see L. B. Paton, *Esther,* ICC (Edinburgh: T. & T. Clark, 1908) 51-54.

52. M. A. Dieulafoy, *L'Acropole de Suse,* 4 vols. (Paris: Hatchetee, 1893).

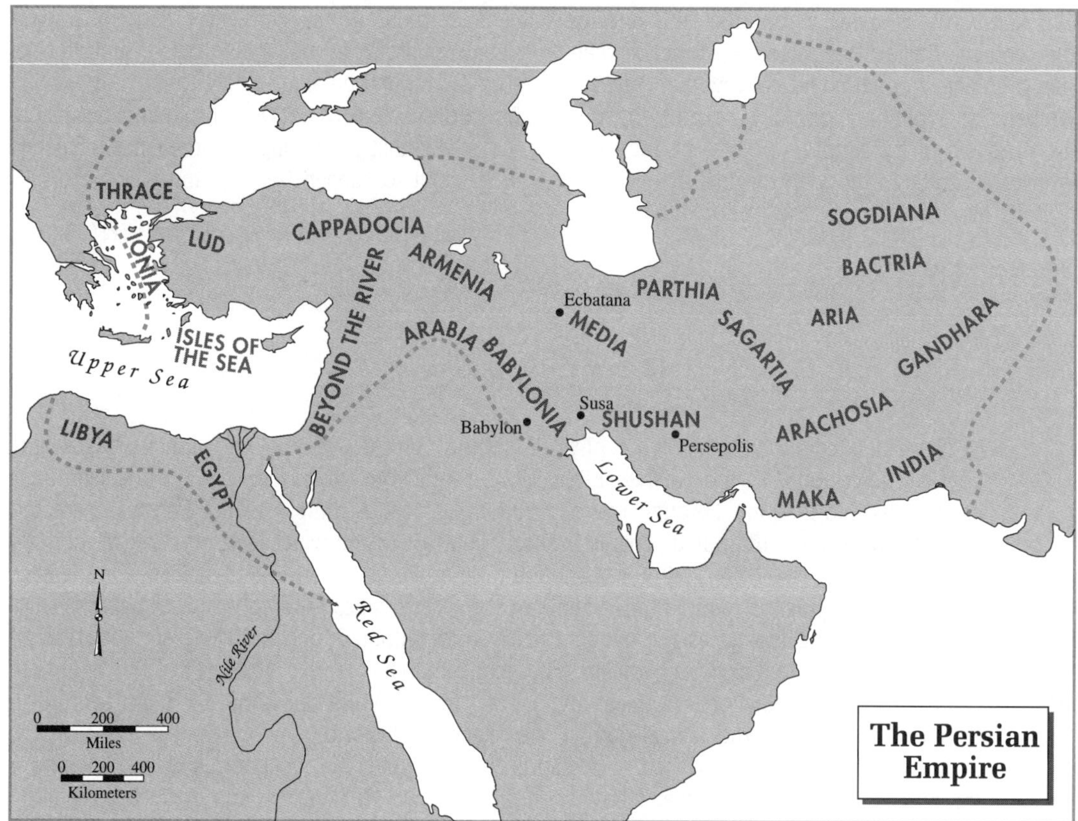

1:5-9. This suspicion is confirmed by the description of the second banquet. This banquet is for the people of Susa, both the great, the palace officials, and the small, the regular people. The description of the garden of the king's palace, where the banquet is held, is meant to convey the opulence of the palace and the wealth of Xerxes. Several of the words occur only here in the Hebrew Bible, and they are piled up, one on top of the other, making an impression of luxury and richness but not creating a very coherent picture.[53] Verses 7-8 place a great deal of emphasis on the drink, in keeping with the Persian notoriety for heavy drinking bouts. In fact, v. 8 in the Hebrew informs us that the drinking was "according to the law" and that "there was no compelling," but "each man could do according to his will," a difficult verse to render into acceptable English. We know from Herodotus[54] that usually the king set the pace of drinking; when he drank, everybody drank. However, at this banquet "there was no compelling." Most commentators resolve the difficulty by taking the Hebrew word דת (*dāt*) to mean here "a special ruling"—that is, for this particular banquet the normal rule was suspended, and each man could drink as much or as little as he wanted.[55] The word *dāt* recurs throughout the book of Esther, always referring to a royal decision; the author is letting the reader know that everything in this court, including drinking, proceeds according to the whims of the king.

Finally, v. 9 introduces the second important character in the story, Queen Vashti. The name "Vashti," which comes from the Persian word *vahista* ("best"), is unattested in extra-biblical sources; Xerxes' queen was Amestris,[56] and she remained queen throughout his reign. The introduction of the unknown Vashti is the first clue to the vigilant reader that, despite its veneer of historicity, the book of Esther is a story. Vashti,

53. Werner Dommershausen suggests that the author uses Persian loan words to create an exotic effect. See his *Die Estherrolle,* SBM 6 (Stuttgart: Katholisches Bibelwerk, 1968) 146. The use of Persian words here also reinforces the story's historical verisimilitude.

54. Herodotus 1.33.

55. See, e.g., C. A. Moore, *Esther,* AB 7B (Garden City, N.Y.: Doubleday, 1971) 7-8.

56. Herodotus 7.61, 9.109-13.

like Ahasuerus, is giving a banquet—this one for the women—inside the palace. Historically, Persian men and women could eat together, but the women left when the drinking began.[57] It suits the purposes of the author to have the men and women separate as the story begins.

Berg has pointed out the importance of the banquet motif in the story of Esther.[58] Banquets signal important events (1:3-9; 3:15), indicate closure (2:18), and provide settings to move the action forward (5:5-8; 6:14–7:10). A banquet is a signal to the reader that something important has happened or is about to happen (see also Introduction).

57. Ibid., 5.18, 9.110.

58. Sandra Beth Berg, *The Book of Esther*, SBLDS 44 (Chico: Scholars Press, 1979) 31-57.

REFLECTIONS

The extended description of the physical setting contrasts greatly with the usually scanty physical descriptions in the Hebrew Bible. Why, then, does the author give all this seemingly extraneous information? Through the description, we get a glimpse of the Persian character: ostentatious, showy, unbridled. This is in direct contrast to the usual Jewish values of modesty and self-restraint (see Prov 11:2-4).[59] Although disapproval is never directly voiced, the message is clear: Such opulence, while immediately awe-inspiring, hides an empty and probably corrupt core. This will be proved as the events of the story unfold. Much the same sort of criticism can be leveled at contemporary society: The "consumerism" of the latter half of the twentieth century substitutes for deeper ethical and moral values. While the implied criticism found in Esther does not strike the radical note of the rejection of worldly goods found in the teaching of Jesus ("Sell all that you own and distribute the money to the poor, and you will have treasure in heaven; then come, follow me" [Luke 18:22 NRSV]), the author does wish us to recognize the ultimate unimportance of wealth.

59. See Jon D. Levenson, *Esther*, OTL (Louisville: Westminster/John Knox, 1997) 45.

ESTHER 1:10-22, THE DOWNFALL OF VASHTI

NIV

10On the seventh day, when King Xerxes was in high spirits from wine, he commanded the seven eunuchs who served him—Mehuman, Biztha, Harbona, Bigtha, Abagtha, Zethar and Carcas— 11to bring before him Queen Vashti, wearing her royal crown, in order to display her beauty to the people and nobles, for she was lovely to look at. 12But when the attendants delivered the king's command, Queen Vashti refused to come. Then the king became furious and burned with anger.

13Since it was customary for the king to consult experts in matters of law and justice, he spoke with the wise men who understood the times 14and were closest to the king—Carshena,

NRSV

10On the seventh day, when the king was merry with wine, he commanded Mehuman, Biztha, Harbona, Bigtha and Abagtha, Zethar and Carkas, the seven eunuchs who attended him, 11to bring Queen Vashti before the king, wearing the royal crown, in order to show the peoples and the officials her beauty; for she was fair to behold. 12But Queen Vashti refused to come at the king's command conveyed by the eunuchs. At this the king was enraged, and his anger burned within him.

13Then the king consulted the sages who knew the laws[a] (for this was the king's procedure toward all who were versed in law and custom,

[a] Cn: Heb *times*

NIV

Shethar, Admatha, Tarshish, Meres, Marsena and Memucan, the seven nobles of Persia and Media who had special access to the king and were highest in the kingdom.

15“According to law, what must be done to Queen Vashti?” he asked. “She has not obeyed the command of King Xerxes that the eunuchs have taken to her.”

16Then Memucan replied in the presence of the king and the nobles, “Queen Vashti has done wrong, not only against the king but also against all the nobles and the peoples of all the provinces of King Xerxes. 17For the queen’s conduct will become known to all the women, and so they will despise their husbands and say, ‘King Xerxes commanded Queen Vashti to be brought before him, but she would not come.’ 18This very day the Persian and Median women of the nobility who have heard about the queen’s conduct will respond to all the king’s nobles in the same way. There will be no end of disrespect and discord.

19“Therefore, if it pleases the king, let him issue a royal decree and let it be written in the laws of Persia and Media, which cannot be repealed, that Vashti is never again to enter the presence of King Xerxes. Also let the king give her royal position to someone else who is better than she. 20Then when the king’s edict is proclaimed throughout all his vast realm, all the women will respect their husbands, from the least to the greatest.”

21The king and his nobles were pleased with this advice, so the king did as Memucan proposed. 22He sent dispatches to all parts of the kingdom, to each province in its own script and to each people in its own language, proclaiming in each people’s tongue that every man should be ruler over his own household.

NRSV

14and those next to him were Carshena, Shethar, Admatha, Tarshish, Meres, Marsena, and Memucan, the seven officials of Persia and Media, who had access to the king, and sat first in the kingdom): 15“According to the law, what is to be done to Queen Vashti because she has not performed the command of King Ahasuerus conveyed by the eunuchs?” 16Then Memucan said in the presence of the king and the officials, “Not only has Queen Vashti done wrong to the king, but also to all the officials and all the peoples who are in all the provinces of King Ahasuerus. 17For this deed of the queen will be made known to all women, causing them to look with contempt on their husbands, since they will say, ‘King Ahasuerus commanded Queen Vashti to be brought before him, and she did not come.’ 18This very day the noble ladies of Persia and Media who have heard of the queen’s behavior will rebel against[a] the king’s officials, and there will be no end of contempt and wrath! 19If it pleases the king, let a royal order go out from him, and let it be written among the laws of the Persians and the Medes so that it may not be altered, that Vashti is never again to come before King Ahasuerus; and let the king give her royal position to another who is better than she. 20So when the decree made by the king is proclaimed throughout all his kingdom, vast as it is, all women will give honor to their husbands, high and low alike.”

21This advice pleased the king and the officials, and the king did as Memucan proposed; 22he sent letters to all the royal provinces, to every province in its own script and to every people in its own language, declaring that every man should be master in his own house.[b]

[a] Cn: Heb *will tell* [b] Heb adds *and speak according to the language of his people*

COMMENTARY

1:10-12. The satirical tone of the book of Esther comes to the forefront in this passage. It raises several questions: Why does the king summon Vashti? Why does she refuse to come? Why does the king need to consult his advisers? The Hebrew text quite clearly indicates that the king summons Vashti when he is drunk—that is, “when the heart of the king was good in wine”—thereby implying that his actions were not quite rational and that her refusal to obey was justified.[60] He sends seven eunuchs (eunuchs are important functionaries in the Persian hierarchy, as well as in harem life) to fetch her, all listed by name, which seems to be an attempt to give the text an air of historical verisimilitude. The figure seven, a number signifying a complete or finished group, recurs throughout the chapter; Vashti is summoned on the seventh day, the king sends seven eunuchs to fetch her, and, in v. 14, he consults with seven nobles.

The king sends the eunuchs to bring Vashti, wearing the royal crown, before the assembly in order to display her beauty before the assembled company. The king has already displayed his wealth and his generosity; what remains but his beautiful wife? However, Vashti refuses.

The Hebrew text gives no reason or justification for Vashti's refusal of a direct command from the king. Her refusal is shocking in its simplicity and directness; the all-powerful king who rules from India to Ethiopia, whose riches and power are immense, has been disobeyed—by his wife![61] However, her reason for refusing is still enigmatic. Is it because the king is drunk? Interpreters have offered several reasons. Josephus informs us that she refused to come because Persian law forbade wives to be seen by strangers, but his contention is historically inaccurate.[62] The rabbis infer, from the command that she wear the royal crown, that she was meant to wear *only* the royal crown—in other words, to appear naked, wearing only the crown.[63] However, in the Hebrew Vashti's refusal remains unexplained.

1:13-22. The king is enraged by her refusal; he has been publicly shamed in front of his court.[64] However, rather than confront Vashti directly, which we might expect, he turns to his advisers to determine what should be done "according to the law." The text's exaggerated emphasis on the law is apparent for the second time in the chapter: First, drinking is done according to law; now the king, in a dispute with his wife, must proceed according to law. This respect for the law will appear with more important consequences later in the story. The men the king consults are "wise men" who "know the times." The term "the times" (העתים *hā'ittîm*) may connote astrology (see Isa 47:12-13; Dan 2:27; 5:15; see also 1 Chr 12:32, with reference to the tribe of Issachar), but that phrase is in apposition to "all those who know law [דת *dāt*] and judgment [דין *dîn*]," so it probably simply refers to those who are knowledgeable about Persian customs, both legal and traditional. The author once more supplies us with a list of Persian names; some of these names occur extra-biblically, while others do not; none of them can be identified with any known historical figures (the AT omits them altogether). The use of the number seven here indicates that the author is familiar with the Persian court: Seven noblemen helped to defeat the false Smerdis in his conspiracy against Darius and thereafter enjoyed special privileges in the Persian court, such as unchecked access to the king.[65] They were the chief noblemen of the Persian court, so it is proper that the king should consult them.

The response of Memucan, one of the advisers, seems out of proportion to the crime. What has been a matter of personal disobedience suddenly becomes an affair of state, affecting all husbands and wives and threatening the stability of the kingdom. It is possible that Memucan is afraid Vashti is plotting a palace coup, but it is more likely that the author means for us to laugh; the pompous Persians turn a personal affront, which could be easily resolved, into a national crisis. The dignity of Persian men is so precarious that the actions of one woman threaten the whole house of cards. The king must take action not only within his own household, but throughout the entire kingdom as well; not only against Vashti, but

60. Josephus, in his attempt to improve the portrait of the king, leaves out any mention of drunkenness. See Louis Feldman, "Josephus' Portrait of Ahasuerus," *Australian Biblical Review* 42 (1994) 17-38.

61. The theme of obedience/disobedience, especially by a wife, runs throughout the book and features prominently in the turning point of the story. See Berg, *The Book of Esther,* 71-82.

62. See Herodotus 9.110 and Neh 2:6 for the presence of women, even royal wives, at banquets.

63. *Meg., Tg. Esth I, Tg. Esth II.* The rabbis are not sympathetic to Vashti, whom they identify as the granddaughter of Nebuchadnezzar, the Babylonian emperor who destroyed Jerusalem in 587 BCE. In fact, the Megilloth, not satisfied that the shameless Vashti would refuse to appear naked, adds that she had become leprous! None of this is implied in the Hebrew text.

64. The concept of honor/shame is important in ancient Mediterranean cultures and often informs the behavior of characters in ways our own culture does not expect. "Honor" and "shame" are attributes applied to the individual from the outside, by the society: A man gains honor by his behavior, while a woman avoids shame by hers. Ahasuerus has been shamed by Vashti's disobedience; on the other hand, the text may imply that Vashti would be shamed by appearing publicly at the banquet, a seemingly insoluble dilemma. For a further discussion of honor and shame in Esther, see Lillian R. Klein, "Honor and Shame in Esther," in *A Feminist Companion to Esther, Judith and Susanna,* ed. Athalya Brenner (Sheffield: Sheffield Academic, 1995) 149-75. See also Timothy S. Laniak, "From the Margin to the Middle: The Pattern of Shame and Honor in the Book of Esther" (unpublished Ph.D. diss., Harvard University, 1997).

65. Herodotus 3.84.

also against all women; and not only for the sake of his own dignity, but for the peace and stability of all families. It is difficult to respect such silliness.

Memucan advises the king to make a law banishing Vashti and stripping her of her royal status (v. 19). The irony, of course, is that Vashti is forbidden to do precisely what she refused to do: appear before the king. The verse also introduces a concept that will prove important later in the story: the irrevocability of Persian law. According to Memucan, once a law has been promulgated by the king, it cannot be revoked. Such a rule goes against any principle of good government and common sense, and, indeed, does not seem historically to have been true of Persian law.[66] However, the concept appears elsewhere in Jewish literature (Dan 6:8-9, 12, 15), and the author of Esther will use it as an important plot device.

The king decides to implement this advice, and letters to that effect are sent throughout the kingdom (v. 22). The Persians maintained an excellent postal system, necessary in such a vast empire; various characters will utilize it throughout the story. What is interesting about the letters is that they do not mention Vashti at all; instead, they declare that every man should be master in his own house (a command from the king, who is not!) and should "speak according to the language of his people."[67] Note that the NRSV omits this final clause (presumably because of the difficulties of its interpretation) and that the NIV places it before the first clause. The decree itself is unenforceable and laughable; as Fox puts it, the Persian postal system "is put to service in the dissemination of inanity."[68]

Thus Vashti disappears from the scene, opening the door for the appearance of Esther and the main plot of the book.

66. See Herodotus 9.109.

67. In the Persian Empire, many languages were spoken; in such a setting, language becomes an important indicator of ethnicity. Nehemiah forces Jews who had married non-Jewish women to repudiate their wives, one of the reasons being that their children spoke the language of their mothers and could not speak Hebrew (Neh 13:23-27).

68. Michael V. Fox, *Character and Ideology in the Book of Esther: Studies in Biblical Personalities* (Columbia: University of South Carolina Press, 1991) 23.

REFLECTIONS

It seems difficult at first to pan any theological gold out of the first chapter of Esther. After all, the story is about Persian characters, set in a pagan court, with no glimmer of religion anywhere. However, the chapter does introduce two themes that this commentary will pursue: (1) the role and status of women and (2) power.

1. The character of Vashti the Queen serves as a foil to Esther the Queen, and very different fates await each. Vashti is queen and seems to function autonomously within the sphere of women; in 1:9 she gives a separate banquet for women. However, the extent of her power and autonomy swiftly becomes clear: The minute she opposes her husband the king, the entire machinery of the state descends on her head, and she loses all status and power. To many modern commentators, Vashti is a feminist hero, opposing the male power structure with what little independence she has.[69] It is easy to see why she is a more attractive character than is the pliant Esther. However, in the story Vashti fails, and Esther succeeds. What message is the author trying to convey? Can we reconcile that message to our differing ideas about the status and role of women in society? Further reflection is called for.

2. The theme of power—who has it, who receives it, who loses it—will recur throughout the story of Esther. In this section, the all-powerfulness of Ahasuerus is revealed as a sham; he does not even have power over his own domestic arrangements. First his wife successfully opposes him, and then he must turn to his advisers to tell him what to do about it. It is not enough to declare that one has power, the author is saying. To truly have power, one must have the accompanying wisdom and skill to exercise it.

69. Alice Laffey, *An Introduction to the Old Testament: A Feminist Perspective* (Philadelphia: Fortress, 1988) 214-15; Timothy K. Beal, "Tracing Esther's Beginnings," and Bea Wyler, "Esther: The Incomplete Emancipation of a Queen," in Brenner, *A Feminist Companion to Esther, Judith and Susanna,* 87-110, 115-18.

ESTHER 2:1-23

ESTHER BECOMES QUEEN

OVERVIEW

This section introduces the main protagonists, Esther and Mordecai, and explains how the young Jewish girl Esther becomes the Persian queen. Esther is a beautiful, malleable young woman (the orphan who makes good); while her cousin Mordecai is presented as the model of the righteous and wise man.

ESTHER 2:1-4, THE SEARCH FOR A NEW QUEEN

NIV

2 Later when the anger of King Xerxes had subsided, he remembered Vashti and what she had done and what he had decreed about her. [2]Then the king's personal attendants proposed, "Let a search be made for beautiful young virgins for the king. [3]Let the king appoint commissioners in every province of his realm to bring all these beautiful girls into the harem at the citadel of Susa. Let them be placed under the care of Hegai, the king's eunuch, who is in charge of the women; and let beauty treatments be given to them. [4]Then let the girl who pleases the king be queen instead of Vashti." This advice appealed to the king, and he followed it.

NRSV

2 After these things, when the anger of King Ahasuerus had abated, he remembered Vashti and what she had done and what had been decreed against her. [2]Then the king's servants who attended him said, "Let beautiful young virgins be sought out for the king. [3]And let the king appoint commissioners in all the provinces of his kingdom to gather all the beautiful young virgins to the harem in the citadel of Susa under custody of Hegai, the king's eunuch, who is in charge of the women; let their cosmetic treatments be given them. [4]And let the girl who pleases the king be queen instead of Vashti." This pleased the king, and he did so.

COMMENTARY

"After these things" indicates an indeterminate length of time. It must be shortly after the events in chap. 1, for Ahasuerus's anger has passed; as we shall see, his emotions tend to change rapidly. Now he remembers Vashti. With love? Regret? Loneliness? The Hebrew text does not supply an answer, although Josephus supplies "with regret," because the king was fond of Vashti.[70] Interestingly, the LXX reads "the king remembered Vashti *no longer*"; thus he was ready to find another wife. The Hebrew does not seem to carry this connotation, for the king also remembers what Vashti had done and "what had been decreed against her." The passive construction in the Hebrew (the NRSV correctly reflects this) deflects blame from the king onto his advisers, a pattern we shall see again.

Josephus's interpretation of the king's emotional state may well be correct, because the servants ("young men" [נערים *nĕʿārîm*], not the noble advisers of chap. 1) quickly propose a scheme to banish Vashti from the king's thoughts

70. Josephus *Antiquities of the Jews* XI.195.

as well as from his courts. Young women are to be sought, and one of them will become the new queen. The only characteristics they must have are beauty and youth; the word translated as "virgins" is בתולות (*bĕtûlôt*), which actually means "young women of marriageable age," although most girls moved very quickly from the onset of puberty into marriage.[71] They are to come from all over the kingdom to be placed in the harem (or women's quarters) in the royal palace of Susa, under the care of Hegai, an official of the palace bearing the title "King's Eunuch." Each young woman is to be given "cosmetic treatments," an oblique hint at the sensuality of the Persian court. Finally, the girl who "pleases the king" the most, a deliberately vague phrase that echoes Memucan's advice in 1:19, will be queen instead of Vashti. Some translations render the Hebrew תמלך (*timlōk*) as "reign," but "reign" implies power; it is not clear whether the queen has power of her own or is simply the king's wife. Vashti attempted to exercise independent power and fell; there is no reason to assume that a young girl (13-14 years old), chosen for her ability to "please" the king, will wield any power of her own. Therefore, "be queen" seems the best translation in the present context; however, the author's irony may be at work here, since Esther eventually does "reign." Ahasuerus, once again relying on the advice of others, readily adopts the plan.

Two things should be noted. First, it is clear that in reality this story could not have taken place, since the Persian king was limited by law to marriage with a woman from one of the seven noble Persian families.[72] The author of Esther is clearly drawing on legendary motifs; the stories of King Shekriya and Scheherazade in *The Thousand and One Nights* and, from Jewish tradition, King David and Abishag the Shunammite (1 Kgs 1:1-4) immediately come to mind.[73] Second, there is no sense of coercion in the text; the young men (and the author) assume that the young women will wish to enter the king's harem; in any case, the women are not consulted. On this matter the king has power over his subjects, and he will exercise it. There is a contest for the girl who pleases the king the most (i.e., is best in bed; this is a sexual contest), and the winner will become queen.[74] (See Reflections at 2:5-7.)

71. For a discussion of the meaning of the term בתולה (*bĕtûlâ*), see Peggy L. Day, *"From the Child Is Born the Woman: The Story of Jephthah's Daughter," in Gender and Difference in Ancient Israel,* ed. P. L. Day (Minneapolis: Fortress, 1989) 58-74.

72. Herodotus 3.84.

73. Michael V. Fox, *Character and Ideology in the Book of Esther,* 28, points out that Esth 2:2*b* is verbally dependent on 1 Kgs 1:2*a*.

74. Fox makes this point strongly in ibid., 28.

ESTHER 2:5-7, THE INTRODUCTION OF ESTHER AND MORDECAI

NIV

[5]Now there was in the citadel of Susa a Jew of the tribe of Benjamin, named Mordecai son of Jair, the son of Shimei, the son of Kish, [6]who had been carried into exile from Jerusalem by Nebuchadnezzar king of Babylon, among those taken captive with Jehoiachin[a] king of Judah. [7]Mordecai had a cousin named Hadassah, whom he had brought up because she had neither father nor mother. This girl, who was also known as Esther, was lovely in form and features, and Mordecai had taken her as his own daughter when her father and mother died.

[a]6 Hebrew *Jeconiah,* a variant of *Jehoiachin*

NRSV

5Now there was a Jew in the citadel of Susa whose name was Mordecai son of Jair son of Shimei son of Kish, a Benjaminite. [6]Kish[a] had been carried away from Jerusalem among the captives carried away with King Jeconiah of Judah, whom King Nebuchadnezzar of Babylon had carried away. [7]Mordecai[b] had brought up Hadassah, that is Esther, his cousin, for she had neither father nor mother; the girl was fair and beautiful, and when her father and her mother died, Mordecai adopted her as his own daughter.

[a] Heb *a Benjamite* [6]who [b] Heb *He*

COMMENTARY

These three verses interrupt the flow of the narrative, yet they are necessary for the story because they introduce the two main characters, Esther and Mordecai. Their parenthetical character, similar to Ezra 2:2 and Neh 7:1, makes the introductions more conspicuous.

Mordecai, who bears a Babylonian name with the theophorous element Marduk,[75] is introduced first. He is identified first as a Jew, now in the post-exilic period of ethnic ("of the nation of Israel") rather than tribal ("of the tribe of Judah") designation, which will be Mordecai's primary epithet throughout the book. Next, the text states that he is in the citadel (not the city) of Susa, which implies that he is a court official (this is made plain in the LXX, Add. A 2). Finally, his genealogy is given: son of Jair, son of Shimei, son of Kish. The identity of these ancestors is open to question. Jair is probably Mordecai's father, but Shimei and Kish may be more remote ancestors. Shimei is known in the biblical tradition as a member of the house of Saul (thus a Benjaminite) who cursed David as he fled from Jerusalem (2 Sam 16:5-14), while Kish is the father of Saul, first king of Israel (1 Sam 9:1; 14:51). If these are the figures the author of Esther wishes to make the ancestors of Mordecai, then two connections with Saul have been established, connections that will be important later on. Finally, Mordecai's tribe, Benjamin, is given.

Verse 6 presents a problem. It begins with the relative pronoun (אשׁר *'ăšer*), "who have been carried captive." The person referred to had been exiled with King Jeconiah (or Jehoiachin), the last king of Judah, in 597 BCE, which implies his nobility (2 Kgs 24:10-12). However, if the person referred to is Mordecai, at the time of this story he would be extremely old, at least 113![76] The NRSV solves the dilemma by identifying the "who" of v. 6 with Kish; but if Kish is the father of Saul, as seems likely for reasons to be made clear, this identification would be incorrect. The author seems to have made a blunder, perhaps thinking that Ahasuerus was the direct successor of Nebuchadnezzar, or at least he seems to have telescoped history; Mordecai's importance and royal connections are more important than the relatively minor matter of his age.

Esther is introduced in v. 7 as the ward of Mordecai. She has both a Hebrew name, "Hadassah" (הדסה *hădassâ*, meaning "myrtle"; this name appears only here in MT Esther and not in the Greek versions), and a Persian name, "Esther" (meaning "star," but some commentators also connect it with the Babylonian goddess Ishtar). "Esther" (אסתר *'str* in its consonantal form) also means "I will hide" in Hebrew, and the rabbis took this as a reference to Esther's concealment of her Jewish identity. The practice of having two names, a Jewish name and a name of one's place of exile, was common among Jews of the post-exilic period (see Dan 1:7).

Esther is an orphan, adopted "as a daughter" by Mordecai, whose relationship to her is not explained at this point. The LXX and *Meg.* 13*a* state that Mordecai took her "as a wife," which would make her entry into the king's harem heinous (and parallel with the kidnapping of Sarah, wife of Abraham, by Pharaoh in Gen 12:10-20; cf. *The Genesis Apocryphon*), but the Hebrew is perfectly clear and fits better with the pattern of the story, which accepts Esther's entry into the king's harem as a matter of course. Esther's status as an orphan mirrors the Jewish people's status as exiles: marginalized and powerless. This is the first clue that Esther is to be a role model. The only other thing we learn about Esther at this time is that she is beautiful (lit., "shapely of form and good of appearance"), thus meeting the one criterion for entrance into the king's harem.

Thus far the reader has been led to believe that Mordecai was the main protagonist of the story, with Esther playing a secondary role; his ethnicity, his public status, his genealogy, and his links with nobility are emphasized, while all that is revealed about Esther is that she is a beautiful orphan. However, it should be remembered that the book is named after Esther, not Mordecai.

75. "Theophorous" means containing a reference to divinity, usually a divine name. For example, the name "Jonathan" in Hebrew (יהונתן *yĕhônātān*) contains the divine name "YHWH."

76. Lewis B. Paton, *Esther,* ICC (Edinburgh: T. & T. Clark, 1908) 168-69. The LXX omits the phrase concerning the exile; the AT does not contain the verse.

REFLECTIONS

The theme of power appears again in these two sections with the juxtaposing of the power of the king and his court, who can disrupt the lives of every family in the empire at will by requiring their daughters to enter his harem, and the powerless status of Mordecai and Esther, an exile and an orphan respectively. The author passes by the dislocation of Esther's life without comment; the comfort of a young girl is nothing beside the desire of the king! We should pause, however, and reflect on the havoc that power can wreak on the lives of the powerless. The examples in our own time are legion: the forced exile of the Armenians by the Turks, which resulted in Armenian genocide; the removal to ghettos and concentration camps (followed by mass murder) of millions of Jews and others in the Holocaust; and the internment of Japanese Americans in prison camps by the American government during World War II. The author of Esther uses the juxtaposition of power and powerlessness as ironic foreshadowing; by the end of the story, the powerless exile and the orphan will control the Persian Empire. For modern readers, the picture of numerous girls being ripped away from their families and forced into the king's harem cannot be resolved so comfortably.

ESTHER 2:8-18, ESTHER IS CHOSEN QUEEN

NIV

[8]When the king's order and edict had been proclaimed, many girls were brought to the citadel of Susa and put under the care of Hegai. Esther also was taken to the king's palace and entrusted to Hegai, who had charge of the harem. [9]The girl pleased him and won his favor. Immediately he provided her with her beauty treatments and special food. He assigned to her seven maids selected from the king's palace and moved her and her maids into the best place in the harem.

[10]Esther had not revealed her nationality and family background, because Mordecai had forbidden her to do so. [11]Every day he walked back and forth near the courtyard of the harem to find out how Esther was and what was happening to her.

[12]Before a girl's turn came to go in to King Xerxes, she had to complete twelve months of beauty treatments prescribed for the women, six months with oil of myrrh and six with perfumes and cosmetics. [13]And this is how she would go to the king: Anything she wanted was given her to take with her from the harem to the king's palace. [14]In the evening she would go there and in the morning return to another part of the harem to the care of Shaashgaz, the king's eunuch who was in charge of the concubines. She would

NRSV

[8]So when the king's order and his edict were proclaimed, and when many young women were gathered in the citadel of Susa in custody of Hegai, Esther also was taken into the king's palace and put in custody of Hegai, who had charge of the women. [9]The girl pleased him and won his favor, and he quickly provided her with her cosmetic treatments and her portion of food, and with seven chosen maids from the king's palace, and advanced her and her maids to the best place in the harem. [10]Esther did not reveal her people or kindred, for Mordecai had charged her not to tell. [11]Every day Mordecai would walk around in front of the court of the harem, to learn how Esther was and how she fared.

12The turn came for each girl to go in to King Ahasuerus, after being twelve months under the regulations for the women, since this was the regular period of their cosmetic treatment, six months with oil of myrrh and six months with perfumes and cosmetics for women. [13]When the girl went in to the king she was given whatever she asked for to take with her from the harem to the king's palace. [14]In the evening she went in; then in the morning she came back to the second harem in custody of Shaashgaz, the king's eunuch,

NIV

not return to the king unless he was pleased with her and summoned her by name.

[15]When the turn came for Esther (the girl Mordecai had adopted, the daughter of his uncle Abihail) to go to the king, she asked for nothing other than what Hegai, the king's eunuch who was in charge of the harem, suggested. And Esther won the favor of everyone who saw her. [16]She was taken to King Xerxes in the royal residence in the tenth month, the month of Tebeth, in the seventh year of his reign.

[17]Now the king was attracted to Esther more than to any of the other women, and she won his favor and approval more than any of the other virgins. So he set a royal crown on her head and made her queen instead of Vashti. [18]And the king gave a great banquet, Esther's banquet, for all his nobles and officials. He proclaimed a holiday throughout the provinces and distributed gifts with royal liberality.

NRSV

who was in charge of the concubines; she did not go in to the king again, unless the king delighted in her and she was summoned by name.

15When the turn came for Esther daughter of Abihail the uncle of Mordecai, who had adopted her as his own daughter, to go in to the king, she asked for nothing except what Hegai the king's eunuch, who had charge of the women, advised. Now Esther was admired by all who saw her. [16]When Esther was taken to King Ahasuerus in his royal palace in the tenth month, which is the month of Tebeth, in the seventh year of his reign, [17]the king loved Esther more than all the other women; of all the virgins she won his favor and devotion, so that he set the royal crown on her head and made her queen instead of Vashti. [18]Then the king gave a great banquet to all his officials and ministers—"Esther's banquet." He also granted a holiday[a] to the provinces, and gave gifts with royal liberality.

[a] Or *an amnesty*

COMMENTARY

2:8-11. Esther, along with all the other young women of Susa (according to Josephus, there were four hundred girls),[77] is taken into the harem and placed in the charge of Hegai. Notice that in the Hebrew text there is no hint of protest on the part of either Esther or Mordecai. The king's law is proclaimed, and they obey it. This obedience to a seemingly immoral command troubled the rabbis, who claimed that Esther was taken by force or that Mordecai tried to hide her; however, these claims import moral standards into the text that do not apply in the situation the author is describing; it does not trouble the author (perhaps because his story is fictional) that a Jewish girl is about to become the concubine of the Gentile king. In v. 9, Esther's first action is recorded: She "wins" (נשׂא *nāśā'*) the favor of Hegai. The active construction is important; she does not "find" (מצא *māṣā'*) favor, but actively earns it. The result is positive: Hegai seems to treat her especially well; she receives her cosmetic treatments "quickly," as well as special food, seven maids from the palace, and the best place in the harem. This is Esther's first step on the road to political power, and she has negotiated it wisely and reaped the rewards. The mention of food is significant: Esther does not seem to eat kosher food, but just what is provided for her by Hegai. This is in contrast to Daniel, another Jew in a foreign court, who insists on obtaining kosher food (Dan 1:8-17). Both the LXX and the rabbis attempt to remedy this problem by having Esther demand, and get, kosher food (see Add. C).

It would have been difficult, within the confines of the Hebrew story, however, for Esther to demand kosher food, since v. 10 informs us that she did not reveal her ethnic background, "for Mordecai had commanded that she was not to tell." This implies that there is nothing in Esther's everyday behavior that would reveal that she was Jewish; in other words, she was not observant. No judgment of her is implied, either; the fact is

77. Josephus *Antiquities of the Jews* XI.201.

simply passed over in silence. The reason for Mordecai's command is not given; this is the second unanswered question in the text (the reason for Vashti's refusal being the first). Some consider it a matter of political expediency,[78] but it may simply be a convenient plot device.[79] It may also imply that it was dangerous to be a Jew in the Persian court. In any case, Esther is triumphantly established in the harem, and every day Mordecai, who as a courtier would have access to the palace, checks on her welfare. How Mordecai could have inquired after her every day without revealing his identity as her foster father, and thus revealing her Jewishness, is not stated.

2:12-14. These verses outline the process by which all the girls were taken to the king. The process took twelve months, "according to the custom of women." Although דת (*dāt*) usually carries the force of law in our sense, here it seems to connote "custom" or perhaps "decree." This is the process that has been established, and no one can hasten it or bypass it.[80] Thus Esther will spend a full year in beauty treatments before being seen by the king, in spite of Hegai's favor. Six months are spent being massaged with oil of myrrh, and six months are given to perfumes and cosmetics. The details of this regimen are unclear to the modern reader, although some cosmetic burners and many perfume vials have been found in excavations in the Middle East.[81] It may be imagined as well that the women were instructed in court etiquette and possibly the sexual arts of pleasing the king. At the end of the year, each woman was brought to the king for one night. It is clear from the text, although not explicitly stated, that the purpose of this night was to have sexual intercourse, for in the morning the woman was returned to a different harem, the harem of concubines (פילגשים *pîlagšîm*; there is no mistaking the sexual connotation of the term). She would not see the king again unless summoned by name. The author here displays his knowledge of Near Eastern harem customs, well-known from the later Ottoman Empire. Although the women of the harem were sequestered and dependent upon male favor, a woman could wield enormous power from within the walls of the palace, especially if she were the queen and/or the mother of the heir. Persian history is speckled with tales of harem intrigue; Xerxes himself was killed in a harem coup. Therefore, although the women had no hand in selecting their lot, they did have the potential of acquiring power and influence.

2:15-18. When Esther's turn comes (v. 15) for her night with the king, her importance is heightened by giving her a genealogy. She is the daughter of Abihail, the uncle of Mordecai. Abihail (אביחיל *'ăbîḥayil*, "my father is mighty") does not seem to be connected with any of the other Abihails in the biblical text (Num 3:25; 1 Chr 2:29; 5:14; 11:18), but his relationship to Mordecai assures the reader that Esther is of the same noble blood and, therefore, worthy to be queen. Her relationship to Mordecai is also clarified; she is his cousin as well as his adopted daughter. She continues her wise course of action; allowed to take whatever she wants with her to the king, she takes only what Hegai advises. Presumably Hegai, the "King's Eunuch," knows what the king prefers. Again, there is no negative judgment on the part of the author; both he and the reader are rooting for Esther to win the contest and become queen. It is clear that she should, since she "wins favor in the eyes of all who see her."

Esther is taken to the king in the seventh year of his reign. Four years have elapsed since the downfall of Vashti. Now events move quickly, and the parallelism of Esther's rise and Vashti's fall is obvious. The king "loves" (יאהב *ye'ĕhab*; the NRSV is correct; the NIV's "was attracted to" is too weak) Esther, whereas at Vashti his "anger burned"; Esther wins (active once again) his devotion, and he sets the royal crown on her head (the crown Vashti refused to wear) and makes her queen "instead of Vashti." Finally, he gives a banquet in honor of Esther, which contrasts with the second and third banquets in chap. 1. Vashti fell at a banquet; Esther completes her rise at a banquet. The banquet motif here signals the satisfactory closure of an episode.

In v. 18 the king shows his generosity to the entire empire by remitting their taxes (or possibly forced labor), as he did at the beginning of chap.

78. See, e.g., Paton, *Esther.*

79. Carey A. Moore, *Esther,* AB 7B (Garden City, N.Y.: Doubleday, 1971) 28.

80. For a different view of the significance of the word *dāt*, see Kristin de Troyer, "An Oriental Beauty Parlour: An Analysis of Esther 2:8-18 in the Hebrew, the Septuagint and the Second Greek Text," in *A Feminist Companion to Esther, Judith and Susanna,* ed. Athalya Brenner (Sheffield: Sheffield Academic, 1995) 47-70.

81. See W. F. Albright, "The Lachish Cosmetic Burner and Esther 2:12," in Carey A. Moore, *Studies in the Book of Esther* (New York: Ktav, 1982) 361-68.

1 by entertaining them, once again forming an inclusio. The whole incident has been satisfactorily concluded; the vacancy created by the rebellious Vashti has been filled by the pliant and pleasing Esther, and the changeable Ahasuerus is once again content. However, two loose threads remain for the author to unravel: Esther's Jewishness remains undisclosed, and Mordecai's position at court, as well as the court's knowledge of his relationship to Esther, is indeterminate.

REFLECTIONS

1. This passage is troubling to the modern reader, and particularly troubling to women. Hundreds of young girls are rounded up, their wishes not consulted or even considered, placed in a strange locale away from their family and friends; subjected, willingly or unwillingly, to a series of "treatments"; and then given one night for the sexual performance of their life, all for the pleasure of one man! What makes it even worse is that the text, contrary to expectations, does not adopt a condemnatory attitude, but rather accepts the process as part of the status quo. In fact, the heroine (whose place in Scripture would seem to imply that she should be a role model) is applauded for her success in the process and her eventual triumph in the contest. It is difficult not to take the position of L. B. Paton, who remarked: "Esther, for the chance of winning wealth and power, takes her place in the herd of maidens who become concubines of the king. . . . Morally Esther falls far below the general level of the Old Testament."[82] However, such a dismissal of Esther's character would be doing the book a disservice. Even though we, as inheritors of Western culture, may decry the moral standards of an earlier era and, as inhabitants of the late twentieth century, deplore that era's treatment of women, it is unfair to judge the entire value of the biblical book by those standards. After all, the text of the Hebrew Bible is littered with stories most Christians and Jews consider of dubious morality (e.g., the story of Lot's daughters, Gen 19:30-38; the rape of the women of Jabesh-Gilead and Shiloh, Judges 21), and we do not discard them. Esther's actions must be judged within the social and cultural parameters of her story, and within those parameters she acts prudently and wisely, thereby protecting herself, her kinsman, and, ultimately, her people.

2. Another theme that will be followed throughout this commentary is raised in this passage: Jewish identity, assimilation, and persecution. Esther's Jewish identity is clearly derived from her ethnicity, and not from her practice, since she appears to be fully assimilated to a Gentile life-style (in spite of the efforts of the Septuagint and the rabbis). Mordecai, while identified as a Jew, also betrays no hint of Jewish practice. His Jewish identity does not seem to have stood in the way of his court position or of Esther's becoming queen. Rather, each seems to have followed the advice of Jeremiah: "Thus says the LORD of hosts, the God of Israel, to all the exiles whom I have sent into exile from Jerusalem to Babylon: Build houses and live in them; plant gardens and eat what they produce. . . . Seek the welfare of the city where I have sent you into exile, and pray to the LORD on its behalf, for in its welfare you will find your welfare" (Jer 29:4-5, 7 NRSV). Jews have wrestled for centuries with the problem of assimilation vs. maintaining their Jewish identity, and Christians have leveled charges of exclusivism and pride against them. In the Holocaust, the most highly assimilated Jewish community in history, the German Jews, was destroyed, a victim of Christian anti-Semitism and indifference. The assimilation of the German Jews did not save them. The United States is home to the largest, and now most assimilated, community of Jews in the diaspora, yet troubling indications of anti-Semitism surface in America as well. Esther 2:10 may likewise indicate that, no matter how much one assimilates, it may be dangerous to be openly Jewish in the Persian court. Jewish experience has not changed significantly in 2,500 years.

82. Paton, *Esther*, 96.

ESTHER 2:19-23, MORDECAI DISCOVERS THE EUNUCHS' PLOT

NIV

[19]When the virgins were assembled a second time, Mordecai was sitting at the king's gate. [20]But Esther had kept secret her family background and nationality just as Mordecai had told her to do, for she continued to follow Mordecai's instructions as she had done when he was bringing her up.

[21]During the time Mordecai was sitting at the king's gate, Bigthana[a] and Teresh, two of the king's officers who guarded the doorway, became angry and conspired to assassinate King Xerxes. [22]But Mordecai found out about the plot and told Queen Esther, who in turn reported it to the king, giving credit to Mordecai. [23]And when the report was investigated and found to be true, the two officials were hanged on a gallows.[b] All this was recorded in the book of the annals in the presence of the king.

[a]*21* Hebrew *Bigthan,* a variant of *Bigthana* [b]*23* Or *were hung* (or *impaled*) *on poles;* similarly elsewhere in Esther

NRSV

19When the virgins were being gathered together,[a] Mordecai was sitting at the king's gate. [20]Now Esther had not revealed her kindred or her people, as Mordecai had charged her; for Esther obeyed Mordecai just as when she was brought up by him. [21]In those days, while Mordecai was sitting at the king's gate, Bigthan and Teresh, two of the king's eunuchs, who guarded the threshold, became angry and conspired to assassinate[b] King Ahasuerus. [22]But the matter came to the knowledge of Mordecai, and he told it to Queen Esther, and Esther told the king in the name of Mordecai. [23]When the affair was investigated and found to be so, both the men were hanged on the gallows. It was recorded in the book of the annals in the presence of the king.

[a] Heb adds *a second time* [b] Heb *to lay hands on*

COMMENTARY

Verse 19 opens with what Paton has termed a *crux interpretum,* a second gathering of the maidens.[83] The phrase is awkward in Hebrew, beginning with an infinitive construct after a series of converted imperfects. It makes no sense in the story line—since Esther has been made queen, there is no need for a second collection of young women. The LXX (and Josephus) solves the problem by omitting the phrase. The NRSV translation attempts to smooth over the difficulty by omitting the word שֵׁנִית (*šēnît,* "a second time"), while the NIV includes it. Many explanations have been put forward to solve the problem, among them that the king, to arouse Esther's jealousy, demanded new concubines or that the courtiers, seeking to supplant Esther, introduced the king to new women. Fox opts for the explanation that the gathering refers to the second harem, the harem of the concubines mentioned in 2:14, and views the word בתולות (*bĕtûlôt,* "virgins" or "young maidens") as a slip of the authorial tongue. Moore emends "second" (*šēnît*) to "various" (שׁנות *šōnôt*) and claims it refers to the general time period, while Clines suggests that *šēnît* could mean "further" or "secondly," referring to a second event that occurred at the time of the gathering of the maidens—namely, the eunuchs' plot.[84] Cazelles, taking a literary-critical approach, views the phrase as a leftover fragment indicating two original sources.[85] Clines's explanation seems the most satisfactory, since it does not involve emenda-

83. Ibid., 186.

84. Fox, *Character and Ideology in the Book of Esther,* 38; Moore, *Esther,* 29-30; and D. J. A. Clines, *The Esther Scroll: The Story of the Story,* JSOTSup 30 (Sheffield: JSOT, 1984) 291. For a summary of the various views, see Paton, *Esther,* 186.

85. Henri Cazelles, "Note sur la composition du rouleau d'Esther," in *Lex tua veritas. Festschrift für Hubert Junker,* ed. H. Gross and F. Mussner (Trier: Paulinus Verlag, 1961) 26.

tion, but the fact remains that in the present form of the book the phrase makes no sense.

The text passes on to Mordecai, described as "sitting in the king's gate"; in other words, he is a royal courtier (שׁער [*šaʿar*, "gate"] refers to the royal court in its entirety; the LXX specifically states that Mordecai "served in the king's court").[86] However, rather than proceeding with the narrative, v. 20 inserts another parenthetical comment—that Esther had still not revealed her Jewishness or her kinsfolk, because she was obedient to Mordecai "as when he brought her up." Two things should be noticed. One, although the Targums and the LXX insist that Esther obeyed Jewish law while in the palace, this would have been impossible for her to do while continuing to conceal her ethnic identity. Second, she places her first loyalty with her adopted father rather than with her husband, thus disobeying the usual rules of patrilocal kinship, but obeying the demands of ethnic loyalty.[87] Therefore, Esther and Mordecai, rather than Esther and the king, continue to be the story's primary focus of partnership and loyalty.

Two eunuchs, Bigthan and Teresh, plot to overthrow the king (v. 21), with whom they are angry. The reason for their anger is not given and is not important for the story; but these types of court intrigues were not unusual in Achaemenid Persia. Xerxes and Artaxerxes II Ochus, for instance, were each killed in palace coups. This plot, however, is foiled by Mordecai, who reports it to Esther, who reports it to the king. This activity foreshadows their later partnership to foil Haman's genocidal scheme. The Hebrew text does not report how Mordecai learns of the plot; according to the LXX's treatment of the incident in Add. A, he overhears it (see the Commentary on Add. A). Mordecai seems to have easy access to Esther, who in turn, at the beginning of her marriage, has easy access to the king. Esther informs the king in Mordecai's name, but since her relationship to Mordecai is undisclosed, her action creates a minor anomaly. Finally, the matter is investigated (a sharp contrast to the king's usually impetuous procedure), punishments are meted out ("hanged on the gallows" may refer to impaling on a stake rather than hanging),[88] and Mordecai's name is duly recorded in the royal annals. It is very clear, however, that Mordecai is not rewarded for his good deed, a loose thread the author will exploit later. This is negligence on the king's part; Herodotus reports that the Persian monarchs were very diligent in handing out rewards, reporting the existence of a list of the "King's Benefactors" in the royal archives.[89] The entire incident is missing from the AT, probably to smooth out the previous reporting of the plot of the eunuchs in Addition A.[90]

Chapters 1–2 constitute a prelude to the main plot, about to begin in chapter 3. Chapter 1 safely removed the former queen Vashti from the scene and introduced the impetuous, mercurial character of Ahasuerus. Chapter 2 introduced the Jewish heroine and hero, Esther and Mordecai; made Esther queen; installed Esther in the palace and Mordecai in the court; and indebted the king to Mordecai. Now, with all the characters in place and the setting prepared, the main narrative is about to begin.

86. See Fox, *Character and Ideology in the Book of Esther,* 38-39, for further references.

87. This type of ethnic loyalty is usually rewarded in the biblical text. See the story of Jael, who is never explicitly identified as an Israelite, in Judges 4. A counterexample is Ruth, who is praised for abandoning her people, the Moabites, and throwing in her lot with Israel.

88. Herodotus 3.125, 159; 4.43.

89. Ibid., 3.139-41.

90. Fox, *Character and Ideology in the Book of Esther,* 40. Clines, *The Esther Scroll,* 105, points out that this incident establishes Mordecai's loyalty before his conflict with Haman. Jon D. Levenson, *Esther,* OTL (Louisville: Westminster/John Knox, 1997) 65, brings to light the connections between this incident and the Joseph story.

REFLECTIONS

Mordecai appears in this vignette as a righteous man performing a good deed without the thought of reward. Even after the rebels are executed, Mordecai does not seem to expect a reward, nor does Esther request one for him. They simply do what is right and then go on about their business. This behavior will prove a sharp contrast to the later actions of Haman, who wants the reward without having done the good deed (6:6-9). The author, without being explicit, presents Mordecai and Esther to the reader as models of wise and righteous conduct.

ESTHER 3:1-15

HAMAN'S PLOT TO DESTROY THE JEWS

OVERVIEW

This section introduces the main antagonist and the main conflict. Haman the Agagite is "the enemy of the Jews," and his scheme is no less than genocide. From here the plot moves quickly to its denouement.

ESTHER 3:1-6, CONFLICT BETWEEN MORDECAI AND HAMAN

NIV

3 After these events, King Xerxes honored
Haman son of Hammedatha, the Agagite,
elevating him and giving him a seat of honor
higher than that of all the other nobles. 2All the
royal officials at the king's gate knelt down and
paid honor to Haman, for the king had commanded this concerning him. But Mordecai would
not kneel down or pay him honor.
3Then the royal officials at the king's gate asked
Mordecai, "Why do you disobey the king's command?" 4Day after day they spoke to him but he
refused to comply. Therefore they told Haman
about it to see whether Mordecai's behavior
would be tolerated, for he had told them he was
a Jew.
5When Haman saw that Mordecai would not
kneel down or pay him honor, he was enraged.
6Yet having learned who Mordecai's people were,
he scorned the idea of killing only Mordecai.
Instead Haman looked for a way to destroy all
Mordecai's people, the Jews, throughout the
whole kingdom of Xerxes.

NRSV

3 After these things King Ahasuerus promoted Haman son of Hammedatha the
Agagite, and advanced him and set his seat above
all the officials who were with him. 2And all the
king's servants who were at the king's gate bowed
down and did obeisance to Haman; for the king
had so commanded concerning him. But Mordecai did not bow down or do obeisance. 3Then the
king's servants who were at the king's gate said
to Mordecai, "Why do you disobey the king's
command?" 4When they spoke to him day after
day and he would not listen to them, they told
Haman, in order to see whether Mordecai's words
would avail; for he had told them that he was a
Jew. 5When Haman saw that Mordecai did not
bow down or do obeisance to him, Haman was
infuriated. 6But he thought it beneath him to lay
hands on Mordecai alone. So, having been told
who Mordecai's people were, Haman plotted to
destroy all the Jews, the people of Mordecai,
throughout the whole kingdom of Ahasuerus.

COMMENTARY

Verse 1 introduces the fourth main character, Haman the Agagite. An uncertain amount of time has passed; but if the events in these verses are followed quickly by the action in vv. 7-11, then we are now in the twelfth year of Ahasuerus's reign, and five years have passed since Esther became queen. The king has a new favorite, whom he has promoted to the top of the palace hierarchy. Irony comes into play again: Mordecai, the king's benefactor, is unrewarded, while Haman, who has, as far as we know, done nothing, is rewarded with the highest office in the land. Haman, like Mordecai in 2:5, is given a genealogy; and that genealogy is an ominous one for the Jews. Haman is an Agagite, a descendant of Agag, king of the Amalekites, the hereditary enemies of the Jews (Exod 17:8-16; Num 24:20). Saul's encounter with Agag caused him to lose the kingship (1 Sam 15:8-33). Thus Haman, the descendant of Agag, and Mordecai, the kinsman of Saul, are natural enemies. In case the reader does not perceive the ominous implication of Haman's ancestry, the versions supply various substitutes for the term "Agagite," all pointing in the same dark direction. Josephus describes Haman as an Amalekite, and thus an enemy of the entire Jewish nation. And Deut 25:17-19 pronounces a curse on the Amalekites, demanding that they be totally destroyed by the Israelites. The LXX translates the term in two different ways, first by Βουγαῖον (*Bougaion*), probably a corruption of האגגי (*hā'ăgāgî*), but also possibly related to the Persian *Bagohi*, rendered by Josephus as *Bagoses*, a name or title of a notorious Persian general in Jerusalem who desecrated the Temple.[91] The second term, "Macedonian," is unrelated to Agagite, but refers to Alexander the Great and his successors, who at various times during the Hellenistic period (when the LXX was translated; see Commentary on Addition F 11) oppressed the Jews. The AT also uses "Macedonian," but MSS 93a corrupts "Agagite" to "Gogite," thereby creating an allusion to Israel's "enemy from the north" in Ezekiel 38–39. What all these names and titles indicate is that no good can come to the Jews from Haman's promotion.

In fact, trouble starts immediately. The king orders that all members of the court bow down before Haman—in other words, perform the ritual of proskynesis. Mordecai refuses to obey this ruling.

Mordecai's refusal to bow to Haman, like Vashti's refusal to appear before the king, is mysterious. Is it because he is Jewish? Some commentators have taken the final clause of v. 4, "for he had told them that he was a Jew," as referring to Mordecai's refusal to bow.[92] However, that clause comes too late in the grammatical structure to refer to Mordecai's refusal, and it makes no sense historically. Jews in similar situations bowed to their superiors (see, e.g., the sons of Jacob to Joseph, Gen 42:6), and there is no (Jewish) law against it. Further, Mordecai could not have functioned as a royal courtier had he made a general refusal to bow. Therefore, he must be refusing to bow to Haman in particular. The versions supply various reasons for this refusal: The LXX (Add. C 7) claims that Haman demanded *divine* honors, which Mordecai would not render.[93] The Targum states that Haman wore an idol pinned to his breast; if Mordecai bowed down to him, he would be guilty of idolatry. Various commentators have also speculated concerning the reason: Paton puts it down to Mordecai's arrogance and petty self-seeking,[94] but Fox points out that this interpretation does not correspond to Mordecai's portrayal elsewhere as a wise courtier.[95] However, it should be noted that Mordecai's actions are not those of a wise courtier; rather, he and his people are put in grave danger, from which they must be extricated by Esther. Camp notes, "Mordecai himself is depicted as proud and somewhat fanatical, refusing to bow before Haman, the king's favorite."[96] Thus Mordecai's refusal to bow before Haman, which sets in motion the main plot of the story, is left unexplained.[97]

Mordecai's fellow servants question him concerning his refusal and, unable to receive a satis-

91. Josephus *Antiquities of the Jews* 11.297. See Sidnie A. White, "Bagoas," in *Anchor Bible Dictionary*, 6 vols., ed. D. N. Freedman (New York: Doubleday, 1992) 1:567. Karen H. Jobes, *The Alpha-Text of Esther: Its Character and Relationship to the Masoretic Text*, SBLDS 153 (Atlanta: Scholars Press, 1996) 125, suggests a "phonetic wordplay" between the terms *bougaios* and *bagoas*. See also the appearance of the name "Bagoshe" (Aramaic) in *4QTales of the Persian Court*. See Sidnie White Crawford, "Has Esther Been Found at Qumran? 4QProto-Esther and the Esther Corpus," *RQ* 17 (1996) 307-25.

92. E.g., Lewis B. Paton, *Esther*, ICC (Edinburgh: T. & T. Clark, 1908) 196.

93. *Tar.* 1.

94. Paton, *Esther*, 213.

95. Michael V. Fox, *Character and Ideology in the Book of Esther: Studies in Biblical Personalities* (Columbia: University of South Carolina Press, 1991) 43.

96. Claudia Camp, "The Three Faces of Esther: Traditional Woman, Royal Diplomat, Authenticator of Tradition," *Academy* 38 (1982) 20.

97. See Sidnie White, "Esther: A Feminine Model for Jewish Diaspora," in *Gender and Difference in Ancient Israel*, ed. Peggy L. Day (Minneapolis: Fortress, 1989) 169.

factory answer, finally report to Haman, "because he [Mordecai] had informed them that he was a Jew." The author implies that the other servants see this as a contest of wills between Haman the Agagite and Mordecai the Jew, and they pit the two against each other to see who will prevail. Again, the motive for their behavior is not clear. Are they hostile to Mordecai for reporting the eunuchs' plot or because he is a Jew? The answer is not clear, but the conflict has suddenly become more than personal.

Haman evidently had not noticed Mordecai's insult until then, but now that it has been brought to his attention, he is furious. The last time the word for "anger" (חמה *ḥēmâ*) appeared in the text, it referred to the king, and the consequence was the banishment of Vashti (1:12). Haman's fury does not bode well for Mordecai. However, personal revenge is not enough for Haman. After finding out Mordecai's ethnicity (which is not a secret, unlike Esther's), Haman decides to destroy all the Jews in the entire empire (which, according to 1:1, encompasses the then-known world). This implied racial hostility is brought out by the versions; as Josephus states, "for he naturally hated the Jews, because his own race, the Amalekites, had been destroyed by them."[98] Dommershausen notes that Haman's desire to wipe out all the Jews is a reversal of the holy war command in 1 Sam 15:3, thereby strengthening the argument that Haman is motivated by racial hostility.[99]

98. Josephus *Antiquities of the Jews* 11.212.

99. Werner Dommershausen, *Die Estherrolle,* SBM 6 (Stuttgart: Katholisches Bibelwerk, 1968) 62.

REFLECTIONS

The theme of racial hostility is emphasized in this chapter, particularly by the epithets given to the main characters: Agagite and Jew. This racial hostility allows a personal quarrel to become a national crisis. Haman seems to feel that Mordecai's insult is motivated by his Jewishness. He resolves, therefore, to wipe out the entire Jewish people, evidently assuming that all Jews would behave in a similar fashion. Generalizations such as these have fueled fires of ethnic and racial conflict in many parts of the world throughout history. The conflict in South Africa in the twentieth century serves as a good example of such thinking. The system of apartheid introduced in South Africa beginning in 1913 was based solely on race; the governing assumption was that persons of darker complexions were inferior to those of lighter ones. Archbishop Desmond Tutu denounced the evil of apartheid with these words:

> The Bible declares right at the beginning that human beings are created in the image and likeness of God. I showed why this fact endows each person with a unique and infinite value, a person whose very hairs are numbered. And what makes any human being valuable therefore is not any biological characteristic. No, it is the fact that he or she is created in the image of and likeness of God. Apartheid exalts a biological quality, which is a total irrelevancy, to the status of what determines the value, the worth of a human being. Why should skin color or race be any more useful as a criterion than, say, the size of one's nose? What has the size of my nose to do with whether I am intelligent? It has no more to do with my worth as a human being than the color of my eyes.[100]

Tutu explicitly states what the author of Esther implies: The oppression of people based on race or ethnic group is evil. Races and ethnic groups exist. But there is no reason, as we will see by the end of the book of Esther, that they cannot *co*exist peacefully and equitably.

100. Desmond Tutu, *The Rainbow People of God* (New York: Doubleday, 1994) 64.

ESTHER 3:7-11, HAMAN'S PLOT

NIV

[7]In the twelfth year of King Xerxes, in the first month, the month of Nisan, they cast the *pur* (that is, the lot) in the presence of Haman to select a day and month. And the lot fell on[a] the twelfth month, the month of Adar.

[8]Then Haman said to King Xerxes, "There is a certain people dispersed and scattered among the peoples in all the provinces of your kingdom whose customs are different from those of all other people and who do not obey the king's laws; it is not in the king's best interest to tolerate them. [9]If it pleases the king, let a decree be issued to destroy them, and I will put ten thousand talents[b] of silver into the royal treasury for the men who carry out this business."

[10]So the king took his signet ring from his finger and gave it to Haman son of Hammedatha, the Agagite, the enemy of the Jews. [11]"Keep the money," the king said to Haman, "and do with the people as you please."

[a]7 Septuagint; Hebrew does not have *And the lot fell on.* [b]9 That is, about 375 tons (about 345 metric tons)

NRSV

7In the first month, which is the month of
Nisan, in the twelfth year of King Ahasuerus, they
cast Pur—which means "the lot"—before Haman
for the day and for the month, and the lot fell on
the thirteenth day[a] of the twelfth month, which
is the month of Adar. [8]Then Haman said to King
Ahasuerus, "There is a certain people scattered
and separated among the peoples in all the provinces of your kingdom; their laws are different
from those of every other people, and they do not
keep the king's laws, so that it is not appropriate
for the king to tolerate them. [9]If it pleases the
king, let a decree be issued for their destruction,
and I will pay ten thousand talents of silver into
the hands of those who have charge of the king's
business, so that they may put it into the king's
treasuries." [10]So the king took his signet ring
from his hand and gave it to Haman son of
Hammedatha the Agagite, the enemy of the Jews.
[11]The king said to Haman, "The money is given
to you, and the people as well, to do with them
as it seems good to you."

[a] Cn Compare Gk and verse 13 below: Heb *the twelfth month*

COMMENTARY

3:7. This verse presents an explanation for the origin of the Festival of Purim, the ostensible reason for the writing of the book of Esther and the reason for its inclusion in the canon. The scene takes place in the month of Nisan, an ironic gesture on the part of the author, for Nisan (a Babylonian month name; the old Hebrew equivalent is אביב [*'ābîb*]) is the month of the Passover and the exodus, the festival of salvation for the Jews (Deut 16:1-8). Here, however, it foreshadows not salvation but destruction, for Haman is having פור (*pûr*) cast for him, evidently by Persian diviners. *Pûr* is a borrowing from Old Babylonian *pūrū,* meaning "stone" or "lot," which appears to refer to the stones thrown to determine an auspicious day. These lots were used in the ancient world to determine the will of the gods; the high priest in Israel cast Urim and Thummim to determine God's will (e.g., Exod 28:30; Num 27:21; 1 Sam 14:41). Haman is trying to determine a day and a month—but for what? The Hebrew is almost untranslatable, but the LXX attempts to make sense of it by supplying "so as to destroy the race of Mordecai" (both the NRSV and the NIV are heavily reliant on the LXX). It is also possible that Haman is trying to ascertain a lucky day to go to the king with his request. However, the text in later chapters seems to assume that Haman is determining an auspicious day to slaughter the Jews, for the month of Adar, where the lot falls, is the date set to carry out the massacre (the LXX supplies "the thirteenth day"). This verse, as garbled as it is, appears intrusive in its context and may be a later addition, intended to tie the Festival of Purim more firmly to the story of Mordecai and Haman.[101]

3:8-10. Verse 8 finds Haman before the king. Haman lays out his charge, constructing a story made up of truths, half-truths, and outright lies.[102] He says that Jews are "scattered" and "separated" among all the peoples of the empire. That is true, according to contemporary sources. Jews lived throughout the Persian Empire, but the Persian Empire historically was extremely tolerant of multiethnic diversity.[103] It is a half-truth that their laws are different from those of every other people, for the Jews keep the Torah, their own special set of commandments—but they also obey the laws of whatever country they are in. Finally, it is a lie that they do not keep the king's law; this is witnessed by the behavior of Esther and Mordecai, who scrupulously obey the Persian law, while not paying particular attention, at least on Esther's part, to Jewish law. Haman offers no proof for his accusations, which, as Fox points out, are the epitome of what would later be recognized as anti-Semitic rhetoric.[104] Nor does Ahasuerus ask for any. The king colludes with Haman's policy of "don't ask, don't tell." If he knows it is the Jews whom Haman wishes to destroy, he may recoil from killing people he knows, such as Mordecai the Jew, "who sits in the king's gate."[105] It is easier not to know, especially when Haman follows up his request for a death warrant with a huge bribe. Ten thousand talents is an enormous sum, probably the equivalent of 375 tons of silver; the annual income of the Persian king was only 14,560 talents.[106] Notice Haman's rhetorical skill in v. 9 in employing a passive construction—"let a decree be used"—rather than an active one—"let the king issue." In this way, Ahasuerus does not have to take responsibility for a genocide in his empire, and he will become substantially richer. The king has so far not responded to Haman, no questions, no protest. In v. 10 he does respond, with an action: He gives his signet ring, the symbol of royal authority, to Haman. This act gives Haman the power to do whatever he wants (cf. Gen 41:42, where Pharaoh gives his signet ring to Joseph). Haman is identified here for the first time as "the enemy of the Jews." What was implied by his ancestry is made clear by his actions: He is the enemy who will actively work for Jewish destruction in the midst of Gentile indifference and passivity, symbolized by the king.

3:11. Ahasuerus speaks for the first time. The NRSV gives an exact translation of a cryptic phrase in Hebrew: "the money is given to you." Does the king give the money back to Haman, thereby exonerating himself from the guilt of accepting a bribe? The NIV (following the LXX) certainly accepts that understanding: "keep the money." Moore translates, "Well, it's your money"—in other words, do with it as you will.[107] It seems unlikely that the king turned down the money; in 4:7 Mordecai tells Esther how much Haman paid for the destruction of the Jews, implying that the king acepted it. In 7:4, Esther declares that the Jews have been "sold" into destruction. Ahasuerus certainly has no qualms about handing this unknown people over to Haman; once again he has not asked about their identity or proof of their crimes. The king, therefore, is not an anti-Semite, as is Haman, but is simply thoughtless and lazy, characteristics that are just as dangerous to the Jews as is Haman's evil. Clines has noted a parallel between this episode and the Vashti episode: Both are cases of disobedience against a royal edict, and the royal advisers, Memucan/Haman, respond in a way completely out of proportion to the offense, while the king unquestioningly acquiesces to their advice.[108]

101. See Carey A. Moore, *Esther,* AB 7B (Garden City, N.Y.: Doubleday, 1971) 37; Fox, *Character and Ideology in the Book of Esther,* 47. However, Hans Bardtke, *Das Buch Esther, Kommentar zum Alten Testament* (Gütersloh: Mohn, 1963) 243-44, disagrees.

102. Fox, *Character and Ideology in the Book of Esther,* 47-48.

103. See, e.g., the Murashu archives from the fifth century BCE, which indicate that Jews owned land in the neighborhood of Nippur, while a Jewish garrison existed on the Egyptian island of Elephantine, also in the fifth century. The term "Judean" seems to be an ethnic, rather than a religious, designation at Elephantine. See M. Dandamayev, "Babylonia in the Persian Age," and Morton Smith, "Jewish Life in the Persian Period," in *The Cambridge History of Judaism,* Introduction: *The Persian Period,* ed. W. D. Davies and L. Finkelstein (Cambridge: Cambridge University Press, 1984).

104. Fox, *Character and Ideology in the Book of Esther,* 47.

105. Ibid., 48.

106. Moore, *Esther,* 38.

107. Ibid., 40.

108. David J. A. Clines, *Ezra, Nehemiah, Esther,* NCBC (Grand Rapids: Eerdmans, 1984) 295.

REFLECTIONS

The charges that Haman levels against the Jews are the same type of charges leveled against the Jews from the beginning of the diaspora until today. Difference is seen as either mysterious and thus dangerous to the majority culture, or as hostile to the host culture. Josephus, in first-century Rome, had to defend the Jews against the charge of *amixia,* or "non-mingling," in his work *Against Apion.* As early as 38 CE, there were anti-Jewish riots in Alexandria, a center of Hellenistic learning and culture. The history of Christianity is stained with anti-Semitism. The expulsion of Jews from England in 1290 and from Spain in 1492 are only two examples. Because the Jews are perceived as different from the Gentile (whether Christian or not) culture in which they live, they often have become the target of bigotry from the majority population. This bigotry can take the form of active hostility, like that of Haman, or passive indifference, like that of Ahasuerus. Most people choose the path of indifference, but the result is the same: the destruction of innocent human beings.

ESTHER 3:12-15, HAMAN'S PLOT IS CARRIED OUT

NIV

12Then on the thirteenth day of the first month the royal secretaries were summoned. They wrote out in the script of each province and in the language of each people all Haman's orders to the king's satraps, the governors of the various provinces and the nobles of the various peoples. These were written in the name of King Xerxes himself and sealed with his own ring. 13Dispatches were sent by couriers to all the king's provinces with the order to destroy, kill and annihilate all the Jews—young and old, women and little children—on a single day, the thirteenth day of the twelfth month, the month of Adar, and to plunder their goods. 14A copy of the text of the edict was to be issued as law in every province and made known to the people of every nationality so they would be ready for that day.

15Spurred on by the king's command, the couriers went out, and the edict was issued in the citadel of Susa. The king and Haman sat down to drink, but the city of Susa was bewildered.

NRSV

12Then the king's secretaries were summoned on the thirteenth day of the first month, and an edict, according to all that Haman commanded, was written to the king's satraps and to the governors over all the provinces and to the officials of all the peoples, to every province in its own script and every people in its own language; it was written in the name of King Ahasuerus and sealed with the king's ring. 13Letters were sent by couriers to all the king's provinces, giving orders to destroy, to kill, and to annihilate all Jews, young and old, women and children, in one day, the thirteenth day of the twelfth month, which is the month of Adar, and to plunder their goods. 14A copy of the document was to be issued as a decree in every province by proclamation, calling on all the peoples to be ready for that day. 15The couriers went quickly by order of the king, and the decree was issued in the citadel of Susa. The king and Haman sat down to drink; but the city of Susa was thrown into confusion.

COMMENTARY

In this section, Haman sets the official wheels of the Persian Empire in motion to carry out his plot. The scribes of the king, official court functionaries, are called together. Again, we glimpse the vast bureaucracy of the Persian Empire, which must be opposed by two small individuals. To emphasize the official nature of what is being done, the author gives the date, the thirteenth of the first month, Nisan. This date is not accidental: Thirteen is an unlucky number in both Babylonian and Persian lore, while in the Jewish calendar, the fourteenth day of Nisan begins the Passover. Salvation minus one day equals destruction.[109] The language of v. 12 emphasizes that this is an edict of the king; it is written in the name of Ahasuerus and sealed with his signet ring (which he has given to Haman). The edict is sent to the satraps (a Persian loan word; satrapies were the largest geographical entities within the Persian Empire, which never had more than thirty-one);[110] the governors, who ruled over provinces and cities (e.g., Tattenai, the governor of the province "Beyond the River" in Ezra 5:3, 6; 6:6, 13); and the princes, who are leaders of ethnic groups (e.g., Sheshbazzar, the "prince of Judah" in Ezra 1:8). It is sent to every province, every people in their own language. Historically, Persian officialdom functioned in several languages: Persian, Aramaic, and Akkadian.[111] However, they did not cater to every small language pocket in the empire (cf. Ezra 6:2-5, where the decree of Cyrus is written in Aramaic, not Hebrew). Haman appears to be saturating the empire with his decree, another case of the author's ironic hyperbole.

Verse 13 gives the content of the decree sent throughout the empire by the efficient Persian postal system. The Hebrew piles up words of destruction: "to destroy," "to slay," "to annihilate." All Jews are to be destroyed—men, women, children, young, old—no one is exempt. And then, the final indignity: Their goods are to be plundered. This is both a foreshadowing of events to come and a reminiscence of the paradigmatic salvific event, the exodus. At the time of the exodus, when the Jews were saved, they took the goods of the Egyptians, who gave them voluntarily in order to be saved from destruction (Exod 12:33-36). The destruction is to take place on one day, the thirteenth of Adar, which is almost a year away. It is puzzling within the story that Haman waits a whole year to destroy the Jews. However, if the date of Purim was fixed and originally separate from the Esther story (see Introduction), and if the author wished to retain the allusion to the exodus by setting his story in the month of Nisan, then the somewhat artificial gap may be explained. Verse 14, which calls on everyone to be ready, presumes that people would be willing, even eager, to destroy the Jews. The riders of the postal system "hasten" out (cf. chap. 1, where the decree concerning Vashti is sent, but without the same urgency), and the decree is published in the citadel of Susa. The decree is called a דת (*dāt*) as in 1:15, which again emphasizes its royal, official character. This is not simply a desire of Haman's but the law of the land. Once again, as in chap. 1, a personal slight has been interpreted as a threat to the stability of the ruling regime and is turned into an empire-wide crisis. This time, however, it is not humorous, but deadly serious.[112]

The reactions of three groups—the king, Haman, and the people of Susa—are contrasted at the end of v. 15: The king and Haman sit down to a feast (banquet #5, see *Fig.* 9, "The Banquets in Esther," 857), but the city (as opposed to the citadel) of Susa "was confused." Haman is triumphant, and the king is indifferent; so far the Gentiles present no hope for the Jews. However, the common inhabitants of Susa are confused; one can assume that they do not understand the reason for the decree and may be reluctant to carry it out. There is hope for the Jews here. This accords with the book of Esther's generally more positive portrayal of Gentiles than in later books,

109. The practice of using significant numbers was common in the ancient world; e.g., the famous number 666 in Rev 13:18 signifies, among other things, the threefold lack of perfection (seven being a perfect number).

110. A. T. Olmstead, *The History of the Persian Empire* (Chicago: University of Chicago Press, 1948) 59.

111. E.g., the Behistun Inscription, erected by Xerxes' father, Darius, which celebrates, in Perisan, Elamite, and Akkadian, Darius's victory over the magi at the beginning of his reign. This inscription was copied into Aramaic at Elephantine, for the use of the Jewish mercenaries there. See ibid. 116-18.

112. See Fox, *Character and Ideology in the Book of Esther,* 56.

such as 3 Maccabees. Gentiles as a whole are not bent on destruction of the Jews, although individuals may be, and thus vigilance is always necessary.

REFLECTIONS

1. The responses of the three groups to the edict of destruction—triumph, indifference, and bewilderment—mirror the reactions of people today to acts of genocide throughout the world: triumph on the part of the perpetrators; indifference by most people not directly affected; and bewilderment from people sensitive enough to be appalled by the violence but powerless to do anything about it. In the book of Esther, all three reactions lead to the same result: destruction for the victims. Action is called for—action to save—but from whence the action will come is unclear.

2. The theme of power returns: Haman now has power. Unlike the foolish Ahasuerus, who is unable to wield the power he supposedly has, Haman proves quite competent in using it. Although power is now being used, it is not being used wisely. The biblical tradition approves of power only when it is used to govern well; such was Solomon's request in 1 Kings 29. Therefore, Haman's power, according to biblical norms, should not last long.

ESTHER 4:1-17

MORDECAI TURNS TO ESTHER

OVERVIEW

The focus of the story now turns to Esther and Mordecai. The fate of the Jews hangs on their courage and resourcefulness, especially that of Esther. It is striking that the author continues to avoid any mention of God, even in this moment of extreme danger for the Jewish people. It is righteous human action that must save the day.

ESTHER 4:1-3, MORDECAI'S REACTION TO HAMAN'S DECREE

NIV

4 When Mordecai learned of all that had
been done, he tore his clothes, put on
sackcloth and ashes, and went out into the city,
wailing loudly and bitterly. 2But he went only as
far as the king's gate, because no one clothed in
sackcloth was allowed to enter it. 3In every province to which the edict and order of the king
came, there was great mourning among the Jews,
with fasting, weeping and wailing. Many lay in
sackcloth and ashes.

NRSV

4 When Mordecai learned all that had been
done, Mordecai tore his clothes and put
on sackcloth and ashes, and went through the
city, wailing with a loud and bitter cry; 2he went
up to the entrance of the king's gate, for no one
might enter the king's gate clothed with sackcloth. 3In every province, wherever the king's
command and his decree came, there was great
mourning among the Jews, with fasting and weeping and lamenting, and most of them lay in
sackcloth and ashes.

COMMENTARY

The edict has been published in Susa, but Mordecai knows more; he knows *all* that Haman has done, as will be clear later in the chapter. How he knows this is not stated, any more than how he learned of the plot of the eunuchs in chap. 2. Mordecai's immediate response to the news of Haman's decree is shock and grief. He enacts the typical gestures of mourning: tearing his clothes (Gen 37:29, Reuben for Joseph); putting on sackcloth, a rough cloth made of some type of coarse material such as goat hair (Gen 37:34, Jacob for Joseph); putting ashes on his head (2 Sam 13:19, Tamar after her rape by Amnon); and weeping loudly and publicly (a function usually performed by women, but see 2 Sam 18:33, where David weeps over Absalom). The LXX adds the phrase "an innocent people is condemned to death!" All these gestures are usually reserved for mourning over the dead; it is as if Mordecai is mourning in advance over his own death and the deaths of his people. However, these gestures can also be efficacious in turning away divine wrath. For example, when the people of Nineveh hear God's pronouncement of doom from the mouth of Jonah, they tear their clothes and sit in sackcloth and ashes, for which gestures of repentance God forgives them (Jonah 3:6-9). However, the Ninevites also fast and pray, religious gestures that are not performed by Mordecai (although the Jews do fast in v. 3). This is in keeping with the rest of the book of Esther, from which obvious religious gestures are omitted (see Introduction). Therefore, Mordecai's actions seem more pessimistic, almost hopeless. One wonders whether Mordecai is simply grief-stricken or whether he might also be guilt-stricken, since it is his actions that have brought disaster upon the Jews. However, Mordecai nowhere in the Hebrew text expresses any guilt feelings (but see LXX Add. C, where he vigorously denies the unstated charge that his pride has caused destruction), nor does the author ever ascribe any guilt to him. Mordecai's gestures are mirrored by all the Jews throughout the empire when word of the decree reaches them. Again, the motivation for their actions is not stated. The obvious motive, petitioning God to act on their behalf, is glaringly absent.[113] In v. 2, Mordecai is unable to enter the palace dressed as a mourner, possibly because he is considered ritually unclean, although there is no extra-biblical evidence to support this custom in the Persian court. (See Reflections at 4:4-17.)

113. Several commentators have suggested that v. 3 should be placed immediately after 3:15 (see OL), but the verse serves a clear literary purpose here: By having the Jews echo the actions of Mordecai, the idea that Mordecai is the representative Jew in the story is emphasized.

ESTHER 4:4-17, DIALOGUE BETWEEN ESTHER AND MORDECAI

NIV

4When Esther's maids and eunuchs came and
told her about Mordecai, she was in great distress.
She sent clothes for him to put on instead of his
sackcloth, but he would not accept them. 5Then
Esther summoned Hathach, one of the king's
eunuchs assigned to attend her, and ordered him
to find out what was troubling Mordecai and why.
6So Hathach went out to Mordecai in the open
square of the city in front of the king's gate.
7Mordecai told him everything that had happened
to him, including the exact amount of money
Haman had promised to pay into the royal treasury for the destruction of the Jews. 8He also gave
him a copy of the text of the edict for their
annihilation, which had been published in Susa,
to show to Esther and explain it to her, and he
told him to urge her to go into the king's presence
to beg for mercy and plead with him for her
people.
9Hathach went back and reported to Esther
what Mordecai had said. 10Then she instructed
him to say to Mordecai, 11"All the king's officials
and the people of the royal provinces know that
for any man or woman who approaches the king
in the inner court without being summoned the

NRSV

4When Esther's maids and her eunuchs came
and told her, the queen was deeply distressed;
she sent garments to clothe Mordecai, so that he
might take off his sackcloth; but he would not
accept them. 5Then Esther called for Hathach, one
of the king's eunuchs, who had been appointed
to attend her, and ordered him to go to Mordecai
to learn what was happening and why. 6Hathach
went out to Mordecai in the open square of the
city in front of the king's gate, 7and Mordecai told
him all that had happened to him, and the exact
sum of money that Haman had promised to pay
into the king's treasuries for the destruction of the
Jews. 8Mordecai also gave him a copy of the
written decree issued in Susa for their destruction,
that he might show it to Esther, explain it to her,
and charge her to go to the king to make supplication to him and entreat him for her people.
9Hathach went and told Esther what Mordecai
had said. 10Then Esther spoke to Hathach and
gave him a message for Mordecai, saying, 11"All
the king's servants and the people of the king's
provinces know that if any man or woman goes
to the king inside the inner court without being
called, there is but one law—all alike are to be

NIV

king has but one law: that he be put to death. The only exception to this is for the king to extend the gold scepter to him and spare his life. But thirty days have passed since I was called to go to the king."

[12]When Esther's words were reported to Mordecai, [13]he sent back this answer: "Do not think that because you are in the king's house you alone of all the Jews will escape. [14]For if you remain silent at this time, relief and deliverance for the Jews will arise from another place, but you and your father's family will perish. And who knows but that you have come to royal position for such a time as this?"

[15]Then Esther sent this reply to Mordecai: [16]"Go, gather together all the Jews who are in Susa, and fast for me. Do not eat or drink for three days, night or day. I and my maids will fast as you do. When this is done, I will go to the king, even though it is against the law. And if I perish, I perish."

[17]So Mordecai went away and carried out all of Esther's instructions.

NRSV

put to death. Only if the king holds out the golden scepter to someone, may that person live. I myself have not been called to come in to the king for thirty days." [12]When they told Mordecai what Esther had said, [13]Mordecai told them to reply to Esther, "Do not think that in the king's palace you will escape any more than all the other Jews. [14]For if you keep silence at such a time as this, relief and deliverance will rise for the Jews from another quarter, but you and your father's family will perish. Who knows? Perhaps you have come to royal dignity for just such a time as this." [15]Then Esther said in reply to Mordecai, [16]"Go, gather all the Jews to be found in Susa, and hold a fast on my behalf, and neither eat nor drink for three days, night or day. I and my maids will also fast as you do. After that I will go to the king, though it is against the law; and if I perish, I perish." [17]Mordecai then went away and did everything as Esther had ordered him.

COMMENTARY

4:4-6. After a marked absence, Esther reappears in the narrative. For the first time, we have a scene in which she is the central character. Esther as queen has her own entourage of maids and eunuchs who keep her informed about the goings-on in the palace. They also know that Mordecai is her relative; therefore, they must know that she, like Mordecai, is a Jew, and yet her identity remains a secret from the king. The maids and eunuchs now tell her what Mordecai is doing. Her response comes in the form of an unusual Hebrew word, ותתחלחל (*wattitḥalḥal*, "and she writhed"), which occurs in this conjugation only here in Esther. In the active conjugations it means "to dance," but in the reflexive sense it means "to writhe in anguish" and can be connected with the pain of childbirth. For example, the verb occurs in poetic texts, one concerning Sarah as the mother of Israel (Isa 51:2) and one portraying Yahweh as "bringing forth" Israel in travail (Deut 32:18). Mordecai's behavior seems to cause Esther intense distress, and she rushes to respond to news of her cousin's state, but not by inquiring the reason for his actions, as one might expect. Instead, she sends him clothes in place of his sackcloth, which he refuses. Her motivation is open to question. Does she wish to relieve his distress?[114] If so, fresh clothes will not help, since Mordecai's outward appearance is merely a reflection of his inner turmoil. Does she wish to enable him to enter the palace, since those dressed in sackcloth are not allowed in? Or does she simply want him to stop his embarrassing behavior? Only after he refuses her solution does she send Hathach the eunuch to find out why Mordecai is behaving this way. Hathach, a new character, appears to be one of the palace eunuchs assigned to Esther. She seems to rely on his discretion, for the ensuing dialogue is intimate,

114. See Sidnie White, "Esther: A Feminine Model for Jewish Diaspora," in *Gender and Difference in Ancient Israel,* ed. Peggy L. Day (Minneapolis: Fortress, 1989) 169.

even confrontational, yet conducted entirely through a third party. No one, neither Esther nor her servants, seems yet to know about Haman's decree, even though it has been posted in the citadel of Susa (3:15). This indicates the kind of sheltered life Esther leads inside the harem and her dependence on the discretion and loyalty of her maids and eunuchs. The dialogue between Mordecai and Hathach takes place in the main city square (a place often associated with rites of mourning; see Jer 48:37-38), in full view of the public. Mordecai, it would seem, is not at this point concerned about discretion.

4:7-8. In these verses, Mordecai demonstrates that he knows the secrets of the palace. He knows the details of Haman's bargain with the king, including the bribe of ten thousand talents. He even has a copy of the decree, which he sends to Esther. Interestingly, the assumption is that both Esther and Mordecai are literate, a fact that might go unnoticed by the modern reader. Mordecai also has a plan of action, which he does not hesitate to communicate to Esther, since, as was stated in 2:20, "Esther obeyed Mordecai just as when she was brought up by him." He assumes that she will obey him now and repair promptly to the king to undo the threat Haman has posed to the Jews. In fact, in the LXX, Mordecai recalls Esther's obligation to him: "Remembering your humble station when you were supported by my hand. . . . Call upon the Lord, and speak to the king concerning us, and save us from death" (the LXX's mention of prayer is typical of that version's attempt to remedy the Hebrew's silence concerning God and religious practice).

4:9-17. The dialogue continues in this passage. Mordecai has assumed Esther's obedience to his command in v. 8, so her first response is something of a shock: She refuses to fall in with his plan. Esther has now been queen for five years and is steeped in palace etiquette (which she has already demonstrated by sending Mordecai clothes in v. 4), and her first response to Mordecai indicates that she cannot obey his command for reasons of palace protocol. *Everyone* (including presumably Mordecai) knows that to appear before the king unsummoned is to court instant death, and she has not been summoned for thirty days. Therefore, she implies, it is obvious that she cannot carry out Mordecai's plan. It is unclear whether Esther's statement is historically accurate. Josephus accepts it as such, but claims that it applies only to the royal family (to avert the danger of a palace coup?) and supplies the colorful note that men with axes surround the king on his throne to prevent unauthorized access.[115] However, Herodotus is ambivalent on the subject. According to him, in the tradition of the Medes, unannounced entry before the king was unlawful,[116] but a petitioner might send in a message and request an audience. Esther does not even suggest doing this, leading to the conclusion that this may be a convenient plot device on the part of the author. It is part of the irony of the book that the first queen, Vashti, is banished for refusing to appear before the king when summoned, while the second queen, Esther, is asked to risk death by appearing before the king unsummoned. Also, the fact that Esther has not been summoned for thirty days indicates that her influence is at a low ebb, and she has no reason to believe that her intervention would be efficacious.

Many biblical leaders—for example Moses (Exod 4:10-13), Barak (Judg 4:8), and Jeremiah (Jer 1:6), all male—attempted to excuse themselves when called upon for drastic action on behalf of the Jews.[117] The author all but abandons the presence of the go-between to emphasize the importance and intensity of this dialogue. Mordecai is not prepared to excuse Esther so easily. He takes a severe tone, first reminding her that she is Jewish and that the decree applies to her as well. She is not safe in the palace, for it is from the palace that the danger emanates. Then, in v. 14, he threatens her: If she does not act, the Jews will receive succor elsewhere, but she and her family (which means Mordecai) will perish. The expression "relief and deliverance will rise for the Jews from another quarter" has excited much commentary, for it may contain an oblique reference to God. The AT, in fact, reads, "God will be their aid and their deliverance," while Josephus and the Targums have taken "quarter" in their MT source as a reference to God.[118] This is a

115. Josephus *Antiquities of the Jews* 11.204.

116. Herodotus 1.99; 3.72, 77, 84, 118, 140.

117. Fox suggests that these figures attempted to excuse themselves "out of feelings of personal unworthiness," rather than from Esther's concern for "personal safety." See Michael V. Fox, *Character and Ideology in the Book of Esther: Studies in Biblical Personalities* (Columbia: University of South Carolina Press, 1991) 62. However, their protests contain a strong element of avoidance of danger, or at least personal discomfort.

118. Josephus *Antiquities of the Jews* XI.227; *Tar.* 1; *Tar.* 2.

plausible interpretation, but it may also simply refer to another human[119] who will help instead of the unwilling Esther. In any case, there seems to be an assumption that something, probably divine providence, is working to save the Jews, whether directly or through human action, and that Esther should choose to cooperate with it. This saves the book from the charge of irreligiosity; God works in the background, through human action. In fact, Mordecai implies ("who knows?") that Esther's ascent to the throne was providential, in order to save the Jews; so if she does not act, she will be disobeying God's unspoken plan.[120] Mordecai, even though he is usually obedient to Persian law, believes that in a conflict between Persian law and the Jewish people, Esther's loyalty must reside with her people.

Esther responds swiftly to Mordecai's pleas. Now that she has been persuaded to act on behalf of the Jews, she quickly comes up with her own plan and carries it out. She begins to give commands, not only to her servants but to Mordecai as well; and she expects to be obeyed. All the Jews in Susa are to gather and observe a three-day fast, while Esther and her maids (it is unlikely that Esther's maids are Jewish) also fast. Fasting, which is an act of petition (2 Sam 12:16-17; Jonah 3:7), is the only overtly religious act in the book of Esther. (Ironically, if the fast did take place, it would have coincided with the beginning of Passover, in direct violation of Jewish law, which forbids fasting on Passover [Exod 12:1-10].) However, since God is not mentioned (although the AT explicitly states that the fasting is directed toward God), its religious character is muted. Thematically, the fast stands in direct contrast to the banquets that occur throughout the book and, in particular, to Haman's feast with Ahasuerus before the fast and to Esther's banquets with the king and Haman after the fast. After the fast, Esther will go to the king, although she again reminds Mordecai that it is against the law for her to do so unbidden. However, she is reconciled to the danger and makes one of the most poignant statements in the book, "If I perish, I perish." Esther's status, even after having been queen for five years, remains precarious and her relationship with her husband is still uncertain. Esther's position as a woman in a male court is analogous to that of the Jews in the Gentile world, with the possibility of danger ever present under the surface. Esther has no guarantee that she will be successful. However, at this point she has taken responsibility for her own fate and has put the welfare of her people first, an action of which the author resoundingly approves. Mordecai is also satisfied; he leaves to carry out Esther's orders.

Mordecai's action in v. 17 signals the radical transformation the character of Esther has undergone in the last three chapters. When Esther was introduced in chap. 2, she was an orphan girl with nothing to recommend her but beauty of face and form. She was passive and obedient, obeying Mordecai, obeying Hegai, and "pleasing" everyone around her. She charmed the king, not least, one supposes, because she was pliant, unlike the spirited Vashti. Even after her marriage, she continued to obey Mordecai. She is not a character from whom we should expect great things. Now, however, she is transformed. She does not obey orders; she gives them. She is active, a risk-taker, not passively compliant. She is a queen, a figure of royal authority, such that even Mordecai hurries to obey her. Now she is a character in whom the reader can trust. Esther has taken charge, and we can rest assured that the danger to the Jews will be averted, no matter what pitfalls lie ahead.

119. So Fox, *Character and Ideology in the Book of Esther,* 63, and David J. A. Clines, *Ezra, Nehemiah, Esther,* NCBC (Grand Rapids: Eerdmans, 1984) 302.

120. Levenson states that the phrase "who knows" "prefaces a guarded hope that penitential practice may induce God to relent from his harsh decree, granting deliverance where destruction had been expected (cf. 2 Sam 12:22, Joel 2:14, and Jonah 3:9)." See Jon D. Levenson, *Esther,* OTL (Louisville: Westminster/John Knox, 1997) 81.

REFLECTIONS

The actions of Esther in chapter 4 present us with an all-too-human portrait of a person's response when faced with a demand for action in a situation that she neither created nor asked for—a resounding "No!" Often life locates us in situations where we are capable of taking action on behalf of some oppressed person or people, but with possible negative consequences for ourselves. Esther's consequences are clear and absolute: She faces death. The consequences for us may be less absolute but nonetheless devastating—loss of job, family rupture, embarrassment, to name only a few. It is difficult at such times to overcome the self-centeredness of our everyday lives in order to discern God's call. In chapter 4, the writer acknowledges the difficulty of discerning that call. Mordecai does not know that Esther can or will be able to help—his use of "who knows?" and "perhaps" recognizes the uncertainty of the situation. But Mordecai is convinced of two things: Help will come for the Jews from somewhere, whether from God or from humans, and Esther, given her favorable circumstances, must act. If she does not, she (and her family) will be held responsible for her cowardice. This statement more than anything else in the book of Esther implies belief in the activity of divine providence, even though God remains unmentioned. The author of Esther has captured in a short two verses the dilemma of the average believer: How does one find the courage and faith to do what is right in the face of divine and human ambiguity? Esther's example may give us courage to reach beyond ourselves and act on behalf of others, placing our trust in God.

ESTHER 5:1–8:2

HAMAN'S PLANS ARE THWARTED

ESTHER 5:1-8, ESTHER ACTS: THE FIRST BANQUET

NIV

5 On the third day Esther put on her royal
robes and stood in the inner court of the
palace, in front of the king's hall. The king was
sitting on his royal throne in the hall, facing the
entrance. [2]When he saw Queen Esther standing
in the court, he was pleased with her and held
out to her the gold scepter that was in his hand.
So Esther approached and touched the tip of the
scepter.

[3]Then the king asked, "What is it, Queen
Esther? What is your request? Even up to half the
kingdom, it will be given you."

[4]"If it pleases the king," replied Esther, "let the
king, together with Haman, come today to a
banquet I have prepared for him."

[5]"Bring Haman at once," the king said, "so that
we may do what Esther asks."

So the king and Haman went to the banquet
Esther had prepared. [6]As they were drinking wine,
the king again asked Esther, "Now what is your
petition? It will be given you. And what is your
request? Even up to half the kingdom, it will be
granted."

[7]Esther replied, "My petition and my request
is this: [8]If the king regards me with favor and if
it pleases the king to grant my petition and fulfill
my request, let the king and Haman come tomorrow to the banquet I will prepare for them. Then
I will answer the king's question."

NRSV

5 On the third day Esther put on her royal
robes and stood in the inner court of the
king's palace, opposite the king's hall. The king
was sitting on his royal throne inside the palace
opposite the entrance to the palace. [2]As soon as
the king saw Queen Esther standing in the court,
she won his favor and he held out to her the
golden scepter that was in his hand. Then Esther
approached and touched the top of the scepter.
[3]The king said to her, "What is it, Queen Esther?
What is your request? It shall be given you, even
to the half of my kingdom." [4]Then Esther said,
"If it pleases the king, let the king and Haman
come today to a banquet that I have prepared for
the king." [5]Then the king said, "Bring Haman
quickly, so that we may do as Esther desires." So
the king and Haman came to the banquet that
Esther had prepared. [6]While they were drinking
wine, the king said to Esther, "What is your
petition? It shall be granted you. And what is your
request? Even to the half of my kingdom, it shall
be fulfilled." [7]Then Esther said, "This is my petition and request: [8]If I have won the king's favor,
and if it pleases the king to grant my petition and
fulfill my request, let the king and Haman come
tomorrow to the banquet that I will prepare for
them, and then I will do as the king has said."

COMMENTARY

The language of this scene is laconic, almost anticlimactic (cf. the LXX's Add. D, which presents a much more dramatic and moving scenario). These eight verses are carefully structured, in a request/grant of request/offer form (ABCA'B'C'A) designed to create maximum suspense in the reader.[121]

5:1. After her three-day fast, Esther clothes herself in "royalty" (מלכות *malkût*). Although clothes are meant, the author's word choice conveys that her royal status is no longer bestowed on her from outside, but has become a personal quality. In contrast to Vashti, who refused to wear the royal crown before the king, Esther makes sure that she is adorned with all the proper paraphernalia before approaching Ahasuerus. One is reminded of her first night with the king, when she took only what Hegai advised her—advice that proved to be correct. We should admire Esther; if she is forced to play her hand within the male power structure of the palace, she is determined to play it well. After dressing appropriately, Esther sets out for the throne room, located in the inner palace, evidently some distance from her own apartments. The narrator, in marked contrast to Add. D and Josephus,[122] gives us no insight into Esther's inner state; she simply walks to the throne room.

5:2-5. Although in chap. 4 Esther had informed Mordecai that her life would be at risk if she approached the king, when the king sees her she immediately wins his approbation, and he extends the scepter to her. As in chap. 2, when she first meets Ahasuerus, Esther once more actively "gains" (נשׂאה *nāśĕʾâ*) his favor (the NIV's "he was pleased" is misleading, for it takes away the active nature of Esther). Esther touches the head of the scepter, acknowledging the king's favor. She is given the title "queen" several times in this section, both by the narrator and by the king, emphasizing her elevated and favored position. However, if she loses that favor, her fate could be the same as Vashti's—and the Jews will be destroyed. She is playing a dangerous game.

Ahasuerus realizes that something urgent must have made Esther risk her life, for he immediately asks what her request is and promises to grant it. The phrase "up to half of the kingdom" is formulaic,[123] and both he and Esther know it is not to be taken literally; however, he certainly does mean to encourage her. We now expect Esther to fall on her knees and beg for the lives of her people, but instead she invites the king to a dinner party! Her request may seem anticlimactic, but in reality it is part of a clever stratagem. In the society of the ancient Near East, as indeed in Middle Eastern societies today, one never makes one's major request right away. Rather, through a series of minor requests that are granted, the road is paved for the major request. Therefore, as Clines points out, Esther's invitation is the first exchange in a play of courtesies.[124] By getting Ahasuerus to accept her hospitality, Esther obligates him to her and makes it more likely that he will grant her next, larger request. The inclusion of Haman is likewise strategic: She will have her enemy in her own territory and under obligation to her, rather than as a free agent in the court. The king, by granting her request (v. 5), thereby obligates himself to her and realizes that he is doing so.

5:6-8. The banquet scene, as a recurring motif, signals to the reader that something important is about to happen. The king and Haman are safely ensconced in Esther's apartments, and they have reached the drinking course, which we know from chap. 1 puts the king in an expansive mood. Ahasuerus once more asks Esther for her request, thereby indicating that he realizes the dinner invitation was not the real request. Now is surely the time for Esther to plead for the Jews, but instead she asks Ahasuerus to a second banquet! This second banquet is puzzling to readers and commentators alike. Verse 7, Esther's reply to Ahasuerus's questions, forms an ellipsis: "And Esther replied, and she said, 'My request and my petition. . . .' " Is she hesitating?[125] Perhaps weigh-

121. Fox, *Character and Ideology in the Book of Esther*, 69-70.
122. Josephus *Antiquities of the Jews* XI.235.

123. See Herodotus 9.109; see also Mark 6:23.
124. David J. A. Clines, *The Esther Scroll: The Story of the Story*, JSOTSup 30 (Sheffield: JSOT, 1984) 304.
125. See P. Haupt, "Critical Notes on Esther," *AJSL* 24 (1907–8) 97-186, esp. 140.

ing her chances for success? Her language in v. 8 is elaborate and courtly, implying a major request, but culminates only in an invitation to a second banquet. Cazelles sees this as evidence for two separate sources, but there is no second plot or telling of the story to support this.[126] Rather, by looking at the language of v. 8, it becomes clear that Esther is being very careful to make it impossible for the king not to grant her request. First, she flatters him ("if I have found favor"; notice that Esther gives the credit for her favor to Ahasuerus, although the narrator consistently gives it to her). Next she appeals to his judgment ("if it is good to the king"). Finally she delivers the closing punch, "to give my request and to carry out my petition." The king will prove his favor by coming to her banquet the next day, where she will finally "do as the king asks"—that is, make her petition. In other words, by coming to the second banquet, the king promises to do whatever she asks.[127] She has successfully backed him into a corner, and he has allowed it to happen.

126. Henri Cazelles, "Note sur la composition du rouleau d'Esther," in *Lex tua veritas. Festschrift für Hubert Junker,* ed. H. Gross and F. Mussner (Trier: Paulinus Verlag, 1961) 27.

127. Clines, *The Esther Scroll,* 305.

The continued presence of Haman, whose voice is noticeably silent, is mysterious. The rabbis give various reasons for his attendance, such as that Esther was acting in accordance with Prov 25:21 ("If your enemies are hungry, give them bread to eat; and if they are thirsty, give them water to drink" [NRSV]), that she was still keeping her Jewishness secret, that she wished to make the king jealous, or that she was setting a trap for Haman and wanted him on hand.[128] Modern commentators, too, have tried to discern Esther's motive, theorizing that she wanted to lull Haman into a false sense of security, that she wanted to make the king jealous, or that she was trying to force the king to choose between her and Haman.[129] It seems most likely that Esther wishes to neutralize Haman and preclude counteraction on his part by having him present for her petition, which she now has gotten the king to promise to grant. So far, things seem to be going entirely Esther's way, but the narrator is about to remind us that the danger has not yet passed.

128. For a good discussion of the rabbinic commentators, see Fox, *Character and Ideology in the Book of Esther,* 72.

129. See Carey A. Moore, *Esther,* AB 7B (Garden City, N.Y.: Doubleday, 1971) 56, for complete references.

REFLECTIONS

Here, for the first time, we see power exercised by a Jewish character. Esther, as was noted in chap. 2, has three disadvantages in the power game: She is a woman, she is Jewish, and she is an orphan. However, her exercise of power marks the first time in the book that power has been used wisely, for a legitimate end: the deliverance of the Jews. Although the author of Esther does not, as usual, mention God, the reader should recall that in biblical tradition God does use powerless women to carry out divine purposes. One thinks of Ruth the Moabite, who becomes the ancestor of the great King David (Ruth 4:13-22), and Mary of Nazareth, who, in Luke 1:46-48, states, "My soul magnifies the Lord, and my spirit rejoices in God my Savior, for he has looked with favor on the lowliness of his servant" (NRSV).

ESTHER 5:9-14, HAMAN BUILDS A GALLOWS FOR MORDECAI

NIV

[9]Haman went out that day happy and in high spirits. But when he saw Mordecai at the king's gate and observed that he neither rose nor showed fear in his presence, he was filled with rage against Mordecai. [10]Nevertheless, Haman restrained himself and went home.

Calling together his friends and Zeresh, his wife, [11]Haman boasted to them about his vast wealth, his many sons, and all the ways the king had honored him and how he had elevated him above the other nobles and officials. [12]"And that's not all," Haman added. "I'm the only person Queen Esther invited to accompany the king to the banquet she gave. And she has invited me along with the king tomorrow. [13]But all this gives me no satisfaction as long as I see that Jew Mordecai sitting at the king's gate."

[14]His wife Zeresh and all his friends said to him, "Have a gallows built, seventy-five feet[a] high, and ask the king in the morning to have Mordecai hanged on it. Then go with the king to the dinner and be happy." This suggestion delighted Haman, and he had the gallows built.

a *14* Hebrew *fifty cubits* (about 23 meters)

NRSV

9Haman went out that day happy and in good spirits. But when Haman saw Mordecai in the king's gate, and observed that he neither rose nor trembled before him, he was infuriated with Mordecai; [10]nevertheless Haman restrained himself and went home. Then he sent and called for his friends and his wife Zeresh, [11]and Haman recounted to them the splendor of his riches, the number of his sons, all the promotions with which the king had honored him, and how he had advanced him above the officials and the ministers of the king. [12]Haman added, "Even Queen Esther let no one but myself come with the king to the banquet that she prepared. Tomorrow also I am invited by her, together with the king. [13]Yet all this does me no good so long as I see the Jew Mordecai sitting at the king's gate." [14]Then his wife Zeresh and all his friends said to him, "Let a gallows fifty cubits high be made, and in the morning tell the king to have Mordecai hanged on it; then go with the king to the banquet in good spirits." This advice pleased Haman, and he had the gallows made.

COMMENTARY

Although the narrator told us nothing about Esther's inner state when she appeared before the king, he fully reveals Haman's state of mind as he leaves Esther's first banquet. Verse 9*a* shows that Haman has reached the pinnacle of his glory, and he knows it. But his reaction to Mordecai's refusal to honor him is entirely out of proportion to the slight (note that Mordecai has returned to his customary station and mode of behavior). Haman, like Ahasuerus, the other Gentile male in the story, is ruled by his emotions; the phrase "good of heart" recalls Ahasuerus's emotional state in 1:10, which had disastrous consequences for Vashti. The female characters and the Jewish characters are more pragmatic and sensible (Mordecai allows his emotions to escape publicly only once (4:1), and Esther only after her personal danger is past (8:3); they are, therefore, ultimately successful.[130] However, in v. 10, Haman "restrains himself" and, once in his own house, gathers together his friends and family. This is the first mention of the Agagite's family, and it emphasizes the threat that Haman poses to the Jews: Not only

130. The "wrath of Haman" is a well-known negative example in later periods. For example, Dante, in *The Purgatorio,* uses Haman as an example of wrath in the Fourth Cornice, the "Reign of Wrath": "Next, down like rain, a figure crucified fell into my high fantasy, his face fierce and contemptuous even as he died. Nearby him great Ahasuerus stood, Esther his wife, and the just Mordecai whose word and deed were always one in good." Dante, *The Purgatorio,* trans. John Ciardi (London: New English Library, 1957) 179.

is he himself a threat, but his heirs are as well, as all Amalekites are enemies to the Jews.

Mordecai's behavior in v. 9 is enigmatic. He has, presumably, carried out Esther's command concerning the fast and has once again taken up his court position. He continues his seemingly reckless behavior toward Haman; indeed, the narrator emphasizes this fact by using the words "rise" (קם *qām*) and "tremble" (זע *zā'*) to indicate Mordecai's continued defiance of Haman. Is Mordecai so convinced of Esther's success? As Moore points out, Mordecai is acting in a "needlessly rash" way.[131] It seems questionable whether Mordecai will even live until Esther's next banquet.

Indeed, that is Haman's purpose in calling his friends and family together. First, he indulges in some boasting, recalling his wealth (which must be vast, since in 3:9 he promised Ahasuerus 10,000 talents), his many sons,[132] and his honor from the king. Finally, he mentions the capstone: He alone dines privately with the king and queen. It is clear that Haman has no idea that Esther is Jewish or that she is related to Mordecai. Esther has successfully dissembled, and that will prove to be Haman's undoing.

Everything he recounts should make Haman ecstatic; however, he gets no pleasure from any of it ("all this does me no good") so long as Mordecai continues to function in the palace. The emphasis in v. 13 is placed on Mordecai the *Jew,* reminding the reader that this is not simply a personal quarrel, but an ethnic conflict with far greater consequences. What is Haman to do?

Zeresh, Haman's wife, comes up with a solution. Zeresh is a new character, another female playing a typical role: that of wife. Like the other females in the book, she thinks independently and leads the weaker Haman into action in response to her suggestions. She gives him the solution to his dilemma; his other (male) advisers, appearing as an afterthought in the sentence structure, merely acquiesce to her suggestion. This is exquisite irony on the part of the author, who began the tale with the unenforceable decree that "every man should be master in his own house" (1:22).

Zeresh's solution is a simple one—get rid of Mordecai! Haman was so busy plotting his grandiose revenge on all the Jews that he failed to find a solution to his immediate problem: continued disrespect by Mordecai. Again, a female character, even one on the enemy's side, proves the more astute and sensible thinker. Once Mordecai is out of the picture, Haman can freely enjoy all the rewards of his position, including the second banquet with the queen. The size of the gallows is part of the author's ironic hyperbole; "fifty cubits high" would be (as the NIV has it) approximately seventy-five feet. The language implies hanging, although Levenson, Clines, and others argue that this gallows is instead a pole for impaling the victim.[133] Haman finds the scheme good and arranges for the gallows to be made. In spite of Esther's recent success, things continue to look grim for Mordecai and the Jews. Haman still has the power to act against them.

131. Moore, *Esther,* 60. Targum I makes it even more rash by having Mordecai taunt Haman.

132. According to Herodotus 1.136, the Persians valued having many sons, as did the Jews.

133. Levenson, *Esther,* 93; Clines, *Ezra, Nehemiah, Esther,* 306.

REFLECTIONS

In this chapter in particular the influence from the wisdom tradition is strong, and the contrast between Esther and Haman is instructive. Esther has become the model of the wise courtier. From the beginning of the story, she has heeded the advice of others. She has acted as the Proverbs suggest: "Fools think their own way is right, but the wise listen to advice" (Prov 12:15 NRSV). She is careful in her speech: "Those who guard their mouths preserve their lives; those who open wide their lips come to ruin" (Prov 13:3 NRSV). And she does not antagonize those in power: "A king's wrath is a messenger of death, and whoever is wise will appease it" (Prov 16:14 NRSV). Rather, she manipulates the king into agreeing to her request in advance, much like the "wise woman of Tekoa" does to David in 2 Sam 14:4-17. She epitomizes the saying of Ecclesiastes: "Better is the end of a thing than its beginning; the patient in spirit are better than the proud in spirit" (7:8 NRSV). Haman, on the other hand, with his anger and pride, is the living example of the proverbial fool: "A fool gives full vent to anger, but the wise quietly holds it back," "A person's pride will bring humiliation, but one who is lowly in spirit will obtain honor," and "Better to be poor and walk in integrity, than to be crooked in one's ways even though rich" (Prov 29:11, 23; 28:6 NRSV). Finally, Haman should be reminded, "Do not boast about tomorrow, for you do not know what a day may bring" (Prov 27:1 NRSV).

To anyone familiar with the wisdom tradition, Haman's downfall seems more and more assured. It is not difficult to realize whom we are meant to emulate. Esther has, indeed, become a model through her wise conduct, not only for the diaspora Jews, but also for the contemporary reader who may have to work within a system that often rewards unethical behavior. The book of Esther reminds us that even when God appears to be absent (not even mentioned by name!), God can be most present, working through willing followers.

ESTHER 6:1-11, HAMAN'S HUMILIATION

NIV

6 That night the king could not sleep; so he ordered the book of the chronicles, the record of his reign, to be brought in and read to him. 2 It was found recorded there that Mordecai had exposed Bigthana and Teresh, two of the king's officers who guarded the doorway, who had conspired to assassinate King Xerxes.

3 "What honor and recognition has Mordecai received for this?" the king asked.

"Nothing has been done for him," his attendants answered.

4 The king said, "Who is in the court?" Now Haman had just entered the outer court of the palace to speak to the king about hanging Mordecai on the gallows he had erected for him.

5 His attendants answered, "Haman is standing in the court."

"Bring him in," the king ordered.

6 When Haman entered, the king asked him, "What should be done for the man the king delights to honor?"

Now Haman thought to himself, "Who is there that the king would rather honor than me?" 7 So he answered the king, "For the man the king delights to honor, 8 have them bring a royal robe the king has worn and a horse the king has ridden, one with a royal crest placed on its head. 9 Then let the robe and horse be entrusted to one of the king's most noble princes. Let them robe the man the king delights to honor, and lead him

NRSV

6 On that night the king could not sleep, and he gave orders to bring the book of records, the annals, and they were read to the king. 2 It was found written how Mordecai had told about Bigthana and Teresh, two of the king's eunuchs, who guarded the threshold, and who had conspired to assassinate[a] King Ahasuerus. 3 Then the king said, "What honor or distinction has been bestowed on Mordecai for this?" The king's servants who attended him said, "Nothing has been done for him." 4 The king said, "Who is in the court?" Now Haman had just entered the outer court of the king's palace to speak to the king about having Mordecai hanged on the gallows that he had prepared for him. 5 So the king's servants told him, "Haman is there, standing in the court." The king said, "Let him come in." 6 So Haman came in, and the king said to him, "What shall be done for the man whom the king wishes to honor?" Haman said to himself, "Whom would the king wish to honor more than me?" 7 So Haman said to the king, "For the man whom the king wishes to honor, 8 let royal robes be brought, which the king has worn, and a horse that the king has ridden, with a royal crown on its head. 9 Let the robes and the horse be handed over to one of the king's most noble officials; let him[b] robe the man whom the king wishes to honor, and let him[b] conduct the man on horseback

[a] Heb *to lay hands on* [b] Heb *them*

NIV	NRSV
on the horse through the city streets, proclaiming before him, 'This is what is done for the man the king delights to honor!'" [10]"Go at once," the king commanded Haman. "Get the robe and the horse and do just as you have suggested for Mordecai the Jew, who sits at the king's gate. Do not neglect anything you have recommended." [11]So Haman got the robe and the horse. He robed Mordecai, and led him on horseback through the city streets, proclaiming before him, "This is what is done for the man the king delights to honor!"	through the open square of the city, proclaiming before him: 'Thus shall it be done for the man whom the king wishes to honor.'" [10]Then the king said to Haman, "Quickly, take the robes and the horse, as you have said, and do so to the Jew Mordecai who sits at the king's gate. Leave out nothing that you have mentioned." [11]So Haman took the robes and the horse and robed Mordecai and led him riding through the open square of the city, proclaiming, "Thus shall it be done for the man whom the king wishes to honor."

COMMENTARY

6:1-5. Esther's plan is proceeding, and Haman's plot against Mordecai is prepared when something happens that nobody could have predicted. The king is gripped by insomnia and orders that the royal records be read to him. Is it mere coincidence that the king cannot sleep, or is it divine providence? The Hebrew text leaves the question open, but the LXX, the AT, and Josephus make it very clear that God caused the king's sleeplessness.[134] This motif of royal sleeplessness, followed by some dramatic incident, also appears in Dan 6:18 and 3 Esdr 3:3. The "book of the remembrances of the things of the days" is the royal annals, mentioned also in 2:23. The Persian Empire, like most bureaucracies, kept vast archives that could be consulted as the need arose. For example, in Ezra 6:1-5 Darius searches the royal archives to discover the decree of Cyrus concerning the Temple in Jerusalem. So when the annals are read to him, Ahasuerus hears the passage concerning Mordecai's life-saving deed, recounted in 2:21-23. Is it coincidence that this particular passage is read? Once again, the MT does not say. Mordecai's lack of reward for his good deed, reported in v. 3, reflects badly on the king and must be remedied. The Persian emperors often bestowed the special title *orosangai,* "benefactor of the king," on someone as a reward for good deeds.[135] Mordecai, however, has received neither title nor reward. In fact, what should have been his has gone to Haman, who, as far as the text reveals, has done nothing to deserve his honors.

The king, who is incapable of doing anything without the advice of others, inquires concerning who is in the court. Presumably, it is very early, the end of the king's sleepless night. Again, is it coincidence or providence that Haman, overly eager to exact revenge on Mordecai, is in the courtyard? The text leaves it to the reader to decide. Haman, like Esther (5:1), is "standing" in the courtyard, waiting to be received by the king. The chapter will consistently draw attention to the contrast between Esther's audience with the king and that of Haman.

6:6. A series of what Dommershausen and Fox have termed "multiple silences" now begins:[136] The king does not say who is to be honored; Haman does not know it is Mordecai; the king does not know that Haman and Mordecai are enemies; and Haman does not tell the king the real situation. Add to this Esther's silence concerning her Jewishness and her relation to Mordecai, and Haman is caught in a trap of his own making.

134. Josephus, with his flair for the melodramatic, states: "But God mocked Haman's wicked hopes; and knowing what was to happen, he rejoiced at the event, for that night he deprived the king of sleep" (*Antiquities of the Jews* XI.247). *4QTales of the Persian Court* has a similar scene, but "the temper of the king was stretched."

135. Herodotus 8.85.

136. Werner Dommershausen, *Die Estherrolle,* SBM 6 (Stuttgart: Katholisches Bibelwerk, 1968) 86; Michael V. Fox, *Character and Ideology in the Book of Esther: Studies in Biblical Personalities* (Columbia: University of South Carolina Press, 1991) 78.

His ego will bring about his own humiliation. Indeed, the jaws of the trap are beginning to close now. The author takes great delight in Haman's egocentricity and subsequent humiliation; we are called upon to sit back and chuckle with him.

6:7-10. The king, in his question to Haman, uses the expression "the man whom the king delights to honor." This phrase, an ironic foreshadowing for both Haman and Mordecai, will be repeated by Haman four times in his reply. He presumes it is he, although he has done nothing to deserve praise. When he begins his reply in v. 7, he repeats the phrase, savoring it. This creates an anacoluthon, indicating a pause for thought, such as Esther used in 5:7.[137] The contrast is instructive, however; Esther uses the pause to create the illusion of humility ("if I have won the king's favor"), while Haman's pause is followed by his grandiloquent plan. Haman's eloquence in vv. 8-9 is extraordinary, for what he is requesting is no less than royal honors for himself. The honors he requests (cf. the LXX and Josephus)[138] are modeled on those given to Joseph in Gen 41:42-43, where Joseph receives linen garments, rides in the second royal chariot, and is hailed wherever he goes. However, again the contrast is significant: Joseph's honor is deserved, while Haman's imagined honor is not. The royal clothing reflects status and could be worn only by those entitled to it; Esther puts on "royalty" when she goes unsummoned to the king (5:1). The giving of royal clothes may reflect genuine Persian custom; Xerxes' daughter-in-law Artaynte requests, and gets, from the infatuated monarch a special robe made for him by Queen Amestris. This request later results in tragedy for Artaynte, much as it does for Haman.[139] The royal horse could be ridden only by the king. The crown on the horse has given trouble to commentators (some have assumed that a crown the king had worn must be meant), but seems to be solved by Assyrian reliefs showing horses wearing tall pointed headdresses (assuming the custom remained the same in Persia).[140] The "man whom the king delights to honor" is to be robed and set on the horse by one of the "princes of the king, the nobles," probably a member of the seven noble Persian families referred to in chap. 1, whom the upstart Haman has displaced. Finally, this noble is to proclaim to the entire city the honor given to the man by the king. This is an unusually high honor Haman has concocted!

As he has done before, the king immediately and without reflection accepts the advice; the trap is sprung on Haman. This literary device of the author's resembles that of 2 Sam 12:1-7 and 14:1-17, where David equally quickly responds to advice; there, however, the trap is sprung on David himself, and he is caught in his own web. Here Haman, not the king, has woven the web of his own downfall. The author has turned what was probably a familiar type of tale on its head. It is Mordecai who is to be honored, not Haman. What is more, the king calls him Mordecai the *Jew,* heaping humiliation upon Haman. This also indicates that the king does not connect the edict of destruction he so blithely approved with the Jews, another example of the "multiple silences" of the text.

6:11. Haman obeys the king. The report of his action mirrors what Haman says in vv. 8-9, but very laconically; and we do not get any insight into Haman's emotions or Mordecai's reaction to this extraordinary event.[141] As before, the Greek tradition attempts to remedy this. The AT adds:

> And Haman said to Mordecai, "Take off the sackcloth!" And Mordecai was troubled, like one who is dying; and in distress he took off the sackcloth. But then he put on the splendid garments, and he thought he beheld an omen, and his heart was to the Lord; and he was speechless.[142]

Josephus tells us that Haman was "confounded in his mind" and "in tears."[143] The rabbis add the interesting note that Haman's daughter, seeing Haman and Mordecai from her roof and supposing that Haman was riding and Mordecai leading him, emptied her chamber pot on Haman's head.

137. An anacoluthon is a syntactical inconsistency or incoherence within a sentence. The deliberate use of the construction creates "space" in a sentence.

138. Josephus *Antiquities of the Jews* XI.254-255.

139. Herodotus 9.110-11.

140. See Cary A. Moore, *Esther,* AB 7B (Garden City, N.Y.: Doubleday, 1971) 65.

141. Bernhard W. Anderson, "The Book of Esther," *IB,* 12 vols. (Nashville: Abingdon, 1954) 3:860, argues that the author omits any dialogue between Mordecai and Haman because he is more interested in plot than character. Fox, *Character and Ideology in the Book of Esther,* 78, however, claims that there is no dialogue because "Haman gritted his teeth and did what he had to do."

142. Translation according to Moore, *Esther,* 65.

143. Josephus *Antiquities of the Jews* XI.256.

When she discovered what she had done, she killed herself by jumping from the roof.[144] All these comments, however, are additions to the terse account of the Hebrew.

144. *Meg.* 16a.

REFLECTIONS

Although this section, like the rest of Hebrew Esther, does not mention God, the author seems to assume the working of divine providence both in the "coincidences" of the plot and in the behavior of the characters. A well-timed sleepless night for the king, Mordecai's previously righteous behavior, and Haman's enormous ego all combine to bring about Mordecai's elevation and Haman's humiliation. Unfortunately, the narrative does not help us to distinguish between mere coincidence and the action of God. The characters certainly are not able to discern the difference: Haman is a fool; Esther is absent; and Mordecai registers no reaction to his fantastic rise in the king's favor. Only the reader might be able to see in these events more than just coincidence, but the narrator is silent on the point. The same dilemma arises when trying to discern true prophecy; according to Deuteronomy, "if a prophet speaks in the name of the LORD but the thing does not take place or prove true, it is a word that the LORD has not spoken" (18:22 NRSV). The hand of God in events is ambiguous; a person must act without sure knowledge.

The behavior of Haman in this passage functions as an object lesson in the perils of pride and self-seeking. One is reminded of the teaching of Jesus in Luke 14:7-11, where he instructs people not to elevate themselves, but to humble themselves, so that others may honor them. Haman is a negative example of this teaching, causing his own humiliation by reaching above himself, whereas Esther and Mordecai do not seek honor; rather, honor is given to them by others.

ESTHER 6:12-13, HAMAN IS WARNED BY HIS ADVISERS

NIV

12Afterward Mordecai returned to the king's gate. But Haman rushed home, with his head covered in grief, 13and told Zeresh his wife and all his friends everything that had happened to him.

His advisers and his wife Zeresh said to him, "Since Mordecai, before whom your downfall has started, is of Jewish origin, you cannot stand against him—you will surely come to ruin!"

NRSV

12Then Mordecai returned to the king's gate, but Haman hurried to his house, mourning and with his head covered. 13When Haman told his wife Zeresh and all his friends everything that had happened to him, his advisers and his wife Zeresh said to him, "If Mordecai, before whom your downfall has begun, is of the Jewish people, you will not prevail against him, but will surely fall before him."

COMMENTARY

After the extraordinary event that has just occurred, Mordecai simply returns to his customary station in the court. The narrator, as usual, gives no insight into his thoughts or emotions, for the focus is now on Haman. In one of the several reversals in the course of the story, Haman is now observing the rituals of mourning, as Mordecai did in 4:1-3. Mordecai was mourning for the anticipated death of the Jews; Haman is in mourning not only for his own humiliation, but also (although he does not yet know it) for his own death, an excellent example of the author's ironic foreshadowing. Haman turns again to his friends (also called "his wise men" [חכמיו *ḥăkāmāyw*]; however, unlike the "wise men" of 1:13, these advisers speak with wisdom) and his wife, Zeresh, but they do not give him sympathy as they did in 5:14; in fact, they counsel giving up. The expression "if Mordecai is of the Jewish people" is rhetorical; everyone knows Mordecai is a Jew, and the text constantly gives him that epithet. Zeresh (in the tradition of the wise woman; cf. 2 Sam 14:4-17; 20:14-22) is speaking here with the voice of the author. Haman cannot, according to them, defeat the Jewish Mordecai. Why? Because Haman is an Agagite—and thus cursed? Because the Jews are divinely protected? Once Haman's associates recognize that he has begun to fall, his doom in the story is sealed; we have reached the turning point of the book. Haman the Agagite cannot defeat Mordecai the Jew. As Levenson astutely observes, "Actions seem to come out of nowhere in this tale, but they gradually link together to form an immensely positive and meaningful pattern of Jewish deliverance: if the term 'theology' means anything in reference to the book of Esther, that is its theology."[145] However, we still await the action of the one appointed to bring about salvation: Queen Esther.

145. Jon D. Levenson, *Esther,* OTL (Louisville: Westminster/John Knox, 1997) 95.

REFLECTIONS

Haman is a sterling example of the foolish man warned against in the wisdom literature. Proverbs 26:27 warns, "Whoever digs a pit will fall into it, and a stone will come back on the one who starts it rolling" (NRSV). Haman brings about his own downfall by not obeying the precepts of wisdom. Wisdom assumes that God rewards those who act wisely and punishes those who do not. The focus is on human action, rather than divine intervention; God does not have to be mentioned, since the righteous moral program will work itself out without direct divine action. Who is the epitome of the wise courtier? Mordecai is one possible example, but he does not always act wisely (see Commentary on 3:1-6). Esther, however, from beginning to end of the story, is a model of wise counsel, patience, and modesty, using the circumstances at her disposal not to further herself but to aid her people. That she and her cousin Mordecai end up in the highest position in the empire (except for the king) is just reward for her righteous behavior, but she does not seek it. What she does seek, the salvation of the Jews, is the ethical centerpiece of the book. It is not right to murder an innocent people; it is right to seek to prevent that. This may seem to be stating the obvious, but self-interest often stands in the way of people's doing what is right. Esther overcame her self-interest in 4:16, and hers is a moral as well as a political victory.

ESTHER 6:14–7:10, ESTHER'S SECOND BANQUET

NIV

14While they were still talking with him, the king's eunuchs arrived and hurried Haman away to the banquet Esther had prepared.

7 So the king and Haman went to dine with Queen Esther, 2and as they were drinking wine on that second day, the king again asked, "Queen Esther, what is your petition? It will be given you. What is your request? Even up to half the kingdom, it will be granted."

3Then Queen Esther answered, "If I have found favor with you, O king, and if it pleases your majesty, grant me my life—this is my petition. And spare my people—this is my request. 4For I and my people have been sold for destruction and slaughter and annihilation. If we had merely been sold as male and female slaves, I would have kept quiet, because no such distress would justify disturbing the king.[a]"

5King Xerxes asked Queen Esther, "Who is he? Where is the man who has dared to do such a thing?"

6Esther said, "The adversary and enemy is this vile Haman."

Then Haman was terrified before the king and queen. 7The king got up in a rage, left his wine and went out into the palace garden. But Haman, realizing that the king had already decided his fate, stayed behind to beg Queen Esther for his life.

8Just as the king returned from the palace garden to the banquet hall, Haman was falling on the couch where Esther was reclining.

The king exclaimed, "Will he even molest the queen while she is with me in the house?"

As soon as the word left the king's mouth, they covered Haman's face. 9Then Harbona, one of the eunuchs attending the king, said, "A gallows seventy-five feet[b] high stands by Haman's house. He had it made for Mordecai, who spoke up to help the king."

The king said, "Hang him on it!" 10So they hanged Haman on the gallows he had prepared for Mordecai. Then the king's fury subsided.

[a]4 Or *quiet, but the compensation our adversary offers cannot be compared with the loss the king would suffer* [b]9 Hebrew *fifty cubits* (about 23 meters)

NRSV

14While they were still talking with him, the king's eunuchs arrived and hurried Haman off to the banquet that Esther had prepared.

7 1So the king and Haman went in to feast with Queen Esther. 2On the second day, as they were drinking wine, the king again said to Esther, "What is your petition, Queen Esther? It shall be granted you. And what is your request? Even to the half of my kingdom, it shall be fulfilled." 3Then Queen Esther answered, "If I have won your favor, O king, and if it pleases the king, let my life be given me—that is my petition—and the lives of my people—that is my request. 4For we have been sold, I and my people, to be destroyed, to be killed, and to be annihilated. If we had been sold merely as slaves, men and women, I would have held my peace; but no enemy can compensate for this damage to the king."[a] 5Then King Ahasuerus said to Queen Esther, "Who is he, and where is he, who has presumed to do this?" 6Esther said, "A foe and enemy, this wicked Haman!" Then Haman was terrified before the king and the queen. 7The king rose from the feast in wrath and went into the palace garden, but Haman stayed to beg his life from Queen Esther, for he saw that the king had determined to destroy him. 8When the king returned from the palace garden to the banquet hall, Haman had thrown himself on the couch where Esther was reclining; and the king said, "Will he even assault the queen in my presence, in my own house?" As the words left the mouth of the king, they covered Haman's face. 9Then Harbona, one of the eunuchs in attendance on the king, said, "Look, the very gallows that Haman has prepared for Mordecai, whose word saved the king, stands at Haman's house, fifty cubits high." And the king said, "Hang him on that." 10So they hanged Haman on the gallows that he had prepared for Mordecai. Then the anger of the king abated.

[a] Meaning of Heb uncertain

COMMENTARY

6:14–7:4. Esther 6:14 is a transitional verse carrying us from one scene to the next. The presence of the eunuchs reflects the royal convention of having guests escorted to the palace (recall that eunuchs are sent to escort Vashti to the king's banquet, 1:10-11). How different must Haman's emotional state be from that of the first banquet! He is losing control of events; the text conveys this by having him rush to Esther's banquet, subtly indicating that she is now in control. However, it is important to keep several things in mind. Although we the readers have been assured that Haman will ultimately fall, the outcome is still in doubt. Esther, as far as the text reveals, has no knowledge of Mordecai's honor and Haman's humiliation. As far as she (and the Jews) is concerned, the edict against the Jews still stands, Haman is still the vizier, and the danger is as acute as ever. Esther's actions must be viewed against that backdrop.

The scene of the second banquet opens in the same way as the first banquet. Esther is referred to as "queen," both by the narrator and by the king, emphasizing her status above Haman. When the guests reach the wine course, the king repeats his offer to Esther for the third time, in exactly the same language as before. Now is the moment for Esther to speak! The AT adds here, "Esther was uneasy about speaking because the enemy was right in front of her, but God gave her the courage for the challenge," supplying both Esther's emotional state and God's unseen action. However, the MT is ambiguous on both counts. Esther responds to the king, using the proper courtly phrases; notice that the phrase "found favor" (מצאתי חן *māṣā'tî ḥēn*) rather than "gained favor" (נשׂאה חן *nāśĕ'â ḥēn*) is used. Esther may, according to the narrator, actively gain favor, but when she speaks to the king she gives all the credit to him. She matches the words of the king's offer in her speech, "petition" and "request," but her request is a bombshell—her life and her people. The parallelism of the sentence ("petition" = "life"; "request" = "people") equates the two; Esther is now fully identified with the Jews. She indicates, however, by the order of her request that she realizes what will be more important to Ahasuerus—her own life. This king, ruled by his own selfish concerns, would be much more affected by the loss of his wife than by the slaughter of an entire group of his subjects. In v. 4, Esther gains steam; she declares that the Jews have been sold, a not-so-veiled allusion to the king's acceptance of Haman's bribe. She is careful, however, to make the verb impersonal ("we have been sold") so as not to make a direct accusation of the king. She goes on to repeat the verbs of the decree in 3:13: "to destroy, to slay, and to annihilate." The final clause of her accusation is a bit strange; the Hebrew is uncertain, and translations differ.[146] Is she really saying that slavery would be acceptable? Or is she just playing a rhetorical game? The last phrase in Hebrew, as it stands in the Masoretic Text, is almost untranslatable: "for there is not distress equivalent [שׁוה *šōweh*; the same word that Haman used in 3:8] in injury [*hapax legomenon*] to the king." Is she talking about financial loss or just unpleasantness? What Esther seems to be saying, and what the versions support, is, "If we had only been sold into slavery, I would keep silent, for it would not be worth bothering the king about."[147] Note the parallel to Haman's "it is not worthwhile for the king to leave them alone" (3:8).[148] Everything in this court must be put in terms of what benefit it brings to the king.

7:5. Ahasuerus's reaction is astonishment. He appears to have no idea what she is talking about and obviously does not connect it with Haman's decree of destruction, which he approved in chap. 3. Why should he? He never inquired as to the identity of the people he was condemning to death, and by handing over his signet ring, he gave Haman the power to do as he pleased. Ahasuerus is now paying the penalty for his laziness and ignorance by facing the shame of his failure to protect his wife.[149] He demands to know the culprit.

146. For a complete discussion see Lewis B. Paton, *Esther,* ICC (Edinburgh: T. & T. Clark, 1908) 261-62.

147. This agrees with Moore's understanding. See Moore, *Esther,* 70.

148. See Fox, *Character and Ideology in the Book of Esther,* 46.

149. See Klein's study of Ahasuerus's character in the context of honor and shame in Lillian R. Klein, "Honor and Shame in Esther," in *A Feminist Companion to Esther, Judith and Susanna,* ed. Athalya Brenner (Sheffield: Sheffield Academic, 1995) 153-56. See also Timothy S. Laniak, "From the Margin to the Middle: The Pattern of Shame and Honor in the Book of Esther" (unpublished Ph.D. diss., Harvard University, 1997) 130-41.

7:6. The climax of the scene comes with Esther's ringing accusation: "A man, an adversary and an enemy! This wicked Haman!" At last the masks are off, the secrets revealed: Haman the Agagite is the blood enemy of Esther the Jew, and the king is forced to choose between the two. (It is still not clear what Ahasuerus himself realizes; Esther has not directly stated that she is Jewish, and Ahasuerus apparently did not know the identity of the people he had condemned to death.) In fact, the wording of the text allies the king and the queen against Haman; for the author, the choice has already been made. Haman, for his part, is dumbfounded (the NRSV's "terrified" better conveyes the Hebrew [נבעת *nib'at*] here). Esther has indeed successfully dissembled; until the moment of the accusation, neither the king nor Haman had an inkling of her purpose.

7:7. The king is once again "full of wrath." Why does he leave the room and go into the garden? Is it because he is presented with an unhappy choice, between Haman his favorite and Esther his queen? The AT, in which Esther notes that Haman is "your friend," certainly understands it this way. Or is he bewildered about what to do? This king, remember, never acts without advice (1:13-15; 2:2-4; 6:6), and now his advisers are pitted against each other. Haman, on the other hand, does the natural thing and begs for mercy from the queen by falling on her couch, where she is reclining while eating. Here is the supreme irony for Haman: He, who wished to slay all Jews because Mordecai refused to bow to him, must now bow to a Jew!

7:8. When Ahasuerus returns and sees Haman prostrate at Esther's feet, he accuses Haman of attempting to rape her. The accusation seems ridiculous under the circumstances. What could Haman possibly gain by ravishing the queen, who has just accused him of trying to kill her, with her husband nearby? The entire scene is farcical; after being accused of attempted murder, pompous Haman is forced to plead for mercy. The king's reaction is equally comic; he sees, not a plea for mercy, but an attempted rape! These characters continue to be self-centered in the extreme: Haman is (understandably) concerned for his own life, while the king sees only a threat to his honor. However unreal the accusation of rape may seem to the reader, it serves as a convenient excuse to prompt the king to do something. After all, it would be difficult for him to punish Haman for doing something that he had been given permission to do in the first place. What is more, the king had accepted a large bribe. However, if Haman is accused of raping the queen, then the king is free from all obligation to him. The minute the king makes the accusation, it is all over; the face of Haman is covered, a gesture of humiliation and mourning. Who the "they" are is unclear; it is probably the ever-present but silent servants.

7:9-10. In v. 9 a eunuch, the otherwise unidentified Harbonah, who must have been present throughout the scene, proves helpful again. He recalls the gallows Haman had erected for Mordecai, who, as Harbonah reminds the king, "spoke good concerning the king." This actually constitutes a second charge against Haman: plotting to kill the king's benefactor (Mordecai's relationship to Esther is still unrevealed). Ahasuerus needs no further prompting; he again makes a snap decision at the leading of others. Haman is hoisted on his own petard,[150] and, finally, "the wrath of the king subsided." This may be the greatest irony of the book. The last time that happened, a queen had been banished, and Ahasuerus had second thoughts, thus setting in motion the events of the book. Is there a possibility that he will again regret his hasty action?

150. Josephus draws out the moral by adding a personal comment: "Wherefore I am moved to marvel at the Deity and to recognize his wisdom and justice, for not only did He punish Haman's wickedness, but also caused the penalty which had been contrived against another to fall upon Haman himself, and thus He has given others an opportunity to learn and know that whatever mischief a man prepares against another, he has, without knowing it, first stored up for himself" (*Antiquities of the Jews* XI.268).

REFLECTIONS

This passage raises the question of our culture's expectations for the appropriate behavior and role of women. Esther is usually applauded for her courage in accusing Haman to the king, but all too often she is condemned for not seeking mercy for him and remaining silent when he is condemned. As Paton says, "Her character would have been more attractive if she had shown pity toward a fallen foe."[151] But is Esther cruel or merely sensible? If Mordecai had behaved in such a way, would he have been condemned? Probably not. Esther is condemned for her behavior because she is a woman, and women "aren't supposed to behave like that." However, Esther is locked in a life-and-death struggle not of her own making—and the outcome seems to be the life of either the Jews or Haman. There are other examples of biblical women who themselves kill the enemy of the Israelites/Jews: Jael hammers a tent peg through the head of Sisera in Judg 4:17-22, and Judith cuts off the head of Holofernes (Jdt 13:6-10). These women are the subjects of universal praise. Esther's action is indirect: She does not kill Haman, but silently acquiesces to his death. Haman is not, it must be remembered, an innocent victim. He has already issued a decree of annihilation of the Jews and has built a gallows for Mordecai. Mercy, in those circumstances, would not be wise but foolhardy, leaving the fate of the Jews unresolved. Mercy, in any case, is not Esther's to grant, since Haman's crime is not just against her, but against all the Jews.

151. Paton, *Esther,* 264.

ESTHER 8:1-2, ESTHER'S TRIUMPH

NIV

8 That same day King Xerxes gave Queen Esther the estate of Haman, the enemy of the Jews. And Mordecai came into the presence of the king, for Esther had told how he was related to her. 2The king took off his signet ring, which he had reclaimed from Haman, and presented it to Mordecai. And Esther appointed him over Haman's estate.

NRSV

8 On that day King Ahasuerus gave to Queen Esther the house of Haman, the enemy of the Jews; and Mordecai came before the king, for Esther had told what he was to her. 2Then the king took off his signet ring, which he had taken from Haman, and gave it to Mordecai. So Esther set Mordecai over the house of Haman.

COMMENTARY

These two verses finish the events of the very busy day, which began with the king's insomnia, and tie up a few loose ends. Esther and Mordecai's relationship is finally made public. Ahasuerus gives to Esther (again her royal title "queen" is emphasized) the "house" (בית [*bayit*] here in the sense of all belongings, as the NIV translates) of Haman. Evidently the property of criminals is confiscated by the state.[152] Also, women must have had certain rights of property ownership.[153] Ahasuerus, continuing on his impulsive course, takes his signet ring, which has evidently just been confiscated from Haman before his death, and gives it to Mordecai, thereby conferring royal power upon him. Esther

152. Herodotus 3.128-129.

153. See ibid., 9.109, where Xerxes offers to give Artaynte cities, gold, and armies under her personal control.

also places Mordecai over her new possession, Haman's property. He becomes the overseer, but she still owns it (note that the AT has the king give Haman's property directly to Mordecai, which serves to denigrate Esther and elevate Mordecai in the story). Mordecai receives his position and wealth only because he is related to Esther, no matter what his personal merits—an important comment on the status of women in the MT text.

This scene is also, in effect, the pivotal point; the greatest reversal in the story has taken place. Esther/Mordecai and Haman have switched places. Haman is dead, and his wealth and position now belong to Esther and Mordecai respectively.

REFLECTIONS

If the book of Esther were a movie, the screen would now fade to black and the credits would roll. The happy ending has been achieved; the villain is dead, the king and queen are reunited, and the hero has been rewarded. Now they can all live happily ever after. Life, however, is not a movie, and the author of Esther recognizes that. The king's character is unchanged; he has not admitted wrongdoing or responsibility. Esther and Mordecai are triumphant now, but their status is dependent on the whim of this mercurial king. The Jews, all but forgotten in this last section, are still under threat; the law of the Medes and the Persians cannot be changed. The sensitive reader will recognize that precariousness of the "happy ending." This recognition leads to a reflection on the changeable nature of human fortune. The author seems to be suggesting that ultimate security does not lie with human institutions. The natural (if unspoken) response to this human condition is that ultimate security rests with God.

ESTHER 8:3-17[154]

THE UNDOING OF HAMAN'S PLOT

OVERVIEW

Even though Haman's downfall has been achieved and Esther is triumphant, a major problem remains. Haman's edict remains in force, and, according to the conventions of the law of the Medes and the Persians, cannot be changed (see Commentary on 1:10-22); the genocide is still scheduled to take place on the thirteenth of Adar.

154. Note that the NIV verses correspond to those of the MT.

ESTHER 8:3-8, ESTHER PETITIONS THE KING

NIV

3Esther again pleaded with the king, falling at his feet and weeping. She begged him to put an end to the evil plan of Haman the Agagite, which he had devised against the Jews. 4Then the king extended the gold scepter to Esther and she arose and stood before him.

5"If it pleases the king," she said, "and if he regards me with favor and thinks it the right thing to do, and if he is pleased with me, let an order be written overruling the dispatches that Haman son of Hammedatha, the Agagite, devised and wrote to destroy the Jews in all the king's provinces. 6For how can I bear to see disaster fall on my people? How can I bear to see the destruction of my family?"

7King Xerxes replied to Queen Esther and to Mordecai the Jew, "Because Haman attacked the Jews, I have given his estate to Esther, and they have hanged him on the gallows. 8Now write another decree in the king's name in behalf of the Jews as seems best to you, and seal it with the king's signet ring—for no document written in the king's name and sealed with his ring can be revoked."

NRSV

3Then Esther spoke again to the king; she fell at his feet, weeping and pleading with him to avert the evil design of Haman the Agagite and the plot that he had devised against the Jews. 4The king held out the golden scepter to Esther, 5and Esther rose and stood before the king. She said, "If it pleases the king, and if I have won his favor, and if the thing seems right before the king, and I have his approval, let an order be written to revoke the letters devised by Haman son of Hammedatha the Agagite, which he wrote giving orders to destroy the Jews who are in all the provinces of the king. 6For how can I bear to see the calamity that is coming on my people? Or how can I bear to see the destruction of my kindred?" 7Then King Ahasuerus said to Queen Esther and to the Jew Mordecai, "See, I have given Esther the house of Haman, and they have hanged him on the gallows, because he plotted to lay hands on the Jews. 8You may write as you please with regard to the Jews, in the name of the king, and seal it with the king's ring; for an edict written in the name of the king and sealed with the king's ring cannot be revoked."

COMMENTARY

There is a paragraph marking in the Hebrew after the end of v. 2, signaling a major break in the action. Does this indicate that v. 3 begins a whole new scene? The verb (ותוסף *wattôsep*, "and she did again" or "and she added to do") probably indicates that this scene is happening on the same day as the events of the preceding scene. It does not seem to be, contra Paton,[155] a second unsummoned audience; why would Esther need to risk her life again? Further, Esther "speaks" (תדבר *tĕdabbēr*) rather than "comes" (באה *bā'â*) again. Although the king extends his scepter to Esther in v. 4, this should be taken as a sign of encouragement rather than clemency.

In this scene, Esther is again the principal actor; Mordecai, while evidently present (v. 7), says nothing the whole time. Esther begins by falling before the king's feet, as Haman fell at her feet to his undoing. Notice that she has no trouble bowing before the king, thereby indicating that Mordecai's refusal to bow before Haman was not unwillingness to bow generally, but to bow before Haman the Agagite in particular. She weeps, which is the first sign of emotion she has shown in the Hebrew text (cf. the Greek versions; one suspects a bit of playacting here, since Esther has been so cool and collected until now), and then she "implores" (ותתחנן *wattitḥannen*) him, a verb used of the entreaties of people in desperate straits (see Gen 42:21; 2 Kgs 1:13). All of the verbs indicate the severity of the situation; even with Haman gone, the Jews are in danger as long as the edict is still in force. This may imply that others besides Haman are eager to put his scheme into action. Esther is the only one who can make the king act to avert the danger.

Esther begins her speech with the longest preamble of any of her petitions, adding two new clauses, "if the thing seems right before the king" and "if I have his approval," to her previous formula; and she makes it intensely personal. "If I have found favor," and "if I am good in his eyes" suggest that the king would be carrying out her wishes as a personal favor to her, as a sign of his affection, not because it is morally right. This is exactly the right type of appeal to make to this emotional and mercurial monarch! The expression "let an order be written" is an impersonal construction, divesting the king of personal responsibility; Esther is doing precisely what Haman had done earlier. In v. 6, she does not claim to be in personal danger, as she did in 7:3, for that would now be an insult to the king. But she does argue that it would cause her personal grief if the Jews were destroyed (the NRSV's "kindred" is a better translation of מולדתי [*môladtî*] than the NIV's "family," since it is more encompassing). Her argument is clear: The king should foil the plot of Haman (called by his full patronymic in v. 5) in order to avoid personal pain for his queen. This is not an ethical argument, but an emotional one; most important, it will work.

Ahasuerus responds in v. 7. He is given the title "king" (מלך *melek*), Esther is called "queen" (מלכה *malkâ*), and Mordecai is called "the Jew" (היהודי *hayyĕhûdî*). The last title has ceased to be a mere ethnic designation and has become an epithet of high dignity, equivalent to "king" and "queen." The king seems to take a defensive tone, pointing out that Haman has been hanged and his property handed over to Esther, "because he sent his hand against the Jews." This is not the reason given for Haman's execution in 7:8, where he is accused of assaulting Esther; however, it would appear that with Haman dead Ahasuerus would like to consider the whole problem solved. Unfortunately, since the original edict is irrevocable, the problem is not solved, as Ahasuerus acknowledges in the next verse. The king turns over complete responsibility to Esther and Mordecai; the "you" (plural) is in the emphatic position in the sentence, indicating that they, not him, are to remedy the situation. He gives them permission to write a new command in the king's name and seal it with his signet ring "as it is good in your eyes." He is again avoiding responsibility, even though, as he acknowledges at the end of v. 8, whatever is so written is irrevocable. Thus the game of the Persian court has not changed, although the players have; what Esther and Mordecai do will be for the benefit of the Jews, whereas what Haman did was against them. But the underlying problem

155. Lewis B. Paton, *Esther*, ICC (Edinburgh: T. & T. Clark, 1908) 279.

that enabled these things to occur has not altered. The dilemma for Esther and Mordecai is now this: If Haman's decree, written in the king's name and sealed with the king's ring, is irrevocable, how can the Jews be saved?

REFLECTIONS

The still-precarious position of Esther and the Jews, hinted at in the last passage, is fully recognized here. Esther, weeping at the feet of the king, becomes a symbol for the Jews; she is a powerless woman dependent on a powerful man. The Jews are a powerless people in exile dependent on a powerful government. Esther uses the one weapon she can count on: her feminine charms. Modern women may cringe at the spectacle of Esther weeping at the king's feet. Esther, however, is a realist. If feminine charms work to avert the threatened massacre, she will use them. The moral underpinning of her action is sound. Modern Western women (and men) may eschew Esther's means, but she remains a powerful role model for the oppressed and downtrodden, whether because of gender or ethnicity.

ESTHER 8:9-14, MORDECAI WRITES AN EDICT

NIV

[9]At once the royal secretaries were summoned—on the twenty-third day of the third month, the month of Sivan. They wrote out all Mordecai's orders to the Jews, and to the satraps, governors and nobles of the 127 provinces stretching from India to Cush.[a] These orders were written in the script of each province and the language of each people and also to the Jews in their own script and language. [10]Mordecai wrote in the name of King Xerxes, sealed the dispatches with the king's signet ring, and sent them by mounted couriers, who rode fast horses especially bred for the king.

[11]The king's edict granted the Jews in every city the right to assemble and protect themselves; to destroy, kill and annihilate any armed force of any nationality or province that might attack them and their women and children; and to plunder the property of their enemies. [12]The day appointed for the Jews to do this in all the provinces of King Xerxes was the thirteenth day of the twelfth month, the month of Adar. [13]A copy of the text of the edict was to be issued as law in every province and made known to the people of every nationality so that the Jews would be ready on that day to avenge themselves on their enemies.

[a]9 That is, the upper Nile region

NRSV

9The king's secretaries were summoned at that time, in the third month, which is the month of Sivan, on the twenty-third day; and an edict was written, according to all that Mordecai commanded, to the Jews and to the satraps and the governors and the officials of the provinces from India to Ethiopia,[a] one hundred twenty-seven provinces, to every province in its own script and to every people in its own language, and also to the Jews in their script and their language. [10]He wrote letters in the name of King Ahasuerus, sealed them with the king's ring, and sent them by mounted couriers riding on fast steeds bred from the royal herd.[b] [11]By these letters the king allowed the Jews who were in every city to assemble and defend their lives, to destroy, to kill, and to annihilate any armed force of any people or province that might attack them, with their children and women, and to plunder their goods [12]on a single day throughout all the provinces of King Ahasuerus, on the thirteenth day of the twelfth month, which is the month of Adar. [13]A copy of the writ was to be issued as a decree in every province and published to all peoples, and the Jews were to be ready on that day to take revenge on their enemies. [14]So the couriers,

[a] Or *Nubia*; Heb *Cush* [b] Meaning of Heb uncertain

NIV	NRSV
14The couriers, riding the royal horses, raced out, spurred on by the king's command. And the edict was also issued in the citadel of Susa.	mounted on their swift royal steeds, hurried out, urged by the king's command. The decree was issued in the citadel of Susa.

COMMENTARY

8:9-10. This section opens with a puzzling time delay.[156] The events of the last sections, beginning with 3:7, have taken place in the first month, Nisan, in the twelfth year of Ahasuerus's reign. Now, however, v. 9 tells us that we are in the third month, Sivan, on the thirteenth day. Why the delay between the last scene and this one? The LXX has Nisan instead of Sivan, but this is clearly a harmonizing change, since there does not seem to be a scribal error in Hebrew. Paton supposes that the intervening time is filled with the events of 4:1–8:2; this is possible, but that would necessitate a wide gap between Haman's casting of the lot and his seeking an audience before the king or a gap between that audience and the writing of his edict, neither of which is mentioned in the text (although they are not precluded).[157] Clines notes that there is exactly a seventy-day difference between the date in 3:7 and this one (the first month; the third month, on the thirteenth day, allowing twenty-eight days per month), and sees this as a veiled allusion to the seventy years of exile.[158] This is possible, but more subtle than the author usually is. The delay remains inexplicable.

In this section Mordecai is the one giving instructions, in obvious contrast to Haman (Esther has momentarily disappeared, since the author wishes to emphasize the Haman/Mordecai contrast). The language of these verses reproduces that of both Haman's decree in 3:12-15 and the decree against Vashti in 1:22. Scribes are gathered together, and their writing is according to *Mordecai's* command (cf. 3:12). The edict is addressed to the satraps, the governors, and the princes (cf. 3:12) of the provinces from India to Ethiopia, 127 in total (see 1:1). However, there is a major difference: Mordecai's decree is also written to the *Jews,* and they are singled out and given pride of place. The decree is written in every group's own language (cf. 1:22; 3:12), and it is especially emphasized that, unlike before, it is specifically written to the Jews in their "script and their language" (i.e., Hebrew). The decree is signed in the name of Ahasuerus and sealed with his ring (cf. 3:12), and it is sent by the official Persian postal system (cf. 1:22; 3:13; the Hebrew is uncertain here, but has to do with the type of horses used). The narrator is emphasizing that this is an official decree, the same as Haman's; it becomes part of the law of the Medes and the Persians and, therefore, is irrevocable.

8:11-13. The content of the decree is given in these verses. The Jews receive permission to defend themselves, which they evidently were not allowed to do before. They may "destroy, kill, and annihilate" (cf. 3:13) any ethnic or provincial force, any adversaries, including women and children (cf. 3:13), and take their booty (cf. 3:13). This is to occur in one day, on the thirteenth of Adar (cf. 3:13), which is now nine months away. The edict assumes that there would be many people, enough to form "forces," willing to attack the Jews; thus the Jews must gather together to repel them. This decree effectively neutralizes Haman's decree without revoking it, which is not allowed; it will now be a fair fight between two opposing forces. The text emphasizes that a copy of the decree is made "law" (דת *dāt,* 3:14) in every province; this goes beyond Haman's actions in emphasizing the legality of the decree. Is there an assumption that some enemies might contest it (cf. Ezra 5:4–6:12, where the provincial governors attempt to contest, with Darius, a decree of Cyrus concerning the Jews)? The couriers go forth

156. Michael V. Fox, *Character and Ideology in the Book of Esther: Studies in Biblical Personalities* (Columbia: University of South Carolina Press, 1991) 96-97.

157. Paton, *Esther,* 272.

158. David J. A. Clines, *Ezra, Nehemiah, Esther,* NCBC (Grand Rapids: Eerdmans, 1984) 316.

in haste (cf. 3:15) and quickly; the extra verb adds urgency to the narrative.

8:14. The chapter ends with the same phrase that 3:15 ended with and returns the action to Susa. The echoing that takes place throughout the decree emphasizes the wisdom doctrine of retributive justice, but the inclusion of women and children in the counterdecree has been criticized by some as "bloodthirstiness."[159] Gordis proposes an interesting solution to the moral dilemma: that the last phrase of Mordecai's decree is a "citation" of Haman's decree, so that "women and children" refer to Jewish women and children who might be attacked according to the terms of Haman's decree. Mordecai's decree thus simply allows the (male) Jews to defend themselves and their women and children.[160] The Hebrew, however, does not clearly identify to whom the women and children belong, so that Gordis's solution is not certain. It is also possible that the author viewed the enemies of the Jews as falling under the ban of holy war (Deut 20:16-17).[161]

159. E.g., Paton, *Esther,* 274; Carey A. Moore, *Esther,* AB 7B (Garden City, N.Y.: Doubleday, 1971) 80, 83.

160. R. Gordis, "Studies in the Esther Narrative," *JBL* 95 (1976) 49-53.

161. So Berhard W. Anderson, "Esther," *IB,* 3:886.

REFLECTIONS

It may seem strange that a law would have to be made allowing the Jews to defend themselves; indeed, the whole project of neutralizing Haman's decree, rather than revoking it, is almost comical. However, it is true that sometimes people get so caught up in legalism and seeking to be law-abiding that they lose sight of the moral ground on which the law should be based. If the law says to attack the Jews, then we should attack the Jews whether we want to or not. If the law does not say the Jews can defend themselves, then they cannot, no matter what the natural response would be. We saw examples of this type of behavior during the Holocaust. As the Nazis passed more and more stringent laws relegating the Jews to second-class citizenship and then to death, most Germans, even those who would later claim that they were not anti-Semites, continued to obey and even to cooperate with the authorities in their eagerness to be law-abiding. In the trial of Adolf Eichmann, for example, Eichmann claimed as his defense that he was simply "following orders"—that is, obeying the law of the land. He did not feel responsible for determining the morality of that law.[162] His behavior resulted in the deaths of millions of people. The attitude exemplified by Eichmann denies the principle that morality ultimately rests in God and that humans are called to be moral because they are created by God.

In Judaism, the law is not good in and of itself. Rather, it is good because it was given by God; its purpose is to make Israel "a holy nation" (Lev 19:2). Therefore, Mordecai and Esther are justified in their attempt to overturn a legal decree, for that decree violates the higher law of God, which views each human life as precious. Immanuel Kant agreed with this position when he claimed that any social law that denies the intrinsic moral worth of the individual violates the "categorial imperative" that we should always treat human beings as ends in themselves.[163] This principle, if applied, protects the minority within a majority culture. Or, as Jesus more simply and vividly put it, "In everything do to others as you would have them do to you; for this is the law and the prophets" (Matt 7:12 NRSV).

162. Hannah Arendt, *Eichmann in Jerusalem: A Report on the Banality of Evil,* rev. ed. (New York: Penguin, 1994) 135-50.

163. Immanuel Kant, *The Foundations of the Metaphysics of Morals,* trans. L. W. Beck (New York: Macmillan, 1990). Arendt, *Eichmann in Jerusalem,* 136, notes that Eichmann himself declared that he had ceased to live by Kant's moral principles.

ESTHER 8:15-17, MORDECAI'S APPEARANCE

NIV

[15]Mordecai left the king's presence wearing royal garments of blue and white, a large crown of gold and a purple robe of fine linen. And the city of Susa held a joyous celebration. [16]For the Jews it was a time of happiness and joy, gladness and honor. [17]In every province and in every city, wherever the edict of the king went, there was joy and gladness among the Jews, with feasting and celebrating. And many people of other nationalities became Jews because fear of the Jews had seized them.

NRSV

15Then Mordecai went out from the presence of the king, wearing royal robes of blue and white, with a great golden crown and a mantle of fine linen and purple, while the city of Susa shouted and rejoiced. [16]For the Jews there was light and gladness, joy and honor. [17]In every province and in every city, wherever the king's command and his edict came, there was gladness and joy among the Jews, a festival and a holiday. Furthermore, many of the peoples of the country professed to be Jews, because the fear of the Jews had fallen upon them.

COMMENTARY

The threat to the Jews now averted, Mordecai appears in his new role as second to the king. The author once again recalls, through similar wording, previous scenes. Mordecai, who was dressed in sackcloth in 4:1, now wears "royal robes" as Esther did and as Haman had wished to do (5:1; 6:8; cf. Joseph, who "went out from the presence of Pharaoh" [Gen 41:46]). The robes are made of the same type of cloth that decorated the royal pavilion in 1:6. Mordecai wears a "crown" (or "turban" [עטרה *'ăṭārâ*]) of gold, as Vashti refused to do in 1:11. Mordecai thus combines in his person identifying markers associated with every main character except the king. Mordecai gains exactly what Haman wanted. (Esther's absence from the scene is notable. The text, slipping back into its androcentric world, is unable to give her the credit and recognition she deserves as the true heroine of the story.) The result is that the people of Susa, who in 3:15 were confused, now shout and rejoice. There is no hint of anti-Semitism here, or even expectation of it. Haman was the Jews' enemy because he was an Agagite, not because he was a Gentile. Verse 16 gives the joyous reaction of the Jews to the glory of Mordecai. The NIV translation of the Hebrew is paraphrastic: The term "light" (אורה *'ôrâ*) is parallel to other words of gladness and contrasts with the gloom of mourning in chap. 4 (see also Add. A; Job 12:25; Pss 97:11; 112:4).

Outside of the city of Susa, the Jews of the provinces rejoice over the decree with feasting and a holiday (this contrasts sharply with the king and Haman's feast after his decree in 3:15). Finally, the narrator states that "many from the people of the land became Jews (מתיהדים *mityahădîm*), for fear (פחד *paḥad*) of the Jews fell upon them." What is the significance of these words? The NRSV translates *mityahădîm* as "professed to be Jews," thereby skirting the question of whether those Gentiles actually converted. The LXX is blunt: "they were circumcised." However, in the relatively secular, or at least non-practicing, atmosphere of this book, what would it mean to "become a Jew"? It would have to be an ethnic rather than religious change, since religious practice seems to play no part in Jewish identity in the book of Esther. Also, what is the nature of the fear that falls upon them? Is it physical, the result of the superior forces of the Jews and a desire to be on the winning side? Or is it spiritual, a recognition that God is on the side of the Jews?[164] The sense is unclear, but the meaning comes through: The ultimate triumph for any minority people is to have the majority want to

164. Fox, *Character and Ideology in the Book of Esther,* 104-6; Clines, *Ezra, Nehemiah, Esther,* 319.

join them. However, as Clines notes, the phrase adds an "almost surrealist" end to the chapter.[165]

At the end of this chapter, with the plot of Haman averted and Mordecai firmly ensconced in power, we feel we have reached the end of the story. In fact, several scholars have raised the possibility that the original form of the story of Esther (proto-Esther) ended here. Indeed, the AT ends at v. 12 (AT 8:7). With the loose ends of the story tied up and the author recalling various earlier scenes in his grand climactic chapter, it is highly likely that proto-Esther ended here and that chaps. 9 and 10 were added by the author of the MT to tie the story in with the Festival of Purim.[166]

165. David J. A. Clines, *The Esther Scroll: The Story of the Story,* JSOTSup 30 (Sheffield: JSOT, 1984) 318.

166. See ibid., esp. chap. 5, and Michael V. Fox, *The Redaction of the Books of Esther,* SBLMS 40 (Atlanta: Scholars Press, 1991) 110-11.

REFLECTIONS

The parallelism between the appearance of Mordecai and the appearance of Joseph in Gen 41:42 is surely not accidental. The reader who recognizes the parallel knows that God enabled Joseph to reach the pinnacle of success; the suggestion is that God is also behind Mordecai's phenomenal success. The implication of God's guiding hand in the success of Mordecai must be teased out, but there is no other way for a faithful Jew to understand the text. God is, after all, the protector of Israel (e.g., Pss 44:1-8; 46:1-11; 68:1-10). So why should not God's unspoken protection be seen in the events of the book of Esther? Although it is unspoken, that theology of salvation permeates the book.

Mordecai's glorification may further be understood typologically by Christians. The New Testament emphasizes the glorification of Jesus (in human terms a humble peasant) by the hand of God, particularly in the scenes of the transfiguration (Matt 17:1-8; Mark 9:2-8; Luke 9:26-36) and the ascension (Luke 24:50-53). In Revelation, the lamb (symbolizing Christ) is glorified by God to reign in heaven (5:11-14). An important difference to bear in mind is that in the Christian tradition glorification takes place in anticipation of martyrdom (the transfiguration) or as a result of martyrdom (the ascension, Revelation). Mordecai's glorification takes place after he helps to *avert* martyrdom. There is no exultation of the martyr's status in the story of Esther.

ESTHER 9:1–10:3

THE BATTLES OF ADAR AND THE FESTIVAL OF PURIM

OVERVIEW

Commentators debate whether chaps. 9–10 originally belonged to the book of Esther.[167] The AT, in particular, does not contain the following items found in the MT: an extended battle report, the second day of battle and celebration, the etiology of Purim, and the epilogue in 10:1-3. Instead, the AT contains a much shorter ending, which includes Esther asking the king's permission to put her enemies to death (including Haman's sons) and Mordecai issuing a decree annulling Haman's previous decree and commanding the Jews to celebrate. For these reasons, Torrey argued that 8:21 of the AT represented the original ending of his posited Aramaic original source of Esther.[168] Clines has suggested that the proposed Semitic source of the AT (the "proto-AT") ended at 8:17, when the king puts Mordecai in charge of the kingdom's affairs, and that the extant ending of the AT developed independently from that of the MT. Fox argues that the proto-AT actually concluded at 8:38 (excluding Add. E) with the decree of Mordecai. Jobes, on the other hand, argues that the present ending of the AT is a shortened version of the MT's ending, supplemented by material from the LXX.[169] In the MT itself, the various sections of chap. 9 often do not fit well together, and some of them may be secondary. The fact that the versions leave out various parts of chap. 9 (see pericope headings below) is a further argument for the secondary, redactional character of chap. 9. However, it is difficult to determine the original or secondary character of any single component section. In this commentary the text is divided into units, some of which may have been interpolated into the present narrative. See textual studies of the versions for further information.

Regardless of the conclusion one reaches concerning the details of the redaction of the endings of the three extant versions, it seems clear that the original story of Esther (proto-Esther, no longer extant) did not contain either a battle report or an etiology of Purim, but rather ended with the triumph of Esther and Mordecai within the Persian court. This would give the original story more of the character of a royal courtier tale, as found in Daniel 2–6.[170] This understanding of the nature of proto-Esther may also be supported by *4QTales of the Persian Court,* a similar type of tale that apparently never departs from its court setting (see Introduction).

However, as the MT version of Esther now stands, it is a unified whole, as Berg has convincingly shown.[171] The various themes continue in chaps. 9–10, including the all-important theme of reversal; and the most important structural motif, that of banquets, would be incomplete without the inclusion of the Purim feasts in chap. 9 (see *Fig.* 9: "The Banquets in Esther," 857). Therefore, MT Esther must be treated as a unified literary work, with chaps. 9–10 as integral parts of the whole.

167. The following remarks are dependent upon Clines, *The Esther Scroll,* 74-92; Fox, *The Redaction of the Books of Esther;* Karen H. Jobes, *The Alpha-Text of Esther: Its Character and Relationship to the Masoretic Text,* SBLDS 153 (Atlanta: Scholars Press, 1996) 195-233.

168. C. C. Torrey, "The Older Book of Esther," *HTR* XXXVII (1944) 7, 14.

169. Jobes, *The Alpha-Text of Esther,* 203.

170. Lawrence M. Wills, *The Jew in the Court of the Foreign King,* HDR 26 (Minneapolis: Fortress, 1990) 153.

171. Sandra Beth Berg, *The Book of Esther: Motifs, Themes, and Structure,* SBLDS 44 (Missoula, Mont.: Scholars Press, 1979) 31-47.

ESTHER 9:1-5, THE FIRST BATTLE

NIV

9 On the thirteenth day of the twelfth month, the month of Adar, the edict commanded by the king was to be carried out. On this day the enemies of the Jews had hoped to overpower them, but now the tables were turned and the Jews got the upper hand over those who hated them. [2]The Jews assembled in their cities in all the provinces of King Xerxes to attack those seeking their destruction. No one could stand against them, because the people of all the other nationalities were afraid of them. [3]And all the nobles of the provinces, the satraps, the governors and the king's administrators helped the Jews, because fear of Mordecai had seized them. [4]Mordecai was prominent in the palace; his reputation spread throughout the provinces, and he became more and more powerful.

[5]The Jews struck down all their enemies with the sword, killing and destroying them, and they did what they pleased to those who hated them.

NRSV

9 Now in the twelfth month, which is the month of Adar, on the thirteenth day, when the king's command and edict were about to be executed, on the very day when the enemies of the Jews hoped to gain power over them, but which had been changed to a day when the Jews would gain power over their foes, [2]the Jews gathered in their cities throughout all the provinces of King Ahasuerus to lay hands on those who had sought their ruin; and no one could withstand them, because the fear of them had fallen upon all peoples. [3]All the officials of the provinces, the satraps and the governors, and the royal officials were supporting the Jews, because the fear of Mordecai had fallen upon them. [4]For Mordecai was powerful in the king's house, and his fame spread throughout all the provinces as the man Mordecai grew more and more powerful. [5]So the Jews struck down all their enemies with the sword, slaughtering, and destroying them, and did as they pleased to those who hated them.

COMMENTARY

The action of this chapter is set on the thirteenth of Adar, the day appointed by Haman for the destruction of the Jews. Nine months have passed since Mordecai's edict was sent throughout the empire. As Paton exclaims, "Lively times are to be expected."[172] These verses bring to a climax two of the major themes of the book: ironic reversal and power. Verse 1 brings the theme of ironic reversal to its climax by putting emphasis on the fact that the tables have turned (נהפוך הוא *nahăpôk hû'*) on the enemies of the Jews (the identity of these enemies is unclear, but they seem to be numerous). Anti-Semitism is accepted as a fact of life, unlike in earlier chapters, where anti-Semitism occurred because of a blood feud rather than natural antipathy between Jew and Gentile (although there have been hints of it along the way, such as the assumption of Haman's original decree that plenty of Gentiles would be willing to kill Jews). In 9:1, the enemies of the Jews "hope to dominate them," but that is changed so that the Jews will dominate the enemies (the NIV is paraphrastic but captures the sense). The Jews not only slay their enemies, but also become more powerful than they. In v. 2, the Jews gather together against those who would attack them, and "no one is able to withstand them [איש לא-עמד לפניהם *'îš lō' 'āmad lipnêhem*]." The LXX is again blunt in its translation, "no one resisted them," making it seem as if the Jews encountered no opposition. The NRSV's "no one could withstand them" (NIV, "no one could stand against them") probably better captures the sense of an inevitable, but not effortless, victory. The action, in fact, seems more aggressive than defensive, since there is no clear mention of a Gentile attack, but that instead "fear" (פחד *paḥad*) falls upon them. The fear here is clearly physical, but

172. Paton, *Esther,* 282.

it is also a more generalized fear of the new power that the formerly oppressed minority has. The action of the larger groups (v. 3) is reflected in the behavior of their leaders. The princes (NRSV, "officials"; NIV, "nobles") of the provinces, the satraps, the governors, and "the doers of the king's work" (a new phrase, possibly indicating a later redactor; this is a different order from earlier chapters, with the leaders of other ethnic groups, who might conceivably have opposed the Jews, placed first) help the Jews because of their fear of Mordecai. Here the fear is political, since Mordecai has now become second in the kingdom. The kind of aid given is not specified. Mordecai has certainly reached the epitome of greatness; the idiom "the man Mordecai" in v. 4 implies importance, since it is elsewhere applied to Moses, the leader of the Jews *par excellence* (e.g., in the story of the rebellion of Aaron and Miriam [Num 12:1-15] Moses is referred to as "the man Moses" [v. 3]; most significantly, Exod 11:3 reads "the man Moses was very great" in the sight of the Egyptian [Gentile] court). The Jews are victorious (v. 5), smiting their enemies with the "edge of the sword" (מכת-חרב *makkat ḥereb*; never used as an idiom for self-defense); this indicates again aggressive action on the part of the Jews against their enemies (the LXX omits this verse). This is the climax to the theme of power. Haman and his unnamed minions sought power over Mordecai and the Jews. Now the Jews and Mordecai have power over them.

REFLECTIONS

These verses, with their matter-of-fact recounting of wholesale slaughter, may be difficult for the reader to accept. They are certainly part of the reason why Martin Luther fulminated against the book of Esther: "I am so hostile to this book that I wish it did not exist, for it Judaizes too much, and has too much heathen naughtiness."[173] It is particularly difficult to reconcile the events of these verses with Christian notions of forgiveness and universalism. As Anderson says, "This is a case of do unto others as they would have done to you."[174] It is important, however, not to see these verses as a reflection of an actual historical event, but rather as the wishful thinking of an oppressed minority (cf. Psalm 137, a lament over the Babylonian exile, which ends with the children of the Babylonians being smashed against a rock). The focus is on the victory, not the slaughter. The Jews have not sought violence, but it has found them; and they must meet it or be destroyed (martyrdom is never considered by the author as an option, nor is it a desirable thing within the Jewish tradition). In the process, the Jews have moved from being a fearful and mourning people to a powerful and feared people (cf. similar sentiments in Psalms 124; 129). Those who wished to destroy the Jews are instead themselves destroyed. The Jews thus become the image of Esther, who changes from a silent, pliable girl into a strong and decisive woman.

173. Martin Luther, *Tischreden,* W. A. xxii, 2080, as quoted by Paton, *Esther,* 96.
174. Anderson, *IB,* 3:828.

ESTHER 9:6-10, THE BATTLE IN SUSA

NIV

6In the citadel of Susa, the Jews killed and destroyed five hundred men. 7They also killed Par-
shandatha, Dalphon, Aspatha, 8Poratha, Adalia,
Aridatha, 9Parmashta, Arisai, Aridai and Vaizatha,
10the ten sons of Haman son of Hammedatha, the

NRSV

6In the citadel of Susa the Jews killed and destroyed five hundred people. 7They killed Parshan-
datha, Dalphon, Aspatha, 8Poratha, Adalia,
Aridatha, 9Parmashta, Arisai, Aridai, Vaizatha,
10the ten sons of Haman son of Hammedatha, the

NIV	NRSV
enemy of the Jews. But they did not lay their hands on the plunder.	enemy of the Jews; but they did not touch the plunder.

COMMENTARY

9:6. The narrator now switches from the provinces to Susa. Even though we are told in 8:15 that the city of Susa rejoiced at Mordecai's ascendancy, the Jews still find 500 men to slaughter (there is no mention of women and children). This is a very large number for a city the size of Susa. Fox suggests, probably correctly, that it is hyperbolic.[175] Further, the verse does not say that the fighting took place in the city of Susa, but in the citadel of Susa. Does this mean that there was fighting within the palace, indicating hostility to the Jews within the Persian bureaucracy? Moore finds it unlikely that the king would tolerate fighting within the palace.[176] However, since in 3:15 the city of Susa was in consternation over Haman's decree, indicating sympathy for the Jews, it seems most likely that hostility to the Jews in Susa would have been found among Haman's cohorts in the bureaucracy. The scene as a whole is rather surrealistic: The enemies are evidently so hostile to the Jews that they act in spite of the fact that Mordecai the Jew is firmly in control in the palace.

9:7-10a. These verses announce the slaughter of the ten sons of Haman. The principle of retributive justice is strongly at work here; the children share in the punishment of the father. It is also possible that the author assumes that, in the nine months since Mordecai's decree, the sons of Haman have been attempting to carry out their father's program to overthrow Mordecai. Hence, they would be the leaders of the enemy forces. This completes Haman's downfall. He boasted of his position, his wealth, and his numerous sons in 5:11. First he lost his wealth to Esther and his position to Mordecai; now even his sons, his posterity, are lost. The names of Haman's sons are all Persian but otherwise unknown; they are probably included, like the other lists of names in 1:10, 14, to give the narrative an air of historical verisimilitude.[177] (The names in the MT are arranged in columns, for reasons that are not clear; cf. Josh 12:9-23.)

9:10b. Finally, the author reports that the Jews took no plunder, in spite of the fact that they had permission to do so (8:11), as did their Gentile counterparts in Haman's decree (3:13). This is a vivid contrast to Saul in his battle with Agag and the Amalekites (1 Samuel 15), where, in spite of the ban of holy war, he took booty and thus lost his throne. The Jews do not make that mistake again! Rather, they place themselves in the camp of the righteous Abraham, who, in his victory over the kings of the plain, took no plunder (Gen 14:22-24).

The Jews' victory appears effortless (no Jewish losses are mentioned); yet, it is not attributed to God. No reason is given for the enemies' hostility—it just *is,* a natural fact of life.

175. Michael V. Fox, *Character and Ideology in the Book of Esther: Studies in Biblical Personalities* (Columbia: University of South Carolina Press, 1991) 110.

176. Carey A. Moore, *Esther,* AB 7B (Garden City, N.Y.: Doubleday, 1971) 87.

177. Lewis B. Paton, *Esther,* ICC (Edinburgh: T. & T. Clark, 1908) 70-71.

REFLECTIONS

The notion that Gentiles are naturally hostile to Jews is a "fact" that Jews have seen borne out in their history over the centuries. Christian literature is rife with anti-Semitism, beginning with the Gospels' ill-starred attempts to shift the entire blame for Jesus' execution from the Romans onto the Jewish elders in Jerusalem. John Chrysostom's sermons against the Jews continued the tradition among the Church Fathers. Even today, the spurious *Protocols of the*

Elders of Zion can be downloaded from the Internet. It is not surprising, therefore, that a "happy ending" to a Jewish story about an averted genocide should include the deaths of their enemies. The Christian, reading the book of Esther as Scripture, should resolve to build a world in which such a "happy ending" would not be necessary because the threat would not exist in the first place.

ESTHER 9:11-15, THE FOURTEENTH OF ADAR

NIV

11The number of those slain in the citadel of Susa was reported to the king that same day. 12The king said to Queen Esther, "The Jews have killed and destroyed five hundred men and the ten sons of Haman in the citadel of Susa. What have they done in the rest of the king's provinces? Now what is your petition? It will be given you. What is your request? It will also be granted."

13"If it pleases the king," Esther answered, "give the Jews in Susa permission to carry out this day's edict tomorrow also, and let Haman's ten sons be hanged on gallows."

14So the king commanded that this be done. An edict was issued in Susa, and they hanged the ten sons of Haman. 15The Jews in Susa came together on the fourteenth day of the month of Adar, and they put to death in Susa three hundred men, but they did not lay their hands on the plunder.

NRSV

11That very day the number of those killed in the citadel of Susa was reported to the king. 12The king said to Queen Esther, "In the citadel of Susa the Jews have killed five hundred people and also the ten sons of Haman. What have they done in the rest of the king's provinces? Now what is your petition? It shall be granted you. And what further is your request? It shall be fulfilled." 13Esther said, "If it pleases the king, let the Jews who are in Susa be allowed tomorrow also to do according to this day's edict, and let the ten sons of Haman be hanged on the gallows." 14So the king commanded this to be done; a decree was issued in Susa, and the ten sons of Haman were hanged. 15The Jews who were in Susa gathered also on the fourteenth day of the month of Adar and they killed three hundred persons in Susa; but they did not touch the plunder.

COMMENTARY

Some scholars have found this a difficult set of verses to interpret because of their bloodthirsty tone; these objections are similar to those raised to the preceding section. Gerlemann claims that these verses owe their existence only to the need to explain the historical fact of a later two-day festival.[178] In fact, vv. 11-15 are not well integrated into the flow of the narrative, since the king's question and Esther's response are, as far as one can tell, completely unmotivated. In v. 11 the king, for the first time in the narrative, receives accurate information in a timely fashion. The report is of the 500 Gentiles who have been killed in the citadel (v. 6). There is no mention of any Jewish loss of life; the implication is that there was none. The king then does something he has never done before: He takes the initiative. He reports to Esther the 500 dead and the killing of the ten sons of Haman. Is his tone one of wonderment, amazement, horror, or ingratiation?[179] He expresses no emotion concerning the battle losses. The king then asks Esther for her "petition and request" and promises that he will give it to her, using almost exactly the same

178. Gilles Gerleman, "Studien zu Esther: Stoff—Struktur—Stil—Sinn," in Carey A. Moore, *Studies in the Book of Esther* (New York: Ktav, 1982) 308-49.

179. Fox, *Character and Ideology in the Book of Esther*, 112, believes that admiration is the only possible tone.

vocabulary he used in chaps. 6–7. It is not clear why he does this; he has already given her a free hand, and her objective has been fulfilled. This whole exchange, like the second day of killing that follows it, seems redundant.[180]

Esther's response (v. 13) is also unexpected. Her opening phrase, "if it please the king," is almost abrupt compared to the long and elaborate formula she used in 8:5.[181] This may indicate that she is feeling more confident and secure in her position now that the king has effectually ceded control of events to her (it may also indicate the hand of a different author). She requests that the Jews of Susa be allowed to continue their slaughter a second day and that the corpses of the ten sons of Haman be defiled by public exposure. Although the NRSV and the NIV have "hanged on the gallows," it is clear that a corpse's impalement on a stake is meant, since the ten sons of Haman are already dead, as reported in vv. 7-10. The use of the same phrase in 2:23; 5:14; and 6:9-10 may indicate that public impalement is meant there as well. Public exposure of a corpse is the ultimate degradation in the Hebrew tradition (Deut 21:22-23; 1 Sam 31:10-12). The principle of intergenerational retribution is at work in the treatment of the sons of Haman; their father's corpse was hanged and exposed, so theirs must be as well.

The king does exactly as Esther asks, and the Jews, in words parallel to v. 2, slay another 300 men. Again, emphasis is placed on the fact that they took no plunder. It is unclear why the Susan Jews need a second day, except to bring the story into line with the two-day festival. History here arises from custom, explaining why Susan Jews (or urban Jews?) celebrate the fifteenth rather than the fourteenth of Adar.

180. Paton, *Esther,* 287, sees it as not merely redundant, but reflecting "a malignant spirit of revenge."

181. D. N. Freedman, as reported by Moore, *Esther,* 88, noted that the use of the single phrase forms an inclusio with the same phrase in Esther's first request in 5:4, thus bringing her string of requests to a close.

REFLECTIONS

It is unfortunate that Esther's reappearance in the narrative should be in such a bloodthirsty guise, but this is in keeping with the tone of the rest of the chapter, which is motivated by desire for revenge for past oppression. Since the book of Esther is a product of a society and a worldview that accepted violence motivated by ethnic or religious causes, it would be unlikely for Esther to deviate from this worldview. Fox terms Esther's action in this section as "punitive and precautionary"; the enemies of the Jews must be eliminated before they can act again.[182] Once more, the reader should not condone the violence, but deplore the necessity for it; according to the story, the Jews in Susa have no fewer than 810 enemies willing to murder them. This time, thanks to the skill and wit of Esther and Mordecai, the Jews are safe—but this will not always be the case. Self-preservation through violence is accepted as a necessity in the world in which the author lives (his matter-of-fact tone throughout this section so indicates), but that is not the ideal.

182. Fox, *Character and Ideology in the Book of Esther,* 112.

ESTHER 9:16-19, THE JEWS CELEBRATE

NIV

16Meanwhile, the remainder of the Jews who were in the king's provinces also assembled to protect themselves and get relief from their enemies. They killed seventy-five thousand of

NRSV

16Now the other Jews who were in the king's provinces also gathered to defend their lives, and gained relief from their enemies, and killed seventy-five thousand of those who hated them;

NIV

them but did not lay their hands on the plunder.
17This happened on the thirteenth day of the
month of Adar, and on the fourteenth they rested
and made it a day of feasting and joy.
18The Jews in Susa, however, had assembled
on the thirteenth and fourteenth, and then on the
fifteenth they rested and made it a day of feasting
and joy.
19That is why rural Jews—those living in villages—observe the fourteenth of the month of
Adar as a day of joy and feasting, a day for giving
presents to each other.

NRSV

but they laid no hands on the plunder. 17This was
on the thirteenth day of the month of Adar, and
on the fourteenth day they rested and made that
a day of feasting and gladness.
18But the Jews who were in Susa gathered on
the thirteenth day and on the fourteenth, and
rested on the fifteenth day, making that a day of
feasting and gladness. 19Therefore the Jews of the
villages, who live in the open towns, hold the
fourteenth day of the month of Adar as a day for
gladness and feasting, a holiday on which they
send gifts of food to one another.

COMMENTARY

9:16.[183] According to this verse, the reason for the fighting on the thirteenth of Adar was self-defense ("the Jews gathered to stand for their lives"), harking back to Mordecai's decree in 8:11. Verse 16 follows very well after v. 10, omitting the section concerning the second day of fighting in Susa—a further indication that vv. 11-15 may be secondary. According to the text, the Jews in the provinces have slain 75,000 Gentiles, an enormous, hyperbolic number. The versions recognize the unreal quality of this number and reduce it, the LXX to 15,000 and the AT to 10,107 (a mysteriously exact figure). However, the huge number is also an indication of the widespread anti-Semitism that the author believed lurked in the provinces, and against which the Jews had to defend themselves. For the fourth time, the narrator emphasizes that the Jews took no spoils.

9:17-19. These verses give the historical basis for the celebration of the Festival of Purim. In v. 17, the theme of the feasts reappears; the Jews of the provinces fight on the thirteenth of Adar and rest on the fourteenth, celebrating with feasts. According to v. 18, the Jews in Susa (which becomes the representative for all walled cities) fight on the thirteenth and fourteenth, then celebrate on the fifteenth with a feast. Verse 19 makes it clear that this festival originated in the villages, in the countryside; it is a Jewish holiday belonging to the diaspora (the LXX glosses the verse by noting that urban Jews celebrate on the fifteenth). This must have been the situation that obtained in the author's (or perhaps a redactor's) time; originally Purim was a one-day festival, the day of celebration determined by one's place of residence. It is certainly a "good day," consisting of feasting, rejoicing, and sending gifts to others.[184] All of these actions recall motifs mentioned earlier in the story. These latter two feasts mirror the two feasts of Ahasuerus in 1:2, 4. The rejoicing that accompanies these feasts contrasts with the mourning that occurred following the decree of Haman (4:3). And finally, the "portions" (מנות *mānôt*) of food that the Jews send to one another recall the special "portion" that Hegai gives to Esther after she wins his favor (2:9), arguably the one incident (coincidence?) that set all the other events in the story in motion. There is no mention of prayers, sacrifices in the Temple, or any other ceremonial actions that ordinarily accompany festivals prescribed in the Torah (cf. Lev 23:4-44); it is, in keeping with the rest of the book, a seemingly secular festival. Respite from fighting is celebrated, not victory; it is safety, not slaughter, that is celebrated. This festival is the whole point of the book of Esther as it now stands, although its historical antecedents are very cloudy (see Introduction).[185]

183. These verses are omitted by the AT.

184. See Sandra Beth Berg, *The Book of Esther: Motifs, Themes, and Structure,* SBLDS 44 (Missoula, Mont.: Scholars Press, 1979) 45.

185. 2 Macc 15:13 mentions Adar 14 as "the Day of Mordecai," evidently a minor celebration. Is this the same as Purim? See Introduction.

ESTHER 9:20-32, THE LETTERS OF PURIM

OVERVIEW

The purpose for the letters written by Mordecai and Esther is to establish the Festival of Purim. The author is trying to account for the fact that Purim is not a festival decreed by Moses in the Torah. By whose authority does it exist? This is not a unique problem to the author of Esther; several festivals celebrated in contemporary Judaism are not legislated in the Torah. The most obvious comparison to Purim is Hanukkah, a festival commemorating the victory of Judas Maccabeus over the Seleucids in 164 BCE, as recounted in 1 Maccabees 4 and 2 Macc 10:1-8. However, Hanukkah commemorates an actual event in Jewish history; Purim, as has been demonstrated in this commentary, does not. The author solves this problem by artificially tying the Festival of Purim to the fictitious, but popular, story of Esther and Mordecai and by inserting the letters found here, giving the festival written sanction. A similar process is also found at Qumran, where the text 4QReworked Pentateuch interpolates legislation concerning the Wood Festival and the New Oil Festival, post-exilic, non-Mosaic festivals, into Leviticus 23.[186]

186. E. Tov and S. White, "4QReworked Pentateuch: 4Q364-367, with an appendix on 4Q365a," in *Discoveries in the Judaean Desert XIII* (Oxford: Oxford University Press, 1994) esp. 290-96.

Esther 9:20-28, Mordecai's Letter

NIV

20Mordecai recorded these events, and he sent letters to all the Jews throughout the provinces of King Xerxes, near and far, 21to have them celebrate annually the fourteenth and fifteenth days of the month of Adar 22as the time when the Jews got relief from their enemies, and as the month when their sorrow was turned into joy and their mourning into a day of celebration. He wrote them to observe the days as days of feasting and joy and giving presents of food to one another and gifts to the poor.

23So the Jews agreed to continue the celebration they had begun, doing what Mordecai had written to them. 24For Haman son of Hammedatha, the Agagite, the enemy of all the Jews, had plotted against the Jews to destroy them and had cast the *pur* (that is, the lot) for their ruin and destruction. 25But when the plot came to the king's attention,[a] he issued written orders that the evil scheme Haman had devised against the Jews should come back onto his own head, and that he and his sons should be hanged on the gallows. 26(Therefore these days were called Purim, from the word *pur*.) Because of everything

a25 Or *when Esther came before the king*

NRSV

20Mordecai recorded these things, and sent letters to all the Jews who were in all the provinces of King Ahasuerus, both near and far, 21enjoining them that they should keep the fourteenth day of the month Adar and also the fifteenth day of the same month, year by year, 22as the days on which the Jews gained relief from their enemies, and as the month that had been turned for them from sorrow into gladness and from mourning into a holiday; that they should make them days of feasting and gladness, days for sending gifts of food to one another and presents to the poor. 23So the Jews adopted as a custom what they had begun to do, as Mordecai had written to them.

24Haman son of Hammedatha the Agagite, the enemy of all the Jews, had plotted against the Jews to destroy them, and had cast Pur—that is "the lot"—to crush and destroy them; 25but when Esther came before the king, he gave orders in writing that the wicked plot that he had devised against the Jews should come upon his own head, and that he and his sons should be hanged on the gallows. 26Therefore these days are called Purim, from the word Pur. Thus because of all that was written in this letter, and of what they

NIV

written in this letter and because of what they had seen and what had happened to them, [27]the Jews took it upon themselves to establish the custom that they and their descendants and all who join them should without fail observe these two days every year, in the way prescribed and at the time appointed. [28]These days should be remembered and observed in every generation by every family, and in every province and in every city. And these days of Purim should never cease to be celebrated by the Jews, nor should the memory of them die out among their descendants.

NRSV

had faced in this matter, and of what had happened to them, [27]the Jews established and accepted as a custom for themselves and their descendants and all who joined them, that without fail they would continue to observe these two days every year, as it was written and at the time appointed. [28]These days should be remembered and kept throughout every generation, in every family, province, and city; and these days of Purim should never fall into disuse among the Jews, nor should the commemoration of these days cease among their descendants.

COMMENTARY

9:20-22.[187] Mordecai writes in his own name, rather than in the name of the king, a report of the king's decree of the festival; but here the letter is addressed only to the Jews. He seems to be writing as a fellow Jew making a request, not as an official declaring the law (דת *dāt*), in marked contrast to all other decrees issued in the book. As Fox points out, Mordecai is taking a bold step by inaugurating a new Jewish holiday.[188]

The section begins with Mordecai recording "these things" (הדברים האלה *haddĕbārîm hā'ēlleh*). To what does "these things" refer? The Jewish commentator Rashi believed that it referred to the events of the book of Esther. However, the phrase probably refers to the events just narrated, since elsewhere Mordecai makes no claim to authorship of the book. A summary of "these things" would appear to be found in vv. 24-26*a*. The locations to which Mordecai's letter is sent are described differently from previous chapters: "near and far" rather than "from India to Ethiopia," for example, possibly indicating the secondary character of this section.

Notice that Mordecai does not write to begin a yearly celebration, but to confirm one that is already taking place. The fourteenth and fifteenth of Adar now become the days of a yearly celebration. This differs from v. 19, where provincial Jews celebrated on the fourteenth and Susan Jews on the fifteenth. Mordecai seems to be requesting that all Jews everywhere celebrate both days. Verse 22 gives a clear reason for the celebration: the fact that the Jews had rest and reversal of fortune. Again the theme of reversal is highlighted. Their salvation through their own efforts is to be celebrated, not the slaughter of their enemies (if the victory was to be celebrated, the festival would fall on Adar 13 and 14). The manner of celebrating is an echo of v. 19, with the exception of the added injunction to give gifts to the poor. This may be a post-exilic emphasis; Neh 8:10-12, which contains directions for Rosh Hashanah, also emphasizes sending food to the poor, and Tobit invites the poor to his Pentecost feast (Tob 2:2). Yet, no mention is made of any overtly religious practice.

9:23-26. The Jews then confirm the holiday (v. 23) by accepting what they had already begun to do and what Mordecai had requested that they do.[189] This establishment of the holiday is evidently a three-part, reciprocal process: (1) The holiday is unofficially celebrated; (2) Mordecai writes a letter to make it official; and (3) the Jews affirm it. Verses 24-26*a* give a "precis" of events, slightly changed from the actual events of the

187. The AT omits vv. 23-26, and the OL omits vv. 24-27.
188. Fox, *Character and Ideology in the Book of Esther,* 117.

189. Jon D. Levenson, *Esther,* OTL (Louisville: Westminster/John Knox, 1997) 126, notes that this action on the part of the people is similar to that of the Israelites at Sinai when they affirmed the obligations of the covenant (Exod 24:3-8).

book: Haman the Agagite, now the enemy of all the Jews, devises a plot to destroy them (Mordecai's role in this is not recounted; if Mordecai is the actual author of the letter, he may prefer to pass over his own, not very edifying, actions in silence) and casts "lots" (פור *pûr*) "to harass [המם *hummām*; note the assonance of *hummām* with Haman] and annihilate them." This is a different function for the *pûr* from that in chap. 3, probably indicating that the history of the name "Purim" and its connection to the festival were only imperfectly understood by this redactor. Haman's evil plot is turned back upon him. The king, rather than Esther, is given credit for foiling the scheme; Fox sees this heaping of credit on the king as further proof of Mordecai's skills as a courtier, but it is also proof of the androcentric bias of the text.[190] The Hebrew of v. 25 does not contain the name "Esther," but rather an unspecified feminine suffix, which may be the otherwise unmentioned Esther (so NRSV) or the plot itself (so NIV). The LXX makes the suffix masculine, thus referring to the plot. Finally, Haman and his sons are hanged (Moore points out that these events are telescoped, since the hanging of father and sons seems to take place at the same time),[191] with no mention of the tremendous slaughter recounted in earlier parts of the chapter. In spite of the valiant efforts of v. 26, it remains unclear why the days are called Purim. The verse does not clarify why the word is plural, since Haman only cast *pûr* (singular); nor does it explain why the holiday is named after an action of the enemy Haman. The holiday and its name existed before the book of Esther, and the author never manages successfully to tie the events of the book and the name together.

9:27-28. The Jews agree to celebrate Purim yearly, "in all their generations" (בכל־דור ודור *bĕkōl-dôr wādôr*) and by "family" (משפחה *mišpāḥâ*), the first time in Esther that these two terms appear.[192] The author is here (unintentionally?) revealing his distance in time from the events narrated; Purim was already an established holiday at the time of writing. The purpose of this material is probably to convince those not already celebrating Purim of the historical validity of the festival. Notice the reference to "all who joined them"—that is, converts. This is an oblique reference to "those who became Jews" in 8:17. It is difficult to escape the sense that v. 28, which spells out the reason for the book of Esther, sounds like an ending: Purim will always be celebrated and will never be forgotten.

190. Fox, *Character and Ideology in the Book of Esther*, 120.
191. Moore, *Esther*, 120.

192. Lev 23:14, 21, 31, 41, 43 uses the term *dôr*, "generation," to emphasize that the Mosaic festivals are to be celebrated in perpetuity.

REFLECTIONS

Purim has proved to be a festival of enduring popularity, sometimes compared to the Christian celebration of Mardi Gras, which it resembled in its emphasis on feasting and hilarity (although the reasons for the two celebrations are very different). Purim begins on the fourteenth of Adar (usually sometime in March in the Western calendar), but is preceded by a minor fast, the Fast of Esther, on the thirteenth of Adar, during which observant Jews fast from sunup until sundown (this fast day came into existence c. 700–750 CE). On the fourteenth of Adar, the Scroll (*mĕgillat*) of Esther is read publicly in the congregation. In some traditions, this reading is accompanied by sound effects from the congregation. For example, there will be shouting and stamping of feet whenever Haman's name is mentioned. The fifteenth of Adar was originally celebrated as a feast day in towns walled in the time of Joshua. This was later extended to all cities, and now a two-day festival is generally kept by all. In Jerusalem there has also been a tradition of a three-day festival.

In every Jewish tradition, Purim is characterized by feasting at home and sending gifts of food to others. Charitable giving is also emphasized. It is now customary for Purim parties to be held, especially for children, for which the celebrants wear costumes, dressing up as Mordecai, Esther, Ahasuerus, and Vashti. This has led to some comparison with the American celebration of Halloween, but the comparison is superficial at best. Altogether, Purim is a delightful, well-beloved holiday.[193]

193. For further information, see Hayyim Schauss, *The Jewish Festivals: History and Observance* (New York: Schocken, 1938) 237-71.

Esther 9:29-32, Esther's Letter

NIV

[29]So Queen Esther, daughter of Abihail, along with Mordecai the Jew, wrote with full authority to confirm this second letter concerning Purim. [30]And Mordecai sent letters to all the Jews in the 127 provinces of the kingdom of Xerxes—words of goodwill and assurance— [31]to establish these days of Purim at their designated times, as Mordecai the Jew and Queen Esther had decreed for them, and as they had established for themselves and their descendants in regard to their times of fasting and lamentation. [32]Esther's decree confirmed these regulations about Purim, and it was written down in the records.

NRSV

29Queen Esther daughter of Abihail, along with the Jew Mordecai, gave full written authority, confirming this second letter about Purim. [30]Letters were sent wishing peace and security to all the Jews, to the one hundred twenty-seven provinces of the kingdom of Ahasuerus, [31]and giving orders that these days of Purim should be observed at their appointed seasons, as the Jew Mordecai and Queen Esther enjoined on the Jews, just as they had laid down for themselves and for their descendants regulations concerning their fasts and their lamentations. [32]The command of Queen Esther fixed these practices of Purim, and it was recorded in writing.

COMMENTARY

These verses probably were originally separate and focused on Esther; the mention of Mordecai (always referred to as "the Jew Mordecai") should be viewed as an interpolation. If the name "Mordecai" is removed from v. 29, what is left is a separate letter from Queen Esther.[194] Esther is given her title and her patronymic; she is both queen and Jew, and she writes with full authority (more in keeping with the "law" [דת *dāt*] of the Persian chancellery) to establish what Mordecai could only request. "This second letter of Purim" must refer to Mordecai's letter, but the referent of "second" is unclear, since there has been, so far, only one letter. Therefore, "second" may be a later gloss, mistakenly referring to Esther's letter. The first words in v. 30 simply are "and he sent letters [וישלח ספרים *wayyišlaḥ sĕpārîm*]." The "he" may refer to Mordecai or may be a scribal or editorial change, with the original text reading "and *she* sent letters," referring to Esther.[195] It is unlikely that Mordecai is also sending the letter, since he is referred to in the third person in v. 31. Verse 30 more clearly imitates the language of earlier passages in which letters were sent by repeating the phrase "one hundred and twenty-seven provinces" (1:1; 8:9). In v. 31, Esther "gives orders" that the days of Purim be observed, mandating a two-day festival. It is possible that "in their approved seasons" reflects some confusion about the time of the festival. Fox suggests removing "and Queen Esther" from v. 31 as a later gloss, because she is here confirming Mordecai's instructions. That this section is referring to Mordecai's letter is confirmed by the fact that Esther's letter seems to allude to the Jews' confirmation of the festival, explicitly requested in v. 21 (the same verb, "impose" [קים *qiyyam*, in the piel], is used).

194. The remarks on this section are heavily dependent on Fox's emended text and his comments, arguing that this section can be viewed as a separate letter from Esther alone. See Fox, *Character and Ideology in the Book of Esther*, 123-27.

195. See ibid., 125, 286.

The mention of fasts and lamentations in v. 31 is confusing in the context; the Hebrew is clearly not referring to fasts and lamentations associated with Purim,[196] but to other holy days.[197] The text simply seems to be saying: "Just as you take upon yourselves non-Mosaic fasts, so also you can take upon yourselves non-Mosaic festivals." This may be a hidden reference to one salient objection to the Festival of Purim: It was not legislated in the Torah. Verse 32 makes clear that the authority of Esther the Persian queen establishes Purim. This authorization of a festival by a woman who is the queen of a foreign empire and whose personal commitment to Judaism is, in the eyes of later readers, at least suspect may explain the confused state of the text. There may have been objection to this "foreign" feast in some circles (Judean?); thus an effort was made to show that Mordecai the *Jew,* and the Jews themselves, not the suspect Esther, established the Festival of Purim. Thus was Esther's hard-won authority partially removed.

196. Contra Paton, *Esther,* 301; Moore, *Esther,* 96-97.

197. In the present Jewish calendar the thirteenth of Adar is a minor fast known as Esther's Fast. But according to Ibn Ezra, "fasting and lamentations" refers to other holy days, like the Ninth of Ab, established (by prophetic word) in Zech 8:18-19.

REFLECTIONS

Esther has made her last appearance in her story. Her character has undergone rapid change and growth, from passive girl to powerful woman. She has been identified as a role model for Jews living in the diaspora, and it is time to ask whether she has been successful in that role. As a woman living in a patriarchal, androcentric culture, she has been completely successful, using the male power structure, beginning with Hegai and ending with Ahasuerus, to achieve her goals. As a Jew, a member of a minority community within a foreign empire, she has succeeded beyond all expectations, bringing her cousin Mordecai to power and achieving safety and security for the Jews. She has played her part with wisdom and skill throughout and has chosen to act according to what the author assumes, but does not state, is the will of God. As such, she is a role model for Jews living in dispersion and, indeed, for any oppressed minority. Some of the circumstances of her day are now in our day rightly condemned as wrong, such as the use of women as sexual objects and the use of violence to reach political ends. However, those were the realities that people in the author's time (and often in our own) had to face. Within those constraints, Esther is wholly admirable. She should be embraced as a heroine working to further God's will in the world.

ESTHER 10:1-3, APPENDIX CONCERNING MORDECAI

NIV

10 King Xerxes imposed tribute throughout the empire, to its distant shores. [2]And all his acts of power and might, together with a full account of the greatness of Mordecai to which the king had raised him, are they not written in the book of the annals of the kings of Media and Persia? [3]Mordecai the Jew was second in rank to King Xerxes, preeminent among the Jews, and held in high esteem by his many fellow Jews,

NRSV

10 King Ahasuerus laid tribute on the land and on the islands of the sea. [2]All the acts of his power and might, and the full account of the high honor of Mordecai, to which the king advanced him, are they not written in the annals of the kings of Media and Persia? [3]For Mordecai the Jew was next in rank to King Ahasuerus, and he was powerful among the Jews and popular with his many kindred, for he sought the good of

NIV	NRSV
because he worked for the good of his people and spoke up for the welfare of all the Jews.	his people and interceded for the welfare of all his descendants.

COMMENTARY

These verses may be a secondary addition (the AT does not contain them), written to give the book a more "fitting" conclusion. It can also be argued that they more convincingly tie chap. 9 to the rest of the book, since the glorification of Mordecai in these verses forms (with 8:1-2, the appearance of Mordecai in glory) an envelope for the fighting and letters in chap. 9.

10:1. Ahasuerus imposes a tax on his kingdom (this might be a corvée of labor, such as Solomon imposed in 1 Kgs 5:13). It is imposed on "the earth and the islands of the sea"—in other words, the known world, which is practically coextensive with the Persian Empire. The reason why the tax is imposed is not clear. When the king married Esther, he gave relief from taxes (2:18). Is he reimposing them here? This is possible, but not confirmed.[198]

10:2-3. The book's final verses are concerned with the greatness of Mordecai and the king (note the disappearance of Esther). Their greatness is recounted in formulaic language (cf. the descriptions of Azariah in 2 Kgs 15:1-6 and of Hezekiah in 2 Kgs 20:21-22) and is recorded in the royal chronicles, as is proper (cf. 2:23). Mordecai is not just generally great, however; he uses his greatness for the benefit of his fellow Jews, which, according to the message of the book, is how power is supposed to be used: for the benefit of others and not for self-aggrandizement. Although only the Jews are mentioned as beneficiaries of Mordecai's high office, the assumption of the text seems to be that his rule is beneficial to the entire empire and that no one suffers because he is Jewish. Here is another parallel to the Joseph story (Gen 47:13-26), where Joseph saves all of Egypt from famine. Again, that is the way government should act—for the benefit of all and the detriment of none. Mordecai is a living example of the wise ruler in action.

The major themes of the book—reversal, power, and escape from persecution—have been brought to closure. Although Ahasuerus is still on the throne, the pomposity and buffoonery of his court in chap. 1 have been replaced by the good and wise government of Mordecai in chap. 10. Mordecai's position has changed from threatened subordinate to all-powerful ruler, and the Jews have moved from the threat of annihilation to the beneficence of Mordecai's rule. Power, which was so important in chap. 1 that Ahasuerus had to banish Vashti to prove that he had it, has proved to be ephemeral in the hands of unworthy recipients. Only those worthy through strength of character (exemplified by the virtues of wisdom, modesty, and patience) have proved to be able to keep it (the exception to this is the king, who has hereditary power). Power, therefore, is not an end in itself but the reward of good character. Finally, the Jews have escaped from the sentence of genocide and achieved their goal, which was to live peacefully and securely within the Persian Empire. As Levenson states, "The scene with which the Masoretic Esther closes is one for which Jewish communities in the Diaspora have always longed: Jews living in harmony and mutual good will with the Gentile majority."[199]

198. D. Daube, "The Last Chapter of Esther," *JQR* 37 (1946–47) 139-47, has argued that the tax was a "peaceful substitute" for the plunder Ahasuerus would have received if Haman's plot had succeeded. However, there is no hint of this rather negative reason in the text.

199. Levenson, *Esther,* 133-34.

THE ADDITIONS TO ESTHER

INTRODUCTION, COMMENTARY, AND REFLECTIONS
BY
SIDNIE WHITE CRAWFORD

THE ADDITIONS TO ESTHER

INTRODUCTION

The so-called Additions to Esther, found in the Greek versions of Esther (LXX and AT), make the book of Esther a very different literary work from that in the Hebrew Bible (MT). The additions add drama, plumb the emotional depths of the characters, add information to fill in the gaps of the the MT, and, most important, supply an overt religious element that is lacking in the MT. To fully appreciate the LXX version of Esther, it is helpful to read it in its entirety, as it is found in the apocrypha of the NRSV. For the purposes of this commentary, however, each Addition will be treated separately. The Additions are not all from the same author, nor were they all composed in the same language. Josephus, who was certainly familiar with LXX, does not use all the Additions (e.g., he does not include Add. A), perhaps indicating that he did not know them all or did not consider them original.[1]

The most striking change in the LXX version of Esther is the addition of religious elements. The additions continually mention God, and the LXX redactor introduces the name of God within the (translated) text of the MT:

"to fear God and obey his commandments" (2:20)
"call upon the Lord" (4:8)
"and the Lord drove sleep from the king that night" (6:1)
"for God is with him" (6:13).

Also, the Additions contain a dream sent by God (Addition A), prayers by Mordecai and

1. Josephus *Antiquities of the Jews* Book XI.

Esther, fasting explicitly directed toward God, a manifest concern for keeping the purity laws, especially those concerning food and marriage, a mention of the Temple (all in Addition C), and a Gentile acknowledgment of the power of the God of Israel (Addition E).[2] The effect of all these changes is that God becomes the hero of the Greek story, and the importance of human action is greatly lessened; the LXX redactor makes clear to the reader that God acts to save the Jews and that, because of God's protective concern for the Jews, the outcome of the crisis is never in doubt.

This change in emphasis also leads to changes in the main human characters, Mordecai and Esther. Mordecai, as the recipient of the dream sent by God, becomes a typical biblical hero, like Joseph or Daniel, and is the chief human character in the drama. Esther, on the other hand, loses status from her portrayal in the MT: She becomes a romantic and emotional heroine, as in the Hellenistic romance novel, and, as such, is less attractive to modern readers.[3]

(See the annotated bibliography for the Hebrew book of Esther.)

2. Carey A. Moore, *Daniel, Esther and Jeremiah: The Additions,* AB 44 (Garden City, N.Y.: Doubleday, 1977) 158-59.

3. For LXX Esther as a Hellenistic romance novel, see Lawrence M. Wills, *The Jew in the Court of the Foreign King,* HDR 26 (Minneapolis: Fortress, 1990) 197.

OUTLINE OF THE ADDITIONS TO ESTHER

I. Esther Addition A 1-17, Mordecai's Dream and the Eunuchs' Plot

- A. A 1-11, Mordecai's Dream
- B. A 12-17, The Plot of the Eunuchs

II. Esther Addition B 1-7, The Letter of Haman

III. Esther Addition C 1-30, The Prayers of Esther and Mordecai

- A. C 1-11, The Prayer of Mordecai
- B. C 12-30, The Prayer of Esther

IV. Esther Addition D 1-16, Esther Appears Before the King

V. Esther Addition E 1-24, Mordecai's Letter

VI. Esther Addition F 1-11, The End of the Greek Esther

- A. F 1-10, The Interpretation of Mordecai's Dream
- B. F 11, The Colophon of the Greek Esther

ESTHER ADDITION A 1-17 (AT 1:1-18; VG 11:2–12:16)[4]

MORDECAI'S DREAM AND THE EUNUCHS' PLOT

OVERVIEW

Addition A was composed in a Semitic language (Hebrew or Aramaic). This Addition probably dates to the late second century BCE, after the time of the Maccabean wars. Gentiles, according to Addition A, have become completely hostile to the Jews, such that their only hope of salvation lies with God.

4. The various numbering systems of the Greek texts are based on *The Old Testament in Greek,* vol. 3, Part I: *Esther, Judith, Tobit,* ed. A. E. Brooke, N. McLean, H. S. J. Thackeray (London: Cambridge University Press, 1940).

ESTHER ADDITION A 1-11, MORDECAI'S DREAM

NAB

1 1 In the second year of the reign of the great King Ahasuerus, on the first day of Nisan, Mordecai, son of Jair, son of Shimei, son of Kish, of the tribe of Benjamin, had a dream. 2 He was a Jew residing in the city of Susa, a prominent man who served at the king's court, 3 and one of the captives whom Nebuchadnezzar, king of Babylon, had taken from Jerusalem with Jeconiah, king of Judah.

4 This was his dream. There was noise and tumult, thunder and earthquake—confusion upon the earth. 5 Two great dragons came on, both poised for combat. They uttered a mighty cry, 6 and at their cry every nation prepared for war, to fight against the race of the just. 7 It was a dark and gloomy day. Tribulation and distress, evil and great confusion, lay upon the earth. 8 The whole race of the just were dismayed with fear of the evils to come upon them, and were at the point of destruction. 9 Then they cried out to God, and as they cried, there appeared to come forth a great river, a flood of water from a little spring. 10 The light of the sun broke forth; the lowly were exalted and they devoured the nobles.

NRSV

ADDITION A

1[a] [2]In the second year of the reign of Artaxerxes the Great, on the first day of Nisan, Mordecai son of Jair son of Shimei[b] son of Kish, of the tribe of Benjamin, had a dream. [3]He was a Jew living in the city of Susa, a great man, serving in the court of the king. [4]He was one of the captives whom King Nebuchadnezzar of Babylon had brought from Jerusalem with King Jeconiah of Judea. And this was his dream: [5]Noises[c] and confusion, thunders and earthquake, tumult on the earth! [6]Then two great dragons came forward, both ready to fight, and they roared terribly. [7]At their roaring every nation prepared for war, to fight against the righteous nation. [8]It was a day of darkness and gloom, of tribulation and distress, affliction and great tumult on the earth! [9]And the whole righteous nation was troubled; they feared the evils that threatened them,[d] and were ready to perish. [10]Then they cried out

a Chapters 11.2—12.6 correspond to chapter A 1-17 in some translations. b Gk *Semeios* c Or *Voices* d Gk *their own evils*

NAB

11 Having seen this dream and what God intended to do, Mordecai awoke. He kept it in mind, and tried in every way, until night, to understand its meaning.

NRSV

to God; and at their outcry, as though from a tiny spring, there came a great river, with abundant water; [11]light came, and the sun rose, and the lowly were exalted and devoured those held in honor.

12Mordecai saw in this dream what God had determined to do, and after he awoke he had it on his mind, seeking all day to understand it in every detail.

COMMENTARY

Addition A opens with a date formula. The story is set in the reign of Artaxerxes, probably Artaxerxes I, the son of Xerxes (465–424 BCE), and takes place in the second year of his reign, one year earlier than the opening scene of the MT (understanding the change of kings from Xerxes to Artaxerxes). It begins on the first day of Nisan, which, as we have seen in MT Esther (3:12; 8:9), strikes a note of salvation as it is the month of the exodus and Passover; this is also the time of the spring new year festival in Babylonian, Persian, and Second Temple Jewish calendars. Mordecai, who is clearly the central human character of Greek Esther, is introduced and his full genealogy given. It is appropriate to give his full genealogy when he is introduced, but if this were part of the original book of Esther, it would be unnecessary to repeat it in 2:5 (an indication of the secondary character of Add. A). The first thing Mordecai does in Greek Esther is to have a dream. This places him in the company of two other visionaries on whom he is modeled: Joseph and Daniel. Like theirs, Mordecai's visionary capacity is understood as a gift from God. He is then further identified as a palace functionary (something alluded to but never openly stated in the MT) and as one of the exiles brought to Babylon in 597 BCE (again, a point of unclarity in the MT). If Mordecai was brought to Babylon as a young man in 597, in the second year of Artaxerxes I he would have been approximately 175 years old—an incredibly venerable person!

Mordecai's dream is recounted in vv. 4-10. Chaos is consuming the earth. Two dragons appear, roaring and ready to fight. Both chaos and the dragon are major symbols found in apocalyptic imagery.[5] Chaos, the upheaval of the natural order, signals the absence of God and the breakdown of the social order (cf. Isa 34:9-11; Joel 2:2-3). The word "dragon" (δράκων *drakōn*) encompasses a wide range of terrifying, yet real, beasts in the LXX, such as the jackal in Jer 9:11, and mythical animals such as Leviathan (Job 26:13; Ps 74:12-13 [LXX 73:12-13]), while in apocalyptic literature it becomes a major symbol of evil (Rev 12:3; 2 Bar 29:3-8). Thus it is clear that Mordecai's dream is a bad omen. A problem in the decoding of their appearance here in Esther, however, is that the dragons do not symbolize real beasts or nations (which are separately mentioned in v. 7), but humans. Further, there is not just one, but two, which is an anomaly; and the second is meant to symbolize Mordecai, one of the heroes of the book. The symbolism of "dragon" does not fit the (positive) character of Mordecai, so the author's choice of it is mysterious.

At the roaring of the dragons, the nations, as separate entities, prepare to fight. These nations will battle against the righteous nation, certainly to be identified with Israel (Wis 16:23; 18:7). This symbolism in Add. A turns the LXX version of Esther into an apocalyptic struggle between other nations and Israel (cf. Joel 2:2, 10-11; Zeph 1:15), not a conflict between individuals, as in Hebrew Esther. It should be noted that in the AT and the

5. "Apocalyptic" is an adjective derived from the noun "apocalypse" (ἀποκάλυψις *apokalypsis*) and refers loosely to a group of themes, concepts, and motifs that frequently appear in works classified as apocalypses. These themes include divine intervention in human history, eschatological judgment by God, otherworldly conflicts, and visions. See Mitchell Reddish, *Apocalyptic Literature: A Reader* (Nashville: Abingdon, 1990) 28.

OL, the nations are ready to fight and are afraid, but their hostility is not directed toward Israel. Verses 8-9 sum up the vision in apocalyptic tones (cf. Joel 2:2; Matt 24:29). Israel is ready to perish from fear. There is no salvation on the human horizon. This dream sets the battle upon the cosmic stage, among the otherworldly powers, rather than on the human stage in a court conflict.[6]

The response, then, must come from the cosmic realm, from God, who responds to Israel's cry (see Exod 3:7-9, where God responds to Israel's cry by sending the human savior Moses). This first mention of God in LXX Esther signals the major difference between the Hebrew and the Greek versions: the presence of God as an active character in the drama. God's salvation, however, is enigmatic; a mighty river comes from a tiny spring, and light and sun follow. Water and light are symbols of salvation in Israelite literature (Zech 14:7-8; Wis 5:6). The referents of the symbols used here are not transparent; "spring" must symbolize Esther, but how the river achieves salvation is not explained, nor are the dragons ever destroyed. However, it is clear that God acts to save Israel, for it is stated that the lowly (exiled Israel) will "devour" the esteemed, a typical Jewish eschatological scenario (cf. Luke 1:52-53). Mordecai, like Joseph and Daniel, is puzzled as to the meaning of his dream. Mordecai may be troubled, but the reader is not meant to be; like Joseph's dream about his brothers (Gen 37:5-8), Mordecai's dream foreshadows the action to come. Therefore, the reader is reassured from the beginning of the book that everything will turn out well, for God's plan is at work. God becomes the main character in the LXX edition of Esther. God is the real hero; everything that happens is a result of the divine plan and maneuverings.

6. For a thorough discussion of the apocalyptic genre see John Collins, *The Apocalyptic Imagination* (New York: Crossroad, 1984) esp. chaps. 1 and 3. The transformation of the book of Esther from court tale (MT) to apocalyptic drama (LXX) is similar to the transformation that takes place in the book of Daniel, where the literary character of chapters 2–6 as royal courtier tales has been transformed by their inclusion in the apocalyptic book of Daniel.

REFLECTIONS

The absolute conflict between the nations and Israel in the LXX is far more severe than the sporadic and occasional hostility between Gentile and Jew, interspersed with episodes of goodwill, found in the MT. This is a product of the historical period of the LXX, during which the Hellenistic empires were, in their later period, far less tolerant of Jewish monotheism and ethnic solidarity than the Persians had been.[7] It is also, perhaps, far more typical of the Jewish experience in the diaspora than is the scenario of MT Esther. In later times, Western Christendom in particular has been radically intolerant of Jewish "otherness." Since the message of LXX Esther reassures the Jews that God will defend them, Christians are called to reexamine their past vis-à-vis the Jews and to consider a different, more tolerant path in the future.

God is vividly present from the very first verses of LXX Esther and is seen unabashedly as the deliverer of the Jews. This brings Esther into conformity with the general biblical theology in which God intervenes in the events of history for Israel's benefit. The LXX redactor had no doubts about the hints in MT Esther: It was God who delivered the Jews, with Mordecai and Esther acting as divine instruments.

7. See, e.g., V. Tcherikover, *Hellenistic Civilization and the Jews* (New York: Jewish Publication Society, 1959).

ESTHER ADDITION A 12-17, THE PLOT OF THE EUNUCHS

NAB

12 Mordecai lodged at the court with Bagathan and Thares, two eunuchs of the king who were court guards. 13 He overheard them plotting, investigated their plans, and discovered that they were preparing to lay hands on King Ahasuerus. So he informed the king about them, 14 and the king had the two eunuchs questioned and, upon their confession, put to death. 15 Then the king had these things recorded; Mordecai, too, put them into writing. 16 The king also appointed Mordecai to serve at the court, and rewarded him for his actions.

17 Haman, however, son of Hammedatha the Agagite, who was in high honor with the king, sought to harm Mordecai and his people because of the two eunuchs of the king.

A, 1.13; B, 1: (*Basileuontos*) *Assuerou*: so LXX^L, Vet Lat; cf MT 1, 1.
A, 12: (*meta*) *Bagathan (kai*) *Thares*: cf MT 2, 21; 6, 2.
A, 17: (*Aman Amadathou*) *agagaios*: cf MT 3, 1.10; etc.

NRSV

12 Now Mordecai took his rest in the courtyard with Gabatha and Tharra, the two
eunuchs of the king who kept watch in the
courtyard. 2He overheard their conversation and
inquired into their purposes, and learned that they
were preparing to lay hands on King Artaxerxes;
and he informed the king concerning them. 3Then
the king examined the two eunuchs, and after
they had confessed it, they were led away to
execution. 4The king made a permanent record of
these things, and Mordecai wrote an account of
them. 5And the king ordered Mordecai to serve
in the court, and rewarded him for these things.
6But Haman son of Hammedatha, a Bougean, who
was in great honor with the king, determined to
injure Mordecai and his people because of the
two eunuchs of the king.

END OF ADDITION A

COMMENTARY

These verses, more than any others in LXX Esther, are in conflict with MT Esther. They repeat, with variations, the episode found in Esth 2:21-23. If this material in Add. A were original, then Esth 2:21-23 would be redundant; however, it is more likely that A 12-17 comes from a later redactor. There is also a time conflict; this episode takes place before Esther becomes queen, while Esth 2:21-23 takes place after she has become queen. It is not possible that these are two separate episodes; the plot, the characters, and the result are the same. (Other conflicts will be pointed out as we move through the verses.) Finally, neither the OL nor Josephus contains these verses, indicating their lack of originality.

The names of the two eunuchs, Gabatha and Tharra, are probably corruptions of the Hebrew names Bigthan and Teresh and are otherwise unidentified. Mordecai overhears their plot (v. 12), thus clearing up an ambiguity in MT 2:21. He then informs the king himself, rather than going through Esther, as in Esth 2:22. Of course, since Esther is not yet the queen, it is impossible for her to inform the king, but this is a blatant contradiction of the MT. The king, as in the MT, takes direct action, and the eunuchs are executed.

As in the MT, the king makes a record of these events, although it is not titled "the book of the annals." The NRSV's 12:4*b,* where Mordecai also writes an account, is derived from the AT, but its purpose is not clear. Mordecai is ordered to serve in the court, but according to Add. A 2, Mordecai already serves in the court, an internal contradiction. Mordecai is also rewarded by the king, an appropriate action on the king's part; however, now MT 6:1-11 is entirely superfluous because Mordecai has already been rewarded.

The last verse of this section reveals its real purpose: to introduce Haman and to explain his enmity toward Mordecai. Haman is called the son of Hammadatha, as in the MT, but he is identified as a Bougaion. This may be a corruption of "Agagite," but it may also be a reference to the Aramaic בגוהי (*bagōhî*), the name of a notorious eunuch under Artaxerxes I who desecrated the Temple. It is also possible that *bagōhî* is a eunuch's title, rather than a name;[8] the implication would then be that Haman was a eunuch, but this is contradicted by the fact that he had children. In any case, "Bougaion" (Βουγαῖον) is clearly a term of opprobrium. The AT has "Macedonian" rather than "Bougaion"; this refers to the successors of Alexander the Great, who conquered the Persian Empire in 332 BCE. The Persians and the Greeks were long-standing enemies; Xerxes had attempted to conquer the Greek mainland and was defeated at Salamis and Plateia, and Artaxerxes continued to have trouble with the Athenians.[9] Referring to Haman as a Macedonian thus makes him an enemy infiltrator of the Persian court. Further, in the Hellenistic period, the Macedonians, in the form of the Seleucid emperors beginning with Antiochus IV Epiphanes, became the major enemies of the Jews.[10] There can be no doubt that Haman is an enemy both to the Jews and to the Persians; indeed, the verse implies that, despite his "great honor" with the king, he was behind the plot of the eunuchs. Therefore, his enmity toward Mordecai stems from the fact that Mordecai foiled his plot to assassinate the king, rather than from Mordecai's failure to bow to him. This clears up the ambiguity of the conflict between Haman and Mordecai in the MT, since a reference to the conflict between Saul and Agag may not have been clear to a Greek-speaking Jewish audience. It also explains the inclusion of this episode at the beginning of the book.

Addition A consists of two separate episodes, neither of which is original to proto-Esther and may be the work of different authors.[11] The dream may have circulated separately before its inclusion in the Esther story; its imagery and symbols do not quite fit the events of the story, as its interpretation in Add. F reveals. The episode of the eunuchs' plot, however, is intrinsic to the story of Esther and Mordecai; its inclusion here, with its obvious reworkings, appears to be the work of a clumsy redactor.

8. *4QTales of the Persian Court* contains the name "Bagoshe," belonging to an opponent of the protagonist, Bagasraw. "Bagoshe" resembles both "Bagohi" and Josephus's spelling of the name, "Bagoas." The proliferation of "bagohis," all in reference to Persian officials, gives support to the idea that the word is a title of an officer of the Persian Empire. See Josephus *Antiquities of the Jews* VII.1, and Papyrus #30 from the Jewish colony at Elephantine.

9. A. T. Olmstead, *The History of the Persian Empire* (Chicago: University of Chicago Press, 1948) 250-59, 302-13.

10. Daniel 7–12, Jubilees, Judith, and the books of the Maccabees, all dating from the second and first centuries BCE, reflect this conflict. The fact that the AT also reflects it is a probable indication of the date of the AT.

11. Moore, *Daniel, Esther, and Jeremiah: The Additions,* 180. Jon D. Levenson, *Esther,* OTL (Louisville: Westminster/John Knox, 1997) 41, suggests that Add. A may reflect a "variant telling" of the Esther story.

ESTHER ADDITION B 1-7 (AT 4:14-18; VG 13:1-7)

THE LETTER OF HAMAN

NAB

B 1 This is a copy of the letter:
"The great King Ahasuerus writes to the satraps of the hundred and twenty-seven provinces from India to Ethiopia, and the governors subordinate to them, as follows: 2 When I came to rule many peoples and to hold sway over the whole world, I determined not to be carried away with the sense of power, but always to deal fairly and with clemency; to provide for my subjects a life of complete tranquillity; and by making my government humane and effective as far as the borders, to restore the peace desired by all men. 3 When I consulted my counselors as to how this might be accomplished, Haman, who excels among us in wisdom, who is outstanding for constant devotion and steadfast loyalty, and who has gained the second rank in the kingdom, 4 brought it to our attention that, mixed in with all the races throughout the world, there is one people of bad will, which by its laws is opposed to every other people and continually disregards the decrees of kings, so that the unity of empire blamelessly designed by us cannot be established.

5 "Having noted, therefore, that this most singular people is continually at variance with all men, lives by divergent and alien laws, is inimical to our interests, and commits the worst crimes, so that stability of government cannot be obtained, 6 we hereby decree that all those who are indicated to you in the letters of Haman, who is in charge of the administration and is a second father to us, shall, together with their wives and children, be utterly destroyed by the swords of their enemies, without any pity or mercy, on the fourteenth day of the twelfth month, Adar, of the current year; 7 so that when these people, whose present ill will is of long standing, have gone down into the nether world by a violent death

NRSV

ADDITION B

13 [a]This is a copy of the letter: "The Great King, Artaxerxes, writes the following to the governors of the hundred twenty-seven provinces from India to Ethiopia and to the officials under them:

2"Having become ruler of many nations and master of the whole world (not elated with presumption of authority but always acting reasonably and with kindness), I have determined to settle the lives of my subjects in lasting tranquility and, in order to make my kingdom peaceable and open to travel throughout all its extent, to restore the peace desired by all people.

3"When I asked my counselors how this might be accomplished, Haman—who excels among us in sound judgment, and is distinguished for his unchanging goodwill and steadfast fidelity, and has attained the second place in the kingdom—
4pointed out to us that among all the nations in the world there is scattered a certain hostile people, who have laws contrary to those of every nation and continually disregard the ordinances of kings, so that the unifying of the kingdom that we honorably intend cannot be brought about.
5We understand that this people, and it alone, stands constantly in opposition to every nation, perversely following a strange manner of life and laws, and is ill-disposed to our government, doing all the harm they can so that our kingdom may not attain stability.

6"Therefore we have decreed that those indicated to you in the letters written by Haman, who is in charge of affairs and is our second father, shall all—wives and children included—be utterly destroyed by the swords of their enemies, without pity or restraint, on the fourteenth day of the

[a] Chapter 13.1-7 corresponds to chapter B 1-7 in some translations.

NAB	NRSV
on one same day, they may at last leave our affairs stable and undisturbed for the future."	twelfth month, Adar, of this present year, [7]so that those who have long been hostile and remain so may in a single day go down in violence to Hades, and leave our government completely secure and untroubled hereafter." END OF ADDITION B

COMMENTARY

The inclusion of a copy of Haman's letter, which comes between 3:13 and 3:14 of the MT, stands in the tradition of including other copies of Persian decrees and letters in the Hebrew Bible (e.g., Ezra 1:2-4; 4:17-22; 6:3-12; 7:11-28).[12] The purpose of including it is to lend the narrative an air of historical veracity. The original language of this Addition is Greek; this is shown by its flowery rhetorical style and lack of the Semitic constructions usually found in Septuagintal Greek.[13] In content the letter is similar to another Greek composition, the letter of King Ptolemy Philopator, found in 3 Macc 3:12-29. The letter in 3 Maccabees reflects the anti-Semitism common throughout the Hellenistic Empire.

Verses 1-3. The extent of Artaxerxes' kingdom, described in v. 1, agrees with MT 1:1, as does the otherwise unknown 127 provinces. The word τοπάρχης (*toparchēs*, "governor") signifies the governor of a district. The preamble emphasizes the king's good intentions, but it is clearly disingenuous—what monarch has ever claimed not to want to bring peace and prosperity to his or her kingdom? The identity of the counselors is unknown, although the wise men of MT 1:13-14 may be meant. The grand rhetoric concerning Haman's goodness and wisdom is ironic—an unusual touch for the LXX redactor, who does not ordinarily imitate the ironic tone of the MT (recall that Haman is writing the decree!).

Verses 4-5. These verses contain the reasons for the decree. The anti-Semitism expressed is much more blunt than Haman's corresponding rhetoric in MT 3:8: The Jews are hostile; their laws (the Torah) are contrary to every other nation's; they do not obey the king's ordinances; and they follow a "perverse" law and are ill-disposed to the imperial government. This is typical of the heightened rhetoric of a Greek composition and may also reflect the Jews' experience of more extensive anti-Semitism during this period (cf. 3 Macc 3:13-29). Their destruction, according to Haman, is crucial to the stability of the kingdom.

Verses 6-7. The Jews are never identified by name, in keeping with MT Esther; however, one wonders how the identity of the intended victims is to be made known. The date, the fourteenth of Adar (v. 6), may be a copyist's error or may reflect confusion over the date or the reason for the celebration of Purim. If Purim is understood by the LXX redactor as a celebration of the defeat of the enemies, rather than as rest from the threat of destruction as in MT, then the original date of destruction must be the same as the date of the celebration. The writer of 2 Macc 15:36 refers to the fourteenth of Adar as the "Day of Mordecai," which may indicate some knowledge in the second century BCE of the festival that was later known as Purim. The mention of Hades in v. 7 indicates the letter's Greek origin.

12. See also Second Targum to Esther, which likewise includes a (different) copy of Haman's letter.

13. For a complete discussion of the rhetorical style, see C. A. Moore, "On the Origins of the LXX Additions to the Book of Esther," *JBL* 92 (1973) 382-93, and Moore, *Daniel, Esther, and Jeremiah: The Additions,* AB 44 (Garden City, N.Y.: Doubleday, 1977) 193.

REFLECTIONS

Unfortunately, between the time of the writing of MT Esther and the writing of LXX Esther, the nature of the charges leveled against the Jews had grown in strength and violence. That pattern has continued into the twentieth century: The Jews have been accused of forming a worldwide economic cabal, of drinking blood, of sacrificing Christian babies, and of corrupting Christian women.[14] None of these charges has been proved true, but that has not stopped some Christians (and some Muslims as well) from believing them. *The Protocols of the Elders of Zion,* a scurrilous diatribe against the Jews, first circulated in czarist Russia, is still available in the United States. Christians, as a group, have not had the will to condemn anti-Semitism as wrong and to fight against it. This would not surprise the redactor of LXX Esther, since he did not believe, as did the author of MT Esther, that it was possible for Jews and Gentiles to live together harmoniously. He believed, rather, that Jews will survive only with the active and overt intervention of God.

14. See Malcolm Hay, *Europe and the Jews: The Pressure of Christendom over 1900 Years* (Chicago: Academy Chicago Publishers, 1992), and Jacob Katz, *From Prejudice to Destruction: Anti-Semitism, 1700–1933* (Cambridge, Mass.: Harvard University Press, 1980).

ESTHER ADDITION C 1-30

THE PRAYERS OF ESTHER AND MORDECAI

OVERVIEW

This Addition, which follows MT 4:17, adds in the LXX tradition what was perceived as a lack in MT Esther: prayer and direct reference to God. The prayers are paraphrased by Josephus, indicating that they were present in his tradition.[15] This Addition, although now found only in Greek, was probably originally a Semitic composition. There exists in a late medieval manuscript an Aramaic version of Mordecai's prayer, containing similar passages in identical sequence. Moore suggests that the two compositions are related through the same original Hebrew text.[16] In addition, *4QTales of the Persian Court* contains a prayer by an unknown protagonist that contains similarities to Mordecai's prayer (see Introduction).

15. Josephus *Antiquities of the Jews* XI.239-253.

16. Moore, *Daniel, Esther, and Jeremiah: The Additions,* 205-7.

ESTHER ADDITION C 1-11 (AT 5:12-17; Vg 13:8-18), THE PRAYER OF MORDECAI

NAB

C Mordecai went away and did exactly as
Esther had commanded. 1 Recalling all that
the LORD had done, he prayed to him 2 and said:
"O Lord God, almighty King, all things are in your
power, and there is no one to oppose you in your
will to save Israel. 3 You made heaven and earth
and every wonderful thing under the heavens. 4
You are LORD of all, and there is no one who can
resist you, LORD. 5 You know all things. You
know, O LORD, that it was not out of insolence
or pride or desire for fame that I acted thus in
not bowing down to the proud Haman. 6 Gladly
would I have kissed the soles of his feet for the
salvation of Israel. 7 But I acted as I did so as not
to place the honor of man above that of God. I
will not bow down to anyone but you, my LORD.
It is not out of pride that I am acting thus. 8 And
now, LORD God, King, God of Abraham, spare

NRSV

ADDITION C

13 [8] [a]Then Mordecai[b] prayed to the Lord,
calling to remembrance all the works of
the Lord.

9He said, "O Lord, Lord, you rule as King over
all things, for the universe is in your power and
there is no one who can oppose you when it is
your will to save Israel, [10]for you have made
heaven and earth and every wonderful thing under heaven. [11]You are Lord of all, and there is no
one who can resist you, the Lord. [12]You know all
things; you know, O Lord, that it was not in
insolence or pride or for any love of glory that I
did this, and refused to bow down to this proud

[a] Chapters 13.8—15.16 correspond to chapters C 1-30 and D 1-16 in some translations. [b] Gk *he*

NAB

your people, for our enemies plan our ruin and
are bent upon destroying the inheritance that was
yours from the beginning. 9 Do not spurn your
portion, which you redeemed for yourself out of
Egypt. 10 Hear my prayer; have pity on your
inheritance and turn our sorrow into joy: thus we
shall live to sing praise to your name, O LORD. Do
not silence those who praise you."
11 All Israel, too, cried out with all their
strength, for death was staring them in the face.

NRSV

Haman; 13for I would have been willing to kiss
the soles of his feet to save Israel! 14But I did this
so that I might not set human glory above the
glory of God, and I will not bow down to anyone
but you, who are my Lord; and I will not do these
things in pride. 15And now, O Lord God and King,
God of Abraham, spare your people; for the eyes
of our foes are upon us[a] to annihilate us, and they
desire to destroy the inheritance that has been
yours from the beginning. 16Do not neglect your
portion, which you redeemed for yourself out of
the land of Egypt. 17Hear my prayer, and have
mercy upon your inheritance; turn our mourning
into feasting that we may live and sing praise to
your name, O Lord; do not destroy the lips[b] of
those who praise you."
18And all Israel cried out mightily, for their
death was before their eyes.

[a] Gk *for they are eying us* [b] Gk *mouth*

COMMENTARY

Mordecai begins his prayer by addressing God in the language of praise typical of other Hebrew Bible prayers: God is ruler of the cosmos, creator of all things, and protector of Israel (e.g., Psalms 8, 19, and 21). In vv. 5-7 the question of Mordecai's motive in refusing to bow to Haman, which was unclear in the Hebrew text (see Commentary on 3:1-6), is explained: Mordecai refused to bow to Haman, not because of his own pride, but because he will bow only to God. Therefore, according to his own explanation, Mordecai is acquitted of wrongdoing, a charge not so easily dismissed in the Hebrew text. Mordecai, in fact, claims that, left to himself, he would have been willing to kiss the soles of Haman's feet, the ultimate act of homage in the Persian court, but his sense of God's honor would not allow him to do so. His protestation does not reflect the actual practice of the Jews, who refused to worship other gods, but freely paid homage to human beings, including foreigners, and may be slightly self-defensive (see Commentary on 3:1-6).

Mordecai closes his prayer with references to God's historical acts in the life of Israel, references lacking in MT Esther. He refers to God as the God of Abraham, thereby invoking the covenant of Genesis 15 and 17; he reminds God that Israel is God's "inheritance," the chosen people (see, e.g., Deut 32:9). He mentions the exodus from Egypt, the paradigmatic salvific event in Israel's history, which is only obliquely alluded to in MT Esther by the mention of the month of Nisan (3:12; 8:9). Finally, Mordecai requests that his petition be granted so that Israel can escape death and continue to praise God, in keeping with the biblical notion that it is only the living who can praise God (see Ps 30:8-10 for similar language). The whole thrust of Mordecai's prayer is that God is the only one capable of saving Israel, and Israel trusts in God's protection as God's special possession—all sentiments missing in the MT. In fact, the word κύριος (*kyrios*, "Lord"), the Greek translation of יהוה (*Yahweh*), the proper name of God, is repeated eight times in the eight verses of the prayer, emphasizing God's special relationship with Israel. All Israel joins with Mordecai's prayer "as loudly as they could" in v. 11.

Mordecai's prayer counteracts the charge of the book of Esther's irreligiosity by placing LXX Esther squarely within the framework of Israel's covenant theology as expressed both in the historical and the prophetic traditions in the Hebrew Bible and in the psalms. The prayer, which is sincere and moving, expresses the faith that was implicit in MT Esther: It is God's plan that the Jews should survive, for they are God's chosen people. However, in the MT this is hardly hinted at, let alone made explicit; only in the actions of the characters, who act in the face of seemingly insurmountable odds, is the author's theology visible. The LXX makes this implied theology explicit, thereby making the book more palatable to a pious audience (but also removing the suspense in the process).

REFLECTIONS

Mordecai's prayer in Add. C is one of the first instances of "reflection" on MT Esther that we possess. Some readers might feel an emptiness at the heart of MT Esther as a biblical book: Where is the faith that should direct Mordecai's actions? The answer is given here: Mordecai's faith is based on the covenant between God and Israel, represented by Abraham and the exodus. Mordecai recalls the scriptural tradition of Israel and concludes that God will not abandon the Jews, even though the circumstances look very bleak. His prayer is mirrored by the prayers of Jews and Christians every day, when they turn to Scripture for comfort, hope, and reassurance.

ESTHER ADDITION C 12-30 (AT 5:18-29; Vg 14:1-19), THE PRAYER OF ESTHER

NAB

12 Queen Esther, seized with mortal anguish, likewise had recourse to the LORD. 13 Taking off her splendid garments, she put on garments of distress and mourning. In place of her precious ointments she covered her head with dirt and ashes. She afflicted her body severely; all her festive adornments were put aside, and her hair was wholly disheveled.

14 Then she prayed to the LORD, the God of Israel, saying: "My LORD, our King, you alone are God. Help me, who am alone and have no help but you, 15 for I am taking my life in my hand. 16 As a child I was wont to hear from the people of the land of my fore-fathers that you, O LORD, chose Israel from among all peoples, and our fathers from among all their ancestors, as a lasting heritage, and that you fulfilled all your promises to them. 17 But now we have sinned in your sight, and you have delivered us into the hands of our enemies, 18 because we worshiped their gods. You are just, O LORD. 19 But now they are

NRSV

14 Then Queen Esther, seized with deadly anxiety, fled to the Lord. [2]She took off her splendid apparel and put on the garments of distress and mourning, and instead of costly perfumes she covered her head with ashes and dung, and she utterly humbled her body; every part that she loved to adorn she covered with her tangled hair. [3]She prayed to the Lord God of Israel, and said: "O my Lord, you only are our king; help me, who am alone and have no helper but you, [4]for my danger is in my hand. [5]Ever since I was born I have heard in the tribe of my family that you, O Lord, took Israel out of all the nations, and our ancestors from among all their forebears, for an everlasting inheritance, and that you did for them all that you promised. [6]And now we have sinned before you, and you have handed us over to our enemies [7]because we glorified their gods. You are righteous, O Lord! [8]And now they are not satisfied that we are in bitter slavery, but they have covenanted with their idols [9]to abolish

NAB

not satisfied with our bitter servitude, but have
undertaken 20 to do away with the decree you
have pronounced, and to destroy your heritage;
to close the mouths of those who praise you, and
to extinguish the glory of your temple and your
altar; 21 to open the mouths of the heathen to
acclaim their false gods, and to extol an earthly
king forever.

22 "O LORD, do not relinquish your scepter to
those that are nought. Let them not gloat over
our ruin, but turn their own counsel against them
and make an example of our chief enemy. 23 Be
mindful of us, O LORD. Manifest yourself in the
time of our distress and give me courage, King of
gods and Ruler of every power. 24 Put in my
mouth persuasive words in the presence of the
lion and turn his heart to hatred for our enemy,
so that he and those who are in league with him
may perish. 25 Save us by your power, and help
me, who am alone and have no one but you, O
LORD.

"You know all things. 26 You know that I hate
the glory of the pagans, and abhor the bed of the
uncircumcised or of any foreigner. 27 You know
that I am under constraint, that I abhor the sign
of grandeur which rests on my head when I
appear in public; abhor it like a polluted rag, and
do not wear it in private. 28 I, your handmaid,
have never eaten at the table of Haman, nor have
I graced the banquet of the king or drunk the
wine of libations. 29 From the day I was brought
here till now, your handmaid has had no joy
except in you, O LORD, God of Abraham. 30 O
God, more powerful than all, hear the voice of
those in despair. Save us from the power of the
wicked, and deliver me from my fear."

C. 20: (*kai*) *thysiastēriou* (*sou*): so several MSS, LXX^{L}.

NRSV

what your mouth has ordained, and to destroy
your inheritance, to stop the mouths of those who
praise you and to quench your altar and the glory
of your house, 10to open the mouths of the nations
for the praise of vain idols, and to magnify forever
a mortal king.

11"O Lord, do not surrender your scepter to
what has no being; and do not let them laugh at
our downfall; but turn their plan against them,
and make an example of him who began this
against us. 12Remember, O Lord; make yourself
known in this time of our affliction, and give me
courage, O King of the gods and Master of all
dominion! 13Put eloquent speech in my mouth
before the lion, and turn his heart to hate the
man who is fighting against us, so that there may
be an end of him and those who agree with him.
14But save us by your hand, and help me, who
am alone and have no helper but you, O Lord.
15You have knowledge of all things, and you know
that I hate the splendor of the wicked and abhor
the bed of the uncircumcised and of any alien.
16You know my necessity—that I abhor the sign
of my proud position, which is upon my head on
days when I appear in public. I abhor it like a
filthy rag, and I do not wear it on the days when
I am at leisure. 17And your servant has not eaten
at Haman's table, and I have not honored the
king's feast or drunk the wine of libations. 18Your
servant has had no joy since the day that I was
brought here until now, except in you, O Lord
God of Abraham. 19O God, whose might is over
all, hear the voice of the despairing, and save us
from the hands of evildoers. And save me from
my fear!"

END OF ADDITION C

COMMENTARY

Esther's prayer, like Mordecai's, serves to add a theological element to the narrative and also allows the reader to view Esther in a new light: as a pious Jewish female (the word "Lord" appears nine times in her prayer). As such, her character is more in keeping with the accepted Jewish norms of the Hellenistic period. Esther is completely reliant on others and, in this moment of extreme crisis, on God; she "flees to the Lord." All of the author's theological ideas are biblical; there are no new insights, as might be argued are present in MT Esther. The prayer itself is reminiscent of Dan 9:3-19, from approximately the same period in time. Daniel, like Esther, is fasting and wears sackcloth and ashes; he confesses Israel's sins and petitions for God's aid.[17]

The scene opens with Esther repeating all the gestures of mourning—sackcloth and ashes—in which Mordecai engaged (4:1). Esther goes even further, however; she puts dung on her head as well, a gesture testified to in the HB (Mal 2:3) only in cases of extremity. Thus disfigured, she begins her prayer.

Esther addresses God not only as the true king (as opposed to Artaxerxes), but also as the helper of the distressed. She will repeatedly stress two aspects of God's character: power and mercy. She also immediately makes her prayer personal; God must help her, for no one else can, and she is *in extremis* (reminiscent of Elijah's prayer during his struggle against Ahab and Jezebel, 1 Kgs 19:9-14). In v. 16, she reminds God of the covenant and of God's special relationship with Israel (the OL here contains a 134-word addition reciting the mighty acts of God). According to the LXX, Esther has received her knowledge from her family's tribe, but according to the AT she learned "from my father's book," thus implying the existence of the Torah. According to Esther, the Jews are in trouble because of idolatry (vv. 17-18); this is a typical deuteronomic formula and must refer to the Babylonian exile (2 Kgs 21:10-15; 23:26-27).[18] Such prayer is formulaic; there is no mention of idolatry in the book of Esther, in which the Jews are innocent victims of Haman's enmity. Verses 18-21 make the conflict into one not between humans but between Yahweh and the other gods, similar to the cosmic conflict in Add. A; the Jews exist as Yahweh's people and are threatened by the gods of other peoples, who are implacably hostile. The mention of "house and altar" is the only reference to the Temple in the book of Esther and may indicate a wider audience than the eastern diaspora, since MT Esther makes no mention of any of the cultic institutions of Israel. The expression "turn their plan against them" recalls the major theme of reversal in MT Esther.

In v. 23, Esther turns from the general situation to her own role in it. She needs courage and eloquent speech and, unlike MT Esther, is not reliant upon her own resources, but upon God. The "lion"—i.e., the king—is a symbol of anger, strength, ferocity, and judgment (cf. Prov 20:2). Lions appear constantly as a symbol of royalty in Assyrian and Persian reliefs, and in biblical thought the royal tribe of Judah is portrayed as a lion (Gen 49:9).

Esther, like Mordecai, claims her own innocence and answers the objections raised against her portrayal in the MT by protesting her piety (vv. 25-29). She hates intercourse with a non-Jew; there is a very strong strand in Jewish thought against intermarriage (see Deut 7:3-4; Ezra 10:2; Neh 13:23-27), although there is a counterstrand that does not condemn it (the book of Ruth). Esther keeps the dietary laws, and she has not "drunk the wine of libations"—i.e., wine poured out in offering to the gods. In other words, she has not participated in pagan worship practices. In fact, she keeps herself generally separate from the heathen. Although these claims are necessary in order for Esther to demonstrate her piety, obviously she would not be able to live in this fashion and keep her Jewish identity secret, a necessary plot device. The description of her crown as a "filthy rag" is particularly sharp; the Greek term ῥάκος καταμηνίων (*rakos katamēniōn*) is better translated as "menstruous rag." In Jewish tradition, menstrual blood is ritually unclean and should not be touched (Lev 15:19-24). Esther's whole life as queen is, in fact, miserable to her. Josephus, since he is attempting to present a portrait of Esther that will be attractive to his Gentile audience, omits these verses (they are also lacking in OL).

Esther ends her prayer on a personal note, asking once again for courage, which is appropriate, for now she must act.

17. Ibid., 214-15. Moore notes that there are no linguistic similarities between Esther's prayer and the Greek version of Daniel's prayer.

18. The prayer in *4QTales of the Persian Court* also refers to idolatry.

REFLECTIONS

Esther appears in these verses as a much more pious, and much more typical, biblical heroine. She more closely resembles the pious Judith, who likewise prays to God, covered in sackcloth and ashes, for aid during her crisis (Jdt 9:1-14) and keeps the dietary laws while in a heathen camp (Jdt 12:1-4). However, by her cleverness Judith avoids intercourse with a Gentile (Jdt 13:1-10); the redactor of LXX Esther, on the other hand, cannot avoid the fact that Esther is married to a Gentile king. The best he can do is to have her declare her hatred of the situation, but then it is unclear how she would have been able to fool the king so thoroughly.

The redactor's emphasis on Esther's separateness, for reasons of purity, from the Gentile court around her is exactly the kind of behavior that has made the Jews vulnerable to charges of hostility toward other cultures. However, this charge should be seen as insecurity on the part of the accusers, since the Jews do no harm to the greater community by keeping special dietary restrictions or practicing endogamy. Since God enjoins the Jews to keep the law, then any attempt to obstruct Jewish practice should be understood as a violation of God's will.

The author's theological understanding emerges in Esther's prayer, as it does in Mordecai's: God is ruler of all, righteous yet merciful. Israel is God's chosen people; yet they can be punished for sinning. However, when faced with true repentance, God is merciful and, further, always comes to the aid of the helpless in distress. Finally, the author of the prayer believes that nothing can be accomplished without God's help. These beliefs need no explanation, since they permeate the biblical text and are shared by the faithful in all times.

ESTHER ADDITION D 1-16 (AT 6:1-12; VG 5:4-19)

Esther Appears Before the King

NAB

D 1 On the third day, putting an end to her prayers, she took off her penitential garments and arrayed herself in her royal attire. 2 In making her state appearance, after invoking the all-seeing God and savior, she took with her two maids; 3 on the one she leaned gently for support, 4 while the other followed her, bearing her train. 5 She glowed with the perfection of her beauty and her countenance was as joyous as it was lovely, though her heart was shrunk with fear. 6 She passed through all the portals till she stood face to face with the king, who was seated on his royal throne, clothed in full robes of state, and covered with gold and precious stones, so that he inspired great awe. 7 As he looked up, his features ablaze with the height of majestic anger, the queen staggered, changed color, and leaned weakly against the head of the maid in front of her. 8 But God changed the king's anger to gentleness. In great anxiety he sprang from his throne, held her in his arms until she recovered, and comforted her with reassuring words. 9 "What is it, Esther?" he said to her. "I am your brother. Take courage! 10 You shall not die because of this general decree of ours. 11 Come near!" 12 Raising the golden scepter, he touched her neck with it, embraced her, and said, "Speak to me."

13 She replied: "I saw you, my lord, as an angel of God, and my heart was troubled with fear of your majesty. 14 For you are awesome, my lord, though your glance is full of kindness." 15 As she said this, she fainted. 16 The king became troubled and all his attendants tried to revive her.

NRSV

Addition D

15 On the third day, when she ended her prayer, she took off the garments in which she had worshiped, and arrayed herself in splendid attire. [2]Then, majestically adorned, after invoking the aid of the all-seeing God and Savior, she took two maids with her; [3]on one she leaned gently for support, [4]while the other followed, carrying her train. [5]She was radiant with perfect beauty, and she looked happy, as if beloved, but her heart was frozen with fear. [6]When she had gone through all the doors, she stood before the king. He was seated on his royal throne, clothed in the full array of his majesty, all covered with gold and precious stones. He was most terrifying.

7Lifting his face, flushed with splendor, he looked at her in fierce anger. The queen faltered, and turned pale and faint, and collapsed on the head of the maid who went in front of her. [8]Then God changed the spirit of the king to gentleness, and in alarm he sprang from his throne and took her in his arms until she came to herself. He comforted her with soothing words, and said to her, [9]"What is it, Esther? I am your husband.[a] Take courage; [10]You shall not die, for our law applies only to our subjects.[b] Come near."

11Then he raised the golden scepter and touched her neck with it; [12]he embraced her, and said, "Speak to me." [13]She said to him, "I saw you, my lord, like an angel of God, and my heart was shaken with fear at your glory. [14]For you are wonderful, my lord, and your countenance is full of grace." [15]And while she was speaking, she fainted and fell. [16]Then the king was agitated, and all his servants tried to comfort her.

End of Addition D

---

[a] Gk *brother* [b] Meaning of Gk uncertain

COMMENTARY

This Addition, which follows immediately after Add. C, replaces Esth 5:1-2 in the MT. It is a much better dramatic scene than that in the MT, which is rather anticlimactic. This Addition is the dramatic climax of the Greek Esther and has some of the elements of a Hellenistic romance.[19] In it God, the real hero of Greek Esther, gets full credit for the positive outcome. Addition D probably had a Semitic source text, possibly the same as Add. C.

Addition D begins on the third day, in accordance with the fast that Esther requested in 4:16. After putting aside the sackcloth she wore in Add. C, she dresses to exploit her best weapon: her beauty. Unlike the MT, where Esther relies on no one but herself, in this scene she again invokes God's help (placing emphasis once more on prayer) and takes with her two maids for support. Esther is evidently a great actress; she looks happy, even though she is petrified (recall that in Add. C she claimed to "loathe the bed of the uncircumcised"; that may be true, but the king is not aware of it!). In vv. 2-5, Esther is the epitome of royal feminine beauty, while in v. 6 the king is the epitome of royal masculine power.[20] The two forces stand juxtaposed.

While in the MT this scene was rather disappointing because Esther's acceptance by the king seemed so cut and dried, and she seemed not to be in danger, the LXX exploits the dramatic potential of the situation to the full. The king is fiercely angry; both the AT and the OL compare him to a bull, a metaphor for rage. As we saw in chap. 1, the rage of this king is cause for alarm. Esther is, in fact, so terrified that she faints. She has failed completely; she has been neither courageous nor eloquent of speech. This is in contrast to MT Esther, where she is completely successful. This major difference in the two Esthers makes the LXX character "a delicate Victorian," much less appealing to the female reader than MT Esther, who has the strength of character to act calmly in spite of tremendous danger. If the LXX emphasizes the danger, it also emphasizes Esther's feminine "weakness."[21]

Esther's failure enables the true hero to act. God gets the credit for making the king do a complete turnaround; the theme of reversal, now clearly the result of God's activity, reappears. Whereas earlier the king seemed about to kill Esther, now he comforts and reassures her. He reminds her that he is her husband (the Greek word is "brother [αδελφος *adelphos*], meaning "close kinsman"; cf. Cant 4:9-10; 5:1-2) and informs her that the law does not apply to her. Does this mean that all the suspense has been for nothing? Evidently not, for he still touches her neck with the scepter.

Esther now seems to have the power of eloquent speech, for she compares the king to an angel of God and confesses her terror. Her use of the phrase "angel of God" is a little strange under the circumstances, since the king is not supposed to know that she is Jewish, but this may be asking for a little too much on the part of the redactor. Esther then faints again, leaving the reader a bit suspicious: Is her emotion genuine or melodramatic? In any case, it has the desired effect upon the king.

Moore points out the similarities, mentioned above, of Adds. C and D to the book of Judith, an apocryphal work written in Palestine in the late second century BCE.[22] Both contain pious Jewish women who exploit their beauty to overcome, with God's help, Gentile enemies for the sake of their people. It is probable that the book of Judith (whose main character may have been created in reaction to the too-secular Esther) influenced the redactor of LXX Esther. Levenson suggests that "both heroines reflect an ideal of womanhood widespread in late Second Temple Judaism."[23]

19. Elements of the Hellenistic romance include a beautiful heroine in danger, a fainting scene, and rescue by a powerful male. See Linda Day, *Three Faces of a Queen: Characterization in the Books of Esther,* JSOTSup 186 (Sheffield: Sheffield Academic, 1995) 214-21.

20. For a description of a Persian monarch enthroned in state, see A. T. Olmstead, *The History of the Persian Empire* (Chicago: University of Chicago Press, 1948) 282-83.

21. Michael V. Fox, *Character and Ideology in the Book of Esther: Studies in Biblical Personalities* (Columbia: University of South Carolina Press, 1991) 272. See also Day, *Three Faces of a Queen,* 170-77.

22. Moore, *Daniel, Esther, and Jeremiah: The Additions,* 220-22.

23. Jon D. Levenson, *Esther,* OTL (Louisville: Westminster/John Knox, 1997) 88.

REFLECTIONS

Again in Addition D the redactor of LXX Esther wants to ensure that the reader understands that God, only subtly alluded to in the MT, is present and orchestrating each event of the story. What was left to the perception of the faithful reader of the MT is spelled out by the LXX: God causes the king to accept Esther at the crucial moment. The two versions may be compared to the way in which a person might perceive the same event while it is happening and again at a later date: While the event is happening, things may appear to be coincidences, and events seem to happen at random. Someone might speak of having "good luck" or describe an event as "serendipitous." Later, the same event, viewed as part of a whole from the perspective of faith, may be seen as God's acting throughout to bring the event to its proper conclusion. Good luck becomes a blessing; serendipity becomes grace. The LXX Esther, which perceives the finger of God in the king's reaction, thus is a later retrospective on MT Esther.

ESTHER ADDITION E 1-24 (AT 8:22-32; VG 16:1-24)

MORDECAI'S LETTER

NAB

16 1 The following is a copy of the letter: "King Ahasuerus the Great to the governors of the provinces in the hundred and twenty-seven satrapies from India to Ethiopia, and to those responsible for our interests: Greetings!

2 "Many have become the more ambitious the more they were showered with honors through the bountiful generosity of their patrons. 3 Not only do they seek to do harm to our subjects; incapable of bearing such greatness, they even begin plotting against their own benefactors. 4 Not only do they drive out gratitude from among men; with the arrogant boastfulness of those to whom goodness has no meaning, they suppose they will escape the vindictive judgment of the all-seeing God.

5 "Often, too, the fair speech of friends entrusted with the administration of affairs has induced many placed in authority to become accomplices in the shedding of innocent blood, and has involved them in irreparable calamities 6 by deceiving with malicious slander the sincere good will of rulers. 7 This can be verified in the ancient stories that have been handed down to us, but more fully when one considers the wicked deeds perpetrated in your midst by the pestilential influence of those undeserving of authority. 8 We must provide for the future, so as to render the kingdom undisturbed and peaceful for all men, 9 taking advantage of changing conditions and deciding always with equitable treatment matters coming to our attention.

10 "For instance, Haman, son of Hammedatha, a Macedonian, certainly not of Persian blood, and very different from us in generosity, was hospitably received by us. 11 He so far enjoyed the good will which we have toward all peoples that he was proclaimed "father of the king,' before whom everyone was to bow down; he attained the rank second to the royal throne. 12 But, unequal to

NRSV

ADDITION E

16 [a]The following is a copy of this letter: "The Great King, Artaxerxes, to the governors of the provinces from India to Ethiopia, one hundred twenty-seven provinces, and to those who are loyal to our government, greetings.

2"Many people, the more they are honored with the most generous kindness of their benefactors, the more proud do they become, 3and not only seek to injure our subjects, but in their inability to stand prosperity, they even undertake to scheme against their own benefactors. 4They not only take away thankfulness from others, but, carried away by the boasts of those who know nothing of goodness, they even assume that they will escape the evil-hating justice of God, who always sees everything. 5And often many of those who are set in places of authority have been made in part responsible for the shedding of innocent blood, and have been involved in irremediable calamities, by the persuasion of friends who have been entrusted with the administration of public affairs, 6when these persons by the false trickery of their evil natures beguile the sincere goodwill of their sovereigns.

7"What has been wickedly accomplished through the pestilent behavior of those who exercise authority unworthily can be seen, not so much from the more ancient records that we hand on, as from investigation of matters close at hand.[b] 8In the future we will take care to render our kingdom quiet and peaceable for all, 9by changing our methods and always judging what comes before our eyes with more equitable consideration. 10For Haman son of Hammedatha, a Macedonian (really an alien to the Persian blood, and quite devoid of our kindliness), having become our guest, 11enjoyed so fully the goodwill that we

[a] Chapter 16.1-24 corresponds to chapter E 1-24 in some translations.
[b] Gk *matters beside* (your) *feet*

NAB

this dignity, he strove to deprive us of kingdom
and of life; 13 and by weaving intricate webs of
deceit, he demanded the destruction of Mordecai,
our savior and constant benefactor, and of Esther,
our blameless royal consort, together with their
whole race. 14 For by such measures he hoped
to catch us defenseless and to transfer the rule of
the Persians to the Macedonians. 15 But we find
that the Jews, who were doomed to extinction
by this arch-criminal, are not evildoers, but rather
are governed by very just laws 16 and are the
children of the Most High, the living God of
majesty, who has maintained the kingdom in a
flourishing condition for us and for our forebears.

17 "You will do well, then, to ignore the letter
sent by Haman, son of Hammedatha, 18 for he
who composed it has been hanged, together with
his entire household, before the gates of Susa.
Thus swiftly has God, who governs all, brought
just punishment upon him.

19 "You shall exhibit a copy of this letter
publicly in every place, to certify that the Jews
may follow their own laws, 20 and that you may
help them on the day set for their ruin, the
thirteenth day of the twelfth month, Adar, to
defend themselves against those who attack them.
21 For God, the ruler of all, has turned that day
for them from one of destruction of the chosen
race into one of joy. 22 Therefore, you too must
celebrate this memorable day among your designated feasts with all rejoicing, 23 so that both
now and in the future it may be, for us and for
loyal Persians, a celebration of victory, and for
those who plot against us a reminder of destruction.

24 "Every city and province, without exception, that does not observe this decree shall be
ruthlessly destroyed with fire and sword, so that
it will be left not merely untrodden by men, but
even shunned by wild beasts and birds forever."

NRSV

have for every nation that he was called our father
and was continually bowed down to by all as the
person second to the royal throne. 12But, unable
to restrain his arrogance, he undertook to deprive
us of our kingdom and our life,[a] 13and with
intricate craft and deceit asked for the destruction
of Mordecai, our savior and perpetual benefactor,
and of Esther, the blameless partner of our kingdom, together with their whole nation. 14He
thought that by these methods he would catch us
undefended and would transfer the kingdom of
the Persians to the Macedonians.

15"But we find that the Jews, who were consigned
to annihilation by this thrice-accursed man, are not
evildoers, but are governed by most righteous laws
16and are children of the living God, most high, most
mighty,[b] who has directed the kingdom both for us
and for our ancestors in the most excellent order.

17"You will therefore do well not to put in execution the letters sent by Haman son of Hammedatha,
18since he, the one who did these things, has been
hanged at the gate of Susa with all his household—for
God, who rules over all things, has speedily inflicted
on him the punishment that he deserved.

19"Therefore post a copy of this letter publicly
in every place, and permit the Jews to live under
their own laws. 20And give them reinforcements,
so that on the thirteenth day of the twelfth month,
Adar, on that very day, they may defend themselves against those who attack them at the time
of oppression. 21For God, who rules over all
things, has made this day to be a joy for his chosen
people instead of a day of destruction for them.

22"Therefore you shall observe this with all
good cheer as a notable day among your com-
memorative festivals, 23so that both now and
hereafter it may represent deliverance for you[c] and
the loyal Persians, but that it may be a reminder
of destruction for those who plot against us.

24"Every city and country, without exception,
that does not act accordingly shall be destroyed
in wrath with spear and fire. It shall be made not
only impassable for human beings, but also most
hateful to wild animals and birds for all time.

END OF ADDITION E

---

[a] Gk *our spirit* [b] Gk *greatest* [c] Other ancient authorities *read for us*

COMMENTARY

This Addition, which follows MT 8:12, serves the same function as does Addition B, giving the narrative an air of historical verisimilitude by rendering the actual text of the decree. Like Add. B, Add. E's original language was Greek; they are probably the products of the same author. Josephus paraphrases Add. E, while the Targums have their own versions of the king's letter.

Verse 1. Addition E's opening is similar, but not identical, to the opening of Add. B. The key difference is the expression "those loyal to our government," implying that there are those who are not loyal to the government. It is addressed to the 127 provinces from India to Ethiopia (1:10)—that is, the entire empire.

Verses 2-6. These verses contain a series of truisms concerning the corruption of power. Power without humility breeds arrogance and contempt (Prov 22:4); of course, the letter is referring to Haman. It is strange that Artaxerxes, by all historical accounts a faithful Zoroastrian, mentions the Jewish God; but recall that it is Mordecai who is writing. Like other Hellenistic stories (such as Daniel or Judith), it follows the conventional style in which the piety of the Jewish protagonist causes the conversion, or at least the acknowledgment of the power of the Jewish God, of the Gentile king or hero (Dan 2:47; 3:28-29; 4:1-3, 34-37; 6:26-27; Jdt 14:10). These verses also provide the king with an excuse: He was misled by one whom he considered a friend (this may be both a technical term and a sarcastic one), even though he himself was benevolent.

Verses 7-11. The letter now turns from general truths to the matter at hand. "More ancient records" probably refers to public monuments rather than to private records. Verse 8 recalls Add. B, in which the king desired to secure peace and quiet in the empire, indicating the same author. Verse 9, with its hint that the king did not do his job properly, is an indication that this is not a genuine royal edict—an ancient Near Eastern monarch would not have admitted weakness to his subjects! Haman is identified as a Macedonian (AT, "Bougaion"), and Macedonia is the subject of an overt racial slur (recall that the Persians and the Macedonians were enemies). Haman's honors are also recited (reminiscent of Add. B).

Verses 12-14. Haman's deception of the king in MT 3:8-11 is recalled, but it is not the destruction of the Jews per se that is condemned, but rather the destruction of Mordecai and Esther, which would cause direct injury to the king. The use of the term "savior" (σωτήρ *sōtēr*) in reference to Mordecai may be jarring in the light of its present christological overtones, but it was a common title for the Hellenistic emperors (e.g., Antiochus I Soter), and points to the Hellenistic date of this Addition. In v. 12, Haman is accused of seeking to destroy the king as well; this is not part of the plot of MT Esther, where Haman has no idea of the connection between Mordecai, Esther, and the king, but it is part of the LXX, where in Add. A Haman is behind the plot of the eunuchs. The ultimate end of Haman's scheme is revealed in v. 14: Haman would hand over the Persian Empire to the Macedonians! This makes no sense within the story world of Esther, but, in the wider historical context of the LXX, that is precisely what happened. The Macedonians, under Alexander the Great, conquered the Persian Empire, much to the detriment of both the Persians and the Jews.

Verses 15-16. God is given credit for Persian success; recall that under Persian rule the Jews were relatively unmolested. The description of Jewish law as "most righteous" reflects the sentiments of the author and should be contrasted with Haman's accusations in MT 3:8 and Add. B 4.

Verses 17-18. The point of the letter is reached in these verses, which essentially annul Haman's edict. This is contrary to what happens in MT Esther, where the Jews are given permission to defend themselves against the law of the Medes and the Persians, which cannot be revoked. The idea of annulment, however, agrees in substance with the AT at 8:16. The instruction not to execute Haman's decree should preclude the need for the slaughter in chap. 9, since that was supposed to be defensive in nature. However, it appears that by the time the LXX edition was redacted, chap. 9 was already part of Hebrew Esther. The author handles this contradiction by including the mention in v. 20 of the possibility that the Jews might still be attacked on the thirteenth of Adar.

Verse 18 also contains contradictions to MT chap. 9, which Add. E is supposedly anticipating. Haman is hanged at the gates of Susa, rather than at his own home. His whole family is hanged with him, contrary to the MT, which places the deaths of his sons months later. These differences might imply different sources or simply the work of a careless redactor.

Verses 19-20. These verses contain commands that would bring joy to the Jewish reader. The Jews are to be allowed to live under their own laws, a major issue in the Hellenistic period. Under the Persians, each ethnic group was allowed to be self-governing, provided they obeyed their Persian overlords. At the beginning of the Hellenistic period, under the Ptolemies until 198 BCE and then under the Seleucids until 175 BCE, the Jews were also allowed to govern themselves by the Torah. However, during the reign of Antiochus IV Epiphanes in 175, that privilege was revoked, and from then on the Jews were constantly engaged in a struggle to follow both the law of the land and their own law. The inclusion of this provision in v. 19 points to a date after 175 BCE.

Verses 21-22. Not only are the Gentiles to leave the Jews alone, but also they are to aid them (v. 20); according to v. 22, they are also to celebrate Purim (the celebration is enjoined for Adar 13, contra MT). This indicates a level of Jewish-Gentile cooperation not envisioned in other documents of the period (v. 22 is omitted by the AT and Josephus). This cooperation is in obedience to God, who made this day joyful for the "chosen people," a phrase not likely to be found in a genuine Persian edict.

Verses 23-24. The threats at the end are typical of royal edicts (e.g., the Behistun inscription), and the style is mimicked in Jewish literature that preserves royal decrees (e.g., 3 Macc 3:29). This language is also reminiscent of Isa 34:10, 13-15:

From generation to generation it shall lie waste;
  no one shall pass through it forever and ever.
. . . .
Thorns shall grow over its strongholds,
  nettles and thistles in its fortresses.
It shall be the haunt of jackals,
  an abode for ostriches.
Wildcats shall meet with hyenas,
  goat-demons shall call to each other;
there too Lilith shall repose,
  and find a place to rest.
There shall the owl nest and lay and hatch and brood
    in its shadow;
there too the buzzards shall gather,
  each one with its mate. (NRSV)

REFLECTIONS

We should be both heartened and distressed by Addition E—heartened, because the author envisions a level of Jewish and Gentile cooperation rarely seen. The Jews live by their own laws, as do the Gentiles; but the Gentiles help the Jews and even celebrate their holidays with them, all for the honor of God. However, the author indulges in a blatant racial slur against the Macedonians, indicating that the lessons of one situation do not necessarily carry over to the next one.

ESTHER ADDITION F 1-11 (AT 8:53-59; VG 10:4-13; 11:1)

THE END OF THE GREEK ESTHER

ADDITION F 1-10 (AT 8:53-58; Vg 10:4-13), THE INTERPRETATION OF MORDECAI'S DREAM

NAB

F 1 Then Mordecai said: "This is the work of God. 2 I recall the dream I had about these very things, and not a single detail has been left unfulfilled— 3 the tiny spring that grew into a river, the light of the sun, the many waters. The river is Esther, whom the king married and made queen. 4 The two dragons are myself and Haman. 5 The nations are those who assembled to destroy the name of the Jews, 6 but my people is Israel, who cried to God and was saved.

"The LORD saved his people and delivered us from all these evils. God worked signs and great wonders, such as have not occurred among the nations. 7 For this purpose he arranged two lots: one for the people of God, the second for all the other nations. 8 These two lots were fulfilled in the hour, the time, and the day of judgment before God and among all the nations. 9 God remembered his people and rendered justice to his inheritance.

10 "Gathering together with joy and happiness before God, they shall celebrate these days on the fourteenth and fifteenth of the month Adar throughout all future generations of his people Israel."

NRSV

ADDITION F

4[a]And Mordecai said, "These things have come from God; 5 for I remember the dream that I had concerning these matters, and none of them has failed to be fulfilled. 6 There was the little spring that became a river, and there was light and sun and abundant water—the river is Esther, whom the king married and made queen. 7 The two dragons are Haman and myself. 8 The nations are those that gathered to destroy the name of the Jews. 9 And my nation, this is Israel, who cried out to God and was saved. The Lord has saved his people; the Lord has rescued us from all these evils; God has done great signs and wonders, wonders that have never happened among the nations. 10 For this purpose he made two lots, one for the people of God and one for all the nations, 11 and these two lots came to the hour and moment and day of decision before God and among all the nations. 12 And God remembered his people and vindicated his inheritance. 13 So they will observe these days in the month of Adar, on the fourteenth and fifteenth[a] of that month, with an assembly and joy and gladness before God, from generation to generation forever among his people Israel."

[a] Chapter 10.4-13 and 11.1 correspond to chapter F 1-11 in some translations. [a] Other ancient authorities lack *and fifteenth*

COMMENTARY

This addition, which comes at the end of MT Esther, is a partner to Add. A, which introduced the Greek Esther. It contains the interpretation of the dream found in Add. A. Like Add. A, it was originally composed in Hebrew or Aramaic. Moore suggests that the dream was originally a separate entity that circulated independently and that when it was later adapted into the Esther story, its interpretation, based on the Esther story, was added.[24] Neither the dream nor its interpretation fits very well in the Esther story, and some of the elements of the interpretation vary among the versions. It is possible that Adds. A and F had a Palestinian provenance, given their strong anti-Gentile sentiment, characteristic of Jewish literature from Palestine in this period.

Verse 1 opens with Mordecai (again, not Esther, making Mordecai the main human character) giving his final valediction of the events that have just been narrated. God is given the credit for everything that has happened, which is the main point of the LXX version of Esther. Mordecai realizes, in retrospect, that his dream foreshadowed the events and proceeds to interpret them. Some of the elements of the interpretation are obvious: The two dragons are Mordecai and Haman; the nations are the hostile Gentiles; and the righteous nation is the Jews. Notice that the hostile Gentiles gather to destroy the "name" of the Jews—that is, to destroy them so thoroughly that even their name will be forgotten. This reflects the very human fear that somehow one's life will be blotted out, because there is no one to remember it. Here the fear is not individual, but that of an ethnic group. Ironically, this fear that Israel's name will be blotted out is the mirror image of Moses' command in Deut 25:17-19 that Amalek's (the tribe of Haman) name be utterly blotted out.

Other elements of the interpretation are not so obvious, however. According to the LXX, Esther is the river, while the tiny spring, the light (but cf. 8:16), and the sun are unaccounted for. It is not clear why Esther is the river and not the spring, or what the river has to do with resolving the conflict. In the AT, the tiny spring is Esther, the river is the enemies of the Jews, and the light and the sun are manifestations of God. This explanation for the spring and the river makes even less sense, for why would the enemies of the Jews come forth from Esther? Further, how is the conflict between the dragons resolved? What this shows is that the dream was not originally part of the story of Esther and only awkwardly relates to it.

The dream was selected, however, because it makes the main point of the Greek version very clearly. The Jews are saved because they cried out to God. The source of salvation is God, not human action, as could be argued in the MT. What is more, the story reflects the eternal, cosmic struggle between Jew and Gentile, in which God is on the side of the Jews. This is emphasized in v. 7, in which the nations are divided into lots, one lot for the Jews and one for everyone else. The lots are an obvious allusion to Purim (Esth 3:7; 9:24), but also are used a good deal in Jewish literature from Palestine during the Hellenistic period in a figurative sense to mean "portion" or "destiny." In the *Community Rule* from Qumran, one's "lot," or destiny, is either for good or for evil. In the *War Scroll,* the battles of the eschatological age are divided into "lots," belonging either to God or to Belial, with the final "lot" going to God.[25] Here "lots" seems to mean "portions," and Israel is God's portion (Deut 32:9). In ultimate conflicts, such as the one just recorded, God will vindicate Israel. This is comforting if you are on the right side. In the cosmic conflict between Jew and Gentile, of which the book of Esther is but one incident, the Jews, according to the redactor, will be vindicated.

As a result, the Festival of Purim should always be celebrated as a memorial to God's vindication, not as a celebration of human victory. It is here a two-day festival (although some Greek MSS omit "the fifteenth"). It is not just a diaspora festival, but a festival everywhere, as befits a commemoration of a cosmic victory.

24. Carey A. Moore, *Daniel, Esther, and Jeremiah: The Additions,* AB 44 (Garden City, N.Y.: Doubleday, 1977) 248-49.

25. F. García Martínez, *The Dead Sea Scrolls Translated: The Qumran Texts in English* (Leiden: E. J. Brill, 1992) 3-32, 95-122.

REFLECTIONS

The "us" versus "them" mentality displayed in the book of Esther, particularly pointedly here and in Add. A, may make us uncomfortable, especially since the hostility seems aimed at some contemporary readers of the book. In fact, this mentality has left the book of Esther open to a lot of criticism over the centuries (see Introduction). It is important to remember the historical circumstances that led to that way of thinking, and the subsequent persecutions the Jews have had to endure throughout their history, as a tool to understanding the theology of the book of Esther. The important lesson for the contemporary reader to take away from this passage is that God is on the side of the oppressed. If we are in the position of oppressor, we can be sure that God will not vindicate us.

By sandwiching the story of Esther between the episodes of Mordecai's dream and its interpretation, the redactor makes clear that God is constantly and thoroughly in control of events. Thus when persecution occurs, even to those who, like Esther and Mordecai, are pious, the reader may find strength in the hope that God is working to carry out the divine purpose. MT Esther is, perhaps, more honest in alluding to the fact that not every evil situation is rectified (see Introduction, but LXX Esther makes the hope that motivates the characters in the MT a reality in Mordecai's statement, "These things have come from God").

ESTHER ADDITION F 11 (AT 8:59; Vg 11:1), THE COLOPHON OF THE GREEK ESTHER

NRSV

11 [1]In the fourth year of the reign of Ptolemy
and Cleopatra, Dositheus, who said that he
was a priest and a Levite,[a] and his son Ptolemy
brought to Egypt[b] the preceding Letter about
Purim, which they said was authentic and had
been translated by Lysimachus son of Ptolemy,
one of the residents of Jerusalem.

END OF ADDITION

[a] Or *priest, and Levitas* [b] Cn: Gk *brought in*

COMMENTARY

This colophon,[26] one of very few attested in Jewish literature of the Hellenistic period, purports to answer the questions of the date and provenance of the Greek version of Esther; in fact, however, it raises more questions than it answers. According to the colophon, which is a note appended to a manuscript in order to authenticate it, the "letter about Purim" was brought to Egypt in the fourth year of the reign of Ptolemy and Cleopatra. All the emperors of Ptolemaic Egypt were named Ptolemy, so the search must be narrowed to one who reigned at least four years and had a wife named Cleopatra. There are three possibilities:

26. Only one AT MSS contains this verse.

Ptolemy VIII, Soter II, in 114 BCE
Ptolemy XII, in 77 BCE
Ptolemy XIV, in 48 BCE[27]

The most likely possibility seems to be Ptolemy XII, bringing the Greek Esther into Egypt in 77 BCE and putting its composition sometime in the late second century BCE, a date I have argued for on other grounds (see the Commentary on Add A). Who brought it? A man named Dositheus and his son Ptolemy. Both are Greek names, indicating Greek-speaking Jews. The colophon states that Dositheus "said" that he was a priest and a Levite. Does this indicate suspicion of his veracity? The equivalence of priest and Levite, which are usually distinct categories, is ambiguous. Where did Dositheus and Ptolemy bring their book? The Greek simply says "brought in"; the NRSV supplies "to Egypt," implying that they brought it to Alexandria, which had one of the largest Jewish communities in the world at that time. What did they bring? The "preceding Letter about Purim," which must have included the whole of MT Esther plus Addition F, which includes this colophon, and Addition A, which goes with Add. F. It did not necessarily include the other Additions, although we cannot be certain. Note that by 77 BCE the festival was called Purim and was known in Judea. Why did they bring it? They claimed it was "authentic," which implies the existence of other, "inauthentic" versions. The AT existed in a previous form (see Introduction), the proto-AT, which ended before chap. 9 and did not contain the LXX Additions. Is this the "inauthentic" version that was circulating in Egypt and that Dositheus and Ptolemy wished to supplant?[28] If so, why did they wish to supplant it? It is also possible to understand "authentic" as referring to Purim itself. The letter would thus be an attempt to answer objections that Purim was an "inauthentic" holiday.

The colophon claims that this "letter of Purim" was translated by Lysimachus, son of Ptolemy. Is this the same Ptolemy mentioned earlier? Is Lysimachus the grandson of Dositheus, "the Priest and Levite"? Is this version supposed to be official in some way? It may have been, but since we cannot identify Lysimachus, Ptolemy, or Dositheus, we do not know the source of their authority. Further, it is unclear what it means to be a "resident" of Jerusalem. It does not imply that Lysimachus was born there; rather, it connotes the presence of a community of Greek-speaking Jews, originally from Alexandria but now living in Jerusalem. It is possible that these Jews came in contact with a Hebrew book of Esther, certainly containing chaps. 1–10 and possibly containing Adds. A, C, D, and F, which had a Semitic source. Recognizing that this version differed from the one with which they were familiar in Alexandria, the proto-AT, they translated it into Greek and took it back to Alexandria to introduce it to the Jewish community there. Because it supposedly came from Jerusalem, it bore a certain authority; and its presence caused the proto-AT to go through a process of editing to conform to this Addition. It may have been in this period that Adds. B and E, more likely of Egyptian provenance, were added to both versions.[29] While this process is admittedly speculative, it does account for the differences that have been noted between the AT and the LXX, and between the Greek versions and the MT.

27. E. J. Bickerman, "The Colophon of the Greek Book of Esther," *JBL* 63 (1944) 339-62.

28. See also Linda Day, *Three Faces of a Queen: Characterization in the Books of Esther*, JSOTSup 186 (Sheffield: Sheffield Academic, 1995) 231, who argues that "the A text is possibly the product of a Jewish community within the diaspora setting which is more integrated with non-Jews and more Hellenized in thought and behavior." I would argue that Alexandria fits this description nicely.

29. The good rhetorical Greek of Adds. B and E, which argues for their composition in a primarily Greek-speaking milieu, and their similarities to 3 Maccabees, which most commentators agree was composed in Egypt, make a strong case for Egyptian provenance. See George W. E. Nickelsburg, *Jewish Literature Between the Bible and the Mishnah* (Philadelphia: Fortress, 1981) 169-72.

REFLECTIONS

The colophon to Esther reflects in microcosm the problems of acceptance the book of Esther has had in various communities throughout the centuries. The missing theological obviousness in MT Esther had to be rectified by LXX Esther before it was accepted in Judea (although not everywhere in Judea, if its absence at Qumran is indicative). An "inauthentic" Greek version was supplanted by an "authentic" one. The book of Esther had trouble gaining canonical status in both Judaism and Christianity. Even after its place in the canon was secure, it was the object of vitriol, as evidenced by Martin Luther's comments about it.[30]

Today various groups again would like to reject Esther.[31] Why is this book so hard for the faithful to accept as part of the Bible? It may be because Esther offers no easy answers. The world according to Esther is not a comfortable and easy place: In MT Esther, God is hidden, and humans must live with theological ambiguity. In LXX Esther, hostility between peoples is an accepted fact, and life is a constant struggle. Just for these reasons, however, the book of Esther speaks most profoundly to the twenty-first century. Life is difficult; people are trapped in hostile situations; God often seems hidden. Faithful people are called to live in ambiguity, hoping, like Esther and Mordecai, that they have come to their situation "for such a time as this." Ultimately we must believe that "relief and deliverance . . . will arise" from God. That is the fundamental message of hope that the book of Esther contains.

30. Martin Luther, *Tischreden,* W. A. xxii, 2080, as quoted in Lewis B. Paton, *Esther,* ICC (Edinburgh: T. & T. Clark, 1908) 96.
31. See, e.g., Alice Laffey, *An Introduction to the Old Testament: A Feminist Perspective* (Philadelphia: Fortress, 1988).

THE BOOK OF TOBIT

INTRODUCTION, COMMENTARY, AND REFLECTIONS

BY

IRENE NOWELL, O.S.B.

THE BOOK OF
TOBIT

INTRODUCTION

The book of Tobit tells the story of a good man named Tobit who seems to suffer without cause. In performing an act of charity, burying a dead man, he is struck with blindness and made dependent on his wife. He is so aggrieved by a quarrel with her that he prays to die. Meanwhile, in another city, a young woman named Sarah also prays to die because she has been married seven times, and each husband has died on the wedding night. God hears their prayers and sends the angel Raphael to heal them each of their distress.

Tobit remembers some money he has deposited in another city and sends his son Tobiah to get it. Tobiah and Tobit hire a guide, the angel Raphael in disguise, who not only leads Tobiah to the house of Raguel, Sarah's father, but also helps Tobiah catch a fish whose parts will be useful in healing both his father and Sarah. Raphael instructs Tobiah to ask for Sarah's hand in marriage. Tobiah burns the parts of the fish to drive away the demon who is killing Sarah's husbands; then he and Sarah pray and sleep happily through the night. Meanwhile Raguel, fearing the death of another son-in-law, has dug a grave. When he and his wife, Edna, discover that Tobiah and Sarah are well, they hold a fourteen-day wedding feast. Raphael, who has gone after Tobit's money, returns to the feast with Gabael, who has held the money in deposit.

Tobiah's parents are worried sick, however, because their son is late in returning. So Tobiah and his wife set out with Raphael on the return journey. As soon as Tobiah sees his father, he uses the remaining parts of the fish to heal his blindness. When the two men attempt to pay the guide, Raphael reveals his identity and instructs them to praise God.

Tobit's song of praise is the last and longest prayer in this book, which contains prayers or blessings by every character except Anna, Tobit's wife, and Raphael. After a long and happy life, Tobit calls for Tobiah and Sarah, along with their children, to give them a final instruction. After their deaths, Tobiah gives both his parents and his parents-in-law honorable burials. Finally Tobiah himself dies at the age of 117.

TEXT AND LANGUAGE

The origins of the book of Tobit are somewhat murky. The book is available to us in three Greek recensions, several fragments of four Aramaic and one Hebrew manuscript, the Old Latin version, and the Latin Vulgate. The presence of Aramaic and Hebrew manuscripts at Qumran led to the conclusion that the original language was Semitic, although whether Hebrew or Aramaic is debatable. Most scholars lean toward Aramaic.[1]

The Qumran manuscripts are fragmentary, however. Thus for a primary text one of the Greek recensions is necessary. There are three Greek recensions: G^{I}, represented by two manuscripts, Vaticanus (B) and Alexandrinus (A); G^{II}, represented by the Sinaiticus MS, and G^{III}, preserved in MSS 44, 106, and 107. G^{II} has a strong Semitic flavor, many narrative details, and is substantially longer than the others. It has two major gaps, however—4:7-19 and 13:6-10. G^{I} is written in a more idiomatic Greek and is shorter and more concise than G^{II}. G^{III} is fragmentary, preserved only from 6:9 to 13:8.[2]

The Old Latin version (VL) represents G^{II} and is useful in correcting and reconstructing S. The Vulgate, Jerome says, was translated rapidly (in one day!) from an Aramaic version. Much of it is dependent on VL. Therefore, it is of less value textually than VL. However, it does provide some interesting interpretations of the story. The Qumran manuscripts support the priority of G^{II}, which will be used as the primary text for this commentary, corrected by the Qumran manuscripts and by the Old Latin, and supplemented by G^{I} where gaps are identified.

DATE

Speculation concerning the date of the book of Tobit has ranged from the seventh century BCE to the third century CE, with a definite preference for the third to second centuries BCE. There are several reasons to support this date with regard to *terminus a quo.* The confusion concerning historical and geographical data in seventh-century Assyria excludes an early date for the book. The title "law of Moses" or "book of Moses" (Tob 6:13; 7:11-13) became current after the writing of the books of Chronicles (4th cent. BCE; cf. 2 Chr 23:18; 25:4; 30:16). The author of Tobit presumes the authority of the prophets as proclaimers of God's Word (14:4). The prophets were canonized around 200 BCE. The

1. See, e.g., J. A. Fitzmyer, "The Aramaic and Hebrew Fragments of Tobit from Qumran Cave 4," *CBQ* 57 (1995) 671. See also C. A. Moore, *Tobit,* AB 40A (Garden City, N.Y.: Doubleday, 1996) 33-39, for further discussion.

2. See R. Hanhart, *Tobit,* Septuaginta; Vetus Testamentum Graecum 8/5 (Göttingen: Vandenhoeck & Ruprecht, 1983) 29-36.

fact that the Jews did not accept the book of Tobit in their canon also indicates a late date for the work.

The Maccabean revolt provides the *terminus ad quem.* There is no evidence in Tobit of the turmoil caused by the persecution begun by Antiochus IV Epiphanes (175–164). The emphasis on endogamy, a practice that died out in the first century BCE, the absence of comment on resurrection of the dead, whether belief or non-belief, and the discovery of copies of the book at Qumran support a *terminus ad quem* in the second century. Fitzmyer suggests that the Aramaic in the Qumran fragments represents the period between the end of the second century BCE and the beginning of the second century CE.[3] The most probable date for the writing of the book of Tobit, then, is between 200 and 180 BCE.

PLACE

The most difficult question concerning the origin of the book of Tobit concerns place. Palestine, Egypt, and Mesopotamia have been suggested as possibilities. Assyria and Persia are usually rejected because of the inaccurate geographical references. The eastern diaspora is a stronger possibility.

The other major area of the diaspora, Egypt, is also possible. Some connections exist between Tobit and the Elephantine papyri (5th cent. BCE). One source of Tobit is the story of Ahiqar (see the section "The Story of Ahiqar," below), an Aramaic copy of which was found at Elephantine. The marriage contract discovered among the same papyri is very similar to the words of Raguel at the wedding of Sarah and Tobiah.[4] Yet there are also several arguments against Egypt. It seems unlikely that a story written in Aramaic would originate in second-century Egypt. Upper Egypt appears to be a faraway place when the demon is banished there (Tob 8:3).

The third possibility is Palestine. The chief objection to this locale is the setting of the story in the diaspora. Nonetheless, the interest in Jerusalem and its cult may indicate Palestinian provenance. The evidence does not allow a definite conclusion concerning the place of origin of our book.

CANONICAL STATUS

The book of Tobit is not included in the Hebrew Scriptures and thus is not a part of the Old Testament in the Protestant tradition. It is, however, contained in the Septuagint, the ancient Greek translation of Jewish holy books, and was translated by Jerome and included in the Latin Vulgate. Thus it remains part of the Old Testament canon for Roman Catholics and for the Orthodox churches.

3. Fitzmyer, "The Aramaic and Hebrew Fragments of Tobit from Qumran Cave 4," 667.

4. See "Contract of Mibtahiah's Third Marriage," *ANET* 222; see also R. Vattioni, "Studi e note sul libro di Tobia," *Aug* 10 (1940) 277.

GENRE

The book of Tobit is a work of narrative prose with several prayers in poetic form. The question of its historicity has been widely debated. There are several arguments against its literal historicity. First, inaccuracies appear in the report of Assyrian history. Sargon II (721–705) is missing from the recital of kings in chapter 1, perhaps echoing 2 Kgs 17:1-6 and 18:9-13, in which Sargon is not mentioned. The Assyrian king responsible for the deportation of Naphtali from Galilee, the deportation that presumably included Tobit, was Tiglath-Pileser III (745–727), not Shalmaneser V as Tob 1:2 states. Second, the first-person narrative in the opening chapters may signal questionable historicity. Authors of antiquity sometimes used first-person narrative to make the teller of the tale, and not the author, responsible for its truth.[5] However, Miller argues that the redactors of texts such as Tobit, the Genesis Apocryphon, and Nehemiah preserved the first-person narrative whenever it was available precisely because it was valued as "original autobiography."[6] Third, the religious principles of the book are more consistent with the period of the author (2nd cent. BCE) than the period in which the story is set (8th–7th cents. BCE). Thus, while there may be a historical nucleus to the book, its primary function is not the telling of history. Rather, it has a didactic purpose: to teach and illustrate basic principles of religious faith.

The book of Tobit bears many characteristics of a "romance" that is cast as a successful quest.[7] The genre, however, is affected by the biblical context. The book also has many features of the Hebrew short story, as defined by Campbell.[8] Its characters are ordinary people whose everyday lives become signs of the working of God's providence. The religious purpose of the author is shown by the subject matter and by the use of biblical models and imagery. It is, however, a late example of the genre. A folktale element predominates, and the distinction between legend and Hebrew short story is blurred.

Hence, the book of Tobit belongs to a mixed genre, created to respond to the needs of the post-exilic community to which its author belonged, a genre shared with Esther, Judith, and Susanna.[9] Overall, the book of Tobit is best described as a Hebrew romance.

Other literary forms appear in the book, specifically poetic prayers (3:2-6, 11-15; 8:5-8, 15-17; 11:14-15; 13:1-18)[10] and wisdom speeches (4:3-21; 12:6-10; 14:3-11). The wisdom speeches, which contain several proverbs, may also be classified as farewell discourses.[11]

5. B. E. Perry, *The Ancient Romances: A Literary-Historical Account of Their Origins* (Berkeley: University of California Press, 1967) Appendix 3, 325-26.

6. J. E. Miller, "The Redaction of Tobit and the Genesis Apocryphon," *JSP* 8 (1991) esp. 56-57.

7. See N. Frye, *Anatomy of Criticism* (Princeton, N.J.: Princeton University Press, 1957) 187-93; R. Scholes and R. Kellogg, *The Nature of Narrative* (New York: Oxford University Press, 1966) 228.

8. E. F. Campbell, Jr., "The Hebrew Short Story: A Study of Ruth," in *A Light unto My Path, Festschrift for J. M. Myers*, ed. H. N. Bream, R. D. Heim, and C. A. Moore (Philadelphia: Temple University Press, 1974) 91.

9. See O. Loretz, "Roman und Kurzgeschichte in Israel," *Wort und Botschaft des Alten Testaments*, ed. J. Schreiner (Würzburg: Echter, 1969) 325.

10. For an excellent analysis of the prayers found in the book, see P. J. Griffin, "The Theology and Function of Prayer in the Book of Tobit" (Ph.D. diss., The Catholic University of America, 1984).

11. A. A. Di Lella, "The Deuteronomic Background of the Farewell Discourse in Tob 14:3-11," *CBQ* 41 (1979) 380n. 1.

SOURCES FOR THE PLOT

The Grateful Dead. The plot of the center section of Tobit, the travelogue (chaps. 5–12), is derived from the folktale "The Grateful Dead."[12] The basic story of the Grateful Dead, as found in a widespread collection of folktales, concerns a man who impoverishes himself to ransom and bury a corpse that is being mistreated by the dead man's creditors. Shortly thereafter, when the poor man is on a journey, he is joined by a stranger who offers to be his servant in return for half of whatever the hero might acquire.

At this point the folktales diverge. The version best known in the Near East and in Eastern Europe is the form that is related to the book of Tobit. In this form the tale is combined with the tale of "The Monster in the Bridal Chamber." The hero in this combination of tales is advised by the stranger to marry a wealthy princess whose former bridegrooms have all perished in the bridal chamber. The stranger then keeps watch on the wedding night and slays the serpent that emerges from the mouth of the princess to kill the hero. Subsequently, the stranger demands half the bride as his payment, but as he threatens to divide the bride with his sword (or actually does), another serpent(s) comes out of the bride, and she is freed from enchantment. The stranger then reveals himself as the grateful dead man whom the hero had buried.[13]

Several similarities exist between this story and the plot of Tobit. Tobit is impoverished because of his practice of burying the dead. His son Tobiah (the hero has been divided into two characters of similar name) is accompanied on a journey by a mysterious stranger who advises him to marry a bride whose husbands have all died on the wedding night. Through the advice and service of the stranger, Tobiah survives the wedding night, and the bride is freed from enchantment. The stranger is offered payment of half the goods acquired on the journey (not, however, half the bride). He then reveals his identity and disappears.

The Story of Ahiqar. A second major source for the plot is the story of Ahiqar (NAB; NRSV, "Ahikar"), who appears in the book of Tobit in four passages (1:21-22; 2:10; 11:18; 14:10). The story seems to have been written originally in Aramaic sometime in the sixth century BCE.[14] Fragments of the story in Aramaic were found at Elephantine and have been dated to the fifth century BCE. The story of Ahiqar appears in several languages: Syriac, Arabic, Armenian, and Slavonic, and fragments in Ethiopic and Greek. These versions are much later than the Aramaic fragments.

The story of Ahiqar consists of a narrative portion and a set of proverbs. The narrative tells the story of the life of Ahiqar, a royal official at the courts of Sennacherib and Esarhaddon. Because he is childless, Ahiqar adopts Nadin,[15] his nephew, and trains him

12. See K. Simrock, *Der Gute Gerhard und die dankbaren Todten* (Bonn: Marcus, 1856) 131-32; G. H. Gerould, *The Grateful Dead,* publications of the Folklore Society 60 (London: D. Nutt, 1980; reprinted, Folcroft, Pa.: Folcroft Library Editions, 1973) 7.

13. See S. Thompson, *The Folktale* (New York: Dryden, 1946) 50-53, for the basic synopsis. See Gerould, *The Grateful Dead,* 47-75, for a description of folktales from several places that demonstrate the combination he calls the Grateful Dead and the Poison Maiden.

14. J. M. Lindenberger, *The Aramaic Proverbs of Ahiqar* (Baltimore: Johns Hopkins University Press, 1983) 16-20.

15. This spelling of the name is found in the Qumran fragments 4QTob[d], 11:18.

to succeed to his royal position. But Nadin, treacherous and ungrateful, accuses Ahiqar of disloyalty to the king. Ahiqar is condemned to death, but is secretly rescued by the executioner whose life Ahiqar had saved earlier. He remains hidden in a cave under his own house until the king, challenged to a contest of wisdom by the pharaoh of Egypt, expresses the wish that Ahiqar still lived. Thereupon Ahiqar emerges from hiding, answers the pharaoh's challenge, and is restored to his former honor. Meanwhile, Nadin is imprisoned and dies.[16] The proverbs of Ahiqar are probably older than the narrative and were presumably added to the story to strengthen the impression of Ahiqar's wisdom.

Similarities between the story of Ahiqar and the book of Tobit can be seen both in content and in literary form. The life of Ahiqar resembles in broad strokes the life of Tobit. Both are faithful men who are unjustly plunged into darkness, but who, because of righteousness, are saved from death and restored to life. The story of Ahiqar is told in first-person narrative, similar to the beginning of the book of Tobit. The wisdom speech of Tobit to his son Tobiah (4:3-21) echoes proverbs in the story of Ahiqar.

General knowledge of the story of Ahiqar is presumed by the author of the book of Tobit. Ahiqar is made a relative of Tobit (1:21), ostensibly to enhance Tobit by connecting him with such a renowned sage. Ahiqar uses his position to help Tobit in his distress (1:21-22; 2:10). He and Nadin come to rejoice in Tobit's joy (11:18). In the final reference to Ahiqar, Tobit recounts a synopsis of Ahiqar's life (14:10-11).

Just as the journey of Tobiah (the central section) rests on the outline of the folktale combination of the "Grateful Dead"/"Monster in the Bridal Chamber," so also the life of Tobit (chaps. 1–4; 13–14; the frame) rests on the outline of the story of Ahiqar. The influence of these two sources clarifies the interweaving of first-person narrative, wisdom sections and prayers, and the theme of innocent suffering and vindication with the folktale quest for a bride.

These two sources, however, are insufficient to explain the motivations and the progress of the plot in the book of Tobit. The book is permeated with biblical themes and principles. Folktale elements from the "Grateful Dead"/"Monster in the Bridal Chamber" have been changed in conformity with the tenets of biblical faith. The grateful dead man has been replaced by an angel. The hero is now represented by two figures: the father-hero and the son-hero. The father-hero buries the dead out of respect for biblical injunctions (e.g., Deut 21:23) and is both tested and rewarded for his fidelity. The son-hero wins the bride, not because he buried the dead, but because he has a right to her by Mosaic law (Tob 6:12-13; 7:10; cf. Num 36:8-9). The marriage is planned in heaven (Tob 6:18; 7:11). The bride is delivered from the demon by God, who sends an angel to instruct the hero in exorcism and prayer (6:17-18; 8:2-9). The angel demands no payment but is offered half of the recovered money (12:15).

Modifications have also been made in the borrowing from Ahiqar. Ahiqar himself has

16. See the synopsis of this story in Lindenberger, *The Aramaic Proverbs of Ahiqar,* 3-4. See also J. R. Harris in F. C. Conybeare, J. R. Harris, and A. S. Lewis, *The Story of Ahikar* (London: C. J. Clay & Sons, 1898) viii-x.

been made a Jew. The figure of the son differs in the two stories. In Ahiqar, Nadin is an adopted son; in Tobit, Tobiah is a natural son. Nadin is a classic example of the ungrateful son; Tobiah is an example of the devoted, faithful son. The just man in the two stories is vindicated for different reasons. Tobit is vindicated simply because he is righteous; Ahiqar is vindicated because of a specific form of righteousness, almsgiving.

The Joseph Story. L. Ruppert proposes the Joseph story (Genesis 37; 39–50) as the link between extra-biblical sources and the biblical tradition that is fundamental to the book of Tobit.[17] The Joseph story, the basic biblical analogue to Tobit, is the third and most significant element that must be considered in outlining its plot. In the Joseph story, as in the book of Tobit, an elderly father sends a beloved son (Benjamin), whom he entrusts to a companion (Reuben or Judah; Gen 42:37; 43:8-9), on a dangerous journey to a distant land to obtain relief from a current need. The travelers recognize that the father's life is so bound up in that of the son that if the son should die, the father would go down to the nether world in grief (Gen 44:30-31; cf. Tob 6:15).

Upon his arrival the son meets a near relative (Joseph/Raguel) who inquires about his father's health (Gen 45:3; Tob 7:4-5). After the close kinship is revealed, the travelers are welcomed with tearful embraces (Gen 45:14-15; cf. Tob 7:6-8; Gen 43:27-30).[18] Meanwhile, although the father (or mother; note that in Tobit it is Edna who inquires concerning Tobit's health) fears the son's death (Gen 37:33-35; 43:14; cf. Tob 10:4, 7), the son escapes danger (Gen 39:1-6; 44:1–45:3; cf. Tob 6:3-4; 8:2-9) and is reunited with the father (Gen 46:30; cf. Tob 11:9-10).[19] With tearful embraces the father (or mother) proclaims readiness to die (Gen 46:30; Tob 11:9; cf. Tob 11:14). As the story draws to a close, the father summons his son(s) and grandchildren to his deathbed, asks for an honorable burial, and makes a statement about the future and about return to the homeland (Gen 47:27–48:2, 15-22; cf. Gen 50:24; Tob 14:3-8; 13:5). There is a final poetic speech by the father concerning the future (Genesis 49; Tobit 13).[20]

Biblical Type Scenes. In addition to the outline from part of the Joseph story, the central scene of the book of Tobit has another biblical analogue. Tobiah's betrothal (7:1-17), including the preceding departure from the father (5:17-22) and subsequent departure from the bride's home (10:7-13), is modeled on the biblical type scene of betrothal.[21] The two betrothal scenes closest in pattern to Tob 7:1-17 are Isaac's (Gen 34:1-67) and Jacob's (Gen 29:1-30). Genesis 29:4-6 appears almost verbatim in Tob 7:3-5 (see Commentary). In addition, each passage is linked to Tobit by a particular key word. The link to Isaac's

17. L. Ruppert, "Zur Function der Achikar-Notizen im Buch Tobias," *BZ* 20 (1976) 232-37. For the links between Ahiqar and the Joseph story, see also S. Niditch and R. Doran, "The Success Story of the Wise Courtier: A Formal Approach," *JBL* 96 (1977) 179-93.

18. G. Priero, *Tobia,* ed. S. Garofalo, 2nd ed., La Sacra Bibbia (Turin: Marietti, 1963) 37, comments on the frequency of tears in Tobit (e.g., 2:7; 3:1, 10; 5:18; 7:6-8, 16; 9:6; 10:4, 7; 11:9, 14). They are, perhaps, an echo of the frequent tears in the Joseph story (Gen 37:35; 42:30; 45:14-15; 47:29; 50:1, 17).

19. Note that in the Joseph story two beloved sons are separated from the father and are feared dead, Joseph and Benjamin. In the book of Tobit there is only one, Tobiah.

20. Ruppert, "Zur Function der Achikar-Notizen im Buch Tobias," 114-15.

21. R. Alter, *The Art of Biblical Narrative* (New York: Basic Books, 1981) 51.

betrothal scene is εὐοδόω (*euodoō*, "prosper," "make successful"). The link to Jacob's betrothal scene is ὑγιαίνω (*hygiainō*, "to be well"). The scenes are also similar in structure.

Two points of correspondence link Tobiah's betrothal scene with that of Moses (Exod 2:15-21): the number seven (a folktale element) and the name of the father-in-law. Seven daughters meet Moses at the well. The father of Moses' future bride is named Raguel (or Reuel). Moses' departure from his father-in-law (Exod 4:18*a*) also resembles the corresponding scenes in Tobit (10:11) and in Genesis (24:54-61).

The Book of Job. A final pattern influencing the book of Tobit appears in the book of Job. The structure of the two books is similar. Each book contains a "framing" section that sets the stage in the beginning and summarizes the situation at the end (Job 1:1–2:13; 42:7-17; Tob 1:1–3:17; 12:1–14:15). The central action is set into this frame (Job 3:1–42:6; Tob 4:1–11:18). The progress of Tobit's life is modeled on that of Job. Each man suffers bodily affliction, even though he is righteous (Job 2:7; 27:6; Tob 1:3; 2:10); each is grieved by the sharp words of a wife (Job 2:9-10; Tob 2:14–3:1) and prays for death (Job 7:15; Tob 3:2-6). After his testing, each man is vindicated and rewarded (Job 42:7-17; Tob 14:1-3). Imagery of light and darkness is prevalent in both books. More than a quarter of the occurrences of the words אור (*ʾôr*, "light") and חשך (*ḥōšek*, "darkness") in the Hebrew Bible are in the book of Job. The story of Tobit moves from light to darkness and back to light.

Conclusion. The outline of the plot of the book of Tobit is shaped by several sources. Extra-biblical literature has contributed the patterns of two folktales—the "Grateful Dead"/"Monster in the Bridal Chamber," and the story of Ahiqar—which form respectively a basis for the central travelogue and for the framing story of the just, guiltless man who suffers but is finally vindicated. Biblical literature has contributed four elements: The story of Joseph functions as a pattern for incorporating the story of Tobit into the flow of salvation history; the betrothal scene from the ancestor stories serves as a model for the central scene in Tobit; the book of Job provides a model for the structure of the book of Tobit, the life of its principal character, and its basic imagery; and finally, the story is set in, and permeated by, a context of faith. As Zimmermann says, "The woof comes from the folklore of mankind, and the warp and the pattern, the vitality and the color, come from the religious experience of the Jewish people."[22]

It is not similarities to a pattern, however, but the variations that are significant.[23] The differences between the book of Tobit and the folktales derive largely from the biblical context. The differences between the book of Tobit and its biblical models can be attributed to the influences of a different time and a different historical situation. The location differs from the ancestor stories. The need for burial of the dead, though a prominent theme in Genesis,[24] arises from a different cause. The essence of a just life—fear of God and charity

22. F. Zimmermann, *The Book of Tobit: An English Translation with Introduction and Commentary,* Dropsie College Edition, JAL (New York: Harper and Bros., 1958) 12.

23. Alter, *The Art of Biblical Narrative,* 52.

24. I. Abrahams, "Tobit and Genesis," *JQR* 5 (1893) 348-50, was the first to point out the connection between Tobit and Genesis in the concentration on burial.

toward others—remains constant, but the ways in which justice is enacted differ for the characters in Tobit, who lived in exile, from the ancestors, who lived in Egypt and among the Canaanites. The outline of the plot of Tobit derives from several sources; however, the unique expression of this particular plot reflects the needs and preoccupations of the second-century diaspora.[25]

LITERARY ARTISTRY

The Narrator. There are two narrators in the book of Tobit: the first-person narrator of 1:3–3:1 and the third-person narrator of 3:17 through the end of the book. A bridge consisting of two prayers and the introduction of two new characters connects them, but it is unclear whether Tobit remains the narrator in the bridge.[26] The third-person narrator is unobtrusive, reliable, omniscient, and brief. The first-person narrator, by contrast, is more limited in perspective, less knowledgeable and less neutral.[27]

Dialogue and Reticence. The bulk of the story in the book of Tobit is carried by dialogue. Alter suggests the analysis of (1) the characters' own speech, particularly the first reported speech; (2) contrasting dialogue between characters; and (3) the discontinuity between speech and reticence.[28] The first reported speech of each character, with the exception of Raphael and Sarah, occurs in the first scene in which that character appears. The first speech is significant as a revelation of character (see Commentary on 2:13-14; 5:4-5). Comparing the speech of various characters is also instructive regarding character. For example, Tobit speaks with greater breadth than does Anna, who speaks in short questions. Also, Tobiah asks many questions and speaks with the haste of youth, whereas Raphael makes long speeches and is generally a vehicle of information (a fitting task for an angel).

The economy of the biblical author is most evident in the reticence of the characters. The most striking example is Sarah, whose only words are spoken in prayer (3:11-15; 8:8). Several times characters simply disappear from a scene (e.g., Tobiah in 2:3-8; 5:10–6:6; 7:11*b*–8:3; 8:20-21; Raphael in 7:9-17; 10:7-13; 11:9-15).

A frequent feature of dialogue shared in common by all speakers is inclusion—that is, beginning and ending a speech with the same word or phrase (e.g., "take courage" [θάρσει *tharsei*] in 5:10; "welcome" [ὑγιαίνων ἔλθοις *hygiainōn elthois*] in 5:14; "child" [παιδίον *paidion*] in 5:17; "will leave in good health/return in good health" [ὑγιαίνων πορεύσεται/ὑποστρέψει ὑγιαίνων *hygiainōn poreusetai/hypostrepsei hygiainōn*] in 5:21-22; "eat and drink" [φάγε καὶ πίε *phage kai pie*] in 7:10-11; "take courage, daughter" [θάρσει θύγατερ *tharsei thygater*] in 7:17; "take courage, child" [θάρσει παιδίον *tharsei paidion*] in 8:21; "my child has perished" [ἀπώλετο τὸ παιδίον μου *apōleto to paidion*

25. See O. Loretz, "Roman und Kurzgeschichte in Israel," *Wort und Botschaft des Alten Testaments*, ed. J. Schreiner (Würzburg: Echter, 1969) 324-25.

26. J. E. Miller, "The Redaction of Tobit and the Genesis Apocryphon," *JSP* 8 (1991) 54-55.

27. See D. McCracken, "Narration and Comedy in the Book of Tobit," *JBL* 114 (1995) 403-9. I am grateful to McCracken for correcting my oversimplification regarding the differences between the two narrative voices.

28. R. Alter, *The Art of Biblical Narrative* (New York: Basic Books, 1981) 182-83.

mou] in 10:4, 7; "how much shall I pay him?" [πόσον αὐτῷ δώσω τόν μισθόν/πόσον αὐτῷ ἔτι δῶ μισθόν *poson autō dōsō ton misthon/poson autō eti dō misthon*] in 12:2-3).

Irony. There are two major and several minor types of irony in the book of Tobit. The basic conflict of the book—the problem that the apparent consequence of doing good is not prosperity but suffering—is an example of the "general irony of events."[29] The veiled identity of Raphael constitutes an example of the second major type of irony, "dramatic irony," in which the readers know what the characters do not.[30] Raguel's digging of the unnecessary grave (8:9-18) is also an example of dramatic irony. The "irony of self-betrayal" is evident in the contradiction between Anna's words and her actions, for she continues to watch the road even though she declares that Tobiah is dead. Irony carries the main theme of the book of Tobit: God blesses the righteous and punishes the wicked; yet God remains free. This final type of irony may be called "divine irony."

Imagery and Key Words. The book is built on a basic opposition between death and life. Only chap. 9 has no mention of death or burial. In addition to words referring specifically to death and life, the concept is imaged through the opposition between night and day, darkness and light, blindness and vision. Tobit's blindness is the physical symbol of the opposition between light and darkness, life and death. It ranks him with sinners as well as with the dead.

A group of abstract terms supports the basic opposition of death and life. Key words on the positive side of the opposition center around healing: health and wellness, safety and salvation, mercy and prosperity are frequently mentioned. With these gifts comes joy. The prayers are particularly filled with expressions of joy. The negative side of the opposition is represented by two clusters of words. The main characters experience and fear distress and reproach. Their distress has two consequences: grief and prayer for deliverance.

One of the major tenets of the book is that these contrasting realities of life and death, suffering and health, joy and sorrow, are in God's hands. The life-and-death opposition manifested in the characters' lives is reflected in the portrait of Jerusalem in the final chapters. For a time, Jerusalem will be desolate, but at the proper time it will be rebuilt.

Another set of key words serves to describe the characters in the book. Four adjectives are used consistently to describe Tobit: "noble/beautiful" (καλός *kalos*); "good" (ἀγαθός *agathos*); "righteous" (δίκαιος *dikaios*); and "charitable/merciful" (ἐλεήμων *eleēmōn*). The cognate nouns of two of these words, "charity" and "righteousness," along with "truth/fidelity" (ἀλήθεια *alētheia*), form an inclusio that frames the book (1:3; 14:9). Tobit exhorts Tobiah and his children, and also the whole people, to these virtues. These words appear also in descriptions of Raphael (5:14, 22) and in his exhortation to Tobit and Tobiah (12:6-8, 11). They describe not only the character of Tobit, but also the nature of God (3:2; 13:6). Thus the four key words characterize God, God's messenger, and the human characters in the book. God is noble and good, just and merciful. The messengers sent

29. D. C. Muecke, *Irony* (London: Methuen & Co., 1970) 67.
30. Ibid., 64-66.

by God to assist human beings manifest the same qualities. Human beings, in response, are called to be noble and good, just and merciful.

Two further images in the book serve as symbols. The fish that attempts to swallow Tobiah's foot (6:3) is a symbol of death (see Commentary on 6:3-4). The number seven is a symbol of completion. Sarah loses seven bridegrooms.[31] Tobiah is the eighth husband; he ends the sorrow brought by the previous seven. He is adjured to bring joy to her heart, beginning with the fourteen-day (twice seven) wedding feast (8:20). Then the two return home to celebrate another seven happy days (11:18). Their children number seven sons (14:3). The messenger of God's providence, sent to bring God's healing and joy to this family, is Raphael, one of the seven angels who stand before God (12:15).

THEOLOGY

The Providence of God. A basic premise of the book is that God cares for human beings. God's plan shapes human history, affecting both individual lives and national destinies. Individual lives are woven together in a common journey. The circle of interwoven lives widens from the individual (Tobit) to the larger family, to the whole people, and finally to all nations who will come to Jerusalem.

The agents of God's providence are an angel, human beings, and natural objects and events. The developed figure of the angel (messenger) is one of the major contributions of the book of Tobit to Old Testament theology. The angel Raphael functions as guide and protector, conveyor of information, mediator of prayer, and one who tests. His words and identity, however, are veiled and ambiguous. God's work through him is not immediately obvious to the other characters in the story.

The primary agents of God's providence in this book are human persons. The clearest example is found in the actions of Tobiah. Through his obedience, God heals both Tobit and Sarah. God's providence is also shown through natural materials, such as the medicinal properties of the fish organs.

The Justice of God. The book of Tobit also asserts that God is just. The understanding of God's justice is expressed in the theory of retribution: God rewards the just and punishes the wicked. The apparent contradiction of this theory, found in the suffering of the just man Tobit, generates the conflict of the plot. How can God be just if the apparent consequence of doing good is not prosperity but suffering? Only at the end is it clear that Tobit's unflinching faith is justified: The wicked are indeed punished (the destruction of Nineveh), and the just are rewarded (the prosperity of Tobit and his family).

The Freedom of God. Although Tobit ultimately receives reward, the story of his life demonstrates that the doctrine of retribution is not a simple equation. The concept of God in this book is not that of a deterministic fate, but of a personal God who is merciful and just, caring and provident, and who blesses the righteous out of the depths of divine freedom.

31. J. Craghan lists seven calamities for Tobit also. See Craghan, *Esther, Judith, Tobit, Jonah, Ruth,* OTM 16, ed. C. Stuhlmueller and M. McNamara (Wilmington, Del.: Michael Glazier, 1982) 138.

The Virtuous Life. The book of Tobit provides a guide and an example for human living. The virtuous life is demonstrated first of all in three sets of relationships in family life: the relationship between parents and children; the marriage relationship; and respect for women. The relationship between parents and children is characterized by instruction, obedience, respect, and love.

There are several examples of the faithful and supportive marriage relationship. The relationships between husband and wife for each of the three married couples differ, but love is expressed in each. The interaction between Tobit and Anna is the liveliest of the three and portrays both positive and negative sides of the relationship. The relationship between Raguel and Edna is less obvious, but there is evidence of mutual interdependence and support. The relationship between Tobiah and Sarah is set firmly upon trust in God's plan and obedience to God's law. It begins with prayer, in which marriage is seen as a gift from God. Raguel, Edna, and Tobit all express the hope that marriage will bring joy, and they regard children as a blessing. They recognize marriage not only as a bond between two people, but also as a bond between families.

The respect for women shown throughout the book is also an element of virtuous family life. The three female characters are carefully drawn and are given significant roles and distinct personalities. Sarah, although the most silent and passive character in the story, reveals in her prayer that she is strong in self-knowledge, capable of deliberation, and has been instructed in the law and in prayer. She is "sensible and beautiful" (6:12). Edna, who never appears without Raguel, has a more limited role and autonomy than Anna. Nonetheless both women are respected by their husbands and are contributing members of their families. Tobit's grandmother Deborah is honored for her instruction of the young Tobit. Women are regarded as competent persons, capable of relating to God through prayer and obedience to the law, capable of providing help and support to their husbands, capable of instructing and guiding their children. They do not, however, have public responsibilities in either the economic or the religious sphere. They are seen primarily in relationship to their families.[32]

Two virtues are expressed not only within the family, but also within the wider kinship group. The first is ἐλεημοσύνη (*eleēmosynē*), which is translated as "almsgiving," "charity," or "mercy." This virtue, mentioned in the inclusio that frames the book (1:3; 14:9), is linked to the major statement of the book that God rewards the just and punishes the wicked. What God rewards is almsgiving.[33] The second virtue exercised within the kinship group is hospitality. Raguel, whose character is modeled on that of Abraham, is

32. See B. Bow and G. W. E. Nickelsburg, "Patriarchy with a Twist: Men and Women in Tobit," in *Women Like This: New Perspectives on Jewish Women in the Greco-Roman World,* ed. Amy-Jill Levine (Atlanta: Scholars Press, 1991) 127-43.

33. See P. J. Griffin, "A Study of *Eleēmosynē* in the Bible with Emphasis upon Its Meaning and Usage in the Theology of Tobit and Ben Sira" (MA thesis, The Catholic University of America, 1982), for a thorough treatment of the structural and narrative significance of *eleēmosynē* in the book of Tobit. He notes that the word *eleēmosynē* appears more often in the book of Tobit than in any other OT book (22 times, compared to 13 times in Sirach; 7 times in Proverbs; 4 times in Isaiah; 3 times in Psalms; twice each in Deuteronomy, the Song of Songs, Baruch, and Daniel; and once in Genesis), and that its semantic development is one of the major contributions of the book of Tobit to OT theology. P. Deselaers defines *eleēmosynē* as "community building activity" (*solidarische handeln*). See Deselaers, *Das Buch Tobit: Studien zu seiner Entstehung, Komposition, und Theologie,* OBO 43 (Freiburg [Schwiez]/Göttingen: Universtätsverlag/Vandenhoeck und Ruprecht, 1982) 348-58.

the primary example of the hospitable person. The hospitality of Tobit can be seen in the alacrity with which he greets Raphael (5:10), his joyous welcome of his daughter-in-law Sarah (11:17), and the feasts he hosts (2:2; 11:17-18). Tobiah follows his father's example in inviting Gabael to join the wedding feast in Ecbatana (9:2, 5-6).

Both *eleēmosynē* and hospitality are limited in the book of Tobit to one's own kindred and people (1:3, 8, 16-18; 2:2-3; 4:17). The diaspora setting of the story helps to explain the limitation to the covenant community. Survival as a people depended on mutual support. Fear of being led astray or contaminated by non-believers encouraged exclusivity. Yet the separation from non-Jews, though evident in matters of food (1:10-11) and marriage (1:9; 4:12-13), does not extend to contempt for other peoples, such as appears in Ezra–Nehemiah or the books of Maccabees.

The relationship of the righteous person to God is characterized by observance of the law and the practice of prayer. Tobit himself is the primary example of faithful observance (1:6-11). He exhorts his son to the same careful observance (chap. 4). Observance of the law is expected not only with regard to detailed external practices, but also through an inner spirit of piety toward God and charity toward neighbor. The relationship with God is to be characterized by fear (4:21; 14:6), love (14:7), and sincerity (4:6; 13:6; 14:7). The habit of prayer is the most pervasive expression of inner devotion to God.[34] The book has been called "a school of prayer";[35] the frequency of prayer and its incorporation at major turning points of the plot indicate its importance. The story is a graphic illustration that prayer is answered. The continual turning to God in prayer indicates that God is the real hero and principal actor of the book. The virtuous life, learned through prayer and the law, is modeled on God, who is righteous, merciful, and truthful.[36]

34. See P. J. Griffin, "The Theology and Function of Prayer in the Book of Tobit" (Ph.D. diss., The Catholic University of America, 1984).

35. J. Goettmann, "Le livre des conseils ou le miroir du Juste engagé dans le monde," *BVC* 21 (1958) 36.

36. See A. A. Di Lella, "The Deuteronomic Background of the Farewell Discourse in Tob 14:3-11," *CBQ* 41 (1979) 386-87.

BIBLIOGRAPHY

Craghan, John. *Esther, Judith, Tobit, Jonah, Ruth.* OTM 16. Edited by C. Stuhlmueller and M. McNamara. Wilmington, Del.: Michael Glazier, 1982. A theological commentary for a general audience, highlighting literary criticism.

Dancy, John C., W. J. Fuerst, and R. J. Hammer. *The Shorter Books of the Apocrypha.* Edited by P. R. Ackroyd et al. Cambridge: Cambridge University Press, 1972. Translation and brief commentary for the general reader.

Fitzmyer, J. A. *Tobit: Qumran Cave 4, xiv.* DJD 19. Edited by M. Broshi et al. Oxford: Clarendon, 1995. Critical edition of the Qumran fragments with a thorough analysis.

Hanhart, R. *Tobit.* Septuaginta, Vetus Testamentum Graecum 8/5. Göttingen: Vandenhoeck & Ruprecht, 1983. The critical edition of the Greek recensions.

Moore, Carey A. *Tobit.* AB 40A. Garden City, N.Y.: Doubleday, 1996. A new translation and comprehensive commentary, based on both the Greek recensions and the Qumran fragments.

Nickelsburg, G. W. E. "Tobit." In *Harper's Bible Commentary.* Edited by J. L. Mays. New York: Harper & Row, 1988. Analysis of literary, religious, and social aspects of the book, plus commentary.

OUTLINE OF TOBIT

I. Tobit 1:1–3:17, Distress in Ecbatana and Nineveh

A. 1:1-22, Tobit's Virtuous Life
B. 2:1–3:6, Tobit's Distress and Prayer
C. 3:7-15, Sarah's Distress and Prayer
D. 3:16-17, God's Answer to Both: Raphael

II. Tobit 4:1–6:1, Preparation for the Journey to Media

A. 4:1-21, Tobit's Instructions to His Son
B. 5:1–6:1, The Hiring of a Guide

III. Tobit 6:2-18, The Journey to Media

A. 6:2-9, Catching the Fish
B. 6:10-18, Raphael's Instructions

IV. Tobit 7:1–11:18, Resolution and Recovery

A. 7:1–8:21, Sarah's Healing
B. 9:1-6, Recovery of the Money
C. 10:1–11:18, Tobit's Healing

V. Tobit 12:1–14:15, All's Well That Ends Well

A. 12:1-22, Revelation of Raphael's Identity
B. 13:1-17, Tobit's Prayer
C. 14:1-15, Epilogue

TOBIT 1:1–3:17

DISTRESS IN ECBATANA AND NINEVEH

OVERVIEW

The first section of the book of Tobit introduces readers to the main characters and to the conflict that drives the plot. This is a story of two families: Tobit's family in Nineveh, and Raguel's family in Ecbatana. The title character, Tobit, is described as a scrupulously virtuous man who is struck with blindness while performing a virtuous act, burying the dead. His wife, Anna, is an industrious woman with a sharp tongue. They have one child, their son, Tobiah. The first member of Raguel's family to be introduced is Sarah, the daughter of Raguel and Edna. She is in great distress because a demon, Asmodeus, keeps killing her bridegrooms. The prayers of Sarah and Tobit bring another major character into the story, the angel Raphael. Raphael is commissioned by God to bring healing to both. Finally, God is an actor behind the scenes throughout the book.

Two plots are introduced in this opening section. The first plot develops in three sequences. The first sequence begins with the statement of Tobit's character: "he has walked on the paths of truth and righteousness." This statement gives rise to questions: How is his righteousness manifested? What will be his reward? These two questions are answered almost immediately. Tobit performs acts of charity, especially burying the dead. His reward seems to be blindness. The second sequence begins with the announcement that Tobit has married Anna, a woman of his own kindred. Anna and their son, Tobiah, will be major actors in the following story. The third sequence begins with the news that Tobit has gone to Media and deposited money there. The question raised by this sequence is, What will happen to the money? The second main plot begins with the introduction of Sarah. Her distress gives rise to the question, How will she be delivered? The plots join in 3:16-17 with the answer to the prayers of Tobit and Sarah. Raphael has been sent, but now the question remains: How will he function? Two new questions are also posed: How will Tobit be healed? How will Tobiah meet and marry Sarah?

The conflict of the story arises from the suffering of Sarah and Tobit. Each character seems to be afflicted unjustly. The theory of retribution, which is described most fully in Deuteronomy 28, holds that righteous people will be blessed by God, while wicked people will be punished. Both Sarah and Tobit seem to be righteous. Why, then, are they afflicted? Does their suffering suggest that God is not just, and the theory does not hold? How can this conflict be resolved?

The resolution to the conflict is suggested already at the end of this first section. In answer to the prayers of Tobit and Sarah, God sends the angel Raphael to heal them both. Thus the suspense of the story resides not in whether they will be healed, but in how they will be healed.

Other major elements of the book are mentioned in the first section:

(1) Prayer is a major theme throughout the book. Six substantial prayers are woven into the plot. Five of the characters turn to God in prayer.

(2) Acts of charity (almsgiving) are presented as the chief element of Tobit's righteousness. These acts also are the primary support of Tobit's hope for a happy life. Anna challenges Tobit precisely on this point when she asks what good his righteous deeds have done him (2:14). God's apparent disregard of Tobit's faithfulness in charitable acts is the reason for the despair in his prayer.

(3) An angel is commissioned as a minister of God's providence.

(4) The inclusion not only of individual characters, but also of two families, suggests the importance of marriage and family life.

TOBIT 1:1-22, TOBIT'S VIRTUOUS LIFE

NAB

1 1 This book tells the story of Tobit, son of Tobiel, son of Hananiel, son of Aduel, son of Gabael of the family of Asiel, of the tribe of Naphtali, 2 who during the reign of Shalmaneser, king of Assyria, was taken captive from Thisbe, which is south of Kedesh Naphtali in upper Galilee, above and to the west of Asser, north of Phogor.

3 I, Tobit, have walked all the days of my life on the paths of truth and righteousness. I performed many charitable works for my kinsmen and my people who had been deported with me to Nineveh, in Assyria. 4 When I lived as a young man in my own country, Israel, the entire tribe of my forefather Naphtali had broken away from the house of David and from Jerusalem. This city had been singled out of all Israel's tribes, so that they all might offer sacrifice in the place where the temple, God's dwelling, had been built and consecrated for all generations to come. 5 All my kinsmen, like the rest of the tribe of my forefather Naphtali, used to offer sacrifice on all the mountains of Galilee as well as to the young bull which Jeroboam, king of Israel, had made in Dan.

6 I, for my part, would often make the pilgrimage alone to Jerusalem for the festivals, as is prescribed for all Israel by perpetual decree. Bringing with me the first fruits of the field and the firstlings of the flock, together with a tenth of my income and the first shearings of the sheep, I would hasten to Jerusalem 7 and present them to the priests, Aaron's sons, at the altar. To the Levites who were doing service in Jerusalem I

The translation of Tobit is based on Codex Sinaiticus, which best reflects the Semitic original of the book. The edition of Brooke, McLean, and Thackeray was used, which also contains the shorter recension (Codices B, A, and most of the cursives) and the third recension (Codices 44, p. and d.). The notes which follow indicate the deviations from LXX^{S}.

1, 1: Omit *tou Raphaēl tou Ragouēl:* so LXX (all other MSS), Vet Lat, P.

1, 2: *Shalmaneser:* so Vet Lat, V, P. LXX corrupt.

1, 3: (*eporeuomēn kai*) *dikaiosynēs* (*pasas*): so LXX (most MSS), Vet Lat, P.

1, 4: Omit *tou patros mou* after *Daueid:* so Vet Lat (*poleōs tēs*) *eklegeisēs:* so LXX^{B,A,}, Vet Lat, P.

1, 5: (*Dan*) *kai* (*epi*): so Vet Lat;^{MSS}.

1, 7: (*akrodryōn*) *edidoun:* so LXX$^{Sc.a}$; cf Vet Lat; *tou sitou kai tou oinou kai elaiou* (in that order): so LXX$^{Sc.a}$, Vet Lat; (*roōn*) *kai tōn sykōn:* so LXX$^{Sc.a}$, Vet Lat.

NRSV

1 This book tells the story of Tobit son of Tobiel son of Hananiel son of Aduel son of Gabael son of Raphael of the descendants[a] of Asiel, of the tribe of Naphtali, 2who in the days of King Shalmaneser[b] of the Assyrians was taken into captivity from Thisbe, which is to the south of Kedesh Naphtali in Upper Galilee, above Asher toward the west, and north of Phogor.

3I, Tobit, walked in the ways of truth and righteousness all the days of my life. I performed many acts of charity for my kindred and my people who had gone with me in exile to Nineveh in the land of the Assyrians. 4When I was in my own country, in the land of Israel, while I was still a young man, the whole tribe of my ancestor Naphtali deserted the house of David and Jerusalem. This city had been chosen from among all the tribes of Israel, where all the tribes of Israel should offer sacrifice and where the temple, the dwelling of God, had been consecrated and established for all generations forever.

5All my kindred and our ancestral house of Naphtali sacrificed to the calf[c] that King Jeroboam of Israel had erected in Dan and on all the mountains of Galilee. 6But I alone went often to Jerusalem for the festivals, as it is prescribed for all Israel by an everlasting decree. I would hurry off to Jerusalem with the first fruits of the crops and the firstlings of the flock, the tithes of the cattle, and the first shearings of the sheep. 7I would give these to the priests, the sons of Aaron, at the altar; likewise the tenth of the grain, wine, olive oil, pomegranates, figs, and the rest of the fruits to the sons of Levi who ministered at Jerusalem. Also for six years I would save up a second tenth in money and go and distribute it in Jerusalem. 8A third tenth[d] I would give to the orphans and widows and to the converts who had attached themselves to Israel. I would bring it and give it to them in the third year, and we would eat it according to the ordinance decreed concerning it in the law of Moses and according to the instructions of Deborah, the mother of my father

[a] Other ancient authorities lack *of Raphael son of Raguel of the descendants* [b] Gk *Enemessaros* [c] Other ancient authorities read *heifer* [d] *A third tenth* added from other ancient authorities

NAB

would give the tithe of grain, wine, olive oil, pomegranates, figs, and other fruits. And except for sabbatical years, I used to give a second tithe in money, which each year I would go and disburse in Jerusalem. 8 The third tithe I gave to orphans and widows, and to converts who were living with the Israelites. Every third year I would bring them this offering, and we ate it in keeping with the decree of the Mosaic law and the commands of Deborah, the mother of my father Tobiel; for when my father died, he left me an orphan.

9 When I reached manhood, I married Anna, a woman of our own lineage. By her I had a son whom I named Tobiah. 10 Now after I had been deported to Nineveh, all my brothers and relatives ate the food of heathens, 11 but I refrained from eating that kind of food. 12 Because of this wholehearted service of God, 13 the Most High granted me favor and status with Shalmaneser, so that I became purchasing agent for all his needs. 14 Every now and then until his death I would go to Media to buy goods for him. I also deposited several pouches containing a great sum of money with my kinsman Gabael, son of Gabri, who lived at Rages, in Media. 15 But when Shalmaneser died and his son Sennacherib succeeded him as king, the roads to Media became unsafe, so I could no longer go there.

16 During Shalmaneser's reign I performed many charitable works for my kinsmen and my people. 17 I would give my bread to the hungry and my clothing to the naked. If I saw one of my people who had died and been thrown outside the walls of Nineveh, I would bury him. 18 I also buried anyone whom Sennacherib slew when he returned as a fugitive from Judea during the days of judgment decreed against him by the heavenly King because of the blasphemies he had uttered. In his rage he killed many Israelites, but I used

1, 8: Omit *auta* 1°; read instead *tēn dekatēn tēn tritēn:* so Vet Lat^{MSS}; cf P. *Tōbiēl* (*tou patros*) *mou:* so Vet Lat; cf LXX^{B,A}, P, and 1, 1.

1, 9: *Annan:* so LXX^{B,A}, Vet Lat, P.

1, 10: *kai* (*meta to aichmalōtisthēnai*) *me eis Nineuē* (*kai pantes*): so with Vet Lat, P; cf LXX^{MSS}. LXX^{S} corrupt; cf 1, 3.

1, 13.15.16: *Shalmaneser:* so Vet Lat, V, P. LXX corrupt; cf 1,2.

1, 14: *Gabaēlǭ*: so LXX$^{Sc.a,B,A}$; cf 4, 1. (*adelphǭ*) *mou* (*tǭ*) *tou* (*Gabrei*): cf Vet Lat and 4, 20. (*en*) *Ragois* (*tēs Mēdias*): so with LXX^{B,A}, P; cf 4, 1 and Vet Lat.

1, 16: *kai* (*tois ek tou genous mou*): conj; cf 1, 3 and LXX^{MSS}, Vet Lat, P.

NRSV

Tobiel,[a] for my father had died and left me an orphan. 9 When I became a man I married a woman,[b] a member of our own family, and by her I became the father of a son whom I named Tobias.

10 After I was carried away captive to Assyria and came as a captive to Nineveh, everyone of my kindred and my people ate the food of the Gentiles, 11 but I kept myself from eating the food of the Gentiles. 12 Because I was mindful of God with all my heart, 13 the Most High gave me favor and good standing with Shalmaneser,[c] and I used to buy everything he needed. 14 Until his death I used to go into Media, and buy for him there. While in the country of Media I left bags of silver worth ten talents in trust with Gabael, the brother of Gabri. 15 But when Shalmaneser[c] died, and his son Sennacherib reigned in his place, the highways into Media became unsafe and I could no longer go there.

16 In the days of Shalmaneser[c] I performed many acts of charity to my kindred, those of my tribe. 17 I would give my food to the hungry and my clothing to the naked; and if I saw the dead body of any of my people thrown out behind the wall of Nineveh, I would bury it. 18 I also buried any whom King Sennacherib put to death when he came fleeing from Judea in those days of judgment that the king of heaven executed upon him because of his blasphemies. For in his anger he put to death many Israelites; but I would secretly remove the bodies and bury them. So when Sennacherib looked for them he could not find them. 19 Then one of the Ninevites went and informed the king about me, that I was burying them; so I hid myself. But when I realized that the king knew about me and that I was being searched for to be put to death, I was afraid and ran away. 20 Then all my property was confiscated; nothing was left to me that was not taken into the royal treasury except my wife Anna and my son Tobias.

21 But not forty[d] days passed before two of Sennacherib's[e] sons killed him, and they fled to the mountains of Ararat, and his son Esar-haddon[f] reigned after him. He appointed Ahikar, the son

[a] Lat: Gk *Hananiel* [b] Other ancient authorities add *Anna* [c] Gk *Enemessaros* [d] Other ancient authorities read either *forty-five* or *fifty* [e] Gk *his* [f] Gk *Sacherdonos*

NAB

to take their bodies by stealth and bury them; so when Sennacherib looked for them, he could not find them. 19 But a certain citizen of Nineveh informed the king that it was I who buried the dead. When I found out that the king knew all about me and wanted to put me to death, I went into hiding; then in my fear I took to flight. 20 Afterward, all my property was confiscated; I was left with nothing. All that I had was taken to the king's palace, except for my wife Anna and my son Tobiah.

21 But less than forty days later the king was assassinated by two of his sons, who then escaped into the mountains of Ararat. His son Esarhaddon, who succeeded him as king, placed Ahiqar, my brother Anael's son, in charge of all the accounts of his kingdom, so that he took control over the entire administration. 22 Then Ahiqar interceded on my behalf, and I was able to return to Nineveh. For under Sennacherib, king of Assyria, Ahiqar had been chief cupbearer, keeper of the seal, administrator, and treasurer; and Esarhaddon reappointed him. He was a close relative—in fact, my nephew.

1, 19: Omit *kai* before *'ote* and replace it before *ephobēthēn*: so P.
1, 21.22; 2, 1: *Esarhaddon*: cf 2 Kgs 19, 37. LXX, Vet Lat, P corrupt.

NRSV

of my brother Hanael[a] over all the accounts of his kingdom, and he had authority over the entire administration. 22Ahikar interceded for me, and I returned to Nineveh. Now Ahikar was chief cupbearer, keeper of the signet, and in charge of administration of the accounts under King Sennacherib of Assyria; so Esar-haddon[b] reappointed him. He was my nephew and so a close relative.

[a] Other authorities read *Hananael* [b] Gk *Sacherdonos*

COMMENTARY

1:1-2. The first two verses of the book begin with the title character and give the setting of the story. The name of the main character in the Qumran fragments is "Tobi" (טובי *ṭwby*), which is probably a shortened form of "Tobiah," the name of his son.[37] Tobit is introduced with a five-member genealogy. The names are all theophoric—that is, they contain the name of God, אל (*'ēl*). For example, Tobi-el means "God is my good"; Hanani-el, "God has shown mercy": Rapha-el, "God heals." These names in Tobit's genealogy suggest the piety of his family.

Tobit's tribe is also identified. Naphtali is a northern tribe; its territory runs from the south end of the Sea of Galilee northward to the Huleh basin. In the eighth century BCE the Assyrians took over Galilee, including the territory of Naphtali. Many of the leading citizens were taken captive into Assyria. The sorrow of this captivity is described by the eighth-century prophet Isaiah (Isa 9:1[8:23]). But Isaiah also holds out hope for the people: "The people who walked in darkness have seen a great light" (Isa 9:2[9:1]).

The book begins as historical annals do, with "the book of the deeds" (βίβλος λόγων *biblos logōn*; cf. LXX 3 Kgdms 14:29; 15:7, 23, 31; 16:5, 14, 20, 27). Some of the historical information in the title, however, is incorrect. The author has confused Tiglath-pileser III (745–727 BCE), the Assyrian ruler who deported the citizens of Galilee, with his successor, Shalmaneser V (727–722 BCE), who began the siege of Samaria, the capital

37. The name has been given a Greek ending in both major recensions (Τωβιθ in G[II]; Τωβιτ in G[I]). See J. A. Fitzmyer, "Tobit," in *Qumran Cave 4, XIV: Parabiblical Texts,* Part 2, DJD 19, ed. Magen Broshi et al. (Oxford: Clarendon, 1995) 51-52. The name is found in Tob 7:2, 4.

city of the northern kingdom. Shalmaneser's successor, Sargon II (722–705 BCE), defeated the northern kingdom, destroyed the capital city, and took captive the ten tribes of Israel.

1:3. The story of Tobit begins with a first-person narrative that continues until the scene changes to the house of Raguel in Ecbatana (3:6). Tobit describes himself with three words that will characterize him throughout the book: truth (αλήθεια *alētheia*), righteousness (δικαιοσύνη *dikaiosynē*), and charity (ελεημοσυνη *eleēmosynē*). These character traits are illustrated by the practices of his youth (vv. 4-9), his continued fidelity when he was taken into captivity (vv. 10-15), and the specific charitable act of burying the dead (vv. 16-22).

1:4-5. Tobit is a living example of fidelity to the law of God as it is laid out in Deuteronomy. The book of Deuteronomy requires that worship be centralized in the Jerusalem Temple and that all sacrifices be offered there (Deut 12:11-14). When the ten northern tribes separated from Judah in the tenth century BCE, their king, Jeroboam, did not want his people to continue worshiping in Jerusalem. The Temple was a strong reminder of the power of David and Solomon; the temple liturgy encouraged support of the Davidic monarchy, which continued to rule in Judah. So Jeroboam built two alternate shrines for the people of his kingdom—one in Bethel and one in Dan. Since he had no ark of the covenant, he installed golden bulls (or calves) in each of the shrines, presumably as pedestals for the God of Israel. These bulls are always judged to be idolatrous by the authors of the books of Kings, who are from the southern kingdom, Judah (see 1 Kgs 12:27-31). In fact, they may well have been occasions for idol worship by the Israelites in the north. Tobit claims that, even though he lived in the north and was a citizen of the northern kingdom of Israel, he never participated in the worship at Dan. He even claims that he went alone to Jerusalem to worship.

Another historical incongruity appears in Tobit's statement that he had been living at the time of the division of Israel into two kingdoms (922 BCE). Since Tiglath-pileser's deportation of the Israelites to Assyria took place at the end of the eighth century, that would make Tobit a very old man, indeed!

1:6-7. Deuteronomy also prescribes certain festivals that must be celebrated in Jerusalem: Passover, Weeks, and Booths (Deut 16:1-17). Tobit claims that he went faithfully to Jerusalem for the festivals and offered the required tithes (vv. 6-7).

❖ ❖ ❖ ❖

EXCURSUS: TITHES

Tithes (the contribution of a tenth of one's income) are prescribed in several places in the law. In Leviticus a tithe of crops and animals is required in order to support the priesthood and maintain the Jerusalem Temple (Lev 27:30-33). In the legislation in Numbers (Num 18:21-24, 30-32), which precedes the centralization of worship prescribed in Deuteronomy, the tithe is intended to support local worship—the Levites and the local sanctuaries—and possibly also for upkeep of the levitical cities (Joshua 21) in the time of David. A tenth of this tithe was to be given to the Jerusalem sanctuary (Num 18:25-29). When Deuteronomy abolished the local sanctuaries and minimized the service of the Levites, the tithe was to be used for a sacrifice and festal banquet at the Temple in Jerusalem (Deut 14:22-26). Every third year, however, the same tithe was to be used for the relief of the poor in the home area of the giver (Deut 14:18-29; cf. Deut 26:12). Thus on years one, two, four, and five of the seven-year sabbatical cycle, the pilgrim brought the tithe in kind or in money to Jerusalem; in years three and six, the tithe was stored for the needy—strangers, orphans, widows, and landless Levites.

In the post-exilic period, however, when the entire Pentateuch became normative, the three passages were interpreted as referring to three different tithes. Thus the first fruits of crops and the firstborn of animals were to go to the priests in the Temple (Lev 27:26-27, 30-33), and the first tithe of crops and animals to the Levites (Num 18:21-24). The "second tithe" was intepreted in two ways. Either the tithe for the banquet (Deut 14:22-26) was replaced by the "poor tithe" (Deut 14:28-29) in the third and sixth years, or the "poor tithe" was levied over and above the banquet tithe in those years, thus becoming a "third tithe." Josephus, a first-century CE Jewish historian, regarded the "poor tithe" as a "third tithe."[38]

The situation in the book of Tobit is complicated further by a discrepancy between the two major recensions of the book. G^I mentions a "third" (τὴν τρίτην *tēn tritēn*) which is specified in the Old Latin as a "third tithe" (*et tertii ad decimationem*). G^{II} describes the tithe of "the third year" (ἐν τῷ τρίτῳ ἔτει *en tō tritō etei*). Whether Tobit is giving two tithes or three, he is scrupulously careful to follow the law concerning tithes.

38. Josephus *Antiquities of the Jews* 4.8.22.

❖ ❖ ❖ ❖

1:8. Tobit credits his grandmother Deborah with teaching him the law to which he is so faithful. She is the first of several strong women to appear in this book. Tobit's respect for her authority mirrors the advice of Ben Sira, whose book was written about the same time as the book of Tobit: "The Lord . . . confirms a mother's right over her children" (Sir 3:2 NRSV; cf. Sir 3:4, 6, 10). Tobit will follow her example in instructing his own son and grandchildren (4:3-21; 14:3-11).

1:9. Tobit also follows the custom of endogamy, marriage within the tribe and clan. The custom seems to be based on the laws concerning the daughters of Zelophehad, in whose case there was no male heir to guarantee the retention of the ancestral property within the tribe and clan (Num 27:5-11; 36:2-12). In order to keep the heritage within the ancestral tribe, these women were required to marry within the clan: "Every daughter who possesses an inheritance in any tribe of the Israelites shall marry one from the clan of her father's tribe, so that all Israelites may continue to possess their ancestral inheritance" (Num 36:8). The custom is also based on the example of the ancestors. Abraham sends a servant back to his kindred in Mesopotamia to find a wife for his son Isaac (Gen 24:3-4). Rebekah and Isaac give similar instructions to their son Jacob (Gen 27:46–28:5). In the post-exilic period interpretation of the law, marriage within Judaism is encouraged as a protection against the false worship of the Gentiles. The custom is carried to the extreme by Nehemiah, who forces the returning exiles to divorce their non-Jewish wives (Neh 13:23-30; cf. Neh 10:31). Tobit is very careful in his observance of this custom. He marries not only within Judaism, not only within his tribe and clan, but also within his "ancestral family" (πατριά *patria*). Deselaers considers *patria* to represent the "ancestral house," a unit even smaller than the clan.[39]

1:10-11. Tobit's fidelity to the law, practiced so earnestly in his homeland, continues after he is deported to Assyria. The example he gives concerns the dietary laws, an observance that gained significance during the exilic period. Tobit implies that he has kept the dietary laws found in the Pentateuch concerning clean and unclean food (see Lev 11:1-47; Deut 14:3-21), the prohibition against eating blood (Lev 7:26-27; 17:10-14; Deut 12:23-25; 15:23), and the avoidance of food sacrificed to idols (Exod 34:15). Again Tobit describes himself as the only one who remains faithful to the law.

1:12-13. Now Tobit asserts his belief in the theory of retribution. Because he is faithful, God rewards him. Tobit's good fortune consists in obtaining a position of responsibility in the Assyrian court as the procurator for King Shalmaneser. This is a position of great trust for a man who is a deportee from a defeated country. He travels from Nineveh, in modern Iraq, to Media (the land of the Medes), in modern Iran, to buy for him.

39. P. Deselaers, *Das Buch Tobit, Studien zu seiner Entstehung, Komposition, und Theologie,* OBO 43 (Freiburg [Schwiez]/Göttingen: Universtätsverlag/Vandenhoeck und Ruprecht, 1982) 309-15.

❖ ❖ ❖ ❖

EXCURSUS: THEORY OF RETRIBUTION

The theory of retribution is expressed most clearly in Deuteronomy 28. A series of blessings that apply to every situation in life is listed as a reward for obedience to God's commandments (Deut 28:1-14). A series of curses that correspond exactly to the blessings and expand upon them is listed as a consequence of disobedience (Deut 28:15-68). The theory is illustrated throughout the historical books of Joshua–2 Kings. When the people are faithful, they are successful; when they sin, they are defeated (e.g., Josh 7:1–8:29; Judg 3:7-11). The theory holds for individuals also: David's sin leads to his punishment (2 Sam 11:1–12:15).

Neither in Deuteronomy nor in the book of Tobit, however, is retribution an automatic or impersonal equation. Blessing comes when it is undeserved (see Deut 7:7-8). The author of Deuteronomy continually emphasizes the dangers to Israel of attributing blessing and prosperity to their own power or merits (see Deut 8:17-18; 9:4-6). The election of Israel is the free choice of a loving God who chooses them as a special people for no reason other than love of their ancestors (see, e.g., Deut 4:32-40; 7:6-11; 10:15; 23:6). A corollary to God's undeserved blessing is that no punishment is without hope. If the people return to the Lord and obey, God will have mercy on them (Deut 30:1-10).

In addition to undeserved blessing, however, Israel also experiences what seems to be undeserved suffering (Deut 8:2, 5). This "testing," according to Deuteronomy, is for the purposes of discovering the people's fidelity (8:3) and of showing them that the blessings are gifts from God and are not earned by their own power (Deut 8:16-17). Tobit believes in the theory of retribution, but he seems dangerously close to attributing his good fortune to his own merits.

❖ ❖ ❖ ❖

1:14. Another historical incongruity appears here. Tobit lives in Nineveh and works for the king. This is not implausible, since there were four great cities in the heartland of Assyria: Nineveh, Asshur, Calah, and Arbela. But Nineveh was not established as the capital city until the reign of Sennacherib, twenty or more years after the reign of Shalmaneser V.

Tobit also gains prosperity in his new position. He is able to deposit in savings ten talents worth of silver. The exact value of this deposit is impossible to calculate, but a talent is usually considered the equivalent of three thousand shekels. Thus ten talents is a large sum of money.

1:15. Shalmaneser V (726–722) was in fact succeeded, not by Sennacherib, but by Sargon II (721–705), who was not in the direct line of succession. The book of Tobit seems to be dependent on 2 Kings, which mentions Shalmaneser (18:9) and Sennacherib (18:13), but not Sargon. Only Isaiah (Isa 20:1) mentions Sargon.

Sargon II began a dynasty that lasted until the end of the Assyrian Empire in 612 BCE. He was succeeded by his son Sennacherib in 705. A change in political power always stirred up hope in occupied countries, and widescale revolt often followed the death of a powerful ruler. Sargon spent most of his reign reconquering the territory won by his father, Tiglath-pileser III, and adding new territory to the empire. The Medes were involved in the struggle against Urartu. It is possible that this unrest made the roads to Media unsafe, as Tobit reports.

1:16-17. At this point in the narrative Tobit begins to recount his acts of charity (*eleēmosynē*). After listing two common works of mercy, feeding the hungry and clothing the naked, he describes in detail his primary work of burying the dead. His account indicates that life for the Israelite exiles in Assyria was already precarious under Shalmaneser, even though Tobit himself holds a position of trust. Bodies of the exiles were simply thrown out and left unburied. To be left unburied was an abomination for Jews.

Burial of the dead as a practice of charity is a theme found also in Genesis. Jacob makes his proper burial a sign of Joseph's charity and fidelity toward him (Gen 47:29).[40] Burial is the specific practice of charity that receives the most attention in the book of Tobit (e.g., 1:18-20; 2:3-8; 4:3-4, 17; 6:15; 14:1-13). In the Greco-Roman period, burial, rather than cremation, was the customary practice among the Jews. They considered it a work of mercy to bury not only family members but also strangers, even non-Jews.[41]

1:18-20. Shalmaneser's successor, Sennacherib, ruled Assyria for twenty-four years (705–681). During the reign of Hezekiah, king of Judah, Sennacherib laid siege to Jerusalem at least once and perhaps twice. Although he defeated and sacked several other Judean cities, notably Lachish, he did not destroy Jerusalem. According to 2 Kgs 18:14-16, Hezekiah paid him a large tribute. It is possible that this payment relates to a first invasion in 701, which Sennacherib himself reports, claiming that he "shut up Hezekiah like a bird in a cage." In 2 Kgs 19:35-36, the story is told that, when Sennacherib was encamped opposite the Ethiopian troops under King Tirhakah (2 Kgs 19:9), who had come to help Hezekiah, a disaster struck the Assyrian army and Sennacherib returned home in disgrace. Is this the same invasion or a later one? The presence of Tirhakah, whose reign did not begin until 690, the occurrence of two differing reasons for Sennacherib's departure, and the announcement of his death (681 BCE) immediately following (2 Kgs 19:37) argue for two invasions—one in 701 and the other at a later date, but before 687, when Hezekiah died.[42]

Josephus also reports the incident.[43] He tells three stories of Sennacherib's disgrace from different sources. Two concern Sennacherib's siege of Pelusium; the third concerns Jerusalem. In the first instance, Sennacherib departs because of fear of Tirhakah. In the second, he leaves because mice have chewed up the bows and armor of his soldiers. In the third, he retreats because God has sent a pestilence into the camp (cf. the angel of the Lord in 2 Kgs 19:35). Josephus reports Sennacherib's death immediately following the third story.

Tobit relates that Sennacherib's anger against the Israelites was great because of his forced retreat from Jerusalem. For this reason he executed many of them and left them unburied. Thus the need for Tobit's charitable act of burying the dead increases. This action puts Tobit himself in danger of death. He saves his life by fleeing but loses all his property except the money that has been deposited with Gabael in Media. He and his family are reduced to temporary poverty.

1:21-22. Sennacherib was assassinated, apparently, by two of his sons. A third son, Esarhaddon, who claimed to be in hiding at the time of the assassination, took the Assyrian throne (680–669 BCE) and established peace at home and in the territories. The book of Tobit, which is apparently dependent upon 2 Kings for its historical information, has telescoped the events even further than has 2 Kings. Tobit reports that Sennacherib was killed less than forty days after his return from Jerusalem.

The succession of Esarhaddon is good news for Tobit. Through the good word of his nephew Ahiqar, Tobit is allowed to return to Nineveh. Ahiqar is modeled on the wise man of the same name who was active at court during the reigns of Sennacherib and Esarhaddon (see Introduction).

40. This is one of three occurrences of ἐλεημοσύνη (*eleēmosynē*) in the Pentateuch. The other two occurrences (Deut 6:25; 24:13) are renderings of צדקה (*ṣĕdāqâ*). All three connote a characteristic of a person. See P. J. Griffin, "The Theology and Function of Prayer in the Book of Tobit" (Ph.D. diss., The Catholic University of America, 1984) 8-10.

41. See *t. Meg.* 3:16; *t. Git.* 3:14. See also Zeev Weiss, "Social Aspects of Burial in beth She'arim: Archaeological Finds and Talmudic Sources," in *The Galilee in Late Antiquity,* ed. Lee I. Levine (Cambridge, Mass.: Harvard University Press, 1992) 365.

42. "Mesopotamia," *ABD* 4:743-47.

43. Josephus *Antiquities of the Jews* 10.1.4-5.

REFLECTIONS

1. The overwhelming impression conveyed by Tobit's report of his youth is that of a man scrupulously faithful to the law. Even when observance becomes difficult because of the division of the kingdom, Tobit remains faithful. Even when his neighbors and family transfer their allegiance and change their practices, Tobit perseveres. The plurality of modern society presents constant challenges to believers who strive to remain faithful to their religious belief and practices. It is sometimes difficult to find a supportive community to encourage one in worshiping regularly and helping the poor. Tobit suffers from the lack of such a community.

2. A gnawing suspicion arises that Tobit is overly careful. His interpretation of the law seems too literal. "He alone" is better than all his kindred. If there is a suggestion that perhaps two or even three tithes are called for, Tobit is there with his offering. He marries not just within Judaism, but within his ancestral family.

Tobit's letter-of-the-law fidelity prepares the reader for the challenge that will come to his faith. Is he relying on external practices to earn a reward from God? Or is a loving relationship with God the source of his fidelity and reward enough? Is he capable of enduring ambiguity, the test of suffering and the uncertainty that comes in its wake? Or will he crumble in despair?

These questions confront everyone who strives to lead a holy life. Is security or love the motive for faithful observance? Only love is strong enough to sustain us to the end.

3. The theory of retribution is alive and well in the late twentieth century. How often does one hear (or think), "Why me? What did I do to deserve this?" It comes to mind when good things happen. In *The Sound of Music,* Maria sings "Somewhere in my youth or childhood, I must have done something good!" She is expressing the theory of retribution, that good things happen to us because we have been good. It does not seem to occur to her that something good could happen simply as a free gift of God. More often, however, the question "Why me?" is provoked, not by blessing, but by suffering. "When bad things happen to good people," to cite Kushner's title, we want a reason, an explanation.[44]

The assumption that retribution—good or bad—is an automatic equation (good behavior = blessing; bad behavior = suffering) is both immature and a denial of basic tenets of the Christian faith. It is left over from our childhood, when our parents disciplined us with reminders of this theory. It also regards suffering simply as punishment for sin. It is undoubtedly true that there is a connection between sin and suffering. But the connection is not simple. It is not always the sinner who suffers; sometimes innocent people suffer for the sins of others. Sometimes suffering is not caused by sin at all, but is simply a part of human life. No human being, no matter how holy, lives a life free of suffering.

There is a further danger in Christianity: identifying suffering as a badge of true holiness. The center of Christian faith is the death and resurrection of Jesus Christ. We believe that the sinless one took on the sins of all humanity. "God made him to be sin who knew no sin, so that in him we might become the righteousness of God" (2 Cor 5:21). We also believe that we are called to complete in our bodies what is lacking in the sufferings of Christ (see Col 1:24). This is the great reversal, the redemption of human suffering that gives it meaning. But this is not an automatic equation. Just as it is not possible to say that anyone who suffers must be a sinner, neither is it possible to say that anyone who suffers must be holy.

So it is perilous to see the theory of retribution as automatic. Doing so causes us to make false judgments: Sufferers are sinners; the prosperous are holy (or the reverse). It also causes us to deny God's freedom. God is free to give good gifts to us whether we deserve them or not. God is free to forgive our sins without charge. God is also free to allow us to suffer, to

44. Harold S. Kushner, *When Bad Things Happen to Good People* (New York: Schocken, 1981).

allow human life to take its course, whether we deserve it or not. Human beings are also free to accept blessings with thanksgiving, free to accept suffering in patience and hope (and the reverse). Tobit is about to learn both aspects of this freedom.

4. Tobit is described as a righteous man because he does merciful works. The seven corporal works of mercy in Christian tradition are these: Feed the hungry, give drink to the thirsty, clothe the naked, shelter the stranger, visit the sick, minister to prisoners, and bury the dead (see Matt 25:35-36). These works are expressions of a living faith in action. Too often we take the easy route, exercising compassion at a distance by writing a check or dropping off a bag of clothes. Tobit's example shows us that sometimes it is necessary to experience other people's misery firsthand. What people need is not only financial help but also a human touch. There are countless opportunities to serve in food kitchens or to work in homeless shelters. Prisoners are in need of visitors, as well as education and religious services. These "hands-on" works of mercy are not easy. We may experience scorn and rejection. We may be repulsed by dirt and disease. Perseverance in the works of mercy, however, has a surprising reward. Those whom we serve begin in turn to teach us the amazing compassion of God.

5. Burying the dead remains one of the corporal works of mercy. In normal situations most people are not compelled actually to dig graves for abandoned corpses (although this may be necessary in war-torn areas). However, it is certainly a duty of families to arrange for the proper burial of their dead, and a responsibility of the state when the deceased has no family.

What is "proper burial" of the dead? In North American culture much money is spent in the denial of death. The body is made to look as lifelike as possible. Elaborately decorated caskets are sometimes purchased. The casket is lowered into the grave only after the family has left. Huge memorial markers may be installed. The question is not whether the body of a human being should be honored. It certainly should. All human beings are created in the image of God and destined for resurrection, body and soul. The question is one of emphasis. How can we as a culture learn to face and ritualize the reality of death? Only an honest recognition of that reality allows us to believe with grateful awe in the reality of resurrection.

TOBIT 2:1–3:6, TOBIT'S DISTRESS AND PRAYER

NAB

2 1 Thus under King Esarhaddon I returned
to my home, and my wife Anna and my
son Tobiah were restored to me. Then on our
festival of Pentocost, the feast of Weeks, a fine
dinner was prepared for me, and I reclined to eat.
2 The table was set for me, and when many
different dishes were placed before me, I said to
my son Tobiah: "My son, go out and try to find
a poor man from among our kinsmen exiled here
in Nineveh. If he is a sincere worshiper of God,
bring him back with you, so that he can share
this meal with me. Indeed, son, I shall wait for
you to come back."

2, 2: (*memnētai*) *tou theou* (*en*): so Vet Lat, V. LXX^{B,A} and P read *tou kyriou.*

NRSV

2 Then during the reign of Esar-haddon[a] I
returned home, and my wife Anna and my
son Tobias were restored to me. At our festival
of Pentecost, which is the sacred festival of weeks,
a good dinner was prepared for me and I reclined
to eat. 2When the table was set for me and an
abundance of food placed before me, I said to my
son Tobias, "Go, my child, and bring whatever
poor person you may find of our people among
the exiles in Nineveh, who is wholeheartedly
mindful of God,[b] and he shall eat together
with me. I will wait for you, until you come
back." 3So Tobias went to look for some poor
person of our people. When he had returned he said,

[a] Gk *Sacherdonos* [b] Lat: Gk *wholeheartedly mindful*

NAB

3 Tobiah went out to look for some poor kinsman of ours. When he returned he exclaimed, "Father!" I said to him, "What is it, son?" He answered, "Father, one of our people has been murdered! His body lies in the market place where he was just strangled!" 4 I sprang to my feet, leaving the dinner untouched; and I carried the dead man from the street and put him in one of the rooms, so that I might bury him after sunset. 5 Returning to my own quarters, I washed myself and ate my food in sorrow. 6 I was reminded of the oracle pronounced by the prophet Amos against Bethel:

"Your festivals shall be returned into
mourning,
And all your songs into lamentation."

7 And I wept. Then at sunset I went out, dug a grave, and buried him.

8 The neighbors mocked me, saying to one another: "Will this man never learn! Once before he was hunted down for execution because of this very thing; yet now that he has escaped, here he is again burying the dead!" 9 That same night I bathed, and went to sleep next to the wall of my courtyard. Because of the heat I left my face uncovered. 10 I did not know there were birds perched on the wall above me, till their warm droppings settled in my eyes, causing cataracts. I went to see some doctors for a cure, but the more they anointed my eyes with various salves, the worse the cataracts became, until I could see no more. For four years I was deprived of eyesight, and all my kinsmen were grieved at my condition. Ahiqar, however, took care of me for two years, until he left for Elymais.

11 At that time my wife Anna worked for hire at weaving cloth, the kind of work women do. 12 When she sent back the goods to their owners, they would pay her. Late in winter she finished the cloth and sent it back to the owners. They paid her the full salary, and also gave her a young goat for the table. 13 On entering my house the goat began to bleat. I called to my wife and said: "Where did this goat come from? Perhaps it was stolen! Give it back to its owners; we have no

2, 6: (*pasai 'ai*) *ōdai*: so Vet Lat^{MSS}; cf Am 8, 10 in LXX.
2, 8: *epezētēthē:* so LXX^{Sa}, Vet Lat.
2, 11: (*ēritheueto*) *' iston epoichomenē* (*en*): so with Vet Lat, P^{MSS}; cf V.

NRSV

"Father!" And I replied, "Here I am, my child." Then he went on to say, "Look, father, one of our own people has been murdered and thrown into the market place, and now he lies there strangled." 4Then I sprang up, left the dinner before even tasting it, and removed the body[a] from the square[b] and laid it[a] in one of the rooms until sunset when I might bury it.[a] 5When I returned, I washed myself and ate my food in sorrow. 6Then I remembered the prophecy of Amos, how he said against Bethel,[c]

"Your festivals shall be turned into
mourning,
and all your songs into lamentation."

And I wept.

7When the sun had set, I went and dug a grave and buried him. 8And my neighbors laughed and said, "Is he still not afraid? He has already been hunted down to be put to death for doing this, and he ran away; yet here he is again burying the dead!" 9That same night I washed myself and went into my courtyard and slept by the wall of the courtyard; and my face was uncovered because of the heat. 10I did not know that there were sparrows on the wall; their fresh droppings fell into my eyes and produced white films. I went to physicians to be healed, but the more they treated me with ointments the more my vision was obscured by the white films, until I became completely blind. For four years I remained unable to see. All my kindred were sorry for me, and Ahikar took care of me for two years before he went to Elymais.

11At that time, also, my wife Anna earned money at women's work. 12She used to send what she made to the owners and they would pay wages to her. One day, the seventh of Dystrus, when she cut off a piece she had woven and sent it to the owners, they paid her full wages and also gave her a young goat for a meal. 13When she returned to me, the goat began to bleat. So I called her and said, "Where did you get this goat? It is surely not stolen, is it? Return it to the owners; for we have no right to eat anything stolen." 14But she said to me, "It was given to me as a gift in addition to my wages." But I did

[a] Gk *him* [b] Other ancient authorities lack *from the square*
[c] Other ancient authorities read *against Bethlehem*

NAB

right to eat stolen food!" 14 But she said to me, "It was given to me as a bonus over and above my wages." Yet I would not believe her; and told her to give it back to its owners. I became very angry with her over this. So she retorted: "Where are your charitable deeds now? Where are your virtuous acts? See! Your true character is finally showing itself!"

3 1 Grief-stricken in spirit, I groaned and wept aloud. Then with sobs I began to pray:

2 "You are righteous, O Lord,
and all your deeds are just;
All your ways are mercy and truth;
you are the judge of the world.
3 And now, O Lord, may you be mindful of me,
and look with favor upon me.
Punish me not for my sins,
nor for my inadvertent offenses,
nor for those of my fathers.

"They sinned against you,
4 and disobeyed your commandments.
So you handed us over to plundering, exile, and death,
till we were an object lesson, a byword, a reproach
in all the nations among whom you scattered us.

5 "Yes, your judgments are many and true
in dealing with me as my sins
and those of my fathers deserve.
For we have not kept your commandments,
nor have we trodden the paths of truth before you.

6 "So now, deal with me as you please,
and command my life breath to be taken from me,
that I may go from the face of the earth into dust.
It is better for me to die than to live,
because I have heard insulting calumnies,
and I am overwhelmed with grief.

3, 4: (*parēkousan*): so LXX$^{Sc.a,B,A}$, P.
3, 5: (*mou*) *kai tōn paterōn mou* : so LXX$^{Sc.a,B,A}$, Vet Lat, P; haplog.

NRSV

not believe her, and told her to return it to the owners. I became flushed with anger against her over this. Then she replied to me, "Where are your acts of charity? Where are your righteous deeds? These things are known about you!"[a]

3 Then with much grief and anguish of heart I wept, and with groaning began to pray:
2 "You are righteous, O Lord,
and all your deeds are just;
all your ways are mercy and truth;
you judge the world.[b]
3 And now, O Lord, remember me
and look favorably upon me.
Do not punish me for my sins
and for my unwitting offenses
and those that my ancestors committed before you.
They sinned against you,
4 and disobeyed your commandments.
So you gave us over to plunder, exile, and death,
to become the talk, the byword, and an object of reproach
among all the nations among whom you have dispersed us.
5 And now your many judgments are true
in exacting penalty from me for my sins.
For we have not kept your commandments
and have not walked in accordance with truth before you.
6 So now deal with me as you will;
command my spirit to be taken from me,
so that I may be released from the face of the earth and become dust.
For it is better for me to die than to live,
because I have had to listen to undeserved insults,
and great is the sorrow within me.
Command, O Lord, that I be released from this distress;
release me to go to the eternal home,
and do not, O Lord, turn your face away from me.
For it is better for me to die
than to see so much distress in my life
and to listen to insults."

[a] Or *to you*; Gk *with you* [b] Other ancient authorities read *you render true and righteous judgment forever*

NAB

"Lord, command me to be delivered from
such anguish;
let me go to the everlasting abode;
Lord, refuse me not.
For it is better for me to die
than to endure so much misery in life,
and to hear these insults!"

COMMENTARY

Tobit's first-person narrative now moves from the general summary of his good life to a specific story of his burying the dead. This specific act of charity results, even if indirectly, in the suffering that will afflict him throughout most of the book. This suffering constitutes the conflict of the book: Why is this good man afflicted? This question is asked by Anna, Tobit's wife (2:14), and by Tobit himself in his lament (3:6).

The Vulgate adds a comparison between Tobit and Job:

> Now this trial the Lord therefore permitted to happen to him, that an example might be given to posterity of his patience, as also of holy Job. . . . For as the kings insulted holy Job, so his relatives and kindred mocked him, saying, "Where is your hope, for which you gave alms and buried the dead?" (2:12, 15-16)

By implication, Anna is compared to Job's wife. Moore notes, however, that this is a false comparison, since Job's wife was angry with God, whereas Anna is angry with Tobit.[45]

2:1-2. The family of Tobit prepares to celebrate one of the three great pilgrimage festivals of Judaism, the Feast of Weeks. This feast, like the other two (Passover/Unleavened Bread and Booths), is a celebration of harvest. The Feast of Weeks is observed at the beginning of the wheat harvest (May/June). Its date is set by Deuteronomy as seven weeks (or fifty days) after the offering of the first fruits of the barley harvest—that is, after the Feast of Unleavened Bread (Lev 23:15-16; Deut 16:9-10). The fifty-day count gives the Greek name to the feast, πεντηκοστή (*pentēkostē*, "Pentecost," "fiftieth"). Because Passover is connected to the historical event of the exodus from Egypt, the Feast of Weeks became associated with the historical context of the covenant-making on Mt. Sinai (see Exod 19:1).

Because Tobit is in exile, he cannot make the pilgrimage to Jerusalem as Deuteronomy required (Deut 16:16). But he is careful to observe the other prescription for the celebration: "All shall give as they are able, according to the blessing of the LORD your God that he has given you" (Deut 16:17 NRSV; see also Deut 16:11, 14). He decides to share his festival meal with a poor Israelite as his offering to the Lord.

Tobiah is sent to find a poor person. Tobit teaches his son the law of God by example. Tobit's practice of charitable acts agrees with the advice of his contemporary, Ben Sira.[46] His sharing of the festival meal replaces his offering of the customary sacrifice. Ben Sira says that "one who gives alms sacrifices a thank offering" (Sir 35:4 NRSV). The recipient of Tobit's alms will be a faithful Israelite. Ben Sira advises one to give to "a brother or a friend" (Sir 29:10 NRSV), to a person who is devout rather than to a sinner (Sir 12:1-7).

2:3-6. Instead of finding a poor Israelite to share the meal, Tobiah finds the body of an Israelite in need of burial. The man seems to have been executed, killed in the marketplace. Moore points out that ἐστραγγάληται (*estrangalētai*) should be rendered as "exposed" instead of "strangled."[47] The corpse has not been buried but instead has been put on public display (cf. Esth 9:13).

45. Carey A. Moore, *Tobit,* AB 40A (Garden City, N.Y.: Doubleday, 1996) 135.

46. See P. J. Griffin, "A Study of *Eleēmosynē* in the Bible with Emphasis upon Its Meaning and Usage in the Theology of Tobit and Ben Sira" (MA thesis, The Catholic University of America, 1982), for a thorough analysis of the concept in both books.

47. Moore, *Tobit,* 128.

Tobit's action is predictable. The burial becomes the focus of his entire effort. His festival dinner is sandwiched between preparations for the burial and the burial itself. The occasion reminds him of a saying of the prophet Amos (Amos 8:10) concerning the approaching day of judgment against Israel. The citation points up the irony of the situation. Amos's oracle decries wealthy Israelites who are exploiting the poor. Tobit, on the other hand, seems to have had his feast turned to mourning precisely because he is helping the poor.

2:7-8. The burial becomes the occasion for further mockery by his neighbors. No one else seems to care that fellow Israelites are lying unburied. Rather, the one man who is tending to this duty is scorned for his actions. His characteristic act of charity seems to result in curse, not in blessing.

2:9. After the burial Tobit washes himself and sleeps outside, perhaps because of ritual uncleanness from contact with a corpse. According to pentateuchal legislation, Tobit will remain unclean for seven days as a consequence of burying the dead. Ritual washing is called for on the third and seventh days, but only on the seventh day is the uncleanness removed. Anything Tobit touches will also become unclean and have the power to communicate uncleanness. It would seem that Tobit's house, though not the place of the man's death, could well be considered unclean also, since the corpse was probably kept there until evening. Josephus reports the Jewish custom that "after the funeral the house and its inhabitants must be purified."[48] Tobit's attempts to comply with the ritual even in exile constitute a further example of his rigorous observance of the spirit of the law as well as of the letter.

48. Josephus *Against Apion* 2.26 205.

EXCURSUS: UNCLEANNESS AND PURIFICATION

According to Num 19:11-22 there are several consequences of contact with a dead body. They include the following: (1) A person who touches a human corpse is unclean for seven days. The ritual for purification calls for washing on the third and seventh days with lustral water—i.e., water in which the ashes of the red heifer have been mixed. (2) The tent in which a person dies is unclean for seven days. The tent as well as all the vessels and persons in it must be sprinkled with lustral water on the third and seventh days. (3) Anything touched by an unclean person also becomes unclean and renders unclean anyone else who then touches it. (4) The person who remains unclean defiles the sanctuary of the Lord and shall be cut off from the community.

Further questions are raised by the circumstances: Was lustral water for purification available to the Israelites in Nineveh? Apparently ashes of the red heifer were saved after the destruction of the Temple in 70 CE and until the Amoraic period (3rd–4th cents. CE),[49] but their availability in Nineveh is questionable. Was this legal purification necessary chiefly for entrance into the Temple or for participation in the temple liturgy? If so, the exiles had no immediate legal need for purification.

49. See "Purity and Impurity, Ritual," *EncJud* 13. 1406.

2:10. The attitude toward Tobit's medical condition reflects a traditional belief. Although it is unknown whether scales on the cornea are ever caused by hot bird droppings, Tobit's blindness is attributed to natural causes. Nonetheless, medical assistance is useless to him. Every attempt to heal him drives him further into darkness (cf. the woman with a hemorrhage in Mark 5:26; Luke

8:43). Only God has the power to heal.[50] Ben Sira advises that one honor physicians because their services are needed, but also remember that "their gift of healing comes from the Most High" (Sir 38:1-15).

2:11. Anna goes to work outside the home in order to earn money the family needs for sustenance and survival. It appears that the work she did was weaving, an assumption that is made specific in the Old Latin version. In ancient Mesopotamia, women of the lower classes were employed by the temples and the palace in various occupations—cooking, baking, cleaning, spinning, and weaving.[51] Woven cloth was made from both goat hair and sheep's wool; it was dyed and fashioned into various items of clothing. Because of her family's need, Anna becomes the Bible's first working mother.

2:12. Anna is a capable and independent woman. There is indication that she is good at her job. Her employers not only pay her full wages, but also give her a bonus. The bonus, a young goat, becomes the occasion for the first dialogue between Tobit and his wife.

2:13-14. This dialogue is revealing of the characters of both Anna and Tobit. Dependent on her wage-earning ability, the blind Tobit strikes out at his wife with the suspicion that her bonus is stolen goods. His suspicion reveals both the pain of the helpless man and his extreme concern for obedience to the law. This scene is still part of the first-person narrative. As narrator, Tobit reports his anger and disbelief, but he gives no indication that his suspicion against Anna is justified.

Initially Anna answers Tobit's suspicion with a simple explanation (2:14*a*). In the face of his persistent disbelief and anger, however, she turns the conversation to her own advantage by attacking him on a vulnerable point. His trust in the justice of God to reward good deeds seems to have been in vain. Either his apparent good works are false, or he has been betrayed by God (2:14*b*). In either case, he is now forced to depend on her. The economy of speech by the narrator in this scene is noteworthy. There is no comment about Anna's emotional state. It is revealed entirely by her words.

Anna has now raised the critical question concerning the theory of retribution and Tobit's trust in it. If virtue is truly rewarded with blessing and, conversely, if suffering is a sign of wickedness, then how can the suffering Tobit claim to be a virtuous man? If the blessings are not there, perhaps the righteousness does not exist either.

3:1-2. Prayer is one of the strongest and most pervasive elements in the book of Tobit.[52] The title character Tobit prays at three significant points in his life: (1) when he has reached a point of despair because of his blindness and his dependence on his wife; (2) when he is healed; and (3) when he realizes that God has sent an angel to help him. He also exhorts his son to pray (4:5, 19), and later also his grandchildren (14:9). The immediate cause of this first prayer is Tobit's argument with Anna. Her attack on his virtue and his motivation is the final blow, leading him to pray for death.

Tobit begins in traditional fashion by focusing first on God. His concept of God emphasizes the same virtues that are predicated of himself in the introduction (1:3): righteousness (δικαιοσύνη *dikaiosynē*), charity/mercy (ἐλεημοσύνη *eleēmosynē*), and truth (ἀλήθεια *alētheia*). Just as these virtues are demonstrated through Tobit's actions, so also Tobit asserts that they are demonstrated through God's actions. God's deeds are righteous; God's ways are mercy and truth. These three virtues characterize God's judgment of the whole world. Whatever Tobit's own distress may be, he acknowledges that it is not a reflection of malice or capriciousness in God.

3:3-4. Tobit then turns to the possible causes of his suffering. Although he has earlier asserted that he is also righteous, charitable, and true, he is aware of his sinfulness and the sinfulness of his people. His sins may be unwitting, but they offend the justice of God. He regards himself not as an individual before God, but as a member of God's people. Since the people have been sinful, he shares in their guilt and in their punishment.

Tobit recognizes that only God can remedy his situation. He begs God to remember him and to

50. See Bernd Kollmann, "Göttliche Offenbarung magisch-parmakologischer Heilkunst im Buch Tobit" *ZAW* 106 (1994) 291.

51. Rikvah Harris, "Women," *ABD* 6:949.

52. For my analysis of the prayers in the book I am greatly dependent on P. J. Griffin, "The Theology and Function of Prayer in the Book of Tobit" (Ph.D. diss., The Catholic University of America, 1984).

look upon him. God's remembering is not simply recollection. It brings divine mercy into one's life (see Noah in Gen 8:1; the Israelites in Exod 2:24; Hannah in 1 Sam 1:19). For God to look upon a person also implies divine mercy. Tobit asks God to look upon him with favor.

3:5-6. In keeping with his belief in the theory of retribution (God punishes the wicked and rewards the just), Tobit acknowledges God's right to exercise strict justice. But Tobit is deeply wounded by grief. His long-term grief over his illness has been brought to a crisis by the argument with his wife, Anna. He suffers crushing anguish. He can think of only one way that God's mercy might be exercised for him. So, even as he prays that God might act according to the divine will, he asks to be allowed to die. It has not occurred to him that God might mercifully give him a happy life. There is no indication that death is the only response Tobit will accept, but it is the only one that he can imagine.

❖ ❖ ❖ ❖

EXCURSUS: BELIEFS ABOUT DEATH

In his prayer for death, Tobit follows the example of some of Israel's ancestors. When Moses is overwhelmed by the people's murmuring in the desert, he prays: "If this is the way you are going to treat me, put me to death at once—if I have found favor in your sight—and do not let me see my misery" (Num 11:15 NRSV). When Elijah is fleeing from the wrath of Jezebel, he prays: "It is enough; now, O LORD, take away my life, for I am no better than my ancestors" (1 Kgs 19:4 NRSV). In his anger over God's mercy toward Nineveh, Jonah says, "It is better for me to die than to live" (Jonah 4:8 NRSV).

None of these people pray for death in the hope of eternal life. Their prayers are simply pleas to be released from present suffering. Tobit's prayer makes clear that he has no hope for life after death. Once God takes his life breath, he expects simply to return to dust. His "eternal home" will be the grave.

Belief in resurrection and in meaningful life after death began to emerge only with the latest OT texts. Israel had encountered the cult of the dead in Egypt, and perhaps also in Mesopotamia, and had rejected the tendency to idolatry that sprang from it. Only in the middle of the second century BCE did a concept of resurrection develop. Even so, both concept and details were hotly contested. Did resurrection apply only to the righteous (2 Macc 7:14), or would there be a general resurrection of righteous and wicked alike (Dan 12:2)? Did resurrection include the body (2 Macc 7:11, 22-23), or did it apply only to an immortal soul (Wis 3:1-4; 9:15)? The controversy over resurrection of the dead also is evident in the NT. The Sadducees attempt to show the foolishness of such a belief when they challenge Jesus with the story of the woman with seven husbands (Mark 12:18-27). Paul escapes his enemies when he turns a trial against him into an argument over belief in resurrection (Acts 23:6-10).

The author of the book of Tobit does not believe in resurrection. Rather, he believes in Sheol (Greek, Hades), a shadowy existence that can best be described as suspended animation (3:10; 4:19; 13:2). In Sheol there is neither pain nor pleasure, neither joy nor sorrow. There is no ranking of persons by power or wealth—only the radical equality brought about by death (Job 3:11-19). One joins one's ancestors in the family grave and persists there (e.g., Gen 15:15; 1 Kgs 11:21; 1 Chr 17:11; Ps 49:19). There is no agreement on whether God can or cannot be found in Sheol (see Pss 6:5; 139:8).

❖ ❖ ❖ ❖

REFLECTIONS

1. Tobit will not eat his festival dinner until he can share it with a poor person. Some churches take up collections for the poor during penitential seasons, such as Lent, and at festival times, both religious and secular, such as Thanksgiving and Christmas. Are there other celebrations that might remind us to share the gifts we have been given with those who have less? What a response to consumerism it would be if each of us celebrated our birthdays by giving a gift to the poor.

2. Tobit not only teaches his son the observance of the law, but also shows it to him in practice. Thus his son has a living example to follow. Moreover, Tobit involves him in the charitable act. My father used to say that there are three ways to teach someone how to tie a knot: (1) Tell her how; (2) take a string and show her how; (3) give her a string and let her do it as you describe and demonstrate. Only the third way is effective for long-term learning. Tobit shows himself to be a good teacher as he involves Tobiah in his charitable act.

3. Tobit does everything he can to be cured. Sickness and suffering are not simply to be endured; every reasonable effort must be made to relieve the situation. The skill of physicians and the knowledge of pharmacists are gifts from God to be used in the improvement of human life. However, no human being can cure every illness; no human being can forever escape death. In the end, life and death, sickness and health, are in the hand of God.

Great suffering may also lead to prayer for death. There comes a time when death, even if it means oblivion, is preferred to a life of agony. Tobit, however, does not take matters into his own hands. Instead, he asks God for death. He does not attempt suicide, but it is clear that if death comes to him he will not resist it. Our society struggles with the arrival of death. Physician-assisted suicide, which is often a response to extreme suffering, is an attempt to hasten the arrival of death. Advance directives, on the other hand, are instructions not to resist death by extraordinary means when there is no hope for a reasonable quality of life in the future. For Christians, this decision to allow death to arrive is shaped by respect for God's gift of life in the present, courage to share in the sufferings of Christ (Phil 3:10), and faith that, having died with him, we will also share in Christ's resurrection (Rom 6:10).

4. Women have been severely criticized for working outside the home and not staying home to care for house and children. Paradoxically, women on welfare have been criticized for not having outside jobs. It is a no-win situation in our society. The story of Anna illustrates that such mistrust and criticism are millennia old. However, in this book, which is so concerned with family values, Anna also demonstrates that a working mother is not necessarily destructive of the family. In fact, her employment sustains the family.

5. Tobit suspects his wife of stealing, or at least of accepting stolen goods. The virtue of kindness that he exercises in public seems to falter at home. His distress at his own situation leads him to lash out at the one person who is his primary support. This is an all-too-common response to frustration and stress. Because we cannot or will not deal with the primary cause of our stress, we take it out on those who have little or nothing to do with it. Often the victims of our reaction are those closest to us, those whom we assume will not abandon us. In the worst case, this projection of anger onto an innocent victim explodes into domestic violence, either verbal or physical.

TOBIT 3:7-15, SARAH'S DISTRESS AND PRAYER

NAB

7 On the same day, at Ecbatana in Media, it so happened that Raguel's daughter Sarah also had to listen to abuse, from one of her father's maids. 8 For she had been married to seven husbands, but the wicked demon Asmodeus killed them off before they could have intercourse with her, as it is prescribed for wives. So the maid said to her: 'You are the one who strangles your husbands! Look at you! You have already been married seven times, but you have had no joy with any one of your husbands. 9 Why do you beat us? Because your husbands are dead? Then why not join them! May we never see a son or daughter of yours!"

10 That day she was deeply grieved in spirit. She went in tears to an upstairs room in her father's house with the intention of hanging herself. But she reconsidered, saying to herself: "No! People would level this insult against my father: 'You had only one beloved daughter, but she hanged herself because of ill fortune!' And thus would I cause my father in his old age to go down to the nether world laden with sorrow. It is far better for me not to hang myself, but to beg the Lord to have me die, so that I need no longer live to hear such insults."

11 At that time, then, she spread out her hands, and facing the window, poured out this prayer:

"Blessed are you, O Lord, merciful God!
Forever blessed and honored is your holy name;
may all your works forever bless you.
12 And now, O Lord, to you I turn my face
and raise my eyes.
13 Bid me to depart from the earth,
never again to hear such insults.

14 "You know, O Master, that I am innocent
of any impure act with a man,
15 And that I have never defiled my own name

3, 7: Omit *tautē*; read (*En tē*) *autē* (*'ēmera*): so LXX^{B,A}, Vet Lat, P, V.
3, 8: (*ei 'ē*) *apopnigousa*: so LXX^{B,A}, Vet Lat, P. (*ouk*) *ōnastēs*: so LXX^{B*,A}, Vet Lat, P.
3, 11: *kyrie 'o theos* (*eleēmōn*): so Vet Lat; cf LXX^{B,A}. (*sou*) *to ' agion kai entimon*: so LXX^{B,A}, Vet Lat, P.
3, 12: (*nyn*) *kyrte*: so LXX$^{B, A,}$ Vet Lat, P, V. (*prosōpon mou*) *dedōka*: so LXX $^{B, A}$, P; cf Vet Lat and Dn 9, 3 (MT and LXX).

NRSV

7On the same day, at Ecbatana in Media, it also happened that Sarah, the daughter of Raguel, was reproached by one of her father's maids. 8For she had been married to seven husbands, and the wicked demon Asmodeus had killed each of them before they had been with her as is customary for wives. So the maid said to her, "You are the one who kills[a] your husbands! See, you have already been married to seven husbands and have not borne the name of[b] a single one of them. 9Why do you beat us? Because your husbands are dead? Go with them! May we never see a son or daughter of yours!"

10On that day she was grieved in spirit and wept. When she had gone up to her father's upper room, she intended to hang herself. But she thought it over and said, "Never shall they reproach my father, saying to him, 'You had only one beloved daughter but she hanged herself because of her distress.' And I shall bring my father in his old age down in sorrow to Hades. It is better for me not to hang myself, but to pray the Lord that I may die and not listen to these reproaches anymore." 11At that same time, with hands outstretched toward the window, she prayed and said,

"Blessed are you, merciful God!
Blessed is your name forever;
let all your works praise you forever.
12 And now, Lord,[c] I turn my face to you,
and raise my eyes toward you.
13 Command that I be released from the earth
and not listen to such reproaches any more.
14 You know, O Master, that I am innocent
of any defilement with a man,
15 and that I have not disgraced my name
or the name of my father in the land of my exile.
I am my father's only child;
he has no other child to be his heir;
and he has no close relative or other kindred
for whom I should keep myself as wife.
Already seven husbands of mine have died.

[a] Other ancient authorities read *strangles* [b] Other ancient authorities read *have had no benefit from* [c] Other ancient authorities lack *Lord*

NAB

or my father's name in the land of my
exile.

"I am my father's only daughter,
and he has no other child to make his heir,
Nor does he have a close kinsman or other
relative
whom I might bide my time to marry.
I have already lost seven husbands;
why then should I live any longer?
But if it please you, Lord, not to slay me,
look favorably upon me and have pity on
me;
never again let me hear these insults!"

3, 15: (*kyrie*) *epiblepsai ep'eme kai eleēsai me kai mēketi akousai me oneidismon*: so with Vet Lat; cf $LXX^{B, A}$, P. LXX^{S} corrupt.

NRSV

Why should I still live?
But if it is not pleasing to you, O Lord, to take
my life,
hear me in my disgrace."

COMMENTARY

In the next section the scene shifts from Tobit's house in Nineveh to Raguel's house in Ecbatana. The two scenes are parallel: Each consists of (1) hard words and grief (2:13–3:1, 7-9); (2) prayer for death (3:2-6, 12-15); (3) God's acceptance of the prayer (3:16); and (4) the consequence of the prayer (3:17). The events in Ecbatana not only parallel those in Nineveh, but also are simultaneous ("on the same day" [ἐν τῇ ἡμέρα ταύτῃ *en tē hēmera tautē*, 3:7], "on that day" [ἐν τῇ ἡμέρα ἐκείνῃ *en tē hēmera ekeinē*, 3:10], "at that very time" [ἐν αὐτῷ τῷ καιρῳ *en autō tō kairō*, 3:11, 16-17]).

In v. 17 it becomes evident that the narrative voice has changed. From 1:3 to 3:1 the narrator is Tobit himself; from 3:17 to the end of the book, the story is told by a third-person narrator. Between 3:1 and 3:17 appears a bridge containing the prayer of Tobit (Tobit speaking in the first-person) and the introduction of Sarah and her prayer (possibly still Tobit telling the story from hindsight). But in 3:17, Tobit is spoken of in the third-person.[53]

53. See J. E. Miller, "The Redaction of Tobit and the Genesis Apocryphon," *JSP* 8 (1991) 54-55. He compares this narrative shift with the Genesis Apocryphon and concludes that in both works the first-person narrative was highly valued but fragmentary.

There are significant differences between the two narrative voices. The third-person narrator has greater freedom of movement than the first-person narrator, can report thoughts and feelings of other characters, and observes actions even when characters seem to be alone. Tobit the narrator reveals no other character's thoughts and feelings—only his own. He tells the story of the conflict between Tobit (the character) and Anna with objectivity and realizes the truth that Anna was indeed given the goat that the character Tobit suspected had been stolen. But Tobit the narrator is not always reliable. In emphasizing his own fidelity to God's law, he announces that he alone went to Jerusalem to worship (1:6), a fact that Tobit the character later contradicts (5:14). Thus the third-person narrator is omniscient and reliable. The first-person narrator is neither.[54]

3:7. Another main character is introduced in this section: Sarah, daughter of Raguel. Her name, which means "lady" or "gentlewoman," links her to the ancestral story of Sarah, wife of Abraham. Like Abraham's wife, the Sarah of this story is kept from those for whom she is not destined (3:8; 6:18; cf. Gen 12:10-20; 20:1-18). Through

54. D. McCracken, "Narration and Comedy in the Book of Tobit," *JBL* 114 (1995) 403-9.

Tobiah, she will become the mother of sons who are the hope of the future people of God (Tob 14:3; cf. Gen 17:19, 21).

Ecbatana, the home of Raguel's family, is the ancient capital of Media. The site of modern Hamadan is Iran; it is located in the Zagros mountains about 325 miles southeast of Nineveh.

3:8-9. Echoing the final word of Tobit's prayer (ὀνειδισμός *oneidismos*, "reproach"), the narrator reports the distress of Sarah, who is "reproached" by her father's maids. The same word will recur as the reason for her prayer for death (v. 10) and twice in the prayer itself (vv. 13, 15).[55]

Sarah is afflicted by the demon Asmodeus, who keeps killing her bridegrooms. The story of her affliction is repeated five times in the course of the narrative. In each telling, the emphasis shifts and the suspense heightens. In this section, the narrator (v. 8) presents the basic facts in a simple and straightforward fashion: (1) Sarah has been married to seven men (2) whom the demon Asmodeus has killed (3) before the marriages could be consummated. The taunts of the maids (vv. 8-9) repeat the first and last points—seven husbands, dead before the consummation of the marriages. But the maids twist the facts of the second point in order to deepen Sarah's grief. They accuse her of murdering the men and seem to know nothing of the demon Asmodeus. They point out Sarah's childless state and the likelihood that she will remain so. Sarah will repeat the story in her prayer (v. 15); Tobiah (6:14-15) and Raguel (7:11) will recount the same events with additional details.

The name of the demon is perhaps derived from the Persian *aeshma daeva,* "demon of wrath."[56] The role of the demon in the story is related to the folktale "The Monster in the Bridal Chamber" (see Introduction). The hero in this tale is advised by a stranger to marry a wealthy princess whose former bridegrooms have all perished in the bridal chamber. On the wedding night, a serpent emerges from the mouth of the bride-princess to kill the hero. The stranger kills the serpent and frees the bride from her affliction. In the book of Tobit, Sarah will be freed from her affliction through the assistance of the angel Raphael (8:3).

Seven, the number of Sarah's dead husbands, is significant throughout the book. In the Bible it signifies completion or fullness. Sarah has already had a complete number of chances at marriage; she should expect no more. Tobiah will be outside the number, one more than can be expected. Her marriage to him will be sheer gift.

3:10. Sarah is the most silent character in the book of Tobit. After listening to the cutting abuse of the maids, to which she makes no reply, she retires to an upstairs room with the intention of hanging herself. As she deliberates over her decision, we are allowed to overhear her interior monologue.

Sarah contemplates suicide as a solution to her distress. Suicide is not directly prohibited in the OT. Those who commit suicide when faced with military defeat, imminent capture, or disgrace are not condemned for their actions: e.g., Saul and his armor bearer (1 Sam 31:4-5); Ahithophel (2 Sam 17:23); Zimri (1 Kgs 16:18); Razis (2 Macc 14:41-46). The prohibition of suicide, however, is implied in the prohibition concerning bloodshed (Gen 9:4-6) and the command not to kill (Exod 20:13). Sarah ultimately rejects suicide out of love for her father, who would suffer for her action. Instead, she pleads with God either to take her life or to end her suffering.

3:11-13. Sarah, like Tobit, is sorely aggrieved by abuse, enough so to consider death. But she is capable of deliberation and strong enough to abandon her life to God rather than to cause grief for others. She understands the proper formula for prayer. She faces the window, no doubt toward Jerusalem (see Dan 6:11), spreads out her hands in the traditional gesture, and begins with the formula, "Blessed are you" (v. 11; cf. Dan 3:26, 52; Jdt 13:17). She blesses God and calls upon all creation to help her give praise. She puts her trust in the mercy and holiness of God.[57] She moves almost immediately from the invocation to the heart of her plea. Her whole body is involved in the prayer—hands, face, eyes. Having rejected suicide, she asks God for death in order to be delivered from her distress.

55. G. W. E. Nickelsburg, "Tobit," in *Harper's Bible Commentary,* ed. James L. Mays (New York: Harper & Row, 1988) 794.

56. For more on Asmodeus, see Carey A. Moore, *Tobit,* AB 40A (Garden City, N.Y.: Doubleday, 1996) 154. Moore also points to the ongoing debate about the origin of the name "Asmodeus" (147). It is possible that the name derives from Hebrew שמד (*šmd*), "to destroy."

57. 4QTob[a] confirms the reading of "your holy name" in 3:11 (שמך קדישא *šmk qdyš'*), which also appears in G[I], in the Old Latin, and in the Syriac.

3:14-15. Sarah calls upon God again, this time with the title "Master" (δέσποτα *despota*), connoting subservience before the all-powerful God. Sarah recognizes God's holiness; she also knows her own: She is "innocent of any defilement with a man"; she has never disgraced either her own name or that of her father. In accordance with the theory of retribution, she should be able to expect reward from God. But now she has no hope. There is no one else with whom to make a proper marriage; she cannot perform the daughterly duty of providing Raguel with an heir. All she wants is deliverance from her misery. She prays for death, but she also allows for the fact that God might "look favorably" upon her, "have mercy" on her, and silence the reproaches she has endured. She is willing to accept any response from God that relieves her of her anguish.[58]

It is instructive to compare her prayer with that of Tobit. The author has skillfully contrasted the prayer of an older man with that of a young woman. Tobit recalls the historical situation of exile and the sins of his ancestors before asking God to take his life. Sarah, although she begins her prayer with a traditional formula of blessing, moves almost immediately to her own situation. Tobit asks God not to turn away from him (v. 6); Sarah turns toward God. She also gives God greater freedom in dealing with her. Tobit says to God, "Deal with me as you will," but then presents only one alternative: "Command my spirit to be taken from me" (v. 6). Sarah presents the same solution, "Command that I be released from the earth" (v. 13), but also allows for another possibility (v. 15).

Interior monologue and prayer are the two most reliable witnesses to the inner life. Thus this scene reveals several things about Sarah's character. She has a clear understanding of who she is. She knows that her father loves her (vv. 10, 15). She also knows her own integrity and innocence (vv. 14-15). She expects to abide by the custom of marriage within the kinship group; however, she is well aware of the empty future ahead for her if there is no eligible man to marry. There are no other possibilities for her life. "Why should I still live?" she cries (v. 15).

58. The end of 3:15 in G^{I} is corrupt. G^{I} and VL, representing the recension G^{II}, indicate that she asks God to "look favorably" upon her and "have mercy" on her so that she might "never again listen to such reproaches."

REFLECTIONS

Belief in demons does not play a major role in modern religious consciousness. We are, however, very aware of evil in the world and in our own lives. The demon in this story has left Sarah hopeless. She has lost seven husbands and can expect no more. Evil still has power to render people hopeless. Some men and women feel trapped in abusive marriages. Parents who are unemployed despair of being able to feed themselves and their children. Floods or tornadoes, as they destroy a lifetime of work and precious keepsakes, crush a family's hopes. People caught in an oppressive political system fear for their lives if they attempt reform.

In the fight against evil, we are challenged to act even when the situation seems hopeless. We are called to help others—to staff shelters, to work in relief programs, to join the struggle for justice and peace. We also recognize, however, that in the end evil can be overcome only with God's help. We are also called to pray.

Sarah's prayer is a courageous cry in the face of despair. Her belief that God cares, that God is both powerful and merciful, keeps her from committing suicide. Our own daily prayer, "Deliver us from evil," gives us courage to do what we can against evil and strengthens our faith that in all things we conquer because of him who has loved us (Rom 8:37).

TOBIT 3:16-17, GOD'S ANSWER TO BOTH: RAPHAEL

NAB	NRSV
16 At that very time, the prayer of these two suppliants was heard in the glorious presence of Almighty God. 17 So Raphael was sent to heal them both: to remove the cataracts from Tobit's eyes, so that he might again see God's sunlight; and to marry Raguel's daughter Sarah to Tobit's son Tobiah, and then drive the wicked demon Asmodeus from her. For Tobiah had the right to claim her before any other who might wish to marry her. In the very moment that Tobit returned from the courtyard to his house, Raguel's daughter Sarah came downstairs from her room. 3, 16: (*tou*) *megalou* (*theou*): so P; cf Vet Lat V, LXX^{B,A}	16At that very moment, the prayers of both of them were heard in the glorious presence of God. 17So Raphael was sent to heal both of them: Tobit, by removing the white films from his eyes, so that he might see God's light with his eyes; and Sarah, daughter of Raguel, by giving her in marriage to Tobias son of Tobit, and by setting her free from the wicked demon Asmodeus. For Tobias was entitled to have her before all others who had desired to marry her. At the same time that Tobit returned from the courtyard into his house, Sarah daughter of Raguel came down from her upper room.

COMMENTARY

The prayers of Tobit (vv. 2-6) and Sarah (vv. 11-15), which occur simultaneously, are also answered simultaneously. The answer to both prayers joins the two main plots, the sequence dependent on Tobit's charitable deeds, leading to his blindness, and the sequence culminating in Sarah's affliction by the demon Asmodeus. Each sequence has ended with a prayer. Both prayers are heard, and Raphael is sent in answer to heal Tobit's blindness, to free Sarah from Asmodeus, and to marry her to Tobiah.

Scholars often point out that these verses destroy the suspense by telling the reader the outcome of the plot in advance. However, creating suspense is not the main purpose of this story. Its main purpose is to show God's action in the lives of ordinary believers. These verses serve that purpose well.

First, God's action is revealed by the fact that God hears. The confidence of Tobit and Sarah that God will pay attention to their cries is well founded. Second, God acts indirectly through a mediator, sending an angel to answer both prayers. Third, God intends a surprise. Sarah fears that there are no other potential husbands. Tobiah has not so much as thought of marriage. No one has prayed for the angel's third task. It is simply a gift from God.

REFLECTIONS

It is often difficult to believe that God hears and answers prayer. We pray intensely, and nothing seems to happen. Tobit and Sarah do not know that their prayers have been answered. Tobit is still blind, still smarting from Anna's sharp words. Sarah is still unmarried, still bruised by the maid's words. Many events will happen before their suffering is relieved. But both prayers have been answered: The angel is already on the way.

TOBIT 4:1–6:1

PREPARATION FOR THE JOURNEY TO MEDIA

OVERVIEW

What will happen to the money Tobit deposited with Gabael? This question, generated by the exposition of the plot (1:14-15), now introduces the sequence concerning a journey into Media. Tobit begins the sequence by remembering the money (4:1). He decides to send Tobiah to Media for it (4:2) and informs him of his decision (4:3, 20). The decision to send Tobiah to Media hints at the answer to another question raised in the exposition: How will Tobiah (NRSV, Tobias) meet and marry Sarah?

Tobiah's response to information concerning the money is twofold. He agrees to go to Media (5:1), but he poses two complications: First, how will he identify himself to Gabael (5:2)? Tobit solves this problem by telling him about the signatures (5:3). The second complication will bring Raphael into the picture. Responding to Tobiah's objection that he does not know the way to Media, Tobit instructs him to find a trustworthy guide (5:2-3). The guide Tobiah finds is Raphael (5:4). This fact forms the initial answer to the question of how Raphael will function.

Several facts about Raphael move the sequence forward. He knows the way to Rages and is acquainted with Gabael (5:6). Raphael's expertise, coupled with the uprightness of his supposed family (5:13-14), convinces Tobit to approve him as a guide. Tobit's approval leads immediately to the departure of Tobiah and his guide (5:15-17). But in spite of the guide's good qualifications, Tobiah's parents worry (5:18–6:1): Will he return safely? Meanwhile the reader learns two other facts about Raphael that contribute to the plot. Tobit has asked about Raphael's family and character and been satisfied with the answers. The reader also learns that Raphael's origins are upright and that he is trustworthy, but for another reason: He is an angel of God (5:4). Thus the reader has a better grasp of the truth of Tobit's reassurance to Anna than does Tobit himself. It is true, as he says, that an angel accompanies Tobiah (5:17, 22). The other piece of information, which at this point is more significant to the reader than to the characters, is that Raphael knows the way to Ecbatana (5:6). This fact also contributes a partial answer to the question of how Tobiah will meet and marry Sarah.

Three remaining questions have been generated by this sequence (4:1–6:1): Will Tobiah get the money? Will he meet and marry Sarah? Will he return safely? Two questions untouched by the sequence remain from the exposition: How will Sarah be delivered from Asmodeus? How will Tobit be healed?

TOBIT 4:1-21, TOBIT'S INSTRUCTIONS TO HIS SON

NAB

4 1 That same day Tobit remembered the money he had deposited with Gabael at Rages in Media, and he thought, 2 "Now that I have asked for death, why should I not call my son Tobiah and let him know about this money before I die?" 3 So he called his son Tobiah; and when he came, he said to him: "My son, when I die, give me a decent burial. Honor your mother, and do not abandon her as long as she lives. Do whatever pleases her, and do not grieve her spirit in any way. 4 Remember, my son, that she went through many trials for your sake while you were in her womb. And when she dies, bury her in the same grave with me.

5 "Through all your days, my son, keep the Lord in mind, and suppress every desire to sin or to break his commandments. Perform good works all the days of your life, and do not tread the paths of wrongdoing. 6 For if you are steadfast in your service, your good works will bring success, not only to you, but also to all those who live uprightly.

7 "Give alms from your possessions. Do not turn your face away from any of the poor, and God's face will not be turned away from you. 8 Son, give alms in proportion to what you own. If you have great wealth, give alms out of your abundance; if you have but little, distribute even some of that. But do not hesitate to give alms; 9 you will be storing up a goodly treasure for yourself against the day of adversity. 10 Almsgiving frees one from death, and keeps one from going into the dark abode. 11 Alms are a worthy offering in the sight of the Most High for all who give them.

4, 3: (*autǭ*) *paidion ean apothanō* (*thapson*): so with Vet Lat; cf LXX^{B,A}. P. V.

4, 6: (*dioti*) *poiountos sou* (*alētheian*) *euodiai esontai soi* (*en tois ergois*) *sou*: Cf Vet Lat. LXX^{B,A}. P.

4, 7-19a: From LXX^{B} corrected principally by LXX^{A} and Vet Lat. These vv are missing from LXX^{S}.

4, 7: Omit *kai mē phthonesatō . . . eleēmosynēn* (inserted here from v. 16): so LXX^{71,P}. Vet Lat. P. V.

4, 8: (*'ōs soi 'yparchei*) *paidion 'outōs poiei eleēmosynēn. Ean plēthos soi 'yparchę̄* (*kata to plēthos poiēson ex autōn eleēmosynēn. ean oligon soi 'yparchę̄ kata to oligon*) *dos kai* (*mē*): so with Vet Lat; cf V.

NRSV

4 That same day Tobit remembered the money that he had left in trust with Gabael at Rages in Media, 2 and he said to himself, "Now I have asked for death. Why do I not call my son Tobias and explain to him about the money before I die?" 3 Then he called his son Tobias, and when he came to him he said, "My son, when I die,[a] give me a proper burial. Honor your mother and do not abandon her all the days of her life. Do whatever pleases her, and do not grieve her in anything. 4 Remember her, my son, because she faced many dangers for you while you were in her womb. And when she dies, bury her beside me in the same grave.

5 "Revere the Lord all your days, my son, and refuse to sin or to transgress his commandments. Live uprightly all the days of your life, and do not walk in the ways of wrongdoing; 6 for those who act in accordance with truth will prosper in all their activities. To all those who practice righteousness[b] 7 give alms from your possessions, and do not let your eye begrudge the gift when you make it. Do not turn your face away from anyone who is poor, and the face of God will not be turned away from you. 8 If you have many possessions, make your gift from them in proportion; if few, do not be afraid to give according to the little you have. 9 So you will be laying up a good treasure for yourself against the day of necessity. 10 For almsgiving delivers from death and keeps you from going into the Darkness. 11 Indeed, almsgiving, for all who practice it, is an excellent offering in the presence of the Most High.

12 "Beware, my son, of every kind of fornication. First of all, marry a woman from among the descendants of your ancestors; do not marry a foreign woman, who is not of your father's tribe; for we are the descendants of the prophets. Remember, my son, that Noah, Abraham, Isaac, and Jacob, our ancestors of old, all took wives from

[a] Lat [b] The text of codex Sinaiticus goes directly from verse 6 to verse 19, reading *To those who practice righteousness* [19] *the Lord will give good counsel.* In order to fill the lacuna verses 7 to 18 are derived from other ancient authorities

NAB

12 "Be on your guard, son, against every form of immorality, and above all, marry a woman of the lineage of your forefathers. Do not marry a stranger who is not of your father's tribe, because we are sons of the prophets. My boy, keep in mind Noah, Abraham, Isaac, and Jacob, our fathers from of old; all of them took wives from among their own kinsmen and were blessed in their children. Remember that their posterity shall inherit the land. 13 Therefore, my son, love your kinsmen. Do not be so proudhearted toward your kinsmen, the sons and daughters of your people, as to refuse to take a wife for yourself from among them. For in such arrogance there is ruin and great disorder. Likewise, in worthlessness there is decay and dire poverty, for worthlessness is the mother of famine.

14 "Do not keep with you overnight the wages of any man who works for you, but pay him immediately. If you thus behave as God's servant, you will receive your reward. Keep a close watch on yourself, my son, in everything you do, and discipline yourself in all your conduct. 15 Do to no one what you yourself dislike. Do not drink wine till you become drunk, nor let drunkenness accompany you on your way.

16 "Give to the hungry some of your bread, and to the naked some of your clothing. Whatever you have left over, give away as alms; and do not begrudge the alms you give. 17 Be lavish with your bread and wine at the burial of the virtuous, but do not share them with sinners.

18 "Seek counsel from every wise man, and do not think lightly of any advice that can be useful. 19 At all times bless the Lord God, and ask him to make all your paths straight and to grant success to all your endeavors and plans. For no pagan nation possesses good counsel, but the Lord himself gives all good things. If the Lord chooses, he raises a man up; but if he should decide otherwise, he casts him down to the deepest recesses of the nether world. So now, my son,

4, 13: (*sou*) *tou mē* (*labein*): so Vet Lat.
4, 14: (*ergasētai*) *soi* (*para soi . . .*): so LXX^{MSS}; cf. Vet Lat, V.
4, 17: (*sou*) *kai to oinon sou:* so with Vet Lat, V; haplog.
4, 19: (*boulēn*) *agathēn . . . (agatha).* ʿ *On an thelē̦ kyrios* ʿ *ypsoi (kai* ʿ*on an*): so with Vet Lat^{MSS}. Rest of v as in LXX^{S}, but omit *kyrios* before *tapeinoi:* so Vet Lat. (*entolas*) *mou* (*kai*): so LXX^{B,A}, Vet Lat.

NRSV

among their kindred. They were blessed in their children, and their posterity will inherit the land. [13]So now, my son, love your kindred, and in your heart do not disdain your kindred, the sons and daughters of your people, by refusing to take a wife for yourself from among them. For in pride there is ruin and great confusion. And in idleness there is loss and dire poverty, because idleness is the mother of famine.

14"Do not keep over until the next day the wages of those who work for you, but pay them at once. If you serve God you will receive payment. "Watch yourself, my son, in everything you do, and discipline yourself in all your conduct. [15]And what you hate, do not do to anyone. Do not drink wine to excess or let drunkenness go with you on your way. [16]Give some of your food to the hungry, and some of your clothing to the naked. Give all your surplus as alms, and do not let your eye begrudge your giving of alms. [17]Place your bread on the grave of the righteous, but give none to sinners. [18]Seek advice from every wise person and do not despise any useful counsel. [19]At all times bless the Lord God, and ask him that your ways may be made straight and that all your paths and plans may prosper. For none of the nations has understanding, but the Lord himself will give them good counsel; but if he chooses otherwise, he casts down to deepest Hades. So now, my child, remember these commandments, and do not let them be erased from your heart.

20"And now, my son, let me explain to you that I left ten talents of silver in trust with Gabael son of Gabrias, at Rages in Media. [21]Do not be afraid, my son, because we have become poor. You have great wealth if you fear God and flee from every sin and do what is good in the sight of the Lord your God."

NAB

keep in mind my commandments, and never let him be erased from your heart.

20 "And now, son, I wish to inform you that I have deposited a great sum of money with Gabri's son Gabael at Rages in Media. 21 Do not be discouraged, my child, because of our poverty. You will be a rich man if you fear God, avoid all sin, and do what is right before the Lord your God."

4, 20: (*en*) *Ragois*: so LXX^{B,A}, Vet Lat, P, V: cf notes on 1, 14.

COMMENTARY

Chapter 4 is Tobit's farewell discourse to Tobiah.[59] The farewell discourse is a speech usually given when a person is about to die, addressed to that person's descendants or followers as a kind of legacy or inheritance. The farewell discourse may include the announcement of the speaker's departure; a reminder of the past; an exhortation to be faithful to God's commandments and to one another; a prediction of the future; a blessing of peace and joy; and a promise that God will remain with the hearers. Several of the major figures in Israel's history are reported to have given farewell discourses: Jacob (Gen 47:29–49:33); Moses (the whole book of Deuteronomy); Joshua (Joshua 22–24); David (1 Chronicles 28–29). There are three farewell discourses in the book of Tobit: two by Tobit (4:3-21; 14:3-11) and one from Raphael (12:6-10).[60]

4:1-2. Tobit assumes that, since he has asked God for death, death is imminent. There are two important matters to attend to before he dies: the money deposited with Gabael (cf. 1:14) and the instruction to be given to his son, Tobiah. Tobit takes care of these things in reverse order.

4:3-4. Tobit has instructed Tobiah by example; now he instructs him also by word. In teaching his son, Tobit is following the example of his grandmother Deborah (1:8). His instruction begins with an exhortation to care for Tobit and Anna, Tobiah's parents. Tobit, who is so attuned to death and burial, wants to be sure that the proper rituals are performed for him. Tobiah is also instructed to honor his mother.

This section resembles the biblical wisdom literature, especially the Wisdom of Ben Sira, a book written about the same time as the book of Tobit. The responsibility of parents to instruct their children and of children to heed that instruction is a frequent wisdom theme. Ben Sira says, "He who teaches his son will make his enemies envious,/ and will glory in him among his friends./ When the father dies he will not seem to be dead,/ for he has left behind him one like himself" (Sir 30:3-4 NRSV; see also Prov 13:24; 19:18; 22:15; 23:13-14; 29:15, 17; Sir 7:23-24; 30:1-13). Proverbs advises the child to heed the instruction: "My child, do not forget my teaching,/ but let your heart keep my commandments;/ for length of days and years of life/ and abundant welfare they will give you" (Prov 3:1-2 NRSV; see also Prov 1:8-9; 2:1-5; 4:1-13, 20-22; 5:1-2; 7:1-4; 13:1; 19:27; 23:22-25).

The instruction to honor one's mother is especially significant: "With all your heart honor your father,/ and do not forget the birth pangs of your

59. Verses 7-19*b* are missing from the Siniaticus MS, the primary representative of the Greek recension G^{II}. They appear in the other major Greek recension (G^{I}), which is based on the MS Vaticanus and Alexandrinus (B, A). Translations are usually supplemented from the Old Latin version (VL) and an eleventh-century CE manuscript, MS 319, which represent the recension G^{I}. Fragments of two Qumran manuscripts contain a few verses of this section (4QTob^{a} has v. 7, and 4QTob^{e} has vv. 7-9). See J. A. Fitzmyer, *Tobit: Qumran Cave 4, xiv,* DJD, ed. M. Broshi et al. (Oxford: Clarendon, 1995) 1-2.

60. See A. A. Di Lella, "The Deuteronomic Background of the Farewell Discourse in Tob 14:3-11," *CBQ* 41 (1979) 380-89. For a thorough and careful analysis of this chapter, see M. Rabenau, *Studien zum Buch Tobit,* BZAW (Berlin: Walter de Gruyter, 1994) 27-66.

mother./ Remember that it was of your parents you were born;/ how can you repay what they have given to you?" (Sir 7:27-28 NRSV; cf. Prov 6:20; 10:1; 15:20; 19:26; 20:20; 30:17; Sir 3:1-16). Children are to be particularly solicitous when the parents are old: "My child, help your father in his old age,/ and do not grieve him as long as he lives;/ even if his mind fails, be patient with him;/ because you have all your faculties do not despise him" (Sir 3:12-13 NRSV).

Echoes of the Pentateuch also appear in this section. In Jacob's farewell discourse, he requests proper burial from his sons (Gen 47:29-31). The command in the decalogue to honor parents is singled out for emphasis by a motive clause, "that you may have a long life in the land" (Exod 20:12; Deut 5:16). The primary pentateuchal influence, however, is Deuteronomy, in which the duty of parents to instruct their children is emphasized. Israel is exhorted to teach the children the saving deeds of God (Deut 4:9; see also Deut 4:10; 6:1-2). The great commandment to love God is to be drilled into the children (Deut 6:7; see also Deut 11:19-20). Much important instruction is to be given as a response to the question of children: "When your son asks you . . ." (Deut 6:20-21; see also Deut 32:7). In the closing chapters of Deuteronomy, the injunction to educate the children regarding God's law appears twice (Deut 31:12-13; 32:46).

4:5-6. Tobit gives Tobiah a general rule for life: Remember God and keep the law; do good and avoid evil. To remember God is to seek God's presence actively in one's life. Awareness of God's presence then forms the foundation for discerning and doing what is good. Faithfulness to this way of life, according to the theory of retribution, results in reward.

4:7. Tobit tells Tobiah of a way in which the practice of righteousness is to be enfleshed—giving alms. He returns to the image he used in his prayer (3:6) of God's face being turned away. Tobit links the relationship with God to one's relationship to the poor. God's response to Tobiah will mirror Tobiah's response to the poor.

4:8. Tobit enunciates a principle of moderation. Alms are to be given in proportion to the resources of the giver.

4:9-11. Tobit lists the benefits of giving alms. Alms, rather than impoverishing the giver, actually are a way of storing treasure against the day of need. When Tobit says that alms are a way of escaping death, he is not declaring a belief in life after death. There is no evidence of this belief in the book. Rather, he is asserting the conviction that alms will protect the giver from premature death, a strong statement in the mouth of one who expects to die soon! Alms also are equivalent to offering sacrifice, a practice unavailable to the Israelites in exile.

❖ ❖ ❖ ❖

EXCURSUS: ALMSGIVING

Almsgiving (ἐλεημοσύνη *eleēmosynē*) is perhaps the most significant virtue in the book of Tobit (see Introduction).[61] The development of the concept conveyed by this word is one of the major contributions of this book to OT theology. Griffin describes four categories of meaning for *eleēmosynē* in this book: (1) "as charitable deed" (e.g., 1:16; 14:10; cf. 1:3; 2:14); (2) "as monetary alms and almsgiving" (e.g., 4:8*b,* 16-17; 12:8); (3) "as characteristic of a person," specifically Tobit (7:7; cf. 9:6; 14:11); (4) "as characteristic of God" (3:2; 13:6).[62] The third and fourth categories represent most of the usage in the OT, with the exception of the later books Ben Sira and Daniel. The first two categories represent NT usage. The book of Tobit (along with Ben Sira), in which all four meanings are represented, stands at the midpoint of the development of the word. The active expression of *eleēmosynē* in charitable deeds and monetary alms predominates in this book. Tobit specifies his charitable deeds as feeding the

61. For a full treatment of the structural and narrative significance of *eleēmosynē* in the book of Tobit, see P. J. Griffin, "A Study of *Eleēmosynē*," in the Bible with Emphasis Upon Its Meaning and Usage in the Theology of Tobit and Ben Sira" (MA thesis, The Catholic University of America, 1982) 61-62.

62. Ibid., 2-5.

hungry, clothing the naked, and burying the dead (1:1-17). He enjoins the same acts of *eleēmosynē* on his son (4:3-4, 16-17).[63]

The basic principles regulating almsgiving are the same in Tobit and Deuteronomy, although the concept is not as fully developed in the latter. Alms are to be given willingly (Deut 15:10; see Tob 4:8, 16) and in proportion to one's income (Deut 16:17; see also Deut 15:14; Tob 4:8, 16). Charity to the needy is restricted to those within the community (4:17; see Deut 14:29; 16:14).

Ben Sira, however, is most similar to the book of Tobit in the theology regarding almsgiving. According to Ben Sira, giving alms delivers the giver from sin (Sir 3:30-31; see Tob 12:9-10) and is a worthy offering before God (Sir 34:18–35:4; see Tob 4:11). The almsgiver is saved from premature death and destruction (Sir 29:10-13; 40:17, 24; see Tob 4:10; 12:9; 14:10). The giving of alms is limited, however, to the righteous (Sir 12:1-7; see Tob 4:17). The amount to be given is to be decided according to the means of the giver, but without fear or hesitation (Sir 18:15-18; 35:9-10; see Tob 4:8, 16).[64]

63. Ibid., 19, 60.
64. Ibid., 67-76.

❖ ❖ ❖ ❖

4:12-13. Marriage is an important theme in the book of Tobit, both the blessing of it and the necessity for a proper attitude toward it. In his catalog of virtues, Tobit includes respect for marriage. First, he instructs his son to be faithful to the sexual demands of marriage and to avoid fornication. Then he teaches his son the proper way to find a wife.

Endogamy, marriage within the kinship group, is understood by Tobit as a requirement, taught both by the law (Exod 34:15-6) and by the examples of the ancestors. Abraham, whose wife may have been related to him (Gen 20:12), insists that his servant "not get a wife for [his] son from the daughters of the Canaanites" but go to Abraham's own homeland to find a wife for Isaac (Gen 24:3-4). Rebekah and Isaac give similar instructions to their son Jacob (Gen 27:46–28:5). Nothing is said in the Pentateuch concerning kinship between Noah and his wife. For this information, the book of Tobit depends on a tradition found in the book of *Jubilees* (4.33).[65] Tobit himself married within his own family (ἐκ τοῦ σπέρματος τῆς πατριᾶς ἡμων *ek tou spermatos tēs patrias hēmōn*, 1:9). According to Tobit, refusal to follow the example of the ancestors in this very important matter will result in disaster for young Tobiah. Tobit ignores the fact, however, that both Joseph (Gen 41:45) and Moses (Exod 2:21; see Num 12:1) married foreign wives.

The way to find a proper wife was hotly debated in the centuries following the Babylonian exile. The strongest condemnation of marriage to foreigners appears in the books of Ezra and Nehemiah (Ezra 9:1-4; Neh 13:23-27). Ezra demands that men divorce their foreign wives (Ezra 10:1-44). By contrast, the book of Ruth, which may have been written in the post-exilic period, tells the story of a foreign wife who becomes the great-grandmother of King David.

4:14. As he approaches the end of his discourse, Tobit presents a collection of maxims to guide his son in his relationship toward others, toward himself, and toward God. He is to be honest in his dealings with others, especially those who work for him (Ben Sira also advises justice toward laborers [Sir 7:20], asserting that withholding wages is equivalent to murder [Sir 34:26-27]). Again, Tobit equates one's relationship to God with that to one's neighbor; to act justly toward the laborer is to serve God. Tobiah must also be just toward himself. His life is to be based on wisdom and discipline.[66] His actions will bring reward, according to the theory of retribution.

65. See J. Gamberoni, "Das 'Gesetz des Mose' im Buch Tobias," in *Studien zum Pentateuch: Festschrift for W. Kornfield,* ed. G. Braulik (Wien/Freiburg: Herder, 1977) 230; R. H. Pfeiffer, *History of New Testament Times* (New York: Harper and Bros., 1949) 267.

66. Verse 14 of the Old Latin (VL) has a phrase that is missing in Greek (BA): "be wise in all that you say [*esto sapiens in omnibus sermonibus tuis*]."

4:15. The Golden Rule, "what you hate, do not do to anyone," is to guide Tobiah's actions. He is to avoid drunkenness, the enemy of discipline and wisdom. Ben Sira similarly advises against excessive drinking: "Let not winedrinking be the proof of your strength" (Sir 31:25; see also Sir 31:26-31).

4:16-17. The principles regarding almsgiving reappear: giving according to one's means; giving to the just but not to sinners. Even the dead and those who mourn them are to be cared for. The command to "place bread on the grave of the righteous" seems to speak of offering food to the dead.[67] Because this practice is expressly forbidden by Deuteronomy (Deut 26:14; see Ps 106:28)—one of the main sources for the theology of the book of Tobit—it probably refers to gifts of food for the mourners (see Jer 16:7; Ezek 24:17, 22).[68]

4:18. Tobiah must recognize that he is not self-sufficient. He is to seek out the wise and accept any useful advice. Again Tobit reflects the same principles as does Ben Sira, who counsels the young to wear away the doorstep of the wise (Sir 6:36; cf. Sir 6:32-35).

4:19. With regard to God, Tobiah is to be generous in praise. He is to expect help and reward from God; on the other hand, he is to accept whatever God sends. Thus the theory of retribution is both affirmed (v. 14) and questioned (v. 19). Tobiah's faith is to be founded on the memory of God's goodness to the chosen people and on the commandments of his father.

Tobit's instruction in vv. 14-19 echoes the proverbs that are part of the story of Ahiqar (see Introduction). Tobit exhorts Tobiah, "Do not drink wine to the point of drunkenness or let drunkenness go with you on your way. . . . Pour out your bread on the grave of the righteous but do not give to sinners" (vv. 15, 17).[69] Ahiqar says, "My son, it is better to remove stones with a wise man than to drink wine with a fool. My son, pour out thy wine on the graves of the righteous rather than drink it with evil men."[70] One of the Aramaic proverbs in Ahiqar states: "If you desire, my son, to be [exalted, cast yourself down before God], who casts down the exalted person and e[xalts the humble person]."[71] This proverb can be compared to v. 19: "If [the Lord] chooses otherwise, he casts down to deepest Hades."[72]

4:20-21. Finally Tobit comes to the practical point of his speech to Tobiah, the recovery of the money that has been deposited with Gabael. He informs his son of the amount and location of the money and adds a moral instruction to the practical information. The theory of retribution, which is the reward in this present life, is again affirmed: Faithfulness to God will bring Tobiah great wealth. Faithfulness to God is defined by three elements. First, Tobiah is to fear God, to maintain loving reverence in his relationship to God. The second and third elements are the negative and positive consequences of fear of the Lord: avoiding sin and doing good. Tobit's sentiment is a common wisdom theme. It appears in Psalm 34:

Come, O children, listen to me;
  I will teach you the fear of the LORD.
Which of you desires life,
  and covets many days to enjoy good?
. . . .
Depart from evil, and do good;
  seek peace and pursue it."
(Ps 34:11-12, 14 NRSV; see also Ps 37:27; Prov 3:7; 14:16; Sir 21:2)

67. The Greco-Roman practice was to eat a feast at the grave in honor of the dead on the day of burial, on the ninth day after the funeral, and then at the end of the period of mourning to pour out a libation on the grave. See Tacitus *Annals* 6.5; Petronius *Satyricon* 65. See also J. M. C. Toynbee, *Death and Burial in the Roman World* (Ithaca: Cornell University Press, 1971) 50-51.

68. See Carey A. Moore, *Tobit,* AB 40A (Garden City, N.Y.: Doubleday, 1996) 173, for a full discussion of this issue.

69. Translation mine, more literal to show the relationship to Ahiqar. The Old Latin (OL) and the Vulgate read, "Pour out your wine [*vinum tuum*] and your bread."

70. Syr 2:9-10[A]. See F. C. Conybeare, J. R. Harris, and A. S. Lewis, "The Story of Ahikar," *APOT* 2.730. Much discussion has centered on this verse as a means to explain the incomplete reading in Tobit 4:17[B]: "pour out your bread." See, e.g., D. C. Simpson, "The Book of Tobit," *APOT* 1.191. This parallel only appears in versions of Ahiqar that are later than Tobit. See, e.g., Sefire 5,7, in J. A. Fitzmyer, *The Aramaic Inscriptions of Sefire,* BibOr 193 (Rome: Pontifical Biblical Institute, 1967) 96-97): "you must not gi[ve th]em food." Fitzmyer goes on to say: "The verb must come from the root נסך (*nsk*) which normally means to 'pour a libation.' But it is used here in a generic sense with לחם (*leḥem,* "bread") and means 'to provide food.' F. Rosenthal (*BASOR* 158 [1960] 29, n. 3), compares Akkad. *nasaku,* 'throw down food, meals.' Cf. Dn 2:46" (ibid., 108).

71. *Story of Ahiqar,* col. x, 11. 149-50; Sachau, pl. 47[B]: text in A. Cowley, *Aramaic Papyri of the Fifth Century B.C.* (Oxford: Clarendon, 1923) 217; translation mine. References to the Aramaic text of the story of Ahiqar are traditionally numbered according to the system of E. Sachau, *Aramäische Papyrus und Ostraka aus einer jüdischen Militär-Kolonie zu Elephantine* (Leipzig: J. C. Hinrichs, 1911).

72. The Old Latin (VL) has the additional phrase, "whomever he wishes, he raises [*quem ergo voluerit ipse allevat*]."

REFLECTIONS

1. Caring for elderly parents is a great concern in our society. People are living longer today than at any time in history. Adults do not ordinarily continue to live with parents in the family home, especially after marriage. The elderly often are left alone after the death of a spouse, and they frequently face economic anxiety and frail health. Their sons and daughters, the "sandwich generation," are burdened with their own children, homes, jobs, and economic needs. Tobit instructs his son never to abandon his mother. Presumably he would include himself if he were not so certain of his imminent death. How can we be faithful to Tobit's instruction? How can society help? How can the church help? The growing trend toward complexes for assisted living, where older people have both privacy and the opportunity for convenient health care, communal meals, recreation, and sometimes also religious services, is a partial solution. Home health care and Meals on Wheels serve some of the needs of the elderly. Situations where nursing home care is a necessity place a strong obligation on family members to visit frequently. Are there other solutions?

2. The instruction of children is perhaps more vital now than at any time in history. Children are more mobile, have more money, and develop a social life outside the family at a very early age. The crucial responsibility of parents to instill values and to provide support is difficult. Tobit teaches Tobiah both by example and by word. His teaching did not begin only when he believed his death to be imminent, however. This responsibility for children's instruction from infanthood on is another area in which parents need the help of society and the church.

3. The word *almsgiving* is rarely used in modern American English. Hopefully the concept is not so rare. When my mother went into a nursing home, her mail began to come to me. Hardly a day passes that I do not receive at least one or two appeals for charitable contributions. The frequency of the appeals indicates to me that someone must be answering them. Other ways of giving alms are also available. People who have more energy than money help with projects such as Habitat for Humanity, which provides low-cost housing for the needy. Soup kitchens and shelters are staffed by volunteers and are supported by contributions of food and bedding as well as money. Major fund drives, such as United Way, organize our charitable contributions. The Salvation Army and the St. Vincent de Paul Society help us turn our crowded closets into "clothing the naked."

The list of possibilities is long. Tobit's exhortation gives us the guidelines: Give willingly; give according to what you have—little or much; and rejoice that your gift has become a treasure, an excellent offering in the presence of God. Christians believe that almsgiving does not merely save them from premature death, but leads to eternal life. In the Gospel of Luke, Jesus says that the treasure is not for this life only: "Sell your belongings and give alms. Provide money bags for yourselves that do not wear out, an inexhaustible treasure in heaven that no thief can reach nor moth destroy" (see Luke 12:33).

4. The Golden Rule is stated here in the negative, rather than in the positive as in the Gospels ("Do to others as you would have them do to you" [Matt 7:12; Luke 6:31]). This saying has long been the "rule" for believers. It is based on the commandment "you shall love your neighbor as yourself" (Lev 19:18). Leviticus adds: "You shall love the alien as yourself, for you were aliens in the land of Egypt" (Lev 19:34 NRSV). The sabbath commandment in Deuteronomy prescribes rest even for slaves, because the Israelites are to remember that they were once slaves in Egypt (Deut 5:15).

Robert Fulghum says that everything he needed to know he learned in kindergarten.[73]

73. Robert Fulghum, *All I Really Need to Know I Learned in Kindergarten: Uncommon Thoughts on Common Things* (New York: Villard, 1988).

Most of us learned the Golden Rule at least that early. It really is everything we need to know. Tobit's whole instruction can be summarized with this simple sentence. Paul tells us that it is, in fact, the whole law: "Owe no one anything, except to love one another; for the one who loves another has fulfilled the law" (Rom 13:8).

5. Just and prompt payment of laborers is an issue of social justice that has intensified in the modern world. In *Rerum Novarum* (1891), Pope Leo XIII promoted the recognition of workers as partners with management in the production of goods.[74] The Vatican II document *Gaudium et Spes* states that "remuneration for work should guarantee one the opportunity to provide a dignified livelihood for oneself and one's family on the material, social, cultural, and spiritual level."[75]

Capitalism is not a good in itself; profit cannot be the only or even the primary goal. Justice toward all, especially toward the more vulnerable members of society, is both Tobit's demand of Tobiah and the demand placed on all who would be faithful to God's teaching.

6. Tobit does not forbid his son to drink wine; rather, he advises his son to avoid drunkenness. There are two issues here: moderation and addiction. Moderation is the exercise of discipline recommended by Tobit. I have heard asceticism defined as "taking only what one needs." Saint Benedict advised his followers to practice moderation in all things.[76] The other issue is addiction, the enslavement to something. Addiction is an illness that can only be healed with help. For example, Alcoholics Anonymous provides lifelong support to those who suffer from alcohol addiction.

7. Tobit advises Tobiah to "seek advice from every wise person." The practice of spiritual direction has a long history among believers. It is rooted in the wisdom tradition of the instruction of a "son" (disciple) by an elder. In the Christian tradition it flowered among the desert fathers and mothers and continued especially in monasticism. Today many people seek out a "wise person" who will help them look at their lives honestly in order to see both the direction in which God is leading them and the pitfalls that lie in the way. Tobit's advice is an affirmation of the communal nature of faith. We do not go to God alone, but as a community, each helping the other.

74. *Rerum Novarum* 1, 6, 26, 28. See *Contemporary Catholic Social Teaching* (Washington, D.C.: VSCC, 1991) for a modern reprint of the encyclical.

75. *Gaudium et Spes* 67.2. See *The Documents of Vatican II*, ed. Walter M. Abbott, S. J. (New York: Herder & Herder, 1966), for an English translation.

76. RB 48.9; cf. 40.6. See *RB 1980: The Rule of St. Benedict*, ed. Timothy Fry et al. (Collegeville, Minn.: Liturgical Press, 1981).

TOBIT 5:1–6:1, THE HIRING OF A GUIDE

NAB

5 1 Then Tobiah replied to his father Tobit: "Everything that you have commanded me, father, I will do. 2 But how shall I be able to obtain the money from him, since he does not know me nor do I know him? What can I show him to make him recognize me and trust me, so that he will give me the money? I do not even know which roads to take for the journey into

5, 2: *to argyrion* (*labein*): so LXX[B,A], Vet Lat, P; cf V.

NRSV

5 Then Tobias answered his father Tobit, "I will do everything that you have commanded me, father; 2but how can I obtain the money[a] from him, since he does not know me and I do not know him? What evidence[b] am I to give him so that he will recognize and trust me, and give me the money? Also, I do not know the roads to Media, or how to get there." 3Then Tobit

[a] Gk *it* [b] Gk *sign*

NAB

Media!" 3 Tobit answered his son Tobiah: "We exchanged signatures on a document written in duplicate; I divided it into two parts, and each of us kept one; his copy I put with the money. Think of it, twenty years have already passed since I deposited that money! So now, my son, find yourself a trustworthy man who will make the journey with you. We will, of course, give him a salary when you return; but get back that money from Gabael."

4 Tobiah went to look for someone acquainted with the roads who would travel with him to Media. As soon as he went out, he found the angel Raphael standing before him, though he did not know that this was an angel of God. 5 Tobiah said to him, "Who are you, young man?" He replied, "I am an Israelite, one of your kinsmen. I have come here to work." Tobiah said, "Do you know the way to Media?" 6 The other replied: "Yes, I have been there many times. I know the place well and I know all the routes. I have often traveled to Media; I used to stay with our kinsman Gabael, who lives at Rages in Media. It is a good two days' travel from Ecbatana to Rages, for Rages is situated at the mountains, Ecbatana out on the plateau." 7 Tobiah said to him, "Wait for me, young man, till I go back and tell my father; for I need you to make the journey with me. I will, of course, pay you." 8 Raphael replied, "Very well, I will wait for you; but do not be long."

9 Tobiah went back to tell his father Tobit what had happened. He said to him, "I have just found a man who is one of our own Israelite kinsmen!" Tobit said, "Call the man, so that I may find out what family and tribe he comes from, and whether he is trustworthy enough to travel with you, son." Tobiah went out to summon the man saying, "Young man, my father would like to see you."

10 When Raphael entered the house, Tobit greeted him first. Raphael said, "Hearty greetings to you!" Tobit replied: "What joy is left for me any more? Here I am, a blind man who cannot see God's sunlight, but must remain in darkness, like the dead who no longer see the light! Though alive, I am among the dead. I can hear a man's

5, 6: (*en*) *Ragois* (*tēs*): so Vet Lat, V; cf note on 1, 14. (*Ekbatanōn eis*) *Ragas:* so Vet Lat.

NRSV

answered his son Tobias, "He gave me his bond and I gave him my bond. I[a] divided his in two; we each took one part, and I put one with the money. And now twenty years have passed since I left this money in trust. So now, my son, find yourself a trustworthy man to go with you, and we will pay him wages until you return. But get back the money from Gabael."[b]

4 So Tobias went out to look for a man to go with him to Media, someone who was acquainted with the way. He went out and found the angel Raphael standing in front of him; but he did not perceive that he was an angel of God. 5 Tobias[c] said to him, "Where do you come from, young man?" "From your kindred, the Israelites," he replied, "and I have come here to work." Then Tobias[d] said to him, "Do you know the way to go to Media?" 6 "Yes," he replied, "I have been there many times; I am acquainted with it and know all the roads. I have often traveled to Media, and would stay with our kinsman Gabael who lives in Rages of Media. It is a journey of two days from Ecbatana to Rages; for it lies in a mountainous area, while Ecbatana is in the middle of the plain." 7 Then Tobias said to him, "Wait for me, young man, until I go in and tell my father; for I do need you to travel with me, and I will pay you your wages." 8 He replied, "All right, I will wait; but do not take too long."

9 So Tobias[d] went in to tell his father Tobit and said to him, "I have just found a man who is one of our own Israelite kindred!" He replied, "Call the man in, my son, so that I may learn about his family and to what tribe he belongs, and whether he is trustworthy enough to go with you."

10 Then Tobias went out and called him, and said, "Young man, my father is calling for you." So he went in to him, and Tobit greeted him first. He replied, "Joyous greetings to you!" But Tobit retorted, "What joy is left for me any more? I am a man without eyesight; I cannot see the light of heaven, but I lie in darkness like the dead who no longer see the light. Although still alive, I am among the dead. I hear people but I cannot see them." But the young man[d] said, "Take courage; the time is near for God to heal you; take cour-

[a] Other authorities read *He* [b] Gk *from him* [c] Gk *He* [d] Gk *he*

NAB

voice, but I cannot see him." Raphael said, "Take courage! God has healing in store for you; so take courage!" Tobit then said: "My son Tobiah wants to go to Media. Can you go with him to show him the way? I will of course pay you, brother." Raphael answered: "Yes, I can go with him, for I know all the routes. I have often traveled to Media and crossed all its plains and mountains; so I know every road well." 11 Tobit asked, "Brother, tell me, please, what family and tribe are you from?" 12 Raphael said: "Why? Do you need a tribe and a family? Or are you looking for a hired man to travel with your son?" Tobit replied, "I wish to know truthfully whose son you are, brother, and what your name is."

13 Raphael answered, "I am Azariah, son of Hananiah the elder, one of your own kinsmen." 14 Tobit exclaimed: "Welcome! God save you, brother! Do not be provoked with me, brother, for wanting to learn the truth about your family. So it turns out that you are a kinsman, and from a noble and good line! I knew Hananiah and Nathaniah, the two sons of Shemaiah the elder; with me they used to make the pilgrimage to Jerusalem, where we would worship together. No, they did not stray from the right path; your kinsmen are good men. You are certainly of good lineage, and welcome!"

15 Then he added: "For each day you are away I will give you the normal wages, plus expenses for you and for my son. If you go with my son, 16 I will even add a bonus to your wages!" Raphael replied: "I will go with him; have no fear. In good health we shall leave you, and in good health we shall return to you, for the way is safe." 17 Tobit said, "God bless you, brother." Then he called his son and said to him: "My son, prepare whatever you need for the journey, and set out with your kinsman. May God in heaven protect you on the way and bring you back to me safe and sound; and may his angel accompany you for safety, my son."

Before setting out on his journey, Tobiah kissed his father and mother. Tobit said to him, "Have a safe journey." 18 But his mother began to weep.

5, 12: (*phylēs*) *kai patrias; ē zēteis misthion ʽos symporeusetai meta tou ʽuiou sou*: cf LXX^{B,A}, P, Vet Lat, V.
5, 14: *Nathanian*: so Vet Lat^{MSS}; *Semaiou*: so LXX^{MSS}, P, Vet Lat^{MSS}.

NRSV

age." Then Tobit said to him, "My son Tobias wishes to go to Media. Can you accompany him and guide him? I will pay your wages, brother." He answered, "I can go with him and I know all the roads, for I have often gone to Media and have crossed all its plains, and I am familiar with its mountains and all of its roads."

11 Then Tobit[a] said to him, "Brother, of what family are you and from what tribe? Tell me, brother." 12 He replied, "Why do you need to know my tribe?" But Tobit[a] said, "I want to be sure, brother, whose son you are and what your name is." 13 He replied, "I am Azariah, the son of the great Hananiah, one of your relatives." 14 Then Tobit said to him, "Welcome! God save you, brother. Do not feel bitter toward me, brother, because I wanted to be sure about your ancestry. It turns out that you are a kinsman, and of good and noble lineage. For I knew Hananiah and Nathan,[b] the two sons of Shemeliah,[c] and they used to go with me to Jerusalem and worshiped with me there, and were not led astray. Your kindred are good people; you come of good stock. Hearty welcome!"

15 Then he added, "I will pay you a drachma a day as wages, as well as expenses for yourself and my son. So go with my son, 16 and[d] I will add something to your wages." Raphael[e] answered, "I will go with him; so do not fear. We shall leave in good health and return to you in good health, because the way is safe." 17 So Tobit[a] said to him, "Blessings be upon you, brother."

Then he called his son and said to him, "Son, prepare supplies for the journey and set out with your brother. May God in heaven bring you safely there and return you in good health to me; and may his angel, my son, accompany you both for your safety."

Before he went out to start his journey, he kissed his father and mother. Tobit then said to him, "Have a safe journey."

18 But his mother[f] began to weep, and said to Tobit, "Why is it that you have sent my child away? Is he not the staff of our hand as he goes in and out before us? 19 Do not heap money upon

[a] Gk *he* [b] Other ancient authorities read *Jathan* or *Nathaniah* [c] Other ancient authorities read *Shemaiah* [d] Other ancient authorities add *when you return safely* [e] Gk *He* [f] Other ancient authorities add *Anna*

NAB

She said to Tobit: "Why have you decided to send
my child away? Is he not the staff to which we
cling, ever there with us in all that we do? 19 I
hope more money is not your chief concern!
Rather let it be a ransom for our son! 20 What
the Lord has given us to live on is certainly
enough for us." 21 Tobit reassured her. "Have no
such thought. Our son will leave in good health
and come back to us in good health. Your own
eyes will see the day when he returns to you safe
and sound. 22 So, no such thought; do not worry
about them, my love. For a good angel will go
with him, his journey will be successful, and he
will return unharmed." 1 Then she stopped weeping.

NRSV

money, but let it be a ransom for our child. 20For
the life that is given to us by the Lord is enough
for us." 21Tobit[a] said to her, "Do not worry; our
child will leave in good health and return to us in
good health. Your eyes will see him on the day
when he returns to you in good health. Say no
more! Do not fear for them, my sister. 22For a good
angel will accompany him; his journey will be
successful, and he will come back in good health."

6 1So she stopped weeping.

The young man went out and the angel went
with him;

[ae] Gk *He*

COMMENTARY

Following the long speech of chap. 4 the action resumes. The primary purpose of chap. 5 is to introduce the angel Raphael, who will act as a guide for the young Tobiah. The reader is already prepared for Raphael's appearance. He has been sent in answer to the prayers of Tobit and Sarah to heal them both (3:17). Now the reader discovers how Raphael will function: as a guide on the journey.

Raphael is a main character in the scenes of preparation, journeying (chap. 6), and conclusion (chap. 12). In these scenes, his identity as an angel is kept clearly before us. The narrator introduces him as the angel Raphael (5:4). After the lengthy negotiation over identity and trustworthiness, we are reminded (ironically) by the unsuspecting Tobit that an angel travels with Tobiah (5:17, 22). The narrator continues to refer to Raphael as "the angel" throughout the journey (6:2, 4, 7). But as soon as the travelers approach Ecbatana, Raphael's angelic character fades from sight. We are not reminded of it again until the revelation speech in chap. 12.

5:1-2. In his response to his father's long speech, Tobiah presents several anticipated difficulties. He seems somewhat helpless. He does not know how to get the money; he does not know how he will be recognized by Gabael. He does not even know how to get to Media. This uncertainty contributes to the impression of Tobiah as an inexperienced young man. He is not unwilling, however, to go on the journey. His questions show that he has already taken the task upon himself, and he accepts and acts upon the answers his father gives him.

5:3. The experienced father reassures his worried son. First he tells Tobiah what he must present to Gabael in order to get the money. The matter of the signed bond is somewhat confusing in the text. Apparently, according to a practice known in the ancient world, the document was written in duplicate on the same parchment or papyrus. Then the document was torn or cut in half. Tobit took his half home and put Gabael's half with the money. Tobit will now give Tobiah the half in his possession, so that he can claim the money (see 9:2).

Tobit deals with Tobiah's other difficulty by instructing him to find a trustworthy guide who will travel with him and show him the way to Media. Although this difficulty seems secondary to the task of regaining the money, the money will become secondary as the plot progresses and the instructions of the guide will become primary.

5:4. The appearance of Raphael in this scene gives several clues to his angelic status. First, Tobiah simply finds Raphael standing in front of him. The immediacy suggests an angelic appearance. Raphael is an ironic character, one "who poses as less than he is" and "who understates things."[77] As a character, he is an example of dramatic irony, in which the readers know what the characters do not.[78] The narrator sets up the ironic situation by informing the reader that Tobiah "did not perceive that he was an angel of God."

5:5. Raphael claims to be an Israelite; the reader knows that he is an angel. His subsequent announcement of his purpose, "I have come here to work," is also ironic. The reader knows what his task is (3:17), but Tobiah does not.

5:6. Raphael knows exactly what Tobiah needs, and he claims extraordinary knowledge. He knows Media well. He knows all the routes, all its plains, all its roads, and he knows that the way is safe (5:6, 10, 16). Raphael knows the very kinsman Tobiah intends to visit, and he knows the distance to Ecbatana, which Tobiah does not intend to visit but will. In fact, however, Raphael's knowledge of geography is not very good. Rages is approximately 185 miles from Ecbatana. The distance took Alexander's army eleven days to cover.[79] Perhaps an angel moves more swiftly! also, Ecbatana is not situated on a plain, but has a higher altitude than Rages.

5:7-8. Tobiah politely begins to negotiate with the potential guide, but the young man still needs the approval of his father. In fact, his father will pay the wages. The aura of haste that surrounds Raphael is another characteristic that hints at his angelic status. He agrees to wait, but insists that Tobiah not be long (see also 8:3; 9:1-6; 11:3).

5:9. When Tobiah informs Tobit that he has found a possible guide, Tobit's response reveals his love for his son. He wants to know Raphael's lineage and his trustworthiness. His concern for strict religious observance, which he will deduce from Raphael's supposed family, is emphasized again. Only a man who can be trusted both to know and to observe the law of God is worthy to be his son's companion.

The irony continues in this section. Raphael's name, like Tobit's, is ironic in the context of the story. He plays upon the meaning of his name, "God heals," saying to Tobit, "Take courage! God's healing is near."

5:10. Tobit's grief and constant awareness of his blindness spill out in his very first words to Raphael: "What joy is left for me?" His treatment of the unknown Raphael is notable for its reverence. Tobit greets Raphael first, although the latter appears to be the younger, since Tobiah addresses Raphael as "young man" (vv. 5, 7, 9).

5:11-12. Raphael seems reluctant to reveal his identity to Tobit. This is a common theme in angelic appearances. Both the angel who wrestles with Jacob (Gen 32:30) and the angel who announces Samson's impending birth (Judg 13:18) refuse to reveal their names. Tobit's characteristic gentleness is again revealed as he turns aside a sharp remark (v. 12) by repeating without rancor his question concerning Raphael's family and by asking pardon for his persistence.

5:13. The pseudonym Raphael uses to mask his identity is also an ironic revelation of his function. He tells Tobit, "I am Azariah [YHWH has helped], son of Hananiah [YHWH is merciful]." The statement is true, but not in the sense that Tobit understands it.

5:14. Tobit's own words are also ironic. Twice he has expressed his desire for a true answer concerning Raphael's identity (vv. 12, 14). When Raphael does answer him, Tobit exclaims, "Welcome!" (lit., "May you come in wellness!"). The word ὑγιαίνω (*hygiainō*, "to be well") is subsequently picked up by Raphael (v. 16) and becomes an ironic echo of the angel's name and function. Tobit concludes that Azariah (Raphael) is of good lineage. Indeed!

5:15-16. Tobit's business arrangements with Raphael demonstrate Tobit's justness and his generosity. He states clearly what the salary will be, and he promises a bonus if the travelers return safely. Raphael answers Tobit with a typical angelic answer, "Fear not" (cf. Gen 21:17; Dan 10:12; Luke 1:13, 30; 2:10; Acts 27:24). Then he repeats the key word *hygiainō* ("to be well"). This word, which occurs only forty times in the whole Septuagint, appears twenty-five times in the book of Tobit. Eight of the occurrences are in vv. 16-22 (translated "good health" or "safe"). A key theme of the book is healing, "to be well."

77. Edwin Good, *Irony in the Old Testament* (Sheffield: Almond, 1981), 14. See also Aristotle *Ethics* 4.7.14 1127b; N. Frye, *Anatomy of Criticism* (Princeton, N.J.: Princeton University Press, 1957) 40.

78. D. C. Muecke, *The Compass of Irony* (London: Methuen, 1969), 104-5; see also D. C. Muecke, *Irony* (London: Methuen & Co., 1970) 64-66.

79. See Arrian, *Anabasis Alexandri*, trans. P. A. Brunt, LCL (Cambridge, Mass.: Harvard University Press, 1976) 3:20.

5:17. Tobit, the man of prayer, pronounces a blessing upon Raphael and upon his son, Tobiah. His prayer for Tobiah is another example of irony. Tobit's prayer for a good angel to accompany his son has already been answered. The readers know this, but he does not.

5:18-20. The final character to appear in this section is Anna, the mother. Again she reveals the immediacy of her emotions. She has been described as a woman inclined to passion and despair.[80] As her son, Tobiah, leaves, she makes a scene, weeping and complaining that Tobit is sending him away.

Anna follows the pattern set in the dialogue of chap. 2. As soon as the immediate subject of her worry is stated, she turns the conversation to an attack on Tobit, accusing him of preferring money to the life of their son. She strikes again at Tobit's trust in God's providence, implying that she is content with what God sends, but that he apparently is not.

The personal pronouns are significant in this and subsequent scenes. Anna, identified by the narrator as "his [Tobiah's] mother," says to Tobit, "Why is it that *you* have sent *my* child away?" (v. 18, italics added). After a single mention of "our child" (v. 19), she continues to refer to Tobiah as "my child" (10:4, 7) until he returns from the journey that has worried her so much.

5:21–6:1. Tobit responds to his wife's worry with assurance. His words are deeply ironic. He repeats the religious cliché with which he bade farewell to Tobiah, "a good angel will go with him." He does not know how true his statement is. The scene closes with an incredible economy of detail. After Tobit's comforting words, the narrator tells us, Anna stops weeping.

80. W. Dommershausen, *Der Engel, die Frauen, das Heil: Tobias, Ester, Judit,* SKK 17 (Stuttgart: Katholische Bibelwerk, 1970) 9.

REFLECTIONS

1. The Letter to the Hebrews warns us not to neglect hospitality, because through it some have entertained angels unawares (Heb 13:2). Tobit welcomes Raphael with respect even though he sees him simply as a man in search of a job. There is a fascination with "angels in disguise" in popular culture. Stories abound in which an ordinary person—night nurse, postal worker, tow-truck driver, cleaning woman—is recognized later as an angel. The angel is known because he or she brings a message (*angel* means "messenger"). The message may give encouragement to do the right thing even though it is hard. It may provide comfort in the face of sickness or death. It may be a warning that one's life has taken a wrong turn. In the last analysis, the message is always, "God loves you."

2. Wellness is a popular theme in our society. There are wellness workshops and wellness retreats. Books promise to teach us wellness. Exercise machines and health clubs promise to lead us there.

What is wellness? What does it mean to be a truly healthy human being? The word *health* has to do with wholeness. A healthy person is a "whole" person. Our experience teaches us that wholeness does not, however, always mean the absence of disease or injury. Wholeness has far more to do with the integrity of a person's spirit. The Special Olympics give us a glimpse of those who may not be physically sound but whose courage and joy testify to their health and wholeness.

The challenge of wellness comes in the recognition that we do not have absolute control over our lives. We do what we can to maintain physical health—eating wisely, exercising, resting—and spiritual health—prayer, companionship, the practice of virtue. But we only do this well if we accept our own situation honestly—our strengths, our weaknesses, the accidents or diseases that may afflict us. True wellness is a consequence of humility, the recognition that life and health are gifts from God.

3. The book of Tobit portrays God's providence working subtly in the midst of ordinary life. The angel sent to help Tobit and Sarah seems to be an ordinary human being. A common fish is the means of healing. Even the ordinary speech of the characters reveals the hidden work of God. Both Tobit and Raphael use the customary greeting: "Well-come." Tobit assures Anna of Tobiah's safety with the pious wish, "An angel goes with him." Part of the irony in this story comes from the characters' unconscious use of these terms and phrases.

Many of our common English words also conceal religious concepts. "Good-bye" is a contraction of "God be with you." "Holiday" comes from "holy day." We use phrases out of habit: "God bless you," "God keep you." We wish each other well without knowing it with "farewell" and "welcome." A brief moment of attention to our language may also reveal to us the hidden work of God.

TOBIT 6:2-18

THE JOURNEY TO MEDIA

OVERVIEW

The book of Tobit bears some characteristics of the romance. A common form of the romance is the successful quest, which falls into three main stages: the dangerous journey, the mortal struggle, and the exaltation of the hero. The hero may embark on the journey for several reasons—e.g., to rescue a bride from a perilous situation or to obtain hidden treasure. Frequently the struggle involves a dragon-killing theme—e.g., victory over a serpent or water monster, such as Leviathan. After the hero passes through the symbolic death of the struggle, the conquered sea monster may become the source of life for him or for others. Throughout the quest, the romantic hero moves in a double world. He is human, not divine, but extraordinary events happen in his favor. The ordinary laws of nature yield to his marvelous actions. At the successful completion of the quest, a "new society" may form around the hero and heroine. This new society is often inaugurated by a festive ritual, such as a wedding or a banquet.[81]

In the book of Tobit the central movement of the plot is a quest for money (4:1-2, 20–5:3), which becomes a quest for a bride (6:10-18; cf. 4:12-13). The hero, Tobiah, embarks on a dangerous journey. He conquers a water animal (6:3-6), which becomes a means of life and healing (8:2-3; 11:10-14). With the help of an angel, he survives a mortal struggle with a demon (8:2-3; cf. 6:17-18). During the quest the angel's assistance puts the hero in touch with a world beyond ordinary human experience. The story ends with a description of the happy and prosperous life of the hero and his bride after the successful completion of the quest (14:1-2, 11-15). The wedding signals the hope for the "new society," the new Jerusalem whose future citizens are symbolized in their seven sons (13:9-18; 14:3).

The journey falls into two segments, each dealing with one of the questions generated by preparation for the journey. It begins with the last question from the previous sequence: Will Tobiah return safely? On the first night of the journey he is attacked by a fish, which attempts to swallow his foot (6:3). By heeding Raphael's encouragement and advice, he conquers the fish (6:4); in obedience to Raphael's instructions, he sets aside its gall, heart, and liver for future use (6:5-6). Raphael's repsonse to Tobiah's inquiry concerning these strange instructions suggests an answer to the two questions that have been ignored since the exposition: How will Tobit be healed? The fish's gall can restore sight (6:9). How will Sarah be delivered from Asmodeus? The burning of the fish's heart and liver will drive away demons (6:8).

The second segment of the journey begins as the travelers approach Ecbatana (6:10). The repetition of this place-name, which occurs in 3:7 (see also 5:6) hints that this section will deal with the question of whether Tobiah will meet and marry Sarah. Raphael introduces the subject immediately and advises Tobiah of his right to marry Sarah (6:11-13). In response, Tobiah objects. He has heard of Sarah's affliction and of the deaths of the previous bridegrooms (6:14-15). Again he raises the question that concluded the previous sequence: Will I return safely? Raphael urges him to twofold obedience: First, he should obey his father's will and marry a woman from his own family (6:16), and, second, he should obey Raphael's instructions and, with prayer and the burning of the fish's liver and heart, deliver Sarah from Asmodeus (6:17-18). Thus the fish, which represents the first threat to his safe return, becomes the first assurance of his safety. Tobiah's

81. N. Frye, *Anatomy of Criticism* (Princeton, N.J.: Princeton University Press, 1957) 187-93.

response is assent and intense love for Sarah. The question is answered: How will Sarah be delivered from Asmodeus?

The four major questions treated by this sequence have collapsed into two: Will Tobiah marry Sarah, escape death, and deliver her? Will Tobiah return safely and heal Tobit? The only question left untreated in this sequence is whether Tobiah will get the money. That question is intensified, since the action seems to be shifting toward Ecbatana and away from Rages.

TOBIT 6:2-9, CATCHING THE FISH

NAB

6 2 When the boy left home, accompanied by the angel, the dog followed Tobiah out of the house and went with him. The travelers walked till nightfall, and made camp beside the Tigris River. 3 Now when the boy went down to wash his feet in the river, a large fish suddenly leaped out of the water and tried to swallow his foot. He shouted in alarm. 4 But the angel said to him, "Take hold of the fish and don't let it get away!" The boy seized the fish and hauled it up on the shore. 5 The angel then told him: "Cut the fish open and take out its gall, heart, and liver, and keep them with you; but throw away the entrails. Its gall, heart, and liver make useful medicines." 6 After the lad had cut the fish open, he put aside the gall, heart, and liver. Then he broiled and ate part of the fish; the rest he salted and kept for the journey. 7 Afterward they traveled on together till they were near Media. The boy asked the angel this question: "Brother Azariah, what medicinal value is there in the fish's heart, liver, and gall?" 8 He answered: "As regards the fish's heart and liver, if you burn them so that the smoke surrounds a man or a woman who is afflicted by a demon or evil spirit, the affliction will leave him completely, and no demons will ever return to him again. 9 And as for the gall, if you rub it on the eyes of a man who has cataracts, blowing into his eyes right on the cataracts, his sight will be restored."

6, 6: (*'ēlismenon*) *eis tēn 'odon* : conj; cf Vet Lat, V.
6, 7: The third Greek recension begins here and continues to 13, 8.
6, 12: (*patēr autēs*) *agapą autēn*: so LXX^{MSS}, Vet Lat.
6, 13: (*ek*) *Ragōn* : so LXX^{MSS}, Vet Lat, P. (*apax*) *o* (*men*): so Vet Lat.
6, 15: (*egō*) *apo tou daimoniou toutou* (*'oti*) *philei autēn kai* (*autēn*): so with Vet Lat; cf LXX^{MSS}.
6, 16: (*labe*) *autēn:* so with Vet Lat.
6, 17: (*labe*) *to 'ēpar*: so Vet Lat; cf 8, 2.

NRSV

[2]and the dog came out with him and went along with them. So they both journeyed along, and when the first night overtook them they camped by the Tigris river. [3]Then the young man went down to wash his feet in the Tigris river. Suddenly a large fish leaped up from the water and tried to swallow the young man's foot, and he cried out. [4]But the angel said to the young man, "Catch hold of the fish and hang on to it!" So the young man grasped the fish and drew it up on the land. [5]Then the angel said to him, "Cut open the fish and take out its gall, heart, and liver. Keep them with you, but throw away the intestines. For its gall, heart, and liver are useful as medicine." [6]So after cutting open the fish the young man gathered together the gall, heart, and liver; then he roasted and ate some of the fish, and kept some to be salted.

The two continued on their way together until they were near Media.[a] [7]Then the young man questioned the angel and said to him, "Brother Azariah, what medicinal value is there in the fish's heart and liver, and in the gall?" [8]He replied, "As for the fish's heart and liver, you must burn them to make a smoke in the presence of a man or woman afflicted by a demon or evil spirit, and every affliction will flee away and never remain with that person any longer. [9]And as for the gall, anoint a person's eyes where white films have appeared on them; blow upon them, upon the white films, and the eyes[b] will be healed."

[a] Other ancient authorities read *Ecbatana* [b] Gk *they*

COMMENTARY

6:2. A trio departs from Nineveh on the journey: the angel, the boy, and a dog. The narrator continues to remind us that the guide is really an angel in disguise. The dog (which reappears in 11:4) is probably a feature of underlying folktale.

They camp the first night along the Tigris River. In the story this marks the end of a long day, which began with the payment of Anna's wages (2:12). The geography is confused. Nineveh lies on the eastern side of the Tigris River; the travelers intend to travel farther east to Ecbatana (and Rages). There is no need for them to backtrack to the river.

❖ ❖ ❖ ❖

EXCURSUS: DAY AND NIGHT

The terms "day" (ἡμέρα *hēmera*) and "night" (νύξ *nux*) are significant in this story of blindness and sight. The distribution of the terms signals the flow of the plot. The word "day" occurs primarily at the beginning and end of the book (14 times in the first five chaps., 14 times in chaps. 8–11, and 4 more times in chaps. 12–14, but not at all in 6:1–8:18. The word "night" occurs almost exclusively in this central section (10 times in chaps. 6–8, and once in 10:7 [Anna weeps all night]; it occurs only one other time, when Tobit is afflicted with blindness in 2:9). Of the ten occurrences between chapters 6 and 8, seven refer to the wedding night of Tobiah and Sarah. Of the three remaining uses, two refer to the wedding nights of the previous bridegrooms (6:14; 7:11) and one to the travelers' first night on the journey. Thus the following pattern emerges:

	1:1–6:1	6:2–8:18	8:19–11:18	12:1–14:15
day	14x	——	14x	4x
night (wedding)	——	7x	——	——
night (other)	1x	3x	1x	——

The story begins with Tobit walking "all the *days* of his life" in truth and righteousness (1:3). He buries a man on Pentecost after *sunset* (2:4, 7) and is then plunged into night (2:9). Tobiah joins him in a journey into night—a night that begins with the journey into Media (6:2) and ends in Ecbatana as the servants fill in a grave before dawn (8:18). "Night," which had begun as a word of sorrow (2:9; 6:14; 7:11), gradually becomes a word of joy (6:11, 13, 16; 7:10-11): "They slept the whole night" (8:9). Anna, however, does not yet know of the transition from night to day. She still keeps watch by *day,* goes home at *sunset,* and weeps all *night* (10:7). But her sunset has already been conquered by the dawn in Ecbatana. Tobiah's journey into night (6:1–8:18) has resulted in a return to daylight both for Sarah, whose previous wedding *nights* ended in disaster (6:14; 7:11), but who now celebrates a fourteen-*day* wedding feast (8:20; 10:7), and for Tobit, who celebrates his return to light by another seven-*day* feast with the newlyweds (11:18). The final chapters of the book tell of the happy length of *days* of them all.

❖ ❖ ❖ ❖

6:3-4. A very large fish leaps out of the water and attempts to swallow Tobiah's foot. In G^I the fish attempts to swallow Tobiah whole! The fish serves as a symbol of the power of death. The struggle with the fish occurs at night, a traditional time for the dominance of evil. This night is the first on the journey that will lead Tobiah to risk death in order to deliver Sarah from Asmodeus. The fish symbolizes not only the beginning of this struggle with death, but also the means to life. Once it is conquered, its vital parts become for Tobiah the means to heal both his bride and his father. Thus the fish recalls the traditional association of water and water monsters with chaos, which, once conquered, become the means for creation (e.g., Gen 1:2; Job 38:8-11; 40:25–41:26; Pss 74:13-15; 89:10-11; 104:25-26; 107:23-30; Isa 27:1-3; 51:9-11).[82]

6:5. The procedure described here concerning the parts of the fish to be used for each healing is repeated twice more for each healing, suggesting the folktale "law of three" and increasing anticipation of the actual events. In answer to Tobiah's question, Raphael tells him what will happen when the fish's heart and liver are burned (v. 8). In response to Tobiah's fear, Raphael makes the instruction specific to him: "When you go into the bridal chamber . . ." (vv. 17-18). The final repetition describes Tobiah's actions on the wedding night (8:2-3). Each repetition grows more specific in detail until Sarah's deliverance is accomplished. The initial instructions for Tobit's healing also are given by Raphael in response to Tobiah's question (v. 9). The two repetitions in chap. 11 (11:7-8, 11-13) increase in specific detail. When each healing finally occurs, the reader knows exactly what to expect.

6:6. Tobiah follows Raphael's instructions precisely, a continuing sign of his trusting obedience. He then eats part of the fish. It will become important to note that there is no mention that Raphael also ate (cf. 12:19). Finally, Tobiah salts the fish. This may simply be a reference to a common means of preserving food, but it may also reflect the belief that salt is a purifying agent that can drive away evil influences, thus removing the deathly quality of the fish and enhancing its life-giving properties.[83]

6:7-9. Raphael now assumes his role as messenger. In answer to Tobiah's question, he tells him how to use the parts of the fish for healing. His reply indicates that he knows who has which affliction. In the instruction regarding evil spirits he mentions "a man or a woman"; in the instruction regarding eye ailments he simply mentions "a man" or "a person" (ἄνθρωπος *anthrōpos*). The reader knows that it is a woman who is afflicted by a demon and a man who is blind. (See Reflections at 6:10-18.)

82. See also *Enûma elish* 4.31-146, in *ANET*, 66-67.

83. See F. Zimmermann, *The Book of Tobit: An English Translation with Introduction and Commentary*, Dropsie College Edition, JAL (New York: Harper and Bros., 1958) 80-81.

TOBIT 6:10-18, RAPHAEL'S INSTRUCTIONS

NAB

10 When they had entered Media and were getting close to Ecbatana, 11 Raphael said to the boy, "Brother Tobiah!" He answered, "Yes, what is it?" Raphael continued: "Tonight we must stay with Raguel, who is a relative of yours. He has a daughter named Sarah, 12 but no other child. Since you are Sarah's closest relative, you before all other men have the right to marry her. Also, her father's estate is rightfully yours to inherit. Now the girl is sensible, courageous, and very

NRSV

10When he entered Media and already was approaching Ecbatana,[a] 11Raphael said to the young man, "Brother Tobias." "Here I am," he answered. Then Raphael[b] said to him, "We must stay this night in the home of Raguel. He is your relative, and he has a daughter named Sarah. 12He has no male heir and no daughter except Sarah only, and you, as next of kin to her, have before ll other men a hereditary claim on her. Also it is

[a] Other ancient authorities read *Rages* [b] Gk *he*

NAB

beautiful; and her father loves her dearly." 13 He continued: "Since you have the right to marry her, listen to me, brother. Tonight I will ask the girl's father to let us have her as your bride. When we return from Rages, we will hold the wedding feast for her. I know that Raguel cannot keep her from you or let her become engaged to another man; that would be a capital crime according to the decree in the Book of Moses, and he knows that it is your right, before all other men, to marry his daughter. So heed my words, brother; tonight we must speak for the girl, so that we may have her engaged to you. And when we return from Rages, we will take her and bring her back with us to your house."

14 Tobiah objected, however: "Brother Azariah, I have heard that this woman has already been married seven times, and that her husbands died in their bridal chambers. On the very night they approached her, they dropped dead. And I have heard it said that it was a demon who killed them. 15 So now I too am afraid of this demon. Because he loves her, he does not harm her; but he does slay any man who wishes to come close to her. I am my father's only child. If I should die, I would bring my father and mother down to their grave in sorrow over me. And they have no other son to bury them!"

16 Raphael said to him: "Do you not remember your father's orders? He commanded you to marry a woman from your own family. So now listen to me, brother; do not give another thought to this demon, but marry Sarah. I know that tonight you shall have her for your wife! 17 When you go into the bridal chamber, take the fish's liver and heart, and place them on the embers for the incense. 18 As soon as the demon smells the odor they give off, he will flee and never again show himself near her. Then when you are about to have intercourse with her, both of you first rise up to pray. Beg the Lord of heaven to show you mercy and grant you deliverance. But do not be afraid, for she was set apart for you before the world existed. You will save her, and she will go with you. And I suppose that you will have children by her, who will take the place of brothers for you. So do not worry."

When Tobiah heard Raphael say that she was

NRSV

right for you to inherit her father's possessions. Moreover, the girl is sensible, brave, and very beautiful, and her father is a good man." 13He continued, "You have every right to take her in marriage. So listen to me, brother; tonight I will speak to her father about the girl, so that we may take her to be your bride. When we return from Rages we will celebrate her marriage. For I know that Raguel can by no means keep her from you or promise her to another man without incurring the penalty of death according to the decree of the book of Moses. Indeed he knows that you, rather than any other man, are entitled to marry his daughter. So now listen to me, brother, and tonight we shall speak concerning the girl and arrange her engagement to you. And when we return from Rages we will take her and bring her back with us to your house."

14Then Tobias said in answer to Raphael, "Brother Azariah, I have heard that she already has been married to seven husbands and that they died in the bridal chamber. On the night when they went in to her, they would die. I have heard people saying that it was a demon that killed them. 15It does not harm her, but it kills anyone who desires to approach her. So now, since I am the only son my father has, I am afraid that I may die and bring my father's and mother's life down to their grave, grieving for me—and they have no other son to bury them."

16But Raphael[a] said to him, "Do you not remember your father's orders when he commanded you to take a wife from your father's house? Now listen to me, brother, and say no more about this demon. Take her. I know that this very night she will be given to you in marriage. 17When you enter the bridal chamber, take some of the fish's liver and heart, and put them on the embers of the incense. An odor will be given off; 18the demon will smell it and flee, and will never be seen near her any more. Now when you are about to go to bed with her, both of you must first stand up and pray, imploring the Lord of heaven that mercy and safety may be granted to you. Do not be afraid, for she was set apart for you before the world was made. You will save her, and she will go with you. I presume that you

[a] Gk *he*

NAB	NRSV
his kinswoman, of his own family's lineage, he fell deeply in love with her, and his heart became set on her.	will have children by her, and they will be as brothers to you. Now say no more!" When Tobias heard the words of Raphael and learned that she was his kinswoman,[a] related through his father's lineage, he loved her very much, and his heart was drawn to her. [a] Gk *sister*

COMMENTARY

6:10-11. Raphael announces that they are staying in Ecbatana at the house of Raguel. This has been the real goal of the journey all along (cf. 3:17; 5:6), though Tobiah has thought that they were heading for Rages.

The second long day of this story (6:10–8:18) is hastened on its way by the constant repetition of "night," ("this very night," vv. 11, 13, 16; 7:10-11). Suspense builds as attention is continually drawn to Sarah's eighth wedding night: "Tonight we must stay with Raguel" (v. 11); "Tonight I will ask the girl's father" (v. 13); "Tonight we must speak for the girl" (v. 13; see also 7:10-11).

6:12-13. Raphael continues to supply information as he exhorts Tobiah to marry Sarah. The exchange between Tobiah and Raphael is a virtual monologue by Raphael, punctuated by only a single objection from Tobiah. The marriage of Tobiah and Sarah will be founded on Tobiah's obedience to the message the angel brings. Raphael tells Tobiah that he, as the closest relative, has the right to marry her. He even states that Raguel would incur the death penalty for refusing the marriage, a penalty mentioned nowhere else with regard to endogamy.

6:14-15. Tobiah's speech manifests the qualities characteristic of him in the first section of the book. He speaks with the haste of youth; short clauses often linked by "and" come tumbling out without apparent order. But his speech makes up in passion what it lacks in organization. He musters all the arguments he knows to avoid what he fears is a life-threatening marriage.

Tobiah's speech contains the fourth repetition of the story of Sarah's seven previous husbands (see 3:8-9, 15). It contains all three of the basic facts told by the narrator (3:8): (1) Sarah has been married to seven husbands; (2) the wicked demon Asmodeus has killed them; (3) they have died before the marriage could be consummated. But Tobiah's own preoccupation is evident in his fourfold repetition that the bridegrooms have died: "her husbands died in the bridal chambers . . . they died . . . it was a demon who killed them . . . it kills any man who desires to approach her" (vv. 14-15). Finally Tobiah expresses his real fear: "If *I* should die" (v. 15, italics added). The demon's motive for killing Sarah's bridegrooms appears in the Qumran manuscript 4QTob[a], Greek MS 319, and the Old Latin: It is in love with her.

6:16-18. Raphael instructs Tobiah in the means to free Sarah from the demon Asmodeus—means that include not only the use of the fish entrails but also prayer. (It seems that Tobiah has already forgotten what he learned about the fish at the Tigris.) Raphael also declares that Sarah was set apart for Tobiah before the world existed. They are to be gifts to each other. Tobiah will save her from her affliction, and she will be his companion and the mother of his children.

Throughout the journey Tobiah obeys Raphael. He follows Raphael's curious instructions concerning the fish (vv. 3-6), and he allows Raphael to persuade him concerning marriage to Sarah. The willingness to marry a kinswoman also accords with his father's command (4:12-13). Having heard all of the angel's words, Tobiah immediately falls in love with Sarah—a strange comment to our modern ears. Tobiah loves her because she has been designated by God for him and because she is the means for his obedience to his father. Tobiah's love is an act of the will, not a movement of the emotions.

REFLECTIONS

1. Guided by an angel of God, Tobiah journeys into night and is threatened by a monster of chaos. Obedient to the angel's instructions, he conquers the watery monster and saves its life-giving parts. Through his obedience, not only he but also his father and his future wife will be brought from night into day. Christian life is often called the Way (see Acts 9:2; 18:25-26; 19:9, 23; 24:4, 14, 22). Living a Christian life can be described as a successful quest. We, too, go into night and are threatened by death and evil. But, like Tobiah, we are not alone. In various ways God leads us on the journey. Through obedience we and those whose lives we touch will be brought from night into eternal day. Our obedience is modeled on Christ, who is himself the Way (John 14:6).

2. The fish, symbol of chaos, becomes a means to life. The sage in the Wisdom of Solomon says that "God did not make death," there is "no destructive poison" in the creatures of the earth (Wis 1:13-14 NRSV). The poison results from being swallowed by created things, enslaved by them. How many healing drugs are death-dealing when used in excess! Tamed and applied wisely, however, they can restore life.

TOBIT 7:1–11:18

RESOLUTION AND RECOVERY

OVERVIEW

The three questions remaining at the end of the journey will be answered in the three-part resolution. Resolution 1 focuses on the question with which the journey ended: Will Tobiah meet Sarah, escape death, and deliver her from Asmodeus?

The arrival of Tobiah and Raphael at Ecbatana and at Raguel's house (7:1-2) commences the sequence of resolution 1. Tobiah's revelation of his kinship with Raguel (7:5), implying his right to Sarah (see 7:10), leads to his request that Raphael ask Raguel for Sarah as Tobiah's bride (7:9). Raguel overhears and objects in words similar to Tobiah's earlier words (7:11; cf. 6:14). Tobiah's insistence and his refusal to eat lead Raguel to agree to the betrothal (7:11). The betrothal itself has several consequences. First, the banquet continues, and Sarah and the bridal chamber are prepared (7:14-17). Subsequently, Tobiah is led to Sarah (8:1). He remembers Raphael's dual instructions (8:2). He burns the heart and liver of the fish, which results in the expulsion of the demon and his binding by Raphael (8:2-3). He prays with Sarah (8:4-8), and both survive the night and sleep peacefully (8:9). Thus the first major question (Will Tobiah marry Sarah, escape death, and deliver her from the demon?) is answered positively.

Between resolutions 1 and 2 appears a transitional sequence. Raguel, anticipating a negative answer to the question of Tobiah's survival, digs a grave for him (8:9-10). His discovery that Tobiah is still alive (8:14) has a threefold result: Raguel prays in thanksgiving (8:15-17); he has his servants fill in the grave (8:18), thus ending all reference to the death of Sarah's husbands; and he joyfully prepares a wedding feast (8:19).

The enforced delay caused by the wedding feast (8:19) leads directly into the two final sequences of the resolution. Because he cannot leave Ecbatana, Tobiah sends Raphael to collect the money (9:1-3). Here is the first mention of the money since the departure (5:19). The question of the money is resolved with dispatch. Raphael goes to Rages (9:5), obtains the money with the aid of the signed bond (cf. 5:3), and brings Gabael to the wedding feast, along with the money (9:6). The second major question of the resolution (Will Tobiah get the money?) has also been answered positively.

One question remains: Will Tobiah return safely and heal Tobit? The question is intensified because the enforced delay in Ecbatana has caused his parents to worry (10:1-7). At last Tobiah, Raphael, and Sarah depart for Nineveh (10:7–11:1). Armed with the gall of the fish and Raphael's repeated instruction (11:4, 7), Tobiah arrives, is announced by his mother (11:5-6), and heals his father (11:10-14). As a consequence of his healing, Tobit prays in thanksgiving (11:14-15) and in his joy becomes the cause of joy for the city (11:16-18). Sarah's arrival increases the joy (11:17), and the wedding feast is celebrated again (11:18). The final question is answered. Tobiah has returned safely with both money and bride and has healed his father. The grief of the exposition (3:1, 10) has been turned to the joy of the resolution. The challenge concerning Tobit's reward for charitable deeds (2:14) has also been answered.

TOBIT 7:1–8:21, SARAH'S HEALING

NAB

7 1 When they entered Ecbatana, Tobiah said, "Brother Azariah, lead me straight to our kinsman Raguel." So he brought him to the house of Raguel, whom they found seated by his courtyard gate. They greeted him first. He said to them, "Greetings to you too, brothers! Good health to you, and welcome!" When he brought them into his home, 2 he said to his wife Edna, "This young man looks just like my kinsman Tobit!" 3 So Edna asked them, "Who are you, brothers?" They answered, "We are of the exiles from Naphtali at Nineveh." 4 She said, "Do you know our kinsman Tobit?" They answered, "Indeed we do!" She asked, "Is he well?" 5 They answered, "Yes, he is alive and well." Then Tobiah exclaimed, "He is my father!" 6 Raguel sprang up and kissed him, shedding tears of joy. 7 But when he heard that Tobit had lost his eyesight, he was grieved and wept aloud. He said to Tobiah: "My child, God bless you! You are the son of a noble and good father. But what a terrible misfortune that such a righteous and charitable man should be afflicted with blindness!" He continued to weep in the arms of his kinsman Tobiah. 8 His wife Edna also wept for Tobit; and even their daughter Sarah began to weep.

9 Afterward, Raguel slaughtered a ram from the flock and gave them a cordial reception. When they had bathed and reclined to eat, Tobiah said to Raphael, "Brother Azariah, ask Raguel to let me marry my kinswoman Sarah." 10 Raguel overheard the words; so he said to the boy: "Eat and drink and be merry tonight, for no man is more entitled to marry my daughter Sarah than you, brother. Besides, not even I have the right to give her to anyone but you, because you are my closest relative. But I will explain the situation to you very frankly. 11 I have given her in marriage to seven men, all of whom were kinsmen of ours, and all died on the very night they approached her. But now, son, eat and drink. I am sure the

7, 1: *elthete:* so Vet Lat; cf LXX^{MSS}.

7, 2: *Tōbeith:* so LXX^{MSS}, Vet Lat, P.

7, 7: (v. 6: *eklausen*). *kai akousas ʿoti Tōbeith apōlesen tous ophthalmous ʿ eautou, elypēthē kai eklausen.* (*Kai elalēsen*): so with LXX^{B}, P; haplog.

7, 9: Omit *kai enipsanto:* so Vet Lat; variant of *elousanto.*

NRSV

7 Now when they[a] entered Ecbatana, Tobias[b] said to him, "Brother Azariah, take me straight to our brother Raguel." So he took him to Raguel's house, where they found him sitting beside the courtyard door. They greeted him first, and he replied, "Joyous greetings, brothers; welcome and good health!" Then he brought them into his house. 2He said to his wife Edna, "How much the young man resembles my kinsman Tobit!" 3Then Edna questioned them, saying, "Where are you from, brothers?" They answered, "We belong to the descendants of Naphtali who are exiles in Nineveh." 4She said to them, "Do you know our kinsman Tobit?" And they replied, "Yes, we know him." Then she asked them, "Is he[c] in good health?" 5They replied, "He is alive and in good health." And Tobias added, "He is my father!" 6At that Raguel jumped up and kissed him and wept. 7He also spoke to him as follows, "Blessings on you, my child, son of a good and noble father!"[d] O most miserable of calamities that such an upright and beneficent man has become blind!" He then embraced his kinsman Tobias and wept. 8His wife Edna also wept for him, and their daughter Sarah likewise wept. 9Then Raguel[b] slaughtered a ram from the flock and received them very warmly.

When they had bathed and washed themselves and had reclined to dine, Tobias said to Raphael, "Brother Azariah, ask Raguel to give me my kinswoman[e] Sarah." 10But Raguel overheard it and said to the lad, "Eat and drink, and be merry tonight. For no one except you, brother, has the right to marry my daughter Sarah. Likewise I am not at liberty to give her to any other man than yourself, because you are my nearest relative. But let me explain to you the true situation more fully, my child. 11I have given her to seven men of our kinsmen, and all died on the night when they went in to her. But now, my child, eat and drink, and the Lord will act on behalf of you both." But Tobias said, "I will neither eat nor drink anything

[a] Other ancient authorities read *he* [b] Gk *he* [c] Other ancient authorities add *alive and* [d] Other ancient authorities add *When he heard that Tobit had lost his sight, he was stricken with grief and wept. Then he said,* [e] Gk *sister*

NAB

Lord will look after you both." Tobiah answered,
"I will eat or drink nothing until you set aside
what belongs to me."

Raguel said to him: "I will do it. She is yours
according to the decree of the Book of Moses.
Your marriage to her has been decided in heaven!
Take your kinswoman; from now on you are her
love, and she is your beloved. She is yours today
and ever after. And tonight, son, may the Lord of
heaven prosper you both. May he grant you mercy
and peace." 12 Then Raguel called his daughter
Sarah, and she came to him. He took her by the
hand and gave her to Tobiah with the words:
"Take her according to the law. According to the
decree written in the Book of Moses she is your
wife. Take her and bring her back safely to your
father. And may the God of heaven grant both of
you peace and prosperity." 13 He then called her
mother and told her to bring a scroll, so that he
might draw up a marriage contract stating that he
gave Sarah to Tobiah as his wife according to the
decree of the Mosaic law. Her mother brought
the scroll, and he drew up the contract, to which
they affixed their seals.

14 Afterward they began to eat and drink. 15
Later Raguel called his wife Edna and said, "My
love, prepare the other bedroom and bring the
girl there." 16 She went and made the bed in the
room, as she was told, and brought the girl there.
After she had cried over her, she wiped away the
tears and said: 17 "Be brave, my daughter. May
the Lord of heaven grant you joy in place of your
grief. Courage, my daughter." Then she left.

8 1 When they had finished eating and drinking, the girl's parents wanted to retire.
They brought the young man out of the dining
room and led him into the bedroom. 2 At this
point Tobiah, mindful of Raphael's instructions,
took the fish's liver and heart from the bag which
he had with him, and placed them on the embers
for the incense. 3 The demon, repelled by the
odor of the fish, fled into Upper Egypt; Raphael
pursued him there and bound him hand and foot.
Then Raphael returned immediately. 4 When the
girl's parents left the bedroom and closed the door

7, 13: (*nomou*) *kai ēnegken ˈē mētēr autēs kai egrapse kai esphragisanto*: so LXX[P]; cf LXX[MSS], Vet Lat.

8, 3: Place *anō* after *ta*: so LXX[d,P], P, Vet Lat; (*kai*) *ēlthen* (*parachrēma*): so Vet Lat.

NRSV

until you settle the things that pertain to me." So
Raguel said, "I will do so. She is given to you in
accordance with the decree in the book of Moses,
and it has been decreed from heaven that she be
given to you. Take your kinswoman;[a] from now
on you are her brother and she is your sister. She
is given to you from today and forever. May the
Lord of heaven, my child, guide and prosper you
both this night and grant you mercy and peace."
12Then Raguel summoned his daughter Sarah.
When she came to him he took her by the hand
and gave her to Tobias,[b] saying, "Take her to be
your wife in accordance with the law and decree
written in the book of Moses. Take her and bring
her safely to your father. And may the God of
heaven prosper your journey with his peace."
13Then he called her mother and told her to bring
writing material; and he wrote out a copy of a
marriage contract, to the effect that he gave her
to him as wife according to the decree of the law
of Moses. 14Then they began to eat and drink.

15Raguel called his wife Edna and said to her,
"Sister, get the other room ready, and take her
there." 16So she went and made the bed in the
room as he had told her, and brought Sarah[c]
there. She wept for her daughter.[c] Then, wiping
away the tears,[d] she said to her, "Take courage,
my daughter; the Lord of heaven grant you joy[e]
in place of your sorrow. Take courage, my daughter." Then she went out.

8 When they had finished eating and drinking they wanted to retire; so they took the
young man and brought him into the bedroom.
2Then Tobias remembered the words of Raphael,
and he took the fish's liver and heart out of the
bag where he had them and put them on the
embers of the incense. 3The odor of the fish so
repelled the demon that he fled to the remotest
parts[f] of Egypt. But Raphael followed him, and at
once bound him there hand and foot.

4When the parents[g] had gone out and shut the
door of the room, Tobias got out of bed and said
to Sarah,[c] "Sister, get up, and let us pray and
implore our Lord that he grant us mercy and
safety." 5So she got up, and they began to pray

[a] Gk *sister* [b] Gk *him* [c] Gk *her* [d] Other ancient authorities read *the tears of her daughter* [e] Other ancient authorities read *favor* [f] Or *fled through the air to the parts* [g] Gk *they*

NAB

behind them, Tobiah arose from bed and said to
his wife, "My love, get up. Let us pray and beg
our Lord to have mercy on us and to grant us
deliverance." 5 She got up, and they started to
pray and beg that deliverance might be theirs. He
began with these words:

"Blessed are you, O God of our fathers;
praised be your name forever and ever.
Let the heavens and all your creation
praise you forever.
6 You made Adam and you gave him his wife
Eve
to be his help and support;
and from these two the human race
descended.
You said, 'It is not good for the man to be
alone;
let us make him a partner like himself.'
7 Now, Lord, you know that I take this wife of mine
not because of lust,
but for a noble purpose.
Call down your mercy on me and on her,
and allow us to live together to a happy
old age."

8 They said together, "Amen, amen," 9 and
went to bed for the night.

But Raguel got up and summoned his servants.
With him they went out to dig a grave, 10 for
he said, "I must do this, because if Tobiah should
die, we would be subjected to ridicule and insult."
11 When they had finished digging the grave,
Raguel went back into the house and called his
wife, 12 saying, "Send one of the maids in to see
whether Tobiah is alive or dead, so that if necessary we may bury him without anyone's knowing
about it." 13 She sent the maid, who lit a lamp,
opened the bedroom door, went in, and found
them sound asleep together. 14 The maid went
out and told the girl's parents that Tobiah was
alive, and that there was nothing wrong. 15 Then
Raguel praised the God of heaven in these words:

8, 6: (*Adam kai*) *edōkas* (*autǭ*): so LXX (all other MSS), Vet Lat, V.
8, 7: (*nyn*) *kyrie sy ginōskeis 'oti* (*ouchi*): so LXX[MSS], Vet Lat, V. (*synkatagērasai*) (*'ygiainontas:* so Vet Lat; cf P, V.
8, 13: (*apesteil*) *en . . .* (*'ēps*) *en . . .* (*ēnoix*) *en:* so with Vet Lat; cf LXX[MSS], P. Omit *kai 'ypnountas:* so LXX[MSS], Vet Lat, P; variant of preceding word.
8, 15: (*eulogēs*) *en . . .* (*eip*) *en:* so with LXX[MSS], Vet Lat; (*eulogią*) *'agią kai* (*katharą*): so Vet Lat[MSS]; (*se*) *pantes 'oi eklektoi sou eulogeitōsan se* (*eis*): so Vet Lat (1 MS); cf LXX[MSS], Vet Lat[MSS]. P: haplog.

NRSV

and implore that they might be kept safe. Tobias[a]
began by saying,

"Blessed are you, O God of our ancestors,
and blessed is your name in all generations
forever.
Let the heavens and the whole creation bless
you forever.
6 You made Adam, and for him you made his
wife Eve
as a helper and support.
From the two of them the human race has
sprung.
You said, 'It is not good that the man should
be alone;
let us make a helper for him like himself.'
7 I now am taking this kinswoman of mine,
not because of lust,
but with sincerity.
Grant that she and I may find mercy
and that we may grow old together."

8 And they both said, "Amen, Amen." 9 Then they
went to sleep for the night.

But Raguel arose and called his servants to him,
and they went and dug a grave, 10 for he said, "It
is possible that he will die and we will become
an object of ridicule and derision." 11 When they
had finished digging the grave, Raguel went into
his house and called his wife, 12 saying, "Send one
of the maids and have her go in to see if he is
alive. But if he is dead, let us bury him without
anyone knowing it." 13 So they sent the maid, lit
a lamp, and opened the door; and she went in
and found them sound asleep together. 14 Then the
maid came out and informed them that he was
alive and that nothing was wrong. 15 So they
blessed the God of heaven, and Raguel[b] said,

"Blessed are you, O God, with every pure
blessing;
let all your chosen ones bless you.[c]
Let them bless you forever.
16 Blessed are you because you have made me
glad.
It has not turned out as I expected,
but you have dealt with us according to your
great mercy.
17 Blessed are you because you had compassion
on two only children.

[a] Gk *He* [b] Gk *they* [c] Other ancient authorities lack this line

NAB

"Blessed are you, O God, with every holy and
pure blessing!
Let all your chosen ones praise you;
let them bless you forever!
16 Blessed are you, who have made me glad;
what I feared did not happen.
Rather you have dealt with us
according to your great mercy.
17 Blessed are you, for you were merciful
toward two only children.
Grant them, Master, mercy and deliverance,
and bring their lives to fulfillment
with happiness and mercy."
18 Then he told his servants to fill in the grave
before dawn.
19 He asked his wife to bake many loaves of
bread; he himself went out to the herd and picked
out two steers and four rams which he ordered
to be slaughtered. So the servants began to prepare the feast. 20 He summoned Tobiah and made
an oath in his presence, saying: "For fourteen days
you shall not stir from here, but shall remain here
eating and drinking with me; and you shall bring
joy to my daughter's sorrowing spirit. 21 Take, to
begin with, half of whatever I own when you go
back in good health to your father; the other half
will be yours when I and my wife die. Be of good
cheer, my son! I am your father, and Edna is your
mother; and we belong to you and to your beloved now and forever. So be happy, son!"

8, 20: (*Tōbeian kai*) *ōmosen autǭ kai eipen* (*deka*): so LXX^{d,p}, Vet Lat; cf 9, 3: 10, 7.

NRSV

Be merciful to them, O Master, and keep them
safe;
bring their lives to fulfillment
in happiness and mercy."
18Then he ordered his servants to fill in the grave
before daybreak.
19After this he asked his wife to bake many
loaves of bread; and he went out to the herd and
brought two steers and four rams and ordered
them to be slaughtered. So they began to make
preparations. 20Then he called for Tobias and
swore on oath to him in these words:[a] "You shall
not leave here for fourteen days, but shall stay
here eating and drinking with me; and you shall
cheer up my daughter, who has been depressed.
21Take at once half of what I own and return in
safety to your father; the other half will be yours
when my wife and I die. Take courage, my child.
I am your father and Edna is your mother, and
we belong to you as well as to your wife[b] now
and forever. Take courage, my child."

[a] Other ancient authorities read *Tobias and said to him* [b] Gk *sister*

COMMENTARY

The events ending this second long day of the story (6:10–8:18) concern not only the deliverance of Sarah from the demon that has been afflicting her, but also the joining of two families. The significance of family is evident, first, in the scene in which the travelers arrive. The recognition of Tobiah as Tobit's son is a cause of great joy. Second, the close family relationship gives reason both for the marriage to happen and for Raguel's hesitation out of fear for Tobiah's life. Finally, the marriage itself is the joining not only of Tobiah and Sarah, but also of their families.

Tobiah's betrothal to Sarah (7:1-17), including the preceding departure from his father (5:17-22) and subsequent departure from the bride's home (10:7-13), is modeled on the biblical type scene of betrothal. Elements that recur in the betrothal type scene (e.g., Gen 24:1-61; 29:1-14; Exod 2:15-22) are a traveler, one or more young women, a well, the drawing of water, a sense of haste, and a meal.[84] Not all of these elements appear in this scene.

84. See R. Alter, *The Art of Biblical Narrative* (New York: Basic Books, 1981) 51-61.

7:1-2. When the travelers arrive in Ecbatana, Tobiah puts his newfound love for Sarah into action. He orders his guide, Raphael, to bring him immediately to the house of Raguel. Raphael complies with dispatch.

Raguel, whose name means "friend of God," shows in this scene the characteristic virtues of another friend of God, Abraham. Abraham is noted for his hospitality, entertaining angels unawares (Gen 18:1-15; cf. Gen 19:1), and for his fatherhood, both of a beloved child and of a host of nations (Gen 17:4-5). Raguel is also generous in hospitality. As soon as he has greeted Tobiah and Raphael, he brings them into his home and introduces them to his family.

"Raguel" is also the name of Moses' father-in-law (spelled "Reuel" in most translations; Exod 2:18; Num 10:29) and of an archangel in *1 Enoch* 20:4; see also *1 Enoch* 23:4).[85] Tobiah has been instructed by his father to follow the example of the ancestors in finding a wife from his own kindred. He has not only done that, but has also found a father-in-law worthy of his ancestors.

7:3-5. The scene of welcome is based primarily on Jacob's betrothal (Gen 29:1-30). In Genesis, Jacob, the son sent by his father to find a proper bride (Gen 28:1-5), arrives in Haran and greets a group of shepherds. When Tobiah and Raphael arrive at the house of Raguel, they have the following conversation with Edna:

Gen 29:4-6	Tob 7:3-5
Jacob said to them, "Brothers, where do you come from?" They said, "We are from Haran."	Edna asked them and said to them, "Where are you from, brothers?" And they said to her, "We are descendants of Naphtali exiled to Nineveh."
He said to them, "Do you know Laban son of Nahor?" They said, "We know him."	And she said to them, "Do you know Tobit our brother?" And they said to her, "We know him."
He said to them, "Is he well?" "He is well," they replied.	And she said to them, "Is he well?" And they said to her, "He is alive and well."

85. *APOT* 2.210, 204.

The two betrothal scenes are linked by the key word ὑγιαίνω (*hygiainō*, "to be well"). This concept is highly significant for the book of Tobit. About two-thirds of the occurrences of the word in the Septuagint are found in the book of Tobit.[86] The two passages also fall into a similar pattern. The traveler is greeted with embraces when he makes himself known as a relative (Gen 29:12-13; see Tob 7:6). He loves his prospective bride (Gen 29:18; see Tob 6:18), who is beautiful (Gen 29:17; see Tob 6:12). The father of the bride is reluctant to agree to the marriage (Gen 29:23-27; see Tob 7:10-11), and in both cases seven is a significant number. Laban requires Jacob to serve seven years for Leah and seven more for Rachel (Gen 29:20, 27); Raguel is reluctant to agree to Tobiah's marriage to Sarah because of the deaths of seven previous husbands (Tob 7:11). Jacob serves a total of fourteen years; Tobiah and Sarah have a fourteen-day wedding feast (Tob 8:20).

The betrothal scene of Tobiah also resembles the betrothal scene of Isaac (Gen 24:1-67). The two scenes are linked by structure and vocabulary. In both scenes, the father sends someone (servant or son) to find a bride from his own kindred (Gen 24:3-4; see Tob 4:12-13), although Tobit is unaware that this is the purpose of his son's journey. The man in whose care the future bride is found prepares a meal for the traveler (Gen 24:33; see Tob 7:9), but the traveler refuses to eat until the betrothal has been arranged (Gen 24:33; see Tob 7:11). The host yields, recognizing that the marriage has been decided by the Lord (Gen 24:50; see Tob 7:11). He gives the woman to the traveler, saying, "Take her with you" (Gen 24:51; see Tob 7:12). When the host wants to delay the travelers, the servant/son asks, "Let me go back to my master/father" (Gen 24:56; see Tob 10:7); the return journey follows immediately.

The key word εὐοδόω (*euodoō*, "to prosper, make successful") also links the two scenes. The word occurs seven times in the Septuagint of Genesis 24 (LXX Gen 24:12, 21, 27, 40, 42, 48, 56). It appears in the words of Abraham, who sends his servant (Isaac's surrogate) to find a bride for his son from his kindred. It occurs in the

86. There are 48 occurrences of ὑγιαίνω (*hygiainō*) in the Septuagint; of these, 25 are in the Sinaiticus recension of Tobit and 8 in the recension represented by Vaticanus and Alexandrinus. There are only 15 additional occurrences in the Septuagint.

prayers and hopes of the servant and in the servant's account of his mission. In the book of Tobit, *euodoō* is found in Tobit's hope for his son's journey. In the wedding ceremony, Raguel prays for Tobiah and Sarah: "May the Lord of heaven prosper you both" (v. 11; see also v. 12). At their departure, Raguel repeats his prayer (10:11), and Edna extends the hope for prosperity to them all (10:12). Finally, the word occurs in Tobiah's own account of his journey (10:13; 11:15).

7:6-8. The theory of retribution surfaces again in Raguel's exclamation concerning Tobit. He repeats the adjectives used throughout the work to describe Tobit, "good and noble, upright and charitable" (cf. 1:3; 9:6; 14:2). He bewails the disaster that has befallen Tobit in his blindness. How is it that such a good person could be overtaken by suffering rather than prosperity (cf. 2:14)?

The scene is filled with tears. Raguel weeps; Edna weeps; Sarah weeps. They weep for joy at recognizing a relative. They weep in sorrow over Tobit's misfortune.

7:9. From this point on Raguel, the host, seems continually occupied with banquets. The first of these feasts is spread in welcome of the two travelers. The scene echoes Genesis 18, where Abraham and Sarah prepare a feast for God in the person of three strangers.

The marriage scene presents the crisis in Tobiah's development into a mature person. He has already begun to take control of the action by his command that Raphael bring him to the house of Raguel (v. 1). As they recline to eat, Tobiah gives Raphael another command: "Ask Raguel to let me marry my kinswoman Sarah" (v. 9). This statement reveals several things about Tobiah at this crucial moment. He is not yet ready to take his life in his own hands and ask in his own name; he is still dependent on Raphael, the guardian appointed by his father. But that relationship is changing. Although he asks Raphael to make the request, he has made his own decision and is beginning to act on it with dispatch.

7:10-14. Raguel is caught in a dilemma regarding his daughter. He knows that he must obey the Mosaic law (as interpreted in his time) and marry her to a near kinsman (see 6:12-13). According to the decision rendered regarding the daughters of Zelophehad (Num 36:5-12), the daughters of a man who has no sons must marry into a clan of their own ancestral tribe, lest their heritage pass from one tribe to another.

But, according to the Qumran text 4QTob[b], Raguel loves Sarah dearly. He is aggrieved over the misfortune of the seven previous bridegrooms, and he repeats the story for the fifth and final time. Like the maids (3:8-9), he knows nothing of Asmodeus. But he adds yet another note to increase the suspense: All of the other bridegrooms, like Tobiah, were kinsmen. Raguel also knows nothing of Raphael's angelic status and his advice. And he is concerned for good reason. Perhaps even the keenness of his hearing can be attributed to his fearful anticipation of Tobiah's question.

The next statement Tobiah makes signals the turning point in the depiction of his character. At this moment he takes responsibility for his own life and decisions: "I will neither eat nor drink anything until you settle what belongs to me" (v. 11). From here on Tobiah is in charge of his own actions. He is ready to become the instrument of healing. In spite of his reluctance, Raguel is persuaded by Tobiah's persistence to agree to an immediate marriage.

The terms "brother" (ἀδελφός *adelphos*) and "sister" (ἀδελφή *adelphē*) are terms of endearment, expressing the intimate relationship between husband and wife or between lovers (see Cant 4:9-10, 12; 5:1-2; 8:1). Tobit uses the term "sister" for Anna (5:22; 10:6), as do Raguel for Edna (7:15) and Tobit for Sarah (8:4, 7). Both of Sarah's parents call her Tobiah's "sister" (8:21; 10:12). The term contributes to the idea that marriage joins not only two individuals, but also two families.

The marriage ceremony itself consists of several elements: First, the father gives the bride to her prospective husband, joining their hands (i.e., giving her hand in marriage). Second, there is an oral statement of the marriage, in which the father proclaims the marriage and declares it to be in accordance with the law of Moses; the father also blesses the couple. Third, a written contract is completed. Finally, a meal is eaten. All members of the family are involved in the ceremony. The father and the bride have major roles; the bride's mother brings the material for the written contract.

The formula pronounced by Raguel, "Take your sister; from now on you are her brother and she is your sister, given to you from this day and forever" (v. 11), echoes the ancient marriage formula found at Elephantine. It is unusual, however, that the father rather than the bridegroom makes the statement. In the "Contract of Mibtahiah's Third Marriage" (5th cent. BCE), the formula reads: "She is my wife and I am her husband from this day forever."[87]

The ceremony is permeated with references to the law and customs concerning marriage. Raphael has already exhorted Tobiah to marry Sarah in accord with his father's command (6:16). He states that Raguel must give Sarah to Tobiah under pain of death, "according to the decree in the Book of Moses" (6:13). Raguel reiterates this obligation (v. 10) and refers to "the decree of the book of Moses" twice in the marriage ceremony (vv. 11-12). The written contract also states that "he gave Sarah to Tobiah as his wife according to the decree of the Mosiac law" (v. 13).

The marriage ceremony is reminiscent of Israel's covenant theology, for the relationship between husband and wife is one image used by the prophets to describe the covenant (see, e.g., Hosea 2; Jer 2:2). The marriage formula is echoed by the covenant formula: "I will be your God; you will be my people" (see Jer 30:22; Ezek 36:28). The Sinai covenant is also sealed by a meal (Exod 24:1-2, 9-11). Eating together, sharing the same food, is a sign of sharing the same life.

7:15-17. Edna prepares her daughter for her eighth wedding night. She is a strong mother. She exhorts her daughter to courage in what seems to be an impossible situation. Twice she uses a word that appeared in connection with both healings, θάρσει (*tharsei*, "take courage"). The word occurs six times—first in Raphael's encouragement of Tobit (5:10), twice in this scene at the beginning of the wedding night (v. 17), twice at the conclusion of the wedding night (8:21), and once as Tobiah prepares to heal his father (11:11). Edna also pronounces a blessing over her daughter.

8:1. When the meal is finished, Tobiah is led to the bedroom, the site of his impending confrontation with Asmodeus. Apparently Sarah is already there (7:15-17).

8:2. Tobiah's chief action in the remainder of the book is healing. He follows Raphael's instructions regarding the fish's liver and heart. The notion that foul odors would drive away demons was common in the ancient world. Josephus reports that a certain Jewish exorcist named Eleazar drove demons out of people by holding a ring in which an aromatic herb was embedded to the nose of the one afflicted.[88] The practice, which comes from the tradition of folk medicine, is magical. In the book of Tobit, however, the magical nature is muted; it is recommended by an angel along with prayer as only one part of a complicated remedy.

8:3. The second part of the remedy requires the assistance of the angel. As soon as the demon is repelled by the foul odor, Raphael follows him to Egypt and binds him there. Upper Egypt is the southern part of that country. Except for the Nile Valley and the Mediterranean coastal fringe, Egypt is primarily desert, and demons were believed to live in desert places. The angel protects the human beings by taking the demon back where he belongs and preventing any further access to them. Raphael returns immediately, another indication of the haste that characterizes the angel.

8:4. The third part of the remedy is also given to Tobiah through Raphael's instruction. Tobiah and Sarah are to pray together. The prayer indicates that the banishing of the demon is not due to magic, but to the power of God.

8:5. Tobiah's prayer reveals that he is a worthy son of his father. He begins by blessing God with a threefold invocation.[89] The invocation is similar to Sarah's prayer (3:11), moving from God, to God's name, and then to God's works. But like his father, Tobiah will connect his story to that of his people, so he invokes God as the "God of the ancestors." He recognizes God as the God of both the past and the future, faithful to the ancestors and blessed forever.

87. *ANET*, 222. See Carey A. Moore, *Tobit*, AB 40A (Garden City, N.Y.: Doubleday, 1996) 225-33, for an analysis of ancient marriage practices.

88. Josephus *Antiquities of the Jews* 8.2.5. For a fuller treatment, see B. Kollmann, "Heilkunst im Buch Tobit," *ZAW* 106 (1994) 292-93. See also R. Pautrel and M. Lefebvre, "Trois textes de Tobie sur Raphaël," *RSR* 39 (1951) 120; G. J. Botterweck, "גר," *TDOT* 3:135.

89. See P. J. Griffin, "The Theology and Function of Prayer in the Book of Tobit" (Ph.D. diss., The Catholic University of America, 1984) esp. 174-85.

8:6. Tobiah then recalls an example from the Word of God that is appropriate to his situation (Gen 2:18-24; see also Gen 2:6). He acknowledges God as the creator, especially of human beings, and as the originator of marriage. From the mention of creation in v. 5, he moves to the creation story and aligns himself with the very beginning of the history of his people (see 3:3-5). In recalling the story of Adam and Eve, he cites three elements: God recognized that human beings should not be alone; the woman was created as help and support for the man; and the man and the woman are the parents of all the living. These elements he regards as the foundation of his own marriage. It is not good for him or for Sarah to be alone; they need each other. God has given them to each other. He hopes that Sarah will be his help—a help like himself. They are each the only child of faithful parents in exile. They are both obedient and honor God's law. They are even related. Suitable partners for each other, they hope also to follow the example of Adam and Eve and have children.

It is instructive to note what part of the story Tobiah leaves out. There is no mention of the tree of the knowledge of good and evil or of the strain in the relationship between Adam and Eve after they eat the fruit of that tree. His recalling of the creation story shows his hope for a positive marriage experience.

8:7. Tobiah's prayer reveals his respect for his new wife and his hopes for a long and happy marriage. He also believes in his own goodness. He knows that his marriage is based on obedience and faith, and not on lust. Obedience is the foundation of his love for Sarah (see 6:18). He asks for a blessing on the marriage bond sworn between them. He prays that God will be merciful to them and that they may grow old together. This is also a prayer for protection from the demon that has so recently been banished. Both he and Sarah have faced death and are now willing to pray for life. The Old Latin (VL) adds the request: "Bless us with children."

8:8. Sarah proclaims her agreement by saying, "Amen, Amen." These are the only words she speaks in the presence of another human being.

8:9a. A reasonable assumption in this verse is that Tobit and Sarah consummate their marriage. Jerome's Latin translation of the book of Tobit, however, adds a comment that Tobiah and Sarah did not consummate the marriage for three nights.[90] Tobiah says to her: "Sarah, get up and let us pray to God today and tomorrow and the next day. For these three nights we are joined to God; when the third night is over, we will be joined to each other. For we are the children of saints, and we must not be joined together like pagans who do not know God" (vv. 4-5). This interpretation is found nowhere else in the textual tradition. The Vulgate text, however, inspired the medieval Christian practice of the "Tobias-nights," three days of continence after the wedding before the marriage was consummated.

8:9*b*-10. Raguel's fear that Sarah's eighth bridegroom will meet the same fate as the previous seven is not allayed by the prayers and blessings of the marriage ceremony. While Tobiah and Sarah are sleeping peacefully, he gets up to dig the eighth grave. His fear is inspired not only by love for his daughter, but also by sensitivity about his own honor. Sarah has already recognized the importance of honor to her father (3:10). We glimpse it in the motive he gives for his secret gravedigging: If necessary, Tobiah might be buried "without anyone knowing about it." Otherwise, he says, "we would become an object of ridicule and derision."

Raguel's digging of the unnecessary grave for Tobiah is an example of dramatic irony. There is a disparity of understanding between readers and characters. We know the grave is unnecessary, but Raguel does not. A further ironic touch appears in Raguel's presumption that he can bury Tobiah without anyone's knowing about it. Will the guide ask no questions? Will his parents never miss him? Have the neighbors not noticed the arrival of the strangers?

8:11-14. In this scene Raguel and Edna appear together. The tenderness of Raguel's feeling is suggested by the fact that he cannot bring himself to check the situation. Instead, he asks his wife to send a maid to report on Tobiah's condition. The request indicates Edna's authority over the maids.

8:15. Upon hearing the good news that their

90. *Sarra exsurge deprecemus Deum hodie et cras et secundum cras quia istis tribus noctibus Deo vingimur terteia autem transacta nocte in nostro erimus coniugio filii quippe sanctorum sumus et non possumus ita coniungi sicut et gentes quae ignorant Deum.* Vg 8:4-5.

son-in-law is alive and sleeping peacefully, Raguel and Edna turn to prayer.[91] This prayer is usually attributed to Raguel alone (as the Greek in G^I suggests and the Old Latin states directly), and it seems to be the prayer of an individual. But G^{II} clearly says, "They blessed . . . they said."

This prayer, like those of Sarah and Tobiah, contains a threefold blessing. In contrast to the previous prayers, however, the invocation comes, not in the first strophe, but at the beginning of each strophe. Also in contrast to the previous prayers, God is addressed directly, "Blessed are you." The first strophe also calls God's people to bless the Lord.

8:16. After the blessing, the second strophe reports the current situation. Raguel (and Edna) had feared that this eighth bridegroom would die, but God has prevented that tragedy. They recognize that their good fortune is due to the mercy and compassion of God and that God has power to protect people. They acknowledge that God's ways are surprising.

8:17. The third strophe turns to thanksgiving and petition. God is addressed as "Master" (δέσποτα *despota*). Raguel and Edna ask God to care for their daughter and son-in-law, to be merciful to them, to keep them safe, and to give them full lives. God has already acted in compassion and mercy; to be consistent, God should continue to do so. They also seem to play on God's compassion by referring to Tobiah and Sarah as "two only children." Just as the prayer of Tobiah flowed from the context of marriage, so also the prayer of Raguel and Edna represents the petition of parents for their offspring.

8:18-20. Raguel orders the grave to be filled in and plans a second banquet more generous than the first. He prepares a fourteen-day wedding feast, twice as long as the ordinary celebration. His primary motivation is love for his daughter. He instructs his new son-in-law to bring joy to her spirit. The introduction to this banquet suggests even more strongly the parallel between Raguel and Abraham (cf. v. 19 with Gen 18:6-7).

8:21. Raguel tells Tobiah of his right to inherit Raguel's estate, a point Raphael had made on the journey (6:12). The inheritance will be received in two portions: half now, half when Raguel and Edna die. The right to inherit is set within the context of family. The marriage of Tobiah and Sarah has joined the families of Tobit and Raguel, the effect of which is that their property also becomes common. The property of both families will now come to the children of both families, and since they are the only children, Tobiah and Sarah will inherit all of the property.

The word that introduces both healings (θάρσει *tharsei*, "take courage") is repeated by Raguel at the end of his talk with Tobiah.

91. See Griffin, "The Theology and Function of Prayer in the Book of Tobit" esp. 186-204.

REFLECTIONS

1. Blessing is a sharing of God's life and power. In Gen 1:28, God blesses human beings with the power to participate in creation and the responsibility of caring for it. The genealogy in Genesis 5 is evidence of the effectiveness of God's blessing. God also blessed the ancestors—Abraham, Isaac, and Jacob—with children (Gen 17:15-17; 26:3; 28:13-15). Human beings are also empowered to bestow God's blessing. Isaac blessed Jacob (Gen 28:1-4). Rebekah's family blessed her (Gen 24:60). Jacob blessed his sons and through them the whole people (Gen 49:1-28).

The blessing of children by their parents has been a custom in many homes. But it is not just solemn occasions that call for blessing. Blessings are appropriate when one leaves the house, at bedtime, before an important event, at celebrations. Blessing is a sharing of God's life and power. It symbolizes the gift of life that parents have given their children; it symbolizes the gift of life that comes from God. Blessing renews the familys bond with one another and with God.

2. Tobiah is the chief minister of healing in the book. He prepares himself for this task by prayer, obedience, and love. All three of these preparations are other-centered. Through prayer, he recognizes that the power to heal belongs to God and that he is only the minister of that power. His obedience puts into action the recognition that the wisdom to heal belongs to God. This wisdom may be passed from one human being to another (or be communicated by an angel!), but its origin is in God. Tobiah's love for Sarah and for his father turns his focus totally toward them, and not to his own aggrandizement.

Power, love, and wisdom are demanded of those who exercise ministry in the Christian community today. The Holy Spirit bestows these gifts (see 2 Tim 1:7) so that the ministry of Christ may continue in the world. The person called to ministry must always remember that these gifts come from God. In a spirit of humility and obedience, faithful ministers will listen to God's Word in Scripture and in the voices of the needy as well. They will act, trusting in God's strength rather than in their own. They will lead others to grateful praise of God.

3. Marriage is a solemn undertaking. The marriage of Tobiah and Sarah begins in a ceremony of blessing. Both parents speak a blessing over the couple. The various forms for blessing a bride and groom in a modern wedding echo the prayer of Tobiah in recalling God's plan of mutual support in the creation of Adam and Eve and in praying for children and a happy old age.

The marriage of Tobiah and Sarah is founded on prayer and community. In their prayer (8:5-8), marriage is construed as a gift from God, dependent upon God for success and perseverance. It is seen as part of God's plan, reaching back to Adam and Eve, and as a participation in God's creation. Their marriage contributes to the ongoing life of God's people. It symbolizes the relationship between God and the people and the love of Christ for the church (Eph 5:31). When the broader focus is lost and a wedding is seen as a private event involving only two people, the creative, world-building power of marriage also is lost. Married people are a living symbol of the church and thus are cocreators with God.

4. God surprises us all with great generosity. In the Gospel of Luke, when the angel tells Zechariah, the father of John the Baptist, that he will have a son (Luke 1:13), Zechariah doubts the angel's word. Vincent McCorry, in *More Blessed Than Kings*,[92] has observed that this was not because Zechariah did not believe that God could give him a son, but because he doubted that God *would!* Raguel does not doubt that power of God to care for his family. His prayer is evidence of that. But he does not believe that God *will* care for his daughter and her eighth bridegroom. When Raguel realizes his mistake, his response his noteworthy. He is not embarrassed; he does not offer excuses. In genuine humility, he turns to God in surprised thanksgiving. Raguel is a worthy model to teach us how to respond to God's generous gifts.

92. Vincent P. McCorry, *More Blessed Than Kings* (Westminster, Md.: Newman, 1954) 14-15.

TOBIT 9:1-6, RECOVERY OF THE MONEY

NAB

9 1 Then Tobiah called Raphael and said to
him: 2 "Brother Azariah, take along with
you four servants and two camels and travel to
Rages. Go to Gabael's house and give him this
bond. Get the money and then bring him along
with you to the wedding celebration. 4 For you
know that my father is counting the days. If I

NRSV

9 Then Tobias called Raphael and said to
him, 2"Brother Azariah, take four servants
and two camels with you and travel to Rages. Go
to the home of Gabael, give him the bond, get
the money, and then bring him with you to the
wedding celebration. 4For you know that my
father must be counting the days, and if I delay

NAB	NRSV
should delay my return by a single day, I would cause him intense grief. 3 You witnessed the oath that Raguel has sworn; I cannot violate his oath." 5 So Raphael, together with the four servants and two camels, traveled to Rages in Media, where they stayed at Gabael's house. Raphael gave Gabael his bond and told him about Tobit's son Tobiah, and that he had married and was inviting him to the wedding celebration. Gabael promptly checked over the sealed moneybags, and they placed them on the camels. 6 The following morning they got an early start and traveled to the wedding celebration. When they entered Raguel's house, they found Tobiah reclining at table. He sprang up and greeted Gabael, who wept and blessed him, exclaiming: "O noble and good child, son of a noble and good, upright and charitable man, may the Lord grant heavenly blessing to you and to your wife, and to your wife's father and mother. Blessed be God, because I have seen the very image of my cousin Tobit!"	even one day I will upset him very much. 3 You are witness to the oath Raguel has sworn, and I cannot violate his oath."[a] 5 So Raphael with the four servants and two camels went to Rages in Media and stayed with Gabael. Raphael[b] gave him the bond and informed him that Tobit's son Tobias had married and was inviting him to the wedding celebration. So Gabael[c] got up and counted out to him the money bags, with their seals intact; then they loaded them on the camels.[d] 6 In the morning they both got up early and went to the wedding celebration. When they came into Raguel's house they found Tobias reclining at table. He sprang up and greeted Gabael,[e] who wept and blessed him with the words, "Good and noble son of a father good and noble, upright and generous! May the Lord grant the blessing of heaven to you and your wife, and to your wife's father and mother. Blessed be God, for I see in Tobias the very image of my cousin Tobit."
9, 5: (*auta*) *epi tas kamēlous:* so with LXX^{d,p}, Vet Lat^{MSS}, P. 9, 6: Omit *sou* after *patri*: so Vet Lat; cf LXX^{d,p}, P.	a In other ancient authorities verse 3 precedes verse 4 b Gk *He* c Gk *he* d Other ancient authorities lack *on the camels* e Gk *him*

COMMENTARY

9:1-2. The original purpose of the journey, at least in the minds of Tobit and Tobiah, was to recover the money Tobit had deposited with Gabael (1:14; 4:1-2, 20). Now Tobiah is prevented from accomplishing that goal by his marriage, which in fact was God's purpose for the journey. So Tobiah sends his faithful guide to recover the money and to bring Gabael to the wedding.

9:3-4. Tobiah knows that his journey will already be longer than he anticipated, and he does not want to lengthen the delay. He knows well that his father will be expecting him on a certain day and will grieve when he does not arrive. His concern is well founded (cf. 10:1-7).

The fourteen-day wedding feast is the longest stretch of time in the story. The progress of the feast is not recounted, but the sense of its length is indicated by the repeated reference to counting the days. Tobiah tells Raphael that Tobit is counting the days (9:4). The narrator tells the reader that Tobit is, indeed, counting the days (10:1). Thus, although the length of telling time for the fourteen-day wedding feast is short (8:19–10:7, only 16 verses), the sense of its length is conveyed psychologically by the notion of counting days and the sevenfold repetition of the word "day" between the two ends of the fourteen-day feast (8:19; 10:7*b*).

9:5. The pace of the interlude, Raphael's journey to get the money, is extremely rapid. There is no indication of the length of the two-way journey. An uninformed reader might assume that Raphael traveled to Rages one day and returned with Gabael the next. The distance to Rages, however, is approximately 185 miles. An angel might be able to cover the distance in a day, but what of the servants and camels and Gabael on the return journey? It is virtually impossible for the travelers to have reached Ecbatana before the wedding feast ended.

Gabael acknowledges the signed bond with no comment and immediately presents the money in sealed bags. Thus Tobiah's concern about how to demonstrate his right to the money is unfounded (5:2). The signed agreement between Tobit and Gabael is recognized as valid.

Raphael's other purpose in making the journey is to convey information. He informs Gabael of Tobiah's marriage and invites him to the wedding feast.

9:6. When the travelers return to Raguel's house, Gabael greets Tobiah with the key words that describe Tobit's character: "good and noble, righteous and charitable" (καλοῦ καὶ ἀγαθου, δικαίου καὶ ἐλεημοποιοῦ *kalou kai agathou, dikaiou kai eleēmopoiou*). He proclaims Tobiah to be "the very image" of his father; he is also "good and noble" (see 1:3; 7:7; 14:2). Gabael adds another blessing to the many already showered on this marriage. He, too, recognizes the familial implications of the union and extends the blessing to Sarah's parents. This is clear in the Old Latin text: "the father and mother of your wife [*patri et matri uxoris tuae*]." Siniaticus reads: "your father and your wife's mother." (See Reflections at 10:1–11:18.)

TOBIT 10:1–11:18, TOBIT'S HEALING

NAB

10 1 Meanwhile, day by day, Tobit was keeping track of the time Tobiah would need to go and to return. When the number of days was reached and his son did not appear, 2 he said, "I wonder what has happened. Perhaps he has been detained there; or perhaps Gabael is dead, and there is no one to give him the money." 3 And he began to worry. 4 His wife Anna said, "My son has perished and is no longer among the living!" And she began to weep aloud and to wail over her son: 5 "Alas, my child, light of my eyes, that I let you make this journey!" 6 But Tobit kept telling her: "Hush, do not think about it, my love; he is safe! Probably they have to take care of some unexpected business there. The man who is traveling with him is trustworthy, and is one of our own kinsmen. So do not worry over him, my love. He will be here soon." 7 But she retorted, "Stop it, and do not lie to me! My child has perished!" She would go out and keep watch all day at the road her son had taken, and she ate nothing. At sunset she would go back home to wail and cry the whole night through, getting no sleep at all. Now at the end of the fourteen-day wedding celebration which Raguel had sworn to hold for his daughter, Tobiah went to him and said: "Please let me go, for I know that my father

10, 7: (*ouk*) *egeueto* (*ouden*) *os:* so Vet Lat; cf LXX[MSS], P.

NRSV

10 Now, day by day, Tobit kept counting how many days Tobias[a] would need for going and for returning. And when the days had passed and his son did not appear, [2]he said, "Is it possible that he has been detained? Or that Gabael has died, and there is no one to give him the money?" [3]And he began to worry. [4]His wife Anna said, "My child has perished and is no longer among the living." And she began to weep and mourn for her son, saying, [5]"Woe to me, my child, the light of my eyes, that I let you make the journey." [6]But Tobit kept saying to her, "Be quiet and stop worrying, my dear;[b] he is all right. Probably something unexpected has happened there. The man who went with him is trustworthy and is one of our own kin. Do not grieve for him, my dear;[b] he will soon be here." [7]She answered him, "Be quiet yourself! Stop trying to deceive me! My child has perished." She would rush out every day and watch the road her son had taken, and would heed no one.[c] When the sun had set she would go in and mourn and weep all night long, getting no sleep at all.

Now when the fourteen days of the wedding celebration had ended that Raguel had sworn to observe for his daughter, Tobias came to him and said, "Send me back, for I know that my father

[a] Gk *he* [b] Gk *sister* [c] Other ancient authorities read *and she would eat nothing*

NAB

and mother do not believe they will ever see me again. So I beg you, father, let me go back to my father. I have already told you how I left him." 8 Raguel said to Tobiah: "Stay, my child, stay with me. I am sending messengers to your father Tobit, and they will give him news of you." 9 But Tobiah insisted, "No, I beg you to let me go back to my father."

10 Raguel then promptly handed over to Tobiah Sarah his wife, together with half of all his property: male and female slaves, oxen and sheep, asses and camels, clothing, money, and household goods. 11 Bidding them farewell, he let them go. He embraced Tobiah and said to him: "Good-bye, my son. Have a safe journey. May the Lord of heaven grant prosperity to you and to your wife Sarah. And may I see children of yours before I die!" 12 Then he kissed his daughter Sarah and said to her: "My daughter, honor your father-in-law and your mother-in-law, because from now on they are as much your parents as the ones who brought you into the world. Go in peace, my daughter; let me hear good reports about you as long as I live." Finally he said goodbye to them and sent them away.

13 Then Edna said to Tobiah: "My child and beloved kinsman, may the Lord bring you back safely, and may I live long enough to see children of you and of my daughter Sarah before I die. Before the Lord, I entrust my daughter to your care. Never cause her grief at any time in your life. Go in peace, my child. From now on I am your mother, and Sarah is your beloved. May all of us be prosperous all the days of our lives." She kissed them both and sent them away in peace.

14 When Tobiah left Raguel, he was full of happiness and joy, and he blessed the Lord of heaven and earth, the King of all, for making his journey so successful. Finally he said goodbye to Raguel and his wife Edna, and added, "May I honor you all the days of my life!"

11 1 Then they left and began their return journey. When they were near Kaserin,

10, 12: *kai ephilēsen Sarran tēn thygatera autou kai eipen autę̄ thygater tima* (*ton pentheron sou*) *kai tēn pentheran sou* (*'oti*): so with Vet Lat; cf LXX[p]; P. (*zōēs sou*) *badize* (*paidion*): so Vet Lat.

10, 13: (*autou kai*) *eulogēsen Ragouēl kai Ednan tēn gynaika autou kai* (*eipen*) *genoito moi timan 'ymas* (*pasas . . . zōēs*) *mou:* conj; cf LXX[MSS], P, Vet Lat; LXX[S] corrupt.

11, 1: *kai exēlthon kai eporeuthēsan tēn 'odon autōn* (*kai 'ōs*): so with P; cf LXX[d,p,44], Vet Lat; haplog.

NRSV

and mother do not believe that they will see me again. So I beg of you, father, to let me go so that I may return to my own father. I have already explained to you how I left him." [8]But Raguel said to Tobias, "Stay, my child, stay with me; I will send messengers to your father Tobit and they will inform him about you." [9]But he said, "No! I beg you to send me back to my father." [10]So Raguel promptly gave Tobias his wife Sarah, as well as half of all his property: male and female slaves, oxen and sheep, donkeys and camels, clothing, money, and household goods. [11]Then he saw them safely off; he embraced Tobias[a] and said, "Farewell, my child; have a safe journey. The Lord of heaven prosper you and your wife Sarah, and may I see children of yours before I die." [12]Then he kissed his daughter Sarah and said to her, "My daughter, honor your father-in-law and your mother-in-law,[b] since from now on they are as much your parents as those who gave you birth. Go in peace, daughter, and may I hear a good report about you as long as I live." Then he bade them farewell and let them go. Then Edna said to Tobias, "My child and dear brother, the Lord of heaven bring you back safely, and may I live long enough to see children of you and of my daughter Sarah before I die. In the sight of the Lord I entrust my daughter to you; do nothing to grieve her all the days of your life. Go in peace, my child. From now on I am your mother and Sarah is your beloved wife.[c] May we all prosper together all the days of our lives." Then she kissed them both and saw them safely off. [13]Tobias parted from Raguel with happiness and joy, praising the Lord of heaven and earth, King over all, because he had made his journey a success. Finally, he blessed Raguel and his wife Edna, and said, "I have been commanded by the Lord to honor you all the days of my life."[d]

11 When they came near to Kaserin, which is opposite Nineveh, Raphael said, [2]"You are aware of how we left your father. [3]Let us run ahead of your wife and prepare the house while they are still on the way." [4]As they went on

[a] Gk *him* [b] Other ancient authorities lack parts of *Then . . . mother-in-law* [c] Gk *sister* [d] Lat: Meaning of Gk uncertain

NAB

just before Nineveh, 2 Raphael said: "You know how we left your father. 3 Let us hurry on ahead of your wife to prepare the house while the rest of the party are still on the way." 4 So they both went on ahead and Raphael said to Tobiah, "Have the gall in your hand!" And the dog ran along behind them.

5 Meanwhile, Anna sat watching the road by which her son was to come. 6 When she saw him coming, she exclaimed to his father, "Tobit, your son is coming, and the man who traveled with him!"

7 Raphael said to Tobiah before he reached his father: "I am certain that his eyes will be opened. 8 Smear the fish gall on them. This medicine will make the cataracts shrink and peel off from his eyes; then your father will again be able to see the light of day." 9 Then Anna ran up to her son, threw her arms around him, and said to him, "Now that I have seen you again, son, I am ready to die!" And she sobbed aloud. 10 Tobit got up and stumbled out through the courtyard gate. Tobiah went up to him 11 with the fish gall in his hand, and holding him firmly, blew into his eyes. "Courage, father," he said. 12 Next he smeared the medicine on his eyes, 13 and it made them smart. Then, beginning at the corners of Tobit's eyes, Tobiah used both hands to peel off the cataracts. When Tobit saw his son, he threw his arms around him 14 and wept. He exclaimed, "I can see you, son, the light of my eyes!" Then he said:

"Blessed be God,
and praised be his great name,
and blessed be all his holy angels.
May his holy name be praised
throughout all the ages,
15 Because it was he who scourged me,
and it is he who has had mercy on me.
Behold, I now see my son Tobiah!"

11, 4: (*autois*) *'o kyōn* (*ek tōn opisō*) *autōn:* cf LXX^{MSS}, Vet Lat. Omit *kai tou 'uiou autēs*: cf other Vrs; LXX^{8} corrupt.
11, 9: (*anedramen*) *Anna (kai*): so LXX^{MSS}, Vet Lat^{MSS}.
11, 11: (*epi*) *tous ophthalmous autou* (*kai eped*) *a* (*ken*): so Vet Lat; cf LXX^{MSS}, P.
11, 12.13: (*autou*) *ta leukōmata* (*apo*): so Vet Lat; cf LXX^{MSS}, P. (*kai*) *eiden ton 'uion autou kai* (*epesen*): so Vet Lat; cf LXX^{MSS}, P; haplog.
11, 14: (*genoito to onoma*) *to 'agion* (*autou*) *eulogēton* (*eis pantes tous aiōnas*): so Vet Lat; omit the rest: dittog.
11, 15: (*me*) *kai autos ēleēsen me:* so Vet Lat; cf LXX^{B,A}; haplog. (*eisēlthen*) *Tōbeith . . .* (*en 'olǭ tǭ*) *stomati;* so Vet Lat (1 MS); cf LXX^{d,p,44}.

NRSV

together Raphael[a] said to him, "Have the gall ready." And the dog[b] went along behind them.

5 Meanwhile Anna sat looking intently down the road by which her son would come. 6 When she caught sight of him coming, she said to his father, "Look, your son is coming, and the man who went with him!"

7 Raphael said to Tobias, before he had approached his father, "I know that his eyes will be opened. 8 Smear the gall of the fish on his eyes; the medicine will make the white films shrink and peel off from his eyes, and your father will regain his sight and see the light."

9 Then Anna ran up to her son and threw her arms around him, saying, "Now that I have seen you, my child, I am ready to die." And she wept. 10 Then Tobit got up and came stumbling out through the courtyard door. Tobias went up to him, 11 with the gall of the fish in his hand, and holding him firmly, he blew into his eyes, saying, "Take courage, father." With this he applied the medicine on his eyes, 12 and it made them smart.[c] 13 Next, with both his hands he peeled off the white films from the corners of his eyes. Then Tobit[l] saw his son and[d] threw his arms around him, 14 and he wept and said to him, "I see you, my son, the light of my eyes!" Then he said,

"Blessed be God,
and blessed be his great name,
and blessed be all his holy angels.
May his holy name be blessed[e]
throughout all the ages.
15 Though he afflicted me,
he has had mercy upon me.[f]
Now I see my son Tobias!"

So Tobit went in rejoicing and praising God at the top of his voice. Tobias reported to his father that his journey had been successful, that he had brought the money, that he had married Raguel's daughter Sarah, and that she was, indeed, on her way there, very near to the gate of Nineveh.

16 Then Tobit, rejoicing and praising God, went out to meet his daughter-in-law at the gate of Nineveh. When the people of Nineveh saw him coming, walking along in full vigor and with no

[a] Gk *he* [b] Codex Sinaiticus reads *And the Lord* [c] Lat: Meaning of Gk uncertain [d] Other ancient authorities lack *saw his son and* [e] Codex Sinaiticus reads *May his great name be upon us and blessed be all the angels* [f] Lat: Gk lacks this line

NAB

Then Tobit went back in, rejoicing and praising
God with full voice. Tobiah told his father that
his journey had been a success; that he had
brought back the money; and that he had married
Raguel's daughter Sarah, who would arrive
shortly, for she was approaching the gate of
Nineveh.

16 Rejoicing and praising God, Tobit went
out to the gate of Nineveh to meet his daughter-
in-law. When the people of Nineveh saw him
walking along briskly, with no one leading him
by the hand, they were amazed. 17 Before them
all Tobit proclaimed how God had mercifully
restored sight to his eyes. When Tobit reached
Sarah, the wife of his son Tobiah, he greeted her:
"Welcome, my daughter! Blessed be your God for
bringing you to us, daughter! Blessed are your
father and your mother. Blessed is my son Tobiah,
and blessed are you, daughter! Welcome to your
home with blessing and joy. Come in, daughter!"
That day there was joy for all the Jews who lived
in Nineveh. 18 Ahiqar and his nephew Nadab
also came to rejoice with Tobit. They celebrated
Tobiah's wedding feast for seven happy days, and
he received many gifts.

11, 17: (*patēr sou*) *kai ‘ē mētēr sou:* so LXX^MSS, Vet Lat, P.
11, 18: *Nadab ‘o exadelphos* (*autou*): cf LXX^MSS, Vet Lat. (*Tōbein*) *kai ēchthē ‘o gamos Tōbeia met’ euphrosynēs ‘epta ‘ēmeras kai edothē autǭ dōra polla* : cf LXX^MSS, Vet Lat, P, V.

NRSV

one leading him, they were amazed. 17 Before
them all, Tobit acknowledged that God had been
merciful to him and had restored his sight. When
Tobit met Sarah the wife of his son Tobias, he
blessed her saying, "Come in, my daughter, and
welcome. Blessed be your God who has brought
you to us, my daughter. Blessed be your father
and your mother, blessed be my son Tobias, and
blessed be you, my daughter. Come in now to
your home, and welcome, with blessing and joy.
Come in, my daughter." So on that day there was
rejoicing among all the Jews who were in
Nineveh. 18 Ahikar and his nephew Nadab were
also present to share Tobit's joy. With merriment
they celebrated Tobias's wedding feast for seven
days, and many gifts were given to him.[a]

[a] Other ancient authorities lack parts of this sentence

COMMENTARY

The final question posed by the exposition—Will Tobiah return safely and heal Tobit?—is answered in the affirmative in this section. The distress of Tobit and Anna keeps the tension alive. However, the reader is now assured by Tobiah's success in delivering Sarah from the demon that he can also use Raphael's advice to heal his father. The departure from Ecbatana is a long Near Eastern farewell. It serves to reiterate the emphasis on family and to continue the spirit of grateful joy that surrounds the wedding feast.

The last major scene of the resolution is told slowly, with careful detail and repetition, pointing to the careful construction of the scene. The procedure to be followed with the parts of the fish is given twice more (11:6-8, 11-13; see 6:9). Each telling provides a fuller account. The description of the healing process alternates with the parents' welcome and gradually takes precedence.

Detail and repetition slow the climax of the scene, and the alternation in perspective presents it in a style suggestive of cinematic technique (in which the action is seen first from the angle of one camera, and then from another).[93] In what follows, note that the perspective of Tobiah and Raphael appears in the passages on the left, the perspective of Anna and Tobit in the passages on

93. B. F. Kawin, *Telling It Again and Again: Repetition in Literature and Film* (Ithaca: Cornell University Press, 1972), discusses several examples of this cinematic technique.

the right. The passages on the left emphasize the healing process; the passages on the right emphasize the welcoming. Tobit's eyes are the major focus of the passages on the left, and the act of seeing is the major motif of those on the right. Both perspectives merge at the end of the passage:

Raphael said to [Tobiah],
"Have the *gall* in your hand!" (11:4).
Meanwhile *Anna* sat watching the road . . .
When she saw him coming,
she exclaimed to his father,
"*Tobit,* your son is coming" (11:5-6).
Raphael said to Tobiah,
"I am certain that his eyes will be opened.
Smear the fish *gall* on them.
This *medicine* will make the cataracts
shrink and peel off from his eyes;
then your father will again be able
to see the light of day" (11:7-8).

Then *Anna* ran up to her son,
threw her arms around him, and said to him,
"Now that I have seen you again, son,
I am ready to die!" And *she sobbed* aloud.
Tobit got up and stumbled out
through the courtyard gate (11:9-10).

Tobiah went up to him
with the fish *gall* in his hand,
and holding him firmly,
blew into his eyes.
"Courage, father," he said.
Next he smeared the *medicine* on his eyes,
and it made them smart.
Then, beginning at the corners of Tobit's eyes,
Tobiah used both hands to peel off the cataracts.

When Tobit saw his son,
he *threw his arms around him* and *wept,*
he exclaimed, "I can see you, son,
the light of my eyes!" (11:10-14)

The return journey gives Raphael one more chance to instruct Tobiah. The arrival in Nineveh reveals the great love uniting all the members of Tobit's family. Their joy increases even more with Tobit's healing and his welcome of Sarah. The moment is punctuated by yet another prayer.

10:1-3. The relationship between Tobit and Anna is artfully portrayed in this scene as both worry about the delay of their son. Tobit's interior monologue reveals his own concern. He rehearses all the things that might have gone wrong. He wonders whether Gabael is dead, when his real fear is that Tobiah is dead.

10:4-5. Anna is the more vocal of the two parents. As Tobit's worry mounts over Tobiah's delay, hers does as well. In contrast to Tobit's silence, she begins to weep and wail. Now not only does she refer to Tobiah as "my child," but she also takes the responsibility for his absence, a responsibility she had previously laid at Tobit's feet (5:18): "Woe to me, my child, the light of my eyes, that *I* let you make this journey" (italics added). Tobit's reassurance is not as effective in silencing her as it was when the journey began. She continues to wail and cry the whole night. The Old Latin (VL) and one of the Greek manuscripts (LXX^{d}, recension G^{III}) indicate that she also stopped eating.

10:6. Anna expresses Tobit's real worry. He, however, does not confess his concern to her. Rather, he replies to her gently and with reassurance. Ironically, he mentions that something unexpected may have happened. It is certainly true that none of the characters except Raphael expected the marriage that is causing Tobiah's delay.

10:7-9. Anna's worry over Tobiah has the peculiar mix of despair and hope so often characteristic of mothers. Even as she repeats "my child has perished," she stations herself near the road to watch for his return. This juxtaposition of maternal hope and despair is reminiscent of Rebekah, who sends one son away to keep the other from killing him (Gen 27:42-45); of Hannah as she grieves over her barrenness, yet has the courage to pray (1 Sam 1:7-11); and of the Shunammite woman as she doubts and hopes in Elisha's promise of a son and as she prays for the life of that son (1 Kgs 4:16-17, 28-30).

Anna's sharp tongue is again in evidence, and, as before, the target of her words is her husband, Tobit. She turns his reassurance into a retort and insists that his hope (which her actions reveal that she also holds) is in vain. Tobit suffers not only from her cutting words, but also from her sleeplessness and loss of appetite.

The departure scene reveals both Tobiah's care for his parents and Raguel's characteristic hospitality. Tobiah insists on leaving, in spite of Raguel's urging that he remain. Tobiah has already recognized that his parents are worried (9:4). He knows that Tobit is counting the days, as indeed he is (9:4; 10:1). Tobiah knows also that Anna (along with Tobit) does not believe that he will return alive (v. 7; cf. v. 3).

10:10. The warmth of Raguel's nature is demonstrated by his tender farewells to his daughter and new son-in-law. He is a rich man, with servants, slaves, flocks, and herds. He is also a generous man. He gives lavish and frequent feasts, and he does not hesitate to give Tobiah half of everything he owns when the newlyweds depart. He has kept his promise with regard to the inheritance (8:21).

10:11-13. This is the most extended and affectionate of the departure/arrival scenes and the only one in which there is genuine interaction between Tobiah and the other characters (cf. 5:17-22; 7:1-8). Raguel bids him a fatherly farewell with a prayer for his safety and prosperity. Edna entrusts her beloved daughter, Sarah, to him. Both Raguel and Edna address him as their own son.

Raguel is a concerned father. He exhorts Sarah to honor Tobiah's parents as her own and to live a life worthy of a good reputation. Edna, too, is concerned for her daughter. She exhorts her new son-in-law concerning responsibility for his wife and her happiness.

Edna hopes to see her motherhood extended in grandchildren. The expectations of the older generation concerning the marriage of Tobiah and Sarah are instructive. In addition to the expectation of marriage within law and custom (see 1:9; 4:12-13; 7:10-11) is the hope that their marriage will bring joy (v. 12; see 8:20; 11:17). Children are seen as a blessing in marriage. Everyone concerned with the wedding of Tobiah and Sarah hopes to see their children (vv. 11-12; see 6:18; 13:16; 14:3, 9, 11).

Tobiah responds to these blessings with a pledge of honor and a feeling of happiness and joy, which overflows in thanksgiving to God.[94]

11:1-4. The return journey is summarized in one verse (v. 1). Raphael, who seems always to be in a hurry (cf. 5:8), hastens Tobiah on the last stage of the journey by preparing him for his second act of healing. Raphael was sent to heal both Tobit and Sarah (3:17). However, God's providence is manifested chiefly through human agents. Through his obedience to Raphael's instructions, Tobiah is enabled to be the instrument of God's healing. The dog, a remainder of the story's folktale origin, appears only at the beginning and end of the journey (see 6:2).

11:5-6. The two great loves of Anna's life are her husband and her son. Since Tobiah's departure, Anna has been referring to him as "my child" (5:18; 10:4, 7). Now she watches the road by which "her son" is to come. The welcome scene reveals Anna's tenderness toward her husband. Aware of his worry and inability to see, she turns to Tobit (who is with her as she watches the road) and says "Tobit, *your* son is coming."

11:7-8. God's providence in the healing of Tobit is manifested through natural materials. (The heart, liver, and gall of the fish are medicines that correspond to ancient healing lore.) Fish gall was used in Assyria as a medicine for eye ailments.[95] The use of gall from other animals, especially pigs and turtles, is also known from Egypt. The medicinal use and preparation of gall is also discussed by Pedanius Dioskurides, Pliny, and Galen.[96]

11:9-10. When her son finally comes, Anna embraces him and declares with tears that her life has reached its fulfillment. He is alive; now she is ready to die. The scene is reminiscent of Jacob's greeting to Joseph, whom he had supposed was dead (Gen 46:29-30). Tobit also loves his son. As soon as he hears the news of Tobiah's arrival, the blind man gets up and stumbles out through the gate.[97]

11:11-12. Tobit is afflicted with blindness due to a thickening or whitening of the cornea, a condition often treated with gall. Tobit reports that his eyes sting or smart.[98] The effectiveness of

94. The textual situation of the final sentence is complex. The Old Latin is the clearest: "I have been commanded by the Lord to honor you all the days of my life" (*Iniunctum est mihi a Domino honorari uos omnibus diebus uitae uestrae*). G^{I} reads, "He blessed Raguel and Edna his wife" (κατευλόγει *Ραγουὴλ* καὶ *Ἔδναν* την γυναῖκα αὐτοῦ *kateulogei Ragouēl kai Ednan tēn gynaika autou*). But G^{II} (Sinaiticus) omits this sentence. G^{I} lacks the following sentence, but G^{II} is corrupt. It reads, "May it be successful for you to honor them all the days of your life" (Εὐοδώθη σοι τιμᾶν αὐτοὺς πάσας τὰς ἡμέρας τῆς ζωῆς αὐτῶν *Euodōthē soi timan autous pasas tas hēmeras tēs zōēs autōn*).

95. W. von Soden, "Fischgalle als Heilmittel für die Augen," *AfO* 21 (1966) 81-82.

96. See Bernd Kollmann, "Göttliche Offenbarung magisch-parmakologischer Heilkunst im Buch Tobit" *ZAW* 106 (1994) 293-97, for a detailed treatment of ancient medical use of gall.

97. The Qumran fragment 4QTob[e] specifies that he went "to meet his son."

98. This is clear in the Old Latin *momordit;* the Greek text is corrupt.

the gall in healing is directly related to its caustic, heat-producing properties. The medical knowledge of eye diseases and their remedies is amazingly accurate in the book of Tobit.[99]

11:13-15a. Tobit's response to the healing is first an expression of delight in the son who is truly the "light of his eyes."[100] Then this man of prayer turns immediately to God. His prayer is an ecstatic outburst of joy.[101] He begins with a triple blessing: He blesses God, God's name, and God's angels. Four times he uses the word εὐλογέω (*eulogeō*, "to bless"). Twice he mentions God's angels, even as he unknowingly stands in the presence of the angel sent by God to help him. Despite its brevity, the prayer contains the basic principle of Tobit's life and of the book: God afflicts, and God has mercy.[102] Blessed be God! His exclamation closes as it opened, with delight in seeing his son Tobiah.

11:15b. The scene ends with a summary that echoes Raphael's commission in 3:17. In one sentence Tobiah relates the successful resolution to two of the three questions left at the end of the journey: Will Tobiah meet Sarah, marry her, and deliver her from Asmodeus? Will Tobiah recover the money? The scene itself has answered the third question: Will Tobiah return safely and heal Tobit? Meanwhile Tobit[103] continues blessing God and rejoicing.

11:16-18. Tobit's welcome of Sarah and the simple reference to another seven-day feast end this scene speedily. His welcoming of Sarah reveals his joy and his concept of marriage. He continues to shower blessings everywhere. The root word "bless" (*eulogeō*) appears six times during his welcome. He blesses Sarah, her parents,[104] his son, and God. He also recognizes Sarah as his daughter, thus emphasizing the family connections brought about by marriage. He calls her "daughter" four times in this short speech. Tobit also repeats the key word ὑγιαίνω (*hygiainō*, "be well," "well-come") twice in his greeting of Sarah.

From here to the end, the characteristic tone of the book is joyful. Tobit cannot stop rejoicing and praising God (11:15-16). When he announces God's gift to him, all the Jews in Nineveh also rejoice. At the wedding feast, Ahiqar and his nephew Nadin[105] join in the general rejoicing. According to all of the reliable textual witnesses except G^{II} (G^{I}, VL, Syriac, Vulgate), everyone celebrates with joy for seven more days.

99. Kollmann, "Göttliche Offenbarung magisch-parmakologischer Heilkunst im Buch Tobit" 297.

100. The Hebrew fragment 4QTob[e] supports the reading of VL and G^{I} in 11:13 that, when the films were removed from his eyes, "and he saw his son" ([בנו] וירא את *wyrʾ ʾt* [*bnw*]).

101. See P. J. Griffin, "The Theology and Function of Prayer in the Book of Tobit" (Ph.D. diss., The Catholic University of America, 1984) esp. 206-23.

102. "He has had mercy on me" appears in G^{I} (ἠλέησάς με *ēleēsas me*) and VL (*ipse misertus est mei*), but not in G^{II}.

103. It is clear in VL that Tobit, not Tobiah (as G^{II}), rejoices.

104. G^{II} mentions only Sarah's father, but G^{I} and VL include her mother.

105. "Nadin" is the correct spelling of the name of Ahiqar's nephew, as testified by 4QTob[d] frg. 2. The Greek and Latin MSS have a variety of spellings.

REFLECTIONS

1. The older generation looks forward to the children of Tobiah and Sarah with delight. The love that holds their marriage together must bear fruit in some way. The joy that surrounds their marriage will be redoubled by the gift of life to others. Children are a gift in marriage; the outward turning of the energy that comes from mutual support is a necessity. This truth is not simple. Some couples are unable to have children. Their struggle to conceive and the sometimes interminable wait to adopt can cause great suffering. Some couples decide for good reason not to have children. There may be other concerns: health; economic distress; other family pressures. Some, on the other hand, remain childless out of selfishness. They are truly barren. Some who have children abuse or neglect them. The trust placed in them by God and society is betrayed; the gift is destroyed.

2. A painting by the nineteenth-century artist Jean-François Millet is titled *Waiting*. It portrays an old woman, her back to the observer, leaning forward into the road, down which she looks intently. To her right an old man, apparently blind, hesitates in a doorway. The painting is an interpretation of Anna and Tobit waiting for Tobiah. The painter was scorned for portraying biblical characters as nineteenth-century French peasants, but his message is very clear: The parents are still waiting for their beloved child.

All parents worry about their children, some more than others. Raising children is an awesome responsibility. The challenge of balancing the need to protect them with the need to give them freedom is ever present. In the end, parents must recognize that they exercise this responsibility in the name of God, who gave their children life. God alone can care for them in every situation.

3. Our mobile society causes us to say good-bye to loved ones with increasing frequency. The farewell at Ecbatana is permeated with blessings and expressions of love. Those kissed with tenderness at the beginning of the journey are instructed to stretch out their love toward those who wait for them at its end. God is entrusted with the responsibility of caring for the departing ones, for those left behind, and for those who await their arrival. Here is a model for our frequent good-byes.

4. In the story the angel instructs Tobiah to use methods of healing known to the medical community of his time. Ben Sira exhorts us to "honor physicians for their services" (Sir 38:1 NRSV; see also Sir 38:2-8). God works through natural means, through the power of created elements and the knowledge and skill of human beings. There are two ways we can strive to be healed of our ills, and both are necessary: Pray to God and seek the services of competent medical personnel (see Sir 38:9-15).

Tobit's immediate response to his healing is grateful prayer. Jesus praises the leper who returns to give thanks for his cure and grieves over the nine who do not (Luke 17:17-18). It is easy to turn to God in prayer when we are in need and to forget to return in praise when God answers our prayer. Tobit is an example for us of genuine gratitude.

5. Dom Columba Marmion, a nineteenth-century Belgian Benedictine, said that joy is a sign and a consequence of the presence of God.[106] The irrepressible joy of the last chapters of the book of Tobit is certainly a sign of God's presence and power. The characters in this story allow God to work in them and through them. They do not hinder God's action by resistance. Therefore, God's blessing and love can flow into them and through them to others. The only possible response is genuine joy.

106. Columba Marmion, *Christ the Ideal of the Monk: Spiritual Conferences on the Monastic and Religious Life*, trans. by a nun of Tyburn convent (St. Louis: B. Herder, 1926) 104-5, 130.

TOBIT 12:1–14:15

ALL'S WELL THAT ENDS WELL

OVERVIEW

A few loose ends remain to be tied up in the final chapters. The reader knows that Raphael is an angel, but the characters do not. The offer of wages for him (12:1-5), far exceeding the promise in 5:15-16, leads to Raphael's refusal of payment and the revelation of his identity (12:15). The main themes of the plot are reiterated in his exhortation (12:6-10): God, who rewards charitable deeds, is just and deserving of praise. Raphael then summarizes the plot and his function in it (12:12-14), exhorting Tobit and Tobiah to pray in thanksgiving (12:17-20). Raphael's exhortation is followed by Tobit's song of praise (13:1-18).

The story has returned to its original calm. The epilogue (14:1-15) reports the permanent state of prosperity of the characters and their final end, thus reinforcing the claim of the plot that God rewards charitable deeds.

TOBIT 12:1-22, REVELATION OF RAPHAEL'S IDENTITY

NAB

12 1 When the wedding celebration came to an end, Tobit called his son Tobiah and said to him, "Son, see to it that you give what is due to the man who made the journey with you; give him a bonus too." 2 Tobiah said: "Father, how much shall I pay him? It would not hurt me at all to give him half of all the wealth he brought back with me. 3 He led me back safe and sound; he cured my wife; he brought the money back with me; and he cured you. How much of a bonus should I give him?" 4 Tobit answered, "It is only fair, son, that he should receive half of all that he brought back." 5 So Tobiah called Raphael and said, "Take as your wages half of all that you have brought back, and go in peace." 6 Raphael called the two men aside privately and said to them: "Thank God! Give him the praise and the glory. Before all the living, acknowledge the many good things he has done for you, by blessing and

12, 6: (*exomologeisthe*) *kai auton megalynete kai autō exomologeisthe* (*enōpion*): so with Vet Lat (1 MS); cf LXX[MSS]; haplog.

NRSV

12 When the wedding celebration was ended, Tobit called his son Tobias and said to him, "My child, see to paying the wages of the man who went with you, and give him a bonus as well." [2]He replied, "Father, how much shall I pay him? It would do no harm to give him half of the possessions brought back with me. [3]For he has led me back to you safely, he cured my wife, he brought the money back with me, and he healed you. How much extra shall I give him as a bonus?" [4]Tobit said, "He deserves, my child, to receive half of all that he brought back." [5]So Tobias[a] called him and said, "Take for your wages half of all that you brought back, and farewell."

6Then Raphael[a] called the two of them privately and said to them, "Bless God and acknowledge him in the presence of all the living for the good things he has done for you. Bless and sing praise to his name. With fitting honor declare to all people the deeds[c] of God. Do not be slow to

a Gk *he* b Gk *words*; other ancient authorities read *words of the deeds*

NAB

extolling his name in song. Before all men, honor
and proclaim God's deeds, and do not be slack
in praising him. 7 A king's secret it is prudent to
keep, but the works of God are to be declared
and made known. Praise them with due honor.
Do good, and evil will not find its way to you.
8 Prayer and fasting are good, but better than
either is almsgiving accompanied by righteousness. A little with righteousness is better than
abundance with wickedness. It is better to give
alms than to store up gold; 9 for almsgiving saves
one from death and expiates every sin. Those who
regularly give alms shall enjoy a full life; 10 but
those habitually guilty of sin are their own worst
enemies. 11 "I will now tell you the whole truth;
I will conceal nothing at all from you. I have
already said to you, 'A king's secret it is prudent
to keep, but the works of God are to be made
known with due honor.' 12 I can now tell you
that when you, Tobit, and Sarah prayed, it was I
who presented and read the record of your prayer
before the Glory of the Lord; and I did the same
thing when you used to bury the dead. 13 When
you did not hesitate to get up and leave your
dinner in order to go and bury the dead, 14 I
was sent to put you to the test. At the same time,
however, God commissioned me to heal you and
your daughter-in-law Sarah. 15 I am Raphael, one
of the seven angels who enter and serve before
the Glory of the Lord."

16 Stricken with fear, the two men fell to the
ground. 17 But Raphael said to them: "No need
to fear; you are safe. Thank God now and forever.
18 As for me, when I came to you it was not out
of any favor on my part, but because it was God's
will. So continue to thank him every day; praise
him with song. 19 Even though you watched me
eat and drink, I did not really do so; what you
were seeing was a vision. 20 So now get up from
the ground and praise God. Behold, I am about
to ascend to him who sent me; write down all

12, 8: (*proseuchē meta*) *nēsteias* (*kai*): so LXX (all other MSS), Vet Lat, V. (*dikaiosynēs*) *'yper amphotera. Agathon to oligon meta dikaiosynēs* (*mallon ē ploutos*): so with Vet Lat (1 MS); cf LXX^{MSS}; haplog.

12, 9: *gar* (*ek*): so LXX^{MSS}, Vet Lat, V.

12, 12: (*kyriou*) *kai anegnōn:* so Vet Lat.

12, 14: (*iasasthai*) *se:* so LXX^{MSS}, Vet Lat.

12, 18: Omit *meth' 'ymōn* before *alla:* so LXX^{U}, Vet Lat: dittog.

12, 19: *etheōreite:* so LXX^{U}, Vet Lat. (*ephagon*) *oude epion:* so LXX^{MSS}; cf P.

12, 20: (*nyn*) *anastēte ek* (*tēs gēs kai*): so LXX^{d,p}, Vet Lat^{MSS}; cf P.

NRSV

acknowledge him. 7It is good to conceal the secret
of a king, but to acknowledge and reveal the
works of God, and with fitting honor to acknowledge him. Do good and evil will not overtake
you. 8Prayer with fasting[a] is good, but better than
both is almsgiving with righteousness. A little with
righteousness is better than wealth with wrongdoing.[b] It is better to give alms than to lay up
gold. 9For almsgiving saves from death and purges
away every sin. Those who give alms will enjoy
a full life, 10but those who commit sin and do
wrong are their own worst enemies.

11"I will now declare the whole truth to you
and will conceal nothing from you. Already I have
declared it to you when I said, 'It is good to
conceal the secret of a king, but to reveal with
due honor the works of God.' 12So now when
you and Sarah prayed, it was I who brought and
read[c] the record of your prayer before the glory
of the Lord, and likewise whenever you would
bury the dead. 13And that time when you did not
hesitate to get up and leave your dinner to go
and bury the dead, 14I was sent to you to test
you. And at the same time God sent me to heal
you and Sarah your daughter-in-law. 15I am
Raphael, one of the seven angels who stand ready
and enter before the glory of the Lord."

16The two of them were shaken; they fell face
down, for they were afraid. 17But he said to them,
"Do not be afraid; peace be with you. Bless God
forevermore. 18As for me, when I was with you,
I was not acting on my own will, but by the will
of God. Bless him each and every day; sing his
praises. 19Although you were watching me, I really
did not eat or drink anything—but what you saw
was a vision. 20So now get up from the ground,[d]
and acknowledge God. See, I am ascending to
him who sent me. Write down all these things
that have happened to you." And he ascended.
21Then they stood up, and could see him no more.
22They kept blessing God and singing his praises,
and they acknowledged God for these marvelous
deeds of his, when an angel of God had appeared
to them.

[a] Codex Sinaiticus *with sincerity* [b] Lat [c] Lat: Gk lacks *and read*
[d] Other ancient authorities read *now bless the Lord on earth*

NAB

these things that have happened to you." 21 When Raphael ascended, they rose to their feet and could no longer see him. 22 They kept thanking God and singing his praises; and they continued to acknowledge these marvelous deeds which he had done when the angel of God appeared to them.

COMMENTARY

Chapter 12 consists primarily of Raphael's farewell discourse. (See the Commentary on 4:1-21 for a description of the farewell discourse form.) Raphael's farewell discourse includes the following elements of the form: the announcement of his departure (v. 20); a reminder of the past (esp. vv. 12-14); and an exhortation to be faithful to God's commandments and to one another (esp. vv. 6-10). The only prediction is the promise that "those who give alms will enjoy a full life" (v. 9). Two other elements that are ordinarily found in the form are a blessing of peace and joy and a promise that God will abide with the hearers. Raphael's presence has itself been a blessing and a sign that God remains with Tobit and Tobiah. The idea of blessing is reversed as Raphael reminds them repeatedly to bless God (vv. 6, 17-18, 20), which they promptly do (v. 22).

In the book of Tobit, Raphael's role as a symbol of the providence of God is threefold: He has prepared Tobiah for the two healings; he has guided Tobiah on the way; and he continues to inspire and encourage the spirit of prayer. But because God heals (the meaning of Raphael's name) and because the providence of God leaves room for human freedom, Raphael leaves the main action to the human characters throughout the book. He continually fades from sight as they make use of his instructions and preparations. Thus it is no surprise that when his mission is over, he ascends to God; and Tobit and Tobiah can no longer see him (v. 21). Raphael's mission has been successful. They are healed; they have found the way; and they turn in thanksgiving to God (v. 18).

12:1. Tobit had promised Raphael a drachma a day for guiding Tobiah to Media and had also suggested the possibility of a bonus if they returned safely (5:10, 15-16). Tobit also exhorted Tobiah to pay promptly the wages of those who worked for him (4:14). Consistently he has practiced what he preaches, and this scene is no exception. As soon as the wedding feast is over, he summons Tobiah to pay Raphael both wages and bonus.

12:2-3. Tobiah's response reveals his gratitude, his humility, and his generosity. In a string of short clauses he lists the gifts of Raphael: guidance, the two healings, the return of the money. Humbly he gives credit to Raphael for the two healings, although the angel had only given the instructions. Tobiah does not mention his own part in carrying out Raphael's instructions.

12:4-5. Tobiah has suggested that he might give Raphael half of the riches they have brought back, and Tobit agrees to the suggestion. When Raphael is summoned, Tobiah makes the offer (the Greek texts omit the name, but the Old Latin identifies Tobiah as the one who makes the offer). The concept of giving half the wealth is a remnant of the story's folktale background. In the tale of "The Grateful Dead," a stranger (the ghost of the grateful dead man) offers to serve and guide the traveler for half of whatever he may acquire. In the book of Tobit, half the wealth signifies Tobit's and Tobiah's generosity.

Tobiah ends his offer to Raphael with the customary blessing, "Go in health." Thus in this story of healing the key word, ὑγιαίνω (*hygiainō*, "to be well"), appears for the last time in the farewell to the angel whose name is "God heals."

12:6-7a. Raphael does not directly refuse payment. Rather, he delivers a wisdom speech, instructing the two men in the basic principles of a good life: prayer, almsgiving, and the theory of retribution. These themes constitute the theological pillars of the book. Raphael begins with an instruction concerning prayer. He reminds the men that prayers of praise and thanksgiving can never be offered in isolation. None of us alone can muster enough strength to give God fitting praise. Thus, in the tradition of the psalms, hymns are ordinarily addressed to others who might join in praising God. Twice Raphael tells them to proclaim to "all the living" what God has done for them. Then, to help them remember, he gives them a little proverb contrasting God's work and a king's secret. Wisdom entails knowing which to hide and which to proclaim.

12:7b-10. Raphael's final statement about prayer ("prayer with fasting is good")[107] is embedded in the beginning of an exhortation concerning almsgiving ("better than both is almsgiving"). His words about almsgiving are based on the theory of retribution. Thus all three themes are linked together.

First, Raphael states the positive principle of retribution: "Do good and evil will not overtake you." Then he illustrates what "doing good" means through the primary example of almsgiving. The benefits of almsgiving are many: It is truly life-giving; it sustains life better than wealth does; it preserves life by cleansing one from sin; and it saves one from death and ensures a full life. Raphael closes this part of his speech with the negative side of retribution: "Those who sin and do evil are their own worst enemies."

The book of Sirach, written in the same century as the book of Tobit, also emphasizes the benefits of almsgiving. Giving alms delivers one from sin (Sir 3:30-31) and saves one from death (Sir 29:10-13; 40:17, 24).[108]

12:11-14. In the second part of his farewell, Raphael finally reveals to Tobit and Tobiah his angelic identity. He sets his revelation under the rubric of the proverb he had given the two men earlier concerning the proclamation of the works of God. Raphael also practices what he preaches.

Raphael eases into the revelation of his identity first by describing his mission. He identifies three of his functions: mediating prayer, testing, and healing. He tells Tobit and Tobiah what the reader has known since 3:17: He was sent, specifically in answer to their prayer, to heal Tobit and Sarah.

Raphael does not perform the healings himself. Rather, his name declares that it is God who heals. In fact, Tobiah performed the actions that led to both healings. The angel has only been the messenger between God and human agents.

Raphael's role as one who tests is not developed in the book. Several possibilities of testing suggest themselves: (1) He is somehow implicated in Tobit's having become blind (2:3-10); (2) he tests Tobit by not revealing his identity (5:11-14); (3) he tests the obedience and trust of Tobiah in the incidents with the fish, the marriage, and the healings. These possibilities, however, remain in the realm of speculation. Since so much of the book echoes Genesis, the suggestion of "angel as one who tests" may be based on the model of the angel with whom Jacob wrestled (Gen 33:24-25).

Raphael's statements concerning healing and testing provide a necessary caution concerning the theory of retribution. In this theory, the good are rewarded, and the wicked are punished. But Raphael says that he was sent to put Tobit to the test precisely because of his good deed of burying the dead. It seems that doing good results in suffering rather than in blessing. But "at the same time" (*ἅμα hama*; a word suggesting the introduction of Raphael in chap. 3), he is also sent to heal Tobit and Sarah. Suffering and healing come simultaneously from God. This ambiguity is a major part of the book's message. Only from God's perspective can blessing and suffering be understood.

Raphael functions as a mediator of prayer throughout the book. He is sent in answer to prayer (3:16-17). He instructs Tobiah to pray on the wedding night (6:18). He urges Tobit and Tobiah to pray in thanksgiving (12:6-7, 17-20). Now he reveals that he presents prayers before the glory of the Lord (v. 12).

12:15. Finally, Raphael proclaims his true name and identity. He is one of the seven "angels of the presence." In the OT, angels (or heavenly beings) surround the throne of God (see 1 Kgs 22:19; Job 1:6; 2:1; Ps 89:5-7). The book of

107. G^{II} reads "prayer with truth" (προσευχὴ μετὰ ἀληθείας *proseuchē meta alētheias*), but G^{I} reads "with fasting" (μετά νηστείας *meta nēsteias*) and is supported by the Old Latin (*cum ieiunio*).

108. See P. J. Griffin, "A Study of *Eleēmosynē* in the Bible with Emphasis upon Its Meaning and Usage in the Theology of Tobit and Ben Sira" (Ma thesis, The Catholic University of America, 1982) 68-76.

Revelation describes seven angels (or spirits) standing before the throne of God (Rev 1:4; 4:5; 8:2).

The names of three of these angels are known to us from the Bible: Gabriel (Dan 8:16; 9:21; Luke 1:19, 26); Michael (Dan 10:13, 21; 12:1; Jude 9; Rev 12:7); and Raphael (only in the book of Tobit). The apocryphal book *1 Enoch* (dating back to at least the 3rd cent. BCE) lists the following six names: Uriel, Raphael, Raguel, Michael, Saraqael, and Gabriel (*1 Enoch* 20:1-8). One of the Greek fragments of Enoch, discovered at Akhmim at the end of the nineteenth century, adds the name of Remiel. Both Akhmim fragments add a final phrase: "Seven names of archangels."[109]

12:16-17. The response of Tobit and Tobiah to Raphael's revelation of his angelic identity is typical of the OT: They fall on their faces (see Gen 18:2; 19:1; Num 22:31; Judg 13:20; Dan 8:17). Raphael's encouragement is also a typical angelic response, "Do not fear" (see Gen 21:17; Luke 1:13, 30).

12:18-20. A theology of angels is further developed in Raphael's final words. He insists that he is only a messenger; thanks and praise are due to God, not to him. Worship of angels is forbidden by the NT (Col 2:18; Rev 22:8-9), just as worship of the "host of heaven" was forbidden by the OT (see Deut 4:19; 17:3; Jer 8:1-2). He also describes himself as a spirit. What seemed to them to be evidence of a body—eating and drinking—was only illusion.[110] The spiritual nature of angels is suggested also in the NT (see Matt 22:30 and par.; Heb 1:14).

12:21-22. Once they have recovered from their fear, Tobit and Tobiah cannot stop praising and thanking God. Like the disciples after Jesus' ascension, they continually bless God in joy (see Luke 24:52-53). God's care of them has been revealed through God's messenger, an angel.

109. See *The Apocryphal Old Testament,* ed. H. F. D. Sparks (Oxford: Clarendon, 1984) 174, 208; G. W. E. Nickelsburg, "Tobit and Enoch: Distant Cousins with a Recognizable Resemblance," ed. D. J. Lull, SBLSP 27 (Atlanta: Scholars Press, 1988) 54-68.

110. The statement that he ate nothing appears in G[II] (οὐκ ἔφαγον οὐθέν *ouk ephagon outhen*). The Qumran text 4QTob[a] says that he drank nothing (אשתית א[ל] [*l*]ʾ ʾ*š tyt*). G[I] contains both (οὐκ ἔφαγον οὐδὲ ἔπιον *ouk ephagon oude epion*).

REFLECTIONS

1. Generosity to those who work for us is made difficult by the impersonalization of much of today's labor. When the worker is a housekeeper, a cook, a gardener, or someone else with whom we interact personally, it is much easier to give an appropriate bonus, gift, or helping hand. How can we discover ways (other than the ubiquitous Christmas bonus) to be generous to other workers in our technological society?

Tobiah lists all the good things brought to him by Raphael. The acknowledgment of a worker's value and achievement is often worth more than monetary reward. Tobit and Tobiah also meet with Raphael in person. What has largely contributed to the success of many companies is the personal attention paid to the workers and their needs. Perhaps there is a way, within the structure of modern business, for supervisors on each level to be empowered to share a worker's evaluation and to give a bonus.

2. Raphael instructs Tobit and Tobiah to praise God with thanksgiving. A habit of prayer that begins with thanksgiving is not just a good idea—it is a recipe for happiness. But this habit must be learned; it is not our natural inclination. There are about twice as many laments as there are hymns in the book of Psalms. Almost all the requests for prayer that come to the minister have to do with trouble: Someone is sick or has lost a job. It seems we are eager to pray when we are in need, but forget to praise God when good things happen to us.

The habit of giving thanks to God leads to the awareness that alone we can never muster enough strength to give God fitting praise. We need others to help us. The psalms teach us how to ask: We call faithful people (Ps 149:1), all nations and peoples (Ps 117:1), everything that has breath (Ps 150:6). Psalm 148 provides the longest list: "fire and hail, snow and mist, storms, winds, mountains, hills, fruit trees and cedars, wild beasts and tame, snakes and birds, princes, judges, rulers, subjects, men, women, old and young" (see Ps 148:8-12).

"It is good to conceal the secret of a king, but to acknowledge and reveal the works of God" (Tob 12:7). Raphael calls us also to proclaim to all the world the good things God has done for us.

3. Prayer, fasting, and almsgiving are three pillars of righteous living in Jewish tradition. Christians, too, declare days of fasting and prayer. Many churches keep the tradition of almsgiving, providing places for food, clothing, and money to be collected for the poor. Lent is a special time for these practices.

Raphael's words teach us that the three practices cannot be separated: "Prayer with fasting is good, but better than both is almsgiving with righteousness" (12:8). Prayer without action is empty, a soul without a body. Fasting by itself is a work of pride, proving one's self-discipline. Charitable giving without the other two is cold; the gift has never touched the giver's life. Raphael shows us that genuine prayer will lead us to share God's concern for the poor. That concern will urge us to fast, to take only what we need so that we will have something to share with the poor.

TOBIT 13:1-17, TOBIT'S PRAYER

NAB

13 1 Then Tobit composed this joyful prayer:
Blessed be God who lives forever,
because his kingdom lasts for all ages.
2 For he scourges and then has mercy;
he casts down to the depths of the netherworld,
and he brings up from the great abyss.
No one can escape his hand.

3 Praise him, you Israelites, before the Gentiles,
for though he has scattered you among them,
4 he has shown you his greatness even there.
Exalt him before every living being,
because he is the Lord our God,
our Father and God forever.
5 He scourged you for your iniquities,
but will again have mercy on you all.
He will gather you from all the Gentiles
among whom you have been scattered.

13, 1: (*kai*) *egrapsen Tōbeith tēn proseuchēn tautēn eis aggalliasin kai* (*eipen*): so with LXX^{d,p}; cf LXX^{MSS}, Vet Lat, P; haplog. (*aiōna*) *'oti eis pantas tous aiōnas* (*'ē*): so LXX^{d,p}, Vet Lat; haplog.
13, 2: Omit *tēs gēs:* so Vet Lat; cf 4, 19.
13, 4: (*kathoti autos*) *kyrios 'o* (*theos 'ēmōn . . . patēr 'ēmōn kai*) *theos* (*eis*): so with Vet Lat.
13, 5: *emastigōsen:* so LXX^{d,p}, Vet Lat; (*eleēsei*) *kai synaxei 'ymas* (*ek pantōn*): so Vet Lat; cf LXX^{MSS}.

NRSV

13 Then Tobit[a] said:
"Blessed be God who lives forever,
because his kingdom[b] lasts throughout all ages.
2 For he afflicts, and he shows mercy;
he leads down to Hades in the lowest regions of the earth,
and he brings up from the great abyss,[c]
and there is nothing that can escape his hand.
3 Acknowledge him before the nations,
O children of Israel;
for he has scattered you among them.
4 He has shown you his greatness even there.
Exalt him in the presence of every living being,
because he is our Lord and he is our God;
he is our Father and he is God forever.
5 He will afflict[d] you for your iniquities,
but he will again show mercy on all of you.
He will gather you from all the nations
among whom you have been scattered.
6 If you turn to him with all your heart and with all your soul,
to do what is true before him,

a Gk *he* b Other ancient authorities read *forever, and his kingdom* c Gk *from destruction* d Other ancient authorities read *He afflicted*

NAB

6 When you turn back to him with all your heart,
to do what is right before him,
Then he will turn back to you,
and no longer hide his face from you.

So now consider what he has done for you,
and praise him with full voice.
Bless the Lord of righteousness,
and exalt the King of the ages.

In the land of my exile I praise him,
and show his power and majesty to a sinful nation.
"Turn back, you sinners! do the right before him:
perhaps he may look with favor upon you
and show you mercy.

7 "As for me, I exalt my God,
and my spirit rejoices in the King of heaven.
8 Let all men speak of his majesty,
and sing his praises in Jerusalem."

9 O Jerusalem, holy city,
he scourged you for the works of your hands,
but will again pity the children of the righteous.
10 Praise the Lord for his goodness,
and bless the King of the ages,
so that his tent may be rebuilt in you with joy.
May he gladden within you all who were captives;
all who were ravaged may he cherish within you
for all generations to come.

11 A bright light will shine to all parts of the earth;

13, 6a: Omit *kai en ʿolȩ̄ tȩ̄ psychȩ̄ ʿymōn:* so Vet Lat; cf P.
13, 6i-10b: From LXX[B], corrected principally by the other LXX[MSS] and by Vet Lat. These vv were omitted by LXX[S] because of haplog occasioned by homoeoteleuton (*ton basilea tōn aiōnōn* in 6h and in 10b).
13. 6j: *ethnei*: so LXX[MSS], Vet Lat.
13, 7: *egō* (*ton theon*): so LXX[d,p]. *ton basilea:* so LXX (all other MSS) Omit *kai* before *agalliasetai:* so LXX[d,p], *tēn megalōsynēn autou* belong in v 8 as object of *legetōsan:* cf Vet Lat.
13, 9: (*polis*) ʿ*agia* : so LXX[MSS], Vet Lat. *emastigōsen se:* so Vet Lat, V. (*erga tōn*) *cheirōn:* so LXX (2 MSS). Vet Lat. V.
13, 10c-f: (*skēnē*) *autou:* so LXX[MSS], V. en (*soi meta*): so LXX[MSS], Vet Lat, V. (*talaipōrous*) *eis* (*pasas tas geneas*): so LXX[MSS], Vet Lat; cf V.
13, 11: (*makrothen*) ʿ*ēxei soi* (*kai katoik*) *oi . . .* (*onoma*) *kyriou tou theou* (*kai*): so Brev. Mozarabicum; cf Vet Lat[MSS], LXX[MSS], V.

NRSV

then he will turn to you
and will no longer hide his face from you.
So now see what he has done for you;
acknowledge him at the top of your voice.
Bless the Lord of righteousness,
and exalt the King of the ages.[a]
In the land of my exile I acknowledge him,
and show his power and majesty to a nation of sinners:
'Turn back, you sinners, and do what is right before him;
perhaps he may look with favor upon you and show you mercy.'
7 As for me, I exalt my God,
and my soul rejoices in the King of heaven.
8 Let all people speak of his majesty,
and acknowledge him in Jerusalem.
9 O Jerusalem, the holy city,
he afflicted[b] you for the deeds of your hands,[c]
but will again have mercy on the children of the righteous.
10 Acknowledge the Lord, for he is good,[d]
and bless the King of the ages,
so that his tent[e] may be rebuilt in you in joy.
May he cheer all those within you who are captives,
and love all those within you who are distressed,
to all generations forever.
11 A bright light will shine to all the ends of the earth;
many nations will come to you from far away,
the inhabitants of the remotest parts of the earth to your holy name,
bearing gifts in their hands for the King of heaven.
Generation after generation will give joyful praise in you;
the name of the chosen city will endure forever.
12 Cursed are all who speak a harsh word against you;

[a] The lacuna in codex Sinaiticus, verses 6b to 10a, is filled in from other ancient authorities [b] Other ancient authorities read *will afflict* [c] Other ancient authorities read *your children* [d] Other ancient authorities read *Lord worthily* [e] Or *tabernacle*

NAB

many nations shall come to you from afar,
And the inhabitants of all the limits of the earth,
drawn to you by the name of the Lord God,
Bearing in their hands their gifts for the King of heaven.
Every generation shall give joyful praise in you,
and shall call you the chosen one,
through all ages forever.

12 Accursed are all who speak a harsh word against you;
accursed are all who destroy you
and pull down your walls,
And all who overthrow your towers
and set fire to your homes;
but forever blessed are all those who build you up.

13 Go, then, rejoice over the children of the righteous,
who shall all be gathered together
and shall bless the Lord of the ages.
14 Happy are those who love you,
and happy those who rejoice in your prosperity.

Happy are all the men who shall grieve over you,
over all your chastisements,
For they shall rejoice in you
as they behold all your joy forever.

15 My spirit blesses the Lord, the great King;
16 Jerusalem shall be rebuilt as his home forever.
Happy for me if a remnant of my offspring survive
to see your glory and to praise the King of heaven!

The gates of Jerusalem shall be built with sapphire and emerald,
and all your walls with precious stones.

13, 12: (*erousin*) *soi* (*logon*): conj. (*aiōna* ʻ*oi*) *oikodomountes* (*se*): so Vet Lat, V.
13, 16: (*oikodomēthēsetai*) *palin* (*oikos*): so Vet Lat.

NRSV

cursed are all who conquer you
and pull down your walls,
all who overthrow your towers
and set your homes on fire.
But blessed forever will be all who revere you.[a]
13 Go, then, and rejoice over the children of the righteous,
for they will be gathered together
and will praise the Lord of the ages.
14 Happy are those who love you,
and happy are those who rejoice in your prosperity.
Happy also are all people who grieve with you
because of your afflictions;
for they will rejoice with you
and witness all your glory forever.
15 My soul blesses[b] the Lord, the great King!
16 For Jerusalem will be built[c] as his house for all ages.
How happy I will be if a remnant of my descendants should survive
to see your glory and acknowledge the King of heaven.
The gates of Jerusalem will be built with sapphire and emerald,
and all your walls with precious stones.
The towers of Jerusalem will be built with gold,
and their battlements with pure gold.
The streets of Jerusalem will be paved
with ruby and with stones of Ophir.
17 The gates of Jerusalem will sing hymns of joy,
and all her houses will cry, 'Hallelujah!
Blessed be the God of Israel!'
and the blessed will bless the holy name forever and ever."

[a] Other ancient authorities read *who build you up* [b] Or *O my soul, bless* [c] Other ancient authorities add *for a city*

NAB

The towers of Jerusalem shall be built with gold,
and their battlements with pure gold.
17 The streets of Jerusalem shall be paved
with rubies and stones of Ophir;
18 The gates of Jerusalem shall sing hymns of gladness,
and all her houses shall cry out, "Alleluia!"

"Blessed be God who has raised you up!
may he be blessed for all ages!"
For in you they shall praise his holy name forever.

13, 17: *Ophir:* LXX has *Soupheir;* cf 1 Kgs 10, 11; 2 Chr 9, 10; Is 13, 12 in MT and LXX.

13, 18: (*theos*) ‘*os* ‘*ypsōsen se:* so LXX^{MSS}, V^{MSS}; Cf Vet Lat. After *se* read *kai eulogētos eis pantas tous aiōnas,* ‘*oti en soi* (*eulogēsousin to onoma*) *autou* (*to* ‘*agion* : so Vet Lat^{MSS}.

COMMENTARY

Chapter 13 is the last and longest prayer in this book of prayer.[111] It can be considered in two parts: (1) Tobit's praise of God's justice and mercy and gratitude for his healing (vv. 1-8) and (2) Tobit's meditation on the new Jerusalem (vv. 9-18).[112]

13:1-8. These verses comprise the prayer of an individual who has been delivered from the deepest distress and affliction (see 3:2-6). The prayer is couched, however, in general terms and phrases that draw from the wealth of biblical prayers. Thus, like the prayers of Hannah (1 Sam 2:1-10) and Jonah (Jonah 2:30-10), it becomes a prayer of thanksgiving for all who are delivered from distress.

In this way Tobit himself becomes a model for his people Israel. He can bear witness that the God who chastises also shows mercy, that the One who leads down to the darkness of Sheol also leads out into the light. He can also assert that the God who has scattered the people will again gather them. For this reason, Tobit calls his kindred to turn to God and join in his praise.

This prayer has elements of both the songs of thanksgiving and the hymns. As in songs of thanksgiving, the memory of Tobit's own affliction and deliverance is very near. He expresses his intention to give thanks and praise to God. However, no detailed description of his distress appears. The general phrases concerning God's deliverance resemble the hymn, as do the repeated calls to give praise and the list of reasons for praise.

Just as the story of Tobit's life exhibits the basic principles of deuteronomic theology in narrative form, so also this prayer exemplifies much of deuteronomic theology in the language of prayer. The concept of joy permeates Deuteronomy (e.g., Deut 12:7; 14:26; 16:11; see Tob 13:1, 7). The theory of retribution is a deuteronomic concept (Deuteronomy 28). If the people obey God, they will have long life in the land; if they disobey, they choose death and doom (Deut 30:17-20; see Tob 13:5). The living God gives people a choice between life and death (v. 1). Deuteronomy exhorts the people to turn back to God with their whole heart and soul (Deut 30:2, 10; see Tob 13:6). In Deuteronomy, Israel is required to wor-

111. For a thorough analysis, see P. J. Griffin, "The Theology and Function of Prayer in the Book of Tobit" (Ph.D. diss., The Catholic University of America, 1984) 224-348. His strophic structure differs from mine.

112. The text of G^{II} is incomplete. It is supplemented by G^{I} from v. 6*i* ("I give praise in the land of my captivity") through v. 10*b* ("and bless the king of the ages").

ship God in the place the Lord chooses—that is, Jerusalem (e.g., Deut 12:5, 11, 14). In his youth, Tobit was faithful to the cult in Jerusalem (1:6-8). Now confident of a return from exile, he exhorts his people to praise God again in Jerusalem (v. 8).

Weitzman uses the allusion in Tobit 13 to Deuteronomy 32 (cf. Tob 13:2 with Deut 32:39; Tob 13:6 with Deut 32:20) to link Tobit 12–13 with Deuteronomy 31–32, the farewell speech and song of Moses. He concludes that the biblical allusions in the book of Tobit move from the beginning of the Pentateuch (the betrothal scenes from Genesis, the similarity between Raguel and Abraham, the Joseph story) to its end (Deuteronomy). He also notes that the allusions all come from scenes that take place outside the land of Israel. The farewell speech and the Song of Moses occur just before the people's entrance into the land. Thus the biblical allusion to the whole Pentateuch reinforces the content of Tobit's life story and his song. Tobit's life is lived according to the Torah from beginning to end. His song promises that the banishment from the land of Israel will soon end.[113]

After the title, the first section can be divided into four strophes: (1) invocation and call to prayer (vv. 1*b*-2); (2) reasons for praise (vv. 3-5); (3) call to conversion (v. 6*a-h*); (4) Tobit as example of one who praises God (vv. 6*i*-8). Strophe 1 is a general, third-person statement concerning God. Strophes 2 and 3 are in the second person, directed to the hearers. Strophe 2 begins and ends with a statement about being scattered among the nations. Strophe 3 has an inner unity owing to the repetition of "whole heart," "whole soul," "whole voice." It ends with an echo of strophe 1 ("bless," "king of the ages"). Strophe 4 is Tobit's own, first-person declaration of praise. He repeats the notion of God's kingship from strophes 1 and 3. The whole poem is bound together by the repetition of the key words of blessing and praise: εὐλογητός/εὐλογέω (*eulogētos/ eulogeō*, "bless") in vv. 1 and 6; ἐξομολογέω (*exomologeō*, "give thanks/acknowledge") in vv. 3, 6, 8; ὑψόω (*hypsoō*, "exalt") in vv. 4, 6-7.

The second section of Tobit's prayer (vv. 9-17) can be considered in four units: (1) the call to Jerusalem, vv. 9-11; (2) curses and blessings, vv. 12-14; (3) Tobit's own prayer, vv. 15-16*d;* (4) the new Jerusalem, vv. 16*e*-18. The division is based on content. The poetic structure is not clear, and the lengths of the units vary. Each unit contains a call to praise God (vv. 10, 13, 15, 18).

The key word "bless/blessed" recurs frequently in this second part of Tobit's prayer (*eulogeō* in vv. 10, 13, 15, 18; *eulogētos* in vv. 12, 18). Two repeated terms connoting the breadth of the prayer are "all" (πᾶς *pas*; see also vv. 4-5) and "forever/ages" (αἰών *aiōn*; see also vv. 1, 4, 6). All who are captives, all who are distressed for all generations will be comforted (v. 10). All who despise, hate, revile, destroy, overthrow Jerusalem will be cursed (v. 12). All the children of the righteous will be gathered together (v. 13). All who grieve over all Jerusalem's afflictions will behold all its joy (v. 14). All of Jerusalem's walls will be built of precious stones; it will stand as God's house for all ages (v. 16). Its light will shine to all the ends of the earth, and people from all the ends of the earth will come to give praise (v. 11). All its houses will sing, "Hallelujah," as God is praised for all the ages (v. 18).

The hope for the new Jerusalem is everlasting. God will cherish the distressed within it for all generations forever (*aiōn*). Those who stand in awe of Jerusalem will be blessed forever (v. 12), and those who rejoice over it will see its joy forever (v. 14). Jerusalem will be rebuilt as God's house forever (v. 16), for God is King and Lord of "forever" (vv. 10, 13), whose name will be blessed forever and ever (vv. 11, 18).

Tobit's description of Jerusalem as the hope of the future reflects the vision of Israel's prophets. Jerusalem will be rebuilt with precious stones (Isa 54:11-12) and will be the source of great light (Isa 60:1-3), which many nations will come to see (Isa 60:1-14; see also Mic 4:2; Zech 8:22). Those who love Jerusalem will rejoice (Isa 66:10, 14), while those who do not serve Jerusalem will be destroyed (Isa 60:12). In the prophets' glorious vision of the future, the scattered will be gathered again (Isa 35:1-10; 52:1-12; Jer 31:7-14), and the blind will be restored to sight (Isa 35:5; 42:16; 58:8, 10). The new Jerusalem upon which Tobit builds his hope is the one the prophets have described.

In Tobit's final prayer, his personal character

113. S. Weitzman, "Allusion, Artifice, and Exile in the Hymn of Tobit," *JBL* 115 (1996) 49-61.

traits are raised to a public and national level. He, an ordinary man, a model of the true Israelite, is willing to present himself as an example for his people. His trust in God's justice and mercy is strong enough not only to support his own life, but also to demand an equal trust from his nation. His love of Jerusalem flows through his whole life, allowing him to identify with it to such an extent that he can recognize its sorrow as his sorrow, and hope for its joy as he has known joy. His awareness of his responsibility to make public proclamation in thanksgiving for God's gifts to him (see 12:6-7, 18-20) leads him to call all his people to join in his hymn of grateful praise. Even as he recognizes that his life is dependent on the pleasure of God (see 3:6), he knows that his life makes a difference. He is set up as an example, and he is called to exhort and instruct not only his son and his grandchildren, but all the kindred of his nation and finally all humanity (vv. 8, 11).

13:1a. Tobit wrote his prayer with joy. The concept of joy occurs frequently in the book of Tobit: He complains that because of his affliction he has no joy (5:10); God brings joy to Raguel and Sarah by means of Tobiah (8:16, 20); joy returns to Tobit (11:15-16) and to all the Jews of Nineveh through God's mercy (11:17-18). The prayers are particularly filled with expressions of joy: Raguel's (8:16-17) and Tobit's (13:1, 7, 10-11, 13-14).

13:1b-2. Tobit begins his prayer with *eulogētos* ("blessed"). This word begins four other major prayers in the book: Sarah's (3:11); Tobiah's (8:5); Raguel's (8:15); and Tobit's (11:14). Tobit praises the living God and, as Raphael had exhorted him, calls his people to praise God before all other living beings (see 12:6). He proclaims that God and God's kingdom are eternal (see 3:11; 8:5, 15; 11:14).

In the second verse of his prayer, Tobit announces the theme of the whole prayer: God is just in everything, both in chastisement and in mercy. This theme appears throughout the book. The earlier prayers ask God for mercy (3:15; 8:7, 17); the later prayers praise God for righteousness in both punishment and mercy (11:15; 13:2, 5, 9; cf. 14:5).

God's power and presence extend to all places. Nothing can escape the One who leads down to Sheol/Hades and back again. In his counsel to Tobiah (4:19), Tobit reminded his son of the power of God. Tobit knows of it from his own experience. He considered himself as good as dead (5:10), but God's mercy restored him to the light (11:14-15). These ideas appear frequently in other biblical prayers as well—for example, the Song of Hannah (1 Sam 2:6), the prayer of Jonah (Jonah 2:3, 7), and some psalms (e.g., Pss 30:4; 86:13). The idea is echoed also in the book of Wisdom (Wis 16:13, 15).

13:3-5. Each strophe of this poem builds on the preceding one. In the second strophe, the general statements of strophe 1 concerning God's righteousness and power are applied specifically to exiled Israel. Tobit is an example for the exiled nation, which also seems as good as dead (see Ezek 37:1-14). Thus the second strophe begins with a summons to the dispersed Israelites to praise God among the nations where they have been scattered. Even there they remain in God's hand, and they must proclaim God's greatness before all the living (12:6; see Deut 32:3; Sir 39:15). Proclaiming God's deeds among the nations also is a frequent theme in the psalms (see Pss 9:12; 96:3; 105:1).

Who do they proclaim? Their God is the Lord, the eternal God (see Pss 18:32; 40:6; 71:19; 77:14). This God is "our Father." The concept of God as the father of the people Israel begins with Exod 4:22: "Israel is my son, my firstborn" (see Hos 11:1; Jer 31:9). The title "my father" appears in Jer 3:4 and Sir 51:10. However, most references to God as "our Father" appear in prayers of the post-exilic period (Isa 63:16; 64:7; see also Sir 23:1, 4; Wis 14:3).[114]

Israel, however, has not been exiled simply for the purpose of proclaiming God before the nations. The people must recognize God's righteousness in their chastisement (see 3:2-5). God as father disciplines disobedient children (see Prov 13:24; Sir 30:1), but will again have mercy and gather them together (see Ps 104:46; Jer 23:3; Ezek 36:24).

13:6a-h. The third strophe builds on the second. Since it is God who chastises and has mercy, exiles and gathers, Israel can hope for mercy only by turning to God. This is the great prophetic cry

114. See Angelika Strotmann, *"Mein Vater Bist Du!" (Sir 51, 10): Zur Bedeutung der Vaterschaft Gottes in kanonischen und nicht kanonischen frühjüdischen Schriften,* FTS 39 (Frankfurt am Main: Josef Knecht, 1991).

of שׁוב (*šûb*, "turn"; e.g., Isa 31:6; Jer 3:12, 14, 22; Hos 14:2-3). When Israel turns, God, too, will turn (Zech 1:3; Mal 3:7); never again will God's face be hidden (see Ps 30:8).

Israel, however, must act in wholeness and in truth (see 4:6; 14:9). With open eyes, Israel must see God's action, bless God's righteousness, and exalt the One who rules over all times and places (Pss 145:13; 146:10). Again Tobit is the example. He walks in truth and righteousness (1:3). Both his eyes and his heart have been opened to God's light (11:13-15, 17). He praises God's righteousness (3:2).

13:6i-8. In the final strophe of the first section, Tobit declares his own praise of God. He, the true Israelite, gives himself as an example to the nation. He has called Israel to praise with four imperatives: "acknowledge/give thanks" (*exomologeō*) in vv. 3 and 6; "recount/show" (ὑποδείκνυμι *hypodeiknymi*) in v. 4;[115] "bless" (*eulogeō*) in v. 6; and "exalt" (*hypsoō*) in vv. 4 and 6. He repeats two of these verbs and a related verb in his own recital of praise: "acknowledge/give thanks" (*exomologeō*) in v. 6; "declare/show" (δείκνυμι *deiknymi*) in v. 6; "exalt" (*hypsoō*) in v. 7. He who has suffered adversity praises God and proclaims God's greatness. He who has called Israel to declare God's majesty before the nations himself declares God's strength and majesty before his own sinful nation, Israel.

Tobit repeats the call to turn and act in righteousness. In words echoing the "perhaps" of Joel 2:14, he declares his confidence in God's mercy (see also Amos 5:15; Jonah 3:9). Perhaps God will relent and act mercifully (lit., "do alms" [ποιήσει ἐλεημοσύνην *poiēsei eleēmosynēn*]).

Three linked words of the book appear in these last two strophes. If Israel acts in "truth" (ἀλήθεια *alētheia*, v. 6) and "righteousness" (δικαιοσύνη *dikaiosynē*, v. 6), the Lord of righteousness (*dikaiosynē*, v. 6) will show "mercy" (ἐλεημοσύνη *eleēmosynē*, v. 6) to them. The book itself is framed by an inclusio of these three words (1:3; 14:9; see also 3:2).

Tobit ends the first section in the same spirit of joy with which he began. He concludes this prayer made "in the land of his exile" by calling for prayer "in Jerusalem" to the God who rules all space, "the king of heaven."

13:9-11. In the first unit of the second section, Tobit suggests that the pattern of his own story offers hope to Jerusalem, destroyed and depopulated. He repeats the terms "afflict" (μαστιγόω *mastigoō*) and "have mercy" (ἐλεέω *eleeō*) from his general description of God and from his call to the exiled Israelites (see vv. 2, 5). He refers to God as "King of the ages" and "King of heaven," echoing his initial statement about God and his final petition (see vv. 2, 7). He emphasizes again the need for righteousness (see v. 6), and just as he called the exiled Israelites to give thanks and bless God, so, too, now he calls the city to do the same.[116]

The theme of retribution undergirds the unit. The powerful God, King of the ages, who punished Jerusalem for wickedness, will restore the city and its righteous citizens. Restoration comes, however, not only because of the renewed righteousness of the people, but also because of the mercy of God. The central concern of the section is introduced: Jerusalem, God's holy city, must be restored and the Temple rebuilt. Then the Israelites will be comforted, and all nations will be drawn to the city to worship God. The theme of joy continues to permeate the prayer.

13:12-14. The second unit begins with curses and ends with beatitudes. The list of curses varies in the textual witnesses. The Qumran text 4QTob[a] and the Old Latin offer the fullest text:

Cursed be all who despise you and revile you;
cursed be all who hate you
and speak a harsh word against you;
cursed be all who destroy you
and pull down your walls.[117]

115. The Qumran text 4QTob[e] and G[I] have an imperative at the beginning of 13:4. G[II], however, has the third-person verb, "He has shown."

116. There are a couple of textual problems: In 13:9, G[I] (G[II] is not available) reads, "works of your children [τὰ ἔργα τῶν υἱῶν *ta erga tōn huiōn*]," whereas the Old Latin reads "works of your hands [*in operibus manuum tuarum*]." In 13:10, G[I] reads, "Give thanks to the Lord worthily [ἀγαθός *agathos*]," where 4QTob[a] reads, "with righteousness [בקושטא הודי *bqwšṭ*ʾ *hwdy*]." In 13:11, where G[II] reads "your holy name [τὸ ὄνομα το ἅγιον σου *to onoma to hagion sou*; i.e., Jerusalem's]," G[I] and the Old Latin have the name of God (G[I]: τὸ ὄνομα κυρίου τοῦ θεοῦ [*to onoma kyriou tou theou*]; VL: *ad nomen Dei mei*).

117. The first line of the curses is found only in the Qumran text 4QTob[a] ([כי] ארי[רין כ]ל [די] ביזין ול די עלי ʾ*ryryn kl dy byzyn wl dy* ʿ*ly ky*) and the Old Latin (*Maledicti omnes qui spernunt te, et omnes qui blasphemant te*). G[II] has only lines 3-5 (ἐπικατάρατοι πάντες οἵ ἐροῦσιν λογον σκληρόν ἐπικατάρατοι ἔσονται πάντες οἱ καθαιρουντες σε καὶ κατασπῶντες τὰ τείχη σου *epikataratoi pantes, hoi erousin logon sklēron, epikataratoi esontai pantes hoi kathairountes se kai kataspōntes ta teichē sou*). G[I] has only line 2 (ἐπικατάρατοι πάντες οἱ μισοῦντες σε *epikataratoi pantes hoi misountes se*).

Anyone who has destroyed Jerusalem in the past or who does so in the future comes under this curse.

Cursing does not dominate the unit, however—blessing does. The beatitudes that end the unit are anticipated in v. 12 with a blessing on those who stand in awe of Jerusalem. In G^{II}, the same term used for "fear" of the Lord (οἱ φοβούμενοί σε *hoi phoboumenoi se*) is here applied to God's city. (In G^{I}, the blessing is for those who "love" the city [οἱ ἀγαπῶντές σε *hoi agapōntes se*].) The city is then called to rejoice over the people who will be gathered again within it to bless God (see vv. 3-5, 10, 18). God is named "Lord of the ages" (see "King of the ages" in v. 10).

The beatitudes balance the curses, and the theme of joy recurs. Along with a threefold exclamation, "Happy are (μακάριοι *makarioi*)," is a threefold statement of joy: Those who rejoice (χαρήσονται *charēsontai*) in Jerusalem's peace and those who once grieved over its afflictions now will rejoice (*charēsontai*) and behold Jerusalem's joy (χαράν *charan*) forever.[118]

13:15-16d. In the third unit Tobit breaks in as the singer of the prayer. Here the call to praise is to himself ("my soul" [ἡ ψυχή μου *hē psychē mou*]). He calls himself to bless the Lord, "the great King" (see "king" in vv. 6-7, 10 and "kingdom" in v. 1). His reason for praise echoes the reason he has given to Jerusalem: The city will be rebuilt as the house of God (see v. 10). He speaks a beatitude over himself, a prayer that his descendants will see the restored city and themselves give thanks to "the King of heaven" (see v. 7).

13:16e-17. The fourth unit is a description of the new Jerusalem. The name of the city is repeated four times, as if Tobit cannot let go of the delight of its name (see "name" in v. 11). The promise of rebuilding from vv. 10 and 16 is fulfilled in Tobit's vision. Gates, walls, towers, and streets will be made of gold and precious stones. As if answering the call to prayer, even the gates and the houses will sing hymns and cry out, "Hallelujah" (see Ps 24:7, 9).

Tobit ends his prayer just as he began it, with a call to praise: "Blessed be God . . . for all ages!"[119] This call is addressed to the new Jerusalem, wherein God's name will be blessed forever.[120] Jerusalem remains the place where God has chosen to set the divine name (see Deut 12:5, 11).

118. G^{I} reads Jerusalem's "glory" (δόξαν *doxan*). See G^{II} 13:16, where Tobit's descendants see Jerusalem's "glory."

119. "For all ages" appears in 4QTob[a] (עלמיא [עלם] [*ʿlm*] *ʿlmyʾ*) and the Old Latin (*im omnia saecula saeculorum*).

120. 4QTob[a] and VL begin the last line with "for in you" (דביכי *dbyky*; quoniam in te).

REFLECTIONS

1. Tobit believes that, just as his suffering mirrors that of his community, so also his healing is a sign of hope for it. Christians have been taught that together we are the body of Christ, that "if one member suffers, all suffer together with it; if one member is honored, all rejoice together with it" (1 Cor 12:26 NRSV). It is impossible for Christians to celebrate eucharist without being joined to one another. In the Liturgy of the Word we tell the story that gives us a common identity. We recite the creed that expresses our common belief. As we pray in petition for those in need and in thanksgiving for those who have been blessed, we acknowledge that their pain and joy are also ours. We share the meal that expresses the sharing of our lives. If we eat and drink without discerning the body (i.e., Christ in one another), we eat and drink judgment on ourselves (see 1 Chr 11:29). Finally, we are set forth to live the mystery we have celebrated: our oneness in Christ Jesus.

2. In Christian theology the new Jerusalem is also the hope of the future. The book of Revelation describes a glorious city in which "there shall be no more death or mourning, wailing or pain" (see Rev 21:4). The glory of God will be its light (Rev 21:23); the river of life-giving water will flow from God's throne (Rev 22:1). God will be so present there that a temple will no longer be needed (Rev 21:22). There all the faithful will see God's face and praise God's name forever (Rev 22:3-4).

The new Jerusalem is an image of the life that awaits God's faithful people. The reality of this new life is impossible to describe. "Eye has not seen, and ear has not heard" what God has prepared (see 1 Cor 2:9). We know two things: This new life has been won for us by Christ, and our delight will be the sharing of God's presence with one another.

TOBIT 14:1-15, EPILOGUE

NAB

14 14 1 Tobit died peacefully at the age of a hundred and twelve, and received an honorable burial in Nineveh. 2 He was sixty-two years old when he lost his eyesight, and after he recovered it he lived in prosperity, giving alms and continually blessing God and praising the divine Majesty.

3 Just before he died, he called his son Tobiah and Tobiah's seven sons, and gave him this command: "Son, take your children 4 and flee into Media, for I believe God's word which was spoken by Nahum against Nineveh. It shall all happen, and shall overtake Assyria and Nineveh; indeed, whatever was said by Israel's prophets, whom God commissioned, shall occur. Not one of all the oracles shall remain unfulfilled, but everything shall take place in the time appointed for it. So it will be safer in Media than in Assyria or Babylon. For I know and believe that whatever God has spoken will be accomplished. It shall happen, and not a single word of the prophecies shall prove false.

"As for our kinsmen who dwell in Israel, they shall all be scattered and led away into exile from the Good Land. The entire country of Israel shall become desolate; even Samaria and Jerusalem shall become desolate! God's temple there shall be burnt to the ground and shall be desolate for a while. 5 But God will again have mercy on them and bring them back to the land of Israel.

14, 3: (*autou kai*) *tous* ʽ*epta* ʽ*uious autou kai:* so Vet Lat; Qumran Ms; cf V, LXX[MSS]; haplog.

14, 4: *Athour* (*kai Nineuē*): so Vet Lat; cf v 15. (*gē Israēl pant*) *es diaskorpisthēsontai* (*kai*): so Vet Lat; cf LXX[MSS] and 3, 4; 13, 5. (*theou en*) *autē̜* (*kauthēsetai*) *kai estai erēmos* (*mechri*): so with Vet Lat; cf LXX[MSS x].

14, 5: (*oikodomēthēsetai*) *kai eis pantas tas geneas tou aiōnas oikodomēthēsetai* (*kathōs*): so with Vet Lat; cf LXX[MSS], P; haplog.

NRSV

14 So ended Tobit's words of praise.

2 Tobit[a] died in peace when he was one hundred twelve years old, and was buried with great honor in Nineveh. He was sixty-two[b] years old when he lost his eyesight, and after regaining it he lived in prosperity, giving alms and continually blessing God and acknowledging God's majesty.

3 When he was about to die, he called his son Tobias and the seven sons of Tobias[c] and gave this command: "My son, take your children 4 and hurry off to Media, for I believe the word of God that Nahum spoke about Nineveh, that all these things will take place and overtake Assyria and Nineveh. Indeed, everything that was spoken by the prophets of Israel, whom God sent, will occur. None of all their words will fail, but all will come true at their appointed times. So it will be safer in Media than in Assyria and Babylon. For I know and believe that whatever God has said will be fulfilled and will come true; not a single word of the prophecies will fail. All of our kindred, inhabitants of the land of Israel, will be scattered and taken as captives from the good land; and the whole land of Israel will be desolate, even Samaria and Jerusalem will be desolate. And the temple of God in it will be burned to the ground, and it will be desolate for a while.[d]

5 "But God will again have mercy on them, and God will bring them back into the land of Israel; and they will rebuild the temple of God, but not like the first one until the period when the times of fulfillment shall come. After this they all will return from their exile and will rebuild Jerusalem

[a] Gk *He* [b] Other ancient authorities read *fifty-eight* [c] Lat: Gk lacks *and the seven sons of Tobias* [d] Lat: Other ancient authorities read *of God will be in distress and will be burned for a while*

NAB

They shall rebuild the temple, but it will not be like the first one, until the era when the appointed times shall be completed. Afterward all of them shall return from their exile, and they shall rebuild Jerusalem with splendor. In her the temple of God shall also be rebuilt; yes, it will be rebuilt for all generations to come, just as the prophets of Israel said of her. 6 All the nations of the world shall be converted and shall offer God true worship; all shall abandon their idols which have deceitfully led them into error, 7 and shall bless the God of the ages in righteousness. Because all the Israelites who are to be saved in those days will truly be mindful of God, they shall be gathered together and go to Jerusalem; in security shall they dwell forever in the land of Abraham, which will be given over to them. Those who sincerely love God shall rejoice, but those who become guilty of sin shall completely disappear from the land.

9 "Now, children, I give you this command: serve God faithfully and do what is right before him; you must tell your children to do what is upright and to give alms, to be mindful of God and at all times to bless his name sincerely and with all their strength.

8 "Now, as for you, my son, depart from Nineveh; do not remain here. 10 The day you bury your mother next to me, do not even stay overnight within the confines of the city. For I see that people here shamelessly commit all sorts of wickedness and treachery. Think, my son, of all that Nadab did to Ahiqar, the very one who brought him up: Ahiqar went down alive into the earth! Yet God made Nadab's disgraceful crime rebound against him. Ahiqar came out again into the light, but Nadab went into the everlasting darkness, for he had tried to kill Ahiqar. Because Ahiqar had given alms to me, he escaped from the deadly trap Nadab had set for him. But Nadab himself fell into the deadly trap, and it destroyed him. 11 So, my children, note well what almsgiving does, and also what wickedness does—it kills! But now my spirit is about to leave me." 12 They placed him on his bed and he died; and he received an honorable burial. When Tobiah's

14, 10: (*poiēsai*) *moi:* conj; cf 2, 10.
14, 12: (*gynē autou*) *kai ʿoi ʿuioi autou* (*eis*): so with LXX^{MSS}; cf Vet Lat, P; haplog.

NRSV

in splendor; and in it the temple of God will be rebuilt, just as the prophets of Israel have said concerning it. [6]Then the nations in the whole world will all be converted and worship God in truth. They will all abandon their idols, which deceitfully have led them into their error; [7]and in righteousness they will praise the eternal God. All the Israelites who are saved in those days and are truly mindful of God will be gathered together; they will go to Jerusalem and live in safety forever in the land of Abraham, and it will be given over to them. Those who sincerely love God will rejoice, but those who commit sin and injustice will vanish from all the earth. [8,9]So now, my children, I command you, serve God faithfully and do what is pleasing in his sight. Your children are also to be commanded to do what is right and to give alms, and to be mindful of God and to bless his name at all times with sincerity and with all their strength. So now, my son, leave Nineveh; do not remain here. [10]On whatever day you bury your mother beside me, do not stay overnight within the confines of the city. For I see that there is much wickedness within it, and that much deceit is practiced within it, while the people are without shame. See, my son, what Nadab did to Ahikar who had reared him. Was he not, while still alive, brought down into the earth? For God repaid him to his face for this shameful treatment. Ahikar came out into the light, but Nadab went into the eternal darkness, because he tried to kill Ahikar. Because he gave alms, Ahikar[a] escaped the fatal trap that Nadab had set for him, but Nadab fell into it himself, and was destroyed. [11]So now, my children, see what almsgiving accomplishes, and what injustice does—it brings death! But now my breath fails me."

Then they laid him on his bed, and he died; and he received an honorable funeral. [12]When Tobias's mother died, he buried her beside his father. Then he and his wife and children[b] returned to Media and settled in Ecbatana with Raguel his father-in-law. [13]He treated his parents-in-law[c] with great respect in their old age, and buried them in Ecbatana of Media. He inherited both the property of Raguel and that of his father

[a] Gk *he*; other ancient authorities read *Manasses* [b] Codex Sinaiticus lacks *and children* [c] Gk *them*

NAB

mother died, he buried her next to his father. He then departed with his wife and children for Media, where he settled in Ecbatana with his father-in-law Raguel. 13 He took respectful care of his aging father-in-law and mother-in-law; and he buried them at Ecbatana in Media. Then he inherited Raguel's estate as well as that of his father Tobit. 14 He died at the venerable age of a hundred and seventeen. 15 But before he died, he heard of the destruction of Nineveh and saw its effects. He witnessed the exile of the city's inhabitants when Cyaxares, king of Media, led them captive into Media. Tobiah praised God for all that he had done against the citizens of Nineveh and Assyria. Before dying he rejoiced over Nineveh's destruction, and he blessed the Lord God forever and ever. Amen.

14, 15: *Kyaxarēs:* all the Vrs are corrupt.

NRSV

Tobit. [14]He died highly respected at the age of one hundred seventeen[a] years. [15]Before he died he heard[b] of the destruction of Nineveh, and he saw its prisoners being led into Media, those whom King Cyaxares[c] of Media had taken captive. Tobias[d] praised God for all he had done to the people of Nineveh and Assyria; before he died he rejoiced over Nineveh, and he blessed the Lord God forever and ever. Amen.[e]

[a] Other authorities read other numbers [b] Codex Sinaiticus reads *saw and heard* [c] Cn: Codex Sinaiticus *Ahikar*, other ancient authorities read *Nebuchadnezzar and Ahasuerus* [d] Gk *He* [e] Other ancient authorities lack *Amen*

COMMENTARY

At its end, the story returns to its original calm. The epilogue (14:1-15) reports the permanent state of prosperity of the characters and their final end, thus reinforcing the claim of the plot (and the theory of retribution) that God rewards charitable deeds.

Tobit's final instruction to Tobiah (vv. 3-11) is the third and final farewell discourse of the book (see chaps. 4 and 12).[121] It has several of the elements of the farewell discourse: Tobit announces his imminent death (v. 11); he recalls the past and predicts the future; he recalls the words of the prophets concerning the exile and predicts that they will indeed be fulfilled (vv. 4-7); he also recalls the story of Ahiqar (v. 10). He exhorts his children and grandchildren to keep God's commandments and to be virtuous and honest (v. 9). He wants to protect his children and grandchildren from the destruction he is sure will overwhelm Nineveh (vv. 9-10).

14:1-2. The end of Tobit's life is a confirmation of the truth of the theory of retribution. He, a just man, is richly blessed. He enjoys a full old age[122] with prosperity, and he lives to see his grandchildren, seven in number,[123] signifying a perfect fullness. Deuteronomy promises these rewards to the just (e.g., Deut 4:40; 5:29; 6:1-2; 11:21; 30:19-20). Tobit is like Job, who, although he suffered for a time, "lived one hundred and forty years, and saw his children, and his children's children, four generations . . . and Job died, old and full of days" (Job 42:16-17 NRSV). The description of the righteous person in Psalm 112 promises powerful and blessed descendants, wealth, and riches (Ps 112:1-3). Wisdom herself gives long life, riches, and honor (Prov 3:16; 8:18): "The reward for humility and fear of the LORD is riches and honor and life" (Prov 22:4 NRSV).

121. See A. A. Di Lella, "The Deuteronomic Background of the Farewell Discourse in Tob 14:3-11," *CBQ* 41 (1979) 380-89.

122. There is a textual problem concerning Tobit's age when he lost his eyesight (14:2). The Qumran texts (4QTob[a] and 4QTob[e]), along with the Old Latin and G[I], indicate that he was fifty-eight years old when he lost his eyesight. G[II] alone says that he was sixty-two.

123. The number "seven" for Tobiah's sons comes from the Old Latin (*septem filios eius*). Fitzmyer also restores 4QTob[a] and 4QTob[c] to read "seven," although he acknowledges they could also read "six," which is what G[I] reads (τοὺς ἕξ υἱούς *tous hex huious*). G[II] does not mention Tobit's grandchildren. See J. A. Fitzmyer, "The Aramaic and Hebrew Fragments of Tobit from Qumran Cave 4," *CBQ* 57 (1995) 663; J. A. Fitzmyer, *Tobit: Qumran Cave 4, xiv*, DJD 19, ed. M. Broshi et al. (Oxford: Clarendon, 1995) 29-31, 57-59.

14:3-8. Tobit exhorts his son to trust the Word of God, spoken through the prophets (vv. 3-4, 8). He has already demonstrated his familiarity with the Word of God and his habit of looking to that Word to shed light on his own life. When the joy of his Pentecost feast turned to mourning, he recalled the appropriate words of the prophet Amos (Tob 2:6; cf. Amos 8:10). Now he exhorts his son to believe God's Word and to act on it. Tobiah will live to see his father's faith justified (v. 15). (The author, writing in the 2nd cent. BCE, already knows that Assyria was defeated and Nineveh destroyed.)

Tobit cites Nahum, a seventh-century prophet whose whole work consists of rejoicing over the fall of Nineveh in 612 BCE. The Greek recension G^{I} reads "Jonah" instead of Nahum. Jonah is a fictional work about a prophet who is sent by God to Nineveh. When, after some resistance to God's call, he finally goes to Nineveh, his words are instrumental in converting the whole city. God, who had intended to punish the Ninevites, instead forgives them, much to Jonah's chagrin. Tobit's whole message is changed if one reads "Jonah" instead of "Nahum." Tobiah would have no need to leave Nineveh. All its citizens would turn to God, and God would turn to them in blessing instead of destruction.

Tobit's vision of the restoration of Israel echoes the prophets and the books of Ezra–Nehemiah. Jeremiah describes a vision of the restored Jerusalem and its faithful population (Jer 31:7-14; 33:6-22). Ezekiel envisions the Lord's return to a glorious new temple, built according to the pattern of the old one (Ezek 43:1-5; see also Ezek 40:1–42:20). The prophet Haggai had the singular commission to tell the returned exiles to rebuild the destroyed Temple, and within a few months the work began. However, Haggai remarks that to those who "saw this house in its former glory" the new Temple seemed like nothing (Hag 2:3). Ezra also reports the weeping of the old men who had seen the former Temple (Ezra 3:12-13).

14:9. After his discourse on the prophetic word, Tobit instructs his son and grandchildren in righteous living as he had earlier instructed his son (4:3-21) and as his grandmother had instructed him (1:8). His exhortation includes those virtues of which his own life has been an example: truth, righteousness, almsgiving (1:3), and mindfulness of God and prayer (see 3:2-6; 5:17; 11:14-15; 13:1-18). Not only are his son and his grandchildren to live such lives, but they also are to exhort their children as he has done for Tobiah and for them.

14:10-11a. Tobit concludes by telling a little story to illustrate his belief that "almsgiving frees one from death, and keeps one from going into the dark abode" (4:10; see also 14:11), just as he, the almsgiver, has been freed from darkness (11:14). (For a synopsis of the story of Ahiqar, see the Introduction.) This incident is itself an example of theology of narrative—that is, telling a story in order to inculcate virtue in the midst of a book that is doing the same thing. Throughout the book, the instructions of the father to the son are embodied for the son in the actions of the father. For Tobiah, Tobit's actions speak as loudly as his words.

14:11b-14. Tobit, who had risked everything to give honorable burial to others (1:17-20; 2:7-10), is himself buried with honor. After Anna's death, she is buried next to Tobit. Raguel and Edna are buried in Ecbatana. Finally, the death of Tobiah is reported. Thus this book, which is preoccupied with death and the ceremonies surrounding it,[124] closes with the deaths of all the main characters except Sarah and Raphael.

Tobit assumes the responsibility for the care of his parents and his wife's parents in their old age and for their honorable burial. He is again obedient to his father, but now it is the obedience of the grown man, responsible for his own actions. He heeds his father's instruction in carrying out the proper burial of Tobit and in burying his mother next to his father (see 4:3-4). He also obeys his father by leaving Nineveh immediately after the death of Anna (see v. 10). He is an example of filial love.

Tobiah's life also testifies to the validity of the theory of retribution. Like his father, he is a just man. He lives a long life, dying at the age of 117. He is also prosperous, having inherited the estates of both Tobit and Raguel, and he has a full number of descendants: seven sons.

In his prayer on their wedding night, Tobiah

124. In this book of 244 verses, 53 verses, or almost 22 percent, contain one or more words referring to death or burial. (This count applies to G^{II}. Where there are lacunae in G^{II} in chaps. 4 and 13, this count applies to G^{I}.) Chapter 9 is the only chapter that does not mention death.

had asked that he and Sarah might grow old together. There is a hint of the patriarchal background of the book in the fact that the death of Sarah, the most silent character, is not even reported. This gap, however, also allows the reader to assume that she did not die young. Surely an early death would have been mentioned. It would seem that Tobiah's prayer was answered.

14:15. The final verse of the book announces the destruction of Nineveh. Alter describes one of the functions of narration as providing a "chronicle of public events and context of meaning."[125] The chronicle of public events is minimal in Tobit, occurring only in chaps. 1 and 14. The title of the book situates the beginning of the story in the reign of Shalmaneser. The succession of Assyrian kings is briefly (and incorrectly) noted, and a few pertinent events during each reign are mentioned (1:15, 18, 21). The story of Tobit's early days is woven into this brief chronicle.

From the last mention of the reign of Esarhaddon in 2:1 until this final chapter, the book is silent concerning public events in Assyria. In chap. 14, the fall of Nineveh to Cyaxares,[126] king of Media, is reported. This public event is also woven into the lives of Tobit and Tobiah. Tobit predicts Nineveh's fall, relying on the prophet's word. Tobiah, having heeded the warning and left Nineveh, rejoices over its fall.

The chronicle of events does not simply provide a historical backdrop for the story of Tobit. It also provides a subtle context for interpretation. Assyria, personified in its kings, was wicked. These kings were responsible for the exile, suffering, and death of many of God's people. Tobit is an example of those who suffered under their rule. His virtue grew under the distress they caused. But, as his life witnesses to the truth that God rewards the righteous, the fate of Nineveh testifies that God punishes the wicked. For this reason, Tobiah rejoices (v. 15). The narrative economy is striking. Nineveh and its rulers appear only at the beginning and end of the story. But even this subtle reference to the wicked city and its fall provides an effective contrast to the story of the just man set in its midst.

125. R. Alter, *The Art of Biblical Narrative* (New York: Basic Books, 1981) 75-81.

126. The name of the conqueror of Nineveh is confused in the various translations: G^{II} and the Old Latin seem to be reading the name "Ahiqar." G^{I} reads: "Nebuchadnezzar and Ahasuerus." In fact, Nineveh fell to Nabopolasar of Babylon and Cyaxares of Media in 612 BCE.

REFLECTIONS

1. A certain psychological exercise recommends that a person write his or her own epitaph. What do you want to be remembered for? It might be equally revealing to consider what you would want to say in your farewell discourse. What would you want to remember? What would you want to recommend to your survivors? For what would you give thanks to God? Tobit had two chances to give a farewell discourse. Some of us might not have a chance to give even one!

2. The commandment to honor one's parents is not so much a command for children to obey parents as it is a command for adults to care for their aged parents. Tobiah and Sarah give a worthy example to follow of caring for parents in their old age. Ben Sira promises a reward for this solicitude:

Help your father in his old age,
  and do not grieve him as long as he lives;
even if his mind fails, be patient with him;
  because you have all your faculties do not despise him.
For kindness to a father will not be forgotten,
  and will be credited to you against your sins;
in the day of your distress it will be remembered in your favor;
  like frost in fair weather, your sins will melt away.

> Whoever forsakes a father is like a blasphemer,
> and whoever angers a mother is cursed by the Lord. (Sir 3:12-16 NRSV)

Care for aged parents is of increasing concern in modern society. As Social Security and Medicare falter, the burden on the family increases. The community, the church, and the extended family share responsibility as we strive to honor this commandment.

3. In the book of Tobit, the chronicle of public events provides a contrast to the lives of faithful people. Nineveh falls in disgrace; Tobit lives a long and virtuous life. The man who was once punished for having buried outcasts is now buried with honor. The story of Tobit is told to illustrate the theory of retribution: The good are blessed, and the wicked are punished. But the story also teaches that retribution is not always obvious: The good may suffer for awhile, and the wicked may prosper. People who strive to be faithful to God's way continue to be challenged by this apparent injustice. Christian faith in the resurrection postpones the day of reckoning and puts retribution out of sight. Nonetheless, innocent suffering continues to be a stumbling block. The book of Tobit teaches a hard truth: Reward and punishment are in the hands of God. Eternal life is not won by the righteous; it is God's gift.

THE BOOK OF JUDITH

INTRODUCTION, COMMENTARY, AND REFLECTIONS
BY
LAWRENCE M. WILLS

THE BOOK OF JUDITH

INTRODUCTION

The book of Judith is a Jewish novel, likely written in about 100 BCE, that celebrates the victory over a foreign power by the hand of a woman. Although never part of Jewish Scriptures, it did become part of the Christian Bible, now consigned to the apocrypha. The anonymous author probably wrote in Hebrew, although there is no copy of a Hebrew original still in existence, and no fragments or quotations of it were discovered among the Dead Sea Scrolls.

It falls naturally into two parts. In the first part (chaps. 1–7), Nebuchadnezzar, king of the Assyrians, is engaged in a major campaign against Arphaxad, king of the Medes. Many of the nations to the west refuse to ally with Nebuchadnezzar, but he proceeds against Arphaxad nevertheless and defeats him easily. He then turns against the nations who spurned him, which include Judea and Samaria, and commissions his general Holofernes to mobilize vast numbers of troops to invade these nations, moving inexorably toward Judea. His forces pause below the mountain village of Bethulia, which must be taken in order for him to move through its pass and proceed on to take Jersualem; and he commences a siege that cuts off the water to the village. The first part thus ends with a pause in the action, as the Israelites contemplate the disaster that is about to befall them.

In the second part (chaps. 8–16), Judith is introduced as a beautiful, wealthy, and pious Jewish widow who has lived a life of prayer and fasting in a special tent or booth on the roof of her estate. She emerges from this relative seclusion to put into motion a plan to thwart the enemy advance. She leaves Bethulia with her favorite maid and goes to the enemy camp. There she captivates Holofernes and his soldiers and lies to manipulate

Holofernes to her ends. Hoping to seduce Judith, Holofernes drinks wine until he is quite drunk and passes out, whereupon Judith takes this opportunity to slice off his head with his own sword. Carrying the head with them, she and her maid return to their village, display the head on the wall, and instruct the villagers to attack the Assyrians the next day. When the Assyrians see that their general has been beheaded, they flee and are decisively beaten by the Israelites.

Popular among both Jews and Christians over the centuries, the story of Judith has nevertheless suffered from strongly ambivalent reactions in the modern period. The interest in biblical history and "higher criticism" that developed in the nineteenth century left Judith out of the picture. By genre, it seemed like a romance or fiction; as history, it was—and is—suspect; in its theology, it was unremarkable; in its depiction of moral character, it presented a heroine who was often considered either morally tainted or decidedly dangerous. As a result, the book of Judith has been viewed as offensive, ludicrous, or—worst of all—irrelevant for biblical theology. Only with the rise of feminist studies of the Bible and an interest in the female characters has a new appreciation for the book developed. This interest has remained strong and has produced a wealth of new studies and a much more positive appreciation for Judith.

HISTORICAL SITUATION AND DATE

Judith begins with a dating formula (using the year of the reign of a major king) that is like the accounts in the biblical history books (1 Kgs 15:1; 16:15, 29; 2 Kgs 12:1; 13:1); yet, the first personage encountered, Nebuchadnezzar, king of the Assyrians, is clearly implausible. Nebuchadnezzar was king of the Babylonian Empire, not the Assyrian, and since both Nebuchadnezzar and the Assyrian Empire were well known to Jews, an accidental error is inconceivable. This one historical impossibility is followed by a number of other difficulties. In the first two chapters alone, we meet the presumably important King Arphaxad of the Medes, who is unknown to history, and geographical problems of all sorts arise with the place-names: Some are unknown; some are in the wrong place. Perhaps most serious of all, however, is what we find at 5:18-19. Achior has faithfully recounted Israelite and Jewish history, but then proceeds to describe events that occurred *after* both Nebuchadnezzar and the Assyrians had long since disappeared. The audience would clearly have been aware of the historical and geographical inaccuracies and would likely have understood the book accordingly as a work of fiction. Some scholars have sought to solve this problem by arguing that the two parts of the book (the military campaigns of chaps. 1–7 and the response of Judith in chaps. 8–16) are of unequal value historically and that there is still a historical kernel to the book, or that to avoid persecution the book makes use of fictitious personages to refer to contemporary leaders, much as the members of the Qumran sect referred to Romans as Kittim. This is not likely, however, because the entire work bespeaks a period of triumph and freedom from external oppression, not a secret text of hope in a time of adversity.

The earliest known references to the story of Judith come in the first century CE. The book probably influenced the description of Deborah in the *Biblical Antiquities* of the author known as Pseudo-Philo,[1] and the first reference by name to the story of Judith is by Clement of Rome, a Christian author who wrote near the end of the first century. He incorporates the story positively, with no hint of a concern about the historical problem, and when Judith is quoted by the later Christian fathers, there is likewise no question as to the historicity of the text. Judith is not quoted as scripture by Jews, but is the subject of legendary treatment, and no one among Jewish authors objects or comments on the reliability of the text. Through the medieval period Judith is treated as a revered figure, but rarely does anyone raise any historical questions. When we come to Martin Luther, however, we encounter a very modern-sounding criticism. In his preface to the book of Judith, he writes, "It hardly squares with the historical accounts of the Holy Scriptures, especially Jeremiah and Ezra."[2] His solution to this problem is also very modern and has in fact become the accepted scholarly consensus: "Some people think this is not an account of historical events but rather a beautiful religious fiction. . . . Such an interpretation strikes my fancy, and I think that the poet deliberately and painstakingly inserted the errors of time and name in order to remind the reader that the book should be taken and understood as that kind of a sacred, religious composition."

Although the stated historical setting in the era of the Assyrian Empire still pushed some scholars to argue for an early dating—that is, before the exile in 587 BCE—most now focus on evidence that it was written at a much later period. There are terms and personages that correspond to the period of the Persian rule of Judea (539–332 BCE) and other terms and ideas that correspond to the period of Greek rule (332–165 BCE) or to the period of the independent Judea under the Maccabees (or Hasmoneans; 165–63 BCE), when Greek customs were still influential in Jewish life. Moore has conveniently listed the terms and names in each category, the most important of which are given here.[3] For dating in the Persian period, we note especially that in 350 and 343 BCE there were invasions of the west by Artaxerxes III Ochus of Persia that were similar in scope to the fictitious invasion by Nebuchadnezzar and Holofernes. He came as far as Egypt (see Jdt 1:10). More imortant, he had a general named Holofernes and a counselor, probably a eunuch, named Bagoas (cf. Jdt 12:11). Thus the connections to Judith are very strong and suggest at least that the memory of this invasion fired the imagination of the author of Judith. In addition, there are a number of terms that

1. Richard I. Pervo, "Aseneth and Her Sisters: Women in Jewish Narrative and in the Greek Novels," in *"Women Like This": New Perspectives on Jewish Women in the Greco-Roman World,* ed. Amy-Jill Levine (Atlanta: Scholars Press, 1991) 159 n. 71.

2. Martin Luther, *Luther's Works,* 55 vols. (Philadelphia: Muhlenberg, 1960) 35:337-38.

3. Carey A. Moore, *Judith,* AB 40 (Garden City, N.Y.: Doubleday, 1985) 50-55, 67-70.

are associated with the Persian era, even though they might also have lingered in the popular consciousness long afterward.

There are no precisely datable Greek terms or ideas, but several motifs—the wearing of garlands and olive wreaths, the worship of a king as a god, and people reclining instead of sitting at table—could have entered in any time after 332 BCE. Some of the most convincing datable motifs arise in connection with the Hasmoneans (the dynastic name of the Maccabees), who achieved independence from the Greeks (Seleucids) in 165 BCE. The high priest as a political and military leader, the ascendancy of the Jerusalem council, and the close similarity between the exhibiting of Holofernes' head and the exhibiting of the head of Nicanor after he had been defeated by Judah the Maccabee (1 Macc 7:43-50; 2 Macc 15:30-32) all speak for a date after the Maccabean revolt.

Even more important for consideration, the *ideals* expressed in Judith correspond closely to the ideals of the later Hasmonean rulers, especially John Hyrcanus I (135–104 BCE) and Alexander Janneus (103–78 BCE). Hyrcanus in 107 BCE annexed Samaria, the provincial designation of the northern half of the old kingdom of Israel. He thus realized a Hasmonean dream of reestablishing the approximate borders of David's and Solomon's united Israel.[4] A dating of the book in this period would even provide a possible origin of "Nebuchadnezzar, king of the Assyrians." Assyria in biblical prophecies was often read as Syria in the literature of this period; thus "Nebuchadnezzar king of the Assyrians" could have been read as a satirical reference to "Antiochus, king of the Syrians," from whom the Maccabees had gained their independence.[5] In the process of annexing Samaria, John Hyrcanus also destroyed the Samaritan temple on Mt. Gerizim, and so rid the land of cult practices not strictly based on the hegemony of Jerusalem. This illuminates Judith's otherwise very odd statement in 8:18-20 that the Jews had successfully rooted out the worship of "gods made with hands." Further, the conversion of Achior, though it would find some precedents in ancient Jewish tradition, would be more comprehensible in the light of John Hyrcanus's move to convert the Idumaeans to Judaism by force. One could argue that the forced annexation of Samaria and the forced conversion of Idumaeans would not lead to such warm relations as are depicted in Judith, but to the Hasmoneans the annexation and conversion would be seen as liberation, and this is precisely why Judith is at such pains to *idealize* them. The boldness of Judith's affirmations make most sense in a situation where unity is imposed. The book of Judith thus idealizes Samaria and Judea together as "Israel" and does not have, as some scholars have suggested, a hidden Samaritan identity. To be sure, other scholars argue that the author of Judith is secretly opposed to the rule of the Hasmoneans, but the agreements with the Hasmonean rulers far outweigh the

4. Lee I. A. Levine, "The Age of Hellenism: Alexander the Great and the Rise and Fall of the Hasmonean Kingdom," in *Ancient Israel: A Short History from Abraham to the Roman Destruction of the Temple,* ed. Hershel Shanks (Englewood Cliffs, N.J.: Prentice Hall, 1988) 186-89.

5. George W. E. Nickelsburg, *Jewish Literature Between the Bible and the Mishnah* (Philadelphia: Fortress, 1981) 109.

possible challenges within the text.[6] Even if Judith were a subversive text within the Hasmonean kingdom, that would still at least date the text in the period that is here proposed.

It has also been suggested that the author was a Samaritan because of the importance of the regions of Samaria, a Sadducee because of the coordination of Judith's practices with the temple administration, or a Pharisee because of the practices of fasting and prayer.[7] Arguing against the first two possibilities are the idealized union of Judea and Samaria into "Israel" (noted above) and the Hasmonean idealization of the high priesthood as a governing office. Whether the author was a Pharisee is impossible to determine, but it should be noted that the practices of the protagonist provide a parallel to the development of fasting, penitence, and prayer of the Pharisees and others in the Judaism of this period. It is likely, then, that the anonymous author lived in Palestine and wrote in Hebrew near the end of the second century BCE. A narrative tradition that may have arisen in the Persian period was possibly utilized, which would explain the Persian parallels;[8] but the concerns of the author clearly point to a composition in the later historical context.

GENRE

Although Judith was included as part of the canon of the Christian Bible as a historical text and was so understood by many, in the modern world a number of scholars have considered it a novel or a romance (the terms are essentially interchangeable) on the analogy of Greek novels. The classicist Ulrich von Wilamowitz judged it a novel, as did Ruth Stiehl, Franz Altheim, and Moses Hadas.[9] Although the Jewish texts are shorter than their Greco-Roman counterparts, they are earlier and should perhaps be considered important parts of a broad international literary development that includes, in addition to the main Greek and Roman novels, smaller novels that arise from various indigenous ethnic groups of the Hellenistic world.[10]

6. Arguing for the subversive position of Judith over against the Hasmonean rulers are André Lacocque, *The Feminine Unconventional: Four Subversive Figures in Israel's Tradition* (Minneapolis: Fortress, 1990) 41, and Jan Willem van Henten, "Judith as Alternative Leader: A Rereading of Judith 7–13," in *A Feminist Companion to Esther, Judith and Susanna*, ed. Athalya Brenner (Sheffield: Sheffield Academic, 1995) 243-44. Moore, *Judith*, 67-70, is in agreement with the position adopted here.

7. See Moore, *Judith*, 70-71; Toni Craven, *Artistry and Faith in the Book of Judith* (Chico, Calif.: Scholars Press, 1983) 118-20.

8. Nickelsburg, *Jewish Literature Between the Bible and the Mishnah*, 108-9.

9. Ulrich von Wilamowitz et al., *Die griechische und lateinische Literatur und Sprache*, 3rd ed. (Leipzig: Teubner, 1912) 189; Ruth Stiehl and Franz Altheim, *Die aramäische Sprache unter den Achaimeniden* (Frankfurt am Main: Vittorio Klostermann, 1963) 200; Moses Hadas, *Hellenistic Culture: Fusion and Diffusion* (New York: Norton, 1959) 165-66.

10. J. R. Morgan and Richard Stoneman, *Greek Fiction: The Greek Novel in Context* (London: Routledge, 1994); Lawrence M. Wills, *The Jewish Novel in the Ancient World* (Ithaca: Cornell University Press, 1995). Greek novels can be found in B. P. Reardon, *Collected Ancient Greek Novels* (Berkeley: University of California Press, 1989), and William F. Hansen, *Anthology of Ancient Greek Popular Literature* (Bloomington: Indiana University Press, 1998).

Some scholars have emphasized the similarity of Judith to oral folk narratives and have pressed this category as a genre designation.[11] While this similarity is very important (see below), the present shape of Judith is like the other written novels of the period. To be sure, Jewish novels sometimes developed out of pre-existing narratives, which may in turn have been derived from oral legends. The development from oral legend to novel can be seen in the combination of originally independent stories in Daniel 1–6 with the visions of Daniel 7–12 to form a larger whole, and then later in the addition of the Prayer of Azariah and the Song of the Three Jews and Susanna to form the apocryphal version of Daniel. The development toward the novel can also be discerned in certain other contemporary Jewish works, such as *Testament of Joseph* from the *Testaments of the Twelve Patriarchs, Testament of Job,* and *Testament of Abraham,* which begin to take on a novelistic coloring as a keener interest in description and character development gives rise to an expansion of the narrative. Other contemporary texts seem to be like histories in that they do not appear to be intended as fictions, and yet they also tend toward an exciting narration of the protagonists' personal situations: 2 Maccabees, 3 Maccabees, Artapanus, and the *Tobiad* Romance, and *Royal Family of Adiabene* from Josephus's *Antiquities of the Jews* 12.154-236, 20.17-96.[12] The novelistic developments should be seen as experiments that push toward the creation of a new art form. In addition to the more obvious elements of the novel, such as rousing action, international sweep, wealth, danger, sex, violence, and use of dialogue, more subtle themes are woven into the text that include the use of everyday characters, domestic settings, and the exploration of the interior life of psychology and emotion. In addition, in both the Greek and the Jewish novels, there is a strong focus on the female protagonist. But while the Greek novels of antiquity portray a young couple in love, separated by challenging circumstances, in the Jewish novels a vulnerable woman is often more alone at the center. She is often directly involved with her extended family, but she faces the trials of life and death alone.

The character of Judith has similarities to two types of characters in Greek novels. In some ways, such as in respect to her beauty, wealth, and piety, she is like the young heroines; in terms of being a self-directed and commanding figure and a widow, she is also like some of the Greek widows.[13] The widows, however, are not generally depicted positively, but are sexually driven, powerful, and sinister, controlling the protagonists' lives. Jerome makes a comparison between Gentile widows and Christian widows that is illuminating: "Gentile widows are wont to paint their faces with rouge and white lead, to flaunt in silk dresses, to deck themselves in gleaming jewels, to wear gold necklaces, to hang from their pierced ears the costliest Red Sea pearls, and to reek of musk."[14] Jerome's

11. Mary P. Coote, "Response," in Luis Alonso-Schökel, *Narrative Structures in the Book of Judith* (Berkeley, Calif.: Center for Hermeneutical Studies in Hellenistic and Modern Culture, 1974) 21-26; Pamela Milne, "What Shall We Do with Judith? A Feminist Reassessment of a Biblical Heroine," *Semeia* 62 (1993) 37-58.

12. Wills, *The Jewish Novel in the Ancient World,* 16-30, 185-211. A good English translation of some of the non-canonical Jewish texts listed here, with scholarly introductions, can be found in James H. Charlesworth, *The Old Testament Pseudepigrapha,* 2 vols. (Garden City, N.Y.: Doubleday, 1985).

13. Achilles Tatius *Leucippe and Clitophon* 5-8; Heliodorus *An Ephesian Story* 7-8.

14. Jerome *Epistle* 127.3, quoted in Pervo, "Aseneth and Her Sisters," 156-57.

stereotype is thus similar to that of the Greek novels; it is all the more striking, then, that Judith does all these things as well, albeit in the service of God, and is seen positively throughout. Another similarity to the Greek novels is the fact that the female protagonist is so much more engaging and active than the male protagonists. This aspect is also found as a genre trait in the Greek novels,[15] but is emphasized even more in Judith. Still, there is one important way in which Judith differs from the Greek and the Jewish novels: the invulnerability of the heroine. The Greek and Jewish novels all feature a vulnerable heroine, and usually a vulnerable hero as well, but Judith is not buffeted by events. She is more like the male hero of epic.

The classical historian Moses Hadas was so convinced that Judith is related to the Greek novels that he objected to just those aspects of the text that are dissimilar to the other novels. A story of a Greek widow in Plutarch, *Amatorius* 2, for example, is very similar to Judith. She remains chaste and curries the favor of a powerful man who she secretly knows killed her husband. Finally she poisons both the suitor and herself and dies triumphantly. In the Greek novel *An Ephesian Tale* by Xenophon of Ephesus, the beautiful young Anthia must also kill a suitor who is trying to rape her. The tragic ending in Plutarch seems appropriate in Greek narrative, and the innocent and threatened heroine in Xenophon seems appropriate as well, but the author of Judith is judged by Hadas to have missed the point of the genre. "What makes the Judith story awkward is the mixed atmosphere of piety and license; the erotic has come in [as in the Greek novels], and shows its leering face despite the author's efforts to smother it in piety. If the constraints of the religious motivation (in itself admirable) are removed, the story would spring back into the pattern of Greek romance."[16] We will turn again below to the heroic Judith, and can perhaps explain the source of the problem as Hadas sees it.

A remaining issue concerning the Jewish novels is whether they were considered historically true or were treated in the ancient world as fictitious, as scholars now often consider them to be. Although many of the known novelistic works were eventually canonized as part of the Christian Bible, it is not clear that these writings were all considered historical at the time of their writing. Several of them contain an obvious historical error that would likely have been easily recognized as such by the audience: Esther becomes a Jewish queen of Persia; in Dan 5:31 Babylon falls to "Darius the Mede" (Darius was a famous Persian king); Tob 14:15 refers to Xerxes king of Media (Xerxes was also a famous Persian king); and in *Joseph and Aseneth*, Joseph rises to become pharaoh until a young prince reaches maturity. Judith's Nebuchadnezzar, king of the Assyrians, is simply another example of this phenomenon, even though it may be the most outrageous historical mistake of all. The audience would have understood why these two evil empires were combined in Judith, and would have applauded it, but they would never have been fooled into thinking this

15. David Konstan, *Sexual Symmetry: Love in the Ancient Novel and Related Genres* (Princeton: Princeton University Press, 1994).

16. Hadas, *Hellenist Culture*, 169.

was a retelling of actual historical events. It is this aspect of these novels that helps to define their genre and distinguish them from other prose narratives, like the Gospels.

LITERARY ASPECTS OF JUDITH

The literary qualities of Judith are significant, but it is often a challenge to describe the attractions of a work of "popular," as opposed to "classical," literature.[17] Popular novels have a function to entertain, perhaps to instruct, but are often perceived as falling short of the higher criteria of excellence that have been arrived at in the study of "classical" literature. Still, it is unfair, and ultimately inaccurate, to apply the standards of classical literature rigidly to popular literature. The latter will come up short, and the essential nature of such literature, and its positive qualities and social function may be missed. Just as the moral ideals in Judith were questioned by commentators in the modern period, so also the literary qualities of the book have often been dismissed by those who misperceived its literary genre and function. These criticisms fall into two categories: the disproportionate length of the first part concerning the rise of the military threat to Bethulia and the rhetorical excesses of the whole.

Cowley, who appreciated other literary qualities about the book, took the author to task for creating a first half that takes too long to come to the introduction of the heroine.[18] Dancy was less kind: "Dramatically [the first half] is spoiled by tedious descriptions and confusions, stylistically by exaggerations and empty rhetoric."[19] Even Alonso-Schökel, who set the tone for the literary-critical approaches, denigrated the first part in favor of the second.[20] It seems that most critics were unappreciative of the first part and failed to recognize its contribution to the narrative as a whole. The first part, which is not quite half of the book (even if the Song of Judith at the end is omitted), does *seem* to be longer; actually, the greater share of attention is devoted to the events in the second part. The reader's impression is that the first part is taken up with military movements and engagements, but it is really mostly talk. The talk is, first of all, a way of revealing the characters of Nebuchadnezzar and Holofernes and how they will try to attain world domination, but it is also a means to introduce Achior into the story, his view of the role of Israel in history, the reactions of the Israelites to the crisis, and what is religiously at stake. But these are far from plodding; they develop all the issues of the context of Judith's decisive act. And since Judith was probably read as entertainment, it simply would not do to have the climactic scene arrive too soon.

On the question of the rhetorical excesses, in general, these were perhaps noted most emphatically by Pfeiffer: "The turgid style, the patent exaggerations, the stately pomp and ceremony throughout, unrelieved by a sense of humor, give to the book a baroque rather

17. Wills, *The Jewish Novel in the Ancient World* 1-39, 212-45; Hansen, *Anthology of Ancient Greek Popular Literature*, 3-13.
18. Arthur E. Cowley, "The Book of Judith," in *APOT* 1:242-43.
19. J. C. Dancy, *The Shorter Books of the Apocrypha*, CBC (Cambridge: Cambridge University Press, 1972) 68.
20. Alonso-Schökel, *Narrative Structures in the Book of Judith*, 5.

than a classic appearance."[21] It is quite revealing of his lack of sympathy for the genre that he says that the book of Judith does not have a sense of humor. Quite the opposite is the case.

In response to these criticisms, it is important to see popular literature in its proper context. It is precisely the goal of the author of Judith to impress the reader with an unrestrained exuberance and to have an immediate impact. The author of Judith makes an art of excess: the descriptions of the troops, the artificial geographical sweep, the pillage and destruction, the gory central scene—all of these serve to keep the reader riveted. This is the same approach that is found in other novelistic works, both Jewish and Greek. It should also be noted that the author of Judith did not work with established models of what the novel genre should look like; the novel was a bold experiment, only in the first stages of development. Nonetheless, the author had introduced innovative improvements over the other novels. Whereas some of the more primitive novels of this period were characterized by duplicated scenes (the Additions to Esther) or separate small narratives strung together (the Additions to Daniel), Judith attains a length that is larger than the other novels of the apocrypha, and yet maintains a smooth, taut narrative. To be sure, there are two different movements to the story, but there is a logical relationship between them, and the author exercises many literary gifts. In many ways, Judith is the best constructed of the Jewish novels.

Toni Craven made a major breakthrough in the literary appreciation of the whole of the book when she identified certain aspects of the function of the first part.[22] There are many parallels and contrasts between the first part of the book and the second and, in addition, parallels and contrasts within each part. This results in a complex and intentional structuring of the two parts that greatly enriches the reading experience, *once one is prepared for such a reading.* Some of the most important correspondences can be represented thus:

First half
- A Campaign against disobedient nations; the people surrender (1:1–3:10)
  - B Israel is "greatly terrified"; Joakim prepares for war (4:1-15)
    - C Holofernes talks with Achior; Achior is expelled (5:1–6:13)
    - C′ Achior is received in Bethulia; Achior talks with the people (6:14-21)
  - B′ Holofernes prepares for war; Israel is "greatly terrified" (7:1-5)
- A′ Campaign against Bethulia; the people want to surrender (7:6-32)

Second half
- A Introduction of Judith (8:1-8)
  - B Judith plans to save Israel (8:9–10:9*a*)

21. Robert H. Pfeiffer, *History of New Testament Times* (New York: Harper and Bros., 1949) 299.
22. Toni Craven, *Artistry and Faith in the Book of Judith* (Chico, Calif.: Scholars Press, 1983) 60-62.

C Judith and her maid leave Bethulia (10:9*b*-10)
D Judith overcomes Holofernes (10:11–13:10*a*)
C′ Judith and her maid return to Bethulia (13:10*b*-11)
B′ Judith plans to destroy Israel's enemy (13:12–16:20)
A′ Conclusion about Judith (16:21-25)

Craven's discernment of the pattern of parallels and contrasts allows a much more sympathetic—and ultimately enjoyable—reading of the first half of the book. Each half is in the form of a chiasm—that is, a structure that resembles the Greek letter *chi*, or X, and in which motifs in the first half are repeated in the second, except reversed.[23] This allows each part to have an effective center, yet move to a culmination. The first part ends with a calm that is not a resolution; it is the dread of Holofernes' attack. The question hanging over the Jews is, "Who is lord, Nebuchadnezzar or God?" The second part removes the Israelites' fear of Holofernes and answers that question resoundingly, "God is Lord and works even through the hand of a woman." The structuring of the narrative is simple and complex at the same time. There are numerous structural relationships, yet they point to a single overall arc: rising action, denouement, falling action. Although Craven's findings have strongly influenced the present commentary on Judith, the outline followed in this commentary has been altered slightly from hers. The text has been broken up into more equal sizes that reflect content more than literary structure.

In addition to the pattern of balanced parallels and oppositions of motifs that Craven analyzed, we can detect several other important narrative operations as well. First, there is a typical hero pattern in the novel. This common cross-cultural narrative structure usually portrays a male hero, sometimes withdrawn from society, who comes forward when the community is threatened by a larger-than-life monster and slays it. At this point, there are essentially two resolutions of the story: either a comic one or a tragic one. In the comic resolution (usually associated with myths and fairy tales), the hero returns to a celebration with the community, and peace and fertility are restored to the land. In the tragic ending (usually associated with epic poetry and tragedy), the hero either dies in the process or returns to a community in which he cannot really participate. Judith can easily be seen as an adaptation of the hero pattern: In the beginning, she is outside of society in the tent on her roof. She comes out of seclusion to "arm" herself in beautiful garments, moves forward to engage the monster, slays the monster, and returns to a celebration of the community. The ending is closer to the comic resolution, although this question will be taken up again in regard to the ending of the work (see Commentary on 16:21-25). The similarity of Judith to heroic narratives has been noted by various scholars. Coote has suggested the cross-cultural tale pattern more typical of the heroine called "wife disguised as a man frees

23. On chiasm see also Adele Berlin, "Introduction to Hebrew Poetry," *The New Interpreter's Bible,* 12 vols. (Nashville: Abingdon, 1994) 4:310, and using the language of "concentric construction," Michael Kolarcik, S.J., "The Book of Wisdom," *NIB,* 5:443-46.

her husband," which depicts a faithful wife (here, Judith is a "wife" of Israel) who disguises herself as a man to rescue her husband.[24] However, it seems more likely that what we see in Judith is not a female pattern such as this, but a more radical adaptation of a male warrior-hero pattern. The role reversal in Judith and the flouting of normal sexual taboos is much stronger than in most heroine tales of disguise.[25]

The hero pattern is a broad and varied phenomenon, occurring in all parts of the world, and it has attracted the attention of scholars who see the possibility of isolating a "monomyth," a single narrative structure that is the model of all hero tales worldwide. While this goal may never be attained in detail, it is clear that there are common patterns of the hero narrative and that comparing Judith with some of the reconstructions of cross-cultural patterns could be instructive. The best-known attempt to isolate a single pattern with variations is that of Joseph Campbell.[26] His summary of the typical hero story pattern—and the vast majority of the narratives he cites concern male heroes—is as follows (slightly simplified): The mythological hero, setting forth from his hut or castle, proceeds to the threshold of adventure. There he encounters a shadow presence that guards the passage. The hero may defeat or conciliate this power and go alive into the kingdom of the dark. Beyond the threshold the hero journeys through a world of unfamiliar, yet strangely intimate, forces, some of which severely threaten him. When he arrives at the nadir of the mythological world, he undergoes a supreme ordeal and gains his reward. The triumph may be represented as the hero's theft of the boon he came to gain. The final work is that of return; the hero reemerges from the kingdom of dread. The boon that he brings restores the world.

The elements of the narrative are very similar to the book of Judith: the departure of the hero, the crossing of the threshold into a dark region of danger (see below on the gates of Bethulia as a threshold), the trials of the hero and the slaying of a monster (in this case, Holofernes), the stealing of a great boon to humanity (the head of Holofernes), the return of the hero, the reentry into society by crossing the threshold again, and the restoration of peace. What we have in the case of Judith is a hero narrative cast in a more realistic setting that brings down to earth many of the elements of the story pattern. Further, Campbell's analysis helps us to understand why some of the characters of Judith are so one-dimensional. The literary or theological value of the book of Judith is not contained in the development of Judith's character or in an analysis of evil as embodied in Holofernes.

24. Mary P. Coote, "Response," in Luis Alonso-Schokel, *Narrative Structures in the Book of Judith* (Berkeley, Calif.: Center for Hermeneutical Studies in Hellenistic and Modern Culture, 1974) 21-26.

25. Pamela Milne, "What Shall We Do with Judith?" A Feminist Reassessment of a Biblical Heroine," *Semeia* 62 (1993) 37-58, also looks to the male hero narrative pattern isolated by Heda Jason, "Ilja of Murom and Tzar Kalin: A Proposal for a Model for the Narrative Structure of an Epic Struggle," *Slavica Hierosylimitana* 5-6 (1981) 47-55. An interesting study of the "female hero" in modern literature also explores the adaptation of the male hero pattern in modern novels about women. See Carol Pearson and Katherine Pope, *The Female Hero in American and British Literature* (New York: Bowker, 1981).

26. Joseph Campbell, *The Hero with a Thousand Faces* (New York: Pantheon, 1949) esp. 245-46. On Judith as a heroic quest, see Mary Garrard, "Judith," in *Artemisia Gentileschi: The Image of the Female Hero in Italian Baroque Art* (Princeton, N.J.: Princeton University Press, 1989) 281.

The complexity that usually makes characters interesting is not present. Judith does not grow as a character and is not mixed of good and evil qualities. It is emphasized that she is wise, virtuous, and capable; but she does not discover anything about herself (cf. in this regard Esther 4). She is like the figures of myth, who are likewise often one-dimensional. The hero of myth is born fully formed in his heroic traits. The remarkable virtues of this person, according to Campbell, are more predestined than achieved in the course of life. Thus both the hero and the monster reach their end by destiny. There is very little need to create multidimensional characters.

The hero pattern is thus the overarching structure for the book of Judith, but contained within it are interesting smaller structures as well that serve to illuminate important segments of the departure and return of the hero. One of these is the preparation of Judith, or her transition out of her life of quietism in chap. 8 (see the Overview of chaps. 8–16). It is best described as what anthropologists would call a "rite of passage," a ritually marked transition that involves separation from society, a liminal period in which normal markers of social order, such as age, class, gender, or status, are obliterated and sacred information is imparted, and incorporation or aggregation back into the social order with a new status.[27] At 8:11-27, Judith has scolded the rulers of Bethulia for being weak willed and has told them that she has a plan to deliver them. She then must prepare herself, and enters into a state of ritual cleansing and self-abnegation in which she uncovers her mourning garments, prays, bathes, and then reclothes herself in rich apparel and cosmetics. The scene is remarkably similar to the central prayer scenes of the female protagonists in the Additions to Esther and *Joseph and Aseneth*.[28] At a turning point near the middle of the narrative, the female protagonist turns to prayer and begins a process of penitence and self-abasement. She condemns her beauty, puts on sackcloth as a garment of mourning, prays, and afterward reclothes herself in beautiful garments and emerges to perform her mission (see also the much less stylized scenes in Tob 3:10-15 and Sus 22-23).

This scene is related to Jewish penitential theology that developed in the post-exilic period, already found, for instance, in Nehemiah 9, Daniel 9, some of the psalms, and Baruch and the Prayer of Manasseh in the apocrypha, and emerging later in Jas 4:8-10. The themes emphasized in these texts differ, as do the content of their prayers. Still, in all the Jewish novels except Judith, the introspective female protagonist is buffeted and psychologically tested.[29] The amount of space devoted to this issue and the depth of the psychological interest vary from Susanna (the least attention) to *Joseph and Aseneth* (the most), but it is interesting that Judith is not psychologically buffeted despite her situation. Moore compares the prayer in Judith with that of Add. Esth 14:1-19,[30] but misses this

27. Arnold van Gennep, *The Rites of Passage* (Chicago: University of Chicago Press, 1960); Victor Turner, "Betwixt and Between: The Liminal Period in Rites de Passage," in *The Forest of Symbols: Aspects of Ndembu Ritual* (Ithaca: Cornell University Press) 93-111.

28. Lawrence M. Wills, *The Jewish Novel in the Ancient World* (Ithaca: Cornell University Press, 1995) 224-32; Alice Bach, *Women, Seduction and Betrayal in Biblical Narrative* (New York: Cambridge University Press, 1997) 202-3.

29. Wills, *The Jewish Novel in the Ancient World,* 147-48.

30. Carey A. Moore, *Judith,* AB 40 (Garden City, N.Y.: Doubleday, 1985) 195-97.

crucial difference. Neither does Judith show any penitence. Esther, and even more so Aseneth, purifies herself by a penitence that involves an abject self-abasement. The rituals of mourning are incorporated, which would be typical in the Bible in a moment of crisis, but Esther goes beyond this; it has become a quasi-ascetic repudiation of those aspects of her body associated with her beauty: "Instead of costly perfumes she covered her head with ashes and dung, and she utterly humbled her body; every part that she loved to adorn she covered with her tangled hair" (Add. Esth 14:2). The heroines' awareness of sin, associated with their bodies, is overwhelming in Esther and *Joseph and Aseneth.* Yet Judith knows nothing of this. Even her fasts do not appear to have an explicit penitential aspect. Judith undergoes an experience of transformation without being transformed. The author takes up the paradigm and the literary pattern of the buffeted Jewish heroine who is penitent and prayerful, but gives her no recognition of sin. She is simply perfect as she is.

In addition, another important segment of the hero's quest, crossing the threshold into the sphere of darkness and danger and returning again,[31] is marked very clearly in the narrative as an important passage as well. Craven notes in her structural arrangement of Judith a correspondence between the departure of Judith and her maid through the gates of Bethulia at 10:9*b*-10 and their return at 13:10*b*-11. These corresponding scenes contain a number of important, ritualized elements. When Judith, with the help of her maid, has prepared for her quest by means of the dressing scene, she commands the town elder Uzziah, "Order the gate of the town to be opened." Accompanying her departure is a series of gestures of Uzziah and the townspeople that are typical of the departure scenes in heroic poetry (see Commentary on 10:6-10). When the two return again she also says, "Open, open the gate!" which marks clearly the return of the hero and her incorporation back into the safety of the known village. Although there is still a battle to be fought when she returns, the immediate danger to her—and especially to her honor as a pious Jewish woman—is while she is in the liminal period between her going and coming. This is also the period in which she flaunts her sexuality, engages in deceit and manipulation, and murders Holofernes. It is also the dramatic center of the book.

Aside from these structural elements of the novel, there are also certain aspects of the literary style that deserve attention. Judith utilizes a number of techniques that enliven the narrative: anticipation of future events; retardation and acceleration of plot; vivid visual description; and irony and humor. Concerning the anticipation of events that appear later in the text, we must assume that the story of Judith was well known, whether from oral tradition or from written narratives, such as the present text. This would be quite likely if, as discussed above, an older narrative tradition from the Persian period was at the core of the present Hasmonean-era text. Anticipation is a way of building suspense about future events, but it also introduces a kind of irony—that is, a perception on the part of the audience about what they think will happen that is different from the perspective of the characters. The anticipation in Judith is sometimes suspenseful, sometimes ironic and

31. Campbell, *Hero with a Thousand Faces,* 90-91.

humorous. It is suspenseful when Achior's exile to the village of Bethulia anticipates his witness there to the events that are about to unfold. It is ironic and humorous when statements that are made take on a different meaning in the light of anticipated events, such as Holofernes' blustery statement to Achior: "You shall not see my face again until I take revenge on this race!" (6:5). Anticipation can often be seen in the irony of many of the statements in Judith's and Holofernes' dialogue (e.g., 11:6; 12:4).

The retardation and acceleration of the plot are among the most effective techniques of the author, creating excellent pacing of the narrative. This is often accomplished by the alternation of narrative and dialogue, action and rest, and alternation of location, but most often by the use of vivid description.[32] The audience fully anticipates the beheading of Holofernes—they know that is what the story is about—to such an extent that the amount of text that goes before it has surprised many critics. Just as the Gospel of Mark has been characterized as a passion story with a long introduction,[33] so also Judith is a beheading with a long introduction. With this in mind, one can see chaps. 1–7 as a series of episodes that use retardation and acceleration, in addition to alternation of types of discourse, to set the stage for the climactic decapitation. Chapter 1 launches immediately into a military drama between two great world powers, followed by a rest (1:16). The narrative moves again into a brisk description of military events and another rest (3:10). Israel's response to war follows, which is described almost like military preparations (4:1-15). There are several extended dialogues following (5:1–6:9), after which there are intrigues that involve a combination of vivid description with some retardation of the plot and dialogue, as Achior is expelled from Holofernes' camp and welcomed into Bethulia (6:10–7:18). In 10:11-23 we find a similar combination of vivid description, plot retardation, and dialogue as Judith reverses the direction of Achior's movement and goes from Bethulia to Holofernes' camp.[34] From 11:1 to 12:18 there is dialogue, and then at the climactic scene in Holofernes' tent, we find slight retardation of the plot as Judith approaches Holofernes (12:19–13:7), and then acceleration of the plot as Judith beheads Holofernes, collects the head and the tent canopy, moves through the camp, climbs up the mountain and back to Bethulia, all in three verses (13:8-10)! The military campaign at the end of Judith (15:1-7) is also told in the same quick, bold strokes as the military campaigns at the beginning of Judith.

If there is one literary device that most characterizes the book of Judith, however, it would be irony. In this respect Judith is in good company; irony is at the center of the Gospel of John, the book of Jonah, and Plato's portrait of Socrates.[35] The irony is ubiquitous in Judith and plays on several levels.[36] On the broadest level, it is found in the unexpected

32. On alternation of location, see Craven, *Artistry and Faith in the Book of Judith,* 61; on description, see Alonso-Schökel, *Narrative Structures in the Book of Judith,* 7.

33. Martin Kähler, *The So-Called Historical Jesus and the Historic, Biblical Christ* (Philadelphia: Fortress, 1964) 80.

34. On the "exchange" of Achior and Judith, see Adolfo Roitman, "Achior in the Book of Judith: His Role and Significance," in *"No One Spoke Ill of Her": Essays on Judith,* ed. James C. VanderKam (Atlanta: Scholars Press, 1992) 31-45.

35. Moore, *Judith,* 78-85.

36. See Gail R. O'Day, "The Gospel of John," *NIB,* 9:566, 813-15.

development that the great Assyrian general Holofernes is felled by the hand of a woman. This is the central irony that underlies the structure of the book as a whole, and it is referred to often, both in Judith's prayer in chap. 9, and in the Song of Judith in chap. 16. The irony spills over into the dialogue, creating an extended train of ironic utterances, as characters time and again speak words that have one meaning for them and another for the audience. Judith, who is very clever, seems to be uttering double entendres intentionally, playing with Holofernes as a cat plays with a mouse. But Holofernes is also prone to making pronouncements that will come back to haunt him; he is too obtuse to realize what is going on around him. The two strands of ironic statements—Judith's and Holofernes'—thus proceed simultaneously through much of the novel. Related to this is the discrepancy between Holofernes' self-understanding and the pitiable end for which he is destined. His bloated self-image clouds his judgment, so that he not only sees in himself what he wants to see, but also he sees in Judith only what he chooses. If Holofernes had been clever enough to catch Judith's irony, he would have been clever enough to avoid her trap, even get the best of her. But he was not. Surrounding these larger ironies are smaller examples that are still significant. Nebuchadnezzar claims to be "lord of the whole world" (2:5); yet the narrative confirms that God is lord, and this will be proved, not on the great battlefields or in the famous cities of the ancient Near East, but outside the tiny mountain village of Bethulia. Also Achior, though an Ammonite, is more stalwart in his defense of Israel than is Uzziah, one of the rulers of Bethulia. We may note one last example of irony that also relates to the moral evaluation of Judith: She is fastidious about the observance of kosher laws, and yet she violates Jewish views of the permissible actions of a pious widow. This irony lies at the center of Judith's liminal actions.

BIBLICAL PARALLELS

The reader familiar with the Bible will immediately recognize in Judith parallels to many biblical stories. The text is indeed a rich tapestry of biblical allusions. The most important of these are listed and analyzed by Dubarle,[37] and here the most important ones will be mentioned. In addition to the explicit references to Abraham, Isaac, and Jacob (Jdt 8:25-27) and to Simeon (Jdt 9:2-4), there are evident influences of narrative motifs from many biblical texts.

The fact that the main character is a woman naturally attracts our attention to biblical stories that focus on female characters. The general theme of the ruse of a woman recurs in biblical literature, from Rebekah's manipulation to secure the birthright for her son Jacob in Genesis 27, to Tamar's ruse to have sex with her father-in-law in order to raise up a child in the name of her dead husband in Genesis 38.[38] Rahab the prostitute's aid to the two spies sent into Jericho (Joshua 2; 6:22-25) bears more than a passing resemblance

37. A. M. Dubarle, *Judith: Formes et sens des diverses traditions,* 2 vols. (Rome: Pontifical Biblical Institute, 1966) 1:137-64.

38. Esther Fuchs, "Who Is Hiding the Truth? Deceptive Women and Biblical Androcentrism," in *Feminist Perspectives on Biblical Scholarship,* ed. Adela Yarbro Collins (Chico, Calif.: Scholars Press, 1985) 137-44.

to parts of Judith. It is not simply that Judith also "plays the harlot" with Holofernes; Rahab, like Achior, is also a non-Israelite who joins Israel, and her speech (Josh 2:9-14) is very similar to Achior's speech in Judith 5. At several points in the HB there is an execution of a warrior by a woman, which was considered a shameful form of death. In Judg 9:50-55, Abimelech is killed by a woman who drops a millstone upon him. Emphasized here is that Abimelech does not want to die at the hand of a woman, a mark of shame that is found also in Jdt 16:5 (see also 2 Sam 4:5-12; 20:14-22).

The most important of the parallels to women in active roles, however, is the story of Deborah the prophet in Judges 4–5, and especially the role of Jael in murdering the general Sisera. In Judges 4, the prose version of the story, King Jabin of Canaan has sent his general Sisera to attack the Israelites. Deborah the prophet instructs Barak to lead the Israelites out to fight Sisera. She promises Barak that the Lord will defeat Sisera and adds, "The LORD will sell Sisera into the hand of a woman." Barak routs the forces of Sisera, but Sisera himself takes refuge in the tent of Jael. He lies down, and while he is sleeping, Jael takes a tent peg and drives it through his head. Judges 5 is then a victory song of Deborah in celebration. The most obvious similarities to Judith are the heroism of a woman who gives courage to her people in a time of oppression by a foreign power, her call to arms to the men to defend themselves, and also the murder scene in which a woman—now not Deborah but Jael—kills the general of the foreign king. More specifically we may note that both women are very strong, patriotic people and that the execution scenes both take place in a tent while the general is incapacitated and lying down.[39] The victory song of Judith is partly modeled on the Song of Deborah and also on Moses' Song of the Sea in Exodus 15. In a fascinating development, we also see that a first-century CE retelling of Bible history, Pseudo-Philo's *Biblical Antiquities* 30-31, modifies the story of Deborah by adding elements evidently drawn from Judith.[40] The influence of the stories has now moved in the opposite direction!

There are similarities as well to male warriors and leaders in the Bible. Judith is not only like Deborah, but she is also like the other judges and prophets who arise when God hears the prayers of the people (Jdt 4:13; cf. Judg 2:11-23), to give the land rest from oppression for a number of years afterward (Jdt 16:25; cf. Judg 3:11, 30; 5:31).[41] We note, for example, Ehud's killing of Eglon, king of Moab (Judg 3:12-30). Once Ehud has assassinated the king in his inner chamber, Ehud leaves the doors closed so that the servants are pacing without, wondering what is taking the king so long. This is played to comic effect, just as is the analogous scene in Jdt 14:14-18.

39. Sidnie Ann White, "In the Steps of Jael and Deborah: Judith as Heroine," in *"No One Spoke Ill of Her": Essays on Judith*, ed. James C. VanderKam (Atlanta: Scholars Press, 1992) 5-16.

40. Richard I. Pervo, "Aseneth and Her Sisters: Women in Jewish Narrative and in the Greek Novels," in *"Women Like This": New Perspectives on Jewish Women in the Greco-Roman World,* ed. Amy-Jill Levine (Atlanta: Scholars Press, 1991) 159n. 71.

41. White, "In the Steps of Jael and Deborah," 12; Jan Willem van Henten, "Judith as Alternative Leader: A Rereading of Judith 7–13," in *A Feminist Companion to Esther, Judith and Susanna*, ed. Athalya Brenner (Sheffield: Sheffield Academic, 1995) 243-44.

Other texts have left their mark on Judith, not just in the similarity of the motifs, but in the use of words as well: Abram's (Abraham's) pursuit of the captors of Lot in Genesis 14 (cf. Judith 15), the motif of the complaining of the people in Exodus 17 (cf. Judith 7), the story of David and Goliath in 1 Samuel 17 (cf. Judith 13), the bluster of Nebuchadnezzar in Daniel 2–4 and the insistence that the king be worshiped as a god in Daniel 6 (cf. Judith 2), and the repentance in sackcloth, even for the cattle, in Jonah 3:5-8 (cf. Jdt 4:10). Some of these parallels may result from the oral circulation of good story motifs, but others are either much too close to be independent or use similar words. Thus the essence of Judith is not a literary rendition of an originally oral story, as may be the case for Tobit, Esther, or Daniel 1–6. Judith uses broad folklore themes, to be sure, but the parallels reveal an author at work who is borrowing heavily from a number of biblical texts and weaving them together into a unified story. Dubarle likens this process to the "anthological style" of other post-exilic Jewish works and of such Christian texts as Luke 1–2.[42] It would be wrong, however, to say that Judith is an imaginative interpretation that simply mines and develops a number of biblical passages. For one thing, non-Jewish traditions can also be postulated that are in many cases just as close as the biblical: the Ugaritic epic of Aqhat, for example, tells the story of the woman Paghat, who, enraged over the death of her brother Aqhat, avenges him by inebriating his murderer and slaying him while he is on his bed.[43] The use of written texts in the composition of another written text does not preclude the use also of motifs and themes from oral tradition,[44] but what is important here is that Judith is not just the sum total of the myriad motifs that it appears to borrow, now strung together. It uses these many building blocks, and yet still reflects the single vision of a talented author who communicates the exuberance of Judith's freedom in a new genre, the novel.

42. Dubarle, *Judith,* 1:137-64.
43. *ANET,* 155.
44. Susan Niditch, *Oral World and Written Word: Ancient Israelite Literature* (Louisville: Westminster/John Knox, 1996) 8-24.

BIBLIOGRAPHY

Commentaries:

Cowley, Arthur E. "The Book of Judith." In *APOT* 1:242-67. An older translation with introduction and notes, it is still valuable.

Dancy, J. C. *The Shorter Books of the Apocrypha.* CBC. Cambridge: Cambridge University Press, 1972. Includes an excellent, but somewhat dated, short commentary on Judith.

Enslin, Morton S., and Solomon Zeitlin. *The Book of Judith.* JAL VIII. Leiden: Brill, 1972. Greek text and English translation with notes. Formerly a standard treatment, it was written before the important contributions of literary and feminist studies. It is still quite valuable.

Moore, Carey A. *Judith.* AB 40. Garden City, N.Y.: Doubleday, 1985. The major commentary in English. Clearly written, with a wealth of historical and geographical information, it incorporated the literary and feminist scholarship that was available at the time of its publication.

Studies on Judith:

Alonso-Schökel, Luis. *Narrative Structures in the Book of Judith.* Berkeley, Calif.: Center for Hermeneutical Studies in Hellenistic and Modern Culture, 1974. A pioneering literary study of Judith, important both for its focus on the literary structures of the text and for the responses included in it by Mary P. Coote and Alan Dundes that pressed folklore parallels to Judith.

Bal, Mieke. "Head Hunting: 'Judith' on the Cutting Edge of Knowledge." *JSOT* 63 (1994) 3-34. Reprinted in Brenner, *A Feminist Companion.* A provocative and insightful feminist interpretation of artistic depictions of Judith that illuminates the biblical text as well.

Brenner, Athalya, ed. *A Feminist Companion to Esther, Judith and Susanna.* Sheffield: Sheffield Academic, 1995. Part of a series of volumes of previously published feminist analyses of biblical texts.

Craven, Toni. *Artistry and Faith in the Book of Judith.* Chico, Calif.: Scholars Press, 1983. With Alonso-Schökel, Craven launched the recent wave of literary-critical studies.

Elder, Linda Bennett. "Judith." In Elisabeth Schüssler Fiorenza, ed. *Searching the Scriptures.* Vol. 2. New York: Crossroad, 1993–94. Focuses on the many sides of Judith's role as a woman in the story.

Garrard, Mary. "Judith." In *Artemisia Gentileschi: The Image of the Female Hero in Italian Baroque Art.* Princeton: Princeton University Press, 1989. This brilliant analysis connects the various Renaissance and Baroque paintings of Judith to the psychological and interpretive issues that are present in the ancient text as well.

Jacobus, Mary. "Judith, Holofernes, and the Phallic Woman." In *Reading Women: Essays in Feminist Criticism.* New York: Columbia University Press, 1986. One of the best essays on the psychological and sexual issues in Judith. Like Garrard, Jacobus incorporates an analysis of visual images as a means of sensitizing the reader to the issues in the biblical text as well.

Lacocque, André. *The Feminine Unconventional: Four Subversive Figures in Israel's Tradition.* Minneapolis: Fortress, 1990. A theologically engaging consideration of the "subversive" side of seemingly domesticated biblical narratives about women.

Levine, Amy-Jill. "Sacrifice and Salvation: Otherness and Domestication in the Book of Judith." In *"No One Spoke Ill of Her": Essays on Judith.* Edited by James C. VanderKam. Atlanta: Scholars Press, 1992. One of the most provocative and thoughtful readings on the symbolism of Judith's reversal of typical male/female gender codes.

McNeil, Brian. "Reflections on the Book of Judith." *The Downside Review* 96 (1978) 199-207. A Roman Catholic reflection on the place of Judith in the church's teachings.

Milne, Pamela. "What Shall We Do with Judith? A Feminist Assessment of a Biblical 'Heroine.' " *Semeia* 62 (1993) 37-58. An excellent and balanced reflection on whether Judith should be considered a feminist work.

Pervo, Richard I. "Aseneth and Her Sisters: Women in Jewish Narrative and in the Greek Novels." In *"Women Like This": New Perspectives on Jewish Women in the Greco-Roman World.* Edited by Amy-Jill Levine. Atlanta: Scholars Press, 1991. Draws many parallels between the Jewish novels and the Greek and includes interesting insights on Judith.

Skehan, Patrick. "The Hand of Judith." *CBQ* 25 (1963) 94-110. Argues strongly that the Song of Judith was modeled on the Song of the Sea in Exodus 15 and that both were used in celebrations of Passover.

Stocker, Margarita. *Judith, Sexual Warrior: Women and Power in Western Culture.* New Haven: Yale University Press, 1998. Excellent on the appropriation of Judith in the Reformation-era debates and in art.

VanderKam, James C., ed. *"No One Spoke Ill of Her": Essays on Judith.* Atlanta: Scholars Press, 1992. Excellent essays by Amy-Jill Levine, Sidnie White Crawford, Nira Stone, Adolfo Roitman, Carey Moore, and Patrick Skehan.

Wills, Lawrence M. *The Jewish Novel in the Ancient World.* Ithaca: Cornell University Press, 1995. The first book-length study to bring all the Jewish novels and related literature together into one genre analysis.

OUTLINE OF JUDITH

I. Judith 1:1–7:32, Nebuchadnezzar Threatens the West and Israel

A. 1:1–2:13, The Rising Threat of Nebuchadnezzar Against the West

1:1-16, Nebuchadnezzar's Campaign Against Arphaxad
2:1-13, Nebuchadnezzar Commissions Holofernes to Destroy the Nations Who Did Not Ally with Him

B. 2:14–7:32, Holofernes' Campaign Narrows to a Siege of Bethulia

2:14-28, Campaign Initiated Against Disobedient Nations
3:1-10, The People of the Seacoast Surrender
4:1-15, Israel Prays and Prepares for War
5:1-21, Achior Tells Holofernes of Israel's History
5:22–6:21, Holofernes Responds by Expelling Achior, Who Is Received in Bethulia
7:1-18, Holofernes Prepares for War and Places Bethulia Under Siege
7:19-32, The People Despair and Want to Surrender

II. Judith 8:1–16:25, Judith Arises to Rescue Her People

A. 8:1-8, Introduction of Judith

B. 8:9–10:10, Judith Resolves to Save Israel

8:9-36, Judith Addresses the Citizens of Bethulia
9:1-14, Judith Purifies Herself and Prays
10:1-10, Judith Emerges from Prayer to Go Forth

C. 10:11–13:10*a*, Judith Overcomes Holofernes

10:11-23, Judith Enters the Enemy Camp and Is Taken to Holofernes
11:1-23, Judith's Dialogue with Holofernes
12:1-20, For Three Days Judith Lives in Holofernes' Camp
13:1-10*a*, Judith Beheads Holofernes

D. 13:10*b*–15:7, Judith Returns to Bethulia and Initiates Counterattack

13:10*b*-20, Judith and Her Maid Return to Bethulia
14:1-10, Judith Issues Orders and Achior Converts
14:11–15:7, The Assyrians Discover Holofernes' Headless Body and Are Put to Flight

E. 15:8–16:25, Celebration and Conclusion

15:8-13, All of Israel Celebrates
15:14–16:17, Judith's Victory Song
16:18-20, Thanksgiving Offerings
16:21-25, Memorial of Judith

JUDITH 1:1–7:32

NEBUCHADNEZZAR THREATENS THE WEST AND ISRAEL

OVERVIEW

The book of Judith can be divided into two parts, the first of which (1:1–7:32) describes a threat to the Israelites that arises from Nebuchadnezzar, king of the Assyrians, and his general Holofernes. Nebuchadnezzar had demanded that all the nations of the west ally with him to defeat Arphaxad, king of the Medes. Although many of the nations refuse to join him, he defeats Arphaxad nevertheless. The first chapter thus begins with a description of battles on the eastern horizon between two great nations, the Assyrians and the Medes. Once the Medes have been conquered, Nebuchadnezzar turns to conquer the nations who spurned his request. This group of nations, those to the west of Assyria, includes Judea and Samaria. He commissions his general Holofernes to muster an army of huge proportions and to attack each nation in turn, accepting as allies those who choose to surrender and laying waste those who do not. Israel will not capitulate, and begs God for help as they await the assault of Holofernes from the north. Standing between Jerusalem and the path of the Assyrians is a series of mountain villages, which are quickly fortified as the first line of defense.

The first half of Judith thus presents a tremendous sweep of nations and battles, military threats, the intrigue of stratagems, abject demonstrations of humility on the part of Israel, and the delivery of Israel's newfound ally, Achior, to Judith's village. All of the issues of the first half come to bear on a single village in the mountains forty miles north of Jerusalem. It ends on a note of calm before the storm, with the Israelite people in despair.

JUDITH 1:1–2:13, THE RISING THREAT OF NEBUCHADNEZZAR AGAINST THE WEST

OVERVIEW

Like modern action movies, Judith leaps immediately into a rousing action scene that is only preparatory to the longer military campaigns to follow. The presence of a "chapter 1," set chronologically well before the main action of the story, is not unusual in the literature of this period (see, e.g., Esther 1, Tobit 1, Matthew 1–2, and Luke 1–2). The function of this introduction is not simply to engage the reader with exciting action—although that is an important element of popular literature; the carefully orchestrated rising action serves to dramatize, first, that Nebuchadnezzar is apparently invincible, since even the great king Arphaxad is defeated by him, and second, that Nebuchadnezzar is bent on world domination and will not stop his expansion until the entire subcontinent is under his control.

Judith 1:1-16, Nebuchadnezzar's Campaign Against Arphaxad

NAB

1 1 It was the twelfth year of the reign of Nebuchadnezzar, king of the Assyrians in the great city of Nineveh. At that time Arphaxad ruled over the Medes in Ecbatana. 2 Around this city he built a wall of blocks of stone, each three cubits in height and six in length. He made the wall seventy cubits high and fifty thick. 3 At the gates he raised towers of a hundred cubits, with a thickness of sixty cubits at the base. 4 The gateway he built to a height of seventy cubits, with an opening forty cubits wide for the passage of his chariot forces and the marshaling of his infantry. 5 Then King Nebuchadnezzar waged war against King Arphaxad in the vast plain, in the district of Ragae. 6 To him there rallied all the inhabitants of the mountain region, all who dwelt along the Euphrates, the Tigris, and the Hydaspes, and King Arioch of the Elamites, in the plain. Thus many nations came together to resist the people of Cheleoud.

7 Now Nebuchadnezzar, king of the Assyrians, sent messengers to all the inhabitants of Persia, and to all those who dwelt in the West: to the inhabitants of Cilicia and Damascus, Lebanon and Anti-Lebanon, to all who dwelt along the seacoast, 8 to the peoples of Carmel, Gilead, Upper Galilee, and the vast plain of Esdraelon, 9 to all those in Samaria and its cities, and west of the Jordan as far as Jerusalem, Bethany, Chelous, Kadesh, and the River of Egypt; to Tahpanhes, Raamses, all the land of Goshen, 10 Tanis, Memphis and beyond, and to all the inhabitants of Egypt as far as the borders of Ethiopia.

11 But the inhabitants of all that land disregarded the summons of Nebuchadnezzar, king of the Assyrians, and would not go with him to the war. They were not afraid of him but regarded him as a lone individual opposed to them, and turned away his envoys emptyhanded, in disgrace.

The translation is based on the LXX as in Brooke-McLean, *The Old Testament in Greek* (Cambridge, Eng., 1940), unless as otherwise noted here.

1, 4: (*dynameōs*) '*armatōn* (*autou*): so LXX[S], P, Vet Lat.
1, 6: ('*yiōn*) *Cheleoud:* so LXX[S]; a garbled form of Chaldaiō*n*? Cf 2, 23.
1, 8: (*pedion*) *Esdrēlōn:* so LXX[S].
1, 11: ('*ōs anēr*) '*eis:* so LXX[S,A].

NRSV

1 It was the twelfth year of the reign of Nebuchadnezzar, who ruled over the Assyrians in the great city of Nineveh. In those days Arphaxad ruled over the Medes in Ecbatana. [2]He built walls around Ecbatana with hewn stones three cubits thick and six cubits long; he made the walls seventy cubits high and fifty cubits wide. [3]At its gates he raised towers one hundred cubits high and sixty cubits wide at the foundations. [4]He made its gates seventy cubits high and forty cubits wide to allow his armies to march out in force and his infantry to form their ranks. [5]Then King Nebuchadnezzar made war against King Arphaxad in the great plain that is on the borders of Ragau. [6]There rallied to him all the people of the hill country and all those who lived along the Euphrates, the Tigris, and the Hydaspes, and, on the plain, Arioch, king of the Elymeans. Thus, many nations joined the forces of the Chaldeans.[a]

7Then Nebuchadnezzar, king of the Assyrians, sent messengers to all who lived in Persia and to all who lived in the west, those who lived in Cilicia and Damascus, Lebanon and Antilebanon, and all who lived along the seacoast, [8]and those among the nations of Carmel and Gilead, and Upper Galilee and the great plain of Esdraelon, [9]and all who were in Samaria and its towns, and beyond the Jordan as far as Jerusalem and Bethany and Chelous and Kadesh and the river of Egypt, and Tahpanhes and Raamses and the whole land of Goshen, [10]even beyond Tanis and Memphis, and all who lived in Egypt as far as the borders of Ethiopia. [11]But all who lived in the whole region disregarded the summons of Nebuchadnezzar, king of the Assyrians, and refused to join him in the war; for they were not afraid of him, but regarded him as only one man.[b] So they sent back his messengers empty-handed and in disgrace.

12Then Nebuchadnezzar became very angry with this whole region, and swore by his throne and kingdom that he would take revenge on the whole territory of Cilicia and Damascus and Syria, that he would kill with his sword also all the inhabitants of the land of Moab, and the people

[a] Syr: Gk *Cheleoudites* [b] Or *a man*

NAB

12 Then Nebuchadnezzar fell into a violent rage
against all that land, and swore by his throne and
his kingdom that he would avenge himself on all
the territories of Cilicia and Damascus and Syria,
and also destroy with his sword all the inhabitants
of Moab, Ammon, the whole of Judea, and those
living anywhere in Egypt as far as the borders of
the two seas.
13 In the seventeenth year he proceeded with
his army against King Arphaxad, and was victorious in his campaign. He routed the whole force
of Arphaxad, his entire cavalry and all his chariots,
14 and took possession of his cities. He pressed
on to Ecbatana and took its towers, sacked its
marketplaces, and turned its glory into shame. 15
Arphaxad himself he overtook in the mountains
of Ragae, ran him through with spears, and utterly
destroyed him. 16 Then he returned home with
all his numerous, motley horde of warriors; and
there he and his army relaxed and feasted for a
hundred and twenty days.

1, 12: (*pasan tēn*) *Ioudaian:* so LXX^{S,A}, P, Vet Lat.
1, 15: (*'eōs tēs 'ēmeras*) *tautas:* so LXX^{S}, P, Vet Lat.
1, 16: (*autos*) *kai pas 'o symmiktos autou plēthos andrōn polemistōn poly sphodra kai ēn ekei rathymōn kai euōchoumenos* (*autos kai 'ē dynamis*): so LXX^{S}; cf LXX^{A}; LXX^{B} skips from one *autos* to the next.

NRSV

of Ammon, and all Judea, and every one in Egypt,
as far as the coasts of the two seas.
13In the seventeenth year he led his forces
against King Arphaxad and defeated him in battle,
overthrowing the whole army of Arphaxad and
all his cavalry and all his chariots. 14Thus he took
possession of his towns and came to Ecbatana,
captured its towers, plundered its markets, and
turned its glory into disgrace. 15He captured Arphaxad in the mountains of Ragau and struck him
down with his spears, thus destroying him once
and for all. 16Then he returned to Nineveh, he
and all his combined forces, a vast body of troops;
and there he and his forces rested and feasted for
one hundred twenty days.

COMMENTARY

1:1-4. The book of Judith opens in a way that is typical of the history books of the Bible, by dating the events described to the year in the reign of the major king (see 1 Kgs 15:1; 16:15, 29; 2 Kgs 12:1; 13:1). However, although the reader is perhaps meant to think of the genre of history writing, it is mock history that is likely intended, for Nebuchadnezzar is identified as the king "who ruled over the Assyrians in the great city of Nineveh." The historical Nebuchadnezzar ruled, not the Assyrians, whose capital was indeed in Nineveh, but the Babylonians. Both empires were remembered as being oppressive to the Israelite and Jewish people: The Assyrians had destroyed the northern kingdom of Israel and deported the leading citizens in 721 BCE, and Nebuchadnezzar and his Babylonian army had defeated Jerusalem and the southern kingdom of Judah (later called Judea) in 586 BCE, when he also destroyed the Temple and deported many citizens to Babylon (see esp. 2 Kings 24–25; Jer 39:1–40:6). Because Assyria and Babylon were considered the two "evil empires" of Israelite and Jewish history, there is no question that both the author and the audience would have been aware of the error of combining them; this was doubtless a signal within the writing that the novel that followed, though as rousing as military history, was meant ironically and even humorously. It would be all the more satisfying if the two evil empires could be merged into one figurehead that would march forward only to be defeated by the stratagems of an Israelite woman.

No sooner has an impossible combination of empires appeared on the stage of "history" than it is met by another fictitious king created for this role: "Arphaxad who ruled over the Medes in Ecbatana." There is no known king of the Medes by that name, but neither would the reader expect such a figure to exist based on the playful combination of Nebuchadnezzar and the Assyrians just encountered. The irony of this fictitious king would have been surprising for another reason as well: The mighty Assyrians, who in this book will crush Arphaxad and the Medes in 1:13-15, were actually defeated by the Medes in 612 BCE.

The might of Arphaxad's kingdom is quickly communicated by means of a description of Ecbatana's city walls; the dimensions of the walls and towers go far beyond any fortifications that were likely built for that city. The size of the gates is emphasized to provide an opportunity for the author to conjure for the audience the awesome image of Arphaxad's troops passing through. This is just the first of many examples of how the author uses description to bring forth an exciting narrative that is almost "cinematic" in what it evokes. Ecbatana figures historically and accurately in Ezra 6:2 and appears in Tob 3:7 as the home of Sarah, the woman who will marry Tobit's son. Thus the city is part of the eastern home of diaspora Jews and would have been a known entity to the audience. Perhaps more important for the literary technique here is the historian Polybius's remark[45] that exaggerated descriptions of the palace, as here in Judith, were common in sensationalist histories. The author has in just a few lines plunged us into a dramatic world of the clash of great nations. At this point we might compare a similar effect achieved in a very different way in the Additions to Esther. Whereas MT Esther began as a court narrative with a description of the pomp and splendor of the great Persian palace, the Additions begin by recounting a dream that came to Mordecai:

> Noises and confusion, thunders and earthquake, tumult on the earth! Then two great dragons came forward, both ready to fight, and they roared terribly. At their roaring every nation prepared for war, to fight against the righteous nation. (Add. Esth A 5–7 NRSV)

We later learn that the two dragons are Mordecai and Haman and that the nations are those arrayed against Israel. Thus in this Addition the scope of the worldwide danger is communicated in a portentous dream that borrows from apocalyptic imagery.

The book of Judith, which reflects in general an excellent and exciting plot development, opens in a way that seems quite awkward. The long opening sentence (broken up by most translations into several sentences) sets the scene by drawing the reader immediately into the high drama of the narrative. A long run-on sentence is used to describe two great nations pitted against each other, but what do they have to do with Israel? We are not told until the next chapter. The book of Esther employs a similar technique of beginning with a long description and a run-on sentence, but there the drama is more court intrigue, here it is the threat of external military campaigns (see also the Commentary on Jdt 8:1-3).

1:5-6. The lists of peoples and lands serves to communicate the worldwide extent of the war that is threatened. They sometimes seem repetitive to the modern reader, or at least unknown and confusing, but this should not detract from our ability to appreciate the literary effects of the treatment of nations and places. Here the great plain on the border of Ragau is in Persia; Ragau (Rages), like Ecbatana, is an important city in Tobit. The famous regions of Persia, near the Tigris and Euphrates rivers, are a stirring setting for the action about to take place. The fortunes of the Jews are thus seen in an international context, and in the company of the major nations of the world. This "global" focus was also known to the prophets (e.g., Amos and Isaiah), but here the nations are not simply condemned from afar; rather, they become characters in a drama, much as Nineveh and Assyria do in Jonah. Throughout Judith, some of the geographical sites are unknown, some anachronistic (such as Persia, which only arose as a world power a century after the Assyrians had been defeated), some simply located incorrectly. The technique of piling up the list of nations is similar to the description of the court festivities in Esther 1; so also is the sweep of lands, seemingly from one end of the world to the other, which Esth 1:1 accomplishes in one short clause.

1:7-10. Nebuchadnezzar's power and reach are awe inspiring; the progress of his messengers moves methodically from east to west, ultimately

45. Polybius *History* 10.27.7-8.

passing through the region of Judea to Egypt, as far as Ethiopia. Most of the geographical entities are well-known, well-established areas of the major nations. The author is clearly trying to convey the sense of doom as the shadow of Nebuchadnezzar's might moves over the land (cf. the image of Assyria as a great world tree in Ezek 31:2-9 and the use of the tree or vine overshadowing the earth in Herodotus).[46] Since in the reader's mind Nebuchadnezzar would be associated with Babylon, it is also relevant to note a Babylonian inscription that may have influenced Daniel 4: "Under Babylon's everlasting shadow, I have gathered all the peoples in peace." Judith does not use a tree metaphor here, but the sense of a shadow across the land, whether understood negatively or positively, is similar in the different passages, and the idea of eastern empires would have conjured such notions.

Samaria and Jerusalem are mentioned only in passing here, a small part of the blur of nations that are being encompassed. This is quite deliberate, as the "real" geographical focus of the narrative, Jerusalem, is intentionally submerged in the list of nations, creating the illusion that *world* history is at stake, which will, as the story proceeds, become more narrowly focused on the area of Syria-Palestine, then on Judea and Samaria, then on Bethulia as the gateway to Judea, then on one woman from the village of Bethulia. "Samaria" was the name given to Israel, the northern half of Israel/Judah, when it became a province under the Assyrians, Babylonians, Persians, and Greeks. The names of the regions of Samaria and Judea reflect the political realities of the post-exilic period, when the former was the name of the province occupying the land that was once northern Israel, and the latter the area of the older southern kingdom of Judah, the temple-state governed from Jerusalem. It will be quite revealing to follow the disappearance of these two real-world terms and their replacement by the more idealized "Israel" for both of these areas, implying a united Israel (see Commentary on 4:1-15). The use of "Israel" as the ideal term for the region is not unusual, but it is carried through more systematically and creatively in Judith than is usually the case elsewhere.

46. Herodotus *Histories* 1.108; 7.19.

1:11-12. The nations, like Arphaxad, have underestimated Nebuchadnezzar. He was, of course, considered by the author of Judith to be a mere mortal, but still no ordinary man—he is the arch adversary and should neither be underestimated nor overestimated. The nations shame him by snubbing his messengers. Nebuchadnezzar's rage is based not only on a desire for world domination, but also on a desire for revenge. The dramatic tension is thus also increased, as negotiation or coexistence—short of complete capitulation—is becoming less likely.

Part of the important cultural background of the book of Judith is the ancient Mediterranean concept of honor and shame. In ancient cultures, honor and shame were important and very public aspects of a person's or a nation's standing, quite different from our modern, more internalized values of self-esteem (positive) and guilt (negative). Symbols of honor and shame and ritual ways of honoring or shaming another person are interwoven into the biblical texts, but modern readers are apt to disregard these elements as mere externals.[47] Honor and shame are certainly at issue here and will be a constant in this book (2:14; 4:12; 5:21; 8:22-23; 9:2). Judith, for example, will not just kill Holofernes, but will reverse his threat of shame upon him and the Assyrians. Interestingly, the list of nations whose lot has been combined with Judea's includes the Ammonites and the Moabites, nations with a very checkered history of involvement with Israel and Judah, raising the question for the next segment of the story: Will these peoples remain practical allies, or will some reveal their past nature and go over to the side of the enemy? They reappear in the narrative at 5:2.

1:13-16. The "seventeenth year" probably evokes the career of the historical Nebuchadnezzar of Babylon, who was known to have captured Jerusalem in the eighteenth year of his reign (Jer 32:1). The reader would thus imagine that this Nebuchadnezzar had cleared the way to move toward Jerusalem in the following year. Nebuchadnezzar runs Arphaxad through in the mountains of Rages, much as Alexander the Great had

47. D. D. Gilmore, ed., *Honor and Shame and the Unity of the Mediterranean* (Washington, D.C.: American Anthropological Association, 1987); Timothy S. Laniak, *Shame and Honor in the Book of Esther* (Atlanta: Scholars Press, 1998).

forced Darius of Persia to retreat from Ecbatana and flee into the mountains. The great city of Ecbatana is destroyed, but as noted above, it is also shamed. The greatness of Arphaxad and Ecbatana were described above, but Nebuchadnezzar has here easily defeated him without the help of those nations he invited to ally with him. The might of Nebuchadnezzar is thus even more dramatically demonstrated.

The feasting is an appropriate way to bring chap. 1 to a close. The action has moved very swiftly and with much slaughter; the feasting allows a temporary lull as the reader makes a transition to the next major movement of the story. There will be other such rests to allow for transitions to new movements in the story (see Commentary on 2:28).

Judith 2:1-13, Nebuchadnezzar Commissions Holofernes to Destroy the Nations Who Did Not Ally with Him

NAB

2 1 In the eighteenth year, on the twenty-second day of the first month, there was a discussion in the palace of Nebuchadnezzar, king of the Assyrians, about taking revenge on the whole world, as he had threatened. 2 He summoned all his ministers and nobles, laid before them his secret plan, and urged the total destruction of those countries. 3 They decided to do away with all those who had refused to comply with the order he had issued.

4 When he had completed his plan, Nebuchadnezzar, king of the Assyrians, summoned Holofernes, general in chief of his forces, second to himself in command, and said to him: 5 "Thus says the great king, the lord of all the earth: Go forth from my presence, take with you men of proven valor, a hundred and twenty thousand infantry and twelve thousand cavalry, 6 and proceed against all the land of the West, because they did not comply with the order I issued. 7 Tell them to have earth and water ready, for I will come against them in my wrath; I will cover all the land with the feet of my soldiers, to whom I will deliver them as spoils. 8 Their slain shall fill their ravines and wadies, the swelling torrent shall be choked with their dead; 9 and I will deport them as exiles to the very ends of the earth.

10 "You go before me and take possession of all their territories for me. If they surrender to you, guard them for me till the day of their punishment. 11 As for those who resist, show

2, 5: (*anabatais*) *chiliadas* (*deka dyo*): so LXX[A]; cf LXX[S,Bab], *and* v 15.
2, 7: (*kai*) *apaggeleis autois* (*etoimazein*): so LXX[S,A,Bab].

NRSV

2 In the eighteenth year, on the twenty-second day of the first month, there was talk in the palace of Nebuchadnezzar, king of the Assyrians, about carrying out his revenge on the whole region, just as he had said. [2]He summoned all his ministers and all his nobles and set before them his secret plan and recounted fully, with his own lips, all the wickedness of the region.[a] [3]They decided that every one who had not obeyed his command should be destroyed.

4When he had completed his plan, Nebuchadnezzar, king of the Assyrians, called Holofernes, the chief general of his army, second only to himself, and said to him, [5]"Thus says the Great King, the lord of the whole earth: Leave my presence and take with you men confident in their strength, one hundred twenty thousand foot soldiers and twelve thousand cavalry. [6]March out against all the land to the west, because they disobeyed my orders. [7]Tell them to prepare earth and water, for I am coming against them in my anger, and will cover the whole face of the earth with the feet of my troops, to whom I will hand them over to be plundered. [8]Their wounded shall fill their ravines and gullies, and the swelling river shall be filled with their dead. [9]I will lead them away captive to the ends of the whole earth. [10]You shall go and seize all their territory for me in advance. They must yield themselves to you, and you shall hold them for me until the day of their punishment. [11]But to those who resist show no mercy, but hand them over to slaughter and plunder throughout your whole region. [12]For as I

[a] Meaning of Gk uncertain

NAB

them no quarter, but deliver them up to slaughter and plunder in each country you occupy.
12 For as I live, and by the strength of my kingdom, what I have spoken I will accomplish by my power.
13 Do not disobey a single one of the orders of your lord; fulfill them exactly as I have commanded you, and do it without delay."

NRSV

live, and by the power of my kingdom, what I have spoken I will accomplish by my own hand.
13 And you—take care not to transgress any of your lord's commands, but carry them out exactly as I have ordered you; do it without delay."

COMMENTARY

The menace that is threatening in chap. 1 is made explicit here: Nebuchadnezzar announces his designs on "the whole region," a phrase used eight times in the first two chapters.[48] The summoning of all of Nebuchadnezzar's ministers and nobles, and the decision that everyone who had not obeyed his command should be destroyed are similar to certain parts of Daniel 1–6 (cf. esp. Dan 2:2-5; 3:2-9; 6:6-8). In the case of Daniel 1–4, it is also Nebuchadnezzar who is the offending king. Daniel was evidently one of the influences on the book of Judith (see Introduction). Regarding Nebuchadnezzar's second-in-command, Holofernes, there is also a likely historical origin for the name that is here used in a very unhistorical way. When Artaxerxes III Ochus of Persia invaded Asia Minor and Egypt, including Judea, in 350 and 343 BCE, his general was named Holofernes, who in turn had an officer named Bagoas, which is the name of Holofernes' officer in Jdt 12:11. These names, probably known from this campaign of Artaxerxes III, were used for the officers of this invading army.

Another indication that we are not in the realm of history but in that of imaginative literature is the repeated characterization of Nebuchadnezzar as "lord." This motif is introduced here for the first time, but will be built on later in the narrative until it takes on ironic and even comic dimensions in chaps. 11–13. The word "lord" in Greek, κύριος (*kyrios*), would have multiple uses, always denoting the clear superior in a hierarchical relation—for example, ruler as opposed to subject, master as opposed to slave, husband as opposed to wife, or in the case of gods, "lord of heaven," and so on. As such, it was adopted by Greek-speaking Jews as the standard word to translate the divine name YHWH. Thus in Judith we find the intentional double meaning of "lord" as God and "lord" as earthly superior. Only the arrogant and deluded Holofernes will mistake Judith's references to the divine Lord for references to himself and Nebuchadnezzar as earthly lords. Whenever the word appears, there is usually an ironic wink to the audience concerning this double meaning. Other language associated with God is then also used to extend this characterization of Nebuchadnezzar's divine self-concept. With this in mind, we can detect a string of Jewish divine terms applied by Nebuchadnezzar to himself: "Thus says the Great King, the lord of the whole earth. . . . For as I live, and by the power of my kingdom. . . . Take care not to transgress any of your lord's commands." The divine pretensions of Nebuchadnezzar are here not stated explicitly—he does not require worship as a god, even though Holofernes will require this for him at 3:8. However, to the Jewish audience his words here will reverberate as sentences associated with God. Further, Nebuchadnezzar's statement (v. 12) that he will accomplish this by his own hand sets up a contrast with Judith's later statement that God will deliver the Jews through her hand (8:33; 12:4). Although, strictly speaking, it is Holofernes who takes on the traits of the blustery tyrant, demanding worship for Nebuchadnezzar as a god, the tradition of Nebuchadnezzar in Daniel would probably have made this association automatic.

Dialogues such as this also point to one of the important patterns of the work: the structural opposition between the protagonists and the an-

48. Carey A. Moore, *Judith,* AB 40 (Garden City, N.Y.: Doubleday, 1985) 127.

tagonists (see the Introduction). Just as Holofernes is a servant of Nebuchadnezzar, and will demand worship of him as a god, so also Judith is a servant of God, and demands proper worship of God by the Bethulians.[49] This set of contrasting correspondences will be extended further when we see that Holofernes has a faithful attendant in Bagoas, and Judith in her unnamed maid.

A number of images of Nebuchadnezzar's threatened campaign would have resonances for the audience. According to Herodotus,[50] earth and water were Persian symbols of surrender and humility.[51] The hyperbole of the rhetoric concerning the number of troops is typical of the Assyrians' boasting in Judith; but interestingly, according to the author the reality is said to match their rhetoric, for the images of how many troops they marshal into the field is often enormous. In 2:19-20, it is said that even those who accompanied the troops were like a "swarm of locusts, like the dust of the earth—a multitude that could not be counted." The threatened deportation would remind the readers of both the Assyrian deportation when the north was defeated by Sargon II in 721 BCE and the deportations by Nebuchadnezzar of Babylon in 597 and 587 BCE that gave rise to the exile. The divine language associated with Nebuchadnezzar and his harsh rhetoric here would also call to mind for the reader the language of God's covenant in Deuteronomy. In chaps. 5, 8, and 9, Achior and Judith articulate the basic premises of deuteronomic theology, which holds that if Israel obeys God's commands, it will prosper; if it disobeys God's commands, it will suffer. Here Nebuchadnezzar presents a worldly version of that theology, in which he arrogates to himself the prerogatives of God. The message that Nebuchadnezzar had sent ahead was accepted by some, rejected by most. Now he has a new message for those who rejected an alliance with him; in vv. 10-11 those who yield will be held "until the day of their punishment"—an almost eschatological sense of his judgment on the nations. Those who resist will be slaughtered and plundered. Nebuchadnezzar's final words to Holofernes that he should obey his lord's commands also sound somewhat like God's words to Moses in Deut 6:1-3.

49. Toni Craven, *Artistry and Faith in the Book of Judith* (Chico, Calif.: Scholars Press, 1983) 53-59. According to W. D. Davies and Dale Allison, *The Gospel According to Saint Matthew,* ICC, 3 vols. (Edinburgh: T. & T. Clark, 1988–97) 1:193, Matthew 1–2 poses an analogous question, "Who is king, Herod or Jesus?"

50. Herodotus *Histories* 6.48.2.

51. Moore, *Judith,* 133.

REFLECTIONS

The book of Judith challenges the modern reader's notion of what constitutes "biblical literature." Concerning its genre, Morton S. Enslin said, "The story of Judith is an example of Jewish fiction at its best."[52] But even those people who grant that not every part of the Bible is historically accurate may have difficulty allowing for deliberate *fiction* in the Bible. The book of Judith is written in the style of history—its opening mimics the introduction of historical epochs in the biblical history books—and yet it immediately turns history on its head by introducing the chief antagonist as "Nebuchadnezzar who ruled over the Assyrians."

Are there other fictions in the Bible? Is Tobit or Esther a fiction? Do even the Gospels and the book of Acts bear a distant relationship to the Jewish novels and the Greek and Roman novels? We are left to our own inferences about how the different texts might have been read, but whereas the Gospels and Acts were never seen as fictions, some of the texts that share similar literary techniques probably were: for example, Susanna, Esther, Judith, and Tobit. They were probably written and read as edifying entertainments and only later included as part of the canonical literature of Jews (in the case of Esther) and Christians (in regard to all four texts), and accepted as sacred history. The significance of the texts must be judged from a number of different perspectives, including that of the imaginative symbolism that underlies such writings as Job, Jonah, Esther, the parables of Jesus, and Judith.

52. Morton S. Enslin and Solomon Zeitlin, *The Book of Judith,* JAL VIII (Leiden: Brill, 1972) 38.

There seems to have been in the ancient world a less clear, or at least a less explicit, distinction between history and fiction. In the Hebrew Bible the journalistic notion of objectivity was not the criterion for judging truthfulness, but rather, the overall claim of the text on one's belief system. Plato has been credited with introducing the idea into Western thought that true statements are ones that correspond to the world.[53] But with this notion in Jewish, Greek, and Latin literature came the idea that seemingly realistic narrative could be written—what looked like a history or a biography—that was yet intentionally an invented world, a story of "what if."

Connected with the category of fiction, both in the ancient world and in our own, is the category of entertainment, and here, too, Judith may challenge typical ideas of what is appropriate to a "biblical" text. The description of events in Judith, as noted in the Introduction, is often almost cinematic and is paced so as to create tension and excitement. The pleasure in reading is not unique to Judith; it is a part of the appreciation of most of the books of the Bible. Yet Judith seems to accentuate the entertaining aspects of storytelling and to deemphasize the larger theological themes.

The modern reader's reactions to this emphasis on entertainment over theology might run along two lines. First, is this sort of literature appropriate for inclusion in the Bible? Second, even if it is appropriate, does it communicate a theological message that can speak to readers and worshipers in the twenty-first century? The answer to the first question might simply be that the wide variety of literary genres in the Bible, most of which are imaginative and not strictly historical, argues for a broad view of what is "appropriate." Paradox, irony, satire, sarcasm, parable, humor, myth—these types of discourse are also in the Bible, and they often create unreal worlds as a means of communicating unusual experiences. The answer to the second question is perhaps more difficult. Does Judith retain any theological significance for modern readers if it is understood as a fictitious work of literature? At the time of its composition, as well as today, the application of Judith does not lie in its journalistic account of a military campaign, but in the values it communicates to its readers. Truth for this text, as in Esther and Tobit, lies not in the facts of history, but in the creation of community and the inculcation of values. What is clearest in this invented world is ethnic and religious identity and—more explicitly than in Esther—reverence and trust in God and a model for the penitential theology and spirituality of the community.

53. Northrop Frye, *The Secular Scripture* (Cambridge, Mass.: Harvard University Press, 1976) 17-20.

JUDITH 2:14–7:32, HOLOFERNES' CAMPAIGN NARROWS TO A SIEGE OF BETHULIA

OVERVIEW

Although the first chapter demonstrated the power of these two great nations, it is only in the chapters that follow that it becomes clear what the threat is for Judea and Israel. Holofernes' campaign will take up the next six chapters. It is an account that includes military campaigns, theological discussions, and intrigues of shifting loyalties. Although often deprecated in relation to chaps. 8–16, many significant themes are raised and important plot developments introduced. The narrative moves methodically from the broadest possible perspective to a focus on the nations to the west (including Judea and Samaria). Then, as the vast armies move inexorably toward the Mediterranean, the focus narrows once again to the area north of Jerusalem, and then to the tiny mountain village of Bethulia, which overlooks a pass through the mountains that the Assyrians will have to take to reach Jerusalem and beyond. The first part of the book of Judith will conclude with the Bethulians' being besieged and in despair, fainting from thirst.

As noted in the Introduction, there are structural parallels and oppositions in the first part of Judith that can be summarized thus:

A Campaign against disobedient nations; the people surrender (2:14–3:10)
- B Israel is "greatly terrified"; Joakim prepares for war (4:1-15)
  - C Holofernes talks with Achior; Achior is expelled (5:1–6:13)
  - C′ Achior is received in Bethulia; Achior talks with the people (6:14-21)
- B′ Holofernes prepares for war; Israel is "greatly terrified" (7:1-5)

A′ Campaign against Bethulia; the people want to surrender (7:6-32)[54]

This chiastic pattern (i.e., like a Greek *chi*, or X, which crosses and reverses itself; the last items are like the first, but in the opposite order) gives a satisfying structure to the first part that ties together the worldwide military drama and the tribulation of the people of tiny Bethulia. (Since some of these passages are only a few verses, they are subsumed under larger sections in the commentary that follows.) At the center of this chiasm is the long dialogue between Holofernes and Achior, in which Achior reveals himself to be an eloquent spokesman for Judaism and the most heroic figure of this half of the book. Achior is literally and figuratively at the center of the first part of Judith. Craven also points out that at the center of this chiasm, in the dialogue between Holofernes and Achior, lies the central question of the narrative, "What god is there except Nebuchadnezzar?"[55] It is not until the center of the chiasm in the second part, when Judith overcomes Holofernes (10:11–13:10*a*), that this question is given a resounding answer.

54. Toni Craven, *Artistry and Faith in the Book of Judith* (Chico, Calif.: Scholars Press, 1983) 60-63.

55. Ibid., 60-63.

Judith 2:14-28, Campaign Initiated Against Disobedient Nations

NAB

14 So Holofernes left the presence of his lord, and summoned all the princes, and the generals and officers of the Assyrian army. 15 He mustered a hundred and twenty thousand picked troops, as his lord had commanded, and twelve thousand mounted archers, 16 and grouped them into a complete combat force. 17 He took along a very large number of camels, asses, and mules for their baggage; innumerable sheep, cattle, and goats for their food supply; 18 abundant provisions for each man, and much gold and silver from the royal palace.

19 Then he and his whole army proceeded on their expedition in advance of King Nebuchadnezzar, to cover all the western region with their chariots and cavalry and regular infantry. 20 A huge, irregular force, too many to count, like

NRSV

14So Holofernes left the presence of his lord, and summoned all the commanders, generals, and officers of the Assyrian army. 15He mustered the picked troops by divisions as his lord had ordered him to do, one hundred twenty thousand of them, together with twelve thousand archers on horseback, 16and he organized them as a great army is marshaled for a campaign. 17He took along a vast number of camels and donkeys and mules for transport, and innumerable sheep and oxen and goats for food; 18also ample rations for everyone, and a huge amount of gold and silver from the royal palace.

19Then he set out with his whole army, to go ahead of King Nebuchadnezzar and to cover the whole face of the earth to the west with their chariots and cavalry and picked foot soldiers. 20Along with them went a mixed crowd like a

NAB

locusts or the dust of the earth, went along with them.

21 After a three-day march from Nineveh, they reached the plain of Bectileth, and from Bectileth they next encamped near the mountains to the north of Upper Cilicia. 22 From there Holofernes took his whole force, the infantry, calvary, and chariots, and marched into the mountain region. 23 He devastated Put and Lud, and plundered all the Rassisites and the Ishmaelites on the border of the desert toward the south of Chaldea.

24 Then, following the Euphrates, he went through Mesopotamia, and battered down every fortified city along the Wadi Abron, until he reached the sea. 25 He seized the territory of Cilicia, and cut down everyone who resisted him. Then he proceeded to the southern borders of Japheth, toward Arabia. 26 He surrounded all the Midianites, burned their tents, and plundered their sheepfolds. 27 Descending to the plain of Damascus at the time of the wheat harvest, he set fire to all their fields, destroyed their flocks and herds, despoiled their cities, devastated their plains, and put all their youths to the sword.

28 The fear and dread of him fell upon all the inhabitants of the coastland, upon those in Sidon and Tyre, and those who dwelt in Sur and Ocina, and the inhabitants of Jamnia. Those in Azotus and Ascalon also feared him greatly.

2, 28: (*katoikountas*) *Sour:* so LXX[Bab], [Sab].

NRSV

swarm of locusts, like the dust[a] of the earth—a multitude that could not be counted.

21They marched for three days from Nineveh to the plain of Bectileth, and camped opposite Bectileth near the mountain that is to the north of Upper Cilicia. 22From there Holofernes[b] took his whole army, the infantry, cavalry, and chariots, and went up into the hill country. 23He ravaged Put and Lud, and plundered all the Rassisites and the Ishmaelites on the border of the desert, south of the country of the Chelleans. 24Then he followed[c] the Euphrates and passed through Mesopotamia and destroyed all the fortified towns along the brook Abron, as far as the sea. 25He also seized the territory of Cilicia, and killed everyone who resisted him. Then he came to the southern borders of Japheth, facing Arabia. 26He surrounded all the Midianites, and burned their tents and plundered their sheepfolds. 27Then he went down into the plain of Damascus during the wheat harvest, and burned all their fields and destroyed their flocks and herds and sacked their towns and ravaged their lands and put all their young men to the sword.

28So fear and dread of him fell upon all the people who lived along the seacoast, at Sidon and Tyre, and those who lived in Sur and Ocina and all who lived in Jamnia. Those who lived in Azotus and Ascalon feared him greatly.

[a] Gk *sand* [b] Gk *he* [c] Or *crossed*

COMMENTARY

2:14-20. Holofernes' campaign is not told with a historian's eye for strategy and detail, but with a storyteller's ear for image and emotion. The lists of officers, soldiers, and livestock are intended to convey the enormousness of the armies, culminating in images that seem almost cinematic ("like a swarm of locusts, like the dust of the earth"). Alonso-Schökel notes this aspect of the author's descriptive ability, and Hägg sees this same quality in the Greek novel.[56] Further, when the author says that Holofernes' army was organized "as a great army is marshaled for a campaign," he seems to signal a humorous and ironic tone, as if to say, "this fiction is just like the real thing." The suspicion that there is a humorous tone here is partially confirmed in the next verse, where we learn of the auxiliary animals and provisions. Whenever the troops are described, there is always a barely restrained excess or comic hyperbole of the auxiliary peoples, animals, or baggage (2:20; 7:2, 18). The Assyrian auxiliary crowds are also referred to as a "mixed crowd," a sarcastic epithet that may reflect the policy of the Hasmoneans to purify the religion, and therefore the

56. Luis Alonso-Schökel, *Narrative Structures in the Book of Judith* (Berkeley, Calif.: Center for Hermeneutical Studies in Hellenistic and Modern Culture, 1974) 7; Tomas Hägg, *The Novel in Antiquity* (Berkeley: University of California Press, 1983) 55-56.

peoples, of the land of Israel (see Introduction), which Judith herself seems to echo in 8:18. It is possible that the descriptions are also modeled on the stories of Israel's deliverers in the book of Judges. In the cycle of stories about Gideon (Judges 6–8), the Midianites and the Amalekites are mighty nations oppressing Israel from the east: "For they and their livestock would come up, and they would even bring their tents, as thick as locusts; neither they nor their camels could be counted; so they wasted the land as they came in" (Judg 6:5 NRSV). However, this description of the livestock and tents has a definite role in Judges 6, and the devastation of the livestock is like that of locusts; in Judith the role of these images does not make as much sense on the realistic level but is exaggerated and repeated, probably for comic effect. Aside from this literary effect, one may wonder if the size of the Assyrian army is to be contrasted to what in the author's time was the proud tradition of the Maccabees, who had fought a guerrilla campaign using small bands of troops against the vast armies of the Seleucid kings. The Maccabees, it is also to be noted, between sorties hid in the mountains like those near Judith's village.

2:21-27. The hyperbolic description of troops, auxiliary personnel, and provisions just mentioned is also matched by the excessive detail of the geographical movements. The campaign that has been promised is now realized with destructive force. Many nations and peoples are defeated, and the cruelty of Holofernes is depicted as well. The description of the campaign builds in intensity from v. 14 to v. 27, as it moves from the gathering of officials and soldiers, animals and equipment, to the movements of the campaign and a first mention of plundering (v. 23), to wholesale slaughter and destruction (v. 27). Every conceivable kind of destruction is listed as a drumbeat to increase the sense of a plague of locusts upon the land, as v. 20 suggested. The slaughter and plundering carried out by Nebuchadnezzar is in itself not out of line with the policy of holy war in the ancient Near East, which was adapted in some traditions in Israel (especially in Deut 7:1-2; 20:1-20, although it is not clear that this command was ever carried out as such). It is not even clear that Judith is opposed to this principle (see Commentary on 5:14-16 for Achior's account of the destruction caused by Israel's conquest). Here, however, the specter of the ancient Near Eastern holy war is bearing down upon the land of Judea.

The author uses good storytelling technique in describing the campaigns, providing details and magnifying the size of the armies gathered. In terms of the author's perspective, it is "from the bottom looking up"—that is, the proud but small kingdom of Judea looking up at the magnitude of the great worldwide empires. If one compares the fifth-century BCE Greek historian Herodotus on the military movements of the Eastern empires, one finds a much more equal perspective, even though the Persian armies were much larger than the Greek. Herodotus communicates the perspective of one who fundamentally believes that the Greeks were a world-class empire; the book of Judith is written from the perspective that the Jews were in danger of being swept under a rug. Perhaps midway between the "bottom-up" perspective of Judith and the "equal perspective" of Herodotus is the adventurous tone of the *Alexander Romance,* a historical novel written in Egypt in about 200 BCE that gives a similar list of known and unknown nations allied against Egypt and communicates a similar sense of foreboding: "It is not just one nation that is advancing upon us but millions of people. Advancing on us are Indians, Nokimaians, Oxydrakai, Iberians, Kauchones, Lelapes, Bosporoi, Bastranoi, Azanoi, Chalybes, and all the other great nations of the East, armies of innumerable warriors advancing against Egypt."[57] In addition to the obvious similarity with Judith, this passage is interesting because it also depicts the same invasion of the west that likely influenced Judith's account, that of the Persian king Artaxerxes III Ochus, whose general and eunuch were named Holofernes and Bagoas respectively (see Introduction and Commentary on 2:1-13).

2:28. While "fear and dread" fall on the people here, in 15:2 Judith will cause "dread and fear" to fall on the Assyrians.[58] In the tradition of the exodus (Exod 15:15-16) and in Rahab's recounting of it (Josh 2:9), the nations tremble in fear at God's mighty acts. After the pounding crescendo of the previous verses, the author astutely inserts a pause, comparable to the pauses at 1:16; 3:10;

57. *Alexander Romance* 1:2.
58. Craven, *Artistry and Faith in the Book of Judith,* 54.

6:21; and 7:32. The effect of the description, whether intended or not, is to make the situation of these non-Israelite cities as sympathetic as those of Israel. We almost forget as the story progresses—or the author would like us to forget—that not only is Judith saving her village or Israel as a whole, but also she is saving that part of the world that has not already been destroyed by Holofernes. Holofernes' campaign is truly a scourge upon the land, and it has the potential to create a sort of kinship of oppressed peoples. However, whatever kinship is created seems to evaporate when some of the peoples of the region quickly surrender and become allies of Holofernes.

The list of seven cities is intriguing. Moore notes that seven is a number signifying completeness in biblical literature, and perhaps the number is more significant than the names of the cities.[59] Five of the cities were famous and known well to Judeans: Sidon and Tyre (Matt 15:31; Acts 21:3-4; 27:3), Jamnia (1 Macc 4:15; 5:58), Azotus or Ashdod (Josh 13:3; 1 Macc 4:15), and Ascalon or Ashkelon (1 Macc 10:86); Sur and Ocina are unknown. The known cities would have been important centers of competition with Judea. When John Hyrcanus I (134–104 BCE) expanded his kingdom, Azotus and Jamnia came under Hasmonean control, while Sidon, Tyre, and Ascalon remained independent. Moore also raises, but wisely dismisses, the theory that since Gaza is missing from the list, Judith must have been written after Alexander Janneus destroyed the city in 96 BCE. The evidence of the text simply cannot be pressed to such a specific conclusion. (See Reflections at 3:1-10.)

59. Carey A. Moore, *Judith*, AB 40 (Garden City, N.Y.: Doubleday, 1985) 139-41.

Judith 3:1-10, The People of the Seacoast Surrender

NAB

3 1 They therefore sent messengers to him to sue for peace in these words: 2 "We, the servants of Nebuchadnezzar the great king, lie prostrate before you; do with us as you will. 3 Our dwellings and all our wheat fields, our flocks and herds, and all our encampments are at your disposal; make use of them as you please. 4 Our cities and their inhabitants are also at your service; come and deal with them as you see fit."

5 After the spokesmen had reached Holofernes and given him this message, 6 he went down with his army to the seacoast, and stationed garrisons in the fortified cities; from them he impressed picked troops as auxiliaries. 7 The people of these cities and all the inhabitants of the countryside received him with garlands and dancing to the sound of timbrels. 8 Nevertheless, he devastated their whole territory and cut down their sacred groves, for he had been commissioned to destroy all the gods of the earth, so that every nation might worship Nebuchadnezzar alone, and every people and tribe invoke him as a god. 9 At length Holofernes reached Esdraelon in the neighborhood of Dothan, the approach to the main

NRSV

3 They therefore sent messengers to him to sue for peace in these words: 2"We, the servants of Nebuchadnezzar, the Great King, lie prostrate before you. Do with us whatever you will. 3See, our buildings and all our land and all our wheat fields and our flocks and herds and all our encampments[a] lie before you; do with them as you please. 4Our towns and their inhabitants are also your slaves; come and deal with them as you see fit."

5The men came to Holofernes and told him all this. 6Then he went down to the seacoast with his army and stationed garrisons in the fortified towns and took picked men from them as auxiliaries. 7These people and all in the countryside welcomed him with garlands and dances and tambourines. 8Yet he demolished all their shrines[b] and cut down their sacred groves; for he had been commissioned to destroy all the gods of the land, so that all nations should worship Nebuchadnezzar alone, and that all their dialects and tribes should call upon him as a god.

9Then he came toward Esdraelon, near Dothan, facing the great ridge of Judea; 10he

[a] Gk *all the sheepfolds of our tents* [b] Syr: Gk *borders*

NAB	NRSV
ridge of the Judean mountains; 10 he set up his camp between Geba and Scythopolis, and stayed there a whole month to refurbish all the equipment of his army.	camped between Geba and Scythopolis, and remained for a whole month in order to collect all the supplies for his army.

COMMENTARY

3:1-4. There is a stark contrast between the former haughtiness and smugness of the peoples of the seacoast toward Nebuchadnezzar's messengers in 1:11 and their abject and total surrender here. There they underestimated him as "only one man"; here they overestimate him and prostrate themselves before his power, almost as if he were a god (v. 8). There is clearly a fearful and emotional response to the destruction they have witnessed; all of the categories of property that the peoples of the coast are willing to surrender to Nebuchadnezzar in v. 3 were mentioned in 2:24-27 as part of Nebuchadnezzar's path of destruction. (It is a part of this storyteller's technique to describe events by listing categories.) There is also a contrast between their immediate capitulation and the reaction of the Israelites in chaps. 4 and 7. Although the latter do not stand up to Judith's tough standards (8:9-27), they are still a good deal more resilient than the peoples of the coast. It was the common practice in the ancient Near East to deport and relocate conquered peoples and in the Greco-Roman world to enslave them (although neither practice would rule out the other). Much of Greek language of resistance to foreign monarchs was based on the notion of freedom versus slavery; nations should fight to the death to avoid enslavement to foreign nations just as individual citizens should do as well.[60] One of the accompanying elements of the war between Greece and Persia was the desire to liberate Greek colonies in Asia Minor from enslavement to Persian rule. Aesop presents a fable of the two roads presented to people: the rough, thorny, and dangerous path that leads to freedom and the smooth, level, pleasant path that leads to slavery.[61] Thus the book of Judith dramatizes the Greco-Roman notion of freedom in addition to the biblical tradition of national independence through loyalty to God as found in Isa 10:24-27; 30:1-7.

3:5-8. Surprisingly, when Holofernes does arrive in the seacoast towns, his is a bloodless takeover. He garrisons troops in the cities, and the inhabitants welcome him enthusiastically with the same festivities—garlands and dances with tambourines—that will be used in the Bethulians' victory celebration in 15:12-13. Some invading armies in the ancient world were greeted as liberators, as was Cyrus of Persia (see Isa 45:1-8); but after chap. 2, the mild actions of Holofernes and the positive reactions of the cities are most unexpected. Holofernes' only destruction mentioned for these cities is in regard to religious institutions: He destroys the shrines and sacred groves. Ironically, according to Judith herself (8:18-20), this is precisely what the Israelites have done in their own nation, and this is what the later Hasmonean kings also do in converting people by force and destroying the Samaritan temple on Mt. Gerizim. For the coastal cities, however, it appears to be a sort of deal with the devil: the loss of their religious freedom in exchange for peace with Holofernes. These were the terms that the early Maccabees faced when they chose to fight. Presumably, we are to see a lack of moral fiber in these people of the coast, neighbors of Israel. They have taken the easy road to slavery rather than the challenging road to freedom.

Holofernes institutes a policy of destroying the shrines and sacred groves of the conquered peoples, presumably to show that the Jerusalem Temple will be destroyed as well. "Sacred groves" probably refers to the somewhat vague references in the HB to the wooden poles used in the worship of the goddess Asherah. They were destroyed in various reforms in an attempt to centralize worship in Jerusalem (1 Kgs 14:15; 2 Kgs 18:4). Greek sacred groves are probably not intended. Daniel 3 also presents an imaginative

60. Orlando Patterson, *Freedom* (New York: Basic Books, 1992).
61. *Life of Aesop* 94.

story in which Nebuchadnezzar requires worship of a golden statue, and in Daniel 6 an edict is passed that no one may pray to anyone, human or divine, except King Darius. Language used in the Daniel stories, especially Daniel 3, has evidently influenced the author here, for not only is there a requirement of exclusive veneration involving Nebuchadnezzar, but also in both texts the various peoples and languages of the land are emphasized (see Dan 4:1). However, whereas Daniel dramatizes the requirement—or at least the attraction—of worshiping foreign gods in foreign lands, it says nothing of the destruction by Nebuchadnezzar of other cult centers on principle.

3:9-10. When Holofernes finally reaches Judea—once again, the name of Judea is submerged in the list until the very end, and mentioned as if an afterthought—there is another pause in the action for rest and to collect bounty. This prepares the audience for the next transition in the narrative. Although many geographical names in Judith are unknown or appear to be mentioned incorrectly, many others, especially as we move closer to Jerusalem, are known and descriptive for the account. The plain of Esdraelon (the Greek form of "Jezreel") lies between the hills of Galilee to the north and those of Samaria and Judea to the south. It is thus a good resting place for the expeditionary forces. Gaba lay on the western end of the plain near the Mediterranean, and Scythopolis on the eastern, near the Jordan River. Dothan was near the plain to the south. Holofernes would thus have been poised about forty miles north of Jerusalem, awaiting the proper moment to take the mountain passes and proceed on his course. This would also place Holofernes very near the spot where Jael had slain Sisera, the closest biblical model for the actions of Judith.[62]

62. Morton Enslin and Solomon Zeitlin, *The Book of Judith,* JAL VIII (Leiden: Brill, 1972) 77.

REFLECTIONS

Ernst Haag argued that Judith is a parabolic narrative, that it is not intended to be a real history, but a story that stands for another truth: the workings of God and Israel.[63] In his view, Nebuchadnezzar becomes a transhistorical figure who stands for those who would oppose Israel. But there is more to this symbol as well. In Judith, and to a lesser extent in Daniel, Nebuchadnezzar represents worldly power run amok. Worldly power, whether in Judith's day or our own, becomes reduced to the ego of the tyrant if it is unchecked by broader religious or ethical concerns. And at a time when the dominant nations were coming from the west and not the east, Nebuchadnezzar could also stand for the power and attraction of the Hellenistic culture that threatened to transform the texture of religious life. After all, the peoples of the seacoast had capitulated willingly and welcomed the Assyrians with dance. Although Nebuchadnezzar may appear one-dimensional, he is all-encompassing enough to allow us to see in him all the forces that oppose a faith in God, whether religious, worldly, or emanating from within the concerns and desires of our everyday life. Nebuchadnezzar is not Satan—for that one would have to look elsewhere in the Bible and not in Judith. But Nebuchadnezzar is the titanic force of the world that can overwhelm those who are unprepared.

Craven shows that in this text Nebuchadnezzar is also characterized through his relationship with Holofernes; they are in a lord/servant relationship that mirrors that of God and Judith.[64] In Nebuchadnezzar and Holofernes, we find a pair of personalities who model worldly power for the reader. Nebuchadnezzar is, first of all, a powerful king who is victorious in great battles, but he is also a vengeful despot who tries to destroy every country that spurned his invitation to an alliance. This can be seen as the outward manifestation of a powerful world leader. But it is in Holofernes' treatment of his king that we begin to see the psychological seductions of power as well. Holofernes not only vanquishes nations and secures their loyalty for his king,

63. Ernst Haag, *Studien zum Buch Judith: Seine theologische Bedeutung und literarisches Eigenart* (Trier: Paulinus, 1963).
64. Craven, *Artistry and Faith in the Book of Judith,* 109.

but he also violently removes all their forms of worship and requires them to worship his lord, Nebuchadnezzar (3:8).

The story suggests that such monstrous egos as that of Nebuchadnezzar seem to find their Holoferneses, people who will crush others to enlarge the stature of those whom they admire. Nebuchadnezzar only gave orders to defeat the rebellious nations (2:4-13), but Holofernes finds it necessary to demand that Nebuchadnezzar alone be worshiped as a god. He seems to need it more than Nebuchadnezzar does. Thus Nebuchadnezzar becomes a distant tyrant, but Holofernes is the willing mouthpiece of the king's interests. In this we find a fascinating insight into the pyramid of power relationships and perceive that unhealthy, unbalanced, ungrounded leaders will readily find servants who have no identity without them. "What god is there except Nebuchadnezzar?" asks Holofernes (6:2). Nebuchadnezzar is "lord of the whole earth." As Craven notes, the book of Judith counters this claim with the argument that God is the lord of the whole earth, and God can prove it by the hand of a single woman.[65]

Further, in contrast to the Assyrian pyramid of power relationships, the model of balanced, functional relationships—relationships that are grounded in the worship of God—is found among the Israelites. The community's coming together in prayer at a time of crisis is what is portrayed in 4:6-15, and it is this demonstration that receives God's response. This community will endure and not capitulate as the peoples of the seacoast did. The parable, then, that Haag sees in Judith is a parable for our day as well. It is a parable about power, about the contrasting models of worldly power and divine power, and about the psychological relationships that follow from each model: a dysfunctional model of the veneration of false gods and the functional model of a community turning to God in a period of crisis.

65. Ibid., 109.

Judith 4:1-15, Israel Prays and Prepares for War

NAB

4 1 When the Israelites who dwelt in Judea
heard of all that Holofernes, commander in
chief of Nebuchadnezzar, king of the Assyrians,
had done to the nations, and how he had despoiled all their temples and destroyed them, 2
they were in extreme dread of him, and greatly
alarmed for Jerusalem and the temple of the LORD,
their God. 3 Now, they had lately returned from
exile, and only recently had all the people of Judea
been gathered together, and the vessels, the altar,
and the temple been purified from profanation. 4
So they sent word to the whole region of Samaria,
to Kona, Beth-horon, Belmain, and Jericho, to
Choba and Aesora, and to the valley of Salem. 5
The people there posted guards on all the summits
of the high mountains, fortified their villages, and
since their fields had recently been harvested,
stored up provisions in preparation for war.

6 Joakim, who was high priest in Jerusalem in
those days, wrote to the inhabitants of Bethulia

NRSV

4 When the Israelites living in Judea heard
of everything that Holofernes, the general
of Nebuchadnezzar, the king of the Assyrians, had
done to the nations, and how he had plundered
and destroyed all their temples, 2they were therefore greatly terrified at his approach; they were
alarmed both for Jerusalem and for the temple of
the Lord their God. 3For they had only recently
returned from exile, and all the people of Judea
had just now gathered together, and the sacred
vessels and the altar and the temple had been
consecrated after their profanation. 4So they sent
word to every district of Samaria, and to Kona,
Beth-horon, Belmain, and Jericho, and to Choba
and Aesora, and the valley of Salem. 5They immediately seized all the high hilltops and fortified
the villages on them and stored up food in preparation for war—since their fields had recently
been harvested.

6The high priest, Joakim, who was in Jerusalem

NAB

[and Betomesthaim], which is on the way to Esdraelon, facing the plain near Dothan, 7 and instructed them to keep firm hold of the mountain passes, since these offered access to Judea. It would be easy to ward off the attacking forces, as the defile was only wide enough for two abreast. 8 The Israelites carried out the orders given them by Joakim, the high priest, and the senate of the whole people of Israel, which met in Jerusalem.

9 All the men of Israel cried to God with great fervor and did penance— 10 they, along with their wives, and children, and domestic animals. All their resident aliens, hired laborers, and slaves also girded themselves with sackcloth. 11 And all the Israelite men, women, and children who lived in Jerusalem prostrated themselves in front of the temple building, with ashes strewn on their heads, displaying their sackcloth covering before the LORD. 12 The altar, too, they draped in sackcloth; and with one accord they cried out fervently to the God of Israel not to allow their children to be seized, their wives to be taken captive, the cities of their inheritance to be ruined, or the sanctuary to be profaned and mocked for the nations to gloat over.

13 The LORD heard their cry and had regard for their distress. For the people observed a fast of many days' duration throughout Judea, and before the sanctuary of the LORD Almighty in Jerusalem. 14 The high priest Joakim, and all the priests in attendance on the LORD who served his altar, were also girded with sackcloth as they offered the daily holocaust, the votive offerings, and the free-will offerings of the people. 15 With ashes upon their turbans, they cried to the LORD with all their strength to look with favor on the whole house of Israel.

4, 9: Omit second *en ekteneią megalę̄*: so LXX[S]; dittog.

NRSV

at the time, wrote to the people of Bethulia and Betomesthaim, which faces Esdraelon opposite the plain near Dothan, 7ordering them to seize the mountain passes, since by them Judea could be invaded; and it would be easy to stop any who tried to enter, for the approach was narrow, wide enough for only two at a time to pass.

8So the Israelites did as they had been ordered by the high priest Joakim and the senate of the whole people of Israel, in session at Jerusalem. 9And every man of Israel cried out to God with great fervor, and they humbled themselves with much fasting. 10They and their wives and their children and their cattle and every resident alien and hired laborer and purchased slave—they all put sackcloth around their waists. 11And all the Israelite men, women, and children living at Jerusalem prostrated themselves before the temple and put ashes on their heads and spread out their sackcloth before the Lord. 12They even draped the altar with sackcloth and cried out in unison, praying fervently to the God of Israel not to allow their infants to be carried off and their wives to be taken as booty, and the towns they had inherited to be destroyed, and the sanctuary to be profaned and desecrated to the malicious joy of the Gentiles.

13The Lord heard their prayers and had regard for their distress; for the people fasted many days throughout Judea and in Jerusalem before the sanctuary of the Lord Almighty. 14The high priest Joakim and all the priests who stood before the Lord and ministered to the Lord, with sackcloth around their loins, offered the daily burnt offerings, the votive offerings, and freewill offerings of the people. 15With ashes on their turbans, they cried out to the Lord with all their might to look with favor on the whole house of Israel.

COMMENTARY

4:1-5. Now the "Israelites," or more specifically the "Israelites living in Judea," are mentioned for the first time. However, the word of Holofernes' conquests also goes out to "every district of Samaria" (v. 4). The term "Israelites" in the narrow sense applied to inhabitants of the north who were conquered by the Assyrians in 721 BCE, although the term also communicates the ideal self-image of both Jews and Samarians (see Matt 10:6; John 1:31, 47; 2 Cor 11:22; Phil 3:5). Samaria was the resettled capital and the province of the old northern kingdom; the mixed ethnic and religious makeup of that region was a source of friction with the Jews of Jerusalem, and this friction had boiled over into conflicts on a number of occasions (see Ezra 4; Nehemiah 4; and Commentary on 1:7-10). John Hyrcanus I, who ruled Jerusalem from 135 to 104 BCE, finally subdued Samaria and destroyed the Samaritan temple on Mt. Gerizim. This did not end hostilities between Jews and Samaritans, as the NT indicates (Luke 10:29-37; 17:11-19; John 4:9), but it did place control of Samaria in Jewish hands. Unlike the other cities of the region, the Samaritan cities and Judea do not seek terms of peace, but brace for war. It is, indeed, surprising that Samaria is portrayed so positively, essentially in alliance with Judea. It is possible, as Moore suggests, that the positive view of Samaria indicates that Judith was written after Samaria was annexed, rather than before when tensions might have been high.[66] Other scholars have argued that the annexation would hardly improve relations, but only pacify the resistance; but the author probably romanticized the notion of a united "Israel," as David and Solomon had constituted it, and this common cause of Samaria and Judea reflects that. The book of Judith may represent a fictionalized and romanticized vision of what John Hyrcanus enforced by the sword. Despite the ambiguity of the geographical term "Israel," from this point on it will dominate as the common designation for the defenders of Bethulia and Jerusalem.

In the parenthesis of v. 3 it is explained that the people of Judea "had only recently returned from the exile" and rededicated their Temple with the returned vessels, an event that occurred two hundred years after the fall of the north to Assyria. We have seen such inaccuracies before, and once again it appears to be a deliberate merging of two separate historical epochs. One may wonder why v. 3 was added, since it calls attention to the historical problems and hardly adds information necessary for the reader's understanding of the narrative. Regardless of how clumsy it seems, it has been taken as evidence for a Persian-era dating for Judith, since it states that the Israelites had only *recently* returned. However, it is probably not a direct reference to the return from the Babylonian exile, but reverberates with the experience of the audience, who, after the Maccabean revolt, had also only recently rededicated the Temple. (Note especially the reference to "the sacred vessels and the altar and the temple which had been consecrated after their profanation"; see also 1 Macc 4:36-61; 2 Macc 10:1-8.)

Judith, as the widow who is an unexpected heroine of faith, is often compared to the widow and her seven sons who are martyred in 2 Maccabees 7, but there is a further important parallel with 2 Maccabees that comes out at this point: the connection to "temple propaganda."[67] In different ways, the novel Judith and the novelistic history 2 Maccabees keep the Temple and its sanctity in sight in the narrative at all times. Although the action for most of the remainder of the book will take place near Judith's village of Bethulia, Jerusalem is constantly in mind; in fact, the author and the original audience may have been in that city. (This argues against the hidden Samaritan origin of Judith that some scholars have suggested, despite the references that might point in that direction.) Both Judith and 2 Maccabees dramatize a struggle over the Temple that God watches over, even though God intervenes directly only in 2 Maccabees. In the Introduction it was noted that there is irony concerning miracles in such texts: The novels generally lack the miraculous intervention of God or depict only minor miracles, as at Add. Esth 15:8, while the novelistic histories often contain quite dramatic miracles.

4:6. Once again, a historical name, "Joakim," is probably pressed into service inaccurately. A high priest named Joakim is mentioned in Neh 12:26, but he would not have had the broad powers over political and military affairs that this Joakim possesses.[68] In the days of the Davidic monarchy, the king and the high priest had always coexisted. After the exile, Judah/Judea was officially a province of the Persian and then successively of two of the Greek empires, the Ptolemaic and the Seleucid. Once again, a governor and a

66. Moore, *Judith,* 67-70.

67. Robert Doran, *Temple Propaganda: The Purpose and Character of 2 Maccabees* (Washington, D.C.: Catholic Biblical Association, 1981).

68. Moore, *Judith,* 150.

high priest coexisted in the administration of the Temple and the province. When the Maccabees achieved a victory in dealing with the Seleucid rulers in 165 BCE, they did not immediately establish a separate kingdom, but rather an independently governed province of the Seleucid Empire. One of the Maccabee brothers, Jonathan, took on the office of high priest in 152, and this became the basis of Hasmonean politics thereafter.[69] Simon, his brother and successor, finally declared full independence from the Seleucids in 141 BCE and took on two other titles, *ethnarchēs* (ἐθνάρχης, "leader of the people") and *stratēgos* (στρατήγος,"general of the army"). His impressive coronation as high priest is recounted in 1 Maccabees 14, along with a hymn praising his accomplishments. Like Judith, he is described as a deliverer of Israel on the model of the judges (see the Introduction on parallels between Judith and Deborah). Following Simon, John Hyrcanus I was also named high priest, leader of the people, and general. The broad powers of Joakim thus match those of the Hasmonean high priests from Jonathan to John Hyrcanus (152–104 BCE).

Judith's village, Bethulia, is named for the first time in this verse. The site is unknown and probably fictitious, but it is clearly in Samaritan territory.[70] Lest it be inferred, however, that this text retains a hidden allegiance to Samaritans, the Jerusalem Temple and the high priest are strongly emphasized at vv. 3-8. It is more likely that the desire to re-create a romanticized vision of the united Israel of David and Solomon motivates the author.

4:7. As noted regarding 3:9-10, Holofernes' army is resting in the plain of Esdraelon, facing the mountains of Samaria as the only obstacle to their southern advance. Joakim's orders to fortify the passes are thus good strategy, although it may seem a hopeless gesture. The narrowness of the passes, only wide enough for two to pass at a time, does not imply that Holofernes' invading armies can be held back, but that Holofernes has no choice but to take the passes first to ensure that his vast armies can be moved through the mountains.

4:8-11. Joakim wrote letters to all "Israelites" to pray and fast, much as Esther in time of danger gives a directive to all the Jews living in Susa to pray and fast as well (Esth 4:16). Interestingly, in Esther, Jerusalem and Judea are never mentioned. In Judith, Jerusalem is the center for the community, and diaspora Jews are never mentioned. Sackcloth and ashes were ritual signs of mourning in ancient Israel, but they were also signs of penitence or protest (Esth 4:1-2; 2 Macc 3:19).[71] The penitential theology assumed in v. 9 reflects an important development in post-exilic Judaism that culminates in early Christian asceticism. The pattern of sin/punishment/repentance/salvation found in Deuteronomy 28–32 gives rise to the inclusion of penitential prayers in post-exilic texts (Nehemiah 9; Dan 9:4-19; Bar 1:1-3).[72] Although the only fast required by Jewish law in the HB is the one-day fast on the Day of Atonement (Lev 16:29-30), fasting was evidently an integral part of the post-exilic penitential theology, where it is also sometimes associated with sackcloth and ashes (Neh 1:4; 9:1; Dan 9:3). It may have arisen originally as a response to the destruction and the exile (Zech 7:3-5).

The public scene of wailing and tribulation is very similar to other passages from this period, such as 2 Macc 3:14-21 and 3 Macc 1:16-21. These scenes are almost interchangeable, but Judith does emphasize the sackcloth and ashes more (cf. 2 Macc 3:19 and 3 Macc 1:18 in this regard), while 2 and 3 Maccabees emphasize more the public consternation. That they "humbled themselves" is also part of the religious experience of the penitential theology. Humility is not considered a positive virtue in Greek thought; it is understood as a negative idea of humiliation or shame in the continuum of honor and shame. In Hebrew thought, there is a positive tradition of God watching over the humble: "For you deliver a humble people, but the haughty eyes you bring down" (Ps 18:27 NRSV); "Toward the scorners he is scornful, but to the humble he shows favor" (Prov 3:34 NRSV). There is also a tradition con-

69. Lee I. A. Levine, "The Age of Hellenism: Alexander the Great and the Rise and Fall of the Hasmonean Kingdom," in *Ancient Israel: A Short History from Abraham to the Roman Destruction of the Temple,* ed. Hershel Shanks (Englewood Cliffs, N.J.: Prentice Hall, 1988) 185-87.

70. Carey A. Moore, *Judith,* AB 40 (Garden City, N.Y.: Doubleday, 1985) 69.

71. See Harvey Guthrie, "Fast, Fasting," *IDB* 2:241; Gary A. Anderson, *A Time to Mourn, a Time to Dance: The Expression of Grief and Joy in Israelite Religion* (University Park: Pennsylvania State University Press, 1991).

72. Rodney Alan Werline, *Penitential Prayer in Second Temple Judaism: The Development of a Religious Institution* (Atlanta: Scholars Press, 1998).

necting humility with true wisdom: "The wisdom of the humble lifts their heads high, and seats them among the great" (Sir 11:1 NRSV). The NT also picks up the Hebrew tradition: "Humble yourselves before the Lord, and he will exalt you" (Jas 4:10). This remains a virtue in the Christian as well as the Jewish religion,[73] and Judith is in fact known later in Christian tradition as a symbol of humility who vanquishes arrogance.

The meaning of "senate [γερουσία *gerousia*] of the whole people [δῆμος *dēmos*] of Israel" has caused some problems for scholars. It is a common expression in the Greek world for the city council that represented the free citizens, or *dēmos,* of a city. For Jews, however, was it the same as the Sanhedrin, mentioned in the NT, in Josephus, and in rabbinic literature? These sources do not agree on the role of the Sanhedrin; the NT and Josephus see it as a council headed by the high priest or ruler that oversaw political and administrative matters of Jerusalem, while the rabbinic sources limit its oversight to religious questions. The former was probably the case in the period of Judith, and the *gerousia* here probably refers to such an administrative Sanhedrin. The Greek word συνέδριον (*synedrion*) that is the basis of the Hebrew term סנהדרין (*Sanhedrîn*), is used in its feminine form at 6:1 for Holofernes' war council. Here it is significant that the *gerousia* of the high priest and the senate of the "whole people of Israel" is followed to the letter. The perspective of the author is that the high priest sits as head of the government of the Temple, of Jerusalem, and of the Israelite people—a likely perspective of someone who was a full supporter of the Hasmonean rulers (see 1 Macc 12:6).

There is, perhaps, another message in this passage, however: The actions carried out by the high priest in the Jerusalem Temple and by the mass of Israelites in the outlying regions are not simply a coordinated response; they are essentially liturgical. That is, the timing and orchestration of the fasting, praying, and wearing of sackcloth appear to be a coordinated practice that may reflect religious observances at the time of the author. We will see that Judith times her prayer to coincide with the incense offering in the Temple in Jerusalem (9:1), and here as well we may detect signs that it is not simply a coordinated vigil, but more of a liturgical act: Every man in Israel, it is stated, prayed to God and humbled himself with fasting, and they all, including slaves and cattle, put sackcloth around their waists, and those living in Jerusalem knelt before the Temple, put ashes on their heads, and spread their sackcloth out before the Lord (cf. Judith's practice in 9:1). Finally, they draped the altar with sackcloth and prayed. It is not clear that any of this represents an actual liturgical practice as much as it does a liturgical ideal, or sense of Israel's engaging in penitential prayer *together.*

Two things are unusual about the penitential theology, however. First, Judith will later pray without so much as a hint of her own penitence (chap. 9). Unlike Esther in Additions to Esther or Aseneth in *Joseph and Aseneth,* Judith does not repent of her sins; nor does she repent on behalf of Israel. Second, it is not only the men and women who are draped in sackcloth, but also the children, resident aliens, slaves, and cattle! Is this a symbol of the completeness of Israel's penitence, or is it intended to be as humorous to the ancient reader as it is to the modern? Craven, probably correctly, takes it to be the latter, as we find the same motif used at Jonah 3:8, most likely also in a humorous way.[74] Still, is it meant to be satirical as well as humorous? Is the practice of the excessive use of sackcloth meant to be satirized? At Matt 6:16-18, Jesus condemns the outward show of the fasting of the "hypocrites," a term Matthew usually applies to the Pharisees. Zechariah 7:3-5 may have been critical of the show of fasting as well. In Judith, however, the prayers of the Israelites are answered, and it is because they have fasted (v. 13). Further, Judith will be described as a devout woman who regularly fasts and wears sackcloth. True, this is precisely the ritual asceticism that she stops performing to take up her task of defeating Holofernes, and it is not explicitly stated that she goes back to these practices at the end (16:21-25); but there is no indication that there is anything wrong with these practices or that she has somehow transcended them. It is more likely that in the high spirits of the book, the excesses are intended to be humorous, but there does not seem to be a clear satire of the acts themselves.

73. See *1 Clement* 13:3, 56:1.

74. Toni Craven, *Artistry and Faith in the Book of Judith* (Chico, Calif.: Scholars Press, 1983) 115.

4:12-15. The inheritance in v. 12 is the land of Israel as a promise from God, which resulted from the conquest of Canaan (Deut 26:1; Josh 11:23; cf. Jdt 8:22; 9:12; 13:5; 16:21). This is, perhaps, more evidence that the author affirms a notion of an ideal Israel.

It is surprising that the readers are told in v. 13 that "the Lord heard their prayers," since this is precisely the question that the residents of Bethulia must grapple with in 7:23-31. The dramatic tension, therefore, would seem to be lessened by this intimation that all will be well. The tension about *whether* the Jews will be saved does not seem to be a strong factor in the reader's interest, however; the tension appears to build around *how* Judith will risk her dignity and keep it at the same time in order to save her people. The book of Judges also states that God heard the cries of the Israelites and sent them deliverers (e.g., Judg 3:9, 15); in the Introduction it is noted that Judith is like one of the judges—sent by God to deliver the people in distress. It should be noted, however, that the text does not explicitly say that God sent Judith or raised her up as a deliverer. God hears the prayers of the Israelites, but Judith appears to act more independently than the judges. It is also interesting that other novels of this period anticipate a happy ending in the narrative by informing the reader that God has heard the prayers of the pious and has foreordained a happy ending (see Tob 3:16-17 and the Greek novel by Xenophon of Ephesus, *Ephesian Tale* 1.6, where an oracle predicts that the young protagonists will be separated but reunited). (See Reflections at 5:1-21.)

Judith 5:1-21, Achior Tells Holofernes of Israel's History

NAB

5 1 It was reported to Holofernes, commander in chief of the Assyrian army, that the Israelites were ready for battle, and had blocked the mountain passes, fortified the summits of all the higher peaks, and placed roadblocks in the plains. 2 In great anger he summoned all the rulers of the Moabites, the generals of the Ammonites, and all the satraps of the seacoast 3 and said to them: "Now tell me, you Canaanites, what sort of people is this that dwells in the mountains? Which cities do they inhabit? How large is their army? In what does their power and strength consist? Who has set himself up as their king and the leader of their army? 4 Why have they refused to come out to meet me along with all the other inhabitants of the West?"

5 Then Achior, the leader of all the Ammonites, said to him: "My lord, hear this account from your servant; I will tell you the truth about this people that lives near you [that inhabits this mountain region]; no lie shall escape your servant's lips.

6 "These people are descendants of the Chaldeans. 7 They formerly dwelt in Mesopotamia, for they did not wish to follow the gods of their

5, 5: (*peri*) *toutou* (*laou*): so LXX^{A}, P, Vet Lat, V.

NRSV

5 It was reported to Holofernes, the general of the Assyrian army, that the people of Israel had prepared for war and had closed the mountain passes and fortified all the high hilltops and set up barricades in the plains. 2In great anger he called together all the princes of Moab and the commanders of Ammon and all the governors of the coastland, 3and said to them, "Tell me, you Canaanites, what people is this that lives in the hill country? What towns do they inhabit? How large is their army, and in what does their power and strength consist? Who rules over them as king and leads their army? 4And why have they alone, of all who live in the west, refused to come out and meet me?"

5Then Achior, the leader of all the Ammonites, said to him, "May my lord please listen to a report from the mouth of your servant, and I will tell you the truth about this people that lives in the mountain district near you. No falsehood shall come from your servant's mouth. 6These people are descended from the Chaldeans. 7At one time they lived in Mesopotamia, because they did not wish to follow the gods of their ancestors who were in Chaldea. 8Since they had abandoned the ways of their ancestors, and worshiped the God

NAB

forefathers who were born in the land of the Chaldeans. 8 Since they abandoned the way of their ancestors, and acknowledged with divine worship the God of heaven, their forefathers expelled them from the presence of their gods. So they fled to Mesopotamia and dwelt there a long time. 9 Their God bade them leave their abode and proceed to the land of Canaan. Here they settled, and grew very rich in gold, silver, and a great abundance of livestock. 10 Later, when famine had gripped the whole land of Canaan, they went down into Egypt. They stayed there as long as they found sustenance, and grew into such a great multitude that the number of their race could not be counted. 11 The king of Egypt, however, rose up against them, shrewdly forced them to labor at brickmaking, oppressed and enslaved them. 12 But they cried to their God, and he struck the land of Egypt with plagues for which there was no remedy. When the Egyptians expelled them, 13 God dried up the Red Sea before them, 14 and led them along the route to Sinai and Kadesh-barnea. First they drove out all the inhabitants of the desert; 15 then they settled in the land of the Amorites, destroyed all the Heshbonites by main force, crossed the Jordan, and took possession of the whole mountain region. 16 They expelled the Canaanites, the Perizzites, the Jebusites, the Shechemites, and all the Gergesites; and they lived in these mountains a long time.

17 "As long as the Israelites did not sin in the sight of their God, they prospered, for their God, who hates wickedness, was with them. 18 But when they deviated from the way he prescribed for them, they were ground down steadily, more and more, by frequent wars, and finally taken as captives into foreign lands. The temple of their God was razed to the ground, and their cities were occupied by their enemies. 19 But now that they have returned to their God, they have come back from the Dispersion wherein they were scattered, and have repossessed Jerusalem, where their sanctuary is, and have settled again in the mountain region which was unoccupied.

20 "So now, my lord and master, if these people are at fault, and are sinning against their God, and if we verify this offense of theirs, then

NRSV

of heaven, the God they had come to know, their ancestors[a] drove them out from the presence of their gods. So they fled to Mesopotamia, and lived there for a long time. 9Then their God commanded them to leave the place where they were living and go to the land of Canaan. There they settled, and grew very prosperous in gold and silver and very much livestock. 10When a famine spread over the land of Canaan they went down to Egypt and lived there as long as they had food. There they became so great a multitude that their race could not be counted. 11So the king of Egypt became hostile to them; he exploited them and forced them to make bricks. 12They cried out to their God, and he afflicted the whole land of Egypt with incurable plagues. So the Egyptians drove them out of their sight. 13Then God dried up the Red Sea before them, 14and he led them by the way of Sinai and Kadesh-barnea. They drove out all the people of the desert, 15and took up residence in the land of the Amorites, and by their might destroyed all the inhabitants of Heshbon; and crossing over the Jordan they took possession of all the hill country. 16They drove out before them the Canaanites, the Perizzites, the Jebusites, the Shechemites, and all the Gergesites, and lived there a long time.

17"As long as they did not sin against their God they prospered, for the God who hates iniquity is with them. 18But when they departed from the way he had prescribed for them, they were utterly defeated in many battles and were led away captive to a foreign land. The temple of their God was razed to the ground, and their towns were occupied by their enemies. 19But now they have returned to their God, and have come back from the places where they were scattered, and have occupied Jerusalem, where their sanctuary is, and have settled in the hill country, because it was uninhabited.

20"So now, my master and lord, if there is any oversight in this people and they sin against their God and we find out their offense, then we can go up and defeat them. 21But if they are not a guilty nation, then let my lord pass them by; for their Lord and God will defend them, and we shall become the laughingstock of the whole world."

[a] Gk *they*

NAB

we shall be able to go up and conquer them. 21
But if they are not a guilty nation, then your lordship should keep his distance; otherwise their LORD and God will shield them, and we shall become the laughingstock of the whole world."

COMMENTARY

5:1-4. The Moabites and the Ammonites are now on Holofernes' side, although at 1:12 they were listed as nations under the threat of the Assyrian advance. Presumably, just as other nations succumbed to the fear of the Assyrians (3:1-8), so also did the Moabites and the Ammonites. They had a very mixed history of relations with Israel (Gen 19:30-38) and fought on the side of the historical Nebuchadnezzar against Jerusalem (2 Kgs 24:2); more recently, the Maccabees had fought against the Ammonites (1 Macc 5:6). One tradition (Deut 23:3-6) had emphasized the distinction between Israel and these neighbors and excludes them and their descendants from entry into the assembly of the Lord. Holofernes in v. 3 addresses them with the ethnic term "Canaanites," which was ordinarily used at a much earlier period. However, it still occurs in the post-exilic period as a designation for the neighboring peoples, probably (though not necessarily) in a pejorative way (Zech 14:41). The negative attitude had worked its way into the vocabulary of Judaism; one title for Satan, Beelzebul, "Lord of the Flies," was derived from the Canaanite deity Baalzebul, or "Baal the Prince." At any rate, the negative tradition regarding the Moabites and the Ammonites seems to be reflected here, subsumed under the umbrella category "Canaanites." If the book of Judith idealizes the golden age of united Israel, it also taps into the ancient notion of the surrounding peoples as Canaanites, whom the Israelites are to conquer to acquire a new inheritance. The same anachronism is taken up by Matt 15:21-28 when Jesus heals a Canaanite woman, but there it may be utilized to undercut an ancient antagonism rather than accentuate it. Still, note that Achior, an Ammonite, will arise as a friend of Israel and a convert to Judaism.

As the expedition has come closer and closer to Jerusalem, the list of nations involved has shrunk; only names such as Assyrians, Moabites, Ammonites, and Canaanites are mentioned now in the list of nations, and the list of allies—or at any rate, fellow victims—has disappeared. Even Samaria as a separate entity (see Commentary on 4:1-15) is no longer mentioned. The world has been reduced to Israel and the ancient mortal enemies. The "governors of the coastland" would also include the cities mentioned in 2:28 who surrendered in 3:1-8. The ethnic origins of some of these cities would be directly or indirectly related to the Canaanites, but the generalization that Holofernes makes in v. 3 is more a catchall for the author's perspective than an attempt to designate the cities correctly.

The variety of nations has subtly changed over the course of the novel. Samaria and Judea, the usual names for their regions at the time of the composition of the book, have gradually disappeared as designations of geographical areas and have been replaced by Israel. Samaria is not used after chap. 2, and Judea is rarely used after chap. 4 (once in 8:21 and once in 11:19 in conversation with Holofernes). Israel is the ancient and traditional name of David's kingdom, and it was still used as a proud affirmation by Jews; but its use in Judith appears to be an invocation of the golden age, a designation that has intentionally swallowed up both halves of the old kingdom and negated the historical tensions. Another older term, "Hebrew," is used at 10:12 and 14:15, and the older term "Judah," rather than "Judea," is used at 14:7. When Holofernes looks for a term with which to insult Achior by associating him with the Israelites, he calls him an Ephraimite, using another ancient term for Israel. At the same time, the enemies of Israel are becoming somewhat more clearly drawn, with designations that also come from the golden age of Israelite history. The Moabites and the Ammonites begin as victim-nations along with Judea, on the direct path of Holofernes' campaign; later they will ally with Holofernes and will be called Canaanites. Thus old terms for Israel's neighbors, Moabites and Ammonites, are replaced by an even more archaic term from the early history of Israel that is more negative (Deut 7:1). Joining this group later are the sons of Esau, or Edomites (7:8, 18), yet another ancient enemy of the Israelites. Out of a plethora of national names, the essence of the conflict has now been distilled into its ancient opponents: Israel on one side and the Canaanites, Moabites, Ammonites, and Edomites on the other. The process is not unlike that at Esth 3:1, where the audience learns that Haman is an Agagite, an Amalekite and an ancient enemy of the Israelites (1 Samuel 15); however, this tension is only alluded to in Esther, while it is played upon constantly in Judith.

The series of questions Holofernes asks does not convey a realistic picture of what a military strategist might ask, and the Jewish audience would already know the answers. However, they serve a dramatic function in pointing to the larger themes that will dominate the book. The questions move in a progression from those that are immediate, concrete, and realistic (e.g., "How large is their army?") to broader issues that are also capable of double meanings (e.g., "In what does their power and strength consist?"). The final questions point to a reflection on the ultimate theological and ethical affirmations of Israel: "Who rules over them as king?" "Why have they alone refused to come out and meet me?" The reader would naturally see these as theological questions, with an answer that sets Israel apart from the other nations: God is king, and this allegiance precludes the reverence of any other king (cf. 3:8). Holofernes asks about worldly kings and powers, while the audience understands that the true king and commander is God. Here we find another example of the irony mentioned above at 2:1-4, which comes to dominate much of the dialogue here and later in the book. The opponents understand terms on a mundane level, while the audience perceives that they refer to God. (See the Introduction for a discussion and comparison of this kind of irony; see also chaps. 11–13.)

Does the irony in Holofernes' question—that is, the implication for the reader that no one was king of Israel except God—imply that Judith was written at a time when the leader did not claim this title? Before the foundation of David's dynasty, the Israelite league of tribes held that God's kingship should suffice for Israel; there should be no permanent king or dynasty (1 Samuel 8; 12). This view was supplanted by, or coexisted with, a belief in the Davidic monarchy. It is clear that the Maccabees did not begin by designating themselves king, but perhaps revivified the old league belief in the ideal—if not the reality—of the charismatic prophet (1 Macc 14:41-42) and the Maccabees as successors to the judges as deliverers. At some point, however, they took on the title of king as well, in addition to the titles of high priest, ethnarch (leader of the people), and strategos (general of the army; see Commentary on 4:6). It is certain that Judas Aristobulus I (104–103) and the leaders after him called themselves king, but it is unlikely that John Hyrcanus I (135–104 BCE) did. Although it would be a weak argument to assert that the irony in Holofernes' question implies that Judith was written at a time in which there was no king, it is true that Judith affirms the religious and political power of the high priest and may undercut the role of an earthly king, a theory of government compatible with that of the Hasmoneans between 152 BCE (the assumption of the title of high priest) and 104 BCE (the assumption of the title of king).

5:5-21. Although various derivations and meanings for Achior's name have been suggested, such as the Hebrew "light is my brother," it is almost certainly the case that it is a slightly altered form of "Ahikar."[75] In the ancient Near Eastern *Story of Ahikar,* Ahikar is an Assyrian court adviser who is falsely accused, imprisoned, and marked for execution, but who is later vindicated to save the kingdom through his wise counsel. A version of the story dating from about 400 BCE was found among the texts of a Jewish military colony at Elephantine in Egypt, and we find that Ahikar was easily adapted to new ethnic roles: He is a Jewish courtier in Tob 1:21-22; 2:10; 14:10,

75. Henri A. Cazelles, "Le personnage d'Achior dans le livre de Judith," *RSR* 39 (1951) 125-37.

and his story is assimilated to Aesop in Greek tradition. Although in Judith he has become an Ammonite general and is not described as the wise man of tradition, it would be wrong to conclude that he cannot be modeled on "Ahikar the wise." Just as Judith is a woman of action, so also Achior, to be treated heroically, must be depicted as a man of action. Achior's conversion is also prompted by the needs of the story. As a wise and brave man, he must naturally in this novel come to see the truth about God that is revealed in Israelite history. He embodies the type of the "righteous Gentile," such as Balaam (Numbers 22–24), Rahab (Joshua 2–6), and Naaman (2 Kings 5),[76] and like the first of these, places himself in danger by uttering true words—one might almost say prophecies (cf. 6:2)—about the Israelites.

Achior, a non-Jew, thus becomes a very important character in this overwhelmingly Jewish book. As an "objective" observer, he can recite Israelite history and the mighty acts of God in a way that sounds even more impressive. He also puts it in terms of "deuteronomic theology," the view of God associated with Deuteronomy and the deuteronomistic history, which holds that if Israel abides in God's laws, God will bless them, and if Israel disobeys God's laws, God will punish them. Achior's explanation of Israelite history makes it much easier for Judith to explain to Holofernes at 11:9-15 that she has betrayed her people because they have abandoned God and as a result are doomed. In addition, Achior, who has met Holofernes, will later be in a position to identify the severed head in Judith's possession as that of Holofernes. The form of Achior's speech is the recitation of the mighty acts of God in bringing the Israelites to the promised land (Deuteronomy 1–3; 26:5-10); yet, while it is positive in regard to Israelite history, it still retains the appearance of objectivity. It is ironic, for instance, that he mentions the abandonment of the Chaldean gods, which might have been seen by the Jewish audience as part of the same ancient Near Eastern polytheism as the Ammonite gods. Thus the "creedal" aspect of Abraham's separation from Chaldean polytheism would have been recognized by Judith's audience. Likewise, the violent conquest of Canaan (Josh 11:16-23) is not described from the Ammonite point of view (although in the tradition the Hebrews did not displace the Ammonites and the Moabites; Deut 2:9-19).

Despite the fact that the Jewish audience would have heard the creedal aspects of Achior's speech, there is still an attempt to represent his speech at times from an outsider's perspective. Abraham was supposedly expelled from his homeland, instead of separating himself by choice. The story of Exodus is told in vv. 10-12, but rather than having Moses *lead* the Hebrews out of slavery, the Egyptians *expel* them. This is in agreement with the view often expressed in the contemporary Greek historians on Jewish history. The technique of putting into the mouths of Gentiles some of the anti-Jewish prejudices of the time is also utilized in the Additions to Esther 13, where the content of Haman's anti-Jewish decree, lacking in MT Esther, is given in a very plausible way. There is a further dramatic function of Achior's speech here, found in his introduction. He tells Holofernes, "I will tell you the truth about this people. . . . No falsehood shall come from your servant's mouth." Since Achior and Judith will become partnered in the narrative as the only two people brave enough to stand up to Holofernes, Achior's words here evoke a comparison with Judith's words at 11:5. There she will offer the same assurances, but she will be lying.

The list of five nations in v. 16 is an abbreviation of the usual list of six nations (Exod 3:8; Josh 9:1; Judg 3:5) or seven nations that are to be conquered, even wiped out, in the conquest of Canaan (Deut 7:1-2; Josh 3:10). "Shechemites" does not appear in the older lists; Shechem was a Samaritan city captured by John Hyrcanus I. Shechemites may be included here to show that they were a people conquered as part of the conquest, or because Judith (in 9:2) will invoke the revenge of Simeon and Levi on Shechem for the rape of Dinah (Genesis 34).

The deuteronomic theology is stated clearly in vv. 17-19; with the perspective of hindsight, the fall of Israel and Judah is directly laid to the sins of the people (although the entire focus is on the fall of Judah only). Jeremiah reflects this theology as well (Jeremiah 26–35), but he lived at the center of the crisis and counseled an adjustment on the part of the defeated people to the effects

76. Moore, *Judith*, 158.

of their sins. Texts such as Daniel 1–6 likewise indicate an attempt to understand life in exile. But v. 19 indicates a different period in Jewish religious life, a realized goal of life in God's temple-city. It likely represents the heady, aggressive policy of the Hasmonean rulers some years after the Maccabean revolt and the rededication of the Temple. The historical impossibility of Nebuchadnezzar king of the Assyrians is made glaringly obvious here: The events described, deportation and destruction of the Temple, were accomplished by Nebuchadnezzar, king of Babylon.

Achior concludes in vv. 20-21 by giving the counsel that in his mind is inescapable: If the people of Judea can be found to be sinning, then attack; they will surely fall. If they have not sinned, they will be invincible; the Assyrians will be routed and shamed. At this point Achior can be seen to be the mouthpiece of unconscious prophecy, similar to the role of Balaam in Numbers 22–24 or of the high priest Caiaphas in John 11:47-53. Holofernes will also sarcastically refer to this speech (6:2) as prophecy, although the audience knows that is precisely what it is. Phrases in the conclusion of Achior's speech ("let my lord pass by them," "their lord and god") set up the comparison between Nebuchadnezzar as lord and God as Lord that will later be used by Judith to create a series of ironic statements that are understood in one way by Holofernes and in another way by the audience. In both cases Achior plays this part unknowingly, addressing Holofernes with a clear meaning, while Judith will later be deliberately deceptive.

REFLECTIONS

1. Achior here provides a marvelous opportunity for the reader to hear the essence of Israelite history as told from an outsider's perspective. His account is positive and affirming of Israelite tradition, and it inevitably makes the modern reader wonder how his or her religious community would be described by an outsider. The book of Judith in general is about the military defense of the community; this scene is about the theological defense of the community as well.

Here the perspective of the author is that the values of Israel, which are grounded in the actions of Israel's God, shine out beyond its borders and are recognized by anyone who has eyes to see this. In other words, the grounding in God is what sets Israel on a firmer basis, and it is not up to Israelites to trumpet its cause; it is self-evident. This, according to the author, is in sharp contrast to the other peoples round about, who have embraced Nebuchadnezzar as a god. The author seems to suggest, across the centuries, that if you want your own religious community to be thought of well, it is not a matter of public relations or bragging; it is a matter of grounding your faith in God in such a way that its integrity is self-evident. A religious faith that affects the lives of its adherents is bound to be noticed.

2. The essence of Israelite theology was wrapped up in history, and Achior's recounting of Israelite history also focuses on the important principle of deuteronomic theology. The peace and prosperity of Israel before the exile, the destruction of Jerusalem by the Babylonians during the exile, and the restoration of Israel after the exile could all be explained by this theory of history. Further, the author of Judith could also explain the peace and independence of Judea after the Maccabean revolt by recourse to this theology. The victories of the Hasmonean rulers confirmed the author's view that Israel's successes were a reward from God.

In our time, however, this kind of thinking comes under closer scrutiny. Does God choose one nation over another? Will God always reward the righteous nation with peace and prosperity? Does deuteronomic theology have a danger of becoming the self-fulfilling prophecy of the "winners"? With a more complex view of history, most religious people today would see peace and prosperity as both blessing from God and awesome responsibility. Most would recognize that the moral standing of modern nations is shot through with contradictions, blind spots, unrealized dreams of freedom, dignity, and equality. The deuteronomic theology of more than two millennia ago seems far too simplistic. And yet it still challenges us, as Achior's speech implies, to ground the community of faith in a relationship with God regardless of the consequences and to hope for God's blessings as a result.

Judith 5:22–6:21, Holofernes Responds by Expelling Achior, Who Is Received in Bethulia

NAB

22 Now when Achior had concluded his recommendation, all the people standing round about the tent murmured; and the officers of Holofernes and all the inhabitants of the seacoast and of Moab alike said he should be cut to pieces. 23 "We are not afraid of the Israelites," they said, "for they are a powerless people, incapable of a strong defense. 24 Let us therefore attack them; your great army, Lord Holofernes, will swallow them up."

6 1 When the noise of the crowd surrounding the council had subsided, Holofernes, commander in chief of the Assyrian army, said to Achior, in the presence of the whole throng of coast-land peoples, of the Moabites, and of the Ammonite mercenaries: 2 "Who are you, Achior, to prophesy among us as you have done today, and to tell us not to fight against the Israelites because their God protects them? What god is there beside Nebuchadnezzar? He will send his force and destroy them from the face of the earth. Their God will not save them; 3 but we, the servants of Nebuchadnezzar, will strike them down as one man, for they will be unable to withstand the force of our cavalry. 4 We will overwhelm them with it, and the mountains shall be drunk with their blood, and their plains filled with their corpses. Not a trace of them shall survive our attack: they shall utterly perish, says King Nebuchadnezzar, lord of all the earth; for he has spoken, and his words shall not remain unfulfilled. 5 As for you, Achior, you Ammonite mercenary, for saying these things in a moment of perversity you shall not see my face after today, until I have taken revenge on this race of people from Egypt. 6 Then at my return, the sword of

6, 1: (*allophylōn*) *kai enantion pantōn tōn 'yiōn Mōab kai enantion misthōntōn Ammon:* cf Vet Lat (Munich MS), LXX[A], and v 2.

6, 2: Omit *kai pros pantas 'yious Mōab kai 'oi misthōtoi Ephraim:* cf LXX[A] and v 1.

NRSV

22When Achior had finished saying these things, all the people standing around the tent began to complain; Holofernes' officers and all the inhabitants of the seacoast and Moab insisted that he should be cut to pieces. 23They said, "We are not afraid of the Israelites; they are a people with no strength or power for making war. 24Therefore let us go ahead, Lord Holofernes, and your vast army will swallow them up."

6 When the disturbance made by the people outside the council had died down, Holofernes, the commander of the Assyrian army, said to Achior[a] in the presence of all the foreign contingents:

2"Who are you, Achior and you mercenaries of Ephraim, to prophesy among us as you have done today and tell us not to make war against the people of Israel because their God will defend them? What god is there except Nebuchadnezzar? He will send his forces and destroy them from the face of the earth. Their God will not save them; 3we the king's[b] servants will destroy them as one man. They cannot resist the might of our cavalry. 4We will overwhelm them;[c] their mountains will be drunk with their blood, and their fields will be full of their dead. Not even their footprints will survive our attack; they will utterly perish. So says King Nebuchadnezzar, lord of the whole earth. For he has spoken; none of his words shall be in vain.

5"As for you, Achior, you Ammonite mercenary, you have said these words in a moment of perversity; you shall not see my face again from this day until I take revenge on this race that came out of Egypt. 6Then at my return the sword of my army and the spear[d] of my servants shall pierce your sides, and you shall fall among their wounded. 7Now my slaves are going to take you

[a] Other ancient authorities add *and to all the Moabites* [b] Gk *his*
[c] Other ancient authorities add *with it* [d] Lat Syr: Gk *people*

NAB

my army or the spear of my servants will pierce your sides, and you shall fall among their slain. 7 My servants will now conduct you to the mountain region, and leave you at one of the towns along the ascent. 8 You shall not die till you are destroyed together with them. 9 If you still cherish the hope that they will not be taken, then there is no need for you to be downcast. I have spoken, and my words shall not prove false in any respect."

10 Then Holofernes ordered the servants who were standing by in his tent to seize Achior, conduct him to Bethulia, and hand him over to the Israelites. 11 So the servants took him in custody and brought him out of the camp into the plain. From there they led him into the mountain region till they reached the springs below Bethulia. 12 When the men of the city saw them, they seized their weapons and ran out of the city to the crest of the ridge; and all the slingers blocked the ascent of Holofernes' servants by hurling stones upon them. 13 So they took cover below the mountain, where they bound Achior and left him lying at the foot of the mountain; then they returned to their lord.

14 The Israelites came down to him from their city, loosed him, and brought him into Bethulia. They haled him before the rulers of the city, 15 who in those days were Uzziah, son of Micah of the tribe of Simeon, Chabris, son of Gothoniel, and Charmis, son of Melchiel. 16 They then convened all the elders of the city; and all their young men, as well as the women, gathered in haste at the place of assembly. They placed Achior in the center of the throng, and Uzziah questioned him about what had happened. 17 He replied by giving them an account of what was said in the council of Holofernes, and of all his own words among the Assyrian officers, and of all the boasting threats of Holofernes against the house of Israel.

18 At this the people fell prostrate and worshiped God; and they cried out: 19 "LORD, God of heaven, behold their arrogance! Have pity on the lowliness of our people, and look with favor this day on those who are consecrated to you."

6, 6: (*kai*) *'ē logchē* (*tōn therapontōn*): so Vet Lat, P. (*'otan*) *epistrepsō:* so LXX^{S,A,Bab}.

6, 12: Omit the first *epi tēn koryphēn tou orous:* so 2 LXX^{MSS}, Vet Lat, P; dittog.

NRSV

back into the hill country and put you in one of the towns beside the passes. [8]You will not die until you perish along with them. [9]If you really hope in your heart that they will not be taken, then do not look downcast! I have spoken, and none of my words shall fail to come true."

10Then Holofernes ordered his slaves, who waited on him in his tent, to seize Achior and take him away to Bethulia and hand him over to the Israelites. [11]So the slaves took him and led him out of the camp into the plain, and from the plain they went up into the hill country and came to the springs below Bethulia. [12]When the men of the town saw them,[a] they seized their weapons and ran out of the town to the top of the hill, and all the slingers kept them from coming up by throwing stones at them. [13]So having taken shelter below the hill, they bound Achior and left him lying at the foot of the hill, and returned to their master.

14Then the Israelites came down from their town and found him; they untied him and brought him into Bethulia and placed him before the magistrates of their town, [15]who in those days were Uzziah son of Micah, of the tribe of Simeon, and Chabris son of Gothoniel, and Charmis son of Melchiel. [16]They called together all the elders of the town, and all their young men and women ran to the assembly. They set Achior in the midst of all their people, and Uzziah questioned him about what had happened. [17]He answered and told them what had taken place at the council of Holofernes, and all that he had said in the presence of the Assyrian leaders, and all that Holofernes had boasted he would do against the house of Israel. [18]Then the people fell down and worshiped God, and cried out:

19"O Lord God of heaven, see their arrogance, and have pity on our people in their humiliation, and look kindly today on the faces of those who are consecrated to you."

20Then they reassured Achior, and praised him highly. [21]Uzziah took him from the assembly to his own house and gave a banquet for the elders; and all that night they called on the God of Israel for help.

[a] Other ancient authorities add *on the top of the hill*

NAB

20 Then they reassured Achior and praised him highly. 21 Uzziah brought him from the assembly to his home, where he gave a banquet for the elders. That whole night they called upon the God of Israel for help.

COMMENTARY

5:22–6:1. Although Achior's words will seem eminently sensible to the audience, the hubris of Holofernes and his allies blinds them from turning away. The question of Holofernes in 5:4, "In what does their power and strength consist?" was ironic, because the audience knew that the answer was "in God." The peoples of the seacoast and the Moabites are oblivious to this truth, and as a result they have accepted the worship of Nebuchadnezzar as god. Nebuchadnezzar's power consists in his armies, in which they have placed their hopes.

Holofernes' tent is mentioned for the first time, but it will be the dramatic setting for many of the dialogues to come, and especially for the meeting of Holofernes and Judith. The meeting here is called a "council" (συνέδριον *synedrion*), a term used elsewhere for Holofernes' meetings, unlike the γερουσία (*gerousia*), used for the city council meeting of the high priest in Jerusalem (4:8). The term *synedrion* is the Greek word from which the Hebrew סנהדרין (*Sanhedrîn*) is derived, but in Greek usage it usually means "meeting," and especially "war council," as it does here (cf. 2 Macc 14:5).

6:2-4. "Mercenaries of Ephraim" is an odd expression. Ephraim appears in some of the lists of the northern tribes of Israel, but the term also came to be used to represent the northern tribes as a whole. In Holofernes' mouth, it is likely a sarcastic attempt to associate Achior the Ammonite with the people he appears to be championing. As noted above, it is another use of an archaic term to re-create the golden age of heroes and villains of Israelite history. The term "mercenaries" (μισθωτοί *misthōtoi*) might also be better translated more contemptuously as "hirelings" or "hired workers," representing the class hierarchy of honor and shame that would have prevailed at this time.

"Who is god but Nebuchadnezzar?" makes explicit the contrast that underlies the entire book. Further, Holofernes' identification of himself as one of "Nebuchadnezzar's servants" should be compared with Judith's reference to herself as Holofernes' servant a number of times (11:5, 10, 16-17; 12:4), although her words often allow for the possibility that she is referring to herself as a servant of God. Holofernes—perhaps appropriately from his point of view—talks about this "god" Nebuchadnezzar in a strangely detached way when he says, "He will send his forces." Holofernes is actually the bearer of the full might of Nebuchadnezzar's army; it is he who is sending his forces. Holofernes seems to understand his role as an agent of his god's will, much as Judith understands her own role. Holofernes also makes his pronouncement using biblical idioms for prophecy: "he has spoken" and "none of his words shall be in vain." Holofernes is precisely a false prophet; he believes truly in his god and the words of his god, and he delivers his prophetic oracle as a biblical prophet would. He is not a false mouthpiece for a true god (cf. 1 Kgs 22:13-28; Jeremiah 28), but a true mouthpiece for a false god (cf. Isa 44:9-20; Wis 13:1–15:17; Letter of Jeremiah; Bel and the Dragon). It is again troubling for the modern reader, however, to find that the closest parallels to Nebuchadnezzar's policy of destruction should be found in the "holy war" passages of the HB.

6:5-13. Holofernes' sarcasm is evident here as

he speaks of "this race that came out of Egypt." As noted in the Commentary on 5:5, this was what pagan historians knew of Israelite history, and so the author's depiction of Holofernes' words would have the ring of verisimilitude. Holofernes quite humorously tells Achior, "You shall not see my face" until he exacts his revenge on Bethulia, but the audience knows that the next time Achior sees Holofernes' head it will be severed from the rest of his body. Although Achior speaks in a truthful manner without any ironic double meanings, Holofernes will often accidentally make statements that are susceptible to two layers of meaning, and Judith will intentionally use language in this way. Holofernes' words have a way of coming true that he does not intend, precisely because he is speaking unwisely. In Esther 6, Haman unwisely and unintentionally suggests to the king a reward that will fall to his nemesis, Mordecai. The wisdom tradition counseled against rash proclamations: "The wise of heart will heed commandments, but a babbling fool will come to ruin" (Prov 10:8 NRSV) and "The talk of fools is a rod for their backs, but the lips of the wise preserve them" (Prov 14:3 NRSV). This is a tradition from which Holofernes and Haman could have profited.

Holofernes emphasizes that his servants will kill Achior and that his slaves will exile him to one of the villages. Since Achior was the leader of the Ammonites, this is intentionally an attempt to shame him. With his parting words, Holofernes cannot help giving another unconscious prophecy: "If you really hope they will not be taken, do not look downcast!" Things look bleak for Achior, but the audience knows that he will be deposited in safe hands and that Holofernes is giving Achior good advice: Achior does hope they will not be taken, and he has reason to be happy. Holofernes closes with another formula of prophecy, "I have spoken, and none of my words shall fail to come true."

6:14-21. The description of the servants depositing Achior at the foot of the hill on which Bethulia sat and the Bethulians admitting him to their town takes up a considerable number of verses, more verses, in fact, than some of the military campaigns of the first two chapters. This section is very important in the structure of the work; as noted in the Overview at 2:14, this passage is at the center of the chiasm of the first part of Judith, and it corresponds to and is a reversal of the dialogue between Holofernes and Achior and the rejection of the latter's advice. It is also a narrative break from the talk of the last two chapters and shows the shift of focus from the campaigns of nations to the experiences of a few individuals, who are now seen to be very important. Achior's movement—unintentional as it is—is very significant, and in addition to being coordinated with previous passages (5:1–6:13), it is balanced and contrasted with passages to come concerning Judith: He moves from Holofernes' camp to Bethulia, she from Bethulia to Holofernes' camp. He presented the deuteronomic theology in truth; she will present it as part of a lie. He will convert from paganism to follow the God of Israel; she will feign an abandonment of God to join Holofernes' god.[77] Furthermore, Achior's movement allows the reader an effective transition from Holofernes' camp to the interior of Bethulia. Uzziah's banquet (a festive occasion?) may seem out of place, but it is a sign of hospitality that Achior has now been ritually welcomed, and it balances the banquet that Judith will receive when she changes places with Achior and is accepted into Holofernes' tent (12:10-20). Further, it provides another rest in the story before the next narrative movement (see Commentary on 2:28).

77. Adolfo Roitman, "Achior in the Book of Judith: His Role and Significance," in *"No One Spoke Ill of Her:" Essays on Judith*, ed. James C. VanderKam (Atlanta: Scholars Press, 1992) 31-45.

REFLECTIONS

That pagan kings demanded worship as gods is today a stereotype of ancient polytheism, but this practice was not common in the ancient world. It was the practice in Egypt, but not in Assyria, Babylon, or Persia. Greek kings and Roman emperors often received divine honors in Egypt or in the east, but seldom in Greece and Rome. Even where reverence of the king was practiced, political and military domination in the ancient world almost never entailed the outlawing of the conquered people's religion; religious persecution was not considered an expedient of military strategy. Polytheism allowed for a pluralism of religious observances, and so requiring the religious reverence of the king, or of any other cult (such as Isis and Serapis in Egypt), did not entail the elimination of the conquered people's own religious traditions. Only in the Maccabean revolt and its aftermath do we find religious persecution and the outlawing of a local religious tradition as a means of political control. In this text we have another case of a later historical development read back into the earlier period. (Esth 8:17 likewise reflects a form of forcible conversion that was not known in earlier centuries.)

This introduces us to the irony that we have lived with in the West for so many centuries, and still do: The idea of a monotheistic God often gives rise to the notion that only one concept of God can be permitted. If there is one God, there can be only one religion. Conflict and persecution then follow in the interest of realizing the vision of one community under one God. Polytheistic cultures, on the other hand, have generally felt free to recognize gods of other cultures, even to embrace them or harmonize them—"My god X must be the same as your god Y." To blame monotheism for religious persecution would be simplistic, however. Polytheistic cultures engage in conflict and persecution as well; they simply do not use "one community under one God" as their rallying cry and are not as likely to oppose local religious institutions as a means of political domination.

In the heat of this novel the reader almost forgets that the violent suppression of local religious worship had its closest parallel not only in what the Jews had actually experienced a few decades earlier under the Greek Seleucids, a religious persecution that had provoked the Maccabean revolt, but also in what the successors of the Maccabees had done to the various ethnic groups that lived within the borders of a renewed Israel. The description here is unsettlingly close to the program of the Jewish ruler John Hyrcanus, almost as if it were based upon it. Hyrcanus destroyed the Samaritan temple on Mt. Gerizim, rid the land of other competing cults, and forcibly converted many people to Judaism. The parallel to the administration of Judea may have been intended; the religious persecution by Holofernes culminates in the declaration, "What god is there except Nebuchadnezzar?" (6:2). That of Hyrcanus would have been similar, except that it culminated in "What God is there except the Lord?"

For us, the lessons of history must be faced, and we need look no further each day than the headlines concerning conflicts on different continents. The persecuted often become the persecutors, seething with the need to reverse the memory of persecution, inflicting a just destruction on the former perpetrators. And this, of course, is the theme of Judith. The way out is not easy, but it is clear that the chain of memory and reversal is a powerful motive for violence, and it is the responsibility of communities of faith to examine closely the power of justification, the religious rallying cries that will be given for the next reversal.

Judith 7:1-18, Holofernes Prepares for War and Places Bethulia Under Siege

NAB

7 1 The following day Holofernes ordered his whole army, and all the allied troops that had come to his support, to move against Bethulia, seize the mountain passes, and engage the Israelites in battle. 2 That same day all their fighting men went into action. Their forces numbered a

NRSV

7 The next day Holofernes ordered his whole army, and all the allies who had joined him, to break camp and move against Bethulia, and to seize the passes up into the hill country and make war on the Israelites. [2]So all their warriors marched off that day; their fighting forces

NAB

hundred and seventy thousand infantry and twelve thousand horsemen, not counting the baggage train or the men who accompanied it on foot—a very great army. 3 They encamped at the spring in the valley near Bethulia, and spread out in breadth toward Dothan as far as Balbaim, and in length from Bethulia to Cyamon, which faces Esdraelon.

4 When the Israelites saw how many there were, they said to one another in great dismay: "Soon they will devour the whole country. Neither the high mountains nor the valleys and hills can support the mass of them." 5 Yet they all seized their weapons, lighted fires on their bastions, and kept watch throughout the night.

6 On the second day Holofernes led out all his cavalry in the sight of the Israelites who were in Bethulia. 7 He reconnoitered the approaches to their city and located their sources of water; these he seized, stationing armed detachments around them, while he himself returned to his troops.

8 All the commanders of the Edomites and all the leaders of the Ammonites, together with the generals of the seacoast, came to Holofernes and said: 9 "Sir, listen to what we have to say, that there may be no losses among your troops. 10 These Israelites do not rely on their spears, but on the height of the mountains where they dwell; it is not easy to reach the summit of their mountains. 11 Therefore, sir, do not attack them in regular formation; thus not a single one of your troops will fall. 12 Stay in your camp, and spare all your soldiers. Have some of your servants keep control of the source of water that flows out at the base of the mountain, 13 for that is where the inhabitants of Bethulia get their water. Then thirst will begin to carry them off, and they will surrender their city. Meanwhile, we and our men will go up to the summits of the nearby mountains, and encamp there to guard against anyone's leaving the city. 14 They and their wives and children will languish with hunger, and even before the sword strikes them they will be laid low in the streets of their city. 15 Thus you will render them dire punishment for their rebellion and their refusal to meet you peacefully."

7, 2: (*chōris tēs aposkeuēs*) *kai* (*tōn andrōn*): so LXX[S,A].
7, 3: (*mēkos*) *apo* (*Baityloua*): so LXX[S,A].
7, 17: (*parabolē 'yion*) *Mōab*: so 1 LXX[MS], Vet Lat, P; cf v 18.

NRSV

numbered one hundred seventy thousand infantry and twelve thousand cavalry, not counting the baggage and the foot soldiers handling it, a very great multitude. 3They encamped in the valley near Bethulia, beside the spring, and they spread out in breadth over Dothan as far as Balbaim and in length from Bethulia to Cyamon, which faces Esdraelon.

4When the Israelites saw their vast numbers, they were greatly terrified and said to one another, "They will now strip clean the whole land; neither the high mountains nor the valleys nor the hills will bear their weight." 5Yet they all seized their weapons, and when they had kindled fires on their towers, they remained on guard all that night.

6On the second day Holofernes led out all his cavalry in full view of the Israelites in Bethulia. 7He reconnoitered the approaches to their town, and visited the springs that supplied their water; he seized them and set guards of soldiers over them, and then returned to his army.

8Then all the chieftains of the Edomites and all the leaders of the Moabites and the commanders of the coastland came to him and said, 9"Listen to what we have to say, my lord, and your army will suffer no losses. 10This people, the Israelites, do not rely on their spears but on the height of the mountains where they live, for it is not easy to reach the tops of their mountains. 11Therefore, my lord, do not fight against them in regular formation, and not a man of your army will fall. 12Remain in your camp, and keep all the men in your forces with you; let your servants take possession of the spring of water that flows from the foot of the mountain, 13for this is where all the people of Bethulia get their water. So thirst will destroy them, and they will surrender their town. Meanwhile, we and our people will go up to the tops of the nearby mountains and camp there to keep watch to see that no one gets out of the town. 14They and their wives and children will waste away with famine, and before the sword reaches them they will be strewn about in the streets where they live. 15Thus you will pay them back with evil, because they rebelled and did not receive you peaceably."

16These words pleased Holofernes and all his

NAB

16 Their words pleased Holofernes and all his ministers, and he ordered their proposal to be carried out. 17 Thereupon the Moabites moved camp, together with five thousand Assyrians. They encamped in the valley, and held the water supply and the springs of the Israelites. 18 The Edomites and the Ammonites went up and encamped in the mountain region opposite Dothan; and they sent some of their men to the south and to the east opposite Egrebel, near Chusi, which is on Wadi Mochmur. The rest of the Assyrian army was encamped in the plain, covering the whole countryside. Their enormous store of tents and equipment was spread out in profusion everywhere.

NRSV

attendants, and he gave orders to do as they had said. [17]So the army of the Ammonites moved forward, together with five thousand Assyrians, and they encamped in the valley and seized the water supply and the springs of the Israelites. [18]And the Edomites and Ammonites went up and encamped in the hill country opposite Dothan; and they sent some of their men toward the south and the east, toward Egrebeh, which is near Chusi beside the Wadi Mochmur. The rest of the Assyrian army encamped in the plain, and covered the whole face of the land. Their tents and supply trains spread out in great number, and they formed a vast multitude.

COMMENTARY

7:1-5. It is not until chap. 7 that the climactic battle is ready to be joined. The enormousness of Holofernes' army is impressed upon the reader, with a description that is very visual. It is what the citizens of Bethulia see that strikes fear in their hearts. The author again notes the auxiliary soldiers and supplies as a way of indicating not only the size of the army, but also its unwieldiness. Although it is a fearsome sight to the Israelites, to the audience it is also a bloated giant, waiting to be slaughtered. Once again, despite the fact that the Bethulians will lack the resolve that Judith demands, they are still far braver than the nations of the coastlands mentioned in 2:18–3:8, who not only surrender at the sight of the Assyrians, but abandon their religious traditions as well.

7:6-18. Holofernes has arrayed his troops for the most visual effect to terrify the Israelites, and he is preparing for battle. Joining the neighboring groups with whom Israel had had dicey relations in the past are the chieftains of the Edomites. This was another group who would have had ancient bad associations for the Israelites. The progenitor of the Edomites was Esau (Genesis 25–33), whose animosity toward Jacob was considered to be indicative of the relations between their progeny. There was a more recent association, however, in that in the author's day the Edomites were known as Idumeans, and John Hyrcanus had forcibly converted many of this group to Judaism. One of those converted was the grandfather of Herod the Great, so their status was not marginal; still, at the end of the second century BCE, when the conversion was probably a recent event, this reference would have appeared divisive.

It is significant that the neighboring nations are not just allied with Holofernes; they lead the attack. Their suggestion is a clever stratagem, and it is they who take the initiative in securing the mountaintops around Bethulia, ensuring that their stratagem will work (7:13, 17-18). Unlike Achior's advice, the advice from these neighboring peoples is malicious in intent and, though clever in the short term, from the audience's point of view lacks the insight that Achior possessed about the bigger picture of Israel's fortunes. An artful and novelistic use of description is in evidence here as the Assyrians move to engage and outsmart the Israelites.

Judith 7:19-32, The People Despair and Want to Surrender

NAB

19 The Israelites cried to the LORD, their God, for they were disheartened, since all their enemies had them surrounded, and there was no way of slipping through their lines. 20 The whole Assyrian camp, infantry, chariots, and cavalry, kept them thus surrounded for thirty-four days. All the reservoirs of water failed the inhabitants of Bethulia, 21 and the cisterns ran dry, so that on no day did they have enough to drink, but their drinking water was rationed. 22 Their children fainted away, and the women and youths were consumed with thirst and were collapsing in the streets and gateways of the city, with no strength left in them.

23 All the people, therefore, including youths, women, and children, went in a crowd to Uzziah and the rulers of the city. They set up a great clamor and said before the elders: 24 "God judge between you and us! You have done us grave injustice in not making peace with the Assyrians. 25 There is no help for us now! Instead, God has sold us into their power by laying us prostrate before them in thirst and utter exhaustion. 26 Therefore, summon them and deliver the whole city as booty to the troops of Holofernes and to all his forces; 27 we would be better off to become their prey. We should indeed be made slaves, but at least should live, and not have to behold our little ones dying before our eyes and our wives and children breathing out their souls. 28 We adjure you by heaven and earth, and by our God, the LORD of our forefathers, who is punishing us for our sins and those of our forefathers, to do as we have proposed, this very day."

29 All in the assembly with one accord broke into shrill wailing and loud cries to the LORD their God. 30 But Uzziah said to them, "Courage, my brothers! Let us wait five days more for the LORD our God, to show his mercy toward us; he will not utterly forsake us. 31 But if those days pass without help coming to us, I will do as you say." 32 Then he dispersed the men to their posts, and they returned to the walls and towers of the city;

7, 28: (*kata ta ʿamartēmata tōn paterōn ʿēmōn*) *tou poiēsai* (*kata ta rēmata*): so 1 LXX[MS], P; cf Vet Lat, Ethiopic, and v 30f.

NRSV

19The Israelites then cried out to the Lord their God, for their courage failed, because all their enemies had surrounded them, and there was no way of escape from them. 20The whole Assyrian army, their infantry, chariots, and cavalry, surrounded them for thirty-four days, until all the water containers of every inhabitant of Bethulia were empty; 21their cisterns were going dry, and on no day did they have enough water to drink, for their drinking water was rationed. 22Their children were listless, and the women and young men fainted from thirst and were collapsing in the streets of the town and in the gateways; they no longer had any strength.

23Then all the people, the young men, the women, and the children, gathered around Uzziah and the rulers of the town and cried out with a loud voice, and said before all the elders, 24"Let God judge between you and us! You have done us a great injury in not making peace with the Assyrians. 25For now we have no one to help us; God has sold us into their hands, to be strewn before them in thirst and exhaustion. 26Now summon them and surrender the whole town as booty to the army of Holofernes and to all his forces. 27For it would be better for us to be captured by them.[a] We shall indeed become slaves, but our lives will be spared, and we shall not witness our little ones dying before our eyes, and our wives and children drawing their last breath. 28We call to witness against you heaven and earth and our God, the Lord of our ancestors, who punishes us for our sins and the sins of our ancestors; do today the things that we have described!"

29Then great and general lamentation arose throughout the assembly, and they cried out to the Lord God with a loud voice. 30But Uzziah said to them, "Courage, my brothers and sisters![b] Let us hold out for five days more; by that time the Lord our God will turn his mercy to us again, for he will not forsake us utterly. 31But if these days pass by, and no help comes for us, I will do as you say."

32Then he dismissed the people to their vari-

[a] Other ancient authorities add *than to die of thirst* [b] Gk *Courage, brothers*

NAB	NRSV
the women and children he sent to their homes. Throughout the city they were in great misery.	ous posts, and they went up on the walls and towers of their town. The women and children he sent home. In the town they were in great misery.

COMMENTARY

7:19-22. Cutting off the water supply has had its effect: The Israelites cry out to God, but now their courage has failed, and they begin to despair. Although it was stated in the Introduction that the depiction of emotion was common in both Jewish and Greek novelistic literature, this description of the sufferings of the Jews in Bethulia is actually very restrained when compared to other texts (e.g., 2 Macc 3:14-21 and the even more extreme account in 3 Maccabees 4).

7:23-28. The Bethulians complain to Uzziah much as the Israelites complained to Moses during the exodus. In Exodus 15–17 there are three episodes in which the Israelites seem to have quickly forgotten God's former miracles and complain about their new trials (see also Deut 6:16). One of these episodes, Exod 17:1-7, contains several parallels to the book of Judith, if we also look ahead to Judith's reaction to this scene. The texts tell a similar story: There is a lack of water; the Israelites complain to their leader and say that it would have been better to be a slave; there is a critique of their testing of God; the leader calls on God; the leader delivers the people; and there is an issue over the acclamation, "the Lord is with us."[78] A crucial difference is that the function of the leader in Judith is divided between Uzziah and Judith; she steps up here to take the role of leader from the recognized male authority in the community.

7:29-31. Uzziah, whose name means "the Lord is my power," is much more resolute than the townspeople, but he fashions a compromise that Judith will later find unacceptable: If God has not sent rain within five days, they will surrender.

7:32. A calm pervades the town of Bethulia, but it is the calm of despair. Nevertheless, it is an effective narrative transition much like the pauses that have come before at junctures in the story (see Commentary on 2:28).

78. Jan Willem van Henten, "Judith as Alternative Leader: A Rereading of Judith 7–13," in *A Feminist Companion to Esther, Judith and Susanna,* ed. Athalya Brenner (Sheffield: Sheffield Academic, 1995) 235.

JUDITH 8:1–16:25

JUDITH ARISES TO RESCUE HER PEOPLE

OVERVIEW

A bit less than halfway through the novel, Judith is finally introduced. She will now dominate the second half of the book, not just in the sense that she is the principal character, center stage most of the time—although indeed she is—but also in the sense that she is the deliverer of Israel when none of the men will step forward. We will meet her in her estate, where she spends most of her days in seclusion, but she will come forward to address the elders of Bethulia. She will pray and prepare herself to do battle with Holofernes with the best weapons at her disposal: her beauty, her courage, and her ability to manipulate through deceit.

The structural outline of the whole of Judith given in the Introduction attempts to divide the content of the narrative at important transition points, but within that overall outline there are other structural patterns at work that will be pointed out in the Commentary. These include the overall pattern of the heroic quest, within which we find two specially noted rites of passage, one involving the special preparation of the heroine in prayer, fasting, and clothing, and one involving the departure across the threshold of the city from known and safe space to unknown and unsafe space, the slaying of Holofernes, and the return across the threshold back to the city. Toni Craven's discovery of clearly marked structural patterns of parallels and contrasts in the first part and in the second part allows us to discern these and other important dynamics of the narrative as part of a chiastic structure. For the second part, her outline can be summarized thus:

- A Introduction of Judith (8:1-8)
  - B Judith plans to save Israel (8:9–10:8)
    - C Judith and her maid leave Bethulia (10:9-10)
      - D Judith overcomes Holofernes (10:11–13:10*a*)
    - C′ Judith and her maid return to Bethulia (13:10*b*-11)
  - B′ Judith plans to destroy Israel's enemy (13:12–16:20)
- A′ Conclusion about Judith (16:21-25)

In the second part there is a center that is more discretely set off from the rest of the chiastic structure than was the case in the first part: the heroine's slaying of the "monster" who threatens Israel.

JUDITH 8:1-8, INTRODUCTION OF JUDITH

NAB

8 1 Now in those days Judith, daughter of Merari, son of Joseph, son of Oziel, son of Elkiah, son of Ananias, son of Gideon, son of Raphain, son of Ahitob, son of Elijah, son of Hilkiah, son

8, 1: Omit *'yiou Ox:* so 2 LXX[MSS]; dittog. of *'yiou Ozeīēl;* (*'yiou 'Elkeia*) *'yiou Ananiou 'yiou Gedeōn 'yiou Raphain 'yiou Achitōb* (*'yiou Eleiou*): so most LXX[MSS]. (*'yiou Sarasadai*) *'yiou Symeōn* (*'yiou Israēl*): cf 9, 2; Nm 1, 6; 2, 12; 7, 36.

NRSV

8 Now in those days Judith heard about these things: she was the daughter of Merari son of Ox son of Joseph son of Oziel son of Elkiah son of Ananias son of Gideon son of Raphain son of Ahitub son of Elijah son of Hilkiah son of Eliab son of Nathanael son of Salamiel son of Sarasadai son of Israel. [2]Her husband Manasseh,

NAB

of Eliab, son of Nathanael, son of Salamiel, son
of Sarasadai, son of Simeon, son of Israel, heard
of this. 2 Her husband, Manasseh, of her own
tribe and clan, had died at the time of the barley
harvest. 3 While he was in the field supervising
those who bound the sheaves, he suffered sunstroke; and he died of this illness in Bethulia, his
native city. He was buried with his forefathers in
the field between Dothan and Balamon. 4 The
widowed Judith remained three years and four
months at home, 5 where she set up a tent for
herself on the roof of her house. She put sackcloth
about her loins and wore widow's weeds. 6 She
fasted all the days of her widowhood, except
sabbath eves and sabbaths, new moon eves and
new moons, feastdays and holidays of the house
of Israel. 7 She was beautifully formed and lovely
to behold. Her husband, Manasseh, had left her
gold and silver, servants and maids, livestock and
fields, which she was maintaining. 8 No one had
a bad word to say about her, for she was a very
God-fearing woman.

8, 3: (*epi tous desmeuontas ta dragmata:* so LXX^S,A^.
8, 6: (*pronoumēniōn*) *kai noumēniōn* (*kai 'eortōn*): so several LXX^MSS^.
8, 7: (*kai*) *emeinen* (*ep' autōn*): so several LXX^MSS^.

NRSV

who belonged to her tribe and family, had died
during the barley harvest. 3For as he stood overseeing those who were binding sheaves in the
field, he was overcome by the burning heat, and
took to his bed and died in his town Bethulia. So
they buried him with his ancestors in the field
between Dothan and Balamon. 4Judith remained
as a widow for three years and four months 5at
home where she set up a tent for herself on the
roof of her house. She put sackcloth around her
waist and dressed in widow's clothing. 6She fasted
all the days of her widowhood, except the day
before the sabbath and the sabbath itself, the day
before the new moon and the day of the new
moon, and the festivals and days of rejoicing of
the house of Israel. 7She was beautiful in appearance, and was very lovely to behold. Her husband
Manasseh had left her gold and silver, men and
women slaves, livestock, and fields; and she maintained this estate. 8No one spoke ill of her, for
she feared God with great devotion.

COMMENTARY

The second part of Judith begins stylistically in a way very similar to the first. In both halves a principal character is named, after which there is a long and seemingly awkward digression to describe a second, weaker character, before the main narrative resumes, recounting the deeds of the principal character.[79] In chap. 1 Nebuchadnezzar is introduced by a long sentence that is largely taken up with a parenthesis on Arphaxad, before Nebuchadnezzar's exploits are resumed in 1:5. In chap. 8, Judith is introduced by a long sentence that is given over to a parenthesis on her genealogy, and only after a description of her husband's death is her background taken up again.

Judith hears about the events and comes to the fore in response to a crisis, like a hero or heroine of folklore or like one of the deliverers of Israel in the book of Judges. The name "Judith" is the feminine equivalent of "Judah" or "Judas," from which the province name "Judea" is derived ("Judah" [יהודה *yĕhûdâ*] in Hebrew became "Judea" [Ἰουδαία *Ioudaia*] in Greek). It is from the word "Judean" that the English word "Jew" ultimately derives; her name thus means "Jewess." Assuming that the name was invented for the character, it could have been chosen to be emblematic of the ideal herione—that is, it communicates the fact that the Jews would be saved by a heroic "Jewess." It is also possible that it evokes the name of one of the heroes of the Maccabean revolt, Judah the Maccabee. This seems even more likely when we consider the close parallels between Judah the Maccabee's de-

79. Morton Enslin and Solomon Zeitlin, *The Book of Judith,* JAL VIII (Leiden: Brill, 1972) 58, 112.

feat of Nicanor (1 Macc 7:47; 2 Macc 15:35; see Commentary on 14:1-4). The name of Judith certainly argues against the possibility of a Samaritan origin for the book, unless the protagonist's name has been changed.

Judith's genealogy is given in some detail—the only extended genealogy for a woman in the Bible (though Matthew 1 includes women in the genealogy of Jesus). Genealogies are common in the Bible, both in early texts and in late ones (*Jub* 4:1-33; Tob 1:1-2; Matt 1:1-17; Luke 3:23-38), and they may serve a different function in the two cases.[80] In early texts they are used to tie together a larger patriarchal history, or what has been called the "primal history." Israelite history is, in effect, the history of one long genealogy; Abraham's family and their genealogies anchor the parts of that history to one idealized lineage. The late genealogies function to tie individuals back in to the primal history as a means of authenticating their identity. The hero or heroine must have proper credentials, but may be a "loner" all the same. This is found in hero legends cross-culturally. The names in Judith's genealogy are unremarkable in general, but two things are significant. First, the genealogy is traced back to Israel. This is another indication that the author intends to idealize the reconstitution of a united Israel and not just Judea as a Hellenistic temple-state, even if the actual achievement of the Hasmoneans was closer to the latter. Second, there are connections in the genealogy to Simeon (Salamiel and Sarasadai are his grandson and son, Num 1:6), which would be relevant for Judith's later affirmation of the role of Simeon in avenging the rape of Dinah (Jdt 9:2).

It is also significant that while Judith is identified by her genealogy, her husband, Manasseh, is not; in fact, he is identified in relation to Judith. This is very unusual and points to an important aspect of the second half of the book: the reversal of expected gender roles. Manasseh, through his loss of genealogy, is already depicted in a passive way, but there may be more. Are we to infer from the description of his death that he died most unheroically—that is, in bed, brought low by a sunstroke? Holofernes will also die in his bed in a most undignified way.[81] Judith is characterized in opposition to the men around her, first her husband, and later, the town leaders of Bethulia and Achior. She is aggressive and active, like a male warrior, while they are weak willed, passive, "feminine" by most cultures' standards. As noted in the Introduction, the male protagonists of the Greek novels are also generally passive compared to the female, but this is carried much further in the book of Judith.

Judith's character is demonstrated by the heroic vigilance she brings to everyday piety. After the death of her husband, Judith observes the ritual mourning of the widow for three years and four months, much longer than was required by Jewish law.[82] In addition, she fasts each day except for the holidays on which fasting is not allowed, and sets up a tent on her roof for her prayer and fasts. In Jewish practice it was forbidden to visit graves on sabbaths and festivals, and her mourning practices are likewise not performed on these days; she comes down from her tent into her quarters (10:2). Her piety is thus prodigious and will sound similar to later Christian asceticism.[83]

She was also a beautiful woman, very wealthy and secure in her social position. These two traits, great beauty and wealth, are always the characteristics of the heroine in the Greek novels, and for the Jewish novels as well: Judith, Susanna, Esther, and Aseneth are all described in this way. The author of Judith makes good use of detail, and we note here that the wealth of Manasseh, and now of Judith, is spelled out in categories. They are the same that were used to emphasize the size and extent of Holofernes' army: gold and silver (2:18), slaves (2:20), livestock (2:17), and fields (3:3). Is the author trying to suggest that just as Holofernes controls a vast army and its auxiliaries, so also, in an analogous way, Judith administers her own empire? It certainly does help to characterize our protagonist as a woman with a commanding presence and a will to succeed, and the analogy to Holofernes' vast power is probably intended. Further, Judith maintains the

80. Robert R. Wilson, "Old Testament Genealogies in Recent Research," *JBL* 94 (1975) 169-89.

81. Amy-Jill Levine, "Sacrifice and Salvation: Otherness and Domestication in the Book of Judith," in *"No One Spoke Ill of Her": Essays on Judith,* ed. James C. VanderKam (Atlanta: Scholars Press, 1992) 105-17.

82. Roland de Vaux, *Ancient Israel,* 2 vols. (New York: McGraw-Hill, 1965) 1:40.

83. The connection to asceticism has been probed by scholars. See Lawrence M. Wills, *The Jewish Novel in the Ancient World* (Ithaca: Cornell University Press, 1995) 15, 123, 139, 228-44.

estate after Manasseh's death, like the "capable wife" of Prov 31:10-31, who excels not only in domestic crafts and running a household, but in buying fields and planting vineyards as well. Although one may wonder how Judith can administer a large estate while praying and fasting in her tent, the person responsible on a daily basis may be her servant, "who was in charge of all she possessed" (v. 10). Still, we need hardly look for a realistic answer; the capable wife of Proverbs 31 also does seemingly impossible things. But although Judith is described so positively, it is interesting that she does not seek a new husband or enter into a levirate marriage to raise up a son for her dead husband, as Jewish law would require (Deut 25:5-10). Judith is simply not a typical model of Jewish womanhood. To be sure, there are other traces in this period of a Jewish piety that allows for celibacy and voluntary childlessness. The Qumran sectarians and the Therapeutae (fem., Therapeutrides) described by Philo in *On the Contemplative Life* encouraged celibacy, and Wis 3:13–4:6 seems to encourage a celibate spirituality. In early Christianity as well, celibacy for some is presumed in 1 Corinthians 7; 1 Tim 5:14; and perhaps Matt 19:12.

Moore also raises another question: Why is the character Judith a widow and not a virgin or a married woman?[84] Here we probably have to concede that even Judith could not rise above all social conventions of ancient Judaism. The risk to her dignity in approaching Holofernes was great, and perhaps titillating to the audience; but for a virgin or a married woman to place herself in that kind of jeopardy would be quite another matter. A young unmarried woman was under the strict control and protection of her father and his family until she married, and then that control was passed over to her husband. An attack on a young woman in ancient society was an affront to the man who had charge of her and was a shame to him as much as it was to her. A widow, on the other hand, was no longer under the control and protection of a man. Widows and orphans were among the most vulnerable social categories in ancient Israel because they were not under the protection of any male relative; as a result, the prophets often felt compelled to take up the cause of the unattached widows and orphans. Judith herself retained a wealthy estate, but if a widow was not wealthy, she might find herself without protection. Even the levirate law, which might have the effect of allowing a widow at least temporary support from her dead husband's brother, is not intended for *her* welfare, but to raise a son for the deceased husband. As a result of these structural aspects of Jewish culture, the fact that Judith is a widow becomes almost a necessity. A young virgin or a married woman could never be depicted in such an unprotected position without causing severe discomfort in the audience; only a widow could be depicted in so flagrant a violation of decorum. The unprotected nature of even a wealthy widow's situation may still be in evidence, however, in the fact that the author must emphasize that even though she was unattached, "no one spoke ill of her." The quotation in the introduction from Jerome on Gentile widows indicates the social reproach that might attach to an unprotected widow. Judith, because "she feared God with great devotion," maintained an impeccable reputation even though she will later flout many commandments and conventions associated with Jewish piety.

Judith spends most of her days fasting in seclusion in a tent or booth on the roof of her house. Is her tent intended to call to mind Sukkot (the Jewish Festival of Booths), the tabernacle in the wilderness wanderings (also a σκηνη *skēnē* in Greek), a synagogue, or none of these? There are important parallels with each. The restoration of observances during Sukkot in Ezra 3:4-5 includes the same offerings mentioned at Jdt 4:14: daily burnt offerings, regular burnt offerings, new moon and festival offerings, freewill offerings (see also Lev 23:33-38), and the booths of the Festival of Sukkot could be constructed on roofs (Neh 8:13-18). The tabernacle, or tent of meeting (Exodus 25–26), in addition to being the locus for the worship of the Israelites during their wanderings, was also a paradigm for the Temple. Since Judith's prayer is timed to correspond to the temple sacrifices (9:1), this parallel is suggestive. Her prayer in the tent is also similar to the prayers in synagogues, but the synagogue as a place for prayer and study, rather than for a public meeting, may not have come into being until after the writing of Judith. Although there are similarities to each

84. Carey A. Moore, *Judith*, AB 40 (Garden City, N.Y.: Doubleday, 1985) 180.

of these forms of sacred space and worship, none of them appears to be clearly in mind to the exclusion of the others.

There is one other possibility that should be considered. Lying behind Judith's practice of fasting and praying at the same time that the priests in the Jerusalem Temple were offering sacrifices is likely a development of ancient Jewish worship that occurred away from the Temple. The huge provisions for the temple sacrifices in Jerusalem were presented each month by one of the twelve tribes on a rotating basis. In addition, a form of local worship was instituted in the land of each tribe during the period of their responsibility. A pillar was erected by each tribe, and for four days during that month people from the tribe came together at the pillar to fast and pray. The prayers and readings of the temple service were also read in the local communities. The similarity to Judith's practice is obvious: A local worship experience that involves fasting and mourning rites takes place at a time that coincides with the priestly rituals in Jerusalem. To be sure, Judith's practice is not limited to the period of her tribe's provision of animals and crops. However, pious Jews evidently began to pray and fast in the public square on a regular basis year-round, a practice that may have been the actual forerunner of the synagogue. This evolved further into a twice-weekly prayer and fast among the Pharisees, although it is not clear whether they alone performed it in this way. The Mishnah, a collection of Jewish laws compiled in about 200 CE, limits the practice to prayer only,[85] but that implies that other aspects had also been involved. Tertullian, a Christian theologian writing at the end of the second century CE, describes—albeit critically—the practice of public prayer, fasting, and wearing of sackcloth: "A Jewish fast is universally celebrated; while neglecting the temples [meaning synagogues?], in every open place they continue to send prayer up to heaven. And though by dress and ornamentation of mourning they disgrace the duty, still they do affect a faith in abstinence."[86] Judith's prayer and fasting, not tied to an annual rotation, represent a continuous practice that is more like this latter development. It is still timed to coincide with a Jerusalem temple observance, but like the personal piety of the Pharisees, it is carried out continuously. Her activities are by no means identical to these practices, but this fictitious representation of her extreme piety is probably influenced by actual local practices.

85. Sidney B. Hoenig, "The Ancient City-Square: The Forerunner of the Synagogue," *ANRW* 2.19.1 (1979) 448-76.
86. Tertullian *On Fasting* 16.

JUDITH 8:9–10:10, JUDITH RESOLVES TO SAVE ISRAEL

Judith 8:9-36, Judith Addresses the Citizens of Bethulia

NAB

9 When Judith, therefore, heard of the harsh words which the people, discouraged by their lack of water, had spoken against their ruler, and of all that Uzziah had said to them in reply, swearing that he would hand over the city to the Assyrians at the end of five days, 10 she sent the maid who was in charge of all her things to ask Uzziah, Chabris, and Charmis, the elders of the city, to

8, 10: (*ekalesen*) *Ozeian kai* (*Chabrein*): so a few LXX^{MSS}, Vet Lat, P; cf v. 28.

NRSV

9When Judith heard the harsh words spoken by the people against the ruler, because they were faint for lack of water, and when she heard all that Uzziah said to them, and how he promised them under oath to surrender the town to the Assyrians after five days, 10she sent her maid, who was in charge of all she possessed, to summon Uzziah and[a] Chabris and Charmis, the elders of her town. 11They came to her, and she said to them;

[a] Other ancient authorities lack *Uzziah* (*see verses 28 and 35*)

NAB

visit her. 11 When they came, she said to them:
"Listen to me, you rulers of the people of Bethulia.
What you said to the people today is not proper.
When you promised to hand over the city to our
enemies at the end of five days unless within that
time the LORD comes to our aid, you interposed
between God and yourselves this oath which you
took. 12 Who are you, then, that you should have
put God to the test this day, setting yourselves in
the place of God in human affairs? 13 It is the
LORD Almighty for whom you are laying down
conditions; will you never understand anything?
14 You cannot plumb the depths of the human
heart or grasp the workings of the human mind;
how then can you fathom God, who has made
all these things, discern his mind, and understand
his plan?

"No, my brothers, do not anger the LORD our
God. 15 For if he does not wish to come to our
aid within the five days, he has it equally within
his power to protect us at such time as he pleases,
or to destroy us in the face of our enemies. 16 It
is not for you to make the LORD our God give
surety for his plans.

"God is not man that he should be moved
by threats,
nor human, that he may be given an
ultimatum.

17 "So while we wait for the salvation that
comes from him, let us call upon him to help us,
and he will hear our cry if it is his good pleasure.
18 For there has not risen among us in recent
generations, nor does there exist today, any tribe,
or clan, or town, or city of ours that worships
gods made by hands, as happened in former days.
19 It was for such conduct that our forefathers
were handed over to the sword and to pillage,
and fell with great destruction before our enemies.
20 But since we acknowledge no other god but
the LORD, we hope that he will not disdain us or
any of our people. 21 If we are taken, all Judea
will fall, our sanctuary will be plundered, and God
will make us pay for its profanation with our life's
blood. 22 For the slaughter of our kinsmen, for
the taking of exiles from the land, and for the
devastation of our inheritance, he will lay the guilt
on our heads. Wherever we shall be enslaved

8, 11: (*ean mē*) *meta pente ʿēmeras:* so 1 LXX[MS], Vet Lat, P; cf V.

NRSV

"Listen to me, rulers of the people of Bethulia!
What you have said to the people today is not
right; you have even sworn and pronounced this
oath between God and you, promising to surrender the town to our enemies unless the Lord turns
and helps us within so many days. 12Who are you
to put God to the test today, and to set yourselves
up in the place of[a] God in human affairs? 13You
are putting the Lord Almighty to the test, but you
will never learn anything! 14You cannot plumb the
depths of the human heart or understand the
workings of the human mind; how do you expect
to search out God, who made all these things,
and find out his mind or comprehend his thought?
No, my brothers, do not anger the Lord our God.
15For if he does not choose to help us within these
five days, he has power to protect us within any
time he pleases, or even to destroy us in the
presence of our enemies. 16Do not try to bind the
purposes of the Lord our God; for God is not like
a human being, to be threatened, or like a mere
mortal, to be won over by pleading. 17Therefore,
while we wait for his deliverance, let us call upon
him to help us, and he will hear our voice, if it
pleases him.

18"For never in our generation, nor in these
present days, has there been any tribe or family
or people or town of ours that worships gods made
with hands, as was done in days gone by. 19That
was why our ancestors were handed over to the
sword and to pillage, and so they suffered a great
catastrophe before our enemies. 20But we know
no other god but him, and so we hope that he
will not disdain us or any of our nation. 21For if
we are captured, all Judea will be captured and
our sanctuary will be plundered; and he will make
us pay for its desecration with our blood. 22The
slaughter of our kindred and the captivity of the
land and the desolation of our inheritance—all
this he will bring on our heads among the Gentiles, wherever we serve as slaves; and we shall
be an offense and a disgrace in the eyes of those
who acquire us. 23For our slavery will not bring
us into favor, but the Lord our God will turn it
to dishonor.

24"Therefore, my brothers, let us set an example for our kindred, for their lives depend upon

[a] Or *above*

NAB

among the nations, we shall be a mockery and a
reproach in the eyes of our masters. 23 Our
enslavement will not be turned to our benefit, but
the LORD our God will maintain it to our disgrace.

24 "Therefore, my brothers, let us set an example for our kinsmen. Their lives depend on us,
and the defense of the sanctuary, the temple, and
the altar rests with us. 25 Besides all this, we
should be grateful to the LORD our God, for putting
us to the test, as he did our forefathers. 26 Recall
how he dealt with Abraham, and how he tried
Isaac, and all that happened to Jacob in Syrian
Mesopotamia while he was tending the flocks of
Laban, his mother's brother. 27 Not for vengeance
did the LORD put them in the crucible to try their
hearts, nor has he done so with us. It is by way
of admonition that he chastises those who are
close to him."

28 Then Uzziah said to her: "All that you have
said was spoken with good sense, and no one can
gainsay your words. 29 Not today only is your
wisdom made evident, but from your earliest
years all the people have recognized your pru-
dence, which corresponds to the worthy disposi-
tions of your heart. 30 The people, however, were
so tortured with thirst that they forced us to speak
to them as we did, and to bind ourselves by an
oath that we cannot break. 31 But now, God-fearing woman that you are, pray for us that the LORD
may send rain to fill up our cisterns, lest we be
weakened still further."

32 Then Judith said to them: "Listen to me! I
will do something that will go down from generation to generation among the descendants of
our race. 33 Stand at the gate tonight to let me
pass through with my maid; and within the days
you have specified before you will surrender the
city to our enemies, the LORD will rescue Israel
by my hand. 34 You must not inquire into what
I am doing, for I will not tell you until my plan
has been accomplished." 35 Uzziah and the rulers
said to her, "Go in peace, and may the LORD God
go before you to take vengeance upon our enemies!" 36 Then they withdrew from the tent and
returned to their posts.

NRSV

us, and the sanctuary—both the temple and the
altar—rests upon us. 25In spite of everything let
us give thanks to the Lord our God, who is putting
us to the test as he did our ancestors. 26Remember
what he did with Abraham, and how he tested
Isaac, and what happened to Jacob in Syrian
Mesopotamia, while he was tending the sheep of
Laban, his mother's brother. 27For he has not tried
us with fire, as he did them, to search their hearts,
nor has he taken vengeance on us; but the Lord
scourges those who are close to him in order to
admonish them."

28Then Uzziah said to her, "All that you have
said was spoken out of a true heart, and there is
no one who can deny your words. 29Today is not
the first time your wisdom has been shown, but
from the beginning of your life all the people have
recognized your understanding, for your heart's
disposition is right. 30But the people were so
thirsty that they compelled us to do for them what
we have promised, and made us take an oath that
we cannot break. 31Now since you are a God-fearing woman, pray for us, so that the Lord may
send us rain to fill our cisterns. Then we will no
longer feel faint from thirst."

32Then Judith said to them, "Listen to me. I
am about to do something that will go down
through all generations of our descendants.
33Stand at the town gate tonight so that I may go
out with my maid; and within the days after
which you have promised to surrender the town
to our enemies, the Lord will deliver Israel by my
hand. 34Only, do not try to find out what I am
doing; for I will not tell you until I have finished
what I am about to do."

35Uzziah and the rulers said to her, "Go in
peace, and may the Lord God go before you, to
take vengeance on our enemies." 36So they returned from the tent and went to their posts.

COMMENTARY

8:9-20. The news of the town meeting comes to Judith while she is in seclusion. Judith does not simply appear or emerge from her tent ready to do battle. Presumably, out of modesty she does not come out of her home to meet the magistrates, even though it is a time of crisis. Soon her actions will be quite different, but at this point she sends her favorite slave. This woman will figure prominently in the unfolding narrative (see 10:2). Judith immediately proceeds to upbraid the magistrates. Just as Holofernes had addressed his war councils in the first part of the story, so also she addresses the elders of Bethulia. This underscores the fact that a significant amount of the second part will be taken up with dialogue as well. She makes several points in addressing them. Her first charge is that it was wrong to test God by imposing a time limit within which to act. If the human realm is impossible to comprehend, she reasons, how can people fathom God's actions? God is free to come to their aid at any point—if God so chooses. There is a close Greek parallel to this motif, the Lindus chronicle, in which the Greek city of Lindus, besieged by Darius of Persia, prays to Athena to bring rain within five days. Rain does come, and Darius realizes that Lindus enjoys divine protection and passes it by. This is clearly intended to be a positive assessment of the city's prayer. The author of Judith has taken this tradition and challenged it: Fervent prayer is not sufficient before God, but a strict humility before God's decrees is called for. It is often thought that this is one of the key theological ideas in Judith, but it is not clear whether the author is really concerned about this theologically or whether it is more of a narrative device. It characterizes Judith as a more valiant soldier of virtue than the other citizens of Bethulia. The testing of God here is not as serious a case as the creation of a golden calf while Moses was on Mt. Sinai (Exodus 32) or the complaints of the people in the wilderness during the exodus (Exodus 15–17; Numbers 11; see Commentary on 7:23-28). It could also be said to have been caused by more extreme conditions. Still, Judith does not entertain any pleas of mitigating circumstances (v. 30).

Her next point is sometimes missed in a quick reading of her speech. Having noted that God is free to choose, Judith asserts that the residents of Bethulia can yet be confident that God will come to their aid because there is no longer anyone among them who worships idols. For Judith this is the criterion of the deuteronomic theology by which God grants either favor or punishment. How is she so sure that the worship of idols has been removed from the land? At the time of the composition of Judith the Hasmonean kings had succeeded in pacifying the land and, more important, had destroyed the Samaritan temple on Mt. Gerizim, expanded the borders to approximately the size of the united Israel under David and Solomon, and converted by force peoples such as the Idumeans. The author must have seen the Hasmonean settlement of the country as the successful expulsion of idol worship.

8:21-23. If God chooses not to help, the stakes are very high: Bethulia is the only fortified town standing between the Assyrians and their entry into Judea. If idol worship has been eradicated from the land, Judith reasons, it is difficult to imagine God allowing the devastation of Judea—and the devastation and servitude will this time be permanent, not as before in Egypt or in the exile. Presumably, two related views are being emphasized simultaneously: Although God operates with a free will that cannot be tested or limited, God shows favor to those who remain faithful. The devastation that would result from an Assyrian invasion is not described in terms of human suffering as it is elsewhere, but in terms of the resulting shame: The Temple will be desecrated, and the Israelites will become an offense and a disgrace serving as slaves among the Gentiles. This time the slavery will have no salvific resolution as it did in Egypt, followed by the exodus, or in the exile, followed by the restoration. This time it will be permanent and will result in utter dishonor and shame (see Commentary on 1:11-12).

8:24-27. Judith turns from indicative to imperative. God's rescue of the people Israel does not come about on its own; the citizens of Bethulia must act. Judith provides a compelling theological understanding of the Bethulians' situation: They should not put God to the test; rather, God is "testing" them (the same Greek word [πειράζω *peirazō*] is used in both cases), just as God tested Abraham, Isaac, and Jacob, the three patriarchs. There are many tests that could be associated with Abraham, Isaac, and Jacob, the greatest of which would be God's demand that Abraham sacrifice Isaac (Genesis 22), but the reference may be to the collective endurance of the three major patriarchs (cf. Heb 11:8-21). In this text, a specific example is given regarding only Jacob—that is, his sojourn to Paddan-aram ("Syrian Mesopotamia") to find a wife from among the daughters of Laban (Genesis 28–31). Whereas the people had decided that God was punishing them for their sins (7:28), or simply abandoning them (7:30), Judith insists that God is testing their mettle. These views are found in other texts that the Bethulians might have drawn on. That God punishes the Jews for their sins was the basis of the deuteronomic theology, even if, as Second Isaiah and Jeremiah insisted, the punishment was only temporary. A similar view was expressed in Judith's day in 2 Macc 5:17-20. However, God's teaching and discipline are also found in early biblical traditions (Deut 8:5; Ps 94:12; Prov 3:11-12), but became much more strongly emphasized after the exile, and especially in the period contemporary with Judith (Sir 6:18-22; 1 Cor 11:32; 2 Cor 6:9; Heb 12:5-11; Jas 1:2-4; *1 Clement* 56). God's testing is often compared to teaching and discipline: "God is found by those who do not put him to the test, and manifests himself to those who do not distrust him. . . . When his power is tested, it exposes the foolish" (Wis 1:2-3). And "Having been disciplined a little, the righteous will receive great good, because God tested them and found them worthy of himself" (3:5; see also Sir 2:1-6). Thus the patriarchs are like the righteous: tested and found worthy of God.

8:28-29. The wisdom of Judith and the approval of her character by everyone are emphasized. Still, there are questions about the precise nature of her wisdom. On the one hand, while she is on her estate she is like the capable wife of Proverbs 31, but on the other hand, when she proceeds out to engage Holofernes, she is not. One must, therefore, distinguish clearly between "wisdom" and "cleverness."[87] Jacob, for example, was clever, even a "trickster," in his dealings with others, but never is he described as wise. Joseph, on the other hand, is described as "discreet and wise" (Gen 41:39); he can interpret dreams and knows enough to retreat from the advances of Potiphar's wife (Genesis 39–41). Other figures in the HB tend to fall into one paradigm or the other—that is, wisdom as piety or wisdom as cleverness. There are wise women in the HB who are clever, such as the wise woman of Tekoa (2 Sam 14:1-7) and the wise woman of Abel (2 Sam 20:14-22). On the other hand, Daniel is wise and pious (Dan 1:20; 4:15; 5:11-16). Judith seems to combine the two paradigms; she is wise and righteous, like Joseph, but she is very clever in dealing with evil and uses deceit as one of her best weapons, like Jacob. She is a trickster, but not for her own ends; unlike Jacob, she is a trickster in the service of others.

8:30-36. Uzziah wants Judith to pray for the people because she is a redeemer for them, a mediator between the people and God. Moses was earlier considered a mediator figure, as were the prophets at times; this was probably the original meaning of Deut 18:15-18. Even a woman could be so depicted: Deborah and Jael team up to deliver Israel in a narrative that has greatly influenced the author of Judith (see Introduction). Uzziah wants Judith to pray for rain to relieve their thirst and allow them to hold out longer; it does not occur to him at this point that Judith is capable of removing the threat of Holofernes altogether (but note v. 35). Judith, however, has bigger plans than bringing rain. She instructs Uzziah to stand by, but informs him that she means to deliver Israel by her hand. Judith will not divulge her plan, but she does prepare the reader for the heroic importance of her deed "for endless generations" and that it will be a memorial to her, as the conclusion implies (16:21-25). She speaks with a conviction and authority that does not allow for second-guessing. Uzziah responds accordingly by endorsing her command, but he is taking his strength from her, more so than was the case of Barak and Deborah (Judges 4–5).

87. Susan Niditch, *Underdogs and Tricksters: A Prologue to Biblical Folklore* (San Francisco: Harper & Row, 1987) 93-125; Lawrence M. Wills, *The Jew in the Court of the Foreign King: Ancient Jewish Court Legends* (Minneapolis: Fortress, 1990) 23-38.

Uzziah is pliant with Judith as he was with the people of Bethulia. He admits that the people forced him to make an oath that will test God. His excuse is similar to that of Aaron after the making of the golden calf (Exod 32:22). The oath is presumably inviolable because it was a solemn vow to God (7:28), but in folktales and traditional literature the inviolability of an oath is often also an important narrative device that forces the actions of the protagonists (see Josh 9:19-20; Judges 11; Esth 1:19; 8:8; Dan 6:8, 12). Here, rather than demanding that the magistrates rescind the oath, Judith presumes its inviolability and must work quickly to save the Bethulians before the five days are up. The tension of the story is thus maintained, as she must operate with a ticking clock in the background.

REFLECTIONS

The Bethulians, including their leader Uzziah, are prepared to capitulate if God does not intervene within a set time. The urgent petitions of the Israelites in Jerusalem were earlier said to be heard by God (4:13), but the Bethulians remain in doubt. Although Judith rebukes them for testing God, is she being too demanding? Are we to experience the outrage that Judith feels toward the weakness of the Bethulians, or should we be sympathetic toward these decent and ordinarily pious people who have been placed in an extreme situation? The catastrophe that apparently awaited them would probably give pause to most people and likewise force them to consider surrendering as the other nations had done. Judith is not gentle in response to their actions, however, since to her mind they tested God much as the Israelites had murmured against Moses in the wilderness wanderings.

Perhaps both here and in the exodus narrative the modern reader experiences some of the doubt that is in the hearts of the Israelites. The reader knows how the two stories will end, but can also imagine not having the courage of Moses or Judith. Real human beings rarely exhibit perfect courage or certainty. These writings seem to recognize that, for at the same time that such scenes exhort the readers to greater courage, they also allow us to experience doubt in a situation where we know all will end well. Although some of Judith's cocksureness may seem less than humble to modern readers, the book of Judith explores the issue of courage and trust from three different perspectives. First, Judith expresses absolute trust. In upbraiding the Bethulians, she argues that they should leave their fate in God's hands: "Let us call upon him to help us, and he will hear our voice, if it pleases him" (8:17). The Israelites in Jerusalem also turn to the Lord in prayer and fasting, and their plea is so urgent that they even put sackcloth on their cattle—a comic touch, but surely one that reflects their sincerity. Where there are heartfelt pleas among the Israelites, God responds (4:13). Even the Ammonite Achior seems to get it when it comes to Israelite history: "As long as they did not sin against their god they prospered. . . . Their Lord and God will defend them" (5:17, 21).

Trust in God is the operative mode for Judith, for the Israelites in Jerusalem, and even for Achior, but not for the Bethulians, whose perspective exhibits the second kind of trust, which is imperfect. Their resilience had a limit, and they transfer their anxieties onto God by setting a time limit within which to act.

And if the Bethulians are to be the "sympathetic sinners" in the text—those whom we cannot really condemn just for being human—there is another group whose capitulation is not sympathetic and who display a third level of trust. The "people who lived along the seacoast" (2:28) not only succumb to their fears, with none of the tension or soul-searching that the Bethulians exhibit, but also demonstrate that they have readily abandoned their gods and dance before Holofernes with garlands and tambourines (3:1-8). Surely this is the opposite of trust in their gods; their allegiance was so ephemeral that they could watch their gods be destroyed, accept Nebuchadnezzar as their new "deity," and celebrate the transformation.

It is not necessary, then, to say that we should be like Judith. We are probably more like the Bethulians, and will remain so. But the text invites us to see three levels of trust and to embrace a life that is oriented toward a sincere trust in God. While Judith's position in regard to the Bethulians may seem overly strict, it is the larger theme of trust in God to which the book ultimately points.

Modern North American readers will probably never be trapped under siege in a mountain village as a general and his mighty army choke off all hope, but the text serves to affirm the need of trust in God in seemingly impossible situations. And those will occur. Whether someone tests God or offers a prayer that imposes a time limit on God is not important; that is probably not as serious as Judith makes it out to be. But in the text her strong reaction serves to put the theme of trust—sincere trust—into sharper relief.

Judith 9:1-14, Judith Purifies Herself and Prays

NAB

9 1 Judith threw herself down prostrate,
with ashes strewn upon her head, and
wearing nothing over her sackcloth. While the
incense was being offered in the temple of God
in Jerusalem that evening, Judith prayed to the
LORD with a loud voice: 2 "LORD, God of my
forefather Simeon! You put a sword into his hand
to take revenge upon the foreigners who had
immodestly loosened the maiden's girdle, shame-
fully exposed her thighs, and disgracefully violated
her body. This they did, though you forbade it. 3
Therefore you had their rulers slaughtered; and
you covered with their blood the bed in which
they lay deceived, the same bed that had felt the
shame of their own deceiving. You smote the
slaves together with their princes, and the princes
together with their servants. 4 Their wives you
handed over to plunder, and their daughters to
captivity; and all the spoils you divided among
your favored sons, who burned with zeal for you,
and in their abhorrence of the defilement of their
kinswoman, called on you for help.

5 "O God, my God, hear me also, a widow. It
is you who were the author of those events and
of what preceded and followed them. The present,
also, and the future you have planned. Whatever
you devise comes into being; 6 the things you
decide on come forward and say, "Here we are!'
All your ways are in readiness, and your judgment
is made with foreknowledge.

7 "Here are the Assyrians, a vast force, priding

9, 2: (*'oi elysan*) *mitran* (*parthenou*): conj; iotacism; cf *mētran* at end of v.

9, 3: (*kai dynastas epi*) *therapousin* (*autōn*): conj., cf v 10.

NRSV

9 Then Judith prostrated herself, put ashes
on her head, and uncovered the sackcloth
she was wearing. At the very time when the
evening incense was being offered in the house
of God in Jerusalem, Judith cried out to the Lord
with a loud voice, and said,

2"O Lord God of my ancestor Simeon, to
whom you gave a sword to take revenge on those
strangers who had torn off a virgin's clothing[a] to
defile her, and exposed her thighs to put her to
shame, and polluted her womb to disgrace her;
for you said, 'It shall not be done'—yet they did
it; 3so you gave up their rulers to be killed, and
their bed, which was ashamed of the deceit they
had practiced, was stained with blood, and you
struck down slaves along with princes, and
princes on their thrones. 4You gave up their wives
for booty and their daughters to captivity, and all
their booty to be divided among your beloved
children who burned with zeal for you and ab-
horred the pollution of their blood and called on
you for help—O God, my God, hear me also—
a widow.

5"For you have done these things and those
that went before and those that followed. You
have designed the things that are now, and those
that are to come. What you had in mind has
happened; 6the things you decided on presented
themselves and said, 'Here we are!' For all your
ways are prepared in advance, and your judgment
is with foreknowledge.

7"Here now are the Assyrians, a greatly in-

[a] Cn: Gk *loosed her womb*

NAB

themselves on horse and rider, boasting of the
power of their infantry, trusting in shield and
spear, bow and sling. They do not know that

8 " 'You, the LORD, crush warfare;
Lord is your name.'

"Shatter their strength in your might, and crush
their force in your wrath; for they have resolved
to profane your sanctuary, to defile the tent where
your glorious name resides, and to overthrow with
iron the horns of your altar. 9 See their pride,
and send forth your wrath upon their heads. Give
me, a widow, the strong hand to execute my plan.
10 With the guile of my lips, smite the slave
together with the ruler, the ruler together with
his servant; crush their pride by the hand of a
woman.

11 "Your strength is not in numbers, nor does
your power depend upon stalwart men; but you
are the God of the lowly, the helper of the
oppressed, the supporter of the weak, the protector of the forsaken, the savior of those without
hope.

12 "Please, please, God of my forefather, God
of the heritage of Israel, LORD of heaven and earth,
Creator of the waters, King of all you have created, hear my prayer! 13 Let my guileful speech
bring wound and wale on those who have
planned dire things against your covenant, your
holy temple, Mount Zion, and the homes your
children have inherited. 14 Let your whole nation
and all the tribes know clearly that you are the
God of all power and might, and that there is no
other who protects the people of Israel but you
alone."

9, 14: (*kai epi pan to ethnos sou kai*) *pasas phylas.*

NRSV

creased force, priding themselves in their horses
and riders, boasting in the strength of their foot
soldiers, and trusting in shield and spear, in bow
and sling. They do not know that you are the
Lord who crushes wars; the Lord is your name.
8Break their strength by your might, and bring
down their power in your anger; for they intend
to defile your sanctuary, and to pollute the tabernacle where your glorious name resides, and to
break off the horns[a] of your altar with the sword.
9Look at their pride, and send your wrath upon
their heads. Give to me, a widow, the strong hand
to do what I plan. 10By the deceit of my lips strike
down the slave with the prince and the prince
with his servant; crush their arrogance by the
hand of a woman.

11"For your strength does not depend on numbers, nor your might on the powerful. But you
are the God of the lowly, helper of the oppressed,
upholder of the weak, protector of the forsaken,
savior of those without hope. 12Please, please, God
of my father, God of the heritage of Israel, Lord
of heaven and earth, Creator of the waters, King
of all your creation, hear my prayer! 13Make my
deceitful words bring wound and bruise on those
who have planned cruel things against your covenant, and against your sacred house, and against
Mount Zion, and against the house your children
possess. 14Let your whole nation and every tribe
know and understand that you are God, the God
of all power and might, and that there is no other
who protects the people of Israel but you alone!"

[a] Syr: Gk *horn*

COMMENTARY

The Jewish novels of this period each have scenes that focus on the prayers and interior thoughts of a significant female character. Susanna has a moment of decision in which she must choose whether to capitulate to the demands of the wicked elders to lie with them or to preserve her virtue, even at the risk of being wrongly convicted and put to death for adultery. The young Sarah in the book of Tobit laments her continuing ill fortune that seven of her fiancés have died on their wedding night, and prays for death. Esther in the Additions confesses to God her repugnance at the situation she finds herself in, and Aseneth in *Joseph and Aseneth* enters into a state of penitence and prayer that lasts for seven days. Similarly Judith has her scene of ritual preparation and prayer. All of these novels have in common the focus on the woman's experience of reflection and decision, but three of them, Additions to Esther, *Joseph and Aseneth,* and Judith, have developed a type scene that is much more dramatic and formulaic.[88] It is presented as a marked transition that is similar to what anthropologists call a "rite of passage" (see Introduction). Arnold van Gennep and Victor Turner divide rituals that mark important human transitions into three distinct stages: separation, liminal period, and incorporation or aggregation. The separation is the marked movement from normal or mundane time and space to the liminal period, a special status that is more in touch with the divine. It is sacred time and space, not marked by the usual everyday indications of time, space, social order, gender, and so on. Last comes incorporation, in which the person moves back into mundane time and space, often with a new status or changed disposition. In Judith each part is marked by clear outward indicators of role or status: The woman begins in the clothing of wealth and position; takes off these clothes (separation); clothes herself in the garments of mourning, which eliminate the indicators of social or gender roles; and begins to pray; then she bathes and reclothes herself in new garments similar to the old, but even more splendid (incorporation).[89] When Judith emerges from her ritualized prayer and reclothes herself, her actions are also very similar to those of Esther and Aseneth. At Add. Esth 15:1 we read, "On the third day, when she had ended her prayer, she took off the garments in which she had worshiped, and arrayed herself in splendid attire." This same scene is found in other Jewish novels and is sometimes greatly expanded, as in *Joseph and Aseneth,* where the heroine repents of her idolatry by covering herself in ashes mixed with her tears for seven days. Men are sometimes also depicted engaging in the rituals of mourning or protest, as Mordecai does in Esther 4, but the woman's scene of grief and self-abasement is more heartrending and penitential. This rite works perfectly to demarcate in narrative form the process of penitence, and it was likely well established in the literary tradition of Judaism (Neh 9:1). Even if the other known Jewish novels were composed later than Judith, there was still a developing penitential novelistic tradition of which Judith was one part, evidenced also by the insertion of the Prayer of Azariah and Susanna into the book of Daniel.

9:1. Judith begins here by prostrating herself, putting ashes on her head, and uncovering the sackcloth that she is presumably wearing under her widow's garments (see 8:5). This seems strange as a mourning custom, but she is presumably exposing her true state of pious self-abnegation—that is, the customs of mourning have become a form of ascetic spirituality. Sackcloth was a coarse, dark cloth woven from the hair of goats and camels. Turner notes that in the liminal state the person undergoing a rite of passage is often colored dark in some way, which is identified with the earth, and is allowed to become filthy.[90] We are reminded that the mourning ritual, which was a marked rite of passage in Israel, included, in addition to the wearing of sackcloth, the covering of the head in ashes, and in Add. Esth 14:2 with dung. Thus the usual ritual of mourning in Israel seemed to include that aspect of liminal symbolism that Turner suggests represents a dissolution of normal distinctions and an identification with undifferentiated earth.

Sackcloth and ashes are symbols of the grief of mourning, which Judith is exhibiting here to enter into a state of purification and prayer. Compare the parallel moment in Additions to Esther:

> Then Queen Esther, seized with deadly anxiety, fled to the Lord. She took off her splendid apparel and put on the garments of distress and mourning, and instead of costly perfumes she covered her head with ashes and dung, and she utterly humbled her body; every part that she loved to adorn she covered with her tangled hair. (Add. Esth 14:1-2 NRSV)

Esther then proceeds to a deeply felt prayer and is penitent over her sin and the sin of her people. Judith, however, is not penitent. She never mentions her own sin, nor in her prayer does she mention the sin of her fellow Israelites—that comes up only in her upbraiding of the elders and

88. Lawrence M. Wills, *The Jewish Novel in the Ancient World* (Ithaca: Cornell University Press, 1995) 224-32; Alice Bach, *Women, Seduction, and Betrayal in Biblical Narrative* (New York: Cambridge University Press, 1997) 201-3.

89. Arnold van Gennep, *The Rites of Passage* (Chicago: University of Chicago Press, 1960); Victor Turner, "Betwixt and Between: The Liminal Period in Rites de Passage," in *The Forest of Symbols: Aspects of Ndembu Ritual* (Ithaca: Cornell University Press, 1967) 93-111.

90. Turner, "Betwixt and Between," 96, 107.

in her lie to Holofernes. Judith does not have a rending self-examination as Esther and Aseneth do, but like them she has crossed the threshold into the liminal state of a profound ritual, where she can meet God more directly. Her ritual has prepared her for a relationship with God that is more direct than is the case for the other Bethulians. As a result, what we seem to have in Judith is a merging of two quite different narrative paradigms: the male hero pattern and the pattern of the penitential Jewish woman. The latter is drained of its original content and pressed into the service of a new theme where it works quite well: The beautiful woman of Israel, like a warrior, readies herself for the quest by stripping away her old garments, praying, bathing, and reclothing herself in the special armor that she is called upon to wear: beguiling clothes, jewelry, and cosmetics.

The timing of her prayer is quite significant, coinciding as it does with the evening incense offering in the Temple in Jerusalem (Exod 30:7-8). We may note by comparison that in John 19:14 it is stated that Jesus' crucifixion occurred at the same moment that the Passover lambs were slaughtered in the Temple. This aligns Judith's practices with those in the Temple, although her actions, even those up to this point, have not been strictly orthodox (her lack of a levirate marriage, her mourning beyond the period required by law). This seems to point to a contradiction in her observance of Jewish law, but this was probably not a difficulty for the ancient reader of the book of Judith. It is not presumed by the audience that this is a normal practice for Jews; rather, in the narrative world of this book the protagonist follows the dictates of her heartfelt piety and is not bound by the ordinary codes of conduct. It is actually in the nature of the Jewish and Christian novels for the protagonists to engage the spirit of the law without always conforming to the letter. Thecla, for instance, in the early Christian *Acts of Paul and Thecla* (34), actually baptizes herself because she thinks she is about to die.

9:2-10. Although Judith's genealogy at 8:1 did not explicitly mention Simeon (except in some ancient MSS), here she makes explicit what was implied there (see Commentary on 8:1): She is descended from Simeon, one of the twelve sons of Jacob and ancestor of the tribe of Simeon. She takes up the most important story associated with Simeon, his revenge on Shechem for the rape of his sister Dinah (Genesis 34). Just as Mattathias, the father of the Maccabee brothers, is likened to Phineas because of the latter's zeal for executing idolaters (Num 25:6-15), so also Judith takes up the cause of a patriarchal avenger. Simeon and his brothers, outraged after Shechem raped their sister Dinah, deceitfully agreed that he could marry her on condition that all the males of Shechem's clan be circumcised. They consented, but while they were still sore, Simeon and Levi came upon them unawares, killed all the males, and took Dinah back with them. The other sons of Jacob then plundered the city, took women and children and livestock, and returned to Jacob. In Gen 34:30 and 49:5-7 Jacob condemns the violent spirit of Simeon and Levi because it will create trouble with the peoples of the land. Judith, however, adopts Simeon as a positive model. She takes up the same cause as Simeon's (v. 4) and sets out a plan of revenge that will be modeled on his. In Judith's view, God orchestrated Simeon's revenge out of a shared sense of outrage. The description of the revenge is gruesome: the slaughter of the males, the taking of the women and enslavement of the daughters, the plundering of the spoils—all this in Judith's view is a justified response for the rape of Dinah.

The violence is not really different from the Genesis account of the slaughter by the sons of Jacob, but here it is all God's doing (v. 5). To be sure, Judith was not the only ancient source to take a positive view of the revenge on Shechem. *Jubilees* 30 and *Testament of Levi* affirm the role of Simeon and Levi, and *Joseph and Aseneth* 23 notes Simeon's violent spirit without condemning it. God's action against the Shechemites thus is not considered by the author of Judith to be a brazen and reckless act on the part of Simeon as it is in Genesis, but part of God's judgment on Shechem for the rape of Dinah. God was acting as "redeemer" (גֹּאֵל *gō'ēl*) through Simeon; God struck down "slaves along with princes," which, along with v. 10, seems to be an echo of God's judgment in Isa 24:2. Judith's belief that it is God's doing appears to be based on the assumption that God wills all actions and events. The very fact that it happened indicates that God orchestrated it; wisdom texts sometimes express a similar opinion concerning natural phenomena

(Job 38:35; Bar 3:34) and, in a general way, historical events (Wisdom 10–19).

Judith emphasizes that unlike the warriors Simeon and Levi, revenge in this case is left in the hands of a widow (v. 4). She returns to this theme in v. 9, and in v. 10 entreats God to destroy Holofernes and his army by the hand of a female. Judith here picks up another motif from the book of Judges, for at Judg 9:53 Abimelech is shamed because he is mortally wounded by a woman and is later known for this (2 Sam 11:21). In a world conscious of honor and shame, for a warrior to be killed by a woman was a great shame.

According to Judith, the rape of Dinah was a pollution of "their blood" (vv. 2, 4), and the point of this emphasis is well taken: The Assyrians intend to defile and pollute the sanctuary in Jerusalem. There is a clear parallelism and contrast, with the implication that Assyria is "raping" Jerusalem. This is perhaps not an unusual metaphor for conquest, but the book of Judith draws it out in specific ways. Looking back, the Assyrian rape of Jerusalem is like Shechem's rape of Dinah; and looking forward, the Assyrians will knock the horns off the altar with their swords (v. 8), just as Judith will decapitate Holofernes. By the parallel Judith draws, she is developing the notion that she will be the *gō'ēl* of Jerusalem, the raped woman. In ancient Israel, the *gō'ēl* was the male family member whose responsibility it was to avenge an attack on any other family member. In the patriarchal period of clans, tribes, and extended families, it was accepted that the "avenger of blood" (גאל הדם *gō'ēl haddām*) would achieve justice for wronged parties; but this function was also regulated and contained by the safeguard of "cities of refuge," into which the avenger of blood could not go to attack the perpetrator of the offense (Num 35:19; Deut 19:6). The concept of *gō'ēl* stands behind the revenge on Shechem, and it stands behind Judith as well as does a concept of extended-family solidarity: "Not only members of a clan, but also their possessions, form an organic unity, and every disruption of this unity is regarded as intolerable and as something which must be restored or repaired."[91] The king can be a *gō'ēl* of the poor who are oppressed (Ps 72:14), and God can act as a *gō'ēl* as well (Jer 50:34). Judith here presents herself to God as the only available *gō'ēl* (although this word or its equivalent is not used), all the men having fallen away.

Judith, in vv. 6*b*-8*a*, quotes a line that is evidently from the Greek translation of Exod 15:3, part of Moses' Song of the Sea, which he sang after the death of Pharaoh and his armies. She takes up this line again in her victory song at 16:2. Several terms in v. 11 ("helper," "protector," "savior") are also influenced by the Song of the Sea (Exod 15:2), where they occur in the same order.[92]

Judith intimates to God—and to the audience—what her weapon of choice will be: "the deceit of my lips." Deceit is not an expedient that she falls back on as a last resort when she is in Holofernes' presence, but the very basis of her plan from the beginning. It is a weapon of power that will allow God, through her, to strike down "slaves along with princes, and princes on their thrones" (v. 3). The power of deceit was recognized in wisdom teachings roughly contemporary with Judith (see Jas 3:5-12; cf. Wis 1:8; Matt 12:36-37), but it is usually viewed by the pious as unequivocally negative. Judith clearly intends to use the weapon for good, but in the liminal state of this novel, she is clearly reversing the accepted standards of Jewish ethics.

9:11-14. Judith here takes up the language of humility. The positive valuation of the humble is unusual, though not unknown, in Greek and Roman culture. The *Life of Aesop,* a Greek novel roughly contemporary with Judith, champions Aesop as a humble satirist of the wealthy, a role for him that was generally recognized in Greek culture. Aesop was one of the seven sages, but he had to sit on a footstool. Diogenes Laertius notes that when Chilo asked Aesop what Zeus was doing, Aesop answered, "He is lowering what is high, and exalting what is low."[93] Still, humility in Greek and Roman culture remained more of a novelty than a central theological value. In Jewish culture, it is a common theme in the psalms: "For you deliver a humble people, but the haughty eyes you bring down" (Ps 18:27 NRSV; see also Pss 10:18; 138:6; 146:7-9). It is also present in the

91. Helmer Ringgren, *TDOT,* 2:351.

92. Carey A. Moore, *Judith,* AB 40 (Garden City, N.Y.: Doubleday, 1985) 192.

93. *Lives,* Chilo 2.

Magnificat of Mary in Luke 1:46-55 and its model, the Song of Hannah in 1 Sam 2:1-10. It is from v. 11, and from her remark on her low status as a woman and a widow, that some have found a theology of humility in the book of Judith.[94] There are, however, problems with this judgment. This prayer shows proper piety on Judith's part, but if the book was written during the expansion of the Hasmonean rulers, the humility may ring somewhat hollow. Granted, this may be confusing the author's situation and that of the fictional character Judith, who lived, after all, in a situation of persecution; but the piety of humility does not seem as genuine in one so triumphalistic. The talented author of Judith is probably not attempting to create a humble heroine or articulate a theology of humility. Judith is merely being characterized as the perfect heroine; the humble Jewish widow is capable of decapitating the mighty Assyrian general. As Moore says in regard to this question, "If most, or at least many, of the important ideas of Judaism exist in Judith, that is all they really do, that is, they do not seem alive and vibrant."[95]

94. Brian McNeil, "Reflections on the Book of Judith," *Downside Review* 96 (1978) 200.

95. Moore, *Judith,* 195.

REFLECTIONS

The book of Judith has remained popular over the centuries, perhaps more popular in the pre-modern period than in the modern. For Jews, Judith was a military heroine associated with Hanukkah, but for Christians she often represented virtues, especially penitence. Chartres Cathedral depicts her as she was often known, as putting ashes on her head. Although Judith's penitential actions are dramatically displayed, she seems unaware of any sins she might have commited. She could be characterized as what Stendahl has called a "robust conscience."[96]

The tendency in Judaism of this period and in early Christianity was to "raise the stakes" of sin. Sin was a more pressing part of religious life; it could keep one from approaching God with a pure heart, and it could separate one group or "sect" of Jews or Christians from another. The washings that Judith practices are not unrelated to the baptism Christians have instituted "for the forgiveness of sins" (Mark 1:4). But is Judith being hypocritical in taking up the practices of penitence without the self-examination? People sometimes conceive of their sin as the individual transgressions of daily life, or in terms of the larger picture of a doctrine of sin that defines the individual in relation to God. It is often difficult to reconcile the consciousness of everyday sins with theological beliefs about the origin and nature of sin. The book of Judith at first seems not to be much help here, because it shows Judith as far removed from her fellow citizens, who display human weakness and sin before God. But the book of Judith portrays a kind of spirituality, arising just before the beginnings of Christianity, that emphasized the cleansing from sin as a prelude to turning to God in prayer. This "penitential theology" has been a form of spirituality for those who might themselves be considered far from sin, the penitence of the righteous. The practices Judith undertakes are thus not intended simply to cleanse her from sinful acts; they are a form of worship in which one can approach God. Perhaps she is not being hypocritical, but is simply "at home" in this form of prayer. Sin, and the response to sin, becomes a way of defining the relationship of the human to God.

A central pastoral concern today, however, is to address the problem of sin in such a way as to recognize the different reactions of parishioners. Some feel comfortable with a doctrine of sin that defines the person as sinful before God or with a penitential spirituality that is conducive to this worship experience, while a fascination or obsession with sin can for others mask psychological problems of guilt, shame, and even unresolved conflicts from the past. The

96. Krister Stendahl, "The Apostle Paul and the Introspective Conscience of the West," *HTR* 56 (1963) 199-215, reprinted in his *Paul Among Jews and Gentiles* (Philadelphia: Fortress, 1976) 78-96.

book of Judith presents the "comfortable" model of penitential spirituality of her period, but it does not address this second problem, which is for the modern reader often the harder question.

Judith 10:1-10, Judith Emerges from Prayer to Go Forth

NAB

10 1 As soon as Judith had thus concluded, and ceased her invocation to the God of Israel, 2 she rose from the ground. She called her maid and they went down into the house, which she used only on sabbaths and feast days. 3 She took off the sackcloth she had on, laid aside the garments of her widowhood, washed her body with water, and anointed it with rich ointment. She arranged her hair and bound it with a fillet, and put on the festive attire she had worn while her husband, Manasseh, was living. 4 She chose sandals for her feet, and put on her anklets, bracelets, rings, earrings, and all her other jewelry. Thus she made herself very beautiful, to captivate the eyes of all the men who should see her.

5 She gave her maid a leather flask of wine and a cruse of oil. She filled a bag with roasted grain, fig cakes, bread and cheese; all these provisions she wrapped up and gave to the maid to carry.

6 Then they went out to the gate of the city of Bethulia and found Uzziah and the elders of the city, Chabris and Charmis, standing there. 7 When these men saw Judith transformed in looks and differently dressed, they were very much astounded at her beauty and said to her, 8 "May the God of our fathers bring you to favor, and make your undertaking a success, for the glory of the Israelites and the exaltation of Jerusalem."

Judith bowed down to God. Then she said to them, 9 "Order the gate of the city opened for me, that I may go to carry out the business we discussed." So they ordered the youths to open the gate for her as she requested. 10 When they did so, Judith and her maid went out. The men of the city kept her in view as she went down the mountain and crossed the valley; then they lost sight of her.

10, 5: (*kai artōn*) *kai tyrou:* so a few LXX[MSS], Vet Lat, P, V.

NRSV

10 When Judith[a] had stopped crying out to the God of Israel, and had ended all these words, 2she rose from where she lay prostrate. She called her maid and went down into the house where she lived on sabbaths and on her festal days. 3She removed the sackcloth she had been wearing, took off her widow's garments, bathed her body with water, and anointed herself with precious ointment. She combed her hair, put on a tiara, and dressed herself in the festive attire that she used to wear while her husband Manasseh was living. 4She put sandals on her feet, and put on her anklets, bracelets, rings, earrings, and all her other jewelry. Thus she made herself very beautiful, to entice the eyes of all the men who might see her. 5She gave her maid a skin of wine and a flask of oil, and filled a bag with roasted grain, dried fig cakes, and fine bread;[b] then she wrapped up all her dishes and gave them to her to carry.

6Then they went out to the town gate of Bethulia and found Uzziah standing there with the elders of the town, Chabris and Charmis. 7When they saw her transformed in appearance and dressed differently, they were very greatly astounded at her beauty and said to her, 8"May the God of our ancestors grant you favor and fulfill your plans, so that the people of Israel may glory and Jerusalem may be exalted." She bowed down to God.

9Then she said to them, "Order the gate of the town to be opened for me so that I may go out and accomplish the things you have just said to me." So they ordered the young men to open the gate for her, as she requested. 10When they had done this, Judith went out, accompanied by her maid. The men of the town watched her until she had gone down the mountain and passed through the valley, where they lost sight of her.

[a] Gk *she* [b] Other ancient authorities add *and cheese*

COMMENTARY

10:1-5. Once Judith's prayer is finished, she rises to move forward with her plan. She is moving from the liminal period into the third phase of this rite of passage, incorporation. Judith's bathing can be compared to the similar scenes in the other Jewish novels, where the heroines emerge from the liminal state, bathe, and redress themselves for their new mission in life. In other cultures, traditions of the hero often include special scenes in which the hero dresses for battle or dons special armor before proceeding to the greatest test of valor. The hero usually has at his side a faithful servant who is instrumental in outfitting him.[97] Here also Judith, with the help of her maid, puts on the special armor that will be necessary for her great conflict. Her new identity is as a rich and beautiful seductress—one might even say a courtesan. She takes off her sackcloth and mourning garments, bathes, anoints herself with perfume, beautifies her hair, and puts on a full assortment of jewelry. Her beautification here includes the very items that Esther in the Additions condemned in herself. In fact, the listing of the items of beautification is very complete—ointment, combing, tiara, festive attire, sandals, anklets, bracelets, rings, earrings, and "all her other jewelry." Judith uses every means at her disposal to entice men, and Esther is not the only person to speak negatively of such cosmetics. At Isa 3:16-24, the wealthy daughters of Zion are condemned for wearing just such makeup, and the listing of items is very similar to Judith's. Judith clearly is threatening to violate the normal standards of clothing for pious Jewish women. She emerges from this a changed woman—or to be more exact, her true nature is now revealed. Now her beauty is so great that each man she meets is awestruck. This is very similar to the way Esther and Aseneth are described after they emerge from their prayer scenes.

Judith's vegetarian diet ensures a strict conformity with kosher food laws, just as Daniel and his three friends remained kosher by eating only vegetables in the court of Nebuchadnezzar (Dan 1:8). Like the beautiful clothes, the food also signifies that Judith has ritually left the confines of her tent and given up her fasts. The food may also have another role. If the book of Judith really is like the hero's quest, then her kosher food becomes almost like a magical charm or protective substance that, along with her bathing, keeps her from becoming polluted by contact with Holofernes.

The maid may seem at first to be an incidental character in the book, but she is actually quite integral. She functions as Judith's lieutenant in much the same way that Bagoas will for Holofernes. But there is something more subtle at play here as well. She is a loyal servant who does Judith's every bidding, and she will be freed by Judith at the end; yet she is never named and never speaks. She takes her identity entirely from Judith and joins in Judith's great service for others, but in a very subordinate way. She never establishes a personality of her own. The maid represents, from the point of view of the slave owner, the ideal slave, a motif also encountered in the Greek novels and in Esth 15:2-3.[98] Yet, on the other hand, as the counterpart to Holofernes' servant Bagoas, she is seen to be characterized quite positively in contrast to him; whereas Bagoas is talkative, gullible, and subservient, the maid is calm, deliberate, and loyal. One is the contrasting image of the other. In addition, since the maid is an effective assistant at just the moment Judith needs her (13:9-10), she becomes forever identified with her mistress's brave act and is often depicted in paintings alongside Judith. As Bal points out, Judith and the maid are both focused in the paintings; they *know* what Holofernes, Bagoas, and the Assyrian soldiers do not know.[99] In some paintings, such as those by Michelangelo and Artemisia Gentileschi, Judith and her maid are depicted as partners, while in others, there is an unmistakable suggestion that the maid represents the darker side of Judith: The maid is ugly and forbidding, sometimes more closely identified with the deed, while Judith can stand tall, beautiful, and pure (see the paintings by Sandro Bot-

97. Albert B. Lord, *The Singer of Tales* (New York: Atheneum, 1976) 86-91; C. M. Bowra, *Heroic Poetry* (London: Macmillan, 1952) 188-97.

98. Jennifer A. Glancy, "The Mistress-Slave Dialectic: Paradoxes of Slavery in Three LXX Narratives," *JSOT* 72 (1996) 71-87.

99. Mieke Bal, "Head Hunting: 'Judith' on the Cutting Edge of Knowledge," *JSOT* 63 (1994) 27.

ticelli, Michelangelo Caravaggio, and Antiveduto Grammatica).[100] Stocker also notes that the maid is sometimes depicted as the older version of Judith herself, a *memento mori,* or reminder of mortality and death, which also serves to underscore the fleeting nature of the power Judith derives from her beauty.[101]

10:6-10. The development of novelistic description in Judith is remarkable, especially as it is sometimes done with considerable subtlety. In this passage, we find, first of all, retardation of plot—that is, a simple act, Judith and her maid leaving Bethulia, is drawn out by the addition of a number of small details to add texture and to increase the narrative tension the audience is feeling. The interchanges between Judith and her maid, on the one hand, and the elders and the young men at the gate, on the other hand, are played out in a series of verbal and physical exchanges. The scene becomes almost ceremonial as Judith and her maid find the elders, receive Uzziah's blessing, bow down, ask the elders to open the gate, wait for them to have the order executed, and exit as the men watch her trail off into the valley. Alonso-Schökel has rightly called this last effect "cinematographic";[102] the ritualism and detail make the entire scene come to life before the eyes much like an American western film.

According to Bowra, a standard feature of heroic quest traditions is that upon departure a blessing of the gods is invoked for the hero's safe travel, often by an elderly figure.[103] Such an episode is probably what we see here in Uzziah's blessing of Judith at the gates. This is part of the large structural pattern of the quest of the hero, but at this point there is also introduced a second rite of passage. It follows the preceding one and encompasses the period between the time when Judith moves out of Bethulia toward Holofernes' camp and when she returns. Campbell talks of the hero's passing over the threshold between the known world and the unknown into the region where the monster resides.[104] It is significant that Judith walks out at night, which connotes here the unknown place of danger. We should also recall that the word "liminal" comes from the Latin word *limen,* or "threshold," which is both literally and figuratively what is here being marked. In Craven's structural division of Judith, she also notes the importance of these two gate scenes. They hold corresponding places in the chiasm, both before and after the longer section of Judith's vanquishing of Holofernes.[105] After praying and preparing herself through the rite of passage above, she has one last dialogue with Uzziah and, as she is ready to proceed to the next passage, gives a command to "order the gate of the town to be opened." Upon her return in 13:11 she again says, "Open, open the gate!" The gates are a marked portal through which she enters into a new zone. It is not simply the zone of the warrior, since she will continue to act as a warrior, a general, and a strategist on the model of Deborah when she returns in chaps. 14–15. The zone she is in while she is between the gates—a liminal period between the thresholds—is one of being sexually provocative, treacherous, deceitful, and murderous. She meets her nemesis and greatest challenge, Holofernes, while in this zone, and Judith's violations of Jewish taboos for female behavior occur during this period; her challenge to gender roles is located in this zone. It is important to note that although Judith is beautiful both inside and outside this zone, she lies only while she is inside it. Within this zone, nearly every word out of her mouth is deceptive, provocative, flattering, and deceitful.

That people are struck by Judith's beauty is constantly emphasized (10:7, 14, 19, 23), which is also a standard, even required motif of the Greek novels. In the Greek novels this usually

100. For photographs of paintings depicting Judith, see Nira Stone, "Judith and Holofernes: Some Observations on the Development of the Scene in Art, in James C. VanderKam, ed., *"No One Spoke Ill of Her": Essays on Judith* (Atlanta: Scholars Press, 1992) 73-93; Moore, *Judith*; Mary Garrard, "Judith," in *Artemisia Gentileschi: The Image of the Female Hero in Italian Baroque Art* (Princeton: Princeton University Press, 1989); Mary Jacobus, "Judith, Holofernes, and the Phallic Woman," in *Reading Women: Essays in Feminist Criticism* (New York: Columbia University Press, 1986); and Bal, "Head Hunting."

101. Margarita Stocker, *Judith, Sexual Warrior: Women and Power in Western Culture* (New Haven: Yale University Press, 1998) 33. It should be noted, however, that since in the ancient text the maid is not in the inner chamber with Judith at the moment of the decapitation, any inclusion of the maid in that scene in later paintings is an editorial change.

102. Luis Alonso-Schökel, *Narrative Structures in the Book of Judith* (Berkeley, Calif.: Center for Hermeneutical Studies in Hellenistic and Modern Culture, 1974) 7.

103. C. M. Bowra, *Heroic Poetry* (London: Macmillan, 1952) 184-86.

104. Joseph Campbell, *The Hero with a Thousand Faces* (New York: Pantheon, 1949) 90-91.

105. Toni Craven, *Artistry and Faith in the Book of Judith* (Chico, Calif.: Scholars Press, 1983) 62-63.

places the heroine in jeopardy as one man after another tries to press his attentions upon her, but in Judith it is the means she will use to gain the upper hand.

The text in v. 8 says, "She bowed down to God," even though it is not clear why she does so at this point. It could be taken as another pious gesture, but Moore accepts an emendation of the text that would read, "She bowed down to them"—i.e., the men—as she took her departure.[106] This is less abrupt, and she makes a similar bow upon being admitted to the presence of Holofernes (10:23). The two bows are somewhat at odds with her commanding personality, but that might be just the point. They are balanced actions that show her social graces as she moves to take control of the situation. (See Reflections at 11:1-23.)

106. Moore, *Judith,* 201-2.

JUDITH 10:11–13:10*a*, JUDITH OVERCOMES HOLOFERNES

Judith 10:11-23, Judith Enters the Enemy Camp and Is Taken to Holofernes

NAB

11 As Judith and her maid walked directly across the valley, they encountered the Assyrian outpost. 12 The men took her in custody and asked her, "To what people do you belong? Where do you come from, and where are you going?" She replied: "I am a daughter of the Hebrews, and I am fleeing from them, because they are about to be delivered up to you as prey. 13 I have come to see Holofernes, the general in chief of your forces, to give him a trustworthy report; I will show him the route by which he can ascend and take possession of the whole mountain district without a single one of his men suffering injury or loss of life."

14 When the men heard her words and gazed upon her face, which appeared wondrously beautiful to them, they said to her, 15 "By coming down thus promptly to see our master, you have saved your life. Now go to his tent; some of our men will accompany you to present you to him. 16 When you stand before him, have no fear in your heart; give him the report you speak of, and he will treat you well." 17 So they detailed a hundred of their men as an escort for her and her maid, and these conducted them to the tent of Holofernes.

18 When the news of her arrival spread among

NRSV

11As the women[a] were going straight on through the valley, an Assyrian patrol met her
12and took her into custody. They asked her, "To what people do you belong, and where are you coming from, and where are you going?" She replied, "I am a daughter of the Hebrews, but I am fleeing from them, for they are about to be handed over to you to be devoured.
13I am on my way to see Holofernes the commander of your army, to give him a true report; I will show him a way by which he can go and capture all the hill country without losing one of his men, captured or slain."

14When the men heard her words, and observed her face—she was in their eyes marvelously beautiful—they said to her,
15"You have saved your life by hurrying down to see our lord. Go at once to his tent; some of us will escort you and hand you over to him.
16When you stand before him, have no fear in your heart, but tell him what you have just said, and he will treat you well."

17They chose from their number a hundred men to accompany her and her maid, and they brought them to the tent of Holofernes.
18There was great excitement in the whole camp, for her

a Gk *they*

NAB

the tents, a crowd gathered in the camp. They came and stood around her as she waited outside the tent of Holofernes, while he was being informed about her. 19 They marveled at her beauty, regarding the Israelites with wonder because of her, and they said to one another, "Who can despise this people that has such women among them? It is not wise to leave one man of them alive, for if any were to be spared they could beguile the whole world."

20 The guard of Holofernes and all his servants came out and ushered her into the tent. 21 Now Holofernes was reclining on his bed under a canopy with a netting of crimson and gold, emeralds and other precious stones. 22 When they announced her to him, he came out to the antechamber, preceded by silver lamps; 23 and when Holofernes and his servants beheld Judith, they all marveled at the beauty of her face. She threw herself down prostrate before him, but his servants raised her up.

NRSV

arrival was reported from tent to tent. They came and gathered around her as she stood outside the tent of Holofernes, waiting until they told him about her. 19They marveled at her beauty and admired the Israelites, judging them by her. They said to one another, "Who can despise these people, who have women like this among them? It is not wise to leave one of their men alive, for if we let them go they will be able to beguile the whole world!"

20Then the guards of Holofernes and all his servants came out and led her into the tent. 21Holofernes was resting on his bed under a canopy that was woven with purple and gold, emeralds and other precious stones. 22When they told him of her, he came to the front of the tent, with silver lamps carried before him. 23When Judith came into the presence of Holofernes[a] and his servants, they all marveled at the beauty of her face. She prostrated herself and did obeisance to him, but his slaves raised her up.

[a] Gk *him*

COMMENTARY

10:11-16. Interestingly, the retardation of plot in the preceding scene is followed by the sudden jolt of the present one. There is finally a meeting of Israelites and Assyrians, which has been threatened for most of the book, and the Assyrians appear to be in the commanding position. Judith's plan, which up to now has only been hinted at, is beginning to be realized. The reader sees Judith at work on the enemy, and in her first words she is already lying. The Assyrian soldiers, also struck by her beauty, usher her along with a comical show of respect. The Assyrians begin to speak in an extended irony in which almost every line can be understood in two ways, depending upon whether the "lord" referred to is Holofernes or God: "You have saved your life by hurrying down to see our lord . . . some of us . . . will hand you over to him [lit., deliver you into his hands]." The audience at this point would have been aware of each reference and would not have missed the ironic distance between the show of the troops and their apparent obtuseness about the meaning of their own words. The obtuseness of the characters is an important part of the comic irony in the Gospel of John as well (see John 3:4; 4:11; 9:25).

10:17-23. Here also a vivid description enlivens the narrative. One can almost see the hubbub and excitement spread through the camp as men not only are struck by her beauty, but also marvel at what it indicates about Israelites in general. The soldiers draw the conclusion that the audience would want them to draw: that Israelite women—and therefore men as well—are superior to any on earth. This means of affirming ethnic superiority is typical of much of the writing of this period, both in the dominant Greek and Roman culture, and of the various indigenous peoples. It is found in a very similar way in *Joseph and Aseneth* 1:4-5, where it is said that Aseneth was "tall and comely, and more beautiful than any young woman on earth. Indeed, she bore little resemblance at all to Egyptian women, but was in every way more like the women of the Hebrews: as tall as Sarah, as comely as Rebecca, as beautiful as Rachel." The *Genesis Apocryphon* (20:2-6) from Qumran is equally complimentary in regard to Sarah.

We first encounter Holofernes in a tent that is parallel to Judith's tent, but rather than a retreat for righteous fasting and praying, it is a palace in miniature, sumptuously decorated with precious stones. It is probably not meant to be effeminate, as its appearance may strike the modern reader, although this is not implausible considering the way Holofernes will later be "unmanned." Enslin suggests that there may be evident here contempt for the luxury of the Eastern despot and his finery.[107] One similarity to Judith's tent that does remain is that Holofernes is generally secluded in it. He meets with his officers in the tent, and while alive always appears in it. This tent has two chambers, and his bedchamber, covered with a canopy, is where he hopes to take Judith to bed and where he will later die. The canopy that covers the bed and separates the chambers will also be of great importance later.

One might wonder whether the structure of the tent is significant. It has at least two chambers, the inner sleeping chamber, separated from the outer chamber by the specially decorated canopy. Is this structure intended to call to mind the Temple in Jerusalem, albeit as a sort of mirror image? The Second Temple consisted of a series of concentric courts, with the Temple itself standing at the center and the altar just outside facing it. Within the Temple was the holy of holies, or inner sanctum, and like the bedchamber of Holofernes' tent, it was separated by a curtain from the rest of the Temple. The curtain was richly decorated, with some of the same colors as those of Holofernes' curtain (Exod 26:31). The curtained area of the Temple was entered only once a year on the Day of Atonement, and then only by the high priest. Judith will enter Holofernes' inner sanctum to kill him, just as the high priest enters the holy of holies, and one might say that she will "sacrifice" him. At this last point the parallel breaks down, however, because the sacrifice on the Day of Atonement is carried out on the altar in front of the Temple, and only some of the blood is carried into the holy of holies. Still, the parallel is suggestive, for the curtain of the Temple was quite symbolic of its integrity and sanctity; in early Christianity, it became a powerful symbol of the access Christ had created to the realm of God (Matt 27:51; Hebrews 9–10). (See Reflections at 11:1-23.)

107. Morton Enslin and Solomon Zeitlin, *The Book of Judith,* JAL VIII (Leiden: Brill, 1972) 133-34. See also Horace *Epodes* 9.16 concerning the bed canopy of Marc Antony.

Judith 11:1-23, Judith's Dialogue with Holofernes

NAB

11 1 Then Holofernes said to her: "Take courage, lady; have no fear in your heart! Never have I harmed anyone who chose to serve Nebuchadnezzar, king of all the earth. 2 Nor would I have raised my spear against your people who dwell in the mountain region, had they not despised me and brought this upon themselves. 3 But now tell me why you fled from them and came to us. In any case, you have come to safety. Take courage! Your life is spared tonight and for the future. 4 No one at all will harm you. Rather, you will be well treated, as are all the servants of my lord, King Nebuchadnezzar."

5 Judith answered him: "Listen to the words

NRSV

11 Then Holofernes said to her, "Take courage, woman, and do not be afraid in your heart, for I have never hurt anyone who chose to serve Nebuchadnezzar, king of all the earth. 2Even now, if your people who live in the hill country had not slighted me, I would never have lifted my spear against them. They have brought this on themselves. 3But now tell me why you have fled from them and have come over to us. In any event, you have come to safety. Take courage! You will live tonight and ever after. 4No one will hurt you. Rather, all will treat you well, as they do the servants of my lord King Nebuchadnezzar."

5Judith answered him, "Accept the words of

NAB

of your servant, and let your handmaid speak in your presence! I will tell no lie to my lord this night, 6 and if you follow out the words of your handmaid, God will give you complete success, and my lord will not fail in any of his undertakings. 7 By the life of Nebuchadnezzar, king of all the earth, and by the power of him who has sent you to set all creatures aright! not only do men serve him through you; but even the wild beasts and the cattle and the birds of the air, because of your strength, will live for Nebuchadnezzar and his whole house. 8 Indeed, we have heard of your wisdom and sagacity, and all the world is aware that throughout the kingdom you alone are competent, rich in experience, and distinguished in military strategy.

9 "As for Achior's speech in your council, we have heard of it. When the men of Bethulia spared him, he told them all he had said to you. 10 So then, my lord and master, do not disregard his word, but bear it in mind, for it is true. For our people are not punished, nor does the sword prevail against them, except when they sin against their God. 11 But now their guilt has caught up with them by which they bring the wrath of their God upon them whenever they do wrong; so that my lord will not be repulsed and fail, but death will overtake them. 12 Since their food gave out and all their water ran low, they decided to kill their animals, and determined to consume all the things which God in his laws forbade them to eat. 13 They decreed that they would use up the first fruits of grain and the tithes of wine and oil which they had sanctified and reserved for the priests who minister in the presence of our God in Jerusalem: things which no layman should even touch with his hands. 14 They have sent messengers to Jerusalem to bring back to them authorization from the council of the elders; for the inhabitants there have also done these things. 15 On the very day when the response reaches them and they act upon it, they will be handed over to you for destruction.

16 "As soon as I, your handmaid, learned all this, I fled from them. God has sent me to perform with you such deeds that people throughout the

11, 7: (*zēsontai*) *epi* (*Nabouchodonosor*): so several LXX^{MSS}.
11, 14: (*tous*) *metakomisontas* (*autois*): so a few LXX^{MSS}, Vet Lat.

NRSV

your slave, and let your servant speak in your presence. I will say nothing false to my lord this night. [6]If you follow out the words of your servant, God will accomplish something through you, and my lord will not fail to achieve his purposes. [7]By the life of Nebuchadnezzar, king of the whole earth, and by the power of him who has sent you to direct every living being! Not only do human beings serve him because of you, but also the animals of the field and the cattle and the birds of the air will live, because of your power, under Nebuchadnezzar and all his house. [8]For we have heard of your wisdom and skill, and it is reported throughout the whole world that you alone are the best in the whole kingdom, the most informed and the most astounding in military strategy.

[9]"Now as for Achior's speech in your council, we have heard his words, for the people of Bethulia spared him and he told them all he had said to you. [10]Therefore, lord and master, do not disregard what he said, but keep it in your mind, for it is true. Indeed our nation cannot be punished, nor can the sword prevail against them, unless they sin against their God.

[11]"But now, in order that my lord may not be defeated and his purpose frustrated, death will fall upon them, for a sin has overtaken them by which they are about to provoke their God to anger when they do what is wrong. [12]Since their food supply is exhausted and their water has almost given out, they have planned to kill their livestock and have determined to use all that God by his laws has forbidden them to eat. [13]They have decided to consume the first fruits of the grain and the tithes of the wine and oil, which they had consecrated and set aside for the priests who minister in the presence of our God in Jerusalem—things it is not lawful for any of the people even to touch with their hands. [14]Since even the people in Jerusalem have been doing this, they have sent messengers there in order to bring back permission from the council of the elders. [15]When the response reaches them and they act upon it, on that very day they will be handed over to you to be destroyed.

[16]"So when I, your slave, learned all this, I fled from them. God has sent me to accomplish with you things that will astonish the whole world

NAB

world will be astonished on hearing of them. 17
Your handmaid is, indeed, a God-fearing woman,
serving the God of heaven night and day. Now I
will remain with you, my lord; but each night
your handmaid will go out to the ravine and pray
to God. He will tell me when the Israelites have
committed their crimes. 18 Then I will come and
let you know, so that you may go out with your
whole force, and not one of them will be able to
withstand you. 19 I will lead you through Judea,
till you come to Jerusalem, and there I will set
up your judgment seat. You will drive them like
sheep that have no shepherd, and not even a dog
will growl at you. This was told me, and announced to me in advance, and I in turn have
been sent to tell you."
20 Her words pleased Holofernes and all his
servants; they marveled at her wisdom and exclaimed, 21 "No other woman from one end of
the world to the other looks so beautiful and
speaks so wisely!" 22 Then Holofernes said to
her: "God has done well in sending you ahead of
your people, to bring victory to our arms, and
destruction to those who have despised my lord.
23 You are fair to behold, and your words are
well spoken. If you do as you have said, your God
will be my God; you shall dwell in the palace of
King Nebuchadnezzar, and shall be renowned
throughout the earth."

NRSV

wherever people shall hear about them. 17Your
servant is indeed God-fearing and serves the God
of heaven night and day. So, my lord, I will
remain with you; but every night your servant
will go out into the valley and pray to God. He
will tell me when they have committed their sins.
18Then I will come and tell you, so that you may
go out with your whole army, and not one of
them will be able to withstand you. 19Then I will
lead you through Judea, until you come to Jerusalem; there I will set your throne.[a] You will drive
them like sheep that have no shepherd, and no
dog will so much as growl at you. For this was
told me to give me foreknowledge; it was announced to me, and I was sent to tell you."
20Her words pleased Holofernes and all his
servants. They marveled at her wisdom and said,
21"No other woman from one end of the earth to
the other looks so beautiful or speaks so wisely!"
22Then Holofernes said to her, "God has done well
to send you ahead of the people, to strengthen our
hands and bring destruction on those who have
despised my lord. 23You are not only beautiful in
appearance, but wise in speech. If you do as you
have said, your God shall be my God, and you shall
live in the palace of King Nebuchadnezzar and be
renowned throughout the whole world."

[a] Or *chariot*

COMMENTARY

11:1-8. Holofernes is as gracious to Judith as she is to him. He does not treat her as a member of a conquered people, but immediately presses her to find out why she has abandoned her village. Judith begins her speech by asking him to "accept the words of your slave," as if it were a humble petition addressed to God. In a way, it is, as the next sentence continues the double-layered reference to "my lord": "I will say nothing false *to my lord* this night." Judith is equivocating with the truth; she will lie to one lord while being truthful with the other. She must use her two cultivated weapons, her beauty and her deceptive tongue (9:10), to distract and manipulate her oppressor: "If you follow out the words of your servant, God will accomplish something through you, and my lord will not fail to achieve his purposes." One might argue that here the double entendre gets Judith into a moral gray area when she says, "I will say nothing false to my lord this night." However, we must understand her intention: Her lies to Holofernes are a form of "truth" to God, since they serve God. This skates very close to lying to God, but that is precisely the point. For the audience, the exhilaration in reading Judith consists in skating close to the edge of moral violations. It is a release of moral tensions. Moore points out that to gain Holofernes' trust, Judith swears by what is holy to him—that is, the name of Nebuchadnezzar—and broadly praises Nebuchadnezzar.[108] Her flattery of Holofernes is shameless and almost as much a violation of the truth as is her lying: "Not only do human beings serve Nebuchadnezzar because of you, but also the animals of the field and the cattle and the birds of the air will live." In the book of Daniel, the king's protection of the animal kingdom is associated with Nebuchadnezzar both in the words of Daniel himself (Dan 2:37-38) and in Nebuchadnezzar's own grandiose self-image (Dan 4:12). The power of Nebuchadnezzar is elsewhere understood to be a gift of God, and strictly temporary (Jer 27:4-7).

11:9-15. Other than her maid, Judith has only one ally in her stratagem, and that is Achior. Without realizing it—although one might suspect the workings of God—Achior has helped to set up the situation that will lead to the Assyrians' downfall. In chap. 5 he presented the deuteronomic principle that could establish the vulnerability of the Israelites: If they have sinned, then their God will not protect them. Judith reiterates this principle and draws a firm conclusion: Now they have sinned and are about to fall to Holofernes. Judith spins a complicated scenario of the practices of the Bethulians that will violate God's laws. The content of her words is clearly directed to the reading audience; it refers to practices that can only really be understood within the context of Jewish laws concerning temple practices. That God could not countenance a violation in the light of the desperation of the Bethulians' situation is part of Judith's deception. The accommodation of God's law to times of crisis was certainly an accepted view in the Hasmonean state (1 Macc 2:32-41). Also, the violation at hand is carefully chosen to show a deference to the priesthood in Jerusalem. This is the real focus of the religious world of the author and audience of Judith. On the assumption that the author is not trying to present a list of violations of Jewish law that Holofernes would understand, but rather a list that the audience would understand, it appears that killing their livestock might have meant slaughtering the animals without draining the blood thoroughly as Lev 17:10-14 required (see also Acts 15:20). This, at any rate, is what the Latin versions understood by it. Since this is a part of the priestly office in Jerusalem, it matches the other violations. In their desperation, the Bethulians are eating the firstfruits and tithes of wine and oil that should have been reserved for the priests. These are precisely the same offerings that are mentioned at 1 Macc 3:49 when the Maccabee rebels hold an alternative temple service at Mizpeh before the capture and rededication of the Jerusalem Temple. The strictness of observance is emphasized by saying that the people could not so much as touch the offerings once they had been consecrated. Tobit 1:6-8 also presents an idealized view of a pious diaspora Jew bringing his offerings to Jerusalem.

The Bethulians are not acting alone, however. Judith's lie incriminates Jerusalem as well, because even there the council has allowed the citizens to do these things; more to the point, the Jerusalem council is prepared to give its permission to Bethulia as well. Bethulia is waiting for messengers to return from Jerusalem, which provides a specific point in time for their transgression to be complete in God's eyes. The precise time line imposed on the action is parallel to the time line that the Bethulians had imposed upon themselves by making a vow to surrender if God had not brought rain within five days. Although Judith says she must pray to learn when the Israelites have violated God's laws, the audience would recognize that the time line for this made-up offense is the same as that for the Bethulians' actual offense.

11:16-18. Judith states her conclusion about these violations of law with a sentence that is a marvelous double entendre: "God has sent me to accomplish with you things that will astonish the world." The polytheistic religion of the ancient Near East would have held that a people's strength in war was related to the strength of their gods; but monotheism in Israel, and especially the deuteronomic theology, held that Israel's setbacks were not because God was weak, but because God was stronger than all nations and had willed for Israel to be overrun. Thus Judith says that God will inform her when the violation has occurred and will collude with the foreign nations to punish Israel. This theology would be laughable to a real adherent of the Assyrian gods, and in fact Holofernes had rejected it when it was spoken by Achior (5:20–6:4). However, Holofernes readily accepts

108. Carey A. Moore, *Judith,* AB 40 (Garden City, N.Y.: Doubleday, 1985) 209.

it from Judith. Sensing an easy victory over her sexually and over her people as well, he need not quibble over theology.

11:19-23. Judith's language in v. 19 is laden with images from the prophets. Just as Achior spoke like a prophet, and as Nebuchadnezzar had as well, so also does Judith speak. In form her words are like an "oracle of salvation" from Second Isaiah (the section of Isaiah written during the exile, Isaiah 40–55. Isaiah 40:3-4, for example, familiar to Christians from its use in the Gospels (Matt 3:3; Mark 1:2; Luke 3:4-6; John 1:23), prophesies that a way will be made for the Lord through the desert to Jerusalem (see also Isa 35:8-10; 42:16; 51:11). Likewise, Judith, in an audacious affirmation of her own role, says, "There I will set your throne," which is similar to what God promises to David in 2 Sam 7:13 and Ps 89:4. "You will lead them like sheep without a shepherd" picks up a common motif in the HB that is found also in the NT (Ezek 34:8; Zech 10:2; 13:7; Matt 9:36; 26:31). Shepherds are also likened to watchdogs that do not bark in Isa 56:10-11, an image that Judith uses here as well. When Achior had said these same things by "prophecy" (5:21; 6:2), Holofernes condemned him. Here, however, Holofernes and his retinue marvel at Judith's wisdom (vv. 20-21). This, too, is ironic, because her wisdom consists in cleverness, the cleverness required to lie to them successfully and convince them that she is giving them wise advice.

Holofernes once again unknowingly speaks words that condemn his own cause, "God has done well to send you . . . to bring destruction on those who have despised my lord." His statement that "your god shall be my god" has caused trouble for scholars. It is the same statement that Ruth makes to Naomi in Ruth 1:16 when Ruth becomes an Israelite. But does Holofernes mean this? In the narratives of this period pagan kings, even oppressive ones, sometimes come to confess the God of Israel (Dan 2:47; 3:28-29; 4:34-37; 2 Maccabees 3; see also 2 Kgs 5:17). Still, Holofernes is being effusive and overly solicitous, but he is hardly converting to a worship of Israel's God. Perhaps he means that Judith will adopt his god, especially if, as he assumes, she will become a wife or courtesan of Nebuchadnezzar. Alternatively, perhaps Holofernes is again unknowingly accurate in his statement. If Judith does as she has promised, her God will be his God—in judgment. At any rate, the passage is probably intentionally ambiguous to show that Holofernes is swept up in the commonality of their purpose. It is, after all, only the audience who understands the meaning of Holofernes' words, and not he himself. Holofernes sums up his list of unintentional prophecies by affirming that Judith will be "renowned throughout the whole world," which the audience knows to be most decidedly true.

REFLECTIONS

From the time Judith leaves the gates of Bethulia until the time she returns, there are two constant motifs: (1) the Assyrians, struck by her beauty, will stumble over themselves in trying to cater to her requests, and (2) Judith all the while will be speaking in comic and ironic utterances. Although there have been comic elements before, they dominate the text for nearly three chapters. All good comedy works with tensions within the audience and effects a release of tensions, and Judith is no exception. It is effective partly because it creates and sustains a comic situation of the pious heroine taking a sojourn outside of her seclusion and respectability to flout social conventions, entice the lustful Holofernes, walk through the menacing enemy troops, and return to the safety of her village. What is interesting about Judith is that it represents the most extended use of comedy in the Bible and combines both the "low" and "high" comedy of burlesque and satire.

This is one of the aspects of Judith that make it very "modern." We can also sense the tensions in our society over sexual taboos that give rise to a comedy of release, and we are aware in our own time of the political implications of comedy in constructing a world (or a new world) with certain values "tested" and then reinstated. By discerning the relation of

Judith's comedy to its political affirmation, we are reminded of this process in our day. Comedy draws us in and entertains us, testing our community values and rebuilding community at the same time. In Judith we can see this in the portrayal of a woman who flouts the prevailing codes of conduct and is ultimately returned to her modest and pious life.

When we talk of examining public values, groping for direction in the new day of the twenty-first century, making intelligent choices in the face of daunting new ethical dilemmas, we rarely think of that kind of discourse that is all around us and that comments on our perplexity the most directly—comedy. The positive and negative effects of comedy are felt by all members of our community alike, and in forms that are constant influences on our lives—television, film, literature, theater. The bold example of Judith reminds us that just as comedy represented a commentary on the political and religious situation of its day, so also the comedy of our own day is the most ubiquitous means of commenting on our disjointed world. And it is not just a "secular" commentary; included in its subject matter are the values of our society and the religious beliefs as well. Just as it is incumbent upon us to ask who the prophets are of our day, we must also address the question of who the Judiths are, for that is where we will find a mirror of the tensions and changes within our society.

Judith 12:1-20, For Three Days Judith Lives in Holofernes' Camp

NAB

12 1 Then he ordered them to lead her into
the room where his silverware was kept,
and bade them set a table for her with his own
delicacies to eat and his own wine to drink. 2
But Judith said, "I will not partake of them, lest
it be an occasion of sin; but I shall be amply
supplied from the things I brought with me." 3
Holofernes asked her: "But if your provisions give
out, where shall we get more of the same to
provide for you? None of your people are with
us." 4 Judith answered him, "As surely as you,
my lord, live, your handmaid will not use up her
supplies till the LORD accomplishes by my hand
what he has determined."

5 Then the servants of Holofernes led her into
the tent, where she slept till midnight. In the
night watch just before dawn, she rose 6 and sent
this message to Holofernes, "Give orders, my lord,
to let your handmaid go out for prayer." 7 So
Holofernes ordered his bodyguard not to hinder
her. Thus she stayed in the camp three days. Each
night she went out to the ravine of Bethulia,
where she washed herself at the spring of the
camp. 8 After bathing, she besought the LORD, the
God of Israel, to direct her way for the triumph
of his people. 9 Then she returned purified to the

NRSV

12 Then he commanded them to bring her in
where his silver dinnerware was kept, and
ordered them to set a table for her with some of
his own delicacies, and with some of his own
wine to drink. 2But Judith said, "I cannot partake
of them, or it will be an offense; but I will have
enough with the things I brought with me."
3Holofernes said to her, "If your supply runs out,
where can we get you more of the same? For
none of your people are here with us." 4Judith
replied, "As surely as you live, my lord, your
servant will not use up the supplies I have with
me before the Lord carries out by my hand what
he has determined."

5Then the servants of Holofernes brought her
into the tent, and she slept until midnight. Toward
the morning watch she got up 6and sent this
message to Holofernes: "Let my lord now give
orders to allow your servant to go out and pray."
7So Holofernes commanded his guards not to
hinder her. She remained in the camp three days.
She went out each night to the valley of Bethulia,
and bathed at the spring in the camp.[a] 8After
bathing, she prayed the Lord God of Israel to
direct her way for the triumph of his[b] people.

[a] Other ancient authorities lack *in the camp* [b] Other ancient authorities read *her*

NAB

tent, and remained there until her food was brought to her toward evening.

10 On the fourth day Holofernes gave a banquet for his servants alone, to which he did not invite any of the officers. 11 And he said to Bagoas, the eunuch in charge of his household: "Go and persuade this Hebrew woman in your care to come and to eat and drink with us. 12 It would be a disgrace for us to have such a woman with us without enjoying her company. If we do not entice her, she will laugh us to scorn."

13 So Bagoas left the presence of Holofernes, and came to Judith and said, "So fair a maiden should not be reluctant to come to my lord to be honored by him, to enjoy drinking wine with us, and to be like one of the Assyrian women who live in the palace of Nebuchadnezzar." 14 She replied, "Who am I to refuse my lord? Whatever is pleasing to him I will promptly do. This will be a joy for me till the day of my death."

15 Thereupon she proceeded to put on her festive garments and all her feminine adornments. Meanwhile her maid went ahead and spread out on the ground for her in front of Holofernes the fleece Bagoas had furnished for her daily use in reclining at her dinner. 16 Then Judith came in and reclined on it. The heart of Holofernes was in rapture over her, and his spirit was shaken. He was burning with the desire to possess her, for he had been biding his time to seduce her from the day he saw her. 17 Holofernes said to her, "Drink and be merry with us!" 18 Judith replied, "I will gladly drink, my lord, for at no time since I was born have I ever enjoyed life as much as I do today." 19 She then took the things her maid had prepared, and ate and drank in his presence. 20 Holofernes, charmed by her, drank a great quantity of wine, more than he had ever drunk on one single day in his life.

12, 10: (*eis tēn*) *klēsin:* so a few LXX^{MSS}.

NRSV

9Then she returned purified and stayed in the tent until she ate her food toward evening.

10On the fourth day Holofernes held a banquet for his personal attendants only, and did not invite any of his officers. 11He said to Bagoas, the eunuch who had charge of his personal affairs, "Go and persuade the Hebrew woman who is in your care to join us and to eat and drink with us. 12For it would be a disgrace if we let such a woman go without having intercourse with her. If we do not seduce her, she will laugh at us."

13So Bagoas left the presence of Holofernes, and approached her and said, "Let this pretty girl not hesitate to come to my lord to be honored in his presence, and to enjoy drinking wine with us, and to become today like one of the Assyrian women who serve in the palace of Nebuchadnezzar." 14Judith replied, "Who am I to refuse my lord? Whatever pleases him I will do at once, and it will be a joy to me until the day of my death." 15So she proceeded to dress herself in all her woman's finery. Her maid went ahead and spread for her on the ground before Holofernes the lambskins she had received from Bagoas for her daily use in reclining.

16Then Judith came in and lay down. Holofernes' heart was ravished with her and his passion was aroused, for he had been waiting for an opportunity to seduce her from the day he first saw her. 17So Holofernes said to her, "Have a drink and be merry with us!" 18Judith said, "I will gladly drink, my lord, because today is the greatest day in my whole life." 19Then she took what her maid had prepared and ate and drank before him. 20Holofernes was greatly pleased with her, and drank a great quantity of wine, much more than he had ever drunk in any one day since he was born.

COMMENTARY

12:1-9. Although Holofernes has intentions to wine and dine Judith, she resists and, in complete control of the situation, imposes on him her own requirements. She will eat the food she has brought with her so as not to break any kosher laws. Holofernes has no objection; he is even solicitous of her needs throughout. The supplies she and her maid have brought are sufficient for the period up until the time "the Lord carries out by my hand what he has determined." The careful adherence to kosher dietary laws, so careful that in some cases it becomes a strict vegetarianism, is found in the novelistic literature of this period (Dan 1:8-16; Add. Esth 14:17; Tob 1:10-11; 2 Macc 5:27).

Judith is remarkably free to move about as she pleases, which once again demonstrates her control of those who have been struck by her beauty. She arranges for an opportunity to go outside the camp to pray, which also establishes a pattern of her leaving very early each morning so that she will ultimately be able to escape.[109] Judith's departure each day also allows her to bathe. This is probably not principally meant for erotic effect, although Susanna's bathing or Bathsheba's bathing (2 Sam 11:2) might suggest that. Verse 9, however, emphasizes that Judith returned purified, so ritual observance must be the purpose of her bath. In the ritual of the Day of Atonement, the high priest bathes before he puts on the special linen garments in which he will perform the sacrifice and the scapegoat ritual. Judith also puts on special garments after bathing, but they are hardly the special linen garments of the high priest. Other forms of bathing in Judaism are perhaps more relevant. Baptism was practiced in a number of contexts at the turn of the first century BCE. For John the Baptist, baptism was described as being for repentance, and for Christians in general it was a ceremony for converts. In both of these cases, baptism was evidently a single ceremony and was not repeated. Jews may have practiced baptism for converts at this time, but the evidence for this practice does not go back any earlier than the first century CE. The Qumran sect provides a much closer parallel to Judith's bathing. The *Manual of Discipline* connects bathing with repentance, but unlike the baptism of John the Baptist, the number of cisterns at Qumran indicate that bathing was a more common, if not a constant, practice. Ritual bathing had evidently become a part of the increased notion of purity at Qumran, and was also part of the Pharisaic ideas of keeping food pure when coming in contact with Gentiles.[110] At the end of the menstrual period a Jewish woman would bathe, but presumably only once (Lev 15:19-24), and that does not appear to be the point of this motif. It is more likely that it is an idealized notion of purification derived from the requirement that a woman and a man must bathe after having sexual intercourse (Lev 15:18). Although Judith has not had sexual intercourse with Holofernes, her presence in his sleeping quarters and in his thoughts renders her symbolically unclean (cf. Matt 5:27-28). In this fictional world, she bathes in order to cleanse herself from even the insinuation of sexual intercourse. Perhaps her bathing is now simply a regular part of her personal devotion, paralleling the bathing that she performed at the end of her prayer in 10:3.

109. Moore, *Judith*, 219.

12:10-20. Holofernes' banquet includes servants only and not soldiers, a fortunate or providential detail if Judith is to be able to accomplish her plan. That Judith remains in control of Holofernes and the other persons around her is seen in the odd combination of phrases used by Holofernes: "Go and persuade her," "it would be a disgrace," "if we do not seduce her, she will laugh at us." On one hand, Holofernes displays the bravado of one who thinks he will soon have sex with Judith, whether she is agreeable or not; on the other hand, he awaits her word and has yet to say no to a single one of her unusual requests. Judith's personal power over Holofernes is only magnified by her insinuations that he will have his way with her. His excitement is growing at the same time that he treats her with more deferential respect, making the scene even more humorous and ironic, and ultimately making Holofernes appear weaker. Bagoas is also little more than a comic character. Despite the fact that the name "Bagoas" was associated with a powerful counselor in the invasion army of Antiochus III Ochus (see Commentary on 2:1-13), he functions only as an attendant to Holofernes, lacking even the quiet resolve of Judith's maid.

The ambiguity of the word "eunuch" (εὐνοῦχος *eunouchos*) may also be played upon here. The primary meaning, a castrated official who oversees

110. James VanderKam, *The Dead Sea Scrolls Today* (Grand Rapids: Eerdmans, 1994) 170; Louis Finkelstein, *The Pharisees: The Sociological Background of Their Faith*, 2 vols. (New York: Jewish Publication Society, 1966) 1:121-28.

the king's harem, was broadened to include any counselor in the royal court (for both meanings, cf. Esth 2:3; Isa 56:3-4; and Matt 19:12 with 2 Chr 18:8). Bagoas is called a eunuch in Judith, and this name was a common one for eunuchs in the Persian courts.[111] As Holofernes' attendant and go-between with Judith, which aspect of Bagoas are we seeing, a powerful counselor or a keeper of the harem, a harem that will now include Judith? Perhaps both are intended in a humorous way: Bagoas sees himself as a powerful counselor, but he is really a keeper of the harem who fetches women for the general's pleasure. As a eunuch, he seems to have desires for Judith, but only because he identifies so completely with Holofernes.

His words to Judith are suggestive without being crude, reflecting his and Holofernes' view of Judith's status—that is, as an ornament in Holofernes' harem, and soon to be an ornament in Nebuchadnezzar's, but one who deserves the respect befitting her beauty and status. Bagoas invites her to become like the Assyrian courtesans, a compliment in his eyes compared with her provincial origins as a "Hebrew woman." But for Judith to become an Assyrian courtesan is for the readers another threat to her purity. In the later Greek novels the hero and heroine are forced by circumstances to become "other" to their aristocratic Greek status. They are abducted and dragged across the eastern Mediterranean, lose their identity and status, are almost forced into prostitution, are forced to become slaves or enter marriages with wealthy men or women who lust after them, and so on. The descent into becoming "other" has been noted as a principal threat by which the protagonists are buffeted, and this is a theme of the other Jewish novels, Susanna, Additions to Esther, Tobit, and *Joseph and Aseneth* as well. But even though Judith is faced with the prospect of descending into the "other," she is never buffeted. Here the threat is stated as clearly as anywhere: A pious Jewish widow may be forced into having sexual relations with an Assyrian general and taken to a palace of Nebuchadnezzar to become like one of the Assyrian courtesans. Yet Judith is in absolute control of the situation. The tension is humorous and not really felt; as a result, Judith can even stoke the fires of Holofernes' desire by answering in an extremely suggestive way herself: "Whatever pleases Nebuchadnezzar I will do at once, and it will be a joy to me until the day of my death." Her words here are yet another example of double entendre, which by now seems to be her only mode of discourse in the Assyrian camp. This gives credence to the view that a rite of passage is initiated in her passing out of the gates of Bethulia, and ending when she reenters the gates at 13:11 (see Introduction and Commentary on 10:6-10). Between these points Judith is almost always lying or equivocating with the truth, and she is almost always speaking in her own special form of discourse, which consists of references on two levels at once. This is the gift of the "deceitful tongue" that she prayed for in 9:10.

Since all of Judith's violations of taboos of female behavior occur at the center of this novel, in a zone where the most important action occurs, one might assume that the novel encourages this illicit behavior, or at least decreases the distinction between acceptable and unacceptable behavior in a pious Jewish woman. If it is true, however, that Judith enters into a sort of liminal state, then Turner's theories about the liminal period suggest just the opposite. He notes the monstrous and animalistic features of masks worn by various peoples during the liminal state in their initiation ceremonies.[112] Another anthropologist has concluded that "primitive" people made little distinction between human and animal, and therefore in the liminal state the human could slide over into the animal. Turner disagrees, and holds the opposite view: The animal forms humans take on in the liminal state serve precisely to impose clear distinctions between the different orders of reality as encountered in everyday life. In the same way, by allowing the pious behavior of a woman to pass over into the liminal state to impious behavior, the book of Judith effectively teaches a rigid distinction between the two, a distinction that would be maintained in the non-liminal state.

The puzzling detail of the lambskins (v. 15) may be simply an element added for atmosphere, an indication of Holofernes' generous hospitality,

111. Pliny *Natural History* 13.41.

112. Victor Turner, "Betwixt and Between: The Liminal Period in Rites de Passage," in *The Forest of Symbols: Aspects of Ndembu Ritual* (Ithaca: Cornell University Press, 1967) 96, 107.

or it may suggest a special precaution to avoid ritual contamination. Menstrual impurity can be communicated by a woman to beds and mats (Lev 15:20-23); perhaps these special lambskins are held to protect Judith from impure contact, moving, as it were, in the opposite direction—that is, from her environment onto her.

Now Judith is reclining with Holofernes at dinner, and on this night he expects to ravish her. Judith seems to be cooperative, even excited herself, but for an entirely different reason. Her apparent cooperation could only excite Holofernes all the more, for although Judith eats and drinks what her maid has prepared, Holofernes now commences drinking wine in a celebratory mood—in fact, more than he has ever drunk in a day. He is indeed out of his mind with desire, which has clearly clouded his thinking. He believes himself to be in control and intends to seduce her with wine, but it is he who is under her control and who is becoming drunk instead.[113] The description of the mythical opponent as given by Campbell could be used to describe Holofernes or Nebuchadnezzar: "The tyrant is proud, and therein lies his doom. He is proud because he thinks of his strength as his own; thus he is in the clown role, as a mistaker of shadow for substance; it is his destiny to be tricked."[114]

113. Luis Alonso-Schökel, *Narrative Structures in the Book of Judith* (Berkeley, Calif.: Center for Hermeneutical Studies in Hellenistic and Modern Culture, 1974) 12.

114. Joseph Campbell, *The Hero with a Thousand Faces* (New York: Pantheon, 1949) 337.

Judith 13:1-10*a*, Judith Beheads Holofernes

NAB

13 1 When it grew late, his servants quickly withdrew. Bagoas closed the tent from the outside and excluded the attendants from their master's presence. They went off to their beds, for they were all tired from the prolonged banquet. 2 Judith was left alone in the tent with Holofernes, who lay prostrate on his bed, for he was sodden with wine. 3 She had ordered her maid to stand outside the bedroom and wait, as on the other days, for her to come out; she said she would be going out for her prayer. To Bagoas she had said this also.

4 When all had departed, and no one, small or great, was left in the bedroom, Judith stood by Holofernes' bed and said within herself: "O LORD, God of all might, in this hour look graciously on my undertaking for the exaltation of Jerusalem; 5 now is the time for aiding your heritage and for carrying out my design to shatter the enemies who have risen against us." 6 She went to the bedpost near the head of Holofernes, and taking his sword from it, 7 drew close to the bed, grasped the hair of his head, and said, "Strengthen me this day, O God of Israel!" 8 Then with all her might she struck him twice in the neck and cut off his head. 9 She rolled his body off the bed and took the canopy from its supports. Soon

NRSV

13 When evening came, his slaves quickly withdrew. Bagoas closed the tent from outside and shut out the attendants from his master's presence. They went to bed, for they all were weary because the banquet had lasted so long. 2But Judith was left alone in the tent, with Holofernes stretched out on his bed, for he was dead drunk.

3Now Judith had told her maid to stand outside the bedchamber and to wait for her to come out, as she did on the other days; for she said she would be going out for her prayers. She had said the same thing to Bagoas. 4So everyone went out, and no one, either small or great, was left in the bedchamber. Then Judith, standing beside his bed, said in her heart, "O Lord God of all might, look in this hour on the work of my hands for the exaltation of Jerusalem. 5Now indeed is the time to help your heritage and to carry out my design to destroy the enemies who have risen up against us."

6She went up to the bedpost near Holofernes' head, and took down his sword that hung there. 7She came close to his bed, took hold of the hair of his head, and said, "Give me strength today, O Lord God of Israel!" 8Then she struck his neck twice with all her might, and cut off his head.

NAB

afterward, she came out and handed over the head of Holofernes to her maid, 10 who put it into her food pouch; and the two went off together as they were accustomed to do for prayer.

13, 10: (*kata ton ethismon autōn*) *epi tēn proseuchēn:* so LXX[S,A].

NRSV

9Next she rolled his body off the bed and pulled down the canopy from the posts. Soon afterward she went out and gave Holofernes' head to her maid, 10who placed it in her food bag.

Then the two of them went out together, as they were accustomed to do for prayer.

COMMENTARY

The climactic scene is prepared for in some detail: Bagoas dismisses the servants and closes the tent from the outside. Judith's maid will stand outside the bedchamber—that is, the inner chamber of the tent, which was covered with the rich canopy (10:21). Judith alone remains in the inner chamber with Holofernes, who is now passed out drunk on his bed. The beheading scene, however, is told quickly, having been anticipated for twelve chapters. Her prayer invokes the power of God to come to the aid of Jerusalem, another indication that this book does not have a hidden Samaritan orientation.

Judith's actions are charged with sexual imagery, as many scholars have noted.[115] First, the vertical bedpost is a phallic symbol upon which Holofernes has hung his sword, another phallic symbol. Holofernes' head is now beside the post, but because he is drunk, he has lost his virility and potency, just at the time when he expected to demonstrate them. Judith grasps him by the hair of his head, and praying again for strength, with two strokes severs his head from his body, an act that many commentators have viewed as a symbolic castration; at first impotent, he is now unmanned. She dethrones him by rolling him off the bed, and she takes the canopy from the posts. If the name "Bethulia" means virgin and Holofernes intended to rape the virgin, then the process has now been reversed and Judith has "raped" Holofernes by penetrating his inner chamber, "deflowering" him, and breaking his canopy. A confirmation of the importance of the canopy, if not its sexual meaning as Holofernes' "hymen," is the fact that Judith will present it as a votive offering in the Temple in Jerusalem (16:19). If this reading of sexual symbolism seems more than what was intended by the author, it should be noted that sexual symbolism such as this is not unusual in popular tales,[116] although it may have been more unconscious than deliberate. Some scholars, to be sure, do not find sexual images present in the narrative,[117] but this text, perhaps more than any other in the OT, is capable of being interpreted in these terms.

Among the biblical passages that have likely influenced the author of Judith is the struggle between David and Goliath (1 Samuel 17). In preparation for his encounters with Goliath, David takes off the armor of Saul, which is a symbol of strength, and chooses the weapons of the weak: five smooth stones taken from a riverbed. Thus he affirms the power of the weak just as Judith does. He places the stones in his pouch as he marches out, just as Judith has placed in her pouch her kosher food, a necessary "weapon" for her stay in Holofernes' camp. Finally, David's utterance to Goliath is similar to Judith's language, although David has no need for double entendre: "This very day the LORD will deliver you into my hand, and I will strike you down and cut off your head" (1 Sam 17:46 NRSV). David first strikes Goliath in the head with a stone to subdue him, then, lacking a sword of his own, David, like

115. Alan Dundes, "Response," in Alonso-Schökel, *Narrative Structures,* 28-29; Amy-Jill Levine, "Sacrifice and Salvation: Otherness and Domestication in the Book of Judith," in *"No One Spoke Ill of Her": Essays on Judith,* ed. James C. VanderKam (Atlanta: Scholars Press, 1992); Mary Jacobus, "Judith, Holofernes, and the Phallic Woman," in *Reading Women: Essays in Feminist Criticism* (New York: Columbia University Press, 1986) 110-36; Margarita Stocker, *Judith, Sexual Warrior: Women and Power in Western Culture* (New Haven: Yale University Press, 1998) 3-23.

116. Bruno Bettelheim, *The Uses of Enchantment: The Meaning and Importance of Fairy Tales* (New York: Vintage, 1977) 232-33, 268-73, 289-92; Erich Fromm, *Forgotten Language: An Introduction to the Understanding of Dreams, Fairy Tales and Myths* (New York: Grove, 1957) 240-41.

117. Moore, *Judith,* 72-73, 240.

Judith, stands over his adversary, takes his sword, and cuts off his head. When the enemy forces saw that their leader had been beheaded, they fled.

The food pouch, which had before represented Judith's special care in remaining kosher, now becomes the trophy pouch containing Holofernes' head and canopy. The grisly irony of this fact has attracted much attention, because in many of the paintings of Judith decapitating Holofernes, she appears with her maid, and it is their secret pact to carry home his head in a pouch that seems to connect them in the reader's memory, even though the maid is not present in the story when Judith actually beheads Holofernes. The meticulous practices of the two women have bound them together until today. The act is quickly concluded in the text in just a few verses, and their escape from the Assyrian camp and their retracing of the steps back up the mountainside to Bethulia is almost instantaneous. Everything in the book has prepared for this moment, and so it was not necessary to dwell on it. The quick release of tension flows as a result of Judith's act, and it is a credit to the pacing of the narrative that the author seems to speed up or slow down the action in just the right places.

REFLECTIONS

The book of Judith has provoked very different moral valuations in artists, theologians, and commentators over the centuries. Many Victorian-era writers and some later writers have strongly questioned the morality of Judith's position. What is more surprising are the authors who are far from being Victorian prudes who nonetheless find Judith threatening. Sigmund Freud was quite interested in Judith, but he participated in the typical evaluation of his day and demoted her from a brilliant and strong-willed heroine to a petulant woman who, like a moth to light, was brought within Holofernes' bedchamber and was actually raped by Holofernes as a result. She takes up his own sword and beheads him only in revenge for his violation of her.[118]

Yet, interestingly, commentators in the ancient world reveal no defensiveness about Judith whatsoever. *First Clement,* the earliest known Jewish or Christian work to mention Judith, saw her unequivocally as a heroine of the faith. It is perhaps by finding in Judith a symbol of something else that Christians and Jews could accommodate her with so little reservation. Other Christian authors have championed her cause, praising her virtues of celibacy and fasting. She has consistently appeared in Christian reflection as a military heroine, as a symbol of virtue (usually chastity or humility), or as a symbol of the virgin Mary victorious over Satan. Reading of part of the Song of Judith (chap. 16) occurs in the lectionary passages associated with Mary and with Joan of Arc.[119] Jews likewise elevate her as a heroine associated with the values of the Maccabean revolt. She has continually been depicted with Hanukkah menorahs, a holiday associated with a miracle at the time of the Maccabean revolt. In art as well, Judith was early on consistently depicted as positive, whether as a military heroine or as a saintly, pious heroine of virtue.[120]

How do we account for this difference between the positive early attitudes toward Judith's actions and the often unsettled or even negative views in the modern period? The key seems to be in locating precisely when the change occurred, and it illuminates the ambivalent modern

118. See Mary Jacobus, "Judith, Holofernes, and the Phallic Woman," in *Reading Women: Essays in Feminist Criticism* (New York: Columbia University Press, 1986).

119. Brian McNeil, "Reflections on the Book of Judith," *The Downside Review* 96 (1978).

120. Some of the important examples of artistic depictions can be seen in Nira Stone, "Judith and Holofernes: Some Observations on the Development of the Scene in Art, in *"No One Spoke Ill of Her": Essays on Judith,* ed. James C. VanderKam (Atlanta: Scholars Press, 1992) 73-93; Moore, *Judith*; Mary Garrard, "Judith," in *Artemisia Gentileschi: The Image of the Female Hero in Italian Baroque Art* (Princeton: Princeton University Press, 1989); Mary Jacobus, "Judith, Holofernes, and the Phallic Woman," in *Reading Women: Essays in Feminist Criticism* (New York: Columbia University Press, 1986); and Mieke Bal, "Head Hunting: 'Judith' on the Cutting Edge of Knowledge," *JSOT* 63 (1994).

reactions to her character. The Christian artistic representations of Judith began to change unmistakably around 1600.[121] The Renaissance artists around 1500 still portrayed Judith positively, but by 1600, a certain ambivalence entered into the depictions, as can be seen in Cristofaro Allori's painting of 1607: a calm and beautiful Judith with a face as smooth as an egg holds Holofernes' head by the hair at her side, her fingers clenched into a tight fist. It is like a trophy that she has effortlessly yanked out by the roots. By this time, a number of other Renaissance painters began to portray Judith sadistically or Holofernes sympathetically, as if to suggest now that their identification with Holofernes as a man was stronger than their hatred of him as an enemy of God. Particularly to be noted in this category are Michelangelo Caravaggio and Bernardo Cavallino. Not surprisingly, Christian theologians also by this time, but evidently not before, began to condemn the book more forthrightly. Capellus (Louis Cappel), a French Huguenot Protestant, writing in 1689, called it "a most silly fable invented by a most inept, injudicious, impudent and clownish Hellenist."[122]

Two factors probably entered in at this period to change drastically the common perception of Judith. First is the introduction of a kind of realism. While Judith was a sort of Joan of Arc figure, no matter how outrageous, she was heroic and a defender of the faith. But Luther's historical observations (see Introduction), still quite positive, signal the beginnings of a realistic concern to bring Judith into the known world, where she simply became too dangerous and unsettling for many people's sensibilities. When the unreal, liminal state of Judith's actions were seen as occurring in the real world in real time, the crucial distinction was lost and a threat to good order was perceived in her actions. Second, as Stocker shows, Judith became a common biblical figure in arguments on both sides of the Reformation debates.[123] The many ruling queens in the monarchies of Europe at this time gave rise to a so-called gynecocratic (rule by women) controversy, and in that context Judith could easily be taken up as a heroine or a villain, depending on one's loyalties for or against a queen.

Because Judith is such a strong female character, the question of the moral evaluation of her actions is intimately bound up with the question of whether the work should be considered feminist. Recent commentators have disagreed on this, and feminist scholars have disagreed as well.[124] The answer to this question may depend on what century one is referring to. From the time of its composition to the sixteenth century, Judith's act was portrayed warmly and positively by male religious leaders. She was a heroine of the church and the synagogue. It does not seem appropriate to call this Judith a feminist creation. When society changed, however, and Judith came to be viewed as a more flesh-and-blood figure, she was perceived as threatening to good order and her achievement was called into question by male commentators. By the simple criterion of the challenge to male order, this Judith can be considered feminist.

121. Jacobus, "Judith, Holofernes, and the Phallic Woman."

122. Quoted in Carey A. Moore, *Judith,* AB 40 (Garden City, N.Y.: Doubleday, 1985) 46.

123. Margarita Stocker, *Judith, Sexual Warrior: Women and Power in Western Culture* (New Haven: Yale University Press, 1998) 67-119.

124. Pamela Milne is a good example of a scholar who is not comfortable with the designation of Judith as feminist. See Milne, "What Shall We Do with Judith? A Feminist Assessment of a Biblical 'Heroine,' " *Semeia* 62 (1993) 37-58. Stocker, *Judith, Sexual Warrior,* argues forcefully that the character represents an uncontainable burst of freedom. It should be noted, however, that Stocker's book is much stronger on the art and literature of the early modern period, when Judith becomes more charged, and less successful in addressing the ancient Jewish text.

JUDITH 13:10*b*–15:7, JUDITH RETURNS TO BETHULIA AND INITIATES COUNTERATTACK

Judith 13:10*b*-20, Judith and Her Maid Return to Bethulia

NAB

They passed through the camp, and skirting the ravine, reached Bethulia on the mountain. As they approached its gates, 11 Judith shouted to the guards from a distance: "Open! Open the gate! God, our God, is with us. Once more he has made manifest his strength in Israel and his power against our enemies; he has done it this very day." 12 When the citizens heard her voice, they quickly descended to their city gate and summoned the city elders. 13 All the people, from the least to the greatest, hurriedly assembled, for her return seemed unbelievable. They opened the gate and welcomed the two women. They made a fire for light; and when they gathered around the two, 14 Judith urged them with a loud voice: "Praise God, praise him! Praise God, who has not withdrawn his mercy from the house of Israel, but has shattered our enemies by my hand this very night." 15 Then she took the head out of the pouch, showed it to them, and said: "Here is the head of Holofernes, general in charge of the Assyrian army, and here is the canopy under which he lay in his drunkenness. The LORD struck him down by the hand of a woman. 16 As the LORD lives, who has protected me in the path I have followed, I swear that it was my face that seduced Holofernes to his ruin, and that he did not sin with me to my defilement or disgrace."

17 All the people were greatly astonished. They bowed down and worshiped God, saying with one accord, "Blessed are you, our God, who today have brought to nought the enemies of your people." 18 Then Uzziah said to her: "Blessed are you, daughter, by the Most High God, above all the women on earth; and blessed be the LORD God, the creator of heaven and earth, who guided your blow at the head of the chief of our enemies. 19 Your deed of hope will never be forgotten by those who tell of the might of God. 20 May God make this redound to your everlasting honor, rewarding you with blessings, because you risked

NRSV

They passed through the camp, circled around the valley, and went up the mountain to Bethulia, and came to its gates. [11]From a distance Judith called out to the sentries at the gates, "Open, open the gate! God, our God, is with us, still showing his power in Israel and his strength against our enemies, as he has done today!"

12When the people of her town heard her voice, they hurried down to the town gate and summoned the elders of the town. [13]They all ran together, both small and great, for it seemed unbelievable that she had returned. They opened the gate and welcomed them. Then they lit a fire to give light, and gathered around them. [14]Then she said to them with a loud voice, "Praise God, O praise him! Praise God, who has not withdrawn his mercy from the house of Israel, but has destroyed our enemies by my hand this very night!"

15Then she pulled the head out of the bag and showed it to them, and said, "See here, the head of Holofernes, the commander of the Assyrian army, and here is the canopy beneath which he lay in his drunken stupor. The Lord has struck him down by the hand of a woman. [16]As the Lord lives, who has protected me in the way I went, I swear that it was my face that seduced him to his destruction, and that he committed no sin with me, to defile and shame me."

17All the people were greatly astonished. They bowed down and worshiped God, and said with one accord, "Blessed are you our God, who have this day humiliated the enemies of your people."

18Then Uzziah said to her, "O daughter, you are blessed by the Most High God above all other women on earth; and blessed be the Lord God, who created the heavens and the earth, who has guided you to cut off the head of the leader of our enemies. [19]Your praise[a] will never depart from the hearts of those who remember the power of

[a] Other ancient authorities read *hope*

NAB

your life when your people were being oppressed, and you averted our disaster, walking uprightly before our God." And all the people answered, "Amen! Amen!"

NRSV

God. [20]May God grant this to be a perpetual honor to you, and may he reward you with blessings, because you risked your own life when our nation was brought low, and you averted our ruin, walking in the straight path before our God." And all the people said, "Amen. Amen."

COMMENTARY

13:10b-17. Judith's call to open the gates corresponds to her request to open the gates at 10:9 and marks an important point in Judith's heroic quest: She has moved out of her tent of isolation, traveled forth to meet the dragon, slayed it, and now returns. Her words also serve multiple functions; in addition to marking her return across the threshold of the gates, they also take up the language of an enthronement psalm or a victory ode (see Commentary on 16:1-17).[125] Compare Ps 24:7: "Lift up your heads, O gates! and be lifted up, O ancient doors! that the King of glory may come in" (NRSV). Her call as she returns, "God our God is with us," is similar to the psalm, and the continuation of her words in v. 14, "Praise God, who has not withdrawn his mercy from the house of Israel" also resounds like a victory ode. The literal gates of Bethulia, then, become like the figurative gates of the psalms (which are themselves based on the actual gates of the Temple). A longer victory song is to come in chap. 16.

In the meantime, she must demonstrate to her fellow citizens her first victory over the Assyrians. Producing the head of Holofernes is certainly dramatic, and the canopy represents another important trophy of her conquest. She further emphasizes the reversal and shame for Holofernes by stating, "The Lord has struck him down by the hand of a woman." This statement is also made in Judith's prayer at 9:10, and it echoes the tradition of another woman deliverer, the unnamed wise woman of Abel (2 Sam 20:14-22). It is also difficult not to connect her words "my *face* that seduced him to his destruction" with the fact that his face is in her hand. One is left with the image of her face and his, with the beauty of Judith's face vanquishing the power of Holofernes. Like Hamlet holding up the skull of Yorick, Judith in a more macabre situation can sum up this relationship between Holofernes and herself; the image of Judith's face juxtaposed with Holofernes' is certainly the one that many artists have chosen to depict. Judith is also quick to assure the Bethulians that Holofernes had not defiled her. It would have been hard for them to believe that she could have gotten close enough to Holofernes to chop off his head and still escape his advances. Although they have not seen what the audience has seen, they still believe her word.

13:18-20. Uzziah's blessing on Judith is very similar to the blessing of Jael for having killed Sisera in the Song of Deborah (Judg 5:24), and also the blessing of Mary at Luke 1:42. In each case the woman blessed is the "most blessed of women." The blessings of Judith and Jael come after a great victory, and in this they are also like Melchizedek's blessing of Abram (Abraham) at Gen 14:19-20. The latter contains several parallels to Uzziah's blessing: "Blessed be Abram by God Most High, maker of heaven and earth; and blessed be God Most High, who has delivered your enemies into your hand!" As in Judith, we find here a double blessing—of the individual and of God—and they both bring in the themes of creation and deliverance from enemies. Uzziah continues with an assurance that the memory of Judith's deed will live on forever, a theme that will close the book as a whole (see Commentary on 16:21-25). Judith's act is acclaimed by Uzziah and the people of Bethulia, and like Judith herself, they balance the credit for the deed between Judith and God. Still, her heroism is being praised,

125. Luis Alonso-Schökel, *Narrative Structures in the Book of Judith* (Berkeley, Calif.: Center for Hermeneutical Studies in Hellenistic and Modern Culture, 1974) 12.

and memory of it will last forever. This last point is crucial for the heroic paradigm, as every culture must sing the praises of its heroes long after they are gone; the end of the book of Judith will be taken up with this theme. The people then authenticate Uzziah's words with "Amen! Amen!" (See Reflections at 14:1-10.)

Judith 14:1-10, Judith Issues Orders and Achior Converts

NAB

14 1 Then Judith said to them: "Listen to me, my brothers. Take this head and hang it on the parapet of your wall. 2 At daybreak, when the sun rises on the earth, let each of you seize his weapons, and let all the able-bodied men rush out of the city under command of a captain, as if about to go down into the plain against the advance guard of the Assyrians, but without going down. 3 They will seize their armor and hurry to their camp to awaken the generals of the Assyrian army. When they run to the tent of Holofernes and do not find him, panic will seize them, and they will flee before you. 4 Then you and all the other inhabitants of the whole territory of Israel will pursue them and strike them down in their tracks. 5 But before doing this, summon for me Achior the Ammonite, that he may see and recognize the one who despised the house of Israel and sent him here to meet his death."

6 So they called Achior from the house of Uzziah. When he came and saw the head of Holofernes in the hand of one of the men in the assembly of the people, he fell forward in a faint. 7 Then, after they lifted him up, he threw himself at the feet of Judith in homage, saying: "Blessed are you in every tent of Judah; and in every foreign nation, all who hear of you will be struck with terror. 8 But now, tell me all that you did during these days." So Judith told him, in the presence of the people, all that she had been doing from the day she left till the time she began speaking to them. 9 When she finished her account, the people cheered loudly, and their city resounded with shouts of joy. 10 Now Achior, seeing all that the God of Israel had done, believed firmly in him. He had the flesh of his foreskin circumcised, and he has been united with the house of Israel to the present day.

NRSV

14 Then Judith said to them, "Listen to me, my friends. Take this head and hang it upon the parapet of your wall. [2]As soon as day breaks and the sun rises on the earth, each of you take up your weapons, and let every able-bodied man go out of the town; set a captain over them, as if you were going down to the plain against the Assyrian outpost; only do not go down. [3]Then they will seize their arms and go into the camp and rouse the officers of the Assyrian army. They will rush into the tent of Holofernes and will not find him. Then panic will come over them, and they will flee before you. [4]Then you and all who live within the borders of Israel will pursue them and cut them down in their tracks. [5]But before you do all this, bring Achior the Ammonite to me so that he may see and recognize the man who despised the house of Israel and sent him to us as if to his death."

6So they summoned Achior from the house of Uzziah. When he came and saw the head of Holofernes in the hand of one of the men in the assembly of the people, he fell down on his face in a faint. [7]When they raised him up he threw himself at Judith's feet, and did obeisance to her, and said, "Blessed are you in every tent of Judah! In every nation those who hear your name will be alarmed. [8]Now tell me what you have done during these days."

So Judith told him in the presence of the people all that she had done, from the day she left until the moment she began speaking to them. [9]When she had finished, the people raised a great shout and made a joyful noise in their town. [10]When Achior saw all that the God of Israel had done, he believed firmly in God. So he was circumcised, and joined the house of Israel, remaining so to this day.

COMMENTARY

14:1-4. Judith's cleverness does not end with the decapitation of Holofernes, or with her quick escape, but extends to the stratagem by which she will use Holofernes' head to defeat his entire army. Judith orchestrates some clever stagecraft to manipulate the Assyrian soldiers into discovering the headless corpse of Holofernes at the most effective moment possible. She again demonstrates complete authority over the Bethulians, and also complete control over the enemy. Hanging the head of the leader of the enemy is encountered elsewhere in the Bible (1 Sam 17:54; 31:9-10; 2 Kgs 10:7-8; Matt 14:8). It perhaps originated in the procession of trophies; a famous bas-relief in the Arch of Titus in Rome depicts the procession through Rome of the trophies taken from Jerusalem after the destruction of the city and the Temple. Prominent among them is a menorah, the symbol of the Jewish religion. Aside from the close parallels to David's decapitation and exhibition of Goliath's head, there are even closer and more contemporary parallels in Judas Maccabeus's defeat of the Seleucid general Nicanor in 1 Macc 7:47 and 2 Macc 15:35: "Judas hung Nicanor's head from the citadel, a clear and conspicuous sign to everyone of the help of the Lord." This example is especially significant since the name of Judith may be inspired by the name of Judas Maccabeus (see Introduction), and also because this treatment of Nicanor's head was part of the introduction of an annual festival celebrating his defeat, called Nicanor's Day. In other words, the memory of this deed is celebrated continually just as the memory of Judith's is said to be (13:19-20; 16:23).

14:5-10. Judith's language in summoning Achior indicates that she is not simply interested in authenticating the identity of Holofernes' head. As already noted, the issues of honor and shame are prominent in Judith, as they are in Esther and other texts in the Bible. Holofernes had shamed Israel because he "despised" it and also because he sent Achior to Bethulia "as if to his death." By bringing Achior in to identify the head of Holofernes, Judith begins the process of reversing the balance of honor and shame, which must be done publicly. Achior's reaction is dramatic, even more dramatic than that of the Bethulians in 13:17. However, he escaped from close contact with Holofernes and had known the man face-to-face. Further, his stronger reaction—he actually collapses—convincingly confirms beyond doubt that the head is indeed that of Holofernes. In addition, it dramatizes the fulfillment of Holofernes' foolhardy prediction that "you shall not see my face again from this day until I take revenge on this race" (6:5). It is very ironic that Achior immediately faints at the sight of Holofernes' head, since Judith had been so bold and nerveless both in taking it and in handling it.[126] Thus their expected gender roles have been reversed; and this is unusual in Jewish novels (cf., e.g., Esther fainting as she comes before the king, Add. Esth 15:7).

Achior blesses Judith, as did Uzziah and the people in chap. 13. One is reminded of the many blessings that occur in the final chapters of Tobit, but there the number of blessings is perhaps exaggerated for comic effect. In Judith the blessings match the drama and heroism of the moment. Achior's blessing is interesting in that it is not what we would expect from an Ammonite: "Blessed are you in every tent of Judah." This signals Achior's perception of the power and benevolence of Israel's God, which he had interpreted for Holofernes in chap. 5. Achior also characterizes Judith as a heroic *warrior*: "those who hear your name will be alarmed." It is not simply that Judith has found an opportunity at this juncture in history to save her people; she is a heroine for the ages, capable of striking fear in the hearts of other enemies as well. But it is significant that Achior as well recognizes that the deliverance comes from both Judith and God: "When Achior saw all that the God of Israel had done, he believed firmly in God." Although Judith credits God alone, neither Judith nor God is forgotten in any of the blessings by the others. It is sufficient evidence of God's power and protection that Achior believes in God and is circumcised and joins Israel. Since Achior (or Ahikar) is a Jewish courtier in Tobit, it may be that these two novels share a tradition of the appropriation

126. Moore, *Judith*, 235.

of the famous Assyrian courtier Ahikar (see Commentary on 5:5-21).

That Achior, an Ammonite, was circumcised appears to violate Jewish law, which forbids the admission of an Ammonite or a Moabite to the tenth generation (Deut 23:3). Was Achior past the tenth generation?[127] Like Ruth, a Moabite, was Achior granted a special dispensation? It is probably simply the case that this Jewish novel allows for a romanticized, but fictionalized, entry of the famous Achior into the Israelite fold, as in Tobit. The same novel that could demonize "Nebuchadnezzar the king of the Assyrians" could idealize "Achior the Ammonite."

127. So Toni Craven, *Artistry and Faith in the Book of Judith* (Chico, Calif.: Scholars Press, 1983) 103n. 68.

REFLECTIONS

Achior's conversion is one of the warmer moments in a book marked by satire and humor. It is briefly but provocatively told. The reason for his conversion is stated simply: "Achior saw all that the God of Israel had done." We are prepared for this conversion, however, by the relatively long speech of Achior in chap. 5.

Any scene of conversion brings to the fore issues of the meaning of religion for the audience, whether ancient or modern. It may be helpful to pause and consider other biblical accounts of conversion, for they reflect some significant differences from each other, and yet all contribute to a picture of conversion that is very modern. First of all, there is the moving depiction of Ruth's conversion, which is addressed to her mother-in-law, Naomi, as Ruth's representative of the Israelite faith: "Where you go, I will go. . . . Your people shall be my people, and your God my God" (Ruth 1:16 NRSV). Ruth, like Achior, is from an excluded ethnic group that had been an enemy of Israel. Both of their descriptions are short but somehow profound. And neither convert chooses at this time to state abstract articles of faith—they are entering a community that comes under the protection of a different understanding of God from the one they have known. Other conversion scenes include Abraham, who is the first to become a worshiper of God (Genesis 12); this becomes the coming-to-faith paradigm for Jews and Christians. The personal encounter with God marks it as different from Achior's and Ruth's, but it is in this respect similar to the description of Paul's experience of the risen Lord in Acts 9. One other example may be helpful. The Ethiopian eunuch in Acts 8:26-40 is reading Isaiah, but is instructed by Philip concerning "the good news about Jesus." This is the only one of these scenes in which someone is catechized or instructed as preparation to conversion.

The various scenes focus on different aspects of conversion: direct encounter with God, joining a new community, catechesis. Which of these is the most important? Like all good literature, the various examples are more suggestive than descriptive in a journalistic way. By combining them, one would begin to get a fuller notion of the nature of what the new faith meant to those in the story, and what a new faith may mean for us today.

Before we turn from this scene of conversion, however, we should remember that different aspects of conversion are not just relevant for those who have converted; they also express the core beliefs of a religion and provide the psychological and reflective experience of coming to a new understanding of faith, even for those who have lived within a particular religion all their lives. In this core one usually sees the whole represented: The God of history is also the God of mercy, of life, of community, of creation. Coming to a new faith and renewing an old faith may be similar processes, and most people's religious lives involve a number of "conversions" in the form of changes and renewals.

Achior's own conversion scene, though quite simple, also implies more than meets the eye. He has already shown that he knows Israel's history, and he is finally convinced to convert by the dramatic rescue of Israel through the hand of Judith. The brevity of the scene challenges the modern reader to ask, What is the core that would define *my* faith? What would make me convert? What would be the cinching evidence before our eyes that what God did in the past God is also doing today? Being manifest in nature? Transforming the world? Creating community? Bringing about justice? Entering into people's lives? The story of the conversion of Achior can raise questions that address the very definition of the core of the religious life of people in the present world, both those who have converted and those who have not.

Judith 14:11–15:7, The Assyrians Discover Holofernes' Headless Body and Are Put to Flight

NAB

11 At daybreak they hung the head of Holofernes on the wall. Then all the Israelite men took up their arms and went to the slopes of the mountain. 12 When the Assyrians saw them, they notified their captains; these, in turn, went to the generals and division leaders and all their other commanders. 13 They came to the tent of Holofernes and said to the one in charge of all his things, "Waken our master, for the slaves have dared come down to give us battle, to their utter destruction." 14 Bagoas went in, and knocked at the entry of the tent, presuming that he was sleeping with Judith. 15 As no one answered, he parted the curtains, entered the bedroom, and found him lying on the floor, a headless corpse. 16 He broke into a loud clamor of weeping, groaning, and howling, and rent his garments. 17 Then he entered the tent where Judith had her quarters; and, not finding her, he rushed out to the troops and cried: 18 "The slaves have duped us! A single Hebrew woman has brought disgrace on the house of King Nebuchadnezzar. Here is Holofernes headless on the ground!"

19 When the commanders of the Assyrian army heard these words, they rent their tunics and were seized with consternation. Loud screaming and howling arose in the camp.

15 1 On hearing what had happened, those still in their tents were amazed, 2 and overcome with fear and trembling. No one kept ranks any longer; they scattered in all directions, and fled along every road, both through the valley and in the mountains. 3 Those also who were stationed in the mountain district around Bethulia took to flight. Then all the Israelite warriors overwhelmed them.

NRSV

11As soon as it was dawn they hung the head of Holofernes on the wall. Then they all took their weapons, and they went out in companies to the mountain passes. [12]When the Assyrians saw them they sent word to their commanders, who then went to the generals and the captains and to all their other officers. [13]They came to Holofernes' tent and said to the steward in charge of all his personal affairs, "Wake up our lord, for the slaves have been so bold as to come down against us to give battle, to their utter destruction."

14So Bagoas went in and knocked at the entry of the tent, for he supposed that he was sleeping with Judith. [15]But when no one answered, he opened it and went into the bedchamber and found him sprawled on the floor dead, with his head missing. [16]He cried out with a loud voice and wept and groaned and shouted, and tore his clothes. [17]Then he went to the tent where Judith had stayed, and when he did not find her, he rushed out to the people and shouted, [18]"The slaves have tricked us! One Hebrew woman has brought disgrace on the house of King Nebuchadnezzar. Look, Holofernes is lying on the ground, and his head is missing!"

19When the leaders of the Assyrian army heard this, they tore their tunics and were greatly dismayed, and their loud cries and shouts rose up throughout the camp.

15 When the men in the tents heard it, they were amazed at what had happened. [2]Overcome with fear and trembling, they did not wait for one another, but with one impulse all rushed out and fled by every path across the plain and through the hill country. [3]Those who had camped in the hills around Bethulia also took to flight. Then the Israelites, everyone that was a

NAB

4 Uzziah sent messengers to Betomasthaim, to Choba and Kona, and to the whole country of Israel to report what had happened, that all might fall upon the enemy and destroy them. 5 On hearing this, all the Israelites, with one accord, attacked them and cut them down as far as Choba. Even those from Jerusalem and the rest of the mountain region took part in this, for they too had been notified of the happenings in the camp of their enemies. The Gileadites and the Galileans struck the enemy's flanks with great slaughter, even beyond Damascus and its territory. 6 The remaining inhabitants of Bethulia swept down on the camp of the Assyrians, plundered it, and acquired great riches. 7 The Israelites who returned from the slaughter took possession of what was left, till the towns and villages in the mountains and on the plain were crammed with the enormous quantity of booty they had seized.

15, 4: (*eis Baitomasthaim kai*) *Choba* (*kai*) *Chona*: cf 4, 4.

NRSV

soldier, rushed out upon them. 4Uzziah sent men to Betomasthaim[a] and Choba and Kola, and to all the frontiers of Israel, to tell what had taken place and to urge all to rush out upon the enemy to destroy them. 5When the Israelites heard it, with one accord they fell upon the enemy,[b] and cut them down as far as Choba. Those in Jerusalem and all the hill country also came, for they were told what had happened in the camp of the enemy. The men in Gilead and in Galilee outflanked them with great slaughter, even beyond Damascus and its borders. 6The rest of the people of Bethulia fell upon the Assyrian camp and plundered it, acquiring great riches. 7And the Israelites, when they returned from the slaughter, took possession of what remained. Even the villages and towns in the hill country and in the plain got a great amount of booty, since there was a vast quantity of it.

[a] Other ancient authorities add *and Bebai* [b] Gk *them*

COMMENTARY

14:11-18. The Bethulians follow Judith's orders to the letter, and the Assyrians respond exactly as she predicted. The Assyrians at first are rousing their troops with the full expectation that they will destroy "these slaves." The story is told with some retardation of the plot, as the reader is treated to a full description of the Assyrian camp in preparation, knowing that they are about to discover what has happened. The message that the Israelites have appeared to challenge the mighty Assyrians is sent up the chain of command to a character we have come to know very well, Bagoas. He is hesitant to disturb Holofernes from what he assumes will be his satisfied repose with Judith. Bagoas's reaction to seeing Holofernes' headless body is not very different from Achior's reaction to seeing Holofernes' head, although it has the opposite import for their lives. The author of Judith does not dwell on Bagoas's reaction, but shows its consequences. The reversal of honor and shame is spelled out: "The slaves have tricked us! One Hebrew woman has brought disgrace on the house of King Nebuchadnezzar." But the reversal is more dramatically—and humorously—brought home by Bagoas's concluding remarks, the last we shall hear from him: "Holofernes is lying on the ground, and his head is missing!"

14:19–15:7. The Assyrians somewhat surprisingly believe Bagoas when he tells them that their leader has lost his head, and they immediately fly into a panic. The description of panic and consternation is similar to others in contemporary literature, such as 2 Macc 3:14-21 and 3 Macc 1:16-29, but the present text is less wordy, depicting in just a few verses the scattering of the Assyrian troops. The key to the routing of the Assyrians is seen in one sentence, "Overcome with fear and trembling, they did not wait for one another"—that is, because of their stark fear there was no unit of soldiers left to turn against the vastly outnumbered Bethulians; rather, all fled separately. The panic and routing of the Assyrians is not based on the appearance of an angel or any other kind of apparition, as it is, for example, in 2 Maccabees 3–4. The Vulgate does mention the appearance of an angel, as does Judas Maccabeus concerning the routing of Nicanor's troops (1 Macc 7:40-42).[128] Word was quickly sent to the nearby Israelite villages, who attacked the flanks of the retreating Assyrians. The villages mentioned are unknown, perhaps fictitious, introduced to give the local color of the area around the fictitious town of Bethulia. Well-known regions are then brought into the picture, Gilead and Galilee, as they join in inflicting heavy casualties until the Assyrians had gotten beyond the borders of Israel. The author has probably been influenced by the story of Abram (Abraham) pursuing the captors of Lot in Genesis 14, for in the LXX version Choba and Damascus appear, and the clause "they fell upon" them is rendered in the same way. This is another indication that the present author is working with the biblical text and not just oral-traditional models.

128. Moore, *Judith*, 1985) 234.

The revenge of the Israelites on the retreating Assyrians is noted, although figures are not given as they are in Esth 9:16. The plundering of the Assyrian camp is also emphasized, in contrast to Esth 9:10, 15-16, where it is stated that the Jews did not touch the plunder. Judith turns over to the Temple all the items that she has received from the spoils (16:19; cf. Josh 6:19, 24), but the other Israelites keep their plunder for themselves. First Maccabees 7:44-47 may have provided a model for this description, as it describes the enemy troops fleeing while being attacked on both flanks by Jews from the surrounding villages, followed by the plundering of the soldiers. The triumph and reversal in Esther are also very similar, in that in both texts, there is first the removal of the immediate danger (execution of Holofernes, execution of Haman), then a broader revenge on the multitude of followers.

REFLECTIONS

It is generally a problem for the modern reader that a large part of the idea of deliverance in the Hebrew Bible involves taking vengeance on the enemies. One need only compare the beautiful first words of Ps 137:1, 4-5:

> By the rivers of Babylon—
> there we sat down and there we wept
> when we remembered Zion
>
> . . . .
>
> How could we sing the LORD's song
> in a foreign land?
> If I forget you, O Jerusalem,
> let my right hand wither! (NRSV)

with the same psalm's conclusion:

> O daughter Babylon, you devastator!
> Happy shall they be who pay you back
> what you have done to us!
> Happy shall they be who take your little ones
> and dash them against the rock! (Ps 137:8-9 NRSV)

The expression of this kind of revenge seems horrifying. We have difficulty endorsing this kind of revenge, even though it has been in the twentieth century that the worst forms of violence have been unleashed by the nations that have laid claim to being the most "advanced." We rightly have reservations about the expression of vengeance, and must reflect on the use of power in order to balance it wisely against past wrongs.

The total destruction of a city, including the killing of all its inhabitants and the taking of all its property, was condoned in the ancient Near East and also in the Hebrew Bible. The "holy war" idea, or total ban, was part of the conquest theme; when the Israelites took possession of the promised land they were to destroy the cities totally, killing all the inhabitants and destroying the property and livestock (Deut 7:1-2; 20:16-18; Josh 6:19, 24). A partial ban was in effect against cities outside the promised land. According to this less stringent policy, all males in the city would be killed, but the women and children would be taken as slaves and the spoils collected and kept (Deut 20:10-15). Although these brutal policies were considered acceptable in the ancient Near East, it is disturbing to encounter them in our own Holy Scriptures. However, it is not clear that they were ever enforced as such. Some of the nations that God instructed the Israelites to annihilate in the programmatic statements about the conquest (e.g., Deut 7:1-2) were archaic names at the time of writing and not real nations that the Israelites would have known; others were still in existence, and so therefore had clearly not been destroyed. One of the messages of the text may be that because they were not annihilated, the peoples remained in the land to cause problems for the centralization of Israelite worship thereafter. As destructive as the Israelite wars were, the language of holy war is a language of hyperbole, often told looking back at an idealized time. It is also sometimes suggested that the conquest of Canaan took place at a "primitive" time in Israel's history and was a necessary part of God's ordained plan to provide a land of inheritance for the descendants of Abraham. As a result, the violence of the settlement is partially mitigated.

What may be more important, however, for interpreting this aspect of Judith is its genre. The book of Judith is an entertaining, high-spirited, and perhaps fictitious novel. The level of violence is not really the difference between the early and late texts, but the "seriousness" of the early texts and the belief that the violence was divinely authorized. The modern reader often feels unsure whether the comic nature of Judith (and also of Esther) excuses the violence as an extended happy ending or merely makes such violent notions of revenge more palatable. The effect of a text like Judith is to create one-dimensional characters representing good and evil, which then permits a one-dimensional solution to the problem of revenge: It is justified in an absolute way because the enemy is so deserving of such a punishment. It is this aspect that should give us pause as we consider the effects of perceiving our enemies to be one-dimensional figures. It is only a short step from perceiving a one-dimensional enemy to justifying a one-dimensional—that is, total—notion of revenge. As the technological means of exercising a total ban on a city or a nation have been brought into existence, the imperative falls upon us all the more urgently to discern the multidimensionality of those who might oppose us.

JUDITH 15:8–16:25, CELEBRATION AND CONCLUSION

Judith 15:8-13, All of Israel Celebrates

NAB

8 The high priest Joakim and the elders of the Israelites, who dwelt in Jerusalem, came to see for themselves the good things that the LORD had done for Israel, and to meet and congratulate Judith. 9 When they had visited her, all with one accord blessed her, saying:

"You are the glory of Jerusalem,
the surpassing joy of Israel;

NRSV

8Then the high priest Joakim and the elders of the Israelites who lived in Jerusalem came to witness the good things that the Lord had done for Israel, and to see Judith and to wish her well.
9When they met her, they all blessed her with one accord and said to her, "You are the glory of Jerusalem, you are the great boast of Israel, you are the great pride of our nation! 10You have done

NAB

You are the splendid boast of our people.
10 With your own hand you have done all this;
You have done good to Israel,
and God is pleased with what you have
wrought.
May you be blessed by the LORD Almighty
forever and ever!"
And all the people answered, "Amen!"
11 For thirty days the whole populace plundered the camp, giving Judith the tent of Holofernes, with all his silver, his couches, his dishes,
and all his furniture, which she accepted. She
harnessed her mules, hitched her wagons to them,
and loaded these things on them.
12 All the women of Israel gathered to see her;
and they blessed her and performed a dance in
her honor. She took branches in her hands and
distributed them to the women around her. 13
and she and the other women crowned themselves with garlands of olive leaves. At the head
of all the people, she led the women in the dance,
while the men of Israel followed in their armor,
wearing garlands and singing hymns.

15, 10: (*kai*) *eudokēsen* (*ep' autois*): so almost all LXX^{MSS}.
15, 11: (*epethēken epi*) *tas 'ēmionous:* so a few LXX^{MSS}, Vet Lat, P.

NRSV

all this with your own hand; you have done great
good to Israel, and God is well pleased with it.
May the Almighty Lord bless you forever!" And
all the people said, "Amen."
11All the people plundered the camp for thirty
days. They gave Judith the tent of Holofernes and
all his silver dinnerware, his beds, his bowls, and
all his furniture. She took them and loaded her
mules and hitched up her carts and piled the
things on them.
12All the women of Israel gathered to see her,
and blessed her, and some of them performed a
dance in her honor. She took ivy-wreathed wands
in her hands and distributed them to the women
who were with her; 13and she and those who
were with her crowned themselves with olive
wreaths. She went before all the people in the
dance, leading all the women, while all the men
of Israel followed, bearing their arms and wearing
garlands and singing hymns.

COMMENTARY

That Bethulia has been tied by strong bonds to Jerusalem and the temple officials there has been emphasized often in Judith, and here the bonds are especially tight. The high priest Joakim and "the elders of the Israelites who lived in Jerusalem" come to Bethulia to witness and acclaim the actions of the local citizens. They give Judith her second blessing, which is also confirmed with the "Amen!" of the people. Verse 9 has been used in the Roman Catholic liturgy regarding the virgin Mary and Joan of Arc. The Israelites celebrate by plundering the enemy camp for thirty days. This will resonate in the reader's mind with the thirty-day rest that Holofernes enjoyed while he collected supplies before turning toward the Israelites (3:10). Holofernes' last rest before setting his face against the Israelites is thus balanced by the celebration of the plundering of his camp, in which his supplies are dispossessed. All of the riches of Holofernes' own tent are given to Judith, which she loads onto her carts and mules to take, as we learn in 16:19, to the Temple in Jerusalem.

The women of Israel bless Judith and dance a special dance in her honor. There is a strong tradition in Israel of women dancing and singing victory songs and dances. The Song of Miriam at Exod 15:21 is sung after the pharaoh and his troops are drowned in the Red Sea. It follows immediately upon the Song of the Sea, which is quoted in Judith's song in chap. 16. More typical of the victory songs is probably the song sung by the women after David slew Goliath (1 Sam 18:6): "The women came out of all the towns of Israel, singing and dancing . . . with tambourines, with songs of joy, and with musical instruments" (NRSV). The tambourine is also known from ancient depictions found in archaeological excavations; it was a small hand drum without the metal rattles found on modern tambourines. The dance of Jephthah's daughter and her companions is an interesting parallel because it also comes after a victory; yet, in this case it is also a lament because Jephthah has vowed to sacrifice as a thank offering the first person who comes out to meet him, who, unfortunately, is his daughter (Judg 11:29-40). Since the daughter's virginity is emphasized, and since the dance is said to become an annual dance for the daughters of Israel, the sacrifice of the daughter seems to have become a special part of women's spirituality. These passages provide some of the cultural background of victory songs and dances. In most cases, they are sung by women; and Cross and Freedman argue that Moses' Song of the Sea was originally attributed to Miriam as well (as it is now at Exod 15:21).[129] What is unusual is the use of wands and olive wreaths, which was originally a Greek practice. However, 2 Macc 10:7 and 3 Macc 7:16 indicate that during the Hasmonean period they had been adapted to Jewish practice as well.

129. F. M. Cross and D. N. Freedman, "The Song of Miriam," *JNES* 14 (1955) 237-50.

Judith 15:14–16:17, Judith's Victory Song

NAB

14 Judith led all Israel in this song of thanksgiving, and the people swelled this hymn of praise:

16 [1] "Strike up the instruments,
a song to my God with timbrels,
chant to the LORD with cymbals;
Sing to him a new song,
exalt and acclaim his name.
2 For the LORD is God; he crushes warfare,
and sets his encampment among his people;
he snatched me from the hands of my persecutors.

3 "The Assyrian came from the mountains of the north,
with the myriads of his forces he came;
Their numbers blocked the torrents, their horses covered the hills.
4 He threatened to burn my land,
put my youths to the sword,
Dash my babes to the ground,
make my children a prey,
and seize my virgins as spoil.

5 "But the LORD Almighty thwarted them,
by a woman's hand he confounded them.

16, 1: (*psalmon*) *kainon,* (*'ypsoute*): so LXX^{A} and a few other LXX^{MSS}.
16, 2: (*Kyrios,*) *'o titheis* (*parembolas autou*): so a few LXX^{MSS}, P, V.
16, 4: (*emprēsein ta*) *'oria* (*mou*): so LXX^{S,A}. (*kai tas parthenous*) *mou* (*skyleusai*): so LXX^{S,A}.
16, 5: (*en cheiri thēleias*) *katēschynen autous:* so a few LXX^{MSS}, Vet Lat, P; cf V.

NRSV

14Judith began this thanksgiving before all Israel, and all the people loudly sang this song of praise.

16 [1]And Judith said,
Begin a song to my God with tambourines,
sing to my Lord with cymbals.
Raise to him a new psalm;[a]
exalt him, and call upon his name.
[2] For the Lord is a God who crushes wars;
he sets up his camp among his people;
he delivered me from the hands of my pursuers.
[3] The Assyrian came down from the mountains of the north;
he came with myriads of his warriors;
their numbers blocked up the wadis,
and their cavalry covered the hills.
[4] He boasted that he would burn up my territory,
and kill my young men with the sword,
and dash my infants to the ground,
and seize my children as booty,
and take my virgins as spoil.

[5] But the Lord Almighty has foiled them
by the hand of a woman.[b]
[6] For their mighty one did not fall by the hands of the young men,

[a] Other ancient authorities read *a psalm and praise* [b] Other ancient authorities add *he has confounded them*

NAB

6 Not by youths was their mighty one struck down,
nor did titans bring him low,
nor huge giants attack him;
But Judith, the daughter of Merari,
by the beauty of her countenance disabled him.
7 She took off her widow's garb
to raise up the afflicted in Israel.
She anointed her face with fragrant oil;
8 with a fillet she fastened her tresses
and put on a linen robe to beguile him.
9 Her sandals caught his eyes,
and her beauty captivated his mind.
The sword cut through his neck.

10 "The Persians were dismayed at her daring,
the Medes appalled at her boldness.
11 When my lowly ones shouted, they were terrified;
when my weaklings cried out, they trembled;
at the sound of their war cry, they took to flight.
12 The sons of slave girls pierced them through;
the supposed sons of rebel mothers cut them down;
they perished before the ranks of my LORD.

13 "A new hymn I will sing to my God.
O LORD, great are you and glorious,
wonderful in power and unsurpassable.
14 Let your every creature serve you;
for you spoke, and they were made,
You sent forth your spirit, and they were created;
no one can resist your word.
15 The mountains to their bases, and the seas, are shaken;
the rocks, like wax, melt before your glance.

"But to those who fear you,
you are very merciful.
16 Though the sweet odor of every sacrifice is a trifle,
and the fat of all holocausts but little in your sight,
one who fears the LORD is forever great.

16, 12: *paides:* so with LXX[A]; cf LXX[B], 1 Sm 20, 30.

NRSV

nor did the sons of the Titans strike him down,
nor did tall giants set upon him;
but Judith daughter of Merari
with the beauty of her countenance undid him.

7 For she put away her widow's clothing
to exalt the oppressed in Israel.
She anointed her face with perfume;
8 she fastened her hair with a tiara
and put on a linen gown to beguile him.
9 Her sandal ravished his eyes,
her beauty captivated his mind,
and the sword severed his neck!
10 The Persians trembled at her boldness,
the Medes were daunted at her daring.

11 Then my oppressed people shouted;
my weak people cried out,[a] and the enemy[b] trembled;
they lifted up their voices, and the enemy[b] were turned back.
12 Sons of slave-girls pierced them through
and wounded them like the children of fugitives;
they perished before the army of my Lord.

13 I will sing to my God a new song:
O Lord, you are great and glorious,
wonderful in strength, invincible.
14 Let all your creatures serve you,
for you spoke, and they were made.
You sent forth your spirit,[c] and it formed them;[d]
there is none that can resist your voice.
15 For the mountains shall be shaken to their foundations with the waters;
before your glance the rocks shall melt like wax.
But to those who fear you
you show mercy.
16 For every sacrifice as a fragrant offering is a small thing,
and the fat of all whole burnt offerings to you is a very little thing;
but whoever fears the Lord is great forever.

[a] Other ancient authorities read *feared* [b] Gk *they* [c] Or *breath*
[d] Other ancient authorities read *they were created*

NAB

17 "Woe to the nations that rise against my
people!
the LORD Almighty will requite them;
in the day of judgment he will punish
them:
He will send fire and worms into their flesh,
and they shall burn and suffer forever."

16, 17: (*en ʿēmerą kriseōs*) *episkepsetai autous:* so 1 LXX, Vet Lat, P, V. (*kai*) *kauthēsontai* (*en aistēsei*): so 1 LXX^{MS}, Vet Lat, P. V.

NRSV

17 Woe to the nations that rise up against my
people!
The Lord Almighty will take vengeance on
them in the day of judgment;
he will send fire and worms into their flesh;
they shall weep in pain forever.

COMMENTARY

The book of Judith concludes with a hymn of thanksgiving, just as does Tobit. The interrelation of prose narrative and hymnic praise is common in the HB and the apocryphal books, but it is practically unknown in Greek literature.[130] Important examples include Moses' Song of the Sea in Exodus 15, the juxtaposition of Judges 4 and 5, Deuteronomy 32–33, 2 Samuel 22, Jonah 2, and the insertion of the Prayer of Azariah and the Song of the Three Jews in the Additions to Daniel. The structure of the hymn has been debated, as has its authorship. Is the song made of disparate parts? If so, were they composed by different authors and inserted at this point in the narrative? Was the story of Judith told in song before the prose narrative was written, as was likely the case with the Song of Deborah in Judges 5? We shall consider these questions as we analyze each of the parts in turn.

Two theories have been suggested for the structure of the Song of Judith. Jansen proposed that the song is composed of three separate hymnic fragments: (1) vv. 1-4, introduction to a thanksgiving psalm; (2) vv. 5-12, account of the story of Judith; and (3) vv. 13-17, enthronement hymn.[131] Jansen asserts that parts of the Song of Judith may pre-date the book of Judith, but it is now a purely literary composition—that is, it may have arisen from hymnic traditions, but it is now a written piece that functions within the book of Judith. Particularly suggestive about this theory is the observation that not only are there differences between the three sections in terms of theme, but also vv. 5-12 contain unmistakable references to the story of Judith. Craven argues instead that this arrangement imposes artificial breaks in the text and that there are motifs that join these sections together. A better analysis, in her mind, would be the following: (1) vv. 1-2, hymnic introduction; (2) vv. 3-12, narration of the epic event; (3) vv. 13-17, hymnic response. This structure has similarities to Moses' Song of the Sea in Exodus 15.[132] Here it will be argued that Craven's structure is ultimately more helpful, although the structure of the song is still somewhat irregular, and some of Jansen's observations should not be overlooked. Skehan also argues that there is a general patterning of the Song of Judith on Moses' Song of the Sea in Exodus 15.[133] There is, first of all, an important parallel between Jdt 16:2 and Exod 15:3 in the LXX version: "For the Lord is a God who crushes wars." In Judith's prayer at 9:2, she quoted a bit more of this passage, so the allusion to Exodus 15 is virtually certain. Further, in Exodus the hand of God finds expression in the hand of Moses, and this is similar to the emphasis on the hand of Judith in this book. The association of the Song of the Sea with Miriam also introduces a women's festival.

However, it is possible that Skehan (and Craven

130. André Lacocque, *The Feminine Unconventional: Four Subversive Figures in Israel's Tradition* (Minneapolis: Fortress, 1990); see also Steven Weitzman, *Song and Story in Biblical Narrative: The History of a Literary Convention in Ancient Israel* (Bloomington: Indiana University Press, 1997).

131. H. Ludin Jansen, "La composition du chant de Judith," *AcOr* 15 (1936) 63-71; see also Carey A. Moore, *Judith*, AB 40 (Garden City, N.Y.: Doubleday, 1985) 252-57.

132. Toni Craven, *Artistry and Faith in the Book of Judith* (Chico, Calif.: Scholars Press, 1983) 105-12.

133. Patrick Skehan, "The Hand of Judith," *CBQ* 25 (1963) 94-110.

following him) have overemphasized the relationship with the Song of the Sea. Even if Exodus 15 was alluded to in the Song of Judith, many other parallels in HB psalms can be detected, especially in vv. 13-17. Further, concerning the parallel between Miriam and Judith, as we have seen it was typical for women to be involved in the victory song. To be sure, there is one clear allusion to Exod 15:3 in the Song of Judith, but the author of Judith constantly includes words and phrases from biblical passages without the parallel necessarily carrying over to the entire chapter. There is really very little verbal or thematic agreement between the Song of Judith and the Song of the Sea that is not also present in the so-called enthronement psalms. These hymns sing the worship of God, who is victorious in a cosmic battle, and, as a result, rules or is enthroned in heaven. God is praised by those who have been saved and metes out punishment upon those who opposed God. The parallel to Moses' Song of the Sea will thus be noted without an assumption that Judith's song is modeled on it.

15:14. Judith is at the center of the book and of the song, and her position here as deliverer of "all Israel" is emphasized. Here we may compare the gathering and confession of the people in Ezra 10 and Nehemiah 8–9. In both cases it is a ceremonial gathering that is understood to represent all the people.

16:1-9. The song begins in a way typical of the victory songs in the HB, with a reference to tambourines and cymbals (see Commentary on 15:12). There is typical parallelism of lines—that is, in each of the pairs of lines, the second line repeats or parallels some of the motifs of the first:

Begin a *song* to my God with *tambourines,*
  sing to my Lord with *cymbals.*
Raise to him a new *psalm;*
  exalt him, and *call* upon his name.

"Song" and "tambourines" in the first line correspond to "sing" and "cymbals" in the second, while "raise" and "psalm" in the third line correspond in idea to "exalt" and "call" in the fourth line. This can be schematized as an AABB pattern, in which the first two lines have parallel terms or motifs, and the last two lines have different parallel terms or motifs.[134] Consider also the AABB pattern in v. 3, with the following parallel motifs: the Assyrian came down/came down with myriads; their numbers blocked/their cavalry covered. As is often the case with Hebrew poetry, however, such neat parallelism is not maintained throughout the poetic composition. We find three roughly parallel lines in v. 2 and five in v. 4. Contrast this with the Song of the Sea, in which parallelism is used in a fairly consistent way. One rhetorical effect in the Song of Judith that does come through strongly, however, is the parallel use of a motif over a number of lines that is resolved with a strong exclamation. Note the AAAAA pattern in v. 4, which culminates in "But the Lord Almighty has foiled them by the hand of a woman" in v. 5; the AAA pattern in v. 6, which is followed by "but Judith . . . with the beauty of her countenance undid him"; and an even stronger crescendo, the AAAAAA pattern in vv. 7-9*a,* which climaxes in v. 9*b:* "and the sword severed his neck!" The loosely constructed stanzas utilize a series of parallel motifs, leading to a climactic affirmation of Judith's heroic act.

We also detect in this section a number of motifs that were found in Judith's prayer in chap. 9: the God who crushes wars, v. 2 and the myriad warriors and cavalry in v. 3 occur also at 9:7; the threat to the women and children in v. 4 occurs in 9:2 (but also, ironically, in Judith's boast of what Simeon had done to the Shechemites in 9:4); and the reprise that God delivered the Israelites by the hand of a woman in v. 5 occurs at 9:10. One subtle difference, however, is that the theme of chap. 9 is that Judith will act by deceit, while in chap. 16 she has overcome Holofernes through her beauty.

16:10. There is no ready explanation for the reference to the Persians and the Medes. The Medes were destroyed in chap. 1 by Nebuchadnezzar, and so would presumably be viewed more sympathetically; and the Persians were mentioned earlier as one of the nations addressed by Nebuchadnezzar. The Persians and the Medes are often referred to together in texts of this period (e.g., Ezra 6:2; Esth 1:19; 10:2; Dan 5:28; 6:7), and so a conventional combining of their names would not be too surprising. But it is also quite likely

134. See Adele Berlin, "Introduction to Hebrew Poetry," *NIB* (Nashville: Abingdon, 1994) 4:303-8.

that, since the core of the book of Judith may have arisen in the Persian period and referred to a Persian invasion (see Introduction), that background of the book has remained here in the song. That the Persians "trembled" and the Medes "were daunted" are motifs from the divine warrior hymns (see Commentary on 16:13-17).

16:11-12. In these two verses the author emphasizes the victory of the oppressed or the humble (ταπεινός [*tapeinos*] can be translated either way) over the haughty. This was a theme of Judith's prayer in chap. 9 (esp. 9:11; see Commentary there). In the psalms and elsewhere there is often a reversal of the oppressed and haughty in the eyes of God, but in Judith it is a military victory as well. Judith has reversed the shame that Holofernes intended to inflict upon Israel and has inflicted it upon him: "Sons of slave-girls pierced them through." This hyperbole emphasizes that a woman has killed Holofernes and that tiny Bethulia has routed the mighty Assyrian army, but the image that it was accomplished by the sons of slave girls is intended to be one of shame.

16:13-17. This last section of the Song of Judith has a fairly consistent structure. After the introductory call to worship, each verse is a stanza composed of two central parallel lines. The parallel motifs are as follows: v. 13, "great"/"wonderful"; v. 14, "spoke and made"/"sent forth spirit and formed"; v. 15, "mountains shaken"/"rocks melt"; v. 16, "sacrifice is a small thing"/"fat of offerings is a little thing"; v. 17, "Lord will take vengeance"/"he will send fire and worms." In each verse there is a summary line after the two parallel lines (taking the first line of v. 14 as the summary line of v. 13). The only exception to this pattern is the transitional line at the beginning of v. 17, "Woe to the nations. . . ." Each stanza has parallels in hymnic traditions, many found together in one psalm or another.

Reference to the "new song" in v. 13 is a common call to worship in the book of Psalms (e.g., Pss 13:3; 40:4; 96:1; 149:1; cf. Isa 42:10).[135] In regard to the connection between prose narrative and song in the biblical tradition, Weitzman notes a connection between the songs embedded in narrative, such as the Song of Judith, and the psalms: "Just as the Psalms were thought of as the prayers and songs of biblical heroes uttered at significant moments in their lives, so too the songs in biblical narrative were reread and rewritten in light of biblical psalmody." Thus, although the influence of Exodus 15 and Judges 5 on Judith 16 can be assumed, these are by no means the only influences, or even the main influences.

The creation by God's Word (v. 14) is a common motif, found in Genesis 1 ("And God said, let there be . . ."), and in the enthronement psalms as well. Psalm 33:6 states: "By the word of the LORD the heavens were made, and all their host by the breath of his mouth" (NRSV).

The shaking of the mountains and the melting of the rocks (v. 15), or expressions like these, are often present in enthronement psalms as well (see Psalm 99:1: "The LORD is king; let the people tremble! He sits enthroned upon the cherubim; let the earth quake!" [NRSV]). These motifs are sometimes part of that adaptation of the enthronement psalm called the divine warrior hymn, in which God must defeat enemies in heaven in order to be enthroned.[136] Psalm 18:7 is particularly dramatic in this regard: "Then the earth reeled and rocked; the foundations also of the mountains trembled and quaked, because he was angry" (NRSV). We find the motif of the earth quaking even when a human king is enthroned (1 Kgs 1:38-40).

The apparent critique of sacrifice in v. 16 has raised questions for some scholars, who wonder how such a devoted observer of Jewish cultic practices as Judith could question the value of sacrifice. One need only look down two verses to v. 18, the prolific sacrifices of the people, to find a striking contradiction to this verse. However, although sharp language about an overreliance on sacrifice is present in the HB (e.g., Ps 50:8-15; Hos 6:6, quoted in Matt 9:13; 12:7), the closest parallel to this passage is in Ps 40:6: "Sacrifice and offering you do not desire, but you have given me an open ear. Burnt offering and sin offering you have not required" (NRSV). It is, perhaps, the

135. Steven Weitzman, *Song and Story in Biblical Narrative: The History of a Literary Convention in Ancient Israel* (Bloomington: Indiana University Press, 1997) 73.

136. Paul D. Hanson, *The Dawn of Apocalyptic* (Philadelphia: Fortress, 1975) 300-316; Susan Niditch, *Oral World and Written Word: Ancient Israelite Literature* (Louisville: Westminster/John Knox, 1996) 21-24.

remnants of an older psalm, or at least the effect of the psalm genre, that provokes this sentiment here, not a sudden and quite isolated desire by the author of the book of Judith to caution the readers about insincere sacrifice.

Ideas similar to this summary line ("whoever fears the Lord is great forever") are also found in one of the psalms mentioned above, Ps 33:18-19:

> Truly the eye of the LORD is on those who fear him,
> on those who hope in his steadfast love,
> to deliver their soul from death,
> and to keep them alive in famine. (NRSV)

This particular example is interesting because it includes not only the motif of the protection of those who fear God, but also the protection from death that could give rise to the hyperbole in Judith of being "great forever."

The motif of judgment (v. 17) also finds a parallel in enthronement psalms. The positive praise of God in some of the psalms turns to announcement of God's terrible presence for those in heaven or on earth who oppose God (cf. Ps 96:13: "He is coming to judge the earth. He will judge the world with righteousness" [NRSV]). The day of judgment in Judith might seem too eschatological for the hymns of praise, but the harsh judgment of the wicked can sometimes be found where God's victory is seen eschatologically as the victory over the enemies in heaven and on earth, as in Isa 24:21, 23:

> On that day the LORD will punish
> the host of heaven in heaven,
> and on earth the kings of the earth.
> . . . . . .
> The LORD of hosts will reign
> on Mt. Zion and in Jerusalem. (NRSV)

Isaiah 66:24 contains this as well as other important parallels to v. 17 in Judith:

> And they shall go out and look at the dead bodies of the people who have rebelled against me; for their worm shall not die, their fire shall not be quenched, and they shall be an abhorrence to all flesh. (NRSV)

These examples push us to consider whether the book of Judith at this point is also expressing an eschatological, even apocalyptic, notion of the day of judgment. This idea has been argued by some scholars, but opposed by Enslin,[137] who suggests that the author is simply reusing common traditions. This is probably the case, if only because there is nothing in the Song of Judith, or in the book as a whole, to match this notion; only 9:4-5 even approaches it. Verse 17 may use the same terms as in Isaiah 66, and may even capture the sense of apocalyptic judgment, but it stands alone in the book of Judith in this regard. It is likely used in its present position as a final warning of extreme judgment to come upon those, like Nebuchadnezzar, who rise up "against my people."[138] Worms as a punishment is found elsewhere in this period (Isa 14:11; Sir 7:17; Acts 12:23; *Testament of Job* 20), but there may be a particular allusion here to the death of Antiochus IV Epiphanes, the tyrant opposed in the Maccabean revolt, as recounted in 2 Macc 9:9.

Several aspects of vv. 13-17 indicate that this section may have been an independent enthronement psalm that was appropriated by the author of Judith to be used at this point in the novel: It contains many parallels to other enthronement psalms, the structure is different from vv. 1-12, and there is no reference to the narrative about Judith. Craven argues that two references to the fear of God in vv. 15-16 represent the culmination of the song and of the book as a whole.[139] Although Nebuchadnezzar had laid claim in 2:5 to being the "lord of all the earth," the author affirms here that the lordship of God is the true religion. To be sure, within the present structure of the song, these lines function in this way; but the fear of God is also a common motif in the enthronement psalms, and so it is quite possible that we have here a fragment of a pre-existing psalm. (See Reflections at 16:21-25.)

137. Morton Enslin and Solomon Zeitlin, *The Book of Judith,* JAL VIII (Leiden: Brill, 1972) 175n. 17.
138. Craven, *Artistry and Faith in the Book of Judith,* 110.
139. Ibid., 109.

Judith 16:18-20, Thanksgiving Offerings

NAB

18 The people then went to Jerusalem to worship God; when they were purified, they offered their holocausts, free-will offerings, and gifts. 19 Judith dedicated, as a votive offering to God, all the things of Holofernes that the people had given her, as well as the canopy that she herself had taken from his bedroom. 20 For three months the people continued their celebration in Jerusalem before the sanctuary, and Judith remained with them.

NRSV

18When they arrived at Jerusalem, they worshiped God. As soon as the people were purified, they offered their burnt offerings, their freewill offerings, and their gifts. 19Judith also dedicated to God all the possessions of Holofernes, which the people had given her; and the canopy that she had taken for herself from his bedchamber she gave as a votive offering. 20For three months the people continued feasting in Jerusalem before the sanctuary, and Judith remained with them.

COMMENTARY

The entourage of people from Bethulia makes a pilgrimage to Jerusalem to bring offerings; it appears that both the women and the men in 15:12-13 have made the journey. They purify themselves to make the offerings—but is it because they have touched dead bodies (Num 19:11-22), or is it another example of the special piety reflected in Judith's earlier asceticism? The answer is not clear. The offerings they bring are nearly identical to those offered by the high priest Joakim in 4:14 at the height of the crisis. A requirement of the ban, or חרם (*ḥērem*; mentioned in the Reflections at 14:19–15:7), is that the property of a defeated city is to be offered to God (see Josh 6:19, 24). Judith presents the inner canopy that she took from Holofernes' tent as a special votive offering. The offering of significant items of defeated warriors is known from elsewhere (for example, David's offering of the sword of Goliath, 1 Sam 21:9), but Judith offers, not Holofernes' sword of power, but the canopy of his inner sanctum, which she penetrated to slay him. Even in death Holofernes is unmanned and shamed. The three-month celebration is exaggerated, but should be seen as a literary motif, and not intended as realistic. One should note, however, that it is still festive—that is, sacred time—and it is emphasized that Judith remains with them during this period. (See Reflections at 16:21-25.)

Judith 16:21-25, Memorial of Judith

NAB

21 When those days were over, each one returned to his inheritance. Judith went back to Bethulia and remained on her estate. For the rest of her life she was renowned throughout the land. 22 Many wished to marry her, but she gave herself to no man all the days of her life from the time of the death and burial of her husband, Manasseh. 23 She lived to be very old in the house of her husband, reaching the advanced age

16, 23: Trsp *kai aphēken tēn abran autēs eleutheran* to the end of v 24: so 1 LXX[MS], Vet Lat, P.

NRSV

21After this they all returned home to their own inheritances. Judith went to Bethulia, and remained on her estate. For the rest of her life she was honored throughout the whole country. 22Many desired to marry her, but she gave herself to no man all the days of her life after her husband Manasseh died and was gathered to his people. 23She became more and more famous, and grew old in her husband's house, reaching the age of one hundred five. She set her maid free. She died in Bethulia, and they buried her in the cave of

NAB

of a hundred and five. She died in Bethulia, where they buried her in the tomb of her husband, Manasseh; 24 and the house of Israel mourned her for seven days. Before she died, she distributed her goods to the relatives of her husband, Manasseh, and to her own relatives; and to the maid she gave her freedom.

25 During the life of Judith and for a long time after her death, no one again disturbed the Israelites.

16, 25: Omit *amēn:* so $LXX^{S,A}$.

NRSV

her husband Manasseh; [24]and the house of Israel mourned her for seven days. Before she died she distributed her property to all those who were next of kin to her husband Manasseh, and to her own nearest kindred. [25]No one ever again spread terror among the Israelites during the lifetime of Judith, or for a long time after her death.

COMMENTARY

Judith returns to her wealthy estate, but it is not clear that she returns to the same conditions of her ascetic discipline as described in 8:2-4. Levine points out the differences in the description here: Judith returns to her estate, but not necessarily to her tent; she no longer communes directly with God, but rather returns to contact with the society of Bethulia, even though she does not accept any of the many marriage proposals.[140] She has evidently given up her special life of spirituality, but does not totally integrate into society. As can be seen in other cultures, it is common for the hero not to be able to integrate into society. The lack of integration, therefore, should not surprise us; but the lack of isolation, the lack of a special spiritual life does. Perhaps the author intentionally is choosing to be ambiguous about Judith's precise relations to society, as she becomes memorialized. A similar technique can be detected at two important memorializing scenes in the NT. At Mark 16:8, the resurrection of Jesus is prepared for but never confirmed; the original text of Mark ends on a searching but ambiguous note: "They said nothing to anyone, for they were afraid" (NRSV). Similarly, but less often noted, the memorializing of Paul at the end of Acts is ambiguous. Paul expounds to the Jewish leaders of Rome his message about Jesus, and some are convinced, while others are not. Paul condemned "this people's" unbelief, but we are not told what became of those who believed, or whether there was any change of heart; rather, it is simply said that he continued preaching for two years "with all boldness and without hindrance." Thus the open-ended conclusion about the person being memorialized is more a norm than an exception in these texts.

What is emphasized is that she was greatly honored as a heroine both in life (v. 21) and in death (vv. 23-25). Her beauty is still irresistible, and her fame only increases. She gives away her wealth and frees her maid as benevolent gestures that, like the ancient code of honor, would establish her role as patroness. Thus she dies with an enormous store of honor and patronage, befitting the death and memorializing of the heroine.[141] Her strength and independence as a woman—to the extent that in her genealogy she even takes precedence over her husband, Manasseh (8:1)—is now subtly brought back under control by the placing of her body in her husband's burial cave.

140. Amy-Jill Levine, "Sacrifice and Salvation: Otherness and Domestication in the Book of Judith," in *"No One Spoke Ill of Her": Essays on Judith,* ed. James C. VanderKam (Atlanta: Scholars Press, 1992) 27.

141. Lawrence M. Wills, *The Quest of the Historical Gospel: Mark, John, and the Origin of the Gospel Genre* (London: Routledge, 1997) 40-41.

The Pandora's box that was opened is now safely closed.

The last line, "No one ever again spread terror among the Israelites," is probably modeled on Judg 5:31: "The land had rest forty years" (see also Judg 3:11, 30). Within the book of Judith, however, it concludes the structural outline of the second half of the book by mirroring a line from the introduction of Judith: "No one spoke ill of her, for she feared God with great devotion" (8:8).

REFLECTIONS

The ending of the book of Judith is so positive concerning the memory of her that it raises the question of the position of Judith among the heroes of Judaism. Was she an intermediator figure, like Moses? Was she like one of the prophets or judges? Was she described in a way parallel to the Maccabean warriors and martyrs? In the Greek and Roman world, the heroes of the culture were honored in death and were thought to have lasting positive effects long afterward. Temples and monuments can still be found that attest to the strength of this tradition, and it likely influenced the later Christian devotion to saints' tombs and the Jewish reverence for the graves of the rabbis. Reverence for the dead and the cult of dead ancestors may have also existed in ancient Israel, although evidence for this in some cases arises from the fact that it was vigorously condemned. Some special reverence for the revered dead must have remained, however, for even in the New Testament we see at issue the reverence for the tombs of the prophets (Matt 23:27).

Today as well it is partly through such memorializing experiences that a community—whether a local community or a whole nation—comes together and its values are reaffirmed. A memorial ceremony is a liturgy that enacts the community's response to the death of a hero and the community's creation of a memory of that person. The collective memory becomes more "real" in some cases than the actual person's life, and it is reaffirmed in further memorials over the years. The somber reverence that today attaches to national cemeteries, monuments, and statues is vivid proof that we are addressing here a powerful part of a society's consciousness of its past.

What, then, is the nature of the remembrance of Judith? Judith is honored during her lifetime, and she is buried in the cave of her husband, Manasseh, which may evoke for the readers Abraham's purchase of the cave of Machpelah for Sarah's burial. Throughout we have noted how Judith is depicted like one of the judges, who were raised up by God when the people cried out for help. In the book of Judith, God also hears the prayers of the Israelites (4:13), and, like the judges, Judith brings peace to the land for many years (16:25). Judith is clearly described as having an elevated place in the memory of Israel, stated as positively, for example, as that of Mordecai in Esth 10:3. But whereas Mordecai is described as a benefactor of Jews, he is not memorialized as directly, expecially not in terms of his death and burial. There was no cult described at the tomb of Judith as there was for Greek and Roman heroes, but her memory is kept and her tomb marked, as with the judges.

What kinds of values are memorialized in Judith? She is a more complex hero than is usually the case. She explicitly says that she uses deceit and beauty, but she is also a military heroine who coolly decapitates an enemy general and directs a major military attack. Her piety and her relation to God are the first priority in her life, and yet are the first things she risks losing—in appearance at any rate—in the interest of saving her people. In Judith, however, it is not just the individual heroine who is being memorialized, but the collective heroism of Israel and the collective religious values as well. Heroes are seen as partially responsible for our present well-being, and yet we do not just receive them as they are; we often ignore their inconsistencies and project onto them a loftier vision of what we think people are capable of. Abraham Lincoln, for example, possessed many fine qualities as a leader, but his memory in popular culture also became shaped by the values society projected onto him. And like the judges or Judith, Lincoln's memory in popular culture takes on quasi-religious overtones, as his tomb is venerated as an American icon. In the collective memory, then, Judith becomes larger than life, even if she is a fictional character, and reminds us of the ways that our own heroes have been idealized as well.

Transliteration Schema

HEBREW AND ARAMAIC TRANSLITERATION

Consonants:

א	=	ʾ	ט	=	ṭ	פ or ף	=	p
ב	=	b	י	=	y	צ or ץ	=	ṣ
ג	=	g	כ or ך	=	k	ק	=	q
ד	=	d	ל	=	l	ר	=	r
ה	=	h	מ or ם	=	m	שׂ	=	ś
ו	=	w	נ or ן	=	n	שׁ	=	š
ז	=	z	ס	=	s	ת	=	t
ח	=	ḥ	ע	=	ʿ			

Masoretic Pointing:

Pure-long			Tone-long			Short			Composite *shewa*		
◌ָה	=	â	◌ָ	=	ā	◌ַ	=	a	◌ֲ	=	ă
◌ֵי or ◌ֶי	=	ê	◌ֵ	=	ē	◌ֶ	=	e	◌ְ or ◌ֱ	=	ĕ
◌ִ or ◌ִי	=	î				◌ִ	=	i			
◌ֹ or ◌וֹ	=	ô	◌ֹ	=	ō	◌ָ	=	o	◌ֳ	=	ŏ
◌ֻ or ◌וּ	=	û				◌ֻ	=	u			

GREEK TRANSLITERATION

α	=	a	ι	=	i	ρ	=	r
β	=	b	κ	=	k	σ or ς	=	s
γ	=	g	λ	=	l	τ	=	t
δ	=	d	μ	=	m	υ	=	y
ϵ	=	e	ν	=	n	φ	=	ph
ζ	=	z	ξ	=	x	χ	=	ch
η	=	ē	ο	=	o	ψ	=	ps
θ	=	th	π	=	p	ω	=	ō

INDEX OF MAPS, CHARTS, AND ILLUSTRATIONS

INDEX OF EXCURSUSES

ABBREVIATIONS

BCE	Before the Common Era
CE	Common Era
c.	circa
cf.	compare
chap(s).	chapter(s)
d.	died
Dtr	deuteronomic historian
esp.	especially
fem.	feminine
HB	Hebrew Bible
lit.	literally
l(l).	line(s)
LXX	Septuagint
masc.	masculiine
MS(S)	manuscript(s)
MT	Masoretic Text
n.(n.)	note(s)
NT	New Testament
OL	Old Latin
OT	Old Testament
par.	parallel(s)
pl(s).	plate(s)
v(v).	verse(s)
Vg	Vulgate

Names of Biblical Books

Gen
Exod
Lev
Num
Deut
Josh
Judg
1–2 Sam
1–2 Kgs
Isa
Jer
Ezek
Hos
Joel
Amos
Obad
Jonah
Mic
Nah
Hab
Zeph
Hag
Zech
Mal
Ps (Pss)
Job
Prov
Ruth
Cant
Eccl
Lam
Esth
Dan
Ezra
Neh
1–2 Chr
1–4 Kgdms
Add Esth
Bar
Bel
1–2 Esdr
4 Ezra
Jdt
Ep Jer
1–4 Macc
Pr Azar
Pr Man
Sir
Sus
Tob
Wis
Matt
Mark
Luke
John
Acts
Rom
1–2 Cor
Gal
Eph
Phil
Col
1–2 Thess
1–2 Tim
Titus
Phlm
Heb
Jas
1–2 Pet
1–3 John
Jude
Rev

Names of Dead Sea Scrolls and Related Texts

Q	Qumran
1Q, 2Q, etc.	Numbered caves of Qumran, yielding written material; followed by abbreviation of biblical or apocryphal book
4QSam^{a}	First copy of Samuel from Qumran Cave 4
4QTob	Copy of Tobit from Qumran Cave 4

4Q550	*4QProto-Esther*[a-f]
11QTemple	*Temple Scroll* from Qumran Cave 11

Targumic Material

Tg. Esth I, II	First or second Targum of Esther

Orders and Tractates in Mishnaic and Related Literature

b. 'Arak.	Babylonian Talmud *'Arakin*
t. Git.	Tosepta *Giṭṭin*
b. Ḥul.	Babylonian Talmud *Ḥullin*
b. Meg.	Babylonian Talmud *Megilla*
t. Meg.	Tosepta *Megilla*

Other Rabbinic Works

Rab.	*Rabbah* (following abbreviation of biblical book—e.g., *Gen. Rab.* = *Genesis Rabbah*)

Commonly Used Periodicals, Reference Works, and Serials

AB	Anchor Bible
ABD	Anchor Bible Dictionary
AcOr	*Acta Orientalia*
AfO	*Archiv fur Orientforschung*
AJSL	*American Journal of Semitic Languages and Literature*
ANEP	J. B. Pritchard (ed.), *Ancient Near East in Pictures*
ANET	J. B. Pritchard (ed.), *Ancient Near Eastern Texts*
ANRW	*Aufstieg und Niedergang der römischen Welt*
APOT	R. H. Charles (ed.), *Apocrypha and Pseudepigrapha of the OT (2 vols., 1913)*
Aug	*Augustinianum*
BA	*Biblical Archaeologist*
BASOR	*Bulletin of the American Schools of Oriental Research*
BDB	F. Brown, S. R. Driver, and C. A. Briggs, *Hebrew and English Lexicon of the Old Testament*
BEATAJ	Beiträge zur Erforschung des Alten Testaments und des antiken Judentu
BEvT	Beiträge zur evangelischen Theologie
BHS	*Biblia hebraica stuttgartensia*
BHT	Beiträge zur Historischen Theologie
Bib	*Biblica*
BJS	Brown Judaic Studies
BR	*Biblical Research*
BVC	*Bible et vie chrétienne*
BWANT	Beiträge zur Wissenschaft vom Alten (und Neuen) Testament
BZ	*Biblische Zeitschrift*
BZAW	Beihefte zur *ZAW*
CBC	Cambridge Bible Commentary
CBQ	*Catholic Biblical Quarterly*
ConBOT	Coniectanea biblica, Old Testament
DJD	Discoveries in the Judaean Desert
EI	*Encyclopaedia of Islam*
EncJud	C. Roth (ed.), *Encyclopaedia Judaica* (16 vols., 1971–72)
ETL	*Ephemerides theologicae lovanienses*
FOTL	Forms of Old Testament Literature
FTS	Frankfurter Theologische Studien
GNB	Good News Bible
HALAT	W. Baumgartner, et al., *Hebräisches und aramäisches Lexikon zum Alten Testament*
HAT	Handbuch zum Alten Testament
HDR	Harvard Dissertations in Religion
HeyJ	*Heythrop Journal*
HSM	Harvard Semitic Monographs
HTR	*Harvard Theological Review*
IB	*Interpreter's Bible*
ICC	International Critical Commentary
IEJ	*Israel Exploration Journal*
JAL	Jewish Apocryphal Literature

JANESCU	*Journal of the Ancient Near Eastern Society of Columbia University*
JBL	*Journal of Biblical Literature*
JNES	*Journal of Near Eastern Studies*
JQR	*Jewish Quarterly Review*
JSOT	*Journal for the Study of the Old Testament*
JSOTSup	*Journal for the Study of the Old Testament*—Supplement Series
JSP	*Journal for the Study of the Pseudepigrapha*
JSS	*Journal of Semitic Studies*
KAT	Kommentar zum Alten Testament
KPG	Knox Preaching Guides
NAB	New American Bible
NCB	New Clarendon Bible
NEB	New English Bible
NIB	*New Interpreter's Bible*
NIV	New International Version
NJB	New Jerusalem Bible
NRSV	New Revised Standard Verion
OBO	Orbis biblicus et orientalis
OBT	Overtures to Biblical Theology
OTL	Old Testament Library
OTM	Old Testament Message
OTS	*Oudtestamentische Studiën*
RB	*Revue biblique*
REB	Revised English Bible
RSR	*Recherches de science religieuse*
RSV	Revised Standard Version
SBL	Society of Bibilical Literature
SBLDS	SBL Dissertation Series
SBLMS	SBL Monograph Series
SBLSP	SBL Seminar Papers
SBLWAW	SBL Writings of the Ancient World
SBM	Stuttgarter biblische Monographien
SBT	Studies in Biblical Theology
SJOT	*Scandinavian Journal of the Old Testament*
SKK	Stuttgarter Kleiner Kommentar
SNTSMS	Society for New Testament Studies Monograph Series
SOTSMS	Society for Old Testament Study Monograph Series
TDOT	G. J. Botterweck and H. Ringgren (eds.), *Theological Dictionary of the Old Testament*
TNK	Tanakh (Jewish Publication Society Version)
TQ	*Theologische Quartalschrift*
TynBul	*Tyndale Bulletin*
VT	*Vetus Testamentum*
VTSup	*Vetus Testamentum,* Supplements
WBC	Word Biblical Commentary
WTJ	*Westminster Theological Journal*
ZAW	*Zeitschrift für die alttestamentliche Wissenschaft*